Stedman's *Pocket* Medical Dictionary

Williams & Wilkins

BALTIMORE • PHILADELPHIA • HONG KONG
LONDON • MUNICH • SYDNEY • TOKYO

A WAVERLY COMPANY

Editor: William R. Hensyl
Associate Editor: Harriet Felscher
Aide: Gertrude A. Wilder
Design: Joanne Janowiak
Production: Raymond E. Reter

Copyright ©, 1987
Williams & Wilkins
428 East Preston Street
Baltimore, MD 21202, U.S.A.

Printed in the United States of America.

Library of Congress Cataloging-in-Publication Data
Stedman, Thomas Lathrop, 1853-1938.
  Pocket medical dictionary.
  Derived from: Stedman's medical dictionary, 24th ed. c1982.
  1. Medicine — Dictionaries. I. Stedman, Thomas Lathrop,
1853-1938. Medical dictionary. II. Title: Pocket medical dictionary.
III. Title. [DNLM: 1. Dictionaries, Medical. W 13 S812m]
R121.S8   1986   610'.3'21   86-32395
ISBN 0-683-07921-2

CONTENTS

PREFACE

The vocabulary of *STEDMAN'S POCKET MEDICAL DICTION-ARY* is derived from the popular 24th Edition of *STEDMAN'S MEDICAL DICTIONARY* and is intended for students and practitioners in the health professions who find the parent volume too comprehensive or unwieldy for their everyday needs. This abridged edition has attempted to retain the valuable essentials and useful features of the larger book in a more compact and convenient size.

STEDMAN'S POCKET MEDICAL DICTIONARY is a selectively edited abridgment whose content has benefited from the ongoing review of the vocabulary of the parent dictionary by its 38 consultants, who represent the major medical specialties and subspecialties. Each term was evaluated initially for its appropriateness as an entry, to provide a balance between older terminology still in use and newer terminology warranting inclusion, and then for the scope of its definition, to avoid an unnecessary sacrifice of content for brevity. The important etymologic content in the parent dictionary was retained as vocabulary entries for prefixes, suffixes, and combining forms, and as derivational information accompanying the terms in the vocabulary. Thus, the dictionary's user is able to ascertain how a term is spelled, pronounced, constructed, and defined.

The user is urged to read carefully the following section, "How To Use This Dictionary." An understanding of the principles of this dictionary's organization, format, and style will not only save time through an efficient search for information but also will increase the amount of information obtained. Hindsight, especially after preparation of first editions, reveals what might have been done differently or better. We welcome and encourage suggestions from users of this dictionary as to how best to improve the usefulness of *STEDMAN'S POCKET MEDICAL DICTIONARY* in subsequent editions.

William R. Hensyl
Managing Editor, Dictionaries
Williams & Wilkins

HOW TO USE
THIS DICTIONARY

Organization of the Vocabulary

In general this dictionary has followed the traditional format of specialty dictionaries by grouping multi-word terms in an index-like arrangement under the principal governing *noun* as the main entry. The advantages of such categorization of information will be obvious to the experienced user, but initially may be confusing to the novice who in seeking a multiple-word term fails to first look for it under the *noun*.

Alphabetization

Single-word terms are alphabetized letter by letter as main entries. Punctuation (such as hyphens), numbers, Greek letters, and italicized prefixes are disregarded in alphabetization. Compound words that are usually written closed-up as one word, or that are hyphenated words, are treated as main entries; however, there are sufficient spelling variations and usages to warrant looking under the noun for a subentry listing if a main entry listing is not found. Multiple-word terms are similarly alphabetized as subentries under their noun main entry word, but disregard the abbreviated main entry word (singular or plural) or spelled-out Latin plurals that are part of the term, as well as any prepositions, conjunctions, articles, and the possessive in eponyms. Eponyms are always treated as subentries.

Main Entry and Subentry Format

Main entries typically begin with the boldface term and any abbreviation or symbol in parenthesis, followed by its pronunciation in parenthesis, and its derivation in brackets. Synonyms begin the definition and are separated by semicolons; if numerous, they are listed at the end of the definition and are preceded by "also called". When a term has more than one definition, each definition is preceded by a boldface number. Cross-references are located at the end of the definition.

Subentries are treated similarly, except that few require pronunciation and/or derivation because their principal words are carried either as main entries in the vocabulary or are sufficiently commonplace as to not require an entry.

> **capacity** (kă-pas'ĭ-tī) [L. *capax*, able to contain; fr. *capio*, to take]. **1.** The potential cubic contents of a cavity or receptacle. **2.** Ability; power do do.
>
>   **buffer c.**, the amount of hydrogen ion (or hydroxyl ion) required to bring about a specific pH change in a specified volume of a buffer. See also buffer *value*.
>
>   **functional residual c. (FRC)**, functional residual air; the volume of gas remaining in the lungs at the end of a normal expiration; it is the sum of expiratory reserve volume and residual volume.
>
>   **residual c.**, residual *volume*.
>
>   **respiratory c.**, vital *c*.
>
>   **vital c. (VC)**, respiratory *c*.; the greatest volume of air that can be exhaled from the lungs after a maximum inspiration.

Cross-references are of two types: synonym and informational. A synonym as a main entry or a subentry uses the defined term with which it is synonymous as the cross-reference rather than duplicate that term's definition; when the cross-reference is to a multiple-word term (subentry), its noun main entry word is italicized. Informational cross-reference entries are identified by "see" or "see also" and similarly have the noun main entry word italicized if the referred-to term is a subentry.

Abbreviations and symbols as entries are treated as synonym cross-references to the terms they represent.

Pronunciation

A simplified phonetic spelling showing pronunciation and syllabification is given in parentheses following the boldface entry term. A prime (') follows stressed syllables. Primes are also used in boldface entry terms where phonetic pronunciation is not needed or to indicate the stressed syllable of Latin words in subentry terms.

Vowels, in most words, have their sounds determined by syllabification: *long,* if the vowel occurs at the end of a syllable; *short,* if the vowel is followed by a consonant. Where this general rule is applicable, diacritical marks have been omitted. For exceptions, the diacritical marks used are restricted to two: the macron (-) for long sound, the breve (˘) for short sounds. The breve is also used arbitrarily for half-long or slurred enunciations, examples of which are shown in the accompanying key.

ă as in *a*ppoint, temper*a*ture	ĭ as in phob*i*a, *y* as in heav*y*
ăr as in c*a*re, f*a*re	ĭr *as in* mi*rr*or
ĕ as in *e*ffect, en*e*my	ŏ as in *o*ccur
ĕr as in m*e*rry	

Consonants follow standard prononunications, but the following should be noted:

dh for *th* as in *th*is, *th*e
ĭ   for *y* as in heav*y*
j   for *g* as in *g*em
zh for *z* as in a*z*ure, *s* as in mea*s*ure

In some words the initial sound is not that of the initial letter(s), or the initial letter(s) is not sounded or has a different sound, as in the following examples:

*ae*robe (ăr'ōb)
*ei*meria (i-me'rĭ-ah)
*g*nathic (nath'ik)
*k*nuckle (nuk'l)
*oe*dipism (ed'ĭ-pizm)

*ph*thalein (thal'e-in)
*p*neumonia (nu-mo'nĭ-ah)
*p*sychology (si-kol'o-jĭ)
*p*tosis (to'sis)
*x*anthoma (zan-tho'mah)

Abbreviations

Ar.	Arabic	Mediev. L., Med. L.	Medieval Latin
A.S.	Anglo-Saxon		
c., ca.	L. *circa*, about	Modl. L.	Mo lern Latin
cf.	L. *confer*, compare	NA	Nomina Anatomica
Eng.	English	neut., ntr.	neuter
e.g.	L. *exempli gratia*, for example	obs.	obsolete
		O.E.	Old English
Fr.	French	O.Fr.	Old Fench
fr.	from	Pers.	Persian
G.	Greek	Pg.	Portuguese
Gael.	Gaelic	p.	participle
gen.	genitive	pl.	plural
Ger.	German	pp.	perfect participle passive
Hind.	Hindu		
i.e.	L. *id est*, that is	priv.	privative, negative
Ind.	Indian	*q.v.*	L. *quod vide*, which see
It.	Italian		
Jap.	Japanese	sing.	singular
L.	Latin	Sp.	Spanish
L.L.	Late Latin	thr.	through
M.E.	Middle English	U.S.	United States

A

α Alpha, first letter of the Greek alphabet; used to denote the first in a series, as in chemistry to designate the order of components of isomeric compounds or of carbon atoms.

A Ampere; adenosine or adenylic acid in polynucleotides; absorbance (usually capitalized italic); alveolar *gas* (subscript).

Å Angstrom.

a Total *acidity;* area;, asymmetric; atto-; specific absorption *coefficient* (usually italic); systemic arterial blood (subscript).

a-, an- [G. alpha, privative or negative, inseparable prefix, usually *an-* before a vowel]. Prefix equivalent to the L. *in-* and E. *un-;* not, without, -less.

AA Amino acids or aminoacyl.

ab- [L. *ab*, from]. **1.** Prefix signifying from, away from, off. **2.** Prefix applied to electrical units in the CGS-electromagnetic system to distinguish them from units in the CGS-electrostatic system (prefix stat-) and those in the more commonly used SI system (no prefix).

abap'ical. Opposite the apex.

abarognosis (ab-ar-og-no'sis) [G. *a-* priv. + *baros*, weight, + *gnōsis*, knowledge]. Loss of sense of weight.

abasia (ă-ba'zĭ-ah) [G. *a-* priv. + *basis*, step]. Inability to walk.

  a.-asta'sia, see astasia-abasia.

  atactic a., ataxic a., difficulty in walking due to ataxia of the legs.

  choreic a., a. related to abnormal movements of the legs.

  paralytic a., a. related to inability to move the leg muscles.

  paroxysmal trepidant a., a. related to spasticity of the legs.

  spastic a., a. due to spastic contraction of the muscles.

  a. trep'idans, a. due to trembling of the legs.

abasic, abatic (ă-ba'sik, ă-bat'ik). Denoting abasia.

abax'ial, abax'ile. **1.** Lying outside the axis of any body or part. **2.** Situated at the opposite extremity of the axis of a part.

abdomen (ab-do'men; ab'do-men) [L. *abdomen*, etym. uncertain] [NA]. Belly; venter (1); the part of the trunk that lies between the thorax and the pelvis. The a. does not include the vertebral region posteriorly but is considered by some anatomists to include the pelvis. It contains the greater part of the abdominal cavity, cavum abdominis, and is divided by arbitrary planes into nine regions. See also *regiones* abdominis, under regio.

  acute a., surgical a.; any serious intra-abdominal condition attended by pain, tenderness, and muscular rigidity, and implying the need for any emergency operation.

  carinate a., a sloping of the sides with prominence of the central line of the a.

  navicular a., scaphoid a.; a condition in which the anterior abdominal wall is sunken and presents a concave contour.

  scaphoid a., navicular a.

  surgical a., acute a.

abdomin-. See abdomino-.

abdom'inal. Relating to the abdomen.

abdomino-, abdomin- [L. *abdomen*]. Combining forms denoting relationship to the abdomen.

abdominocentesis (ab-dom'ĭ-no-sen-te'sis) [abdomino- + G. *kentēsis*, puncture]. Peritoneocentesis.

abdominocyesis (ab-dom'ĭ-no-si-e'sis) [abdomino- + G. *kyēsis*, pregnancy]. **1.** Abdominal *pregnancy.* **2.** Secondary abdominal *pregnancy.*

abdominocystic (ab-dom-ĭ-no-sis'tik) [abdomino- + G. *kystis*, bladder]. Abdominovesical.

abdom'inogen'ital. Relating to the abdomen and the genital organs.

abdom'inohysterec'tomy. Abdominal *hysterectomy.*

abdom'inohysterot'omy. Abdominal *hysterotomy.*

abdominoplasty (ab-dom'ĭ-no-plas-tĭ) [abdomino- + G. *plassō*, to form]. An operation performed on the abdominal wall for esthetic purposes.

abdominos'copy [abdomino- + G. *skopeō*, to examine]. Peritoneoscopy.

abdom'inoscro'tal. Relating to the abdomen and the scrotum.

abdom'inothorac'ic. Relating to both abdomen and thorax.

abdom'inovag'inal. Relating to both abdomen and vagina.

abdom'inoves'ical. Abdominocystic; relating to the abdomen and urinary bladder, or to the abdomen and gallbladder.

abduce (ab-dūs'). Abduct.

abdu'cens oc'uli. *Musculus* rectus lateralis.

abdu'cent [L. *abducens*]. Abducting; drawing away.

abduct (ab-dukt'). Abduce; to move away from the median line.

abduction (ab-duk'shun) [L. *abductio*]. **1.** Movement away from the median line. **2.** Monocular rotation (duction) of the eye toward the temple. **3.** A position resulting from such movement.

abduc'tor. A muscle that draws a part away from the median line.

aber'rancy. Aberration.

aber'rant [L. *aberrans*]. **1.** Wandering off; said of certain ducts, vessels, or nerves taking an unusual course. **2.** Differing from the normal; in botany or zoology, said of certain atypical individuals in a species. **3.** Ectopic (1).

aberration (ab-er-a'shun) [L. *aberratio*]. Aberrancy. **1.** A straying from the normal situation. **2.** Deviant development or growth.

chromatic a., chromatism (2); the difference in focus or magnification of an image arising because of a difference in the refraction of different wavelengths composing white light.

chromosome a., any deviation from the normal number or morphology of chromosomes.

coma a., the distortion of image formation created when a bundle of light rays enters an optical system not parallel to the optic axis.

curvature a., lack of spatial correspondence causing the image of a straight extended object to appear curved.

dioptric a., spherical a.

distortion a., the faulty formation of an image arising because the magnification of the peripheral part of an object is different from that of the central part when viewed through a lens.

lateral a., in spherical a., the distance between paraxial focus of central rays on the optic axis.

longitudinal a., in spherical a., the distance separating the focus of paraxial and peripheral rays on the optic axis.

meridional a., an a. produced in the plane of a single meridian of a lens.

monochromatic a., a defect in optical image arising because of the nature of lenses; the main types are spherical, coma, curvature, and distortion a., and astigmatism of oblique pencils.

optical a., failure of rays from a point source to form a perfect image after traversing an optical system.

spherical a., dioptric a.; a monochromatic a. occurring in refraction at a spherical surface in which the paraxial and peripheral rays focus along the axis at different points.

abetalipoproteinemia (a-ba'tā-lip'o-pro'tēn-e'mĭ-ah). Bassen-Kornzweig syndrome; a disorder characterized by an absence of plasma lipoproteins having a density less than 1.063, presence of acanthocytes in blood, retinal pigmentary degeneration, malabsorption, engorgement of upper intestinal absorptive cells with dietary triglycerides, and neuromuscular abnormalities; autosomal recessive inheritance.

abiosis (ab-ĭ-o'sis) [G. a- priv. + biosis, life]. **1.** Nonviability. **2.** Absence of life. **3.** Abiotrophy.

abiot'ic. Incompatible with life.

abiotrophy (ab-ĭ-ot'ro-fĭ) [G. a- priv. + bios, life, + trophē, nourishment]. Abiosis (3); premature loss of vitality or degeneration of certain cells or tissues, usually of genetic etiology; generic term applied to hereditary degenerative diseases.

abir'ritant. 1. Abirritative; soothing; relieving irritation. **2.** An agent possessing this property.

abirrita'tion [L. ab, from, + irrito, pp. -atus, to irritate]. The diminution or abolition of reflex or other irritability in a part.

abir'ritative. Abirritant (1).

ablate (ab-lāt') [L. ab-latus, taking away]. To remove, or to destroy the function of.

abla'tion [L. see ablate]. Removal of a body part or the destruction of its function, as by a surgical procedure, morbid process, or noxious substance.

ablepharia, ablepharon (a-blef-a'rĭ-ah, a-blef'ă-ron) [G. a- priv. + blepharon, eyelid]. Congenital absence, partial or complete, of the eyelids.

ablepsia, ablepsy (ă-blep'sĭ-ah, ă- blep'sĭ) [G. a- priv. + blepō, to see]. Blindness.

abner'val. Abneural (1); away from a nerve; denoting specifically a current of electricity passing through a muscular fiber in a direction away from the point of entrance of the nerve fiber.

abneural (ab-nu'ral) [L. ab, away from, + G. neuron, nerve]. **1.** Abnerval. **2.** Away from the neural axis.

abnormal'ity [L. ab, from, + norma, rule]. An anomaly, deformity, malformation, or difference from the usual.

abo'rad, abo'ral [L. ab, from, + os(or-), mouth]. In a direction away from the mouth; opposite of orad.

abort [L. aborto, to miscarry]. **1.** To expel an embryo or fetus before it is viable. **2.** To arrest a disease in its earliest stages. **3.** To arrest in growth or development; to cause to remain rudimentary.

abortient (ă-bor'shent). Abortifacient (1).

abortifacient (ă-bor-tĭ-fa'shent) [L. abortus, abortion, + facio, to make]. **1.** Abortient; abortigenic; abortive (3); producing abortion. **2.** An agent that produces abortion.

abortigenic (ă-bor-tĭ-jen'ik) [L. abortus, abortion, + genesis, production]. Abortifacient (1).

abortion (ă-bor'shun). **1.** Expelling an embryo or fetus prior to being viable. **2.** The arrest of any action or process before its normal completion.

criminal a., termination of pregnancy without medical or legal justification.

habitual a., three or more consecutive, spontaneous a.'s at about the same stage of pregnancy.

incomplete a., a. in which part of the products of conception remains in the uterus.

induced a., a. brought on purposefully by drugs or mechanical means.

infected a., a. complicated by sepsis.

missed a., a. in which the fetus dies but is retained in utero for two months or longer.

septic a., an infectious a. complicated by fever, endometritis, and parametritis.

spontaneous a., a. occurring naturally.

therapeutic a., a. induced because of the mother's physical or mental health, or to prevent birth of a deformed child or a child resulting from rape.

abor'tionist. One who performs a.'s, especially criminal a.'s.

abor'tive [L. abortivus]. **1.** Not reaching completion; not fully developed or completed its course. **2.** Rudimentary. **3.** Abortifacient (1).

abor'tus [L.]. The product of an abortion.

abrachia (ă-bra'kĭ-ah) [G. a- priv. + brachiōn, arm]. Congenital absence of arms.

abrachiocephalia (ă-bra′kĭ-o-sĕ-fa′lĭ-ah) [G. *a*- priv. + *brachiōn*, arm, + *kephalē*, head]. Abrachiocephaly.

abrachiocephaly (ă-bra′kĭ-o-sef′ă-li) [G. *a*- priv. + *brachiōn*, arm, + *kephalē*, *head*]. Abrachiocephalia; acephalobrachia; congenital absence of arms and head.

abrade (ă-brād′) [L. *ab-rado*, to scrape off]. **1.** To wear away by mechanical action. **2.** To scrape away the surface layer from a part.

abrasion (ă-bra′zhun) [see abrade]. **1.** An excoriation or circumscribed removal of the superficial layers of skin or mucous membrane. **2.** A scraping away of a portion of the surface. **3.** Grinding; in dentistry, the wearing away of tooth substance.

abra′sive. 1. Causing abrasion. **2.** Any material used to produce abrasion.

abra′siveness. 1. The property of a substance that causes surface wear by friction. **2.** The quality of being able to scratch or abrade another material.

abreaction (ab-re-ak′shun). In freudian psychoanalysis, an episode of emotional release or catharsis associated with the bringing into conscious recollection previously repressed unpleasant experiences.

abruptio placentae (ab-rup′she-o plă-sen′te) [L. to break off]. Premature detachment of a normally situated placenta.

abscess (ab′ses) [L. *abscessus*, a going away]. **1.** A circumscribed collection of pus appearing in acute or chronic, localized infection, and associated with tissue destruction and, frequently, swelling. **2.** A cavity formed by liquefaction necrosis within solid tissue.

  alveolar a., an a. in the dentoalveolar process, either in a lateral periodontal or periapical periodontal position.

  amebic a., tropical a.; an area of liquefaction necrosis of the liver or other organ containing amebae, usually following amebic dysentery.

  appendiceal a., periappendiceal a.; an intraperitoneal a. resulting from extension of infection in acute appendicitis, especially with perforation of the appendix.

  Bezold's a., an a. deep in the neck associated with suppuration in the mastoid tip cells.

  Brodie's a., a chronic a. of bone surrounded by dense fibrous tissue and sclerotic bone.

  cold a., an a. without heat or other usual signs of inflammation.

  collar-button a., shirt-stud a.

  crypt a.'s, a.'s in crypts of Lieberkühn of the large intestinal mucosa; a characteristic feature of ulcerative colitis.

  dentoalveolar a., an a. confined to the dentoalveolar process investing a tooth root.

  diffuse a., a collection of pus not circumscribed by a well defined capsule.

  dry a., the remains of an a. after the pus is absorbed.

  Dubois a.'s, thymic a.'s; small cysts of the thymus containing polymorphonuclear leukocytes but lined by squamous epithelium.

  fecal a., stercoral a.

  gas a., an a. containing gas caused by *Enterobacter aerogenes*, *Escherichia coli*, or other gas-forming microorganisms.

  gummatous a., syphilitic a.; an a. due to the softening and breaking down of a gumma, especially in bone.

  metastatic a., a secondary a. formed, at a distance from the primary focus, as a result of the transportation of pyogenic bacteria by the lymph or blood stream.

  migrating a., wandering a.

  miliary a., one of a number of minute collections of pus, widely disseminated throughout an area or the whole body.

  Munro's a., Munro's *microabscess.*

  Pautrier's a., Pautrier's *microabscess.*

  perforating a., an a. that breaks down tissue barriers to enter adjacent areas.

  periappendiceal a., appendiceal a.

  periarticular a., an a. surrounding a joint, not usually involving it.

  peritonsillar a., quinsy; extension of tonsillar infection beyond the capsule with abscess formation usually above and behind the tonsil.

  phlegmonous a., circumscribed suppuration characterized by intense surrounding inflammatory reaction which produces induration and thickening of the affected area.

  Pott's a., a tuberculous a. of the spine.

  psoas a., an a., usually tuberculous, originating in tuberculous spondylitis and extending through the iliopsoas muscle to the inguinal region.

  pyemic a., septicemic a.; a hematogenous a. resulting from pyemia, septicemia, or bacteremia.

  residual a., an a. recurring at the site of a former a. resulting from persistence of microbes and pus.

  ring a., an acute purulent corneal inflammation in which a central necrotic area is surrounded by an annular girdle of leukocytic infiltration at the corneal periphery, often progressing to panophthalmitis.

  satellite a., an a. with intimate relationship to a parent a.

  septicemic a., pyemic a.

  shirt-stud a., collar-button a.; two a.'s connected by a narrow channel, usually formed by rupture through an overlying fascia.

  stellate a., a star-shaped necrotic area surrounded by epithelioid cells, seen within swollen inguinal lymph nodes in lymphogranuloma venereum.

  stercoral a., fecal a.; a collection of pus and feces.

  stitch a., an a. around a stitch or suture.

  syphilitic a., gummatous a.

  thymic a.'s, Dubois a.'s.

  tropical a., amebic a.

tuberculous a., an a. caused by the tubercle bacillus.

wandering a., migrating a.; an a. occurring at a distance from the primary focus of disease, pus burrowing along fascial planes or other structures.

abscission (ab-sĭ'shun) [L. *ab-scindo,* pp. *-scissus,* to cut away from]. Cutting away.

abscopal (ab-sko'pal, -skop'al). Denoting the remote effect that irradiation of tissue has on nonirradiated tissue.

absence (ab'sens) [L. *absentia*]. Petit mal; petit mal epilepsy; paroxysmal attacks of brief clouding of consciousness that may be unaccompanied (simple a.) or accompanied (complex a.) by other abnormalities.

complex a., paroxysmal impairment of consciousness accompanied by abnormalities such as atonia, automatisms, autonomic phenomena, hypertonicity, myoclonus, retrocursive movements, tussive or sternutatory episodes, and vasomotor changes.

pure a., simple a.

simple a., pure a.; a brief clouding of consciousness accompanied by the abrupt onset of 3/sec spikes and waves.

subclinical a., transient impairment of mentation, without overt manifestations, demonstrable only by psychological testing, and accompanied by an outburst of 3/sec spike and wave complexes.

Absid'ia. A genus of fungi (family Mucoraceae) commonly found in nature; thermophilic species survive in compost piles at temperatures exceeding 45°C and may cause phycomycosis in humans.

absorb (ab-sorb') [L. *ab-sorbeo,* to suck in]. **1.** To take in by absorption. **2.** To reduce the intensity of transmitted light.

absorb'able. Capable of being absorbed.

absorb'ance (*A*). Absorbancy; absorbency; optical density; extinction (2); in spectrophotometry, equal to 2 minus the log of the percentage transmittance of light.

absorb'ancy. Absorbance.

absorbefacient (ab-sor-bĕ-fa'shunt) [L. *ab-sorbeo,* to suck in, + *facio,* to make]. **1.** Causing absorption. **2.** Any substance possessing such quality.

absorb'ency. Absorbance.

absorb'ent. **1.** Absorptive; having the power to absorb, soak up, or take into itself a gas, liquid, light rays, or heat. **2.** Any substance possessing such power.

absorp'tion. Taking in, incorporation, or reception of gases, liquids, light, or heat.

absorp'tive. Absorbent (1).

abstinence (ab'stĭ-nens) [L. *abs- tineo,* to hold back]. Refraining from indulgence in certain foods, drink, or drugs, or from sexual intercourse.

abstraction (ab-strak'shun). **1.** Distillation or separation of the volatile constituents of a substance. **2.** Exclusive mental concentration; absent-mindedness. **3.** Malocclusion in which the teeth or associated structures are lower than their normal occlusal plane. See odontoptosis. **4.** The process of selecting a certain aspect of a concept from the whole.

abter'minal [L. *ab,* from + *terminus,* end]. In a direction away from the end and toward the center; denoting the course of an electrical current in a muscle.

abulia (ă-bu'lĭ-ah) [G. *a-* priv. + *boulē,* will]. Loss or impairment of the ability to perform voluntary actions or to make decisions.

abu'lic. Relating to, or suffering from, abulia.

abuse (ă-būs'). **1.** Misuse, wrong use, especially excessive use, of anything. **2.** Injurious, harmful, or offensive treatment.

abutment (ă-but'ment). In dentistry, a natural tooth or implanted tooth substitute, used for the support or anchorage of a fixed or removable prosthesis.

Ac Actinium; acetate.

a.c. L. *ante cibum,* before meals.

AC/A Accommodative convergence-accommodation *ratio.*

acalculia (ă-kal-ku'lĭ-ah) [G. *a-* priv. + L. *calculo,* to reckon]. A form of aphasia characterized by inability to do mathematical calculations.

acamp'sia [G. *a-* priv. + *kamptō,* to bend]. Stiffening or rigidity of a joint.

acan'tha [G. *akantha,* a thorn. AC-]. A spine or spinous process.

acanthamebiasis (ă-kan-thă-me-bi'ă- sis). Infection by amebae of the genus *Acanthamoeba* that may result in a necrotizing dermal or tissue invasion, or a fulminating and usually fatal primary amebic meningoencephalitis.

Acanthamoeba (ă-kan-thă-me'bah) [G. *akantha,* thorn, spine, + Mod. L. *amoeba*]. A free-living ameba found in soil, sewage, and water, several species of which cause acanthomebiasis.

acanthesthesia (ă-kan-thes-the'zĭ-ah) [G. *akantha,* thorn, + *aisthēsis,* sensation]. Paresthesia in which there is a sensation as of a pinprick.

acan'thion [G. *akantha,* thorn]. The tip of the anterior nasal spine.

acantho- [G. *akantha,* thorn]. Combining form denoting relationship to a spinous process, or meaning spiny or thorny.

Acanthoceph'ala [acantho- + G. *kephalē,* head]. The thorny-headed worms; a phylum of obligatory parasites without an alimentary canal, characterized by an anterior introvertible spiny proboscis; in the adult stage they are parasites of vertebrates, but the larval stage is passed in invertebrates.

acanthocephaliasis (ă-kan'tho-sef-ă-li'ă-sis) Infection with a species of Acanthocephala.

acan'thocheil'onemi'asis. Infection by Acanthocheilonema perstans (Dipetalonema perstans).

Acanthocheilonema (ă-kan'tho-ki-lo-ne'mah) [acantho- + G. *cheilos,* lip, + *nēma,* thread]. A genus of filarial worm parasitic in man, now part of the genus *Dipetalonema.*

acan'thocyte [acantho- + G. *kytos,* cell]. Acanthrocyte; an erythrocyte characterized by multiple spiny cytoplasmic projections and in acanthocytosis.

acan'thocyto'sis. Acanthrocytosis; a rare condition in which the majority of erythrocytes are acanthocytes; a regular feature of abetalipoproteinemia.

acanthoid (ă-kan'thoyd). Spine-shaped.

acantholysis (ak-an-thol'ĭ-sis) [acantho- + G. *lysis,* loosening]. Separation of individual prickle cells from their neighbor, as in conditions such as pemphigus vulgaris and keratosis follicularis.

acanthoma (ak-an-tho'mah) [acantho- + G. *-oma,* tumor]. A tumorous hypertrophy of epidermal squamous cells that may be malignant, benign, or even non-neoplastic.

acanthosis (ak-an-tho'sis) [acantho- + G. *-osis,* condition]. Hyperacanthosis; an increase in the thickness of the prickle cell layer of the epidermis.

  a. ni'gricans, keratosis nigricans; an eruption of velvet warty benign growths and hyperpigmentation occurring in the skin of the axillae, neck, anogenital area, and groins; in adults it is associated with internal malignancy or reticulosis; a benign (juvenile) type occurs in children. See also pseudoacanthosis nigricans.

acanthot'ic. Pertaining to or characteristic of acanthosis.

acan'throcyte. Acanthocyte.

acan'throcyto'sis. Acanthocytosis.

acap'nia [G. *a-* priv. + *kapnos,* smoke]. Absence of carbon dioxide in the blood. See also hypocapnia.

acar'dia [G. *a-* priv. + *kardia,* heart]. Congenital absence of the heart; a condition sometimes occurring in the smaller parasitic member of conjoined twins when its partner monopolizes the placental blood supply.

acariasis (ak'ar-i'ă-sis). Acaridiasis; acarinosis; any disease caused by mites, usually a skin infestation. See also mange; scabies.

acar'icide [Mod. L. *acarus,* a mite, fr. G. *akari* + L. *caedo,* to cut, kill]. **1.** Destructive to acarids, or mites. **2.** An agent having this property.

ac'arid G. *akari,* mite]. A mite of the family Acaridae.

Acar'idae. A family (order Acarina) of exceptionally small mites, usually 0.5 mm or less, abundant in dried fruits and meats, grain, meal, and flour; frequently a cause of severe dermatitis among persons hypersensitized by frequent handling of infested products.

acar'idi'asis. Acariasis.

Acari'na [G. *akari,* a mite]. An order of Arachnida that includes the mites and ticks.

ac'arine. A member of the order Acarina.

acarinosis (ak'ă-rĭ-no'sis) Acariasis.

ac'aroder'mati'tis [G. *akari,* mite, + *derma* (*dermat-*), skin]. A skin inflammation or eruption produced by a mite.

ac'aroid [G. *akari,* mite, + *eidos,* resemblance]. Resembling a mite.

ac'aropho'bia [G. *akari,* mite, + *phobos,* fear]. Morbid fear of small parasites, small particles, or of itching.

Ac'arus [G. *akari,* mite]. A genus of mites (family Acaridae).

  A. folliculo'rum, *Demodex folliculorum.*

  A. scabie'i, *Sarcoptes scabiei.*

  A. triti'ci, *Pediculoides ventricosus.*

acar'yote. Akaryocyte.

acatalasemia (a-kat'ă-la-se'mĭ- ah). Acatalasia; anenzymia catalasia; Takahara's disease; hereditary absence or low levels of catalase in the blood, often manifest by recurrent infection or ulceration of the gums and related oral structures.

acatalasia (a-kat-ă-la'zĭ-ah). Acatalasemia

acatamathesia (ă-kat-ă-mă-the'zĭah) [G. *a-* priv. + *katamathēsis,* a thorough knowledge or understanding]. Loss of the faculty of understanding.

acatapha'sia [G. *a-*priv. + *kataphasis,* affirmation]. Loss of the power to correctly formulate a statement.

acathec'tic. Relating to acathexia.

acathex'ia [G. *a-* priv. + *kathexis,* a holding in]. Abnormal loss of bodily secretions.

acathex'is [G. *a-* priv. + *kathexis,* retention]. A mental disorder in which certain objects or ideas fail to arouse an emotional response in the individual.

acathisia (ă-kă-thiz'ĭ-ah) [G. *a-* priv. + *kathisis,* a sitting]. Akathisia.

accel'erant. Accelerator.

accel'erator [L. *accelerans,* pres. part. of *ac-celero,* to hasten, fr. *celer,* swift]. Accelerant. **1.** Anything that increases rapidity of action or function. **2.** In physiology, a nerve, muscle, or substance that quickens movement or response. **3.** A catalytic agent used to hasten a chemical reaction.

  linear a., a device that produces high energy photons (x-rays) on charged particles for use in radiation therapy.

  proserum prothrombin conversion a. (PPCA), *factor* VII.

  prothrombin a., *factor* V.

  serum a., *factor* VII.

  serum prothrombin conversion a. (SPCA), *factor* VII.

accentuator (ak-sent'u-a-tor) [L. *accentus,* accent, fr. *cano,* to sing]. A substance, such as aniline, the presence of which allows a combination between a tissue or histologic element and a stain that might otherwise be impossible.

acceptor (ak-sep'tor) [L. *ac-cipio,* pp. *-ceptus,* to accept]. A compound that will take up a chemical group from another compound (donor).

accessory (ak-ses'o-rĭ) [L. *accessorius*]. Supernumerary; auxiliary; denoting certain muscles, nerves, glands, etc.

acclima'tion. Acclimatization; physiological adjustment of an individual to a different climate, especially to a change in environmental temperature or altitude.

accommodation (ă-kom′o-da′shun) [L. *ac -commodo*, pp. *-atus*, to adapt, fr. *modus*, a measure]. The act or state of adjustment or adaptation.

absolute a., a. of an eye independent of its fellow.

amplitude of a., the difference in refractivity of the eye at rest and when fully accommodated.

histologic a., change in shape of cells to meet altered physical conditions, as the flattening of cuboidal cells in cysts as a result of pressure.

negative a., adjustment of the lens for distant vision by relaxation of the ciliary muscles.

positive a., a. for near vision by contraction of the ciliary muscles.

range of a., the distance between an object viewed with minimal refractivity of the eye and one viewed with maximal accommodation.

relative a., quantity of a. required for single binocular vision for any specified distance, or for any particular degree of convergence.

accom′modative. Relating to accommodation.

accrementition (ă-kre-men-tish′un) [L. *accresco*, pp. *-cretus*, to increase]. **1.** Reproduction by budding or germination. **2.** Accretion (1).

accre′tio cor′dis. Adhesion of the pericardium to adjacent extracardiac structures.

accretion (ă-kre′shun) [L. *accretio*, fr. *ad*, to, + *crescere*, to grow]. **1.** Accrementition (2); increase by addition to the periphery of material of the same nature as that already present; *e.g.*, the manner of growth of crystals. **2.** In dentistry, foreign material (usually plaque or calculus) collecting on the surface of a tooth or in a cavity. **3.** A growing together.

acel′lular [G. *a*- priv. + L. *cellula*, a small chamber]. Noncellular. **1.** Devoid of cells. **2.** A term applied to unicellular organisms that do not become multicellular and are complete within a single cell unit; frequently applied to protozoans to emphasize their complete organization within a single cell.

acelom (a-se′lom) [G. *a*- priv. + *koilōma*, hollow (celom)]. Acelomate; lacking a true celom or body cavity lined with mesothelium.

acel′omate. Acelom.

acenesthesia (ă-se-nes-the′zĭ-ah) [G. *a*- priv. + *koinos*, common, + *aisthēsis*, feeling]. Absence of the normal sensation of physical existence, or of the consciousness of visceral functioning.

acentric (a-sen′trik) [G. *a*- priv. + *kentron*, center]. Without a center; in genetics, denoting a chromosome fragment without a centromere.

acepha′lia, aceph′alism. Acephaly.

acephalobrachia (ă-sef′al-o-bra′kĭ-ah) [G. *a*- priv. + *kephalē*, head, + *brachiōn*, arm]. Abrachiocephaly.

aceph′alocar′dia [G. *a*- priv. + *kephalē*, head, + *kardia*, heart]. Absence of head and heart in a parasitic conjoined twin.

acephalocheiria, acephalochiria (ă-sef′al-o -ki′rĭ-ah) [G. *a*- priv. + *kephalē*, head, + *cheir*, hand]. Congenital absence of head and hands.

acephalocyst (ă-sef′al-o-sist) [G. *a*- priv. + *kephalē*, head, + *kystis*, bladder]. A hydatid cyst with no daughter cyst; a sterile hydatid.

aceph′alogaste′ria. Congenital absence of head, thorax, and abdomen in a parasitic twin with pelvis and legs only.

aceph′alopo′dia [G. *a*- priv. + *kephalē*, head, + *pous*, foot]. Congenital absence of head and feet.

acephalorrachia (ă-sef′al-o-rak′ĭ- ah) [G. *a*- priv. + *kephalē*, head, + *rhachis*, spine]. Congenital absence of head and spinal column.

aceph′alosto′mia [G. *a*- priv. + *kephalē*, head, + *stoma*, mouth]. Congenital absence of the greater part of the head, with the presence of a mouthlike opening.

aceph′alothora′cia [G. *a*- priv. + *kephalē*, head, + *thorax*, chest]. Congenital absence of head and thorax.

aceph′alous. Headless.

aceph′aly [G. *a*- priv. + *kephalē*, head]. Acephalia; acephalism; absence of a head.

acer′vuline [Mod. L. *acervulus*, a little heap]. Occurring in clusters; aggregated.

acer′vulus [Mod. L. dim. of L. *acervus*, a heap]. Brain *sand*.

acet-, aceto-. Combining forms denoting the two-carbon fragment of acetic acid.

acetabula (as-ĕ-tab′u-lah) Plural of acetabulum.

acetab′ular. Relating to the acetabulum.

ac′etab′ulec′tomy [acetabulum + G. *ektomē*, excision]. Excision of the acetabulum.

ac′etab′uloplas′ty [acetabulum + G. *plassō*, to fashion]. Restorative surgery of the acetabulum.

acetab′ulum, gen. **acetab′uli**, pl. **acetab′ula** [L. a shallow vinegar vessel or cup] [NA]. Cotyloid cavity; cotyle (2); a cup-shaped depression on the external surface of the hip bone, in which the head of the femur fits.

acetal (as′ĕ-tal). Product of the addition of two moles of alcohol to one of an aldehyde.

acetal′dehyde. Acetic aldehyde; ethaldehyde; ethanal; CH_3CHO; an intermediate in yeast fermentation of carbohydrate and in alcohol metabolism.

acetaminophen (ă-set-ă-me′no-fen). *N*-Acetyl-*p*-aminophenol; antipyretic and analgesic.

acetan′ilid. *N*-Phenylacetamide; $C_6H_5NHCOCH_3$; analgesic and antipyretic.

ac′etate (Ac). CH_3–CO–O–; a salt or ester of acetic acid.

acetic acid. Ethanoic acid; CH_3COOH; characteristic component of vinegar; **diluted a. a.** contains 6% w/v of a. a.; **glacial a. a.** contains 99% absolute a. a.

aceto-. See acet-.

acetoace′tic acid. Diacetic acid; CH_3COCH_2COOH; a ketone body formed in excess and appearing in the urine in starvation or diabetes.

acetoacetyl-CoA. Acetoacetylcoenzyme A; intermediate in the oxidation of fatty acids.

ac′etoacetylcoen′zyme A. Acetoacetyl-CoA.

acetohex'amide. 1-[(p-Acetylphenyl)sulfonyl]-3-cyclohexylurea; an oral hypoglycemic agent that stimulates pancreatic insulin secretion.

acetone (as'e-tōn). Dimethylketone; CH_3COCH_3; a compound with solvent properties, abnormal amounts of which occur in urine and blood of diabetics, sometimes imparting an ethereal odor to the urine and breath.

acetone'mia [acetone + G. haima, blood]. Presence of acetone or ketone bodies in relatively large amounts in the blood.

acetonu'ria [acetone + G. ouron, urine]. Excretion in the urine of abnormal amounts of acetone, an indication of incomplete oxidation of large amounts of fat; commonly occurs in diabetic acidosis.

acetyl (as'ē-til). CH_3CO-; an acetic acid molecule from which the hydroxyl group has been removed.

acet'ylase. Any enzyme catalyzing acetylation or deacetylation; usually called acetyltransferases.

acetylation (ă-set-ĭ-la'shun). Formation of an acetyl derivative.

acetylcholine (ACh) (as-ē-til-kō'lēn). $CH_3CO-OCH_2CH_2\overset{+}{N}(CH_3)_3$; the acetic ester of choline, liberated from preganglionic and postganglionic endings of parasympathetic fibers and from preganglionic fibers of the sympathetic nervous system as a result of nerve injuries, whereupon it acts as a neurotransmitter on the effector organ.

acetylcholinesterase (as'ē-til-ko-lin-es'ter -ās). Cholinesterase that hydrolyzes acetylcholine within the central nervous system and at peripheral neuroeffector junctions.

acetyl-CoA. CoAS~COCH_3; acetylcoenzyme A; condensation product of coenzyme A and acetic acid; intermediate in transfer of two-carbon fragment in its entrance into the tricarboxylic acid cycle.

ac'etylcoen'zyme A. Acetyl-CoA.

acet'ylene. HC≡CH; a colorless explosive gas; anesthetic in concentrations of 40 volumes percent.

ac'etylsalicyl'ic acid. Aspirin.

acetyltrans'ferase. Transacetylase; any enzyme transferring acetyl groups from one compound to another.

AcG, ac-g Accelerator globulin.

Ach Abbreviation for acetylcholine.

achalasia (ă-kal-a'-zī-ah) [G. a- priv. + chalasis, a slackening]. Failure to relax; referring especially to visceral openings or sphincter muscles.

    esophageal a., cardiospasm; loss of motor innervation causing an obstruction to develop in the terminal esophagus just proximal to the cardioesophageal junction; the upper esophagus becomes dilated and filled with retained food.

ache (āk). A persistent fixed pain.

acheilia, achilia (ă-ki'lī-ah) [G. a- priv. + cheilos, lip]. Congenital absence of the lips.

acheilous, achilous (ă-ki'lus). Characterized by or relating to acheilia.

acheiria, achiria (ă-ki'rī-ah) [G. a- priv. + cheir, hand]. 1. Congenital absence of the hands. 2.

Anesthesia in, with loss of the sense of possession of, one or both hands; a condition sometimes noted in hysteria.

acheiropody, achiropody (a-ki-rop'o-dī) [G. a- priv. + cheir, hand, + podos, foot]. Congenital absence of the hands and feet.

acheirous, achirous (ă-ki'rus). Characterized by or relating to acheiria.

achilia (ă-ki'lī-ah). Acheilia.

achillobursitis (ă-kil'o-bur-si'tis). Inflammation of a bursa beneath the tendo calcaneus.

achillodynia (ă-kil-o-din'īah) [Achilles (tendon) + G. odynē, pain]. Pain due to achillobursitis.

achillorrhaphy (ă-kil-or'ă-fī) [Achilles (tendon) + G. rhaphē, a sewing]. Suture of the tendo calcaneus.

achillotenotomy (ă-kil'o-ten-ot'o-mī) [Achilles (tendon) + G. tenōn, tendon, + tomē, a cutting]. Achillotomy.

achillotomy (ă-kil-ot'o-mī) [Achilles (tendon) + G. tomē, incision]. Achillotenotomy; division of the tendo calcaneus.

achlorhydria (a-klor-hi'drī-ah) [G. a- priv. + chlorhydric (acid)]. Absence of hydrochloric acid from the gastric juice.

acholia (ă-ko'lī-ah) [G. a- priv. + cholē, bile]. Suppressed secretion of bile.

achol'ic. Without bile.

acholuria (a-ko-lu'rĭah) [G. a- priv. + cholē, bile, + ouron, urine]. Absence of bile pigments from the urine in certain cases of jaundice.

acholuric (a-ko-lu'rik). Without bile in the urine.

achondrogenesis (ă-kon'dro-jen'ē-sis) [G. a- priv., + chondros, cartilage, + genesis, origin]. Dwarfism characterized by various bone aplasias and hypoplasias of the extremities, normal or enlarged skull, and short trunk with delayed ossification of the lower spine; autosomal recessive inheritance.

achondroplasia (ă-kon-dro-pla'zī-ah) [G. a- priv. + chondros, cartilage, + plasis, a molding]. Achondroplasty; osteosclerosis congenita; an abnormality of conversion of cartilage into bone; a type of chondrodystrophy resulting in dwarfism apparent at birth, with short extremities but normal trunk; due to mutation or to autosomal dominant inheritance.

achondroplas'tic. Relating to achondroplasia.

achondroplasty (ă-kon'dro-plas-tī). Achondroplasia.

achromacyte (ă-kro'mă-sit). Achromocyte.

achromasia (ak-ro-ma'sī-ah) [G. achrōmos, colorless]. 1. Pallor associated with the hippocratic facies of extremely severe and chronic illness. 2. Achromia.

achromatic (a-kro-mat'ik) [G. a- priv. + chrōma, color]. 1. Colorless. 2. Not decomposing white light. 3. Not staining readily.

achro'matin. The weakly staining components of the nucleus.

achromatinic (ă-kro-mă-tin'ik). Relating to or containing achromatin.

achromatism (ă-kro'mă-tizm). 1. The quality of being achromatic. 2. Annulment of chromatic aberration by combining glasses of different refractive indexes and different dispersion.

achromatocyte (a-kro-mat'o-sīt). Achromocyte.

achromatolysis (ă-kro-mă-tol'ĭ-sis). Dissolution of the achromatin of a cell or of its nucleus.

achromatophil (ă-kro-mat'o-fil) [G. *a*- priv. + *chrōma*, color, + *philos*, fond]. Achromophil. **1.** Achromophilic; achromophilous; not being colored by the histologic or bacteriologic stains. **2.** A cell or tissue that cannot be stained in the usual way.

achromatopsia, achromatopsy (ă-kro-mă-top'sĭ-ah, ă-kro'mă-top-sī) [G. *a*- priv. + *chrōma*, color, + *opsis*, vision]. Achromatic vision; monochromatism (2); a severe congenital deficiency in color perception, often associated with nystagmus and reduced visual acuity.

achromatosis (ă-kro-mă-to'sis) [G. *a*- priv. + *chrōma*, color]. Achromia.

achromatous (ă-kro'mă-tus). Colorless.

achromaturia (ă-kro-mă-tu'rĭ-ah) [G. *a*- priv. + *chrōma*, color, + *ouron*, urine]. Passage of colorless or very pale urine.

achro'mia [G. *a*-priv. + *chrōma*, color]. Achromasia (2); achromatosis. **1.** Deficiency of natural pigmentation, congenital or acquired. **2.** Lack of capacity to accept stains in cells or tissue.

achro'mic. Colorless.

achromocyte (ă-kro'mo-sīt) [G. *a*- priv. + *chrōma*, color, + *kytos*, hollow (cell)]. A hypochromic, crescent-shaped erythrocyte, probably resulting from artifactual rupture of a red cell with loss of hemoglobin. Also called achromatocyte; achromacyte; ghost or phantom corpuscle.

achro'mophil. Achromatophil.

achromophil'ic, achromoph'ilous. Achromatophil (1).

achylia (ă-ki'lĭ-ah) [G. *a*- priv. + *chylos*, juice]. **1.** Absence of gastric juice or other digestive secretions. **2.** Absence of chyle.

achylous (ă-ki'lus) [G. *achylos*, without juice]. **1.** Lacking in gastric juice or other digestive secretion. **2.** Having no chyle.

acid (as'id) [L. *acidus*, sour]. **1.** A compound yielding hydrogen ion in a polar solvent (*e.g.*, in water); a.'s form salts by replacing all or part of the hydrogen with an electropositive element or radical. An a. containing one displaceable atom of hydrogen in the molecule is called **monobasic**; one containing two such atoms, **dibasic**; and one containing more than two, **polybasic**. **2.** Sour; sharp to the taste. For individual acids, see specific names.

   inorganic a., an a. made up of molecules not containing organic radicals.

   organic a., an a. made up of molecules containing organic radicals.

acidaminuria (as'id-am-ĭ-nu'rĭ-ah). Aminoaciduria.

acide'mia [acid + G. *haima*, blood]. An increase in the hydrogen ion concentration of the blood or a fall below normal in pH.

acid-fast. Denoting bacteria that are not decolorized by acid- alcohol after having been stained.

acid'ify. 1. To render acid. **2.** To become acid.

acid'ity. 1. The state of being acid. **2.** The acid content of a fluid.

acidophil (ă-sid'o-fil) [acid + G. *philos*, fond]. A histolytic structure with an affinity for acid dyes.

acidophilic as'ĭ-do-fil'ik, ă-sid'o-fil-ik). Oxychromatic; having an affinity for acid dyes.

acido'sis [acid + G. *-ōsis*, condition]. A state characterized by actual or relative decrease of alkali in body fluids in proportion to the acid content, the pH of body fluids may be normal or decreased.

   compensated a., a. in which the pH of body fluids is normal due to compensation by respiratory or renal mechanisms.

   diabetic a., decreased pH and bicarbonate concentration in the body fluids caused by accumulation of ketone bodies in diabetes mellitus.

   metabolic a., decreased pH and bicarbonate concentration of the body fluids caused either by the accumulation of excess acids stronger than carbonic acid or by abnormal losses of fixed base from the body.

   renal tubular a., a clinical syndrome characterized by inability to excrete acid urine and by low plasma bicarbonate and high plasma chloride concentrations, often with hypokalemia.

   respiratory a., a. caused by retention of carbon dioxide, due to inadequate pulmonary ventilation or hypoventilation, with decrease in blood pH unless compensated by renal retention of bicarbonate.

acid'ulous. Acid or sour.

acidu'ria [acid + G. *ouron*, urine]. **1.** Excretion of an acid urine. **2.** Excretion of an abnormal amount of any specified acid. Individual types of a. are listed by specific name.

acidu'ric [acid + L. *duro*, to endure]. Pertaining to bacteria that tolerate an acid environment.

acinar (as'ĭ-nar). Acinic; pertaining to the acinus.

acini (as'ĭ-ne). Plural of acinus.

acinic (ă-sin'ik). Acinar.

acin'iform [L. *acinus*, grape, + *forma*, shape]. Acinous.

ac'ini'tis. Inflammation of an acinus.

ac'inose. Acinous.

acinous (as'ĭ-nus). Aciniform; acinose; resembling an acinus or grape-shaped structure.

acinus, gen. and pl. **acini** (as'ĭ-nus, -ne) [L. berry, grape] [NA]. One of the minute grape-shaped secretory portions of an acinous gland. See also alveolus.

   liver a., the area of liver parenchyma that has as its central axis a terminal branch of the portal vein, hepatic artery, and bile duct; composed of segments of several hepatic lobules.

   pulmonary a., that part of the airway consisting of a terminal bronchiole and all of its branches.

ac'lasis [G. *a-* priv. + *klasis,* a breaking away, a fragment]. A state of continuity between normal and abnormal tissue.

   diaphysial a., hereditary multiple *exostoses.*

aclas'tic [G. *a-* priv. + *klastos,* broken in pieces]. Nonrefractive; not refracting the rays of light.

acleistocardia (ă-klīs-to-kar'dī-ah) [G. *a-* priv. + *kleistos,* closed, + *kardia,* heart]. Patency of the foramen ovale of the heart.

acmesthesia (ak-mes-the'zī-ah) [G. *acmē,* point, + *aisthēsis,* sensation]. **1.** Sensitivity to pinprick. **2.** A cutaneous sensation of a sharp point.

acne (ak'ne) [probably a corruption (or copyist's error) of G. *akmē,* point of efflorescence]. An inflammatory follicular, papular, and pustular eruption involving the sebaceous apparatus.

   chlorine a., chloracne.

   a. congloba'ta, severe cystic a., characterized by cystic lesions, abscesses, communicating sinuses, and thickened, nodular scars.

   cystic a., a. in which the predominant lesions are cysts and deep-seated scars.

   a. erythemato'sa, rosacea.

   a. indura'ta, deeply seated a., with large papules and pustules, large scars, and hypertrophic scars.

   a. kerato'sa, an eruption of papules consisting of horny plugs projecting from the hair follicles, accompanied by inflammation.

   a. medicamento'sa, acneform a. caused or exacerbated by several classes of drugs, *e.g.,* antiepileptic, halogens, steroids, tuberculostatic.

   a. papulo'sa, a. vulgaris in which the papular lesions predominate.

   a. puncta'ta, a condition that resembles chloracne in that black central comedones are present in all the lesions.

   a. pustulo'sa, a. vulgaris in which the pustular lesions predominate.

   a. rosa'cea, rosacea.

   a. variolifor'mis, a pyogenic infection involving follicles occurring chiefly on the forehead and temples; involution of the umbilicated and crusting lesions is followed by scar formation.

   a. vulga'ris, an eruption, predominantly of the face, upper back, and chest, comprised of comedones, cysts, papules, and pustules on an inflammatory base; occurs primarily during puberty and adolescence.

ac'neform. Acneiform; resembling acne.

acnegenic (ak-ne-jen'ik). Causing or exacerbating lesions of acne.

acneiform (ak-ne'ĭ-form). Acneform.

ac'onite. The dried root of *Aconitum napellus* (monkshood or wolfsbane) containing a powerful and rapid acting poison, aconitine.

cis-aconitic acid. Dehydration product of citric acid; intermediate in the tricarboxylic acid cycle.

acon'itine. Acetylbenzoylaconine; the poisonous active principle (alkaloid) of aconite.

acorea (ă-ko-re'ah) [G. *a-* priv. + *korē,* pupil]. Congenital absence of the pupil.

acousmatamnesia (ă-kooz-mă-tam-ne'sī-ah) [G. *akousma,* something heard, + *amnēsia,* forgetfulness]. A loss of memory for sounds.

acoustic (ă-koos'tik). Relating to hearing or the perception of sound.

acoustics (ă-koos'tiks) [G. *akoustikos,* relating to hearing]. The science concerned with sounds and their perception.

ACP Acyl carrier protein.

acquired (ă-kwīrd') [L. *ac-quiro* (*adq-*), to obtain]. Denoting a disease, predisposition, etc., that is not congenital but has developed after birth.

acquisition (ak'wĭ-zish'un). In psychology, the empirical demonstration of an increase in the strength of the conditioned response in successive trials of pairing the conditioned and unconditioned stimulus.

acral (ak'ral) [G. *akron,* extremity]. Relating to or affecting peripheral parts, *e.g.,* limbs, fingers, ears.

acra'nia [G. *a-* priv. + *kranion,* skull]. Congenital complete or partial absence of the skull.

acra'nial. Relating to acrania.

acrid (ak'rid) [L. *acer* (*acr-*), pungent]. Sharp; pungent; biting; irritating.

ac'ridine. Dibenzo[*b,e*]pyridine; a dye, dye intermediate, and antiseptic precursor derived from coal tar and irritating to skin and mucous membranes.

acrit'ical [G. *a-* priv. + *kritikos,* critical]. **1.** Not critical; not marked by crisis. **2.** Indeterminate, especially concerning prognosis.

acro- [G. *akron,* extremity, *akros,* extreme]. A combining form denoting extreme, extremity, tip, end, peak, topmost.

acroagnosis (ak'ro-ag-no'sis). [acro- + G. *agnōsia,* a not knowing]. Absence of acrognosis or of limb sensibility.

acroanesthesia (ak'ro-an-es-the'zī-ah) [acro- + G. *an-*priv. + *aisthēsis* sensation]. Anesthesia of one or more of the extremities.

acroataxia (ak'ro-ă-tak'sī-ah) [acro- + ataxia]. Ataxia affecting the distal portion of the extremities: hands and fingers, feet, and toes, in contrast to proximoataxia.

acroblast (ak'ro-blast) [acro- + G. *blastos,* germ]. A component of the developing spermatid, composed of numerous Golgi elements and containing the proacrosomal granules.

acrobrachycephaly (ak'ro-brak-ĭ-sef'ă-lĭ) [acro- + G. *brachys,* short, + *kephale,* head]. A type of craniosynostosis in which there is premature closure of the coronal suture, resulting in abnormally short anteroposterior diameter of the skull.

acrocepha'lia. Oxycephaly.

acrocephal'ic. Oxycephalic.

acrocephalopolysyndactyly (ak'ro-sef'al-o-pol'ĭ-sin-dak'tĭ-lĭ). Carpenter's syndrome; congenital malformation in which oxycephaly, brachysyndactyly of hand, and preaxial polydactyly of feet are associated with mental retardation.

acrocephalosyndactyly (ak'ro-sef'al-o-sin-dak'tĭ-lĭ) [acrocephaly + G. *syn*, together, + *daktylos*, finger]. Acrocephalosyndactylia; acrocephalosyndactylism; acrodysplasia; a congenital syndrome characterized by peaked head, due to premature closure of skull sutures, associated with fusion or webbing of digits; autosomal dominant inheritance.

   type I a., Apert's syndrome; a. with the second through fifth digits fused into one mass with a common nail; often accompanied by moderately severe acne vulgaris of the forearms; autosomal dominant inheritance.

   type II a., Apert-Crouzon syndrome; a. with facial characteristics of Crouzon disease, with extremely hypoplastic maxilla; fusion of digits is less severe, with thumb and fifth finger usually separate; autosomal dominant inheritance.

   type III a., Chotzen syndrome; mild acrocephaly, asymmetry of the skull, and soft tissue syndactyly of the second and third fingers and toes, often with other minor bony abnormalities; autosomal dominant inheritance.

   type V a., Pfeiffer syndrome; a. with broad short thumbs and great toes, often with duplication (polydactyly) of the great toes and variable syndactyly of other digits; autosomal dominant inheritance.

acroceph'alous. Oxycephalic.

acrocephaly (ak'ro-sef'ă-lĭ) [acro- + G. *kephalē*, head]. Oxycephalic.

acrochordon (ak-ro-kor'don) [acro- + G. *chordē*, cord]. Skin *tag*.

acrocyanosis (ak'ro-si-an-o'sis) [acro- + G. *kyanos*, blue, + *-osis*, condition]. A circulatory disorder in which the hands, and less commonly the feet, are persistently cold, blue, and sweaty; milder forms are closely allied to chilblains.

ac'rocyanot'ic. Characterized by acrocyanosis.

ac'rodermati'tis [acro- + G. *derma*, skin, + *-itis*, inflammation]. Inflammation of the skin of the extremities.

   a. chron'ica atroph'icans, a gradually progressive dermatitis appearing first on the feet, hands, elbows or knees, and comprised of indurated, erythematous plaques that become atrophic, giving a tissue-paper appearance of the involved sites.

   a. contin'ua, a. perstans; dermatitis repens; Hallopeau's disease (1); a sterile pustular eruption of the fingers and toes, variously attributed to dyshidrosis, pustular psoriasis, and bacterial infection.

   a. enteropath'ica, a genetic malabsorption (zinc) defect, commencing as a skin eruption on an extremity or around one of the orifices of the body, followed by loss of hair and diarrhea or other gastrointestinal disturbances.

   a. per'stans, a. continua.

ac'rodermato'sis [acro- + G. *derma*, skin, + *-osis*, condition]. Any cutaneous affection involving the more distal portions of the extremities.

acrodolichomelia (ak'ro-dol'ĭ-ko-me'lĭ-ă) [acro- + G. *dolichos*, long, + *melos*, limb]. Abnormal growth of the hands and feet.

acrodynia (ak-ro-din'ĭ-ah) [acro- + G. *adynē*, pain]. **1.** A disease of infants caused almost exclusively by mercury poisoning and manifested by erythema of the extremities, chest, and nose, polyneuritis, and gastrointestinal symptoms. Also known as erythredema; pink or Swift's disease; dermatopolyneuritis. **2.** In adults, a syndrome comprised by anorexia, photophobia, sweating, and tachycardia, associated with mercury ingestion.

acrodysplasia (ak'ro-dis-pla'zĭ-ah) [acro- + dysplasia]. Acrocephalosyndactyly.

acroesthesia (ak-ro-es-the'zĭ-ah) [acro- + G. *aisthēsis*, sensation]. **1.** Extreme degree of hyperesthesia. **2.** Hyperesthesia of one or more of the extremities.

acrogeria (ak-ro-je'rĭ-ah) [acro- + G. *gerōn*, old]. A congenital reduction or loss of subcutaneous fat and collagen of the hands and feet, giving the appearance of premature senility.

acrognosis (ak-rog-no'sis) [acro- + G. *gnōsis*, knowledge]. Cenesthesia in relation to the extremities; sensory perception of the limbs and their several parts.

acrokeratoelastoidosis (ak'ro-ker'ă-to-e-las-toy-do'-sis). Familial hyperkeratotic yellow nodules of the palms and soles, with disorganization of elastic fibers.

acrokerato'sis verruciform'is [acro- + keratosis; L. *verruca*, a wart, + *forma*, form]. A genodermatosis, probably related to keratosis follicularis, characterized by warty excrescences of the hands and feet.

acrokinesia (ak'ro-ki'ne-zĭ-ah). Acrocinesia.

ac'romegal'ic. Pertaining to acromegaly.

acromegaly (ak'ro-meg'al-ĭ) [acro- + G. *megas*, large]. A disorder marked by progressive enlargement of the head and face, hands and feet, and thorax, due to excessive secretion of growth hormone by the anterior lobe of the pituitary gland.

acromelalgia (ak-ro-mel-al'jĭ-ah) [acro- + G. *melos*, limb, + *algos*, pain]. A vasomotor neurosis marked by redness, pain, and swelling of the fingers and toes, headache, and vomiting; probably the same as erythromelalgia.

acromel'ic [acro- + G. *melos*, limb]. Affecting the terminal part of a limb.

acrometagenesis (ak'ro-met-ă-jen'ĕ- sis) [acro- + G. *meta*, beyond, + *genesis*, origin]. Abnormal development of the extremities resulting in deformity.

acro'mial. Relating to the acromion.

acro'mioclavic'ular. Scapuloclavicular (1); relating to the acromion and the clavicle; denoting the articulation between the clavicle and the scapula and its ligaments.

acro'miocor'acoid. Coracoacromial.

acro'miohu'meral. Relating to the acromion and the humerus.

acro'mion [G. *akrōmion*, fr. *akron*, tip, + *ōmos*, shoulder] [NA]. Acromial process; the lateral end of the spine of the scapula which projects as a broad flattened process overhanging the glenoid fossa, articulates with the clavicle, and gives attachment to part of the deltoid and of the trapezius muscles.

acro′mioscap′ular. Relating to the acromion and the scapula.

acro′miothora′cic. Thoracoacromial; relating to the acromion and the thorax.

acrom′phalus [acro- + G. *omphalos,* umbilicus]. Abnormal projection of the umbilicus.

acromyotonia (ak′ro-mi-o-to′nĭ-ah) [acro- + G. *mys,* muscle, + *tonos,* tension]. Acromyotonus; myotonia affecting the extremities only, resulting in spasmodic deformity of the hand or foot.

acromyot′onus. Acromyotonia.

acroneurosis (ak′ro-nu-ro′sis). Any neuropathy, usually vasomotor in nature, of the extremities.

acro-osteolysis (ak′ro-os-te-ol′ĭ-sis). A congenital condition manifested by palmar and plantar ulcerating lesions with osteolysis; a. can be acquired by exposure to vinyl chloride.

acropachyderma (ak′ro-pak-ĭ-der′mah) [acro- + G. *pachys,* thick, + *derma,* skin]. Thickening of the skin of the face, scalp, and extremities together with clubbing of the fingers and deformities of the limb bones.

ac′roparal′ysis. Paralysis of one or more extremities.

acroparesthesia (ak′ro-păr-es-the′zĭ-ah) [acro- + *paresthesia*]. **1.** Paresthesia (numbness, tingling, and other abnormal sensations) of one or more of the extremities. **2.** An extreme degree of paresthesia.

acrop′athy [acro- + G. *pathos,* disease]. Hereditary clubbing of the digits without an associated progressive disease; autosomal dominant inheritance.

acropho′bia [acro- + G. *phobos,* fear]. A morbid dread of heights.

ac′roscleroder′ma [acro- + G. *sklēros,* hard, + *derma,* skin]. Acrosclerosis.

acrosclerosis (ak′ro-sklē-ro′sis). Acroscleroderma; sclerodactyly; stiffness and tightness of the skin of the fingers, with atrophy of the soft tissue and osteoporosis of the distal phalanges of the hands and feet; a form of progressive systemic sclerosis occurring with Raynaud's phenomenon.

acrosome (ak′ro-sōm) [acro- + G. *soma,* body]. Acrosomal *cap.*

acrot′ic [G. *a-* priv. + *krotos,* a striking]. Denoting acrotism.

ac′rotism [G. *a-* priv. + *krotos,* a striking]. Absence or imperceptibility of the pulse.

acrotrophoneurosis (ak′ro-trof′o-nu-ro′sis). A trophoneurosis of one or more of the extremities.

ACTH Adrenocorticotropic *hormone.*

    big ACTH, a form of ACTH produced by certain tumors; it is a larger and more acidic molecule than, is not immunochemically distinguishable from, and does not exert any of the biological effects characteristic of little ACTH.

    little ACTH, term coined to denote conventional ACTH when contrasted with big ACTH.

actin (ak′tin). One of the protein components into which actomyosin can be split; exists in a fibrous form (F-actin) or a globular form (G-actin).

actin′ic [G. *aktis* (*aktin-*), a ray]. Relating to the chemically active rays of the electromagnetic spectrum.

actin′ium [G. *aktis,* a ray]. An element, symbol Ac, atomic no. 89, that possesses no stable isotopes and exists in nature only as a disintegration product of uranium and thorium.

actino- [G. *aktis* (*aktin-*), a ray, beam]. A combining form meaning a ray, as of light; applied to any form of radiation or to any structure with radiating parts. See also *radio-.*

ac′tinodermati′tis [actino- + G. *derma,* skin, + *-itis,* inflammation]. **1.** Inflammation of the skin produced by exposure to sunlight. **2.** Adverse reaction of skin to radiation therapy.

Actinomyces (ak′tĭ-no-mi′sēz) [actino- + G. *mykēs,* fungus]. A genus of nonmotile, nonsporeforming, anaerobic to facultatively anaerobic bacteria (family Actinomycetaceae); pathogenic for man and/or other animals; type species is *A. bovis.*

    A. bo′vis, a species causing actinomycosis in cattle.

    A. israe′lii, a species causing human actinomycosis and, occasionally, infections in cattle.

Actinomycetaceae (ak′tĭ-no-mi′se-ta′se-e). A family of nonsporeforming, nonmotile, ordinarily facultatively anaerobic bacteria (order Actinomycetales) containing Gram-positive, non-acid fast, predominantly diphtheroid cells that tend to form branched filaments.

Actinomycetales (ak′tĭ-no-mi′se-ta′lēz). An order of bacteria consisting of moldlike, rod-shaped, clubbed or filamentous forms with decided tendency to true branching.

actinomycete (ak′tĭ-nō-mi′sēt). A member of the genus *Actinomyces.*

actinomy′cin. A group of antibiotic agents isolated from several species of *Streptomyces* (originally *Actinomyces*) that are active against Gram-positive bacteria, fungi, and neoplasms.

actinomycoma (ak′tĭ-no-mi-ko′mah) [actino- + G. *mykēs,* fungus, + *-oma,* tumor]. A swelling caused by an actinomycete.

ac′tinomyco′sis [actino- + G. *mykēs,* fungus, + *-osis,* condition]. A disease primarily of cattle and man, caused by *Actinomyces bovis* in cattle and by *A. israelii* and *Arachnia propionica* in man, that produces chronic destructive abscesses or granulomas. In man, a. commonly affects the cervicofacial area, abdomen, or thorax; in cattle, the lesion is commonly found in the mandible.

ac′tinomycot′ic. Relating to actinomycosis.

ac′tinother′apy. In dermatology, ultraviolet light therapy.

action (ak′shun) [L. *actio,* to do]. **1.** Performance of any of the vital functions, the manner of such performance, or the result of the same. **2.** Exertion of any force or power, physical or chemical.

cumulative a., cumulative *effect.*

sparing a., the manner in which a nonessential nutritive component, by its presence in the diet, lowers the requirement for an essential component.

specific a., a. of a drug or a method of treatment which has a direct and especially curative effect upon a disease.

specific dynamic a. (SDA), increase of heat production caused by the ingestion of food, especially of protein.

ac'tivator. 1. That which renders another substance active or that accelerates a process or reaction. **2.** The fragment, produced by chemical cleavage of a proactivator that induces the enzymic activity of another substance.

activ'ity. 1. In electroencephalography, the presence of neurogenic electrical energy. **2.** In physical chemistry, an ideal concentration for which the law of mass action will apply perfectly.

blocking a., the phenomenon of repression or elimination of electrical activity in the brain because of the arrival of a sensory stimulus.

insulin-like a. (ILA), a measure of substances, usually in plasma, that exert biologic effects similar to those of insulin in various bioassays.

optical a., the ability of a compound in solution to rotate the plane of polarized light either clockwise or counterclockwise.

plasma renin a. (PRA), estimation of renin in plasma by measuring the rate of formation of angiotensin I or II.

specific a., radioactivity per unit mass of the stated element or compound.

ac'tomy'osin. A protein complex composed of the globulin myosin and actin in the micellae of the muscle fiber; the essential contractile substance of muscle.

acuity (ă-ku'ĭ-tĭ) [thr. Fr. fr. L. *acuo,* pp. *acutus,* sharpen]. Sharpness, clearness, distinctness, especially in vision.

acu'leate [L. *aculeātus,* pointed, fr. *acus,* needle]. Pointed; covered with sharp spines.

acu'minate [L. *acumino,* pp. *-atus,* to sharpen]. Pointed; tapering to a point.

ac'upuncture [L. *acus,* needle, + puncture]. An Oriental procedure in which specific areas associated with peripheral nerves are pierced with fine needles to produce surgical anesthesia, relieve pain, and promote therapy.

acute (ă-kūt') [L. *acutus,* sharp]. **1.** Of short and sharp course, not chronic; said of a disease. **2.** Sharp; pointed at the end.

acyanot'ic. Characterized by absence of cyanosis.

acyl (as'il). An organic radical derived from an organic acid by the removal of the carboxylic hydroxyl group.

acylam'idase. Amidase.

ac'ylase. Amidase.

acyl·CoA. Acylcoenzyme A; $RCH_2CO{\sim}SCoA$; condensation product of a carboxylic acid and coenzyme A, and metabolic intermediate of importance, notably in the oxidation of fat.

acylcoenzyme A (as'il-ko-en'zīm). Acyl-CoA.

ac'yltrans'ferases. Transacylases; enzymes catalyzing the transfer of an acyl group from an acyl-CoA to various acceptors.

acys'tia [G. *a-* priv. + *kystis,* bladder]. Congenital absence of the urinary bladder.

ad- [L. *ad,* to]. Prefix denoting increase, adherence, or motion toward, and sometimes with an intensive meaning.

-ad [L. *ad,* to]. Suffix in anatomical nomenclature having the significance of the English -ward; denoting toward or in the direction of.

adactyl'ia, adac'tylism. Adactyly.

adac'tylous. Without fingers or toes.

adactyly (a-dak'tĭ-lĭ) [G. *a-* priv. + *daktylos,* digit]. Adactylia; adactylism; congenital absence of fingers or toes.

adamantino'ma. Ameloblastoma.

adaman'toblast Ameloblast.

adaman'toblasto'ma. Ameloblastoma.

adamanto'ma. Ameloblastoma.

Adam's apple. Laryngeal *prominence.*

adaptation (ad-ap-ta'shun) [L. *ad-apto,* pp. *-atus,* to adjust]. **1.** Acquisition of modifications fitting a plant or animal to life in a new environment or under new conditions. **2.** An advantageous change in function or constitution of an organ or tissue to meet new conditions. **3.** Adjustment of the pupil and retina to varying degrees of illumination. **4.** A property of certain receptors through which they become less responsive or cease to respond to repeated or continued stimuli the intensity of which is kept constant. **5.** The fitting, condensing, or contouring of a restorative material, foil, or shell to a tooth or cast so as to be in close contact.

dark a., scotopic a.; the adjustment of the eye occurring under reduced illumination in which the sensitivity to light is greatly increased.

light a., photopic a.; the adjustment of the eye occurring under increased illumination in which the sensitivity to light is reduced.

photopic a., light a.

retinal a., adjustment of the eye to the degree of illumination.

scotopic a., dark a.

adaptom'eter. A device for determining the course of ocular dark adaptation and for measuring the minimum light threshold.

ad'dict. A person who is habituated to a substance or practice, especially one considered harmful.

addiction (ad-dik'shun) [L. *ad-dico,* pp. *-dictus,* consent]. Habitual psychological and physiological dependence on a substance or practice which is beyond voluntary control.

additive (ad'ĭ-tĭv). A substance not essentially part of a material but that is deliberately added to fulfill some specific purpose.

adduct (ă-dukt) [L. *ad-duco*, pp. *-ductus*, to bring toward]. **1.** To draw toward the median line. **2.** An addition product, or complex, or one part of the same.

adduc'tion. 1. Movement of a limb toward the median line, or beyond it. **2.** Monocular rotation (duction) of the eye toward the nose. **3.** A position resulting from such movement.

adduc'tor. A muscle that draws a part toward the median line.

adelomorphous (ă-del-o-mor'fus) [G. *adēlos*, uncertain, not clear, + *morphē*, shape]. Of not clearly defined form.

aden-. See adeno-.

adenal'gia [aden- + G. *algos*, pain]. Adenodynia; pain in a gland.

ad'enase. Adenine deaminase; see deaminases.

aden'dric. Adendritic.

adendrit'ic [G. *a-* priv. + *dendron*, tree]. Adendric; without dendrites.

adenec'tomy [aden- + G. *ektomē*, excision]. Excision of a gland.

ad'enecto'pia [aden- + G. *ek*, out of, + *topos*, place]. Presence of a gland elsewhere than in its normal anatomical position.

adenemphraxis (ad'ĕ-nem-frak'sis) [aden- + G. *emphraxis*, stoppage]. Obstruction to the discharge of a glandular secretion.

aden'iform. Adenoid (1).

ad'enine. 6-Aminopurine; a major purine found in both RNA and DNA, and also in various free nucleotides of importance to the body.

  a. deoxyribonucleotide, deoxyadenylic acid.

  a. nucleotide, adenylic acid.

adeni'tis [aden- + *-itis*, inflammation]. Inflammation of a lymph node or of a gland.

adeniza'tion. Conversion into glandlike structure.

adeno-, aden- [G. *adēn*, gland]. Combining forms denoting relation to a gland.

adenoacanthoma (ad'ĕ-no-ak-an-tho'mah). Adenoid squamous cell carcinoma; a malignant neoplasm consisting chiefly of glandular epithelium (adenocarcinoma), usually well differentiated, with foci of metaplasia to squamous (or epidermoid) neoplastic cells.

adenoameloblastoma (ad'ĕ-no-am'el-o-blast-o'mah). Ameloblastic adenomatoid tumor; adenomatoid odontogenic tumor; a benign tumor, usually in the maxilla of young people, composed of ducts lined by cuboidal or columnar cells.

ad'enoblast [adeno- + G. *blastos*, germ]. A proliferating embryonic cell with the potential to form glandular parenchyma.

adenocarcinoma (ad'ĕ-no-kar'sĭ-no'mah) Glandular cancer or carcinoma; a malignant neoplasm of epithelial cells in glandular or glandlike pattern.

  acinic cell a., an a. arising from secreting cells of a racemose gland, particularly the salivary glands.

  papillary a., an a. containing finger-like processes of vascular connective tissue covered by neoplastic epithelium, projecting into cysts or the cavity of glands or follicles.

adenocellulitis (ad'ĕ-no-sel'u-li'tis). Inflammation of a gland and of the adjacent cellular tissue.

adenochondroma (ad'ĕ-no-kon-dro'mah) [adeno- + G. *chondros*, cartilage, + *-oma*, tumor]. Pulmonary *hamartoma*.

ad'enocysto'ma Adenoma in which the neoplastic glandular epithelium forms cysts.

ad'enocyte [adeno- + G. *kytos*, a hollow (cell)]. A gland cell.

adenodynia (ad'ĕ-no-din'ĭah) [adeno- + G. *odynē*, pain]. Adenalgia.

ad'enofibro'ma. A benign neoplasm composed of glandular and fibrous tissues.

ad'enofi'bromyo'ma. Adenomatoid *tumor.*

ad'enofibro'sis. Sclerosing *adenosis.*

adenogenous (ad-en-oj'en-us) Having an origin in glandular tissue.

adenohypophysial (ad'ĕ-no-hi-po-fiz'ĭal). Relating to the adenohypophysis.

adenohypophysis (ad'ĕ-no-hi-pof'ĭsis) [NA]. Official alternative name for *lobus anterior hypophyseos.*

ad'enoid [adeno- + G. *eidos*, appearance]. **1.** Adeniform; lymphoid (2); glandlike; of glandular appearance. **2.** See adenoids.

ad'enoidec'tomy [adenoid + G. *ektomē*, excision]. Surgical removal of adenoid growths in the nasopharynx.

ad'enoidi'tis. Inflammation of nasopharyngeal lymphoid tissue.

ad'enoids. Adenoid disease (1); hypertrophy of the pharyngeal tonsil resulting from chronic inflammation.

adenolymphocele (ad'ĕ-no-lim'fo-sĕl) [adeno- + L. *lympha*, spring water, + G. *kēlē, tumor*]. Cystic dilation of a lymph node following obstruction of the efferent lymphatic vessels.

ad'enolympho'ma. Papillary cystadenoma lymphomatosum; Warthin's tumor; a benign glandular tumor usually arising in the parotid gland and composed of two rows of eosinophilic epithelial cells, which are often cystic and papillary, together with a lymphoid stroma.

adenol'ysis [adeno- + G. *lysis*, destruction]. Enzymatic destruction or dissolution of glandular tissue.

adeno'ma [adeno- + G. *-oma*, tumor]. An ordinarily benign neoplasm of epithelial tissue in which the tumor cells form glands or glandlike structures in the stroma.

  acidophil a., eosinophil a.

  adnexal a., an a. arising in, or forming structures resembling, skin appendages.

  apocrine a., papillary *hidradenoma.*

  basophil a., pituitary basophil a.

bronchial a., a slowly growing benign, or malignant but slowly progressing, polypoid epithelial tumor of bronchial mucosa; of two histological types, the carcinoid and the cylindromatous.

chromophil a., a pituitary basophil or an eosinophil a.

chromophobe a., a tumor of the chromophobe cells of the anterior pituitary body.

eosinophil a., acidophil a.; a tumor of the eosinophilic chromophil cells of the anterior pituitary body, associated with gigantism and acromegaly.

papillary cystic a., an a. in which the lumens of the acini are frequently distended by fluid, and the neoplastic epithelial elements tend to form irregular, fingerlike projections.

papillary a. of large intestine, villous a.

pituitary basophil a., basophil a.; a tumor of the basophilic cells of the anterior pituitary body, associated with Cushing's syndrome.

sebaceous a., a benign tumor of sebaceous tissue, having a more progressive growth and less mature structure than in sebaceous gland hyperplasia.

a. seba'ceum, a hamartoma occurring on the face, composed of fibrovascular tissue and appearing as an aggregation of red or yellow papules which may be associated with tuberous sclerosis.

villous a., papillary a. of the large intestine; usually a solitary sessile, often large, tumor of colonic mucosa composed of mucinous epithelium covering delicate vascular projections.

adeno'matoid Resembling an adenoma.

adenomato'sis Development of multiple glandular overgrowths.

familial polyendocrine a., the presence of functioning tumors in more than one endocrine gland, commonly the pancreatic islands and parathyroid glands, often associated with peptic ulcers and gastric hypersecretion (Zollinger-Ellison syndrome); dominant inheritance.

pulmonary a., a neoplastic diesase in which the alveoli and distal bronchi are filled with mucus and mucus secreting columnar epithelial cells; characterized by abundant, extremely tenacious sputum, chills, fever, cough, dyspnea, and pleuritic pain.

adeno'matous. Relating to adenoma, and to some types of glandular hyperplasia.

adenomere (ad'ē-no-mēr) [adeno- + G. *meros*, part]. A structural unit in the parenchyma of a developing gland.

ad'enomyo'ma. A benign neoplasm of muscle (usually smooth muscle) with glandular elements; occurs most frequently in uterus and uterine ligaments.

ad'enomy'osarco'ma. Wilms *tumor.*

ad'enomyo'sis. The ectopic occurence or diffuse implantation of adenomatous tissue in muscle (usually smooth muscle).

adenop'athy [adeno- + G. *pathos*, suffering]. Swelling of or abnormal enlargement in the lymph nodes.

adenopharyngitis (ad'ē-no-fār-in-ji'tis). Inflammation of the adenoids and the pharyngeal lymphoid tissue.

ad'enophleg'mon (ad'ē-no-fleg'mon) [adeno- + G. *phlegmonē*, inflammation]. Acute inflammation of a gland and the adjacent connective tissue.

adenosalpingitis (ad'ē-no-sal-pin-ji'tis). *Salpingitis isthmica nodosa.*

ad'enosarco'ma. A malignant neoplasm arising simultaneously or consecutively in mesodermal tissue and glandular epithelium of the same part.

aden'osine (A, Ado). Ribofuranosyladenine; a condensation product of adenine and D-ribose; a nucleoside found among the hydrolysis products of all nucleic acids and of the various adenine nucleotides.

a. diphosphate, adenosine 5'-diphosphate.

a. monophosphate (AMP), adenylic acid, specifically adenosine 5'-phosphate.

a. phosphate, adenylic acid, specifically adenosine 5'-phosphate.

a. triphosphatase (ATPase), an enzyme in muscle (myosin) and elsewhere that catalyzes the release of the terminal phosphate group of adenosine triphosphate.

a. triphosphate, adenosine 5'-triphosphate.

adenosine 3',5'-cyclic phosphate. An activator of phosphorylase kinase, formed in muscle from ATP by adenylate cyclase and broken down to 5'-AMP by a phosphodiesterase; sometimes referred to as "the second messenger." Also called cyclic adenylic acid, cyclic phosphate, cyclic AMP.

adenosine 5'-diphosphate (ADP). Adenosine diphosphate; a condensation product of adenosine with pyrophosphoric acid; formed from ATP by the hydrolysis of the terminal phosphate group of the latter compound.

adenosine 5'-triphosphate (ATP). Adenosine triphosphate; adenosine (5)O–(PO$_2$H)$_2$; immediate precursors of adenine nucleotides in RNA.

adeno'sis. Any generalized glandular disease.

fibrosing a., sclerosing a.

sclerosing a., fibrosing a. adenofibrosis; a nodular benign breast lesion occurring most frequently in relatively young women and consisting of hyperplastic distorted lobules of acinar tissue with increased collagenous stroma.

adenot'omy [adeno- + G. *tomē,* a cutting]. Incision of a gland.

ad'enotonsillec'tomy. Operative removal of tonsils and adenoids.

Adenoviridae (ad'ē-no-vīr'ĭ-de). A family of double-stranded DNA-containing viruses, of which there are more than 80 antigenic types (species); it develops in nuclei of infected cells and causes diseases of the respiratory tract and conjunctiva.

ad'enovi'rus [G. *adēn*, gland, + virus]. Adenoidal-pharyngeal-conjunctival or A-P-C virus; any virus of the family Adenoviridae.

ad'enyl. The radical or ion of adenine.

aden'ylate. Salt or ester of adenylic acid.

a. cyclase, 3',5'-cyclic AMP synthetase; enzyme acting on ATP to form 3',5'-cyclic AMP.

a. kinase, adenylic acid kinase; a phosphotransferase that catalyzes the phosphorylation of one molecule of ADP by another, yielding ATP and AMP.

adenyl'ic acid. Adenosine monophosphate or phosphate; adenine nucleotide; a condensation product of adenosine and phosphoric acid; a nucleotide found among the hydrolysis products of all nucleic acids.

ader'mia [G. *a*- priv. + *derma,* skin]. Congenital absence of skin.

ader'mogen'esis [G. *a*- priv. + *derma,* skin, + *genesis,* production]. Failure or imperfection in the regeneration of the skin, especially the imperfect repair of a cutaneous defect.

ADH Antidiuretic *hormone.*

adhesion (ad-he'zhun) [L. *adhesio,* to stick to]. **1.** Conglutination (1); the process of adhering or uniting of two surfaces or parts, especially the union of the opposing surfaces of a wound. **2.** In the plural, inflammatory bands that connect opposing serous surfaces.

  primary a., *healing* by first intention.
  secondary a., *healing* by second intention.

adhesiot'omy. Surgical section or lysis of adhesions.

adhe'sive. 1. Relating to, or having the characteristics of, an adhesion. **2.** Any material that adheres to a surface or causes adherence between surfaces.

adiadochokinesis (ă-di'ă-do-ko-kin-e'sis) [G. *a*- priv. + *diadochos,* successive, + *kinēsis,* movement]. Inability to perform rapid alternating movements.

adiaphoresis (a'di-ă-fo-re'sis, a-di'ă-) [G. *a*- priv. + *diaphorēsis,* perspiration]. Anhidrosis.

a'diaphoret'ic. Anhidrotic.

adiaphor'ia [G. *a*- priv. + *dia,* through, + *phoros,* bearing]. A failure to respond to stimulation after a series of previously applied stimuli.

adip-, adipo- [L. *adeps,* fat]. Combining form relating to fat.

adipocele (ad'ĭ-po-sēl) [adipo- + G. *kēlē,* tumor]. Lipocele.

adipocel'lular. Relating to both fatty and cellular tissues, or to connective tissue with many fat cells.

adipoceratous (ad-ĭ-po-ser'ă-tus). Relating to adipocere.

adipocere (ad'ĭ-po-sēr) [adipo- + G. *cera,* wax]. A fatty substance of waxy consistency into which dead animal tissues are sometimes converted.

adipocyte (ad'ĭ-po-sīt). Fat *cell.*

ad'ipogen'esis. Lipogenesis.

ad'ipogen'ic, adipog'enous. Lipogenic.

ad'ipoid [adipo- + G. *eidos,* resemblance]. Lipoid.

ad'ipoki'nin. Adipokinetic hormone; an anterior pituitary hormone that brings about mobilization of fat from adipose tissue.

ad'ipokinet'ic. Denoting an agent that causes mobilization of stored lipid.

ad'iponecro'sis. Necrosis of fat, such as may be seen in hemorrhagic pancreatitis.

a. neonato'rum, *sclerema* neonatorum.

ad'ipose. Fatty; relating to fat.

adipo'sis [adipo- + G. *-osis,* condition]. Lipomatosis; liposis (1); pimelosis (1); an excessive local or general accumulation of fat in the body.

  a. cardia'ca, fatty *heart* (2).

  a. doloro'sa, Dercum's disease; a condition characterized by a deposit of symmetrical nodular or pendulous masses of fat in various regions of the body, with discomfort or pain.

  a. tubero'sa sim'plex, a condition resembling a. dolorosa, in which the fat occurs in small masses on the abdomen or on the extremities; these masses are sensitive to the touch and may be spontaneously painful.

adipos'ity. Obesity.

ad'iposu'ria [adipo- + G. *ouron,* urine]. Lipuria.

aditus, pl. **aditus** (ad'ĭ-tus) [L. access, fr. *ad-eo,* pp. *-itus,* go to] [NA]. An entrance to a cavity or channel.

ad'juvant [L. *ad-juvo,* to give aid to]. **1.** A substance added to a drug product formulation which affects the action of the active ingredient in a predictable way. **2.** In immunology, a vehicle used to enhance antigenicity; *e.g.,* a suspension of minerals on which antigen is adsorbed; or water-in-oil emulsion in which antigen solution is emulsified in mineral oil (Freund's incomplete a.), sometimes with the inclusion of killed mycobacteria (Freund's complete a.) to further enhance antigenicity.

adner'val. Adneural. **1.** Lying near a nerve. **2.** In the direction of a nerve; said of an electric current passing through muscle toward the nerve.

adneu'ral. Adnerval.

adnexa, sing. **adnexum** (ad-nek'sah, -sum) [L. connected parts, appendages]. Annexa; appendages; parts accessory to the main organ or structure.

adnex'al. Annexal; relating to adnexa.

adnexum (ad-nek'sum). Singular of adnexa.

Ado 18 Adenosine.

adolescence (ad'o-les'ens) [L. *adolescentia*]. Period between puberty and attaining complete growth and maturity.

adolescent (ad'o-les'ent). Pertaining to the period or state of adolescence.

adoral (ad-o'ral) [L. *ad,* to, + *os* (*or-*), mouth]. Near or directed toward the mouth.

ADP Adenosine 5'-diphosphate.

adren-, adrenal-, adreno- [L. *ad,* toward, + *ren,* kidney]. Combining forms relating to the adrenal gland.

adrenal (ă-dre'nal) [L. *ad,* to, + *ren,* kidney]. **1.** Near or upon the kidney. **2.** An adrenal gland or separate tissue thereof.

  accessory a., adrenal rest; an island of cortical tissue separate from the adrenal gland, usually found in the retroperitoneal tissues, kidney, or genital organs.

adrenalectomy (ă-dre-nal-ek′to-mĭ) [adrenal + G. *ektomē*, excision]. Suprarenalectomy; removal of one or both adrenal glands.

adrenaline (ă-dren′ă-lin, -lēn). Epinephrine.

adrenalinemia (ă-dren′al-ĭ-ne′mĭah) [adrenaline + G. *haima*, blood]. The presence of notable or excessive amounts of epinephrine (adrenaline) in the circulation.

adrenalinuria (ă-dren′al-ĭnu′rĭ-ah) [adrenaline + G. *ouron*, urine]. The presence of epinephrine (adrenaline) in the urine.

adrenalitis (ă-dre-nal-i′tis). Inflammation of the adrenal gland.

adrenalopathy (ă-dre-năl′op′ă-thĭ) [adrenal + G. *pathos*, suffering]. Adrenopathy; any pathologic condition of the adrenal glands.

adrenergic (ă-drĕ-ner′jik) [adren- + G. *ergon*, work]. **1.** Relating to nerve cells or fibers of the autonomic nervous system that employ norepinephrine as their neurotransmitter. **2.** Relating to drugs that mimic the actions of the sympathetic nervous system.

adrenic (ă-dre′nik). Relating to the adrenal gland.

adreno-. See adren-.

adrenoceptive (ă-dren-o-sep′tiv). Referring to chemical sites in effectors with which the adrenergic mediator unites.

adrenocortical (ă-dre-no-kor′tĭ-kal). Pertaining to adrenal cortex.

adrenocorticomimetic (ă-dre′no-kor′tĭ-ko-mĭ-met′ik). Mimicking adrenocortical function.

adrenocorticotropic, adrenocorticotrophic (ă-dre′-no-kor′tĭ-ko-tro′pik, -tro′fik) [adrenal cortex + G. *trophē*, nurture; *tropē*, a turning]. Adrenotrophic; adrenotropic; affecting growth or activity of adrenal cortex.

adrenocorticotropin, adrenocorticotrophin (ă-dre′-no-kor′tĭ-ko-tro′pin, -fin). Adrenocorticotropic *hormone*.

adrenogenic (ă-dre-no-jen′ik). Adrenogenous; of adrenal origin.

adrenogenous (ă-drĕ-noj′ĕ-nus). Adrenogenic.

adrenoleukodystrophy (ALD) (ă-dre′no-lu′ko-dis′-tro-fĭ). An X-linked recessive disorder affecting boys, characterized by chronic adrenocortical insufficiency, skin hyperpigmentation, and leukodystrophy, and causing intellectual and neurological disturbances due to myelin degeneration.

adrenolytic (ă-dren-o-lit′ik) [adreno- + G. *lysis*, loosening, dissolution]. Denoting antagonism to or inhibition of the action of epinephrine, norepinephrine, and related sympathomimetics.

adrenomegaly (ă-dre-no-meg′ă-lĭ) [adreno- + G. *megas*, big]. Enlargement of the adrenal glands.

adrenomimetic (ă-dre′no-mĭ-met′ik) [adreno- + G. *mimētikos*, imitative]. Having an action similar to that of epinephrine and norepinephrine, which are liberated from the adrenal medulla and adrenergic nerves.

adrenopathy (ă-dre-nop′ă-thĭ). Adrenalopathy.

adrenoreceptors (ă-dre′no-re-sep′torz). Adrenergic *receptors*.

adrenotoxin (ă-dre-no-tok′sin). A substance toxic to the adrenal glands.

adrenotrophic, adrenotropic (ă-dre-no-tro′fik, -tro′-pik). Adrenocorticotropic.

adrenotrophin, adrenotropin (ă-dre-no-tro′fin, -tro′-pin). Adrenocorticotropic *hormone*.

adsorb′ [L. *ad*, to, + *sorbeo*, to suck in]. To take up by adsorption.

adsor′bent. 1. A substance that adsorbs. **2.** In pharmacology, a substance endowed with the property of attaching other substances to its surface without any chemical action. **3.** An antigen or antibody used in immune adsorption.

adsorption (ad-sorp′shun) [L. *ad*, to, + *sorbeo*, to suck up]. The property of a substance to attract and hold to its surface a gas, liquid or a substance in solution or in suspension.

immune a., (1) removal of antibody from antiserum by use of specific antigen; after aggregation has occurred, the antigen-antibody complex is separated either by centrifugation or by filtration; (2) removal of antigen by specific antiserum in a similar manner.

adter′minal. In a direction toward the nerve endings, muscular insertions, or the extremity of any structure.

adult (ă-dult′). Fully grown and mature; a fully grown individual.

adul′tera′tion. The alteration of any substance by the deliberate addition of a component not ordinarily part of that substance; usually used to imply that the substance is debased as a result.

adul′terant. An impurity; an additive that is considered to have an undesirable effect.

advancement (ad-vans′ment). A surgical procedure in which a tendinous insertion or a skin flap is severed from its attachment and sutured to a point farther forward.

adventitia (ad-ven-tish′yah) [L. *adventicius*, coming from abroad, foreign]. The outermost covering of any organ or structure which is properly derived from without and does not form an integral part of such organ or structure; specifically, the outer coat of an artery.

adventitial (ad-ven-tish′al). Adventitious (3); relating to the adventitia of an organ or structure.

adventitious (ad-ven-tish′us). **1.** Coming from without. **2.** Accidental. **3.** Adventitial.

ae-. For words so beginning and not found here, see under e-.

Aedes (a-e′dēz) [G. *aēdēs*, unpleasant, unfriendly]. A widespread genus of small mosquitos frequently found in tropical and subtropical regions; includes **A. aegyp′ti**, the yellow fever mosquito, a species that is also the vector of dengue viruses.

aer-, aero- [G. *aēr* (L. *aer*), air]. Combining form denoting relationship to air or gas.

aeration (ăr-a'shun). **1.** Airing. **2.** Saturating a fluid with air or other gas. **3.** The change of venous into arterial blood in the lungs.

aero-. See aer-.

aer'obe [aero- + G. *bios,* life]. **1.** An organism that can live and grow in the presence of free oxygen. **2.** An organism that can use oxygen as a final electron acceptor in a respiratory chain.

 obligate a., one that cannot live or grow in the absence of free oxygen.

aerobic (ăr-o'bik). **1.** Relating to an aerobe. **2.** Aerophilic; aerophilous; living in air.

aerobiosis (ăr-o-bi-o'sis) [aero- + G. *biōsis,* mode of living]. Existence in an atmosphere containing oxygen.

aerobiotic (ăr-o-bi-ot'ik). Relating to aerobiosis.

aerocele (ăr'o-sēl) [aero- + G. *kēlē,* tumor]. Distention of a small natural cavity with gas.

aerocolpos (ăr-o-kol'pos) [aero- + G. *kolpos,* womb (vagina)]. Distention of the vagina with gas.

aerodermectasia (ăr'o-der-mek-ta'zĭ-ah) [aero- + G. *derma,* skin, + *ektasis,* a stretching out]. Subcutaneous *emphysema.*

aerodontalgia (ăr-o-don-tal'jĭ-ah) [aero- + G. *odous,* tooth, + *algos,* pain]. Dental pain caused by either increased or reduced atmospheric pressure.

aerodynam'ics [aero- + G. *dynamis,* force]. The study of air and other gases in motion, the forces that set them in motion, and the results of such motion.

aeroemphysema (ăr'o-em-fĭ-se'mah). Decompression *sickness.*

aerogen (ăr'o-jen). A gas-forming microorganism.

aerogenesis (ăr-o-jen'ĕ-sis) [aero- + G. *genesis,* production]. The production of gas.

aerogenic, aerogenous (ăr-o-jen'ik, -oj'en-us). Gas-forming.

aeropathy (ăr-op'ă-thī) [aero- + G. *pathos,* suffering]. Any morbid state induced by a pronounced change in the atmospheric pressure.

aerophagia, aerophagy (ăr-o-fa'jĭ-ah, ăr-of'ă-jĭ) [aero- + G. *phagein,* to eat]. Penumophagia; the excessive swallowing of air.

aerophil, aerophile (ăr'o-fil, -fīl) [aero- + G. *philos,* fond]. **1.** Air-loving. **2.** An aerobic organism, especially an obligate aerobe.

aerophil'ic. Aerobic.

aeroph'ilous. Aerobic.

aerophobia (ăr-o-fo'bĭ-ah) [aero- + G. *phobos,* fear]. Abnormal and extreme dread of fresh air or of air in motion.

aeropiesotherapy (ăr-o-pi-e'so-thēr'ă-pī) [aero- + G. *piesis,* pressure, + *therapeia,* medical treatment]. The treatment of disease by means of compressed (or rarified) air.

aerosinusi'tis. Barosinusitis; inflammation of the paranasal sinuses caused by a difference in pressure within the sinus relative to ambient pressure, secondary to obstruction of the sinus orifice.

aerosol (ăr'o-sol). **1.** A liquid agent or solution dispersed in air in the form of a fine mist for therapeutic, insecticidal, and other purposes. **2.** Pharmaceutical a.; a product packaged under pressure and containing therapeutically active ingredients intended for topical application and for introduction into body orifices.

aerotitis media (ăr-o-ti'tis me'dĭ-ah) [aero- + G. *ous,* ear, + suffix *-itis,* inflammation]. Barotitis media; an acute or chronic traumatic inflammation of the middle ear caused by a reduction in pressure in the air in the tympanic cavity relative to ambient pressure, secondary to eustachian tube obstruction.

aescula'pian [L. *Aesculapius,* G. *Asklēpios,* the god of medicine]. Esculapian; relating to Aesculapius, the art of medicine, or medical practitioner.

afeb'rile. Apyretic.

afetal (ă-fe'tal). Without relation to a fetus or intrauterine life.

affect (af'fekt [L. *affectus,* state of mind]. Emotional feeling tone and mood attached to a thought, including its external manifestations.

affec'tion. 1. Feeling; love. **2.** A disease; an abnormal condition of body or mind.

affec'tive. Pertaining to emotion, feeling, sensibility, or a mental state.

af'ferent [L. *afferens,* fr. *af-fero,* to bring to]. Toward a center, denoting certain arteries, veins, lymphatics, and nerves.

affinity (ă-fin'ĭ-tĭ) [L. *affinis,* neighboring]. **1.** In chemistry, the force that impels certain atoms to unite with certain others to form compounds. **2.** The selective staining of a tissue by a dye or the uptake of a dye, chemical, or other substance selectively by a tissue.

afibrillar (a-fi'brĭ-lar). Denoting a biological structure that does not contain fibrils.

afibrin'ogene'mia. The absence of fibrinogen in the plasma.

 congenital a., a rare disorder of blood coagulation in which little or no fibrinogen can be found in plasma; autosomal recessive inheritance.

AFP α-Fetoprotein.

af'terbirth. Secundines; the placenta and membranes that are extruded from the uterus after birth.

af'terhear'ing. Aftersound.

afterimage (af'ter-im'ij). Persistence of the image after the object has disappeared or the eyes are closed.

afterimpression (af'ter-im-presh'un). Aftersensation.

af'terload. 1. The arrangement of a muscle so that, in shortening, it lifts a weight from an adjustable support or otherwise does work against a constant opposing force to which it is not exposed at rest. **2.** The load or force thus encountered in shortening.

af'terpains. Painful cramplike contractions of the uterus occurring after childbirth.

afterperception (af'ter-per-sep'shun). Appreciation of a stimulus after it has ceased to act.

afterpotential (af'ter-po-ten'shal). Small changes in electrical potential in a stimulated nerve which follow the main (spike) potential; consists of an initial negative deflection followed by a positive deflection in the oscillograph record.

af'tersensa'tion. Afterimpression; a sensation persisting after its original cause has ceased to act.

af'tersound. Afterhearing; the subjective sensation of a sound after the cause of the sound has ceased.

af'tertaste. A taste persisting after contact of the tongue with the substance has ceased.

Ag Silver (argentum); antigen.

agalactia (ă-gal-ak'shĭ-ah) [G. *a-* priv. + *gala* (*galakt-*), milk]. Agalactosis; absence of milk in the breasts after childbirth.

agal'acto'sis. Agalactia.

agalac'tous. Relating to agalactia.

agalorrhea (ā-gal-ŏ-re'ah) [G. *a-* priv. + *gala*, milk, + *rhoia*, a flow]. Absence of the secretion or flow of milk.

agam'ic. Agamous; denoting nonsexual reproduction, as by fission, budding, etc.

agam'maglob'uline'mia. Absence of, or extremely low levels of, the gamma fraction of serum globulin; sometimes used loosely to denote absence of immunoglobulins in general. See also hypogammaglobulinemia.

agamous (ag'ă-mus) [G. *agamos,* unmarried]. Agamic.

aganglion'ic. Without ganglia.

agangliono'sis. Absence of ganglion cells, as from the myenteric plexus as a characteristic of congenital megacolon.

agar (ah'gar, a'gar) [Bengalese]. A polysaccharide, derived from various red algae, used as a solidifying agent in culture media.

agar'ic [G. *agarikon,* a kind of fungus]. The dried fruiting body of the mushroom, *Polyporus officinalis* (family Polyporaceae), occurring in the form of brownish or whitish light masses, which contains agaric acid.

agar'ic, agaric'ic, or **agaricin'ic acid.** Agaricin; α-hexadecylcitric acid; α-cetylcitric acid; obtained from agaric and responsible for the anhidrotic action of the mushroom.

agar'icin. Agaric acid.

agas'tric [G. *a-* priv. + *gastēr,* belly]. Without stomach or digestive tract.

age (āj) [F. *âge,* L. *aetas*]. **1.** The period that has elapsed since the birth of a living being. **2.** To grow old; to gradually develop changes in structure which are not due to preventable disease or trauma and which are associated with an increased probability of death.

achievement a., the relationship between the chronologic age and the age of proficiency, as established by standard achievement tests.

chronologic a., (1) calendar a. or a record of time elapsed since birth; **(2)** a child's a., expressed in years and months, used as a measurement against which to evaluate the mental a.

mental a., a measure, expressed in years and months, of a child's relative intelligence as determined by standard intelligence tests.

agen'esis [G. *a-* priv. + *genesis,* production]. Absence, failure of formation, or imperfect development of any part.

agenet'ic. Pertaining to or characterized by agenesis.

agenitalism (a-jen'ĭ-tal-izm). Congenital absence of genitals.

agen'oso'mia [G. *a-* priv. + *genos,* sex, + *soma,* body]. Defective formation or absence of the genitalia in a fetus, accompanied by eventration.

agent (a'jent) [L. *ago,* pres. p. *agens* (*agent-*), to perform]. An active force or substance capable of producing an effect.

adrenergic blocking a., a compound that selectively blocks or inhibits responses to sympathetic adrenergic nerve activity (sympatholytic a.) and to epinephrine, norepinephrine, and other adrenergic amines (adrenolytic a.); two distinct classes exist, α- and β-adrenergic receptor blocking a.'s.

adrenergic neuronal blocking a., a drug that prevents the responses evoked by sympathetic nerve impulses; it does not inhibit the responses of the adrenergic receptors to circulating epinephrine, norepinephrine, and other adrenergic amines.

alkylating a's, cytotoxic a.'s, such as nitrogen mustards, ethylenimines, and alkyl sulfonates, that alkylate cellular constituents, including cross-linking and cycloalkylation of portions of DNA, of DNA to protein, or of protein to protein.

antianxiety a., minor tranquilizer; a functional category of drugs useful in the treatment of anxiety and able to reduce anxiety at doses that do not cause excessive sedation.

antipsychotic a., major tranquilizer; a functional category of neuroleptic drugs that are helpful in the treatment of psychosis and have a capacity to ameliorate thought disorder.

blocking a., a drug that blocks transmission at an autonomic receptor site, autonomic synapse, or neuromuscular junction.

Eaton a., *Mycoplasma pneumoniae.*

ganglionic blocking a., an a. that impairs the passage of impulses in autonomic ganglia.

initiating a., see promoting a.

neuromuscular blocking a., a compound which, by virtue of its actions on the neuromuscular junction, inhibits the ability of motor nerve stimuli to produce skeletal muscle contraction.

nondepolarizing neuromuscular blocking a., a compound that paralyzes skeletal muscle primarily by inhibiting transmission of nerve impulses at the neuromuscular junction rather than by affecting the membrane potention of motor endplate or muscle fibers.

Pittsburgh pneumonia a., A Gram-negative species of bacteria (*Legionella micadei*) that is a cause of pneumonia.

promoting a., an a., by itself noncarcinogenic, that enhances tumor production in a tissue previously exposed to subcarcinogenic doses of a carcinogen (the latter then is called an initiating a.).

Agent Orange. A defoliant consisting of a mixture of two chlorophenoxyacetic acids and the contaminant dioxin; its teratogenic and carcinogenic effects are controversial.

ageusia (ă-gu'sĭ-ah) [G. *a.* priv. + *geusis*, taste]. Loss of the sense of taste.

agglutinant (ă-glu'tĭ-nant) [L. *ad*, to + *gluten*, glue]. A substance that holds parts together or causes agglutination.

agglutination (ă-glu'tĭ-na'shun) [L. *ad*, to, + *gluten*, glue]. **1.** The process by which suspended bacteria, cells, or other particles of similar size are caused to adhere and form into clumps. **2.** Adhesion of the surfaces of a wound.

bacteriogenic a., the clumping of erythrocytes as a result of effects of bacteria or their products.

cold a., a. of red blood cells by their own serum or by any other serum when the blood is cooled below body temperature.

group a., a. by antibodies specific for minor (group) antigens common to several bacteria, each of which possesses its own major specific antigen.

agglu'tinative. Causing, or able to cause, agglutination.

agglu'tinin. 1. An antibody that causes clumping or agglutination of the bacteria or other cells which either stimulated the formation of the a., or contain immunologically similar, reactive antigen. **2.** A substance, other than a specific agglutinating antibody, that causes organic particles to agglutinate.

chief a., major a.

cold a., an a. associated with cold agglutination.

cross-reacting a., group a.

group a., cross-reacting a.; a specific for a group antigen.

H a., an a. that is formed as the result of stimulation by, and which reacts with, the thermolabile antigen(s) in the flagella of motile strains of microorganisms.

major a., chief a.; a. present in greatest quantity in an antiserum and evoked by the most dominant of a mosaic of antigens.

minor a., partial a.; a. present in an antiserum in lesser concentration than the major a.

O a., an a. that is formed as the result of stimulation by, and that reacts with, the relatively thermostable antigen(s) in the cell bodies of microorganisms.

partial a., minor a.

saline a., complete antibody; an anti-Rh antibody that causes agglutination of Rh + erythrocytes when they are suspended either in saline or in a protein medium.

serum a., incomplete antibody; an anti-Rh antibody which coats Rh + erythrocytes; the cells do not agglutinate when suspended in saline, but do agglutinate when suspended in serum or other protein media.

agglutin + ogen [agglutinin + G. *-gen*, production]. Agglutogen; an antigenic substance that stimulates the formation of specific agglutinin.

agglu'tinogen'ic. Agglutogenic; capable of causing the production of an agglutinin.

agglu'tinophil'ic [agglutination + G. *phileō*, to love]. Readily undergoing agglutination.

agglu'togen. Agglutinogen.

agglu'togen'ic. Agglutinogenic.

aggregate (ag're-gāt) [L. *ag-grego*, pp. *-atus*, to add to]. **1.** To collect together in a mass or cluster. **2.** The total of individual units making up a mass or cluster.

aggrega'tion. A mass or cluster of independent but similar units.

aggression (ă-gresh'un). A domineering, forceful, or assaultive verbal or physical action toward another person as the motor component of the affects of anger, hostility, or rage.

aging (a'jing). **1.** The process of growing old, especially by failure of replacement of cells in sufficient number to maintain function. **2.** The gradual deterioration of a mature organism resulting from time-dependent, irreversible changes in structure that are intrinsic to the particular species, and which eventually lead to decreased ability to cope with the stresses of the environment, thereby increasing the probability of death.

aglossia (ă-glos'ĭ-ah) [G. *a-* priv. + *glōssa*, tongue]. Congenital absence of the tongue.

aglossostomia (ă-glos-os'to-mĭah) [G. *a-* priv. + *glōssa*, tongue, + *stoma*, mouth]. Congenital absence of the tongue and mouth opening.

aglutition (a-gloo-tish'un). Dysphagia.

agly'cosu'ric. Relating to aglycosuria.

aglycosuria (a-gli-ko-su'rĭ-ah). Absence of carbohydrate in urine.

agnathia (ag-na'thĭ-ah) [G. *a-* priv. + *gnathos*, jaw]. Congenital absence of the lower jaw, usually accompanied by approximation of the ears.

agnathous (ag'na-thus). Relating to agnathia.

agnogenic (ag'no-jen'ik)]G. *a-* priv. + *gnosis*, knowledge, + *genesis*, origin]. Idiopathic (1).

agnosia (ag-no'sĭ-ah) [G. ignorance; from *a-* priv. + *gnōsis*, knowledge]. Lack of sensory-perceptual ability to recognize impressions from one or more of the senses.

-agogue, -agog [G. *agōgos*, leading forth]. Suffix indicating a promoter or stimulant of.

agon'adal. Relating to the absence of gonads.

ag'onist [G. *agōn*, a contest]. **1.** Denoting a muscle in a state of contraction, with reference to its opposing muscle, or antagonist. **2.** A drug capable of combining with receptors to initiate drug actions; possesses affinity and intrinsic activity.

agoraphobia (ag'o-ră-fo'bĭ-ah) [G. *agora*, marketplace, + *phobos*, fear]. An irrational fear of leaving the familiar setting of home.

-agra [G. *agra*, a seizure]. Suffix meaning sudden onslaught of acute pain.

agram′matism [G. *agrammatos*, unlearned]. A form of aphasia characterized by inability to construct a grammatical or intelligible sentence.

agran′ulocyte [G. *a-* priv. + L. *granulum*, granule, + G. *kytos*, cell]. A nongranular leukocyte.

agran′ulocyto′sis. An acute condition characterized by pronounced leukopenia with great reduction in the number of polymorphonuclear leukocytes; infected ulcers are likely to develop in mucous membranes and in the skin.

agran′uloplas′tic [G. *a-* priv. + L. *granulum*, granule, + G. *plastikos*, formative]. Capable of forming nongranular cells, and incapable of forming granular cells.

agraph′ia [G. *a-* priv. + *graphō*, to write]. Anorthography; logagraphia; loss of the ability to write or express thoughts in writing.

agraph′ic. Relating to or marked by agraphia.

ague (a′gu) [Fr. *aigu*, acute]. **1.** Archaic term for malarial fever. **2.** A chill.

agyria (ă-ji′rĭ-ah) [G. *a-* priv. + *gyros*, circle]. Lissencephalia; lissencephaly; lack of convolutional pattern in the cerebral cortex due to defect of development.

AHF Antihemophilic *factor*.

AHG Antihemophilic *globulin*.

AID Donor of heterologous (artificial) insemination.

AIDS Acquired immunodeficiency syndrome; a disease that compromises the competency of the immune system, characterized by persistent lymphadenopathy and various opportunistic infections, such as *Pneumocystis carinii* pneumonia, cytomegalovirus, disseminated histoplasmosis, candidiasis, and isosporiasis, and malignancies such as Kaposi's sarcoma; the etiologic agent is HTLV-III, transmissible by body fluids such as blood and semen.

AIH Homologous (artificial) insemination.

ailurophobia (i-loo-ro-fo′bĭ-ah) [G. *ailouros*, cat, + *phobos*, fear]. Morbid fear of or aversion to cats.

air (ār) [G. *aēr*; L. *aer*]. The atmosphere, a mixture of gases in the following approximate percentages by volume after water vapor has been removed: oxygen, 20.94; nitrogen 78.03; argon and other rare gases, 0.99; carbon dioxide, 0.04. Formerly used to mean any respiratory gas, regardless of its composition.

　　alveolar a., alveolar *gas*.

　　complemental a., inspiratory reserve *volume*.

　　complementary a., inspiratory *capacity*.

　　functional residual a., functional residual *capacity*.

　　reserve a., expiratory reserve *volume*.

　　residual a., residual *volume*.

　　supplemental a., expiratory reserve *volume*.

　　tidal a., tidal *volume*.

air′way. 1. Any part of the respiratory tract through which air passes during breathing. **2.** In anesthesia or resuscitation, a device for correcting obstruction to breathing.

akaryocyte (a-kăr-ĭ-o-sīt) [G. *a-* priv. + *karyon*, kernel, + *kytos*, a hollow (cell)]. Acaryote; akaryote; a cell without a nucleus (karyon), such as the erythrocyte.

akaryote (a-kăr′ĭ-ōt) [G. *a-* priv. + *karyon*, kernel]. Akaryocyte.

akathisia (a-kă-thiz′i-ah) [G. *a-* priv. + *kathisis*, a sitting]. Acathisia; a syndrome characterized by an inability to remain in a sitting posture, with motor restlessness and a feeling of muscular quivering.

akerato′sis. Deficiency or absence of the horny tissue.

akinesia (a-ki-ne′sĭ-ah) [G. *a-* priv. + *kinēsis*, movement]. Akinesis. **1.** Absence or loss of the power of voluntary motion. **2.** The postsystolic interval of rest of the heart.

akine′sic. Akinetic.

akinesis (a-ki-ne′sis). Akinesia.

akinesthesia (a-kin′es-the′zĭ-ah) [G. *a-* priv. + *kinēsis*, motion, + *aisthēsis*, sensation]. Absence of the sense of perception of movement; absence of the muscular sense.

akinet′ic. Akinesic; relating to or suffering from akinesia.

Al Aluminum.

ALA δ-Aminolevulinic acid.

Ala Alanine or its mono- or diradical.

alacrima (a-lak′rĭ-mah) [G. *a-* priv. + L. *lacrima*, tear]. Congenital deficiency or absence of tears.

ala, gen. and pl. **alae** (a′lah, a′le) [L. wing] [NA]. Any winglike or expanded structure.

　　a. ma′jor os′sis sphenoida′lis [NA], the greater wing of the sphenoid bone.

　　a. mi′nor os′sis sphenoida′lis [NA], the lesser wing of the sphenoid bone.

　　a. na′si [NA], the outer more or less flaring wall of each nostril.

ala′lia [G. *a-* priv. + *lalia*, talking]. Loss of the power of speech through impairment in the articulatory apparatus.

al′anine (Ala). 2- or α-Aminopropionic acid; $CH_3CH(NH_2)COOH$; one of the amino acids occurring widely in proteins.

al′anine am′inotrans′ferase (ALT). (Serum) glutamic-pyruvic transaminase; an enzyme transferring amino groups from L-alanine to 2-ketoglutarate, or the reverse (from L-glutamate to pyruvate).

al′anyl. The acyl radical of alanine.

a′lar. 1. Relating to a wing; winged. **2.** Axillary. **3.** Relating to the ala of such structures as the nose, sphenoid, sacrum.

alba (al′bah) [fem. of L. *albus*, white]. **1.** White. **2.** *Substantia* alba.

al′bicans, pl. **albican′tia** [L.]. **1.** White. **2.** *Corpus* albicans.

albiduria (al-bĭ-du′rĭ-ah) [L. *albidus*, whitish, + G. *ouron*, urine]. Albinuria; the passing of pale or white urine of low specific gravity.

albinism (al′bĭ-nizm) [L. *albus*, white]. Congenital leukoderma or leukopathia; an inherited deficiency or absence of pigment in the skin, hair, and eyes, or eyes only, due to tyrosene abnormality in production of melanin.

albi'no [L. *albus,* white]. An individual with albinism.

albinot'ic. Pertaining to albinism.

albinu'ria. Albiduria.

albuginea (al-bu-jin'e-ah) [L. albugineous]. A white fibrous tissue layer.

albu'men [L. the white of egg]. Egg *albumin.*

albu'min [L. *albumen* (*-min-*), the white of egg]. A type of simple protein widely distributed throughout the tissues and fluids of plants and animals.

blood a., serum a.

egg a., ovalbumin; albumen; white of egg; the chief protein occurring in the white of egg, resembling in many respects serum a.

iodinated 125 **I serum a.,** a sterile, buffered, isotonic solution prepared to contain not less than 10 mg of radioiodinated normal human serum albumin per ml, and adjusted to provide not more than 1 mCi of radioactivity per ml; used as a diagnostic aid in determining blood volume and cardiac output.

iodinated 131 **I human serum a.,** a sterile, buffered, isotonic solution prepared to contain not less than 10 mg of radioiodinated normal human serum a. per ml, and adjusted to provide not more than 1 mCi of radioactivity per ml; used as a diagnostic aid in the measurement of blood volume and cardiac output.

macroaggregated a. (MAA), conglomerates of human serum a. in a suspension; usually refers to particles 10 to 50 μm in size; used as a radiolabeled agent for lung scanning.

normal human serum a., a sterile preparation of serum a. obtained by fractionating blood plasma proteins from healthy persons; used as a transfusion material and to treat edema due to hypoproteinemia.

serum a., blood a.; seralbumin; the a. present in the blood plasma and in serous fluids; the principal protein in plasma.

albu'minoid. 1. Resembling albumin. **2.** Any protein. **3.** Scleroprotein; a simple type of protein present in horny and cartilaginous tissues and in the lens of the eye.

albu'minous. Relating in any way to albumin; containing or consisting of albumin.

albuminuria (al-bu'mĭ-nu'rĭ-ah) [albumin + G. *ouron,* urine]. Proteinuria (2); the presence of protein in urine, cheifly albumin but also globulin; usually indicative of disease, but sometimes resulting from a temporary or transient dysfunction, in contrast to a truly pathologic condition.

albuminu'ric. Relating to, characterized by, or suffering from albuminuria.

alcap'ton. Homogentisic acid.

alcaptonu'ria. Alkaptonuria

al'cohol [Ar. *al,* the, + *kohl,* fine antimonial powder, the term being applied first to a fine powder, then, to anything impalpable (spirit)]. **1.** One of a series

of organic chemical compounds in which a hydrogen (H) attached to carbon is replaced by a hydroxyl (OH), yielding $>$C-OH. **2.** Ethanol; ethyl alcohol; CH_3CH_2OH; a liquid containing 92.3% by weight, corresponding to 94.9% by volume, at 15.56°, of C_2H_5OH. It has been used in beverages and as a solvent, vehicle, and preservative; externally as a rubefacient, coolant, and disinfectant.

absolute a., (1) anhydrous a.; 100% a., water having been removed; (2) dehydrated a.; a. with a minimum admixture of water, at most 1%.

denatured a., ethyl a. rendered unfit for consumption as a beverage by the addition of one or several chemicals; used in industry.

dihydric a., one containing two OH groups in its molecule; *e.g.,* ethylene glycol.

monohydric a., an a. containing one OH group.

primary a., an a. characterized by the univalent radical, $-CH_2OH.$

secondary a., an a. characterized by the bivalent atom group, $>$CHOH.

tertiary a., an a. characterized by the trivalent atom group, $>$COH.

trihydric a., an a. containing three OH groups; *e.g.,* glycerol.

alcohol'ic. 1. Relating to, containing, or produced by alcohol. **2.** A person addicted to the use of a. beverages in excess.

alcoholism (al'ko-hol-izm). Alcohol abuse, dependence, or addiction; chronic heavy drinking or intoxication resulting in impairment of health, dependency as a coping mechanism, and increased adaptation to the effects of alcohol requiring increasing doses to achieve and sustain a desired effect.

acute a., intoxication (2); a temporary mental disturbance with muscular incoordination and paresis, induced by the ingestion of alcoholic beverages in toxic amounts.

chronic a., a pathologic condition, affecting chiefly the nervous and gastroenteric systems, caused by the habitual use of alcoholic beverages in toxic amounts.

alcoholysis (al-ko-hol'ĭ-sis) [alcohol + G. *lysis,* dissolution]. The splitting of a chemical bond with the addition of the elements of alcohol at the point of splitting.

ALD Adrenoleukodystrophy.

aldehyde (al'dĕ-hīd). A compound containing the radical $-CH=O$, reducible to an alcohol (CH_2OH), oxidizable to an acid (COOH); *e.g.,* acetaldehyde.

aldopen'tose. A monosaccharide, *e.g.,* ribose, with five carbon atoms, of which one is a (potential) aldehyde group.

al'dose. A monosaccharide potentially containing the characteristic group of the aldehydes, $-CHO.$

aldos'terone. $11\beta,21$-Dihydroxy-3,30-dioxo-4-pregnen-18-al ($11\rightarrow18$ lactone); a steroid hormone produced by the adrenal cortex; its major action is to facilitate potassium exchange for sodium in the distal renal tubule, causing sodium reabsorption and potassium and hydrogen loss.

aldos'teronism. Hyperaldosteronism; a disorder caused by excessive secretion of aldosterone.

primary a., Conn's syndrome; an arenocortical disorder caused by excessive secretion of aldosterone and characterized by headaches, nocturia, polyuria, fatigue, hypertension, hypokalemic alkalosis, potassium depletion, hypervolemia, and decreased plasma renin activity; may be associated with small benign adrenocortical ademonas.

secondary a., pathological a. resulting not from a defect intrinsic to the adrenal cortex but from a stimulation of secretion caused by extra-adrenal disorders; it is associated with increased plasma renin activity and occurs in heart failure, nephrotic syndrome, cirrhosis, and hypoproteinemia.

alecithal (ă-les'ĭ-thal) [G. *a-* priv. + *lekithos,* yolk]. Denoting ova with little or no yolk.

aleukemia (ă-lu-ke'mĭ-ah) [G. *a-* priv. + *leukos,* white, + *haima,* blood]. **1.** Literally, a lack of leukocytes in the blood. Generally used to indicate varieties of leukemic disease in which the white blood cell count in circulating blood is normal or even less than normal (*i.e.,* no leukocytosis), but a few young leukocytes are observed; sometimes used more restrictedly for unusual instances of leukemia with no leukocytosis and no young forms in the blood. **2.** Leukemic changes in bone marrow associated with a subnormal number of leukocytes in the blood.

aleuke'mic. Pertaining to aleukemia.

aleukemoid (ă-lu-ke'moyd). Resembling aleukemia symptomatically.

aleukia (ă-lu-kĭ'-ah) [G. *a-* priv. + *leukos,* white]. **1.** Absence or extremely decreased number of leukocytes in circulating blood; sometimes also termed aleukemic myelosis. **2.** Obsolete name for thrombocytopenia.

aleukocytic (ă-lu-ko-sit'ik). Manifesting absence or extremely reduced numbers of leukocytes in blood or lesions.

aleukocytosis (ă-lu-ko-si-to'sis) [G. *a-*priv. + *leukos,* white, + *lytos,* a hollow (cell)]. Absence or great reduction (relative or absolute) of the number of white blood cells in circulating blood (*i.e.,* an advanced degree of leukopenia), or the lack of leukocytes in an anatomical lesion.

alexia (ă-lek-sĭ'-ah) [G. *a-* priv. + *lexis,* a word or phrase]. Visual aphasia (1); loss of the ability to grasp the meaning of written or printed words and sentences. Called also **optical, sensory,** or **visual a.,** in distinction to **motor a.** (anarthria), in which there is loss of the power to read aloud although the significance of what is written or printed is understood.

alex'ic. Pertaining to alexia.

algae (al'je) [pl. of L. *alga,* seaweed]. A division of cellular cryptogamous plants, including seaweeds.

al'gal. Resembling or pertaining to algae.

alge-, algesi-, algo- G. *algos, pain*]. Combining forms meaning pain.

algesia (al-je'zĭ-ah) [G. *algēsis,* a sense of pain]. Algesthesia.

alge'sic. Algetic.

algesim'eter. Algesiometer.

algesiogenic (al-je-zĭ-o-jen'ik) [G. *algēsis,* sense of pain, + *-gen,* production]. Algogenic; pain-producing.

algesiometer (al-je'sĭ-om'ĕ-ter) [G. *algēsis,* sense of pain, + *-metron,* measure]. Algesimter; algometer; odynometer; an instrument for measuring the degree of sensitivity to a painful stimulus.

algesthesia (al-jes-the'ze-ah) [G. *algos,* pain, + *aisthēsis,* sensation]. Algesia. **1.** The appreciation of pain. **2.** Hypersensitivity to pain.

algesthe'sis. Algesthesia.

alget'ic. Alegesia. **1.** Painful, or relating to or causing pain. **2.** Relating to hypersensitivity to pain.

-algia [G. *algos,* pain]. Suffix meaning pain or painful condition.

algicide (al'jĭ-sīd) [algae, + L. *caedo,* to kill]. A chemical active against algae.

algo-. See alge-.

algogen'ic. Algesiogenic.

algom'eter alo- + G. metron, measure]. Algesiometer.

algophilia (al-go-fil'ĭ-ah) [algo- + G. *phileō,* to love]. Pleasure experienced in the thought of pain in others or in oneself.

algopho'bia [algo- + G. *phobos,* fear]. Abnormal fear of or sensitiveness to pain.

al'gorithm. The written steps in protocol for management of health care problems.

algovascular (al-go-vas'ku-lar) [G. *algos,* pain]. Algiovascular; relating to changes in the lumen of the blood vessels occuring under the influence of pain.

alienation (āl'yen-a'a'shun) [L. *alieno,* pp. *-atus,* to make strange]. A condition characterized by lack of meaningful relationships to others and sometimes resulting in depersonalization and estrangement from others.

alienia (a-li-e'nĭ-ah) [G. *a-* priv. + L. *lien,* spleen]. Absence of the spleen.

al'iform [L. *ala,* + *forma,* shape]. Wing-shaped.

alimentary (al'ĭ-men'tă-rĭ) [L. *alimentarius,* fr. *alimentum,* nourishment]. Relating to food or nutrition, or to the organs of digestion.

alimenta'tion. Providing nourishment; see also feeding.

alinasal (al'ĭ-na'sal) [L. *ala,* + *nasus,* nose]. Relating to the alae nasi, or flaring portions of the nostrils.

aliphat'ic [G. *aleipar* (*aleiphat-*), fat, oil]. **1.** Fatty. **2.** Denoting the acyclic carbon compounds, most of which belong to the fatty acid series.

aliphatic acids. The acids of nonaromatic hydrocarbons, *i.e.,* acetic, propionic, butyric (and other) acids; the so-called fatty acids, of the formula R-COOH, where R is a nonaromatic (aliphatic) hydrocarbon.

aliquant (al'ĭ-kwant). In chemistry and immunology, pertaining to a portion that results from dividing the whole in a manner that some is left after the a.'s (equal in volume or weight) have been apportioned.

aliquot (al'ĭ-kwot). In chemistry and immunology, pertaining to a portion of the whole; loosely, any one of two or more samples of something, of the same volume or weight.

alisphenoid (al-ĭ-sfe'noyd) [L. *ala*, + *sphēn*, wedge]. Relating to the greater wing of the sphenoid bone.

aliz'arin. A red dye made synthetically from anthracene, used in the manufacture of dyes and as an indicator.

alkale'mia [alkali + G. *haima*, blood]. A decrease in H-ion concentration of the blood or a rise in pH, irrespective of alterations in the level of bicarbonate ion.

alkalescent (al-kal-es'ent). Slightly alkaline; becoming alkaline.

alkali, pl. **alkalis** or **alkalies** (al'kă-li, -līz) [Ar., *al*, the, + *qaliy*, soda ash]. A strongly basic substance yielding hydroxide ions (OH-) in solution; *e.g.*, sodium hydroxide, potassium hydroxide.

al'kaline. Relating to or having the reaction of an alkali.

alkalin'ity. The condition of being alkaline.

alkalinu'ria [alkaline + G. *ouron*, urine]. Alkaluria; the passage of alkaline urine.

al'kaloid. Any one of hundreds of plant products distinguised by basic reactions, now restricted to heterocyclic nitrogen-containing and often complex structures possessing pharmacological activity; *e.g.*, atropine, nicotine, caffeine, cocaine. For medicinal purposes the salts of a.'s are usually used.

alkalo'sis. A pathophysiological disorder characterized by H-ion loss or base excess in body fluids (metabolic a.), or caused by CO_2 loss due to hyperventilation (respiratory a.).

   compensated a., a. in which there is a rise in bicarbonate but the pH of body fluids approaches normal due to compensatory mechanisms of the body.

   metabolic a., an a. associated with an increased arterial plasma bicarbonate concentration; the base excess and standard bicarbonate are both elevated.

   respiratory a., a. resulting from abnormal loss of CO_2 produced by hyperventilation, either active or passive, with concomitant reduction in arterial plasma bicarbonate concentration.

   uncompensated a., a., usually related to a rise in the bicarbonate concentration, in which the pH of body fluids is elevated because of lack of the compensatory mechanisms of compensated a.

alkalot'ic. Relating to alkalosis.

alkalu'ria. Alkalinuria.

al'kane. The general term for a saturated acylic hydrocarbon.

alkap'ton [alkali + G. *kaptein*, to suck up greedily]. Homogentisic acid.

alkaptonuria (al-kap-tŏ-nu'rĭah) [alkapton + G. *ouron*, urine]. Alcaptonuria; homogentisuria; the excretion of homogentisic acid (alkapton) in the urine due to an inherited disorder of phenylalanine and tyrosine metabolism; the urine turns dark if allowed to stand or if an alkali is added; autosomal recessive inheritance.

al'kene. An acyclic hydrocarbon containing one double bond; *e.g.*, ethylene.

alk'enyl. The radical of an alkene.

al'kide. Alkyl (2).

al'kyl. **1.** A hydrocarbon radical of the general formula C_nH_{2n+1}. **2.** Alkide; a compound, such as tetraethyl lead, in which a metal is combined with alkyl radicals.

al'kylation. Substitution of an alkyl radical for a hydrogen atom.

ALL Acute lymphocytic leukemia.

allachesthesia (al-ă-kes-the'sĭ-ah) [G. *allachē*, elsewhere, + *aisthēsis*, sensation]. A condition in which a sensation is referred to a point other than that to which the stimulus is applied.

   optical a., visual *allesthesia*.

allantiasis (al'an-ti'ă-sis) G. *allas* (*allant-*), sausage]. Sausage poisoning, due to botulism in most cases.

allanto-, allant- [G. *allas*, sausage]. Combining forms for allantois, allantoid.

allantochorion (al-lan-to-ko'rĭ-on). Extraembryonic membrane formed by the fusion of the allantois and chorion.

allanto'ic. Relating to the allantois.

allan'toid [allanto- + G. *eidos*, appearance]. **1.** Sausage-shaped. **2.** Relating to, or resembling, the allantois.

allantoin (al-an'to-in). 5-Ureidohydantoin; a substance present in the allantoic fluid, the urine of the fetus, and elsewhere; also an oxidation product of uric acid and the end product of purine metabolism in animals other than man and the other primates.

allantoinuria (al-lan'to-in-u'rĭ-ah) [allantoin + G. *ouron*, urine]. Urinary excretion of allantoin; normal in most mammals, abnormal in man.

allantois (al-an'to-is) [allanto- + G. *eidos*, appearance]. In man, a vestigial fetal membrane developing from the yolk sac.

allele (ă-lēl') [G. *allēlōn*, reciprocally]. Allelomorph; any one of a series of two or more different genes that may occupy the same position or locus on a specific chromosome.

alle'lemor'phic. Allelic.

alle'lic. Allelomorphic; relating to an allele.

allelomorph (al-e'lo-morf) [G. *allēlōn*, reciprocally, + *morphē*, shape]. Allele.

alle'lotaxis, alle'lotaxy [G. *allēlōn*, reciprocally, + *taxis*, an arranging]. Development of an organ from a number of embryonal structures or tissues.

allergen (al'er-jen) [allergy + G. *-gen*, producing]. Antigen.

allergen'ic. Antigenic.

aller'gic. Relating to any response stimulated by an allergen (antigen).

allergist (al'er-jist). One who specializes in the treatment of allergies.

allergy (al'er-jī) [G. *allos*, other, + *ergon*, work]. **1.** Acquired (induced) sensitivity; the immunologic state induced in a susceptible subject by an antigen (allergen), characterized by a marked change in reactivity. On the subject's initial contact with it, the antigen is seemingly inert immunologically, but after a latent period the subject becomes sensitive, even to antigen that persists from the initial inoculation, and thereafter, the specific antigen evokes a reaction within minutes or hours, the severity of which depends upon quantitative relationships and route of entrance of antigen. **2.** An acquired hypersensitivity to certain drugs and biologic preparations.

  atopic a., see atopy.

  contact a., cutaneous reaction caused by direct contact with an antigen to which the person is hypersensitive.

  delayed a., a type IV allergic reaction; so called because in a sensitized subject the reaction becomes evident only several or more hours after contact with the antigen, reaches its peak after 36 to 48 hours, then recedes slowly.

  immediate a., a type I allergic reaction; so called because in a sensitized subject the reaction becomes evident usually within minutes after contact with the antigen, reaches its peak within an hour or so, then rapidly recedes.

  latent a., a. that causes no signs or symptoms but can be revealed by means of certain immunologic tests with specific allergens.

  physical a., excessive response to factors in the environment, such as heat or cold.

  polyvalent a., allergic response manifested simultaneously for several or numerous specific allergens.

allesthesia (al-es-the'zī-ah) [G. *allos*, other, + *aisthēsis*, sensation]. Allocheiria; allochiria; allachesthesia in which the sensation of a stimulus in one limb is referred to the opposite limb.

  visual a., optical allachesthesia; a disorder characterized by the transposition of images from one half-field to the opposite.

allo- [G. *allos*, other]. Prefix meaning "other," differing from the normal or usual.

alloantibody (al-o-an'tī-bod-ī). An antibody specific for an alloantigen. Isoantibody is sometimes used in this sense.

alloantigen (al-o-an'tī-jen). An antigen that occurs in some, but not in other members of the same species. Isoantigen is sometimes used in this sense.

allobar'bital. 5,5-Diallylbarbituric acid; a sedative and hypnotic.

allocheiria, allochiria (al'o-ki'rī-ah) [allo- + G. *cheir*, hand]. Allesthesia.

allochromasia (al-o-kro-ma'zī-ah) [allo- + G. *chrōma*, color]. Change of color of the skin or hair.

allocortex (al'o-kor'teks) [allo- + L. *cortex*, bark (cortex)]. See *cortex* cerebri.

allodynia (al-o-din'ī̆ah) [allo- + G. *odynē*, pain]. The distress resulting from painful stimuli.

alloerotic (al'o-e-rot'ik). Heteroerotic; pertaining to or characterized by alloerotism.

alloerotism, alloeroticism al-o-ĕr'o-tizm, -er-ot'ī̆-sizm) [allo- + G. *erōs*, love]. Heteroerotism; sexual attraction toward another person.

al'logene'ic, al'logen'ic. Pertaining to different gene consitutions within the same species, in contradistinction to isogeneic and heterogeneic.

al'lograft. Allogeneic graft or homograft; a graft from an allogeneic donor of the same species as the recipient.

alloker'atoplasty. The replacement of opaque corneal tissue with a transparent prosthesis, usually acrylic.

allola'lia [allo- + G. *lalia*, talking]. Any speech defect due to disease affecting the speech center.

allom'erism [allo- + G. *meros*, part]. A characteristic of substances that differ in chemical composition but have the same crystalline form.

allomorphism (al-o-mor'fizm) [allo- + G. *morphē*, form]. **1.** A change of shape in cells due to mechanical causes. **2.** Similarity of chemical composition, but a difference in form, especially of crystalline minerals.

allopath'ic. Relating to allopathy.

allop'athy [allo- + G. *pathos*, suffering]. A therapeutic system in which a disease is treated by producing a second condition that is incompatible with or antagonistic to the first.

al'loplast [allo- + G. *plastos*, formed]. **1.** A graft of an inert metal or plastic material. **2.** An inert foreign body used for implantation into tissues.

al'loplasty. The repair of defects by allotransplantation.

alloploid (al'o-ployd) [allo- + -ploid, *q.v.*]. Relating to a hybrid individual or cell with two or more sets of chromosomes derived from two different ancestral species.

alloploidy (al-o-ploy'dī). The condition of a hybrid individual or cell having two or more sets of chromosomes derived from two different ancestral species.

allopsychic (al-o-si'kik) [allo- + G. *psychē*, mind]. Denoting the mental processes in their relation to the outer world.

all or none. See Bowditch's *law*.

allorhythmia (al-ŏ-rith'mī-ah) [allo- + G. *rhythmos*, rhythm]. An irregularity in the cardiac rhythm that repeats itself again and again.

allorhythmic (al-ŏ-rith'mik). Relating to or characterized by allorhythmia.

al'losome [allo- + G. *sōma*, body]. Heterochromosome; heterotypical chromosome; one of the chromosomes differing in appearance or behavior from the ordinary chromosomes, or autosomes, and sometimes unequally distributed among the germ cells.

alloster'ic. Pertaining to or characterized by allosterism.

allosterism, allostery (al-los'ter-ism, -ter-ī). The influencing of an enzyme activity by a change in the conformation of the enzyme, brought about by the noncompetitive binding of a nonsubstrate at a site (the allosteric site) other than the active site of the enzyme.

al'lotransplanta'tion. Removal of tissue from one individual and grafting it into another of the same species.

allotrichia circumscripta (al-o-trik'ī-ah sir-kum-skrip'tah) [allo- + G. *thrix,* hair, + L. *circumscriptio,* a boundary]. Woolly-hair *nevus.*

al'lotrope [allo- + G. *tropos,* a turning]. A substance in one of the allotropic forms that the element may assume.

allotro'phic [allo- + G. *trophē,* nourishment]. Having an altered nutritive value.

allotrop'ic. 1. Relating to allotropy. **2.** In psychiatry, denoting a type of personality characterized by a preoccupation with the reactions of others.

allot'ropy, allot'ropism [allo- + G. *tropos,* a turning]. The existence of certain elements, such as phosphorus and carbon, in several different forms with unlike physical properties.

allotype (al'o-tīp). Any one of the genetically determined antigenic differences within a given class of immunoglobulin which occur among members of the same species.

allotypic (al-o-tip'ik). Pertaining to an allotype.

alloxure'mia [alloxan + G. *haima,* blood]. Presence of purine bases in the blood.

alloxu'ria [alloxan + G. *ouron,* urine]. Presence of purine bodies in the urine.

allyl (al'il). The monovalent radical (CH$_2$= CHCH$_2$-).

al'oe. Dried juice from the leaves of plants of the genus *Aloe* (family Liliaceae), from which are derived various pharmaceutical preparations.

alogia (ă-lo'jĭ-ah) [G. *a-* priv. + *logos,* speech]. **1.** Aphasia. **2.** Speechlessness due to mental deficiency or mental confusion.

alopecia (al-o-pe'shī-ah) [G. *alōpekia,* a disease like fox mange]. Baldness; loss of hair.

  a. area'ta, a. circumscripta; a. of unknown etiology characterized by circumcribed, noninflamed areas of baldness on the scalp, eyebrows, and bearded portion of the face.

  a. cap'itis tota'lis, a. progressing to involve the entire scalp.

  cicatricial a., a. cicatrisa'ta, a. produced by scar formation as in certain dermatoses.

  a. circumscrip'ta, a. areata.

  a. congenita'lis, congenital a., congenital baldness; absence of all hair at birth.

  a. heredita'ria, male pattern a. or baldness; patterned a.; a. resulting from sex-influenced dominant inheritance, with androgen stimulation required to produce hair loss in heterozygous individuals; homozygous females may have minor hair loss without androgen stimulation.

  a. limina'ris fronta'lis, hair loss at the hair line; may be associated with seborrheic dermatitis but is commonly caused by friction or other trauma.

  male pattern a., a. hereditaria.

  a. medicamento'sa, diffuse hair loss, most notably of the scalp, caused by administration of various types of drugs.

  patterned a., a. hereditaria.

  a. pityro'des, a loss of hair, of the body as well as of the scalp, accompanied by an abundant branlike desquamation.

  a. symptomat'ica, a. occurring in the course of various constitutional or local diseases, or following prolonged febrile illness.

  a. tota'lis, total loss of hair of the scalp either at one time or within a very short period of time.

  a. universa'lis, total loss of hair from all parts of the body.

alopecic (al-o-pe'sik). Relating to alopecia.

Al'phavirus. A genus of viruses (family Togaviridae) formerly classified as group A arboviruses.

ALS Antilymphocyte *serum.*

ALT Alanine aminotransferase.

alternans (awl-ter'nanz [L.]. Alternating; often used substantively for alternation of the heart.

  auscultatory a., alternation in the intensity of heart sounds or murmurs in the presence of a regular cardiac rhythm as a result of alternation of the heart.

  concordant a., right ventricular and pulmonary artery a. occur simultaneously with peripheral pulsus a.

  discordant a., right ventricular and pulmonary artery a. are present with peripheral pulsus a., but the strong beat of the right ventricle coincides with the weak beat of the left and vice versa.

  electrical a., electrical *alternation* of the heart.

  pulsus a., see under pulsus.

alternation (awl-ter-na'shun). The occurrence of two things or phases in succession and recurrently.

  concordant a., a. in either the mechanical or electrical activity of the heart, occurring in both systemic and pulmonary circuits.

  discordant a., a. in cardiac activities of either the systemic or the pulmonic circuits, but not of both.

  electrical a. of heart, a disorder in which the ventricular complexes are regular in time but of alternating pattern; a. of P waves occurs rarely.

  a. of heart, mechanical a., a disorder in which contractions of the heart are regular in time but are alternately stronger and weaker.

al'um. A double sulfate of aluminum and of an alkaline earth element or ammonium; chemically, any one of the double salts formed by a combination of a sulfate of aluminum, iron, manganese, chromium, or gallium with a sulfate of lithium, sodium, potassium, ammonium, cesium, or rubidium; markedly astringent and used as styptics.

alu'minated. Containing alum.

alumino'sis. A pneumonconiosis occurring in workers exposed to alum.

aluminum [L. *alumen,* alum]. A metallic element; symbol Al, atomic no. 13, atomic weight 26.98; in various compounds, used as an astringent, antiperspirant, antiseptic, and antipyretic.

alvei (al've-i). Plural of alveus.

alveoalgia (al've-o-al'jĭ-ah) [alveolus + G. *algos,* pain]. Dry socket; alveolalgia; sequela to tooth extractions in which the blood clot in the socket disintegrates, leading to an empty socket that becomes secondarily infected.

alveolal'gia. Alveoalgia.

alve'olar. Relating to an alveolus.

alveolec'tomy [alveolus + G. *ektomē,* excision]. Surgical excision of a portion of the dentoalveolar process, for recontouring the alveolar ridge at the time of tooth removal to facilitate a dental prosthesis.

alveoli (al-ve'o-li). Plural of alveolus.

alveolin'gual. Alveololingual.

alveoli'tis. 1. Inflammation of alveoli. **2.** Inflammation of a tooth socket (alveolus dentalis).

  acute pulmonary a., acute inflammation involving the pulmonary alveoli, which may result in necrosis with hemorrhage into the lungs; may be associated with glomerulonephritis, in Goodpasture's syndrome.

  extrinsic allergic a., hypersensitivity pneumonitis; pneumoconiosis resulting from hypersensitivity due to repeated inhalation of organic dust, usually specified according to occupational exposure.

alveolo- [L. *alveolus, q. v.*]. Combining form denoting relation to an alveolus or to the alveolar process.

alveoloclasia (al-ve'o-lo-kla'zĭ-ah) [alveolo- + G. *klasis,* breaking]. Destruction of the alveolus.

alve'oloden'tal. Relating to the alveoli and the teeth.

alve'olola'bial. [alveolo- + Mediev. L. *labialis,* relating to a lip]. Relating to the labial or outer surface of the alveolar processes.

alveololingual (al-ve'o-lo-ling'gwal). Alveolingual; relating to the lingual or inner surface of the alveolar process.

alve'olopal'atal. Referring to the palatal surface of the alveolar process.

alve'oloplas'ty [alveolo- + G. *plassō,* to form]. Alveoplasty; surgical preparation of the alveolar ridges for the reception of dentures; shaping and smoothing of socket margins after extraction of teeth with subsequent suturing to insure optimal healing.

alveolot'omy [alveolo- + G. *tomē,* incision]. Incision of the alveolar process to allow drainage of pus from a periapical or other intraosseous abscess.

alve'olus, gen. and pl. **alve'oli** [L. dim. of *alveus,* trough, a hollow sac, cavity] [NA]. A small cell or cavity; a sac-like dilation.

  a. denta'lis [NA], dental a.; tooth socket; a socket in the alveolar process of the maxilla or mandible, into which each tooth fits and is attached by means of the periodontal membrane.

alve'olus, gen. and pl. **alve'oli** alveoli pulmo'nis [NA], pulmonary alveoli; air cells (1); terminal dilations of the bronchioles where gas exchange is thought to occur.

alveoplas'ty. Alveoloplasty.

al'veus, pl. **al'vei** L. tray, trough, cavity]. A channel or trough.

alymphia (ă-lim'fī-ah). Absence or deficiency of lymph.

alymph'ocyto'sis. Absence or great reduction of lymphocytes.

alymphoplasia (ă-lim'fo-pla'zĭ-ah). Aplasia or hypoplasia of lymphoid tissue.

  Nezelof type of thymic a., cellular *immunodeficiency* with abnormal immunoglobulin synthesis.

  thymic a., thymic hypoplasia, with absence of Hassell's corpuscles and deficiency of lymphocytes in the thymus and usually in lymph nodes, spleen, and gastrointestinal tract.

Am Americium.

amacrine (am'ă-krin) [G. *a-* priv. + *makros,* long, + *is* (*in-*), fiber]. **1.** A cell or structure lacking a long, fibrous process. **2.** Denoting such a cell or structure.

amal'gam [G. *malagma,* a soft mass]. An alloy of an element or a metal with mercury. In dentistry, primarily of two types: silver-tin alloy, containing small amounts of copper and zinc, and a second type containing more copper (12 to 30% by weight); used for filling teeth and making dies.

Amanita (am-ă-ni'tah) [G. *amanitai,* fungi]. A genus of fungi, many members of which are highly poisonous.

  A. musca'ria, a toxic species of mushroom that contains muscarine, which produces psychosis-like states and other symptoms caused by muscarine.

  A. phalloi'des, a species of mushroom containing poisonous principles including phalloidine and amanitin, which cause gastroenteritis, hepatic necrosis, and renal necrosis.

amarine (am'ă-rin) [L. *amarus,* bitter]. A name applied to various bitter principles derived from plants; especially to a poisonous substance, 2,4,5-triphenylimidazoline, obtained from oil of bitter almond.

amas'tia [G. *a-* priv. + *mastos,* breast]. Amazia; congenital absence of one or both breasts.

amastigote (ă-mas'tĭ-gōt) [G. *a-* priv. + *mastix,* whip]. Leishman-Donovan *body.*

amaurosis (am-aw-ro'sis) [G. *amauros,* dark, obscure, + *-osis,* condition]. Blindness, especially that occurring without apparent change in the eye itself; *e.g.,* from a cortical lesion.

  a. congeni'ta of Leber, an autosomal recessive cone-rod abiotrophy causing blindness or severely reduced vision at birth, frequently with keratoconus.

  a. fu'gax, a temporary blindness that may result from a transient ischemia due to carotid artery insufficiency or to centrifugal force.

amaurotic (am-aw-rot'ik). Relating to or suffering from amaurosis.

ama'zia. Amastia.

ambageusia (am-bă-gu'sĭ-ah) [L. *ambo*, both, + G. *a-* priv. + *geusis*, taste]. Loss of taste from both sides of the tongue.

ambi- [L. *ambo*, both]. Prefix meaning round; all (both) sides.

am'bidexter'ity, ambidex'trism. Ability to use either hand with equal ease.

ambidex'trous [ambi- + L. *dexter*, right]. Having equal facility in the use of both hands.

ambient (am'bĭ-ent) [L. *ambiens*, going around]. Surrounding, environing; pertaining to the air, noise, temperature, etc., in which an organism or apparatus functions.

ambilat'eral [ambi- + L. *latus*, side]. Relating to both sides.

ambilevous (am-bĭ-le'vus) [ambi- + L. *laevus*, left]. Awkward in the use of either hand.

ambisex'ual. Bisexual.

ambiv'alence [ambi- + L. *valentia*, strenth]. Coexistence of antithetical attitudes or emotions toward a given person or thing; in psychiatry, often refers to simultaneous love and hate toward the same person.

ambiv'alent. Relating to or characterized by ambivalence.

ambly- [G. *amblys*, dull]. Combining form denoting dullness, dimness.

amblyaphia (am-blĭ-a'fĭ-ah) [ambly- + G. *haphē*, touch]. Diminution in tactile sensibility.

amblygeustia (am-blĭ-gūs'tĭ-ah) [ambly- + G. *geusis*, taste]. A blunted sense of taste.

Amblyomma (am-blĭ-om'ah) [ambly- + G. *omma*, eye, vision]. A genus of ornate, hard ticks (family Ixodidae). *A. americanum*, the Lone-Star tick, and *A. cajennense* are important pests and vectors of Rocky Mountain spotted fever.

amblyopia (am-blĭ-o'pĭ-ah) [G. *amblyōpia*, dimness of vision, fr. *amblys* dull, + *ōps*, eye]. Dimness of vision; partial loss of sight.

amblyo'pic. Relating to, or suffering from, amblyopia.

amblyoscope (am'blĭ-o-skōp) [amblyopia + G. *skopeō*, to view]. A reflecting stereoscope used for measuring or training binocular vision, and for stimulation of vision in the amblyopic eye.

ambo- [G. *ambo*, both]. Prefix meaning round; all (both) sides.

am'boceptor [ambo- + L. *capio*, to take]. The anti-sheep erythrocyte antibody used in the hemolytic system of complement-fixation tests.

ambulant (am'bu-lant). Ambulatory.

ambulatory (am'bu-lă-tor-e) [L. *ambulo*, p.p. *-atus*, to walk]. Ambulant; walking about or able to walk about; not confined to bed.

ameba, pl. **amebae, amebas** (ă-me'bah, -be, -bahs). Common name for *Amoeba* and similar naked, lobose, sarcodine protozoa.

amebiasis (am-e-bi'ă-sis) [ameba + G. *-iasis*, condition]. Amebiosis; amebism; infection with *Entamoeba histolytica* or other pathogenic amebas.

ame'bic. Relating to, resembling, or caused by amebas.

amebici'dal. Destructive to amebas.

amebicide (ă-me'bĭsĭd) [ameba + L. *caedo*, to kill]. Any agent that causes the destruction of amebas.

ame'biform [ameba + L. *forma*, shape]. Of the shape or appearance of an ameba.

amebiosis (ă-me'bi-o'sis). Amebiasis.

ame'bism. Amebiasis.

amebocyte (ă-me'bo-sĭt) [ameba, + *kytos*, cell]. **1.** A cell with ameboid movement. **2.** An *in vitro* tissue culture blood cell.

ame'boid [ameba + G. *eidos*, appearance]. **1.** Resembling an ameba in appearance or characteristics. **2.** Of irregular outline with peripheral projections; denoting the outline of a form of colony in plate culture.

amebo'ma [ameba + G. *-oma*, tumor]. Amebic granuloma; a nodular, tumor-like focus of proliferative inflammation sometimes developing in chronic amebiasis, especially in the wall of the colon.

amebula, pl. **amebulae** (ă-me'bu-lah, -le) [fr. *amoibē*, a change, alteration]. The excysted young amebas of *Entamoeba* species and their immediate progeny.

ameburia (am'e-bu'rĭah) [ameba + G. *ouron*, urine]. Presence of amebas in the urine.

amel'ia [G. *a-* priv. + *melos*, a limb]. Congenital absence of one or more limbs.

amel'oblast [Early E. *amel*, enamel, + G. *blastos*, germ]. Adamantoblast; enamel cell; one of the cells of the inner layer of the enamel organ of a developing tooth, concerned with the formation of enamel.

am'elobas'todonto'ma. Ameloblastic *odontoma*.

am'eloblas'tofibro'ma. Ameloblastic *fibroma*.

am'eloblasto'ma. Adamantinoma; adamantoblastoma; adamantoma; an epithelial odontogenic tumor comprised chiefly of epithelial cell aggregates that mimic the enamel organ and which are characterized by peripheral cells reminiscent of ameloblasts that encircle a central group of cells resembling the stellate reticulum.

am'eloden'tinal. Dentinoenamel.

amelogenesis (am'el-o-jen'ē-sis). Enamelogenesis; the production and development of enamel.

a. imperfec'ta, enamelogenesis imperfecta; enamel dysplasia; a group of hereditary defects characterized by faulty metabolism in either of two steps of enamel formation: defective matrix formation leads to enamel hypoplasia; defective maturation leads to enamel hypocalcification.

amenorrhea (ă-men-o-re'ah) [G. *a-* priv. + *mēn*, month, + *rhoia*, flow]. menostasis; menostasia; absence or abnormal cessation of the menses.

primary a., a. in which the menses have never occurred.

secondary a., any a. in which the menses appeared at puberty but have been suppressed.

amenorrhe′al, amenorrhe′ic. Relating to, accompanied by, or due to amenorrhea.

amentia (ă-men′shĭ-ah) [L. madness, fr. *ab*, from, + *mens*, mind]. **1.** Mental *retardation*. **2.** Dementia.

amential (ă-men′shĭ-al). Pertaining to amentia.

American Law Institute rule. See under rule.

americium (am′ē-ris′ĭ-um). An element obtained by the bombardment of uranium with neutrons; symbol Am, atomic no. 95.

ame′tria [G. *a-* priv. + *mētra*, uterus]. Congenital absence of the uterus.

ametrometer (am′ē-trom′ē-ter) [ametropia + G. *metron*, measure]. An appliance for measuring the degree of ametropia.

ametropia (am′ē-tro′pĭ-ah) [G. *ametros*, disproportionate, fr. *a-* priv. + *metron*, measure, + *ōps*, eye]. A condition in which there is some error of refraction in consequence of which parallel rays, with the eye at rest, are not focused on the retina.

ametro′pic. Relating to, or suffering from, ametropia.

-amic. Suffix denoting a compound related to or derived from an amide.

amicro′bic. Not microbic; not related to or caused by microorganisms.

am′idase. Acylase; acylamidase; an enzyme that catalyzes the hydrolysis of monocarboxylic amides to free acid plus NH_3.

am′idases. Amidohydrolases.

amide (am′id, am′īd). A substance that may be regarded as being derived from ammonia through the substitution of one or more of the hydrogen atoms by acyl groups; $R-CO-NH_2$. The replacement of one hydrogen atom constitutes a **primary**, that of two hydrogen atoms a **secondary,** and that of three atoms a **tertiary a.**

amidine (am′ĭ-din). The monovalent radical – $C(NH)-NH_2$.

amido-. A prefix denoting the amide radical, $R-CO-NH-$ or $R-SO_2-NH-$, etc.

amidohydrolases (am′ĭ-do-hi′dro-la′ses). Amidases; deaminidases; deamidizing enzymes; enzymes hydrolyzing C–N bonds of amides.

amim′ia [G. *a-* priv. + *mimos*, a mimic]. Loss of the power to express ideas by gestures or signs.

am′inate. To combine with ammonia.

am′ine. A substance that may be derived from ammonia by the replacement of one or more of the hydrogen atoms by hydrocarbon or other radicals. The substitution of one hydrogen atom constitutes a **primary a.;** that of two atoms a **secondary a.;** that of three atoms a **tertiary a.;** that of four atoms a **quaternary ammonium ion,** a positively charged ion which is isolated only in association with a negative ion. A.'s form salts with acids.

adrenergic a., sympathomimetic a.

adrenomimetic a. sympathomimetic a.

pressor a., pressor *base*.

sympathetic a., sympathomimetic a.

sympathomimetic a., adrenergic, adrenomimetic, or sympathetic a.; an agent that evokes responses similar to those produced by adrenergic nerve activity.

amino-. A prefix denoting a compound containing the radical group, $-NH_2$.

amino acid (AA). An organic acid in which one of the CH hydrogen atoms has been replaced by NH_2.

a. a. dehydrogenases, enzymes catalyzing the oxidative deamination of amino acids to the corresponding keto acids.

essential a. a.'s, α -amino acids required by animals that must be supplied in the diet (*i.e.,* cannot be synthesized by the animal) either as free a. acids or in proteins.

nonessential a a.'s, those a. a.'s that may be synthesized by the organism and thus are not required as such in the diet.

a. a. oxidases, enzymes oxidizing, with O_2, L-and D-amino acids respectively, to the corresponding keto acids, $NH_3$and H_2O_2.

α-amino acid. An amino acid of the general formula $R-CHNH_2-COOH$ (*i.e.,* NH_2 in the α position); L forms are the hydrolysis products of proteins.

aminoacidemia (am′ĭ-no-as-ĭ-de′mĭ-ah) [amino acid + G. *haima*, blood]. Excessive amounts of specific amino acids in the blood.

aminoaciduria (am′ĭ-no-as-ĭ-du′rĭ-ah) [amino acid + G. *ouron*, urine]. Acidaminuria; hyperaminoaciduria; excretion of amino acids in urine, especially in excessive amounts.

aminoacyl (AA) (am′ĭ-no-as′il). The radical formed from an amino acid by removal of OH from a COOH group.

aminoacylase (am′ĭ-no-as′ĭ-las) . Enzyme catalyzing hydrolysis of a wide variety of *N*-acyl amino acids to the amino acids.

p-**am′inobenzo′ic acid (PABA).** A factor (vitamin B_x) in the vitamin B complex, a part of all folic acids and required for its formation; neutralizes the bacteriostatic effects of the sulfonamides.

γ-**am′inobutyr′ic acid (GABA).** $NH_2(CH_2)_3COOH$; a constituent of the central nervous system suggested as a transmitter of inhibitory nerve impulses.

p-**am′inohippu′ric acid (PAH).** *N*-(4-Aminobenzoyl) glycine; used in renal function tests.

δ-**am′inolevulin′ic acid(ALA).** $NH_2CH_2COCH_2CH_2-COOH$; an acid formed by δ-aminoevulinic synthase from glycine and succinyl-coenzyme A; as a precursor of porphobilinogen, an important intermediate in the biosynthesis of hematin.

aminolysis (am-ĭ-nol′ĭ-sis). Replacement of a halogen in an alkyl or aryl molecule by an amine radical, with elimination of hydrogen halide.

am′inopep′tidases. α-Aminoacyl-peptide hydrolases; enzymes catalyzing the breakdown of a peptide, removing the amino acid at the amino end of the chain; found in intestinal juice.

aminopherases (am′ĭ-nof′er-ās). Aminotransferases.

p-aminosalicylic acid (PAS, PASA) (am'ĭ-no-sal-ĭ-sil'ik). 4-Amino-2-hydroxybenzoic acid; a bacteriostatic agent against tubercle bcilli, used as an adjunct to streptomycin.

α-am'inosuccin'ic acid. Aspartic acid.

am'inotrans'ferases. Aminopherases; transaminases; enzymes transferring amino groups between an α-amino acid to (usually) a 2-keto acid.

aminuria (am'ĭ-nu'rĭ-ah) [amine + G. *ouron*, urine]. Excretion of amines in urine.

amito'sis [G. *a*-priv. + mitosis]. Direct division of the nucleus and cell, without the complicated changes in the former that occur in the ordinary process of cell reproduction.

amitot'ic. Relating to or marked by amitosis.

AML Acute myelogenous leukemia.

ammone'mia. Ammoniemia.

ammonia (ă-mo'nĭ-ah). A volatile gas, NH_3, very soluble in water, forming the base, NH_4OH, combining with acids to form ammonium compounds.

ammonia-lyases. Enzymes removing ammonia or an amino compound nonhydrolytically by rupture of a C–N bond, leaving a double bond.

ammoniemia (am-mo-ni-e'mĭ-ah) [ammonia + G. *haima*, blood]. Ammonemia; presence of ammonia or some of its compounds in the blood.

ammonio-, Combining form indicating an ammonium group.

ammo'nium. The radical, NH_4+, formed by combination NH_3 and $H+$; behaves as a univalent metal in forming ammonium compounds.

ammoniu'ria [ammonia + G. *ouron*, urine]. Excretion of urine that contains an excessive amount of ammonia.

ammon'niated. Containing or combined with ammonia.

am'monol'ysis [ammonia + G. *lysis*, dissolution]. The breaking of a chemical bond with the addition of the elements of ammonia ($NH_2$and H) at the point of breakage.

amnesia (am-ne'zĭ-ah) [G. *amnēsia*, forgetfulness]. Disturbance in memory of information stored in long term memory, in contrast to short term memory, manifested by total or partial inability to recall past experiences.

anterograde a., a. in reference to events occurring after the trauma or disease that caused the condition.

retrograde a., a. in reference to events that occurred before the trauma or disease that caused the condition.

amne'siac. One suffering from loss of memory.

amne'sic. Amnestic (1); relating to or affected with amnesia.

amnes'tic. 1. Amnesic. 2. Agent causing amnesia.

amnio- [G. *amnion, q.v.*]. Combining form relating to the amnion.

amniocentesis (am'nĭ-o-sen-te'sis) [amnio- + G. *kentēsis*, puncture]. Transabdominal aspiration of fluid from the amniotic sac.

amniochorial, amniochorionic (am'nĭ-o-ko'rĭ-al, rĭ-on'ik). Relating to both amnion and chorion.

amniogenesis (am'nĭ-o-jen'ĕ-sis) [amnio- + G. *genesis*, production]. Formation of the amnion.

amniography (am-nĭ-og'ră-fĭ) [amnio- + G. *graphō*, to write]. Roentgenography of the amniotic sac after the injection of an opaque, water-soluble solution into the sac.

amnioma (am-nĭ-o'mah) [amnio- + G. *-oma*, tumor]. A broad flat tumor of the skin resulting from antenatal adhesion of the amnion.

amnion (am'nĭ-on) [G. the membrane around the fetus]. Amniotic sac; the innermost of the membranes enveloping the embryo *in utero* and filled with the amniotic fluid.

a. nodo'sum, squamous metaplasia of amnion; nodules in the a. that consist of typical stratified squamous epithelium.

amnion'ic. Amniotic; relating to the amnion.

amnionitis (am'nĭ-o-ni'tis) [amnion + G. *-itis*, inflammation]. Inflammation resulting from infection of the amnion, usually resulting from premature rupture of the membranes and often associated with neonatal infection.

amniorrhea (am-nĭ-o-re'ah) [amnio- + G. *rhoia*, flow]. The escape of amniotic fluid.

amniorrhexis (am-nĭ-ŏ-rek'sis) [amnio- + G. *rhēxis*, rupture]. Rupture of the amnion.

am'nioscope. An endoscope for studying amniotic fluid through the intact amniotic sac.

amnioscopy (am-nĭ-os'ko-pĭ) [amnio- + G. *skopeō*, to view]. Examination of the amniotic fluid in the lowest part of the sac by means of an endoscope introduced through the cervical canal.

amniot'ic. Amnionic.

amniotome (am'nĭ-o-tōm) [amnio- + G. *tomē*, cutting]. An instrument for puncturing the fetal membranes.

amniot'omy. Artificial rupture of the fetal membranes as a means of inducing or expediting labor.

A-mode. In diagnostic ultrasound, a one-dimensional presentation of a reflected sound wave in which echo amplitude (A) is displayed along the vertical axis and time of rebound (depth) along the horizontal axis; the echo information is presented from interfaces along a single line in the direction of the sound beam.

Amoeba (ă-me'bah) [Mod. L. fr. G. *amoibē*, change]. A genus of naked, lobose, pseudopod-forming protozoa of the class Sarcodina (or Rhizopoda). The typical parasites of man are now placed in the genera *Entamoeba, Endolimax, Iodamoeba,* and *Dientamoeba.*

a'morph. An allele that has no phenotypically recognizable product and the existence of which is inferred by negative evidence.

amorphia, amorphism (ă-mor'fĭ-ah, -fizm) [G. *a*-priv. + *morphē*, form]. The condition of being amorphous.

amorphous (ă-mor'fus). **1.** Without definite shape or visible differentiation in structure. **2.** Not crystallized.

amoxicillin (a-mok-sĭ-sil'in). A semisynthetic penicillin antibiotic with an antimicrobial spectrum similar to that of ampicillin.

AMP Adenosine monophosphate (adenylic acid); specifically, the 5'-phosphate unless modified by a numerical prefix.

amph-. See amphi-, and ampho-.

amphet'amine. α-Methylphenethylamine; 1-phenyl-2-aminopropane; (phenylisopropyl)amine; $C_6H_5CH_2CH(NH_2)CH_3$; a powerful synthetic CNS stimulant closely related in its structure and action to ephedrine and other sympathomimetic amines; used as the sulfate.

amphi- [G. *amphi*, two-sided]. Combining form meaning on both sides, surrounding, double.

amphiarthrodial (am'fĭ-ar-thro'dĭ-al). Relating to amphiarthrosis.

amphiarthrosis (am'fĭ-ar-thro'sis) [amphi- + G. *arthrōsis*, joint]. *Articulatio* cartilaginis.

amphibar'ic [amphi- + G. *baros*, pressure]. Denoting a pharmacologic material that may lower or elevate arterial blood pressure, depending on the dose.

amphicen'tric [amphi- + G. *kentron*, center]. Centering at both ends, said of a rete mirabile that begins by the vessel breaking up into a number of branches and ends by the branches joining again to form the same vessel.

amphistome (am-fis'tōm) [amphi- + G. *stoma*, mouth]. Common name for any trematode of the genus *Paramphistomum*.

amphitrichate, amphitrichous (am-fĭ-trī'kăt, am-fit'rĭ-kus) [amphi- + G. *thrix*, hair]. Having a flagellum or flagella at both extremities of a microbial cell; denoting certain microorganisms.

ampho- [G. *amphō*, both]. Combining form meaning on both sides, surrounding, double.

amphocyte (am'fo-sit). Amphophil (2).

amphophil, amphophile (am'fo-fil, -fīl) [ampho- + G. *philos*, fond]. **1.** Amphophilic; amphophilous; having an affinity for both acid and for basic dyes. **2.** Amphocyte; a cell that stains readily with either acid or basic dyes.

amphophil'ic, amphoph'ilous. Amphophil (1).

amphoric (am-for'ik) [G. *amphora*, a jar]. Denoting the sound heard in percussion and auscultation resembling the noise made by blowing across the mouth of a bottle.

amphoteric (am-fo-tēr'ik) [G. *amphoteroi* (pl.), both, fr. *amphō*, both]. Having two opposite characteristics, especially having the capacity or reacting as either an acid or a base.

amphoter'icin B. $C_{46}H_{73}NO_{20}$; an amphoteric polyene antibiotic prepared from *Streptomyces nodosus;* also a nephrotoxic antifungal agent.

amphotericity (am'fo-tēr-is'ĭ-tĭ). Amphoterism.

amphoterism (am-fot'er-izm). Amphotericity; the property of being amphoteric.

ampicillin (am'pĭ-sĭ'lin). An acid-stable semisynthetic penicillin derived from 6-aminopenicillanic acid, with a broader spectrum of antimicrobial action than penicillin G, inhibiting the growth of Gram-positive and Gram-negative bacteria; not resistant to penicillinase.

ampul, ampule (am'pūl) [L. *ampulla, q.v.*]. A hermetically sealed container, usually made of glass, containing a sterile medicinal solution, or powder to be made up in solution, to be used for subcutaneous, intramuscular, or intravenous injection.

ampulla, gen. and pl. **ampullae** (am-pul'lah, -e) [L. a two-handled bottle] [NA]. A saccular dilation of a canal or duct.

a. chy'li, *cisterna* chyli.

a. duc'tus deferen'tis [NA], a. of vas deferens; Henle's a.; the dilation of the duct where it approaches its fellow just before it is joined by the duct of the seminal vesicle.

duodenal a., (1) a. duodeni; **(2)** a. hepatopancreatica.

a. duode'ni [NA], duodenal a. (1); the dilated portion of the superior part of the duodenum. See also duodenal *cap.*

Henle's a., a. ductus deferentis.

a. hepat'opancreat'ica [NA], duodenal a. (2); Vater's a.; the dilation within the major duodenal papilla that normally receives both the common bile duct and the main pancreatic duct.

a. lactif'era, *sinus* lactiferi.

a. membrana'cea, pl. **ampullae membrana'ceae** [NA], **membranous a.,** a nearly spherical enlargement of one end of each of the three semicircular ducts, anterior, posterior, and lateral, where they connect with the utricle; each contains a neuroepithelial crista.

a. os'sea, pl. **ampullae os'seae** [NA], **osseous a.,** a circumscribed dilation of one extremity of each of the three bony semicircular canals, anterior, posterior, and lateral; each contains a membranous a.

a. rec'ti [NA], **rectal a.,** a dilated portion of the rectum just above the anal canal.

Thoma's a., a dilation of the arterial capillary beyond the sheathed artery of the spleen.

a. tu'bae uteri'nae [NA], **a. of uterine tube,** the wide portion of the uterine (fallopian) tube near the fimbriated extremity.

a. of vas deferens, a. ductus deferentis.

Vater's a., a. hepatopancreatica.

ampul'lar. Relating in any sense to an ampulla.

ampullitis (am-pul-li'tis). Inflammation of any ampulla, especially of the dilated extremity of the vas deferens.

amputation (am-pu-ta'shun) [L. *amputatio*, to cut around, prune]. The cutting off of a limb or part of a limb, the breast, or a projecting part.

central a., a. in which the flaps are so united that the scar runs across the end of the stump.

Chopart's a., mediotarsal a.; a. through the midtarsal joint; *i.e.*, between the tarsal navicular and the calcaneocuboid joints.

cineplastic a., cineplastics; kineplastics; a. of an extremity whereby the muscles and tendons are so arranged in the stump that they are able to execute independent movements and to communicate motion to a specially constructed prosthetic apparatus.

circular a., a. performed by a circular incision through the skin, the muscles being similarly divided higher up, and the bone higher still.

congenital a., intrauterine a.; spontaneous a. (1); a. produced *in utero;* formerly attributed to the pressure of constricting bands, now regarded as the result of an intrinsic deficiency of embryonic tissue.

consecutive a., an a. formerly performed during or following suppuration.

a. in continuity, a. through a segment of a limb, not at a joint.

double flap a., a. in which a flap is cut from the soft parts on either side of the limb.

Dupuytren's a., a. of arm at shoulder joint.

elliptical a., circular a. in which the sweep of the knife is not exactly vertical to the axis of the limb.

flap a., flap operation (1); an a. in which flaps of the muscular and cutaneous tissues are made to cover the end of the bone.

flapless a., an a. without any tissue to cover stump.

Gritti-Stokes a., supracondylar a. of the femur, the patella being preserved and applied to the end of the bone, its articular cartilage being removed so as to obtain union.

Hey's a., a. of the foot in front of the tarsometatarsal joint.

interpelviabdominal a., hemipelvectomy.

interscapulothoracic a., a. of the arm with removal of the scapula and a portion of the clavicle on the same side.

intrauterine a., congenital a.

Larrey's a., a. at shoulder joint.

Lisfranc's a., a. of the foot at the tarsometatarsal joint, the sole being preserved to make the flap.

mediotarsal a., Chopart's a.

oblique a., a. in which the line of section through an extremity is at other than a right angle.

oval a., a. in which the flaps are obained by oval incisions through the skin and muscle.

periosteoplastic a., subperiosteal a.

Pirogoff's a., a. of the foot, the lower articular surfaces of the tibia and fibula being sawn through and ends covered with a portion of the os calcis which has also been sawn through from above posteriorly downward and forward.

pulp a., pulpotomy.

racket a., a circular or slightly oval a. in which a long incision is made in the axis of the limb.

root a., radectomy; radiectomy; radisectomy; surgical removal of one or more roots of a multi-rooted tooth, the remaining root canal(s) usually being treated endodontically.

spontaneous a., (1) congenital a.; (2) a. as the result of a pathologic process rather than from external trauma.

Stokes' a., a modification of Gritti's a. in that the line of section of the femur is slightly higher.

subperiosteal a., periosteoplastic a.; a. in which the periosteum is stripped back from the bone and replaced afterward, forming a periosteal flap over the cut end.

Syme's a., a. of the foot at the ankle joint, the malleoli being sawed off, and a flap being made with the soft parts of the heel.

Teale's a., (1) a. of the forearm in its lower half, or of the thigh, with a long posterior rectangular flap and a short anterior one; (2) a. of the leg, with a long anterior rectangular flap and a short posterior one.

transverse a., a. in which the line of section through the extremity is at right angles to the long axis.

traumatic a., a. resulting from accidental or nonsurgical injury.

Tripier's a., a modification of Chopart's a., in that a part of the calcaneus is also removed.

am'putee. A person with an amputated limb.

amu Atomic mass *unit.*

amu'sia [G. *a*- priv. + *mousa*, music]. A form of aphasia characterized by loss of the faculty of musical expression or of the recognition of simple musical tones.

amyelia (ă-mi-e'lĭ-ah) [G. *a*- priv. + *myelos*, marrow]. Congenital absence of the spinal cord, found only in association with anecephaly.

amyelic (ă-mi-e'lik). Amyelous.

amyelinated (ă-mi'ĕ-lĭ-na'ted). Unmyelinated.

amyelination (ă-mi'ĕ-lĭ-na'shun). Loss of the myelin sheath of a nerve.

amyelinic (ă-mi'ĕ-lin'ik). Unmyelinated.

amyeloic, amyelonic (ă-mi-ĕ-lo'ik, ă-mi-ĕ-lon'ik) [G. *a*- priv. + *myelos*, marrow]. **1.** Amyelous. **2.** Terms sometimes used in hematology to indicate the absence of bone marrow, or the lack of functional participation of bone marrow, in hemopoiesis.

amyelous (ă-mi'ĕ-lus). Amyelic; amyeloic (1); amyelonic (1); without spinal cord.

amygdala, gen. and pl. **amygdalae** (ă-mig'dă-lah, -le) [L. fr. G. *amygdalē*, almond; in Mediev. & Mod. L. a tonsil]. **1.** *Corpus* amygdaloideum. **2.** Denoting the tonsilla cerebelli, as well as the lymphatic tonsils (pharyngeal, palatine, lingual, laryngeal, and tubal).

amyg'dalin. Amygdaloside; a glucoside present in almonds and seeds of other plants of the family Rosaceae.

amyg'daline. 1. Relating to an almond. **2.** Relating to a tonsil, or to an amygdala. **3.** Tonsillar.

amyg'daloid [amygdala + G. *eidos*, appearance]. Resembling an almond or a tonsil.

amyg'daloside. Amygdalin.

amyl-. See amylo-.

a'myl. Pentyl; the radical formed from a pentane, C_5H_{12}, by removal of one H; several isomeric forms exist.

a. nitrite, $C_5H_{11}NO_2$; used as a vasodilator in angina pectoris and as an antidote in cyanide poisoning.

amylaceous (am'ĭ-la'shus). Starchy.

am'ylase. One of a group of starch-splitting or amylolytic enzymes that cleave starch, glycogen, and related polysaccharides, all α-1,4-glucans.

amylasu'ria. Diastasuria; the excretion of amylase (sometimes termed diastase) in the urine.

am'ylin. The cellulose of starch; the insoluble envelope of starch grains.

amylo-, amyl- [G. *amylon,* starch]. Combining form indicating starch or polysaccharide nature or origin.

am'ylogen'ic. Amyloplastic; producing starch.

amylogenesis (am'ĭ-lo-jen'ĕ-sis) [amylo- + G. *genesis,* production]. Amylosynthesis; the biosynthesis of starch.

am'ylohydrol'ysis. Amylolysis.

am'yloid [amylo- + G. *eidos,* resemblance]. Any of a group of chemically diverse proteins that appears microscopically homogeneous, but is composed of linear nonbranching aggregated fibrils arranged in sheets when seen under the electron microscope; occurs characteristically as pathologic extracellular deposits in the walls of blood vessels (amyloidosis), especially in association with reticuloendothelial tissue; the chemical nature of the proteinaceous fibrils is dependent upon the underlying disease process.

amyloido'sis [amyloid + G. *-osis,* condition]. A disease of unknown cause characterized by the extracellular accumulation of amyloid in various organs and tissues of the body.

familial a., A heritable type of a. associated with familial Mediterranean fever, Muckle-Wells syndrome, cold hypersensitivity, various patterns of neuropathy, or amyloid deposits in various organs.

focal a., nodular a.

nodular a., focal a.; amyloid tumor; of a. in which amyloid occurs as small masses or nodules beneath the skin or mucous membranes.

primary a., a form of a., sometimes familial, not associated with other recognized disease.

secondary a., a. occurring in association with another chronic disease.

senile a., a common form of a. in elderly people, usually mild and limited to the heart.

amylol'ysis [amylo- + G. *lysis,* dissolution]. Amylohydrolysis; hydrolysis of starch into sugar.

amylopec'tin. A branched-chain polyglucose (glucan) in starch.

am'ylopectino'sis [amylopectin + G. *-osis,* condition]. Glycogenosis due to deficiency of brancher enzyme.

am'yloplas'tic. Amylogenic.

amylorrhea (am-ĭ-lor-re'ah) [amylo- + G. *rhoia,* flow]. Passage of undigested starch in the stools.

am'ylose. Unbranched polyglucose (glucan) in starch, similar to cellulose.

am'ylosu'ria. Amyluria; excretion of starch in the urine.

am'ylosyn'thesis. Amylogenesis.

amylo-1,6-glucosidase. Dextrin 6α-glucosidase; an enzyme hydrolyzing α-1,6 links (branch points) in chains of 1,4-linked α-glucose residues.

amylu'ria. Amylosuria.

amyoesthesia, amyoesthesis (ă-mi'o-es-the'zĭ-ah, -the'sis) [G. *a-* priv. + *mys,* muscle, + *aisthēsis,* perception]. Loss of muscle sensation.

amyoplasia (ă-mi-o-pla'zĭ-ah) [G. *a-* priv. + *mys,* muscle, + *plasis,* a molding]. Deficient formation of muscle tissue.

a. congen'ita, *arthrogryposis* multiplex congenita.

amyostasia (ă-mi'o-sta'zĭ-ah) [G. *a-* priv. + *mys,* muscle, + *stasis,* standing]. Difficulty in standing, due to muscular tremor or incoordination.

amy'ostat'ic. Showing muscular tremors.

amyosthenia (ă-mi'os-the'nĭ-ah) [G. *a-* priv. + *mys,* muscle, + *sthenos,* strength]. Muscular weakness.

amyosthen'ic. Relaating to or causing muscular weakness.

amy'otaxy, amyotax'ia [G. *a-* priv. + *mys,* muscle, + *taxis,* order]. Muscular ataxia.

amyoto'nia [G. *a-* priv. + *mys,* muscle, + *tonos,* tone]. Myatonia.

a. congen'ita, Oppenheim's disease or syndrome; myatonia congenita; atonic pseudoparalysis of congenital origin observed especially in infants and characterized by absences of muscular tone only in muscles innervated by the spinal nerves.

amyotrophia (ă-mi-o-tro'fĭ-ah). Amyotrophy.

amyotro'phic. Relating to muscular atrophy.

amyotrophy (ă-mi-ot'ro-fĭ) [G. *a-* priv. + *mys,* muscle, + *trophē,* nourishment]. Amyotrophia; muscular wasting or atrophy.

amyous (am'ĭ-us) [G. *a-* priv. + *mys,* muscle]. Lacking in muscular tissue, or in muscular strength.

amyxia (ă-mik'sĭ-ah) [G. *a-* priv. + *myxa,* mucus]. Absence of mucus.

amyxorrhea (ă-mik-sor-re'ah) [G. *a-* priv. + *myxa,* mucus, + *rhoia,* flow]. Absence of the normal secretion of mucus.

an-. See a-.

ana- [G. *ana,* up]. Prefix meaning up, toward, apart; distinguished from *an-,* which is *a*-privative with *n* before a vowel.

anabiosis (an-ă-bi-o'sis) [G. a reviving, fr, *ana,* again, + *biōsis,* life]. Resuscitation after apparent death.

anabiot'ic. 1. Resuscitating; restorative. **2.** A revivifying remedy; a powerful stimulant.

anabol'ic. Relating to or promoting anabolism.

anab'olism [G. *anabolē,* a raising up]. The process of assimilation of nutritive matter and its converion into living substance. This includes synthetic processes and requires energy. *Cf.* catabolism.

anab'olite. Any substance formed as a result of anabolic processes.

anacidity (an'ă-sid'ĭ-tĭ). Absence of acidity; denoting especially absence of hydrochloric acid in the gastric juice.

anaclasis (ă-nak'lă-sis) [G. a bending back, reflection]. 1. Reflection of light or sound. 2. Refraction of the ocular media. 3. Forcible flexion of a joint to break up the adhesion in fibrous ankylosis.

anaclit'ic [G. *ana*, toward, + *klinein*, to lean]. Leaning or depending upon; in psychoanalysis, relating to the dependence of the infant on the mother or mother substitute.

anacrot'ic. Anadicrotic; referring to the upstroke or ascending limb of the arterial pulse tracing.

anacrotism (ă-nak'ro-tizm) [G. *ana*, up, + *krotos*, a beat]. Anadicrotism; peculiarity of the pulse wave as in anacrotic pulse.

anacusis (an'ă-ku'sis) [G. *an-* priv. + *akousis*, hearing]. Anakusis; total loss or absence of the ability to perceive sound as such.

anadicrot'ic. Anacrotic.

anadicrotism (an-ă-dik'ro-tizm) [G. *ana*, up, + *di-krotos*, double beating]. Anacrotism.

andre'nalism. Complete lack of adrenal function.

anaerobe (an'ăr-ōb, an-ăr'ōb) [G. *an-*priv. + *aēr*, air, + *bios*, life]. A microorganism that can live and grow in the absence of free oxygen.

  facultative a., one able to live or grow in the presence or absence of free oxygen.

  obligate a., one that will live or grow only in the absence of free oxygen.

anaerobic (an-ăr-o'bik). 1. Relating to an anaerobe. 2. Living without oxygen.

anaerobiosis (an-ăr-o-bi-o'sis) [G. *an-* priv. + *aēr*, air, + *biōsis*, way of living]. Existence in an oxygen-free atmosphere.

anaerogen'ic [G. *an-* priv. + *aēr*, air, + *-gen*, producing]. Not producing gas.

anagen (an'ă-jen) [G. *ana*, up, + *-gen*, producing]. Growth phase of hair cycle.

anaku'sis. Anacusis.

a'nal. Relating to the anus.

analbumine'mia [G. *an-*priv. + albumin, *q.v.*, + G. *haima*, blood]. Absence of albumin from the serum.

analep'tic [G. *analēptikos*, restorative]. 1. Invigorating; restorative. 2. An agent that so acts. 3. A central nervous system stimulant.

analgesia (an-al-je'zĭ-ah) [G. insensibility, fr. *an-*priv. + *algēsis*, sensation of pain]. A condition in which nociceptive stimuli are perceived by are not interpreted as pain; usually accompanied by sedation without loss of consciousness.

  a. al'gera, a. dolorosa; spontaneous pain in a part, associated with loss of sensibility.

  conduction a., sensory denervation in a portion of the body (regional anesthesia), produced by pharmacological means.

  a. doloro'sa, a. algera.

  spinal a., sensory denervation produced by injection of local anesthetic into the subarachnoid space; a euphemism for spinal anesthesia.

surface a., topical *anesthesia*.

analgesic (an-al-je'zik). 1. Analgetic (1); a compound capable of producing analgesia. 2. Antalgic; characterized by reduced response to painful stimuli.

analget'ic. 1. Analgesic (1). 2. Associated with altered pain perception.

anal'ity. Referring to the psychic organization derived from, and characteristic of, the anal period of psychosexual development.

anallergic (an-al-lur'jik). Not allergic.

an'alog. Analogue.

analogous (ă-nal'o-gus). Resembling functionally, but having a different origin or structure.

analogue (an'ă-log) [G. *ana-logos*, analogous]. Analog. 1. One of two organs or parts in different species of animals or plants, that differ in structure or development but are similar in function. 2. A compound that resembles another in structure, such as an isomer.

anal'ysand. In psychoanalysis, the person being analyzed.

analysis, pl. **analyses** (ă-nal'ĭ-sis) [G. a breaking up, fr. *ana*, up + *lysis*, a loosening]. 1. The breaking up of a chemical compound into simpler elements; a process by which the composition of a substance is determined. 2. The separation of any compound substance or concept into the parts composing it. 3. See psychoanalysis. 4. Applied in electroencephalography to the estimation or recording of the components of a complex wave form in terms of their frequency and amplitude.

  bite a., occlusal a.

  blood gas a., the direct electrode measurement of the partial pressure of oxygen and carbon dioxide in blood.

  content a., any of a variety of techniques for classification and study of the verbal products of normal or of psychologically disabled individuals.

  gasometric a., the determination of structure or quantity of a substance by means of gaseous derivatives.

  gastric a., measurement of pH and acid output of stomach contents; basal acid output can be determined by collecting the overnight gastric secretion or by a 1-hr collection; maximal acid output is determined following injection of histamine; output is measured by titration with a strong base.

  gravimetric a., quantitative a. by weighing separately each constituent as such or in a form of known constitution.

  occlusal a., bite a.; a study of the relations of the occlusal surfaces of opposing teeth and their effect upon related structures.

  qualitative a., the determination of the nature, as opposed to the quantity, of the elements entering into the composition of any substance.

  quantitative a., the determination of the amount, as well as the nature, of each of the elements composing a substance.

spectrophotometric a., spectrophotometry; determination of structure and/or quantity by means of light absorption.

transactional a., a psychotherapy system involving a systematic understanding of the qualities of interpersonal interactions in the treatment sessions.

volumetric a., quanititative a. by the addition of graduated amounts of a standard test solution to a solution of a known amount of the substance analyzed, until the reaction is just at an end; depends upon stoichiometric nature of the reaction between test solution and unknown.

an'alyst. 1. One who makes analytical determinations. **2.** Short term for psychoanalyst.

an'alyte. Any substance or chemical constituent that is analyzed.

analyt'ical. 1. Relating to analysis. **2.** Relating to psychoanalysis.

an'alyzer, an'alyzor. 1. The prism in a polariscope by means of which the polarized light is examined. **2.** The neural basis of the conditioned reflex (Pavlov); includes all the sensory side of the reflex arc and its central connections. **3.** An instrument attached as a separate unit to the electroencephalographic apparatus to determine the frequency and amplitude components of a particular channel of the record. **4.** Any instrument that performs an analysis.

anamne'sis [G. *anamnēsis*, recollection]. **1.** The act of remembering. **2.** The medical history of a patient.

anamnes'tic. 1. Relating to the anamnesis or previous medical history of a patient. **2.** Mnemonic; assisting the memory.

anangioplasia (an-an'ji-o-pla'zi-ah) [G. *an-* priv. + *angeion,* vessel, + *plassō,* to form]. Imperfect vascularization of a part due to nonformation of vessels, or vessels with inadequate caliber.

anan'gioplas'tic. Relating to, characterized by, or due to anangioplasia.

anaphase (an'ă-fāz) [G. *ana,* up, + *phasis,* appearance]. The stage of mitosis or meiosis in which the chromosomes move from the equatorial plate toward the poles of the cell.

anaphia (an-a'fi-ah, an-af'i-ah) [G. *an-* priv. + *haphē,* touch]. Absence of the sense of touch.

anaphoria (an'ă-fo'ri-ah) [G. *ana,* up, + *phoros,* bearing]. Anatropia; a tendency of the eyes, when in a state of rest, to turn upward.

anaphrodisia (an-af'ro-diz'i-ah) [G. insensibility to love, from *an-* priv. + *Aphroditē,* goddess of love]. Rarely used term denoting absence of sexual feeling.

anaph'rodis'iac. 1. Relating to anaphrodisia (absence of sexual feeling). **2.** An agent that lessens or abolishes sexual desire.

an'aphylac'togen'esis. The production of anaphylaxis.

an'aphylac'togen'ic. Producing anaphylaxis; pertaining to substances that result in an individual becoming susceptible to anaphylaxis.

an'aphylac'toid [anaphylaxis + G. *eidos,* resemblance]. Resembling anaphylaxis.

anaphylactic (an-ă-fi-lak'tik). Relating to anaphylaxis; manifesting extremely great sensitivity to foreign protein or other material.

anaphylac'togen. Any substance (antigen) capable of rendering an individual susceptible to anaphylaxis; a substance (antigen) that will cause an anaphylactic reaction in such a sensitized individual.

anaphylatoxin (an-ă-fil'ă-tok'sin) [anaphylaxis + toxin]. Anaphylotoxin. A substance postulated to be the immediate cause of anaphylactic shock and which is assumed to result from the *in vivo* combination of specific antibody and the specific sensitizing material, when the later is injected as a shock dose in a sensitized animal.

anaphylaxis (an-ă-fi-lak'sis) [G. *ana,* away from, back from, + *phylaxis,* protection]. The immediate transient kind of immunologic (allergic) reaction characterized by contraction of smooth muscle and dilation of capillaries due to release of pharmacologically active substances (histamine, bradykinin, serotonin, and slow-reacting substance), classically initiated by the combination of antigen (allergen) with mast cell-fixed, cytophilic antibody (chiefly IgE); the reaction can be initiated, also, by relatively large quantities of serum aggregates (antigen-antibody complexes, and other) that seemingly activate complement leading to production of anaphylatoxin.

active a., reaction following inoculation of antigen in a subject previously sensitized to the specific antigen, in contrast to passive a.

antiserum a., passive a.

generalized a., systemic a.; the immediate response, involving smooth muscles and capillaries throughout the body of a sensitized individual, that follows intravenous (and occasionally intracutaneous) injection of antigen (allergen).

local a., the immediate, transient kind of response that follows the injection of antigen (allergen) into the skin of a sensitized individual and is limited to the area surrounding the site of inoculation.

passive a., antiserum a.; a reaction resulting from inoculation of antigen in an individual previously inoculated intravenously with specific antiserum from another individual.

systemic a., generalized a.

anaphyl'otox'in. Anaphylatoxin.

anaplasia (an-ă-pla'si-ah) [G. *ana,* again, + plasis, a molding]. Loss of structural differentiation, especially as seen in most, but not all, malignant neoplasms.

anaplas'tic. 1. Relating to anaplasty. **2.** Characterized by or pertaining to anaplasia. **3.** Growing without form or structure.

anapophysis (an'ă-pof'i-sis) [G. *ana,* back, + *apophysis,* offshoot]. An acessory spinal process of a vertebra, found especially in the thoracic or lumbar vertebrae.

anap'tic. Relating to anaphia.

anarith'mia [G. *an-* priv. + *arithmos*, number]. Aphasia marked by inability to count or use numbers.

anar'thria [G. fr. *an-arthos*, without joints; (of sound) inarticulate]. Loss of the power of articulate speech.

anasarca (an'ă-sar'kah) [G. *ana*, through, + *sarx* (*sark-*), flesh]. A generalized infiltration of edema fluid into subcutaneous connective tissue.

anasar'cous. Characterized by anasarca.

anas'tomose. 1. To open one structure into another directly or by connecting channels, said of blood vessels, lymphatics, and hollow viscera; also incorrectly applied to nerves. **2.** To unite by means of an anastomosis, or connection between formerly separate structures.

anastomo'sis, pl. **anastomo'ses** [G. *anastomōsis*, from *anastomoō*, to furnish with a mouth]. **1.** A natural communication, direct or indirect, between two blood vessels or other tubular structures; also incorrectly applied to nerves. **2.** Operative union of two hollow or tubular structures. **3.** An opening created by surgery, trauma, or disease between two or more normally separate spaces or organs.

    antiperistaltic a., an a. diverting the normal flow of contents.

    a. arteriaoveno'sa [NA], **arteriovenous a., arteriolovenular a.;** vessels through which blood is shunted from arterioles to venules without passing through the capillaries.

    Billroth I and **II a.,** Billroth's *operations* I and II.

    conjoined a., the joining together of two small blood vessels by side-to-side elliptical a. to create a single larger stoma for subsequent end-to-end a.

    cruciate a., crucial a., an a. between branches of the perforating, gluteal and circumflex femoral arteries located behind the upper part of the femur.

    heterocladic a., a. between branches of different arteries.

    H-graft a., a side-to-side grafting of adjacent vessels which utilizes a straight connecting conduit.

    homocladic a., a. between branches of the same artery.

    intestinal a., enteroenterostomy.

    isoperistaltic a., an a. allowing flow of contents in the same and natural direction.

    postcostal a., logitudinal a. of intersegmental arteries giving rise to the vertebral artery.

    precostal a., longitudinal a. of intersegmental arteries giving rise to thyrocervical and costocervical trunks.

    Riolan's a., a. of the superior and inferior mesenteric arteries.

    Roux-en-Y a., a. of the distal end of the divided jejunum to the stomach, bile duct, or another structure, with implantation of the proximal end into the side of the jejunum at a suitable distance below the first a.

    termino-terminal a., a. of the central end of an artery with the peripheral end of the corresponding

vein, and the peripheral end of the artery with the central end of the vein.

anastomot'ic. Pertaining to an anastomosis.

anatomical (an'ă-tom'ĭ-kal). **1.** Relating to anatomy. **2.** Structural.

anat'omist. A specialist in the science of a anatomy.

anatomy (ă-nat'o-mĭ) [G. *anatomē*, dissection, from *ana*, apart, + *tomē*, a cutting]. **1.** The morphologic structure of an organism. **2.** The science of the morphology or structure of organisms.

    applied a., the practical application of anatomical knowledge to diagnosis and treatment.

    comparative a., the comparative study of animal structure in regard to homologous organs or parts.

    dental a., that branch of gross a. concerned with the morphology of teeth, their location, position, and relationships.

    developmental a., a. of the structural changes of an individual from fertilization to adulthood; includes embryology, fetology, and postnatal development.

    functional a., physiologic a.

    general a., the study of gross and microscopic structures as well as of the composition of the body, its tissues and fluids.

    gross a., macroscopic a.; general a. studied without the use of the microscope.

    macroscopic a., gross a.

    microscopic a., the branch of a. in which the structure of cells, tissues, and organs is studied with the light microscope. See histology.

    pathologic a., anatomical *pathology.*

    physiologic a., functional a.; a. studied in its relation to function.

    radiological a., the study of the body through x-ray imaging.

    regional a., topographic a.; a. of certain related parts or divisions of the body.

    special a., a. of certain definite organs or organ systems concerned in the performance of special functions.

    surface a., the study of the configuration of the surface of the body, especially in its relation to deeper parts.

    surgical a., applied a. in reference to surgical diagnosis and treatment.

    topographic a., regional a.

    ultrastructural a., the ultramicroscopic study of structures too small to be seen with a light microscope.

    veterinary a., a. of domestic animals.

anatricrotic (an'ă-tri-krot'ik). Characterized by anatricrotism.

anatricrotism (an'ă-trik'ro-tizm) [G. *ana*, up, + *tri-*, thrice, *krotos*, beating]. The condition of the pulse manifesting itself by a triple beat on the ascending limb of the sphygmographic tracing.

anatro'pia [G. *ana*, up, + *tropē*, a turning]. Anaphoria.

anchorage (ang'kor-ij) [L. *ancora*, fr. G. *ankyra*, anchor]. **1.** Operative fixation of loose or prolapsed abdominal or pelvic organs. **2.** The part to which anything is fastened; in dentistry, a tooth or an implanted tooth substitute to which a fixed or removable partial denture, crown, or restorative material is retained. **3.** The nature and degree of resistance to displacement offered by an anatomical unit when used for the purpose of effecting tooth movement.

ancillary (an'sĭ-lĕr-ĭ) [L. *ancillaris*, relating to a maid servant]. Auxiliary, accessory, or secondary.

ancip'ital, ancip'itate, ancip'itous [L. *anceps*, two-headed]. Two-headed; two-edged.

anconad (an'ko-nad) [G. *ankōn*, elbow, + L. *ad*, to]. Toward the elbow.

an'conal, anco'neal [G. *ankōn*, elbow]. Relating to the elbow.

anconitis (an'ko-ni'tis) [G. *ankōn*, elbow, + *-itis*, inflammation]. Inflammation of the elbow joint.

ancylo-. See ankylo-.

Ancylostoma (an-sĭ-los'to-mah) [G. *ankylos*, curved, hooked, + *stoma*, mouth]. A genus of nematodes that are parasitic in the duodenum, they attach themselves to villi in the mucous membrane, suck blood, and may cause a state of anemia, especially in cases of malnutrition.

  A. brazilien'se, a species normally an intestinal parasite of dogs and cats but also found in man as a cause of human cutaneous larva migrans.

  A. cani'num, a species common in dogs, but also occurring in human skin as a cause of cutaneous larva migrans.

  A. duodena'le, the Old World hookworm, a species widespread in temperate areas, in contrast to the more tropical distribution of the New World hookworm, *Necator americanus;* the cause of ancylostoamiasis.

an'cylostomat'ic. Referring to hookworms of the genus *Ancylostoma.*

ancylostomiasis (an'sĭ-lo-sto-mi'ăsis). Uncinariasis; hookworm disease caused by *Ancylostoma duodenale,* producing eosinophilia, anemia, emaciation, dyspepsia, and, in children with severe long-continued infections, swelling of the abdomen with mental and physical maldevelopment.

ancyroid (an'sĭ-royd) [G. *ankyra*, anchor, + *eidos*, resemblance]. Ankyroid; shaped like the fluke of an anchor.

andro- [G. *anēr* (gen. andros), male]. Combining form meaning masculine; pertaining to the male of the species.

an'droblasto'ma. 1. Sertoli cell tumor; a testicular tumor microscopically resembling fetal testis, with varying proportions of tubular and stromal elements; the tubules contain Sertoli cells, which may cause feminization. **2.** Arrhenoblastoma.

an'drogen. Testoid (2); a generic term for an agent, usually a hormone, that stimulates the activity of the accessory sex organs of the male, encourages the development of male sex charcteristics, or prevents the changes in the latter that follow castration; natural a.'s are steroid derivatives of androstane.

androgen'ic. Testoid (1); relating to an androgen; having a masculinizing effect.

androgynism (an-droj'ĭ-nizm). Female *pseudohermaphroditism.*

androgynous (an-droj'ĭ-nus). Pertaining to androgyny.

androgyny (an-droj'ĭ-nĭ) [andro- + G. *gynē,* woman]. Female *pseudohermaphroditism.*

an'droid [andro- + G. *eidos,* resemblance]. Resembling a man in form and structure.

andropho'bia [andro- + G. *phobos,* fear]. Morbid fear of men or of the male sex.

an'drostane. Parent hydrocarbon of the androgenic steroids.

androstanediol (an-dro-stăn'di-ol). 5α-Androstane-3β,17β-diol; an androgen.

androstanedione (an-dro-stăn'di-ōn). 5α-Androstane-3,17-dione; an androgen.

androstene (an'dro-stēn). Androstane with an unsaturated (−CH=CH−) bond in the molecule.

androstenediol (an-dro-stēn'di-ol). 5-Androsten-3β,17β-diol; an androgen differing from androstanediol in the possession of a double bond between C-5 and C-6.

androstenedione (an-dro-stēn'di-ōn). 4-Androstene-3,17-dione; androstanedione with a double bond between C-4 and C-5; an androgenic steroid of weaker biological potency than testosterone; secreted by the testis, ovary, and adrenal cortex.

andros'terone. 3α-Hydroxy-5α-androstan-17-one; steroid metabolite, found in male urine, having weak androgenic potency.

anectasis (an-ek'tă-sis) [G. *an-* priv. + *ektasis,* dilation]. Primary *atelectasis.*

anemia (ă-ne'mĭ-ah) [G. *anaimia,* fr. *an-* priv. + *haima,* blood]. Any condition in which the number of red blood cells per mm3, the amount of hemoglobin in 100 ml of blood, and the volume of packed red blood cells per 100 ml of blood are less than normal; clinically, generally pertaining to the concentration of oxygen-transporting material in a designated volume of blood, in contrast to total quantities.

  achrestic a. [G. *a-*priv. + *chrēsis,* a using], a form of chronic progressive macrocytic a. in which the changes in bone marrow and circulating blood closely resemble those of pernicious a.

  aplastic a., a. characterized by a greatly decreased formation of erythrocytes and hemoglobin, and usually associated with pronounced granulocytopenia and thrombocytopenia, as a result of hypoplastic or aplastic bone marrow.

  autoallergic hemolytic a. (cold-antibody type), a. caused by hemaglutinating cold autoantibody. See also cold hemagglutinin *disease.*

  autoallergic hemolytic a. (warm-antibody type), acquired hemolytic a. due to serum autoantibodies that react with the patient's red blood cells, antigenic specificity being chiefly in the Rh complex.

congenital a., *erythroblastosis* fetalis.

congenital hemolytic a., hereditary *spherocytosis*.

congenital hypoplastic a., erythrogenesis imperfecta; a normocytic normochromic a. resulting from congenital hypoplasia of the bone marrow; the marrow is grossly deficient in erythroid precursors but other elements are normal.

Cooley's a., *thalassemia* major.

crescent cell a., sickle cell a.

drepanocytic a., sickle cell a.

false a., pseudoanaemia.

Fanconi's a., Fanconi's or congenital pancytopenia; a type of idiopathic refractory a. characterized by pancytopenia, hypoplasia of the bone marrow, and congenital anomalies, occurring in members of the same family.

hemolytic a., a. resulting from abnormal destruction of erythrocytes in the body.

hyperchromic a., a. characterized by an increase in the ratio of the weight of hemoglobin to the volume of the erythrocyte, *i.e.*, the mean corpuscular hemoglobin concentration is greater than normal.

hypochromic a., a. characterized by a decrease in the ratio of the weight of hemoglobin to the volume of the erythrocyte, *i.e.*, the mean corpuscular hemoglobin concentration is less than normal.

hypoplastic a., progressive nonregenerative a. resulting from greatly depressed, inadequately functioning bone marrow; as the process persists, aplastic a. may occur.

iron deficiency a., a form of hypochromic microcytic a. due to dietary lack of iron loss as a result of chronic bleeding.

Lederer's a., a form of acute acquired hemolytic a. associated with abnormal hemolysins, and sometimes with hemoglobinuria.

macrocytic a., a. in which the average size of circulating erythrocytes is greater than normal.

malignant a., pernicious a.

megaloblastic a., a. in which there is a predominant number of megaloblasts, and relatively few normoblasts, among the hyperplastic erythroid cells in the bone marrow (as in pernicious a.).

metaplastic a., pernicious a. in which the various formed elements in the blood are changed.

microcytic a., a. in which the average size of circulating erythrocytes is smaller than normal.

microdrepanocytic a., sickle cell-thalassemia disease; a., clinically resembling sickle cell a., in which individuals are heterozygous for both the sickle cell gene and a thalassemia gene.

myelophthisic a., myelopathic a., leukoerythroblastosis.

neonatal a., *erythroblastosis* fetalis.

normochromic a., a. in which the concentration of hemoglobin in the erythrocytes is within the normal range.

normocytic a., a. in which the erythrocytes are normal in size.

pernicious a., malignant a.; a chronic progressive a. of older adults thought to result from a defect of the stomach, with atrophy and associated lack of an "intrinsic" factor, resulting in malabsorption of vitamin B_{12}; characterized by greatly decreased red blood cell counts, low levels of hemoglobin, numerous macrocytic erythrocytes, and hypo- or achlorhydria, in association with a predominant number of megaloblasts and relatively few normoblasts in the bone marrow.

refractory a., any of a group of anemic conditions in which there is persistent, frequently advanced a. that is not successfully treated by any means except blood transfusions, and that is not associated with another primary disease.

sickle cell a., crescent cell or drepanocytic a.; drepanocytosis; meniscocytosis; sickle cell syndrome; a. characterized by the presence of crescent- or sickle-shaped erythrocytes in peripheral blood, excessive hemolysis, and active hemopoiesis; hemoglobin is abnormal, up to 85% or more being sickle cell hemoglobin (Hb S) and the remainder fetal hemoglobin (Hb F); individuals are homozygous for the sickle cell gene, while those heterozygous for this gene have sickle cell trait.

sideroblastic a., sideroachrestic a., refractory a. characterized by the presence of sideroblasts in the bone marrow.

spherocytic a., hereditary *spherocytosis*.

splenic a., Banti's *syndrome*.

trophoneurotic a., a. presumably resulting from a profound nervous shock.

tropical a., various syndromes frequently observed in persons in tropical climates, usually resulting from nutritional deficiencies or hookworm disease.

ane'mic. Pertaining to or characterized by anemia.

anemophobia (an'e-mo-fo'bĭ-ah) [G. *anemos*, wind, + *phobos*, fear]. Morbid fear of wind or drafts.

anencephal'ic, anenceph'alous. Relating to anencephaly.

anencephaly (an'en-sef'ă-lĭ) [G. *an-* priv. + *enkepholas*, brain]. Markedly defective development of the brain, together with absence of the bones of the cranial vault and the cerebral and cerebellar hemispheres, and with only a rudimentary brain stem and some traces of basal ganglia present.

anephric (ă-nef'rik). Lacking kidneys.

an'ergas'tic. Pertaining to or characterized by anergasia.

anerga'sia [G. *an-* priv. + *ergasia*, work]. Absence of psychic activity as the result of organic brain disease.

anergic (an-er'jik). Relating to, or marked by, anergy.

anergy (an'er-jĭ) [G. *an-* priv. + *energeia*, energy, from *ergon*, work]. Absence of sensitivity reaction in a subject to substances that would be antigenic (immunogenic, allergenic) in most other subjects.

anerythroplasia (an-e-rith′ro-pla′zĭ-ah) [G. *an-* priv. + erythro(cyte) + G. *plasis,* a molding]. A condition in which there is no formation of red blood cells.

anerythroplastic (an-e-rith′ro-plas′tik). Pertaining to or characterized by anerythroplasia.

anesthekinesia (an-es′the-kĭ-ne′zĭ-ah) [G. *an-* priv. + *aisthēsis,* sensation, + *kinēsis,* movement]. Anesthecinesia; combined sensory and motor paralysis.

anesthesia (an′es-the′zĭ-ah) [G. *anaisthēsia,* fr. *an-* priv. + *aisthēsis,* sensation]. A state characterized by loss of sensation, the result of pharmacological depression of nerve function or of neurological disease.

   balanced a., a technique of general a. based on the concept that administration of a mixture of small amounts of several neuronal depressants summates the advantages but not the disadvantages of the individual components of the mixture.

   basal a., parenteral administration of one or more sedatives to produce a state of depressed consciousness short of a general a.

   block a., conduction a.

   caudal a., regional a. by injection of local anesthetic into the epidural space via the sacral hiatus.

   cerebral a., loss of sensation due to a lesion of the cerebral cortex or other parts of the cerebrum.

   circle absorption a., inhalation a. in which a circuit with carbon dioxide absorbent is used for complete (closed) or partial (semiclosed) rebreathing of exhaled gases.

   closed a., inhalation a. in which there is total rebreathing of all exhaled gases, except CO_2 which is absorbed.

   conduction a., block a.; regional a. in which local anesthetic solution is injected about nerves to inhibit nerve transmission.

   dissociated a., loss of sensation for pain and temperature without loss of tactile sense.

   dissociative a., a form of general a., but not necessarily complete unconsciousness, characterized by catalepsy, catatonia, and amnesia, especially that produced by phenylcyclohexylamine compounds, including ketamine.

   a. doloro′sa, severe spontaneous pain occurring in an anesthetic zone.

   endotracheal a., inhalation anesthetic technique in which anesthetic and respiratory gases pass through a tube placed in the trachia via the mouth or nose.

   epidural a., regional a. produced by injection of local anesthetic solution into the peridural space.

   general a., loss of ability to perceive pain associated with loss of consciousness, produced by intravenous or inhalation anesthetic agents.

   girdle a., a. distributed as a band encircling the abdomen.

   glove a., loss of sensation in the area that would be covered by a glove.

   infiltration a., local a.

   inhalation a., general a. resulting from breathing of anesthetic gases or vapors.

   insufflation a., maintenance of inhalation a. by delivery of anesthetic gases or vapors directly to the airway of a patient spontaneously breathing room air.

   intranasal a., (1) insufflation a. in which an inhalation anesthetic is added to inhaled air passing through the nose or nasopharynx; (2) a. of nasal passages by infiltration and topical application of local anesthetic solution to nasal mucosa.

   intraoral a., (1) insufflation a. in which an inhalation anesthetic is added to inhaled air passing through the mouth; (2) regional a. of the mouth and associated structures when local anesthetic solutions are used by topical application to oral mucosa, by local infiltration, or as nerve blocks.

   intravenous a., general a. in which venipuncture is used as a means of injecting central nervous system depressants into the circulation.

   local a., infiltration a.; regional a. produced by direct infiltration of local anesthetic solution into the operative site.

   muscular a., loss of the muscle sense, or of the ability to determine the position of a limb or to recognize a difference in weights.

   nerve block a., conduction a. in which local anesthetic solution is injected about peripheral nerves.

   nonrebreathing a., a technique for inhalation a. in which valves exhaust all exhaled air from the circuit.

   olfactory a., anosmia.

   open drop a., inhalation a. by vaporization of a liquid anesthetic placed drop by drop on a gauze mask covering the mouth and nose.

   rebreathing a., a technique for inhalation a. in which a portion or all of the gases that are exhaled are subsequently inhaled after carbon dioxide has been absorbed.

   rectal a., general a. following instillation into the rectum of liquid inhalation anesthetics or intravenous anesthetics.

   refrigeration a., cryoanesthesia.

   regional a., use of local anesthetic solution(s) to produce circumscribed areas of loss of sensation.

   retrobulbar a., injection of a local anesthetic behind the eye to produce sensory denervation of the eye.

   saddle block a., a form of spinal a. limited in area to the buttocks, perineum, and inner surfaces of the thighs.

   segmental a., loss of sensation limited to an area supplied by one or more spinal nerve roots.

   semi-closed a., inhalation a. using a circuit in which a portion of the exhaled air is exhausted from the circuit and a portion is rebreathed following absorption of carbon dioxide.

   semi-open a., inhalation a. in which a portion of inhaled gases is derived from an anesthesia circuit while the remainder consists of room air.

spinal a., (1) sensory denervation produced by injection of local anesthetic solution(s) into the spinal subarachnoid space; (2) loss of sensation produced by disease of the spinal cord.

splanchnic a., visceral a.; loss of sensation in those areas of the visceral peritoneum innervated by the splanchnic nerves.

stocking a., loss of sensation in the area that would be covered by a stocking.

surgical a., (1) a. administered for the purpose of permitting performance of an operative procedure. (2) loss of sensation with muscle relaxation adequate for surgery.

tactile a., loss or impairment of the sense of touch.

thermal a., thermic a., loss of heat sense.

topical a., surface analgesia; superficial loss of sensation in mucous membranes or skin, produced by direct application of local anesthetic solutions, ointments, or jellies.

traumatic a., loss of sensation resulting from nerve injury.

unilateral a., hemianesthesia.

visceral a., splanchnic a.

an'esthesiol'ogist. A physician specializing solely in anesthesiology and related areas.

anesthesiology (an'es-the-zī-ol'o -jī) [anesthesia + G. *logos*, treatise]. The medical specialty concerned with the pharmacological, physiological, and clinical basis of anesthesia and related fields, including resuscitation, intensive respiratory care, and pain.

anesthet'ic. **1.** Anesthetic agent; a compound that reversibly depresses neuronal function, producing loss of ability to perceive pain and/or other sensations. **2.** Collective designation for anesthetizing agents administered to an individual subject at a particular time. **3.** Characterized by loss of sensation or capable of producing loss of sensation. **4.** Associated with or due to the state of anesthesia.

general a., a compound that produces loss of sensation and loss of consciousness.

inhalation a., a gas or a liquid with a vapor pressure great enough to produce general anesthesia when breathed.

intravenous a., a compound that produces anesthesia when injected into the circulation via venipuncture.

local a., a compound that, when applied directly to mucous membranes or when injected about nerves, produces loss of sensation by inhibiting nerve excitation or conduction.

primary a., the compound that contributes most to loss of sensation when a mixture of anesthetics is administered.

secondary a., a compound that contributes to, but is not primarily responsible for, loss of sensation when two or more anesthetics are simultaneously administered.

anes'thetist. One who administers an anesthetic; *e.g.*, an anesthesiologist, a physician who is not an anesthesiologist, a nurse anesthetist.

anes'thetiza'tion. The act of producing loss of sensation.

anes'thetize. To produce loss of sensation.

anetoderma (an-e-to-der'mah) [G. *anetos, relaxed*, + *derma*, skin]. Atrophoderma characterized by circumscribed translucent lesions in which the skin becomes baglike and wrinkled.

an'euploid'y. State of having an abnormal number of chromosomes not an exact multiple of the haploid number.

aneuploid (an'u-ployd) [G. *an-* priv. + euploid]. Characterized by aneuploidy.

aneurysm (an'u-rizm) [G. *aneurysma (mat-)*, a dilation, fr. *eurys*, wide]. Circumscribed dilation of an artery, or a blood-containing tumor connecting directly with the lumen of an artery.

arteriosclerotic a., atherosclerotic a., the commonest type of a., occuring in the abdominal aorta and other large arteries in the elderly; due to weakening of the media by severe atherosclerosis.

arteriovenous a., a dilated arteriovenous shunt.

bacterial a., an a. caused by the growth of bacteria within the vascular wall, usually following impaction of a septic embolus.

berry a., a small saccular a. of a cerebral artery that resembles a berry.

a. of Charcot, a small round nodular a. of a small artery or arteriole of the cerebral cortex or basal ganglia, occurring more frequently in hypertensive persons.

cirsoid a., racemose a.; dilation of a group of blood vessels due to congenital malformation with arteriovenous shunting.

compound a., an a. in which some of the coats of the artery are ruptured, others intact.

dissecting a., splitting or dissection of an arterial wall by blood entering through an intimal tear or by interstitial hemorrhage.

false a., (1) pulsating, encapsulated hematoma in communication with the lumen of the ruptured vessel; (2) pseudoaneurysm.

fusiform a., an elongated spindle-shaped dilation of an artery.

mycotic a., one caused by the growth of fungi within the vascular wall, usually following impaction of a septic embolus.

racemose a., cirsoid a.

saccular a., sacculated a., a saclike bulging on one side of an artery.

supraclinoid a., an intracranial a. of the internal carotid artery, occurring above the clinoid bone.

syphilitic a., an a., usually involving the thoracic aorta, resulting from tertiary syphilitic aortitis.

varicose a., a blood-containing sac, communicating with both an artery and a vein.

aneurysmal (an-u-riz'mal). Aneurysmatic; relating to an aneurysm.

aneurysmatic (an-u-riz-mat'ik). Aneurysmal.

aneurysmectomy (an-u-riz-mek'to-mī) [aneurysm + G. *ektomē*, excision]. Excision of an aneurysm.

aneurysmoplasty (an-u-riz'mo-plas-tĭ) [aneurysm + G. *plassō,* to form]. Endoaneurysmorrhaphy; endoaneurysmoplasty; treatment of an aneurysm by opening the sac and suturing its walls to restore the normal dimension to the lumen of the artery. See also aneurysmorrhaphy.

aneurysmorrhaphy (an'u-riz-mor'ă-fĭ) [aneurysm + G. *raphē,* suture]. Closure by suture of the sac of an aneurysm to restore the normal lumen dimensions.

aneurysmotomy (an'u-riz-mot'o-mĭ) [aneurysm + G. *tomē,* incision]. Incision into the sac of an aneurysm.

ANF Antinuclear *factor.*

angi-. See angio-.

angiasthenia (an'jĭ-as-the'nĭ-ah) [angio- + G. *astheneia,* weakness]. Vascular instability.

angiectasia, angiectasis (an-jĭ-ek-ta'sĭ-ah, -ek'tă-sis) [angio- + G. *ektasis,* a stretching]. Dilation of a lymphatic or blood vessel.

angiectat'ic [angio- + G. *ektatos,* capable of extension]. Marked by the presence of dilated blood vessels.

angiectomy (an-jĭ-ek'to-mĭ) [angio- + G. *ektomē,* excision]. Excision of a section of a blood vessel.

angiectopia (an-jĭ-ek-to'pĭ-ah) [angio- + G. *ektopos,* out of place]. Abnormal location of a blood vessel.

angiitis (an-jĭ-i'tis) [angio- + G. *-itis,* inflammation]. Vasculitis; inflammation of a blood vessel (arteritis, phlebitis) or of a lymphatic vessel (lymphangitis).

angina (an'jĭ-nah, an-ji'nah) [L. quinsy]. **1.** Sore throat from any cause. **2.** A severe contricting pain; commonly referring to a. pectoris.

abdominal a., intestinal a.; intermittent abdominal pain, frequently occurring at a fixed time after eating, caused by inadequacy of the mesenteric circulation from arteriosclerosis or other arterial disease.

a. cru'ris, intermittent claudication of the leg.

intestinal a., abdominal a.

Ludwig's a., cellulitis of the submandibular spaces, usually spreading to involve the sublingual and submental spaces.

a. pec'toris, stenocardia; severe constricting pain in the chest, often radiating from the precordium to the left shoulder and down the arm, due to ischemia of the heart muscle, usually caused by coronary disease.

Prinzmetal's a., a form of a. pectoris, different in that the pain is not precipitated by cardiac work, is of longer duration, is usually more severe, and is associated with unusual electrocardiographic manifestations including elevated ST segments in leads.

Vincent's a., an ulcerative infection of the tonsils and pharynx caused by fusiform and spirochetal organisms; usually associated with necrotizing ulcerative gingivitis.

anginal (an'jĭ-nal). Relating to angina in any sense.

anginiform (an-jin'ĭ-form). Resembling angina.

anginoid (an'jin-oid). Resembling angina, especially angina pectoris.

an'ginose, an'ginous. Relating to angina.

angio-, angi- [G. *angeion,* vessel]. Combining forms relating to blood or lymph vessels.

an'gioblast [angio- + G. *blastos,* germ]. **1.** A cell taking part in blood vessel formation. **2.** The primordial mesenchymal tissue from which embryonic blood cells and vascular endothelium are differentiated.

an'gioblasto'ma. Hemangioblastoma.

an'giocar'diokinet'ic, an'giocar'diocinet'ic [angio- + G. *kardia,* heart, + *kinēsis,* movement]. Causing dilation or contraction in the heart and blood vessels.

an'giocardi'tis [angio- + G. *kardia,* heart, + *-itis,* inflammation]. Inflammation of the heart and blood vessels.

angiocardiogram (an'jĭ-o-kar'dĭ-o-gram). The x-ray image produced by angiocardiography.

angiocardiography (an'jĭ-o-kar-dĭ-og'ră-fĭ) [angio- + G. *kardia,* heart, + *graphō,* to write]. X-ray imaging of the heart and great vessels made visible by the intravenous injection of a radiopaque solution.

angiocardiopathy (an'jĭ-o-kar-dĭ-op'ă-thĭ) [angio- + G. *kardia,* heart, + *pathos,* disease]. Disease affecting both heart and blood vessels.

angiodysplasia (an'jĭ-o-dis-pla'zĭ-ah). Degenerative dilation of the normal vasculature.

angiodystrophy, angiodystrophia (an'jĭ-o -dis'tro-fĭ, -dis-tro'fĭ-ah) [angio- + G. *dys-,* bad, + *trophē,* nourishment]. A nutritional disorder associated with marked vascular changes.

angioedema (an'jĭ-o-e-de'mah). Angioneurotic *edema.*

angiofibro'ma. Telangiectatic *fibroma.*

an'giofibro'sis. Fibrosis of the walls of blood vessels.

angiogen'ic. 1. Relating to angiogenesis. **2.** Of vascular origin.

angioglioma (an'jĭ-o-gli-o'mah). A mixed glioma and angioma.

angiogram (an'jĭ-o-gram [angio- + G. *gramma,* a writing]. Radiogram obtained in angiography.

angiography (an-jĭ-og'ră-fĭ) [angio- + G. *graphō,* to write]. Radiography of vessels after the injection of a radiopaque material.

an'giohemophil'ia. von Willebrand's *disease.*

angiohyalinosis (an'jĭ-o-hi'al -ĭ-no'sis) [angio- + G. *hyalos,* glass, + *-osis,* condition]. Hyaline degeneration of the walls of the blood vessels.

angioid (an'jĭ-oyd) [angio- + G. *eidos,* resemblance]. Resembling blood vessels.

an'giokerato'ma [angio- + G. *keras,* horn, + *-ōma,* tumor]. Telangiectatic wart; an intradermal cavernous hemangioma, over which there is a wartlike thickening of the horny layer of the epidermis.

an'giokerato'sis. The occurrence of multiple angiokeratomas.

angiokinesis (an'jĭ-o-kin-e'sis) [angio- + G. *kinēsis*, movement]. Vasomotion.

an'giokinet'ic. Vasomotor.

angioleiomyoma (an'jĭ-o-li'o-mi-o'mah). Vascular *leiomyoma*.

an'giolip'ofibro'ma. Angiofibrolipoma.

an'giolipo'ma. a lipoma that contains an unusually large number or foci of vascular channels.

an'giolith [angio- + G. *lithos*, stone]. An arteriolith or phlebolith.

an'giolith'ic. Relating to an angiolith.

angiol'ogy [angio- + G. *logos*, treatise, discourse]. The science concerned with the blood vessels and lymphatics in all their relations.

an'giolu'poid [angio- + L. *lupus*, wolf, + G. *eidos*, resemblance]. A sarcoid-like eruption of the skin in which the granulomatous, telangiectatic papules are distributed over the nose and cheeks.

angiolysis (an-jĭ-ol'ĭsis) [angio- + G. *lysis*, destruction]. Obliteration of a blood vessel, such as occurs in the newborn infant after tying of the umbilical cord.

angioma (an-jĭ-o'mah) [angio- + G. *-ōma*, tumor]. A swelling or tumor due to proliferation with or without dilation of the blood vessels (hemangioma) or lymphatics (lymphangioma).

    cavernous a., cavernous *hemangioma*.

    cherry a., senile *hemangioma*.

    a. serpigino'sum, essential telangiectasia (2); the presence of rings of red dots on the skin, which tend to widen peripherally, due to proliferation, with subsequent atrophy, of the superficial capillaries.

    telangiectatic a., a. composed of dilated vessels.

an'giomato'sis. A condition characterized by multiple angiomas.

    encephalofacial s., Sturge-Weber *syndrome*.

    encephalotrigeminal a., Sturge-Weber *syndrome*.

    retinocerebral a., Lindau's *disease*.

angiomatoid (an-jĭ-o'mă-toid). Resembling a tumor of vascular origin.

angio'matous. Relating to or resembling an angioma.

an'giomeg'aly [angio- + G. *megas*, large]. Enlargement of blood vessels or lymphatics.

an'giomy'osarco'ma. A myosarcoma that has an unusually large number of proliferated, frequently dilated vascular channels.

an'giomyo'ma [angio- + G. *mys*, muscle, + suffix *-ōma*, tumor]. Vascular *leiomyoma*.

angiomyolipoma (an'jĭ-o-mi'o-lĭ-po'mah) [angio- + G. *mys*, muscle, + *lipos*, fat, + *-oma*, tumor]. A benign neoplasm of adipose tissue (lipoma) in which muscle cells and vascular structures are fairly conspicuous.

angiomyoneuroma (an'jĭo-mi'o-nu-ro'mah). Glomus *tumor*.

angioneurectomy (an'jĭ-o-nu-rek'to-mĭ) [angio- + G. *neuron* nerve, + *ektomē*, excision]. Exsection of the vessels and nerves of a part.

an'gioneurede'ma [angio- + G. *neuron*, nerve, + *oidēma*, a swelling]. Edema due to an angioneurosis, or vasomotor disorder.

an'gioneu'romyo'ma. Glomus *tumor*.

angioparalysis (an'jĭ-o-pă-ral'ĭ-sis). Vasoparalysis.

angioparesis (an'jĭ-o-pă-re'sis, par'ē-sis). Vasoparesis.

angiopath'ic. Relating to angiopathy.

angiop'athy [angio- + G. *pathos*, suffering]. Any disease of the blood vessels or lymphatics.

an'gioplas'ty [angio- + G. *plassō*, to form]. Reconstruction of a blood vessel.

    percutaneous transluminal coronary a., an operation for enlarging a narrowed coronary arterial lumen by peripheral introduction of a balloon-tip catheter and dilating the lumen on withdrawal of the inflated catheter tip.

angiopoiesis (an'jĭ-o-poy-e'sis) [angio- + G. *poiesis*, making]. Vasifaction; vasoformation; the formation of blood or lymphatic vessels.

angiopoietic (an'jĭ-o-poy-et'ik). Vasifactive; vasoformative; relating to angiopoiesis.

an'giopressure. Pressure on a vessel for the arrest of bleeding.

angiorrhaphy (an-jĭ-or'ă-fĭ) [angio- + G. *raphē*, a seam]. Suture repair of any vessel, especially of a blood vessel.

an'giosarco'ma. A rare malignant neoplasm occurring most often in the breast and skin, and believed to originate from the endothelial cells of blood vessels; microscopically composed of closely packed round or spindle-shaped cells, some of which line small spaces resembling vascular clefts.

angioscotoma (an'jĭ-o-sko-to'mah) [angio- + G. *skotōma*, dizziness, vertigo]. Cecocentral scotoma; ribbon-shaped defect of the visual fields caused by the retinal vessels overlying photoreceptors.

an'gioscotom'etry. Measurement or projection of an angioscotoma pattern.

an'giospas'tic. Vasospastic.

angiospasm (an'jĭ-o-spazm) Vasospasm.

angiostaxis (an'jĭ-o-stak'sis) [angio- + G. *staxis*, a trickling, fr. *stazō*, to drip]. **1.** Oozing of blood. **2.** Hemophilia.

an'giosteno'sis [angio- + G. *stenōsis*, a narrowing]. Narrowing of one or more blood vessels.

angios'trophy [angio- + G. *strophē*, a twist]. Twisting the cut end of a blood vessel to arrest bleeding.

an'giotelec'tasis, an'giotel'ecta'sia [angio- + G. *telos*, end, + *ektasis*, a stretching out]. Dilation of the terminal arterioles, venules, or capillaries.

angioten'sin. A family of decapeptides with vasoconstrictive activity, produced by enzymatic action of renin upon angiotensinogen.

    a. I, a decapeptide formed from angiotensinogen, a reaction catalyzed by renin; a peptidase cleaves two more residues to yield a. II, the physiologically active form.

a. II, an octapeptide formed from a. I; a potent vasopressor agent and the most powerful stimulus for production and release of aldosterone.

a. amide, a synthetic substance closely related to the naturally occurring a. II; a potent vasopressor.

angiotin′sinase. The enzyme that degrades angiotensin II.

angiotensin′ogen. Angiotensin precursor; a tetradecapeptide converted by renin to angiotensin I.

an′gioto′nia. Vasotonia

angiot′omy [angio- + G. *tomē,* cutting]. Sectioning of a blood vessel, or the creation of an opening into a vessel prior to its repair.

an′gioton′ic. Vasotonic.

angiotribe (an′jĭ-o-trib) [angio- + G. *tribō,* to bruise]. A strong forceps used to crush the end of a blood vessel, together with the tissue in which it is embedded, to arrest hemorrhage.

an′giotrip′sy [angio- + G. *tripsis,* friction, bruising]. Vasotripsy; use of an angiotribe to arrest hemorrhage.

angiotrophic (an′jĭ-o-trof′ĭk) [angio- + G. *trophē,* nourishment]. Vasotrophic; relating to the nutrition of the blood vessels or lymphatics.

angle (ang′gl) [L. *angulus*]. The figure or space formed by the junction of two lines or planes. For a.'s not listed below, see the descriptive term.

acromial a., *angulus* acromialis.

alpha a., (1) the a. between the visual and optic axes as they cross at the nodal point of the eye; (2) the a. between the visual line and the major axis of the corneal ellipse.

a. of anomaly (abnormality), in strabismus, the degree of deviation from parallelism in an eye

axial a., an a. formed by two surfaces of a body, the line of union of which is parallel with its axis, as in the axial a.'s of a tooth.

cavosurface a., the a. formed by the junction of a cavity wall and the surface of the tooth.

a. of convergence, the a. that the visual axis makes with the medial line when a near object is viewed.

costal a., *angulus* costae.

a. of eccentricity, in strabismus, the a. between the line of fixation and the line of normal foveal fixation.

filtration a., *angulus* iridocornealis.

gamma a., the a. formed between the line joining the fixation point to the center of the eye and the optic axis.

incisal guide a., the a. formed with the horizontal plane by drawing a line in the sagittal plane between incisal edges of the maxillary and mandibular central incisors when the teeth are in centric occlusion.

iridocorneal a., a. of iris, *angulus* iridocornealis.

a. of jaw, *angulus* mandibulae.

kappa a., the a. between the pupillary axis and the visual axis: positive when the pupillary axis is nasal to the visual axis: negative when the pupillary axis is temporal to the visual axis.

a. of mandible, *angulus* mandibulae.

mesial a., the a. formed by the meeting of the mesial with the labial (or buccal) or lingual surface of a tooth.

meter a., unit of ocular convergence; the amount of convergence required to view binocularly an object 1 meter distant and exerting 1 diopter of accommodation.

pelvivertebral a., the a. made by the pelvis with the general axis of the trunk or spine.

point a., the junction of three surfaces of the crown of a tooth, or of the walls of a cavity.

pubic a., *angulus* subpubicus.

sternal a., *angulus* sterni.

sternoclavicular a., the a. formed by the junction of the clavicle with the sternum.

subpubic a., *angulus* subpubicus.

a. of torsion, the amount of rotation of a long bone along its axis or between two axes, measured in degrees.

venous a., the junction of the internal jugular and subclavian veins, toward which converge the external and the anterior jugular and the vertebral veins, the thoracic duct in the left a. and the right lymphatic duct in the right.

visual a., the a. formed at the retina by the meeting of lines drawn from the periphery of the object seen.

ang′strom (Å). A unit of wavelength, 10^{-10}, equivalent to 0.1 nm.

ang′ula′tion. Formation of an angle; an abnormal angle or bend in an organ.

an′gulus, gen. and pl. **an′guli** [L.] [NA]. An angle or corner.

a. acromia′lis [NA], acromial angle; the prominent angle at the junction of the posterior and lateral borders of the acromion.

a. cos′tae [NA], costal angle; the rather abrupt change in curvature of the body of a rib posteriorly, such that the neck and head of the rib are directed upward.

a. iridocornea′lis [NA], **a. ir′idis,** angle of the iris; iridocorneal or filtration angle; the acute angle between the iris and the cornea at the periphery of the anterior chamber of the eye.

a. mandib′ulae [NA], angle of the mandible or jaw; the angle formed by the lower margin of the body and the posterior margin of the ramus of the mandible.

a. sphenoida′lis os′sis parieta′lis [NA], the anterior inferior angle of the parietal bone.

a. ster′ni [NA], sternal angle; the angle between the manubrium and the body of the sternum.

a. subpu′bicus [NA], subpubic or pubic a.; the a. formed by the inferior rami of the pubic bones.

anhedonia (an-he-do′nĭ-ah) [G. *an-* priv. + *hedonē,* pleasure]. Absence of pleasure from the performance of acts that would ordinarily be pleasurable.

anhidrosis (an-hi-dro′sis) [G. *an-* priv. + *hidrōs,* sweat]. Anidrosis; adiaphoresis; ischidrosis; absence of sweating.

anhidrotic (an-hi-drot'ik). Adiaphoretic; antihydrotic; antisudorific. **1.** Relating to, or characterized by, anhidrosis. **2.** An agent that reduces, prevents, or stops sweating. **3.** Denoting a reduction or absence of sweat glands.

anhy'drase. An enzyme that catalyzes the removal of water from a compound. Most such enzymes are now known as hydrases, hydro-lyases, or dehydratases.

anhydration (an'hi-dra'shun). Dehydration (1).

anhy'dride. An oxide that can combine with water to form an acid or that is derived from an acid by the abstraction of water.

anhydro- [G. *an-* priv., + *hydōr,* water]. Prefix denoting the removal of water.

anhydrous (an-hi'drus). Containing no water, especially water of crystallization.

anile (an'il) [L. *anilis,* fr. *anus,* an old woman]. In one's dotage.

anilide (an'ĭ-lid). An *N*-acyl aniline; *e.g.,* acetanilide.

an'ilinc'tion, an'ilinc'tus [L. *anus* + *linctio*(*lingere*), licking]. Sexual stimulation by licking or kissing the anus.

aniline (an'ĭ-lin, -lēn) [Ar. *an-nil,* indigo]. Aminobenzene; $C_6H_5(NH_2)$; the parent substance of many synthetic dyes; formally derived from benzene by the substitution of $-NH_2$ for one of the hydrogen atoms.

an'ilinism, an'ilism. Chronic aniline poisoning characterized by gastric and cardiac weakness, vertigo, muscular depression, intermittent pulse, and cyanosis.

anil'ity [L. *anilitas,* fr. *anus,* an old woman]. Dotage.

anima (an'ĭ-mah) [L. air, breath, soul]. **1.** The soul or spirit. **2.** In jungian psychology, the inner self, in contrast with the outer aspect of the personality (persona); a female archtype in a man. See also animus.

animal [L.]. **1.** A living, sentient organism that has membranous cell walls, requires oxygen and organic foods, and is capable of voluntary movement as distinguished from a plant or mineral. **2.** One of the lower a. organisms as distinguished from man.

animation (an'ĭ-ma'shun) [L. *animo,* pp. *-atus,* to make alive; *anima,* breath, soul]. **1.** The state of being alive. **2.** Liveliness; high spirits.

  suspended a., a temporary state resembling death, with cessation of respiration; may also refer to certain forms of hibernation in animals or to endospore formation by some bacteria.

an'imus [L. *animus,* breath, rational soul in man, intellect, conscious power, will, disposition]. **1.** An animating or energizing spirit. **2.** Intention to do something; disposition. **3.** In psychiatry, a spirit of active hostility or grudge. **4.** The ideal image toward which a person strives. **5.** In jungian psychology, a male archtype in a woman. See also anima.

anion (an'ĭ-on). An ion that carries a negative charge, going therefore to the positively charged anode; in salts, the acid radicals are a.'s.

anion exchange. The process by which an anion in a mobile (liquid) phase exchanges with another anion previously bound to a solid, positively charged phase, the latter being an anion exchanger.

aniridia (an'ĭ-rid'ĭ-ah). Congenital absence of all but the root of the iris.

anisakiasis (an-ĭ-să-ki'ă-sis) [G. *anisos,* unequal, + *akis,* a point, + *-iasis,* condition]. Infection of the intestinal wall by larvae of *Anisakis marina,* characterized by intestinal eosinophilic granuloma and symptoms like those of septic ulcer or tumor.

Anisakis (an-ĭ-sa'-kis) [G. *anisos,* unequal, + *akis,* a point]. Genus of nematodes (family Anisakidae) that includes many common parasites of marine fish-eating birds and marine mammals.

aniseikonia (an'ĭ-si-ko'nĭ-ah) [G. *anisos,* unequal, + *eikōn,* an image]. Unequal retinal image; a relative difference in size or shape of ocular images.

aniso- [G. *anisos,* unequal]. Combining form meaning unequal or dissimilar.

anisoaccommodation (an-i'so-ă-kom-o-da'shun) [aniso- + L. *accommodare,* to adapt]. Variation between the two eyes in accommodation capacity.

anisochromatic (an-i'so-kro-mat'ik). Not uniformly of one color.

anisocoria (an-i'so-ko'rĭ-ah) [aniso- + G. *korē,* pupil]. Unequal size of the pupils.

anisocytosis (an-i'so-si-to'sis) [aniso- + G. *kytos,* cell, + *-osis,* condition]. Considerable variation in the size of cells that are normally uniform, especially with reference to red blood cells.

anisodactylous (an-i'so-dak'tĭ-lus). Relating to anisodactyly.

anisodactyly (an-i'so-dak'tĭ-lī) [aniso- + G. *daktylon,* finger]. Unequal length in corresponding fingers.

anisogamy (an'ĭ-sog'ă-mī) [aniso- + G. *gamos,* marriage]. Fusion of two gametes unequal in size or form; fertilization as distinguished from isogamy or conjugation.

anisognathous (an-ĭ-sog'nă-thus) [aniso- + G. *gnathos,* jaw]. Having a maxilla and mandible of abnormal relative size.

anisokaryosis (an-i'so-kar-ĭ-o'sis) [aniso- + G. *karyon,* nut (nucleus), + *-osis,* condition]. Variation in size of nuclei, greater than the normal range for a tissue.

anisomastia (an-i'so-mas'tĭ-ah) [aniso- + G. *mastos,* breast]. Asymmetrical breasts.

anisomelia (an-i'so-me'lĭ-ah) [aniso- + G. *melos,* limb]. Inequality of two paired limbs.

anisometropia (an-i'so-mě-tro'pĭ-ah) [aniso- + G. *metron,* measure, + *ōps,* sight]. Difference in the refractive power of the eyes.

ani'sometrop'ic. Relating to anisometropia.

anisomyopia (an-i'so-mi-o'pĭ-ah) Unequal myopia in the two eyes.

anisopiesis (an-i-so-pi-e'sis) [aniso- + G. *piesis,* pressure]. Unequal arterial blood pressure on the two sides of the body.

anisosphygmia (an-i-so-sfig'mĭ-ah) [aniso- + G. *sphygmos*, pulse]. Difference in volume, force, or time of the pulse in the corresponding arteries on two sides of the body, *e.g.*, the two radials, or femorals.

anisosthenic (an-i-sos-then'ik) [aniso- + G. *sthenos*, strength]. Of unequal strength; denoting two muscles or groups of muscles either paired or antagonists.

anisoton'ic [aniso- + G. *tonus*, tension]. Not having equal tension; having unequal osmotic pressure.

anisotro'pine methylbromide. 8-Methyltropinium bromide 2-propylvalerate; anticholinergic, intestinal antispasmodic.

ankle (ang'kl). **1.** The joint between the leg and foot in which the tibia and fibula above articulate with the talus below. **2.** The region of the a. joint. **3.** Talus.

ankylo- [G. *ankylos*, bent, crooked; *ankylosis*, stiffness or fixation of a joint]. Combining form meaning bent, crooked, stiff, or fixed.

ankyloblepharon (ang'kĭ-lo-blef'ă-ron) [ankylo- + G. *blepharon*, eyelid]. Blepharisynechia.

ankyloglossia (ang'kĭ-lo-glos'ĭ-ah) [ankylo- + G. *glóssa*, tongue]. Tongue-tie.

ankylopoietic (ang'kĭ-lo-poy-et'ik). Forming ankylosis.

ankyloproctia (ang'kĭ-lo-prok'shĭ-ah) [ankylo- + G. *próktos*, anus]. Imperforation or stricture of the anus.

an'kylosed. Stiffened; bound by adhesions; denoting a joint in a state of ankylosis.

ankylosis (ang'kĭ-lo'sis) [G. *ankylosis*, stiffening of a joint]. Stiffening or fixation of a joint as the result of a disease process, with fibrous or bony union across the joint.

　　artificial a., arthrodesis.

　　bony a., synostosis.

　　extracapsular a., spurious a.; stiffness of a joint due to induration or ossification of the surrounding tissues.

　　false a., fibrous a.

　　fibrous a., false a.; pseudankylosis; stiffening of a joint due to the presence of fibrous bands between and about the bones forming the joint.

　　intracapsular a., stiffness of a joint due to the presence of bony or fibrous adhesions between the articular surfaces of the joint.

　　spurious a., extracapsular a.

　　true a., synostosis.

an'kylot'ic. Characterized by or pertaining to ankylosis.

an'kyroid. Ancyroid.

anlage, *pl.* **anla'gen** (ahn'lah-guh) [Ger. hereditary factor]. **1.** Primordium. **2.** In psychoanalysis, genetic predisposition to a given trait or personality characteristic.

annec'tent [L. *an-necto*, pres. p. *-nectnes*, pp. *-nexus*, to join to]. Connected with; joined.

annex'a. Adnexa.

annex'al. Adnexal.

an'nular [L. *anulus*, ring]. Ring-shaped.

an'nuloplasty [L. *anulus*, ring, + G. *plassó*, to form]. Reconstruction of an incompetent (usually mitral) cardiac valve.

annulorrhaphy (an-u-lor'a-fi) [L. *anulus*, ring, + G. *raphē*, seam]. Closure of a hernial ring by suture.

an'nulus. See anulus.

anococcygeal (a-no-kok-sij'e-al). Relating to both anus and coccyx.

anodontia (an-o-don'shĭ-ah) [G. *an-* priv. + *odous*, tooth]. Congenital absence of teeth.

anodyne (an'o-dīn) [G. *an-* priv. + *odynē*, pain]. A compound less potent than an anesthetic or a narcotic but capable of relieving pain.

a'nogen'ital. Relating to both the anal and the genital regions.

anomalad (a-nom'ă-lad) [see anomaly]. A malformation together with its subsequently derived structural changes.

anomaly (ă-nom'ă-lī) [G. *anōmalia*, irregularity]. Deviation from the average or norm; anything structurally unusual or irregular or contrary to a general rule.

　　Alder's a., coarse azurophilic granulation of leukocytes, especially granulocytes.

　　Chediak-Steinbrinck-Higashi a., Chediak-Steinbrinck-Higashi *syndrome*.

　　developmental a., an a. established during intrauterine life.

　　Ebstein's a., Ebstein's disease; congenital downward displacement of the tricuspid valve into the right ventricle.

　　Hegglin's a., May-Hegglin a., a disorder in which neutrophils and eosinophils contain basophilic structures known as Döhle or Amato bodies and in which there is faulty maturation of platelets, with thrombocytopenia.

　　Pelger-Huët nuclear a., congenital inhibition of lobulation of the nuclei of neutrophilic leukocytes; not associated with disease, but may be confused with leukocyte "shift to left;" autosomal dominant inheritance.

an'omer. One of two sugar molecules that are epimeric at the hemiacetal carbon atom (carbon-1 in aldoses, carbon-2 in ketoses); *e.g.*, α-D-glucose and β-D-glucose.

ano'mia [G. *a-* priv. + *ōnoma*, name]. Nominal *aphasia.*

anonychia, anonychosis (an-o-nik'ĭ-ah, an-o-ni-ko'sis) [G. *an-*priv. + *onyx*(*onych-*), nail]. Congenital absence of the nails.

Anopheles (an-of'ĕ-lēz) [G. *anóphelēs*, useless, harmful, fr. *an-* priv. + *ōpheleō*, to be of use]. A genus of mosquitoes (family Culicidae, subfamily Anophelinae) containing over 90 species, many of which are vectors of malaria.

anoph'eline. Referring to the *Anopheles* mosquito.

anophthalmia, anophthalmos, anophthalmus (an-of-thal'mĭ-ah, -mus) [G. *an-* priv. + *ophthalmos*, eye]. Complete absence of tissues of the eyes.

a'noplasty. Reconstructive surgery on the anus.

anorchia, anorchidism, anorchism (an-or'kĭ-ah, -kĭ-dizm, -kizm) [G. *an-* priv. + *orchis*, testis]. Absence of the testes.

anorectal (a'no-rek'tal). Relating to both anus and rectum.

anorectic, anoretic, (an-o-rek'tik, -ret'ik). **1.** Causing, or characterized by, anorexia. **2.** An agent so acting.

anorexia (an-o-rek'sĭah) [G. fr. *an-* + *orexis*, appetite]. Diminished appetite; aversion to food.

 a. nervo'sa, a personality disorder manifested by extreme aversion to food, usually occurring in young women, resulting in extreme weight loss, amenorrhea, and constitutional disorders.

anorex'iant. A drug, process, or event that leads to anorexia.

anorex'ic. Relating to or suffering from anorexia nervosa.

anorexigenic (an'o-rek-sĭ-jen'ik). Promoting or causing anorexia.

anorthog'raphy [G. *an-* priv. + *orthos*, straight, + *graphō*, to write]. Agraphia.

a'noscope. A short speculum for examining the anal canal and lower rectum.

anosigmoidoscopy (a'no-sig-moyd-os'ko-pī). Endoscopy of the anus, rectum and sigmoid colon.

anosmia (an-oz'mĭah) [G. *an-* priv. + *osmē*, sense of smell]. Olfactory anesthesia; loss of the sense of smell.

anosmic (an-oz'mik). Relating to anosmia.

anosognosia (ă-no'sog-no'sĭ-ah) [G. *a-* priv. + *nosos*, disease, + *gnōsis*, knowledge]. Ignorance, real or feigned, of the presence of disease, specifically of paralysis.

anosogno'sic. Relating to anosognosia.

a'nospi'nal. Relating to the anus and the spinal cord.

anostosis (an'os-to'sis) [G. *an-* priv. + *osteon*, bone]. Failure of ossification.

anotia (an-o'shī-ah) [G. *an-* priv. + *ous*, ear]. Congenital absence of one or both ears.

a'noves'ical. Relating to both anus and urinary bladder.

anov'ular, anov'ulatory. Not related to or coincident with ovulation.

anovula'tion. Suspension or cessation of ovulation.

anoxemia (an'ok-se'mĭ-ah) [G. *an-*priv. + oxygen + G. *haima*, blood]. Absence of oxygen in arterial blood.

anoxia (an-ok'sĭ-ah) [G. *an-* priv. + oxygen + *-ia*, condition]. Absence of oxygen in inspired gases, arterial blood, or tissues.

 anemic a., anemic *hypoxia.*

 anoxic a., hypoxic *hypoxia.*

 diffusion a., diffusion *hypoxia.*

 histotoxic a., a. due to the inability of tissue cells to utilize oxygen; its tension in arterial and capillary blood is usually greater than normal.

 stagnant a., ischemic *hypoxia.*

ansa, gen. and pl. **ansae** (an'sah, -se) [L. loop, handle] [NA]. Any anatomical structure in the form of a loop or an arc.

 a. cervica'lis [NA], **cervical a.,** a loop in the cervical plexus consisting of fibers from the first three cervical nerves, some of which accompany the hypoglossal nerve for a short distance.

 a. lenticula'ris [NA], **lenticular a.,** the tortuous efferent pathway of the globus pallidus.

 ansae nervo'rum spina'lium, loops of the spinal nerves, connecting branches between the ventral branches of the spinal nerves.

 a. peduncula'ris [NA], **peduncular a.,** a complex nerve fiber bundle curving around the medial edge of the internal capsule and connecting the anterior part of the temporal lobe with the mediodorsal nucleus of the thalamus.

 a. subcla'via [NA], **subclavian a.,** the cord connecting the middle and cervical stellate sympathetic ganglia, forming a loop around the subclavian artery.

an'sate. Ansiform.

an'siform [L. *ansa*, handle, + *forma*, shape]. Ansate; in the shape of a loop or arc.

ant-. See anti-.

antac'id. Antiacid. Neutralizing an acid.

antag'onism [G. *anti*, against, + *agōnizomai*, to fight]. Mutual resistance; denoting mutual opposition in action between muscles, drugs, diseases, or physiologic processes or between drugs and diseases or drugs and physiologic processes.

antag'onist. Something opposing or resisting the action of another; denoting certain muscles, drugs, etc., that tend to neutralize or impede the action or effect of others.

antal'gic. Analgesic (2).

ante- [L. *ante*, before]. Prefix denoting before. See also pre-, pro-.

antebrachial (an'te-bra'kĭ-al). Relating to the forearm.

antebrachium (an-te-bra'kĭ-um) [ante- + L. *brachium*, arm] [NA]. Forearm.

antecedent (an-te-se'dent) [L. *antecedo*, to go before]. A precursor.

 plasma thromboplastin a. (PTA), *factor* XI.

antecu'bital]ante- + L. *cubitum*, elbow]. In front of the elbow.

antefebrile (an'te-feb'ril) [ante- + L. *febris*, fever]. Antipyretic.

anteflexion (an'te-flek'shun). A bending forward; a sharp forward curve or angulation; denoting especially a forward bend in the uterus at the junction of corpus and cervix.

antemor'tem [L. acc. case of *mors* (*mort-*), death]. Before death.

antena'tal [ante- + L. *natus*, birth]. Prenatal.

antepar'tum [ante- + L. *pario*, pp. *partus*, to bring forth]. Before labor or childbirth.

antepyret'ic [ante- + G. *pyretos,* fever]. Antefebrile; before the occurrence of fever.

ante'rior [L.]. **1.** Before, in relation to time or space. **2** [NA]. Ventral (2); in human anatomy, denoting the front surface of the body; often used to indicate the position of one structure relative to another. **3.** Near the head or rostral end of certain embryos.

antero-. A prefix denoting anterior.

an'terograde [L. *gradior,* pp. *gressus,* to step, go]. Moving forward.

an'teroinfer'ior. In front and below.

an'terolat'eral. In front and away from the middle line.

an'terome'dial. In front and toward the middle line.

an'terome'dian. In front and in the central line.

an'teroposte'rior. Relating to both front and rear.

an'terosupe'rior. In front and above.

antever'sion [ante- + Mediev. L. *versio,* a turning]. Turning forward, inclining forward as a whole without bending.

antevert'ed. Tilted forward; in a position of anteversion.

anthelix (ant'he-liks, an'the-liks)]anti- + G. *helix,* coil] [NA]. Antihelix; an elevated ridge of cartilage anterior and roughly parallel to the posterior portion of the auricle helix.

anthelmin'thic. Anthelmintic (1).

anthelmintic (ant'hel-min'tik, an'thel-) [anti- + G. *helmins,* worm]. **1.** Anthelminthic; helminthagogue; helminthic; vermifuge; an agent that destroys or expels intestinal worms. **2.** Vermifugal; having the power to destroy or expel intestinal worms.

anthracic (an-thras'ik). Relating to anthrax.

an'thracoid [G. *anthrax,* carbuncle, + *eidos,* resemblance]. **1.** Resembling a carbuncle or cutaneous anthrax. **2.** Resembling anthrax.

anthracosilicosis (ah'thră-ko-sil'ĭ-ko'sis). Accumulation of carbon and silica in the lungs from inhaled coal dust.

anthraco'sis. Accumulation of carbon from inhaled smoke or coal dust in the lungs.

an'thrax [G. *anthrax* (*anthrak-*), charcoal, coal, a cabuncle]. Carbuncle (2); a disease occurring in man from infection of subcutaneous tissues with *Bacillus anthracis;* marked by hemorrhage and serous effusions in the organs and cavities in the body and by extreme prostration. Primary forms are pulmonary, gastroenteric or intestinal, and cutaneous.

an'thropo- [G. *anthrōpos,* man]. A combining form meaning human, or denoting some relationship to man.

anthropoid (an'thro-poyd) [G. *anthrōpo- eidēs,* man-like]. Resembling man in structure and form.

anthropol'ogy [anthropo- + G. *logos,* treatise]. The branch of science concerned with man's origins and development.

anthropomet'ric. Relating to anthropometry.

anthropom'etry [anthropo- + G. *metron,* measure]. The branch of anthropology concerned with comparative measurements of the human body and its parts.

anthropomorphism (an'thro-po-mor'fizm) [anthropo- + G. *morphē,* form]. Attribution of human characteristics to nonhuman creatures or inanimate objects.

anthropophilic (an'thro-po-fil'ik) [anthropo- + G. *phileō,* to love]. Human-seeking or -preferring, especially with reference to the preference of a parasite for a human host over an animal host.

anthropozoonosis (an'thro-po-zo'o-no'sis) [anthropo- + G. *zōon,* animal, + *nosis,* disease]. A zoonosis maintained in nature by animals and transmissible to man.

anti- [G. *anti,* against]. Prefix signifying against, opposing, or, in relation to symptoms and diseases, curative; also to denote an antibody (immunoglobulin) specific for the thing indicated; *e.g.,* antitoxin (antibody specific for a toxin).

antiac'id. Antacid.

an'tiadrener'gic. Denoting an agent that annuls or antagonizes the effects of the sympathetic nervous system.

antiagglu'tinin. A specific antibody that inhibits or destroys the action of an agglutinin.

an'tian'tibody. Antibody specific for another antibody.

antianaphylaxis (an'tĭ-an-ă-fi-lak'sis). Desensitization (1).

antiandrogen (an'ti-an'dro-jen). Any substance capable of preventing full expression of the biological effects of androgenic hormones on responsive tissues.

an'tiane'mic. Pertaining to factors or substances that prevent or correct anemic conditions.

an'tiantitox'in. An antiantibody that inhibits or counteracts the effects of an antitoxin.

antianxiety (an-tĭ-ang-zi'ĕ-tĭ). **1.** An antianxiety *agent.* **2.** Denoting the actions of such an agent.

antibacterial (an'tĭ-bak-tēr'ĭ-al). Destructive to or preventing the growth of bacteria.

antibio'sis [anti- + G. *biōsis,* life]. **1.** An association of two organisms which is detrimental to one of them. **2.** Production of an antibiotic by bacteria or other organisms inhibitory to other living things.

antibiot'ic. 1. A chemical substance derived from a mold or bacteria that inhibits the growth of other microorganisms. **2.** Relating to such an action.

broad spectrum a., an a. having a wide range of activity against both Gram-positive and Gram-negative organisms.

antibody (an'tĭ-bod'ĭ). **1.** Generally, any body or substance, soluble or cellular, which is evoked by the stimulus provided by the introduction of antigen and which reacts specifically with antigen in some demonstrable way. **2.** One of the classes of globulins (immunoglobulins) present in the blood serum or body fluids as a result of antigenic stimulus or occurring "naturally." Different genetically inherited determinants, Gm (found on IgG H chains),

Am (found in IgA H chains), and Km (found on K-type L chains) control the antigenicity of the antibody molecule; subclasses are denoted either alphabetically or numerically (*e.g.,* G3mb1 or G3m5).

anaphylactic a., cytotropic a.

antinuclear a., an a. showing an affinity for cell nuclei.

blocking a., (1) a. which, in certain concentrations, does not cause precipitation after combining with specific antigen, and which, in this combined state, "blocks" activity of additional a. added to increase the concentration to a level at which precipitation would ordinarily occur; **(2)** the IgG class of immunoglobulin which combines specifically with an atopic allergen but does not elicit a type I allergic reaction, the combined IgG a. "blocking" available IgE class (reaginic) a. activity.

complement-fixing a., an a. that combines with and sensitizes antigen leading to the activation of complement, sometimes resulting in lysis.

complete a., saline *agglutinin.*

cross-reacting a., (1) a. specific for group antigens, *i.e.,* those with identical functional groups; **(2)** a. for antigens that have functional groups of closely similar, but not identical, chemical structure.

cytotropic a., cytophilic a., anaphylactic a.; a. that has an affinity for certain kinds of cells, in addition to and unrelated to its specific affinity for the antigen that induced it, because of the properties of the Fc portion of the heavy chain.

heterocytotropic a., a cytotropic a. (chiefly of the IgG class) similar in activity to homocytotropic a., but having an affinity for cells of a different species rather than for cells of the same or a closely related species.

homocytotropic a., reaginic a.; a. of the IgE class which has an affinity for tissues (notably mast cells) of the same or a closely related species and that, upon combining with specific antigen, triggers the release of pharmacological mediators of anaphylaxis from the cells to which it is attached.

incomplete a., serum *agglutinin.*

inhibiting a., univalent a.

natural a., normal a.

neutralizing a., a form of a. that reacts with an infectious agent (usually a virus) and destroys or inhibits its infectivity and virulence.

normal a., natural a.; a demonstrable in the serum or plasma of various persons or animals not known to have been stimulated by specific antigen, either artifically or as the result of naturally occurring contact.

reaginic a., homocytotropic a.

anticholinergic (an'tĭ-kol-in-er'jik). Antagonistic to the action of parasympathetic or other cholinergic nerve fibers.

anticholinesterase (an'tĭ-kol-in-es'ter-ās). A drug that inhibits or inactivates acetylcholinesterase.

anticli'nal [anti- + G. *klinō,* to incline]. Inclined in opposite directions, as two sides of a pyramid.

anticoagulant (an'tĭ-ko-ag'u-lant). Preventing coagulation.

antico'don. The trinucleotide sequence complementary to a codon, the complementarity principle arising from Watson-Crick base-pairing.

anticom'plement. A substance that combines with a complement and so neutralizes its action by preventing its union with the antibody.

an'ticonvul'sant, an'ticonvul'sive. Preventing or arresting convulsions.

antidepres'sant. Counteracting depression.

antidiuresis (an'tĭ-di-u-re'sis). Reduction of urinary volume.

antidiuret'ic. An agent that reduces the output of urine.

an'tido'tal. Relating to or acting as an antidote.

an'tidote [anti- + G. *dotos,* what is given]. An agent that neutralizes a poison or counteracts its effects.

chemical a., a substance that unites with a poison to form an innocuous chemical compound.

mechanical a., a substance that prevents the absorption of a poison.

physiologic a., an agent that produces systemic effects opposing those of a given poison.

antidrom'ic [anti- + G. *dromos,* a running]. Relating to propagation of an impulse along an axon in a direction the reverse of the normal.

antiemetic (ant'tĭ-e-met'ik) [anti- + G. *emetikos,* emetic]. Preventing or arresting vomiting.

antienzyme (an-tĭ-en'zīm). An agent or principle that retards, inhibits, or destroys the activity of an enzyme; may be an inhibitory enzyme or an antibody to an enzyme.

antiestrogen (an'tĭ-es'tro-jen). Any substance capable of preventing full expression of the biological effects of estrogenic hormones on responsive tissues, either by producing antagonistic effects on the target tissue or by merely inhibiting estrogenic effects.

antifebrile (an'tĭ-fe'bril) [anti- + L. *febris,* fever]. Antipyretic (1).

anti'fibrinol'ysin. Antiplasmin.

an'tigen'ic. Allergenic; immunogenic; having the properties of an antigen (allergen).

antigen (Ag) (an'tĭ-jen) [anti(body) + G. *-gen,* producing]. Allergen; immunogen; any substance that, as a result of coming in contact with appropriate tissues of an animal body, induces a state of sensitivity and/or resistance to infection or toxic substances after a latent period and which reacts in a demonstrable way with tissues and/or antibody of the sensitized subject *in vivo* or *in vitro.*

Australia a., Au a., hepatitis-associated a.

blood group a., generic term for any inherited antigen found on the surface of erythrocytes that determines a blood grouping reaction with specific antiserum; a.'s of the ABO and Lewis blood groups may be found also in saliva and other body fluids.

capsular a., an a. found only in the capsules of certain microorganisms.

carcinoembryonic a. (CEA), oncofetal a.; a glycoprotein constituent of the glycocalyx of embryonic entodermal epithelium, generally absent from adult cells with the exception of some carcinomas in which it may also be detected in the patient's serum.

cholesterinized a., cardiolipin to which cholesterol has been added.

complete a., any a. capable of stimulating the formation of antibody with which it reacts *in vivo* or *in vitro*, as distinguished from incomplete a. (hapten).

conjugated a., conjugated *hapten.*

flagellar a., the heat-labile a.'s associated with bacterial flagella.

group a.'s, a.'s that are shared by related genera of microorganisms.

H a., the a. in the flagella of motile bacteria.

hepatitis-associated a. (HHA), hepatitis B a., Australia a.; Au a.; a term used for the surface a. of hepatitis B virus before its nature was established. See hepatitis B surface a.

hepatitis B core a. (HB$_c$Ag), the a. found in the core (seemingly the nucleocapsid) of the Dane particle (seemingly the hepatitis B virus) and also in hepatocyte nuclei in hepatic B infections.

hepatitis B e a. (HBe, HB$_e$Ag), an a., or group of a.'s associated with hepatitis B infection and distinct from the surface a. (HB$_s$Ag) and the core a. (HB$_c$Ag).

hepatitis B surface a. (HB$_s$Ag), a. of the small (20nm) spherical and filamentous forms of hepatitis B a., and a surface a. of the larger (42 nm) Dane particle (seemingly the hepatitis B virus).

heterogenetic a., heterophil a., an a. possessed by a variety of different phylogenetically unrelated species. *e.g.* the various organ- or tissue-specific a.'s, the alpha- and beta-crystalline protein of the lens of the eye, and Forssman a.

human lymphocyte a.'s (HLA), the system designation for the gene products of at least four linked loci (A, B, C, and D) on the sixth human chromosome; these a.'s have been shown to have a strong influence on human allotransplantation, transfusions in refractory patients, and certain disease associations; more than 50 alleles are recognized, most of which are at loci HLA-A and HLA-B.

incomplete a., hapten.

mumps skin test a., a sterile suspension of killed mumps virus in isotonic sodium chloride solution, used to determine susceptibility to mumps or to confirm a tentative diagnosis.

O a., somatic a. of nonmotile bacteria.

oncofetal a., carcinoembryonic a.

organ-specific a., tissue-specific a.; a heterogenetic antigen with specificity for a particular organ, whether of a single species or of many species.

partial a., hapten.

sensitized a., the complex formed when a. combines with specific antibody; so called because the a., by the mediation of antibody, is rendered sensitive to the action of complement.

somatic a., an a. located in the body of a bacterium.

species-specific a., antigenic components in the tissues and fluids of members of a species of animal, by means of which various species may be immunologically distinguished.

T a.'s, tumor a.'s.

tissue-specific a., organ specific a.

tumor a.'s, T a.'s; neonantigens; a.'s present in tumors induced by certain types of adenoviruses (papovaviruses) or in cells transformed *in vitro* by those viruses.

tumor-specific transplantation a.'s (TSTA), surface a.'s of DNA tumor virus-transformed cells, which elicit an immune rejection of the virus-free cells when transplanted into an individual that has been immunized against the specific cell-transforming virus.

V a., viral a. that is intimately associated with the virus particle, is protein in nature, has multiple antigenicities, and is strain-specific.

antigenemia (an'tĭ-jĕ-ne'mĭ-ah) [antigen + G. *haima*, blood]. Persistence of antigen in circulating blood.

antigenicity (an'tĭ-jĕ-nis'ĭtĭ). Immunogenicity; the state or property of being antigenic.

antihe'lix. Anthelix.

an'tihemagglu'tinin. A substance (including antibody) that inhibits or prevents the effects of hemagglutinin.

an'tihemol'ysin. A substance (including antibody) that inhibits or prevents the effects of hemolysin.

an'tihemolyt'ic. Preventing hemolysis.

antihemorrhagic (an-tĭ-hem-or-raj'ik). Hemostatic; arresting hemorrhage.

antihidrotic (an'tĭ-hi-drot'ik). Anhidrotic.

antihis'tamines. Drugs having an action antagonistic to that of histamine.

an'tihistamin'ic. Tending to neutralize or antagonize the action of histamine or to inhibit its production in the body.

antihor'mones. Substances that inhibit or prevent the usual effects of certain hormones, and which, in certain instances, are specific antibodies.

an'tihyperten'sive. Indicating a drug or mode of treatment that reduces high blood pressure.

anti-inflam'matory. Reducing inflammation by acting on body mechanisms, without directly antagonizing the causative agent.

antilewisite (an-tĭ-lu'ĭ-sit). Dimercaprol.

antilith'ic [anti- + G. *lithos*, stone]. Anticalculous; preventing the formation of calculi or promoting their dissolution.

antily'sin. An antibody that inhibits or prevents the effects of lysin.

antimere (an'tĭ-mēr) [anti- + G. *meros,* a part]. **1.** A segment of an animal body formed by planes cutting the axis of the body at right angles. **2.** One of the symmetrical parts of a bilateral organism. **3.** The right or left half of the body.

an'timetab'olite. A substance that competes with, replaces, or antagonizes a particular metabolite.

antimicrobial (an'tĭ-mi-kro'bĭ-al). Tending to destroy microbes, to prevent their development, or to prevent their pathogenic action.

antimon'goloid. Denoting an obliquity of the palpebral fissures laterally downward, in contrast to the laterally upward slant seen in Mongolian races.

an'timony. Stibium; a metallic element, symbol Sb, atomic no. 51, atomic weight 121.77, valences $+3$, $+5$.

an'timycot'ic [anti- + G. *mykēs,* fungus]. Antagonistic to fungi.

antineoplastic (an'tĭ-o-plas'tik). Preventing the development, maturation, or spread of neoplastic cells.

antin'ion [anti- + G. *inion,* nape of the neck]. The space between the eyebrows; the point on the skull opposite the inion.

an'tiparasit'ic. Destructive to parasites.

an'tipedic'ulot'ik. Destructive to lice.

an'tiperistal'sis. Reversed *peristalsis.*

an'tiperistal'tic. 1. Relating to antiperistalsis. **2.** Impeding or arresting peristalsis.

antiplasmin (an-tĭ-plaz'min). Antifibrinolysin; a substance that inhibits or prevents the effects of plasmin; found in plasma and some tissues, especially the spleen and liver.

an'tiport [anti- + L. *porto,* to carry]. Coupled transport of two different molecules or ions through a membrane in opposite directions by a common carrier mechanism (antiporter).

an'tiprothrom'bin. An anticoagulant that inhibits or prevents the conversion of prothrombin into thrombin.

an'tiprurit'ic. Preventing or relieving itching.

antipsychotic (an'tĭ-si-kot'ik). **1.** An antipsychotic *agent.* **2.** Denoting the actions of such an agent.

an'tipyret'ic [anti- + G. *pyretos,* fever]. Antifebrile; antithermic; reducing fever.

antipyrot'ic [anti- + G. *pyrōtikos,* burning, inflaming]. Relieving the pain and promoting the healing of superficial burns.

an'tiscorbu'tic. Preventing or relieving scurvy.

an'tise'rum. Immune serum; serum that contains demonstrable antibody or antibodies specific for one (**monovalent a., specific a.**) or more (**polyvalent a.**).

antisecretory (an'tĭ-se-kre'to-rĭ). Inhibitory to secretion, as of certain drugs that reduce or suppress gastric secretion.

antisep'sis [anti- + G. *sēpsis,* putrefaction]. Prevention of infection by inhibiting the growth of infectious agents. See also *disinfection.*

antisep'tic. Relating to or capable of effecting antisepsis.

antisialagogue (an-tĭ-si-al'ă-gog) [anti- + G. *sialon,* saliva, + *agōgos,* drawing forth]. An agent that diminishes or arrests the flow of saliva.

antisialic (an-tĭ-si-al'ik). Reducing the flow of saliva.

antiso'cial. Behaving in violation of the social or legal norms of society.

an'tispasmod'ic. Preventing or relieving convulsions or spasms.

antistreptococcic (an'tĭ-strep-to-kok'sik). Destructive to streptococci or antagonistic to their toxins.

antisudorific (an'tĭ-su'dor-if'ik). Anhidrotic.

antithe'nar. Hypothenar (1).

antither'mic [anti- + G. *thermē,* heat]. Antipyretic (1).

antithrom'bin. Any substance that inhibits or prevents the effects of thrombin in such a manner that blood does not coagulate.

antitox'ic. Neutralizing the action of a poison; specifically, relating to an antitoxin.

antitoxin (an'tĭ-tok'sin) [anti- + G. *toxicon,* poison]. Antibody formed in response to antigenic poisonous substances of biologic origin, such as bacterial exotoxins, phytotoxins, and zootoxins. Generally, a. refers to whole, or globulin fraction, of serum from animals (usually horses) immunized by injections of the specific toxoid.

 botulism a., a. specific for a toxin of one or another strain of *Clostridium botulinum.*

 diphtheria a., a. specific for the toxin of *Corynebacterium diphtheriae.*

 gas gangrene a., a. specific for the toxin of one or more species of *Clostridium* that cause gaseous gangrene and associated toxemia.

 normal a., serum that is capable of neutralizing an equivalent quantity of normal toxin solution.

 scarlet fever a., a. specific for the erythrogenic toxin of strains of group A β-hemolytic streptococci.

 staphylococcus a., a preparation from native serum containing antitoxin globulins or their derivatives that specifically neutralize the properties of the α-toxin of *Staphylococcus aureus.*

 tetanus a., a. specific for the toxin of *Clostridium tetani.*

 tetanus and gas gangrene a.'s, a solution of antitoxic substances obtained from animals immunized against the toxins of *Clostridium tetani, C. perfringens,* and *C. septicum.*

antitra'gus [G. *anti,* opposite, + *tragos,* a goat, the tragus] [NA]. A projection of the auricle posterior to the tragus from which it is separated by the intertragic notch.

antitreponemal (an'tĭ-trep-o-ne'mal). Treponemicidal.

antitro'pic. Bilaterally symmetrical, but in an opposite location (as in a mirror image), *e.g.,* the right thumb in relation to the left thumb.

antityp'sic. Antitryptic.

α-1-antitryp'sin. A glycoprotein that is the major protease inhibitor of human serum; it is synthesized in the liver and is genetically polymorphic due to the presence of over 20 alleles.

antitryp'tic. Antitripsic; possessing properties of antitrypsin.

antitus'sive [anti- + L. *tussis*, cough]. Relieving a cough.

antiven'in. An antitoxin specific for an animal or insect venom.

antivi'ral. Opposing a virus, weakening or abolishing its action.

antivi'tamin. A substance that prevents a vitamin from exerting its typical biological effects; most a.'s have chemical structures similar to vitamins and appear to function as competitive antagonists.

antra (an'trah) Plural of antrum.

an'tral. Relating to an antrum.

antrec'tomy [antrum + G. *ektomē*, excision]. **1.** Removal of the walls of an antrum. **2.** Removal of the antrum (pyloric half) of the stomach.

antro- [L. *antrum*, from G. *antron*, a cave]. Combining form denoting relationship to any antrum.

an'troduodenec'tomy. Surgical removal of the antrum of the stomach and the ulcer-bearing part of the duodenum.

antrona'sal. Relating to a maxillary sinus and the corresponding nasal cavity.

an'troscope [antro- + G. *skopeō*, to view]. An instrument for examination of a cavity, specifically the maxillary sinus.

antros'copy. Examination by means of an antroscope.

antros'tomy [antro- + G. *stoma*, mouth]. Formation of an opening into an antrum.

antrot'omy [antro- + G. *tomē*, incision]. Incision through the wall of an antrum.

an'trotympan'ic. Relating to the mastoid antrum and the tympanic cavity.

an'trum, pl. **an'tra** [L. fr. G. *antron*, a cave] **1** [NA]. Any nearly closed cavity, particularly one with bony walls. **2.** The pyloric end of the stomach, partially shut off, during digestion, from the cardiac end (fundus) by the prepyloric sphincter.

  a. of Highmore, *sinus* maxillaris.

  a. mastoid'eum [NA], **mastoid a.**, tympanic a.; a cavity in the petrous portion of the temporal bone, communicating posteriorly with the mastoid cells and anteriorly with the epitympanic recess of the middle ear.

  maxillary a., *sinus* maxillaris.

  a. pylor'icum [NA], **pyloric a.**, a bulging of the pyloric end of the stomach wall along the greater curvature when the organ is distended. See antrum (2).

  tympanic a., a. mastoideum.

an'ulus, pl. **an'uli** [L.] [NA]. A circular or ring-shaped structure. See also ring.

  a. conjuncti'vae [NA], conjunctival ring; a narrow ring at the junction of the periphery of the cornea with the conjunctiva.

  a. inguina'lis profun'dus [NA], deep inguinal ring; the opening in the transversalis fascia through which the ductus deferens (or round ligament in the female) enters the inguinal canal.

  a. inguina'lis superficia'lis [NA], superficial inguinal ring; the slit-like opening in the aponeurosis of the external oblique muscle of the abdominal wall through which the spermatic cord (round ligament in the female) emerges from the inguinal canal.

  a. tympan'icus [NA], ring; tympanic bone; in the fetus, a bony ring at the medial end of the cartilaginous external acoustic meatus, to which is attached the tympanic membrane.

  a. umbilica'lis [NA], umbilical ring; an opening in the linea alba through which pass the umbilical vessels in the fetus; in adult, its site is indicated by the navel.

anuresis (an-u-re'sis) [G. *an-* priv. + *ourēsis*, urination]. Inability to pass urine.

anuret'ic. Relating to anuresis.

anu'ria. Absence of urine formation.

anu'ric. Relating to anuria.

a'nus, pl. **a'nus** [L.] [NA]. The lower opening of the digestive tract through which fecal matter is expelled.

  imperforate a., anal *atresia*.

an'vil. Incus.

anxiety (ang'zi'ē-tĭ) [L. *anxietas*]. In psychoanalysis, apprehension of danger and dread accompanied by restlessness, tension, tachycardia, and dyspnea unattached to a clearly identifiable stimulus.

  separation a., in psychiatry, a child's apprehension or fear associated with his removal from or loss of a parent or significant person.

aorta, pl. **aortae** (a-or'tah, a-or'te) [Mod. L. fr. G. *aortē*, from *aeirō*, to lift up] [NA]. A large artery that is the main trunk of the systemic arterial system, arising from the base of the left ventricle and ending at the left side of the body of the fourth lumbar vertebra by dividing to form the right and left common iliac arteries. Its parts are: 1) ascending a., 2) aortic arch; and 3) descending a., which is divided into the thoracic a. and abdominal a.

aor'tal. Aortic.

aortal'gia [aorta + G. *algos*, pain]. Pain assumed to be due to aneurysm or other pathologic conditions of the aorta.

aor'tic. Aortal; relating to the aorta or the a. orifice of the left ventricle of the heart.

aorti'tis. Inflammation of the aorta.

aor'tocor'onary. Relating to the aorta and the coronary arteries.

aor'togram. X-ray image of aorta after the injection of contrast medium.

aortography (a-or-tog'rǎ-fĭ) [aorta + G. *graphō*, to write]. Radiographic visualization of the aorta and its branches by injection of contrast media.

aortopathy (a-or-top'ǎ-thĭ) [aorta + G. *pathos*, suffering]. Disease affecting the aorta.

aortorrhaphy (a-or-tor'ă-fĭ) [aorta + G. *rhaphē*, seam]. Suture of the aorta.

aortosclerosis (a-or'to-skle-ro'sis). Arteriosclerosis of the aorta.

aortotomy (a-or-tot'o-mĭ) [aorta + G. *tomē*, a cutting]. Incision of the aorta.

apallesthesia (ă-pal-es-the'zĭ-ah) [G. *a*-priv. + *pallo*, to tremble, quiver, + *aisthēsis*, feeling]. Pallanesthesia.

aparalytic (a-păr'ă-lit'ik). Not paralyzed; without paralysis.

ap'athet'ic. Exhibiting apathy; indifferent.

ap'athism. A sluggishness of reaction, the opposite of erethism.

ap'athy [G. *apatheia*, fr. *a*-priv. + *pathos*, suffering]. Absence of emotion; indifference; insensibility.

APC Aspirin, phenacetin, and caffeine; used as an analgesic and antipyretic.

apel'lous [G. *a*-priv. + L. *pellis*, skin]. **1.** Without skin. **2.** Without foreskin; circumcised.

aperiodic (a-pe'rĭ-od'ik). Not occurring periodically.

aperistal'sis. Absence of peristalsis.

apertognathia (ă-per-to-nath'ĭ-ah) [L. *apertus*, open, + G. *gnathos*, jaw]. Open bite (2); a type of malocclusion characterized by premature posterior occlusion and absence of anterior occlusion.

aperture (ap'er-tür) [L. *apertura*, an opening]. **1.** An opening; orifice. **2.** The diameter of the objective of a microscope.

a'pex, pl. **ap'ices** [L. summit or tip] [NA]. The extremity of a conical or pyramidal structure.

Apgar score. Evaluation of a newborn infant's physical status by assigning numerical values (0 to 2) to each of five criteria: heart rate, respiratory effort, muscle tone, response to stimulation, and skin color.

aphagia (ă-fa'jĭ-ah) [G. *a*-priv. + *phagein*, to eat]. Dysphagia.

aphakia (ă-fa'kĭ-ah) [G. *a*- priv. + *phakos*, lentil, anything shaped like a lentil]. Absence of the lens of the eye.

apha'kial, apha'kic. Denoting aphakia.

aphalangia (a-fă-lan'jĭ-ah) [G. *a*- priv. + *phalanx*, *q.v.*]. Absence of a digit; specifically of one or more of the phalanges of a finger or toe.

aphasia (ă-fa'zĭah) [G. speechlessness, fr. *a*- priv. + *phasis*, speech]. Alogia (1); logagnosia; logamnesia; logasthenia; impaired or absent communication by speech, writing, or signs, due to dysfunction of brain centers in the dominant hemisphere.

   acoustic a., auditory a.

   amnestic a., amnesic a., inability to find or remember words.

   anomic a., nominal a.

   associative a., conduction a.

   ataxic a., motor a.

   auditory a., acoustic a.; impairment in comprehension of the auditory forms of language and communication in the presence of normal hearing.

   Broca's a., motor a.

   conduction a., associative a.; a. in which the subject can speak and write in a way, but skips or repeats words or substitutes one word for another, the lesion being in the association tracts connecting the various language centers.

   expressive a., motor a.

   global a., total a.; loss of all forms of communication.

   impressive a., sensory a.

   jargon a., a. in which the patient talks in nonsense syllables or in which several words are run together as one.

   mixed a., a mixture of motor and sensory a.

   motor a., ataxic, expressive, or Broca's a.; a. in which the power of expression by writing, speaking, or signs is lost.

   nominal a., anomic a.; anomia; a. in which the patient has difficulty in recalling or is unable to recall the names of persons and things.

   receptive a., sensory a.

   sensory a., impressive or receptive a.; loss of the ability to comprehend written (or printed) or spoken words.

   total a., global a.

   visual a., (1) alexia; (2) improperly used as a synonym for anomia.

apha'siac, apha'sic. Relating to or suffering from aphasia.

aphonia (ă-fo'nĭ-ah) [G. *a*- priv. + *phōnē*, voice]. Loss of the voice in consequence of disease or injury of the organ of speech.

aphon'ic. Relating to or suffering from aphonia.

aphrasia (ă-fra'zĭ-ah) [G. *a*- priv. + *phrasis*, speaking]. Inability to speak, from any cause.

aphrodis'iac. 1. Increasing sexual desire. **2.** Anything that arouses or increases sexual desire.

aphtha, pl. **aphthae** (af'thah, af'the) [G. ulceration]. **1.** In the singular, a minute ulcer on a mucous membrane, often covered by a gray or white exudate. **2.** In the plural, small white spots associated with small ulcerations on the mucous membrane of the mouth.

   Bednar's aphthae, a traumatic affection of the newborn consisting of two yellow, flattened, slightly elevated patches, often ulcerated, one on either side of the median raphe of the palate.

aphthoid (af'thoyd). Resembling aphthae.

aphthosis (af-tho'sis). Any condition characterized by the presence of aphthae.

aphthous (af'thus). Characterized by or relating to aphthae or aphthosis.

aphylaxis (a-fi-lak'sis) [G. *a*- priv. + *phylaxis*, guarding]. Nonimmunity; lack of protection against disease.

apical (ap'ĭ-kal). **1.** Relating to the apex of a pyramidal or pointed structure. **2.** Situated nearer to the apex of a structure in relation to a specific reference point.

apicectomy (ap'ĭ-sek'to-mĭ) [L. *apex*, summit or tip, + G. *ektomē*, excision]. Opening and exenteration of air cells in the apex of the petrous part of the temporal bone.

ap'ices. Plural of apex.

apicitis (ap'ĭ-si'tis). Inflammation of the apex of a structure or organ.

apico- [L. *apex,* summit or tip]. Combining form relating to any apex.

apicoectomy (ap'ĭ-ko-ek'to-mĭ) [apico- + G. *ektomē,* excision]. Root resection; surgical removal of a dental root apex.

apicolysis (ap-ĭ-kol'ĭ-sis) [apico- + G. *lysis,* destruction]. Surgical collapse of the upper portion of the lung to allow medial displacement of the apex.

apicotomy (ap-ĭ-kot'o-mĭ) [apico- + G. *tomē,* a cutting]. Incision into an apical structure.

aplacen'tal. Without a placenta; denoting the monotremes (which lay eggs and have no placenta) and the marsupials (which have a transitory simple yolk-sac placenta).

aplanatic (ă-plă-nat'ik) [G. *a-* priv. + *planētos,* wandering]. Free from chromatic or spherical aberration.

aplasia (ă-pla'zĭ-ah) [G. *a-* priv. + *plasis,* a molding]. **1.** Defective development or congenital absence of an organ or tissue. **2.** In hematology, incomplete, retarded, or defective development, or a cessation of the usual regenerative process.

    a. axia'lis extracortica'lis, Merzbacher-Pelizaeus *disease.*

    a. cu'tis congen'ita, congenital absence or deficiency of a localized area of skin, with the base of the defect covered by a thin translucent membrane, most often a single area near the vertex of the scalp.

aplas'tic. Pertaining to aplasia, or conditions characterized by defective regeneration, as in a. anemia.

apnea (ap'ne-ah) [G. *apnoia,* want of breath]. Absence of breathing.

    sleep-induced a. a. resulting from failure of the respiratory center to stimulate adequate respiration during sleep.

apneic (ap'ne-ik). Related to or suffering from apnea.

apneumia (ap-nu'mĭ-ah) [G. *a-* priv. + *pneumō,* lung]. Congenital absence of the lungs.

apo- [G. *apo,* away from, off]. Combining form meaning, usually, separated or derived from.

apocrine (ap'o-krin) [G. *apo-krinō,* to separate]. See apocrine *gland.*

apodal, apodous (a-po'dal, ap'o-dus) [G. *a-* priv. + *pous,* foot]. Denoting apodia.

apodia, apody (a-po'dĭ-ah, ap'o-dĭ) [G. *a-* priv. + *pous,* foot]. Congenital absence of feet.

apoenzyme (ap'o-en-zīm). The protein portion of an enzyme as contrasted with the nonprotein portion (coenzyme) or prosthetic portion.

apofer'ritin. A protein in the intestinal wall that combines with a ferric hydroxide-phosphate compound to form ferritin, the first stage in the absorption of iron.

apolipoprotein (ap'o-lip-o-pro'tēn). The protein component of lipoprotein complexes.

aponeurectomy (ap'nu-rek'to-mĭ). Excision of an aponeurosis.

aponeurorrhaphy (ap'o-nu-ror'ă-fĭ) [aponeurosis + G. *rhaphē,* suture]. Fasciorrhaphy.

aponeurosis, pl. **aponeuroses** (ap'o-nu-ro'sis, -sēz) G. the end of the muscle where it becomes tendon, fr. *apo,* from, + *neuron,* sinew] [NA]. A fibrous sheet or expanded tendon, giving attachment to muscular fibers and serving as the means of origin or insertion of a flat muscle.

ap'oneurosi'tis. Inflammation of an aponeurosis.

ap'oneurot'ic. Relating to an aponeurosis.

aponeurotomy (ap'o-nu-rot'o-mĭ). Incision of an aponeurosis.

apophysial, apophyseal (ă-po-fiz'e-al). Relating to or resembling an apophysis.

apophysis, pl. **apophyses** (ăpof'ĭ-sis, -sēz) [G. an offshoot]. An outgrowth or projection, especially one from a bone; bony process or outgrowth that lacks an independent center of ossification.

apophysitis (ă-pof-ĭ-si'tis). Inflammation of any apophysis.

apoplec'tic. Relating to, suffering from, or predisposed to apoplexy.

apoplexy (ap'o-plek-sĭ) [G. *apoplēxia*]. **1.** Classical but obsolete term for stroke. **2.** An effusion of blood into a tissue or organ.

ap'orepres'sor. Inactive *repressor.*

apostax'is [G. a trickling down]. A slight hemorrhage, or bleeding by drops.

apos'thia [G. *a-* priv. + *posthē,* foreskin]. Congenital absence of the prepuce.

apparatus, pl. **apparatus** (ap-ă-ra'tus, -rat'us) [L. equipment, fr. *ap-paro,* pp. *-atus,* to prepare]. **1.** A collection of instruments adapted for a special purpose or an instrument made up of several parts. **2.** [NA]. A system; the group of glands, ducts, blood vessels, muscles, or other anatomical structures concerned in the performance of some function.

appendage (ă-pen'dij) [L. *appendix, q.v.*]. Any part, subordinate in function or size, attached to a main structure.

appendectomy (ap'pen-dek'to-mĭ) [appendix + G. *ektomē,* excision]. Appendicectomy; surgical removal of the vermiform appendix.

appen'dical. Appendiceal.

appendiceal (ap-pen-dis'ĭ-al). Appendical; relating to an appendix.

appendicectomy (ap-pen'dĭ-sek'to-mĭ). Appendectomy.

appendicitis (ă-pen-dĭsi'tis) [appendix + G. *-itis,* inflammation]. Inflammation of the vermiform appendix.

appendico- [L. *appendix,* appendage]. Combining form relating, usually, to the vermiform appendix.

appen'dicolithi'asis [appendico- + G. *lithos,* stone]. The presence of concretious in the vermiform appendix.

appendicolysis (ă-pen-dĭ-kol'ĭ-sis) [appendico- + G. *lysis*, a loosening]. Surgical freeing of the appendix from adhesions.

appendicos'tomy [appendico- + G. *stoma*, mouth]. Surgical opening into the intestine through the tip of the appendix vermiformis, previously attached to the anterior abdominal wall.

appendicular (ap-pen-dik'u-lar). 1. Relating to an appendix or appendage. 2. Relating to the limbs.

appen'dix, pl. **appen'dices** [L. appendage, fr. *appendo* (*adp-*), to hang something on]. 1 [NA]. An appendage. 2. Specifically, the appendix vermiformis.

  a. epiplo'ica, pl. **appen'dices epiplo'icae** [NA], one of a number of little processes or sacs of peritoneum, generally distended with fat, projecting from the serous coat of the large intestine, except the rectum.

  a. vermifor'mis [NA], a wormlike intestinal diverticulum extending from the blind end of the cecum and ending in a blind extremity.

appercep'tion [L. *ad*, to, + *per-cipio*, pp. *-ceptus*, to take wholly, perceive]. 1. Comprehension; conscious perception; the full apprehension of any psychic content. 2. The process of referring the perception of ideas to one's own personality.

appercep'tive. Relating to, involved in, or capable of apperception.

appetite (ap'ĕ-tīt) [L. *ad-peto*, pp. *-petitus*, to seek after, desire]. A desire or longing to satisfy any conscious physical or mental need.

applanation (ap'lan-a'shun) [L. *ad*, toward, + *planum*, plane]. In tonometry, the flattening of the cornea by pressure. See also applanation *tonometer.*

applanom'etry. Use of an applanation tonometer.

appliance (ăpli'ans). A device used to provide function to a part, or for therapeutic purposes. See also prosthesis.

ap'plicator [L. *ap-plico*, to attach to]. A slender rod at one end of which is attached a pledget of cotton or other substance for making local application to any accessible surface.

appliqué or **accolé form.** Terms applied to the manner in which the ring stage of *Plasmodium falciparum* parasitizes the marginal portion of erythrocytes.

apposition (ap'o-zish'un) [L. *ap-pono*, pp. *-positus*, to place at or to]. 1. The putting in contact of two substances. 2. The condition of being placed or fitted together. 3. The relationship of fracture fragments to one another.

approx'imate [L. *ad*, to, + *proximus*, nearest]. To bring close together. In dentistry: 1. Proximate, denoting the contact surfaces, either mesial (proximal) or distal, of two adjacent teeth. 2. Close together; denoting the teeth in the human jaw.

approxima'tion. In surgery, bringing tissue edges into desired apposition for suturing.

aprac'tic. Apraxic.

aprag'matism [G. *a-* priv. + pragmatism, *q.v.*]. An interest in theory or dogmatism rather than practical results.

apraxia (ă-prak'sĭ-ah) [G. *a-* priv. + *pratto*, to do]. 1. A disorder of voluntary movement, consisting in partial or complete incapacity to execute purposeful movements, without impairment of muscular power, sensibility, and coordination. 2. A psychomotor defect in which one is unable to properly use a known object.

aprax'ic. Apractic; marked by or pertaining to apraxia.

aproctia (ă-prok'shĭ-ah) [G. *a-* priv. + *prōktos*, anus]. Absence or imperforation of the anus.

aprosopia (ap'ro-so'pĭah) [G. *a-* priv. + *prosōpon*, face]. Congenital absence of the greater part or all of the face, usually associated with other malformations.

aptyalia (ap-ti-a'le-ah). Asialism.

aptyalism (ap-ti'al-ism) [G. *a-* priv. + *ptyalon*, saliva]. Asialism.

APUD [*a*mine *p*recursor *u*ptake, *d*ecarboxylase]. Proposed designation for a group of cells in different organs secreting polypeptide hormones. Cells in this group have certain biochemical characteristics in common: they contain amines, take up precursors of these amines *in vivo*, and contain amino-acid decarboxylase.

apyret'ic. Afebrile; nonfebrile; without fever.

apyrexia (a-pi-rek'sĭ-ah) [G. *a-* priv. + *pryexis*, fever]. Absence of fever.

aquaphobia (ak'wah-fo'bĭ-ah) [L. *aqua*, water, + G. *phobos*, fear]. Morbid fear of water.

aqueduct (ak'we-dukt). Aqueductus.

aqueduc'tus, pl. **aqueduc'tus** [L. fr. *aqua*, water, + *ductus*, a leading] [NA]. Aqueduct; a conduit or canal.

  a. cer'ebri [NA], cerebral aqueduct; sylvian aqueduct; a canal about 3/4 inch long, lined with ependymal cells, leading downward through the mesencephalon from the third to the fourth ventricle.

  a. coch'leae [NA], official alternate term for *ductus* perilymphaticus.

aqueous (ak'we-us, a'kwe-us). Watery; of, like, or containing water.

Ar Argon.

arachnephobia (ă-rak-ne-fo'bĭah) [G. *arachne*, spider, + *phobos*, fear]. Arachnophobia; morbid fear of spiders.

Arachnida (ă-rak'nĭ-dah) [G. *arachne*, spider]. A class of arthropods consisting of spiders, scorpions, harvestmen, mites, ticks, and allies.

arachnidism (ă-rak'nĭ-dizm). Systemic poisoning following the bite of a spider.

arachnitis (ar-ak-ni'tis). Arachnoiditis.

arachnodactyly (ă-rak-no-dak'tĭ-lĭ) [G. *arachnē*, spider, + *daktylos*, finger]. Abnormally long and slender hands and fingers, and often feet and toes; a characteristic of Marfan's syndrome and Achard syndrome.

arachnoid (ar-ak'noyd) [G. *arachnē*, spider, cobweb, + *eidos*, resemblance]. Resembling a cobweb; denoting specifically the arachnoidea covering the brain and spinal cord.

arachnoidea, arachnoi'des (ar-ak-noyd'iäh) [Mod. L. *arachnoideus, -ea*, fr. G. *arachnē*, spider, + *eidos*, resemblance] [NA]. Arachnoid membrane; a delicate fibrous membrane forming the middle of the three coverings of the brain (**a. enceph'ali**) and spinal cord (**a. spina'lis**); it is closely applied to the outer membrane, the dura mater, from which it is separated only by the subdural cleft, but between it and the inner layer, the pia mater, lies the subarachnoid space.

arachnoiditis (ä-rak'noy-di'tis). Arachnitis; inflammation of the arachnoid membrane and subarachnoid space.

arachnopho'bia [G. *arachne*, spider + *phobos*, fear]. Arachnephobia.

arborescent (ar-bo-res'ent). Dendriform.

arboriza'tion [L. *arbor*, tree]. Ramification, denoting especially: (**1**) the terminal branching of nerve fibers or blood vessels; (**2**) the leaflike pattern formed under certain conditions by a dried smear of cervical mucus.

ar'borize. Ramify.

ar'bovi'rus, ar'borvi'rus [*ar*thropod *bo*rne virus]. A large, heterogenous group of RNA viruses divisible into groups on the basis of characteristics of the virions; most are associated with arthropods which may serve as vectors. Although about 75 species can infect man, only about 45 species produce disease; apparent infections may be separated into three clinical syndromes: undifferentiated type fevers (systemic febrile disease), hemorrhagic fevers, and encephalitides.

arc [L. *arcus*, a bow]. A curved line or segment of a circle.

  reflex a., the route followed by nerve impulses in the production of a reflex act, from the periphery through the afferent nerve to the nervous system and thence through the efferent nerve to the effector organ.

arch-, arche-, archi-, archo- [G. *archē*, origin, beginning]. Combining forms meaning primitive, or ancestral; also first, or chief.

arch [thru O. Fr. fr. L. *arcus*, bow]. In anatomy, any vaulted or archlike structure. See arcus.

  abdominothoracic a., the line of the false ribs on either side with the lower end of the sternum, marking roughly the boundry line between the abdomen and thorax.

  aortic a., a. of aorta, *arcus* aortae.

  aortic a.'s, a series of arterial channels encircling the embryonic pharynx in the mesenchyme of the branchial a.'s. There are potentially 6 pairs: in mammals, pair 5 is poorly developed or absent, pairs 1 and 2 are functional only in very young embryos; pair 3 is involved in the formation of the carotids;

a. 4 on the left is incorporated in the a. of the aorta; the 6th a.'s form the proximal part of the pulmonary arteries.

  branchial a.'s, visceral or pharyngeal a.'s; typically, six a.'s that transiently appear in the higher vertebrates and give rise to specialized structures in the head and neck; in the lower vertebrates they bear gills.

  Corti's a., the a. formed by the junction of the heads of the inner and outer pillar cells in the organ of Corti.

  costal a., *arcus* costalis.

  dental a., the curved composite structure of the natural dentition and the risidual ridge, or the remains thereof after the loss of some or all of the natural teeth. See arcus dentalis inferior and superior.

  fallen a.'s, a breaking down of the a.'s of the foot, either longitudinal or transverse or both; the resulting deformity is flat foot or spread foot or both.

  a.'s of foot, *arcus* pedis; *arcus* plantaris.

  hemal a.'s, three or four V-shaped bones located ventral to the bodies of the third to sixth coccygeal vertebrae; usually enclose the ventral caudal artery and vein.

  hyoid a., the second branchial a.

  mandibular a., mandibular process; the first postoral a. in the branchial a. series.

  neural a., *arcus* vertebrae.

  a. of palate, the vaulted roof of the mouth.

  palatoglossal a., *arcus* palatoglossus.

  palatopharyngeal a., *arcus* palatopharyngeus.

  palmar a., *arcus* palmaris.

  pharyngeal a.'s, branchial a.'s.

  plantar a., *arcus* plantaris.

  postoral a., the series of branchial a.'s caudal to the mouth; the first is the mandibular, the second is the hyoid; caudal to the hyoid the a.'s are unnamed, and designated only by their postoral number.

  primitive costal a.'s, a.'s formed in the thoracic region of the vertebral column in the embryo from the costal processes or costal elements which give rise to the ribs.

  pubic a., *arcus* pubis.

  superciliary a., *arcus* superciliaris.

  supraorbital a., *margo* supraorbitalis.

  tendinous a., *arcus* tendineus.

  vertebral a., *arcus* vertebrae.

  visceral a.'s, branchial a.'s.

  zygomatic a., *arcus* zygomaticus.

archenteron (ark-en'ter-on) [G. *archē*, beginning, + *enteron*, intestine]. Gastrocele (1).

archeokinetic (ar-ke-o-kin-et'ik) [G. *archaios*, ancient, + *kinētikos*, relating to movement]. Denoting a primitive type of motor nerve mechanism such as is found in the peripheral and the ganglionic nervous systems.

archetype (ar'ke-tīp) [G. *archetypos*, first molded, fr. *arche*, first, + *typiō*, to beat, stamp]. A primitive structural plan from which various modifications have evolved.

ar'ciform. Arcuate.

arcta'tion [L. *arto* (improp. *arcto*), pp. *-atus*, to tighten]. A narrowing, contraction, stricture, or coarctation.

arcuate (ar'ku-āt) [L. *arcuatus*, bowed]. Arciform; arched; having the shape of a bow.

arcuation (ar-ku-a'shun). A bending or curvature.

arcus, pl. **arcus** (ar'kus) [L. a bow] [NA]. Any structure resembling a bent bow or an arch.

a. adipo'sus, a. cornealis.

a. aor'tae [NA], aortic arch; arch of the aorta; the curve between the ascending and descending portions of the aorta; it lies behind the manubrium sterni and gives off the brachiocephalic trunk, the left common carotid, and the left subclavian arteries.

a. cornea'lis, an opaque, grayish ring at the periphery of the cornea just within the sclerocorneal junction, of frequent occurrence in the aged; it results from a deposit of fatty granules in, or hyaline degeneration of, the lamellae and cells of the cornea. Also called a. adiposis, juvenilis, or senilis; anterior embryotoxon; gerontoxon.

a. costa'lis [NA], costal arch; that portion of the inferior aperture of the thorax formed by the cartilages of the seventh to tenth ribs.

a. denta'lis infe'rior [NA], inferior dental arch; mandibular dentition; the teeth supported by the alveolar part of the mandible.

a. denta'lis supe'rior [NA], superior dental arch; maxillary dentition; the teeth supported by the alveolar process of the two maxillae.

a. juveni'lis, a. cornealis.

a. palatoglos'sus palatoglossal arch; one of a pair of ridges or folds of mucous membrane passing from the soft palate to the side of the tongue and enclosing the palatoglossus muscle.

a. palatophryn'geus [NA], palatopharyngeal arch; one of a pair of ridges or folds of mucous membrane passing downward from the posterior margin of the soft palate to the lateral wall of the pharynx and enclosing the palatopharyngeus muscle.

a. palma'ris [NA], palmar arch; (1) deep, the arterial arch located deep to the long flexor tendons in the hand, formed by the radial artery in conjunction with the deep palmar branch of the ulnar artery; (2) superficial, the arterial arch in the hand located superficial to the long flexor tendons, formed principally by the ulnar artery and usually completed by a communication with the superficial palmar branch of the radial artery.

a. pe'dis [NA], arch of foot; (1) longitudinal, consisting of a medial longitudinal arch, including the calcaneus, talus, navicular, three cuneiform bones, and the three medial metatarsals, and a lateral longitudinal arch formed by calcaneus, cuboid and two lateral metatarsals; (2) transverse, formed by the proximal parts of the metatarsal bones, the three cuneiform bones, and the cuboid.

a. planta'ris [NA], plantar arch (1); the arterial arch formed by the lateral plantar artery running across the bases of the metatarsal bones and anastomosing with the dorsal artery of the foot.

a. pu'bis [NA], pubic arch; the arch formed by the inferior rami of the pubic bones.

a. seni'lis, a. cornealis.

a. supercilia'ris [NA], superciliary arch; a fullness extending laterally from the glabella on either side, above the orbital margin of the frontal bone.

a. tendin'eus [NA], tendinous arch; a fibrous band arching over a vessel or nerve as it passes through a muscle, and protecting it from injurious compression.

a. tendin'eus fas'ciae pel'vis [NA], tendinous arch of the pelvic fascia; a linear thickening of the superior fascia of the pelvic diaphragm extending posteriorly from the body of the pubis alongside the bladder (and vagina in the female) and giving attachment to the supporting ligaments of the pelvic viscera.

a. ver'tebrae [NA], vertebral arch; neural arch; the posterior projection from the body of a vertebra that encloses the vertebral foramen.

a. zygomat'icus [NA], zygomatic arch; zygoma (2); the arch formed by the temporal process of the zygomatic bone that joins the zygomatic process of the temporal bone.

ARDS Adult respiratory distress *syndrome*.

area, pl. **areae** (ăr'e-ah, -e) [L. a courtyard] **1** [NA]. Any circumscribed surface or space. **2.** All of the part supplied by a given artery or nerve. **3.** A part of an organ having a special function.

association a.'s, association *cortex*.

auditory a., auditory *cortex*.

Broca's a., Broca's *center*.

Brodmann's a.'s, a.'s of the cerebral cortex mapped out on the basis of the cortical cytoarchitectural patterns.

a. of cardiac dullness, a triangular a. determined by percussion of the front of the chest; corresponds to the part of the heart not covered by lung tissue.

embryonal a., embryonic a., the a. of the blastoderm on either side of, and immediately cephalic to the primitive streak where the component cell layers have become thickened.

excitable a., motor *cortex*.

frontal a., frontal *cortex*.

germinal a., a. germinati'va, the place in the blastoderm where the embryo begins to be formed.

Kiesselbach's a., an a. on the anterior portion of the nasal septum rich in capillaries and often the seat of nosebleed.

macular a., the portion of the retina used for central vision; the center area of the fovea centralis retinae appears free of vessels and is much reduced in thickness.

motor a., motor *cortex*.

postcentral a., the cortex of the postcentral gyrus.

precentral a., the cortex of the precentral gyrus.

prefrontal a., see frontal *cortex.*

premotor a., premotor *cortex.*

Rolando's a., motor *cortex.*

sensorimotor a., the precentral and postcentral gyri of the cerebral cortex.

silent a., any a. of the cerebral or cerebellar surface, lesion of which occasions no definite sensory or motor symptoms.

a. subcallo'sa [NA], **subcallosal a.,** *gyrus* subcallosus.

trigger a., any point or circumscribed a., irritation of which will give rise to functional action or disturbance elsewhere.

visual a., visual *cortex.*

Wernicke's a., Wernicke's *center.*

areflexia (a-re-flek'sĭ-ah). Absence of reflexes.

Arenaviridae (ă-re'nă-vir'ĭ-de) [L. *arēna* (*harēna*), sand]. A family of RNA viruses that includes *Arenavirus,* lymphocytic choriomeningitis virus, Lassa virus, and the Tacaribe virus complex.

Arenavirus (ă-re'nă-vi'rus). The single genus of viruses in the family Arenaviridae.

areola, pl. **areolae** (ă-re'o-lah, ă-re'o-le) [L. dim of *area*]. **1** [NA]. Any small area. **2.** One of the spaces or interstices in areolar tissue. **3.** A. **mammae. 4.** A pigmented, depigmented, or erythematous zone surrounding a papule, pustule, wheal, or cutaneous neoplasm.

a. mam'mae [NA], **a. papillaris,** areola (3); a circular pigmented area surrounding the nipple which is dotted with little projections due to the presence of glands beneath.

Chaussier's a., a ring of indurated tissue surrounding the lesion of cutaneous anthrax.

are'olar. Relating to an areola.

Arg Arginine or its mono- or diradical.

Ar'gas. A genus of soft ticks (family Argasidae), some species of which usually infest birds but may attack man.

argas'id. Common name for members of the family Argasidae.

Argasidae (ar-gas'ĭ-de). Family of ticks (superfamily Ixodoidea, order Acarina), the soft ticks, so called because of their wrinkled, leathery, tuberculated appearance that fills out when the tick is engorged with blood. A. contains about 85 species in 4 genera: *Argas, Ornithodoros, Otobius,* and *Antricola.*

argentaffin (ar-jen'tă-fin) [L. *argentum,* silver, + *affinitas,* affinity]. Pertaining to cells or tissue elements that reduce silver ions in solution, thereby becoming stained brown or black.

ar'gentaffino'ma. Carcinoid *tumor.*

argentophil, argentophile (ar-jen'to-fil, -fil). Argyrophil.

ar'ginase. An enzyme of the liver that catalyzes the hydrolysis of arginine to ornithine and urea; a key enzyme of the urea cycle.

ar'ginine (Arg). 2-Amino-5-guanidinovaleric acid; one of the amino acids occurring among the hydrolysis products of protein.

argininosuccinic acid (ar-jĭ-nin'o-suk-sin'ik). $HOOC-CH_2CH(COOH)-NH-C(NH)-NH(CH_2)_3$ $CHNH_2-COOH$; formed as an intermediate in the conversion of citrulline to arginine in the urea cycle, in a reaction involving aspartic acid and adenosine triphosphate.

argininosuccinicaciduria (ar-jĭ-nin'o-suk-sin'ik-as-ĭ-du'rĭah). A possibly heritable disorder characterized by excessive urinary excretion of argininosuccinic acid, epilepsy, ataxia, mental retardation, liver disease, and friable, tufted hair.

ar'gon [G. ntr. of *argos,* lazy]. A gaseous element, symbol Ar, atomic no. 18, atomic weight 39.95, present in the atmosphere; one of the inert or noble gases.

argyria (ar-jir'ĭ-ah, ar-ji'rĭ-ah) [G. *argyros,* silver]. Argyrism; silver poisoning; a slate-gray or bluish discoloration of the skin and deep tissues due to the deposit of insoluble albuminate of silver.

argyr'ic. Relating to argyria.

argyrism (ar'jir-izm). Argyria.

argyrophil, argyrophile (ar-ji'ro-fil, -fil) [G. *argyros,* silver, + *philos,* fond]. Argentophil, argentophile; pertaining to tissue elements capable of impregnation with silver and of being made visible after a reducing agent is used.

arhinia (ă-rin'ĭ-ah). Arrhinia.

ariboflavinosis (a-ri'bo-fla-vĭ-no'sis). Properly hyporiboflavinosis; a condition produced by a deficiency of riboflavin in the diet, marked by chilosis or angular stomatitis and magenta tongue.

arm [L. *armus,* fore-quarter of an animal; G. *harmos,* a shoulder joint]. The segment of the superior limb between the shoulder and the elbow; commonly used to mean the whole superior limb.

armamenta'rium [L. an arsenal, fr. *armamenta,* implements]. The therapeutic means (drugs, instruments, etc.) available to the health practitioner for the practice of his profession.

Armil'lifer [O. Fr. *armille,* fr. L. *armilla,* a bracelet]. A genus of Pentastomida (order Porocephalida, family Porocephalidae); adults are found in the lungs of reptiles and the larvae or nymphs in many mammals, including man.

aromatic (ar-o-mat'ik) [G. *arōmatikos,* fr. *arōma,* spice, sweet herb]. **1.** Having an agreeable, somewhat pungent, spicy odor. **2.** One of a group of vegetable drugs having a fragrant odor and slightly stimulant properties.

arrec'tor, pl. **arrecto'res** [L. that which raises]. Erector.

arrest [O.Fr. *arester,* fr. LL. *adresto,* to stop behind]. **1.** To stop; check; restrain. **2.** A stoppage; an interference with or a checking of the regular course of a disease or symptom, or the performance of a function. **3.** Inhibition of a developmental process, usually the ultimate stage of development.

cardiac a., a loss of effective cardiac function, which results in cessation of circulation.

epiphysial a., early and premature fusion between epiphysis and diaphysis.

maturation a., cessation of complete differentiation of cells at an immature stage.

sinus a., cessation of cardiac sinus activity; the ventricles may continue to beat under A-V nodal or idioventricular control.

arrhenoblastoma (ă-re'no-blas-to'mah) [G. *arrhēn*, male, + *blastos*, germ, + *-ōma*, tumor]. Androblastoma (2); gynandroblastoma (1); a rare ovarian tumor that produces masculinization and often contains tubules and luteinized cells.

arrhinia (ă-rin'ĭ-ah) [G. *a*-priv. + *rhis* (*rhin*-), nose]. Arhinia; absence of the nose.

arrhythmia (ă-rith'mĭ-ah) [G. *a*- priv. + *rhythmos*, rhythm]. Loss of rhythm; denoting especially an irregularity of the heart beat.

cardiac a., see cardiac *dysrhythmia.*

sinus a., irregularity of the heart beat, the beat being under the control of its normal pacemaker, the sinus (S-A) node.

arrhyth'mic. Marked by loss of rhythm; pertaining to arrhythmia.

arrhythmogenic (ă-rith-mo-jen'ik) [G. *a*- priv. + *rhythmos*, rhythm, + *-gen*, production]. Capable of inducing arrhythmias.

arsenate (ar'sĕ-nāt). A salt of arsenic acid.

arseni'asis. Arsenicalism; chronic arsenical poisoning.

arsenic (ar'sĕ-nik) [Mod. L. fr. G. *arsenikon*, fr. *arsēn*, strong]. **1.** An element, a steel-gray metal, symbol As, atomic no. 33, atomic weight 74.9; forms a number of poisonous compounds, some of which are used in medicine. **2.** Relating to the element arsenic, or one of its compounds; denoting especially arsenic acid.

arsenic acid. H_3AsO_4; hydrate of arsenic oxide or arsenic pentoxide, As_2O_5, which forms arsenates with certain bases.

arsen'ical, arsen'ic. Relating to or containing arsenic.

arsen'icalism. Arseniasis.

ar'tefact. Artifact.

arteri-, See arterio-.

arteria, gen. and pl. **arteriae** (ar-tēr'ĭ-ah, ar-tēr'ĭ-e) [L. from G. *artēria*, the windpipe; later, an artery as distinct from a vein] [NA]. Artery; a blood vessel conveying blood in a direction away from the heart. With the exception of the pulmonary and umbilical arteries, the arteries convey red or aerated blood.

a. alveola'ris infe'rior [NA], inferior alveolar artery; *origin,* maxillary artery; *distribution,* through mandibular canal to lower teeth; *branches,* mylohyoid, mental, dental.

a. alveola'ris supe'rior [NA], superior alveolar artery; **(1)** anterior *origin,* infraorbital artery; *distribution,* upper incisors and canine teeth, maxillary sinus; **(2)** posterior *origin,* maxillary artery; *distribution,* molar and premolar teeth, gingiva.

a. angula'ris [NA], angular artery (1); the terminal branch of facial; *distribution,* muscles and skin of side of nose; *anastomoses,* lateral nasal, and dorsal artery of nose and palpebrals from ophthalmic.

a. appendicula'ris [NA], appendicular artery; branch of ileocolic that supplies vermiform appendix.

a. arcua'ta [NA], arcuate artery; *origin,* dorsalis pedis; *branches,* deep plantar, dorsal metatarsals and dorsal digitals.

arte'riae arcua'tae renis [NA], arcuate arteries of kidney; branches of interlobar arteries of kidney which at junction of the cortex and medulla turn and run at right angles to parent stem and approximately parallel to surface of kidney.

arte'riae il'ei [NA], ileal arteries; intestinal arteries (1); *origin,* superior mesenteric; *distribution,* ileum; *anastomoses,* other branches of superior mesenteric.

a. ascen'dens [NA], ascending artery; branch of ileocolic that communicates with a branch of right colic and supplies ascending colon.

arteriae atria'les [NA], atrial arteries; branches of right and left coronary arteries distributed to muscle of atria.

a. auricula'ris [NA], auricular artery; **(1)** posterior, *origin,* external carotid; *branches,* muscular, posterior tympanic, auricular, occipital, and stylomastoid; **(2)** deep, *origin,* maxillary; *distribution,* articulation of jaw, parotid gland, and external acoustic meatus; *anastomoses,* branches of superficial temporal and posterior auricular.

a. axilla'ris [NA], axillary artery; continuation of subclavian in axilla, becoming brachial in arm; *branches,* superior thoracic, thoracoacromial, lateral thoracic, subscapular, circumflex humeral, posterior and anterior.

a. basila'ris [NA], basilar artery; union of the two vertebral arteries, running from lower to upper border of the pons; *branches,* anterior spinal, two inferior cerebellars, and labyrinthine, pontine, and superior cerebellar.

a. brachia'lis [NA], brachial artery; *origin,* continuation of axillary; *branches,* profunda brachii, superior ulnar collateral, inferior ulnar collateral, muscular, and nutrient; bifurcates at elbow into radial and ulnar.

a. brachia'lis superficia'lis [NA], superficial brachial artery; an occasional variation in which the brachial artery lies superficial to median nerve in arm.

a. bucca'lis [NA], buccal artery; *origin,* maxillary; *distribution,* buccinator muscle, skin, and mucous membrane of cheek; *anastomoses,* buccal branch of facial.

a. bul'bi pe'nis [NA], artery of bulb of penis; branch of internal pudendal artery which supplies bulb of penis.

a. bul'bi vestib'uli [NA], artery of bulb of vestibule; branch of internal pudendal in the female that supplies bulb of vestibule.

a. cana'lis pterygoi'dei [NA], artery of pterygoid canal; tiny artery in pterygoid canal connecting maxillary and internal carotid.

a. carot'is [NA], carotid artery; (1) common, *origin*, right from brachiocephalic, left from arch of aorta; runs upward in neck and divides opposite upper border of thyroid cartilage into *terminal branches*, external and internal carotid; (2) external, *origin*, common carotid; *branches*, superior thyroid, lingual, facial, occipital, posterior auricular, ascending pharyngeal, and *terminal branches*, maxillary and superficial temporal; (3) internal, arises from common carotid opposite upper border of thyroid cartilage, and terminates in middle cranial fossa by dividing into anterior and middle cerebral.

a. celia'ca, *truncus* celiacus.

a. centra'lis ret'inae [NA], central artery of retina; branch of ophthalmic which penetrates optic nerve behind eye to enter it at optic papilla in retina; divides into superior and inferior temporal and nasal branches.

a. cer'ebri [NA], cerebral artery; (1) anterior, one of two terminal branches of internal carotid; divided into two parts, supplying branches to thalamus and corpus striatum and to cortex of medial parts of frontal and parietal lobes; (2) middle, one of two terminal branches of the internal carotid; divided into three parts, supplying perforating branches to internal capsule, thalamus, and corpus, striatum, to insula and adjacent cortical areas, and large part of central cortical convexity; (3) posterior, formed by bifurcation of basilar; divided into three parts, supplying part of thalamus and hypothalamus, thalamus, cerebral peduncles, and choroid plexuses of lateral and third ventricles, and cortex of temporal and occipital lobes.

a. cerebel'li infe'rior [NA], inferior cerebellar artery; (1) anterior, *origin*, basilar; *distribution*, lower surface of lateral lobes of cerebellum; *anastomoses*, posterior inferior cerebellar; (2) posterior, *origin*, vertebral; *distribution*, medulla, choroid plexus, and cerebellum; *anastomoses*, superior cerebellar and anterior inferior cerebellar.

a. cerebel'li supe'rior [NA], superior cerebellar artery; *origin*, basilar; *distribution*, upper surface of cerebellum and colliculi; *anastomoses*, posterior inferior cerebellar.

a. cervica'lis [NA], cervical artery; (1) ascending, *origin*, inferior thyroid; *distribution*, muscles of neck and spinal cord; *anastomoses*, branches of vertebral, occipital, ascending pharyngeal, and deep cervical; (2) deep, *origin*, costocervical trunk; *distribution*, posterior deep muscles of neck; *anastomoses*, branches of occipital, ascending cervical, and vertebral.

a. choroi'dea [NA], choroidal artery; (1) anterior, *origin*, internal carotid or middle cerebral artery;

distribution, optic tract, crus cerebri, uncus, hippocampus, globus pallidus, posterior part of internal capsule, geniculate bodies of thalamus, and choroid plexus in inferior horn of lateral ventricle; (2) posterior, one of several branches of posterior cerebral that supply choroid plexus of body of lateral ventricle and third ventricle.

a. cilia'ris ante'rior [NA], anterior ciliary artery; one of several arteries derived from muscular branches of ophthalmic which perforate anterior part of sclera and anastomose with posterior ciliary arteries.

a. cilia'ris poste'rior [NA], posterior ciliary artery; (1) short, one of several ciliary branches of ophthalmic distributed to choroid coat of eye; (2) long, one of two branches of ophthalmic to the iris, at outer and inner margins of which they anastomose.

a. circumflex'a fem'oris [NA], circumflex a. of thigh; (1) lateral, *origin*, profunda femoris; *distribution*, hip joint, thigh muscles; *anastomoses*, medial circumflex femoral, inferior gluteal, superior gluteal, popliteal; (2) medial, *origin*, profunda femoris; *distribution*, hip joint, muscles of thigh; *anastomoses*, inferior gluteal, superior gluteal, lateral circumflex femoral.

a. circumflex'a hu'meri [NA], circumflex humeral artery; (1) anterior, *origin*, axillary; *distribution*, shoulder joint and biceps muscle; *anastomoses*, posterior circumflex humeral; (2) posterior, *origin*, axillary; *distribution*, muscles and structures of shoulder joint; *anastomoses*, anterior circumflex humeral, suprascapular, thoracoacromial, and profunda brachii.

a. circumflex'a il'ium [NA], circumflex iliac artery; (1) deep, *origin*, external iliac; *distribution*, muscles and skin of lower abdomen, sartorius and tensor fasciae latae; *anastomoses*, lumbar, epigastric, gluteal, iliolumbar, and superficial circumflex iliac; (2) superficial, *origin*, femoral; *distribution*, inguinal lymph nodes and integument of that region; sartorius, and tensor fasciae latae muscles; *anastomoses*, deep circumflex iliac.

a. circumflex'a scap'ulae [NA], circumflex scapular artery; *origin*, subscapular; *distribution*, muscles of shoulder and scapular region; *anastomoses*, branches of suprascapular and transverse cervical.

a. col'ica [NA], colic artery; (1) right, *origin*, superior mesenteric, sometimes by a common trunk with ileocolic; *distribution*, ascending colon; *anastomoses*, middle colic, ileocolic; (2) middle, *origin*, superior mesenteric; *distribution*, transverse colon; *anastomoses*, right and left colic; (3) left, *origin*, inferior mesenteric; *distribution*, descending colon and splenic flexure; *anastomoses*, middle colic, sigmoid.

a. collatera'lis me'dia [NA], middle collateral artery; posterior terminal branch of the profunda brachii, anastomosing with the arteries which form the articular network of the elbow.

a. collatera'lis radia'lis [NA], radial collateral artery; anterior terminal branch of profunda brachii, anastomosing with radial recurrent.

a. collatera'lis ulna'ris [NA], ulnar collateral artery; (1) inferior, *origin*, brachial; *distribution*, arm muscles at back of elbow; *anastomoses*, ulnar recurrent, anterior and posterior, superior ulnar collateral, profunda brachii, and recurrent interosseous; (2) superior, *origin*, brachial; *distribution*, elbow joint; *anastomoses*, posterior ulnar recurrent and inferior ulnar collateral.

a. com'itans ner'vi ischiad'ici [NA], companion artery to sciatic nerve; *origin*, inferior gluteal; *distribution*, sciatic nerve; *anastomoses*, branches of profunda femoris.

a. commu'nicans [NA], communicating artery; (1) anterior, short vessel joining the two anterior cerebral arteries and completing circle of Willis anteriorly; (2) posterior, *origin*, internal carotid; *distribution*, optic tract, crus cerebri, interpeduncular region, and hippocampal gyrus; *anastomoses*, with posterior cerebral to form the circle of Willis.

a. conjunctiva'lis [NA], conjunctival artery; (1) anterior, one of a number of small branches of anterior ciliary arteries that supplies conjunctiva; (2) posterior, one of a series of branches from tarsal arterial arches that supplies conjunctiva.

a. corona'ria [NA], coronary artery; (1) right, *origin*, right aortic sinus; *distribution*, passes around right side of heart in coronary sulcus, giving branches to right atrium and ventricle, including atrioventricular branches and posterior interventricular branch; (2) left, *origin*, left aortic sinus; *distribution*, divides into two major branches, anterior interventricular which descends in anterior interventricular sulcus, and circumflex branch which passes to diaphragmatic surface of left ventricle; gives atrial, ventricular, and atrioventricular branches.

a. cremaster'ica [NA], cremasteric artery; external spermatic artery; *origin*, inferior epigasteric; *distribution*, coverings of spermatic cord; *anastomoses, external pudendal, spermatic, and perineal a.*

a. cys'tica [NA], cystic artery; *origin*, right branch of hepatic; *distribution*, gall bladder and visceral surface of the liver.

a. digita'lis dorsa'lis [NA], dorsal digital artery; one of collateral digital branches of dorsal metatarsal arteries in foot, and of dorsal metacarpal arteries in hand.

a. digita'lis palma'ris [NA], palmar digital artery; (1) common, one of three arteries arising from superficial palmar arch and running to interdigital clefts where each divides into two proper palmar digital arteries; (2) proper, collateral digital artery; artery that passes along side of each finger.

a. digita'lis planta'ris [NA], plantar digital artery; (1) common, one of four arteries arising from a superficial plantar arch and which unite with plantar metatarsal arteries; (2) proper, one of digital branches of plantar metatarsal arteries.

a. dorsa'lis clitori'dis [NA], dorsal artery of clitoris; one of two terminal branches of internal pudendal artery in the female.

a. dorsa'lis na'si [NA], dorsal artery of nose; *origin*, ophthalmic; *distribution*, skin of side of nose; *anastomoses*, angular.

a. dorsa'lis pe'dis [NA], dorsal artery of foot; continuation of anterior tibial; *branches*, lateral tarsal, arcuate, dorsal metatarsal; *anastomoses*, with the lateral plantar to form the plantar arch.

a. dorsa'lis pe'nis [NA], dorsal artery of penis; dorsal terminal branch of internal pudendal artery in the male.

a. duc'tus deferen'tis [NA], artery of ductus deferens; *origin*, anterior division of internal iliac, or sometimes superior vesical; *distribution*, ductus deferens, seminal vesicles, testicle, ureter; *anastomoses*, testicular, cremasteric branch of inferior epigastric.

a. epigas'trica [NA], epigastric artery; (1) inferior, *origin*, external iliac; *branches*, cremasteric, muscular and pubic; *anastomoses*, superior epigastric obturator; (2) superficial, *origin*, femoral; *distribution*, inguinal glands and integument of lower abdomen; *anastomoses*, inferior epigastric, superficial circumflex iliac and external pudendal; (3) superior, *origin*, medial terminal branch of internal thoracic; *distribution*, abdominal muscles and integument, falciform ligament; *anastomoses*, inferior epigastric.

a. episclera'lis [NA], episcleral artery; one of many small branches of anterior ciliary arteries that perforate sclera behind cornea to supply iris and ciliary body.

a. ethmoida'lis [NA], ethmoidal artery; (1) anterior, *origin*, ophthalmic; *distribution*, cerebral membranes in anterior cranial fossa, anterior ethmoidal cells, frontal sinus, anterior upper part of nasal mucous membranes, skin of dorsum of nose; (2) posterior, *origin*, ophthalmic; *distribution*, posterior ethmoidal cells and upper posterior part of lateral wall of nasal cavity.

a. facia'lis [NA], facial artery; external maxillary artery; *origin*, external carotid; *branches*, ascending palatine, tonsillar and glandular branches, submental, inferior labial, superior labial, masseteric, buccal, and lateral nasal branches, and angular.

a. femora'lis [NA], femoral artery; *origin*, continuation of external iliac, beginning at inguinal ligament; *branches*, external pudendal, superficial epigastric, superficial circumflex iliac, profunda femoris, descending genicular, terminating in the popliteal at the upper part of the popliteal space.

a. gas'trica dex'tra [NA], right gastric artery; *origin*, hepatic; *distribution*, pyloric portion of stomach on the lesser curvature; *anastomoses*, left gastric.

a. gas'trica sinis'tra [NA], left gastric artery; *origin*, celiac; *distribution*, lesser curvature of stomach, abdominal part of esophagus, and, frequently, a portion of left lobe of liver; *anastomoses*, esophageal, right gastric.

arte′riae gas′tricae bre′ves [NA], short gastric arteries; vasa brevia; four or five small arteries given off from splenic, passing to greater curvature of stomach, and anastomosing with other arteries in that region.

a. gastroduodena′lis [NA], gastroduodenal artery; *origin,* hepatic; terminal *branches,* right gastroepiploic, superior pancreaticoduodenal.

a. gastroomenta′lis dex′tra [NA], gastroomental artery; or gastroepiploic artery; **(1)** right, *origin,* gastroduodenal; *distribution,* greater curvature and walls of stomach and greater omentum; *anastomoses,* frequently unites with left gastroepiploic, and branches from this arch anastomose with branches of right and left gastric; **(2)** left, *origin,* splenic; *distribution,* greater curvature of stomach and greater omentum, frequently joining right gastroepiploic.

a. ge′nus descen′dens [NA], descending artery of knee; *origin,* femoral; *distribution,* knee joint and adjacent parts; *anastomoses,* medial superior genicular, medial inferior genicular, lateral superior genicular, lateral circumflex femoral, and anterior tibial recurrent.

a. ge′nus infe′rior [NA], inferior artery of knee; **(1)** lateral, *origin,* popliteal; *distribution,* knee joint; *anastomoses,* lateral superior genicular and anterior tibial recurrent (and posterior); **(2)** medial, *origin,* popliteal; *distribution,* knee joint; *anastomoses,* anterior and posterior tibial recurrent and medial superior genicular.

a. ge′nus me′dia [NA], middle artery of knee; *origin,* popliteal; *distribution,* synovial membrane and cruciate ligaments of knee joint.

a. ge′nus supe′rior [NA], superior artery of knee; **(1)** lateral, *origin,* popliteal; *distribution,* knee joint; *anastomoses,* lateral circumflex femoral, third perforating, anterior tibial recurrent, lateral inferior genicular; **(2)** medial, *origin,* popliteal; *distribution,* knee joint; *anastomoses,* descending genicular, lateral superior genicular.

a. glu′tea [NA], gluteal artery; **(1)** inferior, *origin,* internal iliac; *distribution,* hip joint and gluteal region; *anastomoses,* branches of internal pudendal, lateral sacral, superior gluteal, obturator, medial and lateral circumflex femoral; **(2)** superior, *origin,* internal iliac; *distribution,* gluteal region; *anastomoses,* lateral sacral, inferior gluteal, internal pudendal, deep circumflex iliac, lateral circumflex femoral.

a. gy′ri angula′ris [NA], artery of angular gyrus; angular artery; **(2)** last branch of terminal part of middle cerebral artery distributed to parts of temporal parietal and occipital lobes.

a. helici′na [NA], helicine artery; one of coiled arteries in erectile tissue of penis.

a. hepat′ica [NA], hepatic artery; **(1)** common, *origin,* celiac; *branches,* right gastric, gastroduodenal, and proper hepatic; **(2)** proper, *origin,* common hepatic; *branches,* right and left hepatic.

a. hyaloi′dea [NA], hyaloid artery; terminal branch of primitive ophthalmic which forms in embryo an extensive ramification in primary vitreous and vascular tunic around lens; usually atrophied by birth.

a. ileocol′ica [NA], ileocolic artery; *origin,* superior mesenteric, often by common trunk with right colic; *distribution,* terminal part of ileum, cecum, vermiform appendix, and ascending colon; *anastomoses,* right colic and ileal.

a. ili′aca [NA], iliac artery; **(1)** common, one of two terminal branches of abdominal aorta; opposite lumbosacral articulation, becomes internal iliac and also gives off external iliac; **(2)** external, *origin,* common iliac; *branches,* inferior epigastric, deep circuflex iliac; becomes femoral at inguinal ligament; **(3)** internal, the hypogastric artery; *origin,* common iliac; *branches,* iliolumbar, lateral sacral, obturator, superior gluteal, inferior gluteal, umbilical, superior vesical, inferior vesical, middle rectal; usually divides into anterior and posterior, the anterior terminating in internal pudendal, the posterior in superior gluteal.

a. iliolumba′lis [NA], iliolumbar artery; *origin,* internal iliac; *distribution,* pelvic muscles and bones; *anastomoses,* deep circumflex iliac, obturator, lumbar.

a. infraorbita′lis [NA], infraorbital artery; *origin,* maxillary; *distribution,* upper canine and incisor teeth, inferior rectus and inferior oblique muscles, lower eyelid, lacrimal sac, and upper lip; *anastomoses,* branches of ophthalmic, facial, superior labial, transverse facial, and buccinator.

a. intercosta′lis [NA], intercostal artery; **(1)** anterior, *origin,* costocervical trunk; *distribution,* structures of first and second intercostal spaces; *anastomoses,* anterior intercostal branches of internal thoracic; **(2)** posterior, one of nine pairs of arteries arising from thoracic aorta and distributed to nine lower intercostal spaces, spinal column, spinal cord, and muscles and integument of back; anastomose with branches of musculophrenic, internal thoracic, superior epigastric, subcostal and lumbar.

arte′riae interloba′res [NA], interlobar arteries; branches of segmental arteries of the kidney; run between renal lobes and give rise to arcuate arteries.

arteriae interlobula′res [NA], interlobular arteries; arteries that pass between lobules of an organ; **a. i. hepatis,** terminal branches of hepatic passing between hepatic lobules; **a. i. renis,** branches of interlobar arteries of kidney passing outward through cortex and supplying glomeruli.

a. interos′sea [NA], interosseous artery; **(1)** anterior, *origin,* common interosseous, *distribution,* deep parts of forearm anteriorly; *anastomoses,* posterior interosseous; **(2)** common, *origin,* ulnar; *branches,* anterior and posterior interosseous; **(3)** posterior, *origin,* common interosseous; *distribution,* deep parts of forearm posteriorly; **(4)** recurrent, origin, posterior interosseous; *distribution,* elbow joint; *anastomoses,* branches of profunda brachii and inferior ulnar collateral.

arteriae jejuna'les [NA], jejunal arteries; intestinal arteries (2); *origin,* superior mesenteric; *distribution,* jejunum; *anatomoses,* by a series of arches with each other and with ileal arteries.

a. labia'lis [NA], labial artery; **(1)** inferior, *origin,* facial; *distribution,* structures of lower lip; *anastomoses,* artery from opposite side, mental and sublabial; **(2)** superior, *origin,* facial; *distribution,* structures of upper lip and by septal branch, anterior and lower part of nasal septum; *anastomoses,* artery of opposite side and sphenopalatine.

a. labyrin'thi [NA], artery of the labyrinth; internal auditory artery; branch of basilar artery that enters labyrinth through internal acoustic meatus.

a. lacrima'lis [NA], lacrimal artery; *origin,* ophthalmic; *distribution,* lacrimal gland, lateral and superior rectus muscles, superior eyelid, forehead, and temporal fossa.

a. laryn'gea [NA], laryngeal artery; **(1)** inferior, *origin,* inferior thyroid; *distribution,* muscles and mucous membrane of larynx; *anastomoses,* superior laryngeal; **(2)** superior, *origin,* superior thyroid; *distribution,* muscles and mucous membrane of larynx; *anastomoses,* cricothyroid branch of superior thyroid and terminal branches of inferior larnygeal.

a. liena'lis [NA], lienal or splenic artery; *origin,* celiac trunk; *branches,* pancreatic, left gastroepiploic, short gastric, and splenic.

a. ligamen'ti tere'tis u'teri [NA], artery of round ligament of uterus; *origin,* inferior epigastric; *distribution,* round ligament.

a. lingua'lis [NA], lingual artery; *origin,* external carotid; *distribution,* under surface of tongue, terminates as a. profunda linguae; *branches,* suprahyoid and dorsal lingual branches and sublingual artery.

a. lumba'lis [NA], lumbar artery; one of four or five pairs; *origin,* abdominal aorta; *distribution,* lumbar vertebrae, muscles of back, abdominal wall; *anastomoses,* intercostal, subcostal, superior and inferior epigastric, deep circumflex iliac, and iliolumbar.

a. lumba'lis i'ma [NA], lowest lumbar artery; *origin,* middle sacral; *distribution,* sacrum and iliac muscle; *anastomosis,* circumflex iliac artery.

a. luso'ria, an abnormally placed artery or vascular ring producing dysphagia by pressure on the esophagus.

a. malleola'ris ante'rior [NA], anterior malleolar artery; **(1)** lateral, *origin,* anterior tibial; *distribution,* ankle joint; *anastomoses,* peroneal, lateral tarsal; **(2)** medial, *origin,* anterior tibial; *distribution,* ankle joint and neighboring integument; *ankle joint and neighboring integument; anastomoses,* branches of posterior tibial.

a. masseter'ica [NA], masseteric artery; *origin,* maxillary; *distribution,*deep surface of masseter mus-

cle; *anastomoses,* branches of transverse facial and masseteric branches of facial.

a. maxilla'ris [NA], maxillary artery; internal maxillary artery; *origin,* external carotid; *branches,* deep auricular, anterior tympanic, middle meningeal, inferior alveolar, masseteric, deep temporal, buccal, superior posterior alveolar, infraorbital, descending palatine, artery of pterygoid canal, sphenopalatine.

a. media'na [NA], median artery; *origin,* anterior interosseous; *distribution,* accompanies median nerve to palm; *anastomoses,* branches of superficial palmar arch.

a. menin'gea [NA], meningeal artery; **(1)** anterior; *origin,* anterior ethmoidal; *distribution,* meninges in anterior cranial fossa; *anastomoses,* branches of middle meningeal and branches of internal carotid and lacrimal; **(2)** middle, *origin,* maxillary; *branches,* petrosal, ganglionic, superior tympanic, frontal and parietal; *distribution,* to parts mentioned and through terminal branches to anterior and middle cranial fossae; *anastomoses,* meningeal branches of occipital, ascending pharyngeal, ophthalmic and lacrimal, stylomastoid, accessory meningeal branch of maxillary, and deep temporal; **(3)** posterior, *origin,* ascending pharyngeal; *distribution,* dura mater of posterior cranial fossa; *anastomoses,* branches of middle meningeal and vertebral.

a. menta'lis [NA], mental artery; teminal branch of inferior alveolar; *distribution,* chin; *anastomosis,* inferior labial artery.

a. mesenter'ica [NA], mesenteric artery; **(1)** inferior; *origin,* aorta; *branches,* left colic, sigmoid, superior rectal; *anastomoses,* middle colic and middle rectal; **(2)** superior, *origin,* aorta; *branches,* inferior pancreaticoduodenal, jejunal, ileal, ileocolic, appendicular, right colic, middle colic; *anastomoses,* superior pancreaticoduodenal and left colic.

a. metacar'pea [NA], metacarpal artery; **(1)** dorsal, one of three branches of posterior carpal arch, running in back of second, third, and fourth interosseous muscles; **(2)** palmar, one of three arteries springing from deep palmar arch and running in three medial interosseous spaces; anastomose with the dorsal metacarpal arteries.

a. metatar'sea [NA], metatarsal artery; **(1)** dorsal, one of three branches of arcuate supplying three lateral toes and lateral side of second toe through dorsal digital; **(2)** plantar; one of four branches of plantar arch that divide into plantar digital arteries to supply toes.

a. musculophren'ica [NA], musculophrenic artery; *origin,* lateral terminal branch of internal thoracic,; *distribution,* diaphragm and intercostal muscles; *anastomoses,* branches of pericardiacophrenic, inferior phrenic, and posterior intercostal arteries.

arte'riae nasa'les posterio'res latera'les [NA], posterior lateral nasal arteries; branches of sphenopalatine that supply posterior parts of conchae and lateral nasal wall.

a. nasa'lis poste'rior sep'ti [NA], posterior septal artery of nose; branch of sphenopalatine that supplies nasal septum and accompanies nasopalatine nerve.

a. nutri'cia [NA], nutrient artery; an artery of variable origin that supplies the medullary cavity of a long bone.

a. obturato'ria [NA], obturator artery; *origin*, anterior division of internal iliac; *distribution*, ilium, pubis, obturator and adductor muscles; *anastomoses*, iliolumbar, inferior epigastric, medial circumflex femoral; *branches*, pubic, acetabular, anterior, and posterior.

a. obturato'ria accesso'ria [NA], accessory obturator artery; pubic branch of inferior epigastric when it contributes a significant supply through obturator canal.

a. occipita'lis [NA], occipital artery; *origin*, external carotid; *branches*, sternocleidomastoid, and muscular, meningeal, auricular, occipital, mastoid, and descending.

a. occipita'lis latera'lis [NA], lateral occipital artery; one of terminal branches of posterior cerebral; supplies, by several branches, lateral portions of temporal lobe.

a. occipita'lis media'lis [NA], medial occipital artery; one of terminal branches of posterior cerebral; distributed, by several branches, to posterior corpus callosum and medial and superolateral portions of occipital lobe, including the visual cortex.

a. ophthal'mica [NA], ophthalmic artery; *origin*, internal carotid; *branches*, ciliary, central artery of retina, anterior meningeal, lacrimal, conjunctival, episcleral, supraorbital, ethmoidal, palpebral, dorsal nasal, and supratrochlear.

a. ova'rica [NA], ovarian artery; *origin*, aorta; *distribution*, ureter, ovary, ovarian ligament and uterine tube; *anastomoses*, uterine.

a, palati'na [NA], palatine artery; **(1)** ascending, *origin*, facial; *distribution*, lateral walls of pharynx, tonsils, auditory tubes, and soft palate; *anastomoses*, tonsillar branch of facial, dorsal lingual, and descending palatine; **(2)** descending, *origin*, maxillary; *distribution*, soft palate, gums, and bones and mucous membrane of hard palate; *anastomoses*, sphenopalatine, ascending palatine, ascending pharyngeal, and tonsillar branches of facial; **(3)** greater, anterior branch of descending palatine artery, supplying gums and mucous membrane of hard palate; **(4)** lesser, one of several posterior branches of descending palatine in greater palatine canal, distributed to soft palate and tonsil.

arte'riae palpebra'les [NA], palpebral arteries; branches of the ophthalmic supplying upper and lower eyelids, consisting of two sets, *lateral* and *medial.*

a. pancreat'ica [NA], pancreatic artery; **(1)** dorsal, *origin*, splenic; *distribution*, head and body of pancreas; *anastomoses*, superior pancreaticoduode-

nal; **(2)** inferior, *origin*, dorsal pancreatic; *distribution*, body and tail of pancreas; *anastomoses*, pancreatica magna; **(3)** great, *origin*, splenic; *distribution*, tail of pancreas; *anastomoses*. inferior and caudal pancreatic arteries.

a. pancreat'icoduodena'lis [NA], pancreaticoduodenal artery; **(1)** inferior, one of two arteries, anterior and posterior; *origin*, superior mesenteric; *distribution*, head of pancreas, duodenum; *anastomoses*, superior pancreaticoduodenal; **(2)** superior, artery; one of two arteries, anterior and superior; *origin*, gastroduodenal; *distribution*, head of pancreas, duodenum, common bile duct; *anastomoses*, inferior pancreaticoduodenal, splenic.

arte'riae perforan'tes [NA], perforating arteries; *origin*, a. profunda femoris; *distribution*, as three or four vessels that pass through adductor magnus to posterior and lateral parts of thigh.

a. pericardiacophren'ica [NA], pericardiacophrenic artery; *origin*, internal thoracic; *distribution*, pericardium, diaphragm, and pleura; *anastomoses*, musculophrenic, inferior phrenic, mediastinal and pericardial branches of the internal thoracic.

a. perinea'lis [NA], perineal artery; *origin*, internal pudendal; *distribution*, superficial structures of perineum; *anastomoses*, external pudendal arteries.

a. pero'nea [NA], peroneal artery; fibular artery; *origin*, posterior tibial; *distribution*, soleus, tibialis posterior, flexor longus hallucis, peroneal muscles, inferior tibiofibular articulation, and ankle joint; *anastomoses*, anterior lateral malleolar, lateral tarsal, lateral plantar, dorsalis pedis.

a. pharyn'gea ascen'dens [NA], ascending pharyngeal artery; *origin*, external carotid; *distribution*, wall of pharynx and soft palate.

a. phren'ica [NA], phrenic artery; **(1)** inferior, *origin*, first paired branch from abdominal aorta inferior to diaphragm; *distribution*, diaphragm; *anastomoses*, superior phrenic, internal thoracic, and musculophrenic; **(2)** superior, one of a pair of small arteries given off from thoracic aorta just superior to diaphragm; *distribution*, diaphragm; *anastomoses*, musculophrenic, pericardiacophrenic, and inferior phrenic.

a. planta'ris [NA], plantar artery; **(1)** lateral, larger of two terminal branches of posterior tibial; *distribution*, forms plantar arch and through it supplies sole of foot and plantar surfaces of toes; *anastomoses*, medial plantar, dorsalis pedis; **(2)** medial, one of the terminal branches of the posterior tibial; *distribution*, medial side of the sole of the foot; *anastomoses*, dorsalis pedis, lateral plantar.

a. poplit'ea [NA], popliteal artery; continuation of femoral in popliteal space, bifurcating at lower border of popliteus muscle into anterior and posterior tibial; *branches*, lateral and medial superior genicular, middle genicular, lateral and medial inferior genicular, and sural arteries.

a. prin'ceps pol'licis [NA], principal artery of thumb; *origin*, radial; *distribution*, palmar surface and sides of thumb; *anastomoses*, arteries on dorsum of thumb.

a. profun'da bra'chii [NA], deep brachial artery; *origin*, brachial; *distribution*, humerus and muscles and integument of arm; *anastomoses*, radial recurrent, recurrent interosseous, ulnar collateral, posterior circumflex humeral.

a. profun'da clitori'dis [NA], deep artery of clitoris; deep terminal branch of the pudendal artery in the female; supplies crus of clitoris.

a. profun'da fem'oris [NA], deep artery of thigh; *origin*, femoral; *branches*, lateral circumflex femoral, medial circumflex femoral, perforating.

a. profun'da lin'guae [NA], deep artery of tongue; ranine artery; termination of lingual; *distribution*, muscles and mucous membrane of under surface of tongue.

a. profun'da pe'nis [NA], deep artery of penis; *origin*, terminal branch of internal pudendal; *distribution*, corpus cavernosum of penis.

arte'riae puden'dae exter'nae [NA], external pudendal arteries; *origin*, femoral; *distribution*, skin over pubis, skin over penis, scrotum, or labium majus; *anastomoses*, dorsal artery of penis or clitoris, posterior scrotal or labial arteries.

a. puden'da inter'na [NA], internal pudendal artery; *origin*, internal iliac; *branches*, inferior rectal, perineal, posterior scrotal (or labial), urethral, artery of bulb of penis (or of vestibule), deep artery of penis (or clitoris), dorsal artery of penis (or clitoris).

a. pulmona'lis [NA], pulmonary artery; (1) right; one of two branches of pulmonary trunk, passing transversely across mediastinum to enter hilus of right lung; branches are distributed with the bronchi; (2) left, enters hilus of left lung; branches accompany segmental and subsegmental bronchi.

a. radia'lis [NA], radial artery; *origin*, brachial; *branches*, radial recurrent, dorsal metacarpal, dorsal digital, princeps, pollicis, palmar metacarpal, and muscular, carpal, and perforating.

a. radia'lis in'dicis [NA], radial index artery; *origin*, radial; *distribution*, radial side of index finger.

a. recta'lis [NA], rectal artery; (1) inferior, *origin*, internal pudendal; *distribution*, anal canal, muscles and skin of the anal region, and skin of the buttock; *anastomoses*, middle rectal, perineal, and gluteal; (2) middle, *origin*, internal iliac; *distribution*, middle portion of rectum; *anastomoses*, superior and inferior rectal; (3) superior, *origin*, inferior mesenteric; *distribution*, upper part of rectum; *anastomoses*, middle and inferior rectal.

a. recur'rens radia'lis [NA], radial recurrent artery; *origin*, radial; *distribution*, ascends around lateral side of elbow joint; *anastomoses*, radial collateral, interosseous recurrent.

a. recur'rens tibia'lis [NA], tibial recurrent artery; (1) anterior, branch of anterior tibial which ascends to supply front and sides of knee joint; (2) posterior, branch of posterior tibial artery which ascends anterior to popliteus muscle, anastomoses with branches of popliteal artery and sends a twig to tibiofibular joint.

a. recur'rens ulna'ris [NA], recurrent ulnar artery; *origin*, ulnar artery; *distribution*, two branches, anterior and posterior, pass medially in front of and behind the elbow joint; *anastomoses*, superior and inferior ulnar collateral.

a. rena'lis [NA], renal artery; *origin*, aorta; *branches*, segmental, ureteral, and inferior suprarenal; *distribution*, kidney.

arte'riae re'nis [NA], arteries of kidney; branches of renal artery that supply kidney; usually five, they give off interlobar, arcuate and interlobular arteries in sequence.

a. sacra'lis [NA], sacral artery; (1) lateral, one of two arteries that arises from internal iliac; supplies muscles and skin in the area and sends branches into sacral canal; (2) median, *origin*, back of abdominal aorta just above bifurcation; *distribution*, lower lumbar vertebrae, sacrum, and coccyx; *anastomoses*, lateral sacral, superior and middle rectal.

arte'riae sigmoi'deae [NA], sigmoid arteries; *origin*, inferior mesenteric; *distribution*, descending colon and sigmoid flexure; *anastomoses*, left colic, superior rectal.

a. sphe'nopalati'na [NA], sphenopalatine artery; *origin*, maxillary; *distribution*, posterior portion of lateral nasal wall and septum; *anastomoses*, branches of descending palatine, superior labial, and infraorbital.

a. spina'lis [NA], spinal artery; (1) anterior, *origin*, vertebral; *distribution*, spinal cord and pia mater; *anastomoses*, branches of intercostal and lumbar arteries; (2) posterior, *origin*, vertebral; *distribution*, medulla, spinal cord, and pia mater; *anastomoses*, spinal branches of intercostal arteries.

a. stylomastoi'dea [NA], stylomastoid artery; *origin*, posterior auricular; *distribution*, external acoustic meatus, mastoid cells, semicircular canals, stapedius muscle, and vestibule; *anastomoses*, tympanic branches of internal carotid and ascending pharyngeal, and auditory branch of basilar.

a. subcla'via [NA], subclavian artery; *origin*, right from brachiocephalic, left from arch of aorta; *branches*, vertebral, thyrocervical trunk, internal thoracic; costocervical trunk, descending scapular; it is directly continuous with the axillary.

a. subcosta'lis [NA], subcostal artery; *origin*, thoracic aorta; *distribution*, inferior to twelfth rib similar to posterior intercostal arteries.

a. sublingua'lis [NA], sublingual artery; *origin*, lingual; *distribution*, extrinsic muscles of tongue, sublingual gland, mucosa of region; *anastomoses*, artery of opposite side and submental.

a. submenta'lis [NA], submental artery; *origin*, facial; *distribution*, mylohyoid muscle, submandibular and sublingual glands, and structures of lower lip; *anastomoses*, inferior labial, mental branch of inferior dental and sublingual.

a. subscapula'ris [NA], subscapular artery; *origin,* axillary; *branches,* circumflex scapular, thoracodorsal; *distribution,* muscles of shoulder and scapular region; *anastomoses,* branches of transverse cervical, suprascapular, lateral thoracic, and intercostals.

a. supraorbita'lis [NA], supraorbital artery; *origin,* ophthalmic; *distribution,* frontalis muscle and scalp; *anastomoses,* branches of superficial temporal and supratrochlear.

a. suprarena'lis [NA], suprarenal artery; **(1)** inferior, *origin,* renal; *distribution,* suprarenal gland; **(2)** middle, *origin,* aorta; *distribution,* suprarenal gland; *anastomoses,* superior and inferior suprarenal; **(3)** superior, *origin,* inferior phrenic artery; *distribution,* suprarenal gland.

a. suprascapula'ris [NA], suprascapular artery; transverse scapular artery; *origin,* thyrocervical trunk; *distribution,* clavicle, scapula, muscles of shoulder, and shoulder joint; *anastomoses,* transverse cervical circumflex scapular.

a. supratrochlea'ris [NA], supratrochlear artery; frontal artery; *origin,* ophthalmic; *distribution,* anterior portion of scalp; *anastomoses,* branches of supraorbital.

a. sura'lis [NA], sural artery; one of four or five arteries arising from popliteal; *distribution,* muscles and integument of calf; *anastomoses,* posterior tibial, medial and lateral inferior genicular.

a. tar'sea [NA], tarsal artery; **(1)** lateral, *origin,* dorsalis pedis; *distribution,* tarsal joints and extensor digitorum brevis muscle; *anastomoses,* arcuate, peroneal, lateral plantar, anterior lateral malleolar; **(2)** medial, one of two small branches of dorsalis pedis; *distribution,* medial malleolar network.

a. tempora'lis [NA], temporal artery; **(1)** middle, *origin,* superficial temporal; *distribution,* temporal fascia and muscle; *anastomoses,* branches of maxillary; **(2)** deep (anterior and posterior), *origin,* maxillary; *distribution,* temporal muscle; *anastomoses,* branches of superficial temporal, lacrimal, and middle meningeal; **(3)** superficial, *origin,* terminal branch of the external carotid; *branches,* transverse facial, middle temporal, orbital, parotid, anterior auricular, frontal, and parietal.

a. testicula'ris [NA], testicular artery; internal spermatic artery; *origin,* aorta; *branches,* ureteral, cremasteric, epididymal; *distribution,* testicle and parts designated by branches; *anastomoses,* branches of renal, inferior epigastric, deferential.

a. thora'cica [NA], thoracic artery; **(1)** internal, the internal mammary artery; *origin,* subclavian; *branches,* pericardiacophrenic, anterior intercostal, sternal, mediastinal, thymic, bronchial, muscular, and perforating branches, and bifurcates into the musculophrenic and superior epigastric; **(2)** lateral, the external mammary artery; *origin,* axillary; *distribution,* muscles of chest and mammary gland; **(3)** superior, *origin,* axillary; *distribution,* muscles of

chest; *anastomoses,* branches of suprascapular, internal thoracic, and thoracoacromial.

a. thoracoacromia'lis [NA], thoracoacromial or acromiothoracic artery; *origin,* axillary; *distribution,* muscles and skin of shoulder and upper chest; *anastomoses,* branches of superior thoracic, internal thoracic, lateral thoracic, posterior and anterior circumflex humeral, and suprascapular.

a. thoracodorsa'lis [NA], thoracodorsal artery; *origin,* subscapular; *distribution,* muscles of upper part of back; *anastomoses,* branches of lateral thoracic.

a. thyroi'dea [NA], thyroid artery; **(1)** lowest, an inconstant artery; *origin,* arch of aorta or brachiocephalic artery; *distribution,* thyroid gland; **(2)** inferior, *origin,* thyrocervical trunk; *branches,* ascending cervical, inferior laryngeal, and muscular, esophageal, and tracheal; **(3)** superior, *origin,* external carotid; *branches,* infrahyoid, superior laryngeal, sternocleidomastoid, cricothyroid and two terminal branches.

a. tibia'lis [NA], tibial artery; **(1)** anterior, *origin,* popliteal; *branches,* posterior and anterior tibial recurrent, lateral and medial anterior malleolar, dorsalis pedis, lateral tarsal, medial tarsal, arcuate, dorsal metatarsal, and dorsal digital; **(2)** posterior, *origin,* popliteal; *branches,* peroneal, nutrient of fibula, lateral and medial posterior malleolar, nutrient of tibia, medial and lateral plantar.

a. transver'sa col'li [NA], transverse cervical artery; transverse artery of neck; *origin,* thyrocervical trunk; *branches,* superficial (superficial cervical) and deep (descending scapular).

a. transver'sa facie'i [NA], transverse facial artery; *origin,* superficial temporal; *distribution,* parotid gland, parotid duct, masseter muscle, and overlying skin; *anastomoses,* infraorbital and buccal branches of maxillary, and buccal and masseteric branches of facial.

a. tympan'ica [NA], tympanic artery; **(1)** anterior, *origin,* maxillary; *distribution,* middle ear; *anastomoses,* tympanic branches of internal carotid and ascending pharyngeal stylomastoid; **(2)** inferior, *origin,* ascending pharyngeal; *distribution,* middle ear; *anastomoses,* tympanic branches of other arteries; **(3)** posterior, *origin,* stylomastoid; *distribution,* middle ear; *anastomoses,* other tympanic arteries; **(4)** superior, *origin,* middle meningeal; *distribution,* middle ear; *anastomoses,* other tympanic arteries.

a. ulna'ris [NA], ulnar artery; *origin,* brachial; *branches,* ulnar recurrent, interosseous, dorsal and palmar carpal, deep palmar, and superficial palmar arch with its digital branches.

a. umbilica'lis [NA], umbilical artery; before birth, a continuation of common iliac; after birth, obliterated between bladder and umbilicus, forming medial umbilical ligament (remaining portion, between internal iliac and bladder, gives off superior vesical arteries).

a. urethra'lis [NA], urethral artery; *origin,* perineal artery; *distribution,* membranous urethra.

a. uteri'na [NA], uterine artery; *origin,* internal iliac; *distribution,* uterus, upper part of vagina, round ligament, and part of uterine tube; *anastomoses,* ovarian, vaginal, inferior epigastric.

a. vagina'lis [NA], vaginal artery; *origin,* internal iliac; *distribution,* vagina, base of bladder, rectum; *anastomoses,* uterine, internal pudendal.

arte'riae ventricula'res [NA], ventricular arteries; branches of right and left coronary arteries distributed to muscle of ventricles.

a. vertebra'lis [NA], vertebral artery; first branch of subclavian artery, divided into four parts: 1) prevertebral, before it enters foramen of transverse process of sixth cervical vertebra; 2) transverse, in transverse foramina of first six cervical vertebrae; 3) atlas, running along posterior arch of atlas; 4) intercranial, within cranial cavity to union with artery from other side to form basilar artery.

a. vesica'lis [NA], vesical artery; **(1)** inferior, *origin,* internal iliac; *distribution,* base of bladder, ureter, and (in the male) seminal vesicles, ductus deferens, branches; prostate; *anastomoses,* middle rectal, and other vesical branches. **(2)** superior, *origin,* umbilical; *distribution,* bladder, urachus, ureter; *anastomoses, other vesical branches.*

a. zygomat'icoorbita'lis [NA], zygomatico-orbital artery; *origin,* superficial temporal, sometimes middle temporal; *distribution,* orbicularis oculi muscle and portions of orbit; *anastomoses,* lacrimal and palpebral branches of ophthalmic.

arte'rial. Relating to one or more arteries or to the entire system of arteries.

arteriarctia (ar-tēr-ĭ-ark'ĭ-ah) [L. *arteria,* artery, + *arcto,* to constrict]. Vasoconstriction of the arteries.

arteri'asis. Generalized arteriosclerosis.

arteriectasis, arteriectasia (ar-tēr-ĭ-ek'tă-sis, -ek-ta'zĭ-ah) [L. *arteria,* artery, + G. *ektasis,* distention]. Vasodilation of the arteries.

arteriectomy (ar-tēr-ĭ-ek'to-mĭ) [L. *arateria,* artery, + G. *ektomē,* excision]. Excision of part of an artery.

arterio-, arteri- [L. *arteria,* fr. G. *artēria,* artery]. Combining forms meaning artery.

arterioatony (ar-tēr'ĭ-o-at'o-nĭ) [arterio- + G. *antonia,* atony]. A relaxed state of the arterial walls.

arteriocapillary (ar-tēr'ĭ-o-cap'il-lār-ĭ). Relating to both arteries and capillaries.

arteriogram (ar-tēr'ĭ-o-gram) [arterio- + G. *gramma,* something written]. X-ray image of an artery after injection of contrast medium into it.

arteriog'raphy [arterio- + G. *graphō,* to write]. Visualization of an artery or arteries by x-rays after injection of a radiopaque contrast medium.

arteriola, pl. **arteriolae** (ar-tēr-ĭo'lah, ar-tēr-ĭ-o'le) [Mod. L. dim. of *arteria,* artery] [NA]. Arteriole; a minute artery with a muscular wall; a terminal artery continuous with the capillary network.

arterio'lae rec'tae [NA], straight vessels into which the efferent arteriole of the juxtamedullary glomeruli divides; they arise at the bases of the pyramids, run through the renal medulla toward the apex of each pyramid, then reverse direction back toward the base of the pyramid.

arterio'lar. Of or pertaining to an arteriole or the arterioles collectively.

arteriole (ar-tēr'ĭ-ōl). Arteriola.

afferent glomerular a., a branch of an interlobular artery of the kidney that conveys blood to the glomerulus.

capillary a., a minute artery that terminates in a capillary.

efferent glomerular a., the vessel that carries blood from the glomerular capillary network to the capillary bed of the proximal convoluted tubule.

arteriolith (ar-tēr'ĭ-o-lith) [L. *arteria,* artery, + G. *lithos,* a stone]. A calcareous deposit in an arterial wall or thrombus.

arteriolitis (ar-tēr'ĭ-o-li'tis) [L. *arteriola,* arteriole, + G. *-itis,* inflammation]. Inflammation of the wall of arterioles.

arteriolo- [L. *arteriola,* arteriole]. Combining form relating to arterioles.

arteriolonecrosis (ar-tērĭ-o'lo-nĕ-kro'sis) [L. *arteriola,* arteriole, + G. *nekrōsis,* a killing]. Necrosis in the media of arterioles.

arteriolonephrosclerosis (ar-tēr'ĭ-o'lo-nef'ro-sklē-ro'sis). Arterial *nephrosclerosis.*

arteriolosclerosis (ar-tērĭ-o'lo-sklē-ro'sis). Arteriolar sclerosis; arteriosclerosis affecting mainly the arterioles.

arteriomo'tor. Causing changes in the caliber of an artery; vasomotor with special reference to the arteries.

arteriomy'omato'sis [arterio- + G. *mys,* muscle, + *-oma,* tumor, + *-osis,* condition]. Thickening of the walls of an artery by an overgrowth of muscular fibers arranged irregularly, intersecting each other without any definite relation to the axis of the vessel.

arterionephrosclerosis (ar-tēr'ĭ-o-nef'ro-sklē-ro'sis). Arterial *nephrosclerosis.*

arteriop'athy [arterio- + G. *pathos,* suffering]. Any disease of the arteries.

hypertensive a., arterial degeneration resulting from hypertension.

arterioplasty (ar-tēr'ĭ-o -plas-tĭ) [arterio- + G. *plassō,* to form]. Surgical reconstruction of the wall of an artery.

arteriopressor (ar-tēr'ĭ-o-pres'sor) Causing increased arterial blood pressure.

arteriorrhaphy (ar-tēr'ĭ-or'ă-fĭ) [arterio- + G. *rhaphē,* seam]. Suture of an artery.

arteriorrhexis (ar-tēr'ĭ-o-rek'sis) [arterio- + G. *rhēxis,* rupture]. Rupture of an artery.

arteriosclerosis (ar-tēr'ĭ-o-sklē-ro'sis) [arterio- + G. *sklērōsis,* hardness]. Arterial or vascular sclerosis; hardening of the arteries; types generally recognized are: atherosclerosis, Mönckeberg's a., hypertensive a., and arteriolosclerosis.

hypertensive a., progressive increase in muscle and elastic tissue of arterial walls, resulting from hypertension.

Mönckeberg's a., Mönckeberg's sclerosis or calcification; arterial sclerosis involving the peripheral arteries, especially of the legs of older people, with deposition of calcium in the medial coat.

a. oblit′erans, a. producing narrowing and occlusion of the arterial lumen.

senile a., a. as a result of advanced age.

arteriosclerotic (ar-tēr′ĭ-o-sklĕ-rot′ik). Relating to or affected by arteriosclerosis.

arteriospasm (ar-tēr′ĭ-o-spazm). Spasm of one or more arteries.

arteriostenosis (ar-tēr′ĭo-sten-o′sis) [arterio- + G. *stenōsis,* a narrowing]. Narrowing of the caliber of an artery, either temporary, through vasoconstriction, or permanent, through arteriosclerosis.

arteriot′omy [arterio- + G. *tomē,* incision]. Surgical incision into the lumen of an artery.

arteriot′ony [arterio- + G. *tonos,* tension]. Blood *pressure.*

arteriovenous (AV) (ar-tēr′ĭ-o -ve′nus). Relating to both an artery and a vein or to both arteries and veins in general; both arterial and venous.

arteritis (ar-ter-i′tis) [L. *arteria,* artery, + G. *-itis,* inflammation]. Inflammation involving an artery.

cranial a., giant cell a., temporal a.

a. oblit′erans, obliterating a., *endarteritis* obliterans.

rheumatic a., a. due to rheumatic fever; Aschoff bodies are frequently found in the adventitia of small arteries, especially in the myocardium, and may lead to fibrosis and constriction of lumens.

temporal a., cranial or giant cell a.; panarteritis with medial necrosis and multinucleated giant cells in temporal, retinal, or intracerebral arteries; occurs in elderly persons and may be manifested by constitutional symptoms, severe bitemporal headache, and ocular symptoms including sudden loss of vision in one eye.

artery (ar′ter-ĭ) [L. *arteria,* fr. G. *artēria*]. Arteria.

accessory obturator a., *arteria* obturatoria accessoria.

acromiothoracic a., *arteria* thoracoacromialis.

alveolar a.'s, see *arteria* alveolaris inferior and superior.

angular a., (1) *arteria* angularis; (2) *arteria* gyri angularis.

appendicular a., *arteria* appendicularis.

arcuate a., *arteria* arcuata. **arcuate a.'s of kidney,** *arteriae* arcuatae renis.

ascending a., *arteria* ascendens. **ascending pharyngeal a.,** *arteria* pharyngea ascendens.

atrial a.'s, *arteriae* atriales.

auricular a., *arteria* auricularis.

axillary a., *arteria* axillaris.

basilar a., *arteria* basilaris.

brachial a., see *arteria* brachialis, profunda brachii, and brachialis superficialis.

buccal a., *arteria* buccalis.

a. of bulb of penis, *arteria* bulbi penis. **a. of bulb of vestibule,** *arteria* bulbi vestibuli.

carotid a., *arteria* carotis.

caudal pancreatic a., *arteria* caudae pancreatis.

cavernous a.'s, a number of small branches of internal carotid a. that supply trigeminal ganglion and walls of cavernous and petrosal sinuses.

celiac a., *truncus* celiacus.

central a. of retina, *arteria* centralis retinae.

cerebellar a., *arteria* cerebelli inferior and superior.

cerebral a., *arteria* cerebri.

cervical a.'s, see *arteria* cervicalis; *anteria* transverse colli.

choroidal a., *arteria* choroidea.

ciliary a.'s, see *arteria* ciliaris anterior and posterior.

circumflex a.'s, see *arteria* circumflexia femoris, humeri, ilium, and scapulae.

a.'s of clitoris, see *arteria* dorsalis clitoris; *arteria* profunda clitoris.

colic a., *arteria* colica.

collateral a., (1) one that runs parallel with a nerve or other structure; (2) one through which a collateral circulation is established. See *arteria* collateralis media, radialis, and ulnaris.

communicating a., one that connects two larger a.'s. See *arteria* communicans.

companion a. to sciatic nerve, *arteria* comitans nervi ischiadici.

conjunctival a., *arteria* conjunctivalis.

coronary a., see *arteria* coronaria.

cortical a.'s, branches of the anterior, middle and posterior cerebral a.'s that supply the cerebral cortex.

costocervical a., *truncus* costocervicalis.

cremasteric a., *arteria* cremasterica.

cystic a., *arteria* cystica.

deep a. of clitoris, *arteria* profunda clitoridis. **deep a. of penis,** *arteria* profunda penis. **deep a. of thigh,** *arteria* profunda femoris. **deep a. of tongue,** *arteria* profunda linguae.

digital a.'s, see *arteria* digitalis dorsalis, palmaris, and plantaris.

dorsal a. of clitoris, *arteria* dorsalis clitoridis. **dorsal a. of foot,** *arteria* dorsalis pedis. **dorsal a. of nose,** *arteria* dorsalis nasi. **dorsal a. of the penis,** *arteria* dorsalis penis.

a. of ductus deferens, *arteria* ductus deferentis.

end a., terminal a.; an a. with insufficient anastomoses to maintain viability of the tissue supplied if occlusion of the a. occurs.

epigastric a., *arteria* epigastrica.

episcleral a., *arteria* episcleralis.

ethmoidal a., *arteria* ethmoidalis.

facial a., *arteria* facialis.

femoral a., *arteria* femoralis.

fibular a., *arteria* peronea.

frontal a., *arteria* supratrochlearis.

gastric a.'s, see *arteriae* gastricae breves; *arteria* dextra and sinistra.

gastroduodenal a., *arteria* gastroduodenalis.

gastroomental a.'s, gastroepiploic a.'s, *arteria* gastroomentalis.

genicular a.'s, see *arteria* genus descendens, inferior, media, and superior.

gluteal a., *arteria* glutea.

helicine a., *arteria* helicina.

hepatic a., *arteria* hepatica.

hyaloid a., *arteria* hyaloidea.

hypogastric a., *arteria* iliaca, internal.

ileal a.'s, *arteriae* ilei.

ileocolic a., *arteria* ileocolica.

iliac a., *arteria* iliaca.

iliolumbar a., *arteria* iliolumbalis.

infraorbital a., *arteria* infraorbitalis.

innominate a., *truncus* brachiocephalicus.

intercostal a., *arteria* intercostalis.

interlobar a.'s, *arteriae* interlobares.

interlobular a.'s, *arteriae* interlobulares.

internal auditory a., *arteria* labyrinthi.

interosseous a., *arteria* interossea .

intestinal a.'s, see *arteriae* ilei; *arteriae* jejunales.

jejunal a.'s, *arteriae* jejunales.

a.'s of kidney, *arteriae* renis.

a.'s of knee, see *arteria* genus entries.

labial a., *arteria* labialis.

a. of labyrinth, *arteria* labyrinthi.

lacrimal a., *arteria* lacrimalis.

laryngeal a., *arteria* laryngae.

lingual a., *arteria* lingualis.

lumbar a.'s, see *arteria* lumbalis and lumbalis ima.

macular a.'s, see *arteriolae* maculares inferior and superior.

malleolar a., *arteria* malleolaris anterior.

mammary a.'s, *arteria* thoracica.

masseteric a., *arteria* masseterica.

maxillary a., see *arteria* facialis maxillaris.

median a., *arteria* mediana.

medullary a.'s of brain, branches of the cortical a.'s which penetrate to and supply the white matter of the cerebrum.

meningeal a., *arteria* meningea.

mental a., *arteria* mentalis.

mesenteric a., *arteria* mesenterica.

metacarpal a., *arteria* metacarpea.

metatarsal a., *arteria* metatarsia.

musculophrenic a., *arteria* musculophrenica.

a.'s of nose, see *arteria* dorsalis nasi; *arteria* nasalis posterior septi; *arteriae* nasales posteriores.

nutrient a., *arteria* nutricia.

obturator a., *arteria* obturatoria.

occipital a., see *arteria* occipitalis, occipitalis lateralis and medialis.

ophthalmic a., *arteria* ophthalmica.

ovarian a., *arteria* ovarica.

palatine a., *arteria* palatina.

palpebral a.'s, *arteriae* palpebrales.

pancreatic a., *arteria* pancreatica.

pancreaticoduodenal a., *arteria* pancreaticoduodenalis.

a.'s of penis, see *arteria* dorsalis penis; *arteria* profunda penis.

perforating a.'s, *arteriae* perforantes.

pericardiacophrenic a., *arteria* pericardiacophrenica.

perineal a., *arteria* perinealis.

peroneal a., *arteria* peronea.

phrenic a., *arteria* phrenica.

plantar a., *arteria* plantaris.

popliteal a., *arteria* poplitea.

principal a. of thumb, *arteria* princeps pollicis.

a. of pterygoid canal, *arteria* canalis pterygoidei.

pudendal a.'s, see *arteria* pudenda interna; *arteriae* pudendae externae.

pulmonary a., *truncus* pulmonalis. See also *arteria* pulmonalis.

radial a., *arteria* radialis. radial index a., *arteria* radialis indicis.

ranine a., *arteria* profunda linguae.

rectal a., *arteria* rectalis.

recurrent a.'s, see *arteria* recurrens radialis, tibialis anterior and posterior, ulnaris.

renal a., *arteria* renalis.

a. of round ligament of uterus, *arteria* ligamenti teretis uteri.

sacral a., *arteria* sacralis.

sigmoid a.'s, *arteriae* sigmoideae.

spermatic a.'s, see *arteria* cremasterica and testicularis.

sphenopalatine a., *arteria* sphenopalatina.

spinal a., *arteria* spinalis.

splenic a., *arteria* lienalis.

stylomastoid a., *arteria* stylomastoidea.

subclavian a., *arteria* subclavia.

subcostal a., *arteria* subcostalis.

sublingual a., *arteria* sublingualis.

submental a., *arteria* submentalis.

subscapular a., *arteria* subscapularis.

supraorbital a., *arteria* supraorbitalis.

suprarenal a., *arteria* suprarenalis.

suprascapular a., *arteria* suprascapularis.

supratrochlear a., *arteria* supratrochlearis.

sural a., *arteria* suralis.

tarsal a., *arteria* tarsea.

temporal a., *arteria* temporalis.

terminal a., end a.

testicular a., *arteria* testicularis.

thoracic a., *arteria* thoracica.

thoracoacromial a., *arteria* thoracoacromialis.

thoracodorsal a., *arteria* thoracodorsalis.

thyroid a., *arteria* thyroidea.

tibial a., *arteria* tibialis.

transverse cervical a., *arteria* transversa colli.

transverse facial a., *arteria* transversa faciei. transverse a. of neck, *arteria* transversa colli. transverse scapular a., *arteria* suprascapularis.

tympanic a., *arteria* tympanica.

ulnar a., *arteria* ulnaris.

umbilical a., *arteria* umbilicalis.

urethral a., *arteria* urethralis.

uterine a., *arteria* uterina.

vaginal a., *arteria* vaginalis.

ventricular a.'s, *artriae* ventriculares.

vertebral a., *arteria* vertebralis.

vesical a., *arteria* vesicalis.

zygomatico-orbital a., *arteria* zygomaticoorbitalis.

arthr-. See arthro-.

arthralgia (ar-thral′jĭ-ah) [G. *arthron*, joint, + *algos*, pain]. Arthrodynia; severe pain in a joint, especially one not inflammatory in character.

arthral′gic. Arthrodynic; relating to or affected with arthralgia.

arthrec′tomy [G. *arthron*, joint, + *ektomē*, excision]. Exsection of a joint.

arthrit′ic. Relating to arthritis.

arthritide (ar′thrĭ-tēd) [Fr.]. A skin eruption of assumed gouty or rheumatic origin.

arthritis, pl. **arthritides** (ar-thri′tis, ar-thrit′ĭ-dēz) [G. fr. *arthron*, joint, + *-itis*, inflammation]. Articular rheumatism; inflammation of one or more joints.

   atrophic a., a. without new bone formation, usually rheumatoid.

   chronic absorptive a., a. accompanied by pronounced resorption of bone with shortening and deformity, especially of the hands; when extreme, also termed a. mutilans.

   a. defor′mans, rheumatoid a.

   gouty a., inflammation of the joints (especially of the great toe) in gout.

   hypertrophic a., osteoarthritis.

   juvenile rheumatoid a., Still's disease; polyarticular joint disease associated with lymph node and splenic enlargement, occurring in infants and young children.

   Lyme a., the arthritic manifestation of Lyme disease.

   a. mu′tilans, rheumatoid a. in which osteoporosis occurs with destruction of the joint cartilages and pronounced deformities, chiefly of the hands and feet.

   psoriatic a., the concurrence of psoriasis and a., resembling rheumatoid a. but thought to be a specific disease entity.

   rheumatoid a., a. deformans; rheumatoid disease; a chronic and progressive systemic disease, especially common in women, affecting connective tissue; a. is the dominant clinical manifestation, accompanied by thickening of articular soft tissue, with extension of synovial tissue over articular cartilages, which become eroded, leading to deformities and disability.

   suppurative a., pyarthrosis; purulent synovitis; acute inflammation of synovial membranes, with purulent effusion into a joint, due to bacterial infection.

arthro-, arthr- [G. *arthron*, joint]. Combining forms denoting a joint or articulation.

arthrocele (ar′thro-sēl) [arthro- + G. *kēlē*, hernia, tumor]. **1.** Hernia of the synovial membrane through the capsule of a joint. **2.** Any swelling of a joint.

arthrocentesis (ar′thro-sen-te′sis) [arthro- + G. *kentēsis*, puncture]. Aspiration into a joint; withdrawel of fluid through a puncture needle.

arthrochondritis (ar′thro-kon-dri′tis) [arthro- + G. *chondros*, cartilage, + *-itis*, inflammation]. Inflammation of an articular cartilage.

arthrocla′sia [arthro- + G. *klasis*, a breaking]. Forcible breaking up of the adhesions in ankylosis.

arthrod′esis [arthro- + G. *desis*, a binding together]. Artificial ankylosis; syndesis; surgical stiffening of a joint.

arthro′dia [G. *arthrōdia*, a gliding joint, fr. *arthron*, joint, + *eidos*, form]. *Articulatio* plana.

arthro′dial. Relating to arthrodia.

arthrodynia (ar-thro-din′ĭ-ah) [arthro- + G. *odynē*, pain]. Arthralgia.

arthrodyn′ic. Arthralgic.

arthrodysplasia (ar′thro-dis-pla′zĭ-ah) [arthro- + G. *dys*, bad, + *plasis*, a molding]. Abnormal joint development.

ar′throendos′copy. Arthroscopy.

ar′throgram. An x-ray of a joint; usually infers the introduction of a contrast agent into the joint capsule.

arthrography (ar-throg′rā-fĭ) [arthro- + G. *graphō*, to describe]. Radiography of a joint.

arthrogryposis (ar′thro-grĭ-po′sis) [arthro- + G. *gryphōsis*, a crooking]. A congenital defect of the limbs characterized by contractures, flexion, and extension.

   a. mul′tiplex congen′ita, amyoplasia congenita; limitation of range of joint motion and contractures present at birth, usually involving multiple joints.

ar′throlith [arthro- + G. *lithos*, stone]. A loose body in a joint.

arthrol′ysis [arthro- + G. *lysis*, a loosening]. Restoration of mobility in stiff and ankylosed joints.

arthrom′eter. Goniometer (2).

arthrom′etry [arthro- + G. *metron*, measure]. Measurement of the range of movement in a joint.

arthro-ophthalmopathy (ar′thro-of′thal -mop′ă-thǐ) [arthro- + ophthalmo- + G. *pathos*, suffering]. Disease affecting joints and eyes.

   hereditary progressive a., Stickler syndrome; progressive myopia and abnormal epiphysial development in the vertebrae and long bones, inherited as an autosomal dominant trait.

arthrop′athy [arthro- + G. *pathos*, suffering]. Disease affecting a joint.

   neuropathic a., neuropathic *joint*.

   tabetic a., Charcot's joint; a neuropathic joint commonly associated with tabes dorsalis or diabetic neuropathy.

arthrophyma (ar-thro-fi′mah) [arthro- + G. *phyma*, swelling, tumor]. An articular tumor or swelling.

ar'throplasty [arthro- + G. *plassō*, to form]. **1.** Creation of an artificial joint. **2.** Surgical restoration of the integrity and functional power of a joint.

ar'thropod [arthro- + G. *pous*, foot]. A member of the phylum Arthropoda.

Arthrop'oda [arthro- + G. *pous*, foot]. A phylum of the Metazoa that includes the classes Crustacea (crabs, shrimps, crayfish, lobsters), Insecta, Arachnida (spiders, scorpions, mites, ticks), Chilopoda (centipedes), Diplopoda (millipedes), Merostomata (horseshoe crabs), and various other groups.

arthropyosis (ar'thro-pi-o'sis) [arthro- + G. *pyōsis*, suppuration]. Suppuration in a joint.

arthrosclerosis (ar'thro-skle-ro'sis) [arthro- + G. *sklērōsis*, hardening]. Stiffness of the joints.

ar'throscope. An endoscope for examining joint interiors.

arthros'copy [arthro- + G. *skopeō*, to view]. Arthroendoscopy; endoscopic examination of the interior of a joint.

arthro'sis. 1 [G. *arthrōsis*, a jointing]. A joint. **2** [arthro- +G. *-osis*, condition]. A trophic degenerative affection of a joint.

arthros'tomy [arthro- + G. *stoma*, mouth]. Establishment of a temporary opening into a joint cavity.

arthrosynovitis (ar'thro-sin-o-vi'tis). Inflammation of the synovial membrane of a joint.

arthrot'omy [arthro- + G. *tomē*, a cutting]. Synosteotomy; cutting into a joint.

arthroxesis (ar-throk'se-sis) [arthro- + G. *xesis*, a scraping]. Removal of diseased tissue from a joint by scraping.

artic'ular. Relating to a joint.

articulate [L. *articulo*, pp. *-atus*, to articulate]. (ar-tik'u-lit). **1.** Articulated. **2.** Capable of speaking distinctly and connectedly. (ar-tik'u-lāt). **3.** To join or connect together loosely to allow motion between the parts. **4.** To speak distinctly and connectedly.

artic'ulated. Articulate (1); jointed.

articula'tio, pl. **articulationes** (ar-tik -u-la'shĭ-o, -la-shĭ-o'nēz) [L. a forming of vines]. Articulation (1); joint; in anatomy, the place of union, usually movable, between two or more bones. Joints are classified into three general morphological types: cartilaginous, fibrous, and synovial.

a. bicondyla'ris [NA], bicondylar joint; a joint in which two rounded surfaces of one bone articulate with shallow depressions on another bone.

articulatio'nes carpometacar'peae [NA], carpometacarpal joints; joints between the carpal and metacarpal bones.

a. cartilag'inis [NA], cartilaginous joint; movable joint (2); synarthrodial joint (2); amphiarthrosis; a joint in which the apposed bony surfaces are united by cartilage, either a synchondrosis or a symphysis.

a. compos'ita [NA], compound joint; a joint composed of three or more skeletal elements.

a. cox'ae [NA], hip joint; the ball-and-socket joint between the head of the femur and the acetabulum.

a. cu'biti [NA], cubital or elbow joint; a compound hinge joint between the humerus and the bones of the forearm.

a. ellipsoi'dea [NA], ellipsoidal or condylar joint; a modified biaxial ball-and-socket joint in which the joint surfaces are elongated or ellipsoidal.

a. fibro'sa [NA], synarthrodia; fibrous joint; synarthrodial joint (1); immovable joint; a union of two bones by fibrous tissue such that there is no joint cavity and little motion possible; types of fibrous joints are sutura, syndesmosis, and gomphosis.

a. ge'nus [NA], knee joint; a compound condylar joint consisting of the joint between the condyles of the femur and the condyles of the tibia, and the articulation between femur and patella.

a. hu'meri [NA], shoulder joint; a ball-and-socket joint between the head of the humerus and the glenoid cavity of the scapula.

articulatio'nes intercar'peae [NA], intercarpal or carpal joints; joints between the carpal bones.

articulatio'nes intermetacar'peae [NA], intermetacarpal joints; joints between the bases of the second, third, fourth, and fifth metacarpal bones.

articulatio'nes intermetatar'seae [NA], intermetatarsal joints; joints between the bases of the five metatarsal bones.

articulatio'nes interphalan'geae [NA], interphalangeal, digital, or phalangeal joints; hinge joints between the phalanges of the fingers or toes.

articulatio'nes intertar'seae [NA], intertarsal or tarsal joints; joints that unite the tarsal bones.

articulatio'nes ma'nus [NA], joints of the hand: radiocarpal, intercarpal, carpometacarpal, intermetacarpal, metacarpophalangeal, and interphalangeal joints.

articulatio'nes metacarpophalan'geae [NA], metacarpophalangeal joints; spheroid joints between the heads of the metacarpals and the bases of the proximal phalanges.

articulationes metatarsophalan'geae [NA], metatarsophalangeal joints; spheroid joints between the heads of the metatarsals and the bases of the proximal phalanges of the toes.

articulatio'nes pe'dis [NA], joints of the foot: talocrural, intertarsal, tarsometatarsal, intermetatarsal, metatarsophalangeal, and interphalangeal joints.

a. pla'na [NA], plane, arthroidial, or gliding joint; arthrodia; a synovial joint in which the opposing surfaces are nearly planes and in which there is only a slight, gliding motion.

a. radiocar'pea [NA], radiocarpal or wrist joint; the joint between the distal end of the radius and its articular disk and the proximal row of carpal bones, except the pisiform bone.

a. sellar'is [NA], saddle joint; a biaxial joint in which the double motion is effected by the opposition of two surfaces, each of which is concave in one direction and convex in the other; as in the carpometacarpal articulation of the thumb.

a. sim'plex [NA], simple joint; a joint composed of two bones only.

a. spheroi'dea [NA], spheroid, cotyloid, enarthrodial, or ball-and-socket joint; enarthrosis; a multiaxial joint in which a sphere on the head of one bone fits into a rounded cavity in the other bone, as in the hip joint.

a. synovia'lis [NA], diarthrodial or synovial joint; movable joint (1); diarthrosis; a joint in which the opposing bony surfaces are covered with a layer of hyaline cartilage or fibrocartilage; some degree of free movement is possible.

a. tal'ocalca'neonavicula'ris [NA], talocalcaneonavicular joint; a ball-and-socket joint, part of the transverse tarsal joint, formed by the head of the talus articulating with the navicular bone and the anterior part of the calcaneus.

a. talocrural'is [NA], ankle or mortise joint; a hinge joint between the tibia and fibula above and the talus below.

a. tar'si transver'sa [NA], transverse tarsal joint; Chopart's joint; the joint between the talus and calcaneus posteriorly and the navicular and cuboid bones anteriorly.

articulatio'nes tarsometatar'seae [NA], tarsometatarsal joints; Lisfranc's joints; the three joints between the tarsal and metatarsal bones: a medial joint between the first cuneiform and first metatarsal, an intermediate joint between the second and third cuneiforms and corresponding metatarsals, and a lateral joint between the cuboid and fourth and fifth metatarsals.

a. temporomandibula'ris [NA], temporomandibular or mandibular joint; the joint between the head of the mandible and the mandibular fossa and articular tubercle of the temporal bone.

a. trochoid'ea [NA], trochoid, rotary, or pivot joint; a joint in which a section of a cylinder of one bone fits into a corresponding cavity on the other, as in the proximal radioulnar articulation.

articula'tion [L. *articulatio, q.v.*]. **1.** Articulatio. **2.** A joining or connecting together loosely so as to allow motion between the parts. **3.** Distinct connected speech or enunciation. **4.** In dentistry, the contact relationship of the occlusal surfaces of the teeth during jaw movement. **5.** Placement of artificial teeth on a denture base so that the teeth approximate normal position and contact.

artic'ulator. In dentistry, a mechanical device which represents the temporomandibular joints and jaw members to which maxillary and mandibular casts may be attached.

ar'tifact [L. *ars,* art, + *facio,* pp. *factus,* to make]. Artefact. **1.** Anything, especially in a histologic specimen or a graphic record, caused by the technique used and not a natural occurrence, but merely incidental. **2.** A skin lesion produced or perpetuated by self-inflicted action.

artifactitious (a,'ti-fak-tish'us). Produced by an artifact.

aryl (ăr'il). An organic radical derived from an aromatic compound by removing a hydrogen atom.

arytenoid (ăr-ĭ-te'noyd) [G. *arytainoeides,* ladleshaped]. Denoting a cartilage (cartilago arytenoidea) and a muscle (musculus arytenoideus) of the larynx.

arytenoidectomy (ăr'ĭ-te-noy-dek'to-mĭ) [arytenoid + G. *ektomē,* excision]. Excision of an arytenoid cartilage.

arytenoiditis (ă-rit'ĕ-noy-di'tis). Inflammation of an arytenoid cartilage.

ar'ytenoi'dopex'y [arytenoid + G. *pēxis,* fixation]. Surgical fixation of cartilages or muscles of arytenoids.

As Arsenic.

asbes'tos [G. unquenchable]. A fibrous natural material, composed of calcium and magnesium silicates, used for thermal insulation and fireproofing.

asbesto'sis. Pneumoconiosis due to inhalation of asbestos particles; sometimes complicated by pleural mesothelioma or bronchial carcinoma.

ASC Alterered state of consciousness.

ascariasis (as'kă-ri'ă-sis) [G. *askaris,* an intestinal worm, + *-iasis,* condition]. Disease caused by infection with *Ascaris* or related ascarid nematodes.

ascaricide (as-kăr'ĭ-sid) [ascarid + L. *caedo,* to kill]. Causing the death of ascarid nematodes.

as'carid. 1. Any nematode of the family Ascarididae. **2.** Pertaining to such nematodes.

Ascarididae (as-kă-rid'ĭ-de) [G. *askaris,* an intestinal worm]. A family of large intestinal roundworms (superfamily Ascaridoidea) that includes the genus *Ascaris.*

Ascaris (as'kă-ris) [G. *askaris,* an intestinal worm]. A genus of large roundworms parasitic in the small intestine of man and many other vertebrates.

A. lumbricoi'des, one of the commonest human parasites causing symptoms such as restlessness, fever, and sometimes diarrhea; the similar species, *A. suum* (or *A. lumbricoides suum*) is common in swine.

Aschelminthes (ask-hel-min'thēz). Nemathelminthes; a phylum of the Metazoa, including the class Nematoda and other roundworms, that are nonsegmented, bilaterally symmetric, and cylindric or filiform, with a pseudocele body cavity and rounded or pointed ends.

ascites (ă-si'tēz) [L. fr. G. *askos,* a bag, + *-ites, q.v.*]. Hydroperitoneum; accumulation of serous fluid in the peritoneal cavity.

chylous a., chyloperitoneum; presence in the peritoneal cavity of a milky fluid containing suspended fat.

hemorrhagic a., bloody or blood-stained serous fluid in the peritoneal cavity.

ascitic (ă-sit′ik). Relating to ascites.

Ascomycetes (as′ko-mi-se′tēz) [G. *askos*, a bag, + *mykēs*, mushroom]. A class of fungi characterized by the presence of asci and ascospores, and two distinct reproductive phases (sexual or perfect stage and asexual or imperfect stage).

ascor′bate. A salt or ester of ascorbic acid.

ascor′bic acid. Vitamin C; 2,3-didehydro-L-*threo*-hexono-1,4-lactone; the antiscorbutic vitamin, specifically preventing scurvy; a strong reducing agent, also used as an antioxidant in foodstuffs.

-ase. Termination denoting an enzyme suffixed to the name of the substance (substrate) upon which the enzyme acts; enzymes named before the convention was established generally have an *-in* ending.

asema′sia [G. *a*- priv. + *sēmasia*, the giving of a signal]. Asymbolia (2).

ase′mia [G. *a*-priv. + *sēma*, sign]. Asymbolia (2).

asepsis (ă-sep′sis) [G. *a*-priv. + *sēpsis*, putrefaction]. A condition in which living pathogenic organisms are absent; a state of sterility.

asep′tic. Marked by or relating to asepsis.

asex′ual. 1. Without sex, as in a. reproduction. **2.** Having no sexual desire or interest.

asi′alism, asia′lia [G. *a*- priv. + *sialon*, saliva]. Aptyalism; aptyalia; diminished or arrested secretion of saliva.

Asn Asparagine, or its mono- or diradical.

asocial (a-so′shul). Not social; indifferent to social rules or customs; withdrawn from society.

Asp Aspartic acid or its radical forms.

aspar′aginase. 1. An enzyme catlyzing the hydrolysis of asparagine to aspartic acid and ammonia. **2.** The enzyme from *Escherichia coli,* used in the treatment of acute leukemia and other neoplastic diseases.

asparagine (Asn) (as-par′ă-jin). αAmino-β-succinamic acid; $NH_2COCH_2CH(NH_2)COOH$; the β-amide of aspartic acid, a nonessential amino acid occurring in proteins.

aspar′tase. *Aspartate* ammonia-lyase.

aspar′tate. A salt or ester of aspartic acid.

    a. aminotransferase (AST), glutamic-oxaloacetic transaminase; an enzyme catalyzing transfer of an amine group from glutamic acid to oxaloacetic acid, forming αketoglutaric acid and aspartic acid, or vice versa.

    a. ammonia-lyase, aspartase; an enzyme catalyzing the conversion of aspartic acid to fumaric acid, splitting out ammonia.

aspar′tic acid (Asp). αAminosuccinic acid; $HOOC–CH_2–CH(NH_2)–COOH$; one of the amino acids occurring in proteins.

as′pect [L. *aspectus*]. **1.** Appearance; looks. **2.** The side of an object that is directed in any designated direction.

aspergilloma (as′per-jil-o′mah). **1.** An infectious granuloma caused by *Aspergillus.* **2.** A variety of bronchopulmonary aspergillosis; a ball-like mass of *Aspergillis fumigatus* colonizing an existing cavity in the lung.

aspergillosis (as-per-jil-o′sis).p Presence of any species of *Aspergillus* in the tissues or on a mucous surface and the symptoms produced thereby.

Aspergillus (as-per-jil′us) [Mediev L. a sprinkler]. A genus of fungi (class Ascomycetes) that contains many species, a number of them with black, brown, or green spores. Few species are pathogenic; *e.g., A. fumigatus,* a species that yields the antibiotics fumigacin and fumigatin, and is the common cause of aspergillosis.

aspermatism, aspermia (a-sper′mă-tizm, -mĭ-ah) [G. *a*- priv. + *sperma,* seed]. Lack of secretion or of expulsion of semen following ejaculation.

asphyx′ia′tion. The production of, or the state of, asphyxia.

asphyxia (as-fik′sĭ-ah) [G. *a*- priv. + *sphyzō,* to throb]. Imparied or absent exchange of oxygen and carbon dioxide on a ventilatory basis; combined hypercapnia and hypoxia or anoxia.

    a. liv′ida, a. neonatorum in which the skin is cyanotic, but the heart is strong and the reflexes are preserved.

    local a., stagnation of the circulation, sometimes resulting in local gangrene especially of the fingers.

    a. neonato′rum, a. occurring in the newborn.

    traumatic a., extravasation of blood into the skin and conjunctivae, produced by a sudden mechanical increase in venous pressure; common in those who have been hanged and seen occasionally in crush injuries.

asphyx′ial. Relating to asphyxia.

asphyx′iate. To induce asphyxia.

aspirate (as′pĭ-rāt) [L. *a-spiro,* pp. *-atus,* to breathe on, give the H sound]. **1.** A sound having the breathing character of the letter *h.* **2.** To take in or remove by aspiration. **3.** The substance removed by aspiration.

aspira′tion. 1. Removal, by suction, of a gas or fluid. **2.** Inspiratory sucking into the airways of fluid or foreign body, as of vomitus. **3.** Surgical technique for cataract, requiring a small corneal incision, severance of the lens capsule, fragmentation of the lens material, and aspiration with a needle.

as′pirator. An apparatus for removing fluid by aspiration from any of the body cavities; consists usually of a hollow needle or trocar and cannula, connected by tubing with a container vacuumized by a syringe or reversed air (suction) pump.

as′pirin. Acetylsalicylic acid; $C_6H_4(OCOCH_3)\text{-}COOH$; a widely used analgesic, antipyretic, and anti-inflammatory agent.

asple′nia. Absence of the spleen.

asplen′ic. Having no spleen.

assassin bug [Fr., fr. It. *assassino,* fr. Ar. *hashshāshin,* those addicted to hashish]. Insect of the family Reduviidae (order Hemiptera) that inflicts irritating, painful bites in animals and man; vectors of American trypanosomiasis.

assay (as'sā, ă-sā'). **1.** Analysis; test of purity; trial. **2.** To examine; to subject to analysis.

biologic a., bioassay.

competitive binding a., general term for an a. in which a binder competes for labeled versus unlabeled ligand (analyte).

complement binding a., a test for the detection of immune complexes.

enzyme-linked immunosorbent a. (ELISA), an *in vitro* competitive binding a. in which an enzyme and its substrate serve as the indicator system rather than a radioactive substance; in positive tests, the two yield a colored or other easily recognizable substance.

immunochemical a., immunoassay.

assimila'tion [L. *as-simile,* pp. *-atus,* to make alike]. **1.** Incorporation of digested materials from food into the tissues of the organism. **2.** Amalgamation and modification of newly perceived information and experiences into the existing cognitive structure.

association (ă-so'sĭ-a'shun) [L. *as-socio,* pp. *-sociatus,* to join to]. **1.** Union; connection of persons, things, or ideas by some common factor. **2.** A functional connection of two ideas, events, or psychological phenomena that is established through learning or experience.

clang a., psychic a.'s resulting from sounds; often encountered in the manic phase of manic-depressive psychosis.

free a., an investigative psychoanalytic technique in which the patient verbalizes, without reservation or censor, the passing contents of his mind; the verbalized conflicts that emerge constitute resistances that are the basis of the psychoanalyst's interpretations.

AST *Aspartate* aminotransferase.

astasia (ă-sta'zĭ-ah) [G. unsteadiness]. Inability, through muscular incoordination, to stand.

asta'sia-aba'sia. Blocq's disease; inability to either stand or walk in the normal manner as a symptom of conversion hysteria.

astat'ic. Pertaining to astasia.

as'tatine [G. *astatos,* unstable]. An artificial radioactive element of the halogen series; symbol At, atomic number 85.

asteatosis (ă-ste-ă-to'sis) [G. *a-* priv. + *stear* (*steat*), fat]. Diminished or arrested action of the sebaceous glands.

as'ter [Mod. L. fr. G. *astēr,* a star]. Astrosphere.

astereognosis (ă-stĕr'e-og-no'sis) [G. *a-* priv. + *stereos,* solid, + *gnōsis,* knowledge]. Inability to judge the form of an object by touch.

aste'rion [G. *asterios,* starry]. Junction of the lambdoid, occipitomastoid and parietomastoid sutures.

asterixis (ă-ster-ik'sis) [G. *a-* priv. + *stērixis,* fixed position]. Flapping tremor; an abnormal tremor consisting of involuntary jerking movements, especially in the hands; commonly called a "liver flap" because of its frequent occurrence in patients with impending hepatic coma, although also seen in other forms of metabolic encephalopathy.

aster'nal [G. *a-* priv. + *sternon,* chest]. **1.** Not related to or connected with the sternum. **2.** Without a sternum.

aster'nia. Congenital absence of a sternum.

asthenia (as-the'nĭ-ah) [G. *astheneia,* weakness]. Weakness or debility.

neurocirculatory a., Da Costa's or effort syndrome; irritable or soldier's heart; a syndrome of functional nervous and circulatory irregularities characterized by increased susceptibility to fatigue, palpitation, dyspnea, rapid pulse, precordial pain, and anxiety; observed especially in soldiers on active duty.

asthen'ic. Relating to asthenia.

asthenocoria (as-the'no-ko'rĭ-ah) [G. *astheneia,* weakness, + *korē,* pupil of the eye]. Slow reaction of the pupil to a light stimulus.

astheno'pia [G. *astheneia,* weakness, + *ōps,* eye]. Eyestrain; subjective symptoms of ocular fatigue, discomfort, lacrimation, and headaches arising from use of the eyes.

accommodative a., a. due to errors of refraction and excessive contraction of the ciliary muscle.

muscular a., a. due to imbalance of the extrinsic ocular muscles.

asthenop'ic. Relating to asthenopia.

asthe'nosper'mia [G. *astheneia,* weakness, + *sperma,* seed, semen]. Loss or reduction of motility of spermatozoa.

asthma (az'mah) [G.]. Originally, a term used to mean "difficult breathing"; now used to denote bronchial a.

bronchial a., a condition of the lungs in which there is widespread narrowing of airways, varying over short periods of time either spontaneously or as a result of treatment, due in varying degrees to contraction (spasm) of smooth muscle, edema of the mucosa, and mucus in the lumen of the bronchi and bronchioles; caused by the local release of spasmogens and vasoactive substances in the course of an allergic process.

cardiac a., the bronchoconstriction being secondary to the pulmonary congestion and edema of left ventricular failure.

asthmatic (az-mat'ik). Relating to or suffering from asthma.

astigmatic (as'tig-mat'ik). Relating to astigmatism.

astigmatism (ă-stig'mă-tizm) [G. *a-* priv. + *stigma* (*stig- mat-*), a point]. Astigmia. **1.** A lens or optical system having different curvatures in different meridians. **2.** A condition of unequal curvatures along the different meridians in one or more of the refractive surfaces of the eye, in consequence of which the rays from a luminous point are not focused at a single point on the retina.

compound hyperopic a., a. in which all meridians are hyperopic but to different degrees.

compound myopic a. (M + Am), a. in which all meridians are myopic but to different degrees.

corneal a., a. due to a defect in the curvature of the corneal surface.

hyperopic a., a. in which one meridian is hyperopic and the one at right angle to it is without a refractive error.

irregular a., a. in which different parts of the same meridian have different degrees of curvature.

lenticular a., a. due to defect in the curvature, position, or index of refraction of the lens.

mixed a., a. in which one meridian is hyperopic while the one at right angle to it is myopic.

myopic a., a. in which one meridian is myopic and the one at right angle to it is without refractive error.

regular a., a. in which the curvature in each meridian is equal throughout its course, and the meridians of greatest and least curvature are at right angles to each other.

astigmatom'eter, astigmom'eter. An instrument for measuring the degree and determining the variety of astigmatism.

astigmatom'etry, astigmom'etry. Determination of the form and measurement of the degree of astigmatism.

astigmat'oscope, astig'moscope. An instrument for detecting and measuring the degree of astigmatism.

astigmatos'copy, astigmos'copy. Use of the astigmatoscope.

astig'mia. Astigmatism.

astomia (ă-sto'mĭ-ah) [G. *a*-priv. + *stoma*, mouth]. Congenital absence of a mouth.

astrag'alar. Relating to the astragalus or talus.

astrag'alec'tomy [astragalus, + G. *ektomē*, excision]. Removal of the astragalus (talus).

astrag'alus [G. *astragalos*, ball of the ankle joint]. Talus.

as'tral. Relating to an astrosphere.

astriction (as-trik'shun). **1.** Astringent action. **2.** Compression for the arrest of hemorrhage.

astringent (as-trin'jent) [L. *astringens*]. Causing contraction of the tissues, arrest of secretion, or control of bleeding.

as'troblast [G. *astron*, star, + *blastos*, germ]. A primitive cell developing into an astrocyte.

as'troblasto'ma. Grade II or grade III astrocytoma; a relatively poorly differentiated glioma composed of young, immature, neoplastic cells of the astrocytic series, frequently arranged radially about small blood vessels.

as'trocyte [G. *astron*, + *kytos*, hollow (cell)]. Astroglia; macroglia; Dieters' cell (2); one of the large neuroglia cells of nervous tissue.

fibrous a., stellate cell with long processes found in the white substance of the brain and spinal cord and characterized by having bundles of fine filaments in its cytoplasm.

protoplasmic a., one form of a., found in gray substance, having few fibrils and numerous branching processes.

astrocyto'ma [G. *astron*, star, + *kytos*, cell, + *-oma*, tumor]. A relatively well differentiated glioma composed of neoplastic cells that resemble one of the types of astrocytes, with varying amounts of fibrillary stroma.

grade I a., solid or cystic a. of high differentiation.

grade II a., grade III a., astroblastoma.

grade IV a., glioblastoma.

astrog'lia [G. *astron*, star, + neuroglia]. Astrocyte.

astrosphere (as'tro-sfēr) [G. *astron*, star, + *sphaira*, ball]. Aster; attraction sphere; a set of radiating fibrils extending outward from the cytocentrum and centrosphere of a dividing cell.

asymbolia (a'sim-bo'lĭ-ah) [G. *a*-priv. + *symbolon*, an outward sign]. **1.** A loss of the ability to appreciate by touch the form and nature of an object. **2.** Asemasia; asemia; a form of aphasia in which the significance of signs is not appreciated.

asymmet'ric. Not symmetrical; denoting a lack of symmetry between two or more like parts.

asym'metry. Want of symmetry; disporportion between two or more like parts.

asymptomat'ic. Without symptoms, or producing no symptoms.

asynclitism (ă-sin'klĭ-tizm) [G. *a*-priv. + *syn-klino*, to incline together]. Obliquity; absence of synclitism or parallelism between the axis of the presenting part of the child and the pelvic planes in childbirth.

anterior a., Nägele *obliquity.*

posterior a., Litzmann *obliquity.*

asyndesis (ă-sin'de-sis) [*a*-priv. + *syn*, together, + *desis*, binding]. A disorder in which separate ideas or thoughts cannot be joined into a coherent concept.

asynechia (a-sĭ-nek'ĭ-ah) [G. *a*-priv. + *synechia*, continuity]. Discontinuity of structure.

asynergia, asynergy (ă-sin-ur'jĭ-ah, ă-sin'ur-je) [G. *a*-priv. + *syn*, with, + *ergon*, work]. Lack of cooperation or working together of parts that normally act in unison.

a'syner'gic. Characterized by asynergia.

asystemat'ic. Not systematic; not relating to one system or set or organs.

asystole (ă-sis'to-le) [G. *a*-priv. + *systolē*, a contracting]. Cardiac standstill; absence of contractions of the heart.

asystol'ic. 1. Relating to asystole. **2.** Not systolic. At Astatine.

atac'tic. Ataxic.

at'avism [L. *atavus*, a remote ancestor]. Appearance in an individual of characteristics presumed to have been present in some remote ancestor; reversion to an earlier biological type.

atavis'tic. Relating to atavism.

ataxia (ă-tak'sĭ-ah) [G. *a*-priv. + *taxis*, order]. Dyssynergia; incoordination; inability to coordinate the muscles in voluntary movement.

Friedreich's a., hereditary spinal a.

hereditary cerebellar a., a disease of later childhood and early adult life, marked by ataxic gait, hesitating and explosive speech, nystagmus, and sometimes optic neuritis.

hereditary spinal a., Friedreich's a.; sclerosis of the posterior and lateral columns of the spinal cord, occurring in children and marked by a. in the lower extremities, extending to the upper, followed by paralysis and contractures; autosomal recessive inheritance.

motor a., inability to perform coordinated muscular movements.

a. telangiecta'sia, a familial single-gene autosomal recessive disease characterized by progressive cerebellar a., with oculocutaneous telangiectases, proneness to pulmonary infections, and immunodeficiency.

ataxiaphasia (ă-tak'sĭ-ă-fa'zĭ-ah) [G. *a-*priv. + *taxis,* order, + *phasis,* an affirmation, speech]. Inability to form connected sentences, although single words may perhaps be used intelligibly.

atax'ic. Atactic; relating to or marked by ataxia.

atax'iophe'mia [G. *a-*priv. + *taxis,* order, + *phēmē,* voice, speech]. Incoordination of the muscles of speech.

-ate. Termination used to denote a salt or ester of an "-ic" acid.

atelectasis (at'e-lek'tă-sis) [G. *atelēs,* incomplete, + *ektasis,* extension]. Absence of gas from a part or the whole of the lungs, due to failure of expansion or resorption of gas from the alveoli.

primary a., anectasis; nonexpansion of the lungs after birth, as in stillborn infants and in liveborn infants who die before respiration is established.

secondary a., pulmonary collapse, particularly of infants, due to hyaline membrane disease or elastic recoil of the lungs while dying from other causes.

atelectat'ic. Relating to atelectasis.

ate'lia. Ateliosis.

ateliosis (ă-te'lĭ-o'sis) [G. *atelēs,* incomplete, + *-osis,* condition]. Atelia; incomplete development of the body or any of its parts, as in infantilism and dwarfism.

ateliot'ic. Marked by ateliosis.

atelo- [G. *atelēs,* incomplete, fr. *a-*priv. + *telos,* end, fulfillment]. Combining form meaning incomplete or imperfect.

athe'lia [G. *a-* priv. + *thēlē,* nipple]. Congenital absence of the nipples.

ather'mic. Apyretic.

athero- [G. *athere,* gruel]. Combinig form relating to the deposit of gruel-like, soft, pasty materials.

atheroembolism (ath'er-o-em'bo-lizm). Cholesterol *embolism.*

atherogenesis (ath'er-o-jen'ĕ-sis). Formation of atheroma, important in the pathogenesis of arteriosclerosis.

atherogen'ic. Initiating, increasing, or accelerating atherogenesis.

athero'ma [G. *athērē,* gruel, + *-ōma,* tumor]. Lipid deposits in the intima of arteries, producing a yellow swelling on the endothelial surface, characteristic of atherosclerosis.

athero'matous. Relating to or affected by atheroma.

atherosclero'sis (ath'er-o-sklĕ-ro'sis). Arteriosclerosis characterized by irregularly distributed lipid deposits in the intima of large and medium-sized arteries; associated with fibrosis and calcification, and present to some degree in the middle-aged and elderly.

ath'etoid. Resembling athetosis.

atheto'sic, athetot'ic. Pertaining to, or marked by, athetosis.

atheto'sis [G. *athetos,* without position or place]. A constant succession of slow, writhing, involuntary movements of flexion, extension, pronation, and supination of the fingers and hands, and sometimes of the toes and feet.

athrepsia, athrepsy (ă-threp'sĭ-ah, ath'rep-sĭ) [G. *a-*priv. + *threpsis,* nourishment]. Marasmus.

athrep'tic. Relating to athrepsia.

athymia (ă-thi'mĭ-ah) [G. *a-* priv. + *thymos,* mind, also thymus]. **1.** Absence of affect or emotivity; morbid impassivity. **2.** Athymism; absence of the thymus gland or its secretion.

athy'mism. Athymia (2).

athy'roidism, athy'rea; athyro'sis. Absence of the thyroid gland or suppression of its secretion.

athyrot'ic. Relating to athyroidism.

atlan'tad. Toward the atlas.

atlan'tal. Relating to the atlas.

atlanto-, atlo- [G. *atlas, q.v.*]. Combining forms relating to the atlas.

atlan'toax'ial. Atloaxoid; pertaining to the atlas and the axis; denoting the joint between the two vertebrae.

at'las [*Atlas,* G. myth. char.] [NA]. First cervical vertebra, articulating with the occipital bone and rotating around the dens of the axis.

atlo-. See atlanto-.

atloax'oid. Atlantoaxial.

atm Standard *atmosphere.*

atmo- [G. *atmos,* vapor]. Prefix denoting steam or vapor, or derived by action of same.

at'mosphere [atmo- + G. *sphaira,* sphere]. **1.** Any gas surrounding a given body; a gaseous medium. **2.** A unit of air pressure, **standard a. (atm),** at mean sea level, equivalent to 1,013,250 dynes/cm² or 101,325 pascals (newtons/m² in SI).

at'om [G. *atomos,* indivisible, uncut]. The ultimate particle of an element, once believed to be as indivisible as its name indicates; now known to be composed of subatomic particles, notably protons, neutrons and electrons, the first two comprising most of the mass of the atomic nucleus.

atom'ic. Relating to an atom.

at'omizer. A device used to reduce liquid medication to a spray or aerosol.

aton'ic. Relaxed; without normal tone or tension.

at'ony, ato'nia [G. *atonia,* languor]. Relaxation, flaccidity, or lack of tone or tension.

at'open. The causative agent of atopy.

atopic (ă-top'ĭk). Relating to or marked by atopy.

atopognosia, atopognosis (ă-top-og-no'zĭ-ah, -no'sis) [G. *a*- priv. + *topos*, place, + *gnōsis*, knowledge]. Inability to locate a sensation properly.

atopy (at'o-pĭ) [G. *atopia*, strangeness, fr. *a*- priv. + *topos*, a place]. Type I allergic reaction, specifically one with strong familial tendencies, caused by allergens such as pollens, foods, dander, insect venoms, and associated with the Prausnitz-Küstner (IgE class) antibody.

atoxic (a-tok'sik). Not toxic.

ATP Adenosine 5'-triphosphate.

ATPase Adenosine triphosphatase.

atresia (ă-tre'zĭ-ah) [G. *a*- priv. + *trēsis*, a hole]. Absence of a normal opening or normally patent lumen.

  anal a., a. a'ni, imperforate anus; proctatresia; congenital absence of an anal opening due to the presence of a membranous septum or to complete absence of the anal canal.

  aortic a., congenital absence of the normal valvular orifice into the aorta.

  biliary a., a. of the major bile ducts, causing cholestasis and jaundice.

  follicular a., a. follic'uli, a normal process affecting the ovarian primordial follicles in which death of the ovum results in cystic degeneration followed by cicatricial closure.

  intestinal a., an obliteration of the lumen of the small intestine involving the ileum, jejunum, or duodenum.

  mitral a., congenital absence of the normal mitral valve orifice.

  pulmonary a., congenital absence of the normal valvular orifice into the pulmonary artery.

  tricuspid a., congenital lack of the tricuspid orifice.

  vaginal a., colpatresia; imperforation or occlusion of the vagina, or adhesion of the walls of the vagina.

atret'ic, atre'sic. Imperforate; relating to atresia.

atreto- [G. *atrētos*, imperforate]. Prefix denoting lack of opening of the part named.

atria (ā-trī'ah). Plural of atrium.

atrial (a'trī-al). Relating to an atrium.

atrichia (ă-trik'ĭ-ah) [G. *a*- priv. + *thrix* (*trich*-), hair]. Artrichosis; absence of hair, congenital or acquired.

atrichosis (ă-trī-ko'sis). Atrichia.

atrichous (ă-trik'us). Without hair.

atrio- [L. *atrium*, *q.v.*]. Combining form relating to an atrium.

a'triomeg'aly [atrio- + G. *megas*, great]. Enlargement of the atrium of the heart.

atrioseptopexy (a'trī-o-sep'to-pek-sī) [atrio- + L. *septum*, partition, + G. *pexis*, fixation]. A closed surgical technique for repairing atrial septal defects.

atrioseptoplasty (a'trī-o-sep'to-plas-tī) [atrio- + L. *septum*, partition, + G. *plassō*, to form]. Surgical repair of an atrial septal defect.

atrioseptostomy (a'trī-o-sep-tos'to-mī) [atrio- + L. *septum*, partition, + G. *stoma*, mouth]. Establish-

ment of a communication between the atria of the heart.

atrioventricular (A-V) (a'trī-o-ven'trik'u-lar). Relating to both the atria and the ventricles of the heart.

atrium, pl. **atria** (a'trī-um, a'trī-ah) [L. entrance hall] **1** [NA]. A chamber or cavity to which are connected several chambers or passageways. **2. A.** cordis. **3.** That part of the tympanic cavity that lies immediately deep to the eardrum. **4. A.** meatus medii. **5.** In the lung, a subdivision of the alveolar duct from which alveolar sacs open.

  a. cor'dis [NA], the upper chamber of each half of the heart.

  a. dex'trum [NA], a. of the right side of the heart which receives the blood from the venae cavae and coronary sinus.

  a. of heart, a. cordis.

  left a., a. sinistrum.

  right a., a. dextrum.

  a. sinis'trum [NA], a. of the left side of the heart which receives the blood from the pulmonary veins.

atroph'ede'ma. Angioneurotic *edema*.

atro'phia [G. fr. *a*- priv. + *trophē*, nourishment]. Atrophy.

atrophic (ă-trof'ik). Denoting atrophy.

atrophied (at'ro-fēd). Characterized by atrophy.

atrophoderma (at'ro-fo-der'mah). Atrophy of the skin which may occur in discrete localized areas or widespread areas.

at'rophodermato'sis. Any cutaneous affection in which a prominent symptom is skin atrophy.

atrophy (at'ro-fī) [G. *atrophia*, fr. *a*- priv. + *trophē*, nourishment]. Atrophia; a wasting of tissues, as from death and reabsorption of cells, diminished cellular proliferation, pressure, ischemia, malnutrition, decreased function, or hormonal changes.

  acute yellow a. of the liver, Rokitansky's disease (1); extensive and rapid death of parenchymal cells of the liver, sometimes with fatty degeneration.

  familial spinal muscular a., infantile muscular a.

  gyrate a. of choroid and retina, a slowly progressive a. of the choriocapillaris, pigmentary epithelium, and sensory retina, with irregular confluent atrophic areas with an associated ornithenuria; autosomal recessive inheritance.

  infantile muscular a., infantile progressive spinal muscular a., familial spinal muscular a.; progressive muscular wasting due to degeneration of motor neurons in anterior horns of the spinal cord, with onset usually in the first year; autosomal recessive inheritance.

  juvenile muscular a., slowly progressive proximal muscular weakness with fasciculation and wasting, lower motor neuron disease, and onset usually between 2 and 17 years; autosomal recessive inheritance is usual.

  Leber's hereditary optic a., degeneration of the optic nerve and papillomacular bundle with resulting rapid loss of central vision; age of onset is variable, most often seen in males.

linear a., *striae* cutis distensae.

olivopontocerebellar a., a progressive neurologic disease characterized by loss of neurons in the cerebellar cortex, basis pontis, and inferior olivary nuclei; results in ataxia, tremor, involuntary movement, and dysarthria; dominant or recessive inheritance.

peroneal muscular a., Charcot-Marie-Tooth disease; fasicular degeneration characterized by slowly progressive wasting of distal muscles of the extremities, usually involving the legs before the arms; autosomal dominant, autosomal recessive, and X chromosome-linked recessive types exist, with severity related to genetic type.

Pick's a., Pick's disease (2); circumscribed a. of the cerebral cortex.

progressive muscular a., Duchenne-Aran, Aran-Duchenne, or Cruveilier's disease; a. of the cells of the anterior cornua of the spinal cord, resulting in a slow progressive wasting and paralysis of the muscles of the extremities and of the trunk.

spinal a., *tabes* dorsalis.

Sudeck's a., acute a. of a bone, commonly one of the carpal or tarsal bones, following a slight injury such as a sprain.

yellow a. of the liver, see acute yellow a. of the liver.

at'ropine. *dl*-Hyoscyamine; $C_{17}H_{23}NO_3$; alkaloid obtained from *Atropa belladonna*; antispasmodic, antisudorific, anticholinergic, and mydriatic.

attack. Occurrence of some disease or episode, often with a dramatic onset.

transient ischemic a. (TIA), a sudden loss of neurological function with complete recovery within hours, as the result of cerebral vascular impairment.

vagal a., vasovagal a., vasovagal syncope; a paroxysmal condition marked by a slow pulse, fall in blood pressure, and sometimes convulsions; thought to be due to sudden stimulation of the vagus nerve mediated through receptors in the carotid sinus, the aortic arch, or the heart.

attenua'tion [L. *at-tenuo*, pp. *-tenuatus*, to make thin or weak]. 1. Dilution; thinning. 2. Diminution of virulence in a strain of an organism, obtained through selection of variants which occur naturally or experimentally. 3. Reduction or weakening. 4. Loss of energy of an ultrasonic beam as it propagates through a medium.

at'tic. Epitympanum; tympanic attic; upper portion of the tympanic cavity above the tympanic membrane which contains the head of the malleus and the body of the incus.

atticot'omy [attic + G. *tomē*, incision]. Operative opening into the tympanic attic.

at'titude [Mediev. L. *aptitudo*, fr. L. *aptus*, fit]. 1. Posture; position of the body and limbs. 2. Manner of acting. 3. In social or clinical psychology, a relatively stable and enduring predisposition or set to behave or react in a certain way.

atto- (a) [Danish *atten*, eighteen]. Prefix denoting one quintillionth (10^{-18}).

attraction (ă-trak'shun) [L. *at-traho*, pp. *-tractus*, to draw toward]. The tendency of two bodies to approach each other.

capillary a., the force that causes fluids to rise up very fine tubes or through the pores of a loose material.

chemical a., the force impelling atoms of different elements or molecules to unite to form new substances or compounds.

attrition (ă-trish'un) [L. *at-tero*, pp. *-tritus*, to rub against, rub away]. Wearing away by friction or rubbing as the loss of tooth structure caused by the abrasive character of food or from bruxism.

at wt Atomic *weight*.

atypical (a-tip'ĭ-kal) [G. *a-* priv. + *typikos*, conformed to a type]. Not typical; not corresponding to the normal form or type.

Au [L. *aurum*, gold]. Gold.

audile (aw'dil). Relating to audition.

audio- [L. *audio*, to hear]. Combining form relating to hearing.

au'dioanalge'sia. Analgesia produced by sound or sounds.

aud'iogen'ic [audio- + G. *genesis*, production]. Caused by sound, especially a loud noise.

au'diogram [audio- + G. *gramma*, a drawing]. The graphic record drawn from the results of hearing tests with the audiometer.

audiol'ogist. A specialist in evaluation, habitation, and rehabilitation of those whose communication disorders center in whole or in part in the hearing function.

audiol'ogy. The study of hearing disorders through the identification and measurement of hearing function loss as well as the rehabilitation of persons with hearing impairments.

audiom'eter [audio- + G. *metron*, measure]. An electrical instrument for measuring the threshold of hearing for pure tones of frequencies generally varying from 200 to 8000 Hz (recorded in terms of decibels); also records thresholds for lists of spoken words and discrimination percentage for phonetically balanced word lists.

audiom'etry. Use of the audiometer.

audiovisual (aw'dĭ-o-vizh'u-al). Pertaining to a communication or teaching technique that combines both audible and visible symbols.

audition (aw-dish'un). Hearing.

au'ditory [L. *audio*, pp. *auditus*, to hear]. Pertaining to the sense of hearing or to the organs of hearing.

aura, pl. au'rae (aw'rah) [L. breeze, odor, gleam of light]. A peculiar sensation felt by the patient immediately preceding an epileptic attack; called auditory, epigastric, vertiginous, etc., according to its seat or nature.

au'ral. 1. Relating to the ear (auris). 2. Relating to an aura.

auranti'asis cu'tis [L. *aurantium*, orange, + *-iasis*, condition; *cutis*, skin]. Carotenosis cutis.

auri- [L. *auris*, ear]. Combining form denoting the ear. See also ot-, oto-.

au'ric. Relating to gold (aurum).

auricle (aw'rĭ-kl). Auricula.

atrial a., *auricula* atrii.

auricula, pl. **auric'ulae** (aw-rik'u-lah) [L. the external ear. dim. of *auris*, ear] [NA]. Auricle; pinna (1); the projecting shell-like structure on the side of the head constituting, with the external acoustic meatus, the external ear.

a. a'trii [NA], atrial auricle; a small conical pouch projecting from the upper anterior portion of each atrium of the heart.

auric'ular. Relating to the ear, or to an auricle in any sense.

auric'ulotem'poral. Relating to the auricle or pinna of the ear and the temporal region.

auris, pl. **aures** (aw'ris, aw'rēz) [L.] [NA]. Ear.

auriscope (aw'rĭ-skōp) [L. *auris*, ear, + *skopeō*, to view]. Otoscope.

aurum (aw'rum) [L.]. Gold.

auscult (aws-kult'). Auscultate.

auscultate (aws'kul-tāt) [L. *ausculto*, pp. *-atus*, to listen to]. Auscult; to perform auscultation.

ausculta'tion. Listening to the sounds made by the various body structures as a diagnostic method.

immediate a., direct a., a. by application of the ear to the surface of the body.

mediate a., a. using a stethoscope.

auscul'tatory. Relating to auscultation.

aut-. See auto-.

autarcesis (awt'ar-se'sis) [G. *autos*, self, + *arkesis*, a warding off]. Innate *immunity*.

aute'cic, aute'cious [G. *autos*, same, + *oikion*, house]. Denoting a parasite that infects, throughout its entire existence, the same host.

autism (aw'tizm) [G. *autos*, self]. A tendency to morbid self-absorption at the expense of regulation by outward reality.

infantile a., Kanner's syndrome; severe emotional disturbance of childhood characterized by inability to form meaningful interpersonal relationships; believed by some to be a form of childhood schizophrenia.

autis'tic. Pertaining to or suffering from autism.

auto-, aut- [G. *autos*, self]. A prefix meaning self, same.

au'toagglu'tinin. An agglutinating autoantibody.

au'toagglutina'tion. 1. Nonspecific agglutination or clumping together of cells (*e.g.*, bacteria, erythrocytes, and the like) due to physical-chemical factors. **2.** The a. of a person's red blood cells in his own serum, as a consequence of specific autoantibody.

autoallergic (aw'to-al-ler'jik). Pertaining to autoallergy.

au'toal'lergy. An altered reactivity in which antibodies (autoantibodies) are produced against one's own tissues, causing a destructive rather than a protective effect.

au'toan'tibody. An antibody that has affinity for one or other tissue of the subject in whom the antibody was formed.

autocatalysis (aw'to-kă-tal'ĭ-sis). A reaction in which one or more of the products formed acts to catalyze the reaction; beginning slowly, the rate of such a reaction rapidly increases. *Cf.* chain *reaction.*

au'tocatalyt'ic. Relating to autocatalysis.

autochthonous (aw-tok'thon-us) [auto- + G. *chthon*, land, ground, country]. **1.** Native to the place inhabited; aboriginal. **2.** Originating in the place where found; said of a disease originating in the part of the body where found, or of a disease acquired in the place where the patient is.

autoclasis, autoclasia (aw-tok'lă-sis, -to-kla'zĭ-ah) [auto- + G. *klasis*, breaking]. **1.** A breaking up or rupturing from intrinsic or internal causes. Progressive immunologically induced tissue destruction.

au'toclave [auto- + L. *clavis*, a key, in the sense of self-locking]. **1.** An apparatus for sterilization by steam under pressure. **2.** To sterilize in an autoclave.

autocytol'ysin. Autolysin.

autocytolysis (aw'to-si-tol'ĭ-sis). Autolysis.

autocytotox'in. A cytotoxic autoantibody.

au'todiges'tion. Autolysis.

autoecholalia (aw'to-ek-la'lĭ-ah) [auto- + echolalia, *q.v.*]. Repetition of some or all the words in one's own statements.

autoerotic (aw-to-er-ot'ik). Pertaining to autoerotism.

autoerotism (aw-to-er'o-tizm) [auto- + G. *erōtikos*, relating to love]. Autoeroticism. **1.** Sexual arousal or gratification using one's own body, as in masturbation. **2.** Sexual self-love, in contrast with alloerotism.

autog'amous. Relating to or characterized by autogamy.

autogamy (aw-tog'ă-mĭ) [auto- + G. *gamos*, marriage]. Self-fertilization in which fission of the cell nucleus occurs without division of the cell, the two pronuclei so formed reuniting to form the synkaryon.

autogenesis (aw'to-jen'ĕ-sis) [auto- + G. *genesis*, production]. **1.** The origin of living matter within the organism itself. **2.** In bacteriology, the process by which vaccine is made from bacteria obtained from the patient's own body.

autogenet'ic, autogen'ic. Autogenous (1); relating to autogenesis.

autogenous (aw-toj'en-us) [G. *autogenēs*, self-produced]. **1.** Autogenetic. **2.** Originating within the body, *i.e.*, endogenous; applied to vaccines prepared from bacteria obtained from the infected person.

au'tograft. Autotransplant; autologous or autoplastic graft; tissue or an organ transferred by grafting into a new position in the body of the same individual.

au'tohemagglutina'tion. Autoagglutination of erythrocytes.

autohemol'ysin. An autoantibody that (with complement) causes lysis of erythrocytes in the same person or animal in whose body the lysin is formed.

autohemol'ysis. Hemolysis occurring in certain diseases as a result of an autohemolysin.

au'tohemother'apy. Treatment of disease by the withdrawal and reinjection of the patient's own blood.

autoimmunity (aw'to-im-mu'nĭtĭ). In immunology, the condition in which one's own tissues are subject to deleterious effects of the immunological system.

au'toimmuniza'tion. Induction of autoimmunity.

autoinfec'tion. Autoreinfection. **1.** Reinfection by microbes or parasitic organisms on or within the body that have already passed through an infective cycle, such as a succession of boils, or a new infective cycle with production of a new generation of larvae and adults. **2.** Self-infection by direct contagion, as with parasite eggs passed in the infectious state transmitted by fingernails.

autoinfu'sion. Forcing the blood from the extremities, as by the application of a bandage or pressure device, in order to raise the blood pressure and fill the vessels in the vital centers.

au'toinoc'ula'tion. A secondary infection originating from a focus of infection already present in the body.

au'tointoxica'tion. Self-poisoning as the result of absorption of the waste products of metabolism, decomposed matter from the intestine, or the products of dead and infected tissue as in gangrene.

autoisolysin (aw-to-i-sol'ĭ-sin). An antibody that (with complement) causes lysis of cells in the person or animal in whose body the lysin is formed, as well as in others of the same species.

autokeratoplasty (aw'to-kĕr'ă-to -plas-tĭ) [auto- + G. *keras*, horn, + *plassō*, to fashion]. Grafting of corneal tissue from one eye to the other eye.

autokinesia, autokinesis (aw-to-kin-e'sĭ-ah, aw-to-kin-e'sis) [auto- + G. *kinēsis*, movement]. Voluntary movement.

autokinet'ic. Relating to autokinesis.

autol'ogous [auto- + G. *logos*, relation]. **1.** Occurring naturally and normally in a certain type of tissue or a specific structure of the body. **2.** Sometimes used to indicate a neoplasm derived from cells that occur normally in that site, *e.g.*, a squamous cell carcinoma in the esophagus. **3.** In transplantation, referring to a graft in which the donor and recipient areas are in the same individual.

autol'ysate. The complex of substances resulting from autolysis.

autol'ysin. Autocytolysin; an antibody that (with complement) causes lysis of the cells and tissues in the body of the person (or animal) in whom the lysin is formed.

autol'ysis [auto- + G. *lysis*, dissolution]. Autocytolysis, autodigestion. **1.** Enzymatic digestion of cells (especially when dead or degenerate) by enzymes present within them (autogenous). **2.** Destruction of cells as a result of a lysin formed in those cells or

others in the same organism.

autolyt'ic. Pertaining to or causing autolysis.

autom'atism. Telergy. **1.** The state of being independent of the will or of central innervation, as the heart's action. **2.** An act performed without intent or conscious exercise of the will, often without realization of its ocurrence. **3.** A condition in which one is consciously or unconsciously, but involuntarily, compelled to the performance of certain acts.

autonom'ic [G. *autonomos*, fr. *autos*, self, + *nomos*, law]. **1.** Functionally independent; not under voluntary control. **2.** Relating to the autonomic nervous system.

autonomotropic (aw'to-nom-o-trop'ĭk) [autonomic + *trepein*, to turn]. Acting on the autonomic nervous system.

au'to-oxida'tion. Autoxidation; the direct combination of a substance with molecular oxygen at ordinary temperatures.

autophagia (aw-to-fa'jĭ-ah) [auto- + G. *phagein*, to eat]. **1.** Biting one's own flesh. **2.** Segregation and disposal of damaged organelles within a cell. **3.** Maintenance of the nutrition of the whole body by metabolic consumption of some of the body tissues.

autopha'gic. Relating to or characterized by autophagia.

autoplas'tic. Relating to autoplasty.

autoplas'ty. Repair of defects by autotransplantation.

au'topsy [G. *autopsia*, seeing with one's own eyes]. Postmortem examination; necropsy; an examination of a dead body for the purpose of determining the cause of death or of studying the pathologic changes present.

autoradiograph (aw'to-ra'dĭ-o-graf) Radioautograph; reproduction of the distribution and concentration of radioactivity in a tissue or other substance made by placing a photographic emulsion on the surface of, or in close proximity to, the substance.

au'toradiog'raphy. Radioautography; the process of producing an autoradiograph.

au'toregula'tion. **1.** The tendency of the blood flow to an organ or part to remain at or return to the same level despite changes in the pressure in the artery which conveys blood to it. **2.** In general, any biologic system equipped with inhibitory feedback systems such that a given change tends to be largely or completely counteracted.

    heterometric a., a. of the strength of contraction of the ventricle that occurs in direct relation to the end-diastolic fiber length in accordance with Starling's law of the heart.

    homeometric a., a. of strength of contraction of the ventricle by mechanisms or agents that do not depend upon change in the end-diastolic fiber length.

autoreinfection (aw'to-re-in-fek'shun). Autoinfection.

au'toreproduc'tion. Replication (2); the ability of a gene or virus, or nucleoprotein molecule generally, to bring about the synthesis of another molecule like itself from smaller molecules within the cell.

autosepticemia (aw'to-sep-tĭ-se'mĭ-ah) [auto- + G. *sēpsis*, decay, + *haima*, blood]. Septicemia apparently originating from microorganisms existing within the individual and not introduced from without.

au'tose'rum. Serum obtained from the patient's own blood and administered to him.

au'tosite [auto- + G. *sitos*, food]. That member of abnormal, unequal (conjoined) twins that is able to live independently and nourish the other member (parasite) of the pair.

autoso'mal. Pertaining to an autosome.

au'tosome [auto- + G. *sōma*, body]. Any chromosome other than a sex chromosome, normally occurring in pairs in somatic cells and singly in gametes.

autosuggestion (aw'to-sug-jes'chun). **1.** Constant dwelling upon an idea or concept, thereby inducing some change in the mental or bodily functions. **2.** Reproduction in the brain of impressions previously received which become then the starting point of new acts or ideas.

autotopagnosia (aw'to-top-ag-no'zĭ-ah) [auto- + G. *topos*, place, + agnosia, *q.v.*]. Inability to recognize any part of the body.

autotox'ic. Autopoisonous; relating to autointoxication.

autotox'in. Any poison originating within the body upon which it acts.

au'totransfu'sion. Transfusing back into the body of blood removed.

autotrans'plant. Autograft.

au'totransplantātion. Performance of an autograft.

autotroph (aw'to-trōf) [auto- + G. *trophē*, nourishment]. A microorganism which uses only inorganic materials as its source of nutrients; carbon dioxide serves as the sole carbon source.

autotroph'ic. Pertaining to an autotroph.

au'tovac'cina'tion. A second vaccination with virus from a vaccine sore on the same individual.

autoxidation (aw-tok-sĭ-da'shun). Auto-oxidation.

auxano-, aux-, auxo- [G. *auxanō*, to increase]. Prefix denoting relation to increase.

auxanogram (awk-san'o-gram) [auxano- + G. *gramma*, something written]. A plate culture of bacteria in which variable conditions are provided in order to determine the effect of these conditions on the growth of the bacteria.

auxanograph'ic. Pertaining to auxanogram or auxanography.

auxanog'raphy. The study, using auxanograms, of the effects of different conditions on the growth of bacteria.

aux'aton'ic. Denoting the condition when a contracting muscle shortens against an increasing load.

auxesis (awk-se'sis) [G. increase]. Increase in size, especially as in hypertrophy.

auxetic (awk-set'ik) [G. *auxētikos*, promoting growth]. Relating to anxesis.

auxilytic (awk'sĭ-lit'ik) [G. *auxō*, to increase, + *lysis*, dissolution]. Increasing the destructive power of a lysin, or favoring lysis.

auxo-. See auxano-.

auxotroph (awk'so-trōf) [auxo- + G. *trophē*, nourishment]. A mutant microorganism that requires some nutrient not required by the organism (prototroph) from which the mutant was derived.

auxotrophic (awk'so-trof'ik, -tro'fik). Pertaining to an auxotroph.

A-V Arteriovenous; atrioventricular.

avas'cular. Nonvascular; without blood or lymphatic vessels.

avas'culariza'tion. 1. Expulsion of blood from a part. **2.** Loss of vascularity, as by scarring.

a'vian [L. *avis*, bird]. Pertaining to birds.

avir'ulent. Not virulent.

avi'tamino'sis. Properly hypovitaminosis, a deficiency disease state resulting from an inadequate supply of one or more vitamins in the diet.

avoirdupois (av'er-dĕ-poyz') [Fr. to have weight, corrupted fr. O. Fr. *avoir*, property, + *de*, of, + *pois*, weight]. A system of weights in which 16 ounces make a pound equivalent of 453.6 g.

AVP Antiviral *protein.*

avulsion (ă-vul'shun) [L. *a-vello*, pp. *-vulsus*, to tear away]. A tearing away or forcible separation.

AW Atomic *weight.*

Ax Axis.

axenic (a-zen'ik) [G. *a-* priv. + *xenos*, foreign]. Sterile, denoting especially a pure culture or "germ-free" animals.

axes (ak'sēz). Plural of axis.

ax'ial. 1. Axile; relating to an axis. **2.** Relating to or situated in the central part of the body (head and trunk). **3.** In dentistry, relating to or parallel with the long axis of a tooth.

axif'ugal [L. *axis + fugio*, to flee from]. Axofugal; extending away from an axis or axon.

ax'ile. Axial (1).

axilla, gen. and pl. **axillae** (ak'sil'ah, ak-sil'e) [L.]. *Fossa* axillaris.

ax'illary. Alar (2); relating to the axilla.

axio- [L. *axis*]. Combining form relating to an axis. See also axo-.

ax'ioplasm. Axoplasm.

ax'iover'sion. Abnormal inclination of the long axis of a tooth.

axip'etal [L. *axis + peto*, to seek]. Centripetal (2).

axis, pl. **axes (Ax)** (ak'sis, ak'sēz) [L. axle, axis]. **1.** A straight line passing through a spherical body between its two poles, and about which the body may revolve. **2.** The central line of the body or any of its parts. **3** [NA]. Epistropheus; vertebra dentata; the second cervical vertebra. **4.** An artery that divides, immediately upon its origin, into a number of branches.

basibregmatic a., a line extending from the basion to the bregma.

basicranial a., a line drawn from the basion to the midpoint of the sphenoethmoidal suture.

basifacial a., facial a.; a line drawn from the subnasal point to the midpoint of the sphenoethmoidal suture.

biauricular a., a straight line joining the two auricularia.

cephalocaudal a., the long a. of the body.

cerebrospinal a., the brain and spinal cord.

electrical a., the general direction of the electromotive force developed in the heart during its activation, usually represented in the frontal plane.

facial a., basifacial a.

frontal a., the transverse a. of the eyeball, a line running transversely through the center of the globe of the eye.

optic a., the a. of the eye connecting the anterior and posterior poles; usually diverges from the visual a. by 5 degrees or more.

pelvic a., plane of pelvic canal; a hypothetical curved line joining the center point of each of the four planes of the pelvis.

principal optic a., a line passing through the center of the lens of a refracting system at right angles to its surface.

sagittal a., (1) the anteroposterior a. of the eyeball; **(2)** in dentistry, the line around which the working condyle rotates in the frontal plane during mandibular movement.

secondary a., any ray passing through the optical center of a lens.

visual a., line of vision; the straight line extending from the object seen, through the center of the pupil, to the macula lutea of the retina.

axo- [G. *axōn*, axis]. Combining form meaning axis, usually relating to an axon.

axoaxonic (ak'so-ak-son'ik). Referring to the synaptic contact between the axon of one nerve cell and that of another.

axodendrit'ic. Referring to the synaptic relationship of an axon with a dendrite.

axof'ugal [axo- + L. *fugio*, to flee]. Axifugal.

ax'olem'ma [axo- + G. *lemma*, husk]. Mauthner's sheath; the delicate plasma membrane of the axon.

axol'ysis [axo- + G. *lysis*, dissolution]. Destruction of the axon of a nerve.

axom'eter. Axonometer; an instrument for determining the axis of a spectacle lens.

axon (ak'son) [G. *axōn*, axis]. The single one among a nerve cell's processes that under normal conditions conducts nervous impulses away from the cell body and its remaining cell processes (dendrites). A relatively even filamentous process varying in thickness that, in contrast to dendrites, can extend far away from the parent cell body. With some exceptions, nerve cells can synaptically transmit impulses to other nerve cells or to effector cells exclusively by way of the synaptic terminals of their a.

ax'onal. Pertaining to an axon.

axoneme (ak'so-nēm) [axo- + G. *nēma*, a thread]. **1.** The central thread running in the axis of the chromosome. **2.** Axial *filament.*

axonog'raphy. Electroaxonography; the recording of electrical changes in axons.

axonom'eter. Axometer.

axonotme'sis [axo- + G. *tmēsis*, a cutting]. Interruption of the axons of a nerve followed by complete degeneration of the peripheral segment, without severance of the supporting structure of the nerve.

axop'etal [axo- + L. *peto*, to seek]. Extending in a direction toward an axon.

ax'oplasm. Axioplasm; neuroplasm of the axon.

axosomat'ic [axo- + G. *sōma*, body]. Referring to the synaptic relationship of an axon with a nerve cell body.

aze'otrope [G. *a-* priv. + *zeein*, to boil, + *tropos*, a turning]. A mixture of two liquids that boils without change in proportion of the two liquids, either in the liquid or the vapor phase.

azo-. Prefix denoting the presence in a molecule of the group $-N=N-$. See also diazo-.

azo'ic [G. *a-* priv. + *zōikos*, relating to an animal]. Containing no living things; without organic life.

azole (az'ōl). Pyrrole.

azoospermia (a-zo-o-sper'mĭ-ah) [G. *a-* priv. + *zōon*, animal, + *sperma*, seed]. **1.** Absence of living spermatozoa in the semen. **2.** Failure of spermatogenesis.

azote'mia [azote + G. *haima*, blood]. Uremia.

azotem'ic. Relating to azotemia.

azoturia (az-o-tu'rĭ-ah) [azote + G. *ouron*, urine]. An increased elimination of urea in the urine.

azotu'ric. Relating to the urinary excretion of nitrogen.

azure (azh'ūr). A term for a group of basic blue methylthionine or phenothiazine dyes (a. A, B, C, I, and II); used as biological stains, especially in blood and nuclear stains.

az'ures'in. A complex of azure A and carbacrylic resin; used as an indicator for the detection of gastric achlorhydria without intubation.

azurophil, azurophile (azh'u-ro-fil, -fil) [azure + G. *philos*, fond]. Staining readily with an azure dye, denoting especially the hyperchromatin and reddish purple granules of certain blood cells.

az'ygogram. X-ray image obtained by azygography.

azygography (az'i-gog'ră-fĭ). Radiography of the azygos venous system after injection of contrast medium.

azygos (az'i-gos) [G. *a-* priv. + *zygon*, a yoke]. An unpaired (azygous) anatomical structure.

azygous (az'i-gus, ă-zi'gus) [L. *azygos*]. Unpaired; single.

B

β Beta, second letter of the Greek alphabet; used to denote the second in a series, as in chemistry to designate the order of components of isomeric compounds or of carbon atoms.

B Boron; as a subscript, refers to barometric pressure.

b As a subscript refers to blood.

Ba Barium.

Babesia (bă-be′zĭ-ah) [V. *Babès*]. A genus of protozoa (family Babesiidae) characterized by multiplication in host red blood cells to form pairs and tetrads; causes babesiosis (piroplasmosis) in most types of domestic animals; several species cause malaria-like disease in splenectomized or normal people; known vectors are ixodid or argasid ticks.

babesiosis (bă-be′zĭ-o′sis). Piroplasmosis: a highly pathogenic disease of domestic animals caused by infection with a species of *Babesia;* characterized by fever, malaise, listlessness, severe anemia, and hemoglobinuria.

baby. An infant; a newborn child.

  blue b., a child born cyanotic because of congenital cardiac or pulmonary defect causing incomplete oxygenation of the blood.

  collodion b., a newborn child with lamellar ichthyosis; the skin, at birth, is bright red, shiny, translucent, and drawn tight, giving a distorted appearance (as if painted with collodion) of immobilization of the face.

baccate (bak′āt) [L. *bacca,* berry]. Berry-like

bacciform (bak′sĭ-form) [L. *bacca,* berry]. Berry-shaped.

Bacillaceae (bă-sil-la′se-e). A family of aerobic or facultatively anaerobic, chemoheterotrophic, sporeforming, ordinarily motile bacteria (order Eubacteriales) containing Gram-positive rods; some species are pathogenic. Ordinarily two genera, *Bacillus* and *Clostridium,* are included.

bacillar, bacillary (bas′il-ar, bas′il-a-rī). Rod-shaped; consisting of rods or rodlike elements.

Bacille bilié de Calmette-Guérin (BCG) [Fr.]. Calmette-Guérin bacillus; an attenuated strain of *Mycobacterium bovis* used in the preparation of BCG vaccine.

bacille′mia [bacillus + G. *haima,* blood]. Presence of rod-shaped bacteria in the circulating blood.

bacilli (bă-sil′i) Plural of bacillus.

bacil′liform [L. *bacillus,* a rod, + *forma,* form]. Rod-shaped.

bacil′lin. An antibiotic substance produced by *Bacillus subtilis.*

bacillosis (bas′ĭ-lo′sis). A general infection with bacilli.

bacilluria (bas-ĭ-lu′rĭ-ah) [bacillus + G. *ouron,* urine]. Presence of bacilli in the urine.

Bacil′lus [L. dim of *baculus,* rod, staff]. A genus of aerobic or facultatively anaerobic, chemoheterotrophic, sporeforming, ordinarily motile bacteria (family Bacillaceae) containing Gram-positive rods; found primarily in soil; a few species are animal pathogens; some produce antibodies.

bacil′lus, pl. **bacil′li** [L. dim. of *baculus,* a rod, staff]. General term for any member of the genus *Bacillus;* formerly used to refer to any rod-shaped bacterium.

  Bang's b., *Brucella abortus.*
  Bordet-Gengou b., *Bordetella pertussis.*
  Calmette-Guérin b., Bacille bilié de Calmette-Guérin.
  comma b., *Vibrio cholerae.*
  Ducrey's b., *Haemophilus ducreyi.*
  Flexner's b., *Shigella flexneri.*
  Friedländer's b., *Klebsiella pneumoniae.*
  Gärtner's b., *Salmonella enteritidis.*
  gas b., *Clostridium perfringens.*
  Hansen's b., *Mycobacterium leprae.*
  Klebs-Loeffler b., *Corynebacterium diphtheriae.*
  Koch's b., (1) *Mycobacterium tuberculosis,* (2) *Vibrio cholerae.*
  Koch-Weeks b., *Haemophilus influenzae.*
  Morgan's b., *Proteus morganii.*
  Pfeiffer's b., *Haemophilus influenzae.*
  Shiga-Kruse b., *Shigella dysenteriae.*
  Sonne b., *Shigella sonnei.*
  tubercle b., *Mycobacterium tuberculosis.*
  typhoid b., *Salmonella typhi.*

bacitra′cin. An antibacterial polypeptide of known chemical structure isolated from cultures of a member of the *Bacillus subtilis* group; active against hemolytic streptococci, staphylococci, and several types of Gram-positive, aerobic, rod-shaped organisms; usually applied locally.

backache (bak′āk). Nonspecific term used to describe back pain, generally below cervical level.

back′bone. *Columna vertebralis.*

back′cross. Mating of an individual heterozygous for one or more gene pairs to an individual homozygous for the same gene pairs.

bacteremia (bak-tēr-e′mĭ-ah) [bacteria + G. *haima,* blood]. Bacteriemia; presence of viable bacteria in the circulating blood.

bacteria (bak-tēr′ĭ-ah). Plural of bacterium.

bacte′rial. Relating to bacteria.

bacterici′dal. Bacteriocidal; causing the death of bacteria.

bactericide (bak′tēr′ĭ-sīd) [bacteria + L. *caedo,* to kill]. An agent that destroys bacteria.

bacterid (bak′ter-id) [bacteria + *-id* (1)]. **1.** A recurrent or persistent eruption of discrete, sterile pustules of the palms and soles, thought to be an allergic response to infection at a remote site. **2.** A dissemination of a previously localized bacterial skin infection.

bacteriemia (bak-tēr-ĭ-e′mĭ-ah). Bacteremia.

bacterio- [see bacterium]. Combining form relating to bacteria.

bacte′rioci′dal. Bactericidal.

bacte′rioci′din. Antibody having bactericidal activity.

bacte′riocin′ogens. Bacteriocinogenic *plasmids.*

bacte′riocins. Proteins produced by certain bacteria possessing bacteriocinogenic plasmids which exert a lethal effect on closely related bacteria.

bacteriogenic (bak-tēr′ĭ-o-jen′ik). Caused by bacteria.

bacteriolog′ic, bacteriolog′ical. Relating to bacteria or to bacteriology.

bacteriol′ogist. One who primarily studies or works with bacteria.

bacteriology (bak-tēr-ĭ-ol′o-jĭ) [bacterio- + G. *logos,* study]. The branch of science concerned with the study of bacteria.

bacteriol′ysin. Specific antibody that combines with bacterial cells (*i.e.,* antigen) and, when adequate complement is available, causes lysis or dissolution of the cells.

bacteriolysis (bak-tēr-ĭ-ol′ĭ-sis) [bacterio- + G. *lysis,* dissolution]. The dissolution of bacteria, as by specific antibody and complement.

bacteriolyt′ic. Pertaining to lysis of bacteria; manifesting the ability to cause dissolution of bacterial cells.

bacteriopexy (bak-tēr′ĭ-o-pek′sĭ) [bacterio- + G. *pēxis,* fixation]. Immobilization of bacteria by phagocytic cells.

bacteriophage (bak-tēr′ĭ-o-fāj) [bacterio- + G. *phagein,* to eat]. Phage; a virus with specific affinity for bacteria, found in association with essentially all groups of bacteria; like other viruses they contain either RNA or DNA; their relationships to the host bacteria are rather specific and, as in the case of temperate b., may be genetically intimate; they are named after the bacterial species, group, or strain for which they are specific.

defective b., a temperate b. mutant whose genome does not contain all of the normal components and cannot become fully infectious virus, yet can replicate indefinitely in the bacterial genome as defective probacteriophage.

mature b., the complete, infective form of b.

temperate b., b. whose genome incorporates with, and replicates with, that of the host bacterium.

vegetative b., the form of b. in which the b. nucleic acid (lacking its coat) multiplies freely within the host bacterium, independently of bacterial multiplication.

virulent b., a b. that regularly causes lysis of the bacteria that it infects; it may exist only as a vegetative or mature b.

bacteriop′sonin. An opsonin acting upon bacteria, as distinguished from a hemopsonin which affects red blood corpuscles.

bacterio′sis. A localized or generalized bacterial infection.

bacte′riostat′ic Inhibiting or retarding the growth of bacteria.

Bacterium (bak-tēr′ĭ-um). A generic name no longer used in bacteriology; organisms formerly placed in the genus have been transferred to other genera.

bacterium, pl. **bacteria** (bak-tēr′ĭ-um, -ah) [Mod. L. fr. G. *baktērion,* dim. of *baktron,* a staff]. A prokaryotic microorganism that differs from blue-green bacteria (blue-green algae) primarily in that the blue-green bacteria perform photosynthesis accompanied by oxygen evolution and have a photosynthetic pigment system that includes chlorophyll α and β-carotene.

lysogenic b., (1) a b. in the symbiotic condition in which its genome includes the genome (probacteriophage) of a temperate bacteriophage; **(2)** formerly, a pseudolysogenic bacterial strain (*i.e.,* a "carrier" strain of bacteriophage of low infectivity).

bacteriuria (bak-tēr-ĭ-u′rĭ-ah). Presence of bacteria in the urine.

Bacteroides (bak′ter-oy′dēz) [G. *bacterion* + *eidos,* form]. A genus of obligately anaerobic, non-sporeforming bacteria (family Bacteroidaceae, order Eubacteriales) containing Gram-negative rods; some species are pathogenic to man and other animals.

B. frag′ilis, a species that is one of the predominant organisms in the lower intestinal tracts of man and other animals; also found in specimens from appendicitis, peritonitis, rectal abscesses, pilonidal cysts, surgical wounds, and lesions of the urogenital tract.

B. melaninogen′icus, a species found in the mouth, feces, infections of the mouth, soft tissue, respiratory tract, urogenital tract, and the intestinal tract; pathogenic, but ordinarily in association with other organisms.

bacteroidosis (bak′ter-oy-do′sis). Infection with *Bacteroides.*

bag [A.S. *baelg*]. A pouch; sac; receptacle.

Ambu b., proprietary name for a self-reinflating b. used with positive pressure respiration during resuscitation, foam rubber being built into the walls of the b. so that its shape is automatically restored after compression with air or oxygen drawn into the b.

breathing b., reservoir b.; a collapsible reservoir from which gases are inhaled and into which gases may be exhaled during general anesthesia or artificial ventilation.

colostomy b., a b. worn over an artificial anus to collect feces.

Douglas b., a large b. for the collection of expired air for several minutes to determine oxygen consumption in man under many conditions of actual work.

Politzer b., a pear-shaped rubbr b. used for forcing air through the eustachian tube.

reservoir b., breathing b.

b. of waters, common term for the amniotic sac and contains amniotic fluid.

bagassosis (bag-ă-so′sis). Extrinsic allergic alveolitis following exposure to sugar cane fiber (bagasse).

BAL British anti-Lewisite.

balan-. See balano-.

bal′ance [L. *bi-,* twice, + *lanx,* dish, scale]. **1.** Scales; an apparatus for weighing. **2.** The normal state of action and reaction between two or more parts or organs of the body. **3.** Quantities, concentrations, and proportionate amounts of bodily constituents. **4.** The difference between intake and outgo.

acid-base b., the normal b. between acid and base in the blood plasma, expressed in the hydrogen ion concentration, pH.

electrolyte b., usual designation for the bodily content of sodium and potassium and the concentrations of these ions in extracellular and intracellular fluids.

fluid b., water b.; b. in the intake and loss of water.

nitrogen b., the difference between total nitrogen ingested and the total nitrogen excreted by an organism; in an adult, presumably not growing, this should be zero at a given intake or above; during growth, as in children, the b. is positive (more is taken in than is excreted); in starvation, malnutrition, certain febrile diseases, and injuries, the b. may become negative (imbalance).

water b., fluid b.

balan'ic [G. *balanos*, acorn, glans]. Relating to the glans penis or glans clitoridis.

balani'tis [G. *balanos*, acorn, glans, + *-itis*, inflammation]. Inflammation of the glans penis or glans clitoridis.

balano-, balan- [G. *balanos*, acorn, glans]. Combining forms relating to the glans penis.

bal'anoplasty. Any reparative operation upon the glans penis.

balanoposthitis (bal'an-o-pos-thi'tis) [balano- + G. *posthē*, prepuce, + *-itis*, inflammation]. Inflammation of the glans penis and overlying prepuce.

balanopreputial (bal'an-o-pre-pu'shi-al). Relating to the glans penis and the prepuce.

balanorrhagia (bal'an-ō-ra'ji-ah) [balano- + G. *rhēgnymi*, to burst forth]. A running discharge from the glans penis.

bal'antidi'asis. A disease caused by the presence of *Balantidium coli* in the large intestine; characterized by diarrhea, dysentry, and occasionally ulceration.

Balantid'ium [G. *balantidion*, dim of *ballantion*, a bag]. A genus of trichostome ciliates (family Balantidiidae) found in the digestive tract of vertebrates and invertebrates. *B. coli*, a large parasitic species; found in the cecum or large intestine, swimming actively in the lumen; usually harmless in man but may invade and ulcerate the intestinal wall, producing balantidiasis.

bald'ness. Alopecia.

ball. 1. A round mass; see bezoar. **2.** In veterinary medicine, a large pill or bolus.

food b., phytobezoar.

b. of foot, the padded portion of the sole at the anterior extremity of the metatarsus, upon which the weight rests when the heel is raised.

fungus b., a compact mass of fungal mycelium and cellular debris residing within a lung cavity; such cavities may be produced by bacterial as well as mycotic infectious agents, but are usually produced by *Aspergillus fumigatus* or, more rarely, by *A. niger*.

See also aspergilloma (2).

hair b., trichobezoar.

ballismus (bal-iz'mus) [G. *ballismos*, a jumping about]. The occurrence of lively jerking or shaking movements, especially as observed in chorea.

ballistocardiogram (bal-is-to-kar'di-o- gram) [G. *ballō*, to throw, + *kardia*, heart, + *gramma*, something written]. A record of the body's recoil caused by cardiac contraction and the ejection of blood into the aorta; may be used as a basis for calculating the cardiac output in man.

ballis'tocar'diograph (BCG). Instrument for taking a ballistocardiogram.

ballis'tocardiog'raphy. 1. The graphic recording of movements of the body imparted by ballistic forces of cardiac contraction and ejection of blood. **2.** The study and interpretation of ballistocardiograms.

balloon. An inflatable spherical or ovoid device used to retain tubes or catheters in, or provide support to, various body structures.

ballottement (bal-ot-moń') [Fr. *balloter*, to toss up]. **1.** A maneuver in physical examination to estimate the size of an organ not near the surface, particularly when there is ascites, by a flicking motion of the hand or fingers. **2.** An infrequently used method of diagnosis of pregnancy: with the tip of the forefinger in the vagina, a sharp tap is made against the lower segment of the uterus; the fetus, if present, is moved upward and will be felt to strike against the wall of the uterus.

balm [L. *balsanum*, fr. G. *balsamon*, the balsam tree]. **1.** An ointment, especially a fragrant one. **2.** A soothing or healing medication.

bancrofti'asis, bancrofto'sis. Infection with *Wuchereria bancrofti*.

band. 1. Any appliance or part of an apparatus that encircles or binds a part of the body. **2.** Any ribbon-shaped or cordlike anatomical structure that encircles or binds another structure or that connects two or more parts.

A b.'s, the dark-staining anisotropic cross striations occurring in the myofibrils of muscle fibers.

chromosome b., an area of darker or contrasting staining across the width of a chromosome. See banding.

H b., the paler area in the center of the A b. of a striated muscle fiber.

I b., a light b. on each side of the Z line of striated muscle fibers.

iliotibial b., *tractus* iliotibialis.

M b., M *line.*

matrix b., a metal or plastic b. secured around the crown of a tooth to confine restorative material to be adapted into a prepared cavity.

Z b., Z *line.*

bandage (band'dij). **1.** A piece of cloth or other material applied to a body part to make compression, absorb drainage, prevent motion, retain surgical dressings, etc. **2.** To cover a body part by application of a b.

adhesive b., a dressing of plain absorbent gauze affixed to plastic or fabric coated with a pressure-sensitive adhesive.

Barton's b., a figure-of-8 b. supporting the fractured mandible below and arteriorly.

capeline b. [L. *capella*, a cap], a b. covering the head or an amputation stump like a cap.

cravat b., a b. made by bringing the point of a triangular b. to the middle of the base and then folding lengthwise to the desired width.

demigauntlet b., a gauntlet b. that covers only the hand, leaving the fingers exposed.

Desault's b., a b. for fracture of the clavicle; the elbow is bound to the side, with a pad placed in the axilla.

elastic b., a b. containing stretchable material; used to make local pressure.

figure-of-8 b., a b. applied alternately to two parts, usually two segments of a limb above and below the joint, in such a way that the turns describe the figure 8.

gauntlet b., a figure-of-8 b. covering the hand and fingers.

many-tailed b., Sculetus' b.; a large oblong cloth, the ends of which are cut into narrow strips, and applied to the thorax or abdomen with the strips being tied or overlapped and pinned.

plaster b., a roller b. impregnated with plaster of Paris and applied moist; used to make a rigid dressing for a fracture or diseased joint.

roller b., a strip of material, of variable width, rolled into a compact cylinder to facilitate its application.

Scultetus b., many-tailed b.

spica b. [L. *spica*, ear of grain], successive strips of material applied to the body and the first part of a limb, or to the hand and a finger, which overlap slightly, and create a fancied resemblance to an ear of wheat.

spiral b., an oblique b. encircling a limb, the successive turns overlapping those preceding.

suspensory b., a bag of expansile fabric for supporting the scrotum and its contents.

T-b., a b. of two strips of cloth attached at right angles; used for retaining dressings, as on the perineum.

triangular b., a piece of cloth cut in the shape of a right-angled triangle, used as a sling.

Velpeau b., a b. which serves to immobilize arm to chest wall, with the forearm positioned obliquely across and upward on front of chest.

band'ing. The process of differential staining of metaphase chromosomes of cultured cells to reveal the characteristic patterns of bands that permit identification of individual chromosome pairs; each of the 22 pairs of human chromosomes and the X and Y chromosomes has an identifying b. pattern.

bar. 1. The international unit of pressure equal to 1 megadyne (10_6 dyne) per sq. cm or 0.987 atmosphere. 2. A metal segment of greater length than

width which serves to connect two or more parts of a removable partial denture. 3. A segment of tissue or bone which unites two or more similar structures.

median b. of Mercier, a prominent band of fibromuscular tissue involving the interureteric ridge of the urinary bladder, occasionally resulting in significant urinary obstruction.

Mercier's b., *plica* interureterica.

terminal b., the attachment between epithelial cells consisting of the zonula occludens and zonula adherens.

baragnosis (băr-ag-no'sis) [G. *baros*, weight + *a-* priv., + *gnōsis*, a knowing]. Impairment of the ability to differentiate among weights or pressures.

bar'bital. 5,5-Diethylbarbituric acid; a hypnotic and sedative.

barbit'urates. Derivatives of barbituric acid that are CNS depressants; used as tranquilizers and hypnotics.

barbitu'ric acid. 2,4,6-Trioxohexahydropyrimidine; a crystalline dibasic acid from which barbital and other barbiturates are derived.

bar'biturism. Chronic poisoning by any of the derivatives of barbituric acid.

barbotage (bar-bo-tahzh') [Fr. *barboter*, to dabble]. A method of spinal anesthesia in which a portion of the anesthetic solution is injected into the cerebral spinal fluid; cerebral spinal fluid is then aspirated into the syringe and a second portion of the contents of the syringe is injected; this process is repeated until the entire contents of the syringe are injected.

baresthesia (băr-es-the'zī-ah) [G. *baros*, weight, + *aisthēsis*, sensation]. Pressure *sense.*

baresthesiometer (băr'es-the'zī-om'ē-ter) [G. *baros*, weight, + *aisthēsis*, sensation, + *metron*, measure]. An instrument for measuring the pressure sense.

bariatric (băr-ĭ-at'rik). Relating to bariatrics.

bariatrics (băr-ĭ-at'riks) [G. *baros*, weight, + *iatreia*, medical treatment]. That branch of medicine or surgery concerned with the management of obesity and allied diseases.

barium (băr'ĭ-um, ba'rĭ-um) [G. *barys*, heavy]. A metallic, alkaline, divalent earth element; symbol Ba, atomic weight 137.36, atomic no. 56.

b. hydroxide, $Ba(OH)_2$; a caustic compound combined with calcium hydroxide in a carbon dioxide absorbent; used in anesthetic circuits.

b. sulfate, $BaSO_4$; given orally or rectally as a suspension for x-ray visualization of the gastrointestinal tract.

baro- [G. *baros*, weight]. Combining form relating to weight or pressure.

baroceptor (băr'o-sep-tor). Baroreceptor.

barophilic (băr'o-fil'ik) [G. *baros*, weight, + *phileō*, to love]. Thriving under high environmental pressure; applied to microorganisms.

baroreceptor (băr'o-re-sep'tor). Baroceptor; pressoreceptor; sensory nerve ending in the wall of the auricles of the heart, vena cava, aortic arch, and carotid sinus, sensitive to stretching of the wall resulting from increased pressure from within, and functioning as the elicitation point of central reflex mechanisms that tend to reduce that pressure.

bar'osinusi'tis [G. *baros*, weight, pressure + sinusitis]. Aerosinusitis.

bar'ostat. A pressure-regulating device or structure, such as the baroreceptors of the carotid sinus and aortic arch.

barotax'is [G. *baros*, weight, + *taxis*, order]. Reaction of living tissue to changes in pressure.

baroti'tis me'dia. Aerotitis media.

barotrauma (băr'o-traw'mah) [G. *baros*, weight, + trauma]. Injury, generally to the middle ear or paranasal sinuses, resulting from imbalance between ambient pressure and that within the affected cavity.

barrier (băr'rĭ-er). **1.** An obstacle or impediment. **2.** In psychiatry and social psychiatry, a conflictual agent that blocks resolving behavior.

 blood-air b., the material intervening between alveolar air and the blood; consists of a nonstructural film or surfactant, alveolar epithelium, basement lamina, and endothelium.

 blood-aqueous b., a membrane of the capillary bed of the ciliary body that permits two-way transfer of fluids between the aqueous chamber and the blood stream.

 blood-brain b., blood-cerebrospinal fluid b., a selective mechanism opposing the passage of most large-molecular compounds from the blood to the cerebrospinal fluid and brain tissue.

 placental b., the tissue intervening between fetal and maternal blood in the placenta; acts as a selective membrane regulating the passage of substances from the maternal to the fetal blood.

bartholinitis (bar-to-lin-i'tis). Inflammation of a vulvovaginal (Bartholin's) gland.

Bartonel'la [A. L. *Barton*]. A genus of bacteria (family Bartonellaceae, order Rickettsiales) that multiply in fixed-tissue cells and in erythrocytes, and reproduce by binary fission; they are found in man and in arthropod vectors.

 B. bacillifor'mis, a species found in the blood and epithelial cells of lymph nodes, spleen, and liver in Oroya fever, and in blood and eruptive elements in verruga peruana.

bartonello'sis. A disease caused by *Bartonella bacilliformis* and transmitted by the bite of the sandfly, *Phlebotomus verrucarum.* It occurs in three forms: 1) Oroya fever (Carrion's disease), a generalized, acute, febrile, systemic infection, frequently fatal; 2) verruga peruana, a chronic form of the disease followed by nodular eruptions; 3) a combination (or sequence) of these.

baryto-. Prefix indicating the presence of barium in a mineral.

ba'sad. In a direction toward the base of any object or structure.

ba'sal. 1. Situated nearer the base of a pyramid-shaped organ in relation to a specific reference point. **2.** In physiology, denoting the lowest level

possible.

base [L. and G. *basis*]. **1.** Basis; the lower part or bottom; the part opposite the apex; the foundation. **2.** In pharmacy, the chief ingredient of a mixture. **3.** In chemistry, an electropositive element (cation) that unites with an anion to form a salt; a compound ionizing to yield hydroxyl ion. **4.** Brønsted b; any molecule or ion that combines with hydrogen ion.

 Brønsted b., base (4).

 denture b., (1) that part of a denture which rests on the oral mucosa and to which teeth are attached; (2) that part of a complete or partial denture which rests upon the basal seat and to which teeth are attached.

 b. of heart, *basis* cordis.

 b. of lung, *basis* pulmonis.

 pressor b., pressor amine; (1) one of several products of intestinal putrefaction believed to cause functional hypertension when absorbed; (2) any alkaline substance that raises blood pressure.

 b. of skull, *basis* cranii.

 b. of stapes, *basis* stapedis.

base pair. Nucleoside or nucleotide pair; the complex of two heterocyclic nucleic acid bases, one a pyrimidine and the other a purine, brought about by hydrogen bonding; the essential element in the structure of DNA.

baseplate (bās'plāt). A temporary form representing the base of a denture; used for making maxillomandibular (jaw) relation records and for the arrangement of teeth.

ba'sial. Relating to a basis or the basion.

basi-, basio-, baso- [G. and L. *basis*, base]. Combining forms meaning base, or basis.

ba'sic. Relating to a base.

basicity (ba-sis'ĭ-tĭ). **1.** The valence or combining power of an acid, or the number of replaceable atoms of hydrogen in its molecule. **2.** The quality of being basic.

Basidiobolus (bă-sid'ĭ-o-bo'lus) [Mod. L. *basidium*, dim. of G. *basis*, base, + L. *bolus*, fr. G. *bolos*, lump or clod]. A genus of fungi belonging to the class Phycomycetes (Zygomycetes). *B. haptosporus* has been isolated from cases of entomophthoramycosis basidibolae in man, especially in Indonesia, tropical Africa, and Southeast Asia.

ba'sifa'cial. Relating to the lower portion of the face.

ba'sihy'al, basihy'oid. The base or body of the hyoid bone.

basilar (bas'ĭ-lar). Relating to the base of a pyramidal or broad structure.

ba'silat'eral. Relating to the base and one or more sides of any part.

ba'silem'ma [basi- + G. *lemma*, rind]. Basement *membrane.*

basio-. See basi-.

ba'sion [G. *basis*, a base] [NA]. The middle point on the anterior margin of the foramen magnum, opposite the opisthion.

basip'etal [basi- + L. *peto*, to seek]. In a direction toward the base.

basipho'bia [G. *basis*, a stepping, + *phobos*, fear]. A morbid fear of walking.

basis [L. and G.] [NA]. Base (1).

  b. cor'dis [NA], base of the heart; that part of the heart formed mainly by the left atrium but to a small extent by the posterior part of the right atrium; it is directed backward and to the right and is separated from the vertebral column by the esophagus and aorta.

  b. cra'nii [NA], base of the skull; the inferior aspect is the **b. c. externa** [NA], or norma basilaris; the interior aspect on which the brain rests is the **b. c. interna** [NA].

  b. pulmo'nis [NA], base of the lung; the lower concave part of the lung that rests upon the convexity of the diaphragm.

  b. stape'dis [NA], base of the stapes; footplate (1); the flat portion of the stapes that fits in the oval window.

basisphenoid (ba'sĭ-sfe'noyd). Relating to the base or body of the sphenoid bone; denoting the independent center of ossification in the embryo that forms the posterior portion of the body of the sphenoid bone.

baso-. See basi-.

basoerythrocyte (ba'so-e-rith'ro-sīt). A red blood cell that manifests changes of basophilic degeneration, such as basophilic stippling, punctate basophilia or basophilic granules.

basoerythrocytosis (ba'so-e-rith'ro-si-to'sis). An increase of red blood cells with basophilic degenerative changes, frequently observed in diseases characterized by prolonged hypochromic anemia.

basolat'eral.   Basal and lateral; term used with reference to one of the two major subdivisions of the corpus amygdaloideum, the other subdivision being the corticomedial group of nuclei.

basophil, basophile (ba'so-fil, -fīl) [baso- + G. *phileō*, to love]. **1.** A cell with granules that stain specifically with basic dyes. **2.** Basophilic.

ba'sophil'ia. Basophilism. **1.** More than the usual number of basophilic leukocytes in the circulating blood or an increase in the proportion of parenchymatous basophilic cells in an organ. **2.** Basophilic erythrocytes in circulating blood, as in certain instances of leukemia, advanced anemia, malaria, and plumbism.

ba'sophil'ic. Basophil (2); denoting tissue components having an affinity for basic dyes under specific pH conditions.

basophilism (ba-sof'ĭ-lizm). Basophilia.

bath [A.S. *baeth*]. **1.** Immersion of the body or any of its parts in water or any other yielding or fluid medium; or application of such medium in any form to all or part of the body. **2.** The apparatus used in giving a b. of any form, qualified according to the medium used, temperature of the medium, form in which the medium is applied, medicament added to the medium, and part bathed.

  colloid b., a b. prepared by adding soothing agents to the b. water.

  contrast b., a b. in which a part is immersed alternately in hot and cold water.

  douche b., local application of water in the form of a jet or stream.

  needle b., a shower in which water is projected against the body in the shape of many very fine jets.

  sitz b. [Ger. *sitzen*, to sit], immersion of only the hips and buttocks in the b.

  sponge b., a b. in which the body is washed with a wet sponge or cloth.

bathmotro'pic [G. *bathmos*, threshold, + *tropē*, a turning]. Influencing nervous and muscular excitability in response to stimuli.

batho- [G. *bathos*, depth]. Combining form relating to depth. See also bathy-.

bathopho'bia [G. *bathos*, depth, + *phobos*, fear]. Morbid fear of deep places, or of looking into deep places.

bathy- [G. *bathys*, deep]. Combining form relating to depth. See also batho-.

bath'yanesthe'sia [G. *bathys*, deep, + *an-* priv., + *aisthēsis*, sensation]. Loss of deep or mesoblastic sensibility.

bathyesthesia (bath'ĭ-es-the'zĭ-ah) [G. *bathys*, deep, + *aisthēsis*, sensation]. General term for all subcutaneous sensation.

bathyhyperesthesia (bath-ĭ-hi'per-es-the'zĭ-ah) [G. *bathys*, deep, + *hyper*, above, + *aisthēsis*, sensation]. Exaggerated sensitiveness of muscular tissues and other deep structures.

bathyhypesthesia (bath-ĭ-hip'es-the'zĭ-ah) [G. *bathys*, deep, + *hypo*, under, + *aisthēsis*, sensation]. Impaired sensitiveness of muscular tissues and other deep structures.

BBOT Abbreviation for 2,5[bis-2-(5-*t*-butylbenzoxazolyl)]thiophene.

BCG Bacille bilié de Calmette-Guérin; ballistocardiograph.

BCNU Carmustine.

Be Beryllium.

beaded (be'ded). **1.** Marked by numerous small rounded projections, often arranged in a row like a string of beads. **2.** Applied to a series of noncontinuous bacterial colonies along the line of inoculation in a stab culture. **3.** Denoting stained bacteria in which more deeply stained granules occur at regular intervals in the organism.

bearing down. The expulsive effort of a parturient woman in the second stage of labor.

beat [A.S. *beatan*]. **1.** To strike; to throb or pulsate. **2.** A stroke, impulse, or pulsation, as of the heart or pulse.

  apex b., the visible and/or palpable pulsation made by the apex of the left ventricle as it strikes the chest wall in systole, normally in the left fifth intercostal space.

automatic b., in contrast to forced b., an ectopic b. that arises *de novo* and is not precipitated by the preceding b.

capture b., the cardiac cycle resulting when, after a period of atrioventricular (A-V) dissociation, the atria regain control of the ventricles.

ectopic b., a cardiac b. originating elsewhere than at the sinoatrial node.

escape b., escaped b., an automatic b., usually arising from the A-V node or ventricle, occurring *after* the next expected normal b. has defaulted.

forced b., (1) a premature b. supposedly precipitated in some way by the preceding normal b. to which it is coupled; (2) an extrasystole caused by artificial stimulation of the heart.

fusion b., the atrial or ventricular complex in the electrocardiogram when either atria or ventricles are activated by two simultaneously invading impulses.

heart b., a complete cardiac cycle, including spread of the electrical impulse and the consequent mechanical contraction.

becquerel (Bq) (bek'rel) [Antoine *Becquerel*, French physicist, 1852–1908]. A unit of measurement of radioactivity, equal to 1 disintegration per second; 1 millicure = 37 mBq.

bed. In anatomy, a base or structure that supports another structure.

capillary b., the capillaries considered collectively and their volume capacity.

nail b., *matrix* unguis.

bed'bug. *Cimex lectularius.*

Bedso'nia. Generic name formerly used for organisms now placed in the genus *Chlamydia;* occasionally used as a common term denoting species of *Chlamydia.*

bed'sore. Decubitus *ulcer.*

bed-wetting. Enuresis.

beha'vior. 1. Any response emitted by or elicited from an organism. 2. Any mental or motor act or activity. 3. Specifically, parts of a total response pattern.

beha'vioral. Pertaining to behavior.

beha'viorism. Behavioral psychology; a branch of psychology that attempts to formulate, through systematic observation and experimentation, the laws and principles which underlie the behavior of man and animals; its major contributions have been made in the areas of conditioning and learning.

bel [A. G. *Bell*]. Unit expressing the relative intensity of a sound; the logarithm (to the base 10) of the ratio of the power of the sound to that of a reference sound. Ordinarily, the reference sound is assumed to be one with a power of 10^{-16} watts per sq cm, approximately the threshold of a normal human ear at 1000 Hz.

belch'ing. [A.S. *baelcian*]. Eructation.

belladon'na [It. *bella*, beautiful, + *donna*, lady]. Deadly nightshade; *Atropa belladonna* (family Solanaceae); a perennial herb whose leaves and root contain atropine and related alkaloids which are anticholinergic; used as a powder and tincture.

belly (bel'ĭ) [O.E. *belig*, bag]. 1. The abdomen. 2. Venter (2). 3. Popularly, the stomach or womb.

belonephobia (bel'o-ne-fo'bĭ-ah) [G. *belonē*, needle, + *phobos*, fear]. Morbid fear of needles, pins, and other sharp-pointed objects.

bends [fr. convulsive posture of those so afflicted]. Decompression *sickness.*

benign (be-nīn) [thru O. Fr. fr. L. *benignus*, kind]. Denoting the mild character of an illness or the nonmalignant character of a neoplasm.

benz-. Combining form denoting association with benzene.

benzan'threne. 1,2-Benzanthracene; a carcinogenic hydrocarbon.

ben'zene. Coal tar naphtha; $(CH)_6$; a highly toxic hydrocarbon from light coal tar oil used as the basic structure in the aromatic compounds of all chemistry and as a solvent.

benzetho'nium chloride. A synthetic quaternary ammonium compound, one of the cationic class of detergents; germicidal and bacteriostatic.

ben'zidine. $NH_2C_6H_4C_6H_4NH_2$; used to detect sulfates in water analysis, or for the identification of blood.

benzin, benzine. *Petroleum* benzin.

benzoate (ben'zo-āt). A salt or ester of benzoic acid.

ben'zocaine. $NH_2C_6H_4-COO(C_2H_5)$; the ethyl ester of *p*-aminobenzoic acid; a topical anesthetic agent.

benzodiazepine (ben'zo-di-az'ĕ-pēn). Parent compound for the synthesis of a number of psychoactive compounds having a common molecular configuration and similar pharmacologic activity; *e.g.*, diazepam, chlordiazepoxide.

benzo'natate. An antitussive agent related chemically to tetracaine.

benzosul'fimide. Saccharin.

benzothi'adi'azides. A class of diuretics that increase the excretion of sodium and chloride and an accompanying volume of water, independent of alterations in acid-base balance; most of the compounds in this group are analogues of 1,2,4-benzo-thiadiazine-1,1-dioxide. See also benzthiazide.

benzoyl (ben'zo-il). The benzoic acid radical, C_6H_5CO-.

benzyl (ben'zil). The hydrocarbon radical, $C_6H_5CH_2-$.

benzyl'ic. Relating to or containing benzyl.

benzyl'idene. The hydrocarbon radical, $C_6H_5-CH=$.

ben'zylpenicill'in. *Penicillin* G.

beriberi (ber'ĭ-ber'ĭ) [Singhalese, extreme weakness]. Endemic neuritis; a specific polyneuritis resulting mainly from a deficiency of thiamin in the diet; sensory nerves are likely to be affected more than motor nerves, symptoms beginning in the feet and working upward, with the hands affected later.

berkelium (berk'lĭ-um) [*Berkeley*, Calif., city where first prepared]. An artificial transuranium radioactive element; symbol Bk, atomic no. 97.

Berlin blue. Prussian blue; $Fe_4(Fe(CN)_6)_3$; a dye used to color injection masses for blood vessels and lymphatics, and in staining of siderocytes.

berylliosis (bĕ-ril-ĭ-o'sis). Beryllium poisoning characterized by the occurrence of granulomatous fibrosis, especially of the lungs, from inhalation of beryllium salts.

beryl'lium. A white metal element belonging to the alkaline earths; symbol Be, atomic weight 9.013, atomic no. 4.

bestiality (bes'tĭ-al'ĭ-tĭ). Sexual relations with an animal.

betacism (ba'tă-sizm) [G. *bēta*, the second letter of the alphabet]. A defect in speech in which the sound of *b* is given to other consonants.

betaine (ba'tă-in). $(CH_3)_3N-CH_2COO-$; an oxidation product of choline and a transmethylating intermediate in metabolism.

betameth'asone. 9α-Fluoro-16β-methylprednisolone; a semisynthetic glucocorticoid with anti-inflammatory effects and toxicity similar to those of cortisol; for systemic and topical therapy, its actions are similar to those of prednisone, but more potent.

betatron (ba'tă-tron). A circular electron accelerator that is a source of either high energy electrons or x-rays.

betazole hydrochloride (ba'tă-zōl). An analogue of histamine that stimulates gastric secretion with less tendency to produce the side-effects seen with histamine; used in place of histamine to measure gastric secretory response.

bezoar (be'zōr) [Pers. *padzahr*, antidote]. A concretion formed in the alimentary canal of animals, and occasionally man; according to the substance forming the ball, it may be termed trichobezoar (hairball), trichophytobezoar (hair and vegetable fiber mixed), or phytobezoar (foodball).

Bi Bismuth.

bi- [L.]. Prefix meaning twice or double, referring to double structures, dual actions, etc. See also di- and bis-.

bi'artic'ular. Diarthric.

bicam'eral [bi- + L. *camera*, chamber]. Having two chambers; denoting especially an abscess divided by a more or less complete septum.

bicap'sular. Having a double capsule.

bicar'bonate. HCO_3-; the ion remaining after the first dissociation of carbonic acid.

    standard b., the plasma b. concentration of a sample of whole blood that has been equilibrated at 37°C with a carbon dioxide pressure of 40 mm Hg and an oxygen pressure greater than 100 mm Hg; abnormally high or low values indicate metabolic alkalosis or acidosis, respectively.

bicar'diogram. The composite curve of an electrocardiogram representing the combined effects of the right and left ventricles.

bicel'lular. Having two cells or subdivisions.

biceps (bi'seps) [bi- + L. *caput*, head]. Bicipital.

bicip'ital [bi- + L. *caput*, head]. Biceps; two-headed, denoting a biceps muscle.

bicon'cave. Concavoconcave; concave on two sides; denoting especially a form of lens.

bicon'vex. Convexoconvex; convex on two sides; denoting especially a form of lens.

bicor'nous, bicor'nuate, bicor'nate [bi- + L. *cornu*, horn]. Two-horned; having two processes or projections.

bicro-. Pico- (2).

bi'cron. Picometer.

bicuspid (bi-kus'pid) [bi- + L. *cuspis*, point]. Having two points, prongs, or cusps.

b.i.d. L. *bis in die*, twice a day.

bidactyly (bi-dak'tĭ-lĭ) [bi- + G. *daktylos*, finger]. An abnormality in which only the first and fifth digits are present.

bi'fid [L. *bifidus*, cleft in two parts]. Split or cleft; separated into two parts.

bifocal (bi-fo'kal). Having two foci.

bifo'rate [bi- + L. *foro*, pp. *-atus*, to bore, pierce]. Having two openings.

bifur'cate, bifur'cated [bi- + L. *furca*, fork]. Forked; two-pronged; having two branches.

bifurca'tion. A forking; a division into two branches.

bigeminy (bi-jem'ĭ-nĭ) [bi- + L. *geminus*, twin]. Twinning; pairing; especially, the occurrence of heart beats in pairs.

bilat'eral [bi- + L. *latus*, side]. Relating to, or having, two sides.

bile [L. *bilis*]. Gall; the yellowish brown or green fluid secreted by the liver and discharged into the duodenum where it aids in the emulsification of fats, increases peristalsis, and retards putrefaction.

Bilhar'zia [T. *Bilharz*]. An early name for *Schistosoma*, the genus of trematode worms causing animal and human blood fluke disease.

bilharzi'asis. Schistosomiasis.

bili- [L. *bilis*, bile]. Combining form relating to bile.

bil'iary. Bilious (1); relating to bile.

biligen'esis. Bile production.

biligen'ic. Bile-producing.

bilious (bil'yus). **1.** Biliary; relating to bile. **2.** Relating to or suffering from biliousness.

bil'iousness. An imprecisely delineated congestive disturbance with anorexia, coated tongue, constipation, headache, dizziness, pasty complexion, and, rarely, slight jaundice; assumed to result from hepatic dysfunction.

bilirachia (bil-ĭ-ra'kĭ-ah) [bili- + G. *rachis*, spine]. Bile in the spinal fluid.

bilirubin (bil-ĭ-ru'bin) [bili- + L. *ruber*, red]. A red bile pigment found as sodium bilirubinate (soluble), or as an insoluble calcium salt in gallstones; formed from hemoglobin during normal and abnormal destruction of erythrocytes by the reticuloendothelial system.

    direct reacting b., conjugated b., the fraction of serum b. that has been conjugated with glucuronic acid in the liver cell to form b. diglucuronide; so called because it reacts directly with the Erlich diazo reagent.

indirect reacting b., unconjugated b., the fraction of serum b. that has not been conjugated with glucuronic acid in the liver cell; so called because it reacts with the Erlich diazo reagent only when alcohol is added.

bilirubinemia (bil-ĭ-ru-bin-e′mĭ-ah) [bilirubin + G. *haima,* blood]. Presence of bilirubin in the blood, where normally present in relatively small amounts; usually used in relation to increased concentrations observed in various pathologic conditions where there is excessive destruction of erythrocytes or interference with the mechanism of excretion in the bile.

biliru′binoids. Generic term denoting intermediates in the conversion of bilirubin to stercobilin by reductive enzymes in intestinal bacteria; most are found in normal urine and feces.

biliru′binu′ria [bilirubin + G. *ouron,* urine]. Bilirubin in the urine.

biliuria (bil-ĭ-u′rĭ-ah) [bili- + G. *ouron,* urine]. Choluria; choleuria; presence of various bile salts, or bile, in the urine.

biliver′dine, biliver′din. Dehydrobilirubin; a green bile pigment formed from the oxidation of bilirubin.

bilo′bate. Having two lobes.

bilob′ular. Having two lobules.

biloc′ular, biloc′ulate [bi- + L. *loculus,* dim. of *locus,* a place]. Having two compartments or spaces.

biman′ual [bi- + L. *manus,* hand]. Relating to, or performed by, both hands.

bimas′toid. Relating to both mastoid processes.

bi′nary [L. *binarius,* consisting of two, fr. *bini,* double]. Denoting two.

binau′ral [L. *bini,* a pair, + *auris,* ear]. Binotic; relating to both ears.

bind′er. A broad bandage, especially one encircling the abdomen.

obstetrical b., a garment covering the abdomen from the ribs to the trochanters, affording support after childbirth or, rarely, during childbirth.

binocular (bin-ok′u-lar) [L. *bini,* paired, + *oculus,* eye]. Adapted to the use of both eyes; said of an optical instrument.

binomial (bi-no′mĭ-al) [bi- + G. *nomos,* name]. Consisting of two terms or names; *e.g.,* species names of organisms.

binotic (bin-o′tik) [L. *bini,* a pair, + G. *ous* (ōt-), ear]. Binaural.

binov′ular [L. *bini,* pair, + Mod. L. *ovulum,* dim. of L. *ovum,* egg]. Relating to or derived from two ova.

binuclear, binucleate (bi-nu′kle-ar, bi-nu′kle-āt). Having two nuclei.

binu′cleolate. Having two nucleoli.

bio- [G. *bios,* life]. Combining form denoting life.

bioacoustics (bi′o-ă-kus′tiks). The science concerned with the effects of sound fields or mechanical vibrations in living organisms.

bioassay (bi-o-as′a). Determination of the potency or concentration of a compound by its effect upon animals, isolated tissues, or microorganisms.

bioavailability (bi′o-ă-vāl′ă-bil′ĭ-tĭ). Physiological availability of a given amount of a drug, as distinct from its chemical potency.

biochem′ical. Relating to biochemistry, or physiological chemistry.

biochemistry (bi-o-kem′is-trĭ). Biological or physiological chemistry; the chemistry of living organisms and of the changes occurring therein.

biocidal (bi-o-si′dal) [bio- + L. *caedo,* to kill]. Destructive of life; particularly pertaining to microorganisms.

bi′odegrada′tion. Biotransformation.

bi′odegradable. Denoting a substance that can be chemically degraded or decomposed by natural effectors, *e.g.,* weather, soil bacteria, plants, animals.

biofeed′back. A training technique that enables an individual to gain some element of voluntary control over autonomic body functions; based on the learning principle that a desired response is learned when received information (feedback) indicates that a specific thought complex or action has produced the desired response.

biogenesis (bi′o-jen-′ĕ-sis) [bio- + G. *genesis,* origin]. The now generally accepted view that life originates only from preexisting life and not from nonliving material.

biogenet′ic. Relating to biogenesis.

bi′oinstrument. A sensor or device usually attached to or embedded in body tissue to record and to transmit physiologic data to a receiving and monitoring station.

biokinet′ics [bio- + G. *kinēsis,* motion]. The study of the growth changes and movements that developing organisms undergo.

biologic, biological (bi′o-loj′ik, -loj′ĭ-kal). Relating to biology.

biologist (bi-ol′o-jist). A specialist or expert in biology.

biology (bi-ol′o-jĭ) [bio- + G. *logos,* study]. The science concerned with the phenomena of life and living organisms.

cellular b., cytology.

molecular b., that aspect of b. concerned with biological phenomena in terms of molecular (or chemical) interactions; it differs from biochemistry in that the latter is concerned primarily with the chemical behavior of biologically important substances and analogues thereof, and differs from general biology or parts thereof in its emphasis on chemical interactions, especially those involved in the replication of DNA, its "transcription" into RNA, and its "translation" into or expression in protein, *i.e.,* in the chemical reactions connecting genotype and phenotype.

oral b., that aspect of b. devoted to the study of biological phenomena associated with the oral cavity in health and disease.

radiation b., that field of science which studies the biological effects of ionizing radiation on living systems.

bi'omass. The total weight of all living things in a given area, biotic community, species population, or habitat; a measure of total biotic productivity.

bi'ome. The total complex of biotic communities occupying and characterizing a particular area or zone; *e.g.*, desert, grassland, deciduous forest.

biomechan'ics. The science of the action of forces, internal or external, on the living body.

biomed'ical. 1. Pertaining to those aspects of the natural sciences, especially the biologic and physiologic sciences, that relate to or underlie medicine. **2.** Biological and medical, *i.e.*, encompassing both the science(s) and the art.

biometrician (bi-o-mĕ-trish'an). One who specalizes in the science of biometry.

biom'etry. The statistical analysis of biological data.

biomi'croscope. Slitlamp; in ophthalmology, an instrument consisting of a microscope combined with a rectangular light source.

biomicroscopy (bi-o-mi-kros'ko-pī). **1.** Microscopic examination of living tissue in the body. **2.** Examination of structures of the eye by use of a slitlamp combined with a binocular microscope.

bionecrosis (bi-o-ne-kro'sis). Necrobiosis.

bion'ics [bio- + electronics]. The science of biologic functions and mechanisms as applied to electronic chemistry, such as computers, employing various aspects of physics, mathematics, and chemistry.

biopharmaceutics (bi'o-far-mă-su'tiks). The study of the physical and chemical properties of a drug, and its dosage form, as related to the onset, duration, and intensity of drug action.

biophys'ics. 1. The study of biological processes and materials by means of the theories and tools of physics. **2.** The study of physical processes occurring in organisms.

bi'opsy [bio- + G. *opsis*, vision]. **1.** The process of removing tissue from living patients for diagnostic examination. **2.** A specimen so obtained.

aspiration b., needle b.

brush b., b. obtained by passing a bristled catheter into suspected areas of disease and removing cells that are entrapped in the bristles.

endoscopic b., b. obtained by instruments passed through an endoscope or obtained by a needle introduced under endoscopic guidance.

excision b., excision of tissue for gross and microscopic examination in such a manner that the entire lesion is removed.

incision b., removal of only a part of a lesion by cutting into it.

needle b., aspiration b.; removal of the specimen for b. by aspirating it through an appropriate needle or trocar that pierces the skin, or the external surface of an organ, and into the underlying tissue to be examined.

open b., surgical incision or excision of the region from which the b. is taken.

punch b., removal of a small cylindroid specimen for b. by means of a special instrument that either directly pierces the organ, or through the skin or a small incision in it.

biorhythm (bi'o-rith'm) [bio- + G. *rhythmos*, rhythm]. A biologically inherent cyclic variation or recurrence of an event or state, such as the sleep cycle, circadian rhythms, periodic diseases.

bioso'cial. Involving the interplay of biological and social influences.

bi'ospectrom'etry [bio- + L. *spectrum*, an image, + G. *metron*, measure]. Clinical spectrometry; the spectroscopic determination of the types and amounts of various substances in living tissue or fluid from a living body.

bi'ospectros'copy [bio- + L. *spectrum*, image, + G. *skopeō*, to examine]. Clinical spectroscopy; the spectroscopic examination of specimens of living tissue, including fluids removed therefrom.

biosphere (bi'o-sfēr) [bio- + G. *sphaira*, sphere]. All the regions in the world where living organisms are found.

biostatis'tics. The science of statistics applied to biological or medical data.

biosynthesis (bi-o-sin'the-sis). Formation of a chemical compound by enzymes, either in the organism (*in vivo*) or by fragments or extracts of cells (*in vitro*).

biosystem (bi'o-sis'tem). A living organism or any complete system of living things that can, directly or indirectly, interact with others.

biota (bi-o'tah) [Mod. L. fr. G. *bios*, life]. The collective flora and fauna of a region.

biotelemetry (bi-o-tel-em'ĕ-trī). Technique of monitoring vital processes and transmitting data without wires to a point remote from the subject.

biot'ic. Pertaining to life.

bi'otin. *cis*-Tetrahydro-2-oxothieno[3,4-*d*]imidazoline-4-valeric acid; a component of the vitamin B_2 complex occurring in or required by most organisms.

biotope (bi'o-tōp) [G. *bios*, life, + *topos*, place]. The smallest geographical area providing uniform conditions for life; the physical part of an ecosystem.

biotoxicol'ogy. The study of poisons produced by living organisms.

biotox'in. Any toxic substance formed in an animal body, and demonstrable in its tissues or body fluids, or both.

biotransforma'tion. Biodegradation; conversion within an organism of molecules from one form to another; refers especially to drugs and other xenobiotics, a change often associated with change in pharmacologic activity.

bi'otype. 1. A population or group of individuals composed of the same genotype. **2.** In bacteriology, former name for biovar.

bi'ovar. A group (infrasubspecific) of bacterial strains distinguishable from other strains of the same species on the basis of physiological characters.

bi'paren'tal. Having two parents, male and female.

bip'arous [bi- + L. *pario,* to give birth]. Bearing two offspring.

bipen'nate, bipen'niform [bi- + L. *penna,* feather]. Denoting a muscle with a central tendon toward which the fibers converge on either side like the barbs of a feather.

biphenyl (bi-fen'il). Diphenyl; phenylbenzene; an aromatic hydrocarbon; polychlorinated b.'s are industrial carcinogens.

bipo'lar. 1. Having two poles; denoting those nerve cells in which the branches project from two, usually opposite, points. 2. Relating to both ends or poles of a bacterial or other cell.

bi'potential'ity. The capability of differentiating along two developmental pathways.

biramous (bi-ra'mus) [bi- + L. *ramus,* branch]. Having two branches.

birefringence (bi-re-frin'jens). Double *refraction.*

birefringent (bi-re-frin'jent). Refracting twice; splitting a ray of light in two.

birth. Passage of offspring from the uterus to the outside world; the act of being born.

  premature b., the b. of an infant after the period of viability but before full term.

birth'mark. Nevus (1).

bis- [L.]. Prefix signifying two or twice. In chemical terminology, used to denote the presence of two identical but separated complex groups in one molecule. See also bi-.

bis'albu'mine'mia. A genetic polymorphism characterized by the presence of two kinds of serum albumin that differ in mobility on electrophoresis.

2,5-bis[2-(5-*t*-butylbenzoxazolyl)]thiophene(BBOT). A scintillator used in radioactivity measurements by scintillation counting.

bisex'ual. Ambisexual. 1. Having gonads of both sexes. 2. Denoting an individual who engages in both heterosexual and homosexual relations.

bisferious (bis-fe'rī-us) [L. *bis,* twice, + *ferio,* to strike]. Striking twice; said of the pulse.

bishydrox'ycoum'arin. Dicumarol.

bisiliac (bis-il'ī-ak). Relating to any two corresponding iliac parts or structures, as the iliac bones or iliac fossae.

bismuth (biz'muth) [Ger. *Wismut*]. A trivalent metallic element, chemical symbol Bi, atomic no. 83, atomic weight 209; several of its salts are used in medicine, some of which contain BiO^+, rather than Bi^{3+}, and carry the prefix sub-.

bismutho'sis. Chronic bismuth poisoning.

bis'muthyl. The group BiO^+, that behaves chemically as the ion of a univalent metal; its salts are the oxysalts or subsalts of bismuth.

1,4-bis(5-phenyloxazol-2-yl)benzene (POPOP). A liquid scintillation agent used in radioisotope measurement.

bistoury (bis'tu-rī) [Fr. *bistouri,* fr. *bisorit,* dagger]. A long, narrow-bladed knife, straight or curved on the edge, sharp or blunt pointed; used for opening abscesses, slitting sinuses and fistulas, etc.

bisul'fate. Acid sulfate; disulfate; a salt containing HSO_4^-.

bisul'fide. 1. Disulfide (1). 2. A compound of the anion HS^-; an acid sulfide.

bisul'fite. A salt or ion of HSO_3^-.

bitar'trate. A salt or anion resulting from the neutralization of one of tartaric acid's two acid groups.

bite [A.S. *bitan*]. 1. To incise or seize with the teeth. 2. A wound or puncture of the skin made by animal or insect. See bites. 3. Jargon for terms such as interocclusal record, checkbite, maxillomandibular registration, denture space, and interarch distance.

bite'plate, bite'plane. A removable appliance that incorporates a plane of acrylic designed to occlude with the opposing teeth.

bites [see bite]. Puncture or laceration of the skin by animals or insects, with reactions as the result of mechanical injury, injection of toxic material, injection of antigenic substance capable of inducing and eliciting allergic sensitization, introduction of otherwise saprophytic flora, invasion of the tissue by the organism, or transmission of disease.

bite'wing. See bitewing *radiograph.*

bitrochanteric (bi-tro-kan-ter'ik). Relating to two trochanters, either to the two trochanters of one femur or to both great trochanters.

biuret (bi'u-ret'). Carbamoylurea; $NH(CONH_2)_2$; derivative of urea obtained by heating, eliminating NH_3 between two ureas.

bivalence, bivalency (bi-va'lens, bi-va'len-sī). Divalence; divalency; the state of being bivalent (1).

bivalent (bi-va'lent, biv'ă-lent) [bi- + L. *valere,* to have power]. 1. Divalent; having a combining power equal to two atoms of hydrogen. 2. In cytology, a structure consisting of two paired homologous chromosomes, each split into two sister chromatids, as seen during the pachytene stage of prophase in meiosis.

biven'tral [bi- + L. *venter,* belly]. Digastric (1).

Bk Berkelium.

black'head. Comedo.

black'out. Temporary loss of consciousness due to decreased blood flow to the brain.

blad'der [A.S. *blaedre*]. Vesica (1).

  atonic b., a large, dilated, and nonemptying b.; usually due to disturbance of innervation or to chronic obstruction.

  autonomic b., involuntary spontaneous or induced periodic reflex emptying of the b.

  nervous b., a b. condition in which there is a need to urinate frequently but with failure to empty the b. completely.

  neurogenic b., defective functioning of bladder due to impaired innervation.

reflex neurogenic b., an abnormal condition of b. function whereby the b. is cut off from upper motor neuron control, but the lower motor neuron arc is still intact.

uninhibited neurogenic b., a condition, either congenital or acquired, of abnormal b. function whereby normal inhibitory control of detruser function by the central nervous system is impaired or underdeveloped, resulting in precipitant or uncontrolled micturition and/or aneuresis.

urinary b., vesica urinaria.

blad'derworm. Cysticercus.

-blast [G. blastos, germ]. Suffix indicating an immature precursor cell of the type indicated by the preceding word.

blaste'ma [G. a sprout]. **1.** The primordial cellular mass from which an organ or part is formed. **2.** A cluster of cells competent to initiate the regeneration of a damaged or ablated structure.

blastem'ic. Relating to the blastema.

blasto- [G. blastos, germ]. Combining form pertaining to the process of budding (and the formation of buds) by cells or tissue.

blastocele (blas'to-sēl) [blasto- + G. koilos, hollow]. Cleavage or segmentation cavity; the cavity in the blastula of a developing embryo.

blastoce'lic. Relating to a blastocele.

blastocyst (blas'to-sist) [blasto- + G. kystis, bladder]. Blastodermic vesicle; the modified blastula stage of mammalian embryos, consisting of the inner cell mass and a thin trophoblast layer enclosing the blastocele.

blastocyte (blas'to-sīt) [blasto- + G. kytos, cell]. An undifferentiated blastomere of the morula or blastula stage of an embryo.

blastocyto'ma. Blastomoma.

blas'toderm, blastoder'ma [blasto- + G. derma, skin]. Germ or germinal membrane; the thin disk-shaped cell mass of a young embryo and its extraembryonic extensions over the surface of the yolk; when fully formed, all three of the primary germ layers (ectoderm, endoderm, and mesoderm) are present.

blastoder'mal, blastoder'mic. Relating to the blastoderm.

blas'todisk. 1. The disk of active cytoplasm at the animal pole of a telolecithal egg. **2.** The blastoderm, especially in very young stages when its extent is small.

blastogenesis (blas'to-jen'ē-sis) [blasto- + G. genesis, origin]. **1.** Reproduction of unicellular organisms by budding. **2.** Development of an embryo during cleavage and germ layer formation. **3.** Transformation of small lymphocytes of human peripheral blood in tissue culture into large, morphologically primitive blastlike cells capable of undergoing mitosis.

blastogenet'ic, blastogen'ic. Relating to blastogenesis.

blasto'ma [blasto- + G. -oma, tumor]. Blastocytoma; carcinosarcoma of embryonal type; a neoplasm composed chiefly or entirely of immature undifferentiated cells (i.e., blast forms), with little or virtually no stroma.

blas'tomere [blasto- + G. meros, part]. One of the cells into which the egg divides after its fertilization.

Blastomyces dermatitidis (blas-to-mi'sēz der-mă-tit'ĭ-dis) [blasto- + G. mykēs, fungus]. A species of dimorphic fungus that causes blastomycosis; its perfect state is Ajellomyces dermatitidis.

blastomycosis (blas'to-mi-ko'sis). A chronic granulomatous and suppurative disease, caused by Blastomyces dermatitidis, that originates as a respiratory infection and disseminates, usually with pulmonary, osseous, and cutaneous involvement predominating. Formerly called North American b.

South American b., paracoccidioidomycosis.

blastopore (blas'to-pōr) [blasto- + G. poros, opening]. The opening into the archenteron formed by the invagination of the blastula to form a gastrula.

blastospore (blas'to-spōr) [blasto- + G. sporos, seed]. A thallospore formed by budding, as in the yeasts.

blas'tula [G. blastos, germ]. An early stage of an embryo formed by the rearrangement of the blastomeres of the morula to form a hollow sphere.

blas'tular. Pertaining to the blastula.

blastula'tion. Formation of the blastula or blastocyst.

bleb. A large flaccid vesicle.

bleed'ing. Losing blood as a result of rupture or severance of blood vessels.

dysfunctional uterine b., uterine b. due to an endocrine imbalance rather than to any organic disease.

occult b., see occult blood.

blem'ish. A small circumscribed alteration of the skin considered to be unesthetic but insignificant.

blennadeni'tis [G. blennos, mucus, + adēn, gland, + -itis, inflammation]. Inflammation of the mucous glands.

blenno-, blenn- [G. blennos, mucus]. Combining form relating to mucus.

blennogen'ic [blenno- + G. -gen, to produce]. Muciparous.

blennogenous (blen-oj'en-us). Muciparous.

blennoid (blen'oyd) [blenno- + G. eidos, resemblance]. Muciform.

blennorrhagia (blen'o-ra'jĭ-ah) [blenno- + G. rhēgnymi, to burst forth]. Blennorrhea.

blennorrhagic (blen-o-raj'ik). Blennorheal.

blennorrhea (blen'o-re'ah) [blenno- + G. rhoia, a flow]. Blennorrhagia. **1.** Myxorrhea; any mucous discharge, especially from the urethra or vagina. **2.** An obsolete term for gonorrhea.

blennorrhe'al. Blennorrhagic; relating to blennorrhea.

blennostasis (blen-os'tă-sis) [blenno- + G. stasis, standing]. Diminution or suppression of secretion from the mucous membranes.

blennostat'ic. Relating to blennostasis.

blennu'ria [blenno- + G. *ouron*, urine]. Mucus in the urine.

bleomy'cin sulfate. An antineoplastic antibiotic obtained from *Streptomyces verticillus.*

blephar-. See blepharo-.

blepharadenitis (blef'ar-ad-ĕ-ni'tis) [blephar- + G. *adĕn*, gland, + *-itis*, inflammation]. Blepharoadenitis; inflammation of the meibomian glands or the marginal glands of Moll or Zeis.

blepharectomy (blef'ar-ek'to-mī) [blepharo- + G. *ektomē*, excision]. Excision of all or part of an eyelid.

blepharedema (blef'ar-ē-de'mah). Edema of the eyelids, causing swelling and often a baggy appearance.

blepharitis (blef'ă-ri'tis) [blepharo- + G. *-itis*, inflammation]. Inflammation of the eyelids.

bleph'aroadeni'tis. Blepharadenitis.

blepharoadenoma (blef'ar-o-ad-ĕ-no'mah) [blepharo- + G. *adĕn*, gland, + *-oma*, tumor]. A glandular tumor, or adenoma, of the eyelid.

blepharo-, blephar- [G. *blepharon*, eyelid]. Combining forms meaning eyelid.

blepharochalasis (blef'ar-o-kal'ă-sis) [blepharo- + G. *chalasis*, a slackening]. Redundancy of the upper eyelids so that a fold of skin hangs down, often concealing the tarsal margin when the eye is open.

bleph'aroconjunctivi'tis. Inflammation of the palpebral conjunctiva.

blepharokeratoconjunctivitis (blef'ar-o-ker'ă-to-kon-junk'tī-vi'tis). Inflammation involving the margins of the lids, cornea, and conjunctiva.

blepharon'cus (blef'ar-ong'kus) [blephar- + G. *onkos*, a mass]. A tumor of the eyelid.

blepharophimosis (blef'ar-o-fī-mo'sis) [blepharo- + G. *phimōsis*, an obstruction]. Blepharostenosis; decrease in palpebral aperture without fusion of lid margins.

bleph'aroplas'tic. Relating to blepharoplasty.

blepharoplasty (blef'ar-o-plast-tī) [blepharo + G. *plassō*, to form]. Tarsoplasty; surgical correction of a defect in the eyelid.

blepharoplegia (blef'ar-o-ple'jī-ah) [blepharo- + G. *plēgē*, stroke]. Paralysis of an eyelid.

blepharoptosis (blef'ar-o-to'sis, op'to-sis) [blepharo- + G. *ptōsis*, a falling]. Drooping of the upper eyelid.

blepharorrhaphy (blef-ar-or'ă-fī) [blepharo- + G. *rhaphē*, seam]. Tarsorrhaphy.

bleph'arospasm. Spasmodic winking, or contraction of the orbicularis palpebrarum muscle.

bleph'arostat [blepharo- + G. *statos*, fixed]. An instrument used to hold the eyelids apart.

bleph'arosteno'sis [blepharo- + G. *stenōsis*, a narrowing]. Blepharophimosis.

blepharosynechia (blef'ar-o-sin-ek'ĭ-ah) [blepharo- + G. *synecheia*, continuity, fr, *syn-echō*, to hold together]. Ankyloblepharon; adhesion of the eyelids to each other or to the eyeball.

blepharot'omy [blepharo- + G. *tomē*, incision]. Surgical cutting of an eyelid.

blind. Unable to see; without useful sight.

blind'ness. Typhlosis; loss of the sense of sight; absolute b. connotes no light perception.

color b., hereditary or acquired; partial or complete, deficiency of color perception.

cortical b., loss of sight due to an organic lesion in the visual cortex.

day b., hemeralopia.

flash b., temporary loss of vision produced when retinal light-sensitive pigments are bleached by light more intense than that to which the retina is physiologically adapted at that moment.

functional b., loss of vision related to conversion hysteria.

legal b., generally, visual acuity of less than 6/60 or 20/200 using Snellen test types, or visual field restriction to 20 degrees or less.

night b., nyctalopia.

river b., ocular *onchocerciasis.*

snow b., severe photophobia secondary to ultraviolet keratoconjunctivitis.

blis'ter. A fluid-filled vesicle under or within the epidermis.

blood b., a b. containing blood, resulting from a minor pinch or crushing injury.

fever b., herpes simplex of the lips.

fly b., a cantharidal b. caused by discharge of a vesicating body fluid by certain beetles.

blis'tering. Vesiculation (1).

bloat, bloating (blōt). Abdominal distention from swallowed air or intestinal gas from fermentation.

block [Fr. *bloquer*]. **1.** To obstruct; to arrest passage through. **2.** A condition in which the passage of a nervous impulse is arrested, wholly or in part, temporarily or permanently. **3.** Atrioventricular b.

anterograde b., conduction b. of an impulse traveling anywhere in its ordinary direction, from the sinoatrial node toward the ventricular myocardium.

atrioventricular (A-V) b., block (3); impairment of the normal conduction between atria and ventricles.

bundle-branch b., intraventricular b. due to interruption of conduction in one of the two main branches of the bundle of His and manifested in the electrocardiogram by marked prolongation of the QRS complex.

depolarizing b., skeletal muscle paralysis associated with loss of polarity of the motor endplate, as occurs following administration of succinylcholine.

field b., regional anesthesia produced by infiltration of a local anesthetic solution into the tissues surrounding an operative field.

intra-atrial b., impaired conduction through the atria, manifested by widened and often notched P waves in the electrocardiogram.

intraventricular (I-V) b., delayed conduction within the ventricular conducting system or myocardium, including bundle-branch and peri-infarction b.'s, and the hemiblocks.

nerve b., interruption of the passage of impulses through a nerve by the injection of alcohol or local anesthetic solutions.

nondepolarizing b., skeletal muscle paralysis unaccompanied by changes in polarity of the motor endplate, as occurs following administration of tubocurarine.

peri-infarction b., an electrocardiographic abnormality associated with an old myocardial infarct and caused by delayed activation of the myocardium in the region of the infarct; characterized by an initial vector directed away from the infarcted region with terminal vector directed toward it.

phase I b., inhibition of nerve impulse transmission across the myoneural junction associated with depolarization of the motor endplate, as in the muscle paralysis produced by succinylcholine.

phase II b., inhibition of nerve impulse transmission across the myoneural junction unaccompanied by depolarization of the motor endplate, as in the muscle paralysis produced by tubocurarine.

retrograde b., impaired conduction backward from the ventricles or A-V node into the atria.

sinus, sinoatrial, or **sinoauricular (S-A) b.,** failure of the impulse to leave the sinus node.

spinal b., (1) pathologic obstruction of the flow of cerebrospinal fluid in the spinal subarachnoid space; (2) inaccurate term for spinal anesthesia.

stellate b., injection of local anesthetic solution in the vicinity of the stellate ganglion.

Wilson, b., the commonest form of right bundle-branch b., characterized in lead I by a tall slender R wave followed by a wider S wave of lower voltage.

block′ade. 1. Intravenous injection of large amounts of colloidal dyes or other substances whereby the reaction of the reticuloendothelial cells to other influences is temporarily prevented. **2.** Arrest of transmission at autonomic synaptic junctions, autonomic receptor sites, or myoneural junctions by a drug.

adrenergic b., selective inhibition by a drug of the responses of effector cells to adrenergic sympathetic nerve impulses (sympatholytic) and to epinephrine and related amines (adrenolytic).

cholinergic b., (1) inhibition by a drug of nerve impulse transmission at autonomic ganglionic synapses (ganglionic b.), at postganglionic parasympathetic effector cells (*e.g.,* by atropine), and at myoneural junctions (myoneural b.); (2) inhibition of a cholinergic agent.

ganglionic b., inhibition of nerve impulse transmission at autonomic ganglionic synapses by drugs such as nicotine or hexamethonium.

myoneural b., inhibition of nerve impulse transmission at myoneural junctions by a drug such as curare.

narcotic b., the use of drugs to inhibit the effects of narcotic substances.

blood (blud) [A.S. blōd]. The "circulating tissue" of the body; the fluid and its suspended formed elements that are circulated through the heart, arteries, capillaries, and veins by means of which oxygen and nutritive materials are transported to tissues, and carbon dioxide and various metabolic products are removed for excretion; b. consists of plasma in which are suspended erythrocytes, leukocytes, and platelets.

arterial b., b. that is oxygenated in the lungs, is found in the left chambers of the heart and in the arteries, and is relatively bright red.

occult b., b. in the feces in amounts too small to be seen but detectable by chemical tests.

venous b., b. that has passed through the capillaries of various tissues (except the lungs), is found in the veins, right chambers of the heart, and pulmonary arteries, and is usually dark red as a result of a lower content of oxygen.

whole b., b. drawn from a selected donor under rigid aseptic precautions; contains citrate ion or heparin as an anticoagulant.

blood bank. A place, usually a separate part or division of a hospital laboratory, in which blood is collected from donors, typed, and often separated into several components for transfusion to recipients.

blood count. Calculation of the number of red (RBC) or white (WBC) blood cells in a cubic millimeter of blood, by means of counting the cells in an accurate volume of diluted blood; also, the determination of the percentages of various types of leukocytes, *i.e.,* a differential count, as observed in a stained film of blood.

complete b. c. (CBC), a combination of the following determinations: red blood cell count, white blood cell count, erythrocyte indices, hematocrit, and differential blood count.

differential white b. c., an estimate of the percentage of white blood cell types which make up the total white blood cell count.

Schilling's b. c., Schilling's index; a method of counting blood in which the polymorphonuclear neutrophils are separated into four groups according to the number and arrangement of the nuclear masses in these cells.

blood group. A system of genetically determined antigens or agglutinogens located on the surface of the erythrocyte, each group determined by a series of two or more genes that are allelic or at least very closely linked on a single chromosome; because of the antigen differences existing between individuals, blood groups are important with respect to blood transfusions, maternal-fetal blood group incompatibilities, and tissue and organ transplantation. See also blood type.

blood grouping. Blood typing; the classification of blood samples by means of appropriate laboratory tests according to their agglutination reactions with respect to one or more blood groups. In general, a suspension of erythrocytes to be tested is exposed to a known specific antiserum; agglutination of the erythrocytes indicates that they possess the antigen for which the antiserum is specific, while absence of agglutination indicates absence of the antigen.

blood'letting. Removing blood, usually from a vein; formerly used as a general remedial measure, but used now in congestive heart failure and polycythemia.

blood'shot. Locally congested, the smaller blood vessels of the part, *e.g.*, the conjunctiva, being dilated and visible.

bloodstream. The flowing blood as it is encountered in the organism, as distinguished from blood which has been removed from the organism or sequestered in a part.

blood type. The specific reaction pattern of erythrocytes of an individual to the antisera of one blood group; *e.g.*, the ABO blood group consists of four major blood types, O, A, B, and AB, depending on agglutination of erythrocytes by neither, one, the other, or both anti-A and anti-B testing sera. The blood type is the genetic phenotype of the individual for one blood group system and may vary in detail with the number of different antisera available for testing.

blood typing. Blood grouping.

blood vessel. A tube (artery, capillary, vein, or sinus) conveying blood.

blush. A sudden and brief redness of the face and neck due to emotion.

B-mode. A two-dimensional diagnostic ultrasound presentation of echo-producing interfaces in a single plane; the intensity of the echo is represented by modulation of the brightness (B) of the spot, and the position of the echo is determined from the position of the transducer and the transit time of the acoustical pulse.

BMR Basal metabolic *rate*.

body (bod'ĭ) [A.S. *bodig*]. **1.** The head, neck, trunk, and extremities. **2.** The material part of man, as distinguished from the mind and spirit. **3.** The principal mass of any structure. **4.** A thing; a substance. See also corpus; soma.

acetone b., ketone b.

aortic b., *glomus* aorticum.

Aschoff b.'s, a form of granulomatous inflammation characteristically observed in acute rheumatic carditis, consisting of fibrinoid change in connective tissue, lymphocytes, occasional plasma cells, and peculiar histiocytes.

asteroid b., **(1)** an eosinophilic inclusion resembling a star with delicate radiating lines, occuring in a vacuolated area of cytoplasm of a multinucleated giant cell; especially frequent in sarcoidosis, but occurs also in other granulomas; **(2)** a structure that is characteristic of sporotrichosis when found in the skin or secondary lesions of this mycosis.

Auer b.'s. rod-shaped structures of uncertain nature in the cytoplasm of immature myeloid cells,

especially myeloblasts, in acute myelocytic leukemia.

Babès-Ernst b.'s, metachromatic granules; intracellular granules, present in many species of bacteria, which possess a strong affinity for nuclear stains.

Barr chromatin b., sex *chromatin*.

basal b., basal granule; an elongated b. situated at the apical margin of a cell; has nine peripheral triplomicrotubules continuous with the peripheral diplomicrotubules of each cilium or flagellum.

Bollinger b.'s, relatively large, spheroid or ovoid, usually somewhat granular, acidophilic, intracytoplasmic inclusion b.'s observed in the infected tissues of birds with fowlpox; when b.'s are ruptured large numbers of fowlpox virus particles are released.

Cabot's ring b.'s, ring-shaped or figure-8 structures, staining red with Wright's stain, found in red blood cells in severe anemias.

Call-Exner b.'s, small fluid-filled spaces between granulosal cells in ovarian follicles and in ovarian tumors of granulosal origin; may form a rosette-like structure.

carotid b., *glomus* caroticum.

cavernous b., see *corpus* cavernosum clitoridis; *corpus* cavernosum penis.

cell b., the part of the cell containing the nucleus.

chromaffin b., paraganglion.

chromatin b., the genetic apparatus of bacteria.

ciliary b., *corpus* ciliare.

Councilman (hyaline) b., an eosinophilic globule, seen in the liver in yellow fever, derived from necrosis of a single hepatic cell.

cytoplasmic inclusion b.'s, see inclusion b.'s.

Döhle b.'s, discrete round or oval b.'s found in neutrophils of patients with infections, burns, trauma, pregnancy, or cancer.

Donovan b., Leishman-Donovan b.

Ehrlich's inner b., Heinz-Ehrlich b., a round oxyphil b. found in the red blood cell in case of hemocytolysis due to a specific blood poison.

foreign b., anything in the tissues or cavities of the b. that has been introduced there from without.

geniculate b., see *corpus* geniculatum laterale; *corpus* geniculatum mediale.

Heinz-Ehrlich b., Ehrlich's inner b.

Highmore's b., *mediastinum* testis.

Howell-Jolly b.'s, spherical or ovoid eccentrically located granules occasionally observed in the stroma of circulating erythrocytes, more frequently and in greater numbers after splenectomy.

hyaline b.'s, homogeneous eosinophilic inclusions in the cytoplasm of epithelial cells; in renal tubules they represent droplets of protein reabsorbed from the lumen.

hyaloid b., *corpus* vitreum.

immune b., early term for antibody.

inclusion b.'s, distinctive structures frequently formed in the nucleus and/or cytoplasm in cells infected with certain filtrable viruses, observed especially in nerve, epithelial, or endothelial cells. **Nuclear inclusion b.'s** are usually acidophilic and are of two morphologic types: 1) granular, hyaline, or amorphous b.'s of various sizes, occurring in such diseases as herpes simplex infection or yellow fever; 2) more circumscribed b.'s, frequently with several in the same nucleus (and no reaction in adjacent tissue), occurring in such diseases as Rift Valley fever and poliomyelitis. **Cytoplasmic inclusion b.'s** may be: 1) acidophilic, relatively large, spherical or ovoid, and somewhat granular, as in variola or vaccinia, rabies, and molluscum contagiosum; 2) basophilic, relatively large, complex combinations of viral and cellular material, as in trachoma, psittacosis, and lymphopathia venereum.

intercarotid b., *glomus* caroticum.

ketone b., acetone b.; one of a group of ketones, including acetoacetic acid, its reduction product, β-hydroxybutyric acid, and its decarboxylation product, acetone; high in tissues and body fluids in ketosis.

Lafora b., an intraneuronal inclusion b. composed of acid mucopolysaccharides, seen in familial myoclonus epilepsy.

lateral geniculate b., *corpus* geniculatum laterale.

Leishman-Donovan b., amastigote; Donovan b.; the intracytoplasmic, nonflagellated leishmanial form of certain intracellular flagellates, such as species of *Leishmania* or the intracellular form of *Trypanosoma cruz;* originally used for *Leishmania donovani* parasites in infected spleen or liver cells in kala azar.

Mallory b.'s, large, poorly defined accumulations of eosinophilic material in the cytoplasm of damaged hepatic cells in certain forms of cirrhosis and marked fatty change especially due to alcoholism.

malpighian b.'s, *folliculi* lymphatici lienales.

mamillary b., *corpus* mamillare.

medial geniculate b., *corpus* geniculatum mediale.

metachromatic b.'s, concentrated deposits primarily of polymetaphosphate, occurring in many bacteria as well as in algae, fungi, and protozoa, which differ in staining properties from the surrounding protoplasm.

Michaelis-Gutmann b., a rounded homogenous or concentrically laminated b. containing calcium and iron; found within macrophages in the bladder wall in malakoplakia.

multilamellar b., cytosome (2).

Negri b.'s, eosinophilic, sharply outlined, pathognomonic inclusion b.'s found in the cytoplasm of certain nerve cells containing the virus of rabies, especially in Ammon's horn of the hippocampus.

Nissl b.'s, Nissl *substance.*

nuclear inclusion b.'s, see inclusion b.'s.

pacchionian b.'s, *granulationes* arachnoideales.

paraaortic b.'s, *corpora* paraaortica.

parabasal b., in certain parasitic flagellates, a distinct structure near the nucleus, probably equivalent to the metazoan Golgi apparatus.

Paschen b.'s, particles of virus observed in relatively large numbers in squamous cells of the skin in variola (smallpox) or vaccinia.

pineal b., *corpus* pineale.

polar b., one of the two small cells formed by the ovum during its maturation: the first is usually released just prior to ovulation; the second not until after the ovum has been discharged from the ovary and penetrated by a sperm cell.

psammoma b.'s, (1) mineralized b.'s occurring in the meninges, choroid plexus, and in certain meningiomas; **(2)** brain *sand;* **(3)** calcospherite.

quadrigeminal b.'s, *corpora* quadrigemina.

restiform b., *pedunculus* cerebellaris inferior.

Russell b.'s, small, spherical, intracytoplasmic hyaline b.'s that occur frequently in plasma cells in chronic inflammation.

b. of stomach, *corpus* ventriculi.

striate b., *corpus* striatum.

trachoma b.'s., intracytoplasmic forms found in the conjunctival epithelial cells in the acute phase of trachoma, less frequently in later stages.

vitreous b., *corpus* vitreum.

wolffian b., mesonephros.

Wolf-Orton b.'s, intranuclear inclusion b.'s of nonviral origin found in cells of malignant neoplasms, especially those of glial cell origin.

boil [A.S. *byl,* a swelling]. Furuncle.

bo'lus [L. fr. G. *bōlos,* lump, clod]. **1.** A very large pill, usually of soft consistency. **2.** A masticated morsel of food ready to be swallowed.

intravenous b., a large volume of fluid given intravenously and rapidly at one time for immediate response.

bond. In chemistry, the force holding two neighboring atoms in place and resisting their separation. An **electrovalent b.** consists of the attraction between oppositely charged groups; a **covalent b.** results from the sharing of one, two, or three pairs of electrons by the bonded atoms.

conjugated double b.'s, two double b.'s separated by one single b.

coordinate b., semipolar b.

disulfide b., the –S–S– link binding two peptide chains (or different parts of one peptide chain); occurs as part of the molecule of the amino acid, cystine, and is important as a structural determinant in many protein molecules.

double b., a covalent b. resulting from the sharing of two pairs of electrons; *e.g.,* $CH_2 = CH_2$ (ethylene).

high energy phosphate b., see high energy *phosphates.*

hydrogen b., a b. arising from the sharing of a H atom, covalently bound to N or O, with another N or O; such b.'s link purines on one strand to pyrimidines in the other strand of nucleic acids, thus maintaining double-stranded structures.

peptide b., the common link (–CO–NH–) between amino acids in proteins, actually a form of amide linkage, formed by elimination of H_2O between the –CO–OH of one amino acid and the H_2N of another.

simipolar b., coordinate b.; a b. in which the two electrons shared by a pair of atoms belonged originally to only one of the atoms; often represented by a small arrow pointing toward the electron receiver; *e.g.,* nitric acid, $O(OH)N \rightarrow O$.

single b., a covalent b. resulting from the sharing of one pair of electrons; *e.g.,* $CH_3 - CH_3$ (ethane).

triple b., a covalent b. resulting from the sharing of three pairs of electrons; *e.g.,* $CH \equiv CH$ (acetylene).

bone [A.S. *bān*]. A hard connective tissue consisting of cells in a matrix of ground substance and collagen fibers; the fibers are impregnated with mineral substance, chiefly calcium phosphate and carbonate, which comprises about 67% by weight of adult bone. For anatomical definitions of bones as part of the animal skeleton, see under os.

ankle b., talus.

breast b., sternum.

brittle b.'s, *osteogenesis* imperfecta.

b.'s of digits, *ossa* digitorum pedis and manus.

calf b., fibula.

cancellous b., *substantia* spongiosa.

capitate b., *os* capitatum.

carpal b.'s, *ossa* carpi. See carpus (2).

cartilage b., endochondral b.

collar b., clavicula.

compact b., *substantia* compacta.

cortical b., *substantia* corticalis.

cranial b.'s, *ossa* cranii.

cuboid b., *os* cuboideum.

cuneiform b., *os* cuneiforme and *os* triquetrum.

elbow b., ulna.

endochondral b., cartilage b.; a b. that develops in a cartilage after the latter is partially or entirely destroyed.

ethmoid b., *os* ethmoidale.

facial b.'s, *ossa* faciei.

flat b., *os* planum.

frontal b., *os* frontale.

hamate b., *os* hamatum.

heel b., calcaneus.

hip b., *os* coxae.

hollow b., *os* pneumaticum.

hyoid b., *os* hyoideum.

iliac b., *os* ilium.

incisive b., *os* incisivum.

innominate b., *os* coxae.

intermaxillary b., *os* incisivum.

irregular b., *os* irregulare.

ischial b., *os* ischii.

jaw b., maxilla or, especially, mandibula.

jugal b., *os* zygomaticum.

lacrimal b., *os* lacrimale.

lamellar b., b. in which the tubular lamellae are formed that are characterized by having collagen fibers arranged in a parallel, spiral manner.

long b., *os* longum.

lunate b., *os* lunatum.

malar b., *os* zygomaticum.

marble b.'s, osteopetrosis.

mastoid b., *processus* mastoideus (1).

membrane b., a b. developed within a connective tissue membrane, as contrasted with endochondral b.

multangular b., see *os* trapezium and trapezoideum.

nasal b., *os* nasale.

navicular b., *os* naviculare.

nonlamellar b., woven b.

occipital b., *os* occipitale.

palatine b., *os* palatinum.

parietal b., *os* parietale.

perichondral b., periosteal b., in the development of a long b., a collar or cuff of osseous tissue forms in the perichondrium of the cartilage model; the connective tissue membrane of this perichondral b. then becomes periosteum.

petrosal b., petrous b., *pars* petrosa ossis temporalis.

pisiform b., *os* pisiforme.

pneumatic b., *os* pneumaticum.

premaxillary b., *os* incisivum.

pubic b., *os* pubis.

pyramidal b., *os* triquetrum.

reticulated b., woven b.

rider's b., ossification of the tendon of the adductor longus from strain in horseback riding.

scaphoid b., *os* scaphoideum.

scroll b.'s, see *concha* nasalis inferior, media, superior, and suprema.

semilunar b., *os* lunatum.

sesamoid b., *os* sesamoideum. See also *ossa* digitorum manus and pedis.

shin b., tibia.

short b., *os* breve.

sphenoid b., *os* sphenoidale.

spongy b., (1) *substantia* spongiosa; (2) one of the turbinated b.'s.

sutural b.'s, *ossa* suturarum.

tarsal b.'s, *ossa* tarsus.

temporal b., *os* temporale.

thigh b., *os* femoris.

trabecular b., *substantia* spongiosa.

trapezium b., *os* trapezium.

trapezoid b., *os* trapezoideum.

triangular b., *os* trigonum.

triquetral b., *os* triquetrum.

turbinated b.'s, see *concha* nasalis inferior, media, superior, and suprema.

tympanic b., *anulus* tympanicus.

unciform b., *os* hamatum.

wedge b., see *os* cuneiforme mediale and laterale.

wormian b.'s, *ossa* suturarum.

woven b., nonlamellar or reticulated b.; bony tissue characteristic of the embryonal skeleton in which the collagen fibers of the matrix are arranged irregularly in the form of interlacing networks.

zygomatic b., *os* zygomaticum.

bonelet (bōn´let). Ossiculum.

boos´ter. See under dose.

bo´rate. A salt of boric acid.

bo´rax. *Sodium* borate.

borborygmus, pl. **borborygmi** (bor´bo-rig´mus, -rig´mi) [G. *borborygmos*, rumbling in the bowels]. Rumbling or gurgling noises produced by movement of gas in the alimentary canal, and audible at a distance.

bor´der. The part of a surface that forms its outer boundary, as an edge, margin, or process.

brush b., an epithelial surface consisting of microvilli, such as occur on the cells of the proximal tubule of the nephron.

striated b., the free surface of the columnar absorptive cells of the intestine formed by microvilli, giving the appearance of parallel striations with the light microscope.

vermilion b., the red margin of the upper and lower lip that commences at the exterior edge of the intraoral labial mucosa and extends outward, terminating at the extraoral labial cutaneous junction.

Bordetella [J. *Bordet*]. A genus of strictly aerobic bacteria (family Brucellaceae) that contain minute Gram-negative coccobacilli and are parasites and pathogens of the mammalian respiratory tract. The type species, B. *pertussis* (Bordet-Gengou bacillus), causes whooping cough.

bo´ric acid. H_3BO_3; a very weak acid, used as an antiseptic dusting powder, in saturated solution as a collyrium, and with glycerin in aphthae and stomatitis.

bo´rism. Symptoms caused by the ingestion of borax or any compound of boron.

bo´ron. A nonmetallic trivalent element, symbol B, atomic weight 10.81, atomic no. 5; forms borates and boric acid.

Borrelia (bor-re´lĭ-ah, bor-rel´ĭ-ah) [A. *Borrell*]. A genus of parasitic bacteria (family Treponemataceae), some of which are transmitted by the bites of arthropods. Some species cause relapsing fever.

boss. **1.** A protuberance; a circumscribed rounded swelling. **2.** The prominence of a kyphosis, or humpback.

bos´selated [Fr. *bosseler*, to emboss]. Marked by numerous bosses or rounded protuberances.

bot´fly. Robust hairy fly of the order Diptera whose larvae produce a variety of myiasis conditions in man and various domestic animals.

Bothriocephalus (both´rĭ-o-sef´al-us) [G. *bothrion*, dim. of *bothros*, pit or trench, + *kephalē*, head]. A genus of pseudophyllid tapeworms with both plerocercoid and adult stages in fishes; sometimes historically confused with *Diphyllobothrium*.

botryoid (bot´rĭ-oyd) [G. *botryoeidēs*, like a bunch of grapes (*botrys*)]. Staphyline; uviform; having numerous rounded protuberances resembling a bunch of grapes.

bots [Gael. *boiteag*, maggot]. The larvae of several species of botflies.

bot´uline. Botulinus *toxin*.

botulism (bot´u-lizm) [L. *botulus*, sausage]. Intoxication due to the ingestion of *Clostridium botulinum* toxin in improperly canned or preserved food; characterized by paralysis.

boubas (bo-oo´bahs) [native Brazilian word]. Yaws.

bougie (bu-zhē´) [Fr. candle]. A cylindrical instrument, usually somewhat flexible and yielding, used for calibrating or dilating constructed areas in tubular organs, such as the urethra or rectum; sometimes containing a medicament for local application.

bulbous b., a b. with a bulb-shaped tip, some of which are shaped like an acorn or an olive.

elbowed b., a b. with a sharply angulated bend near its tip.

filiform b., a very slender b. usually used for exploration of strictures or sinus tracts of small diameter.

following b., a flexible tapered b. with a screw tip which is attached to the tailing end of a filiform b., to allow progressive dilation of a passage.

bougienage (boo-zhe-nazh´). Examination or treatment of the interior of any canal by the passage of a bougie or cannula.

bouton (boo-ton´) [Fr. button]. **1.** Button, pustule, or knoblike swelling. **2.** Boil, as the tropical sore of cutaneous *leishmaniasis*.

terminal b.'s, b.'s terminaux, axon *terminals*.

bovine (bo´vīn, -vin) [L. *bos* (*bov-*), ox]. Relating to cattle.

bow´el [through the Fr. from L. *botulus*, sausage]. The intestine.

bowleg (bo´leg). *Genu* varum.

BP Blood *pressure; British Pharmacopoeia*.

b.p. Boiling *point*.

Br Bromine.

brace. An orthosis or orthopedic appliance that supports or holds in correct position any movable part of the body and that allows motion of the part, in contrast to a splint, which prevents motion of the part.

braces (bra´sez). Colloquialism for orthodontic appliances.

bra´chia. Plural of brachium.

bra´chial. Relating to the arm.

brachialgia (bra-kĭ-al´jĭ-ah) [L. *brachium*, arm, + *algos*, pain]. Pain in the arm.

brachio- [L. *brachium*, arm]. Combining form meaning 1) arm, 2) radial.

brachiocephalic (bra´kĭ-o-sĕ-fal´ik). Relating to both arm and head.

bra´chiocru´ral. Relating to both arm and thigh.

bra′chiocu′bital. Relating to both arm and elbow or to both arm and forearm.

brachium, pl. **brachia** (bra′kĭ-um, brak′ĭ-um; -ah) [L. arm, prob. akin to G. *brachiōn*]. [NA]. **1.** The arm, specifically the segment of the upper limb between the shoulder and the elbow. **2.** An armlike structure.

   b. collic′uli inferio′ris [NA], a fiber bundle passing from the inferior colliculus on either side of the brain stem along the lateral border of the superior colliculus to the posterior part of the thalamus where it enters the medial geniculate body; forms part of the major ascending auditory pathway.

   b. collic′uli superio′ris [NA], a band of fibers of the optic tract extending past the lateral geniculate body to terminate in the superior colliculus and pretectal region.

   b. conjuncti′vum cerebel′li, *pedunculus* cerebellaris superior.

   b. pon′tis, *pedunculus* cerebellarais medius.

brachy- [G. *brachys,* short]. Combining form meaning short.

brachybasia (brak-ĭ-ba′sĭ-ah) [brachy- + G. *basis,* a stepping]. The shuffling gait characteristic of partial paraplegia.

brachycardia (brak-ĭ-kar′dĭ-ah). Bradycardia.

brachycheilia, brachychilia (brak′ĭ-ki′lĭ-ah) [brachy- + G. *cheilos,* lip]. Abnormally short lips.

brachydactyly (brak-ĭ-dak′tĭ-lĭ) [brachy- + G. *daktylos,* finger]. Abnormal shortness of the fingers.

brachygnathia (brak-ĭna′thĭ-ah) [brachy- + G. *gnathos,* jaw]. Bird face; abnormal shortness or recession of the mandible.

brach′ymetacar′pia. Abnormal shortening of the metacarpals, especially the 4th and 5th.

brachymetatarsia (brak′ĭ-met-ătar′sĭ-ah). Abnormal shortness of the metatarsals.

brachyphalangia (brak′ĭ-fa-lan′jĭ-ah) [brachy- + phalanx]. Abnormal shortness of the phalanges.

brachysyndactyly (brak′ĭ-sin-dak′tĭ-lĭ) [brachy- + syndactyly]. Abnormal shortness of fingers or toes combined with a webbing between the adjacent digits.

brachytherapy (brak-ĭ-ther′ă-pĭ). Radiotherapy in which the source of irradiation is placed close to the surface of the body or within a body cavity.

brady- [G. *bradys,* slow]. Combining form meaning slow.

bradyarrhythmia (brad′ĭ-ă-rith′mĭ-ah) [brady- + G. *a-* priv. + *rhythmos,* rhythm]. Any disturbance of the heart's rhythm resulting in a rate under 60 beats per minute.

bradyarth′ria [brady- + G. *arthroō,* to utter distinctly]. Bradyglossia (2); bradylalia; bradylogia; a form of dysarthria characterized by an abnormal slowness or deliberation in speech.

bradycardia (brad-ĭ-kar′dĭ-ah) [brady- + G. *kardia,* heart]. Brachycardia; oligocardia; slowness of the heart beat, usually defined as a rate under 60 beats per minute.

bradycar′dic. Relating to or characterized by bradycardia.

bradydiastole (brad-ĭ-di-as′to-le). Prolongation of the diastole of the heart.

bradyesthesia (brad-ĭ-es-the′zĭ-ah) [brady- + G. *aisthēsis,* sensation]. Retardation in the rate of transmission of sensory impressions.

bradyglos′sia [brady- + G. *glōssa,* tongue]. **1.** Slow or difficult tongue movement. **2.** Bradyarthria.

brad′yki′nin [brady- + G. *kinein,* to move]. Kallidin I; the nonapeptide Arg-Pro-Pro-Gly-Phe-Ser-Pro-Phe-Arg, produced from a decapeptide (kallidin II; bradykininogen) that is produced from a_2-globulin by kallikrein, normally present in blood in an inactive form, and similar to trypsin in action; one of a number of the plasma kinins and a potent vasodilator, also one of the physiologic mediators of anaphylaxis released from cytotroic antibody-coated mast cells following reaction with antigen (allergen) specific for the antibody.

bradykinesia (brad-ĭ-kin-e′zĭ-ah) [brady- + G. *kinēsis,* movement]. Extreme slowness in movement.

bradykinet′ic. Characterized by or pertaining to slow movement.

brad′ykinin′ogen. Kallidin II.

bradyla′lia [brady- + G. *lalia,* speech]. Bradyarthria.

bradylex′ia [brady- + G. *lexis,* word]. Abnormal slowness in reading.

bradylo′gia [brady- + G. *logos,* word]. Bradyarthria.

bradypnea (brad-ip-ne′ah, brad-ĭ-) [brady- + G. *pnoē,* breathing]. Abnormal slowness of respiration; specifically, a low respiratory frequency.

bradysper′matism. Absence of ejaculatory force, so that the semen trickles away slowly.

bradysphygmia (brad-ĭ-sfig′mĭ-ah) [brady- + G. *sphygmos,* pulse]. Slowness of the pulse, as in bradycardia.

bradystal′sis [G. *bradys,* slow, + (*peri*) *stalsis,* contracting around]. Slow bowel motion.

bradyto′cia [brady- + G. *tokos,* childbirth]. Tedious labor; slow delivery.

bradyuria (brad-ĭ-u′rĭ-ah) [brady- + G. *ouron,* urine]. Slow micturition.

brain [A.S. *braegen*]. Encephalon.

brain′case. The cranium in its restricted sense, the part of the skull that encloses the brain.

brain′stem, brain stem. Originally, the entire unpaired subdivision of the brain, composed of the rhombencephalon, mesencephalon, and diecephalon as distinguished from the telencephalon, the only paired subdivision. More recently, the rhombencephalon plus mesencephalon, distinguishing that complex from the prosencephalon (diencephalon plus telencephalon), exclusively to the rhombencephalon.

brain′washing. Inducing a person to modify his attitudes and behavior in certain directions by conditioning through various forms of pressure or torture.

bran. A by-product of the milling of wheat, containing approximately 20% of indigestible cellulose; a bulk cathartic, usually taken in the form of cereal or special bran products.

branch. An offshoot; in anatomy, one of the primary divisions of a nerve or blood vessel. See also ramus.

Branhamel'la [Sara *Branham*]. A genus of aerobic, nonmotile, nonsporeforming bacteria (family Neisseriaceae) containing Gram-negative cocci, and occurring in the mucous membranes of the upper respiratory tract. The type species, *B. catarrhalis,* occasionally causes disease.

breast [A.S. *breōst*]. **1.** The anterior surface of the thorax. See also chest. **2.** The mamma.
   chicken b., *pectus* carinatum.
   funnel b., *pectus* excavatum.
   pigeon b., *pectus* carinatum.

breath [A.S. *braeth*]. **1.** The respired air. **2.** An inspiration.

breath'ing. The alternate inhalation and exhalation of air.
   apneustic b., a series of slow, deep inspirations, each one held for 30 to 90 seconds, after which the air is suddenly expelled by the elastic recoil of the lung.
   constant positive pressure b. (CPPB), inhalation and exhalation of respiratory gases that are under a small constant positive pressure relative to the ambient pressure.
   glossopharyngeal b., respiration unaided by the usual primary muscles of respiration, the air being forced into the lungs by use of the tongue and muscles of the pharynx.
   intermittent positive pressure b. (IPPB), artificial respiration produced by the intermittent inflation of the lungs by positive pressure applied to a reservoir bag; exhalation usually is passive.
   positive-negative pressure b. (PNPB), inflation of the lungs with positive pressure and deflation with negative pressure by an automatic ventilator.
   shallow b., b. with abnormally low tidal volume.

breech [A.S. *brēc*]. The nates.

bregma (breg'mah) [G. the forepart of the head]. [NA]. The point on the skull corresponding to the junction of the coronal and sagittal sutures.

bregmat'ic. Relating to the bregma.

brevicol'lis [L. *brevis,* short, + *collum,* neck]. Shortness of the neck.

bridge. 1. The upper part of the ridge of the nose formed by the nasal bones. **2.** One of the threads of protoplasm that appears to pass from one cell to another. **3.** Fixed partial *denture.*
   cell b.'s, cytoplasmic b.'s, intercellular b.'s.
   intercellular b.'s, 36 cell or cytoplasmic b.'s; slender cytoplasmic strands connecting adjacent cells; in the epidermis and other stratified squamous epithelia the b.'s are processes separated by a desmosome; true b.'s exist between incompletely divided germ cells.

removable b., removable partial *denture.*

bridge'work. Partial *denture.*

brilliant green. An indicator dye that changes from yellow to green at pH 0.0 to 2.6; also used as a topical antiseptic and as a selective bacteriostatic agent in culture media.

brim. The rim of the superior strait of the pelvis.

brisement forcé (brēz-moñ'for-sa') [Fr. forcible breaking]. The forcible breaking or manipulation of a joint or joints, as with the adhesions in ankylosis.

British anti-Lewisite (BAL). Dimercaprol.

broach. A dental instrument for removing the pulp of a tooth or exploring the canal.

bro'mate. Salt or anion of bromic acid.

bro'mated. Brominated; combined or saturated with bromine or any of its compounds.

brom-, bromo- [G. *brōmos,* a stench]. Prefix indicating presence of bromine in a compound.

bro'melain, bro'melin [C. *Bromelius* (*Bromel*) Swedish botanist, 1639–1705]. One or a group of peptide hydrolases obtained from pineapple; used in tenderizing meats and in producing hydrolysates of proteins; orally administered in the treatment of inflammation and edema of soft tissues associated with traumatic injury.

brom'hidro'sis. Bromidrosis.

bro'mide. The anion Br-; salt of HBr.

bromidrosis (brom'ĭ-dro'sis) [G. *brōmos,* a stench, + *hidrōs,* perspiration]. Bromhidrosis; osmidrosis; fetid or foul smelling perspiration.

bro'minated. Bromated.

bromine (bro'mēn, -min). An element, symbol Br, atomic no. 35, atomic weight, 79.9; unites with hydrogen to form hydrobromic acid, which reacts with many metals to form bromides, some of which are used in medicine.

bro'mism, Bro'minism. Chronic bromide intoxication characterized by headache, mental inertia, occasionally violent delirium, muscular weakness, cardiac depression, an acneform eruption, a foul breath, anorexia, and gastric distress.

bromo-. See brom-.

bro'moder'ma [bromide + G. *derma,* skin]. An acneform or granulomatous eruption due to hypersensitivity to bromide.

bromosulfophthalein (BSP) (bro'mo-sul'fo-thal'e-in, -fthal'e-in). Sulfobromophthalein.

bromphenir'amine maleate. 2-[*p*-Bromo-α-(2-dimethylaminoethyl)benzyl]pyridine maleate; an antihistamine.

bromsulfophthalein (brom-sul'fo-thal'e-in, -fthal'e-in). Sulfobromophthalein.

bronch-, bronchi-. See broncho-.

bronchi (brong'kī). Plural of bronchus.

bronchial brong'kĭ-al). Relating to the bronchi and the bronchial tubes.

bronchiectasic (brong-kĭ-ek-ta'zik). Bronchiectatic.

bronchiectasis (brong-kĭ-ek'tă-sis) [bronchi- + G. *ektasis,* a stretching]. Chronic dilation of bronchi or bronchioles as a sequel of inflammatory disease or obstruction.

bronchiectatic (brong-kĭ-ek-tat'ĭk). Bronchiectasic; relating to bronchiectasis.

bronchiloquy (brong-kil'o-kwĭ) [bronchi- + L. *loquor*, to speak]. Bronchophony.

bronchiocele (brong'kĭ-o-sēl). Bronchocele.

bronchiogenic (brong-kĭ-o-jen'ĭk). Bronchogenic; of bronchial origin; emanating from the bronchi.

bronchiole (brong'kĭ-ōl). Bronchiolus.

respiratory b.'s, the smallest b.'s that connect the terminal b.'s to alveolar ducts.

terminal b., the end of the conducting airway; the lining is simple columnar or cuboidal epithelium without mucous goblet cells; most of the cells are ciliated but a few nonciliated serious secreting cells occur.

bronchiolectasis (brong'kĭ-o-lek'tă-sis) [bronchiole + G. *ektasis*, a stretching]. Bronchiectasis involving the bronchioles.

bronchioli (brong-ki'o-lī). Plural of bronchiolus.

bronchiolitis (brong-kĭ-o-li'tis). Inflammation of the bronchioles, often associated with bronchopneumonia.

bronchiolo- [L. *bronchiolus*]. Combining form relating to the bronchiolus.

bronchiolus, pl. **bronchioli** (brong-ki'o-lus, brong-ki'o-lī) [Mod. L. dim. of *bronchus*] [NA]. Bronchiole; one of the finer subdivisions of the bronchial tubes, with no cartilage in its wall, but relatively abundant smooth muscle and elastic fibers.

bronchiosteno'sis. Bronchostenosis.

bronchit'ic. Relating to bronchitis.

bronchitis (brong-ki'tis). Inflammation of the mucous membrane of the bronchial tubes.

chronic b., b. characterized by cough, hypersecretion of mucus, and expectoration of sputum over a long period of time, associated with increased vulnerability to bronchial infection.

fibrinous b., pseudomembranous b.; inflammation of the bronchial mucous membrane, accompanied by a fibrinous exudation which often forms a cast of the bronchial tree.

obliterative b., fibrinous b. in which the exudate is not expectorated but becomes organized, obliterating the affected portion of the bronchial tubes.

pseudomembranous b., fibrinous b.

broncho- [G. *bronchos,* windpipe]. Combining form denoting bronchus.

bronchoalveolar (brong-ko-al-ve'o-lar). Bronchovesicular.

bronchocavernous (brong-ko-kav'er-nus). Relating to a bronchus or bronchial tube and a pulmonary pathologic cavity.

bronchocele (brong'-ko-sēl) [broncho- + G. *kēlē*, hernia]. Bronchiocele; circumscribed dilation of a bronchus.

bronchoconstrictor (brong-ko-kon-strik'tor). Causing a reduction in caliber of a bronchus or bronchial tube.

bronchodilatation (brong'ko-dil-ă-ta'shun). Increase in caliber of the bronchi and bronchioles.

bronchodilator (brong-ko-di-la'tor) Causing an increase in caliber of a bronchus or bronchial tube.

bron'choesophagol'ogy [broncho- + G. *oisophagos,* esophagus, + *logos,* study]. The specialty concerned with peroral endoscopic examination of the esophagus and tracheobronchial tree.

bron'choesophagos'copy. Examination of the tracheobronchial tree or esophagus through appropriate endoscopes.

bronchofiberscope (brong-ko-fi'ber-skōp). A fiberoptic endoscope particularly adapted for visualization of the trachea and bronchi.

bronchogenic (brong-ko-jen'ik). Bronchiogenic.

bron'chogram. The radiogram obtained at bronchography.

bronchography (brong-kog'ră-fĭ) [broncho- + G. *graphē,* a drawing]. Radiographic examination of the tracheobronchial tree by the injection of a radiopaque material.

broncholith (brong'ko-lith) [broncho- + G. *lithos,* stone]. Bronchial calculus; a hard concretion in a bronchus or bronchial tube.

bron'cholithi'asis. Bronchial inflammation or obstruction caused by broncholiths.

bronchomalacia (brong'ko-mă-la'shĭ-ah) [broncho- + G. *malakia,* a softening]. Degeneration of elastic and connective tissue of bronchi and trachea.

bronchomo'tor. Causing a change in caliber, dilation, or contraction of a bronchus or bronchiole.

bronchomycosis (brong-ko-mi-ko'sis) [broncho- + G. *mykēs,* fungus]. Any fungus disease of the bronchial tubes or bronchi.

bronchophony (brong-kof'o-nĭ) [broncho- + G. *phōnē,* voice]. Bronchiloquy; exaggerated vocal resonance heard over a bronchus surrounded by consolidated lung tissue.

bronchoplasty (brong'ko-plas-tĭ). [broncho- + G. *plassō,* to form]. Surgical alteration of the configuration of a bronchus.

bronchopneumonia (brong'ko-nu-mo'nĭ-ah). Bronchial pneumonia; acute inflammation of the walls of the smaller bronchial tubes, with irregular areas of consolidation due to spread of the inflammation into peribronchiolar alveoli and the alveolar ducts.

bronchopulmonary (brong-ko-pul'mo-něr-ĭ). Relating to the bronchial tubes and the lungs.

bronchorrhaphy (brong-kor'ă-fĭ) [broncho- + G. *raphē,* a seam]. Suture of a wound of the bronchus.

bronchorrhea (brong'ko-re'ah) [broncho- + G. *rhoia,* a flow]. Excessive secretion of mucus from the bronchial mucous membrane.

bronchoscope (brong'ko-skōp) [broncho- + G. *skopeō,* to view]. An endoscope for inspecting the interior of the tracheobronchial tree, either for diagnostic purposes (including biopsy) or for the removal of foreign bodies.

bronchoscopy (brong-kos'ko-pĭ). Inspection of the interior of the tracheobronchial tree through a bronchoscope.

bronchospasm (brong'ko-spazm). Contraction of smooth muscle in the walls of the bronchi and bronchioles, causing narrowing of the lumen.

bron'chospirog'raphy. Use of a single lumen endobronchial tube for measurement of ventilatory function of one lung.

bronchospirom'eter [broncho- + L. *spiro*, to breathe, + G. *metron*, measure]. A device for measurement of rates and volumes of air flow into each lung separately, using a double lumen endobronchial tube.

bron'chospirom'etry. Use of a bronchiospirometer.

bronchostaxis (brong'ko-stak'sis) [broncho- + G. *staxis*, a dripping]. Hemorrhage from the bronchi.

bronchostenosis (brong-ko-sten-o'sis). Bronchiostenosis; chronic stenosis or narrowing of a bronchus.

bronchostomy (brong-kos'to-mĭ) [broncho- + G. *stoma*, mouth]. Surgical formation of a new opening into a bronchus.

bronchotomy (brong-kot'o-mĭ). Incision of a bronchus.

bronchotracheal (brong-ko-tra'kĭ-al). Relating to the bronchi and trachea.

bronchovesicular (brong-ko-ves-ik'u-lar). Bronchoalveolar; relating to the bronchial tubes and alveoli in the lungs.

bronchus, pl. **bronchi** (brong'kus, brong'kĭ) [Mod. L. fr. G. *bronchos*, windpipe] [NA]. One of the primary subdivisions of the trachea that convey air to and from the lungs; the right and left main bronchi in turn form lobar, segmental, and subsegmental bronchi. In structure the intrapulmonary bronchi have a lining of pseudostratified ciliated columnar epithelium, and a lamina propria with abundant longitudinal networks of elastic fibers. There are spirally arranged bundles of smooth muscle, abundant mucoserous glands, and in the outer part of the wall irregular plates of hyaline cartilage.

brow [A.S. *brū*]. **1.** The eyebrow. **2.** Frons.

brow'lift. An operation to elevate the eyebrows and thereby remove excess skin folds or fullness in the upper eyelids.

Brucella (bru-sel'lah) [Sir David *Bruce,* British surgeon, 1855–1931]. A genus of encapsulated, nonmotile bacteria (family Brucellaceae) containing short, rod-shaped to coccoid, Gram-negative cells; they are parasitic, invading all animal tissues and causing infection of the genital organs, the mammary gland, and the respiratory and intestinal tracts, and are pathogenic for man and various species of domestic animals. The type species is *B. melitensis.*

  B. abor'tus, Bang's bacillus; a species that causes abortion in cows, mares, and sheep, undulant fever in man, and a wasting disease in chickens.

  B. meliten'sis, a species that causes brucellosis in man, abortion in goats, and a wasting disease in chickens; it may infect cows and hogs and be excreted in their milk; the type species of the genus *B.*

  B. su'is, a species causing abortion in swine, brucellosis in man, and a wasting disease in chickens; may also infect horses, dogs, cows, monkeys, goats, and laboratory animals.

Brucellaceae (bru-sel-a'se-e). A family of bacteria (order Eubacteriales) containing small, coccoid to rod-shaped, Gram-negative cells which occur singly, in pairs, in short chains, or in groups; these organisms are parasites and pathogens which affect warm-blooded animals, including man. The type genus is *Brucella.*

brucellosis (bru-sel-o'sis). Undulant fever; Mediterranean fever (1); an infectious disease caused by species of *Brucella* and characterized by fever, sweating, weakness, aches, and pains; transmitted to man by direct contact with diseased animals or through ingestion of infested meat, milk, or cheese.

Brugia (bru'jĭ-ah). A genus of filarial worms transmitted by mosquitoes to man, primates, felid carnivores, and a number of other mammals. *B. malayi,* is an important agent of human filariasis and elephantiasis in Southeast Asia and Indonesia.

bruise (brūz). **1.** Contusion (2); and injury usually producing a hematoma without rupture of the skin. **2.** Contusion (1).

bruit (bru-e') [Fr.]. An auscultatory sound, especially an abnormal one.

  aneurysmal b., blowing murmur heard over an aneurysm.

  carotid b., any b. produced by blood flow in a carotid artery.

  thyroid b., vascular murmur heard over hyperactive thyroid gland.

bruxism (bruk'sizm) [G. *brucho,* to grind the teeth]. A clenching of the teeth, resulting in rubbing, gritting, or grinding together of the teeth, usually during sleep.

BSP Bromosulfophthalein.

BTU British thermal *unit.*

bu'ba ma'dre. Mother *yaw.*

bubas (bu'bahs). Yaws.

bu'bo [G. *boubōn,* the groin, a swelling in the groin]. Inflammatory swelling of one or more lymph nodes in the groin; the confluent mass of nodes suppurates.

  climatic b., venereal *lymphogranuloma.*

  indolent b., an indurated enlargement of an inguinal node.

  malignant b., the b. associated with bubonic plague.

  tropical b., venereal *lymphogranuloma.*

  venereal b., an enlarged gland in the groin associated with any venereal disease, especially chancroid.

bubonal'gia [G. *boubōn,* groin, + *algos,* pain]. Pain in the groin.

bubon'ic. Relating in any way to a bubo.

bubonocele (bu-bon'o-sēl) [G. *boubōn*, groin, + *kēlē*, tumor]. Inguinal hernia, especially one in which the knuckle of intestine has not yet emerged from the external abdominal ring.

bucar'dia [G. *bous*, ox, + *kardia*, heart]. Cor bovinum; extreme hypertrophy of the heart.

buc'cal. Pertaining to, adjacent to, or in the direction of the cheek.

bucca, pl. **buccae** (buk'ah, buk'e) [L.] [NA]. The cheek.

bucco- [L. *bucca*, cheek]. Combining form relating to the cheek.

buccogingival (buk'o-jin'jī-val). Relating to the cheek and the gum.

buc'cola'bial. 1. Relating to both cheek and lip. **2.** In dentistry, referring to that aspect of the dental arch or those surfaces of the teeth in contact with the mucosa of lip and cheek, the surfaces opposite the lingual surfaces.

buccolingual (buk'o-ling'wal). Pertaining to the cheek and the tongue.

buccopharyngeal (buk'o-fā-rin'jī-al). Relating to both cheek or mouth and pharynx.

buccoversion (buk'o-ver-zhun). Malposition of a posterior tooth from the normal line of occlusion toward the cheek.

bud. A structure that resembles the b. of a plant.

  end b., tail b.

  limb b., an ectodermally covered mesenchymal outgrowth on the embryonic flank giving rise to either the forelimb or hindlimb.

  tail b., end b.; the rapidly proliferating mass of cells at the caudal extremity of the embryo.

  taste b., one of a number of flask-shaped cell nests located in the epithelium of papillae of the tongue and also in the soft palate, epiglottis, and posterior wall of the pharynx; it consists of sustentacular, gustatory, and basal cells between which the intragemmal sensory nerve fibers terminate.

  tooth b., the primordial structures from which a tooth is formed; the enamel organ, dental papilla, and the dental sac enclosing them.

bud'ding. Gemmation.

buf'fer. 1. A mixture of an acid and its conjugate base (salt) that, when present in a solution, reduces any changes in pH that would otherwise occur in the solution when acid or alkali is added to it. **2.** To add a b. to a solution and thus give it the property of resisting a change in pH when it receives a limited amount of acid or alkali.

bulb [L. *bulbus*, a bulbous root]. Bulbus; any globular or fusiform structure.

  aortic b., *bulbus* aortae.

  b. of corpus spongiosum, *bulbus* penis.

  dental b., the papilla, derived from mesoderm, that forms the part of the primordium of a tooth which is situated within the cup-shaped enamel organ.

  end b., one of the oval or rounded bodies in which the sensory nerve fibers terminate in mucous membrane.

  b. of eye, *bulbus* oculi.

  hair b., *bulbus* pili.

  olfactory b., *bulbus* olfactorius.

  b. of penis, b. of urethra, *bulbus* penis.

  b. of vestibule, *bulbus* vestibuli.

bul'bar. 1. Bulb-shaped; resembling or relating to a bulb. **2.** Relating to the rhombencephalon (pons, cerebellum, and medulla oblongata).

bul'bi. Plural of bulbus.

bulbi'tis. Inflammation of the bulbous portion of the urethra.

bulbo- [L. *bulbus*, bulb]. Combining form relating to a bulb or bulbus.

bulboid (bul'boyd) [bulbo- + G. *eidos*, resemblance]. Bulb-shaped.

bulbospi'nal. Spinobulbar; relating to the medulla oblongata and spinal cord, particularly to nerve fibers interconnecting the two.

bulbourethral (bul'bo-u-re'thral). Urethrobulbar; relating to the bulbus penis and the urethra.

bul'bus, pl. **bul'bi** [L. a plant bulb] [NA]. Bulb.

  b. aor'tae [NA], aortic bulb; the dilated first part of the aorta containing the aortic semilunar valves and the aortic sinuses.

  b. oc'uli [NA], bulb of the eye; the eyeball, without its appendages.

  b. olfacto'rius [NA], olfactory bulb; the grayish expanded anterior extremity of the olfactory tract that lies on the cribriform plate of the ethmoid and receives the olfactory filaments.

  b. pe'nis [NA], bulb of penis, urethra, or corpus spongiosum; the expanded posterior part of the corpus spongiosum penis lying in the interval between the crura of the penis.

  b. pi'li [NA], hair bulb; the lower expanded extremity of the hair that fits like a cap over the papilla pili at the bottom of the hair follicle.

  b. vestib'uli [NA], bulb of the vestibule; a mass of erectile tissue on either side of the vagina united anterior to the urethra.

bulimia (bu-lim'ī-ah) [G. *bous*, ox, + *limos*, hunger]. Hyperorexia; a personality disorder characterized by episodic bouts of eating characterized by uncontrolled, rapid, and great amounts of ingested food followed by physical discomfort and feelings of guilt, self-disgust, and depression.

bulim'ic. Relating to bulimia.

bulla, pl. **bul'lae** (bul'ah, -e) [L. bubble]. **1.** A large vesicle appearing as a circumscribed area of separation of the epidermis from the subepidermal structure, or as a circumscribed area of separation of epidermal cells, caused by the presence of serum, sometimes mixed with blood, or occasionally by a substance injected intra- or subepidermally. **2.** [NA]. A bubble-like structure.

bullous (bul'us). Relating to, of the nature of, or marked by, bullae.

BUN Blood urea *nitrogen*.

bundle. A structure composed of a group of fibers; *e.g.*, a fasciculus.

   atrioventricular (A-V) b., *truncus* atrioventricularis.

   ground b.'s, *fasciculi* proprii.

   His b., b., of His, *truncus* atrioventricularis.

   medial forebrain b., a fiber system coursing longitudinally through the lateral zone of the hypothalamus, connecting the latter reciprocally with the midbrain tegmentum and with various components of the limbic system; it also carries fibers from norepinephrin- and serotonin-containing cell groups in the brainstem to the hypothalamus and cerebral cortex, as well as dopamine-carrying fibers from the substantia nigra to the caudate nucleus and putamen.

   Vicq d'Azyr's b., *fasciculus* mamillothalamicus.

bunion (bun'yun) [O.F. *buigne*, bump on the head]. A localized swelling at either the medial or dorsal aspect of the first metatarsophalangeal joint, caused by an inflammatory bursa.

bunionectomy (buy-yun-ek'to-mĭ). Excision of a bunion.

buphthalmia, buphthalmos, buphthalmus (bŭf-thal'mĭ-ah, -thal'mos, -thal'mus) [G. *bous*, ox, + *ophthalmos*, eye]. Congenital glaucoma; an affection of infancy, marked by an increase of intraocular fluid with enlargement of the eyeball.

bupiv'acaine. *dl*-1-Butylpipecoloxylidide; a potent, long-acting local anesthetic used in regional anesthesia.

bur. A rotary cutting instrument used in dentistry for excavating decay, shaping cavity forms, and any reduction of tooth structure. See also burr.

buret, burette (bu-ret') [Fr.]. A graduated glass tube with a tap as its lower end, used for measuring liquids in volumetric chemical analyses.

burn [A.S. *baernan*]. A lesion caused by heat or any cauterizing agent, including friction, electricity, and electromagnetic energy. Division of burns into three degrees is recognized for geographical designation: **first degree b.,** involving only the epidermis and causing erythema and edema without vesiculation; **second degree b.,** involving the epidermis and dermis and usually forming blisters that may be superficial or deep dermal necrosis, but with epithelial regeneration extending from the skin appendages; **third degree b.,** destruction of the entire skin; deep ones extend into subcutaneous fat, muscle, or bone and often cause much scarring.

bur'nisher [O.F. *burnir*, to polish]. An instrument for smoothing and polishing the surface or edge of a dental restoration.

burr. A drilling tool for enlarging a trephine hole in the cranium. See also bur.

bur'sal. Relating to a bursa.

bursa, pl. **bursae** (bur'sah, bur'se) [Mediev. L., a purse] [NA]. A closed sac or envelope lined with synovia and containing fluid, usually found or

formed in areas subject to friction.

   Achilles b., b. tendinis calcanei.

   b. anseri'na [NA], **anserine b.,** the b. between the tibial collateral ligament of the knee joint and the tendons of the sartorius, gracilis and semitendinosus muscles.

   Boyer's b., b. retrohyoidea.

   Calori's b., a b. between the arch of the aorta and the trachea.

   b. of gastrocnemius, b. subtendinea musculi gastrocnemii.

   gluteofemoral b., b. intermusculares musculi gluteorum.

   iliac b., b. subtendinea iliaca.

   b. intermuscula'res mus'culi gluteo'rum [NA], **intermuscular gluteal b.,** gluteofemoral b.; two or three small bursae between the tendon of the gluteus maximus and the linea aspera.

   b. ischiad'ica mus'culi glu'tei max'imi [NA], **ischial b.,** the b. between the gluteus maximus muscle and the tuberosity of the ischium.

   Luschka's b., b. pharyngea.

   b. mus'culi semimembrano'si [NA], b. of the semimembranosus; the b. between the muscle, the head of the gastrocnemius, and the knee joint.

   b. omenta'lis [NA], **omental b.,** lesser peritoneal cavity, an isolated portion of the peritoneal cavity lying dorsal to the stomach and extending craniad to the liver and diaphragm and caudad into the greater omentum; it opens into the general peritoneal cavity at the epiploic foramen.

   b. pharynge'a [NA], **pharyngeal b.,** Luschka's b.; a cystic notochordal remnant found inconstantly in the posterior wall of the nasopharynx at the lower end of the pharyngeal tonsil.

   popliteal b., *recessus* subpopliteus.

   prepatellar b., b. subcutanea prepatellaris.

   b. retrohyoi'dea [NA], **retrohyoid b.,** Boyer's b.; a b. between the posterior surface of the body of the hyoid bone and the thyrohyoid membrane.

   b. of semimembranosus, b. musculi semimembranosi.

   b. subacromia'lis [NA], **subacromial b.,** the b. between the acromion and the capsule of the shoulder joint.

   b. subdeltoid'ea [NA], **subdeltoid b.,** the b. between the deltoid muscle and the capsule of the shoulder joint, may be combined with the subacromial b.

   b. subtendin'ea ilia'ca [NA], iliac b.; the subtendinous iliac b. at the insertion of the iliopsoas muscle into the lesser trochanter.

   b. subtendin'eae mus'culi gastrocne'mii [NA], b. of gastrocnemius; the subtendinous b. of the gastrocnemius, consisting of a lateral and a medial b. between the heads of the gastrocnemius and capsule of the knee joint.

   b. subtendin'ea mus'culi infraspinat'i [NA], the b. located between the tendon of the infraspinatus and the capsule of the shoulder joint.

b. suprapatella'ris [NA], **suprapatellar b.,** a large b. between the lower part of the femur and the tendon of the quadriceps femoris muscle, usually communicating with the cavity of the knee joint.

b. synovia'lis [NA], **synovial b.,** a sac containing synovial fluid which occurs at sites of friction, as between a tendon and a bone over which it plays, or subcutaneously over a bony prominence.

b. ten'dinis calca'nei [NA], **b. of tendo calcaneus,** Achilles b.; the b. between the tendo calcaneus and the upper part of the posterior surface of the calcaneum.

bursec'tomy [bursa + G. *ektomē*, excision]. Surgical removal of a bursa.

bursi'tis. Bursal synovitis; inflammation of a bursa; specific types of b. are named after the bursa involved.

bur'solith [bursa + G. *lithos*, stone]. A calculus formed in a bursa.

bursop'athy. Any disease of a bursa.

bursot'omy [bursa + G. *tomē*, a cutting]. Incision through the wall of a bursa.

bu'tacaine sulfate. 3-(Dibutylamino)-1-propanol *p*-aminobenzoate sulfate; a local anesthetic.

butam'ben. *Butyl* aminobenzoate.

bu'tane. C_4H_{10}; a gaseous hydrocarbon present in natural gas; various isomers are known, many of which are anesthetically active, as is b. itself.

butter [L. *butyrum*, G. *boutyron*, prob. fr. *bous*, cow, + *tyron*, cheese]. A soft solid having a consistency like that of butter.

but'tocks. Nates.

but'ton [Middle Fr. *boton*, a bud, probably fr. L. *bottire*, to thrust]. A knob-like structure, lesion (as in yaws and cutaneous leishmaniasis), or device.

but'tonhole. 1. A short straight cut made through the wall of a cavity or canal. **2.** The contraction of an orifice down to a narrow slit, as in b. stenosis.

bu'tyl. A radical of butane; C_4H_9-.

butyraceous (bu'tir-a'shĭ-us). Butyrous; buttery in consistence.

bu'tyrate. A salt or ester of butyric acid.

butyr'ic acid. An acid of unpleasant odor occurring in butter, cod liver oil, sweat, and many other substances.

bu'tyroid. Resembling or having the consistency of butter.

butyrophe'none. One of a group of derivatives of 4-phenylbutylamine that have neuroleptic activity.

bu'tyrous. Butyraceous.

butyryl (bu'tĭ-ril). The radical of butyric acid, C_3H_7CDO-.

by'pass. A surgically created shunt or auxiliary flow through a diversionary channel.

aortoiliac b., a shunt uniting the aorta and iliac artery to relieve obstruction of the lower abdominal aorta, its bifurcation, and the proximal iliac branches.

aortorenal b., a shunt between the aorta and the distal renal artery, to circumvent an obstruction of the renal artery.

cardiopulmonary b., diversion of the blood flow returning to the heart through a pump oxygenator (heart-lung machine) and then returning it to the arterial side of the circulation; used in operations upon the heart to maintain extracorporeal circulation.

coronary b., shunting of blood from the aorta to branches of the coronary arteries, to increase the flow beyond the local obstruction.

gastric b., high division of the stomach, anastomosis of the small upper pouch of the stomach to the jejunum, and closure of the distal part of the stomach; used for treatment of morbid obesity.

jejunoileal b., jejunoileal shunt; anastomosis of the upper jejunum to the terminal ileum for treatment of morbid obesity.

byssinosis (bis'ĭ-no'sis) [G. *byssos*, flax, + *-osis*, condition]. A pneumoconiosis of cotton, flax, and hemp workers, characterized by symptoms (especially wheezing) most severe at the beginning of each work week.

C

C Large *calorie;* carbon; Celsius; centigrade; cylindrical *lens;* cytidine; when followed by a subscript, indicates renal clearance of a substance; compliance, or concentration.

c Small *calorie; centi-;* as a subscript, refers to blood *capillary.*

CA Cancer; carcinoma; *cytosine* arabinoside.

Ca Calcium; cathode; cathodal.

ca Latin *circa* (about, approximately).

cac-, caci-. See caco-.

cachectic (kă-kek'tik). Relating to or suffering from cachexia.

cachet (kă-sha') [Fr. a seal]. A seal-shaped capsule or wafer for enclosing powders of disagreeable taste.

cachexia (kă-kek'sĭ-ah) G. *kakos*, bad, + *hexis*, a habit of body]. A general lack of nutrition and wasting occurring in the course of a chronic disease or emotional disturbance.

c. hypophyseopri'va, a condition following total removal of the hypophysis cerebri, marked by a fall of body temperature, electrolyte imbalance, and hypoglycemia, followed by coma and death.

hypophysial c., pituitary c., Simmonds' *disease.*

c. strumipri'va, c. thyropri'va, myxedema resulting from loss of thyroid tissue.

cachinnation (kak-ĭ-na'shun) [L. *cachinnare*, to laugh immoderately and loudly]. Laughter without apparent cause, often found in schizophrenia.

caco-, caci-, cac- [G. *kakos*, bad]. Combining forms meaning bad or ill.

cacogeusia (kak-o-gu'sĭ-ah) [caco- + G. *geusis*, taste]. A bad taste.

cacomelia (kak-o-me′lĭ-ah) [caco- + G. *melos*, limb]. Congenital deformity of one or more limbs.

cacos′mia [cac- + G. *osmē*, sense of smell]. Subjective perception of disagreeable odors that do not exist.

cacumen, pl. **cacumina** (kak-u′men, -mĭ-nah) [L. summit]. The top or apex, as of a plant or an anatomical structure.

cacu′minal. Relating to a cacumen.

cadaver (kă-dav′er) [L. fr. *cado*, to fall]. Corpse; a dead body.

cadav′eric. Relating to a cadaver.

cadav′erine. $H_2N(CH_2)_5NH_2$; a foul-smelling diamine formed by bacterial decarboxylation of lysine.

cadav′erous. Having the pallor and appearance of a corpse.

cad′mium [L. *cadmia*, G. *kadmeia* or *kadmia*, an ore of zinc, calamine]. A metallic element, symbol Cd, atomic no. 48, atomic weight 112.40, resembling tin in appearance and zinc in its chemical relations; its salts are poisonous and little used in medicine.

caduceus (kă-du′se-us) [L. the staff of Mercury]. A staff with two oppositely twined serpents and surmounted by two wings; symbol of the medical profession and emblem of the U.S. Army Medical Corps; veterinary medicine uses a single serpent. See also staff of Aesculapius.

cae-. For words beginning, see under ce-.

caffeine (kaf′ēn). 1,3,7-Trimethylxanthine; an alkaloid obtained from the dried leaves of *Thea sinensis*, tea, or the dried seeds of *Coffea arabica*, coffee; used as a diuretic and circulatory and respiratory stimulant.

caffeinism (kaf′ēn-izm). Chronic coffee poisoning, characterized by palpitation, dyspepsia, irritability, and insomnia.

Cal Large *calorie*.

cal Small *calorie*.

cal′amine. Zinc oxide with a small amount of ferric oxide or basic zinc carbonate suitably colored with ferric oxide; used in dusting powders, lotions, and ointments, as a mild astringent and protective agent for skin disorders.

cal′amus scripto′rius [L. writing pen]. Arantius' ventricle; the inferior, reed-like part of the rhomboid fossa; the narrow lower end of the fourth ventricle between the two clavae.

calcaneal, calcanean (kal-ka′ne-al, -ka′ne-an). Relating to the calcaneus or heel bone.

calcaneo- [L. *calcaneum*, heel]. Combining form relating to the calcaneus.

calca′neoapoph′ysi′tis. Inflammation at the posterior part of the os calcis, at the insertion of the Achilles tendon.

calca′neoastrag′aloid. Relating to the calcaneus, or os calcis, and the astragalus, or talus.

calca′neocu′boid. Relating to the calcaneus and the cuboid bone.

calcaneodynia (kal-ka′ne-o-din′ĭ-ah) [calcaneo- + G. *odynē*, pain]. Painful *heel*.

calca′neonavic′ular, calca′neoscaph′oid. Relating to the calcaneus and the navicular (scaphoid) bone.

calca′neotib′ial. Relating to the calcaneus and the tibia.

calca′neum [L. the heel]. Calcaneus.

calcaneus, gen. and pl. **calcanei** (kal-ka′neus, -ka′ne-i) [L. the heel (another form of *calcaneum*)] [NA]. Calcaneum; heel bone; the largest of the tarsal bones; it forms the heel and articulates with the cuboid anteriorly and the talus above.

calcar (kal′kar) [L. spur, cock's spur]. Spur. **1** [NA]. A small projection from any structure; internal spurs (septa) at the level of division of arteries and confluence of veins when branches or roots form an acute angle. **2.** A dull spine or projection from a bone. **3.** A horny outgrowth from the skin.

calca′reous [L. *calcarius*, pertaining to lime, fr. *calx*, lime]. Chalky; relating to or containing lime or calcium, or calcific material.

cal′carine. **1.** Relating to a calcar. **2.** Spur-shaped.

calcariuria (kal-kar-ĭ-u′rĭ-ah) [L. *calcarius*, of lime, + G. *ouron*, urine]. Excretion of calcium salts in the urine.

calces (kal′sēz). Plural of calx.

calcic (kal′sik). Relating to lime.

calcicosis (kal-sĭ-ko′sis). Pneumoconiosis from the inhalation of limestone dust; sometimes called marble cutter's phthisis.

calcif′erol. Ergocalciferol.

calcifica′tion [L. *calx*, lime, + *facio*, to make]. Calcareous infiltration. **1.** Deposition of insoluble calcium salts. **2.** A process in which tissue or noncellular material in the body becomes hardened as the result of precipitates or larger deposits of insoluble calcium salts, normally occurring only in the formation of bone and teeth.

  dystrophic c., c. occurring in degenerated or necrotic tissue.

  metastatic c., c. occurring in nonosseous, viable tissue whose cells secrete acid materials and the alteration in pH seems to cause precipitation of calcium salts in these sites.

  Mönckeberg's c., Mönckeberg's *arteriosclerosis*.

  pathologic c., c. occurring in excretory or secretory passages as calculi, and in tissues other than bone and teeth.

  pulp c., calcified nodules or amorphous deposits in the pulp of a tooth.

cal′cify. To deposit or lay down calcium salts, as in the formation of bone.

calcino′sis [calcium + -*osis*, condition]. A condition characterized by the deposition of calcium salts in nodular foci in various tissues other than the parenchymatous viscera.

  c. circumscrip′ta, localized deposits of calcium salts in the skin and subcutaneous tissues, usually surrounded by a zone of granulomatous inflammation.

reversible c., c. sometimes observed in patients who constantly ingest large quantities of milk and alkaline medicines.

c. universa'lis, diffuse deposits of calcium salts in the skin and subcutaneous tissues, connective tissue, and other sites; may be associated with dermatomyositis.

calcipexic (kal-sĭ-pek'sik). Related or pertaining to calcipexis.

calcipexis, calcipexy (kal-sĭ-pek'sis, kal'sĭ-pek-sĭ) [calcium + G. pēxis, a fixing]. Fixation of calcium in the tissues.

calciphilia (cal-sĭ-fil'ĭ-ah) [calcium + G. phileō, to love]. A condition in which the tissues manifest an unusual affinity for, and fixation of, calcium salts circulating in the blood.

cal'ciphylax'is. A condition of induced systemic hypersensitivity in which tissues respond to appropriate challenging agents with a sudden, but sometimes evanescent, local calcification (Selye).

calcipriv'ic. Deprived of calcium.

calcito'nin. See thyrocalcitonin.

calcium (kal'sĭ-um) [Mod. L. fr. L. calx, lime]. A metallic dyad element; symbol Ca, atomic no. 20, atomic weight 40.09, density 1.54, melting point 810°; many of its salts have medicinal uses.

c. gluceptate, c. glucoheptonate; used as a nutrient.

calcium group. The metals of the alkaline earths: beryllium, magnesium, calcium, strontium, barium, and radium.

calciuria (kal'sĭ-u're-ah). Urinary excretion of calcium.

calcodynia (kal-ko-din'ĭ-ah) [L. calx, heel, + G. odynē, pain]. Painful heel.

calcospherite (kal-ko-sfēr'ĭt) [L. calx, lime, + G. sphaira, sphere]. Psammoma bodies (3); a tiny, spheroidal, concentrically laminated body containing accretive deposits of calcium salts.

cal'culary. Calculous.

cal'culi. Plural of calculus.

calculosis (kal-ku-lo'sis) [L. calculus, small stone, + -osis, condition]. The tendency to form calculi or stones.

cal'culous. Calcary; lithous; relating to calculi.

calculus, gen. and pl. **calculi** (kal'ku-lus, -li) [L. a pebble, a calculus]. Stone (1); a concretion formed in any part of the body, most commonly in the passages of the biliary and urinary tracts; usually composed of salts of inorganic or organic acids, or of other material such as cholesterol.

alternating c., combination c.; a urinary c. comprised of successive layers of different composition.

apatite c., a c. in which the crystalloid component consists of calcium fluophosphate.

combination c. alternating c.

coral c., stag-horn c.

cystine c., a soft variety of urinary c. composed of cystine.

decubitus c., a c. formed in the urinary tract, as a result of long immobilization.

dendritic c., stag-horn c.

dental c., (1) calcified deposits formed around the teeth; they may appear as subgingival or supragingival c.; (2) tartar (2).

encysted c., pocketed c.; a urinary c. enclosed in a sac developed from the wall of the bladder.

fibrin c., a urinary c. formed largely from fibrinogen in blood.

hematogenetic c., serumal c.

matrix c., putty-like urinary c. containing calcium salts, composed chiefly of an organic matrix consisting of a mucoprotein and a sulfated mucopolysaccharide, and usually associated with chronic infection.

oxalate c., a hard urinary c. of calcium oxalate; some are covered with minute sharp spines, whereas others are smooth.

pocketed c., encysted c.

stag-horn c., coral or dendritic c.; a c. occurring in the renal pelvis, with branches extending into the infundibula and calices.

calefa'cient [L. calefacio, fr. caleo, to be warm, + facio, to make]. Making warm or hot; causing a sense of warmth in the part to which applied.

calf, pl. **calves** (kaf, kavz) [Gael. kalpa]. Sura.

cal'iber [Fr. calibre]. The diameter of a tube.

cal'ibrate. 1. To graduate or standardize any measuring instrument. **2.** To measure the diameter of a tube.

calibrator (kal'ĭ-bra-tor). A standard or reference material or substance used to standardize or calibrate an instrument or laboratory procedure.

caliceal (kal'ĭ-se'al). Relating to a calix.

calicectasis (kal-ĭ-sek'tă-sis) [calix + G. ektasis, dilation]. Caliectasis; pyelocaliectasis; dilation of the calices, usually due to obstruction or infection.

calicectomy (kal-ĭ-sek'to-mĭ) [calix + G. ektomē, excision]. Caliectomy; excision of a calix.

calices (kal'ĭ-sēz). Plural of calix.

calicoplasty (kal'ĭ-so-plas-tĭ) [calix + G. plassō, to form]. Surgical revision of a calix, usually designed to increase its lumen at the infundibulum.

calicotomy (kal-ĭ-sot'o-mĭ) [calix + G. tomē, a cutting]. Incision into a calix, usually for removal of a calculus.

caliculus, pl. **caliculi** (kă-lik'u-lus, -li) [L. dim. from G. kalyx, the cup of a flower]. A bud-shaped or cup-shaped structure.

califor'nium [California, state and university where first prepared]. An artificial transuranium element, symbol Cf, atomic no. 98.

caliorrhaphy (ka'lĭ-or-ă-fĭ) [calix + g. raphē, suture, seam]. **1.** Suturing of a calix. **2.** Reconstructive surgery performed upon a dilated or obstructed calix to improve urinary drainage.

cal'ipers [a corruption of caliber]. An instrument used for measuring diameters, as of the pelvis.

calisthen'ics [G. *kalos*, beautiful, + *sthenos*, strength]. The systematic use of various exercises to preserve health and increase physical strength.

calix, pl. **calices** (ka'liks, kal'ĭ-sēz) [L. fr. G. *kalyx*, the cup of a flower]. [NA]. Calyx; a flower-shaped or funnel-shaped structure; specifically, one of the branches or recesses of the pelvis of the kidney into which the orifices of the malpighian renal pyramids project.

Calliphora (kă-lif'o-rah) [G. *kalli*, beauty, + *phoros*, bearing]. A genus of blowfies, the bluebottle flies, the larvae of which feed on dead flesh; *C. vomitoria* and *C. vicina* are common species in the U.S.

callo'sal. Relating to the corpus callosum.

callos'ity [L. fr. *callosus*, thick skinned]. Callus (1); keratoma (1); poroma (1); tyloma; a circumscribed thickening of the keratin layer of the epidermis as a result of friction or intermittent pressure.

callous (kal'us). Relating to a callus or callosity.

callus (kal'us) [L. hard skin]. **1.** Callosity. **2.** The hard bonelike substance that develops between and around the ends of a fractured bone.

calmodulin (kal-mod'u-lin) [calcium + modulate]. A eukaryotic protein that binds calcium ions, thereby becoming the agent for many, if not most or all, of the cellular effects ascribed to calcium ions.

cal'omel. Mercurous chloride; an intestinal antiseptic and laxative.

calor (ka'lor) [L.]. Heat, as one of the four signs of inflammation (c., rubor, tumor, dolor) enunciated by Celsus.

calor'ic [L. *calor*, heat]. **1.** Relating to a calorie. **2.** Relating to heat.

calorie (kal'o-rī) [L. *calor*, heat]. A unit of heat content or energy; being replaced by the joule, the SI unit equal to 0.24 calorie. See also British Thermal *Unit*.

  gram c., small c.

  kilogram c. (kcal), large c.

  large c. (C, Cal), kilogram c.; kilocalorie; the quantity of energy required to raise the temperature of 1 kg of water 1°C.

  mean c., $1/100$ of the energy required to raise the temperature of 1 g of water from 0°C. to 100°C.

  small c. (c, cal), gram c.; the quantity of energy required to raise the temperature of 1 g of water 1°C.

calorigen'ic. 1. Capable of generating heat. **2.** Thermogenetic (2); stimulating metabolic production of heat.

calorim'eter [L. *calor*, heat, + G. *metron*, measure]. An apparatus for measuring the amount of heat liberated in a chemical reaction.

cal'orimet'ric. Relating to calorimetry.

calorim'etry. Measurement of the amount of heat given off by a reaction or group of reactions (as by an organism).

calvaria, pl. **calvariae** (kal-va'rĭ-ah, -va'rĭ-e) [L. a skull]. [NA]. Skullcap; roof of the skull, the upper domelike portion of the skull.

calva'rium. Incorrectly used for calvaria.

calx, gen. **cal'cis**, pl. **cal'ces. 1** [L. limestone]. Lime (2). **2** [L. heel]. Heel; the posterior rounded extremity of the foot.

calyces (kal'ĭ-sēz). Plural of calyx.

Calym'matobacte'rium [G. *kalymma*, hood, veil, + *bakterion*, rod]. A genus of nonmotile bacteria (family Brucellaceae) containing Gram-negative, pleomorphic rods with single or bipolar condensations of chromatin. The type species, *C. granulomatis*, causes granulomatous lesions in man, particularly in the inguinal region.

calyx, pl. **calyces** (ka'liks, kal'ĭ-sēz) [G. cup of a flower]. Calix.

camera, pl. **camerae, cameras** (kam'er-ah, -e) [L. a vault]. [NA]. In anatomy, any chamber or cavity, such as one of the chambers of the heart, or eye.

  c. ante'rior bul'bi [NA], anterior chamber of the eye; the space between the cornea and the iris, filled with a watery fluid (aqueous humor) and communicating through the pupil with the posterior chamber.

  c. oc'uli, see c. anterior bulbi; c. posterior bulbi.

  c. poste'rior bul'bi [NA], posterior chamber of the eye; the ringlike space, filled with aqueous humor, between the iris, the crystalline lens, and the ciliary body.

  c. vi'trea bul'bi [NA], vitreous chamber of the eye; the large space between the lens and the retina; it is filled with the vitreous body.

cAMP Adenosine 3':5'-cyclic phosphate (cyclic AMP).

cam'phor [mediev. L. fr. Ar. *kāfure*]. A ketone distilled from the bark and wood of the Asian evergreen tree, *Cinnamomum camphora;* also prepared synthetically from oil of turpentine; used as a stimulant, carminative, expectorant, and diaphoretic.

campimeter (kam-pim'ĕ-ter) [L. *campus*, field, + G. *metron*, measure]. A portable, hand-held type of tangent screen used to measure central visual field.

campim'etry. Investigation of the visual field by means of a campimeter.

camptocormia (kamp'to-kor'mĭ-ah) [G. *kamptos*, bent, + *kormos*, trunk of a tree]. A conversion reaction or hysterical condition in which the patient is bent completely forward and is unable to straighten up.

camptodactyly, camptodactylia (kamp-to-dak'tĭ-lī, -dak-til'ĭ-ah) [G. *kamptos*, bent, + *daktylos*, finger]. Campylodactyly.

camptome'lia [G. *kamptos*, bent, + *melos*, limb]. A bending of the limbs, producing a fixed deformity.

camptospasm (kamp'to-spazm). A nervous or hysterical forward bending of the trunk. See also nodding *spasm*.

Campylobacter (kam'pĭ-lo-bak'ter) [G. *campylos*, curved, + *baktron*, staff or rod]. A genus of motile bacteria containing Gram-negative, nonspore-forming, spirally curved rods with a single polar flagellum at one or both ends of the cell. The type species, *C. fetus*, contains various subspecies that can cause human infections as well as abortion in sheep and cattle.

campylodactyly (kam'pĭ-lo-dak'tĭ-lĭ) [G. *campylos,* curved, + *daktylos,* finger]. Camptodactylia; camptodactyly; permanent flexion of one or both interphalangeal joints of one or more fingers, usually the little finger.

canal (kă-nal') [L. *canalis*]. A duct, channel or tubular structure.

adductor c., *canalis* adductorius.

Alcock's c., *canalis* pudendalis.

alimentary c., digestive *tract.*

anal c., *canalis* analis.

Arnold's c., a bony c. in the petrous portion of the temporal bone through which passes the lesser petrosal nerve.

arterial c., *ductus* arteriosus.

atrioventricular c., the c. in the embryonic heart leading from the common sinuatrial chamber to the ventricle.

auditory c., *meatus* acusticus externus.

birth c., parturient c.

carotid c., *canalis* caroticus.

cervical c., *canalis* cervicis uteri.

cochlear c., *canalis* spiralis cochleae.

condylar c., condyloid c., *canalis* condylaris.

Corti's c., Corti's *tunnel.*

crural c., *canalis* femoralis.

dentinal c.'s, *canaliculi* dentales.

facial c., *canalis* facialis.

femoral c., *canalis* femoralis.

haversian c.'s, vascular c.'s in osseous tissue.

Hirschfeld's c.'s., interdental c.'s.

Hunter's c., *canalis* adductorius.

hypoglossal c., *canalis* hypoglossalis.

incisive c., incisor c., *canalis* incisivus.

infraorbital c., *canalis* infraorbitalis.

inguinal c., *canalis* inguinalis.

interdental c.'s, Hirschfeld's c.'s; c.'s that extend vertically through alveolar bone between roots of mandibular and maxillary incisor and maxillary bicuspid teeth.

interfacial c.'s, intercellular spaces occurring in relation to intercellular bridges in stratified squamous epithelium.

musculotubal c., *canalis* musculotubarius.

nasolacrimal c., *canalis* nasolacrimalis.

Nuck's c., see *processus* vaginalis peritonei.

nutrient c., *canalis* nutricius.

obturator c., *canalis* obturatorius.

optic c., *canalis* opticus.

parturient c., birth c.; the cavity of the uterus and the vagina through which the fetus passes.

portal c.'s, the spaces in the substance of the liver which are occupied by connective tissue and the ramifications of the bile ducts, portal vein, hepatic artery, nerves, and lymphatics.

pterygoid c., *canalis* pterygoideus.

pterygopalatine c., *canalis* palatinus major.

pudendal c., *canalis* pudendalis.

pulp c., *canalis* radicis dentis.

pyloric c., *canalis* pyloricus.

root c. of tooth, *canalis* radicis dentis.

sacral c., *canalis* sacralis.

Schlemm's c., *sinus* venosus sclerae.

semicircular c.'s., see *canales* semicirculares ossei.

spinal c., *canalis* vertebralis.

spiral c. of the cochlea, *canalis* spiralis cochleae.

spiral c. of modiolus, *canalis* spiralis modioli.

tarsal c., *sinus* tarsi.

tympanic c., *canaliculus* tympanicus.

urogenital c., urethra.

vertebral c., *canalis* vertebralis.

vestibular c., *scala* vestibuli.

Volkmann's c.'s, vascular c.'s in bone which, unlike those of the haversian system, are not surrounded by concentric lamellae of bone; they run for the most part transversely, perforating the lamellae of the haversian system, and communicate with the c.'s of that system.

Wirsung's c., *ductus* pancreaticus.

cana'les. Plural of canalis.

canalic'ular. Relating to a canaliculus.

canalic'uli. Plural of canaliculus.

canaliculi'tis [L. canaliculus + G. *-itis,* inflammation]. Inflammation of the lacrimal duct.

canalic'uliza'tion. The formation of small canals or channels in tissue.

canaliculus, pl. **canaliculi** (kan-ă-lik'u-lus, -lĭ) [L. dim. fr. *canalis,* canal]. [NA]. A small canal or channel.

biliary c., bile c., one of the intercellular channels that occurs between liver cells.

bone c., the c. interconnecting bone lacunae with one another or with a haversian canal.

c. coch'leae [NA], **cochlear c.,** a minute canal in the temporal bone that passes from the cochlea inferiorly to open in front of the medial side of the jugular fossa; contains the perilymphatic duct.

canalic'uli denta'les [NA], dentinal canals or tubules; a minute, wavy, branching tubes or canals in the dentin which contain dentinal fibers and extend radially from the pulp to the dentoenamel junction.

intercellular c., one of the fine channels between adjoining secretory cells.

intracellular c., a fine canal formed by invagination of the cell membrane into the cytoplasm of a cell.

c. lacrima'lis [NA], **lacrimal c.,** lacrimal duct; a curved canal beginning at the punctum lacrimale in the margin of each eyelid near the medial commissure and running transversely medially to empty with its fellow into the lacrimal sac.

c. mastoid'eus [NA], **mastoid c.,** the canal that extends from the jugular fossa laterally through the mastoid process and transmits the auricular branch of the vagus.

c. tympan'icus [NA], **tympanic c.,** a minute canal passing from the petrous portion of the temporal bone between the jugular fossa and carotid canal to the floor of the tympanic cavity; transmits the tympanic branch of the glossopharyngeal nerve.

canalis, pl. **canales** (kan-a'lis, -lēz) [L.]. [NA].A canal or channel.

c. adductor'ius [NA], adductor or Hunter's canal; the space in the thigh between the vastus medialis and adductor muscles through which the femoral vessels pass.

c. ana'lis [NA], anal canal; the terminal portion of the alimentary canal, extending from the pelvic diaphragm to the anal orifice.

c. car'pi [NA], carpal tunnel; the space deep to the flexor retinaculum of the wrist through which the median nerve and the flexor tendons of the fingers and thumb pass.

c. carot'icus [NA], carotid canal; a passage through the petrous part of the temporal bone which transmits the internal carotid artery and plexuses of veins and autonomic nerves.

c. cerv'icis u'teri [NA], cervical canal; a fusiform canal extending from the isthmus of the uterus to the opening of the uterus into the vagina.

c. condyla'ris [NA], condylar or condyloid canal; posterior condyloid foramen; the opening through the occipital bone posterior to the condyle on each side which transmits the occipital emissary vein.

c. facia'lis [NA], facial canal; the bony passage in the temporal bone through which the facial nerve passes to reach the stylomastoid foramen.

c. femora'lis [NA], femoral or crural canal; the medial compartment of the femoral sheath.

c. hypoglossa'lis [NA], hypoglossal canal; anterior condyloid foramen; the canal through which the hypoglossal nerve emerges from the skull.

c. incisi'vus [NA], incisive or incisor canal; one of several bony canals leading from the floor of the nasal cavity into the incisive fossa on the palatal surface of the maxilla; they convey the nasopalatine nerves and branches of the greater palatine arteries.

c. infraorbita'lis [NA], infraorbital canal; a canal running beneath the orbital margin of the maxilla from the infraorbital groove, in the floor of the orbit, to the infraorbital foramen; transmits the infraorbital artery and nerve.

c. inguina'lis [NA], inguinal canal; the obliquely directed passage through the layers of the lower abdominal wall that transmits the spermatic cord in the male and the round ligament in the female.

c. musculotuba'rius [NA], musculotubal canal; a canal beginning at the petrous portion of the temporal bone and passing to the tympanic cavity; it is divided into two canals; one for the auditory (eustachian) tube, the other for the tensor tympani muscle.

c. nasolacrima'lis [NA], nasolacrimal canal; the bony canal formed by the maxilla, lacrimal bone, and inferior concha which transmits the nasolacrimal duct from the orbit to the inferior meatus of the nose.

c. nutri'cius [NA], nutrient canal; a canal in the shaft of a long bone or in other locations in irregular bones through which the nutrient artery enters.

c. obturato'rius [NA], obturator canal; the opening in the superior part of the obturator membrane through which the obturator nerve and vessels pass from the pelvic cavity into the thigh.

c. op'ticus [NA], optic canal or foramen; the short canal through the lesser wing of the sphenoid bone at the apex of the orbit through which pass the optic nerve and the ophthalmic artery.

cana'les palati'ni mino'res [NA], canals for the lesser palatine nerves located in the posterior part of the palatine bone.

c. palati'nus ma'jor [NA], pterygopalatine canal; the c. formed between the maxilla and palatine bones which transmits the descending palatine artery and the greater palatine nerve.

c. pterygoi'deus pterygoid canal; an opening through the pterygoid process of the sphenoid bone through which pass the artery, vein, and nerve of the pterygoid canal.

c. pudenda'lis [NA], pudendal or Alcock's canal; the space within the obturator fascia lining the lateral wall of the ischiorectal fossa that transmits the pudendal vessels and nerves.

c. pylor'icus pyloric canal; the aboral segment of the stomach that succeeds the antrum and ends at the gastroduodenal junction.

c. rad'icis den'tis [NA], root canal of a tooth; pulp canal; the chamber of the dental pulp lying within the root portion of a tooth.

c. sacra'lis [NA], sacral canal; the continuation of the vertebral canal in the sacrum.

cana'les semicircula'res os'sei [NA], bony semicircular canals; the three bony tubes in the labyrinth of the ear within which the membranous semicircular ducts are located; they lie in planes at right angles to each other and are known as **canales semicirculares anterior, posterior,** and **lateralis.**

c. spira'lis coch'leae [NA], spiral canal of the cochlea; cochlear canal; the winding tube of the bony labyrinth which is divided incompletely into two compartments by a winding shelf of bone.

c. spira'lis modio'li [NA], spiral canal of the modiolus; the space in the modiolus in which the spiral ganglion of the cochlear nerve lies.

c. vertebra'lis [NA], vertebral or spinal canal; the canal that contains the spinal cord, spinal meninges, and related structures; formed by the vertebral foramina of successive vertebrae of the articulated vertebral column.

canaliza'tion. Formation of canals or channels in any tissue.

cancellated, cancellous (kan'sel-āt-ed, -sē-lus) [L. *cancello,* to make a lattice work]. Denoting bone that has a lattice-like or spongy structure.

cancel'lus, pl. **cancel'li** [L. a grating, lattice]. A lattice-like structure, such as spongy bone.

cancer(CA) (kan'ser) [L. a crab, a cancer]. Any of various types of malignant neoplasms, most of which invade surrounding tissues, may metastasize to several sites, and are likely to recur after attempted removal and to cause death of the patient unless adequately treated.

cancer à deux [Fr. *deux*, two]. Carcinomas occurring at approximately the same time, or in fairly close succession, in two persons who live together.

cancerophobia (kan'ser-o-fo'bī-ah) [cancer, + G. *phobos*, fear]. Carcinophobia; morbid fear of acquiring a malignant growth.

cancerous (kan'ser-us). Relating to or pertaining to a malignant neoplasm, or being afflicted with such a process.

cancra (kang'krah). Plural of cancrum.

cancriform (kang'krī-form). Cancroid (1); resembling cancer.

cancroid (kang'kroyd) [cancer + G. *eidos*, resemblance]. **1.** Cancriform. **2.** Obsolete term for a malignant neoplasm that manifests a lesser degree of malignancy than that frequently observed with other types of carcinoma or sarcoma.

cancrum, pl. **cancra** (kang'krum, -krah) [Mod. L. fr. L. *cancer*(*cancr*-), cancer]. A gangrenous, ulcerative, inflammatory lesion.

can'dela (cd) [L.]. Candle; the SI unit of luminous intensity, 1 lumen per square meter.

candici'din. A fungistatic and fungicidal polyene antibiotic agent derived from a soil actinomycete similar to *Streptomyces griseus;* used in the treatment of vaginal candidiasis.

Can'dida [L. *candidus*, dazzling white]. A genus of yeastlike fungi commonly found in nature. The gastrointestinal tract is the source of the most important species, *C. albicans*, which is ordinarily a part of the normal flora, but which becomes pathogenic when there is a disturbance in the balance of flora; resulting disease states vary from limited to generalized cutaneous or mucocutaneous infections, to severe and fatal systemic disease including endocarditis, septicemia, and meningitis.

candide'mia [*Candida* + G. *haima*, blood]. Presence of *Candida* in the peripheral blood.

candidiasis (kan-dī-di'äsis). Moniliasis; infection with, or disease caused by, *Candida.*

candle (kan'dl). Candela.

candle-meter. Lux.

canine (ka'nin) [L. *caninus*]. **1.** Relating to a dog. **2.** Relating to the c. teeth. **3.** A c. (cuspid) tooth.

canities (kan-ish'e-ēz) [L. fr. *canus*, hoary, gray]. A gradual dilution of pigment in hairs, producing a range of colors from normal to white, and perceived as gray.

canker (kang'ker) [L. *cancer*]. An ulcerative sore, especially of the oral mucosa or lip, as in stomatitis.

can'nabinoids. Organic substances present in *Cannabis sativa*, having a variety of pharmacologic properties; *e.g.*, cannabidiol, cannabinol, tetrahydrocannabinol.

can'nabis [L. fr. G. *kannabis*, hemp]. Marijuana; marihuana; bhang, charas; ganja; hashish; the dried flowering tops of the pistillate hemp plants of *Cannabis sativa* var. *indica* (family Moraceae) containing isomeric cannabinoids. Preparations of c. are smoked or ingested to induce psychotomimetic effects; formerly used as a sedative and analgesic.

can'nabism. Poisoning by preparations of cannabis.

cannula (kan'u-lah) [L. dim. of *canna*, reed]. A tube such as one inserted into a cavity by means of a trocar filling its lumen, after which the trocar is withdrawn; the c. remains as a channel for the transport of fluid.

cannula'tion, cannuliza'tion. Insertion of a cannula.

can'thal. Relating to a canthus.

canthec'tomy [G. *kanthos*, canthus, + *ektomē*, excision]. Excision of a canthus.

can'thi. Plural of canthus.

canthi'tis. Inflammation of a canthus.

canthol'ysis [G. *kanthos*, canthus, + *lysis*, loosening]. Canthoplasty (1).

can'thoplasty [G. *kanthos*, canthus, + *plassō*, to form]. **1.** Cantholysis; lengthening the palpebral fissure by cutting through the external canthus. **2.** Surgical restoration of the canthus in case of pathologic or traumatic defect.

canthorrhaphy (kan-thor'ă-fī) [G. *kanthos*, canthus, + *rhaphē*, suture]. Suture of the eyelids at either canthus.

canthot'omy [G. *kanthos*, canthus, + *tomē*, incision]. Slitting of the canthus.

can'thus, pl. **can'thi** [G. *kanthos*, corner of the eye]. The angle at either corner of the eye.

cap. Any structure that resembles a protective covering for the head.

    acrosomal c., head c.; acrosome; a thin covering over the anterior part of the nucleus of the spermatozoon, derived from the acrosomal granule.

    cradle c., colloquialism for seborrheic dermatitis of the scalp of the newborn.

    duodenal c., pyloric c.; the first portion of the duodenum, as seen in a roentgenogram or by fluoroscopy.

    enamel c., the enamel covering the crown of a tooth.

    head c., acrosomal c.

    pyloric c., duodenal c.

capacitation (kă-pas'ī-ta'shun) [L. *capacitas*, fr. *capax*, capable of]. The process occurring in the female genital tract whereby spermatozoa acquire the ability to fertilize ova, characterized by loss of the acrosome cap by spermatozoa and an increase in their respiratory metabolism and content of DNA.

capacity (kă-pas'ī-tĭ) [L. *capax*, able to contain; fr. *capio*, to take]. **1.** The potential cubic contents of a cavity or receptacle. See also volume. **2.** Ability; power to do.

    diffusing c. (D, followed by subscripts indicating location and chemical species), the amount of oxygen taken up by pulmonary capillary blood per minute per unit average oxygen pressure gradient between alveolar gas and pulmonary capillary blood; units are: ml/min/mm Hg; also applied to other gases such as carbon monoxide.

functional residual c. (FRC), functional residual air; the volume of gas remaining in the lungs at the end of a normal expiration; expiratory reserve volume plus residual volume.

heat c., thermal c.; the quantity of heat required to raise the temperature of a system 1°C.

inspiratory c., complementary air; the volume of air that can be inspired after normal expiration; tidal volume plus inspiratory reserve volume.

maximum breathing c. (MBC), maximum voluntary ventilation; the volume of air breathed when breathing as deeply and as quickly as possible for 15 seconds.

oxygen c., the maximum quantity of oxygen that will combine chemically with the hemoglobin in a unit volume of blood; normally it amounts to 1.34 ml of O_2 per gm of Hb or 20 ml of O_2 per 100 ml of blood.

residual c., residual *volume.*

respiratory c., vital c.

thermal c., heat c.

total lung c. (TLC), inspiratory c. plus functional residual c., the volume of air contained in the lungs at the end of maximal inspiration; also equals vital c. plus residual volume.

vital c. (VC), respiratory c.; the greatest volume of air that can be exhaled from the lungs after maximum inspiration.

cap'illarecta'sia [capillary + G. *ektasis,* extension]. Dilation of the capillary blood vessels.

capillar'iomo'tor. Vasomotor, with special reference to the capillaries.

capillaritis (kap'ĭ-lăr-i'tis). Inflammation of a capillary or capillaries.

capillar'ity. The rise of liquids in narrow tubes.

cap'illarop'athy. Microangiopathy; any disease of the capillaries.

cap'illary [L. *capillaris,* relating to hair]. **1.** Resembling a hair; fine; minute. **2.** A capillary vessel. **3.** Relating to a blood or lymphatic c. vessel.

arterial c., a c. opening from an arteriole or metarteriole.

blood c., (c, as a subscript), a vessel about 8 μm in diameter whose wall consists of endothelium and its basement membrane; with the electron microscope, fenestrated c.'s and continuous c.'s are distinguished.

continuous c., a blood c., found in muscle, in which small vesicles (caveolae) are numerous and pores are absent.

fenestrated c., a blood c., found in renal glomeruli, intestinal villi, and some glands, in which ultramicroscopic pores of variable size occur.

lymph c., the beginning of the lymphatic system of vessels; it is lined with flattened endothelium and has a lumen of variable caliber.

venous c., a c. opening into a venule.

capil'lus, pl. **capil'li** [L. hair]. [NA]. A hair of the head.

capistra'tion [L. *capistrum,* muzzle]. Paraphimosis (1).

capita (kap'ĭ-tah). Plural of caput.

cap'itate [L. *caput(capit-),* head]. Head-shaped; having a rounded extremity.

capitel'lum [L. dim. of *caput,* head]. **1.** Capitulum. **2.** The small or radial head of the humerus.

capit'ium [L. *caput,* head]. A bandage for the head.

capitonnage (kap'ĭ-to-nahzh) [Fr. *capitonnage,* upholstering]. Surgical closure of a cyst cavity.

capitula (kă-pit'u-lah). Plural of capitulum.

capit'ular. Relating to a capitulum.

capitulum, pl. **capitula** (kă-pit'u-lum, -lah) [L. dim. of *caput,* head]. [NA]. Capitellum (1); a small head or rounded articular extremity of a bone. See also caput.

cap'rate. A salt or ester of capric acid.

***n-* cap'ric acid.** $CH_3(CH_2)_8COOH$; a fatty acid found among the hydrolysis products of fat in goat's milk, cow's milk, and other substances.

cap'roate. 1. A salt or ester of caproic acid. **2.** USAN-approved contraction for hexanoate, $CH_3-(CH_2)_4COO-$.

***n-* capro'ic acid.** $CH_3(CH_2)_4COOH$; a fatty acid found among the hydrolysis products of fat in butter and some other substances.

caproyl (kap'ro-il). The radical of caproic acid.

caproylate (kap'ro-ĭ-lāt). A salt or ester of caproic acid.

cap'rylate. A salt of ester of caprylic acid.

capryl'ic acid. $CH_3(CH_2)_6COOH$; a fatty acid found among the hydrolysis products of fat in butter and other substances.

capsid (kap'sid). See virion.

capsomer(e) (kap'so-mēr). A subunit of the protein coat or capsid of a virus particle.

capsula, pl. **capsulae** (kap'su-lah, -le) [L. dim. of *capsa,* a chest or box]. [NA]. Capsule (1). **1.** A membranous structure, usually dense collagenous connective tissue, that envelops an organ, a joint or any other part. **2.** An anatomical structure resembling a capsule or envelope.

c. articula'ris [NA], articular or joint capsule; a sac enclosing a joint, formed by an outer fibrous membrane and an inner synovial membrane.

c. exter'na [NA], external capsule; a thin lamina of white substance separating the claustrum from the putamen.

c. fibro'sa [NA], the fibrous capsule of an organ.

c. f. perivascula'ris, perivascular fibrous capsule; Glisson's capsule; a layer of connective tissue ensheathing the hepatic artery, portal vein, and bile ducts as these ramify within the liver. **c. f. re'nis,** fibrous capsule of the kidney; a fibrous membrane ensheathing the kidney.

c. glomer'uli [NA], Bowman's capsule; malpighian capsule (1); the expanded beginning of a renal tubule.

c. inter'na [NA], internal capsule; a layer of white matter separating the caudate nucleus and thalamus on the medial side from the more laterally situated lentiform nucleus (globus pallidus and putamen); the major route by which the cerebral cortex is connected with the brainstem and spinal cord. Laterally it is directly continuous with the corona radiata which forms a major part of the cerebral hemisphere's white matter; caudally and medially it continues as the crus cerebri which contains, among others, the pyramidal tract.

c. len'tis [NA], lenticular capsule; the capsule enclosing the lens of the eye.

cap'sular. Relating to any capsule.

capsule (kap'sūl) **1.** Capsula. **2.** A fibrous tissue layer enveloping a tumor, especially if benign. **3.** A solid dosage form in which the drug is enclosed in a soluble container or "shell."

    articular c., *capsula articularis.*

    auditory c., auditory cartilage; the cartilage that, in the embryo, surrounds the developing auditory vesicle.

    bacterial c., a layer of slime of variable composition which covers the surface of some bacteria.

    Bowman's c., *capsula glomeruli.*

    cartilage c., the basophilic matrix in hyaline cartilage surrounding the lacunae in which lie the cartilage cells.

    external c., *capsula externa.*

    fibrous c. of kidney, *capsula fibrosa renis.*

    Gerota's c., *fascia renalis.*

    Glisson's c., *capsula fibrosa perivascularis.*

    internal c., *capsula interna.*

    joint c., *capsula articularis.*

    lenticular c., *capsula lentis.*

    malpighian c., (1) *capsula glomeruli;* (2) a thin fibrous membrane enveloping the spleen and continued over the vessels entering at the hilus.

    nasal c., the cartilage around the developing nasal cavity of the embryo.

    optic c., the concentrated zone of mesenchyme around the developing optic cup; the primordium of the sclera of the eye.

    otic c., the cartilage c. surrounding the inner ear mechanism of the embryo; it later becomes bony.

    perivascular fibrous c., *capsula fibrosa perivascularis.*

    Tenon's c., *vagina bulbi.*

capsulitis (kap-su-li'tis). Inflammation of the capsule of an organ or part.

    adhesive c., frozen shoulder; a condition in which there is restriction of glenohumeral and scapulothoracic motion, and pain both on motion and at rest; not caused by infection or neoplasm.

cap'sulolentic'ular. Referring to the lens of the eye and its capsule.

cap'suloplasty [L. *capsula,* capsule, + G. *plassō,* to fashion]. Plastic surgery of a capsule, more specifically the capsule of a joint.

capsulorrhaphy (kap-su-lor'ă-fī) [L. *capsula,* capsule, + *raphē,* suture]. Suture of a tear in any capsule; specifically, suture of a joint capsule to prevent recurring dislocation of the articulation.

capsulot'omy [L. *capsula,* capsule, + G. *tomē,* a cutting]. Incision through a capsule, especially the capsule of the lens in the extracapsular cataract operation.

cap'ture. A taking, a catch, such as control of the atria after a period of independent beating, as in complete A-V block, by the retrograde impulse.

caput, gen. **cap'itis,** pl. **capita** (kap'ut, ka'put; kap'ĭ-tah) [L.]. Head. **1** [NA]. The upper or anterior extremity of the animal body, containing the brain and the organs of sight, hearing, taste, and smell. **2** [NA]. The upper, anterior, or larger extremity, expanded or rounded, of any body, organ, or other anatomical structure. **3.** That end of a muscle which is attached to the less movable part of the skeleton.

    c. medu'sae [*Medusa,* G. myth. character], Medusa head; (1) Cruveilhier's sign; varicose veins radiating from the umbilicus, seen in the Cruveilhier-Baumgarten *syndrome;* (2) dilated ciliary arteries girdling the corneoscleral limbus in absolute glaucoma.

    c. succeda'neum, an edematous swelling formed on the presenting portion of the scalp of an infant during birth; the effusion overlies the periosteum and consists of serum.

carb-, carba-, carbo-. Prefixes indicating the attachment of a group containing a carbon atom.

car'bamate. Carbamoate; a salt or ester of carbamic acid; forms the basis of urethane hypnotics.

carbam'ic acid. A hypothetical acid, NH_2–COOH, forming carbamates; the acyl radical is carbamoyl.

car'bamide. Urea.

car'bamino com'pound. Any carbamic acid derivative formed by the combination of carbon dioxide with a free amino group to form an *N*-carboxy group, –NH–COOH, as in hemoglobin forming carbaminohemoglobin.

car'baminohemoglo'bin. Hb-NHCOOH; carbon dioxide bound to hemoglobin by means of a reactive amino group on the latter; approximately 20% of the total content of carbon dioxide in blood is combined with hemoglobin in this manner.

carbamoate (kar'bă-mo-āt). Carbamate.

carbamoyl (kar-bam'o-il). Carbamyl; the acyl radical, NH_2–CO–, the transfer of which plays an important role in certain biochemical reactions.

car'bamoyltrans'ferases. Transcarbamoylases; enzymes transferring carbamoyl groups from one compound to another.

car'bamolu'rea. Biuret.

car'bamyl. Carbamoyl.

carbenicil'lin disodium. Disodium salt of 6-(α-carboxy-α-phenylacetamido)-penicillanic acid (α-carboxybenzyl penicillin); a semisynthetic form of penicillin.

car'binol. *Methyl* alcohol.

carbo-. See carb-.

car'bobenzox'y (Cbz, Z). Benzyloxcarbonyl.

carbocation (kar-bo-kat'ĭ-on). See carbonium.

carbohy'drases. A generic term for enzymes that hydrolyze carbohydrates.

carbohy'drates. Saccharides; class name for the aldehydic or ketonic derivative of polyhydric alcohols, the name being derived from the fact that the most common examples of such compounds have formulas that may be written $C_n(H_2O)_n$ (e.g., glucose, $C_6(H_2O)_6$; sucrose, $C_{12}(H_2O)_{11}$), although they are not true hydrates; includes compounds with relatively small molecules, such as the simple sugars (monosaccharides, disaccharides, etc.), as well as macromolecular substances (starch, glycogen, cellulose polysaccharides, etc.).

carbohydratu'ria. Excretion of one or more carbohydrates in the urine.

carbol-fuchsin (kar'bol-fook'sin). See Ziehl's *stain*.

carbol'ic acid. Phenol.

carbolu'ria [carbolic acid + G. *ouron,* urine]. Presence of phenol (carbolic acid) in the urine.

car'bon [L. *carbo,* coal]. A nonmetallic tetravalent element, symbol C, atomic no. 6, atomic weight 12.01, with two natural isotopes, ^{12}C and ^{13}C (the former, set at 12.00000, being the standard for all molecular weights), and two artificial radioactive isotopes, ^{11}C and ^{14}C. It occurs in two pure forms, diamond and graphite; in impure form in charcoal, coke, and soot; in the atmosphere as CO_2; and in compounds found in all living tissues.

    c. dioxide, (1) CO_2; the product of the combustion of c. with an excess of air; (2) in concentrations not less than 99.0% by volume of CO_2, used as a respiratory stimulant.

    c. monoxide, CO; a colorless, odorless, poisonous gas formed by incomplete combustion of c.; its toxic action is due to its strong affinity for hemoglobin and cytochrome, reducing oxygen transport and blocking oxygen utilization.

    c. tetrachloride, tetrachloromethane; CCl_4; a colorless mobile liquid having a characteristic etheral odor resembling that of chloroform. See also tetrachloroethane.

car'bonate. A salt of carbonic acid; $CO_3 =$.

car'bonyl. The characteristic group, –CO–, of the ketones, aldehydes, and organic acids.

carboxy-. Combining form indicating addition of CO or CO_2.

carbox'yhemoglo'bin (HbCO). A fairly stable union of carbon monoxide with hemoglobin. Formation of c. prevents the normal transfer of carbon dioxide and oxygen during the circulation of blood; thus, increasing levels of c. result in various degrees of asphyxiation, including death.

carbox'yhemoglobine'mia. The presence of carboxyhemoglobin in the blood.

carbox'yl. The characterizing group (–COOH) of certain organic acids.

carbox'ylase. One of several carboxy-lyases, trivially named carboxylases or decarboxylases, catalyzing the addition of CO_2 to all or part of another molecule to create an additional –COOH group.

carboxyla'tion. Addition of CO_2 to an organic acceptor, as in photosynthesis, to yield a –COOH group; catalyzed by carboxylases.

carbox'yltrans'ferases. Transcarboxylases; enzymes transferring carboxyl groups from one compound to another.

carbox'ypep'tidases. Hydrolases removing the amino acid at the free carboxyl end of a polypeptide chain.

carbuncle (kar'bung-kl) [L. *carbunculus,* dim. of *carbo,* a live coal, a carbuncle]. **1.** Deep-seated pyogenic infection of several contiguous hair follicles, with formation of connecting sinuses; often preceded or accompanied by fever, malaise, and prostration. **2.** Anthrax (1).

carbun'cular. Relating to a carbuncle.

carbunculo'sis. Occurrence of several carbuncles simultaneously or within a short period of time.

carcino-, carcin- [G. *karkinos,* crab, cancer]. Combining form relating to cancer.

carcinogen (kar'sĭ-no -jen). Any cancer-producing substance.

car'cinogen'esis [carcino- + G. *genesis,* generation]. The origin of production of cancer, including carcinomas and other malignant neoplasms.

car'cinogen'ic. Causing cancer.

car'cinolyt'ic [carcino- + G. *lytikos,* causing a solution]. Destructive to the cells of carcinoma.

carcinoma (CA) (kar-sĭ-no'mah) [G. *karkinōma,* fr. *karkinos,* cancer, + *-oma,* tumor]. Any of the various types of malignant neoplasm derived from epithelial tissue, occurring more frequently in the skin and large intestine in both sexes, the bronchi, stomach, and prostate gland in men, and the breast and cervix in women; c.'s are identified histologically on the basis of invasiveness and the changes that indicate anaplasia.

    adenoid cystic c., cylindromatous c.; a histologic type of c. characterized by large epithelial masses containing round glandlike spaces or cysts, frequently containing mucus and bordered by layers of epithelial cells without intervening stroma, forming a cribriform pattern; occurs most commonly in salivary glands as a cylindroma.

    adenoid squamous cell c., adenoacanthoma.

    alveolar cell c., bronchiolar c.

    basal cell c., basal cell epithelioma; a slow-growing, locally invasive, but rarely metastasizing neoplasm derived from basal cells of the epidermis or hair follicles.

    basal squamous cell c., basosquamous c., a c. of the skin which in structure and behavior is considered transitional between basal cell and squamous cell c.

bronchiolar c., bronchiolo-alveolar c., alveolar cell c.; a c., thought to be derived from epithelium of terminal bronchioles, in which the neoplastic tissue extends along the alveolar walls and grows in small masses within the alveoli, involving the lung in a fairly uniformly diffuse, frequently massive manner, or in a nodular or lobular manner.

bronchogenic c., squamous cell or oat cell c. which arises in the mucosa of the large bronchi and produces a persistent productive cough or hemoptysis; local growth causes bronchial obstruction and malignant tumor cells metastasize early to the thoracic lymph nodes and to other organs via the blood stream.

colloid c., mucinous c.

cylindromatous c., adenoid cystic c.

embryonal c., a malignant neoplasm of the testis, composed of large anaplastic cells with indistinct cellular borders, amphophilic cytoplasm, and ovoid, round, or bean-shaped nuclei that may have multiple large nucleoli; may be malignant teratomas without differentiated elements.

epidermoid c., squamous cell c.

giant cell c., a malignant epithelial neoplasm characterized by unusually large anaplastic cells.

hepatocellular c., malignant *hepatoma.*

Hürthle cell c., see Hürthle cell *tumor.*

c. in si'tu, a lesion observed most commonly in stratified squamous epithelium and characterized by cytologic changes of the type associated with invasive c., but with the pathologic process limited to the lining epithelium and without histologic evidence of extension to adjacent structures.

large cell c., an anaplastic c., particularly bronchogenic, composed of cells which are much larger than those in oat cell (small cell) c. of the lung.

medullary c., a malignant neoplasm consisting chiefly of neoplastic epithelial cells, with only a scant amount of fibrous stroma.

melanotic c., melanoma.

mesometanephric c., mesonephroma.

mucinous c., colloid c. or cancer; a variety of adenocarcinoma in which the neoplastic cells secrete conspicuous quantities of mucin.

oat cell c., small cell c. (2); an anaplastic, highly malignant, and usually bronchogenic c. composed of small ovoid cells with very scanty cytoplasm.

papillary c., a malignant neoplasm characterized by the formation of numerous, irregular, finger-like projections of fibrous stroma covered with a surface layer of neoplastic epithelial cells.

scirrhous c., fibrocarcinoma; a hard fibrous c. resulting from a desmoplastic reaction by the stromal tissue to the presence of the neoplastic epithelium.

signet ring cell c., a poorly differentiated adenocarcinoma composed of cells with a cytoplasmic droplet of mucus that compresses the nucleus to one side along the cell membrane; arises most frequently

in the stomach, occasionally in the large bowel or elsewhere.

c. sim'plex, (1) any form of c. in which the relative proportions of stroma and neoplastic epithelial cells are not unusual; **(2)** a c. lacking any identifiable microscopic pattern, such as glandular structure.

small cell c., (1) an anaplastic c. composed of small cells; **(2)** oat cell c.

spindle cell c., a c. composed of elongated cells, frequently a poorly differentiated squamous cell c. which may be difficult to distinguish from a sarcoma.

squamous cell c., epidermoid c.; a malignant neoplasm that is derived from stratified squamous epithelium, but that may also occur in sites where glandular or columnar epithelium is normally present.

transitional cell c., a malignant neoplasm derived from transitional epithelium, occurring chiefly in the urinary bladder, ureters, or renal pelves.

villous c., a form of c. in which there are numerous, closely packed, papillary projections of neoplastic epithelial tissue.

carcinomatosis (kar'sĭ-nō-mă-to'sis). Carcinosis; a condition resulting from widespread dissemination of carcinoma in multiple sites in various organs or tissues of the body; sometimes also used in relation to involvement of a relatively large region of the body.

carcino'matous. Pertaining to or manifesting the characteristic properties of carcinoma.

carcinopho'bia. Cancerophobia.

carcinosarcoma (kar'sĭ-no-sar-ko'mah). Sarcocarcinoma; a malignant neoplasm that contains elements of carcinoma and sarcoma so extensively intermixed as to indicate neoplasia of epithelial and mesenchymal tissue. See also collision *tumor.*

c. of embryonal type, blastoma.

renal c., Wilms *tumor.*

carcino'sis. Carcinomatosis.

cardi-. See cardio-.

car'dia [G. *kardia,* heart]. The cardiac part of the stomach; the area of the stomach close to the esophageal opening (cardiac opening) which containes the cardiac glands.

car'diac [L. *cardiacus*]. Pertaining to the heart or to the esophageal opening of the stomach.

cardial'gia [cardi- + G. *algos,* pain]. **1.** Heartburn; an uncomfortable burning sensation in the stomach. **2.** Cardiodynia.

cardiasthenia (kar-dĭ-as-the'nĭ-ah) [cardi- + G. *astheneia,* weakness]. Weakness in the action of the heart.

cardiectasia (car'dĭ-ek-ta'zĭ-ah) [cardi- + G. *ektasis,* a stretching]. Dilation of the heart.

cardio-, cardi- [G. *kardia,* heart]. Combining forms relating to the heart or to the esophageal opening of the stomach.

car'dioaccel'erator. That which quickens the heart beat.

car'dioac'tive. Influencing the heart.

cardioangiology (kar-dĭ-o-an-jĭ-ol'o-jĭ) [cardio- + G. *angeion*, vessel, + *logos*, study]. The science concerned with the heart and blood vessels.

car'dioaor'tic. Relating to the heart and the aorta.

car'dioarte'rial. Relating to the heart and the arteries.

cardiocele (kar'dĭ-o-sēl) [cardio- + G. *kētē*, hernia]. Herniation or protrusion of the heart through an opening in the diaphragm, or through a wound.

car'diocente'sis [cardio- + G. *kentēsis*, puncture]. Paracentesis of the heart.

cardiochalasia (kar'dĭ-o-kă-la'zĭ-ah). Achalasia of the gastric cardia.

cardiocirrhosis (kar'dĭ-o-sĭ-ro'sis). Cardiac *cirrhosis.*

car'diodio'sis [cardio- + G. *diōsis*, a spreading open]. Maneuver of dilating the gastric cardia.

car'diodyn'ia [cardio- + G. *odynē*, pain]. Cardialgia (2); pain in the heart.

car'diodynam'ics. The mechanics of the heart's action, including its movement and the forces thus generated.

car'diogen'ic. Of origin in the heart.

car'diogram [cardio- + G. *gramma*, a diagram]. The graphic tracing made by the stylet of a cardiograph; generally, any recording derived from the heart, such prefixes as apex-, echo-, electro-, phono-, or vector- being understood.

car'diograph [cardio- + G. *graphō*, to write]. An instrument for recording graphically the movements of the heart.

cardiog'raphy. Use of the cardiograph.

  ultrasound c., echocardiography.

car'diohepat'ic. Relating to the heart and the liver.

car'dioinhib'itory. Arresting or slowing the action of the heart.

car'diokinet'ic [cardio- + G. *kinēsis*, movement]. Influencing the action of the heart.

car'diolith [cardio- + G. *lithos*, stone]. Cardiac calculus; a concretion in the heart, or an area of calcareous degeneration in its walls or valves.

cardiol'ogist. Physician specializing in the diagnosis and treatment of heart disease.

cardiol'ogy [cardio- + G. *logos*, study]. The medical specialty concerned with the heart and its diseases.

cardiolysis (kar-dĭ-ol'ĭ-sis) [cardio- + G. *lysis*, loosening]. An operation for breaking up the adhesions in chronic mediastinopericarditis.

cardiomalacia (kar'dĭ-o-mă-la'shĭ-ah) [cardio- + G. *malakia*, softness]. Softening of the walls of the heart.

car'diomeg'aly [cardio- + G. *megas*, large]. Macrocardia; megalocardia; enlargement of the heart.

car'diomotil'ity. Movements of the heart.

cardiomuscular (kar'dĭ-o-mus'ku-lar). Pertaining to the musculature of the heart.

cardiomyoliposis (kar'dĭ-o-lī-po'sis) [cardio- + G. *mys*, muscle, + *lipos*, fat, + *-osis*, condition]. Fatty degeneration of the myocardium.

cardiomyopathy (kar'dĭ-o -mi-op'ă-thĭ) [cardio- + G. *mys*, muscle, + *pathos*, disease]. Myocardiopathy; disease of the myocardium.

car'dioneph'ric. Cardiorenal.

cardioneural (kar'dĭ-o-nu'ral) [cardio- + G. *neuron*, nerve]. Relating to the nervous control of the heart.

cardioneurosis (kar'dĭ-o-nu-ro'sis). Cardiac *neurosis.*

cardio-omentopexy (kar'dĭ-o-o-men'to-pek-sĭ) [cardio- + omentum, + G. *pēxis*, fixation]. Surgical attachment of omentum to the heart to improve its blood supply.

cardiop'athy [cardio- + G. *pathos*, disease]. Any disease of the heart.

cardiopericardiopexy (kar'dĭ-o-pĕr-ĭ-kar'dĭ-o-pek-sĭ) [cardio- + pericardium + G. *pēxis*, fixation]. An operation to increase the blood supply to the myocardium by spreading sterile magnesium silicate within the pericardial sac to cause an adhesive pericarditis and an increase in blood supply to develop through the stimulation of interarterial coronary anastomoses and pericardial collaterals.

cardiopericarditis (kar'dĭ-o-pĕr-ĭ-kar-di'tis). Inflammation of both myocardium and pericardium.

car'diopho'bia. Morbid fear of heart disease.

car'dioplas'ty [cardio- + G. *plassō*, to fashion]. Esophagogastroplasty.

cardioplegia (kar'dĭ-o-ple'jĭ-ah) [cardio- + G. *plēgē*, stroke]. **1.** Paralysis of the heart. **2.** Elective temporary stopping of cardiac activity as by injection of chemicals, selective hypothermia, or electrical stimuli.

cardiople'gic. Relating to cardioplegia.

cardioptosia (kar'dĭ-op-to'sĭ-ah) [cardio- + G. *ptōsis*, a falling]. A condition in which the heart is unduly movable and displaced downward.

car'diopul'monary. Relating to the heart and lungs.

cardiopyloric (kar'dĭ-o-pi-lor'ik, -pī-lor'ik). Relating to the cardiac and pyloric extremities of the stomach.

car'diore'nal. Cardionephric; nephrocardiac; relating to the heart and the kidney.

cardiorrhaphy (kar-dĭ-or'ă-fĭ) [cardio- + G. *rhaphē*, suture]. Suture of the heart wall.

cardiorrhexis (kar-dĭ-o-rek'sis) [cardio- + G. *rhēxis*, rupture]. Rupture of the heart wall.

cardioschisis (kar-dĭ-os'kĭ-sis) [cardio- + G. *schisis*, a division]. Surgical division of adhesions between the heart and the pericardium or the chest wall.

car'diospasm. Esophageal *achalasia.*

cardiosphygmograph (kar'dĭ-o-sfig'mo-graf) [cardio- + G. *sphygmos*, pulse, + *graphō*, to write]. An instrument for recording graphically the movements of the heart and the radial pulse.

cardiotachometer (kar'dĭ-o-tă-kom'ĕ-ter) [cardio- + G. *tachos*, rapidity, + *metron*, measure]. An instrument for measuring the rapidity of the heart beat.

cardiot'omy [cardio- + G. *tomē*, incision]. **1.** Incision of the heart wall. **2.** Incision of the cardiac end of the stomach.

car'dioton'ic [cardio- + G. *tonos*, tension]. Exerting a favorable, so-called tonic, effect upon the action of the heart.

cardiotopometry (kar'dĭ-o-to-pom'ĕ-trĭ) [cardio- + G. *topos*, place, + *metron*, measure]. Determination of the area of cardiac dullness.

car'diotox'ic [cardio- + G. *toxikon*, poison]. Having a deleterious effect upon the action of the heart, due to poisoning of the cardiac muscle or of its conducting system.

car'diovalvot'omy. Cardiovalvulotomy.

cardiovalvulitis (kar'dĭ-o-val-vu-li'tis). Inflammation of the heart valves.

cardiovalvulotomy (kar'dĭ-o-val-vu-lot'o-mĭ) [cardio- + Mod. L. *valvula*, a little valve, *tomē*, a cutting]. Cardiovalvotomy; surgical correction of valvular stenosis by cutting or excising a part of a heart valve.

car'diovas'cular [cardio- + L. *vasculum*, vessel]. Relating to the heart and the blood vessels, or the circulation.

car'diover'sion. Restoration of the heart's rhythm to normal by electrical countershock.

car'dioverter. Machine used to perform cardioversion.

cardi'tis. Inflammation of the heart. See myocarditis.

caries (kăr-ēz) [L. dry rot]. **1.** A localized progressively destructive disease of the teeth which starts at the enamel with the apparent dissolution of the inorganic components by organic acids that are produced in immediate proximity to the tooth by the enzymatic action of masses of microorganisms (in the bacterial plaque) on carbohydrates; this initial demineralization is followed by an enzymatic destruction of the protein matrix with subsequent cavitation and direct bacterial invasion. **2.** Obsolete term for destruction or necrosis of bone.

carina, pl. **carinae** (kări'nah, -ri'ne) [L. the keel of a boat]. An anatomical structure forming a projecting central ridge.

car'inate. Keel-shaped, relating to or resembling a carina.

cario-. Combining form relating to caries.

cariogen'esis. The process of producing caries; the mechanism of caries production.

cariogen'ic. Producing caries; usually said of diets.

cariogenic'ity. Potential for caries production.

cariol'ogy. The study of dental caries and cariogenesis.

carious (kăr'ĭ-us). Relating to or affected with caries.

carmin'ative [L. *carmino*, pp. *-atus*, to card wool; special Mod. L. use, to expel wind]. Preventing the formation or causing the expulsion of flatus.

carmine (kar'min, kar'mēn) [Mediev. L. *carminus*]. Red coloring matter produced from coccinellin, treatment of which with alum forms an aluminum lake of carminic acid, the essential consituuent; used in histologic stains.

carmin'ophil [carmine + G. *phileō*, to love]. Staining readily with carmine dyes.

car'nitine. A trimethylammonium (betaine) derivative of γ-amino-β-hydroxybutyric acid; a thyroid inhibitor found in muscle, liver, and meat extracts; an acyl carrier with respect to the mitochondrial membrane, thus stimulating fatty acid oxidation and synthesis.

car'otenase. β-Carotene 15,15'-dioxygenase.

car'otene. A class of carotenoids, yellow-red pigments (lipochromes), widely distributed in plants and animals, that include precursors of the vitamins A; closely related in structure to the xanthophylls and lycopenes and to the open chain squalene, a C_{30} compound.

β-carotene-15, 15'-dioxygenase. Carotenase; an enzyme converting β-carotene to retinalehyde, adding O_2.

carotene'mia. Xanthemia; carotene in the blood, especially pertaining to increased quantities, which sometimes cause a pale yellow-red pigmentation of skin that may resemble icterus.

carot'enoid. 1. Resembling carotene, having a yellow color. **2.** One of the carotenoids.

carot'enoids. Generic term for a class of carotenes and their oxygenated derivates (xanthophylls); c. may be formally derived from the acyclic $C_{40}H_{56}$ structure by hydrogenation, dehydrogenation, oxidation, cyclization, or combinations of these. Included as c. are some compounds arising from certain rearrangements or degradations of the carbon skeleton, but not retinol and related C_{20} compounds.

caroteno'sis cu'tis. Aurantiasis cutis; yellow coloration of the skin caused by an increase in carotene content.

carot'icotympan'ic. Relating to the carotid canal and the tympanum.

carot'id [G. *karōtides*, the carotid arteries, fr. *karoō*, to put to sleep (because compression of the c. artery results in unconsciousness)]. Pertaining to any c. structure.

carot'igram. Tracing of the carotid pulse.

carot'odyn'ia [carotid + G. *odynē*, pain]. Pain caused by pressure on the carotid artery.

car'pal. Relating to the carpus.

carpec'tomy [G. *karpos*, wrist, + *ektomē*, excision]. Exsection of a portion or all of the carpus.

carphen'azine maleate. A phenothiazine tranquilizer of the piperazine group, functionally classified as an antipsychotic agent, but also possesses antiemetic, adrenolytic, anticholinergic, and dopamineblocking actions.

carpocar'pal. Mediocarpal (2).

car'pometacar'pal. Relating to both carpus and metacarpus.

carpopedal (kar'po-ped'al) [G. *karpos*, wrist, + L. *pes*(*ped*-), foot]. Relating to the wrist and the foot, or the hands and feet.

carpoptosis, carpoptosia (kar-pop-to'sis, -to'zĭ-ah) [G. *karpos*, wrist, + *ptōsis*, a falling]. Wrist-drop.

carpus, pl. **carpi** (kar'pus, kar'pi) [Mod. L. fr. Gr. *karpos*] [NA]. **1.** The wrist proper, the proximal segment of the hand consisting of the carpal bones and associated soft parts. **2.** The carpal bones, which articulate proximally with the radius and indirectly with the ulna, and distally with the five metacarpal bones.

car'rier. 1. An individual with an asymptomatic condition that is capable of being transmitted to other individuals. **2.** Any chemical capable of accepting an atom, radical, or subatomic particle from one compound, then passing it to another. **3.** A substance having chemical properties closely related to or indistinguishable from those of a radioactive tracer and which engages in the process being performed or studied.

cartilage (kar'tĭ-lij) [L. *cartilago*, gristle]. Cartilage; a connective tissue characterized by its nonvascularity and firm consistency; consists of cells (chondrocytes), interstitial substance (matrix) of fibers, and a ground substance (chondromucoid). There are three kinds of the c.: hyaline c., elastic c., and fibrocartilage.

alar c.'s, see *cartilago* alaris major and minor.

arthrodial c., articular c., *cartilago* articularis.

arytenoid c., *cartilago* arytenoidea.

auditory c., auditory *capsule.*

auricular c., *cartilago* auriculae.

connecting c., interosseous c.; the c. in a cartilaginous joint such as the symphysis pubis.

corniculate c., *cartilago* corniculata.

costal c., *cartilago* costalis.

cricoid c., *cartilago* cricoidea.

cuneiform c., *cartilago* cuneiformis.

diarthrodial c., *cartilago* articularis.

elastic c., yellow c.; c. in which the cells are surrounded by a territorial capsular matrix outside of which is an interterritorial matrix containing elastic fiber networks in addition to the collagen fibers and ground substance.

ensiform c., *processus* xiphoideus.

epiglottic c., *cartilago* epiglottica.

epiphysial c., *cartilago* epiphysialis.

floating c., a loose piece of c. within a joint cavity, detached from the articular c. or from a meniscus.

hyaline c., c. having a frosted glass appearance; in mature c. the cells are present in isogenous groups and the interstitial substance contains fine collagenous fibers obscured by the ground substance (chondromucoid).

innominate c., *cartilago* cricoidea.

interarticular c., *discus* articularis.

interosseous c., connecting c.

intervertebral c., *discus* intervertebralis.

investing c., *cartilago* articularis.

lateral c. of nose, *cartilago* nasi lateralis.

mandibular c., Meckel's c., a c. bar in the mandibular arch that forms a temporary supporting structure in the embryonic mandible; its proximal end gives rise to the cartilaginous primordium of the malleus.

c. of nasal septum, *cartilago* septi nasi.

permanent c., c. that remains as such and does not become converted into bone.

precursory c., temporary c.

secondary c., c., such as that in certain joints which undergoes a direct transformation into bone.

semilunar c., one of the articular menisci of the knee joint. See *meniscus* lateralis and medialis.

slipping rib c., subluxation of costal c., usually at junction with sternum, causing pain and audible click.

temporary c., precursory c.; c. that normally becomes replaced by bone, to form a part of the skeleton.

thyroid c., *cartilago* thyroidea.

tracheal c.'s, *cartilagines* tracheales.

vomerine c., vomeronasal c., *cartilago* vomeronasalis.

xiphoid c., *processus* xiphoideus.

Y c., Y-shaped c., the connecting c. for the ilium, ischium, and pubis; extends through the acetabulum.

yellow c., elastic c.

cartila'gines. Plural of cartilago.

cartilaginoid (kar-tĭ-laj'ĭ-noyd). Chondroid (1).

cartilaginous (kar-tĭ-laj'ĭ-nus). Chondral; relating to or consisting of cartilage.

cartila'go, pl. **cartila'gines** [L. gristle] [NA]. Cartilage.

cartila'gines ala'res mino'res [NA], lesser alar cartilages; the two to four cartilaginous plates of the wing of the nose posterior to the c. alaris major.

c. ala'ris ma'jor [NA], greater alar cartilage; one of a pair of cartilages that form the tip of the nose.

c. articula'ris [NA]; articular, arthrodial, diarthrodial, or investing cartilage; the cartilage covering the articular surfaces of the bones forming a synovial joint.

c. arytenoi'dea [NA], artenoid cartilage; one of a pair of small pyramidal laryngeal cartilages that articulate with the lamina of the cricoid cartilage and give attachment to the posterior part of the corresponding vocal ligament and to several muscles.

c. auric'ulae [NA], auricular cartilage; the cartilage of the auricle.

c. cornicula'ta [NA], corniculate cartilage; a conical nodule of elastic cartilage surmounting the apex of each arytenoid cartilage.

c. costa'lis [NA], costal cartilage; the cartilage forming the anterior continuation of a rib.

c. cricoi'dea [NA], cricoid or innominate cartilage; the lowermost of the laryngeal cartilages, expanded into a nearly quadrilateral plate (lamina) posteriorly.

c. cuneifor'mis [NA], cuneiform cartilage; a small rod of elastic cartilage in the aryepiglottic fold above the corniculate cartilage.

c. epiglot'tica [NA], epiglottic cartilage; a thin lamina of elastic cartilage forming the central portion of the epiglottis.

c. epiphysia'lis epiphysial cartilage or plate; the disk of cartilage between the shaft and the epiphysis of a long bone during its growth.

c. na'si latera'lis [NA], lateral cartilage of the nose; the cartilage located in the lateral wall of the nose above the alar cartilage.

c. sep'ti na'si [NA], cartilage of the nasal septum; a thin cartilaginous plate located between vomer, perpendicular plate of the ethmoid, and nasal bones to complete the nasal septum anteriorly.

c. thyroid'ea [NA], thyroid cartilage; the largest of the cartilages of the larynx, formed of two approximately quadrilateral plates (laminae) joined anteriorly at an angle; the prominence so formed constituting the laryngeal prominence (Adam's apple).

cartila'gines trachea'les [NA], tracheal cartilages or rings; the 16 to 20 incomplete rings of hyaline cartilage forming the skeleton of the trachea.

c. vomeronasa'lis [NA], vomeronasal or vomerine cartilage; a narrow strip of cartilage located between the lower edge of the cartilage of the nasal septum and the vomer.

caruncle (kăr'ung-kl). Caruncula; a small fleshy protuberance, or any similar structure.

hymenal c., one of the numerous tabs or projections surrounding the orifice of the vagina after rupture of the hymen.

lacrimal c., a small reddish body at the medial angle of the eye, containing modified sebaceous and sweat glands.

sublingual c., a papilla on each side of the frenulum linguae marking the opening of the submandibular (Wharton's) duct.

urethral c., a small, fleshy, sometimes painful growth from the mucous membrane usually occurring at the meatus of the female urethra.

caruncula, pl. **carun'culae** (kă-rung'ku-lah, -lē) [L. a small fleshy mass, fr. *caro,* flesh]. [NA]. Caruncle.

caryo- [G. *karyon,* nut, kernel]. See karyo-.

cascade (kas-kād') [Fr. fr. It. *cascare,* to fall]. A series of sequential interactions, as of a physiological process, which once initiated continues to the final one; each interaction is activated by the preceding one, sometimes with cumulative effect.

case [L. *casus,* an occurrence]. An instance of disease with its attendant circumstances; not synonymous with "patient".

caseation (ka-se-a'shun) [L. *caseus,* cheese]. A form of coagulation necrosis in which the necrotic tissue resembles cheese and contains a mixture of protein and fat that is absorbed very slowly; occurs particularly in tuberculosis.

casein (ka'se-in, ka'sēn). The principal protein of cow's milk and the chief constituent of cheese; used as a constituent of some glues.

caseous (ka'se-us). Pertaining to or manifesting the gross and microscopic features of tissue affected by caseation.

cast. 1. An object formed by the solidification of a liquid poured into an impression or mold. **2.** The rigid encasement of a part, as with plaster or a plastic, for purposes of immobilization. **3.** An elongated or cylindroid mold formed in a tubular structure that may be observed in histologic sections or in material such as urine or sputum; results from inspissation of fluid material secreted or excreted in the tubular structures, and named after the constituents (blood, epithelial, hyaline, etc.).

cast brace. A specially designed plaster cast incorporating hinges and other brace components; used in the treatment of fractures to promote early activity and early joint motion.

cas'tor oil. A fixed oil expressed from the seeds of *Ricinus communis* (family Euphorbiaceae); a purgative.

castrate (kas'trāt) [L. *castro,* pp. *-atus,* to deprive of generative power]. To remove the testicles or ovaries.

castra'tion [see castrate]. **1.** Sterilzation (2); removal of the testicles or ovaries. **2.** In psychiatry, usually the fantasied loss of the penis by the female or fear of its actual loss by the male.

CAT Computerized axial *tomography.*

cata- [G. *kata,* down]. Combining form meaning down. For words so beginning and not found here, see also kata-.

cat'abiot'ic [cata- + G. *biōtikos,* relating to life]. Used up in the carrying on of the vital processes other than growth, or in the performance of function, referring to the energy derived from food.

catabol'ic. Relating to catabolism.

catab'olism [G. *katabolē,* a casting down]. The breaking down in the body of complex chemical compounds into simpler ones, often accompanied by the liberation of energy. *Cf.* anabolism.

catab'olite. Any product of catabolism.

catacrot'ic. Denoting catacrotism.

catacrotism (kă-tak'ro-tizm) [cata- + G. *krotos,* beat]. A condition of the pulse in which there are one or more secondary expansions of the artery following the main beat, producing secondary upward waves on the downstroke of the pulse tracing.

cat'adicrot'ic. Denoting catadicrotism.

catadicrotism (kat'ă-di'kro-tizm) [cata + G. *di-,* two, + *krotos,* beat]. A condition of the pulse marked by two minor expansions of the artery following the main beat, producing two secondary upward waves on the downstroke of the pulse tracing.

catagen (kat'ă-jen). An intermediate phase of the hair cycle during which proliferation ceases and regression of the hair follicle occurs.

catagenesis (kat-ă-jen'ĕ-sis) [cata- + G. *genesis,* production]. Involution.

cat'alase. A hemoprotein catalyzing the decomposition of hydrogen peroxide to water and oxygen.

cat'alepsy [G. *katalēpsis*, a seizing]. A morbid state in which there is a waxy rigidity of the limbs that may be placed in various positions which will be maintained for a time; there is irresponsiveness to stimuli, the pulse and respiration are slow, and the skin is pale.

catalept'ic. Relating to or characteristic of catalepsy.

catalep'toid. Simulating or resembling catalepsy.

catalysis (kă-tal'ĭ-sis) [G. *katalysis*, dissolution]. The effect that a catalyst exerts upon a chemical reaction.

cat'alyst. That which accelerates a chemical reaction but is not consumed or changed permanently thereby.

catalyt'ic. Relating to or effecting catalysis.

cat'alyze. To act as a catalyst.

catamnesis (kat-am-ne'sis) [cata- + G. *mnēmē*, memory]. The medical history of a patient after an illness; the follow-up history.

catamnes'tic. Related to catamnesis.

catapha'sia [cata- + G. *phasis*, a saying]. A disorder of speech in which there is an involuntary repetition several times of the same word. See also echolalia.

cataph'ora [G. a falling down]. Semicoma, or somnolence interrupted by intervals of partial consciousness.

cataphylaxis (kat-ă-fi-lak'sis) [cata- + G. *phylaxis*, protection]. A deterioration in the natural defense mechanisms by which the body resists infectious disease.

catapla'sia, catapla'sis [cata- + G. *plasis*, a molding]. A degenerative change in cells or tissues that is the reverse of the constructive or developmental change as in a return to an earlier or embryonic stage.

cataplec'tic. 1. Developing suddenly. **2.** Pertaining to cataplexy.

cataplexy (kat'ă-plek-sĭ) [cata- + G. *plēxis*, a blow, stroke]. A transient attack of extreme generalized muscular weakness, often precipitated by an emotional state such as laughing heartily.

cataract (kat'ă-rakt) [L. *cataracta*, fr. G. *katarrhak-iēs*, a downrushing, a waterfall]. A loss of transparency of the lens of the eye, or of its capsule.

    annular c., a. congenital c. in which a central white membrane replaces the nucleus.

    atopic c., a c. associated with atopic dermatitis.

    axillary c., a type of hereditary c. with opacities deep and central.

    black c., a c. in which the lens is hardened and dark brown.

    blue c., a coronary c. of bluish color.

    capsular c., a c. in which the opacity affects the capsule only.

    capsulolenticular c., a c. in which both the lens and its capsule are involved.

    coronary c., peripheral cortical developmental c. occurring just after puberty; transmitted as a hereditary dominant characteristic.

    cortical c., a c. in which the opacity affects the cortex of the lens.

    cupuliform c., a common form of senile c. often confined to a region just within the posterior capsule.

    diffuse c., congenital central c. with involvement of the embryonic nucleus and surrounding lens.

    fibroid c., fibrinous c., a sclerotic hardening of the capsule of the lens, following exudative iridocyclitis.

    galactose c., a neonatal c. associated with galactosemia, *q. v.*

    glaucomatous c., a nuclear opacity usually seen in absolute glaucoma.

    gray c., a c. of gray color, usually seen in senile, mature, or cortical c.

    hypermature c., a c. in which the lens becomes either dehydrated and flattened or liquid and soft, with the nucleus at the bottom of the capsule.

    immature c., a stage of partial lens opacification.

    juvenile c., a soft c. occurring in a child or young adult.

    lamellar c., zonular c.; a c. in which the opacity is limited to certain of the layers of the lens external to the nucleus.

    lenticular c., a c. in which the opacity is confined to the substance of the lens.

    mature c., a c. in which the entire lens substance is opaque.

    membranous c., a secondary c. composed of the remains of the thickened capsule with more or less degenerated lens substance.

    Morgagni's c., a hypermature c. in which the cortex becomes soft and of a milky opacity while the hard dark nucleus sinks.

    nuclear c., a c. involving the nucleus only.

    polar c., a capsular c. limited to a certain area over the anterior or posterior pole of the lens.

    primary c., a c. occurring independently of any other disease of the eye.

    progressive c., a c. in which the opacification process progresses to involve the entire lens.

    pyramidal c., a cone-shaped anterior polar c.

    secondary c., (1) a c. that accompanies or follows some other eye disease such as glaucoma; (2) a c. occurring in the remains of the lens or capsule after a cataract extraction.

    senile c., c. occurring spontaneously in old age.

    siliculose c., siliquose c., calcareous degeneration of the capsule of the lens.

    subcapsular c., a c. in which the opacities are concentrated beneath the capsule.

    vascular c., a congenital c. in which the degenerated lens is replaced with mesodermal tissue.

    zonular c., lamellar c.

cat'aractogen'ic. Cataract-producing.

catarac'tous. Relating to a cataract.

catarrh (kă-tahr') [G. *katarrheō*, to flow down]. Old term for inflammation of a mucous membrane; popularly, chronic rhinitis.

catarrhal (kă-tah'ral). Relating to catarrh.

catastalsis (kat-ă-stal'sis) [G. *kata-stellō*, to put in order, check]. A contraction wave resembling ordinary peristalsis but not preceded by a zone of inhibition.

catastal'tic. Inhibitory; restricting; restraining.

catato'nia [G. *katatonos*, stretching down, depressed, fr. *kata,* down, + *tonos,* tone]. A syndrome characterized by periods of physical rigidity, negativism, excitement, and stupor.

cataton'ic. Relating to, or characterized by, catatonia.

catatricrotic (kat'ă-tri-krot'ik). Denoting catatricrotism.

catatricrotism (kat'ă-tri'kro-tizm) [cata- + G. *tri-,* three, + *krotos,* beat]. A condition of the pulse marked by three minor expansions of the artery following the main beat, producing three secondary upward waves on the downstroke of the pulse tracing.

catechol (kat'ĕ-kol). Pyrocatechol.

cat'echolam'ines. Pyrocatechols with an alkylamine side chain; *e.g.*ĕpinephrine, norepinephrine, dopa.

cat'gut [probably from *kit,* a small violin, through confusion with kit, a small cat]. An absorbable surgical suture material made from the collagenous fibers of the submucosa of certain animals.

catharsis (kă-thar'sis) [G. purification, fr. *katharos,* pure]. **1.** Purgation. **2.** Release or discharge of emotional tension or anxiety by psychoanalytically guided emotional reliving of past, especially repressed, events.

cathar'tic. 1. Relating to catharsis. **2.** An agent causing active movement of the bowels.

cathectic (kă-thek'tik). Pertaining to cathexis.

cath'eter [G. *kathetēr,* fr. *kathiēmi,* to send down]. A tubular instrument for the passage of fluid from or into a body cavity, especially one designed to be passed through the urethra into the bladder to drain it of retained urine.

  balloon-tip c., a tube with a balloon at its tip that can be inflated or deflated; the inflated balloon may facilitate passage of the tube through a blood vessel (propelled by the bloodstream) or to occlude the vessel.

  Bozeman-Fritsch c., a slightly curved double-current uterine c. with several openings at the tip.

  brush c., a ureteral c. with a finely bristled brush tip which is endoscopically passed into the ureter or renal pelvis and which brushes cells from the surface of suspected tumors.

  cardiac c., intracardiac c.

  Carlens c., endobronchial tube; a double lumen, flexible c. for bronchospirometry and for isolation of a portion of the lung to control passage of secretions into the remainder of the tracheobronchial tree while the patient is under general anesthesia.

  female c., a short, nearly straight c. for passage into the female bladder.

  Fogarty c., a c. with an inflatable balloon near its tip; used to remove arterial emboli and thrombi

from major veins and to remove stones from the biliary ducts.

  Foley c., a c. with a retaining balloon.

  Gouley's c., a solid curved steel instrument grooved on its inferior surface so that it can be passed over a guide through a urethral stricture.

  indwelling c., a c. left in place in the bladder.

  intracardiac c., cardiac c.; a c. that can be passed into the heart via a vein or artery, to withdraw samples of blood, measure pressures within the heart's chambers or great vessels, and inject contrast media.

  Nélaton c., a flexible c. of red rubber.

  pacing c., a cardiac c. with one or two electrodes at its tip which, when connected to a pulse generator and properly positioned in the right atrium or ventricle, will artificially pace the heart.

  Phillips c., a c. with a filiform guide for the urethra.

  self-retaining c., a c. so constructed that it remains in urethra and bladder until removed.

  Swan-Ganz c., a thin (5 Fr), very flexible, flow-directed c. using a balloon to carry it through the heart to a pulmonary artery; when it is positioned in a small arterial branch, pulmonary wedge pressure is measured in front of the temporarily inflated and wedged balloon.

  two-way c., a double-channel c. used for irrigation.

  vertebrated c., a c. made of several segments moving on each other like the links of a chain.

  winged c., a soft rubber c. with little flaps at each side of the beak to retain it in the bladder.

catheteriza'tion. Passage of a catheter.

cath'eterize. To pass a catheter.

cathexis (kă-thek'sis) [G. *kathexis,* a holding in, retention]. Attachment of libido to a specific idea or object.

cation (kat'i-on) [G. *katiōn,* going down]. An ion carrying a charge of positive electricity, therefore going to the negatively charged cathode.

cation exchange. The process by which a cation in a liquid phase exchanges with another cation present as the counter-ion of a negatively charged polymer, the latter being a cation exchanger.

caudad (kaw'dad). **1.** In a direction toward the tail. **2.** Situated nearer the tail in relation to a specific reference point; opposite of craniad.

caudal (kaw'dal) [Mod. L. *caudalis*]. Pertaining to the tail.

cauda, pl. **caudae** (kaw'dah, -de) [L. a tail] [NA]. Any tail, or tail-like structure, or tapering or elongated extremity of an organ or other part.

  c. equi'na [L. horse's tail] [NA], the bundle of spinal nerve roots running through the lower part of the subarachnoid space within the vertebral canal below the first lumbar vertebra; comprises the roots of all the spinal nerves below the first lumbar.

  c. pancre'atis [NA], tail of the pancreas, the left extremity of the pancreas within the lienorenal ligament.

cauda'tum. *Nucleus* caudatus.

caul (kawl) [Gaelic, *call*, a veil]. Veil (2); the amnion forming the bag of waters, sometimes delivered unruptured with the baby; a piece of amnion capping the baby's head when born.

caumesthesia (kaw-mes-the'zĭ-ah) [G. *kauma*, heat, + *aisthēsis*, sensation]. A sense of heat irrespective of the temperature of the air.

causalgia (kaw-zal'jĭah) [G. *kausis*, burning + *algos*, pain]. Persistent severe burning sensation of the skin, usually following direct or indirect (vascular) injury of sensory fibers of a peripheral nerve, accompanied by cutaneous changes (temperature and sweating).

caustic (kaws'tik) [G. *kaustikos*, fr. *kaiō*, to burn]. Pyrotic (2). Exerting an effect resembling a burn.

cauterant (kaw'ter-ant). Cauterizing.

cauteriza'tion. The act of cauterizing.

cauterize (kaw'ter-īz). To apply a cautery; to burn with an actual or potential cautery.

cautery (kaw'ter-ĭ) [G. *kautērion*, a branding iron]. An agent or device used for scarring, burning, or cutting the skin or tissues by means of heat, electric current, or caustic chemicals.

   actual c., a c., such as electrocautery or a hot iron, acting directly through heat and not by chemical means.

   bipolar c., a c. using high frequency electrical current passed through tissue from an active to a passive electrode.

   monopolar c., a c. using high frequency electrical current passed from a single electrode, where the cauterization occurs, the patient's body serving as a ground.

   potential c., virtual c., an agent, such as potassium hydroxide, that forms an eschar by chemical means.

cava (ka'vah). Plural of cavum. See also *Vena* cava.

cav'agram. Cavogram.

ca'val. Relating to a vena cava.

caveo'la, pl. **caveo'lae** [L.]. A small pocket, vesicle, or recess communicating with the outside of a cell and extending inward, indenting the cytoplasm and the cell membrane; may be pinched off to form free vesicles within the cytoplasm.

caverna, pl. **caver'nae** (kă-ver'nah) [L.] [NA]. An anatomical cavity.

caverniloquy (kav'er-nil'o-kwiĭ) [L. *caverna*, cavern, + *loqui*, to talk]. Low pitched pectoriloquy heard over a lung cavity.

caverni'tis. Cavernositis; inflammation of the corpus cavernosum penis.

cavernosi'tis. Cavernitis.

cavernos'tomy [L. *caverna*, cavern, + G. *stoma*, mouth]. Surgical opening of any cavity to establish drainage.

cav'ernous. Relating to a cavern or a cavity; containing many cavities.

cav'itary. 1. Relating to a cavity, or having a cavity or cavities. **2.** Denoting any animal parasite that has an enteric canal or body cavity and that lives within the host's body.

cav'itas, pl. **cavita'tes** [Mod. L.]. A cavity.

cavita'tion. Formation of a cavity, as in the lung in tuberculosis.

cavitis (ka-vi'tis). Celophlebitis.

cavity (kav'ĭ-tĭ) [L. *cavus*, hollow]. **1.** A hollow space within a body structure. **2.** Lay term for the loss of tooth structure due to dental caries.

   abdominal c., the space bounded by the abdominal walls, diaphragm, and pelvis which contains the major part of the organs of digestion, the spleen, the kidneys, and the suprarenal glands; arbitrarily separated from the pelvic cavity by a plane across the superior aperature of the pelvis.

   amniotic c., the fluid-filled c. surrounding the developing embryo.

   axillary c., axilla.

   buccal c., *vestibulum* oris.

   cleavage c., blastocele.

   cotyloid c., acetabulum.

   cranial c., intracranial c.

   glenoid c., glenoid fossa (1); the hollow in the head of the scapula that receives the head of the humerus to make the shoulder joint.

   intracranial c., cranial c.; the space within the skull.

   lesser peritoneal c., *bursa* omentalis.

   medullary c., the marrow c. in the shaft of a long bone.

   nasal c., the cavity on either side of the nasal septum, lined with ciliated respiratory mucosa, extending from the naris anteriorly to the choana posteriorly, and communicating with the paranasal sinuses through their orifices in the lateral wall.

   oral c., mouth (1); the area bounded by the lips and cheeks, teeth and gums, and isthmus of the fauces.

   orbital c., orbita.

   pelvic c., the space bounded at the sides by the bones of the pelvis, above by the superior aperture of the pelvis, and below by the pelvic diaphragm; contains the pelvic viscera.

   pericardial c., the potential space between the parietal and the visceral layers of the serous pericardium.

   peritoneal c., greater peritoneal sac; the interior of the peritoneal sac, normally only a potential space between the parietal and visceral layers of the peritoneum.

   pleural c., the potential space between the parietal and visceral layers of the pleura.

   pulp c., the central hollow of a tooth including the root canal.

   segmentation c., blastocele.

   tension c., an expanding lung abscess.

   thoracic c., the space within the thoracic walls, bounded below by the diaphragm and above by the neck.

   trigeminal c., Meckel's *space.*

tympanic c., tympanum; an air chamber in the temporal bone containing the ossicles; it is lined with mucous membrane and is continuous with the auditory tube anteriorly and the tympanic antrum and mastoid air cells posteriorly.

uterine c., the space within the uterus extending from the cervical canal to the openings of the uterine tubes.

cav′ogram. Cavagram; an angiogram of a vena cava.

cavog′raphy. Venacavography.

ca′vosur′face. Relating to a cavity and the surface of a tooth.

cavum, pl. **ca′va** (ka′um) [L. ntr. of adj. *cavus*, hollow] [NA]. A hollow space, hole, or cavity.

CBC Complete *blood count*.

CBG Corticosteroid-binding *globulin*.

cc Cubic centimeter.

CCNU Lomustine.

Cd Cadmium.

cd Candela.

CDC Centers for Disease Control.

cDNA Complementary DNA.

CDP Cytidine 5′-diphosphate.

Ce Cerium.

CEA Carcinoembryonic *antigen*.

cec-. See ceco-.

ceca (se′kah). Plural of cecum.

cecal (se′kal). **1.** Relating to the cecum. **2.** Ending blindly or in a cul-de-sac.

cecectomy (se-sek′to-mĭ) [ceco- + G. *ektomē*, excision]. Typhlectomy; excision of the cecum.

cecitis (se-si′tis). Typhlitis; inflammation of the cecum.

ceco-, cec- [L. *caecum*, cecum]. Combining forms denoting the cecum. See also typhlo-.

cecocolostomy (se′ko-ko-los′to-mĭ). Surgical anastomosis between cecum and colon.

cecoileostomy (se′ko-il-e-os′to-mĭ). Ileocecostomy.

cecopexy (se′ko-pek′sĭ) [ceco- + G. *pexis*, fixation]. Typhlopexy; an operation for anchoring a movable cecum.

cecoplication (se′ko-pli-ka′shun) [ceco- + L. *plico*, pp. *-atus*, to fold]. Operative reduction in size of a dilated cecum by making folds or tucks in its wall.

cecorrhaphy (se-kor′ă-fĭ) [ceco- + G. *rhaphe*, suture]. Typhlorrhaphy; suture of the cecum.

cecosigmoidostomy (se′ko-sig-moy-dos′to-mĭ) Surgical formation of a communication between the cecum and the sigmoid colon.

cecostomy (se-kos′to-mĭ) [ceco- + G. *stoma*, mouth]. Typhlostomy; surgical formation of a cecal fistula.

cecot′omy [ceco- + G. *tome*, incision]. Typhlotomy; incision into the cecum.

cecum, pl. **ceca** (se′kum, se′kah) [L. ntr. of *caecus*, blind]. [NA]. **1.** Blind gut; the cul-de-sac, about 6 cm in depth, lying below the terminal ileum forming the first part of the large intestine. **2.** Any similar structure ending in a cul-de-sac.

cefadroxil (sef-ă-drok′sil). A semisynthetic broad spectrum antibiotic substance derived from cephalosporin; used orally and has an antimicrobial spectrum similar to that of cephalothin.

cefoxitin sodium (se-fok′sĭ-tin). A semisynthetic antibiotic substance structurally and pharmacologically similar to the cephalosporins; used by injection and has an antimicrobial spectrum similar to that of cephalothin.

-cele [G. *kēlē*, tumor, hernia]. Suffix denoting a swelling or hernia.

ce′liac [G. *koilia*, belly]. Relating to the abdominal cavity.

celio- [G. *koilia*, belly]. Combining form denoting relationship to the abdomen. See also celo-.

celiocentesis (se′lĭ-o-sen-tē′sis) [celio- + G. *kentēsis*, puncture]. Peritoneocentesis.

ce′lioenterot′omy [celio- + G. *enteron*, intestine, + *tomē*, incision]. Opening into the intestine through an incision in the abdominal wall.

ce′liogastrot′omy [celio- + G. *gastēr*, stomach, + *tomē*, incision]. Abdominal section with incision of the stomach.

ce′liomy′osi′tis [celio- + G. *mys*, muscle, + *-itis*, inflammation]. Inflammation of the abdominal muscles.

celioparacentesis (se′lĭ-o-par-ă-sen-te′sis) [celio- + G. *parakentēsis*, a puncture for dropsy]. Peritoneocentesis.

celiop′athy [celio- + G. *pathos*, disease]. Any abdominal disease.

celiorrhaphy (se-lĭ-or′ă-fĭ)) [celio- + G. *rhaphē*, seam]. Laparorrhaphy; suture of a wound in the abdominal wall.

celios′copy [celio- + G. *skopeō*, to view]. Peritoneoscopy.

celiot′omy [celio- + G. *tomē*, incision]. Laparotomy (2); abdominal section; ventrotomy; transabdominal incision into the peritoneal cavity.

vaginal c., opening the peritoneal cavity through the vagina.

celi′tis [G. *koilia*, belly, + *-itis*, inflammation]. Any inflammation of the abdomen.

cell [L. *cella*, a storeroom, a chamber]. **1.** A minute structure, the living, active basis of all plant and animal organization, composed of a mass of protoplasm enclosed in a delicate membrane and containing a nucleus. **2.** A small closed or partly closed cavity.

   A c.'s, alpha c.'s.

   acid c., parietal c.

   acinar c., acinous c., any secreting c. lining an acinus, especially applied to the c.'s of the pancreas which furnish pancreatic juice, to distinguish them from the c.'s of the islets of Langerhans.

   adipose c., fat c.

   adventitial c., pericyte.

   air c.'s, (1) *alveoli* pulmonis; (2) air-containing spaces in the skull bones.

alpha c.'s, A c.'s; (1) acidophil c.'s that constitute about 35% of the c.'s of the anterior lobe of the hypophysis; there are two varieties, one elaborates somatotrophic hormone, the other, mammotrophic hormone; (2) c.'s of the islets of Langerhans believed to secrete glucagon.

alveolar c.'s, (1) thin epithelial c.'s lining alveoli of lung; (2) c.'s lining a secretory alveolus.

ameboid c., a c., such as a leukocyte, having ameba-like movements and power of locomotion.

anaplastic c., (1) a c. that has reverted to an embryonal state; (2) an undifferentiated c., characteristic of malignant neoplasms.

Anitschkow c., cardiac *histiocyte.*

antigen-sensitive c., antigen-responsive c., a small lymphocyte that, although not itself an immunologically activated c., responds to antigenic (immunogenic) stimulus by a process of division and differentiation that results in the production of immunologically activated cells.

APUD c.'s, See APUD.

argentaffin c.'s, enteroendocrine c.'s.

auditory receptor c.'s, columnar c.'s in the epithelium of the organ of Corti, having hairs. See Corti's c.'s.

B c.'s, (1) beta c.'s; (2) B *lymphocyte.*

band c., stab or staff c.; any c. of the granulocytic (leukocytic) series that has a nucleus which could be described as a curved or coiled band, no matter how marked the indentation, if it does not completely segment the nucleus into lobes connected by a filament.

basal c., a c. of the deepest layer of an epithelium.

basket c., (1) a neuron enmeshing the cell body of another neuron with its terminal axon ramifications; (2) myoepithelial c.'s with branching processes which occur basal to the secretory c.'s of certain salivary gland and lacrimal gland alveoli.

beaker c., goblet c.

beta c.'s, B c.'s (1); (1) basophil c.'s of anterior lobe of hypophysis that contain basophil granules and are believed to furnish gonadotrophic hormones; (2) the predominant c.'s of the islets of Langerhans; they furnish insulin.

Betz c.'s, large pyramidal c.'s in the motor area of the precentral gyrus of the cerebral crotex.

bipolar c., a neuron having two processes.

blast c., an immature precursor c.

branchial c.'s, cartilage c.'s forming the branchial apparatus.

centroacinar c., Langerhans' c. (2); a nonsecretory c. of a pancreatic ductule that occupies the lumen of an acinus.

chief c., (1) pinealocyte; (2) in the parathyroid gland, a dark, clear, or transitional c.; the clear c. has abundant glycogen, the others a varying content of fine granules; (3) zymogenic c.

chromaffin c., a c. that stains with chromic salts, especially in the adrenal medulla and paraganglia of sympathetic nervous system.

chromophobe c.'s, in the adenohypophysis, c.'s without specific granules so that the cytoplasm is essentially unstained after the usual histological procedures.

clear c., (1) a c. in which the cytoplasm appears empty with the light microscope, as in eccrine sweat glands and in the parathyroid glands when the glycogen is unstained; (2) any c., particularly a neoplastic one, containing abundant glycogen or other material which is not stained by hematoxylin or eosin, so that the c. cytoplasm is very pale in routinely stained sections.

columnar c., a c. taller than it is broad, usually epithelial.

cone c. one of the two types of visual receptor c.'s of the retina, essential for visual acuity and color vision; the second type is the rod c.

Corti's c.'s, cochlear hair c.'s.

daughter c., one of the c.'s resulting from the division of a mother c.

decidual c., an enlarged, ovoid connective tissue c. appearing in the endometrium of pregnancy.

Deiters' c.'s, (1) phalangeal c.'s; (2) astrocytes.

delta c., (1) a variety of c. in the anterior lobe of the hypophysis that has basophilic granules. (2) a c. of the islets of the pancreas, with fine granules that stain with aniline blue.

dendritic c.'s, in embryonic ectoderm, c.'s of neural crest origin with extensive processes; they early develop melanin.

Downey c., the atypical lymphocyte of infectious mononucleosis.

dust c., coniophage; an alveolar phagocyte that contains carbon or other foreign particles; occurs in the lumen or interalveolar septum of pulmonary alveoli.

enteroendocrine c.'s, enterochromaffin c.'s, argentaffin c.'s; c.'s with granules which may be either argentaffinic or argyrophilic; such c.'s, scattered in the digestive tract, are of several varieties and are believed to produce such hormones as gastrin, serotonin, glucagon, and perhaps other substances.

ependymal c., a c. lining the central canal of the spinal cord (pyramidal shape) or one of the brain ventricles (cuboidal shape).

epithelioid c., (1) a nonepithelial c. having certain characteristics of epithelium; (2) large mononuclear histiocytes having certain epithelial characteristics, particularly in tubercles where they are polygonal and have eosinophilic cytoplasm.

ethmoidal c.'s, numerous small airfilled c.'s in the ethmoid labyrinth.

fat c., adipose c.; adipocyte; a connective tissue c. distended with one or more fat globules, the cytoplasm usually being compressed into a thin envelope, with the nucleus at one point in the periphery.

foam c.'s, c.'s with abundant, pale-staining, finely vacuolated cytoplasm, usually histiocytes which have ingested or accumulated material that dissolves during tissue preparation, especially lipids.

follicular c., an epithelial c. lining a follicle, such as that of the thyroid or ovary.

ganglion c., gangliocyte; a neuron the c. body of which is located outside the limits of the brain and spinal cord, hence forming part of the peripheral nervous system; ganglion c.'s are either (1) the pseudounipolar c.'s of the sensory spinal and cranial nerves (sensory ganglia), or (2) the peripheral multipolar motor neurons innervating the viscera (visceral or autonomic ganglia).

Gaucher c.'s, finely and uniformly vacuolated large c.'s containing kerasin and derived from the reticuloendothelial system, characteristic of Gaucher's disease.

germ c., sex c.

germinal c., a c. from which other c.'s are proliferated.

ghost c., (1) a dead c. in which the outline remains visible, but without other cytoplasmic structures or stainable nucleus; (2) an erythrocyte after loss of its hemoglobin.

giant c., a c. of large size, often with many nuclei.

glia c.'s, neuroglia c.'s; see neuroglia.

glomerulosa c., a c. of the zona glomerulosa of the adrenal cortex that is the source of aldosterone.

goblet c., beaker c.; an epithelial c. that has been distended with mucin, and when this is discharged as mucus a crateriform or goblet-shaped shell remains.

Golgi's c.'s, type I: nerve c.'s whose axons leave the gray matter of which they form part; type II: c.'s with short axons which ramify in the gray matter.

granule c.'s, nerve cell bodies in the external and internal granular layers of the cerebral cortex and in the granular layer of the cerebellar cortex.

granulosa c., a c. of the membrana granulosa lining the vesicular ovarian follicle which becomes a luteal c. after ovulation.

gustatory c.'s, taste c.'s.

hair c.'s, sensory epithelial c.'s present in the organ of Corti, in the maculae and cristae of the membranous labyrinth of the ear, and in taste buds; characterized by having long stereocilia or kinocilia (or both) which, with the light microscope, appear as fine hairs.

"hairy" c.'s, medium sized leukocytes which have features of reticuloendothelial c.'s but which may be a variety of B-lymphocyte; found in leukemic reticuloendotheliosis (hairy cell leukemia).

HeLa c.'s, the first continuously cultured human malignant c.'s, derived from a cervical carcinoma of a patient, Henrietta Lacks; used in the cultivation of viruses.

helper c., a T-lymphocyte that helps cell-mediated cytotoxicity and induces B-lymphocytes to secrete immunoglobin.

HEMPAS c.'s, the abnormal erythrocytes of type II congenital dyserythropoietic anemia.

Hensen's c., one of the supporting c.'s in the organ of Corti, immediately to the outer side of the c.'s of Deiters.

heteromeric c., commissural c.

hilus c.'s, c.'s in the hilus of the ovary which produce androgens; they are thought to be the ovarian counterpart of the interstitial c.'s of the testis.

hobnail c.'s, c.'s characteristic of a mesonephroma; a round expansion of clear cytoplasm projects into the lumen of neoplastic tubules, but the basal part of the c. containing the nucleus is narrow.

Hortega c.'s, microglia.

Hürthle c., a large, granular eosinophilic c. derived from thyroid follicular epithelium by accumulation of mitochondria, e.g., in Hashimoto's disease.

I c., inclusion c., a cultured skin fibroblast containing membrane-bound inclusions.

interstitial c.'s, (1) Leydig's c.'s; c.'s between the seminiferous tubules of the testis, believed to furnish the male sex hormone; (2) c.'s derived from the theca interna of atretic follicles of the ovary; (3) pineal c.'s similar to glial c.'s with long processes.

islet c., one of the c.'s of the pancreatic islets.

juvenile c., metamyelocyte.

juxtaglomerular c.'s, c.'s located at or near the vascular pole of a renal glomerulus which produce renin and form a component of the juxtaglomerular complex.

killer c.'s, K c.'s, null c.'s.

Kupffer c.'s, stellate reticuloendothelial c.'s lining the hepatic sinusoids.

Langerhans' c.'s, (1) dendritic c.'s in the epidermis, which appear rod- or racket-shaped in section, with a clear cytoplasm and a central linear striated density; (2) centroacinar c.'s.

L.E. c., lupus erythematosus c.; a polymorphonuclear leukocyte containing an amorphous round body that is a phagocytosed nucleus from another cell plus serum antinuclear globulin (IgG) and complement.

Leydig's c.'s, interstitial c.'s (1).

lupus erythematosus c., L.E. c.

luteal c., lutein c., a c. of the corpus luteum of the ovary.

mast c., labrocyte; mastocyte; a connective tissue c. that contains coarse, basophilic, metachromatic granules; the c. is believed to contain heparin and histamine.

mastoid c.'s, mastoid *sinuses*.

mirror-image c., (1) a cell whose nuclei have identical features and are placed in the cytoplasm in similar fashion; (2) a binucleate form of Reed-Sternberg c. often found in Hodgkin's disease.

mother c., a c. which, by division, gives rise to two or more daughter c.'s.

mucoserous c.'s, glandular c.'s intermediate in histologic characteristics between serous and mucous c.'s.

mucous c., a c. secreting mucus; *e.g.,* a goblet c.

multipolar c., a nerve c. with a number of dendrites arising from the c. body.

myoid c.'s, peritubular contractile c.'s.

natural killer c.'s, NK c.'s; blood lymphocytes from humans which lyse target c.'s (tumor or virus-infected c.'s) without involvement of antibody or complement.

neurilemma c.'s, neurolemma c.'s, Schwann c.'s.

nevus c., the c. of a pigmented cutaneous nevus which differs from a melanocyte in that it lacks dendrites.

Niemann-Pick c., Pick c.

NK c.'s, natural killer c.'s.

null c.'s, killer or K c.'s; cytotoxic c.'s involved in c.-mediated immune responses; they appear to be the T lymphocytes of the "suppressor" subset with receptors for the Fc portion of IgG molecules, and lyse IgG-coated "target" c.'s without the mediation of complement.

oat c., a short, bluntly spindle-shaped c. that contains a relatively large, hyperchromatic nucleus, frequently observed in some forms of undifferentiated bronchogenic carcinoma.

olfactory receptor c.'s, the receptors for smell; very slender nerve c.'s, with large nuclei and surmounted by six to eight long, sensitive cilia in the olfactory epithelium at the roof of the nose.

oxyntic c., parietal c.

oxyphil c.'s, oxyphil (1); c.'s of the parathyroid gland which increase in number with age; the cytoplasm contains numerous mitochondria and stains with eosin. Similar c.'s, and the thyroid, and in the latter are also called Hürthle c.'s.

Paget's c.'s, pagetoid c.'s, relatively large, neoplastic epithelial c.'s with hyperchromatic nuclei and palely staining cytoplasm; in Paget's disease of the breast, such c.'s occur in neoplastic epithelium in the ducts and in the epidermis of the nipple, areola, and adjacent skin.

Paneth's granular c.'s, granular c.'s located in the fundus of intestinal glands of the small intestine and appendix.

parafollicular c.'s, c.'s rich in mitochondria which are present between follicles or interspersed among follicular c.'s; the source of thyrocalcitonin.

parietal c., acid or oxyntic c.; one of the c.'s of the gastric glands which lies upon the basement membrane covered by the chief c.'s and secretes hydrochloric acid which reaches the lumen of the gland through fine canals (canaliculi).

peptic c., zymogenic c.

peritubular contractile c.'s, myoid c.'s; flattened c.'s that surround seminiferous tubules which have certain characteristics of smooth muscle c.'s.

phalangeal c.'s, Deiters' c.'s (1); the supporting c.'s of the organ of Corti, attached to the basement membrane and receiving between their free extremities the hair c.'s.

photoreceptor c.'s, rod and cone c.'s of the retina.

Pick c., Niemann-Pick c.; a relatively large, rounded or polygonal, mononuclear c., with indistinctly or palely staining, foamlike cytoplasm that contains numerous droplets of sphingomyelin; characteristic of Niemann-Pick disease.

plasma c., plasmocyte; plasmacyte; an ovoid c. with an eccentric nucleus having chromatin arranged radially; the cytoplasm is strongly basophilic because of abundant RNA in its endoplasmic reticulum; plasma c.'s are derived from B-lymphocytes and are active in the formation of antibodies.

polychromatic c., polychromatophil c., a primitive erythrocyte in bone marrow, with basophilic material as well as hemoglobin (acidophilic) in the cytoplasm.

prickle c., one of the c.'s of the stratum spinosum of the epidermis; so called because of the intercellular bridges.

Purkinje's c.'s, Purkinje's corpuscles; large nerve c.'s of the cerebellar cortex with a piriform cell body and dendrites arranged in a plane transverse to the folium.

pyramidal c.'s, neurons of the cerebral cortex which, in sections perpendicular to the cortical surface, exhibit a triangular shape with a long apical dendrite directed toward the surface of the cortex; there are also lateral dendrites, and a basal axon which descends to deeper layers.

red blood c. (RBC), erythrocyte.

Reed-Sternberg c., a large transformed lymphocyte, generally regarded as pathognomonic of Hodgkin's disease, with a pale-staining acidophilic cytoplasm and one or two large nuclei showing marginal clumping of chromatin and unusually conspicuous, deeply acidophilic nucleoli.

reticular c., a c. with processes making contact with those of similar c.'s to form a network which along with that of reticular fibers form the stroma of bone marrow and lymphatic tissues.

Rieder c.'s, abnormal myeloblasts in which the nucleus may be widely and deeply indented or may be a bi- or multi-lobate structure; observed in acute leukemia.

rod c., rod (2). See also retina.

Schwann c.'s, neurolemma or neurilemma c.'s; c.'s of ectodermal origin that compose a continuous envelope around each nerve fiber of peripheral nerves; comparable to the oligodendroglia of the brain and spinal cord; like the latter, they may form membranous expansions that wind around axons and thus form the axon's myelin sheath.

segmented c., a polymorphonuclear leukocyte matured beyond the band c. so that two or more lobes of the nucleus occur.

sensitized c., (1) a c., or bacterium, that has combined with specific antibody to form a complex capable of reacting with complement components; (2) a small "committed, " c. derived, by division and differentiation, from a transformed lymphocyte.

serous c., a c. especially of the salivary gland that secretes a watery or thin albuminous fluid.

Sertoli c.'s, elongated c.'s in the seminiferous tubules to which spermatids are attached during spermiogenesis.

sex c., germ c., a spermatozoon or an ovum.

Sézary c., an atypical mononuclear c. seen in the peripheral blood in the Sézary syndrome; it has large, convoluted nucleus and scanty cytoplasm containing PAS -positive vacuoles.

sickle c., drepanocyte; meniscocyte; an abnormal crescentic erythrocyte characeristic of sickle c. anemia, resulting from an inherited abnormality of hemoglobin (hemoglobin S) that causes decreased solubility at low oxygen tension.

signet ring c.'s, c.'s containing a cytoplasmic droplet of mucus that compresses the nucleus to one side of the c.; found in certain adenocarcinomas.

somatic c.'s, the c.'s of an organism, other than the sex c.'s.

spindle c., a fusiform c., such as those in the deeper layers of the cerebral cortex.

squamous c., a flat scalelike epithelial c.

stab c., staff c., band c.

stellate c. a star-shaped c., such as an astrocyte or Kupffer c., that has many filaments extending radially.

stem c., a c. whose daughter c.'s may differentiate into other c. types.

strap c., an elongated tumor c. of uniform width which may show cross-striations; found in rhabdomyosarcoma.

T c., T *lymphocyte.*

target c., (1) an erythrocyte in target c. anemia, with a dark center surrounded by a light band which again is encircled by a darker ring; such c.'s also appear after splenectomy; (2) a c. selectively affected by a particular agent.

tart c., a monocyte with an engulfed nucleus in which the structure is still well preserved.

taste c.'s, gustatory c.'s; darkly staining c.'s in a taste bud that appear to have fine hairs extending into the gustatory pore and stand in synaptic contact with sensory nerve fibers of the facial, glossopharyngeal, or vagus nerves.

tendon c.'s, elongated fibroblastic c.'s arranged in rows between the collagenous tendon fibers.

Touton giant c., a xanthoma c. in which the multiple nuclei are grouped around a small island of nonfoamy cytoplasm.

transducer c., in neurology, any c. equipped to respond to a mechanical, thermal, photic, or chemical stimulus by generating an electrical impulse that is synaptically transmitted to a sensory neuron in contact with the c.

tufted c., a particular type of c. in the olefactory bulb comparable to the bulb's mitral c. with respect to afferent and efferent relationships, but smaller and more superficially located.

vasoformative c., angioblast (1).

Virchow's c.'s, (1) the lacunae in osseous tissue containing the bone c.'s; also the bone c.'s themselves; (2) corneal *corpuscles.*

virus-transformed c., a c. that has been genetically changed to a tumor c., the change being heriditarily transmitted to daughter c.'s.

visual receptor c.'s, the rod and cone c.'s of the retina.

wandering c., ameboid c. (1).

white blood c. (WBC), leukocyte.

zymogenic c., peptic c.; a c. that secretes an enzyme; specifically a chief c. of a gastric gland or an acinar c. of the pancreas.

cellula, pl. **cellulae** (sel'u-lah, -le) [L. a small chamber, dim. of *cella*, storeroom]. 1 [NA]. Cellule; in gross anatomy, a small but macroscopic compartment. 2. In histology, a cell.

cel'lular [L. *cellula*, dim. of *cella*, storeroom]. 1. Relating to, derived from, or composed of cells. 2. Having numerous compartments or interstices.

cellular'ity. The degree, quality, or condition of cells that are present.

cel'lulase. An enzyme catalyzing the hydrolysis of cellulose to cellobiose; found in a variety of microorganisms in soil and in the digestive tracts of herbivores.

cellule (sel'ūl). Cellula (1).

cel'lulici'dal [cellula + L. *caedo*, to kill]. Destructive to cells.

cellulif'ugal [cellula + L. *fugio*, to flee]. Moving from, or extending in a direction away from, a cell or cell body; denoting certain cells repelled by other cells, or processes extending from the body of a cell.

cellulip'etal [cellula + L. *peto*, to seek]. Moving toward, or extending in a direction toward, a cell or cell body.

cellulite (sel'u-lit). Colloquial term for deposits of fat and other material believed to be trapped in pockets beneath the skin.

celluli'tis. Inflammation of cellular or connective tissue.

dissecting c, *perifolliculitis* abscedens et suffodiens.

pelvic c., parametritis.

cel'lulose. A polysaccharide (polyglucose) made up of cellobiose residues which form the basis of vegetable fiber.

oxidized c., (1) cellulosic acid in the form of an absorbable gauze; used as a hemostatic in operations where ligation is not feasible because it has a pronounced affinity for hemoglobin and produces an artifical clot; (2) a sterile, absorbable substance prepared by the oxidation of cotton.

celo-. 1 [G. *koilōma*, hollow (celom)]. Combining form relating to the celom. 2 [G. *kēlē*, hernia]. Combining form meaning hernia. 3 [G. *koilia*, belly]. Combining form relating to the abdomen. See also celio-.

celom, celoma (se'lom, se-lo'mah) [G. *koilōma*, a hollow]. Coelom. **1.** The cavity between the splanchnic and somatic mesoderm in the embryo. **2.** The general body cavity in the adult.

celom'ic. Relating to the celom, or body cavity.

celophlebitis (se-lo-flē-bi'tis) [G. *koilos*, hollow, + phlebitis]. Cavitis; inflammation of a vena cava.

celoschisis (se-los'kī-sis) [G. *koilia*, belly, + *schisis*, a fissure]. Gastroschisis.

ce'loscope [G. *koilos*, hollow, + *skopeō*, to view]. An optical device for examining the interior of a body cavity.

celos'copy. Examination of any body cavity with an optical instrument.

celosomia (se-lo-so'mīah) [G. *kēlē*, hernia, + *sōma*, body]. Congenital protrusion of the abdominal or thoracic viscera, usually with defect of the sternum and ribs as well as of the abdominal walls.

celotomy (se-lot'o-mī) [G. *kēlē*, hernia, + *tomē*, incision]. Herniotomy.

celozo'ic [G. *koilos*, hollow, + *zoikos*, pertaining to animals]. Inhabiting any of the cavities of the body; applied to certain parasitic protozoa, chiefly gregarines.

cement (se-ment') [L. *cementum*]. **1.** Cementum. **2.** In dentistry, a nonmetallic material used for luting, filling, permanent or temporary restorative purposes, or as an adherent sealer in attaching various dental restorations.

cemen'ticle. A calcified spherical body, composed of cementum lying free within the periodontal membrane, attached to the cementum or imbedded within it.

cement'oblast [L. *cementum*, cement, + G. *blastos*, germ]. One of the cells concerned with the formation of the layer of cementum on the roots of teeth.

cemen'toblasto'ma. A benign odontogenic tumor of functional cementoblasts which elaborate cementum or cementum-like tissue upon the tooth root.

cementoclasia (se'men-to-kla'zī-ah) [L. *cementum*, cement, + G. *klasis*, fracture]. Destruction of cementum by cementoclasts.

cement'oclast [L. *cementum*, cement, + G. *klastos*, broken]. One of the multinucleated giant cells, identical with osteoclasts, that are associated with the destruction of cementum.

cement'ocyte [L. *cementum*, cement, + G. *kytos*, cell]. A cell with numerous processes, present in the secondary cementum of the tooth.

cementoma (se-men-to'mah) [L. *cementum*, cement, + G. *-ōma*, tumor]. An unusual dysplastic or reactive change initiated in the periapical region of affected teeth; may be comprised of a fibrocellular stroma, of fibrocellular stroma with scattered foci of cementum-like tissue, or predominately of cementum-like tissue.

cementum (se-men'tum) [L. *caementum*, rough quarry stone, fr. *caedo*, to cut]. [NA]. Cement (1); a layer of modified bone covering the dentin of the root and neck of a tooth which blends with the fibers of the periodontal membrane.

cenesthesia (se-nes-the'zī-ah) [G. *koinos*, common, + *aisthēsis*, sensation]. The general sense of bodily existence; the sensation caused by the functioning of the internal organs.

cenesthe'sic, cenesthet'ic. Relating to cenesthesia.

ceno-. **1** [G. *koinos*, common]. Combining form meaning shared in common. **2** [G. *kainos*, new]. Combining form meaning new or fresh. **3** [G. *kenos*, empty]. Rarely used combining form denoting emptiness.

ce'nosite [G. *koinos*, common, + *sitos*, food]. Coinosite; a facultative commensal organism; one that can sustain itself apart from its usual host.

censor (sen'sor) [L. a judge, critic, fr. *censeo*, to value, judge]. The psychic barrier which, according to psychoanalytic theory, prevents certain unconscious thoughts and wishes from coming to consciousness unless they are so cloaked or disguised as to be unrecognizable.

cen'ter [L. *centrum;* G. *kentron*]. **1.** The middle point of a body; loosely, the interior of a body. **2.** A group of nerve cells governing a specific function.

Broca's c., Broca's area; motor speech c.; a small posterior part of the inferior frontal gyrus of the left hemisphere, identified as an essential component of the motor mechanisms governing articulated speech.

ciliospinal c., the preganglionic motor neurons in the first thoracic segment of the spinal cord which give rise to the sympathetic innervation of the dilator muscle of the eye's pupil.

epiotic c., the c. of ossification of the petrous part of the temporal bone that appears posterior to the posterior semicircular canal.

germinal c. of Flemming, secondary *nodule.*

medullary c., the great mass of white matter composing the interior of the cerebral hemisphere.

motor speech c., Broca's c.

optic c., the point in the lens of the eye where light rays cross each other in proceeding from the cornea to the retina.

ossification c., the spot where bone begins to form in a specific bone or part of a bone: **primary o. c.** is the first site of formation in the shaft of a long bone; **secondary o. c.** is a c. of formation appearing later, usually in an epiphysis.

ossific c., the area of earliest destruction of cartilage prior to onset of ossification.

respiratory c., the region in the medulla oblongata concerned with integrating afferent information to determine the signals to the respiratory muscles.

sensory speech c., Wernicke's c.

speech c.'s, see Broca's c.; Wernicke's c.

Wernicke's c., Wernicke's area; sensory speech c.; a large region of the parietal and temporal lobes of the left cerebral hemisphere, thought to be essential for understanding and formulating coherent, propositional speech.

Centers for Disease Control (CDC). The federal facility for disease eradication, epidemiology, and education headquartered in Atlanta, Georgia, which encompasses the Center for Infectious Diseases, Center for Environmental Health, Center for Health Promotion and Education, Center for Prevention Services, Center for Professional Development and Training, and Center for Occupational Safety and Health. Formerly named Center for Disease Control (1970), Communicable Disease Center (1946).

centesis (sen-te'sis) [G. *kentēsis*, puncture, fr. *kenteō*, to prick, pierce]. Puncture; when used as a suffix, usually denotes paracentesis.

centi- (**c**) [L. *centum*, one hundred]. A prefix used in the metric system to signify one one-hundredth (10–2).

cen'tigrade (C) [L. *centum*, one hundred, + *gradus*, step, degree]. Consisting of 100 degrees. See centigrade *scale.*

cen'tigram. One hundredth of a gram; 0.1543 grain.

centiliter (sen'tĭ-le-ter). One hundredth of a liter; ten milliliters; 162.3 minims.

cen'timeter (cm). One hundredth of a meter; 0.3937 inch.

cubic c. (cc), one thousandth of a liter; one milliliter.

cen'timorgan (cM). See morgan.

centinor'mal. One hundredth normal (0.01 N); denoting the concentration of a solution.

centipoise (sen'tĭ-poyz). One hundredth of a poise.

cen'tistoke. A unit of kinematic viscosity equal to one hundredth of a stoke.

centra (sen'trah). Plural of centrum.

cen'trad. Toward the center.

centraphose (sen'tră-fōz) [G. *kentron*, center, + *a-* priv. + *phōs*, light]. Centrophose.

cen'trencephal'ic. Relating to the center of the encephalon.

centric (sen'trik). Pertaining to a center.

centriciput (sen-tris'ĭ-put) [L. *centrum*, center, + *caput*, head]. Central portion of the upper surface of the skull, between the occiput and the sinciput.

centrif'ugal [L. *centrum*, center, + *fugio*, to flee]. Denoting a direction outward (away) from an axis of rotation.

centrifuga'tion. Subjection to sedimentation, by means of the centrifuge, of solids suspended in a fluid.

centrifuge (sen'trĭ-fūj). 18 **1.** An apparatus by means of which particles in suspension in a fluid may be separated by centrifugal force. **2.** To subject to centrifugation.

cent'rilob'ular. At or near the center of a lobule, *e.g.*, of the liver.

centriole (sen'trĭ-ōl) [G. *kentron*, a point, center]. Usually paired tubular organelles lying in the cytocentrum and having a wall having nine triple microtubules; may be multiple and numerous in cells such as the giant cells of bone marrow.

centrip'etal [L. *centrum*, center, + *peto*, to seek]. Axipetal; denoting the direction of the force pulling an object toward an axis of rotation.

centro- [G. *kentron*, center]. Combining form relating to a center.

centrokinesia (sen'tro-kin-e'sĭ-ah) [centro- + G. *kinēsis*, movement]. Movement excited by a stimulus of central origin.

centrokinet'ic. 1. Relating to centrokinesia. **2.** Excitomotor.

centromere (sen'tro-mēr) [centro- + G. *meros*, part]. Kinetochore; the nonstaining primary constriction of a chromosome which is the point of attachment of the spindle fiber, is concerned with chromosome movement during cell division, divides the chromosome into two arms, and is constant for a specific chromosome.

centrophose (sen'tro-fōz) [centro- + G. *phōs*, light]. Centraphose; a subjective sensation of darkness originating in the eye or central visual system.

cen'trosome [centro- + G. *sōma*, body]. Cytocentrum.

centrosphere (sen'tro-sfēr) [centro- + G. *sphaira*, a ball, sphere]. Astrocele; the specialized, often gelated cytoplasm of the cytocentrum from which the astral fibers (microtubules) extend during mitosis.

centrostal'tic [centro- + G. *stallein*, set forth, fetch]. Relating to the center of motion.

centrum, pl. **centra** (sen'trum, sen'trah) [L. fr. G. *kentron*]. [NA]. A center of any kind, especially an anatomical center.

cephal-. See cephalo-.

cephalad (sef'ă-lad). Craniad (1); in a direction toward the head.

cephalalgia (sef'al-al'jĭ-ah) [cephal- + G. *algos*, pain]. Headache.

cephaledema (sef'al-ĕ-de'mah). Edema of the head.

cephalexin (sef-ă-lek'sin). A broad spectrum antibiotic derived from cephalosporin.

cephalhematocele (sef'al-he-mat'o-sēl) [cephal- + G. *haima*, blood, + *kēlē*, tumor]. Cephalohematocele; a cephalhematoma communicating with the cerebral sinuses.

cephalhematoma (sef'al-he-mă-to'mah) [cephal- + G. *haima*, blood, + *-ōma*, tumor]. Cephalohematoma; a blood cyst of the scalp in a newborn infant, due to an effusion of blood beneath the pericranium.

cephalhydrocele (sef-al-hi'dro-sēl) [cephal- + G. *hydōr*, water, + *kēlē*, tumor]. An extracranial serous cyst.

cephalic (sĕ-fal'ik). Cranial (1).

cephalin (sef'ă-lin). A group of phosphatidic esters resembling lecithin but containing ethanolamine or serine in the place of choline, now known as phosphatidylethanolamine and phosphatidylserine; widely distributed in the body, especially in the brain and spinal cord, and used as a local hemostatic and as a reagent in liver function test.

cephalitis (sef-ă-li'tis). Encephalitis.

cephalo-, cephal- [G. *kephalē*, head]. Combining forms denoting the head.

cephalocele (sef'ă-lo-sēl). Encephalocele.

cephalocentesis (sef'ă-lo-sen-te'sis) [cephalo- + G. *kenetēsis*, puncture]. Passage of a hollow needle or trocar and cannula into the brain to drain an abscess or the fluid of a hydrocephalus.

cephalodynia (sef'ă-lo-din'ĭ-ah) [cephalo- + G. *odynē*, pain]. Pain in the head.

cephalogly'cin. A semisynthetic broad spectrum antibiotic produced from cephalosporin.

cephalogyric (sef-ă-lo-ji'rik) [cephalo- + G. *gyros*, a circle]. Relating to circular movements of the head.

cephalohematocele (sef'ă-lo-he-mat'o-sēl). Cephalhematocele.

cephalohematoma (sef'ă-lo-he-mă-to'mah). Cephalhematoma.

cephalomegaly (sef'ă-lo-meg'ă-lĭ). [cephalo- + G. *megas*, great]. Enlargement of the head.

cephalomeningitis (sef'ă-lo-men-in-ji'tis) [cephalo- + G. *mēninx* [mening-], membrane]. Inflammation of the membranes of the brain.

cephalometer (sef-ă-lom'ĕ-ter) [cephalo- + G. *metron*, measure]. Cephalostat; an instrument used to position the head to produce oriented, reproducible lateral and posterior-anterior headfilms.

cephalometrics (sef-ă-lo-met'riks) [cephalo- + G. *metron*, measure]. **1.** The scientific measurement of the bones of the cranium and face, utilizing a fixed, reproducible position for lateral radiographic exposure of skull and facial bones. **2.** A scientific study of the measurements of the head with relation to specific reference points; used for evaluation of facial growth and development, including soft tissue profile.

cephalometry (sef-ă-lom'ĕ-trĭ) [cephalo- + G. *metron*, measure]. Any measurement of the living head.

cephalomo'tor. Relating to movements of the head.

cephalopathy (sef-ă-lop'ă-thĭ) [cephalo- + G. *pathos*, suffering]. Encephalopathy.

ceph'alopel'vic. Pertaining to the size of the fetal head in relation to the maternal pelvis.

cephaloridine (sef'ă-lor'ĭ-dēn). A broad spectrum antimicrobial produced from chemically modified cephalosporin.

cephalospor'in. One of several antibiotic substances obtained from *Cephalosporium acremonium, C. salmosynnematum*, and other fungi. Antibiotic activity is due to the 7-aminocephalosporanic acid portion of the molecule; addition of side chains have produced semisynthetic broad spectrum antibiotics with greater antibacterial activity.

cephalosporinase (sef'ă-lo-spor'ĭ-nās). Penicillinase.

cephalostat (sef'ă-lŏ-stat) [cephalo- + G. *statos*, stationary]. Cephalometer.

ceph'alothin. 7-(Thiophene-2-acetamido)cephalosporanic acid; chemically modified cephalosporin; a broad spectrum antibiotic.

cephalothoracic (sef'ă-lo-tho-ras'ik). Relating to the head and the chest.

cephapirin sodium (sef-ă-pi'rin). A semisynthetic broad spectrum antibiotic substance derived from cephalosporin; used by injection and has an antimicrobial spectrum similar to that of cephalothin.

cephradine (sef'ră-dēn). A semisynthetic broad spectrum antibiotic substance derived from cephalosporin; used orally and by injection, and has an antimicrobial spectrum similar to that of cephalothin.

-ceptor [L. *capio*, pp. *captus*, to take]. Suffix meaning taker or receiver.

ceramidase (ser-am'ĭ-dās). An enzyme that cleaves ceramides into sphingosine and fatty acids.

cer'amide. Generic term for a class of sphingolipid, *N*-acyl (fatty acid) derivatives of a long chain base or sphinoid (*e.g.*, sphinganine or sphingosine).

cerat-, cerato-. See kerat-; kerato-.

Ceratophyllus (sĕr'ă-tof'ĭ-lus) [cerat- (kerat-) + G. *phyllos*, leaved]. A genus of fleas (family Ceratophyllidae) found in temperate climates.

cercaria, pl. **cerca'riae** (ser-ka'rĭ-ah, -rĭ-ē) [G. *kerkos*, tail]. The free-swimming trematode larva that emerges from its host snail and may penetrate the skin of a final host, encyst on vegetation or in or on fish, or penetrate and encyst in various arthropod hosts.

cer'ci. Plural of cercus.

cerclage (sair-klazh') [Fr. an encircling, hooping, banding]. **1.** Binding together the ends of an obliquely fractured bone or the fragments of a broken patella, brought into close apposition, by an encircling wire loop or a ring. **2.** Operation for retinal detachment in which the choroid and retinal pigment epithelium are brought into contact with the detached sensory retina by a taut encircling silicone band around the sclera. **3.** Placement of a nonabsorbable suture around an incompetent cervical os.

cercocystis (ser-ko-sis'tis) [G. *kerkos*, tail, + *kystis*, bladder]. A specialized form of tapeworm cysticercoid larva that develops within the vertebrate host villus rather than in an invertebrate host.

ce'rea flexibil'itas [L.]. "Waxy flexibility," in which the limb remains where placed; often seen in catatonia.

cerebellar (sĕr'e-bel'ar). Relating to the cerebellum.

cerebelli'tis. Inflammation of the cerebellum.

cerebello- [L. *cerebellum*]. Combining form relating to the cerebellum.

cerebellum, pl. **cerebel'la** (sĕr-e-bel'um, -bel'ah) [L. dim. of *cerebrum*, brain]. [NA]. The large posterior brain mass lying above the pons and medulla and beneath the posterior portion of the cerebrum; consists of two lateral hemispheres united by a narrow middle portion, the vermis.

cerebr-. See cerebro-.

cerebral (sĕr'ĕ-bral, sĕ-re'bral). Relating to the cerebrum.

cerebration (sĕr-e-bra'shun). Activity of the mental processes, conscious or unconscious.

cerebri-. See cerebro-.

cerebriform (sĕ-re'brĭ-form) [cerebri- + L. *forma*, shape, appearance, nature]. Resembling the external fissures and convolutions of the brain.

cerebritis (sĕ-r-e-bri'tis). Nonlocalized inflammation of the brain without suppuration.

cerebro-, cerebr-, cerebri- [L. *cerebrum*, brain]. Combining forms relating to the cerebrum.

cerebro'ma. Encephaloma.

cer'ebromala'cia. Encephalomalacia.

cerebromeningitis (sĕr'bro-men-in-ji'tis). Meningoencephalitis.

cerebropathy (sĕ-r-e-brop'ă-thĭ). Encephalopathy.

cerebrosclerosis (sĕr'e-bro-skle-ro'sis) [cerebro- + g. *sklērōsis*, hardening]. Encephalosclerosis of the cerebral hemispheres.

cer'ebroside. Galactolipid; galactolipin; a class of glycosphingolipid; specifically, a monoglycosylceramide found in the myelin sheath of nerve tissue.

cer'ebrosido'sis. Gaucher's *disease*.

cer'ebro'sis. Encephalosis.

cerebrospinal (sĕr'e-bro-spi-nal, sĕ-re'bro-). Relating to the brain and the spinal cord.

cer'ebrospi'nant. Acting upon the cerebrospinal system.

cer'ebrot'omy [cerebro- + G. *tomē*, incision]. Incision of the brain substance.

cer'ebrovas'cular. Relating to the blood supply to the brain, particularly with reference to pathologic changes.

cerebrum, pl. **cerebrums, cerebra** (sĕr'e-brum, sĕ-re'brum) [L. *brain*]. [NA]. Originally, the largest portion of the brain, including practically all parts within the skull except the medulla, pons, and cerebellum; now, usually only the parts derived from the telencephalon and includes mainly the cerebral hemispheres (cerebral cortex and basal ganglia).

cerium (se'rĭum) [named after the planetoid *Ceres*]. A metallic element, symbol Ce, atomic no. 58, atomic weight 140.12.

certifi'able. 1. That which can or must be certified; said of infectious, industrial, and other diseases that are required by law to be reported to health authorities. **2.** Denoting a person showing disordered behavior of sufficient gravity to justify involuntary mental hospitalization.

certifica'tion. 1. The reporting to health authorities of notifiable disease. **2.** The attainment of board certification in a specialty. **3.** The court procedure by which a person is committed to a mental institution. **4.** Involuntary mental hospitalization.

ceruloplasmin (sĕ-roo'lo-plaz'min) [L. *caeruleus*, dark blue]. A blue, copper-containing α-globulin of blood plasma, believed to play a part in erythropoiesis and O_2 reduction.

cerumen (sĕ-roo'men) [L. *cera*, wax]. Earwax; the brownish yellow, waxy secretion (a modified sebum) of the ceruminous glands of the external auditory meatus.

ceru'minal. Relating to cerumen.

ceruminolytic (sĕ-roo'mĭ-no-lit'ik) [cerumen, *q.v.*, + G. *lysis*, a loosening]. One of several substances instilled into the external auditory canal to soften wax.

ceru'mino'sis. Excessive formation of cerumen.

ceru'minous. Relating to cerumen.

cervical (ser'vĭ-kal) [L. *cervix(cervic-)*, neck]. Relating to a neck, or cervix, in any sense.

cervicectomy (ser-vĭ-sek'to-mĭ) [cervix + G. *ektomē*, excision]. Trachelectomy; excision of the cervix uteri.

cervices (ser'vĭ-sēz). Plural of cervix.

cervicitis (ser-vĭ-si'tis). Trachelitis; inflammation of the mucous membrane, frequently involving also the deeper structures, of the cervix uteri.

cervico- [L. *cervix*, neck]. Combining form relating to a cervix, or neck, in any sense.

cervicobrachial (ser'vĭ-ko-bra'kĭ-al). Relating to the neck and the arm.

cer'vicodyn'ia [cervico- + G. *odynē*, pain]. Trachelodynia; neck pain.

cer'vicofa'cial. Relating to the neck and the face.

cervico-occipital (ser'vĭ-ko-ok-sip'ĭ-tal). Relating to the neck and the occiput.

cer'vicoplasty. Plastic surgery on the cervix uteri or on the neck.

cervicothoracic (ser'vĭ-ko-tho-ras'ik). Relating 1) to the neck and thorax, 2) to their transition, 3) to the disk between the 7th cervical vertebra and 1st thoracic vertebra, and 4) to the fusion of these vertebrae.

cervicotomy (ser-vĭ-kot'o-mĭ) [cervico- + G. *tomē*, incision]. Trachelotomy; incision into the cervix uteri.

cer'vicoves'ical. Relating to the cervix uteri and the bladder.

cervix, pl. **cervices** (ser'viks, ser'vĭ-sēz) [L. neck]. [NA]. **1.** Collum. **2.** Any necklike structure.

   c. u'teri [NA], neck of the uterus or womb; the lower part of the uterus extending from the isthmus of the uterus into the vagina.

   c. ves'icae urina'riae [NA], neck of the urinary bladder; the lowest part of the bladder formed by the junction of the fundus and the inferolateral surfaces.

cesium (se'zĭ-um) [L. *caesius*, bluish gray]. A metallic element, symbol Cs, atomic no. 55, atomic weight 132.91; a member of the alkali metal group.

Cestoda (ses-to'dah) [G. *kestos*, girdle]. A subclass of tapeworms (class Cestoidea), containing the typical members of this group, including the segmented tapeworms that parasitize man and domestic animals.

ces'tode, ces'toid. Common name for tapeworms of the class Cestoidea or its subclasses, Cestoda and Eucestoda.

Cestoidea (ses-toy'dĭ-ah) [G. *kestos*, girdle, + *eidos*, form]. The tapeworms; a class of platyhelminth flatworms characterized by lack of an alimentary canal and, in typical forms, by a strobilate or segmented body with a scolex or holdfast organ at one end; adult worms are vertebrate parasites, usually found in the small intestine.

ce'tyl. The univalent alcohol radical, $C_{16}H_{33}-$, of cetyl alcohol (hexadecanol).

Cf Californium.

CG Chorionic *gonadotropin.*

CGS, cgs Centimeter-gram-second.

chafe (chāf) [Fr. *chauffer,* to heat, fr. L. *calefacio,* to make warm]. To cause irritation of the skin by friction.

chago'ma. The skin lesion in acute Chagas disease.

chain (chān) [L. *catena*]. **1.** In chemistry, a series of atoms held together by one or more covalent bonds. **2.** In bacteriology, a linear arrangement of living cells that have divided in one plane and remain attached to each other.

    A c., a polypeptide component of insulin containing 21 amino acids; the amino-acid composition is a function of species.

    B c., a polypeptide component of insulin containing 30 amino acids; the amino-acid composition is a function of species.

    heavy c., a polypeptide c. of high molecular weight, as the γ, α, or μ c.'s in immunoglobulin.

    light c., a polypeptide c. with low molecular weight, as the κ or λ c.'s in immunoglobulin.

    side c., a c. of atoms linked to a benzene ring, or any closed c. compound.

chalasia, chalasis (kā-la'zī-ah, -la'sis) [G. *chalaō,* to loosen]. Inhibition and relaxation of any previously sustained contraction of muscle, usually of a synergic group of muscles.

chalazion, pl. **chala'zia** (kal-a'zī-on, -zī-ah) [G. dim. of *chalaza,* a sty]. Meibomian or tarsal cyst; a chronic inflammatory granuloma in the tarsus of the eyelid, due to inflammation of a meibomian gland.

chalcosis (kal-ko'sis) [G. *chalkos,* copper, brass]. **1.** Chronic copper posioning. **2.** A deposit of fine particles of copper in the lungs or other parts.

chalicosis (kal-e-ko'sis) [G. *chalix,* gravel]. A pneumonoconiosis caused by the inhalation of dust incident to the occupation of stone cutting.

chalone (ka'lōn). Originally, a hormone that inhibits rather than stimulates. Now, any one of a number of mitotic inhibitors elaborated by a tissue and active within that tissue rather than, like hormones, on another tissue; a reversible tissue-specific mitotic inhibitor.

chalybeate (kal-ib'e-āt) [G. *chalyps*(*chalyb-*), steel]. Impregnated with or containing iron salts.

chamber (chām'ber) [L. *camera*]. A compartment or enclosed space.

    anterior c. of the eye, *camera* anterior bulbi.

    aqueous c.'s, the anterior and posterior c.'s of the eye containing the aqueous humor.

    counting c., a special, standardized glass slide used for counting cells (especially erythrocytes and leukocytes) and other particulate material in a measured volume of fluid; such slides are frequently known as hemocytometers.

    hyperbaric c., a c. employing high-pressure oxygenation.

    ionization c., a c. for detecting ionization of the enclosed gas; used for determining intensity of ionizing radiation.

    posterior c. of the eye, *camera* posterior bulbi.

    pulp c., that portion of the pulp cavity which is contained in the crown or body of the tooth.

    vitreous c. of the eye, *camera* vitrea bulbi.

chancre (shang'ker) [Fr. indirectly from L. *cancer*]. Hard c., or ulcer; syphilitic ulcer (1); the primary lesion of syphilis, a hard, nonsensitive, dull red papule or area of infiltration that begins at the site of infection after an interval of 10 to 30 days; the center usually becomes eroded or breaks down into an ulcer that heals slowly after 4 to 6 weeks.

    hard c., chancre.

chan'criform. Resembling chancre.

chancroid (shang'kroyd) [chancre + G. *eidos,* resemblance]. Soft chancre or ulcer; venereal ulcer; an infectious venereal ulcer at the site of infection by *Haemophilus ducreyi,* beginning after an incubation period of 3 to 5 days.

chancroid'al. Relating to or of the nature of chancroid.

chancrous (shang'krus). Characterized by having a chancre.

chapped (chapt) [M.E. *chap,* to chop, split]. Having or pertaining to skin that is dry, scaly, and fissured, owing to the action or to the excess rate of evaporation of moisture from the skin surface.

character (kăr'ak-ter). Characteristic (1); an attribute, trait, or definite and distinct structural feature of an animal or plant.

    acquired c., a c. developed as a result of environmental influences.

    dominant c., an inherited c. determined by a dominant gene.

    inherited c., mendelian c., a single attribute of an animal or plant that is transmitted from generation to generation in accordance with genetic principle.

    primary sex c.'s the sex glands, testes or ovaries, and the accessory sex organs.

    recessive c., an inherited c. determined by a recessive gene.

    secondary sex c.'s, those c.'s peculiar to the male or female, *e.g.,* the beard of men and the breasts of women, which develop at puberty.

    sex-linked c., an inherited c. determined by sex-linked gene.

characteristic (kăr'ak-ter-is'tik). **1.** Character. **2.** Pertaining to or of a character.

char'coal. Carbon obtained by heating or burning organic material with restricted access of air. Activated c. is the residue from destructive distillation of various organic materials, treated to increase its adsorptive power; used in diarrhea, as an antidote, and in purification processes in industry and research.

charlatan (shar'lă-tan). A quack; a fraud claiming knowledge and skills not possessed.

char'ley horse. Colloquialism for localized pain or muscle stiffness following a contusion of a muscle.

chart. 1. A recording, in tabular form, of clinical data relating to a case. 2. In optics, symbols of graduated size for measuring visual acuity, or test types for examining far or near vision; *e.g.*, Snellen's test type.

Ch.B. Chirurgiae Baccalaureus, Bachelor of Surgery.

Ch.D. Chirurgiae Doctor, Doctor of Surgery.

cheek [A.S. *ceáce*]. Bucca; mala (1); gena; the side of the face forming the lateral wall of the mouth.

cheil-. See cheilo-.

cheilalgia, chilalgia (ki-lal'jĭ-ah) [cheil- + G. *algos*, pain]. Pain in the lip.

cheilectomy, chilectomy (ki-lek'to-mĭ) [cheil- + G. *ektomē*, excision]. 1. Excision of a portion of the lip. 2. Chiseling away bony irregularities on the lips of a joint cavity that interfere with movements of the joint.

cheilectropion, chilectropion (ki-lek-tro'pĭ-on) [cheil- + G. *ektropos*, a turning out]. Eversion of the lips or a lip.

cheilitis, chilitis (ki-li'tis) [cheil- + G. *-itis*, inflammation]. Inflammation of the lips or of a lip, with redness and the production of fissures radiating from the angles of the mouth. See also cheilosis.

cheilo-, cheil- [G. cheilos, lip]. Combining forms denoting relationship to the lips. See also chilo-; chil-.

cheiloplasty, chiloplasty (ki'lo-plas-tĭ) [cheilo- + G. *plassō*, to form]. Plastic surgery of the lips.

cheilorrhaphy, chilorrhaphy (ki-lor'ă-fĭ) [cheilo- + G. *raphē*, suture]. Suturing of the lip.

cheiloschisis, chiloschisis (ki-los'kĭ-sis) [cheilo- + G. *schisis*, cleft]. Cleft *lip*.

cheilosis, chilosis (ki-lo'sis) [cheil- + G. *-osis*, condition]. Angular stomatitis seen in riboflavin deficiency and other B-complex deficiencies; begins with a small fissure, without much inflammation, and accumulation of dried serum, and may eventuate in deep fissures.

cheilostomatoplasty, chilostomatoplasty (ki-lo-sto'mă-to-plas-tĭ) [cheilo- + G. *stoma*, mouth, + *plassō*, to form]. Plastic surgery of the lips and mouth.

cheilotomy, chilotomy (ki-lot'o-mĭ) [cheilo- + G. *tomē*, incision]. Incision into the lip.

cheiro- [G. *cheir*, hand]. Combining forms meaning hand. See also chiro-.

cheirognostic, chirognostic (ki-rog-nos'tik) [cheiro- + G. *gnostikos*, perceptive]. Able to recognize the hand, or to distinguish between right and left.

cheirokinesthesia, chirokinesthesia (ki'ro-kin-es-the'zĭ-ah) [cheiro- + G. *kinēsis*, movement, + *aisthēsis*, sensation]. Subjective sensation of movement of the hands.

cheirokinesthetic (ki'ro-kin-es-thet'ik). Relating to cheirokinesthesia.

cheiromegaly, chiromegaly (ki-ro-meg'ă-lĭ) [cheiro- + G. *megas*, large]. Macrocheiria.

cheiroplasty, chiroplasty (ki'ro-plas-tĭ) [cheiro- + G. *plassō*, to form]. A plastic operation upon the hand.

cheiropodalgia, chiropodalgia (ki'ro-po-dal'jĭ-ah) [cheiro- + G. *pous*, foot, + *algos*, pain]. Pain in the hands and in the feet.

cheiropompholyx, chiropompholyx (ki-ro-pom'fo-liks) [cheiro- + G. *pompholyx*, a bubble, fr. *pomphos*, a blister]. Dyshidrosis.

cheirospasm, chirospasm (ki'ro-spazm) [cheiro- + G. *spasmos*, spasm]. Spasm of the muscles of the hand, as in writers' cramp.

chelate (ke'lāt). 1. To effect chelation. 2. Pertaining to chelation. 3. A complex formed through chelation.

chelation (ke-la'shun) [G. *chēlē*, claw]. Complex formation involving a metal ion and two or more polar groupings of a single molecule; *e.g.*, in heme, the Fe^{2+} ion is chelated by the porphyrin ring. Chelation can be used to remove an ion from participation in biological reactions, as in the chelation of Ca^{2+} of blood by EDTA, which thus acts as an anticoagulant.

chem-. See chemo-.

chem'exfolia'tion. A chemosurgical technique designed to remove acne scars or treat chronic skin defects caused by exposure to sunlight.

chem'ical. Relating to chemistry, to the mutual relations and interaction of the elements, and to the phenomena resulting therefrom.

chem'ist. 1. One educated in and practicing the science of chemistry. 2. British term for pharamacist.

chemistry (kem'is-trĭ) [G. *chēmeia*, alchemy]. The science concerned with the atomic composition of substances, with the elements and their reactions, and with the formation, decomposition and properties of molecules.

   inorganic c., c. concerned with compounds not involving covalent bonds.

   organic c., c. concerned with covalently linked atoms, centering around carbon compounds of this type; originally, and still including, the c. of natural (organic) products.

chemo-, chem- [G. *chēmeia*, alchemy]. Combining forms relating to chemistry.

chemoautotroph (kem'-aw'to-trōf) [chemo- + G. *autos*, self, + *trophikos*, nourishing]. Chemolithotroph; an organism that depends on chemicals for its energy and principally on carbon dioxide for its carbon.

chemoautotrophic (kem'o-aw'to-trof'ik). Chemolithotrophic; pertaining to a chemoautotroph.

chemobiot'ic. A combination of an antibiotic with a chemotherapeutic agent; *e.g.*, penicillin plus sulfanilamide.

chem'ocautery. Any substance that destroys tissue upon application.

chem'odecto'ma. Aortic body, carotid body, or glomus jugulare tumor; nonchromaffin paraganglioma; a relatively rare, usually benign, neoplasm originating in the chemoreceptor tissue of the carotid body, glomus jugulare, and aortic bodies, consisting of rounded or ovoid hyperchromatic cells that tend to be grouped in an alveolus-like pattern within a scant to moderate amount of fibrous stroma and a few large, thin-walled vascular channels.

chem'odectomato'sis. Multiple tumors of perivascular tissue of carotid body or presumed chemoreceptor type, which have been reported in the lungs as minute neoplasms.

chem'okine'sis [chemo- + G. *kinēsis,* movement]. Stimulation of an organism by a chemical.

chem'okinet'ic. Referring to chemokinesis.

chemolithotroph (kem'o-lith'o-trof). Chemoautotroph.

chemolithotrophic (kem'o-lith-o-trof'ik). Chemoautotrophic.

chemoluminescence (kem'o-lku-min-es'ens). Light produced by chemical action.

chemonucleolysis (kem'o-nu-kle-ol'ĭ-sis). The enzymatic dissolution of the nucleus pulposus by injection of chymopapain; used in the treatment of intervertebral disk lesions.

chemoorganotroph (kem'o-or'gă-no-trof) [chemo- + G. *organon,* organ, + *trophē,* nourishment]. An organism that depends on organic chemicals for its energy and carbon.

chemoorganotrophic (kem'o-or-gan-o-trof'ik). Pertaining to a chemoorganotroph.

chemoprophylaxis (kem'o-pro-fī-lak'sis) [chemo- + prophylaxis]. Prevention of disease by use of chemicals or drugs.

chem'orecep'tor. Any cell that is activated by a change in its chemical milieu and thereby originates a flow of nervous impulses.

chem'ose'rotherapy. Combination of treatment with serum and drugs.

chem'osen'sitive. Capable of perceiving changes in the chemical composition of the environment, *e.g.,* changes in the oxygen and carbon dioxide content of the blood.

chemosis (ke-mo'sis) [G. *chēmē,* a yawning]. Edema of the bulbar conjunctiva, forming a swelling around the cornea.

chem'osurgery. Excision of diseased tissue after it has been fixed *in situ* by chemical means.

chemosyn'thesis. The formation of definite compounds by chemical action.

chemotac'tic. Relating to chemotaxis.

chemotaxis (kem-o-tak'sis) [chemo- + G. *taxis,* orderly arrangement]. Chemotropism; attraction of living protoplasm to chemical stimuli, whereby the cells are attracted (**positive c.**) by acids, alkalies, or other bodies exhibiting chemical properties.

chem'other'apy. Treatment of disease by means of chemical substances or drugs.

chem'otherapeu'tic. Relating to chemotherapy.

chemotic (ke-mot'ic). Relating to chemosis.

chemotropism (kem-o-trōp'izm) [chemo- + G. *tropos,* direction, turn]. Chemotaxis.

cher'ubism [Hebr. *kerubh,* cherub]. A familial multilocular fibro-osseous disease, with enlargment of the jaw bones in young children (producing the characteristc facies) that tends to regress in adult life.

chest [A.S. *cest,* a box]. The thorax, especially the anterior aspect. See also breast.

    barrel c., a c. permanently the shape of a barrel during full inspiration, *i.e.,* with increased anteroposterior diameter and usually some degree of kyphosis, seen in cases of emphysema.

    flail c., flapping chest wall; loss of stability of thoracic cage following fracture of sternum and/or ribs.

    flat c., a c. in which the anteroposterior diameter is less than the average.

    funnel c., *pectus* excavatum.

chiasm (ki'azm) [G. *chiasma,* two crossing lines, fr. the letter *chi,* X]. **1.** A decussation or crossing of two tracts, such as tendons or nerves. **2.** The crossing of intertwined chromosomes during prophase.

    optic c., optic decussation; a flattened quadrangular body in front of the tuber cinereum and infundibulum, the point of crossing or decussation of the fibers of the optic nerves.

chick'enpox. Varicella.

chig'ger. The six-legged larva of *Trombicula* species and other members of the family Trombiculidae; a bloodsucking stage of mites that includes the vectors of scrub typhus.

chigoe (chig'o). Common name for *Tunga penetrans.*

chil-. See chilo-.

chilalgia. Cheilalgia.

chilblain [chill + A.S. *blegen,* a skin lesion]. Erythema pernio; erythema, itching, and burning, especially of the dorsa of the fingers and toes, and of the heels, nose, and ears on exposure to extreme cold (usually associated with high humidity).

child'bearing. Pregnancy and parturition.

child'birth. Parturition; the process of labor and delivery in the birth of a child. See also birth, accouchement.

child'hood. The period of life between infancy and puberty.

chilectomy (ki-lek'to-mi). Cheilectomy.

chilectropion (ki-lek-tro'pī-on). Cheilectropion.

chilitis (ki-li'tis). Cheilitis.

chill [A.S. *cele,* cold]. A feeling of cold, with shivering and pallor, accompanied by an elevation of temperature in the interior of the body.

chilo-, chil- [G. *cheilos,* lip]. Combining form denoting relationship to the lips. See also cheilo-; cheil-.

chiloplasty (ki-lo-plas'ti). Cheiloplasty.

chilorrhaphy (ki-lor'ă-fĭ). Cheilorrhaphy.

chiloschisis (ki-los'kĭ-sis). Cheiloschisis.

chilosis (ki-lo'sis). Cheilosis.

chilostomatoplasty (ki-lo-sto'mah-plas-tĭ). Cheilostomatoplasty.

chilotomy (ki-lot'ŏ-mĭ). Cheilotomy.

chimera (ki-mēr'ah, kĭ-) [L. *chimoera*, fr. G. *chimaira*, a fabulous monster]. **1.** One who has received a transplant of genetically and immunologically different tissue, such as bone marrow. **2.** Twins with two immunologically different types of erythrocytes. **3.** Sometimes used as a synonym for mosaic.

chimeric (ki-mer'ik). **1.** Relating to a chimera. **2.** Composed of parts of different origin, or seemingly incompatible.

chin [A.S. *cin*]. Mentum; the prominence formed by the anterior projection of the mandible, or lower jaw.

chirality (ki-ral'ĭ-tĭ) [G. *cheir*, hand]. The property of nonidentity of an object with its mirror image; used in chemistry with respect to stereochemical isomers.

chiro-, chir- [G. *cheir*, hand]. Combining forms denoting the hand. See also cheiro-.

chirognostic (ki-rog-nos'tik). Cheirognostic.

chirokinesthesia (ki'ro-kin-es-the'zĭ-ah). Cheirokinesthesia.

chiromegaly (ki-ro-meg'ă-l ĭ). Cheiromegaly.

chiroplasty (ki'ro-plas-tĭ) . Cheiroplasty.

chiropodalgia (ki'ro-po-dal'jĭ-ah). Cheiropodalgia.

chiropodist (ki-rop'o-dist) [chiro- + G. *pous*, foot]. Podiatrist.

chiropody (ki-rop'o-dĭ). Podiatry.

chiropompholyx (ki-ro-pom'fo-liks). Dyshidrosis.

chiropractic (ki-ro-prak'tik) [chiro- + G. *praktikos*, efficient]. The science that utilizes the recuperative powers of the body and the relationship between the musculoskeletal structures and functions of the body, particularly of the spinal column and the nervous system, in the restoration and maintenance of health.

chiropractor (ki-ro-prak'tor). One licensed and certified to practice chiropractic.

chirospasm (ki'ro-spazm). Cheirospasm.

chirurgical (ki-rur'jĭ-kal). Obsolete term for surgical.

chitin (ki'tin). A polymer of *N*-acetyl-D-glucosamine, similar in structure to cellulose, comprising the horny substance in the exoskeleton of beetles, crabs, certain microorganisms.

chitinous (ki'tin-us). Of or relating to chitin.

Chlamydia (klă-mid'ĭ-ah) [G. *chlamys*, cloak]. *Miyagawanella;* the single genus of the family Chlamydiaceae, which includes all the agents of the psittacosis-lymphogranuloma-trachoma disease groups; two species are recognized, *C. psittaci* and *C. trachomatis* (the type species).

C. psitta'ci, a species that causes psittacosis, ornithosis, and pneumonitis, abortion, encephalomyelitis, and enteritis in various animals.

C. tracho'matis, a species that causes trachoma, inclusion conjunctivitis, lymphogranuloma venereum, nonspecific urethritis, and proctitis; the type species of the genus *C.*

Chlamydiaceae (klă-mid'ĭ-a'se-e). A family of the order Chlamydiales that includes the agents of the psittacosis-lymphogranuloma-trachoma group; small, coccoid, Gram-negative bacteria that resemble rickettsiae but which differ from them significantly by possessing a unique, obligately intracellular developmental cycle. These organisms are now placed in a single genus, *Chlamydia,* the type genus of the family.

chlamydial (klă-mid'ĭ-al) . Relating to or caused by *Chlamydia.*

chlamydospore (klam'ĭ-do-spōr) [G. *chlamys,* cloak, + *sporos,* seed]. In filamentous fungi, a thick-walled, terminal or intercalary cell containing stored food but also able to function as a thallospore; common in dermatophytes and other fungi that are pathogenic for man.

chloasma (klo-az'mah) [G. *chloazō,* to become green]. Melanoderma or melasma characterized by the occurrence of extensive brown patches of irregular shape and size on the skin of the face and elsewhere; such pigmented patches are also called the mask of pregnancy, and are associated most commonly with pregnancy, menopause, and use of oral contraceptives.

chloracne (klor-ak'ne). Chlorine acne; an acne-like eruption due to prolonged contact with certain chlorinated compounds (naphthalenes and diphenyls).

chlorambucil (klor-am'bu-sil). { *p*-[bis(2-Chloroethyl)amino]phenyl}butyric acid; a nitrogen mustard derivative that depresses lymphocytic proliferation and maturation.

chloramphen'icol. D-(-)-*threo*- 2,2-Dichloro-*N*-[β-hydroxy-α-(hydroxy-methyl)-*p*- nitrophenethyl]-acetamide; an oral antibiotic.

chlo'rate. A salt of chloric acid.

chlor-, chloro- [G. *chloros,* green]. Combining form denoting 1) green; 2) association with chlorine. See also chloro-.

chlor'dane. A chlorinated hydrocarbon used as an insecticide; may be absorbed through the skin with resultant severe toxic effects.

chlore'mia. 1. Chlorosis. **2.** Hyperchloremia.

chlorhy'dria. Hyperchlorhydria.

chlor'ide. A compound containing chlorine, especially salts of hydrochloric acid.

chlor'idu'ria. Chloruresis.

chlo'rinated. Containing chlorine.

chlor'ine. A gaseous element; symbol Cl, atomic no. 17, atomic weight 35.46; a halogen used as a disinfectant and bleaching agent because of its oxidizing power.

chlorine group. The halogens.

chlor'ite. A salt of chlorous acid, containing the radical ClO_2-.

chloro-. See chlor-.

chlor'oform [chlor(ine) + form(yl)]. Methylene trichloride; CHCl₃; used by inhalation to produce general anesthesia; also used as a solvent.

chlor'oformism. Habituation to chloroform inhalation, or the symptoms caused thereby.

chloroleukemia (klo'ro-lu-ke'mǐ-ah) [chloro- + G. *leukos,* white, + *haima,* blood]. Chloroma.

chloro'ma [chloro- + G. *-ōma,* tumor]. Chloroleukemia; chloromyeloma; development of multiple, localized green masses of abnormal cells (in most instances, myeloblasts), especially in relation to the periosteum of the skull, spine, and ribs.

chloromyeloma (klo'ro-mi-ē-lo'mah) [chloro- + G. *myelos,* marrow, + *-ōma,* tumor]. Chloroma.

chlorophe'nol. One of several substitution products obtained by the action of chlorine on phenol; an antiseptic.

chlo'rophyll. The porphyrin derivative (phorbin) found in photosynthetic organisms as the light-absorbing, green pigments that, in living plants, convert light energy into oxidizing and reducing power, thus fixing CO_2 and evolving O_2.

chloropriv'ic. Deprived of the chlorides or hydrochloric acid.

chloroprocaine hydrochloride (klo'ro-pro'kān). β-Diethylaminoethyl-2-chloro-4-aminobenzoate hydrochloride; a local anesthetic.

chloropsia (klo-rop'sǐ-ah) [chloro- + G. *opsis,* eyesight]. A condition in which all objects appear to be colored green, as may occur in digitalis intoxication.

chlor'oquine. 7-Chloro-4-(4-diethylamino-1-methylbutylamino)quinoline; an antimalarial also used in the treatment of hepatic amebiasis and for certain skin diseases.

chloro'sis [chloro- + *-osis,* condition]. Chloremia (1); a form of chronic hypochromic microcytic (iron deficiency) anemia, characterized by a reduction in hemoglobin out of proportion to the decreased number of red blood cells; observed chiefly in females from puberty to the third decade and usually associated with deficiency in iron and protein.

chlorot'ic. Pertaining to or having characteristics of chlorosis.

chlorpro'mazine. 10-(3-Dimethylaminopropyl)-2-chlorophenothiazine; a phenothiazine antipsychotic agent with antiemetic, antiadrenergic, and anticholinergic actions.

chlorpro'pamide. 1-(*p*-Chlorophenylsulfonyl)-3-propylurea; an orally effective hypoglycemic related chemically and pharmacologically to tolbutamide.

chlorprothixene (klor-pro-thik'sēn). 2-Chloro-9-(3-dimethylamino-propylidene)thiaxanthene; an antipsychotic of the thioxanthene group; also possesses antiemetic, adrenolytic, spasmolytic, and antihistaminic actions.

chlor'tetracy'cline. A naphthacene derivative, obtained from *Streptomyces aureofaciens,* used as an antibiotic.

chloruresis (klor-u-re'sis). Chloruria; chloriduria; excretion of chloride in the urine.

chloruretic (klor'u-ret'ik). Increasing the excretion of chloride in the urine.

choluʹria. Chloruresis.

choana, pl. **choanae** (ko'an-ah, ko-a'ne) [Mod. L. fr. G. *choanē,* a funnel] [NA]. The posterior naris; the opening into the nasopharynx of the nasal cavity on either side.

choke. To prevent respiration by compression or obstruction of the larynx or trachea.

chokes. A manifestation of caisson disease or altitude sickness characterized by dyspnea, coughing, and choking.

chol-. [G. *cholē,* bile]. Combining form denoting relationship to bile.

cholagogic (kol-ă-goj'ik). Cholagogue (2).

cholagogue (kol'ă-gog) [chol- + G. *agōgos,* drawing forth]. **1.** An agent that promotes the flow of bile into the intestine, especially as a result of contraction of the gallbladder. **2.** Cholagogic; relating to such an agent or effect.

chola'ic acid. Taurocholic acid.

cholangeitis (ko-lan-je-i'tis). [chol- + G. *angeion,* vessel, + *-itis,* inflammation]. Cholangitis.

cholangiectasis (ko-lan'jǐ-ek'tă-sis) [chol- + G. *angeion,* vessel, + *ektasis,* a stretching]. Dilation of the bile ducts, usually a sequel to obstruction.

cholangiocarcinoma (ko-lan'jǐ-o-kar-sǐ-no'mah). An adenocarcinoma of the intrahepatic bile ducts.

cholangioenterostomy (ko-lan'jǐ-o-en-ter-os'to-mǐ). Surgical anastomosis of bile duct to intestine.

cholangiofibrosis (ko-lan'jǐ-o-fi-bro'sis) [chol- + G. *angeion,* vessel, + fibrosis]. Fibrosis of the bile ducts.

cholangiogastrostomy (ko-lan'jǐ-o-gas-tros'to-mǐ) [chol- + G. *angeion,* vessel, + *gastēr,* belly, + *stoma,* mouth]. Formation of a communication between a bile duct and the stomach.

cholangiogram (ko-lan'jǐ-o-gram). Radiographic image of the bile ducts obtained by cholangiography.

cholangiography (ko-lan-jǐ-og'ră-fǐ) [chol- + G. *angeion,* vessel, + *graphō,* to write]. Radiographic examination of the bile ducts.

cholangiole (ko-lan'jǐ-ōl) [chol- + G. *angeion,* vessel, + *-ole,* dim. suffix]. A ductule occurring between a bile canaliculus and an interlobular bile duct.

cholangiolitis (ko-lan'jǐ-o-li'tis). Inflammation of the small bile radicles or cholangioles.

cholangioma (ko-lan-jǐ-o'mah) [chol- + G. *angeion,* vessel, + *-oma,* tumor]. A neoplasm of bile duct origin, especially within the liver; may be either benign or malignant (cholangiocarcinoma).

cholangiopancreatography (ko-lan'jǐ-o-pan'kre-ă-tog'ră-fǐ). Radiographic examination of the bile ducts and pancreas.

 endoscopic retrograde c. (ERCP), a method of c. using an endoscope to inspect the pancreatic duct and common bile duct; may also involve biopsy or introduction of contrast material for radiographic examination.

cholangioscopy (ko-lan-jĭ-os'ko-pĭ) [chol- + G. *angeion*, vessel, + *skopeō*, to examine]. Examination of bile ducts utilizing a cystoscope or fiberoptic endoscope.

cholangiostomy (ko-lan-jĭos'to-mĭ) [chol- + G. *angeion*, vessel, + *stoma*, mouth]. Formation of a fistula into a bile duct.

cholangiotomy (ko-lan-jĭ-ot'o-mĭ) [chol- + G. *angeion*, vessel, + *tomē*, incision]. Incision into a bile duct.

cholangitis (ko-lan-ji'tis) [chol- + G. *angeion*, vessel, + *-itis*, inflammation]. Cholangeitis; Inflammation of a bile duct.

cholanopoiesis (ko'lă-no-poy-e'sis) [chol- + G. *anō*, upward, + *poiēsis*, making]. Synthesis by the liver of cholic acid or its conjugates, or of natural bile salts.

cholanopoietic (ko'lă-no-poy-et'ik). Pertaining to or promoting cholanopoiesis.

cho'late. A salt or ester of a cholic acid.

chole- [G. *cholē*, bile]. Combining form relating to bile. See also cholo-.

cho'lecalcif'erol. Vitamin D₃; an antirachitic, oil-soluble vitamin.

cholecyanin (ko-le-si'an-in). Bilicyanin.

cho'lecys'tokinet'ic. Promoting emptying of the gallbladder.

cholecyst (ko'le-sist). *Vesica fellea*, the gallbladder.

cholecystagogic (ko'le-sis-tă-goj'ik). Stimulating activity of the gallbladder.

cholecystagogue (ko'le-sis'tă-gog) [chole- + G. *kystis*, bladder, + *agōgos*, leader]. A substance that stimulates activity of the gallbladder.

cholecystectasia (ko'le-sis-tek-ta'zĭ-ah) [chole- + G. *kystis*, bladder, + *ektasis*, extension]. Dilation of the gallbladder.

cholecystectomy (ko'le-sis-tek'to-mĭ) [chole- + G. *kystis*, bladder, + *ektomē*, excision]. Surgical removal of the gallbladder.

cholecystenterostomy (ko'le-sist-en-ter-os'to-mĭ) [chole- + G. *kystis*, bladder, + *enteron*, intestine, + *stoma*, mouth]. Formation of a direct communication between the gallbladder and the intestine.

cholecystic (ko-le-sis'tik). Relating to the gallbladder.

cholecystis (ko-le-sis'tis) [chole- + G. *kystis*, bladder]. *Vesica fellea*, the gallbladder.

cholecystitis (ko-le-sis-ti'tis) [chole- + G. *kystis*, bladder, + *-itis*, inflammation]. Inflammation of the gallbladder.

cholecystocolostomy (ko-le-sis'to-ko-los'to-mĭ) [chole- + G. *kystis*, bladder, + *kolon*, colon, + *stoma*, mouth]. Establishment of a communication between the gallbladder and the colon.

cholecystoduodenostomy (ko-le-sis'to-du-o-de-nos'to-mĭ) [chole- + G. *kystis*, bladder, + L. *duodenum* + G. *stoma*, mouth]. Establishment of a communication between the gallbladder and the duodenum.

cholecystogastrostomy (ko-le-sis'to-gas-tros'to-mĭ) [chole- + G. *kystis*, bladder, + *gastēr*, stomach, + *stoma*, mouth]. Establishment of a communication between the gallbladder and the stomach.

cholecystogram (ko-le-sis'to-gram). Radiographic image of the gallbladder obtained by cholecystography.

cholecystog'raphy [chole- + G. *kystis*, bladder, + *grapho*, to write]. Visualization of the gallbladder by x-rays after the administration of a radiopaque substance that is excreted by the liver and concentrated by the normal gallbladder.

cholecystoileostomy (ko-le-sis'to-il-e-os'to-mĭ) [chole- + G. *kystis*, bladder, + ileum + G. *stoma*, mouth]. Establishment of a communication between the gallbladder and the ileum.

cholecystojejunostomy (ko-le-sis'to-jĕ-ju-nos'to-mĭ) [chole- + G. *kystis*, bladder, + jejunum, + G. *stoma*, mouth]. Establishment of a communication between the gallbladder and the jejunum.

cholecystokinin (ko'le-sis-to-kin'in). A polypeptide hormone liberated by the upper intestinal mucosa on contact with gastric contents; stimulates the contraction of the gallbladder.

cholecystolithiasis (ko-le-sis'to-lĭ-thi'ă-sis) [chole- + G. *kystis*, bladder, + *lithos*, stone]. Presence of one or more gallstones in the gallbladder.

cho'lecystop'athy. Disease of the gallbladder.

cholecystopexy (ko-le-sis'to-pek-sĭ) [chole- + G. *kystis*, bladder, + *pēxis*, fixation]. Suture of the gallbladder to the abdominal wall.

cholecystorrhaphy (ko-le-sis-tor'ă-fĭ) [chole- + G. *kystis*, bladder, + *rhaphē*, sewing]. Suture of the incised or ruptured gallbladder.

cholecystosonography (ko-le-sis'to-so-nog'ră-fĭ). Ultrasonic examination of the gallbladder.

cholecystostomy (ko-le-sis-tos'to-mĭ) [chole- + G. *kystis*, bladder, + *stoma*, mouth]. Establishment of a fistula into the gallbladder.

cholecystotomy (ko'le-sis-tot'o-mĭ) [chole- + G. *kystis*, bladder, + *tomē*, incision]. Incision into the gallbladder.

choledoch-. See choledocho-.

choledochal (ko-le-dok'al, ko-led'o-kal). Relating to the common bile duct.

choledochectomy (ko'led-o-kek'to-mĭ) [choledoch- + G. *ektomē*, excision]. Surgical removal of a portion of the common bile duct.

choledochitis (ko'led-o-ki'tis) [choledoch- + G. *-itis*, inflammation]. Inflammation of the common bile duct.

choledocho-, cholodoch- [G. *cholēdochos*, containing bile, fr. *cholē*, bile, + *dechomai*, to receive]. Combining forms relating to the common bile duct.

choledochoduodenostomy (ko-led'o-ko-du'o-de-nos'to-mĭ) [choledocho- + duodenum + G. *stoma*, mouth]. Surgical formation of a communication between the common bile duct and the duodenum.

choledochoenterostomy (ko-led'o-ko-en-ter-os'to-mĭ) [choledocho- + G. *enteron*, intestine, + *stoma*, mouth]. Surgical establishment of a communication between the common bile duct and any part of the intestine.

choledochojejunostomy (ko-led'o-ko-jĕ-ju-nos'to-mĭ). Anastomosis between the common bile duct and the jejunum.

choledocholithiasis (ko-led'o-ko-lith-i'ă-sis). Presence of a gallstone in the common bile duct.

choledocholithotomy (ko-led'o-ko-lĭ-thot'o-mĭ) [choledocho- + G. *lithos*, stone, + *tomē*, incision]. Incision of the common bile duct for the extraction of an impacted gallstone.

choledochoplasty (ko-led'o-ko-plas-tĭ). Plastic surgery on the common bile duct.

choledochorrhaphy (ko-led-o-kor'ră-fĭ) [choledocho- + G. *rhaphē*, suture]. Suturing together the divided ends of the common bile duct.

choledochostomy (ko-led-o-kos'to-mĭ) [choledocho- + G. *stoma*, mouth]. Establishment of a fistula into the common bile duct.

choledochotomy (ko-led-o-kot'o-mĭ) [choledocho- + G. *tomē*, incision]. Incision into the common bile duct.

choledochous (ko-led'o-kus). Containing or conveying bile.

choleic (ko-le'ĭk). Cholic.

chole'ic acids. Compounds of bile acids and sterols.

cholelith (ko'le-lith) [chole- + G. *lithos*, stone]. Gallstone.

cholelithiasis (ko'le-lĭă-sis). Presence of concretions in the gallbladder or bile ducts.

cholelithotomy (ko'le-lĭthot'o-mĭ) [chole- + G. *lithos*, stone, + *tomē*, incision]. Operative removal of a gallstone.

cholelithotripsy (ko-le-lith'o-trip-sĭ) [chole- + G. *lithos*, stone, + *tripsis*, a rubbing]. Crushing of a gallstone.

cholemesis (ko-lem'e-sis) [chole- + G. *emesis*, vomiting]. Vomiting of bile.

cholemia (ko-le'mĭ-ah). [chole- + G. *haima*, blood]. Presence of bile salts in the circulating blood.

chole'mic. Relating to cholemia.

cho'leperitone'um. Bile in the peritoneum, which may lead to peritonitis.

cholepoiesis (ko'le-poy-e'sis) [chole- + G. *poiēsis*, a making]. Formation of bile.

cholepoietic (ko'le-poy-et'ĭk). Relating to cholepoiesis.

cholera (kol'er-ah) [L. a bilious disease, fr. G. *cholē*, bile]. Asiatic c.; an acute epidemic infectious disease caused by *Vibrio cholerae*, occurring chiefly in Asia, characterized by profuse watery diarrhea, extreme loss of fluid and electrolytes, and prostration.

choleraic (kol'er-a'ik). Relating to cholera.

choleresis (kol-er-e'sis). Secretion of bile as opposed to the expulsion of bile by the gallbladder.

choleretic (ko-ler-et'ĭk). 1. Relating to choleresis. 2. An agent, usually a drug, that stimulates the liver to increase output of bile.

choleriform (kol'er-ĭform). Choleroid; resembling cholera.

cholerine (kol'er-ēn). A mild form of diarrhea seen during epidemics of cholera.

choleroid (kol'er-oyd). Choleriform.

cholerrhagic (kol-e-raj'ik). Referring to the flow of bile.

cholestasia, cholestasis (ko-les-ta'sĭ-ah, -les'tă-sis) [chole- + G. *stasis*, a standing still]. An arrest in the flow of bile.

cholestat'ic. Tending to diminish or stop the flow of bile.

cholesteatoma (ko-les'te-ă-to'mah) [chole- + steatoma]. Pearl tumor; a tumor-like mass of keratinizing squamous epithelium and cholesterol in the middle ear, usually resulting from chronic otitis media, with squamous metaplasia or extension of squamous epithelium inward to line an expanding cystic cavity that may involve the mastoid and erode surrounding bone.

cholesteremia (ko-les-ter-e'mĭ-ah) [cholesterol + G. *haima*, blood]. Cholesterolemia.

cholesterol (ko-les'ter-ol). 5-Cholesten-3β-ol; the most abundant steroid in animal tissues, especially in bile and gallstones; used as an emulsifying agent.

cholesterolemia (ko-les'ter-ol-e'mi-ah) [cholesterol + G. *haima*, blood]. Cholesteremia; presence of enhanced quantities of cholesterol in the blood.

cholesterolosis (ko-les'ter-ol-o'sis). Cholesterosis. 1. A condition resulting from a disturbance in metabolism of lipids, characterized by deposits of cholesterol in tissue, as in Tangier disease. 2. Cholesterol crystals in the anterior chamber of the eye; it occurs in aphakia with associated retinal separation.

cholesteroluria (ko-les'ter-ol-u'rĭ-ah). Excretion of cholesterol in urine.

cholestero'sis. Cholesterolosis.

choleuria (ko-le-u'rĭah). Biliuria.

cholic (kol'ik). Choleic; relating to the bile.

cho'lic acid. Trivial name for a family of steroids comprising the bile acids (or salts), generally in conjugated form. Biologically, they are derived from cholesterol and display varying degrees of oxidation and orientation at positions 3, 7, aand 12; these oxidations and orientations distinguish the several c.a.'s.

choline (ko'lēn). (2-Hydroxyethyl)trimethylammonium ion; $HOCH_2CH_2N(CH_3)_3+$; found in most animal tissues either free or in combination as lecithin (phosphatidylcholine) or acetate (acetylcholine) or cytidine diphosphate (cytidinediphosphocholine); included in the vitamin B complex. Several of its salts are used in medicine.

c. acetyltransferase, an enzyme catalyzing the condensation of choline and acetyl-coenzyme A, forming acetylcholine.

c. kinase, an enzyme which, in the presence of ATP, catalyzes formation of phosphocholine from c.

cholinergic (kol-in-er'jik) [choline + G. *ergon*, work]. 1. Relating to nerve cells or fibers that employ acetylcholine as their neurotransmitter. **2.** Denoting an agent that mimics their action.

cholinesterase (ko-lin-es'ter-ās). One of a family of enzymes capable of catalyzing the hydrolysis of acylcholines and a few other compounds. See also acetylcholinesterase.

chol'inocep'tive. Referring to chemical sites in effector cells with which acetylcholine unites to exert its actions.

chol'inolyt'ic. Preventing the action of acetylcholine.

chol'inomimet'ic. Having an action similar to that of acetylcholine, the substance liberated by cholinergic nerves.

cholinoreactive (kol'in-o-re-ak'tiv). Responding to acetylcholine and related compounds.

chol'inorecep'tors. See cholinergic *receptors.*

cholo-. See chole-.

choloyl (ko'lo-il). The radical of cholic acid or cholate.

choluria (ko-lu'rĭ-ah) [G. *cholē,* bile, + *ouron,* urine]. Biliuria.

chondral (kon'dral) [G. *chondros,* cartilage]. Cartilaginous.

chondralgia (kon-dral'jĭ-ah) [G. *chondros,* cartilage, + *algos,* pain]. Chondrodynia.

chondrectomy (kon-drek'to-mī) [G. *chondros,* cartilage, + *ektomē,* excision]. Excision of cartilage.

chondrification (kon'drĭ-fĭ-ka'shun) [G. *chondros,* cartilage, + L. *facio,* to make]. Conversion into cartilage.

chondrio-. See chondro-.

chondritis (kon-dri'tis) [G. *chondros,* cartilage, + *-itis,* inflammation]. Inflammation of cartilage.

chondro-, chondrio- [G. *chondrion,* grit, gristle, cartilage]. Combining forms meaning, or relating to, **1)** cartilage or cartilaginous, **2)** granular or gritty substance.

chondroblast (kon'dro-blast) [chondro- + G. *blastos,* germ]. Chondroplast; a cell of growing cartilage tissue.

chon'droblasto'ma. A tumor arising in the epiphyses of long bones in young males; consists of highly cellular tissue resembling fetal cartilage.

chondrocalcinosis (kon'dro-kal-sĭ-no-sis) [chondro- + calcium + G. *-osis,* condition]. Calcification of cartilage.

articular c., pseudogout; a disease characterized by calcified deposits, free from urate and consisting of calcium hypophosphate crystals, in synovial fluid, articular cartilage, and adjacent soft tissue; leads to goutlike attacks of pain and swelling of the involved joints.

chondroclast (kon'dro-klast) [chondro- + G. *klastos,* broken in pieces]. A multinucleated cell concerned in the reabsorption of cartilage.

chondrocostal (kon-dro-kos'tal) [chondro- + L. *costa,* rib]. Relating to the costal cartilages.

chondrocranium (kon-dro-kra'nĭ-um) [chondro- + G. *kranion,* skull]. The cartilaginous parts of the developing skull.

chondrocyte (kon'dro-sīt) [chondro- + G. *kytos,* a hollow (cell)]. A connective tissue cell that occupies a lacuna within the cartilage matrix.

chondrodynia (kon-dro-din'ĭ-ah) [chondro- + G. *odyne,* pain]. Chondralgia; pain in cartilage.

chondrodysplasia (kon'dro-dis-pla'zĭ-ah) [chondro- + G. *dys,* bad, + *plasis,* a molding]. Chondrodystrophy.

chondrodystro'phia. Chondrodystrophy.

chondrodystrophy (kon-dro-dis'tro-fī) [chondro- + G. *dys,* bad, + *trophe,* nourishment]. Chondrodysplasia; chondrodystrophia; a disturbance in the development of the cartilage primordia of the long bones, involving especially the region of the epiphysial plates, and resulting in arrested growth of the long bones.

chondrofibroma (kon'dro-fi-bro'mah). Chondromyxoid *fibroma.*

chondrogenesis (kon-dro-jen'ĕ-sis) [chondro- + G. *genesis,* origin]. Chondrosis; the formation of cartilage.

chondroid (kon'droyd) [chondro- + G. *eidos,* resemblance]. **1.** Cartilaginoid; resembling cartilage. **2.** Uncharacteristically developed cartilage which is primarily cellular with capsules thin or lacking and with a basophilic matrix.

chondrolysis (kon-drol'ĭ-sis). Disappearance of articular cartilage as the result of lysis or dissolution of cartilage.

chondroma (kon-dro'mah) [chondro- + G. *-ōma,* tumor]. A benign neoplasm derived from mesodermal cells that form cartilage.

chondromalacia (kon-dro-mă-la'shĭ-ah) [chondro- + G. *malakia,* softness]. Abnormal softening of cartilage.

chondromatosis (kon'dro-mă-to'sis). Presence of multiple tumor-like foci of cartilage.

chondromatous (kon-dro'mă-tus). Pertaining to or manifesting the features of a chondroma.

chon'dromere [chondro- + G. *meros,* part]. A cartilage unit of the axial skeleton developing within a single metamere of the body; a primordial cartilaginous vertebra together with its costal component.

chondromyxoma (kon'dro-mik-so'mah). Chondromyxoid *fibroma.*

chondro-osseous (kon'dro-os'e-us). Relating to cartilage and bone either as a mixture of the two tissues or as a junction between the two.

chon'dro-osteodys'trophy. Osteochondrodystrophy; osteochondrodystrophia term used for a group of disorders of bone and cartilage which includes Morquio syndrome and similar conditions.

chondropathy (kon-drop'ă-thī) [chondro- + G. *pathos,* suffering]. Any disease of cartilage.

chondrophyte (kon'dro-fīt) [chondro- + G. *phytos,* a growth]. An abnormal cartilaginous mass that develops at the articular surface of a bone.

chondroplast (kon'dro-plast) [chondro- + G. *plastos,* formed]. Chondroblast.

chondroplasty (kon'dro-plas-tǐ) [chondro- + G. *plassō*, to form]. Reparative or plastic surgery of cartilage.

chondroporosis (kon'dro-po-ro'sis) [chondro- + L. *porosus*, porous]. A condition of cartilage in which spaces appear, either normal (in the process of ossification) or pathologic.

chondrosarcoma (kon'dro-sar-ko'mah). A malignant neoplasm derived from cartilage cells, occurring most frequently in pelvic bones or near the ends of long bones.

chondrosis (kon-dro'sis). Chondrogenesis.

chondrosternal (kon-dro-ster'nal). **1.** Relating to a sternal cartilage. **2.** Relating to the costal cartilages and the sternum.

chon'droster'nosplas'ty. Correction of malformations of sternum.

chondrotomy (kon-drot'o-mǐ) [chondro- + G. *tomē*, a cutting]. Division of cartilage.

chondroxiphoid (kon-dro-zif'oyd) [chondro- + G. *xiphos*, sword, + *eidos*, appearance]. Relating to the xiphoid cartilage.

chord- [G. *chordē*,]. Combining form meaning cord. See also cord-.

chorda, pl. **chordae** (kor'dah, -de) [L., cord]. **1.** A tendon. **2** [NA]. A tendinous or a cordlike structure.

    chor'dae tendin'eae [NA], tendinous cords; the tendinous strands running from the papillary muscles to the atrioventricular valves (mitral and tricuspid).

    c. tym'pani [NA], cord of the tympanum, a nerve given off from the facial nerve in the facial canal to join the lingual branch of the mandibular nerve; conveys taste sensation from the anterior two-thirds of the tongue and carries parasympathetic preganglionic fibers to the submandibular and sublingual salivary glands.

chordal (kor'dal). Relating to any chorda or cord.

Chorda'ta [L. *chorda*, re G. *chordē*, a string]. The phylum of animals with a notochord in the adult or at a stage in their development.

chor'date. An animal of the phylum *Chordata*.

chordee (kor-de') [Fr. corded]. **1.** Painful erection of the penis in gonorrhea or Peyronie's disease, with curvature resulting from lack of distensibility of the corpus cavernosum urethrae. **2.** Ventral curvature of the penis, most apparent on erection, as seen in hypospadias due to congenital shortness of the urethra.

chorditis (kor-di'tis) [G. *chordē*, cord, + *-itis*, inflammation]. Inflammation of a cord; usually a vocal cord.

chordo'ma [(noto)chord + G. *-oma*, tumor]. A rare solitary neoplasm of skeletal tissue in adults, thought to be derived from remnants of the notochord.

chordoskeleton (kor-do-skel'ĕ-ton). The part of the skeleton in the embryo that develops in relation with the notochord.

chordot'omy. Cordotomy.

chorea (ko-re'ah) [L. fr. G. *choreia*, a choral dance]. **1.** Irregular, spasmodic, involuntary movements of the limbs or facial muscles. **2.** Sydenham's c.

    hereditary c., Huntington's c., a chronic disorder characterized by choreic movements in the face and extremities, accompanied by a gradual loss of the mental faculties ending in dementia; autosomal dominant inheritance.

    Sydenham's c., c. (2); an acute toxic or infective disorder of the nervous system, usually associated with acute rheumatic fever, occurring in young persons and characterized by involuntary, irregular, jerky movement of the muscles of the face, neck, and limbs; they are intensified by voluntary effort but disappear in sleep.

choreal (ko-re'al). Relating to chorea.

choreic (ko-re'ik). Relating to or of the nature of chorea.

choreiform (ko-re'ǐ-form). Choreoid.

choreo- [see chorea]. Combining form relating to chorea.

choreoathetoid (ko're-o-ath'e-toyd). Pertaining to or characterized by choreoathetosis.

choreoathetosis (ko're-o-ath-e-to'sis) [choreo- + G. *athetos*, unfixed, + *-ōsis*, condition]. Abnormal movements of body of combined choreic and athetoid pattern.

choreoid (ko're-oyd). Choreiform; resembling chorea.

choreophrasia (ko're-o-fra'zǐ-ah) [choreo- + G. *phrasis*, speaking]. Continual repetition of meaningless phrases.

chorio- [G. *chorion*, membrane]. Combining form relating to any membrane, but especially that which encloses the fetus.

chorioadenoma (ko'rǐ-o-ad-ĕ-no'mah). A benign neoplasm of the chorion, especially with hydatidiform mole formation.

    c. destru'ens, hydatidiform mole in which there is an unusual degree of invasion of the myometrium or its blood vessels, causing hemorrhage, necrosis, and occasionally rupture the uterus.

chorioallantoic (ko'rǐ-o-al-an-to'ik). Pertaining to the chorioallantois.

chorioallantois (ko'rǐ-o-ă-lan'to-is). The extraembryonic membrane formed by the fusion of the allantois with the serosa or false chorion.

chorioamnionitis (ko'rǐ-o-am'nǐ-o-ni'tis). See amnionitis.

chorioangioma (ko'rǐ-o-an-jǐ-o'mah) [chorion + angioma]. A benign tumor of placental blood vessels (hemangioma), usually of no clinical significance; large tumors may be associated with placental insufficiency or hydramnios.

choriocapillaris (ko'rǐ-o-kap-ǐ-la'ris). *Lamina* choroidocapillaris.

choriocarcinoma (ko'rǐ-o-kar-sǐ-no'mah). Chorioepithelioma; trophoblastoma; a highly malignant neoplasm derived from syncytial trophoblasts and cytotrophoblasts which forms irregular sheets and cords, which are surrounded by irregular "lakes" of blood; villi are not formed.

choriocele (ko'rĭ-o-sēl) [chorio- + G. *kēlē*, hernia]. A hernia of the choroid coat of the eye through a defect in the sclera.

chorioepithelioma (ko'rĭ-o-ep-ĭ-the-lĭ-o'mah). Choriocarcinoma.

chorioid-, chorioido-. See choroid-, choroido-.

chorioma (ko-rĭ-o'mah). Rarely used term for a benign or malignant tumor of chorionic tissue.

choriomeningitis (ko'rĭ-o-men-in-ji'tis). Cerebral meningitis in which there is marked cellular infiltration of the meninges, often with a lymphocytic infiltration of the choroid plexuses, particularly of the third and fourth ventricles.

chorion (ko'rĭ-on) [G. *chorion*, membrane enclosing the fetus]. The multilayered outermost fetal membrane; consisting of extraembryonic somatic mesoderm and trophoblast; on the maternal surface it possesses villi that are bathed by maternal blood; as pregnancy progresses part of the c. becomes the definitive placenta.

chorionepithelioma (ko'rĭ-on-ep-ĭ-the-lĭ-o'mah). Choriocarcinoma.

chorionic (ko-rĭ-on'ik). Relating to the chorion.

chorioretinal (ko'rĭ-o-ret'in-al). Retinochoroid; relating to the choroid coat of the eye and the retina.

chorioretinitis (ko'rĭ-o-ret-in-i'tis). Choroidoretinitis; retinochoroiditis, inflammation of the choroid and retina.

chorista (ko-ris'tah) [G. *chōristos*, separated]. A focus of tissue that is histologically normal *per se*, but not in the organ or structure in which it is located.

choristoma (ko-ris-to'mah) [G. *chōristos*, separated, + -ōma]. A mass formed by maldevelopment of tissue of a type not normally found at that site.

choroid (ko'royd) [G. *choroeidēs*, a false reading for *chorioeidēs*, like a membrane]. 1. Resembling the chorion, the corium, or any membrane. 2. Choroidea.

choroidal (ko-roy'dal). Choroid (1); especially relating to the choroidea.

choroidea (ko-royd'e-ah) [see choroid] [NA]. Choroid (2); the middle, vascular tunic of the eye lying between the retina and the sclera.

choroideremia (ko'roy-der-e'mĭ-ah) [choroid + G. *erēmia*, absence]. 1. Congenital absence of the choroid of the eye. 2. Progressive degeneration of the choroid in males, beginning with peripheral pigmentary retinopathy, followed by atrophy of the retinal pigment epithelium and of the choriocapillaris, night blindness, progressive constriction of visual fields, and finally complete blindness; X chromosome-linked inheritance.

choroiditis (ko-roy-di'tis). Inflammation of the choroid.

choroido-. Combining form relating to the choroid.

choroidoiritis (ko-roy'do-i-ri'tis). Inflammation of the choroid coat and the iris.

choroidopathy (ko-roy-dop'ă-thĭ). Noninflammatory degeneration of the choroid.

choroidoretinitis (ko-roy'do-ret-in-i'tis). Chorioretinitis.

chroidocyclitis (ko-roy'do-si-kli'tis) [choroido- + G. *kyklos*, circle]. Inflammation of the choroid coat and the ciliary body.

chrom-, chromat-, chromato-, chromo- [G. *chrōma*, color]. Combining forms meaning color.

chro'maffin [chrom- + L. *affinis*, affinity]. Chromophil (3); pheochrome (1); giving a brownish yellow reaction with chromic salts; denoting certain cells in the medulla of the adrenal glands and in paraganglia.

chromaffinoma (kro'maf-in-o'mah). Chromaffin tumor; a neoplasm composed of chromaffin cells derived from primitive sympathogonia, and occurring in the medullae of adrenal glands, the organs of Zuckerkandl, or the paraganglia of the thoracolumbar sympathetic chain.

chromaffinopathy (kro'maf-in-op'ă-thĭ) [chromaffin + G. *pathos*, suffering]. Any pathologic condition of chromaffin tissue.

chromat-. See chrom-.

chro'mate. A salt of chromic acid.

chromat'ic. Of or pertaining to color or colors; produced by, or made in, a color or colors.

chro'matid [G. *chrōma*, color, + -id(2)]. Each of the two strands formed by longitudinal duplication of a chromosome that becomes visible during prophase of mitosis or meiosis; the two c.'s are joined by the still undivided centromere, but after the centromere has divided at metaphase and the two c.'s have separated, each c. becomes a chromosome.

chro'matin [G. *chrōma*, color]. The genetic material of the nucleus, consisting of deoxyribonucleoprotein and occurring in two forms during the phase between mitotic divisions: 1) as heterochromatin, seen as coiled, condensed, readily stainable clumps; 2) as euchromatin, dispersed lightly staining or nonstaining threads. During mitotic division the c. condenses and is seen as chromosomes.

sex c., Barr c. body; a small condensed mass of c. representing an inactivated X-chromosome, usually located at the periphery of the interphase nucleus just inside the nuclear membrane; the number of sex c. bodies per nucleus is one less than the number of X-chromosomes.

chro'matism [G. *chrōma*, color]. 1. Abnormal pigmentation. 2. Chromatic *aberration*.

chromato-. See chrom-.

chromatogenous (kro-mă-toj'en-us) [chromato- + -gen, producing]. Producing color; causing pigmentation.

chromat'ogram. The record produced by chromatography.

chro'matograph'ic. Pertaining to chromatography.

chromatography (kro-mă-tog'ră-fĭ) [chromato- + G. *graphō*, to write]. Absorption c.; separation of chemical substances and particles by differential movement through a two-phase system. The mixture of materials to be separated is percolated through a column or sheet of some suitable chosen absorbent. The substances least absorbed are least retarded and emerge the soonest; those more strongly absorbed emerge later.

absorption c., chromatography.

column c., a form of partition c. in which one phase is liquid (aqueous) which flows down a column packed with the second phase, a solid.

gas c., c. in which the moving phase is a mixture of gases or vapors, which are separated in the process by their differential adsorption on a stationary phase.

gas-liquid c. (GLC), gas c., with the stationary phase being liquid rather than solid.

liquid-liquid c., c. in which both the moving phase and the stationary (or reverse-moving) phase are liquids.

paper c., partition c. in which the moving phase is a liquid and the stationary phase is paper.

partition c., separation of similar substances by repeated divisions between two immiscible liquids, so that the substances, in effect, cross the partition between the liquids in opposite directions.

thin-layer c. (TLC), c. through a thin layer of cellulose or similar inert material supported on a glass or plastic plate.

chromatolysis (kro-mă-tol′ĭ-sis) [chromato- + G. *lysis,* dissolution]. Chromolysis; hypochromatosis; disintegration of the granules of chromophil substance (Nissl bodies) in a nerve cell body, which may occur after exhaustion of the cell or damage to its peripheral process.

chromatolyt′ic. Relating to chromatolysis.

chromat′ophil, chromat′ophile. Chromophil.

chro′matophil′ia. Chromophilia.

chromatophil′ic. Chromophilic.

chromatopho′bia. Chromophobia.

chromatophore (kro-mat′o-fōr) [chromato- + G. *phoros,* bearing]. **1.** A colored plastid found in certain forms of protozoa. **2.** A pigment-bearing phagocyte. **3.** Chromophore.

chromato′psia [chromato- + G. *opsis,* vision]. Chromatic vision; a specific response of the eye to color in which all objects appear abnormally colored.

chromatu′ria [chromato- + G. *ouron,* urine]. Abnormal coloration of the urine.

chrome (krōm). Chromium, especially as a source of pigment.

chromesthesia (kro-mes-the′zĭ-ah) [G. *chrōma,* color, + *aisthēsis,* sensation]. **1.** The color sense. **2.** A condition in which another sensation, such as taste or smell, is excited by the perception of color.

chromidro′sis, chromhidrosis [G. *chrōma,* color, + *hidros,* sweat]. Excretion of sweat containing pigment.

chro′mium. A metallic element, symbol Cr, atomic no. 24, atomic weight 52.01.

chromo-. See chrom-.

chro′moblast. [chromo- + G. *blastos,* germ]. An embryonic cell with the potentiality of developing into a pigment cell.

chromocystoscopy (kro′mo-sis-tos′ko-pī) [chromo- + G. *kystis,* bladder, + *skopeō,* to view]. Cystochromoscopy.

chromocyte (kro′mo-sīt) [chromo- + G. *kytos,* cell]. Any pigmented cell, such as a red blood corpuscle.

chromogen (kro′mo-jen). **1.** A substance, itself without definite color, that may be transformed into a pigment. **2.** microorganism that produces pigment.

chromogenesis (kro-mo-jen′ĕ-sis) [chromo- + G. *genesis,* production]. Production of coloring matter or pigment.

chromogen′ic. Relating to a chromogen or to chromogenesis.

chromol′ysis. Chromatolysis.

chromomere (kro′mo-mēr) [chromo- + G. *meros,* a part]. **1.** A condensed segment of a chromonema. **2.** Granulomere.

chro′momyco′sis [chromo- + G. *mykēs,* fungus, + *-osis,* condition]. A localized chronic mycosis of skin and subcutaneous tissues, characterized by skin lesions so rough and irregular as to present a cauliflower-like appearance; caused by several dematiaceous fungi.

chromone′ma, pl. **chromone′mata** [chromo- + G. *nema,* thread]. The coiled filament which extends the entire length of a chromosome and on which the genes are located.

chromophil, chromophile (kro′mo-fil, kro′mo-fīl) [chromo- + G. *phileō,* to love]. Chromatophil; chromatophile. **1.** Chromophilic. **2.** A cell or any histologic element that stains readily. **3.** Chromaffin.

chro′mophil′ia [chromo- + G. *phileō,* to love]. Chromatophilia; the property possessed by most cells of staining readily with appropriate dyes.

chromophil′ic. Chromatophilic; chromophil (1); staining readily; denoting certain cells and histologic structures.

chro′mophobe [chromo- + G. *phobos,* fear]. Chromophobic; resistant to stains, staining with difficulty or not at all.

chro′mopho′bia [chromo- + G. *phobos,* fear]. Chromatophobia; resistance to stains, denoting certain cells and histologic structures.

chromopho′bic [chromo- + *phobos,* fear]. Chromophobe.

chromophore (kro′mo-fōr) [chromo- + G. *phoros,* bearing]. Chromatophore (3); color radical; the atomic grouping upon which the color of a substance depends.

chromophor′ic. **1.** Relating to a chromophore. **2.** Producing or carrying color; denoting certain microorganisms.

chromophose (kro′mo-phōz) [chromo- + G. *phōs,* light]. A subjective sensation of a spot or patch of color.

chromop′sia. Chromatopsia.

chro'moso'mal. Pertaining to chromosomes.

chromosome (kro'mo-sōm) [chromo- + G. *sōma*, body]. A structure (normally 46 in man) in the cell nucleus that is the bearer of genes; it has the form of a delicate chromatin filament during interphase, contracts to form a compact cylinder segmented into two arms by the centromere during metaphase and anaphase stages of cell divison, and is capable of reproducing its physical and chemical structure through successive cell divisions. In the case of microbes, the c. is prokaryotic, not being enclosed within a nuclear membrane and not being subject to a mitotic mechanism.

  acrocentric c., a c. with the centromere placed very close to one end so that the shorter arm is very small, often with a satellite.

  bivalent c., a pair of c.'s temporarily united.

  Christchurch (Ch¹) c., an abnormal small acrocentric c. (no. 21 or 22) with complete or almost complete deletion of the short arm; found in leukocytes in some cases of chronic lymphocytic leukemia, also in some normal relatives of patients.

  fragile X c., an X c. with a fragile site near the end of the long arm, resulting in the appearance of an almost detached fragment.

  heterotypical c., allosome.

  homologous c.'s, members of a single pair of c.'s.

  metacentric c., a c. with a centrally placed centromere that divides the c. into two arms of approximately equal length.

  Philadelphia (Ph¹) c., an abnormal minute c. formed by a rearrangement of c.'s 9 and 22; found in leukocytes of many cases of chronic myelocytic leukemia.

  ring c., a c. with ends joined to form a circular structure, the normal form of the c. in certain bacteria.

  sex c.'s, the pair of c.'s responsible for sex determination, designated X and Y; females have two X c.'s, whereas males have one X and one Y c.

  X c., Y c., see sex c.'s.

chro'mosome map'ping. The process of determining the position of specific genes on specific chromosomes and constructing a diagram of each chromosome showing the relative positions of genes.

chronaxie, chronaxy (kro'nak-sī) [G. *chronos*, time, + *axia*, value]. A time chracteristic; a measurement of excitability of nervous or muscular tissue: the shortest duration of an effective electrical stimulus having a strength equal to twice the minimum strength required for excitation.

chronic (kron'ik) [G. *chronos*, time]. Of long duration; denoting a disease of slow progress and long continuance.

chrono- [G. *chronos,* time]. Combining form relating to time.

chron'obiol'ogy [chrono- + G. *bios*, life, + *logos*, study]. That aspect of biology concerned with the timing of biological events, especially repetitive or cyclic phenomena in individual organisms.

chronotropic (kron-o-trop'ik). Affecting the rate of rhythmic movements such as the heart beat.

chronotropism (kron-ot'ro-pizm) [chrono- + G. *tropē*, turn, change]. Modification of the rate of a periodic movement, *e.g.*, the heart beat, through some external influence.

chrys-, chryso- [G. *chrysos*, gold]. Combining form meaning gold. See also auro-.

chrysiasis (krī-si'äsis) [G. *chrysos*, gold]. Chrysoderma; a permanent slate-gray discoloration of the skin and sclera resulting from deposition of gold in the connective tissue of the skin and eye after therapeutic administration of gold salts.

chrysoderma (kris'o-der'mah) [G. *chrysos*, gold, + *derma*, skin]. Chrysiasis.

Chrysomyia (kris-o-mi'yah) [G. *chrysos*, gold, + *myia*, fly]. A genus of myiasis-producing fleshflies (family Calliphoridae) including the Old World screw worm, *C. bezziana.*

Chrysops (kris'ops) [G. *chrysos*, gold, + *ōpos*, eye]. The deer fly, a genus of biting flies with about 80 North American species. *C. discalis* is a vector of *Francisella tularensis* in the United States; *C. dimidata, C. distinctipenis,* and *C. silacea* are vectors of *Loa loa.*

chrysotherapy (kris-o-thĕr'ă-pī) [G. *chrysos*, gold]. Treatment of disease by the administration of gold salts.

chyl-. See chylo-.

chylangioma (ki'lan-jī-o'mah) [chyl- + G. *angeion*, vessel, + *-oma*, tumor]. A mass of prominent, dilated lacteals and larger intestinal lymphatic vessels.

chyle (kīl) [G. *chylos*, juice]. A turbid, white or pale yellow fluid taken up by the lacteals from the intestine during digestion and carried by the lymphatic system via the thoracic duct into the circulation.

chylemia (ki-le'mī-ah) [chyl- + G. *haima*, blood]. Presence of chyle in the circulating blood.

chylifaction (ki-lī-fak'shun) [chyl- + L. *facio*, to make]. Chylopoiesis.

chylifactive (ki-lī-fak'tiv). Chylopoietic.

chyliferous (ki-lif'er-us) [chyl- + L. *fero*, to carry]. Chylophoric; conveying chyle.

chylification (ki'lī-fi-ka'shun). Chylopoiesis.

chyliform (ki'lī-form). Resembling chyle.

chylo-, -chyl [G. *chylos*, juice, chyle]. Combining form relating to chyle.

chylocele (ki'lo-sēl) [chylo- + G. *kēlē*, tumor]. A cystlike lesion resulting from the effusion of chyle into the tunica vaginalis propria and cavity of the tunica vaginalis testis.

chyloderma (ki-lo-der'ma) [chylo- + G. *derma*, skin]. *Elephantiasis* scroti.

chylomediastinum (ki'lo-me-dī-as-ti'num). Abnormal presence of chyle in the mediastinum.

chylomicron, pl. **chylomicra, chylomicrons** (ki-lo-mi'kron, -mi'krah) [chylo- + G. *micros*, small]. A microscopic particle of fat occurring in chyle, especially numerous after a meal of fat, and also in blood.

chylomicronemia (ki'lo-mi-kro-ne'mĭ-ah). Presence of chylomicrons, especially an increased number, in the circulating blood.

chylopericardium (ki'lo-per-ĭ-kar'dĭ-um). A milky pericardial effusion resulting from obstruction of the thoracic duct or from trauma.

chyloperitoneum (ki'lo-per-ĭ-to-ne'um). Chylous *ascites.*

chylophoric (ki-lo-for'ik) [chylo- + G. *phoros,* bearing]. Chyliferous.

chylopneumothorax (ki'lo-nu'mo-tho'raks). Free chyle and air in the pleural space.

chylopoiesis (ki'lo-poy-e'sis) [chylo- + G. *poiesis,* a making]. Chylifaction; chylification; formation of chyle in the intestine and its absorption by the lacteals.

chylopoietic (ki'lo-poy-et'ik). Chylifactive; relating to chylopoiesis.

chylosis (ki-lo'sis). Formation of chyle from the food in the intestine, its absorption by the lacteals, and its mixture with the blood and conveyance to the tissues.

chylothorax (ki-lo-tho'raks). Accumulation of milky chylous fluid in the pleural space, usually on the left.

chylous (ki'lus). Relating to chyle.

chyluria (ki-lu'rĭ-ah) [chyl- + G. *ouron,* urine]. Presence of chyle in the urine; a form of albiduria.

chyme (kĭm) [G. *chymos,* juice]. The semifluid mass of partly digested food passed from the stomach into the duodenum.

chymification (ki'mĭ-fĭ-ka'shun) [G. *chymos,* juice, + L. *facio,* to make]. Chymopoiesis.

chymopoiesis (ki'mo-poy-e'sis) [G. *chymos,* juice, chyme, + *poiesis,* a making]. Chymification; production of chyme, the physical state of the food (semifluid) brought about by digestion in the stomach.

chymosin (ki'mo-sin). Renin; a proteinase structurally homologous with pepsin present as such (or as a zymogen) in the chief cells of the gastric tubules.

chymotryp'sin. A proteinase of the gastrointestinal tract, preferentially cleaving carboxyl links of hydrophobic amino acids; synthesized in the pancreas as chymotrypsinogen; proposed for use in the treatment of inflammation and edema associated with trauma and to facilitate intracapsular cataract extraction.

chy'motrypsin'ogen. Precursor of chymotrypsin in the pancreas.

Ci Curie.

C.I. Color *index;* Colour Index.

cicatrectomy (sik'ă-trek'to-mĭ) [L. *cicatrix,* scar, + G. *ektomē,* excision]. Excision of a scar.

cicatrices (sik-ă-tri'sēz) Plural of cicatrix.

cicatricial (sik-ă-trish'al). Epulotic (1); relating to scar.

cicatrix, pl. **cicatrices** (sik'ă-triks, sĭ-ka'triks; sik-ă-tri'sēz) [L.]. Scar.

cicat'rizant. Epulotic (2); causing or favoring cicatrization.

cicatrization (sik'ă-trĭ-za'shun). **1.** Epulosis; the process of scar formation. **2.** Healing of a wound otherwise than by first intention.

-cide, -cidal [L. *caedo,* to kill]. Suffix denoting an agent that kills or destroys.

cili-. See cilio-.

cilia (sil'ĭ-ah). Plural of cilium.

ciliarotomy (sil'ĭ-ăr-ot'o-mĭ). Surgical division of the zona ciliaris.

ciliary (sil'ĭ-ă-rĭ) [Mod. L. *ciliaris,* relating to or resembling an eyelid or eyelash]. Relating to any cilia or hairlike processes; the eyelashes; certain structures of the eyeball.

Ciliata (sil-ĭ-a'tah) [L. *cilium,* eyelid]. Ciliates; a class of Protozoa whose members bear cilia or structures derived from them, such as cirri or membranelles; typical members, such as *Paramecium,* reproduce by conjugation.

cil'iated. Having cilia.

ciliates (sil'ĭ-āts). Ciliata.

ciliectomy (sil-ĭ-ek'to-me). Cyclectomy.

cilio-, cili- [L. *cilium,* eyelid]. Combining forms relating to cilia or meaning ciliary.

cil'ioret'inal. Pertaining to the ciliary body and the retina.

cilioscleral (sil'ĭ-o-skle'ral). Relating to the ciliary body and the sclera.

cil'iospi'nal. Relating to the ciliary body and the spinal cord.

cilium, pl. **cilia** (sil'ĭ-um, -ah) [L. eyelid]. **1** [NA]. Eyelash; one of the stiff hairs projecting from the margin of the eyelid. **2.** A motile extension of a cell surface, *e.g.,* of certain epithelial cells, containing nine longitudinal double microtubules arranged in a peripheral ring, together with a central pair.

cillo'sis [Mod. L., spelling influenced by Fr. *ciller,* to wink]. Spasmodic twitching of an eyelid.

cimet'idine. A histamine analogue and antagonist used to treat peptic ulcer and hypersecretory conditions by blocking histamine receptor sites, thus inhibiting gastric acid secretion.

Ci'mex lectula'rius [L. *cimex,* bug, L. *lectulus,* a bed]. Bedbug; a biting member of the family Cimicidae that produces a characteristic pungent odor from thoracic stink glands and is a household pest.

cin-. See cine-.

cine- [G. *kineō, fut. kinēsō,* to move]. Combining forms denoting movement; when spelled this way, usually relating to motion pictures. See also kin-; kine-.

cineangiocardiography (sin'e-an'jĭ-o-kar-dĭ-og'ră-fĭ). Motion pictures of the passage of a contrast medium through chambers of the heart and great vessels.

cineangiography (sin'e-an-jĭ-og'ra-fĭ). Motion picutres of the passage of a contrast medium through blood vessels.

cinefluorography (sin'e-flūr-og'ră-fī). The taking of motion pictures of fluoroscopic views, especially of the heart and great vessels or gastrointestinal tract, after the administration of a contrast medium.

cineplastics (sin-e-plas'tiks). Cineplastic *amputation*.

cineradiography (sin'e-ra-dī-og'ră-fī). Radiography of an organ in motion.

cinerea (sin-e'rĭ-ah) [L. fem. of *cinereus*, ashy, fr. *cinis*, ashes]. The gray matter of the brain and other parts of the nervous system.

cinereal (sin-e're-al). Relating to the cinerea.

cingulate (sin'gu-lāt). Relating to a cingulum.

cingulectomy (sin-gu-lek'to-mī) [cingulum + G. *ektomē*, excision]. See cingulotomy.

cingulotomy (sin-gu-lot'o-mī) [cingulum + G. *tomē*, a cutting]. Formerly, a unilateral or bilateral surgical excision of the anterior half of the cingulate gyrus (cingulectomy), but now electrolytic destruction of the cortex and white matter of the cingulate gyrus and the anterior corpus callosum.

cingulum, gen. **cin'guli**, pl. **cingula** (sin'gu-lum, -lah) [L. girdle, fr. *cingo*, to surround] [NA]. **1.** A structure that has the form of a belt or girdle. **2.** A well marked fiber bundle passing longitudinally in the white matter of the gyrus cinguli (collateral gyrus); composed largely of fibers from the anterior thalamic nucleus to the cingulate and parahippocampal gyri, but also contains association fibers connecting these gyri with the frontal cortex, and their various subdivisions with each other.

circadian (ser'kă-de'an, ser-ka'dī-an) [L. *circa*, about, + *dies*, day]. Relating to biologic variations or rhythms with a cycle of about 24 hours.

circinate (sur'sĭ-nāt) [L. *circinatus*, made round]. Circular; ring-shaped.

circle (sur'kl) [L. *circulus*]. **1.** A ring-shaped structure or group of structures. **2.** A line or process with every point equidistant from the center.

    defensive c., the addition of a secondary disease limiting or arresting the progress of the primary affection, the two affections exerting a reciprocally antagonistic action.

    Haller's c., a network of branches of the short ciliary arteries on the sclera around the point of entrance of the optic nerve.

    vicious c., the mutually accelerating action of two independent diseases, or of a primary and secondary affection.

    c. of Willis, an anastomotic "circle"at the base of the brain, formed, in order from before backward, by the anterior communicating artery, the two anterior cerebral, the two internal carotid, the two posterior communicating, and the two posterior cerebral arteries.

circulation (sur-ku-la'shun) [L. *circulatio*]. Movements in a circle, or through a circular course or one which leads back to the same point.

    collateral c., c. maintained in small anastomosing vessels when the main artery is obstructed.

    compensatory c., c. established in dilated collateral vessels when the main artery of the part is obstructed.

    enterohepatic c., c. of substances such as bile salts which are absorbed from the intestine and carried to the liver, where they are secreted into the bile and again enter the intestine.

    extracorporeal c., c. of blood outside of the body through a heart-lung machine, artificial kidney, etc.

    placental c., c. of blood through the placenta during intrauterine life, serving the needs of the fetus for aeration, absorption, and excretion.

    portal c., c. of blood to the liver from the small intestine via the portal vein.

    pulmonary c., passage of blood from the right ventricle through the pulmonary artery to the lungs and back through the pulmonary veins to the left atrium.

    systemic c., c. of blood through the arteries, capillaries, and veins of the general system, from the left ventricle to the right atrium.

cir'culatory. 1. Relating to circulation. **2.** Sanguiferous.

circulus, pl. **circuli** (sur'ku-lus, -li) [L. dim. of *circus*, circle]. **1** [NA]. Any ringlike structure. **2.** A circle formed by connecting arteries, veins, or nerves.

circum- [L. around]. Prefix denoting a circular movement, or a position surrounding the part indicated by the word to which it is joined. See also peri-.

circumcise (sir'kum-sīz). To perform circumcision.

circumcision (sur-kum-sizh'un) [L. *circumcido*, to cut around]. **1.** Peritomy (2); the operation of removing part or all of the prepuce. **2.** The cutting around an anatomical part.

circumduc'tion [circum- + L. *duco*, pp. *ductus*, to draw]. Movement of a part in a circular direction.

cir'cumflex [circum- + L. *flexus*, to bend]. Bowed; like the arc of a circle.

circumscribed (sur'kum-skrībd) [circum- + L. *scribo*, to write]. Bounded by a line; limited or confined.

circumstantiality (sur'kum-stan-shī-al'ĭ-tī) [L. *circum-sto*, pr. p. *-stans*, to stand around]. A disturbance in the thought process characterized by an excessive amount of detail (circumstances) that is often tangential, elaborate, and irrelevant.

circumval'late [circum- + L. *vallum*, wall]. Denoting a structure surrounded by a wall.

circumvol'ute [L. *circum-volvo*, pp. *-volutus*, to roll around]. Twisted around; rolled about.

cirrhosis (sĭr-ro'sis) [G. *kirrhos*, tawny, + *-osis*, condition]. Fibroid or granular induration; progressive disease of the liver characterized by diffuse damage to hepatic parenchymal cells, with nodular regeneration, fibrosis, and disturbance of normal architecture; associated with failure in the function of hepatic cells and interference with blood flow in the liver, frequently resulting in jaundice, portal hypertension and ascites.

alcoholic c., c. that frequently develops in chronic alcoholism, characterized in an early stage by enlargement of the liver due to fatty change with mild fibrosis, and later by Laënnec's c. with contraction of the liver.

biliary c., c. due to biliary obstruction, which may be a primary intrahepatic disease or secondary to obstruction of extrahepatic bile ducts.

cardiac c., pseudocirrhosis; cardiocirrhosis; an extensive fibrotic reaction within the liver as a result of prolonged congestive heart failure.

cholangiolitic c., c. in which there is diffuse inflammation of the cholangioles, with inflammation, fibrosis, and regeneration; characterized by chronicity, relapses, and febrile episodes.

fatty c., early nutritional c., especially in alcoholics, in which the liver is enlarged by fatty change, with mild fibrosis.

Laënnec's c., portal c.; c. in which normal liver lobules are replaced by small regeneration nodules, sometimes containing fat, separated by a fairly regular framework of fine fibrous tissue strands (hobnail liver).

necrotic c., postnecrotic c.

portal c., Laënnec's c.

posthepatitic c., active chronic *hepatitis.*

postnecrotic c., necrotic c.; c. characterized by necrosis involving whole lobules, with collapse of the reticular framework to form large scars; may follow viral or toxic necrosis, or develop as a result of ischemic necrosis in the course of dietary deficiencies.

toxic c., c. of the liver resulting from chronic poisoning.

cirrhotic (sĭ-rot'ik). Relating to or affected with cirrhosis.

cirsectomy (sur-sek'to-mĭ) [G. *kirsos,* varix, + *ektomē,* excision]. Excision of a section of a vericose vein.

cirsoid (sur'soyd) [G. *kirsos,* varix, + *eidos,* appearance]. Varicoid.

cis- [L.]. **1.** Prefix meaning on this side, on the near side; opsite of trans-. **2.** In genetics, denoting the location of two or more genes on the same chromosome of a homologous pair. **3.** In organic chemistry, a form of isomerism in which similar functional groups are attached on the same side of the plane that includes two adjacent, fixed carbon atoms.

cistern (sis'tern) [L. *cisterna*]. Cisterna.

cisterna, gen. and pl. **cister'nae** (sis-ter'nah, -ter'ne) [L. an undergound reservoir for water]. Cistern. **1** [NA]. Any cavity or enclosed space serving as a reservoir, especially for chyle, lymph, or cerebrospinal fluid. **2.** An ultramicroscopic space occurring between the membranes of the flattened sacs of the endoplasmic reticulum, the Golgi complex, or the two membranes of the nuclear envelope.

cister'nal. Relating to a cisterna.

cisternography sis'tern-og'rā-fī). The radiographic study of the basal cisterns of the brain after the subarachnoid introduction of an opaque or other contrast medium, or a radiopharmaceutical.

cistron (sis'tron). The smallest functional unit of heredity; a length of chromosomal DNA associated with a single biochemical function, essentially equivalent to the gene.

citrate (sit'rāt, si'trāt). A salt or ester of citric acid.

cit'ric acid. 2-Hydroxypropane-1,2,3-tricarboxylic acid; the acid of citrus fruits, widely distributed in nature and a key intermediate in intermediary metabolism; its salts (citrates) are used as anticoagulants because they bind calcium ions.

citrul'line. α-Amino-δ-ureidovaleric acid; an amino acid formed from ornithine in the course of the urea cycle.

citrulline'mia. A disease of amino acid metabolism in which citrulline concentrations in blood, urine, and cerebrospinal fluid are elevated; manifested clinically by vomiting, ammonia intoxication, and mental retardation beginning in infancy; autosomal recessive inheritance.

cit'rullinu'ria. Enhanced urinary excretion of citrulline; a manifestation of citrullinemia.

Cl Chlorine.

cladosporiosis (klad'o-spo-rī-o'sis). Infection with *Cladosporium.*

Cladospor'ium [G. *klados,* a branch, + *sporos,* seed]. A genus of fungi commonly isolated in soil or plant residues. *C. carrionii* is a cause of chromomycosis in man; *C. wernekii* is the causative agent of tinea nigra.

clairvoyance (klār-voy'ans) [Fr.]. Perception of objective events (past, present, or future) not ordinarily discernible except by normal means (the senses); a type of extrasensory perception.

clamp. An instrument for compression or grasping of a structure.

clarif'icant [L. *clarus,* clear, + *facio,* to make]. That which clears a turbid liquid.

clasp. A part of a removable partial denture which acts as a direct retainer and/or stabilizer for the denture.

class [L. *classis,* a class, division]. In biologic classification, the next division below the phylum (or subphylum) and above the order.

classifica'tion. A systematic arrangement into classes or groups.

adansonian c. [*Adanson,* Michel, naturalist, 1727–1806], the c. of organisms based on giving equal weight to every character of the organism; applied in numerical taxonomy.

Angle's c. of malocclusion, a c. of different types of malocclusion, based on the mesiodistal relationship of the permanent molars upon their eruption and locking, and comprised of three classes: I, normal relationship of the jaws; II, distal relationship of the mandible; III, mesial relationship of the mandible.

Caldwell-Moloy c., a c. of the variations in the female pelvis (gynecoid, android, anthropoid, and platypelloid pelvis), based on the type of posterior and anterior segments of the inlet.

Dukes c., a c. into three stages of the extent of spread of operable carcinoma of the large intestine in surgical specimens.

Jansky's c., the c. of the blood groups of the human race into I, II, III, and IV, now designated, respectively, as O, A, B, and AB.

Lancefield c., a serologic c. dividing hemolytic streptococci into groups (A to O) which bear a definite relationship to their sources based upon precipitation tests depending upon group-specific substances that are carbohydrate in nature.

Salter-Harris c., the c. of epiphysial fractures into five groups (I to V), according to different prognoses regarding the effects of the injury on subsequent growth and subsequent deformity of the epiphysis.

clastic (klas'tik) [G. *klastos,* broken]. Breaking up into pieces, or exhibiting a tendency so to break or divide.

clastogenic (klas-to-jen'ik). [G. *klasma,* a fragment, + *genos,* birth]. Capable of causing breakage of chromosomes.

clastothrix (klas'to-thriks) [G. *klastos,* broken, + *thrix,* hair]. *Trichorrhexis* nodosa.

cla'thrates. A type of inclusion compound in which small molecules are trapped in the cage-like lattice of macromolecules.

claudication (klaw-dĭ-ka'shun) [L. *claudicatio,* fr. *claudico,* to limp]. Limping, usually referring to intermittent c.

intermittent c., Charcot's syndrome; myasthenia angiosclerotica; a condition caused by ischemia of the muscles due to sclerosis with narrowing of the arteries; characterized by attacks of lameness and pain, brought on by walking.

claudicatory (klaw'dĭ-kă-to-rĭ). Relating to claudication, especially intermittent claudication.

claustra (klaw'strah). Plural of claustrum.

claus'tral. Relating to the claustrum.

claustrophobia (klaw-stro-fo'bĭ-ah) [L. *claustrum,* an enclosed space, + G. *phobos,* fear]. Morbid fear of being in a closed place.

claustrum, pl. **claustra** (klaw'strum, klaw'strah) [L. barrier]. One of several anatomical structures bearing a fancied resemblance to a barrier. Specifically [NA], a thin, vertically placed lamina of gray matter lying close to the outer portion (putamen) of the lenticular nucleus, from which it is separated by the external capsule.

clava (kla'vah) [L. a club]. *Tuberculum* nuclei gracilis.

clavicle (klav'ĭ-kl). Clavicula.

clavicotomy (klav-ĭ-kot'o-mĭ) [clavicle + G. *tomē,* incision]. Surgical division of the clavicle.

clavicula, pl. **clavic'ulae** (klă-vik'u-lah) [L. *clavicula,* a small key] [NA]. Clavicle; collar bone; a doubly curved long bone that forms part of the shoulder girdle; its medial end articulates with the manubrium sterni, its lateral end with the acromion of the scapula.

clavic'ular. Relating to the clavicle.

clavus (kla'vus) [L. a nail, wart, corn]. **1.** Corn; heloma; a small conical callosity caused by pressure over a bony prominence, usually on a toe. **2.** A condition resulting from healing of a granuloma of the foot in yaws, in which a core falls out, leaving an erosion.

claw'hand. Atrophy of the interosseous muscles of the hand with hyperextension of the metacarpophalangeal joints and flexion of the interphalangeal joints.

clear'ance (C with a subscript indicating the substance removed). Removal of a substance from the blood, expressed as the volume flow of arterial blood or plasma that would contain the amount of substance removed per unit time; measured in ml/min.

creatinine c., the volume of serum or plasma that would be cleared of creatinine by one minute's excretion of urine.

inulin c., a method for determining the rate of filtration in the renal glomeruli, since inulin is completely filterable through them and is neither excreted nor reabsorbed by the renal tubules.

p-**aminohippuric acid c.,** a test of renal plasma flow using *p*-aminohippuric acid (PAH) which, if injected intravenously to achieve low plasma concentrations, is almost totally cleared by the kidneys.

urea c., the volume of plasma or blood that would be completely cleared of urea by one minute's excretion of urine.

cleavage (klēv'ij). **1.** Segmentation (2); a series of cell divisions occurring in the ovum immediately following its fertilization. **2.** Scission (2); the splitting of a complex molecule into two or more simpler molecules. **3.** The linear clefts in the skin, indicating the direction of the fibers in the dermis.

cleft. A fissure.

branchial c.'s, a bilateral series of slitlike openings into the pharynx through which water is drawn by aquatic animals; sometimes loosely applied to the branchial ectodermal grooves of mammalian embryos.

synaptic c., the space between the axolemma and the postsynaptic surface. See also synapse.

visceral c., any c. between two branchial (visceral) arches in the embryo.

cleid-. See cleido-.

cleidal, clidal (kli'dal). Relating to the clavicle.

cleido-, cleid- [G. *kleis,* clavicle]. Combining forms relating to the clavicle. See also clido-, clid-.

cleidocostal, clidocostal (kli-do-kos'tal) [cleido- + L. *costa,* rib]. Relating to the clavicle and a rib.

cleidocranial, clidocranial (kli'do-kra'nĭ-al) [G. *kleis,* clavicle, + *kranion,* cranium]. Relating to the clavicle and the cranium.

-cleisis [G. *kleisis,* a closing]. Suffix meaning closure.

click. A slight sharp sound, as that heard during cardiac systole.

cli'dal. Cleidal.

clido-, clid- [G. *kleis*, clavicle]. Combining forms relating to the clavicle. See also cleido-, cleid-.

cli'docos'tal. Cleidocostal.

cli'docra'nial. Cleidocranial.

climacteric (kli-mak'ter-ik, kli-mak-ter'ik) [G. *klimaktēr*, rung of a ladder]. A period of life occurring in women, encompassing termination of the reproductive period, and characterized by endocrine, somatic, and transitory psychologic changes culminating in menopause.

climax (kli'maks) [G. *klimax*, staircase]. **1.** The height of a disease; the stage of greatest severity. **2.** Orgasm.

clinical (klin'ĭ-kl). **1.** Relating to the bedside of a patient or to the course of his disease. **2.** Denoting the symptoms and course of a disease, as distinquished from the laboratory findings of anatomical changes.

clinician (klin-ish'un). A health professional engaged in clinical practice, as distinguished from an academician.

clinicopathologic (klin'ĭ-ko-path-o-loj'ik). Pertaining to the signs and symptoms manifested by a patient, and also the results of laboratory studies, as they relate to the findings in the gross and histologic examination of tissue.

clino- [G. *klinō*, to slope, incline, or bend]. Combining form denoting a slope or bend.

clinocephaly (kli'no-sef'ă-lĭ) [clino- + G. *kephalē*, head]. Concavity of the upper surface of the skull, presenting a saddle-shaped appearance in profile.

clinodactyly (kli'no-dak'tĭ-lĭ) [clino- + G. *daktylos*, finger]. Permanent deflection of one or more fingers.

clinoscope (kli'no-skōp) [clino- + G. *skopeō*, to view]. An instrument for measuring cyclophoria.

clithrophobia (klĭth-ro-fo'bĭ-ah) [G. *kleithron*, a bolt, + *phobos*, fear]. Morbid dread of being locked in.

clit'oridec'tomy [clitoris + G. *ektomē*, excision]. Removal of the clitoris.

clitoriditis (klit'o-rĭ-di'tis) [clitoris + G. -*itis*, inflammation]. Clitoritis; inflammation of the clitoris.

clit'orism. Prolonged and usually painful erection of the clitoris; the analogue of priapism.

clitoris, pl. **clitorides** (klit'o-ris, kli'to-ris) [G. *kleitoris*]. [NA]. A small erectile body situated at the most anterior portion of the vulva and projecting between the branched extremities of the labia minora, which form its prepuce and frenulum; homologue of the penis in the male except that it is not perforated by the urethra and does not possess a corpus spongiosum.

clitori'tis. Clitoriditis.

clit'oromeg'aly [clitoris + G. *megas*, great]. An enlarged clitoris.

clivus, pl. **cli'vi** (kli'vus) [L. slope] [NA]. A downward sloping surface.

CLL Chronic lymphocytic leukemia.

cloaca (klo-a'kah) [L. sewer]. In early embryos, the entodermally lined chamber into which hindgut and allantois empty.

cloacal (klo-a'kal). Pertaining to the cloaca.

clo'nal. Pertaining to a clone.

clone [G. *klōn*, slip, cutting used for propagation]. Progeny derived from a single organism or cell by asexual reproduction, all having identical characteristics.

clon'ic. Of the nature of clonus, marked by alternate contraction and relaxation of muscle.

clonicity (klon-is'ĭ-tĭ). The state of being clonic.

clon'icoton'ic. Both clonic and tonic; said of certain forms of muscular spasm.

cloning (klōn'ing). The transplantation of a nucleus from a somatic cell to an ovum, which then develops into an embryo (clone).

clon'ism. A long continued state of clonic spasms.

clonogen'ic. Arising from or consisting of a clone.

clonorchiasis (klo-nor-ki'ă-sis). A disease caused by *Clonorchis sinensis* that affects the distal bile ducts after transmission by ingestion of raw, smoked, or undercooked fish repeated infection induces an intense proliferative and granulomatous condition with considerable tissue pathology.

Clonor'chis sinen'sis. The Oriental liver fluke, a species of trematodes (family Opisthorchiidae) which in the Far East causes clonorchiasis.

clon'ospasm. Clonus.

clonus (klo'nus) [G. *klonos*, a tumult]. Clonospasm; a form of movement marked by contractions and relaxations of a muscle, occurring in rapid succession, after forcible extension or flexion of a part.

clostrid'ial. Relating to any bacterium of the genus *Clostridium*.

Clostridium (klos-trid'ĭ-um) [G. *klōstēr*, a spindle]. A genus of anaerobic, sporeforming, motile bacteria (family Bacillaceae) containing Gram-positive rods. The type species is *C. butyricum*.

C. bifermen'tans, a species found in putrid meat and gaseous gangrene, and in soil, feces, and sewage; pathogenicity varies from strain to strain.

C. botuli'num, a species that occurs widely in nature and is a frequent cause of food poisoning (botulism); six main types, A to F, characterized by antigenically distinct but pharmacologically similar, very potent neurotoxins.

C. histoly'ticum, a species found in wounds, where it induces necrosis of tissue by producing a cytolytic exotoxin.

C. no'vyi, a species consisting of three types: A, B, and C; type A causes gaseous gangrene and necrotic hepatitis.

C. parabotuli'num, a species containing organisms formerly referred to as *C. botulinum* types A and B; produces a powerful exotoxin and is pathogenic for man and other animals.

C. perfrin'gens, *C. welchii,* gas bacillus; a species that is the chief causative agent of gas gangrene and may also be involved in causing enteritis, appendicitis, food poisoning, and puerperal fever.

C. tet'ani, a species that causes tetanus; produces a potent exotoxin (neurotoxin) which is intensely toxic for man and other animals.

C. welch'ii, *C. perfringens.*

clot. 1. To coagulate. 2. A soft, nonrigid, insoluble mass formed when blood or lymph gels.

chicken fat c., c. formed *in vitro* or postmortem from leukocytes and plasma of sedimented blood.

currant jelly c., a jelly-like mass of red blood cells and fibrin formed by the *in vitro* or postmortem clotting of whole or sedimented blood.

laminated c., a c. formed in a succession of layers such as occurs in the natural course of an aneurysm.

passive c., a c. formed in an aneurysmal sac consequent to the cessation of circulation through the aneurysm.

clot'tage. Blocking of any canal or duct by a blood clot.

club'bing. A condition affecting the fingers and toes in which the extremities of the digits are broadened and the nails are shiny and abnormally curved longitudinally.

club'foot. *Talipes* equinovarus.

club'hand. Talipomanus.

clump'ing. The massing together of bacteria or other cells suspended in a fluid.

cluneal (klu'ne-al). Pertaining to the clunes.

clunes (klu'nēz) [pl. of L. *clunis,* buttock]. [NA]. Nates.

clysis (kli'sis) [G. *klysis,* a drenching by a clyster]. 1. Infusion of fluid for therapeutic purposes. 2. Formerly, use of an enema or irrigation of any body space or cavity by fluids. 3. Suffix denoting injection.

clyster (klis'ter) [G. *klystēr,* fr. *klysō,* to wash out]. Old term for enema.

C.M. Chirurgiae Magister, Master in Surgery.

Cm Curium.

cM Centimorgan.

cm Centimeter.

CMI Cell-mediated *immunity.*

CML Chronic myelogenous leukemia.

CMP Cytidine 5'-phosphate (or for any cytidine monophosphate).

CNS Central nervous *system.*

Co Cobalt.

co-. See con-.

CoA Coenzyme A.

coacervate (ko-as'er-vät). A cluster of molecules; generic term indicating an aggregate of colloidal particles, aggregates separated out of an emulsion (coacervation) by the addition of some third component (coacervating agent).

coagglutinin (ko-ă-glu'tĭ-nin). A substance that *per se* does not agglutinate an antigen, but does result in agglutination of antigen that is appropriately coated with univalent antibody.

coag'ula. Plural of coagulum.

coag'ulable. Capable of being coagulated or clotted.

coagulant (ko-ag'u-lant). Coagulative; causing, stimulating, or accelerating coagulation, especially with reference to blood.

coag'ulate [L. *coagulo,* pp. *-atus,* to curdle]. To clot or curdle; to change from the liquid state to a solid or gel.

coagulation (ko-ag-u-la'shun). 1. Clotting; the process of changing from liquid to solid, especially of blood. 2. A clot or coagulum.

disseminated intravascular c. (DIC), a hemorrhagic syndrome which occurs following the uncontrolled activation of clotting factors and fibrinolytic enzymes throughout small blood vessels; fibrin is deposited, platelets and clotting factors are consumed, and fibrin degradation products inhibit fibrin polymerization, resulting in tissue necrosis and bleeding.

coag'ulative. Coagulant.

coagulop'athy. A disease affecting the coagulability of the blood.

consumption c., a disorder in which marked reductions develop in blood concentrations of platelets with exhaustion of the coagulation factors in the peripheral blood as a result of disseminated intravascular coagulation.

coagulum, pl. **coagula** (ko-ag'u-lum, -lah) [L. a means of coagulating, rennet]. A clot or a curd; a soft insoluble mass formed when a sol is coagulated.

coalescence (ko-ă-les'ens). Concrescence.

coaptation (ko-ap-ta'shun) [L. *co-apto,* pp. *-aptatus,* to fit together]. Joining together or fitting of two surfaces, as the edges of a wound or the ends of a broken bone.

coarct (ko-arkt') [L. *co-arcto,* pp. *-arctatus,* to press together]. Coarctate (1); to restrict or press together.

coarc'tate. 1. Coarct. 2. Pressed together.

coarctation (ko-ark-ta'shun). A constriction, stricture, or stenosis.

reversed c., aortic arch syndrome in which blood pressure in the arms is lower than in the legs.

coat. The outer covering or enveloping layer(s) of an organ or part. See also tunica.

buffy c., the upper, lighter portion of the blood clot (coagulated plasma and white blood cells), occurring when coagulation is delayed so that the red blood cells have had time to settle; the portion of centrifuged anticoagulated blood which contains leukocytes and platelets.

cobal'amin. A general term for compounds containing the dimethylbenzimidazolylcobamide nucleus of vitamin B_{12}.

cobalt (ko'bawlt) [Ger. *kobalt*]. A steel-gray metallic element, symbol Co, atomic no. 27, atomic weight 58.93; a constituent of vitamin B_{12}; some of its radioisotopes are used diagnostically and therapeutically.

cocaine (ko-kān). Benzoylmethylecgonine; an alkaloid obtained from the leaves of *Erythroxylon coca* (family Erythroxylaceae) and other species of *Erythroxylon*, or by synthesis from ecgonine or its derivatives; has moderate vasoconstrictor activity and pronounced psychotropic effects; salts are used as a topical anesthetic.

cocar'cinogen. A substance that works symbiotically with a carcinogen in the production of cancer.

coccal (kok'al). Relating to cocci.

cocci (kok'si). Plural of coccus.

Coccidia (kok-sid'ĭ-ah) [Mod. L. fr. G. *kokkos*, berry]. A subclass of protozoa (class Sporozoa that includes the genera *Eimeria* and *Isospora* (family Eimeriidae).

coccid'ia. Plural of coccidium.

coccidial (kok-sid'ĭ-al). Relating to coccidia.

coccidioidal (kok-sid-ĭ-oy'dal). Denoting to the disease or to the infecting organism of coccidioidomycosis.

Coccidioides (kok-sid-ĭ-oy'dēz) [coccidium + G. *eidos*, resemblance]. A genus of fungi, a single species of which, *C. immitis*, causes coccidioidomycosis.

coccidioidin (kok'sid-ĭ-oy'din). A sterile solution containing the by-products of growth of *Coccidioides immitis;* used as an intracutaneous skin test for coccidioidomycosis.

coccidioidoma (kok'sid-ĭ-oy-do'mah). A benign localized residual granulomatous lesion or scar in a lung following primary coccidioidomycosis.

coccidioidomycosis (kok'sid-ĭ-oy'do-mi-ko'sis) [coccidioides + G. *mykēs*, fungus, + *-osis*, condition]. A respiratory mycosis due to *Coccidioides immitis*. Lesions orginate in the upper respiratory tract and lungs, and may disseminate to other visceral organs, bones, joints, skin, and subcutaneous tissues; acquired by inhaling dust particles containing arthrospores.

coccidiosis (kok-sid-ĭ-ō'sis). Any disease due to a species of coccidia.

coccidium, pl. **coccidia** (kok-sid'ĭ-um, -ĭ-ah) [Mod. L. dim. of G. *kokkos*, berry]. Common name given to protozoan parasites of the family Eimeriidae.

coc'cobac'illary. Relating to a coccobacillus.

coccobacillus (kok'o-bă-sil'us) [G. *kokkos*, berry]. A short, thick bacterial rod of the shape of an oval or slightly elongated coccus.

coc'coid [G. *kokkos*, berry, + *eidos*, resemblance]. Resembling a coccus.

coccus, pl. **cocci** (kok'us, kok'si) [G. *kokkos*, berry]. A bacterium of round, spherodial, or ovoid form.

coccalgia (kok-sĭ-al'jĭ-ah) [coccyx 'G. *algos*, pain]. Coccygodynia.

coccydyn'ia. Coccygodynia.

coccygeal (kok-sij'e-al). Relating to the coccyx.

coccygectomy (kok-sĭ-jek'to-mĭ) [coccyx + G. *ektomē*, excision]. Removal of the coccyx.

coccygodynia (kok'sĭ-go-din'ĭah) [coccyx + G. *odynē*, pain]. Coccalgia; coccydynia; coccyodinia pain in the coccygeal region.

coccygotomy (kok-sĭ-got'o-mĭ) [coccyx + G. *tomē*, a cutting]. Operation for freeing the coccyx from its attachments.

coccyodynia (kok'sĭ-o-din-ĭ-ah). Coccygodynia.

coccyx, gen. **coc'cygis**, pl. **coc'cyges** (kok'siks) [G. *kokkyx*, a cuckoo, the coccyx]. *Os* coccygis.

cochlea, pl. **cochleae** (kok'le-ah, le-e) [L. snail shell]. [NA]. A cone-shaped cavity in the petrous portion of the temporal bone, forming one of the divisions of the labyrinth and consisting of a spiral canal around a central core of sponge bone (modiolus).

cochlear (kok'le-ar). Relating to the cochlea.

cochleitis (kok-le-i'tis). Cochlitis.

cochleovestibular (kok'le-o-ves-tib'u-lar). Relating to the cochlea and the vestibule of the ear.

Cochliomyia (kok-lĭ-o-mi'yah). A genus of fleshflies (family Calliphoridae) whose larvae develop in decaying flesh or carrion in wounds or sores (myiasis). *C. hominivorax*, the screw-worm fly, is a serious pest of livestock and is known to attack man.

cochlitis (kok-li'tis). Cochleitis; inflammation of the cochlea.

cock'tail. Mixed drink.

Brompton c., Brompton m. [*Brompton* Chest Hospital, London England, where developed], a mixture of morphine and cocaine usually used for analgesia in terminal cancer patients.

lytic c., a mixture of drugs injected intravenously to produce sedation, analgesia, amnesia, hypotension, hypothermia, and blockade of sympathetic and parasympathetic nervous systems during surgical anesthesia.

codeine (ko'dēn) [G. *kōdeia*, head, poppy head]. Methylmorphine; obtained from opium but usually made from morphine; a narcotic analgesic and antitussive; dependence may develop, but less liable to produce addiction than morphine.

codominant (ko-dom'ĭ-nant). In genetics, denoting an equal degree of dominance of two genes, both being expressed in the phenotype of the individual.

co'don. Triplet (3); a sequence of three nucleotides in a strand of DNA or RNA that provides genetic code information for a specific amino acid.

coe-. For words so beginning, and not found here, see ce-.

coefficient (ko-ĕ-fish'ent) [L. *co-* + *efficio*(*exfacio*), to accomplish]. Expression of the amount or degree of any quality possessed by a substance, or of the degree of physical or chemical change normally occurring in that substance under stated conditions.

absorption c., (1) the milliliters of a gas at standard temperature and pressure that will saturate 100 ml of liquid; (2) the amount of light absorbed in passing through 1 cm of a 1 mol solution of a given substance, expressed as a constant in Beer's law.

Bunsen's solubility c. (α), the milliliters of gas STPD dissolved per milliliter of liquid and per atmosphere (760 mm Hg) partial pressure of the gas at any given temperature.

diffusion c., the mass of material diffusing across a unit area in unit time under a concentration gradient of unity.

extraction c., the percentage of a substance removed from the blood or plasma in a single passage through a tissue.

filtration c., a measure of a membrane's permeability to water: the volume of fluid filtered in unit time through a unit area of membrane per unit pressure difference.

Ostwald's solubility c., (γ), the milliters of gas dissolved per milliliter of liquid and per atmosphere (760 mm of Hg) partial pressure of the gas at any given temperature.

phenol c., Rideal-Walker c.

reflection c. (σ), a measure of the relative permeability of a particular membrane to a particular solute, calculated as the ratio of observed osmotic pressure to that calculated from van't Hoff's law; also equal to 1 minus the ratio of the effective pore areas available to solute and to solvent.

Rideal-Walker c., phenol c.; a figure expressing the disinfecting power of a substance, obtained by dividing the figure indicating the degree of dilution of the disinfectant that kills a microorganism in a given time by that indicating the degree of dilution of phenol which kills the organism in the same space of time.

Coelenterates (se-len'ter-āts). One of the major phyla of invertebrates, to which such forms as jellyfish belong.

coelom. Celom.

coeno-. See ceno-.

coenzyme. (ko-en'zīm). A substance that enhances or is necessary for the action of enzymes; c.'s are of smaller molecular size, are dialyzable and relatively heat-stable, and are usuaally easily dissociable from the protein portion of the enzyme.

coenzyme A (CoA). A coenzyme containing pantothenic acid, adenosine 3'-phosphate 5'-pyrophosphate, and 2-aminoethanethiol; involved in the transfer of acyl groups, notable in transacetylations.

coenzyme Q. Quinones with isoprenoid side chains that mediate electron transfer between cytochromes.

coeur en sabot (ker-en-sah-bo') [Fr. wooden-shoe heart]. Descriptive term for the radiographic configuration of the heart in the tetralogy of Fallot, in which the elevated apex combined with a transverse rectangular enlargment.

co'factor. A prosthetic group, such as heme, coenzymes, and inorganic ions such as magnesium ion, essential for enzyme action.

cognition (kog-nĭ'shun) [L. *cognitio*]. A generic term embracing the quality of knowing, which includes perceiving, recognizing conceiving, judging, sensing, reasoning, and imagining.

cognitive (kog'nĭ-tiv). Pertaining to cognition.

cohesion (ko-he'zhun) [L. *co-haereo,* pp. *-haesus,* to stick together]. The attraction between molecules or masses that holds them together.

co'hort. A defined population group followed prospectively in an epidemiological study.

coin'osite. Cenosite.

coital (ko'ĭ-tal). Pertaining to coitus.

coition (ko-ish'un) [L. *co-eo,* pp. *-itus,* to come together]. Coitus.

coitus (ko'ĭ-tus) [L.]. Copulation (1); coition; sexual intercourse; sexual union between male and female.

c. interrup'tus, onanism (1).

c. reserva'tus, c. in which ejaculation is delayed or suppressed.

col. A crater-like area of the interproximal oral mucosa joining the lingual and buccal interdental papillae.

cold. A virus infection involving the upper respiratory tract; characterized by lack of fever, watery nasal discharge, and sneezing.

colectomy (ko-lek'to-mĭ) [G. *kolon,* colon, + *ektomē,* excision]. Excision of a segment or all of the colon.

colibacillemia (ko'li-bas-il-le'mĭ-ah) [colibacillus + G. *haima,* blood]. Presence of *Escherichia coli* in the circulating blood.

colibacilluria (ko'li-bas-il-u'rĭ-ah) [colibacillus + G. *ouron,* urine]. Coliuria; presence of *Escherichia coli* in aseptically or "cleanly" voided urine.

colibacillus, pl. **colibacilli** (ko'li-bă-sil'us). See *Escherichia coli.*

colic (kol'ik) [G. *kōlikos,* relating to the colon]. **1.** Relating to the colon. **2.** Spasmodic pains in the abdomen. **3.** Paroxysms of pain, with crying and irritiability in young infants, due to a variety of causes, such as swallowing of air, emotional upset, or overfeeding.

col'icin. Bacteriocin produced by strains of *Escherichia coli* and by other enterobacteria (*Shigella* and *Salmonella*) that carry the necessary plasmids.

colicky (kol'ĭ-kĭ). Relating to or affected by colic.

coliform (ko'lĭ-form, kol'ĭ-form). Denoting Gram-negative, fermentative rods that inhabit the intestinal tract of man and other animals; sometimes used to refer to all enteric bacteria, or only to lactose-fermenting enteric bacteria.

co'lipase [co- + lipase]. A small protein in pancreatic juice that is essential for the efficient action of pancreatic lipase.

coliphage (ko'lĭ-fāj, kol'ĭ-fāj). A bacteriophage with an affinity for one or another strain of *Escherichia coli.*

colitis (ko-li'tis) [G. *kolon,* colon, + *-itis,* inflammation]. Inflammation of the colon.

amebic c., inflammation of the colon in amebiasis.

granulomatous c., changes, identical to those of regional enteritis, involving the colon.

mucous c., myxomembranous c., an affection of the mucous membrane of the colon, characterized by colicky pain, constipation or diarrhea, sometimes alternating, and the passage of mucous or slimy pseudomembranous shreds and patches.

pseudomembranous c., pseudomembranous *enterocolitis.*

ulcerative c., a chronic disease of unknown cause, characterized by ulceration of the colon and rectum, with bleeding, mucosal crypt abscesses, and inflammatory pseudopolyps; frequently causes anemia, hypoproteinemia, and electrolyte imbalance; less frequently complicated by perforation or carcinoma of the colon.

co'litoxe'mia. A condition resulting from the toxic effects of *Escherichia coli* or its products (or both) in the circulating blood.

coliuria (ko-lĭ-u'rĭ-ah). Colibacilluria.

colla (kol'ah). Plural of collum.

collagen (kol'lă-jen) [G. *koila,* glue, + *-gen,* producing]. Ossein; the major protein of the white fibers of connective tissue, cartilage, and bone; high in glycine, alanine, proline, hydroxyproline, low in sulfur, and has no tryptophan.

collagenase (kol'lă-jĕ-nās). An enzyme that catalyzes the hydrolysis of collagen.

collagenation (kol'lă-jĕ-nās). 1. Replacement of tissues or fibrin by collagen. 2. Synthesis of collagen by fibroblasts.

collagen'ic. Collagenous.

collagenolytic (kol-laj'ĕ-no-lit'ik). Causing the lysis of collagen, gelatin, and other proteins containing proline.

collagenoses (kol-laj-ĕ-no'sēz). Collagen *diseases.*

collagenous (kol-laj'ĕ-nus). Collagenic; producing or containing collagen.

collapse (ko-laps') [L. *col-labor,* pp. *-lapsus,* to fall together]. 1. A condition of extreme prostration, similar to hypovolemic shock and due to the same causes. 2. A falling together of the walls of a structure or the failure of a system.

collat'eral. 1. Indirect, subsidiary or accessory to the main thing; side by side. 2. A side branch of a nerve axon or blood vessel.

collic'ulec'tomy. Excision of the colliculus seminalis.

colliculi'tis. Inflammation of the urethra in the region of the colliculus seminalis.

colliculus, pl. **colliculi** (kol-lik'u-lus, -li) [L. mound, dim. of *collis,* hill] [NA]. A small elevation above the surrounding parts.

c. semina'lis [NA], **seminal c.,** an elevated portion of the urethral crest upon which open the two ejaculatory ducts and the prostatic utricle.

collima'tion [L. *collineare,* to direct in a straight line]. The process, in radiology, of restricting and confining the x-ray beam to given area and, in nuclear medicine, of restricting the detection of emitted radiations from a given area of interest.

colliquation (kol'lĭ-kwa'shun) [L. *col-,* together, + *liquo,* pp. *liquatus,* to cause to melt]. 1. Excessive discharge of fluid. 2. Softening. 3. Degeneration of tissue.

colliquative (kol-lik'wă-tiv). Denoting a discharge, liquid in character and excessive in amount.

collo'dion. A liquid made by dissolving pyroxylin in ether and alcohol; on evaporation it leaves a glossy contractile film, except when mixed with camphor and castor oil (flexible c.); used as a protective for cuts or as a vehicle for the local application of medicinal substances.

colloid (kol'loyd) [G. *kolla,* glue, + *eidos,* appearance]. 1. Aggregates of atoms or molecules in a finely divided state (submicroscopic), dispersed in a gaseous, liquid, or solid medium, and resisting sedimentation, diffusion, and filtration, thus differing from precipitates. 2. Colloidin; a homogeneous material of glue-like consistency, less fluid than mucoid or mucinoid, found in the cells and tissues in a state of c. degeneration. 3. The stored secretion within follicles of the thyroid gland.

colloid'al. Relating to a colloid.

colloi'din. Colloid (2).

collum, pl. **colla** (kol'um, kol'ah) [L.]. 1 [NA]. Neck (1); cervix (1); the body part between the shoulders or thorax and the head. 2. A constricted or necklike portion of a structure.

col'lutory [L. *colluere,* to rinse]. Mouthwash.

collyrium (kol-lĭr'ĭ-um) [G. *kollyrion,* poultice, eye salve]. Originally, any preparation for the eye; now, an eyewash.

colo- [G. *kolon,* colon]. Combining form relating to the colon.

colobo'ma [G. *kolobōma,* lit., the part taken away in mutilation]. Any defect, congenital, pathologic, or artifical, especially of the eye.

colocentesis (ko'lo-sen-te'sis) [colo- + G. *kentēsis,* a puncture]. Colopuncture; surgical puncture of the colon to relieve distention.

colocholecystostomy (ko'lo-ko-le-sis-tos'to-mĭ). Cholecystocolostomy.

co'locolos'tomy [colon + colon + G. *stoma,* mouth]. Establishment of a communication between two noncontinuous segments of the colon.

co'loenteri'tis. Enterocolitis.

colon (ko'lon) [G. *kolon*] [NA]. The division of the large intestine extending from the cecum to the rectum.

c. ascen'dens [NA], **ascending c.,** the portion of the c. between the ileocecal orifice and the right colic flexure.

c. descen'dens [NA], **descending c.,** the part of the c. extending from the left colic flexure to the pelvic brim.

iliac c., that portion of the descending c. which lies in the left iliac fossa, between the crest of the left ilium and the pelvic brim.

irritable c., a tendency to colonic hyperperistalsis, sometimes with colicky pains and diarrhea.

c. sigmoi'deum [NA], **sigmoid c.,** sigmoid flexure; the part of the c. describing an S-shaped curve between the pelvic brim and the third sacral segment, continuous with the rectum.

c. transver′sum [NA], transverse c., the part of the c. between the right and left colic flexures, extending transversely across the abdomen.

colonalgia (ko-lon-al′jĭ-ah) [colon + G. *algos*, pain]. Pain in the colon.

colon′ic. Relating to the colon.

co′lonop′athy. Colopathy; any disordered condition of the colon.

colonorrhagia (ko-lon-or-ra′jĭ-ah). Colorrhagia.

colonorrhea (ko′lon-or-re′ah). Colrrhea.

colon′oscope. An elongated endoscope, usually fiberoptic.

colonos′copy [colon + G. *skopeō*, to view]. Visual examination of the inner surface of the colon by means of a colonoscope.

col′ony [L. *colonia*, a colony]. A discrete group of organisms, as a group of cells growing on a solid nutrient surface.

colop′athy. Colonopathy.

colopexos′tomy [colo- + G. *pēxis*, fixation, + *stoma*, mouth]. Establishment of an artificial anus by opening into the colon after its fixation to the abdominal wall.

colopexot′omy [colo- + G. *pēxis*, fixation, + *tomē*, incision]. Incision into the colon after its fixation to the abdominal wall.

colopexy (kol′o-pek-sĭ) [colo- + G. *pēxis*, fixation]. Attachment of a portion of the colon to the abdominal wall.

coloplication (ko′lo-plĭ-ka′shun) [colo- + Mod. L. *plica*, fold]. Reduction of the lumen of a dilated colon by making folds or tucks in its walls.

coloproctitis (ko-lo-prok-ti′tis) [colo- + G. *prōktos*, anus (rectum), + *-itis*, inflammation]. Colorectitis; inflammation of both colon and rectum.

co′loproctos′tomy [colo- + G. *prōktos*, anus (rectum), + *stoma*, mouth]. Colorectostomy; establishment of a communication between the rectum and a discontinuous segment of the colon.

coloptosis, coloptosia (ko-lop-to′sis, -to′sĭ-ah) [colo- + G. *ptōsis*, a falling]. Downward displacement, or prolapse, of the colon, especially of the transverse portion.

co′lopunc′ture. Colocentesis.

color (kul′or) [L.]. 1. That aspect of the appearance of objects and light sources that may be specified as to hue, lightness (brightness), and saturation. 2. That portion of the visible electromagnetic spectrum specified as to wavelength, luminosity, and purity.

col′orectal. Relating to the colon and rectum, or to the entire large bowel.

colorectitis (ko′lo-rek-ti′tis). Coloproctitis.

colorectostomy (ko′lo-rek-tos′to-mĭ). Coloproctostomy.

colorim′etry. A procedure for quantitative chemical analysis, based on comparison of the color developed in a solution of the test material with that in a standard solution; the two solutions are observed simultaneously in a colorimeter, and quantitated on the basis of the absorption of light.

colorrhagia (ko-lo-ra′je-ah) [colo- + G. *rhēgnymi*, to burst forth]. Colonorrhagia; an abnormal discharge from the colon.

color′rhaphy [colo- + G. *rhaphē*, suture]. Suture of the colon.

colorrhea (ko-lo-re′ah) [colo- + G. *rhoia*, a flow]. Colonorrhea; diarrhea thought to originate from the process confined to or affecting chiefly the colon.

colos′copy [colo- + G. *skopeō*, to view]. Visual examination of the colon during laparotomy by use of a sterilized endoscope.

colosigmoidostomy (ko′lo-sig-moy-dos′ko-pĭ). Establishment of an anastomosis between any other part of the colon and the sigmoid colon.

colostomy (ko-los′to-mĭ) [colo- + G. *stoma*, mouth]. Establishment of an artificial cutaneous opening into the colon.

colos′tric. Relating to the colostrum.

colostrorrhea (ko′los-tror-re′ah) [colostrum + G. *rhoia*, flow]. An abnormally profuse secretion of colostrum.

colostrum (ko-los′trum) [L.]. Foremilk; the first milk secreted at the termination of pregnancy, differing from the milk secreted later by containing more lactalbumin and lactoprotein, and also being rich in antibodies which confer passive immunity to the newborn.

colot′omy [colo- + G. *tomē*, incision]. Incision into the colon.

Colour Index (C.I.). A publication concerned with the chemistry of dyes, each of which listed therein is identified by a five-digit C.I. number, *e.g.*, methylene blue is C.I. 52015.

colp-. See colpo-.

colpal′gia [colp- + G. *algos*, pain]. Vaginodynia.

colpatresia (kol-pă-tre′zĭ-ah) [colp- + G. *atrētos*, imperforate]. Vaginal *atresia*.

colpec′tasis, colpecta′sia [colp- + G. *aktasis*, stretching]. Distention of the vagina.

colpec′tomy [colp- + G. *ektomē*, excision]. Vaginectomy.

colpi′tis [colp- + G. *-itis*, inflammation]. Vaginitis.

colpo-, colp- [G. *kolpos*, any fold or hollow; specifically, the vagina]. Combining forms denoting the vagina. See also vagino-, vagin-.

colpocele (kol′po-sēl) [colpo- + G. *kēlē*, hernia]. 1. Vaginocele; a hernia projecting into the vagina. 2. Colpoptosis.

colpocleisis (kol-po-kli′sis) [colpo- + G. *kleisis*, closure]. Surgical obliteration of the lumen of the vagina.

col′pocysti′tis [colpo- + G. *kystis*, bladder, + *-itis*, inflammation]. Inflammation of both vagina and bladder.

colpocys′tocele [colpo- + G. *kystis*, bladder, + *kēlē*, hernia]. Cystocele.

col′pocys′toplasty [colpo- + G. *kystis*, bladder, + *plassō*, to mold]. Plastic surgery to repair the vesicovaginal wall.

colpodynia (kol-po-din'ĭ-ah) [colpo- + G. *odynē*, pain]. Vaginodynia.

col'pohyperpla'sia [colpo- + hyperplasia]. Thickening of the vaginal mucous membrane.

col'pomicros'copy. Direct observation and study of cells in the vagina and cervix magnified *in vivo*, in the undistrubed tissue, by means of a special microscope.

colpoperineoplasty (kol'po-pĕr-ĭ-ne'o-plas-tĭ) [colpo- + perineum, + G. *plassō*, to form]. Vaginoperineoplasty.

colpoperineorrhaphy (kol'po-pĕr-ĭ-ne-or'ă-fĭ) [colpo- + perineum, + G. *rhaphē*, sewing]. Vaginoperineorrhaphy.

colpopexy (kol'po-pek-sĭ) [colpo- + G. *pēxis*, fixation]. Vaginofixation.

col'poplasty [colpo- + G. *plassō*, to form]. Vaginoplasty.

colpopoiesis (kol'po-poy-e'sis) [colpo- + G. *poiēsis*, a making]. Surgical construction of an artificial vagina.

colpoptosis, colpoptosia (kol-pop-to'sis, kol-po-to'sis, -to'sĭ-ah) [colpo- + G. *ptōsis*, a falling]. Colpocele (2); prolapse of the vaginal walls.

colporrhagia (kol-po-ra'jĭ-ah) [colpo- + G. *rhēgnymi*, to burst forth]. Vaginal hemorrhage.

colporrhaphy (kol-por'ă-fĭ) [colpo- + G. *rhaphē*, suture]. Repair of a rupture of the vagina by freshening and suturing the edges of the tear.

colporrhexis (kol-po-rek'sis) [colpo- + G. *rhēxis*, rupture]. Vaginal laceration; tearing of the vaginal wall.

col'poscope. An endoscopic instrument that magnifies cells of the vagina and cervix *in vivo* to allow direct observation and study of these tissues.

colpos'copy [colpo- + G. *skopeō*, to view]. Examination of vagina and cervix by means of an endoscope.

colpospasm (kol'po-spazm). Spasmodic contraction of the vagina.

colposteno'sis [colpo- + G. *stenōsis*, narrowing]. Narrowing of the lumen of the vagina.

colpostenot'omy [colpo- + G. *stenōsis*, narrowing, + *tomē*, incision]. Surgical correction of colpostenosis.

colpot'omy [colpo- + G. *tomē*, incision]. Vaginotomy.

colpoxerosis (kol-po-ze-ro'sis) [colpo- + G. *xērōsis*, dryness]. Abnormal dryness of the vaginal mucous membrane.

columella, pl. **columellae** (kol'u-mel'lah, -mel'e) [L. dim. of *columna*, column]. Columnella; a column, or a small column.

column (kol'um) [L. *columna*]. A part or structure in the form of a pillar or cylindric funiculus. See also fasciculus.

  anal c.'s, *columnae anales.*

  anterior c. of spinal cord, *columna anterior.*

  dorsal c. of spinal cord, *columna posterior.*

  gray c.'s, *columnae griseae.*

  lateral c. of spinal cord, *columna lateralis.*

  posterior c. of spinal cord, (1) *columna posterior;* (2) clinically, the term often refers to the funiculus posterior of the spinal cord's white matter.

  rectal c.'s, *columnae anales.*

  renal c.'s, *columnae renales.*

  spinal c., vertebral c., *columna vertebralis.*

  ventral c. of spinal cord, *columna anterior.*

columna, pl. **columnae** (kol-um'nah, -um'ne) [L.]. [NA]. Column.

  colum'nae ana'les [NA], anal or rectal columns; a number of vertical ridges in the mucous membrane of the upper half of the anal canal.

  c. ante'rior [NA], anterior or ventral column of the spinal cord; the ventrally oriented ridge of gray matter in each half of the spinal cord; contains the motor neurons innervating the skeletal musculature of the trunk, neck, and extremities.

  c. for'nicis [NA], that part of the fornix, consisting primarily of fibers originating in the hippocampus, that is the direct continuation of the corpus fornicis.

  columnae gris'eae [NA], gray columns; the three masses of gray matter (c. anterior, posterior, and lateralis) that extend longitudinally through the center of each lateral half of the spinal cord; in transverse sections these columns appear as gray horns and are commonly called ventral or anterior, dorsal or posterior, and lateral horn, respectively.

  c. latera'lis [NA], lateral column of spinal cord; a slight protrusion of the gray matter of the spinal cord into the lateral funiculus of either side, especially marked in the thoracic region where it encloses preganglionic motor neurons of the sympathetic division of the autonomic nervous system.

  c. poste'rior [NA], posterior or dorsal column of the spinal cord; the dorsolaterally oriented ridge of gray matter in each lateral half of the spinal cord.

  colum'nae rena'les [NA], renal columns; the prolongations of cortical substance separating the pyramids of the kidney.

  c. vertebra'lis [NA], vertebral or spinal column; spine (2); backbone; rachis; the series of vertebrae that extend from the cranium to the coccyx, providing support and forming a flexible bony case for the spinal cord.

columnel'la [L. dim. of *columna*, a column; another form of *columella*]. Columella.

com-. See con-.

coma (ko'mah) [G. *kōma*, deep sleep]. A state of profound unconsciousness from which one cannot be roused.

  diabetic c., Kussmaul's c.; c. that develops in severe and inadequately treated case of diabetes mellitus; results from reduced oxidative metabolism of the central nervous system that, in turn, stems from severe ketoacidosis.

  hepatic c., c. occurring in advanced cirrhosis, hepatitis, poisoning, or other severe liver disease.

  Kussmaul's c., diabetic c.

metabolic c., c. as the result of disorders of the neuronal mechanisms of energy transfer or of impairment or deprivation of the energy sources.

co'matose. In a state of coma.

combus'tible. Capable of rapid combination with oxygen, or of burning.

combus'tion [L. *comburo*, pp. *-bustus*, to burn up]. Burning; the rapid oxidation of any substance accompanied by the production of heat and light.

comedo, pl. **comedo'nes** (kom'e-do, ko-me'do) [L. a glutton, fr. *com-edo*, to eat up]. Blackhead; a plug of sebaceous matter, capped with a blackened mass of epithelial debris, filling the pilosebaceous orifice.

come'docarcino'ma. A form of carcinoma of the breast in which plugs of necrotic malignant cells may be expressed from the ducts.

comes, pl. **comites** (ko'mēz, kom'ī-tēz) [L. a companion]. A blood vessel accompanying another vessel or a nerve.

commen'sal. Pertaining to or characterized by commensalism.

commen'salism. [L. *con-*, with together, + *mensa*, table]. A symbiotic relationship in which one organism derives benefit and the other is unharmed.

comminuted (kom'ī-nu-ted) [L. *com-minuo*, pp. *-minutus*, to make smaller, break into pieces]. Broken into fragments; denoting especially a fractured bone.

comminution (kom-ī-nu'shun). A breaking into fragments.

commissu'ra, pl. **commissu'rae** [L. a joining together, seam]. [NA]. Commissure. **1.** Angle or corner of the eye, lips, or labia. **2.** A bundle of nerve fibers passing from one side to the other in the brain or spinal cord.

   c. ante'rior [NA], anterior commissure; a round bundle of nerve fibers that crosses the midline of the brain near the anterior limit of the third ventricle; its fibers pass in part to the olfactory bulbs and also interconnects the left and right temporal lobes.

   c. poste'rior cer'ebri [NA], posterior cerebral commissure; a thin band of white matter, crossing from side to side beneath the habenula of the pineal body and over the entrance to the cerebral aqueduct; largely composed of fibers interconnecting the left and right pretectal region and related cell groups of the midbrain.

   commissu'rae supraop'ticae [NA], supraoptic commissures; the commissural fibers that lie above and behind the optic chiasm.

commissu'ral. Relating to a commissure.

com'missure. Commissura.

   anterior c., *commissura* anterior.

   c. of the cerebral hemispheres, *corpus* callosum.

   posterior cerebral c., *commissura* posterior cerebri.

   supraoptic c.'s, *commissurae* supraopticae.

commissurot'omy. **1.** Surgical division of any commissure, fibrous band, or ring. **2.** Midline *myelotomy.*

commun'icable. Capable of being communicated or transmitted.

commu'nica'tion [L. *communicatio*]. In anatomy, a joining or connecting, said of fibrous, solid structures, *e.g.,* tendons and nerves.

compensa'tion [L. *com-penso*, pp. *-atus*, to weigh together, counterblance]. **1.** A process in which a tendency for a change in a given direction is counteracted by another change so that the original change is not evident. **2.** An unconscious mechanism by which one tries to make up for fancied or real deficiencies.

compen'satory. Relating to or characterized by compensation.

compe'tence. **1.** The quality of being competent or capable of performing an allotted function. **2.** Integrity; especially the normal tight closure of a cardiac valve. **3.** In psychiatry, the ability to distinguish right from wrong and to manage one's own affairs.

complaint (kom-plānt'). A disorder, disease, or symptom, or the description of it.

com'plement [L. *complementum,* that which completes]. A serum protein complex, the activity of which is effected by a series of interactions resulting in enzymatic cleavages and which can follow one or the other of at least two pathways. In the case of immune hemolysis, the complex comprises nine components (designated C1 through C9) which react in a definite sequence and the activation of which is effected by the antigen-antibody complex. An alternative pathway (see properdin *system*) is activated by factors other than antigen-antibody complexes and involves components other than C1, C4, and C2 in the activation of C3. See also component of c.

complementarity (kom'plē-men-tār'ī-tī). The degree of similarity of base sequences between DNA and RNA molecules; the degree of affinity, or fit, of antigen and antibody combining sites.

com'plementa'tion. **1.** Functional interaction between two defective viruses permitting replication under conditions inhibitory to the single virus. **2.** Interaction between two genetic units, one or both of which are defective, permitting the organism containing these units to function normally, whereas it could not do so if one unit were absent.

complex (kom'pleks) [L. *complexus,* woven together]. **1.** An organized constellation of feelings, thoughts, perceptions, and memories which may be in part unconscious and may strongly influence associations and attitudes. **2.** In chemistry, the relatively stable combination of two or more compounds into a larger molecule without covalent binding. **3.** A composite of chemical or immunological structures. **4.** An entity made up of three or more interrelated components. **5.** A group of individual structures known or believed to be anatomically, embryologically, or physiologically related.

anomalous c., in the electrocardiogram, a c. differing significantly from the physiologic type in the same heart and lead.

atrial c., the P wave in the electrocardiogram.

avian leukosis-sarcoma c., avian leukosis-sarcoma virus; a division of the RNA tumor viruses (subfamily Oncovirinae), causing the avian leukemia-sarcoma c. of diseases and subgrouped according to antigenic characteristics and growth in defined types of tissue culture cells.

Cain c. [*Cain,* biblical personage], extreme envy or jealousy of a brother, leading to hatred.

castration c., castration anxiety; **(1)** a child's fear of injury to the genitals by the parent of the same sex as punishment for unconscious guilt over oedipal feelings; **(2)** unconscious fear of injury from those in authority.

Diana c. [*Diana,* L. myth. character], adoption of masculine traits and behavior in a female.

Eisenmenger's c., combination of ventricular septal defect with pulmonary hypertension and consequent right-to-left shunt through the defect, with or without an associated overriding aorta.

Electra c. [*Electra,* G. myth. character], female counterpart of the Oedipus c.

femininity c., the unconscious fear, in boys and men, of castration at the hands of the mother with resultant identification with the aggressor and envious desire for breasts and vagina.

Golgi c., a c. of parallel, flattened saccules, vesicles, and vacuoles that lies adjacent to the nucleus of a cell and is concerned with intracellular formation of secretory products.

immune c. antigen combined with specific antibody, to which complement may also be fixed, and which may precipitate or remain in solution.

inferiority c., a sense of inadequacy which is expressed in extreme shyness, diffidence, or timidity, or as a compensatory reaction in exhibitionism or aggressiveness.

Jocasta c. [*Jocasta,* G. myth. character], a mother's libidinous fixation on a son.

Lear c. [*Lear,* Shakespearean character], a father's libidinous fixation on a daughter.

Oedipus c. [*Oedipus,* G. myth. character], a developmentally distinct group of associated ideas, aims, instinctual drives, and fears generally observed in male children 3 to 6 years old; in female children, referred to as the Electra c. During this period, coinciding with the peak of the phallic phase of psychosexual development, the child's sexual interest is attached primarily to the parent of the opposite sex and is accompanied by aggressive feelings toward the parent of the same sex.

primary c., the typical lesions of primary pulmonary tuberculosis, consisting of a small peripheral focus of infection, with hilar or paratracheal lymph node involvement.

QRS c., the principal deflection in the electrocardiogram, representing ventricular depolarization.

superiority c., term sometimes given to the compensatory behavior, *e.g.,* aggressiveness, self-assertion, associated with inferiority c.

symptom c., see syndrome; complex (1).

VATER c., acronym for vertebral defects, anal atresia, tracheo esophageal fistula with esophageal atresia, renal defects, and radial dysplasia; associated with Fanconi's anemia.

ventricular c., the QRST wave in the electrocardiogram.

complexion (kom-plek′shun) [L. *complexio,* a combination, (later) physical condition]. The color, texture, and general appearance of the skin of the face.

compliance (C) (kom-pli′ans). **1.** A measure of the ease with which a structure or substance may be deformed, usually a measure of the ease with which a hollow organ may be distended. **2.** The degree of adherence by a patient to a prescribed regimen.

complica′tion. A morbid process or event occurring during a disease which is not an essential part of the disease, although it may result from it or from independent causes.

component of complement. Any one of the nine distinct protein units (designated C1 through C9 and distributed in the α, β, and γ electrophoretic partitions of normal serum) that effect the immunological activites long associated with complement.

com′pos men′tis [L. possessed of one's mind]. Of sound mind; sane; usually used in its opposite form, *non compos mentis.*

com′pound [thru O. Fr., fr. L. *compono*]. **1.** In chemistry, a substance formed by the covalent or electrostatic union of two or more elements, generally differing entirely in physical characteristics from any of its components. **2.** In pharmacy, denoting a preparation containing several ingredients.

acyclic c., open chain c.; an organic c. in which the chain does not form a ring.

aromatic c., a cyclic c. characterized by the presence of conjugated double bonds within the ring.

closed chain c., cyclic c.

cyclic c., closed chain c.; any c. in which the constituent atoms, or any part of them, form a ring; used mainly in organic chemistry where numerous c.'s contain rings of carbon atoms or carbon atoms plus one or more atoms of other types.

inorganic c., a c. in which the atoms or radicals are held together by electrostatic forces rather than covalent bonds.

open chain c., acyclic c.

organic c., a c. composed of atoms held together by covalent (shared electron) bonds.

saturated c., a c. in which all the atoms of the molecule are connected by single bonds.

unsaturated c., organic c.'s containing double or triple bonds, thus capable of adding other atoms to become saturated without loss of any atom.

comprehen′sion. Apperception (1).

com′press [L. *com-primo*, pp. *-pressus*, to press together]. A pad of gauze or other material applied for local pressure.

compression (kom-presh′un). A squeezing together; exertion of pressure on a body in such a way as to tend to increase its density.

compres′sor. A muscle, contraction of which causes compression of any structure.

compulsion (kom-pul′shun) [L. *com- pello* pp. *-pulsus*, to drive together, compel]. Uncontrollable thoughts or impulses to perform an act, often repetitively, as an unconscious mechanism to avoid unacceptable ideas and desires which, by themselves, arouse anxiety.

compul′sive. Influenced by compulsion.

con- [L. *cum*, with, together]. Prefix denoting with, together, in association; appears as com- before p, b, or m, and as co- before a vowel.

conarium (ko-na′rī-um) [G. *kōnarion*(dim. of *kōnos*, core), the pineal body]. *Corpus* pineale.

cona′tion [L. *conātio*, an undertaking, effort]. The conscious tendency to act; in human context, usually an aspect of mental process, historically aligned with cognition and affection, but more recently used in the wider sense of impulse, desire, purposive striving.

con′ative. Pertaining to conation.

concave (kon′kāv) [L. *concavus*, arched or vaulted]. Having a depressed or hollowed surface.

concav′ity. A hollow or depression, with evenly curved sides, on any surface.

conca′vocon′cave. Concave on two opposing surfaces.

conca′vocon′vex. Concave on one surface and convex on the opposite surface.

concentration (kon-sen-tra′shun) [L. *con-*, together, + *centrum*, center]. **1.** A preparation made by extracting a crude drug, precipitating from the solution, and drying. **2.** Increasing the strength of a fluid by evaporation. **3.** The quantity of a substance per unit volume or weight. In renal physiology, symbol U for urinary c., P for plasma c.; in respiratory physiology, symbol C for amount per unit volume in blood, F for fractional c. (mole fraction or volume per volume) in dried gas; subscripts indicate location and chemical species.

   mean cell hemoglobin c. (MCHC), the average hemoglobin c. in a given volume of packed red cells, calculated from the hemoglobin therein and the hematocrit, in erythrocyte indices.

concentric (kon-sen′trik). Having a common center, such that two or more spheres, circles, or segments of circles are within one another.

con′cept [L. *conceptum*, something undertood]. Conception (1). **1.** An abstract idea or notion. **2.** An explanatory variable or principle in a scientific system.

concep′tion [L. *conceptio*; see concept]. **1.** Concept. **2.** The act of forming a general idea or notion. **3.** The act of conceiving, or becoming pregnant; the fertil-

ization of the oocyte (ovum) by a spermatozoon.

concept′ual. Relating to the formation of ideas, to mental conceptions.

concep′tus. The products of conception (3); *i.e.*, embryo and membranes.

concha, pl. **conchae** [kon′kah, kon′ke) [L. a shell]. [NA]. In anatomy, a structure comparable to a shell in shape.

   c. auric′ulae [NA], the large hollow or floor of the auricle, between the anterior portion of the helix and the antihelix.

   nasal c., *crista* ethmoidalis.

   c. nasa′lis infe′rior [NA], **inferior c.,** inferior turbinated bone; a thin bony plate with curved margins, on the lateral wall of the nasal cavity, separating the middle from the inferior meatus.

   c. nasa′lis me′dia [NA], **middle c.,** middle turbinated bone; a thin bony plate with curved margins, projecting from the lateral wall of the nasal cavity and separating the superior meatus from the middle meatus.

   c. nasa′lis supe′rior [NA], **superior c.,** superior turbinated bone; a thin bony plate with curved margins, projecting from the lateral wall of the nasal cavity and separating the superior meatus from the sphenoethmoidal recess.

   c. nasa′lis supre′ma [NA], **supreme c.,** supreme, highest, or fourth turbinated bone; a small c. frequently present on the posterosuperior part of the lateral nasal wall; it overlies the supreme nasal meatus.

   con′chae sphenoida′les [NA], **sphenoidal conchae,** paired ossicles of pyramidal shape, the bases forming the roof of the nasal cavity.

conchitis (kon-ki′tis). Inflammation of any concha.

con′clina′tion. Incycloduction.

concres′cence [see concrement]. Coalescence; the growing together of originally separate parts.

concretio cordis (kon-kre′shī-o kor′dis). Internal adhesive pericarditis; extensive adhesion between parietal and visceral layers of the pericardium with partial or complete obliteration of the pericardial cavity.

concre′tion [L. *cum*, together, + *crescere*, to grow]. Aggregation or formation of solid material.

concus′sion [L. *concussio*, fr. *con-cutio*, pp. *-cussus*, to shake violently]. **1.** A violent shaking or jarring. **2.** An injury of a soft structure, as the brain, resulting from a blow or violent shaking.

   brain c., a clinical syndrome, due to trauma of the head, characterized by immediate and transient impairment of neural function, such as alteration of consciousness, disturbance of vision and equilibrium, etc.

   spinal c., sudden transient loss of function of the spinal cord, caused by trauma but without permanent gross damage.

condensa′tion [L. *con-denso*, pp. *-atus*, to make thick, condense]. **1.** Compression; making more solid or dense. **2.** Change of a gas to a liquid, or of a liquid to a solid. **3.** In psychoanalysis, an unconscious mental process in which one symbol stands for a number of others. **4.** In dentistry, the process of packing a filling material into a cavity.

condenser. 1. An apparatus for cooling a gas to a liquid, or a liquid to a solid. **2.** In dentistry, an instrument for packing a material into a cavity of a tooth. **3.** The simple or compound lens on a microscope that is used to supply the illumination necessary for visibility of the specimen under observation.

condition (kon-dish'un). **1.** To train. **2.** A certain response elicited by a specifiable stimulus or emitted in the presence of certain stimuli with reward of the response during prior occurrence. **3.** Referring to several classes of learning in the behavioristic branch of psychology.

conditioning (kon-dish'un-ing). The process of acquiring, developing, educating, establishing, learning, or training new responses in both respondent and operant behavior; refers to a change in the frequency or form of behavior as a result of the influence of the environment.

condom. A sheath or cover for the penis to prevent conception or infection during coitus.

conduc'tance. 1. A measure of conductivity; the ratio of the current flowing through a conductor to the difference in potential between the ends of the conductor; the reciprocal of resistance. **2.** The ease with which a fluid or gas enters and flows through a conduit, air passage, or respiratory tract; the flow per unit pressure difference.

conduction (kon-duk'shun) [L. *con-duco*, pp. *ductus*, to lead, conduct]. Transmission or conveyance of certain forms of energy, such as heat, sound, or electricity, from one point to another, without evident movement in the conducting body.

   air c., atmospheric transmission of sound to the inner ear through the external auditory canal and via structures of the middle ear.

   atrial c., intra-atrial c.

   atrioventricular (A-V) c., forward c. of the cardiac impulse from atria to ventricles via the A-V node, represented in the electrocardiogram by the P-R interval.

   bone c., transmission of sound to the inner ear through vibrations applied to the bones of the skull.

   intra-atrial c., atrial c.; c. of the cardiac impulse through the atrial myocardium, represented by the P wave in the electrocardiogram.

   intraventricular c., ventricular c.; c. of the cardiac impulse through the ventricular myocardium, represented by the QRS complex in the electrocardiogram.

   nerve c., transmission of an impulse along a nerve fiber.

   saltatory c., c. in which the nerve impulse jumps from one node of Ranvier to the next.

   synaptic c., c. of a nerve impulse across a synapse.

   ventricular c., intraventricular c.

conductiv'ity. Capacity for conduction.

conduc'tor. 1. A probe or sound with a groove along which a knife is passed in slitting open a sinus or fistula; a grooved director. **2.** That which possesses conductivity.

conduit. A channel for passage of fluids.

condu'plicate [L. *con-*, with, + *duplico*, pp. *-atus*]. Folded upon itself lengthwise.

con'dylar. Relating to a condyle.

con'dylarthro'sis [G. *kondylos*, condyle, + *arthrōsis*, a joining]. A joint formed by condylar surfaces.

condyle (kon'dil) [G. *kondylos*, knuckle of a joint]. Condylus; the rounded articular surface at the extremity of a bone.

condylec'tomy [G. *kondylos*, condyle, + *ektomē*, excision]. Excision of a condyle.

con'dyloid [G. *kondylōdēs*, like a knuckle]. Relating to or resembling a condyle.

condylo'ma [G. *kondylōma*, a knob]. A wartlike excrescence.

   c. acumina'tum, a projecting warty growth on the external genitals or at the anus, consisting of fibrous overgrowths covered by thickened epithelium, due to infection by a human papovavirus. Also called verruca acuminata; fig, genital, moist, pointed, or venereal wart.

   flat c., c. latum.

   giant c., Buschke-Löwenstein tumor; a large type of c. acuminatum found in the preputial sac of the penis of uncircumcized men; tends to extend deeply and recur.

   c. la'tum, flat c.; a secondary syphilitic eruption of flat-topped papules, occurring in groups covered by a necrotic layer of epithelial detritus, and secreting a seropurulent fluid; found wherever contiguous folds of skin produce heat and moisture.

condylo'matous. Relating to a condyloma.

condylot'omy [G. *kondylos*, condyle, + *tomē*, incision]. Division, without removal, of a condyle.

con'dylus [L. knuckle of a joint]. [NA]. Condyle.

-cone. Suffix denoting the cusp of a tooth in the maxilla.

cone [G. *kōnos*, cone]. **1.** Conus (1); a figure having a circular base with sides inclined so as to meet at a point above. **2.** One of the photoreceptors in the retina. See retinal c.'s.

   arterial c., *conus* arteriosus.

   c. of light, light reflex (3); a bright triangular area seen on illuminated inspection of the tympanic membrane.

   medullary c., *conus* medullaris.

   retinal c.'s, the photosensitive, outward-directed, cone-shaped process of a cone cell, one of the two types of photoreceptor cell of the retina (the other being the rods), essential for sharp vision and for color vision.

   twin c., two retinal c.'s fused together.

conex'us, pl. **conex'us** [L.] [NA]. A connecting structure.

confabula'tion [L. *con-fabular*, pp. *-fabulatus*, to talk together]. Making up of tales and recitals and a readiness to give a fluent answer to any question put; a symptom of presbyophrenia.

confection [L. *confectio*, to prepare]. Electuary; a pharmaceutical preparation consisting of a drug mixed with a sweetener.

configura'tion. 1. The general form of the body and its parts. **2.** In chemistry, the spatial arrangement of atoms in a molecule.

confinement [L. *confine* (ntr.), a boundary]. Lying-in (1); giving birth to a child.

conflict. Tension or stress experienced by an organism when satisfaction of a need, drive, or motive is thwarted by the presence of other attractive or unattractive needs, drives, or motives.

con'fluence [L. *confluens*]. A flowing or running together; a joining.

   c. of the sinuses, a meeting place, at the internal occipital protuberance, of the superior sagittal, straight, occipital, and two transverse sinuses of the dura mater.

con'fluent. Relating to or characterized by confluence.

conforma'tion. Spatial arrangement of a molecule achieved by rotation of groups about single covalent bonds, without breaking any covalent bonds; the latter restriction differentiates c. from configuration, where a bond or bonds must be broken in going from one form to another.

confu'sion. A mental state in which reactions to environmental stimuli are inappropriate; a state in which one is bewildered, perplexed, or disoriented.

congener (kon'je-ner) [L. *con-*, with, + *genus*, race]. **1.** One of two or more things of the same kind, as of organisms with respect to classification. **2.** One of two or more muscles with the same function.

congenital (kon-jen'ĭ-tal) [L. *congenitus*, born with]. Existing at birth; may be either hereditary or due to some influence occurring during gestation, even up to the moment of birth.

congested (kon-jes'ted). Denoting conjestion.

congestion (kon-jes'chun) [L. *congestio*, a bringing together, a heap]. Presence of an abnormal amount of fluid in the vessels or passages of a part or organ; especially, of blood due either to increased afflux or to obstruction of return flow.

   active c., c. due to an increased flow of arterial blood to a part.

   functional c., physiologic c.; hyperemia occurring during functional activity of an organ.

   hypostatic c., hypostasis (2); c. due to pooling of venous blood in a dependent part.

   passive c., c. due to partial stagnation of blood in capillaries and venules due to obstruction or slowing of the venous drainage.

   physiologic c., functional c.

congestive (kon-jes'tiv). Characterized by congestion.

conglo'bate [L. *con-globo*, pp. *-atus*, to gather into a *globus*, ball]. Formed in a single, rounded mass.

conglom'erate [L. *con-glomero*, pp. *-atus*, to roll together]. Composed of several parts aggregated into one mass.

conglu'tinant [L. *con-glutino*, pp. *-atus*, to glue together]. Adhesive, promoting the union of a wound.

conglutina'tion. 1. Adhesion (1). **2.** Agglutination of antigen(erythrocyte)-antibody-complement complex by normal bovine serum and other colloidal materials.

Congo red. An acid dye used as an indicator in testing for free hydrochloric acid in gastric contents, as a laboratory aid in the diagnosis of amyloidosis, and as a histologic stain for amyloid.

co'ni. Plural of conus.

con'ic, con'ical. Resembling a cone.

-conid. Suffix denoting the cusp of a tooth in the mandible.

co'niofibro'sis [G. *konis*, dust, + fibrosis]. Fibrosis produced by dust, especially of the lungs by inhaled dust.

co'niophage. Dust *cell.*

conio'sis [G. *konis*, dust]. Any disease or morbid condition caused by dust.

coniza'tion. Excision of a cone of tissue; *e.g.,* mucosa of the cervix.

con'jugant [L. *con-jugo*, to join]. A member of a mating pair of organisms or gametes undergoing conjugation.

conjuga'ta [L. fem. of *conjugatus*, joined together] [NA], Conjugate (2).

con'jugate [L. *conjugatus*, joined together]. **1.** Conjugated; joined or paired. **2.** The distance from the promontory of the sacrum to the upper edge of the pubic symphysis. Also called conjugate or anteroposterior diameter, internal or true conjugate; conjugate (2).

   diagonal c., false c. (1); the anteroposterior dimension of the inlet that measures the clinical distance from the promontory of the sacrum to the lower margin of the symphysis pubis.

   effective c., false c. (2); the internal c. measured from the nearest lumbar vertebra to the symphysis, in spondylolisthesis.

   external c., the distance in a straight line between the depression under the last spinous process of the lumbar vertebrae and the upper edge of the symphysis pubis.

   false c., (1) diagonal c.; (2) effective c.

   internal c., conjugate (2).

   obstetric c., the diameter that represents the shortest diameter through which the head must pass in descending into the superior strait and measures, radiographically, the distance from the promontory of the sacrum to a point on the inner surface of the symphysis a few millimeters below its upper margin.

   true c., conjugate (2).

conjugate acid-base pair. In protonic solvents, two molecular species differing only in the presence or absence of a hydrogen ion; the basis of buffer action.

con'jugated. Conjugate (1).

conjuga'tion [L. *con-jugo*, pp. *-jugatus*, to join together]. **1.** The union of two unicellular organisms or of the male and female gametes of multicellular forms by which genetic material is exchanged, followed by partition. **2.** The combination, especially in the liver, of certain toxic substances formed in the intestine, drugs, or steroid hormones with glucuronic or sulfuric acid; a means by which the biological activity of certain chemical substances can be terminated.

conjuncti'va, pl. **conjuncti'vae** [L. fem. of *conjunctivus,* from *conjungo,* pp. *-junctus,* to bind together]. Tunica conjunctiva; the mucous membrane covering the anterior surface of the eyeball and lining the lids.

conjuncti'val. Relating to the conjunctiva.

conjunctivi'tis. Inflammation of conjunctiva.

   acute contagious c., acute epidemic c., pinkeye (1); an acute c. marked by intense hyperemia and profuse mucopurulent discharge; caused by *Haemophilus aegypticus.*

   allergic c., atopic c., a conjunctival reaction to a substance producing an allergic response, either immediate or delayed.

   calcareous c., a common condition in which the palpebral conjunctiva displays minute yellow concretions due to products of cellular degeneration in Henle's glands.

   contagious granular c., trachoma.

   gonococcal c., severe c. caused by gonococci and marked by intensely swollen, congested conjunctiva, swollen eyelids, and profuse purulent discharge.

   granular c., trachomatous c.

   inclusion c., swimming pool c.; a benign follicular c. caused by *Chlamydia oculogenitale.*

   infantile purulent c., *ophthalmia* neonatorum.

   spring c., vernal c.

   swimming pool c., inclusion c.

   trachomatous c., granular c.; a chronic infection of the conjunctiva characterized by conjunctival follicles and subsequent cicatrization. See also trachoma.

   vernal c., spring c.; a chronic bilateral conjunctival inflammation with photophobia and intense itching that recurs seasonally during warm weather.

conjunctivo'ma. A homeoplastic tumor of the conjunctiva.

conjunctivoplasty (kon-jungk-ti'vo-plas-ti, konjungk'ti-vo-). Plastic operation on the conjunctiva.

consanguineous (kon-sang-gwin'e-us) [L. *cum,* with, + *sanguis,* blood]. Related by blood.

consanguinity (kon-sang-gwin'i-ti) [L. *consanguinitas,* blood relationship]. Blood relationship; kinship because of common ancestry.

conscious (con'shus) [L. *conscius,* knowing]. **1.** Aware; having present knowledge or perception of oneself, one's acts and surroundings. **2.** Denoting something occurring with the perceptive attention of the individual, as a c. act or idea, as distinguished from automatic or instinctive.

consciousness (con'shus-nes) [L. *con-scio,* to know, to be aware of]. The state of being conscious (1).

consensual L. *con-, with,* + *sensus,* sensation]. Reflex (2); denoting what is done in response to a stimulus without the cooperation of the will.

conserv'ative. Denoting treatment by gradual, limited, or well- established procedures, as opposed to radical.

consolidation [L. *consolido,* to make thick, condense]. Solidification into a firm dense mass; applied especially to inflammatory induration of a normally aerated lung due to the presence of cellular exudate in the pulmonary alveoli.

constant. A quantity which, under stated conditions, does not vary with changes in the environment.

   Avogadro's c., Avogadro's *number.*

   Michaelis or **Michaelis-Menten c.,** the concentration of the substrate at which half the maximum velocity of a reaction is achieved.

   newtonian c. of gravitation (G), a universal c. relating the gravitational force, f, attracting two masses, m_1 and m_2, toward each other when they are separated by a distance, r, in the equation: $f = G(m_1m_2/r^2)$; the value of 6.6732×10^{-8} dyne cm^2gm^{-2}.

   sedimentation c., the c. s in Svedberg's equation for estimating the molecular weight of a protein from the rate of movement in a centrifugal field; s, with dimensions of time per unit of field force, is usually between 1×10^{-13} and 200×10^{-13} second. The Svedberg unit (S) is fixed at 1×10^{-13} second and is often used to describe the sedimentation rate of macromolecules.

constipate [L. *con-stipo,* pp. *-atus,* to press togethr]. To cause a sluggishness in the action of the bowels.

constipated. Suffering from constipation.

constipation. A condition in which bowel movements are infrequent or incomplete.

constitution [L. *constitutio,* constitution, disposition]. **1.** The physical makeup of the body, including the mode of performance of its functions, the activity of its metabolic processes, the manner and degree of its reactions to stimuli, and its power of resistance to the attack of pathogenic organisms. **2.** In chemistry, the number and kind of atoms in the molecule and the relation they bear to each other.

constitutional. 1. Relating to the constitution. **2.** General; relating to a system as a whole; not local.

constriction (kon-strik'shun) [L. *con-stringo,* pp. *-strictus,* to draw together]. **1.** Binding or contraction of a part. **2.** A subjective sensation as if the body or any part were tightly bound or squeezed.

constrictor (kon-strik'tor) [L. fr. *constringo,* to draw together]. **1.** Anything that binds or squeezes a part. **2.** A muscle the action of which is to narrow a canal, as a sphincter.

consultant [L. *consulto*, pp. *-atus*, to deliberate, ask advice]. **1.** A physician or surgeon who does not take actual charge of a patient, but acts in an advisory capacity to the personal attendant. **2.** A member of a hospital staff who has no active service but stands ready to advise in any case, at the request of the attending physician or surgeon.

consultation. Meeting of two or more health professionals to evaluate the nature and progress of disease in a particular patient and to establish diagnosis, prognosis, and therapy.

consumption [L. *con-sumo*, pp. *-sumptus*, to take up wholly, use up, waste]. **1.** The using up of something, especially the rate at which it is used. **2.** Obsolete term for a wasting of the tissues of the body, usually tuberculous.

contact [*con-tingo*, pp. *-tactus*, to touch]. **1.** The touching or apposition of two bodies. **2.** A person who has been exposed to contagion.

contactant. Any of a heterogeneous group of allergens that elicit manifestations of induced sensitivity (hypersensitivity) by direct contact with skin or mucosa.

contact with reality. Correctly interpreting external phenomena in relation to the norms of one's social or cultural milieu; this ability is impaired in some psychoses.

contagion (kon-ta'jun) [L. *contagio;* fr. *contingo*, to touch closely]. Transmission of disease by contact with the sick, or the disease so transmitted. The term originated long before development of modern ideas of infectious disease and has since lost much of its significance, being included under the more inclusive term "communicable disease."

contagious. Communicable; relating to contagion; transmissible by contact with the sick.

contagiousness. Communicableness; the quality of being contagious.

contam'inant. An impurity; that which causes contamination.

contamina'tion [L. *contamino*, pp. *-atus*, to stain, defile]. **1.** Rendering harmful or unsuitable, as by the presence of radioactive substance. **2.** In chemistry or pharmacy, the presence of any extraneous material that renders a substance or preparation impure.

con'tent [L. *contentus*, fr. *con-tineo*, pp. *-tentus*, to hold together, contain, fr. *teneo*, to hold]. **1.** That which is contained within something else, usually contents. **2.** In psychology, the form of a dream as presented to consiousness.

    latent c., the hidden, unconscious meaning of thoughts or actions, especially in dreams or fantasies.

    manifest c., those elements of fantasy and dreams which are consciously available and reportable.

contiguity (kon-tĭ-gu'ĭ-tĭ) [L. *contiguus*, touching, fr. *contingo*, to touch]. Contact without actual continuity.

contig'uous. Adjacent or in actual contact.

con'tinence [L. *continentia*]. Moderation, temperance, or self-restraint.

continu'ity [L. *continuus*, continued]. Absence of interruption, a succession of parts intimately united. A single bone of the skull has the quality of *continuity* in all its parts; a cranial suture is marked by *contiguity* of the bones entering into its formation.

contra- [L.]. Prefix signifying opposed, against. See also counter-.

con'tra-ap'erture. Counteropening.

contracep'tion. Prevention of conception or impregnation.

contracep'tive [L. *contra*, against, + conceptive]. Relating to any measure or agent designed to prevent conception or that so used.

    "combination" oral c., a mixture of a steroid having progestational activity and an estrogen; one such pill is taken daily for approxiamtely 21 days of each menstrual cycle.

    intrauterine c., see under device.

    oral c., any orally effective preparation designed to prevent conception.

    "sequential" oral c., a preparation providing two types of medication; the first, containing only an estrogen, is taken daily from the 5th to approximately the 19th day of the menstrual cycle; the second, containing an estrogen and a semisynthetic progestational steroid, is taken daily from the 20th to the 24th days of the cycle.

contract [L. *con-traho*, pp. *-tractus*, to draw together]. **1** (kon-trakt'). To shorten; to become reduced in size; in the case of muscle, either to shorten or to undergo an increase in tension. **2.** To acquire by contagion or infection. **3** (kon'trakt). An explicit, bilateral commitment by psychotherapist and patient to a defined course of action to attain the goal of the psychotherapy.

contrac'tile. Having the property of contracting.

contractil'ity. The ability or property of a substance, especially of muscle, of shortening, or becoming reduced in size, or developing increased tension.

contrac'tion [L. *contractio*, to draw together]. **1.** A shortening or increase in tension; denoting the normal function of muscular tissue. **2.** A shrinkage or reduction in size. **3.** Heart beat, as in premature c.

    carpopedal c., carpopedal *spasm.*

    escaped ventricular c., an escaped beat arising in the ventricle.

    fibrillary c.'s, c.'s occurring spontaneously in individual muscle fibers, seen commonly a few days after damage to the motor nerves supplying the muscle.

    hourglass c., constriction of the middle portion of a hollow organ, such as the stomach or the gravid uterus.

    hunger c.'s, strong c.'s of the stomach associated with hunger pains.

    idiomuscular c., myoedema.

myotatic c., a reflex c. of a skeletal muscle that occurs as a result of stimulation of the stretch receptors in the muscle, *i.e.,* as part of a myotatic reflex.

paradoxical c., a tonic c. of the anterior tibial muscles when a sudden passive dorsal flexion of the foot is made.

postural c., maintenance of muscular tension (usually isometric) sufficient to maintain posture.

tonic c., sustained contraction of a muscle, as employed in the maintenance of posture.

uterine c., rhythmic activity of the myometrium associated with menstruation, pregnancy, or labor.

contrac′ture [L. *contractura,* fr. *con-traho,* to draw together]. A permanent muscular contraction due to tonic spasm or fibrosis, or to loss of muscular equilibrium, the antagonists being paralyzed.

Dupuytren's c., a disease of the palmar fascia resulting in thickening and c. of fibrous bands on the palmar surface of the hand and fingers.

ischemic c. of the left ventricle, stone heart; irreversible contraction of the left ventricle of the heart as a complication of cardiopulmonary bypass.

organic c., c., usually due to fibrosis within the muscle, that persists whether the subject is conscious or unconscious.

Volkmann's c., tissue degeneration produced by ischemia leading to a late c. involving muscles, tendons, fascia, and other soft tissues; caused by interference with blood flow.

contrafissura (kon′trǎ-fĭ-shūr′ah) [L. *contra,* against, counter, + *fissura,* fissure]. Fracture by contrecoup; fracture of a bone, as in the skull, at a point opposite that where the blow was received.

contraindication (kon′trǎ-in-dĭ-ka′shun). Any special symptom or circumstance that renders the use of a remedy or the carrying out of a procedure inadvisable.

contralat′eral [L. *contra,* opposite, + *latus,* side]. Heterolateral; relating to the opposite side, as when pain is felt or paralysis occurs on the side opposite that of the lesion.

contrecoup (kawn-tr-ku′) [Fr. counter-blow]. Denoting the manner of a contrafissura, as in the skull, at a point opposite that at which the blow was received.

control′ [Mediev. L. *contrarotulum,* a counterroll for checking accounts, fr. L. *rotula,* dim. of *rota,* a wheel]. **1.** To verify an experiment by means of another with the crucial variable omitted. **2.** A standard against which experimental observations can be compared and evaluated. **3.** Regulation of maintenance of a function, action, reflex, etc.

birth c., (1) restriction of the number of offspring by means of contraceptive measures; (2) projects, programs, or methods to control reproduction by either improving or diminishing fertility.

quality c., c. of laboratory analytical error by monitoring analytical performance with control sera and maintaining error within ±2 SD of mean control values.

stimulus c., use of conditioning techniques to bring target behavior under environmental c.

contu′sion [L. *contusio,* a bruising]. **1.** Bruise (2); any injury caused by a blow in which the skin is not broken. **2.** Bruise (1).

co′nus, pl. **co′ni** [L. fr. G. *kōnos,* cone]. 1[NA]. Cone. **2.** Posterior staphyloma in myopic choroidopathy.

c. arterio′sus [NA], arterial cone; infundibulum (4); the left or anterior portion of the cavity of the right ventricle of the heart, which terminates in the pulmonary artery.

c. medulla′ris [NA], medullary cone; the tapering lower extremity of the spinal cord.

convalescence [L. *con-valesco,* to grow strong]. A period between the end of an illness, operation, or injury and the patient's recovery.

convalescent. Pertaining to convalescence.

convection [L. *con-veho,* pp. *-vectus,* to carry or bring together]. Conveyance of heat in liquids or gases by movement of the heated particles.

convergence [L. *con-vergo,* to incline together]. **1.** The tending of two or more objects toward a common point. **2.** The direction of the visual lines to a near point.

negative c., slight divergence of the visual axes when c. is at rest, as when looking at the far point of normal vision or during sleep.

positive c., inward deviation of the visual axes even when c. is at rest, as in cases of convergent squint.

convergent. Tending toward a common point.

conversion (kon-ver′zhun) [L. *con-verto,* pp. *-versus,* to turn around, to change]. **1.** Change; transmutation. **2.** Transformation of an emotion into a physical manifestation, as in hysteria. **3.** In virology, lysogenic c.; the acquisition, by bacteria, of a new property associated with presence of a prophage.

convertase C3. The complexed and activated fourth and second (C42a) components of complement that activate the third component (C3).

conver′tin. Factor VII.

convex [L. *convexus,* vaulted, arched, convex]. Applied to a surface that is evenly curved or bulging outward, the segment of a sphere.

convex′ocon′cave. Convex on one surface and concave on the opposite surface.

convex′ocon′vex. Biconvex.

convolution [L. *convolutio*]. **1.** A coiling or rolling of an organ by infolding upon itself. **2.** Specifically, a gyrus of the cerebral or cerebellar cortex.

convulsion [L. *convulsio,* fr. *con-vello,* pp. *-vulsus,* to tear up]. An involuntary spasm or series of jerkings of the muscles.

clonic c., a c. in which the contractions are intermittent, the muscles alternately contracting and relaxing.

febrile c., a c. in infancy or early childhood, associated with fever.

salaam c.'s, nodding *spasm.*

static c., saltatory *spasm.*

tonic c., one in which muscle contraction is sustained.

convulsive. Relating to convulsions; marked by or producing convulsions.

coordination (ko-or'dĭ-na'shun) [L. *co-*, together, + *ordino*, pp. *-atus*, to arrange, fr. *ordo(ordin-)*, arrangement, order]. A harmonious working together, especially of several muscles or muscle groups in the execution of complicated movements.

cope. In psychiatry and psychology, to confront a challenge, conflict, or anxiety with intent to resolve.

copper [L. cuprum, orig. *Cyprium*, after *Cyprus*, where mined]. A metallic element, symbol Cu, atomic no. 29, atomic weight 63.55; several cupric salts are used in medicine.

copremesis (kop-rem'ă-sis) [G. *kopros*, dung, + *emesis*]. Fecal *vomiting.*

copro- [G. *kopros*, dung]. Combining form denoting filth or dung, usually used in referring to feces. See also scato-, sterco-.

cop'roan'tibodies. Antibodies occurring in the intestinal content that are formed by plasma cells in the intestinal mucosa and consist chiefly of the IgA class.

coprolag'nia [copro- + G. *lagneia*, lust]. A form of sexual perversion in which the thought or sight of excrement causes pleasurable sensation.

coprola'lia [copro- + G. *lalia*, talk]. Involuntary utterance of vulgar or obscene words.

cop'rolith [copro- + G. *lithos*, stone]. Fecalith; stercolith; a hard mass consisting of inspissated feces.

coprol'ogy [copro- + G. *logos*, study]. Scatology (1).

copro'ma [copro- + G. *-ōma*, tumor]. Fecaloma; stercoroma; accumulation of inspissated feces in the colon or rectum giving the appearance of an abdominal tumor.

coprophagy (ko-prof'ă-jĭ) [copro- + G. *phagein*, to eat]. Scatophagy.

cop'rophil, coprophil'ic. 1. Denoting bacteria, protozoa, etc. occurring in fecal matter. 2. Relating to coprophilia.

coprophil'ia [copro- + G. *philos*, fond]. 1. Attraction of microorganisms for fecal matter. 2. In psychiatry, a morbid attraction to (with a sexual element) fecal matter.

copropho'bia [copro- + G. *phobos*, fear]. Morbid abhorrence of defecation and feces.

coproporphyrin (kop-ro-por'fi-rin). One of two porphyrin compounds found normally in feces as a decomposition product of bilirubin.

coprosta'sis [copro- + G. *stasis*, a standing]. Fecal impaction.

coprozoa (kop-ro-zo'ah) [copro- + G. *zōon*, animal]. Protozoa that can be cultivated in fecal matter, although not necessarily living in feces within the intestine.

coprozoic (kop-ro-zo'ik). Relating to coprozoa.

cop'ula [L. a bond, tie]. A narrow part connecting two structures.

copula'tion [L. *copulatio*, a joining]. 1. Coitus. 2. In protozoology, conjugation between two cells that do not fuse but separate after mutual fertilization.

coracoacromial (kor'ă-ko-ă-kro'mĭ-al). Acromiocoracoid; relating to the coracoid and acromial processes.

cor'acoclavic'ular. Scapuloclavicular (2); relating to the coracoid process and the clavicle.

cor'acohu'meral. Relating to the coracoid process and the humerus.

cor'acoid [G. *korakōdēs*, like a crow's beak]. Shaped like a crow's beak, denoting a process of the scapula.

cord-. For words beginning thus, not found here, see chord-.

cord [L. *chorda*, a string]. In anatomy, any long, ropelike structure.

false vocal c., *plica* vestibularis.

genital c., one of a pair of mesenchymal ridges bulging into the caudal part of the celom of a young embryo and connecting the mesonephric (wolffian) and paramesonephric or female (müllerian) duct.

gonadal c.'s, columns of germinal and follicle cells penetrating centripetally into the embryonic ovarian cortex.

spermatic c., *funiculus* spermaticus.

spinal c., *medulla* spinalis.

tendinous c.'s, *chordae* tendineae.

testicular c., *funiculus* spermaticus.

true vocal c., *plica* vocalis.

umbilical c., *funiculus* umbilicalis.

cor'date. Heart-shaped.

cordec'tomy [G. *chordē*, cord, + *ektomē*, excision]. Excision of a part or whole of a cord, as of a vocal cord.

cor'diform [L. *cor(cord-)*, heart, + *forma*, shape]. Heart-shaped.

cordopexy (kord'o-pek-sĭ) [G. *chordē*, cord, + *pēxis*, fixation]. Surgical fixation of a cord, as of one or both vocal cords for the relief of laryngeal stenosis.

cordot'omy [G. *chordē*, cord, + *tomē*, a cutting]. Chordotomy. 1. Any operation on the spinal cord. 2. Division of tracts of the spinal cord.

corecleisis, coreclisis (kor-e-kli'sis) [G. *korē*, pupil, + *kleisis*, a closing]. Occlusion of the pupil.

core-, coreo-, coro- [G. *korē*, pupil]. Combining forms relating to the pupil.

corecta'sia, corec'tasis [G. *korē*, pupil, + *ektasis*, a stretching out]. Pathologic dilation of the pupil.

corec'tomedial'ysis [G. *korē*, pupil, + *ektomē*, excision, + *dialysis*, a loosening]. A peripheral iridectomy to form an artificial pupil.

corecto'pia [G. *korē*, pupil, + *ektopos*, out of place]. Eccentric location of the pupil so that it is not in the center of the iris.

corelysis (ko-re-li'sis) [G. *korē*, pupil, + *lysis*, a loosening]. Loosening of adhesions between the capsule of the lens and the iris.

coremor'phosis [G. *korē*, pupil, + *morphōsis*, formation]. Formation of an artificial pupil.

coreo-. See core-.

cor'eoplasty [G. *korē*, pupil, + *plassō*, to form]. Coroplasty; Correction of a deformed or occluded pupil.

corepexy (kor-pek'sĭ) [G. *korē*, pupil, + *pēxis*, a fixing in place]. Corepraxy.

corepraxy (kor-prak'sĭ) [G. *korē*, pupil, + *praxis*, action]. Corepexy; an operation to centralize an eccentric pupil.

co'repres'sor. A homeostatic mechanism for regulating enzyme production in repressible enzyme systems; a molecule, usually a product of a specific enzyme pathway, that combines with inactive repressor (produced by a regulator gene) to form active repressor, which then attaches to an operator gene site and inhibits activity of the structure genes controlled by the operator.

cor, gen. **cordis** [L.] [NA]. Heart.

  c. adipo'sum, fatty heart (2).

  c. bilocula're, a heart in which the interatrial and interventricular septa are absent or incomplete.

  c. bovi'num, bucardia.

  c. pulmona'le, (1) **chronic c. p.,** hypertrophy of the right ventricle resulting from disease of the lungs; (2) **acute c. p.,** dilation and failure of the right side of the heart due to pulmonary embolism.

  c. triatria'tum, a heart with three atrial chambers, the left atrium being subdivided by a transverse septum with a single small opening which separates the openings of the pulmonary veins from the mitral valve.

  c. trilocula're, three-chambered heart due to absence of the interatrial or of the interventricular septum.

co'rium, pl. **co'ria** [L. skin, hide, leather] [NA]. Dermis; cutis vera; a superficial, thin layer that interdigitates with the epidermis, the stratum papillare, and a deeper thick layer of dense, irregular connective tissue, the stratum reticulare; contains blood and lymphatic vessels, nerves and nerve endings, glands, and, except for glabrous skin, hair follicles.

corn [L. *cornu*, horn, hoof]. Clavus.

  hard c., heloma durum; the usual form of c. over a toe joint.

  soft c., heloma molle; a c. formed by pressure between two toes, the surface being macerated and yellowish in color.

cor'nea [L. fem. of *corneus*, horny] [NA]. Transparent tissue constituting the anterior sixth of the outer wall of the eye.

  conical c., keratoconus.

cor'neal. Relating to the cornea.

corneosclera (kor'ne-o-skle'rah). The combined cornea and sclera when considered as forming the external coat of the eyeball.

cor'neoscle'ral. Pertaining to the cornea and sclera.

cor'neous [L. corneus, fr. *cornu*, horn]. Horny.

cornic'ulate [L. *corniculatus*, horned]. Resembling a horn or having horn-shaped appendages.

cornic'ulum [L. dim. of *cornu*, horn]. A cornu of small size.

cornifica'tion [L. *cornu*, horn, + *facio*, to make]. Keratinization.

cor'nu, gen. **cor'nus,** pl. **cor'nua** [L. horn, hoof]. A horn. **1** [NA]. Any structure resembling a horn in shape or composed of horny substance. **2.** the major subdivisions of the lateral ventricle in the cerebral hemisphere (frontal horn, occipital horn, temporal horn).

  c. ammo'nis, Ammon's *horn.*

  c. ante'rius [NA], anterior or ventral horn; **(1)** the anterior division of the lateral ventricle of the brain, extending forward from Monro's foramen; **(2)** the anterior or ventral gray column of the spinal cord in cross section.

  c. poste'rius [NA], posterior or dorsal horn; **(1)** the posterior or occipital division of the lateral ventricle of the brain, extending backward into the occipital lobe; **(2)** the posterior or dorsal gray column of the spinal cord in cross section.

cor'nua. Plural of cornu.

cor'nual. Relating to a cornu.

coro- [G. *korē*, pupil]. See core-.

coro'na, pl. **coro'nae** [L. garland, crown] [NA]. Crown (1); any structure, normal or pathologic, resembling or suggesting a crown or a wreath.

  c. glan'dis [NA], the prominent posterior border of the glans penis.

  c. radia'ta [NA], radiate crown; a fan-shaped fiber mass on the white matter of the cerebral cortex, composed of the widely radiating fibers of the internal capsule.

cor'onad. In a direction toward any corona.

cor'onal. Relating to a corona.

cor'onari'tis. Inflammation of coronary artery or arteries.

cor'onary [L. *coronarius*, fr. *corona*, a crown]. **1.** Relating to or resembling a crown. **2.** Encircling; denoting various anatomical structures, as the arteries of the heart; by extension, a heart attack.

Coronaviridae (kŏ-ro'nă-vīr'ĭ-de). A family of single-stranded RNA-containing viruses of medium size, some of which cause upper respiratory tract infections in man; they resemble myxoviruses except for the petal-shaped projections which give an impression of the solar corona. *Coronavirus* is the only recognized genus.

Coro'navi'rus. The single recognized genus in the family Coronaviridae.

coro'navi'rus. Any virus of the family Coronaviridae.

cor'oner [L. *corona*, a crown]. An official whose duty it is to investigate sudden, suspicious, or violent death to determine the cause; In some communities, the office has been replaced by that of medical examiner.

coronoidectomy (kor'on-oyd-ek'to-mĭ). Surgical removal of the coronoid process of the mandible.

cor'oplasty. Coreoplasty.

corot'omy. Iridotomy.

cor'pora. Plural of corpus.

corpo'real. Pertaining to the body, or to a corpus.

corpse [L. *corpus,* body]. Cadaver.

cor'pulence, cor'pulency [L. *corpulentia,* magnification of *corpus,* body]. Obesity.

cor'pus, gen. **cor'poris,** pl. **cor'pora** [L. body] [NA]. **1.** The human body, consisting of head, neck, trunk, and limbs. **2.** Any body or mass. **3.** The main part of an organ or other anatomical structure.

c. al'bicans [NA], albicans (2); a retrogressed c. luteum characterized by increasing cicatrization and shrinkage of the cicatricial core with a hyalinized lutein zone surrounding the central plug of scar tissue.

c. amygdaloi'deum [NA], amygdala (1); amygdaloid nucleus; a rounded mass of gray matter in the anterior portion of the temporal lobe of the cerebrum; its major efferent fiber connections are with the hypothalamus and mediodorsal nucleus of the thalamus; also reciprocally associated with the cortex of the temporal lobe.

c. amyla'ceum, pl. **cor'pora amyla'cea,** one of a number of small ovoid or rounded, sometimes laminated, bodies resembling a grain of starch and found in nervous tissue, in the prostate, and in pulmonary alveoli; apparently derived from degenerated cells or proteinaceous secretions.

c. callo'sum [NA], commissure of the cerebral hemispheres; the commissural plate of nerve fibers interconnecting the cortical hemispheres, with the exception of most of the temporal lobes which are interconnected by the anterior commissure.

c. caverno'sum clitor'idis [NA], cavernous body of the clitoris; one of the two parallel columns of erectile tissue forming the body of the clitoris.

c. caverno'sum pe'nis [NA], cavernous body of the penis; one of two parallel columns of erectile tissue forming the dorsal part of the body of the penis.

c. cilia're [NA], ciliary body; a thickened portion of the tunica vasculosa of the eye between the choroid and the iris; consists of three parts: orbiculus ciliaris, corona ciliaris, and musculus ciliaris.

c. coccy'geum [NA], coccygeal body; glomus coccygeum; an arteriovenous anastomosis supplied by the middle sacral artery and located on the pelvic surface of the coccyx.

c. fimbria'tum, *fimbria* hippocampi.

c. genicula'tum latera'le [NA], lateral geniculate body; the lateral one of a pair of small oval masses that protrude slightly from the posteroinferior aspects of the thalamus; its main (dorsal) subdivision serves as a processing station in the major pathway from the retina to the cerebral cortex, receiving fibers from the optic tract and giving rise to the geniculocalcarine radiation to the visual cortex in the occipital lobe.

c. genicula'tum media'le [NA], medial geniculate body; the medial one of a pair of prominent cell groups in the posteroinferior parts of the thalamus; it functions as the last of a series of processing stations along the auditory conduction pathway to the cerebral cortex, receiving the brachium of the inferior colliculus and giving rise to the auditory radiation to the auditory cortex in the superior temporal gyrus.

c. hemorrhag'icum, a c. luteum hematoma, the lining of which is formed by the thinned-out lutein zone; gradual resorption of the blood elements leave a cavity filled with a clear fluid (c. luteum cyst).

c. lu'teum, [NA], the yellow endocrine body formed in the ovary in the site of a ruptured ovarian follicle, immediately after ovulation. If pregnancy does not occur, it is called a **c. spurium,** which undergoes progressive retrogression to a c. albicans; in the event of pregnancy, the **c. verum** becomes even larger and persists to the fifth or sixth month of pregnancy before beginning to retrogress.

c. mamilla're [NA], mamillary body; a small, round, paired cell group that protrudes into the interpeduncular fossa from the inferior aspect of the hypothalamus; receives a major bundle of hippocampal fibers from the fornix and projects fibers to the anterior thalamic nuclei and into the tegmentum of the brainstem.

c. oliva're, oliva.

cor'pora paraaor'tica [NA], paraaortic bodies; organs of Zuckerkandl; small masses of chromaffin tissue found near the sympathetic ganglia along the abdominal aorta; more prominent during fetal life.

c. pinea'le [NA], pineal body or gland; conarium; a small, unpaired, flattened glandular structure attached to the region of the posterior and habenular commissures and lying in the depression between the two superior colliculi; despite its attachment to the brain, it appears to receive nerve fibers exclusively from the peripheral autonomic nervous system.

cor'pora quadrigem'ina, quadrigeminal bodies; the colliculus inferior and colliculus superior, together forming the lamina tecti mesencephali.

c. spongio'sum pe'nis [NA], the median column of erectile tissue located between the ventral to the two corpora cavernosa penis; posteriorly it expands into the bulbus penis and anteriorly it terminates as the enlarged glans penis.

c. spongio'sum ure'thrae mulie'bris, the submucous coat of the female urethra, containing a venous network that insinuates itself between the muscular layers, giving to them an erectile nature.

c. stria'tum [NA], striate body; the caudate and lentiform nuclei considered as one structure, a striate appearance on section being caused by slender fascicles of myelinated fibers.

c. ventric'uli [NA], body of the stomach; the part of the stomach that lies between the fundus above and the pyloric antrum below.

c. vit'reum [NA], vitreous (2); vitreum; vitreous or hyaloid body; a transparent jelly-like substance filling the interior of the eyeball behind the lens; composed of a delicate network enclosing in its meshes a watery fluid.

corpuscle (kor'pus-l) [L. *corpusculum*, dim. of *corpus*, body]. **1.** Corpusculum. **2.** A blood cell.

articular c.'s, *corpuscula* articularia.

bulboid c.'s, *corpuscula* bulboidea.

corneal c.'s, Virchow's cells (2); connective tissue cells found between the laminae of fibrous tissue in the cornea.

genital c.'s, *corpuscula* genitalia.

ghost c., achromocyte.

Golgi-Mazzoni c., an encapsulated sensory nerve ending similar to a pacinian c. but simpler in structure.

Hassall's concentric c.'s, thymus c.'s; small bodies of flattened epithelial cells arranged around a granular nucleated c., found in the medulla of the lobules of the thymus.

lamellated c.'s, *corpuscula* lamellosa.

lymph c., lymphatic c., lymphoid c., a mononuclear type of leukocyte formed in lymph nodes and other lymphoid tissue, and also in the blood.

malpighian c., (1) *corpusculum* renis; **(2)** *folliculus* lymphaticus lienalis.

Meissner's c., *corpusculum* tactus.

Merkel's c., *meniscus* tactus.

pacinian c.'s, *corpuscula* lamellosa.

phantom c., achromocyte.

Purkinje's c.'s, Purkinje's *cells.*

red c., erythrocyte.

renal c., *corpusculum* renis.

Ruffini's c.'s, sensory end-structures in the subcutaneous connective tissues of the fingers, consisting of an ovoid capsule within which the sensory fiber ends with numerous collateral knobs.

tactile c., *corpusculum* tactus.

thymus c., Hassall's concentric c.

white c., any type of leukocyte.

corpus'cular. Relating to a corpuscle.

corpus'culum, pl. **corpus'cula** [NA]. Corpuscle (1); a small mass or body.

corpus'cula articula'ria [NA], articular corpuscles; encapsulated nerve terminations within joint capsules.

corpus'cula bulboi'dea [NA], bulboid corpuscles; nerve terminals in skin, mouth, conjunctiva, and other parts; consist of a laminated capsule of connective tissue enclosing the terminal ending of an afferent nerve fiber.

corpus'cula genita'lia [NA], genital corpuscles; special encapsulated nerve endings found in the skin of the genitalia and nipple.

corpus'cula lamello'sa [NA], lamellated or pacinian corpuscles; small oval bodies in the skin of the fingers, in the mesentery, tendons, and elsewhere, formed of concentric layers of connective tissue with a soft core in which the axon of a nerve fiber runs, splitting up into a number of fibrils that terminate in bulbous enlargements: they are sensitive to pressure.

c. re'nis, pl. **corpus'cula re'nis** [NA], renal corpuscle; malpighian corpuscle (1); the tuft of glomerular capillaries and the capsula glomeruli that encloses it.

c. tac'tus, pl. **corpus'cula tac'tus** [NA], tactile or Meissner's corpuscle; one of numerous oval bodies found in the papillae of the corium, especially that of the fingers and toes; consists of a connective tissue capsule in which the axon fibrils terminate around and between epithelioid cells.

corrective [L. *cor-rigo(conr-*), pp. *-rectus,* to set right]. Counteracting, modifying, or changing what is undesirable or injurious.

correspondence. In optics, the point on each retina that has the same visual direction; when stimulated, a single image is seen.

anomalous c., a condition, frequent in strabismus, in which corresponding retinal points do not have the same visual direction; the fovea of one eye corresponds with an extrafoveal area of the fellow eye.

dysharmonious c., a type of anomalous retinal c. in which the angle of the visual direction of the two retinas is less than the objective angle of the strabismus.

harmonious c., a type of anomalous retinal c. in which the angle of the visual direction of the two retinas is equal to the objective angle of strabismus.

cor'rin [fr. *core(* of vitamin B_{12} molecule)]. The cyclic system of four pyrrole rings forming **corrinoids,** the central structure of the vitamins B_{12} and related compounds, differing from porphyrin in that two of the pyrrole rings are directly linked.

corro'sive. Causing gradual deterioration of a substance as by biochemical or chemical reaction.

corrugator [L. *cor-rugo(conr-*), pp. *-atus,* to wrinkle, fr. *ruga,* a wrinkle]. A muscle that draws together the skin, causing it to wrinkle.

cor'tex, gen. **cor'ticis,** pl. **cor'tices** [L. bark] [NA]. The outer portion of an organ as distinguished from the inner, or medullary, portion.

adrenal c., c. glandulae suprarenalis.

association c., association areas; expanses of the cerebral c. that are not sensory or motor in the customary sense, and instead are thought to be involved in advanced stages of sensory information processing, multisensory integration, or sensorimotor integration.

auditory c., auditory area; the region of the cerebral c. that receives auditory data from the medial geniculate body.

c. cerebel'li [NA], **cerebellar c.,** the thin gray surface layer of the cerebellum, consisting of an outer molecular layer (including a single layer of Purkinje cells, the ganglionic layer), and an inner granular layer.

c. cer'ebri [NA], cerebral c., the layer of gray matter covering the entire surface of the cerebral hemisphere, characterized by a laminar organization of its cellular and fibrous components such that its nerve cells are stacked in defined layers varying in number from one, as in the archicortex of the hippocampus, to five or six in the larger neocortex. From the surface inward, the layers are: molecular or plexiform layer, outer granular layer, pyramidal cell layer, inner granular layer, inner pyramidal layer (ganglionic layer), and multiform cell layer. This multilaminate organization is typical of the neocortex (homotypic c.; isocortex), which covers the largest part of the cerebral hemisphere; the more primordial heterotypic c. or allocortex has fewer cell layers. A form of c. intermediate between isocortex and allocortex, the juxtallocortex, covers the ventral part of the cingulate gyrus and the entorhinal area of the parahippocampal gyrus. On the basis of local differences in the arrangement of nerve cells (cytoarchitecture), areas in the cerebral c. can be classified in functional terms into three categories: motor c., having a poorly developed inner granular layer (agranular c.) and prominent pyramidal cell layers; sensory c., characterized by a prominent inner granular layer (granular c. or koniocortex) and comprising the somatic sensory c., auditory c., and visual c.; and association c., the vast remaining expanses of the cerebral c.

frontal c., frontal area; c. of the frontal lobe of the cerebral hemisphere.

c. glan'dulae suprarena'lis [NA], adrenal c.; the outer part of the adrenal gland, consisting of three zones: zona glomerulosa, zona fasciculata, and zona reticularis; yields various steroid hormones.

heterotypic c., allocortex. See c. cerebri.

homotypic c., isocortex. See c. cerebri.

motor c., motor, excitable, or Rolando's area; the region of the cerebral c. influencing movements of the face, neck and trunk, and arm and leg.

c. re'nis [NA], renal c., the part of the kidney containing the glomeruli and the proximal and distal convoluted tubules.

sensory c., formerly denoting specifically the somatic sensory c., but now referring collectively to the somatic sensory, auditory, visual, and olfactory regions of the cerebral c.

somatic sensory c., somatosensory c., the region of the cerebral c. receiving the somatic sensory data from the ventrobasal nucleus of the thalamus; represents the primary cortical processing mechanism for sensory information originating at the body surfaces and in deeper tissues.

visual c., visual area; the region of the cerebral c. occupying the entire surface of the occipital lobe and receiving the optic or visual data from the lateral geniculate body of the thalamus.

cor'tical. Relating to a cortex.

cor'tices. Plural of cortex.

corticifugal (kor-tĭ-sif'u-gal) [L. cortex, rind, bark, + fugio, to flee]. Passing in a direction away from the outer surface, especially nerve fibers conveying impulses away from the cerebral cortex.

corticipetal (kor-tĭ-sip'e-tal) [L. cortex, rind, bark, + peto, to seek]. Passing in a direction toward the outer surface, especially nerve fibers conveying impulses toward the cerebral cortex.

cor'ticobul'bar. Connecting cortex and motor cranial nuclei in the medulla.

cor'ticoid. A principle having an action similar to that of a steroid hormone of the adrenal cortex.

cor'ticolib'erin. Corticotropin-releasing hormone.

corticosteroid. (kor'tĭ-ko-stěr'oid). A steroid produced by the adrenal cortex; a corticoid containing steroid.

cortices'terone. $11\beta,21$-Dihydroxy-4-pregnene-3,20-dione; a steroid obtained from the adrenal cortex that induces some deposition of glycogen in the liver, sodium conservation, and potassium excretion.

corticotroph (kor'tĭ-ko-trof). A cell of the adenohypophysis that produces adrenocorticotropic hormone.

corticotro'pin, corticotro'phin [G. tropē, a turning; trophē, nourishment]. Adrenocorticotropic hormone.

cor'tisol. Hydrocortisone.

cortisone (kor'ti-son) [Hench's acronym for corticosterone]. $17\alpha,21$-Dihydroxy-4-pregnene-3,11,20 trione; a steroid isolated from the adrenal cortex that exhibits no biological activity until it is converted to hydrocortisone (cortisol); acts upon carbohydrate metabolism (glucocorticoid), and influences the nutrition and growth of connective (collagenous) tissues.

corusca'tion [L. corusco, to flash]. A subjective sensation of a flash of light before the eyes.

corymbiform (kŏ-rim'bĭ-form) [L. corymbus, cluster, garland]. Denoting the flower-like clustering configuration of skin lesions in granulomatous diseases.

Corynebacterium (kŏ-ri'ne-bak-tēr'ĭ-um) [G. coryne, a club, + bacterium, a small rod]. A genus of nonmotile, aerobic to anaerobic bacteria (family Corynebacteriaceae) containing irregularly staining Gram-positive rods. The type species, C. diphtheriae, the Klebs-Loeffler bacillus, causes diphtheria and produces a powerful exotoxin causing degeneration of various tissues.

coryza (kŏ-ri'zah) [G.]. Acute rhinitis.

cory'zavi'rus. See Rhinovirus.

cosme'sis [G. kosmēsis, an adorning]. A concern in therapeutics, especially in surgical operations, for the appearance of the patient.

cosmet'ic. 1. Relating to cosmesis. 2. Relating to the use of cosmetics.

cosmet'ics. Composite term for a variety of camouflages applied to the skin, hair, and nails for purposes of beautifying them in accordance with cultural dictates.

cosmopol'itan [G. *kosmos*, universe, + *polis*, city-state]. In the biological sciences, a term denoting worldwide distribution.

cos'ta, pl. **cos'tae** [L.]. 1[NA]. Rib; one of the 24 elongated curved bones forming the main portion of the bony wall of the chest. 2. Basal rod; a rodlike internal supporting organelle that runs along the base of the undulating membrane of certain flagellate parasites.

c. cervica'lis [NA], cervical rib; a supernumerary rib articulating with a cervical vertebra, usually the seventh, but not reaching the sternum anteriorly. See also cervical rib *syndrome.*

cos'tae fluitan'tes [NA], floating ribs; the two lower ribs on either side that are not attached anteriorly.

cos'tae spu'riae [NA], false ribs; the five lower ribs on either side that do not articulate directly with the sternum.

cos'tae ve'rae [NA], true ribs; the seven upper ribs on either side whose cartilages articulate directly with the sternum.

costal. Relating to a rib.

costal'gia [L. *costa*, rib, + G. *algos*, pain]. Pleurodynia.

costec'tomy [L. *costa*, rib, + G. *ektomē*, excision]. Excision of a rib.

costo- [G. *costa*, rib]. Combining form relating to the ribs.

costochondral (kos-to-kom'dral). Relating to the costal cartilages.

costochondritis (kos'to-kon-dri'tis) [costo- + G. *chondros*, cartilage, + *-itis*, inflammation]. Inflammation of one or more costal cartilages, characterized by pain of the anterior chest wall that may radiate.

costoclavic'ular. Relating to the ribs and the clavicle.

costocor'acoid. Relating to the ribs and the coracoid process of the scapula.

costogen'ic. Arising from a rib.

costoscap'ular. Relating to the ribs and the scapula.

costoscapula'ris. *Musculus* serratus anterior.

costoster'nal. Pertaining to the ribs and the sternum.

costoster'noplasty [costo- + G. *sternon*, chest, + *plassō*, to fashion]. Surgical correction of a malformation of the anterior chest wall.

costot'omy [costo- + G. *tomē*, a cutting]. Division of a rib.

costotransverse (kos-to-trans-vurs'). Relating to the ribs and the transverse processes of the vertebrae articulating with them.

cos'totransversec'tomy. Excision of a proximal portion of a rib and the articulating transverse process.

costover'tebral. Vertebrocostal (1); relating to the ribs and the bodies of the thoracic vertebrae with which they articulate.

costoxiphoid (kos-to-zi'foyd). Relating to the ribs and the xiphoid cartilage of the sternum.

cosyntropin (ko-sin-tro'pin). A synthetic corticotrophic agent, comprising the first 24 amino-acid residues of human ACTH, which sequence retains the full biologic activity of the complete ACTH; the remaining 15 residues differ among species and confer specific immunologic properties.

cothromb'oplas'tin. *Factor VII.*

cotransport (ko-trans'port). Transport of one substance across a membrane, coupled with the simultaneous transport of another substance across the same membrane in the same direction.

cotyle'don [G. *kotylēdon*, any cup-shaped hollow]. A unit of the placenta made up of trophoblastic cells, fibrous tissue, and abundant blood vessels, visible on the maternal surface as an irregularly shaped lobe circumscribed by depressed areas; fetal vessels traverse the villous structures and are in close contact with the maternal blood of the intervillous space where gaseous and metabolic exchange occurs.

cot'yloid [G. *kotylē*, a small cup, + *eidos*, appearance]. Cup-shaped; cuplike; relating to the cotyloid cavity or acetabulum.

couching [Fr. *coucher*, to lay down, to put to bed]. Abaissement; an outmoded operation for cataract, consisting in displacing the lens into the vitreous cavity out of the line of vision.

cough. 1. A sudden explosive forcing of air through the glottis, occurring immediately on opening of the previously closed glottis, and excited by mechanical or chemical irritation of the trachea or bronchi, or by pressure from adjacent structures. **2.** To force air through the glottis by a series of expiratory efforts.

dry c., a c. not accompanied by expectoration; a non-productive c.

productive c., a c. accompanied by expectoration.

reflex c., a c. excited reflexly by irritation in some distant part, as the ear or the stomach.

whooping c., pertussis.

coulomb (Q) (ku-lom') [C. A. de *Coulomb*, Fr. physicist, 1736–1806]. The amount of electricity delivered by a current of 1 ampere in 1 second; equal to 1/96,500 faraday.

count. An enumeration or accounting.

Addis c., quantitative enumeration of the red blood c., white blood c., and casts in a 12-hr urine specimen; used to follow the progress of known renal disease.

Arneth c., the percentage distribution of polymorphonuclear neutrophils, based on the number of lobes in the nuclei (from 1 to 5).

blood c., see *blood count.*

counter- [L. *contra*, against]. Combining form meaning opposite, opposed, against. See also contra-.

counter. A device that counts.

automated differential leukocyte c., an instrument using digital imaging or cytochemical techniques to differentiate leukocytes.

electronic cell c., an automatic blood cell c.; some types are capable of multiple simultaneous measurements on each blood sample, *e.g.*, leukocyte count, red cell count, hemoglobin, hematocrit, and red cell indices.

Geiger-Müller c., an instrument for measuring radioactivity by counting the emission of radioactive particles.

scintillation c., scintillascope; scintillator; an instrument used to detect radioactivity.

whole-body c., shielding and instrumentation, usually involving more than one detector, designed to evaluate the total-body burden of various gamma-emitting nuclides.

counterconditioning (kown'ter-kon-dish'un-ing). Any of a group of specific behavior therapy techniques in which a second conditioned response is instituted for the express purpose of counteracting or nullifying a previously conditioned or learned response.

coun'terexten'sion. Countertraction.

counterimmunoelectrophoresis (cown'ter-im'u-no-e-lek'tro-fo-re'sis). A modification of immunoelectrophoresis in which antigen and antibody, moving in opposite directions, form precipitates in the area between the cells where they meet in concentrations of optimal proportions.

coun'terincis'ion. A second incision adjacent to a primary incision.

counterir'ritant. 1. An agent that produces counterirritation. **2.** Relating to or producing counterirritation.

counterirrita'tion. Revulsion; irritation or mild inflammation of the skin produced to relieve an inflammation of the deeper structures.

coun'teropening. Contra-aperture; counterpuncture; a second opening made at the dependent part of an abscess or other cavity containing fluid, which is not draining satisfactorily through a previously made opening.

coun'terpuncture. Counteropening.

coun'tershock. An electric shock applied to the heart to terminate a disturbance of its rhythm.

coun'terstain. A second stain of different color, having affinity for tissues, cells, or parts of cells other than those taking the primary stain, used to render more distinct the parts taking the first stain.

countertraction. Counterextension; resistance, or back-pull, made to extension on a limb.

coun'tertransfer'ence. In psychoanalysis, the analyst's transference of his emotional needs and feelings toward the patient.

coun'tertrans'port. Transport of one substance across a membrane, coupled with the simultaneous transport of another substance across the same membrane in the opposite direction.

couple. To copulate; denoting especially performance of coitus by the lower animals.

coup'ling. Bigeminal rhythm; usually the result of the repeated pairing of a normal sinus beat with a ventricular extrasystole.

covalent (ko'va-lent). Denoting an interatomic bond characterized by the sharing of 2, 4, or 6 electrons.

cowper'ian. Relating to or described by William Cowper.

cowperi'tis. Inflammation of Cowper's gland.

coxa, pl. **coxae** [L]. **1.** Os coxae. **2**[NA]. Hip or hip joint.

c. mag'na, enlargement and deformation of femoral head; usually a sequela of avascular necrosis.

c. pla'na. Legg-Calvé-Perthes *disease.*

c. val'ga, alteration of the angle made by the axis of the femoral neck to the axis of the femoral shaft, the angle tending to approach 180° degrees.

c. va'ra, alteration in angulation of neck to shaft of femur so that it approaches 90° or less.

coxal'gia [L. *coxa,* hip, + G. *algos,* pain]. Coxodynia.

Coxiel'la [H.R. *Cox,* U.S. bacteriologist, *1907]. A genus of filterable parasitic bacteria (order Rickettsiales) containing small rod-shaped or coccoid, Gram-negative cells. The type species, *C. burnetii,* causes Q fever in man.

coxodyn'ia [L. *coxa,* hip, + G. *odynē,* pain]. Coxalgia; pain in the hip joint.

coxofem'oral. Relating to the hip bone and the femur.

cox'otuber'culo'sis. Tuberculous hip-joint disease.

coxsackievirus (kok-sak'ī-vi-rus) [*Coxsackie,* N.Y., where first isolated]. A group of picornaviruses included in the genus *Enterovirus* and responsible for a variety of symptoms and infections in man. They are divided antigenically into two groups (A and B), each of which includes a number of serological types.

CPAP Constant positive airway *pressure.*

CPPB Constant positive pressure *breathing.*

CPR Cardiopulmonary *resuscitation.*

cps Cycles per second.

CR Conditioned *reflex;* crown-rump *length.*

Cr Chromium; creatinine.

cradle (kra'dl). A frame used to keep the bedclothes from pressing on a fractured or wounded part.

cramp. 1. A painful spasm. **2.** A professional neurosis, qualified according to the occupation of the sufferer; *e.g.,* writer's c.

heat c.'s, muscle spasm induced by hard work in intense heat, accompanied by severe pain.

intermittent c., tetany.

crani-. See cranio-.

crania (kra'nī-ah). Plural of cranium.

craniad (kra'nī-ad). **1.** Cephalad. **2.** Situated nearer the head in relation to a specific reference point; opposite of caudad.

cranial (kra'nī-al). **1.** Cephalic; relating to the cranium or head. **2.** Superior.

craniectomy (kra-nī-ek'to-mī) [G. *kranion,* skull, + *ektomē,* excision]. Excision of a portion of the skull.

cranio-, crani- [G. *kranion,* skull]. Combining forms denoting relation to the cranium.

craniocele (kra'nī-o-sēl) [cranio- + G. *kēlēo,* hernia]. Encephalocele.

craniocerebral (kra'nĭ-o-sĕr'e-bral). Relating to the skull and the brain.

craniocleidodysostosis (kra'nĭ-o-kil'do-dis-os-to'sis) [cranio- + G. *kleis,* clavicle, + dysostosis]. Cleidocranial *dysostosis.*

craniofacial (kra'nĭ-o-fa'shal). Relating to both the face and the cranium.

cra'niofenes'tria [cranio- + L. *fenestra,* window]. Craniolacunia; incomplete formation of the bones of the vault of the fetal skull so that there are nonossified areas in the calvarium.

craniolacunia (kra'nĭ-o-lă-ku'nĭ-ah) [cranio- + L. *lacuna,* cleft, + *-ia,* condition]. Craniofenestria.

craniomalacia (kra'nĭ-o-mal-a'shĭ-ah) [cranio- + G. *malakia,* softness]. Softening of the bones of the skull.

craniopathy (kran-ĭ-op'ă-thĭ) [cranio- + G. *pathos,* suffering]. Any pathological condition of the cranial bones.

    metabolic c., Morgagni's *syndrome.*

craniopharyngeal (kra'nĭ-o-fă-rin'je-al). Relating to the cavity of the skull and to the pharynx.

craniopharyngioma (kra'nĭ-o-fărin-jĭ-o'mah). A neoplasm, usually cystic, that develops from the nests of epithelium derived from Rathke's pouch.

cra'nioplasty [cranio- + G. *plassō,* to form]. Operative repair of a defect or deformity of the skull.

cra'niopunc'ture. Surgical puncture of the skull.

craniorrhachischisis (kra'nĭ-o-ră-kis'kĭ-sis) [cranio- + G. *rhachis,* spine, + *schisis,* a cleaving]. Congenitally unclosed skull and spinal column.

cra'niosa'cral. Denoting the cranial and sacral origins of the parasympathetic division of the autonomic nervous system.

cranioschisis (kra-nĭ-os'kĭ-sis) [cranio- + G. *schisis,* a cleavage]. Congenital failure of the skull to close mid-dorsally, usually accompanied by grossly defective development of the brain.

craniosclerosis (kra'nĭ-o-skle-ro'sis) [cranio- + G. *skleros,* hard, + *-osis,* condition]. Thickening of the skull.

cra'niospi'nal. Relating to the cranium and spinal column.

cra'niosteno'sis [cranio- + G. *stenōsis,* a narrowing]. Premature closure of cranial sutures resulting in malformation of the skull.

craniosynostosis (kra'nĭ-o-sin'os-to'sis) [cranio- + synostosis]. Premature ossification of the skull and obliteration of the sutures.

craniotabes (kra'nĭ-o-ta'bēz) [cranio- + L. *tabes,* a wasting]. A disease marked by the presence of areas of thinning and softening in the bones of the skull, usually of symphilitic or rachitic origin.

craniotomy (kra-nĭot'o-mĭ) [cranio- + G. *tomē,* incision]. Opening into the skull, either by creation of a bone flap or by trephination.

craniotympanic (kra'nĭ-o-tim-pan'ik). Relating to the skull and the middle ear.

cranium, pl. **crania** (kra'nĭum, ah) [Mediev. L. fr. G. *kranion*] [NA]. Skull; the bones of the head

collectively. In a more limited sense, the brain pan, the bony case containing the brain, excluding the bones of the face.

CRD Chronic respiratory *disease.*

cream (krēm) [L. *cremor,* thick juice, broth]. **1.** The upper fatty layer which forms in milk on standing or which is separated from it by centrifugalization; contains about the same amount of sugar and protein as milk, but from 12 to 40% more fat. **2.** A semisolid emulsion of either the oil-in-water or the water-in-oil type, ordinarily intended for topical use.

crease (krēs). See fold.

creatinase (kre'ă-tĭ-nās). An enzyme catalyzing the hydrolysis of creatine to sarcosine and urea.

creatine (kre'ă-tēn, -tin). *N*-(Aminoiminomethyl)-*N*-methylglycine; occurs in urine, generally as creatinine, and in muscle generally as phosphocreatine.

    c. kinase, an enzyme catalyzing the transfer of phosphate from phosphocreatine to ADP, forming creatine and ATP; of importance in muscle contraction.

    c. phosphate, Phosphocreatine.

creatinemia (kre-ă-tĭ-ne'mĭ-ah) [creatine + G. *haima,* blood]. Abnormal concentrations of creatine in peripheral blood.

creatininase (kre-at'ĭ-nin-ās). An amidohydrolase catalyzing the conversion of creatine to creatinine, with participation of ATP.

creatinine (Cr) (kre-at'ĭ-nēn, -nin). A component of urine and the final product of creatine catabolism; formed by the dephosphorylative cyclization of phosphocreatine to form the internal anhydride of creatine.

creatinuria (kre-ă-tĭ-nu'rĭ-ah) [creatine + G. *ouron,* urine]. Urinary excretion of increased amounts of creatine.

cremasteric (kre-mas-tĕr'ik) [G. *kremastēr,* a suspender]. Relating to the cremaster muscle.

cremnocele (krem'no-sēl) [G. *krēmnos,* overhanging cliff + *kēlē,* hernia]. Labial hernia; a protrusion of intestine into a labium majus.

crena, pl. **crenae** (kre'nah, kre'ne) [L. a notch] [NA]. A notch; a cleft; one of the notches into which the opposing projections fit in the cranial sutures.

cre'nate, cre'nated [L. *crena,* a notch]. Notched; indented; denoting the outline of a shriveled red blood cell, as observed in a hypertonic solution.

crenocyte (kre'no-sit) [L. *crena,* a notch, + G. *kytos,* a hollow (cell)]. A red blood cell with serrated, notched edges.

crep'itant. Relating to or characterized by crepitation.

crepita'tion [L. *crepitus, q.v.*]. Crepitus (1). **1.** Crackling; the quality or sound of a rale which resembles noise heard on rubbing hair between the fingers. **2.** The sensation felt on placing the hand over the seat of a fracture when the broken ends of the bone are moved, or over tissue, in which gas gangrene is present. **3.** Noise or vibration produced by rubbing bone or irregular cartilage surfaces together as by movement of patella against femoral condyles in arthritis and other conditions.

crepitus (krep′ĭ-tus) [L. fr. *crepo*, to rattle]. **1.** Crepitation. **2.** A noisy discharge of gas from the intestine.

crescent (kres′ent) [L. *cresco*, pp. *cretus*, to grow]. **1.** A shape like that of the moon in its first quarter; a demilune or meniscus. **2.** The figure made by the gray columns or cornua on cross-section of the spinal cord.

    malarial c., sickle form; the male or female gametocyte(s) of *Plasmodium falciparum*, whose presence in human red blood cells is diagnostic of falciparum malaria.

    myopic c., a white or grayish white crescentic area in the fundus of the eye to the temporal side of the optic disk, due to atrophy of the choroid, permitting the sclera to become visible.

crescentic (kres-sen′tik). Shaped like a crescent.

cre′sol red. An acid-base indicator with pK value of 8.3; yellow at pH values below 7.4, red above 9.0.

crest [L. *cresta*]. A ridge, especially a bony ridge. See also crista.

    ampullary c., *crista* ampullaris.

    anterior lacrimal c., *crista* lacrimalis anterior.

    ethmoidal c., *crista* ethmoidalis.

    external occipital c., *crista* occipitalis externa.

    frontal c., *crista* frontalis.

    iliac c., *crista* iliaca.

    infratemporal c., *crista* infratemporalis.

    internal occipital c., *crista* occipitalis interna.

    intertrochanteric c., *crista* intertrochanterica.

    nasal c., *crista* nasalis.

    neural c., a band of neuroectodermal cells that lie dorsolateral to the developing spinal cord, where they separate into clusters of cells that develop into dorsal-root ganglion cells, autonomic ganglion cells, chromaffin cells of the adrenal medulla, neurolemmal cells (Schwann cells), or integumentary pigment cells.

    obturator c., *crista* obturatoria.

    palatine c., *crista* palatina.

    posterior lacrimal c., *crista* lacrimalis posterior.

    pubic c., *crista* pubica.

    sacral c., *crista* sacralis.

    sphenoid c., *crista* sphenoidalis.

    supramastoid c., *crista* supramastoidea.

    supraventricular c., *crista* supraventricularis.

    tibial c., *margo* anterior tibiae.

    urethral c., *crista* urethralis.

    vestibular c., *crista* vestibuli.

cresyl blue (brilliant) (kres′il). $C_{17}H_{20}N_3OCl$; a basic oxazin dye used for staining the reticulum in young erythrocytes; also used in vital staining.

cre′tin [Fr. *crétin*]. An individual exhibiting cretinism.

cre′tinism. Infantile hypothyroidism; congenital myxedema; stunting of bodily growth and of mental development that may arise from thyroid agenesis or inadequate maternal intake of iodine during gestation.

cre′tinoid. Resembling a cretin; presenting symptoms similar to those of cretinism.

cre′tinous. Relating to cretinism or a cretin.

crevice (krev′is) [Fr. *crevasse*]. A crack or small fissure, especially in a solid substance.

    gingival c., subgingival space; the space between the surface of a tooth and the free gingiva.

crevicular (krĕ-vik′u-lar). Relating to a crevice, especially the gingival crevice.

CRH Corticotropin-releasing *hormone*.

cribra (kri′brah, krib′rah). Plural of cribrum.

crib′rate. Cribriform.

cribra′tion. The condition of being numerously pitted or perforated.

crib′riform [L. *cribrum*, a sieve, + *forma*, form]. Cribrate; polyporous; sievelike; containing many perforations.

cribrum, pl. **cribra** (kri′brum, krib′rum; -brah) [L. a sieve]. *Lamina* cribrosa ossis ethmoidalis.

cricoarytenoid (kri′ko-ăr-ĭ-te′noyd). Relating to the cricoid and arytenoid cartilages.

cricoid (kri′koyd) [L. *cricoideus*, fr. G. *krikos*, a ring, + *eidos*, form]. Ring-shaped; denoting the c. cartilage.

cricoidectomy (kri′koy-dek′to-mĭ) [cricoid + G. excision]. Excision of the cricoid cartilage.

cricopharyngeal (kri′ko-fă-rin′je-al). Relating to the cricoid cartilage and the pharynx.

cricothyroid (kri-ko-thi′royd). Relating to the cricoid and thyroid cartilages.

cricothyrotomy (kri′ko-thi-rot′o-mĭ) [cricoid + thyroid + G. *tomē*, incision]. Intercricothyrotomy; inferior laryngotomy; incision through the skin and cricothyroid membrane for relief of respiratory obstruction; used prior to tracheotomy in certain emergency respiratory obstructions.

cricotomy (kri-kot′o-mĭ) [cricoid + G. *tomē*, incision]. Division of the cricoid cartilage.

crinogenic (krin′o-jen′ik) [G. *krinō*, to separate, + -*gen*, to produce]. Causing secretion; stimulating a gland to increased function.

crinophagy (krin-of′ă-jĭ). Disposal of excess secretory granules by lysosomes.

crisis, pl. **crises** (kri′sis, -sēz) [G. *krisis*, separation, crisis]. **1.** Sudden change, usually for the better, in the course of an acute disease, in contrast to the gradual improvement by lysis. **2.** Paroxysmal pain in an organ or circumscribed region of the body occurring in the course of tabes dorsalis.

    addisonian c., adrenal c., acute adrenocortical *insufficiency.*

    Dietl's c., paroxysmal attacks of lumbar and abdominal pain with nausea and vomiting resulting from kinking of the ureter in persons with wandering kidney.

    identity c., a disorientation concerning one's sense of self and role in society, often of acute onset and related to a particular and significant event in one's life.

sickle cell c., protean acute symptoms developing recurrently in patients with sickle cell anemia; caused by vascular occlusion or hemolysis and may follow infection, dehydration, or hypoxia from blood loss or high altitudes.

therapeutic c., a turning point leading to positive or negative change in psychiatric treatment.

thyrotoxic c., thyroid c., thyroid storm; the exacerbation of symptoms that occurs in thyrotoxicosis following shock or injury or after thyroidectomy.

crista, pl. **cristae** (kris'tah, kris'te) [L. crest] [NA]. A ridge, crest, or elevated line projecting from a level or evenly rounded surface. See also **crest.**

c. ampulla'ris [NA], ampullary crest; an elevation on the inner surface of the ampulla of each semicircular duct; filaments of the vestibular nerve pass through to reach hair cells on its surface.

cristae cu'tis [NA], epidermal or skin ridges; ridges of the epidermis of the palms and soles, where the sweat pores open.

c. ethmoida'lis [NA], ethmoidal crest; nasal concha; (1) a ridge on the upper part of the nasal surface of the maxilla that gives attachment to the anterior portion middle nasal concha; (2) a ridge on the medial surface palatine bone to which the middle nasal concha attaches posteriorly.

c. fronta'lis [NA], frontal crest; a ridge arising at the termination of the sagittal sulcus on the cerebral surface of the frontal bone and ending at the foramen caecum.

c. gal'li [NA], the triangular midline process of the ethmoid bone extending upward from the cribriform plate and giving attachment to the falx cerebri.

c. ilia'ca [NA], iliac crest; the long, curved upper border of the ilium.

c. infratempora'lis [NA], infratemporal crest; a rough ridge marking the angle of union of the temporal and infratemporal surfaces of the greater wing of the sphenoid bone.

c. intertrochanter'ica [NA], intertrochanteric crest; the rounded ridge that connects the greater and lesser trochanters of the femur posteriorly and marks the junction of the neck and shaft of the bone.

c. lacrima'lis ante'rior [NA], anterior lacrimal crest; a vertical ridge on the lateral surface of the frontal process of the maxilla that forms part of the medial margin of the orbit.

c. lacrima'lis poste'rior [NA], posterior lacrimal crest; a vertical ridge on the orbital surface of the lacrimal bone which, together with the anterior lacrimal crest, bounds the fossa for the lacrimal sac.

c. media'lis [NA], medial crest; a ridge of bone, on the posterior surface of the fibula, separating the attachment of the posterior tibial muscle from that of the flexor hallucis longus and soleus muscles.

c. nasa'lis [NA], nasal crest; the midline ridge in the floor of the nasal cavity, formed by the union of the paired maxillae and palatine bones, to which the vomer is attached.

c. obtura'ria [NA], obturator crest; a ridge that extends from the pubic tubercle to the acetabular notch, giving attachment to the pubofemoral ligament of the hip joint.

c. occipita'lis exter'na [NA], external occipital crest; a ridge extending from the external occipital protuberance to the border of the foramen magnum.

c. occipita'lis inter'na [NA], internal occipital crest; a ridge running from the internal occipital protuberance to the posterior margin of the foramen magnum, giving attachment to the falx cerebelli.

c. palati'na [NA], palatine crest; a transverse ridge near the posterior border of the bony palate, located on the inferior surface of the horizontal lamina of the palatine bone.

c. pu'bica [NA], pubic crest; the rough anterior border of the body of the pubis, continuous laterally with the pubic tubercle.

c. sacra'lis [NA], sacral crest; one of five rough irregular ridges on the posterior surface of the sacrum; the unpaired **c. sacralis mediana** is formed by the fused spinous processes of the upper four sacral vertebrae; the **cristae sacrales intermediae** are formed by the fusion of articular processes of all the sacral vertebrae; the **cristae sacrales laterales,** rough ridges lying lateral to the sacral foramina, represent the fused transverse processes of sacral vertebrae.

c. sphenoida'lis [NA], sphenoid crest; a vertical ridge in the midline of the anterior surface of the sphenoid bone that articulates with perpendicular plate of the ethmoid bone.

c. supramastoi'dea [NA], supramastoid crest; the ridge that forms the posterior root of the zygomatic process of the temporal bone.

c. supraventricula'ris [NA], supraventricular crest; the internal muscular ridge that separates the conus arteriosus from the remaining part of the cavity of the right ventricle of the heart.

c. urethra'lis [NA], urethral crest; (1) in the female, a conspicuous longitudinal fold of mucosa on the posterior wall of the urethra; (2) in the male, a longitudinal fold on the posterior wall of the urethra extending from the uvula of the bladder through the prostatic urethra.

c. vestib'uli [NA], vestibular crest; an oblique ridge on the inner wall of the vestibule of the labyrinth, bounding the spherical recess above and posteriorly.

crithid'ia [Mod. L. fr. G. *krithidion,* dim. of *krithē,* a barley]. Stage of development of certain flagellate parasites of vertebrates in the insect host, such as the multiplying form of the agent of African sleeping sickness in the tsetse fly host, or the agent of Chagas disease in the triatomine bug.

CRL Crown-rump *length.*

cross'bite. An abnormal relation of one or more teeth of one arch to the opposing tooth or teeth of the other arch due to labial, buccal, or lingual deviation of tooth position, or to abnormal jaw position.

cross-eye. Alternative spelling for crossed *eyes.*

crossing-over of genes. The reciprocal exchange of material between two paired chromosomes during meiosis, resulting in the transfer of a block of genes from each chromosome to its homologue.

cross-matching, crossmatching. 1. A test for incompatibility between donor and recipient blood, carried out prior to transfusion to avoid potentially lethal hemolytic reactions between the donor's red blood cells and antibodies in the recipient's plasma, or the reverse; incompatibility is indicated by clumping of red blood cells and contraindicates use of the donor's blood. **2.** In allotransplantation of solid organs, a test for identification of antibody in the serum of potential allograft recipients which reacts directly with the lymphocytes or other cells of a potential allograft donor; presence of antibodies usually contraindicates the transplantation.

croup (kroop) [Scots, probably from A.S. *kropan,* to cry aloud]. **1.** Laryngotracheobronchitis in infants and young children caused by parainfluenza virus types 1 and 2. **2.** Any affection of the larynx in children, characterized by difficult and noisy respiration and a hoarse cough.

croupous (kroo'pus). Relating to croup; marked by a fibrinous exudation.

crowd'ing. A condition in which the teeth are crowded, assuming altered positions such as bunching, overlapping, displacement in various directions, torsiversion, etc.

crown [L. *corona*]. **1.** Corona. **2.** In dentistry, that part of a tooth that is covered with enamel or an artificial substitute for that part.

　c. of the head, the topmost part of the head.

　radiate c., *corona* radiata.

crown'ing. 1. Preparation of the natural crown of a tooth and covering the prepared crown with a veneer of suitable dental material. **2.** That stage of childbirth when the fetal head has negotiated the pelvic outlet and the largest diameter of the head is encircled by the vulvar ring.

CRP Cross-reacting protein. See CAP.

cruces (kru'sēz). Plural of crux.

cruciate (kru'shi-at) [L. *cruciatus*]. Shaped like, or resembling, a cross.

crura (kru'rah). Plural of crus.

crural (kru'ral). Relating to the leg or thigh, or to any crus.

crus, gen. **cruris,** pl. **crura** (krŭs, kru'ris, -rah) [L.] [NA]. **1.** The leg, that part between the knee and the ankle. **2.** Any anatomical structure resembling a leg; in the plural, a pair of diverging bands or elongated masses.

　c. cer'ebri [NA], cerebral peduncle; the massive bundle of corticofugal nerve fibers passing longitudinally over the ventral surface of the midbrain on each side of the midline.

　c. clitor'idis [NA], **c. of the clitoris,** the continuation on each side of the corpus cavernosum of the clitoris which diverges from the body posteriorly and is attached to the pubic arch.

　cru'ra diaphrag'matia [NA], **crura of the diaphragm,** the muscular origins of the diaphragm from the bodies of the upper lumbar vertebrae that pass the aorta upward to the central tendon.

　c. for'nicis [NA], **c. of the fornix,** that part of the fornix that rises in a forward curve behind the thalamus to continue forward as the corpus fornicis below the corpus callosum.

　c. pe'nis [NA], **c. of penis,** the posterior portion of the corpus cavernosum penis attached to the ischiopubic ramus.

crust [L. *crusta*]. **1.** An outer layer or covering. **2.** A scab.

　milk c., seborrhea of the scalp in an infant.

crutch [A. S. *cryce*]. A device used singly or in pairs to assist in walking, when the act is impaired, by transferring weight-bearing to the upper extremity.

crux, pl. **cru'ces** (kruks, kru'sēz) [L.]. Cross.

　c. of the heart, the area of junction of the walls of the four chambers of the heart.

　cru'ces pilo'rum [NA], crosslike figures formed by hairs growing from two directions that meet and then separate in a direction perpendicular to the original orientation.

cry-. See cryo-.

cryalgesia (kri-al-je'zĭ-ah) [G. *kryos,* cold, + *algos,* pain]. Crymodynia; pain caused by cold.

cryanesthesia (kri'an-es-the'zĭ-ah) [G. *kryos,* cold, + *an-* priv, + *aisthēsis,* sensation]. Loss of sensation of perception of cold.

cryesthesia (kri-es-the'zĭ-ah) [G. *kryos,* cold, + *aisthēsis,* sensation]. **1.** Subjective sensation of cold. **2.** Sensitivity to cold.

crymo- [G. *krymos,* cold]. Combining form relating to cold.

crymodynia (kri-mo-din'ĭ-ah) [crymo- + G. *odynē,* pain]. Cryalgesia.

crymophilic (kri-mo-fil'ik) [crymo- + G. *philos,* fond]. Cryophilic; preferring cold; denoting microorganisms which grow best at low temperatures.

crymophylactic (kri'mo-fī-lak'tik) [crymo- + G. *phylaxis,* a guarding against]. Cryophylactic; resistant to cold; said of certain microorganisms which are not destroyed even by freezing temperatures.

crymother'apy. Cryotherapy.

cryo-, cry- [G. *kryos,* cold]. Combining form relating to cold.

cryoanesthesia (kri'o-an-es-the'zĭ-ah). Refrigeration anesthesia; localized application of cold as means of producing regional anesthesia.

cryocautery (kri'o-kaw-ter-ĭ). Any substance or a low temperature instrument that causes destruction of tissue by freezing.

cry'oextrac'tion. Removal of cataract by using a cryoprobe to extract the lens by freezing contact.

cryofibrinogen (kri'o-fi-brin'o-jen). An abnormal type of fibrinogen rarely found in human plasma; precipitated upon cooling, but redissolves when warmed to room temperature.

cry'ofibrin'ogene'mia. Presence in the blood of cryofibrinogens.

cryogenic (kri-o-jen'ik) [cryo- + G. -gen, producing]. Producing, or relating to the production of, low temperatures.

cryoglob'ulin. Abnormal plasma proteins (paraproteins) characterized by precipitating, gelling, or crystallizing when serum or solutions of them are cooled; distinguished from Bence Jones proteins by their larger molecular weight.

cry'oglobuline'mia. Presence of abnormal quantities of cryoglobulin in the blood plasma.

cryolysis (kri-ol'ĭ-sis) [cryo- + G. lysis, dissolution]. Destruction by cold.

cryopathy (kri-op'ă-thĭ) [cryo- + G. pathos, suffering]. A condition in which exposure to cold is an important factor.

cryopexy (kri'o-pek-sĭ) [cryo- + G. pēxis, a fixing in place]. In retinal separation surgery, sealing the sensory retina to the pigment epithelium and choroid by a cryoprobe applied to the sclera.

cryophilic (kri-o-fil'ik) [cryo- + G. philos, fond]. Crymophilic.

cry'ophylac'tic. Crymophylactic.

cry'oprecip'itate. Precipitate that forms when soluble material is cooled, especially that formed in normal blood plasma which has been subjected to cold precipitation and which is rich in factor VIII.

cry'oprobe. An extremely cold instrument used in cryosurgery.

cryopro'tein. A protein that precipitates from solution when cooled and redissolves upon warming.

cryoscopy (kri-os'ko-pĭ) [cryo- + G. skopeō, to examine]. Determination of the freezing point of a fluid, usually blood or urine, compared with that of distilled water.

cry'osur'gery. An operation in which decreased temperature is used.

cry'otherapy. Crymotherapy; the use of cold in the treatment of disease.

cry'otol'erant. Tolerant of very low temperatures.

crypt-. See crypto-.

crypt [L. crypta, fr. G. kryptos, hidden]. A pitlike depression or tubular recess.

   dental c., the space filled by the dental follicle.

   enamel c., the narrow, mesenchymally filled space between the dental lodge and an enamel organ.

   c.'s of the iris, pits near the pupillary margin of the anterior surface of the iris.

   Lieberkühn's c.'s, glandulae intestinales.

   Morgagni's c.'s, sinus anales.

   synovial c., a diverticulum of the synovial membrane of a joint.

   tonsillar c., one of the variable number of deep recesses that extend into the palatine and pharyngeal tonsils.

cryptectomy (krip-tek'to-mĭ) [crypt, + G. ektomē, excision]. Excision of a tonsillar or other crypt.

cryptesthesia (krip-tes-the'zĭ-ah) [G. kryptos, concealed, + aisthesis, sensation, perception]. Subconscious perception; intuition; awareness of facts or occurrences not ordinarily perceptible to the senses.

cryptic (krip'tik) [G. kryptikos]. Hidden; occult.

crypti'tis. Inflammation of a follicle or glandular tubule, particularly in the rectum.

crypto-, crypt- [G. kryptos, hidden, concealed]. Combining form relating to a crypt, or meaning hidden, obscure, without apparent cause.

cryptococcosis (krip'to-kok-o'sis). Busse-Buschke disease; an acute, subacute, or chronic infection by Cryptococcus neoformans, causing a pulmonary, systemic, or meningeal mycosis.

Cryptococcus (krip-to-kok'us) [crypto- + G. kokkos, berry]. A genus of yeastlike fungi that reproduce by budding. C. neoformans is a species that causes cryptococcosis.

cryptogen'ic [crypto- + G. genesis, origin]. Of obscure, indeterminate etiology or origin.

cryp'tolith [crypto- + G. lithos, stone]. A concretion in a gland follicle.

cryptomenorrhea (krip'to-men-o-re'ah) [crypto- + G. mēn, month, + rhoia, flow]. Occurrence each month of the general symptoms of the menses without any flow of blood, as in cases of imperforate hymen.

cryptomerorachischisis (krip'to-me'ro-ră-kis'kĭ-sis) [crypto- + G. meros, part, + rachis, spine, + schisis, cleavage]. Spina bifida occulta.

cryptophthalmia, cryptophthalmus (krip-tof-thal'mĭ-ah, -thal'mus) [crypto- + G. ophthalmos, eye]. Congenital absence of eyelids with skin passing continuously from forehead onto cheek over a rudimentary eye.

cryptopo'dia [crypto- + G. pous, foot]. Swelling of the lower part of the leg and the foot, in such a way that there is great distortion and the sole seems to be a flattened pad.

cryptorchidectomy (krip'tor-kĭ-dek'o-mĭ) [crypto- + G. orchis, testis, + ektomē, excision]. Surgical removal of an undescended testis.

cryptorchidism (krip-tor'kĭ-dizm). Cryptorchism.

cryptorchidopexy (krip-tor'kĭdo-pek-sĭ) [crypto- + G. orchis, testis, + pēxis, fixation]. Orchiopexy.

cryptorchism (krip-tor'kizm). Cryptorchidism; failure of descent of a testis.

cryp'tosporidio'sis. Infection with members of the genus Cryptosporidium, characterized by chronic protracted diarrhea.

Cryp'tosporid'ium. A genus of parasitic coccidian sporozoans (family Cryptosporiidae, suborder Eimeriina) that infect epithelial cells of the gastrointestinal tract in vertebrates and flourish under conditions of intense immunosuppression in man.

cryptozygous (krip-toz'ĭ-gus) [crypto- + G. zygon, yoke]. Having a narrow face as compared with the width of the cranium, so that, when the skull is viewed from above, the zygomatic arches are not visible.

crystal (kris'tal) [G. *krystallos*, clear ice, crystal]. A solid of regular shape and, for a given compound, characteristic angles, formed when an element or compound solidifies.

blood c's, hematoidin.

Charcot-Leyden c.'s, c's in the shape of elongated double pyramids, formed from eosinophils, found in the sputum in bronchial asthma and in other exudates or transudates containing eosinophils.

Virchow's c.'s, hematoidin frequently observed in extravasated blood in tissues.

crys'tallin. A globulin in the lens of the eye.

crys'talline. **1.** Clear; transparent. **2.** Relating to a crystal or crystals.

crys'talliza'tion. Assumption of a crystalline form when a vapor or liquid becomes solidified, or a solute precipitates from solution.

crys'talloid. **1.** Resembling a crystal, or being such. **2.** A body which in solution can pass through a semipermeable membrane, as distinguished from a colloid, which cannot do so.

crystalluria (kris'tal-lu'rī-ah). Excretion of crystalline materials in the urine.

crystal violet. A dye that, as variable mixtures of c.v., gentian violet, or methyl violet B, can be tetra-, penta-, and hexamethyl-*p*-rosanilin; used to treat burns, wounds, fungal infections of skin and mucous membranes, pinworm, and certain fluke infections, and as a stain in histology.

Cs Cesium.

CSF Cerebrospinal *fluid.*

CT Computed *tomography.*

Ctenocephalides (te'no-sef-al'ī-dēz) [G. *ktenodēs,* like a cockle, + *kephalē,* head]. A genus of fleas. *C. canis* (dog flea) and *C. felis* (cat flea) are ectoparasites of household pets.

CTP Cytidine 5'-triphosphate.

Cu Copper (cuprum).

cubital (ku'bĭ-tal). Relating to the elbow or to the ulna.

cubitus, pl. **cubiti** (ku'bĭ-tus, -ti) [L. elbow] [NA]. **1.** Elbow (1). **2.** Ulna.

c. val'gus, deviation of the extended forearm to the outer (radial) side of the axis of the limb.

c. va'rus, deviation of the extended forearm to the inward (ulnar) side of the axis of the limb.

cuboid, cuboidal (ku'boyd, ku-boy'dal) [G. *kybos,* cube, + *eidos,* resemblance]. Resembling a cube.

cuff. A bandlike structure encircling a part.

musculotendinous c., rotator c. of the shoulder, the upper half of the capsule of the shoulder joint reinforced by the tendons of insertion of the supraspinatus, infraspinatus, teres minor, and subscapularis muscles.

cul-de-sac, pl. **culs-de-sac** (kul-dĕ-sak') [Fr. bottom of a sack]. A blind pouch or tubular cavity closed at one end.

Douglas c., *excavatio* rectouterina.

culdocentesis (kul'do-sen-te'sis) [cul-de-sac + G. *kentesis,* puncture]. Aspiration of fluid from the

cul-de-sac (rectouterine excavation) by puncture of the vaginal vault near the midline between the uterosacral ligaments.

culdoplasty (kul'do-plas-tĭ) [cul-de-sac + G. *plasso,* to fashion]. A surgical procedure to remedy relaxation of the posterior fornix of the vagina.

culdoscope (kul'do-skōp). An endoscopic instrument used in culdoscopy.

culdoscopy (kul-dos'ko-pĭ) [cul-de-sac + G. *skopeō,* to view]. Introduction of an endoscope through the posterior vaginal wall to view the rectovaginal pouch and pelvic viscera.

Culex (ku'leks) [L. gnat]. A genus of mosquitoes (family Culicidae) including over 2000 species that are worldwide in distribution and vectors for a number of diseases of man and of domestic and wild animals.

culicidal (ku-lī-si'dal) [L. *culex,* gnat, + *caedo,* to kill]. Destructive to mosquitoes.

culicide (ku'lī-sī). An agent that destroys mosquitoes.

culicifuge (ku-lis'ī-fūj) [L. *culex,* gnat + *fugo,* to drive away]. A gnat or mosquito repellant.

Culicoides (ku-lī-koy'dēz) [L. *culex,* gnat]. A genus of minute biting gnats or midges.

cultiva'tion [Mediev. L. *cultivo,* pp. -*atus,* fr. L. *colo,* pp. *cultus,* to till]. Culture.

culture (kul'tūr) [L. *cultura,* tillage, fr. *colo,* pp. *cultus,* to till]. Cultivation. **1.** The propagation of microorganisms on or in media of various kinds. **2.** A mass of microorganisms on or in a medium.

cell c., the maintenance or growth of dispersed cells in a medium after removal from the body.

neotype c., neotype *strain.*

organ c., maintenance or growth of tissues, organ primordia, or the parts or whole of an organ *in vitro* in such a way as to allow differentiation or preservation of the architecture or function.

pure c., a c. consisting of the descendants of a single cell.

slant c., slope c., a c. made on the slanting surface of a medium which has been solidified in a test tube inclined from the perpendicular so as to give a greater area than that of the lumen of the tube.

smear c., a c. obtained by spreading material presumed to be infected on the surface of a solidified medium.

stab c., a c. produced by inserting an inoculating needle with inoculum down the center of a solid medium contained in a test tube.

stock c., a c. of a microorganism maintained solely for the purpose of keeping the microorganism in a viable condition by subculture, as necessary, into fresh medium.

streak c., a c. produced by lightly stroking an inoculating needle or loop with inoculum over the surface of a solid medium.

tissue c., maintenance of live tissue after removal from the body, by placing in a vessel with a sterile nutritive medium.

type c., type *strain.*

cumulative (ku'mu-la-tiv). Tending to accumulate or pile up, as with certain drugs that may have a c. effect.

cuneate (ku'ne-āt), **cuneiform** (ku'ne-ĭ-form) [L. *cuneus*, wedge]. Wedge-shaped.

cuneocuboid (ku'ne-o-ku'boyd). Relating to the lateral cuneiform and the cuboid bones.

cu'neonavic'ular. Relating to the cuneiform and the navicular bones.

cuneus, pl. **cu'nei** (ku'ne-us, ku'ne-i) [L. wedge] [NA]. That region of the medial aspect of the occipital lobe of each cerebral hemisphere that is bounded by the parietooccipital fissure and the calcarine fissure.

cuniculus, pl. **cunic'uli** (ku-nik'u-lus) [L. a rabbit; an underground passage]. The burrow of the itch mite in the epidermis.

cunnilingus (kun-ĭ-ling'gus) [L. *cunnus*, pudendum, + *lingo*, to lick]. Cunnilinction; cunnilinctus; licking or kissing of the vulva or clitoris as a type of oral-genital sexual activity.

cup [A. S. *cuppe*]. An excavated or cup-shaped structure, either anatomical or pathologic. 2. Cupping *glass.*

eye c., a small oval receptacle intended to facilitate the application of a liquid medicament to the external eye.

glaucomatous c., a deep depression of the optic disk caused by glaucoma.

optic c., ocular c., the double-walled c. formed by the invagination of the embryonic optic vesicle; its inner component becomes the sensory layer of the retina, its outer layer, the pigment layer.

physiologic c., a funnel-shaped excavation of the optic disk.

cu'pola. Cupula.

cup'ping. 1. Formation of a hollow, or cup-shaped excavation. 2. Application of a c. glass.

cu'pric. Pertaining to copper, particularly to copper in the form of a doubly charged positive ion.

cupula, pl. **cu'pulae** (ku'pu-lah) [L. dim. of *cupa*, a tub] [NA]. Cupola; a cup-shaped or domelike structure.

cu'pulogram. A graphic representation of vestibular function relative to normal performance.

curare (ku-rah're) [S. Am.]. An extract of various plants, especially *Strychnos toxifera, S. castelnaei, S. crevauxii,* and *Chondodendron tomentosum,* that produces nondepolarizing paralysis of skeletal muscle by blocking transmission at the myoneuronal junction; used clinically (*e.g.,* as *d*-tubocurarine) to provide muscle relaxation during operations.

curar'iform. Denoting a drug having an action like curare.

curative (kūr'ă-tiv). Tending to heal or cure.

cure (kūr) [L. *curo*, to care for]. 1. To heal; to make well. 2. A restoration to health. 3. A special method or course of treatment.

curet (ku-ret'). Curette.

curetment (ku-ret'ment). Curettage.

curettage (ku-rĕ-tahzh'). Curettement; curetment; a scraping, usually of the interior of a cavity or tract, for the removal of new growths or other abnormal tissues, or to obtain material for tissue diagnosis.

periapical c., (1) removal of a cyst or granuloma from its pathologic bony crypt, utilizing a curette; (2) the removal of tooth fragments and debris from sockets at the time of extraction or of bone sequestra subsequently.

subgingival c., apoxesis; removal of subgingival calculus, ulcerated epithelial and granulomatous tissues found in periodontal pockets.

curette (ku-ret') [Fr.]. Curet. 1. An instrument in the form of a loop, ring, or scoop with sharpened edges used for curettage. 2. To use a c.

curettement (ku-ret'ment). Curettage.

curie (Ci) (ku'rī) [Pierre (1859–1906) and Marie (1867–1934) *Curie,* French chemists and physicists]. A unit of measurement of radioactivity, 3.70 × 10^{10} disintegrations per second.

curium (ku're-um) [see curie]. An artificial element, atomic no. 96, symbol Cm.

current (kur'rent) [L. *currens,* pres. p. of *curro,* to run]. A stream or flow of fluid, air or electricity.

action c., an electrical c. induced in muscle fibers when they are effectively stimulated, normally followed by contraction.

axial c., the central, rapidly moving portion of the blood stream in an artery.

curvature (kur'vă-tūr) [L. *curvatura,* fr. *curvo,* pp. *-atus,* to bend, curve]. A bending or flexure.

angular c., a gibbous deformity, *i.e.,* a sharp angulation of the spine, occurring in Pott's disease.

greater c. of stomach, the border of the stomach to which the greater omentum is attached.

lesser c. of stomach, the border of the stomach to which the lesser omentum is attached.

spinal c., see kyphosis; lordosis; scoliosis.

curve (kurv) [L. *curvo,* to bend]. 1. A curvature; a nonangular continuous bend. 2. A graphic representation, by means of a continuous line of shifting direction, that might be otherwise presented by a table of figures.

alignment c., the line passing through the center of the teeth laterally in the direction of the c. of the dental arch.

Barnes c., a c. corresponding in general with Carus c., the segment of a circle whose center is the promontory of the sacrum.

Carus c., an imaginary curved line, obtained from a mathematical formula, indicating the outlet of the pelvic canal.

Frank-Starling c., Starling's c.

Friedman c., hours of labor plotted against cervical dilation in centimeters.

c. of occlusion, (1) a curved surface which makes simultaneous contact with the major portion of the incisal and occlusal prominences of the existing teeth; (2) the c. of a dentition on which the occlusal surfaces lie.

Price-Jones c., a distribution c. of the measured diameters of red blood cells; it is to the right of the normal c. (indicating large diameters) in instances of pernicious anemia and other forms in which macrocytes are present, and to the left (indicating smaller diameters) in iron deficiency and other forms of microcytic anemia.

Starling's c., Frank-Starling c.; cardiac output plotted against atrial pressure; with increasing venous return and atrial pressure the output proportionately increases until further increments overload the heart and the output falls.

tension c., the direction of the trabeculae in cancellous bone tissue adapted to resist stress.

Traube-Hering c.'s, Traube-Hering waves; slow oscillations in blood pressure usually extending over several respiratory cycles; related to variations in vasomotor tone.

whole body titration c., graphic representation of the *in vivo* changes in hydrogen ion, PA CO_2 and bicarbonate that occur in arterial blood in response to primary acid base disturbances.

cush'ingoid. Resembling the signs and symptoms of Cushing's disease or syndrome.

cushion (kŏŏsh'un). In anatomy, any structure resembling a pad or c.

atrioventricular canal c.'s, endocardial c.'s, a pair of mounds of embryonic connective tissue covered by endothelium, bulging dorsally and ventrally into the embryonic atrioventricular canal, that grow together and fuse to divide the canal into right and left atrioventricular orifices.

Passavant's c., a prominence on the posterior wall of the nasal pharynx formed by contraction of the superior constrictor of the pharynx during swallowing.

cusp (kusp) [L. *cuspis,* point]. **1.** In dentistry, a conical elevation arising on the surface of a tooth from an independent calcification center. **2.** A leaflet of one of the heart's valves.

cuspal (kus'pal). Pertaining to a cusp.

cuspid (kus'pid) [L. *cuspis,* point]. **1.** Cuspidate; having but one cusp. **2.** *Dens* caninus.

cus'pidate. Cuspid (1).

cutaneous (ku-ta'ne-us) [L. *cutis,* skin]. Relating to the skin.

cut'down. Venostomy; dissection of a vein for insertion of a cannula or needle for the administration of intravenous fluids or medication.

cuticle (ku'tĭ-kl) [L. *cuticula,* dim. of *cutis,* skin]. **1.** An outer thin layer, usually horny. **2.** The layer, sometimes chitinous in invertebrates, which occurs on the surface of epithelial cells. **3.** Epidermis.

cu'tireac'tion [L. *cutis,* skin, + reaction]. Cutaneous reaction; inflammatory reaction in the case of a skin test in a sensitive (allergic) subject.

cutis (ku'tis) [L.] [NA]. Skin; the membranous protective covering of the body, consisting of epidermis and corium (dermis).

c. anseri'na, contraction of the arrectores pilorum muscles produced by cold, fear, or other stimulus, causing the orifices of hair follicles to become prominent.

c. hyperelas'tica, Ehlers-Danlos *syndrome.*

c. lax'a, pachydermatocele (1); a congenital condition characterized by an excessive amount of skin hanging in folds; vascular anomalies may be present; inheritance is either dominant or recessive, the latter sometimes in association with pulmonary emphysema.

c. marmora'ta, a pink marble-like mottling of the skin on exposure to cold; also associated with debilitating diseases.

c. rhomboida'lis nu'chae, geometric configurations of the skin of the back of the neck as a result of aging or prolonged exposure to sunlight.

c. ve'ra, corium.

c. ver'ticis gyra'ta, a congenital condition in which the skin of the scalp is hypertrophied and thrown into folds forming anterior to posterior furrows.

cu'tisec'tor [L. *cutis,* skin, + *sector,* a cutter]. **1.** An instrument for cutting small pieces of skin for grafting. **2.** An instrument used to remove a section of skin for microscopic examination.

CVA Cerebrovascular accident, older classical term for stroke.

CVP Central venous *pressure.*

cyan-. See cyano-.

cy'anide. A compound containing the radical –CN or ion (CN)–; some c. compounds are extremely poisonous.

cyanmethemoglobin (si'an-met-he'mo-glo-bin). A relatively nontoxic compound of cyanide with methemoglobin, formed when methylene blue is administered in cases of cyanide poisoning.

cy'anmetmy'oglobin. Compound in which a cyanide group is bound to the iron atom (Fe^{3+}) of metmyoglobin.

cyano-, cyan- [G. *kyanos,* a dark blue mineral]. **1.** Combining form meaning blue. **2.** Chemical prefix frequently used in naming compounds that contain the cyanide group, CN, as part of the molecule.

Cyanobacteria (si'ă-no-bak-tēr'ĭ-ah). Cyanophyceae; a division of the kingdom Procaryotae consisting of unicellular or filamentous bacteria that are either nonmotile or possess a gliding motility, reproduce by binary fission, and perform photosynthesis with the production of oxygen; formerly referred to as blue-green algae.

cy'anocobal'amin. Vitamin B_{12}; a complex of cyanide and cobalamin; a hematopoietic agent apparently identical with the antianemia factor of liver.

cyanophil, cyanophile (si'an-o-fil, -fīl) [cyano- + G. *philos,* fond]. A cell or element that is differentially colored blue by a staining procedure.

cyanophilous (si-ă-nof'ĭ-lus). Readily stainable with a blue dye.

Cyanophyceae (si'ă-no-fi'se-e) [cyano- + G. *phykos,* seaweed]. Cyanobacteria.

cyanop'sia (si-ă-nop'sĭ-ah) [cyano- + G. *opsis*, vision]. A condition in which all objects appear blue; may temporarily follow cataract extraction.

cyanosed (si'ă-nozd). Cyanotic.

cyanose tardive (se'ă-nōs-tar-dēv') Tardive cyanosis; cyanosis that is slow to appear; applied to the potentially cyanotic group of congenital heart diseases with an abnormal communication between systemic and pulmonary circulations; cyanosis is absent while the shunt is from left to right, but if the shunt reverses, as after exercise or late in the course of the disease, cyanosis appears.

cyanosis (si-ă-no'sis) [G. dark blue color, fr. *kyanos*, blue substance]. A dark bluish or purplish coloration of the skin and mucous membrane due to deficient oxygenation of the blood, evident when reduced hemoglobin in the blood exceeds 5 g per 100 ml.

compression c., c. due to severe compression of the thorax or abdomen, resulting in a venous reflex that causes c., edema, and petechial hemorrhages over the head, neck, and upper part of the chest; the conjunctiva and retinas are similarly affected.

enterogenous c., apparent c. caused by the absorption of nitrites or other toxic materials from the intestine with formation of methemoglobin or sulfhemoglobin; the skin color change is due to the chocolate color of methemoglobin.

tardive c., cyanose tardive.

cyanot'ic. Cyanosed; relating to or marked by cyanosis.

cybernetics (si'ber-net'iks) [G. *kybernētica*, things pertaining to control or piloting]. **1.** Comparative study of computers and the nervous system, with intent to explain the functioning of the brain. **2.** The science of control and communication in both living and nonliving systems.

cycl-. See cyclo-.

cyclamate (si'klă-māt). A salt or ester of cyclamic acid, a sweetening agent; *e.g.*, calcium cyclamate; sodium cyclamate.

cyclarthrodial (si-klar-thro'dĭal). Relating to a cyclarthrosis.

cyclarthrosis (si-klar-thro'sis) [cyclo- + G. *arthrōsis*, articulation]. A rotary, or trochoid, joint.

cy'clase. An enzyme that forms a cyclic compound.

cycle (si'kl) [G. *kyklos*, circle]. **1.** A recurrent series of events. **2.** A recurring period of time.

carbon dioxide c., carbon c., the circulation of carbon as CO_2 from the expired air of animals and decaying organic matter to plant life where it is synthesized (through photosynthesis) to carbohydrate material, from which, as a result of catabolic processes in all life, it is again ultimately released to the atmosphere as CO_2.

cardiac c., the complete round of cardiac systole and diastole with the intervals between, or commencing with any event in the heart's action to the moment when that same event is repeated.

cell c., the cyclic biochemical and structural events occurring during rapid growth of cells such as in tissue culture; the c. is divided into periods called: G_0, Gap_1 (G_1), synthesis (S_1), Gap_2 (G_2), and mitosis (M).

citric acid c., tricarboxylic acid c.

Cori c., the phases in the metabolism of carbohydrate: glycogenolysis in the liver; passage of glucose into the circulation; deposition of glucose in the muscles as glycogen; and glycogenolysis during muscular activity and conversion to lactate, which is converted to glycogen in the liver.

dicarboxylic acid c., that portion of the tricarboxylic acid c. involving the dicarboxylic acids: succinic, fumaric, malic, and oxaloacetic acids.

estrous c., the series of physiologic uterine, ovarian, and other changes that occur in higher animals: proestrus, estrus, postestrus, and anestrus or diestrus.

fatty acid oxidation c., a series of reactions involving acyl-coenzyme A compounds, whereby these undergo beta oxidation and thioclastic cleavage, with the formation of acetylcoenzyme A; the major pathway of fatty acid catabolism in living tissue.

Krebs c., tricarboxylic acid c.

Krebs-Henseleit c., urea c.

menstrual c., the period in which an ovum matures, is ovulated, and enters the uterine lumen via the fallopian tubes; ovarian hormonal secretions effect endometrial changes such that, if fertilization occurs, nidation will be possible; in the absence of fertilization, ovarian secretions wane, the endometrium sloughs, and menstruation begins; day 1 of the c. is that day on which menstrual flow begins.

nitrogen c., the series of events in which the nitrogen of the atmosphere is fixed and made available for plant and animal life and then returned to the atmosphere: nitrifying bacteria convert N_2 and O_2 and NO_2- and NO_3-, the latter being absorbed by plants and converted to protein; if plants decay, the nitrogen is in part given up to the atmosphere, and the remainder is converted by microorganisms to ammonia, nitrites, and nitrates; if the plants are eaten by animals, their excreta or bacterial decay return the nitrogen to the soil and air.

ovarian c., the normal sex c. which include development of an ovarian (graafian) follicle, rupture of the follicle and discharge of the ovum, and formation and regression of a corpus luteum.

reproductive c., the c. which begins with conception and extends through gestation and parturition.

tricarboxylic acid c., citric acid or Krebs c.; the main source of energy in the mammalian body and the end toward which carbohydrate, fat, and protein metabolism all point; a series of reactions, beginning and ending with oxaloacetic acid, during the course of which a two-carbon fragment is completely oxidized to carbon dioxide and water with the production of twelve high-energy phosphate bonds. So called because the first four substances involved (citric acid, cis-aconitic acid, isocitric acid, and oxalosuccinic acid) are all tricarboxylic acids; from oxalosuccinate, the others are, in order, α-ketoglutarate, fumarate, L-malate and oxaloacetate, which condenses with acetyl-CoA (from fatty acid degradation) to form citrate (citric acid) again.

urea c., Krebs–Hanseleit c.; the sequence of chemical reactions, occurring in the liver, that results in the production of urea; the key reaction is the hydrolysis of arginine, by arginase, to ornithine and urea; ornithine is then converted to citrulline by a carbamoylation reaction involving glutamic acid and then to arginine again by an amination reaction involving aspartic acid.

cyclectomy (si-klek'to-mĭ, sik-lek'to-mĭ) [cyclo- + G. ektomē, excision]. Ciliectomy; excision of a portion of the ciliary body.

cyclencephaly (si-klen-sef'ă-lĭ) [cyclo- + G. enkephalos, brain]. Cyclocephaly; in a malformed fetus, poor development and a varying degree of fusion of the two cerebral hemispheres.

cycles per second (cps). The number of successive compressions and rarefactions per second of a sound wave; a measure of pitch or frequency, synonymous with hertz.

cyclic (si'klik, sik'lik). **1.** Occurring periodically. **2.** In chemistry, continuous, without end.

cyclic AMP (cAMP). Adenosine 3':5'-cyclic phosphate.

3':-cyclic AMP synthetase. *Adenylate* cyclase.

cyclicot'omy. Cyclotomy.

cyclitis (si-kli'tis) [G. kyklos, circle (ciliary body), + -itis, inflammation]. Inflammation of the ciliary body.

cyclo-, cycl- [G. kyklos, circle]. **1.** Combining form relating to a circle or cycle, or denoting association with the ciliary body. **2.** Chemical combining form indicating a continuous molecule, without end, or formation of such a structure between two parts of a molecule.

cyclocephaly (si-klo-sef'ă-lĭ) [cyclo- + G. kephalē, head]. Cyclencephaly.

cyclochoroiditis (si'klo-ko-royd-i'tis). Inflammation of the ciliary body and the choroid coat of the eye.

cyclocryotherapy (si'klo-kri'o-thěr'ă-pĭ). Application of a freezing probe to the sclera in the region of the ciliary body in treatment of glaucoma.

cyclodialysis (si'klo-di-al'ĭ-sis) [cyclo- + G. dialysis, separation]. Heine's operation; establishment of a communication between the anterior chamber and the suprachoroidal space in order to reduce intraocular pressure in glaucoma.

cy'clodiather'my. Diathermy applied to the ciliary region in treatment of glaucoma.

cyclokerati'tis. Inflammation of both the ciliary body and the cornea.

cyclopenta[α]phenanthrene. Phenanthrene, to the α side of which a three-carbon fragment is fused; as

the perhydro (saturated) derivative, it is the basic structure of the steroids.

cyclopep'tide. A polypeptide lacking terminal $-NH_2$ and $-COOH$ groups by virtue of their combination to form another peptide link.

cyclophor'ases. The group of enzymes in mitochondria catalyzing the complete oxidation of pyruvic acid to carbon dioxide and water; those enzymes and coenzymes involved in the tricarboxylic acid cycle.

cyclophoria (si'klo-fo'rĭ-ah) [cyclo- + G. phora, movement]. Tendency of the eyes to rotate around their sagittal axes, the movement being prevented by visual fusional impulses.

minus c., incyclophoria.

plus c., excyclophoria.

cyclophotocoagulation (si'klo-fo'to-ko-ag-u-la'shun) [cyclo- + photocoagulation]. Photocoagulation with a laser through the pupil to selectively destroy individual ciliary processes; used in glaucoma.

cyclo'pia [G. Kyklōps, fr. kyklos, circle, + ōps, eye]. Synophthalmia; a congenital defect in which the two orbits merge to form a single cavity containing one eye; usually combined with cyclencephaly.

cycloplegia (si-klo-ple'jĭ-ah) [cyclo- + G. plēgē, stroke]. Paralysis of accommodation; loss of power in the ciliary muscle of the eye.

cyclople'gic. Relating to cycloplegia; paralyzing the ciliary muscle and thus the power of accommodation.

cyclo'sis [G. fr. kykloō, to move around]. Movement of the protoplasm and contained plastids within the protozoan cell.

cyclothymic (si-klo-thi'mik) [cyclo- + G. thymos, rage]. Denoting a disorder marked by swings of mood, from elation to depression, within normal limits.

cyclotomy (si-klot'o-mĭ) [cyclo- + G. tomē, incision]. Cyclicotomy; cutting the ciliary muscle.

cyclotropia (si-klo-tro'pĭ-ah) [cyclo- + G. tropē, a turn, turning]. A meridional deviation around the anterior-posterior axis of one eye with respect to the other.

Cyd Cytidine.

cyesis (si-e'sis) [G. kyēsis]. Pregnancy.

cylindroadenoma (sil'in-dro-ad-ĕ-no'mah). Cylindroma.

cyl'indroid [G. kylindrōdēs, fr. kylindros, roll, cylinder, + eidos, appearance]. False cast.

cylindroma (sil-in-dro'mah) [G. kylindros, cylinder -oma, tumor]. Cylindroadenoma; a histologic type of epithelial neoplasm, frequently malignant, characterized by islands of neoplastic cells embedded in a hyalinized stroma formed from ducts of glands, especially in salivary glands, skin, and bronchi.

cylindruria (sil-in-dru'rĭ-ah). Presence of renal casts in the urine.

cymbocephalic, cymbocephalous (sim-bo-sĕ-fal'ik, sef'ă-lus) [G. kymbē, the hollow of a vessel, a boat-shaped structure, + kephalē, head]. Denoting a boat-shaped skull with a depression of the upper surface.

cynanche (sin-ang'ke) [L. fr. G. *kynanchē*, dog quinsy, sore throat]. Sore *throat*.

cy'nopho'bia [G. *kyōn*, dog, + *phobos*, fear]. Morbid fear of dogs.

Cys Cysteine.

cyst-. See cysto-.

cyst (sist) [G. *kystis*, bladder]. **1.** A bladder. **2.** An abnormal sac containing gas, fluid, or a semisolid material, with a membranous lining.

   adventitious c., pseudocyst (1).

   aneurysmal bone c., a solitary benign osteolytic lesion in a long bone or a vertebra, consisting of blood-filled spaces separated by fibrous tissue and causing swelling, pain, and tenderness.

   arachnoid c., a fluid-filled c. lined with arachnoid membrane, frequently situated near the lateral aspect of the fissure of Sylvius.

   Baker's c., a collection of synovial fluid that has escaped from the knee joint or a bursa and formed a new synovial-lined sac in the popliteal space.

   Bartholin's c., a c. arising from the major vestibular gland or its ducts.

   Blessig's c.'s, peripheral cystoid degeneration of the sensory retina.

   blood c., hemorrhagic c.

   blue dome c., (1) one of a number of small dark blue nodules or c.'s in the vaginal fornix to retained menstrual blood in endometriosis affecting this region; **(2)** a benign retention c. of the mammary gland in fibrocystic disease.

   Boyer's c., a subhyoid c.

   chocolate c., c. of the ovary with intracavitary hemorrhage and formation of a hematoma containing old brown blood.

   choledochal c., c. originating from common bile duct; usually becomes apparent early in life as a right upper abdominal mass in association with jaundice.

   daugther c., a secondary c. usually multiple, derived from a mother c.

   dentigerous c., a c. arising from odontogenic epithelium (reduced dental epithelium or dental lamina) after the completion of crown formation.

   dermoid c., dermoid (2); dermoid tumor; a tumor consisting of displaced ectodermal structures along lines of embryonic fusion, the wall being formed of epithelium-lined connective tissue, including skin appendages, and containing keratin, sebum, and hair; a common benign cystic teratoma of the ovary.

   echinococcus c., hydatid c.

   epidermal c., a c. formed of a mass of epidermal cells which, as a result of trauma, has been pushed beneath the epidermis.

   epidermoid c., c. of the dermis, comprised of encysted keratin and sebum and lined by a keratinizing epithelium resembling the epidermis; may be derived from a sebaceous cyst or epidermal metaplasia of the lining epithelium.

   exudation c., a c. resulting from distention of a closed cavity, such as a bursa, by an excessive secretion of its normal fluid contents.

   follicular c., a cystic graafian follicle.

   granddaughter c., a tertiary c. sometimes developed within a daughter c., as in the hydatid cyst of *Echinococcus.*

   hemorrhagic c., blood c.; hematocele (1); hematocyst; a c. containing blood or resulting from the encapsulation of a hematoma.

   hydatid c., echinococcus c.; hydatid (1); a c. formed by the larval stage of *Echinococcus granulosus;* may be unilocular or osseous.

   meibomian c., chalazion.

   morgagnian c., *appendix* vesiculosa.

   mother c., parent c.; the echinococcus c. from the inner, or germinal, layer, from which secondary c.'s containing scoleces (daughter c.'s) are developed; sometimes tertiary c.'s (granddaughter c.'s) are developed within the daughter c.'s; occurs most frequently in the liver.

   multilocular c., a c. containing several compartments formed by membranous septa.

   myxoid c., ganglion (2).

   nabothian c., nabothian follicle; a retention c. that develops when a mucous gland of the cervix uteri is obstructed, often developing in chronic inflammation of the cervix.

   odontogenic c., a c. that may be derived from a variety of sources of odontogenic epithelium.

   osseous hydatid c., a morphological form of hydatid c. caused by *Echinococcus granulosus,* and found in the long bones or the pelvic arch of man if the embryo is filtered out in bony tissue; in this site no limiting membrane forms and the c. grows in an uncontrolled fashion, producing cancellous structures and inducing fracture, followed by spread to new sites.

   ovarian c., a cystic tumor of the ovary, usually retricted to benign c.'s.

   parasitic c., a c. formed by the larva of a parasite, such as a hydatid c.

   parent c., mother c.

   periapical periodontal c., radicular c.; a c. about the root of a nonvital tooth, usually the sequela of dental caries-inflammatory pulpal disease.

   pilar c., sebaceous c.

   radicular c., periapical periodontal c.

   retention c., a c. resulting from some obstruction to the excretory duct of a gland.

   sebaceous c., pilar c.; steatocystoma (2); wen; a common c. of the skin and subcutis containing sebum and keratin which is lined by pale-staining stratified epithelial cells derived from the pilosebaceous follicle.

   serous c., a c. containing clear serous fluid, such as a hygroma.

   solitary bone c., unicameral bone c.; osteocystoma; a unilocular c. containing serous fluid and lined with a thin layer of connective tissue, occurring usually in the shaft of a long bone in growing children.

sterile c., a hydatid c. without brood capsules or viable scoleces.

sublingual c., ranula (2).

synovial c., ganglion (2).

tarry c., a c. or collection of old blood having a tarry or black, sticky appearance; usually due to endometriosis.

tarsal c., chalazion.

tubular c., tubulocyst.

unicameral bone c., solitary bone c.

unilocular c., unicameral c., a c. having a single sac.

vitellointestinal c., a small red sessile or pedunculated tumor at the umbilicus of an infant, due to persistence of a segment of the vitellointestinal (omphalomesenteric) duct.

wolffian c., a c. arising from any mesonephric structure.

cyst'adeno'ma. Cystoadenoma; a histologically benign neoplasm derived from glandular epithelium, in which cystic accumulations of retained secretions are formed.

papillary c., an adenoma of the epididymis or collecting ducts and rete of the testis.

papillary c. lymphomato'sum, adenolymphoma.

cystad'enocarcino'ma. A malignant neoplasm derived from glandular epithelium, in which cystic accumulations of retained secretions are formed; develops frequently in the ovaries, where pseudomucinous and serous types are recognized.

cystal'gia [cyst- + G. *algos*, pain]. Pain in the urinary bladder.

cystathi'onase. Cystathionine γ-lyase.

cystathi'onine. An intermediate in the conversion of methionine to cysteine; cleaved by cystathionase to yield cysteine.

cystathionine γ-lyase. Cystathionase; a liver enzyme, requiring pyridoxal phosphate as coenzyme, that catalyzes the hydrolysis of cystathionine to cysteine and 2-ketobutyrate.

cys'tathi'oninu'ria. A heritable disorder characterized by inability to metabolize cystathionine normally, with development of elevated concentrations of the amino acid in blood, tissue and urine; mental retardation is an associated condition.

cystectasia, cystectasy (sist-ek-ta'sĭ-ah, sis-tek'ta-sĭ) [cyst- + G. *ektasis*, a stretching]. Dilation of the bladder.

cystec'tomy [cyst- + G. *ektomē*, excision]. **1.** Excision of the gallbladder or of the urinary bladder. **2.** Removal of a cyst.

cyste'ic acid. An oxidation product of cysteine, and a precursor of taurine and isethionic acid.

cysteine (Cys) (sis'te-in). 2-Amino-3-mercaptopropionic acid; an α-amino acid found in most proteins; especially abundant in keratin.

cysti-. See cysto-.

cystic (sis'tik). **1.** Relating to the urinary bladder or gallbladder. **2.** Relating to a cyst. **3.** Containing cysts.

cysticercosis (sis'tĭ-sur-ko'sis). Disease caused by encystment of cysticercus larvae in subcutaneous, muscle, or central nervous system tissues; results from the hatching of the eggs of *Taenia solium* in the intestines or by accidental ingestion of eggs from human feces.

cysticercus, pl. **cysticerci** (sis-ti-sur'kus, -sur'si) [G. *kystis*, bladder, + *kerkos*, tail]. Bladderworm; the larval form of certain *Taenia* species.

cys'tiform. Cystoid (1).

cys'tine. 3,3'-Dithiobis(2-aminopropionic acid); an oxidation product of cysteine; sometimes occurs as a deposit in the urine, or forming a vesical calculus.

cystinemia (sis-tĭ-ne'mĭ-ah) [cystine + g. *haima*, blood]. Presence of cystine in blood.

cystinosis (sis-tĭ-no'sis). Cystine storage disease; the most common of a group of disease with characteristic renal tubular dysfunction disorders, termed collectively Fanconi's *syndrome* (2); a recessive hereditary disease of early childhood characterized by deposits of cystine crystals throughout the body; abnormality in cystine metabolism; associated with a marked generalized aminoaciduria, glycosuria, polyuria, chronic acidosis, hypophosphatemia with vitamin D-resistant rickets, and often with hypokalemia.

cystinuria (sis-tĭ-nu'rī-ah) [cystine + G. *ouron*, urine]. Excessive urinary excretion of cystine, along with lysine, arginine, and ornithine, as a result of a defect in renal tubular reabsorption.

cystistax'is [cysti- + G. *staxis*, trickling]. Cystostaxis; oozing of blood from the mucous membrane of the bladder.

cystitis (sis-ti'tis) [cyst- + G. *-itis*, inflammation]. Inflammation of the urinary bladder.

c. cys'tica, c. characterized by the formation of cysts derived from glandlike invaginations of transitional epithelium.

follicular c., chronic c. characterized by small mucosal nodules due to lymphocytic infiltration with formation of lymphoid follicles.

c. glandula'ris, chronic c. with glandlike invaginations of transitional epithelium.

interstitial c., a chronic inflammatory condition of unknown etiology involving the mucosa and muscular tissue of the bladder, resulting in reduced bladder capacity.

cysto-, cysti-, cyst- [G. *kystis*, bladder]. Combining forms relating to the bladder; the cystic duct; a cyst.

cystoadenoma (sis'to-ad-ĕ-no'mah). Cystadenoma.

cystocarcinoma (sis'to-kar-sĭ-no'mah). Cystoepithelioma; a carcinoma in which cystic degeneration has occurred.

cystocele (sis'to-sēl) [cysto- + G. *kēlē*, hernia]. Colpocystocele; vesicocele; herniation of the bladder.

cystochromoscopy (sis'to-kro-mos'ko-pĭ) [cysto- + G. *chrōma*, color + *skopeō*, to view]. Chromocystoscopy; examination of the interior of the bladder after administration of a colored dye to aid in the identification or study of the function of the ureteral orifices.

cystoelytroplasty (sis-to-el'ĭ-tro-plas-tĭ) [cysto- + G. *elytron*, sheath, + *plassō*, to form]. Surgical repair of a vesicovaginal fistula.

cystoepithelioma (sis'to-ep-ĭ-the-lĭ-o'mah). Cystocarcinoma.

cystofibro'ma. A fibroma in which cysts or cystlike foci have formed.

cys'togram. An x-ray image produced by cystography.

cystog'raphy [cysto- + G. *graphō*, to write]. Radiography of the bladder following injection of a radiopaque substance.

cystoid [cysto- + G. *eidos*, appearance]. **1.** Cystiform; cystomorphous; bladder-like, resembling a cyst. **2.** A tumor resembling a cyst, with fluid, granular, or pultaceous contents, but without capsule.

cys'tolith [cisto- + G. *lithos*, stone]. A vesical calculus; a urinary calculus formed or lodged in the bladder.

cystolithectomy (sis'to-lĭ-thek'to-mĭ) [cysto- + G. *lithos*, stone, + *ektomē*, excision]. Cystolithotomy.

cystolithiasis (sis-to-lĭ-thi'a-sis) [cysto- + G. *lithos*, stone, + *-iasis*, condition]. Presence of a vesical calculus.

cystolith'ic. Relating to a vesical calculus.

cystolithotomy (sis'to-lĭ-thot'o-mĭ) [cysto- + G. *lithos*, stone, + *tomē*, incision]. Cystolithectomy; removal of a stone from the bladder through an incision in its wall.

cystoma (sis-to'mah) [cyst- + G. *-oma*, tumor]. A cystic tumor; a new growth containing cysts.

cystometer (sis-tom'ĕ-ter) [cysto- + G. *metron*, measure]. A device for studying bladder function by measuring capacity, sensation, intravesical pressure, and residual urine.

cystometrogram (sis-to-met'ro-gram) [cysto- + G. *metron*, measure, + *gramma*, a writing]. The graphic record produced by a cystometer.

cystometrography (sis'to-mĕ-trog'ră-fĭ). Cystometry; measurement of bladder function, as by a cystometer.

cystometry (sis-tom'ĕ-trĭ) [see cystometer]. Cystometrography.

cystomor'phous [cysto- + G. *morphē*, form]. Cystoid (1).

cystopanendoscopy (sis'to-pan-en-dos'ko-pĭ) [cysto- + panendoscope]. Inspection of the interior of the bladder and urethra by an endoscope introduced retrograde through the urethra and into the bladder.

cystoparal'ysis. Cystoplegia.

cys'topexy [cysto- + G. *pēxis*, fixation]. Surgical attachment of the gallbladder or of the urinary bladder to the abdominal wall or to other supporting structures.

cys'toplasty [cysto- + G. *plassō*, to form]. Surgical repair of a defect in the urinary bladder.

cystoplegia (sis-to-ple'jĭ-ah) [cysto- + G. *plēgē*, a stroke]. Cystoparalysis; paralysis of the bladder.

cystoproctostomy (sis'to-prok-tos'to-mĭ) [cysto- + G. *prōktos*, anus, + *stoma*, mouth]. Vesicorectostomy.

cystoptosis, cystoptosia (sis-to-to'sis, -to'zĭ-ah) [cysto- + G. *ptōsis*, a falling]. Prolapse of the vesical mucous membrane into the urethra.

cystopyelitis (sis'to-pi-el-i'tis) [cysto- + G. *pyelos*, trough (pelvis), + *-itis*, inflammation]. Inflammation of both the bladder and the pelvis of the kidney.

cystopyelonephritis (sis-to-pi'el-o-nĕ-fri'tis) [cysto- + G. *pyelos*, trough (pelvis), + *nephros*, kidney, + *-itis*, inflammation]. Inflammation of the bladder, the pelvis of the kidney, and the kidney substance.

cystorectostomy (sis'to-rek-tos'to-mĭ) [cysto- + rectum + G. *stoma*, mouth]. Vesicorectostomy.

cystorrhaphy (sis-tor'ă-fĭ) [cysto- + *raphē*, a sewing]. Suture of a wound or defect in the urinary bladder.

cystorrhea (sis'to-re-ah) [cysto- + G. *rhoia*, a flow]. A mucous discharge from the bladder.

cys'tosarco'ma. A sarcoma in which the formation of cysts or cystlike foci has occurred.

cys'toscope [cysto- + G. *skopeō*, to examine]. Lithoscope; a lighted tubular endoscope for examining the interior of the bladder.

cystos'copy. Inspection of the interior of the bladder by means of a cystoscope.

cystostax'is. Cystistaxis.

cystostomy (sis-tos'to-mĭ) [cysto- + G. *stoma*, mouth]. Formation of an opening into the urinary bladder or gallbladder.

cys'totome. 1. An instrument for incising the urinary bladder or gallbladder. **2.** A surgical instrument used for incising the capsule of a cataractous lens.

cystotomy (sis-tot'o-mĭ) [cysto- + G. *tomē*, incision]. Vesicotomy; incision into urinary bladder or gallbladder.

    suprapubic c., epicystotomy; opening into the bladder through an incision above the symphysis pubis.

cystoureteritis (sis'to-u-re-ter-i'tis). Inflammation of the bladder and of one or both ureters.

cystoureterogram (sis'to-u-re'ter-o-gram). A radiograph of the bladder and ureter.

cystoureterography (sis'to-u-re'ter-og'ră-fĭ). Radiography of the bladder and ureter.

cystourethritis (sis'to-u-re-thri'tis). Inflammation of the bladder and of the urethra.

cystourethrography (sis'to-u-re-throg'ră-fĭ). Radiography of the bladder and urethra after visualization by means of a radiopaque substance.

cystourethroscope (sis-to-u-re'thro-skōp). An instrument combining the uses of a cystoscope and a urethroscope, whereby both the bladder and urethra can be visually inspected.

Cyt Cytosine.

cyt-. See cyto-.

-cyte. See cyto-.

cy'tidine (C, Cyd). Cytosine ribonucleoside; 1-β-D-ribofuranosylcytosine; a major component of ribonucleic acids.

cytidine 5'-diphosphate (CDP). Ester, at the 5'position, between cytidine and diphosphoric acid.

cytidine 5'-triphosphate (CTP). Ester, at the 5'position, between cytidine and triphosphoric acid.

cytidyl'ic acid. Cytidine phosphate (five are possible, depending on the site of attachment of the phosphate to the ribosyl OH's); a constituent of ribonucleic acids.

cyto-, cyt- [G. *kytos*, a hollow (cell)]. Combining forms meaning cell; as a suffix, -cyte.

cytoarchitecture (si'to-ar' kĭ-tek-chŭr). Arrangement of cells in a tissue; commonly refering to the arrangement of nerve-cell bodies in the brain, especially the cerebral cortex.

cytocentrum (si-to-sen'trum) [cyto- + G. *kentron*, center]. Centrosome; a zone of cytoplasm, usually located near the nucleus, that contains one or two centrioles but is devoid of other organelles.

cytochalasins (si-to-kal-a'zinz) [cyto- + G. *chalasis*, a relaxing]. A group of substances derived from molds that interfere with the division of cytoplasm, inhibit cell movement, and cause extrusion of the nucleus.

cytochemistry (si'to-kem-is-trĭ). Histochemistry; study of intracellular distribution of chemical components and their activities.

cytochrome (si'to-krōm) [cyto- + G. *chrōma*, color]. A class of hemoprotein whose principal biological function is electron and/or hydrogen transport by virtue of a reversible valency change of the heme iron; classified in four groups. (*a*, *b*, *c*, *d*) according to spectrochemical characteristics.

cytoci'dal [cyto- + L. *caedo*, to kill]. Causing the death of cells.

cy'tocide [cyto- + L. *caedo*, to kill]. An agent that is destructive to cells.

cytoclasis (si-tok'lă-sis) [cyto- + G. *klasia*, a breaking]. Fragmentation of cells.

cytoclas'tic. Relating to cytoclasis.

cytodiagno'sis. Diagnosis of a pathologic process by means of microscopic study of cells.

cytogenesis (si-to-jen'ĕ-sis) [cyto- + G. *genesis*, origin]. The origin and development of cells.

cy'togenet'icist. A specialist in cytogenetics.

cy'togenet'ics. The branch of genetics concerned with the structure and function of the cell, especially the chromosomes.

cytogen'ic. Relating to cytogenesis.

cytogenous (si-toj'en-us). Cell-forming.

cy'toglucope'nia [cyto- + glucose + G. *penia*, poverty]. Intracellular deficiency of glucose.

cytoid (si'toyd) [cyto- + G. *eidos*, resemblance]. Resembling a cell.

cytokinesis (si-to-kin-e'sis) [cyto- + G. *kinēsis*, movement]. Changes occurring in the protoplasm of the cell outside of the nucleus during cell division.

cytolog'ic. Relating to cytology.

cytol'ogist. A specialist in cytology.

cytology (si-tol'o-jĭ) [cyto- + G. *logos*, study]. Cellular biology; the study of the anatomy, physiology, pathology, and chemistry of the cell.

  exfoliative c., the examination, for diagnostic purposes, of cells denuded from a lesion and recovered from the sediment of the exudate, secretions, or washings from the tissue.

cytol'ysin. An antibody that, in association with complement, effects partial or complete destruction of an animal cell.

cytolysis (si-tol'ĭ-sis) [cyto- + G. *lysis*, loosening]. Dissolution of a cell.

cytolysosome (si-to-li'so-sōm). A variety of secondary lysosome that contains mitochondria, ribosomes, or other organelles.

cytolyt'ic. Pertaining to cytolysis; possessing a solvent or destructive action on cells.

cytomeg'alovi'rus. A group of species-specific herpetoviruses infecting man and other animals and causing enlargement of cells of various organs and development of characteristic inclusions in the cytoplasm or nucleus.

cytometaplasia (si'to-met-ă-pla'zĭah) [cyto- + G. *metaplasis*, transformation]. Change of form or function of a cell, other than that related to neoplasia.

cytometer (si-tom'ĕ-ter) [cyto- + G. *metron*, measure]. A standardized glass slide or small glass chamber of known volume, used in counting and measuring cells, especially blood cells.

cytometry (si-tom'ĕ-trĭ). The counting of cells, especially blood cells, using a cytometer or hemocytometer.

cytomorphology (si'to-mor-fol'o-jĭ). The study of the structure of cells.

cytomorphosis (si'to-mor-fo'sis) [cyto- + G. *morphōsis*, a shaping]. The changes that the cell undergoes during the various stages of its existence.

cytopath'ic. Pertaining to a diseased condition of a cell.

cytopathogenic (si'to-path-o-jen'ik). Pertaining to an agent or substance that causes a diseased condition in cells.

cy'topathol'ogist. A physician, usually skilled in anatomical pathology, who is specially trained and experienced in cytopathology.

cytopathologic, cytopathological (si'to-path-o-loj'ik, -ik-al). Relating to cytopathology; denoting the changes in cells caused by disease.

cytopathology (si'to-pă-thol'o-jĭ). 1. The medical science and subspecialty concerned with studies and diagnoses of health and disease by microscopic examination and evaluation of cellular specimens. 2. Sometimes used as a synonym for cellular *pathology*.

cytope'nia [cyto- + G. *penia,* poverty]. A reduction, *i.e.,* hypocytosis, or a lack of cellular elements in the circulating blood.

cytophagous (si-tof'ă-gus). Devouring, or destructive to, cells.

cytophagy (si-tof'ă-jĭ) [cyto- + G. *phagein,* to devour]. Ingestion of other cells by the phagocytes.

cytophilic (si-to-fil'ik) [cyto- + G. *philos,* fond]. Cytotropic.

cy'tophylac'tic. Relating to cytophylaxis.

cytophylaxis (si-to-fi-lak'sis) [cyto- + G. *phylaxis,* a guarding]. Protection of cells against lytic agents.

cytoplasm [cyto- + G. *plasma,* thing formed]. The substance of a cell exclusive of the nucleus; contains various organelles and inclusions within a colloidal protoplasm.

cytoplas'mic. Relating to the cytoplasm.

cytosine (Cyt) (si'to-sēn). 4-Amino-2(1*H*)-pyrimidinone; a pyrimidine found in nucleic acids.

  c. arabinoside (CA), incorrect term for arabinosylcytosine.

  c. ribonucleoside, cytidine.

cytosis (si-to'sis) [cyto- + G. *-osis,* condition]. A condition in which there is more than the usual number of cells; frequently used with a prefixed combining form as a means of describing certain features pertaining to cells.

cy'toskel'eton. The tonofilaments, keratin, or other filaments serving to act as supportive cytoplasmic elements, especially of certain epithelial cells.

cytosol (si'to-sol) [cyto- + "sol, " abbrev. of soluble]. The cytoplasm minus the mitochondria and endoplasmic reticulum components.

cy'tosome [cyto- + G. *sōma,* body]. **1.** The cell body exclusive of the nucleus. **2.** Multilamellar body; one of the osmiophilic bodies that have concentric lamellae and occur in the great alveolar cells of the lung.

cytostasis (si-tos'tă-sis) [cyto- + G. *stasis,* standing]. The slowing of movement and accumulation of blood cells in the capillaries, as in a region of inflammation.

cytostat'ic. Characterized by cytostasis.

cytotac'tic. Relating to cytotaxis.

cytotaxis (si-to-tak'sis) [cyto- + G. *taxis,* arrangement]. The attraction or repulsion of cells for one another.

cytothesis (si-toth'ĕ-sis) [cyto- + G. *thesis,* a placing]. The repair of injury in a cell; the restoration of cells.

cytotox'ic. Detrimental or destructive to cells; pertaining to the effect of noncytophilic antibody on specific antigen, frequently but not always, mediating the action of complement.

cytotoxicity (si'to-tok-sis'ĭ-tĭ). The quality or state of being cytotoxic.

cytotoxin (si'to-tok'sin) [cyto- + G. *toxikon,* poison]. A specific substance, usually with reference to antibody, that inhibits or prevents the functions of cells, or causes destruction of cells, or both.

cytotrophoblast (si-to-trof'o-blast). The inner layer of the trophoblast.

cytotropic (si-to-trop'ik). Cytophilic; having an affinity for cells.

cytotropism (si-tot'ro-pizm) [cyto- + G. *tropos,* a turning]. Affinity for cells, especially the ability of viruses to localize in and damage specific cells.

cytozo'ic. Living in a cell; denoting certain parasitic protozoa.

cytozoon (si-to-zo'on) [cyto- + G. *zōon,* animal]. A protozoan cell or organism.

cytu'ria [G. *kytos,* cell, + *ouron,* urine]. Passage of cells in unusual numbers in the urine.

D

δ, Δ Delta.

D Vitamin D potency of cod liver oil; deuterium; in optics, diopter and dexter (right); dihydrouridine in nucleic acids; diffusing capacity; as a subscript, refers to dead space.

D-. Prefix indicating a chemical compound to be sterically related to D-glyceraldehyde, the basis of stereochemical nomenclature.

d Deci-.

d Deuterium.

d- Prefix indicating a chemical compound to be dextrorotatory.

-d Suffix indicating a deuterium-containing compound; Subscripts indicate the number of such atoms.

2,4-D (2,4-Dichlorophenoxy)acetic acid.

dacry-. See dacryo-.

dacryagogue (dak'rĭ-ă-gog) [dacry- + G. *agōgos,* drawing forth]. An agent that stimulates the lacrimal gland to secretion, promoting the flow of tears.

dacryo-, dacry- [G. *dakryon,* tear]. Combining forms relating to tears, or to the lacrimal sac or duct.

dacryoadenalgia (dak-rĭ-o-ad-en-al'jĭ-ah) [dacryo- + G. *adēn,* gland, + *algos,* pain]. Pain in a lacrimal gland.

dacryoadenitis (dak-rĭ-o-ad-ĕni'tis) [dacryo- + G. *adēn,* gland, + *-itis,* inflammation]. Inflammation of a lacrimal gland.

dacryoblennorrhea (dak'rĭ-o-blen-or-re'ah) [dacryo- + G. *blenna,* mucus, + *rhoia,* flow]. Dacryocystoblennorrhea; chronic discharge of mucus from a lacrimal sac.

dacryocele (dak'rĭ-o-sēl). Dacryocystocele.

dacryocyst (dak'rĭ-o-sist) [dacryo- + G. *kystis,* sac]. *Saccus* lacrimalis.

dacryocystalgia (dak'rĭ-o-sis-tal'jĭ-ah) [dacryocyst + G. *algos,* pain]. Pain in the lacrimal sac.

dacryocystectomy (dak'rĭ-o-sis-tek'to-mĭ) [dacryocyst + G. *ektomē,* excision]. Surgical removal of the lacrimal sac.

dacryocystitis (dak'rĭ-o-sis-ti'tis) [dacryocyst + G. *-itis,* inflammation]. Inflammation of the lacrimal sac.

dacryocystoblennorrhea (dak'rĭ-o-sis'to-blen-or-re'ah). Dacryoblennorrhea.

dacryocystocele (dak'rĭ-o-sis'to-sēl) [dacryocyst + G. *kēlē*, hernia]. Dacryocele; protrusion of the lacrimal sac.

dacryocystoptosis (dak'rĭ-o-sis'top-to'sis) [dacryocyst + G. *ptōsis*, a falling]. Downward displacement of the lacrimal sac.

dacryocystorhinostenosis (dak'rĭ-o-sis'to-ri'no-stē-no'sis). Obstruction to the nasolacrimal duct.

dacryocystorhinostomy (dak'rĭ-o-sis'tor-ri-nos'to-mĭ) [dacryocyst + G. *rhis(rhin-), nose, + stoma, mouth]. Surgical anastomosis between the lacrimal sac and the nasal mucosa through an opening in the lacrimal bone.

dacryocystotomy (dak'rĭ-o-sis-tot'o-mĭ) [dacryocyst + G. *tomē, incision]. Incision of the lacrimal sac.

dacryohemorrhea (dak'rĭ-o-hem-o-re'ah) [dacryo- + G. *haima*, blood, + *rhoia*, flow]. Shedding of bloody tears.

dacryolith (dak'rĭ-o-lith) [dacryo- + G. *lithos*, stone]. Lacrimal calculus; ophthalmolith; a concretion in the lacrimal apparatus.

dacryolithiasis (dak'rĭ-o-lĭ-thi'ă-sis). Formation and presence of dacryoliths.

dacryoma (dak'rĭ-o'mah) [dacryo- + G. *-ōma*, tumor]. **1.** A cyst formed by the accumulation of tears in an obstructed lacrimal duct. **2.** A tumor of the lacrimal apparatus.

dacryops (dak'rĭ-ops) [dacryo- + G. *ōps*, eye]. **1.** Excess of tears in the eye. **2.** A cyst of a tear duct of the lacrimal gland.

dacryopyorrhea (dak'rĭ-o-pi-o-re'ah) [dacryo- + G. *pyon*, pus, + *rhoia*, flow]. Discharge of tears containing pus.

dacryopyosis (dak-rĭ-o-pi-o'sis) [dacryo- + G. *pyōsis*, suppuration]. Suppuration in the lacrimal sac or duct.

dacryorrhea (dak'rĭ-o-re'ah) [dacryo- + G. *rhoia*, flow]. Excessive flow of tears.

dacryoscintography (dak'rĭ-o-sin-tog'ră-fĭ) [dacryo- + L. *scintilla*, spark, + G. *graphō*, to write]. A test to determine the patency of the lacrimal passages using a radioactive isotope and a gamma camera.

dacryosolenitis (dak'rĭ-o-so-len-i'tis) [dacryo- + G. *sōlēn*, a channel, + *-itis*, inflammation]. Inflammation of the lacrimal or nasal duct.

dacryostenosis (dak'rĭ-o-stē-no'sis) [dacryo- + G. *stenōsis*, narrowing]. Stricture of a lacrimal or nasal duct.

dacryosyrinx (dak'rĭ-o-sĭr'inks) [dacryo- + G. *syrinx*, pipe]. An abnormal opening into a tear duct or the lacrimal sac.

dactyl-. See dactylo-.

dactyl (dak'til) [G. *daktylos*]. Digit.

dactylitis (dak-til-i'tis). Inflammation of one or more fingers.

dactylo-, dactyl- [G. *daktylos*, finger]. Combining forms relating to the fingers, and sometimes to the toes.

dactylocampsis (dak'tĭ-lo-kamp'sis) [dactylo- + G. *kampsis*, bending]. Permanent flexion of the fingers.

dactylogrypposis (dak'tĭ-lo-grĭ-po'sis) [dactylo- + G. *grypōsis*, a crooking]. Contraction of the fingers.

dactylomegaly (dak'tĭ-lo-meg'ă-lĭ) [dactylo- + G. *megas*, large]. Megadactyly.

dactylus, pl. **dactyli** (dak'tĭ-lus, -li) [G. *daktylos*]. Digitus.

dalton (dawl'ton) [J. *Dalton*, Br. chemist, 1766–1844]. A unit of mass equal to $1/_{12}$ the mass of a carbon-12 atom; 1.0000 in the atomic mass scale; numerically but not dimensionally, equal to molecular weight.

dam [A.S. *fordemman*, to stop up]. Any barrier to the flow of fluid; especially, in surgery and dentistry, a sheet of thin rubber arranged so as to shut off the part operated upon from the access of fluid.

dAMP Deoxyadenylic acid.

dan'der. Scales from skin, hair, or feathers; may cause an allergic reaction in sensitive persons.

dan'druff. Seborrhea sicca (2); the presence, in varying amounts, of scales in the scalp hair, due to the normal branny exfoliation of the epidermis.

DANS 1-Dimethylaminonaphthalene-5-sulfonic acid; a green fluorescing compound used in immunohistochemistry to detect antigens.

Darrow red [Mary A. *Darrow*, U.S. stain technologist, 1894–1973]. A basic oxazin dye, $C_{18}H_{14}N_3O_2Cl$, used as a substitute for cresyl violet acetate in the staining of Nissl substance.

dar'tos [G. skinned or flayed, fr. *derō*, to skin]. See tunica dartos.

darwin'ian. Relating to or described to Charles Darwin.

db, dB Decibel.

DC Dental Corps.

D.C. Doctor of Chiropractic.

D & C Dilation and curettage.

dCMP Deoxycytidylic acid.

D.D.S. Doctor of Dental Surgery.

DDT Dichlorodiphenyltrichloroethane.

de- [L. *de*, from, away]. Prefix, often privative or negative, denoting away from, cessation.

D & E Dilation and evacuation.

deacylase (de-as'il-ās). A member of the subclass of esterases, lipases, lactonases, and hydrolases; any enzyme catalyzing the hydrolytic cleavage of an acyl group (R–CO–) in an ester linkage.

deaf (def) [A.S. *deáf*]. Unable to hear; hearing indistinctly; hard of hearing.

deafferentation (de-af'er-en-ta'shun) [L. *de*, from, + afferent]. A loss of the sensory nerve fibers from a portion of the body.

deafmutism (def'mu'tizm). Inability to speak, due to congenital or early acquired profound deafness.

deaf'ness. General term for loss of the ability to hear, without designation of the degree of loss or the cause.

acoustic trauma d., noise-induced hearing loss, due to changes in the organ of Corti secondary to overexposure to high intensity noise levels.

central d., d. due to disease in the auditory system of the brainstem or hemispheres.

conductive d., hearing impairment caused by interference with sound or vibratory energy in the external canal, middle ear, or ossicles.

cortical d., d. resulting from a lesion of the cerebral cortex.

functional d., psychogenic d.

psychogenic d., functional d.; hearing loss of a hysterical or functional type without evidence of organic cause or malingering; often follows severe psychic shock.

sensorineural d., hearing loss due to lesions or dysfunction of the cochlea or retrocochlear nerve tracts and centers, as opposed to conductive d.

dealcoholization (de-al′ko-hol-ĭ-za′shun). Removal of alcohol from a fluid.

deamidases (de-am′ĭ-da-sez). Amidohydrolases.

deamidation, deamidization (de-am-ĭ-da′shun, -dĭ-za′shun). Hydrolytic removal of an amide group.

deaminases (de-am′ĭ-na-sez). Enzymes catalyzing simple hydrolysis of C–NH$_2$ bonds of purines, pyrimidines, and pterins, usually named in terms of the substrate.

deamination, deaminization (de-am-ĭ-na′shun, -nĭ-za′shun). Removal, usually by hydrolysis, of the NH$_2$ group from an amino compound.

dearterialization (de-ar-te′rĭ-al-i-za′shun). Changing the character of arterial blood to that of venous blood; *i.e.,* deoxygenation of blood.

death (deth) [A.S. *dēath*]. Cessation of life. In multicellular organisms, a gradual process at the cellular level, with tissues varying in their ability to withstand deprivation of oxygen; in higher organisms, a cessation of integrated tissue and organ functions; in man, manifested by the loss of heart beat, by the absence of spontaneous breathing, and by cerebral d.

black d., term applied to the worldwide epidemic of pneumonic plague in the 14th century, of which some 60 million persons are said to have died.

cerebral d., brain d., in the presence of cardiac activity, the permanent loss of cerebral function, manifested clinically by absence of purposive responsiveness to external stimuli, absence of cephalic reflexes, apnea, and an isoelectric electroencephalogram for at least 30 minutes in the absence of hypothermia and poisoning by central nervous system depressants.

crib d., sudden death *syndrome.*

local d., d. of a part of the body or of a tissue by necrosis.

somatic d., systemic d., d. of the entire body, as distinguished from local d.

deband′ing. Removal of fixed orthodontic appliances.

debilitating (dĕ-bil′ĭ-ta-ting) [L. *debilitas,* fr. *debilis,* weak]. Causing weakness.

débridement (da-brēd-moń′) [Fr. unbridle]. Excision of devitalized tissue and foreign matter from a wound.

debt (det) [L. *debitum,* debt]. That which is owed; a liability to be rendered.

oxygen d., the extra oxygen, taken in by the body during recovery from exercise, beyond the resting needs of the body; sometimes used as if synonymous with oxygen deficit.

deca- (dk) [G. *deka,* ten]. Prefix in the metric system to signify ten.

decalcifica′tion [L. *de-,* away, + *calx*(*calc-*), lime, + *facio,* to make]. **1.** Removal of lime salts from bones and teeth, either *in vitro* or as a result of a pathologic process. **2.** Precipitation of calcium from blood as by oxalate or flouride, or the conversion of blood calcium to an un-ionized form as by citrate, thus preventing or delaying coagulation.

decal′cifying. Relating to that which causes decalcification.

de′capacita′tion. Prevention of capacitation by spermatozoa, and thus of their ability to fertilize ova.

decapitation (de-kap-ĭ-ta′shun) [L. *de-,* away, + *caput,* head]. Removal of a head.

decapsulation (de-kap-su-la′shun). Incision and removal of a capsule or enveloping membrane, as of the kidney.

decarbox′ylase. An enzyme that removes a molecule of carbon dioxide from a carboxylic group.

decarboxyla′tion. A reaction involving the removal of a molecule of carbon dioxide from an organic compound, usually a carboxylic acid.

decay (de-ka′) [L. *de,* down, + *cado,* to fall]. **1.** Destruction of an organic substance by slow combustion or gradual oxidation. **2.** Putrefaction. **3.** To deteriorate; to undergo slow combustion or putrefaction. **4.** In dentistry, caries. **5.** In psychology, loss of information which was registered by the senses and processed into the short term memory system. **6.** Loss of radioactivity with time.

decerebrate (de-sĕr′ĕ-brāt). **1.** To cause decerebration. **2.** Denoting an animal so prepared, or a patient whose brain has suffered an injury which results in neurologic function comparable to a decerebrate animal.

decerebration (de-sĕr′ĕ-bra′shun). Removal of the brain above the lower border of the corpora quadrigemina or a complete section of the brain at about this level or somewhat below, or destroying the function of the cerebrum by tying the common carotid arteries and the basilar artery at about the middle of the pons.

de′cholest′eroliza′tion. Therapeutic reduction of the cholesterol concentration of the blood.

deci- (d) [L. *decimus,* tenth]. Prefix in the metric system to signify one-tenth (10$_{-1}$).

decibel (db, dB) (des′ĭ-bel) [L. *decimus,* tenth, + bel]. One-tenth of a bel; unit for expressing the relative loudness of sound on a logarithmic scale.

decidua (de-sid'u-ah) [L. *deciduus,* falling off]. *Membrana* decidua.

d. basa'lis [NA], d. serotina; the area of endometrium between the implanted chorionic vesicle and the myometrium, which becomes the maternal part of the placenta.

d. capsula'ris [NA], d. reflexa; the layer of endometrium overlying the implanted chorionic vesicle which becomes progressively more attenuated as the chorionic vesicle enlarges.

d. menstrua'lis, the succulent mucous membrane of the nonpregnant uterus at the menstrual period.

d. parieta'lis, [NA], d. vera; uteroepichorial membrane; the altered mucous membrane lining the main cavity of the pregnant uterus elsewhere than at the site of attachment of the chorionic vesicle.

d. polypo'sa, d. parietalis showing polypoid projections of the endometrial surface.

d. reflex'a, d. capsularis.

d. serot'ina, d. basalis.

d. spongio'sa, the portion of the d. basalis attached to the myometrium.

d. ve'ra, d. parietalis.

decidual (de-sid'u-al). Relating to the decidua.

deciduation (de-sid-u-a'shun) [L. *deciduus,* falling off]. The shedding of endometrial tissue during menstruation.

deciduitis (de-sid-u-i'tis). Inflammation of the decidua.

deciduoma (de-sid-u-o'mah). Placentoma; an intrauterine mass of decidual tissue, probably the result of hyperplasia of decidual cells retained in the uterus. It is doubtful that d. is a true neoplasm.

Loeb's d., a mass of decidual tissue produced in the uterus in the absence of a fertilized ovum, by means of mechanical or hormonal stimulation.

d. malig'num, a term formerly used for chorioadenoma.

deciduosis (de-sid-u-o'sis). Changes in tissues other than in the body of the uterus resembling those which occur in the endometrium during pregnancy.

deciduous (de-sid'u-us) [L. *deciduus,* falling off]. 1. Not permanent; denoting that which eventually falls off. 2 (abbreviated D in dental formulas). In dentistry, often used to designate the first or primary dentition. See *dens* deciduus.

declination (dek-lĭ-na'shun) [L. *declinatio,* a bending aside]. 1. A bending, sloping, or other deviation from a normal vertical position. 2. In ophthalmology, deflection of the vertical meridian of the eye to one or the other side in consequence of rotation of the eyeball in its anteroposterior axis;

declive (de-klīv') [L. *declivis,* sloping downward] [NA]. Declivis; the posterior sloping portion of the monticulus of the vermis of the cerebellum.

decli'vis. Declive.

de'compensa'tion. 1. A failure of compensation in heart disease. 2. The appearance or exacerbation of a mental disorder due to failure of defense mechanisms.

decomposition (de'kom-po-zish'un). Decay; disintegration; lysis.

decompression (de'kom-presh'un) [L. *de-,* from, down, + *com-primo,* pp. *-pressus,* to press together, fr. *premo,* to press]. Removal of pressure.

cardiac d., pericardial d.; incision into the pericardium to relieve pressure due to blood or other fluid in the pericardial sac.

cerebral d., removal of a piece of the cranium, usually in the subtemporal region, with incision of the dura, to relieve intracranial pressure.

nerve d., release of pressure on a nerve trunk by the surgical excision of constricting bands or widening of the bony canal.

pericardial d., cardiac d.

spinal d., removal of pressure upon the spinal cord as by a tumor, cyst, hematoma, or bone.

decongestant, decongestive (de-kon-jes'tant, -tiv). Having the property of reducing congestion.

de'contamina'tion. Removal or neutralization of toxic substances, radioactive materials, etc.

decortica'tion (de'kor-tĭ-ka'shun) [L. *decortico,* pp. *-atus,* to deprive of bark]. 1. Removal of the cortex, or external layer, beneath the capsule from any organ or structure. 2. Surgical removal of the residual clot and/or newly organized scar tissue that form after a hemothorax or neglected empyema.

decrudescence (de-kru-des'ens) [L. *de,* from, + *crudesco,* to become worse]. Abatement of the symptoms of disease.

decubital (de-ku'bĭ-tal). Relating to a decubitus ulcer.

decubitus (de-ku'bĭ-tus) [L. *decumbo,* to lie down]. 1. The position of the patient in bed, as dorsal d., lateral d. 2. A decubitus ulcer.

decus'sate [L. *decusso,* pp. *-atus,* to make in the form of an X]. 1. To cross. 2. Crossed like the arms of an X.

decussatio, pl. **decussationes** (de-kus-sa'shĭ-o, -o'nēz) [L. (see decussate)]. [NA]. Decussation. 1. In general, any crossing over or intersection of parts. 2. Intercrossing of two homonymous fiber bundles as each crosses over to the opposite side of the brain in the course of its ascent or descent through the brainstem or spinal cord.

d. lemnisco'rum, [NA], decussation of medial lemniscus; intercrossing of the fibers of the left and right medial lemniscus ascending from the nuclei gracilis and cuneatus, immediately rostral to the level of the decussation of the pyramidal tracts in the medulla oblongata.

d. pedunculo'rum cerebella'rium superio'rum [NA], decussation of superior cerebellar peduncles; intercrossing of the left and right superior cerebellar peduncles in the tegmentum of the mesencephalon.

d. pyram'idum, [NA], pyramidal or motor decussation; intercrossing of the bundles of the pyramidal tracts at the lower border region of the medulla oblongata.

decussatio'nes tegmen'ti, [NA], tegmental decussations; collective term denoting 1) the dorsal tegmental decussation (fountain or Meynert's decussation) of the left and right tectospinal and tectobulbar tracts, and 2) the ventral tegmental decussation (rubrospinal or Forel's decussation) of the left and right rubrospinal and rubrobulbar tracts; both are located in the mesencephalon.

decussation (de-kus-sa'shun). Decussatio.

Forel's d., see *decussationes* tegmenti.

fountain d., see *decussationes* tegmenti.

d. of medial lemniscus, *decussatio* lemniscorum.

Meynert's d., see *decussationes* tegmenti.

motor d., *decussatio* pyramidum.

optic d., *chiasma* opticum.

pyramidal d., *decussatio* pyramidum.

rubrospinal d., see *decussationes* tegmenti.

d. of superior cerebellar peduncles, *decussatio* pedunculorum cerebellarium superiorum.

tegmental d.'s, *decussationes* tegmenti.

de'differentia'tion. 1. The return of parts to a more homogeneous state. **2.** The process by which mature, differentiated cells or tissues are the sites of origin of immature, undifferentiated elements of the same type, as in fibroma that becomes a fibrosarcoma.

de-epicar'dializa'tion. Surgical destruction of the epicardium, usually by the application of phenol, designed to promote collateral circulation to the myocardium.

def, DEF Decayed, extraction indicated due to caries, or *filled;* designation used in dental examinations of deciduous (lower case letters) or permanent (capital letters) teeth, to describe the caries history.

defecate (def'ē-kāt). To perform defecation.

defecation (def-ē-ka'shun) [L. *defaeco,* pp. *-atus,* to remove the dregs]. Movement (3); the discharge of feces from the rectum.

de'fect. An imperfection or malformation.

aortic septal d., a small congenital opening between the aorta and pulmonary artery just above the similunar valves.

atrial septal d., a d. in the septum between the atria of the heart, due to failure of the foramen primum or secundum to close normally.

congenital ectodermal d., incomplete development of the epidermis and skin appendages; the skin is smooth and hairless, the facies abnormal, and the teeth and nails may be affected; sweating may be deficient.

fibrous cortical d., nonosteogenic fibroma; a common small d. in the cortex of a bone, usually the lower femoral shaft of a child, filled with fibrous tissue.

filling d., abnormal contour of any part of the gastrointestinal tract, seen by x-ray after contrast medium is introduced, indicating tumor or foreign body.

ventricular septal d., a congenital d. in the septum between the cardiac ventricles, usually resulting from failure of the spiral septum to close the interventricular foreamen.

defective (de-fek'tīv) [L. *defectivus;* fr. *facio,* to do, fail, lack]. Denoting an imperfection or malformation; lacking in some physical or mental quality.

defense (de-fens') [L. *defendo,* to ward off]. Methods used to control anxiety.

def'erent [L. *deferens,* pres. p. of *defero,* to carry away]. Carrying away.

def'erentec'tomy [(ductus) deferens, + G. *ektomē,* excision]. Vasectomy.

deferential (def'er-en'shal). Relating to the ductus deferens.

def'erenti'tis. Vasitis; inflammation of the ductus deferens.

defervescence (de-fer-ves'ens) [L. *de-fervesco,* to cease boiling]. Falling of an elevated temperature; abatement of fever.

defibrillation (de'fib-rī-la'shun). Arrest of fibrillation of the cardiac muscle (atrial or ventricular) with restoration of the normal rhythm.

defib'rillator. That which arrests fibrillation of the ventricular muscle and restores the normal heart beat.

defibrination (de'fi-brī-na'shun). Removal of fibrin from blood, usually by means of constant agitation.

deficiency (de-fish'en-sī) [L. *deficio,* to fail, fr. *facio,* to do]. A lacking; something wanting. See also the disease or the substance involved.

antitrypsin d., d. of α_1-antitrypsin, a glycoprotein of the postalbumin region of human serum, which may be moderate or severe; autosomal recessive inheritance.

familial high density lipoprotein d., Tangier *disease.*

galactokinase d., an inborn error of metabolism due to congential d. of galactokinase, resulting in increased blood galactose concentration and cataracts; autosomal recessive inheritance.

glucosephosphate isomerase d., phosphohexose isomerase d.; an enzyme d. characterized by chronic nonspherocytic hemolytic anemia; autosomal recessive inheritance.

immunological, immune, or **immunity d.,** immunodeficiency.

LCAT d., a rare condition characterized by corneal opacities, anemia, proteinuria, and very low levels of *l*ecithin *c*holesterol *a*cyl*t*ransferase activity.

phosphohexose d., glucosephosphate isomerase d.

pseudocholinesterase d., a heritable disorder manifested by exaggerated responses to drugs ordinarily hydrolyzed by serum pseudocholinesterase.

pyruvate kinase d., a disorder in which essentially no pyruvate kinase is formed and characterized by hemolytic anemia; autosomal recessive inheritance.

deficit (def'ī-sit) [L. *deficio,* to fail]. The result of temporarily consuming something faster than it is being replenished.

base d., a decrease in the total concentration of blood buffer base, indicative of metabolic acidosis or compensated respiratory alkalosis.

oxygen d., the difference between oxygen uptake of the body during early stages of exercise and during a similar duration in a steady state of exercise; sometimes considered as the formation of the oxygen debt.

pulse d., absence of palpable pulse waves in a peripheral artery for every heart beat, as is often seen in atrial fibrillation.

deflection (de-flek'shun) [L. *de-flecto*, pp. *-flexus*, to bend aside]. **1.** A moving to one side. **2.** In the electrocardiogram, a deviation of the curve from the isoelectric base line; any wave or complex of the electrocardiogram.

deflu'vium [L. fr. *de-fluo*, pp. *-fluxus*, to flow down]. Defluxion.

defluxion (de-fluk'shun) [L. *defluxio, de-fluo*, pp. *-fluxus*, to flow down]. Defluvium. **1.** A falling down or out, as of the hair. **2.** A flowing down or discharge of fluid.

de'forma'tion [L. *de-formo*, pp. *-atus*, to deform]. **1.** An alteration in shape and/or structure of a previously normally formed part. **2.** Deformity.

deform'ity. Deformation (2); a deviation from the normal shape or size, resulting in disfigurement.

Arnold-Chiari d., elongation of the cerebellar tonsils and drawing of the cerebellum into the fourth ventricle, together with smallness of the medulla and pons and internal hydrocephalus; frequently associated with spina bifida.

gunstock d., a form of cubitus varus resulting from condylar fracture at the elbow in which the axis of the extended forearm is not continous with that of the arm but is displaced toward midline.

Åkerlund d., indentation (incisura) with niche of duodenal cap as seen radiologically.

lobster-claw d., a hand or foot, with the medial digits missing or fused so that it suggests the shape of a lobster claw; usually autosomal dominant inheritance.

Madelung's d., inferior radioulnar subluxation due to a curvature of the lower extremity of the radius with concavity anterior.

reduction d., a congenital skeletal shortening or deficiency of one or more limbs.

silver-fork d., the d. resembling the curve of the back of a fork seen in Colles' fractures.

torsional d., in orthopedics, a d. caused by rotation of a portion of an extremity with relationship to the long axis of the entire extremity.

degen'erate [L. *de*, from, + *genus*, (*gener*-), race]. **1.** To decline to a lower level of mental, physical, or moral qualities. **2.** Denoting such a state or one with such qualities.

degeneration (de-jen-er-a'shun) [L. *degeneratio*]. **1.** Deterioration; a declining to a lower level of mental, physical, or moral qualities. **2.** A retrogressive pathologic change in cells or tissues, in consequence of which the functions may be impaired or destroyed.

adipose d., fatty d.

albuminoid d., albuminous d., cloudy *swelling*.

amyloid d., waxy d. (1); infiltration of amyloid between cells and fibers of tissues and organs.

ascending d., (1) retrograde d. of a severed nerve fiber; *i.e.,* toward the nerve cell of the fiber; (2) d. cephalad to a severed or injured spinal cord.

atheromatous d., focal accumulation of lipid material (atheroma) in the intima and subintimal portion of arteries, eventually resulting in fibrous thickening or calcification.

calcareous d., deposition of insoluble calcium salts in tissue that has degenerated and become necrotic, as in dystrophic calcification.

caseous d., caseous *necrosis*.

colloid d., a d. similar to mucoid d., in which the material is inspissated.

Crooke's hyaline d., replacement of cytoplasmic granules of basophil cells of the anterior pituitary by homogenous hyaline material; a characteristic finding in Cushing's syndrome.

descending d., (1) orthograde (wallerian) d. of a severed nerve fiber; *i.e.,* distal to the section; (2) d. caudal to the level of section or injury of the spinal cord.

elastotic d., elastoid d., elastosis (2).

familial pseudoinflammatory macular d., macular d. with sudden development of a central scotoma in one eye followed rapidly by a similar lesion in the opposite eye; autosomal dominant inheritance.

fascicular d., muscular d. due to atrophy of motor neurons in the cord or brainstem.

fatty d., adipose d.; pimelosis (2); steatosis; abnormal formation of microscopically visible droplets of fat in the cytoplasm of cells, as a result of injury.

fibrinoid d., fibrinous d., a process resulting in poorly defined, deeply acidophilic, homogeneous, refractile deposits with some staining reactions that resemble fibrin, occurring in connective tissue, blood vessel walls, and other sites.

fibroid d., fibrous d., a reparative process in which cells and foci of tissue previously affected with degenerative processes, and necrosis, are replaced by cellular fibrous tissue.

glassy d., hyaline d.

gray d., d. of the white substance of the spinal cord, the fibers of which lose their myelin sheaths and become darker in color.

hepatolenticular d., Wilson's disease (1); a disorder of copper metabolism characterized by cirrhosis, d. in the basal ganglia of the brain, and deposition of green pigment in the periphery of the cornea; autosomal recessive inheritance.

heredomacular d., a group of hereditary disorders involving predominately the posterior portion of the ocular fundus due to degeneration in the sensory retina, retinal pigment epithelium, Bruch's membrane, choroid, or a combination of these tissues.

hyaline d., glassy d.; a group of several degenerative processes that affect various cells and tissues, resulting in the formation of rounded masses ("droplets") or relatively broad bands of substances that are homogeneous, translucent, refractile, and moderately to deeply acidophilic.

hydropic d., cloudy *swelling.*

mucoid d., myxomatosis (1); a conversion of any of the connective tissues into a gelatinous or mucoid substance.

orthograde d., wallerian d.

parenchymatous d., cloudy *swelling.*

reticular d., severe epidermal edema resulting in multilocular bullae.

secondary d., wallerian d.

spongy d., Canavan's disease; a rare, recessively transmitted, fatal brain disease of infancy characterized by progressive paralysis, blindness, and megalencephaly; also with extensive spongiform demyelination of the cerebral hemispheres.

subacute combined d. of the spinal cord, Putnam-Dana syndrome; a subacute or chronic disorder of the spinal cord characterized by a slight to moderate degree of gliosis in association with spongiform degeneration of the posterior and lateral columns.

transsynaptic d., atrophy of nerve cells following damage to the axons that make synaptic connection with them.

vitelliform d., vitelliruptive d., a cystic form of heredomacular d. in Best's disease, with the macular region of each eye occupied by a bright orange-yellow deposit followed by scarring; autosomal dominant inheritance.

wallerian d., orthograde or secondary d.; d of a nerve fiber separated from its trophic center, the nerve cell characterized by proliferation of the nucleus of the interannular segment and by segmentation of the myelin, ending in atrophy and destruction of the axon.

waxy d., (1) amyloid d.; **(2)** Zenker's d.

Zenker's d., waxy d. (2); Zenker's necrosis; a form of severe hyaline d. or necrosis in skeletal muscle, occurring in severe infections.

degen'erative. Relating to degeneration.

deglov'ing. Intraoral surgical exposure of the anterior mandible used in various orthognathic surgical operations.

deglutition (de-glu-tish'un) [L. *de-glutio,* to swallow]. The act of swallowing.

degradation (deg-rǎ-da'shun) [L. *degradatus,* degrade]. The change of a chemical compound into a less complex compound.

degree [Fr. *degré;* L. *gradus,* a step]. **1.** One of the divisions on the scale of a thermometer, barometer, etc. See subentries under scale. **2.** Division of a circle equal to $1/_{360}$ of its circumference. **3.** A position or rank within a graded series.

degusta'tion [L. *degustatio,* fr. *de-gusto,* pp. *-atus,* to taste]. **1.** The act or function of tasting. **2.** The sense of taste.

dehiscence (de-his'ens) [L. *dehiscere,* to split apart or open]. A bursting open, splitting, or gaping along natural or sutured lines.

dehy'drase. Former name for dehydratase.

dehy'dratase. A class of lyases (hydro-lyases) that remove H and OH as H_2O from a substrate, leaving a double bond, or add a group to a double bond by the elimination of water from two substances to form a third.

dehydration (de-hi-dra'shun) [L. *de,* from + G. *hydōr(hydr-),* water]. **1.** Anhydration; deprivation of water. **2.** Reduction of water content. **3.** Exsiccation (2). **4.** Desiccation.

dehydro-. Prefix used in the names of those chemical compounds that differ from other and more familiar compounds in the absence of two hydrogen atoms.

7-dehy'drocholes'terol. 5,7-Cholestadien-3β-ol; a sterol in skin and other animal tissues that upon activation by ultraviolet light becomes antirachitic and is then referred to as vitamin D_3 (cholecalciferol).

dehy'drochol'ic acid. 3,7,12-Trioxo-5β-cholan-24-oic acid; has a stimulating effect upon the secretion of bile by the liver (choleretic) and improves the absorption of essential food materials in states associated with deficient bile formation.

11-dehydrocorticosterone. 21-Hydroxy-4-pregnene-3,11,20-trione; a metabolite of corticosterone found in the adrenal cortex.

dehy'dro-3-epiandros'terone. 3β-Hydroxy-5-androstene-17-one; a weakly androgenic steroid secreted largely by the adrenal cortex, but also by the testes; one of the principal components of urinary 17-ketosteroids.

dehydrogenase (de-hi'dro-jen-ās). Trivial name for those enzymes that catalyze removal of hydrogen from certain metabolites (hydrogen donors) and transfer it to other substances (hydrogen acceptors); the first metabolite is oxidized, the second reduced.

dehy'drogena'tion. **1.** Removal of a pair of hydrogen atoms from a compound, by the action of enzymes (dehydrogenases) or other catalysts. **2.** Removal of hydrogen from the lungs by breathing oxygen in a semiclosed or nonrebreathing system for several minutes prior to the induction of inhalation anesthesia.

déjà vu (da-zhah-vu') [Fr. already seen]. See under phenomenon.

dejection (de-jek'shun) [L. *dejectio,* fr. *de-jicio,* pp. *-jectus,* to cast down]. **1.** Depression (3). **2.** Discharge of excrementitious matter. **3.** The matter so discharged.

deka-. See deco-.

delacrimation (de'lak-rī-ma'shun) [L. *delacrimation,* fr. *lacrimo,* pp. *-atus,* to weep]. Excessive secretion of tears.

de'lamina'tion [L. *de,* from, + *lamina,* a thin plate]. A division into separate layers.

de-lead (de-led'). To cause the mobilization and excretion of lead deposited in the bones and other tissues, as by the administration of a chelating agent or acid salts.

deleterious (de-le-te'rĭus) [G. *dēlētērios,* fr. *dēleomai,* to injure]. Injurious; noxious; harmful.

deletion of chromosomes. A chromosome aberration resulting from breakage of a chromosome, failure of refusion of the segments, and loss of a fragment.

deliquescence (del-ĭ-kwes'ens) [L. *de-liquesco,* to melt or become liquid]. The process of becoming damp or liquid by absorbing water from the atmosphere, said of certain salts.

delir'ious. In a state of delirium.

delir'ium [L. fr. *deliro,* to be crazy]. A condition of extreme mental, and usually motor, excitement marked by defective perception, impaired memory, and a rapid succession of confused and unconnected ideas, often with illusions and hallucinations.

   posttraumatic d., a form of posttraumatic neuropsychologic disorder with disturbed consciousness, agitation, hallucinations, delusions, and/or disorientation.

   d. tre'mens, a form of acute insanity due to alcoholic withdrawal and marked by sweating, tremor, atonic dyspepsia, restlessness, anxiety, precordial distress, mental confusion, and hallucinations.

deliv'er [thru O. Fr. fr. L. *de-* + *liber,* free]. **1.** To assist a woman in childbirth. **2.** To extract from an enclosed place, as the child from the womb, foreign body, tumor, etc.

deliv'ery. Passage of the child and the fetal membranes through the genital canal into the external world.

   forceps d., assisted birth of the child by an instrument designed to grasp the head of the child; **high f. d.** occurs before engagement has taken place; **low f. d.** occurs when the fetal head is clearly visible, the skull has reached the perineal floor, and the sagittal suture is in the anteroposterior diameter of the pelvis; **midforceps d.** before the criteria of low forceps d. have been met, but after engagement has taken place.

   postmortem d., extraction of the fetus after the death of its mother.

   premature d., birth of a fetus before its proper time.

delle (del'eh). The central, lighter-colored portion of the erythrocyte, as observed in a stained film of blood.

del'len [D. *delle,* low ground, pit]. Shallow, clearly defined excavations at the margin of the cornea, due to localized dehydration.

delta [the G. letter Δ, Δ (capital) or δ (lower case)]. **1.** Denoting the fourth in a series (usually δ). **2.** In anatomy, a triangular surface. **3.** In chemistry, Δ is used to denote an unsaturated (double) bond between carbon atoms, with superscripts indicating the positional number of the affected carbon atoms.

deltoid (del'toyd) [G. *deltoeidēs,* shaped like the letter *delta*]. **1.** Resembling the Greek letter delta (Δ); triangular. **2.** *Musculus* deltoideus.

delusion (de-lu'zhun) [L. *de-ludo,* pp. *-lusus,* to deceive]. A false belief or wrong judgment held with conviction despite incontrovertible evidence to the contrary.

   d. of grandeur, a d. in which one believes himself possessed of great wealth, intellect, importance, power, etc.

   d. of negation, nihilistic d., a depressive d. in which one imagines that the world and all that relates to it have ceased to exist.

   d. of persecution, a false notion that one is being persecuted; characteristic symptom of paranoid schizophrenia.

   somatic d., a d. having reference to a nonexistent lesion or alteration of some organ or part of the body; sometimes indistinguishable from hypochondriasis.

   systematized d., a d. that is logically founded upon a false premise and embraces a specific sector of one's life.

   unsystematized d., a d. of a group of apparently discrete, disconnected d.'s.

delu'sional. Relating to a delusion or delusions.

dematiaceous (de-mat-ĭ-a'shus). Dark in color, usually olive colored, gray, or black; used frequently to denote dark-colored fungi.

dementia (de-men'she-ah) [L. fr. *de-* priv. + *mens,* mind]. Amentia (2); a general mental deterioration due to organic or psychological factors.

   dialysis d., dialysis encephalopathy *syndrome.*

   paralytic d., d. paralyt'ica, paresis (2).

   posttraumatic d., a form of posttraumatic neuropsychologic disorder with mental impairment.

   d. pre'cox, [L. precocious], any one of the group of psychotic disorders known as the schizophrenias; formerly used to describe schizophrenia as a single entity.

   presenile d., d. preseni'lis, (1) d. developing before old age; (2) Alzheimer's *disease.*

   primary d., d. occurring independently of other forms of psychosis.

   secondary d., chronic d. following and due to a psychosis.

   senile d., an organic brain syndrome associated with aging and marked by progressive mental deterioration, loss of recent memory, lability of affect, difficulty with novel experience, self-centeredness, and childish behavior.

demi- [Fr. fr. L. *dimidius,* half]. Prefix denoting half, lesser. See also hemi-, semi-.

dem'ilune. [Fr. half-moon]. A small body with a form similar to that of a half-moon or a crescent.

demin'eraliza'tion. A loss or decrease of the mineral constituents of the body or individual tissues, especially of bone.

Demodex (dem'o-deks) [G. *dēmos,* tallow, + *dēx,* a woodworm]. A genus of minute follicular parasitic mites (family Demodicidae) that invade the skin and are usually found in the sebaceous glands and hair follicles of man and animals; seldom pathogenic.

demography (de-mog'ră-fĭ) [G. *demos,* people, + *graphō,* to write]. The statisical study of groups of people, their environment, and their geographic distribution.

demucosa'tion. Excision or stripping of the mucosa of any part.

demulcent (de-mul'sent) [L. *de-mulceo,* pp. *-mulctus,* to stroke lightly, to soften]. Soothing; relieving irritation, especially of mucous surfaces.

demyelination, demyelinization (de-mi'ĕ-lĭ-na'shun, de-mi'ĕ-lin-ĭ-za'shun). Destruction or loss of myelin from the medullary sheath of Schwann or of myelin associated with oligodendroglia.

dena'tured. 1. Made unnatural or changed from the normal in any of its characteristics; often applied to proteins or nucleic acids heated or otherwise treated to the point where tertiary structural characteristics are altered. **2.** Adulterated, as by addition of methyl alcohol to ethyl alcohol.

den'driform [G. *dendron,* tree, + L. *forma,* form]. Dendritic (1); dendroid; arborescent; tree-shaped, or branching.

den'drite [G. *dendritēs,* relating to a tree]. Dendron; neurodendrite; neurodendron; one of the two types of branching protoplasmic processes of the nerve cell (the other being the axon).

dendrit'ic. 1. Dendriform. **2.** Relating to the dendrites of nerve cells.

dendroid (den'droyd) [G. *dendron,* tree, + *eidos,* appearance]. Dendriform.

den'dron [G. a tree]. Dendrite.

denervate (de-ner'vāt). To cut off the nerve supply of a part by incision, excision, or local anesthesia.

dengue (den'ga) [Sp. a corruption of "dandy" fever]. A disease of tropical and subtropical regions occurring epidemically, transmitted by an *Aedes* mosquito, and caused by dengue virus. Four grades of severity are recognized: *I,* fever and constitutional symptoms; *II,* grade I plus spontaneous bleeding of skin, gums, or gastrointestinal tract; *III,* grade II plus agitation and circulatory failure; *IV,* profound shock.

denial (de-ni'al). Negation; unconscious defense mechanism used to allay anxiety by denying the existence of important conflicts or troublesome impulses.

denidation (den-ĭ-da'shun) [L. *de,* from, + *nidus,* nest]. Exfoliation of the superficial portion of the mucous membrane of the uterus.

dens, pl. **dentes** (denz, den'tēz) [L.] [NA]. **1.** Tooth. **2.** A toothlike process projecting upward from the body of the axis around which the atlas rotates.

  d. cani'nus, pl. **den'tes cani'ni** [NA], canine, cuspid, or eye tooth; cuspid (2); a tooth having a crown of thick conical shape and a long conical root; there are two canine teeth in each jaw, adjacent to the distal surface of the lateral incisors, in both

deciduous and permanent dentition.

  d. decid'uus, pl. **den'tes decidu'ui** [NA], baby, milk, primary, deciduous, or temporary tooth; deciduous or primary dentition; a tooth of the first set of teeth, 20 in all, that erupts between the mean ages of 6 and 28 months of life.

  d. in den'te, a developmental disturbance in tooth formation resulting from invagination of the epithelium associated with coronal development into the area which was destined to be pulp space.

  d. incisi'vus, pl. **den'tes incisi'vi** [NA], incisor tooth; a tooth with a chisel-shaped crown and a single conical root; there are four in the anterior part of each jaw, in both deciduous and permanent dentitions.

  d. mola'ris, pl. **den'tes mola'res** [NA], molar tooth; molar (2); a tooth having a crown with four or five cusps on the grinding surface, a bifid root in the lower jaw, and three conical roots in the upper jaw; in permanent dentition, there are three on either side behind the premolars; in deciduous dentition, there are two on either side behind the canines.

  d. per'manens, pl. **den'tes permane'tes** [NA], second or permanent tooth; secondary dentition; one of the 32 teeth whose eruptions begin from the 5th to the 7th year, and last until the 17th to the 23rd year, when the last of the wisdom teeth appears.

  d. premola'ris, pl. **den'tes premola'res** [NA], premolar or bicuspid tooth; a tooth usually having two cusps on the grinding surface and a flattened root; there are two on either side between the canine and the molars.

  d. seroti'nus [NA], wisdom tooth; the third molar tooth on each side in each jaw that erupt from the 17th to the 23rd year.

densim'eter [L. *densitas,* density, + G. *metron,* measure]. An instrument for measuring the density of a fluid.

densitom'eter [L. *densitas,* density, + G. *metron,* measure]. **1.** A special form of densimeter for measuring, by virtue of relative turbidity, the growth of bacteria in broth. **2.** An instrument for measuring the density of components separated by electrophoresis or chromatography, utilizing light absorption or reflection.

densitom'etry. A procedure utilizing a densitometer.

density (den'sĭ-tĭ) [L. *densitas,* fr. *densus,* thick]. **1.** The compactness of a substance; the ratio of mass to volume, usually expressed as g/ml (kg/m^{3}in SI units). **2.** The quantity of electricity on a given surface or in a given time per unit of volume.

dent-, denti-, dento- [L. *dens,* tooth]. Combining forms relating to the teeth.

den'tal [L. *dens,* tooth]. Relating to the teeth.

dentalgia (den-tal'jĭ-ah) [L. *dens,* tooth, + G. *algos,* pain]. Toothache.

den'tate [L. *dentatus,* toothed]. Notched; toothed; cogged.

dentes (den'tēz) [L.]. Plural of dens.

denti-. See dent-.

den'ticle [L. *denticulus,* a small tooth]. **1.** A pulpstone. **2.** A slight projection from a hard surface.

dentifrice (den'tĭ-fris) [L. *dentifricium,* fr. *dens,* tooth, + *frico,* pp. *frictus,* to rub]. Any preparation used in the cleansing of the teeth.

dentigerous (den-tij'er-us) [denti- + L. *gero,* to bear]. Arising from or associated with teeth.

den'tila'bial [denti- + L. *labium,* lip]. Relating to the teeth and lips.

dentilingual (den-tĭ-ling'gwal) [denti- + L. *lingua,* tongue]. Relating to the teeth and tongue.

den'tin [L. *dens,* tooth]. Dentinum; the ivory substance forming the mass of a tooth.

   hereditary opalescent d., *dentinogenesis* imperfecta.

   irregular d., tertiary d.

   primary d., d. which forms until the root is completed.

   reparative d., tertiary d.

   sclerotic d., transparent d.; d. characterized by calcification of the dentinal tubules as a result of injury or normal aging.

   secondary d., d. formed by normal pulp function after root end formation is complete.

   tertiary d., irregular or reparative d.; morphologically irregular d. formed in response to an irritant.

   transparent d., sclerotic d.

den'tinal. Relating to dentin.

dentinal'gia [dentin + G. *algos,* pain]. Pain or tenderness of the dentin.

den'tinocemen'tal. Relating to the dentin and cementum of teeth.

dentinoenamel (den'tĭ-no-e-nam'el). Amelodentinal; relating to the dentin and enamel of teeth.

dentinogenesis (den'tĭ-no-jen'ĕ-sis) [dentin + G. *genesis,* production]. The process of dentin formation in the development of teeth.

   d. imperfec'ta, dentinal dysplasia; hereditary opalescent dentin; a defect of dentin formation characterized by translucent or opalescent color of teeth, easy fracturing of enamel, wearing of occlusal surfaces, and staining of exposed dentin. autosomal dominant inheritance.

den'tinoid [dentin + G. *eidos,* resembling]. **1.** Resembling dentin. **2.** Dentinoma.

dentinoma (den'tĭ-no-mah) [dentin + G. *-oma,* tumor]. Dentinoid (2); an odontogenic tumor in which dentin formation has been induced by invading epithelium.

den'tinum [L. *dens,* tooth] [NA]. Dentin.

dentip'arous [denti- + L. *pario,* to bear]. Tooth-bearing.

den'tist. A licensed practitioner of dentistry.

den'tistry. Odontology; the healing science and art concerned with the prevention, diagnosis, and treatment of deformities, diseases, and traumatic injuries of the teeth and orofacial complex.

forensic d., legal d., **(1)** the relation and application of dental facts to legal problems, as in using the teeth for identifying the dead; **(2)** the law in its bearing on the practice of dentistry.

operative d., restorative d., individual restoration of teeth by means of amalgam, synthetic porcelain-like materials, or inlays.

preventive d., a philosophy and method of dental practice that seeks to prevent the initiation, progression, and recurrence of dental caries.

dentition (den-tish'un) [L. *dentitio,* to teethe]. The natural teeth, considered collectively, in the dental arch.

   deciduous d., *dens* deciduus.

   delayed d., delayed eruption of the teeth.

   mandibular d., *arcus* dentalis inferior.

   maxillary d., *arcus* dentalis superior.

   primary d., *dens* deciduus.

   retarded d., d. in which growth phenomena occur later than in the average range of normal variation as a result of some systemic metabolic dysfunction.

   secondary d., *dens* permanens.

dento-. See dent-.

den'toalve'olar. Denoting that portion of the alveolar bone immediately about the teeth; also the functional unity of teeth and alveolar bone.

dentulous (den'tu-lus). Having natural teeth present in the mouth.

denture (den'tūr). An artificial substitute for missing natural teeth and adjacent tissues.

   complete d., full d., a dental prosthesis that is a substitute for the lost natural dentition and associated structures of the maxillae or mandible.

   fixed partial d., bridge (3); a restoration of one or more missing teeth permanently attached to natural teeth or roots which furnish the primary support to the appliance.

   immediate d., a complete or partial d. constructed for insertion immediately following the removal of natural teeth.

   implant d., a d. that receives its stability and retention from a substructure which is partially or wholly implanted under the soft tissues.

   interim d., temporary d.; a dental prosthesis to be used for a short interval of time or to condition the patient to accept an artificial substitute for missing natural teeth.

   overlay d., overdenture; a complete d. supported by both soft tissue and natural teeth that have been altered so as to permit it to fit over them.

   partial d., bridgework; a dental prosthesis that restores one or more, but less than all, of the natural teeth and/or associated parts and is supported by the teeth and/or the mucosa; may be removable or fixed.

   removable partial d., a partial d. that supplies teeth and associated structures on a partially edentulous jaw and can be removed.

   temporary d., interim d.

transitional d., a partial d. used to serve as a temporary prosthesis to which teeth will be added as more teeth are lost, and which will be replaced after postextraction tissue changes have occurred.

trial d., wax model d.; a setup of artificial teeth placed in the patient's mouth to verify esthetics, for the making of records, or for any other operation before final commpletion of the d.

denucleated (de-nu′kle-a-ted). Deprived of a nucleus.

denudation (den-u-da′shun) [L. *de-nudo*, to lay bare]. Depriving of a covering or protecting layer.

deo′dorant [L. *de-* priv. + *odoro*, pp. *-atus*, to give an odor to]. An agent that destroys odors, especially disagreeable odors.

deo′dorizer. A substance that removes malodorous substances or converts them into odorless compounds.

deossification (de-os′ĭ-fĭ-ka′shun) [L. *de*, from, + *os*, bone, + *facio*, to make]. Loss or removal of the mineral constituents of bone.

deoxy-. Prefix (replacing desoxy-) to chemical names of substances containing carbohydrate moieties to indicate replacement of an —OH by an H.

deoxyaden′osine. 2′-Deoxyribosyladenine, a constituent of DNA.

deox′yadenyl′ic acid (dAMP). Adenine deoxyribonucleotide; deoxyadenosine phosphate, a hydrolysis product of DNA, differing from adenylic acid in containing deoxyribose in place of ribose.

deoxycho′lic acid (DOC). 3α, 12α-Dihydroxy-5β-cholanic acid; a bile acid and choleretic.

deox′ycorticos′terone (DOC). 21-Hydroxy-4-pregnene-3,20-dione; an adrenocortical steroid and biosynthetic precursor of corticosterone; a potent mineralocorticoid, with no appreciable glucocorticoid activity.

11-deoxycor′tisone. 17,21-Dihydroxy-4-pregnene-3,20-dione; an adrenocortical steroid, with weak biologic activity, and biosynthetic precursor of cortisol.

deoxycy′tidine. 2′-Deoxyribosylcytosine, a constituent of DNA.

deox′ycytidyl′ic acid. Deoxycytidine phosphate, a hydrolysis product of DNA.

deoxygenation (de′ok-sĭ-jen-a′shun). Removing or depriving of oxygen.

deoxyguan′osine. 2′-Deoxyribosylguanine, a constituent of DNA.

deoxyguanyl′ic acid (dGMP). Guanine deoxyribonucleotide; deoxyguanosine phosphate; a hydrolysis product of DNA.

deoxyribonuclease (DNase, DNAse, DNAase) (de-ok′sĭ-ri-bo-nu′kle-ās). An enzyme (a phosphodiesterase) hydrolyzing phosphodiester bonds in DNA; used in cytochemistry to selectively remove DNA as a control for staining it.

deoxyri′bonucle′ic acid (DNA). Nucleic acid containing deoxyribose as the sugar component and found principally in the chromatin and chromosomes of animal and vegetable cells, usually loosely bound to

protein; considered to be the autoreproducing component of chromosomes and of many viruses, and the repository of hereditary characteristics.

complementary DNA (cDNA), DNA that is complementary to messenger RNA.

deox′yribonu′cleopro′tein (DNP). The complex of DNA and protein in which DNA is usually found upon cell disruption and isolation.

deoxyri′bonu′cleoside. A nucleoside containing 2-deoxyribose; condensation product of deoxyribose with purines or pyrimidines; component of DNA.

deoxyri′bonu′cleotide. A nucleotide component of DNA containing 2-deoxyribose; phosphoric ester of deoxyribonucleoside.

deoxyri′bose. A deoxypentose occurring in DNA and responsible for its name.

deox′ythymidyl′ic acid (dTMP). Thymine deoxyribonucleotide, a component of DNA.

depen′dence [L. *dependeo*, to hang from]. The quality or condition of lacking independence by relying upon, being influenced by, or being subservient to a person or object reflecting a particular need.

deper′sonaliza′tion. A state in which a person loses the feeling of his own identity in relation to others in his family or peer group, or loses the feeling of his own reality.

depigmenta′tion. Loss of pigment; it may be partial or complete.

depilate (dep′ĭ-lāt) [L. *de-pilo*, pp. *-atus*, to deprive of hair]. To remove hair by any means.

depilation (dep-ĭ-la′shun). Epilation.

depilatory (de-pil′ă-to-rĭ). **1.** Epilatory (1). **2.** Epilatory (2); an agent that causes the falling out of hair.

deplumation (de-plu-ma′shun) [L. *de-* priv. + *plumo*, pp. *-atus*, to deprive of feathers]. Falling out or loss of the eyelashes.

depolarization (de-po′lar-ĭ-za′shun). The destruction, neutralization, or change in direction of polarity.

depres′sant [L. *de-primo*, pp. *-pressus*, to press down]. Reducing functional tone or activity.

depressed (de-prest′). **1.** Below the normal level or the level of the surrounding parts, below the normal functional level. **2.** Dejected; lowered in spirits.

depression (de-presh′un). **1.** A sinking below the surrounding level. **2.** A hollow or sunken area. **3.** Dejection (1); a sinking of spirits so as to consitute a clinically discernible condition.

agitated d., d. with excitement and restlessness.

anaclitic d., impairment of an infant's physical, social, and intellectual development following separation from its mother or from a mothering influence; characterized by listlessness, withdrawal, and anorexia.

pacchionian d.'s, pits on the inner surface of the skull, along the course of the superior sagittal sinus, in which are lodged the arachnoidal granulation.

reactive d., a psychotic state occasioned directly by an intensely sad external situation and relieved by the removal of the external situation.

depres′somo′tor. Retarding motor activity.

depres'sor. 1. A muscle that flattens or lowers a part. **2.** Anything that depresses or retards functional activity. **3.** An instrument or device used to push certain structures out of the way during an operation or examination. **4.** Hypotensor; an agent producing decreased blood pressure.

deprivation (dep'rĭ-va'shun). Absence, loss, or withholding of something needed.

 emotional d., lack of adequate and appropriate interpersonal or environmental experiences, or both, usually in the early developmental years.

 sensory d., diminution or absence of usual external stimuli or perceptual opportunities, commonly resulting in psychological distress and aberrant functioning.

depth. Distance from the surface downward.

 anesthetic d., the degree of central nervous system depression produced by a general anesthetic agent; a function of potency of the anesthetic and the concentration in which it is administered.

 focal d., d. of focus, the greatest distance through which an object point can be moved while producing a clear image.

derangement (de-rānj'ment) [Fr.]. **1.** Disordering; a disturbance of the regular order or arrangement. **2.** Mental disturbance or disorder.

derealization (de-re'ă-lĭ-za'shun). An alteration in one's perception of the environment such that things that are ordinarily familiar seem strange, unreal, or two-dimensional.

dereism (de're-izm) [L. *de*, away, + *res*, thing]. Mental activity in fantasy, in contrast to reality.

dereistic (de-re-is'tik). Living in imagination or fantasy.

derencephaly (dĕr-en-sef'ă-lĭ) [G. *derē*, neck, + *enkephalos*, brain]. Cervical rachischisis and anencephaly, a malformation involving an open cranial vault with a markedly defective brain usually crowded back toward bifid cervical vertebrae.

derepression (de're-presh'un). The process in which an inducer, usually a substrate of a specific enzyme pathway, combines with an active repressor (produced by a regulator gene) to deactivate the repressor; results in activation of a previously repressed operator gene and activity of the structural genes controlled by the operator, followed by enzyme production; a homeostatic mechanism for regulating enzyme production in an inducible enzyme system.

derivative (dĕ-riv'ă-tiv). **1.** Something produced by modification of something preexisting. **2.** Specifically, a chemical compound that may be produced from another compound of similar structure in one or more steps.

derm-, derma-, dermat-, dermato-, dermo- [G. *derma*, skin]. Combining forms signifying skin.

dermabrasion (der-mă-bra'zhun). Operative removal of disfigured skin using sand paper, wire brushes, or other abrasive materials.

Der'macen'tor [derm- + G. *kentōr*, a goader]. A characteristically marked genus of hard ticks (family Ixodidae).

 D. anderso'ni, the Rocky Mountain spotted-fever, or wood tick; a species that is the vector of spotted fever in the Rocky Mountain regions, and also transmits tularemia and causes tick paralysis.

 D. variabi'lis, the American dog or wood tick, a species that transmits tularemia and is a principal vector of spotted fever in the central and eastern U.S.

der'mal. Dermatic; dermic; relating to the skin.

dermat-. See derm-.

dermat'ic. Dermal.

dermati'tis, pl. **dermatit'ides** [derm- + G. *-itis,* inflammation]. Inflammation of the skin.

 actinic d., eruption of sensitivity produced by exposure to sunlight, usually of specific electromagnetic energy.

 atopic d., d. characterized by the distinctive phenomena of atopy, including infantile and flexural eczema.

 berloque d., berlock d., a type of photosensitization resulting in deep brown pigmentation on exposure to sunlight after exposure to essential oils in perfume.

 bubble gum d., allergic contact d. developing about the lips in children who chew bubble gum; caused by plastics in the gum substance.

 chemical d., allergic contact d. or primary irritation d. due to application of chemicals; usually characterized by erythema, edema, and vesiculation of the exposed or contacted site.

 contact d., a delayed type of induced sensitivity (allergy) of the skin with varying degrees of erythema, edema, and vesiculation, resulting from cutaneous contact with a specific allergen.

 contact-type d., d. resembling contact d., but caused by an ingested or injected allergen and with a widespread or generalized distribution.

 diaper d., colloquially referred to as diaper rash; d. of thighs and buttocks supposedly due to ammonia produced in decomposing urine in infants' diapers.

 d. exfoliati'va infan'tum or **neonato'rum,** impetigo neonatorum (1); a generalized pyoderma affecting young infants, accompanied by exfoliative d. with constitutional symptoms.

 exfoliative d., pityriasis rubra; Wilson's disease (2); generalized exfoliation with scaling of the skin and usually with erythema (erythroderma).

 d. herpetifor'mis, Duhring's disease; a chronic disease of the skin marked by a severe, extensive, itching eruption of vesicles and papules which occur in groups.

 industrial d., d. resulting from exposure to an agent discharged by an industry into the environment.

infectious eczematoid d., an inflammatory reaction of skin adjacent to the site of a pyogenic infection.

livedoid d., reddish blue mottled condition of skin due to affection of cutaneous vascular apparatus.

meadow d., meadow grass d., phytophlyctodermatitis; a phototoxic reaction to contact with a plant in which the configuration of the eruption is that of the streaky pattern of the plant contact.

d. medicamento'sa, drug *eruption.*

occupational d., d. as a response of allergic sensitization to substances normally encountered in an occupation, or as a reaction of primary irritation.

d. papilla'ris capillit'ii, acne *keloid.*

d. pediculoi'des ventrico'sus, an urticarial eruption caused by the mite *Pediculoides ventricosus,* which infests grain and straw.

d. re'pens [L. creeping]. *acrodermatitis* continua.

schistosome d., swimmer's itch; a sensitization response to repeated cutaneous invasion by cercariae of bird, mammal, or human schistosomes.

seborrheic d., d. seborrhe'ica, dyssebacia; pityriasis alba; a scaly macular eruption that occurs primarily on the face, scalp, interscapular area, pubic area, and about the anus; the lesions are covered with a slightly adherent oily scale.

stasis d., erythema and scaling of the lower extremities due to impaired circulation and other factors, such as nutritional edema.

d. verruco'sa, chromoblastomycosis.

dermato-. See derm-.

dermatoautoplasty (der′mă-to-aw′to-plas-tĭ) [dermato- + G. *autos,* self, + *plassō,* to form]. Autografting of skin taken from another part of the patient's own body.

Dermato'bia [dermato- + G. *bios,* way of living]. A genus of flies (family Oestridae) found in tropical America. *D. hominis,* the human, skin, or warble botfly, is a species whose larvae develop in boil-like cysts in the skin of man, many domestic animals, and some fowl.

dermatocele (der′mă-to-sēl) [dermato- + G. *kēlē,* hernia]. A localized atrophy or herniation of skin that may result from a neurofibroma or a congenital defect.

der′matofibro′ma. A slowly growing benign skin nodule consisting of poorly demarcated cellular fibrous tissue enclosing collapsed capillaries, with scattered hemosiderin-pigmented and lipid macrophages.

der′matofi′brosarco′ma protu′berans. A slow-growing dermal neoplasm consisting of one or several firm nodules usually covered by dark red-blue skin which tends to be fixed to the palpable masses; histologically, resembles a cellular dermatofibroma or a low-grade fibrosarcoma.

dermatoglyphics (der′mă-to-glif′iks) [dermato- + *glyphē,* carved work]. **1.** Configurations of the characteristic ridge patterns of the volar surfaces of the skin; the distal segment of each digit has three

types of configurations: whorl, loop, and arch. See also fingerprint. **2.** The science or study of these configurations or patterns.

dermatographism (der-mă-tog′ră-fizm) [dermato- + G. *graphō,* to write]. Dermographia; dermographism; a form of urticaria in which whealing occurs in the site and in the configuration of stroking.

der′matohet′eroplasty [dermato- + G. *heteros,* another, + *plassō,* to form]. Heterografting of skin from a member of another species.

der′matoho′moplasty [dermato- + G. *homos,* same, + *plastos,* formed]. Homografting of skin from another member of the same species.

dermatol′ogist. A physician who specializes in the diagnosis and treatment of cutaneous lesions and related systemic diseases.

dermatology (der-mă-tol′o-jĭ) [dermato- + G. *logos,* study]. The medical specialty concerned with the study of the skin and the relationship of cutaneous lesions to systemic disease.

dermatolysis (der-mă-tol′ĭ-sis) [dermato- + G. *lysis,* a loosening]. Loosening of the skin or atrophy of the skin by disease.

dermatoma (der-mă-to′mah) [dermato- + G. *-oma,* tumor]. A circumscribed thickening or hypertrophy of the skin.

der′matome [dermato- + *tomē,* a cutting]. **1.** An instrument for cutting thin slices of skin for grafting, or excising small lesions. **2.** The dorsolateral part of an embryonic somite. **3.** The area of skin supplied by cutaneous branches from a single spinal nerve.

dermatomegaly (der′mă-to-meg′ă-lĭ) [dermato- + G. *megas,* large]. A congenital defect in which the skin hangs in folds.

dermatomere (der′mă-to-mēr) [dermato- + G. *meros,* part]. A metameric area of the embryonic integument.

der′matomyco′sis. Dermatophytosis.

dermatomyoma (der′mă-to-mi-o′mah) [dermato- + G. *mys,* muscle, + *-oma,* tumor]. *Leiomyoma* cutis.

dermatomyositis (der′mă-to-mi-o-si′tis) [dermato- + G. *mys,* muscle, + *-itis,* inflammation]. A progressive condition characterized by muscular weakness with a skin rash, typically a purplish-red heliotrope erythema on the face and edema of the eyelids and periorbital tissue.

dermatoneurosis (der′mă-to-nu-ro′sis). Any cutaneous eruption due to emotional stimuli.

der′matopathol′ogy. Histopathology of skin lesions.

dermatopathy (der′mă-top′ă-thĭ) [dermato- + G. *pathos,* suffering]. Dermopathy; any disease of the skin.

Dermatophagoi′des pteronyssi′nus [dermato- + G. *phagein,* to eat]. A common species of cosmopolitan sarcoptiform mites found in house dust and a common contributory cause of atopic asthma.

dermatophylaxis (der′mă-to-fi-lak′sis) [dermato- + G. *phylaxis,* protection]. Protection of the skin against potentially harmful agents.

dermatophyte (der'mă-to-fīt) [dermato- + G. *phyton*, plant]. A fungus that causes infections of the skin, hair, and/or nails.

dermatophytid (der-mă-tof'ĭ-tid) [dermatophyte + -*id*]. An allergic manifestation of dermatophytosis at a site distant from that of the primary fungous infection.

dermatophytosis (der'mă-to-phi-to'sis). Dermatomycosis; infection of the hair, skin, or nails caused by a dermatophyte; characterized by erythema, small papular vesicles, fissures, and scaling.

der'matoplas'tic. Relating to dermatoplasty.

der'matoplas'ty [dermato- + G. *plassō*, to form]. Dermoplasty; repair of defects of the skin, as by skin grafting.

dermatopolyneuritis (der'mă-to-pol'ĭ-nu-ri'tis). Acrodynia (1).

dermatosclerosis (der'mă-to-skle-ro'sis) [dermato- + G. *sclērō*, to harden]. Scleroderma.

dermatosis, pl. **dermatoses** (der-mă-tō'sis, -sēz) [dermato- + G. -*osis*, condition]. Any cutaneous lesion or group of lesions, or eruptions of any type.

   lichenoid d., any chronic skin eruption, characterized by induration and thickening of the skin with accentuation of skin markings.

   d. medicamento'sa, drug *eruption.*

   d. papulo'sa ni'gra, dark brown papular lesions, observed in Blacks, on the face and upper trunk; histologically and clinically resemble seborrheic keratoses.

   progressive pigmentary d., Schamberg's disease; chronic purpura, especially of the legs in men, spreading to form brownish patches; associated microscopically with capillary dilation, diapedesis, and hemosiderosis.

   radiation d., skin changes caused by ionizing radiation, particularly erythema in the acute stage and chronic changes in the epidermis and dermis resembling actinic keratosis.

   seborrheic d., seborrheic *dermatitis.*

   subcorneal pustular d., a pruritic chronic annular eruption of sterile vesicles and pustules beneath the stratum corneum.

der'matother'apy. Treatment of skin diseases.

dermatotropic (der'mă-to-trop'ik) [dermato- + G. *trōpe*, a turning]. Dermotropic; having an affinity for the skin.

der'mic. Dermal.

der'mis [G. *derma*, skin] [NA]. Corium.

dermo-. See derm-.

der'moblast [dermo- + G. *blastos*, germ]. One of the mesodermal cells from which the corium is developed.

dermograph'ia, dermog'raphism. Dermatographism.

dermoid (der'moyd) [derm- + G. *eidos*, resemblance]. **1.** Dermatoid (1). **2.** Dermoid *cyst.*

dermoidectomy (der-moy-dek'to-mĭ) [dermoid + G. *ektomē*, excision]. Surgical removal of a dermoid cyst.

dermop'athy. Dermatopathy.

   diabetic d., small macules and papules of the extensor surfaces of the extremities (most commonly the shins) which become atrophic, hyperpigmented, and occasionally undergo ulceration with scarring.

der'moplasty. Dermatoplasty.

dermotrop'ic. Dermatotropic.

dermovas'cular [dermo- + L. *vasculus*, small vessel]. Pertaining to the blood vessels of the skin.

de'rota'tion [L. *de*, away, + *rotatio*, turning]. **1.** A turning back. **2.** In orthopedics, the correction of a torsional deformity.

des-. See de-.

desat'ura'tion. The act or the result of making something less completely saturated; more specifically, the percentage of total binding sites remaining unfilled.

descemetitis (des'ĕ-mĕ-ti'tis). Inflammation of Descemet's membrane on the posterior surface of the cornea.

descemetocele (des-ĕ-met'o-sēl) [Descemet's membrane + G. *kēlē*, hernia]. Hernia of Descemet's membrane.

descensus (de-sen'sus) [L.]. Descent; a falling.

   d. ab'errans tes'tis, incomplete descent of the testis which comes to rest in the inguinal canal, femoral canal, or perineal region, or under the skin of the penis.

   d. paradox'us tes'tis, descent of the right testis to the left half of the scrotum and the left testis to the right half.

   d. tes'tis [NA], descent of the testis from the abdomen into the scrotum during the seventh and eighth months of intrauterine life.

   d. u'teri, falling of the womb.

descent (de-sent') [L. descensus]. In obstetrics, the passage of the presenting part of the fetus into and through the birth canal.

desen'sitiza'tion. **1.** Antianaphylaxis; reduction or abolition of allergic sensitivity or reactions to the specific antigen (allergen). **2.** The act of removing an emotional complex.

desen'sitize. **1.** To reduce or remove any form of sensitivity. **2.** To effect desensitization.

desiccant (des'ĭ-kant) [L. *de-sicco*, pp. -*siccatus*, to dry up]. Exsiccant; desiccative; drying; causing or promoting dryness.

desiccate (des'ĭ-kāt). Exsiccate; to dry thoroughly; to render free from moisture.

desicca'tion. Exsiccation (1); dehydration (4); the process of being desiccated.

desiccative (des'ĭ-ka-tiv). Desiccant (1).

desm-. See desmo-.

desmitis (dez-mi'tis) [desm- + G. -*itis*, inflammation]. Inflammation of a ligament.

desmo-, desm- [G. *desmos*, a band]. Combining forms meaning fibrous connection or ligament.

desmocranium (dez'mo-kra'nĭ-um). The mesenchymal primordium of the cranium.

desmogenous (dez-moj'ĕ-nus) [desmo- + G. -gen, producing]. Of connective tissue or ligamentous origin or causation.

desmoid (dez'moyd) [desmo- + G. eidos, appearance, form]. 1. Fibrous or ligamentous. 2. Desmoid tumor; a nodule or relatively large mass of unusually firm scarlike connective tissue resulting from active proliferation of fibroblasts, occurring most frequently in the abdominal muscles of women who have borne children.

desmolases (dez'mo-la-sez). Enzymes catalyzing reactions other than those involving hydrolysis.

desmopathy (dez-mop'ă-thī) [desmo- + G. pathos, suffering]. A disease of ligaments.

desmoplasia (dez-mo-pla'zīah) [desmo- + G. plasis, a molding]. Hyperplasia of fibroblasts and disproportionate formation of fibrous connective tissue, especially in the stroma of a carcinoma.

desmoplas'tic. 1. Causing or forming adhesions. **2.** Causing fibrosis in the vascular stroma of a neoplasm.

desmosome (dez'mo-sōm) [desmo- + G. sōma, body]. Macular adherens; a site of adhesion between two cells, consisting of a dense plate separated from a similar structure in the other cell by a thin layer of extracellular material.

desoxy-. See deoxy-.

despeciation (de-spe'shī-a'shun). **1.** Alteration of, or loss of species characteristics. **2.** Removal of species-specific antigenic properties from a foreign protein.

desquamation (des-kwă-ma'shun) [L. desquamo, pp. -atus, to scale off]. The shedding of the epidermis in scales or shreds, or of the outer layer of any surface.

desquamative (des-kwam'ă-tiv). Relating to or marked by desquamation.

desulf'hydrases, desul'furases. Enzymes or groups of enzymes catalyzing the removal of a molecule of H_2S or substituted H_2S from a compound.

DET Diethyltryptamine.

detach'ment. 1. A voluntary or involuntary separation from normal associations or environment. **2.** Separation of a structure from its support.

retinal d., d. of retina, loss of apposition between the sensory retina and the retinal pigment epithelium.

detergent (de-ter'jent) [L. de-tergeo, pp. -tersus, to wipe off]. **1.** Cleansing. **2.** A cleansing or purging agent.

deterioration (de-tēr'ī-o-ra'shun) [L. deterior, worse]. The process or condition of becoming worse.

deter'minant [L. determans, determining, limiting]. A factor that establishes the nature of any given quality.

antigenic d., the particular chemical group of a molecule that determines immunological specificity.

genetic d., genetic marker; any antigenic d. or identifying characteristic particularly those of allotypes.

deter'mina'tion [L. de-termino, pp. -atus, to limit, determine]. **1.** A change, for the better or for the worse, in the course of a disease. **2.** A general move toward a given point. **3.** The measurement or estimation of any quantity or quality in scientific investigation.

determinism (de-ter'mĭ-nizm). The proposition that all behavior is dependent on genetic and environmental influences and independent of free will.

detoxicate (de-tok'sĭ-kāt) [L. de, from, + toxicum, poison]. Detoxify; to diminish or remove the poisonous quality of any substance or the virulence of any pathogen.

detoxica'tion. Detoxification. **1.** Recovery from toxic effects. **2.** Removal of toxic properties. **3.** Metabolic conversion of pharmacologically active principles to pharmacologically less active principles.

detox'ifica'tion. Detoxification.

detox'ify. Detoxicate.

detrition (de-trish'un) [L. de-tero, pp. -tritus, to rub off]. A wearing away by use or friction.

detri'tus [L. (see detrition)]. Matter resulting from or remaining after decomposition or disintegration of a substance.

detru'sor [L. detrudo, to drive away]. A muscle that has the action of expelling a substance.

detumescence (de-tu-mes'ens) [L. de, from, + tumesco, to swell up]. Subsidence of a swelling.

deut-. See deutero-.

deuteranopia (du'ter-ă-no'pī-ah) [G. deuteros, second, + anopia]. A form of dichromatism in which there are two rather than three retinal cone pigments and complete insensitivity to green.

deu'terano'pic. Pertaining to or characterized by deuteranopia.

deuterio-. Prefix indicating "containing deuterium."

deuterium (D, d) (du-tēr'ī-um) [G. deuteros, second]. Hydrogen-2.

deutero-, deuto-, deut- [G. deuteros, second]. Combining forms meaning two, or second (in a series).

Deuteromycetes (du'ter-o-mi-se'tēz). Fungi Imperfecti.

deuteropathic (du'ter-o-path'ik). Relating to a deuteropathy.

deuteropathy (du-ter-op'ă-thī) [deutero- + G. pathos, suffering]. A secondary disease or symptom.

deuteroplasm (du'ter-o-plazm) [deutero- + G. plasma, thing formed]. Deutoplasm.

deuto-. See deutero-.

deutoplasm (du'to-plazm) [deuto- + G. plasma, thing formed]. Deuteroplasm; the nonliving material in the cytoplasm, especially that stored in the ovum as food for the developing embryo, such as lipoid droplets and yolk granules.

devas'culariza'tion [L. de, away, + vasculus, small vessel, + G. izo, to cause]. Occlusion of all or most of the blood vessels to any part or organ.

devel'opment. The act or process of natural progression from a previous, lower, or embryonic stage to a later, more complex, or adult stage.

psychosexual d., maturation and development of the psychic phase of sexuality from birth to adult life through the oral, anal, phallic, latency, and genital phases.

deviance (de'vĭans) [see deviation]. Departure from an accepted norm, role, or rule.

deviation (de-vĭ-a'shun) [L. *devio,* to turn from the straight path]. **1.** Deflection; a turning away or aside from the normal point or course. **2.** An abnormality. **3.** In psychiatry, deviance.

axis d., axis shift; deflection of the electrical axis of the heart to the right or left of the normal.

conjugate d. of the eyes, (1) the turning of eyes equally and simultaneously in the same direction, as occurs normally; (2) a condition in which both eyes are pathologically turned to the same side as a result of either paralysis or muscular spasm.

primary d., the ocular deviation seen in paralysis of an ocular muscle when the nonparalyzed eye is used for fixation.

secondary d., the condition in which the eyes are not directed simultaneously to the same object; seen in paralysis of an ocular muscle when the paralyzed eye is used for fixation.

standard d. (S.D., σ), statistical index of the degree of d. from central tendency; namely, of the variability within a distribution; the square root of the average of the squared deviations from the mean.

device (de-vīs'). A contrivance, usually mechanical, designed to perform a specific function.

contraceptive d., a d. used to prevent pregnancy; *e.g.,* occlusive diaphragm, condom, intrauterine d.

intra-aortic balloon d., an externally and intermittently inflatable balloon placed into the descending aorta and which, on activation during diastole, augments blood pressure and organ perfusion by that pulsatile thrust that then, on deflation, decreases the cardiac work with each systole.

intrauterine d.'s (IUD), intrauterine contraceptive d.'s (IUCD), plastic or metal of various shapes inserted into the uterus to exert a contraceptive effect.

de'viom'eter. A form of strabismometer.

devi'talized. Devoid of life; dead, as a tooth in which the pulp has been destroyed.

dexpan'thenol. D-(+)-2,4-Dihydroxy-*N*-(3-hydroxypropyl)-3,3-dimethylbutyramide; a cholinergic agent and a dietary source of pantothenic acid.

dexter (D) (deks'ter) [L. f. *dextra,* neut. *dextrum*] [NA]. Right.

dextr-. See dextro-.

dex'trad [L. *dexter,* right, + *ad,* to]. Toward the right side.

dex'tral. Right handed; pertaining to dextrality.

dextral'ity. Right-handedness; preference for the right hand in performing manual tasks.

dex'tran. Any of several water-soluble, high molecular weight glucose polymers produced by the action of *Leuconostoc mesenteroides* on sucrose; used in isotonic sodium chloride solution for the treatment of shock, in distilled water for the relief of the edema of nephrosis, and as plasma substitutes or expanders.

dex'tranase. An enzyme hydrolyzing 1,6-α-glucosidic linkages in dextran.

dex'trase. The complex of enzymes that converts dextrose (glucose) into lactic acid.

dex'trin. A mixture of oligo(α-1,4-glucose) molecules formed during the enzymic or acid hydrolysis of starch, amylopectin, or glycogen; on further hydrolysis they are converted into glucose.

limit d., polysaccharide fragments remaining at the end (limit) of exhaustive hydrolysis of amylopectin or glycogen by α-1,4-glucan maltohydrolase, which cannot hydrolyze the α-1,6 bonds at branch points.

dex'trinase. Any of the enzymes catalyzing the hydrolysis of dextrins.

limit d., oligo-1,6-glucosidase.

dextrin dextranase. A glucosyltransferase transferring 1,4-α-D-glucosyl residues, thus catalyzing the synthesis of dextrans from dextrins by glucose transfer.

dextrin 6-α-glucosidase. Amylo-1,6-glucosidase.

dex'trino'sis. Glycogenosis.

debrancher deficiency limit d., type 3 *glycogenosis.*

dextrinu'ria. Passage of dextrin in the urine.

dextro-, dextr- [L. *dexter,* right]. **1.** Prefix meaning right, or toward or on the right side. **2.** Chemical prefix meaning dextrorotatory. See also *d-.*

dextrocardia (deks'tro-kar'dĭ-ah) [dextro- + G. *kardia,* heart]. Displacement of the heart to the right, usually as one of two kinds: 1) dextroposition, in which the heart is simply displaced to the right; 2) cardiac heterotaxia, in which there is complete transposition of the right and left chambers, the heart thus presenting a mirror picture of the normal.

dextrocardia with situs inversus. Displacement of the heart to the right side of the chest with mirror transposition of the cardiac chambers together with transposition of the abdominal viscera.

dextroclination (deks'tro-klĭ-na'shun). Dextrotorsion (2).

dextrocular (deks-trok'u-lar) [dextro- + L. *oculus,* eye]. Right-eyed; denoting one who uses the right eye by preference in monocular work.

dex'trogas'tria [dextro- + G. *gastēr,* stomach]. Displacement of the stomach to the right; usually associated with dextrocardia.

dextrogyration (deks'tro-ji-ra'shun) [dextro- + L. *gyro,* pp. *-atus,* to turn in a circle]. A twisting to the right.

dextrop'edal [dextro- + L. *pes* (*ped-*), foot]. Right-footed; denoting one who uses the right leg in preference to the left.

dextroposition (deks'tro-po-zish'un). Abnormal right-sided location or origin of a normally left-sided structure.

d. of the heart, see dextrocardia.

dextrorotatory (*d-*) (deks'tro-ro'tă-to-rǐ). Denoting certain crystals or solutions capable of giving a clockwise twist to the plane of plane-polarized light.

dex'trose. Glucose.

dex'trosinis'tral [dextro- + L. *sinister*, left]. In a direction from right to left.

dextrotorsion (deks'tro-tor'shun) [dextro- + L. *torsio*, a twisting]. **1.** A twisting to the right. **2.** Dextroclination; in ophthalmology, extorsion of the right eye or intorsion of the left eye.

dextrotropic (deks'tro-trop'ik) [dextro- + G. *tropos*, a turn]. Turning to the right.

dextroversion (deks'tro-ver'zhun) [dextro- + L. *verto*, pp. *versus*, to turn]. **1.** Version (a turning) toward the right. **2.** In ophthalmology, rotation of both eyes to the right.

dGMP Deoxyguanylic acid.

di- [G. *dis*, two]. Prefix denoting two, twice. See also bi-, bis-.

dia- [G. *dia*, through]. Prefix meaning through, throughout, completely.

diabetes (di-ă-be'tēz) [G. *diabētēs*, a compass, a siphon]. Either d. insipidus or d. mellitus, diseases having in common the symptom polyuria; when used without qualification, refers to d. mellitus.

   brittle d., d. in which there is marked spontaneous fluctuation in blood glucose concentrations.

   bronze d., a type of d. associated with hemochromatosis, with iron deposits in the skin, liver, and other viscera, and often with severe liver damage and glycosuria.

   growth-onset d. mellitus, juvenile d.

   d. insip'idus, the chronic excretion of very large amounts of pale urine of low specific gravity, accompanied by extreme thirst; ordinarily results from inadequate output of pituitary antidiuretic hormone.

   d. intermittens, d. mellitus in which there are periods of relatively normal carbohydrate metabolism followed by relapses to the previous diabetic state.

   juvenile d., growth-onset d. mellitus; severe d. mellitus, usually of abrupt onset during the first two decades of life.

   latent d., a mild form of d. mellitus in which the patient displays no overt symptoms, but displays certain abnormal responses to diagnostic procedures, such as an elevated fasting blood glucose concentration or reduced glucose tolerance.

   maturity-onset d., an often mild form of d. mellitus, of gradual onset in obese individuals over the age of 35.

   d. melli'tus [L. sweetened with honey], a metabolic disorder in which carbohydrate utilization is reduced and that of lipid and protein enhanced; caused by deficiency of insulin and is characterized, in more severe cases, by glycosuria, water and electrolyte loss, ketoacidosis, and coma; chronic complications include neuropathy, retinopathy, nephropathy, and generalized degenerative changes

in large and small blood vessels.

   nephrogenic d. insipidus, d. insipidus due to inability of the kidney tubules to respond to antidiuretic hormone; X chromosome-linked inheritance, with full expression in males and partial defect in heterozygous females.

   starvation d., after prolonged fasting, glycosuria following the ingestion of carbohydrate or glucose, because of reduced ouput of insulin or reduced ability to form glycogen.

   subclinical d., a form of d. mellitus evident only under certain circumstances, such as pregnancy or extreme stress; may progress to the latent or overt forms of the disease.

diabet'ic. Relating to or suffering from diabetes.

diabetogenic (di-ă-bet'o-jen'ik, -be'to-jen'ik). Causing diabetes.

diabetogenous (di-ă-bĕ-toj'en-us). Caused by diabetes.

diacetic acid (di-ă-se'tik, -set'ik). Acetoacetic acid.

diac'etylmor'phine. Heroin.

diaclasis (di-ak'lă-sis) [G. *diaklasis*, a breaking up, fr. *dia*, through, + *klasis*, a breaking]. Osteoclasis.

diacritic, diacritical (di'ă-krit'ik, -krit'ĭ-kal) [G. *diakritikos*, able to distinguish]. Distinguishing; diagnostic; allowing of distinction.

di'ad. 1. The transverse tubule and a cisterna in cardiac muscle fibers. **2.** Dyad (1).

diadochokinesia, diadochokinesis (di-ad'o-ko-kǐ-ne'zǐ-ah, -kǐ-ne'sis) [G. *diadochos*, working in turn, + *kinēsis*, movement]. The normal power of alternately bringing a limb into opposite positions, as of flexion and extention or of pronation and supination.

diadochokinetic (di-ad'o-ko-kǐ-net'ik). Relating to diadochokinesia.

diagnose (di-ag-nōs') [G. *diagignōskō*, to distinguish]. To make a diagnosis.

diagnosis (di-ag-no'sis) [G. *diagnōsis*, a deciding]. Determination of the nature of a disease.

   clinical d., d. made from a study of the signs and symptoms of a disease.

   differential d., differentiation (2); determination of which of two or more diseases with similar symptoms is the one from which the patient is suffering.

   d. by exclusion, d. made by excluding those affections to which some of the symptoms belong, leaving only one to which all the symptoms point.

   laboratory d., d. made by a chemical, microscopic, bacteriologic, or biopsy study of secretions, discharges, blood, or tissue.

   physical d., d. made by means of physical examination of the patient.

diagnos'tic. Relating to or aiding in diagnosis.

diagnostician (di-ag-nos-tish'an). An expert in making diagnoses.

diakinesis (di'ă-kǐ-ne'sis) [G. *dia*, through, + *kinēsis*, movement]. The final stage of prophase in meiosis in which the chiasmata present during the diplotene stage disappear and the chromosomes continue to shorten.

dialysance (di-al'ĭsans) [fr. dialysis]. The number of milliliters of blood completely cleared of any substance by an artificial kidney or by peritoneal dialysis in a unit of time; conventional clearance formulas are expressed as mm/min.

dialysate (di-al'ĭ-sāt). Diffusate; that part of the mixture that passes through the dialyzing membrane.

dialysis (di-al'ĭ-sis) [G. a separation]. Diffusion (2); separation of crystalloid from colloid substances (or smaller molecules from larger ones) in a solution by interposing a semipermeable membrane between the solution and water; the crystalloid (smaller) substances pass through the membrane into the water on the other side, the colloids do not.

equilibrium d., in immunology, a method for determination of association constants for hapten-antibody reactions in a system in which the hapten (dialyzable) and antibody (nondialyzable) solutions are separated by semipermeable membranes.

peritoneal d., removal from the body of soluble substances and water by transfer across the peritoneum, utilizing a solution which is intermittently introduced into and removed from the peritoneal cavity.

di'alyzer. A device used in dialysis; a hemodialyzer.

diam'eter [G. *diametros*]. **1.** A straight line connecting two opposite points on the surface of a spherical or cylindrical body, or at the boundary of an opening or foramen, passing through the center of such body or opening. **2.** The distance measured along such a line.

anteroposterior d., conjugate (2).

biparietal d., d. of the fetal head between the two parietal eminences.

conjugate d. of the pelvic inlet, conjugata.

oblique d., a measurement across the pelvic inlet from the sacroiliac joint of one side to the opposite iliopectineal eminence.

occipitofrontal d., d. of the fetal head from the external occipital protuberance to the most prominent point of the frontal bone in the midline.

occipitomental d., d. of the fetal head from the external occipital protuberance to the midpoint of the chin.

suboccipitobregmatic d., d. of the fetal head from the lowest posterior point of the occipital bone to the center of the anterior fontanelle.

trachelobregmatic d., d. of the fetal head from the middle of the anterior fontanelle to the neck.

transverse d., d. of the pelvic inlet measured between the terminal lines.

diapause (di'ă-pawz). A period of biological quiescence or dormancy; an interval in which development is arrested or greatly slowed.

diapedesis (di'ă-pĕ-de'sis) [G. *dia*, through, + *pēdēsis*, a leaping]. Migration (2); the passage of blood, or any of its formed elements, through the intact

walls of blood vessels.

diaphanoscope (di-af'ă-no-skōp) [G. *diaphanēs*, transparent, + *skopeō*, to examine]. An instrument for illuminating the interior of a cavity to determine the translucency of its walls.

diaphanoscopy (di-af-ă-nos'ko-pī). Examination utilizing a diaphanoscope.

diaphemetric (di'ă-fē-met'rik) [G. *dia*, through, + *haphē*, touch, + *metron*, measure]. Relating to the determination of the degree of tactile sensibility.

diaphoresis (di'a-fo-re'sis) [G. *diaphorēsis*]. Perspiration (1).

diaphoret'ic. Relating to or promoting perspiration.

diaphragm (di'ă-fram) [G. *diaphragma*, a partition wall]. **1.** A thin partition separating adjacent regions. **2.** Midriff; the musculomembranous partition between the abdominal and thoracic cavities. **3.** A flexible metal ring covered with a dome-shaped sheet of elastic material used in the vagina to prevent pregnancy.

pelvic d., the paired levator ani and coccygeus muscles together with the fascia above and below them.

urogenital d., a triangular sheet of muscle between the ischiopubic rami, composed of the sphincter urethrae and the deep transverse perineal muscles.

diaphragmatic (di'ă-frag-mat'ik). Relating to the diaphragm.

diaphragmatocele (di'ă-frag-mat'o-sēl) [diaphragm + G. *kēlē*, hernia]. Diaphragmatic *hernia.*

diaphysectomy (di'ă-fī-sek'to-mī) [diaphysis + G. *ektomē*, excision]. Partial or complete removal of the shaft of a long bone.

diaphysial, diaphyseal (di-ă-fiz'ī-al). Relating to the diaphysis.

diaphysis, pl. **diaphyses** (di-af'ĭ-sis, -sēz) [G. a growing between]. [NA]. The shaft of a long bone, as distinguished from the epiphyses, or extremities, and apophyses, or outgrowths.

diaphysitis (di-af-ĭ-si'tis). Inflammation of the shaft of a long bone.

diapiresis (di'ă-pi-rēsis) [G. *diapeirō*, to drive through, fr. *peirō*, to pierce]. Passage of colloidal or other small particles of suspended matter through the unruptured walls of the blood vessels.

diapophysis (di-ă-pof'ĭ-sis) [G. *dia*, through, + *apophysis*, an offshoot]. *Processus* articularis superior.

diarrhea (di-ă-re'ah) [G. *diarrhoia*, fr. *dia*, through, + *rhoia*, a flow, flux]. An abnormally frequent discharge of fluid fecal matter from the bowel.

choleraic d., summer d.

lienteric c., d. in which undigested food appears in the stools.

summer d., choleraic d.; d. of infants in hot weather, usually an acute gastroenteritis due to the presence of a microorganism of the *Shigella* or *Salmonella* groups.

traveler's d., d. of sudden onset occurring sporadically in travelers in all parts of the world, usually during the first week of a trip, and most commonly caused by *Escherichia coli.*

tropical d., tropical *sprue.*

diarrheal, diarrheic (di-ă-re'al, -re'ik). Relating to diarrhea.

diarthric (di-ar'thrik) [G. *di,* two, + *arthron,* joint]. Biarticular; diarticular; relating to two joints.

diarthrosis, pl. **diarthroses** (di-ar-thro'sis, -sēz) [G. articulation]. *Articulatio* synovialis.

diarticular (di-ar-tik'u-lar). Diarthric.

diaschisis (di-as'kĭ-sis) [G. a splitting]. A sudden inhibition of function produced by an acute focal disturbance in a portion of the brain at a distance from the original seat of injury, but anatomically connected with it through fiber tracts.

diascope (di'ă-skōp) [G. *dia,* through, + *skopeō,* to view]. A flat glass plate through which one can examine superficial skin lesions, by means of pressure.

diascopy (di-as'ko-pī) [G. *dia,* through, + *skopeō,* to see]. Examination with a diascope.

diastalsis (di-ă-stal'sis) [G. an arrangement]. The type of peristalsis in which a region of inhibition precedes the wave of contraction, as seen in the intestinal tract.

diastal'tic. Pertaining to diastalsis.

diastase (di'as-tās). A mixture of amylolytic enzymes (principally α- and β-amylases), that converts starch into dextrin and maltose; used to make soluble starches, to aid in digestion of starches in certain types of dyspepsia, and to digest glycogen in histologic sections.

diastasis (di-as'tă-sis) [G. a separation]. **1.** Divarication; any simple separation of normally joined parts. **2.** The latter part of diastole when the blood enters the ventricle slowly and the venous pressure tends to rise.

diastasuria (di-as'tās-u'rī-ah). Amylasuria.

diastat'ic. Relating to a diastasis.

diastema, pl. **diastemata** (di'ă-ste'mah, -ste'mă-tah) [G. *diastēma,* an interval]. **1.** A fissure or abnormal opening in any part, especially if congenital. **2**[NA]. A space between two adjacent teeth in the same dental arch.

diastematocrania (di-ă-ste'mă-to-kra'nĭ-ah) [G. *diastēma,* an interval, + *kranion,* skull]. Congenital sagittal fissure of the skull.

diastematomyelia (di-ă-ste'mă-to-mi-e'lĭ-ah) [G. *diastēma,* interval, + *myelon,* marrow]. Complete or incomplete sagittal division of spinal cord (diplomyelia) by osseous or fibrocartilaginous septum.

diastematopyelia (di-ă-ste'mă-to-pi-e'lĭ-ah) [G. *diastēma,* interval, + *pyelos,* a trough (pelvis)]. Congenital separation between the pubic bones.

di'aster [G. *di-,* two, + *astēr,* star]. The double star figure in mitosis, formed just before the division of the nucleus.

diastole (di-as'to-le) [G. *diastolē,* dilation]. Dilation of the heart cavities, during which they fill with blood; d. alternates rhythmically with systole or

contraction of the heart musculature.

diastol'ic. Relating to diastole.

diataxia (di'ă-tak'sĭ-ah). Ataxia affecting both sides of the body.

diather'mal. Diathermic.

diather'manous [G. *dia-thermaino,* to heat through]. Transcalent; permeable by heat rays.

diather'mic. Diathermal; relating to, characterized by, or affected by diathermy.

diathermy (di'ă-ther-mī) [G. *dia,* through, + *thermē,* heat]. Local elevation of temperature within the tissues, produced by high frequency current, ultrasonic waves, or microwave radiation.

medical d., d. of mild degree causing no destruction of tissue.

short wave d., therapeutic elevation of temperature in the tissues by means of an oscillating electric current of extremely high frequency (10 to 100 million Hz) and short wavelength of 3 to 30 m.

surgical d., electrocoagulation with a high frequency electrocautery, resulting in local tissue destruction.

diathesis (di-ath'ĕ-sis) [G. arrangement, condition]. A constitutional or inborn predisposition to a disease, group of diseases, or anomaly.

diathet'ic. Relating to a diathesis.

diatom'ic. 1. Denoting a compound with a molecule made up of two atoms. **2.** Denoting any ion or atomic grouping composed of two atoms only.

diazepam (di-āz'ĕ-pam). 7-Chloro-1,3-dihydro-1-methyl-5-phenyl-2*H*-1,4-benzodiazepin-2-one; a skeletal muscle relaxant, sedative, and antianxiety agent; also used as an anticonvulsant.

di'azines. A group of synthetic tuberculostatic drugs.

diazo- [G. *di-,* two, + LFr. *azote,* nitrogen. ZO-]. Prefix denoting a compound containing the $-N \equiv N-$ or $-N = N +$ group.

diba'sic. Having two replaceable hydrogen atoms, denoting an acid with two ionizable hydrogen atoms.

dibucaine number (DN). A test for differentiation of one of several forms of atypical pseudocholinesterases that are unable to inactivate succinylcholine at normal rates; based upon per cent inhibition of the enzymes by dibucaine.

DIC Disseminated intravascular *coagulation.*

dicen'tric. Having two centromeres.

dichlorodiphen'yltrichloroeth'ane (DDT). An insecticide that was once very effective, but insect populations rapidly developed tolerance for it; general usage is now widely discouraged because of the toxicity that results from the environmental persistance of this agent.

di(2-chloroethyl)sulfide. Mustard *gas.*

dichlor'oisoproter'enol (DCI). Congener of the adrenergic beta receptor stimulant, isoproterenol; it blocks the responses, involving beta receptors, to epinephrine and other sympathomimetic drugs.

dichorial, dichorionic (di-ko'rĭ-al, di-ko-rĭ-on'ik) [G. *di-*, two, + chorion]. Showing evidence of two chorions, as the placenta of diovular twins.

dichroic (di-kro'ik). Relating to dichroism.

dichroism (di'kro-izm) [G. *di-*, two, + *chrōa*, color]. The property of seeming to be differently colored when viewed from emitted light and from transmitted light.

dichromate (di-kro'māt). A compound containing the radical $Cr_2O_7=$.

dichromatic (di'kro-mat'ik). 1. Having or exhibiting two colors. 2. Relating to dichromatism (2).

dichromatism (di-kro'mă-tizm) [G. *di-*, two, + *chrōma*, color]. 1. State of being dichromatic (1). 2. The abnormality of color vision in which only two of the three retinal cone pigments are present. Also called dichromatopsia; dyschromatopsia; parachromatopsia.

dichromatopsia (di-kro'mă-top'sĭ-ah) [G. *di-*, two, + *chrōma*, color, + *opsis*, vision]. Dichromatism (2).

dicoria (di-ko'rĭ-ah) [G. *di-*, two, + *korē*, pupil]. Diplocoria.

dicrot'ic [G. *dikrotos*, double-beating]. Relating to dicrotism.

dicrotism (di'kro-tizm) [G. *di-*, two, + *krotos*, a beat]. That form of the pulse in which a double beat can be felt at the wrist for each beat of the heart; due to accentuation of the dicrotic wave.

dictyoma (dik-tĭ-o'mah) [G. *dikyton*, net (retina), + *-oma*, tumor]. An epitheliomatous tumor of the nonpigmented layer of the ciliary epithelium.

dicu'marol. Bishydroxycoumarin; 3,3'-methylenebis (4-hydroxycoumarin); an anticoagulant agent that inhibits the formation of prothrombin in the liver.

didactic (di-dak'tik) [G. *didaktikos*, fr. *didaskō*, to teach]. Instructive; denoting medical teaching by lectures or textbooks as distinguished from clinical demonstration with patients.

didactylism (di-dak'tĭ-lizm) [G. *di-*, two, + *daktylos*, finger or toe]. Congenital condition of only two digits on a hand or a foot.

didelphic (di-del'fic) [G. *di-*, two, + *delphys*, womb]. Having or relating to a double uterus.

didym-, didymo- [G. *didymos*, twin]. Combining form denoting relationship to the didymus, testis.

didymalgia (did-ĭ-mal'jĭ-ah) [didym- + G. *algos*, pain]. Orchialgia.

didymitis (did-ĭ-mi'tis) [G. *didymoi*, the testes, + *-itis*, inflammation]. Orchitis.

-didymus, [G. *didymos*, twin]. Termination denoting a conjoined twin, the first element of the word designating the part or parts of the twins which have remained *unfused*; the more common usage is to designate the parts *fused* by use of the suffix -pagus. See also -dymus.

didymus (did'ĭ-mus) [G. *didymoi*, testes]. Testis.

diecious (di-e'shus) [G. *di-*, two, + *oikia*, house]. Applied to animals or plants that are sexually distinct, the individuals being of one or the other sex.

dieldrin (di-el'drin). A chlorinated hydrocarbon used as an insecticide; may cause toxic effects through skin contact, inhalation, or food contamination.

diencephalon, pl. **diencephala** (di-en-sef'ă-lon) [G. *dia*, through, + *enkephalos*, brain] [NA]. That part of the prosencephalon that is composed of the thalamus, the subthalamus, and the hypothalamus.

Dientamoeba fragilis (di-ent-ă-me'bah fraj-ĭ-lis). A species of small ameba parasitic in the large intestine and capable of sometimes causing low grade inflammation with mucous diarrhea and gastrointestinal disturbance.

dieresis (di-er'e-sis) [G. *diairesis*, a division]. *Solution of continuity.*

dieretic (di-er-et'ik). 1. Relating to dieresis. 2. Dividing; ulcerating; corroding.

diestrous (di-es'trus). Pertaining to diestrus.

diestrus (di-es'trus) [G. *dia*, between, + *oistros*, desire]. A period of sexual quiescence intervening between two periods of estrus.

di'et [G. *diaita*, a way of life; a diet]. 1. Food and drink in general. 2. A prescribed course of eating and drinking, in which the amount and kind of food, as well as the times at which it is to be taken, are regulated for therapeutic purposes. 3. Reduction of caloric intake so as to lose weight. 4. To follow any prescribed or specific d.

acid-ash d., a d. consisting largely of meat or fish, eggs, and cereals, but containing a minimal quantity of milk, fruit, and vegetables which, when catabolized, leave an acid residue to be excreted in the urine.

alkaline-ash d., a d. consisting mainly of fruits, vegetables, and milk, with minimal amounts of meat, fish, eggs, cheese, and cereals which, when catabolized, leave an alkaline residue to be excreted in the urine.

balanced d., a d. that furnishes in proper proportions all of the nutrients necessary for adequate nutrition.

bland d., a regular d. omitting foods that irritate the gastrointestinal tract.

diabetic d., a d. suitable for a diabetic patient; with the aim of achieving normoglycemia.

elimination d., a d. designed to detect what foodstuffs cause allergic manifestations by separate and succesive withdrawl of foods from the d. until that which causes the symptoms is discovered.

high calorie d., a d. containing upward of 4000 calories per day.

ketogenic d., a high-fat, low-carbohydrate, and normal protein d.

low calorie d., a d. of 1200 calories or less per day.

smooth d., a d. containing little roughage.

soft d., a normal d. limited to soft easily digestable foods.

dietary (di'ĕ-tĕr-ĭ). Relating to the diet.

dietetic (di'ĕ-tet'ik). **1.** Relating to diet. **2.** Descriptive of food that, naturally or through processing, has a low caloric content.

dietetics (di'ĕ-tet'iks). The branch of therapeutics concerned with food and drink in relation to health and disease.

dieth'ylenetriam'ine pentaace'tic acid (DTPA). Pentetic acid.

dieth'yl e'ther. Anesthetic, ethyl, or sulfuric ether; ethyl oxide; $CH_3CH_2OCH_2CH_3$; a pungent volatile liquid the vapor of which produces inhalation anesthesia.

dieth'yltryp'tamine (DET). A hallucinogenic agent similar to dimethyltryptamine.

dietitian (di'ĕ-tish'un). An expert in dietetics; one versed in the practical application of diet in the prophylaxis and treatment of disease.

dif'ference. The magnitude or degree by which one quantity differs from another of the same kind.

    alveolar-arterial oxygen d., the d. or gradient between the partial pressure of oxygen in the alveolar spaces and the arterial blood: $P_{(A-a)}O_2$.

    arteriovenous carbon dioxide d., the d. in carbon dioxide content (in ml per 100 ml blood) between the arterial and venous bloods.

    arteriovenous oxygen d., the d. in the oxygen content (in ml per 100 ml blood) between arterial and venous blood.

    standard error of d., a statistical index of the probability that a difference between two sample means is greater than zero.

differentiation (dif'er-en-shĭ-a'shun). **1.** Specialization (2); the acquiring or the possession of character or function different from that of the original type. **2.** Differential *diagnosis.*

diffraction (dĭ-frak'shun) [L. *dif-fringo*, pp. *-fractus*, to break in pieces]. Deflection of the rays of light from a straight line in passing by the edge of an opaque body.

diffusate (dĭ-fu'zāt) [L. *dif-fundo*, pp. *-fuscus*, to pour in different directions]. Dialysate.

diffuse (dĭ-fūz') [L. *dif-fundo*, pp. *-fusus*, to pour in different directions]. Spread about, not circumscribed or limited.

diffu'sible. Capable of diffusing; not bound.

diffusion (dĭ-fu'zhun). **1.** Random movement of molecules or ions or small particles in solution or suspension under the influence of brownian (thermal) motion toward a uniform distribution throughout the available volume; relatively rapid among liquids and gases, but very slow among solids. **2.** Dialysis (1).

digastric (di-gas'trik) [G. *di-*, two, + *gastēr*, belly]. **1.** Biventral; having two bellies; denoting especially a muscle with two fleshy parts separated by an intervening tendinous part. **2.** Relating to the d. muscle; denoting a fossa or groove with which it is in relation and a nerve supplying its posterior belly.

digenesis (di-jen'ĕ-sis) [G. *di-*, two, + *genesis*, generation]. Reproduction in distinctive patterns in alternate generations, as seen in the nonsexual (vertebrate) and the sexual (invertebrate) cycles of malarial parasites.

digenetic (di-jĕ-net'ik). **1.** Heteroxenous; pertaining to or characterized by digenesis. **2.** Pertaining to the digenetic fluke.

digest (dī-jest') [L. *digero*, pp. *-gestus*, to force apart, divide, dissolve]. **1.** To soften by moisture and heat. **2.** To hydrolyze or break up into simpler chemical compounds by means of hydrolyzing enzymes or chemical action; denoting the action of the secretions of the alimentary tract upon the food.

diges'tant **1.** Aiding digestion. **2.** Digestive (2); an agent that favors or assists the process of digestion.

digestion (dī-jes'chun, di-) [L. *digestio*, see digest]. The process whereby ingested food is converted into material suitable for assimilation for synthesis of tissues or liberation of energy.

    gastric d., peptic d.,; that part of d., chiefly of the proteins, carried on in the stomach by the enzymes of the gastric juice.

    intestinal d., that part of d. carried on in the intestine, affecting all foodstuffs: starches, fats, and proteins.

    pancreatic d., d. in the intestine by the enzymes of the pancreatic juice.

    peptic d., gastric d.

    primary d., d. in the alimentary tract.

    salivary d., conversion of starch into sugar by the action of salivary amylase.

    secondary d., change in the chyle effected by the action of the cells, whereby the final products of d. are assimilated in the process of metabolism.

digestive (dī-jes'tiv). **1.** Relating to digestion. **2.** Digestant (2).

digit (dij'it) [L. *digitus*]. Dactyl; dactylus; a finger or toe.

    clubbed d.'s, hippocratic, clubbed, or drumstick fingers; a bulbous enlargement of the terminal phalanges produced by clubbing.

digital (dij'ĭ-tal). Relating to or resembling a digit or digits or an impression made by them.

digitalin (dij'ĭ-tal'in, -ta'lin). A standardized mixture of glycosides obtained from digitalis and used as a cardiotonic.

digitalis (dij'ĭ-tal'is, -ta'lis) [L. *digitalis*, relating to the fingers (in allusion to the finger-like flowers)]. Foxglove, a genus of perennial flowering plants (family Schrophulariaceae). *D. lanata* and *D. purpurea* are the main sources of cardioactive steroid glycosides used in the treatment of certain heart diseases, especially heart failure.

digitalization (dij-ĭ-tal-ĭ-za'shun). Administration of digitalis by a dosage schedule until sufficient amounts are present in the body to produce the desired therapeutic effects.

digitate (dij'ĭ-tāt). Marked by a number of finger-like processes or impressions.

digitation (dij'ĭ-ta'shun) [Mod. L. *digitatio*]. A process resembling a finger.

digiti (dij′ĭ-ti) [L.]. Plural of digitus.

digitoxin (dij-ĭ-tok′sin). A secondary cardioactive glycoside obtained from *Digitalis purpurea* and more completely absorbed from the gastrointestinal tract than is digitalis.

digitus, pl. **digiti** (dij′ĭ-tus, -ti) [L.] [NA]. Digit.

diglossia (di-glos′sĭ-ah) [G. *di-*, two, + *glossa*, tongue]. Bifid *tongue.*

digoxin (dĭ-jok′sin). A cardioactive steroid glycoside obtained from *Digitalis lanata.*

diheterozygote (di-het′er-o-zi′gōt) [G. *di-*, two, + heterozygote]. An individual heterozygous for two different gene pairs at two different loci.

dihy′drate. A compound with two molecules of water of crystallization.

dihydro-. Prefix indicating the addition of two hydrogen atoms.

dihydrocodeine (di-hi′dro-ko′dēn). 6-Hydroxy-3-methoxy-*N*-methyl-4,5-epoxymorphinan; a narcotic analgesic derivative of codeine, about one-sixth as potent as morphine.

dihydrofo′lic acid. Intermediate between folic acid and tetrahydrofolic acid, the reduction requiring NADPH.

dihydroorotic acid (di-hi′dro-o-rot′ik). An intermediate in the biosynthesis of pyrimidines.

dihydropteroic acid (di-hi′dro-tĕr-o′ik). Intermediate in the formation of folic acid; a compound of 6-hydroxymethylpterin and *p*-aminobenzoic acid, the combining of which is inhibited by sulfonamides.

dihy′drotestos′terone. Stanolone.

dihydroxy-. Prefix denoting addition of two hydroxyl groups; as a suffix, becomes -diol.

dihydrox′yac′etone. $HOCH_2-CO-CH_2OH$; the simplest ketose; as d. phosphate, one of the intermediates in the glycolytic pathway of glucose catabolism and fat synthesis.

3, 4-dihydrox′yphenylal′anine. Dopa.

diiodide (di-i′o-did). A compound containing two atoms of iodine per molecule.

diiodo-. Prefix indicating two atoms of iodine.

diketone (di-ke′tōn). A molecule containing two carbonyl groups.

diketopiperazines (di-ke′to-pi-pĕr-ă-zēnz). A class of organic compounds with a closed ring structure formed from two α-amino acids by the joining of the α-amino group of each to the carboxyl group of the other, with the loss of two molecules of water.

dilaceration (di-las-er-a′shun) [L. *di-lacero*, pp. *laceratus*, to tear in pieces]. **1.** Discission of a cataractous lens. **2.** A displacement of some portion of a developing tooth which then further developed in its new relation.

dilatation (dil-ă-ta′shun). Dilation.

dil′atator. Dilator.

dilation (di-la′shun) [L. *dilato*, pp. *dilatatus*, to spread out, dilate]. Dilatation. **1.** Physiologic, pathologic, or artifical enlargement of a cavity, canal, blood vessel, or opening. **2.** The act of such enlargement.

dilation and curettage (D & C). Dilation of the cervix and curettement of the endometrium.

dilation and evacua′tion (D & E). Dilation of the cervix and removal of the early products of conception.

di′lator. Dilatator. **1.** An instrument or substance for enlarging a cavity, canal, blood vessel, or opening. **2.** A muscle that opens an orifice or dilates the lumen of a structure; the opening or dilating component of a pylorus.

dil′do, dil′doe. An artificial penis; an object having the approximate shape and size of an erect penis, utilized for sexual pleasure by vaginal insertion.

diluent (dil′u-ent). **1.** Diluting; making weaker or more watery. **2.** That which dilutes the strength of a solution or mixture.

dilution (di-lu′shun) [L. *di-luo*, pp. *-lutus*, to wash away, dilute]. **1.** The act of reducing the concentration of a mixture or solution. **2.** A weakened (diluted) solution.

dime′lia [G. *di-*, two, + *melos*, limb]. Congenital duplication of all or part of a limb.

dimension (dĭ-men′shun). Scope, size, magnitude; in the plural, linear measurements of length, width, and height.

di′mer [G. *di-*, two, + -mer]. A compound or unit produced by the combination of two like molecules without loss of atoms, but usually by elimination of H_2O or a similar small molecule between the two or by simple noncovalent association.

dimercap′rol. Antilewisite; British anti-Lewisite; BAL; 2,3-dimercaptopropanol; $HSCH_2CH(SH)-CH_2OH$; a chelating agent, developed as an antidote for lewisite and other arsenical poisons; also used as an antidote for antimony, bismuth, chromium, mercury, gold, and nickel poisoning.

di′meric. Having the characteristics of a dimer.

2, 5-dimethoxy-4-methylamphetamine (DOM). An hallucinogenic agent chemically related to amphetamine and mescaline, a drug of abuse.

dimeth′yltryp′tamine (DMT). A psychotomimetic agent present in several South American snuffs and in the leaves of *Prestonia amazonica* (family Apocynaceae); produces effects similar to those of LSD, but with more rapid onset, greater likelihood of a panic reaction, and a shorter duration.

dimorphic (di-mor′fik). Dimorphous; relating to or characterized by dimorphism.

dimorphism (di-mor′fizm) [G. *di-*, two, + *morphē*, shape]. Existence in two shapes or forms.

   sexual d., the somatic differences between male and female individuals that arise as a consequence of sexual maturation; including the secondary sexual characters.

dimorphous (di-mor′fus). Dimorphic.

dimple (dim′pl). **1.** An indentation, usually circular and small, in the chin, cheek, or sacral region; probably due to some developmental fault in the subcutaneous connective tissue or in underlying bone. **2.** A depression of similar appearance to a d., resulting from trauma or the contraction of scar tissue. **3.** To cause d.'s.

dimp'ling. 1. Causing dimples. **2.** A condition marked by the formation of dimples, natural or artificial.

2, 4-dinitrophenol (DNP, Dnp) (di-ni′tro-fe′nol). N₂ph-OH; a toxic die chemically related to trinitrophenol (picric acid), used in biochemical studies of oxidative processes.

dinoflagellate (di′no-flaj′e-lāt) [G. *dinos*, whirling, + L. *flagellum*, a whip]. A plantlike flagellate of the subclass Phytomastigophorea, some species of which produce a potent neurotoxin that may cause severe food intoxication following ingestion of parasitized shellfish.

-diol. Suffix form of the prefix dihydroxy-.

diopter (D) (di-op′ter) [G. *dioptra*, a leveling instrument]. The unit of refracting power of lenses, denoting the reciprocal of the focal length expressed in meters.

prism d. (p.d.), the unit of measurement of the deviation of light in passing through a prism, being a deflection of 1 cm at a distance of 1 m.

diop'tric. 1. Relating to dioptrics. **2.** Refractive.

diop'trics. The branch of optics that deals with the refraction of light.

diovulatory (di-o′vu-lă-to′rĭ). Releasing two ova in one ovarian cycle.

dioxide (di-ok′sīde). Binoxide; a molecule containing two atoms of oxygen.

dioxin (di-oks′in). **1.** A ring consisting of two oxygen atoms, four CH groups, and two double bonds; the positions of the oxygen atoms are specified by prefixes. **2.** Popular abbreviation for dibenzo[*b, e*][1,4]dioxin, a contaminant in the herbicide, 2,4,5-T; its potential toxicity and carcinogenicity are controversial.

diox'ygenase. An oxidoreductase that incorporates two atoms of oxygen (from one molecule of O₂) into the (reduced) substrate.

dipep'tidase. An enzyme catalyzing the hydrolysis of a dipeptide to its constituent amino acids.

dipep'tide. A combination of two amino acids by means of a peptide link.

dipep'tidyl carboxypep'tidase. Angiotensin converting enzyme; a hydrolase cleaving C-terminal dipeptides from a variety of substrates, including angiotensin I, which is thus converted to angiotensin II.

Dipetalonema (di-pet′ă-lo-ne′mah) [G. *di-*, two, + *petalon*, leaf, + *nema*, thread]. A large genus of nematode filariae (including the genus *Acanthocheilonema*) transmitted by species of *Culicoides*; it produces microfilariae in blood or tissue fluids, and adults in deep connective tissue, membranes, or visceral surfaces.

D. per'stans, *Acanthocheilonema perstans;* the persistant "filaria" species characterized by unsheathed microfilariae without periodicity in the circulating blood and by adult forms in the peritoneal, pleural, or pericardial cavities.

D. streptocer'ca, *Acanthocheilonema streptocerca;* a species characterized by unsheathed microfilariae without periodicity in the circulating blood and by adult forms in the dermis and subcutaneous tissues.

diphallus (di-fal′us) [G. *di-*, two, + *phallos*, penis]. Bifid penis; a congenital anomaly in which the organs may be symmetrical or placed above the other.

diphasic (di-fa′zik) [G. *di-*, two, + *phasis*, appearance]. Occurring in or referring to two phases or stages.

2, 5-diphenylox'azole (PPO). A scintillator used in radioactivity measurements by scintillation counting.

diphosgene (di-fos′jēn). Trichlormethyl chloroformate; ClCOOCCl₃; a poison gas used in World War I.

1, 3-disphos'phoglyc'erate (1,3-DPG). An intermediate in glycolysis which reacts with ADP to generate ATP and 3-phosphoglycerate.

2, 3-diphos'phoglyc'erate (2,3-DPG). An intermediate in the Rapoport-Luebring shunt, formed between 1,3-DPG and 3-phosphoglycerate; it is an important regulator of the affinity of hemoglobin for oxygen.

diphtheria (dif-the′rĭ-ah) [G. *diphthera*, leather]. A specific infectious disease due to *Corynebacterium diphtheriae* and its toxin, marked by inflammation, with formation of a fibrinous exudate, of the mucous membrane of the throat, the nose, and sometimes the tracheobronchial tree; the toxin produces degeneration in peripheral nerves, heart muscle, and other tissues.

diphthe'rial. Diphtheritic.

diphtheritic (dif′thĕ-rit′ik). Diphtherial; relating to diphtheria, or the membrane characteristic of this disease.

diphtheroid (dif′thĕ-royd) [diphtheria + G. *eidos*, resemblance]. **1.** Pseudodiphtheria; a local infection suggesting diphtheria, caused by a microorganism other than *Corynebacterium diphtheriae.* **2.** Any of the species resembling *Corynebacterium diphtheriae.*

diphyllobothriasis (di-fil′o-both-ri′ă-sis). Infection with *Diphyllobothrium latum,* caused by ingestion of raw or inadequately cooked fish infected with the larva; leukocytosis and eosinophilia may occur.

Diphyllobothrium (di-fil-lo-both′rĭ-um) [G. *di-*, two, + *phyllon*, leaf, + *bothrion*, little ditch]. A large genus of tapeworms (order Pseudophyllidea). *D. latum,* the broad tapeworm, is a species that causes diphyllobothriasis.

diphyodont (dif′ĭ-o-dont) [G. *di-*, two, + *phyō,* to produce, + *odous* (*odont-*), tooth]. Developing two sets of teeth, as occurs in man and most mammals.

diplacusis (dip-lă-ku′sis) [G. *diplous,* double, + *akousis,* a hearing]. A difference of perception of sound by the ears, either in time or in pitch, so that one sound is heard as two.

binaural d., the same sound is heard differently by the two ears.

dysharmonic d., the same sound is heard with a different pitch in each ear.

echo d., sound heard in the affected ear is repeated.

monaural d., one sound is perceived as two in the same ear.

diplegia (di-ple'jĭ-ah) [G. *di-,* two, + *plēgē,* a stroke]. Paralysis of corresponding parts on both sides of the body.

diplo- [G. *diplous,* double]. Combining form meaning double or twofold.

diplobacillus (dip'lo-bă-sil'us). Two rod-shaped bacterial cells linked end to end.

diplobacteria (dip'lo-bak-tēr'ĭ-ah). Bacterial cells linked together in pairs.

diploblas'tic [diplo- + G. *blastos,* germ]. Formed of two germ layers.

diplocar'dia [diplo- + G. *kardia,* heart]. A condition in which the two lateral halves of the heart are more or less separated by a central fissure.

diplococci (dip-lo-kok'si). Plural of diplococcus.

diplococcoid (dip-lo-kok'oyd). Resembling a diplococcus.

Diplococcus (dip-lo-kok'us) [diplo- + G. *kokkos,* berry]. *Streptoccoccus.*

diplococcus, pl. **diplococci** (dip-lo-kok'us, -kok'si) [diplo- + G. *kokkos,* berry]. **1.** Spherical or ovoid bacterial cells joined together in pairs. **2.** Common name of any member of the bacterial genus *Diplococcus.*

diplocoria (dip-lo-ko'rĭ-ah) [diplo- G. *korē,* pupil]. Dicoria; presence of a double pupil in the eye.

diploë (dip'lo-e) [G. *diploē,* fem. of *diplous,* double] [NA]. The central layer of spongy bone between the two layers of compact bone, outer and inner plates, or tables, of the flat cranial bones.

diplogenesis (dip-lo-jen'ĕ-sis) [diplo- + G. *genesis,* production]. Production of a double fetus or of one with some parts doubled.

diplo'ic. Relating to the diploë.

diploid (dip'loyd) [diplo- + G. *eidos* resemblance]. Containing twice the normal gametic number of chromosomes, one member of each chromosome pair derived from the father and one from the mother; the normal chromosome complement (46) of somatic cells in man.

diplomyelia (dip'lo-mi-e'lĭ-ah) [diplo- + G. *myelon,* marrow]. Complete or incomplete doubling of the spinal cord that may or may not be accompanied by a bony septum of the vertebral canal.

diplonema (dip'lo-ne'mah) [diplo- + G. *nema,* thread]. The doubled form of the chromosome strand visible at the diplotene stage of meiosis.

diplopagus (dip-lop'ă-gus) [diplo- + G. *pagos,* something fixed]. General term for conjoined twins, each with fairly complete bodies, although one or more internal organs may be in common.

diplopia (dī-plo'pĭ-ah) [diplo- + G. *ōps,* eye]. Double vision; the condition in which a single object is perceived as two objects.

heteronymous d., crossed d., d. in which the false image is on the same side as the sound eye; due to divergent squint or paralysis of the internal rectus muscle.

homonymous d., direct d., d. in which the false image is on the same side as the affected eye; due to convergent squint or paralysis of the external rectus muscle.

monocular d., monodiplopia; a form of d. in which two objects are seen with the same eye, due to an opacity in the visual axis.

diplosome (dip'lo-sōm) [diplo- + G. *sōma,* body]. The pair of centrioles of mammalian cells.

diploso'mia [diplo- + G. *somā,* body, + *-ia,* condition]. A condition in which twins, seemingly functionally independent, are joined at one or more points.

diplotene (dip'lo-tēn) [diplo- + G. *taenia,* band]. The late stage of prophase in meiosis in which the paired homologous chromosomes begin to repel each other and move apart but are usually held together by regions of crossing or intertwining called chiasmata.

dipro'pyltryp'tamine (DPT). *N,N*-Dipropyltryptamine; a hallucinogenic agent similar to dimethyltryptamine.

dipse'sis [G. *dipsein,* to thirst]. Dipsosis; abnormal or excessive thirst, or a craving for certain unusual forms of drink.

dip'sogen [G. *dipsa,* thirst, + *-gen,* producing]. A thirst-provoking agent.

dipsoma'nia [G. *dipsa,* thirst, + *mania,* madness]. A recurring compulsion to drink alcoholic beverages to excess.

dipso'sis [G. *dipsa,* thirst, + *-osis,* condition]. Dipsesis.

dipsotherapy (dip'so-thĕr-ă-pī). Treatment of certain diseases by abstention, as far as possible, from liquids.

Dip'tera [G. *di-,* two, + *pteron,* wing]. An important order of insects (the two-wing flies and gnats), including many important disease vectors such as the mosquito, tsetse fly, sandfly, and biting midge.

Dipylid'ium cani'num [G. *dipylos,* with two entrances; L. ntr. of *caninus,* pertaining to *canis,* dog]. The commonest species of dog tapeworm, the double-pored tapeworm, the larvae of which are harbored by dog fleas or lice.

direc'tor [L. *dirigo,* pp. *-rectus,* to arrange, set in order]. Staff (2); a smoothly grooved instrument used with a knife to limit the incision of tissues.

Dirofilaria (di-ro-fī-la'rĭ-ah) [L. *dirus,* dread, + *dread,* + *filum,* thread]. A genus of filaria (family Onchocercidae, superfamily Filarioidea), species of which are usually found in mammals other than man; rare examples of human infection are known by *D. magalhaesi, D. repens,* and *D. immitis.*

dirt-eating. Geophagia.

dis- [L. inseparable particle denoting separation, taking apart, sundering in two]. Prefix having the same force as the original Latin preposition.

disabil'ity. Medicolegal term signifying loss of function and earning power.

disa'blement. Medicolegal term signifying loss of function without loss of earning power.

disaccharide (di-sak'ă-rīd). Condensation product of two monosaccharides by elimination of water, usually between an alcoholic OH and a hemiacetal OH.

disaggregation (dis-ag-gre-ga'shun) [L. dis-, separating, + ag-grego, pp. -gregatus, to add to something]. **1.** A breaking up into the component parts. **2.** Inability to coordinate the various sensations and failure to observe their mutual relations.

disarticula'tion [L. dis-, apart, + articulus, joint]. Exarticulation; amputation of a limb through a joint, without cutting of bone.

disassociation (dis-ă-so'sĭ-a'shun). Dissociation (1).

disc. See disk; discus.

disc-. See disco-.

discectomy (dis-sek'to-me) [G. diskos, disk, + ektomē, excision]. Discotomy; excision, in part or whole, of an intervertebral disk.

dis'charge. 1. That which is emitted or evacuated, as an excretion or a secretion. **2.** The activation or firing of a neuron.

dischronation (dis-kro-na'shun) [L. dis-, apart, + G. chronos, time]. A disturbance in the consciousness of time.

disci (dis'ki). Plural of discus.

disciform (dis'ĭ-form). Disk-shaped.

discission (dis-sish'un) [L. di-scindo, pp. -scissus, to tear asunder]. **1.** Incision or cutting through a part. **2.** Specifically, needling, splitting the capsule, and breaking up the substance of the crystalline lens with a knife needle, in cases of soft cataract.

discitis (dis-i'tis). Diskitis; nonbacterial inflammation of an intervertebral disc or disc space.

dis'clina'tion. Extorsion (2).

disco-, disc- [G. diskos, disk]. Combining forms indicating relation to, or similarity to, a disk.

discogenic (dis'ko-gen'ik). Denoting a disorder originating in or from the intervertebral disc.

discography (dis-kog'ră-fī) [disco- + G. graphō, to write]. Radiographic, visualization of intervertebral disk space by injection of contrast media.

discoid (dis'koyd) [disco- + G. eidos, appearance]. Resembling a disk.

discopathy (dis-kop'ă-thī) [disco- + G. pathos, disease]. Disease of a disk, particularly of the intervertebral disk.

    traumatic d., an injury characterized by fissuration, laceration and/or fragmentation of the disc or surrounding ligaments, with or without displacement of fragments against spinal cord, nerve roots, or ligaments.

dis'coplacen'ta. A placenta of discoid shape.

discotomy (dis-kot'o-mĭ) [disco- + G. tomē, incision]. Discectomy.

discrete (dis-krēt) [L. dis-cerno, pp. -cretus, to separate]. Separate; distinct; not joined to or incorporated with another; especially denoting certain lesions of the skin.

discus, pl. **disci** (dis'kus, -ki) [L. fr. G. diskos, a quoit, disk] [NA]. Disk (1); any approximately flat circular surface.

    d. articula'ris [NA], articular disk; interarticular cartilage; interarticular fibrocartilage; a plate or ring of fibrocartilage attached to the joint capsule and separating the articular surfaces of the bones.

    d. intervertebra'lis [NA], intervertebral disk or cartilage; a disk interposed between the bodies of adjacent vertebrae; composed of an outer fibrous part (anulus vibrosus) that surrounds a central gelatinous mass (nucleus pulposus).

    d. ner'vi op'tici [NA], blind spot (3); optic disk or papilla; an oval area of the ocular fundus, devoid of light receptors, where retinal ganglion cell axons converge to form the optic nerve.

    d. prolig'erus, cumulus oophorus.

discutient (dis-ku'she-ent) [L. dis-cutio, pp. -cussus, to shatter]. Scattering or dispersing a pathologic accumulation.

disease (diz-ēz) [Eng. dis- priv. + ease]. **1.** Morbus; illness; sickness; an interruption, cessation, or disorder of body functions, systems, or organs. **2.** A pathologic entity characterized usually by at least two of these criteria: a recognized etiologic agent(s), an identifiable group of signs and symptoms, or consistent anatomical alterations. See also syndrome and subentries.

    ABO hemolytic d. of the newborn, erythroblastosis fetalis due to maternal-fetal incompatibility with respect to an antigen of the ABO blood group.

    Acosta's d., altitude sickness.

    Adams-Stokes d., Adams-Stokes syndrome.

    Addison's d., chronic adrenocortical insufficiency.

    akamushi d., (ak-kă-mu'shĭ) [Jap. aka, red, + mushi, bug], tsutsugamushi d.

    Albers-Schönberg d., osteopetrosis.

    Albright's d., Albright's syndrome (1); polyostotic fibrous dysplasia with irregular brown patches of cutaneous pigmentation and endocrine dysfunction, especially precocious puberty, in girls.

    Almeida's d., paracoccidioidomycosis.

    Alpers' d., poliodystrophia cerebri progressiva infantalis.

    Alzheimer's d., presenile dementia (2); organic dementia occurring usually in persons under 50 years of age, associated with Alzheimer's sclerosis, neurofibrillary degeneration, and senile plaques.

    Andersen's d., type 4 glycogenosis.

    aortoiliac occlusive d., Leriche's syndrome; obstruction of the abdominal aorta and its main branches by atherosclerosis.

    Aran-Duchenne d., progressive muscular atrophy.

    Australian X d., Murray Valley encephalitis.

autoimmune d., a d. resulting from an immune reaction produced by an individual's leukocytes or antibodies acting on the subject's own tissues or extracellular proteins.

Ayerza's d., a condition resembling polycythemia vera but resulting from primary pulmonary arteriosclerosis or primary pulmonary hypertension, characterized by plexiform (weblike) lesions of arterioles.

Bamberger-Marie d., hypertrophic pulmonary *osteoarthropathy.*

Bannister's d., angioneurotic *edema.*

Banti's d., Banti's *syndrome.*

Barlow's d., infantile *scurvy.*

Barraquer's d., progressive *lipodystrophy.*

Basedow's d., Graves d.

Batten-Mayou d., late juvenile type of cerebral *spingolipidosis.*

Bazin's d., *erythema* induratum.

Bechterew's d., *spondylitis* deformans.

Behçet's d., Behçet's *syndrome.*

Benson's d., asteroid *hyalosis.*

Bernhardt's d., *meralgia* paraesthetica.

Besnier-Boeck-Schaumann d., sarcoidosis.

Best's d., heredomacular degeneration occurring during the first few years of life.

Bielschowsky's d., early juvenile type of cerebral *sphingolipidosis.*

Binswanger's d., Binswanger's encephalopathy; organically caused dementia found in chronic hypertensives; is characterized by recurrent edema of cerebral white matter, with secondary demyelination.

Blocq's d., astasia-abasia.

Blount's d., nonrachitic bowlegs in children.

Boeck's d., sarcoidosis.

Bornholm d., [*Bornholm,* island in the Baltic], epidemic *pleurodynia.*

Bourneville's d., tuberous *sclerosis.*

Bourneville-Pringle d., tuberous sclerosis with adenoma sebaceum.

Bowen's d., a precancerous dermatosis or form of intraepidermal carcinoma characterized by the development of pinkish or brownish papules covered with a thickened horny layer.

Breda's d., espundia.

Bright's d., nonsuppurative nephritis with albuminuria and edema, corresponding stages of glomerulonephritis; sometimes used in general reference to unspecified kidney d.

Brill's d., Brill-Zinsser d.

Brill-Symmers d., nodular *lymphoma.*

Brill-Zinsser d., Brill's d.; recrudescent typhus; an endogenous infection associated with the "carrier state" in persons who previously had epidemic typhus fever.

bronzed d., (1) Addison's d.; (2) hemochromatosis.

Buerger's d., *thromboangiitis* obliterans.

Busse-Buschke d., cryptococcosis.

Caffey's d., infantile cortical *hyperostosis.*

caisson d., (ka'son) [Fr. *caisson,* a water-tight box or cylinder containing air under high pressure, used in sinking structural pilings underwater]. decompression *sickness.*

Calvé-Perthes d., Legg-Calvé-Perthes d.

Canavan's d., spongy *degeneration.*

Carrión's d., Oroya *fever.*

cat-scratch d., cat-scratch fever; benign inoculation lymphoreticulosis, an ulceroglandular d. that frequently follows the scratch or bite of a cat, producing regional lymphadenitis, indolent reaction, and benign low grade infection.

celiac d., gluten enteropathy; a disease characterized by sensitivity to gluten and atrophy of the mucosa of the upper small intestine; mainifestations include diarrhea, malabsorption, steatorrhea, and nutritional and vitamin deficiencies.

Chagas d., Chagas-Cruz d., South American *trypanosomiasis.*

Charcot's d., amyotrophic lateral *sclerosis.*

Charcot-Marie-Tooth d., peroneal muscular *atrophy.*

Chédiak-Higashi d., Chédiak-Steinbrinck-Higashi *syndrome.*

Chiari's d., Chiari's *syndrome.*

Christensen-Krabbe d., *poliodystrophia* cerebri progressiva infantalis.

Christian's d., (1) Hand-Schüller-Christian d.; (2) nodular nonsuppurative *panniculitis.*

Christmas d., [surname of child with the d.], *hemophilia* B.

chronic granulomatous d., congenital dysphagocytosis; a congenital defect in the killing of phagocytosed bacteria by polymorphonuclear leukocytes, resulting in increased susceptibility to severe infection; inheritance is usually by X chromosome-linked transmission.

chronic obstructive pulmonary d., general term used for those diseases in which forced expiratory flow is slowed, especially when no etiologic or other more specific term can be applied.

Coats's d., exudative *retinitis.*

Cockayne's d., Cockayne's *syndrome.*

collagen, collagen-vascular d.'s, collagenoses; a group of non-mendelian, although sometimes familial, generalized d.'s affecting connective tissue and frequently characterized by fibrinoid necrosis or vasculitis, included in this group are lupus erythematosus, progressive systemic sclerosis rheumatoid arthritis, rheumatic fever, polyarteritis nodosa, and dermatomyositis. See also connective tissue d.

communicable d., contagious d.; any d. that is transmissible by infection or contagion directly or through the agency of a vector.

Concato's d., polyserositis.

connective-tissue d., a group of generalized d.'s affecting connective tissue, especially d.'s not inherited as mendelian characteristics; rheumatic fever and rheumatoid arthritis were first proposed as such d.'s, and other so-called collagen d.'s have been added.

constitutional d., d. related to diathesis, disposition, or constitution, often inherited as an inborn error of structure or metabolism.

contagious d., communicable d.

Cori's d., type 3 *glycogenosis.*

Cowden's d. [surname of family from which reported], hypertrichosis and gingival fibromatosis from infancy, accompanied by postpubertal fibroadenomatous breast enlargement; papules of the face are characteristic of multiple trichilemmomas.

Creutzfeldt-Jakob d., spastic pseudosclerosis with corticostriatal-spinal degeneration, a form of spongiform encephalopathy caused by a slow virus and characterized by dementia, myoclonus, ataxia, and other neurologic manifestations; progresses rapidly to coma and death.

Crigler-Najjar d., Crigler-Najjar *syndrome.*

Crohn's d., regional *enteritis.*

Crouzon's d., craniofacial *dysostosis.*

Cruveilhier's d., progressive muscular *atrophy.*

Cruveilhier-Baumgarten d., Cruveilhier-Baumgarten *syndrome.*

Cushing's d., Cushing's syndrome associated with a pituitary basophil adenoma.

cystic d. of the breast, fibrocystic d. of the breasts.

cystic d. of renal medulla, the presence of small cysts in the renal medulla associated with anemia, sodium depletion, and chronic renal failure; of two types: autosomal recessive or juvenile type, autosomal dominant or adult type.

cystine storage d., cystinosis.

cytomegalic inclusion d., inclusion body d.; the presence of inclusion bodies within the cytoplasm and nuclei of enlarged cells of various organs or newborn infants dying with jaundice, hepatomegaly, splenomegaly, purpura, thrombocytopenia, and fever; also occurs, at all ages, as a complication of other d.'s in which immune mechanisms are severly depressed.

Darier's d., *keratosis* follicularis.

Darling's d., histoplasmosis.

deficiency d., any d. resulting from lack of calories, proteins, essential amino acids, fatty acids, vitamins, or trace minerals.

degenerative joint d., osteoarthritis.

Déjérine's, Déjérine-Sottas d., hereditary hypertrophic *neuropathy.*

demyelinating d., one of a group of d.'s of unknown cause in which there is extensive loss of the myelin sheaths of nerve fibers, as in multiple sclerosis.

de Quervain's d., fibrosis of the sheath of a tendon of the thumb.

Dercum's d., *adiposis* dolorosa.

Devic's d., *neuromyelitis* optica.

Duchenne's d., (1) obsolete eponym for *tabes* dorsalis; (2) pseudohypertrophic muscular *dystrophy;* (3) progressive bulbar *paralysis.*

Duchenne-Aran d., progressive muscular *atrophy.*

Duhring's d., *dermatitis* herpetiformis.

Dukes d., fourth d.

Ebstein's d., Ebstein's *anomaly.*

Engelmann's d., diaphysial *dysplasia.*

Erb's d., progressive bulbar *paralysis.*

Eulenburg's d., congenital *paramyotonia.*

extrapyramidal d., degenerative d. affecting the corpus striatum or other part of the extrapyramidal system, *e.g.* parkinsonism.

Fabry's d., angiokeratoma corporis diffusum; an X-linked recessive disorder due to deficiency of the enzyme α-galactosidase and characterized by abnormal accumulations of neutral glycolipids in histiocytes in blood vessel walls and by purple skin lesions; death results from renal, cardiac, or cerebrovascular complications.

fibrocystic d. of the breast, cystic d. of the breast; a benign d. common in women of the third, fourth, and fifth decades, characterized by formation, in one or both breasts, of small cysts containing fluid, associated with stromal fibrosis and variable degrees of intraductal epithelial hyperplasia and sclerosing adenosis.

fibrocystic d. of the pancreas, cystic *fibrosis.*

fifth d., *erythema* infectiosum.

Forbes d., type 3 *glycogenosis.*

Fordyce's d., Fordyce's *spots.*

Fothergill's d., (1) trigeminal *neuralgia;* (2) anginose *scarlatina.*

fourth d., Dukes d.; scarlatinella; a mild exanthematous affection of childhood bearing a resemblance to scarlatina analogous to that of German measles to measles.

Fox-Fordyce d., a rare chronic eruption of dry papules and distended ruptured apocrine glands, with follicular hyperkeratosis of the nipples, axillae, and pubic and sternal regions, and with intense pruritus.

Freiberg's d., epiphysial ischemic (aseptic) necrosis of second metatarsal head.

Friedreich's d., *myoclonus* multiplex.

functional d., functional *disorder.*

Gamna's d., a form of chronic splenomegaly characterized by conspicuous thickening of the capsule and the presence of multiple, small, rustlike, brown foci (Gamna-Gandy bodies), which contain iron.

Garré's d., sclerosing *osteitis.*

Gaucher's d., cerebrosidosis; glycocerebroside accumulation in macrophages due to a genetic deficiency of glucocerebrosidase; marked by hepatosplenomegaly, lymphadenopathy, and bone destruction by characteristic cells containing cytoplasmic tubules; autosomal recessive inheritance.

Gierke's d., type 1 *glycogenosis.*

Gilbert's d., familial nonhemolytic *jaundice.*

Gilles de la Tourette d., Gilles de la Tourette's syndrome; motor incoordination with echolalia and coprolalia; a form of tic.

Glanzmann's d., Glanzmann's *thrombasthenia*.

glycogen storage d., glycogenosis.

Goldflam d., *myasthenia* gravis.

graft versus host d., graft versus host reaction; a type of incompatibility reaction of transplanted cells against those host tissues that possess an antigen not possessed by the donor.

granulomatous d., see chronic granulomatous d.

Graves d., Basedow's or Parry's d.; toxic goiter characterized by diffuse hyperplasia of the thyroid gland; a form of hyperthyroidism.

Greenfield's d., late infantile form of metachromatic leukodystrophy.

Günther's d., congenital erythropoietic *porphyria*.

H d., Hartnup d.

Hailey and Hailey d., familial benign chronic *pemphigus*.

Hallopeau's d., (1) *acrodermatitis* continua; (2) *pemphigus* vegetans (2); (3) *lichen* sclerosus et atrophicus.

Hamman's d., Hamman's *syndrome*.

hand-foot-and-mouth d., an exanthematous eruption of the fingers, toes, palms, and soles, accompanied by often painful vesicles and ulceration of the buccal mucous membrane and the tongue and by slight fever; caused by a Coxsackie virus.

Hand-Schüller-Christian d., Schüller's d.; Christian's (2); generalized lipid histiocytosis of bones, especially the skull, with bone destruction by accumulation of cells containing cholesterol esters, and eosinophil leukocytes.

Hansen's d., leprosy (2).

Hartnup d., H d.; a congenital metabolic disorder consisting of aminoaciduria due to a defect in renal tubular absorption of neonatal α-amino acids and urinary excretion of tryptophan derivatives; characterized by a pellagra-like, light-sensitive skin rash with temporaray cerebellar ataxia; autosomal recessive inheritance.

Hashimoto's d., Hashimoto's struma or thyroiditis; struma lymphomatosa; lymphadenoid goiter; diffuse infiltration of the thyroid gland with lymphocytes, resulting in diffuse goiter and progressive destruction of the parenchyma and hypothyroidism.

heavy chain d., the paraproteinemias, characterized by abnormal γ-globulins and associated with malignant disorders of the plasmacytic and lymphoid cell series; globulin fragments resembling, but not identical with, Fc fragment of IgG occur in large quantities in serum and urine.

Heerfordt's d., uveoparotid *fever*.

Heine-Medin d., acute anterior *poliomyelitis*.

hemoglobin d., see *hemoglobin* C; *hemoglobin* H.

hemolytic d. of newborn, *erythroblastosis* fetalis.

hemorrhagic d. of the newborn, a syndrome characterized by spontaneous internal or external bleeding accompanied by hypoprothrombinemia, slightly decreased platelets, and markedly elevated bleeding and clotting times, usually occurring between the 3rd and 6th days of life.

Hers d., type 6 *glycogenosis*.

Hippel's d., Hippel-Lindau d., Lindau's d.

Hirschsprung's d., congenital *megacolon*.

Hodgkin's d., a d. marked by chronic enlargement of the lymph nodes, enlargement of the spleen and often of the liver, by anemia and fever, and by transformed lymphocytes (Reed-Sternberg cells) associated with inflammatory infiltration of lymphocytes and eosinophilic leukocytes and fibrosis; classified into lymphocytic predominant and nodular sclerosing types, mixed cellularity type, and lymphocytic depletion type.

Hodgson's d., dilation of the arch of the aorta associated with insufficiency of the aortic valve.

hoof-and-mouth d., incorrect term for foot-and-mouth d.

hookworm d., see ancylostomiasis; necatoriasis.

Hurler's d., Hurler's *syndrome*.

Hutchinson-Gilford d., progeria.

hyaline membrane d. respiratory distress syndrome of the newborn; a d. seen especially in premature neonates with respiratory distress, characterized post mortem by atelectasis and an eosinophilic membrane lining alveolar ducts and associated with reduced amounts of lung surfactant.

hydatid d., infection with larvae of *Echinococcus*.

Iceland d., epidemic *neuromyasthenia*.

immune complex d., a d. evoked by the deposition of antigen-antibody or antigen-antibody-complement complexes on cell surfaces, with subsequent involvement of breakdown products of complement, platelets, and polymorphonuclear leukocytes, and development of vasculitis.

inclusion body d., cytomegalic inclusion d.

inclusion cell d., *mucolipidosis II*.

infectious d., a d. resulting from the presence and activity of a microbial agent.

insufficiency d., deficiency d.

interstitial d., a d. affecting chiefly the connective-tissue framework of an organ, the parenchyma suffering secondarily.

iron storage d., the storage of excess iron in the parenchyma of many organs, in conditions such as idiopathic hemochromatosis or transfusion hemosiderosis.

Jansky-Bielschowsky d., early juvenile type of cerebral *sphingolipidosis*.

Jensen's d., *retinochoroiditis* juxtapapillaris.

Kashin-Bek d., a form of generalized osteoarthrosis, limited to areas of Asia, believed to result from ingestion of wheat infected with fungus *Fusarium sporotrichiella*.

Katayama d. [Jap. town where the d. is common], *schistosomiasis* japonicum.

Kawasaki d., mucocutaneous lymph node *syndrome*.

Kienböck's d., osteolysis of the lunate bone following trauma to the wrist.

Kimmelstiel-Wilson d., Kimmelstiel-Wilson syndrome; intercapillary glomerulosclerosis; a nodular hyaline deposit in tufts of the glomeruli of the kidneys associated with diabetes, albuminuria, hypertension, and edema of the nephrotic type.

kinky-hair d., Menkes syndrome; a congenital metabolic defect (X-linked recessive) manifested by short, sparse, poorly pigmented kinky hair; associated with failure to thrive, physical and mental retardation, and progressive severe deterioration of the brain.

Klippel's d., arthritic general *pseudoparalysis.*

Köhler's d., epiphysial aseptic necrosis of the tarsal navicular bone or of the patella.

Krabbe's d., globoid cell *leukodystrophy.*

Kufs d., adult type of cerebral *sphingolipidosis.*

Kussmaul's d., *polyarteritis* nodosa.

Kyasanur Forest d., a d. occurring among forest workers in the Kyasanur Forest and in Mysore, India, caused by a group B arbovirus (*Flavivirus*) transmitted chiefly by the tick *Haemaphysalis spinigera;* symptoms include fever, headache, back and limb pains, diarrhea, and intestinal bleeding.

Lafora's d., myoclonus *epilepsy.*

Legg-Calvé-Perthes, Legg-Perthes, or **Legg's d.,** epiphysial aseptic necrosis of the upper end of the femur. Also called pseudocoxalgia; coxa plana; osteochondritis deformans juvenilis; Perthes or Calvé-Perthes d.

Legionnaires d., [American *Legion* convention, 1976, at which many delegates were so affected], legionellosis; an acute infectious d., caused by *Legionella pneumophila,* with prodromal influenza-like symptoms and a rapidly rising high fever, followed by severe pneumonia and production of usually nonpurulent sputum, mental confusion, hepatic fatty changes, and renal tubular degeneration.

Leiner's d., *erythroderma* desquamativum.

Letterer-Siwe d., nonlipid *histiocytosis.*

Lindau's d., (von) Hippel-Lindau or Hippel's d.; retinocerebral angiomatosis; a type of phacomatosis, consisting of hemangiomas of the retina, associated with hemangiomas or hemangioblastomas primarily of the cerebellum and walls of the fourth ventricle, occasionally involving the spinal cord; sometimes associated with cysts or hamartomas of kidney, adrenal, or other organs; autosomal dominant inheritance.

Lutz-Splendore-Almeida d., paracoccidioidomycosis.

Lyme d. [*Lyme,* CT, where first recognized], an inflammatory disorder caused by the spirochete *Borrelia burgdorferi* and transmitted by ixodid ticks, typically occurring during the summer months; the characterizing lesion, erythema chronicum migrans, usually is preceded or accompanied by fever, malaise, fatigue, headache, and stiff neck; neurologic or cardiac manifestations, or arthritis (Lyme arthritis) may occur weeks to months later.

Madelung's d., diffuse symmetrical lipomatosis, or deposit of fatty tissue, on the upper part of the back, shoulders, and neck.

Majocchi's d., *purpura* annularis telangiectodes.

Manson's d., *schistosomiasis* mansoni.

maple syrup urine d. branched chain ketoaciduria; a disorder caused by deficient oxidative decarboxylation of α-keto acid metabolites of leucine, isoleucine, and valine which are present in blood and urine in elevated concentrations, the urine having an odor similar to that of maple syrup; mental and physical retardation are associated; autosomal recessive inheritance.

marble bone d., osteopetrosis.

Marburg virus d., human infection by Marburg virus, causing fever, diarrhea, a maculopapular rash, and disseminated intravascular coagulation with high mortality.

Marchiafava-Bignami d., a degenerative process involving the corpus callosum that occurs predominately in chronic alcoholics.

Marie's d., obsolete eponym for (1) acromegaly; (2) hypertrophic pulmonary *osteoarthropathy;* (3) hereditary cerebellar *ataxia;* (4) ankylosing *spondylitis.*

Marie-Strümpell d., ankylosing *spondylitis.*

McArdle-Schmid-Pearson d., type 5 *glycogenosis.*

Mediterranean-hemoglobin E d., thalassemia with hemoglobin E in the blood.

Ménétrièr's d., hypertrophic gastritis; gastric mucosal hyperplasia, either mucoid or glandular, the latter type may be associated with the Zollinger-Ellison syndrome.

Ménière's d., endolymphatic hydrops; auditory or labyrinthine vertigo; an affection characterized clinically by vertigo, nausea, vomiting, tinnitus, and progressive deafness.

mental d., see mental *illness.*

Merzbacher-Pelizaeus d., Pelizaeus-Merzbacher d.; aplasia axialis extracorticalis; familial degenerative d. of the brain marked by progressive sclerosis of white substance of the frontal lobes, mental deficiency, and vasomotor disorders.

Mikulicz d., benign swelling of the lacrimal, and usually also of the salivary glands in consequence of an infiltration of and replacement of the normal gland structure by lymphoid tissue.

Milroy's d., the congential type of hereditary lymphedema.

Minamata d. [*Minamata* Bay, Japan], a neurological disorder resulting from poisoning by organic mercury compounds and characterized by peripheral paresthesis, dysarthria, ataxia, and loss of peripheral vision.

Mitchell's d., erythromelalgia.

mixed connective-tissue d., d. with features of systemic lupus erythematosus and also of systemic sclerosis or of polymyositis, and with serum antibodies to nuclear ribonucleoprotein.

Möbius d., ophthalmoplegic migraine or periodic oculomotor paralysis.

molecular d., a d. in which there is a single alteration affecting only a particular molecule.

Mondor's d., thrombophlebitis of the thoracoepigastric vein of the breast and chest wall.

Monge's d., chronic mountain *sickness.*

Morgagni's d., Adams-Stokes *syndrome.*

Morquio's d., Morquio-Ullrich d., Morquio's *syndrome.*

Morvan's d., syringomyelia.

motor neuron d., general term including progressive muscular atrophy (infantile, juvenile, and adult), amyotrophic lateral sclerosis, progressive bulbar paralysis, and primary lateral sclerosis; frequently familial.

Nicolas-Favre d., *lymphogranuloma* venereum.

Niemann-Pick d., sphingomyelin lipidosis; lipid histiocytosis with accumulation of phospholipid (sphingomyelin) in histiocytes in the liver, spleen, lymph nodes and bone marrow; cerebral involvement may occur at a late stage, with red macular spots less common than in Tay-Sachs d.; autosomal recessive inheritance.

Norrie's d., congenital bilateral masses of tissue arising from the retina or vitreous and resembling glioma (pseudoglioma), usually with atrophy of iris and development of cataract; X-linked recessive inheritance.

notifiable d., a d. that, by statutory requirements, must be reported to public health authorities at diagnosis because of its importance to human or animal health.

Oguchi's d., congenital nonprogressive night blindness with yellow or gray coloration of fundus; autosomal recessive inheritance.

Ollier's d., enchondromatosis.

Oppenheim's d., *amyotonia* congenita.

organic d., a d. in which there is anatomical change in some tissue or organ.

Ormond's d., idiopathic retroperitoneal *fibrosis.*

Osgood-Schlatter d., Schlatter-Osgood d.; epiphysial aseptic necrosis of the tibial tubercle.

Osler's d., (1) erythremia; (2) hereditary hemorrhagic *telangiectasia.*

Osler-Vaquez d., erythremia.

Owren's d., parahemophilia; a congenital deficiency of factor V, resulting in prolongation of prothrombin time and coagulation time.

Paget's d., (1) osteitis deformans; a generalized skeletal disease, frequently familial, of older persons in which bone resorption and formation are both increased, leading to thickening and softening of bones, and bending of weight-bearing bones; (2) a d. of elderly women, characterized by an infiltrated, somewhat eczematous lesion surrounding and involving the nipple and areola, and associated with subjacent intraductal cancer of the breast and infiltration of the lower epidermis by malignant cells; (3) cancer of the vulva arising from apocrine sweat glands.

Parkinson's d., parkinsonism (1).

Parrot's d., pseudoparalysis in infants, due to syphilitic osteochondritis.

Parry's d., Graves' d.

Pel-Ebstein d., Hodgkin's d. with periodic pyrexia.

Pelizaeus-Merzbacher d., Merzbacher-Pelizaeus d.

Pellegrini's d., Pellegrini-Stieda d., a calcific density in the medial collateral ligament and/or bony growth at the internal condyle of the femur.

pelvic inflammatory d. (PID), acute or chronic inflammation in the pelvic cavity, particularly, suppurative lesions of the female genital tract.

periodic d., any d. in which attacks tend to recur at regular intervals.

Perthes d., Legg-Calvé-Perthes d.

Peyronie's d., a d. of unknown cause in which there are plaques or strands of dense fibrous tissue surrounding the corpus cavernosum of the penis, causing deformity and painful erection.

Pick's d., (1) [F. Pick], a form of multiple serositis (or polyserosis) characterized by chronic congestive hepatomegaly, persistent or recurrent ascites, sometimes recurrent pleural effusion, peritonitis, and pleuritis, occurring in a patient with previous (or concurrent) hyalinizing pericarditis; (2) [A. Pick], Pick's *atrophy.*

pink d., acrodynia (1).

polycystic d. of kidneys, polycystic *kidney.*

Pompe's d., type 2 *glycogenosis.*

Pott's d., tuberculous *spondylitis.*

primary d., a d. that arises spontaneously and is not associated with or caused by a previous disease, injury, or event.

pulseless d., Takayasu's syndrome or d.; a progressive obliterative arteritis of the vessels arising from the arch of the aorta.

Quincke's d., angioneurotic *edema.*

Raynaud's d., idiopathic paroxysmal bilateral cyanosis of the digits, due to arterial and arteriolar contraction, caused by cold or emotion.

Recklinghausen's d., neurofibromatosis.

Recklinghausen's d. of bone, *osteitis* fibrosa cystica.

Reiter's d., Reiter's *syndrome.*

Rendu-Osler-Weber d., hereditary hemorrhagic *telangiectasia.*

rheumatic heart d., d. of the heart resulting from rheumatic fever, chiefly manifested by abnormalities of the valves.

Ritter's d., (1) toxic epidermal *necrolysis;* (2) *iceterus* neonatorum.

Roger's d., a congenital cardiac anomaly consisting of a small isolated defect of the interventricular septum.

Rokitansky's d., (1) acute yellow *atrophy* of the liver; (2) Chiari's *syndrome.*

Schamberg's d., progressive pigmentary *dermatosis.*

Scheuermann's d., osteochondritis deformans juvenilis dorsi; epiphysial aseptic necrosis of vertebral bodies.

Schilder's d., *encephalitis* periaxialis diffusa.

Schlatter-Osgood d., Osgood-Schlatter d.

Schönlein's d., Henoch-Schönlein *purpura.*

Schüller's d., Hand-Schüller- Christian d.

secondary d., (1) a d. that follows and results from an earlier disease, injury, or event; **(2)** a wasting disorder that follows successful transplantation of bone marrow into a lethally irradiated host; frequently severe and is usually associated with fever, anorexia, diarrhea, dermatitis, and desquamation.

serum d., serum *sickness.*

sickle cell C d., a d. resulting from abnormal sickle-shaped erythrocytes, containing both hemoglobin S and hemoglobin C, in response to a lowering of the partial pressure of oxygen; includes anemia, crises due to hemolysis or vascular occlusion, chronic leg ulcers and bone deformities, and infarcts of bone or of the spleen.

sickle cell-thalassemia d., microdrepanocytic *anemia.*

Simmonds d., hypophysial or pituitary cachexia; anterior pituitary insufficiency due to trauma, vascular lesions, or tumors; characterized clinically by asthenia, loss of weight and body hair, arterial hypotension, and manifestations of thyroid, adrenal, and gonadal hypofunction.

sixth d., *exanthema* subitum.

sixth venereal d., *lymphogranuloma* venereum.

slow virus d., a d. that follows a slow, progressive course, such as visna and maedi of sheep, caused by viruses of the subfamily Lentivirinae (family Retroviridae) and subacute sclerosing panencephalitis, seemingly caused by the measles virus.

social d.'s., a term used to designate venereal d.'s., especially gonorrhea and syphilis.

Spielmeyer-Vogt d., Vogt-Spielmeyer d.; late juvenile type of cerebral *sphingolipidosis.*

Steinert's d., myotonic *dystrophy.*

Still's d., juvenile rheumatoid *arthritis.*

Stokes-Adams d., Adams-Stokes *syndrome.*

storage d., accumulation of a specific substance within tissues, generally because of congenital deficiency of an enzyme necessary for further metabolism of the substance.

Strümpell's d., (1) *spondylitis* deformans; **(2)** acute epidemic *leukoencephalitis.*

Strümpell-Marie d., ankylosing *spondylitis.*

Strümpell-Westphal d., pseudosclerosis (2).

Sturge-Weber d., Sturge-Weber *syndrome.*

Sutton's d., (1) [R. L. Sutton], halo *nevus;* **(2)** [R. L. Sutton, Jr.], *periadenitis* mucosa necrotica recurrens.

Swift's d., acrodynia (1).

Takahara's d., acatalasemia.

Takayasu's d., pulseless d.

Tangier d., [island in the Chesapeake Bay where first cases described], a heritable disorder of lipid metabolism characterized by almost complete absence from plasma of high density lipoproteins, and by storage of cholesterol esters in foam cells autosomal recessive inheritance.

Tay-Sachs d., infantile type of cerebral *sphingolipidosis.*

third d., rubella.

Thomsen's d., *myotonia* congenita.

thyrocardiac d., heart d. resulting from hyperthyroidism.

tsutsugamushi d., akamushi d.; scrub or tropica typhus; an acute infectious disease, caused by *Rickettsia tsutsugamushi* and transmitted by *Trombicula akamushi* and *T. deliensis,* that occurs ir harvesters of hemp in some parts of Japan; characterized by fever, painful swelling of the lymphatic glands; a small blackish scab on the genitals, neck or axilla, and an eruption of large, dark red papules

vagabond's d., vagrant's d., parasitic *melanoderma.*

Vaquez d., erythremia.

venereal d., a contagious d. acquired during sexua intercourse; *e.g.,* syphilis, gonorrhea, chancroid.

veno-occlusive d. of the liver, obliterating endo phlebitis of small hepatic vein radicles, associated with ingestion of toxic plant substances in bush tea causes ascites which may progress to cirrhosis.

Vincent's d., necrotizing ulcerative *gingivitis.*

Vogt-Spielmeyer d., Spielmeyer-Vogt d.

von Economo's d., encephalitis lethargica; th basis for postencephalic parkinsonism, suspected t be of viral origin.

von Gierke's d., type 1 *glycogenosis.*

von Hippel-Lindau d., Lindau's d.

von Recklinghausen's d., neurofibromatosis.

von Willebrand's d., angiohemophilia; hereditar pseudohemophilia; vascular hemophilia; a hemor rhagic diathesis characterized by tendency to blee primarily from mucous membranes, prolonge bleeding time, normal platelet count, normal clo retraction, partial and variable deficiency of facto VIII, and possibly a morphologic defect of platelets autosomal dominant inheritance with reduced pene trance and variable expressivity.

Weber-Christian d., nodular nonsuppurative *par niculitis.*

Weil's d., leptospirosis caused by a leptospire an characterized clinically by fever, jaundice, muscula pains, conjunctival congestion, and albuminuria.

Werlhof's d., idiopathic thrombocytopenic *pu pura.*

Wernicke's d., Wernicke's *syndrome.*

Westphal-Strümpell d., pseudosclerosis (2).

Whipple's d., intestinal lipodystrophy; a rare c characterized by steatorrhea, frequently generalize lymphadenopathy, arthritis, fever, and cough.

Wilson's d., (1) [S. A. K. Wilson], hepatolenticular *degeneration;* (2) [Sir W. J. E. Wilson], exfoliative *dermatitis.*

Winiwarter-Buerger d., *thromboangiitis* obliterans.

Wolman's d., a lipidosis caused by deficiency of lysosomal acid lipase acitivity resulting in widespread accumulation of cholesterol esters and triglycerides in viscera with xanthomatosis, adrenal calcification, hepatosplenomegaly, foam cells in bone marrow and other tissues, and vacuolated lymphocytes in peripheral blood; autosomal recessive inheritance.

disengagement (dis-en-gāj'ment) [Fr.]. Emergence of the fetal head from the vulva during childbirth, or ascent of the presenting part from the pelvis after the inlet has been negotiated.

disequilibrium (dis'e-kwĭ-lib'rĭ-um). A lack of equilibrium in any sense.

disgermino'ma. Dysgerminoma.

disimpaction (dis'im-pak'shun). Withdrawal of impaction in a fractured bone.

disinfect (dis'in-fekt'). To destroy pathogenic microorganisms in or on any substance or to inhibit their growth and vital activity.

disinfectant (dis'in-fek'tant). Destroying organisms of putrefaction or disease, or inhibiting their activity.

disinfection (dis'in-fek'shun). The act of disinfecting.

disintegration (dis-in-tĕ-gra'shun). **1.** Loss or separation of the component parts of a substance, such as occurs in catabolism or decay. **2.** Disorganization of psychic processes.

disjugate (dis'ju-gāt) [L. *dis-*, apart, + *jugatus,* yoked]. Not paired in action or joined together.

disjunction (dis-junk'shun) [L. *dis-*, apart, + *junctura,* juncture]. Separation of pairs of chromosomes at the anaphase stage of cell division.

disk [L. *discus;* G. *diskos,* a quoit, disk]. **1.** Discus. **2.** Lamella (2).

articular d., *discus* articularis.

blood d., platelet.

Bowman's d.'s, d.'s resulting from transverse segmentation of striated muscular fiber.

choked d., papilledema.

ciliary d., *orbiculus* ciliaris.

embryonic d., germinal d., germ d., the point in a telolecithal ovum where the embryo begins to be formed.

herniated d., protruded or ruptured d.; protrusion of a degenerated or fragmented intervertebral d. into the intervertebral foramen, compressing the nerve root.

intercalated d., an undulating double membrane separating adjacent cells in cardiac muscle fibers.

intervertebral d., *discus* intervertebralis.

optic d., *discus* nervi optici.

Placido's d., keratoscope.

protruded d., herniated d.

ruptured d., herniated d.

tactile d., *meniscus* tactus.

diskitis (disk-i'tis). Discitis.

disko-. See disco-.

dis'locate. To luxate; to put out of joint.

dislocation (dis-lo-ka'shun) [L. *dislocatio,* fr. *dis-*, apart, + *locatio,* a placing]. Luxation; displacement of an organ or any part; specifically a disturbance or disarrangement of the normal relation of the bones entering into the formation of a joint.

closed d., simple d.; a d. not complicated by an external wound.

compound d., open d.

open d., compound d.; a d. complicated by a wound opening from the surface down to the affected joint.

simple d., closed d.

dismem'ber. To amputate an arm or leg.

dis'mutase. Generic name for enzymes catalyzing the reaction of two identical molecules to produce two molecules in differing states of oxidation or phosphorylation.

disor'der. A disturbance of function, structure, or both.

acute neuropsychologic d., acute brain *syndrome.*

adjustment d.'s, a class of mental d.'s in which the development of symptoms is related to the presence of some environmental stressor.

affective d.'s, a class of mental d.'s characterized by a disturbance in mood.

antisocial personality d., a personality d. characterized by a history of continuous and chronic antisocial behavior with disregard for and violation of the rights of others.

behavior d., general term used to denote mental illness, specifically those mental, emotional, and behavioral subclasses of mental illness for which organic correlates do not exist.

bipolar d., an affective d. characterized by the occurrence of manic episodes or manic episodes alternating with depressive episodes.

borderline personality d., a personality d. characterized by instability in a variety of areas including interpersonal relationships, behavior, mood, and self-image.

character d., a term referring to a group of behavioral d.'s, which has been replaced by a more general term, personality d., of which character d.'s are now a subclass.

cyclothymic d., an affective d. characterized by mood swings including periods of hypomania and depression.

emotional d., see mental *illness.*

functional d., functional disease; a physical d. with no known or detectable organic basis to explain the symptoms.

immunoproliferative d.'s, d.'s in which there is a continuing proliferation of cells of the immunocyte complex associated with autoallergic disturbances and γ-globulin abnormalities, with the implication that the etiologic factor concerned might be immunologic (allergic).

neuropsychologic d., disturbance of mental function due to trauma, associated with one or more of the following manifestations: psychotic, neurotic, behavioral, psychophysiologic, and mental impairment.

personality d., general term for a group of behavioral d.'s, each characterized by usually lifelong, ingrained, maladaptive patterns of deviant behavior, life style, and social adjustment that are different in quality from psychotic and neurotic symptoms; former designations for these personality d.'s were psychopath and sociopath.

posttraumatic stress d., a form of neuropsychologic d., classified as an anxiety d. and characterized by the development of symptoms subsequent to a psychologically traumatic event outside the range of usual human experience.

psychophysiologic d., standard nomenclature used in reference to psychosomatic d.

psychosomatic d., a d. characterized by physical symptoms of psychic origin, usually involving a single organ system innervated by the autonomic nervous system.

substance abuse d.'s, a class of mental disorders in which behavioral changes are associated with regular use of substances that affect the central nervous system.

disor'ganiza'tion. Destruction of an organ or tissue with consequent loss of function.

disorientation (dis'or-ĭ-en-ta'shun) . Loss of the sense of familiarity with one's surroundings; loss of one's bearings.

dispen'sary [L. *dis-penso*, pp. *-atus,* to distribute by weight]. **1.** A physician's office, especially the office of one who dispenses his own medicines. **2.** The office of a hospital apothecary, where medicines are given out on the physicians' orders. **3.** An out-patient department of a hospital.

dispen'satory [L. *dispensator,* a manager, steward; see dispensary], A work originally intended as a commentary on the Pharmacopeia, but now rather a supplement to that work. It contains an account of the sources, mode of preparation, physiologic action, and therapeutic uses of most of the agents, official and nonofficial, used in the treatment of disease.

dispense. To give out medicine and other necessities to the sick; to fill a medical prescription.

disperse (dis-pers'). To dissipate, to cause disappearance of, to scatter, to dilute.

dispersion (dis-per'zhun).[L. *dispersio*]. **1.** The act of dispersing or being dispersed. **2.** The more or less intimate incorporation of the particles of one substance into the mass of another, including solutions, suspensions, and colloidal dispersions. **3.** Colloidal *solution.*

dispireme (di-spi'rēm) [G. *di-,* twice, + *speirēma,* coil, convolution]. The double chromatin skein in the telophase of mitosis.

displacement (dis-plās'ment). **1.** Removal from the normal location or position. **2.** Transfer of impulses from one expression to another, as from fighting to talking.

dissect (dĭ-sekt') [L. *dis-seco,* pp. *-sectus,* to cut asunder]. **1.** To cut apart or separate the tissues of the body for study. **2.** In an operation, to separate the different structures along natural lines by dividing the connective tissue framework.

dissection (dĭ-sek'shun). Necrotomy (1); the act of dissecting.

dissem'inated [L. *dis-semino,* pp. *-atus,* to scatter seed]. Widely scattered throughout an organ, tissue, or the body.

dissimulation (dis-sim-u-la'shun). Concealment of the truth about a situation, especially about a state of health, as by a malingerer.

dissociation (dis-so'sī-a'shun, -shī-a'shun) [L. *dis-socio,* pp. *-atus,* to disjoin, separate]. **1.** Disassociation; separation, or a dissolution of relations. **2.** The change of a complex into a more simple chemical compound by any lytic reaction or by ionization. **3.** An unconscious process by which a group of mental processes is separated from the rest of the thinking processes, resulting in an independent functioning of these processes and a loss of the usual relationships.

atrial d., mutually independent beating of the two atria or of parts of the atria.

atrioventricular (A-V) d., (1) any situation in which atria and ventricles are activated and contract independently, as in complete A-V block; (2) more specifically, the d. between atria and ventricles which results from slowing of the atrial pacemaker or acceleration of the ventricular pacemaker.

electromechanical d., persistence of electrical activity in the heart without associated mechanical contraction; often a sign of cardiac rupture.

longitudinal d., d. between parallel chambers of the heart, as between one atrium and the other or between one ventricle and the other, in contrast to d. between atria and ventricles.

dissolution (dis-o-lu'shun) [L. *dis-solvo,* pp. *-solutus,* to loose asunder, dissolve]. A dissolving.

dissolve (dĭ-zolv'). To change or cause to change from solid to dispersed form by immersion in a fluid of suitable character.

dis'tad. Toward the periphery; in a distal direction.

dis'tal [L. *distalis*]. **1.** Situated away from the center of the body, or from the point of origin; applied to the extremity or distant part of a limb or organ. **2.** In dentistry, away from the median sagittal plane of the face, following the curvature of the dental arch.

dista'lis [NA]. Distal (1, 2).

distance (dis'tans) [L. *distantia,* fr. *di-sto,* to stand apart, be distant]. The measure of space between two objects.

focal d., the d. from the center of a lens to its focus

infinite d., infinity; the limit of distant vision, the rays entering the eyes from an object at that point being practically parallel.

interarch d., vertical d. between the maxillary and mandibular arches under certain conditions of vertical dimensions.

interocclusal d., vertical d. between the opposing occlusal surfaces, assuming the mandible in rest position.

pupillary d., the d. between the major reference points in measuring for fitting of spectacle frames and lenses.

distention, distension (dis-ten'shun) [L. *dis-tendere*, to stretch apart]. The act or state of being distended or stretched.

distichia, distichiasis (dis-tik'ĭ-ah; dis-tĭ-ki'a-sis) [G. *di-*, double, + *stichos*, row]. A congenital, abnormal, accessory row of eyelashes arising from tarsal (meibomian) gland orifices.

dis'tillate. The product of distillation.

distillation (dis'tĭ-la'shun). The volatilization of a liquid by heat and the subsequent condensation of the vapor; a means of separating the volatile from the nonvolatile, or the more volatile from the less volatile, part of a liquid mixture.

distobuccal (dis'to-buk'kal). Relating to the distal and buccal surfaces of a tooth; denoting the angle formed by their junction.

dis'tobuc'co-occlu'sal. Relating to the distal, buccal, and occlusal surfaces of a bicuspid or molar tooth; denoting especially the angle formed by the junction of these surfaces.

dis'tobuc'copul'pal. Relating to the angle formed by the junction of a distal, buccal, and pulpal wall of a cavity.

distocervical (dis'to-ser'vĭ-kal). Relating to the line angle formed by the junction of the distal and cervical (gingival) walls of a cavity.

distoclu'sal. **1.** Relating to or characterized by distoclusion. **2.** Denoting a compound cavity or restoration involving the distal and occlusal surfaces of a tooth. **3.** Denoting the line angle formed by the distal and occlusal walls of a cavity.

distoclusion (dis'to-klu'zhun). A malocclusion in which the mandibular arch articulates with the maxillary arch in a position distal to normal.

distogingival (dis'to-jin'jĭ-val). Relating to the junction of the distal surface with the gingival line of a tooth.

distoincisal (dis'to-in-si'zal). Relating to the angle formed by the junction of the distal and incisal walls of a cavity in an anterior tooth.

distola'bial. Relating to the distal and labial surfaces of a tooth; denoting the angle formed by their junction.

dis'tola'biopul'pal. Relating to the angle formed by the junction of distal, labial and pulpal walls of the incisal part of a cavity.

distolingual (dis-to-ling'gwal). Relating to the distal and lingual surfaces of a tooth; denoting the angle formed by their junction.

distolinguo-occlusal (dis'to-ling'gwo-ŏ-klu'zal). Relating to the distal, lingual, and occlusal surfaces of a bicuspid or molar tooth; denoting especially the angle formed by their junction.

distomiasis (dis-to-mi'ă-sis). Presence in any of the organs or tissues of a fluke formerly known as Distoma or Distomum; in general, infection by any parasitic trematode or fluke.

distomolar (dis'to-mo'lar). A supernumerary tooth located in the region of the third molar tooth.

dis'topul'pal. Relating to the angle formed by the junction of the distal pulpal walls of a cavity.

distortion (dis-tor'shun). **1.** A twisting out of normal shape or form. **2.** A prime mechanism that helps to repress or disguise unacceptable thoughts.

parataxic d., an attitude toward another person based on a distorted evaluation, usually because of an identification of that person with emotionally significant figures in the patient's past life.

distoversion (dis'to-ver-zhun). Malposition of a tooth distal to normal, in a posterior direction following the curvature of the dental arch.

distraction (dis-trak'shun) [L. *dis-traho*, pp. *-tractus*, to pull in different directions]. **1.** Difficulty or impossibility of concentration or fixation of the mind. **2.** Extension of a limb to separate bony fragments or joint surfaces.

distress (dis-tres') [L. *distringo*, to draw asunder]. Mental or physical suffering or anguish.

distribution (dis-trĭ-bu'shun) [L. *dis-tribuo*, pp. *-tributus*, to distribute]. **1.** Passage of the branches of arteries or nerves to the tissues and organs. **2.** The area in which the branches of an artery or a nerve terminate, or the area supplied by such artery or nerve.

dis'trix [G. *dis*, twice, + *thrix*, hair]. Splitting of the hairs at their ends.

disul'fate. Bisulfate.

disul'fide. **1.** Bisulfide (1); a molecule containing two atoms of sulfur to one of the reference element. **2.** A compound containing the –S–S– group, as in cystine.

disulf'iram. Bis(diethylthiocarbamyl)disulfide; an antioxidant that interferes with the normal metabolic degradation of alcohol in the body, resulting in increased acetaldehyde concentrations in blood and tissues; used in the treatment of chronic alcoholism. When a small quantity of alcohol is consumed an unpleasant reaction results.

diterpenes (di-ter'pēnz). Hydrocarbons or their derivatives containing 4 isoprene units, hence containing 20 carbon atoms and 4 branched methyl groups.

diuresis (di'u-re'sis) [G. *dia*, throughout, completely, + *ourēsis*, urination]. Excretion of urine; commonly denotes production of unusually large volumes of urine.

diuret'ic. Promoting the excretion of urine.

diurnal (di-ur'nal) [L. *diurnus,* of the day]. **1.** Pertaining to the daylight hours; opposite of nocturnal. **2.** Repeating once each 24 hours, as a d. rhythm.

divalence, divalency (di-va'lens, di-va'len-sĭ). Bivalence.

divalent (di-va'lent, div'ă-lent). Bivalent (1).

divarication (di-văr-ĭ-ka'shun) [L. *divaricare,* to spread asunder]. Diastasis (1).

divergence (di-ver'jens) [L. *di-,* apart, + *vergo,* to incline]. **1.** A moving or spreading apart or in different directions. **2.** The spreading of branches of the neuron to form synapses with several other neurons.

diver'gent. Moving in different directions; radiating.

diverticu'la. Plural of diverticulum.

diverticu'lar. Relating to a diverticulum.

diverticulectomy (di'ver-tik-u-lek'to-mĭ). Excision of a diverticulum.

diverticulitis (di'ver-tik-u-li'tis). Inflammation of a diverticulum, especially of the small pockets in the wall of the colon which fill with stagnant fecal material and become inflamed.

di'vertic'ulogram. Radiographic image of a diverticulum.

diverticuloma (di'ver-tik-u-lo'mah) [diverticulum + G. *-oma,* tumor]. Development of a granulomatous mass in the wall of the colon.

diverticulo'sis. Presence of a number of diverticula of the intestine.

diverticulum, pl. **diverticula** (di-ver-tik'u-lum, -u-lah) [L. *deverticulum* (or *di-*), a by- road] [NA]. A pouch or sac opening from a tubular or saccular organ, such as the gut or bladder.

    false d., a term denoting a d. of the intestine that passes through a defect in the muscular wall of the gut and thus does not include a layer of muscle in its wall.

    hypopharyngeal d., Zenker's d.; a pulsion d. of the hypopharynx.

    Meckel's d., a blind sac or pouch, the remains of the omphalomesenteric duct of the embryo, located on the ileum a short distance above the cecum and may be attached to the umbilicus.

    Nuck's d., *processus* vaginalis peritonei.

    pharyngoesophageal d., a d. of the posterior pharyngeal wall opening just behind the cricoid cartilage.

    pituitary d., Rathke's pouch; a cup-shaped mass, around the infundibular process of the diencephalon, giving rise to the pars distalis and pars juxtaneuralis of the hypophysis.

    pulsion d., a d. formed by pressure from within, frequently causing herniation of mucosa through the muscularis.

    traction d., a d. formed by the pulling force of contracting bands of adhesion, occurring mainly in the esophagus, from tuberculous hilar or mediastinal lymphadenitis.

    true d., a term denoting a d. that includes all the layers of the wall from which it protrudes.

    vesical d., a d. of the bladder wall; may be either true or false type.

    Zenker's d., hypopharyngeal d.

divi'nyl ether. Vinyl ether; $O(CH = CH_2)_2$; a rapidly acting inhalation anesthetic used principally for induction of anesthesia.

division (dĭ-vizh'un). Separation.

    cleavage d., the rapid mitotic d. of the zygote with decrease in size of individual cells or blastomeres and the formation of a morula.

    direct nuclear d., amitosis.

    equation d., nuclear d. in which each chromosome divides equally.

    indirect nuclear d., mitosis.

    maturation d., see maturation; meiosis.

    multiplicative d., reproduction by simultaneous d. of a mother cell into a number of daughter cells.

divulsion (dĭ-vul'shun) [L. *di-vello,* pp. *-vulvus,* to pull apart]. **1.** Removal of a part by tearing. **2.** Forcible dilation of the walls of a cavity or canal.

divul'sor. An instrument for forcible dilation of the urethra or other canal or cavity.

dixyrazine (di-zir'ă-zēn). 2-[2-[4-(2-Methyl-3(10H-Phenothiazin-10-yl)propyl)-1-piperazinyl]ethoxy]ethanol; a phenothiazine compound used as antipsychotic agent.

dizygotic (di'zi-got'ik) [G. *di-,* two, + *zygotos,* yoked together]. Relating to twins derived from two separate zygotes.

diz'ziness [A. S. *dyzig,* foolish]. Imprecise term commonly used to describe various peculiar subjective symptoms such as faintness, giddiness, light-headedness, or unsteadiness. See also vertigo.

dk Deca-.

DL-. Chemical prefix denoting a substance consisting of equal quantities of the two enantionmorphs, D and L; replaces the older *dl-* as a more exact definition of structure.

dM Decimorgan.

D.M.D. Doctor of Dental Medicine.

dmf, DMF Decayed, missing, or filled; a designation used in dental examinations of deciduous (lower case letters) or permanent (capital letters) teeth, to describe the caries history.

DMSO Dimethyl sulfoxide.

DMT Dimethyltryptamine.

DN Dibucaine number.

DNA Deoxyribonucleic acid.

DNASe, DNAse, DNase Deoxyribonuclease.

DNP **1.** Dnp; 2,4-Dinitrophenol. **2.** Deoxyribonucleoprotein.

Dnp DNP (1).

DNR Do not resuscitate.

D.N.S. Director of Nursing Service(s).

D.O. Doctor of Osteopathy.

DOA Dead on admission (arrival).

DOC 97 Deoxycorticosterone; deoxycholic acid.

docimasia, docimasy (dos-ĭ-ma'zĭ-ah, dos'ĭ-ma-sĭ) [G. *dokimasia,* fr. *dokimazō,* to assay (metals)]. Examination of a newborn infant's lungs to determine whether the baby has breathed or expanded its lungs with air and was therefore born alive.

docimastic (dos-ĭ-mas'tik). Relating to docimasia.

doctor [L. a teacher, fr. *doceo*, pp. *doctus*, to teach]. **1.** Title conferred by a university on one who has followed a prescribed course of study, or given as a mark of distinction; as d. of medicine, d. of laws, philosophy, etc. **2.** A physician, especially one upon whom has been conferred the degree of M.D. by a university or medical school.

dol [L. *dolor*, pain]. A unit measure of pain.

dolicho- [G. *dolichos*, long]. Combining form meaning long.

dolichocephalic (dol'ĭ-ko-sĕ-fal'ik) [dolicho- + G. *kephalē*, head]. Having a disproportionately long head.

dolichoderus (dol'ĭ-ko-dēr'us) [G. *dolichodeiros*, person with long neck]. A person having a disproportionately long neck.

dolichofacial (dol'ĭ-ko-fa'shăl). Dolichoprosopic.

dolichopellic, dolichopelvic (dol'ĭ-ko-pel'ik, -pel'vik) [dolicho- + G. *pellis*, bowl (pelvis)]. Having a disproportionately long pelvis.

dolichoprosopic (dol'ĭ-ko-pros-o'pik) [dolicho- + G. *prosōpikos*, facial]. Dolichofacial; having a disproportionately long face.

do'lor [L.]. Pain, as one of the four signs of inflammation (d., calor, rubor, tumor) enunciated by Celsus.

do'lorif'ic. Pain-producing.

dolorim'etry [L. *dolor*, pain, + G. *metron*, measure]. The measurement of pain.

DOM 2,5-Dimethoxy-4-methylamphetamine.

dom'inance. The state of being dominant.

d. of genes, an expression of the apparent physiologic relationship existing between two or more genes that may occupy the same chromosome locus (alleles); *e.g.*, if a heterozygous individual presents only the hereditary characteristic determined by one gene, while the effect of the other gene is not apparent, the former is said to be dominant and the latter is said to be recessive. D. relationships may in some cases be modified by environmental factors and in a series of multiple alleles, complex d. relationships may exist.

dom'inant [L. pres. p. of *dominor*, pp. *-atus*, to rule]. **1.** Ruling or controlling. **2.** In genetics, denoting an allele possessed by one of the parents of a hybrid which is expressed in the latter to the exclusion of a contrasting allele (the recessive) from the other parent.

Don Juan (wahn) [legendary Spanish nobleman]. In psychiatry, a term used to denote males with compulsive sexual overactivity, usually with a succession of female partners.

do'nor [L. *dono*, pp. *donatus*, to donate, to give]. **1.** An individual from whom blood, tissue, or an organ is taken for transplantation. **2.** A compound that will transfer an atom or a radical to an acceptor. **3.** An atom that readily yields electrons to an acceptor.

hydrogen d., a metabolite from which hydrogen is removed (by a dehydrogenase system) and transferred by a hydrogen carrier to another metabolite, which is thus reduced.

universal d., in blood grouping, a person belonging to group O; *i.e.*, one whose erythrocytes do not contain either agglutinogen A or B and are, therefore, not agglutinated by plasma containing either of the ordinary isoagglutinins, alpha or beta.

don'ovano'sis. Granuloma inguinale, caused by *Calymmatobacterium granulomatis*, which are observed intracellularly (in macrophages in the lesion) at Donovan bodies.

dopa (Dopa, DOPA) (do'pah). 3,4-Dihydroxyphenylalanine; an intermediate in the catabolism of phenylalanine and tyrosine, and in the biosynthesis of norepinephrine, epinephrine, and melanin. The L form (levodopa) is biologically active.

dopamine. 3-Hydroxytyramine; an intermediate in tyrosine metabolism and the precursor of norepinephrine and epinephrine; present in the central nervous system and localized in the basal ganglia (caudate and lentiform nuclei).

dope [Dutch, *doop*, sauce]. Any drug, either stimulating or depressing, administered for its temporary effect or taken habitually.

dor'nase. Obsolete term for deoxyribonuclease. See also streptodornase.

dorsa (dor'sah). Plural of dorsum.

dor'sad [L. *dorsum*, back, + *ad*, to]. Toward or in the direction of the back.

dorsal [Mediev. L. *dorsalis*, fr. *dorsum*, back]. **1.** Pertaining to the back or any dorsum. **2.** In human anatomy, synonymous with posterior (2). **3.** In veterinary anatomy, pertaining to the back or upper surface of an animal; often used to indicate the position of one structure relative to another. **4.** Old term meaning thoracic, in a limited sense; *e.g.*, dorsal vertebrae.

dorsal'gia [L. *dorsum*, back, + G. *algos*, pain]. Pain in the upper back.

dorsiflexion (dor'sĭ-flek'shun). Turning of the foot or the toes upward.

dorsispinal (dor'sĭ-spi'nal). Relating to the spinal column, especially to its dorsal aspect.

dorsocephalad (dor'so-sef'ă-lad) [L. *dorsum*, back, + G. *kephalē*, head, + L. *ad*, to]. Toward the occiput, or back of the head.

dorsolat'eral. Relating to the back and the side.

dorsolum'bar. Referring to the back in the region of the lower thoracic and upper lumbar vertebrae.

dorsoven'trad. In a direction from the dorsal to the ventral aspect.

dor'sum, gen. **dor'si**, pl. **dor'sa** [L. back] [NA]. **1.** The back of the body. **2.** The upper or posterior surface, or the back, of any part.

dosage (do'sij). **1.** The giving of medicine or other therapeutic agent in prescribed amounts. **2.** The determination of the proper dose of a remedy; often incorrectly used for *dose*.

dose [G. *dosis, a giving, fr. didōmi,* fut. *dōsō,* to give]. The quantity of a drug or other remedy to be taken or applied within a given period.

absorbed d., the amount of energy absorbed per unit mass of target, expressed in rads.

air d., the radiation d., expressed in roentgens, delivered at a point in free air.

booster d., a d. given at some time after an initial d. to enhance the effect, said usually of antigens for the production of antibodies.

curative d., the quantity of any substance required to effect the cure of a disease or that will correct the manifestations of a deficiency of a particular factor in the diet.

effective d. (ED), the d. which produces the desired effect; when followed by a subscript (generally "ED_{50}"), it denotes the d. having such an effect on a certain percentage (*e.g.,* 50%) of the test animals.

erythema d., the minimal amount of x-rays or other form of radiation sufficient to produce an erythema after the application; regarded as the full d. that is safe to give at one time.

L d.'s ["L" for *limes*], a group of terms that indicate the relative activity or potency of diphtheria toxin; the L d.'s are distinctly different from the minimal lethal d. and minimal reacting d., inasmuch as the latter two represent the direct effects of toxin, whereas the L d.'s pertain to the combining power of toxin with specific antitoxin.

lethal d. (LD), the d. of a chemical or biologic preparation that is likely to cause death; when followed by a subscript (generally "LD_{50}" or median lethal d.), it denotes the d. likely to cause death in a certain percentage (*e.g.,* 50%) of the test animals.

maximal d., the largest amount of a drug that an adult can take with safety.

maximal permissible d. (MPD), the greatest d. of radiation to which members of a population may be exposed without harmful effects; defined in terms of acute or chronic exposure to organs, systems, regions of, and/or the whole body.

minimal d., the smallest amount of a drug that will produce a physiologic effect in an adult.

minimal infecting d. (MID), the smallest quantity of infectious material regularly producing infection; usually expressed as ID_{50}, the quantity causing infection in 50% of a suitable series of animals or cells (cell cultures).

minimal lethal d. (MLD, mld), the minimal d. of a toxic substance or infectious agent that is lethal, as assayed in various experimental animals, when followed by a subscript (generally "MLD_{50}"), denotes the minimal dose that is lethal to a certain percentage (*e.g.,* 50%) of animals so assayed.

minimal reacting d. (MRD, mrd), the minimal d. of a toxic substance causing a reaction, as manifested in the skin of a series of susceptible test animals.

optimum d., the d. that will produce the desired effect without any untoward symptoms.

skin d., the quantity of radiation delivered to the skin surface.

tolerance d., the largest dose of a remedy that the animal organism will accept without the production of injurious symptoms.

dosim'etry [G. *dosis,* dose, + *metron,* measure]. The accurate determination of dosage.

dot. A small spot.

Gunn's d.'s, Marcus Gunn d.'s, minute, glistening, white or yellowish specks usually seen in the posterior part of the fundus.

Maurer's d.'s, finely granular precipitates or irregular cytoplasmic particles that usually occur diffusely in red blood cells infected with the trophozoites of *Plasmodium falciparum.*

Schüffner's d.'s, Schüffner's granules; fine, round, uniform red or red-yellow d.'s (as colored with Romanovsky stains) characteristically observed in erythrocytes infected with *Plasmodium vivax* and *P. ovale.*

Trantas d.'s, pale, grayish red, uneven nodules of gelatinous aspect at the limbal conjunctiva in vernal conjunctivitis.

do'tage. Anility; the loss of previously intact mental powers, common in old age.

doublet (dub'let). A combination of two lenses designed to correct the chromatic and spherical aberration.

douche (dūsh) [Fr. fr. *doucher,* to pour]. **1.** A current of water, gas, or vapor directed against the surface or projected into a cavity. **2.** An instrument for giving a d. **3.** To apply a d.

D.P. Doctor of Podiatry.

D.P.H. Diploma in Public Health.

D.P.M. Doctor of Podiatric Medicine.

DPN Diphosphopyridine nucleotide.

DPT Dipropyltryptamine.

D.R. *Reaction* of degeneration.

dr.

drachm (dram) [G. *drachmē,* ancient Greek weight, equivalent to about 60 gr]. Dram.

dracontiasis (dra-kon-ti'ă-sis) [G. *drakōn,* drakont-), dragon]. Dracunculiasis; dracunculosis; infection with *Dracunculus medinensis.*

dracun'culi'asis, dracun'culo'sis. Dracontiasis.

Dracunculus (dră-kung'ku-lus) [L. dim. of *draco,* serpent]. A genus of nematodes (superfamily Dracunculoidea) that have some resemblances to true filarial worms. *D. medinensis* is a species of skin-infecting, yard-long parasites, the females of which migrate along fascial planes to subcutaneous tissues, where chronic ulcers are formed in the skin.

draft. Draught; a quantity of liquid medicine ordered as a single dose.

drain [A. S. *drehnian,* to draw off]. **1.** To draw off fluid from a cavity as it forms. **2.** A device, usually in the shape of a tube or wick, for removing fluid as it collects in a cavity, wound, or infected area.

cigarette d., a wick of gauze wrapped in rubber tissue, providing capillary drainage.

Mikulicz d., a d. made of several strings of gauze held together by a single layer of gauze.

stab d., a d. passed into the cavity through a puncture made at a dependent part away from the surgical wound, designed to prevent infection of the wound.

sump d., a d. consisting of an outer tube with a smaller tube within it which is attached to a suction pump; the outer tube has multiple perforations that allow fluid to pass into its interior and be carried away through the suction tube.

drain'age. The continuous withdrawal of fluids from a wound or other cavity.

capillary d., d. by means of a wick of gauze or other material.

closed d., d. of a body cavity via a water- or air-tight system.

dependent d., d. from the lowest part and into a receptacle at a level lower than the structure being drained.

infusion-aspiration d., d. in which antibiotics are continuously infused into a cavity at the same time fluid is being drained (aspirated) from the cavity.

open d., d. allowing air to enter.

postural d., therapeutic d. used in bronchiectasis and lung abscess by placing the patient with the head downward to that the trachea is included downward and below the affected area.

suction d., closed drainage of a cavity, with a suction apparatus attached to the drainage tube.

through d., d. obtained by the passage of a perforated tube, open at both ends, through a cavity; in addition, the cavity can be irrigated by a solution passed through the tube.

tidal d., d. of the urinary bladder by means of an intermittent filling and emptying apparatus.

dram (dr). Drachm; a unit of weight; $1/8$ oz., 60 gr., apothecaries' weight; $1/16$oz., avoirdupois weight.

drape (drāp). 1. To cover parts of the body other than those to be examined or operated upon. 2. The cloth or materials used for such cover.

dream. Ideas or images formed in the mind during sleep.

drepanocyte (drep'ă-no-sit) [G. *drepanē*, sickle, + *kytos*, a hollow (cell)]. Sickle *cell.*

drepanocytic (drep-ă-no-sit'ik). Relating to or resembling a sickle cell.

drep'anocyto'sis [drepanocyte + -*osis*, condition]. Sickle cell *anemia.*

dressing. Material applied, or its application, to a wound for protection, absorbance, drainage, etc.

adhesive absorbent d., a sterile individual d. consisting of a plain absorbent compress affixed to a film of fabric coated with a pressure-sensitive adhesive.

antiseptic d., a sterile d. of gauze impregnated with an antiseptic.

occlusive d., a d. that hermetically seals a wound.

pressure d., a d. by which pressure is exerted on the area covered to prevent the collection of fluids in the underlying tissues; most commonly used after skin grafting and in the treatment of burns.

drip. 1. To flow a drop at a time. 2. A flowing in drops.

intravenous d., continuous introduction of solutions intravenously, a drop at a time.

Murphy d., proctoclysis.

postnasal d., the sensation of excessive mucoid or mucopurulent discharge from the posterior nares.

drive. A basic compelling urge; in psychology, classified as innate (*e.g.,* hunger), learned (*e.g.,* hoarding) and appetitive (*e.g.,* hunger, thirst, sex), or aversive (*e.g.,* fear, pain, grief).

acquired d.'s, secondary d.'s.

learned d., motive.

physiological d.'s, primary d.'s, those d.'s which stem from the biological needs of an organism.

secondary d.'s, acquired d.'s, those d.'s not directly related to biological needs.

drom'ograph [G. *dromos,* a running, + *graphō,* to record]. An instrument for recording the rapidity of the blood circulation.

drom'omania [G. *dromos,* a running, + *mania,* insanity]. Uncontrollable impulse to wander or travel.

dromotropic (drom'o-trop'ik) [G. *dromos,* a running, + *tropē,* a turn]. Influencing the velocity of conduction of excitation, as in nerve or cardiac muscle fibers.

drop [A. S. *droppan*]. 1. To fall, or to be dispensed or poured in globules. 2. A liquid globule. 3. A volume of liquid regarded as a unit of dosage, equivalent in the case of water to about 1 minum. 4. A solid confection in globular form, usually dissolved in the mouth.

drop'sical. Relating to or suffering from dropsy.

dropsy (drop'sĭ) [G. *hydrōps*]. An old term for edema.

drow'siness. Hypnesthesia; a state of impaired awareness associated with a desire or inclination to sleep.

Dr.P.H. Doctor of Pubic Health.

drug. 1. A therapeutic agent; any substance, other than food, used in the prevention, diagnosis, alleviation, treatment, or cure of disease. 2. To give or take a d., usually implying an overly large quantity. 3. To narcotize.

drug-fast. Pertaining to microorganisms that resist or become tolerant to an antibacterial agent.

drug interactions. The pharmacological result, either desirable or undesirable, of drugs interacting with themselves or other drugs, with endogenous physiologic chemical agents; with components of the diet, and with chemicals used in diagnostic tests or the results of such tests.

drum, drumhead. *Membrana* tympani.

drusen (dru'sen [Ger. pl. of *druse*, bump, body]. Hyaline or colloid bodies that contain sialomuccin and cerebroside and are located in degenerated retinal pigment cells.

dT Thymidine.

D.t. Duration *tetany*.

dTDP Thymidine 5'-diphosphate.

dThd Thymidine.

dTMP Deoxythymidylic acid.

DTPA Diethylenetriamine pentaacetic acid.

dTTP Thymidine 5'-triphosphate.

du'alism [L. *dualis*, relating to two]. **1.** In hematology, the concept that blood cells have two origins, *i.e.*, lymphogenous or myelogenous. **2.** The theory that the mind and body are two distinct systems, independent and different in nature.

duct [L. *duco*, pp. *ductus*, to lead]. Ductus; a tubular structure giving exit to the secretion of a gland, or conducting any fluid. See also canal.

aberrant d., *ductulus* aberrans.

accessory pancreatic d., *ductus* pancreaticus accessorius.

alveolar d., (1) *ductulus* alveolaris; (2) the smallest of the intralobular d.'s in the mammary gland; the secretory alveoli open into them.

arterial d., *ductus* arteriosus.

Bartholin's d., *ductus* sublingualis major.

Bellini's d.'s, straight collecting tubules of the kidney.

bile d., biliary d., gall d.; any of the d.'s conveying bile between the liver and the intestine, including the hepatic, cystic, and common bile d.'s.

Botallo's d., *ductus* arteriosus.

branchial d., the lumen of one of the embryonic pharyngeal pouches, elongated and narrowed by later differential growth.

cochlear d., *ductus* cochlearis.

common bile or **gall d.**, *ductus* choledochus.

common hepatic d., *ductus* hepaticus communis.

cystic d., *ductus* cysticus.

deferent d., *ductus* deferens.

efferent d., *ductulus* efferens testis.

ejaculatory d., *ductus* ejaculatorius.

endolymphatic d., *ductus* endolymphaticus.

excretory d., a d. carrying the secretion from a gland or a fluid from any reservoir.

galactophorous d.'s, *ductus* lactiferi.

gall d., bile d.

hepatic d., see *ductus* hepaticus communis, dexter, and sinister.

intercalated d.'s, minute d.'s of glands, such as the salivary and the pancreas, that lead from the acini.

interlobar d., a d. draining the secretion of the lobe of a gland and formed by the junction of a number of interlobular d.'s.

interlobular d., any d. leading from a lobule of a gland and formed by the junction of the fine d.'s draining the acini.

intralobular d., a d. that lies within a lobule of a gland.

lacrimal d., *canaliculus* lacrimalis.

lactiferous d.'s, *ductus* lactiferi.

Luschka's d.'s, glandlike tubular structures in the wall of the gallbladder, especially in the part covered with peritoneum.

lymphatic d., see *ductus* lymphaticus dexter; *ductus* thoracicus.

mamillary d.'s, mammary d.'s, *ductus* lactiferi.

mesonephric d., *ductus* mesonephricus.

metanephric d., the slender tubular portion of the metanephric diverticulum.

milk d.'s, *ductus* lactiferi.

Müller's d., müllerian d., *ductus* paramesonephricus.

nasolacrimal d., *ductus* nasolacrimalis.

omphalomesenteric d., yolk *stalk*.

pancreatic d., *ductus* pancreaticus.

papillary d.'s, the principal straight excretory d.'s in the kidney medulla and papillae whose openings form the area cribrosa.

paramesonephric d., *ductus* paramesonephricus.

paraurethral d.'s, *ductus* paraurethrales.

parotid d., *ductus* parotideus.

perilymphatic d., *ductus* perilymphaticus.

prostatic d.'s, *ductuli* prostatici.

Rivinus d.'s, *ductus* sublinguales minores.

salivary d., secretory d.; a type of intralobular d. found in salivary glands which contributes to the secretion.

Santorini's d., *ductus* pancreaticus accessorius.

secretory d., salivary d.

semicircular d.'s, *ductus* semicirculares.

seminal d., gonaduct (1); any one of the d.'s conveying semen from the epididymis to the urethra, ductus deferens, d. of the seminal vesicles or ejaculatory d.

d. of seminal vesicle, *ductus* excretorius vesiculae seminalis.

spermatic d., *ductus* deferens.

Stensen's d., Steno's d., *ductus* parotideus.

sublingual d., see *ductus* sublingualis major and minor.

submandibular d., submaxillary d., *ductus* submandibularis.

thoracic d., *ductus* thoracicus.

Wharton's d., *ductus* submandibularis.

wolffian d., *ductus* mesonephricus.

ductal (duk'tăl). Relating to a duct.

ductile (duk'til) [L. *ductilis*, capable of being led or drawn]. Pertaining to the property of a material that allows it to be bent, drawn out, or otherwise deformed without breaking.

duct'less. Having no duct; denoting certain glands having only an internal secretion.

ductular (duk'tu-lar). Relating to a ductule.

ductule (duk'tūl). Ductulus.

aberrant d., *ductulus* aberrans.

biliary d.'s, *ductuli* biliferi.

excretory d.'s of lacrimal gland, *ductuli* excretorii glandulae lacrimalis.

prostatic d.'s, *ductuli* prostatici.

ductulus, pl. **ductuli** (duk′tu-lus, -tu-li) [Mod. L. dim. of L. *ductus,* duct] [NA]. Ductule; a minute duct.

d. aber′rans [NA], aberrant ductule or duct; vas aberrans; one of the diverticula of the epididymis.

d. alveola′ris [NA], alveolar duct (1); the part of the respiratory passages beyond a respiratory bronchiole; from it arise alveolar sacs and alveoli.

duc′tuli bilif′eri [NA], biliary ductules; excretory ducts of the liver that connect the interlobular ductules to the right (or left) hepatic duct.

d. ef′ferens tes′tis [NA], efferent duct; one of the small seminal ducts leading from the testis to the head of the epididymis.

duc′tuli excreto′rii glan′dulae lacrima′lis [NA], excretory ductules of the lacrimal gland that open into the superior fornix of the conjunctival sac.

duc′tuli prostat′ici [NA], prostatic ductules or ducts; ductus prostatici; minute canals that receive the prostatic secretion from the glandular tubules and discharge it through openings on either side of the urethral crest in the posterior wall of the urethra.

ductus, pl. **duc′tus** (duk′tus) [L. a leading, fr. *duco,* pp. *ductus, to lead*] [NA]. Duct.

d. arterio′sus [NA], arterial canal or duct; Botallo's duct; a fetal vessel connecting the left pulmonary artery with the descending aorta; after birth, it normally becomes changed into a fibrous cord, the ligamentum arteriosum; occasional failure to close postnatally causes a cardiovascular handicap (patent d. arteriosus) that can be surgically corrected.

d. choled′ochus [NA], common bile or gall duct; a duct formed by the union of the hepatic and cystic ducts; it discharges at the duodenal papilla.

d. cochlea′ris [NA], cochlear duct; scala media; a spirally arranged membranous tube suspended within the cochlea, occupying the lower portion of the vestibular scala; the spiral organ (organ of Corti) occupies the floor of the duct.

d. cys′ticus [NA], cystic duct; the d. leading from the gallbladder; joins the hepatic duct to form the common bile duct.

d. def′erens [NA], deferent duct spermatic duct; vas deferens; spermiduct (1); the secretory duct of the testicle, running from the epididymis, of which it is the continuation, to the prostatic urethra where it terminates as the ejaculatory duct.

d. ejaculato′rius [NA], ejaculatory duct; spermiduct (2); the duct formed by the union of the deferent duct and the excretory duct of the seminal vesicle, which opens into the prostatic urethra.

d. endolymphat′icus [NA], endolymphatic duct; aqueductus vestibuli (2); a small membranous canal, connecting with both saccule and utricle of the membranous labyrinth and terminating in the endolymphatic sac.

d. hepat′icus commu′nis [NA], common hepatic duct; the part of the biliary duct system formed by the confluence of right and left hepatic ducts; joined by the cystic duct to become the common bile duct.

d. hepat′icus dex′ter [NA], right hepatic duct; the duct that transmits bile to the common hepatic duct from the right half of the liver.

d. hepat′icus sinis′ter [NA], left hepatic duct; the duct that drains bile from the left half of the liver, including the left quandrate and caudate lobes.

d. lactif′eri [NA], lactiferous, milk, galactophorous, mamillary, or mammary ducts; galactophores; ducts that drain the lobes of the mammary gland at the nipple.

d. lymphat′icus dex′ter [NA], right lymphatic duct; one of the two terminal lymph vessels, a short trunk formed by the union of the right jugular lymphatic jugular lymphatic vessel and vessels from the lymph nodes of the right superior limb, thoracic wall, and both lungs; it lies on the right side of the root of the neck and empties into the right brachiocephalic vein.

d. mesoneph′ricus [NA], mesonephric or wolffian duct; a duct in the embryo draining the mesonephric tubules; in the male, becomes the ductus deferens; in the female, becomes vestigial.

d. nasolacrima′lis [NA], nasolacrimal duct; the passage leading downward from the lacrimal sac on each side to the anterior portion of the inferior meatus of the nose, through which tears are conducted into the nasal cavity.

d. om′phalomesenter′icus, yolk *stalk.*

d. pancreat′icus [NA], pancreatic duct; Wirsung's canal or duct; the excretory duct of the pancreas which extends through the gland from tail to head where it empties into the duodenum at the greater duodenal papilla.

d. pancreat′icus accesso′rius [NA], accessory pancreatic duct; Santorini's duct; the excretory duct of the head of the pancreas, one branch of which joins the pancreatic duct, the other opening independently into the duodenum at the lesser duodenal papilla.

d. paramesoneph′ricus [NA], paramesonephric duct; Müller's or müllerian duct; one of the embryonic tubes extending along the mesonephros roughly parallel to the mesonephric duct and emptying into the cloaca; in the female, the ducts form the uterine tubes, uterus, and part of the vagina; in the male, vestiges are the vaginal masculina and the appendix testis.

d. paraurethra′les [NA], paraurethral ducts; inconstant ducts along the side of the female urethra that convey the mucoid secretion of the paraurethral glands to the vestibule.

d. parotid′eus [NA], parotid, Steno's, or Stensen's duct; the duct of the parotid gland opening from the cheek into the vestibule of the mouth opposite the neck of the superior second molar tooth.

patent d. arteriosus, see d. arteriosus.

d. perilymphat′icus [NA], perilymphatic duct; cochlear aqueduct; aqueductus cochleae; a fine canal connecting the perilymphatic space of the cochlea with the subarachnoid space.

d. prostat'ici, *ductuli* prostatici.

d. semicircula'res [NA], semicircular ducts; three small membranous tubes that lie within the bony labyrinth, form loops in planes at right angles to each other, and open into the vestibule; each duct has an ampulla at one end within which filaments of the vestibular nerve terminate.

d. sublingua'les mino'res [NA], minor sublingual ducts; Rivinus ducts; small ducts of the sublingual salivary gland which open into the mouth on the surface of the sublingual fold.

d. sublingua'lis ma'jor [NA], major sublingual duct; Bartholin's duct; the duct that drains the anterior portion of the sublingual gland.

d. submandibula'ris, d. submaxilla'ris, [NA], submandibular, submaxillary, or Wharton's duct; the duct of the submandibular salivary gland; it opens at the sublingual papilla near the frenulum of the tongue.

d. thorac'icus [NA], thoracic duct; the largest lymph vessel in the body, beginning at the cisterna chyli at about the level of the second lumbar vertebra, passing through the aortic opening of the diaphragm, and crossing the posterior mediastinum to form the arcus ductus thoracici and discharge into the left brachiocephalic vein at its origin.

d. veno'sus [NA], the continuation, in the fetus of the umbilical vein through the liver to the vena cava inferior.

dull. Not sharp or acute, qualifying the action of the mind, pain, a percussion note, etc.

dull'ness, dul'ness. The character of the sound obtained by percusing over a solid part which is incapable of vibrating.

dumping. See dumping *syndrome.*

duodenal (du'o-de'nal, du-od'ĕ-nal). Relating to the duodenum.

duodenectomy (du'o-dĕ-nek'to-mĭ) [duodenum + G. *ektomē,* excision]. Excision of the duodenum.

duodenitis (du'od-ĕ-ni'tis). Inflammation of the duodenum.

duodeno- [L. *duodenum*]. Combining form relating to the duodenum.

duodenocholangitis (du-o-de'no-ko-lan-ji'tis) [duodeno- + G. *cholē,* bile, + *angeion,* vessel, + *-itis,* inflammation]. Inflammation of the duodenum and common bile duct.

duodenocholecystostomy (du-o-de'no-ko-le-sis-tos'to-mĭ) [duodeno- + G. *cholē,* bile, + *kystis,* bladder, + *stoma,* mouth]. Duodenocystostomy; formation of a fistula between duodenum and gallbladder.

duodenocholedochotomy (du-o-de'no-ko-led-o-kot-'o-mĭ) [duodeno- + G. *cholèdochus,* bile duct, + *tomē,* incision]. Incision into the common bile duct and the adjacent portion of the duodenum.

duodenocystostomy (du-o-de'no-sis-tos'to-mĭ). Duo-denocholecystostomy.

duodenoenterostomy (du-o-de'no-en-ter-os'to-mĭ) [duodeno- + G. *enteron,* intestine, + *stoma,* mouth]. Establishment of communication between the duodenum and another part of the intestinal tract.

duodenojejunostomy (du-o-de'no-jĕ-ju-nos'to-mĭ) [duodeno- + jejunum, + G. *stoma,* mouth]. The operative formation of an artificial communication between the duodenum and the jejunum.

duodenolysis (du'o-dĕ-nol'ĭ-sis) [dudeno- + G. *lysis,* a freeing]. Incision of adhesions to the duodenum.

duodenorrhaphy (du'o-dĕ-nor'ă-fĭ) [duodeno- + G. *rhaphē,* a seam]. Suture of a tear or incision in the duodenum.

duodenoscopy (du'o-dĕ-nos'ko-pĭ) [duodeno- + G. *skopeō,* to examine]. Inspection of the interior of the duodenum through an endoscope.

duodenostomy (du'o-dĕ-nos'to-mĭ) [duodeno- + G. *stoma,* mouth]. Establishment of a fistula into the duodenum.

duodenotomy (du'o-dĕ-not'o-mĭ) [duodeno- + G. *tomē,* incision]. Incision of the duodenum.

duodenum, gen. **duodeni,** pl. **duodena** (du-o-de'num, od'ĕ-num; -de'nah, -od'ĕ-nah) [Mediev. L. fr. L. *duodeni,* twelve] [NA]. The first division of the small intestine, about 25 cm or 12 fingerbreadths (hence the name) in length, extending from the pylorus to the junction with the jejunum at the level of the first or second lumbar vertebra on the left side.

duplication (du-plĭ-ka'shun). A doubling. See also reduplication (2).

d. of chromosomes, a chromosome aberration resulting from unequal crossing over or exchange of segments between two homologous chromosomes; one chromosome of the pair loses a small segment, while the other gains this segment; the chromosome gaining the segment has undergone d. while its homologue has undergone deletion.

dura (du'rah) [L. fem. of *durus,* hard]. Dura mater.

du'ral. Relating to the dura mater.

dura mater (du'rah ma'ter) [L. hard mother]. Dura; pachymeninx; a tough, fibrous membrane forming the outer envelope of the brain and the spinal cord.

D.V.M. Doctor of Veterinary Medicine.

dwarf [A.S. *dweorh*]. Nanus; a markedly undersized person.

asexual d., a d. with deficient sexual development who is beyond the age of puberty.

ateliotic d., a normally proportioned individual of unusually short stature; such d.'s are functionally normal, by currently available criteria, and the cause of this condition is not known.

phocomelic d., a d. in whom the diaphyses of the long bones are extremely short, or in whom the intermediate parts of the limbs are absent.

physiologic d., primordial d., an undersized person, not deformed, whose development has been symmetrical and at a normal rate, but less in extent than that of others.

sexual d., a d. with normal sexual development.

dwarf'ism. Nanism; the condition of being markedly undersized.

   achondroplastic d., see achondroplasia.

   camptomelic d., d. with shortening of the lower limbs, due to anterior bending of the femur and tibia.

   chondrodystrophic d., see chondrodystrophy.

   Laron type d., d. associated with an absence of somatomedin and with high plasma levels of somatotropin.

   mesomelic d., d. with shortness of the forearms and lower legs.

   metatropic d., a congenital skeletal dysplasia characterized by a changing pattern of d. in which there is a lengthening of the trunk (relative to the limbs) at birth but with a subsequent shortening.

   micromelic d., d. with disproportionately short or small limbs.

   pituitary d., Lorain-Lévi syndrome; a rare form of d. caused by the absence of a functional anterior pituitary gland.

Dy Dysprosium.

dy'ad [G. *dyas,* the number two, duality]. **1.** Diad (2); a pair. **2.** A bivalent element. **3.** A pair of persons in an interactional situation. **4.** The double chromosome resulting from the splitting of a tetrad during meiosis.

dye (di) [A.S. *deah, deag*]. A stain or coloring matter; a compound consisting of chromophore and auxochrome groups attached to one or more benzene rings, its color being due to the chromophore and its dyeing affinities to the auxochrome; used for intravital coloration of living cells, staining tissues and microorganisms, and as antiseptics and germicides.

-dymus [g. *-dymos,* fold]. **1.** Suffix combined with number roots; *e.g.,* didymus, tridymus. **2.** An occasionally used shortened form for -didymus.

dynamics (di-nam'iks) [G. *dynamis,* force]. **1.** The science of motion in response to forces. **2.** In psychiatry, the determination of how behavior patterns and emotional rections develop. **3.** In the behavioral sciences, any of the numerous intrapersonal and interpersonal influences or phenomena associated with personality development and interpersonal processes.

dynamo- [G. *dynamis,* force]. Combining form relating to force or energy.

dynamogenesis (di'nă-mo-jen'ĕ-sis) [dynamo- + G. *genesis,* production]. Production of the force, especially of muscular or nervous energy.

dy'namogen'ic. 58 Relating to dynamogenesis.

dynamograph (di-nam'o-graf) [dynamo- + G. *graphō,* to write]. An instrument for recording the degree of muscular power.

dynamometer (di-nă-mom'e-ter) [dynamo- + G. *metron,* measure]. Ergometer; an instrument for measuring the degree of muscular power.

dyne (dīn) [G. *dynamis,* force]. The unit of force in the CGS system, replaced in the SI system by the newton (1 newton = 10^5 dynes), that gives a body of 1 g mass an acceleration of 1 cm/sec²; expressed as F(dynes) = m(grams) × a(cm/sec²).

dynein (dīn'ēn) [dyne + protein]. A protein associated with motile structures, exhibiting adenosine triphosphatase activity; it forms "arms" on the microtubules of cilia and flagella, including human sperm tails.

dys- [G.]. Prefix meaning bad or difficult. *Cf.* dis-.

dysacousia, dysacusia (dis-ă-koo'sī-ah). Dysacusis.

dysacusis (dis-a-koo'sis) [dys- + G. *akousis,* hearing]. Dysacousia; dysacusia. **1.** Any impairment of hearing that is not primarily a loss of ability to perceive sound. **2.** Pain or discomfort in the ear from exposure to sound.

dysaphia (dis-a'fĭ-ah, dis-af'ĭ-ah) [dys- + G. *haphē,* touch]. Impairment in the sense of touch.

dysarteriotony (dis'ar-te-rī-ot'o-nī) [dys- + G. *artēria,* artery, + *tonos,* tension]. Abnormal blood pressure, either too high or too low.

dysarthria (dis-ar'thrĭ-ah) [dys- + G. *arthroō,* to articulate]. Dysarthrosis (1); disturbance of articulation due to emotional stress or to paralysis, incoordination, or spasticity of muscles.

dysar'thric. Relating to difficulty in articulating.

dysarthrosis (dis-ar-thro'sis) [dys- + G. *arthrōsis,* joint]. **1.** Dysarthria. **2.** Malformation of a joint. **3.** A false joint.

dysautonomia (dis'aw-to-no'mĭ-ah) [dys- + G. *autonomia,* self-government]. Abnormal functioning of the autonomic nervous system.

   familial d., Riley-Day syndrome; a congenital syndrome with specific disturbances of the nervous system and aberrations in autonomic nervous system function such as indifference to pain, diminished lacrimation, poor vasomotor control, motor incoordination, labile cardiovascular reactions, hyporeflexia, frequent attacks of bronchial pneumonia, hypersalivation with aspiration and trouble in swallowing, hyperemesis, emotional instability, and an intolerance for anesthetics; autosomal recessive inheritance.

dysbarism (dis'bar-izm) [dys- + G. *baros,* weight]. The symptom complex resulting from exposure to decreased or changing barometric pressure, including all physiologic effects resulting from such changes with the exception of hypoxia, and including the effects of rapid decompression.

dysbasia (dis-ba'zĭ-ah) [dys- + G. *basis,* a step]. **1.** Difficulty in walking. **2.** Difficult or distorted walking that occurs in persons with mental disorders.

dysbu'lia [dys- + G. *boulē,* will]. Weakness and uncertainty of will power.

dysbu'lic. Relating to dysbulia.

dyscephalia, dyscephaly (dis'sĕ-fa'lĭ-ah, -sef'ă-lĭ) [dys- + G. *kephalē,* head]. Dyscephaly; malformation of the head and face.

dyscheiral, dyschiral (dis-ki'ral). Relating to dyscheiria.

dyscheiria, dyschiria (dis-ki'rī-ah) [dys- + G. *cheir*, hand]. A disorder of sensibility in which, although there is no apparent loss of sensation, the patient is unable to tell which side of the body has been touched (acheiria), or refers it to the wrong side (allocheiria), or to both sides (syncheiria).

dyschezia (dis-ke'zī-ah) [dys- + G. *chezō*, to defecate]. Difficulty in defecation.

dyschondrogenesis (dis'kon-dro-jen'ē-sis) [dys- + G. *chondros*, cartilage, + *genesis*, production]. Abnormal development of cartilage.

dyschondroplasia (dis'kon-dro-pla'zī-ah) [dys- + G. *chondros*, cartilage, + *plasis*, a forming]. Enchondromatosis.

dyschondrosteosis (dis'kon-dros-te-o'sis) [dys- + G. *chondros*, cartilage, + *osteon*, bone, + *-osis*, condition]. Leri-Weill syndrome; a bone dysplasia characterized by bowing of the radius, dorsal dislocation of the distal ulna and proximal carpal bones, and mesomelic dwarfism; autosomal dominant inheritance.

dyschromatopsia (dis'kro-mă-top'sī-ah) [dys- + G. *chrōma*, color, + *opsis*, vision]. Dichromatism (2).

dyschromia (dis-kro'mǐah). Any abnormality in the color of the skin.

dyscoria (dis-ko'rī-ah) [dys- + G. *korē*, pupil of eye]. Abnormality in the shape of the pupil.

dyscrasia (dis-kra'zhǐ-ah) [G. bad temperament]. 1. A morbid general state. 2. An old term to indicate disease.

    blood d., a diseased state of the blood; usually refers to abnormal cellular elements of permanent character.

dyscra'sic, dyscrat'ic. Pertaining to or affected with dyscrasia.

dysembryoma (dis'em'brī-o'mah). A teratoid tumor with its tissues showing more irregular arrangement than the typical embryomas.

dysencepha'lia splanchnocys'tica. Meckel syndrome; a malformation syndrome, lethal in the perinatal period, characterized by intrauterine growth retardation, sloping forehead, occipital exencephalocele, ocular anomalies, cleft palate, polydactyly, polycystic kidney, and other malformations; autosomal recessive inheritance.

dysenteric (dis'en-tēr'ik). Relating to or suffering from dysentery.

dysentery (dis'en-tēr-ĭ) [G. *dysenteria*, fr. *dys-*, bad, + *entera*, bowels]. A disease marked by frequent watery stools, often with blood and mucus, abdominal pain, tenesmus, fever, and dehydration.

    amebic d., diarrhea resulting from ulcerative inflammation of the colon, caused chiefly by *Entamoeba hystolytica*.

    bacillary d., d. caused by infection with *Shigella dysenteriae*, *Shigella flexneri*, or other organisms.

    bilharzial d., d. due to infection with *Schistosoma mansoni*, *S. haematobium*, or *S. japonicum*.

    viral d., profuse watery diarrhea due to, or thought to be due to, a virus.

dyserethism (dis-ĕr'e-thizm) [dys- + G. *erethismos*, irritation]. A condition of slow response to stimuli.

dysergia (dis-er'jī-ah) [dys- + G. *ergon*, work]. Lack of harmonious action between the muscles concerned in executing any definite voluntary movement.

dysesthesia (dis-es-the'zī-ah) [G. *dysaisthesia*, fr. *dys-*, hard, difficult, + *aisthēsis*, sensation]. **1.** Impairment of sensation short of anesthesia. **2.** A condition in which a disagreeable sensation is produced by ordinary stimuli.

dysfibrinogenemia (dis'fi-brin'o-jē-ne'mǐ-ah). A familial disorder of qualitatively abnormal fibrinogens; various types are classified according to the major defect, thrombin time, effect on clotting, and symptoms such as bleeding and thrombosis.

dysfunction (dis-funk'shun). Difficult or abnormal function.

    minimal brain d., a mild degree of impaired cerebration which may be manifested by dyslexia, dysgraphia, hyperactivity, and/or mental retardation.

dysgam'maglob'uline'mia. An immunoglobulin abnormality, especially a disturbance of the percentage distribution of γ-globulins.

dysgenesis (dis-jen'ē-sis) [dys- + G. *genesis*, generation]. Defective embryonic development.

    gonadal d., defective gonadal development, varying types and degrees of which have been identified: gonadal aplasia or agenesis, rudimentary gonads, congenitally defective gonads, and true hermaphroditism.

    seminiferous tubule d., a disorder in which the seminiferous tubules exhibit an abnormal cytoarchitecture and extensive hyalinization; the testes are small, and few spermatozoa are formed; a constant feature of Klinefelter's *syndrome*.

dysgen'ic. Denoting a detrimental effect upon hereditary qualities.

dysgerminoma (dis-jer-mǐ-no'mah) [dys- + L. *germen*, a bud or sprout, + G. *-oma*, tumor]. Disgerminoma; a rare malignant neoplasm of the ovary, a counterpart of seminoma of the testis, composed of undifferentiated gonadal germinal cells.

dysgeusia (dis-gu'sī-ah) [dys- + G. *geusis*, taste]. Impairment or perversion of the gustatory sense.

dysgnathia (dis-na'thī-ah) [dys- + G. *gnathos*, jaw]. Any abnormality that extends beyond the teeth and includes the maxilla, mandible, or both.

dysgnathic (dis-nath'ik). Pertaining to or chaaracterized by disgnathia.

dysgnosia (dis-no'sī-ah) [G. *dysgnōsia*, difficulty of knowing]. Any cognitive disorder, *i.e.*, any mental disorder or disease.

dyshematopoiesis (dis-he'mă-to-poy-e'sis) [dys- + G. *haima*(haimat-), blood, + *poiēsis*, making]. Imperfect formation of blood.

dyshidrosis (dis-ĭ-dro'sis) [dys- + G. *hidrōs*, sweat]. Pompholyx; cheiropompholyx; chiropompholyx; a vesicular or vesicopustular eruption that occurs primarily on the hands and feet; the lesions spread peripherally but have a tendency to central clearing.

dyskaryosis (dis-kăr-ĭ-o'sis) [dys- + G. *karyon*, nucleus, + *ōsis*, condition]. Abnormal maturation seen in exfoliated cells which have normal cytoplasm but hyperchromatic nuclei, or irregular chromatin distribution.

dyskaryotic (dis-kăr-ĭ-ot'ik). Pertaining to or characterized by dyskaryosis.

dyskeratoma (dis-kĕr-ă-to'mah) [dys- + G. *keras*, horn, + *-oma*, tumor]. A skin tumor showing dyskeratosis.

   warty d., a benign solitary tumor of the skin, usually of the scalp, face, or neck, with a central keratotic plug; it appears to arise from a hair follicle, and microscopically resembles a lesion of keratosis follicularis but is larger, with more extensive epithelial downgrowth.

dyskeratosis (dis-kĕr-ă-to'sis) [dys- + G. *keras*, horn, + *-osis*, condition]. **1.** Appearance of premature keratinization in individual cells that have not reached the keratinizing surface layer. **2.** Epidermalization of the conjunctival and corneal epithelium.

dyskinesia (dis-kĭ-ne'zĭ-ah) [dys- + G. *kinēsis*, movement]. Difficulty in performing voluntary movements.

   d. al'gera, a hysterical condition in which active movement causes pain.

   biliary d., abnormal mobility (spasm) of the gallbladder or its ducts impairing filling or emptying due to intrinsic or extrinsic disease.

   extrapyramidal d.'s, movement disorders attributed to pathological states of one or the other part of the extrapyramidal motor system, generally characterized by insuppressible, stereotyped, automatic movements that cease only during sleep.

   d. intermit'tens, intermittent disability of the limbs due to impairment of circulation.

   tardive oral d., involuntary movement of the lips or jaw and other dystonic gestures; an extrapyramidal effect of certain psychotropic drug treatments.

dyslalia (dis-la'lĭ-ah, -lal'ĭ-ah) [dys- + G. *lalia*, talking]. Disorder of articulation due to structural abnormalities of the articulatory organs or impaired hearing.

dyslexia (dis-lek'sĭ-ah) [dys- + G. *lexis*, word, phrase]. Incomplete alexia; a level of reading ability markedly below that expected on the basis of the individual's level of over-all intelligence or ability in skills.

dyslochia (dis-lo'kĭ-ah) [dys- + G. *lochia*]. Abnormal puerperal discharge.

dyslogia (dis-lo'jĭ-ah) [dys- + G. *logos*, speaking, reason]. **1.** Impairment in the power of speech in consequence of a central lesion. **2.** Impairment of the reasoning faculty.

dys'mature. **1.** Denoting faulty development or ripening; often connoting structural and/or functional abnormalities. **2.** In obstetrics, denoting an infant whose birth weight is inappropriately low for its gestational age.

dysmaturity (dis-mă-chŭr'ĭ-tĭ). Syndrome of an infant born with relative absence of subcutaneous fat, wrinkling of the skin, prominent fingernails and toenails, and meconium staining of the skin and placental membranes; associated with postmaturity or placental insufficiency.

dysme'lia [dys- + G. *melos*, limb]. A congenital abnormality characterized by missing or foreshortened extremities, sometimes with associated spinal abnormalities.

dysmenorrhea (dis'men-o-re'ah) [dys- + G. *mēn*, month, + *rhoia*, a flow]. Menorrhalgia; difficult and painful menstruation.

   essential d., functional d., intrinsic d., primary d.

   mechanical d., obstructive d.; d. due to an obstruction to the escape of the menstrual blood, as in cervical stenosis.

   membranous d., d. accompanied by an exfoliation of the menstrual decidua.

   obstructive d., mechanical d.

   primary d., essential, functional, or intrinsic d.; d. due to a functional disturbance and to inflammation, new growths, or anatomic factors.

   secondary d., d. due to inflammation, infection, tumor, or anatomical or orthopedic factors.

   spasmodic d., d. accompanied by painful contractions of the uterus.

dysmetria (dis-me'trĭ-ah, -met'rĭ-ah) [dys- + G. *metron*, measure]. A form of dysergia in which one is unable to arrest a muscular movement at the desired point.

dysmim'ia [dys- + G. *mimeomai*, to mimic]. **1.** Impairment of the power of expression by gestures. **2.** Imperfect power of imitation.

dysmnesia (dis-ne'zĭ-ah) [dys- + G. *mnēmē*, memory]. A naturally poor or an impaired memory.

dysmorphism (dis-mor'fizm) [G. *dysmorphia*, badness of form]. Abnormality of shape.

dysmorphogenesis (dis'mor-fo-jen'ĕ-sis) [dys- + G. *morphē*, form, + *genesis*, production]. The process of abnormal tissue formation.

dysmorphology (dis'mor-fol'o-jĭ) [dys- + G. *morphē*, form, + *logos*, study]. The study of, or the general subject of, abnormal development of tissue form.

dysmyotonia (dis'mi-o-to'nĭ-ah) [dys- + G. *mys*, muscle, + *tonos*, tension, tone]. Abnormal muscular tonicity.

dysodontiasis (dis-o-don-ti'ă-sis) [dys- + G. *odous*, tooth, + *-iasis*, condition]. Difficulty or irregularity in the eruption of the teeth.

dysontogenesis (dis'on-to-jen'ĕ-sis) [dys- + G. *ōn*, being, + *genesis*, generation]. Defective development of the individual.

dysontogenetic (dis'on-to-jĕ-net'ik). Characterized by dysontogenesis.

dysorexia (dis-o-rek'sĭ-ah) [dys- + G. *orexis,* appetite]. Diminished or perverted appetite.

dysosmia (dis-oz'mĭ-ah) [dys- + G. *osmē,* smell]. Impaired sense of smell.

dysosteogenesis (dis'os-te-o-jen'ĕ-sis) [dys- + G. *osteon,* bone, + *genesis,* production]. Dysostosis; defective bone formation.

dysostosis (dis-os-to'sis) [dys- + G. *osteon,* bone, + *-osis,* condition]. Dysosteogenesis.

   cleidocranial d., clidocranial d., craniocleidodysostosis; a development defect characterized by absence or rudimentary development of the clavicles, abnormal shape of the skull with depression of the sagittal suture, frontal bosses, many wormian bones, and aplasia or hypoplasis of teeth; autosomal dominant inheritance.

   craniofacial d., Crouzon's disease; cranial stenosis with widening of the skull and high forehead, ocular hypertelorism, exophthalmos, beaked nose, and hypoplasis of the maxilla; usually autosomal dominant inheritance.

   mandibulofacial d., a variable syndrome of malformations primarily of derivatives of the first branchial arch: palpebral fissures slope outward and downward with notches or coloboma in the outer third of the lower lids, bony defects or hypoplasia of malar bones and zygoma, hypoplasia of the mandible, macrostomia with high or cleft palate and malposition and malocclusion of teeth, low-set malformed external ears, atypical hair growth, and occasional pits or clefts between mouth and ear. Also called Franceschetti's syndrome (if complete or nearly complete), or Treacher Collins syndrome (if limited to orbit and malar region).

   metaphysial d., a rare developmental abnormality of the skeleton in which metaphyses of tubular bones are expanded by deposits of cartilage.

   d. mul'tiplex, Hurler's *syndrome.*

   orodigitofacial d., orodigitofacial syndrome; an inherited syndrome with varying combinations of defects of the oral cavity, face, and hands; found only in females, with X-linked dominant inheritance from mother to daughter.

dyspareunia (dis-pă-ru'nĭ-ah) [dys- + G. *pareunos,* lying beside, fr. *para,* beside, + *eunē,* a bed]. The occurrence of pain during sexual intercourse.

dyspep'sia [dys- + G. *pepsis,* digestion]. Gastric indigestion; impaired digestion or "upset stomach" due to some disorder of the stomach.

dyspep'tic. Relating to or suffering from dyspepsia.

dysphagia, dysphagy (dis-fa'jĭ-ah, dis'fă-jĭ) [dys- + G. *phagein,* to eat]. Aglutition; aphagia; odynophagia; difficulty in swallowing.

dysphasia (dis-fa'zĭ-ah) [dys- + G. *phasis,* speaking]. Dysphrasia; lack of coordination in speech, and failure to arrange words in an understandable way; due to cortical lesion.

dysphemia (dis-fe'mĭ-ah) [dys- + G. *phēmē,* speech]. Disorder of phonation, articulation, or hearing due to emotional or intellectual deficits.

dysphonia (dis-fo'nĭ-ah) [dys- + G. *phōnē,* voice]. Difficulty or pain in speaking.

dysphoria (dis-fo'rĭ-ah) [G. extreme discomfort, fr. *dys-,* difficult, bad, + *phora,* a bearing]. A feeling of unpleasantness or discomfort.

dysphrasia (dis-fra'zĭ-ah) [dys- + G. *phrasis,* speaking]. Dysphasia.

dys'pigmenta'tion. Any abnormality in the formation or distribution of pigment, especially in the skin.

dysplasia (dis-pla'zĭah) [dys- + G. *plasis,* a molding]. Abnormal tissue development.

   anhidrotic ectodermal d., congenital absence of sweat glands resulting in heat intolerance, with smooth finely wrinkled skin, sunken nose, malformed and missing teeth, sparse fragile hair; X-linked recessive inheritance.

   anterofacial, anteroposterior or **anteroposterior facial d.,** abnormal growth of the face or cranium in an anterioposterior direction as seen and measured from a cephalogram.

   chondroectodermal d., triad of chondrodysplasia ectodermal d., and polydactyly, with congenital heart defects in over half of patients; autosomal recessive inheritance.

   congenital ectodermal d., congenital ectodermal *defect.*

   cretinoid d., see cretinism.

   dentinal d., *dentinogenesis* imperfecta.

   diaphysial d., Engelmann's disease; progressive, symmetrical fusiform enlargement of the shafts of long bones characterized by formation of excessive new periosteal and endosteal bone and irregular conversion of this cortical bone into cancellous bone.

   enamel d., *amelogenesis* imperfecta.

   d. epiphysia'lis mul'tiplex, a dominantly inherited abnormality of epiphyses characterized by difficulty in walking, pain and stiffness of joints, stubby fingers, and often dwarfism of short-limb type; epiphyses are mottled and irregular, ossification centers are late in appearance and may be multiple, but the vertebrae are normal.

   d. epiphysia'lis puncta'ta, stippled epiphysis; a developmental error of the epiphyses characterized by severe deformities, epiphyses ossified from several discrete centers and with a stippled appearance, and thickened shafts of the long bones.

   faciodigitogenital d., Aarskog-Scott syndrome; a syndrome of ocular hypertelorism, anteverted nostrils, broad upper lip, saddle-bag scrotum, and laxity of ligaments resulting in genu recurvatum, flat feet, and hyperextensible fingers; X-linked inheritance.

   fibrous d. of bone, a disturbance of medullary bone maintenance in which bone undergoing physiologic lysis is replaced by abnormal proliferation of fibrous tissue, resulting in asymmetric distortion and expansion of bone; may be confined to a single bone (monostotic fibrous d.) or involve multiple bones (polyostotic fibrous d.).

hereditary ectodermal d., anhidrotic ectodermal d. with variable hereditary traits.

hidrotic ectodermal d., congenital dystrophy of the nails and hair, with thickened nails, sparse or absent scalp hair, and often associated with keratoderma of the palms and soles.

metaphysial d., a failure of remodeling to normal tubular structure of new bone at the metaphyses of long bones; the ends of long bones appear to be expanded and porotic, with thin cortex.

oculovertebral d., microphthalmia, colobomas or anophthalmia with small orbit, unilateral d. of maxilla, macrostomia with malformed teeth and malocclusion, vertebral malformations, and branched and hypoplastic ribs.

spondyloepiphysial d., a group of conditions characterized by growth insufficiency of the vertebral column, with flattening of vertebrae, and often involving the epiphyses at the hip and shoulder; results in dwarfism of the short trunk type, often also with short extremities; types with dominant, recessive, and X-linked recessive inheritance have been described.

dysplas'tic. Pertaining to or marked by dysplasia.

dyspnea (disp-ne'ah) [G. *dyspnoia,* fr. *dys-,* bad, + *pnoē,* breathing]. Shortness of breath, a subjective difficulty or distress in breathing.

paroxysmal nocturnal d., acute d. appearing suddenly at night, usually waking the patient after an hour or two of sleep; caused by pulmonary congestion and edema which result from left-sided heart failure.

dyspneic (disp-ne'ik). Relating to or suffering from dyspnea.

dyspraxia (dis-prak'sĭ-ah) [dys- + G. *praxis,* a doing]. Impaired or painful functioning in any organ.

dysprosium (dis-pro'sĭ-um). A metallic element of the lanthanide (rare earth) series, symbol Dy, atomic No. 66, atomic weight 162.50.

dysproteinemia (dis-pro'tēn-e'mĭ-ah). An abnormality in plasma proteins, usually in immunoglobulins.

dysproteinem'ic. Relating to dysproteinemia.

dysraphism, dysraphia (dis'rā-fizm, dis-raf'ĭ-ah) [dys- + g. *raphē,* suture]. Defective fusion of a raphe, especially of the neural folds.

dysrhythmia (dis-rith'mĭ-ah) [dys- + G. *rhythmos,* rhythm]. Defective rhythm.

cardiac d., any abnormality in the rate, regularity, or sequence of cardiac activation.

electroencephalographic d., a diffusely irregular brain wave tracing.

dyssebacia (dis-sĕ-ba'shĭ-ah) [dys- + L. *sebum,* grease]. Seborrheic *dermatitis.*

dyspermatism, dysspermia (dis-sper'mă-tizm, dis-sper'mĭ-ah) [dys- + G. *sperma,* seed]. Occurrence of pain or discomfort in the discharge of seminal fluid.

dysstasia (dis-sta'sĭ-ah) [dys- + G. *stasis,* standing]. Difficulty in standing.

dysstatic (dis-stat'ik). Characterized by dysstasia.

dyssynergia (dis-sin-er'jĭ-ah) [dys- + G. *syn,* with, + *ergon,* work]. Ataxia.

d. cerebella'ris myoclon'ica, an affection with symptoms similar to those of d. cerebellaris progressiva, with the addition of myoclonus and epilepsy.

d. cerebellar'is progressi'va, Hunt's *syndrome*(1).

dyssystole (dis-sis'to-le). A defective cardiac systole.

dystaxia (dis-tak'sĭ-ah) [dys- + G. *taxis,* order]. A mild degree of ataxia.

dysthymia (dis-thi'mĭ-ah) [dys- + G. *thymos,* mind, emotion]. Any disorder of mood.

dystocia (dis-to'sĭ-ah) [G. *dystokia,* fr. *dys-,* difficult, + *tokos,* childbirth]. Difficult childbirth.

fetal d., d. due to an abnormality of the fetus.

maternal d., d. caused by an abnormality in the mother.

placental d., retention or difficult delivery of the placenta.

dystonia (dis-to'nĭ-ah) [dys- + G. *tonos,* tension]. Abnormal tonicity in any of the tissues.

d. musculo'rum defor'mans, d. lenticula'ris, progressive torsion spasm of childhood; an affection, occurring especially in children, marked by muscular contractions producing most peculiar distortions of the spine and hips; the musculature is hypertonic when in action, hypotonic when at rest.

dyston'ic. Pertaining to dystonia.

dystopia (dis-to'pĭ-ah) [dys- + G. *topos,* place]. Malposition; faulty or abnormal position of a part or of the body.

dystop'ic. Pertaining to, or characterized by, dystopia. See also ectopic.

dystrophia (dis-tro'fĭ-ah) [L. fr. G. *dys-,* bad, + *trophē,* nourishment]. Dystrophy.

d. adipo'sogenita'lis, adiposogenital dystrophy; a disorder characterized primarily by obesity and genital hypoplasia; when caused by an adenohypophysial tumor it is called Frölich's syndrome; may also be caused by hypothalamic lesions in areas regulating appetite and gonadal development.

d. epithelia'lis cor'neae, Fuchs epithelial *dystrophy.*

d. myoton'ica, myotonic *dystrophy.*

d. un'guium, dystrophy of the nails.

dystrophic (dis-trof'ik). Relating to dystrophy.

dystrophoneurosis (dis-trof'o-nu-ro'sis) [dys- + G. *trophē,* nourishment, + *neuron,* nerve, + *-osis,* condition]. Any nervous disorder associated with faulty nutrition.

dystrophy (dis'tro-fī) [dys- + G. *trophē,* nourishment]. Dystrophia; defective nutrition.

adiposogenital d., *dystrophia* adiposogenitalis.

adult pseudohypertrophic muscular d., Becker type tardive muscular d., muscular d. of late onset, often in the 20's or 30's, with relatively mild course; X-linked recessive inheritance.

childhood muscular d., pseudohypertrophic muscular d.

Duchenne's d., pseudohypertrophic muscular d.

facioscapulohumeral muscular d., Landouzy-Déjérine d.; a relatively benign type of d. commencing in childhood and characterized by wasting and weakness, mainly of the muscles of the face, shoulder girdle, and arms; autosomal dominant inheritance.

Fuchs epithelial dystrophy, dystrophia epithelialis corneae; a condition dependent on a prior endothelial d. of the cornea; begins with a fine spreading central edema, is eventually bilateral, and occurs predominantly in elderly women.

Landouzy-Déjérine d., facioscapulohumeral muscular d.

limb-girdle muscular d., Leyden-Möbius muscular d., a progressive disorder that usually begins in the preadolescent period; manifestations include those of childhood and facioscapulohumeral muscular d.; commonly, the pelvic girdle is most severely involved; autosomal recessive inheritance.

muscular d., myodystrophy; inborn abnormality of muscle associated with dysfunction and ultimately with deterioration.

myotonic d., dystrophia myotonica; myotonia atrophica or dystrophica; Steinert's disease; a chronic, slowly progressing disease, with onset usually in the third decade, marked by atrophy of the muscles, failing vision, lenticular opacities, ptosis, slurred speech, and general muscular weakness; autosomal dominant inheritance.

pseudohypertrophic muscular d., a type of muscular d. occurring in males in childhood; characterized by muscular weakness in the pelvic girdle that spreads with relative rapidity to the musculature of the pectoral girdle, trunk, and extremities, muscular pseudohypertrophy, and contractures of muscle and tendon; X-linked recessive inheritance. Also called childhood muscular d.; pseudohypertrophic muscular paralysis; Duchenne's d., disease (2), or paralysis.

reticular d. of cornea, bilateral, progressive, superficial degeneration of the corneal epithelium and adjacent Bowman's membrane.

dysuria (dis-u′rĭ-ah) [dys- + G. *ouron*, urine]. Difficulty or pain in urination.

dysuric (dis-u′rik). Relating to or suffering from dysuria.

dysversion (dis-ver′zhun) [dys- + L. *verto*, to turn]. A turning in any direction, less than inversion; particularly d. of the optic nerve head (situs inversus of the optic disk).

E

ear [A.S. *éare*]. The organ of hearing: composed of the **external e.,** which includes the auricle and the external acoustic, or auditory, meatus; the **middle e.,** or the tympanic cavity with its ossicles; and the **internal** or **inner e.,** or labyrinth, which includes the semicircular canals, vestibule, and cochlea.

Blainville e.'s, asymmetry in size or shape of the auricles.

Cagot e., (kă-go′) [name of a degenerate race in the Pyrenees among whom physical stigmata are common]. an auricle having no lobulus.

cauliflower e., thickening and induration of the e. with distortion of contours following extravasation of blood within its tissues.

ear′ache. Otalgia; otodynia; pain in the ear.

ear′drum. *Membrana* tympani.

earth (urth) [A.S. *eorthe*]. In chemistry, an insoluble oxide of aluminum or of certain other elements characterized by a high melting point.

alkaline e.'s, any of the elements in the family Be, Mg, Ca, Sr, Ba, Ra, the hyroxides of which are highly ionized, hence alkaline in water solution.

diatomaceous e., a powder made of desiccated diatom material; used as a filtering agent, adsorbent, and abrasive in many chemical operations.

fuller's e. [fr. *fulling*, an old process of cleaning wool, with earth or clay], a refined clay sometimes used as a dusting powder or applied moistened with water as a form of poultice.

rare e.'s, those elements with atomic numbers 57 through 71, often called lanthanides; they closely resemble one another chemically and are thus difficult to separate from each other.

eburnation (e-bur-na′shun) [L. *eburneus*, of ivory]. A change in exposed subchondral bone in degenerative joint disease in which it is converted into a dense, smooth substance like ivory.

ec-. Prefix fr. G. preposition meaning out of, away from.

eccentric (ek-sen′trik) [G. *ek*, out, + *kentron*, center]. **1.** Erratic (1); abnormal or peculiar in ideas, actions, or speech. **2.** Proceeding from a center. **3.** Peripheral.

eccentrochondroplasia (ek-sen′tro-kon-dro-pla′zĭ-ah) [G. *ek*, out + *kentron*, center, + *chondros*, cartilage, + *plasis*, a molding]. Abnormal epiphysial development from eccentric centers of ossification.

ecchondroma (ek-kon-dro′mah) [G. *ek*, from, + *chondros*, cartilage, + *-oma*, tumor]. Ecchondrosis. **1.** A cartilaginous neoplasm arising as an overgrowth from normally situated cartilage, as a mass protruding from the articular surface of a bone. **2.** An enchondroma that has burst through the shaft of a bone and become pedunculated.

ecchondrosis (ek-kon-dro′sis). Ecchondroma.

ecchymoma (ek-ĭ-mo′mah) [G. *ek*, out, + *chymos*, juice, + *-oma*, tumor]. A slight hematoma following a bruise.

ecchymosed (ek′ĭ-mōzd). Characterized by or affected with ecchymosis.

ecchymosis, pl. **ecchymo′ses** (ek-ĭ-mo′sis, -sēz) [G. *ekchymōsis*, ecchymosis, fr. *ek*, out, + *chymos*, juice]. A purplish patch caused by extravasation of blood into the skin, differing from petechiae only in size.

ecchymotic (ek-ĭ-mot′ik). Relating to an ecchymosis.

eccrine (ek′rin) [G. *ek-krino*, to secrete]. **1.** Exocrine (1). **2.** Denoting the flow of sweat.

eccrisis (ek′rĭ-sis) [G. separation]. **1.** The removal of waste products. **2.** Any waste product; excrement.

eccritic (ek-krit′ik). Promoting the expulsion of waste matters.

eccyesis (ek-si-e′sis) [G. *ek*, out, + *kyēsis*, pregnancy]. Ectopic *pregnancy*.

ecdemic (ek-dem′ik) [G. *ekdēmos*, foreign, from home]. Denoting a disease brought into a region from without, not epidemic or endemic.

ECF-A Eosinophil chemotactic *factor* of anaphylaxis.

ECG Electrocardiogram.

ecgonine (ek′go-nēn, -nin). 3β-Hydroxy-1α H,5α H-2β-tropanecarboxylic acid; the important part of the cocaine molecule.

echino-, echin- [G. *echinos*, hedgehog, sea urchin]. Combining forms meaning prickly or spiny.

echinococcosis (ĕ-ki′no-kok′ko′sis). Infection with *Echinococcus;* larval infection is hydatid *disease.*

Echinococcus (ĕ-ki-no-kok′us) [echino- + G. *kokkos*, a berry]. A genus of very small taeniid tapeworms. Adults are found in various carnivores but not in man; larvae, in the form of hydatid cysts, are found in the liver and other organs of ruminants, rodents, and, under certain epidemiological circumstances, man.

echoacousia (ek′o-ă-ku′zĭ-ah) [echo + G. *akouō*, to hear]. A subjective disturbance of hearing in which a sound heard appears to be repeated.

echoaortography (ek′o-a-or-tog′ră-fĭ) [echo + aortography]. Application of ultrasound techniques to the diagnosis and study of the aorta, particularly the abdominal aorta.

echocar′diogram. The ultrasonic record obtained by echocardiography.

echocardiography (ek′o-kar-dĭ-og′ră-fĭ) [echo + cardiography]. Ultrasound cardiography. Use of ultrasound in the diagnosis of cardiovascular lesions and recording of the size, motion, and composition of various cardiac structures.

echoencephalography (ek′o-en-sef-ă-log′ră-fĭ) [echo + encephalography]. Use of reflected ultrasound in the diagnosis of intracranial processes.

echogen′ic. Containing internal interfaces that reflect high frequency sound waves.

echogram (ek′o-gram) [echo + G. *gramma*, a diagram]. Ultrasonic display of reflection techniques appropriate for any field of application, but applied especially to the heart.

echography (ĕ-kog′ră-fĭ) [echo + G. *graphō*, to write]. Ultrasonography.

echolalia (ek′o-la′lĭ-ah) [echo + G. *lalia*, a form of speech]. Involuntary repetition of a word or sentence just spoken by another person.

echomimia (ek′o-mim′ĭ-ah) [echo + G. *mimēsis*, imitation]. Echopathy.

echomotism (ek′o-mo′tizm) [echo + L. *motio*, motion]. Echopraxia.

echopathy (ĕ-kop′ă-thĭ) [echo + G. *pathos*, suffering]. Echomimia; a mental disorder in which the words or actions of another are imitated and repeated by the patient.

echophrasia (ek-o-fra′zĭ-ah) [echo + *phrasis*, speech]. Echolalia.

echopraxia (ek-o-prak′sĭ-ah) [echo + G. *praxis*, action]. echomotism; the involuntary imitation of movements made by another.

ech′ovirus. ECHO *virus.*

eclabium (ek-la′bĭ-um) [G. *ek*, out, + L. *labium*, lip]. Eversion of a lip.

eclampsia (ek-lamp′sĭ-ah) [G. *eklampsis*, a shining forth]. Occurrence of one or more convulsions, not attributable to other cerebral conditions such as epilepsy or cerebral hemorrhage, in a patient with preeclampsia.

   puerperal e., convulsions and coma associated with hypertension, edema, or proteinuria occurring in a woman following delivery.

eclampsism (ek-lamp′sizm). A state in which general signs point to the early occurrence of puerperal eclampsia, but convulsions do not take place.

eclamp′tic. Relating to eclampsia.

eclamptogenic (ek-lamp′to-jen′ik). Causing eclampsia.

ecmnesia (ek-ne′zĭ-ah) [G. *ek*, out, + *mnēsios*, relating to memory]. Loss of memory for recent events.

eco- [G. *oikos*, house, household, habitation]. Combining form denoting relationship to environment.

ecology (e-kol′o-jĭ) [eco- + G. *logos*, study]. The branch of biology concerned with the total complex of interrelationships among living organisms, encompassing the relations of organisms to each other, to the environment, and to the entire energy balance within a given ecosystem.

ecomania (e′ko-ma′nĭ-ah) [eco- + G. *mania*, frenzy]. A syndrome of domineering behavior at home and humility toward persons in authority.

ecosystem (e′ko-sis-tem) [eco- + system]. A biocenosis (biotic community) and its biotope.

ecotaxis (e′ko-tak′sis). The migration of lymphocytes from the thymus and bone marrow into tissues possessing an appropriate microenvironment.

ecphy′ma [G. a pimply eruption]. A warty growth or protuberance.

écraseur (a-krah-zër′) [Fr. *écraser*, to crush]. A snare, especially one of great strength for cutting through the base or pedicle of a tumor.

ECS Electrocerebral silence.

ECT Electroconvulsive (electroshock) *therapy.*

ect-. See ecto-.

ectad (ek′tad) [G. *ektos*, outside, + L. *ad*, to]. Outward.

ectal (ek′tăl) [G. *ektos*, outside]. Outer; external.

-ectasia, -ectasis [G. *ektasis*, a stretching]. Combining form in suffix position used to denote dilation or expansion.

ecta′sia, ec′tasis (ek-ta′zĭ-ah, ek′tă-sis) [G. *ektasis*, a stretching.] Dilation of a tubular structure.

e. cor′dis, dilation of the heart.

hypostatic e., dilation of a blood vessel, usually a vein, in a dependent portion of the body, as in varicose veins of the leg.

mammary duct e., dilation of mammary ducts by lipid and cellular debris in older women; rupture of ducts may result in granulomatous inflammation and infiltration by plasma cells.

ectatic (ek-tat′ik). Relating to or marked by ectasis.

ectental (ek-ten′tal) [G. *ektos*, outside, + *entos*, within]. Relating to both ectoderm and entoderm; denoting the line where these two layers join.

ectethmoid (ekt-eth′moyd) [G. *ektos*, outside, + ethmoid]. *Labyrinthus* ethmoidalis.

ecthyma (ek-thi′mah) [G. a pustule]. A pyogenic infection of the skin due to staphylococci or streptococci and characterized by adherent crusts beneath which ulceration occurs.

ecto-, ect- [G. *ektos*, outside]. Combining forms denoting outer, on the outside. See also exo-.

ectoantigen (ek-to-an′tĭ-jen). Any toxin or other excitor of antibody formation, separate or separable from its source.

ectoblast (ek′to-blast) [ecto- + G. *blastos*, germ]. Ectoderm.

ectocardia (ek-to-kar′dĭ-ah) [ecto- + G. *kardia*, heart]. Exocardia; congenital displacement of the heart.

ectocervical (ek-to-ser′vĭ-kal). Pertaining to the pars vaginalis of the cervix uteri lined with stratified squamous epithelium.

ectoderm (ek′to-derm) [ecto- + G. *derma*, skin]. Ectoblast; the outer layer of cells in the embryo, after the establishing of the primary germ layers.

ectoder′mal, ectoder′mic. Relating to the ectoderm.

ec′todermo′sis. A disorder of any organ or tissue developed from the ectoderm.

ectoentad (ek-to-en′tad). From without inward.

ectoenzyme (ek-to-en′zīm). An enzyme that is excreted externally.

ectogenous (ek-toj′en-us) [ecto- + G. *-gen*, producing]. Exogenous.

ectoglobular (ek-to-glob′u-lar). Not within a red blood cell.

ectomere (ek′to-mēr) [ecto- + G. *meros*, part]. One of the blastomeres destined to take part in forming the ectoderm.

ectomorph (ek′to-morf) [ecto- + G. *morphē*, form]. A constitutional body type or build in which tissues that originated from the ectoderm prevail; from the morphological standpoint, the limbs predominate over the trunk.

ectomorph′ic. Relating to ectomorphs.

-ectomy [G. *ektomē*, excision]. Combining form used as a suffix to denote removal of any anatomical structure. See also -tomy.

ectopagia (ek-to-pa′jĭ-ah) [ecto- + G. *pagos*, something fixed, + *-ia*, condition]. The condition in conjoined twins in which the bodies are joined laterally.

ectopar′asite. A parasite that lives on the surface of the host body.

ectophyte (ek′to-fīt) [ecto- + G. *phyton*, plant]. A plant parasite of the skin.

ectopia (ek-to′pĭ-ah) [G. *ektopos*, out of place, fr. *ektos*, outside, + *topos*, place]. Ectopy; heterotopia (1); congenital displacement of any organ or part of the body.

e. cor′dis, congenital condition in which the heart is exposed on the chest wall because of maldevelopment of the sternum and pericardium.

e. len′tis, displacement of the lens of the eye.

e. pupil′lae congen′ita, marked excentric congenital displacement of the pupil.

e. tes′tis, ectopic *testis.*

ectopic (ek-top′ik) [see ectopia]. **1.** Aberrant (3); heterotopic (1); out of place; said of an organ that is not in its proper position, or of a pregnancy occurring elsewhere than in the cavity of the uterus. **2.** In cardiography, denoting a heart beat that has its origin in a focus other than the sinoatrial node.

ectopy (ek′to-pī). Ectopia.

ectosteal (ek-tos′te-al) [ecto- + G. *osteon* bone]. Relating to the external surface of a bone.

ectostosis (ek′tos-to′sis) [ecto- + G. *osteon*, bone, + *-osis*, condition]. Ossification in cartilage beneath the perichondrium, or the formation of bone beneath the periosteum.

ec′tothrix [ecto- + G. *thrix*, hair]. Fungus spores forming a sheath on the outside of a hair as well as growing within the hair shaft; a characteristic of some of the dermatophytes.

ectozo′on [ecto- + G. *zōon*, animal]. An animal parasite living on the surface of the body.

ectro- [G. *ektrōsis*, miscarriage]. Combining form denoting congenital absence of a part.

ectrocheiry, ectrochiry (ek-tro-ki′rī) [ectro- + G. *cheir*, hand]. Total or partial absence of a hand.

ectrodactyly, ectrodactylia, ectrodactylism (ek-tro-dak′tĭ-lī, -dak-til′ī-ah, -dak′tĭ-lizm) [ectro- + G. *daktylos*, finger]. Congenital absence of one or more fingers or toes.

ectrogen′ic. Relating to ectrogeny.

ectrogeny (ek-troj′en-ī) [ectro- + G. *-gen*, producing]. Congenital absence of any part.

ectromelia (ek-tro-me′lĭ-ah) [ectro- + G. *melos*, limb]. Congenital absence of one or more of limbs.

ectromel′ic. Pertaining to, or characterized by, ectromelia.

ectro′pion [G. *ek*, out, + *tropē*, a turning]. A rolling outward of the margin of a part.

e. u′veae, iridectropium; eversion of the anterior edge of the secondary optic vesicle at the pupillary margin.

ectropody (ek-trop′o-dī) [ectro- + G. *pous*, foot]. Total or partial absence of a foot.

ectrosyndactyly (ek-tro-sin-dak'tĭ-lĭ) [ectro- + G. *syn*, together, + *dactylos*, finger]. A congenital deformity marked by the absence of one or more digits and the fusion of others.

eczema (ek'zĕ-mah) [G. fr. *ekzeō*, to boil over]. Generic term for acute or chronic inflammatory conditions of the skin, typically erythematous, edematous, papular, vesicular, and crusting; followed often by lichenification and scaling, occasionally by duskiness of the erythema, and infrequently hyperpigmentation; often accompanied by sensations of itching and burning.

  allergic e., macular, papular, or vesicular eruption due to an allergic reaction.

  e. herpet'icum, Kaposi's varicelliform eruption; a febrile condition caused by herpesvirus type 1, occurring most commonly in children, consisting of a widespread eruption of vesicles rapidly becoming umbilicated pustules.

  e. margina'tum, *tinea* cruris.

  e. nummula're, discrete, coin-shaped patches of e.

  stasis e., eczematous eruption on legs due to or aggravated by vascular stasis.

  e. vaccina'tum, a form of generalized vaccinia supervening upon an existing atopic dermatitis; characterized by crops of vesicles and vesicopustules appearing on the face, neck, extremities, and trunk, with even minimal atopic involvement; accompanied by a high fever, malaise, and enlargement of the lymph nodes.

eczematoid (ek-sem'ă-toyd). Resembling eczema in appearance.

eczematous (ek-sem'ă-tus). Marked by or resembling eczema.

ED Effective *dose*.

edema (ĕ-de'mah) [G. *oidēma*, a swelling]. An accumulation of an excessive amount of watery fluid in cells, tissues, or serous cavities.

  angioneurotic e., periodically recurring episodes of noninflammatory swelling of skin, mucous membranes, viscera, and brain, of sudden onset and occasionally with arthralgia, purpura, or fever. Also called angioedema; atrophedema; Bannister's, Milton's, or Quincke's disease; giant urticaria; urticaria gigans.

  cardiac e., e. resulting from congestive heart failure.

  cerebral e., brain swelling due to increased volume of the extravascular compartment from the uptake of water in the neuropile and white matter.

  gestational e., the occurrence of a generalized and excessive accumulation of fluid in the tissues due to the influence of pregnancy.

  hereditary angioneurotic e., angioneurotic e. associated with either a deficiency of Cl esterase inhibitor (Cl inactivator) or a functionally inactive form of the inhibitor, either of which permits uncontrolled activation of early complement components and production of a kinin-like factor which induces the angioedema; autosomal dominant inheritance.

  e. neonato'rum, a diffuse, firm e. occuring in the newborn, beginning usually in the legs and spreading upward.

  pitting e., e. that retains for a time the indentation produced by pressure.

  pulmonary e., e. of lungs usually resulting from mitral stenosis or left ventricular failure.

edem'atous. Marked by edema.

eden'tate (ĕ-den'tāt) [L. *edentatus*]. Toothless.

edentulous (e-den'tu-lus) [L. *edentulus*, toothless]. Toothless; without teeth.

edet'ic acid Ethylenediaminetetraacetic acid.

edropho'nium chloride. Dimethylethyl (3-hydroxyphenyl)ammonium chloride; a competitive antagonist of skeletal muscle relaxants (curare derivatives and gallamine triethiodide) used as an antidote for curariform drugs, as a diagnostic agent in myasthenia gravis, and in myasthenic crisis.

EDTA Ethylenediaminetetraacetic acid.

EEG Electroencephalogram.

effect (ĕ-fekt') [L. *ef-ficio*, pp. *effectus*, to accomplish]. The result or consequence of an action.

  abscopal e., a reaction produced following irradiation but occurring outside the zone of actual radiation absorption.

  additive e., an e. wherein two substances or actions used in combination produce a total e. the same as the sum of the individual e.'s.

  Bohr e., the influence exerted by carbon dioxide on the oxygen dissociation curve of blood, *i.e*, the curve is shifted to the right, which means a reduction in the affinity of hemoglobin for oxygen.

  cumulative e., cumulative action; the condition in which repeated administration of a drug may produce e.'s that are more pronounced than those produced by the first dose.

  Doppler e., a change in frequency is observed when the sound and observer are in relative motion away from or toward each other. See also Doppler *shift*.

  experimenter e.'s, the influence of the experimenter's behavior, personality traits, or expectancies on the results of his own research.

  Haldane e., the promotion of carbon dioxide dissociation by oxygenation of hemoglobin.

  position e., a change in the phenotypic expression of one or more genes due to a change in position with respect to other genes; may result from change in chromosome structure or from crossing-over.

  side e., see under S.

  Somogyi e., in diabetes, reactive hyperglycemia following hypoglycemia.

effec'tor [L. producer]. A peripheral tissue that receives nerve impulses and reacts by contraction (muscle) or secretion (gland).

effemination (ef-fem-ĭ-na'shun) [L. *ef-femino*, pp. *-atus*, to make feminine, fr. *ex*, out, + *femina*, woman]. Acquisition of feminine characteristics, either physiologically by women, or pathologically by individuals of either sex.

ef'ferent [L. *efferens*, fr. *effero*, to bring out]. Conducting outward from a given organ or part thereof.

efficiency (ĕ-fish'en-sĭ). **1.** The production of the desired effects or results with minimum waste of time, effort, or skill. **2.** A measure of effectiveness; specifically, the useful work output divided by the energy input.

effloresce (ef-flor-es') [L. *ef-floresco*, to blossom]. To become powdery by losing the water of crystallization on exposure to a dry atmosphere.

effluvium, pl. efflu'via (ĕ-flu'vĭ-um) [L. a flowing out]. **1.** A shedding, especially of hair. **2.** Obsolete term for an exhalation, especially one of bad odor or injurious influence.

effusion (ĕ-fu'zhun) [L. *effusio*, a pouring out]. **1.** The escape of fluid from the blood vessels or lymphatics into the tissues or a cavity. **2.** The fluid so escaped.

egest (e-jest') [L. *e-gero*, pp. *-gestus*, to carry out, discharge]. To discharge unabsorbed food residues from the digestive tract.

egesta (e-jes'tah). Matter that is egested.

egg [A.S. *aeg*]. The female sexual cell or gamete; after fertilization and fusion of the pronuclei it is a zygote. See also oocyte, ovum.

egg cluster. One of the clumps of cells resulting from the breaking up of the gonadal cords in the ovarian cortex; these clumps later develop into primary ovarian follicles.

e'go [L. I]. In psychoanalysis, one of the three components of the psychic apparatus in the freudian structural framework, the other two being the id and superego. Although the e. has some conscious components, many of its functions are learned and automatic. It occupies a position between the primal instincts (pleasure principle) and the demands of the outer world (reality principle), and mediates between the person and external reality, and is also responsible for certain defensive functions to protect the person against the demands of the id and superego.

egobronchophony (e'go-brong-kof'o-nĭ) [G. *aix* (*aig*), goat, + *bronchos*, bronchus, + *phōnē*, voice]. Egophony with bronchophony.

egocentric (e-go-sen'trik) [ego + G. *kentron*, center]. Egotropic; marked by extreme concentration of attention upon oneself; selfish, self-centered.

ego-dystonic (e'go-dis-ton'ik) [ego + G. *dys*, bad, + *tonos*, tension]. Repugnant to or at variance with the aims of the ego.

egomania (e-go-ma'nĭ-ah) [ego + G. *mania*, frenzy]. Extreme self-appeciation or self-content.

egophonic (e-go-fon'ik). Relating to egophony.

egophony (e-gof'o-nĭ) [G. *aix*(aig-), goat, + *phōnē*, voice]. A peculiar broken quality of the voice sounds, like the bleating of a goat, heard about the upper level of the fluid in cases of pleurisy with effusion.

ego-syntonic (e'go-sin-ton'ik) [ego + G. *syn*, together, + *tonos*, tension]. Acceptable to the aims of the ego.

egotropic (e'go-trop'ik) [ego + G. *tropē*, a turning]. Egocentric.

eidometry (i-dop-tom'ĕ-trĭ) [G. *eidos*, form, + *optikos*, referring to vision, + *metron*, measure]. The measurement of the acuteness of form vision.

eikonometer, eiconometer (i-ko-nom'e-ter) [G. *eikon*, image, + *metron*, measure]. **1.** An instrument for determining the magnifying power of a microscope, or the size of a microscopic object. **2.** An instrument for determining the degree of aniseikonia.

Eimeria (i-me'rĭ-ah) [Theodor *Eimer*]. The largest, most economically important, and most widespread genus of the coccidial protozoa (family Eimeriidae, class Sporozoa); highly pathogenic, especially in young domesticated mammals and birds.

einstein (īn'stĭn) [A. *Einstein*, U.S. theoretical physicist, 1879-1955]. A unit of energy equal to 1 mol quantum, hence to 6.02×10^{23} quanta.

einsteinium (in-stīn'ĭ-um) [A. *Einstein* U.S. theoretical physicist, 1879-1955]. Artificial radioactive element, atomic no. 99, atomic symbol at first E, now Es.

ejac'ulate. 1. To expel suddenly, as semen. **2.** Semen expelled in ejaculation.

ejaculatio (e-jak-u-la'shĭ-o) [L.]. Ejaculation.

   e. pre'cox, premature *ejaculation.*

ejaculation (e-jak-u-la'shun) [L. *ejaculatio*]. Emission of seminal fluid.

   premature e., ejaculatio precox; during sexual intercourse, too rapid achievement of climax and e. in the male relative to his own or his partner's wishes.

ejac'ulatory. Relating to an ejaculation.

ejecta (e-jek'ta) [L. ntr. pl. of *ejectus*, pp. of *ejicio*, to throw out]. Ejection (2).

ejection (e-jek'shun) [L. *ejectio*, from *ejicio*, to cast out]. **1.** The act of driving or throwing out by physcial force from within. **2.** Ejecta; that which is ejected.

eka-. Prefix used to denote an undiscovered or just discovered element in the periodic system before a proper and official name is assigned by authorities; *e.g.,* eka-osmium, now plutonium.

EKG Electrocardiogram.

EKY Electrokymogram.

elabora'tion [L. *e-laborō*, pp. *-atus*, to labor, endeavor]. **1.** The process of working out in detail by labor and study. **2.** In psychiatry, the mental process occurring partly during dreaming and partly during the recalling or telling of a dream by means of which the latent (relatively organized) content of the dream is brought into increasingly more coherent and logical order, resulting in the manifest content of the dream.

elas'tance. A measure of the tendency of a hollow viscus to recoil toward its original dimensions upon removal of a distending or compressing force, the recoil pressure resulting from a unit distention or compression of the viscus; the reciprocal of compliance.

elas'tase. A hydrolase hydrolyzing elastin; formed from proelastase and structurally homologous with trypsin and some other serine proteinases.

elas'tic [G. *elastreō*, epic form of *elaunō*, drive, push]. Having the property of returning to the original shape after being distorted.

elas'ticin. Elastin.

elasticity (e-las-tis'ĭ-tĭ). The quality or condition of being elastic.

elas'tin. Elasticin; a yellow, elastic, fibrous mucoprotein that is the major connective tissue protein of elastic structures.

elastofibro'ma. A nonencapsulated slow-growing mass of poorly cellular, collagenous, fibrous tissue and elastic tissue; occurs usually in subscapular adipose tissue of elderly persons.

elasto'ma. Pseudoxanthoma elasticum.

elastorrhexis (e-las-to-rek'sis) [G. *rhēxis*, rupture]. Fragmentation of elastic tissue in which the normal wavy strands appear shredded and clumped.

elasto'sis. 1. Degenerative change in elastic tissue. **2.** Elastoic or elastoid dengeneration; degeneration of collagen fibers, with altered staining properties resembling elastic tissue.

    actinic e., e. colloidalis conglomerata.

    e. colloida'lis conglomera'ta, actinic e.; colloid degeneration of the elastic tissue of the dermis in persons who are repeatedly or constantly exposed to sunlight over a period of many years.

    e. per'forans serpigino'sa, circinate groups of asymptomatic keratotic papules; the epidermis is thickened around a central plug of keratin, overlying an accumulation of elastic tissue.

    senile e., e. seen histologically in the sun-exposed skin of the elderly or in those who have chronic actinic effect.

elbow (el'bo) [A.S. *elnboga*]. **1.** Cubitus (1); the joint between the arm and the forearm. **2.** An angular body resembling a flexed e.

    capped e., shoe *boil.*

    nursemaid's e., Malgaigne's *luxation.*

    tennis e., pain in or near the lateral epicondyle of the humerus, and lateral epicondylitis, as a result of unusual strain (not necessarily from playing tennis).

electro- [G. *ēlektron,* amber (on which static electricity can be generated by friction)]. Prefix denoting electric or electricity.

electroanalgesia (e-lek'tro-an-al-je'zĭ-ah). Analgesia induced by the passage of an electric current.

electroanesthesia (e-lek'tro-an-es-the'zĭ-ah). Anesthesia produced by an electric current.

elec'trobiol'ogy. The science concerned with electrical phenomena in living organisms.

electrocar'diogram (ECG, EKG) [electro- + G. *kardia,* heart, + *gramma,* a drawing]. The graphic record of the heart's action currents obtained with the electrocardiograph.

elec'trocar'diograph. An instrument for recording the potential of the electrical currents that traverse the heart and initiate its contraction.

elec'trocar'diograph'ic. Relating to an electrocardiograph.

elec'trocardiog'raphy. 1. A method of recording electrical currents traversing the heart muscle just previous to each heart beat. **2.** The study and interpretation of electrocardiograms.

electrocauterization (e-lek'tro-caw'ter-i-za'shun). Cauterization by an electrocautery.

electrocautery (e-lek'tro-caw'ter-ĭ). **1.** An instrument for directing a high frequency current through a local area of tissue. **2.** A metal cauterizing instrument heated by electricity.

elec'trocere'bral si'lence (ECS). An electroencephalogram with absence of potentials of cerebral origin over 2 μv from symmetrically placed electrode pairs 10 more centimeters apart, and with interelectrode resistance between 100 and 10,000 ohms.

elec'trochem'ical. Relating to chemical reactions effected by means of electricity and the mechanisms involved.

electrocoagulation (e-lek'tro-ko-ag-u-la'shun). Coagulation produced by an electrocautery.

electrocochleogram (e-lek'tro-kōk'le-o-gram). The record obtained by electrocochleography.

electrocochleography (e-lek'tro-kōk-le-og'rä-fĭ) [electro- + L. *cochlea,* snail shell, + G. *graphō,* to write]. A measurement of the electrical potentials generated in the inner ear as a result of sound stimulation.

elec'trocontractil'ity. The power of contraction of muscular tissue in response to an electrical stimulus.

elec'troconvul'sive. Denoting a convulsive response to an electrical stimulus. See electroshock *therapy.*

elec'trocor'ticogram. The record obained by electrocorticography.

elec'trocorticog'raphy. The technique of surveying the electrical activity of the cerebral cortex.

elec'trode [electro- + G. *hodos,* way]. **1.** One of the two extremities of an electric circuit; one of the two poles of an electric battery or of the end of the conductors connected thereto. **2.** An electrical terminal specialized for a particular electrochemical reaction.

electroder'mal [electro- + G. *derma,* skin]. Pertaining to electric properties of the skin, usually referring to altered resistance.

electrodesiccation (e-lek'tro-des-ĭ-ka'shun) [electro- + L. *desicco,* to dry up]. Destruction of lesions or sealing off of blood vessels by monopolar high frequency electric current.

electrodiagno'sis. Determination of the nature of a disease through observation of changes in electrical irritability.

electrodialysis (e-lek'tro-di-al'ĭ-sis). The removal in an electric field of ions from larger molecules and particles.

electroencephalogram (EEG) (e-lek'tro-en-sef'ă-lo-gram). The record obtained by means of the electroencephalograph.

flat e., isoelectric e., a record indicating the absence of electric potentials of cerebral origin of over 2 microvolts during a period of, at least, 30 minutes, when recording from symmetrically placed electrode pairs 10 or more cm apart and with interelectrode resistances between 100 and 10,000 ohms.

electroencephalograph (e-lek'tro-en-sef'ă-lo-graf) [electro- + G. *encephalon,* brain, + *graphō,* to write]. An apparatus for recording the electric potentials of the brain derived from electrodes attached to the scalp.

electroencephalographic (e-lek'tro-en-sef'ă-lo-graf'ik). Relating to electroencephalography.

electroencephalography (e-lek'tro-en-sef'ă-log'ră-fi). Registration the electrical potentials recorded by an electroencephalograph.

electroendosmosis (e-lek'tro-en-dos-mo'sis). Endosmosis produced by means of an electric field.

elec'trogas'trogram. The record obtained with the electrogastrograph.

elec'trogas'trograph. An instrument used in electrogastrography.

elec'trogastrog'raphy The recording of the electrical phenomena associated with gastric secretion and motility.

elec'trogram. 1. Any record made by an electrical event. 2. In electrophysiology, a recording taken directly from the surface by unipolar or bipolar leads.

His bundle e., an e. recorded from the His bundle during cardiac catheterization.

electrohemostasis (e-lek'tro-he-mos'tă-sis, -he'mo-sta'sis) [electro- + G. *haima,* blood, + *stasis,* halt]. Arrest of hemorrhage by means of the electrocautery.

electroimmunodiffusion (e-lek'tro-im'u-no-dī-fu'z-hun). An immunochemical method that combines electrophoretic separation with immunodiffusion by incorporating antibody into the support medium.

electrokymogram (EKY) (e-lek-tro-ki'mo-gram). The graphic record produced by the electrokymograph.

electrokymograph (e-lek-tro-ki'mo-graf). An apparatus for recording, from changes in the x-ray silhouette, the movements of the heart and great vessels.

electrokymography (e-lek'tro-ki-mog'ră-fi) [electro- + G. *kyma,* wave, + *graphō,* to write]. **1.** The registration of the movements of the heart and great vessels by means of the electrokymograph. **2.** The science and technique of interpreting electrokymograms.

electrolysis (e-lek-trol'ĭ-sis) [electro- + G. *lysis,* dissolution]. **1.** Decomposition of a salt or other chemical compound by means of an electric current. **2.** Destruction of certain body tissues by means of galvanic electricity.

electrolyte (e-lek'tro-līt) [electro- + G. *lytos,* soluble]. Any compound that, in solution, conducts a current in electricity and is decomposed by it; an ionizable substance in solution.

electrolytic (e-lek-tro-lit'ik). Referring to or caused by electrolysis.

electromy'ogram (EMG). The graphic representation produced by an electromyograph.

electromy'ograph. An instrument used in electromyography.

electromyographic (e-lek'tro-mi-o-graf'ik). Relating to electromyography.

electromyography (e-lek'tro-mi-og'ră-fi) [electro- + G. *mys,* muscle, + *graphō,* to write]. A method of recording the electrical currents generated in an active muscle.

elec'tron. One of the negatively charged subatomic particles that, distributed about the positive nucleus, constitute the atom.

elec'tronarco'sis. Production of insensibility to pain by the use of electrical current.

electroneg'ative. Relating to or charged with negative electricity; referring to an element whose uncharged atoms have a tendency to ionize by adding electrons, thus becoming anions.

electroneurography (e-lek'tro-nu-rog'ră-fi). A method of recording the electrical changes and nerve conduction velocities associated with the passing of impulses along peripheral nerves.

electroneuromyography (e-lek'tro-nu'ro-mi-og'ră-fi). A method of measuring changes in a peripheral nerve by combining electromyography of a muscle with electrical stimulation of the nerve trunk carrying fibers to and from the muscle.

electron-volt (eV, ev). The energy imparted to an electron by a potential of 1 volt; equal to $1.6 \times 10_{-12}$ erg in the CGS system, or $1.6 \times 10_{-19}$ joule in the SI system.

electronystagmography (ENG) (e-lek'tro-ni-stag-mog'ră-fi) [electro- + nystagmus + G. *graphō,* to write]. A method of nystagmography based on electro-oculography; skin electrodes are placed at outer canthi to register horizontal nystagmus or above and below each eye for vertical nystagmus.

electro-oculography (EOG) (e-lek-tro-ok'u-log'ră-fi). Oculography using electrodes placed on the skin adjacent to the lateral canthi to measure a standing potential difference between the front and the back of the eyeball.

electropherogram (e-lek-tro-fer'o-gram). Electrophoretogram; the densitometric or colorimetric pattern obtained from filter paper strips on which substances have been separated by electrophoresis; may also refer to the strips themselves.

electrophil, electrophile (e-lek'tro-fil, -fil) [electro- + G. *philos,* fond]. **1.** The electron-attracting atom or agent in an organic reaction. **2.** Electrophilic; relating to an electrophil.

electrophilic (e-lek-tro-fil'ik). Electrophil (2).

electrophoresis (e-lek'tro-fo-re'sis [electro- + G. *phorēsis*, a carrying]. Ionophoresis; phoresis (1); the movement of particles in an electric field toward one or other electric pole, anode, or cathode.

elec'trophoret'ic. Ionophoretic; relating to electrophoresis.

elec'trophoret'ogram. Electropherogram.

electroretinogram (ERG) (e-lek'tro-ret'ĭ-no-gram) [electro- + retina + G. *gramma*, something written]. A record of the retinal action currents produced in the retina by an adequate light stimulus.

electroretinography (e-lek'tro-ret-ĭ-nog'ră-fĭ). The recording and study of the retinal action currents.

electroscission (e-lek'tro-sĭ-shun) [electro- + L. *scissio*, to cleave]. Division of tissues by an electrocautery knife.

elec'troshock. See electroshock *therapy.*

electrosur'gery. Division of tissues by high frequency current applied locally with an instrument or needle.

electrotax'is [electro- + G. *taxis*, orderly arrangement]. Electrotropism; reaction of plant or animal protoplasm to either an anode (negative e.) or a cathode (positive e.).

electrotherapeutics, electrotherapy (e-lek'tro-thĕr-ă-pu'tiks, e-lek'tro-thĕr-ă-pĭ). Use of electricity in the treatment of disease.

electroton'ic. Relating to electrotonus.

electrotonus (e-lek-trot'o-nus, -tro-to'nus) [electro- + G. *tonos*, tension]. Changes in excitability and conductivity in a nerve or muscle cell caused by the passage of a constant electric current.

electrotropism (e-lek-trot'ro-pizm, e-lek'tro-tro'pizm) [electro- + G. *tropē*, a turning]. Electrotaxis.

electuary (e-lek'chu-a-rĭ) [G. *eleikton*, a medicine that melts in the mouth, fr. *eleichō*, to lick up]. Confection.

eledoisin (el-ĕ-doy'sin). An undecapeptide formed in the venom gland of cephalopods of the genus *Eledone;* a cephalotoxin that causes vasodilation and contraction of extravascular smooth muscle.

eleidin (e-le'ĭ-din). A refractile substance related to keratin present in the stratum lucidum of the epidermis.

el'ement [L. *elementum*, a rudiment, beginning]. 1. A substance composed of atoms of only one kind, *i.e.*, of identical atomic number, that therefore cannot be decomposed into two or more substances, and that can lose its chemical property only by union with some other e. 2. An indivisible structure or entity.

    extrachromosomal e., plasmid; a genetic e. that can stably function and replicate while physically separate from the chromosome of the host cell (chiefly bacterial) and that is not essential to the cell's basic functioning.

    insertion sequence e., discrete DNA sequences that are repeated at various sites on a bacterial chromosome, certain plasmids, and bacteriophages, and which can move from one to another site on the chromosome, or to another plasmid in the same bacterium, or to a bacteriophage.

    rare-earth e.'s, see rare *earths.*

    trace e.'s., e.'s present in minute amounts in the body; many are essential in metabolism or for the manufacture of essential compounds.

eleo- [G. *elaion*, oil]. Combining form relating to oil. See also oleo-.

eleoma (el-e-o'mah) [G. *elaion*, oil, + *-oma*, tumor]. Lipogranuloma.

elephantiac (el-ĕ-fan'tĭ-ak). Relating to elephantiasis.

elephantiasis (el-ĕ-fan-ti'ă-sis) [G. fr. *elephas*, elephant]. Hypertrophy and fibrosis of the skin and subcutaneous and lymphoid tissue due to long-standing obstructed circulation in the blood or lymphatic vessels, chiefly by the presence of the filarial worms *Wuchereria bancrofti* or *Brugia malayi.*

    e. neuromato'sa, enlargement of a limb due to diffuse neurofibromatosis of the skin and subcutaneous tissue.

    nevoid e., thickening of skin, usually unilateral, involving a small area or the entire extremity, due to congenital enlargement of lymph vessels and lymph vessel obstruction.

    e. nos'tras, a solid persisting edema of the eyelids and face that follows recurrent erysipelas or sometimes results from injury.

    e. scro'ti, chyloderma; brawny swelling of the scrotum as a result of chronic lymphatic obstruction.

el'evator [L. fr. *e-levo*, pp. *-atus*, to lift up]. 1. An instrument for prying up a sunken part, as the depressed fragment of bone in fracture of the skull, or for elevating tissues. 2. An instrument used to luxate and remove teeth and roots that cannot be engaged by the beaks of a forceps, or to loosen teeth and roots prior to forceps application.

elimina'tion [L. *elimino*, pp. *-atus*, to turn out of doors]. Expulsion; removal of waste material from the body.

ELISA Enzyme-linked immunosorbent *assay.*

elixir (e-lik'ser) [Med. L. fr. Ar. *al-iksir*, the philosopher's stone]. A clear, sweetened, hydroalcoholic liquid intended for oral use; used either as vehicles or for the therapeutic effect of the active medicinal agents.

elliptocyte (ĕ-lip'to-sīt) [G. *elleipsis*, a leaving out, an ellipse, + *kytos*, cell]. Ovalocyte; an elliptical red blood corpuscle found normally in lower vertebrates and in camels.

elliptocytosis (e-lip'to-si-to'sis). Ovalocytosis; a relatively rare hereditary abnormality of hemopoiesis in which 50 to 90% of the red blood cells consist of rod forms and elliptocytes, frequently with an associated hemolytic anemia.

eluant (el'u-ant). Eluent.

el'uate [see elution]. The material washed out of paper or out of a column of adsorbent in chromatography.

el'uent [see elution]. Eluant; a liquid used in the process of elution.

elution (e-lu'shun) [L. *e-luo*, pp. *lutus*, to wash out].
1. Separation, by washing, of one solid from another. **2.** Removal, by means of a suitable solvent, of one material from another that is insoluble in that solvent.

elytro- [G. *elytron*, sheath (vagina)]. Obsolete combining form denoting the vagina. See also colpo-; vagino-.

em-. See en-.

emaciation (e-ma-sĭ-a'shun) [L. *e-macio*, pp. *-atus*, to make thin]. Wasting; becoming abnormally thin from extreme loss of flesh.

emanation (em-ă-na'shun) [L. *-e-mano*, pp. *-atus*, to flow out]. Any substance that flows out or is emitted from a source or origin.

emasculation (e-mas-ku-la'shun) [L. *emasculo*, pp. *-atus*, to castrate]. Castration of the male by removal of the testis and/or penis.

embalm (em-balm') [L. *in*, in, + *balsamum*, balsam]. To treat a dead body with balsams or antiseptics to preserve it from decay.

embole (em'bo-lĭ) [G. *embolē*, insertion]. Emboly; formation of the gastrula by invagination.

embolectomy (em-bo-lek'to-mĭ) [G. *embolos*, a plug (embolus), + *ektomē*, excision]. Removal of an embolus.

em'boli. Plural of embolus.

embol'ic. Relating to an embolus or to embolism.

embolism (em'bo-lizm) [G. *embolisma*, a piece or patch]. Obstruction or occlusion of a vessel by a transported clot or vegetation, a mass of bacteria, or other foreign material (embolus).

  air e., presence of bubbles of air in the vascular system, which may obstruct blood flow; due to entry of air into the venous circulation following trauma or operations.

  cholesterol e., atheroembolism; e. of lipid debris from an ulcerated atheromatous deposit, generally from a large artery to small arterial branches.

  fat e., occurrence of fat globules in the circulation following fractures of a long bone, in burns, in parturition, and in association with fatty degeneration of the liver.

  infective e., pyemic e.

  miliary e., e. occurring simultaneously in a number of capillaries.

  paradoxical e., plugging of a systemic artery by an embolus derived from the venous system which, when it reaches the right side of the heart, is diverted through a septal defect or patent foramen ovale to the arterial side, thus bypassing the pulmonary circulation.

  pulmonary e., e. of pulmonary arteries, most frequently by detached fragments of thrombus from a leg or pelvic vein.

  pyemic e., infective e.; plugging of an artery by an embolus detached from a suppurating thrombus.

  retrograde e., plugging of a vein by a mass carried in a direction opposite to that of the normal blood current.

emboliza'tion. Therapeutic introduction of various substances into the circulation to occlude vessels, either to arrest or prevent hemorrhaging or to defunctionalize a structure or organ.

embolola'lia [G. *embolos*, something thrown in + *lalia*, speaking]. Embolophrasia; interjection of meaningless words in the sentence when speaking.

embolophrasia (em'bo-lo-fra'zĭ-ah) [G. *embolos*, something thrown in, + *phrasis*, phase]. Embololalia.

embolus, pl. **emboli** (em'bo-lus, -lĭ) [G. *embolos*, a plug, wedge or stopper]. A plug, composed of a detached clot or vegetation, mass of bacteria, or other foreign body, occluding a blood vessel (embolism).

  catheter e., coiled worm-shaped platelet and fibrin aggregates produced during vascular catheterization, originating on the catheter or its guide wire.

  saddle e., a large e. that straddles the bifurcation of an artery and so occludes both branches.

em'boly. Embole.

embrasure (em-bra'zhūr) [Fr. an opening in a wall for cannon]. In dentistry, that space adjacent to the interproximal contact area that spreads toward the facial, gingival, lingual, occlusal, or incisal aspect.

embryectomy (em-brĭ-ek'to-mĭ) [embryo- + G. *ektomē*, excision]. Operative removal of the product of conception, especially in ectopic pregnancy.

embryo-, embry- [G. *embryon*, embryo]. Combining forms relating to the embryo.

embryo (em'brĭ-o) [G. *embryon*]. **1.** An organism in the early stages of development. **2.** In man, the developing organism from conception until approximately the end of the second month; developmental stages from this time to birth are commonly designated as fetal. **3.** A primordial plant within a seed.

em'bryocar'dia [embryo- + G. *kardia*, heart]. A condition in which the cadence of the heart sounds resembles that of the fetus, the first and second sounds becoming alike and evenly spaced; a sign of serious myodardial disease.

embryoctony (em-brĭ-ok'to-nĭ) [embryo- + G. *kteinō*, to destroy]. Feticide.

embryogenesis (em'brĭ-o-jen'ĕ-sis) [embryo- + G. *genesis*, production]. That phase of prenatal development involved in the establishing of the characteristic configuration of the embryonic body, usually regarded as extending from the end of the 2nd week, when the embryonic disk is formed, to the end of the 8th week, after which the conceptus is usually spoken of as a fetus.

embryogen'ic, embryogenet'ic. Producing an embryo; relating to the formation of an embryo.

embryogeny (em-brĭ-oj'ĕ-nĭ). The origin and growth of the embryo.

embryol'ogist. One who specializes in embryology.

embryology (em-brĭ-ol'o-jĭ) [embryo- + G. *logos*, study]. The science of the origin and development of the organism from the fertilization of the ovum to the period of extrauterine or extraovular life.

embryo'ma. Embryonal *tumor*.

e. of the kidney, Wilms' *tumor*.

embryonal, embryonic (em'brĭ-o-nal, em-brĭ-on'ik). Of, pertaining to, or in the condition of an embryo.

embryonization (em'brĭ-on-ĭ-za'shun). Reversion of a cell or a tissue to an embryonic form.

embryonoid (em'brĭ-o-noyd) [embryo- + G. *eidos*, appearance]. Resembling an embryo or a fetus.

embryony (em'brĭ-o-nĭ). The condition of being an embryo.

embryopathy (em-brĭ-op'ă-thĭ) [embryo- + G. *pathos*, disease]. Fetopathy (1); a morbid condition in the embryo or fetus.

embryoplas'tic [embryo- + G. *plassō*, to form]. **1.** Producing an embryo. **2.** Relating to the formation of an embryo.

embryotomy (em-brĭ-ot'o-mĭ) [embryo- + G. *tomē*, cutting]. Any operation on the fetus to make possible its removal when delivery is impossible by natural means.

embryotoxon (em'brĭ-o-tok'son) [embryo- + G. *toxon*, bow]. A congenital opacity of the periphery of the cornea.

anterior e., *arcus* cornealis.

posterior e., a developmental atavistic trait marked by a prominent white ring of Schwalbe and iris strands that partially obscure the chamber angle.

embryotroph (em'brĭ-o-trŏf) [embryo- + G. *trophē*, nourishment]. The nutritive material supplied to the embryo during development.

embryotrophic (em'brĭ-o-trof'ik). Relating to any process or agency directed to the nourishment of the embryo.

embryotrophy (em-brĭ-ot'ro-fĭ) [embryo- + G. *trophē*, nourishment]. The nutrition of the embryo.

emed'ullate [L. *e-*, from, + *medulla*, marrow]. To extract any marrow or pith.

em'esis [G. fr. *emeō*, to vomit]. Vomiting. Also used as a combining form in suffix position.

emet'ic [G. *emetikos*, producing vomiting]. Vomitive; vomitory; relating to or causing vomiting.

emetocathartic (em'ĕ-to-kă-thar'tik). Both emetic and cathartic, causing vomiting and purging.

EMF Electromotive *force*.

EMG Electromyogram.

-emia [G. *haima*, blood]. Suffix meaning blood.

emiction (e-mik'shun). Urination.

emigra'tion [L. *e-migro*, pp. *-atus*, to emigrate]. Passage of white blood cells through the endothelium and wall of small blood vessels.

eminence (em'ĭ-nens) [L. *eminentia*, prominence]. A circumscribed prominence or elevation.

e'miocyto'sis [L. *emitto*, to send forth, + G. *kytos*, cell, + *-osis*, condition]. Exocytosis (2).

em'issary. 1. Relating to, or providing, an outlet or drain. **2.** *Vena* emissaria.

emission (e-mish'un) [L. *emissio;* fr. *e-mitto*, to send out]. A discharge; referring usually to a seminal discharge occuring during sleep (nocturnal e.).

emmenagogic (ĕ-men'ă-goj'ik). Relating to or acting as an emmenagogue.

emmenagogue (ĕ-men'ă-gog) [G. *emmēnos*, monthly, + *agōgos*, leading]. Hemagogue (2); an agent that induces or increases menstrual flow.

emmenia (ĕ-men'ĭ-ah) [G. *emmēnos*, monthly]. Menses.

emmenic (ĕ-men'ik). Menstrual.

emmeniopathy (ĕ-men'ĭ-op'ă-thĭ) [G. *emmēnos*, monthly, + *pathos*, suffering]. A disorder of menstruation.

emmetro'pia [G. *emmetros*, according to measure, + *ōps*, eye]. The state of refraction of the eye in which parallel rays, when the eye is at rest, are focused exactly on the retina.

emmetrop'ic. Pertaining to or characterized by emmetropia.

Emmon'sia. A genus of fungi with complex growth cycles. Two species, *E. crescens* and *E. parva*, cause adiaspiromycosis.

emollient (e-mol'yent) [L. *emolliens*, pres. p. of *e-mollio*, to soften]. Soothing to skin or mucous membrane.

emotion (e-mo'shun) [L. *e-moveo*, pp. *-motus*, to move out, agitate]. A strong feeling, aroused mental state, or intense state of drive or unrest directed toward a definite object and evidenced in both behavior and in psychologic changes.

emotional (e-mo'shun-al). Relating to any of the emotions.

empath'ic. Relating to or marked by empathy.

em'pathize. To feel empathy in relation to another person; to put oneself in another's place.

empathy (em'pă-thĭ) [G. *en(em)*, in, + *pathos*, feeling]. **1.** The intellectual and occasionally emotional identification with another person's mental and emotional states, as distinguished from sympathy. **2.** The anthropomorphization or humanizing of objects and feeling oneself as in and part of them.

emperipolesis (em-pĕr'ĭ-po-le'sis) [G. *en(em)*, inside, + *peri*, around, + *poleomai*, to wander about]. Active penetration by one cell into and through larger cell.

emphysema (em-fĭ-se'mah) [G. inflation of stomach]. **1.** The presence of air in the interstices of the connective tissue of a part. **2.** Pulmonary e.; a condition of the lung characterized by increase beyond the normal in the size of air spaces distal to the terminal bronchiole (those parts containing alveoli), with destructive changes in their walls and reduction in their number. Two structural varieties are described: panlobular e. and centrilobular e.

centrilobular e., centri-acinar e., e. affecting the lobules around their central bronchioles, causally related to bronchiolitis.

interlobular e., interstitial e. in the connective tissue septa between the pulmonary lobules.

interstitial e., (1) presence of air in the pulmonary tissues consequent upon rupture of the air cells; **(2)** presence of air or gas in the connective tissue.

intestinal e., *pneumatosis* cystoides intestinalis.

mediastinal e., deflection of air, usually from a ruptured emphysematous bleb in the lung, into the mediastinal tissue.

panlobular e., panacinar e., e. effecting all parts of the lobules, in part, or usually the whole, of the lungs.

pulmonary e., emphysema (2).

subcutaneous e., aerodermectasia; pneumoderma; the presence of air or gas in the subcutaneous tissues.

surgical e., subcutaneous e. from air trapped in the tissues by an operation or injury.

emphysematous (em'fĭ-sem'ă-tus). Relating to or affected with emphysema.

empiric, empirical (em-pīr'ik, -ĭ-kăl) [G. *empeirikos;* fr. *empeiria,* experience]. Founded on practical experience but not proved scientifically, in contrast to rational.

emprosthotonos (em-pros-thot'o-nus) [G. *emprosthen,* forward, + *tonos,* tension]. A tetanic contraction of the flexor muscles, curving the back with concavity forward.

empyema (em-pi-e'mah, -pī) [G. *empyēma,* suppuration]. Pus in a body cavity; when used without qualification, refers to pyothorax.

extradural e., epidural *abscess.*

subdural e., subdural *abscess.*

empyemic (em-pi-e'mik). Relating to empyema.

empyesis (em-pi-e'sis) [G. suppuration]. A pustular eruption.

emulgent (e-mul'jent) [L. *e-mulgeo,* pp. *-mulsus,* to milk or drain out]. Denoting a straining, extracing, or purifying process.

emul'sifier. An agent used to make an emulsion of a fixed oil.

emulsion (e-mul'shun) [Mod. L. fr. *e-mulgeo,* pp. *-mulsus,* to milk or drain out]. A system containing two immiscible liquids in which one is dispersed, in the form of very small globules, throughout the other. That in the form of globules is called the internal phase; the second liquid is called the external phase.

emulsoid (e-mul'soyd). A colloidal dispersion in which the dispersed particles are more or less liquid and exert a certain attraction on and absorb a certain quantity of the fluid in which they are suspended.

en-. Prefix fr. G. preposition meaning in; appears as em- before b, p, and m.

enam'el. The hard, glistening substance covering the exposed portion of the tooth. It is composed of an inorganic portion (about 96%) made up of hydroxyapatite with small amounts of carbonate, magnesium, fluoride, and an organic matrix of

glycoprotein and a keratin-like protein.

mottled e., alterations in e. formation due to excessive fluoride ingestion during tooth formation; varies in appearance from small white opacities to yellow and black spotting.

enam'elogen'esis. Amelogenesis.

enam'elo'ma. A developmental anomaly in which there is a small nodule of enamel below the cementoenamel junction, usually at the bifurcation of molar teeth.

enanthem, enanthema (en-an'them, en-an-the'mah) [G. *en,* in, + *anthēma,* bloom, eruption]. A mucous membrane eruption, especially one occurring in connection with one of the exanthemas.

en'anthem'atous. Relating to an enanthem.

enanthesis (en-an-the'sis) [G. *en,* in, + *anthēsis,* full bloom]. The skin eruption of a general disease, such as scarlatina or typhoid fever.

enarthro'dial. Relating to an enarthrosis.

enarthro'sis [G. *en-arthrōsis,* a jointing where the ball is deep set in the socket]. *Articulatio*spheroidea.

encapsulation (en'kap-su-la'shun) [L. *in* + capsula, dim of *capsa,* box]. Enclosure in a capsule or sheath.

encatarrhaphy (en-kat-ar'ră-fī) [G. *enkatarrhaptō,* to sew in]. Enkatarrhaphy; the artifical implantation of an organ or tissue in a part where it does not naturally occur.

encepahlosclerosis (en-sef'ă-lo-skle-ro'sis) [encephalo- + G. *sklērōsis,* hardening]. A sclerosis, or hardening, of the brain.

encephal-. See encephalo-.

encephalalgia (en-sef-ă-lal'jĭ-ah) [encephalo- + G. *algos,* pain]. Headache.

encephalatroph'ic. Relating to encephalatrophy.

encephalatrophy (en-sef-ă-lat'ro-fī) [encephalo- + G. *a-* priv. + *trophē,* nourishment]. Atrophy of the brain.

encéphale isolé (ahn-sef-al'ē-so-la') [Fr. isolated brain]. An animal with its caudal medulla transected and its respiration maintained artificially. The animal remains alert, has sleep-wake cycles, normal pupillary reactions, and a normal electroencephalogram. *Cf.* cerveau isolé.

encephalic (en-sĕ-fal'ik). Relating to the brain, or to the structures within the cranium.

encephalit'ic. Relating to encephalitis.

encephalitis, pl. **encephalitides** (en-sef-ă-li'tis, -lit'ĭ-dēz) [G. *enkephalos,* brain, + *-itis,* inflammation]. Cephalitis; inflammation of the brain.

acute necrotizing e., an acute form of e., usually caused by herpes simplex virus and affecting largely the temporal lobes and limbic system.

bunyavirus e., e. of abrupt onset, with severe frontal headache and low-grade to moderate fever, caused by virus of the genus *Bunyavirus.*

Coxsackie e., an inflammation of the brain, seen mainly in infants and involving principally the gray matter of the medulla and cord, caused by Coxsackie (B) virus.

herpes e., e. caused by the herpes simplex virus.

inclusion body e., subacute sclerosing leukoencephalitis or panencephalitis; a usually fatal disease that seems to result from persistent measles virus infection and causes varying types of inflammatory reaction in both the white and gray matter; characterized by the presence of Cowdry type A nuclear inclusion bodies.

Japanese B e., an epidemic e. or encephalomyelitis of Japan, Russia (Siberia), and other parts of Asia; due to the Japanese B e. virus of the genus *Flavivirus* (Togaviridae).

lead e., lead *encephalopathy.*

e. lethar'gica, von Economo's *disease.*

Murray Valley e., Australian X disease; a severe e. with a high mortality rate reported as occurring in the Murray Valley of Australia; most severe in children and is ushered in by headache, fever, malaise, drowsiness or convulsions, and rigidity of the neck; extensive brain damage may result; caused by the Murray Valley encephalitis virus, a species of *Flavivirus.*

e. periaxia'lis diffu'sa, Schilder's disease; an affection occurring chiefly in children, marked by progressive dementia, convulsions, failure of hearing, and spastic paralysis followed by rapidly increasing speech defect, gradual loss of sight, and death; the white matter of the brain is confluently demyelinated and degenerated, but the cortex and meninges are not involved.

postvaccinal e., demyelinating e. following vaccination.

secondary e., e. following vaccination for smallpox or during convalescence from measles, mumps, varicella, and certain other infectious diseases, usually of the demyelinating kind.

tick-borne e. (Central European subtype), tick-borne meningoencephalitis caused by a flavivirus closely related to the virus causing the Far Eastern type; transmitted by *Ixodes ricinus,* also by infected raw milk.

tick-borne e. (Eastern subtype), a severe form of e. caused by a flavivirus (Togaviridae) and transmitted by *Ixodes pertulcatus* and *I. ricinus*).

varicella e., e. occurring as a complication of chickenpox.

encephalo-, encephal- [G. *enkephalos,* brain]. Combining forms indicating the brain or some relationship thereto.

encephalocele (en-sef'ă-lo-sēl) [encephalo- + G. *kēlē,* hernia]. Cephalocele; craniocele; bifid cranium; a congenital gap in the skull, usually with herniation of brain substance.

enceph'alogram [encephalo- + G. *gramma,* a drawing]. The record obtained by encephalography.

encephalography (en-sef-ă-log'ră-fī) [encephalo- + G. *graphō,* to write]. Radiographic imaging of the brain.

encephaloid (en-sef'ă-loyd) [encephalo- + G. *eidos,* resemblance]. Resembling brain subtance; denoting a carcinoma of brainlike consistence, with reference to gross features.

encephalolith (en-sef'ă-lo-lith) [encephalo- + G. *lithos,* stone]. Cerebral calculus; a concretion in the brain or one of its ventricles.

encephalo'ma. Cerebroma; herniation of brain substance.

encephalomalacia (en-sef'ă-lo-mă-la'shĭ-ah) [encephalo- + G. *malakia,* softness]. Cerebromalacia; infarction of brain tissue, usually caused by vascular insufficiency.

encephalomenengitis (en-sef'ă-lo-men-in-ji'tis) [encephalo- + G. *mēninx,* membrane, + *-itis,* inflammation]. Meningoencephalitis.

encephalomeningocele (en-sef'ă-lo-mĕ-nin'go-sēl) [encephalo- + G. *mēninx,* membrane, + *kēlē,* hernia]. Meningoencephalocele.

encephalomeningopathy (en-sef'ă-lo-men-in-gop'ă-thī). Meningoencephalopathy.

encephalomere (en-sef'ă-lo-mēr) [encephalo- + G. *meros,* a part]. A neuromere.

encephalom'eter [encephalo- + G. *metron,* measure]. An apparatus for indicating on the skull the location of the cortical centers.

encephalomyelitis (en-sef'ă-lo-mi'ĕ-li'tis) [encephalo- + G. *myelon,* marrow, + *-itis,* inflammation]. An acute inflammation of the brain and spinal cord.

acute disseminated e., a diffuse inflammation of the brain and spinal cord usually caused by a perivascular hypersensitivity response.

benign myalgic e., epidemic *neuromyasthenia.*

granulomatous e., a disease causing necrosis and granulomas in the substance of the brain.

encephalomyelocele (en-sef'ă-lo-mi'ĕ-lo-sēl) [G. *enkephalos,* brain, + *myelon,* marrow, + *kēlē,* hernia]. A congenital defect in the occipital region with herniation of the meninges, medulla, and spinal cord.

encephalomyeloneuropathy (en-sef'ă-lo-mi'ĕ-lo-nu-rop'ă-thī). A disease involving the brain, spinal cord and peripheral nerves.

enceph'alomy'eloradiculi'tis. Inflammation involving the brain, spinal cord, and peripheral nerves.

enceph'alomy'eloradiculop'athy. A disease process involving the brain, spinal cord, and spinal roots.

enceph'alomyelop'athy [G. *enkephalos,* brain, + *myelon,* marrow, + *pathos,* suffering]. Any disease of both brain and spinal cord.

encephalomyocarditis (en-sef'ă-lo-mi'o-kar-di'tis). Associated encephalitis and myocarditis.

encephalon, pl. **encephala** (en-sef'ă-lon, -ă-lah) [G. *enkephalos,* brain, fr. *en,* in, + *kephalē,* head] [NA]. Brain; that portion of the cerebrospinal axis contained within the cranium, comprised of the prosencephalon, mesencephalon, and rhombencephalon.

encephalopathy (en-sef'ă-lop'ă-thĭ) [encephalo- + G. *pathos,* suffering]. Cephalopathy; cerebropathy; any disease of the brain.

  bilirubin e., e. due to the toxic effects of bilirubin, as in kernicterus.

  Binswanger's e., Binswanger's *disease.*

  hepatic e., portal-systemic e.

  hypernatremic e., subarachnoid and subdural effusions in infants with hypernatremic dehydration.

  lead e., lead encephalitis; a rapidly developing e. caused by the ingestion of lead compounds and seen particularly in early childhood; clinical manisfestations are convulsions, delirium, hallucinations, and other cerebral symptoms due to chronic lead poisoning.

  portal-sytemic e., hepatic e.; an e. associated with cirrhosis of the liver, attributed to the passage of toxic nitrogenous substances from the portal to the systemic circulation.

  traumatic e., disturbance of structure of cerebral nerve cells, glia, or intracranial vessels resulting from injury.

  "viral" spongiform e., progressive vacuolation in dendritic and axonal processes and neuronal cell bodies, associated with slow virus infections.

  Wernicke-Korsakoff e., see Wernicke's *syndrome;* Korsakoff's *syndrome.*

  Wernicke's e., Wernicke's *syndrome.*

encephalopuncture (en-sef'ă-lo-punk'chŭr). Surgical puncture of the brain substance.

encephalopyosis (en-sef'ă-lo-pi-o'sis) [encephalo- + G. *pyōsis,* suppuration]. Purulent inflammation of the brain.

encephalorrhagia (en-sef'ă-lo-ra'jĭ-ah) [encephalo- + G. *rhēgnymi,* to burst forth]. Cerebral *hemorrhage.*

encephaloschisis (en-sef-ă-los'kĭ-sis) [encephalo- + G. *schisis,* fissure]. Developmental failure of closure of the rostral part of the neural tube.

encephalosis (en-sef-ă-lo'sis). Cerebrosis; any organic disease of the brain.

encephalotomy (en-sef-ă-lot'o-mĭ) [encephalo- + G. *tomē,* incision]. Dissection or incision of the brain.

enchondroma (en-kon-dro'mah) [Mod. L. fr. G. *en,* in, + *chondros,* cartilage, + *-oma,* tumor]. A benign cartilaginous growth starting within the medullary cavity of a bone originally formed from cartilage.

enchondromato'sis. Asymmetrical chondrodystrophy; dyschondroplasia; Ollier's disease; nonfamilial hamartomatous proliferation of cartilage in the metaphyses of several bones, most commonly of the hands and feet, causing distorted growth in length or pathological fractures.

enchondromatous (en-kon-dro'mă-tus). Relating to or having the elements of enchondroma.

enchondrosarcoma (en-kon-dro-sar-ko'mah). A malignant neoplasm of cartilage cells derived from an enchondroma, or occurring in the same locations.

enclave (en-klāv) [Fr. fr. L. *clavis,* key]. An enclosure; a detached mass of tissue enclosed in tissue of another kind.

enclit'ic [G. *enkilitikos,* leaning on]. Inclined; denoting especially the relation of the planes of the fetal head to those of the pelvis of the mother.

enco'ding. The first of three stages in the memory process, involving processes associated with receiving or briefly registering stimuli through one or more of the senses and modifying that information. A decay process or loss of this information (a type of forgetting) occurs rapidly unless the next stages, storage and retrieval, are activated.

encopre'sis [G. *enkopros,* full of manure]. Involuntary passage of feces.

encys'ted [G. *kystis,* bladder]. Encapsulated by a membranous bag.

end-. See endo-.

endangiitis (end'an-jĭ-i'tis) [endo- + G. *angeion,* vessel, + *-itis,* inflammation]. Endoangiitis; endovasculitis; inflammation of the intima of a blood vessel.

endaortitis (end'a-or-ti'tis). Inflammation of the intima of the aorta.

endarterectomy (end'ar-ter-ek'to-mĭ) [endo- + arterý + G. *ektomē,* excision]. Excision of diseased endothelial lining of an artery and occluding atheromatous deposits, so as to leave a smooth lining.

endarteritis (end'ar-ter-i'tis) [endo- + arteritis]. Endoarteritis; inflammation of the intima of an artery.

  bacterial e., implantation and growth of bacteria with formation of vegetations on the arterial wall, such as may occur in a patent ductus arteriosus or arteriovenous fistula.

  e. oblit'erans, obliterating e., arteritis obliterans; obliterating arteritis; an extreme degree of e. proliferans closing the lumen of the artery.

  e. prolif'erans, chronic e. accompanied by a marked increase of fibrous tissue in the intima.

endaural (end-aw'ral) [endo- + L. *auris,* ear]. Within the ear.

end'brain. Telencephalon.

endem'ic [G. *endēmos,* native, fr. *en,* in, + *dēmos,* the people]. **1.** Present in a community or among a group of people; said of a disease prevailing continually in a region. **2.** Enzootic.

endemoepidemic (en-dem'o-ep-ĭ-dem'ik). Denoting a temporary large increase in the number of cases of an endemic disease.

endergonic (en-der-gon'ik) [endo- + G. *ergon,* work]. Referring to a chemical reaction that takes place with absorption of energy from its surroundings (*i.e.,* becomes cool).

end-feet. axon *terminals.*

endo-, end- [G. *endon,* within]. Prefix indicating within, inner, absorbing, containing. See also ento-.

endoaneurysmoplasty (en'do-an-u-riz'mo-plas-tĭ). Aneurysmoplasty.

endoaneurysmorrhaphy   (en'do-an-u-riz-mor'ă-fĭ) [endo- + G. *aneurysma*, aneurysm, + *raphe*, suture]. Aneurysmoplasty.

endoangiitis (en-do-an-jĭ-i'tis). Endangiitis.

endoappendicitis (en'do-ă-pen-dĭ-si'tis). Simple catarrhal inflammation, limited to the mucosal surface of the vermiform appendix.

endoarteritis (en'do-ar-ter-i'tis). Endarteritis.

en'doblast [endo- + G. *blastos*, germ]. Entoblast; a potential endoderm.

en'docardit'ic. Relating to endocarditis.

endocarditis (en'do-kar-di'tis). Inflammation of the endocardium.

    atypical verrucous e., Libman-Sacks e.

    bacterial e., e. caused by the direct invasion of bacteria and leading to deformity of the valve leaflets; **acute b. e.** is caused by pyogenic organisms such as hemolytic streptococci or staphylococci; **subacute b. e.** is usually due to *Streptococcus viridans* or *S. fecalis.*

    infectious e., infective e., e. due to infection by microorganisms.

    Libman-Sacks e., atypical verrucous or nonbacterial verrucous e.; Libman-Sacks s.; verrucous e. sometimes associated with disseminated lupus erythematosus.

    Löffler's e., Löffler's fibroplastic e., fibroplastic parietal e. with eosinophilia, an e. of obscure cause characterized by progressive congestive heart failure, multiple systemic emboli, and eosinophilia.

    mural e., inflammation of the endocardium other than valvular.

    nonbacterial verrucous e., Libman-Sacks e.

    rheumatic e., e. as part of the acute rheumatic process, recognized clinically by valvular involvement.

    valvular e., inflammation confined to the endocardium of the valves.

    vegetative e., verrucous e., e. associated with the presence of fibrinous clots (vegetations) forming on the ulcerated surfaces of the valves.

endocar'dium, pl. **endocar'dia** [endo- + G. *kardia*, heart]. [NA]. The innermost tunic of the heart, which includes endothelium and subendothelial connective tissue.

endocervical (en'do-ser'vĭ-kal). **1.** Intracervical; within any cervix, specifically within the cervix uteri. **2.** Relating to the endocervix.

endocervicitis (en'do-ser-vĭ-si'tis). Endotrachelitis; inflammation of the mucous membrane of the cervix uteri.

endocervix (en'do-ser'viks). The mucous membrane of the cervical canal.

endocolitis (en'do-ko-li'tis). Simple inflammation of the colon.

endocra'nial. 1. Within the cranium. **2.** Relating to the endocranium.

endocranium (en'do-kra'nĭ-um). The lining membrane of the cranium, or dura mater of the brain.

endocrine (en'do-krin) [endo- + G. *krinō*, to separate]. Secreting internally, most commonly into the systemic circulation; of or pertaining to such secretion or to a gland that furnishes such a secretion.

en'docrinol'ogist. One specializing in endocrinology.

endocrinology (en'do-krĭ-nol'o-jĭ) [endocrine + G. *logos*, study]. The science concerned with internal secretions and their physiologic and pathologic relations.

endocrinoma (en'do-krĭ-no'mah). A tumor with endocrine tissue that retains the function of the parent organ, usually to an excessive degree.

endocrinopathic (en'do-krin-o-path'ik). Relating to endocrinopathy.

endocrinopathy (en'do-krĭ-nop'ă-thĭ). A disorder in the function of an endocrine gland and the consequences thereof.

endocystitis (en'do-sis-ti'tis) [endo- + G. *kystis*, bladder, + *-itis*, inflammation]. Inflammation of the mucous membrane of the bladder.

endocytosis (en'do-si-to'sis) [endo- + *kytos*, cell, + *-osis*, condition]. The process, including pinocytosis and phagocytosis, whereby materials are taken into a cell by the invagination of the plasma membrane, which it breaks off as a boundary membrane of the part engulfed.

en'doderm [endo- + G. *derma*, skin]. Entoderm; hypoblast; the innermost of the three primary germ layers of the embryo, giving rise to the epithelial lining of the primitive gut tract, its glands, and the epithelial component of structures arising as outgrowths from the gut.

endodontia (en-do-don'shĭ-ah). Endodontics.

endodon'tics [endo- + G. *odous*, tooth]. Endodontia; endodontology; a field of dentistry concerned with the prevention, diagnosis, and treatment of diseases and traumatic injuries in the dental pulp and periapical tissues.

endodon'tist. One who specializes in endodontics.

endodontol'ogy. Endodontics.

en'doenteri'tis [endo- + G. *enteron*, intestine, + *-itis*, inflammation]. Inflammation of the intestinal mucous membrane.

endogamy (en-dog'ă-mĭ) [endo- + G. *gamos*, marriage]. Reproduction by conjugation between sister cells, the descendants of one original cell.

endogenous (en-doj'ĕ-nus) [endo- + G. *-gen*, production]. Originating or produced within the organism or one of its parts.

en'dointoxica'tion. Poisoning by an endogenous toxin.

endolymph (en'do-limf) [endo- + L. *lympha*, a clear fluid]. The fluid contained within the membranous labyrinth of the inner ear.

endolym'phic. Relating to endolymph.

endometria (en-do-me'trĭ-ah). Plural of endometrium.

endometrial (en-do-me'trĭ-al). Relating to or composed of endometrium.

endometrioma (en'do-me-trĭ-o'mah). A circumscribed mass of ectopic endometrial tissue in endometriosis.

endometriosis (en'do-me-trĭ-o'sis). Ectopic occurrence of endometrial tissue, frequently forming cysts containing altered blood.

endometritis (en'do-me-tri'tis). Inflammation of the endometrium.

endometrium, pl. **endometria** (en'do-me'trĭ-um, -trĭ-ah) [endo- + G. + *mētra,* uterus]. [NA]. The mucous membrane comprising the inner layer of the uterine wall.

endomitosis (en'do-mi-to'sis). Endopolyploidy.

endomorph (en'do-morf) [endo- + G. *morphē,* form]. A constitutional body type or build in which tissues that orginated in the endoderm prevail; from a morphological standpoint, the trunk predominates over the limbs.

endomorphic (en'do-mor'fik). Relating to, or having the characteristics of, an endomorph.

endomyocardial (en'do-mi'o-kar'dĭ-al). Relating to the endocardium and the myocardium.

en'domy'ocardi'tis. Inflammation of both endocardium and myocardium.

endomysium (en'do-miz'ĭ-um, -mis'ĭ-um) [endo- + G. *mys,* muscle]. The fine connective tissue sheath surrounding a muscle fiber.

endoneuritis (en'do-nu-ri'tis). Inflammation of the endoneurium.

endoneurium (en'do-nu'rĭ-um) [endo- + G. *neuron,* nerve]. Henle's sheath; the delicate connective tissue enveloping individual nerve fibers within a peripheral nerve.

endonuclease (en'do-nu'kle-ās). A nuclease (phosphodiesterase) that cleaves polynucleotides (nucleic acids) at interior bonds, thus producing poly- or oligonucleotide fragments of varying size.

   restriction e., restriction enzyme; one of many e.'s isolated from bacteria that hydrolyze (cut) double-stranded DNA chains at specific (usually hexanucleotide) sequences, thus inactivating a foreign (viral or other) DNA and restricting its activity.

endopar'asite. A parasite living within the body of its host.

endopep'tidase. An enzyme catalyzing the hydrolysis of a peptide chain at points well within the chain, not near termini.

endopericarditis (en'do-pĕr'ĭ-kar-di'tis) [endo- + G. *peri,* around, + *kardia,* heart, + *-itis,* inflammation]. Simultaneous inflammation of the endocardium and pericardium.

endoperimyocarditis (en'do-pĕr'i-mi'o-kar-di'tis) [endo- + G. *peri,* around, + *mys,* muscle, + *kardia,* heart, + *-itis,* inflammation]. Simultaneous inflammation of the heart muscle and of the endocardium and pericardium.

endoperitonitis (en'do-pĕr'ĭ-to-ni'tis). Superficial inflammation of the peritoneum.

endophlebitis (en'do-flĕ-bi'tis) [endo- + G. *phleps* (*phleb-*), vein, + *-itis,* inflammation]. Inflammation of the intima of a vein.

endophthalmitis (en-dof-thal-mi'tis) [endo- + G. *ophthalmos,* eye, + *-itis,* inflammation]. Inflammation of the internal structures of the tissues in the eyeball.

endophyte (en'do-fīt) [endo- + G. *phyton,* plant]. A plant parasite living inside another organism.

endophytic (en-do-fit'ik). **1.** Pertaining to an endophyte. **2.** In dentistry, referring to the growth pattern of oral lesions that invade the lamina propria and submucosa.

en'doplasm. In certain cells, especially motile ones and protozoa, the inner or medullary part of the cytoplasm.

endoplas'mic. Relating to the endoplasm.

endopol'yploid. Relating to endopolyploidy.

endopolyploidy (en'do-pol'ĭ-ploy-dĭ) [endo- + polyploidy]. Endomitosis; the process or state of duplication of the chromosomes without accompanying spindle formation or cytokinesis, resulting in a polyploid nucleus.

endoreduplication (en'do-re-du'plĭ-ka'shun). A form of polyploidy or polysomy characterized by redoubling of chromosomes giving rise to four-stranded chromosomes at prophase and metaphase.

end organ. See under organ.

endorphin (en'dor-fin). One of a family of opioid-like polypeptides originally isolated from the brain but now found in many parts of the body; in the brain, it binds to the same receptors that bind exogenous opiates.

endosalpingitis (en'do-sal-pin-ji'tis) [endo- + G. *salpinx* (*salping-*), tube, + *-itis,* inflammation]. Inflammation of the lining membrane of the eustachian or the fallopian tube.

en'doscope [endo- + G. *skopeō,* to examine]. An instrument for the examination of the interior of a canal or hollow viscus.

endos'copist. A specialist in the use of an endoscope.

endoscopy (en-dos'ko-pĭ) [see endoscope]. Examination of the interior of a canal or hollow viscus by means of an endoscope.

endoskel'eton. The internal bony framework of the body; the skeleton in its usual context.

endosmosis (en-dos-mo'sis). Osmosis in a direction toward the interior of a cell or a cavity.

endosmot'ic. Relating to endosmosis.

en'dospore [endo- + G. *sporos,* seed]. **1.** A resistant body formed within the vegetative cells of some bacteria, particularly those belonging to the genera *Bacillus* and *Clostridium.* **2.** A fungus spore borne within a cell or within the tubular end of a sporophore.

endosteal (en-dos'te-al). Relating to the endosteum.

endosteitis, endostitis (en'dos-te-i'tis, en'dos-ti'tis). Perimyelitis; inflammation of the endosteum or of the medullary cavity of a bone.

endosteoma (en-dos'te-o'mah) [endo- + G. *osteon,* bone, + *-ōma,* tumor]. Endostoma; a benign neoplasm of bone tissue in the medullary cavity of a bone.

endosteum (en-dos'te-um) [endo- + G. *osteon,* bone] [NA]. Medullary membrane; a thin membrane lining the inner surface of bone in the central medullary cavity.

endosto'ma. Endosteoma.

en'dotendin'eum [endo- + L. *tendon,* tendon]. The fine connective tissue surrounding secondary fascicles of a tendon.

endothelia (en'do-the'lĭ-ah). Plural of endothelium.

endothelial (en'do-the'lĭ-al). Relating to the endothelium.

endotheliocyte (en-do-the'lĭ-o-sīt). Endothelial *leukocyte.*

endothelioid (en-do-the'lĭ-oyd). Resembling endothelium.

endothelioma (en'do-the-lĭ-o'mah). A generic term for a group of neoplasms derived from the endothelial tissue of blood vessels of lymphatic channels.

endotheliosis (en'do-the-lĭ-o'sis). Proliferation of endothelium.

endothelium, pl. **endothelia** (en'do-the'lĭ-um, -lĭ-ah) [endo- + G. *thēlē,* nipple]. A layer of flat squamous cells lining especially blood and lymphatic vessels and the heart.

endother'mic. Denoting a chemical reaction during the progress of which there is absorption of heat.

en'dothrix [endo- + G. *thrix,* hair]. A trichophyton (notably *Trichophyton violaceum* and *T. tonsurans*) whose spores and, occasionally, mycelia characteristically invade the interior of the hair shaft.

endotoxemia (en'do-tok-se'mĭ-ah). The presence in the blood of endotoxins, which, if derived from Gram-negative, rod-shaped bacteria, may cause a generalized Shwartzman phenomenon with shock.

endotoxicosis (en'do-tok-sĭ-ko'sis). Poisoning by an endotoxin.

endotox'in. Intracellular toxin. **1.** A bacterial toxin not freely liberated into the surrounding medium. **2.** The complex phospholipid-polysaccharide macromolecules which form an integral part of the cell wall of a variety of relatively avirulent as well as virulent strains of Gram-negative bacteria; they are released only when the of the cell wall is disturbed, are relatively heat-stable, are less potent than most exotoxins, are less specific, and do not form toxoids.

endotracheal (en'do-tra'ke-al). Within the trachea.

endotrachelitis (en'do-trak-el-i'tis). Endocervicitis.

endovasculitis (en'do-vas'ku-li'tis). Endangiitis.

end-piece. The terminal part of the tail of a spermatozoon consisting of the axoneme and the flagellar membrane.

end'plate, end-plate. The ending of a motor nerve fiber in relating to a skeletal muscle fiber.

motor e., the large and complex end-formation by which the axon of a motor neuron establishes synaptic contact with a striated muscle fiber (cell).

end-ti'dal. At the end of a normal expiration.

-ene. A suffix applied to a chemical name indicating the presence of a carbon-carbon double bond.

enema (en'ĕ-mah) [G.]. A substance introduced into the rectum to evacuate the bowel, or to administer drugs or nutrients.

analeptic e., an e. of a pint of lukewarm water with one-half teaspoonful of table salt.

barium e., contrast e., administration of barium as a radiopaque medium, for radiographic study of the lower intestinal tract.

double contrast e., after evacuation of a barium e. and injection of air into the rectum, for finer radiographic study of mucosa of the rectum and colon.

high e., enteroclysis; an e. instilled high up into the colon.

energy (en'er-ji) [G. *energeia,* fr. *en,* in, + *ergon,* work]. Dynamic force; the exertion of power; the capacity to do work.

chemical e., e. liberated by a chemical reaction or absorbed in the formation of a chemical compound.

free e., a thermodynamic function symbolized as *F* or *G* (Gibbs free e.); defined as *H* E *TS,* where *H* is the enthalpy of a system, *T* the absolute temperature, and *S* the entropy; chemical reactions proceed spontaneously in the direction that involves a net decrease in the free e. of the system.

kinetic e., the e. of motion.

potential e., e., existing in a body by virtue of its position or state of existence, which is not being exerted at the time.

enervation (en-er-va'shun) [L. *enervo,* pp. *-atus,* to enervate]. Failure of nerve force; weakening.

ENG Electronystagmography.

engagement (en-gāj'ment). In obstetrics, the mechanism by which the biparietal diameter of the fetal head enters the plane of the inlet.

engorged (en-gorjd') [O. Fr. fr. Mediev. L. *gorgia,* throat, narrow passage, fr. L. *gurges,* a whirlpool]. Congested, distended with fluid.

en'gram [G. *en,* in, + *gramma,* mark]. In the mnemic hypothesis, a physical habit or memory trace made on the protoplasm of an organism by the repetition of stimuli.

engraphia (en-graf'ĭ-ah). Formation of engrams.

enkatar'rhaphy. Encatarrhaphy.

enkephalin (en-kef'ă-lin). A pentapeptide, found in many parts of the brain, which binds to specific receptor sites, some of which may be pain-related opiate receptors.

-enoic. Suffix indicating an unsaturated acid.

e'nol. A compound possessing a hydroxyl group (alcohol) attached to a doubly bonded (ethylenic) carbon atom (–CH=CH(OH)–); as an infix, properly italicized when attached to an otherwise complete name, it is derived as an abbreviation of ethyl *ene* alcoh*ol. (e.g.,* phospho*enol*pyruvate).

e'nolase. An enzyme catalyzing the dehydration of 2-phospho-D-glycerate to phospho*enol*pyruvate.

enophthalmos (en'of-thal'mos) [G. *en*, in, + *ophthalmos*, eye]. Recession of the eyeball within the orbit.

enostosis (en'os-to'sis) [G. *en*, in, + *osteon*, bone, + *-osis*, condition]. A mass of proliferating bone tissue within a bone.

enoyl (e'no-il) [*-ene*, for unsaturation, + *-oyl*, for an acid radical]. The acyl radical of an unsaturated aliphatic acid.

en'siform [L. *ensis*, sword, + *forma*, appearance]. Xiphoid.

enstrophe (en'stro-fe) [G. *en*, in, + *strophē*, a turning]. Entropion (2).

ENT Ear, nose, and throat.

ent-. See ento-.

en'tad [G. *entos*, within, + L. *ad*, to]. Toward the interior.

en'tal [G. *entos*, within]. Relating to the interior; inside.

entamebiasis (ent-ă-me-bi'ă-sis). Infection with *Entamoeba histolytica.*

Entamoeba (ent-ă-me'bah) [G. *entos*, within + *emoibē*, change]. A genus of ameba parasitic in the cecum and large bowel of man and other primates and many domestic and wild mammals and birds. *E. histolytica*, the only distinct pathogen of the genus, causes tropical or amebic dysentery, and hepatic amebiasis.

entasia, entasis (en-ta'zi-ah, en'tă-sis) [G. distention]. Tonic *spasm.*

enter-. See entero-.

en'teral. Within or by way of the intestine, as distinguished from parenteral.

enteralgia (en-ter-al'ji-ah) [entero- + G. *algos*, pain]. Severe abdominal pain accompanying spasm of the bowel.

enterectasis (en-ter-ek'tă-sis) [entero- + G. *ektasis*, a stretching]. Dilation of the bowel.

enterectomy (en-ter-ek'to-mi) [entero- + G. *ektomē*, excision]. Resection of a segment of the intestine.

enterelcosis (en-ter-el-ko'sis) [entero- + G. *helkos*, ulcer]. Ulceration of the bowel.

enteric (en-tĕr'ik) [G. *enterikos*, from *entera*, bowels]. Relating to the intestine.

enteritis (en-ter-i'tis) [entero- + *-itis*, inflammation]. Inflammation of the intestine, especially of the small intestine.

   granulomatous e., regional e.

   mucomembranous e., mucoenteritis (2); an affection of the intestinal mucous membrane characterized by constipation or diarrhea, sometimes alternating, colic, and the passage of pseudomembranous shreds or incomplete casts of the intestine.

   e. necrot'icans, e. with necrosis of the bowel wall caused by *Clostridium welchii.*

   pseudomembranous e., pseudomembranous *enterocolitis.*

regional e., Crohn's disease; distal, regional, or terminal ileitis; granulomatous e.; granulomatous segmented e. of unknown cause, involving the terminal ileum and less frequently other parts of the gastrointestinal tract, characterized by patchy deep ulcers that may cause fistulas, and narrowing and thickening of the bowel by fibrosis and lymphocytic infiltration, with noncaseating tuberculoid granulomas which may also be found in regional lymph nodes.

entero-, enter- [G. *enteron*, intestine]. Combining form relating to the intestines.

en'teroanastomo'sis. Enteroenterostomy.

enterobiasis (en'ter-o-bi'ă-sis). Infection with *Enterobius vermicularis,* the human pinworm.

Enterobius (en-ter-o'bĭ-us) [entero- + G. *bios*, life]. A genus of nematode worms that includes the pinworms (*E. vermicularis*) of man and primates.

enterocele (en'ter-o-sēl) [entero- + G. *kēlē*, hernia]. **1.** A hernial protrusion through a defect in the rectovaginal or vasicovaginal pouch. **2.** An intestinal hernia.

enterocentesis (en'ter-o-sen-te'sis) [entero- + G. *kentēsis*, puncture]. Puncture of the gut with a hollow needle (cannula or trocar) to withdraw substances.

enterocleisis (en-ter-o-kli'sis) [entero- + G. *kleisis*, closing]. Occlusion of the lumen of the alimentary canal.

enteroclysis (en-ter-ok'lĭ-sis) [entero- + G. *klysis*, washing out]. High *enema.*

enterococcus, pl. **enterococci** (en'ter-o-kok'us, -kok'si) [entero- + G. *kokkos*, a berry]. A streptococcus that inhabits the intestinal tract.

enterocolitis (en'ter-o-ko-li'tis) [entero- + G. *kolon*, colon, + *-itis*, inflammation]. Coloenteritis; inflammation of varying extent of the mucous membrane of both small and large intestines.

   antibiotic e., e. caused by oral adminstration of broad spectrum antibiotics, resulting from antibiotic-resistant staphylococci or the overgrowth of yeasts and fungi, when the normal fecal Gram-negative organisms are absent.

   pseudomembranous e., pseudomembranous colitis or enteritis; e. with the formation and passage in the stools of pseudomembranous material; commonly a sequel to prolonged antibiotic therapy.

enterocolostomy (en'ter-o-ko-los'to-mi) [entero- + G. *kōlon*, colon, + *stoma*, mouth]. Establishment of an artificial opening between the small intestine and the colon.

enterocyst (en'ter-o-sist) [entero- + G. *kystis*, bladder]. Enterocystoma; a cyst of the wall of the intestine.

enterocystocele (en'ter-o-sis'to-sēl) [entero- + G. *kystis*, bladder, + *kēlē*, hernia]. A hernia of both intestine and bladder wall.

enterocysto'ma. Enterocyst.

enterodynia (en'ter-o-din'ĭ-ah) [entero- + G. *odynē*, pain]. Enteralgia.

en'teroenteros'tomy. Enteroanastomosis; intestinal anastomosis; establishment of a new communication between two segments of intestine.

en'terogastri'tis [entero- + G. *gastēr*, belly, + *-itis*, inflammation]. Gastroenteritis.

en'terogas'trone. A hormone, obtained from intestinal mucosa, that inhibits gastric secretion and motility.

enterogenous (en-ter-oj'ĕ-nus) [entero- + G. *-gen*, producing]. Of intestinal origin.

en'terohepati'tis [entero- + G. *hēpar* (*hēpat-*), liver, + *-itis*, inflammation]. Inflammation of both the intestine and the liver.

enterohepatocele (en'ter-o-hep'ă-to-sēl) [entero- + G. *hēpar* (*hēpat-*), liver, + *kēlē*, hernia]. Congenital umbilical hernia containing intestine and liver.

enterohydrocele (en'ter-o-hi'dro-sēl). Hydrocele in which the sac contains also a loop of intestine.

enterokinesis (en'ter-o-ki-ne'sis) [entero- + G. *kinēsis*, movement]. Muscular contraction of the alimentary canal, as in peristalsis.

en'terokinet'ic. Relating to, or producing, enterokinesis.

en'terolith [entero- + G. *lithos*, stone]. An intestinal calculus formed of layers surrounding a nucleus of some hard indigestible substance swallowed.

enterolithiasis (en'ter-o-li-thi'ă-sis). Presence of calculi in the intestine.

enterology (en-ter-ol'o-ji) [entero- + G. *logos*, study]. The branch of medical science concerned with the intestinal tract.

enterolysis (en-ter-ol'i-sis) [entero- + G. *lysis*, dissolution]. Division of intestinal adhesions.

en'teromeg'aly [entero- + G. *megas*, great]. Megaloenteron.

enteromerocele (en'ter-o-me'ro-sēl) [entero- + G. *mēros*, thigh, + *kēlē*, hernia]. Femoral *hernia*.

enteromycosis (en'ter-o-mi-ko'sis) [entero- + G. *mykēs*, fungus, + *-osis*, condition]. An intestinal disease of fungal origin.

enteroparesis (en'ter-o-pă-re'sis, -păr'i-sis) [entero- + G. *paresis*, slackening, relaxation]. A state of diminished or arrested peristalsis with flaccidity of the intestinal walls.

en'teropath'ogen'ic. Pathogenic for the alimentary canal.

enterop'athy [entero- + G. *pathos*, suffering]. A disorder of the intestine.

    gluten e., celiac *disease*.

    protein-losing e., increased fecal loss of serum protein, especially albumin, causing hypoproteinemia.

en'teropep'tidase. An intestinal proteolytic enzyme that converts trypsinogen into trypsin.

en'teropexy [entero- + G. *pēxis*, fixation]. Fixation of a segment of the intestine to the abdominal wall.

en'teroplasty [entero- + G. *plassō*, to mold]. Reconstructive operation on the intestine.

enteroplegia (en'ter-o-ple'ji-ah) [entero- + G. *plēgē*, stroke]. See ileus.

enteroptosis, enteroptosia (en'ter-op-to'sis, -to'sīah) [entero- + G. *ptōsis*, a falling]. Abnormal descent of the intestines in the abdominal cavity, usually associated with falling of the other viscera.

enteroptot'ic (en'ter-o-tot'ik). Relating to or suffering from enteroptosis.

enterorrhagia (en'ter-o-ra'ji-ah) [entero- + G. *rhēgnymi*, to burst forth]. Bleeding within the intestinal tract.

enterorrhaphy (en'ter-or'ă-fi) [entero- + G. *rhaphē*, suture]. Suture of the intestine.

enterorrhexis (en'ter-o-rek'sis) [entero- + G. *rhēxis*, rupture]. Rupture of the gut or bowel.

en'terosep'sis [entero- + G. *sēpsis*, putrefaction]. Sepsis occurring in or derived from the alimentary canal.

enterospasm (en'ter-o-spazm) [entero- + G. *spasmos*, spasm]. Increased, irregular, and painful peristalsis.

enterostasis (en-ter-os'tă-sis) [entero- + G. *stasis*, a standing]. Intestinal stasis; a retardation or arrest of the passage of the intestinal contents.

en'terostax'is [entero- + G. *staxis*, a dripping]. Oozing of blood from the mucous membrane of the intestine.

en'terosteno'sis [entero- + G. *stenōsis*, narrowing]. Narrowing of the lumen of the intestine.

enteros'tomy [entero- + G. *stoma*, mouth]. An artificial anus or fistula into the intestine through the abdominal wall.

enterot'omy. Incision into the intestine.

enterotox'in. A cytotoxin specific for the cells of the mucous membrane of the intestine.

en'terotrop'ic [entero- + G. *tropikos*, turning]. Attracted by or affecting the intestine.

Enterovi'rus. A proposed genus of viruses (family Picornaviridae) that includes poliovirus types 1 to 3, coxsackievirus A and B, echoviruses, and the enteroviruses.

enterozo'ic. Relating to an enterozoon.

enterozoon (en'ter-o-zo'on) [entero- + G. *zōon*, animal]. An animal parasite in the intestine.

en'thalpy [G. *enthalpein*, to warm in]. Heat content, symbolized as *H*. A thermodynamic function, defined as $E + PV$, where E is the internal energy of a system, *P* the pressure, and *V* the volume.

en'thesis [G. an insertion, fr. *en*, in, + *thesis*, a placing]. Insertion of synthetic or other nonvital material to replace lost tissue.

enthesitis (en'the-si'tis) [G. *enthetos*, implanted, + *-itis*, inflammation]. Traumatic disease occurring at the insertion of muscles where recurring concentration of muscle stress provokes inflammation with a strong tendency toward fibrosis and calcification.

enthet'ic. 1. Relating to enthesis. **2.** Exogenous.

ento-, ent- [G. *entos*, within]. Prefixes meaning inner, or within. See also endo-.

en'toblast [ento- + G. *blastos*, germ]. Endoblast.

entocele (en'to-sēl) [ento- + G. *kēlē*, hernia]. An internal hernia.

entochoroidea (en'to-ko-roy'de-ah) [ento- + G. *chorioeidēs,* choroid]. *Lamina* chroidocapillaris.

entocor'nea. *Lamina* limitans posterior corneae.

en'toderm [ento- + G. *derma,* skin]. Endoderm.

entoectad (en-to-ek'tad) [G. *entos,* within, + *ektos,* without, + L. *ad,* to]. From within outward.

entomion (en-to'mĭ-on) [G. *entomē,* notch]. The tip of the mastoid angle of the parietal bone.

entomology (en'to-mol'o-jĭ) [G. *entomon,* insect, + *logos,* study]. The science concerned with insects, especially as affecting man.

entop'ic [G. *en,* within, + *topos,* place]. Placed within; occurring or situated in the normal place.

entop'tic [ento- + G. *optikos,* relating to vision]. Within the eyeball.

entoptoscopy (en-top-tos'ko-pĭ) [ento- + G. *optos,* visible, + *skopeō,* to view]. Examination of the interior of the eyeball.

entoret'ina. The layers of the retina from the outer plexiform to the nerve fiber layer inclusive.

entozo'on, pl. **entozo'a** [ento- + G. *zōon,* animal]. An animal parasite inhabiting any of the internal organs or tissues.

entro'pion [G. *en,* in, + *tropē,* a turning]. Inversion or turning inward of a part.

    e. u'veae, iridentropium; inversion of the pupillary margin.

entropy (en'tro-pĭ) [G. *entropia,* a turning towards]. That fraction of heat (energy) content not available for the performance of work, usually because (in a chemical reaction) it has gone to increasing the random motion of the atoms or molecules in the system; thus, e. is a measure of randomness or disorder.

en'typy [G. *entypē,* pattern]. In an early mammalian embryo, the covering by the endoderm of the embryonic and amniotic ectoderm.

enucleate (e-nu'kle-āt). To perform enucleation.

enucleation (e'nu-kle-a'shun) [L. *enucleo,* to remove the kernel, fr. *e* out, + *nucleus,* nut, kernel]. **1.** The entire removal of a tumor or structure (such as the eyeball), without rupture, as one shells out the kernel of a nut. **2.** The removal or destruction of the nucleus of a cell.

enuresis (en-u-re'sis) [G. *en-oureō,* to urinate in]. Bed-wetting; involuntary passage of urine, usually occurring at night or during sleep.

en'velope. In anatomy, a structure that encloses or covers.

    nuclear e., nuclear membrane; the double membrane at the boundary of the nucleoplasm.

    viral e., the outer structure that encloses the nucleocapsids of some viruses.

envenomation (en-ven'om-a'shun). Injection of a poisonous material by sting, spine, bite, or other venom apparatus.

envi'ronment [Fr. *environ,* around]. The milieu; the aggregate of all of the external conditions and influences affecting the life and development of an organism.

enzootic (en-zo-ot'ik) [G. *en,* in, + *zōon,* animal]. Endemic (2); denoting a disease of animals which is indigenous to a certain locality, more precisely, the temporal pattern of occurrence of a disease in a population of animals with only minor changes in its incidence with time.

enzygotic (en-zi-got'ik) [G. *eis*(*en*), one, + zygote]. Derived from a single fertilized ovum, denoting twins so derived.

enzymatic (en-zi-mat'ik). Relating to an enzyme.

enzyme (en'zīm) [G. *en,* in, + *zymē,* leaven]. A protein, secreted by cells, that acts as a catalyst to induce chemical changes in other substances, itself remaining apparently unchanged by the process. E.'s, with the exception of those discovered long ago (*e.g.,* pepsin, emulsin), are generally named by adding -ase to the name of the substrate on which the e. acts (*e.g.,* glucosidase) or the substance activated (*e.g.,* hydrogenase) and/or the type of reaction (*e.g., oxidoreductase, transferase, hydrolase, lyase, isomerase, ligase or synthetase*—these being the six main groups).

    angiotensin converting e., dipeptidyl carboxypeptidase.

    autolytic e., an e. capable of causing autolysis of the cell forming it.

    brancher e., branching e., 1,4-α-glucan branching enzyme.

    deamidizing e.'s, amidohydrolases.

    deaminating e.'s, deaminases.

    debrancher e.'s, debranching e.'s, e.'s that bring about destruction of branches in glycogen; formerly considered to be one enzyme, now known to be a mixture of transferases and hydrolases.

    extracellular e., exoenzyme; an e. performing its functions outside a cell; *e.g.,* the various digestive e.'s.

    induced e., an e. that can be detected in a growing culture of a microorganism, after the addition of a particular substance to the culture medium, that can act on the inducer, and was not detectable prior to the addition.

    inducible e., an e. that is produced only in response to demand created by accumulation or addition of a substrate compound.

    repressible e., an e. that is produced continuously unless production is repressed by excess of a product (corepressor).

    respiratory e., one of those e.'s in tissues that is a part of an oxidation-reduction system accomplishing the conversion of substrates to CO_2 and H_2O and the transfer of the electrons removed to O_2.

    restriction e., restriction *endonuclease.*

enzymology (en'zi-mol'o-jĭ) [enzyme + G. *logos,* study]. The branch of chemistry concerned with the properties and actions of enzymes.

enzymolysis (en'zi-mol'ĭ-sis) [enzyme + G. *lysis,* dissolution]. Splitting or cleavage of a substance into smaller parts by means of enzymatic action; lysis by the action of an enzyme.

enzymopathy (en-zi-mop'ă-thĭ) [enzyme + G. *pathos*, disease]. Disturbance of enzyme function, including genetic deficiency of specific enzymes.

EOG Electro-oculography.

e'osin [G. *ēōs*, dawn]. Sodium salts of 2',4',5',7'-tetrabromofluorescein or 4',5'-dibromo-2',7'-dinitrofluorescein, also known as **e. Y** (for yellowish) or **e. YS**, or **e. I** Bluish, respectively; acid dyes used as cytoplasmic stains and counterstains in histology and in Romanovsky-type blood stains.

eosin'ope'nia [eosino(phil) + G. *penia*, poverty]. Presence of eosinophils in an abnormally small number in the peripheral bloodstream.

eosinophil, eosinophile (e-o-sin'o-fil, -fīl) [eosin + G. *philos*, fond]. Eosinophilic *leukocyte*.

eosinophil'ia. Eosinophilic *leukocytosis*.

    tropical e., e. associated with cough and asthma, caused by occult filarial infection without evidence of microfilaremia, occurring most frequently in India and southeast Asia.

eosinophil'ic. Staining readily with eosin dyes; denoting such cell or tissue elements.

epax'ial [G. *epi*, upon, + L. *axis*, axis]. Above or behind any axis, such as the spinal axis or the axis of a limb.

ependyma (ep-en'dĭ-mah) [G. *ependyma*, an upper garment] [NA]. The cellular membrane lining the central canal of the spinal cord and the brain ventricles.

ependymal (ep-en'dĭ-mal). Relating to the ependyma.

ependymitis (ep-en-dĭ-mi'tis). Inflammation of the ependyma.

ependymoblast (ep-en'dĭ-mo-blast) [ependyma + G. *blastos*, germ]. An embryonic ependymal cell.

ependymocyte (ep-en'dĭ-mo-sīt) [ependyma + G. *kytos*, cell]. As ependymal cell.

ependymoma (ep-en-dĭ-mo'mah). A glioma derived from relatively undifferentiated ependymal cells; the neoplastic cells tend to be arranged radially about blood vessels, to which they are attached by means of fibrillary processes.

ephapse (ef'aps) [G. *ephapsis*, contact]. A place where two or more nerve cell processes touch without forming a typical synaptic contact.

ephaptic (e-fap'tik). Relating to an ephapse.

ephebiatrics (ĕ-fe'bĭ-ȧ'riks) [G. *ephebos*, Athenian youth of military age]. Adolescent *medicine*.

ephe'bic [G. *ephēbikos*, relating to youth, fr. *hēbē*, *youth*]. Relating to the period of puberty or to adolescence.

ephedrine (ĕ-fed'rin, ef'ĕ-drin). 2-Methylamino-1-phenyl-1-propanol; an alkaloid from the leaves of *Ephedra equisetina, E. sinica,* and other species, or produced synthetically; an adrenergic (sympathomimetic) agent with actions similar to those of epinephrine.

ephelis, pl. **ephelides** (ef-e'lis, ef-e'lĭ-dēz) [G.]. Freckle.

epi-. G. preposition, used as a prefix, meaning upon, following, or subsequent to.

epiandros'terone. 3β-Hydroxy-5α-androstan-17-one; inactive isomer of androsterone found in urine and testicular and ovarian tissue.

ep'iblast [epi- + G. *blastos*, germ]. A potential ectoderm.

epiblas'tic. Relating to the epiblast.

epiblepharon (ep'ĭ-blef'ă-ron) [epi- + G. *blepharon*, eyelid]. A congenital horizontal skin near the margin of the eyelid, due to abnormal insertion of muscle fibers. In the upper lid it simulates blepharochalasis; in the lower lid its presence causes an innocuous, and spontaneously disappearing, turning inward of the lashes.

epiboly (ĕ-pib'o-lĭ) [G. *epibolē*, a throwing or laying on]. **1.** In the gastrulation of telolecithal eggs, as a result of differential growth, some of the cells of the primordial outer layer (protoderm) move over the surface toward the lips of the blastopore; when at the blastopore margins, they undergo involution, forming entoderm and mesoderm.

epibul'bar. Upon the eyeball.

epican'thus [epi- + G. *kanthos*, canthus]. Palpebronasal or mongolian fold; a fold of skin extending from the root of the nose to the medial termination of the eyebrow, overlapping the medial angle of the eye; normal in fetal life and in various oriental peoples.

epicar'dia [epi- + cardia]. The portion of the esophagus from where it passes through the diaphragm to the stomach.

epicar'dial. 1. Relating to the epicardia. **2.** Relating to the epicardium.

epicar'dium [epi- + G. *kardia*, heart]. [NA]. *Lamina* visceralis (1).

epicondylalgia (ep'ĭ-kon-dĭ-lal'jĭ-ah) [epicondyle + G. *algos*, pain]. Pain in an epicondyle of the humerus or in the tendons or muscles originating therefrom.

epicondyle (ep-ĭ-kon'dĭl) [epi- + G. *kondylos*, a knuckle]. Epicondylus; a projection from a long bone near the articular extremity above or upon the condyle.

epicondylitis (ep'ĭ-kon-dĭ-li'tis). Infection or inflammation of an epicondyle.

epicondylus, pl. **epicondyli** (ep-ĭ-kon'dĭ-lus, -li) [L.] [NA]. Epicondyle.

epicra'nium [epi- + G. *kranion*, skull]. The muscle, aponeurosis, and skin covering the cranium.

epicrisis (ep-ĭ-kri'sis). A secondary crisis; a crisis terminating a recrudescence of morbid symptoms following a primary crisis.

epicrit'ic [G. *epikritikos*, adjudicatory]. Denoting that component of the somatic sensory modality by which one is enabled to discriminate the finer degrees of touch and temperature stimuli, and to localize them on the body surface.

epicystitis (ep-ĭ-sis-ti'tis) [epi- + G. *kystis*, bladder, + *-itis*, inflammation]. Inflammation of the cellular tissue around the bladder.

epicystotomy (ep′ĭ-sis-tot′o-mĭ) [epi- + G. *kystis*, bladder, + *tomē*, incision]. Suprapubic *cystotomy*.

epidem′ic [epi- + G. *dēmos*, the people]. **1.** A disease attacking many in a community simultaneously; distinguished from endemic, since the disease is not continously present but has been introduced from outside. **2.** A temporary increase in number of cases of an endemic disease.

epidemicity (ep-ĭ-dem-is′ĭ-tĭ). The state of prevailing disease in epidemic form.

ep′idemiol′ogist. An expert or specialist in epidemiology.

epidemiology (ep′ĭ-de-mĭ-ol′jĭ) [G. *epidēmios*, epidemic, + *logos*, study]. **1.** The study of the prevalence and spread of disease in a community. **2.** The field of medicine concerned with determination of specific causes of occurrences of health problems or diseases in a locality.

epider′mal. Epidermic; relating to the epidermis.

epidermalization (ep-ĭ-der′mal-ĭ-za′shun). Squamous *metaplasia.*

epider′mic. Epidermal.

epidermis, pl. **epidermides** (ep-ĭ-derm′is, -derm′ĭ-dēz) [G. *epidermis*, the outer skin] [NA]. Cuticle (3); the outer epithelial portion of the skin (cutis).

epidermi′tis. Inflammation of the epidermis or superficial layers of the skin.

epidermodysplasia (ep-ĭ-der′mo-dis-pla′zĭ-ah) [epidermis + G. *dys-*, bad, + *plasis*, a molding]. Faulty growth or development of the epidermis.

   e. verrucifor′mis, numerous flat warts on the hands and feet, sometimes familial, in which intranuclear viral particles with the appearance of infectious wart virus have been demonstrated.

epider′moid [epidermis + G. *eidos*, appearance]. **1.** Resembling epidermis. **2.** A cholesteatoma or other cystic tumor arising from aberrant epidermic cells.

epidermol′ysis [epidermis + G. *lysis*, loosening]. A condition in which the epidermis is loosely attached to the corium, readily exfoliating or forming blisters.

   e. bullo′sa, a group of inherited chronic noninflammatory skin diseases in which large bullae and erosions result from slight mechanical trauma.

Epidermophyton (ep′ĭ-der-mof′ĭ-ton, -der′mo-fi′ton) [epidermis + G. *phyton*, plant]. A genus of fungi distinguished from *Trichophyton* in that it never invades the hair follicles. *E. floccosum*, is a common cause of tinea pedis.

epididymal (ep-ĭ-did′ĭ-mal). Relating to the epididymis.

epididymectomy (ep′ĭ-did-ĭ-mek′to-mĭ) [epididymis + G. *ektomē*, excision]. Operative removal of the epididymis.

epididymis, pl. **epididymides** (ep-ĭ-did′ĭ-mis, -dĭ-dim′ĭ-dēz) [Mod. L. fr. G. *epididymis*, fr. *epi*, on, + *didymos*, twin, in pl. testes] [NA]. An elongated structure connected to the posterior surface of the testis; the main component is the ductus epididymidis which in the tail and the beginning of the ductus deferens is a reservoir for spermatozoa.

epididymitis (ep-ĭ-did-ĭ-mi′tis). Inflammation of the epididymis.

epididymo-orchitis (ep-ĭ-did′ĭ-mo-or-ki′tis) [epididymis + G. *orchis*, testis]. Simultaneous inflammation of both epididymis and testis.

epididymoplasty (ep-ĭ-did′ĭ-mo-plas-tĭ) [epididymis + G. *plassō*, to form]. Surgical repair of the epididymis.

epididymotomy (ep′ĭ-did-ĭ-mot′o-mĭ) [epididymis + G. *tomē*, a cutting]. Incision into the epididymis.

epididymovasectomy (ep-ĭ-did′ĭ-mo-vă-sek′to-mĭ) [epididymis + vasectomy]. Surgical removal of the epididymis and vas deferens, usually proximal to its entry into the inguinal canal.

epididymovasostomy (ep-ĭ-did′ĭ-mo-vă-sos′to-mĭ) [epididymis + vasostomy]. Surgical anastomosis of the vas deferens to the epididymis.

epidu′ral. Upon (or outside) the dura mater.

epidurog′raphy. Radiographic visualization of the epidural space following the regional instillation of a radiopaque contrast medium.

epiestriol (ep-ĭ-es′trĭ-ol). An epimer of estriol; an estrogenic metabolite found in urine, bile, and the placenta.

epigastral′gia [epigastrium + G. *algos*, pain]. Pain in the epigastric region.

epigas′tric. Relating to the epigastrium.

epigas′trium [G. *epigastrion*] [NA]. Epigastric region; the topographical area of the abdomen located between the costal margins and the subcostal plane.

epigastrocele (ep-ĭ-gas′tro-sēl) [epigastrium + G. *kēlē*, hernia]. A hernia in the epigastric region.

epigenesis (ep-ĭ-jen′ĕ-sis) [epi- + G. *genesis*, creation]. Development of offspring as a result of the union of the ovum and sperm.

ep′igenet′ic. Relating to epigenesis.

epiglot′tic. Relating to the epiglottis.

epiglottidectomy (ep′ĭ-glot′ĭ-dek′to-mĭ) [epiglottis + G. *ektomē*, excision]. Excision of the epiglottis.

epiglottiditis (ep-ĭ-glot-ĭ-di′tis). Epiglottitis.

epiglot′tis [G. *epiglōttis*, fr. *epi*, on, + *glōttis*, the mouth of the windpipe] [NA]. A plate shaped of elastic cartilage at the root of the tongue that serves as a diverter valve over the superior aperture of the larynx during the act of swallowing.

epiglottitis (ep-ĭ-glot-i′tis). Epiglottiditis; inflammation of the epiglottis.

epilate (ep′ĭ-lāt) [L. *e*, out, + *pilus*, a hair]. To extract a hair; to remove the hair from a part by forcible extraction, electrolysis, or loosening at the root by chemical means.

epilation (ep-ĭ-la′shun). Depilation; the act or result of removing hair.

epil′atory. 1. Depilatory (1); having the property of removing hair; relating to epilation. **2.** Depilatory (2).

epilem′ma [epi- *lemma*, husk]. The connective tissue sheath of nerve fibers near their termination.

epilepsy (ep'ĭ-lep-sĭ) [G. *epilēpsia*, seizure]. A chronic disorder characterized by paroxysmal attacks of brain dysfunction due to excessive neuronal discharge, and usually associated with some alteration of consciousness; attacks may remain confined to elementary or complex impairment of behavior or may progress to a generalized convulsion.

focal e., cortical e., an epileptic attack beginning with an isolated disturbance of cerebral function such as a twitching of a limb, a somatosensory or special sense phenomenon, or a disturbance of higher mental function.

generalized e., grand mal e., grand mal; a seizure characterized by loss of consciousness and tonic spasm of the musculature, usually followed by repetitive generalized clonic jerking.

jacksonian e., focal e. with a "march" of the attack usually from distal to proximal limb musculature.

myoclonus e., Lafora's disease; a seizure characterized by sporadic or continuous clonus of muscle groups, familial origin, and association with progressive mental deterioration.

petit mal e., absence.

photogenic e., reflex e. induced by a flickering light.

posttraumatic e., a convulsive epileptic state following and causally related to head injury.

procursive e., a psychomotor attack initiated by whirling or running.

psychomotor e., temporal lobe e.; attacks characterized clinically by impairment of consciousness and amnesia for the episode, often associated with semipurposeful movements of the arms or legs and sometimes with psychic disturbances such as hallucinations.

reflex e., a form of e. in which the attacks are induced by peripheral stimulation.

sensory e., focal e. initiated by a somatosensory phenomenon.

temporal lobe e., psychomotor e.

tonic e., a convulsive attack in which the body is rigid.

epilep'tic. Relating to or suffering from epilepsy.

epilep'tiform. Epileptoid.

epileptogenic, epileptogenous (ep'ĭ-lep-to-jen'ik, toj'ĕ-nus). Causing epilepsy.

epileptoid (ep-ĭ-lep'toyd) [G. *epilēpsia*, seizure, epilepsy, + *eidos*, resemblance]. Epileptiform; resembling epilepsy; denoting certain convulsions, especially of functional nature.

epimandib'ular [epi- + L. *mandibulum*, mandible]. Upon the lower jaw.

epimenorrhagia (ep'ĭ-men-o-ra'jĭ-ah). Too prolonged and too profuse menstruation.

epimenorrhea (ep-ĭ-men-o-re'ah). Too frequent menstruation.

ep'imer [epi- + G. *meros*, part]. One of two molecules differing only in the spatial arrangement about a single carbon atom.

epimerase (ep'ĭ-mer-ās). A class of enzymes catalyzing epimeric changes.

epimere (ep'ĭ-mēr) [epi- + G. *meros*, part]. The dorsal part of the myotome.

epimorpho'sis (ep-ĭ-mor'fo-sis, -mor-fo'sis) [epi- + G. *morphē*, shape]. Regeneration of a part of an organism by growth at the cut surface.

epimysiotomy (ep'ĭ-mis-ĭ-ot'o-mĭ) [epimysium + G. *tomē*, a cutting]. Incision or section of a muscle within its sheath.

epimysium (ep-ĭ-miz'ĭ-um) [epi- + G. *mys*, muscle]. The fibrous envelope surrounding a skeletal muscle.

epinephrine (ep-ĭ-nef'rin). Adrenaline; 3,4-dihydroxy-α[methylaminomethyl]benzyl alcohol; a catecholamine neurohormone of the adrenal medulla that is the most potent stimulant (sympathomimetic) of adrenergic α- and β- receptors, resulting in increased heart rate and force of contraction, vasoconstriction or vasodilation, relaxation of bronchiolar and intestinal smooth muscle, glycogenolysis, lipolysis, and other metabolic effects.

epinephros (ep-ĭ-nef'ros) [epi- + G. *nephros*, kidney]. *Glandula* suprarenalis.

epineural (ep-ĭ-nu'ral). On a neural arch of a vertebrae.

epineurial (ep-ĭ-nu'rĭ-al). Relating to the epineurium.

epineurium (ep-ĭ-nu'rĭ-um) [epi- + G. *neuron*, nerve]. The connective tissue encapsulating a nerve trunk and binding together the fascicles; contains the blood vessels and lymphatics supplying the nerves.

epipharynx (ep'ĭ-făr'ingks) [G. *epi*, on, over, + pharynx]. Nasopharynx.

epiphenomenon (ep'ĭ-fe-nom'e-non). An unusual and unassociated symptom appearing during the course of a disease.

epiphora (e-pif'o-rah) [G. a sudden flow]. Tearing; an overflow of tears upon the cheek, due to imperfect drainage by the tear-conducting passages.

epiphysial, epiphyseal (ep-ĭ-fiz'ĭ-al). Relating to an epiphysis.

epiphysiolysis (ep'ĭ-fiz-ĭ-ol'ĭ-sis) [epiphysis + G. *lysis*, loosening]. Loosening or separation, either partial or complete, of an epiphysis from the shaft of a bone.

epiphysis, pl. **epiphyses** (e-pif'ĭ-sis, -sēz) [G. an excrescence, fr. *epi*, upon, + *physis*, growth] [NA]. A part of a long bone developed from a center of ossification distinct from that of the shaft and separated at first from the latter by a layer of cartilage.

pressure e., A secondary center of ossification in the articular end of a long bone.

stippled e., *dysplasia* epiphysialis punctata.

traction e., a secondary center of ossification at the site of attachment of a tendon.

epiphysitis (e'pif-ĭ-si'tis). Inflammation of an epiphysis.

epipial (ep-ĭ-pi'al). On the pia mater.

epiplo- [G. *epiploon*, omentum]. Combining form relating to the omentum. See also omento-.

epiploic (ep'ĭ-plo'ik). Omental.

epiploon (e-pip'lo-on) [G.]. *Omentum* majus.

episclera (ep-ĭ-skle'rah) [epi- + sclera]. The connective tissue between the sclera and the conjunctiva.

episcle'ral. 1. Upon the sclera. 2. Relating to the episclera.

episcleritis (ep'ĭ-skle-ri'tis). Inflammation of the episcleral or subconjunctival connective tissue. See also scleritis.

episio- [G. *episeion*, pudenda]. Combining form relating to the vulva. See also vulvo-.

episioperineorrhaphy (ĕ-pis'ĭ-o-pĕr'ĭ-ne-or'ă-fĭ) [episio- + G. *perinaion*, perineum, + *rhaphē*, a stitching]. Repair of a ruptured perineum and lacerated vulva, or repair or a surgical incision of the vulva and perineum.

episioplasty (ĕ-pis'ĭ-o-plas-tĭ) [episio- + G. *plassō*, to form]. Repair of a defect of the vulva.

episiorrhaphy (ĕ-pis-ĭ-or'ră-fĭ) [episio- + G. *rhaphē*, a stitching]. Repair of a lacerated vulva or an episiotomy.

episiostenosis (ĕ-pis'ĭ-o-stĕ-no'sis) [episio- + G. *stenōsis*, narrowing]. Narrowing of the vulvar orifice.

episiotomy (ĕ-pis-ĭ-ot'o-mĭ) [episio- + G. *tomē*, incision]. Surgical incision of the vulva to prevent laceration at the time of delivery or to facilitate vaginal surgery.

ep'isome [epi- + G. *sōma*, body (chromosome)]. An extrachromosomal element (plasmid) that may either integrate into the bacterial chromosome of the host or replicate and function stably when physically separated from the chromosome.

epispad'ial. Relating to an epispadias.

epispadias (ep-ĭ-spa'dĭ-as, -spad'ĭ-as) [epi- + G. *spadōn*, a rent]. A malformation in which the urethra opens on the dorsum of the penis.

episplenitis (ep'ĭ-sple-ni'tis). Inflammation of the capsule of the spleen.

epistasis (e-pis'tă-sis) [G. scum; epi- + G. *stasis*, a standing]. 1. Formation of a pellicle or scum on the surface of a liquid, especially as on standing urine. 2. A form of gene interaction whereby one gene masks or interferes with the phenotypic expression of one or more genes at other loci.

epistat'ic. Relating to epistasis.

epistaxis (ep'ĭ-stak'sis) [G. fr. *epistazō*, to bleed at the nose]. Nosebleed; profuse bleeding from the nose.

epister'nal. 1. Over or on the sternum. 2. Relating to the episternum.

epister'num [epi- + L. *sternum*, chest]. *Manubrium* sterni.

epistropheus (ep-ĭ-stro'fe-us) [G. the pivot]. Axis.

epitendineum (ep'ĭ-ten-din'e-um) [L.]. The white fibrous sheath surrounding a tendon.

epithalamus (ep-ĭ-thal'ă-mus) [epi- + thalamus] [NA]. A small dorsomedial area of the thalamus corresponding to the habenula and its associated structures.

ep'ithalax'ia [epithelium + G. *allaxis*, exchange]. Shedding of any surface epithelium, but especially of that lining the intestine.

epithe'lia. Plural of epithelium.

epithe'lial. Relating to or consisting of epithelium.

epithe'lializa'tion. Epithelization; formation of epithelium over a denuded surface.

epithelioid (ep-ĭ-the'lĭ-oyd) [epithelium + G. *eidos*, resemblance]. Resembling or having some of the characteristics of epithelium.

epitheliolytic (ep-ĭ-the'lĭ-o-lit'ik). Destructive to epithelium.

epithelioma (ep'ĭ-the-lĭ-o'mah) [epithelium + G. *-oma*, tumor]. 1. An epithelial neoplasm or harmartoma of the skin, especially of skin appendage orgin. 2. A carcinoma of the skin derived from squamous, basal, or adnexal cells.

  e. adenoi'des cys'ticum, the multiple form of trichoepithelioma.

  basal cell e., basal cell *carcinoma*.

  chorionic e., choriocarcinoma.

  Malherbe's calcifying e., pilomatrixoma.

  malignant ciliary e., adult medulloepithelioma; malignant hyperplasia of ciliary epithelium with frequent involvement of the pigmented layer.

epithelio'matous. Pertaining to epithelioma.

epithelium, pl. **epithelia** (ep-ĭ-the'lĭ-um) [G. *epi*, upon, + *thēlē*, nipple; originally, the thin skin covering the nipples and the papillary layer of the border of lips] [NA]. The purely cellular, avascular layer covering all the free surfaces, cutaneous, mucous, and serous, including the glands and other structures derived therefrom.

  ciliated e., e. having motile cilia on the free surface.

  columnar e., e. formed of a single layer of prismatic cells taller than they are wide.

  cuboidal e., simple e. with cells appearing as cubes in a vertical section but as polyhedra in surface view.

  germinal e., surface e.

  glandular e., e. composed of secretory cells.

  junctional e., a collar of epithelial cells attached to the tooth surface and subepithelial connective tissue found at the base of the gingival crevice.

  laminated e., stratified e.

  olfactory e., pseudostratified e. that contains olfactory, receptor, nerve cells whose axons extend to the olfactory bulb of the brain.

  pseudostratified e., e. that gives a superficial appearance of being stratified because the cell nuclei are at different levels, but in which all cells reach the basement membrane.

  seminiferous e., e. lining the convoluted tubules of the testis where spermatogenesis and spermiogenesis occur.

  simple e., e. having one layer of cells.

  simple squamous e., e. composed of a single layer of flattened scalelike cells.

stratified e., e. composed of a series of layers, the cells of each varying in size and shape; named specifically according to the type of cells at the surface, *e.g.,* stratified squamous e., stratified columnar e.

surface e., germinal e.; **(1)** a layer of celomic epithelial cells covering the gonadial ridges as they are formed on the medial border of the mesonephroi near the root of the mesentery; **(2)** the mesothelial covering of the definitive ovary.

transitional e., stratified e. of several layers, each of which is formed by a transformation of the cells from the layer below.

epithelization (ep-ĭ-the-lĭ-z'shun). Epithelialization.

epitope (ep'ĭ-tōp). An antigenic determinant, in simplest form, of a complex antigenic molecule.

epitrichium (ep-ĭ-trik'ĭ-um) [epi- + G. *trichion,* dim. of *thrix,* (*trich*-), hair]. Periderm.

epitympan'ic. Above, or in the upper part of, the tympanic cavity or membrane.

epitympanum (ep'ĭ-tim'pă-num). The upper part of the tympanic cavity above the tympanic membrane, containing the head of the malleus and the body of the incus.

epizo'ic. Living as a parasite on the skin surface.

epizoology (ep-ĭ-zo-ol'o-jĭ) [epi- + G. *zōon,* animal, + *logos,* study]. Epizootiology.

epizoon, pl. **epizoa** (ep-ĭ-zo'on, -zo'ah) [epi- + G. *zōon,* animal]. An animal parasite living on the body surface.

epizootic (ep'ĭ-zo-ot'ik) [epi- + G. *zōon,* animal]. Denoting a disease attacking a large number of animals simultaneously or the prevalence of a disease among animals, similar to an epidemic among humans.

epizootiology (ep'ĭ-zo-ot'ĭ-ol'o-jĭ) [epi- + G. *zōon,* animal, + *logos,* study]. Epizoology; epidemiology of disease in animal populations.

eponychia (ep-o-nik'ĭah). Infection involving the proximal nail fold.

eponychium (ep-on-nĭk'ĭ-um) [G. *epi,* upon, + *onyx* (*onych*-), nail]. **1.** The condensed eleidin-rich areas of the epidermis preceding the formation of the nail in the embryo. **2** [NA]. Perionychium; nail skin; the epidermis forming the ungual wall behind and at the sides of the nail. **3.** The thin skin adherent to the nail at its proximal portion.

eponym (ep'o-nim) [G. *epōnymos,* named after]. The name of a disease, structure, operation, or procedure, supposedly derived from the name of the person who first discovered or described it.

eponym'ic. 1. Relating to an eponym. **2.** An eponym.

epoophorectomy (ep-o-of'o-rek'to-mĭ) [G. *epi,* upon, + *ōophoros,* bearing eggs, + *ektomē,* excision]. Removal of the epoophoron.

epoophoron (ep-o-of'o-ron) [epi- + G. *ōophoros,* egg-bearing]. [NA]. A collection of rudimentary tubules in the mesosalpinx between the ovary and the uterine tube; the remains of the tubules of the middle portion of the mesonephros (wolffian body).

epox'y. Chemical term describing an oxygen atom bound to two linked carbon atoms and produced from peracids acting on alkenes.

epulis (ep-u'lis) [G. *epoulis,* gumboil]. Persisting inflammatory hyperplasia of the gingiva, a nonspecific growth on the gingiva that may be present at birth as a benign tumor resembling a granular cell myoblastoma.

ep'uloid. A nodule or mass (in the gingival tissue) that resembles an epulis.

epulosis (ep-u-lo'sis) [G. *epoulōsis,* a scarring over]. Cicatrization (1).

epulot'ic. 1. Cicatricial. **2.** Cicatrizant.

equation (e-kwa'zhun) [L. *aequare,* to make equal]. A statement expressing the equality of two things, usually with the use of mathematical or chemical symbols.

Henderson-Hasselbalch e., a formula relating the pH of a solution to the ratio of bicarbonate ion concentration to free carbon dioxide in solution: pH $= pK' + \log$ ([HCO_3-]/[CO_2]). The value of pK' for blood plasma is 6.10 and includes the first dissociation constant of H_2CO_3, the relation between [H_2CO_3] and [CO_2], and other corrections.

Hill's e., $y/100 = Kx^n/(1 + Kx^n)$, where y is the per cent saturation of blood, x the oxygen pressure, and K and n are constants, representing the shape of the oxygen dissociation curve of hemoglobin, which would be hyperbolic if n equaled 1, but which becomes increasingly sigmoid with higher values of n; for human blood, n equals 2.5.

personal e., a slight error in judgment, perceptual response, or action peculiar to the individual and so constant that it is usually possible to allow for it in accepting the person's statements or conclusions, thus arriving at approximate exactness.

equiaxial (e'kwĭ-ak'sĭ-al). Having axes of equal length.

equilibration (e'kwĭ-lĭ-bra'shun). **1.** The act of maintaining an equilibrium or balance. **2.** The act of exposing a liquid to a gas at a certain partial pressure until the partial pressures of the gas within and without the liquid are equal.

occlusal e., the modification of occlusal forms of teeth by grinding with the intent of equalizing occlusal stress, or producing simultaneous occlusal contacts, or of harmonizing cuspal relations.

equilibrium (e-kwĭ-lib'rĭ-um) [L. *aequilibrium,* a horizontal position, fr. *aequus,* equal, + *libra,* a balance]. **1.** The condition of being evenly balanced; a state of repose between two or more antagonistic forces that exactly counteract each other. **2.** Dynamic e.; in chemistry, a state of apparent repose created by two reactions proceeding in opposite directions at equal speed.

dynamic e., equilibrium (2).

nutritive e., physiologic e., condition in which there is a perfect balance between intake and excretion of nutritive material, so that there is no increase or loss in weight.

equine (ē'kwīn) [L. *equinus,* fr. *equus,* horse]. Relating to, derived from, or resembling the horse, mule, ass, or other members of the genus *Equus.*

equinovalgus (e-kwi'no-val'gus, ek'wĭ-no-). *Talipes* equinovalgus.

equinovarus (e-kwi'no-va'rus, ek'wĭ-no-). *Talipes* equinovarus.

equitoxic (e'kwĭ-tok'sik). Of equivalent toxicity.

equivalence, equivalency (e-kwiv'ă-lens, -len-sĭ) [L. *aequus,* equal, + *valentia,* strength (valence)]. The property of an element or radical of combining with or displacing, in definite and fixed proportion, another element or radical in a compound.

equivalent (e-kwiv'ă-lent) [see equivalence]. **1.** Equal in any respect. **2.** Something that is equal in size, weight, force, or any other quality to something else.

    gram e., chemical e., (1) the weight in grams of an element that combines with or replaces 1 g of hydrogen; (2) the atomic or molecular weight in grams of an atom or group of atoms involved in a chemical reaction divided by the number of electrons donated, taken up, or shared by the atom or group of atoms in the course of that reaction; (3) the weight of a substance contained in 1 liter of 1 normal solution (a variant of (1)).

    metabolic e. (MET), the energy expended while in a resting state; approximately the energy expended in burning 3 to 4 ml oxygen per kg (body weight) per minute.

    nitrogen e., the nitrogen content of protein, used in calculating the protein breakdown in the body from the nitrogen excreted in the urine, 1 g of nitrogen being equal to 6.25 g of protein catabolized.

ER Endoplasmic *reticulum.*

Er Erbium.

ERBF Effective renal blood *flow.*

er'bium. A rare earth (lanthanide) element, symbol Er, atomic no. 68, atomic weight 167.26.

ERCP Endoscopic retrograde *cholangiopancreatography.*

erec'tile. Capable of erection.

erection (e-rek'shun) [L. *erectio,* fr. *erigo,* pp. *erectus,* to set up]. The condition of erectile tissue when filled with blood, becoming hard and unyielding; denoting especially this state of the penis.

erector [Mod. L.]. That which raises or makes erect, denoting specifically certain muscles having such action.

erethism (ěr'ĕ-thizm) [G. *erethismos,* irritation]. An abnormal state of excitement or irritation, either general or local.

erethis'mic, erethis'tic, erethit'ic. Marked by or causing erethism.

ERG Electroretinogram.

erg [G. *ergon,* work]. The unit of work in the CGS system; the amount of work done by 1 dyne acting through 1 cm, 1 g cm^2 S^{-2}. One erg equals 10^{-7} joule in the SI system.

ergasia (er-ga'zī-ah) [G. work]. **1.** Any form of activity, especially mental. **2.** The total of functions and reactions of an individual.

ergastoplasm (er-gas'to-plazm) [G. *ergastēr,* a workman, + *plasma,* something formed]. Granular endoplasmic *reticulum.*

ergo- [G. *ergon,* work]. Combining form relating to work.

er'gocalcif'erol. Vitamin D$_2$; calciferol; 9,10-secoergosta-5,7,10(19),22-tetraen-3β-ol; activated ergosterol, the vitamin D of plant origin which arises from ultraviolet irradiation of ergosterol.

ergograph (er'go-graf) [ergo- + G. *graphō,* to write]. An instrument for recording the amount of work done by muscular contractions, or the amplitude of contraction.

ergographic (er-go-graf'ik). Relating to the ergograph and the record made by it.

ergom'eter (er-gom'ĕ-ter) [ergo- + G. *metron,* measure]. Dynamometer.

ergonom'ics [ergo- + G. *nomos,* law]. A branch of ecology dealing with human factors in the design and operations of machines and the physical environment.

ergos'terol. 7,22-Didehydrocholesterol; the most important of the provitamins D$_2$; ultraviolet irradiation converts e. to lumisterol, tachysterol, and vitamin D$_2$.

er'got. Rye smut; the resistant, over-wintering stage of the fungus *Claviceps purpura,* a pathogen of rye grass that transforms the seed of rye into a compact spur-like mass of fungal pseudotissue containing five or more optically isomeric pairs of alkaloids; the levorotary isomers induce uterine contractions, control bleeding, and alleviate certain localized vascular disorders (migraine headaches).

ergotamine (er-got'am-ēn). C$_{33}$H$_{35}$N$_5$O$_5$; an alkaloid from ergot that is a potent stimulant of smooth muscle, particularly of the blood vessels and the uterus, and produces adrenergic blockade (chiefly of the alpha receptors).

ergotism (er'got-izm). Poisoning by a toxic substance contained in the sclerotia of the fungus, *Claviceps purpurea,* growing on rye grass; symptoms are necrosis of the extremities due to contraction of the peripheral vascular bed.

erode (e-rōd') [L. *erodere,* to gnaw away]. **1.** To cause, or to be affected by, erosion. **2.** To remove by ulceration.

erogenous (e-roj'ĕ-nus). Capable of producing sexual excitement when stimulated.

eros (e'ros, ěr'os) [G. love]. In psychoanalysis, the life principle representing all instinctual tendencies toward procreation and life, as opposed to thanatos.

erosion (e-ro'zhun) [L. *erosio,* fr. *erodere,* to gnaw away]. **1.** A wearing away or a state of being worn away, as by friction or pressure. **2.** A shallow ulcer; in the stomach and intestine, an ulcer limited to the mucosa, with no penetration of the muscularis mucosa. **3.** Odontolysis; the wearing away of a tooth by chemical or abrasive action.

ero'sive. Having the property of eroding or wearing away.

erot'ic [G. *erōtikos*, relating to love, fr. *erōs*, love]. Relating to sexual passion; lustful; having the quality to arouse sexual drive.

eroticism (ĕ-rot'ĭ-sizm). Erotism.

erotism (ĕr'o-tizm). Eroticism; a condition of sexual excitement.

erotogenic (ĕr'o-to-jen'ik) [G. *erōs*, love, + *-gen*, production]. Causing sexual excitement.

erotomania (ĕr'o-to-ma'nĭ-ah) [G. *erōs*, love, + *mania*, frenzy]. Excessive or morbid inclination to erotic thoughts and behavior.

erotopath'ic. Relating to erotopathy.

erotopathy (ĕr'o-top'ă-thĭ) [G. *erōs*, love, + *pathos*, suffering]. Any abnormality of sexual impulse.

erotophobia (ĕr'o-to-fo'bĭ-ah) [G. *erōs*, love, + *phobos*, fear]. A morbid aversion to the thought of sexual love and to its physical expression.

ERPF Effective renal plasma *flow.*

eructation (e-ruk-ta'shun) [L. *eructo*, pp. *-atus*, to belch]. Belching; the raising of gas or of a small quantity of acid fluid from the stomach.

eruption (e-rup'shun) [L. *e-rumpo*, pp. *-ruptus*, to break out]. **1.** A breaking out, especially the appearance of lesions on the skin. **2.** A rapidly developing dermatosis of the skin or mucous membranes, especially when appearing as a local manifestation of a general disease; characterized, according to the nature of the lesion, as macular, papular, vesicular, pustular, bullous, nodular, erythematous, etc. **3.** Passage of a tooth through the alveolar process and perforation of the gums.

creeping e., cutaneous *larva migrans.*

drug e., dermatitis or dermatosis medicamentosa; drug rash; any e. caused by the ingestion, injection, inhalation, or insertion of a drug, most often the result of allergic sensitization; reactions to drugs applied to the skin are generally designated as a contact dermatitis.

fixed drug e., a type of drug e. that recurs at a fixed site (or sites) following the administration of a particular drug; the affected areas undergo gradual involution, but flare and enlarge on readministration of the offending drug.

Kaposi's varicelliform e., *eczema* herpeticum.

erup'tive. Characterized by eruption.

ERV Expiratory reserve *volume.*

erysipelas (ĕr-ĭ-sip'ĕ-las) [G. from *erythros*, red, + *pella*, skin]. A specific, acute, inflammatory disease caused by a hemolytic streptococcus and characterized by an eruption, limited to the skin and sharply defined, usually accompanied by severe constitutional symptoms.

erysipelatous (ĕr'ĭ-sĭ-pel'ă-tus). Relating to erysipelas.

erysip'eloid [G. *erysipelas* + *eidos*, resemblance]. A specific, usually self-limiting cellulitis of the hand, caused by *Erysipelothrix rhusiopathiae;* appears as a

dusky erythema at the site of a wound sustained in handling fish or fowl.

Erysipelothrix (ĕr-ĭ-sip'ĕ-lo-thriks, -sĭ-pel'o-thriks) [erysipelas + G. *thrix*, hair]. A genus of bacteria (family Corynebacteriaceae) that are parasitic on mammals, birds, and fish. The type species, *E. rhusiopathiae*, causes swine erysipelas, human erysipeloid, and mouse septicemia, and commonly infects fish handlers.

erythema (ĕr-ĭ-the'mah) [G. *erythēma*, flush]. Inflammatory redness of the skin.

e. ab ig'ne, e. caloricum.

e. annula're, rounded or ringed lesions.

e. annula're centrif'ugum, a chronic recurring erythematous eruption consisting of small and large annular lesions, both discrete and confluent.

e. arthrit'icum epidem'icum, Haverhill *fever.*

e. calor'icum, e. ab igne; a reticulated, pigmented, macular eruption that occurs, mostly on the shins, from exposure to radiant heat.

e. chron'icum mi'grans, a raised erythematous ring with advancing indurated borders and central clearing, radiating from the site of an insect bite; the characteristic skin lesion of Lyme disease.

e. indura'tum, Bazin's disease; recurrent hard subcutaneous nodules that frequently break down and form necrotic ulcers, usually on the calves and less frequently on the thighs or arms of women; are associated with erythrocyanotic changes in cold weather.

e. infectio'sum, fifth disease; a mild infectious disease characterized by an erythematous maculopapular eruption, accompanied by little or no fever.

e. i'ris, herpes iris (1); concentric rings of e. varying in intensity, characteristic of e. multiforme.

e. margina'tum, a variant of e. multiforme seen in rheumatic fever.

e. mi'grans, geographical *tongue.*

e. mi'grans ling'uae, geographical *tongue.*

e. multifor'me, herpes iris (2); an acute eruption of macules, papules, or subdermal vesicles presenting a multiform appearance, the characteristic lesion being the target or iris lesion over the dorsal aspect of the hands and forearms; its origin may be allergic, seasonal, or from drug sensitivity; the eruption may be recurrent or may run a severe course with fatal termination (Stevens-Johnson syndrome).

e. nodo'sum, a dermatosis marked by the sudden formation of painful nodes on the extensor surfaces of the lower extremities, with lesions that are self-limiting, but that tend to recur; associated with arthralgia and fever or may be evidence of drug sensitivity, sarcoidosis, or infections.

e. per'nio, chilblain.

e. tox'icum, flushing of the skin due to allergic reaction to some toxic substance.

e. tox'icum neonato'rum, a common transient eruption of erythema, small papules, and occasionally pustules filled with eosinophil leukocytes overlying hair follicles of the newborn.

erythematous (ĕr-ĭ-them'ă-tus, -the'mă-tus). Relating to or marked by erythema.

erythe'matovesic'ular. Denoting a condition characterized by edema, erythema, and vesiculation, as in allergic contact dermatitis.

erythr-. See erythro-.

erythralgia (ĕr-ĭ-thral'jĭ-ah) [erythro- + G. *algos,* pain]. Painful redness of the skin. See also erythromelalgia.

erythrasma (ĕr-ĭ-thraz'mah) [G. *erythrainō,* to redden]. An eruption of reddish brown pathces, in the axillae and groins especially, due to the presence of *Corynebacterium minutissimum.*

erythredema (ĕ-rith-re-de'mah) [erythro- + G. *oidēma,* swelling]. Acrodynia (1).

erythremia (ĕr-ĭ-thre'mĭ-ah) [erythro- + G. *haima,* blood]. A chronic form of polycythemia of unknown cause; characterized by bone marrow hyperplasia, an increase in blood volume as well as in the number of red cells, redness or cyanosis of the skin, and splenomegaly. Also called Osler's disease (1); Vaquez' or Osler-Vaquez disease; polycythemia rubra or vera.

erythrism (ĕr'ĭ-thrizm) [G. *erythros,* red]. Redness of the hair with a ruddy, freckled complexion.

erythristic (ĕr-ĭ-thris'tik). Relating to or marked by erythrism.

erythro-, erythr- [G. *erythros,* red]. **1.** Combining forms meaning red or denoting relationship to redness. **2.** Prefix denoting the structure of erythrose in a larger sugar; used as such, it is italicized.

erythroblast (ĕ-rith'ro-blast) [erythro- + G. *blastos,* germ]. Originally, a term denoting all forms of human red blood cells containing a nucleus, both pathologic (*i.e.,* megaloblastic) and normal (*i.e.,* normoblastic). Now, the nucleated precursor from which a reticulocyte develops into an erythrocyte.

erythroblastemia (ĕ-rith'ro-blas-te'mĭ-ah) [erythroblast + G. *haima,* blood]. Presence of nucleated red cells in the peripheral blood.

erythroblastopenia (ĕ-rith'ro-blas-to-pe'nĭ-ah) [erythroblast + G. *penia,* poverty]. A primary deficiency of erythroblasts in bone marrow, seen in aplastic anemia.

erythroblastosis (ĕ-rith'ro-blas-to'sis) [erythroblast + *-osis,* condition]. Presence in considerable number of erythroblasts in the blood.

e. feta'lis, fetal e., hemolytic disease of newborn; congenital or neonatal anemia; hemolytic anemia that, in most instances, results from development in the mother of anti-Rh antibody in response to the Rh factor in the (Rh-positive) fetal blood; characterized by many erythroblasts in the circulation, and often generalized edema (hydrops fetalis) and enlargement of the liver and spleen.

eryth'roblastot'ic. Pertaining to erythroblastosis (especially erythroblastosis fetalis).

erythroclasis (ĕr-ith-rok'lă-sis) [erythro- + G. *klasis,* a breaking]. Fragmentation of the red blood cells.

erythroclastic (ĕ-rith'ro-klas'tik). Pertaining to erythroclasis; destructive to red blood cells.

eryth'rocyano'sis [erythro- + G. *kyanos,* blue, + *-osis,* condition]. A condition seen particularly in girls and women in which exposure of the limbs to cold causes them to become swollen and dusky red.

erythrocyte (ĕ-rith'ro-sit) [erythro- + G. *kytos,* cell]. Red blood cell or corpuscle: a mature red blood cell.

erythrocythemia (ĕ-rith'ro-si-the'mĭ-ah) [erythro- + G. *kytos,* cell, + *haima,* blood]. Polycythemia.

erythrocytic (ĕ-rith'ro-sit'ik). Pertaining to an erythrocyte.

erythrocytolysin (ĕ-rith'ro-si-tol'ĭ-sin). Hemolysin (1).

erythrocytolysis (ĕ-rith'ro-si-tol'ĭ-sis) [erythrocyte + G. *lysis,* loosening]. Hemolysis.

erythrocytorrhexis (ĕ-rith'ro-si'to-rek'sis) [erythrocyte + G. *rhēxis,* rupture]. Erythrorrhexis; a partial erythrocytolysis in which particles of protoplasm escape from the red blood cells, which then become crenated and deformed.

erythrocytoschisis (ĕ-rith'ro-si-tos'kĭ-sis) [erythrocyte + G. *schisis,* a splitting]. A breaking up of the red blood cells into small particles that morphologically resemble platelets.

erythrocytosis (ĕ-rith'ro-si-to'sis). Polycythemia, especially that which occurs in response to some known stimulus.

ery'throdegen'erative. Pertaining to or characterized by degeneration of the red blood cells.

erythroderma (ĕ-rith'ro-der'mah) [erythro- + G. *derma,* skin]. Erythrodermatitis; a nonspecific designation for intense and usually widespread reddening of the skin, often preceding, or associated with exfoliation.

congenital ichthyosiform e., ichthyosiform e.; a genodermatosis characterized by diffuse chronic erythema and scale formation with hyperkeratosis of palms and soles, and associated in varying degrees with other defects, including ocular and neural changes.

e. desquamati'vum, Leiner's disease; severe, extensive seborrheic dermatitis in the newborn; frequently occurs in the undernourished, cachectic children.

ichthyosiform e., congenital ichthyosiform e.

maculopapular e., an eruption of macules and papules of reddish color.

e. psoriat'icum, extensive exfoliative dermatitis simulating psoriasis.

eryth'rodermati'tis. Erythroderma.

erythrodontia (ĕ-rith-ro-don'shĭ-ah) [erythro- + G. *odous,* tooth]. Reddish discoloration of the teeth, as may occur in porphyria.

erythrogen'esis imperfec'ta. Congenital hypoplastic *anemia.*

erythrogenic (ĕ-rith'ro-jen'ik) [erythro- + *-gen,* producing]. **1.** Producing red, or causing an eruption or a red color sensation. **2.** Pertaining to the formation of red blood cells.

erythroid (ĕr′ĭ-throyd, ĕ-rith′royd). Reddish in color.

erythrokeratoderma (ĕrith′ro-kĕr-ă-to-der′mah). The association of erythroderma and hyperkeratosis, which may be symptomatic at sites of chronic injury or inherited; symmetrical progressive e. is inherited as an autosomal dominant gene and does not involve the palms and soles.

e. variabi′lis, a dermatosis characterized by hyperkeratotic plaques of bizarre, geographic configuration, associated with erythrodermic areas that may vary in size, shape, and position from day to day; autosomal dominant inheritance.

erythʹrokinetʹics [erythro- + G. *kinēsis,* movement]. A consideration of the kinetics of erythrocytes from their generation to destruction; erythrokinetic studies are sometimes made in cases of anemia to evaluate the balance between erythrocyte production and destruction.

erythroleukemia (ĕ-rith′ro-lu-ke′mĭ-ah). Simultaneous neoplastic proliferation of erythroblastic and leukoblastic tissues.

erythroleukosis (ĕ-rith′ro-lu-ko′sis). A condition resembling leukemia in which the erythropoietic tissue is affected in addition to the leukopoietic tissue.

erythrolysin (ĕr′ĭ-throl′ĭ-sin). Hemolysin (1).

erythrolysis (ĕr′ĭ-throl′ĭ-sis). Hemolysis.

erythromelalgia (ĕ-rith′ro-mel-al′jĭ-ah) [erythro- + G. *melos,* limb, + *algos,* pain]. Mitchell's disease; red neuralgia; paroxysmal throbbing and burning pain in the skin, affecting one or both legs and feet, sometimes one or both hands, accompanied by a dusky mottled redness of the parts; associated with polycythemia vera, thrombocythemia; gout, neurological disease, or heavy-metal poisoning.

erythromycin (ĕrith′ro-mi′sin). An antibiotic agent obtained from cultures of a strain of *Streptomyces erythraeus;* Gram-positive bacteria are in general more susceptible to its action than are Gram-negative bacteria.

erythron (ĕr′ĭ-thron). The total mass of circulating red blood cells, and that part of the hematopoietic tissue from which they are derived.

erythroneocytosis (ĕ-rith′ro-ne′o-si-to′sis) [erythrocyte + G. *neos,* new, + *kytos,* cell, + *-osis,* condition]. Presence in the peripheral circulation of regenerative forms of red blood cells.

erythropenia (ĕ-rith′ro-pe′nĭ-ah) [erythrocyte + G. *penia,* poverty]. Deficiency in the number of red blood cells.

erythrophagia (ĕ-rith′ro-fa′jĭ-ah). Phagocytic destruction of red blood cells.

erythrophagocytosis (ĕ-rith′ro-fag′o-si-to′sis). Phagocytosis of erythrocytes.

erythrophil (ĕ-rith′ro-fil) [erythro- + G. *philos,* fond]. **1.** Erythrophilic; staining readily with red dyes. **2.** A cell or tissue element that stains red.

eryth′rophil′ic. Erythrophil (1).

erythroplakia (ĕ-rith′ro-pla′kĭ-ah) [erythro- + G. *plax,* plate]. A red, velvety plaque-like lesion of mucous membrane which often represents malig-

nant change.

erythroplasia (ĕ-rith′ro-pla′zĭ-ah) [erythro- + G. *plassō,* to form]. Erythema and dysplasia of the epithelium.

e. of Queyrat, carcinoma in situ of the glans penis.

erythropoiesis (ĕ-rith′ro-pov-e′sis) [erythrocyte + G. *poiēsis,* a making]. Formation of red blood cells.

erythropoietic (ĕ-rith′ro-poy-et′ik). Pertaining to or characterized by erythropoiesis.

erythropoietin (ĕ-rith-ro-poy′ĕ-tin). A sialic acid-containing protein that enhances erythropoiesis by stimulating formation of proerythroblasts and release of reticulocytes from bone marrow; secreted by the kidney and possibly by other tissues, and can be detected in human plasma and urine.

erythroprosopalgia (ĕ-rith′ro-pros-o-pal′jĭ-ah) [erythro- + G. *prosōpon,* face, + *algos,* pain]. A disorder similar to erythromelalgia, but with the pain and redness occurring in the face.

erythropsia (ĕ-rith-rop′sĭ-ah) [erythro- + G. *ōps,* eye]. A condition in which all objects appear to be tinged with red.

erythrorrhexis (ĕr′ĭ-thro-rek′sis, ĕ-rith′ro-rek′sis) [erythrocyte + G. *rhēxis,* rupture]. Erythrocytorrhexis.

erythrothrombomonoblastosis (ĕ-rith′ro-throm′bo-mon-o-blas-to′sis) [erythro- + G. *thrombos,* a clot, + mono(cyte) + *blastos,* germ]. A leukemia-like disorder of the hemopoietic system characterized by: 1) initial splenomegaly; 2) various changes in the blood, including thrombocythemia, erythroblastemia, hypochromic anemia, atypical or immature monocytes, increased bone marrow activity; 3) increased metabolic rate; 4) bone atrophy not unlike that in Gaucher's disease.

erythruria (ĕr′ĭ-thru′rĭ-ah) [erythro- + G. *ouron,* urine]. Passage of red urine.

Es Einsteinium.

escape. The situation when a higher pacemaker defaults or A-V conduction fails and a lower pacemaker assumes the functions of pacemaking for one or more beats.

nodal e., e. with the A-V mode as pacemaker.

ventricular e., e. with an ectopic ventricular focus as pacemaker.

eschar (es′kar) [G. *eschara,* a fireplace, a scab caused by burning]. A thick, coagulated crust or slough which develops following a thermal burn or chemical or physcial cauterization of the skin.

escharotic (es-kă-rot′ik) [G. *escharōtikos.* Caustic or corrosive.

escharotomy (es-kă-rot′o-mĭ) [eschar + G. *tomē,* incision]. A surgical incision in a burn eschar to lessen constriction.

Escherichia (esh-er-ik′ĭ-ah). A genus of aerobic, facultatively anaerobic bacteria found in feces; occasionally they are pathogenic to man, causing enteritis, peritonitis, cystitis, etc. The type species, *E. coli,* occurs normally in the intestines of man and other vertebrates, is widely distributed in nature and is a frequent cause of infections of the urogenital tract and of diarrhea in infants.

-esis [G. suffix *-esis*, condition or process]. Suffix meaning condition, action, or process.

esoethmoiditis (es'o-eth-moy-di'tis) [G. *esō*, within, + ethmoid *-itis*, inflammation]. Inflammation of the lining membrane of the ethmoid cells.

es'ogastri'tis [G. *esō*, within, + *gastēr*, stomach, + *-itis*, inflammation]. Catarrhal inflammation of the mucous membrane of the stomach.

esophagalgia (e-sof-ă-gal'jĭ-ah) [esophagus + G. *algos*, pain]. Esophagodynia; pain the the esophagus.

esophageal (e-sof-ă-je'al, e-sŏ-faj'e-al). Relating to the esophagus.

esophagectasis, esophagectasia (e-sof-ă-jek'tă-sis, -jek-ta'zĭ-ah) [esophagus + G. *ektasis*, a stretching]. Dilation of the esophagus.

esophagectomy (e-sof-ă-jek'to-mĭ) [esophagus + G. *ektomē*, excision]. Excision of any part of the esophagus.

esophagi (e-sof'ă-ji, -gi). Plural of esophagus.

esophagism (e-sof'ă-jizm). Esophageal spasm causing dysphagia.

esophagitis (e-sof-ă-ji'tis). Inflammation of the esophagus.

    peptic e., inflammation of the lower esophagus from regurgitation of acid gastric contents, producing substernal pain.

esophagocardioplasty (e-sof'ă-go-kar'dĭ-o-plas-tĭ). A reconstructive operation on the esophagus and cardiac end of the stomach.

esophagocele (e-sof'ă-go-sēl) [esophagus + G. *kēlē*, hernia]. Protrusion of the mucous membrane of the esophagus through a rent in the muscular coat.

esophagodynia (e-sof'ăgo-din'ĭ-ah) [esophagus + G. *odynē*, pain]. Esophagalgia.

esophagoenterostomy (e-sof'ă-go-en-ter-os'to-mĭ) [esophagus + G. *enteron*, intestine, + *stoma*, mouth]. Operative formation of a direct communication between the esophagus and intestine.

esoph'agogas'troanas'tomo'sis. Esophagogastrostomy.

esoph'agogas'troplasty. Cardioplasty; surgical repair of the cardiac sphincter of the stomach.

esoph'agogastrec'tomy. Removal of a portion of the lower esophagus and proximal stomach for treatment of neoplasms or strictures of those organs, especially lesions located at or near the cardioesophageal junction.

esophagogastrostomy (e-sof'ă-go-gas-tros'to-mĭ) [esophagus + G. *gastēr*, stomach, + *stoma*, mouth]. Esophagogastroanastomosis; anastomosis of esophagus to stomach, usually following esophagogastrectomy.

esophagomalacia (e-sof'ă-go-mă-la'shĭ-ah) [esophagus + G. *malakia*, softness]. Softening of the walls of the esophagus.

esophagomyotomy (e-sof'ă-go-mi-ot'o-mĭ) [esophagus + G. *mys*, muscle, + *tomē*, incision]. Treatment of esophageal achalasia by longitudinal division of the lowest part of the esophageal muscle down to the submucosal layer; some muscle fibers of the cardia may also be divided.

esophagoplasty (e-sof'ă-go-plas-tĭ) [esophagus + G. *plassō*, to form]. Surgical repair of a defect in the wall of the esophagus.

esophagoplication (e-sof'ă-go-pli-ka'shun) [esophagus + L. *plico*, to fold]. Reduction in size of a dilated esophagus or of a pouch in the same by making longitudinal folds or tucks in its walls.

esophagoptosis, esophagoptosia (e-sof'ă-gop-to'sis, -to'sĭ-ah) [esophagus + G. *ptōsis*, a falling]. Relaxation and downward displacement of the walls of the esophagus.

esoph'agoscope [esophagus + G. *skopeō*, to examine]. An endoscope for inspecting the interior of the esophagus.

esophagoscopy (e-sof-ă-gos'ko-pĭ) [esophagus + g. *skopeō*, to examine]. Inspection of the interior of the esophagus by means of an endoscope.

esophagospasm (e-sof'ă-go-spazm). Spasm of the walls of the esophagus.

esophagostenosis (e-sof'ă-go-stĕ-no'sis) [esophagus + G. *stenōsis*, a narrowing]. Stricture or a general narrowing of the esophagus.

esophagostomy (e-sof-ă-gos'to-mĭ) [esophagus + G. *stoma*, mouth]. The operative formation of an opening directly into the esophagus from without.

esophagotomy (e-sof-ă-got'o-mĭ) [esophagus + G. *tomē*, an incision]. An incision through the wall of the esophagus.

esophagus, pl. esophagi (e-sof'ă-gus, -ji, -gi) [G. *oisophagos*, gullet] [NA]. The portion of the digestive canal between the pharynx and stomach. It is about 25 cm long and consists of three parts: cervical, from the cricoid cartilage to the thoracic inlet; thoracic from thoracic inlet to the diaphragm; and abdominal, below the diaphragm to the cardiac opening of the stomach.

esophoria (es-o-fo'rĭ-ah) [G. *esō*, inward, + *phora*, a carrying]. A tendency of the eyes to deviate inward.

esophoric (es-o-for'ik). Relating to or marked by esophoria.

esosphenoiditis (es'o-sfe'noyd-i'tis) [G. *esō*, within, + sphenoid + *-itis*, inflammation]. Osteomyelitis of the sphenoid bone.

esotro'pia [G. *esō*, inward, + *tropē*, turn]. Crossed eyes; convergent strabismus; strabismus in which the visual axes converge; may be paralytic or concomitant, monocular or alternating, accomodative or nonaccommodative.

esotrop'ic. Relating to or marked by esotropia.

ESP Extrasensory *perception.*

espundia (es-poon'dĭ-ah) [Sp. fr. L. *spongia*, sponge]. Breda's disease; a type of American leishmaniasis caused by *Leishmania braziliensis* that affects the mucous membranes, particularly in the nasal and oral region, resulting in grossly destructive changes.

ESR Erythrocyte sedimentation *rate;* electron spin *resonance.*

essential (ĕ-sen'shal). **1.** Necessary, indispensable (*e.g.,* e. amino acids). **2.** Characteristic of. **3.** Determining. **4.** Idiopathic, inherent.

es'ter. An organic compound formed by the elimination of H_2O between the –OH of an acid group and the –OH of an alcohol group.

es'terase. A generic term for enzymes that catalyze the hydrolysis of esters.

esterification (es'tĕr-ĭ-fĭ-ka'shun). The process of forming an ester.

es'terol'ysis. The splitting of a chemical bond with the addition of the elements of an ester at the point of splitting.

esthesio- [G. *aesthēsis,* sensation]. Combining form relating to sensation or perception.

esthesiodic (es-the'zĭ-od'ik) [esthesio- + G. *hodos,* way]. Esthesodic; conveying sensory impressions.

esthesiogenesis (es-the'zĭ-o-jen'ĕ-sis) [esthesio- + G. *genesis,* generation]. Production of sensation, especially of nervous erethism.

esthesiogen'ic. Producing a sensation.

esthesiometer (es-the-zĭ-om'ĕ-ter) [esthesio- + G. *metron,* measure]. Tactometer; an instrument for determining the state of tactile and other forms of sensibility.

esthesiom'etry. Measurement of the degree of tactile or other sensibility.

esthesioneurosis (es-the'zĭ-o-nu-ro'sis). Any sensory neurosis; *e.g.,* anesthesia, hyperesthesia, paresthesia.

esthe'siophysiol'ogy. The physiology of sensation and the sense organs.

esthesodic (es-the-zod'ik). Esthesiodic.

esthet'ic [G. *aisthēsis,* sensation]. **1.** Pertaining to the sensations. **2.** Pertaining to esthetics.

esthet'ics. The branch of philosophy dealing with beauty, especially with the components thereof as they relate to appearance.

es'tival [L. *aestivus,* summer (adj.)]. Relating to or occurring in the summer.

estivoautumnal (es'tĭ-vo-aw-tum'nal) [L. *aestivus,* summer, + *autumnalis,* autumnal]. Relating to or occurring in summer and autumn.

estradiol (es-tră-di'ol). 1,3,5(10)-Estratriene-3,17β-diol; the most potent naturally occurring estrogen in mammals, formed by the ovary, the placenta, the testis, and possible the adrenal cortex; therapeutic indications for e. are those typical of an estrogen.

es'trin. Estrogen.

estriol (es'trĭ-ol). A metabolite of estradiol; usually the predominant estrogenic metabolite found in urine.

estrogen (es'tro-jen). Estrin; generic term for any substance, natural or synthetic, that exerts biological effects characteristic of estrogenic hormones, such as estradiol; formed by the ovary, placenta, testes, possibly the adrenal cortex, and certain plants. Besides stimulation of secondary sexual characteristics, they also exert systemic effects, such as growth and maturation of long bones, and are used therapeutically in any disorder attributable to e. deficiency, to prevent or stop lactation, to suppress ovulation, and to ameliorate carcinoma of the breast and of the prostate.

estrogen'ic. 1. Causing estrus in animals. **2.** Having an action similar to that of an estrogen.

estrone (es'trōn). A metabolite of 17β-estradiol, commonly found in urine, with considerably less biological activity than the parent hormone.

ethal'dehyde. Acetaldehyde.

ethanoic acid (eth'ă-no'ik). Acetic acid.

eth'anol. Alcohol (2).

eth'ene. Ethylene.

eth'enyl. Vinyl.

eth'enylben'zene. Styrene.

ether (e'ther) [G. *aithēr,* the pure upper air]. **1.** Any organic compound in which two carbon atoms are independently linked to a common oxygen atom, thus containing the group –C–O–C–. **2.** Loosely used to refer to diethyl e. or an anesthetic e., although a large number of e.'s have anesthetic properties. For individual e.'s, see the specific name.

ethereal (e-the're-al) [g. *aitherios,* etherial, fr. *aithēr,* the upper air]. Relating to or containing ether.

ethical (eth'ĭ-kal). Relating to ethics; in conformity with the rules governing personal and professional conduct.

ethics (eth'iks) [G. *ethikos,* arising from custom, fr. *ethos,* custom]. The science of morality; the principles of proper professional conduct concerning the rights and duties of the health care professional, his patients, and his colleagues.

ethmo- [G. *ēthmos,* sieve]. Combining form meaning ethmoid; relating to the ethmoid bone.

ethmoid (eth'moyd) [G. *ēthmos,* sieve, + *eidos,* resemblance]. Ethmoidal. **1.** Resembling a sieve. **2.** The e. bone, *os* ethmoidale.

ethmoid'al. Ethmoid.

ethmoidectomy (eth-moy-dek'to-mĭ) [ethmo- + G. *ektomē,* excision]. Removal of all or part of the mucosal lining and bony partitions between the ethmoid sinuses.

ethmoiditis (eth-moy-di'tis). Inflammation of the ethmoid sinuses.

ethmotur'binals. The conchae (superior and middle) of the ethmoid bone.

ethnocentrism (eth-no-sen'trizm) [G. *ethnos,* race, tribe, + *kentron,* center of a circle, + ism]. The tendency to evaluate other groups according to the values and standards of one's own ethnic group, especially with the conviction that one's own ethnic group is superior to the other groups.

ethox'y. The monovalent radical, $CH_3CH_2O–$.

eth'yl. The hydrocarbon radical, $CH_3CH_2–$.

  e. alcohol, alcohol (2).

  e. chloride, a very volatile, explosive liquid (under increased pressure); used to produce local anesthesia by superficial freezing, but also a potent inhalation anesthetic.

ethylacetic acid (eth'il-ă-se'tik). Normal *butyric acid.*

eth'ylate. A compound in which the hydrogen of the hydroxyl group of an alcohol is replaced by a metallic atom, usually sodium or potassium.

eth'ylcar'binol. *Propyl* alcohol.

eth'ylene. Ethene; CH_2CH_2; an explosive constituent of ordinary illuminating gas; an inhalation anesthetic, now infrequently used, slightly more potent than nitrous oxide.

eth'ylenedi'aminetet'raace'tic acid (EDTA). Edetic acid; $(HOOC -CH_2)_2N(CH_2)N(CH_2-COOH)_2$; a chelating agent used to remove multivalent cations from solution as chelates. As the sodium salt, it is used as a water softener, to stabilize drugs rapidly decomposed in the presence of traces of metal ions, and as an anticoagulant; as the sodium calcium salt, used to remove radium, lead, strontium, plutonium, and cadmium from the skeleton.

ethyl'idene. The radical $CH_3CH=$.

ethyl'idyne. The radical $CH_3C\equiv$.

eth'ylvi'nyl ether. Vinylethyl ether; $CH_3CH_2OCHCH_2$; a flammable inhalation anesthetic of moderate potency.

ethynodiol (ĕ-thi-no-di'ŏl). 17α-Ethynyl-4-estrene-3β,17β-diol; a semisynthetic steroid with biological effects resembling those of progesterone; administered in combination with an estrogen as an oral contraceptive.

ethynyl (eth'ĭ-nil). Acetenyl; the monovalent radical $HC\equiv C-$.

etidocaine (e-ti'do-cān). $(\underline{+})$-2-(Ethylpropyl-amino)-2',6'-butyroxylidide; a local anesthetic.

etiola'tion [Fr. *étioler*, to blanch]. **1.** Paleness or pallor resulting from deprivation of light. **2.** The process of blanching or making pale by withholding light.

etiologic (e'tĭ-o-loj'ik). Relating to etiology.

etiologist (e'tĭ-ol'o-jist). A specialist in etiology.

etiology (e'tĭ-ol'o-jĭ) [G. *aitia*, cause, + *logos*, treatise, discourse]. The science and study of the causes of disease and their mode of operation.

Eu Europium.

eu-. G. particle used as a prefix, meaning good, well.

Eubacterium (u-bak-tēr'ĭ-um). A genus of anaerobic, nonsporeforming, nonmotile bacteria occurring in the intestinal tract; they attack carbohydrates and may be pathogenic. The type species is *E. foedans.*

euca'ryote. Eukaryote.

eu'caryot'ic. Eukaryotic.

euchlorhydria (u'klor-hi'drĭ-ah). Presence of normal amounts of free hydrochloric acid in the gastric juice.

eucholia (u-ko'lĭ-ah) [eu- + G. *cholē,* bile]. A normal state of the bile in quantity and quality.

euchromatin (u-kro'mă-tin). See chromatin.

eucrasia (u-kra'zĭ-ah) [G. *eukrasia,* good temperament]. **1.** The normal balance in the body of the qualities, functions, and chemical and physical

states. **2.** A condition of reduced susceptibility to certain drugs, articles of diet, etc.

eudiaphoresis (u-di'ă-fo-re'sis) [eu- + G. *diaphorēsis,* perspiration]. Normal, free sweating.

eudiemorrhysis (u'di-ĕ-mor'ĭ-sis) [eu- + G. *dia,* through, + *haima,* blood, + *rhysis,* a flowing]. A free, normal capillary circulation.

eugenic (u-jen'ik). Relating to eugenics.

eugenics (u-jen'iks) [G. *eugeneia,* nobility of birth]. Practices and policies that tend to better the innate qualities of man and to develop them to the highest degree.

euglobulin (u-glob'u-lin). That fraction of the serum globulin less soluble in $(NO_4)_2SO_4$ solution than the pseudoglobulin fraction.

euglycemia (u-gli-se'mĭ-ah) [eu- + G. *glykys,* sweet, + *haima,* blood]. Normoglycemia; normal blood glucose concentration.

euglycemic (u-gli-se'mik). Normoglycemic; denoting euglycemia.

eugnathia (u-na'thĭ-ah, -nath'ĭ-ah) [eu- + G. *gnathos,* jaw]. An abnormality limited to the teeth and their immediate alveolar supports.

eugonic (u-gon'ik) [G. *eugonos,* productive]. Denoting rapid and relatively luxuriant growth of a bacterial culture, especially in reference to that of the human tubercle bacillus (*Mycobacterium tuberculosis*).

eu'karyot'ic. Eucaryotic; pertaining to a eukaryote.

eukaryote (u-kăr'ĭ-ōt) [eu- + G. *karyon,* kernel, nut]. Eucaryote; an organism whose cells contain a limiting membrane around the nuclear material and which undergoes mitosis.

eumetria (u-me'trĭ-ah) [G. moderation, goodness of meter]. Graduation of the strength of nerve impulses to match the need.

eunuch (u'nuk) [G. *eunouchos,* fr. *eunē,* bed, + *echein,* to have, because used as chamberlain]. One whose testes have been removed or have never developed.

eunuchoid (u'nuk-oyd) [G. *eunouchos,* eunuch, + *eidos,* resembling]. Partially resembling, or having the general characteristics of, a eunuch.

eunuchoidism (u'nuk-oyd-izm). Male hypogonadism; a state in which testes are present but fail to function.

    hypergonadotropic e., defective gonadal development or function, or both, resulting from inadequate secretion of pituitary gonadotropins.

    hypogonadotropic e., hypogonadotropic *hypogonadism.*

eupepsia (u'pep'sĭ-ah) [G. fr. *eu,* well, + *pepsis,* digestion]. Good digestion.

eupep'tic. Digesting well; having a good digestion.

euphoretic (u-fo-ret'ik). Euphoriant.

euphoria (u-fo'rĭ-ah) [eu- + G. *pherō,* to bear]. A feeling of well-being, commonly exaggerated and not necessarily well founded.

euphoriant (u-fo'rĭ-ant). Euphoretic; having the capability to produce a sense of well-being (euphoria).

euploid (u'ployd). Relating to euploidy.

euploidy (u'ploy-dĭ) [eu- + G. *-ploos*, -fold]. The state of a cell whose number of chromosomes is an exact multiple of the haploid number normal for the species.

eupnea (ūp-ne'ah) [G. *eupnoia*, fr. *eu*, well, + *pnoia*, breath]. Easy, free respiration, as observed in the normal subject under resting conditions.

eupraxia (u-prak'sĭ-ah) [eu- + G. *praxis*, a doing]. Normal ability to perform coordinated movements.

eurhythmia (u-rith'mĭ-ah) [eu- + G. *rhythmos*, rhythm]. Harmonious body relationships of the separate organs.

europium (u-ro'pĭ-um) [L. *Europa*, Europe]. An element of the rare earth (lanthanide) group, symbol Eu, atomic no. 63, atomic weight 151.96.

eury- [G. *eurys*, wide]. Combining form meaning wide or broad.

eurycephalic, eurycephalous (u'rĭ-sĕ-fal'ik, -sef'ă-lus) [eury- + G. *kephalēs*, head]. Having an unusually broad head.

eurygnathic, eurygnathous (u-rig-nath'ik, -rig'nă-thus) [eury- + G. *gnathos*, jaw]. Having a wide jaw.

euryon (u'rĭ-on) [G. *eurys*, broad]. The extremity, on either side, of the greatest transverse diameter of the head; a point used in craniometry.

euryopia (u-rĭ-o'pĭ-ah) [eury- + G. *ops*, eye]. A wide intraocular distance.

eustachian (u-sta'kĭ-an, u-sta'shĭ-an). Described by or attributed to Eustachio.

eusystole (u-sis'to-le) [eu- + systole]. Normality of the cardiac systole in force and time.

eusystolic (u-sis-tol'ik). Denoting eusystole.

euthanasia (u'thă-na'zĭ-ah) [eu- + G. *thanatos*, death]. 1. A quiet, painless death. 2. The intentional putting to death by artificial means of persons with incurable or painful disease.

euthen'ics [G. *euthenein*, to thrive]. The science concerned with establishing optimum living conditions for plants, animals, or humans, especially through care for proper provisioning and environment.

euthermic (u-ther'mik) [eu- + G. *thermos*, warm]. At an optimal temperature.

eutonic (u-ton'ik) [eu- + G. *tonus*, tone]. Normotonic (1).

eutrophia (u-tro'fĭ-ah) [G. fr. *eu*, well, + *trophē*, nourishment]. A state of normal nourishment and growth.

eutroph'ic. Relating to, characterized by, or promoting eutrophia.

evacuant (e-vak'u-ant). Promoting evacuation.

evacuation (e-vak'u-a'shun) [L. *e-vacuo*, pp. *-vacuatus*, to empty out]. 1. Removal of waste material, especially from the bowels. 2. Stool (2).

evacuator (e-vak'u-a-tor). An instrument for removal of material from a body cavity.

evagination (e-vaj-ĭ-na'shun) [L. *e*, out, + *vagina*, sheath]. The protrusion of some part or organ from its normal position.

evanescent (ev-ă-nes'sent) [L. *e*, out, + *vanescere*, to vanish]. Of short duration.

Evans blue [H.M. *Evans*, U.S. anatomist, 1882–1971]. $C_{34}N_{24}N_6Na_4O_{14}S_4$; a diazo dye used for the determination of the blood volume on the basis of the dilution of a standard solution of the dye in the plasma after its intravenous injection; also used as a vital stain for following diffusion through blood vessel walls.

evap'ora'tion [L. *e*, out, + *vaporare*, to emit vapor]. Volatilization. 1. A change from liquid to vapor form. 2. Loss of volume of a liquid by conversion into vapor.

eventration (e-ven-tra'shun) [L. *e*, out, + *venter*, belly]. 1. Protrusion of omentum and/or intestine through an opening in the abdominal wall. 2. Removal of the contents of the abdominal cavity.
   e. of the diaphragm, extreme elevation of a half or part of the diaphragm, which is usually atrophic and abnormally thin.

eversion (e-ver-shun) [L. *e-everto*, pp. *-versus*, to overturn]. A turning outward, as of the eyelid.

evert [L. *e-verto*, to overturn]. To turn outward.

eV, ev Electron-volt.

evisceration (e-vis-er-a'shun) [L. *eviscero*, pp. *-atus*, to disembowel]. 1. Exenteration. 2. Removal of the contents of the eyeball, leaving the sclera and sometimes the cornea. 3. Disembowelling. 4. Protrusion of the abdominal viscera, *e.g.*, through a defect created by wound dehiscence.

evocation (ev-o-ka'shun, e-vo-) [L. *evoco*, pp. *evocatus*, to call forth]. Induction of a particular tissue produced by the action of an evocator during embryogenesis.

ev'ocator. The substance discharged from a factor in the control of morphogenesis in the early embryo.

evolu'tion [L. *e-volvo*, pp. *-volutus*, to roll out]. A continuing process of change from one state, condition, or form to another.
   biologic e., organic e.; the doctrine that all forms of life have been derived by gradual changes from simpler forms or from a single cell.
   convergent e., evolutionary development of similar structures in two or more species, often widely separated phylogenetically, in response to similarities of environment.
   organic e., biologic e.
   saltatory e., the theory that e. of a new species from an older one may occur as a large "jump," such as a major repatterning of chromosomes, rather than by gradual accumulation of small "steps" or mutations.

evulsion (e-vul'shun) [L. *evulsio*, fr. *e-vello*, pp. *-vulsus*, to pluck out]. A forcible pulling out or extraction.

ex- [L. and G. out of]. Prefix denoting out of, from, away from.

exacerbation (eks′as-er-ba′shun) [L. *ex-acerbo,* pp. *-auts,* to exasperate]. An increase in the severity of a disease or any of its signs or symptoms.

examina′tion. Any investigation or inspection made for the purpose of diagnosis, usually qualified by the method used; *e.g.,* cytologic, physical.

exan′them [G. *exanthēma,* efflorescence; an eruption]. Exanthema.

exanthe′ma [G.]. Exanthem; a skin eruption occurring as a symptom of an acute viral or coccal disease.

   keratoid e., a symptom occurring in the secondary stage of yaws: patches of fine, light colored, furfuraceous desquamation, scattered irregularly over limbs and trunk.

   e. subi′tum, roseola infantum; sixth disease; a viral disease of infants and young children, marked by sudden onset with fever lasting several days (sometimes with convulsions) and followed by a fine macular (sometimes maculopapular) rash.

exanthem′atous. Relating to an exanthema.

exarticula′tion [L. *ex,* out, + *articulus,* joint]. Disarticulation.

excalation (eks′kă-la′shun) [G. *ex,* from, + *chalān,* to abate, release]. Absence, suppression, or failure of development of one of a series of things, as of a digit, vertebra.

excavatio (eks-kă-va′shĭ-o) [L. fr. *ex-cavo,* pp. *-cavatus,* to hollow out, *ex,* out, + *cavus,* hollow] [NA]. Excavation (1).

   e. dis′ci [NA], excavation of the optic disk; physiologic excavation; the normally occurring depression or pit in the center of the optic disk.

   e. rectouteri′na [NA], rectouterine pouch; Douglas cul-de-sac, or pouch; a pocket formed by the deflection of the peritoneum from the rectum to the uterus.

   e. rectovesica′lis [NA], rectovesical pouch; a pocket formed by the deflection of the peritoneum from the rectum to the bladder in the male.

   e. vesicouteri′na [NA], vesicouterine pouch; a pocket formed by the deflection of the peritoneum from the bladder to the uterus in the female.

excavation (eks-kă-va′shun). **1.** Excavatio; a natural cavity, pouch, or recess. **2.** A cavity formed artifically or as the result of a pathologic process.

   atrophic e., an exaggeration of the normal or physiologic cupping of the optic disk (excavatio disci) caused by atrophy of the optic nerve.

   glaucomatous e., glaucomatous *cup.*

   e. of optic disk, physiologic e., *excavatio* disci.

ex′cavator. An instrument like a sharp spoon or curette, used in scraping out pathologic tissue.

excementosis (ek′se-men-to′sis). Outgrowth of cementum or root surface of a tooth.

excentric (ek-sen′trik). Eccentric (2, 3).

excess (ek′ses). That which is more than the usual or specified amount.

   base e., a measure of metabolic alkalosis; the amount of strong acid that would have to be added per unit volume of whole blood to titrate it to pH

7.4 while at 37°C and at a carbon dioxide pressure of 40 mm Hg.

   negative base e., a measure of metabolic acidosis; the amount of strong alkalai that would have to be added per unit volume of whole blood to titrate it to pH 7.4 while at 37°C and at a carbon dioxide pressure of 40 mm Hg.

excipient (ek-sip′ĭ-ent) [L. *excipiens;* pres. p. of *ex-cipio,* to take out]. A more or less inert substance added in a prescription as a diluent or vehicle or to give form or consistency when the remedy is given in pill form.

excise (ek-sīz′). Exsect; to cut out.

excision (ek-sizh′un) [L. *excidere,* to cut out]. **1.** Exsection; operative removal of a portion of a structure or organ. **2.** In molecular biology, a recombination event in which a genetic element is removed.

exci′table. 1. Capable of quick response to a stimulus; having potentiality for emotional arousal. **2.** In neurophysiology, referring to a tissue, cell, or membrane capable of undergoing excitation in response to an adequate stimulus.

excitability (ek-si-tă-bil′ĭ-tĭ). Having the capability of being excitable.

excitation (ek-si-ta′shun). **1.** The act of increasing the rapidity or intensity of the physical or mental processes. See also stimulation. **2.** In neurophysiology, the complete, all-or-none response of a nerve or muscle to an adequate stimulus, ordinarily including propagation of e. along the membranes of the cell or cells involved.

excite′ment. An emotional state characterized by its potential for impulsive or poorly controlled activity.

exci′tomo′tor. Centrokinetic (2); causing or increasing the rapidity of motion.

exclave (eks-klāv′) [L. *ex,* out, + *-clave*(in enclave)]. An outlying, detached portion of a gland or other part, such as the thyroid or pancreas; an acessory gland.

exclusion (eks-klu′zhun) [L. *ex-cludo,* pp. *-clusus,* to shut out]. Surgical isolation of a part or segment without removal from the body.

excoriate (eks-ko′rĭ-āt). To scratch or otherwise denude the skin by physical means.

excoriation (eks-ko′rĭ-a′shun) [L. *excorio,* to skin, strip]. A scratch mark; a linear break in the skin surface, usually covered with blood or serous crusts.

excrement (eks′krē-ment) [L. *ex-cerno,* pp. *-cretus,* to separate]. Waste matter or any excretion cast out of the body; *e.g.,* feces.

excrementitious (eks′krē-men-tish′us). Relating to any cast out waste material.

excrescence (eks-kres′ens) [L. *ex-cresco,* pp. *-cretus,* to grow forth]. Any outgrowth from the surface.

excreta (eks-kre′tah) [L. neut. pl. of *excretus,* pp. of *ex-cerno,* to separate]. Excretion (2).

excrete (eks-krēt′). To eliminate, as waste material, from the body.

excretion (eks-krē'shun) [see excrement]. **1.** The process whereby the undigested residue of food and the waste products of metabolism are eliminated. **2.** Excreta; the product of a tissue or organ that is waste material to be passed out of the body.

ex'cretory. Relating to excretion.

excyclophoria (eks-si-klo-fo'rĭ-ah). Plus cyclophoria; the tendency toward outward rotation of the upper pole of the cornea, prevented by visual fusional impulses.

excystation (ek-sis-ta'shun). Removal from a cyst; denoting the action of certain encysted organisms in escaping from their envelope.

exemia (eks-e'mĭ-ah) [G. *ex*, out of, + *haima*, blood]. A condition in which a considerable portion of the blood is temporarily removed from the general circulating mass, as in shock when there is a great accumulation within the abdomen.

exencephalic (eks'en-sĕ-fal'ĭk). Relating to exencephaly.

exencephaly (eks-en-sef'ă-lĭ) [G. *ex*, out, + *enkephalos*, brain]. A condition in which the skull is defective, the brain being exposed or extruding.

exenteration (eks'en-ter-a'shun) [G. *ex*, out, + *enteron*, bowel]. Evisceration (1); removal of internal organs and tissues, usually radical removal of the contents of a body cavity.

exenteri'tis (eks'en-ter-i'tis) [G. *exō*, on the outside, + enteritis]. Inflammation of the peritoneal covering of the intestine.

exercise (eks'er-sīz). **1.** *Active:* bodily exertion for the sake of restoring the organs and functions to a healthy state or keeping them healthy. **2.** *Passive:* motion of limbs without effort by the individual.

exeresis (eks-er'e-sis) [G. *exairesis*, a taking out]. Excision, or surgical removal of any part or organ; also used as combining form in suffix position.

exergon'ic [exo- + G. *ergon*, work]. Referring to a reaction that takes place with release of energy to its surroundings.

exfoliation (eks'fo-lĭ-a'shun) [L. *exfolatio*, fr. *ex*, out, + *folium*, leaf]. **1.** Detachment and shedding of superficial cells of an epithelium or from any tissue surface. **2.** Scaling or desquamation of the horny layer of epidermis. **3.** Loss of deciduous teeth following physiological loss of root structure. **4.** Extrusion of permanent teeth as a result of disease or loss of their antagonists.

exfoliative (eks-fo'lĭ-a-tiv) [Mod. L. *exfoliativus*]. Marked by exfoliation, desquamation, or profuse scaling.

exhalation (eks-hă-la'shun) [L. *ex-halo*, pp. *-halatus*, to breathe out]. **1.** Expiration; breathing out. **2.** The giving forth of gas or vapor. **3.** Any exhaled or emitted gas or vapor.

ex'hale. 1. Expire (1); to breathe out. **2.** To emit a gas or vapor or odor.

exhaustion (eks-zos'chun) [L. *ex-haurio*, pp. *-haustus*, to draw out, empty]. **1.** Extreme fatigue; inability to respond to stimuli. **2.** Removal of contents; using up

of a supply of anything. **3.** Extraction of the active constituents of a drug by treating with water, alcohol, or other solvent.

heat e., a form of reaction to heat, marked by prostration, weakness, and collapse, resulting from unrecognized or unavoidable dehydration.

exhibitionist (ek'sī-bish'un-ist). One who has a morbid compulsion to expose the genitals to a person of the opposite sex.

exhumation (eks-hu-ma'shun) [L. *ex*, out of, + *humus*, earth]. Disinterment.

exo- [G. *exō*, outside]. Prefix meaning exterior, external, or outward. See also ecto-.

exoantigen (ek'so-an'tĭ-jen). Ectoantigen.

exocar'dia. Ectocardia.

exocrine (ek'so-krin) [exo- + G. *krinō*, to separate]. **1.** Eccrine (1); denoting glandular secretion that is delivered to a surface. **2.** Pertaining to a gland that secretes outwardly through excretory ducts.

exocyto'sis [exo- + G. *kytos*, cell, + *-osis*, condition]. **1.** The appearance of migrating inflammatory cells in the epidermis. **2.** Emiocytosis; the process whereby secretory granules or droplets are released from a cell; the membrane around the granule fuses with the cell membrane, which ruptures, and the secretion is discharged.

ex'odevia'tion. Exophoria or exotropia.

exodontia (eks-o-don'shĭ-ah) [exo- + G. *odous*, tooth]. The branch of dental practice concerned with the extraction of teeth.

exodontist (eks-o-don'tist). One who specializes in the extraction of teeth.

ex'oen'zyme. Extracellular *enzyme*.

exogamy (eks-og'ă-mĭ) [exo- + G. *gamos*, marriage]. Sexual reproduction by means of conjugation of two gametes of different ancestry, as in certain protozoan species.

ex'ogas'trula. An abnormal embryo in which the primitive gut has been everted.

exogenous (eks-oj'ĕ-nus) [exo- + G. *-gen*, production]. Ectogenous; enthetic (2); originating or produced outside of the organism.

exomphalos (eks-om'fă-lus) [G. *ex*, out, + *omphalos*, umbilicus]. Exumbilication. **1.** Protrusion of the umbilicus. **2.** Umbilical *hernia*. **3.** Omphalocele.

exon (eks'on). A portion of DNA that codes for a section of the mature messenger RNA from that DNA, and is therefore expressed ("translated" into protein) at the ribosome.

exonuclease (eks-o-nu'kle-ās). A nuclease that releases one nucleotide at a time, serially, beginning at one end of a polynucleotide (nucleic acid).

exopep'tidase. An enzyme that catalyzes the hydrolysis of the terminal amino acid of a peptide chain.

exophoria (ek-so-fo'rĭ-ah) [exo- + G. *phora*, a carrying]. A tendency of the eyes to deviate outward when fusion is suspended.

exophor'ic. Relating to exophoria.

exophthalmic (eks-of-thal'mĭk). Relating to exophthalmos; marked by prominence of the eyeball.

exophthalmos (eks-of-thal′mos) [G. *ex*, out, + *ophthalmos*, eye]. Protrusion of the eyeballs.

ex′ophyte (ek′so-fīt) [exo- + G. *phyton*, plant]. An exterior or external plant parasite.

exophytic (ek-so-fit′ik). **1.** Pertaining to an exophyte. **2.** In dentistry, referring to the growth pattern of oral lesions that project into the oral cavity. **3.** In oncology, denoting a noninvasive neoplasm that projects out from an epithelial surface.

exoserosis (ek′so-sēr-o′sis). Serous exudation from the skin surface, as in eczema or abrasions.

exoskel′eton. **1.** All hard parts, such as hair, teeth, nails, feathers, dermal plates, scales, etc., developed from the ectoderm or mesoderm in vertebrates. **2.** The outer chitinous envelope of an insect, or the chitinous or calcareous covering of certain Crustacea and other invertebrates.

exosmosis (eks-os-mo′sis). Osmosis from within outward, as from the interior of a blood vessel.

exostosis, pl. **exosto′ses** (eks-os-to′sis) [exo- + G. *osteon*, bone, + *-osis*, condition]. Hyperostosis; poroma (2); a cartilage-capped bony projection arising from any bone that develops from cartilage.

   e. cartilagin′ea, an ossified chondroma arising from the epiphysis or joint surface of a bone.

   hereditary multiple exostoses, diaphysial aclasis; osteochondromatosis; a disturbance of enchondral bone growth in which multiple osteochondromas of long bones appear during childhood, with shortening of the radius and fibula; autosomal dominant inheritance.

   ivory e., a small, hardened, eburnated tumor arising from a bone, usually one of the cranial bones.

exoteric (ek-so-tĕr′ik) [G. *exōterikos*, outer]. Of external origin; arising outside the organism.

ex′other′mic [exo- + G. + *thermē*, heat]. **1.** Denoting a chemical rection attended by the development of heat. **2.** Relating to the external warmth of the body.

exotox′ic. **1.** Relating to an exotoxin. **2.** Relating to the introduction of an exogenous poison or toxin.

exotox′in. Extracellular *toxin;* an antigenic, injurious substance elaborated within the cells of certain Gram-positive bacteria and released into the environment where it is rapidly active in small amounts.

exotro′pia [exo- + G. *tropē,* turn]. Divergent or external strabismus; wall-eye (1); that type of strabismus in which the visual axes diverge; may be paralytic or concomitant, monocular or alternating; constant or intermittent.

expan′sion [L. *ex-pando,* pp. *-pansus,* to spread out]. **1.** An increase in size as of chest or lungs. **2.** The spreading out of any structure, as a tendon.

expectorant (eks-pek′to-rant) [L. *ex,* out, + *pectus,* chest]. Promoting secretion from the mucous membrane of the air passages or facilitating its expulsion.

expec′torate. To spit; to eject saliva, mucus, or other fluid from the mouth.

expectora′tion. **1.** Mucus and other fluids formed in the air passages and the mouth, and expelled by coughing. **2.** Spitting; the expelling from the mouth of saliva, mucus, and other material.

exper′ience. The feeling of emotions and sensations as opposed to thinking; involvement in what is happening rather than abstract reflection on an event or interpersonal encounter.

exper′iment. A test or trial.

   control e., an e. used to check another, to verify the result, or to demonstrate what would have occurred had the factor under study been omitted.

   double blind e., an e. conducted with neither experimenter nor subjects knowing which e. is the control; prevents bias in recording results.

   factorial e.'s, an experimental design in which two or more series of treatments are tried in all combinations.

expiration (eks-pī-ra′shun) [L. *expiro* or *ex-spiro,* pp. *-atus,* to breathe out]. Exhalation (1).

expi′ratory. Relating to expiration.

expire (eks-pīr′). **1.** Exhale (1). **2.** To die.

explant 1 (eks-plant′). To transfer living tissue from an organism to an artificial medium for culture. **2** (eks′plant). Tissue so transferred.

explora′tion [L. *ex-ploro,* pp. *-ploratus,* to explore]. An active examination, usually involving endoscopy or a surgical procedure, to ascertain conditions present as an aid in diagnosis.

explor′atory. Relating to or with a view to exploration.

explo′rer. A sharp, pointed probe used to investigate teeth surfaces in order to detect caries or other defects.

express [L. *ex-premo,* pp. *-pressus,* to press out]. To press or squeeze out.

expres′sion. **1.** Squeezing out; expelling by pressure. **2.** Facies (3); mobility of the features giving a particular emotional significance to the face. **3.** Any act determined by the nature of an individual.

expul′sive [L. *ex-pello,* pp. *-pulsus,* to drive out]. Tending to expel.

exsanguinate (ek-sang′gwĭ-nāt) [L. *ex,* out, + *sanguis* (*-guin*), blood]. **1.** To deprive of blood; to make bloodless. **2.** Exsanguine.

exsanguination (ek-sang′gwĭ-na′shun). Depriving of blood; making exsanguine.

exsanguine (ek-sang′gwin). Exsanguinate (2); deprived of blood.

exsect (ek-sekt′) [L. *ex-seco,* pp. *-sectus,* to cut out]. Excise.

exsection (ek-sek′shun). Excision.

exsiccant (ek-sik′ant) [L. *ex-sicco,* pp. *-siccatus,* to dry up]. Desiccant.

exsiccate (ek′sĭ-kāt). Desiccate.

exsiccation (ek-sĭ-ka′shun). **1.** Desiccation. **2.** Dehydration (3); removal of water of crystallization.

exsorption (ek-sorp′shun) [G. *ex,* out, + *sorbēre,* to suck]. Movement of substances from the blood into the lumen of the gut.

exstrophy (ek'stro-fi) [G. *ex*, out, + *strophē*, a turning]. A congenital turning out or eversion of a hollow organ.

  e. of the bladder, a congenital gap in the anterior wall of the bladder and the abdominal wall in front of it, the posterior wall of the bladder being exposed.

  e. of the cloaca, a developmental anomaly in which an area of intestinal mucosa is interposed between two separate areas of the urinary bladder.

extend [L. *ex-tendo*, pp. *-tensus*, to stretch out]. To straighten a limb, to diminish or extinguish the angle formed by flexion; to place the distal segment of a limb in such a position that its axis is continuous with that of the proximal segment.

exten'sion [L. *extensio*, to stretch out]. 1. The act of bringing the distal portion of a joint in continuity (though only parallel) with the long axis of the proximal portion. 2. A pulling or dragging force exerted on a limb in a distal direction.

  Buck's e., Buck's traction; an apparatus for applying skin traction on the leg through contact between the skin and adhesive tape connected to a suspended weight.

  skeletal e., skeletal *traction.*

exten'sor [L. one who stretches] [NA]. A muscle the contraction of which tends to straighten a limb; the antagonist of a flexor.

exte'riorize. **1.** To direct a patient's interest, thoughts, or feelings into a channel leading outside himself, to some definite aim or object. **2.** To expose an organ temporarily for observation, or permanently for purposes of physiologic experiment.

ex'tern [F. *externe*, outside, a day scholar]. An advanced student or recent graduate who assists in the medical or surgical care of hospital patients, but who lives outside of the institution.

exter'nal [L. *externus*]. Exterior; on the outside or farther from the center.

exteroceptive (eks'ter-o-sep'tiv) [L. *exterus*, outside, + *capere*, to take]. Relating to the exteroceptors; denoting the surface of the body containing the end organs adapted to receive impressions or stimuli from without.

exteroceptor (eks'ter-o-sep'tor) [L. *exterus*, external, + *receptor*, receiver]. One of the peripheral end organs of the afferent nerves in the skin or mucous membrane, which respond to stimulation by external agents.

exterofective (eks'ter-o-fek'tiv) [L. ab. *extero*, from outside, + *affectus*, affected]. Pertaining to the response of the nervous system to external stimuli.

extima (eks'ti-mah) [L. fem. of *extimus*, outermost]. Rarely used term for the adventitia (outer coat) of a blood vessel.

extinction (eks-tingk'shun) [L. *extinguo*, to quench]. **1.** A progressive reduction in the strength of the conditioned response in successive conditioning trials during which only the conditioned stimulus is presented and the unconditioned stimulus is deliberately omitted. **2.** Absorbance.

extinguish (eks-ting'wish) [L. *extinguo*, to quench]. In psychology, to progressively abolish a previously conditioned response.

extirpation (eks-tir-pa'shun) [L. *extirpo*, pp. *-atus*, to root out]. The removal of an organ, in part or completely, or of a diseased tissue.

extorsion (eks-tor'shun) [L. *extorsio*, fr. *ex-torqueo*, pp. *-tortus*, to twist out]. **1.** Outward rotation of a limb or of an organ. **2.** Disclination; positive declination; rotation of the eye temporally around its anteroposterior axis.

extra-. Prefix fr. L. preposition meaning without, outside of.

extracel'lular. Outside a cell.

extracorporeal (eks'trä-kor-po're-al). Outside of, or unrelated to, the body or any anatomical "corpus."

extract. 1 (ek'strakt). A concentrated preparation of a drug obtained by removing the active constituents of the drug with suitable solvents, evaporating all or nearly all of the solvent, and adjusting the residual mass or powder to the prescribed standard. **2** (ek-strakt'). To remove part of a mixture with a solvent.

  allergenic e., allergic e., e. (usually containing protein) from various sources (*e.g.,* food, bacteria, pollen) suspected of specific action in stimulating manifestations of allergy.

extraction (eks-trak'shun) [L. *ex-traho*, pp. *-tractus*, to draw out]. **1.** Removal by withdrawing or pulling out, as a tooth from its alveolus, or a baby from the genital canal in assisted delivery. **2.** The active portion of a drug; the making of an extract.

  serial e., selective e. of certain deciduous or permanent teeth, or both, during the early years of dental development, usually with the eventual e. of the first, or occasionally the second, premolars, to encourage autonomous adjustment of moderate to severe crowding of anterior teeth.

extrac'tives. Substances present in vegetable or animal tissue that can be separated by successive treatment with solvents and recovered by evaporation of the solution.

extrac'tor. An instrument for use in drawing or pulling out any natural part or a foreign body.

extracystic (eks-trä-sis'tik). Outside of, or unrelated to, the gallbladder or urinary bladder or any cystic tumor.

extraembryonic (eks'trä-em-brī-on'ik). Outside the embryonic body; *e.g.,* pertaining to structures concerned with the embryo's protection and nutrition, and discarded at birth without being incorporated into the embryo.

extraphysiologic (eks'trä-fiz-ī-o-loj'ik). Outside of the domain of physiology; more than physiologic, therefore pathologic.

extrasen'sory. Ouside or beyond the ordinary senses; not limited to the senses; *e.g.,* clairvoyance or thought transference.

extrasystole (eks'trä-sis'to-le). Premature systole; an ectopic, usually premature, contraction of the heart;

such beats arise from the atrium, the A-V node, or the ventricle and interrupt the dominant, usually sinus, rhythm; they are in some way dependent on the preceding beat and are therefore "forced" beats.

atrial e., a premature contraction of the heart arising from an ectopic atrial focus.

atrioventricular (A-V) e., e. arising from the "junctional" tissues, either the A-V node or A-V bundle.

atrioventricular (A-V) nodal e., nodal e.; a premature beat arising from the A-V node and leading to a simultaneous or almost simultaneous contraction of atria and ventricles.

infranodal e., ventricular e.

interpolated e., a ventricular e. which, instead of being followed by a compensatory pause, is sandwiched between two consecutive sinus cycles.

nodal e., atrioventricular nodal e.

return e., a form of reciprocal rhythm in which the impulse having arisen in the ventricle ascends toward the atria, but before reaching the atria is reflected back to the ventricles to produce a second ventricular contraction.

ventricular e., infranodal e.; a premature contraction of the ventricle.

extravasate (eks-trav'ă-sāt) [L. *extra*, out of, + *vas*, vessel]. **1.** To exude from or pass out of a vessel into the tissues, said of blood, lymph, or urine. **2.** Extravasation (2); suffusion (4); the substance thus exuded.

extravasation (eks-trav-ă-sa'shun). **1.** The act of extravasating. **2.** Extravasate (2).

ex'traver'sion. Extroversion.

extrem'itas [L. from *extremus*, last, outermost] [NA]. Extremity (1).

extremity (eks-trem'ĭ-tĭ) [L. *extremitas*]. **1.** Extremitas; an end of an elongated or pointed structure. **2.** An arm or a leg.

lower e., inferior or pelvic limb; the hip, thigh, leg, ankle, and foot.

upper e., superior or thoracic limb; the shoulder, arm, forearm, wrist, and hand.

extrinsic (eks-trin'sik) [L. *extrinsecus*, from without]. Originating outside of the part where found or upon which it acts; denoting especially a muscle.

extroversion (eks'tro-ver'zhun) [fr. L. *extra*, outside, + *verto*, pp. *versus*, to turn]. Extraversion. **1.** A turning outward. **2.** A trait involving social intercourse.

ex'trovert. A gregarious person whose chief interests lie outside himself, and who is involved in the affairs of others.

extrude (eks-trood'). To thrust, force, or press out.

extrusion (eks-tru'zhun). **1.** A thrusting or forcing out of a normal position. **2.** The overeruption or migration of a tooth beyond its normal occlusal position.

extubation (eks-tu-ba'shun) [L. *ex*, out, + *tuba*, tube]. Removal of a tube from an organ, structure, or orifice; specifically, the removal of the tube after

intubation of the larynx or trachea.

exuberant (eks-u'ber-ant) [L. *exubero*, to abound, be abundant]. Denoting excessive proliferation or growth, as of a tissue or granulation.

exudate (eks'u-dāt) [L. *ex*, out, + *sudare*, to sweat]. Exudation (2); any fluid that has exuded out of a tissue or its capillaries, specifically because of injury or inflammation.

exudation (eks-u-da'shun). **1.** The act or process of exuding. **2.** Exudate.

exudative (eks-u'dă-tiv). Relating to the process of exudation or to an exudate.

exude (eks-ūd') [L. *ex*, out, + *sudare*, to sweat]. To ooze or pass gradually out of a body structure or tissue; specifically, restricted to a fluid or semisolid that so passes and may become encrusted or infected, because of injury or inflammation.

ex'umbilica'tion [L. *ex*, out, + *umbilicus*, navel]. Exomphalos.

eye [A.S. *eáge*]. Oculus; the organ of vision.

crossed e.'s, esotropia.

dark-adapted e., scotopic e.; an e. that has been in darkness or semidarkness for some time and has undergone regeneration of rhodopsin (visual purple) and dilation of the pupil, which renders it more sensitive to low illumination (a function of the rods).

dominant e., the e. customarily used for monocular tasks.

exciting e., the injured e. in sympathetic ophthalmia.

light-adapted e., photopic e.; an e. that has been exposed to light of relatively high intensity and has undergone adjustments of photochemical change and pupillary constriction (mainly a function of the retinal cones).

photopic e., light-adapted e.

scotopic e., dark-adapted e.

eye'ball. *Bulbus* oculi.

eye bank. A place where corneas of eyes removed immediately after death are preserved for subsequent keratoplasty.

eye'brow. Supercilium (1).

eye'grounds. The fundus of the eye as seen with the ophthalmoscope.

eye'lash. Cilium (1).

eye'lid. Palpebra.

eye'piece. The compound lens at the end of the microscope tube nearest the eye; it magnifies the image made by the objective.

eye'strain. Asthenopia.

eye'wash. Collyrium; a soothing solution for bathing or medicating the eye.

F

F Fractional *concentration*, followed by subscripts indicating location and chemical species; free *energy;* Fahrenheit; faraday; visual *field;* fluorine; force; filial *generation.*

f Respiratory *frequency;* femto-.

Fab See Fab *fragment.*

fabella (fă-bel'lah) [Mod. L. dim of *faba,* bean]. A small sesamoid bone in the tendon of the lateral head of the gastrocnemius muscle.

F.A.C.D. Fellow of the American College of Dentists.

face. Facies (1); the front portion of the head, from forehead to chin.

    hippocratic f., hippocratic *facies.*

    masklike f., Parkinson's *facies.*

    moon f., the round, usually red face, with large jowls, seen in Cushing's disease or in hyperadrenocorticalism.

face-bow. A caliper-like device used to record the relationship of the jaws to the temporomandibular joints; the record may then be used to orient the maxillary cast to the opening and closing axis of the articulator.

face-lift. See rhytidectomy.

facet (fas'et) [Fr. *facette*]. **1.** A small smooth area on a bone or other firm structure. **2.** A worn spot on a tooth, produced by chewing or grinding.

facetectomy (fas-ĕ-tek'to-mĭ) [facet + G. *ektomē,* excision]. Excision of a facet, as of a vertebra.

facial (fa'shal). Relating to the face.

-facient [L. *facio,* to make]. Suffix meaning that which brings about.

facies, pl. **facies** (fa'she-ēz, fash'e-ēz) [L.] **1** [NA]. Face. **2** [NA]. Surface. **3.** Expression (2).

    adenoid f., the open-mouthed and often stupid appearance in children with adenoid hypertrophy, associated with a pinched nose and narrow nares.

    Corvisart's f., the characteristic f. seen in cardiac insufficiency or aortic regurgitation: a swollen, purplish, cyanotic face with shiny eyes and puffy eyelids.

    hippocratic f., hippocratic face; a pinched expression of the face, with sunken eyes, hollow cheeks and temples, relaxed lips, and leaden complexion, observed in one dying after an exhausting illness.

    hurloid f., the coarse gargoyle-like facial appearance characteristically seen in the mucopolysaccharidoses and mucolipidoses.

    Hutchinson's f., the peculiar facial expression produced by the drooping eyelids and motionless eyes in ophthalmoplegia.

    leonine f., leontiasis.

    myasthenic f., the facial expression in myasthenia gravis: drooping of the eyelids and corners of the mouth, and weakness of the muscles of the face.

    Parkinson's f., masklike face; the expressionless or masklike f. characteristic of parkinsonism (1).

    Potter's f., characteristic f. seen in bilateral renal agenesis and other severe renal malformations: ocular hypertelorism, low-set ears, receding chin, and flattening of the nose.

facilitation (fă-sil-ĭ-ta'shun) [L. *facilitas,* fr. *facilis,* easy]. Enhancement or reinforcement of a reflex or other nervous activity by the arrival at the reflex center of other excitatory impulses.

facing (fās'ing). A tooth-colored material used to hide the buccal or labial surface of a gold crown to give the outward appearance of a natural tooth.

facio- [L. *facies,* face]. Combining form relating to the face.

facioplasty (fa'shĭ-o-plas-tĭ) [facio- + G. *plastos,* formed]. Reparative or reconstructive surgery involving the face.

facioplegia (fa'shĭ-o-ple'jĭ-ah) [facio- + G. *plēgē,* a stroke]. Facial *palsy.*

F.A.C.O.G. Fellow of the American College of Obstetricians and Gynecologists.

F.A.C.P. Fellow of the American College of (1) Physicians, (2) Prosthodontists.

F.A.C.R. Fellow of the American College of Radiologists.

F.A.C.S. Fellow of the American College of Surgeons.

F-actin. See under actin.

factitious (fak-tish'us) [L. *factitius,* made by art]. Artificial; self-induced; not natural; produced either unintentionally (accidentally) or deliberately (consciously or unconsciously).

factor (fak'ter) [L. maker, causer, fr. *facio,* to make]. **1.** One of the contributing causes in any action. **2.** One of the components which by multiplication makes up a number or expression. **3.** Gene. **4.** Vitamin or other essential element.

    f. I, in the clotting of blood, fibrinogen.

    f. II, (1) in the clotting of blood, prothrombin; (2) lipoic acid.

    f. III, in the clotting of blood, tissue thromboplastin.

    f. IV, in the clotting of blood, calcium ions.

    f. V, in the clotting of blood, also known as: proaccelerin; plasma accelerator globulin; prothrombin accelerator. Deficiency of this f. leads to a rare hemorrhagic tendency known as parahemophilia or hypoproaccelerinemia, with autosomal recessive inheritance; heterozygous individuals are recognized by reduced levels of f. V but have no bleeding tendency.

    f. VII, in the clotting of blood, also known as: proconvertin; serum prothrombin conversion accelerator; cothromboplastin; serum accelerator. F. VII is known to be involved in: 1) congenital deficiency of f. VII, with purpura and bleeding from mucous membranes, autosomal recessive inheritance; 2) the acquired deficiency of f. VII in association with a deficiency of vitamin K, the neonatal period, and administration of prothrombinopenic drugs; and 3) acquired excess of f. VII in some patients with thromboembolism F. VII accelerates the conversion of prothrombin to thrombin, in the presence of tissue thromboplastin, calcium, and f. V.

f. VIII, in the clotting of blood, also known as: antihemophilic globulin; antihemophilic f.; proconvertin; proserum prothrombin conversion accelerator. Deficiency of f. VIII is associated with classic hemophilia A, an X-linked recessive hemorrhagic tendency that occurs almost exclusively in males; clotting time is prolonged, less thromboplastin is formed, and the conversion of prothrombin is diminished.

f. IX, in the clotting of blood, also known as: Christmas f.; plasma thromboplastin component. Deficiency of this f. causes hemophilia B or Christmas disease, which resembles hemophilia A and is an X-linked recessive defect that leads to a severe hemorrhagic disorder. F. IX is required for the formation of intrinsic blood thromboplastin and affects the amount formed (rather than the rate).

f. X, prothrombinase.

f. XI, in the clotting of blood, also known as plasma thromboplastin antecedent. A component of the contact system absorbed from plasma and serum by glass and similar surfaces. Deficiency of f. XI results in a hemorrhagic tendency and is caused by an autosomal recessive gene.

f. XII, in the clotting of blood, also known as Hageman f. Deficiency of f. XII results in prolongation of the clotting time of venous blood, rarely in a hemorrhagic tendency, and is caused by an autosomal recessive gene.

f. XIII, in the clotting of blood, thrombin catalyzes the conversion of this f. into its active form, fibrinase (also called fibrin-stabilizing f., Laki-Lorand f.), which cross-links subunits of the fibrin clot to form insoluble fibrin.

accelerator f., f. V.

antihemophilic f., f. VIII.

antihemorrhagic f., vitamin K.

antinuclear f. (ANF), a f. present in serum with strong affinity for nuclei and detected by fluorescent antibody technique; present in lupus erythematosus, rheumatic arthritis, and certain other conditions.

antipernicious anemia f. (APA), vitamin B$_{12}$.

Castle's intrinsic f., intrinsic f.; a relatively small mucoprotein secreted by the neck cells of gastric glands and required for adequate absorption of vitamin B$_{12}$; deficient in patients with pernicious anemia.

Christmas f. [surname of child afflicted], f. IX.

clearing f.'s, lipoprotein lipases that appear in plasma during lipemia and catalyze hydrolysis of triglycerides only when the latter are bound to protein and when an acceptor (*e.g.,* serum albumin) is present, thus "clearing" the plasma.

clotting f., coagulation f., various plasma components involved in the clotting process, including, notably, fibrinogen (f. I), prothrombin (f. II), thromboplastin (f. III), and calcium ion (f. IV).

complement chemotactic f., the activated complex of the fifth, sixth, and seventh components of complement (C567) which induces chemotaxis in

the case of polymorphonuclear leukocytes.

coupling f.'s (CF), proteins that restore phosphorylating ability to mitochondria that have lost it, *i.e.,* have become "uncoupled" so that oxidation no longer produces ATP.

eosinophil chemotactic f. of anaphylaxis, (ECF-A), a peptide that is chemotactic for eosinophilic leukocytes and is released from disrupted mast cells.

extrinsic f., dietary vitamin B$_{12}$.

F. f., fertility f., F. *plasmid.*

follicle-stimulating hormone-releasing f. (FRF, FSH-RF), folliberin; follicle-stimulating hormone-releasing hormone; a decapeptide of hypothalamic origin capable of accelerating pituitary secretion of follicle-stimulating hormone.

glycotropic f., insulin-antagonizing f.; a principle in extracts of the anterior lobe of the hypophysis that raises the blood sugar and antagonizes the action of insulin.

gonadotropin-releasing f., gonadoliberin (1); a hypothalamic substance causing release of gonadotropin.

growth hormone-releasing f., (GHRF, GH-RF), somatoliberin.

Hageman f., f. XII.

human antihemophilic f., antihemophilic globulin; a lyophilized concentrate of f. VIII, obtained from fresh normal human plasma; used as a hemostatic agent in hemophilia.

insulin-antagonizing f., glycotropic f.

intrinsic f. (IF), Castle's intrinsic f.

Laki-Lorand f., see f. XIII.

L.E. f.'s, antinuclear immunoglobulins in plasma of persons with disseminated lupus erythematosus, associated with positive L.E. tests.

lethal f., a gene mutation or chromosomal structural change which, when expressed, caused death prior to sexual maturity.

luteinizing hormone/follicle-stimulating hormone-releasing f. (LH/FSH-RF), gonadoliberin (2); the decapeptide from pig hypothalami that induces release of both lutropin and follitropin in constant proportions and thus acts as both luliberin and folliberin.

lymph node permeability f. (LNPF), a substance, released by lymphocytes when stimulated or damaged, that increases capillary permeability and the accumulation of mononuclear cells.

platelet f. 3, a blood coagulation factor derived from platelets; a phospholipid lipoprotein that acts with certain plasma thromboplastin f.'s to convert prothrombin to thrombin.

platelet-aggregating (or- activating) f. (PAF), a substance released from rabbit basophilic leukocytes that causes aggregation of platelets and also is involved in the deposition of immune complexes.

platelet tissue f., thromboplastin.

prolactin-inhibiting f. (PIF), prolactostatin; a substance of hypothalamic origin capable of inhibiting the synthesis and release of prolactin by the anterior pituitary gland.

properdin f. A, a component of the properdin system; a hydrazine-sensitive β_1-globulin, now known to be C3 (third component of complement).

properdin f. B, a normal serum protein and a component of the properdin system.

properdin f. D, a normal serum α-globulin required in the properdin system.

properdin f. E, a serum protein required for activation of C3 (third component of complement).

R f.'s, resistance *plasmids.*

recognition f.'s, f.'s which effect "recognition" of target antigens by polymorphonuclear neutrophil leukocytes; apparently the Fc portion of antibody molecules and the activated third component of complement (C3), for both of which phagocytes have receptor sites.

releasing f. (RF), releasing hormone; a substance of hypothalamic origin capable of accelerating the rate of secretion of a given hormone by the anterior pituitary gland.

resistance f.'s, resistance *plasmids.*

resistance-transfer f., the transfer gene of the resistance plasmid.

rheumatoid f.'s (RF), globulins in the serum of patients with rheumatoid arthritis that enhance agglutination of suspended particles coated with pooled human γ-globulin; seem to be antibodies of the IgG and IgM classes.

slow-reacting f. of anaphylaxis (SRF-A), slow-reacting *substance* (of anaphylaxis).

somatotropin release-inhibiting f. (SRIF), somatostatin.

somatotropin-releasing f. (SRF), somatoliberin.

Stuart f., Stuart-Prower f., prothrombinase.

transfer f., (1) the transfer gene of a conjugative plasmid, especially of the resistance plasmid; **(2)** a substance, free of nucleic acid and antibody, that is obtained from the leukocytes of a person with a delayed-type sensitivity and that will, following injection into the skin of a nonsensitive person, transfer the specific sensitivity to the recipient.

transforming f., the DNA responsible for bacterial transformation.

tumor angiogenic f. (TAF), a substance released by solid tumors which induces formation of new blood vessels to supply the tumor.

facultative (fak'ul-ta'tiv). Able to live under more than one specific set of environmental conditions; with an alternative pathway.

faculty (fak'ul-tĭ). A natural or specialized power of a living organism.

FAD *Flavin* adenine dinucleotide.

failure. Inability to function or perform satisfactorily.

backward heart f., the phenomena of heart f. resulting from passive engorgement of the veins caused by a "backward" rise in pressure proximal to the failing cardiac chambers.

congestive heart f., heart f. (1).

coronary f., acute coronary insufficiency.

forward heart f., the phenomena of heart f. resulting from the inadequate cardiac output, and especially from the consequent inadequacy of renal blood flow with resulting retention of sodium and water.

heart f., (1) congestive heart f.; cardiac or myocardial insufficiency; mechanical inadequacy of the heart to maintain the circulation of blood, with congestion and edema developing in the tissues; **(2)** the resulting clinical syndrome consisting of shortness of breath, pitting edema, enlarged tender liver, engorged neck veins, and pulmonary rales.

left ventricular f., heart f. manifested by signs of pulmonary congestion and edema.

right ventricular f., heart f. manifested by distention of the neck veins, enlargement of the liver, and dependent edema.

faint. 1. Extremely weak; threatened with syncope. **2.** An attack of syncope.

fal'cate. Falciform.

fal'ces. Plural of falx.

falciform (fal'sĭ-form) [L. *falx,* sickle, + *forma,* form]. Falcate; falcular (2); crescentic or sickle-shaped.

falcula (fal'ku-lah) [L. dim. of *falx*]. *Falx* cerebelli.

fal'cular. 1. Relating to the falx cerebelli. **2.** Falciform.

falling of womb. Prolapse of uterus.

fallo'pian. Described by or attributed to Fallopius.

fal'sifica'tion. The deliberate act of misrepresentation so as to deceive.

retrospective f., unconscious distortion of past experience to conform to present psychological needs.

falx, pl. **falces** (falks, fal'sēz) [L. sickle] [NA]. A sickle-shaped structure.

f. cerebel'li [NA], falcula; a short process of dura mater projecting forward from the internal occipital crest below the tentorium; it occupies the posterior cerebellar notch and the vallecula, and bifurcates below into two diverging limbs passing to either side of the foramen magnum.

f. cer'ebri [NA], the scythe-shaped fold of dura mater in the longitudinal fissure between the two cerebral hemispheres.

famil'ial [L. *familia,* family]. Affecting several members of the same family, usually within a single sibship.

fam'ily [L. *familia*]. **1.** A group of blood relatives; strictly, the parents and their children. **2.** In biologic classification, a division between order and tribe or genus.

cancer f., a group of blood relatives in which cancer has been reported; the mode of aggregation may be genetic, as in familial cancer, or due to common exposure to a carcinogenic or oncogenic agent.

fan'tasy [G. *phantasia*, idea, image]. Imagery that is more or less coherent, as in dreams and daydreams, yet unrestricted by reality.

farad (făr'ad) [M. *Faraday*]. A practical unit of electrical capacity, being the capacity of a condenser having a chaarge of 1 coulomb under an electromotive force of 1 volt.

faraday (F) (făr'ă-da) [M. *Faraday*]. 96,500 coulombs, the amount of electricity required to reduce one equivalent of (*e.g.*) silver ion.

far'sight'edness. Hyperopia.

fascia, pl. **fasciae** (fash'ĭ-ah, fash'ĭ-e) [L. a band or fillet] [NA]. A sheet of fibrous tissue that envelops the body beneath the skin; also encloses muscles and muscle groups, and separates their several layers or groups.

broad f., f. lata.

Colles f., f. perinei superficialis.

deep f., a thin fibrous membrane, devoid of fat, that invests the muscles, separating the several groups and the individual muscles, forms sheaths for the nerves and vessels, becomes specialized around the joints to form or strengthen ligaments, envelops various organs and glands, and binds all the structures together into a firm compact mass.

f. endothora'cica, [NA], **endothoracic f.,** the extrapleural f. that lines the wall of the thorax; it extends over the cupula of the pleura as the suprapleural membrane and also forms a thin layer between the diaphragm and pleura.

extraperitoneal f., f. subperitonealis.

f. la'ta [NA], broad f.; the strong f. enveloping the muscles of the thigh.

f. pel'vis, [NA], **f. of the pelvis;** f. that covers the muscles that pass from the interior of the pelvis to the thigh, the pelvic organs, and vessels and nerves in the subperitoneal space.

f. perine'i superficia'lis, [NA], **superficial f. of the perineum,** Colles f.; the membranous layer of the subcutaneous tissue in the urogenital region attaching posteriorly to the border of the urogenital diaphragm, at the sides to the ischiopubic rami, and continuing anteriorly onto the abdominal wall.

f. phrenicopleura'lis, [NA], **phrenicopleural f.,** the thin layer of endothoracic f. intervening between the diaphragmatic pleura and the diaphragm.

f. rena'lis, [NA], **renal f.,** Gerota's capsule; the condensation of the fibroareolar tissue and fat surrounding the kidney to form a sheath for the organ.

Scarpa's f., the deeper, membranous or lamellar part of the subcutaneous tissue of the lower abdominal wall, continuous with the superficial perineal (Colles) f.

f. subperitonea'lis, [NA], **subperitoneal f.,** extraperitoneal f.; the thin layer of f. and adipose tissue between the peritoneum and f. transversalis.

superficial f., *tela* subcutanea.

superficial f. of perineum, f. perinei superficialis.

f. thoracolumba'lis, [NA], **thoracolumbar f.,** the f. that covers the deep muscles of the back.

f. transversa'lis [NA], **transverse f.,** the lining f. of the abdominal cavity, between the inner surface of the abdominal musculature and the peritoneum.

fascial (fash'ĭ-al). Relating to any fascia.

fascicle (fas'ĭ-kl). Fasciculus.

fascicular, fasciculate, fasciculated (fă-sik'u-lar, -u-lāt, -u-lāt-ed). Relating to a fasciculus; arranged in the form of a bundle or collection of rods.

fasciculation (fă-sik-u-la'shun). 1. An arrangement in the form of fasciculi. 2. Involuntary contractions, or twitchings, of groups (fasciculi) of muscle fibers, a coarser form of muscular contraction than fibrillation.

fasciculi (fa-sik'u-li). Plural of fasciculus.

fasciculus, gen. and pl. **fasciculi** fă-sik'u-lus, -u-li) [L. dim. of *facis*, bundle] [NA]. Fascicle; a band or bundle of fibers, usually of muscle or nerve fibers.

f. cunea'tus, [NA], **cuneate f.,** cuneate funiculus; the larger lateral subdivision of the funiculus posterior.

f. dorsolatera'lis, [NA], **dorsolateral f.,** dorsolateral tract; a longitudinal bundle of thin, unmyelinated and poorly myelinated fibers capping the apex of the posterior horn of the spinal gray matter, composed of posterior root fibers and short association fibers that interconnect neighboring segments of the posterior horn.

f. grac'ilis [NA], the smaller medial subdivision of the funiculus posterior.

inferior longitudinal f., f. longitudinalis inferior.

f. latera'lis plex'us brachia'lis [NA], lateral cord of the brachial plexus; formed by the anterior divisions of the superior and middle trunks, it gives off the lateral pectoral nerve and terminates by dividing into the musculocutaneous nerve and the lateral root of the median nerve.

fasciculi longitudina'les pon'tis, the massive bundles of corticofugal fibers passing longitudinally through the pars ventralis pontis; composed of corticopontine, corticobulbar, and corticospinal fibers.

f. longitudina'lis infe'rior [NA], inferior longitudinal f.; a well marked bundle of long association fibers running the whole length of the occipital and temporal lobes of the cerebrum, in part parallel with the inferior horn of the lateral ventricle.

f. longitudina'lis media'lis [NA], medial longitudinal f.; a longitudinal bundle of fibers extending from the upper border of the mesencephalon into the cervical segments of the spinal cord, located close to the midline and ventral to the central gray matter; composed largely of fibers from the vestibular nuclei ascending to the motor neurons innervating the external eye muscles, and descending to spinal cord segments innervating the musculature of the neck.

f. longitudina'lis supe'rior [NA], superior longitudinal f.; a bundle of long association fibers in the lateral portion of the centrum ovale of the cerebral hemisphere, connecting the frontal, occipital, and temporal lobes.

f. mamillothalam'icus, [NA], **mamillothalamic f.,** bundle of Vicq d'Azyr; a compact, thick bundle of nerve fibers that passes dorsalward from the mamillary body on either side to terminate in the anterior nucleus of the thalamus.

medial longitudinal f., f. longitudinalis medialis.

f. media'lis plex'us brachia'lis [NA], medial cord of the brachial plexus; formed by the anterior division of the inferior trunk, it gives off the medial pectoral nerve, the medial brachial cutaneous, medial antebrachial cutaneous, ulnar, and the medial root of the median nerves.

f. poste'rior plex'us brachia'lis [NA], posterior cord of the brachial plexus; formed by the posterior divisions of the upper, middle and lower trunks, it gives rise to the subscapular, thoracodorsal, axillary, and radial nerves.

fascic'uli pro'prii, [NA], **proper fasciculi,** ground bundles; ascending and descending association fiber systems of the spinal cord which lie deep in the anterior, lateral, and posterior funiculi adjacent to the gray matter.

superior longitudinal f., f. longitudinalis superior.

f. uncina'tus, [NA], **uncinate f.,** a band of long association fibers reciprocally connecting the frontal and temporal lobes of the cerebrum.

fasciectomy (fä-shĭ-ek'to-mĭ) [fascia + G. *ektomē,* excision]. Excision of strips of fascia.

fasciitis (fash'ĭ-i-tis). 1. Inflammation in fascia. 2. Reactive proliferation of fibroblasts in fascia.

nodular, proliferative, or **pseudosarcomatous f.,** a tumor-like proliferation of fibroblasts, not thought to be neoplastic, with mild inflammatory exudation occurring in fascia.

fascio- [L. *fascia,* a band or fillet]. Combining form denoting a fascia.

fasciodesis (fash-ĭ-od'ĕ-sis) [fascio- + G. *desis,* a binding together]. Operative attachment of a fascia to another fascia or a tendon.

Fasciola (fä-se'o-lah) [L. dim of *fascia,* a band]. A genus of large digenetic liver flukes (family Fasciolidae, class Trematoda) of mammals. *F. hepatica,* the common liver fluke inhabiting the bile ducts of sheep and cattle, is rarely reported from man, where it may cause considerable biliary damage.

fasciola, pl. **fasciolae** (fä-se'o-lah, -o-lĭ) [L. dim of *fascia,* band, fillet]. A small band or group of fibers.

fasci'olar. Relating to the gyrus fasciolaris.

fascioliasis (fas'ĭ-o-li'ă-sis). Infection with a species of *Fasciola.*

fas'ciolopsi'asis. Parasitization by any of the flukes of the genus *Fasciolopsis.*

Fasciolopsis (fas'ĭ-o-lop'sis) [*Fasciola* + G. *opsis,* form, appearance]. A genus of very large intestinal fasciolid flukes. *F. buski* in a species found in the intestine of man in eastern and southern Asia.

fascioplasty, (fash'ĭ-o-plas-tĭ). A plastic operation on fascia.

fasciorrhaphy (fash-ĭ-or'ră-fĭ) [fascio- + G. *raphē,* suture]. Aponeurorrhaphy; suture of a fascia or aponeurosis.

fasciotomy (fash-ĭ-ot'o-mĭ) [fascio- + G. *tomē,* incision]. Incision through a fascia.

fast [A.S. *foest,* firm, fixed]. 1. Durable; resistant to change; applied to stained microorganisms which cannot be decolorized. 2. To abstain from food.

fastid'ious. In bacteriology, having complex nutritional requirements.

fastigium (fas-tij'ĭ-um) [L. top, as of a gable; a pointed extremity]. 1. Summit of the roof of the fourth ventricle of the brain, an angle formed by the union of the anterior and posterior medullary vela pushing up into the substance of the vermis. 2. The acme or period of full development of a disease.

fat [A.S. *faet*]. 1. Adipose *tissue.* 2. Obese; corpulent. 3. A greasy, soft-solid material, found in animal tissues and many plants, composed of a mixture of glycerol esters; together with oils these make up that class of foodstuffs known as simple lipids.

saturated f., see saturated *fatty acid.*

unsaturated f., see unsaturated *fatty acid.*

fa'tal [L. *fatalis,* of or belonging to fate]. 1. Inevitable. 2. Pertaining to or causing death; denoting especially inevitability or inescapability of death.

fatigability (fat'ĭ-gă-bil'ĭ-tĭ). Condition in which fatigue is easily induced.

fatigue (fä-tēg') [Fr. fr. L. *fatigo,* to tire]. 1. That state following a period of mental or bodily activity characterized by a lessened capacity for work and reduced efficiency of accomplishment when from any cause energy expenditure outstrips restorative processes. 2. Sensation of boredom and lassitude due to absence of stimulation, monotony, or lack of interest in one's surroundings.

fat-pad. An accumulation of somewhat encapsulated adipose tissue.

fat'ty. Oily or greasy; relating in any sense to fat.

fatty acid. Any acid derived from fats by hydrolysis; any long-chain monobasic organic acid.

saturated f. a., a f. a., the carbon chain of which contains no ethylenic or other unsaturated linkages between carbon atoms and is not capable of absorbing any more hydrogen.

unsaturated f. a., a f. a., the carbon chain of which possesses one or more double or triple bonds and is capable of absorbing additional hydrogen.

fauces (faw'sēz) [L. the throat] [NA]. The space between the cavity of the mouth and the pharynx.

faucial (faw'shal). Relating to the fauces.

faucitis (faw-si'tis). Inflammation of the fauces.

fauna (faw'nah) [Mod. L. application of *Fauna,* sister of *Faunus,* a rural deity]. The animal forms of a continent, district, locality, or habitat.

faveolate (fa-ve'o-lāt). Pitted.

faveolus, pl. **faveoli** (fa-ve'o-lus, -o-li) [Mod. L. dim of *favus,* honeycomb]. A small pit or depression.

fa'vid. An allergic reaction in the skin observed in favus.

fa′vism [Ital. *favismo*, from *fava*, bean]. An acute condition following the ingestion of certain species of beans, *e.g.*, *Vicia faba*, or inhalation of the pollen of its flower; characterized by fever, headache, abdominal pain, severe anemia, prostration, and coma, and occurs in certain individuals with genetic erythrocytic deficiency of glucose 6-phosphate dehydrogenase.

favus (fa′vus) [L. honeycomb]. A severe type of chronic ringworm of the scalp and nails caused by three dissimilar dermatophytes, *Trichophyton schönleinii*, *T. violaceum*, and *Microsporum gypseum*.

Fc See Fc *fragment*.

FDA Food and Drug Administration.

Fe Iron.

fear (fēr) [A.S. *faer*]. Apprehension; dread; alarm. F. has an identifiable stimulus, and thus is differentiated from anxiety which has no easily identifiable stimulus.

febrifacient (feb′rĭ-fa′shent) [L. *febris*, fever, + *facio*, to make]. Febrific; causing fever.

febrif′ic. Febrifacient.

febrif′ugal. Febrifuge.

febrifuge (feb′rĭ-fūj) [L. *febris*, fever, + *fugo*, to put to flight]. Febrifugal; antipyretic; reducing fever.

febrile (feb′ril, fe′bril). Feverish; pyretic; relating to fever.

fecal (fe′kal). Relating to feces.

fe′calith [L. *faeces*, feces, + G. *lithos*, stone]. Coprolith.

fe′calo′ma. Coproma.

fe′caloid [L. *faeces*, feces, + G. *eidos*, resemblance]. Resembling feces.

fecaluria (fe′kā-lu′rĭ-ah) [L. *faeces*, feces, + G. *ouron*, urine]. Commingling of feces with urine passed from the urethra in persons with a fistula connecting the intestinal tract and bladder.

feces (fe′sēz) [L., pl. of *faex* (*faec-*), dregs]. Stercus; the matter discharged from the bowel during defecation.

fec′ulent. Excrementitious; fecal; foul.

fecund (fe′kund, fek′und) [L. *fecundus*, fruitful]. Fertile (1).

fecundation (fe′kun-da′shun) [L. *fecundo*, pp. *-atus*, to make fruitful, fertilize]. The act of rendering fertile.

fecun′dity. Pronounced fertility; capability of repeated fertilization.

feed′back. **1.** In a given system, the return, as input, of some of the output, as a regulatory mechanism. **2.** An explanation for the learning of motor skills: sensory stimuli set up by muscle contractions modulate the activity of the motor system.

fella′tio [L.]. The sexual act of taking a penis into the mouth.

fel′on [M.E. *feloun*, malignant]. Whitlow; a purulent infection or abscess involving the bulbous distal end of a finger.

felt′work. **1.** A fibrous network. **2.** A close plexus of nerve fibrils.

fe′male. In zoology, denoting the sex that bears the young or the sexual cell which develops into a new organism.

  genetic f., (1) An individual with a normal female karyotype, including two X chromosomes; (2) an individual whose cell nuclei contain Barr sex chromatin bodies, which are normally present in f.'s and absent in males.

feminism (fem′ĭ-nizm) [L. *femina*, woman]. Possession of feminine characteristics by the male.

feminization (fem′ĭ-nĭ-za′shun). The acquisition of female characteristics by the male. See testicular f. *syndrome*.

fem′oral. Relating to the femur or thigh.

femorocele (fem′or-o-sēl) [L. *femur*, thigh, + G. *kēlē*, hernia]. Femoral *hernia*.

fem′orotib′ial. Relating to the femur and the tibia.

femto- (f) [Danish *femten*, fifteen]. Prefix used in the metric system to signify one-quadrillionth (10^{-15}) of any unit.

fe′mur, pl. **fem′ora,** gen. **fem′oris** [L. thigh]. **1** [NA]. The thigh. **2.** *Os femoris.*

fenestra, pl. **fenestrae** (fē-nes′trah, -tre) [L.]. Window. **1** [NA]. An anatomical aperture, often closed by a membrane. **2.** A specialized opening, as in an instrument.

  f. coch′leae [NA], **f. of the cochlea,** round window; an opening on the medial wall of the middle ear leading into the cochlea, closed in life by the secondary tympanic membrane.

  f. vestib′uli [NA], **f. of the vestibule,** oval window; an oval opening on the medial wall of the tympanic cavity leading into the vestibule, closed in life by the foot of the stapes.

fenes′trated. Having fenestrae or window-like openings.

fen′estra′tion. The presence or making of openings or fenestrae in a part.

fen′tanyl citrate. *N*-(1-phenethyl-4-piperidyl)propionanilide citrate; a narcotic analgesic used as supplementary analgesic agent in general anesthesia.

ferment (fer-ment′). To cause or to undergo fermentation.

fermenta′tion [L. *fermento*, pp. *-atus*, to ferment]. **1.** A chemical change induced in a complex organic compound by the action of an enzyme, whereby the substance is split into more simple compounds. **2.** In bacteriology, the anaerobic dissimilation of substrates with the production of energy and reduced compounds.

ferment′ative. Causing or having the ability to cause fermentation.

fermium (fer′mĭ-um) [E. *Fermi*, It. physicist in U.S., 1901–1954]. Artificial radioactive element, atomic symbol Fm, atomic no. 100.

fern′ing. A term used to describe the pattern of arborization produced by cervical mucus, secreted at midcycle, upon crystallization, which resembles somewhat a fern or a palm leaf.

fer'redox'in. Any of the iron-containing, non-heme proteins found in green plants, algae, and anerobic bacteria and considered, largely because of their low redox potential, to accept the light-produced electron from chlorophyll at the initiation of photosynthesis. F.'s are involved in several oxidation-reduction reactions in living organisms (*e.g*, nitrogen fixation).

ferri- [L. *ferrum*, iron]. Prefix designating the presence in a compound of a ferric ion.

ferric (fĕr'ĭk). Relating to iron, especially denoting a salt containing iron in its higher (triad) valence, Fe^{3+}.

fer'ritin. An iron protein complex containing up to 23% iron, formed by the union of ferric iron with apoferritin; found in the intestinal mucosa, spleen, liver.

ferro- [L. *ferrum*, iron]. Prefix designating the presence of metallic iron or of the divalent ion Fe^{2+}.

fer'rocy'tochrome. Cytochrome *c* (reduced).

ferrokinetics (fĕr-o-kĭ-net'ĭks) [L. *ferrum*, iron, + G. *kinēsis*, movement]. The study of iron metabolism using radioactive iron.

fer'ropro'teins. Proteins containing iron in a prosthetic group, *e.g.*, heme, cytochrome.

ferrous (fĕr'us) [L. *ferreus*, made of iron]. Relating to iron, especially denoting a salt containing iron in its lowest valence, Fe^{2+}.

ferrugination (fĕ-ru'jĭ-na'shun) [L. *ferrugo*, iron-rust]. Deposition of ferric salts in the walls of small blood vessels, typically within the basal ganglia and cerebellum.

ferruginous (fĕ-ru'jĭ-nus) [L. *ferrugineus*, iron rust, rust-colored]. **1.** Iron-bearing; associated with or containing iron. **2.** Of the color of iron rust.

fer'rum [L.]. Iron.

fer'tile [L. *fertilis; fero*, to bear]. **1.** Fecund; fruitful; capable of conceiving and bearing young. **2.** Impregnated; fertilized.

fertil'ity. The state of being fertile; specifically, the ability to produce young.

fer'tiliza'tion. The process that begins with the penetration of the secondary oocyte by the spermatozoon and is completed with the fusion of the male and female pronuclei.

fes'ter [L. *fistula*]. **1.** To ulcerate. **2.** An ulcer. **3.** To form pus or putrefy.

fes'tinant [L. *festino*, to hasten]. Rapid; quick; hastening; accelerating.

festina'tion [L. *festino*, to hasten]. The peculiar acceleration of gait noted in parkinsonism and some other nervous affections.

festoon' [thr. Fr. fr. L. *festum*, festival, hence festive decorations]. **1.** A carving in the base material of a denture that simulates the contours of the natural tissue being replaced by the denture. **2.** A distinguishing characteristic of certain hard tick species, consisting of small rectangular areas separated by grooves along the posterior margin of the dorsum of both males and females.

fe'tal. Relating to a fetus.

feticide (fe'tĭ-sĭd) [L. *fetus* + *caedo*, to kil]. Destruction of the embryo or fetus in the uterus.

fetid (fet'ĭd, fe'tĭd) [L. *foetidus*]. Foul-smelling.

fetish (fet'ish, fe'tish) [Fr. *fétiche*, fr. L. *factitius*, made by art, artificial]. An inanimate object or nonsexual body part that is regarded as endowed with magic or erotic qualities.

fetishism (fet'ish-izm, fe'tish-). The act of worshipping or using for sexual arousal and gratification that which is regarded as a fetish.

fetography (fe-tog'rä-fĭ) [L. *fetus* + G. *graphĭ*, to write]. Radiography of the fetus *in utero*.

fetology (fe-tol'o-jĭ) [L. *fetus* + G. *logos*, study]. The branch of medicine concerned with the study, diagnosis, and treatment of the fetus *in utero*.

fetometry (fe-tom'ē-trĭ) [L. *fetus* + G. *metron*, measure]. Estimation of the size of the fetus, especially of its head, prior to delivery.

fetopathy (fe-top'ä-thĭ) [L. *fetus* + G. *pathos*, suffering, disease]. **1.** Embryopathy. **2.** Disease in a fetus after the third month of pregnancy.

fe'toplacen'tal. Relating to the fetus and its placenta.

fetopro'tein. A fetal protein found in adults; α-f. (AFP) increases in maternal blood during pregnancy and, when detected by amniocentesis, is an important indicator of open neural tube defects; β-f., although a fetal liver protein, has been detected in adult patients with liver disease; γ-f., occurs in various neoplasms.

fe'tor [L. an offensive smell, fr. *feteo*, to stink]. A very offensive odor.

f. ex o're [L. from the mouth], halitosis.

f. hepat'icus, a peculiar odor to the breath in persons with severe liver disease; caused by volatile aromatic substances that accumulate in the blood and urine.

fe'toscope. A fiberoptic endoscope used in fetoscopy.

fetoscopy (fe-tos'ko-pĭ). Use of a fiberoptic endoscope to view the fetus and placenta, and for collection of fetal blood.

fe'tus, pl. **fe'tuses** [L. offspring]. The unborn young of a viviparous animal after it has taken form in the uterus; in man, it represents the product of conception from the end of the eighth week to the moment of birth.

harlequin f., ichthyosis fetalis (1); a severe form of collodian baby in a newborn infant, usually premature; a form of ichthyosiform erythroderma characterized by encasement of the body in grayish brown, often fissured plaques and by grotesque deformity of the face, hands, and feet.

f. papyra'ceus, one of twin f.'s that has died and been pressed flat against the uterine wall by the growth of the living f.

FEV Forced expiratory *volume*.

fe'ver [A.S. *fefer*]. **1.** Pyrexia; a bodily temperature above the normal of 98.6°F (37°C). **2.** A disease in which there is an elevation of the body temperature above the normal.

blackwater f., malarial hemoglobinuria from falciparum malaria.

boutonneuse f., tick typhus in tropical and South Africa, and Asia, caused by *Rickettsia conori.*

camp f., typhus.

cat-scratch f., cat-scratch *disease.*

childbed f., puerperal f.

Colorado tick f., infection caused by Colorado tick f. virus and transmitted to man by *Dermacentor andersoni;* symptoms are mild, there is no rash, and f. is not excessive.

continued f., a f. of some duration in which there are no intermissions or marked remissions in the temperature.

desert f., primary *coccidioidomycosis.*

elephantoid f., lymphangitis and an elevation of temperature marking the beginning of endemic elephantiasis (filariasis).

enteric f., (1) typhoid f.; **(2)** the group of typhoid and paratyphoid A and B f.'s.

entericoid f., a f. neither paratyphoid nor typhoid, but resembling the latter.

epidemic hemorrhagic f., Far Eastern, Korean, or Manchurian hemorrhagic f.; hemorrhagic f. with renal syndrome, a condition characterized by acute onset of headache, chills and high f., sweating, thirst, photophobia, coryza, cough, myalgia, arthralgia, and abdominal pain with nausea and vomiting; this phase lasts from three to six days and is followed by capillary hemorrhages, edema, oliguria, and shock; most varieties are caused by arboviruses (togaviruses, arenaviruses, and possibly bunyaviruses), suspected of being rodent-borne.

familial Mediterranean f., familial paroxysmal *polyserositis.*

Far Eastern hemorrhagic f., epidemic hemorrhagic f.

Fort Bragg f., pretibial f.

Haverhill f. [*Haverhill,* MA, where an epidemic occurred in 1926], erythema arthriticum epidemicum; an infection by *Streptobacillus moniliformis* marked by initial chills and high f., gradually subsiding, by arthritis usually in the larger joints and spine, and by a rash occurring chiefly over the joints and on the extensor surfaces of the extremities. The term Haverhill f. is used to indicate *Streptobacillus moniliformis* infections not associated with rat bite, in contradistinction to rat-bite f.

hay f., a form of atopy characterized by an acute irritative inflammation of the mucous membranes of the eyes and upper respiratory passages accompanied by itching and profuse watery secretion, followed occasionally by bronchitis and asthma; recurs annually at the same or nearly the same time of the year as an allergic reaction to the pollen of trees, grasses, weeds, flowers, etc.

hemorrhagic f., a syndrome that occurs in perhaps 20 to 40% of infections by arboviruses of the hemorrhagic f. group; clinical manifestations are generally indistinguishable from those of the undif-

ferentiated type f.'s caused by other arboviruses or by viruses of other taxonomic groups. The syndrome is associated with high f., scattered petechiae, gastrointestinal tract and other organ bleeding, hypotension, and shock; kidney damage may be severe, especially in epidemic hemorrhagic f., and neurologic signs may appear, especially in the case of the Argentinian-Bolivian types. Etiologic agents are distributed among several taxonomic groups: alphaviruses, flaviviruses, bunyaviruses, and arenaviruses; some types are tick-borne, others mosquito-borne, and some seem to be zoonoses.

jungle f., malaria.

Kew garden f., rickettsialpox.

Korean hemorrhagic f., epidemic hemorrhagic f.

Lassa (hemorrhagic) f., a highly fatal form of epidemic hemorrhagic f. caused by Lassa virus and characterized by high f., sore throat, severe muscle aches, skin rash with hemorrhages, headache, abdominal pain, vomiting, and diarrhea; the multimammate rat *Mastomys natalensis* serves as reservoir, but person-to-person transmission is common.

Manchurian hemorrhagic f., epidemic hemorrhagic f.

Mediterranean f., (1) brucellosis; **(2)** familial paroxysmal *polyserositis.*

Mediterranean exanthematous f., an affection occurring sporadically in the Mediterranean littoral marked by a severe chill with abrupt rise of temperature, pains in the joints, tonsillitis, diarrhea, and vomiting; on the third to fifth day a rash of elevated nonconfluent macules beginning on the thighs and spreading to the entire body; the disease lasts from 10 days to a fortnight and then disappears by rapid lysis without desquamation.

metal fume f., an occupational disease, characterized by malaria-like symptoms, due to inhalation of particles and fumes of metallic oxides.

miliary f., (1) an infectious desease characterized by f., profuse sweating, and the production of sudamina, occurring formerly in severe epidemics; **(2)** miliaria.

milk f., (1) a slight elevation of temperature following childbirth, said to be due to the establishment of the secretion of milk.

mud f., a leptospirosis caused by *Leptospira grippotyphosa.*

Oroya f., Carrion's disease; a specific, acute, febrile, endemic disease of the Peruvian Andes, caused by *Bartonella bacilliformis* and marked by high fever, rheumatic pains, progressive, severe anemia, and albuminuria.

paratyphoid f., an acute infectious disease with symptoms and lesions resembling those of typhoid f., though milder in character; associated with the presence of the paratyphoid bacillus, of which at least three varieties (types A, B, and C) have been described.

parenteric f., one of a group of f.'s clinically resembling typhoid and paratyphoid A and B, but caused by bacteria differing specifically from those of either of these diseases.

parrot f., psittacosis.

pharyngoconjunctival f., an epidemic disease characterized by f., pharyngitis, and conjunctivitis; due to an adenovirus.

phlebotomus f., an infectious but not contagious dengue-like disease occurring in the Balkan Peninsula and other parts of southern Europe, caused by an arbovirus (family Bunyaviridae) apparently introduced by the bite of the sandfly, *Phlebotomus papatasi.*

polymer fume f., a condition marked by f., pain in the chest, and cough caused by the inhalation of fumes given off by a plastic, polytetrafluorethylene, when heated by molding, cutting, or grinding.

pretibial f., Fort Bragg f.; a mild disease characterized by f., moderate prostration, splenomegaly, and a rash on the anterior aspects of the legs; due to *Leptospira autumnalis.*

puerperal f., childbed f.; puerperal sepsis; postpartum sepsis with a rise in f. after the first 24 hours following delivery, but before the 11th postpartum day.

Q f., ["Q" for *query,* because etiologic agent was unkown], a disease caused by a rickettsial organism, *Coxiella burnetii* (*Rickettsia burnetii*); the organism is propagated in sheep and cattle, where it produces no symptoms; human infections occur as a result of contact not only with such animals, but also with humans, air and dust, wild reservoir hosts, and other sources.

rat-bite f., headache, f., lymphangitis, and lymphadenitis following the bite of a rat or other rodent; due either to a spirillum or to *Streptobacillus moniliformis;* the latter resembles Haverhill f., but is contracted from a rat bite.

relapsing f., recurrent f., an acute infectious disease caused by any one of a number of strains of *Borrelia,* transmitted by lice or ticks and marked by a number of febrile attacks lasting about six days and separated from each other by apyretic intervals of about the same length; the microorganism is found in the blood during the febrile periods but not during the intervals, the disappearance being associated with specific antibodies and previously evoked antibodies.

rheumatic f., f. occurring during recovery from infection, usually of the throat, with group A streptococci and is variably associated with acute migratory polyarthritis, Sydenham's chorea, subcutaneous nodules over bony prominences, myocarditis with formation of Aschoff bodies, which may cause acute cardiac failure, and endocarditis which is frequently followed by scarring of valves, causing stenosis or incompetence.

Rocky Mountain spotted f., an acute infectious disease characterized by frontal and occipital headache, intense lumbar pain, malaise, a moderately high continuous f., and a rash on wrists and ankles later spreading to all parts of the body; it occurs in the spring of the year, primarily in the southeast U.S. and the Rocky Mountain region, and is caused by *Rickettsia rickettsi,* transmitted by two or more tick species of the genus *Dermacentor.*

scarlet f., scarlatina.

septic f., septicemia.

South African tick-bite f., a typhus-like f. of South Africa caused by *Rickettsia rickettsii,* and usually characterized by primary eschar and regional adenitis, rigors, and maculopapular rash on the fifth day, often with severe central nervous system symptoms.

spotted f., (1) old term for meningococcal meningitis with petechiae; (2) tick typhus caused by *Rickettsia rickettsii,* such as Rocky Mountain s. f.

swamp f., malaria.

tick f., any infectious disease of man or the lower animals caused by a protozoan blood parasite transmitted through the agency of a tick; *e.g.,* the tick-borne variety of relapsing f., Rocky Mountain spotted f., Colorado tick f.

typhoid f., enteric f. (1); typhoid (2); an acute infectious disease caused by *Salmonella typhi* and characterized by a continued f., physical and mental depression, an eruption of rose-colored spots on the chest and abdomen, tympanites, often diarrhea, sometimes intestinal hemorrhage or performation of the bowel.

undifferentiated type f.'s, illnesses resulting from infection by any one of the arboviruses pathogenic for man, in which the only constant manifestation is f.; rash, lymphadenopathy, or arthralgia, alone, or in combination, may occur in some individuals but not in others.

undulant f., [referring to the wavy appearance of the long temperature curve], brucellosis.

uveoparotid f., Heerfordt's disease; chronic enlargement of the parotid glands and inflammation of the uveal tract accompanied by a long-continued f. of low degree; now recognized as a form of sarcoidosis.

yellow f., a tropical mosquito-borne viral hepatitis, due to yellow f. virus, with an urban form transmitted by *Aedes aegypti,* and a rural, jungle, or sylvatic form from tree-dwelling mammals by various mosquitos of the *Haemogogus* species complex; characterzed clinically by fever, slow pulse, albuminuria, jaundice, congestion of the face, and hemorrhages, especially hematemesis.

FF Filtration *fraction.*

fi′ber [L. *fibra*]. Fibra; a slender thread or filament. In anatomy, refers to 1) extracellular filamentous structures such as collagenic or elastic connective tissue f.'s; 2) the nerve cell axon with its glial envelope; 3) certain elongated, threadlike cells such as muscle cells and the epithelial cells composing the major part of the eye lens.

A f.'s, myelinated nerve f.'s in somatic nerves, measuring 1 to 22 μm in diameter, conducting nerve impulses at a rate of 6 to 120 m/sec.

accelerator f.'s, postganglionic sympathetic nerve f.'s originating in the superior middle and inferior cervical ganglia of the sympathetic trunk, conveying nervous impulses to the heart that tend to increase the rapidity and force of the cardiac pulsations.

adrenergic f.'s, nerve f.'s that transmit nervous impulses to other nerve cells (or smooth muscle or gland cells) by norepinephrine.

afferent f.'s, nerve f.'s that convey impulses to a ganglion or to a nerve center in the brain or spinal cord.

alpha f.'s, large somatic motor or proprioceptive nerve f.'s conducting impulses at rates near 100 m/sec.

arcuate f.'s, nervous or tendinous f.'s passing in the form of an arch from one part to another, such as those connecting adjacent gyri in the cerebral cortex, and the external and internal f.'s of the medulla oblongata.

association f.'s, nerve f.'s interconnecting individual subdivisions of a given brain structure or different segments of the spinal cord.

B f.'s, myelinated nerve f.'s in autonomic nerves, of 2 μm diameter or less, conducting at a rate of 3 to 15 m/sec.

beta f.'s, nerve f.'s having conduction velocities of about 40 m/sec.

C f.'s, unmyelinated f.'s, 0.4 to 1.2 μm in diameter, conducting nerve impulses at a velocity of 0.7 to 2.3 m/sec.

cholinergic f.'s, nerve f.'s that transmit impulses to other nerve cells or to muscle fibers or gland cells by acetylcholine.

collagen f., collagenous f., white f.; an individual f. composed of fibrils and usually arranged in bundles which undergo some branching and are of indefinite length; chemically the f. is a scleroprotein, collagen, which makes up the principal element of irregular connective tissue, tendons, aponeuroses, and most ligaments, and occurs in the matrix of cartilage and osseous tissue.

commissural f.'s, nerve f.'s crossing the midline and connecting the two symmetrical halves of the nervous system.

depressor f.'s, sensory nerve f.'s having pressure-sensitive nerve endings in the wall of certain arteries, and capable of activating blood pressure-lowering brainstem mechanisms when stimulated by an increase in intraarterial pressure.

dietary f.'s, plant polysaccharides and lignin resistant to hydrolysis by the digestive enzymes in humans.

elastic f.'s, yellow f.'s; f.'s 0.2 to 2 μm in diameter and containing elastin which branch and anastomose to form networks and fuse to form fenestrated membranes.

exogenous f.'s, nerve f.'s by which a given region of the central nervous system is connected with other regions; the term applies to both afferent and efferent fiber connections.

gamma f.'s, nerve f.'s that have a conduction rate of about 20 m/sec.

gray f.'s, unmyelinated f.'s.

inhibitory f.'s, nerve f.'s that inhibit the activity of the nerve cells with which they have synaptic connections, or of the effector tissue (smooth muscle, heart muscle, glands) in which they terminate.

intrafusal f.'s, muscle f.'s present within a neuromuscular spindle.

medullated f., myelinated f.

motor f.'s, the f.'s in a mixed nerve that transmit motor impulses.

myelinated f., medullated f.; an axon enveloped by a myelin sheath formed by oligodendroglia cells (in brain and spinal cord) or Schwann cells (in peripheral nerves).

nonmedullated f.'s, unmyelinated f.'s.

osteogenetic f.'s, the f.'s in the osteogenetic layer of the periosteum.

perforating f.'s, bundles of collagenous f.'s that pass into the outer circumferential lamellae of bone or the cementum of teeth.

periodontal membrane f.'s, the collagen f.'s running from the cementum to the alveolar bone, that suspend a tooth in its socket.

precollagenous f.'s, immature, argyrophilic f.'s.

pressor f.'s, sensory nerve f.'s that cause vasoconstriction and rise of blood pressure on stimulation.

projection f.'s, nerve f.'s connecting the cerebral cortex with other centers in the brain or spinal cord.

Purkinje's f.'s, interlacing f.'s formed of modified cardiac muscle cells with central granulated protoplasm containing one or two nuclei and a transversely striated peripheral portion; found beneath the endocardium of the ventricles.

reticular f.'s, argyrophilic, small, branching intercellular f. elements that may be continuous with collagen f.'s.

sudomotor f.'s, postganglionic sympathetic nerve f.'s innervating the sweat glands.

tautomeric f.'s, nerve f.'s of the spinal cord that do not extend beyond the limits of the spinal cord segment in which they originate.

unmyelinated f.'s, gray or nonmedullated f.'s; nerve f.'s (axons) lacking a fatty sheath but in common with others enveloped by a sheath of Schwann cells.

white f., collagen f.

yellow f.'s, elastic f.'s.

fiberop'tic. Pertaining to fiberoptics.

fiberop'tics. An optical system whereby light or an image is conveyed by a compact, coherent bundle of fine flexible glass or plastic fibers.

fi'berscope. An optical instrument that transmits images by fiberoptics.

fibr-. See fibro-.

fibra, pl. **fibrae** (fi'brah, fi'bre) [L.] [NA]. Fiber.

fibremia (fi-bre'mĭ-ah) [fibrin + G. *haima,* blood]. Inosemia (2); fibrinemia; presence of formed fibrin in the blood, causing thrombosis or embolism.

fi'bril [Mod. L. *fibrilla*]. A minute fiber.

fibrilla, pl. **fibrillae** (fi-bril'lah, fi-bril'le) [Mod. L. dim. of L. *fibra,* a fiber]. Fibril.

fibrillar, fibrillary (fi'brĭ-lar, -lăr-ĭ). **1.** Filar (1); relating to a fibril. **2.** Denoting the fine rapid contractions or twitchings of fibers or of small groups of fibers in skeletal or cardiac muscle.

fi'brillate. 1. To make or to become fibrillar. **2.** Fibrillated. **3.** To be in a state of fibrillation (3).

fi'brillated. Fibrillate (2); composed of fibrils.

fibrillation (fi'brĭ-la'shun, fib-rĭ-). **1.** The condition of being fibrillated. **2.** Formation of fibrils. **3.** Exceedingly rapid contractions or twitching of muscular fibrils, but not of the muscle as a whole. **4.** Vermicular twitching, usually slow, of individual muscular fibers, commonly occurs in atria or ventricles of the heart as well as in recently denervated skeletal muscle fibers.

    atrial f., auricular f., f. in which the normal rhythmical contractions of the cardiac atria are replaced by rapid irregular twitchings of the muscular wall; the ventricles respond irregularly to the dysrhythmic bombardment from the atria.

    ventricular f., fine, rapid, fibrillary movements of the ventricular muscle that replace the normal contraction.

fibrillogenesis (fi-bril'o-jen'ĕ-sis). The development of fine fibrils normally present in collagenous fibers of connective tissue.

fi'brin [L. *fibra,* fiber]. An elastic filamentous protein derived from fibrinogen by the action of thrombin, which releases fibrinopeptides A and B from fibrinogen, in coagulation of the blood.

fi'brinase. 1. See *factor* XIII. **2.** Plasmin.

fi'brine'mia. Fibremia.

fibrino- [L. *fibra,* fiber]. Combining form relating to fibrin.

fi'brinocel'lular. Composed of fibrin and cells, as in certain types of exudates resulting from acute inflammation.

fibrinogen (fi-brin'o-jen). Factor I (blood clotting); a globulin of the blood plasma that is converted into fibrin by the action of thrombin in the presence of ionized calcium; produces coagulation of the blood.

fibrinogenemia (fi-brin'o-jĕ-ne'mĭ-ah). Hyperfibrinogenemia.

fibrinogenesis (fi'brĭ-no-jen'ĕ-sis). The formation or production of fibrin.

fibrinogenic, fibrinogenous (fi'brĭ-no-jen'ik, fi'brĭ-noj'ĕ-nus). Pertaining to fibrinogen; producing fibrin.

fibrinogenolysis (fi-brin'o-jen-ol'ĭ-sis). The inactivation or dissolution of fibrinogen in the blood.

fibrin'ogenope'nia [fibrinogen + G. *penia,* poverty]. A less than the normal concentration of fibrinogen in the blood.

fibrinoid (fi'brĭ-noyd) [fibrin + G. *eidos,* resemblance]. **1.** Resembling fibrin. **2.** An acidophilic, homogeneous, refractile, proteinaceous material that is frequently formed in the walls of blood vessels and in connective tissue of patients with certain diseases and is sometimes observed in healing wounds, chronic peptic ulcers, malignant hypertension, and other unrelated conditions.

fi'brinol'ysin. Plasmin.

fibrinolysis (fi'brĭ-nol'ĭ-sis) [fibrino- + G. *lysis,* dissolution]. The hydrolysis of fibrin.

fi'brinopep'tide. One of two peptides (A and B) released from fibrinogen by the action of thrombin.

fi'brinopu'rulent. Pertaining to pus or suppurative exudate that contains a relatively large amount of fibrin.

fi'brinous. Pertaining to or composed of fibrin.

fi'brinu'ria. Passage of urine that contains fibrin.

fibro-, fibr- [L. *fibra,* fiber]. Combining forms denoting fiber.

fibroadenoma (fi'bro-ad-ĕ-no'ma). A benign neoplasm derived from glandular epithelium, in which there is a conspicuous stroma of proliferating fibroblasts and connective tissue elements.

fibroadipose (fi'bro-ad'ĭ-pōz). Relating to or containing both fibrous and fatty structures.

fibroareolar (fi'bro-ă-re'o-lar). Denoting connective tissue that is both fibrous and areolar in character.

fi'broblast. A stellate or spindle-shaped cell with cytoplasmic processes present in connective tissue, capable of forming collagen fibers.

fi'broblas'tic. Relating to fibroblasts.

fi'brocarcino'ma. Scirrhous *carcinoma.*

fi'brocar'tilage. A variety of cartilage that contains visible collagenic fibers.

    circumferential f., a ring of f. around the articular end of a bone, serving to deepen the joint cavity.

    interarticular f., *discus* articularis.

    semilunar f., see *meniscus* lateralis; *meniscus* medialis.

fibrocartilaginous (fi'bro-kar-tĭ-laj'ĭ-nus). Relating to or composed of fibrocartilage.

fi'brocel'lular. Both fibrous and cellular.

fibrochondritis (fi'bro-kon-dri'tis). Inflammation of a fibrocartilage.

fibrochondroma (fi'bro-kon-dro'mah). A benign neoplasm of cartilaginous tissue, in which there is a relatively unusual amount of fibrous stroma.

fi'brocyst (fi'bro-sist). Any cystic lesion that is circumscribed by or situated within a conspicuous amount of fibrous connective tissue.

fi'brocys'tic. Pertaining to or characterized by the presence of fibrocysts.

fibrocystoma (fi'bro-sis-to'mah). A benign neoplasm, usually derived from glandular epithelium, characterized by cysts within a conspicuous fibrous stroma.

fibrodysplasia (fi'bro-dis-pla'zĭ-ah). Abnormal development of fibrous connective tissue.

f. ossif'icans progres'siva, a generalized disorder of connective tissue in which bone replaces tendons, fasciae, and ligaments, autosomal dominant inheritance.

fi'broelas'tic. Composed of collagen and elastic fibers.

fi'broelasto'sis. Excessive proliferation of collagenous and elastic fibrous tissue.

endocardial f., endomyocardial f., a congential condition characterized by thickening of the left ventricular mural endocardium, thickening and malformation of the cardiac valves, subendocardial changes in the myocardium, and hypertrophy of the heart.

fibroenchondroma (fi'bro-en-kon-dro'mah). An enchondroma in which the neoplastic cartilage cells are situated within an abundant fibrous stroma.

fibroepithelioma (fi'bro-ep-ĭ-the-lĭ-o'mah). A skin tumor composed of fibrous tissue intersected by thin anastomosing bands of basal cells of the epidermis.

fi'broid [fibro- + G. *eidos,* resemblance]. **1.** Resembling or composed of fibers or fibrous tissue. **2.** Old term for certain types of leiomyoma, especially those occurring in the uterus. **3.** Fibroleiomyoma.

fibroidectomy (fi'broyd-ek'to-mĭ) [fibroid + G. *ektomē,* excision]. Surgical removal of a fibroid tumor.

fibroleiomyoma (fi'bro-li'o-mi-o'mah). Leiomyofibroma; fibroid (3); a leiomyoma containing non-neoplastic collagenous fibrous tissue, which may make the tumor hard; f.'s usually arise in the myometrium, and the proportion of fibrous tissue increases with age.

fi'brolipo'ma. A lipoma with an abundant stroma of fibrous tissue.

fibroma (fi-bro'mah) [fibro- + G. *-oma,* tumor]. A benign neoplasm derived from fibrous connective tissue.

ameloblastic f., ameloblastofibroma; a benign mixed tumor of odontogenic origin, distinguished by a concomitant neoplastic proliferation of both epithelial and mesenchymal components of the tooth bud without the production of hard tissue.

cementifying f., A form of cementoma occurring in the mandible of older persons and consisting of cellular fibrous tissue containing round or lobulated calcified masses of cementum.

chondromyxoid f., chondrofibroma; chondromyxoma; an uncommon benign bone tumor composed of lobulated myxoid tissue with scanty chondroid foci.

f. myxomato'des, myxofibroma.

nonosteogenic f., fibrous cortical *defect.*

telangiectatic f., angiofibroma; a benign neoplasm of fibrous tissue in which there are numerous, small and large, frequently dilated, vascular channels.

fibromatoid (fi-bro'mă-toyd). A focus, nodule, or mass (of proliferating fibroblasts) that resembles a fibroma, but is not regarded as neoplastic.

fibromatosis (fi-bro-mă-to'sis). **1.** The occurrence of multiple fibromas, with a relatively large distribution. **2.** Abnormal hyperplasia of fibrous tissue.

palmar f., nodular fibroblastic proliferation in the palmar fascia of one or both hands, preceding or associated with Dupuytren's contracture.

plantar f., nodular fibroblastic proliferation in plantar fascia of one or both feet; rarely associated with contracture.

fibro'matous. Pertaining to, or of the nature of, a fibroma.

fi'bromus'cular. Both fibrous and muscular; relating to both fibrous and muscular tissues.

fibromyectomy (fi'bro-mi-ek'to-mĭ). Excision of a fibromyoma.

fibromyoma (fi'bro-mi-o'mah). A leiomyoma that contains a relatively abundant amount of fibrous tissue.

fibromyositis (fi'bro-mi'o-si'tis) [fibro- + G. *mys,* muscle, + *-itis,* inflammation]. Chronic inflammation of a muscle with an overgrowth, or hyperplasia, of the connective tissue.

fibromyxoma (fi'bro-mik-so'mah) [fibro- + G. *mysa,* mucus, + *-oma,* tumor]. A myxoma that contains a relatively abundant amount of mature fibroblasts and connective tissue.

fibronectin (fi-bro-nek'tin) [L. *fibra,* fiber, + *nexus,* interconnection]. A fibrous linking protein; a reticuloendothelial mediated host defense mechanism, impaired by surgery and other trauma, burns, infection, neoplasia, and disorders of the immune system.

plasma f., a circulating α_2-glycoprotein that functions as an opsonin, mediating reticuloendothelial and macrophage clearance of fibrin microaggregates, collagen debris, and bacterial particulates, protecting microvascular perfusion and lymphatic drainage.

fi'broneuro'ma. Neurofibroma.

fi'bropapillo'ma. A papilloma characterized by a conspicuous amount of fibrous connective tissue at the base and forming the cores upon which the neoplastic epithelial cells are massed.

fibroplasia (fi'bro-pla'zĭ-ah) [fibro- + G. *plasis,* a molding]. Production of fibrous tissue, usually implying an abnormal increase of non-neoplastic fibrous tissue.

retrolental f., abnormal replacement of the sensory retina by fibrous tissue and blood vessels, occurring mainly in premature infants placed in a high oxygen environment.

fibroplas'tic [fibro- + G. *plastos,* formed]. Producing fibrous tissue.

fi'broretic'ulate. Relating to or consisting of a network of fibrous tissue.

fi'brosarco'ma. A malignant neoplasm derived from fibrous connective tissue and characterized by immature proliferating fibroblasts or undifferentiated anaplastic spindle cells.

fi′brose′rous. Composed of fibrous tissue with a serous surface; denoting any serous membrane.

fibrosis (fi-bro′sis). Formation of fibrous tissue as a reparative or reactive process.

cystic f. (of the pancreas), fibrocystic disease of the pancreas; mucoviscidosis; Clarke-Hadfield syndrome; a congenital metabolic disorder, inherited as a recessive trait, in which exocrine glands secrete excessively viscid mucus, causing obstruction of passageways (including pancreatic and bile ducts, intestines, and bronchi); the sodium and chloride content of sweat is increased.

endomyocardial f., thickening of the ventricular endocardium by f., involving the subendocardial myocardium, and sometimes the atrioventricular valves, with mural thrombosis.

idiopathic retroperitoneal f., Ormond's disease; f. of retroperitoneal structures commonly involving and often obstructing the ureters.

mediastinal f., idiopathic f. obstructing the superior vena cava or other superior mediastinal structures.

fi′brosi′tis [fibro- + G. *-itis,* inflammation]. **1.** Inflammation of fibrous tissue. **2.** A term used to denote aching, soreness, or stiffness in the absence of objective abnormalities.

fi′brotho′rax, Fibrosis of the pleural space.

fibrot′ic. Pertaining to or characterized by fibrosis.

fi′brous. Composed of or containing fibroblasts, and also the fibrils and fibers of connective tissue formed by such cells.

fibula (fib′u-lah) [L. *fibula* (contr. fr. *figibula*), that which fastens, a clasp, buckle, fr. *figo,* to fix, fasten] [NA]. Calf bone; the lateral and smaller of the two bones of the leg; articulating with the tibia above and the tibia and talus below.

fib′ular [L. *fibularis*]. Relating to the fibula.

fibulocalcaneal (fib′u-lo-kal-ka′ne-al). Relating to the fibula and the calcaneus.

field (fēld) [A.S. *feld*]. A definite area of plane surface, considered in relation to some specific object.

auditory f., the space included within the limits of hearing of a definite sound, as of a tuning fork.

individuation f., the f. within which an organizer can bring about the rearrangement of primordial tissues in such a manner that a complete embryo is formed.

visual f. (F), the area simultaneously visible to one eye without movement; usually measured by means of an arc (perimeter) located 330 mm from the eye.

FIGLU Formiminoglutamic acid.

fig′ure. 1. A form or shape. **2.** A person representing the essential aspects of a particular role.

authority f., a real or projected person in a position of power; during the transference phase of psychoanalysis, the psychoanalyst becomes an authority f.

mitotic f., the microscopic appearance of a cell undergoing mitosis; a cell whose chromosomes are visible with the light microscope.

Purkinje's f.'s, shadows of the retinal vessels, seen as dark lines on a reddish field when a light enters the eye through the sclera in a dark room.

figure and ground. That aspect of perception wherein the perceived is separated into at least two parts, each with different attributes but influencing one another. Figure is the most distinct; ground the least formed; *e.g.,* a bird (figure) seen against the sky (ground).

fila (fi′lah) [L.]. Plural of filum.

filaceous (fi-la′shus) [L. *filum,* a thread]. Filamentous.

fil′ament [L. *filamentum,* fr. *filum,* a thread]. A fibril, fine fiber, or threadlike structure.

actin f., one of the contractile elements in skeletal, cardiac, and muscular fibers; in skeletal muscle the actin f. is about 50 Å wide and 100 μm long; they attach to the transverse Z f.'s.

axial f., axoneme (2); the central f. of a flagellum or cilium; with the electron microscope it is seen as a complex of nine peripheral diplomicrotubules and a central pair of microtubules.

myosin f., one of the contractile elements in skeletal, cardiac, and smooth muscle fibers; in skeletal muscle, the f. is about 100 Å thick and 1.5 μm long.

Z f., the thin zig-zag strand at the Z line or striated muscle fibers to which the actin f.'s attach.

filamen′tous. Filaceous; filar (2). **1.** Filiform (1); threadlike in structure. **2.** Composed of filaments or threadlike structures.

fi′lar [L. *filum,* a thread]. **1.** Fibrillar. **2.** Filamentous.

Filaria (fī-lăr′ĭ-ah). Former genus of nematodes now classified in several genera and species of the family Onchocercidae.

filaria, pl. **filariae** (fī-lăr′ĭ-ah, fī-lăr′ĭ-e) [L. *filum,* a thread]. Common name for nematodes of the family Onchocercidae, which live as adults in the blood, tissue fluids, tissues, or body cavities of many vertebrates.

fila′rial. Pertaining to a filaria (or filariae), including the microfilaria stage.

filariasis (fil-ă-rī′ă-sis). The presence of filariae in the tissues of the body or in blood or tissue fluids (microfilaremia or microfilariosis); death of the adult worms leads to granulomatous inflammation and permanent fibrosis causing obstruction of the lymphatic channels from dense hyalinized scars in the subcutaneous tissues; the most serious consequence is elephantiasis or pachyderma.

filaricidal (fī-lăr-ĭ-sī′dal). Fatal to filariae.

filaricide (fī-lăr′ĭ-sīd) [filaria + L. *caedo,* to kill]. An agent that kills filariae.

filar′iform. 1. Resembling filariae or other types of small nematode worms. **2.** Thin or hairlike.

fil'ial [L. *filialis*, fr. *filius*, son, *filia*, daughter]. Denoting the relationship of offspring to parents.

fil'iform [L. *filum*, thread]. **1.** Filamentous (1). **2.** In bacteriology, denoting an even growth along the line of inoculation, either stroke or stab.

fil'let [Fr. *filet*, a band]. **1.** Lemniscus. **2.** A skein or loop of cord or tape used for making traction on a part of the fetus.

fil'ling. Lay term for a dental restoration.

film. 1. A light-sensitive or x-ray-sensitive substance used in taking photographs or radiographs. **2.** A thin layer or coating.

    absorbable gelatin f., a sterile, nonantigenic, absorbable, water-insoluble, thin sheet of gelatin prepared by drying a gelatin-formaldehyde solution on plates; used in the closure and repair of defects in membranes.

    bitewing f., a special packaging of roentgenographic f. that allows an appendage of one f. package to be held between the occlusal surfaces of the teeth.

    panoramic x-ray f., in dentistry, a radiogram taken to give a panoramic view of the entire upper and lower dental arch as well as the temporomandibular joint.

    plain f., X-ray taken without use of a contrast medium.

fi'lopres'sure [L. *filum*, thread]. Temporary pressure on a blood vessel by a ligature, which is removed when the flow of blood has ceased.

fil'ter [Mediev. L. *filtro*, pp. -*atus*, to strain through felt]. **1.** To pass a fluid through a porous substance that arrests suspended solid particles. **2.** A porous substance through which a fluid is passed in order to separate it from contained particulate matter. **3.** A translucent screen, used in both diagnostic and therapeutic radiology, that permits the passage of certain rays and inhibits the passage of others which have a lower and less desirable energy. **4.** A device used in spectrophotometric analysis to isolate a segment of the spectrum.

fil'trable, fil'terable. Capable of passing through a filter; frequently applied to smaller viruses and some bacteria.

fil'trate [see filter]. Liquid that has passed through a filter.

filtration (fil-tra'shun). Percolation (1); the process of passing a liquid through a filter.

fi'lum, pl. **fi'la** [L. thread] [NA]. A structure of filamentous or threadlike appearance.

    f. du'rae ma'tris spina'lis [NA], the termination of the spinal dura mater, surrounding the f. terminale of the cord, and attached to the deep dorsal sacrococcygeal ligament.

    fi'la radicula'ria [NA], the small, individual fiber fascicles into which the roots of all of the spinal nerves and several cranial nerves (hypoglossus, vagus, oculomotorius) divide in fanlike fashion before entering or leaving the spinal cord or brainstem.

    f. termina'le [NA], terminal f., a long, slender connective tissue strand extending from the extremity of the conus medullaris to the termination of the spinal canal.

fimbria, pl. **fimbriae** (fim'brĭ-ah, fim'brĭ-e) [L. fringe]. **1** [NA]. Any fringelike structure. **2.** Pilus (2).

    f. hippocam'pi [NA], corpus fimbriatum a narrow sharp-edged crest of white fiber matter, continuous with the alveus hippocampi, attached to the medial border of the hippocampus; composed of efferent fibers of the hippocampus that eventually form the fornix, fibers of the hippocampal commissure, and septohippocampal fibers.

    fim'briae tu'bae [NA], irregularly branched or fringed processes surrounding the abdominal opening of the uterine tube, with cilia that beat toward the uterus.

fim'briate, fim'briated. Having fimbriae.

fimbriocele (fim'brĭ-o-sēl) [L. *fimbria*, fringe, + G. *kēlē*, hernia]. A hernia of the corpus fimbriatum of the oviduct.

fin'ger [A.S.]. *Digitus* manus; one of the digits of the hand.

    baseball f., hammer f., mallet f., avulsion of the long finger extensor from the base of the distal phalanx.

    clubbed f.'s, hippocratic f.'s, clubbed *digits*.

    webbed f.'s, two or more f.'s united by a common sheath of skin.

fin'gerprint. 1. An impression of the inked bulb of the distal phalanx of a finger, showing the configuration of the ridges, used as a means of identification. **2.** Any analytical method capable of making fine distinctions between similar compounds.

first aid. Immediate assistance given in the case of injury or sudden illness by a bystander before the arrival of a health care professional.

fission (fish'un) [L. *fissio*, a cleaving]. **1.** The act of splitting, *e.g.,* amitotic division of a cell or its nucleus. **2.** Splitting of the nucleus of an atom.

    binary f., simple f. in which the two new cells are approximately equal in size.

    multiple f., sporulation; division of the nucleus, simultaneously or successively, into a number of daughter nuclei, followed by division of the cell body into an equal number of parts, each containing a nucleus.

    simple f., division of the nucleus and then the cell body into two parts.

fissiparity (fis-ĭ-păr'ĭ-tĭ) [L. *findo*, pp. *fissus*, split; + *pario*, pp. *paritus*, to bring forth]. Schizogenesis.

fissip'arous [L. *fissus; findere*, to cleave, + *pario*, to produce]. Reproducing or propagating by fission.

fissura, pl. **fissurae** (fis-su'rah, -su're) [L. fr. *findo*, to cleave] [NA]. **1.** A deep fissure, cleft, or slit. **2.** In neuroanatomy, a particularly deep sulcus of the surface of the brain or spinal cord.

    fissu'rae cerebel'li [NA], cerebellar fissures; deep furrows between the lobules of the cerebellum.

f. horizonta'lis cerebel'li [NA], horizontal fissure of the cerebellum; a deep cleft encircling the circumference of the cerebellum.

f. ligamen'ti tere'tis [NA], fissure of the round ligament; a cleft on the inferior surface of the liver that lodges the ligamentum teres hepatis.

f. ligamen'ti veno'si [NA], fissure of the venous ligament; a deep cleft on the posterior surface of the liver, between the left and caudate lobes, that lodges the ligamentum venosum.

f. longitudina'lis cer'ebri [NA], longitudinal fissure of the cerebrum; a deep cleft separating the two hemispheres of the cerebrum, but bridged by the corpus callosum and hippocampal commissure.

f. media'na ante'rior [NA], anterior median fissure, the longitudinal groove in the midline of the anterior aspect of the medulla oblongata continuous with the anterior median fissure of the spinal cord and ending at the lower border of the pons in the foramen cecum.

f. orbita'lis supe'rior [NA], superior orbital fissure; foramen lacerum anterius; a cleft between the greater and the lesser wing of the sphenoid through which pass the oculomotor and trochlear nerves, ophthalmic division of the trigeminal nerve, abducens nerve, and ophthalmic veins.

f. petrotympan'ica [NA], petrotympanic or glaserian fissure, a fissure between the tympanic and petrous portions of the temporal bone; transmits the chorda tympani nerve.

f. pri'ma cerebel'li [NA], primary fissure of the cerebellum; a deep V-shaped fissure that marks the superior surface of the cerebellum and demarcates the anterior lobe from the rest of the cerebellum.

f. transver'sa cer'ebri [NA], transverse fissure of the cerebrum; the space between the corpus callosum and fornix above, and the dorsal surface of the thalamus below.

f. tympanomastoid'ea [NA], tympanomastoid or auricular fissure; a fissure separating the tympanic portion from the mastoid portion of the temporal bone; transmits the auricular branch of the vagus nerve.

fissure (fish'ur) [L. *fissura*]. **1.** A deep furrow, cleft, or slit. For anatomical f.'s, see under fissura and sulcus. **2.** In dentistry, a developmental break or fault in the enamel of a tooth.

abdominal f., congenital failure to close the ventral body wall.

anal f., a crack or slit in the mucous membrane of the anus.

anterior median f., *fissura* mediana anterior.

auricular f., *fissura* tympanomastoidea.

Bichat's f., the nearly circular f. corresponding to the medial margin of the pallium, marking the hilus of the cerebral hemisphere.

calcarine f., *sulcus* calcarinus.

caudal transverse f., *porta* hepatis.

cerebellar f.'s, *fissurae* cerebelli.

collateral f., *sulcus* collateralis.

glaserian f., *fissura* petrotympanica.

Henle's f.'s, minute spaces, filled with connective tissue, between the muscular fasciculi of the heart.

hippocampal f., *sulcus* hippocampi.

horizontal f. of cerebellum, *fissura* horizontalis cerebelli.

palpebral f., *rima* palpebrarum.

paracentral f., a curved f. on the medial surface of the cerebral hemisphere, bounding the paracentral gyrus and separating it from the precuneus and gyrus cinguli.

parietooccipital f., *sulcus* parietooccipitalis.

petrotympanic f., *fissura* petrotympanica.

portal f., *porta* hepatis.

posterior median f., *sulcus* medianus posterior.

primary f. of the cerebellum, *fissura* prima cerebelli.

Rolando's f., *sulcus* centralis.

f. of round ligament, *fissura* ligamenti teretis.

superior orbital f., *fissura* orbitalis superior.

sylvian f., f. of Sylvius, *sulcus* lateralis cerebri.

transverse f. of cerebrum, *fissura* transversa cerebri.

tympanomastoid f., *fissura* tympanomastoidea.

f. of venous ligament, *fissura* ligamenti venosi.

fistula, pl. **fistulae** or **fistulas** (fis'tu-lah, -le, lăz) [L. a pipe, tube]. An abnormal passage from a hollow organ to the surface, or from one organ to another.

anal f., a f. opening at or near the anus, usually opening into the rectum above the internal sphincter.

arteriovenous f., an abnormal communication between an artery and a vein, usually resulting in the formation of an arteriovenus aneurysm.

blind f., incomplete f.; a f. that ends in a cul-de-sac, being open at one extremity only.

carotid-cavernous f., arteriovenous communication resulting from rupture of the intracavernous portion of the carotid artery.

complete f., a f. that is open at both ends.

Eck f., transposition of the portal circulation to the systemic by making an anastomosis between the vena cava and portal vein and then ligating the latter close to the liver.

external f., a f. between a hollow viscus and the skin.

fecal f., intestinal f.

gastric f., a fistulous tract from the stomach to the abdominal wall.

horseshoe f., an anal f. partially encircling the anus and opening at both extremities on the cutaneous surface.

incomplete f., blind f.

internal f., a f. between hollow viscera.

intestinal f., fecal or stercoral f.; a tract leading from the lumen of the bowel to the exterior.

parietal f., a f., either blind or complete, opening on the wall of the thorax or abdomen.

reverse Eck f., side-to-side anastomosis of the portal vein with the inferior vena cava and ligation of the latter above the anastomosis but below the hepatic veins; the blood from the lower part of the body is thus directed through the hepatic circulation.

salivary f., an opening between a salivary duct or gland and the cutaneous surface, or into the oral cavity through other than the normal anatomical pathway.

stercoral f., intestinal f.

fistula′tion, fistuliza′tion. Formation of a fistula in a part; becoming fistulous.

fistulectomy (fis-tu-lek′to-mĭ) [fistula + G. *ektomē,* excision]. Syringectomy; excision of a fistula.

fistulotomy (fis-tu-lot′o-mĭ) [fistula + G. *tomē,* incision]. Syringotomy; incision or surgical enlargement of a fistula.

fis′tulous. Relating to or containing a fistula.

fit [A.S. *fitt*]. An acute attack or the sudden appearance of some symptom, such as coughing or a convulsion.

fit′ness. 1. Well-being. **2.** Suitability.

fixa′tion [L. *figo,* pp. *fixus,* to fix, fasten]. **1.** The condition of being stabilized, firmly attached, or set. **2.** Fixing; in histology, rapid killing of tissue elements and their preservation and hardening, to retain as nearly as possible the same relations they had in the living body. **3.** In chemistry, conversion of a gas into solid or liquid form by chemical reactions either with or without the help of living tissue. **4.** In psychoanalysis, the quality of being firmly attached or fixed to a particular person or object, such as a close and paralyzing attachment. **5.** In physiological optics, the coordinated positioning and accommodation of both eyes that results in bringing or maintaining a sharp image of a stationary or moving object on the fovea of each eye.

complement f., f. of complement in a serum by an antigen-antibody combination whereby it is rendered unavailable to complete a reaction in a second antigen-antibody combination for which complement is necessary.

external f., f. of fractured bones by splints, plastic dressings, or transfixion pins.

internal f., stabilization of fractured bony parts by direct f. to one another with surgical wires, screws, pins, plates, or methylmethacrylate.

fix′ative. 1. Serving to fix, bind, or make firm or stable. **2.** A substance used for the preservation of gross and histologic specimens of tissue, or individual cells, usually be denaturing and precipitating or cross-linking the protein constituents.

fix′ing. Fixation (2).

flaccid (flak′sid, flas′id) [L. *flaccidus*]. Relaxed; flabby; without tone.

flagel′la. Plural of flagellum.

flagellar (flă-jel′ar). Relating to a flagellum or to the extremity of a protozoan.

flagellate (flaj′ĕ-lāt). **1.** Possessing one or more flagella. **2.** Common name for a member of the class Mastigophora.

flagellated (flaj′ĕ-la-ted). Possession one or more flagella.

flagellation (flaj-ĕ-la′shun) [L. *flagellatus,* fr. *flagell-āre,* to whip or scourge]. Whipping either one's self or another as a means of arousing or heightening sexual feeling.

flagellosis (flaj-ĕ-lo′sis). Infection with flagellated protozoa in the intestinal or genital tract.

flagellum, pl. **flagella** (flă-jel′um, -ah) [L. dim. of *flagrum,* a whip]. A whiplike locomotory organelle consisting of nine double peripheral microtubules and two single central microtubules; it arises from a deeply staining basal granule, often connected to the nucleus by a fiber, the rhizoplast.

flange. 1. A projecting rim or edge. **2.** That part of the denture base which extends from the cervical ends of the teeth to the border of the denture.

flank. Latus.

flap. 1. A mass or tongue of tissue for transplantation, vascularized by a pedicle or stem; specifically, a pedicle f. **2.** An uncontrolled movement, as of the hands.

advancement f., sliding f.

arterial f., a f. that includes a direct cutaneous artery within its longitudinal axis.

buried f., a f. denuded of both surface epithelium and superficial dermis, and transferred into the subcutaneous tissues.

caterpillar f., waltzed f.; a tubed f. transferred end-over-end (in stages) from the donor area to a distant recipient area.

composite f., compound f., a skin f. incorporating underlying muscle, bone, or cartilage.

cross f., a skin f. transferred from one arm, breast, eyelid, finger, foot, lip, leg, etc. to the other.

delayed f., a f. raised in its donor area in two or more stages to increase its chances of survival after transfer.

direct f., immediate f.; a f. raised completely and transferred at the same stage.

distant f., a f. in which the donor site is distant from the recipient area.

flat f., open f.; a f. in which during transfer the pedicle is left flat or open, *i.e.,* untubed.

free f., an island f. in which the donor vessels are severed proximally, the f. is transported as a free object to the recipient area, and the flap is revascularized by anastomosing its supplying vessels to similar vessels there.

full thickness f., a f. consisting of the full thickness of the mucosa and submucosa or skin and subcutaneous tissues.

hinged f., a turnover f. transferred by lifting it over on its pedicle as though the pedicle was a hinge.

immediate f., direct f.

island f., a f. in which the pedicle consists solely of the supplying artery and vein(s), sometimes plus a nerve.

jump f., a distant f. transferred in stages via an intermediate carrier; *e.g.,* an abdominal f. is attached to the wrist, then at a later stage the wrist is brought to the face.

local f., a f. transferred to an adjacent area.

open f., flat f.

partial-thickness f., split-thickness f.

pedicle f., a f. sustained by a blood-carrying stem from the donor site during transfer.

random pattern f., a f. in which the pedicle blood supply is derived randomly from the network of vessels in the area, rather than from a single longitudinal artery (as in an arterial f.).

rotation f., a pedicle f. rotated from the donor site to an adjacent recipient area, usually as a direct f.

sliding f., advancement f.; a rectangular f. raised in an elastic area, with its free end adjacent to a defect; the defect is covered by stretching the f. longitudinally until the end comes over it.

split thickness f., partial-thickness f.; a f. which consists of part of the mucosa and submucosa but does not include periosteum.

subcutaneous f., a pedicle f. in which the pedicle is denuded of epithelium and buried in the subcutaneous tissue of the recipient area.

tubed f., a f. in which the sides of the pedicle are sutured together to create a tube, with the entire surface covered by skin.

waltzed f., caterpillar f.

flare. A diffuse redness of the skin extending beyond the local reaction to the application of an irritant; due to a vasomotor reaction.

flat'foot. *Talipes* planus.

flatulence (flat'u-lens) [Mod. L. *flatulentus,* fr. L. *flatus,* a blowing]. Presence of an excessive amount of gas in the stomach and intestines.

flat'ulent. Relating to or suffering from flatulence.

fla'tus [L. a blowing]. Gas or air in the gastrointestinal tract which may be expelled through the anus.

flat'worm. A member of the phylum Platyhelminthes, including the free-living Turbellaria and parasitic tapeworms and flukes.

flavin(e) (fla'vin, -vēn). [L. *flavus,* yellow[. **1.** Riboflavin. **2.** A yellow acridine dye, preparations of which are used as antiseptics.

f. adenine dinucleotide (FAD), a condensation product of riboflavin and adenosine diphosphate; the coenzyme of various aerobic dehydrogenases.

f. mononucleotide (FMN), riboflavin 5'-phosphate; a coenzyme involved in the action of various aerobic dehydrogenases.

Fla'vivirus. A genus of viruses (family Togaviridae) formerly classified as group B arboviruses.

Flavobacterium (fla'vo-bak-tēr'ī-um) [L. *flavus,* yellow]. A genus of bacteria (family Achromobacteraceae) that characteristically produce yellow, orange, red, or yellow-brown pigments; found in soil and fresh and salt water; some species are pathogenic. The type species is *F. aquatile.*

flavoenzyme (fla'vo-en'zīm). Any enzyme that possesses a flavin nucleotide as coenzyme.

fla'vopro'tein. A compound protein (enzyme) possessing a flavin as prosthetic group.

flea. An insect of the order Siphonaptera, marked by lateral compression, sucking mouthparts, extraordinary jumping powers, and ectoparasitic adult life in the hair and feathers of warm- blooded animals. Important f.'s include *Ctenocephalides* (*C. felis,* cat f., or *C. canis,* dog f.), *Pulex irritans,* (human f.), *Tunga penetrans* (chigger, chigoe, or sand f.), *Echidonophaga gallinacea* (sticktight f.), *Xenopsylla* (rat f.), and *Ceratophyllus.*

flesh [A.S. *flaesc*]. **1.** The meat of animals used for food. **2.** Muscular *tissue.*

proud f., exuberant granulations in the granulation tissue on the surface of a wound.

flesh'flies. Members of the order Diptera, whose larvae (maggots) develop in putrifying or living tissues.

flex [L. *flecto,* pp. *flexus,* to bend]. To bend; to move a joint in such a direction as to approximate the two parts which it connects.

flexibil'itas ce'rea [L. waxy flexibility]. The peculiar rigidity of catalepsy which may be overcome by slight external force, but which returns at once, holding the limb firmly in the new position.

flexion (flek'shun) [L. *flecto,* pp. *flectus,* to bend]. **1.** The act of flexing or bending. **2.** The condition of being flexed or bent.

flex'or [NA]. A muscle the action of which is to flex a joint.

flexura, pl. **flexu'rae** (flek-shūr'ah, -e) [L. a bending] [NA]. Flexure; a bend, as in an organ or structure.

f. co'li dex'tra [NA], right colic flexure; hepatic flexure; the bend of the colon at the juncture of its ascending and transverse portions.

f. co'li sinis'tra [NA], left colic flexure; splenic flexure; the bend at the junction of the transverse and descending colon.

f. duode'nojejuna'lis [NA], duodenojejunal flexure; an abrupt bend in the small intestine at the junction of the duodenum and jejunum.

flexural (flek'shur-al). Relating to a flexure.

flexure (flek'shur) [L. *flexura*]. Flexura.

caudal f., sacral f.; the bend in the lumbosacral region of the embryo.

cephalic f., cranial or mesencephalic f.; the sharp, ventrally concave bend in the developing midbrain of the embryo.

cervical f., the ventrally concave bend at the juncture of the brainstem and spinal cord in the embryo.

cranial f., cephalic f.

dorsal f., a f. in the mid-dorsal region in the embryo.

duodenojejunal f., *flexura* duodenojejunalis.

hepatic f., *flexura* coli dextra.

left colic f., *flexura* coli sinistra.

lumbar f., the normal ventral curve of the vertebral column in the lumbar region.

mesencephalic f., cephalic f.

pontine f., the dorsally concave curvature of the rhombencephalon in the embryo.

right colic f., *flexura* coli dextra.

sacral f., caudal f.

sacral f. of rectum, *flexura* sacralis recti.

sigmoid f., *colon* sigmoideum.

splenic f., *flexura* coli sinistra.

telencephalic f., a f. appearing in the embryonic forebrain region.

flight into disease. Gain through falling ill or assuming the sick role.

flight into health. In psychoanalysis, the early but often only temporary disappearance of the symptoms that ostensibly brought the patient into therapy; a defense against the anxiety engendered by the prospect of further psychoanalytic exploration of the patient's conflicts.

float'ing. 1. Free or unattached. **2.** Out of the normal position; unduly movable; wandering; denoting an occasional abnormal condition of certain organs.

floccillation (flok-sĭ-la'shun) [Mod. L. *flocculus*]. An aimless plucking at the bedclothes, as if one were picking off threads or tufts of cotton, occuring in the delirium of a fever.

floccose (flok'ōs) [L. *floccus,* a flock of wool]. In bacteriology, denoting growth of short curving filaments or chains, closely but irregularly disposed.

floc'cular. Relating to a flocculus of any sort; specifically to the flocculus of the cerebellum.

floc'culate. To become flocculent.

floc'cula'tion, floc'culence. Precipitation from solution in the form of fleecy masses; the process of becoming flocculent.

flocculent (flok'u-lent). **1.** Resembling tufts of cotton or wool; denoting a fluid, such as the urine, containing numerous shreds or fluffy particles of gray-white or white mucus or other material. **2.** In bacteriology, denoting a fluid culture in which there are numerous colonies either floating in the fluid medium or loosely deposited at the bottom.

flocculus, pl. **flocculi** (flok'u-lus, -li) [Mod. L. dim. of L. *floccus,* a tuft of wool]. **1.** A tuft or shred of cotton or wool or anything resembling it. **2**[NA]. A small lobe of the cerebellum at the posterior border of the brachium pontis anterior to the lobulus biventer and associated with the nodulus of the vernis; together, these two structures compose the vestibular part of the cerebellum.

flood (flud) [A.S. *flōd*]. **1.** To bleed profusely from the uterus, as after childbirth or in cases of menorrhagia. **2.** Colloquialism for a profuse menstrual discharge.

flood'ing. A type of behavior therapy in which the patient, at the beginning of therapy as the therapeutic strategy, imagines the most anxiety producing scene and fully immerses (floods) himself in it.

flora (flo'rah) [L. *Flora,* goddess of flowers, fr. *flos* (*flor-*), a flower]. **1.** Plant life, usually of a certain locality or district. **2.** The various bacterial and other microscopic forms of life inhabiting an individual.

florid (flŏr'id) [L. *floridus,* flowery]. Of a bright red color; denoting certain cutaneous lesions.

flota'tion. A process for separating solids by their tendency to float upon or sink into a liquid.

flow [A.S. *flōwan*]. The movement of a fluid or gas; specifically, the volume of fluid or gas passing a given point per unit of time. In respiratory physiology, the symbol for gas flow is V̇ and for blood flow is Q̇, followed by subscripts denoting location and chemical species. **4.** In rheology, a permanent deformation of a body which proceeds with time.

effective renal blood f. (ERBF), the amount of blood flowing to the parts of the kidney that are concerned with production of constituents of urine.

effective renal plasma f. (ERPF), the amount of plasma flowing to the parts of the kidney that have a function in the production of constituents of urine.

flowers. A mineral substance in a powdery state after sublimation.

flow'meter. A device for measuring velocity or volume of flow of liquids or gases.

fluctuate (fluk'tu-āt) [L. *fluctuo,* pp. *-atus,* to flow in waves]. **1.** To move in waves. **2.** To vary, to change from time to time, as in referring to any quantity or quality.

flu'id [L. *fluridus,* fr. *fluo,* to flow]. **1.** Flowing; liquid; gaseous. **2.** A nonsolid substance, either liquid or gas.

allantoic f., the f. within the allantoic cavity.

amniotic f., a liquid within the amnion that surrounds the fetus and protects it from injury.

cerebrospinal f. (CSF), f. secreted by the choroid plexuses of the ventricles of the brain, filling the ventricles and the subarachnoid cavities of the brain and spinal cord.

extracellular f., (1) the interstitial f. and the plasma, constituting about 20% of the weight of the body; **(2)** sometimes used to mean all f. outside of cells, usually excluding transcellular f.

extravascular f., all f. outside the blood vessels (intracellular, and transcellular f.'s); constitutes about 48 to 58% of the body weight.

interstitial f., the f. in spaces between the tissue cells; constituting about 16% of the weight of the body.

intracellular f., the f. within the tissue cells; constitutes about 30 to 40% of the body weight.

pleural f., the thin film of f. between the visceral and parietal pleurae.

prostatic f., a whitish secretion that is one of the constituents of the semen.

Scarpa's f., endolymph.

seminal f., semen (1).

synovial f., synovia.

transcellular f.'s, f.'s that are not inside cells, but are separated from plasma and interstitial f. by cellular barriers.

flu'idex'tract. Pharmacopeial liquid preparation of vegetable drugs, containing alcohol as a solvent, preservative, or both, and so made that each milliliter contains the therapeutic constitutents of 1g of the standard drug that it represents.

fluidounce (flu'id-owns'). A measure of capacity, containing 8 fluidrams.

fluidrachm, fluidram (flu'ĭ-dram'). A measure of capacity, ¹/₈ of a fluidounce; a teaspoonful.

fluke (flūk) [A.S. *flōc*, flatfish]. Common name for members of the class Trematoda (phylum Platyhelminthes). All f.'s of mammals (subclass Digenea) are internal parasites in the adult stage and are characterized by complex digenetic life cycles involving a snail initial host, in which larval multiplication occurs, and the release of swimming larvae (cercariae) which directly penetrate the skin of the final host, encyst on vegetation, or encyst in or on another intermediate host.

fluor-, fluoro-. Prefixes denoting fluorine.

fluorescein (flūr-es'e-in). 9-(*o*-Carboxyphenyl)-6-hydroxy-3*H*-xanthen-3-one; an orange-red crystalline powder that yields a bright green fluorescence in solution; a nontoxic, water-soluble indicator used to trace water flow.

fluorescence (flūr-es'ens). The emission of a longer wavelength radiation by a substance as a consequence of absorption of energy from a shorter wavelength radiation, continuing only as long as the stimulus is present.

fluorescent (flūr-es'ent). Possessing the quality of fluorescence.

fluoridation (flūr-ĭ-da'shun). Addition of fluorides to the drinking water, usually 1 p.p.m., to reduce incidence of dental decay.

fluoride (flūr'īd). A compound of fluorine with a metal, a nonmetal, or an organic radical; the anion of fluorine.

fluoride number. The per cent inhibition of pseudocholinesterase produced by fluorides; used to differentiate normal from atypical pseudocholinesterases.

fluoridization (flūr'ĭ-dĭ-za'shun). Therapeutic use of fluorides to reduce the incidence of dental decay, as by topical application of fluoride agents to the teeth.

fluorine (flūr'ēn). A gaseous chemical element, symbol F, atomic no. 9, atomic weight 19.00.

fluoro-. See fluor-.

fluorochrome (flūr'o-krōm). Any fluorescent dye used to stain tissues and cells for examination by fluorescence microscopy.

fluorography (flūr'o'ră-fī). Photofluorography.

fluoroscope (flūr'o-skōp) [fluorescence + G. *skopeō*, to examine]. An apparatus for rendering visible the shadows of the x-rays which, after passing through the body examined, are projected on a fluorescent screen.

fluoroscopic (flūr-o-skop'ik). Relating to or effected by means of fluoroscopy.

fluoroscopy (flūr-os'ko-pī). Radioscopy; examination of the tissues and deep structures of the body by x-ray, using the fluoroscope.

fluorosis (flūr-o'sis). A condition caused by an excessive intake of fluorides in drinking water, characterized mainly by mottling of the enamel of the teeth, although the skeletal bones are also affected.

flush. 1. To wash out with a full stream of fluid. **2.** A transient erythema due to heat, exertion, stress, or disease. **3.** Flat, or even with another surface.

flutter [A.S. *flotorian*, to float about]. Agitation; tremulousness.

    atrial f., auricular f., rapid regular atrial contractions occurring usually at rates between 250 and 400 per minute and often producing "saw-tooth" waves in the electrocardiogram.

    diaphragmatic f., rapid rhythmical contractions (average, 150 per minute) of the diaphragm, simulating atrial f. clinically and sometimes electrocardiographically.

    impure f., mixture of atrial flutter (FF) and fibrillation (ff) waves in the electrocardiogram.

    ventricular f., a form of rapid ventricular tachycardia in which the electrocardiographic complexes assume a regular undulating pattern with an absence of distant QRS and T waves.

flutter-fibrillation. An electrocardiographic pattern of atrial activity with features of both fibrillation and flutter.

flux [L. *fluxus*, a flow]. **1.** The discharge of a fluid material in large amount from a cavity or surface of the body. **2.** Material thus discharged from the bowels. **3.**(*J*). Flux density, the moles of a substance crossing through a unit area of a boundary layer or membrane per unit of time.

fly [A.S. *fleōge*]. A two-winged insect in the order Diptera. Typical flies of the housefly type and similar forms are in the family Muscidae.

Fm Fermium.

FMN Flavin mononucleotide.

fo'cal. Relating to a focus.

focus, pl. **foci** (fo'kus, fo'si) [L. a hearth]. **1.** The point at which the light rays meet after passing through a convex lens. **2.** The center, or the starting point, of a disease process.

    Ghon's f., Ghon's *tubercle.*

fog'ging. A method of refraction in which accommodation is relaxed by overcorrection with a convex spherical lens.

fo'late. A salt or ester of folic acid.

fold. 1. A ridge or margin apparently formed by the doubling back of a lamina. See also plica. **2.** In the embryo, a transient elevation or reduplication of tissue in the form of a lamina.

    amniotic f., a f. of amniotic membrane enclosing the vitelline duct and extending from the point of insertion of the umbilical cord to the yolk sac.

    aryepiglottic f., arytenoepiglottidean f., *plica* aryepiglottica.

    circular f.'s, *plicae* circulares.

    Douglas f., *plica* rectouterina.

    epiglottic f., *plica* epiglottica.

    gastric f.'s, *plicae* gastricae.

gluteal f., a prominent f. that marks the upper limit of the thigh from the lower limit of the buttock; coincides with the lower border of the gluteus maximus muscle.

head f., a ventral folding of the cephalic extremity in the embryonic disk, so that the brain lies rostrad to the mouth and pericardium.

interureteric f., *plica* interureterica.

lacrimal f., *plica* lacrimalis.

lateral f.'s, ventral foldings of the lateral margins of the embryonic disk which establish the definitive embryonic body form.

mammary f., mammary *ridge.*

mesonephric f., urogenital *ridge.*

mongolian f., epicanthus.

nail f., a groove in the cutis in which lie the margins and proximal edge of the nail.

neural f.'s, the elevated margins of the neural groove.

palmate f.'s, *plicae* palmatae.

rectouterine f., *plica* rectouterina.

semilunar conjunctival f., *plica* semilunaris conjunctivae.

spiral f. of cystic duct, *plica* spiralis ductus cystici.

tail f., the ventral folding of the caudal extremity of the embryonic disk.

transverse f.'s of rectum, *plicae* transversales recti.

ventricular f., vestibular f., *plica* vestibularis.

vocal f., *plica* vocalis.

fo'lia. Plural of folium.

fo'lic acid. 1. Collective term for pteroylglutamic acids and their oligoglutamic acid conjugates. **2.** Specifically, pteroylmonoglutamic acid, the growth factor for *Lactobacillus casei,* and a member of the vitamin B complex necessary for the normal production of red blood cells; present in peptide linkages in liver, green vegetables, and yeast.

f. a. antagonists, modified pterins such as aminopterin and amethopterin, that interfere with the action of folic acid and thus produce the symptoms of a folic acid deficiency.

f. a. conjugate, folates with three molecules of glutamic acid instead of one (pteropterin) or with seven (pteroylheptaglutamic acid or vitamin B_c conjugate).

folie (fo-le') [Fr. folly]. Old term for madness or insanity.

f. à deux (ă-dü') [Fr. *deux,* two]. double insanity; identical or similar mental disorders affecting two individuals, usually members of the same family living together.

f. du doute (düdūt'), doubting mania; an excessive doubting about all the affairs of life and a morbid scrupulosity in regard to minutiae.

fo'linate. A salt or ester of folinic acid.

folin'ic acid. Citrovorum factor; leucovorin; 5-formyl-5,6,7,8-tetrahydrofolic acid; the compound that acts as formyl group carrier in transformylation reactions.

folium, pl. **folia** (fo'lĭ-um, fo'lĭ-ah) [L. a leaf] [NA]. A broad, thin, leaflike structure, as of the cerebellar cortex.

follib'erin. Follicle-stimulating hormone-releasing *factor.*

follicle (fol'ĭ-kl) [L. *folliculus,* a small sac]. **1.** Folliculus. **2.** Ovarian f.

aggregated lymphatic f.'s, *folliculi* lymphatici aggregati.

dental f., the dental sac with its enclosed developing tooth.

f.'s of the thyroid gland, *folliculi* glandulae thyroideae.

gastric f.'s, *glandulae* gastricae.

gastric lymphatic f., *folliculus* lymphaticus gastricus.

graafian f., vesicular ovarian f.

hair f., *folliculus* pili.

intestinal f.'s, *glandulae* intestinales.

Lieberkühn's f.'s., *glandulae* intestinales.

lingual f.'s, *folliculi* linguales.

lymph f., lymphatic f., *folliculus* lymphaticus.

nabothian f., nabothian *cyst.*

ovarian f., one of the spheroidal cell aggregations in the ovary containing an ovum.

primary ovarian f., an ovarian f. before the appearance of an antrum, marked by developmental changes in the oocyte and follicular cells so that the latter form one or more layers of cuboidal or columnar cells; it becomes surrounded by the theca.

primordial ovarian f., a f. in which the primordial oocyte is surrounded by a single layer of flattened follicular cells.

sebaceous f.'s, *glandulae* sebaceae.

secondary f., vesicular ovarian f.

solitary f.'s, *folliculi* lymphatici solitarii.

splenic lymph f.'s, *folliculi* lymphatici lienales.

vesicular ovarian f., graafian or secondary f.; a f. in which the oocyte attains its full size and is surrounded by the (zona pellucida) at the periphery of the fluid-filled antrum; the follicular cells proliferate and form the membrana granulosa; the theca of the f. develops into internal and external layers.

follicular (fŏ-lik'u-lar). Relating to a follicle or follicles.

folliculi (fŏ-lik'u-li). Plural of folliculus.

folliculitis (fŏ-lik-u-li'tis). An inflammatory reaction in hair follicles.

f. bar'bae, *tinea* sycosis.

f. decal'vans, papular or pustular inflammation of the hair follicles of the scalp, resulting in scarring and loss of hair in the affected area.

f. keloida'lis, acne *keloid.*

f. ulerythemato'sa reticula'ta, erythematous "ice-pick" or pitted scars on the cheeks; a scarring type of folliculitis.

folliculoma (fŏ-lik-u-lo'mah). **1.** Granulosa cell *tumor.* **2.** Cystic enlargement of a graafian follicle.

folliculosis (fŏ-lik-u-lo'sis). Presence of lymph follicles in abnormally great numbers.

folliculus, pl. **folliculi** (fŏ-lik'u-lus, -u-li) [L. a small sac] [NA]. Follicle (1). **1.** A more or less spherical mass of cells usually containing a cavity. **2.** A crypt or minute cul-de-sac or lacuna, such as the depression in the skin, from which the hair emerges.

follic'uli glan'dulae thyroi'deae [NA], follicles of the thyroid gland; the small spherical vesicular components of the thyroid gland lined with epithelium and containing colloid which colloid serves for storage of thyroid hormones.

follic'uli lingua'les [NA], lingual follicles; collections of lymphoid tissue in the mucosa of the pharyngeal part of the tongue posterior to the terminal sulcus, collectively forming the lingual tonsil.

follic'uli lymphat'ici aggrega'ti [NA], aggregated lymphatic follicles; aggregate, agminate, or agminated glands; Peyer's patches or glands; collections of many lymphoid follicles closely packed together, forming oblong elevations on the mucous membrane of the small intestine.

follic'uli lymphat'ici liena'les [NA], splenic lymph follicles; malpighian corpuscles (2); malpighian bodies; small nodular masses of lymphoid tissue attached to the sides of the smaller arterial branches.

follic'uli lymphat'ici solita'rii [NA], solitary follicles, or glands; minute collections of lymphoid tissue in the mucosa of the small and large intestines, especially numerous in the cecum and appendix.

f. lymphat'icus [NA], lymph or lymphatic follicle; lymph nodule; one of the spherical masses of lymphoid cells frequently having a more lightly staining center.

f. lymphat'icus gas'tricus [NA], gastric lymphatic follicle; one of the numerous small masses of lymphoid tissue in the gastric mucosa.

f. pi'li [NA], hair follicle; a deep narrow pit formed by invagination of the epidermis and corium; it contains the root of the hair and the ducts of the sebaceous glands open into it.

fol'litropin. Follicle-stimulating *hormone*.

fomentation (fo'men-ta'shun) [L. *fomento*, pp. *-atus*, to foment]. **1.** A warm application; a poultice. **2.** Application of warmth and moisture in the treatment of disease.

fomes, pl. **fomites** (fo'mĕz, fo'mĭ-tēz) [L. tinder, fr. *foveo*, to keep warm]. A substance, such as clothing, capable of absorbing and transmitting the contagium of disease; usually used in the plural.

fontanel, fontanelle (fon'tă-nel') [Fr. dim. of *fontaine*, fountain, spring]. Fonticulus.

fonticulus, pl. **fonticuli** (fon-tik'u-lus, -li) [L. dim. of *fons (font-)*, fountain, spring] [NA]. Fontanel; one of several membranous intervals at the angles of the cranial bones in the infant: the midline anterior and posterior fontanels, and the paired sphenoidal and mastoid fontanels.

food [A.S. *fōda*]. Aliment; nourishment; what is eaten to supply necessary nutritive elements.

foot [A.S. *fōt*]. **1.** Pes (1); the lower, pedal, podalic, extremity of the leg. **2.** A unit of length, containing 12 inches, equal to 30.48 cm.

athlete's f., *tinea* pedis.

claw f., a condition of the f. characterized by hyperextension at the metatarsophalangeal joint and flexion at the interphalangeal joints, as a fixed contracture.

club f., *talipes* equinovarus.

drop f., see foot-drop.

flat f., *talipes* planus.

immersion f., trench f., a condition resulting from prolonged exposure to damp and cold; the extremity is initially cold and anesthetic, but on rewarming becomes hyperemic, paresthetic, and hyperhidrotic.

foot'candle. Illumination or brightness equivalent to 1 lumen per square foot; replaced in the SI system by the candela (1 lumen per square meter).

foot-drop. Paralysis or weakness of the dorsiflexor muscles of the foot and ankle, as a consequence of which the foot falls and the toes drag on the ground in walking.

foot'plate, foot-plate. 1. *Basis* stapedis. **2.** Pedicel.

foot-pound. The energy expended, or work done, in raising a mass of 1 pound a height of 1 foot, vertically against gravitational force.

foot-poundal. Energy exerted, or work done, when a force of 1 poundal displaces a body 1 foot in the direction of the force.

foramen, pl. **foramina** (fo-ra'men, -ram'ĭ-nah) [L. an aperture, fr. *foro*, to pierce] [NA]. An aperture or perforation through a bone or a membranous structure.

anterior condyloid f., *canalis* hypoglossalis.

anterior palatine foramina, foramina palatina minora.

aortic f., *hiatus* aorticus.

f. ap'icis den'tis [NA], apical dental f., the opening at the apex of the root of a tooth that gives passage to the nerve and blood vessels.

f. ce'cum medullae oblongatae, a small triangular depression at the lower boundary of the pons that marks the upper limit of the median fissure of the medulla oblongata.

conjugate f., a f. formed by the notches of two bones in apposition.

f. epiplo'icum [NA], epiploic f., the passage, below and behind the portal fissure of the liver, connecting the two sacs of the peritoneum.

f. ethmoida'le [NA], ethmoidal f., one of two foramina, anterior and posterior, formed by grooves on either edge of the ethmoidal notch of the frontal bone and similar grooves on the ethmoid bone.

external acoustic f., *porus* acusticus externus.

external auditory f., *porus* acusticus externus; **internal acoustic f.,** *porus* acusticus internus.

great f., f. magnum.

greater palatine f., f. palatinum majus.

f. incisi′vum [NA], **incisive f.,** one of several (usually four) opening of the incisive canals into the incisive fossa.

f. infraorbita′le [NA], **infraorbital f.,** the external opening of the infraorbital canal, on the anterior surface of the body of the maxilla.

internal auditory f., *porus* acusticus internus.

f. interventricula′re [NA], **interventricular f.,** Monro's f.; porta (2); the short, often slitlike passage that, on both the left and right side, connects the third ventricle (in the diencephalon) with the lateral ventricle (in the cerebral hemisphere).

f. intervertebra′le [NA], **intervertebral f.,** one of a number of openings into the vertebral canal bounded by the pedicles of adjacent vertebrae above and below, the vertebral bodies anteriorly, and the articular processes posteriorly.

f. ischiad′icum [NA], **sciatic f.;** one of two foramina, greater and lesser, formed by the sacrospinous and sacrotuberous ligaments crossing the sciatic notches of the hip bone.

f. jugula′re [NA], **jugular f.** a passage between the petrous portion of the temporal bone and the jugular process of the occipital, sometimes divided into two by the intrajugular processes; it contains the internal jugular vein, inferior petrosal sinus, the glossopharyngeal, vagus, and accessory nerves, and meningeal branches of the ascending pharyngeal and occipital arteries.

lesser palatine foramina, foramina palatina minora.

f. mag′num [NA], **great f.;** the large opening in the basal part of the occipital bone through which the spinal cord becomes continuous with the medulla oblongata.

f. mastoi′deum [NA], **mastoid f.,** an opening at the posterior portion of the mastoid process, transmitting a small artery to the dura and an emissary vein to the sigmoid sinus.

f. menta′le [NA], **mental f.,** the anterior opening of the mandibular canal on the body of the mandible lateral to and above the mental tubercle.

Monro′s f., f. interventriculare.

f. nutric′ium [NA], **nutrient f.,** the external opening of the canalis nutricius in a bone.

f. obtura′tum [NA], **obturator f.,** a large, oval or irregularly triangular aperture in the hip bone, the margins of which are formed by the pubis and the ischium; by the obturator membrane, except for a small opening for the passage of the obturator vessels and nerve.

olfactory f., one of the openings in the cribriform plate of the ethmoid bone, transmitting the olfactory nerves.

optic f., *canalis* opticus.

f. ova′le, oval f., (1) [NA], in the fetal heart, the oval opening in the septum secundum; the persistent part of septum primum acts as a valve for this interatrial communication during fetal life and postnatally becomes fused to septum secundum to

close it; (2) [NA], a large oval opening in the greater wing of the sphenoid bone, transmitting the mandibular nerve and a small meningeal artery; (3) valvular incompetence of the f. ovale of the heart; a condition contrasting with probe patency of the f. ovale in that the valvula foraminis ovalis has abnormal perforations in it or is of insufficient size to afford adequate valvular action at the f. ovale prenatally, or effect a complete closure postnatally.

foram′ina palati′na mino′ra [NA], lesser palatine foramina; anterior palatine foramina; openings on the hard palate of palatine canals passing vertically through the tuberosity of the palatine bone and transmitting the smaller palatine nerves and vessels.

f. palati′num ma′jus [NA], greater or posterior palatine f.; an opening in the posterolateral corner of the hard palate opposite the last molar tooth, marking the lower end of the pterygopalatine canal.

f. parieta′le [NA], **parietal f.,** a f. in the parietal bone near the sagittal margin posteriorly; transmits an emissary vein to the superior sagittal sinus.

posterior condyloid f., *canalis* condylaris.

posterior palatine f., f. palatinum majus.

f. proces′sus transver′sus [NA], transverse or vertebroarterial f.; the f. in the transverse process of a cervical vertebra for the passage of the vertebral artery and vein and the sympathetic nerve plexus.

quadrate f., f. venae cavae.

f. rotun′dum [NA], **round f.,** an opening in the greater wing of the sphenoid bone, transmitting the maxillary nerve.

f. sacra′le [NA], **sacral f.,** one of two sets of openings between the fused sacral vertebrae transmitting the sacral nerves: the anterior, pelvis, foramina, transmit ventral branches, the posterior foramina, dorsal, give passage to dorsal branches.

Scarpa′s foramina, two openings in the line of the intermaxillary suture: the anterior f. transmits the left nasopalatine nerve, the posterior the right.

sciatic f., f. ischiadicum.

f. sphenopalati′num [NA], **sphenopalatine f.,** the f. formed from the sphenopalatine notch of the palatine bone in articulation with the sphenoid bone.

f. spino′sum [NA], an opening in the great wing of the sphenoid bone, anterior to the spine, transmitting the middle meningeal artery.

f. stylomastoid′eum [NA], **stylomastoid f.,** an opening on the inferior surface of the petrous portion of the temporal bone, between the styloid and mastoid processes, that transmits the facial nerve and stylomastoid artery.

f. supraorbita′le [NA], **supraorbital f.,** a f. in the supraorbital margin of the frontal bone at the junction of the medial and intermediate thirds.

transverse f., f. processus transversus.

f. ve′nae ca′vae [NA], **f. of the vena cava,** quadrate f.; an opening in the right lobe of the central tendon of the diaphragm which transmits the inferior vena cava and branches of the right phrenic nerve.

f. vertebra'le [NA], **vertebral f.,** the f. formed by the union of the vertebral arch with its body.

vertebroarterial f., f. processus transversus.

Weitbrecht's f., an opening in the articular capsule of the shoulder joint, communicating with the subtendinous bursa of the subscapularis muscle.

f. zygomaticofacia'le [NA], **zygomaticofacial f.,** the opening on the lateral surface of the zygomatic bone, below the orbital margin, that transmits the zygomaticofacial nerve.

f. zygomat'icoorbita'le [NA], **zygomaticoorbital f.,** the common opening on the orbital surface of the zygomatic bone of the canals transmitting the zygomaticofacial and zygomaticotemporal nerves; sometimes each of these canals has a separate opening on the orbital surface.

f. zygomat'icotempora'le [NA], zygomaticotemporal f., the opening, on the temporal surface of the zygomatic bone, of the canal that gives passage to the zygomaticotemporal nerve.

foram'ina. Plural of foramen.

force [L. *fortis,* strong]. Power; strength; that which tends to produce motion in a body.

electromotive f. (EMF), the f. (measured in volts) that causes the flow of electricity from one point to another.

f. of mastication, masticatory f., the motive f. created by the dynamic action of the muscles during the physiologic act of mastication.

occlusal f., the result of muscular f. applied on opposing teeth.

reciprocal f.'s, in dentistry, f.'s whereby the resistance of one or more teeth is utilized to move one or more opposing teeth.

reserve f., the energy residing in an organ or any of its parts above that required for its normal functioning.

forced feeding. Giving nourishment through a nasal tube passed into the stomach of someone unable or unwilling to eat.

for'ceps [L. a pair of tongs]. **1.** An instrument for seizing a structure, and making compression or traction. **2** [NA]. Bands of white fibers (f. major and f. minor) composing the radiation of the corpus callosum to the cerebrum.

alligator f., long f. with a small hinged jaw on the end.

arterial f., locking f. with sloping blades for grasping the end of a blood vessel until a ligature is applied.

axis-traction f., obstetrical f. provided with a second handle so attached that traction can be made in the line in which the head must move in the axis of the pelvis.

bone f., strong f. used for seizing or removing fragments of bone.

bulldog f., f. for occluding a blood vessel.

bullet f., f. with thin curved blades with serrated grasping surfaces, for extracting a bullet from tissues.

capsule f., fine, strong f. used for removing the capsule of the lens in cataract.

clamp f. (rubber dam), rubber dam clamp f.; a f. with pronged jaws designed to engage the jaws of a rubber dam clamp so that they may be separated to pass over the widest buccolingual contour of a tooth.

clip f., a small f. with spring catch to hold a bleeding vessel.

cup biopsy f., slender flexible f. with movable cup-shaped jaws, used to obtain biopsy specimens by introduction through a specially designed endoscope.

cutting f., labitome.

dental f., extracting f.; f. used to luxate teeth and remove them from the alveolus.

dressing f., f. for general use in dressing wounds, removing fragments of necrosed tissue, small foreign bodies, etc.

extracting f., dental f.

hemostatic f., f. with a catch for locking the blades, used for seizing the end of a blood vessel to control hemorrhage.

mosquito f., mosquito *clamp.*

mouse-tooth f., f. with one or two fine points at the tip of each blade, fitting into hollows between the points on the opposite blade.

needle f., needle-holder.

nonfenestrated f., obstetrical f. without fenestrae or openings in the blades, thus facilitating rotation of the head.

obstetrical f., f. used for grasping and making traction on or rotation of the fetal head; they are introduced separately into the genital canal, permitting the fetal head to be grasped firmly but with minimal compression and then are articulated after being placed in correct position.

speculum f., a slender f. for use through a speculum, a form of tubular f.

tenaculum f., f. with jaws armed each with a sharp, straight hook like a tenaculum.

thumb f., spring f. used by compression with thumb and forefinger.

torsion f., f. used for making torsion on an artery to arrest hemorrhage.

tubular f., a long slender f. intended for use through a cannula or other tubular instrument.

vulsella f., vulsellum f., vulsella; vulsellum; f. with hooks at the tip of each blade.

for'cipressure. A method of arresting hemorrhage by compressing a blood vessel with forceps.

fore'arm. Antebrachium; the segment of the superior limb between the elbow and the wrist.

fore'brain. Prosencephalon.

fore'conscious. Denoting memories, not at present in the consciousness, which can be evoked from time to time; or an unconscious mental process which becomes conscious only on the fulfillment of certain conditions.

fore'finger. Index (1).

fore'gut. The cephalic portion of the primitive digestive tube in the embryo. From its entoderm arises the epithelial lining of the pharynx, trachea, lungs, esophagus, and stomach; the first part and cranial half of the second part of the duodenum; and the parenchyma of the liver and pancreas.

fore'head. Frons.

fore'milk. Colostrum.

forensic (fo-ren'sik) [L. *forensis*, of a forum]. Pertaining to, or used in, legal proceedings.

fore'play. Stimulative sexual play preceding sexual intercourse.

fore'skin. Preputium.

fore'waters. Bulging membranes filled with amniotic fluid presenting in front of the fetal head.

-form [L. *-formis*]. Suffix denoting in the form or shape of; equivalent to -oid.

formaldehyde (for-mal'dĕ-hīd) [form(ic) + aldehyde]. H–CHO; a pungent gas used as an antiseptic, disinfectant, and histologic fixative.

formam'idase. Formylase; an enzyme catalyzing the hydrolysis of formylkynurenine to kynurenine and formate, a reaction of significance in tryptophan catabolism.

for'mate. A salt or ester of formic acid; *i.e.*, the monovalent radical HCCOO– or the anion HCOO–.

formatio, pl. **formationes** (for-ma'shi-o, -o'nēz) [L. fr. *formo*, pp. *-atus*, to form] [NA]. A formation; a structure of definite shape or cellular arrangement.

   f. reticula'ris [NA], reticular formation; reticular substance (2); a massive but vaguely delimited neural apparatus composed of closely intermingled gray and white matter extending throughout the length of the spinal cord and upward into the diencephalon; it has extremely complex, largely polysynaptic ascending and descending connections that play a dominant role in the central control of autonomic and endocrine functions, as well as in bodily posture, skeletomuscular reflex activity, and general behavioral states.

formation (for-ma'shun). **1.** Formatio. **2.** That which is formed or the act of giving form and shape.

   concept f., in psychology, learning to conceive and respond in terms of abstract ideas based upon an action or object.

   personality f., the life history associated with the development of individual patterns and of one's individuality.

   reaction f., in psychoanalysis, the development of conscious attitudes and interests that are the opposites of certain unconscious or infantile trends; *e.g.*, excessive cleanliness as a reaction to anal interests.

   reticular f., *formatio* reticularis.

   rouleaux f., pseudoagglutination (2); arrangement of red blood cells in fluid blood (or in diluted suspensions) with their biconcave surfaces in apposi-

tion, thereby forming groups that resemble stacks of coins.

   symptom f., symptom *substitution*.

forme fruste, pl. **formes frustes** (form früst) [Fr. from L. *forma*, form; *frustra*, without effect]. A partial or arrested form of disease.

for'mic acid. H–COOH; the smallest carboxylic acid; a strong caustic.

formication (for'mĭ-ka'shun) [L. *formica*, ant]. A form of paresthesia in which there is a sensation as of ants running over the skin.

formim'inoglutam'ic acid (FIGLU). $HN=CH-NH-CH(COOH)CH_2CH_2COOH$; an intermediate metabolite in the conversion of histidine to glutamic acid.

for'mula, pl. **for'mulas, for'mulae** [L. dim. of *forma*, form]. **1.** A recipe or prescription containing directions for the compounding of a medicinal preparation. **2.** In chemistry, a symbol or collection of symbols expressing the number of atoms of the element or elements forming one molecule of a substance, together with, *e.g.*, information concerning the arrangement of the atoms within the molecule, their electronic structure, their charge, the nature of the bonds within the molecule. **3.** An expression by symbols and numbers of the normal order or arrangement of parts or structures.

   dental f., in tabular form, the number of each kind of teeth (deciduous or permanent) in the jaw.

   empirical f., molecular f., a f. indicating the kind and number of atoms in the molecules of a substance, or its composition, but not the relation of the atoms to each other or the intimate structure of the molecule.

   official f., a f. contained in the Pharmacopeia or the National Formulary.

   rational f., a f. that indicates the constitution as well as the composition of a substance.

   stereochemical f., spatial f., a f. in which the arrangement of the atoms or atomic groupings in space are indicated.

   structural f., a f. in which the connections of the atoms and groups of atoms, as well as their kind and number, are indicated.

   vertebral f., a f. indicating the number of vertebrae in each segment (cervical, thoracic, lumbar, sacral, and coccygeal) of the spinal column; for man it is C. 7, T. 12, L. 5, S. 5, Co. 4 = 33.

for'mulary. A collection of formulas for the compounding of medicinal preparations.

formyl (for'mil). The radical, H–CO–.

formylase (for'mĭ-lās). Formamidase.

formylkynurenine (for'mil-kĭ-nūr'ĕ-nēn). The product of the oxidative cleavage of the indole ring in tryptophan, the intermediate first formed in tryptophan catabolism.

for'nicate. 1 [L. *fornicatus*, arched, fr. *fornix*, vault, arch]. Vaulted or arched; resembling a fornix. **2** [see fornication]. To commit fornication.

fornication (for'nĭ-ka'shun) [L. *fornicatio,* an arched or vaulted basement (brothel)]. Sexual intercourse, especially between unmarried partners.

fornix, gen. **for'nicis,** pl. **for'nices** (for'niks, -nĭ-sis, -sēz) [L. arch, vault]. **1** [NA]. An arch-shaped structure; often the arch-shaped roof (or roof portion) of an anatomical space. **2** [NA]. The compact white fiber bundle by which the hippocampus of each cerebral hemisphere projects to the contralateral hippocampus and to the septum, anterior nucleus of the thalamus, and mamillary body.

fossa, gen. and pl. **fossae** (fos'ah, fos'e) [L. a trench or ditch] [NA]. A depression, usually longitudinal in shape, in the surface of a part.

  f. acetab'uli [NA], **acetabular f.,** a depressed area in the floor of the acetabulum above the acetabular notch.

  adipose fossae, subcutaneous spaces in the breast containing accumulations of fat.

  amygdaloid f., f. tonsillaris.

  f. axilla'ris [NA], **axillary f.,** axilla; armpit; the space below the shoulder joint, bounded by the pectoralis major, the latissimus dorsi, the serratus anterior, and the humerus; contains the axillary artery and vein, the infraclavicular part of the brachial plexus, lymph nodes and vessels, and areolar tissue.

  f. condyla'ris [NA], **condylar f.,** a depression behind the condyle of the occipital bone in which the posterior margin of the superior facet of the atlas lies in extension.

  f. coronoi'dea [NA], **coronoid f.,** a hollow on the anterior surface of the distal end of the humerus, just above the trochlea, in which the coronoid process of the ulna rests when the elbow is flexed.

  f. cra'nii [NA], **cranial f.,** the internal base of the skull in which rest the frontal and temporal lobes of the brain, the hypophysis, the cerebellum, pons, and medulla oblongata.

  f. digas'trica [NA], **digastric f.,** a hollow on the posterior surface of the base of the mandible, on either side of the median plane, giving attachment to the anterior belly of the digastric muscle.

  duodenal fossae, *recessus* duodenalis.

  epigastric f., pit of the stomach; the slight depression in the midline just inferior to the xiphoid process of the sternum.

  gallbladder f., f. vesicae felleae.

  f. glan'dulae lacrima'lis [NA], f. of the lacrimal gland; a hollow in the orbital plate of the frontal bone, formed by the overhanging margin and zygomatic process, lodging the lacrimal gland.

  glenoid f., (1) glenoid *cavity.* (2) f. mandibularis.

  f. hyaloi'dea [NA], **hyaloid f.,** a depression on the anterior surface of the vitreous body in which lies the lens.

  f. hypophysia'lis [NA], **hypophysial f.,** pituitary f.; f. of the sphenoid bone housing the pituitary gland.

  f. incisi'va [NA], **incisive fossa,** the depression in the midline of the bony palate behind the central incisors into which the incisive canals open.

  f. infraclavicula'ris [NA], **infraclavicular f.,** infraclavicular triangle; a triangular depression bounded by the clavicle and the adjacent borders of the deltoid and pectoralis major muscles.

  f. infratempora'lis [NA], **infratemporal f.,** zygomatic f.; the cavity on the side of the skull bounded laterally by the zygomatic arch and ramus of the mandible.

  f. interpeduncula'ris [NA], **interpeduncular f.,** deep depression on the inferior surface of the mesencephalon between the two cerebral peduncles.

  f. jugula'ris, jugular f., (1) [NA] an oval depression near the posterior border of the petrous portion of the temporal bone, medial to the styloid process, in which lies the beginning of the internal jugular vein; (2) the depression in the anterior part of the neck just superior to the jugular notch of the manubrium sterni.

  f. of lacrimal gland, f. glandulae lacrimalis.

  f. mandibula'ris [NA], **mandibular f.,** glenoid f. (2); a deep hollow in the squamous portion of the temporal bone at the root of the zygoma, in which rests the condyle of the mandible.

  f. navicula'ris ure'thrae [NA], **navicular f. of the urethra,** the terminal portion of the urethra in the glans penis.

  f. navicula'ris vestib'ulae vagi'nae, f. vestibuli vaginae.

  f. ova'lis, oval f., (1) [NA] an oval depression on the lower part of the septum of the right atrium, its floor corresponds to the septum primum of the fetal heart; (2) *hiatus* saphenus.

  ovarian f., a depression in the parietal peritoneum of the pelvis that lodges the ovary.

  patellar f. of vitreous, a saucer-shaped depression of the vitreous humor representing the impression of the posterior convexity of the lens of the eye.

  pituitary f., f. hypophysialis.

  f. rhomboi'dea [NA], **rhomboid f.,** the floor of the fourth ventricle of the brain, formed by the ventricular surface of the rhombencephalon.

  f. subarcua'ta [NA], **subarcuate f.,** an irregular depression on the posterior surface of the petrous portion of the temporal bone, above and a little lateral to the internal acoustic meatus.

  f. tempora'lis [NA], **temporal f.,** the space on the side of the cranium bounded by the temporal lines and terminating below at the level of the zygomatic arch.

  f. tonsilla'ris [NA], **tonsillar f.,** amygdaloid f.; the depression between the palatoglossal and palatopharyngeal arches occupied by the palatine tonsil.

  f. vesi'cae fel'leae [NA], gallbladder f.; a depression on the undersurface of the liver anteriorly, between the quadrate and the right lobes, lodging the gallbladder.

f. vestib'uli vagi'nae [NA], **f. of the vestibule of the vagina,** f. navicularis vestibulae vaginae; the portion of the vestibule of the vagina between the frenulum of the pudendal lips and the posterior commissure of the vulva.

Waldeyer's fossae, *recessus* duodenalis inferior and superior.

zygomatic f., f. infratemporalis.

fossette (fō-set') [Fr. dim of *fosse*, a ditch]. **1.** A small fossa. **2.** A deep corneal ulcer of small diameter.

fos'sula, pl. **fos'sulae** [L. dim. of *fossa*, ditch] [NA]. A small fossa.

foulage (fu-lahzh') [Fr. impression]. Kneading and pressure of the muscles, constituting a form of massage.

founda'tion. A base; a supporting structure.

denture f., that portion of the oral structures which is available to support a denture.

fourchette (für-shet') [Fr. dim. of *fourché*, fr. L. *furca,* fork]. *Frenulum* labiorum pudendi.

fovea, pl. **foveae** (fo've-ah, fo've-e) [L. a pit] [NA]. A cup-shaped depression or pit.

f. centra'lis ret'inae [NA], central f., a depression in the center of the macula retinae where only cones are present and blood vessels are lacking.

f. sublingua'lis [NA], sublingual pit; a shallow depression on either side of the mental spine, on the inner surface of the body of the mandible, superior to the mylohyoid line, lodging the sublingual gland.

f. submandibula'ris [NA], submandibular f., the depression on the medial surface of the body of the mandible inferior to the mylohyoid line in which the submandibular gland is lodged.

foveate (fo've-āt). Pitted; having foveas or depressions on the surface.

foveation (fo-ve-a'shun) [L. *fovea,* a pit]. Pitted scar formation as in smallpox, chickenpox, or vaccina.

foveola, pl. **foveolae** (fo-ve'o-lah, fo-ve'o-le) [Mod. L. dim. of L. *fovea,* pit] [NA]. A minute fovea or pit.

foveolar (fo-ve'o-lar). Pertaining to a foveola.

foveolate (fo've-o-lāt, fo-ve'o-lāt). Having minute pits (foveolae) or small depressions on the surface.

FPS, fps Foot-pound-second. See under system, unit.

Fr Francium; abbreviation for French *scale.*

fraction (frak'shun). Quotient of two quantities; an aliquot portion.

blood plasma f.'s, portions of the blood plasma as separated by electrophoresis or other technique.

ejection f. (systolic), the f. of the blood contained in the ventricle at the end of diastole that is expelled during its contraction, *i.e.,* the stroke volume divided by end-diastolic volume, normally 0.67 or greater.

filtration f. (FF), the f. of the plasma entering the kidney that filters into the lumen of the renal tubules, determined by dividing the glomerular filtration rate by the renal plasma flow; normally around 0.17.

human plasma protein f., a sterile solution of selected proteins derived from the blood plasma of adult human donors, containing 4.5 to 5.5 g of protein per 100 ml, of which 83 to 90% is albumin and the remainder is α-and β-globulins; used as a blood volume supporter.

fractionation (frak-shun-a'shun). **1.** To separate components of a mixture. **2.** Protraction of a total therapeutic radiation dose over a period of time, ordinarily days or weeks, in order to minimize untoward radiation effects on normal contiguous tissue.

fracture (frak'cher) [L. *fractura,* a break]. **1.** To break. **2.** A break, especially the breaking of a bone or cartilage.

avulsion f., sprain f.; a f. that occurs when a joint capsule, ligament, or muscle insertion of origin is pulled from the bone as a result of a sprain dislocation or strong contracture of the muscle against resistance; as the soft tissue is pulled away from the bone, a fragment or fragments of the bone may come away with it.

Barton's f., f. dislocation of the radiocarpal joint.

bending f., bending of a long bone due to multiple micro-fractures.

Bennett's f., f. dislocation of the first metacarpal bone at the carpal-metacarpal joint.

blow-out f., a f. of the floor of the orbit, without a fracture of the rim, produced by a blow on the globe with the force being transmitted via the globe to the orbital floor.

f. by contrecoup, contrafissura.

capillary f., hairline f.

closed f., simple f.; one in which skin is intact at site of f.

Colles f., a f. of the lower end of the radius with displacement of the distal fragment dorsally; volar displacement of the distal fragment in the same location is sometimes called a reversed Colles f., or Smith's f.

comminuted f., a f. in which the bone is broken into pieces.

compound f., open f.

craniofacial dysjunction f., LeFort III f.; transverse facial f.; a complex f. in which the facial bones are separated from the cranial bones.

depressed skull f., a f. with inward displacement of a part of the calvarium.

direct f., a f., especially of the skull, occurring at the point of injury.

dislocation f., a f. of a bone near an articulation with its concomitant dislocation from that joint.

double f., a f. in two parts of the same bone.

expressed skull f., a f. with outward displacement of a part of the cranium.

fissured f., linear f.

green-stick f., the bending of a bone with incomplete f. involving the convex side of the curve only.

gutter f., a long, narrow, depressed f. of the skull.

hairline f., capillary f.; a f. without separation of the fragments, the line of break being fine, as seen sometimes in the skull.

hangman's f., a f. or f. dislocation of the cervical spine at the level of C-2 and C-3 and through the pedicles of C-2.

horizontal maxillary f., LeFort I f.; a f. of the facial bones in which there is a horizontal f. at the base of the maxillae above the apices of the teeth.

impacted f., a f. in which one of the fragments is driven into the cancellar tissue of the other fragment.

indirect f., a f., especially of the skull, that occurs at a point not at the site of impact.

intrauterine f., a f. of one or more bones of a fetus occurring before birth.

LeFort I f., horizontal maxillary f. **LeFort II f.,** pyramidal f. **LeFort III f.,** craniofacial dysjunction f.

linear f., fissured f.; a f. running parallel with the long axis of the bone.

longitudinal f., a f. involving the bone in the line of its axis.

march f., a fatigue f. of one of the metatarsals.

multiple f., a f. of several bones occurring simultaneously.

oblique f., a f. the line of which runs obliquely to the axis of the bone.

occult f., a condition in which there are clinical signs of f. but no x-ray evidence; after 3 or 4 weeks, x-ray shows new bone formation.

open f., compound f.; f. in which the skin is perforated and there is an open wound down to the f.

pathologic f., a f. occurring at a site weakened by preexisting disease, especially neoplasm or necrosis, of the bone.

Pott's f., f. of the lower part of the fibula and of the malleolus of the tibia, with outward displacement of the foot.

pyramidal f., LeFort II f.; a f. of the midfacial skeleton with the principal f. lines meeting at an apex at or near the superior aspect of the nasal bones.

silver-fork f., a Colles f. of the wrist in which the deformity has the appearance of a fork in profile.

simple f., closed f.

Smith's f., see Colles f.

spiral f., a f. in which the line of break is helical in the bone.

sprain f., avulsion f.

stellate f., a f. in which the lines of break radiate from a central point.

strain f., the tearing off, by a sudden force, of a piece of bone attached to a tendon, ligament, or capsule; the force may be exogenous or endogenous.

stress f., a fatigue f. occurring usually from sudden, strong, violent, endogenous force; distinct from strain f., in that stress f. is not at the point of connective tissue attachment, but usually at the

point of muscular attachment.

torsion f., a f. resulting from twisting of the limb.

torus f., a deformity in children consisting of a local bulging caused by the longitudinal compression of the soft bone; occurs in the radius or ulna or both.

transverse f., a f. the line of which forms a right angle with the axis of the bone.

transverse facial f., craniofacial dysjunction f.

fragility (frå-jil'ĭ-tĭ) [L. *fragilitas*]. Brittleness; liability to break, burst, or disintegrate.

    f. of the blood, increased susceptibility of the red blood cells to break down when the proportion of the saline content of the fluid is altered.

frag'ment. 1. A small part broken from a larger entity. 2. To break into small parts.

    Fab f., the antigen-binding f. of an immunoglobulin molecule, also called Fab portion or piece.

    Fc f., the crystallizable f. of an immunoglobulin molecule, also called Fc portion or piece.

    one-carbon-f., see under O.

    two-carbon f., see under T.

frambesia (fram-be'zĭ-ah) [Fr. *framboise*, raspberry]. Yaws.

frambesioma (fram-be-zĭ-o'mah) [frambesia + *-oma*, tumor]. Mother *yaw.*

frame. A structure made of parts fitted together.

    Balkan f., Balkan splint; an overhead pole or f., supported on uprights attached to the bed posts or to a separate stand, from which a splinted limb is slung.

    Bradford f., an oblong rectangular f. made of pipe, over which are stretched transversely two strips of canvas; permits trunk and lower extremities to move as a unit.

    Foster f., a reversible bed similar to a Stryker f.

    Stryker f., a f. that holds the patient and permits turning in various planes without individual motion of parts.

    trial f., a type of spectacle f. having variable adjustments, for holding trial lenses during retinoscopy or refraction.

Francisella (fran'sĭ-sel'la̋). A genus of nonmotile, nonsporeforming, aerobic bacteria that contain small, Gram-negative cocci and rods. The type species, *F. tularensis* (*Pasteurella tularensis*), causes tularemia in man.

francium (fran'sĭ-um) [*France*]. Radioactive element of the alkali metal series; symbol Fr, atomic no. 87.

frank. Unmistakable; manifest; clinically evident.

FRC Functional residual *capacity.*

F.R.C.P. Fellow of the Royal College of Physicians.

F.R.C.S. Fellow of the Royal College of Surgeons.

freckle (frek'l) [O. Eng. *freken*]. Ephelis; yellowish or brownish macules developing on the exposed parts of the skin, especially in persons of light complexion, due to an increase in melanin from exposure to the sun.

    Hutchinson's f., melanotic f., *lentigo* maligna.

freeze-drying. Lyophilization.

freezing. Congealing, stiffening, or hardening by exposure to cold.

fremitus (frem'ĭ-tus) [L. a dull roaring sound]. A vibration imparted to the hand resting on the chest or other part of the body.

  hydatid f., hydatid *thrill.*

  pericardial f., vibration in the chest wall produced by the friction of opposing roughened surfaces of the pericardium.

  pleural f., vibration in the chest wall produced by the rubbing together of the roughened opposing surfaces of the pleura.

  rhonchal f., f. produced by vibrations from the passage of air in the bronchial tubes partially obstructed by mucous secretion.

  tactile f., vibration felt with the hand on the chest during vocal f.

  tussive f., a form of f. similar to the vocal, produced by a cough.

  vocal f., the vibration in the chest wall, felt on palpation, produced by the spoken voice.

fre'na. Plural of frenum.

fre'nal. Relating to any frenum.

frenectomy (fre-nek'to-mĭ) [frenum + G. *ektomē*, excision]. Excision of frenum.

frenoplasty (fre'no-plas-tĭ) [frenum + G. *plassō*, to fashion]. Surgical correction of an abnormally attached frenum.

frenotomy (fre-not'o-mĭ) [frenum + G. *tomē*, a cutting]. Division of any frenum, especially of the frenulum linguae.

fren'ulum, pl. **fren'ula** [Mod. L. dim. of L. *frenum*, bridle] [NA]. A small frenum.

  f. clitor'idis [NA], **f. of the clitoris,** the line of union of the inner portions of the labia minora on the undersurface of the glans clitoridis.

  f. la'bii inferio'ris, f. la'bii superio'ris [NA], f. of the lower lip, f. of the upper lip; the folds of mucous membrane extending from the gum to the middle line of the lower and upper lips, respectively.

  f. labio'rum puden'di [NA], f. of the pudendal lips; fourchette; the fold connecting the two labia minora posteriorly.

  f. lin'guae [NA], f. of the tongue; a fold of mucous membrane extending from the floor of the mouth to the midline of the undersurface of the tongue.

  frenula of lips, f. labii inferioris and superioris.

  f. prepu'tii [NA], **f. of the prepuce,** a fold of mucous membrane passing from the undersurface of the glans penis to the deep surface of the prepuce.

  f. of pudendal lips, f. labiorum pudendi.

  synovial frenula, *vincula tendinum.*

  f. of tongue, f. linguae.

fre'num, pl. **fre'na, fre'nums** [L. a bridle, curb]. Bridle (1). **1.** A narrow reflection or fold of mucous membrane passing from a more fixed to a movable part, serving to check undue movement of the part. **2.** An anatomical structure resembling such a fold. See frenum.

freudian (froy'dĭ-an). Relating to or described by Freud.

freudian slip. A mistake which presumably suggests some underlying motive, often sexual or aggressive in nature.

FRF Follicle-stimulating hormone-releasing *factor.*

fri'able [L. *friabilis*, fr. *frio*, to crumble]. **1.** Easily reduced to powder. **2.** In bacteriology, denoting a dry and brittle culture falling into powder when touched or shaken.

friction (frik'shun). **1.** The rubbing of one surface against another. **2.** The force required for relative motion of two bodies that are in contact.

frigid (frij'id) [L. *frigidus*, cold]. **1.** Cold. **2.** Temperamentally, especially sexually, cold or irresponsive.

frigidity (frĭ-jid'ĭ-tĭ). The state of being frigid.

frigolabile (frig'o-la'bil) [L. *frigus*, cold, + *labilis*, perishable]. Subject to destruction by cold.

frigostabile, frigostable (frig'o-sta'bil, -sta'bl) [L. *frigus*, cold, + *stabilis*, stable]. Not subject to destruction by a low temperature.

frog in the throat. A collection of mucus in the larynx causing hoarseness and an inclination to hawk.

frôlement (frol-moñ) [Fr.]. **1.** Light friction or massage with the palm of the hand. **2.** A rustling sound heard in auscultation.

frons, gen. **frontis** [L.] [NA], Forehead; brow (2); the part of the face between the eyebrows and the hairy scalp.

fron'tad. Toward the front.

fron'tal. 1. In front; relating to the anterior part of a body. **2.** Frontalis.

fronta'lis [L.] [NA]. Frontal (2); referring to the frontal (coronal) plane or to the frontal bone or forehead.

fron'toma'lar. Frontozygomatic.

fron'tomax'illary. Relating to the frontal and the maxillary bones.

fron'tona'sal. Relating to the frontal and the nasal bones.

frontooccipital (fron'to-ok-sip'ĭ-tal). Relating to the frontal and the occipital bones, or to the forehead and the occiput.

frontoparietal (fron'to-pă-ri'ĕ-tal). Relating to the frontal and the parietal bones.

fron'totem'poral. Relating to the frontal and the temporal bones.

frontozygomatic (fron'to-zi'go-mat'ik). Frontomalar; relating to the frontal and zygomatic bones.

frost. A deposit resembling that of frozen vapor or dew.

  uremic f., *uridrosis* crystallina.

frost'bite. Local tissue destruction resulting from exposure to extreme cold or contact with extremely cold objects; in mild cases, it results in erythema and slight pain; in severe cases, it can be painless or paresthetic and result in blistering, deep-seated destruction, and gangrene.

frottage (fro-tahzh′) [F., a rubbing]. **1.** The rubbing movement in massage. **2.** Production of sexual excitement by rubbing against someone.

FRS First rank *symptoms.*

F.R.S. Fellow of the Royal Society.

Fru Fructose.

fructo- [L. *fructus*, fruit]. Prefix indicating the fructose configuration.

fructofuranose (fruk-to-fūr′ă-nōs). D-Fructose in furanose form.

β-fruc′tofurano′sidase. Invertase; invertin; sucrase; an enzyme converting β-D-fructofuranosides (*e.g.*, sucrose) to glucose and D-fructose (invert sugar).

fruc′toki′nase. A liver enzyme that catalyzes the reaction of ATP and D-fructose to form fructose 6-phosphate.

fructose (Fru) (fruk′tōs). Fruit sugar; D-*arabino*-2-hexulose; in D form, physiologically the most important of the ketohexoses, and one of the two products of sucrose hydrolysis; metabolized or converted to glycogen in the absence of insulin.

fruc′toside. Fructose in –C–O– linkage where the –C–O– group is the original 2 group of the fructose.

fructosuria (fruk′to-su′rĭ-ah) [G. *ouron*, urine]. Excretion of fructose in the urine.

essential f., a benign, asymptomatic metabolic abnormality due to deficiency of fructokinase in which fructose appears in the blood and urine, but is simply excreted unchanged; autosomal recessive inheritance.

fructosyl-. Prefix indicating fructose in –C–R– linkage through its carbon-2 (R usually C).

frustration (frus′tra′shun) [L. *frustro*, pp. *-atus*, to deceive, disappoint, fr. *frustra* (adv.), in vain]. Used as a physiologic, psychologic, or psychiatric term to indicate the thwarting of or inability to gratify a desire or to satisfy an urge or need.

FSH Follicle-stimulating *hormone.*

FSH-RF Follicle-stimulating hormone-releasing *factor.*

FSH-RH Follicle-stimulating hormone-releasing *hormone.*

fuchsin (fū′sin). A nonspecific term referring to any of several red rosanilin dyes used as stains in histology and bacteriology.

acid f., a mixture of the sodium salts bi- and trisulfonic acids of rosanilin and pararosanilin; used as an indicator dye and for staining of cytoplasm and collagen.

basic f., a mixture of rosanilin and pararosanilin chlorides, used in histology to stain nuclei, mucin, elastic tissue, fuchsinophil granules, and tubercle bacilli, and in histochemistry as the main constituent of Schiff's reagent.

fuchsinophil (fūk′sĭ-no-fil) [fuchsin + G. *philos*, fond]. **1.** Fuchsinophilic; staining readily with fuchsin dyes. **2.** A cell or histologic element that stains readily with fuchsin.

fuchsinophil′ic. Fuchsinophil (1).

fucose (fu′kōs). A methylpentose, the L-configuration of which occurs in the mucopolysaccharides of the blood group substances in human milk (as a polysaccharide), and elsewhere in nature.

fucosidosis (fu′ko-sĭ-do′sis). A metabolic storage disease characterized by accumulation of fucose-containing glycolipids and deficiency of the enzyme α-fucosidase; progressive neurologic deterioration begins after the first year of life, accompanied by spasticity, tremor, and mild skeletal changes; autosomal recessive inheritance.

fugacity (fu-gas′ĭ-tĭ) [L. *fuga*, flight]. The tendency of a fluid, as a result of all forces acting on it, to leave a given site in the body.

-fuge [L. *fuga*, flight]. Suffix meaning flight, denoting the place from which flight takes place or that which is put to flight.

fugue (fūg) [Fr. fr. L. *fuga*, flight]. A period in the past for which one alleges almost complete amnesia, accompanied by life elsewhere with different conduct; afterward, earlier events are remembered but those of the f. period are alleged to be forgotten.

ful′gurant [L. *fulgur*, flashing lightning]. Fulgurating (1); sharp and piercing.

ful′gurating. 1. Fulgurant. **2.** Relating to fulguration.

fulguration (ful-gu-ra′shun) [L. *fulgur*, lightning stroke]. Destruction of tissue by means of a high-frequency electric current.

ful′minant [L. *fulmino*, pp. *-atus*, to hurl lightning]. Occurring suddenly, with lightning-like rapidity, and with great intensity or severity; applied to certain pains, such as those of tabes dorsalis.

ful′minating. Running a speedy course, with rapid worsening.

fu′marate hydratase, fu′marase, An enzyme catalyzing the interconversion of fumaric acid and malic acid, a reaction of importance in the tricarboxylic acid cycle.

fumaric acid (fu-măr′ik). *trans*-Butanedioic acid; an unsaturated dicarboxylic acid occurring as an intermediate in the tricarboxylic acid cycle.

fu′migant [see fumigate]. Any vaporous substance used as a disinfectant or pesticide.

fu′migate [L. *fumigo*, pp. *-atus*, to fumigate]. To expose to the action of smoke or of fumes of any kind as a means of disinfection.

fumiga′tion. The act of fumigating; the use of a fumigant.

fu′ming [L. *fumus*, smoke]. Giving forth a visible vapor, a property of concentrated nitric, sulfuric, and hydrochloric acids.

functio laesa (fungk′shĭ-o le′sah) [L.]. Loss of function, a fifth sign of inflammation added by Galen to those enunciated by Celsus (rubor, tumor, calor, and dolor).

function (fungk′shun) [L. *functio*, fr. *fungor*, pp. *functus*, to perform]. **1.** The special action or physiologic property of an organ or body part. **2.** To perform its special work or office, said of an organ or other body part. **3.** The general properties of any substance, depending on its chemical character and relation to other substances, according to which it may be grouped among acids, bases, alcohols, esters, etc. **4.** A particular reactive grouping in a molecule; *e.g.*, a functional group, is the –OH group of an alcohol.

func'tional. 1. Relating to a function. **2.** Nonorganic, not caused by a structural defect.

fundectomy (fun-dek'to-mĭ) [fundus + G. *ektomē*, excision]. Fundusectomy.

fun'dic. Relating to a fundus.

fun'diform [L. *funda*, a sling, + *forma*, shape]. Looped; sling-shaped.

fundoplication (fun'do-plĭ-ka'shun) [fundus + L. *plico*, to fold]. Suture of the fundus of the stomach around the esophagus to prevent reflux in repair of hiatal hernia.

fun'dus, pl. **fun'di** [L. bottom] [NA]. The bottom or lowest part of a sac or hollow organ; that part farthest removed from the opening or exit.

f. of eye, f. oculi.

f. of gallbladder, f. vesicae felleae.

f. oc'uli, f. of the eye; the portion of the interior of the eyeball around the posterior pole, visible through the ophthalmoscope.

f. of stomach, f. ventriculi.

f. of urinary bladder, f. vesicae urinariae.

f. u'teri [NA], **f. of the uterus,** the upper rounded extremity of the uterus above the openings of the uterine (fallopian) tubes.

f. ventric'uli [NA], f. of the stomach; the portion of the stomach that lies above the cardiac notch.

f. vesi'cae fel'leae [NA], f. of the gallbladder; the wide closed end of the gallbladder situated at the inferior border of the liver.

f. vesi'cae urina'riae [NA], f. of the urinary bladder; the base of the bladder, formed by the posterior wall which is somewhat convex.

fun'duscop'ic. An undesirable term, relating to the visualization of the eyegrounds with the ophthalmoscope.

fundusec'tomy [L. *fundus*, cardia, + G. *ektomē*, excision]. Fundectomy; excision of the fundus of an organ.

fungal (fung'gal). Fungous.

fungate (fung'gāt). To grow exuberantly like a fungus or spongy growth.

fungemia (fun-je'mĭ-ah). Fungal infection disseminated by way of the bloodstream.

Fungi (fun'ji) [L. *fungus*, a mushroom]. A division of plantlike organisms growing in irregular masses, without roots, stems, or leaves, and devoid of chlorophyll or other pigments capable of photosynthesis; they reproduce sexually or asexually (spore formation), and may obtain nutrition as parasites or as saprophytes.

fungi (fun'ji). Plural of fungus.

fungicidal (fun-jĭ-si'dal) [fungus + L. *caedo*, to kill]. Denoting a fungicide.

fungicide (fun'jĭ-sīd). An agent that has a destructive killing action upon fungi.

fungiform (fun'jĭ-form). Shaped like a fungus or mushroom; applied to any structure with a broad, often branched, free portion and a narrower base.

Fungi Imperfecti (fun'ji im-per-fek'ti). Deuteromycetes; a class of fungi in which sexual reproduction is not known or in which one of the mating types has not yet been discovered.

fungistatic (fun-jĭ-stat'ik) [fungus + G. *statos*, standing]. Having an inhibiting action upon the growth of fungi.

fungitoxic (fun'jĭ-tok'sik). Poisonous or in any way deleterious to the growth of fungi.

fungoid (fung'goyd). Resembling a fungus; denoting an exuberant morbid growth on the surface of the body.

fungosity (fung-gos'ĭ-tĭ). A fungoid growth.

fungous (fung'gus). Fungal; relating to a fungus.

fungus, pl. **fungi** (fung'gus, fun'ji) [L. *fungus*, a mushroom]. General term used to encompass the diverse morphological forms of yeasts and molds; originally classified as primitive plants without chlorophyll, the fungi are being placed increasingly in the kingdom Protoetista, along with the algae (all but the blue-green algae), protozoa, and slime molds. Relatively few fungi are pathogenic for man, whereas most plant diseases are caused by fungi.

fission fungi, Schizomycetes.

imperfect f., a f. in which the means of sexual reproduction is not yet recognized; these fungi generally reproduce by means of conidia.

perfect f., a f. possessing both sexual and asexual means of reproduction, and in which both mating forms are recognized.

fu'nic. Relating to the funis, or umbilical cord.

fu'nicle. Funiculus.

funicular (fu-nik'u-lar). Relating to a funiculus.

funiculitis (fu-nik-u-li'tis) [funiculus + G. *-itis*, inflammation]. **1.** Inflammation of a funiculus, especially of the spermatic cord. **2.** Inflammation of that portion of a spinal nerve that lies within the intervertebral canal.

funiculopexy (fu-nik'u-lo-pek-sĭ) [funiculus + G. *pēxis*, a fixing]. Suturing of the spermatic cord to the surrounding tissue in the correction of an undescended testicle.

funiculus, pl. **funiculi** (fu-nik'u-lus, -li) [L. dim. of *funis*, cord] [NA]. A small, cordlike structure composed of several to many longitudinally oriented fibers, vessels, ducts, or combinations thereof.

f. ante'rior [NA], **anterior f.,** a column or bundle of white matter on either side of the anterior median fissure, between that and the anterolateral sulcus.

cuneate f., *fasciculus* cuneatus.

f. latera'lis [NA], **lateral f.,** the lateral white column of the spinal cord between the lines of exit and entrance of the anterior and posterior nerve roots.

f. poste′rior [NA], **posterior f.**, the large wedge-shaped fiber bundle lying between the posterior gray column and the posterior midplane, and composed largely of dorsal root fibers.

f. spermat′icus [NA], spermatic or testicular cord; the cord formed by the ductus deferens and its associated structures extending from the deep inguinal ring through the inguinal canal into the scrotum.

f. umbilica′lis [NA], umbilical cord; funis (1); the definitive connecting stalk between the embryo or fetus and the placenta.

fu′niform [L. *funis*, cord, + *forma*, shape]. Ropelike; cordlike.

fu′nis [L. a rope, cord]. **1.** *Funiculus* umbilicalis. **2.** A cordlike structure.

FUO Fever of unknown origin.

fu′ranose [furan + -ose (1)]. A saccharide unit or molecule containing an oxygen bridge between carbon atoms 1 and 4, or 2 and 5, or 3 and 7; specific examples are preceded by prefixes indicating the configuration, *e.g.*, fructofuranose, ribofuranose.

furcal (fur′kal). Forked.

furcation (fur-ka′shun) [L. *furca*, fork]. **1.** A forking, or a forklike part or branch. **2.** In dental histology, the region of a multirooted tooth at which the roots divide.

furfuraceous (fur-fu-ra′shus) [L. *furfuraceus*, fr. *furfur*, bran]. Pityroid; branny; or composed of small scales; denoting a form of desquamation.

fu′ror epilep′ticus. Attacks of anger to which epileptics are occasionally subject, occurring without apparent provocation and without disturbance of consciousness.

furrow (fur′ro) [A.S. *furh*]. A groove or sulcus.

digital f., one of the grooves on the palmar surface of a finger, at the level of an interphalangeal joint.

genital f., a groove on the genital tubercle in the embryo, appearing toward the end of the second month.

gluteal f., *sulcus* gluteus.

primitive f., the groove in the primitive streak.

furuncle (fu′rung-kl) [L. *furunculus*, a petty thief]. Furunculus; boil; a localized pyogenic infection originating in a hair follicle.

furuncular (fu-rung′ku-lar). Furunculous; relating to a furuncle.

furunculoid (fu-rung′ku-loyd) [furunculus + G. *eidos*, resemblance]. Resembling a furuncle.

furunculosis (fu-rung′ku-lo′sis). A condition marked by the presence of furuncles.

furunculous (fu-rung′ku-lus). Furuncular.

furunculus, pl. **furun′culi** (fu-rung′ku-lus, -ku-li) [L. a petty thief, a boil, dim. of *fur*, a thief]. Furuncle.

fuscin (fus′in) [L. *fuscus*, dusky]. A benzodipyran derivative; the melanin-like pigment of the retinal pigment epithelium.

fusiform (fu′zĭ-form, fu′sĭ-) [L. *fusus*, a spindle, + *forma*, form]. Spindle-shaped; tapering at both ends.

fusimotor (fu′zĭ-mo′tor) [L. *fusus*, spindle, + to move]. Pertaining to the efferent innervation intrafusal muscle fibers by gamma motor neuron.

fusion (fu′zhun) [L. *fusio*, a pouring, fr. *fundo*, pp. *fusus*, to pour]. **1.** Liquefaction, as by melting by heat. **2.** Union, as by joining together. **3.** The blending of slightly different images from each eye into a single perception. **4.** The growth together, as one, of two or more teeth, in consequence of the abnormal union of their formative organs.

centric f., robertsonian *translocation*.

spinal f., **vertebral f.**, spondylosyndesis; an operative procedure to accomplish bone ankylosis between two or more vertebrae.

Fusobacterium (fu′zo-bak-tēr′ĭ-um) [L. *fusus*, a spindle, + *bacterium*]. A genus of bacteria (family Bacteroidaceae) that produce butyric acid as a major metabolic product and are found in cavities of man and other animals; some species are pathogenic. The type species is *F. nucleatum*.

fusocellular (fu-zo-sel′u-lar). Spindle-celled.

fusospirochetal (fu′zo-spi-ro-ke′tal). Referring to the associated fusiform and spirochetal organisms such as those found in the lesions of Vincent's angina.

G

γ Gamma, third letter in the Greek alphabet; used as a symbol to denote the third in a series, fourth carbon in an aliphatic acid, or position 2 removed from the α position in the benzene ring.

G Newtonian *constant* of gravitation; giga-; glucose, as in UDPG; guanosine (or guanylic acid) residues in polynucleotides, as in poly(G).

g Gram.

g A unit of acceleration based on the acceleration produced by the earth's gravitational attraction, where 1 g = 980.6 cm (about 32 ft./sec), per second.

Ga Gallium.

GABA γ-Aminobutyric acid.

G-actin. See under actin.

gad′olin′ium [Johan *Gadolin*, Finnish chemist, 1760–1852]. An element of the lanthanide group, symbol Gd, atomic no. 64, atomic weight 157.25.

gag. 1. To retch; to cause to retch or heave. **2.** To prevent from talking. **3.** An instrument adjusted between the teeth to keep the mouth from closing during operations in the mouth or throat.

gain. Increase; profit.

primary g., alleviation of anxiety derived from conversion of emotional concerns into demonstrably organic illnesses.

secondary g., interpersonal or social advantages gained indirectly from organic illness.

gait (gāt). Manner of walking.

antalgic g., a characteristic g. resulting from pain on weight bearing in which the stance phase of g. is shortened on the affected side.

ataxic g., an unsteady, staggering, or irregular g.

cerebellar g., a staggering g., often with a tendency to fall.

festinating g., see festination.

helicopod g., helicopodia; a g., seen in some conversion reactions or hysterical disorders, in which the feet describe half circles.

hemiplegic g., the walk of hemiplegics characterized by swinging the affected leg in a half circle.

high steppage g., a g. in which the foot is raised high to avoid catching a crooping foot and brought down suddenly in a flapping manner; often seen in peroneal nerve palsy and tabes.

spastic g., a g. characterized by stiffness of legs, feet and toes.

Gal Galactose.

galact-. See galacto-.

galactacrasia (gă-lak'tă-kra'zĭ-ah) [galact- + G. *akrasia,* bad mixture]. Abnormal composition of breast milk.

galactagogue (gă-lak'tă-gog) [galact- + G. *agōgos,* leading]. An agent that promotes the secretion and flow of milk.

galac'tic. Pertaining to milk; promoting the flow of milk.

galacto-, galact- [G. *gala,* milk]. Combining forms indicating milk.

galactobolic (gă-lak-to-bol'ik) [galacto- + G. *bole,* throwing]. Causing the release or ejection of milk from the breast.

galactocele (gă-lak'to-sēl) [galacto- + G. *kēlē,* tumor]. Lactocele; a retention cyst caused by occlusion of a lactiferous duct.

galac'toki'nase. An enzyme (phosphotransferase) that, in the presence of ATP, catalyzes the phosphorylation of galactose to galactose 1-phosphate.

galac'tolip'id. Cerebroside.

galac'tolip'in. Cerebroside.

galactophore (gă-lak'to-fōr) [galacto- + G. *phoros,* bearing]. A milk duct.

galactophoritis (gă-lak'to-fo-ri'tis). Inflammation of the milk ducts.

galactophorous (gal-ak-tof'o-rus). Conveying milk.

galactopoiesis (gă-lak'to-poy-e'sis) [galacto- + G. *poiesis,* forming]. Milk production.

galactopoietic (gă-lak'to-poy-et'ik). Pertaining to galactopoiesis.

galactorrhea (gă-lak-to-re'ah) [galacto- + G. *rhoia,* a flow]. Incontinence of milk; lactorrhea; a continued discharge of milk from the breasts in the intervals of nursing or after weaning.

galactosam'ine. The 2-amino-2-deoxy derivative of galactose, NH_2 replacing the 2-OH group; occurs in various mucopolysaccharides.

galac'tose (Gal). A hexose found (in D form) as a constituent of lactose, cerebrosides, mucoproteins, etc., in galactoside or galactosyl combination.

galactosemia (gă-lak-to-se'mĭ-ah) [galactose + G. *haima,* blood]. An inborn error of galactose metabolism due to congenital deficiency of the enzyme galactosyl-1-phosphate uridyltransferase, resulting in tissue accumulation of galactose 1-phosphate; characterized by nutritional failure, hepatosplenomegaly with cirrhosis, cataracts, mental retardation, galactosuria, aminoaciduria, and albuminuria; autosomal recessive inheritance.

α-galactosidase. Melibiase; an enzyme (a hydrolase) catalyzing the hydrolysis of α-D-galactosides to D-galactose.

β-galactosidase. Lactase; a sugar-splitting enzyme that catalyzes the hydrolysis of lactose into glucose and galactose, and that of other β-D-galactosides; also catalyzes galactotransferase reactions.

galac'tosides. Glycosides of galactose.

galactosis (gal-ak-to'sis) [galacto- + G. *-osis,* condition]. Formation of milk by the lacteal glands.

galac'tosu'ria [galactose + G. *ouron,* urine]. Excretion of galactose in the urine.

galac'tosyl. The glycosyl radical of galactose.

galac'tother'apy. Lactotherapy. **1.** Treatment of disease by means of an exclusive or nearly exclusive milk diet. **2.** Medicinal treatment of a nursing infant by giving to the mother a drug that is excreted in part by the milk.

galacturia (gal-ak-tu'rĭ-ah) [galacto- + G. *ouron,* urine]. Passage of turbid, milklike urine.

galea (ga'le-ah) [L. a helmet]. **1** [NA]. A structure shaped like a helmet; *e.g.,* g. aponeurotica, the aponeurosis connecting the frontalis and occipitalis muscles to form the epicranius. **2.** A form of bandage covering the head.

galenicals (ga-len'ĭ-kalz) [Claudius *Galen*]. **1.** Herbs and other vegetable drugs, as distinguished from the mineral or chemical remedies. **2.** Crude drugs and the tinctures, decoctions, and other preparations made from them, as distinguished from the alkaloids and other active principles. **3.** Remedies prepared according to an official formula.

gall (gawl) [A.S. *gealla*]. Bile.

gallbladder (gawl'blad-der). *Vesica fellea.*

gallium (gal'ĭ-um) [L. *Gallia,* France]. A rare metal, symbol Ga, atomic no. 31, atomic weight 69.7.

gallium-67 (^{67}Ga). A cyclotron-produced radionuclide with a physical half-life of 78 hr and major gamma ray emmisions of 93, 184, and 296 kiloelectron volts; used in the citrate form as a tumor- and inflammation-localizing radiotracer.

gallium-68 (^{68}Ga). A positron emitter with a physcial half-life of 1.13 hr; used in brain scanning.

gal'lon. A measure of liquid capacity containing 4 quarts, 231 cubic inches, or 8.3389 pounds of distilled water; equivalent of 3.7853 liters.

gal'lop. Gallop or cantering rhythm; a triple cadence to the heart sounds at rates of 100 beats per minute or more due to an abnormal third or fourth heart sound being heard in addition to the first and second sounds; usually indicative of a serious disease.

presystolic g., g. rhythm in which the g. sound occurs in late diastole and is an audible fourth heart sound.

protodiastolic g., g. rhythm in which the g. sound occurs in early diastole and is an abnormal third heart sound.

summation g., g. rhythm in which the g. sound is due to superimposition of third and fourth heart sounds; usually indicative of myocardial disease.

systolic g., a triple cadence to the heart sounds in which the extra sound occurs during systole, usually in the form of a systolic "click."

gall'stone. Cholelith; biliary calculus; a concretion in the gallbladder or a bile duct, composed chiefly of cholesterol crystals and occasionally mixed with calcium.

gal'vanochem'ical. Electrochemical.

gamete (gam'ēt) [G. *gametēs*, husband; *gametē*, wife]. **1.** One of two cells undergoing karyogamy or true conjugation. **2.** In heredity, any germ cell, whether ovum, spermatozoon, or pollen cell.

gameto- [see gamete]. Combining form relating to a gamete.

gametocide (gă-me'to-sīd) [gameto- + L. *caedo*, to kill]. An agent destructive to gametes, specifically the malarial gametocytes.

gametocyte (gă-me'to-sīt) [gameto- + G. *kytos*, cell]. A cell capable of dividing to produce gametes; *e.g.*, a spermatocyte or oocyte.

gametogenesis (gam-ĕ-to-jen'ĕ-sis) [gameto- + G. *genesis*, production]. Formation and development of gametes.

gamma-benzene hexachloride. Lindane.

gammopathy (gă-mop'ă-thī). A primary disturbance in immunoglobulin (γ-globulin) synthesis.

gam'ogen'esis [G. *gamos*, marriage, + *genesis*, production]. Sexual reproduction.

ganglia (gang'glī-ah). Plural of ganglion.

ganglial (gang'glī-al). Ganglionic.

gangliate, gangliated (gang'glī-āt, gang'glī-a-ted). Ganglionated; having ganglia.

gangliec'tomy. Ganglionectomy.

gangliform (gang'glī-form). Ganglioform; having the form or appearance of a ganglion.

gangliitis (gang-glī-i'tis). Ganglionitis.

ganglioblast (gang'glī-o-blast) [ganglion + G. *blastos*, germ]. An embryonic cell giving rise to ganglion cells.

gangliocyte (gang'glī-o-sīt). Ganglion *cell.*

gangliocytoma (gang'glī-o-si-to'mah). Ganglioneuroma.

gan'glioform. Ganglioform.

ganglioglioma (gang'glī-o-glī-o'mah). Central *ganglioneuroma.*

gangliolysis (gang-lī-ol'ī-sis). Dissolution or breaking up of a ganglion.

ganglioma (gang-lī-o'mah). Ganglioneuroma.

ganglion, pl. **ganglia, ganglions** (gang'glī-on, -glī-ah, -glī-onz) [G. a swelling or knot] **1** [NA]. Originally, any group of nerve cell bodies in the central or peripheral nervous system; currently, an aggregation of nerve cell bodies located in the peripheral nervous system. **2.** Myxoid or synyovial cyst; a cyst

containing mucopolysaccharide-rich fluid ᵂ· fibrous tissue or, occasionally, muscle or a semiluna. cartilage; usually attached to a tendon sheath in the hand, wrist, or foot.

Acrel's g., **(1)** pseudoganglion on the posterior interosseous nerve on the dorsal aspect of the wrist joint; **(2)** a cyst on a tendon of an extensor muscle at the level of the wrist.

autonomic ganglia, visceral ganglia. See *systema* nervosum autonomicum.

ganglia of autonomic plexuses, ganglia plexuum autonomicorum.

basal ganglia, originally, all of the large masses of gray matter at the base of the cerebral hemisphere; currently, the corpus striatum (caudate and lentiform nuclei) and cell groups associated with the corpus striatum.

gang'lia cardi'aca [NA], **cardiac ganglia,** parasympathetic ganglia of the cardiac plexus between the arch of the aorta and the bifurcation of the pulmonary artery.

carotid g., a small ganglionic swelling on filaments from the internal carotid plexus, on the undersurface of the carotid artery in the cavernous sinus.

gang'lia celia'ca [NA], **celiac ganglia,** semilunar g. (2); the largest and highest group of sympathetic prevertebral ganglia, on the upper part of the abdominal aorta on either side of the celiac artery, and containing the sympathetic neurons whose unmeylinated postganglionic axons innervate the stomach, liver, gallbladder, spleen, kidney, small intestine, and ascending and transverse colon.

g. cervica'le [NA], **cervical g.,** **(1)** inferior, g. cervicothoracium; **(2)** middle, a small and sometimes absent sympathetic g. at the level of the cricoid cartilage; **(3)** superior, uppermost and largest of the ganglia of the sympathetic trunk, near the base of the skull between the internal carotid artery and the internal jugular vein.

g. cer'vicothora'cicum [NA], **cervicothoracic g.,** stellate or inferior cervical g.; a sympathetic trunk g. behind the subclavian artery near the origin of the vertebral artery, at the level of the seventh cervical vertebra, close to the first thoracic g. with which it is usually fused.

g. cilia're [NA], **ciliary g.,** a small parasympathetic g. in the orbit behind the eye that receives preganglionic innervation from the Edinger-Westphal nucleus by way of the oculomotor nerve, and in turn gives rise to postganglionic fibers that innervate the ciliary muscle and the sphincter (narrowing) muscle of the pupil.

coccygeal g., g. impar.

Corti's g., g. spirale cochleae.

dorsal root g., g. spinale.

gasserian g., g. trigeminale.

g. genic'uli [NA], **geniculate g.,** a g. of the intermediate nerve, within the facial canal, containing sensory neurons innervating taste buds on the anterior two-thirds of the tongue.

g. im'par [NA], coccygeal g.; the most inferior unpaired g. of the sympathetic trunk.

g. infe'rius ner'vi glossopharyn'gei [NA], **inferior g. of the glossopharyngeal nerve,** petrosal or petrous g.; the lower of two sensory g.'s on the glossopharyngeal nerve as it traverses the jugular foramen.

g. infe'rius ner'vi va'gi [NA], **inferior g. of the vagus,** a large sensory g. of the vagus, anterior to the internal jugular vein.

jugular g., (1) g. superius nervi glossopharyngei; (2) g. superius nervi vagi.

Ludwig's g., a small collection of parasympathetic nerve cells in the interatrial septum.

gang'lia lumba'lia trun'ci sympath'ici [NA], **lumbar ganglia,** four or more ganglia on the medial border of the psoas major muscle on either side; they form, with the sacral and coccygeal ganglia and their connecting cords, the abdominopelvic sympathetic trunk.

g. mesenter'icum [NA], mesenteric g., (1) inferior, the lowest of the sympathetic prevertebral ganglia, at the origin of the inferior mesenteric artery from the aorta, containing the sympathetic neurons innervating the descending and sigmoid colon; (2) superior, a paired sympathetic g. at the origin of the superior mesenteric artery from the aorta.

g. o'ticum [NA], otic g., otoganglion; an autonomic g. situated just below the foramen ovale medial to the mandibular nerve; its postganglionic fibers are distributed to the parotid gland.

parasympathetic ganglia, those ganglia of the autonomic nervous system composed of cholinergic neurons receiving afferent fibers originating from preganglionic visceral motor neurons in either the brainstem or the middle sacral segments (S2 to S4) of the spinal cord; on the basis of their location with respect to the organs they innervate, these ganglia can be categorized as juxtamural and intramural ganglia.

paravertebral ganglia, ganglia trunci sympathetici.

gang'lia pelvi'na [NA], **pelvic ganglia,** parasympathetic ganglia scattered through the pelvic plexus on either side.

petrosal g., petrous g., g. inferius nervi glossopharyngei.

gang'lia phren'ica [NA], **phrenic ganglia,** several small autonomic ganglia contained in the plexuses accompanying the inferior phrenic arteries.

gang'lia plex'uum autonomico'rum [NA], ganglia of the autonomic plexuses; autonomic ganglia in plexuses of autonomic fibers, as of the sympathetic and the myenteric plexus.

prevertebral ganglia, the sympathetic ganglia (celiac, aorticorenal, superior and inferior mesenteric) lying in front of the vertebral column.

g. pterygopalati'num [NA], **pterygopalatine g.** sphenopalatine g.; a small parasympathetic g. in the upper part of the pterygopalatine fossa whose postsynaptic fibers supply the lacrimal and nasal glands.

gang'lia rena'lia [NA], **renal ganglia,** small scattered sympathetic ganglia along the renal plexus.

gang'lia sacra'lia trun'ci sympath'ici [NA], **sacral ganglia,** three or four ganglia one on either side constituting, with the g. impar and the connecting cords, the pelvic portion of the sympathetic trunk.

semilunar g., (1) g. trigeminale; (2) ganglia celiaca.

sensory g., a cluster of primary sensory neurons forming a swelling in the course of a peripheral nerve or its dorsal root; such nerve cells establish the sole afferent neural connection between the sensory periphery and the central nervous system.

solar ganglia, ganglia celiaca.

sphenopalatine g., g. pterygopalatinum.

g. spina'le [NA], spinal g., dorsal root g.; the g. of the posterior root of each spinal segmental nerve, containing the cell bodies of the pseudounipolar pimary sensory neurons whose peripheral axon branch becomes part of the mixed segmental nerve, while the central axon branch enters the spinal cord as a component of the sensory posterior root.

g. spira'le coch'leae [NA], **spiral g. of the cochlea,** Corti's g.; an elongated g. of bipolar sensory nerve cell bodies on the cochlear part of the vestibulocochlear nerve in the spiral canal of the modiolus; each g. cell issues a peripheral axon that passes to the organ of Corti, and a central axon that enters the rhombencephalon as a component of the inferior (cochlear) root of the eighth nerve.

g. splanch'nicum [NA], **splanchnic g.,** a small sympathetic g. often present in the course of the greater splanchnic nerve.

stellate g., g. cervicothoracicum.

g. submandibula're [NA], **submandibular g., submaxillary g.,** a small parasympathetic g. suspended from the lingual nerve; its postganglionic branches go to the submandibular and sublingual glands; its preganglionic fibers come from the salivary nucleus by way of the chorda tympani.

g. supe'rius ner'vi glossopharyn'gei [NA], **superior g. of the glossopharyngeal nerve,** jugular g. (1); the upper and smaller of two ganglia on the glossopharyngeal nerve as it traverses the jugular foramen.

g. supe'rius ner'vi va'gi [NA], **superior g. of the vagus nerve,** jugular g. (2); a small sensory g. on the vagus as it traverses the jugular foramen.

sympathetic ganglia, those ganglia of the autonomic nervous system composed of adrenergic neurons receiving afferent fibers originating from preganglionic visceral motor neurons in the lateral horn of the thoracic and upper lumbar segments of the spinal cord (Th 1-L 2); on the basis of their location, the sympathetic ganglia can be classified as paravertebral ganglia (ganglia trunci sympathici) and prevertebral ganglia.

ganglia of sympathetic trunk, ganglia trunci sympathici.

gang'lia thorac'ica trun'ci sympath'ici [NA], thoracic ganglia, 11 or 12 ganglia, on either side, at the level of the head of each rib, constituting with the connecting nerve cords the thoracic portion of the sympathetic trunk.

g. trigemina'le [NA], **trigeminal g.,** semilunar g. (1); gasserian g.; the large flattened sensory g. of the trigeminal nerve lying in close relation to the cavernous sinus along the medial part of the middle cranial fossa.

gang'lia trun'ci sympath'ici, [NA], ganglia of the sympathetic trunk; paravertebral ganglia; the clusters of postganglionic nerve cell bodies located at intervals along the sympathetic trunks, including the superior cervical, middle cervical, and cervicothoracic g., the thoracic, lumbar, and sacral ganglia, and the g. impar.

g. tympan'icum [NA], **tympanic g.,** a small g. on the tympanic nerve during its passage through the petrous portion of the temporal bone.

g. vestibula're [NA], **vestibular g.,** a collection of bipolar nerve cell bodies forming a swelling on the vestibular part of the eighth nerve in the internal acoustic meatus; associated with the utriculoampullar and saccular nerves.

gan'gliona'ted. Gangliate.

ganglionectomy (gang'lī-o-nek'to-mī) [ganglion + G. ektomē, excision]. Gangliectomy; excision of a ganglion.

ganglioneuroma (gang'glī-o-nu-ro'mah). Gangliocytoma; ganglioma; neurocytoma; a benign neoplasm composed of mature ganglionic neurons scattered singly or in clumps within a relatively abundant and dense stroma of neurofibrils and collagenous fibers; usually found in the posterior mediastinum and retroperitoneum, sometimes in relation to the adrenal glands.

central g., ganglioglioma; a rare form of glioma composed of nearly mature, slowly growing neuron-like cells, found in the optic chasm or cerebral white matter.

ganglionic (gang-glī-on'ik). Glialial; relating to a ganglion.

ganglionitis (gang'glī-o-ni'tis). Ganglitis; inflammation of a lymphatic or of a nerve ganglion.

ganglionostomy (gang'glī-o-nos'to-mī) [ganglion + G. stoma, mouth]. Making an opening into a ganglion (2).

ganglioplegic (gang'glī-o-ple'jik) [ganglion + G. plēgē, stroke, shock]. Paralyzing an autonomic ganglion, usually for a relatively short period of time.

ganglioside (gang'glī-o-sīd). A glycosphingolipid chemically similar to cerebrosides but containing one or more sialic acid residues; found principally in nerve tissue and spleen.

gangliosidosis (gang'glī-o-si-do'sis). Any disease characterized, in part, by the abnormal accumulation within the nervous system of specific gangliosides.

GM1 g., g. characterized by accumulation of a specific monosialoganglioside (GM1); resembles Tay-Sachs disease; except that visceral mucopolysaccharidosis is also present.

GM2 g., infantile type of cerebral sphingolipidosis.

gangrene (gang'grēn) [G. gangraina, an eating sore]. Mortification; necrosis due to obstruction, loss, or diminution of blood supply; may be localized to a small area or involve an entire extremity or organ, and may be wet or dry.

dry g., mummification (1); g. in which the involved part is dry and shriveled.

gas g., g. occurring in a wound infected with various anaerobic, sporeforming bacteria, especially Clostridium perfringens, and C. oedematiens; crepitation of the surrounding tissues is due to gas liberated by bacterial fermentation and constitutional septic symptoms.

moist g., g. in which the necrosed part is moist and soft.

symmetrical g., g. affecting the extremities of both sides of the body; seen particularly in severe arteriosclerosis, myocardial infarction, and ball-valve thrombus.

wet g., ischemic necrosis of an extremity with bacterial infection, producing cellulitis adjacent to the necrotic areas.

gan'grenous. Mortified; relating to or affected with gangrene.

gap. 1. A hiatus or opening in a structure. 2. An interval or discontinuity in any series or sequence.

air-bone g., the difference between the threshold for hearing acuity by bone conduction and by air conduction.

anion g., the difference between the sum of the measured cations and anions in the plasma or serum calculated as follows: $(Na + K) - (Cl + HCO_3) = < 20$ MMOL/1.

auscultatory g., the period during which sounds indicating true systolic pressure fade away and reappear at a lower pressure point.

gar'gle [thru Old Fr. fr. L. gurgulio, gullet, windpipe]. 1. To rinse the fauces with fluid in the mouth through which expired breath is forced to produce a bubbling effect while the head is held far back. 2. A medicated fluid used for gargling; a throat wash.

gargoylism (gar'goyl-izm) [gargoyle, fr. L. gurgulio, gullet]. The gargoyle-like facies and related characteristics of Hurler's syndrome (autosomal recessive type g.) and Hunter's syndrome (X-linked recessive type g.).

gas. 1. A thin fluid, like air, capable of indefinite expansion but convertible by compression and cold into a liquid and, eventually, solid. 2. To subject to the action of a g.

alveolar g. (symbol subscript A), alveolar air; the g. in the pulmonary alveoli, where O_2-CO_2 exchange with pulmonary capillary blood occurs.

anesthetic g., a compound above its boiling point at room temperature capable of producing general anesthesia upon inhalation.

blood g.'s, a clinical expression for the determination of the partial pressures of oxygen and carbon dioxide in blood.

expired g., (1) any g. that has been expired from the lungs; (2) often used synonymously with mixed expired g.

inert g.'s, noble g.'s.

inspired g. (symbol subscript I), (1) any g. that is being inhaled; (2) specifically, that g. after it has been humidified at body temperature.

laughing g. [so called because its inhalation sometimes excites a hilarious delirum preceding insensibility], nitrous oxide.

mixed expired g., one or more complete breaths of expired g. coming thoroughly mixed from the dead space and the alveoli.

mustard g., $S(CH_2CH_2Cl)_2$; a poisonous vesicating gas introduced in World War I; the progenitor of the so-called nitrogen mustards.

noble g.'s, inert g.'s; zero group in the periodic series: helium, neon, argon, krypton, xenon, and radon.

tear g., a g., such as acetone, benzene bromide, and xylol, that causes irritation of the conjunctiva and profuse lacrimation.

gaseous (gas'e-us). Of the nature of gas.

gasome'tric. Relating to gasometry.

gasom'etry. Determination of the relative proportion of gases in a mixture.

gasse'rian. Relating to or described by Johann L. Gasser.

gas'sing. Poisoning by irrespirable or otherwise noxious gases.

gas'ter [G. *gastēr*, belly] [NA]. Stomach.

gastr-. See gastro-.

gastradenitis (gas'trä-dĕ-ni'tis) [gastr- + G. *adēn*, gland, + *-itis*, inflammation]. Inflammation of the glands of the stomach.

gastral'gia [gastr- + G. *algos*, pain]. Gastrodynia.

gastrectasis, gastrectasia (gas-trek'tă-sis, gas-trek-ta'zī-ah) [gastr- + G. *ektasis*, extension]. Dilation of the stomach.

gastrectomy (gas-trek'to-mĭ) [gastr- + G. *ektomē*, excision]. Excision of a part or all of the stomach.

gas'tric. Relating to the stomach.

gastrinoma (gas-trĭ-no'mah). A gastrin-secreting tumor associated with the Zollinger-Ellison syndrome.

gas'trins. Hormones secreted in the pyloric-antral mucosa of the mammalian stomach that stimulate secretion of HC1 by the parietal cells of the gastric glands.

gastri'tis [gastr- + G. *-itis*, inflammation]. Inflammation, especially mucosal, of the stomach.

atrophic g., chronic g. with atrophy of the mucous membrane and destruction of the peptic glands.

catarrhal g., g. with excessive secretion of mucus.

exfoliative g., g. with excessive shedding of nucosal epithelial cells.

hypertrophic g., Ménétrièr's *disease.*

interstitial g., inflammation of the stomach involving the submucosa and muscle coats.

phlegmonous g., severe inflammation, chiefly of the submucous coat, with purulent infiltration of the wall of the stomach.

polypous g., chronic g. in which there is irregular atrophy of the mucous membrane with cystic glands giving rise to a knobby or polypous appearance of the surface.

pseudomembranous g., g. characterized by the formation of a false membrane.

gastro-, gastr- [G. *gastēr*, stomach]. Combining forms denoting the stomach.

gas'troanastomo'sis. Gastrogastrostomy; anastomosis of the cardiac and antral segments of the stomach.

gas'trocar'diac. Relating to both the stomach and the heart.

gastrocele (gas'tro-sēl) [gastro- + G. *kēlē*, hernia]. 1. Archenteron; the primitive cavity formed by the invagination of the blastula. 2. Hernia of a portion of the stomach.

gastrocnemius (gas-trok-ne'mĭ-us) [G. *gastroknēmia*, calf of the leg]. *Musculus* gastroenemius.

gastrocolic (gas'tro-kol'ik). Relating to the stomach and the colon.

gastrocolitis (gas'tro-ko-li'tis). Inflammation of both stomach and colon.

gastrocolostomy (gas'tro-ko-los'to-mĭ) [gastro- + G. *kōlon*, colon, + *stoma*, mouth]. Establishment of a communication between stomach and colon.

gastrocolotomy (gas'tro-ko-lot'o-mĭ) [gastro- + G. *kōlon*, colon, + *tomē*, incision]. Incision of stomach and colon.

gastroduodenal (gas'tro-du'o-de'nal, -du-od'ĕ-nal). Relating to the stomach and duodenum.

gas'trodu'odeni'tis. Inflammation of both stomach and duodenum.

gas'trodu'odenos'copy [gastro- + duodenum, + G. *skopeō*, to view]. Visualization of the interior of the stomach and duodenum by a gastroscope.

gas'trodu'odenos'tomy [gastro- + duodenum + G. *stoma*, mouth]. Establishment of a communication between the stomach and the duodenum.

gastrodynia (gas-tro-din'ĭ-ah) [gastro- + G. *odynē*, pain]. Gastralgia; a stomach ache.

gastroenteric (gas'tro-en-tĕr'ik). Gastrointestinal.

gastroenteritis (gas'tro-en-ter-i'tis) [gastro- + G. *enteron*, intestine, + *-itis*, inflammation]. Enterogastritis; inflammation of the mucous membrane of both stomach and intestine.

gastroenterocolitis (gas'tro-en'ter-o-ko-li'tis) [gastro- + G. *enteron*, intestine, + *kolon*, colon, + *-itis*, inflammation]. Inflammatory disease involving the stomach and intestines.

gas'troenterol'ogist. A specialist in gastroenterology

gas'troenterol'ogy [gastro- + G. *enteron,* intestine, + *logos,* study]. The medical specialty concerned with the function and disorders of the stomach and intestines.

gas'troenterop'athy [gastro- + G. *enteron,* intestine, + *pathos,* suffering]. Any disorder of the alimentary canal.

gas'troen'teroplas'ty [gastro- + G. *enteron,* intestine, + *plassō,* to form]. Operative repair of defects in the stomach and intestine.

gastroenteroptosis (gas'tro-en-ter-o-to'sis) [gastro- + G. *enteron,* intestine, + *ptōsis,* a falling]. Downward displacement of the stomach and a portion of the intestine.

gas'troenteros'tomy [gastro- + G. *enteron,* intestine, + *stoma,* mouth]. Establishment of a new opening between the stomach and the intestine, either anterior or posterior to the mesocolon.

gas'troenterot'omy [gastro- + G. *enteron,* intestine, + *tomē,* incision]. Section into both stomach and intestine.

gastroepiploic (gas'tro-ep'ĭ-plo'ik). Relating to the stomach and the greater omentum (epiploon).

gastroesophageal (gas'tro-e-sof'ă-je'al) [gastro- + G. *oisophagos,* gullet (esophagus)]. Relating to both stomach and esophagus.

gastroesophagitis (gas'tro-e-sof'ă-ji'tis). Inflammation of the stomach and esophagus.

gas'troesoph'agos'tomy. Establishment of a new opening between esophagus and stomach.

gas'trogastros'tomy. Gastroanastomosis.

gastrogavage (gas-tro-gă-vahzh'). Gavage.

gas'trogen'ic. Deriving from or caused by the stomach.

gas'trohepat'ic [gastro- + G. *hēpar* (*hēpat-*), liver]. Relating to the stomach and the liver.

gastroileitis (gas'tro-il-e-i'tis). Inflammation of the alimentary canal in which the stomach and ileum are preponderantly involved.

gastroileostomy (gas'tro-il-e-os'to-mĭ). A surgical joining of stomach to ileum; a technical error in which the ileum instead of jejunum is selected for the site of a gastrojejunostomy.

gas'trointes'tinal (GI). Gastroenteric; relating to the stomach and intestines.

gastrojejunocolic (gas'tro-je-ju'no-kol'ik). Referring to the stomach, jejunum, and colon.

gastrojejunostomy (gas'tro-je-ju-nos'to-mĭ) [gastro- + jejunum G. *stoma,* mouth]. Establishment of a direct communication between the stomach and the jejunum.

gastrolienal (gas-tro-li'ĕ-nal) [gastro- + L. *lien,* spleen]. Gastrosplenic.

gas'trolith [gastro- + G. *lithos,* stone]. Gastric calculus; a concretion in the stomach.

gastrolithiasis (gas'tro-lĭ-thi'ă-sis). Presence of one or more calculi in the stomach.

gastrolysis (gas-trol'ĭ-sis) [gastro- + G. *lysis,* loosening]. Surgical division of perigastric adhesions.

gastromalacia (gas'tro-mă-la'shĭ-ah) [gastro- + G. *malakia,* softness]. Softening of the walls of the stomach.

gastromegaly (gas'tro-meg'ă-lĭ) [gastro- + G. *megas* (*megal-*), Enlargement of the abdomen or the stomach.

gastromyxorrhea (gas'tro-mik'so-re'ah) [gastro- + G. *myxa,* mucus, + *rhoia,* a flow]. Excessive secretion of mucus in the stomach.

gas'troparal'ysis. Paralysis of the muscular coat of the stomach.

gastroparesis (gas'tro-pă-re'sis) [gastro- + G. *paresis,* a letting go, paralysis]. A slight degree of gastroparalysis.

gastropath'ic. Relating to a disease of the stomach.

gastropathy (gas-trop'ă-thĭ) [gastro- + G. *pathos,* disease]. Any disease of the stomach.

gastropexy (gas'tro-pek-sĭ) [gastro- + G. *pēxis,* fixation]. Surgical attachment of the stomach to the abdominal wall or diaphragm.

gastrophrenic (gas'tro-fren'ik) [gastro- + G. *phrēn,* diaphragm]. Relating to the stomach and the diaphragm.

gas'troplasty [gastro- + G. *plassō,* to form]. Operative repair of a defect in the stomach or lower esophagus.

gastroplication (gas'tro-plĭ-ka'shun) [gastro- + L. *plicare,* to fold]. Gastrorrhaphy (2); reducing the size of the stomach by suturing a longitudinal fold with the peritoneal surfaces in apposition.

gastroptosis (gas-trop-to'sis) [gastro- + G. *ptosis,* a falling]. Descensus ventriculi; downward displacement of the stomach.

gastropul'monary. Pneumogastric.

gastropylorectomy (gas'tro-pi'lo-rek'to-mĭ). Pylorectomy.

gastropyloric (gas'tro-pi-lor'ik). Relating to the stomach as a whole and to the pylorus.

gastrorrhagia (gas-tro-ra'jĭ-ah) [gastro- + G. *rhēgnymi,* to burst forth]. Hemorrhage from the stomach.

gastrorrhaphy (gas-tror'ă-fĭ) [gastro- + G. *rhaphē,* a stitching]. 1. Suture of a perforation of the stomach. 2. Gastroplication.

gastrorrhea (gas-tror-re'ah) [gastro- + G. *rhoia,* a flow]. Excessive secretion of gastric juice or of mucus by the stomach.

gastroschisis (gas-tros'kĭ-sis) [gastro- + G. *schisis,* a fissure]. Celoschisis; a congenital muscular defect in the abdominal wall, not at the umbilical ring, usually with protrusion of the viscera.

gas'troscope [gastro- + G. *skopeō,* to examine]. An endoscope for inspecting the inner surface of the stomach.

gastroscop'ic. Relating to gastroscopy.

gastros'copy. Inspection of the inner surface of the stomach through an endoscope.

gas'trospasm. Spasmodic contraction of the walls of the stomach.

gastrosplen'ic. Gastrolienal; relating to the stomach and the spleen.

gastrostaxis (gas'tro-stak'sis) [gastro- + G. *staxis*, trickling]. Oozing of blood from the mucous membrane of the stomach.

gas'trosteno'sis [gastro- + G. *stenosis*, narrowing]. Diminution in size of the cavity of the stomach.

gastrostolavage (gas-tros'to-lă-vahzh'). Lavage of the stomach through a gastric fistula.

gastrostomy (gas-tros'to-mǐ) [gastro- + G. *stoma*, mouth]. Establishment of a new opening into the stomach.

gastrot'omy [gastro- + G. *tomē*, incision]. Incision into the stomach.

gastrotonometry (gas'tro-to-nom'ĕ-trǐ) [gastro- + G. *tonos*, tension, + *metron*, measure]. Measurement of intragastric pressure.

gastrotropic (gas'tro-trop'ik) [gastro- + G. *tropikos*, turning]. Affecting the stomach.

gastrula (gas'tru-lah) [Mod. L. dim. of G. *gastēr*, belly]. The embryo in the stage of development following the blastula: in lower forms with minimal yolk it is a simple double-layered structure consisting of ectoderm and entoderm enclosing the archenteron which opens to the outside by way of the blastospore; in forms with considerable yolk the configuration of the g. is greatly modified.

gastrula'tion. Tranformation of the blastula into the gastrula; development and invagination of the embryonic germ layers.

gauss (gows) [J. K. F. *Gauss*]. A unit of magnetic field intensity.

gauss'ian. Relating to or described by Johann K.F. Grauss.

gauze (gawz). A bleached cotton cloth of plain weave, used for dressings, bandages, and absorbent sponges.

gavage (gă-vahzh') [Fr. *gaver*, to gorge fowls]. Gastrogavage. **1.** Forced feeding by stomach tube. **2.** Therapeutic use of a high-potency diet.

gaze. The act of looking steadily in one direction for a period of time.

Gd Gadolinium.

Ge Germanium.

gel (jel) [Mod. L. *gelatum*]. **1.** A jelly or the solid or semisolid phase of a colloidal solution. **2.** To form a g. or jelly; to convert a sol into a gel.

 colloidal g., a colloid that has developed resistance to flow because of chemical or thermal change.

 pharmacopeial g., a suspension, in a water medium, of an insoluble drug in hydrated form wherein the particle size approaches or attains colloidal dimensions.

gelatin (jel'ă-tin) [L. *gelo*, pp. *gelatus*, to freeze, congeal]. A derived protein formed from the collagen of tissues by boiling in water.

gelatinize (jĕ-lat'ǐnǐz). **1.** To convert into gelatin. **2.** To become gelatinous.

gelatinous (jĕ-lat'ǐ-nus). **1.** Relating to gelatin. **2.** Jelly-like; resembling gelatin.

gelation (jĕ-la'shun). In colloidal chemistry, transformation of a sol into a gel.

gelo'sis (jĕ-lo'sis) [L. *gelo*, to freeze, congeal, + G. *-osis*, condition]. An extremely firm mass in tissue (especially in a muscle) with a consistency resembling that of frozen tissue.

gemellipara (jem-el-lip'ă-rah) [L. *gemellus*, twin, + *pario*, to bear]. A woman who has given birth to twins.

geminate (jem'ǐ-nāt) [L. *gemino*, pp. *-atus*, to double]. Occurring in pairs.

gemination (jem-ǐ-na'shun) [L. *germinatio*, a doubling]. Embryologic partial division of a primordium.

gemmation (jem-ma'shun) [L. *gemma*, a bud]. Budding; bud fission; a form of fission in which the parent cell does not divide, but puts out a budlike process (daughter cell) of small size, containing its proportion of chromatin, which then separates and begins an independent existence.

gemmule (jem'ūl) [L. *gemmula*, dim. of *gemma*, bud]. A small bud that projects from the parent cell, and finally becomes detached, forming a cell of a new generation.

gen-, -gen [G. *genos*, birth]. **1.** Combining form meaning "producing" or "coming to be." **2.** In chemistry, use as a suffix indicates "precursor of."

gena (je'nah) [L.]. Cheek.

genal (je'nal). Relating to the gena, or cheek.

gender (jen'der). The anatomical sex of an individual.

gene (jēn) [G. *genos*, birth]. Factor (3); the functional unit of heredity that occupies a specific place or locus on a chromosome, is capable or reproducing itself exactly at each cell division, and is capable of directing formation of an enzyme or other protein.

 allelic g., see allele; *dominance* of g.'s.

 autosomal g., a g. located on any chromosome other than a sex chromosome (X or Y).

 histocompatibility g.'s, g.'s that control HLA antigens.

 holandric g., Y-linked g.

 immune response g.'s, g.'s in the HLA-D region of the histocompatibility complex of human chromosome 6 which control the immune response to specific antigens.

 lethal g., a g. that causes death of the organism when in a specified condition, homozygous or heterozygous.

 operator g., a g. with the function of activating the production of messenger-RNA by one or more adjacent structural g.'s; part of the feedback system for determining the rate of production of an enzyme.

 penetrant g., a g. (trait) that in appropriate genotypes is phenotypically manifest.

 pleiotropic g., polyphenic g., a g. that has multiple, apparently unrelated, phenotypic manifestations.

 recessive g., see *dominance* of g.'s.

regulator g., a g. with the function of producing a repressor substance capable of combining with an operator g. and inhibiting the ability of the operator g. to activate one or more structural g.'s, thus preventing the production of a specific enzyme.

repressor g., a g. that prevents a non-allele from being transcribed.

sex-linked g., a g. located on a sex chromosome, in usual usage the X chromosome.

structural g., a g. with the function of determining the structure (amino acid sequence) of a specific protein or peptide.

X-linked g., a g. located on an X chromosome.

Y-linked g., holandric g.; a g. located on a Y chromosome.

genealogy (je-ne-ahl'o-ji) [G. *genea,* descent, + *logos,* study]. History of the descent of a person or family.

gen'era. Plural of genus.

gen'eralist. A general physician or family physician; a physician trained to take care of the majority of nonsurgical diseases, sometimes including obstetrics.

genera'tion [L. *generatio,* fr. *genero,* pp. *-atus,* to beget]. **1.** Reproduction. **2.** A stage in succession of descent; *e.g.,* father, son, and grandson are three g.'s.

asexual g., reproduction by fission, gemmation, or in any other way without union of the male and female cell, or conjugation.

filial g., the offspring resulting from a genetically specified mating: first filial g. (F$_1$), the offspring resulting from mating of parents of contrasting genotypes; second filial g. (F$_2$), the offspring resulting from the mating of two F$_1$ individuals; third filial g. (F$_3$), etc., the offspring in succeeding g.'s of continued inbreeding of F$_2$ descendents.

parental g. (P$_1$), the parents of a mating; parents of the F$_1$ g.

sexual g., reproduction by conjugation, or the union of male and female cells.

gen'erative. Relating to generation.

gen'erator [*generatus,* pp. *generare,* to beget, produce]. An apparatus for conversion of chemical, mechanical, atomic, or other forms of energy into electricity.

aerosol g., a device for producing airborne suspensions of small particles, as for inhalation therapy.

pulse g., in an electronic pacemaker, a device that produces an electrical discharge at regular intervals, which may be modified by a sensory circuit which can reset the time-base for subsequent discharge on the basis of other electrical activity, such as that produced by spontaneous cardiac beating.

gener'ic [L. *genus* (*gener-*), birth]. **1.** Relating to or denoting a genus. **2.** General. **3.** Characteristic or distinctive.

generic name. 1. In chemistry, a noun that indicates the class or type of a single compound; "class" is more appropriate and more often used. **2.** Misnomer

for nonproprietary name. **3.** In the biologic sciences, the first part of the scientific name (Latin binary combination or binomial) of an organism.

genesis (jen'ě-sis) [G.]. An origin or beginning process. Also used as combining form in suffix position.

gene splicing. Splicing (1).

genetic (jě-net'ik). Relating to (1) genetics, and (2) ontogenesis.

genetic code. Genetic information carried by the specific DNA molecule of the chromosomes; specifically, the system whereby particular combinations of three adjacent nucleotides in a DNA molecule control the insertion of particular amino acids in equivalent places in a protein molecule.

geneticist (jě-net'ĭ-sist). A specialist in genetics.

genetics (jě-net'iks) [G. *genesis,* origin or production]. The branch of science concerned with heredity.

clinical g., the means of diagnosis, prognosis, management, and prevention of genetic disease.

medical g., study of the etiology, pathogenesis, and natural history of diseases that are at least partially genetic in origin.

genetotrophic (jě-net'o-trof'ik) [G. *genesis,* origin, + *trophē,* nourishment]. Relating to inherited individual distinctions in nutritional requirements.

genial, genian (jě-ni'al, -ni'an) [G. *geneion,* chin]. Mental (2).

-genic. Suffix denoting producing or forming, produced or formed by.

genicular (jě-nik'u-lar). Commonly used to mean genual.

geniculate (jě-nik'u-lāt) [L. *geniculo,* pp. *-atus,* to bend the knee, fr. *genu,* knee]. **1.** Geniculated; bent like a knee. **2.** Referring to the geniculum of the facial nerve, denoting the ganglion there. **3.** Denoting the corpus geniculatum laterale or mediale.

geniculum, pl. **genicula** (je-nik'u-lum, -lah) [L. dim. of *genu,* knee]. **1** [NA]. A small genu or angular kneelike structure. **2.** A knotlike structure.

-genin. A suffix used to denote the basic steroid unit of the toxic substance, usually a steroid glycoside.

genion (je-ni'on) [G. *geneion,* chin]. The tip of the mental spine, a point in craniometry.

genioplasty (je'ni-o-plas-ti) [G. *geneion,* chin, cheek, + *plassō,* to form]. Mentoplasty.

gen'ital. 1. Relating to reproduction, or generation. **2.** Relating to the organs of reproduction (genitalia). **3.** Relating to or characterized by genitality.

genitalia (jen'ĭ-ta'lĭ-ah) [L. neut. pl. of *genitalis,* genital]. Genital *organs.*

ambiguous external g., external g. not clearly of either sex; most commonly designates external g. that are incompletely masculinized.

external g., the vulva in the female, and the penis and scrotum in the male.

genitality (jen-ĭ-tal'ĭ-ti). In psychoanalysis, a term referring to the genital components of sexuality (penis and vagina), as opposed to orality and

anality — *Organa* genitalia.

gen'itals.

gen'itofem'oral, genitocrural. Relating to the genitalia and the thigh.

genitourinary (GU) (jen-ĭ-to-u'rĭ-na-rĭ). Urogenital; relating to the organs of reproduction and urination.

genocopy (je'no-kop-ĭ). A genotype at one locus that produces a phenotype which stimulates that produced by another.

gen'odermato'sis. A skin condition of genetic origin.

genome (je'nōm, -nom) [gene + chromosome]. 1. A complete set of chromosomes derived from one parent, the haploid number of a gamete. 2. The total gene complement of a set of chromosomes found in higher life forms, or the functionally similar but simpler linear arrangements found in bacteria and viruses.

genospecies (je'no-spe-sēz). A group of organisms in which interbreeding is possible, as evidenced by genetic transfer and recombination.

genote (je'nōt). In microbial genetics, an element of recombination when one of the pair is not a complete chromosome; commonly used as a suffix.

genotype (jen'o-tīp) [G. *genos*, birth, descent, + *typos*, type]. The genetic constitution of an individual; may be used with respect to gene combination at one specified locus or with respect to any specified combination of loci.

genotypical (jen'o-tip'ĭ-kal). Relating to the genotype.

gentamicin, gentamycin (jen-tă-mi'sin). A broad spectrum antibiotic complex, obtained from *Microspora purpurea* and *M. echinospora*, comprised of monospora purpurea and linked to variously methylated purpurosamines and garosamines; inhibits the growth of both Gram-positive and Gram-negative bacteria.

gentianophilic (jen'shan-o-fil'ik) [gentian + G. *philos*, fond]. Staining readily with gentian violet.

gentianophobic (jen'shan-o-fo-bik) [gentian + G. *phobos*, fear]. Not taking a gentian violet stain, or taking it poorly.

gentian violet (jen'shan). Methyl violet; mixtures of tetra-, penta-, and hexamethyl *p*-rosalinin. See crystal violet.

genu, gen. ge'nus, pl. genua (je'nu, jen'u-ah) [L.] [NA]. 1. The knee. 2. Any structure of angular shape resembling a flexed knee.

  g. recurva'tum, back-knee; a condition of hyperextension of the knee, the lower extremity making a curve with concavity forward.

  g. val'gum, knock-knee; tibia valga; a deformity marked by abduction of the leg in relation to the thigh.

  g. va'rum, bowleg; tibia vara; an outward bowing of the legs.

genual (jen'u-al) [L. *genu*, knee]. Genicular; relating to the knee.

genus, pl. genera (je'nus, jen'er-ah) [L. birth, descent]. In natural history classification, the division between the family, or tribe, and the species; a group of species alike in the broad features of their organization but different in detail.

geo- [G. *gē*, earth]. Combining form relating to the earth, or to soil.

geode (je'ōd). A cystlike space (or spaces) with or without an epithelial lining, observed radiologically in subarticular bone, usually in arthritic disorders.

geophagia, geophagism, geophagy (je-o-fa'jĭ-ah, je-of'ă-jism, -of'ă-jĭ) [geo- + G. *phagein*, to eat]. The practice of eating dirt or clay; variously referred to as earth-eating; dirt-eating.

geotrichosis (je'o-trĭ-ko'sis) [geo- + G. *thrix*, hair, + -*osis*, condition]. A systemic mycosis caused by a yeastlike fungi, *Geotrichum candidum*, whose ascribed symptoms are diverse and suggestive of secondary or mixed infections.

geriat'ric. Relating to old age or to geriatrics.

geriatrics (jĕr'ĭ-at'riks) [G. *gēras*, old age, + *iatrikos*, healing]. Presbyiatrics; the branch of medicine concerned with the diseases and problems of the elderly.

germ (jerm) [L. *germen*, sprout, bud, germ]. 1. A microbe; a microorganism. 2. A primordium; the earliest trace of a structure within an embryo.

  enamel g., the enamel organ of a developing tooth.

  tooth g., the enamel organ and dentin papilla, constituting the developing tooth.

germa'nium [L. *Germania*, Germany]. A metallic element, symbol Ge, atomic no. 32, atomic weight 72.59.

germici'dal. Germicide (1).

ger'micide [germ + L. *caedo*, to kill]. 1. Germicidal; destructive to germs or microbes. 2. An agent with this action.

germinal (jer'mĭ-nal). Relating to a germ or (botany) to germination.

germinoma (jer-mĭ-no'mah). A neoplasm of germinal tissue that normally differentiates to form sperm cells or ova.

gero-, geront-, geronto- [G. *gerōn*, old man]. Combining forms denoting old age. See also presby-.

geroderma (jĕr-o-der'mah) [gero- + G. *derma*, skin]. 1. The atrophic skin of the aged. 2. Any condition in which the skin is thinned and wrinkled, resembling the integument of old age.

gerodontics, gerodontology (jĕr-o-don'tiks, -dontol'o-jĭ) [gero- + G. *odous*, tooth]. Dentistry concerned with the problems of the elderly.

geromorphism (jĕr-o-mor'fizm) [gero- + G. *morphē*, form]. A condition of premature senility.

gerontal (jĕ-ron'tal). Relating to old age.

geronto-. See gero-.

gerontol'ogist. A specialist in gerontology.

gerontology (jĕr-on-tol'o-jĭ) [geronto- + G. *logos*, study]. Scientific study of the process and problems of aging.

gerontoxon (jĕr-on-tok'son) [geronto- + G. *toxon*, bow]. *Arcus* senilis.

gestagen (jes'tă-jen). Inclusive term used to denote any substance with progestational effects in the uterus, usually steroid hormones.

gestalt (gĕ-stahlt) [Ger. shape]. A system of phenomena so integrated as to constitute a functional unit with properties not derivable from its parts.

gestalt'ism [see gestalt]. The theory in psychology that the objects of mind come as complete forms or configurations which cannot be split into parts; *e.g.*, a square is perceived as such rather than as four discrete lines.

gestation (jes-ta'shun) [L. *gestatio*, from *gesto*, pp. *gestatus*, to bear]. Pregnancy in viviparous animals.

gestosis, pl. **gestoses** (jes-to'sis, -sēz) [L. *gesto*, to carry, to bear, + G. *-osis*, condition]. Any disorder of pregnancy.

GFR Glomerular filtration *rate.*

GH Growth *hormone.*

GHRF, GH-RF Growth hormone-releasing *factor.*

GHRH, GH-RH Growth hormone-releasing *hormone.*

GI Gastrointestinal; Gingival Index.

giantism (ji'an-tizm). Gigantism.

Giardia (je-ar'de-ah) [Alfred *Giard*, French biologist, 1846–1908]. A genus of parasitic flagellates that parasitize the small intestine of mammals, including most domestic animals and man. *G. lamblia*, the common species in man, is usually asymptomatic except in heavy infections, when it may interfere with absorption of fats and produce flatulence, steatorrhea, and acute discomfort.

giardiasis (je-ar-di'ă-sis). Lambliasis; infection with *Giardia lamblia.*

gibbous (gib'us) [L. *gibbosus*]. Humped; humpbacked.

gibbus (gib'us) [L. a hump]. Extreme kyphosis, hump, or hunch; a deformity of spine in which there is a sharply angulated segment, the apex of the angle being posterior.

giga- (G) [G. *gigas*, giant]. Prefix in the metric system to signify one billion (10⁹).

gigantism (ji'gan-tizm) [G. *gigas*, giant]. Giantism; abnormal size, or overgrowth, of the entire body or of any of its parts.

cerebral g., a syndrome characterized by birth weight and length above the 90th percentile, accelerated growth rate for the first 4 or 5 years without elevation of serum growth hormone levels, then reversion to normal growth rate; characteristic facies with prognathism, hypertelorism, antimongoloid slant, and dolichocephalic skull, plus moderate mental retardation and impaired coordination, are also associated.

eunuchoid g., g. with deficient development of sexual organs and eunuchoid habitus.

pituitary g., g. caused by hypersecretion of pituitary growth hormone; a rare disorder commonly the result of a pituitary adenoma.

giganto- [G. *gigas*, giant]. Combining form meaning huge, or gigantic.

gigantomastia (ji-gan'to-mas'tĭ-ah) [giganto- + G. *mastos*, breast]. Massive hypertrophy of the breast.

gingiva, gen. and pl. **gingivae** (jin'jĭ-vah, -ve) [L.] [NA]. gum (1); the dense fibrous tissue, covered by mucous membrane, that envelops the alveolar processes of the upper and lower jaws and surrounds the necks of the teeth.

alveolar g., gingival tissue supplied to the alveolar bone.

attached g., that part of the oral mucosa firmly bound to the tooth and alveolar process.

free g., that portion of the g. that surrounds the tooth and is not directly attached to the tooth surface.

gingival (jin'jĭ-val). Relating to the gums.

Gingival Index (GI). An index of periodontal disease based upon the severity and location of the lesion.

Gingival-Periodontal Index (GPI). An index of gingivitis, gingival irritation, and advanced periodontal disease.

gingivectomy (jin-jĭ-vek'to-mĭ) [gingiva + G. *ektomē*, excision]. Gum resection; surgical resection of unsupported gingival tissue.

gingivitis (jin-jĭ-vi'tis). [gingiva + G. *-itis*, inflammation]. Inflammation of the gingival tissue.

chronic desquamative g., gingivosis; a diffuse or patchy, often painful erythematous area of the gingiva with loss of stippling; represents an alteration in the connective tissue associated with epithelial atrophy.

fusospirillary g., necrotizing ulcerative g.

necrotizing ulcerative g. (NUG), Vincent's disease; fusospirillary or ulceromembranous g.; trench mouth; an acute, sometimes recurrent lesion of the gingivae characterized by ulceration and necrosis of the gingival margin and destruction of the interdental papillae; commonly associated with fusiform bacilli and spirochetes.

pregnancy g., inflammatory changes in the gingiva which appear during gestation.

ulceromembranous g., necrotizing ulcerative g.

gingivo- [L. *gingiva*]. Combining form relating to the gingivae.

gingivoglossitis (jin'jĭ-vo-glos-si'tis). Inflammation of both the tongue and gingival tissues.

gingivo-osseous (jin'jĭ-vo-os'us). Referring to the gingiva and its underlying bone.

gin'givoplas'ty. Surgical reshaping and recontouring of the gingival tissue to attain esthetic, physiologic, and functional form.

gingivosis (jin-jĭ-vo'sis). Chronic desquamative *gingivitis.*

gingivostomatitis (jin'jĭ-vo-sto'mă-ti'tis) [gingivo- + G. *stoma*, month, + *-itis*, inflammation]. Inflammation of the gingival tissues of the oral cavity.

gingivostomatosis (jin'jĭ-vo-sto'mă-to'sis) [gingivo- + G. *stoma*, mouth, + *-osis*, condition]. Any disease of both the gingiva and portions of the oral mucosa.

ginglyform (jing'glĭ-form, ging-) [G. *ginglymos,* a hinge joint, + L. *forma,* form]. Ginglymoid.

ginglymoarthrodial (jing'glĭ-mo-ar-thro'dĭ-al, ging-). Denoting a joint having the form of both ginglymus and arthrodia, or hinge joint and sliding joint.

ginglymus (jing'glĭ-mus, ging-) [G. *ginglymos*] [NA]. Hinge or ginglymoid joint; a uniaxial joint in which a broad, transversely cylindrical convexity on one bone fits into a corresponding concavity on the other, allowing motion in one plane only, as in the elbow.

gir'dle [A.S. *gyrdel*]. A belt; a zone. See also cingulum (1).

pelvic g., the bony ring formed by the hip bones and the sacrum, to which the lower limbs are attached.

shoulder g., thoracic g., the bony apparatus formed by the manubrium sterni, clavicles, and scapulae, to which the upper limbs are attached.

gitalin (jit'ă-lin). An extract of *Digitalis purpurea* containing a mixture of glycosides and genins; action and uses are similar to those of digitalis; duration is intermediate between that of digitoxin and digoxin.

glabella (glă-bel'ah) [L. *glabellus,* hairless, smooth]. Intercilium. **1** [NA]. A smooth prominence, most marked in the male, on the frontal bone above the root of the nose. **2.** Mesophryon; the most forward projecting point of the forehead in the midline at the level of the supraorbital ridges.

gla'brous, gla'brate [L. *glaber,* smooth]. Smooth or hairless; denoting areas of the body where hair does not normally grow.

gladiolus (glă-di'o-lus, glad'ĭ-o'lus) [L. dim. of *gladius,* a sword]. *Corpus* sterni.

gland [L. *glans,* acorn]. A secreting organ.

accessory g., a small mass of glandular structure, detached from but lying near another and larger g., to which it is similar in structure and probably in function.

acinotubular g., tubuloacinar g.

acinous g., a g. in which the secretory unit (or units) has a grapelike shape and a very small lumen.

adrenal g., *glandula* suprarenalis.

aggregate g.'s, agminate g.'s, agminated g.'s, *folliculi* lymphatici aggregati.

alveolar g., a g. in which the secretory unit (or units) has a saclike form and an obvious lumen.

anterior lingual g., *glandula* lingualis anterior.

apical g., *glandula* lingualis anterior.

apocrine g., a coiled, tubular g. the cells of which were formerly believed to contribute part of their protoplasmic substance to their secretion.

areolar g.'s, *glandulae* areolares.

axillary g.'s, axillary lymph nodes.

Bartholin's g., *glandula* vestibularis major.

bronchial g.'s, *glandulae* bronchiales.

buccal g.'s, *glandulae* buccales.

bulbourethral g., *glandula* bulbourethralis.

cardiac g., a coiled tubular g. located in the cardiac region of the stomach.

celiac g.'s, nodes located along the celiac trunk; they drain lymph from the stomach, duodenum, pancreas, spleen, and biliary tract.

ceruminous g.'s, *glandulae* ceruminosae.

cervical g.'s, (1) *lymphonodi* cervicales anteriores profundi and superficiales; **(2)** *glandulae* cervicales uteri.

ciliary g.'s, *glandulae* ciliares.

circumanal g.'s, *glandulae* circumanales.

compound g., a g. whose larger excretory ducts branch repeatedly into smaller ducts which ultimately drain secretory units.

Cowper's g., *glandula* bulbourethralis.

ductless g.'s, *glandulae* sine ductibus.

duodenal g.'s, *glandulae* duodenales.

eccrine g., a coiled tubular sweat g. (other than apocrine g.'s) that occurs on almost all parts of the body.

endocrine g.'s, *glandulae* sine ductibus.

excretory g., a g. separating excrementitious or waste material from the blood.

exocrine g., a g. from which secretions reach a free surface of the body by ducts.

fundus g.'s, gastric g.'s, *glandulae* gastricae.

genal g.'s, *glandulae* buccales.

hematopoietic g., a blood-forming organ, such as the spleen.

holocrine g., a g. whose secretion consists of disintegrated cells of the g. itself.

intestinal g.'s, *glandulae* intestinales.

jugular g., signal *node.*

lacrimal g., *glandula* lacrimalis.

lymph g., lymph *node.*

mammary g., *glandula* mammaria.

master g., hypophysis.

maxillary g., *glandula* submandibularis.

meibomian g.'s, *glandulae* tarsales.

merocrine g., a g. that is repeatedly functional, not destroyed while secreting.

mixed g., (1) a g. that contains serous and mucous secretory units; **(2)** a g. that is both exocrine and endocrine.

muciparous g., mucous g., *glandula* mucosa.

olfactory g.'s, *glandulae* olfactoriae.

parathyroid g., *glandula* parathyroidea.

paraurethral g.'s, urethral glands in the female.

parotid g., *glandula* parotidea.

Peyer's g.'s, *folliculi* lymphatici aggregati.

pilous g., a sebaceous g. emptying into the hair follicle.

pineal g., *corpus* pineale.

pituitary g., hypophysis.

preputial g.'s, *glandulae* preputiales.

prostate g., prostata.

pyloric g.'s, *glandulae* pyloricae.

racemose g., a g. that has the appearance of a bunch of grapes if viewed as a three-dimensional reconstruction.

Rivinus g., *glandula* sublingualis.

saccular g., a single alveolar g.

salivary g.'s, *glandula* parotidea, sublingualis, and submandibularis.

sebaceous g.'s, *glandulae* sebaceae.

seminal g., seminal vesicle.

sentinel g., a single enlarged lymph node in the omentum that may be an indication of an ulcer opposite to it in the greater or lesser curvature of the stomach.

seromucous g., *glandula* seromucosa.

serous g., *glandula* serosa.

solitary g.'s, *folliculi* lymphatici solitarii.

sublingual g., *glandula* sublingualis.

submandibular g., submaxillary g., *glandula* submandibularis.

sudoriferous g.'s, sweat g.'s, *glandulae* sudoriferae.

suprarenal g., *glandula* suprarenalis.

target g., the effector that functions when stimulated by the internal secretion of another gland or by some other stimulus.

tarsal g.'s, *glandulae* tarsales.

thymus g., thymus.

thyroid g., *glandula* thyroidea.

tubular g., a g. composed of one or more tubules ending in a blind extremity.

tubuloacinar g., acinotubular g.; a g. whose secretory elements are elongated acini.

unicellular g., a single secretory cell such as a mucous goblet cell.

urethral g.'s, *glandulae* urethrales.

uterine g.'s, *glandulae* uterinae.

vaginal g., one of the mucous g.'s in the mucous membrane of the vagina.

vestibular g.'s, *glandula* vestibularis major and *glandulae* vestibulares minores.

vulvovaginal g., *glandula* vestibularis major.

Weber's g.'s, muciparous g.'s at the border of the tongue on either side posteriorly.

Zeis g.'s, sebaceous g.'s opening into the follicles of the eyelashes.

glandes (glan'dēz). Plural of glans.

glandilem'ma [L. *glandula,* gland, + G. *lemma,* sheath]. The capsule of a gland.

glandula, pl. glandulae (glan'du-lah, -du-le) [L. gland, dim, of *glans,* acorn] [NA]. A glandule or small gland.

glan'dulae areola'res [NA], areolar glands; a number of cutaneous glands forming small, rounded projections from the surface of the areola of the mamma.

glan'dulae bronchia'les [NA], bronchial glands; mucous and seromucous glands whose secretory units lie outside of the muscle of the bronchi.

glan'dulae bucca'les [NA], buccal glands; genal glands; numerous racemose, mucous, or serous glands in the submucous tissue of the cheeks.

g. bulbourethra'lis [NA], bulbourethral gland; Cowper's gland; one of two small compound racemose glands, which produce a mucoid secretion, side by side along the membranous urethra just above the bulb of the corpus spongiosum; they discharge through a small duct into the spongy portion of the urethra.

glan'dulae cerumino'sae [NA], ceruminous glands; apocrine sudoriferous glands in the external acoustic meatus.

glan'dulae cervica'les uteri [NA], cervical glands of the uterus; branched mucus-secreting glands in the mucosa of the cervix.

glan'dulae cilia'res [NA], ciliary glands; a number of modified apocrine sudoriferous glands in the eyelids, with ducts that usually open into the follicles of the eyelashes.

glan'dulae circumana'les [NA], circumanal glands; large apocrine sweat glands surrounding the anus.

glan'dulae duodena'les [NA], duodenal glands; small, branched, coiled tubular glands that occur mostly in the submucosa of the first part of the duodenum; they secrete a mucoid substance.

glan'dulae gas'tricae [NA], gastric glands or follicles; fundus glands; branched tubular glands in the mucosa of the fundus and body of the stomach; they contain parietal cells which secrete hydrochloric acid, zymogen cells which produce pepsin, and mucous cells.

glan'dulae glomifor'mes [NA], (1) glomus (2); (2) tubular glands of the skin, the blind extremity of which is coiled in the form of a ball or glomerulus.

glan'dulae intestina'les [NA], intestinal glands or follicles; Lieberkühn's crypts or follicles; tubular glands in the mucous membrane of the small and large intestines.

g. lacrima'lis [NA], lacrimal gland; the gland that secretes tears; consists of separate compound tubuloalveolar serous glands located in the upper lateral part of the orbit.

g. lingua'lis ante'rior [NA], anterior lingual gland; apical gland; one of the small mixed glands deeply placed near the apex of the tongue on each side of the frenulum.

g. mamma'ria [NA], mammary gland; the compound alveolar gland that forms the breast; consists of lobes separated by adipose tissue and fibrous septa, each lobe consisting of many lobules.

g. muco'sa [NA], mucous or muciparous gland; a gland that secretes mucus.

glan'dulae olfacto'riae [NA], olfactory glands; branched tubuloalveolar serous secreting glands in the mucous membrane of the olfactory region of the nasal cavity.

g. parathyroi'dea [NA], parathyroid; one of two small paired endocrine glands (superior and inferior) embedded in the connective tissue capsule on the posterior surface of the thyroid gland; concerned with the metabolism of calcium and phosphorus.

g. parotid'ea [NA], parotid gland; the largest of the salivary glands; a compound acinous gland situated below and in front of the ear, on either side, extending from the angle of the jaw to the zygomatic arch and backward to the sternocleidomastoid muscle; it discharges through the parotid duct.

glan'dulae preputia'les [NA], preputial glands; sebaceous glands of the corona glandis and inner surface of the prepuce.

glan'dulae pylor'icae [NA], pyloric glands; the coiled, tubular mucus-secreting glands of the pylorus.

glan'dulae seba'ceae [NA], sebaceous glands or follicles; numerous holocrine glands in the corium that usually open into the hair follicles and secrete sebum.

g. sero'sa [NA], serous gland; a gland that secretes a watery substance that may or may not contain an enzyme.

g. seromuco'sa [NA], seromucous gland; (1) a gland in which some of the secretory cells are serous and some mucous; (2) a gland whose cells secrete a fluid intermediate between a watery and a viscous, mucoid substance.

glan'dulae sine duc'tibus [NA], ductless or endocrine glands; glands that have no ducts, their secretions being absorbed directly into the blood.

g. sublingua'lis [NA], sublingual gland; Rivinus gland; one of two salivary glands in the floor of the mouth beneath the tongue, discharging through the sublingual ducts.

g. submandibula'ris [NA], submandibular gland; submaxillary or maxillary gland; one of two salivary glands in the neck, located in the space bounded by the two bellies of the digastric muscle and the angle of the mandible; discharges through the submandibular duct.

glan'dulae sudorif'erae [NA], sudoriferous or sweat glands; the coil glands of the skin that secrete the sweat.

g. suprarena'lis [NA], suprarenal or adrenal gland, epinephros; paranephros; a flattened, roughly triangular body upon the upper end of each kidney; a ductless gland furnishing epinephrine and norepinephrine from the medulla and steroid hormones from the cortex.

glan'dulae tarsa'les [NA], tarsal or meibomian glands; sebaceous glands embedded in the tarsal plate of each eyelid, discharging at the edge of the lid near the posterior border.

g. thyroi'dea [NA], thyroid gland; a horseshoe shaped ductless gland in front and to the sides of the upper part of the trachea; it is supplied by branches from the external carotid and subclavian arteries, and its nerves are derived from the middle cervical and cervicothoracic ganglia of the sympathetic system.

glan'dulae urethra'les [NA], urethral glands; numerous mucous glands in the wall of the urethra.

glan'dulae uteri'nae [NA], uterine glands; numerous tubular glands in the uterine mucosa.

glan'dulae vestibula'res mino'res [NA], lesser vestibular glands; a number of minute mucous glands opening on the surface of the vestibule between the orifices of the vagina and urethra.

g. vestibula'ris ma'jor [NA], greater vestibular gland; Bartholin's gland; vulvovaginal gland; one of two mucoid-secreting tubuloalveolar glands on either side of the lower part the vagina; equivalent of the bulbourethral glands in the male.

glan'dular. Glandulous; relating to a gland.

glandule (glan'dūl) [L. *glandula*]. A small gland.

glan'dulous. Glandular.

glans, pl. **glandes** (glanz, glan'dēz) [L. acorn] [NA]. A conical acorn-shaped structure.

g. clitor'idis [NA], a small mass of erectile tissue capping the body of the clitoris.

g. pe'nis [NA], the conical expansion of the corpus spongiosum that forms the head of the penis.

glaser'ian. Relating to or described by Johann H. Glaser.

glass [A.S. *glaes*]. A transparent brittle substance, a compound of silica with oxides of various bases.

cupping g., cup (2); a g. vessel, from which the air has been exhausted by heat or a special suction apparatus, formerly applied to the skin in order to draw blood to the surface.

soluble g., water g., a silicate of potassium or sodium, soluble in hot water but solid at ordinary temperatures; used for fixed dressings.

glasses. 1. Spectacles. 2. Lenses for correcting refractive errors in the eyes.

glaucoma (glaw-ko'mah) [G. *glaukōma*, opacity of the crystalline lens]. A disease of the eye characterized by increased intraocular pressure due to restricted outflow of the aqueous humor through the aqueous veins and Schlemm's canal, excavation and degeneration of the optic disk, and nerve fiber bundle damage producing arcuate defects in the field of vision.

angle-closure g., narrow-angle g.; primary g. in which increased pressure occurs because outflow of the aqueous humor is mechanically prevented by contact of the iris with the trabecular drainage meshwork and peripheral cornea.

combined g., g. with angle-closure and open-angle mechanisms in the same eye.

congenital g., buphthalmos.

narrow-angle g., angle-closure g.

open-angle g., simple g.; primary g. in which the aqueous humor has free access to the trabecular meshwork.

secondary g., g. occurring as a sequel of preexisting ocular disease or injury.

simple g., open-angle g.

glaucomatous (glaw-ko'mă-tus). Relating to glaucoma.

GLC Gas-liquid *chromatography.*

gleet. A slight chronic discharge of thin mucus from the urethra, following gonorrhea.

glenoid (gle'noyd, glen'oyd) [G. *glēnoeidēs,* fr. *glēnē,* socket of joint, + *eidos,* appearance]. Resembling a socket; denoting the articular depression of the scapula entering into the formation of the shoulder joint.

glia (gli'ah) [G. glue]. Neuroglia.

gli'acyte [G. *glia,* glue, + *kytos,* cell]. A neuroglia cell. See neuroglia.

gli'adin. A class of protein separable from wheat and rye glutens; a member of a group of simple proteins, the prolamins, that contains up to 40% of glutamine.

gli'al. Pertaining to glia or neuroglia.

glinglymoid (jing'glī-moyd, ging-) [G. *ginglymos,* a hinge joint, + *eidos,* resembling]. Ginglyform; relating to or resembling a hinge joint.

glio- [G. *glia,* glue]. Combining form meaning glue or gluelike, relating specifically to the neuroglia.

gli'oblasto'ma [glio- + G. *blastos,* germ, sprout, + *-oma,* tumor]. Grade IV astrocytoma; a glioma, consisting chiefly of undifferentiated anaplastic cells frequently arranged radially about an irregular focus of necrosis, that grows rapidly and invades extensively, occurring most frequently in the cerebrum of adults.

glioma (gli-o'mah) [glio- + G. *-oma,* tumor]. Any neoplasm derived from one of the various types of cells that form the interstitial tissue of the brain, spinal cord, pineal gland, posterior pituitary gland, and retina.

gliomato'sis. Neurogliomatosis; neoplastic growth of neuroglial cells in the brain or spinal cord, especially with reference to a relatively large neoplasm or to multiple foci.

glio'matous. Pertaining to or characterized by a glioma.

glioneuroma (gli'o-nu-ro'mah). A ganglioneuroma derived from neurons, with numerous glial cells and fibers in the matrix.

gli'osarco'ma. A glioma consisting of immature, undifferentiated, pleomorphic, spindle-shaped cells with relatively large, hyperchromatic, frequently bizarre nuclei and poorly formed fibrillary processes.

glio'sis. Occurrence of overgrowth or tumors of the neuroglia.

glissoni'tis. Inflammation of Glisson's capsule, or the connective tissue surrounding the portal vein and the hepatic artery and bile ducts.

Gln Glutamine or glutaminyl.

glo'bal. Complete, generalized, overall, or total aspect.

glo'bi. 1. Plural of globus. **2.** Brown bodies sometimes found in the granulomatous lesions of leprosy, in addition to the macrophages that contain the acid-fast bacilli.

glo'bin. The protein of hemoglobin.

glo'boside. A glycosphingolipid, specifically a ceramide tetrasaccharide (tetraglycosylceramide), isolated from kidney and erythrocytes.

globule (glob'ūl) [L. *globulus,* dim. of *globus,* a ball]. **1.** A small spherical body of any kind. **2.** A fat droplet in milk.

glob'ulin [L. *globulus,* globule]. A family of proteins precipitated from plasma (or serum) by half-saturation with ammonium sulfate and which may be further fractionated by separation methods into many subgroups, the main groups being α-, β-, and γ-g.; these differ with respect to associated lipids or carbohydrates and in their content of many physiologically important factors.

accelerator g. (AcG, ac-g), a substance in serum that hastens the conversion of prothrombin to thrombin in the presence of thromboplastin and ionized calcium.

antihemophilic g., **(1)** factor VIII; **(2)** human antihemophilic *factor.*

β_{1C} g., β_{1E} g., β_{1F} g., the third component (C3), fourth component (C4), and fifth component (C5) of complement, respectively.

chickenpox immune g. (human), g. fraction of serum from persons recently recovered from herpes zoster infection; used to prevent infection of high-risk children.

corticosteroid-binding g. (CBG), transcortin.

human gamma g., a preparation of the proteins of liquid human plasma containing the antibodies of normal adults.

immune serum g. (human), a sterile solution of g.'s that contains many antibodies normally present in adult human blood; a passive immunizing agent.

measles immune g. (human), a sterile solution of g.'s derived from the blood plasma of normal adult human donors; prepared from immune serum g. that complies with the measles antibody reference standard; a passive immunizing agent.

pertussis immune g., a sterile solution of g.'s derived from the plasma of adult human donors who have been immunized with pertussis vaccine; used both prophylactically and therapeutically.

plasma accelerator g., factor V.

poliomyelitis immune g. (human), a sterile solution of g.'s that contains those antibodies normally present in adult human blood; a passive immunologic agent that attenuates or prevents poliomyelitis, measles, and infectious hepatitis, and confers temporary but significant protection against paralytic polio.

rabies immune g. (human), g. fraction of pooled plasma of high anti-rabies virus titer from immunized persons.

Rh_0 (D) immune g., a g. fraction of antibody specific for the most common antigen, Rh_0 (D), of the Rh group; used to prevent Rh-sensitization of an Rh-negative woman after delivery of an Rh-positive fetus.

serum accelerator g., a substance in serum that accelerates the conversion of prothrombin to thrombin in the presence of thromboplastin and calcium; produced by the action of traces of thrombin upon plasma accelerator g.

specific immune g. (human), g. fraction of pooled serums (or plasma) selected for high titer of antibodies specific for a particular antigen, or from persons specifically immunized.

tetanus immune g., a sterile solution of g.'s derived from the blood plasma of adult human donors immunized with tetanus toxoid; a passive immunizing agent.

globulinuria (glob'u-lin-u'rĭ-ah). Excretion of globulin in the urine, usually, if not always, in association with serum albumin.

glo'bus, pl. **glo'bi** [L.] [NA]. A round body; sphere; ball.

g. **hyster'icus,** a sensation as of a ball in the throat or as if the throat were compressed; a symptom of hysteria.

g. **pal'lidus** [NA], pallidum; the inner and lighter gray portion of the lentiform or lenticular nucleus.

glo'mal. Relating to or involving a glomus.

glomangioma (glo-man'jĭ-o'mah). Glomus *tumor.*

glomangiosis (glo-man'jĭ-o'sis). The occurrence of multiple complexes of small vascular channels, each resembling a glomus.

glomectomy (glo-mek'to-mĭ) [L. *glomus,* + G. *ektomē,* cutting out]. Excision of a glomus tumor.

glomerular (glo-mĕr'u-lar). Relating to or affecting a glomerulus or the glomeruli.

glomerule (glom'er-ūl). Glomerulus.

glomerulitis (glo-mĕr-u-li'tis). Inflammation of a glomerulus, specifically of the renal glomeruli, as in glomerulonephritis.

glomerulonephritis (glo-mĕr'u-lo-nĕ-fri'tis) [glomerulus + G. *nephros,* kidney, + *-itis,* inflammation]. Glomerular nephritis; renal disease characterized by bilateral inflammatory changes in glomeruli that are not the result of infection of the kidneys.

focal g., g. affecting a small proportion of renal glomeruli, not associated with azotemia, which commonly presents with hematuria and may be associated with acute upper respiratory infection in young males; associated with IgA deposits in the glomerular mesangium, and may also be associated with systemic disease.

lobular g., membranoproliferative g.

membranoproliferative g., lobular g.; chronic g. characterized by mesangial cell proliferation, increase lobular separation of glomeruli, thickening of glomerular capillary walls by nodular subendothelial deposits and increased mesangial matrix, and low serum levels of complement.

membranous g., lipoid nephrosis; g. characterized by diffuse thickening of glomerular capillary basement membranes, due in part to deposits of immunoglobulins, and clinically by an insidious onset of the nephrotic syndrome and failure of disappearance of proteinuria.

glomerulopathy (glo-mĕr-u-lop'ă-thĭ) [glomerulus + G. *pathos,* suffering]. Glomerular disease of any type.

glomerulosclerosis (glo-mĕr'u-lo-skle-ro'sis) [glomerulus + G. *sklērōsis,* hardness]. Hyaline deposits or scarring within the renal glomeruli, a degenerative process occurring in association with renal arteriosclerosis or diabetes.

intercapillary g., Kimmelstiel-Wilson *disease.*

glomerulus, pl. **glomeruli** (glo-mĕr'u-lus, -u-li) [Mod. L. dim. of L. *glomus,* a ball of yarn] [NA]. Glomerule. **1.** A plexus of capillaries. **2.** A tuft formed of capillary loops at the beginning of each uriniferous tubule in the kidney; this tuft with its capsule (Bowman's capsule) constitutes the corpusculum renis (malpighian body). **3.** The twisted secretory portion of a sweat gland. **4.** A cluster of dendritic ramifications and axon terminals in often complex synaptic relationship with each other, surrounded by a glial sheath.

glo'mus [L. *glomus (glomer-),* pl. *glomera,* a ball]. **1** [NA]. A small globular body. **2.** Glandulae glomiformis (1); a richly innervated, highly organized arteriolovenular anastomosis forming a tiny nodular focus in the nailbed, pads of the fingers and toes, ears, hands, and feet and many other organs of the body; functions as a shunt or bypass regulation mechanism in the flow of blood, temperature, and conservation of heat in the part as well as in the indirect control of the blood pressure and other functions of the circulatory system.

g. **aor'ticum,** aortic body; one of the small bilateral structures, similar to the glomus caroticum and attached to a small branch of the aorta near its arch, containing chemoreceptors that respond primarily to decreases in blood oxygen tension.

g. **carot'icum** [NA], carotid or intercarotid body; a small epithelioid structure, located just above the bifurcation of the common carotid artery on each side, consisting of granular principal cells and nongranular supporting cells, a sinusoidal vascular bed and a rich network of sensory fibers of the glossopharyngeal nerve; serves as a chemoreceptor organ responsive to oxygen lack, carbon dioxide excess, and increased hydrogen ion concentration.

g. **choroide'um** [NA], a marked enlargement of the choroid plexus of the lateral ventricle at the junction of the central part with the inferior horn.

g. **coccyge'um,** *corpus* coccygeum.

g. **jugula're,** a microscopic collection of chemoreceptor tissue in the adventitia of the jugular bulb.

gloss-. See glosso-.

glos'sa [G.]. Lingua (1).

glos'sal. Lingual (1).

glossalgia (glos-al'jĭ-ah) [gloss- + G. *algos,* pain]. Glossodynia.

glossec'tomy [gloss- + G. *ektomē,* excision]. Lingulectomy (1); excision or amputation of the tongue.

Glossi'na [G. *glōssa,* tongue]. A genus of bloodsucking Diptera (tsetse flies) confined to Africa that serve as vectors of the pathogenic trypanosomes that cause various forms of African sleeping sickness.

glossi'tis [gloss- + G. -itis, inflammation]. Inflammation of the tongue.

g. area'ta exfoliati'va, geographical *tongue*.

median rhomboid g., a congenital rhomboid or ovoid red area in the dorsal midline of the tongue, just anterior to the circumvallate papillae, which is devoid of lingual papillae and may be fat or nodular.

glosso-, gloss- [G. *glōssa,* tongue]. Combining forms relating to the tongue.

glossocele (glos'o-sēl) [glosso- + G. *kēlē, tumor, hernia*]. Protrusion of the tongue from the mouth, owing to its excessive size.

glossodynia (glos'o-din'ĭ-ah) [glosso- + G. *odynē,* pain]. Glossalgia; a burning or painful tongue.

glossoepiglottic, glossoepiglottidean (glos'o-ep-ĭ-glot'ik, -glŏ-tid'e-an). Relating to the tongue and the epiglottis.

glossohyal (glos-o-hi'al). Hyoglossal.

glossola'lia [glosso- + G. *lalia,* talk, chat]. Unintelligible jargon.

glossopathy (glos-op'ă-thi) [glosso- + G. *pathos,* suffering]. A disease of the tongue.

glossopharyngeal (glos'o-fă-rin'je-al). Relating to the tongue and the pharynx.

glossoplasty (glos'o-plas-tĭ) [glosso- + G. *plassō,* to form]. Reparative or plastic surgery of the tongue.

glossorrhaphy (glos-sor'ă-fĭ) [glosso- + G. *rhaphē,* suture]. Suture of a wound of the tongue.

glossospasm (glos'o-spazm). Spasmodic contraction of the tongue.

glossot'omy [glosso- + G. *tomē,* incision]. Any cutting operation on the tongue.

glossotrichia (glos-o-trik'ĭ-ah) [glosso- + G. *thrix,* hair]. Hairy *tongue.*

glot'tic. Relating to the tongue or to the glottis.

glottis, pl. **glottides** (glot'is, glot'ĭ-dēz) [G. *glōttis,* aperture of the larynx] [NA]. The vocal apparatus of the larynx, consisting of the vocal folds of mucous membrane investing the vocal ligament and vocal muscle on each side, the free edges of which are the vocal cords, and of a median fissure, the rima glottidis.

glotti'tis. Inflammation of the glottic portion of the larynx.

Glu Glutamic acid or glutamyl.

glucagon (glu'kă-gon). A polypeptide hormone secreted by pancreatic alpha cells. It activates hepatic phosphorylase, thereby increasing glycogenolysis; decreases gastric motility and gastric and pancreatic secretions; and increases urinary excretion of nitrogen and potassium.

glucagonoma (glu'kă-gon-o'mah). A glucagon-secreting tumor, usually derived from pancreatic islet cells.

glucan (glu'kan). A polyglucose.

1,4-α-glucan branching enzyme, α-glucan branching glycosyltransferase. Brancher or branching enzyme; a glucanotransferase in muscle that cleaves α-1,4 linkages in glycogen or starch, transferring the fragments into α-1,6 linkages, creating branches in the polysaccharide molecules.

1,4-α-glucan 6-α-glucosyltransferase. An enzyme that transfers an α-glucosyl residue in a 1,4-α-glucan to the primary hydroxyl group of glucose in a 1,4-α-glucan.

4-α-glucanotransferase. A 4-glycosyltransferase converting maltodextrins into amylose and glucose by transferring parts of 1,4-glucan chains to new 4-positions on glucose or other 1,4-glucans.

gluco-. Combining form denoting relationship to glucose. See also glyco-.

glu'cocer'ebroside. Glucosylceramide.

glu'cocor'ticoid. Glycocorticoid. **1.** Any steroid-like compound capable of significantly influencing intermediary metabolism and of exerting a clinically useful anti-inflammatory effect. **2.** Denoting an agent with this type of biological activity.

glucofuranose (glu-ko-fūr'ă-nōs). D-Glucose in furanose form.

glucogenesis (glu-ko-jen'ĕ-sis) [gluco- + G. *genesis,* production]. Glycogenesis.

glucogen'ic. Giving rise to glucose.

glucoki'nase. A hexokinase or phosphotransferase that catalyzes the conversion of glucose to glucose 6-phosphate by ATP.

glu'cokinet'ic. Tending to mobilize glucose; usually evidenced by a reduction of the glycogen stores in the tissues to produce an increase in the concentration of glucose circulating in the blood.

glucolip'ids. Glycolipids that contain glucose as part of the molecule.

gluconeogenesis (glu'ko-ne-o-jen'ĕ-sis). Glyconeogenesis.

glucon'ic acid. The hexonic (aldonic) acid derived from glucose by oxidation of the –CHO group to –COOH.

glu'copro'tein. Glycoprotein in which the sugar is glucose.

glu'copy'ranose. D-Glucose in its pyranose form.

gluco'samine. 2-Amino-2-deoxy-D-glucose; an amino sugar found in chitin, cell membranes, and mucopolysaccharides.

glu'cosans. Anhydrides of glucose; polysaccharides yielding glucose upon hydrolysis.

glu'cose. Dextrose; blood sugar; a dextrorotatory monosaccharide (hexose) found in the free state in fruits and other parts of plants, and combined in glucosides, disaccharides, oligosaccharides, and polysaccharides; the product of complete hydrolysis of cellulose, starch, and glycogen. Free g. occurs in the blood and in the urine in diabetes mellitus.

glucose 6-phosphatase. A liver enzyme catalyzing the hydrolysis of glucose 6-phosphate to glucose and inorganic phosphate.

glucose 6-phosphate dehydrogenase. A pyridinoenzyme (NADP as coenzyme) catalyzing the dehydrogenation (oxidation) of glucose 6-phosphate to 6-phosphogluconolactone, the reaction initiating the Dickens shunt.

glu'cosidases. Enzymes that hydrolyze glucosides to glucose.

glu'coside. A glycoside of glucose.

glucosuria (glu'ko-su'rĭ-ah). Glycosuria (1); the urinary excretion of glucose, usually in enhanced quantities.

glucosylceramide (glu'ko-sil-sĕr'ă-mīd). Glucocerebroside; a neutral glycolipid containing equimolar amounts of fatty acid, glucose, and sphingosine (or a derivative).

glu'cosyltrans'ferase. Any enzyme transferring glucosyl groups from one compound to another.

glucuronate (glu-ku'ro-nāt). A salt or ester of glucuronic acid.

glucuron'ic acid. The uronic acid of glucose in which carbon 6 is oxidized to a carboxyl group; detoxicates or inactivates various substances by conjugation in the liver, the glucuronides so formed being excreted in the urine.

β-glucuron'idase. An enzyme catalyzing the hydrolysis of various β-D-glucuronides, liberating free glucuronic acid.

glucu'ronide. A glycoside of glucuronic acid.

glue-sniffing. Inhalation of fumes from plastic cements, the solvents of which (toluene, xylene, and benzene) induce central nervous system stimulation followed by depression.

glu'tamate. A salt or ester of glutamic acid.

glutam'ic acid (Glu). An amino acid, HOOC–CH_2–CH_2–CH(NH_2)COOH, occurring in proteins.

glutamic-oxaloacetic transaminase (GOT). *Aspartate* aminotransferase.

glutamic-pyruvic transaminase (GPT). *Alanine* aminotransferase.

glutam'inase. An enzyme in kidney and other tissues that catalyzes the breakdown of glutamine to ammonia and glutamic acid.

glutamine (Gln) (glu'tă-mēn, -min; glu-tam'in). Glutaminic acid; the δ-amide of glutamic acid, derived by oxidation from proline in the liver or by the combination of glutamic acid with ammonia; present in proteins, in blood and other tissues, and an important source of urinary ammonia, being broken down in the kidney by the action of the enzyme glutaminase.

glutamin'ic acid. Glutamine.

glutaminyl (Gln) (glu-tam'ĭ-nil). The acyl radical of glutamine.

glutamoyl (glu-tam'o-il). The radical of glutamic acid from which both α-and δ-hydroxyl groups have been removed.

glutamyl (Glu) (glu-tam'il, glu'tă-mil). The radical of glutamic acid from which the α- or the δ-hydroxyl group has been removed.

glutar'ic acid. HOOC$(CH_2)_3$COOH; an intermediate in tryptophan catabolism.

glutathione (glu-tă-thi'ōn). A tripeptide of glycine, cystine, and glutamic acid. **Oxidized g. (GSSG)** acts in cells as a hydrogen acceptor and **reduced g.**

(GSH) acts as a hydrogen donor; oxidized g. is reduced by **g. reductase,** which appears to be a ubiquitous reducing agent involved in many redox reactions.

gluteal (glu'te-al) [G. *gloutos*, buttock]. Relating to the buttocks.

glu'ten [L. *gluten*, glue]. The insoluble protein constituent of wheat and other grains, a mixture of gliadin, glutenin, and other proteins.

glu'teofem'oral. Relating to the buttocks and the thigh.

gluteo-inguinal (glu'te-o-ing'gwĭ-nal). Relating to the buttock and the groin.

glu'tinous. Adhesive; sticky.

glutitis (glu-ti'tis) [G. *gloutos*, buttock, + *-itis*, inflammation]. Inflammation of the muscles of the buttock.

Gly Glycine or glycyl.

gly'can. Polysaccharide.

glycemia (gli-se'mĭ-ah) [G. *glykys*, sweet, + *haima*, blood]. Presence of glucose in the blood.

glyceraldehyde (glis-er-al'dĕ-hīd). $HOCH_2$.CHOH-CHO; a triose; the simplest optically active monosaccharide. The dextrorotatory isomer is taken as the structural reference point for all D compounds; the levorotatory isomer for all L compounds.

glyceric acid (glĭ-sĕr'ik, glis-er-ik). $HOCH_2$CHOH-COOH; the fatty acid analogue of glycerol occurring, particularly in the form of phosphorylated derivatives, as an intermediate in glycolysis.

L-glyceric aciduria. Excretion of L-glyceric acid in the urine; a primary metabolic error due to deficiency of D-glyceric dehydrogenase resulting in excretion of L-glyceric and oxalic acids, leading to the clinical syndrome of oxalosis with frequent formation of oxalate renal calculi.

glyceridases (glis'er-ĭ-dās-ez). Enzymes catalyzing the hydrolysis of glycerol esters.

glyceride (glis'er-id, -īd). An ester of glycerol; usually used in combination with phospho-. Use of mono-, di-, and triglyceride is being replaced by the more precise mono-, di-, and triacylglycerol.

glycerin (glis'er-in). Glycerol.

glycerol (glis'er-ol). Glycerin; $C_3H_5(OH)_3$; a sweet, oily fluid, obtained by the saponification of fats and fixed oils. It is used as a solvent, as an emollient, by injection or in the form of suppository for constipation, orally to reduce ocular tension, and as a vehicle and sweetening agent.

glyceryl (glis'er-il) [G. *hylē*, stuff]. The trivalent radical, $C_3H_5 \equiv$ of glycerol.

gly'cine (Gly). Aminoacetic acid, NH_2–CH_2–COOH, used as a nutrient and dietary supplement, and in solution for irrigation.

g. amidinotransferase, an enzyme catalyzing the transfer of an amidine group from arginine to glycine, forming glycocyamine and ornithine; an important reaction in creatine synthesis.

glycinuria (gli'sĭ-nu'rĭ-ah). Excretion of glycine in the urine.

glyco- [G. *glykys,* sweet]. Combining form denoting relationship to sugars in general.

glycocalyx (gli-ko-ka'liks) [glyco- + G. *kalyx,* husk, shell]. An outer filamentous coating of carbohydrate-rich molecules on the surface of certain cells.

glycocholate (gli-ko-ko'lāt). A salt or ester of glycocholic acid.

glycocholic acid (gli-ko-ko'lik). One of the major bile acid conjugates: *N*-cholylglycine, formed by condensation of the –COOH group of cholic acid and the NH₂ group of glycine.

gly'cocor'ticoid. Glucocorticoid.

glycogen (gli'ko-jen). A glucosan of high molecular weight, resembling amylopectin in structure but more highly branched, found in most tissues of the body, especially those of the liver and muscular tissue; as the principal carbohydrate reserve, it is readily converted into glucose.

glycogenesis (gli-ko-jen'ĕ-sis) [glyco- + G. *genesis,* production]. Glucogenesis; formation of glycogen from glucose by means of glycogen synthase and dextrin dextranase.

glycogenet'ic, glycogen'ic, glycog'enous. Relating to glycogenesis.

glycogenolysis (gli'ko-jĕ-nol'ĭ-sis). The hydrolysis of glycogen to glucose.

glycogenosis (gli'ko-jĕ-no'sis). Glycogen storage disease; dextrinosis; any of the glycogen deposition diseases characterized by abnormal accumulation of glycogen in tissue. Six types (Cori classification) are recognized, depending on the enzyme deficiency involved, all of autosomal recessive inheritance, but with a different gene for each enzyme deficiency.

type 1 g., Gierke's or von Gierke's disease; g. due to glucose 6-phosphatase deficiency resulting in accumulation of excessive amounts of glycogen of normal chemical structure, particularly in liver and kidney.

type 2 g., Pompe's disease; generalized g.; g. due to lysosomal α-1,4-glucosidase deficiency resulting in accumulation of excessive amounts of glycogen of normal chemical structure in heart, muscle, liver and nervous system.

type 3 g., Cori's or Forbes disease; debrancher deficiency limit dextrinosis; g. due to amylo-1,6-glucosidase (debrancher enzyme) deficiency resulting in accumulation of abnormal glycogen with short outer chains in liver and muscle.

type 4 g., Andersen's disease; brancher deficiency amylopectinosis; g. due to brancher enzyme deficiency resulting in accumulation of abnormal glycogen with long inner and outer chains in liver, kidney, muscle, and other tissues.

type 5 g., McArdle-Schmid-Pearson disease; g. due to muscle glycogen phosphorylase deficiency resulting in accumulation of glycogen of normal chemical structure in muscle.

type 6 g., Hers disease; g. due to hepatic glycogen phosphorylase deficiency resulting in accumulation of glycogen of normal chemical structure in liver

and leukocytes.

glycogenous (gli-koj'ĕ-nus). Glycogenetic.

glycol (gli'kol). **1.** A compound containing adjacent alcohol groups. **2.** Ethylene glycol, CH₂OH–CH₂OH, the simplest glycol.

glycolaldehyde (gli-kol-al'dĕ-hīd). Diose; CH₂OH–CHO, the simplest possible sugar; a probable intermediate in the interconversion of serine and glycine.

glycol'ic acid. CH₂OH–COOH; an intermediate in the interconversion of glycine and ethanolamine.

glycolic aciduria. Excessive excretion of glycolic acid in the urine; a primary metabolic defect due to deficiency of 2-hydroxy-3-oxoadipate carboxylase, resulting in excretion of glycolic and oxalic acids, leading to the clinical syndrome of oxalosis.

gly'colip'id. Glycosphingolipid.

glycolyl (gli'ko-lil). The acyl radical of glycolic acid, CH₂OH–CO–, replacing acetyl in some sialic acids.

glycolysis (gli-kol'ĭ-sis) [glyco- + G. *lysis,* a loosening]. Energy-yielding anaerobic conversion of glucose to lactic acid in various tissues, notably muscle.

glycolyt'ic. Relating to glycolysis.

glyconeogenesis (gli'ko-ne-o-jen'ŏ-sis) [glyco- + G. *neos,* new, + *genesis,* production]. Formation of glycogen from noncarbohydrates, such as protein or fat, by conversion of the latter to glucose.

glycopenia (gli-ko-pe'nĭ-ah) [glyco- + G. *penia,* poverty]. A deficiency of any or all sugars in an organ or tissue.

glycopep'tide. A compound containing sugar(s) linked to amino acids (or peptides), with the latter preponderant.

glycophilia (gli-ko-fil'ĭ-ah) [glyko- + G. *phileō,* to love]. A condition in which there is a distinct tendency to develop hyperglycemia, even after the ingestion of a relatively small quantity of glucose.

gly'copro'tein. Glucoprotein; one of a group of protein-carbohydrate compounds (conjugated proteins), among which the most important are the mucins, mucoid and amyloid; sometimes restricted to proteins containing small amounts of carbohydrate, in contrast to mucoids or mucoproteins, usually measured as hexosamine.

glycoptyalism (gli'ko-ti'ă-lizm) [glyco- + G. *ptyalon,* saliva]. Glycosialia.

glycopyr'rolate. 3-Hydroxy-1,1-dimethylpyrrolidinium bromide; a parasympatholytic compound used as premedication prior to general anesthesia, as an antagonist to the bradycardic effects of neostigmine during curare reversal, and as an adjunct in the treatment of peptic ulcer.

glycorrhachia (gli-ko-ra'kĭ-ah) [glyco- + G. *rhachis,* spine]. Presence of sugar in the cerebrospinal fluid.

glycorrhea (gli-ko-re'ah) [glyco- + G. *rhoia,* a flow]. A discharge of sugar from the body, as in glucosuria, especially in unusually large quantities.

glycosecretory (gli'ko-se-kre'to-rī). Causing or involved in the secretion of glycogen.

glycosialia (gli'ko-si-al'ĭ-ah, -a'lĭ-ah) [glyco- + G. *sialon*, saliva]. Glycoptyalism; presence of sugar in the saliva.

glycosialorrhea (gli'ko-si'ă-lo-re'ah) [glyco- + G. *sialon*, saliva, + *rhoia*, a flow]. An excessive secretion of saliva that contains sugar.

gly'coside. The condensation product of a sugar with any other radical involving the loss of the H of the hemiacetal OH of the sugar, leaving the O of this OH as the link.

glycosphingolipid (gli'co-sfing-o-lip'id). Glycolipid; a ceramide linked to one or more sugars via the terminal OH group.

gly'costat'ic. Denoting the property of certain extracts of the anterior hypophysis that permit the body to maintain its glycogen stores in muscle, liver, and other tissues.

glycosuria (gli-ko-su'rĭ-ah) [glyco- + G. *ouron*, urine]. Glycuresis. **1.** Glucosuria. **2.** Urinary excretion of carbohydrates.

  alimentary g., g. developing after the ingestion of a moderate amount of sugar or starch, which normally is disposed of without appearing in the urine.

  renal g., recurring or persistent excretion of glucose in the urine, in association with blood levels that are in the normal range; results from the failure of renal tubules to reabsorb glucose at a normal rate from the glomerular filtrate.

gly'cosyl. The radical resulting from detachment of the OH of the hemiacetal of a saccharide.

gly'cosyltrans'ferase. Any enzyme transferring glycosyl groups from one compound to another.

glycotropic, glycotrophic (gli'ko-trop'ik, -trof'ik) [glyco- + G. *trophē*, nourishment; *tropē*, a turning]. Pertaining to a principle in extracts of the anterior lobe of the pituitary that antagonizes the action of insulin and causes hyperglycemia.

glycuresis (gli-ku-re'sis) [glyco- + G. *ourēsis*, urination]. Glycosuria.

glycu'ronate. A salt or ester of a uronic acid (*e.g.*, glucuronate).

glycyl (Gly) (gli'sil). Univalent acid radical derived from glycine.

gm Former abbreviation for gram.

GMP Guanylic acid.

gnat (nat) [A.S. *gnaet*]. A midge; general term applied to several species of minute insects; British authors sometimes include mosquitoes in this group.

gnath-. See gnatho-.

gnathic (nath'ik) [G. *gnathos*, jaw]. Relating to the jaw or alveolar process.

gnathion (nath'ĭ-on) [G. *gnathos*, jaw] [NA]. The most inferior point of the mandible in the midline.

gnatho-, gnath- [G. *gnathos*, jaw]. Combining form relating to the jaw.

gnathodynamics (nath'o-di-nam'iks) [gnatho- + G. *dynamis*, power]. The study of the relationship of the magnitude and direction of the forces developed by and upon the components of the masticatory system during function.

gnathodynamometer (nath'o-di-nă-mom'ĕ-ter) [gnatho- + dynamometer]. Bite gauge; a device for measuring biting pressure.

gnathological (nath'o-loj'ĭ-kal). Pertaining to gnathodynamics.

gnathoplasty (nath'o-plas-tĭ) [gnatho- + G. *plassō*, to form]. Reparative surgery of the jaw.

Gnathostoma (nă-thos'to-mah) [gnatho- + G. *stoma*, mouth]. A genus of spiruroid nematode worms (family Gnathostomatidae) characterized by several rows of cuticular spines about the head and by multiple-host aquatic life cycles; *G. spinigerum* is a parasite of cats, dogs, and wild carnivores, and occasionally man.

gnathostomiasis (nath-o-sto-mi'ăsis). A migrating edema, or creeping eruption, caused by cutaneous infection by larvae of *Gnathostoma spinigerum*.

gnosia (no'sĭ-ah) [G. *gnōsis*, knowledge]. The perceptive faculty enabling one to recognize the form and the nature of persons and things.

gnotobiology (no'to-bi-ol'o-jĭ) [G. *gnotos*, known, + *bios*, life, + *logos*, study]. The study of animals in the absence of contaminating bacteria, viruses, fungi, and other microorganisms; *i.e.*, of "germ-free" animals.

gnotobiota (no'to-bi-o'tah) [G. *gnotos*, known, + L. *biota*, *q.v.*]. Living colonies or species, assembled from pure isolates.

GnRH Gonadotropin-releasing *hormone*.

goiter (goy'ter) [Fr. from L. *guttur*, throat]. Struma (1); a chronic enlargement of the thyroid gland not due to a neoplasm.

  aberrant g., enlargement of a supernumerary thyroid gland.

  adenomatous g., g. due to the growth of one or more encapsulated adenomas or multiple nonencapsulated colloid nodules within its substance.

  colloid g., g. in which the contents of the follicles increase greatly, causing pressure atrophy of the epithelium so that the gelatinous matter predominates.

  cystic g., g. due to the presence of one or more cysts within the gland.

  diving g., wandering g.; a freely movable g. that is sometimes above and sometimes below the sternal notch.

  exophthalmic g., any of the various forms of hyperthyroidism in which the thyroid gland is enlarged and exophthalmos is present.

  familial g., a group of heritable thyroid disorders in which g. is commonly apparent first during childhood; often associated with skeletal and-/or mental retardation, and with other signs of hyperthyroidism which may develop with age.

  fibrous g., a firm hyperplasia of the thyroid and its capsule.

  follicular g., parenchymatous g.

lingual g., a tumor of thyroid tissue involving the embryonic rudiment at the base of the tongue.

lymphadenoid g., Hashimoto's *disease.*

multinodular g., adenomatous g. with several colloid nodules.

nontoxic g., g. not accompanied by hyperthyroidism.

parenchymatous g., follicular g.; g. in which there is a great increase in the follicles with proliferation of the epithelium.

simple g., thyroid enlargement unaccompanied by constitutional effects, commonly caused by inadequate dietary intake of iodine.

substernal g., g., chiefly of the lower part of the isthmus, palpable with difficulty or not at all.

suffocative g., a g. that by pressure causes extreme dyspnea.

toxic g., g. that forms an excessive secretion, causing signs and symptoms of hyperthyroidism.

wandering g., diving g.

goitrogenic (goy-tro-jen'ik). Causing goiter.

goitrous (goy'trus). Denoting or characteristic of a goiter.

gold. Aurum; a yellow metallic element, symbol Au, atomic no. 79, atomic weight 196.97; compounds are used chiefly in treatment of arthritis.

gomitoli (gom-ĭ'to-lī) [Ital. *gomitolo,* coil]. Intricately coiled and looped capillary vessels present largely in the upper infundibular stem of the stalk of the pituitary gland; they comprise a portion of the pituitary portal circulation.

gomphosis (gom-fo'sis) [G. *gomphos,* bolt, nail, + *-osis,* condition] [NA]. Peg-and-socket joint; a form of fibrous joint in which a peglike process fits into a hole, as the root of a tooth into the socket in the alveolus.

gon'ad [Mod. L. fr. G. *gonē,* seed]. An organ that produces sex cells; the testis or ovary.

gonad-. See gonado-.

indifferent g., the primordial organ in an embryo before its differentiation into testis or ovary.

gon'adal. Relating to a gonad.

gonadectomy (gon-ă-dek'to-mī) [gonado- + G. *ektomē,* excision]. Excision of an ovary or testis.

gonado-, gonad- [G. *gonē,* seed]. Combining forms relating to the gonads.

gonadolib'erin. 1. Gonadotropin-releasing *factor.* **2.** Luteinizing hormone/follicle-stimulating hormone-releasing *factor.*

gon'adop'athy [gonado- + G. *pathos,* suffering]. Disease affecting the gonads.

gonadotroph (go-nad'o-trof, -gon'ă-do-). A cell of the adenohypophysis that affects certain cells of the ovary or testis.

gonadotrophic (gon'ă-do-trof'ik). Gonadotropic.

gonadotrophin (gon'ă-do-tro'fin) [gonado- + G. *trophē, nourishment*]. Gonadotropin.

gonadotropic (gon'ă-do-trop'ik) [gonado- + G. *tropē,* a turning]. Gonadotrophic. **1.** Descriptive of or relating to the actions of a gonadotropin. **2.** Promoting the growth and/or function of the gonads.

gonadotropin (gon'ă-do-tro'pin). Gonadotrophin; gonadototropic hormone; a hormone capable of promoting gonadal growth and function. Such effects, as exerted by a single hormone, are usually limited to discrete functions or histological components of a gonad; most g.'s exert their effects in both sexes, although the effect of a given g. will be very different in males and in females.

anterior pituitary g., pituitary gonadotropic hormone; any g. of hypophysial origin.

chorionic g. (CG), human chorionic g. (HCG), anterior pituitary-like hormone; chorionic gonadotropic hormone; a glycoprotein produced by the placental trophoblastic cells and excreted in the urine of pregnant women; its most important role appears to be stimulation, during the first trimester, of ovarian secretion of the estrogen and progesterone required for the integrity of conceptus; used in the treatment of cryptorchidism and as an aid to conception in women by substituting for endogenous luteinizing hormone.

human menopausal g. (HMG), an injectable preparation, obtained from the urine of menopausal women, with biological activity similar to that of follicle-stimulating hormone but also weakly mimicing the effects of luteinizing hormone; used in conjunction with human chorionic g. to induce ovulation.

gon'aduct [gonado- + duct]. **1.** Seminal *duct.* **2.** Uterine *tube.*

gonalgia (go-nal'jĭ-ah) [G. *gony,* knee, + *algos,* pain]. Pain in the knee.

gonangiectomy (gon-an-jĭ-ek'to-mī) [G. *gonē,* seed, + *angeion,* vessel, + *ektomē,* excision]. Vasectomy.

gonarthritis (gon-ar-thri'tis) [G. *gony,* knee, + *arthron,* joint, + *-itis,* inflammation]. Inflammation of the knee joint.

gonarthrotomy (gon'ar-throt'o-mī) [G. *gony,* knee, + *arthron,* joint, + *tomē,* incision]. Incision into the knee joint.

gonecyst, gonecystis (gon'e-sist, gon-e-sis'tis) [G. *gonē,* seed, + *kystis,* bladder]. Seminal vesicle.

gonecystolith (gon-e-sis'to-lith) [gonecyst + G. *kystis,* bladder, + *lithos,* stone]. A concretion or calculus in a seminal vesicle.

gonio- [G. *gōnia,* angle]. Combining form meaning angle.

goniometer (go-nĭ-om'ĕ-ter) [G. *gōnia,* angle, + *metron,* measure]. **1.** An instrument for measuring angles, as of crystals. **2.** Arthometer; a calibrated device designed to measure the arc or range of motion of a joint.

gonion, pl. **gonia** (go'nĭ-on, go'nĭ-ah) [G. *gōnia,* an angle] [NA]. The lowest posterior and most outward point of the mandible.

go'niopunc'ture. An operation for congenital glaucoma in which a puncture is made in the filtration angle of the anterior chamber.

gonioscope (go'nĭ-o-skōp) [G. *gōnia*, angle + *skopeō*, to examine]. A lens designed to study the angle of the anterior chamber of the eye or to view the retina using a biomicroscope.

gonios'copy. Examination of the angle of the anterior chamber of the eye with a gonioscope or with a contact prism lens and beam illumination from the slitlamp.

goniosynechia (go'nĭ-o-sĭ-nek'ĭ-ah) [G. *gōnia*, angle, + *synechis*, holding together]. Peripheral anterior synechia; adhesion of the iris to the posterior surface of the cornea in the angle of the anterior chamber; associated with angle-closure glaucoma.

goniotomy (go-nĭ-ot'o-mĭ) [G. *gōnia*, angle, + *tomē*, incision]. Surgical opening of Schlemm's canal by way of the angle of the anterior chamber in congential glaucoma.

gonitis (go-ni'tĭs) [G. *gony*, knee, + *-itis*, inflammation]. Inflammation of the knee.

gonocele (gon'o-sēl) [G. *gonē*, seed, + *kēlē*, tumor]. A cystic lesion of the epididymis or rete testis, resulting from obstruction and containing secretions from the testis; g.'s that contain spermatozoa are spermatoceles.

gonocide (gon'o-sīd). Gonococcicide; destructive to gonococci.

gonococcal (gon-o-kok'al). Gonococcic; relating to gonococci.

gonococcemia (gon-o-kok-se'mĭ-ah) [gonococcus + G. *haima*, blood]. Presence of gonococci in the circulating blood.

gonococcic (gon'o-kok'sik). Gonococcal.

gonococcicide (gon-o-kok'sĭ-sid) [gonococcus + L. *caedo*, to kill]. Gonocide.

gonococcus, pl. **gonococci** (gon-o-kok'us, -kok'si) [G. *gonē*, seed, + *kokkos*, berry]. *Neisseria gonorrhoeae.*

gonophore (gon'o-fōr) [G. *gonē*, seed, + *phoros*, bearing]. Any structure serving to store up or conduct the sex cells; an accessory generative organ.

gonorrhea (gon-o-re'ah) [G. *gonorrhoia*, fr. *gonē*, seed, + *rhoia*, a flow]. Specific urethritis; a contagious catarrhal inflammation of the genital mucous membrane transmitted chiefly by coitus and due to *Neisseria gonorrhoeae*; may involve the lower or upper genital tract, especially the uterine tubes, or spread to the peritoneum and other structures by the bloodstream.

gonorrhe'al. Relating to gonorrhea.

Gonyau'lax catanel'la [G. *gony*, knee, + *aulakos*, a furrow]. A marine dinoflagellate protozoan that produces a powerful toxin that accumulates in the tissues of mussels and other filter-feeding shellfish and may cause fatal mussel poisoning in man.

gon'ycamp'sis [G. *gony*, knee, + *kampsis*, a bending or curving]. Ankylosis or any abnormal curvature of the knee.

gorget (gor'jet). A director or guide with wide groove for use in lithotomy.

GOT Glutamic oxaloacetic transaminase, now known as aspartate aminotransferase.

gouge (gowj). A strong curved chisel used in operation on bone.

goundou (gūn'dū) [native name]. A disease, endemic in West Africa, characterized by exotoses from the nasal processes of the maxillary bones, producing a symmetrical swelling on each side of the nose; generally believed to be an osteitis connected with yaws.

gout (gowt) [L. *gutta*, drop]. Arthritis uratica; an inherited metabolic disorder, occurring especially in men, characterized by raised by variable blood uric acid level, recurrent acute arthritis of sudden onset, deposition of crystalline sodium urate in connective tissues and articular cartilage, and progressive chronic arthritis.

latent g., masked g., hyperuricemia without symptoms of gout.

retrocedent g., occurrence of severe gastric, cardiac, or cerebral symptoms during an attack of g., especially when the joint symptoms at the same time suddenly subside.

secondary g., g. resulting from increased nucleoprotein metabolism and uric acid production, in patients with diseases of the blood and bone marrow, and in lead poisoning.

tophaceous g., g. in which deposits of uric acid and urates occur as gouty tophi.

gouty (gow'tĭ). Relating to gout.

GPI Gingival-Periodontal Index.

GPT Glutamic pyruvic transaminase, now known as alanine aminotransferase.

gr Grain.

gra'dient. Rate of change of temperature, pressure, or other variable as a function of distance.

grad'uated. Marked to denote capacity, degrees, percentages, etc.

graft [A.S. *graef*]. **1.** Any free (unattached) tissue or organ for transplantation. **2.** To transplant such structures. See also flap; implant; transplant.

accordion g., a skin g. in which multiple slits have been made so it can be stretched to cover a large area.

allogeneic g., allograft.

autodermic g., a skin autograft.

autologous g., autoplastic g., autograft.

Blair-Brown g., a split-skin g. of intermediate thickness.

cable g., a multiple strand nerve g. arranged as a pathway for regeneration of axons.

chip g., a g. utilizing small pieces of cartilage or bone packed into a bone defect.

composite g., a g. composed of several structures, such as skin and cartilage or a full-thickness segment of the ear.

corneal g., keratoplasty.

delayed g., application of a skin g. after waiting several days for healthy granulations to form.

dermal g., a g. of dermis, made from skin by cutting away a thin split-skin g.

Esser g., inlay g.

fascia g., g. of fibrous tissue, usually the fascia lata.

fascicular g., a nerve g. in which each bundle of fibers is approximated and sutured separately.

free g., a g. transplanted without its normal attachments, or a pedicle, from one site to another.

full-thickness g., a g. of the full thickness mucosa and submucosa or of skin and subcutaneous tissue.

funicular g., a nerve g. in which each funiculus (composed of two or more fasciculi) is approximated and sutured separately.

heterologous g., heteroplastic g., heterospecific g., heterograft.

homologous g., homoplastic g., homograft.

inlay g., Esser g.; a skin g. wrapped (raw side out) around a bolus of dental compound and inserted into a prepared surgical pocket.

isologous g., isoplastic g., isograft.

Ollier g., Ollier-Thiersch g., a thin split-skin g., usually in small pieces.

omental g., a segment of omentum, with its supplying blood vessels, transplanted as a free flap to a distant area and revascularized by arterial and venous anastomoses.

partial-thickness g., split skin g.

periosteal g., a g. of periosteum, usually placed on bare bone.

pinch g., small bits of skin, partial- or full-thickness, removed from a healthy area and seeded in the site to be covered.

punch g.'s, small g.'s of the full-thickness of the scalp, removed with a circular punch and transplanted to a bald area to grow hair.

sieve g., a full-thickness skin g. taken after cutting multiple holes in it with a circular punch, thus leaving islands of skin in the donor area to heal it.

split-skin g., split-thickness g., partial-thickness g.; a g. of portions of the skin or of part of the mucosa and submucosa, but not including the periosteum.

vascularized g., the state of a g. after the recipient vasculature has been connected with the vessels in the g.

white g., rejection of a skin allograft so acute that vascularization never occurs.

grain [L. *granum*]. **1.** Cereal plants; a seed of one of the cereal plants. **2.** A minute hard particle of any substance. **3** (gr). A unit of weight, 1/60 dram, 1/437.5 avoirdupois ounce, 1/480 Troy ounce, 1/5760 Troy pound, 1/7000 avoirdupois pound; equivalent of 0.0648 g.

gram (g). A unit of weight in the metric system, equivalent of 15.432 grains.

-gram [G. *gramma*, character, mark]. Suffix denoting a recording, usually by an instrument.

gram-centimeter. Energy exerted, or work done, when a mass of 1 g is raised a height of 1 cm; equal to 9.807×10^{-5} joules or newton-meters.

gramici′din (gram-ĭ-si′din). One of a group of polypeptides (two of which are known as g. D and g. S

or g. C) produced by *Bacillus brevis* and active against Gram-positive cocci and bacilli as a bacteriostatic; its natural mixture with tyrocidin is tyrothricin.

gram-ion. The weight in grams of an ion that is equal to the sum of the atomic weights of the atoms making up the ion.

gram-meter. A unit of energy equal to 100 gram-centimeters.

gram-molecule. The amount of a substance with a mass of the number of grams of its molecular weight.

Gram-negative, Gram-positive. See Gram's *stain*.

grand mal (grahn-mahl′). Generalized *epilepsy*.

gran′ular. 1. Composed of or resembling granules or granulations. **2.** Denoting particles with strong affinity for nuclear stains, seen in many bacterial species.

granulatio, pl. **granulationes** (gran-u-la′shĭ-o, -shĭ-o′nēz) [L.]. Granulation.

granulatio′nes arachnoidea′les [NA], arachnoid granulations or villi; pacchionian bodies; numerous villus-like projections of the cranial arachnoid through the dura into the superior sagittal sinus or its lateral venous lacunae.

granulation (gran′u-la′shun) [L. *granulatio*]. **1.** Formation into grains or granules; the state of being granular. **2.** A granular mass in or on the surface of any organ or membrane; or one of the individual grains forming the mass. **3.** Formation of minute, rounded, fleshy connective tissue projections on the surface of wound, ulcer, or inflamed tissue surface in the process of healing; one of the fleshy granules composing this surface.

arachnoid g.'s, *granulationes* arachnoideales.

granule (gran′ūl) [L. *granulum*, dim of *granum*, grain]. **1.** A grain; a granulation; minute discrete mass. **2.** A very small pill, usually gelatin coated or sugar coated.

acrosomal g., a proacrosomal g., derived from the Golgi apparatus, that becomes fused into a single g. within the acrosomal vesicle, which adheres to the nuclear envelope of the developing spermatozoon.

alpha g., a g. of an alpha cell.

basal g., basal *body*.

beta g., a g. of a beta cell.

cone g., nucleus of a retinal cell connecting with one of the cones.

Crooke's g.'s, lumpy masses of basophilic material in the basophil cells of the anterior lobe of the pituitary, associated with Cushing's disease, or following the administration of ACTH.

delta g., a g. of a delta cell.

elementary g., hemoconia.

glycogen g., glycogen occurring in cells as beta g.'s which average about 300 Å in diameter, or as alpha g.'s which are aggregates measuring 900 Å.

juxtaglomerular g.'s, stainable osmophilic secretory g.'s present in the juxtaglomerular cells, closely resembling zymogen g.'s.

keratohyalin g.'s, irregularly shaped g.'s in the cells of the stratum granulosum of the epidermis.

Langerhans g., a g. with characteristic plate-like ultrastructure; first reported in Langerhans cells of the epidermis.

membrane-coating g., keratinosome.

Nissl g.'s, Nissl *substance.*

proacrosomal g.'s, small carbohydrate-rich g.'s appearing in vesicles of the Golgi apparatus of spermatids; they coalesce into a single acrosomal g. contained within an acrosomal vesicle.

rod g., the nucleus of a retinal cell connecting with one of the rods.

Schüffner's g.'s, Schüffner's *dots.*

seminal g., one of the minute granule bodies present in the spermatic fluid.

granulo- [L. *granulum,* granule]. Combining form meaning granular, or denoting relationship to granules.

granulocyte (gran'u-lo-sīt) [granulo- + G. *kytos,* cell]. A mature granular leukocyte, including neutrophils, eosinophils, and basophils.

granulocytopenia (gran'u-lo-si-to-pe'nĭ-ah) [granulocyte + G. *penia,* poverty]. Granulopenia; less than the normal number of granular leukocytes in the blood.

granulocytopoietic (gran'u-lo-si-to-poy-et'ĭk) [granulocyte + G. *poieō,* to make]. Granulopoietic.

granulocytosis (gran'u-lo-si-to'sis). A condition characterized by more than the normal number of granulocytes in the circulating blood or in the tissues.

granulo'ma [granulo- + G. *-oma,* tumor]. An indefinite term applied to nodular inflammatory lesions, usually small or granular, firm, persistant, and containing compactly grouped mononuclear phagocytes.

amebic g., ameboma.

apical g., periapical periodontal g.

dental g., periapical periodontal g.

eosinophilic g., a lesion that occurs chiefly as a solitary focus in one bone, although multiple involvement is possible and similar foci may develop in the lung; characterized by numerous histiocytes which may contain Langerhans granules, numerous eosinophils and occasional foci of necrosis.

g. inguina'le, g. venereum; ulcerating g. of the pudenda; a specific g., classified as a venereal disease and caused by *Donovania granulomatis,* with ulcerating granulomatous lesions that occur in the inguinal regions and genitalia.

lethal midline g., malignant g.; a destructive granulomatous lesion usually arising in the nose or paranasal sinuses and ending fatally; distinguished from Wegener's granulomatosis by the absence of angiitis and of involvement of other organs.

lipoid g., g. characterized by aggregates or accumulations of fairly large mononuclear phagocytes that contain lipid; typical cells are derived from the reticuloendothelial system.

lipophagic g., a lesion formed as a result of the inflammatory reaction provoked by foci of necrosis in subcutaneous fat, as in certain types of traumatic injury.

malignant g., lethal midline g.

paracoccidiodal g., paracoccidioidomycosis.

periapical periodontal g., apical or dental g.; a reactive lesion comprised of inflammatory granulation tissue occurring at the periapex of devitalized teeth and usually the sequela of dental caries-inflammatory pulpal disease.

pyogenic g., a small spheroidal or ovoid mass of inflamed, highly vascular granulation tissue, frequently with an ulcerated surface, projecting from the skin.

swimming pool g., a chronic, low grade, infectious, verrucous lesion most commonly seen on the knees and due to an acid-fast bacillus of the genus *Myobacterium.*

g. trop'icum, yaws.

ulcerating g. of the pudenda, g. vene'reum, g. inguinale.

granulomatosis (gran'u-lo-mă-to'sis). Any condition characterized by multiple granulomas.

lymphoid g., a disease related to or a form of Wegener's g., characterized by nodular lower lung lesions which are granulomatous proliferations of lymphocytes, plasma cells, and histiocytes, notably perivascular with destruction of small arteries; the lesions often are fatal and the skin, kidneys, and nervous system are often involved.

g. siderot'ica, g. in which firm, brown foci that contain iron pigment, Gamna nodules, are present in an enlarged spleen.

Wegener's g., a rare lethal disease, occurring mainly in the fourth and fifth decades, characterized by progressive ulceration of the upper respiratory tract, with purulent rhinorrhea, nasal obstruction, and sometimes with otorrhea, hemoptysis, pulmonary infiltration and cavitation, and fever; the underlying condition is a vasculitis affecting small vessels, possibly due to an immune disorder.

granulom'atous. Having the characteristics of a granuloma.

granulomere (gran'u-lo-mēr) [granulo- + G. *meros,* a part]. Chromomere (2); the central part of a blood platelet.

gran'ulope'nia. Granulocytopenia.

gran'uloplas'tic. Forming granules.

granulopoiesis (gran'u-lo-poy-e'sis) [granulo(cyte) + G. *poiēsis,* a making]. Granulocytopoiesis; formation of granulocytes.

granulopoietic (gran'u-lo-poy-et'ik). Pertaining to granulopoiesis.

granulo'sis. A mass of minute granules of any character.

g. ru'bra na'si, erythema, papules, and occasional vesicles of the tip of the nose and extending upward and laterally to the cheeks, resulting from occlusion and chronic inflammation of sweat ducts.

-graph [G. *graphō*, to write]. Suffix designating a recording instrument.

graphanesthesia (graf'an-es-the'zĭ-ah) [G. *graphē*, writing + *anaisthēsia*, fr. *an*-priv. + *aisthēsis*, sensation]. Inability to recognize figures written on the skin.

graphorrhea (graf-o-re'ă) [G. *graphō*, to write, + *rhioa*, flow]. The writing of long lists of meaningless words.

-graphy [G. *graphō*, to write]. Suffix denoting a writing or description.

grattage (gră-tazh') [Fr. scraping]. Scraping or brushing to stimulate the healing process.

grave [L. *gravis*, heavy, grave]. Denoting symptoms of a serious or dangerous character.

grav'el. Small concretions, usually of uric acid, calcium oxalate, or phosphates, formed in the kidney and passed through the ureter, bladder, and urethra.

grav'id. Pregnant.

grav'ida [L. *gravidus* (adj.), fem. *gravida*, fr. *gravis*, heavy]. A pregnant woman, denoted by a Latin numerical prefix for each occurrence; *e.g.*, **primigravida**, a woman in her first pregnancy; **secundigravida**, a woman in her second pregnancy; etc.

gravid'ic. Relating to pregnancy or a pregnant woman.

gravidity (gră-vid'ĭ-tĭ) [L. *graviditas*, pregnancy]. Number of pregnancies.

grav'idocar'diac. Relating to an affection of the heart during pregnancy.

gravimet'ric. Relating to or determined by weight.

gravireceptors (grav'ĭ-re-sep'tors). Highly specialized receptor organs and nerve endings in the inner ear, joints, tendons, and muscles, that give the brain information about body position, equilibrium, direction of gravitational forces, and the sensation of "down" or "up."

gray (Gy). SI unit for a specific absorbed dose of radiation; 10^{-2} Gy = 1 rad.

gregarine (greg'a-rin). Denoting a member of the Gregarinida, an order of sporozoan parasites of annelids and arthropods.

grief. A normal emotional response to an external loss; distinguished from depression since it subsides after a reasonable time.

grind'ing. Abrasion (3).

grinding-in. Correcting occlusal disharmonies by grinding the natural or artificial teeth.

grip. 1. Influenza. **2.** Grasp or clasp.

    devil's g., epidemic *pleurodynia*.

grippe (grip) [Fr. *gripper*, to seize]. Influenza.

gristle (gris'l) [A.S.]. Cartilage.

groin. Inguen; inguinal region; the topographical area of the abdomen related to the inguinal canal, lateral to the hypogastrium (pubic region).

groove. A linear depression or furrow on any surface; a sulcus.

    atrioventricular g., *sulcus* coronarius.

developmental g.'s, developmental lines; fine lines found in the enamel of a tooth that mark the junction of the lobes of the crown in its development.

frontal g.'s, see *sulcus* frontalis.

Harrison's g., a deformity of the ribs which results from the pull of the diaphragm on ribs weakened by rickets or other softening of the bone.

interventricular g., *sulcus* interventricularis.

medullary g., neural g., the gutter-like g. formed in the midline of the embryo's dorsal surface by the progressive elevation of the lateral margins of the neural plate; the ultimate fusion of the left with the right margin forms the neural tube.

g. of nail matrix, *sulcus* matricis unguis.

olfactory g., *sulcus* olfactorius.

pontomedullary g., the transverse g. on the ventral aspect of the brainstem that demarcates the pons from the medulla oblongata; from its bottom the sixth, seventh, and eighth cranial nerves emerge.

posterolateral g., *sulcus* lateralis posterior.

urethral g., the g. on the undersurface of the embryonic penis which ultimately is closed to form the penile portion of the urethra.

group. 1. A number of similar or related objects. **2.** In chemistry, a radical.

characterizing g., a g. of atoms in a molecule that distinguishes the class of substances in which it occurs from all other classes.

control g., a g. of subjects participating in the same experiment as another g. of subjects except for the inclusion of the variable under investigation.

encounter g., a form of psychological sensitivity training that emphasizes the experiencing of individual relationships within the g. and minimizes intellectual and didactic imput; the g. focuses on the present rather than concerning itself with the past or outside problems of its members.

experimental g., a g. of subjects participating in the variable of an experiment, as opposed to the control g.

matched g.'s, a method of experimental control in which subjects in one g. are matched on a one-to-one basis with subjects in other g.'s concerning all organism variables which the experimenter deems important.

prosthetic g., a non-amino acid compound attached to a protein, usually in a reversible fashion, that confers new properties upon the conjugated protein thus produced.

sensitivity training g., a g. in which members seek to develop self-awareness and an understanding of g. processes rather than to obtain therapy for an emotional disturbance.

training g., any g. emphasizing training in self-awareness and group dynamics.

growth. The increase in size of a living being or any of its parts occurring in the process of development.

accretionary g., g. by an increase of intercellular material.

appositional g., g. by the addition of new layers on those previously formed; the characteristic method of g. of rigid materials.

interstitial g., g. from a number of different centers within an area; occurs when the materials are nonrigid.

gryposis (grĭ-po'sis) [G. *grypos*, hooked, + *-osis*, condition]. An abnormal curvature, as of the nails.

GSH Reduced *glutathione.*

GSR Galvanic skin *response.*

GSSG oxidized *Glutathione.*

GTP *Guanosine 5⅜-triphosphate.*

GU Genitourinary.

guanase (gwah'nās). *Guanine* deaminase.

guanine (gwah'nēn, -nin). 2-Amino-6-oxypurine; a major purine occurring in nucleic acids.

  g. deaminase, guanase; a deaminase of the liver that catalyzes the conversion of guanine into xanthine.

  g. deoxyribonucleotide, deoxyguanylic acid.

  g. ribonucleotide, guanylic acid.

guanosine (Guo) (gwah'no-sēn, -sin). 9-β-D-Ribosylguanine; a major consitutent of RNA and of guanine nucleotides.

guanosine 5'-triphosphate (GTP). Immediate precursor of guanine nuleotides in RNA; similar to ATP.

guanylic acid (GMP) (gwă-nil'ik). Guanine ribonucleotide; a major component of ribonucleic acids.

gubernaculum (gu'ber-nak'u-lum) [L. a helm]. A fibrous cord connecting two structures.

  g. den'tis, a connective tissue band uniting the tooth sac with the gum.

  g. tes'tis [NA], a mesenchymal column of tissue that connects the fetal testis to the developing scrotum and is involved in testicular descent.

guide (gīd). Any device or instrument by which another is led into its proper course, *e.g.,* a grooved director, a catheter g.

guillotine (gil'o-tēn) [Fr. instrument for decapitation]. An instrument in the shape of a metal ring through which runs a sliding knifeblade, used in cutting off an enlarged tonsil.

gul'let [L. *gula*, throat]. Throat (1).

gu'losacchar40 ic acid. Glucaric acid.

gum. 1 [A.S. *goma*, jaw]. Gingiva. **2** [L. *gummi*]. The dried exuded sap from a number of trees and shrubs, forming an amorphous brittle mass; usually forms a mucilaginous solution in water.

gum'boil. A gingival abscess.

gumma, pl. **gummas** or **gummata** (gum'ah, ahz, -ă-tah) [L. *gummi*, gum, fr. G. *kommi*]. Gummatous, nodular, or tubercular syphilid; symphiloma; an infectious granuloma characteristic of tertiary syphilis, but observed infrequently; may be solitary or multiple and diffusely scattered; characterized by an irregular central portion that is firm, sometimes partially hyalinized, and consisting of coagulative necrosis.

gummatous (gum'ă-tus). Pertaining to or characterized by the features of a gumma.

Guo Guanosine.

gusta'tion [L. *gustiatio*, fr. *gusto*, pp. *-atus*, to taste]. **1.** The act of tasting. **2.** The sense of taste.

gus'tatory. Relating to gustation, or taste.

gut [A.S.]. ⁱ. The intestine. **2.** Embryonic digestive tube. **3.** Catgut.

gutta-percha (gut'ah-per'chah) [Malay *gatah*, gum, + *percha*, tree]. A temporary filing material in dentistry.

gut'tate. Of the shape of, or resembling, a drop, characterizing certain cutaneous lesions.

guttural (gut'er-al). Throaty; relating to the throat.

gyn-, gyne-, gyneco-, gyno- [G. *gyne*, woman]. Combining forms denoting relationship to a woman.

gynandrism (jĭ-nan'drizm, gi-) [gyn- + G. *anēr* (*andr-*), man]. A developmental abnormality characterized by hypertrophy of the clitoris and union of the labia majora, simulating in appearance the penis and scrotum.

gynandroblastoma (jĭ-nan'dro-blas-to'mah, gi-). **1.** Arrhenoblastoma. **2.** A rare variety of arrhenoblastoma of the ovary, containing the cogranulomatous elements and producing simultaneous androgenic and estrogenic effects.

gynandroid (jĭ-nan'droyd, gi-) [gyn- + G. *anēr* (*andr-*), man, + *eidos,* resemblance]. Exhibiting gynandrism.

gynandromorph (jĭ-nan'dro-morf, gi-). An individual exhibiting gynandromorphism.

gynandromorphism (jĭ-nan-dro-mor'fizm, gi-) [gyn- + G. *anēr* (*andr-*), man, + *morphē*, form]. A combination of male and female characteristics.

gynan'dromor'phous. Having both male and female characteristics.

gynecic (jĭ-ne'sik). Pertaining to or associated with women.

gynecoid (gi'nĕ-koyd, jin'ĕ-) [gyneco- + G. *eidos,* resemblance]. Resembling a woman in form and structure.

gynecologic (gi'nĕ-ko-loj'ik, jin'ĕ-). Relating to gynecology.

gynecologist (gi-nĕ-kol'o-jist, jin-ĕ-). A specialist in gynecology.

gynecology (gi-nĕ-kol'o-jĭ, jin-ĕ-) [gyneco- + G. *logos*, study]. The medical specialty concerned with diseases of the female genital tract, as well as the endocrinology and reproductive physiology of the female.

gynecomastia (gi'nĕ-ko-mas'tĭ-ah, jin'ĕ-) [gyneco- + G. *mastos*, breast]. Excessive development of the male mammary glands, sometimes secreting milk.

gynephobia (gi-nĕ-fo'bĭ-ah, jin'ĕ-) [gyne- + G. *phobos,* fear]. Morbid aversion to women.

gynogenesis (gi-no-jen'ĕ-sis) [gyno- + G. *genesis,* production]. Egg development activated by a spermatozoon, but to which the male gamete contributes no genetic material.

gynoplastics (jin'o-plas-tiks, gi'no-) [gyno- + G. *plassō,* to form]. Reparative or reconstructive surgery of the female genital organs.

gyrate (ji'rāt) [L. *gyro*, pp. *gyratus*, to turn round in a circle, gyrus]. **1.** Of convoluted or ring shape. **2.** To revolve.

gyrectomy (ji-rek'to-mĭ) [G. *gyros*, ring (gyrus), + *ektomē*, excision]. Excision of a cerebral gyrus.

gyri (ji'ri) [L.]. Plural of gyrus.

gyrose (ji'rōs) [G. *gyros*, circle]. Marked by irregular curved lines like the surface of a cerebral hemisphere.

gyrospasm (ji'ro-spazm) [G. *gyros*, circle, + *spasmos*, spasm]. Spasmodic rotary movements of the head.

gyrus, gen. and pl. **gy'ri** (ji'rus, gi'ri) [L. fr. G. *gyros*, circle] [NA]. Convolution (2); one of the prominent, rounded, folded elevations that form the cerebral hemispheres, each consisting of an exposed superficial portion and a portion hidden from view in the wall and floor of the sulcus separating it from the others.

  g. angula'ris [NA], **angular g.,** a folded convolution in the inferior parietal lobule formed by the united posterior ends of the superior and middle temporal gyri.

    annectent g., transitional g.

  gy'ri bre'ves in'sulae [NA], short gyri of insula; several short, radiating gyri converging toward the base of the insula, composing the anterior two-thirds of the insular cortex.

    callosal g., g. cinguli.

    central gyri, gyri precentralis and postcentralis.

  g. cin'guli [NA], **cingulate g.,** callosal g.; a long curved convolution of the medial surface of the cortical hemisphere, arched over the corpus callosum from which it is separated by the deep sulcus corporis callosi; together with the g. parahippocampalis, with which it is continuous behind the corpus callosum, it forms the g. fornicatus.

  g. denta'tus [NA], **dendate g.,** one of the two interlocking gyri composing the hippocampus, the other one being the cornu ammonis.

  g. fornica'tus, the horseshoe-shaped cortical convolution bordering the hilus of the cerebral hemisphere; its upper limb is formed by the g. cinguli, its lower by the g. parahippocampalis.

  g. fronta'lis [NA], **frontal g., (1)** inferior, a broad convolution on the convexity of the frontal lobe of the cerebrum between the inferior frontal sulcus and the sylvian fissure, and divided by branches of the sylvian fissure into three parts; **(2)** middle, a convolution on the convexity of each frontal lobe of the cerebrum running in an anteroposterior direction between the superior and inferior frontal sulci; **(3)** superior, a broad convolution running in an anteroposterior direction on the inner edge of the convex surface and one the mesial surface of each frontal lobe.

  g. fusifor'mis **fusiform g.,** an extremely long convolution extending lengthwise over the ventral aspect of the temporal and occipital lobes.

  Heschl's gyri, gyri temporales transversi.

  hippocampal g., g. parahippocampalis.

  gy'ri in'sulae [NA], the gyri breves and longus insulae.

  g. lingua'lis [NA], **lingual g.,** medial occipitotemporal g.; a short horizontal convolution on the inferomedial aspect of the occipital and temporal lobes, demarcated from the fusiform g. by the deep sulcus collateralis and from the cuneus by the calcarine sulcus; the medial or upper part of the g., forming the lower bank of the calcarine sulcus, corresponds to the inferior half of the area striata or primary visual cortex.

  g. lon'gus in'sulae [NA], **long g. of the insula,** the most posterior and longest of the slender and relatively straight gyri that compose the insula.

    marginal g., the superior frontal g.

    medial occipitotemporal g., g. lingualis.

  gy'ri orbita'les [NA], **orbital gyri,** a number of small, irregular convolutions occupying the concave inferior surface of each frontal lobe of the cerebrum.

  g. par'ahippocampa'lis [NA], **parahippocampal g.,** hippocampal g.; a long convolution on the medial surface of the temporal lobe, forming the lower part of the g. fornicatus; the anterior extreme of the g. curves back upon itself to form the uncus, the major location of the olfactory cortex.

    paraterminal g., g. subcallosus.

  g. postcentra'lis [NA], **postcental g.,** the anterior convolution of the parietal lobe, bounded in front by the central sulcus (fissure of Rolando) and posteriorly by the interparietal sulcus.

  g. precentra'lis [NA], **precentral g.,** the posterior convolution of the frontal lobe bounded posteriorly by the central sulcus and anteriorly by the precentral sulcus.

  g. rec'tus [NA], **straight g.,** a g. running along the medial part of the orbital surface of the frontal lobe of the cerebral hemisphere and bounded laterally by the olfactory sulcus.

    short gyri of the insula, gyri breves insulae.

  g. subcallo'sus [NA], **subcalloual g.,** subcallosal area; peduncle of the corpus callosum; paraterminal g. a slender vertical whiteish band immediately anterior to the lamina terminalis and anterior commissure; the ventral continuation of the septum pellucidum.

    supracallosal g., *indusium* griseum.

  g. supramargina'lis [NA], **supramarginal g.,** a folded convolution capping the posterior extremity of the lateral (sylvian) sulcus; together with the g. angularis, it forms the inferior half of the parietal lobe.

  gy'ri tempora'les transver'si [NA], **transverse temporal gyri,** Heschl's gyri; two or three convolutions running transversely on the upper surface of the temporal lobe bordering on the lateral (sylvian) fissure, separated from each other by the transverse temporal sulci.

  g. tempora'lis [NA], **temporal g., (1)** inferior, a sagittal convolution on the inferolateral border of the temporal lobe of the cerebrum, separated from the middle temporal g. by the inferior temporal sulcus and including the fusiform g.; (2) middle, a longitudinal g. on the lateral surface of the temporal lobe, between the superior and inferior temporal sulci; (3) superior, a longitudinal g. on the lateral surface of the temporal lobe between the lateral (sylvian) fissure and the superior temporal sulcus.

transition g., annectent g.; a small convolution connecting two lobes or two main gyri in the depth of a sulcus.

uncinate g., uncus (2).

H

H Henry; hydrogen; hyperopia or hyperopic.

H+ Hydrogen ion.

h Hecto-.

h Planck's *constant.*

HAA Hepatitis-associated *antigen.*

habena, pl. **habenae** (hă-be'nah, -be'ne) [L. strap]. **1.** A frenum or restricting fibrous band. **2.** Habenula (2).

hab'enal, habe'nar. Relating to a habena.

habenula, pl. **habenulae** (hă-ben'u-lah) [L. See little strap]. **1.** A frenulum. **2.** Habena (2); in neuroanatomy, originally the stalk of the pineal gland, but now the nucleus habenulae, a circumscript cell mass in the dorsomedial thalamus, embedded in the posterior end of the stria medullaris from which it received most of its afferent fibers.

haben'ular. Relating to a habenula, especially the stalk of the pineal body.

hab'it [L. *habeo,* pp. *habitus,* to have]. **1.** An act, behavioral response, practice, or custom established by frequent repetition of the same act. See also addiction. **2.** A basic variable in the study of conditioning and learning used to designate a new response learned either by association or by being followed by a reward or reinforced event.

habitua'tion. **1.** The process of forming a habit, referring generally to psychological dependence on the continued use of a substance to maintain a sense of well-being, which can result in addiction. **2.** The method by which the nervous system reduces or inhibits responsiveness during repeated stimulation.

hab'itus [L. habit]. Physical characteristics of a person.

haem- [G. *haima,* blood]. Combining form meaning blood. See also hem-.

Haemaphysalis (hem'ă-fi'să-lis, he'mă-) [G. *haima,* blood, + *physaleos,* full of wind]. A genus of small inornate ticks that are important vectors of protozoa and viruses.

Haemophilus (he-mof'ĭ-lus) [G. *haima,* blood, + *philos,* fond]. *Hemophilus;* a genus of aerobic to facultatively anaerobic, parasitic bacteria (family Brucellaceae) containing minute, Gram-negative rod-shaped cells. The type species is *H. influenzae.*

H. ducrey'i, Ducrey's bacillus; a species that causes soft chancre (chancroid).

H. influen'zae, Pfeiffer's or Koch-Weeks bacillus; a species that causes acute respiratory infections, acute conjunctivitis, and purulent meningitis; originally considered to be the cause of influenza, it is the type species of the genus *H.*

hafnium (haf'nĭ-um) [L. *Hafniae,* Copenhagen]. A rare chemical element symbol Hf, atomic no. 72, atomic weight 178.50.

hahn'ium (Ha) [Otto *Hahn,* Ger. physical chemist, 1879–1968]. Name and symbol proposed for the artificial element 105.

hair [A.S. *haer*]. **1.** Pilus (1). **2.** One of the fine, hairlike processes of a sensory cell.

auditory h.'s, cilia on the free surface of the auditory cells.

bamboo h., trichorrhexis invaginata; h. with nodules along the shaft caused by intermittent fracturing and telescoping of the h., with intervening lengths of normal h., giving the appearance of bamboo.

bayonet h., a spindle-shaped developmental defect occurring at the tapered end of the hair.

beaded h., monilethrix.

club h., a h. in resting state, prior to shedding, in which the bulb has become a club-shaped mass.

Frey's irritation h.'s, short h.'s of varying degrees of stiffness, set at right angles into the end of a light wooden handle; used for determining the presence and degree of irritability of pressure points in the skin.

ingrown h.'s, pili cuniculati or incarnati; h.'s that grow at abnormally acute angles and in all directions, incompletely clear the follicle, turn back in, and cause formation of pustules and papules.

lanugo h., lanugo.

moniliform h., monilethrix.

stellate h., h. split into several strands at free end.

taste h.'s, clusters of microvilli of the gustatory cells of taste buds.

terminal h., a mature h.

twisted h.'s, *pili* torti.

hair'ball. Trichobezoar.

hair cast. A small, nodular accretion of epithelial cells and keratinous debris, resulting from failure of the internal root sheath to disintegrate, that appears along the hair shaft.

halation (hă-la'shun). Blurring of the visual image by irradiation of light.

half-life. The period during which the radioactivity of a radioactive substance, due to disintegration, is reduced to half of its original value.

biological h.-l., the time taken for one-half of an administered radioactive substance to be lost through biological processes.

effective h.-l., the time required for one-half of an administered dose of radioactivity to be dissipated through a combination of physical decay and biological turnover.

physical h.-l., the time required for a given number of atoms of a specific radionuclide to undergo disintegration.

half-time. The time, in a first-order chemical (or enzymic) reaction, for half of the substance (substrate) to be converted or to disappear.

halfway house. A facility for patients who no longer require the complete facilities of a hospital but are not yet prepared to return to their communities.

halide (hal'īd). A salt or compound of a halogen.

halisteresis (hă-lis-ter-e'sis) [G. *hals,* salt, + *sterēsis,* privation]. A deficiency of lime salts in the bones.

halisteretic (hă-lĭs-ter-et'ĭk). Relating to or marked by halisteresis.

halito'sis [L. *halitus,* breath, + G. *-osis,* condition]. Fetor ex ore; bad breath, especially a foul odor from the mouth.

hal'itus [L. fr. *halo,* to breathe]. Any exhalation, as of a breath or vapor.

Hal'lucal. Relating to the hallux.

hallucination (hă-lu-sĭ'-na'shun) [L. *alucinari,* to wander in mind]. The apparent, often strong subjective sense perception of sight, sound, smell, taste, or touch without basis in external stimuli.

hallucinogen (hă-lu'sĭ-no-jen). A hallucinatory substance whose most prominent pharmacologic action is on the central nervous system eliciting hallucinations, depersonalization, perceptual disturbances, and disturbances of thought processes.

hallucinogenic (hă-lu'sĭ-no-jen'ik). Relating to a hallucinogen.

hallucinosis (hă-lu'sĭ-no'sis). A syndrome, of organic origin, characterized by more or less persistent hallucinations.

hallux, pl. **halluces** (hal'uks, hal'u-sēz) [a Mod. L. form for L. *hallex*(*hallic-*), great toe] [NA]. The great toe, the first digit of the foot.

h. doloro'sus, a condition, usually associated with flatfoot, in which walking causes severe pain in the metatarsophalangeal joint of the great toe.

h. flex'us, h. mal'leus, hammer toe involving the first toe.

h. rig'idus, a condition in which there is stiffness in the first metatarsophalangeal joint, a site of a hypertrophic arthritis.

h. val'gus, deviation of the tip or main axis of the first toe, toward the outer side of the foot.

h. va'rus, deviation of the main axis of the great toe to the inner side of the foot.

halmatogenesis (hal'mă-to-jen'ĕ-sis) [G. *halma,* a spring, leap, + *genesis,* production, generation]. Saltatory variation; a sudden change of type from one generation to another.

ha'lo [G. *halōs*]. 1. A reddish yellow ring surrounding the optic disk, due to a widening out of the scleral ring permitting the deeper structures to show through. 2. An annular flare of light surrounding a luminous body.

anemic h., pale, relatively avascular areas in the skin seen around vascular spiders, cherry angiomas, and sometimes in acute macular eruptions.

glaucomatous h., a yellowish white ring surrounding the optic disk, indicating atrophy of the choroid in glaucoma.

halogen (hal'o-jen) [G. *hals,* salt, + *-gen,* producing]. One of the chlorine group (fluorine, chlorine, bromine, iodine, astatine) of elements which form monobasic acids with hydrogen.

halom'eter. 1. An instrument used to measure the diffraction halo of a red blood cell. 2. An instrument for measuring ocular halos.

halophil, halophile (hal'o-fil, -fīl) [G. *hals,* salt, + *philos,* fond]. A microorganism whose growth is enhanced by or dependent on a high salt concentration.

halophil'ic. Requiring a high concentration of salt for growth.

hal'othane. 2-Bromo-2-chloro-1,1,1-trifluoroethane; a widely used inhalation anesthetic with rapid onset, rapid reversal, and benign effect.

hamartia (ham-ar'shĭ-ah) [G. *hamartion,* a bodily defect]. A localized developmental disturbance characterized by abnormal arrangement and/or combinations of the tissues normally present in the area.

hamar'toblasto'ma [hamartoma + blastoma]. A malignant neoplasm of undifferentiated anaplastic cells thought to be derived from a hamartoma.

hamartoma (ham-ar-to'mah) [G. *hamartion,* a bodily defect, + *-oma,* tumor]. A focal malformation that resembles a neoplasm but results from faulty development in an organ; composed of an abnormal mixture of tissue elements, or an abnormal proportion of a single element, normally present in that site which develop and grow at virtually the same rate as normal components, and are not likely to result in compression of adjacent tissue.

pulmonary h., adenochondroma; h. of the lung, producing a coin lesion composed primarily of cartilage and bronchial epithelium.

ham'mer. Malleus.

ham'string. One of the tendons bounding the popliteal space on either side: **medial h.,** comprises the tendons of the semimembranosus, semitendinosus, gracilis, and sartorius muscles; **lateral h.,** the tendon of the biceps femoris.

ham'ular [L. *hamulus*]. Hook-shaped; unciform.

ham'ulus, gen. and pl. **ham'uli** [L. dim. of hamus, hook] [NA]. Any hooklike structure.

hand [A.S.]. Manus.

accoucheur's h., obstetrical h.; position of the h. in tetany or in muscular dystrophy; the fingers are flexed at the metacarpophalangeal joints and extended at the phalangeal joints, with the thumb flexed and adducted into the palm.

claw h., see clawhand.

cleft h., split h.; a congenital deformity in which the division between the fingers, especially between the third and fourth, extends into the metacarpal region. See also lobster-claw *deformity*.

drop h., wrist-drop.

obstetrical h., accoucheur's h.

split h., cleft h.

writing h., a contraction of the h. muscles in paralysis agitans, bringing the fingers somewhat in the position of holding a pen.

hand'edness. Preference for the use of one hand, most commonly the right, associated with dominance of the opposite cerebral hemisphere; also the result of training or habit.

hand'icap. A physical, mental, or emotional condition that interferes with one's functioning.

hang'nail. A loose tag of epidermis attached at the proximal portion in the medial or lateral nail fold.

haphalgesia (haf-al-je'zĭ-ah) [G. *haphē*, touch, + *algēsis*, sense of pain]. Pain or an extremely disagreeable sensation caused by the merest touch.

haplo- [G. *haplous*, simple, single]. Combining form meaning simple or single.

haploid (hap'loyd) [halpo- + -ploid]. Denoting the number of chromosomes in sperm or ova (23 in man); which is half the number in somatic (diploid) cells.

haploscopic (hap-lo-skop'ik). Relating to a haploscope.

haplotype (hap'lo-tīp) [haplo- + G. *typos*, impression, model]. **1.** The genetic constitution of an individual with respect to one member of a pair of allelic genes; individuals are of the same h. (but of different genotypes) if alike with respect to one allele of a pair but different with respect to the other allele of a pair. **2.** In immunogenetics, that portion of the phenotype determined by closely linked genes inherited as a unit from one parent (*i.e.,* genes located on one of the pair of chromosomes).

hap'ten [G. *haptō*, to fasten, bind]. Incomplete or partial antigen; an antigen that is incapable, alone, of causing the production of antibodies but is capable of combining with specific antibodies.

conjugated h., conjugated antigen; a h. that may cause the production of antibodies when it has been covalently linked to protein.

haptics [G. *haptō*, to grasp, touch]. The science concerned with the tactile sense.

hap'toglo'bin. A group of α_2-globulins in human serum, so called because of their ability to combine with hemoglobin; variant types form a polymorphic system, with α- and β-polypeptide chains controlled by separate genetic loci.

hare-lip. Cleft *lip.*

hashish (hash'ish, -ēsh) [Ar hay]. A form of cannabis that consists largely of resin from the flowering tops and sprouts of cultivated female plants; contains the highest concentration of cannabinols among the preparations derived from cannabis.

haustra (haw'strah) [L.]. Plural of haustrum.

haustral (haw'stral). Relating to a haustrum.

haustration (haw-stra'shun). **1.** Formation of a haustrum. **2.** An increase in prominence of the haustra.

haustrum, pl. **haustra** (haw'strum, -strah) [L. a machine for drawing water]. One of a series of saccules or pouches (so-called because of a fancied resemblance to the buckets on a water wheel); such as sacculations of the colon caused by longitudinal bands that are slightly shorter than the gut so that the latter is shaped into tucks or pouches.

HAV Hepatitis A *virus.*

haversian (ha-ver'shan). Relating to the various osseous structures described by Clopton Havers.

Hb Hemoglobin.

HB$_c$Ag Hepatitis B core *antigen.*

HB$_s$Ag Hepatitis B surface *antigen.*

Hb AS Heterozygosity for hemoglobin A and hemoglobin S, the sickle cell trait.

HBe, HB$_e$Ag Heptitis B e *antigen.*

Hb S Sickle cell *hemoglobin.*

HBV Hepatitis B *virus.*

HCG Human chorionic *gonadotropin.*

HCS Human chorionic somatomammotropic *hormone;* human chorionic *somatomammotropin.*

Hct Hematocrit (2).

HDL High density *lipoprotein.*

He Helium.

head (hed) [A.S. *heáfod*]. Caput.

Medusa h., *caput* medusae.

saddle h., clinocephaly.

head'ache. Cephalalgia; diffuse pain in various parts of the head, not confined to the area of distribution of any nerve.

cluster h., histaminic h.; a migraine variant characterized by recurrent, severe, unilateral orbitotemporal h.'s associated with conjunctival injection.

fibrositic h., h. centered in the occipital region due to fibrositis of the occipital muscles.

histaminic h., cluster h.

migraine h., see migraine.

sick h., migraine.

spinal h., h. following spinal anesthesia; usually frontal or occipital, precipitated by sitting or upright posture and relieved by lying down.

tension h., h. associated with nervous tension, anxiety, etc., often related to chronic contraction of the scalp muscles.

heal (hēl) [A.S. *healan*]. **1.** To restore to health, to cure; especially to cause an ulcer or wound to cicatrize or unite. **2.** To become well, to be cured; to cicatrize or close, said of an ulcer or wound.

heal'ing. 1. Curing; restoring to health; promoting the closure of wounds and ulcers. **2.** The process of a return to health or closing of a wound.

h. by first intention, primary adhesion or union; h. by fibrous adhesion, without suppuration or granulation tissue formation.

h. by second intention, secondary adhesion or union; union of two granulating surfaces accompanied by suppuration and delayed closure.

h. by third intention, the slow filling of a wound cavity or ulcer by granulations, with subsequent cicatrization.

health (helth) [A.S. haelth]. The state of an organism when it functions optimally without evidence of disease or abnormality.

mental h., the absence of mental or behavioral disorder; a state of psychological well-being in which a person has achieved a satisfactory integration of his instinctual drives acceptable to both himself and his social milieu.

public h., the art and science of community health, concerned with statistics, epidemiology, hygiene, and the prevention and eradication of epidemic diseases.

Health Maintenance Organization (HMO). A comprehensive prepaid system of health care with emphasis on the prevention and early detection of disease, and continuity of care.

health'y. Well; in a state of normal functioning; free from disease.

hearing (hēr'ing) [A.S. hēran, hear]. The ability to perceive sound; the sensation of sound as opposed to vibration.

color h., pseudochromesthesia (2); chromatic audition; subjective perception of color produced by certain sounds.

normal h., acusis.

hearing aid. An electronic amplifying device designed to bring sound more effectively into the ear; consists of a microphone, amplifier, and receiver.

hear'ing impair'ment. Hearing loss; a reduction in the ability to perceive sound, ranging from partial to complete deafness.

conductive h. i., hearing loss attributable to interference with the apparatus conducting sound to the inner ear.

sensorineural h. i., hearing loss due to dysfunction of the neural elements involved in the conduction or interpretation of nerve impulses orginating in the cochlea.

hear'ing loss. Hearing impairment. See also deafness.

heart (hart) [A.S. heorte]. Cor; a hollow muscular organ that receives blood from the veins and propels it into the arteries; divided by a musculomembranous septum into two halves, venous and arterial, each of which consists of an atrium and a ventricle.

armored h., calcareous deposits in the pericardium occurring in subacut or chronic inflammation.

athletic h., hypertrophy of the h. supposedly due to overindulgence in athletics.

fatty h., (1) fatty degeneration of the myocardium; (2) adiposis cardiaca; cor adiposum; accumulation of adipose tissue on the external surface of the h. with occasional infiltration of fat between the muscle bundles of the h. wall.

horizontal h., the h.'s electrical axis when directed at approximately $-30°$; recognized in the electrocardiogram when the QRS in lead aVL is positive while that in aVF is negative.

intermediate h., the h.'s electrical axis when directed at approximately $+30°$; recognized in the electrocardiogram when the QRS complexes in both aVL and aVF are mainly positive.

irritable h., neurocirculatory asthenia.

left h., left atrium and left ventricle.

right h., right atrium and right ventricle.

semihorizontal h., the h.'s electrical axis when directed at approximately $0°$; recognized in the electrocardiogram when the QRS complex in lead aVL is positive while that in aVF is isodiphasic.

semivertical h., the h.'s electrical axis when directed at approximately $+60°$; recognized in the electrocardiogram when the ARS complex in lead aVF is positive while that in aVL is isodiphasic.

soldier's h., neurocirculatory asthenia.

stone h., ischemic contracture of the left ventricle.

tobacco h., cardiac irritability marked by irregular action, palpitation, and sometimes pain, occurring as a result of the excessive use of tobacco.

vertical h., the h.'s electrical axis when directed at approximately $+90°$; recognized in the elctrocardiogram when the QRS complex in lead aVL is negative while that in aVF is positive.

heart'burn. Pyrosis.

heat (hēt) [A.S. haete]. A high temperature; the sensation produced by proximity to fire or an incandescent object, as opposed to cold.

conductive h., h. transmitted by direct contact as by an electric pad or hot water bottle.

convective h., h. conveyed by a warm medium, such as air or water, in motion from its source.

conversive h., h. produced in a body by the absorption of waves which are not in themselves hot, such as the sun's rays or infrared radiation.

heat-labile. Destroyed or altered by heat.

prickly h., miliaria rubra.

heatstroke (hēt'strōk). A condition produced by exposure to excessively high temperatures and characterized by headache, vertigo, confusion, and a slight rise in body temperature; collapse and coma, very high fever, tachycardia, and hot dry skin follow in severe cases.

hebephrenia (he-be-fre'nĭ-ah, heb'e-) [G. hēbē, puberty, + phrēn, the mind]. A syndrome characterized by shallow and inappropriate affect, giggling, and silly regressive behavior and mannerisms.

hebet'ic [G. hēbētikos, youthful, fr. hēbē, youth]. Pertaining to youth.

hebetude (heb'ē-tūd) [L. hebetudo, fr. hebeo, to be dull]. Moria (1).

hebiatrics (he'bĭ-at'riks) [G. hēbē, youth, + iatrio, to heal]. Ephebiatrics.

hecateromeric, hecatomeric, hecatomeral (hek'ă-ter-o-mĕr'ik, hek'ă-to-, hek-a-tom'er-al) [G. hekateros, each of two, + meros, part]. Denoting a spinal neuron whose axon divides and gives off processes to both sides of the cord; usually the same as a heteromeric neuron.

hecto- (h) [G. *hekaton*, one hundred]. Prefix used in the metric system to signfy one hundred (102).

hedrocele (hed′ro-sēl) [G. *hedra*, a seat, the fundament, + *kēlē*, hernia]. Prolapse of the intestine through the anus.

heel [A.S. *hēla*]. Calx (2).

    cracked h., *keratoderma* plantare sulcatum.

    painful h., calcodynia; calcaneodynia; a condition in which bearing the weight on the h. causes pain of varying severity.

    prominent h., a condition marked by a tender swelling on the os calcis due to a thickening of the periosteum or fibrous tissue covering the back of the os calcis.

height (hīt). Vertical measurement.

    cusp h., (1) the shortest distance between the tip of a cusp and its base plane; (2) the shortest distance between the deepest part of the central fossa of a posterior tooth and a line connecting the points of the cusps of the tooth.

    h. of contour, the line encircling a tooth or other structure at its greatest bulge or diameter with respect to a selected path of insertion.

hel′ical. [G. *helix*, a coil]. **1.** Helicine (2); relating to a helix. **2.** Helicoid.

hel′icine [G. *helix*, a coil]. **1.** Coiled. **2.** Helical (1).

helicoid (hel′ĭ-koyd) [G. *helix*, a coil, + *eidos*, resemblance]. Helical (2); resembling a helix.

hel′icopo′dia [G. *helix*, a coil, + *pous*, foot]. Helicopod *gait.*

hel′icotre′ma [G. *helix*, a spiral, + *trēma*, a hole] [NA]. A semilunar opening at the apex of the cochlea through which the scala vestibuli and the scala tympani of the cochlea communicate with one another.

heliencephalitis (he-lī-en-sef-al-i′tis) [G. *helios*, sun, + *enkephalos*, brain, + *-itis*, inflammation]. Inflammation of the brain following sunstroke.

he′lium [G. *hēlios*, sun]. A gaseous element, symbol He, atomic no. 2, atomic weight 4.0026; used as a diluent of medicinal gases.

helix, pl. **helices** (he′liks, hel′ĭ-sēz) [L. fr. G. *helix*, a coil]. **1** [NA]. The margin of the auricle; a folded rim of cartilage forming the upper part of the anterior, the superior, and the greater part of the posterior edges of the auricle. **2.** A line in the shape of a coil, (or a spring, or threads on a bolt (but mistakenly applied to a spiral), each point being equidistant from a straight line that is the axis of the cylinder in which each point of the h. lies.

    α-h., the right-handed helical form assumed by many proteins, deduced by Pauling and Corey from x-ray diffraction studies of collagen.

    DNA h., double h., see Watson-Crick h.

    Watson-Crick h., the helical structure assumed by two strands of deoxyribonucleic acid, held together throughout their length by hydrogen bonds between bases on opposite strands.

hel′minth [G. *helmins*, worm]. An intestinal verminform parasite.

helminthagogue (hel-minth′ă-gog) [G. *helmins*, worm, + *agōgos*, leading]. Anthelmintic (1).

helminthemesis (hel-min-them′ĕ-sis) [G. *helmins*, a worm, + *emesis*, vomiting]. The vomiting or expulsion through the mouth of intestinal worms.

helminthiasis (hel′min-thi′ă-sis). The condition of having intestinal vermiform parasites.

helmin′thic. Anthelmintic (1).

helmintho′ma [G. *helmins*, worm, + *-oma*, tumor]. A discrete nodule of granulomatous inflammation (including the healed stage) caused by a helminth or its products.

Helminthospor′ium. A genus of rapidly growing, saprobic fungi that are common laboratory contaminants.

heloma (he-lo′mah) [G. *hēlos*, nail, + *-oma*, tumor]. Clavus (1).

    h. dur′um, hard *corn.*

    h. mol′le, soft *corn.*

helot′omy [heloma + G. *tomē*, cutting]. The surgical treatment of corns.

hem-, hema- [G. *haima*, blood]. Combining forms meaning blood. See also hemat-, hemato-, hemo-.

he′macytom′eter. Hemocytometer.

hemadsorption (hem-ad-sorp′shun). A phenomenon manifested by an agent or substance adhering to or being adsorbed on the surface of a red blood cell.

hemagglutination (he′mă-glu-tĭ-na′shun, hem-). Agglutination of red blood cells which may be immune, as a result of specific antibody either for red blood cell antigens per se or other antigens which coat the red blood cells, or may be nonimmune, as in h. caused by viruses or other microbes.

    passive h., indirect hemagglutination test; passive agglutination in which erythrocytes, usually modifed by mild treatment with tannic acid or other chemicals, are used to adsorb soluble antigen onto their surface, and which then agglutinate in the presence of antiserum specific for the adsorbed antigen.

    viral h., nonimmune agglutination of suspended red blood cells by certain of a wide range of otherwise unrelated viruses, usually by the virion itself but in some instances by products of viral growth, the species of erythrocyte agglutinated differing with the different viruses.

hemagglutinin (he′mă-glu′tĭ-nin, hem-). An antibody or other substance that causes hemagglutination.

hemagogic (he′mă-goj′ik, hem-). Promoting a flow of blood.

hemagogue (he′mă-gog, hem-) [hem- + G. *agogos*, leading]. **1.** An agent that promotes a flow of blood. **2.** Emmenagogue.

he′mal [G. *haima*, blood]. **1.** Relating to the blood or blood vessels. **2.** Ventral to the spinal axis, where the heart and great vessels are located.

hemalum (hēm-al′um). A solution of hematoxylin and alum used as a nuclear stain in histology, especially with eosin as a counterstain.

hem'amebi'asis. Any infection with ameboid forms of parasites in red blood cells, as in malaria.

hemanalysis (hem'ă-nal'ĭ-sis) [G. *haima*, blood, + analysis]. Analysis of the blood, especially with reference to chemical methods.

hemangiectasis (he-man-jĭ-ek'tă-sis) [G. *haima*, blood, + *angeion*, vessel, + *ektasis*, a stretching]. Dilation of blood vessels.

hemangio- [G. *haima*, blood, + *angeion*, vessel]. Combining form relating to the blood vessels.

hemangioblast (he-man'jĭ-o-blast) [hemangio- + G. *blastos*, germ]. A primitive embryonic cell of mesodermal origin that produces cells giving rise to vascular endothelium, reticuloendothelial elements, and blood-forming cells of all types.

hemangioblastoma (he-man'jĭ-o-blas-to'mah). Angioblastoma; a benign, slowly growing, cerebellar neoplasm composed of capillary vessel-forming endothelial cells.

hemangioendothelioblastoma (he-man'jĭ-o-en-do-the'lĭ-o-blas-to'mah) [hemangio- + endothelium + G. *blastos*, germ, + *-oma*, tumor]. Hemangioendothelioma in which the endothelial cells seem to be especially immature forms.

hemangioendothelioma (he-man'jĭ-o-en'do-the-lĭ-o'-mah) [hemangio- + endothelium + G. *-oma*, tumor]. A neoplasm derived from blood vessels, characterized by numerous prominent endothelial cells that occur singly, in aggregates, and as the lining of congeries of vascular tubes or channels.

hemangiofibroma (he-man'jĭ-o-fi-bro'mah). A hemangioma with an abundant fibrous tissue framework.

hemangioma (he-man'jĭ-o'mah) [hemangio- + G. *-oma*, tumor]. A congenital anomaly in which a proliferation of vascular endothelium leads to a mass that resembles neoplastic tissue; most frequently seen in the skin and subcutaneous tissues.

    capillary h., a congenital lesion consisting of numerous, variably sized but predominantly small, closely packed capillaries usually separated only by a thin network of reticulin.

    cavernous h., cavernous angioma; a vascular erectile tumor containing large blood-filled spaces, due to dilation and thickening of the walls of the capillary loops.

    sclerosing h., a dermatofibroma or variety thereof.

    senile h., cherry angioma; a red papule due to weakening of the capillary wall, seen in most persons over 30 years of age.

hemangiomatosis (he-man'jĭ-o-mă-to'sis). Presence of numerous hemangiomas.

hemangiopericytoma (he-man'jĭ-o-pĕr'ĭ-si-to'mah) [hemangio- + pericyte + G. *-oma*, tumor]. A rare vascular, usually benign, neoplasm composed of round and spindle cells presumably derived from the pericytes.

hemangiosarcoma (he-man'jĭ-o-sar-ko'mah). A rare malignant neoplasm characterized by rapidly proliferating, extensively infiltrating, anaplastic cells de-

rived from blood vessels and lining blood-filled spaces.

hemarthrosis (hem'ar-thro'sis) [G. *haima*, blood, + *arthron*, joint]. Blood in a joint or its cavity.

hemat- [G. *haima* (*haimat-*), blood]. Combining form meaning blood. See also hem-, hemato-, hemo-.

hematemesis (he'mă-tem'e-sis) [hemat- + G. *emesis*, vomiting]. Vomiting of blood.

hematencephalon (he'mat-en-sef'ă-lon, hem'at-) [hemat- + G. *enkephalos*, brain]. Cerebral *hemorrhage*.

hemat'ic. 1. Hemic; relating to blood. **2.** Hematinic.

hematidrosis (he'mat-ĭ-dro'sis, hem'at-) [hemat- + G. *hidrōs*, sweat]. Hemidrosis (1); excretion of blood or blood pigment in the sweat.

hematin (hēm'ă-tin). An iron-protoporphyrin differing from heme in that the central iron atom is in the ferric (Fe^{3+}) rather than the ferrous (Fe^{2+}) state; the prosthetic group of methemoglobin.

    h. chloride, hemin.

    reduced h., heme.

hematinemia (hem'ă-tin-e'mĭ-ah) [hematin + G. *haima*, blood]. Presence of heme in the circulating blood.

hematinic (hem'ă-tin'ik). Hematic (2); improving the quality of blood, as by increasing the number of erythrocytes and/or the hemoglobin concentration.

hemato- [G. *haima* (*haimat-*), blood]. Combining form meaning blood. See also hem-, hemat-, hemo-.

hematoblast (hem'ă-to-blast) [hemato- + G. *blastos*, germ]. A primitive, undifferentiated form of blood cell from which erythroblasts, lymphoblasts, myeloblasts, and other immature blood cells are derived; probably identical or closely similar to hemocytoblast and hemohistioblast.

hematocele (hem'ă-to-sēl) [hemato- + G. *kēlē*, tumor]. **1.** Hemorrhagic *cyst*. **2.** An effusion of blood into a canal or a cavity of the body.

hematochezia (hem'ă-to-ke'zĭ-ah) [hemato- + G. *chezō*, to go to stool]. Passage of bloody stools, in contradistinction to melena, or tarry stools.

hematochyluria (hem'ă-to-ki-lu'rĭ-ah) [hemato- + G. *chylos*, juice, + *ouron*, urine]. Presence of blood as well as chyle in the urine.

hematocolpometra (hem'ă-to-kol'po-me'trah) [hemato- + G. *kolpos*, vagina, + *mētra*, womb]. Accumulation of blood in the uterus and vagina.

hematocolpos (hem'ă-to-kol'pos) [hemato- + G. *kolpos*, vagina]. Accumulation of menstrual blood in the vagina.

hematocrit (hem'ă-to-krit) [hemato- + G. *krinō*, to separate]. **1.** A centrifuge or device for separating cells and other particulate elements of the blood from the plasma. **2 (Hct).** The percentage of the volume of a blood sample occupied by cells, as determined by a h.

hematocyst (hem'ă-to-sist). Hemorrhagic *cyst*.

hematocystis (hem'ă-to-sis'tis) [hemato- + G. *kystis*, a bladder]. An effusion of blood into the bladder.

hematocyturia (hem′ă-to-si-tu′rĭ-ah) [hemato- + G. *kytos*, cell, + *ouron*, urine]. Presence of red blood cells in the urine.

hematogenesis (hem′ă-to-jen′ĕ-sis) [hemato- + G. *genesis*, production]. Hemopoiesis.

hematogenic, hematogenous (hem′ă-to-jen′ik, hem-ă-toj′en-us). **1.** Hemopoietic. **2.** Pertaining to anything produced from, derived from, or transported by the blood.

hem′atohis′ton. Globin.

he′matoid [hemato- + G. *eidos*, resemblance]. Resembling blood.

hematoidin (hēm-ă-toy′din). Blood crystals; a pigment derived from hemoglobin and formed intracellularly which contains no iron but is closely related to or similar to bilirubin.

hematol′ogist. A physician specializing in hematology.

hematology (he-mă-tol′o-jĭ, hem-ă-) [hemato- + G. *logos*, study]. The medical specialty concerned with the anatomy, physiology, pathology, symptomatology, and therapeutics related to the blood and blood-forming tissues.

hematolymphangioma (hem′ă-to-limf′an-jĭ-o′mah). A congenital anomaly consisting of numerous, closely packed, variably sized lymphatic vessels and larger channels, in association with a moderate number of blood vessels of a similar types.

hematol′ysis. Hemolysis.

hematolyt′ic. Hemolytic.

he′matom′etry [hemato- + G. *metron*, measure]. Examination of the blood to determine: 1) the total number, types, and relative proportions of various blood cells; 2) the number or proportion of other formed elements; 3) the percentage of hemoglobin.

hematoma (he-mă-to′mah, hem-ă-) [hemato- + G. -*oma*, tumor]. A localized mass of extravasated, usually clotted, blood confined within an organ, tissue, or space.

   epidural h., extradural *hemorrhage.*

   intramural h., a h. in the wall of a structure, such as the bowel or bladder, usually resulting from trauma.

   subdural h., subdural *hemorrhage.*

hematometra (hem′ă-to-me′trah) [hemato- + G. *mētra*, uterus]. Hemometra; a collection or retention of blood in the uterine cavity.

hematomphalocele (hem′at-om-fal′o-sēl) [hemato- + G. *omphalos*, umbilicus, + *kēlē*, hernia]. An umbilical hernia into which an effusion of blood has taken place.

hematomyelia (hem′ă-to-mi-e′lĭ-ah) [hemato- + G. *myelos*, marrow]. Hematorrhachis interna; myelapoplexy; myelorrhagia; hemorrhage into the substance of the spinal cord; usually a posttraumatic lesion but also encountered in instances of spinal cord capillary telangiectases.

hematomyelopore (hem′ă-to-mi′ĕ-lo-pōr) [hemato- + G. *myelos*, marrow, + *poros*, a pore]. Formation of porosites in the spinal cord as a result of hemorrhages.

hem′atopathol′ogy [hemato- + G. *pathos*, suffering, + *pathos*, suffering, + *logos*, study]. Hemopathology; the division of pathology concerned with diseases of the blood and of hemopoietic and lymphoid tissues.

hem′atoplas′tic [hemato- + G. *plassō*, to form]. Hemopoietic.

hematopoiesis (hem′ă-to-poy-e′sis). Hemopoiesis.

hematopoietic (hem′ă-to-poy-et′ik). Hemopoietic.

hematoporphyrin (hēm′ă-to-por′fĭ-rin). A porphyrin resulting from the decomposition of hemoglobin, with a chemical composition that of heme with the iron removed and the two vinyl ($-CH=CH_2$) groups hydrated to hydroxyethyl ($-CHOH-CH_3$).

hematop′sia [hemato- + G. *opsis*, vision]. Hemorrhage into the eye.

hematorrhachis (hem-ă-tor′ă-kis) [hemato- + G. *rhachis*, spine]. A spinal hemorrhage.

   h. exter′na, extradural h., hemorrhage into the spinal canal external to the cord, either within or outside the dura.

   h. inter′na, hematomyelia.

hem′atosal′pinx [hemato- + G. *salpinx*, a trumpet]. A collection of blood in a tube, often associated with a tubal pregnancy.

hematoscheocele (hem-ă-tos′ke-o-sēl) [hemato- + G. *oscheon*, scrotum, + *kēlē*, hernia, tumor]. Accumulation of blood in the scrotal cavity.

hematospermatocele (hem′ă-to-sper′mă-to-sēl). A spermatocele that contains blood.

hem′atostat′ic. 1. Hemostatic. **2.** Due to stagnation or arrest of blood in the vessels of the part.

hematostaxis (hem′ă-to-stak′sis) [hemato- + G. *staxis*, a dripping]. Spontaneous bleeding due to a disease of the blood.

hematos′teon [hemato- + G. *osteon*, bone]. Bleeding in the medullary cavity of a bone.

hem′atotox′ic. Hemotoxic.

hem′atotox′in. Hemotoxin.

hematotrachelos (hem′ă-to-tră-ke′lus) [hemato- + G. *trachēlos*, neck]. Distention of the cervix uteri with accumulated blood.

hem′atotrop′ic. Hemotropic.

hem′atotym′panum. Hemotympanum.

hematoxylin (he-mă-toks′ĭ-lin). A compound, $C_{16}H_{14}O_6 \cdot 3H_2O$, containing the coloring matter of *Haematoxylon campechianum* (logwood), used as a dye in histology and as an indicator.

hemature′sis. Hematuria, especially with reference to unusually large amounts of blood in urine.

hematu′ria [hemato- + G. *ouron*, urine]. Any condition in which the urine contains blood or red blood cells.

   endemic h., *schistosomiasis* haematobium.

   essential h., h. in which the cause and source are not recognized.

   false h., pseudohematuria.

renal h., h. resulting from extravasation of blood into the glomerular spaces, or tubules, or pelves of the kidneys.

urethral h., h. in which the site of bleeding is in the urethra.

vesical h., h. in which the site of bleeding is in the urinary bladder.

heme (hēm). Reduced hematin; the prosthetic, oxygen-carrying, color-furnishing constituent of hemoglobin.

hemeostat′ic. Relating to homeostasis.

hemeralopia (hem′er-al-o′pĭ-ah) [G. *hēmera,* day, + *alaos,* obscure, + *ōps,* eye]. Day blindness; night sight; inability to see as distinctly in a bright light as in a dim one.

hemi- [G.]. Prefix signifying one-half. See also semi-.

hemiachromatopsia (hem′ĭ-ă-kro-mă-top′sĭ-ah) [hemi- + G. *a-* priv. + *chrōma,* color, + *opsis,* vision]. Color *hemianopsia.*

hemiamyosthenia (hem′ĭ-ă-mi′os-the′nĭ-ah) [hemi- + G. *a-* priv. + *mys(myo-),* muscle, + *stheneia,* strength]. Hemiparesis.

hemianalgesia (hem′ĭ-an′al-je′zĭ-ah). Loss of sensibility to pain affecting one side of the body.

hemianencephaly (hem′ĭ-an-en-sef′ă-lĭ). Anencephaly on one side only, or involving one side much more extensively than the other.

hemianesthesia (hem′ĭ-an-es-the′zĭ-ah). Unilateral anesthesia; loss of tactile sensibility on one side of the body.

alternate h., crossed h., h. affecting the head on one side and the body and extremities on the other side.

hemianopsia, hemianopia (hem′ĭ-an-op′sĭ-ah, o′pĭ-ah) [hemi- + G. *an-* priv. + *opsis,* vision]. Loss of vision for one half of the visual field of one or both eyes.

absolute h., h. in which the affected field is totally insensitive to all visual stimuli.

altitudinal h., a defect in the visual field in which the upper or lower half is lost.

binasal h., blindness in the nasal field of vision of both eyes.

bitemporal h., blindness in the temporal field of vision of both eyes.

color h., hemiachromatopsia; loss of color perception in half of each visual field.

complete h., h. involving a full half of the visual field.

congruous h., h. in which the visual field defects in both eyes are completely symmetrical in every respect.

crossed h., heteronymous h., altitudinal h. involving the upper field of one eye and the lower field of the other.

homonymous h., lateral h., loss of sight in the corresponding (right or left) lateral halves of the eyes.

quadrantic h., quadrantanopsia; loss of vision in a quarter section of the visual field of one or both

eyes; if bilateral, it may be homonymous or heteronymous, binasal or bitemporal, or crossed.

unilateral h., uniocular h., loss of sight in half the visual field of one eye.

hem′ianop′tic. Pertaining to hemianopsia.

hemianosmia (hem′ĭ-an-oz′mĭ-ah) [hemi- + G. *an-* priv. + *osmē,* smell]. Loss of the sense of smell on one side.

hemiapraxia (hem′ĭ-ă-prak′sĭ-ah). Apraxia affecting one side of the body.

hem′iatax′ia. Ataxia affecting one side of the body.

hemiathetosis (hem′ĭ-ath′e-to′sis). Athetosis affecting one hand, or one hand and foot, only.

hemiatrophy (hem-ĭ-at′ro-fĭ). Atrophy of one lateral half of a part or of an organ.

hemiballismus, hemiballism (hem′ĭ-bal-iz′mus, -bal′izm) [hemi- + G. *ballismos,* jumping about]. Violent writing and choreic movements involving one side of the body, usually related to a lesion of the subthalamic nucleus of the opposite side of the brain.

hem′iblock. Arrest of the impulse in one of the two main divisions of the left branch of the bundle of His.

he′mic. Hematic (1).

hemicardia (hem-ĭ-kar′dĭ-ah) [hemi- + G. *kardia,* heart]. **1.** One lateral half, including atrium and ventricle, of the heart. **2.** A congenital malformation of the heart in which only two of the usual four chambers are formed.

hem′icen′trum [hemi- + G. *kentron,* center]. One of the two lateral halves of the body of the vertebra.

hemicephalalgia (hem′ĭ-sef-ă-lal′jĭ-ah) [hemi- + G. *kephalē,* head, + *algos,* pain]. Hemicrania (2); the unilateral headache characteristic of typical migraine.

hemicephalia (hem′ĭ-sě-fa′lĭ-ah) [hemi- + G. *kephalē,* head]. Congenital failure of the cerebrum to develop normally; the cerebellum and basal ganglia are usually represented in rudimentary form.

hemichorea (hem′ĭ-ko-re′ah). Chorea involving the muscles on one side of the body.

hem′icolec′tomy [hemi- + G. *kolon,* colon, + *ektomē,* excision]. Removal of the right or left side of the colon.

hemicrania (hem-ĭ-kra′nĭ-ah) [hemi- + G. *kranion,* skull]. **1.** Migraine. **2.** Hemicephalalgia.

hem′icranio′sis. Enlargement of one side of the cranium.

hem′ides′mosomes. Half desmosomes that occur on the basal surface of the stratum basalis of stratified squamous epithelium.

hemidiaphoresis (hem′ĭ-di-ă-fo-re′sis). Hemihidrosis; hemidrosis (2); diaphoresis, or sweating, on one side of the body.

hemidrosis (hem-ĭ-dro′sis). **1.** Hematidrosis. **2.** Hemidiaphoresis.

hemidysesthesia (hem′ĭ-dis-es-the′zĭ-ah). Dysesthesia affecting one lateral half of the body.

hemidystrophy (hem-ĭ-dis'tro-fĭ) [hemi- + G. *dys-*, ill, + *trophē*, nourishment, growth]. Underdevelopment of one lateral half of the body.

hemiectromelia (hem'ĭ-ek-tro-me'lĭ-ah) [hemi- + ectromelia]. Defective development of the limbs on one side of the body.

hemiep'ilepsy. Epilepsy in which the convulsive movements are confined to one side of the body.

hemifa'cial. Pertaining to one side of the face.

hem'igastrec'tomy. Excision of the distal half of the stomach.

hemigeusia (hem'ĭ-gu'sĭ-ah). Hemiageusia.

hem'iglossec'tomy [hemi- + G. *glōssa*, tongue, + *ektomē*, excision]. Surgical removal of one-half of the tongue.

hem'iglossi'tis [hemi- + G. *glōssa*, tongue, + *-itis*, inflammation]. A vesicular eruption on one side of the tongue and the corresponding inner surface of the cheek.

hemignathia (hem-ĭ-nath'ĭ-ah) [hemi- + G. *gnathos*, jaw]. Defective development of one side of the mandible.

hemihidro'sis. Hemidiaphoresis.

hemihypalgesia (hem'ĭ-hi-pal-je'zĭ-ah). Partial loss of sensibility to pain affecting one lateral half of the body.

hemihyperesthesia (hem'ĭ-hi'per-es-the'zĭ-ah). Increased tactile and painful sensibility affecting one side of the body.

hemihyperidrosis (hem'ĭ-hi-per-ĭ-dro'sis) [hemi- + G. *hyper*, over, + *hidrōsis*, sweating]. Excessive sweating confined to one side of the body.

hem'ihyperto'nia [hemi- + G. *hyper*, over, + *tonos*, tone]. Exaggerated muscular tonicity on one lateral half of the body.

hemihypertrophy (hem'ĭ-hi-per'tro-fĭ). Muscular hypertrophy of one side of the face or body.

hemihypesthesia (hem'ĭ-hi-pes-the'zĭ-ah) [hemi- + G. *hypo*, under, + *aesthēses*, sensation]. Diminished sensibility in one lateral half of the body.

hem'ihypoto'nia [hemi- + G. *hypo*, under, + *tonos*, tone]. Partial loss of muscular tonicity on one side of the body.

hem'ilaminec'tomy [hemi- + L. *lamina*, layer, + G. *ektomē*, excision]. Removal of a portion of a vertebral lamina; often used to denote unilateral laminectomy.

hemilaryngectomy (hem'ĭ-lăr-in-jek'to-mĭ) [hemi- + G. *larnyx* (*laryng-*), larynx, + *ektomē*, excision]. Excision of a lateral half of the larynx.

hemilat'eral. Relating to one lateral half.

hemimelia (hem-ĭ-me'lĭ-ah) [hemi- + G. *melos*, limb]. A condition marked by defects in the limbs.

he'min. Hematin chloride; the chloride of heme in which Fe^{2+} has become Fe^{3+} (hematin is the hydroxide).

hemiparanesthesia (hem'ĭ-păr-an-es-the'zĭ-ah). Anesthesia of one lower extremity, or of the lower part of one side of the body.

hemiparaplegia (hem'ĭ-păr-ă-ple'jĭ-ah). Paralysis of one leg.

hemiparesis (hem-ĭ-pă-re'sis, -păr'ĕ-sis). Hemiamyosthenia; slight paralysis affecting one side of the body.

hem'ipelvec'tomy [hemi- + L. *pelvis*, basin (pelvis), + G. *ektomē*, excision]. Interpelviabdominal amputation; amputation of an entire leg together with the os coxae.

hemiplegia (hem-ĭ-ple'jĭ-ah) [hemi- + G. *plēgē*, a stroke]. Paralysis of one side of the body.

   alternating h., crossed h., stauroplegia; h., as the result of a brainstem lesion, occurring on the contralateral side (with reference to the lesion) and a paralysis of a motor cranial nerve on the ipsilateral side.

   contralateral h., paralysis occurring on the side opposite to the causal central lesion.

   facial h., paralysis of one side of the face, the muscles of the extremities being unaffected.

   spastic h., a h. with increased tone in the antigravity muscles of the affected side.

hemiplegic (hem-ĭ-ple'jik). Relating to hemiplegia.

hem'ispasm. A spasm affecting one or more muscles of one side of the face or body.

hemisphere (hem'ĭ-sfēr) [hemi- + G. *sphaira*, ball, globe]. Half of a spherical structure or organ.

   cerebellar h., the large part of the cerebellum lateral to the vermis cerebelli.

   cerebral h., the large mass of the telencephalon, on either side of the midline, consisting of the cerebral cortex and its associated fiber systems, together with the deeper-lying corpus striatum.

   dominant h., the cerebral h. that contains the representation of speech and controls the arm and leg used preferentially in skilled movements.

hemisystole (hem-ĭ-sis'to-le). Systole alternans; contraction of the left ventricle following every second atrial contraction only, so that there is but one pulse beat to every two heart beats.

hemitho'rax. One side of the thorax.

hemiver'tebra. A congenital defect of the spine in which one side of a vertebra fails to develop completely.

hemizygos'ity. The state of having unpaired genes in an otherwise diploid cell; males are normally hemizygous for genes on the X chromosome.

hemizy'gote [hemi- + G. *zytōtos*, yoked (see zygote)]. An individual hemizygous with respect to one or more specified genes.

hemizy'gous. Relating to hemizygosity.

hemo- [G. *haima*, blood]. Combining form signifying blood. See also hem-, hemat-, hemato-.

he'moblast. Hemocytoblast.

he'moblasto'sis. A proliferative condition of the hematopoietic tissues in general.

hemocatheresis (he'mo-kath-er-e'sis) [hemo- + G. *kathairesis*, destruction]. Destruction of the blood cells, especially of erythrocytes (hemocytocatheresis).

he'mocatheret'ic. Pertaining to or characterized by hemocatheresis.

hemocholecyst (he'mo-ko'le-sist) [hemo- + G. *cholē*, bile, + *kystis*, bladder]. **1.** A cyst containing blood and bile. **2.** Nontraumatic hemorrhage or old blood accumulated in the gallbladder.

hemocholecystitis (he'mo-ko'le-sis-ti'tis). Hemorrhagic cholecystitis.

hemochromatosis (he'mo-kro-mă-to'sis) [hemo- + G. *chrōma*, color, + *-osis*, condition]. A disorder of iron metabolism characterized by increased absorption of ingested iron, saturation of iron-binding protein, and deposition of hemosiderin in tissue, particularly in the liver, pancreas, and skin.

primary h., a specific inherited metabolic defect with increased absorption and accumulation of iron on a normal diet; autosomal dominant inheritance with reduced penetrance in females; juvenile h. may represent a homozygous state of the same gene.

secondary h., increased intake and accumulation of iron secondary to known cause, such as oral iron therapy or multiple transfusions.

hemoclasis (he-mok'lă-sis) [hemo- + G. *klasis*, a breaking]. Rupture, dissolution (hemolysis), or other type of destruction of red blood cells.

he'moclas'tic. Pertaining to hemoclasis.

he'moconcentra'tion. Decrease in the volume of plasma in relation to the number of red blood cells; increase in the concentration of red blood cells in the circulating blood.

hemoconia (he-mo-ko'nĭ-ah) [hemo- + G. *konis*, dust]. Small refractive particles in the circulating blood, probably lipid material associated with fragmented stroma from red blood cells.

hemoconiosis (he'mo-ko-nĭ-o'sis). An abnormal amount of hemoconia in the blood.

he'mocyte [hemo- + G. *kytos*, a hollow (cell)]. Any cell or formed element of the blood.

he'mocy'toblast [hemo- + G. *kytos*, cell, + *blastos*, germ]. Mesameboid cell (2); hemoblast; a primitive blood cell derived from embryonic mesenchyme, representing the primitive stem cells of the monophyletic theory of the origin of blood which have the potentiality of developing into erythroblasts, young forms of the granulocytic series, megakaryocytes, etc.

hemocytocatheresis (he'mo-si'to-kă-thĕr'e-sis) [hemo- + G. *kytos*, a hollow (cell), + *kathairesis*, destruction]. Hemolysis, or other type of destruction of red blood cells.

he'mocytol'ysis [hemo- + G. *kytos*, cell, + *lysis*, dissolution]. The dissolution of blood cells, including hemolysis.

he'mocytom'eter [hemo- + G. *kytos*, cell, + *metron*, measure]. Hemacytometer; an apparatus for estimating the number of blood cells in a quantitively measured volume of blood.

hemocytometry (he'mo-si-tom'ĕ-trī). The counting of red blood cells.

he'mocy'totrip'sis [hemo- + G. *kytos*, + *tripsis*, a grinding]. Fragmentation or disintegration of blood cells by means of mechanical trauma.

he'modiagno'sis. Diagnosis by means of examination of the blood.

hemodialysis (he'mo-di-al'ĭ-sis). Dialysis of soluble substances and water from the blood by diffusion through a semipermeable membrane; separation of cellular elements and colloids from soluble substances is achieved by pore size in the membrane and rates of diffusion.

hemodi'alyzer. Artificial kidney; a machine for hemodialysis in acute or chronic renal failure; toxic substances in the blood are removed by exposure to dialyzing fluid across a semipermeable membrane.

he'modilu'tion. Increase in the volume of plasma in relation to red blood cells; reduced concentration of red blood cells in the circulation.

he'modynam'ic. Relating to the physical aspects of the blood circulation.

he'modynam'ics hemo- + G. *dynamis*, power]. The study of the dynamics of the blood circulation.

hemoflagellates (he'mo-flaj'ĕ-lāts) [hemo- + L. *flagellum*, dim of *flagrum*, a whip]. Protozoan flagellates in the family Trypanosomatidae that are parasitic in the blood; they include the genera *Leishmania* and *Trypanosoma*, several species of which are important pathogens.

hemofuscin (he-mo-fus'in). A brown pigment derived from hemoglobin which occurs in urine occasionally along with hemosiderin.

hemogen'esis. Hemopoiesis.

hemogen'ic. Hemopoietic.

he'moglo'bin (Hb). The red respiratory protein of erythrocytes, consisting of approximately 6% heme and 94% globin, that transports oxygen (as oxyhemoglobin, HbO_2) from the lungs to the tissues, where the oxygen is readily released and HbO_2 becomes Hb. In man there are four kinds of normal Hb; embryonic (Hb Gower), fetal (Hb F), and two adult types (Hb A, Hb A_2), each consisting of two alpha globin chains containing 141 amino acid residues, and two of another kind (beta, gamma, delta or epsilon) each containing 146 amino acid residues.

Hb Bart's, a Hb homotetramer found in the early embryo and in β-thalassemia; not effective in oxygen transport.

Hb C, an abnormal Hb with substitution of lysine for glutamic acid at the 6th position of the beta chain; reduces the normal plasticity of erythrocytes; two types cause sickling of erythrocytes similar to Hb S

carbon monoxide h., carboxyhemoglobin.

glycosylated h., any one of four h. fractions (A_{Ia1}, A_{Ia2}, A_{Ib}, or A_{Ic}) which together account for less than 4% of the total h. in blood.

Hb H, homotetramer found only when alpha chain synthesis is depressed; not effective in oxygen transport and is involved in a thalassemia-like syndrome in individuals heterozygous for both severe and mild genes for alpha thalassemia.

Hb M, a group of abnormal Hb's in which a single amino acid substitution favors the formation of methemoglobin in spite of normal quantities of methemoglobin reductase enzyme; heterozygotes have congenital methemoglobinemia.

mean cell h. (MCH), the h. content of the average red cell, calculated from the h. therein and the red cell count, in erythrocyte indices.

muscle h., myoglobin.

oxygenated h., oxyhemoglobin.

reduced h., h. in red blood cells after the oxygen of oxyhemoglobin is released in the tissues.

Hb S, sickle cell h., an abnormal Hb with substitution of valine for glutamic acid at the 6th position of the beta chain. The heterozygous state results in sickle cell trait; homozygous state, sickle cell anemia.

he'moglobine'mia. Presence of free hemoglobin in the blood plasma.

he'moglobinol'ysis [hemoglobin + G. *lysis,* dissolution]. Destruction or chemical splitting of hemoglobin.

hemoglobinopathy (he'mo-glo-bĭ-nop'ă-thĭ) [hemoglobin + G. *pathos,* disease]. A disorder or disease caused by or associated with the presence of abnormal hemoglobins in the blood.

he'moglo'binophil'ic [hemoglobin + G. *phileō,* to love]. Relating to certain microorganisms that cannot be cultured except in the presence of hemoglobin.

hemoglobinuria (he'mo-glo-bĭ-nu'rĭ-ah) [hemoglobin + G. *ouron,* urine]. Presence of hemoglobin in the urine, including certain closely related pigments formed from slight alteration of the hemoglobin molecule, due to the Donath-Lansteiner cold autoantibody; in sufficient quantities, they result in the urine being colored from light red-yellow to fairly dark red.

epidemic h., presence of hemoglobin, or of pigments derived from it, in the urine of young infants, attended with cyanosis, jaundice, and other conditions.

march h., h. occurring after prolonged or heavy physical exercise.

toxic h., h. occurring after the ingestion of various poisons, in certain blood diseases, and in certain infections.

he'moglobinu'ric. Relating to or marked by hemoglobinuria.

he'mogram [hemo- + G. *gramma,* a drawing]. A record of the findings in an examination of the blood, especially with reference to the numbers, proportions, and morphologic features of the formed elements.

he'mohis'tioblast [hemo- + G. *histion,* web, + *blastos,* germ]. A primitive mesenchymal cell believed to be capable of developing into all types of blood cells, including monocytes, and into histiocytes.

he'molith [hemo- + G. *lithos,* stone]. A concretion in the wall of a blood vessel.

he'molymph [hemo- + L. *lympha,* clear water]. The blood and lymph, in the sense of a circulating tissue.

hemolysate (he-mol'ĭ-sāt). The preparation resulting from the lysis of erythrocytes.

hemolysin (he-mol'ĭ-sin). **1.** Erythrocytolysin; erythrolysin; any substance elaborated by a living agent and capable of causing lysis of red blood cells and liberation of their hemoglobin. **2.** A sensitizing (complement-fixing) antibody that combines with red blood cells of the antigenic type that stimulated formation of the h., affecting the cells in such a manner that complement fixes with the antibody-cell union and causes dissolution of the cells, with liberation of their hemoglobin.

hemolysinogen (he'mo-li-sin'o-jen). The antigenic material in red blood cells that stimulates the formation of hemolysin.

hemolysis (he-mol'ĭ-sis) [hemo- + G. *lysis,* destruction]. Erythrolysis; erythrocytolysis; hematolysis; the alteration, dissolution, or destruction of red blood cells in such a manner that hemoglobin is liberated.

he'molyt'ic. Hematolytic; hemotoxic (2); destructive to blood cells, resulting in liberation of hemoglobin.

hemolyze (he'mo-līz). To produce hemolysis or liberation of the hemoglobin from red blood cells.

he'mome'tra. Hematometra.

hemomediastinum (he'mo-me-dĭ-ă-sti'num). Blood in the mediastinum.

hemonephrosis (he'mo-nĕ-fro'sis) [hemo- + G. *nephros,* kidney]. Blood in the pelvis of the kidney.

he'monor'moblast. Erythroblast.

he'mopathol'ogy. Hematopathology.

hemopathy (he-mop'ă-thĭ) [hemo- + G. *pathos,* suffering]. Any abnormal condition or disease of the blood or hemopoietic tissues.

hemopericardium (he'mo-pĕr'ĭ-kar'dĭ-um). Blood in the pericardial sac.

hemoperitoneum (he'mo-pĕr-ĭ-to-ne'um). Blood in the peritoneal cavity.

he'mopex'in. A serum protein related to β-globulins, consisting of sialic acid, mannose, galactose, fructose, and hexosamine; important in binding heme and porphyrins.

hemophil, hemophile (he'mo-fil, -fī) [hemo- + G. *philos,* fond]. Applied to microorganisms growing preferably in media containing blood.

hemophilia (he'mo-fil'ĭ-ah) [hemo- + G. *philos,* fond]. Angiostaxis (2); an inherited disorder of the blood marked by a permanent tendency to hemorrhages, spontaneous or traumatic, due to a defect in the coagulating power of the blood.

h. A., h. due to deficiency of factor VIII; an X-linked recessive condition occurring almost exclusively in males, characterized by prolonged clotting time, decreased formation of thromboplastin, and diminished conversion of prothrombin.

h. B., Christmas disease; a clotting disorder resembling h. A, caused by the hereditary deficiency of factor IX.

vascular h., von Willebrand's *disease.*

hemophiliac (he-mo-fil′ĭ-ak). A person suffering from hemophilia.

hemophilic (he-mo-fil′ik). Relating to hemophilia.

hemophoresis (he′mo-fo-re′sis) [hemo- + G. *phoreō,* to bear]. Blood convection or irrigation of tissues.

hemophthalmia (he′mof-thal′mĭ-ah) [hemo- + G. *ophthalmos,* eye]. An effusion of blood into the eyeball.

he′moplas′tic [hemo- + G. *plassō,* to form]. Hemopoietic.

hemopneumopericardium (he′mo-nu′mo-pĕr-ĭ-kar′dĭ-um). Pneumohemopericardium; the occurrence of blood and air in the pericardium.

hemopneumothorax (he′mo-nu-mo-tho′raks) [hemo- + G. *pneuma,* air, + thorax]. Pneumohemothorax; accumulation of air and blood in the pleural cavity.

hemopoiesis (he′mo-poy-e′sis) [hemo- + G. *poiēsis,* a making]. Hematogenesis; hematopoiesis; hemogenesis; sanguification; formation and development of the various types of blood cells and other formed elements.

hemopoietic (he′mo-poy-et′ik). Hematogenic (1); hematogenous (1); hematopoietic; hematoplastic; hemogenic; hemoplastic; sanguifacient; pertaining to or related to the formation of blood cells.

hemoporphyrin (he-mo-por′fĭ-rin). Hematoporphyrin.

he′moprecip′itin. An antibody that combines with and precipitates soluble antigenic material from erythrocytes.

hemoprotein (he-mo-pro′tēn). Protein linked to a metal-porphyrin compound.

hemoptysis (he-mop′tĭ-sis) [hemo- + G. *ptysis,* a spitting]. The spitting of blood derived from the lungs or bronchial tubes.

hemorrhachis (he-mor′ă-kis). Hematorrhachis.

hemorrhage (hem′ŏ-rij) [G. *haima,* blood, + *rhēgnymi,* to burst forth]. Hemorrhea; bleeding; an escape of blood from the vessels.

cerebral h., encephalorrhagia (1); hematencephalon; h. into the substance of the cerebrum, usually in the region of the internal capsule by the rupture of the lenticulostriate artery.

concealed h., internal h.

extradural h., epidural hematoma; an accumulation of blood between the skull and the dura mater.

internal h., concealed h.; bleeding into organs or cavities of the body.

intracranial h., escape of blood within the cranium due to loss of integrity of vascular channels, frequently leading to formation of a hematoma.

intrapartum h., h. occurring in the course of normal labor and delivery.

parenchymatous h., bleeding into the substance of an organ.

petechial h., punctate h.; capillary h. into the skin, forming petechiae.

postpartum h., h. from the birth canal in excess of 500 ml during the first 24 hours after birth.

primary h., h. immediately after an injury or operation.

punctate h., petechial h.

secondary h., h. at an interval after an injury or an operation.

subdural h., subdural hematoma; extravasation of blood between the dural and arachnoidal membranes.

hemorrhagenic (hem-ŏ-ră-jen′ik) [hemorrhage + G. *genesis,* production]. Causing or producing hemorrhage.

hemorrhagic (hem-ŏ-raj′ik). Relating to or marked by hemorrhage.

hemorrhagins (hem-o-raj′inz, -ra′jins). A group of toxins, found in certain venoms and poisonous material from some plants, that causes degeneration and lysis of endothelial cells in capillaries and small vessels, thereby resulting in numerous small hemorrhages in the tissues.

hemorrhea (hem′o-re-ah) [G. *haimorrhoia,* fr. *haima,* blood, + *rhoia,* a flow]. Hemorrhage.

hemorrhoid (hem′ŏ-royd). Denoting one of the tumors or varices constituting hemorrhoids.

hemorrhoidal (hem-ŏ-roy′dal). **1.** Relating to hemorrhoids. **2.** Denoting certain arteries and veins supplying the region of the rectum and anus.

hemorrhoidectomy (hem′ŏ-roy-dek′to-mĭ) [hemorrhoids + G. *ektomē,* excision]. Surgical removal of hemorrhoids, as by excision of hemorrhoidal tissues or by ligation to produce ischemic necrosis and ultimate ablation of the h.

hemorrhoids (hem′ŏ-roydz) [G. *haimorrhois,* pl. *haimorrhoides,* veins likely to bleed]. Piles; a varicose condition of the external hemorrhoidal veins causing painful swellings at the anus: **external h.,** when the dilated veins form tumors to the outer side of the external sphincter, or are covered by the skin of the anal canal; **internal h.,** when the swollen veins are beneath the mucous membrane within the sphincter.

he′mosal′pinx. Hematosalpinx.

he′mosid′erin. An insoluble protein produced by phagocytic digestion of hematin and found in most tissues, especially in the liver, in the form of granules much larger than ferritin molecules.

he′mosidero′sis. Abnormal accumulation of hemosiderin in tissue.

he′mosper′mia [hemo- + G. *sperma,* seed]. Presence of blood in the seminal fluid.

hemostasis (he-mos′tă-sis, he′mo-sta-sis) [hemo- + G. *stasis,* a standing]. **1.** The arrest of bleeding. **2.** The arrest of circulation in a part. **3.** Stagnation of blood.

he′mostat. **1.** An antihemorrhagic agent. **2.** An instrument for arresting hemorrhage by compression of the bleeding vessel.

he'mostat'ic. Hematostatic (1). **1.** Arresting the flow of blood within the vessels. **2.** Arresting hemorrhage.

hemotherapy (he-mo-thĕr'ă-pī). Treatment of disease by the use of blood or blood derivatives, such as transfusion.

he'mothorax. Blood in the pleural cavity.

he'motox'ic. Hematotoxic. **1.** Causing blood poisoning. **2.** Hemolytic.

he'motox'in. Hematotoxin; any substance that causes destruction of red blood cells; usually referring to substances of biologic origin in contrast to chemicals.

hemotroph (he'mo-trŏf) [hemo- + G. *trophē*, food]. Materials supplied to the embryo through the maternal blood stream.

he'motrop'ic [hemo- + G. *tropos*, a turning]. Hematotropic; pertaining to the mechanism by which a substance in or on blood cells, especially erythrocytes, attracts phagocytic cells.

hemotympanum (he'mo-tim'pă-num). Hematotympanum; presence of blood in the middle ear.

HEMPAS Hereditary erythroblastic multinuclearity associated with positive acidified serum. See HEMPAS *cells.*

henry (H) (hen'rī) [J. *Henry*]. The unit of electrical inductance, when 1 volt is induced by a change in current of 1 ampere/sec.

he'par, gen. **he'patis** [L. borrowed fr. G. *hēpar*, gen. *hēpatos,* the liver] [NA]. The liver.

hep'arin. An anticoagulant principle that is a constituent of various tissues (especially liver and lung) and mast cells; principle and active constituent is a mucopolysaccharide comprised of D-glucuronic acid and D-glucosamine, both sulfated, in 1,4-α linkage. In conjunction with a serum protein cofactor, h. is an antithrombin and an antiprothrombin by preventing platelet agglutination and thus prevents thrombus formation; also enhances activity of clearing factors.

hep'arinize. Therapeutic administration of heparin.

hepat-, hepatico-, hepato- [G. *hēpar* (*hēpat*-), liver]. Combining forms denoting the liver.

hepatalgia (hep-ă-tal'jī-ah) [hepat- + G. *algos*, pain]. Hepatodynia; pain in the liver.

hepatatrophia, hepatatrophy (hep'ă-tă-tro'fī-ah, hep-ă-tat'ro-fī). Atrophy of the liver.

hepatectomy (hep'ă-tek'to-mī) [hepat- + G. *ektomē*, excision]. Excision of liver tissue.

hepat'ic [G. *hēpatikos*]. Relating to the liver.

hepatico-. See hepat-.

hepaticodochotomy (hĕ-pat'ī-ko-do-kot'o-mī). Combined choledochotomy and hepaticotomy.

hepaticoduodenostomy (hĕ-pat'ī-ko-du'o-de-nos'to-mī) [hepatico- + duodenostomy]. Establishment of a communication between the hepatic ducts and the duodenum.

hepaticoenterostomy (hĕ-pat'ī-ko-en-ter-os'to-mī) [hepatico- + enterostomy]. Establishment of a communication between the hepatic ducts and the intestine.

hepaticogastrostomy (hĕ-pat'ī-ko-gas-tros'to-mī) [hepatico- + gastrostomy]. Establishment of a communication between the hepatic duct and the stomach.

hepat'icolithot'omy [hepatico- + G. *lithos*, stone, + *tomē*, a cutting]. Removal of the calculus from a hepatic duct.

hepaticolithotripsy (hĕ-pat'ī-ko-lith'o-trip-sī) [hepatico- + G. *lithos*, stone, + *tripsis*, a rubbing]. Crushing a biliary calculus in the hepatic duct.

hepaticostomy (hĕ-pat-ī-kos'to-mī) [hepatico- + G. *stoma*, mouth]. Establishment of an opening into the hepatic duct.

hepaticotomy (hĕ-pat-ī-kot'o-mī) [hepatico- + G. *tomē*, incision]. Incision into the hepatic duct.

hepatit'ic. Relating to hepatitis.

hepatitis (hep'ă-ti'tis) [hepat- + G. *-itis*, inflammation]. Inflammation of the liver.

  h. A, viral h. type A.

  active chronic h., posthepatitic cirrhosis; h. with chronic portal inflammation that extends into the parenchyma.

  anicteric virus h., a relatively mild h., without jaundice, due to a virus.

  h. B, viral h. type B.

  cholangiolitic h., h. with inflammatory changes around small bile ducts, producing primarily obstructive jaundice.

  infectious h., (IH), viral h. type A.

  lupoid h., jaundice with evidence of liver cell damage and positive L.E. cell tests, but without evidence of systemic lupus erythematosus.

  neonatal h., h. of unknown cause, characterized by onset of obstructive jaundice in the neonatal period, and hepatocellular degeneration with multinucleated giant cell transformation of liver cells.

  non-A, non-B h., h. caused by an infectious agents antigenically different from h. viruses A and B; in the acute stage, it is generally milder than h. B, but a greater proportion of such infections become chronic.

  persistent chronic h., benign chronic h. which may follow acute viral h. A or B, or complicate bowel diseases.

  serum h. (SH), viral h. type B.

  viral h., a disease characterized by fever, nausea, vomiting, and jaundice, associated with inflammation of the liver and necrosis of scattered liver cells; caused by h. A virus, h. B virus, or non-A, non-B virus.

  viral h. type A, infectious h.; virus A h.; h. A; a virus disease with a short incubation period caused by h. virus A; occurs sporadically or in epidemics; transmission is by the fecal-oral route, with necrosis of liver cells characteristic and jaundice a common symptom.

  viral h. type B, serum h.; h. B; a virus disease with a long incubation period caused by h. virus B, usually transmitted by injection of infected blood or blood derivatives or by contaminated instruments; clinically and pathologically, the disease is similar to viral h. type A; however, there is no cross-protective immunity and viral antigen (HBAg) is found in the serum.

hepatization (hep'ă-tĭ-za'shun). Conversion of a loose tissue into a firm mass like the substance of the liver macroscopically, denoting especially such a change in the lungs in the consolidation of pneumonia.

gray h., the second stage of h. in pneumonia, when the yellowish-gray exudate is beginning to degenerate prior to breaking down.

red h., the first stage of h. in which the exudate is blood-stained.

yellow h., the final stage of h. in which the exudate is becoming purulent.

hepato-. See hepat-.

hep'atoblasto'ma. A malignant neoplasm, occurring in children, primarily in the liver, composed of tissue resembling fetal or mature liver cells or bile ducts.

hep'atocarcino'ma. Malignant *hepatoma*.

hepatocele (hep'ă-to-sēl, hĕ, pat'o-sēl) [hepato- + G. *kēlē*, hernia]. Hernia of the liver; protrusion of part of the liver through the abdominal wall or the diaphragm.

hepatocholangiojejunostomy (hep'ă-to-ko-lan'jĭ-o-je-ju-nos'to-mī) [hepato- + G. *cholē*, bile, + *angeion*, vessel, + jejunostomy]. Union of the hepatic duct to the jejunum.

hepatocholangiostomy (hep'ă-to-ko-lan-jĭ-os'to-mī). Creation of an opening into the common bile duct to establish drainage.

hepatocholangitis (hep'ă-to-ko-lan-ji'tis). Inflammation of the liver and biliary tree.

hep'atocys'tic [hepato- + G. *kystis*, bladder]. Relating to the gallbladder, or to both liver and gallbladder.

hep'atocyte. A parenchymal liver cell.

hep'atodyn'ia [hepato- + G. *odynē*, pain]. Hepatalgia.

hepatoenteric (hep'ă-to-en-tĕr'ik) [hepato- + G. *enteron*, intestine]. Relating to the liver and the intestine.

hep'atogas'tric. Relating to the liver and the stomach.

hepatogenic, hepatogenous (hep-ă-to-jen'ik, -toj'en-us) [Of hepatic origin; formed in the liver.

hepatog'raphy [hepato- + G. *graphē*, a writing]. Radiography of the liver.

hepatoid (hep'ă-toyd) [hepato- + G. *eidos*, resemblance]. Resembling the liver.

hep'atolith [hepato- + G. *lithos*, stone]. A concretion in the liver.

hepatolithectomy (hep'ă-to-lĭ-thek'to-mī) [hepato- + G. *lithos*, stone, + *ektomē*, excision]. Removal of a calculus from the liver.

hepatolithiasis (hep'ă-to-lĭ-thi'ă-sis) [hepato- + G. *lithiasis*, presence of a calculus]. Presence of calculi in the liver.

hepatology (hep'ă-tol'o-jī) [hepato- + G. *logos*, study]. The branch of medical science concerned with the liver and its diseases.

hepatolysin (hep-ă-tol'ĭ-sin). A cytolysin that destroys parenchymal cells of the liver.

hepato'ma [hepato- + G. *-oma*, tumor]. See malignant h.

malignant h., hepatocellular carcinoma; hepatocarcinoma; a carcinoma derived from parenchymal cells of the liver.

hepatomalacia (hep'ă-to-mă-la'shĭ-ah) [hepato- + G. *malakia*, softening]. Softening of the liver.

hepatomegaly (hep'ă-to-meg'ă-lĭ) [hepato- + G. *megas*, large]. Megalohepatia; enlargement of the liver.

hepatomelanosis (hep'ă-to-mel'ă-no'sis) [hepato- + G. *melas*, black, + *-osis*, condition]. Deep pigmentation of the liver.

hepatomphalocele (hep'ă-tom-fal'o-sēl, -tom'fă-lo-sēl) [hepato- + omphalocele]. Umbilical hernia with involvement of the liver.

hepatonephric (hep'ă-to-nef'rik). Hepatorenal; relating to the liver and the kidney.

hep'atopath'ic. Damaging the liver.

hepatopathy (hep'ă-top'ă-thī) [hepato- + G. *pathos*, suffering]. A disease of the liver.

hepatopexy (hep'ă-to-pek-sī) [hepato- + G. *pēxis*, fixation]. Anchoring of the liver to the abdominal wall.

hepatopneumonic (hep'ă-to-nu-mon'ik) [hepato- + G. *pneumonikos*, pulmonary]. Hepatopulmonary; relating to the liver and the lungs.

hep'atopor'tal. Relating to the portal system of the liver.

hep'atopul'monary. Hepatopneumonic.

hepatore'nal [hepato- + L. *renalis*, renal, fr. *renes*, kidneys]. Hepatonephric.

hepatorrhaphy (hep-ă-tor'ă-fī) [hepato- + G. *rhaphē*, a suture]. Suture of a wound of the liver.

hepatorrhexis (hep'ă-to-rek'sis) [hepato- + G. *rhēxis*, rupture]. Rupture of the liver.

hepatoscopy (hep'ă-tos'ko-pī) [hepato- + G. *skopeō*, to examine]. Examination of the liver.

hepatosplenitis (hep'ă-to-sple-ni'tis). Inflammation of the liver and spleen.

hepatosplenography (hep'ă-to-sple-nog'ră-fī). Use of contrast dyes to depict the liver and spleen radiographically.

hepatosplenomegaly (hep'ă-to-sple-no-meg'ă-lĭ) [hepato- + G. *splēn*, spleen, + *megas*, large]. Enlargement of the liver and spleen.

hepatosplenopathy (hep'ă-to-sple-nop'ă-thī). Disease of the liver and spleen.

hepatotomy (hep-ă-tot'o-mī) [hepato- + G. *tomē*, incision]. Incision into the liver.

hep'atotox'ic. Damaging or destructive to the liver.

hep'atotox'in. A toxin that is destructive to parenchymal cells of the liver.

hepatotoxemia (hep′ă-to-tok-se′mĭ-ah) [hepato- + G. *toxikon*, poison, + *haima*, blood]. Autointoxication originating in the liver.

hepta- [G. *hepta*, seven]. Prefix denoting seven.

hep′tose. A sugar with 7 carbon atoms in its molecule.

herd. An immunologic concept of an ecologic composite that includes susceptible animal species (including man), vectors, and environmental factors.

hereditary (hĕ-red′ĭ-tĕr-ĭ). Relating to heredity.

heredity (hĕ-red′ĭ-tĭ) [L. *hereditas*, inheritance, fr. *heres* (*hered*-), heir]. **1.** Genetic transmission of characters from parent to offspring. **2.** One's genetic constitution.

heredo- [L. *heres*, an heir]. Prefix denoting heredity.

heredofamilial (hĕr′e-do-fă-mil′ĭ-al). Denoting an inherited condition present in more than one member of a family.

heritability (hĕr-ĭ-tă-bil′ĭ-tĭ) [See heredity]. In genetics, the proportion of phenotypic variance due to variance in genotypes.

hermaphrodite (her-maf′ro-dīt) [G. *Hermaphroditus*, son of *Hermēs* + *Aphroditē*]. An individual with hermaphroditism.

hermaphroditism (her-maf′ro-dĭt-izm). Presence in one individual of both ovarian and testicular tissue.

    bilateral h., true h. with ovotestis on both sides.

    false h., pseudohermaphroditism.

    lateral h., h. which a testis is present on one side and an ovary on the other.

    transverse h., pseudohermaphroditism in which the external genital organs are characteristic of one sex and the gonads are characteristic of the other sex.

    unilateral h., h. in which the doubling of sex characteristics occurs only on one side: ovotestis on one side and either ovary or testis on the other.

hermet′ic. Denoting a container closed or sealed in such a way that it is airtight.

hernia (her′nĭ-ah) [L. rupture]. Rupture (1); the protrusion of a part or structure through the tissues normally containing it.

    abdominal h., laparocele; a h. protruding through or into any part of the abdominal wall.

    Barth's h., a loop of intestine between a persistent vitelline duct and the abdominal wall.

    Béclard's h., femoral h. through the opening for the saphenous vein.

    Bochdalek's h., a dorsolateral diaphragmatic h. associated with a developmental defect in the pleuroperitoneal membrane.

    cerebral h., protrusion of brain substance through a defect in the skull.

    Cloquet's h., a femoral h. perforating the aponeurosis of the pectineus and insinuating itself between this aponeurosis and the muscle, lying behind the femoral vessels.

    complete h., an indirect inguinal h. in which the contents extend into the tunica vaginalis.

    crural h., femoral h.

    diaphragmatic h., diaphragmatocele; protrusion of abdominal contents into the chest through a weakness in the respiratory diaphragm.

    epigastric h., h. through the linea alba above the navel.

    extrasaccular h., sliding h.

    fatty h., pannicular h.

    femoral h., enteromerocele; femorocele; crural h.; h. through the femoral ring.

    gastroesophageal h., a hiatal h. into the thorax.

    Hesselbach's h., h. with diverticula through the cribriform fascia, presenting a lobular outline.

    hiatal h., hiatus h., h. of a part of the stomach through the esophageal hiatus of the diaphragm.

    Holthouse's h., inguinal h. with extension of the loop of intestine along the inguinal ligament.

    incarcerated h., irreducible h.

    incisional h., h. occurring through a surgical incision or scar.

    inguinal h., a h. at the inguinal region: **direct i. h.** involves the abdominal wall between the deep epigastric artery and the edge of the rectus muscle; **indirect i. h.** involves the internal inguinal ring and passes into the inguinal canal.

    interstitial h., a h. in which the protrusion is between any two of the layers of the abdominal wall.

    irreducible h., incarcerated h.; a h. that cannot be reduced without an operation.

    ischiatic h., a h. through the sacrosciatic foramen.

    labial h., cremnocele.

    Littre's h., (1) parietal h.; (2) h. of Meckel's diverticulum.

    lumbar h., a protrusion between the last rib and the iliac crest where the aponeurosis of the transversus muscle is covered only by the latissimus dorsi.

    obturator h., h. through the obturator foramen.

    pannicular h., fatty h.; escape of subcutaneous fat through a gap in a fascia or an aponeurosis.

    paraperitoneal h., a vesical h. in which only a part of the protruded organ is covered by the peritoneum of the sac.

    parietal h., Richter's h.; Littre's h. (1); h. in which only a portion of the wall of the intestine is engaged.

    perineal h., perineocele; a h. protruding through the pelvic diaphragm.

    reducible h., a h. in which the contents of the h. sac can be returned to their normal location by manipulation.

    retrograde h., a double loop h., the central loop of which lies in the abdominal cavity.

    Richter's h., parietal h.

    sciatic h., ischiocele; protrusion of intestine through the great sacrosciatic foramen.

    scrotal h., oscheocele; scrotocele; a complete inguinal h. located in the scrotum.

    sliding h., extrasaccular or slipped h.; a h. in which an abdominal viscus forms part of the sac.

    slipped h., sliding h.

strangulated h., an irreducible h. in which the circulation is arrested.

synovial h., protrusion of a fold of the stratum synoviale through a rent in the stratum fibrosum of a joint capsule.

umbilical h., exomphalos (2); a h. in which bowel or omentum protrudes through the abdominal wall under the skin at the umbilicus.

vesicle h., protrusion of a segment of the bladder through the abdominal wall or into the inguinal canal and into the scrotum.

vitreous h., internal prolapse of the vitreous into the anterior chamber; may follow removal or displacement of the lens from the lenticular space.

her′nial. Relating to hernia.

her′niated. Denoting any structure protruded through a hernial opening.

herniation (her′nĭ-a′shun). Formation of a hernia.

hernio- [L. *hernia,* rupture]. Combining form relating to hernia.

hernioid (her′nĭ-oyd) [hernio- + G. *eidos,* resemblance]. Resembling hernia.

herniology (her′nĭ-ol-o-jĭ) [hernio- + G. *logos,* study]. The aspect of surgery concerned with hernia.

her′nioplasty hernio- + G. *plassō,* to form]. Surgical correction of a hernia.

herniorrhaphy (her′nĭ-or′ă-fĭ) [hernio- + G. *rhaphē,* a seam]. Surgical correction of a hernia by suturing.

herniotomy (her-nĭ-ot′o-mĭ) [hernio- + G. *tomē,* a cutting]. Celotomy; kelotomy; surgical correction of a hernia by cutting.

heroic (he-ro′ik) [G. *hērōïkōs,* pertaining to a hero]. Denoting an aggressive, daring procedure which in itself may endanger the patient but which also has a possibility of being successful, whereas lesser action would result in failure.

heroin (hĕr′o-in). Diacetylmorphine; an addictive alkaloid, $C_{17}H_{17}(OC_2H_3O)_2ON$, prespared from morphine by acetylation.

herpangina (herp-an′jĭ-nah, herp-an-ji′nah). A disease caused by types of coxsackievirus and marked by a sudden onset of fever, loss of appetitie, dysphagia, pharyngitis, and sometimes abdominal pain, nausea, and vomiting; vesiculopapular lesions are present around the fauces and soon ulcerate.

herpes (her′pēz) [G. *herpēs,* a spreading skin eruption, shingles]. Serpigo (2); an eruption of groups of deep-seated vesicles on erythematous bases.

genital h., h. genita′lis, herpetic lesions on the penis of the male or on the cervix, perineum, vagina, or vulva of the female, caused by herpesvirus (herpes simplex virus) type 2.

h. gestatio′nis, a polymorphous, bullous eruption, more common on the extremities than on the trunk, with the appearance of pemphigoid or dermatitis herpetiformis; recurrent during each subsequent pregnancy after onset.

h. i′ris, (1) *erythema* iris; (2) *erythema* multiforme.

neonatal h., herpesvirus type 2 infection transmitted to the newborn infant during passage through an infected birth canal.

h. sim′plex, fever blister; cold sore; a variety of infections caused by h. simplex virus (herpesvirus) types 1 and 2; type 1 infections are marked by the eruption of one or more groups of vesicles on the vermilion border of the lips or at the external nares, type 2 by such lesions on the genitalia; both types commonly are recrudescent and reappear during other febrile illnesses or certain physiologic states.

h. zos′ter, zona (2); zoster; shingles; an infection caused by a herpetovirus (varicella-zoster virus) and characterized by an eruption of groups of vesicles on one side of the body following the course of a nerve due to inflammation of ganglia and dorsal nerve roots resulting from activation of the virus which has been latent; the condition is self-limited but may be accompanied by or followed by severe pain.

Her′pesvi′rus. A genus (family Herpetoviridae) including herpes simplex and closely related viruses.

herpesvirus (her′pēz-vi′rus). 1. Herpes simplex virus; a virus of the genus *Herpesvirus* (family Herpetoviridae), divided into two types: **h. type 1,** the pathogen of herpes simplex in humans, causing acute stomatitis, especially in children, and fever blisters, usually on the lips and external nares; also causes eczema herpeticum and herpetic gingivostomatitis, keratoconjunctivitis, and meningoencephalitis; **h. type 2,** the pathogen of genital herpes and neonatal herpes. 2. Formerly, any virus of the genus *Herpesvirus,* which then included those viruses now grouped in the family Herpetoviridae, now herpetovirus.

herpet′ic. 1. Relating to or characterized by herpes. 2. Relating to a herpetovirus or herpesvirus.

herpet′iform. Resembling herpes.

Herpetoviridae (her′pĕ-to-vĭr′ĭ-de). A family of morphologically similar viruses, all of which contain double-stranded DNA, whose infections produce type A inclusion bodies; only one genus, *Herpesvirus,* has been established. The family includes herpes simplex virus, varicella-zoster virus, cytomegalovirus, and EB virus (which infect man), and many others.

herpetovirus (her′pĕ-to-vi′rus). Any virus belonging to the family Herpetoviridae.

hersage (ār-sahzh′) [Fr. (from L. *hirpex,* a large rake), a harrowing]. Surgical separation of the individual fibers of a nerve trunk.

hertz (**Hz**) [H. R. *Hertz*]. A unit of frequency equivalent to 1 cycle per second.

hesitancy (hez′ĭ-tăn-sĭ). An involuntary delay or inability in starting the urinary stream.

heter-. See hetero-.

heterecious (het-er-e′shī-us) [heter- + G. *oikion,* home]. Metoxenous; having more than one host, said of a parasite passing different states of its existence in different animals.

heterecism (het'er-e-sizm) [heter- + G. *oikion*, home]. Metoxeny (1); the occurrence, in parasite, of two cycles of existence, passed in two different hosts.

heteresthesia (het'er-es-the'zĭ-ah) [heter- + G. *aisthēsis*, sensation]. A change occurring in the degree (either plus or minus) of the sensory response to a cutaneous stimulus as the latter crosses a certain line on the skin's surface.

hetero-, heter- [G. *heteros*, other]. Combining form meaning other, or different.

het'eroagglu'tinin. A form of hemagglutinin that agglutinates the red blood cells of species other than that in which the h. occurs.

heteroantibody (het'er-o-an'tĭ-bod-ĭ). Antibody that is heterologous with respect to antigen.

heteroblas'tic [hetero- + G. *blastos*, germ]. Developing from more than a single type of tissue.

het'erocel'lular. Formed of cells of different kinds.

heterochromatin (het'er-o-kro'mă-tin). See chromatin.

heterochromia (het-er-o-kro'mĭ-ah) [hetero- + G. *chrōma*, color]. A difference in coloration in two structures or two parts of the same structure which are normally alike in color.

heterochromosome (het'er-o-kro'mo-sōm). Allosome.

heterochromous (het'er-o-kro'mus). Having an abnormal difference in coloration.

heterochronia (het-er-o-kro'nĭ-ah) [hetero- + G. *chronos*, time]. The origin or development of tissues or organs at an unusual time or out of the regular sequence.

heterochronic (het-er-o-kron'ik). Hetrochronous.

heterochronous (het-er-ok'ro-nus). Heterochronic; relating to heterochronia.

heterocrine (het'er-o-krin) [hetero- + G. *krinō*, to separate]. Denoting the secretion of two or more kinds of material.

heterocytotropic (het'er-o-si'to-tro'pik, -trop'ik) [hetero- + G. *kytos*, cell, + *tropē* a turning toward]. Having an affinity for cells of a different species.

heterodromous (het-ĕr-ŏd'ro-mus) [hetero- + G. *dromos*, running]. Moving in the opposite direction.

heteroerotic (het'er-o-e-rot'ik). Alloerotic.

heteroerotism (het'er-o-ĕr'o-tizm). Alloeroticism.

het'erogamet'ic [hetero- + G. *gametikos*, connubial]. Relating to production of gametes of contrasting types with respect to sex chromosomes.

heterog'amous. Relating to heterogamy.

heterogamy (het'er-og'ă-mĭ) [hetro- + G. *gamos*, marriage]. 1. Conjugation of unlike gametes. 2. Alternation of generations in which two kinds of sexual generation alternate.

het'erogene'ic, het'erogen'ic. Pertaining to different gene constitutions, especially with respect to different species.

heterogeneity (het'er-o-jĕ-ne'ĭ-tĭ). The state of being heterogeneous.

heterogeneous (het'er-o-je'ne-us). Composed of parts having various and dissimilar characteristics or properties.

heterogenesis (het-er-o-jen'ĕ-sis) [hetero- + G. *genesis*, production]. Production of offspring unlike the parents.

heterogenetic (het'er-o-jĕ-net'ik). Relating to heterogenesis.

heterogenous (het-er-oj'ĕ-nus). Of different or dissimilar origin.

het'erograft. Heterotransplant; heterologous, heteroplastic, heterospecific, or interspecific graft; xenograft; a graft transferred from an animal of one species to one of another species.

heterokinesis (het'er-o-kĭ-ne'sis). Differential distribution of X and Y chromosomes during meiotic cell division.

het'erola'lia [hetero- + G. *lalia*, speech]. Heterophasia; heterophemia; a form of aphasia characterized by habitual substitution of meaningless or inappropriate words for those intended.

het'erolat'eral [hetero- + L. *latus*, side]. Contralateral.

heterologous (het-er-ol'o-gus) [hetero- + G. *logos*, ratio, relation]. 1. Pertaining to cytologic or histologic elements occurring where they are not normally found. 2. Derived from a different species.

heterolysis (het-er-ol'ĭ-sis) [hetero- + G. *lysis*, a loosening]. Dissolution or digestion of cells or protein components from one species by a lytic agent from a different species.

het'erolyt'ic. Pertaining to heterolysis.

heteromeric (het'er-o-mĕr'ik) [hetero- + G. *meros*, part]. 1. Having a different chemical composition. 2. Denoting spinal neurons that have processes passing over to the opposite side of the cord.

heterometaplasia (het'er-o-met-ă-pla'zĭ-ah). Tissue transformation resulting in the production of a tissue foreign to the part where produced.

het'erometro'pia [hetero- + G. *metron*, measure, + *ōps*, eye]. A condition in which the degree of refraction is unlike in the two eyes.

het'eromor'phous. Differing from the normal type.

heteromorphosis (het'er-o-mor-fo'sis) [hetero- + G. *morphōsis*, a molding]. 1. Development of one tissue from a tissue of another kind or type. 2. Embryonic development of tissue or an organ inappropriate to its site.

heteronomous (het-er-on'o-mus) [hetero- + G. *nomos*, law]. 1. Different from the type; abnormal. 2. Subject to the direction or law of another; not self-governing.

heteronomy (het-er-on'o-mĭ) [hetero- + G. *nomos*, law]. The condition or state of being heteronomous.

heteropathy (het-er-op'ă-thĭ) [hetero- + G. *pathos* suffering]. Abnormal sensitivity to stimuli.

heterophagy (het-er-of'ă-jĭ) [hetero- + G. *phagein*, to eat]. Digestion within a cell of a substance phagocytosed from the cell's environment.

heterophasia (het-er-o-fa'zĭ-ah) [hetero- + G. *phasis*, speech]. Heterolalia.

heterophemia (het-er-o-fe'mĭ-ah) [hetero- + G. *phēmē*, a speech]. Heterolalia.

heterophil, heterophile (het'er-o-fil, -fĭl) [hetero- + G. *philos, fond*]. 1. In man, the neutrophil leukocyte. 2. Pertaining to heterogenetic antigens and related antibody.

het'eropho'nia [hetero- + G. *phōnē*, voice]. 1. The change of voice at puberty. 2. Any abnormality in the voice sounds.

heterophoria (het'er-o-fo'rĭ-ah) [hetero- + G. *phora*, movement]. A tendency for deviation of the eyes from parallelism, prevented by binocular vision.

heterophthalmus (het'er-of-thal'mus) [hetero- + G. *ophthalmos*, eye]. A difference in the appearance of the two eyes, as in the color or direction of the visual axes.

Heterophyes (het'er-of'ĭ-ēz) [hetero- + G. *phyē*, stature, form]. A genus of digenetic trematode flukes (family Heterophyidae) parasitic in fish-eating birds and mammals, including man.

heterophyiasis (het'er-o-fi-i'ă-sis). Infection with *Heterophyes*.

het'eropla'sia [hetero- + G. *plasis*, a forming]. 1. Development of cytologic and histologic elements that are not normal for the organ or part in question. 2. Malposition of tissue or a part that is otherwise normal.

het'eroplas'tic. 1. Pertaining to or manifesting heteroplasia. 2. Relating to tissue transplantation from one species to another.

het'eroploid. Relating to heteroploidy.

heteroploidy (het'er-o-ploy'dĭ) [hetero- + -ploid]. The state of an individual or cell possessing a chromosome number other than the normal diploid number (in man, 46).

heteropyknosis (het'er-o-pik-no'sis) [hetero- + G. *pyknos*, dense]. Any state of variable density; usually refers to differences in degree of density between chromosomes of different cells or between individual chromosomes.

heterosexual (het'er-o-sek'shu-ăl). 1. Denoting or characteristic of heterosexuality. 2. One who practices heterosexuality.

heterosexuality (het'er-o-sek'shu-ăl-ĭ-te). Erotic attraction, predisposition, or sexual behavior between persons of the opposite sex.

het'erosugges'tion. Suggestion received from another person.

het'erotax'ia [hetero- + G. *taxis*, arrangement]. Abnormal arrangement of organs or parts of the body in relation to each other.

heterotax'ic. Abnormally placed or arranged.

het'eroto'nia [hetero- + G. *tonos*, tension]. Abnormality or variation in tension or tonus.

het'eroto'pia [hetero- + G. *topos*, place]. 1. Ectopia. 2. In neuropathology, displacement of gray matter, typically into the deep cerebral white matter.

het'erotop'ic. 1. Ectopic (1). 2. Relating to heterotopia (2).

heterotopous (het-er-ot'o-pus). Heterotopic, especially in reference to teratomos composed of tissues that are out of place in the region where found.

het'erotrans'plant. Heterograft.

het'erotransplanta'tion. Transfer of a heterograft.

heterotrichosis (het'er-o-trī-ko'sis) [hetero- + G. *trichōsis*, growth of hair]. Hair growth of variegated color.

heterotroph (het'er-o-trof, -trŏf) [hetero- + G. *trophē*, nourishment]. A microorganism that obtains its carbon, as well as its energy, from organic compounds.

heterotrophic (het'er-o-trof'ik). Relating to a heterotroph.

heterotropia (het'er-o-tro'pĭ-ah) [hetero- + G. *tropē*, a turning]. Strabismus.

heterotypic (het'er-o-tip'ik). Of a different or unusual type or form.

heteroxanthine (het'er-o-zan'thin). 7-Methylxanthine; one of the alloxuric bases in urine, representing end products of purine metabolism.

heteroxenous (het'er-ok'sĕ-nus) [hetero- + G. *xenos*, stranger]. Digenetic (1).

heterozygosity (het'er-o-zi-gos'ĭ-tĭ) [hetero- + G. *zygon*, a yoke]. The state of having different allelic genes at one or more paired loci in homologous chromosomes.

heterozygote (het'er-o-zi'gōt) [hetero- + G. *zygotos*, yoked]. A heterozygous individual.

heterozygous (het'er-o-zi'gus). Relating to heterozygosity.

hetrax'ial. Having mutually perpendicular axes of unequal length.

hexa-, hex- [G. *hex*, six]. Prefixes meaning six.

hex'ad. A sexivalent element or radical.

hexadactyly, hexadactylism (hek'sah-dak'tĭ-lĭ, -lizm) [hexa- + G. *daktylos*, finger]. Presence of six digits on one or both hands or feet.

hex'adecano'ic acid. Palmitic acid.

hexamer (hek'să-mer) [hexa- + G. *meros*, part]. See virion.

hex'ane. A saturated hydrocarbon, C_6H_{14}, of the paraffin series.

hexaploidy (hek'să-ploy-dĭ). See polyploidy.

hex'itol. The polyol (sugar alcohol) obtained on the reduction of a hexose.

hexokinase (hek-so-ki'nās). A phosphotransferase present in yeast, muscle, and other tissues that catalyzes the phosphorylation of glucose and other hexoses to form hexose 6-phosphate.

hex'osam'ine. The amine derivative (NH_2 replacing OH) of a hexose.

hex'osamin'idase. General term for enzymes cleaving *N*-acetylhexose (glucose or galactose) residues from ganglioside-like oligosaccharides; at least four such specific enzymes carrying out this type of reaction are known, each being specific for the configuration and type of sugar.

hex'osans. Polysaccharides with the general formula $(C_6H_{10}O_5)_x$ which, on hydrolysis, yield hexoses.

hex'ose. A monosaccharide containing six carbon atoms in the molecule $(C_6H_{12}O_6)$.

hex'ose phos'phatase. An enzyme catalyzing the hydrolysis of a hexose phosphate to a hexose.

hexose-1-phosphate uridylyltransferase. An enzyme system that catalyzes the interconversion of glucose 1-phosphate and galactose 1-phosphate with simultaneous interconversion of UDPglucose and UDPgalactose.

hexulose (heks'u-lōs). A ketohexose; *e.g.*, fructose.

hex'yl. The radical of hexane, $CH_3(CH_2)_4CH_2—$.

hex'ylcaine hydrochloride. Cyclohexylamino-2-propylbenzoate hydrochloride; a local anesthetic agent suitable for surface application, infiltration, or nerve block.

Hf Hafnium.

Hg Mercury (hydrargyrum).

hiatal (hi-a'tal). Relating to a hiatus.

hiatus, pl. **hiatus** (hi-a'tus) [L. an aperture, fr. *hio,* pp. *hiatus,* to yawn] [NA]. **1.** An aperture or fissure. **2.** A foramen.

 h. aor'ticus [NA], aortic foramen; the opening in the diaphragm through which pass the aorta and thoracic duct.

 h. esophage'us [NA], the opening in the diaphragm, between the central tendon and the h. aorticus, through which pass the esophagus and the two vagus nerves.

 h. saphe'nus [NA], fossa ovalis (2); the opening in the fascia lata inferior to the medial part of the inguinal ligament through which the saphenous vein passes to enter the femoral vein.

 h. semiluna'ris [NA], a groove in the lateral wall of the middle meatus of the nasal cavity, into which the maxillary sinus, the frontonasal duct, and the middle ethmoid cells open.

hibernoma (hi'ber-no'mah) [L. *hibernus,* pertaining to winter, + G. *-oma,* tumor]. A rare type of benign neoplasm in human beings, consisting of brown fat that resembles the fat in certain hibernating animals; individual tumor cells contain multiple lipid deposits.

hiccup, hiccough (hik'up). A diaphragmatic spasm causing sudden inhalation that is interrupted by a spasmodic closure of the glottis, producing the characteristic noise.

hidr-. See hidro-.

hidradenitis (hi-drad-ĕ-ni'tis) [G. *hidrōs,* sweat, + *adēn,* gland, + *-itis,* inflammation]. Inflammation of the sweat glands; more specifically, of the apocrine glands.

 h. suppurati'va, inflammation of the apocrine sweat glands of the perianal, axillary, and genital areas or under the breasts, producing chronic abscesses or sinuses.

hidradenoma (hi-drad-ĕ-no'mah) [G. *hidrōs,* sweat, + *adēn,* gland, + *-oma,* tumor]. A benign neoplasm derived from epithelial cells of sweat glands.

 papillary h., apocrine adenoma; a solitary tumor, cystic and papillary, occurrring usually in the labia majora, composed of epithelium resembling that of apocrine glands.

hidro-, hidr- [G. *hidrōs,* sweat]. Combining forms relating to sweat or sweat glands.

hidrocystoma (hi'dro-sis-to'mah) [hidro- + G. *kystis,* bladder, + *-oma,* tumor]. Syringocystoma; a cystic form of hidradenoma.

hidropoiesis (hi'dro-poy-e'sis) [hidro- + G. *poiēsis,* formation]. Formation of sweat.

hidropoietic (hi'dro-poy-et'ik). Relating to hidropoiesis.

hidroschesis (hi-dros'ke-sis) [hidro- + G. *schesis,* a checking]. Suppression of sweating.

hidro'sis [G. *hidrōs,* sweat, + *-osis,* condition]. Production and excretion of sweat.

hidrot'ic. Relating to or causing hidrosis.

hi'la. Plural of hilum.

hi'lar. Pertaining to a hilus.

hilitis (hi-li'tis). Inflammation of the lining membrane of any hilus.

hil'lock. In anatomy, any small elevation or prominence.

 axon h., the conical area of origin of the axon from the nerve cell body; it contains parallel arrays of microtubules and is devoid of Nissl substance.

hi'lum, pl. **hi'la** [L. a small bit or trifle] [NA]. Porta (1); depression or slitlike opening in an organ where the nerves and vessels enter and leave.

hi'lus [an Eng. variant of L. *hilum*]. Former incorrect NA designation for hilum.

hind'brain. Rhombencephalon.

hind'gut. **1.** The large intestine, rectum, and anal canal. **2.** The caudal or terminal part of the embryonic gut.

hind'water. **1.** *Hydrorrhea gravidae.* **2.** Liquor amnii *in utero* behind the presenting part of the fetus.

hip [A.S. *hype*]. Coxa (2); the lateral prominence of the pelvis from the waist to the thigh; more strictly the h. joint.

hippocam'pal. Relating to the hippocampus.

hippocampus (hip-po-kam'pus) [G. *hippocampos,* seahorse] [NA]. The complex, internally convoluted structure that forms the medial margin of the cortical mantle of the cerebral hemisphere, bordering the choroid fissure of the lateral ventricle, and composed of two gyri (Ammon's horn and the dentate gyrus), together with their white matter; it forms part of the limbic system and, by way of the fornix, projects to the septum, anterior nucleus of the thalamus, and mamillary body.

hippocrat'ic. Relating to, described by, or attributed to Hippocrates.

Hippocratic Oath. An oath demanded of the physician about to enter upon the practice of his profession, the composition of which, though usually attributed to Hippocrates of Cos, is probably an ancient oath of the Aesclepiads. It appears in a book of the hippocratic collections as follows:

"I swear by Apollo the physician, by Aesculapius, Hygeia, and Panacea, and I take to witness all the gods, all the goddesses, to keep according to my ability and my judgment the following Oath:

"To consider dear to me as my parents him who taught me this art; to live in common with him and if necessary to share my goods with him; to look upon his children as my own brothers, to teach them this art if they so desire without fee or written promise; to impart to my sons and the sons of the master who taught me and the disciples who have enrolled themselves and have agreed to the rules of the profession, but to these alone, the precepts and the instruction. I will prescribe regimen for the good of my patients according to my ability and my judgment and never do harm to anyone. To please no one will I prescribe a deadly drug, nor give advice which may cause his death. Nor will I give a woman a pessary to procure abortion. But I will preserve the purity of my life and my art. I will not cut for stone, even for patients in whom the disease is manifest; I will leave this operation to be performed by practitioners (specialists in this art). In every house where I come I will enter only for the good of my patients, keeping myself far from all intentional ill-doing and all seduction, and especially from the pleasures of love with women or with men, be they free or slaves. All that may come to my knowledge in the exercise of my profession or outside of my profession or in daily commerce with men which ought not to be spread abroad, I will keep secret and will never reveal. If I keep this oath faithfully, may I enjoy my life and practice my art, respected by all men and in all times: but if I swerve from it or violate it, may the reverse be my lot."

hip′pus [G. *hippos*, horse, from a fancied suggestion of galloping movements]. Spasmodic, rhythmical pupillary dilation and constriction, independent of illumination, convergence, or psychic stimuli.

hircus, gen. and pl. **hirci** (hur′kus, hur′si) [L. he-goat]. **1.** The odor of the axillae. **2.**[NA]. One of the hairs growing in the axillae. **3.** Tragus (1).

hirsute (hur-sūt′) [L. *hirsutus*, shaggy]. Relating to or characterized by hirsutism.

hirsutism (hur′su-tizm) [L. *hirsutus*, shaggy]. Presence of excessive bodily and facial hair, especially in women.

hirudicide (hĭ-ru′dĭ-sīd) [L. *hirudo*, leech, + *caedo*, to kill]. An agent that kills leeches.

hir′udin [L. *hirudo*, leech]. An antithrombin substance extracted from the salivary glands of the leech that has the property of preventing coagulation of the blood.

Hirudinea (hĭr′u-din′e-ah) [L. *hirudo*, leech]. The leeches, a class of worms (phylum Annelida) that are predatory on invertebrate tissues, or feed on blood and tissue exudates of vertebrates.

Hirudo (hĭ-ru′do) [L. leech]. A genus of leeches (class Hirudinea), including *H. medicinalis*, the species most commonly used in medicine.

His Histidine or histidyl.

histamine (his′tă-mēn). 2-(4-Imidazolyl)ethylamine; a depressor amine derived from histidine by decarboxylation; a powerful stimulant of gastric secretion, constrictor of bronchial smooth muscle, and vasodilator (capillaries and arterioles).

histamine-fast. Indicating the absence of the normal response to histamine, especially in speaking of true gastric anacidity.

his′tamine′mia. Presence of histamine in the circulating blood.

his′taminu′ria. Excretion of histamine in the urine.

his′tidase, his′tidinase. *Histidine* ammonia-lyase.

his′tidine (His). α-Amino-β-(4-imidazolyl)propionic acid; a basic amino acid in proteins.

h. ammonia-lyase, histidase; histidinase; an enzyme catalyzing deamination of histidine to urocanate.

h. decarboxylase, an enzyme catalyzing the decarboxylation of histidine to histamine.

his′tidine′mia. Elevation of blood histidine level and excretion of histidine and related imidazole metabolites in urine due to deficiency of histidase activity; autosomal recessive inheritance.

his′tidinu′ria. Excretion of considerable amounts of histidine in the urine, as in histidinemia.

histidyl (His) (his′tĭ-dil). Radical of histidine.

histio- [G. *histion*, web (tissue)]. Combining form relating to tissue.

his′tioblast [histio- + G. *blastos*, germ]. Histoblast; a tissue-forming cell.

histiocyte (his′tĭ-o-sit) [histio- + G. *kytos*, cell]. Histocyte; a macrophage present in connective tissue. See reticuloendothelial *system*.

cardiac h., Anitschkow cell or myocyte; a large mononuclear cell found in connective tissue of the heart wall in inflammatory conditions, especially in the Aschoff body.

histiocytoma (his′tĭ-o-si-to′mah) [histio- + G. *kytos*, cell, + *-ōma*, tumor]. A tumor composed of histiocytes.

his′tiocyto′sis. Histiocytosis; a generalized multiplication of histiocytes.

kerasin h., Gaucher's *disease*.

lipid h., h. with cytoplasmic accumulation of lipid, either cholesterol (Hand-Schüller-Christian disease), phospholipid (Niemann-Pick disease), or kerasin (Gaucher's disease).

nonlipid h., Letterer-Siwe disease; an acute progressive generalized disease in young children, characterized by a purpuric rash, enlargement of lymph glands and spleen, and invasion of the spleen, liver, and bone marrow by histiocytes.

h. X, histiocytic proliferation of undetermined type, possible Hand-Schüller-Christian d. or eosinophilic granuloma of bone.

histiogenic (his′tĭ-o-jen′ik). Histogenous.

histo- [G. *histos,* web (tissue)]. Combining form relating to tissue.

his′toblast. Histioblast.

his′tochemistry. Cytochemistry.

his′tocompat′ibil′ity. A state of immunologic similarity or identity of tissues sufficient to permit successful transplantation.

histocompatability testing. A testing system for HLA antigens, of major importance in transplantation.

histocyte (his′to-sīt). Histiocyte.

his′tocyto′sis. Histiocytosis.

his′todifferentia′tion. The morphologic appearance of tissue characteristics during development.

histogenesis (his′to-jen′ĕ-sis) [histo- + G. *genesis,* origin]. The origin of a tissue; the formation and development of the tissues of the body.

his′togenet′ic. Relating to histogenesis.

histogenous (his-toj′ĕ-nus) [histo- + G. *-gen,* producing]. Histiogenic; formed by tissues.

histoid (his′toyd) [histo- + G. *eidos,* resemblance]. Histioid. Resembling in structure one of the tissues of the body; sometimes used with reference to the histologic structure of a neoplasm derived from and consisting of a single, relatively simple type of neoplastic tissue that closely resembles the normal.

his′toincompatibil′ity. State of immunologic dissimilarity of tissues sufficient to cause rejection of transplanted tissue.

histolog′ic, histolog′ical. Pertaining to histology.

histologist (his-tol′o-jist). Microanatomist; one who specializes in histology.

histology (his-tol′o-jī) [histo- + G. *logos,* study]. Microanatomy; the science concerned with the minute structure of cells, tissues, and organs in relation to their function.

histolysis (his-tol′ī-sis) [histo- + G. *lysis,* dissolution]. Disintegration of tissue.

histo′ma [histo- + G. *-oma,* tumor]. A benign neoplasm in which the cytologic and histologic elements are closely similar to those of normal tissue from which the neoplastic cells are derived.

his′tometaplas′tic. Stimulating the metaplasia of tissue.

his′tone. One of a number of simple proteins that contains a high proportion of basic amino acids; *e.g.,* the proteins associated with nucleic acids in the nuclei of plant and animal tissues.

histonu′ria. Excretion of histone in the urine.

his′topath′ogen′esis. [histogenesis + pathgenesis]. Abnormal embryonic development or growth of tissue.

his′topathol′ogy. The science concerned with the cytologic and histologic structure of abnormal or diseased tissue.

his′tophysiol′ogy. Microscopic study of tissues in relation to their functions.

hist′oplas′min. An antigenic extract of *Histoplasma capsulatum,* used in immunological tests for histoplasmosis.

Histoplasma capsulatum (his′to-plaz′mah kap-su-la′-tum) [histo- + G. *plasma,* something formed]. A dimorphic fungus species that causes histoplasmosis in man and other mammals.

histoplasmoma (his′to-plaz-mo′mah) [*Histoplasma* + G. *-oma,* tumor]. An infectious granuloma caused by *Histoplasma capsulatum.*

histoplasmosis (his′to-plaz-mo′sis). Darling's disease; an infectious disease caused by *Histoplasma capsulatum* and manifested by a primary benign pneumonitis similar in clinical features to primary tuberculosis; occasionally, the primary disease progresses to produce localized lesions in lung, such as pulmonary cavitation, or the typical disseminated disease of the reticuloendothelial system manifested by fever, emaciation, splenomegaly, and leukopenia.

  presumed ocular h., hemorrhagic chorioretinitis of the macular region associated with peripapillary chorioretinal atrophy and peripheral fundus chorioretinal atrophy.

historrhexis (his-to-rek′sis) [histo- + G. *rhēxis,* rupture]. Breakdown of tissue by some agency other than infection.

his′totome [histo- + G. *tomē,* cut]. Microtome.

histot′omy. Microtomy.

histotox′ic. Relating to poisoning of the respiratory enzyme system of the tissues.

histotroph′ic [histo- + G. *trophē,* nourishment]. Nourishing or favoring the formation of tissue.

histotrop′ic [histo- + G. *tropikos,* turning]. Attracted toward tissues; denoting certain parasites, stains, and chemical compounds.

hives. Urticaria.

Hl Latent *hyperopia.*

HLA Human lymphocyte *antigens.*

Hm Manifest *hyperopia.*

HMG Human menopausal *gonadotropin.*

HMO Health Maintenance Organization.

Ho Holmium.

hoarse [A.S. *hās*]. Having a rough, harsh quality of voice.

holandric (hol-an′drik) [G. *holos,* entire, + *aner,* man]. Related to genes located on the Y chromosome.

hole of retina. A break in the continuity of the inner layers of the retina permitting separation between the stratum pigmenti retinae and the stratum cerebrale retinae.

holism (ho′lizm) [G. *holos,* entire]. In psychology, the approach to the study of a psychlogical phenomenon through the analysis of the phenomenon as a complete entity in itself.

holistic (ho-lis′tik). Pertaining to the characteristics of holism or h. psychologies.

holmium (hol′mĭ-um). An element of the lanthanide group, symbol Ho, atomic no. 67, atomic weight 164.94.

holo- [G. *holos,* whole, entire, complete]. Combining form denoting entirety or relationship to a whole.

hol'oblas'tic [holo- + G. *blastos*, germ]. Denoting the involvement of the entire (isolecithal or moderately telolecithal) ovum in cleavage.

holocrine (hol'o-krin) [holo- + G. *krinō*, to separate]. See holocrine *gland.*

hol'odiastol'ic. Relating to or occupying the entire diastole.

holoendemic (hol'o-en-dem'ik). Endemic in the entire population.

holoenzyme (hol-o-en'zī). The complete enzyme, *i.e.,* apoenzyme plus coenzyme.

hol'ogram [holo- + G. *gramma*, something written]. A three-dimensional image.

hologynic (hol'o-jin'ik) [holo- + G. *gynē*, woman]. Related to sex-limited characters manifest only in females.

holophytic (hol-o-fit'ik) [holo- + G. *phyton*, plant]. Having a plantlike mode of obtaining nourishment; denoting certain photosynthesizing protozoans.

holoprosencephaly (hol'o-pros-en-sef'ă-lī) [holo- + G. *prosō*, forward, + *enkephalos*, brain]. Failure of the forebrain to divide into hemispheres or lobes.

holorachischisis (hol'o-ră-kis'ki-sis) [holo- + G. *rhachis*, spine, + *schisis*, fissure]. Spina bifida of the entire spinal column.

hol'osystol'ic. Pansystolic.

holozoic (hol-o-zō'ik) [holo- + G. *zōon*, animal]. Animal-like in mode of obtaining nourishment, lacking photosynthetic capacity; denoting certain protozoans.

homaxial (ho-mak'sī-al) [G. *homos*, the same, + axis]. Having all the axes alike, as a sphere.

homeo- [G. *homoios,* like]. Combining form meaning the same, or alike. See also homo-.

homeomorphous (ho'me-o-mor'fus) [homeo- + G. *morphē,* shape]. Of similar shape, but not necessarily of the same composition.

ho'meopath. Homeopathist.

homeopathic (ho'me-o-path'ik). Homeotherapeutic (1); relating to homeopathy.

homeopathist (ho-me-op'ă-thist). Homeopath; a medical practitioner of the homeopathic school.

homeopathy (ho-me-op'ă-thī) [homeo- + G. *pathos,* suffering]. A system of therapy developed by Samuel Hahnemann on the theory that large doses of a certain drug given to a healthy person will produce certain conditions which, when occurring spontaneously as symptoms of a disease, are relieved by the same drug in small doses.

homeoplasia (ho'me-o-pla'zī-ah) [homeo- + G. *plasis,* a molding]. Formation of new tissue of the same character as that already existing in the part.

homeoplas'tic. Relating to or characterized by homeoplasia.

homeostasis (ho'me-o-sta'sis) [homeo- + G. *stasis,* a standing]. **1.** The state of equilibrium in the body with respect to various functions and to the chemical compositions of the fluids and tissues. **2.** The processes through which such bodily equilibrium is maintained.

homeotherapeutic (ho'me-o-thĕr-ă-pu'tik). **1.** Homeopathic. **2.** Relating to homeotherapy.

homeother'apy. Treatment or prevention of a disease by means of a product similar to, but not identical with, the active causal agent, as in jennerian vaccination.

hom'igrade. See homigrade *scale.*

homo- [G. *homos,* the same]. Combining form meaning the same or alike. See also homeo-.

ho'mobi'otin. A compound resembling biotin except for the substitution of an oxygen atom for the sulfur and the presence of an additional CH_2 group in the side chain; an active biotin antagonist.

ho'moblas'tic [homo- + G. *blastos,* germ]. Developing from a single type of tissue.

ho'mocar'nosine. N^2-(γ-Aminobutyryl)histidine; h. in brain is formed from γ-aminobutyric acid, which in turn comes from glutamic acid.

homocysteine (ho'mo-sis'te-ēn). $HSCH_2CH_2CHNH_2$-$COOH$; a homologue of cysteine, produced by the demethylation of methionine, and an intermediate in the biosynthesis of cysteine from methionine via cystathionine.

homocystine (ho'mo-sis'tēn). The disulfide resulting from the mild oxidation of homocysteine; an analogue of cystine.

ho'mocys'tinu'ria. A disorder characterized by excretion of homocystine in urine, mental retardation, ectopia lentis, sparse blond hair, genu valgum, convulsive tendency, failure to thrive, thromboembolic episodes, and fatty changes of liver; associated with defective formation of cystathionine synthetase; autosomal recessive inheritance.

homocytotropic (ho'mo-si'to-tro'pik, -trop'ik) [homo- + G. *kytos,* cell, + *tropē,* a turning toward]. Having an affinity for cells of the same or a closely related species.

ho'mogamet'ic [homo- + G. *gametikos,* connubial]. Monogametic; producing only one type of gamete with respect to sex chromosomes.

homogamy (ho-mog'ă-mī) [homo- + G. *gamos,* marriage]. Similarity of husband and wife in a specific trait.

homogeneous (ho-mo-je'ne-us) [homo- + G. *genos,* race]. Of uniform structure or composition throughout.

homogenesis (ho-mo-jen'ĕ-sis) [homo- + G. *genesis,* production]. Reproduction in which the offspring is similar to the parents.

homogenous (ho-moj'ĕ-nus) [homo- + G. *genos,* family, kind]. Having a structural similarity because of descent from a common ancestor.

ho'mogentis'ic acid. Alcapton; alkapton; (2,5-dihydroxyphenyl)acetic acid; an intermediate in tyrosine catabolism, accumulating in those persons suffering a congenital deficiency of the enzyme homogentisate 1,2-dioxygenase and occurring in the urine in alkaptonuria.

homogentisuria (ho'mo-jen-tĭ-su'rī-ah). Alkaptonuria.

ho′mograft. Homologous or homoplastic graft; a tissue or an organ transplanted from one individual to another of the same species, not identical twins; used generally or with respect to animal strains not isogeneic for histocompatibility genes.

    allogeneic h., allograft.

    isogeneic h., syngeneic h., isograft.

ho′molat′eral [homo- + L. *latus,* side]. Ipsilateral.

homologous (ho-mol′o-gus) [see homologue]. Corresponding or alike in certain critical attributes; *e.g.,* of organs or parts corresponding in evolutionary origin and similar to some extent in structure, but not necessarily similar in function, of a single chemical series, differing by fixed increments, of chromosomes or chromosome parts identical with respect to their genetic loci, of serum or tissue derived from members of a single species, or of an antibody with respect to the antigen that produced it.

homologue (hom′o-log) [homo- + G. *logos,* word, ratio, relation]. A member of a homologous pair or series.

homol′ysin. A sensitizing, hemolytic antibody (hemolysin) formed as the result of stimulation by an antigen derived from an animal of the same species.

homol′ysis. Lysis of red blood cells by a homolysin and complement.

homomorphic (ho-mo-mor′fik) [homo- + G. *morphē,* shape, appearance]. Denoting two or more structure of similar size and shape.

homonomous (ho-mon′o-mus) [G. *homonemos,* under the same laws]. Denoting parts, having similar form and structure, arranged in a series, as the digits.

homonymous (ho-mon′ĭ-mus) [G. *homōnymous,* of the same name]. Having the same name or expressed in the same terms.

ho′mophil [homo- + G. *philos,* fond]. Denoting an antibody that reacts only with the specific antigen that induced its formation.

ho′moplas′tic. Similar in form and structure, but not in origin.

ho′moplas′ty. Repair of a defect by a homograft.

homopolymer (ho′mo-pol′ĭ-mer). A polymer yielding a single substance on hydrolysis, or composed of a series of identical radicals.

homorganic (hom′or-gan′ik). Produced by the same organs, or by homologous organs.

ho′moser′ine. 2-Amino-4-hydroxybutyric acid; a hydroxyamino acid differing from serine in the possession of an additional CH_2 group; formed in the conversion of methionine to cysteine.

homosexual (ho′mo-sek′shu-ăl). **1.** Denoting or characteristic of homosexuality. **2.** One who practices homosexuality.

homosexuality (ho′mo-sek-shu-al′ĭ-tĭ). Erotic attraction, predisposition, or sexual behavior between individuals of the same sex, especially past puberty.

    latent h., an erotic inclination toward members of the same sex not consciously experienced or expressed in overt action.

    overt h., homosexual inclinations consciously experienced and expressed in actual homosexual behavior.

ho′moton′ic. Of uniform tension or tonus.

ho′motop′ic [homo- + G. *topos,* place]. Pertaining to or occurring at the same place or part of the body.

ho′motype [homo- + G. *typos,* type]. Any part or organ of the same structure or function as another, especially as a corresponding one on the opposite side of the body.

homotyp′ic, homotyp′ical. Of the same type or form; corresponding to the other one of two paired organs or parts.

ho′movanil′lic acid. A phenol found in human urine, arising through the degradation of tyrosine, dopa, and hydroxytyramine.

homozygosity (ho′mo-zi-gos′ĭ-tĭ) [homo- + G. *zygon,* yoke]. The state of having identical genes at one or more paired loci in homologous chromosomes.

homozygote (ho-mo-zi′gōt) [homo- + G. *zygōtos,* yoke]. A homozygous individual.

homozygous (ho-mo-zi′gus). Relating to homozygosity.

homunculus (ho-mungk′u-lus) [L. dim. of *homo,* man]. An exceedingly minute body which, according to the medical views of the 16th and 17th centuries, was contained in a sex cell; from this infinitely small preformed structure the human body was supposed to be developed.

hook′worm. Common name for bloodsucking nematodes of the family Ancylostomatidae, chiefly members of the genera *Ancylostoma, Necator,* and *Uncinaria.*

hordeolum (hor-de′o-lum) [Mod. L. fr. L. *hordeolus,* a sty in the eye]. Sty; suppurative infection of a marginal gland of the eyelid; may be external, inflammation of the sebaceous gland of an eyelash, or internal, acute purulent infection of a meibomian gland.

hormo′nal. Pertaining to hormones.

hormone (hor′mōn) [G. *hormōn,* pres. part. of *hormaō,* to rouse or set in motion]. A chemical substance, formed in one organ or part of the body and carried in the blood to another organ or part, with specific regulatory effect on functional activity, and sometimes the structure, of just one organ or of various numbers of them. For h.'s not listed below, see specific names.

    adipokinetic h., adipokinin.

    adrenocortical h.'s, cortical h.'s; h.'s secreted by the human adrenal cortex, principally cortisol, aldosterone, and corticosterone; others include several weakly androgenic h.'s.

    adrenocorticotropic h. (ACTH), corticotropin; adrenocorticotropin; adrenotropin; the h. of the anterior lobe of the hypophysis that governs nutrition and growth of the adrenal cortex, stimulates it to functional activity, and also possesses extraadrenal adipokinetic activity. See also big *ACTH;* little

ACTH.

androgenic h., any h. that produces a masculinizing effect.

anterior pituitary-like h., chorionic *gonadotropin.*

antidiuretic h. (ADH), vasopressin.

chorionic gonadotropic h., chorionic *gonadotropin.*

corpus luteum h., progesterone.

cortical h.'s, adrenocortical h.'s.

corticotropin-releasing h. (CRH), corticoliberin; a h. from the hypothalamus that stimulates the anterior pituitary to release adrenocorticotropic h.

follicle-stimulating h. (FSH), follitropin; a glycoprotein h. of the anterior pituitary gland that stimulates the graafian follicles of the ovary and assists subsequently in follicular maturation and the secretion of estradiol, and stimulates the epithelium of the seminiferous tubules and is partially responsible for inducing spermatogenesis.

follicle-stimulating h.-releasing h. (FSH-RH), follicle-stimulating h.-releasing *factor.*

gonadotropic h., gonadotropin.

gonadotropin-releasing h. (GnRH), a h. of the hypothalamus that stimulates anterior pituitary secretion of gonadotropins.

growth h. (GH), somatotropin.

growth h.-releasing h. (GH-RF), somatoliberin.

human chorionic somatomammotropic h. (HCS), human placental *lactogen.*

interstitial cell-stimulating h. (ICSH), luteinizing h.

lactogenic h., prolactin.

luteinizing h. (LH), lutropin; interstitial cell-stimulating h.; a glycoprotein h. stimulating the final ripening of the follicles and the secretion of progesterone by them, their rupture to release the egg, and the conversion of the ruptured follicle into the corpus luteum.

luteinizing h.-releasing h. (LH-RH, LRH), luliberin; a decapeptide h. from the hypothalamus that stimulates the anterior pituitary to release both follicle-stimulating h. and luteinizing h.

luteotropic h. (LTH), luteotropin; an anterior pituitary h. whose action maintains the function of the corpus luteum.

melanocyte-stimulating h. (MSH), intermedin; a peptide h., secreted by the intermediate lobe of the pituitary gland, that causes dispersion of melanin with melanophores (chromatophores), resulting in darkening of the skin by promoting melanin synthesis with melanocytes.

parathyroid h. (PTH), parathyrin; a peptide h., formed by the parathyroid glands, that raises the serum calcium causing bone resorption.

pituitary gonadotropic h., anterior pituitary *gonadotropin.*

pituitary growth h., somatotropin.

placental growth h., human placental *lactogen.*

progestational h., progesterone.

releasing h. (RH), releasing *factor.*

sex h.'s, those steroid h.'s formed by testicular, ovarian, and adrenocortical tissues, and that are androgens or estrogens.

somatotropic h. (STH), somatotropin.

steroid h.'s, those h.'s possessing the cyclopentanoperhydrophenanthrene ring system (steroid nucleus) in their molecules.

thyroid-stimulating h. (TSH), thyrotropic h., thyrotropin.

thyrotropin-releasing h. (TRH), thyroliberin; a tripeptide h. from the hypothalamus that stimulates the anterior pituitary to release thyrotropin.

hormonogenesis (hor'mo-no-jen'ĕ-sis). Hormonopoiesis; the formation of hormones.

hormonogenic (hor'mo-no-jen'ik). Hormonopoietic; pertaining to the formation of a hormone.

hormonopoiesis (hor'mo-no-poy-e'sis) [hormone + G. *poiēsis,* production]. Hormonogenesis.

hormonopoietic (hor'mo-no-poy-et'ik). Hormonogenic.

horn [A.S.]. Cornu.

Ammon's h. G. *Ammōn,* Egyptian deity]. cornu ammonis; one of the two interlocking gyri composing the hippocampus, the other being the gyrus dentatus.

anterior h., *cornu* anterius.

cicatricial h., a keratinous growth projecting outward from a scar.

cutaneous h., a protruding keratotic growth of the skin; the base may show changes of senile keratosis or carcinoma.

dorsal h., posterior h., *cornu* posterius.

pulp h., a prolongation of the pulp extending toward the cusp of a tooth.

ventral h., *cornu* anterius.

horny. Corneous; keratic; keratinous (2); keratoid (1); keroid; of the nature or structure of horn.

horopter (ho-rop'ter) [G. *horos,* limit, + *optēr,* one who sees]. The sum of the points in space, the images of which for a given distance fall on corresponding retinal points.

hos'pice [L. *hospes,* a host, a guest]. An institution that provides a centralized program of palliative and supportive services to dying persons and their families, in the form of physical, psychological, social, and spiritual care.

hospital [L. *hospitalis,* for a guest, fr. *hospes,* a host, a guest]. An institution for the treatment, care, and cure of the sick and wounded, for the study of disease, and for the training of health professionals.

closed h., a h. in which only members of the attending or consulting staff may admit and treat patients.

open h., any h. in which practitioners, not members of the regular staff, are permitted to admit their patients and control their treatment.

proprietary h., a private h. operated as a profit-making business and owned by a corporation, investment group, or physicians primarily for their own patients.

hos'pitaliza'tion. Confinement in a hospital as a patient for diagnostic study and treatment.

host [L. *hospes,* a host]. The organism in or on which a parasite lives, deriving its body substance or nourishment from the h.

definitive h., final h., the h. in which a parasite reaches the adult or sexually mature stage.

intermediate h., intermediary h., the h. in which larval or developmental parasitic stages occur.

paratenic h., an intermediate h. in which no development of the parasite occurs, although its presence may be required as an essential link in the completion of the parasite's life cycle.

reservoir h., the h. of an infection that can also infect man, hence one that serves as a potential source of human reinfection and as a means of sustaining the parasite when it is not infecting man.

hot flash, hot flush. A vasomotor symptom of the climacterium: sudden vasodilation with a sensation of heat, usually involving the face and neck, and upper part of the chest; sweats, often profuse, frequently follow.

HPL Human placental *lactogen.*

Ht Total *hyperopia.*

5-HT 5-Hydroxytryptamine.

HTLV Human T-cell lymphocytotrophic *virus.*

hum. A low continuous murmur.

venous h., a musical murmur, usually continuous, heard on auscultation over the large veins at the base of the neck when an anemic patient is upright and looks to the opposite side; may also be heard over the umbilicus with large portal anastomotic veins.

hu'meral. Relating to the humerus.

hu'merora'dial. Relating to both humerous and radius; denoting especially the ratio of length of one to the other.

hu'meroscap'ular. Relating to both humerus and scapula.

hu'meroul'nar. Relating to both humerus and ulna; denoting especially the ratio of length of one to the other.

hu'merus, gen. and pl. **hu'meri** [L. shoulder] [NA]. The bone of the arm, articulating with the scapula above and the radius and ulna below.

humid'ity [L. *humiditas,* dampness]. The degree of moisture or dampness, as of the air.

absolute h., the weight of water vapor actually present per unit volume of gas or air.

relative h., the actual amount of water vapor present in the air or in a gas, divided by the amount necessary for saturation at the same temperature and pressure; expressed as a percentage.

hu'mor, gen. **humo'ris** [L. correctly, *umor,* liquid] **1**[NA]. Any clear fluid or semifluid hyaline anatomical substance. **2.** One of the elemental body fluids that were the basis of the physiologic and pathologic teachings of the hippocratic school: blood, yellow bile, black bile, and phlegm.

h. aquo'sus [NA], **aqueous h.,** the watery fluid that fills the anterior and posterior chambers of the eye.

ocular h., one of the two h.'s of the eye: aqueous and vitreous.

h. vit'reus [NA], **vitreous h.,** the fluid component of the corpus vitreum.

hu'moral. Relating to a humor.

hump'back, hunch'back. Kyphosis.

hun'ger [A.S.]. **1.** A desire or need for food. **2.** Any appetite, strong desire, or craving.

HVL Half-value *layer.*

hyal-. See hyalo-.

hyalin (hi'ă-lin) [G. *hyalos,* glass]. A clear, eosinophilic, homogeneous substance occurring in degeneration.

hyaline (hi'ă-lin, -lēn) [G. *hyalos,* glass]. Hyaloid; of a glassy, homogeneous, translucent appearance; a characteristic gross and microscopic appearance.

hy'aliniza'tion. Formation of hyalin.

hyalino'sis. Hyaline *degeneration,* especially that of relatively extensive degree.

hyalinu'ria. Excretion of hyalin or casts of hyaline material in the urine.

hyalitis (hi-al-i'tis). Inflammation of the vitreous humor in which the inflammatory changes extend into the avascular vitreous from adjacent structures. See also hyalosis.

suppurative h., purulent vitreous humor due to exudation from adjacent structures.

hyalo-, hyal- G. *hyalos,* glass]. Combining forms meaning glassy, or relating to hyalin.

hyal'ogens. Substances related to mucoids found in structures such as cartilage, vitreous humor, hydatid cysts, etc., and yielding sugars on hydrolysis.

hy'aloid [hyalo- + G. *eidos,* resemblance]. Hyaline.

hyalomere (hi'ă-lo-mēr) [hyalo- + G. *meros,* part]. The clear periphery of a blood platelet.

Hyalomma (hi-ă-lom'mah) [hyalo- + G. *omma,* eye]. An Old World genus of large ixodid ticks that parasitize domestic animals and a wide variety of wild animals; species of *H.* harbor a variety of pathogens of man and animals, and also cause considerable mechanical injury.

hy'alomu'coid. Mucoid present in the vitreous humor.

hyalonyxis (hi'ă-lo-nik'sis) [hyalo- + G. *nyxis,* puncture]. Surgical puncture of the vitreous humor.

hyalophagia (hi'ă-lo-fa'ji-ah) [hyalo- + G. *phagein,* to eat]. Eating or chewing of glass.

hyaloplasm (hi'ă-lo-plazm) [hyalo- + G. *plasma,* thing formed]. The protoplasmic fluid substance of cell.

nuclear h., karyolymph.

hyaloserositis (hi'ă-lo-se-ro-si'tis) [hyalo- + Mod. L. *serosa,* + *-itis,* inflammation]. Inflammation of a serous membrane, with a fibrinous exudate that eventually becomes hyalinized, resulting in a relatively thick, glistening, white or gray-white coating.

hyalosis (hi-al-o'sis) [hyalo- + G. *-osis*, condition].
Degenerative changes in the vitreous humor.

   asteroid h., Benson's disease; numerous small
spherical bodies in solid vitreous; a senile change,
usually unilateral, not affecting vision.

   punctate h., a condition marked by minute
opacities in the vitreous.

hyalosome (hi-al'o-sōm) [hyalo- + G. *sōma*, body].
An oval or round structure within a cell nucleus that
stains faintly but otherwise resembles a nucleolus.

hyalu'ronate. A salt or ester of hyaluronic acid.

hyaluronic acid (HA) (hi'al-u-ron'ik). A mucopolysaccharide forming a gelatinous material in the
tissue spaces, and an intercellular cement substance
throughout the body.

hyaluron'idases. Any of three enzymes (hyaluronog-
glucosaminidase, hyaluronoglucuronidase, and hya-
luronate lyase) that hydrolyze hyaluronic acid; one
or more are present in testis, sperm, bee and snake
venoms, and certain microorganisms.

hybridoma (hi-brid-o'mah) [G. *hybris*, violation,
wantonness, + *-ōma*, tumor]. A tumor of hybrid
cells used in the *in vitro* production of specific
monoclonal antibodies; produced by fusion of an
established tissue culture line of lymphocyte tumor
cells and specific antibody-producing cells.

hydantoin (hi-dan'to-in). Glycocolyl-urea; 2,4-
(3*H*,5*H*)-imidazoledione, derived from urea or from
allantoin; the $NH-CH_2-CO$ group is prototypical
of α-amino acids.

hydatid (hi'dă-tid) [G. *hydatis*, a drop of water, a
hyatid]. **1.** Hydatid *cyst.* **2.** A vesicular structure
resembling an echinococcus cyst.

hydatidiform (hi'dă-tid'ĭ-form). Having the form or
appearance of a hydatid.

hydatidocele (hi-dă-tid'osĕl) [hydatid + G. *kēlē,
tumor*]. A cystic mass composed of one or more
hydatids formed in the scrotum.

hydatidoma (hi'dă-tĭ-do'mah) [hydatid + G. *-oma,*
tumor]. A benign neoplasm in which there is
prominent formation of hydatids.

hydatidosis (hi'dă-tĭ-do'sis). The disease state caused
by the presence of hydatid cysts.

hydatidostomy (hi'dă-tĭ-dos'to-mĭ) [hydatid + G.
stoma, mouth]. Surgical evacuation of a hydatid
cyst.

hydr-. See hydro-.

hydragogue (hi'dră-gog) [hydr- + G. *agōgos*, drawing forth]. Producing a discharge of watery fluid;
denoting a class of cathartics that retain fluids in the
intestine and aid in the removal of edematous fluids.

hydramnion, hydramnios (hi-dram'nĭ-on, -nĭ-os) [G.
hydōr, water, + amnion]. Presence of an excessive
amount of amniotic fluid.

hydranencephaly (hi'dran-en-sef'ă-lĭ) [hydro- + G.
an- priv. + *enkephalos*, brain]. Congenital absence
of the cerebral hemispheres, with the basal ganglia
and remnants of mesencephalon covered by leptomeninges, dura, skull bones, and skin.

hydrargyria, hydrargyrism (hi-drar-jĭr'ĭ-ah, -drar'-
jir-izm) [L. *hydrargyrum*, mercury]. Mercury *poisoning.*

hydrargyrum (hi-drar'jĭ-rum) [G. *hydrargyros,*
quicksilver]. Mercury.

hy'drarthro'dial. Relating to hydrarthrosis.

hydrarthrosis (hi-drar-thro'sis) [hydr- + G. *arthron,*
joint]. Effusion of a serous fluid into a joint cavity.

hy'drase. Hydratase.

hy'dratase. Hydrase; trivial name applied, together
with dehydratase, to certain hydro-lyases, enzymes
catalyzing hydration-dehydration, which belong to
the lyases, enzymes removing groups nonhydrolytically.

hy'drate. An aqueous solvate; a compound crystallizing with one or more molecules of water.

hydra'tion. 1. Addition of water, differentiated from
hydrolysis, where the union with water is accompanied by a splitting of the original molecule and the
water molecule. **2.** Clinically, the taking in of water
to correct a deficit, as in dehydration.

hydremia (hi-dre'mĭ-ah) [hydr- + G. *haima,* blood].
An increase in blood volume as a result of an
increase of plasma, with or without a reduction in
the concentration of protein.

hydrencephalocele (hi-dren-sef'ă-lo-sēl) [hydr- + G.
enkephalos, brain, + *kēlē,* tumor]. Hydrocephalocele; hydroencephalocele; protrusion through a defect in the skull, of brain substance expanded into a
sac containing fluid.

hydrencephalomeningocele (hi'dren-sef'ă-lo-mĕ-
nin'go-sēl). A protrusion through a defect in the
skull of a sac containing meninges, brain substance,
and spinal fluid.

hy'dric. Relating to hydrogen in chemical combination.

hydride (hi'drid, hi'drīd). A compound of hydrogen
in which it assumes a formal negative charge.

hydro-, hydr- [G. *hydōr*, water]. Combining forms
denoting water or association with water; hydrogen.

hydro'a [hydro + G. *ōon*, egg]. Any bullous
eruption.

   h. vaccinifor'me, a hereditary recurrent eruption
of umbilicated bullae, occuring on exposure to the
sun and affecting chiefly male children or young
men.

   h. vesiculo'sum, erythema multiforme with iris or
vesicular lesions.

hydrobleph'aron [hydro- + G. *blepharon*, eyelid].
Edematous swelling of the eyelid.

hydrocalycosis (hi'dro-kal'ĭ-ko'sis) [hydro- + G.
kalyx, cup of a flower]. A rare symptomless
anomaly of the renal calix, which is dilated from
obstruction of the infundibulum.

hydrocar'bon. A compound containing only hydrogen and carbon.

hydrocele (hi'dro-sēl) [hydro- + G. *kēlē,* hernia]. A
collection of serous fluid in a sacculated cavity;
specifically, such a collection in the tunica vaginalis
testis.

hydrocelectomy (hi'dro-se-lek'to-mĭ) [hydrocele + G. *ektomē*, excision]. Excision of a hydrocele.

hydrocephalic (hi'dro-sĕ-fal'ĭk). Relating to hydrocephalus.

hydrocephalocele (hi-dro-sef'ă-lo-sēl). Hydrencephalocele.

hydrocephaloid (hi-dro-sef'ă-loyd). Resembling hydrocephalus.

hydrocephalus (hidro-sef'ă-lus) [hydro- + G. *kephalē*, head]. **1.** Excessive accumulation of fluid dilating the cerbral ventricles, thinning the brain, and causing a separation of cranial bones. **2.** In infants, an accumulation of fluid in the subarachnoid or subdural space.

  communicating h., h. in which there is a connection between ventricles and lumbar cerebrospinal fluid.

  h. ex vac'uo, h. due to loss or atrophy of brain tissue.

  noncommunicating h., obstructive h., h. with ventricular block.

  normal pressure h., occult h., h. due to failure of cerebrospinal fluid to be absorbed by the pacchionian granulations, characterized clinically by progressive dementia, unsteady gait, and usually a normal spinal fluid pressure.

hydrochloric acid (hi-dro-klor'ĭk). HCl; the acid of gastric juice.

hydrochloride (hi-dro-klor'ĭd). A compound formed by the addition of a hydrochloric acid molecule to an amine or related substance.

hydrocholecystis (hi'dro-ko-le-sis'tis) [hydro- + G. *cholē*, bile, + *kystis*, bladder]. Effusion of serous fluid into the gallbladder.

hydrocholeresis (hi'dro-ko-ler-e'sis) [hydro- + G. *cholē*, bile, + *hairesis*, a taking]. Increased output of a watery bile of low specific gravity, viscosity, and solid content.

hy'drocholeret'ic. Pertaining to hydrocholeresis.

hydrocirsocele (hi-dro-sir'so-sēl) [hydro- + G. *kirsos*, varix, + *kēlē*, tumor]. Hydrocele complicated with varicocele.

hydrocol'loid. A gelatinous colloid in unstable equilibrium with its contained water.

hydrocolpocele, hydrocolpos (hi-dro-kol'po-sēl, -kol'-pos) [hydro- + G. *kolpos*, vagina]. Accumulation of mucus or other nonsanguineous fluid in the vagina.

hy'drocor'tisone Cortisol; 17α-Hydroxycorticosterone; a steroid hormone secreted by the adrenal cortex and the most potent of the naturally occurring glucocorticoids.

hy'drocyan'ic acid. Prussic acid; hydrogen cyanide; HCN; a colorless liquid poison with the odor of bitter almonds.

hydrocyst (hi'dro-sist) [hydro- + G. *kystis*, bladder]. A cyst with clear, watery contents.

hy'droenceph'alocele. Hydrencephalocele.

hydrogel (hi'dro-jel). A colloid in which the particles are in the external or dispersion phase and water in the internal or dispersed phase.

hydrogen (hi'dro-jen) [hydro- + G. *-gen,* producing]. A gaseous element, symbol H, atomic no. 1, atomic weight 1.0079.

  h. chloride, a very soluble gas which, in solution, forms hydrochloric acid.

  h. cyanide, hydrocyanic acid.

  heavy h., hydrogen-2.

  h. sulfide, H_2S; a colorless, flammable, toxic gas with a familiar "rotten egg" odor, formed in the decomposition of organic matter containing sulfur.

hydrogen-1 (^1H). Protium; the common hydrogen isotope, making up 99.985% of the hydrogen atoms occurring in nature.

hydrogen-2 (^2H). Heavy hydrogen; deuterium; the isotope of hydrogen of mass number 2; the less common stable isotope of hydrogen making up 0.015% of the h. atoms occurring in nature.

hydrogen-3 (^3H). Tritium; a hydrogen isotope of mass number 3; weakly radioactive, emitting beta particles to become the stable helium-3; half-life, 12.5 years.

hydrogenase (hi'dro-jĕ-nās). Any enzyme that abstracts molecular hydrogen (H_2) from NADH, or adds it to ferricytochrome c_3 or to ferredoxin(s).

hydro'gena'tion. Addition of hydrogen to a compound, especially to an unsaturated fat or fatty acid; thus soft fats or oils are solidified or "hardened."

hydrogen exponent. Logarithm of the hydrogen ion concentration in blood or other fluid; its negative is the pH of that fluid.

hy'drokinet'ic. Pertaining to the motion of fluids and the forces giving rise to such motion.

hy'drolases. Hydrolyzing enzymes cleaving substrates with addition of H_2O at the point of cleavage.

hy'dro-ly'ases. A class of lyases comprising enzymes removing H and OH as water, leading to formation of new double bonds within the affected molecule.

hydrolysate (hi-drol'ĭ-sāt). A solution containing the products of a hydrolysis.

hydrolysis (hi-drol'ĭ-sis) [hydro- + G. *lysis,* dissolution]. A chemical process whereby a compound is cleaved into two or more simpler compounds with the uptake of the H and OH parts of a water molecule on either side of the chemical bond cleaved; effected by the action of acids, alkalies, or enzymes.

hydrolyt'ic. Referring to or causing hydrolysis.

hydro'ma. Hygroma.

hydromeningocele (hi-dro-men-in'go-sēl) [hydro- + G. *mēninx*, membrane, + *kēlē*, hernia]. Protrusion of the meninges of brain or spinal cord through defect in the bony wall, the sac so formed containing fluid.

hydrom'eter [hydro- + G. *mēron*, measure]. Gravimeter; an instrument for determining the specific gravity of a liquid.

hydrometra (hi-dro-me'trah) [hydro- + G. *mētra*, uterus]. Accumulation of thin mucus or other watery fluid in the cavity of the uterus.

hydromet'ric. Relating to hydrometry or hydrometer.

hydrometrocolpos (hi'dro-me'tro-kol'pos) [hydro- + G. *mētra*, uterus, + *kolpos*, vagina]. Distention of uterus and vagina by fluid other than blood or pus.

hydrom'etry. Determination of the specific gravity of a fluid by means of a hydrometer.

hydromicrocephaly (hi'dro-mi'kro-sef'ă-lĭ). Microcephaly associated with an increased amount of cerebrospinal fluid.

hydromor'phone hydrochloride. A synthetic derivative or morphine, with analgesic potency about 10 times that of morphine.

hydromphalus (hi-drom'fă-lus) [hydro- + G. *omphalos*, umbilicus]. A cystic tumor at the umbilicus, most commonly a vitellointestinal cyst.

hydromyelia (hi-dro-mi-e'lĭ-ah) [hydro- + G. *myelos*, marrow]. An increase of fluid in the dilated central canal of the spinal cord, or in congenital cavities elsewhere in the cord substance.

hydromyelocele (hi'dro-mi'ĕ-lo-sēl) [hydro- + G. *myelos*, marrow, + *kēlē*, tumor, hernia]. The protrusion of a portion of cord, thinned out into a sac distended with cerebrospinal fluid, through a spina bifida.

hy'dromyo'ma. A leiomyoma that contains cystlike foci of proteinaceous fluid.

hydronephrosis (hi'dro-nĕ-fro'sis) [hydro- + G. *nephros*, kidney, + *-osis*, condition]. Uronephrosis; dilation of the pelvis and calices of one or both kidneys resulting from obstruction to the flow of urine.

hy'dronephrot'ic. Relating to hydronephrosis.

hydropericarditis (hi'dro-pĕr-ĭ-kar-di'tis). Pericarditis with a large serous effusion.

hydropericardium (hi'dro-pĕr-ĭ-kar'dĭ-um). Noninflammatory accumulation of fluid in the pericardial sac.

hydroperitoneum (hi'dro-pĕr-ĭ-to-ne'um) [hydro- + peritoneum]. Ascites.

hydrophilia (hi-dro-fil'ĭ-ah) [hydro- + G. *philos*, fond]. A tendency of the blood and tissues to absorb fluid.

hydrophilic (hi-dro-fil'ik). Denoting the property of attracting or associating with water molecules, possessed by polar radicals or ions, as opposed to hydrophobic.

hydrophobia (hi-dro-fo'bĭ-ah) [hydro- + G. *phobos*, fear]. Rabies in man, so named from exaggerated folklore depictions.

hydropho'bic. 1. Relating to or suffering from hydrophobia. **2.** Repelling water, as opposed to hydrophilic.

hydrophysometra (hi'dro-fi-so-me'trah) [hydro- + G. *physa*, bellows, wind, + *metra*, uterus]. Presence of fluid and gas in the uterine cavity.

hydropneumatosis (hi'dro-nu-mă-to'sis) [hydro- + G. *pneuma*, breath, spirit]. Combined emphysema and edema; the presence of gas and liquid in the tissues.

hydropneumogony (hi'dro-nu-mo'go-nĭ) [hydro- + G. *pneuma*, air, + *gony*, knee]. Injection of air into a joint to determine the amount of effusion.

hydropneumopericardium (hi-dro-nu'mo-pĕr-ĭ-kar'dĭ-um) [hydro- + G. *pneuma*, air, + pericardium]. Pneumohydropericardium; presence of a serous effusion and of gas in the pericardial sac.

hydropneumoperitoneum (hi-dro-nu'mo-pĕr-ĭ-to-ne'um) [hydro- + G. *pneuma*, air, + peritoneum]. Pneumohydroperitoneum; presence of gas and serous fluid in the peritoneal cavity.

hydropneumothorax (hi'dro-nu-mo-tho'raks) [hydro- + G. *pneuma*, air, + thorax]. Pneumohydrothorax; presence of both gas and fluids in the pleural cavity.

hy'drops [G. *hydrōps*]. Excessive accumulation of clear, watery fluid in any of the tissues or cavities of the body as in ascites, anasarca, edema, etc.

    endolymphatic h., Ménière's *disease.*

    fetal h., h. fetalis, abnormal accumulation of serous fluid in the fetal tissues, as in erythroblastosis fetalis.

hydropyonephrosis (hi'dro-pi'o-nĕ-fro'sis) [hydro- + G. *pyon*, pus, + nephrosis]. Presence of purulent urine in the pelvis and calices of the kidney following obstruction of the ureter.

hydrorrhea (hi-dro-re'ah) [hydro- + G. *rhoia*, flow]. A profuse discharge of watery fluid from any part.

    h. gravida'rum, hindwater (1); discharge of a watery fluid from the vagina during pregnancy.

hydrosal'pinx [hydro- + G. *salpinx*, trumpet]. Accumulation of serous fluid in the fallopian tube.

hydrosarcocele (hi-dro-sar'ko-sēl) [hydro- + G. *sarx*, flesh, + *kēlē*, tumor]. A chronic swelling of the testis complicated with hydrocele.

hydroscheocele (hi-dros'ke-o-sēl) [hydro- + G. *oscheon*, scrotum, + *kēlē*, hernia]. A scrotal hernia complicated with a serous effusion in the sac.

hy'drosol. A colloid in aqueous solution, the particles being in the dispersed or internal phase, with water in the external or dispersion phase.

hydrostat'ic. Relating to the pressure of fluids or to their properties when in equilibrium.

hydrosyringomyelia (hi'dro-sĭr-in'go-mi-e'lĭ-ah) [hydro- + G. *hydōr*, water, + *syrinx*, a tube, + *myelos*, marrow]. Syringomyelia.

hydrotax'is [hydro- + G. *taxis*, *arrangement*]. Movement of cells or organisms in relation to water.

hydrothionemia (hi'dro-thi-o-ne'mĭ-ah) [hydro- + G. *theion*, sulfur, + *haima*, blood]. Presence of hydrogen sulfide in the circulating blood.

hydrothionuria (hi'dro-thi-o-nu'rĭ-ah) [hydro- + G. *theion*, sulfur, + *ouron*, urine]. Excretion of hydrogen sulfide in the urine.

hydrotho'rax. Presence of serous fluid in one or both pleural cavities, usually not associated with inflammatory reactions.

hydrotropism (hi-drot'ro-pizm, -tro'pizm) [hydro- + G. *tropos*, a turning]. The property in growing organisms of turning toward or away from moisture.

hy'drotuba'tion. Injection of liquid medication or saline solution through the cervix into the uterine cavity and fallopian tubes for dilation and medication of the tubes.

hydroureter (hi'dro-u-re'ter, -ūr'e-ter). Uroureter; distention of the ureter with urine due to blockage.

hydrovarium (hi-dro-va'rī-um). A collection of fluid in the ovary.

hydrox'ide. A compound containing a potentially ionizable hydroxyl group; particularly a compound that liberates OH- upon dissolving in water.

hydrox'ocobal'amin. Vitamin B_{12b}, differing from cyanocobalamin (vitamin B_{12}) in the presence of a hydroxyl ion in place of the cyanide ion.

hydroxy-. Prefix indicating addition or substitution of the –OH group to or in the compound whose name follows.

hydrox'yapatite. $3Ca_3(PO_4)_2 \cdot Ca(OH)_2$; a natural mineral structure that the crystal lattice of bones and teeth closely resembles; used in chromatography of nucleic acids.

25-hydrox'ychol'ecalcif'erol. A metabolite of cholecalciferol (vitamin D_3), produced largely in the liver and more potent than the parent vitamin in promoting intestinal absorption of calcium and in curing rickets; also promotes decalcification of bone much as parathyroid hormone.

hydrox'yl. The atom group or radical, OH.

hydrox'ylases. Enzymes catalyzing formation of hydroxyl groups by addition of an oxygen atom, hence oxidizing the substrate.

hydroxyphenyluria (hi-drok'sī-fen-il-u'rī-ah). Urinary excretion of tyrosine and phenylalanine, as a result of ascorbic acid deficiency.

21-hydrox'yproges'terone. Deoxycorticosterone.

hydrox'ypro'line. 4-Hydroxy-2-pyrrolidinecarboxylic acid; an amino acid found among the hydrolysis products of collagen.

hydrox'yproline'mia. A metabolic disorder characterized by enhanced plasma concentrations and urinary excretion of free hydroxyproline, and associated with severe mental retardation; autosomal recessive inheritance.

5-hydroxytryp'tamine (5HT). Serotonin.

3-hydroxyty'ramine. Dopamine.

hydru'ria [hydro- + G. *ouron*, urine]. Polyuria.

hydru'ric. Relating to polyuria.

hygiene (hi'jēn) [G. *hygieinos*, healthful, fr. *hygiēs*, healthy]. The science of health.

    mental h., the science and practice of maintaining and restoring mental health; an interdisciplinary branch of psychiatry.

    oral h., cleaning of oral structures by means of brushing, flossing, irrigating, massaging, or the use of other devices.

hygienic (hi-je'nik, hi-jī-en'ik). Healthful; relating to hygiene; tending to preserve health.

hygienist (hi-je'nist, hi'jī-en-ist). One skilled in the science of health.

    dental h., a licensed, professional auxiliary in dentistry who is both an oral health educator and clinician, and who uses preventive, therapeutic, and educational methods for the control of oral diseases.

hygro-, hygr- [G. *hygros*, moist]. Combining forms meaning moist, relating to moisture or humidity.

hygro'ma [hygro- + G. *-oma*, tumor]. Hydroma; a cystic swelling containing a serous fluid.

hygrom'etry. Psychrometry.

hy'groscop'ic. Capable of readily absorbing and retaining moisture.

hy'men [G. *hymēn*, membrane] [NA]. Virginal membrane; a thin crescentic or annular membranous fold partly occluding the vaginal external orifice of a virgin.

hy'menal. Relating to the hymen.

hymenectomy (hi-mē-nek'to-mī) [G. *hymēn*, membrane, + *ektomē*, excision]. Excision of the hymen.

hymenitis (hi-mē-ni'tis). Inflammation of the hymen.

hymenology (hi'mē-nol'o-jī) [G. *hymēn*, membrane, + *logos*, study]. The branch of anatomy and physiology concerned with the membranes of the body.

hymenotomy (hi-mē-not'o-mī) [G. *hymēn*, membrane, + *tomē*, incision]. Surgical division of a hymen.

hyoepiglottic, hyoepiglottidean (hi'o-ep-ī-glot'ik, -glot-id'e-an). Relating to the hyoid bone and the epiglottis.

hyoglossal (hi'o-glos'al). Glossohyal; relating to the hyoid bone and the tongue.

hyoid (hi'oyd) [G. *hyoeidēs*, shaped like the letter upsilon, ν]. U-shaped or V-shaped.

hyoscine (hi'o-sēn). Scopolamine.

hyoscyamine (hi-o-si'a-mēn). *l*-Tropine tropate; an alkaloid found in hyoscyamus, belladonna, duboisia (duboisine), and stramonium; the levorotatory component of atropine; an antispasmodic, analgesic, and sedative.

hyp-. See hypo-.

hypacusis (hi-pă-ku'sis) [hypo- + G. *akousis*, hearing]. Hypoacusis; hearing impairment attributable to deficiency in the peripheral organs of hearing; may be on a conductive or neurosensory basis.

hy'palbumine'mia [G. *hypo*, under, + albuminemia]. Hypoalbuminemia.

hypalgesia (hi-pal-je'zī-ah) [G. *hypo*, under, + *algēsis*, sense of pain]. Hypoalgesia; decreased sensibility to pain.

hypalgesic, hypalgetic (hi-pal-je'sik, -jet'ik). Relating to hypalgesia; having diminished sensitiveness to pain.

hypamnios (hi-pam′nĭ-os) [G. *hypo*, under, + amnion]. Presence of an abnormally small amount of amniotic fluid.

hypanakinesis (hi-pan′ă-kin-e′sis) [G. *hypo*, under + *anakinēsis*, a to-and-fro movement]. Diminution in the normal gastric or intestinal movements.

hyper- [G. *hyper*, above, over]. Prefix denoting excessive or above the normal. See also **super-**.

hyperacidity (hi′per-ă-sid′ĭ-tĭ). An abnormally high degree of acidity.

hyperactivity (hi′per-ak-tiv′ĭ-tĭ). General restlessness or excessive movement such as that characterizing children with minimal brain dysfunction or hyperkinesis.

hyperacusis (hi′per-ă-ku′sis) [hyper- + G. *akousis*, a hearing]. Abnormal acuteness of hearing due to increased irritability of the sensory neural mechanism.

hy′peradeno′sis [hyper- + G. *adēn*, gland, + *-ōsis*, condition]. Glandular enlargement, especially of the lymphatic glands.

hy′peradipo′sis. An extreme degree of adiposis or fatness.

hy′peradrenocor′ticalism Hypercortisolism; excessive secretion of adrenocortical hormones, usually cortisol.

hyperaldosteronism (hi′per-al-dos′ter-on-izm). Aldosteronism.

hyperalgesia (hi-per-al-je′zĭ-ah) [hyper- + G. *algos*, pain]. Extreme sensitiveness to painful stimuli.

hy′peralge′sic, hy′peralget′ic. Relating to hyperalgesia.

hy′peralimenta′tion. Superalimentation; administration or consumption of nutrients beyond normal requirements.

hyperamylasemia (hi′per-am′ĭ-la-se′mĭ-ah) [hyper- + amylase, + G. *haima*, blood]. Elevated serum amylase, seen as one of the features of acute pancreatitis.

hyperanakinezia, hyperanakinesis (hi′per-an-ă-kĭ-ne′zĭ-ah, -e′sis) [hyper- + G. *anakinēsis*, to-and-fro movement]. Excessive gastric or intestinal movements.

hyperaphia (hi′per-a′fĭ-ah) [hyper- + G. *haphē*, touch]. Tactile hyperesthesia; extreme sensitiveness to touch.

hyperaph′ic. Marked by hyperaphia.

hyperazotemia (hi′per-az′o-te′mĭ-ah). An abnormally large amount of nonprotein nitrogenous matter, especially urea, in the circulating blood.

hyperazoturia (hi′per-az′o-tu′rĭ-ah) [hyper- + Fr. *azote*, nitrogen, + G. *ouron*, urine]. Excretion of an abnormally large amount of nonprotein nitrogenous matter, especially urea, in the urine.

hyperbaric (hi′per-băr′ik) [hyper- + G. *baros*, weight]. **1.** Pertaining to pressure of ambient gases greater than 1 atmosphere. **2.** With respect to solutions, more dense than the diluent or medium.

hyperbarism (hi′per-băr′izm) [hyper- + G. *baros*, weight, + *ismos*, condition]. Disturbances in the body resulting from the pressure of ambient gases at greater than 1 atmosphere.

hyperbetalipoproteinemia (hi′per-ba-tah-lip′o-protēn-e′mĭ-ah). Enhanced concentration of β-lipoproteins in the blood.

familial h., type II familial *hyperlipoproteinemia*.
familial h. and hyperprebetalipoproteinemia, type III familial *hyperlipoproteinemia*.

hy′perbilirubine′mia. An abnormally large amount of bilirubin in the circulating blood.

hypercalcemia (hi′per-kal-se′mĭ-ah). An abnormally high concentration of calcium compounds in the circulating blood; commonly used to indicate an elevated concentration of calcium ions in the blood.

idiopathic h. of infants, persistent h. of unknown cause in very young children, associated with osteosclerosis, renal insufficiency, and sometimes hypertension; may also be associated with supravalvular aortic stenosis, elfin facies, and mental retardation.

hypercalciuria (hi′per-kal-sĭ-u′rĭ-ah). Excretion of abnormally large amounts of calcium in the urine.

hypercapnia (hi-per-kap′nĭ-ah) [hyper- + G. *kapnos*, smoke, vapor]. Hypercarbia; presence of an abnormally large amount of carbon dioxide in the circulating blood.

hy′percar′bia. Hypercapnia.

hypercementosis (hi′per-se-men-to′sis) [hyper- + L. *caementum*, a rough quarry stone, + *-osis*, condition]. An overgrowth of cementum on the root of a tooth which may be caused by localized trauma or inflammation, metabolic dysfunction, or developmental defect.

hyperchloremia (hi′per-klo-re′mĭ-ah). Chloremia (2); an abnormally large amount of chloride ions in the circulating blood.

hyperchlorhydria (hi′per-klōr-hid′rĭ-ah) [hyper- + chlorhydric (acid)]. Chlorhydria; the presence of an abnormal amount of hydrochloric acid in the stomach.

hypercholesteremia (hi′per-ko-les′ter-e′mĭ-ah). Hypercholesterolemia.

hypercholesterolemia (hi′per-ko-les′ter-ol-e′mĭ-ah). Hypercholesteremia; presence of an abnormally large amount of cholesterol in the cells and plasma of the circulating blood.

familial h., type II familial *hyperlipoproteinemia*.
familial h. with hyperlipemia, type III familial *hyperlipoproteinemia*.

hypercholia (hi-per-ko′lĭ-ah) [hyper- + G. *cholē*, bile]. A condition in which an abnormally large amount of bile is formed in the liver.

hy′perchro′mia. Hyperchromatism.

hy′perchro′mic. **1.** Hyperchromatic. **2.** Denoting increase in light absorption.

hyperchromasia (hi′per-kro-ma′sĭ-ah). Hyperchromatism.

hyperchromatic (hi′per-kro-mat′ik) [hyper- + G. *chrōma*, color]. Hyperchromic (1); abnormally highly colored, excessively stained, or overpigmented.

hyperchromatism (hi'per-kro'mă-tizm) [hyper- + G. *chrōma*, color]. Hyperchromasia; hyperchromia. **1.** Excessive pigmentation. **2.** Increased staining capacity, especially of cell nuclei for hematoxylin. **3.** Increased chromatin in cell nuclei.

hyperchromemia (hi'per-kro-me'mĭ-ah) [hyper- + G. *chrōma*, color, + *haima*, blood]. Abnormally high color index of the blood.

hyperchylia (hi-per-ki'lĭ-ah) [hyper- + G. *chylos*, juice]. Excessive secretion of gastric juice.

hyperchylomicronemia (hi'per-ki'lo-mi-kro-ne'mĭ-ah). Increased plasma concentrations of chylomicrons.

    familial h., type I familial *hyperlipoproteinemia*.
    familial h. with hyperprebetalipoproteinemia, type V familial *hyperlipoproteinemia*.

hy'percor'tisolism. Hyperadrenocorticalism.

hypercryalgesia (hi'per-kri-al-je'zĭ-ah) [hyper- + G. *kryos*, cold, + *algēsis*, the sense of pain]. Hypercryesthesia.

hypercryesthesia (hi'per-kri-es-the'zĭ-ah) [hyper- + G. *kryos*, cold, + *aisthēsis*, sensation]. Hypercryalgesia; extreme sensibility to cold.

hypercupremia (hi'per-ku-pre'mĭ-ah) [hyper- + L. *cuprum*, copper, + G. *haima*, blood]. An abnormally high level of plasma copper.

hypercyanotic (hi'per-si'ă-not'ik). Marked by extreme cyanosis.

hypercythemia (hi'per-si-the'mĭ-ah) [hyper- + G. *kytos*, cell, + *haima*, blood]. Hypererythrocythemia; presence of an abnormally high number of red blood cells in the circulating blood.

hypercytosis (hi'per-si-to'sis). An abnormal increase in the number of cells in the circulating blood or the tissues; frequently used synonymously with leukocytosis.

hyperdactyly (hi-per-dak'tĭ-lĭ) [hyper- + G. *daktylos*, finger or toe]. Polydactyly.

hyperdicrotic (hi'per-di-krot'ik). Pronouncedly dicrotic.

hyperechema (hi'per-e-ke'mah) [hyper- + G. *ēchēma*, sound]. Auditory magnification or exaggeration.

hyperemesis (hi'per-em'e-sis) [hyper- + G. *emesis*, vomiting]. Excessive vomiting.

hy'peremet'ic. Marked by excessive vomiting.

hyperemia (hi-per-e'mĭ-ah) [hyper- + G. *haima*, blood]. Presence of an increased amount of blood in a part or organ. See also congestion.

    active h., arterial h., fluxionary h.; due to an increased afflux of arterial blood in dilated capillaries.
    collateral h., increased blood flow through collateral channels when the circulation through the main artery to a part is arrested.
    fluxionary h., active h.
    passive h., venous h.; h. due to an obstruction in the flow of blood from the affected part, the venous radicles becoming distended.

    reactive h., h. following the arrest and subsequent restoration of the blood supply to a part.
    venous h., passive h.

hyperemic (hi-per-e'mik). Denoting hyperemia.

hypereosinophilia (hi'per-e-o-sin-o-fil'ĭ-ah). A greater degree of abnormal increase in the number of eosinophilic granulocytes in the circulating blood or the tissues.

hyperergasia (hi'per-er-ga'zĭ-ah) [hyper- + G. *ergasia*, work]. Increased or excessive functional activity.

hyperergia, hyperergy (hi-per-er'jĭ-ah, -er'gĭ). Hypergia; allergic hypersensitivity.

hyperergic (hi-per-er'jik). Hypergic; relating to hyperergia.

hypererythrocythemia (hi'per-e-rith'ro-si-the'mĭ-ah). Hypercythemia.

hyperesophoria (hi'per-es-o-fo'rĭ-ah) [hyper- + G. *esō*, inward, + *phora*, movement]. A tendency of one eye to deviate upward and inward.

hyperesthesia (hi'per-es-the'zĭ-ah) [hyper- + G. *aisthēsis*, sensation]. Oxyesthesia; abnormal acuteness of sensitivity to sensory stimuli.

hy'peresthet'ic. Marked by hyperesthesia.

hyperexophoria (hi'per-ek-so-fo'rĭ-ah) [hyper- + G. *exō*, outward, + *phora*, movement]. A tendency of one eye to deviate upward and outward.

hy'perexten'sion. Overextension; extension of a limb or part beyond the normal limit.

hy'perferre'mia. High serum iron level.

hyperfibrinogenemia (hi'per-fi-brin'o-jĕ-ne'mĭ-ah). Fibrinogenemia; increased level of fibrinogen in the blood.

hyperfibrinolysis (hi'per-fi-brin-ol'ĭ-sis). Markedly increased fibrinolysis, as in subdural hematomas.

hy'perflex'ion. Flexion of a limb or part beyond the normal limit.

hy'pergalacto'sis [hyper- + G. *gala*, milk, + *-osis*, condition]. Excessive secretion of milk.

hy'pergammaglob'uline'mia. An increased amount of the gamma globulins in the plasma, such as that frequently observed in chronic infectious diseases.

hypergenesis (hi-per-jen'ĕ-sis) [hyper- + G. *genesis*, production]. Excessive development or redundant production of parts or organs of the body.

hy'pergenet'ic. Relating to hypergenesis.

hypergenitalism (hi-per-jen'ĭ-tă-lizm). Abnormally overdeveloped genitalia in adults or for the individual's age.

hypergeusia (hi-per-gu'sĭ-ah, -ju'sĭ-ah) [hyper- + G. *geusis*, taste]. Gustatory hyperesthesia; oxygeusia; abnormal acuteness of the sense of taste.

hypergia (hi-per'jĭ-ah). Hyperergia.

hyper'gic. Hyperergic.

hy'perglan'dular. Characterized by overactivity or increased size of a gland.

hyperglobulia (hi'per-glo-bu'lĭ-ah) [hyper- + L. *globulus*, globule]. Polycythemia.

hyperglobulinemia (hi'per-glob'u-lin-e'mĭ-ah). Abnormally large amounts of globulins in the circulating blood plasma.

hyperglycemia (hi'per-gli-se'mĭ-ah) [hyper- + G. *glykys*, sweet, + *haima*, blood]. Abnormally high concentrations of glucose in the circulating blood, especially with reference to a fasting level.

hyperglyceridemia (hi'per-glis'er-ĭ-de'mĭ-ah). Elevated plasma concentration of glycerides, usually present within chylomicrons, normal if transiently present after a meal containing lipids, but abnormal if a persistent state.

   endogenous h., type IV familial hyperlipoproteinemia or a nonfamilial sporadic variety.

   exogenous h., persistent h. due to retarded rate of removal from plasma of chylomicrons of dietary origin.

hyperglycinemia (hi'per-gli-sin-e'mĭ-ah). Elevated plasma glycine concentration. See also *hyperglycinuria* with hyperglycinemia.

hyperglycinuria (hi'per-gli'sin-u'rĭ-ah). Enhanced urinary excretion of glycine. **H. with hyperglycinemia** is a metabolic disorder generally appearing in the neonatal period and characterized by vomiting, metabolic acidosis, ketonuria, osteoporosis, periodic thrombocytopenia, and neutropenia; autosomal recessive inheritance.

hyperglycogenolysis (hi'per-gli'ko-jĕ-nol'ĭ-sis). Excessive glycogenolysis.

hyperglycorrhachia (hi'per-gli-ko-rak'ĭ-ah) [hyper- + G. *glykys*, sweet, + *rhachis*, spine]. Excessive amounts of sugar in the cerebrospinal fluid.

hyperglycosuria (hi'per-gli-ko-su'rĭ-ah). Persistent excretion of unusually large amounts of glucose in the urine.

hypergonadism (hi-per-gon'ă-dizm). Enhanced secretion of gonadal hormones, with precocious sexual development.

hy'perhe'moglobine'mia. An unusually large amount of hemoglobin in the circulating blood plasma.

hyperhidrosis (hi'per-hi-dro'sis) [hyper- + hidrosis]. Hyperidrosis; polyhidrosis; excessive or profuse sweating.

   gustatory h., excessive sweating of the lips, nose, and forehead after eating certain foods.

hy'perhydra'tion. Overhydration; excess water content of the body.

hyperidrosis (hi'per-ĭ-dro'sis). Hyperhidrosis.

hyperinsulinism (hi'per-in'su-lin'izm). Excessive secretion of insulin by the islets of Langerhans, resulting in hypoglycemia; the symptoms are those of insulin shock, though more chronic in character.

hyperinvolution (hi'per-in'vo-lu'shun). Superinvolution.

hyperisotonic (hi'per-i-so-ton'ik). Hypertonic.

hyperkalemia (hi'per-kă-le'mĭ-ah) [hyper- + Mod. L. *kalium*, potash, + G. *haima*, blood]. Hyperpotassemia; an abnormal concentration of potassium ions in the circulating blood.

hy'perker'atiniza'tion. Hyperkeratosis.

hyperkeratosis (hi'per-kĕr-ăto'sis). Hyperkeratinization; hypertrophy of the horny layer of the epidermis.

hyperketonemia (hi'per-ke-to-ne'mĭ-ah). Elevated concentrations of ketone bodies in blood.

hyperketonuria (hi'per-ke-to-nu'rĭ-ah). Increased urinary excretion of ketonic compounds.

hyperkinemia (hi'per-kĭ-ne'mĭ-ah) [hyper- + G. *kineō*, to move, + *haima*, blood]. Increased volume flow through the circulation; increased circulation rate; supernormal cardiac output.

hyperkinesis, hyperkinesia (hi'per-kĭ-ne'sis, -ne'zĭ-ah) [hyper- + G. *kinēsis*, motion]. Excessive motor function or activity.

hy'perkinet'ic. Pertaining to or characterized by hyperkinesia.

hy'perlacta'tion. Continuance of lactation beyond the normal period.

hyperleukocytosis (hi'per-lu'ko-si-to'sis). An unusually great increase in the number and proportion of leukocytes in the circulating blood or the tissues.

hyperlipemia (hi'per-lip-e'mĭ-ah) [hyper- + G. *lipos*, fat, + *haima*, blood]. Lipemia.

   carbohydrate-induced h., type III and type IV familial *hyperlipoproteinemia.*

   combined fat- and carbohydrate-induced h., type V familial *hyperlipoproteinemia.*

   familial fat-induced h., type I familial *hyperlipoproteinemia.*

hyperlipidemia (hi'per-lip'ĭ-de'mĭ-ah). Lipemia.

hyperlipoidemia (hi'per-lip'oy-de'mĭ-ah). Lipemia.

hyperlipoproteinemia (hi'per-lip'o-pro'tēn-e'mĭ-ah). An increase in the lipoprotein concentration of the blood.

   acquired h., nonfamilial h.; h. that develops as a consequence of some primary disease, such as thyroid deficiency.

   familial h., a group of diseases characterized by changes in concentration of β-lipoproteins and pre-β-lipoproteins and the lipids associated with them. See types I through V familial h.

   type I familial h., familial fat-induced hyperlipemia; familial hyperchylomicronemia; familial hypertriglyceridemia; h. characterized by the presence of large amounts of chylomicrons and triglycerides on a normal diet (disappearance on a fat-free diet), low α- and β-lipoproteins on a normal diet (increase on fat-free diet), decreased plasma postheparin lipolytic activity, and low tissue lipoprotein lipase activity; accompanied by bouts of abdominal pain, hepatosplenomegaly, and eruptive xanthomas; autosomal recessive inheritance.

   type II familial h., familial hyperbetalipoproteinemia or hypercholesterolemia; h. characterized by increased plasma levels of β-lipoproteins, cholesterol, and phospholipids, but normal triglycerides; generalized xanthomatosis and coronary atherosclerosis are associated; autosomal inheritance.

type III familial h., familial hyperbetalipoproteinemia and hyperprebetalipoproteinemia; familial hypercholesterolemia with hyperlipemia; carbohydrate-induced hyperlipemia; h. characterized by increased plasma levels of β-lipoproteins, pre-β-lipoproteins, cholesterol, phospholipids, and triglycerides; hypertriglyderidemia is endogenous, induced by high carbohydrate diet, and glucose tolerance is abnormal; frequently accompanied by eruptive xanthomas and atheromatosis; autosomal recessive inheritance.

type IV familial h., familial hyperprebetalipoproteinemia; familial hypertriglyceridemia; carbohydrate-induced hyperlipemia; h. characterized by increased plasma levels of pre-β-lipoproteins and triglycerides on a normal diet, but normal β-lipoproteins, cholesterol, and phospholipids; hypertriglyceridemia is endogenous, induced by high carbohydrate diet; may be accompanied by abnormal glucose tolerance and susceptibility to ischemic heart disease; probably autosomal recessive inheritance.

type V familial h., familial hyperchylomicronemia with hyperprebetalipoproteinemia; combined fat- and carbohydrate-induced hyperlipemia; h. characterized by increased plasma levels of chylomicrons, pre-β-lipoproteins, and triglycerides, with atherosclerosis, slight elevation of cholesterol on a normal diet, and normal β-lipoproteins; may be accompanied by bouts of abdominal pain, hepatosplenomegaly, susceptibility to atherosclerosis, and abnormal glucose tolerance; probably autosomal recessive inheritance.

hy′perlipo′sis [hyper- + G. *lipos*, fat]. **1.** Excessive adiposity. **2.** An extreme degree of fatty degeneration.

hyperlithuria (hi′per-li-thu′ri-ah). An excessive excretion of uric (lithic) acid in the urine.

hyperlysinemia (hi′per-li′sin-e′mi-ah). Abnormal increase of lysine in the circulating blood; associated with mental retardation, convulsions, anemia and asthenia; autosomal recessive inheritance.

hyperlysinuria (hi′per-li′sin-u′ri-ah). Abnormally high concentrations of lysine in the urine; a form of aminoaciduria.

hy′permas′tia [hyper- + G. *mastos*, breast]. **1.** Polymastia. **2.** Excessively large mammary glands.

hypermenorrhea (hi′per-men-o-re′ah) [hyper- + G. *mēn*, month, + *rhoia*, flow]. Menorrhagia; menostaxis; excessively prolonged or profuse menses.

hy′permetab′olism. Abnormal heat production by the body, as in thyrotoxicosis.

hy′perme′tria [hyper- + G. *metron*, measure]. A manifestation of ataxia characterized by overreaching a desired object or goal.

hypermetropia (hi′per-mē-tro′pi-ah) [hyper- + G. *metron*, measure, + *ōps*, eye]. Hyperopia.

hypermyotonia (hi′per-mi-o-to′ni-ah) [hyper- + G. *mys*, muscle, + *tonos*, tension]. Extreme muscular tonus.

hypermyotrophy (hi′per-mi-ot′ro-fi) [hyper- + G. *mys*, muscle, + *trophē*, nourishment]. Muscular hypertrophy.

hypernatremia (hi′per-nă-tre′mi-ah) [hyper- + *natrium* (q.v.), + G. *haima*, blood]. Abnormally high plasma concentration of sodium ions.

hyperneocytosis (hi′per-ne′o-si-to′sis) [hyper- + G. *neos*, new, + *kytos*, cell, + *-osis*, condition]. Hyperleukocytosis in which there are considerable numbers of immature and young cells.

hyperoncotic (hi′per-on-kot′ik). Indicating an oncotic pressure higher than normal.

hyperonychia (hi′per-o-nik′i-ah) [hyper- + G. *onyx*, (*onych-*), nail]. Hypertrophy of the nails.

hyperopia (H) (hi-per-o′pi-ah) [hyper- + G. *ōps*, eye]. Hypermetropia; farsightedness; the refractive state of the eye in which parallel rays of light would come to focus behind the retina if not intercepted by it.

　absolute h., manifest h. that cannot be overcome by accommodation.

　axial h., h. due to shortening of the anteroposterior diameter of the globe of the eye.

　curvature h., h. due to diminution of convexity of the refracting media of the eye.

　facultative h., manifest h. that can be overcome by an effort of accommodation.

　latent h. (Hl), the difference between total and manifest h.

　manifest h. (Hm), h. that can be measured by convex lenses without paralysis of accommodation.

　total h. (Ht), that which can be determined after complete paralysis of accommodation.

hyperopic (H) (hi′per-o′pik). Pertaining to hyperopia.

hyperorchidism (hi′per-or′ki-dizm) [hyper- + G. *orchis*, testis]. Increased size or functioning of the testes.

hyperorexia (hi′per-o-rek′si-ah) [hyper- + G. *orexis*, appetite]. Bulimia.

hyperorthocytosis (hi′per-or′tho-si-to′sis) [hyper- + G. *orthos*, correct, + *kytos*, cell, + *-osis*, condition]. Hyperleukocytosis in which the relative percentages of the various types of white blood cells are within the normal range and immature forms are not observed.

hyperosmia (hi-per-oz′mi-ah) [hyper- + G. *osmē*, sense of smell]. Olfactory hyperesthesia; an exaggerated or abnormally acute sense of smell.

hyperosmolality (hi′per-oz-mo-lal′i-ti). Increased concentration of a solution expressed as osmoles of solute per kilogram of serum water.

hyperosmolarity (hi′per-oz-mo-lăr′i-ti). An increase in the osmotic concentration of a solution expressed as osmols of solute per liter of solution.

hy′perosmot′ic. Relating to increased osmosis.

hy′perosto′sis [hyper- + G. *osteon*, bone, + *-osis*, condition]. **1.** Hypertrophy of bone. **2.** Exostosis.

　h. cortica′lis defor′mans, marked irregular thickening of the skull and bone cortex, with thickening and widening of the shafts of long bones and elevated serum alkaline phosphatase; autosomal recessive inheritance.

h. frontal'is inter'na, abnormal deposition of bone on the inner aspect of the frontal bone.

generalized cortical h., Van Buchem's *syndrome.*

infantile cortical h., Caffey's disease or syndrome; familial subperiosteal bone formation over many bones, especially the mandible, clavicles, and shafts of long bones, following fever and usually appearing before 6 months of age and disappearing during childhood.

hyperovarianism (hi′per-o-va′ri-an-izm). A condition of sexual precocity due to premature development of the ovaries accompanied by the secretion of ovarian hormones.

hyperoxaluria (hi′per-ok-să-lu′ri-ah). An unusually large amount of oxalic acid or oxalates in the urine.

primary h. and oxalosis, a metabolic disorder characterized by calcium oxalate nephrocalcinosis and nephrolithiasis, plus extrarenal oxalosis; urinary output of oxalic and glycolic acids is greatly increased; frequently produces progressive renal failure and terminal uremia; autosomal recessive inheritance.

hyperoxia (hi′per-ok′si-ah). 1. An excess of oxygen in tissues and organs. 2. A greater oxygen tension than normal, such as that produced by breathing air or oxygen at pressures greater than 1 atmosphere.

hyperparasitism (hi′per-păr′ă-sit-izm). A condition in which a secondary parasite develops within a previously existing parasite.

hyperparathyroidism (hi′per-păr-ah-thi′roy-dizm). An increase in the secretion of the parathyroids, causing generalized osteitis fibrosa cystica, elevated serum calcium, decreased serum phosphorus, and increased excretion of both calcium and phosphorus; due to neoplasms or idiopathic hyperplasia of the parathyroid glands (**primary h.**) or as a result of disordered metabolism (**secondary h.**).

hyperpepsinia (hi-per-pep-sin′i-ah). Excess pepsin in the gastric juice.

hyperperistalsis (hi′per-pĕr′i-stal′sis). Excessive rapidity of the passage of food through the stomach and intestine.

hyperphalangism (hi′per-fă-lan′jizm). Polyphalangism; presence of a supernumerary phalanx in a finger or toe.

hyperphenylalaninemia (hi′per-fen′il-al-a-ni′-ne′mi-ah). Abnormally high blood levels of phenylalanine, which may or may not be associated with elevated tyrosine levels, in newborn infants, associated with the heterozygous state of phenylketonuria, maternal phenylketonuria, or transient deficiency of phenylalanine hydroxylase or *p*-hydroxyphenylpyruvic acid oxidase.

hyperphonesis (hi′per-fo-ne′sis) [hyper- + G. *phōnēsis,* a sounding]. Increase in the percussion sound, or of the voice sound, in ausculation.

hyperphoria (hi-per-fo′ri-ah) [hyper- + G. *phora,* motion]. A tendency of the visual axis of one eye to deviate upward.

hyperphosphatasemia (hi′per-fos′fă-tă-se′mi-ah). Abnormally high content of alkaline phosphatase in the circulating blood.

hyperphosphatasia (hi′per-fos′fă-ta′zi-ah). Elevated alkaline phosphatase, with dwarfism, macrocranium, blue sclerae, and expansion of the diaphyses of tubular bones with multiple fractures; autosomal recessive inheritance.

hyperphosphatemia (hi′per-fos-fă-te′mi-ah). Abnormally high concentration of phosphates in the circulating blood.

hy′perphos′phatu′ria. Increased excretion of phosphates in the urine.

hy′perpigmenta′tion. Excess pigment in a tissue or part.

hyperpituitarism (hi′per-pi-tu′i-tă-rizm). Excessive production of anterior pituitary hormones, especially somatotropin; may result in gigantism or acromegaly.

hyperplasia (hi-per-pla′zi-ah) [hyper- + G. *plasis,* a molding]. An increase in number of cells in a tissue or organ, excluding tumor formation, whereby the bulk of the part or organ is increased.

hyperplasmia (hi-per-plaz′mi-ah). 1. Excessive accumulation of white blood cells (especially of a single type) within various organs and tissues in association with a peripheral white blood cell count within the normal range. 2. An increase in the size of red blood cells as a result of fluid absorption.

hy′perplas′tic. Relating to hyperplasia.

hy′perploid. Relating to hyperploidy.

hyperploidy (hi-per-ploy′di) [hyper- + -ploid]. The state of possessing one or more chromosomes in addition to the normal number.

hyperpnea (hi-perp-ne′ah) [hyper- + G. *pnoē,* breathing]. Respiration that is deeper and more rapid than normal.

hy′perpo′lariza′tion. An increase in polarization of membranes or nerves or muscle cells; the reverse change from that associated with excitatory action.

hyperponesis (hi′per-po-ne′sis) [hyper- + G. *ponos,* toil]. Exaggerated activity within the motor portion of the nervous system.

hy′perpotasse′mia. Hyperkalemia.

hyperpraxia (hi-per-prak′si-ah) [hyper- + G. *praxis,* action]. Excessive activity; restlessness.

hyperprebetalipoproteinemia (hi′per-pre-ba′tah-lip-o-pro′tēn-e′mi-ah). Increased concentrations of pre-β-lipoproteins in the blood.

hy′perprolac′tine′mia. An elevated level of prolactin in the blood, a normal physiological reaction during lactation, but pathological otherwise.

hy′perproline′mia. A metabolic disorder characterized by enhanced plasma proline concentrations and urinary excretion of proline, hydroxyproline, and glycine; autosomal recessive inheritance.

hyperproteinemia (hi′per-pro-tēn-e′mī-ah). An abnormally large concentration of protein in plasma.

hyperproteosis (hi′per-pro-te-o′sis). A condition due to an excessive amount of protein in the diet.

hyperpyretic (hi′per-pi-ret′ik). Hyperpyrexial; relating to hyperpyrexia.

hyperpyrexia (hi′per-pi-rek′sī-ah) [hyper- + G. *pyrexis,* feverishness]. Extremely high fever.

hy′perpyrex′ial. Hyperpyretic.

hyperreflexia (hi′per-re-flek′sī-ah). A condition in which the deep tendon reflexes are exaggerated.

hyperresonance (hi′per-rez′o-nans). Resonance increased above the normal, and often of lower pitch, on percussion of the body.

hy′persaliva′tion. Sialism.

hypersarcosinemia (hi′per-sar-ko-sī-ne′mī-ah). Sarcosinemia.

hy′persecre′tion. Excessive secretion.

hy′persitiveness, hy′persensitiv′ity. 1. Abnormal sensitiveness or sensitivity; a condition in which the response to a stimulus is excessive in degree. **2.** Allergy. "Hypersensitiveness" was introduced into immunologic terminology because of the original misconception that repeated inoculations of toxin-containing preparations produced an increase in the already existing sensitivity to the toxin.

hypersensitization (hi′per-sen-sī-tī-za′shun). The immunological process by which hypersensitiveness (2) is induced.

hypersom′nia [hyper- + L. *somnus,* sleep]. A condition in which one sleeps for an excessively long time, but is normal in the intervals; distinguished from somnolence, in which one is always inclined to sleep.

hy′persple′nism. A condition, or group of conditions, in which the hemolytic action of the spleen is greatly increased.

hypersthenia (hi′per-sthe′nī-ah) [hyper- + G. *sthenos,* strength]. Excessive tension or strength.

hy′persthen′ic. Pertaining to or marked by hypersthenia.

hypersthenuria (hi′per-sthen-u′rī-ah) [hyper- + G. *sthenos,* strength, + *ouron,* urine]. Excretion of urine of unusually high specific gravity and concentration of solutes, resulting usually from loss or deprivation of water.

hypertelorism (hi-per-tel′or-izm) [hyper- + G. *tele,* far off, + *horizō,* to separate]. Abnormal distance between two paired organs.

ocular h., Greig's syndrome; extreme width between the eyes due to an enlarged sphenoid bone; other congenital deformities and mental retardation may be associated.

hy′perten′sive. Characterized by or suffering from abnormally increased blood pressure.

hypertension (hi-per-ten′shun) [hyper- + L. *tensio,* tension]. Persistent high blood pressure.

adrenal h., h. due to pheochromocytoma.

benign h., essential h. that runs a relatively long and symptomless course.

essential h., h. without preexisting renal disease or known cause.

malignant h., severe h. that runs a rapid course, causing necrosis of arteriolar walls, hemorrhagic lesions, and a poor prognosis.

portal h., h. in the portal system as seen in cirrhosis of the liver and other conditions causing obstruction to the portal vein.

pulmonary h., h. in the pulmonary circulation; may be primary or secondary to pulmonary or cardiac disease.

renal h., h. secondary to renal disease.

renovascular h., h. produced by renal arterial obstruction.

hy′perten′sor. Pressor.

hyperthecosis (hi′per-the-ko′sis). Diffuse hyperplasia of the theca cells of the graafian follicles.

hy′perthe′lia [hyper- + G. *thēlē,* nipple]. Polythelia.

hyperthermalgesia (hi′per-ther-mal-je′zī-ah) [hyper- + G. *thermē,* heat, + *algēsis,* pain]. Extreme sensitivity to heat.

hy′perther′mia [hyper- + G. *thermē,* heat]. Therapeutically induced hyperpyrexia.

malignant h., rapid onset of extremely high fever with muscle rigidity, precipitated in genetically susceptible persons, especially by halothane or succinylcholine.

hyperthrombinemia (hi′per-throm-bin-e′mī-ah). An abnormal increase of thrombin in the blood, frequently resulting in a tendency to intravascular coagulation.

hyperthy′mic. Pertaining to hyperthymism.

hyperthymism (hi-per-thi′mizm). Excessive activity of the thymus gland, formerly postulated to be a causal factor in certain instances of unexpected and sudden death.

hyperthyroidism (hi-per-thi′royd-izm). An abnormality of the thyroid gland in which its secretion is usually increased and is no longer under regulatory control of hypothalamic-pituitary centers.

hy′perthyrox′inemia. An elevated thyroxine concentration in blood.

hy′perto′nia [hyper- + G. *tonos,* tension]. Hypertonicity (1); extreme tension of the muscles or arteries.

hy′perton′ic. Hyperisotonic. **1.** Spastic (1); having a greater degree of tension. **2.** Having a greater osmotic pressure than a reference solution.

hypertonicity (hi′per-to-nis′ī-tī). **1.** Hypertonia. **2.** Increased effective osmotic pressure of body fluids.

hypertrichosis (hi′per-trī-ko′sis) [hyper- + G. *trichōsis,* a being hairy]. Growth of hair in excess of the normal.

hypertriglyceridemia (hi′per-tri-glis′er-ī-de′mī-ah). An elevated triglyceride concentration in blood.

familial h., type I or type IV familial *hyperlipoproteinemia.*

hy′pertro′pia [hyper- + G. *tropē,* a turn]. *Strabismus* sursum vergens.

hypertrophic (hi-per-trof′ik). Relating to or characterized by hypertrophy.

hypertrophy (hi-per'tro-fi) [hyper- + G. *trophē*, nourishment]. General increase in bulk of a part or organ, not due to tumor formation; may be restricted to denote greater bulk through increase in size, but not in number, of the individual tissue elements. See also hyperplasia.

   adaptive h., thickening of the walls of a hollow organ when there is obstruction to outflow.

   compensatory h., increase in size of an organ or part of an organ or tissue, when called upon to do additional work or perform the work of destroyed tissue or of a paired organ.

   complementary h., increase in size or expansion of part of an organ or tissue to fill the space left by the destruction of another portion of the same organ or tissue.

   concentric h., thickening of the walls of the heart or any cavity with apparent diminution of the capacity of the cavity.

   eccentric h., thickening of the wall of the heart or other cavity, with dilation.

   physiologic h., functional h., temporary increase in size of an organ or part to provide for a natural increase of function such as occurs in the walls of the uterus and in the mammae during pregnancy.

   vicarious h., h. of an organ following failure of another organ because of a functional relationship between them.

hyperuricemia (hi'per-u-ri-se'mi-ah). Enhanced blood concentrations of uric acid.

hy'perurice'mic. Relating to or characterized by hyperuricemia.

hypervalinemia (hi'per-val-ĭ-ne'mi-ah). Abnormally high plasma concentrations of valine; a common finding in maple syrup urine disease.

hypervascular (hi'per-vas'ku-lar) [hyper- + L. *vas,* a vessel]. Abnormally vascular; containing an excessive number of blood vessels.

hy'perventila'tion. Increased alveolar ventilation relative to metabolic carbon dioxide production, so that alveolar carbon dioxide pressure tends to fall below normal.

hypervitaminosis (hi'per-vi'tă-min-o'sis). A condition resulting from the ingestion of an excessive amount of a vitamin preparation, the symptoms varying according to the particular vitamin implicated.

hypervolemia (hi'per-vo-le'mi-ah) [hyper- + L. *volumen,* volume, + G. *haima,* blood]. Plethora (1); abnormally increased volume of blood.

hy'pervole'mic. Pertaining to or characterized by hypervolemia.

hypesthesia (hi-pes-the'zĭ-ah) [G. *hypo,* under, + *aisthēsis,* feeling]. Hypoesthesia; diminished sensitivity to stimulation.

hypha, pl. **hyphae** (hi'fah, hi'fe) [G. *hyphē,* a web]. A branching tubular cell characteristic of the growth of filamentous fungi; intercommunicating hyphae constitute a mycelium, the visible colony.

hyphedonia (hip-he-do'nĭ-ah) [G. *hypo,* under, + *hēdonē,* pleasure]. A habitually lessened or attenuated degree of pleasure.

hyphe'ma. Hemorrhage into the anterior chamber of the eye.

hyphemia (hi-fe'mĭ-ah) [G. *hypo,* under, + *haima,* blood]. Oligemia.

hyphidrosis (hip-hi-dro'sis). Hypohidrosis.

hypn-. See hypno-.

hypnagogic (hip-nă-goj'ik) [hypno- + G. *agōgos,* leading]. Denoting a transitional state, related to the hypnoidal, preceding the oncome of sleep; applied also to various hallucinations that may manifest themselves at that time.

hypnagogue (hip'nă-gog) [hypno- + G. *agōgos,* leading]. An agent that induces sleep.

hypnapagogic (hip'nap-ă-goj'ik) [hypno- + G. *apo,* from, + *agōgos,* leading]. **1.** Denoting a state similar to the hypnagogic, through which the mind passes in coming out of sleep; denoting also delusion experienced at such time. **2.** Causing wakefulness; preventing sleep.

hypno-, hypn- [G. *hypnos,* sleep]. Combining forms relating to sleep or hypnosis.

hyp'noanal'ysis. Psychoanalysis or other psychotherapy that employs hypnosis as an adjunctive technique.

hypnogenesis (hip-no-jen'ĕ-sis) [hypno- + G. *genesis,* production]. Induction of sleep or of the hypnotic state.

hypnogenic (hip-no-jen'ik). Relating to hypnogenesis.

hypnoidal (hip-noy'dal) [hypno- + G. *eidos,* resemblance]. Resembling hypnosis; denoting the subwaking state, a mental condition intermediate between sleeping and waking.

hyp'nolepsy [hypno- + G. *lēpsis,* a seizing]. Narcolepsy.

hypnosis (hip-no'sis) [G. *hypnos,* sleep, + *-osis,* condition]. An artificially induced trancelike state resembling somnambulism in which the subject is highly susceptible to suggestion, oblivious to all else, and responds readily to the commands of the hypnotist.

hyp'nother'apy. 1. Treatment of disease by inducing prolonged sleep. **2.** Psychotherapeutic treatment by means of hypnotism.

hypnotic (hip-not'ik) [G. *hypnōtikos,* causing one to sleep]. **1.** Causing sleep. **2.** Relating to hypnotism.

hypnotism (hip'no-tizm) [G. *hypnos,* sleep]. **1.** The process or act of inducing hypnosis. **2.** The practice or study of hypnosis.

hyp'notist. One who practices hypnotism.

hyp'notize. To induct one into hypnosis.

hypo- [G. *hypo,* under]. Prefix denoting a location beneath something else; a diminution or deficiency; the lowest, or least rich in oxygen, of a series of chemical compounds. See also sub-.

hypoacidity (hi'po-ă-sid'ĭ-ti). A lower than normal degree of acidity.

hy'poacu'sis. Hypacusis.

hy'poadre'nalism. Reduced adrenocortical function.

hy'poalbumine'mia. Hypalbuminemia; an abnormally low concentration of albumin in blood.

hypoalgesia (hi'po-al-je'zĭ-ah). Hypalgesia.

hypoalimentation (hi'po-al-ĭ-men-ta'shun). A condition of insufficient nourishment.

hypoazoturia (hi'po-az-o-tu'rĭ-ah) [hypo- + Fr. *azote*, nitrogen, + G. *ouron*, urine]. Excretion of abnormally small quantities of nonprotein nitrogenous material (especially urea) in the urine.

hypobaric (hi-po-bǎr'ik) [hypo- + G. *baros*, weight]. **1.** Pertaining to pressure of ambient gases below 1 atmosphere. **2.** With respect to solutions, less dense than the diluent or medium.

hypobarism (hi-po-bǎr'izm). Dysbarism resulting from decreasing barometric pressure on the body without hypoxia.

hypobaropathy (hi'po-bǎr-op'ǎ-thĭ) [hypo- + G. *baros*, weight, + *pathos*, suffering]. Sickness produced by reduced barometric pressure; not always distinguished from hypobarism and altitude sickness.

hy'poblast [hypo- + G. *blastos*, germ]. Endoderm.

hypoblas'tic. Relating to or derived from the hypoblast.

hypocalcemia (hi-po-kal-se'mĭ-ah). Abnormally low levels of calcium in the circulating blood; commonly denotes subnormal concentrations of calcium ions.

hypocalcification (hi'po-kal-sĭ-fĭ-ka'shun). Deficient calcification of bone or teeth.

hypocapnia (hi-po-kap'nĭ-ah) [hypo- + G. *kapnos*, smoke]. Hypocarbia; abnormally low tension of carbon dioxide in the circulating blood.

hypocar'bia. Hypocapnia.

hypochloremia (hi'po-klo-re'mĭ-ah). An abnormally low level of chloride ions in the circulating blood.

hypochlorhydria (hi'po-klŏr-hi'drĭ-ah). An abnormally small amount of hydrochloric acid in the stomach.

hypochloruria (hi'po-klŏr-u'rĭ-ah). Excretion of abnormally small quantities of chloride ions in the urine.

hypocholesterolemia (hi'po-ko-les'ter-ol-e'mĭ-ah). Abnormally small amounts of cholesterol in the circulating blood.

hypochondria (hi-po-kon'drĭ-ah). **1.** Hypochondriasis. **2.** Plural of hypochondrium.

hypochondriac (hi-po-kon'drĭ-ak). **1.** Hypochondriacal. **2.** A victim of hypochondriasis. **3.** Beneath the ribs; relating to the hypochondrium.

hypochondriacal (hi-po-kon-dri'ǎ-kal). Hypochondriac (1); relating to or suffering from hypochondriasis.

hypochondriasis (hi-po-kon-dri'ǎ-sis) [hypochondrium, the site of hypochondria, + *-iasis*, condition]. Hypochondria (1); morbid concern about one's own health and exaggerated attention to any unusual bodily or mental sensations; a false belief that one is suffering from some disease.

hypochondrium, pl. **hypochondria** (hi-po-kon'drĭ-um, -ah) [L. fr. G. *hypochondrion*, abdomen, belly, from *hypo*, under, + *chondros*, cartilage (of ribs)]. The area on each side of the abdomen covered by the costal cartileges, lateral to the epigastrium.

hypochondroplasia (hi'po-kon-dro-pla'zĭ-ah) [hypo- + G. *chondros*, cartilage, + *plasis*, a molding]. Dwarfism similar to but milder than achondroplasia, not seen in the same families or evident until mid-childhood, and with normal skull and facies; autosomal dominant inheritance.

hypochromasia (hi'po-kro-ma'zĭ-ah). Hypochromia.

hypochromatic (hi'po-kro-mat'ik) [hypo- + G. *chrōma*, color]. Hypochromic (1); containing a small amount of pigment, or less than the normal amount for the individual tissue.

hypochromatism (hi-po-kro'mǎ-tizm). **1.** The condition of being hypochromatic. **2.** Hypochromia.

hypochromemia (hi'po-kro-me'mĭ-ah) [hypo- + G. *chrōma*, color, + *haima*, blood]. Anemia characterized by a color index that is less than unity.

hypochromia (hi-po-kro'mĭ-ah) [hypo- + G. *chrōma*, color]. Hypochromasia; hypochromatism (2); an anemic condition in which the percentage of hemoglobin in the red blood cells is less than the normal range.

hypochromic (hi-po-kro'mik). **1.** Hypochromatic. **2.** Denoting decrease in light absorption.

hypochylia (hi-po-ki'lĭ-ah) [hypo- + G. *chylos*, juice]. Deficiency of gastric juice.

hy'pocomplemente'mia. A hereditary or acquired condition of the blood in which one or another component of complement is lacking or reduced in amount.

hypocorticoidism (hi'po-kor'tĭ-koyd-izm). Adrenocortical *insufficiency*.

hypocupremia (hi'po-ku-pre'mĭ-ah) [hypo- + L. *cuprum*, copper, + G. *haima*, blood]. Reduced copper content of the blood.

hypocythemia (hi'po-si-the'mĭ-ah) [hypo- + G. *kytos*, cell, + *haima*, blood]. Abnormally low numbers of red and white cells and other formed elements of the circulating blood, as in aplastic anemia.

hypodactyly (hi-po-dak'tĭ-lĭ) [hypo- + G. *daktylos*, finger, + *-ia*, condition]. Less than the normal number of digits.

Hypoderma (hi'po-der'mah) [hypo- + G. *derma*, skin]. A genus of botflies whose larvae are the cause of cutaneous larva migrans of man.

hy'podermat'ic. Subcutaneous.

hypoder'mic. 1. Subcutaneous. **2.** Hypodermic *injection.* **3.** Hypodermic *syringe.*

hy'poder'mis. Tela subcutanea.

hypodermoclysis (hi'po-der-mok'lĭ-sis) [hypo- + G. *derma*, skin, + *klysis*, a washing out]. Subcutaneous injection of a saline or other solution.

hypodip'sia [hypo- + G. *dipsa*, thirst]. A physiologic condition, perhaps of hypertonicity of body fluids, insufficient to initiate drinking but at times sufficient to sustain drinking when started.

hypodontia (hi´po-don´shǐ-ah) [hypo- + G. *odous,* tooth]. Oligodontia (2); congenitally absent teeth, usually the secondary teeth.

hy´podynam´ic. Possessing or exhibiting subnormal power or force.

hypoeccrisis (hi´po-ek´rǐ-sis) [hypo- + eccrisis]. Reduced excretion of waste matter.

hypoeccritic (hi´po-ĕ-krit´ik). Characterized by hypo-eccrisis.

hypoergia, hypoergy (hi-po-er´jǐ-ah, hi-po-er´jǐ) [hypo- + G. (en) ergeia, from *ergon,* work]. Hyposensitiveness.

hypoesophoria (hi´po-es-o-fo´rǐ-ah) [hypo- + G. *esō,* within, + *phoros,* bearing]. Combined downward and inward deviation of the eyeball.

hypoesthesia (hi´po-es-the´zǐ-ah). Hypesthesia.

hypoexophoria (hi´po-ek-so-fo´rǐ-ah) [hypo- + G. *exō,* without, + *phoros,* bearing]. Combined outward and downward deviation of the eyeball.

hy´poferre´mia. Deficiency of iron in the circulating blood.

hypofibrinogenemia (hi´po-fi-brin´o-jĕ-ne´mǐ-ah). Abnormally low concentration of fibrinogen in the circulating blood plasma.

hypofunction (hi´po-funk´shun). Reduced, low, or inadequate function.

hypogalactia (hi´po-gǎ-lak´shǐ-ah) [hypo- + G. *gala,* milk]. Less than normal milk secretion.

hy´pogalac´tous. Producing or secreting a less than normal amount of milk.

hy´pogam´maglob´uline´mia. Decreased quantity of the gamma fraction of serum globulin; sometimes used loosely to denote a decreased quantity of immunoglobulins.

 transient h. of infancy, transient agammaglobulinemia; a type of primary immunodeficiency that occurs in infants of both sexes, usually before the sixth month of life.

hypoganglionosis (hi´po-gang-lǐ-on-o´sis). A reduction in the number of ganglionic nerve cells.

hypogas´tric. Relating to the hypogastrium.

hypogastrium (hi-po-gas´trǐ-um) [G. *hypogastrion,* lower belly, fr. *hypo,* under, + *gastēr,* belly] [NA]. Pubic region; the lower central area of the abdomen below the umbilicus.

hypogastroschisis (hi´po-gas-tros´kǐ-sis) [hypogastrium + G. *schisis,* cleaving]. Congenital fissure in the hypogastric region.

hypogenesis (hi-po-jen´ĕ-sis) [hypo- + G. *genesis,* origin]. General underdevelopment of parts or organs of the body.

hypogenet´ic. Relating to hypogenesis.

hypogenitalism (hi-po-jen´ǐ-tal-izm). Partial or complete failure of maturation of the genitalia; commonly, a consequence of hypogonadism.

hypogeusia (hi-po-gu´sǐ-ah) [hypo- + G. *geusis,* taste]. A blunting of the sense of taste.

hypoglos´sal [L. *hypoglossus* fr. hypo- + *glossus,* tongue]. Subglossal.

hypoglot´tis [G. *hypoglōsis,* or -*glōttis,* undersurface of tongue]. Ranula (1); the undersurface of the tongue.

hypoglycemia (hi´po-gli-se´mǐ-ah). An abnormally small concentration of glucose in the circulating blood, *i.e.,* less than the minimum of the normal range.

hypoglyce´mic. Pertaining to or characterized by hypoglycemia.

hypoglycogenolysis (hi´po-gli´ko-jĕ-nol´ǐ-sis). Deficient glycogenolysis.

hypoglycorrhachia (hi´po-gli-ko-rak´ǐ-ah) [hypo- + G. *glykys,* sweet, + *rhachis,* spine]. Depressed concentration of sugar in the cerebrospinal fluid.

hypognathous (hi-po-nath´us, hi-pog´nǎ-thus) [hypo- + G. *gnathos,* jaw]. Having a congenitally defectively developed lower jaw.

hypogonadism (hi-po-go´nad-izm). Inadequate gonadal function, as manifested by deficiencies in gametogenesis and/or the secretion of gonadal hormones.

hypogonadotropic (hi-po-gon´ǎ-do-trop´ik). Indicating inadequate secretion of gonadotrophins and the consequence thereof.

hypohidrosis (hi´po-hi-dro´sis). Hyphidrosis; diminished perspiration.

hy´pohidrot´ic. Characterized by diminished sweating.

hy´pokale´mia [hypo- + Mod. L. *kalium,* potassium, + G. *haima,* blood]. Hypopotassemia; an abnormally small concentration of potassium ions in the circulating blood.

hypokinesis, hypokinesia (hi´po-kǐ-ne´sis, -kǐ-ne´zǐ-ah) [hypo- + G. *kinēsis,* movement]. Hypomotility; diminished or slow movement.

hypokinet´ic. Relating to or characterized by hypokinesis.

hypoleydigism (hi-po-li´dig-ism). Subnormal secretion of androgens by the cells of Leydig.

hy´pomagnese´mia. Subnormal plasma concentration of magnesium.

hypomas´tia [hypo- + G. *mastos,* breast]. Atrophy or congenital smallness of the breasts.

hypomenorrhea (hi´po-men-o-re´ah) [hypo- + G. *mēn,* month, + *rhoia,* flow]. A diminution of the flow or a shortening of the duration of menstruation.

hypomere (hi´po-mēr) [hypo- + G. *meros,* part]. **1.** The portion of the myotome that extends ventrolaterally to form body-wall muscle, innervated by the primary ventral branch of a spinal nerve. **2.** The somatic and splanchnic layers of the lateral mesoderm which give rise to the lining of the celom.

hy´pometab´olism. Reduced metabolism; low metabolic rate.

hy´pome´tria [hypo- + G. *metron,* measure]. A manifestation of ataxia characterized by underreaching an object or goal.

hypomnesia (hi-pom-ne´zǐ-ah) [hypo- + G. *mnēmē,* memory]. Impaired memory.

hy'pomorph [hypo- + G. *morphē,* form]. One whose standing height is short in proportion to the sitting height, owing to shortness of limb.

hypomotil'ity. Hypokinesis.

hypomyotonia (hi'po-mi-o-to'nĭ-ah) [hypo- + G. *mys* (*myo-*) muscle, + *tonos,* tension]. Diminished muscular tone.

hypomyxia (hi-po-mik'sĭ-ah) [hypo- + G. *myxa,* mucus]. Diminished secretion of mucus.

hyponatremia (hi'po-nă-tre'mĭ-ah) [hypo- + L. *natrium,* sodium, + G. *haima,* blood]. Abnormally low concentrations of sodium ions in the circulating blood.

hyponeocytosis (hi'po-ne'o-si-to'sis) [hypo- + G. *neos,* new, + *kytos,* cell, + *-osis,* condition]. Leukopenia associated with the presence of immature and young leukocytes (especially in the granulocytic series), *i.e.,* a "shift to the left" in the hemogram.

hyponychial (hi-po-nik'ĭ-al). **1.** Subungual. **2.** Relating to the hyponychium.

hyponychium (hi-po-nik'ĭ-um) [hypo- + G. *onyx,* nail] [NA]. The epithelium of the nail bed, particularly its posterior part in the region of the lunula.

hyponychon (hi-pon'ĭ-kon) [hypo- + G. *onyx,* nail]. An ecchymosis beneath a finger or toe nail.

hypoorthocytosis (hi'po-or'tho-si-to'sis) [hypo- + G. *orthos,* correct, + *kytos,* cell, + *-osis,* condition]. Leukopenia in which the relative numbers of the various types of white blood cells are within the normal range, and no immature cells are found in the circulating blood.

hypopancreatism (hi'po-pan'kre-ă-tizm). A condition of diminished activity of the pancreas.

hypoparathyroidism (hi'po-păr-ah-thi'roy-dizm). Parathyroid insufficiency; a condition due to diminution or absence of the secretion of the parathyroid hormones.

hypophalangism (hi'po-fă-lan'jizm). Congenital absence of one or more of the phalanges of a digit.

hypopharynx (hi'po-făr'inks). Laryngopharynx.

hypophonesis (hi-po-fo-ne'sis) [hypo- + G. *phōnēsis,* a sounding]. In percussion or auscultation, a sound that is diminished or fainter than usual.

hypopho'ria [hypo- + G. *phora,* motion]. A tendency of the visual axis of one eye to sink below that of its normal fellow.

hypophosphatasia (hi'po-fos-fă-ta'zĭ-ah). Abnormally low content of alkaline phosphatase in the circulating blood.

hypophosphatemia (hi'po-fos-fă-te'mĭ-ah). Abnormally low concentrations of phosphates in the circulating blood.

hy'pophos'phatu'ria. Reduced urinary excretion of phosphates.

hypophysectomy (hi-pof-ĭ-sek'to-mĭ). Excision or destruction of the pituitary gland.

hypophysial, hypophyseal (hi-po-fiz'ĭ-al). Relating to a hypophysis.

hypophysioprivic, hypophyseoprivic (hi'po-fiz'ĭ-o-priv'ik) [hypophysis + L. *privus,* deprived of]. Denoting the condition in which the pituitary gland may be absent or functionally inactive, as after hypophysectomy.

hypophysis (hi-pof'ĭ-sis) [G. an undergrowth] [NA]. Pituitary or master gland; an unpaired compound gland suspended from the base of the hypothalamus by a short cordlike extension of the infundibulum; consists of two major subdivisions: 1) a posterior lobe that appears as the bulbous end of the stalk and stores and releases the hormone vasopressin and oxytocin, 2) the larger anterior lobe that, in response to releasing factors, releases into systemic circulation any one (or combination) of a variety of tropic hormones, each of which activates the corresponding endocrine gland and triggers the release of its hormone.

hypopiesis (hi'po-pi-e'sis) [hypo- + G. *piesis,* pressure]. Hypotension (1).

hypopituitarism (hi'po-po-pĭ-tu'ĭ-tă-rizm). A condition due to diminished activity of the anterior lobe of the hypophysis, with inadequate secretion of one or more anterior pituitary hormones.

hypoplasia (hi-po-pla'zĭ-ah) [hypo- + G. *plasis,* a molding]. **1.** Underdevelopment of tissue or an organ, usually due to a decrease in the number of cells. **2.** Atrophy due to destruction of some of the elements and not merely to their general reduction in size.

hypoplas'tic. Pertaining to or characterized by hypoplasia.

hypoploid (hi'po-ployd). Characterized by hypoploidy.

hypoploidy (hi'po-ploy'dĭ). State of having fewer chromosomes than the normal number.

hypopnea (hi-pop'ne-ah) [hypo- + G. *pnoē,* breathing]. Respiration that is shallower, slower, or both, than normal.

hypopo'sia [hypo- + G. *posis,* drinking]. Hypodipsia, with emphasis on tendency to drink rather than on the reduced sensation of thirst.

hypopotassemia (hi'po-pot-ah-se'mĭ-ah). Hypokalemia.

hy'poprax'ia [hypo- + G. *praxis,* action, + *-ia,* condition]. Deficient activity.

hypoproteinemia (hi-po-pro'tēn-e'mĭ-ah). Abnormally small amounts of total protein in the circulating blood plasma.

hypoprothrombinemia (hi'po-pro-throm'bin-e'mĭ-ah). Abnormally small amounts of prothrombin in the circulating blood.

hypoptyalism (hi-po-ti'ă-lizm) [hypo- + G. *ptyalon,* saliva]. Hyposalivation.

hypopyon (hi-po'pĭ-on) [hypo- + G. *pyon,* pus]. Puslike fluid in the anterior chamber of the eye.

hyporeflexia (hi'po-re-flek'sĭ-ah). Diminished or weakened reflexes.

hy'pori'boflavino'sis. See ariboflavinosis.

hy'posal'iva'tion. Hypoptyalism; reduced salivation.

hyposcle'ral. Beneath the sclerotic coat of the eyeball.

hyposecre'tion. Diminished secretion, as by a gland.

hyposen'sitiveness. Hypoergia; hypoergy; subnormal sensitiveness or sensitivity in which the response to a stimulus is unusually delayed or lessened in degree.

hyposmia (hi-poz'mĭ-ah) [hypo- + G. *osmē,* smell]. Diminished sense of smell.

hyposomatotropism (hi'po-so'mă-to-tro'pizm). Deficient secretion of pituitary growth hormone (somatotropin).

hypospa'diac. Relating to hypospadias.

hypospadias (hi-po-spa'dĭ-as) [G. one having the orifice of the penis too low]. A developmental anomaly characterized by a defect in the wall of the urethra so that a part of the canal is open on the undersurface of the penis; also a similar defect in the female in which the urethra opens into the vagina.

hypostasis (hi-pos'tă-sis) [G. *hypo-stasis,* a standing under, sediment]. **1.** Formation of a sediment at the bottom of a liquid. **2.** Hypostatic *congestion.*

hypostat'ic. **1.** Sedimentary; resulting from a dependent position. **2.** Relating to hypostasis.

hyposthenia (hi-pos-the'nĭ-ah) [hypo- + G. *sthenos,* strength]. Weakness.

hyposthenic (hi-pos-then'ik). Weak.

hyposthenuria (hi'pos-the-nu'rĭ-ah) [hypo- + G. *sthenos,* strength, + *ouron,* urine]. Secretion of urine of low specific gravity, due to inability of the tubules of the kidneys to produce a concentrated urine.

hypostomia (hi-po-sto'mĭ-ah) [hypo- + G. *stoma,* mouth]. A form of microstomia in which the oral opening is a small vertical slit.

hy'potel'orism [hypo- + G. *tēle,* far off, + *horizō,* to separate]. Abnormal closeness of the eyes.

hypoten'sion [hypo- + L. *tensio,* a stretching]. **1.** Hypopiesis; subnormal arterial blood pressure. **2.** Reduced pressure or tension of any kind.

induced h., controlled h., deliberate, acute reduction of arterial blood pressure to reduce operative blood loss, either by pharmacologic means during anesthesia and surgery or preoperative withdrawal of blood which is returned to the circulation postoperatively.

orthostatic h., postural h., a form of low blood pressure that occurs when standing.

hypoten'sive. Characterized by low blood pressure or causing a reduction in blood pressure.

hy'poten'sor. Depressor (4).

hy'pothal'amus [hypo- + thalamus] [NA]. The ventral and medial region of the diencephalon forming the walls of the ventral half of the third ventricle; its ventral surface is marked by, from before backward, the optic chiasma, the unpaired infundibulum, and the paired mamillary bodies; prominently involved in the functions of the autonomic nervous system and, through its vascular link with the anterior lobe of the hypophysis, in endo-

crine mechanisms; also appears to play a role in the nervous mechanisms underlying moods and motivational states.

hypothenar (hi'po-the'nar, -poth'ē-nar) [hypo- + G. *thenar,* the palm]. **1[** NA]. Antithenar; the fleshy mass at the medial side of the palm. **2.** Denoting any structure in relation with this part.

hypother'mal. Denoting hypothermia.

hypother'mia [hypo- + G. *thermē,* heat]. A body temperature significantly below 98.6°F (37°C).

accidental h., unintentional decrease in body temperature on exposure to a cold environment.

regional h., perfusion with cold blood or local refrigeration to cool an organ being subjected to ischemia in order to reduce its metabolic requirements.

total body h., deliberate reduction of total body temperature to reduce the general metabolism of the tissues.

hypothesis (hi-poth'e-sis) [L. fr. G. *hypotithenai,* to propose or suppose]. A supposition or assumption advanced as a basis for reasoning or argument, or as a guide to experimental investigation; a tentative theory unsupported by the essential facts that would prove its truth.

Lyon h., that one X-chromosome is inactive during interphase in normal females, and is represented in interphase cell nuclei as the sex chromatin body; as either X-chromosome may be inactivated, females heterozygous for an X-linked mutant gene may show patches of tissue expressing the phenotype of the mutant gene while the majority of tissue remains normal.

Michaelis-Menten h., that a complex is formed between an enzyme and its substrate, which complex then decomposes to yield free enzyme and the reaction products, the latter rate determining the over-all rate of substrate-product conversion. See also Michaelis-Menten *constant.*

Starling's h., that net filtration through capillary membranes is proportional to the transmembrane hydrostatic pressure difference minus the transmembrane oncotic pressure difference; distinguished from Starling's *law* of the heart.

zwitter h., that an ampholytic molecule (*e.g.,* an amino acid) yields, at the isoelectric point, equal numbers of basic and acid ions, thus becoming a zwitterion.

hypothrombinemia (hi'po-throm-bin-e'mĭ-ah). Abnormally small amounts of thrombin in the circulating blood, thereby resulting in bleeding tendency.

hypothymia (hi-po-thi'mĭ-ah) [hypo- + G. *thymos,* mind]. Depression of spirits; the "blues."

hypothy'mic. Pertaining to hypothymia or hypothymism.

hypothy'mism. Inadequate function of the thymus.

hypothy'roid. Marked by reduced thyroid function.

hypothyroidism (hi-po-thi'royd-izm) [hypo- + G. *thyreoeidēs,* thyroid]. Diminished production of thyroid hormone, leading to thyroid insufficiency.

hypoto'nia [hypo- + G. *tonos*, tone]. Hypotonicity (1). **1.** Reduced tension in any part, as in the eyeball. **2.** Relaxation of the arteries. **3.** A condition in which there is diminution or loss of muscular tonicity, in consequence of which the muscles may be stretched beyond their normal limits.

hypoton'ic. 1. Having a lesser degree of tension. **2.** Having a lesser osmotic pressure than a reference solution, ordinarily assumed to be blood plasma or interstitial fluid.

hypotonicity (hi'po-to-nis'ĭ-tĭ). **1.** Hypotonia. **2.** A decreased effective osmotic pressure.

hypotoxicity (hi-po-toks-is'ĭ-tĭ). Reduced toxicity; the quality of being only slightly poisonous.

hypotrichosis [hi'po-trĭ-ko'sis) [hypo- + G. *trichōsis*, hairiness]. A less than normal amount of hair on the head and/or body.

hypotro'pia [hypo- + G. *tropē*, turn]. Downward deviation of the visual axis of one eye.

hy'potympanot'omy [hypo- + G. *tympanon*, tympanum, + *tomē*, incision]. Complete surgical extirpation, without sacrifice of hearing, of small tumors confined to the lower tympanic cavity.

hypotympanum (hi-po-tim'pă-num). The lower part of the tympanic cavity.

hypouricemia (hi'po-u-rĭ-se'mĭ-ah). Reduced blood concentration of uric acid.

hypouricuria (hi'po-u'rĭ-ku'rĭ-ah). Reduced excretion of uric acid in the urine.

hy'poventila'tion. Reduced alveolar ventilation relative to metabolic carbon dioxide production, so that alveolar carbon dioxide pressure tends to rise above normal.

hy'povitamino'sis. Insufficiency of one or more essential vitamins.

hypovolemia (hi'po-vo-le'mĭ-ah) [hypo- + L. *volumen*, volume, + G. *haima*, blood]. Oligemia.

hypovolia (hi'po-vo'lĭ-ah) [hypo- + L. *volumen*, volume]. Diminished water content or volume of a given compartment.

hypoxanthine (hi-pok-san'thin). 6-Oxypurine; purine-6(1*H*)-one; a purine present in the muscles and other tissues and formed during purine catabolism by deamination of adenine.

hypoxemia (hi-pok-se'mĭ-ah) [hypo- + oxygen, + G. *haima*, blood]. Subnormal oxygenation of arterial blood, short of anoxia.

hypox'ia. Subnormal levels of oxygen in air, blood, or tissue, short of anoxia.

   anemic h., anemic anoxia; h. resulting from a decreased concentration of functional hemoglobin or a reduced number of erythrocytes.

   diffusion h., diffusion anoxia; abrupt transient decrease in alveolar oxygen tension when room air is inhaled at the conclusion of a nitrous oxide anesthesia.

   hypoxic h., anoxic anoxia; h. resulting from a defective mechanism of oxygenation in the lungs as by a low tension of oxygen, by abnormal pulmonary function, or by a right-to-left shunt in the heart.

   ischemic h., stagnant anoxia or h.; h. resulting from slower peripheral circulation through the tissues, so that oxygen tension in capillary blood is less than normal, even though the saturation, content, and tension in arterial blood are normal; associated with congestive cardiac failure, shock, and impaired venous return.

hypsarhythmia, hypsarrhythmia (hip'sā-rith'mĭ-ah) [G. *hypsi*, high, + a-priv. + *rhythmos*, rhythm]. The abnormal and characteristically chaotic electroencephalogram commonly found in patients with infantile spasms.

hyster-. See hystero-.

hysteralgia (his-ter-al'jĭ-ah) [hystero- + G. *algos*, pain]. Hysterodynia; metralgia; metrodynia; pain in the uterus.

hysteratresia (his'ter-ă-tre'zĭ-ah). Atresia of the uterine cavity, usually resulting from inflammatory endocervical adhesions.

hysterectomy (his-ter-ek'to-mĭ) [hystero- + G. *ektomē*, excision]. Surgical removal of the uterus.

   abdominal h., abdominohysterectomy; removal of the uterus through an incision in the abdominal wall.

   cesarean h., cesarean section followed by h.

   radical h., complete removal of the uterus, upper vagina, and parametrium.

   supracervical h., subtotal h., removal of the fundus of the uterus, leaving the cervix *in situ.*

   vaginal h., removal of the uterus through the vagina without incising the wall of the abdomen.

hystere'sis [G. *hysterēsis*, a coming later]. Failure of either one of two related phenomena to keep pace with the other; or any situation in which the value of one depends upon whether the other has been increasing or decreasing.

hystereurysis (his'ter-u'rĭ-sis) [hystero- + G. *eurynein*, to dilate]. Dilation of the lower segment and cervical canal of the uterus.

hysteria (his-tēr'ĭ-ah) [G *hystera*, womb, because formerly thought to be of uterine causation]. A diagnostic term, referable to a wide variety of psychogenic symptoms involving disorder of function which may be mental, sensory, motor, or visceral.

   anxiety h., h. characterized by manifest anxiety.

   conversion h., conversion h. neurosis; conversion reaction; h. characterized by the substitution through psychic transformation of physical signs or symptoms for anxiety; generally restricted to such major symptoms as psychic blindness, deafness, or paralysis.

   major h., grande hysterie; a syndrome characterized by a first stage of aura, a second stage of epileptoid convulsions, a third stage of tonic and clonic spasms; a fourth stage of dramatic behavior; and a fifth stage of delirium.

   minor h., a mild form of h. characterized chiefly by subjective pains, nervousness, undue sensitiveness, and sometimes attacks of emotional excitement, but without paralysis or other stigmata.

hysterical (his-těr′ĭ-kal). Relating to or suffering from hysteria.

hysterics (his-těr′iks). An expression of emotion accompanied often by crying, laughing, and screaming.

hystero-, hyster-. 1[G. *hystera*, womb (uterus)]. Combining forms denoting the uterus (see also metra-, metro-, utero-) or hysteria. 2[G. *hysteros*, later]. Combining forms meaning late or following.

hys′terocat′alepsy. Hysteria with cataleptic manifestations.

hysterocele (his′ter-o-sēl) [hystero- + G. *kēlē*, hernia]. 1. An abdominal or perineal hernia containing part or all of the uterus. 2. Protrusion of uterine contents into a weakened, bulging area of uterine wall.

hysterocleisis (his′ter-o-kli′sis) [hystero- + G. *kleisis*, closure]. Operative occlusion of the uterus.

hysterodynia (his′ter-o-din′ĭ-ah) [hystero- + G. *odynē*, pain]. Hysteralgia.

hysteroepilepsy (his′ter-o-ep′ĭ-lep-sī). Hysterical convulsions. See major *hysteria.*

hysterogenic (his′ter-o-jen′ik). Causing hysterical symptoms or reactions.

hys′terogram. 1. A radiograph of the uterus, usually using contrast media. 2. A record of the strength of uterine contractions.

hys′terograph. An apparatus for recording the strength of uterine contractions.

hysterography (his-ter-og′ră-fī) [hystero- + G. *graphō*, to write]. 1. Radiography of a uterine cavity filled with contrast medium. 2. The procedure of recording uterine contractions.

hys′teroid [hystero- + G. *eidos*, resemblance]. Resembling or simulating hysteria.

hys′terolith [hystero- + G. *lithos*, stone]. Uterine *calculus.*

hysterolysis (his-ter-ol′ĭ-sis) [hystero- + G. *lysis*, dissolution]. Breaking up of adhesions between the uterus and neighboring parts.

hysterom′eter [hystero- + G. *metron*, measure]. Uterometer; a graduated sound for measuring the depth of the uterine cavity.

hysteromyoma (his′ter-o-mi-o′mah) [hystero- + G. *mys*, muscle, + *-oma*, tumor]. A myoma of the uterus.

hysteromyomectomy (his′ter-o-mi-o-mek′to-mī) [hysteromyoma + G. *ektomē*, excision]. Operative removal of a uterine myoma.

hysteromyotomy (his′ter-o-mi-ot′o-mī) [hystero- + G. *mys*, muscle, + *tomē*, incision]. Incision into the uterine muscles.

hystero-oophorectomy (his′ter-o-o′o-fo-rek′to-mī) [hystero- + G. *ōon*, egg, + *phoros*, bearing, + *ektomē*, excision]. Surgical removal of the uterus and ovaries.

hysteropathy (his-ter-op′ă-thī) [hystero- + G. *pathos*, suffering]. Any disease of the uterus.

hys′teropexy [hystero- + G. *pēxis*, fixation]. Uteropexy; uterofixation; surgical fixation of a misplaced or abnormally movable uterus.

hys′teroplasty. Uteroplasty.

hysterorrhaphy (his-ter-or′ă-fī) [hystero- + G. *raphē*, suture]. Sutural repair of a lacerated uterus.

hysterorrhexis (his′ter-o-rek′sis) [hystero- + G. *rhēxis*, rupture]. Rupture of the uterus.

hysterosalpingectomy (his′ter-o-sal-pin-jek′to-mī) [hystero- + G. *salpinx*, a trumpet, + *ektomē*, excision]. Surgical removal of the uterus and one or both uterine tubes.

hysterosalpingography (his′ter-o-sal-ping-gog′ră-fī) [hystero- + G. *salpinx*, a trumpet, + *graphō*, to write]. Gynecography; hysterotubography; uterosalpingography; radiography of the uterus and oviducts after the injection of radiopaque material.

hysterosalpingo-oophorectomy (his′ter-o-sal-ping-go-o′of-o-rek′to-mī) [hystero- + G. *salpinx*, trumpet, + *ōon*, egg, + *phoros*, bearing, + *ektomē*, excision]. Excision of the uterus, oviducts, and ovaries.

hysterosalpingostomy (his′ter-o-sal-ping-gos′to-mī [hystero- + G. *salpinx*, trumpet, + *stoma*, mouth]. An operation to restore patency of a tube.

hysteroscope (his′ter-o-skōp) [hystero- + G. *skopeō*, to view]. Uteroscope; an endoscope used in direct visual examination of the uterus.

hysteroscopy (his-ter-os′ko-pī). Uteroscopy; visual instrumental inspection of the uterine cavity.

hys′terospasm. Spasm of the uterus.

hysterot′omy [hystero- + G. *tomē*, incision]. Uterotomy; incision of the uterus.

   abdominal h., abdominohysterotomy; transabdominal incision into the uterus.

   vaginal h., incision into the uterus via the vagina.

hysterotrachelectomy (his′ter-o-trak-el-ek′to-mī) [hystero- + G. *trachēlos*, neck, + *ektomē*, excision]. Surgical removal of the cervix uteri.

hysterotracheloplasty (his′ter-o-trak′el-o-plas-tī) [hystero- + G. *trachēlos*, neck, + *plastos*, formed, shaped]. Plastic repair of the cervix uteri.

hysterotrachelorrhaphy (his′ter-o-trak-el-or′ă-fī) [hystero- + G. *trachēlos*, neck, + *rhaphē*, a seam]. Sutural repair of a lacerated cervix uteri.

hysterotrachelotomy (his′ter-o-trak-el-ot′o-mī) [hystero- + G. *trachēlos*, neck, + *tomē*, incision]. Incision of the cervix uteri.

hysterotubography (his′ter-o-tu-bog′ră-fī). Hysterosalpingography.

Hz Hertz.

I

I Iodine; as a subscript, inspired *gas;* I blood group.

-ia [G. *-ia*, denoting action or an abstract]. Suffix denoting a condition. *Cf.* -ism.

-iasis [G. verb-nominalizing suffix]. Suffix denoting a condition or state, particularly morbid. See also -OSIS.

iatric (i-at′rik) [G. *iatros*, physician]. Pertaining to medicine or to a physician.

iatro- [G. *iatros*, physician]. Combining form denoting relation to physicians, medicine, treatment.

iatrogenic (i-at′ro-jen′ik) [iatro- + G. *-gen*, producing]. Denoting an unfavorable response to therapy, induced by the therapeutic effort itself; formerly used to imply autosuggestion resulting from the physician's discussion, examination, or suggestions.

-ic [L. *-icus*, fr. G. *-ikos*]. **1.** A suffix denoting of or pertaining to. **2.** A chemical suffix denoting that the element to the name of which it is attached is in combination in one of its higher valencies or indicating an acid.

ICD *International Classification of Diseases of the World Health Organization.*

ICDA *International Classification of Diseases, Adapted for Use in the United States;* includes a classification of surgical operations and other therapeutic and diagnostic procedures.

ichor (i′kor) [G. *ichōr*, serum]. A thin, watery discharge from an ulcer or unhealthy wound.

ichoroid (i′ko-royd) [G. *ichōr*, serum, + *eidos*, resemblance]. Denoting a thin, purulent discharge.

ichorous (i′kor-us). Relating to or resembling ichor.

ichorrhea (i′ko-re′ah) [G. *ichōr*, serum, + *rhoia*, a flow]. A profuse ichorous discharge.

ichthyism (ik′thĭ-izm) [G. *ichthys*, fish]. Ichthyotoxism.

ichthyo- [G. *ichthys*, fish]. Combining form relating to fish.

ichthyoid (ik′thĭ-oyd) [ichthyo- + G. *eidos*, resemblance]. Fish-shaped.

ichthyosis (ik-thĭ-o′sis) [ichthyo- + *-osis*, condition]. A congenital disorder of keratinization characterized by dryness and fishskin-like scaling of the skin. Also called alligator or fish skin; i. sauroderma.

   i. feta′lis, harlequin *fetus.*

   lamellar i., a dry form of congenital ichthyosiform erythroderma inherited as an autosomal recessive trait and present at birth; characterized by large, coarse scales over most of the body and thickened palms and soles, and associated with ectropion.

   i. sauroder′ma, ichthyosis.

   i. sim′plex, i. vulgaris.

   i. u′teri, transformation of the columnar epithelium of the endometrium into stratified squamous epithelium.

   i. vulga′ris, i. simplex; a form of i. inherited as an autosomal dominant trait, with onset in childhood of fine scales on the trunk and extremities but not on the flexural areas, and associated with atopy and prominent palmar and plantar markings.

ichthyotic (ik-thĭ-ot′ik). Relating to ichthyosis.

ichthyotoxism (ik′thĭ-o-tok′sizm) [ichthyo- + G. *toxikon*, poison]. Ichthyism; poisoning by fish.

ICP Intracranial *pressure.*

-ics [-ic + -s]. Suffix denoting organized knowledge, practice, or treatment.

ICSH Interstitial cell-stimulating *hormone.*

ictal (ik′tal) [L. *ictus*, a stroke]. Relating to or caused by a stroke or seizure; *e.g.,* epilepsy.

icteric (ik-tĕr′ik) [G. *ikterikos*, jaundiced]. Relating to or marked by icterus (jaundice).

ictero- [G. *ikteros*, icterus, jaundice]. Combining form relating to icterus.

ic′terogen′ic [ictero- + *-gen*, producing]. Causing jaundice.

ic′terohepati′tis [ictero- + G. *hēpar*, liver, + *-itis*, inflammation]. Inflammation of the liver with jaundice as a prominent symptom.

icteroid (ik′ter-oyd) [ictero- + G. *eidos*, resemblance]. Yellow-hued, or seemingly jaundiced.

icterus (ik′ter-us) [G. *ikteros*]. Jaundice.

   i. gra′vis, malignant jaundice; jaundice associated with high fever and delirium, seen in acute yellow atrophy and other destructive diseases of the liver.

   i. neonato′rum, Ritter's disease (2); jaundice of the newborn; either a mild temporary physiologic jaundice, or a severe and usually fatal form due to congenital occlusion of the common bile duct, erythroblastosis fetalis, congenital syphilitic cirrhosis of the liver, or septic pylephlebitis.

   physiologic i., physiologic jaundice; mild jaundice of the newborn due mainly to functional immaturity of the liver.

ictus (ik′tus) [L.]. **1.** A stroke or attack. **2.** A beat.

ICU Intensive care *unit.*

id [L. *id*, that]. **1.** In psychoanalysis, a part of the "psychic or mental apparatus," that is completely in the unconscious realm, unorganized, the reservoir of psychic energy or libido, and under the influence of the primary processes. **2.** A single term for the total of all psychic energy available from the innate drives and impulses in a newborn infant. Through socialization this diffuse, undirected energy becomes channeled in less egocentric and more socially responsive directions (development of the ego from the id).

-id. **1** [G. *-eidēs*, resembling, through Fr. *-id*]. Suffix indicating a state of sensitivity of the skin in which a part remote from the primary lesion reacts ("-id reaction") to substances of the pathogen, giving rise to a secondary inflammatory lesion; the lesion manifesting the reaction is designated by the use of -id as a suffix. **2** [G. *-idion*, a diminutive ending]. Suffix indicating a small or young specimen.

-ide. **1.** Suffix denoting a binary chemical compound; formerly denoted by the qualification, -ureted. **2.** Suffix to a sugar name indicating substitution for the H of the hemiacetal OH.

idea (i-de′ah) [G. semblance]. Any mental image or concept.

autochthonous i.'s, thoughts that suddenly burst into awareness as if they are terribly important, often as if they have come from an outside source.

compulsive i., a fixed and inappropriate i.

dominant i., an i. that governs all the actions and thoughts of the individual.

fixed i., idée fixe; an obsession; an exaggerated notion, belief, or delusion that persists, despite evidence to the contrary, and controls the mind.

i. of reference, the misinterpretation that other people's statements or acts pertain to one's self when, in fact, they do not.

ideal (i-de'al). A standard of perfection.

ego i., the part of the personality that comprises the goals and aims of the self; usually refers to the emulation of significant persons with whom it has identified.

ideation (i-de-a'shun). The formation of ideas.

idea'tional. Relating to ideation.

idée fixe (ē-dā'fēks') [Fr. obsession]. Fixed *idea*.

identification (i-den'tĭ-fĭ-ka'shun) [Mediev. L. *identicus,* fr. L. *idem,* the same, + *facio,* to make]. **1.** In the behavioral sciences, an imitation, sense of oneness, or psychic continuity with another person or group. **2.** In psychoanalysis, an unconscious defense mechanism in which a person incorporates into himself the mental picture of another person and then patterns himself after this person, and thus sees himself as like that person.

iden'tity. The social role of the person and his perception of it.

ego i., the ego's sense of its own identity.

gender i., the anatomical-sexual i. of the person; opposite of gender role.

ideo- [G. *idea,* form, notion]. Combining form pertaining to ideas or ideation. *Cf.* idio- .

ideology (i'de-ol'o-jī; i'de) [ideo- + G. *logos,* study]. The composite system of ideas, beliefs, and attitudes that constitutes an individual's or group's organized view of others.

idio- [G. *idios,* one's own]. Combining form meaning private, distinctive, peculiar to. *Cf.* ideo-.

idioagglutinin (id'ĭ-o-ă-glu'tin-in). An agglutinin that occurs naturally in the blood of a person or an animal, without the injection of a stimulating antigen or the passive transfer of antibody.

idiocy (id'ĭ-o-sī) [G. *idiōteria,* awkwardness, uncouthness]. Obsolete term for a subclass of mental *retardation.*

id'iogram [idio- + G. *gramma,* something written]. **1.** Karyotype. **2.** A diagrammatic representation of chromosome morphology characteristic of a species or population.

idioheteroagglutinin (id'ĭ-o-het'er-o-ă-glu'tin-in) [idio- + G. *heteros,* another, + agglutinin]. An idioagglutinin occurring in the blood of one animal, but capable of combining with the antigenic material from another species.

id'ioheterol'ysin. An idiolysin occurring in the blood of an animal of one species, but capable of combin-

ing with the red blood cells of another species, thereby causing hemolysis when complement is present.

idioisoagglutinin (id'ĭ-o-i'so-ă-glu'tin-in) [idio- + G. *isos,* equal, + agglutinin]. An idioagglutinin occurring in the blood of an animal of a certain species, capable of agglutinating the cells from animals of the same species.

idioisolysin (id'ĭ-o-i-sol'ĭ-sin). An idiolysin occurring in the blood of an animal of a certain species capable of combining with the red blood cells from animals of the same species, thereby causing hemolysis when complement is present.

idiolysin (id-ĭ-ol'i-sin). A lysin that occurs naturally in the blood of a person or an animal, without the injection of a stimulating antigen or the passive transfer of antibody.

id'iopath'ic [idio- + G. *pathos,* suffering]. **1.** Agnogenic; denoting a disease of unknown cause. **2.** Denoting a primary disease.

idiopathy (id'ĭ-op'ă-thī) [idio- + G. *pathos, suffering*]. A primary disease; one arising without apparent extrinsic cause.

idiophrenic (id'ĭ-o-fren'ik) [idio- + G. *phrēn,* mind]. Relating to, or originating in, the mind or brain alone, not reflex or secondary.

idiosyncrasy (id'ĭ-o-sin'kră-sī) [G. *idiosynkrasia,* fr. *idios,* one's own, + *synkrasis,* a mixing together]. An individual mental, behavioral, or physical characteristic or peculiarity.

id'iosyncrat'ic. Relating to or marked by an idiosyncrasy.

idiot (id'ĭ-ot) [G. *idiōtēs,* an ignorant, uncouth person]. Obsolete term for a subclass of mental *retardation,* or an individual classified therein.

idiot-savant [Fr.]. A person of low general intelligence who possesses an unusual faculty in performing certain mental tasks of which most normal persons are incapable.

id'iotype. Idiotypic antigenic determinant; a determinant that confers on an immunoglobulin molecule an antigenic "individuality" that is analogous to the "individuality" of the molecule's antibody activity. It seems to reflect the antigenic properties of the receptor (combining site) that confers specificity of antibody activity.

idioventricular (id-ĭ-o-ven-trik'u-lar). Pertaining to or associated with the cardiac ventricles alone, when dissociated from the atria.

IFN Interferon(s).

Ig Immunoglobulin.

ignipuncture (ig'nī-pungk-chur) [L. *ignis,* fire, + puncture]. The original procedure of closing a retinal break in retinal separation by transfixation of the break with cautery.

IH Infectious *hepatitis.*

ILA Insulin-like *activity.*

Ile Isoleucine or its radical isoleucyl.

ileac (il'e-ak). Relating to ileus or to the ileum.

ileal (il'e-al). Of or pertaining to the ileum.

ileectomy (il-e-ek'to-mĭ) [ileum + G. *ektomē*, excision]. Removal of the ileum.

ileitis (il-e-i'tis). Inflammation of the ileum.

distal, regional, or **terminal i.,** regional *enteritis.*

ileo- [L. *ileum*]. Combining form denoting relationship to the ileum.

ileocecal (il'e-o-se'kal). Relating to both ileum and cecum.

ileocecostomy (il'e-o-se-kos'to-mĭ). Cecoileostomy; anastomosis of ileum to cecum.

il'eocol'ic. Relating to the ileum and the colon.

ileocolitis (il-e-o-ko-li'tis). Inflammation of the mucous membrane of a greater or lesser extent of both ileum and colon.

i. ulcero'sa chron'ica, a chronic form of i. marked by mild intermittent fever, anorexia, anemia, slight diarrhea, dull pain in the inguinal (or iliac) region, and rapid pulse.

ileocolostomy (il'e-o-ko-los'to-mĭ) [ileo- + colostomy]. Surgical establishment of a new communication between the ileum and the colon.

ileocystoplasty (il'e-o-sis'to-plas-tĭ) [ileo- + G. *kystis*, bladder, + *plastos*, molded]. Surgical reconstruction of the bladder involving the use of an isolated intestinal segment to augment bladder capacity.

ileoileostomy (il'e-o-il-e-os'to-mĭ) [ileum + ileum + G. *stoma*, mouth]. Surgical establishment of a communication between two segments of the ileum.

ileojejunitis (il'e-jĕ-ju-ni'tis). A chronic inflammatory condition involving the jejunum and parts or most of the ileum.

ileopexy (il'e-o-pek'sĭ) [ileo- + G. *pēxis*, fixation]. Surgical fixation of ileum.

ileoproctostomy (il'e-o-prok-tos'to-mĭ) [ileo- + G. *prōktos*, anus (rectum), + *stoma*, mouth]. Surgical establishment of a communication between the ileum and the rectum.

ileorrhaphy (il-e-or'ă-fĭ) [ileo- + G. *raphe*, suture]. Suturing the ileum.

ileosigmoidostomy (il'e-o-sig'moyd-os'ko-pĭ) [ileo- + sigmoid + G. *stoma*, mouth]. Surgical establishment of a communication between the ileum and the sigmoid colon.

ileostomy (il'e-os'to-mĭ) [ileo- + G. *stoma*, mouth]. Surgical establishment of a fistula through which the ileum discharges directly to the outside of the body.

ileotomy (il'e-ot'o-mĭ) [ileo- + G. *tomē*, incision]. Incision into the ileum.

ileum (il'e-um) [L. fr. G. *eileō*, to roll up, twist] [NA]. The third portion of the small intestine, extending from the junction with the jejunum to the ileocecal opening.

ileus (il'e-us) [G. *eileos*, intestinal colic, from *eilō*, to roll up tight]. Obstruction of the bowel attended with severe colicky pain, vomiting, and often fever and dehydration.

adynamic i., paralytic i.

dynamic i., spastic i.; obstruction due to spastic contraction of a segment of the bowel.

mechanical i., obstruction of the bowel due to some mechanical cause, *e.g.,* volvulus, gallstone, adhesions.

meconium i., intestinal obstruction in the newborn following inspissation of meconium due to lack of trypsin; associated with cystic fibrosis of pancreas.

occlusive i., complete mechanical blocking of the intestinal lumen.

paralytic i., adynamic i.; nonmechanical obstruction of the bowel from paralysis of bowel wall, usually as a result of localized or generalized peritonitis or shock.

spastic i., dynamic i.

i. subpar'ta, obstruction of the large bowel by pressure of the pregnant uterus.

iliac (il'ĭ-ak). Relating to the ilium.

ilio- [L. *ilium, q.v.*]. Combining form denoting relationship to the ilium.

iliococcygeal (il'ĭ-o-kok-sij'e-al). Relating to the ilium and the coccyx.

il'iofem'oral. Relating to the ilium and the femur.

ilioinguinal (il'ĭ-o-ing'gwĭ-nal). Relating to the iliac region and the groin.

iliolumbar (il'ĭ-lum'bar]. Relating to the iliac and the lumbar regions.

iliopectineal (il'ĭ-o-pek-tin'e-al). Relating to the ilium and the pubis.

iliotrochanteric (il'ĭ-o-tro-kan-ter'ik). Relating to the ilium and the great trochanter of the femur.

ilium, pl. **ilia** (il'ĭ-um, il'ĭ-ah) [L. groin, flank]. *Os* ilium.

ill. 1. In veterinary medicine, a term used in the common names of several diseases. **2.** Not well; sick.

ill'ness. Disease (1).

mental i., mental or emotional disease, disturbance, or disorder; behavioral disorder; a broadly inclusive term, generally denoting one or all of the following: **1)** a disease of the brain, with predominant behavioral symptoms, as in paresis or acute alcoholism; **2)** a disease of the "mind" or personality, evidenced by abnormal behavior; **3)** a disorder of conduct, evidenced by socially deviant behavior.

illusion (ĭ-lu'zhun) [L. *illusio*, to play at, mock]. A false perception; the mistaking of something for what it is not.

illusional (ĭ-lu'zhun-al). Relating to or of the nature of an illusion.

image (im'ij) [L. *imago*, likeness]. The representation or picture of an object made by the rays of light emanating from or reflected from it.

body i., (1) the cerebral representation of all body sensation organized in the parietal cortex; **(2)** one's i. or concept of his own body, in contrast to his actual, anatomic body or to others' concept of it.

false i., the i. in the deviating eye in strabismus.

mental i., a picture of an object not present, produced in the mind by memory or imagination.

motor i., the cerebral i. of possible body movements.

optical i., an i. formed by the refraction or reflection of light.

sensory i., an i. based on one or more types of sensation.

tactile i., an i. of an object as perceived by the sense of touch.

imagery (im'ij-rī). A technique in behavior therapy in which the client or patient is conditioned to use pleasant fantasies to counter the unpleasant feelings associated with anxiety.

imbal'ance [L. *in*-neg. + *bi-lanx*(*-lanc*-), having two scales]. **1.** Lack of equality between opposing forces. **2.** Lack of equality in some aspect of binocular vision, such as strabismus, heterophoria, anisometropia, or aniseikonia.

autonomic i., vasomotor i.; a lack of balance between parasympathetic and parasympathetic nervous systems, especially in relation to the vasomotor disturbances.

sex chromosome i., any abnormal pattern of sex chromosomes; *e.g.,* XXY in men with seminiferous tubule dysgenesis, XO in women with Turner's syndrome.

sympathetic i., vagotonia.

vasomotor i., autonomic i.

imbecile (im'bĕ-sil) [L. *imbecillus,* weak, silly]. Obsolete term for a subclass of mental *retardation.*

imbibition (im-bĭ-bish'un) [L. *im-bibo,* to drink in]. **1.** Absorption of fluid by a solid body without resultant chemical change in either. **2.** Taking up of water by a gel, increasing the size of the gel.

imbricate, imbricated (im'brĭ-kāt, -ka-ted) [L. *imbricatus,* covered with tiles]. Overlaping like shingles.

imidazole (im'id-az'ōl). 1,3-Diaza-2,4-cyclopentadiene; a five-membered heterocyclic compound occurring in histidine.

imide (im'īd). The radical or group, =NH, attached to two −CO− groups.

imido-. Prefix denoting the radical of an imide, formed by the loss of the H of the =NH group.

im'idole. Pyrrole.

I.M., i.m. Intramuscular, or intramuscularly.

-imine. Suffix indicating the group =NH.

imino-. Prefix denoting an imine.

imino acids (im'ī-no, ĭ-me'no). Compounds with molecules containing both an acid group (usually the carboxyl, −COOH) and an imino group (=NH).

iminoglycinuria (im'in-o-gli-sĭ-nu'rĭah). A benign inborn error of amino acid transport; glycine, proline, and hydroxyproline are excreted in the urine.

immersion (ĭ-mer'zhun) [L. *im-mergo,* pp. *-mersus,* to dip in]. **1.** The placing of a body under water or other liquid. **2.** In microscopy, the use of a fluid medium (placed on the slide being examined) in order to exclude air from between the glass slide and the bottom lens of an immersion objective.

immiscible (im-mis'ĭ-bl) [L. *im-misceo,* to mix in (*in* + *misceo*)]. Incapable of mutual solution; *e.g.,* oil and water.

immobilize (im-mo'bĭ-līz) [L. *in*- neg. + *mobilis,* movable]. To render fixed or incapable of moving.

immune (ĭ-mūn') [L. *immunis,* free from service]. **1.** Free from the possibility of acquiring a given infectious disease; resistant to an infectious disease. **2.** Pertaining to the mechanism of sensitization in which the reactivity is so altered by previous contact with an antigen that the responsive tissues respond quickly upon subsequent contact.

immunifacient (im'mu-nĭ-fa'shent) [L. *immunis,* exempt, + *faciens,* making]. Making immune; producing immunity.

immunity (ĭ-mu'nĭ-tĭ) [L. *immunitas* (see immune)]. Insusceptibility; the status or quality of being immune (1).

acquired i., resistance resulting from previous exposure of the individual in question to an infectious agent or antigen; it may be 1) *active* and *specific,* as a result of naturally acquired infection or intentional vaccination (*artificial active i.*) or 2) *passive,* being acquired from transfer of antibodies from another person or from an animal, either naturally, as from mother to fetus, or by intentional inoculation (*artificial passive i.*), and, with respect to the particular antibodies transferred, it is *specific.*

active i., see acquired i.

cellular i., cell-mediated i. (CMI), i. associated with cellular elements (including T-lymphocytes).

general i., i. associated with widely diffused mechanisms that tend to protect the body as a whole, as compared with local i.

genetic i., innate i.

herd i., group i., **(1)** a concept that there is resistance or relative resistance to the spread of infectious disease in a herd or group, irrespective of the presence or absence of a significant degree of i. in the individual members; **(2)** the immunologic status of a population as a whole, determined by the ratio of resistant to susceptible members and their distribution.

humoral i., i. associated with circulating antibodies.

infection i., premunition; the paradoxical immune status in which resistance to reinfection coincides with the persistence of the original infection.

innate i., inherent i., genetic or natural i.; autarcesis; resistance manifested by a species (or by races, families, and individuals in a species) that has not been immunized by previous infection or vaccination; nonspecific and is not stimulated by specific antigens.

local i., a natural or acquired i. to certain infectious agents, as manifested by an organ or a tissue, as a whole or in part.

natural i., innate i.

passive i., see acquired i.

specific i., the immune status in which there is an altered reactivity directed solely against the antigenic determinants that stimulated it.

immunization (im'u-nĭ-za'shun). The process or procedure by which an organism is rendered immune.

im'munize. To render immune.

immuno- [L. *immunis*, immune]. Combining form meaning immune, or relating to immunity.

im'munoad'juvant. See adjuvant (2).

im'munoas'say. Immunochemical assay; detection and assay of hormones, or other substances, by serological (immunological) methods; in most applications the hormone (or other substance) in question serves as antigen, both in antibody production and in measurement of antibody by the test substance.

im'munoblast [immuno- + G. *blastos*, germ]. An antigenically stimulated lymphocyte.

im'munocom'petence. Normal capabilities of the immune system.

immunocompromised (im'mu-no-kom'pro-mizd). Denoting one whose immunologic mechanism is deficient either because of an immunodeficiency disorder or by immunosuppressive agents.

im'munoconglu'tinin. An autoantibody-like immunoglobulin (IgM) formed against their own complement following injection of complement-containing complexes or sensitized bacteria.

immunocyte (im'u-no-sīt) [immuno- + G. *kytos,* cell]. A leukocyte capable, actively or potentially, of producing antibodies.

immunodeficiency (im'u-no-de-fish'en-si). Immunological, immunity, or immune deficiency; a condition resulting from a defective immunological mechanism; may be *primary* (due to a defect in the immune mechanism *per se*) or *secondary* (dependent upon another disease process), *specific* (due to defect in either the B-lymphocyte or the T-lymphocyte system, or both) or *nonspecific* (due to defect in one or another component of the nonspecific immune mechanism).

cellular i., an ill-defined group of sporadic disorders of unknown cause, occurring in either sex, and associated with recurrent bacterial, fungal, protozoal, and viral infections; there is thymic hypoplasia with depressed cellular (T-lymphocyte) immunity combined with defective humoral (B-lymphocyte) immunity, although immunoglobulin levels may be normal.

combined i., i. of both the B-lymphocytes and T-lymphocytes.

common, variable i., i. of unknown cause that may occur at any age in either sex; the total quantity of immunoglobulin is commonly less than 300 mg/dl, with the number of B-lymphocytes frequently within normal limits but with a lack of plasma cells in lymphoid tissue; cellular (T-lymphocyte) immunity may also be abnormal but usually is intact; associated with increased susceptibility to pyogenic infection and, not infrequently, with autoimmune disease.

immunodiffusion (im'u-no-dī-fu'zhun). A technique of study of antigen-antibody reactions by observing precipitates formed by combination of specific antigen and antibodies which have diffused in a gel in which they have been separately placed.

immunoelectrophoresis (im'u-no-e-lek'tro-fo-re'sis). A kind of precipitin test in which the components of one group of immunological reactants (usually a mixture of antigens) are first separated on the basis of electrophoretic mobility in agar or other medium, the separated components then being identified, by means of the technique of double diffusion, on the basis of precipitates formed by reaction with components of the other group of reactants (antibodies).

immunofluorescence (im'u-no-flür-es'ens). The use of fluorescein-labeled antibodies to identify antigenic material specific for the labeled antibody; the specific binding of antibody can be determined microscopically through the production of a characteristic visible light by the application of ultraviolet rays to the preparation.

immunogen (ĭ-mu'no-jen). Antigen.

im'munogenet'ics. The branch of genetics concerned with inheritance of differences in antigens or antigenic responses.

im'munogen'ic. Antigenic.

immunogenicity (im'u-no-jĕ-nis'ĭ-tĭ). 40 Antigenicity.

im'munoglob'ulin (Ig). One of a class of structurally related proteins consisting of two pairs of polypeptide chains, one pair of light (L) [low molecular weight] chains (κ or λ) and one pair of heavy (H) chains (γ, α, or μ, and more recently, δ and ε), all four linked together by disulfide bonds. On the basis of the structural and antigenic properties of the H chains, Ig's are classified (in order of relative amounts present in normal human serum) as IgG (7S in size, 80%), IgA (10 to 15%), IgM (19S, a pentamer of the basic unit, 5 to 10%), IgD (less than 0.1%), and IgE (less than 0.01%). All of these classes are homogeneous and susceptible to amino acid sequence analysis. The large number of possible combinations of L and H chains make up the "libraries" of antibodies of each individual.

im'munohis'tochem'istry. Microscopic localization of specific substances, or receptors for them, within tissues by staining with antibodies labeled with fluorescent or pigmented materials.

immunol'ogist. A specialist in immunology.

immunology (im-u-nol'o-jĭ) [immuno- + G. *logos,* study]. The science concerned with the various phenomena of immunity, induced sensitivity, and allergy.

im'munoprecipita'tion. Immune *precipitation.*

immunosorbent (im'mu-no-sor'bent). An antibody (or antigen) used to remove specific antigen (or antibody) from solution or suspension.

im'munosuppres'sant. Immunosuppressive; denoting an agent that effects immunosuppression.

im'munosuppres'sion. Suppression of immunologic response, usually with reference to grafts or organ transplants, by use of chemical, pharmocologic, physical, or immunologic agents.

immunotransfusion (im'u-no-trans-fu'zhun). An indirect transfusion in which the donor is first immunized by means of injections of an antigen prepared from microorganisms isolated from the recipient; later, the donor's blood is administered to the patient who is then presumably passively immunized by means of antibody formed in the donor.

IMP Inosine monophosphate.

impac'ted [L. *impingo,* pp. *-pactus,* to strike at]. Pressed closely together so as to be immovable; wedged and incapable of spontaneous advance or recession.

impair'ment. Weakening, damage, or deterioration; *e.g.,* as a result of injury or disease.

impal'pable [L. *im-; neg.* + *palpabilis,* that can be felt]. Not capable of being felt.

impatent (im-pa'tent). Not patent; closed.

impe'dance. 1. Total opposition to flow. When flow is steady, i. is simply the resistance, *i.e.,* the driving pressure per unit flow; when flow is changing, i. also includes the factors that oppose changes in flow. 2. The resistance of an acoustic system of being set in motion.

imper'forate. Atretic.

imperforation (im-per-fo-ra'shun) [L. *im-* neg. + *per-foro,* pp. *-auts,* to bore through]. The condition of being atretic, occluded, or closed.

impermeable (im-per'me-ă-bl) [L. *im-permeabilis,* not to be passed through]. Impervious; not permitting passage.

impetiginous (im-pĕ-tij'ĭ-nus). Relating to impetigo.

impetigo (im-pĕ-ti'go) [L. a scabby eruption, fr. *im-peto* (*inp-*), to rush upon, attack]. I. contagiosa; i. vulgaris; a contagious superficial pyoderma, caused by staphylococci and streptococci, that begins with a superficial flaccid vesicle which ruptures and forms a thick yellowish crust.

    bullous i. of the newborn, i. neonatorum (2); usually, widely disseminated bullous lesions appearing soon after birth, caused by infection with staphylococci, occasionally mixed with streptococci.

    i. contagio'sa, impetigo.

    i. herpetifor'mis, a rare pyoderma occurring most commonly in pregnant women; an eruption of small, closely aggregated pustules, developing upon an inflammatory base, accompanied by severe general symptoms.

    i. neonato'rum, (1) *dermatitis* exfoliativa infantum; (2) bullous i. of the newborn.

    i. vulga'ris, impetigo.

implant [L. *im-,* in, + *planto,* pp. *-atus,* to plant, fr. *planta,* a sprout, shoot]. 1(im-plant'). To graft or insert. 2(im'plant). Material inserted or grafted into tissues.

implanta'tion. 1. Attachment of the fertilized ovum (blastocyst) to the endometrium, and its subsequent embedding in the compact layer, occurring six or seven days after fertilization of the ovum. 2. Grafting or inserting of material into tissues.

implosion (im-plo'shun). 1. A type of behavior therapy, similar to flooding, during which the patient is given massive exposure to extreme anxiety-arousing stimuli; the therapist attempts to extinguish the future influence of such unconscious material over the patient's behavior and feelings, and previous avoidance responses to the stimuli are replaced by more appropriate responses. 2. A bursting inward rather than outward.

im'potence, im'potency [L. *impotentia,* inability]. 1. Weakness; lack of power. 2. In the male, inability to achieve or maintain penile erection.

impreg'nate [L. *im-,* in, + *praegnans,* with child]. 1. To fecundate; to cause to conceive. 2. To diffuse or permeate with another substance.

impression (im-presh'un) [L. *impressio,* to press upon]. 1. An indentation or depression made by the pressure of one organ on the surface of another. 2. An effect produced upon the mind by some external object acting through the organs of sense. 3. The negative form of the teeth and/or other tissues of the oral cavity made in a plastic material to reproduce a positive form or cast of the recorded tissues.

imprint'ing. A particular kind of learning characterized by its occurrence in the first few hours of life, and which determines species-recognition behavior.

im'pulse [L. *im-pello,* pp. *-pulsus,* to push against, impel]. 1. A sudden pushing or driving force. 2. A sudden, often unreasoning, determination to perform some act. 3. The action potential of a nerve fiber.

impulsion (im-pul'shun). An abnormal urge to perform certain activity, often unpleasant.

impul'sive. Relating to or actuated by an impulse, rather than controlled by reason.

In Indium.

in- [L.]. 1. Prefix conveying a sense of negation. 2. Prefix denoting in, within, inside. 3. Prefix denoting an intensive action, appearing as im- before b, p, or m.

inac'tivate. To destroy the activity or the effects of an agent or substance.

inan'imate. Not alive.

inanition (in-ă-nish'un) [L. *inanis,* empty]. Exhaustion from lack of food or defect in assimilation.

inappetence (in-ap'ĕ-tens) [L. *in-* neg. + *ap-peto,* pp. *-petitus,* to strive after, long for]. Lack of desire or of craving.

inartic'ulate. 1. Not articulate in the form of intelligible speech. 2. Unable to satisfactorily express oneself in words.

inassim'ilable. Not assimilable; not capable of being appropriated for the nutrition of the body.

in'born. Innate; inherited; implanted during development *in utero.*

in'breed'ing. Mating of individuals that are closely related or have very similar genetic constitutions.

incarcerated (in-kar'ser-a-ted) [L. *in*, in, + *carcero*, pp. *-atus*, to imprison]. Confined; imprisoned; trapped.

incest (in'sest) [L. *incestus*, unchaste, fr. *in-*, not, + *castus*, chaste]. **1.** Sexual relations between persons so closely related by blood as to be prohibited by law or culture.

incestuous (in-ses'tu-us). Pertaining to incest.

incidence (in'sĭ-dens) [L. *incido*, to fall into or upon, to happen]. The number of new cases of a disease in a population over a period of time.

incisal (in-si'zal) [L. *incido*, pp. *-cisus*, to cut into]. Cutting; relating to the cutting edges of the incisor and cuspid teeth.

incise (in-sīz'). To cut with a knife.

incision (in-sizh'un) [L. *incisio*]. A cut; a surgical wound; a division of the soft parts made with a knife.

inci'sive. 1. Cutting; having the power to cut. **2.** Relating to the incisor teeth.

inci'sor [L. *incido*, to cut into]. One of the cutting teeth, or i. teeth, four in number in each jaw at the apex of the dental arch.

incisure (in-si'zhūr) [L. *incisura*]. Notch; an indentation at the edge of any structure.

　Rivinus i., tympanic i., the notch in the superior part of the tympanic ring bridged by the flaccid part of the tympanic membrane.

　Schmidt-Lanterman i.'s, Lanterman's i.'s i.'s, funnel-shaped interruptions in the regular structure of the myelin sheath of nerve fibers, corresponding each to a strand of cytoplasm locally separating the two otherwise fused oligodendroglial (or, in peripheral nerves, Schwann cell) membranes composing the myelin sheath.

inclination (in-klĭ-na'shun) [L. *inclinatio*, a leaning]. **1.** A leaning or sloping, as of the pelvis, the angle which the plane of the pelvic inlet makes with the horizontal plane. **2.** In dentistry, the deviation of the long axis of a tooth from the perpendicular.

inclusion (in-klu'zhun) [L. *inclusio*, a shutting in]. **1.** Any foreign or heterogenous substance contained in a cell or in any tissue or organ, not introduced as a result of trauma. **2.** The process by which a foreign or heterogenous structure is misplaced in another tissue.

　cell i.'s, (1) metaplasm; the nonliving elements of the cytoplasm which are metabolic products of the cell; **(2)** storage materials such as glycogen or fat; **(3)** engulfed material such as carbon or other foreign substances.

incompatible (in-kom-pat'ĭ-bl) [L. *in-* neg. + *con-*, with, + *patior*, pp. *passus*, to suffer]. **1.** Not of suitable composition to be combined or mixed with another agent or substance, without resulting in an undesirable reaction (including chemical alteration or destruction). **2.** Denoting persons who can not freely associate together without resulting anxiety and conflict.

incompetence, incompetency (in-kom'pĕ-tens, -ten-sĭ) [L. *in-*, neg. + *com-peto*, strive after together]. **1.** Insufficiency (2); the quality of being incompetent or incapable of performing the allotted function. **2.** In psychiatry, the mental inability to distinguish right from worng or to manage one's affairs.

incon'stant. 1. Variable; irregular. **2.** In anatomy, denoting a structure that normally may or may not be present.

incon'tinence [L. *in-continentia*, fr. *in-* neg. + *con-tineo*, to hold together]. Incontinentia **1.** Inability to prevent the discharge of excretions, especially of urine or feces. **2.** Lack of restraint; immoderation.

　urge i., involuntary loss of urine associated with an uncontrollable urge to void; usually in association with neurogenic bladder or local irritative bladder conditions.

　urinary stress i., leakage of urine as a result of coughing, straining, or some sudden voluntary movement.

incontinentia (in-kon'tĭ-nen'shĭ-ah) [L.]. Incontinence.

　i. pigmen'ti, Bloch-Sulzberger syndrome; an inherited developmental defect of the skin which may also involve other structures; characterized by pigmented lesions in linear, zebra-stripe, and other bizarre configurations.

incoordination (in'ko-or'dĭ-na'shun) [L. *in-* neg. + coordination]. Ataxia.

increment (in'kre-ment) [L. *incrementum*, increase]. A change in the value of a variable; usually an increase.

incretion (in-kre'shun) [L. *in*, within, + *secernere*, to separate]. The functional activity of an endocrine gland.

incrustation (in'krus-ta'shun) [L. *in-crusto*, pp. *-atus*, to incrust]. **1.** Formation of a crust or a scab. **2.** A coating of some adventitious material or an exudate; a scab.

incubation (in'ku-ba'shun) [L. *incubo*, to lie on]. **1.** Maintenance of controlled environmental conditions for the purpose of favoring growth or development of microbial or tissue cultures or of an artificial environment for an infant, usually a premature or hypoxic one. **2.** Development, without sign or symptom, of an infection from the time it gains entry until the appearance of the first signs or symptoms.

incubator (in'ku-ba'tor). An apparatus in which controlled environmental conditions may be maintained, as for culturing microorganisms or for maintaining a premature infant.

incubus (in'ku-bus) [L. fr. *incubo*, to lie on. CUB⁻]. **1.** Originally, an evil spirit which lay upon and oppressed sleeping persons. **2.** Nightmare.

in'cudal. Relating to the incus.

incudec'tomy [incus + G. *ektomē*, excision]. Removal of the incus of the tympanum.

incudes (in-ku'dēz) [L.]. Plural of incus.

incu'domal'leal. Relating to the incus and the malleus; denoting the articulation between the anvil and the hammer in the middle ear.

incu'dostape'dial. Relating to the incus and the stapes; denoting the articulation between the anvil and the stirrup in the middle ear.

incurvation (in'kur-va'shun). An inward curvature; a bending inward.

incus, gen. **incu'dis,** pl. **incudes** (ing'kus, in-ku'dēz) [L. anvil] [NA]. Anvil; the middle of the three ossicles in the middle ear; it has a body and two limbs or processes at the tip of the long limb is a small knob, processus lenticularis, which articulates with the head of the stapes.

incycloduction (in-si'klo-duk'shun). Conclination; negative declination; intorsion; rotation of the upper pole of one cornea inward.

incyclophoria (in-si'klo-fo'rĭ-ah) [L. *in,* + *cyclo-* + G. *phora,* movement]. Minus cyclophoria; the tendency toward inward rotation of the upper pole of the cornea, prevented by visual fusional impulses.

indanediones (in-dān'ē-di-ōnz). A class of orally effective indirect-acting anticoagulants of which pheninidione is representative.

index, gen. **indicis,** pl. **indexes** or **indices** (in'deks, -dĭ-sis, -dek-sez, -dĭ-sēz) [L. one that points out, an informer]. **1**[NA]. Forefinger; index finger; the second finger (the thumb as the first). **2.** A guide, standard, indicator, symbol, or number denoting the relation in respect to size, capacity, or function, of one part or thing to another.

anesthetic i., ratio of the number of units of anesthetic required for anesthesia to the number of units of anesthetic required to produce respiratory or cardiovascular failure.

Arneth i., an expression based on adding the percentages of polymorphonuclear neutrophils with 1 or 2 lobes in their nuclei, plus one-half the percentage with 3 lobes; the normal value is 60%.

cardiac i., the amount of blood ejected by the heart in a unit of time divided by the body surface area; usually expressed in liters per minute per square meter.

color i., the ratio between the amount of hemoglobin and the number of red blood cells.

dmfs or **DMFS caries i.,** an i. of past caries experience based upon the number of decayed, missing, and filled surfaces of deciduous (lower case letters) or permanent (capital letters) teeth.

erythrocyte indices, calculations for determining the average size, hemoglobin content, and concentration of red blood cells, including mean cell volume, mean cell hemoglobin, and mean cell hemoglobin concentrate.

icterus i., the value that indicates the relative level of bilirubin in serum or plasma; calculated by comparing (in a colorimeter) the intensity of the color of the specimen with that of a standard solution.

leukopenic i., a significant decrease in the white blood count after ingestion of food to which a patient is hypersensitive, a count made during the normal fasting state being used as the basis for evaluation of the postprandial count.

opsonic i., a value that indicates the relative content of opsonin in the blood of a person with an infectious disease, as evaluated *in vitro* in comparison with presumably normal blood.

phagocytic i., the average number of bacteria observed in the cytoplasm of polymorphonuclear leukocytes.

refractive i (*n*), the relative velocity of light in another medium compared to the velocity in air.

saturation i., an indication of the relative concentration of hemoglobin in the red blood cells.

Schilling's i., Schilling's *blood count.*

small increment sensitivity i., see SISI *test.*

stroke work i., a measure of the work done by the heart with each contraction, adjusted for body surface area; equal to the stroke volume of the heart multiplied by the arterial pressure and divided by body surface area.

therapeutic i., the ratio of LD_{50} to ED_{50}, used in quantitative comparison of drugs.

ventilation i., the figure obtained by dividing the ventilation test by the vital capacity.

vital i., the ratio of births to deaths within a population during a given time.

volume i., an indication of the relative size (*i.e.,* volume) of erythrocytes, calculated as follows: hematocrit value, expressed as per cent of normal ÷ red blood cell count, expressed as per cent of normal = volume i.

in'dican. 1. Indoxyl β-D-glucoside, from *Indigofera* species, a source of indigo. **2.** 3-Indoxylsulfuric acid, a substance found (as its salts) in the sweat and in variable amount in the urine, indicative, when in quantity, of protein putrefaction in the intestine (indicanuria).

in'dicanidro'sis [indican + G. *hidrōs,* sweat]. Excretion of indican in the sweat.

indicanuria (in'dĭ-kan-u'rĭ-ah). An increased urinary excretion of indican.

indication (in-dĭ-ka'shun) [L. fr. *in-dico,* to point out]. A suggestion or pointer as to the proper treatment of a disease; it may be furnished by a knowledge of the cause (**causal i.**), by the symptoms present (**symptomatic i.**), or by nature of the disease (**specific i.**).

in'dicator [L. one that points out]. In chemical analysis, a substance that changes color within a certain definite range of pH or oxidation potential, or in any way renders visible the completion of a chemical reaction.

in'dices. Alternative plural of index.

indigestion (in-dĭ-jes'chun). Failure of proper digestion and absorption of food in the alimentary tract, and the consequences thereof.

acid i., thought to represent hyperchlorhydria; often used colloquially as a synonym for pyrosis.

gastric i., dyspepsia.

nervous i., i. caused by emotional factors.

indium (in'dĭ-um) [*indigo*, because it gives a blue line in the spectrum]. A metallic element, symbol In, atomic no. 49, atomic weight 114.82. The radionuclide indium-111 (111In) in chloride form is used as a bone marrow and tumor-localizing tracer; in chelate form, as a cerebrospinal fluid tracer.

individuation (in'dĭ-vid-u-a'shun). 1. The development of the individual from the specific. 2. In jungian psychology, the process by which one's personality is differentiated, developed, and expressed.

indocyanine green (in-do-si'ă-nēn). A tricarbocyanine dye that binds to serum albumin and is used in blood volume determinations and in liver function tests.

indolaceturia (in'dōl-as-ĕ-tu'rĭ-ah). Excretion of an appreciable amount of indolacetic acid in the urine.

indol'amine. An indole or indole derivative containing a primary, secondary, or tertiary amine group (*e.g.,* serotonin).

indole (in'dōl). 2,3-Benzopyrrole; basis of many biologically active substances.

in'dolent [L. *in-* neg. + *doleo,* pr. p. *dolens,* to feel pain]. Inactive; sluggish; painless or nearly so.

indo'lic acids. Metabolites of tryptophan formed within the body or by intestinal microorganisms; principal ones encountered in urine are indoleacetic acid, indoleacetylglutamine, 5-hydroxyindoleacetic acid, and indolelactic acid.

indox'yl. 3-Hydroxyindole; a product of intestinal bacterial degradation of indoleacetic acid, excreted in the urine as indoleacetic acid (conjugated with glycine) or as sulfate (urinary indican) or glucuronide (glucosiduronate).

indoxyluria (in-dok'sil-u'rĭ-ah). The excretion of indoxyl, especially indoxyl sulfate, in the urine; may be associated with indicanuria, inasmuch as hydrolysis of indican results in formation of indoxyl.

indu'cer. A molecule, usually a substrate of a specific enzyme pathway, that combines with active repressor (produced by a regulator gene) to deactivate the repressor; this results in activation of a previously repressed operator gene and initiates activity of the structural genes controlled by the operator, which in turn results in enzyme production; a homeostatic mechanism for regulating enzyme production in an inducible enzyme system.

induction (in-duk'shun) [L. *inductio,* a leading in]. 1. Production or causation. 2. The period from the start of anesthesia to the establishment of a depth of anesthesia adequate for operation. 3. In embryology, the influence exerted by an organizer or evocator on the differentiation of adjacent cells or on the development of an embryonic structure. 4. A modification imposed upon the offspring by the action of environment on the germ cells of one or both parents.

induc'tor. 1. An agent bringing about induction. 2. An evocator. 3. An organizer.

in'durated [L. *in-duro,* pp. *-duratus,* to harden]. Hardened, usually used with reference to soft tissues becoming extremely firm but not as hard as bone.

induration (in-du-ra'shun) [L. *induratio* (see indurated)]. 1. The process of becoming extremely firm or hard, or having such a quality. 2. A focus or region of indurated tissue.

brown i. of the lung, a condition characterized by firmness of the lungs, and a brown color associated with hemosiderin-pigmented macrophages in alveoli, consequent upon long-continued congestion due to heart disease.

cyanotic i., i. related to persistent, chronic venous congestion in an organ or tissue, frequently resulting in fibrous thickening of the walls of the walls of the veins and eventual fibrosis of adjacent tissues.

fibroid i., granular i., cirrhosis.

gray i., a condition occurring in lungs during and after pneumonic processes in which there is failure of resolution; there is a conspicuous increase in fibrous connective tissue in the walls of the alveoli, and also within the alveoli.

red i., a condition observed in lungs in which there is an advanced degree of acute passive congestion, acute pneumonitis, or a similar pathologic process.

in'durative. Pertaining to, causing, or characterized by induration.

indu'sium gris'eum [NA]. Supracallosal gyrus; a thin layer of gray matter on the dorsal surface of the corpus callosum.

inebriant (in-e'brĭ-ant) [see inebriety]. 1. Making drunk; intoxicating. 2. An intoxicant.

inebriation (in-e'brĭ-a'shun) [L. *in-* intensive + *ebrietas,* drunkenness]. Intoxication, as by alcohol.

inert (in-ert') [L. *iners,* unskillful, sluggish]. 1. Slow in action; sluggish. 2. Devoid of active chemical properties. 3. Having no pharmacologic or therapeutic action.

inertia (in-er'shĭ-ah, -er'shah) [L. want of skill, laziness]. 1. The state of a physical body in which it "resists" any force tending to move it from a position of rest or to change its uniform motion. 2. Denoting inactivity or lack of force; lack of mental or physical vigor.

in extre'mis [L. *extremus,* last]. At the point of death.

in'fancy. Babyhood, earliest period of extrauterine life; roughly the first year of life.

in'fant [L. *infans,* not speaking]. A child under the age of 1 year; more specifically, a newborn baby.

liveborn i., the product of a livebirth; an i. who shows evidence of life after birth: breathing, beating of the heart, pulsation of the umbilical cord, or definite movement of voluntary muscles.

post-term i., an i. with a gestational age of 42 completed weeks or more (294 days or more).

preterm i., an i. with gestational age of less than 37 completed weeks (259 completed days).

stillborn i., an i. who shows no evidence of life after birth.

term i., an i. with gestational age of 37 completed weeks (259 completed days) to less than 42 completed weeks (less than 294 completed days).

infan'ticide [infant + L. *caedo*, to kill]. The killing of an infant.

in'fantile. Relating to, or characteristic of, infants or infancy.

infantilism (in-fan'tĭ-lizm). **1.** A state marked by extremely slow development of mind and body. **2.** Childishness as expressed by an adolescent or adult.

sexual i., failure to develop secondary sexual characteristics after the normal time of puberty.

infarct (in'farkt) [L. *in-farcio*, pp. *-fartus*, to stuff into]. Infarction (2); an area of necrosis resulting from a sudden insufficiency of arterial or venous blood supply.

anemic i., white i. (1); an i. in which little or no bleeding into tissue occurs when the blood supply is obstructed.

hemorrhagic i., red i., an i. red in color from infiltration of blood from collateral vessels into the necrotic area.

septic i., an area of necrosis resulting from vascular obstruction due to emboli comprised of clumps of bacteria or infected material.

white i., (1) anemic i.; (2) in the placenta, intervillous fibrin with ischemic necrosis of villi.

infarction (in-fark'shun). **1.** Sudden insufficiency of arterial or venous blood supply due to emboli, thrombi, vascular torsion, or pressure that produces a macroscopic area of necrosis. **2.** Infarct.

myocardial i., cardiac i., i. of an area of the heart muscle, usually as a result of occlusion of a coronary artery.

silent myocardial i., i. that produces none of the characteristic symptoms and signs of myocardial i.

watershed i., cortical i. in an area of blood supply between two major cerebral arteries.

infect (in-fekt') [L. *in-ficio*, pp. *-fectus*, to corrupt, infect]. **1.** To enter, invade, or inhabit another organism, causing infection or contamination. **2.** To dwell internally, endoparasitically, as opposed to infest.

infection (in-fek'shun). Multiplication of parasitic organisms within the body; multiplication of the "normal" flora of the intestinal tract is not considered an i.

cross i., i. spread from one source to another.

droplet i., i. acquired through the inhalation of droplets or aerosols of saliva or sputum containing microorganisms expelled by another person.

endogenous i., i. caused by an infectious agent already present in the body, the previous i. having been inapparent.

focal i., an old term that distinguishes local i.'s (focal) from generalized i.'s (sepsis).

terminal i., an acute i., commonly pneumonic or septic, occurring toward the end of any disease (usually a chronic disease), and often the cause of death.

infectious (in-fek'shus). **1.** Capable of being transmitted by infection, with or without actual contact. **2.** Infective. **3.** Denoting a disease due to the action of a microorganism.

infec'tive. Infectious (2); producing or relating to an infection.

inferior (in-fēr'ĭ-or) [L. lower]. **1.** Situated below or directed downward. **2**[NA]. In human anatomy, situated nearer the soles of the feet in relation to a specific reference point.

infe'rior'ity. The condition or state of being or feeling inadequate or inferior, especially to others similarly situated.

in'fertil'ity. [L. *in*-neg. + *fertilis,* fruitful]. Relative sterility; diminished or absent fertility; does not imply (either in the male or the female) the existence of as positive or irreversible a condition as sterility. In the female, it indicates adequate anatomical structures and equivocal function, with the possibility of pregnancy that may or may not proceed to term.

infest (in-fest') [L. *infesto*, pp. *-atus*, to attack]. **1.** To infect, usually by macroscopic parasites; to invade parasitically. **2.** To dwell externally, ectoparasitically, as opposed to infect.

infesta'tion. The act or process of infesting.

infiltrate (in-fil'trāt) [L. *in* + Mediev. L. *filtro*, pp. *-atus*, to strain through felt]. **1.** To percolate; to enter or cause to enter the pores of a substance, denoting a liquid. **2.** Material that has permeated into the tissues.

infiltration (in-fil-tra'shun). **1.** The act of passing into or interpenetrating a substance, cell, or tissue; said of gases, fluids, or matters held in solution. **2.** The gas, fluid, or dissolved matter that has entered any substance, cell, or tissue.

adipose i., growth of normal adult fat cells in sites where they are not usually present.

calcareous i., calcification.

cellular i., migration of cells from their sources of origin, or direct extension of cells as a result of unusual growth and multiplication, thereby resulting in fairly well defined foci, irregular accumulations, or diffusely distributed individual cells in the connective tissue and interstices of various organs and tissues.

fatty i., abnormal accumulation of fat droplets in the cytoplasm of cells, particularly of fat derived from outside the cells.

infirm (in-firm') [L. *in-firmus*, fr. *in-* neg. + *firmus*, strong]. Weak or feeble because of old age or disease.

infirmary (in-fir'mă-rī) [L. *infirmarium,* see infirm]. A small hospital, especially in a school or college.

infirmity (in-fir'mĭ-tī). A weakness; an abnormal, more or less disabling, condition of mind or body.

inflammation (in-flă-ma'shun) [L. *inflammo,* pp. -*atus,* fr. *in,* in, + *flamma,* flame]. A fundamental pathologic process consisting of a dynamic complex of cytologic and histologic reactions that occur in the affected blood vessels and adjacent tissues in response to an injury or abnormal stimulation caused by a physical, chemical, or biologic agent. The so-called cardinal signs of i. are: *rubor,* redness; *calor,* heat (or warmth); *tumor,* swelling; and *dolor,* pain; a fifth sign, *functio laesa,* inhibited or lost function, is sometimes added. All may be observed in certain instances, but no one of them is necessarily always present.

acute i., any i. that has a fairly rapid onset and then relatively soon comes to a crisis, with clear and distinct termination.

catarrhal i., an inflammatory process that may occur in any mucous membrane and is characterized by hyperemia of the mucosal vessels, edema of the interstitial tissue, enlargement of the secretory epithelial cells, and an irregular layer of viscous, mucinous material on the surface.

chronic i., the antithesis of acute i. which may begin with a relatively rapid onset or in a slow, insidious, and even unnoticed manner, but tends to persist; termination of the pathologic process is indefinite and frequently not recognizable.

exudative i., i. in which the conspicuous or distinguishing feature is an exudate, which may be chiefly serous, serofibrinous, fibrinous, or mucous.

fibrinous i., an exudative i. in which there is a disproportionately large amount of fibrin.

granulomatous i., a form of proliferative i.

proliferative i., an inflammatory reaction in which the distinguishing feature is an actual increase in the number of tissue cells, in contrast to cells exuded from blood vessels.

pseudomembranous i., a form of exudative i. that involves mucous and serous membranes.

purulent i., suppurative i.; an acute exudative i. in which the accumulation of polymorphonuclear leukocytes is sufficiently great that their enzymes cause liquefaction of the affected tissues; the purulent exudate is frequently termed pus.

serous i., an exudative i. in which the exudate is predominantly fluid; relatively few (if any) cells are observed.

subacute i., an i. intermediate in duration between an acute i. and a chronic i.

suppurative i., purulent i.

inflam'matory. Pertaining to, characterized by, resulting from, or becoming affected by inflammation.

infla'tion [L. *inflatio,* fr. *in-flo,* pp. -*flatus,* to blow into, inflate]. Vesiculation (2); distention by a fluid or gas.

inflection, inflexion (in-flek'shun) [L. *in-flecto,* pp. -*flexus,* to bend]. An inward bending.

influenza (in-flu-en'zah) [It. fr. L. *in-fluo,* pr. p. *influens*]. The grippe (grip); the flu; an acute infectious respiratory disease, caused by orthomyxoviruses, in which the inhaled virus attacks the respiratory epithelial cells of susceptible persons and produces a catarrhal inflammation; commonly occurs in epidemics or pandemics which develop quickly, spread rapidly, and involve sizable proportions of the population; characterized by sudden onset, chills, fever of short duration, severe prostration, headache, muscle aches, and a dry cough.

influen'zal. Relating to, marked by, or resulting from, influenza.

Influenzavirus (in-flu-en'ză-vi-rus). The genus of Orthomyxoviridae that comprises the influenza viruses types A and B; each type has a stable nucleoprotein group antigen common to all strains of the type, but distinct from that of the other type.

infor'mosomes. Name suggested for the bodies composed of messenger (informational) RNA and protein that are found in the cytoplasm of animal cells.

infra- [L. below]. Prefix denoting a position below the part denoted by the word to which it is joined. See also **sub-**.

infrabulge (in'fră-bulj). 1. That portion of the crown of a tooth gingival to the height of contour. 2. That area of a tooth where the retentive portion of a clasp of a removable partial denture is placed.

infraclusion (in'fra'-klu'zhun). Infraocclusion; infraversion (3); the state wherein a tooth has failed to erupt to the maxillomandibular plane of interdigitation.

infraction (in-frak'shun) [L. *infractio,* a breaking, fr. *infringere,* to break]. A fracture, especially one without displacement.

inframar'ginal. Below any margin or edge.

inframax'illary. Mandibular.

infraocclusion (in'fră-ŏ-klu'zhun). Infraclusion.

infrapsychic (in'fră-si'kik). Denoting ideas or actions originating below the level of consciousness.

infrared (in'fră-red). Beyond the red end of the spectrum; denoting that section of the electromagnetic spectrum, invisible to the eye, with wavelengths from 7700 nm upward to about 10,000,000 nm.

infrasonic (in-fră-son'ik) [infra- + L. *sonus,* sound]. Pertaining to sounds with frequencies below the human range of hearing.

infraversion (in'fră-ver'shun). 1. A turning (version) downward. 2. Rotation of both eyes downward. 3. Infraclusion.

infundibula (in-fun-dib'u-lah). Plural of infundibulum.

infundibular (in-fun-dib'u-lar). Relating to an infundibulum.

infundibulectomy (in'fun-dib'u-lek'to-mĭ) [infundibulum + G. *ektomē,* excision]. Excision of the infundibulum, especially of hypertrophied myocardium encroaching on the ventricular outflow tract.

infundibuliform (in-fun-dib'u-lĭ-form) [L. *infundibulum,* funnel, + *forma,* form]. Choanoid.

infundibuloma (in'fun-dib'u-lo'mah) [infundibulum + G. *-oma,* tumor]. A piloid astrocytoma arising in tissues adjacent to the third ventricle of the cerebrum.

infundibulum, pl. **infundibula** (in-fun-dib'u-lum, -u-lah) [L. a funnel]. **1** [NA]. A funnel or funnel-shaped structure or passage. **2.** I. tubae uterinae. **3.** The expanding portion of a calix as it opens into the pelvis of the kidney. **4** [NA]. Official alternative name for *conus* arteriosus. **5.** Termination of a bronchiole in the alveolus. **6.** Termination of the cochlear canal beneath the cupola. **7** [NA]. The funnel-shaped, unpaired prominence of the base of the hypothalamus behind the optic chiasm, enclosing the infundibular recess of the third ventricle and continuous below with the stalk of the hypophysis.

   i. ethmoida'le [NA], **ethmoid i.,** a passage from the middle meatus of the nose communicating with the anterior ethmoidal cells and frontal sinus.

   i. hypothal'ami [NA], **hypothalamic i.,** the apical portion of the tuber cinereum extending into the stalk of the hypophysis.

   i. tu'bae uteri'nae [NA], **i. of uterine tube,** infundibulum (2); the funnel-like expansion of the abdominal extremity of the uterine (Fallopian) tube.

infusion (in-fu'zhun) [L. *infusio,* fr. *in-fundo,* pp. *-fusus,* to pour in]. **1.** The process of steeping a substance in water to extract its soluble principles. **2.** A medicinal preparation obtained by steeping the crude drug in water. **3.** The introduction of fluid other than blood into a vein.

ingesta (in-jes'tah) [pl. of L. *ingestum,* ntr. pp. of *in-gero, -gestus,* to carry in]. Solid or liquid nutrients taken into the body.

ingestion (in-jes'chun) [L. *ingestio,* a pouring in]. **1.** Introduction of food and drink into the stomach. **2.** The taking in of particles by a phagocytic cell.

ingestive (in-jes'tiv). Relating to ingestion.

ingravescent (in-grā-ves'ent) [L. *ingravesco,* to grow heavier, fr. *gravis,* heavy]. Increasing in severity.

inguen (ing'gwen) [L.]. Groin.

inguinal (ing'gwĭ-nal). Relating to the groin.

in'guinocru'ral. Relating to the groin and the thigh.

inguinodynia (ing'gwĭ-no-din'ĭ-ah) [L. *inguen* (*inguin-*), groin, + G. *odynē,* pain]. Pain in the groin.

inguinola'bial. Relating to the groin and the labium.

in'guinoper'itone'al. Relating to the groin and the peritoneum.

in'guinoscro'tal. Relating to the groin and the scrotum.

inha'lant [see inhalation]. **1.** That which is inhaled; a remedy given by inhalation. **2.** Insufflation (2); finely powdered or liquid drugs that are carried to the respiratory passages by the use of special devices such as low pressure aerosol containers.

inhalation (in-hă-la'shun) [L. *in-halo,* pp. *-halatus,* to breathe at or in]. **1.** Inspiration; the act of drawing in the breath. **2.** Drawing a medicated vapor in with the breath. **3.** Denoting a solution of a drug or combination of drugs for administration as a nebulized mist intended to reach the repiratory tree.

inhale (in-hāl'). Inspire; to draw in the breath.

inha'ler. 1. Respirator (1). **2.** An apparatus for administering pharmacologicallly active agents by inhalation.

inheritance (in-hĕr'ĭ-tans) [L. *heredito,* inherit, fr. *heres* (*hered-*), an heir]. **1.** Characters or qualities that are transmitted from parent to offspring. **2.** That which is so transmitted.

   codominant i., i. in which two alleles are individually expressed in the presence of one another.

   collateral i., the appearance of characters in collateral members of a family group, as when an uncle and a niece show the same character inherited from a common ancestor; it occurs with recessive characters appearing irregularly, in contrast to dominant characters directly from one generation to the next.

   cytoplasmic i., transmission of characters dependent on self-perpetuating elements not nuclear in origin.

   dominant i., see *dominance* of genes.

   extrachromosomal i., transmission of characters dependent on some factor not connected with the chromosomes.

   mendelian i., See also Mendel's *law.*

   mosaic i., i. in which the paternal influence if dominant in one group of cells and the maternal in another.

   recessive i., see *dominance* of genes.

   sex-linked i., the pattern of inheritance that may result from a mutant gene located on either the X or Y chromosome.

inherited (in-hĕr'ĭ-ted). Inborn; transmitted by inheritance.

inhib'it. To curb or restrain.

inhibition (in-hī-bish'un) [L. *in-hibeo,* pp. *-hibitus,* to keep back]. **1.** Depression or arrest of a function. **2.** In psychoanalysis, the restraining of instinctual or unconscious drives or tendencies, especially if they conflict with one's conscience or with the demands of society. **3.** In psychology, a generic term for a variety of processes associated with the gradual attenuation, masking, and extinction of a previously conditioned response.

   competitive i., selective i.; blocking of the action of an enzyme on its substrate by replacing the latter with a similar but inactive compound, one capable of combining with the active site of the enzyme but not being acted upon or split by it.

   contact i., cessation of replication of dividing cells which come into contact, as in the center of a healing wound.

   feedback i., feedback mechanism; i. of activity by an end product of the action.

   noncompetitive i., a type of enzyme i. in which the inhibiting compound does not compete with the natural substrate for the active site on the enzyme, but inhibits reaction by combining with the enzyme-substrate complex, once the latter has been formed.

reflex i., a situation in which sensory stimuli decrease reflex activity.

selective i., competitive i.

inhib′itor. 1. An agent that restrains or retards physiologic, chemical, or enzymatic action. **2.** A nerve, stimulation of which represses activity.

monoamine oxidase i. (MAOI), any of the hydrazine (-NHNH₂) and hydrazide (-CONHNH₂) derivatives that inhibit several enzymes and raise the brain norepinephrine and 5-hydroxytryptamine levels; used as antidepressant and hypotensive agents.

inhib′itory. Restraining; tending to inhibit.

inion (in′ĭ-on) [G. nape of the neck] [NA]. A point on the external occipital protuberance at the intersection of the midline with a line drawn tangent to the uppermost convexity of the right and left superior nuchal lines.

initis (in-i′tis) [G. *is* (*in-*), fiber, + *-itis,* inflammation]. **1.** Inflammation of fibrous tissue. **2.** Myositis.

inject (in-jekt′) [L. *injicio,* to throw in]. To introduce into the body; denoting a fluid forced into one of the cavities beneath the skin, or into a blood vessel.

injec′ted. 1. Denoting a fluid introduced into the body. **2.** Denoting blood vessels visibly distended with blood.

injection (in-jek′shun) [L. *injicio,* pp. *-jectus,* to throw in]. **1.** Introduction of a medicinal substance or nutrient material into the subcutaneous cellular tissue (*subcutaneous* or *hypodermic*), the muscular tissue (*intramuscular*), a vein (*intravenous*), the rectum (*rectal i.,* clyster, or enema), the vagina (*vaginal i.* or douche), the urethra, or other canals or cavities of the body. **2.** An injectable pharmaceutical preparation. **3.** Congestion or hyperemia.

depot i., an i. of a substance in a vehicle which tends to keep it at the site of i. so that absorption occurs over a prolonged period.

jet i., hypodermic i. of drugs by a small, high-pressure apparatus, without the use of a needle.

lactated Ringer's i., a sterile solution of calcium chloride, potassium chloride, sodium chloride, and sodium lactate in water for injection; used intravenously as a systemic alkalizer and a fluid and electrolyte replenisher.

Ringer's i., a sterile solution of sodium chloride, potassium chloride, and calcium chloride; used intravenously as a fluid and electrolyte replenisher.

injury (in′ju-rĭ) [L. *injuria,* fr. *in-* neg. + *jus (jur), right*]. The damage or wound of trauma.

blast i., tearing of lung tissue or rupture of abdominal viscera without external i., as by the force of an explosion.

closed head i., a head i. in which continuity of the scalp and mucous membranes is maintained.

contrecoup i. of brain, an i. occurring beneath the skull opposite to the area of impact.

coup i. of brain, i. to the brain occurring directly beneath the area of impact.

degloving i., avulsion of the skin of the hand (or foot) in which the part is skeletonized by removal of most or all of the skin and subcutaneous tissue.

hyperextension-hyperflexion i., violence to the body causing the unsupported head to hyperextend and hyperflex the neck rapidly.

open head i., a head i. in which there is a loss of continuity of scalp or mucous membranes; sometimes indicating a communication between the exterior and the intracranial cavity.

whiplash i., popular term for hyperextension-hyperflexion i.'s of the neck.

in′lay. 1. In dentistry, a prefabricated restoration sealed in the cavity with cement. **2.** A graft of bone, skin, or other tissue. **3.** In orthopedics, an orthomechanical device inserted into a shoe.

in′let. A passage leading into a cavity.

innate (in-nāt′) [L. *in-nascor,* pp. *-natus,* to be born in]. Inborn.

innervation (in-er-va′shun) [L. *in,* in, + *nervus,* nerve]. The supply of nerve fibers functionally connected with a part.

innidiation (in′nid-ĭ-a′shun) [L. *in,* in, + *nidus,* nest]. The growth and multiplication of abnormal cells in another location to which they have been transported by means of lymph or the blood stream, or both.

innocent (in′o-sent) [L. *innocens* (*-ent-*), fr. *in,* neg., + *noceo,* to injure]. **1.** Not apparently harmful. **2.** Free from moral wrong.

innocuous (ĭ-nok′u-us) [L. *innocuus*]. Harmless.

innominate (in-nom′in-āt) [L. *innominatus,* fr. *in-* neg. + *nomen* (*nomin-*), name]. Nameless; applied to several anatomical structures.

Ino Inosine.

inoc′ulabil′ity. The quality of being inoculable.

inoc′ulable. 1. Transmissible by inoculation. **2.** Susceptible to a disease transmissible by inoculation.

inoculate (in-ok′u-lāt) [L. *inoculo,* pp. *-atus,* to ingraft]. **1.** To introduce the agent of a disease or other antigenic material into the subcutaneous tissue or a blood vessel or through an abraded or absorbing surface for preventive, curative, or experimental purposes. **2.** To implant microorganisms or infectious material into or upon culture media. **3.** To communicate a disease by transferring its virus.

inoculation (in-ok′u-la′shun). Introduction into the body of the causative organism of a disease.

inoc′ulum. The microorganism or other material introduced by inoculation.

inop′erable. Denoting that which cannot be operated upon, or cannot be corrected or removed by an operation.

in′organ′ic. 1. Originally, not organic; not formed by living organisms; **2.** In chemistry, refers to compounds not containing covalent bonds between atoms.

inosamine (in-ōs′ă-min, -mēn). An inositol in which an –OH group is replaced by an –NH₂ group.

inoscopy (in-os'ko-pĭ) [ino- + G. *skopeō*, to look at]. Microscopic examination of biologic materials after dissecting or chemically digesting the fibrillary elements and strands of fibrin.

inosemia (in-o-se'mĭ-ah) [inose + G. *haima*, blood]. Presence of inositol in the circulating blood. **2.** Fibremia.

in'osine (Ino). 9-β-D-Ribosylhypoxanthine; a nucleoside formed by the deamination of adenosine.

in'osin'ic acid. Inosine phosphate; a mononucleotide found in muscular and other tissues.

myo-**inositol** (in-o'sĭ-tol). 1,2,3,5/4,6-Inositol; the most widely distributed inositol in microorganisms, higher plants, and animals.

inosituria ,7inositol (in'o-si-tu'rĭ-ah) [inositol + G. *ouron*, urine]. Excretion of inositol in the urine.

inotropic (in-o-trop'ik) [ino- + G. *tropos*, a turning]. Influencing the contractility of muscular tissue.

inquest (in'kwest) [L. *in*, in, + *quaero*, pp. *quaisitus*, to seek]. A legal inquiry into the cause of sudden, violent, or mysterious death.

insane (in-sān'). Relating to insanity.

insanity (in-san'ĭ-tĭ) [L. *in*- neg. + *sanus*, sound]. **1.** Now outmoded term, more or less synonymous with severe mental illness or psychosis. **2.** In law, that degree of mental illness which negates the individual's legal responsibility or capacity.

inscription (in-skrip'shun) [L. *inscriptio*]. **1.** The main part of a prescription; that which indicates the drugs and the quantity of each to be used in the mixture. **2.** A mark, band, or line.

insecticide (in-sek'tĭ-sīd) [insect + L. *caedō*, to kill]. An agent that kills insects.

insecurity (in'se-ku'rĭ-tĭ). A feeling of unprotectedness and helplessness.

insemination (in-sem'ĭ-na'shun) [L. *in-semino*, pp. -*atus*, to sow or plant in]. Semination; the deposit of seminal fluid within the vagina, as introduced during coitus.

artificial i., the introduction of semen of the husband (*homologous i.*) or of another (*heterologous i.*) into the vagina otherwise than through the act of coitus.

insenescence (in-sĕ-nes'ens) [L. *insenescere*, to begin to grow old]. The process of becoming senile.

insensible (in-sen'sĭ-bl) [L. *in-sensibilis*, fr. *in*, neg. + *sentio*, pp. *sensus*, to feel]. **1.** Unconscious. **2.** Not appreciable by the senses.

insertion (in-ser'shun) [L. *insertio*, a planting in]. **1.** The attachment of a muscle to the more movable part of the skeleton, as distinguished from origin. **2.** In dentistry, the intraoral placing of a dental prosthesis.

insidius (in-sid'ĭ-us) [L. *insidiosus*, cunning, fr. *in-sidioe* (pl.), an ambush]. Treacherous; stealthy; denoting a disease that progresses with few or no symptoms to indicate its gravity.

insight (in'sĭt). Self-understanding.

in si'tu [L. *in*, in, + *situs*, site]. In position; confined to site or origin.

insoluble (in-sol'u-bl). Not soluble.

insomnia (in-som'nĭ-ah) [L. fr. *in*- priv. + *somnus*, sleep]. Wakefulness, inability to sleep, in the absence of external impediments, during the period when sleep should normally occur.

insomniac (in-som'nĭ-ak). Exhibiting suffering from, tending toward, or producing insomnia.

insorp'tion [L. *in*, in, + *sorbere*, to suck]. Movement of substances from the lumen of the gut into the blood.

inspersion (in-sper'shun, -zhun) [L. *inspersio*, fr. *in-spergo*, pp. -*spersus*, to scatter upon]. Sprinkling with a fluid or a powder.

inspiration (in'spĭ-ra'shun) [L. *inspiratio*, fr. *in-spiro*, pp. -*atus*, to breathe in]. Inhalation (1).

inspiratory (in-spi'ră-to-rĭ). Relating to or timed during inhalation.

inspire (in-spīr'). Inhale.

inspis'sated [L. *in*- intensive + *spisso*, pp. -*atus*, to thicken]. Thickened by evaporation or absorption of fluid.

inspissation (in'spĭ-sa'shun). **1.** The act of thickening by evaporation or by the absorption of fluid. **2.** An increased thickness or diminished fluidity.

in'star [L. form]. Any of the successive nymphal stages in the metamorphosis of insects or the stages of larval change by successive molts.

in'step. The arch, or highest part of the dorsum of the foot.

instillation (in'stĭ-la'shun) [L. *instillatio*, fr. *in-stillo*, pp. -*atus*, to pour in by drops]. The dropping of a liquid on or into a part.

in'stinct [L. *instinctus*, impulse]. **1.** An enduring disposition or tendency of an organism to act in an organized and biologically adaptive manner characteristic of its species. **2.** The unreasoning impulse to perform some purposive action without an immediate consciousness of the end to which that action will lead. **3.** In psychoanalytic theory, the forces assumed to exist behind the tension caused by the needs of the id.

death i., the i. of all living creatures toward self-destruction, death, or a return to the inorganic lifelessness from which they arose.

herd i., tendency or inclination to band together with and share the customs of others of a group, and to conform to the opinions and adopt the views of the group.

life i., the i. of self-preservation and sexual procreation; the basic urge toward preservation of the species.

instinc'tive, instinc'tual. Relating to instinct.

in'strumenta'rium. A collection of instruments and other equipment for an operation or for a medical procedure.

insudate (in'su-dāt) [L. *in*, in, + *sudare*, to sweat]. Fluid swelling within an arterial wall.

insufficiency (in-sŭ-fish'en-sĭ) [L. *in*-, neg. + *sufficientia*, to suffice]. **1.** Lack of completeness of function or power. **2.** Incompetence (1).

acute adrenocortical i., addisonian or adrenal crisis; severe adrenocortical i. resulting from untreated chronic adrenocortical i.; characterized by nausea, vomiting, hypotension, and frequently hyperthermia, hyponatremia, hyperkalemia, and hypoglycemia.

adrenocortical i., hypocorticoidism; loss, to varying degrees, of adrenocortical function.

aortic i., see valvular i.

cardiac i., heart *failure* (1).

chronic adrenocortical i., Addison's disease; adrenocortical i. caused by idiopathic atrophy or destruction of both adrenal glands; characterized by fatigue, decreased blood pressure, weight loss, melanin pigmentation of the skin and mucous membranes, anorexia, and nausea or vomiting.

coronary i., coronarism (1); inadequate coronary circulation leading to anginal pain.

mitral i., see valvular i.

myocardial i., heart *failure* (1).

primary adrenocortical i., adrenocortical i. caused by disease, destruction, or surgical removal of the adrenal cortices.

pulmonary i., see valvular i.

secondary adrenocortical i., adrenocortical i. caused by failure of ACTH secretion resulting from anterior pituitary disease, or by ACTH inhibition resulting from exogenous steroid therapy.

tricuspid i., see valvular i.

valvular i., failure of the cardiac valves to close perfectly, thus allowing regurgitation of blood past the closed valve; named, according to the valve involved: aortic, mitral, pulmonary, or tricuspid i.

velopharyngeal i., anatomical deficiency in the soft palate or superior constrictor muscle, resulting in the inability to achieve velopharyngeal closure.

venous i., inadequate drainage of venous blood from a part, resulting in edema or dermatosis.

insuf'flate [L. *in-sufflo*, to blow on or into]. To blow into; to fill the lungs of an asphyxiated person with air, or to blow a medicated vapor, powder, or anesthetic into the lungs or into any cavity or orifice of the body.

in'sufflation. 1. The act or process of insufflating. **2.** Inhalant (2).

insula, gen. and pl. **insulae** (in'su-lah, -le) [L. island]. **1** [NA]. Island of Reil; an oval region of the cerebral cortex overlying the capsula extrema, lateral to the lenticular nucleus, buried in the depth of the sylvian fissure. **2.** Island. **3.** Any circumscribed body or patch on the skin.

in'sular. Denoting an island-like structure.

insulin (in'su-lin). A peptide hormone secreted by the pancreatic islets of Langerhans that promotes glucose utilization, protein synthesis, and the formation and storage of neutral lipids. Insulins, obtained from various animals and available in a variety of preparation, are used parenterally in the treatment of diabetes mellitus.

insulinase (in'su-lin-ās). An enzyme in liver, kidney, and muscle, capable of inactivating insulin.

insulinemia (in'su-lin-e'mĭ-ah) [insulin + G. *haima*, blood]. Abnormally large concentrations of insulin in the circulating blood.

insulinogenesis (in'su-lin-o-jen'ĕ-sis) [insulin + G. *genesis*, production]. Production of insulin by the islets of Langerhans.

insulinogen'ic, insulogen'ic. Relating to insulinogenesis.

insulinoma (in'su-lin-o'mah). Insuloma; an islet cell adenoma that secretes insulin.

insulitis (in-su-li'tis) [L. *insula*, island, + *-itis*, inflammation]. A histologic change in which the islets of Langerhans are edematous and contain small numbers of leukocytes.

insulo'ma [L. *insula*, island, + suffix *-oma*, tumor]. Insulinoma.

in'sult [LL. *insultus*, fr. L. *insulto*, to spring upon]. An injury, attack, or trauma.

insusceptibility (in'sus-sep'tĭ-bil'ĭ-tĭ) [L. *suscipio*, pp. *-ceptus*, to take upon one]. Immunity.

integration (in-tĕ-gra'shun) [L. *integro*, pp. *-atus*, to make whole]. **1.** The state of being combined, or the process of combining, into a complete and harmonious whole. **2.** In physiology, building up, as by accretion, anabolism, etc. **3.** In molecular biology, a recombination event in which a genetic element is inserted.

integ'rity. Soundness or completeness of structure; a sound or unimpaired condition.

integument (in-teg'u-ment) [L. *integumentum*, a covering]. **1.** *Integumentum commune.* **2.** The rind, capsule, or covering of any body or part.

integumen'tary. Relating to the integument.

integumen'tum commu'ne [NA]. Integument (1); the enveloping membrane of the body; includes, in addition to the epidermis and dermis, all of the derivatives of the epidermis, *i.e.,* hairs, nails, sudoriferous and sebaceous glands, and mammary glands.

intellectualization (in-tel-lek'chu-al-ĭ-za'shun) [L. *intellectus,* perception, discernment]. An unconscious defense mechanism in which reasoning, logic, or attention to intellectual minutiae is used in an attempt to avoid confrontation with an objectionable impulse, affect, or interpersonal situation.

intel'ligence [L. *intelligentia*]. **1.** An individual's aggregate capacity to act purposefully, think rationally, and deal effectively with his environment, especially in relation to the extent of his perceived effectiveness in meeting challenges. **2.** An individual's relative standing on two quantitative indices, measured i. and effectiveness of adaptive behavior.

intention (in-ten'shun) [L. *intentio*, a stretching out]. **1.** An objective. **2.** In surgery, a process or operation.

inter- [L. *inter*, between]. Prefix conveying the meaning of between, among.

in'terbod'y. Between the bodies of two adjacent vertebrae.

intercadence (in-ter-ka'dens) [inter- + L. *cado,* pr. p. *cadens* (*-ent-*), to fall]. Extreme dicrotism; interpolated extrasystole; the occurrence of an extra beat between the two regular pulse beats.

interca'dent. Irregular in rhythm; characterized by intercadence.

intercalary (in-ter'kă-lĕr-ĭ, in'ter-kal'ă-rī) [L. *intercalarius,* concerning an insertion]. Occurring between two others; as in a pulse tracing, an upstroke interposed between two normal pulse beats.

intercalated (in-ter'kă-la-ted) [L. *intercalatus*]. Interposed; inserted between two others.

intercil'ium [inter- + L. *cilium,* eyelid]. Glabella.

intercourse (in'ter-kōrs) [L. *intercursus,* a running between]. Communication or dealings between or among people; interchange of ideas.

    sexual i., coitus.

in'tercri'cothyrot'omy. Cricothyrotomy.

in'tercross. A mating between individuals both heterozygous at a specific locus (loci).

intercur'rent [inter- + L. *curro,* pr. p. *currens* (*-ent-*), to run]. Intervening; said of a disease attacking a person already ill with another malady.

intercuspation (in'ter-kus-pa'shun) [L. *inter,* among, mutually, + cusp]. **1.** The cusp-to-fossa relation of the maxillary and mandibular posterior teeth to each other. **2.** Interdigitation (4); the interlocking or fitting together of the cusps of opposing teeth.

interden'tal [inter- + L. *dens,* tooth]. **1.** Between the teeth. **2.** Denoting the relationship between the proximal surfaces of the teeth of the same arch.

interdentium (in-ter-den'shĭ-um). The interval between any two contiguous teeth.

interdigit (in-ter-dij'it). That part of the sloping extremity of the hand or foot lying between any two adjacent fingers or toes.

interdigitation (in'ter-dij-ĭ-ta'shun) [inter- + L. *digitus,* finger]. **1.** The mutual interlocking of toothed or tonguelike processes. **2.** The processes thus interlocked. **3.** Infoldings or plicae of adjacent cell or plasma membranes. **4.** Intercuspation (2).

in'terface. A surface that forms a common boundary of two bodies.

interference (in-ter-fēr'ens) [inter- + L. *ferio,* to strike]. **1.** The coming together of waves in various media in such a way that the crests of one series correspond to the hollows of the other, the two thus neutralizing each other; or so that the crests of the two series correspond, thus increasing the excursions of the waves. **2.** The condition in which infection of a cell by one virus prevents superinfection by another virus, or in which superinfection prevents effects which would result from infection by either virus alone, even though both viruses persist.

interferon (IFN) (in-ter-fēr'on). A glycoprotein induced in different cell types by appropriate stimuli. At least three types are recognized: IFN-α or leukocyte i., elaborated by leukocytes in response to viral infection or stimulation with double-stranded RNA; IFN-β made by fibroblasts under the same conditions; IFN-γ or immune i., produced by lymphocytes following mitogenic stimulation.

interictal (in'ter-ik'tal) [inter- + L. *ictus,* stroke]. Denoting the interval between convulsions.

interkine'sis [inter- + G. *kinēsis,* movement]. Interphase.

interleu'kin. A class of lymphokine that acts as a T-lymphocyte growth factor.

interlobitis (in'ter-lo-bi'tis). Inflammation of the pleura separating two pulmonary lobes.

intermediate (in'ter-me'dī-āt) [L. *intermedius,* lying between]. **1.** Between two extremes; interposed; intervening. **2.** A substance, formed in the course of chemical reactions, which then proceeds to participate rapidly in further reactions, so that at any given moment it is present in minute concentrations only.

interme'din. Melanocyte-stimulating *hormone.*

intermedius (in-ter-me'dī-us) [L.] [NA]. An element or organ between right and left (or lateral and medial) structures.

intermit'tent. Marked by intervals of complete quietude between two periods of activity.

intern (in'tern or in-tern') [F. *interne,* inside]. An advanced student or recent graduate who assists in the medical or surgical care of hospital patients and who resides within the institution.

inter'nal [L. *internus*]. Interior; away from the surface; often incorrectly used to mean medial.

inter'naliza'tion. Adopting as one's own the standards and values of another person or society.

International System of Units (SI) [Fr. *Système International d'Unités*]. A system of weights and measures designed to cover both the coherent units (basic, supplementary, and derived units) and the decimal multiples and submultiples of these units formed by use of prefixes proposed for general international scientific and technological use. SI proposes seven basic units: meter (m), kilogram (kg), second (s), ampere (A), kelvin (K), candela (cd), and mole (mol) for the basic quantities, length, mass, time, electric current, temperature, luminous intensity, and amount of substance. Supplementary units proposed are radian (rad) for plane angle and steradian (sr) for solid angle. Derived units (*e.g.,* force, power, frequency) are stated in terms of the basic units. Multiples (prefixes) in descending order are: tera -(T, 10^{12}), giga- (G, 10^9), mega- (M, 10^6), kilo- (k, 10^3), hecto- (h, 10^2), deca- (da, 10^1), deci- (d, 10^{-1}), centi (c, 10^{-2}), milli- (m, 10^{-3}), micro- (μ, 10^{-6}), nano- (n, 10^{-9}), pico- (p, 10^{-12}), femto- (f, 10^{-15}), atto- (a, 10^{-18}).

interneurons (in'ter-nu'ronz). Combinations or groups of neurons between sensory and motor neurons which govern coordinated activity.

inter'nist. A physician trained in internal medicine.

in'ternode. Internodal *segment.*

internuclear (in-ter-nu'kle-ar). Between nerve cell groups in the brain or retina.

internuncial (in-ter-nun'sĭ-al) [L. *inter-nuntius* (or *-nuncius*), a messenger between two parties]. **1.** Indicating a neuron functionally interposed between two or more other neurons. **2.** Acting as a medium of communication between two organs.

interoceptive (in'ter-o-sep'tiv) [inter- + L. *capio,* to take]. Relating to the sensory nerve cells innervating the viscera (thoracic, abdominal and pelvic organs, and the cardiovascular system), their sensory end organs, or the information they convey to the spinal cord and the brain.

interoceptor (in'ter-o-sep'tor) [inter- + L. *capio,* to take]. One of the various forms of small sensory end organs (receptors) situated within the walls of the respiratory and gastrointestinal tracts or in other viscera.

interparoxysmal (in'ter-păr'ok-siz'mal). Occurring between successive paroxysms of a disease.

interphase (in'ter-fāz). Interkinesis; the stage between two successive divisions of a cell nucleus; the stage in which the biochemical and physiologic functions of the cell are performed.

interphyletic (in-ter-fi-let'ik) [inter- + G. *phylē,* tribe]. Denoting the transitional forms between two kinds of cells during the course of metaplasia.

inter'preta'tion. 1. In psychoanalysis, the characteristic therapeutic intervention of the analyst. **2.** In clinical psychology, drawing inferences and formulating the meaning in terms of the psychological dynamics inherent in an individual's responses to psychological tests.

interprox'imal. Between adjoining surfaces.

in'terspace. Any space between two similar objects.

interstice, pl. **interstices** (in-ter'stis, -stĭ-sēz) [L. *interstitium,* fr. *sisto,* to stand]. A small area, space, or hole in the substance of an organ or tissue.

interstitial (in-ter-stish'al). Relating to spaces or interstices in any structure.

intertrigo (in-ter-tri'go) [L. a galling of the skin, fr. *inter,* between, + *tero,* to rub]. Dermatitis occurring between folds or juxtaposed surfaces of the skin and caused by sweat retention, moisture, warmth, and concomitant overgrowth of resident microorganisms.

in'terval [L. *inter-vallum,* space between ramparts in a camp, an interval]. A time or space between two periods or objects; a break in a current or the course of a disease; a period of rest between two periods of activity.

   atriocarotid (a-c) i., the time between the beginning of the atrial and that of the carotid waves in a tracing of the jugular pulse.

   A-V i., the time from the beginning of atrial systole to the beginning of ventricular systole as measured from the electrocardiogram.

   cardioarterial (c-a) i., the time between the apex beat of the heart and the radial pulse beat.

   postsphygmic i., postsphygmic period; the interval in the cardiac cycle following the sphygmic period, *i.e.,* from the closure of the semilunar valves to the

opening of the atrioventricular valves.

   P-R i., in the electrocardiogram, the time elapsing between the beginning of the P wave and the beginning of the QRS complex; corresponds to the a-c interval of the venous pulse.

   presphygmic i., presphygmic period; the brief period at the beginning of the ventricular systole during which the pressure rises before the semilunar valves open.

   Q-T i., in the electrocardiogram, the time elapsing from the beginning of the QRS complex to the end of the T wave; represents the total duration of electrical activity of the ventricles.

   sphygmic i., ejection or sphygmic period; the period in the cardiac cycle when the semilunar valves are open and blood is being ejected from the ventricles into the arterial system.

interven'tion. Interference so as to modify a process or situation.

intes'tinal. Relating to the intestine.

intestine (in-tes'tin) [L. *intestinus,* internal; as noun, the entrails]. The digestive tract passing from the stomach to the anus.

   large i., the portion of the digestive tract extending from the ileocecal valve to the anus; comprises the cecum, colon, rectum, and anal canal.

   small i., the portion of the digestive tract between the stomach and the cecum or beginning of the large intestine; consists of the duodenum, jejunum, and ileum.

intima (in'tĭ-mah) [L. fem. of *intimus,* inmost]. *Tunica* intima.

in'timal. Relating to the intima or inner coat of a vessel.

intimitis (in-tĭ-mi'tis) [intima + *-itis,* inflammation]. Inflammation of an intima, as in endangiitis.

in'toe. *Metatarsus* varus.

intol'erance. Abnormal metabolism, excretion, or other disposition of a given substance; term often used to indicate impaired disposal of dietary constituents.

intorsion (in-tor'shun) [L. *in-torqueo,* pp. *tortus,* to twist]. Incycloduction.

intor'tor. Medial rotator; a muscle that turns a part medially.

intoxation (in-tok-sa'shun) [see intoxication]. Poisoning, especially by the toxic products of bacteria or poisonous animals, other than alcohol.

intoxicant (in-tok'sĭ-kant). **1.** Having the power to intoxicate. **2.** An intoxicating agent, such as alcohol.

intoxication (in-tok'sĭ-ka'shun) [L. *in,* in, + G. *toxicon,* poison]. **1.** Poisoning. **2.** Acute *alcoholism.*

intra- [L. within]. Prefix meaning within.

intracatheter (in'tră-kath'ē-ter). A plastic tube, usually attached to the puncturing needle, inserted into a blood vessel for infusion, injection, or pressure monitoring.

intracorporeal (in'tră-kor-po're-al) [intra- + L. *corpus,* body]. **1.** Within the body. **2.** Within any structure anatomically styled a corpus.

intrac'table [L. *in-tractabilis*, fr. *in-* neg. + *tracto*, to draw, haul]. **1.** Refractory (1). **2.** Obstinate (1).

in'trad. Toward the inner part.

intrafilar (in-trah-fī'lar) [intra- + L. *filum*, thread]. Lying within the meshes of a network.

intrafu'sal. Applied to structures within the muscle spindle.

intramedullary (in'tră-med'u-lĕr-ĭ). Within the bone marrow, the spinal cord, or the medulla oblongata.

intrapar'tum [intra- + L. *partus*, childbirth]. During labor and delivery or childbirth.

intrapsychic (in'tră-si-kik). Denoting the psychological dynamics which occur inside the mind without reference to the individual's exchanges with persons or events.

intravasation (in'trav-ă-sa'shun) [intra- + L. *vas*, vessel]. Entrance of foreign matter into a blood vessel.

intra vi'tam [L. *vita*, life]. During life.

intrin'sic [L. *intrinsecus, on the inside*]. **1.** Inherent; belonging entirely to a part. **2.** In anatomy, denoting those muscles of the limbs whose origin and insertion are both in the same limb, distinguished from the extrinsic muscles which have their origin in some part of the trunk outside of the pelvic or shoulder girdle; applied also to the ciliary muscle as distinguished from the recti and other orbital muscles which are on the eyeball.

intro- [L. *intro*, into]. Prefix meaning in or into.

introdu'cer [L. *intro-duco*, to lead into, introduce]. An instrument or stylet for the introduction of a flexible instrument; *e.g.*, a catheter or an endotracheal tube.

introflection, introflexion (in-tro-flek'shun) [intro- + L. *flecto*, pp. *flectus*, to bend]. A bending inward.

intro'itus [L. entrance, fr. *intro-eo*, to go into]. The entrance into a canal or hollow organ, as the vagina.

introjection (in-tro-jek'shun) [intro- + L. *jacere*, to throw]. A psychological defense mechanism involving appropriation of an external happening and its assimilation by the personality, making it a part of the self.

intromission (in-tro-mish'un) [intro- + L. *mitto*, to send]. The insertion or introduction of one part into another.

intromit'tent. Conveying or sending into a body or cavity.

intron (in'tron). A portion of a DNA between two exons that is transcribed into RNA as usual, but does not appear in that RNA after maturation, and so is not expressed (as protein) in protein synthesis.

introspec'tion [intro- + L. *spicere*, to look]. Looking inward; self-scrutinizing; contemplating one's own mental processes.

introspec'tive. Relating to introspection.

introsusception (in'tro-sus-sep'shun). Intussusception.

introversion (in-tro-ver'shun) [intro- + L. *verto*, pp. *versus*, to turn]. **1.** The turning of a structure into itself. **2.** A trait of preoccupation with oneself, in contrast to extraversion.

introvert. **1** (in'tro-vert). One who tends to be introspective and self-centered and who takes small interest in the affairs of others. **2** (in-tro-vert'). To turn a structure into itself.

intubate (in'tu-bāt) L. *in-* in, + *tuba*, tube]. To perform intubation.

intubation (in-tu-ba'shun). The insertion of a tube into any canal or other part.

 endotracheal i., passage of a tube through the nose (**masotrachial i.**) or mouth (**oratracheal i.**) into the trachea for maintenance of the airway during anesthesia or in a patient with an imperilled airway.

intuition. (in-tu-ĭ'shun). Cryptesthesia.

intumesce (in-tu-mes') [L. *in-tumesco*, to swell up]. To swell up; to enlarge.

intumescence (in-tu-mes'ens). **1.** An anatomical swelling, enlargement, or prominence. **2.** The process of enlarging or swelling.

intumescent (in-tu-mes'ent). Enlarging; swelling; becoming enlarged or swollen.

intussusception (in'tus-sus-sep'shun) [L. *intus*, within, + *sus-cipio*, to take up]. Introsusception; the taking up or receiving of one part within another, especially the infolding of one segment of the intestine within another.

intussusceptive (in'tus-sus-sep'tiv). Relating to or characterized by intussusception.

intussusceptum (in'tus-sus-sep'tum). In an intussusception, that part of the bowel which is received within the other part.

intussuscipiens (in'tus-sus-sip'ĭ-enz). In intussusception, that part of the bowel which receives the other part.

in'ulin. A fructose polysaccharide from the rhizome of *Inula helenium* or *elecampane*, and other plants; a hygroscopic powder used by intravenous injection to determine the rate of glomerular filtration.

inunction (in-ungk'shun) [L. *inunctio*, an anointing, fr. *inunguo*, pp. *-unctus*, to smear on]. Anointing; the administration of a drug in ointment form applied with rubbing, with the purpose of causing absorption of the active ingredient.

in u'tero [L.]. Within the womb; not yet born.

invaginate (in-vaj'ĭ-nāt) [L. *in*, in, + *vagina*, a sheath]. To ensheathe, infold, or insert a structure within itself or another.

invagination (in-vaj'ĭ-na'shun). **1.** The ensheathing, infolding, or insertion of a structure within itself or another. **2.** The state of being invaginated.

in'valid [L. *in-* neg. + *validus*, strong]. **1.** Weak; sick. **2.** A sickly person suffering from a disabling but not necessarily completely incapacitating disease.

invasive (in-vās'iv). **1.** Involving puncture, incision, or penetration of the body, as in a diagnostic technique. **2.** Denoting local spread of a malignant neoplasm by infiltration or destruction of adjacent tissue.

inversion (in-ver'shun) [L. *inverto*, pp. *-versus*, to turn upside down, turn about]. **1.** A turning inward, upside down, or in any direction contrary to the existing one. **2.** Conversion of a disaccharide or polysaccharide by hydrolysis into a monosaccharide. **3.** Alteration of a DNA molecule made by removing a fragment, reversing its orientation, and pulling it back into place.

   i. of the uterus, a turning of the uterus inside out, usually following childbirth.

   visceral i., situs inversus.

invertebrate (in-ver'tĕ-brāt). **1.** Not possessed of a spinal, or vertebral, column. **2.** Any such animal.

invert'or [see inversion]. A muscle that inverts or causes inversion or turns a part, such as the foot, inward.

invet'erate [L. *in-vetero,* pp. *-atus,* to render old]. Chronic; long seated; firmly established; said of a disease or of confirmed habits.

inviscation (in-vis-ka'shun) [L. *in,* in, on, + *viscum,* birdlime]. **1.** Smearing with mucilaginous matter. **2.** The mixing of food, during mastication, with the buccal secretions.

in vitro (in ve'tro) [L. in glass]. In an artificial environment, referring to a process or reaction occurring therein, as in a test tube or culture media.

in vivo (in-ve'vo) [L. in the living being]. In the living body, referring to a process or reaction occurring therein.

involucrum, pl. **involucra** (in'vo-lu'krum, -lu'krah) [L. a wrapper, fr. *in-volvo,* to roll up]. An enveloping membrane, *e.g.,* the sheath of new bone that forms around a sequestrum.

invol'untary [L. *in-* neg. + *voluntarius,* willing, fr. *volo,* to wish]. **1.** Independent of the will; not volitional. **2.** Contrary to the will.

involution (in-vo-lu'shun) [L. *in-volvo,* pp. *-volutus,* to roll up]. Catagenesis. **1.** The return of an enlarged organ, as the postpartum uterus, to normal size. **2.** The turning inward of the edges of a part. **3.** In psychiatry, the mental decline associated with later life.

involu'tional. Relating to involution.

iocetamic acid (i'o-se-tam'ik). *N*-Acetyl-*N*-(3-amino-2,4,6-triiodophenyl)-2-methyl-β-alanine; a radiopaque contrast medium.

iodamide (i-o'dă-mīd). α,5-Diacetamide-2,4,6-triiodo-*m*-toluic acid; a radiopaque contrast medium.

i'odide. The negative ion of iodine, I-.

iodimetry (i-o-dim'ĕ-trī) [iodine + G. *metron,* measure]. Determination of the amount of iodine in any compound, or the amount consumed in a reaction, as by an unsaturated compound.

io'dinate. To treat or combine with iodine.

iodine (i'o-dīn) [G. *iōdēs,* violet-like]. A nonmetallic chemical element, symbol I, atomic no. 53, atomic weight 126.91; used as a catalyst, a reagent and stain, a topical antiseptic, internally in thyroid disease, and as an antidote for alkaloidal poisons.

   protein-bound i. (PBI), thyroid hormone in its circulating form, consisting of one or more of the iodothyronines bound to one or more of the serum proteins.

   radioactive i., Usually refers to ^{131}I, ^{125}I, or ^{123}I used as tracers in biology and medicine.

iodine-123 (^{123}I). A radioisotope of iodine with a pure gamma emission and a physical half-life of 13.1 hr, used for studies of thyroid metabolism.

iodine-125 (^{125}I). Radioactive iodine isotope that decays by K-capture with a half-life of 60 days; used as a tracer in thyroid studies and as therapy in hyperthyroidism.

iodine-131 (^{131}I). A radioactive iodine isotope; a beta emitter with a half-life of 8.05 days; used as a tracer in thyroid studies and as therapy in hyperthyroidism and thyroid cancer.

iodine-fast. Denoting hyperthyroidism unresponsive to iodine therapy, which ultimately develops in most cases so treated.

iodinophil, iodinophile (i-o-din'o-fil, -fīl) [iodine + G. *philos,* fond]. **1.** Iodinophilous; staining readily with iodine. **2.** Any histologic element that stains readily with iodine.

iodinophilous (i'o-din-of'ĭ-lus). Iodinophil (1).

iodip'amide. Adipiodone; 3,3'-(adipoyldiimino)-bis[2,4,6-triiodobenzoic acid]; a radiographic contrast medium for the biliary system; used as i. meglumine or i. sodium.

i'odism. Poisoning by iodine, a condition marked by severe coryza, an acneform eruption, weakness, salivation, and a foul breath.

i'odize. To treat or impregnate with iodine.

iodized oil. An iodine addition product of vegetable oils used as radiopaque medium in hysterosalpingography.

io'doder'ma. An eruption of follicular papules and pustules, or a granulomatous lesion, caused by iodine toxicity or sensitivity.

io'dohip'purate sodium. A radiopaque compound used intravenously, orally, or for retrograde urography; when tagged with iodine-131, used to measure renal function externally in radioisotopic renography.

io'dometh'amate sodium. An organic iodine radiopaque compound used in intravenous urography or retrograde pyelography.

iodometry (i-o-dom'ĕ-trī) [iodine + G. *metron,* measure]. Analytical techniques involving titrations in which iodine is either formed or consumed, the sudden appearance or disappearance of iodine marking the end point.

iodophilia (i-o'do-fil'ĭ-ah) [iodine + G. *phileō,* to love]. An affinity for iodine, as manifested by some leukocytes in certain conditions; may be intracellular or extracellular, affecting the particles in the immediate vicinity of the leukocytes.

iodop'sin. Visual violet; a visual pigment composed of 11-*cis*-retinal bound to an opsin, found in the cones of the retina.

io'dopy'racet. 3,5-Diiodo-4-pyridone-*N*-acetate; a radiopaque medium used intravenously in urography; also used to determine the renal plasma flow and the renal tubular excretory mass.

i'odother'apy. Treatment with iodine.

iodu'ria. Urinary excretion of iodine.

i'on [G. *iōn*, going]. An atom or group of atoms carrying a charge of electricity by virtue of having gained or lost one or more valence electrons, usually constituting one of the parts of an electrolyte. Those charged with negative electricity, which travel toward a positive pole (anode) are *anions*, those charged with positive electricity, which travel toward a negative pole (cathode), are *cations*.

 dipolar i.'s, zwitterions; i.'s possessing both a negative charge and a positive charge, each localized at a different point in the molecule which thus has both positive and negative "poles."

ion exchange. The process whereby a small ion, constituting part of a salt or acid or base with an immobilized solid polymeric ion, exchanges position with another small ion of like charge in a surrounding liquid (aqueous) medium.

ion exchanger. A polymer containing numerous charged groups to which mobile ions of opposite charge are attached; if a solution containing other ions of similar charge is passed through a column of the polymer, the new ion may replace (exchange for) the old.

ion'ic. Relating to an ion or ions.

i'oniza'tion. 1. Dissociation into ions, occurring when an electrolyte is dissolved in water. **2.** Iontophoresis.

i'onize. To separate into ions; to dissociate atoms or molecules into electrically charged atoms or radicals.

ionophore (i-on'o-for) [ion + G. *phore*, a bearer]. The compound or substance that forms a complex with an ion and transports it across a membrane.

ionophoresis (i-on'o-fo-re'sis) [ion + G. *phorēsis*, a being borne]. Electrophoresis.

ion'ophoret'ic. Electrophoretic.

iontophoresis (i-on'to-fo-re'sis) [ion + G. *phorēsis*, a being borne]. Ionization (2); introduction into the tissues, by means of an electric current, of the ions of a chosen medicament.

ion'tophoret'ic. Relating to iontophoresis.

iopanoic acid (i-o-pan-o'ik). A radiopaque iodine compound used as a contrast medium in cholecystography.

iophendylate (i-o-fen'dī-lāt). A mixture of isomers of ethyl iodophenylundecylate; an absorbable iodized fatty acid of low viscosity used for roentgenography of the spinal cord, biliary tree, sinuses, and body cavities.

iothal'amate sodium. The sodium salt of iothalamic acid; used as a radiopaque medium.

I.P., i.p., Intraperitoneal, or intraperitoneally.

ipecac (ip'e-kak). The dried root of *Uragoga* (*Cephaelis*) *ipecacuanha* (family Rubiaceae) which has expectorant, emetic, and antidysenteric properties.

i'podate sodium. Sodium 3-[(dimethylaminomethylene)amino]-2,4,6-triiodohydracinnamate; a radiopaque medium.

IPPB Intermittent positive pressure *breathing*.

ipsilat'eral [L. *ipse*, same, + *latus* (*later*-), side]. Homolateral; with reference to a given point, on the same side.

IQ Intelligence *quotient*.

Ir Iridium.

irid-. See irido-.

iridal (i'rī-dal, ĭr-ĭ-dal). Iridial; iridian; iridic; relating to the iris.

iridauxesis (ĭr-id-awk-se'sis) [irido- + G. *auxēsis*, enlargment]. Thickening of the iris following plastic iritis.

iridectomesodialysis (ĭr-ĭ-dek'to-mes'o-di-al'ĭ-sis) [irido- + G. *ektomē*, excision, + *mesos*, middle, + *dialysis*, loosening]. Formation of an artificial pupil by combined excision of iris at its periphery and separation of the adhesions around its inner margin.

iridectomy (ĭr-ĭ-dek'to-mī) [irido- + G. *ektomē*, excision]. Excision of a portion of the iris.

iridectropium (ĭr'ĭ-dek-tro'pĭ-um) [irido- + G. *ektropion*, everted eyelid]. *Ectropion* uveae.

iridemia (ĭr-ĭ-de'mĭ-ah) [irido- + G. *haima*, blood]. Bleeding from the iris.

iridencleisis (ĭr'ĭ-den-kli'sis) [irido- + G. *enkleiō*, to shut in]. Incarceration of a portion of the iris in a wound of the cornea as an operative measure in glaucoma to effect filtration; may also occur accidently.

iridentropium (ĭr'ĭ-den-tro'pĭ-um) [irido- + G. *entropia*, a turning toward]. *Entropion* uveae.

irideremia (ĭr'ĭd-er-e'mĭ'ah) [irido- + G. *erēmia*, absence]. An iris so rudimentary that it seems to be absent.

irides (ĭr'ĭ-dēz) [G.]. Plural of iris.

iridesis (i-rid'e-sis) [irido- + G. *desis*, a binding together]. Iridodesis; ligature of a portion of the iris brought out through an incision in the cornea.

irid'ial, irid'ian, irid'ic. Iridal.

irid'ium. A white, silvery metallic element, symbol Ir, atomic no. 77, atomic weight 192.2.

irido-, irid- [G. *iris* (*irid*-), rainbow]. Combining forms relating to the iris.

iridoavulsion (ĭr'ĭ-do-ă-vul'shun). A tearing away of the iris.

iridocapsulitis (ĭr'ĭ-do-kap-su-li'tis). Iritis with accompanying inflammation of the capsule of the crystalline lens.

iridocele (ĭr'ĭ-do-sēl) [irido- + G. *kēlē*, hernia]. Protrusion of a portion of the iris through a corneal defect.

iridochoroiditis (ĭr'ĭ-do-ko-roy-di'tis). Inflammation of both iris and choroid.

iridocoloboma (ĭr'ĭ-do-kol'o-bo'mah) [irido- + G. *kolobōma*, coloboma]. A coloboma or congenital defect of the iris.

ir'idoconstric'tor. Causing contraction of the pupil; denoting especially the circular muscular fibers of the iris.

iridocyclectomy (ĭr'ĭ-do-si-klek'to-mĭ) [irido- + G. *kyklos*, circle (ciliary body), + *ektomē*, excision]. Removal of the iris and ciliary body for excision of a tumor.

iridocyclitis (ĭr'id-o-si-kli'tis) [irido- + G. *kyklos*, circle (ciliary body), + *-itis*, inflammation]. Inflammation of both iris and ciliary body.

iridocyclochoroiditis (ĭr'ĭ-do-si'klo-ko-royd-i'tis). Inflammation of the iris, involving the ciliary body and the choroid.

iridocystectomy (ĭr'ĭ-do-sis-tek'to-mĭ) [irido- + G. *kystis*, bladder (capsule), + *ektomē*, excision]. An operation for making an artificial pupil when posterior synechiae follow extracapsular extraction of cataract.

iridodesis (ĭr'ĭ-dod'e-sis). Iridesis.

iridodialysis (ĭr'ĭ-do-di-al'ĭ-sis) [irido- + G. *dialysis*, loosening]. A colobomatous defect of the iris due to its separation from its ciliary attachment.

iridodiastasis (ĭr'ĭ-do-di-as'tă-sis) [irido- + G. *diastasis*, a separation]. A colobomatous defect affecting the peripheral border of the iris with an intact pupil.

iridodilator (ĭr'ĭ-do-di-la'tor). Causing dilation of the pupil; applied to the radiating muscular fibers of the iris.

iridodonesis (ĭr'ĭ-do-do-ne'sis) [irido- + G. *doneō*, to shake to and fro]. Agitated motion of the iris.

iridokinesis, iridokinesia (ĭr'ĭ-do-kĭ-ne'sis, -kĭ-ne'zĭ-ah) [irido- + G. *kinēsis*, movement]. The movement of the iris in contracting and dilating the pupil.

ir'idokinet'ic. Iridomotor; relating to the movements of the iris.

iridomalacia (ĭr'ĭ-do-mă-la'shĭ-ah) [irido- + G. *malakia*, softness]. Degenerative softening of the iris.

iridomesodialysis (ĭr'ĭ-do-mes'o-di-al'ĭ-sis) [irido- + G. *mesos*, middle, + *dialysis*, loosening]. Separation of adhesions around the inner margin of the iris.

ir'idomo'tor. Iridokinetic.

iridoncosis (ĭr'ĭ-dong-ko'sis) [irido- + G. *onkos*, mass, + *-ōsis*, condition]. Thickening of the iris.

iridoncus (ĭr'ĭ-dong'kus) [irido- + G. *onkos*, mass]. A tumefaction of the iris.

ir'idoparal'ysis. Iridoplegia.

iridopathy (ĭr-ĭ-dop'ă-thĭ). Pathologic lesions in the iris.

iridoperiphakitis (ĭr'ĭ-do-per'ĭ-fă-ki'tis) [irido- + G. *peri*, around, + *phakos*, lentil (lens)]. Inflammation of the iris and the anterior portion of the capsule of the lens.

iridoplegia (ĭr'ĭ-do-ple'jĭ-ah) [irido- + G. *plēgē*, stroke]. Iridoparalysis; paralysis of the sphincter of the iris.

iridoptosis (ĭr'ĭ-do-to'sis) [irido- + G. *ptosis*, a falling]. Prolapse of the iris.

iridorrhexis (ĭr'ĭ-do-rek'sis) [irido- + G. *rhēxis*, rupture]. Tearing the iris from its peripheral attachment in order to increase the breadth of a coloboma.

iridoschisis (ĭr-ĭ-dos'kĭ-sis) [irido- + G. *schisma*, cleft]. Separation of the anterior layer of the iris from the posterior layer, with ruptured anterior fibers floating in the aqueous.

iridosclerotomy (ĭr'ĭ-do-skle-rot'o-mĭ) [irido- + sclera + G. *tomē*, incision]. An incision involving both sclera and iris.

iridosteresis (ĭr'ĭ-do-stĕ-re'sis) [irido- + G. *sterēsis*, loss]. Loss or absence of all or part of the iris.

iridotasis (ĭr'ĭ-dot'ă-sis) [irido- + G. *tasis*, a stretching]. Surgical stretching of the iris and incarcerating it in the limbal incision; a substitute for iridencleisis in glaucoma.

iridotomy (ĭr'ĭ-dot'o-mĭ) [irido- + G. *tomē*, incision]. Corotomy; iritomy; irotomy; transverse division of some of the fibers of the iris, forming an artificial pupil.

i'ris, pl. **ir'ides** [G. rainbow] [NA]. The anterior division of the vascular tunic of the eye, a disklike diaphragm, perforated in the center (the pupil), attached marginally to the ciliary body; composed of stroma and a double layer of pigmented retinal epithelium from which are derived the sphincter and dilator muscles of the pupil.

irit'ic. Relating to iritis.

iritides (i-rit'ĭ-dēz). Alternate plural of iritis.

iritis (i-ri'tis). Inflammation of the iris.

irit'omy. Iridotomy.

iron (I) (i'ern) [A.S. *iren*]. A metallic element, symbol Fe, atomic no. 26, atomic weight 55.85; occurs in the heme of hemoglobin, myoglobin, transferrin, ferritin, and iron-containing porphyrins, and is an essential component of enzymes such as catalase, peroxidase, and the various cytochromes; its ferric and ferrous salts are used medicinally.

iron-59 (^{59}Fe). An iron isotope; a beta emitter with half-life of 45.1 days; used as a tracer in study of iron metabolism.

irot'omy. Iridotomy.

irradiate (ĭr-ra'dĭ-āt) [see irradiation]. To apply radiation from a source to a structure or organism.

irradiation (ĭr-ra-dĭ-a'shun) [L. *ir-radio* (*in-r*), pp. *-radi- atus*, to beam forth]. **1.** Exposure or subjection to the action of radiant energy for diagnostic or therapeutic purposes. **2.** The spread of nervous effects (impulses) from one area in the brain or cord, or from a tract, to another tract.

irrational (ĭr-rash'un-al) [L. *irrationalis*, without reason]. Not rational; unreasonable (contrary to reason) or unreasoning (not exercising reason).

irreducible (ir-re-du'sĭ-bl). **1.** Not reducible; incapable of being made smaller. **2.** In chemistry, incapable of being made simpler, or of being replaced or hydrogenated or reduced in positive charge.

irresuscitable (ĭr're-sus'ĭ-tăbl). Incapable of being revived.

irrigate (ĭr'ĭ-gāt) [L. *ir-rigo*, pp. *-atus*, to irrigate]. To wash out a cavity or wound with a fluid.

ir'rita'tive. Causing irritation.

ir'ritabil'ity [L. *irritabilitas*, fr. *irrito*, pp. *-atus*, to excite]. The property inherent in protoplasm of reacting to a stimulus.

  myotatic i., the ability of a muscle to contract in response to the stimulus produced by a sudden stretching.

ir'ritable. 1. Capable of reacting to a stimulus. **2.** Tending to react immoderately to a stimulus.

ir'ritant. Irritating; causing irritation.

irrita'tion [L. *irritatio*]. **1.** Extreme incipient inflammatory reaction of the tissues to an injury. **2.** The normal response of nerve or muscle to a stimulus. **3.** Evocation of a normal or exaggerated reaction in the tissues by the application of a stimulus.

irruption (ĭ-rup'shun) [L. *irruptio*, fr. *irrumpo*, to break in]. The act or process of breaking through to a surface.

IRV Inspiratory reserve *volume.*

isauxesis (is-sawk-ze'sis) [G. *isos*, even, + *auxēsis*, increase]. Growth of parts at the same rate as growth of the whole.

ischemia (is-ke'mĭ-ah) [G. *ischō*, to keep back, + *haima*, blood]. Local anemia due to mechanical obstruction (mainly arterial narrowing) of the blood supply.

ischemic (is-ke'mik). Relating to or affected by ischemia.

ischia (is'kĭ-ah). Plural of ischium.

ischiadic (is-kĭ-ad'ik). Sciatic (1).

ischial (is'kĭ-al). Sciatic (1).

ischialgia (is-kĭ-al'jĭ-ah) [G. *ischion*, hip, + *algos*, pain]. **1.** Ischiodynia; pain in the hip; specifically, the ischium. **2.** Sciatica.

ischiatic (is-kĭ-at'ik). Sciatic (1).

ischidrosis (is-ki-dro'sis) [G. *ischō*, to hold back, + *hidrōsis*, perspiration]. Anhidrosis.

ischio- [G. *ischion*, hip-joint, haunch (ischium)]. Combining form relating to the ischium.

ischiocapsular (is-kĭ-o-kap'su-lar). Relating to the ischium and the capsule of the hip joint; denoting that part of the capsule which is attached to the ischium.

ischiocele (is'kĭ-o-sēl) [ischio- + G. *kēlē*, hernia]. Sciatic *hernia.*

ischiococcygeal (is-kĭ-o-kok-sij'e-al). Relating to the ischium and the coccyx.

ischiodynia (is'kĭ-o-din'ĭ-ah) [ischio- + G. *odynē*, pain]. Ischialgia.

ischiofemoral (is-kĭ-o-fem'o-ral). Relating to the ischium and the femur.

ischiofibular (is'kĭ-o-fib'u-lar). Relating to or connecting the ischium and the fibula.

ischionitis (is'kĭ-o-ni'tis). Inflammation of the ischium.

ischiotibial (is'kĭ-o-tib'ĭ-al). Relating to or connecting the ischium and the tibia.

ischiovertebral (is-kĭ-o-ver'te-bral). Relating to the ischium and the vertebral column.

ischium, pl. **ischia** (is'kĭ-um, is'kĭ-ah) [Mod. L. fr. G. *ischion*, hip]. *Os* ischii.

ischuretic (is-ku-ret'ik). Relating to or relieving ischuria.

ischuria (is-ku'rĭ-ah) [G. *ischō*, to keep back, + *ouron*, urine]. Retention or suppression of urine.

island (i'land) [A.S. *īgland*]. Insula (2); in anatomy, any isolated part, separated from the surrounding tissues by a groove, or marked by difference in structure.

  i.'s of Langerhans, islets of Langerhans; cellular masses varying from a few to hundreds of cells lying in the interstitial tissue of the pancreas; they are composed of different cell types which comprise the endocrine portion of the pancreas, and are the source of insulin and glucagon.

  i. of Reil, insula (1).

islet (i'let). A small island.

  i.'s of Langerhans, *islands* of Langerhans.

-ism [G. *-isma*, *-ismos*, noun-forming suffix]. Suffix denoting a condition or disease resulting from or involving, or a practice or doctrine. *Cf.* -ia.

-ismus [L. fr. G. *-ismos*, noun of action suffix]. Suffix customarily used to imply spasm or contraction.

iso- [G. *isos*, equal]. **1.** Prefix meaning equal, like. **2.** In chemistry, prefix indicating "isomer of."**3.** In immunology, prefix designating sameness with respect to species; recently, sameness with respect to genetic constitution of individuals.

isoagglutination (i'so-ă-glu-tĭ-na'shun) [iso- + L. *ad*, to, + *gluten*, glue]. Isohemagglutination; agglutination of red blood cells as a result of the reaction between an isoagglutinin and specific antigen in or on the cells.

isoagglutinin (i'so-ă-glu'tĭ-nin). Isohemagglutinin; an isoantibody that causes agglutination of cells.

isoagglutinogen (i'so-ă-glu-tin'o-jen). An isoantigen that induces agglutination of the cells to which it is attached upon exposure to its specific isoantibody.

i'soam'ylase. A hydrolase that cleaves 1,6- α-glucosidic branch linkages in glycogen, amylopectin, and their β-limit dextrins; part of the complex known as debranching enzyme or debranching factor.

isoantibody (i'so-an'tĭ-bod-ĭ) [G. *isos*, equal]. **1.** An antibody that occurs only in some individuals of a species, and reacts specifically with the corresponding isoantigen; the latter does not occur naturally in the cells of the same individual who has the antibody.

isoantigen (i'so-an'tĭ-jen). **1.** An antigenic substance that occurs only in some individuals of a species, such as the blood group antigens of man. **2.** Sometimes used as a synonym of alloantigen.

isobar (i'so-bar) [iso- + G. *baros*, weight]. **1.** A term applied to one of two or more nuclides having the same total number of protons plus neutrons, but with different distribution. **2.** The line connecting points of equal barometric pressure.

isobaric (i'so-băr'ik). **1.** Having equal weights or pressures. **2.** With respect to solutions, having the same density as the diluent or medium.

i'socel'lular [iso- + L. *cellula,* dim, of *cella,* a storeroom]. Composed of cells of equal size or of similar character.

isochromatic (i'so-kro-mat'ik) [iso- + G. *chrōma,* color]. **1.** Of uniform color. **2.** Denoting two objects of the same color.

isochromatophil (i'so-kro-mat'o-fil) [iso- + G. *chrōma,* color, + *philos,* fond]. Having an equal affinity for the same stain.

i'sochro'mosome. A chromosomal aberration that arises as a result of transverse rather than longitudinal division of the centromere during meiosis; two daughter chromosomes are formed, each lacking one chromosome arm but with the other doubled.

isochronia (i'so-kro'nĭ-ah) [iso- + G. *chronos,* time]. **1.** The state of having the same chronaxie. **2.** Agreement, with respect to time, rate, or frequency, between processes.

isochronous (i-sok'ro-nus). Occurring during the same time.

i'socit'rate dehy'drogenase. Isocitric acid dehydrogenase; one of two enzymes that catalyze the conversion of isocitrate to α-ketoglutarate (2 -oxoglutarate), one of the reactions of the tricarboxylic acid cycle.

i'socit'ric acid. Intermediate in the tricarboxylic acid cycle.

i'soco'ria [iso- + G. *korē,* pupil]. Equality in the size of the two pupils.

isocortex (i-so-kor'teks). Equality in the size of the two pupils. See *cortex cerebri.*

i'socytol'ysin. A cytolysin that reacts with the cells of certain other animals of the same species, but not with the cells of the individual that formed it.

isodactylism (i-so-dak'tĭ-lizm) [iso- + G. *daktylos,* finger]. A condition in which each of the fingers or toes are approximately of equal length.

i'sodynam'ic [iso- + G. *dynamis,* force]. Of equal force or strength; relating to foods or other materials that liberate the same amount of energy on combustion.

isoenergetic (i'so-en-er-jet'ik). Exerting equal force; equally active.

i'soen'zyme. Isozyme.

isoerythrolysis (i'so-ĕ-rith-rol'ĭ-sis). Destruction of erythrocytes by isoantibodies.

isoflu'rane. 1-Chloro-2,2,2-trifluoro-ethyl difluoromethyl ether; a halogenated ether with potent anesthetic action.

isogamete (i-so-gam'ēt) [iso- + G. *gametēs* or *gametē,* husband or wife]. One of two or more similar cells by the conjugation or fusion of which, with subsequent division, reproduction occurs.

isogamy (i-sog'ă-mĭ) [iso- + G. *gamos,* marriage]. Conjugation between two equal gametes, or two individual cells alike in all respects.

isogeneic (i'so-jĕ-ne'ik). Isogenic.

isogenesis (i-so-jen'ĕ-sis) [iso- + G. *genesis,* production]. Identity of morphologic development.

i'sogen'ic. Isogeneic; relating to a group of individuals or a strain of animals genetically alike with respect to specified gene pairs.

isogenous (i-soj'ĕ-nus) [iso- + G. *genos,* family, kind]. Of the same origin, as in development from the same tissue or cell.

i'sograft [iso- + graft]. Syngeneic graft or homograft; isogeneic homograft; isologous or isoplastic graft; a tissue or organ transplanted between genetically identical individuals, or between syngeneic animals which are isogeneic with respect to histocompatibility genes.

isohemagglutination (i'so-he'mă-glu'tĭ-na'shun). [iso- + G. *haima,* blood, + L. *ad,* to + *gluten,* glue]. Isoagglutination.

isohemagglutinin (i'so-he'mă-glu'tĭ-nin). Isoagglutinin.

i'sohemol'ysin. An isolysin that reacts with red blood cells.

isohemolysis (i'so-he-mol'ĭ-sis) [iso- + G. *haima,* blood, + *lysis,* dissolution]. Isolysis in which there is dissolution of red blood cells as a result of the reaction between an isolysin (isohemolysin) and specific antigen in or on the cells.

isohypercytosis (i'so-hi'per-si-to'sis) [iso- + G. *hyper,* above, + *kytos,* cell]. A condition in which the number of leukocytes in the circulating blood is increased, but the relative proportions of the various types are within the usual range.

isohypocytosis (i'so-hi'po-si-to'sis) [iso- + G. *hypo,* below, + *kytos,* cell]. An abnormally small number of leukocytes in the circulating blood, but the relative proportions of the various types (especially the granulocytes) are within the usual range.

isoiconia (i-so-i-ko'nĭ-ah) [iso- + G. *eikōn,* image, + *-ia,* condition]. Equality of the two retinal images.

isoiconic (i-so-i-kon'ik). Marked by or relating to isoiconia.

i'soim'muniza'tion. The development of a significant titer of specific antibody as a result of antigenic stimulation with material contained on or in the red blood cells of another individual of the same species.

i'solate [It. *isolare;* Mediev. L. *insulo,* pp. *-atus,* to insulate]. **1.** To separate; to set apart from others. **2.** To free from chemical contaminants. **3.** In psychoanalysis, to separate experiences or memories from the affects pertaining to them. **4.** That which is isolated.

isola'tion. The act or state of being isolated.

isolecithal (i-so-les'ĭ-thal). Denoting an ovum in which there is a moderate amount of uniformly distributed yolk.

isoleucine (Ile) i-so-lu'sēn). α-Amino-β-methylvaleric acid; an amino acid found in almost all proteins; an isomer of leucine and, like it, a dietary essential.

isologous (i-sol'o-gus) [iso- + G. *logos,* ratio]. Isoplastic; syngeneic; syngenic (1); relating to tissue transplant between identical twins or between syngeneic individuals, isogeneic with respect to histocompatibility genes.

isolysin (i-sol′ĭ-sin). An antibody that combines with, sensitizes, and results in complement-fixation and dissolution of cells that contain the specific isoantigen.

isolysis (i-sol′ĭ-sis) [iso- + G. *lysis,* dissolution]. Lysis or dissolution of cells as a result of the reaction between an isolysin and specific antigen in or on the cells.

i′solyt′ic. Pertaining to, characterized by, or causing isolysis.

isomal′tose. A disaccharide in which two glucose molecules are attached by an α-1,6 link, rather than an α-1,4 link as in maltose.

i′somer [iso- + G. *meros,* part]. **1.** One of two or more substances displaying isomerism. **2.** One of two or more nuclides having the same atomic and mass numbers but differing in energy states for a finite period of time.

isom′erase. A class of enzymes catalyzing the conversion of a substance to an isomeric form.

isomeric (i-so-měr′ik). Relating to or characterized by isomerism.

isom′erism The existence of a chemical compound in two or more forms that are identical with respect to percentage composition but differ as to the position of the atoms within the molecule, and also in physical and chemical properties.

   geometric i., a form of i. displayed by unsaturated or ring compounds where free rotation about a carbon bond is restricted.

   optical i., stereoisomerism involving the arrangement of substituents about an asymmetric carbon atom or atoms so that there is a difference in the behavior of the various isomers with regard to the extent of their rotation of the plane of polarized light.

   structural i., i. involving the same atoms in different arrangements.

isom′eriza′tion. A process in which one isomer is formed from another, as in the action of isomerases.

isomet′ric [iso- + G. *metron,* measure]. **1.** Of equal dimensions. **2.** In physiology, denoting the condition when the ends of a contracting muscle are held fixed so that contraction produces increased tension at constant overall length.

isometro′pia [iso- + G. *metron,* measure, + *ōps* (*ōp*), eye]. Equality in kind and degree of refraction in the two eyes.

isomor′phic. Isomorphous.

isomor′phism [iso- + G. *morphē,* shape]. Similarity of form between two or more organisms or between parts of the body.

isomor′phous. Isomorphic; having the same form or shape, or being morphologically equal.

isop′athy [iso- + G. *pathos,* suffering]. Treatment of disease by means of the causal agent or a product of the same disease; also the treatment of a diseased organ by an extract of a similar organ from a healthy animal.

isophagy (i-sof′ă-jĭ) [iso- + G. *phagein,* to eat]. Autolysis.

isophoria (i′so-fo′rĭ-ah) [iso- + G. *phora,* movement]. A condition in which there is no change or muscular imbalance with changes of direction of gaze.

i′soplas′tic. Isologous.

isoprecipitin (i′so-pre-sip′ĭ-tin) [iso- + precipitin]. An antibody that combines with and precipitates soluble antigenic material in the plasma or serum, or in an extract of the cells, from another member, but not all members, of the same species.

i′soprene. $CH_2=CH-C(CH_3)=CH_2$; an unsaturated five-carbon with a branched chain, which in the plant kingdom is used as the basis for the formation of isoprenoids.

i′sopre′noids. Polymers whose carbon skeletons consist in whole or in large part of isoprene units joined end to end.

isopropyl alcohol (i′so-pro′pil). $(CH_3)_2CHOH$; an isomer of propyl alcohol and a homologue of ethyl alcohol, similar in its properties, when used externally, to the latter, but more toxic when taken internally.

i′soproter′enol hydrochloride. A sympathomimetic β-receptor stimulant possessing the inhibitory properties and the cardiac excitatory, but not the vasoconstrictor, actions of epinephrine.

isopter (i-sop′ter) [iso- + G. *optēr,* observer]. A curve of equal retinal sensitivity in the visual field designated by a fraction, the numerator being the diameter of the white test object, and the denominator, the testing distance.

isorrhea (i-so-re′ah) [iso- + G. *rhoia,* a flow]. Equilibrium of intake and output of water and solutes of the body.

i′sosex′ual. 1. Relating to the existence of characteristics or feelings of both sexes in one person. **2.** Descriptive of somatic characteristics possessed by, or of processes occurring within, an individual that are consonant with the sex of that individual.

isosmotic (i-sos-mot′ik). Having the same total osmotic pressure or osmolality as another fluid (ordinarily intracellular fluid).

Isospora (i-sos′po-rah) [iso- + G. *sporos,* seed]. A genus of coccidia (family Eimeriidae, class Sporozoa), with species parasitic chiefly in mammals. *I. hominis* is a rare species described only from man and capable of causing a mucous diarrhea with anorexia, nausea, and abdominal pain; it is very similar to *I. bigemina* and may prove to be the same species.

isos′pori′asis. Infection with coccidia of the genus *Isospora.*

isosthenuria (i-sos′the-nu′rĭ-ah) [iso- + G. *sthenos,* strength, + *ouron,* urine]. A state in chronic renal disease in which the kidney cannot form urine with a higher or a lower specific gravity than that of protein-free plasma; specific gravity of the urine becomes fixed around 1.010, irrespective of the fluid intake.

i'sother'mal [iso- + G. *thermē*, heat]. Having the same temperature.

i'sotone. One of several nuclides having the same number of neutrons in their nuclei.

isotonia (i'so-to'nĭ-ah) [iso- + G. *tonos*, tension]. A condition of tonic equality, in which tension or osmotic pressure in two substances or solutions is the same.

i'soton'ic. 1. Relating to isotonicity or isotonia. 2. Having equal tension; denoting solutions possessing the same osmotic pressure; more specifically, limited to solutions in which cells neither swell nor shrink. 3. In physiology, denoting the condition when a contracting muscle shortens against a constant load, as when lifting a weight.

isotonicity (i'so-to-nis'ĭ-tĭ). 1. The quality of possessing and maintaining a uniform tone or tension. 2. The property of a solution in being isotonic.

isotope (i'so-tōp) [iso- + G. *topos*, part, place]. Either of two or more nuclides that are chemically identical yet differ in mass number, since their nuclei contain different numbers of neutrons. Individual i.'s are named with the inclusion of their mass number; *e.g.*, carbon-12 (^{12}C).

radioactive i., an i. with a nuclear composition that is unstable; nuclei of such an i. decompose spontaneously by emission of a nuclear electron (β-particle) or helium nucleus (α-ray) and radiation (γ-rays), thus achieving a stable nuclear composition; used as tracers.

stable i., a nonradioactive nuclide; an i. of an element that shows no tendency to undergo radioactive breakdown.

i'sotop'ic. Of identical chemical composition but differing in some physical property, such as atomic weight.

i'sotrop'ic, isot'ropous [iso- + G. *tropē*, a turn]. Having properties the same in all directions.

i'sotype. An antigenic determinant (marker) that occurs in all members of a subclass of an immunoglobulin class.

isotyp'ic. Pertaining to an isotype.

isovalericacidemia (i'so-vă-ler'ik-as'ĭ-de'mĭ-ah). A disorder of leucine metabolism characterized by the excessive production of isovaleric acid upon protein ingestion or during infectious episodes; severe metabolic acidosis results from the large quantities of acid formed; autosomal recessive inheritance.

i'sovolu'mic, i'sovolumet'ric. Occurring without an associated alteration in volume; as when, in early ventricular systole, the muscle fibers initially increase their tension without shortening so that ventricular volume remains unaltered.

i'sozyme. Isoenzyme; one of a group of enzymes that are very similar in catalytic properties, but may be differentiated by variations in physical properties, such as isoelectric point or electrophoretic mobility.

issue (ish'u) [Fr. a going out]. 1. A suppurating or discharging sore, acting as a counterirritant, sometimes maintained by the presence of a foreign body in the tissues. 2. A discharge of pus, blood, or other matter.

isthmectomy (is-mek'to-mĭ) [G. *isthmos*, isthmus, + *ektomē*, excision]. Excision of the midportion of the thyroid.

isthmoparalysis (is'mo-pă-ral'ĭ-sis) [G. *isthmos*, isthmus, + *paralysis*]. Isthmoplegia; paralysis of the velum pendulum palati and the muscles forming the anterior pillars of the fauces.

isthmoplegia (is-mo-ple'jĭ-ah) [G. *isthmos*, isthmus, + *plēgē*, stroke]. Isthmoparalysis.

isthmus, pl. **isth'muses, isth'mi** (is'mus, -mi) [G. *isthmos*]. A constriction or narrow passage connecting two larger parts of an organ or other anatomical structure.

i. of auditory or **eustachian tube,** the narrowest portion of the auditory tube at the junction of the cartilaginous and bony portions.

i. of fauces, the constricted and short space which establishes the connection between the cavity of the mouth and the oral part of the pharynx.

rhombencephalic i., (1) a constriction in the embryonic neural tube delineating the mesencephalon from the rhombencephalon; (2) the anterior portion of the rhombencephalon connecting with the mesencephalon.

i. of thyroid, the central part of the gland joining the two lateral lobes.

i. of uterine tube, the narrow portion of the uterine tube adjoining the uterus.

i. of uterus, an elongated constriction at the junction of the body and cervix of the uterus.

itch [A.S. *gikkan*]. 1. A peculiar irritating sensation in the skin that arouses the desire to scratch. 2. Common name for scabies. 3. Pruritus (2).

bath i., bath *pruritus*.

jock i., *tinea* cruris.

swimmer's i., water i., schistosome *dermatitis*.

itch'ing. Pruritus (1); an uncomfortable sensation of irritation of the skin or mucous membranes which causes scratching or rubbing of the affected parts.

-ite [G. *-itēs*, fem. *-itis*]. 1. Suffix denoting of the nature of, resembling. 2. In chemistry, denoting a salt of an acid that has the termination -ous. 3. In comparative anatomy, a suffix denoting an essential portion of the part to the name of which it is attached.

i'ter [L. *iter* (*itiner*-), a way, road]. A passage leading from one anatomical part to another.

i'teral. Relating to an iter.

-ites [G. *itēs*, m., or *-ites*, n.]. An adjectival suffix to nouns, corresponding to the English -y, -like; the adjective so formed is used without the qualified noun. The feminine form, *-itis* (agreeing with *nosos*, disease), is so often associated with inflammatory disease that it has acquired in most cases the significance of inflammation.

-itis [G. fem of -*ites*]. See -ites.

ITP Idiopathic thrombocytopenic *purpura;* inosine 5'-triphosphate.

ITyr Monoiodotyrosine.

IU International *unit.*

IUCD Intrauterine contraceptive *device.*

IUD Intrauterine *device.*

I-V Intraventricular.

I.V., i.v. Intravenous or intravenously.

Ixodes (ik-so'dēz) [G. *ixōdēs,* sticky, like bird-lime]. A genus of hard ticks (family Ixodidae), many species of which are parasitic on man and animals; severe reactions frequently follow their bites.

ixodiasis (ik-so-di'ă-sis). **1.** Skin lesions caused by the bites of certain ticks; the tick may burrow under the skin, causing some degree of irritation, but in most cases an urticarioid eruption is the only result. **2.** Any disease, such as Rocky Mountain fever, that is transmitted by ticks.

ixod'ic. Relating to or caused by ticks.

ixodid (ik'so-did). Common name for members of the family Ixodidae.

Ixod'idae [G. *ixōdēs,* sticky]. A family of ticks (order Acarnia, suborder Ixodides), the so-called "hard" ticks, species of which transmit many important human and animal diseases and cause tick paralysis.

J

J Joule.

J Flux.

jack'et. 1. A fixed bandage applied around the body in order to immobilize the spine. **2.** In dentistry, a term commonly used in reference to an artificial crown composed of fired porcelain or acrylic resin.

jactitation (jak'tī-ta'shun) [L. *jactatio,* a tossing]. Extreme restlessness or tossing about from side to side.

jan'iceps [L. *Janus,* a Roman diety having two faces, + *caput,* head]. Conjoined twins having their two heads fused together, with the faces looking in opposite directions.

Janus green B. $C_{30}H_{31}N_6Cl$; a basic dye used in histology.

jar'gon [Fr. gibberish]. **1.** Language or terminology peculiar to a specific field, profession, or group. **2.** Paraphasia.

jaundice (jawn'dis) [Fr. *jaune,* yellow]. Icterus; a yellowish staining of the integument, sclerae, and deeper tissues and the excretions with bile pigments, which are increased in the serum.

  acholuric j., j. with excessive amounts of unconjugated bilirubin in the circulatory blood and without bile pigments in the blood.

  cholestatic j., j. produced by inspissated bile or bile plugs in small biliary passages in the liver.

  chronic acholuric, familial, or **hemolytic j.,** hereditary *spherocytosis.*

  chronic idiopathic j., Dubin-Johnson *syndrome.*

  familial nonhemolytic j., Gilbert's disease or syndrome; j. without evidence of liver damage, biliary obstruction, or hemolysis; thought to be due to an inborn error of metabolism.

  hematogenous j., hemolytic j., j. resulting from excessive amounts of hemoglobin released by any process causing hemolysis of erythrocytes.

  hepatocellular j., j. resulting from diffuse injury or inflammation or failure of function of the liver cells.

  hepatogenous j., j. resulting from disease of the liver, as distinguished from that due to blood changes.

  leptospiral j., j. associated with infection by various species of *Leptospira.*

  malignant j., *icterus* gravis.

  mechanical j., *obstructive* j.

  j. of the newborn, *icterus* neonatorum.

  nonobstructive j., any j. in which the main biliary passages are not obstructed, *e.g.,* hemolytic j. or j. due to hepatitis.

  nuclear j., kernicterus.

  obstructive j., mechanical j.; j. resulting from obstruction to the flow of bile into the duodenum.

  physiologic j., physiologic *icterus.*

  regurgitation j., j. due to biliary obstruction, the bile pigment having been secreted by the heptatic cells and then reabsorbed into the blood stream.

  retention j., j. due to insufficiency of the liver in secreting bile pigment or to an excess of bile pigment production.

jaw [A.S. *ceōwan,* to chew]. One of the two bony structures, maxillae or the mandible, in which the teeth are set, forming the framework of the mouth.

  Hapsburg j. and lip, prognathism and pouting lower lip, characteristic of the Hispano-Austrian imperial dynasty.

jejun-. See jejuno-.

jeju'nal. Relating to the jejunum.

jejunectomy (jĕ-ju-nek'to-mĭ) [jejunum + G. *ek-tomē,* excision]. Excision of all or a part of the jejunum.

jejunitis (jĕ-ju-ni'tis). Inflammation of the jejunum.

jejuno-, jejun- [L. *jejunus,* empty]. Combining forms relating to the jejunum.

jeju'nocolos'tomy [jejuno- + colon + G. *stoma,* mouth]. Establishment of a communication between the jejunum and the colon.

jejunoileal (jĕ-ju'no-il'e-al). Relating to the jejunum and the ileum.

jejunoileitis (jĕ-ju'no-il-e-i'tis). Inflammation of jejunum and ileum.

jejunoileostomy (jĕ-ju'no-il-e-os'to-mĭ) [jejuno- + G. *stoma,* mouth]. Surgical establishment of a communication between the jejunum and the ileum.

jejunojejunostomy (jĕ-ju'no-jĕ-ju-nos'to-mĭ) [jejuno- + jejuno- + G. *stoma,* mouth]. An anastomosis between two portions of jejunum.

jejunoplasty (jĕ-ju'no-plas-tĭ) [jejuno- + G. *plastos,* molded]. A corrective surgical procedure on the jejunum.

jejunostomy (jĕ-ju-nos'to-mĭ) [jejuno- + G. *stoma,* mouth]. Surgical establishment of an opening from the abdominal wall into the jejunum, usually with creation of a stoma on the abdominal wall.

jejunotomy (jĕ-ju-not'o-mĭ) [jejuno- + G. *tomē,* incision]. Incision into the jejunum.

jejunum (jĕ-ju'num) [L. *jejunus,* empty] [NA]. The portion of small intestine between the duodenum and the ileum.

jel'ly [L. *gelo,* to freeze]. A semisolid resiliant compound.

    cardiac j., the gelatinous noncellular material between the endothelial lining and the myocardial layer of the heart in very young embryos; later serving as a substratum for cardiac mesenchyme.

    interlaminar j., the gelatinous material between ectoderm and endoderm that serves as the substrate on which mesenchymal cells migrate.

    Wharton's j., the mucous connective tissue of the umbilical cord.

jerk. 1. A sudden pull. **2.** Deep *reflex.*

jet lag. A disturbance of normal circadian rhythm as a result of sub- or supersonic travel through a number of time zones, resulting in fatigue and varied constitutional symptoms.

jig'ger. Common name for *Tunga penetrans.*

joint [L. *junctura*]. Articulatio.

    ankle j., *articulatio* talocruralis.

    arthrodial j., *articulatio* plana.

    ball-and-socket j., *articulatio* spheroidea.

    biaxial j., a j. in which there are two principal axes of movement situated at right angles to each other.

    bicondylar j., *articulatio* bicondylaris.

    bilocular j., a j. in which the intra-articular disk is complete, dividing the j. into two distinct cavities.

    carpal j.'s, *articulationes* intercarpeae.

    carpometacarpal j.'s, *articulationes* carpometacarpeae.

    cartilaginous j., *articulatio* cartilaginis.

    Charcot's j., tabetic *arthropathy.*

    Chopart's j., *articulatio* tarsi transversa.

    cochlear j., spiral j.; a variety of hinge j. in which the elevation and depression, respectively, on the opposing articular surfaces form part of a spiral, flexion being then accompanied by a certain amount of lateral deviation.

    compound j., *articulatio* composita.

    condylar j., *articulatio* ellipsoidea.

    cotyloid j., *articulatio* spheroidea.

    cubital j., *articulatio* cubiti.

    diarthrodial j., *junctura* synovialis.

    digitial j.'s, *articulationes* interphalangeae.

    dry j., a j. affected with atrophic desiccating changes.

    elbow j., *articulatio* cubiti.

    ellipsoidal j., *articulatio* ellipsoidea.

    enarthrodial j., *articulatio* spheroidea.

    false j., pseudarthrosis.

    fibrous j., *articulatio* fibrosa.

    flail j., a j. with loss of function caused by loss of the power to stabilize the j. in any plane within its normal range of motion.

    j.'s of foot, *articulationes* pedis.

    ginglymoid j., ginglymus.

    gliding j., *articulatio* plana.

    j.'s of hand, *articulationes* manus.

    hinge j., ginglymus.

    hip j., *articulatio* coxae.

    hysterical j., a simulation of j. disease, but of emotional origin.

    immovable j., *articulatio* fibrosa.

    intercarpal j.'s, *articulationes* intercarpeae.

    intermetacarpal j.'s, *articulationes* intermetacarpeae.

    intermetatarsal j.'s, *articulationes* intermetatarseae.

    interphalangeal j.'s, *articulationes* interphalangeae.

    intertarsal j.'s, *articulationes* intertarseae.

    knee j., *articulatio* genus.

    Lisfranc's j.'s, *articulationes* tarsometatarseae.

    mandibular j., *articulatio* temporomandibularis.

    metacarpophalangeal j.'s, *articulationes* metacarpophalangeae.

    metatarsophalangeal j.'s, *articulationes* metatarsophalangeae.

    mortise j., *articulatio* talocruralis.

    movable j., (1) *articulatio* synovialis; (2) *articulatio* cartilaginis.

    multiaxial j., polyaxial j.; a j. in which movement occurs in a number of axes.

    neuropathic j., neuropathic arthropathy; destructive j. disease caused by diminished proprioceptive sensation, with gradual destruction of the j. by repeated subliminal injury.

    peg and socket j., gomphosis.

    phalangeal j.'s, *articulationes* interphalangeae.

    pivot j., *articulatio* trochoidea.

    plane j., *articulatio* plana.

    polyaxial j., multiaxial j.

    radiocarpal j., *articulatio* radiocarpea.

    rotary j., rotatory j., *articulatio* trochoidea.

    saddle j., *articulatio* sellaris.

    shoulder j., *articulatio* humeri.

    simple j., *articulatio* simplex.

    spheroid j., *articulatio* spheroidea.

    spiral j., cochlear j.

    synarthrodial j., (1) *articulatio* fibrosa; (2) *articulatio* cartilaginis.

    synchondrodial j., synchondrosis.

    syndesmodial j., syndesmotic j., syndesmosis.

    synovial j., *articulatio* synovialis.

    talocalcaneal j., *articulatio* subtalaris.

    talocalcaneonavicular j., *articulatio* talocalcaneonavicularis.

    tarsal j.'s, *articulationes* intertarseae.

tarsometatarsal j.'s, *articulationes* tarsometatar-seae.

temporomandibular j., *articulatio* temporoman-dibularis.

transverse tarsal j., *articulatio* tarsi transversa.

trochoid j., *articulatio* trochoidea.

uniaxial j., a j. in which movement is around one axis only.

unilocular j., a j. in which an intra-articular disk is incomplete or absent, the j. having but a single cavity.

wedge-and-groove j., schindylesis.

wrist j., *articulatio* radiocarpea.

joule (J) (jūl) [J. P. *Joule*]. The SI unit of energy: the heat generated, or energy expended, by an ampere flowing against an ohm for 1 second; equal to 10⁷ ergs, and to a newton-meter.

ju'ga. Plural of jugum.

ju'gal [L. *jugalis,* yoked together]. **1.** Connecting; yoked. **2.** Relating to the zygomatic bone.

juga'le. Jugal point; a craniometric point at the union of the temporal and frontal processes of the zygomatic bone.

jugular (jug'u-lar) [L. *jugulum,* throat]. **1.** Relating to the throat or neck. **2.** Relating to the j. veins. **3.** A j. vein.

ju'gum, pl. **ju'ga** [L. a yoke]. **1.** Yoke; a ridge or furrow connecting two points. **2.** A type of forceps.

juice (jūs) [L. *jus,* broth]. **1.** The tissue fluid of a plant or animal. **2.** A digestive secretion, such as that secreted by glands of the stomach and intestine.

junction (jungk'shun). Junctura (2).

amelodental j., amelodentinal j., dentinoenamel j.

cementodental j., dentinocemental j., the surface at which the cementum and dentin of the root of a tooth are joined.

dentinoenamel j., amelodental j.; amelodentinal j.; the surface at which the enamel and the dentin of the crown of a tooth are joined.

esophagogastric j., the line at the cardiac orifice of the stomach where there is a transition from the stratified squamous epithelium of the esophagus to the simple columnar epithelium of the stomach.

gap j., nexus; a 20-Å gap between apposed cell membranes that contains subunits in the form of polygonal lattices; believed to mediate electrotonic coupling which allows ionic currents to pass from one cell to another.

mucocutaneous j., the site of transition from epidermis to the epithelium of a mucous membrane.

myoneural j., the synaptic connection of the axon of the motor neuron with a muscle fiber.

sclerocorneal j., *limbus* corneae.

tight j., an intercellular j. in which the outer layers of the cell membranes fuse.

junctura, pl. **junctu'rae** (jungk-tu'rah) [L. a joining]. **1.** Articulatio. **2.** Juncture; junction; the point, line, or surface of union of two parts.

juncture (jungk'chur). Junctura (2).

juxtaepiphysial (juks'tă-ep-ĭ-fiz'ĭ-al). Close to or adjoining an epiphysis.

juxtaglomerular (juks'tă-glo-mĕr'u-lar). Close to or adjoining a renal glomerulus.

jux'tallocor'tex. See *cortex* cerebri.

juxtaposition (juks-tă-po-zish'un) [L. *juxta,* near to, + *positio,* a placing]. A position side by side.

K

K Potassium (kalium); Kelvin.

k Kilo-.

k Rate or velocity constant.

kak-, kako- See caco-.

kal-, kali- [L. *kalium,* potassium]. Combining forms relating to potassium; sometimes *kalio-.*

kala azar (kah'lah-ah-zahr') [Hind. *kala,* black, + *azar,* poison]. Visceral *leishmaniasis.*

kalemia (kă-le'mĭ-ah). Presence of potassium in the blood.

ka'liope'nia [Mod. L. *kalium,* potassium, + G. *penia,* poverty]. Insufficiency of potassium in the body.

ka'liope'nic. Relating to kaliopenia.

ka'lium [Mod. L. fr. Ar. *quali,* potash]. Potassium.

kaliuresis (ka'lĭ-u-re'sis). Kaluresis.

ka'liuret'ic. Kaluretic.

kallak' [Eskimo word meaning skin disease]. A peculiar pustular dermatitis observed among the Eskimos.

kal'lidin, kallidin I. Bradykinin.

kallidin II. Bradykinnogen.

kallikrein (kal-ĭ-kre'in). Kininogenase; an enzyme that can convert a component of the globulin fraction of blood, by proteolysis, to bradykinin or kallidin.

kaluresis (kal-u-re'sis) [Mod. L. *kalium,* potassium, + G. *ouresis,* urination]. Kaliuresis; the increased urinary excretion of potassium.

kal'uret'ic. Kaliuretic; relating to, causing, or characterized by kaluresis.

ka'olino'sis. Pneumonoconiosis caused by the inhalation of clay dust.

karyo- [G. *karyon,* nucleus]. Combining form denoting nucleus.

karyocyte (kăr'ĭ-o-sit) [karyo- + G. *kytos,* cell]. A young, immature normoblast.

karyogamic (kăr-ĭ-o-gam'ik). Relating to or marked by karyogamy.

karyogamy (kăr-ĭ-og'ă-mĭ) [karyo- + G. *gamos,* marriage]. Fusion of the nuclei of two cells, as occurs in fertilization or true conjugation.

karyogenesis (kăr-ĭ-o-jen'ĕ-sis) [karyo- + G. *genesis,* production]. Formation of the nucleus of a cell.

karyogenic (kăr'ĭ-o-jen'ik). Relating to karyogenesis; forming the nucleus.

karyokinesis (kăr'ĭ-o-kĭ-ne'sis) [karyo- + G. *kinesis,* movement]. Mitosis.

kar'yokinet'ic. Mitotic.

karyolymph (kăr´ĭ-o-limf) [karyo- + L. *lympha,* clear water]. Nuclear hyaloplasm; the presumably fluid substance or gel of the nucleus in which stainable elements were believed to be suspended; much formerly considered to be k. is now euchromatin.

karyolysis (kăr-ĭ-ol´ĭ-sis) [karyo- + G. *lysis,* dissolution]. Apparent destruction of the nucleus of a cell by swelling and the loss of affinity of its chromatin for basic dyes.

karyolytic (kăr´ĭ-o-lit´ik). Relating to karyolysis.

karyomorphism (kăr´ĭ-o-mor´fizm) [karyo- + G. *morphē,* form]. **1.** Development of a cell nucleus. **2.** Denoting the nuclear shapes of the cells, especially of the leukocytes.

karyon (kăr´ĭ-on) [G. *karyon,* a nut, kernel]. Nucleus (1).

karyophage (kăr´ĭ-o-fāj) [karyo- + G. *phagein,* to devour]. An intracellular parasite that feeds on the host nucleus.

karyoplasm (kăr´ĭ-o-plazm). Rarely used synonym for nucleoplasm.

karyoplast (kăr´ĭ-o-plast) [karyo- + G. *plastos,* formed]. A cell nucleus surrounded by a narrow band of cytoplasm and a plasma membrane.

karyopyknosis (kăr´ĭ-o-pik-no´sis) [karyo- + G. *pyknos,* thick, crowded, + *-osis,* condition]. Cytologic characteristics of the superficial or cornified cells of stratified squamous epithelium in which there is shrinkage of the nuclei and condensation of the chromatin into structureless masses.

karyorrhexis (kăr´ĭ-o-rek´sis) [karyo- + G. *rhexis,* rupture]. Fragmentation of the nucleus whereby its chromatin is distributed irregularly throughout the cytoplasm; a stage of necrosis usually followed by karyolysis.

karyosome (kăr´ĭ-o-sōm) [karyo- + G. *sōma,* body]. A mass of chromatin often found in the interphase cell nucleus representing a more condensed zone of chromatin filaments.

karyotype (kăr´ĭ-o-tīp). Idiogram (1); the chromosome characteristics of an individual or of a cell line, usually presented as a systemized array of metaphase chromosomes from a photomicrograph of a single cell nucleus arranged in pairs in descending order of size and according to the position of the centromere.

kar´yotyp´ing. Chromosome analysis.

kata- [G. *kata,* down]. Alternative spelling for *cata-*.

kc Kilocycle.

kcal Kilogram *calorie* or kilocalorie.

ke´loid [G. *kēlē,* a tumor (or *kēlis,* a spot), + *eidos,* appearance]. A nodular linear mass of hyperplastic scar tissue, consisting of relatively wide and parallel bands of collagenous fibrous tissue; occurs in the dermis and adjacent subcutaneous tissue, usually after a traumatic injury, surgery, a burn, or severe cutaneous disease such as cystic acne.

    acne k., dermatitis papillaris capillitii; folliculitis keloidalis; a chronic eruption of fibrous papules which develop at the site of follicular lesions, usually on the back of the neck at the hairline.

ke´loido´sis. Multiple keloids.

ke´loplasty [keloid + G. *plassō,* to fashion]. Operative removal of a scar or keloid.

kelotomy (ke-lot´o-mī) [G. *kēlē,* hernia, + *tomē,* incision]. Herniotomy.

Kelvin. See K. *scale.*

Kendall. See Abell-K *method.*

keno- [G. *kenos,* empty]. See ceno- (3).

keph´alin. Cephalin.

ker´asin. A cerebroside found in brain tissue associated with phrenosin and sphingomyelin; yields lignoceric acid, as its characteristic fatty acid, spingosine, and galactose as hydrolysis products.

kerat-. See kerato-.

ker´atan sul´fate. Keratosulfate; a type of sulfated mucopolysaccharide containing D-galactose in place of the uronic acid or hyaluronic acid or chondroitin; found in cartilage, bone, connective tissue, and the cornea.

keratectasia (kĕr´ă-tek-ta´zĭ-ah) [kerato- + G. *ektasis,* extrusion]. Herniation of the cornea.

keratec´tomy [kerato- + G. *ektomē,* excision]. Excision of a portion of the cornea.

kerat´ic [G. *keras* (*kerat-*), horn]. Horny.

ker´atin. A scleroprotein or albuminoid that is present largely in cuticular structures and contains a relatively large amount of sulfur.

ker´atinases. Hydrolases catalyzing the hydrolysis of keratin.

ker´atiniza´tion. Cornification; hornification; keratin formation or development of a horny layer; may also apply to premature formation of keratin.

kerat´inocyte. A cell of the epidermis and parts of the mouth that produces keratin.

kerat´inosome. Membrane-coating granule; a membrane-bound granule located in the upper layers of the stratum spinosum of certain stratified squamous epithelia.

kerat´inous. **1.** Relating to keratin. **2.** Horny.

keratitis (kĕr´ă-ti´tis) [kerato- + *-itis,* inflammation]. Inflammation of the cornea.

    dendriform k., dendritic k., a form of herpetic k.

    herpetic k., herpetic keratoconjuncitivits; inflammation of the cornea (or cornea and conjunctiva) due to herpesvirus type 1.

    interstitial k., parenchymatous k.

    neuroparalytic k., ulceration of the cornea occurring with trigeminal paralysis.

    parenchymatous k., interstitial k.; a chronic inflammation, with cellular infiltration of the middle and posterior layers of the cornea.

    phlyctenular k., an inflammation of the corneal conjunctiva with the formation of small red nodules of lymphoid tissue (phlyctenulae) near the limbus.

    punctate k., precipitate (3).

    sclerosing k., inflammation of the cornea complicating scleritis; characterized by opacification of corneal stroma.

trachomatous k., vascular k. at upper limbus, resulting in pannus.

keratoacanthoma (kĕr'ă-to-ak'an-tho'mah). A rapidly growing tumor usually occurring on exposed areas of the skin, with a central keratin mass that opens on the skin surface; it invades the dermis, but remains localized and usually resolves spontaneously.

keratocele (kĕr'ă-to-sēl) [kerato- + G. *kēlē,* hernia]. Herniation of Descemet's membrane through a defect in the outer layer of the cornea.

keratoconjunctivitis (kĕr'ă-to-kon-jungk'tĭ-vi'tis). Inflammation of the conjunctiva and of the cornea as a phlyctenular hypersensitivity reaction of corneal and conjunctival epithelium to endogenous toxin.

epidemic k., virus k.; rapidly developing follicular conjunctivitis with marked inflammatory symptoms but a scanty exudate; caused by an adenovirus.

herpetic k., herpetic *keratitis.*

superior limbic k., a distinct entity, the essential of which is inflammatory edema of the central area of the superior limbus with upward extension; usually bilateral and distinguished by spontaneous sudden resolution or recurrence.

ultraviolet k., acute k. resulting from exposure to intense ultraviolet irradiation.

virus k., epidemic k.

virus punctate k., k. with all the features of inclusion conjunctivitis, associated with epithelial and subepithelial punctate keratitis.

keratoconus (kĕr'ă-to-ko'nus) [kerato- + G. *kōnos,* cone]. Conical cornea; a conical protrusion of the center of the cornea due to noninflammatory thinning of the stroma; usually bilateral.

keratocyte (kĕr'ă-to-sīt). The fibroblastic stromal cell of the cornea.

keratoderma (kĕr'ă-to-der'mah) [kerato- + G. *derma,* skin]. **1.** Any horny superficial growth. **2.** A generalized thickening of the horny layer of the epidermis.

k. blennorrhag'ica, *keratosis* blennorrhagica.

mutilating k., diffuse k. of the extremities, with the development during childhood of constricting fibrous bands around the middle phalanx of the fingers or toes which may lead to spontaneous amputation; autosomal dominant inheritance.

palmoplantar k., keratosis or ichthyosis palmaris et plantaris; the occurence of symmetrical diffuse or patchy areas of hypertrophy of the horny layer of the epidermis on the palms and soles; a group of ectodermal dysplasias of considerable variety, and either autosomal dominant or recessive inheritance.

k. planta're sulca'tum, cracked heel; hyperkeratosis and fissure formation on the soles.

punctate k., keratosis punctata; horny papules over the palms, soles, and digits which may develop central craters; autosomal dominant inheritance.

keratogenous (kĕr-ă-toj'ĕ-nus). Causing a growth of cells that produce keratin and result in the formation of horny tissue.

ker'atoglo'bus [kerato- + L. *globus,* ball]. Anterior *megalophthalmus.*

keratohyalin (kĕr'ă-to-hi'ă-lin) [kerato- + hyalin]. The substance in the granules of the stratum granulosum of the epidermis.

ker'atoid [kerato- + G. *eidos,* resemblance]. **1.** Horny. **2.** Resembling corneal tissue.

kerato-, kerat- [G. *keras,* horn]. Combining forms denoting the cornea or horny tissue or cells.

keratoleptynsis (kĕr'ă-to-lep-tin'sis) [kerato- + G. *leptynsis,* a making thin]. Surgical removal of the surface of the cornea and replacement by bulbar conjunctiva for cosmetic reasons.

keratoleukoma (kĕr'ă-to-lu-ko'mah) [kerato- + G. *leukos,* white, + *-ōma,* growth]. A white corneal opacity.

keratolysis (kĕr-ă-tol'ĭ-sis) [kerato- + G. *lysis,* loosening]. **1.** Separation or loosening of the horny layer of the epidermis. **2.** A disease characterized by a shedding of the epidermis recurring at more or less regular intervals.

ker'atolyt'ic. Relating to keratolysis.

keratoma (kĕr-ă-to'mah) [kerato- + G. *-oma,* tumor]. **1.** Callosity. **2.** A horny tumor.

keratomalacia (kĕr'ă-to-mā-la'shĭ-ah) [kerato- + G. *malakia,* softness]. Dryness with ulceration and perforation of the cornea, with absence of inflammatory reactions, occurring in cachectic children.

ker'atome. Keratotome.

keratom'eter [kerato- + G. *metron,* measure]. Ophthalmometer; an instrument for measuring the curvature of the anterior corneal surface.

keratom'etry. Measurement of the degrees of corneal curvature in the principal meridians.

keratomileusis (kĕr'ă-to-mi-lu'sis) [G. *keras* (*kerat-*), horn, cornea, + *smileusis,* carving]. Alteration of the refraction of the cornea by removal of a deep corneal lamella, freezing it to grind a new curvature, and then replacing it in the bed from which it was removed.

keratopachyderma (ker'ă-to-pak-ĭ-der'mah) [kerato- + G. *pachys,* thick, + *derma,* skin]. A syndrome of congenital deafness with development of hyperkeratosis of the skin of the palms, soles, elbows, and knees in childhood, and with bandlike constrictions of the fingers; autosomal dominant inheritance.

keratopathy (kĕr-ă-top'ă-thĭ) [kerato- + G. *pathos,* suffering, disease]. A noninflammatory dystrophy of the cornea, as distinguished from keratitis.

band-shaped k., a horizontal, gray, interpalpebral opacity of the cornea, slowly progressing from the limbus.

bullous k., formation of large subepithelial bullae in corneal edema, resulting in intense pain when their rupture exposes corneal nerves.

ker'atoplasty [kerato- + G. *plassō,* to form]. Corneal graft; the removal of a portion of the cornea containing an opacity and the insertion in its place of a piece of the same size and shape.

optic k., transplantation of transparent corneal tissue to replace a leukoma or scar that obstructs vision.

tectonic k., grafting of corneal material on a part where it has been lost, without attempt to restore the transparency.

ker'atoprosthe'sis [kerato- + G. *prosthesis*, addition]. Replacement of the central area of an opacified cornea by acrylic plastic.

keratorhexis, keratorrhexis (kĕr'ă-to-rek'sis) [kerato- + G. *rhexis*, a bursting]. Rupture of the cornea, due to trauma or perforating ulcer.

keratoscleritis (kĕr'ă-to-skle-ri'tis). Inflammation of both cornea and sclera.

keratoscope (kĕr'ă-to-skōp) [kerato- + G. *skopeō*, to examine]. Placido's disk; an instrument marked with lines or circles by means of which the corneal reflex can be observed.

keratoscopy (kĕr-ă-tos'ko-pĭ) [kerato- + G. *skopeō*, to examine]. Examination of the reflections from the anterior surface of the cornea to determine the character and amount of corneal astigmatism.

keratose (kĕr'ă-tōs). Relating to or marked by keratosis.

keratosis (kĕr-ă-to'sis) [kerato- + G. *-osis*, condition]. Any lesion on the epidermis marked by the presence of circumscribed overgrowths of the horny layer.

actinic k., solar k.

k. blennorrhag'ica, keratoderma blennorrhagica; pustules and crusts associated with Reiter's disease.

k. follicula'ris, Darier's disease; a familial eruption, beginning usually in childhood, in which keratotic papules originating from both follicles and intrafollicular epidermis of the trunk, face, scalp, and axillae become crusted and verrucous.

k. palma'ris et planta'ris, palmoplantar *keratoderma.*

k. puncta'ta, punctate *keratoderma.*

seborrheic k., k. seborrhe'ica, superficial, benign, verrucous lesions consisting of proliferating epidermal cells, especially of basal type, enclosing horn cysts.

senile k., solar k., actinic k.; a premalignant warty lesion occurring on the sun-exposed skin of the face or hands in aged light-skinned persons; hyperkeratosis may form a cutaneous horn, and squamous cell carcinoma of low-grade malignancy or basal cell carcinoma may develop.

ker'atosul'fate. Keratan sulfate.

ker'atotome. Keratome; a knife used for incising the cornea.

keratotomy (kĕr'ă-tot'o-mĭ) [kerato- + G. *tomē*, incision]. Incision through the cornea.

ke'rion [G. *kērion*, honeycomb]. A granulomatous secondarily infected lesion complicating fungal infection of the hair; typically, a raised boggy lesion.

kernicterus (ker-nik'ter-us) [Ger. *kern*, kernel (nucleus), + *ikteros, jaundice*]. Nuclear jaundice; a grave form of icterus neonatorum in which a yellow pigment and degenerative lesions are found in the intracranial gray matter.

keroid (kĕr'oyd) [G. *keroeidēs*, horn-like]. Horny.

ket'amine hydrochloride. DL-2-(*o*-Chlorophenyl)-2-(methylamino)cyclohexanone hydrochloride; a parenterally administered anesthetic that produces catatonia, profound analgesia, increased sympathetic activity, and little relaxation of skeletal muscles.

keto-. Combining form denoting a compound containing a ketone group; often replaced by oxo- in systematic nomenclature.

ke'to acid. An acid containing a keto group (-CO-) in addition to the acid group(s).

ketoacidosis (ke'to-as-ĭ-do'sis). Acidosis, *e.g.,* diabetic acidosis, caused by the enhanced production of ketone bodies.

ketoaciduria (ke'to-as-ĭ-du'rĭ-ah). Excretion of urine having an elevated content of ketonic acids.

branched chain k., maple syrup urine *disease.*

ketogenesis (ke-to-jen'ĕ-sis). Production of acetone or other ketones.

ketogenic (ke-to-jen'ik). Giving rise to ketones in metabolism.

ke'tohep'tose. A seven-carbon sugar possessing a ketone group.

ke'tol. A ketone that has an OH group near the CO group.

ke'tole. Indole.

ketole group. Carbon 1 and 2 of a 2-ketose ($HOCH_2CO$-); trans-ketolation from D-xylose 5'-phosphate to C-1 of aldoses is important in various metabolic pathways involving carbohydrates.

ketolytic (ke-to-lit'ik). Causing the dissolution of ketone or acetone substances, referring usually to oxidation products of glucose and allied substances.

ke'tone. A substance with the carbonyl group -CO- linking two carbon atoms.

ketonemia (ke-to-ne'mĭ-ah) [ketone + G. *haima,* blood]. Presence of recognizable concentrations of ketone bodies in the plasma.

ketonuria (ke-to-nu'rĭ-ah). Enhanced urinary excretion of ketone bodies.

ke'tose. A carbohydrate containing the characterizing group of the ketones (-CO-).

ketosis (ke-to'sis) [ketone + *-osis,* condition]. A condition characterized by the enhanced production of ketone bodies, as in diabetes mellitus.

17-ketosteroids (17-KS) (kē-to-stēr'oydz). 17-Oxosteroids; nominally, any steroid with a ketone group on C-17; commonly used to designate urinary C_{19} steroidal metabolites of androgenic and adrenocortical hormones that possess this structural feature.

kg Kilogram.

kidney (kid'nĭ) [A.S. *cwith,* womb, belly, + *neere,* kidney]. One of the two organs in the lumbar region that filters blood and excretes urine.

amyloid k., waxy k.; a k. in which amyloidosis has occurred, usually in association with some chronic illness.

artificial k., hemodialyzer.

cake k., a solid irregularly lobed organ of bizarre shape, usually situated in the pelvis toward the midline, produced by fusion of the renal anlagen.

contracted k., a diffusely scarred k. in which the relatively large amount of abnormal fibrous tissue and ischemic atrophy leads to a significant reduction in the size of the organ.

fatty k., a k. in which there is fatty metamorphosis of the parenchymal cells, especially fatty degeneration.

floating k., wandering k.; the abnormally mobile k. in nephroptosia.

fused k., a single anomalous organ produced by fusion of the renal anlagen.

Goldblatt k., a k. whose arterial blood supply has been compromised, followed by arterial (renovascular) hypertension.

horseshoe k., union of the lower or occasionally the upper extremities of the two k.'s by a band of tissue extending across the vertebral column.

medullary sponge k., cystic disease of the renal pyramids associated with calculus formation and hematuria; differs from cystic disease of the renal medulla in that renal failure does not usually develop.

polycystic k., polycystic disease of the kidneys; a progressive disease characterized by formation of multiple cysts of varying size scattered diffusely throughout both k.'s resulting in compression and destruction of k. parenchyma, usually with hypertension, gross hematuria, and uremia. There are two major types: one with onset in infancy or early childhood, usually with autosomal recessive inheritance; one with onset in adulthood, with autosomal dominant inheritance.

wandering k., floating k.

waxy k., amyloid k.

kilo- (k) [G. *chilioi,* one thousand]. A prefix used in the metric system to signify one thousand (10^3).

kilocalorie (kcal) (kil'o-kal-o-rī). Large *calorie.*

kil'ogram (kg). The SI unit of mass: 1000 g or 1 cubic decimeter of water; equivalent to 15,432 gr., 2.205 lb. avoirdupois, or 2.68 lb. troy.

kil'ogram-me'ter. The energy exerted, or work done, when a mass of 1 kg is raised a height of 1 m; equal to 9.806 joules in the SI system.

kin-, kine- [G. *kinēsis,* movement]. Prefix denoting movement. See also cine-.

kinanesthesia (kin'an-es-the'zī-ah) [G. *kinēsis,* motion, + *an-* priv. + *aisthēsis,* sensation]. A disturbance of deep sensibility in which there is inability to perceive either direction or extent of movement, the result being ataxia.

kinase (ki'nās). 1. An enzyme catalyzing the conversion of a proenzyme to an active enzyme. 2. An enzyme catalyzing the transfer of phosphate groups

to form triphosphates (ATP).

kinematics (kin-ē-mat'iks) [G. *kinēmatica,* things that move]. The science concerned with movements of the parts of the body.

kin'eplastics. Cineplastic *amputation.*

kinesalgia (kin-e-sal'jī-ah) [G. *kinēsis,* motion, + *algos,* pain]. Kinesialgia; pain caused by muscular movement.

kinesi-, kinesio-, kineso- [G. *kinēsis,* motion]. Combining forms relating to motion.

kinesia (kĭ-ne'zī-ah, -sī-ah) [G. *kinēsis,* movement]. Motion *sickness.*

kine'sial'gia. Kinesalgia.

kinesiatrics (kĭ-ne'sī-at'riks) [G. *kinēsis,* movement, + *iatrikos,* relating to medicine]. Kinesitherapy.

kinesics (kĭ-ne'siks). The study of nonverbal bodily motion in communication.

kin'esim'eter [G. *kinēsis,* movement, + *metron,* measure]. Kinesiometer; an instrument for measuring the extent of a movement.

kinesiology (kĭ-ne'sī-ol'o-jī) [G. *kinēsis,* movement, + *-logos,* study]. The science or the study of movement, and the active and passive structures involved.

kinesiometer (kĭ-ne'sī-om'ē-ter). Kinesimeter.

kinesioneurosis (kĭ-ne'sī-o-nu-ro'sis) [G. *kinēsis,* movement]. A functional nervous disease marked by tics, spasms, or other motor disorders.

kinesis (kĭ-ne'sis) [G.]. Motion; as a suffix, used to denote movement or activation.

kinesitherapy (kĭ-ne-sĭ-thĕr'ā-pī). Kinesiatrics; treatment by means of a movement regimen.

kinesthesia (kin-es-the'zī-ah) [G. *kinēsis,* motion, + *aisthēsis,* sensation]. 1. The sense perception of movement; the muscular sense. 2. An illusion of moving in space.

kinesthesiometer (kin'es-the-sĭ-om'ē-ter) [kinesthesia + G. *metron,* measure]. An instrument for determining the degree of muscular sensation.

kin'esthet'ic. Relating to kinesthesia.

kinetic (kĭ-net'ik) [G. *kinētikos*]. Relating to motion or movement.

kinetics (kĭ-net'iks). The study of motion, acceleration, or rate of change.

kineto- [G. *kinētos,* moving, movable]. Combining form relating to motion.

kinetocardiogram (kĭ-ne'to-kar'dī-o-gram). Graphic recording of the vibrations of the chest wall produced by cardiac activity.

kinetocardiograph (kĭ-ne'to-kar'dī-o-graf). A device for recording precordial impulses due to cardiac movement.

kinetochore (kĭ-ne'to-kōr) [kineto- + G. *chōra,* space]. Centromere.

kinetogenic (kĭ-ne'to-jen'ik). Causing or producing motion.

kinetoplast (kĭ-ne'to-plast) [kineto- + G. *plastos,* formed]. An intensely staining, DNA+, rod-shaped structure found in parasitic flagellates near the base of the flagellum, posterior to the basal granule.

ki'nin. One of a number of widely differing substances having pronounced and dramatic physiological effects. Some are plant growth regulators; others are polypeptides, formed in blood by proteolysis secondary to some pathological process, that stimulate visceral smooth muscle but relax vascular smooth muscle, thus producing vasodilation.

kininogen (kĭ-nĭn'o-jen). The globulin precursor of a (plasma) kinin.

kininogenase (kĭ-nĭn'o-jĕ-nās). Kallikrein.

kino- [G. *kineō*, to move]. Combining form relating to movement.

kinocilium (ki-no-sil'ĭ-um) [kino- + cilium]. A cilium, usually motile, having nine peripheral double microtubules and two single central ones.

Klebsiella (kleb-sĭ-el'ah). A genus of bacteria (family Enterobacteriaceae) containing Gram-negative, encapsulated rods which occur singly, in pairs, or in short chains. The type species, *K. pneumoniae*, Friedländer's bacillus, occurs in the intestinal tract of man and other animals, and also in association with several pathologic conditions.

kleptomania (klep-to-ma'nĭ-ah) [G. *kleptō*, to steal, + *mania*, insanity]. A morbid tendency to steal.

klep'toma'niac. A person exhibiting kleptomania.

knee (ne) [A.S. *cneōw*]. **1.** Genu. **2.** A geniculum.

   housemaid's k., prepatellar bursitis; inflammation and swelling of the bursa anterior to the patella, due to traumatism in those who are much on their k.'s.

   locked k., a condition in which the k. is prevented from full motion by an internal derangement of the joint.

kneecap. Patella.

knitting (nit'ing). Nonmedical term denoting the process of union of the fragments of a broken bone or of the edges of a wound.

knock-knee. *Genu* valgum.

knot (not) [A.S. *cnotta*]. **1.** An intertwining of the ends of two cords, tapes, sutures, etc. in such a way that they cannot spontaneously become separated; or a simple twining or infolding in its continuity. **2.** In anatomy or pathology, a node, ganglion, or circumscribed swelling suggestive of a k.

   false k.'s (of umbilical cord), local increases in length or varicosity of the umbilical vein, causing markedly apparent twisting of the cord.

   primitive k., primitive *node*.

   syncytial k., syncytial bud; a localized aggregation of synctiotrophoblastic nuclei in the villi of the placenta during early pregnancy.

   true k. (of umbilical cord), actual intertwining of a segment of umbilical cord; circulation is usually not obstructed.

knuckle (nuk'l). **1.** A joint of a finger when the fist is closed, especially a metacarpophalangeal joint. **2.** A kink or loop of intestine, as in a hernia.

koilonychia (koy-lo-nik'ĭ-ah) [G. *koilos*, hollow, + *onyx* (*onych-*), nail]. Celonychia; spoon nail; a malformation of the nails in which the outer surface is concave.

kolp-. For words beginning thus, see colp-.

kolytic (ko-lit'ik) [G. *kolyō*, to hinder]. Denoting an inhibitory action.

kopro-. For words beginning thus, see copro-.

Kr Krypton.

kraurosis vulvae (kraw-ro'sis vul've [G. *krauros*, dry, brittle]. Leukokraurosis; atrophy and shrinkage of the skin of the vagina and vulva, often accompanied by a chronic inflammatory reaction in the deeper tissues.

krymo-, kryo- [G. *krymos, kryos*, cold]. For words beginning thus, see crymo- and cryo-.

krypton (krip'ton) [G. *kryptos*, concealed]. One of the inert gases, present in small amount in the atmosphere; symbol Kr, atomic no. 36, atomic weight 83.80.

ku'ru [to shiver from fear or cold]. A progressive, fatal form of spongiform encephalopathy endemic to certain Melanesian tribes of New Guinea and probably due to a slow virus.

kv Kilovolt.

kwashiorkor (kwash-shĭ-or'kor) [African, red boy or displaced child]. A disease seen in African natives, particularly very young children, due to severe protein deficiency; characterized by anemia, edema, pot belly, depigmentation of the skin, loss or change in hair color, marked hypoalbuminemia, and bulky stools containing undigested food.

ky-. For words beginning thus and not found below, see cy-.

ky'matism [G. *kyma*, wave]. Myokymia.

kymogram (ki'mo-gram). The graphic curve made by a kymograph.

kymograph (ki'mo-graf) [G. *kyma*, wave, + *graphō*, to record]. An instrument for recording wavelike motions or modulation, as of variations in blood pressure.

kymog'raphy. Use of the kymograph.

kynurenic acid (kin'u-re'nik, -ren'ik). 4-Hydroxyquinoline-2-carboxylic acid; a product of the metabolism of tryptophan.

kynurenine (ki-nu'rĕ-nin, -nēn). 3-Anthraniloylalanine; a product of the metabolism of tryptophan, excreted in the urine in small amounts.

kyphos (ki'fos) [G.]. The hump produced by kyphosis.

ky'phoscolio'sis. Kyphosis combined with scoliosis.

kyphosis (ki-fo'sis) [G. *kyphōsis*, hump-back, fr. *kyphos*, bent, hump-backed]. A deformity of the spine characterized by extensive flexion.

kyphot'ic. Relating to kyphosis.

kyto- [G. *kytos*, a hollow (cell)]. For words beginning thus, see cyto-.

L

λ The 11th letter of the Greek alphabet, lambda, used

as a symbol for wavelength, Ostwald's solubility *coefficient*, and radioactive *constant*.

L Left; liter; inductance; limes, used with a lower case letter or a plus sign (or a subscript letter or plus sign) as a symbol for various doses of toxin.

l Liter.

l- Prefix indicating a chemical compound to be levorotatory.

L- Prefix indicating a chemical compound to be structurally (sterically) related to L-glyceraldehyde.

La Lanthanum.

la belle indifference [Fr.]. A naive, inappropriate lack of emotion or concern for the implications of one's disability, typically seen in persons with conversion hysteria.

la'bia. Plural of labium.

la'bial. Relating to the lips or any labium.

labile (la'bĭl, la'bīl) [L. *labilis*, liable to slip]. Unstable or unsteady; not fixed; characterized by adaptability to alteration or modification.

labil'ity. The state or condition of being labile.

labio- [L. *labium*, lip]. Combining form relating to the lips.

labiocervical (la'bĭ-o-ser'vĭ-kal) [labio- + L. *cervix*, neck]. Relating to the labial or buccal surface of the neck of a tooth.

labiochorea (la'bĭ-o-ko-re'ah) [labio- + G. *choreia*, dance]. A chronic spasm of the lips, interfering with speech.

la'bioclina'tion. Inclination of a tooth more toward the lips than is normal;

labiodental (la'bĭ-o-den'tal) [labio- + L. *dens*, tooth]. Relating to the lips and teeth; denoting certain letters the sound of which is formed by both lips and teeth.

labiogingival (la'bĭ-o-jin'jĭ-val). Relating to the point of junction of the labial border and the gingival line on the distal or mesial surface of an incisor tooth.

labioglossolaryngeal (la'bĭ-o-glos'o-lä-rin'je-al) [labio- + G. *glōssa*, tongue, + larynx]. Relating to the lips, tongue, and larynx.

labioglossopharyngeal (la'bĭ-o-glos'o-fä-rin'je-al) [labio- + G. *glōssa*, tongue, + pharynx]. Relating to the lips, tongue, and pharynx.

la'biograph [labio- + G. *graphō*, to record]. An instrument for recording the movements of the lips in speaking.

la'biomen'tal [labio- + L. *mentum*, chin]. Relating to the lower lip and the chin.

la'biona'sal. Relating to the upper lip and the nose, or to both lips and the nose.

labiopalatine (la'bĭ-o-pal'ä-tīn). Relating to the lips and the palate.

la'bioplace'ment. Positioning of a tooth more toward the lips than normal.

labioplasty (la'bĭ-o-plas-tĭ) [labio- + G. *plasso*, to form]. Plastic operation on a lip.

labioversion (la'bĭ-o-ver-zhun). Malposition of an anterior tooth from the normal line of occlusion toward the lips.

la'bium, gen. **la'bii,** pl. **la'bia** [L.] [NA]. A lip or lip-shaped structure.

  l. ma'jus puden'di, pl. **la'bia majo'ra** [NA], large pudendal lip; one of two rounded folds of integument forming the lateral boundaries of the rima pudendi.

  l. mi'nus puden'di, pl. **la'bia mino'ra** [NA], small pudendal lip; nympha; one of two narrow longitudinal folds of mucous membrane enclosed in the cleft within the labia majora.

  la'bia o'ris [NA], the lips bounding the cavity of the mouth.

la'bor [L. toil, suffering]. The process of expulsion of the fetus and the placenta from the uterus. The **stages of l.** are: **first,** the period of dilation of the os uteri; **second,** that stage of expulsive effort, beginning with the complete dilation of the cervix and ending with delivery of the infant; **third** (placental stage), the period beginning with the delivery of the baby and ending with more or less complete expulsion of the placenta; **fourth,** the period after the birth of the baby during which the membranes and placenta are extruded.

  dry l., l. after spontaneous loss of practically all of the amniotic fluid.

  missed l., occurrence of a few l. pains at the normal term followed by their cessation and the retention of the fetus for an indefinite period.

  precipitate l., l. ending in rapid expulsion of fetus.

  premature l., onset of labor before the 37th completed week of pregnancy dated from the last normal menstrual period.

labra (la'brah) [L.]. Plural of labrum.

la'brum, pl. **la'bra** [L.] [NA]. An edge, rim, or lip-shaped structure.

labyrinth (lab'ĭ-rinth) [G. *labyrinthos*]. **1.** The internal or inner ear, composed of the semicircular ducts, vestibule, and cochlea. **2.** Any group of communicating cavities, cells, or canals.

  ethmoidal l., a mass of air cells with thin bony walls forming part of the lateral wall of the nasal cavity.

  membranous l., an arrangement of communicating membranous sacs, filled with endolymph and surrounded by perilymph, lying within the cavity of the osseous labyrinth; its chief divisions are: sacculus, utriculus, cochlear duct, and semicircular ducts.

  osseous l., bony l.; a series of cavities (cochlea, vestibule, and semicircular canals) in the petrous portion of the temporal bone which lodge the membranous l.

labyrinthectomy (lab'ĭ-rin-thek'to-mĭ) [labyrinth + G. *ektomē*, excision]. Excision of the labyrinth of the ear.

labyrinthine (lab-ĭ-rin'thin). Relating to any labyrinth.

labyrinthitis (lab'ĭ-rin-thi'tis). Otitis interna; inflammation of the labyrinth (the internal ear), sometimes accompanied by vertigo.

labyrinthotomy (lab'ĭ-rin-thot'o-mĭ) [labyrinth + G. *tomē*, incision]. Incision into the labyrinth of the ear.

lac, gen. **lactis** [L. milk] [NA]. **1.** Milk. **2.** Any whitish, milky looking liquid.

lacerated (las'er-a-ted). Torn; rent; having a ragged edge.

laceration (las-er-a'shun) [L. *lacero*, pp. *-atus*, to tear to pieces]. **1.** A torn or jagged wound, or an accidental cut wound. **2.** The process or act of tearing the tissues.

lacertus (lă-ser'tus) [L.] [NA]. A fibrous band or arm related to a muscle.

lacrimal (lak'rĭ-mal) [L. *lacrima*, a tear]. Relating to tears, their secretion, and the organs concerned therewith.

lacrimation (lak-rĭ-ma'shun) [L. *lacrimatio*]. Secretion of tears, especially in excess.

lacrimator (lak'rĭ-ma-tor) [L. *lacrima*, tear]. An agent (such as tear gas) that irritates the eyes and produces tears.

lacrimatory (lak'rĭ-mă-to-rĭ). Causing lacrimation.

lacrimotomy (lak-rĭ-mot'o-mĭ) [L. *lacrima*, tear, + G. *tomē*, incision]. Incision of the lacrimal duct or sac.

lact-, lacti-, lacto- [L. *lac, lactis*, milk]. Combining forms denoting milk.

lactacidemia (lak-tas-ĭ-de'mĭ-ah). Lacticacidemia.

lactacidosis (lak'tas-ĭ-do'sis). Acidosis due to increased lactic acid.

lac'tam, lac'tim. Abbreviations of "lactoneamine" and "lactoneimine," and applied to the tautomeric forms $-NH-CO-$ and $-N=C(OH)-$, respectively, observed in many purines, pyrimidines, and other substances; the latter form accounts for the acidic properties of uric acid, in particular.

lac'tase. β-Galactosidase.

lac'tate. 1. A salt or ester of lactic acid. **2.** To produce milk in the mammary glands.

lactate dehydrogenase (LDH). Four enzymes involved in catalyzing the oxidation of lactate to pyruvate.

lactation (lak-ta'shun) [L. *lactatio*, suckle]. **1.** The production of milk. **2.** The period following childbirth during which milk is formed in the breasts.

lacteal (lak'te-al). **1.** Relating to or resembling milk; milky. **2.** Chyle or lacteal vessel; a lymphatic vessel that conveys chyle from the intestine.

lactescent (lak-tes'ent). Resembling milk; milky.

lacti-. See lact-.

lactic (lak'tik) [L. *lac*(*lact-*), milk]. Relating to milk.

lac'tic acid. 2-Hydroxypropionic acid $CH_3-CHOH-COOH$; a liquid obtained by the action of the lactic acid bacillus on milk or milk sugar; a caustic in concentrated form, used internally to prevent gastrointestinal fermentation.

L-lactic acid. A dextrorotatory form of lactic acid sometimes excreted in the urine after severe muscular exercise.

lacticacidemia (lak'tik-as-ĭ-de'mĭ-ah) [lactic acid + G. *haima*, blood]. Lactacidemia; presence of dextrorotatory lactic acid in the circulating blood.

lactiferous (lak-tif'er-us) [lacti- + L. *fero*, to bear]. Lactigerous; yielding milk.

lactifuge (lak'tĭ-fūj) [lacti- + L. *fugo*, to drive away]. Causing the arrest of the secretion of milk.

lactigenous (lak-tij'en-us) [lacti- + suffix *-gen*, producing]. Producing milk.

lactigerous (lak-tij'er-us) [lacti- + L. *gero*, to carry]. Lactiferous.

lac'tim. See lactam.

lacto-. See lac-.

Lactobacillus (lak'to-bă-sil'us). A genus bacteria (family Lactobacillaceae) containing Gram-positive rods which vary from long and slender cells to short coccobacilli. They ferment glucose, and at least half of the end product is lactic acid. Some organisms are parasitic in many warm-blooded animals, including man, but rarely are pathogenic. The type species is *L. delbrueckii*.

lactocele (lak'to-sēl) [lacto- + G. *kēlē*, tumor]. Galactocele.

lactogen (lak'to-jen) [lacto- + *-gen*, producing]. An agent that stimulates milk production or secretion.

human placental l. (HPL), human chorionic somatomammotropic hormone; human chorionic somatomammotropin; a protein hormone of placental origin; its biological activity weakly mimics that of human pituitary growth hormone and prolactin.

lactogenesis (lak-to-jen'ĕ-sis) [lacto- + G. *genesis*, production]. Milk production.

lactogen'ic. Pertaining to lactogenesis.

lactoglob'ulin. The globulin present in milk; comprises 50–60% of bovine whey protein.

lac'tone. An organic anhydride formed from a hydroxyacid by the loss of water between the $-OH$ and $-COOH$ groups; an internal ester.

lactorrhea (lak-to-re'ah) [lacto- + G. *rhoia*, a flow]. Galactorrhea.

lac'tose. Galactosylglucose; a disaccharide present in mammalian milk and obtained from cow's milk; occurs naturally as α- and β-forms.

lactosuria (lak-to-su'rĭ-ah) [lacto- + G. *ouron*, urine]. Excretion of lactose in the urine.

lac'tother'apy. Galactotherapy.

lac'totro'pin. Prolactin.

lacuna, pl. **lacunae** (lă-ku'nah, -ku'ne) [L. a pit] [NA]. A small space, cavity, or depression. **2.** A gap or defect. **3.** An abnormal space between the strata or between the cellular elements of the epidermis. **4.** Corneal *space*.

cartilage l., cartilage space; a cavity within the matrix of cartilage, occupied by a chondrocyte.

Howship's lacunae, resorption lacunae; tiny depressions, pits, or irregular grooves in bone that is being resorbed by osteoclasts.

intervillous l., one of the blood spaces in the placenta into which the chorionic villi project.

lacunae latera'les [NA], parasinoidal sinuses; lateral expansions of the sinus sagittalis superior of the dura mater, often increasing in width with advancing age.

l. mag'na, a recess on the roof of the fossa navicularis of the penis, formed by a fold of mucous membrane; the valve of the navicular fossa.

osseous l., a cavity in bony tissue occupied by an osteocyte.

resorption lacunae, Howship's lacunae.

trophoblastic l., one of the spaces in the early syncytiotrophoblastic layer of the chorion before the formation of villi; with the differentiation of the chorionic villi they become intervillous spaces, sometimes called intervillous lacunae.

l. vaso'rum [NA], vascular compartment; the medial compartment beneath the inguinal ligament, for the passage to the femoral vessels; it is separated from the l. musculorum by the iliopectineal arch.

lacu'nar. 1. Relating to a lacuna. **2.** Denoting a hiatus or temporary lack of manifestation in a symptom.

lacunule (lă-ku'nŭl) [Mod. L. *lacunula,* dim. of L. *lacuna*]. A very small lacuna.

la'cus, pl. **la'cus** [L. lake]. Lake (1); a small collection of fluid.

l. lacrima'lis [NA], lacrimal lake; the small cistern-like area of the conjunctiva at the medial angle of the eye, in which the tears collect after bathing the anterior surface of the eyeball and the conjunctival sac.

l. semina'lis, seminal lake; the vault of the vagina after insemination.

laetrile (la'ĕ-tril). An allegedly antineoplastic drug consisting chiefly of amygdalin derived from apricot pits.

laev-. For words so beginning see lev-.

lag'ging. Retarded or diminished movement of the affected side of the chest in pulmonary tuberculosis.

lagophthalmia, lagophthalmos (lag'of-thal'mĭ-ah, -thal'mos) [G. *lagōs,* hare, + *ophthalmos,* eye]. A condition in which complete closure of the eyelids over the eyeball is difficult or impossible.

lake (lāk) [A.S. *lacu,* fr. L. *lacus,* lake]. **1.** Lacus. **2.** To cause blood plasma to become red as a result of the release of hemoglobin from the erythrocytes, as when the latter are suspended in water.

capillary l., the total mass of blood contained in capillary vessels.

lacrimal l., *lacus* lacrimalis.

seminal l., *lacus* seminalis.

subchorial l., subchorial *space.*

la'ky. Pertaining to the transparent, bright red appearance of blood serum or plasma, developing as a result of hemoglobin being released from destroyed red blood cells.

lal'ling [G. *laleō,* to chatter]. A form of stammering in which the speech is almost unintelligible.

lalochezia (lal'o-ke'zĭ-ah) [G. *lalia,* speech, + *chezo,* to relieve oneself]. Emotional discharge gained by uttering indecent or filthy words.

laloplegia (lal-o-ple'jĭ-ah) [G. *lalia,* speech, + *plēgē,* a stroke]. Paralysis of the muscles concerned in the mechanism of speech.

lalorrhea (lal'o-re'ah) [G. *lalia,* speech, + *rhoia,* flow]. Excessive flow of words.

lambda (lam'dah) [the 11th letter of the Greek alphabet, λ, Λ]. The craniometric point at the junction of the sagittal and lambdoid sutures.

lamb'doid [lambda + G. *eidos,* resemblance]. Resembling the Greek letter lambda.

Lam'blia intestina'lis. Old term for *Giardia lamblia.*

lambliasis (lam-bli'ă-sis). Giardiasis.

lamella, pl. **lamellae** (lă-mel'ah, -mel'e) [L. dim. of *lamina,* plate, leaf]. **1.** A thin sheet or layer, as occurs in compact bone. **2.** Disk (2); a preparation in the form of a medicated gelatin disk, used as a means of making local applications to the conjunctiva in place of solutions.

articular l., the compact layer of bone on its articular surface that is firmly attached to the overlying articular cartilage.

circumferential l., a bony l. that encircles the outer or inner surface of a bone.

concentric l., haversian l.; one of the tubular layers of bone surrounding the central canal in an osteon.

elastic l., a thin sheet of elastic fibers, as found in a vein or the respiratory tract; not the same as elastic membrane, which usually refers to a condensed mass of fibers, as in an artery.

ground l., interstitial l.

haversian l., concentric l.

interstitial l., intermediate l., ground l.; one of the lamellae of partially resorbed osteons occurring between newer, complete osteons.

vitreous l., *lamina* basalis choroideae.

lamellar (lam'ĕ-lar, lă-mel'ar). **1.** Scaly; arranged in thin plates or scales. **2.** Relating to lamellae.

lamellipodium, pl. **lamellipodia** (lă-mel-ĭ-po'dĭ-um, -ah). A cytoplasmic veil produced on all sides of migrating polymorphonuclear leukocytes.

lamina, pl. **laminae** (lam'ĭ-nah, lam'ĭ-ne) [L.] [NA]. A thin plate or flat layer.

l. ar'cus ver'tebrae [NA], l. of the vertebral arch; neurapophysis; the flattened posterior portion of the vertebral arch from which the spinous process extends.

l. basa'lis [NA], basal l. or ventral plate of the neural tube; the ventral division of the lateral walls of the neural tube in the embryo; contains neuroblasts giving rise to somatic and visceral motor neurons.

l. basa'lis chordi'deae [NA], basal layer of the choroid; vitreal or vitreous lamella; vitreous membrane (3); Bruch's membrane; the inner layer of the choroid in contact with the pigmented layer of the retina.

l. basa'lis cor'poris cilia'ris [NA], basal layer of the ciliary body; the inner layer of the ciliary body, continuous with the basal layer of the choroid.

basilar l., l. basilaris cochleae.

l. basila'ris coch'leae [NA], basilar l. or membrane; the membrane extending from the osseous spiral l. to the basilar crest of the cochlea; forms the greater part of the floor of the cochlear duct and supports the organ of Corti.

l. choroidocapilla'ris [NA], choriocapillary layer; Ruysch's membrane; entochoroidea; the internal layer of the choroid of the eye, composed of a very close capillary network.

l. cribro'sa os'sis ethmoida'lis [NA], cribriform plate of the ethmoid bone; cribrum; a horizontal l. that fits into the ethmoidal notch of the frontal bone and supports the olfactory lobes of the cerebrum, being pierced with numerous openings for the passage of the olfactory nerves.

l. cribro'sa scle'rae, perforated layer of the sclera; the portion of the sclera through which pass the fibers of the optic nerve.

dental l., a band of ectodermal cells growing from the epithelium of the embryonic jaws into the underlying mesenchyme; local buds from the l. give rise to the primordia of the enamel organs of the teeth.

elastic laminae of arteries, elastic layers of arteries; (1) external: the layer of elastic connective tissue lying immediately outside the smooth muscle of the tunica media; (2) internal: a fenestrated layer of elastic tissue of the tunica intima.

elastic laminae of cornea, l. limitans corneae.

l. epithelia'lis [NA], epithelial l., the layer of modified ependymal cells that forms the inner layer of the tela choroidea, facing the ventricle.

l. fus'ca scle'rae [NA], a thin layer of pigmented connective tissue on the inner surface of the sclera, connecting it with the choroid.

l. of lens, one of a series of concentric layers composed of the lens fibers that make up the substance of the lens.

l. lim'itans cor'neae [NA], elastic or limiting layer of the cornea; (1) Bowman's membrane; a basement membrane lying between the outer layer of stratified epithelium and the substantia propria of the cornea; (2) posterior: entocornea; Descemet's membrane; vitreous membrane (1); a basement membrane between the substantia propria and the endothelial layer of the cornea.

l. muscula'ris muco'sae [NA], muscular layer of the mucosa; the thin layer of smooth muscle found in most parts of the digestive tube located outside the l. propria mucosae and adjacent to the tela submucosa.

l. pro'pria muco'sae [NA], the layer of connective tissue underlying the epithelium of a mucous membrane.

l. spira'lis os'sea [NA], spiral l.; a double plate of bone winding spirally around the modiolus and dividing the spiral canal of the cochlea into the scala tympani and scala vestibuli; between the two plates of this l. the fibers of the cochlear nerve reach the spiral organ of Corti.

l. tec'ti mesenceph'ali [NA], tectum mesencephali; the roofplate of the mesencephalon formed by the corpora quadrigemina.

l. vasculo'sa choroi'deae [NA], vascular layer of the choroid; the outer portion of the choroid containing the largest blood vessels.

l. of vertebral arch, l. arcus vertebrae.

l. viscera'lis [NA], visceral layer; (1) epicardium; the inner part of the serous pericardium applied directly on the heart; (2) the inner part of the tunica vaginalis testis applied directly to the testis and epididymis.

vitreal l., vitreous l., l. basalis choroideae.

lam'inagram. A film taken by a laminagraph.

lam'inagraph. A tornographic technique whereby tissues above and below the level of a suspected lesion are blurred out to emphasize a specific area.

laminagraphy (lam'ĭ-nag'ră-fĭ) [lamina + G. graphē, a writing]. Tomography.

lam'inar. 1. Laminated; arranged in plates or laminae. 2. Relating to any lamina.

laminectomy (lam-ĭ-nek'to-mĭ) [L. lamina, layer, + G. ektomē, excision]. Rachiotomy; excision of a vertebral lamina; commonly used to denote removal of the posterior arch.

laminitis (lam-ĭ-ni'tis). Inflammation of any lamina.

laminotomy (lam-ĭ-not'o-mĭ) [L. lamina, layer, + G. tomē, incision]. Division of one or more vertebral laminae.

lamp. An illuminating device; a source of heat or light.

annealing l., an alcohol l. with a soot-free flame used in dentistry to drive off the protective NH_3 gas coating from the surface of cohesive gold foil.

spirit l., an alcohol l., used mainly for heating in laboratory work.

Wood's l., an ultraviolet l. with a nickel oxide filter that passes only light with a maximal wavelength of about 3660 Å; used to detect by fluorescence hairs infected with Microsporum fungi.

lanat'osides A, B, and C. Digilanides A, B, and C; the cardioactive precursor glycosides obtained from Digitalis lanata.

lance (lans) [L. lancea, a slender spear]. 1. To incise a part, as an abscess or boil. 2. A lancet.

lancet (lan'set) [Fr. lancette]. A surgical knife with a small, sharp-pointed, two-edged blade.

lancinating (lan'sĭ-na-ting) [L. lancino, pp. -atus, to tear]. Denoting a sharp cutting or tearing pain.

lan'olin [L. lana, wool, + oleum, oil]. A purified, fatlike substance from the wool of sheep, containing not less than 25% and not more than 30% of water, used as a water-adsorbable ointment base.

lan'thanum [G. lanthanō, to lie hid]. A metallic element, symbol La, atomic no. 57, atomic weight 138.91; first of the rare earth element series (lanthanides).

lanuginous (lă-nu'jĭ-nus). Covered with lanugo.

lanugo (lă-nu'go) [L. down, wooliness; fr. *lana*, wool] [NA]. Lanugo hair; fine, soft, unmedullated fetal or embryonic hair with minute shafts and large papillae.

laparo- [G. *lapara*, flank, loins]. Combining form denoting the loins or, less properly, the abdomen in general.

laparocele (lap'ă-ro-sēl) [laparo- + G. *kēlē*, hernia]. Abdominal *hernia.*

laparorrhaphy (lap-ă-ror'ă-fĭ). Celiorrhaphy.

laparoscope (lap'ă-ro-skōp) [laparo- + G. *skopeō*, to view]. Peritoneoscope.

laparoscopy (lap-ă-ros'ko-pĭ). Peritoneoscopy.

laparotomy (lap'ă-rot'o-mĭ) [laparo- + G. *tomē*, incision]. **1.** Incision into the loin. **2.** Celiotomy.

lapinization (lap'ĭ-nĭ-za'shun) [Fr. *lapin*, rabbit]. Serial passage of a vaccine in rabbits.

lapinized (lap'ĭ-nĭzd) [Fr. *lapin*, rabbit]. Denoting viruses which have been adapted to develop in rabbits by serial transfers in this species.

lard [L. *lardum*]. Adeps (2).

larva, pl. **larvae** (lar'vah, lar've) [L. a mask]. **1.** The wormlike form of an insect or helminth upon issuing from the egg. **2.** The young of fishes or amphibians, often differing in appearance from the adult.

lar'val. 1. Relating to larvae. **2.** Larvate.

lar'va mi'grans [L. *larva*, mask, + *migrare*, to transfer, migrate]. A larval worm, typically a nematode, that wanders in the host tissues but does not develop to the adult stage; usually occurs in abnormal hosts that inhibit normal development of the parasite.

cutaneous l. m., creeping eruption; an advancing serpiginous or netlike tunneling in the skin, with marked pruritus, caused by wandering hookworm larvae not adapted to intestinal maturation in man.

visceral l. m., a disease, chiefly of children, caused by ingestion of infective nematode ova of *Toxocara canis* or less commonly by other ascarid nematodes not adapted to man; the larvae hatch in the intestine, penetrate the gut wall, and wander in the viscera, chiefly the liver, producing a sustained high eosinophilia; may be asymptomatic or may be marked by hepatomegaly, pulmonary infiltration, fever, cough, and hyperglobulinemia.

lar'vate [L. *larva*, mask]. Larval (2); masked or concealed; applied to a disease with undeveloped, absent, or atypical symptoms.

larvicidal (lar-vĭ-si'dal). Destructive to larvae, grubs, caterpillars, etc.

larvicide (lar'vĭ-sĭd) [larva + L. *caedo*, to kill]. An agent that kills larvae.

laryng-. See laryngo-.

laryngeal (lă-rin'je-al). Relating to the larynx.

laryngectomy (lăr-in-jek'to-mĭ) [laryngo- + G. *ektomē*, excision]. Excision of the larynx.

laryngemphraxis (lăr'in-jem-frak'sis) [G. *emphraxis*, a stoppage]. Laryngeal obstruction or closure.

larynges (lă-rin'jēz) [L.]. Plural of larynx.

laryngismus (lăr-in-jiz'mus) [L. fr. G. *larynx*, + *-ismos*, -ism]. Spasmodic narrowing or closure of the rima glottidis.

l. strid'ulus, pseudocroup; a spasmodic closure of the glottis, lasting a few seconds, followed by noisy inspiration.

laryngitic (lăr-in-jit'ik). Relating to or caused by laryngitis.

laryngitis (lăr-in-ji'tis) [laryngo- + G. *-itis*, inflammation]. Inflammation of the mucous membrane of the larynx.

membranous l., a form in which there is a pseudomembranous exudate on the vocal cords.

l. stridulo'sa, catarrhal inflammation of the larynx in children, accompanied by night attacks of spasmodic closure of the glottis, causing inspiratory stridor.

laryngo-, laryng-. Combining forms relating to the larynx.

laryngocele (lă-ring'go-sēl) [laryngo- + G. *kēlē*, hernia]. An air sac communicating with the larynx through the ventricle, often bulging outward into the tissue of the neck, especially during coughing.

laryngofissure (lă-ring'go-fish'ur). Laryngotomy; thyrotomy (2); operative opening into the larynx, generally through the midline.

laryngology (lăr'ing-gol'o-jĭ) [laryngo- + G. *logos*, study]. The branch of medical science concerned with the larynx; the specialty of diseases of the larynx.

laryngoparalysis (lă-ring'go-pă-ral'ĭ-sis). Laryngoplegia; paralysis of the laryngeal muscles.

laryngopathy (lăr'ing-gop'ă-thĭ) [laryngo- + G. *pathos*, suffering]. Any disease of the larynx.

laryngopharyngeal (lă-ring'go-fă-rin'je-al). Relating to both larynx and pharynx or to the laryngopharynx.

laryngopharyngectomy (lă-ring'go-făr'in-jek'to-mĭ). Resection or excision of both larynx and pharynx.

laryngopharyngitis (lă-ring'go-făr-in-ji'tis). Inflammation of the larynx and pharynx.

laryngopharynx (lă-ring'go-făr'ingks). hypopharynx; the part of the pharynx lying below the aperture of the larynx and behind the larynx, extending from the vestibule of the larynx to the esophagus at the level of the inferior border of the cricoid cartilage.

laryngophony (lăr-ing-gof'o-nĭ) [laryngo- + G. *phōnē*, voice]. The voice sounds heard in auscultation of the larynx.

laryngoplasty (lă-ring'go-plas-tĭ) [laryngo- + G. *plassō*, to form]. Reparative or plastic surgery of the larynx.

laryngoplegia (lă-ring'go-ple'jĭ-ah) [laryngo- + G. *plēgē*, stroke]. Laryngoparalysis.

laryngoptosis (lă-ring'go-to'sis) [laryngo- + G. *ptōsis*, a falling]. An abnormally low position of the larynx.

laryngorhinology (lă-ring'go-ri-nol'o-jĭ) [laryngo- + G. *rhis*, nose, + *logos*, study]. The branch of medical science concerned with the larynx and of the nose.

laryngoscope (lă-ring'go-skōp) [laryngo- + G. *skopeō*, to inspect]. Any of several types of illuminated hollow tubes used in examining or operating upon the interior of the larynx through the mouth.

laryngoscopic (lă-ring'go-skop'ik). Relating to laryngoscopy.

laryngoscopy (lăr-ing-gos'ko-pī). Inspection of the larynx by means of the laryngoscope.

laryngospasm (lă-ring'go-spazm). Spasmodic closure of the glottic aperture.

laryngostenosis (lă-ring'go-stě-no'sis) [laryngo- + G. *stenōsis*, a narrowing]. Stricture or narrowing of the lumen of the larynx.

laryngostomy (lăr-ing-gos'to-mī) [laryngo- + G. *stoma*, mouth]. Establishment of a permanent opening from the neck into the larynx.

laryngotomy (lăr-ing-got'o-mī) [laryngo- + G. *tomē*, incision]. Laryngofissure.

laryngotracheal (lă-ring'go-tra'ke-al). Relating to both larynx and trachea.

laryngotracheitis (lă-ring'go-tra-ke-i'tis). Inflammation of both larynx and trachea.

laryngotracheobronchitis (lă-ring'go-tra'ke-o-bron-ki'tis). An acute respiratory infection involving the larynx, trachea, and bronchi. See croup.

laryngotracheotomy (lă-ring'go-tra-ke-ot'o-mī) laryngo- + trachea + G. *tomē*, incision]. An incision through the cricoid cartilage and the upper tracheal rings.

laryngoxerosis (lar-ing'go-ze-ro'sis) [laryngo- + G. *xērōsis*, a drying up]. Abnormal dryness of the laryngeal mucous membrane.

larynx, pl. **larynges** (lăr'ingks, lă-rin'jēz) [Mod. L. fr. G.] [NA]. The organ of voice production; the part of the respiratory tract, between the pharynx and the trachea, consisting of a framework of cartilages and elastic membranes housing the vocal folds and the muscles which control the position and tension of these elements.

lase (lāz). To cut, divide, or dissolve a substance, or to treat an anatomical suture, with a laser beam.

laser (la'zer) [*l*ight *a*mplification by *s*timulated *e*mission of *r*adiation]. A device that concentrates high energies into a narrow beam of visible, coherent (nonspreading), monochromatic light; used in surgery to cut and dissolve tissue.

las'situde [L. *lassitudo*, fr. *lassus;* weary]. A sense of weariness.

latah (lah'tah) [Malay, ticklish]. A nervous affection characterized by an exaggerated physical response to being startled or to unexpected suggestion.

latency (la'ten-sī). **1.** The state of being latent. **2.** In conditioning, the period of apparent inactivity between the time the stimulus is presented and the moment a response occurs.

la'tent [L. *lateo*, pres. p. *latens* (*-ent-*), to lie hid]. Not manifest, but potentially discernible.

laterad (lat'er-ad) [L. *latus*, side, + *ad*, to]. Toward the side.

lat'eral [L. *lateralis*, lateral, fr. *latus*, side]. **1.** On the side. **2.** Farther from the median or midsagittal plane. **3.** In dentistry, a position either right or left of the midsagittal plane.

lateral'ity. In voluntary motor acts, preferential use of members of one side of the body through right or left dominance of the cerebral cortex; **crossed l.** is right dominance of some members and left dominance of others.

latero- [L. *lateralis*, lateral, fr. *latus*, side]. Combining form meaning lateral, to one side, or relating to a side.

laterodeviation (lat'er-o-de-vī-a'shun) [latero- + L. *devio*, to turn aside, fr. *via*, a way]. A bending or a displacement to one side.

lateroduction (lat'er-o-duk'shun) [lactero- + L. *duco*, pp. *ductus*, to lead]. A drawing to one side; denoting a movement of a limb or of the eyeball.

lateroflexion (lat'er-o-flek'shun) [latero- + L. *flecto*, pp. *flexus*, to bend]. A bending or curvature to one side.

laterotorsion (lat'er-o-tor'shun) [latero- + L. *torsio*, a twisting]. A twisting to one side; denoting the turning of the eyeball around its anteroposterior axis.

laterotrusion (lat'er-o-tru'zhun) [latero- + L. *trudo*, pp. *trusus*, to thrust]. The outward thrust given by the muscles of mastication to the rotating mandibular condyle during movement of the mandible.

lateroversion (lat'er-o-ver'shun) [latero- + L. *verto*, pp. *versus*, to turn]. A turning to one side or the other, denoting especially a malposition of the uterus.

lathyrism (lath'ī-rizm) [L. *lathyrus*, vetch]. A disorder characterized by various nervous manifestations, tremors, spastic paraplegia, and parasthesias; prevalent where vetches, *Lathyrus sativus* and allied species, form the main food.

Latrodec'tus [L. *lactro*, servant, robber, + G. *dēktēs*, a biter]. A genus of relatively small spiders, the "widow" spiders, capable of inflicting highly poisonous, neurotoxic, antagonizing bites; they are responsible, along with *Loxosceles* (the brown spider), for most of the severe reactions from spider envenomation.

LATS Long-acting thyroid *stimulator.*

la'tus, gen. **lat'eris,** pl. **lat'era** [L.]. Flank; the side of the body between the pelvis and the ribs.

laudable (law'dă-bl) [L. *laudabilis*, praiseworthy]. Formerly used to describe pus, under the notion that suppuration in a wound favored healing.

laudanum (law'dă-num) [G. *lēdanon*, a resinous gum]. A tincture containing opium.

lauric acid. $CH_3(CH_2)_{10}COOH$; a fatty acid occurring in spermaceti, in milk, and in laurel, coconut, and palm oils.

lavage (lă-vahzh′) [Fr. from L. *lavo*, to wash]. The washing out of a hollow cavity or organ by copious injections and rejections of fluid.

law [A.S. *lagu*]. A principle or rule; a formula expressing a fact or number of facts common to a group of processes or actions. See also principle, theorem.

Allen's l., the more carbohydrate that is taken by a diabetic, the less utilized.

all or none l., Bowditch's l.

Arndt's l., weak stimuli excite physiologic activity, moderately strong ones favor it, strong ones retard it, and very strong ones arrest it.

Behring's l., parenteral administration of serum from an immunized person provides a relative, passive immunity to that disease in a previously susceptible person.

Bell's l., the ventral spinal roots are motor, the dorsal are sensory.

Bernoulli's l., when friction is negligible, the velocity of flow of a gas or fluid through a tube is inversely related to its pressure against the side of the tube; *i.e.,* velocity is greatest and pressure lowest at a point of constriction.

Bowditch's l., all or none l.; any stimulus, however feeble, that will excite a cardiac contraction will produce as powerful a contraction as the strongest stimulus; "minimal stimuli cause maximal pulsations."

Boyle's l., at constant temperature, the volume of a given quantity of gas varies inversely with its absolute pressure.

Charles' l., all gases expand equally on heating, namely, $1/273$ of their volume at 0°C. for every degree Celcius.

l. of contiguity, when two ideas or events have once occurred in close association they are likely to so occur again, the subsequent occurrence of one tending to elicit the other.

Dalton's l., l. of partial pressures; each gas in a mixture of gases exerts a pressure proportionately to the percentage of the gas and independently of the presence of the other gases present.

Donders' l., the rotation of the eyeball is determined by the distance of the object from the median plane and the line of the horizon.

Einthoven's l., in the electrocardiogram, the potential of any wave or complex in lead II is equal to the sum of the potentials of leads I and III.

l. of excitation, a motor nerve responds, not to the absolute value, but to the alteration of value from moment to moment, of the electric current.

Fechner-Weber l., Weber-Fechner l.

Hamburger's l., albumins and phosphates pass from red corpuscles to serum, and chlorides pass from serum to cells when blood is acid; reverse occurs when blood is alkaline.

Hardy-Weinberg l., Hardy-Weinberg *equilibrium.*

l. of the heart, Starling's l.; the energy liberated by the heart when it contracts is a function of the length of its muscle fibers at the end of diastole.

Hellin's l., twins occur once in 89 births, triplets once in 89², and quadruplets once in 89³.

Henry's l., at equilibrium, the amount of gas dissolved in a given volume of liquid is directly proportional to the partial pressure of that gas in the gas phase.

Hilton's l., the nerve supplying a joint supplies also the muscles which move the joint and the skin covering the articular insertion of those muscles.

Hooke's l., the stress applied to stretch or compress a body is proportional to the strain, or change in length thus produced, so long as the limit of elasticity of the body is not exceeded.

l. of independent assortment, Mendel's second l.; different hereditary factors are assorted independently when the gametes are formed (modified by the restriction that linked genes do not assort independently).

l. of inverse square, intensity of radiation is inversely proportional to the square of the distance from the source.

Listing's l., when the eye leaves one object and fixes another, it revolves about an axis perpendicular to a plane cutting both the former and the present lines of vision.

Mendel's l.'s, (1) first l.: l. of segregation; (2) second l.: l. of independent assortment.

Nysten's l., rigor mortis affects first the muscles of the head and spreads toward the hands and feet.

l. of partial pressures, Dalton's l.

Pascal's l., fluids at rest transmit pressure equally in every direction.

Poiseuille's l., in laminar flow, the volume of a homogeneous fluid passing per unit time through a capillary tube is directly proportional to the pressure difference between its ends and to the fourth power of its internal radius, and inversely proportional to its length and to the viscosity of the fluid.

Raoult's l., the vapor pressure of a solution is that of the pure solvent multiplied by the mole fraction of the solvent in the solution.

l. of recapitulation, recapitulation *theory.*

l. of referred pain, pain arises only from irritation of nerves that are sensitive to those stimuli which produce pain when applied to the surface of the body.

l. of segregation, Mendel's first l.; factors that affect development retain their individuality from generation to generation, do not become contaminated when mixed in a hybrid, and become sorted out from one another when the gametes are formed.

l. of similars, see *similia similibus curantur.*

Starling's l., l. of the heart.

Weber-Fechner l., Fechner-Weber l.; the intensity of a sensation varies by a series of equal increments (arithmetically) as the strength of the stimulus is increased geometrically.

Wolff's l., every change in the form and the function of a bone, or in its function alone, is followed by certain definite changes in its internal architecture and secondary alterations in its external conformation.

lawren′cium [E.O. *Lawrence,* U.S. physicist, 1901–1958]. An artificial element; symbol Lr, atomic number 103.

laxative (laks′ă-tiv) [L. *laxo,* pp. *-atus,* to slacken, relax]. **1.** Mildly cathartic; having the action of loosening the bowels. **2.** A mild cathartic; a remedy that moves the bowels slightly without pain or violent action.

layer (la′er). A sheet of some substance lying upon another and distinguished from it.

ameloblastic l., enamel l.; the internal l. of the enamel organ.

bacillary l., l. of rods and cones.

basal l., *stratum* basale.

basal l. of choroid, *lamina* basalis choroideae.

basal l. of ciliary body, *lamina* basalis corporis ciliaris.

choriocapillary l., *lamina* choroidocapillaris.

clear l. of epidermis, *stratum* lucidum.

corneal l., *stratum* corneum.

elastic l.'s of arteries, elastic *laminae.*

elastic l.'s of cornea, *lamina* limitans corneae.

enamel l., ameloblastic l.

ganglionic l. of cerebellar cortex, *stratum* gangliosum cerebelli.

germ l., one of the three primordial cell l.'s (ectoderm, endoderm, mesoderm) established in an embryo during gastrulation and the immediately following stages.

germinative l., *stratum* germinativum.

granular l., *stratum* granulosum.

horny l., *stratum* corneum.

limiting l.'s of cornea, *lamina* limitans corneae.

malpighian l., *stratum* germinativum.

molecular l. of cerebellar cortex, *stratum* moleculare cerebelli.

muscular l. of mucosa, *lamina* muscularis mucosae.

odontoblastic l., a l. of connective tissue cells at the periphery of the dental pulp of the tooth.

osteogenetic l., the inner bone-forming l. of periosteum.

perforated l. of the sclera, *lamina* cribrosa sclerae.

prickle cell l., *stratum* spinosum epidermidis.

Purkinje's l., *stratum* gangliosum cerebelli.

l. of rods and cones, bacillary l.; the l. of the retina containing the visual receptors.

spinous l., *stratum* spinosum epidermidis.

still l., Poiseuille's space; the l. of the blood stream next to the wall in the capillary vessels that flows slowly and transports the white blood cells.

subendocardial l., the loose connective tissue l. that joins the endocardium and myocardium.

subendothelial l., the thin l. of connective tissue lying between the endothelium and elastic lamina in the intima of blood vessels.

vascular l., *lamina* vasculosa choroideae.

vascular l. of choroid, *lamina* vasculosa choroideae.

visceral l., *lamina* visceralis.

LBT Lupus band *test.*

LD Lethal *dose.*

LDH Lactate dehydrogenase.

LDL Low density lipoprotein.

L.E. Left eye; *lupus* erythematosus.

leaching (le′ching) [A.S. *leccan,* to wet]. Lixiviation.

lead (lĕd). Plumbum; a metallic element, symbol Pb, atomic no. 82, atomic weight 207.21.

lead (lĕd). The electrical connection for taking records by means of the electrocardiograph.

bipolar l., a record obtained with two electrodes placed on different regions of the body, each electrode contributing significantly to the record.

chest l.'s, precordial l.'s; bipolar l.'s in which the exploring electrode is on the chest (C) overlying the heart or its vicinity, the indifferent one on the back (CB), left leg (CF), left arm (CL), or right arm (CR).

esophageal l., a record obtained with the exploring electrode lying within the lumen of the esophagus.

limb l., one of the three standard l.'s or one of the unipolar limb l.'s (aVR, aVL, aVF).

precordial l.'s, chest l.'s.

standard l., one of the three original bipolar limb l.'s of the clinical electrocardiogram, designated I, II and III: I records potential difference between the right and left arms; II, the difference between right arm and left leg; III, the difference between left arm and left leg.

unipolar l.'s, those in which the exploring electrode is on the chest in the vicinity of the heart or on one of the limbs, while the other or indifferent electrode is the central terminal.

learn′ing. Generic term for the relatively permanent change in behavior that occurs as a result of practice.

latent l., l. that is not evident to the observer at the time it occurs, but which is inferred from later performance.

rote l., l. of arbitrary relationships, usually by repetition of the l. procedure, without an understanding of the relationships.

lecithal (les′ĭ-thal) [G. *lekithos,* egg yolk]. Having a yolk or pertaining to the yolk of any egg; used especially as a suffix.

lecithin (les′ĭ-thin) [G. *lekithos,* egg yolk]. Phospholipids that, on hydrolysis, yield two fatty acid molecules and a molecule each of glycerophosphoric acid and choline; under the microscope, they appear as irregular elongated particles known as myelin forms; found in nervous tissue, especially in myelin sheaths, in egg yolk and as essential constituents of animal and vegetable cells.

lecithinase (les′ĭ-thin-ās). Phospholipase.

lecithoblast (les'ĭ-tho-blast) [G. *lekithos,* egg yolk, + *blastos,* germ]. One of the cells proliferating to form the yolk-sac entoderm.

lectin (lek'tin). A protein that effects agglutination, precipitation, or other phenomena resembling the action of specific antibody, but that is not an antibody in that it was not evoked by an antigenic stimulus.

leech [A.S. *laece,* physician; a leech]. **1.** A blood-sucking aquatic annelid worm (genus *Hirudo,* class Hirudinea formerly used in medicine for local abstraction of blood. **2.** To treat medically by applying leeches.

left-eyed. Sinistrocular.

left-footed. Sinistropedal.

left'handed. Sinistromanual.

leg. The segment of the inferior limb between the knee and the ankle; commonly used to mean the entire inferior limb.

    milk l., *phlegmasia* alba dolens.

    restless l.'s, restless legs *syndrome.*

-legia [L. *legere,* to read]. Suffix that properly relates to reading, as distinguished from the -lexis and -lexy (G. *legein, lexai,* to speak).

Legionella (le-jun-el'lah). A genus of Gram-negative bacilli that includes the species *L. pneumophila,* the etiologic agent of Legionnaire's disease.

legionellosis (le-jun-el-o'sis). Legionnaires *disease.*

leio- [G. *leios,* smooth]. Combining form meaning smooth.

leioder'mia (li-o-der'mĭ-ah) [leio- + G. *derma,* skin]. Smooth, glossy skin.

leiomyofibroma (li-o-mi'o-fi-bro'ma). Fibroleiomyoma.

leiomyoma (li'o-mi-o'mah) [leio- + G. *mys,* muscle, + *-oma,* tumor]. A benign neoplasm derived from smooth muscle.

    l. cu'tus, dermatomyoma; cutaneous eruption of small painful nodules composed of smooth muscle fibers.

    vascular l., angioleiomyoma; angiomyoma; a markedly vascular l., apparently arising from the smooth muscle of blood vessels.

leiomyosarcoma (li'o-mi'o-sar-ko'mah) [leio- + myosarcoma]. A malignant neoplasm derived from smooth muscle.

Leishmania (lēsh-man'ĭ-ah) [W. B. *Leishman*]. A genus of digenetic, asexual, protozoan flagellates (family Trypanosomatidae) whose species (*L. braziliensis, L. donovani, L. tropica*) are indistinguishable morphologically, but may be separated serologically, on the basis of their sandfly host, by geographic occurrence, and by clinical manifestations of infection (leishmaniasis).

leishmaniasis (lēsh-mă-ni'ă-sis). Infection with a species of *Leishmania* resulting in a clinically ill-defined group of diseases traditionally divided into three major types: visceral l. (kala azar), cutaneous l. (Old World l.), and mucocutaneous l. (American or New World l.). Each is clinically and geographically quite distinct, etiologic agents are morphologically identical, and transmission is by various species of sandfly of the genus *Phlebotomus* or *Lutzomyia.*

    American l., mucocutaneous l.

    cutaneous l., Old World l.; infection with promastigotes of *Leishmania tropica* inoculated into the skin by the bite of the sandfly, *Phlebotomus,* after which an ulcer begins as a papule that enlarges to a nodule and then breaks down into an ulcer. Endemic in parts of Asia Minor, northern Africa, and India.

    mucocutaneous l., New World, American, or nasopharyngeal l.; a variable disease caused by *Leishmania braziliensis,* endemic in Central and South America, and limited to the skin and mucous membranes; lesions resembling the sores of cutaneous l. heal after a time, but later fungating and eroding forms of ulceration may appear on the tongue and buccal or nasal mucosa.

    nasopharyngeal l., mucocutaneous l.

    New World l., mucocutaneous l.

    Old World l., cutaneous l.

    visceral l., kala azar; a chronic disease, occurring in India, Assam, China, the USSR, Kenya, Sudan, and various parts of South America, caused by *Leishmania donovani,* and transmitted by the bite of a sandfly (*Phlebotomus* or *Lutzomyia*); leukopenia, anemia, splenomegaly, and hepatomegaly are characteristic, along with enlargement of lymph nodes, and secondary infections.

lem'moblast [G. *lemma,* husk, + *blastos,* germ]. In an embryo, a cell of the neural crest origin capable of forming a cell of the neurolemma sheath.

lemmocyte (lem'o-sit) [G. *lemma,* husk, + *kytos,* cell]. One of the cells of the neurolemma.

lemniscus, pl. **lemnisci** (lem-nis'kus, -nis'sē) [L. from G. *lēmniskos,* ribbon or fillet] [NA]. Fillet (1); a bundle of nerve fibers ascending from sensory nuclei in the spinal cord and rhombencephalon to the thalamus.

length. Linear distance between two points.

    crown-heel l., the total l. or standing height of an embryo or fetus.

    crown-rump l. (CR, CRL), the l. from the skull vertex to the midpoint between the apices of the buttocks of an embryo or fetus, for an approximation of embryonic or fetal age.

lens (lenz) [L. a lentil]. **1.** A piece of glass or other transparent substance, with one or both surfaces curved, used for convergence or divergence of light. **2** [NA]. A transparent biconvex cellular body lying between the iris and the vitreous, one of the refracting media of the eye.

    achromatic l., a double l. made of two kinds of glass with different dispersive qualities, so that one neutralizes the light dispersion of the other, without interfering with refraction.

    aplanatic l., a l. designed to correct spherical aberration and coma.

astigmatic l., cylindrical l.

biconcave l., concavoconcave l.; a l. that is concave on two opposing surfaces.

biconvex l., convexoconvex l.; a l. with both surfaces convex.

bifocal l., a l. in which one portion is suited for distant vision, the other for reading and near work.

concave l., a diverging minus power lens.

concavoconcave l., biconcave l.

concavoconvex l., a converging meniscus l. that is concave on one surface and convex on the opposite surface.

contact l., a l. that fits over the cornea in direct contact with the sclera or cornea; used to correct refractive errors.

convex l., a converging plus power.

convexoconcave l., a minus power l. having one surface convex and the opposite surface concave, with the latter having the greater curvature.

convexoconvex l., biconvex l.

cylindrical l. (C, cyl.), astigmatic l.; a l. in which one of the surfaces is curved in one meridian and less curved in the opposite meridian.

multifocal l., a l. with segments providing two or more powers.

omnifocal l., a l. for near and distant vision in which the reading portion is a continuously variable curve.

photochromic l., a light-sensitive spectacle l. that automatically darkens in sunlight and clears in reduced light.

planoconcave l., a l. that is flat on one side and concave on the other.

planoconvex l., one that is flat on one side and convex on the other.

safety l., a l. that meets government specifications of impact resistance.

spherical l. (S, sph.), a l. in which all refracting surfaces are spherical.

trial l.'s, a series of cylindrical and spherical l.'s used in testing vision.

trifocal l., a l. with segments of three focal powers: distant, intermediate, and near.

lensec'tomy [lens + G. *ektomē*, excision]. Removal of the lens, usually done by puncture incision through the pars plana in the course of vitrectomy.

lenticonus (len-tǐ-ko'nus) [lens + L. *conus*, cone]. A conical projection of the anterior or posterior surface of the lens, occurring as a developmental anomaly.

lentic'ular [L. *lenticula*, a lentil]. **1.** Relating to or resembling a lens of any kind. **2.** Of the shape of a lentil.

lentic'ulopap'ular. Indicating an eruption with dome-shaped or lens-shaped papules.

lenticulus, pl. **lenticuli** (len-tik'u-lus, -li) [L. dim. of *lens, lentis*, little lens]. An intraocular lens of inert plastic placed in the anterior chamber or behind the iris, or clipped to the iris after cataract extraction.

len'tiform. Lens-shaped.

lentiginosis (len-tij'ǐ-no'sis). Multiple lentigines.

lentiglo'bus [lens + L. *globus*, sphere]. A rare congenital anomaly showing a prominent spheroid elevation on the posterior surface of the lens.

lentigo, pl. **lentigines** (len-ti'go, len-tij'ǐ-nēz) [L. fr. *lens*(*lent-*), a lentil]. A brown macule resembling a freckle, except that the border is usually regular and microscopic proliferation of rete ridges is present.

malignant l., Hutchinson's or melanotic freckle; a brown or black mottled, slowly enlarging lesion usually occurring on the face of older persons; malignant change is frequent, but the resulting melanomas are not highly malignant.

senile l., liver spot; a variably pigmented l. occurring on exposed skin of older Caucasians.

leontiasis (le'on-ti'ă-sis) [G. *leōn* (*leont-*), lion]. Leonine facies; the ridges and furrows on the forehead and cheeks of patients with advanced lepromatous leprosy, giving a leonine appearance.

lep'er [G. *lepra*]. One who has leprosy.

lepidic (lě-pid'ik) [G. *lepis* (*lepid-*), scale, rind]. Relating to scales or a scaly covering layer.

lepothrix (lep'o-thriks) [G. *lepos*, rind, husk, + *thrix*, hair]. Trichomycosis axillaris.

leprechaunism (lep'rě-kawn-izm) [Irish *leprechaun*, elf]. A congenital disorder characterized by extreme growth retardation and emaciation, with grotesque elfin facies and large, low-set ears; autosomal recessive inheritance.

lep'rid [G. *lepra*, leprosy, + *-id*]. Early cutaneous lesion of leprosy.

leproma (lě-pro'mah) [G. *lepros*, scaly, + *-oma*, tumor]. A circumscribed discrete focus of granulomatous inflammation caused by *Mycobacterium leprae*.

lepro'matous. Pertaining to, or characterized by, the features of a leproma.

lep'romin. An extract of tissue infected with *Mycobacterium leprae* used in skin tests to classify the stage of leprosy.

leprosarium (lep-ro-sār'ǐ-um). A hospital especially designed for the care of those suffering from leprosy.

lep'rostat'ic. Inhibiting the growth of *Mycobacterium leprae*.

leprosy (lep'ro-sǐ) [G. *lepra*, from *lepros*, scaly]. **1.** A name given in Biblical times to various cutaneous diseases, especially those of a chronic or contagious nature, that probably embraced psoriasis and leukoderma. **2.** Hansen's disease; chronic granulomatous infection caused by *Mycobacterium leprae*(Hansen's bacillus) which occurs in two principal types: lepromatous and tuberculoid.

anesthetic l., trophoneurotic l.; l. chiefly affecting the nerves, marked by hyperesthesia succeeded by anesthesia, and by paralysis, ulceration, and various trophic disturbances, terminating in gangrene and mutilation.

cutaneous l., tuberculoid l.

lepromatous l., l. in which nodular cutaneous lesions are infiltrated, have ill-defined borders, and are bacteriologically positive, but the lepromin test is negative.

macular l., tuberculoid l. in which the lesions are small, hairless, and dry, and are erythematous in light skin and hypopigmented or copper-colored in dark skin.

nodular l., tuberculoid l.

trophoneurotic l., anesthetic l.

tuberculoid l., cutaneous or nodular l.; a benign, stable, and resistant form in which the lepromin reaction is strongly positive and in which the lesions are erythematous, insensitive, infiltrated plaques with clear-cut edges.

-lepsis, -lepsy [G. *lēpsis,* seizure]. Combining forms denoting seizure.

lepto- [G. *leptos,* slender, delicate]. A combining form meaning light, slender, thin, or frail.

leptocephalous (lep-to-sef′ă-lus) [lepto- + G. *kephalē,* head]. Having an abnormally small head.

leptocyte (lep′to-sīt) [lepto- + G. *kytos,* cell]. A "target" or "Mexican hat" cell, *i.e.,* an unusually thin or flattened red blood cell in which there is 1) a central rounded area of pigmented material, 2) a middle clear zone that contains no pigment, and 3) an outer pigmented rim at the edge of the cell.

lep′tocyto′sis. Presence of leptocytes in the circulating blood.

leptodactylous (lep-to-dak′tĭ-lus) [lepto- + G. *daktylos,* finger]. Having abnormally slender fingers.

leptomeningeal (lep′to-mē-nin′je-al). Pertaining to the leptomeninges.

leptomeninges (lep′to-mē-nin′jēz) [lepto- + G. *mēninges,* membranes]. Piarachnoid; pia-arachnoid; collective term denoting the soft membranes enveloping brain and spinal cord, the pia mater and arachnoidea mater.

leptomeningitis (lep′to-men-in-ji′tis). Pia-arachnitis; inflammation of the leptomeninges.

leptomonad (lep′to-mo′nad). Any member of the genus *Leptomonas.*

Leptomonas (lep′to-mo′nas) [lepto- + G. *monas,* unit]. A genus of parasitic flagellates (family Trypanosomatidae) commonly found in the hindgut of insects.

Leptospira (lep′to-spi′rah) [lepto- + G. *speira,* a coil]. A genus of aerobic bacteria (order Spirochaetales) containing thin, tightly coiled organisms; type species is *L. interrogans,* with over 100 parasitic or saprophytic serovars.

leptospirosis (lep′to-spi-ro′sis). Infection with species of *Leptospira.*

leptospiruria (lep′to-spi-ru′rĭ-ah). The presence of *Leptospira* in the urine.

leptotene (lep′to-tēn) [lepto- + G. *tainia,* band, tape]. Early stage of prophase in meiosis in which the chromosomes contract and become visible as long filaments well separated from each other.

Leptothrix (lep′to-thriks). Invalid name for a genus of organisms that would probably now be classified as actinomycetes, norcardiae, or corynebacteria.

Leptotrichia (lep-to-trik′ĭ-ah) [lepto- + G. *thrix,* hair]. A genus of Gram-negative bacteria that occur in the oral cavity; type species is *L. buccalis.*

lesbian (lez′bĭ-an). **1.** One who practices lesbianism. **2.** Pertaining to or practicing lesbianism.

lesbianism (lez′bĭ-an-izm) [G. *lesbios,* relating to the island of Lesbos]. Sapphism; tribadism; homosexual practices between women.

lesion (le′zhun) [L. *laedo,* pp. *laesus,* to injure]. **1.** A wound or injury. **2.** A pathologic change in the tissues. **3.** One of the individual points or patches of a multifocal disease.

coin l.'s of lungs, term given to solitary round, circumscribed shadows found in the lungs in radiographic examinations; may be caused by tuberculosis, carcinoma, cysts, infarcts, or vascular anomalies.

Ghon's primary l., Ghon's *tubercle.*

Janeway l., a small erythematous or hemorrhagic l. seen in some cases of bacterial endocarditis, usually on the palm or sole.

Mallory-Weiss l., Mallory-Weiss tear; laceration of the gastric cardia, as seen in the Mallory-Weiss syndrome.

le′thal [L. *letalis,* death]. Pertaining to or causing death; denoting especially the causal agent.

lethargy (leth′ar-jĭ) [G. *lēthargis,* drowsiness]. A state of deep and prolonged unconsciousness from which one can be aroused but into which he immediately relapses.

LETS Large external transformation-sensitive fibronectin.

leuc-, leuco-. See leuk-, leuko-.

leucine (lu′sēn). (CH₃)₂CHCH₂Ch(NH₂)COOH; an essential amino acid in protein.

leucinuria (lu-sĭ-nu′rĭ-ah). Excretion of leucine in the urine.

leucovorin (lu-ko-vo′rin). Folinic acid.

leuk-. See leuko-.

leukapheresis (lu′kă-fē-re′sis) [leuko- + G. *aphairesis,* a withdrawal]. Removal of leukocytes from the withdrawn blood, with the remainder retransfused into the donor.

leukemia (lu-ke′mĭ-ah) [leuko- + G. *haima,* blood]. Progressive proliferation of abnormal leukocytes found in hemopoietic tissues, other organs, and usually in the blood in increased numbers; classified by dominant cell type, and by duration from onset to death: duration of **acute l.** is a few months and is associated with symptoms that suggest acute infection, with severe anemia, hemorrhages, and slight enlargement of lymph nodes or spleen; duration of **chronic l.** exceeds one year, with a gradual onset of symptoms of anemia or marked enlargement of spleen, liver, or lymph nodes.

acute promyelocytic l., l. presenting as a severe bleeding disorder, with infiltration of the bone marrow by abnormal promyelocytes and myelocyte, a low plasma fibrinogen, and defective coagulation.

aleukemic l., l. in which abnormal (or leukemic) cells are absent in the peripheral blood.

basophilic l., mast cell l.; granulocytic l. in which there are unusually great numbers of basophilic granulocytes in the tissues and circulating blood.

l. cu'tis, yellow-brown, red, blue-red, or purple, sometimes nodular lesions associated with diffuse infiltrations or massive accumulations of leukemic cells in the skin.

embryonal l., stem cell l.

eosinophilic l., granulocytic l. in which there are conspicuous numbers of eosinophilic granulocytes in the tissues and circulating blood, or in which such cells are predominant.

granulocytic l., myelocytic, myeloid, myelogenous, or myelogenous l.; l. characterized by an uncontrolled proliferation of myelopoietic cells in the bone marrow and in extramedullary sites, and presence of large numbers of immature and mature granulocytic forms in various tissues (and organs) and in the circulating blood.

hairy cell l., leukemic *reticuloendotheliosis.*

leukopenic l., lymphocytic, granulocytic, or monocytic l. in which the total number of white blood cells in the circulating blood is in the normal range, or may be diminished to various levels that are significantly less than normal.

lymphatic l., lymphocytic l.

lymphoblastic l., acute lymphocytic l. in which the abnormal cells are chiefly blast forms of the lymphocytic series, or in which unusually large numbers of immature forms occur in association with adult lymphocytes.

lymphocytic l., lymphoid l., lymphatic l., l. characterized by an uncontrolled proliferation and conspicuous enlargement of lymphoid tissue in various sites and occurrence of increased numbers of cells of the lymphocytic series in the circulating blood and in various tissues and organs.

mast cell l., basophilic l.

megakaryocytic l., myelopoietic disease characterized by a seemingly uncontrolled proliferation of megakaryocytes in the bone marrow, and sometimes by the presence of a considerable number of megakaryocytes in the circulating blood.

micromyeloblastic l., myelocytic l. in which relatively large proportions of micromyeloblasts are found in the circulating blood, bone marrow, and other tissues.

monocytic l., l. characterized by large numbers of monocytes, in addition to larger, apparently related cells formed from the uncontrolled proliferation of the reticuloendothelial tissue; characterized by swelling of gums, oral ulceration, bleeding in skin or mucous membranes, secondary infection, and splenomegaly.

myeloblastic l., granulocytic l. in which there are large numbers of myeloblasts in various tissues (and organs) and in the circulating blood.

myelocytic, myelogenic, myelogenous, or **myeloid l.,** granulocytic l.

plasma cell l., disease characterized by leukocytosis and other signs and symptoms suggestive of l., in association with diffuse infiltrations and aggregates of plasma cells in the spleen, liver, bone marrow, and lymph nodes, and the presence of considerable numbers of plasma cells in the circulating blood.

Rieder cell l., acute granulocytic l. in which the affected tissues and the circulating blood contain relatively large numbers of atypical myeloblasts (Rieder cells) that have the usual, faintly granular, immature type of cytoplasm, and a comparatively mature nucleus with several wide and deep indentations.

stem cell l., embryonal l.; l. in which the abnormal cells are thought to be the precursors of lymphoblasts, myeloblasts, or monoblasts.

subleukemic l., l. in which abnormal cells are present in the peripheral blood, but total leukocyte count is not elevated.

leukemic (lu-ke'mik). Pertaining to, or having the characteristics of, leukemia.

leukemid (lu-kem'id) [leuko- + G. *haima,* blood, + *id*]. Any nonspecific type of cutaneous lesion frequently associated with leukemia, but is not a localized accumulation of leukemic cells.

leukemogen (lu-ke'mo-jen). That which is known to be (or seems to be) a causal factor in the occurrence of leukemia.

leukemogenesis (lu-ke'mo-jen'ĕ-sis) [leukemia + G. *genesis,* production]. Induction, development, and progression of a leukemic disease.

leukemogenic (lu-ke'mo-jen'ik). Pertaining to leukemogenesis or to a leukemogen.

leukemoid (lu-ke'moyd) [leukemia + G. *eidos,* resemblance]. Resembling leukemia in various signs and symptoms.

leukemoid reaction. A moderate, advanced, or sometimes extreme degree of leukocytosis in the circulating blood, closely similar or possible identical to that occurring in various forms of leukemia, but due to some other cause.

leuko-, leuk- [G. *leukos,* white]. Combining forms meaning white.

leukoagglutinin (lu'ko-ă-glu'tĭ-nin). An antibody that agglutinates white blood cells.

leukoblast (lu'ko-blast) [leuko- + G. *blastos,* germ]. Proleukocyte; an immature white blood cell transitional between the lymphoidocyte and the promyelocyte.

granular l., promyelocyte.

leukoblastosis (lu'ko-blas-to'sis). General term for the abnormal proliferation of leukocytes, especially that occurring in myelocytic and lymphocytic leukemia.

leukocidin (lu-ko-si'din) [leukocyte + L. *caedo,* to kill]. A heat-labile substance elaborated by many strains of *Staphylococcus aureus, Streptococcus pyogenes,* and pneumococci which manifests a destructive action on leukocytes, with or without lysis of the cells.

leukocyte (lu'ko-sīt) [leuko- + G. *kytos*, cell]. White blood cell; a type of cell formed in the myelopoietic, lymphoid, and reticular portions of the reticuloendothelial system in various parts of the body, and normally present in those sites and in the circulating blood. L.'s represent three lines of development from primitive elements: myeloid, lymphoid, and monocytic series. On the basis of features observed with various methods of staining, cells of the myeloid series are frequently termed granular l.'s, or granulocytes and consist of three distinct types: neutrophils, eosinophils, and basophils, based on the staining reactions of the cytoplasmic granules.

basophilic l., mast l.; a polymorphonuclear l. characterized by many large, coarse, metachromatic granules that usually fill the cytoplasm and may almost mask the nucleus; unique in that they usually do not occur in increased numbers as the result of acute infectious disease, and their phagocytic qualities are probably not significant.

eosinophilic l., eosinophil; oxyphil (2); a polymorphonuclear l. characterized by many large or prominent, refractile, cytoplasmic granules fairly uniform in size and with nuclei usually larger than those of neutrophils.

granular l., any one of the l.'s of the myeloid series.

mast l., basophilic l.

neutrophilic l., a neutrophilic granulocyte, the most frequent of the polymorphonuclear l.'s, and also the most active phagocyte among the various types of white blood cells.

oxyphilic l., eosinophilic l.

polymorphonuclear l., common term for granulocyte or granular l. because the nucleus is divided into lobes connected by strands of chromatin.

leukocytic (lu-ko-sit'ik). Pertaining to or characterized by leukocytes.

leukocytoblast (lu-ko-si'to-blast) [leukocyte + G. *blastos*, germ]. Any immature cell from which a leukocyte develops.

leukocytogenesis (lu'ko-si-to-jen'ĕ-sis) [leukocyte + G. *genesis*, production]. Formation and development of leukocytes.

leu'kocytol'ysin. Leukolysin; any substance that causes dissolution of leukocytes.

leukocytolysis (lu'ko-si-tol'ĭ-sis) [leukocyte + G. *lysis*, dissolution]. Dissolution or lysis of leukocytes.

leukocytolytic (lu'ko-si-to-lit'ik). Pertaining to, causing, or manifesting leukocytolysis.

leukocytoma (lu'ko-si-to'mah) [leukocyte + G. *-oma*, tumor]. A fairly well circumscribed, nodular, dense accumulation of leukocytes.

leukocytopenia (lu'ko-si-to-pe'nĭ-ah). Leukopenia.

leukocytoplania (lu'ko-si-to-pla'nĭ-ah) [leukocyte + G. *planē*, a wandering]. Movement of leukocytes from the lumens of blood vessels, through serous membranes, or in the tissues.

leukocytopoiesis (lu'ko-si'to-poy-e'sis) [leukocyte + G. *poiēsis*, a making]. Leukopoiesis.

leukocytosis (lu'ko-si'to'sis) [leukocyte + G. *-osis*, condition]. An abnormally large number of leukocytes, as observed in acute infections.

absolute l., an actual increase in the total number of leukocytes in the circulating blood.

eosinophilic l., eosinophilia; a form of relative l. in which the greatest proportionate increase is in the eosinophils.

physiologic l., l. associated with apparently normal situations, not directly related to a pathologic condition.

relative l., an increased proportion of one or more types of leukocytes in the circulating blood, without an actual increase in the total number of white blood cells.

leukocytotactic (lu'ko-si-to-tak'tik). Leukotactic; pertaining to, characterized by, or causing leukocytotaxia.

leukocytotaxia lu-ko-si-to-tak'sĭ-ah) [leukocyte + G. *taxis*, arrangement]. Leukotaxia. **1.** Active ameboid movement of leukocytes, especially the neutrophilic granulocytes, either toward (**positive l.**) or away from (**negative l.**) certain microorganisms as well as various substances frequently formed in inflamed tissue. **2.** The property of attracting or repelling leukocytes.

leukocytotoxin (lu'ko-si-to-tok'sin) [leukocyte + G. *toxikon*, poison]. Leukotoxin; any substance that causes degeneration and necrosis of leukocytes.

leukocyturia (lu'ko-si-tu'rī-ah) [leukocyte + G. *ouron*, urine]. Presence of leukocytes in urine that is recently voided or collected by a catheter.

leukoderma (lu-ko-der'mah). Leukopathia; an absence of pigment, partial or total, in the skin.

l. acquisi'tum centrifu'gum, halo *nevus.*

syphilitic l., a fading of the roseola of secondary syphilis, leaving reticulated depigmented and hyperpigmented areas located chiefly on the sides of the neck.

leukodystrophy (lu-ko-dis'tro-fī) [leuko- + G. *dys*, bad, + *trophē,* nourishment]. Leukoencephalopathy; degeneration of the white matter of the brain characterized by demyelination and glial reaction, probably related to defects of lipid metabolism.

globoid cell l., Krabbe's disease; a metabolic encephalopathy of infancy with rapidly progressive cerebral degeneration, massive loss of myelin, severe astrocytic gliosis, and infiltration of the white matter with characteristic multinucleate globoid cells; metabolically, there is gross deficiency of cerebrosidase (galactosylceramide β-galactosidase); autosomal recessive inheritance.

hereditary cerebral l., Merzbacher-Pelizaeus *disease.*

metachromatic l., a metabolic disorder characterized by myelin loss, accumulation of metachromatic lipids (galactosphingosulfatides) in white matter of central and peripheral nervous systems, a marked excess of sulfatide in white matter and in urine, progressive paralysis and dementia; autosomal recessive inheritance.

leukoedema (lu'ko-ĕ-de'mah). A benign abnormality of the buccal mucosa clinically resembling leukoplakia, consisting of a filmy, opalescent to whitish gray, wrinkled epithelium.

leukoencephalitis (lu'ko-en-sef-ă-li'tis). Encephalitis restricted to the white matter.

    acute epidemic l., Strumpell's disease (2); a disease characterized by acute onset of fever, followed by convulsions, delirium, and coma, and associated with perivascular demyelination and hemorrhagic foci in the CNS.

leukoencephalopathy (lu'ko-en-sef-ă-lop'ă-thĭ) [leuko- + G. *enkephalos*, brain, + *pathos*, suffering]. Leukodystrophy.

leukoerythroblastosis (lu'ko-ĕ-rith'ro-blas-to'sis). Myelophthisic or myelopathic anemia; any anemic condition resulting from space-occupying lesions in the bone marrow; the circulating blood contains immature cells of the granulocytic series and nucleated red blood cells, frequently in numbers disproportionately large in relation to the degree of anemia.

leukoko'ria [leuko- + G. *korē*, pupil]. Reflection from a white mass within the eye, giving the appearance of white pupil.

leukokraurosis (lu'ko-kraw-ro'sis). *Kraurosis* vulvae.

leukolymphosarcoma (lu'ko-lim'fo-sar-ko'mah). Leukosarcoma.

leukol'ysin. Leukocytolysin.

leukoma (lu-ko'mah) [G. whiteness]. A dense, opaque, white opacity of the cornea.

leukomatous (lu-ko'mă-tus). Denoting leukoma.

leukomyelopathy (lu'ko-mi-ĕ-lop'ă-thĭ) [leuko- + G. *myelos*, marrow, + *pathos*, suffering]. Any disease involving the white substance or conducting tracts of the spinal cord.

leukonecrosis (lu'ko-nĕ-kro'sis) [leuko- + G. *nekrōsis*, deadness]. White *gangrene.*

leukonychia (lu-ko-nik'ĭ-ah) [leuko- + G. *onyx*, nail]. Occurrence of white spots or patches under the nails, due to the presence of air bubbles between the nail and its bed.

leukopathia (lu-ko-path'ĭ-ah) [leuko- + G. *pathos*, disease]. Leukoderma.

leukopedesis (lu-ko-pe-de'sis) [leuko- + G. *pēdēsis*, a leaping]. Movement of white blood cells through the walls of capillaries and into the tissues.

leukopenia (lu-ko-pe'nĭ-ah) [leukocyte + G. *penia*, poverty]. Leukocytopenia; any situation in which the total number of leukocytes in the circulating blood is less than normal.

    basophilic l., a decrease in the number of basophilic granulocytes normally present in the circulating blood.

    eosinophilic l., a decrease in the number of eosinophilic granulocytes normally present in the circulating blood.

leukope'nic. Pertaining to leukopenia.

leukoplakia (lu-ko-pla'kĭ-ah) [leuko- + G. *plax, plate*]. Smoker's patches or tongue; a disturbance of keratinization of mucous membrane, variously present as small opalescent patches or as extensive leathery plaques, occasionally ulcerated; may be precancerous.

    l. vul'vae, a patchy white atrophic thickening and keratinization of the vulvar epithelium, often associated with papillary hypertrophy.

leukopoiesis (lu'ko-poy-e'sis) [leuko- + G. *poiēsis*, a making]. Leukocytopoiesis; formation and development of the various types of white blood cells.

leukopoietic (lu'ko-poy-et'ik). Pertaining to or characterized by leukopoiesis.

leukorrhagia (lu-ko-ra'jĭ-ah) [leuko- + G. *rhēgnymi*, to burst forth]. Leukorrhea.

leukorrhea (lu-ko-re'ah) [leuko- + G. *rhoia*, flow]. Leukorrhagia; a discharge from the vagina of white or yellowish viscid fluid containing mucus and pus.

leukosarcoma (lu'ko-sar-ko'mah). Leukolymphosarcoma; a variant of malignant lymphoma in which abnormal immature forms of the lymphocytic series are found in large numbers in the circulating blood in lymphosarcoma.

leukosarcomatosis (lu'ko-sar'ko-mă-to'sis). A condition characterized by numerous widespread nodules or masses of lymphosarcoma, and the presence of similar cells in the circulating blood.

leukosis (lu-ko'sis). Abnormal proliferation of one or more of the leukopoietic tissues.

leukotac'tic. Leukocytotactic.

leukotax'ia. Leukocytotaxia.

leukotax'ine. A cell-free nitrogenous material prepared from injured, acutely degenerating tissue and from inflammatory exudates.

leukotax'is. Leukocytotaxia.

leukotic (lu-kot'ik). Pertaining to, characterized by, or manifesting leukosis.

leukotomy (lu-kot'o-mĭ) [leuko- + G. *tomē*, a cutting]. Incision into the white matter of the frontal lobe of the brain.

leukotox'in. Leukocytotoxin.

leukotrichia (lu-ko-trik'ĭ-ah) [leuko- + G. *thrix*, hair]. Whiteness of the hair.

leukotrienes (lu-ko-tri'ĕnz). Products of arachidonic acid metabolism with postulated physiologic activity, such as mediators of inflammation and roles in allergic reactions.

levallorphan tartrate (lev-al-or'fan). The *N*-allyl analogue of levorphanol, antagonistic to the actions of narcotic analgesics; used in the treatment of respiratory depression due to overdosage of narcotics.

levarter'enol. Norepinephrine.

leva'tor [L. a lifter]. **1.** A surgical instrument for prying up the depressed part in a fracture of the skull. **2.** One of several muscles whose action is to raise the part into which it is inserted.

levo- [L. *laevus*, left]. Prefix denoting left, toward or on the left side.

le'vocar'dia [levo- + G. *kardia*, heart]. Situs inversus of the viscera but with the heart normally situated on the left.

levodopa (le-vo-do'pah). L-Dopa; the biologically active form of dopa; an antiparkinsonian agent.

levoduction (le-vo-duk'shun) [levo- + L. *duco*, pp. *ductus*, to lead]. A rotation of one or both eyes to the left.

levorotation (le'vo-ro-ta'shun) [levo- + L. *rotare*, to turn]. **1.** A turning or twisting to the left; in particular, the counterclockwise twist given the plane of plane-polarized light by solutions of certain optically active substances. **2.** Sinistrotorsion.

le'voro'tatory. Denoting levorotation, or certain crystals or solutions capable of doing so. As a chemical prefix, usually abbreviated *l*-.

levorphanol tartrate (lev-orf'ă-nol). L-3 -Hydroxy- *N*-methylmorphinan tartrate dihydrate; an analgesic similar in action to morphine.

levotorsion (le-vo-tor'shun) [levo- + L. *torsio*, a twisting]. **1.** Sinistrotorsion. **2.** Extorsion of left eye or intorsion of right eye.

levoversion (le-vo-ver'zhun) [levo- + L. *verto*, pp. *versus*, to turn]. **1.** A turning toward the left. **2.** Rotation of both eyes to the left.

-lexis, -lexy [G. *legein, lexai*, to speak]. Suffix that properly relates to speech, although often confused with -legia (L. *legere*, to read).

LH Luteinizing *hormone.*

LH/FSH-RF Luteinizing hormone/follicle-stimulating hormone-releasing *factor.*

LH-RF Luteinizing hormone-releasing *factor.*

LH-RH Luteinizing hormone-releasing *hormone.*

Li Lithium.

libidinous (lǐ-bid'ǐ-nus) [L. *libidinosus*, pleasure, desire, fr. *libet*, it pleases]. Lascivious; erotic; invested with or arousing sexual desire or energy.

libido (lǐ-be'do) [L. lust]. Conscious or unconscious sexual desire.

lice (lis). Plural of !ouse.

lichen (li'ken) [G. *leichēn*]. A discrete flat papule or an aggregate of papules giving a patterned configuration resembling lichens growing on rocks.

   l. myxedemato'sus, a lichenoid eruption of papules or plaques of mucinous edema due to deposit of acid mucopolysaccharides in the skin, in the absence of endocrine disease.

   l. niti'dus, small, minute, asymptomatic, whitish or pinkish flat-topped papules; may coexist with l. planus.

   l. pla'nus, l. ruber planus; eruption of flat-topped, shiny, violaceous papules on flexor surfaces, male genitalia, and buccal mucosa; may form linear groups.

   l. ru'ber pla'nus, l. planus.

   l. sclero'sus et atro'phicus, Hallopeau's disease (3); an eruption consisting of white atrophic papules, discrete or confluent, that may contain a central depression or a black keratotic plug.

   l. scrofuloso'rum, papular *tuberculid.*

   l. sim'plex, a small, intensely pruritic, lichenified area in the skin.

   l. stria'tus, a self-limited papular eruption, occurring primarily in children, in which lesions are arranged in linear groups and usually occur on one extremity.

   tropical l., l. trop'icus, *miliaria* rubra.

   l. urtica'tus, papular urticaria; a type of urticaria occurring in children, in which the lesions are papules, or small papules and vesicles.

lichenification (li'ken-if-ĭ-ka'shun) [lichen + L. *facio*, to make]. Leathery induration and thickening of the skin with hyperkeratosis, due to a chronic inflammation caused by scratching or long-continued irritation.

lichenoid (li'ken-oyd). **1.** Resembling lichen. **2.** Accentuation of normal skin markings observed in cases of chronic eczema.

lidocaine hydrochloride (li'do-kān). A local anesthetic possessing pronounced antiarrhythmic and anticonvulsant properties.

lie. The relation which the long axis of the fetus bears to that of the mother.

   longitudinal l., that relationship in which the long axis of the fetus is longitudinal and roughly parallel to the long axis of the mother.

   oblique l., that relationship in which the fetal axis crosses the maternal axis at an angle other than a right angle.

   transverse l., that relationship in which the long axis of the fetus is transverse or at right angles to that of the mother.

lie detector. Polygraph (2).

lien-, lieno- [L. *lien*, spleen]. Combining form relating to the spleen. See splen-; spleno-.

li'en [L.] [NA]. Spleen.

   l. accesso'rius [NA], accessory spleen; one of the small globular masses of splenic tissue occasionally found in the area of the spleen, in one of the peritoneal folds, or elsewhere.

   l. mo'bilis, floating *spleen.*

lienal (li'ē-nal). Splenic.

lienteric (li-en-tēr'ik). Relating to, or marked by, lientery.

lientery (li'en-tēr-ĭ) [G. *leienteria*, fr. *leios*, smooth, + *enteron*, intestine]. Passage of undigested food in the stools.

life [A.S. *lif*]. **1.** Vitality, the essential condition of being alive; the state of existence characterized by active metabolism. **2.** The existence of organisms.

life-span. 1. The duration of existence of an individual. **2.** The normal or average duration of existence of a given species.

ligament (lig'ă-ment) [L. *ligamentum*, a band]. Ligamentum.

   accessory l.'s, l.'s about a joint, in addition to the articular capsule.

   alveolodental l., periodontal l.

   annular l., one of a number of l.'s encircling various parts, as of the stapes, radius, and trachea.

arcuate l., *ligamentum* arcuatum.

broad l. of the uterus, *ligamentum* latum uteri.

capsular l., thickened portions of the fibrous membrane of an articular capsule.

cardinal l., cervical l. of the uterus.

cervical l. of the uterus, cardinal l.; a fibrous band attached to the uterine cervix and the vault of the lateral fornix of the vagina, continuous with the tissue ensheathing the pelvic vessels.

check l.'s of eyeball, expansions of the sheaths of the medial and lateral rectus muscles of the eyeball which are attached, respectively, to the lacrimal bone; they prevent overaction of these muscles.

collateral l.'s, l.'s on either side of, and acting as a radius of movement of, a hinge joint, as of the elbow, knee, and wrist.

coracoclavicular l., *ligamentum* coracoclaviculare.

costoclavicular l., *ligamentum* costoclaviculare.

costotransverse l., *ligamentum* costotranversarium.

cystoduodenal l., a peritoneal fold that sometimes passes from the gallbladder to the first part of the duodenum.

deltoid l., *ligamentum* deltoideum.

diaphragmatic l. of the mesonephros, urogenital mesentery; that segment of the urogenital ridge which extends from the mesonephros to the diaphragm.

extracapsular l.'s, *ligamenta* extracapsularia.

falciform l., *processus* falciformis.

falciform l. of liver, *ligamentum* falciforme hepatis.

glenohumeral l.'s, *ligamenta* glenohumeralia.

l. of head of femur, *ligamentum* capitis femoris.

iliofemoral l., *ligamentum* iliofemorale.

iliotrochanteric l., see *ligamentum* iliofemorale.

inguinal l., *ligamentum* inguinale.

intracapsular l.'s, *ligamentum* intracapsularia.

lacunar l., *ligamentum* lacunare.

longitudinal l., *ligamentum* longitudinale.

lumbocostal l., *ligamentum* lumbocostale.

medial l., (1) *ligamentum* deltoideum; (2) *ligamentum* mediale.

meniscofemoral l., *ligamentum* meniscofemorale.

nuchal l., *ligamentum* nuchae.

patellar l., *ligamentum* patellae.

pectineal l., *ligamentum* pectineale.

periodontal l., alveolodental l.; periodontal membrane; connective tissue that surrounds the tooth root and attaches it to its bony socket.

phrenicocolic l., *ligamentum* phrenicocolicum.

popliteal l., *ligamentum* popliteum.

Poupart's l., *ligamentum* inguinale.

pulmonary l., *ligamentum* pulmonale.

radiate l. of rib, *ligamentum* capitis costae radiatum.

reflex l., *ligamentum* reflexum.

rhomboid l., *ligamentum* costoclaviculare.

round l., *ligamentum* capitis femoris, *ligamentum* teres hepatis and uteri.

serous l., one of a number of peritoneal folds attaching certain of the viscera to the abdominal wall or to each other.

spring l., a dense fibroelastic l. extending from the calcaneus to the navicular bone to support the head of the talus.

stellate l., *ligamentum* capitis costae radiatum.

sternocostal l., *ligamentum* sternocostale.

suspensory l. of axilla, continuation of the clavipectoral fascia downward to attach to the axillary fascia; maintains the characteristic hollow of the armpit.

suspensory l.'s of breast, *ligamenta* suspensoria mammae.

suspensory l. of eyeball, a thickening of the inferior part of the bulbar sheath which supports the eye within the orbit.

suspensory l. of lens, ciliary zonule.

suspensory l. of ovary, *ligament* suspensorium ovarii.

sutural l., a delicate membrane binding the bones at the cranial sutures.

synovial l., one of the large synovial folds in a joint.

transverse l. of knee, *ligamentum* transversum genus.

transverse l. of perineum, *ligamentum* transversum perinei.

trapezoid l., *ligamentum* trapezoideum.

umbilical l., *ligamentum* umbilicale.

vesicouterine l., a peritoneal fold extending from the uterus to the posterior portion of the bladder.

vocal l., *ligamentum* vocale.

Y-shaped l., *ligamentum* iliofemorale.

ligamentopexy (lig′ă-men-to-pek-sī) [ligament + G. *pēxis*, fixation]. Shortening of any ligament of the uterus.

ligamentous (lig-ă-men′tus). Relating to or of the form or structure of a ligament.

ligamentum, pl. **ligamenta** (lig-ă-men′tum, -men′tah) [L. a band, tie] [NA]Ligament. **1.** A band or sheet of fibrous tissue connecting two or more bones, cartilages, or other structures, or serving as support for fasciae or muscles. **2.** A fold of peritoneum supporting any of the abdominal viscera. **3.** The cordlike remains of a fetal vessel or other structure that has lost its original lumen.

l. arcua′tum latera′le [NA], arcuate ligament; (1) lateral, a thickening of the fascia of the quadratus lumborum muscle, between the transverse process of the first lumbar vertebra and the twelfth rib on either side, that gives attachment to a portion of the diaphragm; (2) medial, a tendinous thickening of the psoas fascia that extends from the body of the first lumbar vertebra to its transverse process on either side; a portion of the diaphragm arises from it; (3) median, a tendinous connection between the crura of the diaphragm that arches in front on the aorta.

l. cap′itis cos′tae radia′tum [NA], radiate ligament of rib; stellate ligament; the ligament connecting the head of each rib to the bodies of the two vertebrae with which it articulates.

l. cap'itis femo'ris [NA], ligament of head of femur; round ligament of femur; a flattened ligament that passes from the fovea in the head of the femur to the borders of the acetabular notch.

l. coracoacromia'le [NA], coracoacromial ligament; the heavy arched fibrous band that passes between the coracoid process and the acromion above the shoulder joint.

l. coracoclavicula're [NA], coracoclavicular ligament; the strong ligament that unites the clavicle to the coracoid process.

l. costoclavicula're [NA], costoclavicular or rhomboid ligament; the ligament that connects the first rib and the clavicle near its sternal end.

l. costotransversa'rium [NA], costotransverse ligament; (1) middle, the ligament that connects the dorsal aspect of the neck of a rib to the ventral aspect of the corresponding transverse process; (2) lateral, the short quadrangular ligament that passes across behind the costotransverse joint from the tip of the transverse process to the posterior surface of the neck of the rib; (3) superior, the fibrous band that extends upward from the neck of a rib to the transverse process of the next higher vertebra.

ligamen'ta crucia'ta ge'nus [NA], cruciate ligaments of knee; anterior and posterior l.'s that pass from the intercondylar area of the tibia to the intercondylar fossa of the femur.

l. deltoi'deum [NA], deltoid ligament; l. mediale (1); medial ligament (1); a ligament consisting of four bands which pass downward from the medial malleolus of the tibia to the tarsal bones.

ligamen'ta extracapsula'ria [NA], extracapsular ligaments; ligaments associated with a synovial joint but separate from and external to its articular capsule.

l. falcifor'me hep'atis [NA], falciform ligament of liver; a crescentic fold of peritoneum extending to the surface of the liver from the diaphragm and anterior abdominal wall.

ligamen'ta glenohumera'lia [NA], glenohumeral ligaments; three fibrous bands that reinforce the anterior part of the articular capsule of the shoulder joint; they are attached to the margin of the glenoid cavity of the scapula and to the anatomic neck of the humerus.

l. iliofemora'le [NA], iliofemoral ligament; Y-shaped ligament; a triangular ligament attached by its apex to the anterior inferior spine of the ilium and rim of the acetabulum, and by its base to the anterior intertrochanteric line of the femur; the strong medial band is attached to the lower part of the intertrochanteric line; the strong lateral part (iliotrochanteric ligament) is fixed to the tubercle at the upper part of this line.

l. inguina'le [NA], inguinal ligament; Poupart's ligament; a fibrous band formed by the inferior border of the aponeurosis of the external oblique

that extends from the anterior superior spine of the ilium to the pubic tubercle.

ligamenta intracapsula'ria [NA], intracapsular ligaments; ligaments located within and separate from the articular capsule of a synovial joint.

l. lacuna're [NA], lacunar ligament; a curved fibrous band that passes horizontally backward from the medial end of the inguinal ligament to the pectineal line, to form the medial boundary of the femoral ring.

l. la'tum u'teri [NA], broad ligament of uterus; the peritoneal fold passing from the lateral margin of the uterus to the wall of the pelvis on either side.

l. longitudin'ale [NA], longitudinal ligament; one of two extensive fibrous bands (anterior and posterior) that interconnect the bodies of the vertebrae by attachment to the intervertebral disks.

l. lumbocosta'le [NA], lumbocostal ligament; a strong band that unites the twelfth rib with the tips of the transverse processes of the first and second lumbar vertebrae.

l. media'le [NA], medial ligament (2); (1) l. deltoideum; (2) the bundle of fibers strengthening the medial part of the articular capsule of the temporomandibular joint.

l. meniscofemora'le [NA], meniscofemoral ligament; one of two bands (anterior and posterior) that extend upward from the lateral meniscus, pass anterior to and posterior to the posterior cruciate ligament, and reach the medial condyle of the femur.

l. nu'chae [NA], nuchal ligament; a sagittal band at the back of the neck, extending from the external occipital protuberance to the posterior border of the foramen magnum, cranially, and to the seventh cervical spinous process, caudally.

l. patel'lae [NA], patellar ligament; a strong flattened fibrous band passing from the apex and adjoining margins of the patella to the tuberosity of the tibia.

l. pectinea'le [NA], pectineal ligament; a thick, strong fibrous band that passes laterally from the lacunar ligament along the pectineal line of the pubis.

l. phrenicocol'icum [NA], phrenicocolic ligament; a triangular fold of peritoneum attached to the left flexure of the colon and to the diaphragm, on which rests the inferior extremity of the spleen.

l. poplite'um [NA], popliteal ligament; (1) arcuate, a broad fibrous band attached above to the lateral condyle of the femur and passing medially and downward in the posterior part of the capsule of the knee joint, arching over the tendon of the popliteus muscle; (2) oblique, a fibrous band that extends across the back of the knee from the insertion of the semimembranosus on the medial condyle of the tibia to the lateral condyle of the upper femur.

l. pulmona'le [NA], pulmonary ligament; the reflection of pleura from the mediastinum to the lung which continues as a two-layered fold below the root of the lung.

l. reflex'um [NA], reflex ligament; a triangular fibrous band extending from the aponeurosis of the external oblique to the pubic tubercle of the opposite side.

l. sternocosta'le [NA], sternocostal ligament; one of the two sets (interarticular and radiate) of chondrosternal ligaments connecting the rib cartilages and the sternum.

ligamen'ta suspenso'ria mam'mae [NA], suspensory ligaments of breast; well developed retinacula cutis that extend from the overlying skin to the fibrous stroma of the mammary gland.

l. suspenso'rium ova'rii [NA], suspensory ligament of ovary; a band of peritoneum that extends upward from the upper pole of the ovary and contains the ovarian vessels and ovarian plexus of nerves.

l. te'res hep'atis [NA], round ligament of liver, the remains of the umbilical vein.

l. te'res u'teri [NA], round ligament of uterus; a fibromuscular band attached to the uterus on either side in front of and below the opening of the fallopian tube and passing through the inguinal canal to the labium majus.

l. transver'sum ge'nus [NA], transverse ligament of knee; a transverse band that passes between the lateral and medial menisci in the anterior part of the knee joint.

l. transver'sum perine'i [NA], transverse ligament of perineum; the thickened anterior border of the urogenital diaphragm, formed by the fusion of its two fascial layers.

l. trapezoi'deum [NA], trapezoid ligament; the lateral part of the coracoclavicular ligament that attaches to the trapezoid line of the clavicle.

l. umbilica'le [NA], umbilical ligament; **(1)** median, the obliterated umbilical artery that persists as a fibrous cord passing upward alongside the bladder to the umbilicus; **(2)** middle, the remnant of the urachus, persisting as a midline fibrous cord between the apex of the bladder and the umbilicus.

l. voca'le [NA], vocal ligament; the band that extends on either side from the thyroid cartilage to the vocal process of the arytenoid cartilage.

ligand (lig'and, li'gand) [L. *ligo,* to bind]. **1.** An organic molecule attached to a central metal ion by multiple coordination bonds. **2.** An organic molecule attached to a tracer element.

li'gase. Generic term for enzymes catalyzing the joining of two molecules coupled with the breakdown of a pyrophosphate bond in ATP or a similar compound.

li'gate [L. *ligo,* pp. *-atus,* to bind]. To apply a ligature.

ligation (li-ga'shun) [L. *ligatio,* fr. *ligo,* to bind]. Application of a ligature.

tubal l., interruption of the continuity of the oviducts, by cutting, cautery, or a device, to prevent future conception.

ligature (lig'a-chūr) [L. *ligatura,* a band or tie]. **1.** A thread, wire, etc. tied tightly around a structure to constrict it. **2.** A wire or other material used to secure an orthodontic attachment or tooth to an archwire.

light (līt) [A.S. *leōht*]. That portion of electromagnetic radiations to which the retina is sensitive.

polarized l., l. in which, as a result of reflection or transmission through certain media, the vibrations are all in one plane, transverse to the ray, instead of in all planes.

Wood's l., ultraviolet l. produced by Wood's lamp.

light'ening. The feeling of decreased abdominal distention during the later weeks of pregnancy following the descent of the fetal head into the pelvic inlet.

limb [A.S. *lim*]. **1.** An extremity; a member; an arm or leg. **2.** A segment of any jointed structure.

inferior l., pelvic l., *membrum* inferius.

phantom l., pseudesthesia (3); the sensation that an amputated l. is still present, often associated with painful paresthesia.

superior l., thoracic l., *membrum* superius.

lim'bic. Relating to a limbus or to the limbic *system.*

limbus, pl. **limbi** (lim'bus, lim'bi) [L. a border] [NA]. The edge, border, or fringe of a part.

l. cor'neae [NA], corneal margin; sclerocorneal junction; the margin of the cornea overlapped by the sclera.

lime (līm). **1.** Fruit of the l. tree, *Citrus medica* (family Rutaceae). **2.** Calx (1); calcium oxide; CaO; an alkaline earth which on exposure to the atmosphere it becomes converted into calcium hydrate and calcium carbonate.

limen, pl. **limina** (li'men, lim'ĭ-nah) [L.] [NA]. Threshold (3); entrance; the external opening of a canal.

l. in'sulae [NA], the band of transition between the anterior portion of the gray matter of the insula and the anterior perforated substance; formed by a narrow strip of olfactory cortex.

l. na'si [NA], a ridge marking the boundary between the nasal cavity proper and the vestibule.

limes (L) (li'mēz) [L.]. A boundary, limit, or threshold.

liminal (lim'ĭ-nal) [L. *limen* (*limin-*), a threshold]. **1.** Pertaining to a threshold. **2.** Pertaining to a stimulus just strong enough to excite a tissue.

linc'ture, linc'tus [L. *lingo,* pp. *linctus,* to lick]. An electuary or a confection; originally a medical preparation taken by licking.

line [L. *linea,* a linen thread, a string]. A mark, strip, or streak. See also linea.

absorption l.'s, dark l.'s in the solar spectrum due to the fact that rays passing from an incandescent body through a cooler medium are absorbed by elements in that medium.

anocutaneous l., *linea* anocutanea.

base l., a l. corresponding to the base of the skull, passing from the infraorbital ridge to the midline of the occiput, cutting the external auditory meatus.

Beau's l.'s, transverse depressions on the fingernails following severe febrile disease, malnutrition, trauma, coronary occlusion, etc.

blood l., a l. of descent or ancestry of several generations.

blue l., a bluish l. along the free border of the gums, occurring in chronic heavy metal poisoning.

cell l., in tissue culture, the cells growing in the first or later subculture from a primary culture.

cement l., the refractile boundary of an osteon or interstitial lamellar system in compact bone.

cervical l., a continuous anatomical irregular curved l. marking the cervical end of the crown of a tooth.

Clapton's l., a greenish discoloration of the dental margin of the gums in cases of chronic copper poisoning.

cleavage l.'s, linear clefts in the skin indicating the special distribution of the subcutaneous fibrous connective tissue bundles.

l. of demarcation, a zone of inflammatory reaction separating a gangrenous area from healthy tissue.

developmental l.'s, developmental *grooves.*

epiphysial l., *linea epiphysialis.*

l. of fixation, a l. joining the object (or point of fixation) with the fovea and passing through the nodal point.

gum l., the position of the margin of the gingiva in relation to the teeth in the dental arch.

Harris l.'s, transverse l.'s seen by x-ray near the epiphyses of the long bones.

Hilton's white l., white l. of anal canal.

His l., a l. extending from the tip of the anterior nasal spine to the hindmost point on the posterior margin of the foramen magnum, dividing the face into an upper and a lower or dental part.

iliopectineal l., *linea terminalis.*

intertrochanteric l., *linea intertrochanterica.*

isoelectric l., the base line of the electrocardiogram.

Kerley-B l.'s, fine horizontal l.'s above the costophrenic angle in the chest x-ray; seen in patients with pulmonary hypertension secondary to mitral stenosis and thought to be due to distention of interlobular lymphatics by edema.

lead l., an irregular dark deposit in the gums, occurring in lead poisoning, which tends to accumulate in areas of chronic inflammation.

M l., M band; a fine l. in the center of the A band in the myofibrils of striated muscle fibers.

mamillary l., nipple l.; a perpendicular l. passing through the nipple on either side.

mammary l., a transverse l. drawn between the two nipples.

median l., (1) anterior: the l. of intersection of the midsagittal plane with the anterior surface of the body; (2) posterior: the l. of intersection of the midsagittal plane with the posterior surface of the body.

milk l., mammary *ridge.*

Nélaton's l., a l. drawn from the anterior superior iliac spine to the tuberosity of the ischium; normally the great trochanter lies in this l., but in cases of iliac dislocation of the hip or fracture of the neck of the femur the trochanter is felt above it.

nipple l., mammillary l.

pectinate l., *linea anocutanea.*

popliteal l., *linea musculi solei.*

Poupart's l., a perpendicular l. passing through the center of the inguinal ligament on either side; it marks off the hypochondriac, lumbar, and iliac from the epigastric, umbilical, and hypogastric regions, respectively.

semilunar l., *linea semilunaris.*

Shenton's l., a curved l. or arch, formed by the top of the obturator foramen and the inner side of the neck of the femur, seen in a radiograph of the normal joint; it is disturbed in congenital dislocation or hip fracture.

Spigelius l., *linea semilunaris.*

sternal l., *linea sternalis.*

terminal l., *linea terminalis.*

vibrating l., the imaginary l. across the posterior part of the palate, marking the division between the movable and immovable tissues.

white l., *linea alba.*

white l. of anal canal, Hilton's white l.; a bluish pink zone in the mucosa of the anal canal below the pectinate l. at the interval between the subcutaneous part of the external sphincter and the lower border of the internal sphincter.

Z l., Z band; one of the cross striations in a muscle fiber which bisects the I band in the myofibrils and occurs at the limits of the sarcomere.

linea, gen. and pl. **lineae** (lin′e-ah, lin′e-e) [L.] [NA]. A line; a long narrow mark, strip, or streak distinguished from the adjacent tissues by color, texture, or elevation.

l. al′ba [NA], white line; a fibrous band running vertically the entire length of the center of the anterior abdominal wall, receiving the attachments of the oblique and transverse abdominal muscles.

l. anocuta′nea [NA], anocutaneous or pectinate line; the line between the simple columnar epithelium of the rectum and the stratified epithelium of the anal canal.

lin′eae atroph′icae, *striae* cutis distensae.

l. epiphysia′lis [NA], epiphysial line; the line of junction of the epiphysis and diaphysis of a long bone where growth in length occurs.

l. intertrochanter′ica [NA], intertrochanteric or spiral line; a rough line that separates the neck and shaft of the femur anteriorly.

l. ni′gra, the l. alba in pregnancy, which then becomes pigmented.

l. semiluna'ris [NA], semilunar line; Spigelius line; the slight groove in the external abdominal wall parallel to the lateral edge of the rectus sheath.

l. sterna'lis [NA], sternal line; a vertical line corresponding to the lateral margin of the sternum.

l. termina'lis [NA], terminal or iliopectineal line; an oblique ridge on the inner surface of the ilium and continued on the pubis; separates the true from the false pelvis.

linear (lin'e-ar). Pertaining to or resembling a line.

lingua, gen. and pl. **linguae** (ling'gwah, ling'gwe) [L. tongue] [NA]. **1.** Glossa; tongue; a mobile mass of muscular tissue covered with mucous membrane, occupying the cavity of the mouth, forming part of its floor, bearing the organ of taste, and assisting in mastication, deglutition, and articulation. **2.** Any tongue-like anatomical structure.

l. geograph'ica, geographical *tongue.*

l. ni'gra, black *tongue.*

l. plica'ta, furrowed *tongue.*

lingual (ling'gwal). **1.** Glossal; relating to the tongue or any tongue-like part. **2.** Next to or toward the tongue.

Linguatula (ling-gwat'u-lah) [L. *linguatulus,* tongued]. A genus of endoparasitic bloodsucking arthropods (family Linguatulidae), commonly known as tongue worms; found in lungs or air passages of a variety of vertebrates, including man, but chiefly in animals that serve as prey.

linguatuliasis (ling-gwat'u-li'ǎ-sis). Infection with *Linguatula.*

linguiform (ling'gwĭ-form). Tongue-shaped

lingula, pl. **lingulae** (ling'gu-lah, -le) [L. dim. of *lingua,* tongue] [NA]. Any of several tongue-shaped processes.

ling'ular. Pertaining to any lingula.

lingulectomy (ling'u-lek'to-mĭ). **1.** Glossectomy. **2.** Excision of the lingular portion of the left upper lobe of the lung.

linguo- [L. *lingua,* tongue]. Combining form relating to the tongue.

linguoclusion (ling-gwo-klu'zhun). Lingual occlusion (1); displacement of a tooth toward the interior of the dental arch, or toward the tongue.

linguopapillitis (ling'gwo-pap-ĭ-li'tis). Small painful ulcers involving the papillae on the tongue margins.

linguoversion (ling'gwo-ver-zhun). Malposition of a tooth lingual to the normal position.

liniment (lin'ĭ-ment) [L. fr. *lino,* to smear]. A liquid preparation for external application or application to the gums, frequently applied by friction to the skin; used as counterirritants, rubefacients, anodynes, or cleansing agents.

linitis (lĭ-ni'tis, li-ni'tis) [G. *linon,* flax, linen cloth, + *-itis,* inflammation]. Inflammation of cellular tissue, specifically of the perivascular tissue of the stomach.

l. plas'tica, originally believed to be an inflammatory condition, but now recognized to be due to infiltrating scirrhous carcinoma causing extensive thickening of the wall of the stomach.

linkage (lingk'ij). **1.** Chemical covalent bond. **2.** Association of genes in inheritance, due to the fact that they are in the same chromosome pair; may be between genes on the same chromosome (cis-l.) or on opposite chromosomes (trans-l.) of a homologous pair.

sex l., a form of inheritance related to sex as a result of the gene concerned being carried on the X chromosome.

linole'ic acid [L. *linum,* flax, + *oleum,* oil]. $CH_3(CH_2)_3(CH_2CH=CH)_2(CH_2)_7COOH$; an unsaturated fatty acid essential in nutrition.

linolen'ic acid. $CH_3(CH_2CH=CH)_3(CH_2)_7COOH$; an unsaturated fatty acid essential in nutrition.

lip-. See lipo-.

lip [A.S. *lippa*]. **1.** Labium oris; one of the two muscular folds with an outer mucosa having a stratified squamous epithelial surface layer which bound the mouth anteriorly. **2.** Any liplike structure bounding a cavity or groove. See also labium; labrum.

cleft l., harelip; cheiloschisis; chiloschisis; a congenital facial deformity of the l. (usually the upper) due to a mesodermal deficiency or failure of merging in one or more of the embryologic processes that form the l.; frequently associated with cleft alveolus and cleft palate.

Hapsburg l., see Hapsburg *jaw.*

large pudendal l., *labium* majus pudendi.

small pudendal l., *labium* minus pudendi.

lip'ase. Any fat-splitting or lipolytic enzyme that cleaves a fatty acid residue from the glycerol residue in a neutral fat or a phospholipid.

lipectomy (lip-ek'to-mĭ) [lipo- + G. *ektomē,* excision]. Surgical removal of fatty tissue, as in cases of adiposity.

lipedema (lip-ě-de'mah) [lipo + G. *oidēma,* swelling]. Chronic swelling, usually of the lower extremities, caused by the widespread, even distribution of subcutaneous fat and fluid.

lipemia (lip-e'mĭ-ah) [lipid + G. *haima,* blood]. Presence of an abnormally large amount of lipids in the circulating blood. Also called hyperlipemia; hyperlipidemia; hyperlipoidemia; lipidemia; lipoidemia.

alimentary l., postprandial l., relatively transient l. occurring after the ingestion of foods with a large content of fat.

l. retina'lis, a creamy appearance of the retinal blood vessels when the lipoids of the blood are over 5%.

lipem'ic. Relating to lipemia.

lip'id [G. *lipos,* fat]. "Fat-soluble," denoting substances extracted from animal or vegetable cells by nonpolar or "fat" solvents; an operational term describing a solubility characteristic, not a chemical substance.

lipidemia (lip-ĭ-de'mĭ-ah). Lipemia.

lipidosis, pl. **lipidoses** (lip-ĭ-do'sis, -sēz) [lipid + G. -osis, condition]. Inborn or acquired disorder of lipid metabolism.

cerebral l., cerebral *sphingolipidosis.*
cerebroside l., Gaucher's *disease.*
glycolipid l., Fabry's *disease.*
sphingomyelin l., Niemann-Pick *disease.*

lipo-, lip- [G. *lipos,* fat]. Combining forms relating to fat or lipid.

lipoarthritis (lip'o-ar-thri'tis) [lipo- + arthritis]. Inflammation of the periarticular fatty tissues of the knee.

lip'oate. A salt or ester of lipoic acid.

lipoatrophy (lip-o-at'ro-fī) [G. *lipos,* fat + *a-,* priv. + *trophe,* nourishment]. Loss of subcutaneous fat.

lip'oblast [lipo- + G. *blastos,* germ]. An embryonic fat cell.

lip'oblasto'ma. 1. Liposarcoma. **2.** A tumor composed of embryonal fat cells separated into distinct lobules, occurring usually in infants.

lipocele (lip-o-sēl) [lipo- + G. *kēlē,* tumor]. Adipocele; presence of fatty tissue, without intestine, in a hernia sac.

lipoceratous (lip-o-sēr'ă-tus). Adipoceratous.

lipocere (lip'o-sēr) [lipo- + L. *cera,* wax]. Adipocere.

lipochondrodystrophy (lip'o-kon'dro-dis'tro-fī). Hurler's *syndrome.*

lipochrome (lip'o-krōm) [lipo- + G. *chroma,* color]. **1.** A pigmented lipid. **2.** Yellow pigments that seem to be identical to carotene and xanthophyll, and frequently found in the serum, skin, adrenal cortex, corpus luteum, and arteriosclerotic plaques, as well as in the liver, spleen, and adipose tissue.

lipocrit (lip'o-krit) [lipo- + G. *krinō,* to separate]. An apparatus and procedure for separating and volumetrically analyzing the amount of lipid in blood or other body fluid.

lipocyte (lip'o-sīt) [lipo- + G. *kytos,* cell]. A fat-storing stellate cell in the perisinusoidal space in the liver.

lipodermoid (lip-o-der'moyd) [lipo- + dermoid]. A congenital, yellowish-white, fatty, benighn tumor located subconjunctivally.

lipodystrophy (lī-po-dis'tro-fī) [lipo- + G. *dys-,* bad, difficult, + *trophe,* nourishment]. Defective metabolism of fat.

congenital total l., l. characterized by almost complete lack of subcutaneous fat, accelerated rate of growth and skeletal development during the first 3 to 4 years of life, muscular hypertrophy, cardiac enlargement, hepatosplenomegaly, hypertrichosis, renal enlargement, hyperlipemia, and hypermetabolism; probably autosomal recessive inheritance.

intestinal l., Whipple's *disease.*

progressive l., Barraquer's disease; a condition characterized by a complete loss of the subcutaneous fat of the upper part of the torso, the arms, neck, and face, sometimes with an increase of fat in the tissues about and below the pelvis.

lipofibroma (lip'o-fi-bro'mah). A benign neoplasm of fibrous connective tissue, with conspicuous numbers of adipose cells.

lipofuscin (lip-o-fus'in). Brown pigment granules representing lipid-containing residues of lysosomal digestion.

lipofuscinosis lip'o-fus-ĭ-no'sis). Abnormal storage of any one of a group of fatty pigments.

ceroid l., late juvenile type of cerebral *sphingolipidosis.*

lipogenesis (lip'o-jen'ĕ-sis) [lipo- + G. *genesis,* production]. Adipogenesis; production of fat, either fatty degeneration or fatty infiltration; also applied to the normal deposition of fat or to the conversion of carbohydrate or protein to fat.

lipogenic (lip-o-jen'ik). Adipogenic; adipogenous; lipogenous; relating to lipogenesis.

lipogenous (lī-poj'ĕ-nus). Lipogenic.

lipogranuloma (lip'o-gran-u-lo'mah). Eleoma; a nodule or focus of granulomatous inflammation (usually of the foreign-body type) in association with lipid material deposited in tissues.

lip'ogran'ulomato'sis. 1. The presence of lipogranulomas. **2.** The local inflammatory reaction to necrosis of adipose tissue.

disseminated l., Farber's syndrome; a form of mucolipidosis developing soon after birth, characterized by swollen joints, subcutaneous nodules, lymphadenopathy, and infiltration of affected cells by PAS-positive lipid.

lipo'ic acid. Factor II (2); 6,8-dithio-*n*-octanoic acid; functions as the amide (lipoamide) in the oxidized (−S−S−) form in the transfer of "active aldehyde," the two-carbon fragment resulting from decarboxylation of pyruvate, from α-hydroxyethylthiamin pyrophosphate to acetyl-CoA, itself being reduced (to the −SH HS−form) in the process.

lipoid (lip'oyd) [lipo- + G. *eidos,* appearance]. Adipoid. **1.** Resembling fat. **2.** Former term for lipid.

lipoidemia (lip'oy-de'mĭ-ah). Lipemia.

lipoidosis (lip-oy-do'sis). Presence of anisotropic lipoids in the cells.

lipolysis (lī-pol'ĭ-sis) [lipo- + G. *lysis,* dissolution]. The splitting up (hydrolysis), or chemical decomposition, of fat.

lipolytic (lip-o-lit'ik). Relating to or causing lipolysis.

lipoma (lī-po'mah) [lipo- + G. *-oma,* tumor]. A benign neoplasm of adipose tissue, comprised of mature fat cells.

lipomatoid (lī-po'mă-toyd) Resembling a lipoma, said of accumulations of adipose tissue not thought to be neoplastic.

lipomatosis (lip'o-mă-to'sis). Adiposis.

lipo'matous. Pertaining to, manifesting the features of, or characterized by the presence of a lipoma.

lipomeningocele (lip'o-mĕ-ning'go-sēl) [lipo- + G. *mēninx,* membrane, + *kēlē,* tumor]. An intraspinal lipoma associated with a spina bifida.

lipomeria (lip-o-me'rī-ah) [G. *leipō*, leave behind, lack, + *meros*, a part]. The congenital absence of a limb or other part.

lipomucopolysaccharidosis (lip'o-mu'ko-pol-ĭ-sak'ā-rī-do'sis). Mucolipidosis I.

lipopenia (lip-o-pe'nī-ah) [lipo- + G. *penia*, poverty]. An abnormally small amount, or a deficiency, of lipids in the body.

lipophage (lip'o-fāj) [G. *lipos*, fat, + *phagein*, to eat]. A cell that ingests fat.

lipophagic (lip-o-fa'jik). Relating to lipophagy.

lipophagy (lip-of'a-jī) [lipo- + G. *phagein*, to eat]. Ingestion of fat by a lipophage.

lipophil (lip'o-fil) [lipo- + G. *philos*, fond of]. **1.** A substance with lipophilic (hydrophobic) properties. **2.** Lipophilic.

lipophilic (lip'o-fil-ik). Lipophil (2); capable of dissolving, of being dissolved in, or of absorbing lipids.

lipopolysaccharide (lip'o-pol-ĭ-sak'ar-id). A compound or complex of lipid and carbohydrate.

lipoprotein (lip'o-pro'te-in, -tēn). Complexes or compounds containing lipid and protein, the form of lipids in plasma. Plasma l.'s migrate electrophoretically with the α- and β-globulins, but are presently characterized by their flotation constants (densities) as follows: chylomicra (< 1.006), very low density (1.006-1.019), low density (1.019-1.063), high density (1.063-1.21), very high density (> 1.21); the last four are often abbreviated as VLD, LD, HD, VHD (followed by L for lipoprotein).

l. lipase, an emzyme reponsible for clearing the milky plasma of alimentary hyperlipemia by hydrolyzing the fats.

α₁-lipoprotein. A lipoprotein fraction of relatively small molecular weight, high density, rich in phospholipids, and found in the α₁-globulin fraction of human plasma.

β₁-lipoprotein. A lipoprotein fraction of relatively large molecular weight, low density, rich in cholesterol, and found in the β-globulin fraction of human plasma.

liposarcoma (lip'o-sar-ko'mah) [lipo- + *sarx*, flesh, + *-oma*, tumor]. Lipoblastoma (1); a malignant neoplasm consisting chiefly of immature, anaplastic lipoblasts of varying sizes (including giant forms), with bizarre nuclei and vacuoles of varying sizes in the cytoplasm, usually in association with a rich network of capillaries.

liposis (lī-po'sis) [lipo- + G. *-osis*, condition]. **1.** Adiposis. **2.** Fatty infiltration, neutral fats being present in the cells.

lip'osol'uble. Fat-soluble.

lip'osuctioning. Removal of subcutaneous fat by high-vacuum pressure; used in body contouring.

lip'otrop'ic. 1. Pertaining to substances preventing or correcting the fatty liver of choline deficiency. **2.** Relating to lipotropy.

lip'otroph'ic. Relating to lipotrophy.

lipotrophy (lī-pot'ro-fī) [lipo- + G. *trophē*, nourishment]. Increase of fat in the body.

lipotropy (lī-pot'ro-pī) [lipo- + G. *tropē*, turning]. **1.** Affinity of basic dyes for fatty tissue. **2.** Prevention of accumulation of fat in the liver. **3.** Affinity of nonpolar substances for each other.

lipovaccine (lip'o-vak'sēn). A vaccine having a vegetable oil as a vehicle.

lipox'idase. Lipoxygenase.

lipox'ygenase (lī-pok'sī-jen-ās). Lipoxidase; an enzyme that catalyzes the oxidation of unsaturated fatty acids with O_2 to yield peroxides of the fatty acids.

lip'ping. Formation of a liplike structure, as at the articular end of a bone in osteoarthritis.

lipuria (lī-pu'rī-ah) [lipo- + G. *ouron*, urine]. Adiposuria; excretion of lipid in the urine.

lipu'ric. Pertaining to lipuria.

liquefacient (lik'wē-fa'shent) [L. *lique-facio*, pres. p. *-faciens*, to make fluid]. Making fluid; causing a solid to become liquid.

liquefaction (lik-wē-fak'shun) [see liquefacient]. The act of becoming liquid; change from a solid to a liquid form.

liquescent (lī-kwes'ent) [L. *liquesco*, to become liquid]. Becoming or tending to become liquid.

liquid (lik'wid) [L. *liquidus*]. **1.** Flowing. **2.** An inelastic fluid, like water, that is neither solid nor gaseous.

liquor (lik'er) [L.]. **1.** Any liquid or fluid. **2.** A term used for certain body fluids. **3.** Pharmacopeial term for any aqueous solution (not a decoction or infusion) of a nonvolatile substance and for aqueous solutions of gases.

lisp'ing. Mispronunciation of the sibilants *s* and *z*.

lissencephalia, **lissencephaly** (lis'en-sē-fa'lī-ah, -sef'ā-lī) [G. *lissos*, smooth, + *enkephalos*, brain]. Agyria.

lissencephalic (lis'en-sē-fal'ik). Pertaining to, or characterized by, lissencephalia.

Listeria (lis-tēr-ī-ah) [Joseph *Lister*]. A genus of parasitic bacteria (family Corynebacteriaceae) containing small, coccoid, Gram-positive rods; found in the feces of man and other animals, on vegetation, and in silage. The type species is *L. monocytogenes*.

lis'terism. Lister's *method*.

liter (l, L) (le'ter) [Fr. fr. G. *litra*, a pound]. A measure of capacity of 1000 cubic centimeters, or 1 cubic decimeter, the equivalent of 1.0567 quarts.

lith-. See litho-.

lithagogue (lith'ā-gog) [litho- + G. *agōgos*, a drawing forth]. Causing the dislodgment or expulsion of calculi, especially urinary calculi.

lithectasy (lī-thek'tā-sī) [litho- + G. *ektasis*, a stretching out]. Urethral extraction of a vesical calculus after a preliminary dilation of this canal.

lithectomy (lī-thek'to-mī) [litho- + G. *ektomē*, excision]. Lithotomy.

lithiasis (lī-thi'ā-sis) [litho- + G. *-iasis*, condition]. Formation of calculi of any kind, especially of biliary or urinary calculi.

lith'ium [Mod. L. fr G. *lithos*, a stone]. An element of the alkali metal group, symbol Li, atomic no. 3, atomic weight 6.940; some of its salts are used medicinally.

litho-, lith- [G. *lithos*, stone]. Combining forms relating to a stone or calculus, or to calcification.

lith'oclast [litho- + G. *klastos*, broken]. Lithotrite.

lithodialysis (lith'o-di-al'ĭ-sis) [litho- + G. *dialysis*, a breaking up]. Fragmentation or solution of a calculus.

lithogenesis (lith-o-jen'ĕ-sis) [litho- + G. *genesis*, production]. Formation of calculi.

lithogenous (li-oj'ĕ-nus). Calculus-forming.

litholapaxy (lĭ-thol'ă-pak-sĭ) [litho- + G. *lapaxis*, an emptying out]. Crushing of a stone in the bladder and washing out the fragments through a catheter.

litholysis (lĭ-thol'ĭ-sis) [litho- + G. *lysis*, dissolution]. Dissolution of urinary calculi.

lithonephritis (lith'o-nĕ-fri'tis) Interstitial nephritis associated with calculus formation.

lithonephrotomy (lith'o-nĕ-frot'o-mĭ) [litho- + G. *nephros*, kidney, + *tomē*, incision]. Incision of the kidney for the removal of a calculus.

lithopedion (lith-o-pe'dĭ-on) [litho- + G. *paidion*, small child]. A retained fetus, usually extrauterine, that has become calcified.

lithoscope (lith'o-skōp) [litho- + G. *skopeō*, to view]. Cystoscope.

lithotomy (lĭ-thot'o-mĭ) [litho- + G. *tomē*, incision]. Lithectomy; cutting for stone; surgical removal of a calculus, especially a vesical calculus.

lithotripsy (lith'o-trip-sĭ) [litho- + G. *tripsis*, a rubbing]. Lithotrity; crushing of a stone in the bladder or urethra.

lith'otrip'tic. 1. Relating to lithotripsy. **2.** An agent that effects the dissolution of a calculus.

lithotriptoscopy (lith'o-trip-tos'ko-pĭ) [litho- + G. *tribō*, to rub, crush, + *skopeō*, to view]. Crushing of a stone in the bladder under direct vision.

lith'otrite [litho- + G. *tero*, pp. *tritus*, to rub]. Lithoclast; an instrument used to crush a stone in the bladder or urethra.

lithotrity (lĭ-thot'rĭ-tĭ). Lithotripsy.

lithous (lith'us). Calculous.

lithuresis (lith'u-re'sis) [litho- + G. *ourēsis*, urination]. Passage of gravel in the urine.

lit'mus. A blue coloring matter obtained from *Roccella tinctoria* and other species of lichens, the principal component of which is azolitmin; used as an indicator (reddened by acids and turned blue by alkalies).

lit'ter [Fr. *litière*; fr. *lit*, bed]. **1.** A stretcher or portable couch for moving the sick or injured. **2.** Brood (1); a group of animals of the same parents, born at the same time.

livedo (lĭ-ve'do) [L. lividness, fr. *liveo*, to be black and blue]. Suggillation (2); a bluish discoloration of the skin, either in limited patches or general.

postmortem l., postmortem lividity; a purple coloration of dependent parts, except in areas of contact pressure, appearing within one half to two hours after death, as a result of gravitational movement of blood within the vessels.

l. reticula'ris, l. racemosa, a purplish network-patterned discoloration of the skin caused by dilation of capillaries and venules due to alteration of a site or changes in underlying larger vessels.

livedoid (liv'e-doyd). Pertaining to or resembling livedo.

liv'er [A.S. *lifer*]. Hepar; jecur; the largest gland of the body, lying beneath the diaphragm in the right hypochondrium and upper part of the epigastrium; it secretes the bile and is also of importance in both carbohydrate and protein metabolism.

fatty l., yellow discoloration of the l. due to fatty degeneration of the parenchymal cells.

frosted l., hyaloserositis of the liver.

hobnail l., in Laënnec's cirrhosis, the contraction of scar tissue and hepatic cellular regeneration which causes a nodular appearance of the l.'s surface.

liv'id [L. *lividus*, being black and blue]. Having a black and blue or a leaden or ashy gray color, as in discoloration from a contusion, congestion, or cyanosis.

lividity (lĭ-vid'ĭ-tĭ). The state of being livid.

postmortem l., postmortem *livedo*.

li'vor [L. a black and blue spot]. The livid discoloration of the skin on the dependent parts of a corpse.

lixiviation (lik'siv-ĭ-a'shun) [L. *lixivius*, made into lye, fr, *lix*, lye]. Leaching; the removal of the soluble constituents of a substance by running water through it.

L.M. Licentiate in Midwifery.

LMA Left mentoanterior *position.*

LMP Left mentoposterior *position.*

LNPF Lymph node permeability *factor.*

load. A departure from normal body content, as of water, salt, or heat; positive l.'s are quantities in excess of the normal; negative l.'s are deficits.

loading (lo'ding). Administration of a substance for the purpose of testing metabolic function.

Loa loa. The African eye worm, a species of the family Onchocercidae (superfamily Filarioidea) indigenous to the western part of equatorial Africa and the causal agent of loiasis; man is the only known definitive host, and parasites are transmitted by *Chrysops* or tabanid flies.

lo'bar. Relating to any lobe.

lo'bate. 1. Divided into lobes. **2.** Lobe-shaped.

lobe [G. *lobos*, lobe]. **1.** Lobus. **2.** A rounded projecting part, as the l. of the ear. See also lobule; lobulus. **3.** One of the larger divisions of the crown of a tooth, formed from a distinct point of calcification.

anterior l. of hypophysis, *lobus* anterior hypophyseos.

caudate l., *lobus* caudatus.

frontal l., *lobus* frontalis cerebri.

left l. of liver, *lobus* hepatis sinister.

occipital l., *lobus* occipitalis cerebri.

parietal l., *lobus* parietalis cerebri.

placental l., the unit of the human placenta, incompletely separated by septa, that contains the fetal cotyledon(s) and the surrounding blood-filled intervillous space.

posterior l. of hypophysis, *lobus* posterior hypophyseos.

quadrate l., (1) *lobus* quadratus; (2) precuneus.

Riedel'l., an occasional tongue-like process extending downward from the right l. of the liver lateral to the gallbladder.

right l. of liver, *lobus* hepatis dexter.

Spigelius l., *lobus* caudatus.

temporal l., *lobus* temporalis.

lobec'tomy [G. *lobos*, lobe, + *ektomē*, excision]. Excision of a lobe of any organ or gland.

lo'bi [L.]. Plural of lobus.

lobitis (lo-bi'tis). Inflammation of a lobe.

lobotomy (lo-bot'o-mĭ) [G. *lobos*, lobe, + *tomē*, a cutting]. **1.** Incision into a lobe. **2.** Division of one or more nerve tracts in a lobe of the cerebrum.

lob'ular. Relating to a lobule.

lob'ulate, lob'ulated. Divided into lobules.

lobule (lob'ūl). Lobulus.

l.'s of epididymis, *lobuli* epididymidis.

hepatic l., *lobulus* hepatis.

portal l. of liver, a polygonal mass of liver tissue that has as its center a portal canal and at its periphery several central hepatic veins.

primary pulmonary l., respiratory l., a unit of pulmonary tissue that includes a respiratory bronchiole, alveolar ducts, sacs, and alveoli.

renal cortical l., *lobulus* corticalis renalis.

lobulus, gen. and pl. **lobuli** (lob'u-lus, u-li) [Mod. L. dim. of *lobus*, lobe] [NA]. Lobule; a small lobe or subdivision of a lobe.

l. cortica'lis rena'lis [NA], renal cortical lobule; one of the subdivisions of the kidney, consisting of the medullary ray and the labyrinth having renal corpuscles and convoluted tubules.

lob'uli epididym'idis [NA], lobules of the epididymis; the coiled portion of the efferent ductules that constitute the head of the epididymis; these join the ductus epididymidis.

l. hep'atis [NA], hepatic lobule; the polygonal histologic unit of the liver consisting of masses of liver cells arranged around a central vein, a terminal branch of one of the hepatic veins; at the periphery are located branches of the portal vein, hepatic artery and bile duct.

lo'bus, gen. and pl. **lo'bi** [LL. fr G. *lobos*] [NA]. Lobe (1); one of the subdivisions of an organ or other part, bounded by fissures, connective tissue, septa, or other structural demarcations.

l. ante'rior hypophys'eos [NA], anterior lobe of the hypophysis; adenohypophysis; consists of a distal, intermediate, and infundibular part. See also hypophysis.

l. az'ygos, a small accessory lobe sometimes found on the upper part of the right lung; it is separated from the rest of the upper lobe by a deep groove lodging the azygos vein.

l. cauda'tus [NA], caudate lobe; Spigelius lobe; a small lobe of the liver situated posteriorly between the sulcus for the vena cava and the fissure for the ligamentum venosum.

l. fronta'lis cer'ebri [NA], frontal lobe; the portion of each cerebral hemisphere anterior to the central sulcus.

l. hep'atis dex'ter [NA], right lobe of the liver; the largest lobe of the liver, separated from the left lobe above and in front by the falciform ligament and from the caudate and quadrate lobes by the sulcus for the vena cava and the fossa for the gallbladder.

l. hep'atis sinis'ter [NA], left lobe of the liver; it is separated from the right lobe above and in front by the falciform ligament, and from the quadrate and caudate lobes by the fissure for the ligamentum teres and the fissure for the ligamentum venosum.

l. occipita'lis cer'ebri [NA], occipital lobe; the posterior, somewhat pyramidal part of each cerebral hemisphere.

l. parieta'lis cer'ebri [NA], parietal lobe; the middle portion of each cerebral hemisphere, separated from the fontal lobe by the central sulcus, from the temporal lobe by the lateral sulcus, and from the occipital lobe only partially by the parietooccipital sulcus on its medial aspect.

l. poste'rior hypophys'eos [NA], neurohypophysis; the posterior lobe of the hypophysis. See hypophysis.

l. quadra'tus [NA], quadrate lobe (1); a lobe on the inferior surface of the liver located between the fossa for the gallbladder and the fissure for the ligamentum teres.

l. tempora'lis [NA], temporal lobe; the lowest of the major subdivisions of the cortical mantle, forming the posterior two-thirds of the ventral surface of the cerebral hemisphere, separated from the frontal and parietal lobes above it by the fissure of Sylvius and arbitrarily delineated from the occipital lobe with which it is continuous posteriorly.

lo'cal [L. *localis*, fr. *locus*, place]. Having reference or confined to a limited part; not general or systemic.

localization (lo'kal-ĭ-za'shun). **1.** Limitation to a definite area. **2.** The reference of a sensation to its point of origin. **3.** The determination of the location of a morbid process.

cerebral l., the mapping of the cerebral cortex into areas and the correlation of the various areas with cerebral function, or the diagnosis of the situation in the cerebrum of a brain lesion from the signs and symptoms manifested by the patient or from a study of the electroencephalogram.

germinal l., the determination in very young embryos of the presumptive areas for specific organs or structures.

localized (lo'kal-īzd). Restricted or limited to a definite part.

lo'cator. An instrument or apparatus for finding the position of a foreign object in tissue.

lochia (lo'kĭ-ah) [G. neut. pl. of *lochios,* relating to childbirth, fr. *lochos,* childbirth]. The discharge from the vagina of mucus, blood, and tissue debris, following childbirth.

lochial (lo'kĭ-al). Relating to the lochia.

lochiometra (lo'kĭ-o-me'trah) [G. *mētra,* womb]. Distention of the uterus with retained lochia.

lochiometritis (lo'kĭ-o-me-tri'tis). Puerperl metritis.

lochioperitonitis (lo'kĭ-o-pĕr'ĭ-to-ni'tis). Puerperal peritonitis.

lochiorrhagia (lo'kĭ-ŏ-ra'jĭ-ah) [lochia + G. *rhēg-nymi,* to burst forth]. Lochiorrhea.

lochiorrhea (lo'kĭ-ŏ-re'ah) [lochia + G. *rhoia,* a flow]. Lochiorrhagia; a profuse flow of the lochia.

loci (lo'si). Plural of locus.

lock'jaw. Trismus.

lo'como'tor, lo'como'tive [L. *locus,* place, + L. *moveo,* pp. *motus,* to move]. Relating to locomotion, or movement from one place to another.

locular (lok'u-lar). Relating to a loculus.

loc'ulate. Containing numerous loculi.

loculation (lok-u-la'shun). **1.** A loculate region in an organ or tissue, or a loculate structure formed between surfaces of organs, mucous or serous membranes, and so on. **2.** The process that results in the formation of a loculus or loculi.

loculus, pl. **loculi** (lok'u-lus, -li) [L. dim. of *locus,* place]. A small cavity or chamber.

locus, pl. **loci** (lo'kus, lo'si) [L.]. A place; usually, a specific site.

log-. See logo-.

logagnosia (log-ag-no'sĭ-ah) [logo- + G. *agnosia,* ignorance]. Aphasia.

logagraphia (log-ă-graf'ĭ-ah) [logo- + G. *a-* priv. + *graphō,* to write]. Agraphia.

logamnesia (log-am-ne'zĭ-ah) [logo + G. *amnēsia,* forgetfulness]. Aphasia.

logaphasia (log-ă-fa'zĭ-ah) [logo- + G. *aphasia,* speechlessness]. Aphasia of articulation.

logasthenia (log-as-the'nĭ-ah) [logo- + G. *astheneia,* weakness]. Aphasia.

-logia. 1 [G. *logos,* discourse, tretise]. Suffix expressing in a general way the study of the subject noted in the body of the word, or a treatise on the same; also -logy, or, with the connecting vowel, -ology. **2** [G. *legō,* to collect]. A suffix signifying collecting or picking.

logo-, log- [G. *logos,* word, discourse]. Combining forms relating to speech, or words.

logoplegia (log-o-ple'jĭ-ah) [logo- + G. *plēgē,* stroke]. Paralysis of the organs of speech.

logorrhea (log-o-re'ah) [logo- + G. *rhoia,* a flow]. Garrulousness.

-logy. See -logia.

loiasis (lo-i'ă-sis). A chronic disease caused by infection with *Loa loa,* which provokes hyperemia and exudation of fluid, and a "creeping" sensation in the tissues with intense itching.

loin (loyn) [Fr. *longe;* E. *lumbus*]. Lumbus.

longevity (lon-jev'ĭ-tĭ). Duration of a particular life beyond the norm for the species.

longitudinal (lon-jĭ-tu'dĭ-nal) [L. *longitudo,* length]. Running lengthwise; in the direction of the long axis of the body or any of its parts.

loop [M.E. *loupe*]. **1.** A curve or complete bend in a cord or other cylindrical body, forming an oval or circular ring. See also ansa.

capillary l.'s, small blood vessels in papillae of the corium.

Henle's l., nephronic l.

nephronic l., Henle's l. or ansa; the U-shaped part of the nephron extending from the proximal to the distal convoluted tubules and consisting of descending and ascending limbs.

l.'s of spinal nerves, *ansae* nervorum spinalium.

lordoscoliosis (lor'do-sko-lĭ'o'sis) [G. *lordos,* bent back, + *skoliōsis,* crookedness]. Combined backward and lateral curvature of the spine.

lordo'sis [G. *lordōsis,* a bending backward]. Hollow or saddle back; an abnormal extension deformity: anteroposterior curvature of the spine, generally lumbar with the convexity looking anteriorly.

lordot'ic. Pertaining to or marked by lordosis.

lotion (lo'shun) [L. *lotio,* a washing, fr. *lavo,* to wash]. Wash; a class of pharmacopeial preparations that are liquid suspensions or dispersions intended for external application.

loupe (lūp) [Fr.]. A magnifying lens.

louse pl. **lice** (lows; līs) [A.S. *lūs*]. Common name for members of the ectoparasitic insect orders Anoplura (sucking lice) and Mallophaga (biting lice).

loxoscelism (loks-os'ĕ-lizm). A clinical illness produced by the brown recluse spider, *Loxosceles reclusus,* of North America; characterized by gangrenous slough at the site of bite, nausea, malaise, fever, hemolysis, and thrombocytopenia.

lozenge (loz'enj) [Fr. *losange,* from *lozangé,* rhombic]. Troche.

L.P.N. Licensed practical *nurse.*

Lr Lawrencium.

L.R.C.P. Licentiate of the Royal College of Physicians.

L.R.C.S. Abbreiation for Licentiate of the Royal College of Surgeons.

LRH Luteinizing hormone-releasing *hormone.*

LSA Left sacroanterior *position.*

L.S.A. Licentiate of the Society of Apothecaries.

LSD Lysergic acid diethylamide.

LSH Lutein-stimulating *hormone.*

LSP Left sacroposterior *position.*

LTH Luteotropic *hormone.*

LTM Long term *memory.*

Lu Lutetium.

lucidity (lu-sid'ĭ-tĭ) [L. *lucidus*, clear]. Clarity, especially mental clarity.

lucifugal (lu-sif'u-gal) [L. *lux*, light, + *fugio*, to flee from]. Avoiding, or repelled by, light.

lucipetal (lu-sip'ĭ-tal) [L. *lux*, light, + *peto*, to seek]. Seeking, or attracted to, light.

lues (lu'ēz) [L. pestilence]. A plague, or pestilence; specifically, syphilis.

luetic (lu-et'ik). Syphilitic.

lulib'erin. Luteinizing hormone-releasing *hormone*.

lumba'go [L. fr. *lumbus*, loin]. Lumbar rheumatism; pain in mid and lower back; a descriptive term not specifying cause.

lum'bar [L. *lumbus*, a loin]. Relating to the loins, or the part of the back and sides between the ribs and the pelvis.

lum'bariza'tion. Sacral development of the fifth lumbar vertebra.

lum'bi [L.]. Plural of lumbus.

lumbocolostomy (lum'bo-ko-los'to-mĭ) [L. *lumbus*, loin, + G. *kolon*, colon, + *stoma*, mouth]. The formation of a permanent opening into the colon via an incision through the lumbar region.

lumbocostal (lum'bo-kos'tal) [L. *lumbus*, loin, + *costa*, rib]. Relating to the lumbar and the hypochondriac regions.

lumboinguinal (lum-bo-ing'guĭ-nal) [L. *lumbus*, loin, + *inguen* (*inguin-*), groin]. Relating to the lumbar and the inguinal regions.

lumbosacral (lum-bo-sa'kral). Sacrolumbar; relating to the lumbar vertebrae and the sacrum.

lumbricidal (lum-brĭ-si'dal). Destructive to lumbricoid (intestinal) worms.

lumbricide (lum'brĭ-sīd) [L. *lumbricus*, worm, + *caedo*, to kill]. An agent that kills lumbricoid (intestinal) worms.

lumbricoid (lum'brĭ-koyd) [L. *lumbricus*, earthworm, + G. *eidos*, resemblance]. 1. Denoting or resembling a roundworm, especially *Ascaris lumbricoides*. 2. Common name for *Ascaris lumbricoides*.

lumbricosis (lum'brĭ-ko'sis). Infestation with lumbricoid (intestinal) worms.

lumbricus (lum'brĭ-kus) [L. earthworm]. Common name for *Ascaris lumbricoides*.

lum'bus, gen. and pl. **lum'bi** [L.] [NA]. Loin; the part of the side and back between the ribs and the pelvis.

lu'men, pl. **lu'mina** [L. light, window]. 1. The space in the interior of a tubular structure, such as an artery or the intestine. 2. The unit of luminous flux; the luminous flux emitted in a solid angle of 1 steradian by a uniform point source of light having a luminous intensity of 1 candela.

lu'minal. Relating to the lumen of a blood vessel or other tubular structure.

luminescence (lu-mĭ-nes'ens) [L. *lumen*, light]. Emission of light from a body without a corresponding amount of heat.

luminiferous (lu-mĭ-nif'er-us) [L. *lumen*, light, + *fero*, to carry]. Producing or conveying light.

luminophore (lu'mĭ-no-fōr) [L. *lumen*, light, + G. *phoros*, bearing]. An atom or atomic grouping that, when present in an organic compound, increases its ability to luminesce.

luminous (lu'mĭ-nus) [L. *lumen*, light]. Emitting light, with or without accompanying heat.

lumirhodopsin (lu'mĭ-ro-dop'sin). An intermediate between rhodopsin and all-*trans*-retinal plus opsin during bleaching of rhodopsin by light.

lumpectomy. Tylectomy.

lu'nar [L. *luna*, moon]. 1. Relating to the moon or to a month. 2. Lunate; semilunar; resembling the moon in shape, especially a half moon.

lu'nate. Lunar (2).

lung [A.S. *lungen*]. Either of the organs of respiration, occupying the cavity of the thorax, in which aeration of the blood takes place; the right l. is slightly larger than the left and is divided into three lobes (upper, middle, and lower or basal), while the left has but two lobes (upper and lower or basal).

bird-breeder's l., bird-fancier's l., extrinsic allergic alveolitis caused by inhalation of particulate avian emanations; sometimes specified by avian species.

black l., a form of pneumoconiosis common in coal miners; characterized by deposit of carbon particles in the lung.

farmer's l., an occupational disease characterized by fever and dyspnea, caused by inhalation of organic dust from moldy hay containing spores of actinomycetes and certain true fungi.

honeycomb l., the radiological and gross appearance of the l.'s resulting from diffuse fibrosis and cystic dilation of bronchioles.

iron l., Drinker *respirator*.

miner's l., anthracosis.

postperfusion l., a condition in which abnormal pulmonary function develops in patients who have undergone cardiac surgery involving the use of an extracorporeal circulation.

quiet l., the collapse of a lung during thoracic operations to facilitate surgical procedure by absence of movement.

shock l., in shock, the development of edema, impaired perfusion, and reduction in alveolar space so that the alveoli collapse.

wet l., the l. in pulmonary edema.

lung'worms. Nematodes that inhabit the air passages of animals, chiefly in the family Metastrongylidae.

lunula, pl. **lunulae** (lu'nu-lah, -le) [L. dim. of *luna*, moon]. 1. [NA]. The pale arched area at the proximal portion of the nail plate. 2. A small semilunar structure.

lu'piform. Lupoid.

lu'poid [L. *lupus*, wolf + G. *eidos*, resemblance]. Lupiform; resembling lupus.

lu'pous. Relating to lupus.

lu'pus [L. wolf]. A term originally used to depict erosion (as if gnawed of the skin, now used with modifying terms designating various diseases.

discoid l. erythemato'sus l. erythematosus in which only cutaneous lesions are present, commonly on the face, as atrophic plaques with erythema, hyperkeratosis, follicular plugging, and telangiectasia.

disseminated l. erythemato'sus, systemic l. erythematosus.

l. erythemato'sus (L.E.), an illness which may be chronic (characterized by skin lesions alone), subacute (characterized by skin lesions that are more disseminate and present more acute features both clinically and histlogically than those seen in the discoid type), or systemic (in which the L.E. cell test may be positive and in which there is almost always involvement of vital structures.

l. erythemato'sus profun'dus, a histologically nonspecific subcutaneous panniculitis giving rise to deep-seated, firm, rubbery nodules that sometimes become ulcerated, usually of the face.

l. hypertroph'icus, l. tumidus; a form of l. vulgaris in which the tubercles are grouped into prominent hypertrophic nodules with deep-seated scarring, usually on the face.

l. milia'ris dissemina'tus fa'ciei, a millet-like papular eruption of the face, associated with a positive anergy to tuberculin and (histopathologically) to tuberculoid structure.

l. per'nio, sarcoid lesions, resembling those of frostbite, involving ears and hands.

systemic l. erythemato'sus (S.L.E.), disseminated l. erythematosus; an inflammatory connective tissue disease with variable features, frequently including fever, weakness and fatigability, joint pains or arthritis resembling rheumatoid arthritis, diffuse erythematous skin lesions on the face, neck, or upper extremities, with liquefaction degeneration of the basal layer and epidermal atrophy, lymphadenopathy, pleurisy or pericarditis, glomerular lesions, anemia, hyperglobulinemia, a positive L.E. cell test, and other evidence of an autoimmune phenomenon.

l. tu'midus, l. hypertrophicus.

l. vulga'ris, cutaneous tuberculosis with characteristic nodular lesions on the face, particularly about the nose and ears.

lu'sus natu'rae [L. a sport of nature]. A conspicuous congenital abnormality.

luteal (lu'te-al) [L. *luteus,* saffron-yellow]. Relating to the corpus luteum.

lutein (lu'te-in) [L. *luteus,* saffron-yellow]. The yellow pigment in the corpus luteum, in the yolk of eggs, or any lipochrome.

luteinization (lu'te-in-ĭ-za'shun). Transformation of the mature ovarian follicle and its theca interna into a corpus luteum after ovulation; the formation of luteal tissue.

lu'teohor'mone. Progesterone.

luteolysis (lu-te-ol'ĭ-sis). Degeneration of destruction of ovarian luteinized tissue.

luteoma (lu-te-o'mah). An ovarian tumor of granulosa or theca cell origin in which luteinization has occurred, producing progesterone effects on the uterine mucosa.

luteotropic, luteotrophic (lu'te-o-trop'ik, -trof'ik). Having a stimulating action on the development and function of the corpus luteum.

luteotropin (lu'te-o-tro'pin). Luteotropic *hormone.*

lutetium, lutecium (lu-te'shī-um) [L. *Lutetia,* Paris]. A rare earth element; symbol Lu, atomic no. 71, atomic weight 174.99.

lutropin (lu'tro-pin). Luteinizing *hormone.*

Lutzomy'ia. A genus of New World sandflies or bloodsucking midges (family Psychodidae) that serve as vectors of leishmaniasis and Oroyo fever; formerly combined with the Old World sandfly genus *Phlebotomus.*

lux (luks) [L. light]. Meter-candle; candle-meter; a SI unit of light or illumination: the reception of a luminous flux of 1 lumen per square meter of surface.

luxation (luks-a'shun) [L. *luxatio*]. **1.** Dislocation. **2.** In dentistry, the dislocation or displacement of the condyle in the temporomandibular fossa, or of a tooth from the alveolus.

Malgaigne's l., l. of head of radius beneath the annular ligament.

Luxol fast blue. Name for a group of closely related copper phthalocyanin dyes used as stains for myelin in nerve fibers.

LVET Left ventricular ejection *time.*

L.V.N. Licensed vocational *nurse.*

Lw Former symbol for lawrencium.

ly'ase. Class name for those enzymes removing groups nonhydrolytically; prefixes such as "hydro-," "ammonia-," etc., are used to indicate the type of reaction.

lycanthropy (li-kan'thro-pī) [G. *lykos,* wolf, + *anthropos,* man]. The delusion that one is a wolf, possibly a mental atavism of the werewolf superstition.

lycopene (li'ko-pēn). Ψ, Ψ-Carotene; red pigment of the tomato that may be considered chemically as the parent substance from which all natural carotenoid pigments are derived.

lycopenemia (li'ko-pě-ne'mī-ah) [lycopene + G. *haima,* blood]. A condition in which there is a high concentration of lycopene in the blood, producing carotenoid-like yellowish pigmentation of the skin, as a result of excessive consumption of tomatoes or lycopene-containing fruits and berries.

lycoperdonosis (li'ko-per-don-o'sis). A persisting pneumonitis following inhalation of spores of the puffballs *Lycoperdon pyriforme* and *L. bovista.*

lying-in. 1. Confinement. **2.** Relating to childbirth.

lymph-. See lympho-.

lymph (limf) [L. *lympha,* clear spring water]. A transparent, sometimes faintly yellow and slightly opalescent fluid that carries varying numbers of white blood cells (chiefly lymphocytes) and a few red blood cells, is collected from the tissues throughout the body, flows in the lymphatic vessels (through the lymph nodes), and is eventually added to the venous blood circulation.

aplastic l., corpuscular l., l. containing a relatively large number of leukocytes, but comparatively little fibrinogen; manifests only slight tendency to become organized.

euplastic l., l. that contains relatively few leukocytes, but a comparatively high concentration of fibrinogen; tends to become organized with fibrous tissue.

inflammatory l., plastic l., euplastic l. that collects on the surface of an acutely inflamed membrane or cutaneous wound.

tissue l., l. derived chiefly from fluid in tissue spaces rather than from the blood.

vaccine l., vaccinia l., l. collected from the vesicles of vaccinia infection, and used for active immunization against smallpox.

lymphaden-. See lymphadeno-.

lymphadenectomy (lim-fad-ě-nek′to-mĭ) [lymphadeno- + G. *ektomē,* excision]. Excision of lymph nodes.

lymphadenitis (lim′fad-ě-ni′tis) [lymphadeno- + G. *-itis,* inflammation]. Lymphnoditis; inflammation of one or more lymph nodes.

lymphadeno-, lymphaden- [L. *lympha,* spring water, + G. *adēn.* gland]. Combining forms relating to the lymph nodes.

lymphadenography (lim′fad-ě-nog′rǎ-fĭ) [lymphadeno- + G. *graphō,* to write]. Radiography after opaque (iodized) oil is injected into the center of an enlarged lymph node.

lymphadenoid (lim-fad′ě-noyd) [lymphadeno- + G. *eidos,* resemblance]. Relating to, or resembling, or derived from a lymph node.

lymphadenoma (lim-fad-ě-no′mah) [lymphadeno- + G. *-oma,* tumor]. **1.** Obsolete term for an enlarged lymph node. **2.** Infrequently used term for Hodgkin's disease.

lymphadenopathy (lim-fad-ě-nop′ǎ-thĭ) [lymphadeno- + G. *pathos,* suffering]. Any disease process affecting lymph nodes.

angioimmunoblastic l., immunoblastic l.; acute or subacute generalized l. in older persons associated with polyclonal hypergammaglobulinemia, anemia, and hepatosplenomegaly, not responding to chemotherapy; enlarged nodes show proliferation of immunoblasts, plasma cells, and capillaries.

dermatopathic l., enlargement of lymph nodes, with proliferation of histiocytes and macrophages containing fat and melanin, secondary to various forms of dermatitis, particularly with pruritus or exfoliation.

immunoblastic l., angioimmunoblastic l.

lymphadenosis (lim-fad-ě-no′sis) [lymphadeno- + G. *-osis,* condition]. The basic underlying proliferative process that results in enlargement of lymph nodes.

lymphagogue (limf′ǎ-gog) [lymph + G. *agōgos,* drawing forth]. An agent that increases the formation and flow of lymph.

lymphangi-. See lymphangio-.

lymphangial (lim-fan′jĭ-al). Relating to a lymphatic vessel.

lymphangiectasis, lymphangiectasia (lim-fan′jĭ-ek′tǎ-sis, -ek-ta′zĭ-ah) [lymphangio- + G. *ektasis,* a stretching]. Lymphectasia; dilation of the lymphatic vessels.

lymphangiectatic (lim-fan′jĭ-ek-tat′ik). Relating to or characterized by lymphangiectasis.

lymphangiectomy (lim-fan-jĭ-ek′to-mĭ) [lymphangio- + G. *ektomē,* excision]. Excision of a lymphatic vessel.

lymphangiitis (lim-fan-jĭ-i′tis). Lymphangitis.

lymphangio-, lymphangi- [L. *lympha,* spring water, + G. *angeion,* vessel]. Combining forms relating to the lymphatic vessels.

lymphangioendothelioma (lim-fan′jĭ-o-en′do-the-lĭ-o′mah). A neoplasm consisting of irregular groups or small masses of endothelial cells, as well as congeries of tubate structures that are thought to be derived from lymphatic vessels.

lymphangiography (lim-fan-jĭ-og′rǎ-fĭ) [lymphangio- + G. *graphō,* to write]. Radiographic visualization of lymph vessels following injection of a contrast medium.

lymphangiology (lim-fan′jĭ-ol′o-jĭ) [lymphangio- + G. *logos,* study]. Lymphology; the branch of medical science concerned with the lymphatic system.

lymphangioma (lim-fan-jĭ-o′mah) [lymphangio- + G. *-oma,* tumor]. A circumscribed nodule or mass of lymphatic vessels or channels that vary in size, are frequently greatly dilated, and are lined with normal endothelial cells; present at birth, or shortly thereafter, and probably represent anomalous development of lymphatic vessels rather than true neoplasms.

cavernous l., conspicuous dilation of lymphatic vessels in a fairly circumscribed region, frequently with the formation of cavities or "lakes" filled with lymph.

cystic l., a condition characterized by a fairly well circumscribed group of several or numerous, cyst-like, dilated vessels or spaces lined with endothelium and filled with lymph.

lymphangiophlebitis (lim-fan′jĭ-o-flě-bi′tis). Inflammation of the lymphatic vessels and veins.

lymphangioplasty (lim-fan′jĭ-o-plas-tĭ) [lymphangio- + G. *plassō,* to form]. Surgical alteration of lymphatic vessels.

lymphangiosarcoma (lim-fan′jĭ-o-sar-ko′mah). An angiosarcoma in which the neoplastic cells originate from the endothelial cells of lymphatic vessels.

lymphangiotomy (lim-fan-jĭ-ot′o-mĭ) [lymphangio- + G. *tomē,* incision]. Incision of lymphatic vessels.

lymphangitis (lim-fan-ji′tis) [lymphangio- + G. *-itis,* inflammation]. Lymphangiitis; inflammation of the lymphatic vessels.

lymphatic (lim-fat′ik) [L. *lymphaticus,* frenzied; Mod. L. use, of or for lymph]. Pertaining to lymph, a vascular channel that transports lymph, or a lymph node.

lymphaticostomy (lim-fat-ĭ-kos'to-mĭ) [lymphatic + G. *stoma*, mouth]. Making an opening into a lymphatic duct.

lymphatism (lim'fă-tizm). An excess in the lymphoid or tonsillar structures.

lymphatitis (lim-fă-ti'tis) [lymphatic + G. *-itis*, inflammation]. Inflammation of the lymphatic vessels or lymph nodes.

lymphatolysis (lim-fă-tol'ĭ-sis) [lymphatic + G. *lysis*, dissolution]. Destruction of the lymphatic vessels, lymphoid tissue, or both.

lymphatolytic (lim'fă-to-lit'ik). Pertaining to or characterized by lymphatolysis.

lymphectasia (lim-fek-ta'zĭ-ah) [lymph + G. *ektasis*, a stretching]. Lymphangiectasis.

lymphedema (limf-ĕ-de'mah) [lymph + G. *oidēma*, a swelling]. Swelling (especially in subcutaneous tissues) as a result of obstruction of lymphatic vessels or lymph nodes and the accumulation of large amounts of lymph in the affected region.

   hereditary l., trophedema; permanent pitting edema, usually confined to the lower extremities, of two types: **1)** congenital (Milroy's disease); **2)** onset at about the age of puberty (Meige's disease) and autosomal dominant inheritance.

lymphemia (lim-fe'mĭ-ah) [lymph(ocyte) + G. *haima*, blood]. Presence of unusually large numbers of lymphocytes, their precursors, or both, in the circulating blood.

lymphenteritis (limf'en-ter-i'tis) [lymph + G. *enteron*, intestine, + *-itis*, inflammation]. Inflammation of the peritoneal covering of the intestine.

lymphnoditis (limf'no-di'tis). Lymphadenitis.

lympho-, lymph- [L. *lympha*, spring water]. Combining forms relating to lymph.

lymphoblast (lim'fo-blast) [lympho- + G. *blastos*, germ]. Lymphocytoblast; a young immature cell that matures into a lymphocyte.

lymphoblas'tic. Pertaining to the production of lymphocytes.

lymphoblastoma (lim'fo-blas-to'mah) [lymphoblast + G. *-oma*, tumor]. A form of malignant lymphoma in which the chief cells are lymphoblasts.

lymphoblastosis (lim'fo-blas-to'sis) [lymphoblast + G. *-osis*, condition]. Presence of lymphoblasts in the peripheral blood.

lymphocyte (lim'fo-sit) [lympho- + G. *kytos*, call]. A white blood cell formed in lymphoid tissue; in normal adults, l.'s comprise approximately 22 to 28% of the total number of leukocytes in the circulating blood.

   B l., B cell (2); an immunologically important l. that is not thymus-dependent, is of short life, and is responsible for the production of immunoglobulins.

   T l., T cell; an immunologically important l. that is thymocytic-derived, is of long life (months to years) and is responsible for delayed-type (cell-mediated) sensitivity.

lymphocythemia (lim'fo-si-the'mĭ-ah). Lymphocytosis.

lymphocytic (lim-fo-sit'ik). Pertaining to or characterized by lymphocytes.

lymphocytoblast (lim-fo-si'to-blast) [lymphocyte, + G. *blastos*, germ]. Lymphoblast.

lymphocytoma (lim'fo-si-to'mah) [lymphocyte + G. *-oma*, tumor]. A circumscribed nodule or mass of mature lymphocytes, grossly resembling a neoplasm.

   benign l. cutis, a skin nodule caused by dense infiltration of the dermis by lymphocytes and histiocytes, often forming lymphoid follicles, separated from the epidermis by a narrow noninfiltrating layer.

lymphocytopenia (lim'fo-si-to-pe'nĭ-ah). Lymphopenia.

lymphocytopoiesis (lim'fo-si-to-poy-e'sis) [lymphocyte + G. *poiēsis*, a making]. Formation of lymphocytes.

lymphocytosis (lim'fo-si-to'sis). Lymphocytic leukocytosis; lymphocythemia; a form of actual or relative leukocytosis in which there is an increase in the number of lymphocytes.

lymphoduct (lim'fo-dukt) [lympho- + L. *ductus*, a leading]. A lymphatic vessel.

lymphoepithelioma (lim'fo-ep'ĭ-the-li-o'mah). A poorly differentiated radio-sensitive squamous cell carcinoma involving lymphoid tissue in the region of the tonsils and nasopharynx.

lymphogen'ic. Lymphogenous (1).

lymphogenous (lim-foj'ĕ-nus). **1.** Lymphogenic; originating from lymph or the lymphatic system. **2.** Producing lymph.

lymphoglandula (lim-fo-glan'du'lah). Lymphonodus.

lymphogranuloma (lim'fo-gran-u-lo'mah) **1.** Old nonspecific term referring to a few basically dissimilar diseases in which the pathologic processes result in granulomas or granuloma-like lesions, especially in various groups of lymph nodes (which then become conspicuously enlarged). **2.** Old term for Hodgkin's disease.

   venereal l., l. vene'reum, a venereal infection usually caused by *Chlamydia,* and characterized by a transient genital ulcer and inguinal adenopathy in the male; in the female, perirectal nodes are involved and rectal stricture is a common occurrence. Also called climatic or tropical bubo; sixth venereal disease; Nicolas-Favre disease.

lymphogranulomatosis (lim-fo-gran'u-lo-mă-to'sis). Any condition characterized by the occurrence of multiple and widely distributed lymphogranulomas.

lymphography (lim-fog'ră-fĭ) [lympho- + *graphō*, to write]. Radiographic delineation of lymph vessels or nodes utilizing injected dyes or radiopaque material.

lymphoid (lim'foyd) [lympho- + G. *eidos*, appearance]. **1.** Resembling lymph or lymphatic tissue, or pertaining to the lymphatic system. **2.** Adenoid (1).

lymphoidectomy (lim-foy-dek'to-mĭ) [lymphoid + G. *ektomē*, excision]. Excision of lymphoid tissue.

lymphokines (lim'fo-kīnz). Soluble substances, released by sensitized lymphocytes on contact with specific antigen, which help effect cellular immunity by stimulating activity of monocytes and macrophages.

lymphokinesis (lim'fo-kĭ-ne'sis) [lympho- + G. *kinēsis*, movement]. **1.** Circulation of lymph in the lymphatic vessels and through the lymph nodes. **2.** Movement of lymph in the semicircular canals.

lymphology (lim-fol'o-jĭ) [lympho- + G. *logos*, study]. Lymphangiology.

lymphoma (lim-fo'mah) [lympho- + G. suffix *-oma*, tumor]. Malignant l.; general term for ordinarily malignant neoplasms of lymph and reticuloendothelial tissues which present as apparently circumscribed solid tumors composed of cells that appear primitive or resemble lymphocytes, plasma cells, or histiocytes; classified by cell type, degrees of differentiation, and nodular or diffuse pattern.

Burkitt's l., a form of malignant l. frequently involving facial bones, ovaries, and abdominal lymph nodes, which are infiltrated by undifferentiated stem cells with scattered pale macrophages containing nuclear debris.

follicular l., nodular l.

malignant l., lymphoma.

nodular l., follicular l.; Brill-Symmers disease; malignant l. characterized by nodules resembling normal lymphoid follicles consisting of small lymphocytoid cells or with variable numbers of larger histiocyte-like cells.

poorly differentiated lymphocytic l, (PDLL), a B-cell l. with nodular or diffuse lymph node or bone marrow involvement by large lymphoid cells.

well differentiated lymphocytic l. (WDLL), essentially the same disease as chronic lymphocytic leukemia, except that lymphocytes are not increased in the peripheral blood; lymph nodes are enlarged and other lymphoid tissue or bone marrow is infiltrated by small lymphocytes.

lymphomatoid (lim-fo'mă-toyd). Resembling a lymphoma.

lymphomatosis (lim'fo-mă-to'sis). Any condition characterized by the occurrence of multiple, widely distributed sites of involvement with lymphoma.

lympho'matous. Pertaining to or characterized by lymphoma.

lymphomyxoma (lim'fo-mik-so'mah) [lympho- + G. *myxa*, mucus, + *-oma*, tumor]. A soft nonmalignant neoplasm that contains lymphoid tissue in a matrix of loose, areolar connective tissue.

lymphopathy (lim-fop'ă-thĭ) [lympho- + G. *pathos*, suffering]. Any disease of the lymphatic vessels or lymph nodes.

lymphopenia (lim-fo-pe'nĭ-ah) [lympho- + G. *penia*, poverty]. Lymphocytopenia; lymphocytic leukopenia; a reduction, relative or absolute, in the number of lymphocytes in the circulating blood.

lymphopoiesis (lim'fo-poy-e'sis) [lympho- + G. *poiēsis*, a making]. Formation of lymphocytes.

lymphopoietic (lim'fo-poy-et'ik). Pertaining to or characterized by lymphopoiesis.

lymphoreticulosis (lim'fo-rĕ-tik-u-lo'sis) Proliferation of the reticuloendothelial cells of the lymph glands.

benign inoculation l., cat-scratch *disease*.

lymphorrhagia (lim-fo-ra'jĭ-ah) [lympho- + G. *rhēgnymi*, to burst forth]. Lymphorrhea.

lymphorrhea (lim-fo-re'ah) [lympho- + G. *rhoia*, a flow]. Lymphorrhagia; an escape of lymph on the surface from ruptured, torn, or cut lymphatic vessels.

lymphorrhoid (lim'fo-royd). A dilation of a lymph channel, resembling hemorrhoid.

lymphosarcoma (lim'fo-sar-ko'mah) [lympho- + G. *sarkōma*, sarcoma]. A diffuse lymphocytic lymphoma.

lymphosarcomatosis (lim'fo-sar-ko-mă-to'sis). A condition characterized by the presence of multiple, widely distributed masses of lymphosarcoma.

lymphostasis (lim-fos'tă-sis) [lympho- + G. *stasis*, a standing still]. Obstruction of the normal flow of lymph.

lymphotaxis (lim-fo-tak'sis) [lympho- + G. *taxis*, orderly arrangement]. Exertion of an effect that attracts or repels lymphocytes.

lymphotoxicity (lim'fo-toks-is'ĭ-tĭ). The potential of an antibody in the serum of an allograft recipient to react directly with the lymphocytes or other cells of an allograft donor to produce a hyperacute type of graft rejection.

lymphotoxin (lim-fo-tok'sin). A lymphokine that lyses or damages many cell types.

lyo- [G. *lyō*, to loosen, dissolve]. Combining form relating to dissolution. See also *lyso-*.

lyophil, lyophile (li'o-fil, -fīl). Lyophilic.

lyophilic (li-o-fil'ik) [lyo- + G. *phileō*, to love]. Lyophil; lyophile; lyotropic; in colloid chemistry, denoting a dispersed phase having a pronounced affinity for the dispersion medium.

lyophilization (li-of'ĭ-lĭ-za'shun). Freeze-drying; the process of isolating a solid substance from solution by freezing the solution and evaporating the ice under the vacuum.

lyophobe (li'o-fōb). Lyophobic.

lyophobic (li-o-fo'bik) [lyo- + G. *phobos*, fear]. Lyophobe; denoting a dispersed phase having but slight affinity for the dispersion medium.

lyotropic (li-o-trop'ik) [lyo- + G. *tropē*, a turning]. Lyophilic.

ly'pressin. 8-Lysine vasopressin; vasopressin containing lysine in position 8; an antidiuretic and vasopressor hormone.

Lys Lysine or its radicals in peptides.

lys- See *lyso-*.

ly'sate. The material (cellular debris and fluid) produced by lysis.

lyse (liz). Lyze; to break up, to disintegrate, to effect lysis.

lysemia (li-se'mĭ-ah) [lyso- + G. *haima*, blood]. Disintegration or dissolution of red blood cells and the occurrence of hemoglobin in the circulating plasma and in the urine.

lysergic acid diethylamide (LSD) (li-sur'jik). Lysergide; a derivative of D-lysergic acid, a cleavage product of alkaline hydrolysis of ergot alkaloids; a hallucinogen and serotonin antagonist.

lysergide (li-ser'jĭd). Lysergic acid diethylamide.

ly'sin. 1. A specific complement-fixing antibody that acts destructively on cells and tissues; various types are designated in accordance with the form of antigen that stimulates its production. **2.** Any substance that causes lysis.

lysine (Lys) (li'sēn). 2,6-Diaminohexanoic acid; $NH_2(CH_2)_4CH(NH_2)COOH$; an α-amino acid found in many proteins; distinguished by an ε-amino group.

lysinemia (li-sĭ-ne'mĭ-ah). Increased concentration of lysine in the blood, associated with mental and physical retardation.

lysin'ogen. An antigen that stimulates the formation of a specific lysin.

lysinogenic (li'sĭ-no-jen'ik). Having the property of a lysinogen.

lysinuria (li'sĭ-nu'rĭ-ah). Presence of lysine in the urine.

lysis (li'sis) [G. dissolution or loosening]. **1.** Gradual subsidence of the symptoms of an acute disease, a form of curative process, distinguished from crisis. **2.** Destruction of red blood cells, bacteria, and other antigens, by a specific lysin.

lyso-, lys- [G. lysis, a loosening or dissolution]. Combining forms relating to lysis, or dissolution. See also lyo-.

lysogen (li'so-jen) [lysin + G. suffix -gen, producing]. **1.** Something capable of inducing lysis. **2.** A bacterium in the state of lysogeny.

lysogenesis (li-so-jen'ĕ-sis). Production of lysins.

lysogenic (li-so-jen'ik). **1.** Causing or having the power to cause lysis, indicating the action of certain antibodies and chemical substances. **2.** Pertaining to bacteria in the state of lysogeny.

lysogenicity (li'so-jĕ-nis'ĭ-tĭ). The property of being lysogenic.

lysogeny (li-soj'ĕ-nĭ The phenomenon of a culture of a bacterial strain being capable of inducing, by means of its contained bacteriophage, general lysis in a culture of another bacterial strain without itself undergoing obvious lysis.

ly'soki'nase. Term proposed for activator agents, such as streptokinase, urokinase, or staphylokinase, that produce plasmin by indirect or multiple-stage action on plasminogen.

lysosome (li'so-sōm) [lyso- + G. soma, body]. A cytoplasmic, membrane-bound particle, 0.5 μm or less in diameter, containing hydrolyzing enzymes.

   primary l.'s, cytoplasmic bodies produced at the Golgi apparatus where hydrolytic enzymes are incorporated; they fuse with phagosomes or pinosomes to become secondary l.'s.

   secondary l.'s, l.'s in which lysis takes place, owing to the activity of hydrolytic enzymes.

lysozyme (li'so-zim). Muramidase; an enzyme destructive to cell walls of certain bacteria.

lyssa (lis'ah) [G. madness]. Old term for rabies.

Lyssavirus (lis'să-vi-rus). A genus of viruses (family Rhabdoviridae) that includes the rabies virus group.

lytic (ly'ik). Pertaining to lysis.

lyze (liz). Lyse.

M

μ [mu, 12th letter of the G. alphabet]. Micro-; micron.

μμ Micromicro-. See pico-.

μm Micrometer.

M Myopia or myopic; mega-; morgan.

M Moles per liter.

m Meter; minim; milli-; mass.

m- meta-.

mμ Millimicron.

ma Milliampere.

MAA Macroaggregated albumin.

Mace, MACE ω-Chloracetophenone (the classical lacrimator) in a light petroleum dispersant and a Freon-like propellant.

macerate (mas'er-āt) [see maceration]. To soften by steeping or soaking.

maceration (mas-er-a'shun) [L. macero, pp. -atus, to soften by soaking]. **1.** Softening by the action of a liquid. **2.** Softening of tissues after death by nonputrefactive (sterile) autolysis.

macrencephaly (mak'ren-sef'ă-lĭ) [macro- + G. enkephalos, brain]. Hypertrophy of the brain.

macro-, macr- [G. makros, large]. Combining form meaning large or long. See also mega-, megalo-.

mac'roam'ylase. A form of serum amylase in which the enzyme is present as a complex joined to a globulin, with a molecular weight that makes renal excretion of the complex not appreciable.

macroamylasemia (mak'ro-am'ĭ-la-se'mĭ-ah) [macroamylase + G. haima, blood]. A form of hyperamylasemia, in which a portion of serum amylase exists as macroamylase.

mac'robiot'ic. 1. Long-lived. **2.** Tending to prolong life.

mac'roblast [macro- + G. blastos, germ]. A large erythroblast.

macroblepharia (mak'ro-blĕ-făr'ĭ-ah) [macro- + G. blepharon, eyelid, + -ia, condition]. The state of having abnormally large eyelids.

macrocardia (mak-ro-kar'dĭ-ah). Cardiomegaly.

macrocephalic, macrocephalous (mak'ro-sĕ-fal'ik, -sef'ă-lus) [macro- + G. kephalē, head]. Megacephalic.

macrocephaly (mak'ro-sef'ă-lĭ) [macro- + G. kephalē, head]. Megacephaly.

macrocheilia, macrochilia (mak-ro-ki'lĭ-ah) [macro- + G. cheilos, lip]. **1.** Abnormally enlarged lips. **2.**

Cavernous lymphangioma of the lip, a permanent swelling of the lip resulting from the presence of greatly distended lymphatic spaces.

macrocheiria, macrochiria (mak-ro-ki'ri'ah) [macro- + G. *cheir,* hand]. Cheiromegaly; chiromegaly; megalocheiria; megalochiria; abnormally large hands.

macrocolon (mak'ro-ko'lon). A sigmoid colon of unusual length; a variety of megacolon.

macrocornea (mak-ro-kor'ne-ah). Megalocornea; an unusually large cornea.

macrocra'nium. An enlarged skull, especially the bones containing the brain, as seen in hydrocephalus.

macrocryoglobulinemia (mak'ro-kri-o-glob'u-lin-e'mi-ah). Presence of cold-precipitating macroglobulins (cold hemagglutinins) in the periheral blood.

macrocyte (mak'ro-sīt) [macro- + G. *kytos,* a hollow (cell)]. A large erythrocyte, such as those observed in pernicious anemia.

macrocythemia (mak'ro-si-the'mi-ah) [macrocyte + G. *haima,* blood]. Macrocytosis; occurence of unusually large numbers of macrocytes in the circulating blood.

macrocytosis (mak'ro-si-to'sis) [macrocyte + G. *-osis,* condition]. Macrocythemia.

macrodac'tyly. Megadactyly.

macrodontia (mak-ro-don'shi-ah). Megalodontia; megadontism; the state of having abnormally large teeth.

macrogamete (mak-ro-gam'ēt) [macro- + G. *gametē,* wife]. The female element in anisogamy, or conjugation of unicellular organisms of unequal size; the larger of the two sex cells, with more reserve material, and usually nonmotile.

macrogametocyte (mak'ro-gă-me'to-sīt). The female gametocyte or mother cell producing the macrogamete.

macrogenitosomia (mak'ro-jen'ĭ-to-so'mi-ah) [macro- + L. *genitalis,* genital, + G. *sōma,* body]. Excessive bodily and genital development.

   m. pre'cox, puberty in which gonadal maturation and adolescent growth spurt in bodily height occur in the first decade of life.

macroglia (mă-krog'li-ah) [macro- + G. *glia,* glue]. Astrocyte.

macroglobulin (mak'ro-glob-u-lin). Plasma globulin that has an unusually large molecular weight, as much as 1,000,000.

mac'roglob'uline'mia. Presence of macroglobulins in the circulating blood.

   Waldenström's m., m. occurring in elderly persons, especially women, characterized by proliferation of cells resembling lymphocytes or plasma cells in the bone marrow, anemia, increased sedimentation rate, and hyperglobulinemia.

mac'roglos'sia [macro- + G. *glōssa,* tongue]. Megaloglossia; pachyglossia; enlargement of the tongue.

macrognathia (mak-ro-na'thi-ah) [macro- + G. *gnathos,* jaw, + *-ia,* condition]. Enlargement or elongation of the jaw.

mac'rolides. A class of antibiotics characterized by molecules made up of large-ring lactones.

macromastia (mak-ro-mas'ti-ah) [macro- + G. *mastos,* breast]. Abnormally large breasts. See also hypermastia.

macromelia (mak-ro-me'li-ah) [macro- + G. *melos,* limb]. Megalomelia; abnormally large size of one or more of the extremities.

macromolecule (mak-ro-mol'e-kūl). A molecule of colloidal size, notably proteins, nucleic acids, and polysaccharides.

mac'romon'ocyte. An unusually large monocyte.

macromyeloblast (mak'ro-mi'ē-lo-blast). An abnormally large myeloblast.

mac'ronor'moblast. 1. A large normoblast. 2. A large, incompletely hemoglobiniferous, nucleated red blood cell with a "cart-wheel" nucleus.

macronucleus (mak-ro-nu'kle-us). A nucleus that occupies a relatively large portion of the cell, or the larger nucleus where two (or more) are present in a cell.

macronychia (mak-ro-nik'ĭ-ah) [macro- + G. *onyx,* nail]. Abnormally large fingernails or toenails.

macropenis (mak-ro-pe'nis). Megalopenis; an abnormally large penis.

macrophage (mak'ro-fāj) [macro- + G. *phagein,* to eat]. Any large ameboid mononuclear phagocytic cell, regardless of origin.

macrophthalmia (mak-rof-thal'mi-ah) [macro- + G. *ophthalmos,* eye]. Megalophthalmus.

macropodia (mak-ro-po'di-ah) [macro- + G. *pous,* foot]. Megalopodia; abnormally large feet.

macropolycyte (mak-ro-pol'ĭ-sīt) [macro- + G. *polys,* many, + *kytos,* cell]. An unusually large polymorphonuclear neutrophilic leukocyte that contains a multisegmented nucleus.

macroprosopia (mak'ro-pro-so'pĭ-ah) [macro- + G. *prosōpon,* face]. A large face out of proportion to the size of the cranial vault.

macrorhinia (mak-ro-rin'ĭ-ah) [macro- + G. *rhis (rhin-),* nose]. Excessive size of the nose.

macroscopic (mak-ro-skop'ik). Relating to macroscopy; visible to the naked eye.

macroscopy (mă-kros'ko-pi) [macro- + G. *skopeō,* to view]. Examination of objects with the naked eye.

macrosig'moid. Enlargement or dilation of the sigmoid colon.

macrosomia (mak-ro-so'mi-ah) [macro- + G. *sōma,* body]. Abnormally large size of the body.

macrostomia (mak-ro-sto'mi-ah) [macro- + G. *stoma,* mouth]. Abnormally large size of the mouth.

macrotia (mak-ro'shi-ah) [macro- + G. *ous,* ear, + *-ia,* condition]. Excessive enlargement of the auricle.

macula, pl. **maculae** (mak'u-lah, -u-le) [L. a spot]. Spot (1); macule. 1 [NA]. A small spot, perceptibly different in color from the surrounding tissue. 2. A small, discolored patch or spot on the skin, neither elevated above nor depressed below the skin's surface.

mac'ulae acus'ticae, see m. sacculi and m. utriculi.

m. adher'ens, desmosome.

m. atroph'ica, an atrophic glistening white spot in the skin.

m. ceru'lea, blue spot (1); a bluish stain on the skin caused by the bites (saliva) of fleas or lice.

m. cor'neae, a moderately dense opacity of the cornea.

m. cribro'sa [NA], one of three areas (inferior, middle, and superior) on the wall of the vestibule of the labyrinth, marked by numerous foramina giving passage to nerve filaments supplying portions of the membranous labyrinth.

m. den'sa, a densely packed collection of special staining cells in the distal tubular epithelium of a nephron, in direct apposition to the juxtaglomerular cells.

m. fla'va, a yellowish spot at the anterior extremity of the rima glottidis where the two vocal folds join.

m. lu'tea, m. ret'inae [NA], yellow spot; an oval area of the sensory retina, temporal to the optic disk, corresponding to the posterior pole of the eye; at its center is the fovea centralis, which contains only retinal cones.

m. sac'culi [NA], the oval neuroepithelial sensory area in the anterior wall of the saccule.

m. utric'uli [NA], the neuroepithelial sensory area in the inferolateral wall of the utricle.

macular, maculate (mak'u-lar, -lāt). **1.** Relating to or marked by macules. **2.** Denoting the retina, especially the macula retinae.

macule (mak'ūl) [L. *macula,* spot]. Macula.

maculocerebral (mak'u-lo-sĕr'ĕ-bral). Denoting a type of nervous disease marked by degenerative lesions in both the retina and the brain.

maculoerythematous (mak'u-lo-ĕr-ĭ-the'mă-tus). Denoting lesions that are erythematous and macular, covering wide areas.

maculopapule (mak'u-lo-pap'ūl). A lesion with a sessile base, that slopes from a papule in the center.

maculopathy (mak-u-lop'ă-thī). Any pathological condition of the macula lutea.

mad'aro'sis [G. a falling off of the eyelashes]. Milphosis.

Madurella (mad-u-rel'ah) [*Madura,* India]. A genus of the Fungi Imperfecti, including a number of species that cause maduromycosis, and two species, *M. grisea* and *M. mycetomi,* that cause mycetoma.

maduromycosis (mad'u-ro-mi-ko'sis). A type of mycetoma caused by a varied group of filamentous or true fungi and characterized by the formation of tumefactions and sinuses, from which serosanguineous or "oily" exudate drains (containing characteristic granules of variable colors).

mag'got. A fly larva or grub.

magistral (maj'is-tral) [L. *magister,* master]. Denoting a preparation compounded according to a physician's prescription.

magma (mag'mah) [G. a soft mass or salve, fr. *massō,* to knead]. **1.** A soft mass left after extraction of the active principles. **2.** A salve or thick paste.

magnesia (mag-ne'zhuh) [see magnesium]. Magnesium oxide.

magnesium (mag-ne'zhĭ-um) [Mod. L. fr. G. *Magnēsia,* a region in Thessaly]. A mineral element, symbol Mg, atomic no. 12, atomic weight 24.31, oxidizing to the alkaline earth magnesia; many of its salts are used medicinally.

m. sulfate, Epsom salts; the active ingredient of most of the natural laxative waters, and a promptly acting cathartic particularly useful in certain poisonings; when applied locally, it has anti-inflammatory action.

magnification (mag'nĭ-fĭ-ka'shun) [L. *magnifico,* pp. *-atus,* to magnify]. **1.** The seeming increase in size of an object viewed under the microscope, expressed by a figure preceded by ×, indicating the number of times its diameter is enlarged. **2.** The increased amplitude of a tracing, as of a muscular contraction.

magnocellular (mag-no-sel'u-lar) [L. *magnus,* large, + cellular]. Composed of cells of large size.

maidenhead (ma'den-hed). Infrequently used term for the intact hymen of a virgin.

main'streaming. Providing the least restrictive environment socially, physically, and educationally for handicapped individuals by introducing them into the natural environment rather than segregating them into homogenous groups in a sheltered environment.

maintainer (mān-ta'ner). A device utilized to hold or keep teeth in a given position.

mal (mahl) [Fr. fr. L. *malum,* an evil]. A disease or disorder.

grand m., generalized *epilepsy.*

m. de mer, seasickness.

petit m., absence.

mal- [L. *malus,* bad]. Combining form meaning ill or bad.

mala (ma'lah) [L. cheek bone]. Cheek.

mal'absorp'tion. Imperfect, inadequate or otherwise disordered gastrointestinal absorption.

malacia (mă-la'shĭ-ah) [G. *malakia,* a softness]. Malacosis; mollities (2); a softening or loss of consistency and contiguity in any of the organs or tissues. Also used as combining form in suffix position.

malacoplakia (mal'ă-ko-pla'kĭ-ah) [G. *malakos,* soft + *plax,* plate, plaque]. A rare lesion in the mucosa of the urinary bladder, characterized by numerous mottled yellow and gray soft plaques and nodules that consist of numerous macrophages and calcospherites (Michaelis-Guttman bodies) which may form around intracellular bacteria.

malacosis (mal'ă-ko'sis). Malacia.

malacotic (mal'ă-kot'ik). Pertaining to or characterized by malacia.

mal'adjust'ment. In the mental health professions, an inability to cope with the problems and challenges of everyday living.

malady (mal'ă-dĭ) [Fr. *maladie*, illness]. Disease; illness; especially a chronic, usually fatal, disease.

malaise (mă-lāz') [Fr. discomfort]. A feeling of general discomfort; an out-of-sorts feeling.

malalignment (mal'ă-lin'ment). Displacement of a tooth or teeth from a normal position in the dental arch.

ma'lar. Relating to the mala, the cheek or cheek bones.

malaria (mă-la'rĭ-ah) [It. *malo* (fem. *mala*), bad, + *aria*, air, referring to the old theory of the miasmatic origin of the disease]. Jungle fever; swamp fever (2); a disease caused by the presence of the sporozoan *Plasmodium* in human or other vertebrate red blood cells, and transmitted to humans by the bite of an infected female mosquito of the genus *Anopheles*, that previously sucked the blood from a person with m.

    acute m., a form of m. that may be intermittent or remittent, consisting of a chill accompanied and followed by fever with its attendant general symptoms, and terminating in a sweating stage; the paroxysms, caused by release of merzoites from infected cells, recur every 48 hours in tertian (vivax) m., every 72 hours in quartan (malariae) m., and at indefinite but frequent intervals, usually about 48 hours, in falciparum (malignant tertian) m.

    chronic m., m. that develops after frequently repeated attacks of one of the acute forms, usually falciparum m.; characterized by profound anemia, enlargement of the spleen, emaciation, mental depression, sallow complexion, edema of ankles, feeble digestion, and muscular weakness.

    falciparum m., malignant tertian m.; m. caused by *Plasmodium falciparum;* 48-hr malarial paroxysms of severe form occur with acute cerebral, renal, or gastrointestinal manifestations in severe cases, chiefly caused by the large number of red blood cells affected and the tendency for infected red cells to become sticky and clump, blocking capillaries.

    malariae m., quartan m.; m. with paroxysms that recur every 72 hours or every fourth day (reckoning the day of the paroxysm as the first); due to the schizogony and invasion of new red blood corpuscles by *Plasmodium malariae*.

    malignant tertian m., falciparum m.

    quartan m., malariae m.

    quotidian m., m. in which the paroxysms occur daily, usually a double tertian, in which there is an infection by two distinct groups of *Plasmodium* sporulating alternately every 48 hours.

    vivax m., tertian m., m. with paroxysms that recur every 48 hours or every third day (reckoning the day of the paroxysm as the first); the fever is induced by release of merozoites and their invasion of new red blood corpuscles.

malarial (mă-lārĭ-al). Pertaining to or affected with malaria.

Malassezia (mal-ă-sa'zĭ-ah) [L. C. *Malassez*]. A genus of fungi. *M. furfur* causes tinea versicolor (pityriasis versicolor).

mal'assimila'tion. Incomplete or faulty assimilation.

mal'ate. A salt or ester of malic acid.

malate dehydrogenase. An enzyme that catalyzes, through NAD or NADP, the dehydrogenation of malate to oxaloacetate or its decarboxylation to pyruvate.

malaxation (mal-ak-sa'shun) [L. *malaxo*, pp. *-atus*, to soften]. **1.** Formation of ingredients into a mass for pills and plasters. **2.** A kneading process in massage.

male (māl) [L. *masculus*, fr. *mas*, male]. **1.** In zoology, denoting the sex to which those belong that produce spermatozoa; an individual of the male sex. **2.** Masculine.

    genetic m., (1) an individual with a normal m. karyotype, including one X and one Y chromosome; (2) an individual whose cell nuclei do not contain Barr sex chromatin bodies (normally present in females and absent in males).

mal'erup'tion. Faulty eruption of teeth.

mal'forma'tion. Failure of proper or normal development; a primary structural defect that results from a localized error of morphogenesis.

mal'function. Disordered, inadequate or abnormal function.

malic acid (mal'ik, ma'lik). Hydroxysuccinic acid; $HOOCCH_2CHOHCOOH$; an acid found in apples and various other tart fruits; an intermediate in the tricarboxylic acid cycle.

malignancy (mă-lig'nan-sĭ). The property or condition of being malignant.

malignant (mă-lig'nant) [L. *maligno*, pres. p. *-ans* (*ant-*), to do anything maliciously]. **1.** Resistant to treatment; occurring in severe form, and frequently fatal; tending to become worse and lead to an ingravescent course. **2.** In reference to a neoplasm, having the property of locally invasive and destructive growth and metastasis.

malinger (mă-ling'ger) [Fr. *malingre*, poor, weakly]. To sham; to feign an illness, usually in order to escape work, excite sympathy, or gain compensation.

malingerer (mă-ling'ger-er). One who feigns illness.

malinterdigitation (mal'in-ter-dij'ĭ-ta'shun). Faulty intercuspation of teeth.

malleable (mal'e-ă-bl) [L. *malleus*, a hammer]. Capable of being shaped by being beaten or by pressure, a property of certain metals.

malleoincudal (mal'e-o-ing'ku-dal). Relating to the malleus and the incus in the typarum.

malleolar (mă-le'o-lar). Relating to one or both malleoli.

malleolus, pl. **malleoli** (mă-le′o-lus, -li) [L. dim. of *malleus,* hammer] [NA]. A rounded bony prominence such as those on either side of the ankle joint.

malleotomy (mal-e-ot′o-mĭ). **1** [malleus + G. *tomē,* incision]. Division of the malleus. **2** [malleolus + G. *tomē,* incision]. Division of the ligaments holding the malleoli in apposition, to permit their separation.

malleus, gen. and pl. **mallei** (mal′e-us, mal′e-i) [L. a hammer] [NA]. Hammer; the largest of the three auditory ossicles, resembling a club, which is attached to the tympanic membrane and articulating with the body of the incus.

malnutrition (mal-nu-trish′un). Faulty nutrition resulting from malassimilation, poor diet, or overeating.

malocclusion (mal′o-klu′zhun). **1.** Any deviation from a physiologically acceptable contact of opposing dentitions. **2.** Any deviation from a normal occlusion.

malonic acid (mă-lo′nik, -lon′ik). Propanedioic acid; $HOOC-CH_2-COOH$; a dicarboxylic acid of importance in intermediary metabolism.

malonyl-CoA (mal′o-nil). Malonylcoenzyme A; the condensation product of malonic acid and coenzyme A, an intermediate in fatty acid synthesis.

malpighian (mahl-pig′ĭ-an). Described by or attributed to Marcello Malpighi.

malposition (mal-po-zish′un). Dystopia.

mal′prac′tice. Mistreatment of a disease or injury through ignorance, carelessness, or criminal intent.

mal′presenta′tion. Faulty presentation of the fetus; presentation of any part other than the occiput.

mal′rota′tion. Failure during embryonic development of normal rotation of all or any portion of the intestinal tract.

maltose (mawl-tōs). 4-(α-D-Glucosido)-D-glucose; a disaccharide formed in the hydrolysis of starch and consisting of two glucose residues bound by a 1,4-α-glycoside link.

ma′lum [L. an evil]. A disease.

malunion (mal-ūn′yun). Incomplete union, or union in a faulty position, after fracture or a wound of the soft parts.

mamil-, mamilli- [L. *mamilla,* nipple]. Combining forms relating to the mamillae. See also mammil-. mammilli-.

mamilla, pl. **mamillae** (mă-mil′ah, mă-mil′e) [L. nipple]. **1.** A small rounded elevation resembling the female breast. **2.** *Papilla mammae.*

mam′illary. Relating to or shaped like a nipple.

mam′illate, mam′illated. Studded with nipple-like projections.

mamilla′tion. **1.** A nipple-like projection. **2.** The condition of being mamillated.

mamil′liform [L. *mamilla,* nipple, + *forma,* form]. Nipple-shaped.

mamma, gen. and pl. **mammae** (mam′ah, mam′e) [L.] [NA]. Breast (2); the organ of milk secretion; one of two hemispheric projections of variable size situated in the subcutaneous layer over the pectoralis major muscle on either side of the chest; rudimentary in the male. See *glandula mammaria.*

mammalgia (mă-mal′jĭ-ah) [L. *mamma,* breast, + G. *algos,* pain]. Mastodynia.

mam′maplasty [L. *mamma,* breast, + G. *plasso,* to form]. Mammoplasty; plastic surgery on the breast to alter its shape, size and/or position.

   augmentation m., plastic surgery to enlarge the breast, often by insertion of an implant.

   reconstructive m., the making of a simulated breast by plastic surgery, to replace the appearance of one that has been removed.

   reduction m., plastic surgery on the breast to reduce its size and (frequently) to improve its shape and position.

mam′mary. Relating to the breasts.

mammectomy (mă-mek′to-mĭ) [L. *mamma,* breast, + *ektomē,* excision]. Mastectomy.

mam′miform [L. *mamma,* breast, + *forma,* form]. Mammose (1); resembling a breast; breast-shaped.

mammil-, mammilli- [L. *mammilla (mamilla),* nipple]. Combining forms relating to the mamillae. See also mamil-, mamilli-.

mammillaplasty (mă-mil′ă-plas-tĭ) [L. *mammilla,* nipple, + G. *plasso,* to form]. Theleplasty; plastic surgery of the nipple and areola.

mammillitis (mam′ĭ-li′tis) [L. *mamilla,* nipple, + G. *-itis,* imflammation]. Inflammation of the nipple.

mammitis (mă-mi′tis) [L. *mamma,* breast, + G. *-itis,* inflammation]. Mastitis.

mammo- [L. *mamma,* breast]. Combining form relating to the breasts.

mammogens I and II (mam′o-jen) [mammo- + G. *-gen,* producing]. Mammogenic *hormones.*

mam′mogram. A radiograph of the breast.

mammography (mă-mog′ră-fĭ) [mammo- + G. *graphō,* to write]. Radiographic examination of the breast.

mam′moplasty [mammo- + G. *plasso,* to mold]. Mammaplasty.

mam′mose. **1.** Mammiform. **2.** Having large breasts.

mammotomy (mă-mot′o-mĭ) [mammo- + G. *tomē,* incision]. Mastotomy.

mammotropic, mammotrophic (mam-o-trop′ik, mam-o-trof′ik) [mammo- + G. *tropos,* a turning]. Having a stimulating effect upon the development, growth, or function of the mammary glands

mandel′ic acid. $C_6H_5CHOHCOOH$; a urinary antibacterial agent (both bactericidal and bacteriostatic).

mandelytropine. Homatropine.

mandible (man′dĭ-bl). Mandibula.

mandibula, pl. **mandibulae** (man-dib′u-lah, -le) [L. a jaw, fr. *mando,* pp. *mansus,* to chew] [NA]. Mandible; jaw bone; submaxilla; a U-shaped bone, forming the lower jaw, articulating by its upturned extremities with the temporal bone on either side.

mandib′ular. Inframaxillary; submaxillary (1); relating to the lower jaw.

mandib'ulofa'cial. Relating to the mandible and the face.

mandib'ulo-oc'ulofa'cial. Relating to the mandible and the orbital part of the face.

man'drel, man'dril [G. *mandra,* the bed in which a ring's stone is set]. **1.** The shaft or spindle to which a tool is attached and by means of which it is rotated. **2.** Mandrin. **3.** In dentistry, an instrument used in a handpiece to hold a disk, stone, or cup used for grinding, smoothing, or finishing.

man'drin [Fr. *mandrin,* mandrel]. Mandrel (2); a stiff wire or stylet inserted in the lumen of a soft catheter to give it shape and firmness while passing through a hollow tubular structure.

maneuver (mă-nu'ver) [Fr. *manoeuvre,* fr. L. *manu operari,* to work by hand]. A planned movement or procedure.

    Bracht m., delivery of a fetus in breech position by which the fetal head is expelled spontaneously.

    Brandt-Andrews m., a method of expressing the placenta by grasping the umbilical cord with one hand and placing the other hand on the abdomen.

    Giffard's m., in breech delivery, a m. to flex the aftercoming head.

    Heimlich m., expulsion of an obstructing bolus of food from the throat by suddenly thrusting the fist into the abdomen between the navel and the rib cage so as to force air up the trachea and dislodge the obstruction.

    key-in-lock m., a method by which obstetrical forceps are used to rotate the fetal head.

    Mauriceau's m., a method of assisted breech delivery in which the infant's body is astraddle the right forearm, and the middle finger of the right hand is in the fetal mouth to maintain flexion while traction is made upon the shoulders by the other hand.

    Pinard's m., in breech delivery, flexion of the leg while wiping it along the other thigh as the foot is brought down and out.

    Prague m., a technique for delivery of the fetus in breech position when the fetal occiput is posterior.

    Scanzoni's m., forceps rotation and traction in a spiral course, with reapplication of forceps for delivery.

    Sellick's m., pressure applied to the cricoid cartilage, to prevent regurgitation during endotracheal intubation in the anesthetized patient.

    Valsalva m., (1) forced expiratory effort with closed nose and mouth to inflate the eustachian tubes and middle ears, as used by persons descending from high altitudes; (2) any forced expiratory effort against a closed airway to increase intrathoracic pressure and thus impede venous return to the right atrium; used to study cardiovascular effects of raised peripheral venous pressure and decreased cardiac filling and cardiac output.

manganese (mang'gă-nēz) [Mod. L. *manganesium, manganum,* an altered form of *magnesium*]. A metallic element, symbol Mn, atomic no. 25, atomic weight 54.94.

mange (mānj) [Fr. *manger,* to eat]. A cutaneous disease of domestic and wild animals caused by any one of several genera of skin-burrowing mites; in man, such infestations are usually referred to as scabies or itch.

mania (ma'nĭ-ah) [G. frenzy]. An emotional disorder characterized by great psychomotor activity, excitement, a rapid passing of ideas, exaltation, and unstable attention.

-mania [G. frenzy]. Combining form used in the suffix position, usually referring to an abnormal love for, or morbid impulse toward, some specific object, place, or action.

maniacal (mă-ni'ă-kal). Manic; relating to or characterized by mania.

manic (man'ik, ma'nik). Maniacal.

manic-depressive. Alternating between epidodes of mania and depression.

man'icy. Behavior characteristic of the manic phase of manic-depressive psychosis.

man'ifesta'tion. Display or disclosure of characteristic signs or symptoms of an illness.

manipulation (mă-nip'u-la'shun) [Mediev. L. *manipulo,* pp. *-atus,* to lead by the hand]. Any manual procedure.

man'nerism. A peculiar or unusual characteristic mode of movement, action, or speech.

man'nitol. The hexahydric alcohol, widespread in plants, derived by reduction of fructose; used in renal function testing to measure glomerular filtration, and intravenously as an osmotic diuretic.

man'nose. An aldohexose obtained from various plant sources.

mannose-1-phosphate guanylyltransferase (GDP). A transferase that catalyzes the transfer of GDP to the mannose of mannose 1-phosphate.

man'nosido'sis. Congenital deficiency of α-mannosidase; associated with mental retardation, kyphosis, enlarged tongue, and vacuolated lymphocytes, with accumulation of mannose in tissues; autosomal recessive inheritance.

manometer (mă-nom'ĕ-ter) [G. *manos,* thin, scanty, + *metron,* measure]. An instrument for indicating the pressure of gases or vapor, or the tension of the blood.

manomet'ric. Relating to a manometer.

manometry (mă-nom'ĕ-trĭ) [see manometer]. Measurement of pressure of gases by means of a manometer.

Mansonella (man'so-nel'ah) [P. *Manson*]. Generic term for *M. ozzardi,* a filarial parasite occurring in areas of Central and South America, and causing mansonelliasis; the life cycle is similar to that of *Wuchereria bancrofti,* man is the only known definitive host, and the intermediate hosts are biting midges of the genus *Culicodes.*

mansonelliasis (man'so-nĕl-i'ă-sis). Infection with *Mansonella ozzardi,* transmitted to man by biting midges of the genus *Culicodes,* in the serous cavities, especially the peritoneal cavity, and in mesenteric and perivisceral adipose tissue.

Mansonia (man-so'nĭ-ah) [*P. Manson*]. A genus of mosquitoes (tribe Culicini) that are vectors of *Brugia malayi* and *Wuchereria bancrofti*.

man'tle. 1. A covering layer. **2.** Pallium.

manubrium, pl. **manubria** (mă-nu'brĭ-um, -ah) [L. Handle] [NA]. The portion of the sternum or of the malleus similar to a handle.

m. mal'lei [NA], handle of the malleus; the portion extending from the neck of the malleus and embedded in the tympanic membrane.

m. ster'ni [NA], episternum; presternum; the upper segment of the sternum occasionally fused with the body of the sternum and forming the sternal angle.

manus, gen. and pl. **manus** (ma'nus) [L] [NA]. Hand; the distal portion of the superior limb, comprised of the carpus, metacarpus, and digits.

MAO Monoamine oxidase.

MAOI Monoamine oxidase *inhibitor.*

marantic (mă-ran'tik) [G. *marantikos,* wasting]. Marasmic.

marasmic (mă-raz'mik). Marantic; relating to or suffering from marasmus.

marasmus (mă-raz'mus) [G. *marasmos,* withering]. Athrepsia; athrepsy; cachexia, especially in young children, commonly due to prolonged dietary deficiency of protein and calories.

margin (mar'jin) [L. *margo,* border, edge]. Margo; the boundary or edge of any surface. See also border; edge.

ciliary m., (1) the border of the iris attached to the ciliary body; **(2)** the tarsal border of an eyelid.

corneal m., *limbus* corneae.

gingival m., (1) the most coronal portion of the gingiva surrounding the tooth; **(2)** the edge of the free gingiva.

m. of safety, the m. between the therapeutic dose and the lethal dose of a drug.

marginal (mar'jĭ-nal). Relating to a margin.

margination (mar'jĭ-na'shun). A phenomenon that occurs during the relatively early phases of an inflammation; as a result of dilation of capillaries and slowing of the blood stream, leukocytes tend to occupy the periphery of the cross-sectional lumen and adhere to the endothelial cells that line the vessels.

marginoplasty (mar'jĭ-no-plas-tĭ). Plastic or reparative surgery of the tarsal border of an eyelid.

margo, pl. **margines** (mar'go, mar'jĭ-nēz) [L] [NA]. Margin.

marihuana (măr'ĭ-wah'nah) [fr. Sp. *Maria-Juana,* Mary-Jane]. Marijuana; marijuana; popular name for the dried flowering leaves of *Cannabis sativa,* which are smoked as cigarettes; in the U.S., m. includes any part of, or any extracts from, the female plant.

mark [A.S. *mearc*]. Any spot, line, or other figure on the cutaneous or mucocutaneous surface, visible through difference in color, elevation, or other peculiarity.

port-wine m. *nevus* flammeus.

strawberry m., strawberry *nevus.*

mark'er. A characteristic or factor by which a cell or molecule can be recognized or identified.

marmorated (mar'mo-ra-ted) [L. *marmoratus,* marbled]. Denoting a streaked appearance of the skin, like marble.

marrow (măr'o) [A.S. *mearh*]. **1.** The soft, fatty substance filling the medullary cavities and spongy extremities of the long bones. **2.** Any soft gelatinous or fatty material resembling the m. of bone. See also medulla.

marsupialization (mar-su'pĭ-al-ĭ-za'shun) [L. *marsupium,* pouch]. Exteriorization of a cyst, or other such enclosed cavity, to create a pouch.

masculine (mas'ku-lin) [L. *masculus,* male]. Relating to or marked by the characteristics of the male sex.

masculinity (mas-ku-lin'ĭ-tĭ). The characteristics of a male.

masculinization (mas'ku-lin-ĭ-za'shun) [L. *masculus,* male]. Attainment of male characteristics.

masculinize (mas'ku-lĭ-nīz). To confer the qualities or characteristics peculiar to the male.

masculinovoblastoma (mas'ku-lin-o'vo-blas-to'mah). An ovarian neoplasm that causes varying degrees of masculinization.

maser (ma'zer) [*m*icrowave *a*mplification by *s*timulated *e*mission of *r*adiation]. See laser.

mask. 1. Any of a variety of disease states producing alteration or discoloration of the skin of the face. **2.** The expressionless appearance seen in certain diseases. **3.** A covering for the mouth amd nose to maintain antiseptic conditions. **4.** A device covering the mouth and nose for administration of inhalation anesthetics or other gases. See also masking.

ecchymotic m., a dusky discoloration of the head and neck occurring when the trunk has been subjected to sudden and extreme compression, as in traumatic asphyxia.

Hutchinson's m., the sensation in tabes dorsalis as if the face were covered with a m. or with cobwebs.

luetic m., a dirty brownish-yellow pigmentation, blotchy in character, resembling that of chloasma, occurring on the forehead, temples, and sometimes cheeks in patients with tertiary syphilis.

mask'ing. 1. In hearing testing, the use of a noise applied to one ear while testing the hearing acuity of the other ear. **2.** In dentistry, an opaque covering used to camouflage the metal parts of a prosthesis.

masochism (maz'o-kizm, mas'o-kizm) [Leopold von Sacher-*Masoch,* Austrian novelist, 1836–1895]. **1.** A form of perversion in which sexual pleasure is heightened in one who is beaten and maltreated. *Cf.* sadism. **2.** A general orientation in life that personal suffering relieves guilt and leads to a reward.

masochist (mas'o-kist). The passive party in the practice of masochism.

mass [L. *massa*, a dough-like mass]. **1.** Massa. **2.** In pharmacy, a soft solid preparation, containing an active medicinal agent, that can be divided and rolled into pills. **3.** One of the seven fundamental SI units, the kilogram.

massa, gen. and pl. **massae** (mas'sah, mas'se) [L.] [NA]. Mass (1); a lump or aggregation of coherent material, as of the atlas.

massage (mă-sahzh') [Fr. from G. *massō*, to knead]. Manipulation of the body by rubbing, pinching, kneading, tapping, etc.

    cardiac m. manual rhythmic compression of the ventricles to maintain the circulation.

    closed chest m., external cardiac m., rhythmic compressiom of the heart between the sternum and spine.

    gingival m., mechanical stimulation of the gingiva by rubbing or pressure.

    open chest m., rhythmic manual compression of the ventricles of the heart with the hand inside the thoracic cavity.

    prostatic m., (1) manual expression of prostatic secretions by digital rectal technique; (2) the emptying of prostatic sini and ducts by repeated downward compression maneuvers.

mas'soth'er'apy [G. *massō*,to knead, + *therapeia*, treatment]. Therapeutic use of massage.

mast-. See masto-.

mastadenitis (mast-ad-ĕ-ni'tis) [masto- + G. *adēn*, gland, + *-itis*, inflammation]. Mastitis.

mastadenoma (mast-ad-ĕ-no'mah) [masto- + G. *adēn*, gland, + *-ōma*, tumor]. A benign neoplasm (adenoma) of the breast

Mastadenovirus (mast'ad-ĕ-no-vi'rus). A genus of the family Adenoviridae, including adenoviruses, with at least 33 antigenic types (species) being infective for man; they can cause respiratory infections, acute follicular conjunctivitis, and epidemic keratoconjunctivitis, but many infections are inapparent.

mastalgia (mas-tal'jĭ-ah) [masto- + G. *algos*, pain]. Mastodynia.

mastatrophy (mas-tat'ro-fĭ) [masto- + atrophy]. Atrophy or wasting of the breasts.

mastectomy (mas-tek'to-mĭ) [masto- + G. *ektomē*, excision]. Mammectomy; excision of the breast.

    extended radical m., excision of the entire breast including the nipple, areola, and overlying skin, plus the pectoral muscles and axillary and internal mammary nodes.

    modified radical m., excision of the entire breast including the nipple, areola, and overlying skin, plus the lymphatic-bearing tissue in the axilla.

    radical m., Halsted's o. (2); excision of the entire breast including the nipple, areola, and overlying skin, plus the pectoral muscles, lymphatic-bearing tissue in the axilla, and various other neighboring tissues.

    simple m., excision of the breast including the nipple, areola, and most of the overlying skin.

    subcutaneous m., excision of the breast tissues, but sparing the skin, nipple, and areola; usually followed by implantation of a prosthesis.

mas'ticate. To chew; to perform mastication.

mastication (mas-tĭ-ka'shun) [L. *mastico*, pp. *-atus*, to chew]. The process of chewing food in preparation for deglutition and digestion.

masticatory (mas'tĭ-kă-to-rĭ). Relating to mastication.

mastigote (mas'tĭ-gōt) [G. *mastix*, a whip]. An individual flagellate.

mastitis (mas-ti'tis) [masto- + G. *-itis*, inflammation]. Mammitis; mastadenitis; inflammation of the breast.

    phlegmonous m., abscess or cellulitis of the breast.

    plasma cell m., a condition of the breasts characterized by tumor-like indurated masses containing numerous plasma cells.

    submammary m., paramastitis; inflammation of the tissues lying deep to the mammary gland.

masto-, mast- [G. *mastos*, breast]. Combining forms relating to the breast.

mastocyte (mas'to-sīt). Mast cell.

mastocytoma (mas'to-si-to'mah) [mastocyte + G. *-oma*, tumor]. A circumscribed accumulation or nodular focus of mast cells, grossly resembling a neoplasm.

mastocytosis (mas'to-si-to'sis) [mastocyte + G. *-osis*, condition]. Urticaria pigmentosa, particularly with mast cell infiltration of viscera as well as skin.

mastodynia (mas-to-din'ĭ-ah) [masto- + G. *odynē*, pain]. Mastalgia; mammalgia; pain in the breast.

mastoid (mas'toyd) [masto- + G. *eidos*, resemblance]. **1.** Resembling a mamma; breast-shaped. **2.** Relating to the m. process, antrum, cells, etc.

mastoidectomy (mas-toy-dek'to-mĭ) [mastoid (process) + G. *ektomē*, excision]. Hollowing out of the mastoid process by curretting, gouging, drilling, or otherwise removing the bony partitions forming the mastoid cells.

mastoideocentesis (mas-toyd'e-o-sen-te'sis) [mastoid + G. *kentēsis*, puncture]. Drilling or chiseling into the mastoid cells and antrum.

mastoiditis (mas-toy-di'tis). Inflammation of any part of the mastoid process.

mastoidotomy (mas-toy-dot'o-mĭ) [mastoid (process) + G. *tomē*, cutting]. Incision into the subperiosteum or the mastoid process of the temporal bone.

mastoncus (mas-tong'kus) [masto- + G. *onkos*, mass]. A tumor or swelling of the breasts.

masto-occipital (mas'to-ok-sip'ĭ-tal). Relating to the mastoid portion of the temporal bone and to the occipital bone.

mastoparietal (mas'to-pă-ri'ĕ-tal). Relating to the mastoid portion of the temporal bone and to the parietal bone.

mastopathy (mas-top'ă-thĭ) [masto- + G. *pathos*, suffering]. Any disease of the breasts.

mastopexy (mas'to-pek-sĭ) [masto- + G. *pēxis*, fixation]. Mazopexy; plastic surgery to affix sagging breasts in a more elevated and normal position, often with some improvement in shape.

mastoplasia (mas-to-pla'zĭ-ah) [masto- + G. *plasis*, a molding]. Mazoplasia; enlargement of the breast.

mastoplasty (mas'to-plas-tĭ) [masto- + G. *plassō*, to form]. Any plastic operation on the breast.

mastoptosis (mas-to-to'sis, mas-to-to'sis) [masto- + G. *ptōsis*, a falling]. Ptosis or sagging of the breast.

mastorrhagia (mas-to-ra'jĭ-ah) [masto- + G. *rhēgnymi*, to burst forth]. Hemorrhage from a breast.

mastoscirrhus (mas-to-skĭr'us). A scirrhous carcinoma of the breast.

mastosquamous (mas'to-skwa'mus). Relating to the mastoid and the squamous portions of the temporal bone.

mastotomy (mas-tot'o-mĭ) [masto- + G. *tomē*, incision]. Mammotomy; incision of the breast.

mas'turbate [L. *masturbari*, pp. *masturbatus*]. To practice masturbation.

masturbation (mas-tur-ba'shun) [L. *masturbatio*]. Erotic stimulation of the genital organs usually resulting in orgasm, achieved by manual or other stimulation exclusive of sexual intercourse.

materia (mă-tēr'ĭ-ah) [L. substance]. Substance; matter.

m. al'ba [L. white matter], accumulation or aggregation of microorganisms, desquamated epithelial cells, blood cells and food debris loosely adherent to oral surfaces.

m. med'ica [L. medical matter], old term for: **(1)** that aspect of medical science concerned with the origin and preparation of drugs, their doses, and their mode of administration; **(2)** any agent used therapeutically.

maternal (mă-ter'nal) [L. *maternus*, fr. *mater*, mother]. Relating to or derived from the mother.

maternity (mă-ter'nĭ-tĭ) [see maternal]. Motherhood.

ma'ting. The pairing of male and female for the purpose of reproduction.

assortative m., m. in which pairing of male and female is not random with respect to one or more specified characters.

random m., m. in which the pairing of male and female with respect to one or more characters occurs with the frequency that would be predicted by chance, based on the frequency of the characters in the population.

matrical (ma'trĭ-kăl). Relating to any matrix.

matrices (ma'trĭ-sēz) [L.]. Plural of matrix.

matricide (mat'rĭ-sid) [L. *mater*, mother, + *caedo*, to kill]. Killing of one's mother.

matrilineal (mat-rĭ-lin'e-al) [L. *mater*, mother, + *linea*, line]. Related to descent through the female line.

matrix, pl. **matrices** (ma'triks, -trĭ-sēz) [L. womb; female breeding animal]. **1.** The womb. **2** [NA]. The formative portion of a tissue. **3.** The intercellular substance of a tissue. **4.** A specially shaped device for holding and shaping the material used in filling a tooth cavity.

bone m., the intercellular substance of bone tissue consisting of collagen fibers, ground substance, and inorganic bone salts.

cartilage m., the intercellular substance of cartilage consisting of fibers and ground substance.

territorial m., the more basophilic area around isogenous groups of cells in the cartilage m.

m. un'guis, nail m., nail bed; keratogenous membrane; the area of the corium on which the nail rests.

mat'ter [L. *materies*, substance]. **1.** Substance. **2.** Pus.

gray m., *substantia grisea.*

white m., *substantia alba.*

maturation (mat-u-ra'shun) [L. *maturatio*, a ripening]. **1.** A stage of cell division in the formation of sex cells during which the number of chromosomes in the germ cells is reduced to one-half the number characteristic of the species. **2.** Achievement of full development or growth. **3.** The developmental changes that lead to maturity.

mature (mă-tūr') [L. *maturus*, ripe]. **1.** Ripe; fully developed. **2.** To ripen; to become fully developed.

maturity (mă-tūr'ĭ-tĭ). A state of full development or completed growth.

maxilla, gen. and pl. **maxillae** (mak-sil'ah, -sil'e) [L. jawbone] [NA]. Upper jaw bone; uppper jaw; an irregularly shaped bone supporting the superior teeth and taking part in the formation of the orbit, hard palate, and nasal cavity.

maxillary (mak'sĭ-lĕr-ĭ). Relating to the maxilla.

maxil'loden'tal. Relating to the upper jaw and its associated teeth.

maxil'lofa'cial. Pertaining to the jaws and face, particularly with reference to specialized surgery of this region.

maxil'lomandib'ular. Relating to the upper and lower jaws.

maxillotomy (mak-sĭ-lot'o-mĭ) [maxilla + G. *tomē*, incision]. Surgical sectioning of the maxilla to allow movement of all or a part of the maxilla into the desired portion.

maximum (mak'sĭ-mum) [L. neuter of *maximus*, greatest]. The greatest amount, value, or degree attained or attainable.

glucose transport m., the maximal rate of reabsorption of glucose from the glomerular filtrate.

transport m., tubular m (Tm), the maximal rate of secretion or reabsorption of a substance by the renal tubules.

mazo-. [G. *mazos*, breast]. Combining form relating to the breast. See also masto-.

mazopexy (ma'zo-pek-sĭ). Mastopexy.

mazoplasia (ma-zo-pla'zĭ-ah). Mastoplasia.

MBC Maximum breathing *capacity.*

Mb, MbCO, MbO₂ Myoglobin and its combinations with CO and O₂.

M.C. *Magister Chirurgiae,* Master of Surgery; Medical Corps.

MCH Mean cell *hemoglobin.*

M.Ch. *Magister Chirurgiae,* Master of Surgery.

MCHC Mean cell hemoglobin *concentration.*

mCi Millicurie.

MCV Mean cell *volume.*

Md Mendelevium.

M.D. *Medicinae Doctor,* Doctor of Medicine.

meal (mēl). Food consumed at regular intervals or at a specified time.

Boyden m., a m. consisting of three or four egg yolks, beaten up in milk and sweetened, used to test the evacuation time of the gallbladder.

test m., bland food given to stimulate gastric secretion before analysis of gastric contents.

mean. A statistical measurement of central tendency or average derived from adding a set of values and then dividing the sum by the number of values.

measles (me'zlz) [D. *maselen*]. Morbilli; rubeola; an acute exanthematous disease caused by measles virus and marked by fever and other constitutional disturbances, a catarrhal inflammation of the respiratory mucous membranes, and a generalized red maculopapular eruption followed by a branny desquamation.

atypical m., the rather severe, unusual clinical manifestations of natural m. virus infection in persons with waning vaccination immunity; an accelerated allergic reaction apparently resulting from an anamnestic antibody response, and is characterized by high fever, a shortened prodromal period, atypical rash, and pneumonia.

German m., three-day m., rubella.

hemorrhagic m., black m., a severe form in which the eruption is dark in color due to an effusion of blood into the skin.

meatal (me-a'tal). Relating to a meatus.

meato-. Combining form relating to a meatus.

meatoplasty (me'ă-to-plas-tĭ). Reparative or reconstructive surgery of a meatus or canal.

meatorrhaphy (me-ă-tor'ă-fĭ) [meato- + G *rhaphē,* suture]. Closing by suture of the wound made by performing a meatomy.

meatoscopy (me-ă-tos'ko-pĭ) [meato- + G. *skopeō,* to view]. Inspection, usually instrumental, of a meatus, especially that of the urethra.

meatotomy (me-ă-tot'o-mĭ) [meato- + G. *tomē,* incision]. Porotomy; an incision made to enlarge a meatus, *e.g.,* of the urethra or ureter.

meatus, pl. **meatus** (me-a'tus) [L. a going, a passage] [NA]. A passage or channel, especially the external opening of a canal.

m. acus'ticus [NA], **acoustic m.,** (1) external: auditory canal; the passage leading inward through the tympanic portion of the temporal bone, from the auricle to the membrana tympani; (2) internal: a canal running through the petrous portion of the temporal bone, giving passage to the facial and vestibulocochlear nerves and the labyrinthine artery and veins.

m. na'si [NA], **nasal m.,** the three passages (inferior, middle, superior) in the nasal cavity formed by the projection of the conchae.

ureteral m., *ostium* ureteris.

mechanical (mĕ-kan'ĭ-kal) [G. *meckanikos,* fr. *mē-chanē,* a contrivance, machine]. **1.** Performed by means of some apparatus, not manually. **2.** Explaining phenomena in terms of mechanics. **3.** Automatic.

mechanics (mĕ-kan'iks) [see mechanical]. The science of the action of forces in promoting motion or equilibrium.

mechanism (mek'ă-nizm) [G. *mēchanē,* a contrivance]. **1.** An arrangement or grouping of the parts of anything that has a definite action. **2.** The means by which an effect is obtained.

defense m., (1) a psychological means of coping with conflict or anxiety, *e.g.,* conversion, denial, dissociation, rationalization, repression, and sublimation; (2) the psychic structure underlying a coping strategy; (3) immunological m.

feedback m., feedback *inhibition.*

gating m., (1) occurrence of the maximum refractory period among cardiac conducting cells approximately 2 mm proximal to the terminal Purkinje fibers in the ventricular muscle, beyond which the refractory period is shortened through a sequence of Purkinje cells, transitional cells, and muscular cells; (2) a m. by which painful impulses may be blocked from entering the spinal cord.

immunological m., defense m. (3); the groups of cells (chiefly lymphocytes and cells of the reticuloendothelial system) that function in establishing active acquired immunity (induced sensitivity, allergy).

proprioceptive m., the m. of sense of position and movement, by which one is able to accurately adjust muscular movements and to maintain our equilibrium.

mechanoreceptor (mek'ă-no-re-sep'tor). A receptor which has the role of responding to mechanical pressures.

meconism (me'ko-nizm) [G. *mēkon,* the poppy]. Opium addiction or poisoning.

meconium me-ko'nĭ-um) [L. fr G *mēkōnion,* dim. of *mēkōn,* poppy]. **1.** The first intestinal discharges of the newborn infant, greenish in color and consisting of epithelial cells, mucus, and bile. **2.** Opium.

media (me'dĭ-ah) [L. fem. of *medius,* middle]. **1.** *Tunica* media. **2.** Plural of medium.

medial (me'dĭ-al) [L. *medialis,* middle]. Relating to the middle or center; nearer to the median or midsagittal plane.

median (me'dĭ-an) [L. *medianus,* middle]. **1.** Central; middle; lying in the midline. **2.** The middle value in a set of measurements; like the mean, a measure of central tendency.

me'diastin'oscope. An endoscope for inspection of the mediastinum through a suprasternal incision.

mediastinal (me'dĭ-as-ti'nal). Relating to the mediastinum.

mediastinitis (me'dĭ-as-tĭ-ni'tis). Inflammation of the cellular tissue of the mediastinum.

mediastinography (me'dĭ-as-tĭ-nog'ră-fĭ) [mediastinum + G. *graphō*, to write]. Radiography of the mediastinum.

mediastinopericarditis (me'dĭ-as-tĭ'no-pĕr'ĭ-kar-di'-tis). Inflammation of the pericardium and of the surrounding mediastinal cellular tissue.

mediastinoscopy (me'dĭ-as-tĭ-nos'ko-pĭ) [mediastinum + G. *skopeō*, to view]. Exploration of the mediastinum through a suprasternal incision.

mediastinotomy (me'dĭ-as-tĭ-not'o-mĭ) [mediastinum + G. *tomē*, incision]. Incision into the mediastinum.

mediastinum (me'dĭ-as-ti'num) [Mediev. L. *mediastinus*, medial] [NA]. **1.** A septum between two parts of an organ or a cavity. **2.** Interpleural or mediastinal space; the median partition of the thoracic cavity, covered by the mediastinal pleura and containing all the thoracic viscera and structures except the lungs; divided arbitrarily into superior, middle, inferior, anterior, and posterior parts.

  m. tes'tis [NA], septum of the testis; Highmore's body; a mass of fibrous tissue continuous with the tunica albuginea, projecting into the testis from its posterior border.

mediate (me'dĭ-it, -āt) [L. *medio*, pp. *-atus*, to divide in the middle]. **1.** Situated between two parts; intermediate. **2.** To effect something by means of an intermediary.

medicable (med'ĭ-kă-bl). Treatable with hope of cure.

medical (med'ĭ-kal) [L. *medicalis*, fr. *medicus*, physician]. Relating to medicine or the practice of medicine.

medic'ament [L. *medicamentum*, medicine]. A medicine; a medicinal application; a remedy.

medicate (med'ĭ-kāt) [L. *medico*, pp. *-atus*, to heal]. **1.** To treat disease by the giving of drugs. **2.** To imbue with a medical substance.

medication (med'ĭ-ka'shun). **1.** The act of medicating. **2.** A medicinal substance, or medicament.

medicinal (mĕ-dis'ĭ-nal). Relating to medicine having curative properties.

medicine [L. *medicina*, fr. *medicus*, physician]. **1.** A drug or remedy. **2.** The art and science of preventing or curing disease. **3.** The study and treatment of general diseases or those affecting the internal parts of the body.

  adolescent m., ephebiatrics; the branch of medicine concerned with the treatment of youth of about 13 to 21 years.

  clinical m., the study and practice of m. in relation to the actual patient.

  experimental m., the scientific investigation of medical problems by experimentation upon animals or by clinical research.

  family m., the medical specialty concerned with providing continuous, comprehensive care to all age groups, from first patient contact to terminal care.

  fetal m., the study of the growth, development, care, and treatment of the fetus, and of the environmental factors that may harm the fetus.

  folk m., treatment of ailments in the home by remedies and simple measures based upon experience and knowledge passed from generation to generation.

  forensic m., legal m.; **(1)** the relation and application of medical facts to legal problems; **(2)** the law in its bearing on the practice of medicine.

  internal m., the medical specialty concerned with nonsurgical diseases of a constitutional nature in adults.

  legal m., forensic m.

  nuclear m., the clinical discipline concerned with the diagnostic, therapeutic, and investigative uses of radionuclides, excluding the therapeutic use of sealed radiation sources.

  patent m., a m., usually of secret composition or patented, advertised to the public.

  perinatal m., the branch of m. concerned with care of the mother and fetus during pregnancy, labor, and delivery, particularly when the mother and/or fetus are ill or at risk of becoming ill.

  physical m., physiatry; the study and treatment of disease mainly by mechanical and other physical methods.

  preventive m., the branch of medical science concerned with the prevention of disease and with promotion of physical and mental health, through study of the etiology and epidemiology of disease processes.

  proprietary m., a medicinal compound the formula and mode of manufacture of which are the property of the maker.

  psychosomatic m., the study and treatment of diseases, disorders, or abnormal states in which psychological processes and reactions are believed to play a prominent role.

  socialized m., the control of medical practice by a government agency, the practitioners being an integral part of the organization from which they receive compensation for their services, and to which the public contributes.

  tropical m., the branch of m. concerned with diseases, mainly of parasitic origin, of tropical countries.

  veterinary m., the field concerned with the diseases and health of animal species other than man.

medico- [L. *medicus*, physician]. Combining form meaning medical.

medicochirurgical (med'ĭ-ko-ki-rur'jĭ-kal) [medico- G. *cheirourgia*, surgery]. Relating to both medicine and surgery, or to both physicians and surgeons.

medicolegal (med'ĭ-ko-le'gal) [medico- + L. *legalis*, legal]. Relating to both medicine and the law.

medio-, medi- [L. *medius,* middle]. Combining forms meaning middle, or median.

mediocarpal (me'di-o-kar'pal). **1.** Relating to the central part of the carpus. **2.** Carpocarpal; denoting the articulation between the two rows of carpal bones.

me'diodor'sal. Relating to the median plane and the dorsal plane.

me'diolat'eral. Relating to the median plane and a side.

me'dionecro'sis. Necrosis of a tunica media.

me'diotar'sal. Tarsotarsal; relating to the middle of the tarsus; denoting the articulations of the tarsal bones with each other.

medium, pl. **media** (me'di-um, -ah) [L. neuter of *medius,* middle]. **1.** A means; anything through which an action is performed. **2.** A substance through which impulses or impressions are transmitted. **3.** Culture m. **4.** The liquid holding a substance in solution or suspension.

    contrast m., any material relatively opaque to x-rays, such as barium, used in radiography to visualize the stomach, intestine, or other organ.

    culture m., a substance used for the cultivation, isolation, identification, or storage of microorganisms.

    dispersion m., external *phase.*

me'dius [L.] [NA]. Middle, denoting an anatomical structure that is between two other similar structures or that is midway in position.

MEDLARS Medical Literature Analysis and Retrieval System, a computerized index system of the U. S. National Library of Medicine.

MEDLINE [MEDLARS-on-line]. A telephone linkage between a number of medical libraries in the United States and MEDLARS for rapid provision of medical bibliographies.

medorrhea (me-dor-re'ah) [G. *medos* (sing.), the bladder, *medea* (pl.), the genitals, + *rhoia,* flow]. Gleet.

medulla, pl. **medullae** (me-dul'ah, dul'e) [L. marrow, fr. *medius,* middle] [NA]. Substantia medullaris (1); any soft marrow-like structure, especially in the center of a part.

    m. glan'dulae suprarena'lis [NA], **m. of adrenal gland,** anastomosing cords of cells in the core of the gland; the cells display a chromaffin reaction because of the presence of epinephrine and norepinephrine in their granules.

    m. of hair shaft, the central axis of some hairs, containing air spaces in white hair, surrounded by the cortex.

    m. no'di lymphat'ici, [NA], **m. of lymph node,** the central portion of a node consisting of cordlike masses of lymphocytes separated by lymph sinuses.

    m. oblonga'ta [NA], myelencephalon; the lowest subdivision of the brainstem, immediately continuous with the spinal cord, extending from the lower border of the decussation of the pyramidal tracts up to the pons.

    m. of kidney, m. renis.

    m. os'sium [NA], bone marrow; the tissue filling the cavities of bones, having a stroma of reticular fibers and cells: **(1) m. o. flava,** yellow bone marrow, in which the meshes of the reticular network are filled with fat; **(2) m. o. rubra,** red bone marrow, in which the meshes contain the developmental stages of erythrocytes, leukocytes, and megakaryocytes.

    m. ren'is [NA], m. of the kidney; the inner, darker portion of the kidney parenchyma consisting of the renal pyramids.

    m. spina'lis [NA], spinal cord; the elongated cylindrical portion of the central nervous system contained in the spinal or vertebral canal.

medul'lar. Medullary.

medullary (med'uh-ler-i, me-dul'er-i, med'u-ler-i). Medullar; relating to the medulla or marrow.

med'ullated. **1.** Having a medulla or medullary substance. **2.** Myelinated.

medullectomy (med-u-lek'to-mi) [medulla + G. *ektome,* excision]. Excision of any medullary substance.

medullization (med'uh-li-za'shun, med'u-). Enlargement of the medullary spaces in rarefying osteitis.

medullo- [L. *medulla*]. Combining form meaning medulla.

medulloarthritis (med-ul'o-ar-thri'tis). Inflammation of the cancellous articular extremity of a long bone.

med'ulloblast. A cell of the neural tube that may develop into nerve cells or neuroglial cells.

med'ulloblasto'ma. A glioma consisting of neoplastic cells that resemble the undifferentiated cells of the primitive medullary tube.

medulloepithelioma (med'uh-lo-ep-i-the-li-o'mah). A primitive rapidly growing glioma, thought to originate from the cells of the embryonic medullary canal, which may occur in the central nervous system or in the ciliary body; in the latter they are referred to as dictyoma or malignant ciliary epithelioma.

mega- (M) [G. *megas,* big]. **1.** Combining form meaning large, oversize. See also macro-, megalo-. **2.** Prefix used in the metric system to signify one million (10⁶).

meg'abacte'rium. A bacterium of unusually large size.

meg'ablad'der. Megalocystis.

megacephalic (meg'a-se-fal'ik). Macrocephalic; macrocephalous; megacephalous; relating to or characterized by megacephaly.

megacephalous (meg-a-sef'a-lus). Megacephalic.

megacephaly (meg'a-sef'a-li) [mega- + G. *kephale,* head]. Macrocephaly; megalocephaly; an abnormally large head.

megacolon (meg-a-ko'lon). Extreme dilation and hypertrophy of the colon.

    congenital m., Hirschsprung's disease; congenital dilation and hypertrophy of the colon due to absence (aganglionosis) or marked reduction (hypoganglionosis) in the number of ganglion cells of the myenteric plexus of the rectum and a varying but continuous length of gut above the rectum.

idiopathic m., m. without distal obstruction or absence of ganglion cells, but with thin musculature.

toxic m., acute nonobstructive dilation of the colon, seen in fulminating ulcerative colitis.

meg'acycle. One million cycles.

megadactyl (meg-ă-dak'til) [mega- + G. *daktylos*, finger]. Denoting large fingers.

megadactyly (meg-ă-dak'tĭ-lĭ) [mega- + G. *daktylos*, digit]. Megalodactyly; macrodactyly; dactylomegaly; enlargement of one or more digits.

megadon'tism. Macrodontia.

megaesophagus (meg'ă-e-sof'ă-gus). Enlargement of the lower portion of the esophagus, as seen in patients with achalasia and Chagas disease.

meg'ahertz (MHz). One million hertz.

megakaryoblast (meg-ă-kăr'ĭ-o-blast). Precursor of a megakaryocyte.

megakaryocyte (meg-ă-kăr'ĭ-o-sīt) [mega- + G. *karyon*, nut (nucleus), + *kytos*, hollow vessel (cell)]. Megalokaryocyte; a large cell with a nucleus that is usually multilobed, normally present in bone marrow but not in the circulating blood; gives rise to blood platelets.

megal- See megalo-.

megalgia (meg-al'jĭ-ah) [megal- + G. *algos*, pain]. Very severe pain.

megalo-, megal-, -megaly [G. *megas* (*megal-*), large]. Combining forms meaning large. See also macro-, mega-.

megaloblast (meg'ă-lo-blast) [megalo- + G. *blastos*, + *germ, sprout*]. A large, nucleated, embryonic type of cell that is a precursor of erythrocytes in an abnormal erythropoietic process observed almost exclusively in pernicious anemia.

megalocardia (meg'ă-lo-kar'dĭ-ah) [megalo- + G. *kardia*, heart]. Cardiomegaly.

megalocephaly (meg'ă-lo-sef'ă-lĭ). Megacephaly.

megalocheiria, megalochiria (meg'al-o-ki'rĭ-ah) [megalo- + G. *cheir*, hand]. Macrocheiria.

meg'alocor'nea. Macrocornea.

megalocystis (meg'ă-lo-sis'tis) [megalo- + G. *kystis*, bladder]. Megabladder; an enlarged or overdistended bladder.

megalocyte (meg'ă-lo-sīt) [megalo- + G. *kytos*, cell]. A large nonnucleated red blood cell.

megalodontia (meg'ă-lo-don'shĭ-ah). Macrodontia.

megaloencephalic (meg'ă-lo-en-sĕ-fal'ik). Denoting an abnormally large brain.

megaloencephalon (meg'ă-lo-en-sef'ă-lon) [megalo- + G. *enkephalos*, brain]. An abnormally large brain.

megaloencephaly (meg'ă-lo-en-sef'ă-lĭ) [megalo- + G. *enkephalon*, brain]. Abnormal largeness of the brain.

megaloenteron (meg'ă-lo-en'ter-on) [megalo- + G. *enteron*, intestine]. Enteromegaly; abnormal largeness of the intestine.

meg'alogas'tria [megalo- + G. *gastēr*, stomach, + -*ia*, condition]. Abnormally large size of the stomach.

megaloglossia (meg'ă-lo-glos'sĭ-ah) [megalo- + G. *glōssa*, tongue]. Macroglossia.

megalohepatia (meg'al-o-hē-pat'ĭ-ah). Hepatomegaly.

megalokaryocyte (meg'ă-lo-kăr'ĭ-o-sit). Megakaryocyte.

megalomania (meg'ă-lo-ma'nĭ-ah) [megalo- + G. *mania*, frenzy]. Morbid overevaluation of oneself or of some aspect of oneself.

megalomaniac (meg'ă-lo-ma'nĭ-ak). A person exhibiting megalomania.

meg'alome'lia. Macromelia.

megalopenis (meg'ă-lo-pe'nis). Macropenis.

megalophthalmus (meg'al-of-thal'mus) [megalo- + G. *ophthalmos*, eye]. Macrophthalmia; megophthalmus; abnormally large eyes ocurring as a developmental anomaly.

anterior m., keratoglobus; m. affecting the anterior segment of the eyeball, with associated changes in the zonular ligament and the lens.

megalopodia (meg'ă-lo-po'dĭ-ah) [megalo- + G. *pous*, foot]. Macropodia.

meg'alosple'nia. Splenomegaly.

megalosyndactyly (meg'ă-lo-sin-dak'tĭ-lĭ) [megalo- + G. *syn*, together, + *daktylos*, finger]. Webbed or fused fingers or toes of large size.

megaloureter (meg'ă-lo-u-re'ter). A congenitally enlarged ureter without evidence of obstruction or infection.

megarectum (meg-ă-rek'tum). Extreme dilation of the rectum.

meg'avolt. A unit of electromotive force, equal to one million volts.

meglumine (meg'lu-mēn). *N*-methylglucamine; its diatrizoate, iodipamide, and iothalamate salts are used as contrast and diagnostic radiopaque media.

megophthalmus (meg'of-thal'mus). Megalophthalmus.

meibomian (mi-bo'mĭ-an). Attributed to or described by Hendrik Meibom.

meibomitis, meibomianitis (mi'bo-mi'tis, mi-bo'mĭ-ă-ni'tis). Inflammation of the meibomian glands.

meio-. For words beginning thus and not found here, see mio-.

meiosis (mi-o'sis) [G. *meiōsis*, a lessening]. Meiotic division; the special process of cell division that results in the formation of gametes, consisting of two nuclear divisions in rapid succession that result in the formation of four gametocytes each containing half the number of chromosomes found in somatic cells.

meiotic (mi-ot'ik). Pertaining to meiosis.

mel-, melo-. 1 [G. *melos*, limb]. Combining form indicating limb. **2** [G. *mēlon*, cheek]. Combining form indicating cheek. **3** [L. *mel, mellis*, honey; G. *meli, melitos*, honey]. Combining form relating to honey or sugar. See also meli-.

melag'ra [G. *melos*, limb, + *agra*, seizure]. Rheumatic or myalgic pains in the arms or legs.

melal'gia [G. *melos*, a limb, + *algos*, pain]. Pain in a limb; specifically, burning pain in the feet extending up the leg and thickening of the walls of the blood vessels with obliteration of the vascular lumina.

melan-, melano- [G. *melas*, black]. Combining forms meaning black or extreme darkness of hue.

melancholia (mel-an-ko'lĭ-ah) [melan- + G. *cholē*, bile]. Melancholy. **1.** A mental disorder marked by apathy and indifference to one's surroundings, mental sluggishness, and depression, **2.** A symptom occurring in other conditions, marked by depression of spirits and by a sluggish and painful process of thought.

   m. attoni'ta, m. stuporosa; in schizophrenia, the catatonic state characterized by immobility and muscular rigidity.

   hypochondriacal m., m. with many associated physical complaints, often with little basis in fact.

   involutional m., depressive disorder of middle life, commonly associated with the male or female climacteric.

   m. stuporo'sa, m. attonita.

melancholy (mel'an-kol-ĭ). Melancholia.

melanedema (mel'an-ĕ-de'mah) [melan- + G. *oidēma*, swelling]. Anthracosis.

melanif'erous [melan- (melanin) + L. *ferro*, to carry]. Containing melanin or other black pigment.

mel'anin [G. *melas* (*melan*-), black]. Any of the dark brown to black polymers of indole 5,6-quinone and/or 5,6-dihydroxyindole 2-carboxylic acid that normally occur in the skin, hair, pigmented coat of the retina, and inconstantly in the medulla and zona reticularis of the adrenal gland.

mel'anism. Unusually marked, diffuse, melanin pigmentation of body hair.

melano-. See melan-.

melanoameloblastoma (mel'ă-no-am'e-lo-blas-to'-mah). Melanotic neuroectodermal *tumor*.

mel'anoblast [melano- + G. *blastos*, germ, sprout]. A cell derived from the neural crest that migrates to various parts of the body during the relatively early phases of embryonic life, and then becomes a mature melanocyte capable of forming melanin.

melanoblastoma (mel'ă-no-blas-to'mah) [melano- + G. *blastos*, germ, sprout, + *-ōma*, tumor]. Melanoma.

mel'anocarcino'ma. Melanoma.

melanocyte (mel'ă-no-sīt) [melano- + G. *kytos*, cell]. A cell located at the dermoepidermal junction having branching processes by means of which melanosomes are transferred to epidermal cells, resulting in pigmentation.

melanocytoma (mel'ă-no-si-to'mah) [megalo + cyto- + G. *-oma*, tumor]. **1.** A pigmented tumor of the uveal stroma. **2.** Usually benign melanoma of the optic disk, appearing in highly pigmented individuals as a small deeply pigmented tumor at the edge of the disk, sometimes extending into the retina and choroid.

mel'anoder'ma [melano- + G. *derma*, skin]. An abnormal darkening of the skin by deposition of excess melanin or of metallic substances.

   parasitic m., vagabond's, vagrant's disease; excoriations and m. caused by scratching the bites of the body louse, *Pediculus corporis*.

   senile m., melasma universale; cutaneous pigmentation occurring in the aged.

mel'anodermati'tis. Excessive deposit of melanin in an area of dermatitis.

mel'anoder'mic. Relating to or marked by melanoderma

melanogen (mĕ-lan'o-jen) [melano- + G. *-gen*, producing]. A colorless substance that may be converted into melanin.

melanogenesis (mel'ă-no-jen'ĕ-sis) [melanin + G. *genesis*, production]. Formation of melanin by living cells.

mel'anoglos'sia [melano- + G. *glōssa*, tongue]. Black *tongue*.

mel'anoid. A dark pigment that resembles melanin; formed from glucosamines in chitin.

melanoleukoderma (mel'ă-no-lu-ko-der'mah) [melano- + G. *leukos*, white, + *derma*, skin]. Marbled, or marmorated, skin.

   m. col'li, syphilitic *leukoderma*.

melanoma (mel'ă-no'mah) [melano- + G. *ōma*, tumor]. Melanotic carcinoma; melanocarcinoma; melanoblastoma; malignant m., a malignant neoplasm derived from cells capable of forming melanin and which frequently metastasizes widely.

   benign juvenile m., a benign, slightly pigmented or red, superficial small skin tumor composed of spindle-shaped, epithelioid, and multinucleated cells; most common in children.

   malignant m., melanoma.

   malignant m. in situ, a m. limited to the epidermis and composed of nests and single atypical cells that may be round with abundant cytoplasm (pagetoid cells).

melanomatosis (mel'ă-no-mă-to'sis) [melanoma + G. *-osis*, condition]. A condition characterized by numerous widespread lesions of melanoma.

melanonychia (mel'ă-no-nik'ĭ-ah) [melano- + G. *onyx* (*onych*-), nail]. Black pigmentation of the nails.

melanophage (mel'ă-no-fāj) [melano- + G. *phagein*, to eat]. Melanophore (1).

melanophore (mel'ă-no-fōr) [melano- + G. *phoros*, bearing]. **1.** Melanophage; in human histology and pathology, a phagocytic cell that contains melanin, but does not form the pigment. **2.** In general biology, a cell capable of forming melanin.

melanoplakia (mel'ă-no-pla'kĭ-ah) [melano- + G. *plax*, plate, plaque]. The occurrence of pigmented patches on the tongue and buccal mucous membrane.

melanosis (mel-ă-no'sis) [melano- + G. *-osis*, condition]. **1.** Abnormal, dark brown or brown-black pigmentation of various tissues or organs, as the result of melanins or other substances that resemble melanin. **2.** Cachexia resulting from widespread metastases of melanoma.

m. co'li, m. of the large intestinal mucosa due to accumulation of pigment within macrophages in the lamina propria.

oculodermal m., Ota's nevus; pigmentation of the conjunctiva and skin around the eye, usually unilateral.

melanosome (mel'ă-no-sōm) [melano- + G. *sōma*, body]. The generally oval pigment granule produced by melanocytes.

mel'anot'ic. 1. Pertaining to the presence of melanin. **2.** Relating to or characterized by melanosis.

melanotroph (mel'ă-no-trof) [melano- + G. *trophē*, nourishment]. A cell of the hypophysis that produces melanocyte-stimulating hormone.

melanuria mel-ă-nu'rĭ-ah) [melano- + G. *ouron*, urine]. Excretion of urine of a dark color, resulting from the presence of melanin or other pigments or from the action of coal tar derivatives.

melanu'ric. Pertaining to or characterized by melanuria.

melasma (mě-laz'mah) [G. a black color, a black spot]. A patchy or generalized pigmentation of the skin.

m. gravida'rum, chloasma occurring in pregnancy.
m. universa'le, senile *melanoderma*.

mel'ato'nin. *N*-Acetyl-5-methoxytryptamine formed by the pineal gland which appears to depress gonadal function.

melena (mel-e'nah) [G. *melaina*, fem. of *melas*, black]. Passage of dark colored, tarry stools, due to the presence of blood altered by the intestinal juices.

meli- [G. *meli*, honey]. Combining form relating to honey or sugar. See also mel- (3).

melioidosis (me'lĭ-oy-do'sis) [G. *mēlis*, a distemper of asses, + *eidos*, resemblance, + *-osis*, condition]. An infectious disease of rodents in India and Southeast Asia that is communicable to man and is caused by *Pseudomonas pseudomallei*; the characteristic lesion is a small caseous nodule that breaks down into an abscess.

melitis (me-li'tis) [G. *mēlon*, cheek, + *-itis*, inflammation]. Inflammation of the cheek.

melo-. See mel-.

meloplasty (mel'o-plas-tĭ) [melo- + G. *plassō*, to form]. Reparative or plastic surgery of the cheek.

melorheostosis (mel'o-re-os-to'sis) [G. *melos*, limb, + *rheos*, stream, + *osteon*, bone, + *-ōsis*]. Rheostosis confined to the long bones.

melotia (mě-lo'shĭ-ah) [G. *mēlon*, cheek, + *ous*, ear]. Congenital displacement of the auricle.

mem'ber [L. *membrum*]. A limb.

mem'bra [L.]. Plural of membrum.

membrana, gen. and pl. **membranae** (mem-bra'nah, -bra'ne) [L.] [NA]. Membrane; a thin sheet or layer of pliable tissue, serving as a covering or envelope of a part, the lining of a cavity, as a partition or septum, or to connect two structures.

m. adventi'tia, (1) *tunica* adventitia; **(2)** *decidua* capsularis.

m. atlantooccipita'lis [NA], atlantooccipital membrane; **(1)** anterior: the fibrous layer that extends from the anterior arch of the atlas to the anterior margin of the foramen magnum.; **(2)** posterior: the fibrous membrane that attaches between the posterior arch of the atlas and the posterior margin of the foramen magnum.

m. decid'ua [NA], deciduous membrane; decidua; the mucous membrane of the pregnant uterus which has already undergone certain changes, under the influence of the ovulation cycle, to fit it for the implantation and nutrition of the ovum.

m. fibro'sa [NA], fibrous membrane; the outer fibrous part of the capsule of a synovial joint which may in places be thickened to form capsular ligaments.

membran'nae intercosta'lia [NA], intercostal membranes; the membranous layers between ribs.

m. pupilla'ris [NA], pupillary membrane; the thin central portion of the iridopupillary lamina occluding the pupil in fetal life.

m. reticula'ris [NA], reticular membrane; the membrane formed by cuticular plates of the cells of the spiral organ of Corti.

m. sero'sa, (1) *tunica* serosa; **(2)** serosa (2).

m. synovia'lis [NA], synovial membrane; synovium; the connective tissue membrane that lines the cavity of a synovial joint and produces the synovial fluid.

m. tecto'ria duc'tus cochlea'ris [NA], tectorial membrane of cochlear duct; Corti's membrane; tectorium (2); a gelatinous membrane that overlies the spiral organ (Corti) in the inner ear.

m. tym'pani [NA], tympanic or drum membrane; drum; drumhead; myrinx; a thin tense membrane forming the greater part of the lateral wall of the tympanic cavity and separating it from the external acoustic meatus; constitutes the boundary between the external and middle ear.

m. tym'pani secunda'ria [NA], secondary tympanic membrane; Scarpa's membrane; the membrane closing the fenestra cochleae or rotunda.

m. vestibula'ris [NA], vestibular membrane; Reissner's membrane; the membrane separating the cochlear duct from the scala vestibuli.

m. vit'rea [NA], vitreous membrane (2); hyaloid membrane; a condensation of fine collagen fibers in places in the cortex of the vitreous body; formerly thought to form a membrane or capsule at its periphery.

m. vitelli'na, yolk membrane; **(1)** vitelline or ovular membrane; the membrane enveloping the egg yolk; **(2)** sometimes used to designate the zona pellucida of a mammalian ovum.

membrane [L. *membrana,* skin or membrane that covers parts of the body]. Membrana.

 allantoid m., allantois.

 alveolodental m., periodontium.

 arachnoid m., arachnoidea.

 atlantooccipital m., *membrana* atlantooccipitalis.

 basement m., basilemma; a thin layer that intervenes between epithelium and connective tissue.

 Bichat's m., the inner elastic m. of arteries.

 Bowman's m., *lamina* limitans corneae (1).

 Bruch's m., *lamina* basalis choroideae.

 Brunn's m., the epithelium of the olfactory region of the nose.

 cell m., plasmalemma; plasma m.; the protoplasmic boundary of all cells which controls permeability and may serve other functions through surface specializations.

 cloacal m., a transitory m. in the caudal area of the ventral wall of the embryo, separating the entodermal from the ectodermal cloaca.

 Corti's m., *membrana* tectoria ductus cochlearis.

 croupous m., false m.

 deciduous m., *membrana* decidua.

 Descemet's m., *lamina* limitans corneae (2).

 diphtheritic m., the false m. forming on the mucous surfaces in diphtheria.

 drum m., *membrana* tympani.

 egg m., the investing envelope of the ovum produced from ovarian cytoplasm, the ovarian follicle, and the lining of the oviduct.

 elastic m., a m. formed of elastic connective tissue fibers, present in the coats of the arteries and elsewhere.

 embryonic m., fetal m.

 enamel m., the internal layer of the enamel organ formed by the enamel cells.

 false m., pseudomembrane; croupous m.; neomembrane; plica (2); a thick, tough fibrinous exudate on the surface of a mucous m. or the skin.

 fenestrated m., an elastic m., as in elastic laminae of arteries.

 fetal m., embryonic m.; a structure or tissue developed from the fertilized ovum but which does not form part of the embryo proper.

 fibrous m., *membrana* fibrosa.

 germ m., germinal m., blastoderm.

 glassy m., (1) the basement m. present between the stratum granulosum and the theca interna of a vesicular ovarian follicle; (2) hyaline m. (2); the basement m. of the hair follicle.

 hyaline m., (1) the thin, clear basement m. beneath certain epithelia; (2) glassy m. (2).

 hyaloid m., *membrana* vitrea.

 hyoglossal m., a delicate fibrous m. that extends between the hyoid bone and the tongue.

 intercostal m.'s, *membranae* intercostalia.

 Jackson's m., a thin vasular m. or veil-like adhesion, covering the anterior surface of the ascending colon from the cecum to the right flexure; it may cause obstruction by kinking of the bowel.

 keratogenous m., *matrix* unguis.

 medullary m., endosteum.

 mucous m., see *tunica* mucosa.

 nuclear m., nuclear *envelope.*

 olfactory m., that part of the nasal mucosa having olfactory receptor cells and Bowman's glands.

 ovular m., *membrana* vitellina (1).

 peridental m., periodontium.

 periodontal m., periodontal *ligament.*

 placental m., the semipermeable layer of tissue separating the maternal from the fetal blood.

 plasma m., cell m.

 postsynaptic m., that part of the plasma m. of a neuron or muscle fiber with which an axon terminal forms a synaptic junction.

 presynaptic m., that part of the plasma m. of an axon terminal that faces the plasma m. of the neuron or muscle fiber with which the axon terminal establishes a synpatic junction.

 pupillary m., *membrana* pupillaris.

 Reissner's m., *membrana* vestibularis.

 reticular m., *membrana* reticularis.

 Ruysch's m., *lamina* choroidocapillaris.

 Scarpa's m., *membrana* tympani secundaria.

 secondary tympanic m., *membrana* tympani secundaria.

 serous m., *tunica* serosa.

 synovial m., *membrana* synovialis.

 tectorial m. of cochlear duct, *membrana* tectoria ductus cochlearis.

 tympanic m., *membrana* tympani.

 undulating m., undulatory m., a locomotory organelle of certain flagellate parasites, consisting of a finlike m. with the flagellar sheath that produces a characteristic rippling movement.

 unit m., a trilaminar m. of membranous cellular structures; observed with the electron microscope.

 vestibular m., *membrana* vestibularis.

 virginal m., hymen.

 vitelline m., *membrana* vitellina (1).

 vitreous m., (1) *lamina* limitans corneae (2); (2) *membrana* vitrea; (3) *lamina* basalis choroideae.

 yolk m., *membrana* vitellina.

 Zinn's m., the anterior layer of the iris.

membra′niform. Membranoid; of the appearance or character of a membrane.

membranocartilaginous (mem′bră-no-kar-tĭ-laj′ĭ-nus). **1.** Partly membranous and partly cartilaginous. **2.** Derived from both membrane and cartilage, denoting certain bones.

membranoid (mem′bră-noyd). Membraniform.

membranous (mem′bră-nus). Hymenoid (1); relating to or of the form of a membrane.

mem′ory [L. *memoria*]. **1.** General term for the recollection of that which was once experienced or learned. **2.** The mental information processing system that receives (registers), modifies, stores, and retrieves informational stimuli; composed of three stages: encoding, storage, and retrieval.

mem′ory [L. *memoria*]. **1.** General term for the recollection of that which was once experienced or learned. **2.** The mental information processing system that receives (registers), modifies, stores, and retrieves informational stimuli; composed of three stages: encoding, storage, and retrieval.

long term m. (LTM), that phase of the m. process which is essentially the permanent storehouse of retained information for future retrieval; material and information in LTM underlies cognitive abilities.

screen m., in psychoanalysis, a consciously tolerable m. that unwittingly serves as a cover for another associated m. which would be emotionally painful if recalled.

short term m, (STM), that phase of the m. process in which stimuli that have been recognized and registered are stored briefly; decay is typically rapid.

menacme (mě-nak′me) [G. *měn*, month, + *akmē*, prime]. The period of life marked by menstrual activity.

menadiol (men′ā-di′ol). Vitamin K$_4$.

menadione (men-ā-di′ŏn). Menaquinone 2-methyl-1,4-naphthoquinone; the root of compounds that are 3-multiprenyl derivatives of m. and known as the menaquinones or vitamins K$_2$.

menaquinone (MK) (men-ā-kwin′ŏn). Menadione.

menarche (mě-nar′ke) [G. *měn*, month, + *archē*, beginning]. The establishment of the menstrual function; the time of the first menstrual period or flow.

menar′cheal, menar′chial. Pertaining to the menarche.

mendelevium (men-dě-le′vĭ-um) [*D. Mendeléeff*] Element no. 101, symbol Md, prepared by bombardment of einsteinium (element no. 99) with alpha particles.

mende′lian. Attributed to or described by Gregor Mendel.

mening-. See meningo-.

meningeal (mě-nin′je-al). Relating to the meninges.

meningeorrhaphy (mě-nin′je-or′ă-fĭ) [G. *měninx* (*měning-*), membrane, + *rhaphē*, suture]. Suture of the cranial or spinal meninges, or of any membrane.

meninges (mě-nin′jēz). Plural of meninx.

meningioma (mě-nin-jĭ-o′mah) [mening- + G. *-oma*, tumor]. A benign encapsulated neoplasm of arachnoidal origin, occurring in adults; tends to occur along the superior sagittal sinus or the sphenoid ridge, or in the vicinity of the optic chiasm.

meningism (men′in-jizm). A condition of irritation of the brain or spinal cord in which the symptoms simulate meningitis, but in which no actual inflammation is present.

meningitic (men′in-jit′ik). Relating to or characterized by meningitis.

meningitis pl. **meningitides** (men-in-ji′tis, -jit′ĭ-dēz) [mening- + G. *-itis*, inflammation]. Inflammation of the membranes of the brain or spinal cord.

basilar m., m. at the base of the brain, due usually to tuberculosis, syphilis, or any low grade chronic granulomatous process.

cerebrospinal m., meningococcal m.

meningococcal m., cerebrospinal m.; an acute infectious disease affecting children and young adults, caused by the meningococcus, *Neisseria meningitidis;* symptoms are headache, vomiting, convulsions, nuchal rigidity, photophobia, cutaneous hyperesthesia, a purpuric or herpetic eruption, and the presence of Kernig's sign.

occlusive m., leptomeningitis causing occlusion of the spinal fluid pathways.

otitic m., infection of the meninges secondary to mastoiditis or otitis media.

serous m., acute m. with secondary external hydrocephalus.

tuberculous m., inflammation of the cerebral leptomeninges marked by the presence of granulomatous inflammation; usually confined to the base of the brain.

meningo-, mening- [G. *měninx*, membrane]. Combining forms relating to meninges.

meningocele (mě-ning′go-sēl) [meningo- + G. *kēlē*, tumor]. Protrusion of the membranes of the brain or spinal cord through a defect in the skull or spinal column.

meningococcemia (mě-ning′go-kok-se′mĭ-ah). The presence of meningococci (*Neisseria meningitidis*) in the circulating blood.

meningococcus, pl. **meningococci** (mě-ning′go-kok′us, -kok′si) [meningo- + G. *kokkos*, berry]. *Neisseria meningitidis.*

meningocortical (mě-ning′go-kor′tĭ-kal). Relating to the meninges and the cortex of the brain.

meningocyte (mě-ning′go-sīt) [meningo- + G. *kytos*, cell]. A mesenchymal epithelial cell of the subarachnoid space.

meningoencephalitis (mě-ning′go-en-sef-ă-li′tis) [meningo- + G. *enkephalos*, brain, + *-itis*, inflammation]. Cerebromeningitis; encephalomeningitis; inflammation of the brain and its membranes.

meningoencephalocele (mě-ning′go-en-sef′ă-lo-sēl) [meningo- + G. *enkephalos*, brain, + *kēlē*, hernia]. Encephalomeningocele; protrusion of the meninges and brain through a congenital defect in the cranium.

meningoencephalomyelitis (mě-ning′go-en-sef′ă-lo-mi-ě-li′tis) [meningo- + G. *enkephalos*, brain, + *myelos*, marrow, + *-itis*, inflammation]. Inflammation of the brain and spinal cord together with their membranes.

meningoencephalopathy (mě-ning′go-en-sef-ă-lop′ă-thĭ) [meningo- + G. *enkephalos*, brain, + *pathos*, suffering]. Encephalomeningopathy; any disorder affecting the meninges and the brain.

meningomyelitis (mě-ning′go-mi-ě-li′tis) [meningo- + G. *myelos*, marrow, + *-itis*, inflammation]. Inflammation of the spinal cord and of its enveloping arachnoid and pia mater, less commonly also of the dura mater.

meningomyelocele (mĕ-ning-go-mi'ĕ-lo-sēl) [meningo- + G. *myelos*, marrow, + *kēlē*, tumor]. Myelomeningocele; myelocystomeningocele; protrusion of the spinal membranes and cord through a defect in the vertebral column.

meningo-osteophlebitis (mĕ-ning'go-os-te-o-flĕ-bi'tis). Inflammation of the veins of the periosteum.

meningopathy (men-ing-gop'ă-thī) [meningo- + G. *pathos*, suffering]. Any disease of the cerebral or spinal meninges.

meningoradicular (mĕ-ning'go-ră-dik'u-lar) [meningo- + L. *radix*, root]. Relating to the meninges and the cranial or spinal nerve roots.

meningoradiculitis (mĕ-ning'go-ră-dik-u-li'tis). Inflammation of the meninges and roots of the nerves.

meningorrhachidian (mĕ-ning'go-ră-kid'ī-an) [meningo- + G. *rhachis*, spine]. Relating to the spinal cord and its membranes.

meningorrhagia (mĕ-ning-go-ra'jī-ah) [meningo- + G. *rhēgnymi*, to burst forth]. Hemorrhage into or beneath the cerebral or spinal meninges.

meningosis (men-ing-go'sis) [meningo- + G. *-ōsis*, condition]. Membranous union of bones, as in the skull of the newborn.

meningovascular (mĕ-ning'go-vas'ku-lar). Concerning the blood vessels in the meninges, or the meninges and blood vessels.

meninx, gen. **meningis**, pl. **meninges** (me'ningks, men'ingks, mĕ-nin'jēz) [Mod. L. fr. G. *mēninx*, membrane]. Any membrane; specifically, one of the membranous coverings of the brain and spinal cord: arachnoidea, dura mater, pia mater.

meniscectomy (men-ĭ-sek'to-mī) [G. *mēniskos*, crescent (meniscus) + *ektomē*, excision]. Excision of a meniscus, usually from the knee joint.

menisci (mĕ-nis'sī). Plural of meniscus.

meniscitis (men-ĭ-si'tis) [G. *mēniskos*, crescent (meniscus), + *-itis*, inflammation]. Inflammation of a fibrocartilaginous meniscus.

meniscocyte (mĕ-nis'ko-sīt) [G. *mēniskos*, a crescent, + *kytos*, a hollow (cell)]. Sickle *cell.*

meniscocytosis (mĕ-nis-ko-si-to'sis) [meniscocyte + G. *-osis*, condition]. Sickle cell *anemia.*

meniscus, pl. **menisci**, (mĕ-nis'kus, mĕ-nis'sī) [G. *mēniskos*, crescent]. **1.** Meniscus *lens.* **2** [NA]. A crescent-shaped structure, as the fibrocartilage in certain joints.

  m. tac'tus [NA], **tactile m.**, tactile disk; Merkel's corpuscle; a specialized tactile sensory nerve ending in the skin characterized by a terminal cuplike expansion of the nerve fiber in contact with a single modified epithelial cell.

meno- [G. *mēn*, month]. Combining form denoting relationship to the menses.

menometrorrhagia (men'o-me-tro-ra'jī-ah) [meno- + G. *mētra*, uterus, + *rhēgnymi*, to burst forth]. Irregular or excessive bleeding during menstruation and between menstrual periods.

menopausal (men'o-paw-zăl). Associated with or occasioned by the menopause.

menopause (men'o-pawz) [meno- + G. *pausis*, cessation]. Permanent cessation of the menses.

menorrhagia (men-o-ra'jī-ah) [meno- + G. *rhēgnymi*, to burst forth]. Hypermenorrhea.

menorrhalgia (men-o-ral'jī-ah) [meno- + G. *algos*, pain]. Dysmenorrhea.

menoschesis (mĕ-nos'ke-sis, men'o-ske'sis) [meno- + G. *schesis*, retention]. Suppression of menstruation.

menostasis (mĕ-nos'tă-sis) [meno- + G. *stasis*, a standing]. Amenorrhea.

menostaxis (men-o-stak'sis) [meno- + G. *staxis*, a dripping]. Hypermenorrhea.

menotro'pins. Extract of postmenopausal urine containing primarily follicle-stimulating hormone.

menses (men'sēz) [L. pl. of *mensis*, month]. Emmenia; a periodic physiologic hemorrhage, occurring at approximately 4-week intervals, and having its source from the uterine mucous membrane; under normal circumstances, the bleeding is preceded by ovulation and predecidual changes in the endometrium. See also menstrual *cycle.*

menstrual (men'stru-al) [L. *menstrualis*]. Emmenic; relating to the menses.

menstruant (men'stru-ant). Menstruating.

menstruate (men'stru-āt) [L. *menstruo,* pp. *-atus,* to be menstruant]. To undergo menstruation.

menstruation (men-stru-a'shun) [see menstruate]. Cyclic endometrial shedding and discharge of a bloody fluid from the uterus during the catamenial period.

  anovular m., menstrual bleeding without the discharge of an ovum.

  retained m., hematocolpos.

  retrograde m., a flow of menstrual blood back through the fallopian tubes.

  vicarious m., bleeding from any surface other than the mucous membrane of the uterine cavity, occurring periodically at the time when the normal m. should take place.

menstruum, pl. **menstrua** (men'stru-um, -stru-ah) [Mediev. L. menstrual fluid (thought to possess markedly solvent properties)]. Solvent (2).

men'tal. 1 [L. *mens* (*ment-*), mind]. Relating to the mind. **2** [L. *mentum,* chin]. Genial; genian; relating to the chin.

mental'ity. The functional condition of the mind; mental activity.

men'thol. *p*-Menthan-3-ol; an alcohol obtained from peppermint oil or other mint oils, or prepared synthetically; used as an antipruritic and topical anesthetic, and as a flavoring agent.

men'toplasty [L. *mentum,* chin + G. *plastos,* formed]. Genioplasty; plastic surgery of the chin, whereby its shape or size is altered.

men'tum, gen. **men'ti** [L.] [NA]. Chin.

mephit'ic [L. *mephitis,* a noxious exhalation]. Foul; poisonous; noxious.

mepivacaine hydrochloride (mĕ-piv′ă-kān). 2,6-Dimethylanilide hydrochloride; local anesthetic agent similar in action to lidocaine.

mEq, meq Milliequivalent.

-mer. **1.** Suffix attached to a prefix such as mono-, di-, tri-, poly-, etc., to indicate the smallest unit of a repeating structure. See polymer. **2.** Suffix denoting a member of a particular group, as in isomer, enantiomer.

meralgia (me-ral′jĭ-ah) [G. *mēros*, thigh, + *algos*, pain]. Pain in the thigh.

m. paraesthet′ica, Bernhardt's disease; paresthesia in the outer side of the lower part of the thigh in the area of distribution of the external cutaneous branch of the femoral nerve.

mercap′tan. Thioalcohol; a class of substances in which the oxygen of an alcohol has been replaced by sulfur.

mercapto-. Prefix indicating the presence of a thiol group, –SH.

mercap′tol(e). A substance derived from a ketone by the replacement of the bivalent oxygen by two thioalkyl groups.

mercapturic acid (mer-kap-tūr′ik). A condensation product of cysteine with aromatic compounds such as bromobenzene; formed biologically via glutathione in the liver and excreted in the urine.

mercurial (mer-ku′rĭ-al). ku′rĭ-al). **1.** Relating to mercury. **2.** Any salt of mercury used medicinally.

mercurialism (mer-ku′rĭ-ă-lizm). Mercury *poisoning*.

mercu′ric. Denoting a salt of mercury in which the ion of the metal is bivalent.

mercurous (mer-ku′rus, mer′ku-rus). Denoting a salt of mercury in which the ion of the metal is univalent.

mercury (mer′ku-rĭ) [L. *Mercurius*, Mercury, Roman deity; Mediev. L. quicksilver, mercury]. Quicksilver; hydrargyrum; a liquid metallic element, symbol Hg, atomic no. 80, atomic weight 200.59; used in scientific instruments; some salts and organic mercurials are used medicinally.

mere-, mero- [G. *mēros*, part]. Combining forms meaning part; also indicating one of a series of similar parts. See also -mer.

merergasia (mer-er-gă′zĭ-ah) [G. *meros*, part, + *ergasia*, work]. A mild form of mental incapacity.

meridian (mĕ-rid′ĭ-an) [L. *meridianus*, pertaining to midday, on the south side, southern]. **1.** A line encircling a globular body at right angles to its equator and touching both poles, or the half of such a circle extending from pole to pole. **2.** In acupuncture, the lines connecting different anatomical sites.

meridional (mĕ-rid′ĭ-o-nal). Relating to a meridian.

mero-. See mere-.

merocele (me′ro-sēl) [G. *mēros*, thigh, + *kele*, hernia]. Femoral *hernia*.

merodiastolic (mĕr′o-di-ă-stol′ik) [mero- + diastole]. Partially diastolic; relating to a part of the diastole of the heart.

merogenesis (mĕr′o-jen′ĕ-sis) [mero- + G. *genesis*, production]. Reproduction by segmentation.

merogenet′ic, merogen′ic. Relating to merogenesis.

merogony (mĕ-rog′o-nĭ) [mero- + G. *gonē*, generation]. **1.** Incomplete development of an ovum which has been disorganized. **2.** A form of asexual multiple fission (schizogony), typical of sporozoan protozoa, in which the nucleus divides several times before the cytoplasm divides; the dividing cell (schizont) breaks up to form daughter cells (merozoites) in this asexual phase of the life cycle.

meromelia (mĕr-o-me′lĭ-ah) [mero- + G. *melos*, a limb]. Partial absence of a free limb (exclusive of girdle).

meromicrosomia (mĕr′o-mi′kro-so′mĭ-ah) [mero- + G. *mikros*, small, + *sōma*, body]. Abnormal smallness of some portion of the body.

mer′omy′osin. A product of the tryptic digestion of myosin; a subunit of myosin; two types are produced: heavy (H) and light (L).

merorachischisis, merorrhachischisis (mĕr′o-ră-kis′kĭ-sis) [mero- + G. *rhachis*, spine, + *schisis*, fissure]. Fissure of a portion of the spinal cord.

merosmia (mĕ-roz′mĭ-ah) [mero- + G. *osmē*, smell]. Inability to perceive certain odors.

merosystolic (mĕr′o-sis-tol′ik) [mero- + systole]. Partially systolic; relating to a portion of the systole of the heart.

merotomy (mĕ-rot′o-mĭ) [mero- + G. *tomē*, incision]. Cutting into parts, as of a cell.

merozoite (mĕr′o-zo′ĭt) [mero- + G. *zōon*, animal]. Endodyocyte (2); the motile infective stage of sporozoan protozoa that results from schizogony or a similar type of asexual reproduction.

merozygote (mĕr-o-zi′gōt) [mero- + *zygōtos*, yoked]. In microbial genetics, an organism that, in addition to its own original genome (endogenote), contains a fragment (exogenote) of a genome from another organism.

mes-. See meso-.

mesad (me′zad) [G. *mesos*, middle, + L. *ad*, to]. Mesiad; passing or extending toward the median plane of the body or of a part.

mesangial (mes-an′jĭ-al). Referring to the mesangium.

mesangium (mes-an′jĭ-um) [mes- + G. *angeion*, vessel]. A central part of the renal glomerulus between capillaries.

mesaortitis (mes′a-or-ti′tis) [mes- + aortitis]. Inflammation of the middle or muscular coat of the aorta.

mesarteritis (mes′ar-ter-i′tis) [mes- + arteritis]. Inflammation of the middle (muscular) coat of an artery.

mesatipellic, mesatipelvic (mĕ-sat′ĭ-pel′ik, -pel′vik) [G. *mesatos*, midmost, + *pellis*, a bowl (pelvis)]. Denoting an individual with a pelvic index between 90 and 95; the superior strait has a round appearance, with the transverse diameter longer than the anteroposterior by 1 cm of less.

mesaxon (mez-ak′son, mes-). The plasma membrane of the neurolemma which is folded in to surround a nerve axon.

mescaline (mes'kă-lēn). 3,4,5-Trimethoxyphenethylamine; the most active alkaloid present in the buttons of a small cactus, *Lophophora williamsii*, which produces psychotomimetic effects similar to those produced by LSD.

mesectoderm (mes-ek'to-derm) [mes- + ectoderm]. **1.** The cells in the area around the dorsal lip of the blastopore where separation of mesoderm and ectoderm is being accomplished. **2.** That part of the mesenchyme derived from ectoderm, especially from the neural crest in the cephalic region in very young embryos.

mesencephalic (mes-en'sě-fal'ik, mez-). Relating to the mesencephalon.

mesencephalitis (mes'en-sef'ă-li'tis). Inflammation of the midbrain (mesencephalon).

mesencephalon (mes-en-sef'ă-lon) [mes- + G. *enkephalos*, brain] [NA]. Midbrain; that part of the brainstem that develops from the middle of the three primary cerebral vesicles of the embryo; in the adult, characterized gross-anatomically by the unique conformation of its roofplate, the lamina tecti mesencephali, and by the paired prominence of the crus cerebri at its ventral surface. Prominent cell groups of the m. include the motor nuclei of the trochlear and oculomotor nerves, the red nucleus, and the substantia nigra.

mesencephalotomy (mes'en-sef-ă-lot'o-mī) [mesencephalon + G. *tomē*, incision]. **1.** The sectioning of any structure in the midbrain, especially of the spinothalamic tracts for the relief of unbearable pain. **2.** A mesencephalic spinothalamic *tractotomy*.

mesenchymal (mě-seng'kī-mal, mes'eng-ki'mal). Relating to the mesenchyme.

mesenchyme (mes'en-kīm) [mes- + G. *enkyma*, infusion]. **1.** An aggregation of mesenchymal cells. **2.** A primordial embryonic tissue consisting of mesenchymal cells, usually stellate in form, supported in a ground substance.

mesenchymoma (mes'en-ki-mo'mah). A neoplasm in which there is a mixture of mesenchymal derivatives, other than fibrous tissue.

mesenter'ic. Relating to the mesentery.

mesenteriopexy (mes'en-tĕr'ĭ-o-pek-sī) [mesentery + G. *pēxis*, fixation]. Mesopexy; fixation or attachment of a torn or incised mesentery.

mesenteriorrhaphy (mes'en-tĕr-ĭ-or'ă-fī) [mesentery + G. *rhaphē*, suture]. Mesorrhaphy; suture of the mesentery.

mesenteriplication (mes'en-tĕr-ĭ-plī-ka'shun) [mesentery + L. *plico*, pp. *-atus*, to fold]. Reducing redundancy of a mesentery by making one or more tucks in it.

mesenteritis (mes'en-tĕr-i'tis). Inflammation of the mesentery.

mesenterium (mes'en-tĕr'ĭ-um) [Mod. L.] [NA]. Mesentery.

mesentery (mes'en-tĕr-ĭ) [Mod. L. *mesenterium*, fr. G. *mesenterion*, fr. G. *mesos*, middle, + *enteron*, intestine]. Mesenterium. **1.** A double layer of

peritoneum attached to the abdominal wall and enclosing in its fold a portion or all of one of the abdominal viscera, conveying to it its vessels and nerves. **2.** The fold of peritoneum encircling the greater part of the small intestines (jejunum and ileum) and attaching it to the posterior abdominal wall.

mesiad (me'zĭ-ad). Mesad.

mesial (me'zĭ-al) [G. *mesos*, middle]. Proximal (2); toward the midline following the curvature of the dental arch.

mesio- [G. *mesos*, middle]. Combining form meaning mesial.

mesiobuccal (me'zĭ-o-buk'al). Relating to the mesial and buccal surfaces of a tooth; denoting especially the angle formed by the junction of these two surfaces.

me'siocer'vical. 1. Relating to the line angle of a cavity preparation at the junction of the mesial and cervical walls. **2.** Pertaining to the area of a tooth at the junction of the mesial surface and the cervical region.

mesioclusion (me'zĭ-o-klu'zhun) Mesial occlusion (2); malocclusion in which the mandibular arch articulates with the maxillary arch in a position mesial to normal.

mesiodens (me'zĭ-o-denz) [mesio- + L. *dens*, tooth]. A supernumerary tooth located in the midline of the anterior maxillae, between the maxillary central incisor teeth.

me'siodis'tal. Denoting the plane or diameter of a tooth cutting its mesial and distal surfaces.

mesiogingival (me'zĭ-o-jin'jĭ-val). Relating to the angle formed by the junction of the mesial surface with the gingival line of a tooth.

me'siola'bial. Relating to the mesial and labial surfaces of a tooth; denoting especially the angle formed by their junction.

mesiolingual (me'zĭ-o-ling'gwal). Relating to the mesial and lingual surfaces of a tooth; denoting especially the angle formed by their junction.

mesiolinguo-occlusal (me'zĭ-o-ling'gwo-o-klu'sal, -zal). Denoting the angle formed by the junction of the mesial, lingual, and occlusal surfaces of a tooth.

mesiolinguopulpal (me'zĭ-o-ling'gwo-pul'pal). Relating to the angle denoting the junction of the mesial, lingual and pulpal surfaces in a tooth cavity preparation.

mesion (me'zĭ-on, mes'ĭ-on). Meson.

mesio-occlusal (me'zĭ-o-o-klu'sal, -zal). Denoting the angle formed by the junction of the mesial and occlusal surfaces of a tooth.

mesio-occlusion (me'zĭ-o-o-klu'zhun). Mesial *occlusion* (1).

mesioversion (me'zĭ-o-ver-zhun). Malposition of a tooth distal to normal, in a posterior direction following the curvature of the dental arch.

mes'merism [F.A. *Mesmer*, Austrian physician, 1733–1815]. A system of therapeutics from which were developed hypnotism and therapeutic suggestion.

meso-, mes- [G. *mesos*, middle]. **1.** Prefix meaning middle, or mean, or used to give an indication of intermediacy. **2.** Prefix designating a mesentery or mesentery-like structure.

mesoappendix (mes'o-ă-pen'diks) [NA]. The short mesentery of the appendix lying behind the terminal ileum.

mesobi'lane. Mesobilirubinogen; a reduced mesobilirubin with no double bonds between the pyrrole rings and, consequently, colorless.

mesobilirubin (mes'o-bil'ĭ-ru'bin). A compound differing from bilirubin only in that the vinyl groups of bilirubin are reduced to ethyl groups.

mesobilirubinogen (mes'o-bil'ĭ-ru-bin'o-jen). Mesobilane.

mes'oblast [meso- + G. *blastos*, germ]. Mesoderm.

mes'oblaste'ma [meso- + G. *blastēma*, a sprout]. All the cells that collectively constitute the early undifferentiated mesoderm.

mes'oblaste'mic. Relating to or derived from the mesoblastema.

mes'oblas'tic. Relating to or derived from the mesoderm (mesoblast).

mesocardia (mes-o-kar'dĭ-ah) [meso- + G. *kardia*, heart]. **1.** Atypical position of the heart in a central position in the chest, as in early embryonic life. **2.** Plural of mesocardium.

mesocardium, pl. **mes'ocar'dia** (mes-o-kar'dĭ-um) [meso- + G. *kardia*, heart]. The double layer of splanchnic mesoderm supporting the embryonic heart in the pericardial cavity.

mesocecal (mes'o-se'kal). Relating to the mesocecum.

mesocecum (mes'o-se'kum) [meso- + cecum]. Part of the mesocolon, supporting the cecum, that occasionally persists when the ascending colon becomes retroperitoneal during fetal life.

mes'ocol'ic. Relating to the mesocolon.

mesocolon (mes'o-ko'lon) [meso- + G. *kolon*, colon] [NA]. The fold of peritoneum attaching the colon to the posterior abdominal wall.

mesocolopexy. (mes'o-ko'lo-pek-sĭ) [meso- + G. *kolon*, colon, + *pēxis*, fixation]. Mesocoloplication; an operation for shortening the mesocolon to correct undue mobility and ptosis.

mesocoloplication (mes'o-ko'lo-plĭ-ka'shun) [meso- + G. *kolon*, colon, + L. *plico*, pp. *-atus*, to fold]. Mesocolopexy.

mes'ocord. A fold of amnion that sometimes binds a segment of the umbilical cord to the placenta.

mes'oderm [meso- + G. *derma*, skin]. Mesoblast; the middle of the three primary germ layers of the embryo; gives origin to all connective tissues, all body musculature, blood, cardiovascular and lymphatic systems, most of the urogenital system, and the lining of the pericardial, pleural, and peritoneal cavities.

mes'oder'mic. Relating to the mesoderm.

mes'odiastol'ic. Middiastolic.

mes'oduode'nal. Relating to the mesoduodenum.

mesoduodenum (mes'o-du'o-de'num, -du-od'ĕ-num). The mesentery of the duodenum.

mesoepididymis (mes-o-ep-ĭ-did'ĭ-mis) [meso- + epididymis]. An occasional fold of the tunica vaginalis binding the epididymis to the testis.

mes'ogas'ter. Mesogastrium.

mes'ogas'tric. Relating to the mesogastrium.

mesogastrium (mes'o-gas'trĭ-um) [meso- + G. *gastēr*, stomach] [NA]. Mesogaster; in the embryo, the mesentery in relation to the dilated portion of the enteric canal, which is the future stomach.

mes'ogen'ic [meso- + G. *-gen*, producing]. Denoting the virulence of a virus capable of inducing lethal infection in embryonic hosts, after a short incubation period, and an inapparent infection in immature and adult hosts.

mesoglia (mĕ-sog'lĭ-ah) [meso- + G. *glia*, glue]. Neuroglial cells of mesodermal origin.

mesogluteal (mes-o-glu'te-al). Relating to the musculus gluteus medius.

mesoileum (mes-o-il'e-um). The mesentery of the ileum.

mesojejunum (mes'o-jĕ-ju'num). The mesentery of the jejunum.

mesolymphocyte (mez-o-lim'fo-sit) [meso- + lymphocyte]. A mononuclear leukocyte of medium size, with a deeply staining large nucleus relatively smaller than that in most of the lymphocytes.

mesomelia (mez-o-me'lĭ-ah) [meso- + G. *melos*, limb]. Abnormally short forearms and lower legs.

mesomere (mes'o-mēr) [meso- + G. *meros*, part]. A blastomere intermediate in size between a macromere and a micromere.

mesometrium (mes-o-me'trĭ-um) [meso- + G. *mētra*, uterus] [NA]. The broad ligament of the uterus, below the mesosalpinx.

mes'omorph [meso- + G. *morphē*, form]. A constitutional body type in which tissues that originate from the mesoderm prevail, with a proportional balance between trunk and limbs.

mes'omorph'ic. Relating to a mesomorph.

meson (mes'on, mē'zon) [G. neuter of *mesos*, middle]. Mesion; an elementary particle having a rest mass intermediate in value between the mass of an electron and that of a proton.

mes'oneph'ric. Relating to the mesonephros.

mesonephroma (mes'o-nĕ-fro'mah). Mesometanephric carcinoma; mesonephric adenocarcinoma; clear cell adenocarcinoma (2); a relatively rare malignant neoplasm of the ovary and corpus uteri, thought to originate in mesonephric structures that become misplaced in ovarian tissue during embryonic development; characterized by a tubular pattern, with focal proliferation of epithelial cells with clear cytoplasm or of the hob-nail type.

mesonephros, pl. **mesonephroi** (mes'o-nef'ros, -roy) [meso- + G. *nephros*, kidney] [NA]. Wolffian body; one of three excretory organs appearing in the evolution of vertebrates; it undergoes regression as an excretory organ but its duct system is retained in the male as the epididymis and ductus deferens.

mesoneuritis (mes'o-nu-ri'tis). Inflammation of a nerve or of its connective tissue without involvement of its sheath.

mesopexy (mes'o-pek-sĭ). Mesenteriopexy.

mesophil, mesophile (mes'o-fil, -fil) [meso- + G. *philos*, fond]. A microorganism with an optimum temperature between 25°C and 40°C, but growing within the limits of 10°C and 45°C.

mes'ophil'ic. Pertaining to a mesophil.

mesophlebitis (mes'o-flē-bi'tis) [meso- + phlebitis]. Inflammation of the middle coat of a vein.

mesophryon (mes-of'rĭ-on) [meso- + Gr. *ophrys*, eyebrow]. Glabella (2).

mes'opor'phyrin. Porphyrin compounds resembling the protoporphyrins except that the vinyl side chains of the latter are reduced to ethyl side chains.

mesorchial (mes-or'kĭ-al). Relating to the mesorchium.

mesorchium (mes-or'kĭ-um) [meso- + G. *orchis*, testis]. **1** [NA]. A fold of tunica vaginalis testis in the fetus supporting the mesonephros and the developing testis. **2.** A fold of tunica vaginalis testis in the adult between the testis and epididymis.

mes'orec'tum. The peritoneal investment of the rectum, covering the upper part only.

mesorrhaphy (mes-or'ă-fĭ). Mesenteriorrhaphy.

mes'osal'pinx [meso- + G. *salpinx*, trumpet] [NA]. The part of the broad ligament investing the fallopian tube.

mesosig'moid. The mesocolon of the sigmoid colon.

mesosigmoiditis (mes'o-sig-moy-di'tis). Inflammation of the mesosigmoid.

mesosigmoidopexy (mes'o-sig-moy'do-pek-sĭ). Surgical fixation of the mesosigmoid.

mes'oster'num [meso- + G. *sternon*, chest]. *Corpus sterni*.

mes'osystol'ic. Midsystolic.

mes'oten'don. Mesotendineum.

mesotendineum (mes'o-ten-din'e-um) [NA]. Mesotendon; the synovial layers that pass from a tendon to the wall of a tendon sheath where tendons lie within osteofibrous canals.

mesothelia (mes-o-the'lĭ-ah). Plural of mesothelium.

mesothe'lial. Relating to the mesothelium.

mesothelioma (mes'o-the-lĭ-o'mah) [mesothelium + G. *-oma*, tumor]. A rare neoplasm, derived from the lining cells of the pleura and peritoneum, which grows as a thick sheet covering the viscera and is composed of spindle cells or fibrous tissue.

mesothelium, pl. **mesothelia** (mes-o-the'lĭ-um, -the'lĭ-ah) [meso- + epithelium]. A single layer of flattened cells forming an epithelium that lines serous cavities.

mesovarium, pl. **mesovaria** (mes-o-va'rĭ-um, -ah) [meso- + L. *ovarium*, ovary]. [NA]. A short peritoneal fold connecting the anterior border of the ovary with the posterior layer of the broad ligament of the uterus.

MET Metabolic *equivalent*.

Met Methionine or its radicals in peptides.

meta- [G. after, between, over]. **1.** Prefix denoting the concept of after, subsequent to, behind, or hindmost, corresponding to *post-*. **2.** Prefix denoting joint action or shareing. **3**(*m-*). In chemistry, a prefix denoting that a compound is formed by two substitutions in the benzene ring separated by one carbon atom. For terms beginning with *meta-*, or *m-*, see the specific name.

metabasis (mĕ-tab'ă-sis) [G. a passing over, change]. A change of any kind in symptoms or course of a disease.

metabiosis (met'ă-bi-o'sis) [meta- + G. *biōsis*, way of life]. Dependence of one organism on another for its existence.

metabol'ic. Relating to metabolism.

metabolism (mĕ-tab'o-lizm) [G. *metabolē*, change]. The sum of the chemical changes occurring in tissue, consisting of anabolism (those reactions that convert small molecules into large) and catabolism (those reactions that convert large molecules into small), including both endogenous large molecules as well as biodegradation of drugs and other xenobiotics.

  basal m., basal metabolic rate; heat production at the lowest level of cell chemistry in the waking state; the minimal amount of cell activity associated with the continuous organic functions of respiration, circulation, and secretion.

metabolite (mĕ-tab'o-līt). Any product of metabolism, especially of catabolism.

metaboli'zable. Capable of taking part in metabolic reactions within the organism.

metacar'pal. Relating to the metacarpus.

metacarpectomy (met'ah-kar-pek'to-mĭ) [metacarpus + G. *ektomē*, excision]. Excision of one or all of the metacarpals.

metacarpophalangeal (met-ă-kar'po-fă-lan'je-al). Relating to the metacarpus and the phalanges; denoting the articulations between them.

metacarpus, pl. **metacarpi** (met-ă-kar'pus, -kar'pi) [meta- + G. *karpos*, wrist] [NA]. The five bones of the hand between the carpus and the phalanges.

metacercaria, pl. **metacercariae** (met'ă-ser-kār'ĭ-ah, -e) [meta- + G. *kerkos*, tail]. The post-cercarial encysted stage in the life history of a fluke, prior to transfer to the definitive host.

metachromasia (met'ă-kro-ma'zĭ-ah) [meta- + G. *chrōma*, color]. **1.** Metachromatism (2); the condition in which a cell or tissue component takes on a color different from the dye solution with which it is stained. **2.** Two or more different colors seen in tissues after staining with the same dye solution.

metachromatic (met'ă-kro-mat'ik). Metachromophil; metachromophile; denoting cells or dyes which exhibit metachromasia.

metachromatism (met-ă-kro'mă-tizm) [meta- + G. *chrōma*, color]. **1.** Any color change, whether natural or produced by basic aniline dyes. **2.** Metachromasia (1).

metachromophil, metachromophile (met-ă-kro'mo-fil, -fīl) [meta- + G. *chrōma*, color, + *philos*, fond]. Metachromatic.

metagenesis (met-ă-jen'ĕ-sis) [meta- + G. *genesis*, production]. *Alternation* of generations.

Metagonimus (met-ă-gon'ĭ-mus) [meta- + G. *gonimos*, productive]. A genus of flukes that encyst on fish and infest various fish-eating animals, including man. *M. yokogawai* is an intestinal fluke widely distributed in the Far East and Balkan states.

metakinesis (met'ă-kĭ-ne'sis) [meta- + G. *kinēsis*, movement]. Separation of the two chromatids of each chromosome and their movement to opposite poles in the anaphase of mitosis.

met'al [L. *metallum*, a mine, a mineral, fr. G. *metallon*, a mine, pit]. One of the electropositive elements, either amphoteric or basic, usually characterized by properties such as luster, malleability, ductility, the ability to conduct electricity, and the tendency to lose electrons in chemical reaction rather than gaining electrons.

   alkali m., one of the members of the family Li, Na, K, Rb, Cs, all of which have highly ionized hydroxides, which are alkalies.

   base m., basic m., a m. that is readily oxidized.

   earth m., an element of the third group of the periodic system.

   rare-earth m., elements of the third group of the periodic system from atomic numbers 57 to 72.

metallo- [see metal]. Combining form relating to metal.

metal'loen'zyme. An enzyme containing a metal (ion) as an integral part of its active structure.

metal'lopor'phyrin. A combination of a porphyrin with a metal, *e.g.,* hematin.

metal'lopro'tein. A protein with a tightly bound metal ion or ions; *e.g.,* hemoglobin.

metallothionein (mē-tal-lo-thi'o-nēn). A small protein, rich in sulfur-containing amino acids, that is synthesized in the liver and kidney in response to the presence of divalent ions, and that binds these ions tightly; of importance in ion transport and detoxification.

met'amer [meta- + suffix -mer, *q.v.*]. A substance, thing, or color that is similar to, but ultimately differentiable from, some other substance, thing, or color.

metamere (met'ă-mēr) [meta- + G. *meros*, part]. One of a series of homologous body segments.

metamer'ic. Relating to or showing metamerism, or occurring in a metamere.

metam'erism. A type of anatomic structure exhibiting serially homologous segments; are in vertebrates, evident in serially repeated vertebrae, ribs, intercostal muscles, and the spinal nerves.

metamorphopsia (met'ă-mor-fop'sĭ-ah) [meta- + G. *morphē*, shape, + *opsis*, vision]. A condition in which objects appear distorted in various ways.

metamorphosis (met'ă-mor'fo-sis, -mor-fo'sis) [G. transformation; *meta*, beyond, over, + *morphē*, form]. Transformation (1); a change in form, structure, or function.

   fatty m., the appearance of microscopically visible droplets of fat in the cytoplasm of cells.

met'amorphot'ic. Relating to or marked by metamorphosis.

metamyelocyte (met-ă-mi'el-o-sīt) [meta- + G. *myelos*, marrow, + *kytos*, cell]. Juvenile cell; a transitional form of myelocyte with nuclear construction intermediate between the mature myelocyte and the two-lobed granular leukocyte.

met'aneph'rine. A catabolite of epinephrine found, together with normetanephrine, in the urine and in some tissues; results from the action of catechol-*O*-methyltransferase on epinephrine; has no sympathomimetic actions.

metanephrogenic (met'ă-nef-ro-jen'ik) [meta- + G. *nephros*, kidney, + *-gen*, producing]. Applied to the more caudal part of the intermediate mesoderm which, under the inductive action of the metanephric diverticulum, has the potency to form metanephric tubules.

metanephros, pl. **metanephroi** (met'ă-nef'ros, -roy) [meta- + G. *nephros*, kidney]. The most caudally located of the three excretory organs appearing in the evolution of the vertebrates, becoming the permanent kidney of mammals.

metaphase (met'ăfāz) [meta- + G. *phasis*, an appearance]. The stage of mitosis or meiosis in which the chromosomes become aligned on the equatorial plate of the cell with the centromeres mutually repelling each other.

metaphrenia (met-ă-fre'nĭ-ah) [meta- + G. *phren*, mind]. The psychology, orientation, or life style of one whose energies have at least temporarily withdrawn from close interpersonal relationships, such as the family, and are directed to practical, gainful interests, such as business.

metaphysial, metaphyseal (met-ă-fiz'ĭ-al). Relating to a metaphysis.

metaphysis, pl. **metaphyses** (mě-taf'ĭ-sis, -sēz) [meta- + G. *physis*, growth] [NA]. The growth zone between the epiphysis and diaphysis during development of a bone.

met'aplas'tic. Pertaining to metaplasia.

metaplasia (met-ă-pla'zĭ-ah) [G. *metaplasis*, transformation]. Abnormal transformation of an adult, fully differentiated tissue of one kind into a differentiated tissue of another kind; an acquired condition.

   apocrine m., alteration of acinar epithelium of breast tissue to resemble apocrine sweat glands, as in fibrocystic disease of the breasts.

   myeloid m., a syndrome characterized by anemia, enlargement of the spleen, nucleated red blood cells and immature granulocytes in the circulating blood, and conspicuous foci of extramedullary hemopoiesis in the spleen and liver. It occurs in some persons who have another disease and is termed *secondary* or *symptomatic myeloid m.;* it also occurs as an apparently primary illness, and is then termed *primary* or *agnogenic myeloid m.,* or *myelofibrosis* or *myeloscle-rosis,* because of the presence of an associated fibrosis of the bone marrow of unknown cause.

squamous m., epidermalization; the transformation of glandular or mucosal epithelium into stratified squamous epithelium.

squamous m. of amnion, *amnion* nodosum.

metaplasm (met′ă-plazm) [meta- + G. *plasma,* something formed]. Cell *inclusions* (1).

metapsychology (met′ă-si-kol′o-jī) [G. *meta,* beyond, transcending, + psychology]. **1.** A systematic attempt to discern and describe what lies beynd the empirical facts and laws of psychology, such as the relations between body and mind. **2.** In psychoanalysis, psychology concerning the fundamental assumptions of the freudian theory of the mind.

metarteriole (met′ar-tēr′ī-ōl) [meta- + arteriole]. One of the small peripheral blood vessels between the arterioles and the true capillaries that contain scattered groups of smooth muscle fibers in their walls.

metarubricyte (met′ă-ru′brī-sīt). An orthochromatic normoblast.

metastasis, pl. **metastases** (mĕ-tas′tă-sis, -sēz) [G. a removing] **1.** The shifting of a disease, or its local manifestations, from one part of the body to another. **2.** In cancer, the appearance of neoplasms in parts of the body remote from the seat of the primary tumor. **3.** Transportation of bacteria from one part of the body to another, through the bloodstream or lymph channels.

metas′tasize. To pass into or invade by metastasis.

met′astat′ic. Relating to metastasis.

met′atar′sal. Relating to the metatarsus or to one of the metatarsal bones.

metatarsalgia (met′ă-tar-sal′jī-ah) [meta- + G. *algos,* pain]. Pain in the forefoot in the region of the heads of the metatarsals.

metatarsectomy (met′ă-tar-sek′to-mĭ) [metarsus + G. *ektomē,* excision]. Excision of the metatarsus.

metatarsophalangeal (met′ă-tar′so-fă-lan′je-al). Relating to the metatarsal bones and the phalanges; denoting the articulations between them.

metatarsus, pl. **metatar′si** (met-ă-tar′sus, -tar′si) [meta- + G. *tarsos,* tarsus] [NA]. The distal portion of the foot between the instep and the toes, having as its skeleton the five metatarsal bones articulating posteriorly with the cuboid and cuneiform bones and distally with the phalanges.

m. la′tus, deformity caused by sinking down of the transverse arch of the foot.

m. va′rus, intoe; fixed deformity of the foot in which the forepart of the foot is rotated on the long axis of the foot, so that the plantar surface faces the midline of the body.

metathalamus (met′ă-thal′ă-mus) [meta- + G. *thalamos,* thalamus] [NA]. The most caudal part of the thalamus, composed of the medial and lateral geniculate bodies.

metathesis (mĕtath′ĕ-sis) [meta- + G. *thesis,* a placing]. **1.** The transfer of a pathologic product from one place to another, where it will cause less inconvenience or injury, when it is not possible or expedient to remove it from the body. **2.** Double decomposition, wherein a compound, A-B, reacts with another compound, C-D, to yield A-C + B-D, or A-D + B-C.

metatrophic (met-ă-trof′ik) [meta- + G. *trophē,* nourishment]. Denoting the ability to undertake anabolism or to obtain nourishment from varied sources, *i.e.,* both nitrogenous and carbonaceous organic matter.

Metazoa (met-ă-zo′ah) [meta- + G. *zōon,* animal]. A subkingdom of the kingdom Animalia, including all multicellular animal organisms in which the cells are differentiated and form tissues.

metazoonosis (met′ă-zo-o-no′sis) [meta- + G. *zōon,* animal, + *nosos,* disease]. A zoonosis that requires both a vertebrate and an invertebrate host for completion of its life cycle.

met′encephal′ic. Relating to the metencephalon.

metencephalon (met-en-sef′ă-lon) [meta- + G. *enkephalos,* brain] [NA]. The anterior of the two major subdivisions of the rhombencephalon (the posterior being the myelencephalon or medulla oblongata), composed of the pons and the cerebellum.

meteorism (me′te-o-rizm) [G. *meteōrismos,* a lifting up]. Tympanites.

meteorotropic (me′te-or-o-trop′ik) [meteorology, the science of the weather, + G. *tropos,* a turning]. Denoting diseases affected in their incidence by the weather.

me′ter (m) [Fr. *metre;* G. *metron,* measure]. A measure of length; the SI unit of length, equivalent to 39.37 inches.

meter-candle. Lux.

metestrus (met-es′trus) [meta- + estrus]. The period between estrus and diestrus in the estrous cycle.

meth-, metho-. Chemical prefixes usually denoting a methyl or methoxy group.

meth′adone hydrochloride. 6-Dimethylamino-4,4-diphenyl-3-heptanone hydrochloride; a synthetic narcotic analgesic similar in action to morphine but with slightly greater potency and longer duration; used orally as a replacement for morphine and heroin and during withdrawal treatment in morphine and heroin addiction.

meth′amphet′amine hydrochloride. *d-N,α*-dimethylphenethylamine hydrochoride; a sympathomimetic agent with greater stimulating effects upon the CNS than does amphetamine.

meth′ane [meth(yl) + *-ane*]. Marsh gas; CH_4; an odorless combustible gas produced by the decomposition of organic matter.

meth′anol. *Methyl* alcohol.

metHb Methemoglobin.

methemalbumin (met′hēm-al-bu′min) An abnormal compound formed in the blood as a result of heme combining with plasma albumin.

methemoglobin (metHb) (met-he'mo-glo'bin). A transformation product of oxyhemoglobin because of the oxidation of the normal FE^{2+} to Fe^{3+}, thus converting ferroprotoporphrin to ferriprotoporphyrin.

methemoglobinemia (met-he'mo-glo-bin-e'mĭ-ah) [methemoglobin + G. *haima*, blood]. Presence of methemoglobin in the circulating blood.

methemoglobinuria (met-he'mo-glo-bin-u'rĭ-ah) [methemoglobin + G. *ouron*, urine]. Presence of methemoglobin in the urine.

methi'onine (Met). 2-Amino-4-(methylthio)butyric acid; an essential amino acid and an important natural source of "active methyl" groups in the body.

metho-. See meth-.

meth'od [G. *methodos*; fr. *meta*, after, + *hodos*, way]. The mode or manner or orderly sequence of events of a process or procedure.

Abbott's m., a m. of treatment of scoliosis by use of a series of plaster jackets applied after partial correction of the curvature by external force.

Abell-Kendall m., a standard m. for estimation of total serum cholesterol that avoids interference by bilirubin, protein, and hemoglobin.

aristotelian m., a m. of study that stresses the relation between a general category and a particular object.

Bier's m., (1) intravenous regional *anesthesia;* (2) treatment of various surgical conditions by reactive hyperemia.

closed circuit m., a m. for measuring oxygen consumption in which the subject rebreathes an initial quantity of oxygen through a carbon dioxide absorber and the decrease in the volume of oxygen being rebreathed is noted.

copper sulfate m., a m. for the determination of specific gravity of blood or plasma in which the blood or plasma is delivered by drops into solutions of copper sulfate graded in specific gravity.

Credé's m.'s, instillation of one drop of a 2% solution of silver nitrate into each eye of the newborn infant, to prevent ophthalmia.

flash m., sterilization of milk by raising it rapidly to a temperature of 178°F. and, after holding it there for a short time, reducing it rapidly to 40°F.

flotation m., any of several procedures for concentrating helminth eggs, when eggs are difficult to find in direct examination, by use of a liquid of sufficiently high specific gravity.

glucose oxidase m., a highly specific m. for measurement of glucose in serum or plasma by reaction with glucose oxidase, in which gluconic acid and hydrogen peroxide are formed.

hexokinase m., the most specific m. for measuring glucose in serum or plasma, wherein hexokinase plus ATP transforms glucose to glucose 6-phosphate plus ADP; glucose 6-phosphate is then reacted with NADP and glucose 6-phosphate dehydrogenase to form NADP which is measured spectrophotometrically.

Jaboulay's m., anastomosis of arteries by splitting the cut ends a short distance and then suturing the flaps together, applying intima to intima.

Lamaze m., a technique of psychoprophylactic preparation for childbirth, designed to minimize the pain of labor.

Lister's m., listerism; antiseptic surgery, as first advocated by Lister in 1867, using carbolic acid as an antiseptic.

micro-Astrup m., an interpolation technique for acid-base measurement, based on pH and the use of the Siggaard-Anderson nomogram to determine the base deficit as an expression of metabolic acidosis and the arterial PCO_2 as an expression of respiratory acidosis or alkalosis.

open circuit m., a m. for measuring oxygen consumption and carbon dioxide production by collecting the expired gas over a known period of time and measuring its volume and composition.

Quick's m., prothrombin *test.*

rhythm m., a natural means of contraception that spaces sexual intercourse to avoid the fertile period of the menstrual cycle.

Westergren m., a procedure for estimating the sedimentation rate of red blood cells in fluid body by mixing venous blood with an aqueous solution of sodium citrate and allowing it to stand in pipet.

methoxy-. Chemical prefix denoting addition of a methoxyl group (CH_3O-).

methoxyflurane (mĕ-thok-sĭ-flūr'ān). 2,2-Dichloro-1,1-difluoroethyl methyl ether; a potent, nonflammable, nonexplosive inhalation anesthetic.

methox'yl. The group $-OCH_3$.

meth'ylate. 1. To mix with methyl alcohol. **2.** To introduce a methyl group. **3.** A compound of a metal ion with methyl alcohol.

methylcellulose (meth'il-sel'u-lōs). A methyl ester of cellulose that forms a colorless liquid when dissolved in water, alcohol, or ether.

meth'ylene. The radical, $-CH_2-$.

m. blue, tetramethylthionine chloride; a basic dye used in histology and microbiology, to track RNA and RNase in electrophoresis, and as an antidote for methemoglobinemia.

Loeffler's m. blue, a stain for diphtheria organisms.

methylmalon'ic aciduria. Excretion of excessive amounts of methylmalonic acid in urine due to deficiency of activity of methylmalonyl-CoA mutase; two types occur: congenital, a metabolic error resulting in severe ketoacidosis developing shortly after birth, with urine that also contains long-chain ketones; autosomal recessive inheritance; acquired, developing in vitamin B_{12} deficiency.

methyl (Me) (meth'il) [G. *methy*, wine, + *hylē*, wood]. The radical, $-CH_3$.

active m., a m. group attached to a quaternary ammonium ion or a tertiary sulfonium ion that can take part in transmethylation reactions.

m. alcohol, wood alcohol; methanol; carbinol; CH_3OH; a flammable, toxic, mobile liquid, used as an industrial solvent, antifreeze, and in chemical manufacture.

m. green, a basic triphenylmethane dye used as a chromatin stain, for differential staining of ribonucleic acid (red) and deoxyribonucleic acid (green), and as a tracking dye for DNA in electrophoresis.

meth'ylol. Hydroxymethyl; the monovalent radical, $-CH_2OH$.

meth'ylpen'tose. A 6-deoxyhexose in which carbon-6 is part of a methyl group.

meth'yltestos'terone. A methyl derivative of testosterone, with the same actions and uses.

meth'yltrans'ferase. Transmethylase; any enzyme tranferring methyl groups from one compound to another.

metMb Metmyoglobin.

metmyoglobin (metMb) (met'mi-o-glo'bin). Myoglobin in which the ferrous ion of the heme prosthetic group is oxidized to ferric ion.

metonymy (mĕ-ton'o-mī) [meta- + G. *ōnyma*, name]. Imprecise or circumscribed labeling of objects or events, said to be characteristic of the language disturbance of schizophrenics.

meto'pic [G. *metōpon*, forehead]. Relating to the forehead or anterior portion of the cranium.

metopoplasty (met'o-po-plas-tī, mĕ-top'o-) [G. *metōpon*, forehead, + *plassō*, to form]. Reparative surgery of the skin or bone of the forehead.

metox'enous [G. *meta*, beyond, + *xenos*, host]. Heterecious.

metox'eny [G. *meta*, beyond, + *xenos*, host]. **1.** Heterecism. **2.** Change of host by a parasite.

metr-, metra-. [G. *mētra*, uterus]. Combining forms denoting the uterus. See also hystero-, utero-.

metra (me'trah) [G. uterus]. Uterus.

metralgia (me-tral'jĭ-ah) [metra- + G. *algos*, pain]. Hysteralgia.

metrato'nia [metra- + G. *a*-priv. + *tonos*, tension]. Atony of the uterine walls after childbirth.

metratrophy, metratrophia (me-trat'ro-fī, me-trătro'fĭ-ah) [metra- + atrophy]. Uterine atrophy.

me'tria [G. *mētra*, uterus]. Pelvic cellulitis or other inflammatory condition in the puerperal period.

met'ric [G. *metrikos*, fr. *metron*, measure]. Quantitative; relating to measurement. See metric *system*.

metritis (me-tri'tis) [G. *mētra*, uterus, + *-itis*, inflammation]. Inflammation of the uterus.

metro- [G. *metra*, uterus]. Combining form relating to the uterus. See also hystero-, utero-.

metrocystosis (me'tro-sis-to'sis) [metro- + G. *kystis*, cyst, + *-osis*, condition]. Formation of uterine cysts.

metrocyte (me'tro-sīt) [G. *mētēr*, mother, + *kytos*, a hollow (cell)]. Mother *cell*.

metrodynia (me-tro-din'ĭ-ah) [metro- + G. *odynē*, pain]. Hysteralgia.

me'trofibro'ma. A fibroma of the uterus.

metrolymphangitis (me'tro-lim-fan-ji'tis) [metro- + lymphangitis]. An inflammation of the uterine lymphatics.

metromalacia (me'tro-mă-la'shĭ-ah) [metro- + G. *malakia*, softness]. Pathologic softening of the uterine tissues.

metroparalysis (me'tro-pă-ral'ĭ-sis) [metro- + paralysis]. Flaccidity or paralysis of the uterine muscle during or immediately after childbirth.

metropathia (me-tro-path'ĭ-ah) [L.]. Metropathy.

m. hemorrhag'ica, abnormal, excessive, often continuous uterine bleeding due to persistence and exaggeration of the follicular phase of the menstrual cycle.

metropath'ic. Relating to or caused by uterine disease.

metropathy (me-trop'ă-thĭ) [metro- + G. *pathos*, suffering]. Metropathia; any disease of the uterus.

metroperitonitis (me'tro-pĕr-ĭ-to-ni'tis) [metro- + peritonitis]. Inflammaation of the uterus involving the peritoneal covering.

metrophlebitis (me'tro-flĕ-bi'tis) [metro- + G. *phleps*, vein, + *-itis*, inflammation]. Inflammation of the uterine veins, usually following childbirth.

me'troplasty. Uteroplasty.

metrorrhagia (me-tro-ra'jĭ-ah) [metro- + G. *rhēgnymi*, to burst forth]. Any irregular, acyclic bleeding from the uterus between periods.

metrorrhea (me-tro-re'ah) [metro- + G. *rhoia*, a flow]. A discharge of mucus or pus from the uterus.

metrosalpingitis (me'tro-sal-pin-ji'tis) [metro- + G. *salpinx*, trumpet (oviduct), + *-itis*, inflammation]. Inflammation of the uterus and of one or both fallopian tubes.

metrosalpingography (me'tro-sal-pin-gog'raf-ī) [metro- + G. *salpinx*, tube, + *graphō*, to write]. Hysterosalpingography.

metroscope (me'tro-skōp) [metro- + G. *skōpeō*, to view]. Hysteroscope.

metrostaxis (me-tro-stak'sis) [metro- + G. *staxis*, a dripping]. A small but continuous uterine hemorrhage.

metrostenosis (me'tro-stĕ-no'sis) [metro- + G. *stenosis*, a narrowing]. A narrowing of the uterine cavity.

metyrapone (mĕ-tīr'ă-pōn). 2-Methyl-1,2-di-3-pyridyl-1-propanone; an inhibitor of adenocortical steroid to determine the ability of the pituitary gland to increase its secretion of corticotropin.

Mev Million electron-volts, or 10^6 ev.

Mg Magnesium.

mg Milligram.

mho (mo) [*ohm* reversed]. Siemens.

mHz Megahertz.

micr-. See micro-.

micracoustic (mi'kră-koo'stik) [micro- + G. *akoustikos*, relating to hearing, fr. *akouō*, to hear]. Microcoustic. **1.** Relating to faint sounds. **2.** Magnifying very faint sounds to make them audible.

micrencephaly (mi-kren-sef'ă-lĭ) [micro- + G. *enkephalos*, brain]. Microencephaly; abnormal smallness of the brain.

micro-, micr- [G. *mikros*, small]. **1.** Prefix denoting smallness. **2.** (μ) Denoting one-millionth (10⁻⁶) of a unit. **3.** Denoting that minimal quantities of the substance to be examined are used. **4.** Combining form meaning microscopic.

microabscess (mi'kro-ab'ses). A very small circumscribed collection of leukocytes in solid tissues.

    Munro's m., Munro's abscess; a microscopic collection of polymorphonuclear leukocytes found in the stratum corneum in psoriasis.

    Pautrier's m., Pautrier's abscess; a microscopic lesion in the epidermis, seen in mycosis fungoides, composed of the same type of mononuclear cells as those that form the infiltrate in the corium.

microaerophilic (mi'kro-ār-o-fil'ik). Microaerophil (2).

microaerophil, microaerophile (mi-kro-ār'o-fil, -fīl) [micro- + G. *aēr*, air, + *philos*, fond]. **1.** An aerobic bacterium that requires oxygen, but less than is present in the air. **2.** Microaerophilic; relating to such an organism.

microanastomosis (mi'kro-ă-nas-to-mo'sis). Anastomosis of minute structures performed under a surgical microscope.

microanatomist (mi'kro-ă-nat'o-mist). Histologist.

microanatomy (mi'kro-ă-nat'o-mĭ). Histology.

microaneurysm (mi-kro-an'u-rizm). Focal dilation of retinal capillaries occuring in diabetes mellitus, retinal vein obstruction, and absolute glaucoma, or of arteriolocapillary junctions in many organs in thrombotic thrombocytopenic purpura.

microangiography (mi'kro-an-jĭ-og'ră-fĭ). Radiography of the finer vessels of an organ after the injection of a contrast medium and enlarging the resulting radiograph.

microangiopathy (mi'kro-an-jĭ-op'ă-thĭ). Capillaropathy.

microbe (mi'krōb) [Fr. fr. G. *mikros*, small, + *bios*, life]. A microscopic or ultramicroscopic organism, including spirochetes, bacteria, rickettsiae, and viruses; such organisms form a biologically distinctive group, in that the genetic material is not surrounded by a nuclear membrane, and mitosis does not occur during replication.

micro'bial, micro'bic. Relating to a microbe or microbes.

microbicidal (mi-kro'bĭ-si'dal). Destructive to microbes.

microbicide (mi-kro'bĭ-sīd) [microbe + L. *caedo*, to kill], An agent destructive to microbes.

mi'crobiol'ogist. One who specializes in microbiology.

microbiologic (mi'kro-bi-o-loj'ik). Relating to microbiology.

microbiology (mi'kro-bi-ol'o-jĭ) [Fr. *microbiologie*]. The science concerned with microscopic and ultramicroscopic organisms.

mi'croblast [micro- + G. *blastos*, sprout, germ]. A small nucleated red blood cell.

microblepharia, microblepharism, microblepharon (mi'kro-blĕ-făr'ĭ-ah, -blef'ăr-izm, -blef'ă-ron) [micro- + G. *blepharon*, eyelid, + *-ia*, condition]. A rare developmental anomaly characterized by eyelids of abnormally short vertical dimension.

mi'crobody. Peroxisome.

microbrachia (mi-kro-bra'kĭ-ah) [micro- + G. *brachiōn*, arm]. Abnormal smallness of the arms.

microcar'dia [micro- + G. *kardia*, heart]. Abnormal smallness of the heart.

microcen'trum [micro- + G. *kentron*, center]. Cytocentrum.

microcephalic (mi'kro-sĕ-fal'ik). Nanocephalous; having an abnormally small head.

microcephaly (mi-kro-sef'ă-lĭ) [micro- + G. *kephalē*, head]. Nanocephaly; abnormal smallness of the head.

microcheilia, microchilia (mi-kro-ki'lĭ-ah) [micro- + G. *cheilos*, lip]. Abnormal smallness of the lips.

microcheiria, microchiria (mi-kro-ki'rĭ-ah) [micro- + G. *cheir*, hand]. Abnormal smallness of the hands.

microcinematography (mi'kro-sin-ĕ-mă-tog'ră-fĭ) [micro- + G. *kinēma*, movement, + *graphō*, to write]. The application of motion pictures taken through magnifying lenses to the study of an organ or system in motion.

mi'crocir'cula'tion. Circulation in the smallest vessels (arterioles, capillaries, and venules).

Micrococcaceae (mi'kro-kok-a'se-e). A family of bacteria (order Eubacteriales) containing Gram-positive spherical cells which occur singly or in pairs, tetrads, irregular masses, or chains; free living, saprophytic, parasitic, and pathogenic species occur. The type genus is *Micrococcus*.

micrococci (mi-kro-kok'si). Plural of micrococcus.

Micrococcus (mi-kro-kok'us) [micro- + G. *kokkos*, berry]. A genus of bacteria (family Micrococcaceae) containing Gram-positive spherical cells that occur in irregular masses, and are saprophytic or parasitic but are not pathogenic. The type species is *M. luteus.*

microcolon (mi'kro-ko-lon). A small colon, often arising from a decreased functional state.

microcoria (mi-kro-ko'rĭah) [micro- + G. *korē*, pupil]. Congenital contraction of the pupil.

microcornea (mi'kro-kor'ne-ah). An abnormally thin and flat cornea.

microcoustic (mi-kro-ku'stik). Micracoustic.

microcurie (μCi) (mi-kro-ku're). A measure of radium emanation, one-millionth of a curie; 3.7 × 10⁴ disintegrations per second.

microcyst (mi'kro-sist). A tiny cyst, such that a magnifying lens is required for observation.

microcyte (mi'kro-sīt) [micro- + G. *kytos*, cell]. Microerythrocyte; a small non-nucleated red blood cell.

microcythemia (mi'kro-si-the'mĭ-ah) [microcyte + G. *haima*, blood]. Microcytosis; presence of many microcytes in the circulating blood.

microcyto'sis. [microcyte + G. *-osis*, condition]. Microcythemia.

microdactyly (mi'kro-dak'tĭ-lĭ) [micro- + G. *dactylos*, finger, toe]. Abnormal smallness or shortness of the fingers or toes.

microdissection (mi'kro-dĭ-sek'shun). Dissection of tissues under magnification, usually done by teasing the tissues apart with needles.

microdontia (mi-kro-don'shĭ-ah) [micro- + G. *odous*, tooth]. A condition in which a single tooth, or pairs of teeth, or the whole dentition may be disproportionately smaller than body build.

mi'crodrep'anocyto'sis [microcytosis + drepanocytosis]. Chronic hemolytic anemia resulting from interaction of the genes for sickle cell anemia and thalassemia.

mi'croenceph'aly. Micrencephaly.

microerythrocyte (mi'kro-ĕ-rith'ro-sīt). Microcyte.

microfibril (mi-kro-fi'bril). A very small fibril, which may be a bundle of still smaller elements, the microfilaments.

microfilament (mi-kro-fil'ă-ment). The finest of the fibrous elements of a cell or tissue.

microfilaremia (mi'kro-fil-ă-re'mĭ-ah). Infection of the blood with microfilariae.

microfilaria, pl. **microfilariae** (mi'kro-fĭ-lăr'ĭ-ah, -e). Embryos of filarial nematodes in the family Onchocercidae.

microgamete (mi-kro-gam'ēt) [micro- + G. *gametēs*, husband]. The smaller motile male element in anisogamy.

microgametocyte (mi-kro-gam'e-to-sīt). The mother cell producing the microgametes.

microgas'tria [micro- + G. *gastēr*, stomach]. Abnormal smallness of the stomach.

microgenia (mi-kro-je'nĭ-ah) [micro- + G. *geneion*, chin]. Abnormal smallness of the chin.

microgenitalism (mi-kro-jen'ĭ-tal-izm). Abnormal smallness of the external genitalia.

microglia (mi-krog'lĭ-ah) [micro- + G. *glia*, glue]. Hortega cells; small neuroglial cells of mesodermal origin which may become phagocytic, hence are considered elements of the reticuloendothelial system.

microgliacyte (mi-kro-gli'ă-sīt) [micro- + G. *glia*, glue, + *kytos*, cell]. A cell, especially an embryonic cell, of the microglia.

microglioma (mi-krog'lĭ-o'mah) [microglia + G. *-oma*, tumor]. An intracranial neoplasm of microglial cell origin that is structurally similar to reticulum cell sarcoma.

microglos'sia [micro- + G. *glōssa*, tongue]. Abnormal smallness of the tongue.

micrognathia (mi-kro-na'thĭ-ah) [micro- + G. *gnathos*, jaw]. Abnormal smallness of the jaws, especially of the mandible.

microgonioscope (mi'kro-go'nĭ-o-skōp) [micro- + G. *gōnia*, angle, + *skopeō*, to examine]. An instrument for measuring minute angles; used in the study of glaucoma.

mi'crogram (μg). One-millionth of a gram.

mi'crograph [micro- + G. *graphō*, to write]. **1.** An instrument that magnifies the microscopic movements of a diaphragm and records them on a moving photographic film.

microgyria (mi-kro-ji'rĭ-ah) [micro- + G. *gyros*, convolution]. Abnormal narrowness of the cerebral convolutions.

microhepatia (mi-kro-hĕ-pat'ĭ-ah) [micro- + G. *hepar*(*hepat*-), liver]. Abnormal smallness of the liver.

microincision (mi'kro-in-sizh'un). Micropuncture; destruction of cellular organelles by laser beam.

mi'croinva'sion. Invasion of tissue immediately adjacent to a carcinoma in situ, the earliest stage of malignant neoplastic invasion.

microliter (μl) (mi'kro-le-ter). One-millionth of a liter.

mi'crolith [micro- + G. *lithos*, stone]. A minute calculus, usually multiple and constituting a coarse sand or gravel.

microlithiasis (mi'kro-lĭ-thi'ă-sis). The formation, presence, or discharge of minute concretions or gravel.

mi'cromanipula'tion. Microdissection, microinjection, and other maneuvers performed with the aid of a microscope.

micromas'tia [micro- + G. *mastos* breast]. A condition in which the breasts are rudimentary and functionless.

micromelia (mi-kro-me'lĭ-ah) [micro- + G. *melos*, limb]. Nanomelia; disproportionately short or small limbs.

micromere (mi'kro-mēr) [micro- + G. *meros*, a part]. A blastomere of small size.

micrometastasis (mi'kro-mĕ-tas'tă-sis). A stage of metastasis when the secondary tumors are too small to be clinically detected.

mi'crometer (μm). Micron; one-millionth of a meter.

microm'eter [micro- + G. *metron*, measure]. A glass slide or lens that is accurately marked for measuring microscopic forms.

microm'etry. Measurement of objects with a micrometer and microscope.

mi'cromi'cro- (μμ). Formerly one-trillionth (10^{-12}); pico- is preferred.

micromyelia (mi'kro-mi-e'lĭ-ah) [micro- + G. *myelos*, marrow]. Abnormal smallness or shortness of the spinal cord.

micromyeloblast (mi-kro-mi'el-o-blast). A small myeloblast, often the predominating cell in myeloblastic leukemia.

mi'cron (μ). Micrometer.

micronod'ular [G. *mikros*, small]. Characterized by the presence of minute nodules; denoting a somewhat coarser appearance than that of a granular tissue or substance.

micronucleus (mi-kro-nu'kle-us). **1.** A small nucleus in a large cell, or the smaller nuclei in cells that have two or more such structures. **2.** The smaller of the two nuclei in ciliates dividing mitotically and bearing specific inheritable material.

micronu'trients. Essential food factors required in only small quantities by the body.

micronychia (mi-kro-nik'ĭ-ah) [micro- + G. *onyx*, nail]. Abnormal smallness of nails.

microorganism (mi'kro-or'gan-izm). A microscopic organism.

micropathol'ogy [micro- + G. *pathos*, suffering, + *logos*, study]. The microscopic study of disease changes.

micrope'nis. Microphallus; an abnormally small penis.

mi'cropha'kia [micro- + G. *phakos*, lens]. Spherophakia.

microphage (mi'kro-fāj) [micro- + phag(ocyte)]. A polymorphonuclear leukocyte that is phagocytic.

microphallus (mi-kro-fal'us). Micropenis.

micropho'nia, microph'ony [micro- + G. *phōnē*, voice]. Hypophonia.

micropho'tograph. A minute photograph of any object, as distinguished from photomicrograph.

microphthalmia, microphthalmos (mi-krof-thal'mĭ-ah, -thal'mos) [micro- + G. *ophthalmos*, eye]. Nanophthalmia; nanophthalmos; abnormal smallness of one or both eyeballs.

microplethysmography (mi'kro-pleth'iz-mog'rā-fĭ) [micro- + plethysmography]. The technique of measuring minute changes in the volume of a part as a result of blood flow into or out of it.

micropo'dia [micro- + G. *pous*, foot]. Abnormally small feet.

microp'sia [micro- + G. *opsis*, sight]. Subjective perception of objects as smaller than they actually are.

mi'cropuncture. Microincision.

microrefractometer (mi'kro-re-frak-tom'ĕ-ter). A refractometer used in the study of blood cells.

microrespirometer (mi'kro-res-pir-om'ĕ-ter). An apparatus for measuring the utilization of oxygen by small particles of isolated tissues or cells or particles of cells.

microscope (mi'kro-skōp) [micro- + G. *skopeō*, to view]. An instrument that gives an enlarged image of an object or substance that is minute or not visible with the naked eye.

    binocular m., a m. having two eyepieces.

    compound m., one consisting of two or more lenses.

    dark-field m., a m. that has a special condenser and objective with a diaphragm or stop such that light is scattered from the object observed, with the result that the object appears bright on a dark background.

    electron m., a visual and photographic m. in which electron beams with wavelengths thousands of times shorter than visible light are utilized in place of light, thereby allowing much greater magnification.

    fluorescent m., see fluorescence *microscopy.*

    infrared m., a m. equipped with infrared transmitting optics that measures the infrared absorption of minute samples with the aid of photoelectric cells; images may be observed with image converters or television.

    operating m., surgical m.

    phase m., a specially constructed m. which employs a special condenser and objective containing a phase-shifting ring whereby small differences in index of refraction are made visible as intensity or contrast differences in the image.

    scanning electron m., a m. in which the object is examined point by point directly by an electron beam, and an image is formed on a television screen.

    simple m., a m. that consists of a single magnifying lens.

    stereoscopic m., a m. having double eyepieces and objectives and thus independent light paths, giving a three-demensional image.

    stroboscopic m., a m. which has a light source that flashes at a constant rate so that an analysis of the motility of an object may be made.

    surgical m., operating m.; a binocular m. used to obtain good visualization of fine structures in the operating field.

    ultraviolet m., a m. having otpics of quartz and fluorite which allow transmission of light waves shorter than those of the visible spectrum.

    x-ray m., a m. in which images are obtained by using x-rays as an energy source and are recorded on a very fine-grained film, or the image is enlarged by projection.

microscop'ic, microscop'ical. 1. Of minute size; visible only with the aid of the microscope. **2.** Relating to a microscope.

microscopy (mi-kros'ko-pĭ). Investigation of minute objects by means of a microscope.

    fluorescence m., a procedure based on the fact that fluorescent materials emit visible light when they are irradiated with ultraviolet or violet-blue visible rays.

    immune electron m., electron m. of viral specimens to which specific antibody has been added.

mi'crosec'ond (μs, μsec). One-millionth of a second.

mi'crosome [micro- + G. *sōma*, body]. One of the small spherical vesicles derived from the endoplasmic reticulum after disruption of cells by centrifugation.

microsomia (mi-kro-so'mĭ-ah) [micro- + G. *sōma*, body]. Nanocormia; abnormal smallness of body, as in dwarfism.

microspectrophotometry (mi'kro-spek'tro-fo-tom'ĕ-trĭ). A technique for characterizing and quantitating nucleoproteins in single cells or cell organelles by their natural absorption spectra (ultraviolet) or after binding stoichiometrically in selective cytochemical staining reactions.

microspectroscope (mi-kro-spek'tro-skōp). An instrument for observing the spectrum of microscopic objects.

microspherocytosis (mi'kro-sfe-ro-si-to'sis). A condition of the blood seen in hemolytic icterus in which small spherocytes are predominant; red blood cells are smaller and more globular than normal.

microsphygmy (mi-kro-sfig'mi) [micro- + G. *sphygmos*, pulse]. A pulse that is difficult to detect manually.

microsplenia (mi-kro-sple'ni-ah). Abnormal smallness of the spleen.

Microsporum (mi-kro-spo'rum) [micro- + G. *sporos*, seed]. A genus of pathogenic fungi causing dermatophytosis.

microsteth'oscope. A stethoscope that amplifies the sounds heard.

microsto'mia [micro- + G. *stoma*, mouth]. Abnormal smallness of the oral aperature.

microsur'gery. Surgical procedures performed under the magnification of a surgical microscope.

microsu'ture. Tiny caliber suture material, often 9-0 or 10-0, with a similar attached needle, for use in microsurgery.

microsyringe (mi'kro-si-rinj', -sir'inj). A hypodermic syringe having a micrometer screw attached to the piston, whereby accurately measured minute quantities of fluid may be injected.

microtia (mi-kro'shi-ah) [micro- + G. *ous*, ear, + *-ia*, condition]. Abnormal smallness of the auricle or pinna of the ear.

mi'crotome. Histotome; an instrument for making sections for examination under the microscope.

microtomy (mi-krot'o-mi) [micro- + G. *tomē*, incision]. Histotomy; section-cutting; the making of thin sections of tissues for examination under the microscope.

Microtrombid'ium [micro- + Mod. L. *trombidium*, a timid one]. A genus of chigger or harvest mites that cause severe itching from the presence of the larval stage in the skin.

mi'crotu'bule. A cylindrical cytoplasmic element of variable length that increases in number during mitosis and meiosis, and occurs widely in plant and animal cells, where it may be related to movement of the chromosomes or chromatids on the nuclear spindle during nuclear division.

microvil'lus, pl. **microvil'li.** One of the minute projections of cell membranes greatly increasing surface area.

mi'crowaves. That portion of the radio wave spectrum of shortest wavelength, including the region with wavelengths of 1 mm to 30 cm (1000 to 300,000 megacycles per second.

microxyphil (mi-krok'si-fil) [micro- + G. *oxys*, acid, + *philos*, fond]. A multinuclear oxyphil leukocyte.

microzoon (mi'kro-zo'on) [micro- + G. *zōon*, animal]. A microscopic form of the animal kingdom.

micrurgical (mi-krer'ji-kal) [micro- + G. *ergon*, work]. Relating to procedures performed on minute structures under a microscope.

miction (mik'shun). Urination.

micturate (mik'tu-rāt) [see micturition]. Urinate.

micturition (mik-tu-rish'un) [L. *micturio*, to desire to make water]. **1.** Urination. **2.** The desire to urinate. **3.** Frequency of urination.

MID Minimal infecting *dose.*

mid- [A.S. *mid*, *midd*]. Combining form meaning middle.

mid'body. Residual interzonal spindle fibers (microtubules) appearing as a granule between daughter cells during telophase of mitosis.

mid'brain. Mesencephalon.

mid'gut. 1. The central portion of the digestive tube; the small intestine. **2.** The portion of the embryonic gut tract between the foregut and the hindgut.

midriff [A.S. *mid*, middle, + *hrif*, belly]. Diaphragma (2).

mid'wife (mid'wif) [A.S. *mid*, with, + *wif*, wife]. A person qualified to practice midwifery, having specialized training in gynecology and child care and the ability to carry out emergency measures in the absence of medical help.

midwifery (mid'wif'ri). Independent care of essentially normal, healthy women and infants by a midwife, antepartally, intrapartally, postpartally, and/or gynecologically, including normal delivery of the infant, with medical consultation, collaborative management, and referral of cases in which abnormalities develop.

migraine (mi'grān) [through O. Fr. fr. G. *hēmi-krania*, pain on one side of the head]. Sick headache; hemicrania (1); a symptom complex occurring periodically and characterized by pain in the head (usually unilateral), vertigo, nausea and vomiting, photophobia, and scintillating appearances of light. Classified as classic m., common m., cluster *headache*, hemiplegic m., ophthalmoplegic m., and ophthalmic m.

mi'grate [L. *migro*, pp. *-atus*, to move from place to place]. To wander; to pass from one part to another, as in an organ or in the body.

migration (mi-gra'shun) [L. *migratio* (see migrate)]. **1.** Passing from place to place, said of certain morbid processes of symptoms. **2.** Diapedesis. **3.** Movement of a tooth or teeth out of normal position. **4.** Movement of molecules during electrophoresis.

mil'ia. Plural of milium.

miliaria (mil-i-ār'i-ah) [L. *miliarius*, relating to millet, fr. *milium*, millet]. Miliary fever (2); an eruption of minute vesicles and papules due to retention of fluid at the mouths of the sweat follicles.

  m. ru'bra, an eruption of papules and vesicles at the mouths of the sweat follicles, accompanied by redness and inflammatory reaction of the skin. Also called strophulus; lichen infantum; tropical lichen; heat rash; prickly heat.

miliary (mil'ĭ-ĕr-ĭ, mil'yă-rĭ) [see miliaria]. **1.** Resembling a millet seed in size (about 2 mm). **2.** Marked by the presence of nodules of millet seed size on any surface.

milieu (mēl-yü) [Fr. *mi*, fr. L. *medius*, middle, + *leiu*, fr. L. *locus*, place]. **1.** Surroundings; environment. **2.** In psychiatry, the social setting of the mental patient.

mil'ium, pl. **mil'ia** [L. millet]. Whitehead; a small subepidermal keratin cyst, usually multiple.

milk [A.S. *meolc*]. **1.** A white liquid, containing proteins, sugar, lipids, secreted by the mammary glands and designed for nourishment of the young. **2.** Any whitish, milky fluid. **3.** A pharmacopeial preparation that is a suspension of insoluble drugs in a water medium. **4.** Stripe (1).

certified m., cow's m. that has not more than the maximal permissible limit of 10,000 bacteria per ml at any time prior to delivery to the consumer, and that must be cooled to 50°F or less and maintained at that temperature until delivery.

certified pasteurized m., cow's m.; that has a maximum permissible limit for bacteria of not more than 10,000 bacteria per ml before pasteurization and not more than 500 bacteria per ml after pasteurization; must be cooled to 45°F or less and maintained at that temperature until delivery.

condensed m., a thick liquid prepared by the partial evaporation of cow's m., with or without the addition of sugar.

m. of magnesia, magnesia magma; an aqueous solution of magnesium hydroxide, used as an antacid and laxative.

skim m., the aqueous (noncream) part of m. from which casein is isolated.

vitamin D m., cow's m. containing 400 USP units of vitamin D per quart.

witch's m., Hexenmilch; a secretion of colostrum-like m. sometimes occurring in the glands of newborn infants of either sex 3 to 4 days after birth and lasting a week or two; due to endocrine stimulation from the mother before birth.

milli- (m) [L. *mille*, one thousand]. Prefix used in the metric system to signify one-thousandth (10^{-3}).

mil'liam'pere (ma). One thousandth of an ampere.

millicurie (mCi) (mil'ĭ-ku're). A unit of radioactivity equivalent to 3.7×10^7 disintegrations per second.

milliequivalent (mEq, meq) (mil'ĭ-e-kwiv'ă-lent). One-thousandth (10^{-3}) equivalent; 10^{-3} mole divided by valence.

mil'ligram (mg). One-thousandth (10^{-3}) of a gram.

milligramage (mil'ĭ-gram-āj). Milligram hour.

milligram hour. Milligramage; a unit of exposure in radium therapy, *i.e.,* the application of 1 mg of radium during 1 hr.

milliliter (ml) (mil'ĭ-le-ter). One-thousandth (10^{-3}) of a liter, 1 cubic centimeter, or about 15 minims.

millimeter (mm) (mil'ĭ-me-ter). One-thousandth (10^{-3}) of a meter, roughly $1/25$ inch.

millimicro-. Prefix sometimes used to signify one-billionth (10^{-9}); nano- is preferred.

millimicron (mμ) (mil'ĭ-mi-kron). One-thousandth (10^{-3}) of a micron; nano-meter is preferred.

millimole (mmol) (mil'ĭ-mōl). One-thousandth (10^{-3}) of a gram-molecule.

milliosmole (mil'ĭ-oz-mōl). One-thousandth (10^{-3}) of an osmole.

mil'lisecond (ms, msec). One-thousandth (10^{-3}) of a second.

mil'livolt (mV). One thousandth (10^{-3}) of a volt.

milphosis (mil-fo'sis) [G. *milphōsis*]. Loss of eyelashes.

mimesis (mĭ-me'sis, mi-me'sis) [G. *mimēsis*, imitation, fr. *mimeomai*, to mimic]. **1.** Hysterical simulation of organic disease. **2.** Symptomatic imitation of one organic disease by another.

mimet'ic [G. *mimētikos*, imitative]. Relating to mimesis.

mimic (mim'ik) [G. *mimikos*, imitating, fr. *mimos*, a mimic]. To imitate or simulate.

mind [A.S. *gemynd*]. **1.** The psyche; the organ or seat of consciousness, remembering, reasoning, and willing. **2.** The organized totality of all mental processes and psychic activities, with emphasis on the relatedness of the phenomena.

mineral (min'er-al) [L. *mineralis*, pertaining to mines, fr. *mino*, to mine]. Any homogeneous inorganic material found in the earth's crust.

mineralocorticoid (min'er-al-o-kor'tĭ-koyd). One of the steroid principles of the adrenal cortex that influences salt (sodium and potassium) metabolism.

mineral oil. A mixture of liquid hydrocarbons obtained from petroleum.

min'ilaparot'omy. A technique for sterilization by surgical ligation of the fallopian tubes, performed through a small suprapubic incision.

min'im [L. *minimus*, least]. **1 (m).** A fluid measure, $1/60$ of a fluidrachm; in the case of water, about one drop. **2.** Smallest; least; the smallest of several similar structures.

minor [L.]. Smaller; lesser; denoting the smaller of two similar structures.

mio- [G. *meiōn*, less]. Combining form meaning less.

miocardia (mi'o-kar-dĭ-ah) [mio- + G. *kardia*, heart]. Systole.

mio'sis [G. *meiosis*, a lessening]. **1.** The period of decline of a disease in which the intensity of the symptoms begins to diminish. **2.** Contraction of the pupil.

miosphygmia (mi-o-sfig'mĭ-ah) [mio- + G. *sphygmos*, pulse]. Fewer pulse beats than heart beats.

miot'ic. 1. Relating to or characterized by miosis. **2.** An agent that causes the pupil to contract.

mire (mēr) [L. *miror*, pp. *-atus*, to wonder at]. One of the test objects in the ophthalmometer, by means of the images of which the amount of astigmatism is calculated.

miryach'it. A nervous affection observed in Siberia; similar to palmus, latah, or the jumper disease of Maine.

misan'dria [G. *miseō,* to hate, + *anēr, andros,* male]. Fear of men.

misanthropy (mis-an'thro-pĭ) [G. *miseō,* to hate, + *anthrōpos,* man]. Aversion to people; hatred of mankind.

miscarriage (mis-kăr'ij). Spontaneous expulsion of the products of pregnancy before the middle of the second trimester.

miscegenation (mis'ĕ-jĕ-na'shun) [L. *misceo,* to mix, + *genus,* descent, race]. Marriage or interbreeding of individuals of different races.

miscible (mis'ĭ-bl) [L. *misceo,* to mix]. Capable of being mixed and remaining so after the mixing process ceases.

mis'diagno'sis. Wrong or mistaken diagnosis.

misogamy (mĭ-sog'ă-mĭ) [G. *miseō,* to hate, + *gamos,* marriage]. Aversion to marriage.

misogyny (mĭ-soj'ĕ-nĭ) [G. *miseō,* to hate, + *gynē,* woman]. Aversion to or hatred of women.

misope'dia, misop'edy [G. *miseō,* to hate, + *pais* (*paid-*), child]. Aversion to or hatred of children.

mite [A.S.]. A minute arthropod of the order Acarina, a vast assemblage of parasitic and (primarily) free-living organisms of which only a small number are of importance as vectors or intermediate hosts of pathogenic agents by directly causing dermatitis or tissue damage, or by causing blood or tissue fluid loss.

mithridatism (mith'rĭ-da-tizm, mith-rid'ă-tizm) [*Mithridates,* King of Pontus (132–63 B.C.), said to have acquired immunity to poison by this means]. Immunity against the action of a poison produced by small and gradually increasing doses of the same.

miticidal (mĭ'tĭ-si'dal). Destructive to mites.

miticide (mĭ'tĭ-sĭd) [mite + L. *caedo,* to kill]. An agent destructive to mites.

mit'igate [L. *mitigo,* pp. *-atus,* to make mild or gentle]. Palliate.

mitochondrial (mit'o-kon'drĭ-al, mi'to-). Relating to mitochondria.

mitochondrion, pl. **mitochondria** (mit'o-kon'drĭ-on, mi'to-; -kon'drĭ-ah) [G. *mitos,* thread, + *chondros,* granule, grits]. An organelle of the cell cytoplasm consisting of two sets of membranes, a smooth continuous outer coat and an inner membrane arranged in tubules or in folds that form platelike double membranes (cristae); the principal energy source of the cell, containing the cytochrome enzymes of terminal electron transport and the enzymes of the citric acid cycle, fatty acid oxidation, and oxidative phosphorylation.

mitogen (mi'to-jen) [mitosis + G. *-gen,* producing]. A substance that stimulates mitosis and lymphocyte transformation.

mitogenesis (mi-to-jen'ĕ-sis) [mitosis + G. *genesis,* origin]. Induction of mitosis in a cell.

mitogenetic (mit'to-jĕ-net-net'ik). Pertaining to the factor or factors causing cell mitosis.

mitogen'ic. Pertaining to a mitogen.

mitosis, pl. **mitoses** (mi-to'sis, -sēz) [G. *mitos,* threat]. Karyokinesis; mitotic or indirect nuclear division; the usual process of cell reproduction consisting of a sequence of modifications of the nucleus (prophase, prometaphase, metaphase, anaphase, telophase) that result in the formation of two daughter cells with exactly the same chromosome and DNA content as that of the original cell.

mitot'ic. Karyokinetic; relating to or marked by mitosis.

mi'tral [L. *mitra,* a coif or turban]. **1.** Relating to the mitral or bicuspid valve. **2.** Shaped like a bishop's miter; denoting a structure resembling the shape of a headband or turban.

mi'traliza'tion. Straightening of the left heart border in the chest x-ray due to increased prominence of the left atrial appendage and/or the pulmonary salient.

mittelschmerz (mit'el-schmĕrts) [Ger. middle pain]. Intermenstrual pain (2); abdominal pain occurring at the time of ovulation, resulting from irritation of the peritoneum by bleeding from the ovulation site.

mix'ture [L. *mixtura* or *mistura*]. **1.** A mutual incorporation of two or more substances, without chemical union, the physical characteristics of each of the components being retained. A **mechanical m.** is a m. of particles or masses distinguishable as such under the microscope or in other ways; a **physical m.** is more intimate m. of molecules, as of gases and many solutions. **2.** In chemistry, a mingling together of two or more substances without the occurrence of a reaction by which they would lose their individual properties, *i.e.,* without permanent gain or loss of electrons. **3.** In pharmacy, a preparation, consisting of a liquid holding an insoluble medicinal substance in suspension by means of some viscid material.

Miyagawanella (me'yă-gah'wă-nel'ah). *Chlamydia.*

MK Menaquinone.

MKS, mks Meter-kilogram-second.

ml Milliliter.

MLD, mld Minimal lethal *dose.*

mm Millimeter.

M-mode. A diagnostic ultrasound presentation of the temporal changes in echoes in which the depth of echo-producing interfaces is displayed along one axis and time (T) is displayed along the second axis, recording motion (M) of the interfaces toward and away from the transducer.

mmol Millimole.

Mn Manganese.

mnemenic, mnemic (ne-men'ik, ne'mik). Relating to memory.

mnemonic (ne-mon'ik). Anamnestic (2).

mnemonics (ne-mon'iks) [G. *mnēmonikos,* mnemonic, pertaining to memory]. The art of improving the memory; a system for aiding the memory.

M.O. Medical Officer.

Mo Molybdenum.

mobilization (mo'bĭ-lĭ-za'shun) [see mobilize]. **1.** Making movable; restoring the power of motion in a joint. **2.** The act of mobilizing; exciting a hitherto quiescent process into physiologic activity.

stapes m., an operation to remobilize the footplate of the stapes to relieve conductive hearing impairment caused by its immobilization through otosclerosis or middle ear disease.

modality (mo-dal'ĭ-tĭ) [Mediev. L. *modalitas,* fr. L. *modus,* a mode]. **1.** Any form of therapeutic intervention. **2.** Various forms of sensation, *e.g.,* touch, vision.

mode [L. *modus,* a measure, quantity]. In a set of measurements, that value which appears most frequently.

modifica'tion. A nonhereditary change in an organism; *e.g.,* one that is acquired from its own activity or environment.

behavior m., the systematic use of principles of conditioning and learning to teach simple skills or to alter undesirable behavior.

modiolus, pl. **modi'oli** (mo-di'o-lus) [L., the nave of a wheel] [NA]. The central cone-shaped core of spongy bone about which turns the spiral canal of the cochlea.

modulation (mod-u-la'shun) [L. *modulari,* to measure off properly]. **1.** The functional and morphologic fluctuation of cells in response to changing environmental conditions. **2.** Systematic variation in a characteristic of a sustained oscillation to code additional information.

moiety (moy'ĭ-te) [M.E. *moite,* a half]. Originally a half, now (loosely) one of two or more parts into which something may be divided.

mol Mole.

mo'lal. Denoting one mole of solute dissolved in 1000 grams of solvent; such solutions provide a definite ratio of solute to solvent molecules.

molal'ity. The concentration of a solution expressed in moles per kilogram of pure solvent.

molal'ity. The concentration of a solution expressed in moles per kilogram of pure solvent.

mo'lar. 1 [L. *molaris,* relating to a mill]. Grinding. **2.** *Dens* molaris. **3** [L. *moles,* mass]. Massive; relating to a mass; not molecular. **4 (M, *M*M).** Denoting a concentration of 1 gram-molecular weight (1 mole) of solute per liter of solution, the common unit of concentration in chemistry. **5.** Denoting specific quantity, *e.g.,* molar volume (volume of 1 mole). **6.** Relating to or associated with hydatidiform mole.

first m., sixth permanent tooth or fourth deciduous tooth in the maxilla and mandible on either side.

second m., seventh permanent or fifth deciduous tooth in the maxilla and mandible on either side.

sixth-year m., the first permanent m.

third m., eighth permanent tooth in the maxilla and mandible on either side.

twelfth-year m., the second permanent m.

molarity (mo-lăr'ĭ-tĭ). The concentration of a solution expressed in moles per liter of solution (mol/l).

mold. 1. A filamentous fungus, generally a circular colony with filaments not organized into large fruiting bodies, such as mushrooms. **2.** A shaped receptacle into which material is pressed or poured in making a cast. **3.** To shape a mass of plastic material according to a definite pattern. **4.** To change in shape; denoting especially the adaptation of the fetal head to the pelvic canal. **5.** In dentistry, the shape of an artificial tooth (or teeth).

mole (mōl). **1** [A.S. *māēl*(L. *macula*), a spot]. *Nevus* pigmentosus. **2** [L. *moles,* mass]. An intrauterine mass formed by the degeneration of the partly developed products of conception. **3 (mol).** The unit of "amount" of substance, one of the seven base SI units, defined as that amount of substance that contains as many "elementary entities" (atoms, molecules, ions, etc.) as there are atoms in 0.0120 kg of carbon-12; 6.0225×10^{23} "elementary entities."

Breus m., an aborted ovum in which the fetal surface of the placenta presents numerous hematomata, there is an absence of blood vessels in the chorion, and the ovum is much smaller than it should be according to the duration of the pregnancy.

hairy m., *nevus* pilosus.

hydatidiform m., hydatid m., a vesicular or polycystic mass resulting from the proliferation of the trophoblast, with hydropic degeneration and avascularity of the chorionic villi.

molecular (mo-lek'u-lar). Relating to molecules.

molecule (mol'ĕ-kūl) [Mod. L. *molecula,* dim. of L. *moles,* mass]. The smallest possible quantity of a di-, tri-, or polyatomic substance that retains the chemical properties of the substance.

molimen, pl. **molim'ina** (mo-li'men, mo'li-men) [L. endeavor]. An effort; the laborious performance of a normal function.

mollities (mol-ish'ĭ-ēz) [L. *mollis,* soft]. **1.** Characterized by a soft consistency. **2.** Malacia (1).

molluscous (mol-us'kus). Relating to or resembling molluscum.

molluscum (mol-us'kum) [L. *molluscus,* soft]. A disease marked by the occurrence of soft rounded tumors of the skin.

m. contagio'sum, an infectious disease of the skin, caused by a virus of the family Poxviridae and characterized by the appearance of small, pearly, umbilicated, papular epithelial lesions which contain numerous inclusion bodies.

molt [L. *muto,* to change]. To cast off feathers, hair, or cuticle; to undergo ecdysis. See also desquamate.

mol wt Molecular *weight.*

molybdenum (mo-lib'dĕ-num) [G. *molybdaina,* a piece of lead; a metal]. A metallic element, symbol Mo, atomic no. 42, atomic weight 95.94.

mon-. See mono-.

monad (mo'nad, mon'ad) [G. *monas,* the number one, unity]. **1.** A univalent element or radical. **2.** A unicellular organism. **3.** In meiosis, the single chromosome derived from a tetrad after the first and second maturation divisions.

mon'arthri'tis. Arthritis of a single joint.

monarthric (mon-ar'thrik). Monarticular.

mon'artic'ular. Monarthric; relating to a single joint.

monas'ter [mono- + G. *astēr*, star]. The single star figure at the end of prophase in mitosis.

mon'atheto'sis. Athetosis affecting one hand or foot.

mon'atom'ic. 1. Relating to or containing a single atom. **2.** Monovalent (1).

monaural (mon-aw'ral) [mono- + L. *auris*, ear]. Pertaining to one ear.

mon'esthet'ic [mono- + G. *aisthēsis*, sense perception]. Relating to a single sense or sensation.

mongo'lian. 1. Mongoloid. **2.** Characteristic of the Mongolian race.

mon'golism [fancied facial appearance resembling that of a Mongol]. Down's *syndrome*.

mon'goloid. Mongolian (1); relating to or characterized by mongolism.

monilethrix (mo-nil'ĕ-thriks) [L. *monile*, necklace, + G. *thrix*, hair]. Beaded or moniliform hair; a condition in which the hairs are brittle and show a series of constrictions, giving the appearance of a string of fusiform beads.

Monilia (mo-nil'ĭ-ah) [L. *monile*, necklace]. Generic term for a large group of molds or fungi commonly known as fruit molds; a few closely related pathogenic organisms formerly classified in this genus are now properly termed *Candida*.

monil'ial. Pertaining to fungi of the genus *Monilia*, but not to the genus *Candida*.

moniliasis (mo-nī-li'ă-sis). Candidiasis.

monil'iform [L. *monile*, necklace, + *forma*, appearance]. Shaped like a string of beads or beaded necklace.

Moniliformis (mo-nil'ĭ-for'mis) [L. *monile*, necklace, + *forma*, appearance]. A genus of the class (or phylum) Acanthocephala, the thorny-headed worms. *M. moniliformis* is a species normally found in rodents and a rare parasite of man.

moniliid (mo-nil'e-id). Minute macular or papular lesions occurring as an allergic reaction to monilial infection.

mon'itor. 1. A device that records specified data for a given series of events, operations, or circumstances. **2.** To check constantly on a specific condition or situation.

mono-, mon- [G. *monos*, single]. Prefix denoting the participation or involvement of a single element or part; equivalent of *uni-*.

mon'oam'ide. A molecule containing one amide group.

mon'oam'ine. A molecule containing one amine group.

monoaminergic (mon'o-am-ĭ-ner'jik) [monoamine + G. *ergon*, work]. Referring to nerve cells or fibers that transmit nervous impulses by the medium of a catecholamine or indolamine.

monoba'sic. Denoting an acid with only one replaceable hydrogen atom, or only one replaced hydrogen atom.

mon'oblast [mono- + G. *blastos*, germ]. An immature cell that develops into a monocyte.

monochorea (mon'o-ko-re'ah). Chorea affecting the head alone or only one extremity.

monochorionic (mon'o-ko-rī-on'ik). Relating to or having a single chorion; denoting monovular twins.

monochromatic (mon'o-kro-mat'ik). **1.** Having but one color. **2.** Indicating a pure spectral color of a single wavelength. **3.** Relating to or characterized by monochromatism.

monochromatism (mon-o-kro'mă-tizm) [mono- + G. *chrōma*, color]. **1.** The state of having or exhibiting only one color. **2.** Achromatopsia.

monochromatophil, monochromatophile (mon'o-kro-mat'o-fil, -fīl) [mono- + G. *chrōma*, color, + *philos*, fond]. **1.** Taking only one stain. **2.** A cell or any histologic element staining with only one kind of dye.

mon'oclo'nal. In immunochemistry, pertaining to a protein from a single clone of cells, all molecules of which are the same; *e.g.*, in the Bence-Jones protein, the chains are all κ or λ.

monocrotic (mon-o-krot'ik) [mono- + G. *krotos*, beat]. Denoting a pulse the curve of which presents no notch in the downward line.

monocrotism (mon-ok'ro-tizm). The state in which the pulse is monocrotic.

monocular (mon-ok'u-lar) [mono- + L. *oculus*, eye]. Relating to, affecting, or visible by, one eye only.

monocyte (mon'o-sīt) [mono- + G. *kytos*, cell]. A relatively large mononuclear leukocyte that normally constitutes 3 to 7% of the leukocytes of the circulating blood and is normally found in lymph nodes, spleen, bone marrow, and loose connective tissue.

monocytopenia (mon'o-si-to-pe'nī-ah) [mono- + G. *kytos*, cell, + *penia*, poverty]. Monocytic leukopenia; diminution in the number of monocytes in the circulating blood.

monocytosis (mon'o-si-to'sis). Monocytic leukocytosis; an abnormal increase in the number of monocytes in the circulating blood.

monodactyly (mon-o-dak'tī-lī) [mono- + G. *daktylos*, digit]. Presence of a single finger on the hand, or a single toe on the foot.

mon'odermo'ma [mono- + G. *derma*, skin, + *-ōma*, tumor]. A neoplasm composed of tissues from a single germinal layer.

monodiplopia (mon'o-dī-plo'pī-ah). Monocular *diplopia*.

monogamet'ic. Homogametic.

monog'amy [mono- + G. *gamos*, marriage]. The marriage or mating system in which each partner has but one mate.

monogenesis (mon-o-jen'ĕ-sis) [mono- + G. *genesis*, origin, production]. **1.** Production of similar organisms in each generation. **2.** Production of young by a single parent as in nonsexual generation and parthenogenesis. **3.** The process of parasitizing a single host, in which the life cycle of the parasite is passed.

monogenet'ic. Monoxenous; relating to monogenesis.

monogenic (mon-o-jen'ik). Relating to a hereditary disease or syndrome, or to an inherited characteristic, controlled by alleles at a single genetic locus.

monogenous (mŏ-noj'ĕ-nus). Asexually produced, as by fission, gemmation, or sporulation.

monoiodotyrosine (ITyr) (mon'o-i-o-do-ti'ro-sēn). 3-Iodotyrosine; tyrosine with one ring H replaced by I; one of the iodinated amino acids present in thyroid hydrolysates.

mon'olay'ers. 1. Films, one molecule thick, formed on water by certain substances, such as proteins and fatty acids, characterized by molecules containing some atom groupings that are soluble in water and other atom groupings that are insoluble in water. **2.** A confluent sheet of cells, one cell deep, growing on a surface in a cell culture.

monolocular (mon'o-lok'u-lar) [mono- + L. *loculus,* a small place]. Unicameral; having one cavity or chamber.

mon'oma'nia [mono- + G. *mania,* frenzy]. An obsession or abnormally extreme enthusiasm for a single idea or subject; a psychosis marked by the limitation of symptoms to a certain group, as the delusion in paranoia.

monomel'ic [mono- + G. *melos,* limb]. Relating to one limb.

mon'omer [mono- + -mer]. **1.** The molecular unit that, by repetition, constitutes a large structure or polymer. **2.** The protein structural unit of a virion capsid. **3.** The protein subunit of a protein composed of several loosely associated such units.

monomeric (mon-o-mĕr'ik) [mono- + G. *meros,* part]. **1.** Consisting of a single part. **2.** In genetics, relating to a hereditary disease or characteristic controlled by genes at a single locus. **3.** Consisting of monomers.

monomolecular (mon'o-mo-lek'u-lar). Referring to a single molecule or single layer of molecules.

monomor'phic mono- + G. *morphē,* shape]. Of one shape; unchangeable in shape.

monomyoplegia (mon'o-mi-o-ple'jĭ-ah) [mono- + G. *mys,* muscle, + *plēgē, a stroke*]. Paralysis limited to one muscle.

monomyositis (mon'o-mi-o-si'tis). Inflammation of a single muscle.

mononeural (mon'o-nu'ral). **1.** Having only one neuron. **2.** Supplied by a single nerve.

mononeuralgia (mon'o-nu-ral'jĭ-ah). Pain along the course of one nerve.

mononeuritis (mon'o-nu-ri'tis). Inflammation of a single nerve.

  m. mul'tiplex, inflammation of several seperate nerves in unrelated portions of the body.

mononeuropathy (mon'o-nu-rop'ă-thī). Disease involving a single nerve.

mon'onu'cleotide. Nucleotide.

mononuclear (mon-o-nu'kle-ar). Having only one nucleus.

mononucleosis (mon'o-nu-kle-o'sis). Presence of abnormally large numbers of mononuclear leukocytes in the circulating blood, especially forms that are not normal.

  infectious m., an acute febrile illness associated with the Epstein-Barr herpetovirus and characterized by fever, sore throat, enlargement of lymph nodes and spleen, and leukopenia that changes to lymphocytosis.

mono'osome [mono- + chromosome]. Accessory *chromosome.*

monooxygenases (mon'o-ok'sĭ-jĕ-na-sez). Oxidoreductases that induce the incorporation of one atom of oxygen from O_2 into the substance being oxidized.

monoparesis (mon'o-pă-re'sis, -păr'e-sis). Paresis affecting a single extremity or part of an extremity.

monoparesthesia (mon'o-păr-es-the'zĭ-ah). Paresthesia affecting a single region only.

monopath'ic Relating to a single disease or to a disease affecting a single part.

monop'athy [mono- + G. *pathos,* suffering]. **1.** A single uncomplicated disease. **2.** A local disease affecting only one organ or part.

monophasia (mon-o-fa'zĭ-ah) [mono- + G. *phasis,* speech]. Inability to speak other than a single word or sentence.

monophasic (mon-o-fa'zik). **1.** Marked by monophasia. **2.** Characterized by only one phase. **3.** Pertaining to a psychiatric disorder with one phase, as opposed to a diphasic disorder like manic-depressive psychosis.

monophthal'mos [mono- + G. *ophthalmos,* eye]. Complete failure of outgrowth of the primary optic vesicle, with absence of ocular tissues; the remaining eye is often maldeveloped.

monophyletic (mon'o-fi-let'ik) [mono- + G. *phylē,* tribe]. Having a single source of origin; derived from one line of descent.

monoplegia (mon-o-ple'jĭ-ah) [mono- + G. *plēgē,* a stroke]. Paralysis of one limb.

monopo'dia [mono- + G. *pous,* foot]. A malformation in which there is only one foot externally recognizable.

monorchidic, monorchid (mon-or-kid'ik, mon-or'-kid). **1.** Having but one testis. **2.** Having apparently but one testis, the other being undescended.

monorchism, monorchidism (mon'or-kizm, mon-or'kĭ-dizm). [mono- + G. *orchis,* testis]. A condition in which only one testis is apparent, the other being absent or undescended.

monosaccharide (mon-o-sak'ă-rīd). A carbohydrate that cannot form any simpler sugar by simple hydrolysis.

monosomia (mon-o-so'mĭ-ah) [mono- + G. *sōma,* body]. A state in which, in conjoined twins, the trunks are comletely merged although the heads remain separate.

monoso'mic. Relating to monosomy.

monosomy (mon'o-so'mĭ) [see monosome]. State of an individual or cell that has lost one member of a pair of homologous chromosomes.

mon'ospasm. Spasm affecting only one muscle or group of muscles, or a single extremity.

monostotic (mon-os-tot'ik) [Mono- + G. *osteon*, bone]. involving only one bone.

monostra'tal [mono- + L. *stratum*, layer]. Composed of a single layer.

mon'osymptomat'ic. Denoting a disease or morbid condition manifested by only one marked symptom.

monosynaptic (mon'o-sĭ-nap'tik). Referring to direct neural connections (those not involving an intermediary neuron).

monother'mia [mono- + G. *thermē*, heat]. Evenness of bodily temperature throughout the day.

monotrichous (mo-not'rĭ-kus). Denoting a microorganism possessing a single flagellum or cilium.

monova'lence. Univalence; a valence of one; the state of being monovalent.

monova'lent. **1.** Monatomic; univalent; having the combining power of an atom of hydrogen; denoting a valence of one. **2.** Pertaining to a monovalent (specific) antiserum.

monox'enous [mono- + G. *xenous*, stranger]. Monogenetic.

monox'ide. Any oxide having only one atom of oxygen (*e.g.*, carbon monoxide, CO).

monozygotic (mon'o-zi-got'ik) [mono- + G. *zygōtos*, yoked]. Denoting twins derived from a single fertilized ovum.

mons, pl. **montes** (monz, mon'tēz) [L. a mountain] [NA]. An anatomical prominence or slight elevation above the general level of the surface.

   m. pu'bis [NA], **m. ven'eris,** pubis (3); the prominence caused by a pad of fatty tisssue over the symphysis pubis in the female.

mon'ster [L. *monstrum*, an evil omen, a prodigy, a wonder, fr. *moneo*, to advise, warn]. Pejorative term for malformed embryos, fetuses, or individuals.

monticulus, pl. **monticuli** (mon-tik'u-lus, -li) [L. dim of *mons,* mountain]. **1.** Any slight rounded projection above a surface. **2.** The central portion of the superior vermis forming a projection on the surface of the cerebellum.

mood. The emotional state of an individual.

mood swing. Oscillation of a person's emotional feeling tone between periods of euphoria and depression.

MOPP A cancer chemotherapy drug consisting of Mustargen (mechlorethamine hydrochloride), Oncovin (vincristine sulfate), procarbozine hydrochloride, and prednisone.

Moraxel'la [V. *Morax*]. A genus of obligately aerobic, nonmotile bacteria, containing Gram-negative coccoids or short rods which usually occur in pairs, that are parasitic on the mucous membranes of man and other mammals. The type species, *M. lacunata,* causes conjunctivitis in man.

mor'bid [L. *morbidus*, ill, fr. *morbus*, disease]. **1.** Diseased or pathologic. **2.** In psychology, abnormal or deviant.

morbid'ity. **1.** A diseased state. **2.** The ratio of sick to well in a community.

morbif'ic]L. *morbus*, disease, + *facio*, to make]. Pathogenic.

morbil'li [Mediev. L. *morbillus*, dim. of L. *morbus,* disease]. Measles.

morbil'liform [see morbilli]. Resembling measles.

Morbil'livirus. A genus of the family Paramyxoviridae that includes the measles, canine distemper, and bovine rinderpest viruses.

mor'bus [L. disease]. Disease (1).

morcellation (mor-sĕ-la'shun) [Fr. *morceler*, to subdivide]. Division into and removal of small pieces, as of a tumor.

mor'dant [L. *mordeo,* to bite]. **1.** A substance capable of combining with a dye and the material to be dyed, thereby increasing the affinity or binding of the dye. **2.** To treat with a m.

mor'gan (M). The unit of map distance in linkage maps of chromosomes, representing a theoretical crossover value of 100% between two loci; usually expressed in centimorgans or decimorgans.

morgue (morg) [Fr.]. Mortuary (2). A building where unidentified dead are kept pending identification before burial or a pending autopsy.

moria (mo'rĭ-ah) [G. *mōria*, folly, fr. *mōros*, stupid, dull]. **1.** Hebetude; rarely used term denoting foolishness or dullness of comprehension. **2.** Rarely used term for a mental state marked by frivolity, joviality, and inveterate tendency to jest.

moribund (mor'ĭ-bund) [L. *moribundus*, dying, fr. *morior*, to die]. Dying; at the point of death.

mo'ron [G. *mōros*, stupid] Obsolete term for a subclass of mental retardation (*q.v.*).

morph-. See morpho-.

morphea (mor-fe'ah) [G. *morphē*, form, figure]. Circumscribed or localized scleroderma; a cutaneous lesion characterized by indurated, slighty depressed plaques of thickened dermal fibrous tissue, of a whitish or yellowish white color surrounded by a pinkish or purplish halo.

morphine (mor'fēn, mor-fēn') [L. *Morpheus*, god of dreams or sleep]. $C_{17}H_{19}NO_3$; the major phenanthrene alkaloid of opium; produces a combination of depression and excitation in the CNS and some peripheral tissues; repeated administration leads to the development of tolerance, physical dependence, and (if abused) psychic dependence; an analgesic that also produces sedation and allays anxiety.

morpho-, morph- [G. *morphē*, form, shape]. Combining forms relating to form, shape, or structure.

morphogenesis (mor-fo-jen'ĕ-sis) [morpho- + G. *genesis*, production]. Differentiation of cells and tissues in the early embryo which results in establishing the form and structure of the various organs and parts of the body.

morphogenetic (mor'fo-jĕ-net'ik). Relating to morphogenesis.

morphologic (mor-fo-loj'ik). Relating to morphology.

morphology (mor-fol'o-jĭ) [morpho- + G. *logos*, study]. The study of the configuration or the structure of animals and plants.

morphometric (mor-fo-mĕ'trik). Pertaining to morphometry.

morphometry (mor-fom'ĕ-trĭ) [morpho- + G. *metron*, measure]. Measurement of the form of organisms or their parts.

morphosis (mor-fo'sis) [G. formation, act of forming]. Mode of development of a part.

mors, gen. **mor'tis** [L.]. Death.

mor'tal [L. *mortalis*, fr. *mors*, death]. **1.** Pertaining to, or causing death. **2.** Destined to die.

mortality (mor-tal'ĭ-tĭ) [L. *mortalitus*, fr. *mors* (*mort-*), death]. **1.** The state of being mortal. **2.** Mortality *rate.*

mor'tar [L. *mortarium*]. A vessel with rounded interior in which crude drugs and other substances are crushed or bruised by means of a pestle.

mortification (mor'tĭ-fĭ-ka'shun) [L. *mors* (*mort-*), death. + *facio*, to make]. Gangrene.

mor'tified. Gangrenous.

mortuary (mor'tu-ĕr-ĭ) [L. *mortuus*, dead]. **1.** Relating to death or burial. **2.** Morgue.

morula (mor'u-lah) [Mod. L. dim. of L. *morus*, mulberry]. The mass of blastomeres resulting from the early cleavage divisions of the zygote.

morulation (mor-u-la'shun). Formation of the morula.

Morulavirus (mor'u-lă-vi-rus) [Mod. L. dim. of L. *morus*, mulberry]. A genus of viruses (family Microviridae) that includes the phage group of bacterial viruses.

mosaic (mo-za'ik) [Mod. L. *mosaicus*, *musaicus*, pertaining to the Muses, artistic]. **1.** Tesselated; inlaid; resembling inlaid work. **2.** Juxtaposition in an organism of genetically different tissues, resulting from somatic mutation (gene mosaicism), an anomaly of chromosome division resulting in two or more types of cells containing different numbers of chromosomes (chromosome mosaicism) or chimerism.

mosaicism (mo-zā'ĭ-sizm). Condition of being mosaic. (2).

mosquito, pl. **mosquitoes** (mus-ke'to, -tōs) [Sp. dim. of *mosca*, fly, fr. L. *musca*, a fly]. A blood-sucking dipterous insect of the family Culicidae, which includes *Aedes, Anopheles, Culex,* and *Stegomyia,* the genera containing most of the species involved in the transmission of pathogens.

mote (mōt) [A.S. *mot*]. A small particle; a speck.

motile (mo'til) [L. *motio*, movement]. **1.** Having the power of spontaneous movement. **2.** Denoting the type of mental imagery in which the person learns and recalls most readily that which he has felt.

motil'ity. The power of spontaneous movement.

mo'tive [L. *moveo*, to move, to set in motion]. **1.** Learned drive; a predisposition, need, or specific state of tension within an individual which arouses, maintains, and directs behavior toward a goal. **2.** The reason attributed to or given by an individual for a behavioral act.

motofacient (mo-to-fa'shĭ-ent) [L. *motus*, motion, + *facio*, to make]. Causing motion; denoting the second phase of muscular activity in which actual movement is produced.

motoneuron (mo'to-nu'ron). Motor *neuron.*

mo'tor [L. a mover, fr. *movere*, to move]. That which imparts movement. **1.** In anatomy and physiology, those neural structures which by the impulses generated and transmitted by them cause muscle fibers or pigment cells to contract, or glands to secrete. **2.** In psychology, the organism's overt reaction to a stimulus (motor response).

mottling (mot'ling) [E. *motley*, variegated in color]. An area of skin comprised of macular lesions of varying shades or colors.

mound'ing. Myoedema.

mount. **1.** To prepare for microscopic examination. **2.** To climb on for purposes of copulation.

mouth [A.S. *mūth*]. **1.** Oral *cavity.* **2.** The opening, usually external, of a cavity or canal.

    tapir m., protrusion of the lips due to weakness of the oral muscle in certain forms of juvenile muscular dystrophy.

    trench m., necrotizing ulcerative *gingivitis.*

mouth'wash. Collutory; a medicated liquid used for cleaning the mouth and treating diseased states of its mucous membranes.

move'ment [L. *moveo*, pp. *motus*, to move]. **1.** The act of motion; said of the entire body or of one or more of its numbers or parts. **2.** Stool. **3.** Defecation.

    ameboid m., m. charcteristic of leukocytes and protozoan organisms of the class Rhizopodea.

    associated m., involuntary m. in a limb corresponding to one voluntarily executed in its fellow.

    brownian m., molecular m.; erratic, nondirectional, zigzag m. observed in certain colloidal solutions and in suspensions of light particulate matter that results from impacting of the larger particles by the molecules in the suspending medium, which are regarded as being in continuous motion.

    choreic m., an involuntary spasmodic twitching or jerking in groups of muscles not associated in the production of definite purposeful m.'s.

    ciliary m., rhythmic sweeping m. of epithelial cell cilia, of ciliate protozoans, or the sculling m. of flagella.

    molecular m., brownian m.

    morphogenetic m., the streaming of cells in the early embryo to form tissues or organs.

    passive m., m. of any joint effected by the hand of another person, or by mechanical means, without participation of the subject himself.

    rapid eye m.'s (REM), symmetrical quick m.'s occurring many times during a single night's sleep, in clusters for 5 to 60 minutes, associated with dreaming.

streaming m., m. characteristic of the protoplasm of leukocytes, amebae, and other unicellular organisms; involves massing of the protoplasm, its extrusion in the form of a pseudopod, and a flow into the latter.

vermicular m., peristalsis.

MPD Maximal permissible *dose.*

Mr Molecular weight *ratio.*

M.R.C.P. Member of the Royal College of Physicians.

M.R.C.S. Member of the Royal College of Surgeons.

MRD, mrd Minimal reacting *dose.*

mRNA Messenger RNA.

MS Multiple *sclerosis.*

ms Millisecond.

msec Millisecond.

MSH Melanocyte-stimulating *hormone.*

M.u. Mache *unit.*

muci-. Combining form for mucus, mucous, or mucin. See also muco-, myxo-.

mucif'erous. Muciparous.

mu'ciform. Blennoid; mucoid (2); resembling mucus.

mucilage (mu'sĭ-lij) [L. *mucilago*]. A pharmacopeial preparation consisting of a solution in water of viscid principles of vegetable substances.

mucilaginous (mu-sĭ-laj'ĭ-nus). Resembling mucilage, *i.e.,* adhesive, viscid, sticky.

mucin (mu'sin). A secretion containing mucopolysaccharides, such as that from mucous glandular cells; also present in the ground substance of connective tissue.

mucinase (mu'sin-ās). Mucopolysaccharidase; a term specifically applied to hyaluronidases, but more loosely to any enzyme that hydrolyzes mucopolysaccharide substances (mucins).

mucinogen (mu'sin-o-jen) [mucin + G. *-gen,* producing]. A glycoprotein that forms mucin through the imbibition of water.

mucinoid (mu'sĭ-noyd). **1.** Mucoid (1). **2.** Resembling mucin.

mucinosis (mu'sĭ-no'sis) [mucin + G. *-osis,* condition]. A condition in which mucin is present in the skin in excessive amounts, or in abnormal distribution.

follicular m., a benign eruption of discrete lesions on the face or scalp in which there are cystic mucinous changes in the pilosebaceous units in the involved area.

papular m., *lichen* myxedematosus.

mucinous (mu'sin-us). Mucoid (3); relating to or containing mucin.

mucip'arous [mucin + L. *pario,* to bring forth, bear]. Muciferous; blennogenic; blennogenous; producing mucus.

muco-. Combining form for mucus, mucous, or mucosa. See also muci-, myxo-.

mucocele (mu'ko-sēl) [muco- + G. *kēlē,* tumor, hernia]. **1.** A mucous polypus. **2.** A retention cyst of the lacrimal sac, paranasal sinuses, appendix, or gallbladder.

mu'cocuta'neous. Relating to mucous membrane and skin; denoting the line of junction of the two at the nasal, oral, vaginal, and anal orifices.

mucoenteritis (mu'ko-en-ter-i'tis). **1.** Inflammation of the intestinal mucous membrane. **2.** Mucomembranous *enteritis.*

mucoepidermoid (mu'ko-ep-ĭ-der'moyd). Denoting a mixture of mucus-secreting and epithelial cells.

mucoid (mu'koyd) [mucus + G. *eidos,* appearance]. **1.** Mucinoid (1); a mucin, mucoprotein, or mucopolysaccharide. **2.** Muciform. **3.** Mucinous.

mucolipidosis, pl. **mucolipidoses** (mu'ko-lip-ĭ-do'sis, -sēz). Any of a group of metabolic storage diseases resembling Hurler's syndrome but with normal urinary mucopolysaccharides, in which symptoms of visceral and mesenchymal sphingolipid and/or glycolipid storage are present; autosomal recessive inheritance.

m. I, lipomucopolysaccharidosis; m. with mild Hurler-like symptoms, mild dysostosis multiplex, and moderate mental retardation.

m. II, inclusion cell disease; m. with severe Hurler-like symptoms, but with normal urinary mucopolysaccharides, vacuolated lymphocytes, and inclusion bodies in cultured fibroblasts.

m. III, m. with mild Hurler-like symptoms, restricted joint mobility, short stature, mild mental retardation, and dysplastic skeletal changes.

m. IV, psychomotor retardation with cloudy corneas and retinal degeneration, with inclusion cells in cultured fibroblasts.

mucolytic (mu-ko-lit'ik) [muco- + G. *lysis,* dissolution]. Capable of dissolving, digesting, or liquefying mucus.

mucomembranous (mu'ko-mem'brā-nus). Relating to a mucous membrane.

muc'operios'teal. Relating to mucoperiosteum.

mucoperiosteum (mu'ko-pĕr-ĭ-os'te-um). Mucous membrane and periosteum so intimately united as to nearly form a single membrane.

mu'copolysac'charidase. Mucinase.

mu'copolysac'charide. A complex of protein and polysaccharide, usually implying that the polysaccharide component is a major part of the complex.

mucopolysaccharidosis (mu'ko-pol-ĭ-sak'ă-rĭ-do'sis). Term embracing a group of diseases that have in common a disorder in metabolism of mucopolysaccharides, with various defects of bone, cartilage, and connective tissue.

type I m., Hurler's *syndrome.*

type IS m., Scheie's *syndrome.*

type II m., Hunter's *syndrome.*

type III m., Sanfilippo's *syndrome.*

type IV m., Morquio's *syndrome.*

type V m., former designation for Scheie's *syndrome.*

type VI m., Maroteaux-Lamy *syndrome.*

type VII m., m. due to β-glucuronidase deficiency.

mucopolysacchariduria (mu′ko-pol-ĭ-sak′ă-rĭ-du′rĭ-ah). The excretion of mucopolysaccharides in the urine.

mu′copro′tein. A protein-polysaccharide complex, usually implying that the protein component is the major part of the complex.

    Tamm-Horsfall m., the matrix of urinary casts derived from the secretion of renal tubular cells.

mu′copu′rulent. Pertaining to an exudate that is chiefly pus, but contains significant proportions of mucous material.

Mu′cor [L. mold]. A genus of fungi (class Phycomycetes, family Mucoraceae), several species of which are pathogenic and may cause mucormycosis (phycomycosis) in man.

mucormycosis (mu′kor-mi-ko′sis). General term denoting conditions occasionally caused by, or associated with, various fungi species in the family Mucoraceae, *e.g.*, *Absidia, Mortierella, Mucor,* and *Rhizopus.*

mucosa (mu-ko′sah) [L. fem. of *mucosus,* mucous]. See *tunica* mucosa.

muco′sal. Relating to the mucosa or mucous membrane.

mucosanguineous, mucosanguinolent (mu′ko-sang-gwin′e-us, -o-lent) [muco- + L. *sanguis,* blood]. Pertaining to an exudate that has a relatively high content of blood and mucus.

mucoserous (mu-ko-sēr′us). Pertaining to an exudate that consists of mucus and serum or a watery component.

mucous (mu′kus) [L. *mucosus,* mucous, fr. *mucus*]. Relating to mucus or a m. membrane.

mucoviscidosis (mu′ko-vis-ĭ-do′sis). Cystic *fibrosis.*

mucus (mu′kus) [L.]. The clear viscid secretion of the mucous membranes, consisting of mucin, epithelial cells, leukocytes, and various inorganic salts suspended in water.

muliebria (mu′lĭ-e′brĭ-ah) [L. neut pl of *muliebris,* relating to *mulier,* a woman]. The female genital organs.

mülle′rian. Attributed to or described by Johannes Müller.

multi- [L. *multus,* much, many]. Prefix denoting many, properly; equivalent of *poly-.* See also pluri-.

mul′tiartic′ular [multi- + L. *articulus,* joint]. Polyarthric; polyarticular; relating to or involving many joints.

multicus′pidate. 1. Having more than two cusps. **2.** A tooth with three or more cusps or projections on the crown; a multicuspid; a molar tooth.

mul′tifid [L. *multus,* much, + *findo,* to cleave]. Divided into many clefts or segments.

multifocal (mul-tĭ-fo′kăl). Relating to or arising from many foci.

mul′tiform. Polymorphic.

multigrav′ida [multi- + L. *gravida,* pregnant]. A pregnant woman who has been pregnant one or more times previously.

multi-infection (mul-tĭ-in-fek′shun). Mixed infection with two or more varieties of microorganisms developing simultaneously.

multilo′bar, multilo′bate, multilobed (mul-tĭ-lōbd′). Having several lobes.

multilob′ular. Having many lobules.

multiloc′ular. Having many compartments or loculi.

multinod′ular, multinod′ulate. Having many nodules.

multinu′clear, multinu′cleated. Polynuclear; polynucleated; having two or more nuclei.

multip′ara [multi- + L. *pario,* to bring forth, to bear]. A woman who has given birth at least two times to an infant, whether alive or dead.

multipar′ity. The condition of being a multipara.

multip′arous. Relating to a multipara.

multipen′nate [multi- + L. *penna,* feather]. Denoting a muscle with several central tendons toward which the muscle fibers converge like the barbs of feathers.

multipo′lar. Having more than two poles; denoting a nerve cell in which the branches project from several points.

multisynaptic (mul′tĭ-sĭ-nap′tik). Polysynaptic.

multiva′lence. The state of being multivalent.

multiva′lent. [multi- + L. *valentia,* power]. Polyvalent (1). **1.** In chemistry, having a combining power of more than one atom of hydrogen. **2.** Efficacious in more than one direction.

mum′mifica′tion [mummy + L. *facio,* to make]. **1.** Dry *gangrene.* **2.** The shrivelling of a dead and retained fetus.

mumps [dialectic Eng. *mump,* a lump or bump]. Epidemic *parotiditis.*

mu′ral [L. *muralis;* fr. *murus,* wall]. Relating to the wall of any cavity.

muram′idase. Lysozyme.

muriat′ic [L. *muriaticus,* pickled in brine]. Hydrochloric; relating to brine.

murine (mu′rin, -rin, -rēn) [L. *murinus,* relating to mice]. Relating to mice and rats (family Muridae).

mur′mur [L.]. A soft sound heard on auscultation of the heart, lungs, or blood vessels. Also used for a variety of other-than-soft sounds, which may be loud, harsh, frictional, etc.

    anemic m., a nonvalvular m. heard on auscultation of the heart and large blood vessels in cases of profound anemia.

    aortic m., a m. produced at the aortic orifice, either obstructive or regurgitant.

    Austin Flint m., Flint's m.

    cardiac m., a m. produced within the heart, at one of its orifices.

    cardiopulmonary m., an innocent extracardiac m., synchronous with the heart's beat but disappearing when the breath is held, due to movement of air in a segment of lung compressed by the contracting heart.

    Carey Coombs m., an apical middiastolic m. occurring in the acute stage of rheumatic mitral valvulitis and disappearing as the valvulitis subsides.

continuous m., a m. heard without interruption throughout systole and into diastole.

crescendo m., a m. that increases in intensity and suddenly ceases.

Cruveilhier-Baumgarten m., a m. heard over collateral veins, connecting portal and caval venous systems, on the abdominal wall.

diastolic m., a m. heard during diastole.

Duroziez m., Duroziez *symptom*.

ejection m., systolic m. ending before the second heart sound and produced by the ejection of blood into aorta or pulmonary artery.

Flint's m., Austin Flint m.; a diastolic m., similar to that of mitral stenosis, heard at the cardiac apex in some cases of free aortic insufficiency.

functional m., innocent or inorganic m.; a cardiac m. not associated with a heart lesion.

Gibson m., machinery m.; the typical continuous rumbling m. of patent ductus arteriosus.

Graham Steell's m., an early diastolic m. of pulmonic insufficiency secondary to pulmonary hypertension, as in mitral stenosis.

hemic m., a cardiac or vascular m. heard in anemic persons who have no valvular lesion.

hourglass m., one in which there are two areas of maximum loudness decreasing to a point midway between the two.

innocent m., inorganic m., functional m.

machinery m., Gibson m.

mitral m., a m. produced at the mitral valve, either obstructive or regurgitant.

obstructive m., a m. caused by narrowing of one of the valvular orifices.

organic m., a m. caused by an organic lesion.

pansystolic m., a m. occupying the entire systolic interval, from first to second sound.

pericardial m., a friction sound, synchronous with the heart movements, heard in certain cases of pericarditis.

presystolic m., a m. heard at the end of ventricular diastole (during atrial systole), usually due to obstruction at one of the atrioventricular orifices.

pulmonary m., pulmonic m., a m. produced at the pulmonary orifice of the heart, either obstructive or regurgitant.

regurgitant m., a m. due to leakage or backward flow at one of the valvular orifices of the heart.

Roger's m., a loud pansystolic m. maximal at the left sternal border, caused by a small ventricular septal defect.

stenosal m., an arterial m. due to narrowing of the vessel from pressure or organic change.

Still's m., an innocent musical m. resembling the noise produced by a twanging string.

systolic m., a m. heard during ventricular systole.

tricuspid m., a m. produced at the tricuspid orifice, either obstructive or regurgitant.

vesicular m., vesicular *respiration*.

Musca (mus'kah) [L. fly]. A genus of flies (family Muscidae, order Diptera) that includes the common housefly, *M. domestica,* a species involved in the mechanical transfer of numerous pathogens.

muscae volitantes (mus'ke vol-ĭ-tan'tē) [L. pl. of *musca,* fly; pres. p. pl. of *volito,* to fly to and fro]. An appearance of moving spots before the eyes.

muscarine (mus'kă-rēn, -rin). A toxin with neurologic effects, isolated from *Amanita muscaria* (fly agaric mushroom) and also present in some other mushroom species; cholinergic substance whose pharmacologic effects resemble those of acetylcholine and postganglionic parasympathetic stimulation (cardiac inhibition, vasodilation, salivation, lacrimation, bronchoconstriction, gastrointestinal stimulation).

muscarin'ic. 1. Having a muscarine-like action, *i.e.,* producing effects that resemble postganglionic parasympathetic stimulation. **2.** An agent that stimulates the postganglionic parasympathetic receptor.

muscle (mus'el) [L. *musculus*]. Tissue consisting predominantly of contractile cells and classified as skeletal, cardiac, or smooth, the latter lacking in transverse striations characteristic of the other varieties. For a gross anatomical description, see musculus.

abductor m.'s, *musculus* abductor hallucis, abductor digiti minimi manus and pedis, and abductor pollicis.

adductor m.'s, *musculus* adductor hallucis and pollicis.

anconeous m., *musculus* anconeus.

antagonistic m.'s, m.'s having an opposite function, the contraction of one neutralizing that of the other.

m. of antitragus, *musculus* antitragicus.

appendicular m., one of the skeletal m.'s of the limbs.

articular m., a m. that inserts directly onto the capsule of a joint, acting to retract the capsule in certain movements. See *musculus* articularis cubuti and genus.

arytenoid m., *musculus* arytenoideus.

auricular m., *musculus* auricularis.

axial m., one of the skeletal m.'s of the trunk or head.

Bell's m., a band of muscular fibers, forming a slight fold in the wall of the bladder, running from the uvula to the opening of the ureter on either side, bounding the trigonum.

biceps m.'s, *musculus* biceps brachii and femoris.

brachial m., *musculus* brachialis.

brachioradial m., *musculus* brachioradialis.

broadest m. of back, *musculus* latissimus dorsi.

bronchoesophageal m., *musculus* bronchoesophageus.

Brücke's m., the part of the ciliary m. formed by the meridional (radiating) fibers.

bulbospongious m., *musculus* bulbospongiosus.

cardiac m., myocardium; m. of the heart, consisting of anastomosing transversely striated m. fibers formed of cells united at intercalated disks.

ceratocricoid m., *musculus* ceratocricoideus.

cheek m., *musculus* buccinator.

chin m., *musculus* mentalis.

ciliary m., *musculus* ciliaris.

coccygeal m., *musculus* coccygeus.

constrictor m. of pharynx, *musculus* constrictor pharyngis.

coracobrachial m., *musculus* coracobrachialis.

corrugator m., *musculus* corrugator supercilii.

cremaster m., *musculus* cremaster.

cricoarytenoid m., *musculus* cricoarytenoideus.

cricothyroid m., *musculus* cricothyroideus.

cruciate m., m. in which the bundles of m. fibers cross in an x-shaped configuration.

cutaneous m., a m. that lies in the subcutaneous tissue and attaches to the skin, with or without a bony attachment; *e.g.,* a m. of expression.

deltoid m., *musculus* deltoideus.

depressor m.'s, *musculus* depressor anguli oris, depressor supercilii, depressor labii inferioris, and depressor septi.

digastric m., (1) a m. with two fleshy bellies separated by a fibrous insertion; (2) *musculus* digastricus.

dilator m., see dilator (2).

elevator m.'s, *musculus* levator prostatae, levator glandulae thyroideae, levator labii superioris, levator labii superioris alaeque nasi, levator anguli oris, levator ani, levator costae, levator palpebrae superioris, levator scapulae, and levator veli palatini.

epicranial m., *musculus* epicranius.

erector m.'s of hairs, *musculi* arrectores pilorum.

erector m. of spine, *musculus* erector spinae.

extensor m. of fingers, *musculus* extensor digitorum.

extensor m.'s of great toe, *musculus* extensor hallucis brevis and longus.

extensor m. of index finger, *musculus* extensor indicis.

extensor m. of little finger, *musculus* extensor digiti minimi.

extensor m. of thumb, *musculus* extensor pollicis.

extensor m.'s of toes, *musculus* extensor digitorum brevis and longus.

fibular m., *musculus* peroneus.

fixator m., a m. that acts as a stabilizer of one part of the body during movement of another part.

flexor m.'s of fingers, *musculus* flexor digitorum profundis and superficialis.

flexor m. of great toe, *musculus* flexor hallucis.

flexor m. of thumb, *musculus* flexor pollicis.

flexor m.'s of toes, *musculus* flexor digitorum brevis and longus.

Gavard's m., oblique fibers in the muscular coat of the stomach.

gemellus m., *musculus* gemellus.

genioglossus m., *musculus* genioglossus.

geniohyoid m., *musculus* geniohyoideus.

gluteus m.'s, *musculus* gluteus maximus, medius, and minimus.

gracilis m., *musculus* gracilis.

great m., *musculus* vastus.

great adductor m., *musculus* adductor magnus.

hamstring m.'s, m.'s at the back of the thigh, comprising the biceps, the semitendinosus, and the semimembranosus.

m.'s of helix, *musculus* helicis major and minor.

hyoglossus m., *musculus* hyoglossus.

iliac m., *musculus* iliacus.

iliococcygeal m., *musculus* iliococcygeus.

iliocostal m., *musculus* iliocostalis.

iliopsoas m., *musculus* iliopsoas.

infraspinous m., *musculus* infraspinatus.

intercostal m., *musculus* intercostalis.

interosseus m.'s, *musculus* interosseus dorsalis manus and pedis, interosseus palmaris, and interosseus plantaris.

interspinal m.'s, *musculi* interspinales.

intertransverse m.'s, *musculi* intertransversarii.

involuntary m.'s, m.'s not under control of the will; except those of the heart, they are smooth m.'s.

ischiocavernous m., *musculus* ischiocavernosus.

Kohlrausch's m., the longitudinal m.'s of the rectal wall.

Landström's m., microscopic m. fibers in the fascia behind and about the eyeball, attached anteriorly to the lids and anterior orbital fascia, which draw the eyeball forward and the lids backward, resisting the pull of the four orbital m.'s.

m.'s of larynx, *musculi* laryngis.

lingual m., *musculus* longitudinalis.

long adductor m., *musculus* adductor longus.

longissimus m.'s, *musculus* longissimus capitis, cervis, and thoracis.

longitudinal m., *musculus* longitudinalis.

long m. of head, *musculus* longus capitis.

long m. of neck, *musculus* longus colli.

lumbrical m.'s, *musculus* lumbricalis manus and pedis.

Marcacci's m., a sheet of smooth m. fibers underlying the areola and nipple of the mammary gland.

masseter m., *musculus* masseter.

multifidus m., *musculus* multifidus.

mylohyoid m., *musculus* mylohyoideus.

nasal m., *musculus* nasalis.

oblique m.'s, *musculus* obliquus capitis, obliquus externus and internus abdominis, and obliquus inferior and superior.

obturator m., *musculus* obturatorius.

occipitofrontal m., *musculus* occipitofrontalis.

omohyoid m., *musculus* omohyoideus.

opposer m.'s, *musculus* opponens pollicis and digiti minimi.

orbicular m.'s, *musculus* orbicularis oculi and oris.

orbital m., *musculus* orbitalis.

palatoglossus m., *musculus* palatoglossus.

palatopharyngeal m., *musculus* palatopharyngeus.

palmar m., *musculus* palmaris.

papillary m., *musculus* papillaris.

pectinate m.'s, *musculi* pectinati.

pectineal m., *musculus* pectineus.

pectoral m., *musculus* pectoralis.

peroneal m., *musculus* peroneus.

piriform m., *musculus* piriformis.

plantar m., *musculus* plantaris.

pleuroesophageal m., *musculus* pleuroesophageus.

popliteal m., *musculus* popliteus.

procerus m., *musculus* procerus.

pronator m.'s, *musculus* pronator quadratus and teres.

psoas m., *musculus* psoas.

pterygoid m., *musculus* pterygoideus.

pubococcygeal m., *musculus* pubococcygeus.

puboprostatic m., *musculus* puboprostaticus.

puborectal m., *musculus* puborectalis.

pubovaginal m., *musculus* pubovaginalis.

pubovesical m., *musculus* pubovesicalis.

pyramidal m., *musculus* pyramidalis.

pyramidal m. of auricle, *musculus* pyramidalis auriculae.

quadrate m.'s, *musculus* quadratus lumborum, quadratus plantae, quadratus femoris, and quadratus labii superioris.

quadriceps m. of thigh, *musculus* quadriceps femoris.

radial extensor m. of wrist, *musculus* extensor carpi radialis.

radial flexor m. of wrist, *musculus* flexor carpi radialis.

rectococcygeal m., *musculus* rectococcygeus.

rectourethral m., *musculus* rectourethralis.

rectouterine m., *musculus* rectouterinus.

rectovesical m., *musculus* rectovesicalis.

rectus m.'s, *musculus* rectus abdominis, rectus capitis anterior, lateralis, and posterior, rectus femoris, and rectus inferior, lateralis, medialis, and superior.

red m., a m. in which small dark fibers predominate; myoglobin and mitochondria are abundant.

Reisseissen's m.'s, microscopic smooth m. fibers in the smallest bronchial tubes.

rhomboid m.'s, *musculus* rhomboideus major and minor.

risorius m., *musculus* risorius.

rotator m.'s, *musculi* rotatores.

Ruysch's m., the muscular tissue of the fundus uteri.

sacrococcygeal m., *musculus* sacrococcygeus.

salpingopharyngeal m., *musculus* salpingopharyngeus.

sartorius m., *musculus* sartorius.

scalene m., *musculus* scalenus.

semimembranosus m., *musculus* semimembranosus.

semispinal m.'s, *musculus* semispinalis capitis, cervicis, and thoracis.

semitendinous m., *musculus* semitendinosus.

serratus m.'s, *musculus* serratus anterior and posterior.

short adductor m., *musculus* adductor brevis.

short flexor m. of little finger, *musculus* flexor digiti minimi brevis manus.

short flexor m. of little toe, *musculus* flexor digiti minimi brevis pedis.

skeletal m., a m. connected at either or both extremities with a bone; consists of elongated, multinucleated, transversely striated skeletal muscle fibers, together with connective tissues, blood vessels, and nerves.

smooth m., one of the m.'s of the internal organs, blood vessels, hair follicles, etc.; although transverse striations are lacking, fine myofibrils occur.

soleus m., *musculus* soleus.

sphincter m., see anatomical *sphincter.*

sphincter m.'s, *musculus* sphincter ductus choledochi and pancreatici, sphincter ani, sphincter pupillae, sphincter pylori, sphincter urethrae, and sphincter vesicae.

spinal m.'s, *musculus* spinalis capitis, cervicis and thoracis.

splenius m.'s, *musculus* splenius capitis and cervicis.

stapedius m., *musculus* stapedius.

sternal m., *musculus* sternalis.

sternocleidomastoid m., *musculus* sternocleidomastoideus.

sternohyoid m., *musculus* sternohyoideus.

sternothyroid m., *musculus* sternothyroideus.

straight m.'s, *musculus* rectus abdominus, rectus capitis anterior, lateralis, and posterior, rectus femoris, and rectus inferior, lateralis, medialis, and superior.

striated m., skeletal or cardiac m. in which cross striations occur in the fibers.

styloglossus m., *musculus* styloglossus.

stylohyoid m., *musculus* stylohyoideus.

stylopharyngeal m., *musculus* stylopharyngeus.

subclavian m., *musculus* subclavius.

subcostal m., *musculus* subcostalis.

subscapular m., *musculus* subscapularis.

supinator m., *musculus* supinator.

supraspinous m., *musculus* supraspinatus.

suspensory m. of duodenum, *musculus* suspensorius duodeni.

synergistic m.'s, m.'s having a similar and mutually helpful function or action.

tarsal m.'s, *musculus* tarsalis.

temporal m., *musculus* temporalis.

temporoparietal m., *musculus* temporoparietalis.

tensor m.'s, *musculus* tensor fasciae latae, tensor veli palatini, and tensor tympani.

teres major m., *musculus* teres major.

teres minor m., *musculus* teres minor.

third peroneal m., *musculus* peroneus tertius.

thyroarytenoid m., *musculus* thyroarytenoideus.

thyroepiglottic m., *musculus* thyroepiglotticus.

thyrohyoid m., *musculus* thyrohyoideus.

tibial m., *musculus* tibialis.

tracheal m., *musculus* trachealis.

m. of tragus, *musculus* tragicus.

transverse m.'s, *musculus* transversus abdominis, transversus linguae, transversus menti, transversus nuchae, transversus perinei profundus and superficialis, and transversus thoracis.

transversospinal m., *musculus* transversospinalis.

trapezius m., *musculus* trapezius.

triangular m., *musculus* depressor anguli oris.

triceps m.'s, *musculus* triceps brachii and surae.

ulnar extensor m. of wrist, *musculus* extensor carpi ulnaris.

ulnar flexor m. of wrist, *musculus* flexor carpi ulnaris.

m. of uvula, *musculus* uvulae.

vertical m. of the tongue, *musculus* verticalis linguae.

vocal m., *musculus* vocalis.

voluntary m., a m. whose action is under the control of the will; all the striated m.'s, except the heart, are voluntary m.'s.

white m., a m. in which large pale fibers predominate; mitochondria and myoglobin are sparse.

zygomatic m., *musculus* zygomaticus.

mus'cle-bound. Said of one whose individual muscles are large or overdeveloped but which function poorly together for concerted action.

muscular (mus'ku-lar). Relating to a muscle or the muscles.

muscula'ris [Mod. L. muscular]. The muscular coat of a hollow organ or tubular structure.

muscularity (mus'ku-lăr'ĭ-tĭ). The state or condition of having well developed muscles.

mus'culature. The aarrangement of the muscles in a part or in the body as a whole.

mus'culoap'oneurot'ic. Relating to muscular tissue and an aponeurosis of origin or insertion.

musculocutaneous (mus'ku-lo-ku-ta'ne-us). Myocutaneous (1); relating to or supplying both muscle and skin.

mus'culomem'branous. Relating to both muscular tissue and membrane.

mus'culoskel'etal. Relating to muscles and to the skeleton.

mus'culoten'dinous. Relating to both muscular and tendinous tissues.

mus'culotrop'ic. Affecting, acting upon, or attracted to muscular tissue.

musculus, gen. and pl. **musculi** (mus'ku-lus, mus'-ku-li) [L. a little mouse, a muscle] [NA]. Muscle; one of the contractile organs of the body by which movements of the various organs and parts are effected; typically, a mass of muscle fibers attached at each extremity by means of a tendon to a bone or other structure. For histologic descriptions, see muscle.

m. abduc'tor dig'iti min'imi ma'nus [NA], abductor muscle of little finger; *origin,* pisiform bone and pisohamate ligament; *insertion,* medial side of base of proximal phalanx of little finger; *nerve supply,* ulnar; *action,* abducts and flexes little finger.

m. abduc'tor dig'iti min'imi pe'dis [NA], abductor muscle of little toe; *origin,* lateral and medial processes of calcanean tuberosity; *insertion,* lateral side of proximal phalanx of fifth toe; *nerve supply,* lateral plantar nerve; *action,* abducts and flexes little toe.

m. abduc'tor hal'lucis [NA], abductor muscle of great toe; *origin,* medial process of tuber calcanei, flexor retinaculum, and plantar aponeurosis; *insertion,* medial side of proximal phalanx of great toe; *nerve supply,* medial plantar; *action,* abducts great toe.

m. abduc'tor pol'licis [NA], abductor muscle of thumb; **(1)** short, *origin,* tubercle of trapezium and flexor retinaculum; *insertion,* lateral side of proximal phalanx of thumb; *nerve supply,* median; *action,* abducts thumb; **(2)** long, *origin,* interosseous membrane and posterior surfaces of radius and ulna; *insertion,* lateral side of base of first metacarpal bone; *nerve supply,* radial; *action,* abducts and assists in extending thumb.

m. adduc'tor bre'vis [NA], short adductor muscle; *origin,* superior ramus of pubis; *insertion,* upper third of medial lip of linea aspera; *nerve supply,* obturator; *action,* adducts thigh.

m. adduc'tor hal'lucis [NA], adductor muscle of great toe; *origin,* the caput transversum from capsules of lateral four metatarsophalangeal joints and caput obliquum from cuneiform and bases of third and fourth metatarsal bones; *insertion,* lateral side of base of proximal phalanx of great toe; *nerve supply,* lateral plantar; *action,* adducts great toe.

m. adduc'tor lon'gus [NA], long adductor muscle; *origin* symphysis and crest of pubis; *insertion,* middle third of medial lip of linea aspera; *nerve supply,* obturator; *action,* adducts thigh.

m. adduc'tor mag'nus [NA], great adductor muscle; *origin,* ischial tuberosity and ischiopubic ramus; *insertion,* linea aspera and adductor tubercle of femur; *nerve supply,* obturator and sciatic; *action,* adducts and extends thigh.

m. adduc'tor pol'licis [NA], adductor muscle of thumb; *origin,* caput transversum from shaft of third metacarpal and caput obliquum from front of base of second metacarpal, trapezoid, and capitate bones; *insertion,* medial side of base of proximal phalanx of thumb; *nerve supply,* ulnar; *action,* adducts thumb.

m. ancone'us [NA], anconeus muscle; *origin,* back of lateral condyle of humerus; *insertion,* olecranon process and posterior surface of ulna; *nerve supply,* radial; *action,* extends forearm and abducts ulna in pronation of wrist.

m. antitrag'icus [NA], muscle of the antitragus; a band of transverse muscular fibers on outer surface of antitragus, arising from border of intertragic notch and inserted into anthelix and cauda helicis.

mus'culi arrecto'res pilo'rum [NA], erector muscles of hairs; bundles of smooth muscle fibers, attached to deep part of hair follicles, passing outward alongside sebaceous glands to papillary layer of corium; *action,* erection of hairs.

m. articula'ris cu'biti [NA], articular muscle of elbow; a small slip of the medial head of triceps that inserts into capsule of elbow joint.

m. articula'ris ge'nus [NA], articular muscle of knee; *origin,* lower fourth of anterior surface of shaft of femur; *insertion,* capsule of knee joint; *nerve supply,* femoral; *action,* retracts suprapatellar bursa.

m. aryepiglot'ticus [NA], fibers of oblique arytenoid muscle that extend from summit of arytenoid cartilage to side of epiglottis; *action,* constricts laryngeal aperture.

m. arytenoi'deus [NA], arytenoid muscle; (1) oblique; *origin,* muscular process of arytenoid cartilage; *insertion,* summit of arytenoid cartilage of opposite side and aryepiglottic fold as far as epiglottis; *nerve supply,* recurrent laryngeal; *action,* narrows rima glottidis; (2) transverse, a band of muscular fibers passing between the two arytenoid cartilages posteriorly; *nerve supply,* recurrent laryngeal; *action,* narrows rima glottidis.

m. auricula'ris [NA], auricular muscle; (1) anterior: *origin,* galea aponeurotica; *insertion,* cartilage of auricle; *action,* draws pinna of ear upward and forward; *nerve supply,* facial; (2) posterior: *origin,* mastoid process; *insertion,* posterior portion of root of auricle; *action,* draws back the pinna; *nerve supply,* facial; (3) superior: *origin,* galea aponeurotica; *insertion,* cartilage or auricle; *action,* draws pinna of ear upward and backward; *nerve supply,* facial.

m. bi'ceps bra'chii [NA], biceps muscle of arm; *origin,* long head from supraglenoidal tuberosity of scapula, short head from coracoid process; *insertion,* tuberosity of radius; *nerve supply,* musculocutaneous; *action,* flexes and supinates forearm.

m. bi'ceps fem'oris [NA], biceps muscle of thigh; *origin,* long head from tuberosity of ischium, short head from lower half of lateral lip of linea aspera; *insertion,* head of fibula; *nerve supply,* long head, tibial, short head, peroneal; *action,* flexes knee and rotates leg laterally.

m. brachia'lis [NA], brachial muscle; *origin,* lower two-thirds of anterior surface of humerus; *insertion,* coronoid process of ulna; *nerve supply,* musculocutaneous and (usually) radial; *action,* flexes forearm.

m. brachioradia'lis [NA], brachioradial muscle; *origin,* lateral supracondylar ridge of humerus; *insertion,* front of base of styloid process of radius; *nerve supply,* radial; *action,* flexes forearm.

m. bronchoesopha'geus [NA], bronchoesophageal muscle; muscular fascicles, arising from the wall of the left bronchus, that reinforce musculature of esophagus.

m. buccina'tor [NA], cheek muscle; *origin,* posterior portion of alveolar portion of maxilla and mandible and pterygomandibular ligament or raphe; *insertion,* orbicularis oris at angle of mouth; *action,* flattens cheek, retracts angle of mouth; *nerve supply,* facial.

m. bulbospongio'sus [NA], (1) in male: *origin,* inferior fascia of urogenital diaphragm, fascia on dorsum of bulb of penis; *insertion,* central tendon of perineum and median raphe on free surface of bulb; *action,* constricts bulbous urethra; (2) in female: *origin,* dorsum of clitoris, corpus cavernosum, and inferior fascia of urogenital diaphragm; *insertion,* central tendon of perineum; *nerve supply,* pudendal; *action,* weak sphincter of vagina.

m. ceratocricoi'deus [NA], ceratocricoid m. a fasciculus from m. cricoarytenoideus posterior inserted into inferior cornu of thyroid cartilage.

m. cilia'ris [NA], ciliary muscle; smooth muscle of the ciliary body, consisting of circular fibers and radiating fibers; *action,* changes shape of lens in process of accommodation.

m. coccyg'eus [NA], coccygeal muscle; *origin,* spine of ischium and sacrospinous ligament; *insertion,* sides of lower part of sacrum and upper part of coccyx; *nerve supply,* third and fourth sacral; *action,* assists in raising and supporting pelvic floor.

m. constric'tor pharyn'gis [NA], constrictor muscle of pharynx; (1) inferior: *origin,* outer surfaces of thyroid and cricoid cartilages; *insertion,* pharyngeal raphe in posterior portion of wall of pharynx; *nerve supply,* pharyngeal plexus; *action,* narrows lower part of pharynx in swallowing; (2) middle: *origin,* stylohyoid ligament, lesser cornu of hyoid bone, and greater cornu of hyoid bone; *insertion,* pharyngeal raphe in posterior wall of pharynx; *nerve supply,* pharyngeal plexus; *action,* narrows pharynx in swallowing; (3) superior: *origin,* medial pterygoid plate, pterygomandibular raphe, mylohyoid line of mandible, and mucous membrane of floor of mouth and side of tongue; *insertion,* pharyngeal raphe in posterior wall of pharynx; *nerve supply,* pharyngeal plexus; *action,* narrows pharynx.

m. coracobrachia'lis [NA], coracobrachial muscle; *origin,* coracoid process of scapula; *insertion,* middle of medial border of humerus; *nerve supply,* musculocutaneous; *action,* adducts and flexes the arm.

m. corruga'tor supercil'ii [NA], corrugator muscle; *origin,* from orbital portion of m. orbicularis oculi and nasal prominence; *insertion,* skin of eyebrow; *action,* draws medial end of eyebrow downward and wrinkles forehead vertically; *nerve supply,* facial.

m. cremas'ter [NA], cremaster muscle; *origin,* from m. obliquus internus and inguinal ligament; *insertion,* cremasteric fascia and pubic tubercle; *action,* raises testicle; *nerve supply,* genitofemoral. In male, muscle envelops spermatic cord and testis; in female, round ligament of uterus.

m. cricoarytenoi'deus [NA], cricoarytenoid muscle; **(1)** lateral: *origin,* upper margin of arch of cricoid cartilage; *insertion,* muscular process of arytenoid; *nerve supply,* recurrent laryngeal; *action,* narrows rima glottidis; **(2)** posterior: *origin,* depression on posterior surface of lamina of cricoid; *insertion,* muscular process of arytenoid; *nerve supply,* recurrent laryngeal; *action,* widens rima glottidis.

m. cricothyroi'deus [NA], cricothyroid muscle; *origin,* anterior surface of arch of cricoid; *insertion,* anterior or straight part passes upward to ala of thyroid, posterior or oblique part passes more outward to inferior cornu of thyroid; *nerve supply,* superior laryngeal; *action,* makes vocal folds tense.

m. deltoi'deus [NA], deltoid muscle; deltoid (2); *origin,* lateral third of clavicle, lateral border of acromion process, lower border of spine of scapula; *insertion,* lateral side of shaft of humerus; *nerve supply,* axillary from fifth and sixth cervical through brachial plexus; *action,* abduction, flexion, extension, and rotation of arm.

m. depres'sor an'guli o'ris [NA], depressor muscle of angle of mouth; triangular muscle; *origin,* lower border of mandible anteriorly; *insertion,* blends with other muscles in lower lip near angle of mouth; *action,* pulls down corners of mouth; *nerve supply,* facial.

m. depres'sor la'bii inferio'ris [NA], depressor muscle of lower lip; *origin,* anterior portion of lower border of mandible; *insertion,* m. orbicularis oris and skin of lower lip; *action,* depresses lower lip; *nerve supply,* facial.

m. depres'sor sep'ti [NA], depressor muscle of septum; a vertical fasciculus from the m. orbicularis oris passing upward along median line of upper lip, and inserted into cartilaginous septum of nose.

m. depres'sor supercil'ii [NA], depressor muscle of eyebrow; fibers of orbital part of m. orbicularis oculi which insert in eyebrow.

m. digas'tricus [NA], digastric muscle (2); m. consisting of two bellies united by central tendon connected to body of hyoid bone; *origin,* by posterior belly from digastric groove medial to mastoid process; *insertion,* by anterior belly into lower border of mandible near midline; *action,* elevates hyoid when mandible is fixed; depresses mandible when hyoid is fixed; *nerve supply,* posterior belly from facial, anterior belly by mylohyoid from mandibular division of trigeminal.

m. dila'tor pupil'lae [NA], dilator of pupil; radial muscular fibers extending from sphincter pupillae to ciliary margin.

m. epicra'nius [NA], epicranial muscle; the galea aponeurotica and muscles inserting into it, *i.e.,* m. occipitofrontalis and m. temporoparietalis.

m. erec'tor spi'nae [NA], erector muscle of spine; *origin,* from sacrum, ilium, and spines of lumbar vertebrae; divides into three columns which insert into ribs and vertebrae with additional muscle slips joining columns at successively higher levels; *action,* extends vertebral column; *nerve supply,* posterior branches of spinal nerves.

m. exten'sor car'pi radia'lis [NA], radial extensor muscle of wrist; **(1)** short, *origin,* lateral epicondyle of humerus; *insertion,* base of third metacarpal bone; *nerve supply,* radial; *action,* extends and abducts wrist radialward; **(2)** long, *origin,* lateral supracondylar ridge of humerus; *insertion,* back of base of second metacarpal bone; *nerve supply,* radial; *action,* extends and abducts wrist radialward.

m. exten'sor car'pi ulna'ris [NA], ulnar extensor muscle of wrist; *origin,* lateral epicondyle of humerus and oblique line and posterior border of ulna; *insertion,* base of fifth metacarpal bone; *nerve supply,* radial; *action,* extends and abducts wrist ulnarward.

m. exten'sor dig'iti min'imi [NA], extensor muscle of little finger; *origin,* lateral epicondyle of humerus; *insertion,* dorsum of proximal, middle, and distal phalanges of little finger; *nerve supply,* radial (posterior interosseous); *action,* extends little finger.

m. exten'sor digito'rum [NA], extensor muscle of fingers; *origin,* lateral epicondyle of humerus; *insertion,* by four tendons into the base of the proximal and middle and base of the distal phalanges; *nerve supply,* radial (posterior interosseous); *action,* extends fingers.

m. exten'sor digito'rum bre'vis [NA], short extensor muscle of toes; *origin,* dorsal surface of calcaneus; *insertion,* by four tendons fusing with those of the extensor digitorum longus, and by a slip attached independently to the base of the proximal phalanx of the great toe; *nerve supply,* deep peroneal; *action,* extends toes.

m. exten'sor digito'rum lon'gus [NA], long extensor muscle of toes; *origin,* lateral condyle of tibia, upper two-thirds of anterior margin of fibula; *insertion,* by four tendons to dorsal surfaces of bases of proximal, middle, and distal phalanges of second to fifth toes; *nerve supply,* deep branch of peroneal; *action,* extends four lateral toes.

m. exten'sor hal'lucis bre'vis [NA], medial belly of m. extensor digitorum brevis, the tendon of which is inserted into base of proximal phalanx of great toe.

m. exten'sor hal'lucis lon'gus [NA], long extensor muscle of great toe; *origin,* lateral surface of tibia and interosseous membrane; *insertion,* base of distal phalanx of great toe; *action,* extends great toe; *nerve supply,* anterior tibial.

m. exten'sor in'dicis [NA], extensor muscle of index finger; *origin,* dorsal surface of ulna; *insertion,* dorsal extensor aponeurosis of index finger; *nerve supply,* radial; *action,* assists in extending the forefinger.

m. exten'sor pol'licis [NA], extensor muscle of thumb; **(1)** short, *origin,* dorsal surface of radius; *insertion,* base of proximal phalanx of thumb; *nerve supply,* radial; *action,* extends and abducts thumb; **(2)** long, *origin,* posterior surface of ulna; *insertion,* base of distal phalanx of thumb; *nerve supply,* radial;

action, extends distal phalanx of thumb.

m. flex'or car'pi radia'lis [NA], radial flexor muscle of wrist; *origin,* medial condyle of humerus; *insertion,* anterior surface of bases of second and third metacarpal bones; *nerve supply,* median; *action,* flexes and abducts wrist radialward.

m. flex'or car'pi ulna'ris [NA], ulnar flexor muscle of wrist; *origin,* humeral head (caput humerale) from medial condyle of humerus, ulnar head (caput ulnare) from olecranon and upper posterior border of ulna; *insertion,* pisiform bone; *nerve supply,* ulnar; *action,* flexes and abducts wrist ulnarward.

m. flex'or dig'iti min'imi brev'is ma'nus [NA], short flexor muscle of little finger; *origin,* hamulus of hamate bone; *insertion,* medial side of proximal phalanx of little finger; *nerve supply,* ulnar; *action,* flexes proximal phalanx of little finger.

m. flex'or dig'iti min'imi brev'is pe'dis [NA], short flexor muscle of little toe; *origin,* base of metatarsal bone of little toe and sheath of m. peroneus longus; *insertion,* lateral surface of base of proximal phalanx of little toe; *nerve supply,* lateral plantar; *action,* flexes proximal phalanx of the little toe.

m. flex'or digito'rum bre'vis [NA], short flexor muscle of toes; *origin,* medial tubercle of calcaneus and central portion of plantar fascia; *insertion,* middle phalanges of four lateral toes; *nerve supply,* medial plantar; *action,* flexes lateral four toes.

m. flex'or digito'rum lon'gus [NA], long flexor muscle of toes; *origin,* middle third of posterior surface of tibia; *insertion,* bases of distal phalanges of four lateral toes; *nerve supply,* tibial nerve; *action,* flexes second to fifth toes.

m. flex'or digito'rum profun'dus [NA], deep flexor muscle of fingers; *origin,* anterior surface of upper third of ulna; *insertion,* base of distal phalanx of each finger; *nerve supply,* ulnar and median; *action,* flexes distal phalanges of fingers.

m. flex'or digito'rum superficia'lis [NA], superficial flexor muscle of fingers; *origin,* humeroulnar head from the medial epicondyle of humerus, medial border of coronoid process, and a tendinous arch between these points, radial head from oblique line and middle third of lateral border of radius; *insertion,* sides of middle phalanx of each finger; *nerve supply,* median; *action,* flexes middle phalanges of fingers.

m. flex'or hal'lucis [NA], flexor muscle of great toe; (1) short, *origin,* medial surface of cuboid and middle and lateral cuneiform bones; *insertion,* sides of base of proximal phalanx of great toe; *nerve supply,* medial and lateral plantar; *action,* flexes great toe; (2) long, *origin,* lower posterior surface of fibula; *insertion,* base of distal phalanx of great toe; *nerve supply,* medial plantar; *action,* flexes great toe.

m. flex'or pol'licis [NA], flexor muscle of thumb; (1) short, *origin,* superficial portion from flexor retinaculum of wrist, deep portion from ulnar side of first metacarpal bone; *insertion,* base of proximal

phalanx of thumb; *nerve supply,* median and ulnar; *action,* flexes proximal phalanx of thumb; (2) long, *origin,* anterior surface of middle third of radius; *insertion,* distal phlanx of thumb; *nerve supply,* median palmar interosseous; *action,* flexes distal phalanx of thumb.

m. gastrocne'mius [NA], *origin,* lateral and medial condyles of the femur; *insertion,* with soleus by tendo calcaneus (achillis) into lower half of posterior surface of calcaneus; *nerve supply;* tibial; *action,* plantar flexion of foot.

m. gemel'lus [NA], (1) inferior: *origin,* tuberosity of ischium; *insertion,* tendon of m. obturator internus; *nerve supply* and *action* rotates thigh laterally; (2) superior: *origin,* ischial spine and margin of lesser sciatic notch; *insertion,* tendon of m. obturator internus; *nerve supply* and *action* rotates thigh laterally.

m. genioglos'sus [NA], genioglossus muscle; one of the paired lingual muscles; *origin,* mental spine of the mandible; *insertion,* lingual fascia beneath the mucous membrane and epiglottis; *nerve supply,* hypoglossal; *action,* depresses and protrudes the tongue.

m. geniohyoi'deus [NA], geniohyoid muscle; *origin,* mental spine of mandible; *insertion,* body of hyoid bone; *action,* draws hyoid forward, or depresses jaw when hyoid is fixed; *nerve supply,* fibers from first and second cervical accompanying hypoglossal.

m. glu'teus max'imus [NA], *origin,* ilium behind posterior gluteal line, posterior surface of sacrum and coccyx, and sacrotuberous ligament; *insertion,* iliotibial band of fascia lata and gluteal ridge of femur; *nerve supply,* inferior gluteal; *action,* extends thigh.

m. glu'teus me'dius [NA], mesogluteus; *origin,* ilium between anterior and posterior gluteal lines; *insertion,* lateral surface of great trochanter; *nerve supply,* superior gluteal; *action,* abducts and rotates thigh.

m. glu'teus min'imus [NA], *origin,* ilium between anterior and inferior gluteal lines; *insertion,* great trochanter of femur; *nerve supply,* superior gluteal; *action,* abducts thigh.

m. grac'ilis [NA], gracilis muscle; *origin,* ramus of pubis near symphysis; *insertion,* shaft of tibia below medial tuberosity; *nerve supply,* obturator; *action,* adducts thigh, flexes knee, rotates leg medially.

m. hel'icis [NA], muscle of helix; (1) major: a narrow band of muscular fibers on the anterior border of the helix arising from the spine and inserted at the point where the helix becomes transverse; (2) minor: a band of oblique fibers covering the crus helicis.

m. hyoglos'sus [NA], hyoglossus muscle; *origin,* body and greater horn of hyoid bone; *insertion,* side of the tongue; *nerve supply,* hypoglossal; *action,* retracts and pulls down side of tongue.

m. ili'acus [NA], iliac muscle; *origin,* iliac fossa; *insertion,* tendon of psoas, anterior surface of lesser trochanter, and capsule of hip joint; *nerve supply,* lumbar plexus; *action,* flexes thigh and rotates it medially.

m. il'iococcyg'eus [NA], iliococcygeal muscle; posterior part of levator ani arising from tendinous arch of levator ani muscle and inserting on anococcygeal ligament and coccyx.

m. iliocosta'lis [NA], iliocostal muscle; lateral division of the erector spinae, having three subdivisions: **m. i. cer'vicis,** *origin,* angles of upper six ribs; *insertion,* transverse processes of middle cervical vertebrae; *action,* extends, abducts, and rotates cervical vertebrae; *nerve supply,* dorsal branches of upper thoracic nerves; **m. i. lumbo'rum,** *origin,* with erector spinae; *insertion,* angles of lower six ribs; *action,* extends, abducts, and rotates lumbar vertebrae; *nerve supply,* dorsal branches of thoracic and lumbar nerves; **m. i. thora'cis,** *origin,* medial side of angles of lower six ribs; *insertion,* angles of upper six ribs; *action,* extends, abducts, and rotates thoracic vertebrae; *nerve supply,* dorsal branches of thoracic nerves.

m. iliopso'as [NA], iliopsoas muscle; a compound muscle, consisting of the m. iliacus and m. psoas major.

m. infraspina'tus [NA], infraspinous muscle; *origin,* infraspinous fossa of scapula; *insertion,* middle facet of great tubercle of humerus; *nerve supply,* suprascapular from fifth to sixth cervical; *action,* extends arm and rotates it laterally.

m. intercosta'lis [NA], intercostal muscle; **(1)** external, each arises from lower border of one rib and is inserted into the upper border of rib below; *action,* contract during inspiration, also maintain tension in intercostal spaces to resist mediolateral movement; *nerve supply,* intercostal; **(2)** internal, each arises from lower border of rib and is inserted into upper border of rib below; *action,* contract during expiration, also maintain tension in intercostal spaces to resist mediolateral movement; *nerve supply,* intercostal; **(3)** innermost, a layer parallel to internal intercostal muscle but separated from it by intercostal vessels and nerves.

m. interos'seus dorsa'lis ma'nus [NA], dorsal interosseus muscle of hand; four in number; *origin,* sides of adjacent metacarpal bones; *insertion,* proximal phalanges and extensor expansion; *nerve supply,* ulnar; *action,* abducts index, abducts or adducts middle finger, abducts ring finger.

m. interos'seus dorsa'lis pe'dis [NA], dorsal interosseus muscle of foot; four muscles; *origin,* from sides of adjacent metatarsal bones; *insertion,* first into medial, second into lateral side of proximal phalanx of second toe, third and fourth into lateral side of proximal phalanx of third and fourth toes; *nerve supply,* lateral plantar; *action,* first adducts second toe; second, third, and fourth abduct second, third, and fourth toes.

m. interos'seus palma'ris [NA], palmar interosseus muscle; three in number; *origin,* first from ulnar side of second metacarpal, second and third from radial sides of fourth and fifth metacarpals; *insertion,* first into ulnar side of index, second and third into radial sides of ring and little fingers; *nerve supply,* ulnar; *action,* adducts fingers toward axis of middle finger.

m. interos'seus planta'ris plantar interosseus muscle; [NA], three muscles; *origin,* the medial side of the third, fourth, and fifth metatarsal bones; *insertion,* corresponding side of proximal phalanx of the same toes; *nerve supply,* lateral plantar; *action,* adducts three lateral toes.

mus'culi interspina'les [NA], interspinal muscles; the paired muscles between spinous processes of adjacent vertebrae: subdivided into cervical, thoracic, and lumbar muscles.

mus'culi intertransversa'rii [NA], intertransverse muscles; paired muscles between transverse processes of adjacent vertebrae: anterior and posterior muscles in cervical region, lateral and medial in lumbar region, and single in thoracic region.

m. ischiocaverno'sus [NA], ischiocavernous muscle; *origin,* ramus of ischium; *insertion,* corpus cavernosum penis (or clitoridis); *nerve supply,* perineal; *action,* compresses crus of penis (or clitoris) forcing blood in its sinus into distal part of corpus cavernosum.

mus'culi laryn'gis [NA], muscles of larynx; intrinsic muscles that regulate length, position and tension of vocal cords and adjust size of openings between aryepiglottic folds, ventricular folds and vocal folds.

m. latis'simus dor'si [NA], broadest muscle of back; *origin,* spinous processes of lower five or six thoracic and the lumbar vertebrae, median ridge of sacrum, and outer lip of iliac crest; *insertion,* with teres major into posterior lip of bicipital groove of humerus; *action,* adducts arm, rotates it medially, and extends it; *nerve supply,* thoracodorsal.

m. leva'tor an'guli o'ris [NA], elevator muscle of angle of mouth; *origin,* canine fossa of maxilla; *insertion,* orbicularis oris and skin at angle of mouth; *action,* raises angle of mouth; *nerve supply,* facial.

m. leva'tor a'ni [NA], elevator muscle of anus; formed by m. puborectalis, m. levator prostatae, m. pubococcygeus, and m. iliococcygeus; *origin,* back of pubis, tendinous arch of levator ani, and spine of ischium; *insertion,* anococcygeal ligament, sides of lower part of sacrum and of coccyx; *nerve supply,* fourth sacral; *action,* draws anus upward in defecation, supports pelvic viscera.

m. leva'tor cos'tae [NA], elevator muscle of rib; **(1)** short: each arises from transverse processes of last cervical and eleven thoracic vertebra and is *inserted* into rib next below; **(2)** long: each is *inserted* into second rib below its origin; *action,* raises rib; *nerve supply,* intercostal.

m. leva'tor glan'dulae thyroi'deae [NA], elevator muscle of thyroid gland; a fasciculus occasionally passing from thyrohyoid muscle to isthmus of thyroid gland.

m. leva'tor la'bii superio'ris [NA], elevator of the upper lip; *origin,* maxilla below infraorbital foramen; *insertion,* orbicularis oris of upper lip; *action,* elevates upper lip; *nerve supply,* facial.

m. leva'tor la'bii superio'ris alae'que na'si [NA], elevator muscle of upper lip and wing of nose; *origin,* root of nasal process of maxilla; *insertion,* ala of nose and m. orbicularis oris of upper lip; *action,* elevates upper lip and wing of nose; *nerve supply,* facial.

m. leva'tor palpe'brae superio'ris [NA], elevator muscle of upper eyelid; *origin,* orbital surface of lesser wing of the sphenoid; *insertion,* skin of eyelid, tarsal plate, and orbital walls; *nerve supply,* oculomotor; *action,* raises upper eyelid.

m. leva'tor prosta'tae [NA], elevator muscle of prostate; most medial fibers of levator ani muscle that extend from pubis into fascia of prostate.

m. leva'tor scap'ulae [NA], elevator muscle of scapula; *origin,* from posterior tubercles of transverse processes of four upper cervical vertebrae; *insertion,* into superior angle of scapula; *action,* raises scapula; *nerve supply,* dorsal nerve of scapula.

m. leva'tor ve'li palati'ni [NA], elevator muscle of soft palate; *origin,* apex of petrous portion of temporal bone and lower part of auditory tube; *insertion,* aponeurosis of soft palate; *nerve supply,* pharyngeal plexus; *action,* raises soft palate.

m. longis'simus cap'itis [NA], longissimus muscle of head; *origin,* from transverse processes of upper thoracic and transverse and articular processes of lower and middle cervical vertebrae; *insertion,* into mastoid process; *action,* keeps head erect, draws it backward or to one side; *nerve supply,* dorsal branches of cervical nerves.

m. longis'simus cer'vicis [NA], longissimus muscle of neck; *origin,* transverse processes of upper thoracic vertebrae; *insertion,* transverse processes of middle and upper cervical vertebrae; *action,* extends cervical vertebrae; *nerve supply,* dorsal branches of lower cervical and upper thoracic nerves.

m. longis'simus thora'cis [NA], longissimus muscle of thorax; *origin,* with iliocostalis and from transverse processes of lower thoracic vertebrae; *insertion,* ribs between angles and tubercles, transverse processes of upper lumbar vertebrae, and accessory processes of upper lumbar and transverse processes of thoracic vertebrae; *action,* extends vertebral column; *nerve supply,* dorsal branches of thoracic and lumbar nerves.

m. longitudina'lis [NA], longitudinal or lingual muscle; **(1)** inferior: an intrinsic muscle of the tongue, cylindrical in shape, occupying the underpart on either side; **(2)** superior: an intrinsic muscle of the tongue, running from base to tip on the dorsum just beneath the mucous membrane.

m. lon'gus cap'itis [NA], long muscle of head; *origin,* anterior tubercles of transverse processes of third to sixth cervical vertebrae; *insertion,* basilar process of occipital bone; *action,* twists or bends neck forward; *nerve supply,* cervical plexus.

m. lon'gus col'li [NA], long muscle of neck; *medial portion* arises from third thoracic to fifth cervical vertebrae and is inserted into second to fourth cervical vertebrae; *superolateral portion* arises from transverse processes of third to fifth cervical vertebrae and is inserted into anterior tubercle of atlas; *inferolateral portion* arises from first to third thoracic vertebrae and is inserted into transverse processes of fifth and sixth cervical vertebrae; *action,* twists and bends neck forward; *nerve supply,* ventral branches of cervical.

m. lumbrica'lis ma'nus [NA], lumbrical muscle of hand (four); *origin,* two lateral, from radial side of tendons of flexor digitorum profundus going to index and middle fingers, two medial, from adjacent sides of second and third, and third and fourth tendons; *insertion,* radial side of extensor tendon on dorsum of each of four fingers; *nerve supply,* median and ulnar; *action,* flexes proximal and extends middle and distal phalanges.

m. lumbrica'lis pe'dis [NA], lumbrical muscle of foot (four); *origin,* first from tibial side of tendon to second toe of flexor digitorum longus; second, third, and fourth from adjacent sides of all four tendons of this m.; *insertion,* tibial side of extensor tendon on dorsum of each of four lateral toes; *nerve supply,* lateral and medial plantar; *action,* flex proximal and extend middle and distal phalanges.

m. masse'ter [NA], masseter muscle; *origin,* inferior border and medial surface of the zygomatic arch; *insertion,* lateral surface of ramus and coronoid process of mandible; *action,* closes jaw; *nerve supply,* masseteric from mandibular division of trigeminal.

m. menta'lis [NA], chin muscle; *origin,* incisor fossa of mandible; *insertion,* skin of chin; *action,* raises and wrinkles skin of chin and pushes up lower lip; *nerve supply,* facial.

m. multif'idus [NA], multifidus muscle; *origin,* from sacrum, sacroiliac ligament, mammillary processes of lumbar vertebrae, transverse processes of thoracic vertebrae, and articular processes of last four cervical vertebrae; *insertion,* into spinous processes of all vertebrae up to and including axis; *action,* rotates vertebral column; *nerve supply,* dorsal branches of spinal nerve.

m. mylohyoi'deus [NA], mylohyoid muscle; *origin,* mylohyoid line of mandible; *insertion,* upper border of hyoid bone and raphe separating muscle from its fellow; *action,* elevates floor of mouth and tongue, depresses jaw when hyoid fixed; *nerve supply,* mylohyoid from mandibular division of trigeminal.

m. nasa'lis [NA], nasal muscle; transverse part arises from the maxilla on each side and passes across bridge of nose; alar part arises from maxilla and attaches to ala of nose; *action*, dilates the nostrils; *nerve supply*, facial.

m. obli'quus cap'itis [NA], oblique muscle of head; **(1)** inferior, *origin*, spinous process of axis; *insertion*, transverse process of atlas; *action*, rotates head; *nerve supply*, suboccipital; **(2)** superior, *origin*, transverse process of atlas; *insertion*, lateral third of inferior nuchal line; *action*, rotates head; *nerve supply*, suboccipital.

m. obli'quus exter'nus abdom'inis [NA], external oblique muscle of abdomen; *origin*, fifth to twelfth ribs; *insertion*, anterior lateral lip of iliac crest, inguinal ligament, and anterior layer of sheath of rectus; *action*, diminishes capacity of abdomen, draws thorax downward; *nerve supply*, ventral branches of lower thoracic nerves.

m. obli'quus infe'rior [NA], inferior oblique muscle; *origin*, orbital plate of maxilla lateral to lacrimal groove; *insertion*, sclera between superior and lateral recti; *nerve supply*, oculomotor; *action*, directs pupil of eye upward and outward; extorsion.

m. obli'quus inter'nus abdom'inis [NA], internal oblique muscle of abdomen; *origin*, iliac fascia deep to lateral part of inguinal ligament, anterior half of crest of ilium, and lumbar fascia; *insertion*, 10th to 12th ribs and sheath of rectus; *action*, diminishes capacity of abdomen, bends thorax forward; *nerve supply*, lower thoracic.

m. obli'quus supe'rior [NA], superior oblique muscle; *origin*, above medial margin of optic canal; *insertion*, by tendon passing through trochlea to sclera between the superior and lateral recti; *nerve supply*, trochlear nerve; *action*, directs pupil of eye downward and outward; intorsion.

m. obtura'rius [NA], obturator muscle; **(1)** external, *origin*, margin of obturator foramen and adjacent external surface of obturator membrane; *insertion*, trochanteric fossa of greater trochanter; *nerve supply*, obturator; *action*, rotates thigh laterally; **(2)** internal, *origin*, pelvic surface of obturator membrane and margin of obturator foramen; *insertion*, medial surface of greater trochanter; *nerve supply*, sacral plexus; *action*, rotates thigh laterally.

m. occipitofronta'lis, [NA], occipitofrontal muscle; a part of m. epicranius; occipital belly arises from occipital bone and inserts into galea aponeurotica; frontal belly arises from galea and inserts into skin of eyebrow and nose; *action*, moves scalp; *nerve supply*, facial.

m. omohyoi'deus [NA], omohyoid m.; has two bellies attached to intermediate tendon; *origin*, by inferior belly from upper border of scapula between superior angle and notch; *insertion*, by superior belly into hyoid bone; *action*, depresses hyoid; *nerve supply*, upper cervical through ansa cervicalis.

m. oppo'nens dig'iti min'imi [NA], opposer muscle of the little finger; *origin*, hamulus of the hamate bone and flexor retinaculum; *insertion*, shaft of fifth metacarpal; *nerve supply*, ulnar; *action*, draws ulnar side of hand toward center of palm.

m. oppo'nens pol'licis [NA], opposer muscle of thumb; *origin*, ridge of trapezium and flexor retinaculum; *insertion*, anterior surface of first metacarpal bone; *nerve supply*, median; *action*, opposes thumb to other fingers.

m. orbicula'ris oc'uli [NA], orbicular muscle of eye; consists of three portions: *external*, arises from frontal process of maxilla and nasal process of frontal bone, encircles aperture of orbit, and is inserted near origin; *internal*, arises from medial palpebral ligament, passes through each eyelid, and is inserted into lateral palpebral raphe; *lacrimal*, arises from posterior lacrimal crest and passes across lacrimal sac to join palpebral portion; *action*, closes eye, wrinkles forehead vertically; *nerve supply*, facial.

m. orbicula'ris o'ris [NA], orbicular muscle of mouth; *origin*, by nasolabial band from septum of nose, by superior incisive bundle from incisor fossa of maxilla, by inferior incisive bundle from lower jaw each side of symphysis; *insertion*, fibers surround mouth between skin and mucous membrane of lips and cheeks, and are blended with other muscles; *action*, closes lips; *nerve supply*, facial.

m. orbita'lis [NA], orbital muscle; a rudimentary nonstriated muscle, crossing infraorbital groove and sphenomaxillary fissure, intimately united with the periosteum of the orbit.

m. palatoglos'sus [NA], palatoglossus muscle; forms anterior pillar of fauces; *origin*, oral surface of soft palate; *insertion*, side of tongue; *nerve supply*, pharyngeal plexus; *action*, raises back of tongue and narrows fauces.

m. palatopharyn'geus [NA], palatopharyngeal muscle; forms posterior pillar of fauces; *origin*, soft palate; *insertion*, posterior border of thyroid cartilage and aponeurosis of pharynx; *nerve supply*, pharyngeal plexus; *action*, narrows fauces, depresses soft palate, elevates pharynx and larynx.

m. palma'ris [NA], palmar muscle; **(1)** short, *origin*, ulnar side of central portion of palmar aponeurosis; *insertion*, skin of ulnar side of hand; *nerve supply*, ulnar; *action*, wrinkles skin on medial side of palm; **(2)** long, *origin*, medial epicondyle of humerus; *insertion*, flexor retinaculum of wrist and palmar fascia; *nerve supply*, median; *action*, tenses palmar fascia and flexes hand and forearm.

m. papilla'ris [NA], papillary muscle; one of the group of myocardial bundles that terminate in the chordae tendineae which attach to the cusps of the atrioventricular valves.

mus'culi pectina'ti [NA], pectinate muscles; prominent ridges of atrial myocardium located on the inner surface of much of the right atrium and both auricles.

m. pectin'eus [NA], pectineal muscle; *origin*, crest of pubis; *insertion*, pectineal line of femur; *nerve supply*, obturator and femoral; *action*, adducts thigh and assists in flexion.

m. pectora'lis [NA], pectoral muscle; (1) greater, *origin*, medial half of clavicle, anterior surface of manubrium, body of sternum, cartilages of first to sixth ribs, and aponeurosis of obliquus externus; *insertion*, crest of greater tubercle of humerus; *action*, adducts and medially rotates arm; *nerve supply*, anterior thoracic; (2) smaller, *origin*, third to fifth ribs at costochondral articulations; *insertion*, tip of coracoid process of scapula; *action*, draws down scapula or raises ribs; *nerve supply*, anterior thoracic.

m. perone'us [NA], peroneal or fibular muscle; (1) short, *origin*, lower two-thirds of lateral surface of fibula; *insertion*, base of fifth metatarsal bone; *nerve supply*, peroneal; *action*, everts foot; (2) long, *origin*, upper two-thirds of outer surface of fibula and lateral condyle of tibia; *insertion*, by tendon passing behind lateral malleolis and across sole of foot to medial cuneiform and base of first metatarsal; *nerve supply*, peroneal; *action*, plantar flexes and everts foot; (3) third, muscle; *origin*, in common with m. extensor digitorum longus; *insertion*, dorsum of base of fifth metatarsal bone; *nerve supply*, deep branch of peroneal; *action*, assists in dorsal flexion of foot.

m. pirifor'mis [NA], piriform muscle; *origin*, margins of pelvic sacral foramina and greater sciatic notch of ilium; *insertion*, upper border of great trochanter; *nerve supply*, sciatic plexus; *action*, rotates thigh laterally.

m. planta'ris [NA], plantar muscle; *origin*, lateral supracondylar ridge of femur; *insertion*, medial margin of tendo Achillis and deep fascia of ankle; *nerve supply*, tibial nerve; *action*, plantar flexion of foot.

m. pleuroesopha'geus [NA], pleuroesophageal muscle; muscular fasciculi, arising from the mediastinal pleura, which reinforce musculature of esophagus.

m. poplite'us [NA], popliteal muscle; *origin*, lateral condyle of femur; *insertion*, posterior surface of tibia; *nerve supply*, tibial; *action*, flexes leg and rotates it medially.

m. proce'rus [NA], procerus muscle; *origin*, from membrane covering bridge of nose; *insertion*, into frontalis; *action*, assists frontalis; *nerve supply*, branch of facial.

m. prona'tor quadra'tus [NA], quadrate pronator muscle; *origin*, distal fourth of anterior surface of ulna; *insertion*, distal fourth of anterior surface of radius; *nerve supply*, anterior interosseous; *action*, pronates forearm.

m. prona'tor te'res [NA], round pronator muscle; *origin*, superficial head from medial epicondyle of humerus, deep head from medial side of coronoid process of ulna; *insertion*, middle of lateral surface of radius; *nerve supply*, median; *action*, pronates forearm.

m. pso'as [NA], psoas muscle; (1) greater, *origin*, bodies of vertebrae and intervertebral disks from 12th thoracic to fifth lumbar, and transverse processes of lumbar vertebrae; *insertion*, lesser trochanter of femur; *nerve supply*, lumbar plexus; *action*, flexes thigh; (2) smaller, an inconstant muscle; *origin*, bodies of 12th thoracic and first lumbar vertebrae and disk between them; *insertion*, iliopubic eminence with iliac fascia; *nerve supply*, lumbar plexus; *action*, assits in flexion of lumbar spine.

m. pterygoi'deus [NA], pterygoid muscle; (1) lateral, *origin*, inferior head from lateral lamina of pterygoid process, superior head from inframtemporal crest and adjacent greater wing of the sphenoid; *insertion*, into pterygoid pit of mandible and articular disk; *action*, brings jaw forward, opens jaw; *nerve supply*, nerve to lateral pterygoid from mandibular division of trigeminal; (2) medial, *origin*, pterygoid fossa of sphenoid and tuberosity of maxilla; *insertion*, medial surface of mandible between angle and mylohyoid groove; *action*, raises mandible closing jaw; *nerve supply*, nerve to medial pterygoid from mandibular division of trigeminal.

m. pubococcy'geus [NA], pubococcygeal muscle; fibers of levator ani, arising from pelvic surface of body of pubis, attaching to coccyx.

m. puboprostat'icus [NA], puboprostatic muscle; smooth muscle fibers within puboprostatic ligament.

m. puborecta'lis [NA], puborectal muscle; part of m. levator ani that passes from body of pubis around anus to form muscular sling at level anorectal junction; relaxes during defecation.

m. pubovagina'lis [NA], pubovaginal muscles; the most medial fibers of levator ani muscle that extend from pubis into lateral walls of vagina.

m. pubovesica'lis [NA], pubovesical muscle; smooth muscle fibers within the pubovesical ligament in the female.

m. pyramida'lis [NA], pyramidal muscle; *origin*, crest of pubis; *insertion*, lower portion of linea alba; *action*, makes linea alba tense; *nerve supply*, last thoracic.

m. pyramida'lis auric'ulae [NA], pyramidal muscle of auricle; an occasional prolongation of fibers of the tragicus to the spina helicis.

m. quadra'tus fem'oris [NA], quadrate muscle of the thigh; *origin*, lateral border of tuberosity of ischium; *insertion*, intertrochanteric ridge; *nerve supply*, sacral plexus; *action*, rotates thigh laterally.

m. quadra'tus la'bii superior'is. quadrate muscle of upper lip; composed of three heads usually described as three muscles: levator labii superioris alaeque nasi, levator labii superioris and zygomaticus minor.

m. quadra'tus lumbo'rum [NA], lumbar quadrate muscle; quadrate muscle of loins, *origin*, iliac crest, iliolumbar ligament, and transverse processes of lower lumbar vertebrae; *insertion*, 12th rib and transverse processes of upper lumbar vertebrae; *action*, abducts trunk; *nerve supply*, upper lumbar.

m. quadra'tus plan'tae [NA], plantar quadrate muscle; quadrate muscle of sole; *origin*, by two heads from the lateral and medial borders of the inferior surface of the calcaneus; *insertion,* tendons of flexor digitorum longus; *nerve supply,* lateral plantar; *action,* assists long flexor.

m. quad'riceps fem'oris [NA], quadriceps muscle of thigh; *origin,* by four head: rectus femoris, vastus lateralis, vastus intermedius, and vastus medialis; *insertion,* patella, and by ligament to tuberosity of tibia; *nerve supply,* femoral; *action,* extends leg; flexes thigh by action of rectus femoris.

m. rectococcyg'eus [NA], rectococcygeal muscle; band of smooth muscle fibers passing from posterior surface of rectum to anterior surface of second or third coccygeal segment.

m. rectourethra'lis [NA], rectourethral muscle; smooth muscle fibers that pass forward from longitudinal muscle layer of rectum to membranous urethra in the male.

m. rectouteri'nus [NA], rectouterine muscle; a band of fibrous tissue and smooth muscle fibers passing between cervix uteri and rectum in rectouterine fold, on either side.

m. rectovesica'lis [NA], rectovesical muscle; smooth muscle fibers in the sacrogenital fold in the male; they correspond to m. rectouterinus.

m. rec'tus abdom'inis [NA], rectus or straight muscle of abdomen; *origin,* crest and symphysis of pubis; *insertion,* xiphoid process and fifth to seventh costal cartilages; *action,* flexes vertebral column, draws thorax downward; *nerve supply,* branches of lower thoracic.

m. rec'tus cap'itis ante'rior [NA], anterior rectus or straight muscle of head; *origin,* transverse process and lateral mass of atlas; *insertion,* basilar process of occipital bone; *action,* turns and inclines head forward; *nerve supply,* first and second cervical.

m. rec'tus cap'itis latera'lis [NA], lateral rectus or straight muscle of head; *origin,* transverse process of atlas; *insertion,* jugular process of occipital bone; *action,* inclines head to one side; *nerve supply,* ventral branch of first cervical.

m. rec'tus cap'itis poste'rior [NA], posterior rectus or straight muscle of head; **(1)** greater, *origin,* spinous process of axis; *insertion,* middle of inferior nuchal line of occipital bone; *action,* rotates and draws head backward; *nerve supply,* dorsal branch of first cervical; **(2)** smaller, *origin,* from posterior tubercle of atlas; *insertion,* medial third of inferior nuchal line of occipital bone; *action,* rotates head and draws it backward, *nerve supply,* dorsal branch of first cervical.

m. rec'tus fem'oris [NA], rectus or straight muscle of thigh; *origin,* anterior inferior spine of ilium and upper margin of acetabulum; *insertion,* common tendon of quadriceps femoris.

m. rec'tus infe'rior [NA], inferior rectus or straight muscle; *origin,* inferior part of anulus tendineus communis; *insertion,* inferior part of sclera of eye; *nerve supply,* oculomotor; *action,* directs pupil downard and medialward; extorsion.

m. rec'tus latera'lis [NA], lateral rectus or straight muscle; abducens oculi; *origin,* lateral part of anulus tendineus communis that bridges superior orbital fissure; *insertion,* lateral part of sclera of eye; *nerve supply,* abducens; *action,* directs pupil laterally.

m. rec'tus media'lis [NA], medial rectus or straight muscle; *origin,* medial part of anulus tendineus communis; *insertion,* medial part of sclera of the eye; *nerve supply,* oculomotor; *action,* directs pupil medialward.

m. rec'tus supe'rior [NA], superior rectus or straight muscle; *origin,* superior part of anulus tendineus communis; *insertion,* superior part of sclera of the eye; *nerve supply,* oculomotor; *action,* directs pupil upward and medialward; intorsion.

m. rhomboi'deus [NA], rhomboid muscle; **(1)** greater, *origin,* spinous processes and corresponding supraspinous ligaments of first four thoracic vertebrae; *insertion,* medial border of scapula below spine; *action,* draws scapula toward vertebral column; *nerve supply,* dorsal nerve of scapula; **(2)** smaller, *origin,* spinous processes of sixth and seventh cervical vertebrae; *insertion,* medial margin of scapula above spine; *action,* draws scapula toward vertebral column and slightly upward; *nerve supply,* dorsal nerve of scapula.

m. riso'rius [NA], risorius muscle; *origin,* from platysma and fascia of masseter; *insertion,* orbicularis oris and skin at corner of mouth; *action,* draws out angle of mouth; *nerve supply,* facial.

mus'culi rotato'res [NA], rotator muscles; a number of short transversospinal muscles chiefly developed in cervical, lumbar, thoracic regions, arising from transverse process of one vertebra and inserted into root of spinous process of next two or three vertebrae above; *action,* rotate vertebral column; *nerve supply,* dorsal branches of spinal.

m. sacrococcyg'eus [NA], sacrococcygeal muscle; an inconstant and poorly developed muscle on the dorsal and ventral surfaces of the sacrum and coccyx.

m. salpingopharyn'geus [NA], salpingopharyngeal muscle; *origin,* medial lamina of cartilaginous part of auditory tube; *insertion,* muscular layer of pharynx in association with m. palatopharyngeus; *nerve supply,* pharyngeal plexus; *action,* assists in elevating pharynx and opening auditory tube during swallowing.

m. sarto'rius [NA], sartorius or tailor's muscle; *origin,* anterior superior spine of ilium; *insertion,* medial border of tuberosity of tibia; *nerve supply,* femoral; *action,* flexes thigh and leg, rotates leg medially and thigh laterally.

m. scale'nus [NA], scalene muscle; **(1)** anterior, *origin,* anterior tubercles of transverse processes of third to sixth cervical vertebrae; *insertion,* scalene tubercle of first rib; *action,* raises first rib; *nerve supply,* cervical plexus; **(2)** medial, *origin,* costotransverse lamellae of transverse processes of second to sixth cervical vertebrae; *insertion,* first rib posterior to subclavian artery; *action,* raises first rib; *nerve supply,* cervical plexus; **(3)** posterior, *origin,* posterior tubercles of transverse processes of fourth to sixth cervical vertebrae; *insertion,* lateral surface of second rib; *action,* elevates second rib; *nerve supply,* cervical and brachial plexuses; **(4)** smallest, an occasional independent muscular fasciculus between scalenus anterior and medius, and having same action and innervation.

m. semimembrano'sus [NA], semimembranosus muscle; *origin,* tuberosity of ischium; *insertion,* medial condyle of tibia and by membrane to tibial collateral ligament of knee joint, popliteal fascia, and lateral condyle of femur; *nerve supply,* tibial; *action,* flexes leg and rotates it medially, tenses capsule of knee joint.

m. semispina'lis cap'itis [NA], semispinal muscle of head; *origin,* transverse processes of five or six upper thoracic and articular processes of four lower cervical vertebrae; *insertion,* occipital bone between superior and inferior nuchal lines; *action,* rotates head and draws it backward; *nerve supply,* dorsal branches of cervical.

m. semispina'lis cer'vicis [NA], semispinal muscle of neck; continuous with m. semispinalis thoracis; *origin,* transverse processes of second to fifth thoracic vertebrae; *insertion,* spinous processes of axis and third to fifth cervical vertebrae; *action,* extends cervical spine; *nerve supply,* dorsal branches of cervical and thoracic.

m. semispina'lis thora'cis [NA], semispinal muscle of thorax; *origin,* transverse processes of fifth to eleventh thoracic vertebrae; *insertion,* spinous processes of first four thoracic and fifth and seventh cervical vertebrae; *action,* extends vertebral column; *nerve supply,* dorsal branches of cervical and thoracic.

m. semitendino'sus [NA], semitendinous muscle; *origin,* ischial tuberosity; *insertion,* medial surface of upper fourth of shaft of tibia; *nerve supply,* tibial; *action,* extends thigh, flexes leg and rotates it medially.

m. serra'tus ante'rior [NA], anterior serratus muscle; *origin,* from center of lateral aspect of first eight to nine ribs; *insertion,* superior and inferior angles and intervening medial margin of scapula; *action,* rotates scapula and pulls it forward, elevates ribs; *nerve supply,* long thoracic from brachial plexus.

m. serra'tus poste'rior [NA], posterior serratus muscle; **(1)** inferior, *origin,* with latissimus dorsi, from spinous processes of two lower thoracic and two upper lumbar vertebrae; *insertion,* into lower borders of last four ribs; *action,* draws lower ribs backward and downward; *nerve supply,* ninth to 12th intercostal; **(2)** superior, *origin,* from spinous processes of two lower cervical and two upper thoracic vertebrae; *insertion,* into lateral side of angles of second to fifth ribs; *nerve supply,* first to

fourth intercostals.

m. sol'eus [NA], soleus muscle; *origin,* posterior surface of head and shaft of fibula, oblique line and medial margin of tibia, and tendinous arch passing between tibia and fibula over popliteal vessels; *insertion,* with gastrocnemius by tendo calcaneus into tuberosity of calcaneus; *nerve supply,* tibial; *action,* plantar flexion of foot.

m. sphincter ampullae hepatopancreat'icae [NA], Oddi's sphincter; the smooth muscle sphincter of the hepatopancreatic ampulla.

m. sphinc'ter a'ni [NA], sphincter muscle of anus; **(1)** external, a fusiform ring of striated muscular fibers surrounding anus, attached posteriorly to coccyx and anteriorly to central tendon of perineum; **(2)** internal, a smooth muscle ring, formed by increase of circular fibers of rectum, situated at upper end of anal canal.

m. sphinc'ter duc'tus choledo'chi [NA], sphincter muscle of the common bile duct; smooth muscle sphincter at terminal end of common bile duct.

m. sphinc'ter duc'tus pancreat'ici, [NA], sphincter muscle of pancreatic duct; smooth muscle sphincter of main pancreatic duct within duodenal papilla.

m. sphinc'ter pupil'lae [NA], sphincter muscle of the pupil; a ring of smooth muscle fibers surrounding pupillary border of the iris.

m. sphinc'ter pylo'ri [NA], sphincter muscle of the pylorus; pyloric sphincter; a thickening of circular layer of gastric musculature encircling gastroduodenal junction.

m. sphinc'ter ure'thrae [NA], sphincter muscle of urethra; *origin,* ramus of pubis; *insertion,* with fellow in median raphe behind and in front of urethra; *nerve supply,* pudendal; *action,* constricts membranous urethra.

m. sphinc'ter vesi'cae, sphincter muscle of the urinary bladder; a vesical sphincter made up of a thickening of middle muscular layer of bladder around urethral opening; although no anular sphincter exists, a sphincteric action is attributed to the bundle of muscles in region of neck of urinary bladder.

m. spina'lis cap'itis [NA], spinal muscle of head; inconstant extension of spinalis cervicis to occipital bone, sometimes fusing with semispinalis capitis.

m. spina'lis cer'vicis [NA], spinal muscle of neck; inconstant or rudimentary muscle; *origin,* spinous processes of sixth and seventh cervical; *insertion,* spinous processes of axis and third cervical vertebra; *action,* extends cervical spine; *nerve supply,* dorsal branches of cervical.

m. spina'lis thora'cis [NA], spinal muscle of thorax; *origin,* spinous processes of upper lumbar and two lower thoracic vertebrae; *insertion,* spinous processes of middle and upper thoracic vertebrae; *action,* supports and extends vertebral column; *nerve supply,* dorsal branches of thoracic and upper lumbar.

m. sple'nus cap'itis [NA], splenius muscle of head; *origin*, from ligamentum nuchae of last four cervical vertebrae and supraspinous ligament of first and second thoracic vertebrae; *insertion*, lateral half of superior nuchal line and mastoid process; *action*, rotates head and extends neck; *nerve supply*, dorsal branches of second to sixth cervical.

m. sple'nius cer'vicis [NA], splenius muscle of neck; *origin*, from supraspinous ligament and spinous processes of third to fifth thoracic vertebrae; *insertion*, posterior tubercles of transverse processes of first and second (sometimes third) cervical vertebrae; *action*, rotates and extends neck; *nerve supply*, dorsal branches of fourth to eighth cervical.

m. stape'dius [NA], stapedius; stapedius muscle; *origin*, internal walls of pyramidal eminence in tympanic cavity; *insertion*, neck of stapes; *action*, draws head of stapes backward; *nerve supply*, facial.

m. sterna'lis [NA], sternal muscle; inconstant muscle, running parallel to sternum across costosternal origin of pectoralis major, and usually connected with sternocleidomastoid and rectus abdominis muscles.

m. sternocleidomastoi'deus [NA], sternocleidomastoid muscle; *origin*, anterior surface of manubrium sterni and sternal end of clavicle; *insertion*, mastoid process and lateral half of superior nuchal line; *action*, turns head obliquely to opposite side; when acting together, flex neck and extend head; *nerve supply*, accessory.

m. sternohyoi'deus [NA], sternohyoid muscle; *origin*, posterior surface of manubrium sterni and first costal cartilage; *insertion*, body of hyoid bone; *action*, depresses hyoid bone; *nerve supply*, upper cervical through ansa cervicalis.

m. sternothyroi'deus [NA], sternothyroid muscle; *origin*, posterior surface of manubrium sterni and first or second costal cartilage; *insertion*, oblique line of thyroid cartilage; *action*, depresses larynx; *nerve supply*, upper cervical through ansa cervicalis.

m. styloglos'sus [NA], styloglossus muscle; *origin*, lower end of styloid process; *insertion*, side and undersurface of tongue; *nerve supply*, hypoglossal; *action*, retracts tongue.

m. stylohyoi'deus [NA], stylohyoid muscle; *origin*, styloid process of temporal bone; *insertion*, hyoid bone by two slips on either side of intermediate tendon of digastric; *action*, elevates hyoid bone; *nerve supply*, facial.

m. stylopharyn'geus [NA], stylopharyngeal muscle; *origin*, root of styloid process; *insertion*, thyroid cartilage and wall of pharynx; *nerve supply*, glossopharyngeal; *action*, elevates pharynx and larynx.

m. subcla'vius [NA], subclavian muscle; *origin*, first costal cartilage; *insertion*, inferior surface of acromial end of clavicle; *action*, fixes clavicle or elevates first rib; *nerve supply*, subclavian from brachial plexus.

m. subcosta'lis [NA], subcostal muscle; one of a number of inconstant muscles having same direction

as intercostales interni, but passing deep to one or more ribs.

m. subscapula'ris [NA], subscapular muscle; *origin*, subscapulara fossa; *insertion*, lesser tuberosity of humerus; *nerve supply*, upper and lower subscapular from fifth and sixth cervical; *action*, rotates arm medially.

m. supina'tor [NA], supinator muscle; *origin*, lateral epicondyle of humerus and supinator ridge of ulna; *insertion*, anterior and lateral surface of radius; *nerve supply*, radial; *action*, supinates forearm.

m. supraspina'tus [NA], supraspinous muscle; *origin*, supraspinous fossa of scapula; *insertion*, great tuberosity of humerus; *nerve supply*, suprascapular from fifth and sixth cervical; *action*, abducts arm.

m. suspenso'rius duode'ni [NA], suspensory muscle of the duodenum; a broad flat band of smooth muscle and fibrous tissue attached to right crus of diaphragm and to duodenum at its junction with jejunum.

m. tarsa'lis [NA], tarsal muscle; **(1)** inferior, poorly developed smooth muscle in the lower eyelid that acts to widen the palpebral fissure; **(2)** superior, a well defined layer of smooth muscle that extends from the aponeurosis of the m. levator palpebrae superioris to the superior tarsus; it is innervated by sympathetic nerves and acts to hold the upper lid in an elevated position.

m. tempora'lis [NA], temporal muscle; *origin*, temporal fossa; *insertion*, anterior border of ramus and apex of coronoid process of mandible; *action*, closes jaw; *nerve supply*, deep temporal branches of mandibular division of trigeminal.

m. temporoparieta'lis [NA], temporoparietal muscle; the part of m. epicranius that arises from lateral part of galea aponeurotica and inserts in cartilage of auricle.

m. ten'sor fas'ciae la'tae [NA], tensor muscle of the fascia lata; *origin*, anterior superior spine and adjacent lateral surface of ilium; *insertion*, iliotibial band of fascia lata; *nerve supply*, superior gluteal; *action*, tenses fascia lata; flexes, abducts and medially rotates thigh.

m. ten'sor tym'pani [NA], tensor muscle of tympanic membrane; *origin*, auditory tube; *insertion*, handle of malleus; *nerve supply*, branches of trigeminal through otic ganglion; *action*, draws handle of malleus medialward and tenses tympanic membrane.

m. ten'sor ve'li palati'ni [NA], tensor muscle of palatine velum; *origin*, scaphoid fossa of sphenoid, auditory tube, and spine of sphenoid; *insertion*, posterior border of hard palate and aponeurosis of soft palate; *nerve supply*, branches of trigeminal nerve through otic ganglion; *action*, tenses soft palate; opens auditory tube.

m. te'res ma'jor [NA], teres major muscle; *origin*, inferior angle and lower third of border of scapula; *insertion*, medial border of intertubercular groove of humerus; *nerve supply*, lower subscapular from fifth and sixth cervical; *action*, adducts and extends arm and rotates it medially.

m. te'res mi'nor [NA], teres minor muscle; *origin*, lateral border of scapula; *insertion*, great tuberosity of humerus; *nerve supply*, axillary from fifth and sixth cervical; *action*, adducts arm and rotates it laterally.

m. thyroarytenoi'deus [NA], thyroarytenoid muscle; *origin*, inner surface of thyroid cartilage; *insertion*, muscular process and outer surface of arytenoid; *nerve supply*, recurrent laryngeal; *action*, shortens vocal cords.

m. thyroepiglot'ticus [NA], thyroepiglottic muscle; *origin*, inner surface of thyroid cartilage in common with m. thyroarytenoideus; *insertion*, aryepiglottic fold and margin of epiglottis; *nerve supply*, recurrent laryngeal; action, depresses base of epiglottis.

m. thyrohyoi'deus [NA], thyrohyoid muscle; a continuation of the sternothyroid; *origin*, oblique line of thyroid cartilage; *insertion*, body of hyoid bone; *action*, approximates hyoid bone to larynx; *nerve supply*, upper cervical passing with hypoglossal.

m. tibia'lis [NA], tibial muscle; **(1)** anterior, *origin*, upper two-thirds of lateral surface of tibia, interosseous membrane, and intermuscular septum; *insertion*, medial cuneiform and base of first metatarsal; *nerve supply*, deep peroneal; *action*, dorsiflexion and inversion of foot; **(2)** posterior, *origin*, soleal line and posterior surface of tibia, the head and shaft of the fibula between the medial crest and interosseous border, and the posterior surface of interosseous membrane; *insertion*, navicular, three cuneiform, cuboid, and second, third, and fourth metatarsal bones; *nerve supply*, tibial; *action*, plantar flexion and inversion of foot.

m. trachea'lis [NA], tracheal muscle; the band of smooth muscular fibers in the fibrous membrane connecting posteriorly the ends of the tracheal rings.

m. tra'gicus [NA], muscle of the tragus; a band of vertical muscular fibers on outer surface of tragus of ear.

m. transversospina'lis [NA], transversospinal muscle; the group of muscles that originate from transverse processes of vertebrae and pass to spinous processes of higher vertebrae; act as rotators and include semispinalis, multifidus, and rotatores.

m. transver'sus abdom'inis [NA], transverse muscle of abdomen; *origin*, seventh to 12th costal cartilages, lumbar fascia, iliac crest, and inguinal ligament; *insertion*, xiphoid cartilage and linea alba and, through falx inguinalis, pubic tubercle and pecten; *action*, compresses abdominal contents; *nerve supply*, lower thoracic.

m. transver'sus lin'guae [NA], transverse muscle of tongue; intrinsic muscle of tongue, fibers of which arise from septum and radiate to dorsum and sides.

m. transver'sus men'ti [NA], transverse muscle of chin; inconstant fibers of m. depresser anguli oris

which continue into neck and cross to opposite side inferior to chin.

m. transver'sus nu'chae [NA], transverse muscle of nape; occasional muscle passing between tendons of trapezius and sternocleidomastoid.

m. transver'sus perine'i profun'dus [NA], deep transverse muscle of perineum; *origin*, ramus of ischium; *insertion*, with its fellow in a median raphe; *nerve supply*, pudendal; *action*, assists sphincter urethrae.

m. transver'sus perine'i superficia'lis [NA], superficial transverse muscle of perineum; an inconstant muscle; *origin*, ramus of ischium; *insertion*, central tendon of perineum; *nerve supply*, pudendal; *action*, draws back and fixes central tendon of perineum.

m. transver'sus thora'cis [NA], transverse muscle of thorax; *origin*, dorsal surface of xiphoid cartilage and of body of sternum; *insertion*, second to sixth costal cartilages; *action*, narrows chest; *nerve supply*, intercostal.

m. trape'zius [NA], trapezius muscle; *origin*, superior nuchal line, external occipital protuberance, ligamentum nuchae, spinous processes of seventh cervical and thoracic vertebrae and corresponding supraspinous ligaments; *insertion*, lateral third of posterior surface of clavicle, medial side of acromion, and upper border of spine of scapula; *action*, draws head to one side or backward, rotates scapula; *nerve supply*, accessory and cervical plexus.

m. tri'ceps bra'chii [NA], triceps muscle of arm; *origin*, long or scapular head from lateral border of scapula below glenoid fossa, lateral head from lateral and posterior surface of humerus below greater tubercle, medial head from posterior surface of humerus below radial groove; *insertion*, olecranon of ulna; *nerve supply*, radial; *action*, extends forearm.

m. tri'ceps su'rae [NA], triceps muscle of calf; gastrocnemius and soleus considered as one muscle.

m. u'vulae [NA], muscle of the uvula; *origin*, posterior nasal spine; *insertion*, forms chief bulk of uvula; *nerve supply*, pharyngeal plexus; *action*, raises uvula.

m. vas'tus [NA], great muscle; **(1)** intermediate, *origin*, anterior surface of shaft of femur; *insertion*, tibial tuberosity; *action*, extends leg; *nerve supply*, femoral; **(2)** lateral, *origin*, lateral lip of linea aspera as far as great trochanter; *insertion*, tibial tuberosity; *action*, extends leg; *nerve supply*, femoral; **(3)** medial, *origin*, medial lip of linea aspera; *insertion*, tibial tuberosity; *action*, extends leg; *nerve supply*, femoral.

m. vertica'lis lin'guae [NA], vertical muscle of tongue; intrinsic muscle of tongue, consisting of fibers that pass from aponeurosis of dorsum to aponeurosis of inferior surface.

m. voca'lis [NA], vocal muscle; *origin*, depression between two laminae of thyroid cartilage; *insertion*, vocal process of arytenoid; *nerve supply*, recurrent laryngeal; *action*, shortens and relaxes vocal cords.

m. zygomat′icus [NA], zygomatic muscle; (1) greater, *origin*, zygomatic bone anterior to temporozygomatic suture; *insertion*, muscles at angle of mouth; *action*, draws upper lip upward and laterally; *nerve supply*, facial; (2) smaller, *origin*, zygomatic bone posterior to zygomaticomaxillary suture; *insertion*, orbicularis oris of upper lip; *action*, draws upper lip upward and outward; *nerve supply*, facial.

mu′sicother′apy. Melodiotherapy; treatment of mental disorders by means of music.

mussitation (mus′ĭ-ta′shun) [L. *mussito*, to murmur constantly]. Movements of the lips as if speaking, but without sound; observed in delirium and in semicoma.

mu′tacism. Mytacism.

mutagen (mu′tă-jen) [L. *muto*, to change, + G. *-gen*, producing]. Any agent that causes production of a mutation.

mu′tagen′esis. Production of a mutation.

mu′tagen′ic. Having the power to cause mutations.

mu′tant. An organism possessing one or more genes that have undergone mutation.

mu′tase. Any enzyme that catalyzes the apparent migration of groups within one molecule, or from one molecule to another.

mutation (mu-ta′shun) [L. *muto*, pp. *-atus*, to change]. **1.** A change in the character of a gene that is perpetuated in subsequent divisions of the cell in which it occurs. **2.** Sudden production of a species, as distinguished from variation.

missense m. [L. *mitto*, to send away], m. in which a base change or substitution results in a codon that causes insertion of a different amino acid into the growing polypeptide chain, giving rise to an altered protein.

point m., m. that involves a single nucleotide; may consist of loss of a nucleotide, substitution of one nucleotide for another, or the insertion of an additional nucleotide.

somatic m., m. occurring in the general body cells (as opposed to the germ cells).

suppressor m., m. that alters the anticodon in a tRNA so that it is complementary to a termination codon, thus suppressing termination of the amino acid chain.

transition m., a point m. involving substitution of one base-pair for another, *i.e.*, replacement of one purine for another and of one pyrimidine for another pyrimidine without change in the purine-pyrimidine orientation.

transversion m., a point m. involving base substitution in which the orientation of purine and pyrimidine is reversed, in contradistinction to transition m.

mute [L. *mutus*]. **1.** Unable or unwilling to speak. **2.** One who does not have the faculty of speech.

mutilation (mu-tĭ-la′shun) [L. *mutilatio*, fr. *mutilo*, pp. *-atus*, to maim]. Disfigurement or injury by removal or destruction of any conspicuous or essential part of the body.

mu′tism [L. *mutus*, mute]. Organic or functional absence of the faculty of speech.

akinetic m., a syndrome characterized by m., loss of voluntary and emotional movement, and apparent loss of emotional feeling; related to lesions of the upper brain stem.

elective m., m. due to hysteria, abnormal inhibition, or emotional causes.

mu′ton. In genetics, the smallest unit of a chromosome in which alteration can be effective in causing a mutation.

mutualism (mu′tu-al-izm). Symbiotic relationship in which both species derive benefit.

mutualist (mu′tu-al-ist) [L. *mutuus*, in return, mutual]. Symbion.

Mv Former symbol for mendelevium.

mV Millivolt.

MVV Maximum voluntary *ventilation*.

MW Molecular *weight*.

my. Myopia.

myalgia (mi-al′jĭ-ah) [G. *mys*, muscle, + *algos*, pain]. Myodynia; pain in a muscle.

epidemic m., epidemic *pleurodynia*.

my′asthe′nia [G. *mys*, muscle, + *astheneia*, weakness]. Muscular weakness.

m. angiosclerot′ica, intermittent *claudication*.

m. gra′vis, Goldflam disease; a chronic progressive muscular weakness, beginning usually in the face and throat, unaccompanied by atrophy; due to a defect in myoneural conduction.

my′asthen′ic. Relating to myasthenia.

myatonia, myatony (mi-ă-to′nĭ-ah, mi-at′o-nĭ) [G. *mys*, muscle, + *a-* priv. + *tonos*, tone]. Amyotonia; abnormal extensibility of a muscle.

m. congen′ita, *amyotonia* congenita.

myatrophy (mi-at′ro-fĭ). Myoatrophy.

mycelia (mi-se′lĭ-ah). Plural of mycelium.

myce′lian. Pertaining to a mycelium.

mycelium, pl. **mycelia** (mi-se′lĭ-um, -ah) [G. *mykēs*, fungus, + *hēlos*, nail, wart]. The mass of hyphae making up a colony of fungi.

my′cete [G. *mykēs*, fungus]. A fungus.

mycetism, mycetis′mus (mi′se-tizm, -tiz′mus) [G. *mykēs*, fungus]. Mushroom poisoning.

mycet-, myceto- [G. *mykēs*, fungus]. Combining forms relating to fungus. See also myco-.

mycetogenetic, mycetogenic (mi-se′to-jĕ-net′ik, -jen-′ik; mi′se-to-) [G. *mykēs*, fungus, + *gennētos*, begotten]. Caused by fungi.

myceto′ma. 1. A chronic infection, usually involving the feet, characterized by the formation of localized lesions with tumefactions and multiple draining sinuses; the exudate contains granules that may be yellow, white, red, brown, or black, depending upon the causative agent. M. is caused by two principal groups of microorganisms: actinomyces and true fungi. **2.** Any tumor produced by filamentous fungi.

my′cid [G. *mykēs*, fungus, + *-id*]. An allergic reaction to a remote focus of mycotic infection.

myco- [G. *mykēs*, fungus]. Combining form relating to fungus. See also mycet-.

my'cobacte'ria Organisms belonging to the genus *Mycobacterium*.

mycobacteriosis (mi'ko-bak-tēr-ĭ-o'sis). Infection with mycobacteria.

Mycobacterium (mi'ko-bak-tēr'ĭ-um) [myco- + bacterium]. A genus of aerobic, nonmotile bacteria (family Mycobacteriaceae) containing Gram-positive rods; parasitic and saprophytic species occur. The type species is *M. tuberculosis.*

M. bal'nei, *M. marinum.*

M. kansas'ii, a species causing a tuberculosis-like pulmonary disease, and various infections.

M. lep'rae, Hansen's bacillus; an obligately parasitic species of man which causes leprous lesions.

M. mari'num, M. balnei; a species causing swimming pool granuloma.

M. scrofula'ceum, a species frequently associated with cervical adenitis in children.

M. tuberculo'sis, Koch's bacillus (1); tubercle bacillus (human); a species that causes tuberculosis in man; it is the type species of the genus *M.*

my'coder'mati'tis. An eruption of mycotic origin.

mycologist (mi-kol'o-jist). A person specializing in mycology.

mycology (mi-kol'o-jĭ) [myco- + G. *logos*, study]. The science and study of fungi.

mycophage (mi'ko-fāj) [myco- + G. *phagein*, to eat]. A virus the host of which is a fungus.

Mycoplasma. (mi'ko-plaz-mah) [myco- + G. *plasma*, something formed (plasm)]. A genus of aerobic to facultatively anaerobic bacteria (family Mycoplasmataceae) containing Gram-negative cells that do not possess a true cell wall, but are bounded by a three-layered membrane; they are parasitic to pathogenic. The type species is *M. mycoides.*

M. hom'inis, a species found in the genital tract and anal canal of man.

M. mycoi'des, a species containing two subspecies, *M. mycoides* subsp. *mycoides,* the type subspecies, and *M. mycoides* subsp. *capri,* which cause pleuropneumonia in cattle and goats; the type species of the genus *M.*

M. pharyn'gis, a species occurring as a commensal in human oropharynx.

M. pneumo'niae, Eaton agent; a species causing primary atypical pneumonia in man.

mycoplasma, pl. **mycoplasmata** (mi-ko-plaz'mah, -plaz'mă-tah). Any member of the genus *Mycoplasma.*

Mycoplasmatales (mi'ko-plaz-mă-ta'lēz). An order of Gram-negative bacteria containing cells which are bounded by a three-layered membrane but which do not possess a true cell wall; pathogenic and saprophytic species occur, including the pleuropneumonia-like *organisms* (PPLO).

mycosis (mi-ko'sis) [myco- + G. *-osis*, condition]. Any disease caused by fungi.

m. fungoi'des, a chronic progressive lymphoma arising in the skin (so-called because tumors in the late stage resemble mushrooms); initially, the disease simulates eczema or other inflammatory dermatoses.

mycot'ic. Relating to a mycosis or to a fungus.

mycotoxicosis (mi'ko-tok-sĭ-ko'sis). Intoxication due to ingestion of preformed substances produced by the action of certain molds on particular foodstuffs, or ingestion of the fungi themselves.

mycotoxins (mi'ko-tok-sinz). Toxic compounds produced by certain mushrooms.

my'covirus. A virus that infects fungi.

mydriasis (mĭ-drī'ă-sis) [G.]. Dilation of the pupil.

mydriatic (mĭ-drī-at'ik). Causing mydriasis or dilation of the pupil.

myectomy (mi-ek'to-mĭ) [G. *mys*, muscle, + *ektomē*, excision]. Exsection of a portion of muscle.

myectopy, myectopia (mi-ek'to-pĭ, -to'pĭ-ah) [G. *mys*, muscle, + *ektopos*, out of place]. Dislocation of a muscle.

myel-, myelo- [G. *myelos*, medulla, marrow]. Combining form denoting relationship to the bone marrow, the spinal cord and medulla oblongata, or the myelin sheath of nerve fibers.

myelapoplexy (mi'el-ap'o-plek'sĭ) [myel- + G. *apoplēxia*, apoplexy]. Hematomyelia.

myelatelia (mi'el-ă-te'lĭ-ah) [myel- + G. *ateleia*, incompleteness]. A developmental defect of the spinal cord.

myele'mia [myel- + G. *haima*, blood]. Myelocytosis.

myelencephalon (mi'el-en-sef'ă-lon) [myel- + G. *enkephalos*, brain] [NA]. *Medulla* oblongata.

my'elin. **1.** The lipoproteinaceous material enveloping the axon of myelinated nerve fibers, composed of regularly alternating layers of lipids and protein. **2.** Droplets of lipid formed during autolysis and postmortem decomposition.

my'elinated. Medullated (2); having a myelin sheath.

myelination, myelinization (mi'ĕ-lĭ-na'shun, mi'el-in-i-za'shun). Acquisition, development, or formation of a myelin sheath around a nerve fiber.

myelinolysis (mi'ĕ-lĭ-nol'ĭ-sis) [myelin + G. *lysis*, dissolution]. Dissolution of the myelin sheaths of nerve fibers.

myelitic (mi-ĕ-lit'ik). Relating to or affected by myelitis.

myelitis (mi-ĕ-li'tis) [myel- + G. *-itis*, inflammation]. Inflammation of the spinal cord, or of the bone marrow.

bulbar m., inflammation of the medulla oblongata.

subacute necrotizing m., a disorder of the lower spinal cord resulting in progressive paraplegia.

myelo-. See myel-.

my'eloblast [myelo- + G. *blastos*, germ]. Premyelocyte; an immature cell in the granulocytic series, occurring normally in bone marrow but not in the circulating blood, which matures into a promyelocyte and then a myelocyte.

my'eloblaste'mia [myeloblast + G. *haima*, blood]. Presence of myeloblasts in the circulating blood.

my'eloblasto'ma [myeloblast + G. *-oma*, tumor]. A nodular focus or circumscribed accumulation of myeloblasts.

my'eloblasto'sis. Presence of unusually large numbers of myeloblasts in the circulating blood, tissues, or both.

myelocele (mi'ĕ-lo-sēl). **1** [myelo- + G. *kēle*, hernia]. Protrusion of the spinal cord in spina bifida. **2** [G. *myelos*, marrow, + *koilia*, a hollow]. The central canal of the spinal cord.

my'elocyst'ic. Pertaining to or characterized by the presence of a myelocyst.

myelocyst (mi'ĕ-lo-sist) [myelo- + G. *kystis*, bladder]. Any cyst that develops from a rudimentary medullary canal in the central nervous system.

myelocystocele (mi'ĕ-lo-sis'to-sēl) [myelo- + G. *kystis*, bladder, + *kēle*, tumor]. Spina bifida containing spinal cord substance.

myelocystomeningocele (mi'ĕ-lo-sis'to-mĕ-ning'go-sēl) [myelo- + G. *kystis*, bladder, + *mēninx* (*mēning*-), membrane, + *kēle*, hernia]. Meningomyelocele.

myelocyte (mi'ĕ-lo-sīt) [myelo- + G. *kytos*, cell]. **1.** A young cell of the granulocytic series, occurring normally in bone marrow but not in circulating blood, which matures into a metamyelocyte. **2.** A nerve cell of the gray matter of the brain or spinal cord.

myelocythemia (mi'ĕ-lo-si-the'mĭ-ah) [myelocyte + G. *haima*, blood]. Presence of myelocytes in the circulating blood, especially in persistently large numbers.

myelocytic (mi'ĕ-lo-sit'ik). Pertaining to or characterized by myelocytes.

myelocytoma (mi'ĕ-lo-si-to'mah) [myelocyte + G. *-oma*, tumor]. A nodular focus or circumscribed, relatively dense accumulation of myelocytes.

myelocytomatosis (mi'ĕ-lo-si'to-mă-to'sis). A form of tumor involving chiefly myelocytes.

myelocytosis (mi'ĕ-lo-si-to'sis) [myelocyte + G. *-osis*, condition]. Myelemia; occurrence of abnormally large numbers of myelocytes in the circulating blood, tissues, or both.

myelodysplasia (mi'ĕ-lo-dis-pla'zĭ-ah) [myelo- + G. *dys*-, difficult, + *plasis*, a molding]. An abnormality in development of the spinal cord.

my'elofibro'sis. See myeloid *metaplasia*.

myelogenesis (mi'ĕ-lo-jen'ĕ-sis). Development of bone marrow.

myelogenetic, myelogenic (mi'ĕ-lo-jen-et'ik, -jen'ik). **1.** Relating to myelogenesis. **2.** Myelogenous; produced by or originating in the bone marrow.

myelogenous (mi'ĕ-lo-loj'ĕ-nus). Myelogenetic (2).

myelogone, myelogonium (mi'ĕ-lo-gōn, -go'nĭ-um) [myelo- + G. *gonē*, seed]. An immature white blood cell of the myeloid series characterized by a relatively large, fairly deeply stained, finely reticulated nucleus that contains palely stained nucleoli, and a scant amount of rimlike, nongranular, moderately basophilic cytoplasm.

myelography (mi-ĕ-log'ră-fī) [myelo- + G. *graphē*, a drawing]. Radiography of the spinal cord after injection of a radiopaque substance into the spinal arachnoid space.

myeloid (mi'ĕ-loyd). **1.** Pertaining to, derived from, or manifesting certain features of the bone marrow. **2.** Sometimes used with reference to the spinal cord. **3.** Pertaining to certain characteristics of myelocytic forms, not necessarily implying origin, in the bone marrow.

my'eloido'sis. General hyperplasia of myeloid tissue.

my'elolipo'ma. Misnomer for certain nodular foci that are not neoplasms, but probably represent accumulations of cells derived from localized proliferation of reticuloendothelial tissue in the blood sinuses of the adrenal glands; grossly, the nodules may seem to be adipose tissue, but actually are foci of bone marrow.

myeloma (mi-ĕ-lo'mah) [myelo- + G. *-oma*, tumor]. A tumor composed of cells derived from hemopoietic tissues of the bone marrow.

   endothelial m., Ewing's *tumor*.

   giant cell m., giant cell *tumor* of bone.

   multiple m., multiple myelomatosis; a clinically characteristic monoclonal gammopathy that occurs more frequently in men than in women and is associated with anemia, hemorrhages, recurrent, infections, and weakness; ordinarily regarded as a malignant neoplasm that originates in bone marrow and involves chiefly the skeleton; clinical features are attributable to the sites of involvement and to abnormalities in formation of plasma protein, the most frequent being: occurrence of Bence Jones proteinuria, great increase in γ-globulin in the plasma, occasional formation of cryoglobulin, and a form of primary amyloidosis.

   plasma cell m., (1) multiple m.; (2) plasmacytoma of bone, usually a solitary lesion and not associated with the occurrence of Bence Jones protein or other disturbances in the metabolism of protein.

my'elomala'cia [myelo- + G. *malakia*, a softness]. Softening of the spinal cord.

my'elomato'sis. The occurrence of myelomas in various sites.

myelomeningocele (mi'ĕ-lo-mĕ-ning'go-sēl) [myelo- + G. *mēninx*, membrane, + *kēle*, hernia]. Meningomyelocele.

my'elomere [myelo- + G. *meros*, part]. A neuromere of the spinal cord.

myeloneuritis (mi'ĕ-lo-nu-ri'tis). Neuromyelitis.

myelonic (mi-ĕ-lon'ik) [G. *myelon*, fr. *myelos*, marrow]. Relating to the spinal cord.

my'elop'etal [myelo- + L. *peto*, to seek]. Proceeding in a direction toward the spinal cord; said of different nerve impulses.

my'elopath'ic. Relating to myelopathy.

myelopathy (mi-ĕ-lop′ă-thĭ) [myelo- + G. *pathos,* suffering]. **1.** Disturbance or disease of the spinal cord. **2.** A disease of the myelopoietic tissues.

myelophthisic (mi′ĕ-lo-tiz′ik, -thiz′ik). Relating to myelophthisis.

myelophthisis (mi-ĕ-lof′thĭ-sis, mi′ĕ-lo-ti′sis, -te′sis) [myelo- + G. *phthisis,* a wasting away]. **1.** Wasting or atrophy of the spinal cord. **2.** Panmyelophthisis; replacement of hemopoietic tissue in the bone marrow by abnormal tissue, usually fibrous tissue or malignant tumors that are most commonly meta-static carcinomas.

my′eloplast [myelo- + G. *plastos,* formed]. Any of the leukocytic series of cells in the bone marrow, especially young forms.

myelopoiesis (mi′ĕ-lo-poy-e′sis) [myelo- + G. *poiēsis,* a making]. Formation of the tissue elements of bone marrow, any of the types of blood cells derived from bone marrow, or both processes.

my′elopoiet′ic. Relating to myelopoiesis.

my′eloprolif′erative. Pertaining to or characterized by unusual proliferation of myelopoietic tissue.

my′eloradic′uli′tis [myelo- + L. *radicula,* root, + G. *-itis,* inflammation]. Inflammation of the spinal cord and nerve roots.

my′eloradic′ulodyspla′sia [myelo- + L. *radicula,* root, + dysplasia]. Congential maldevelopment of the spinal cord and spinal nerve roots.

myeloradiculopathy (mi′ĕ-lo-ră-dik′u-lop′ă-thĭ) [myelo- + L. *radicula,* root, + G. *pathos,* disease]. Radiculomyelopathy; disease involving the spinal cord and nerve roots.

myelorrhagia (mi′ĕ-lo-ra′jĭ-ah) [myelo- + G. *rhēgnymi,* to burst forth]. Hematomyelia.

myelorrhaphy (mi-ĕ-lor′ă-fĭ) [myelo- + G. *rhaphē,* a seam]. Suture of a wound of the spinal cord.

my′elosarco′ma [myelo- + G. *sarx,* flesh, + *-ōma,* tumor]. A malignant neoplasm derived from bone marrow or one of its cellular elements.

my′elosarco′mato′sis. Widespread myelosarcomas.

myelosclerosis (mi′ĕ-lo-sklĕ-ro′sis) [myelo- + G. *sklērōsis,* induration]. See myeloid *metaplasia.*

myelo′sis. 1. Abnormal proliferation of tissue or cellular elements of bone marrow. **2.** Abnormal proliferation of medullary tissue in the spinal cord.

erythremic m., a neoplastic process involving the erythropoietic tissue, characterized by anemia, irregular fever, splenomegaly, hepatomegaly, hemorrhagic disorders, and numerous erythroblasts in all stages of maturation in the circulating blood. Acute and chronic forms are recognized, the former is also called Di Guglielmo's disease and acute erythremia.

my′elot′omy [myelo- + G. *tomē,* incision]. Incision of the spinal cord.

myelotomography (mi′ĕ-lo-to-mog′ră-fĭ). Tomographic depiction of the spinal subarachnoid space filled with contrast media.

myelotoxic (mi′ĕ-lo-tok′sik). **1.** Inhibitory, depressant, or destructive to one or more of the components of bone marrow. **2.** Pertaining to, derived

from, or manifesting the features of diseased bone marrow.

myenteric (mi-en-tĕr′ik). Relating to the myenteron.

myen′teron [G. *mys,* muscle, + *enteron,* intestine]. The muscular coat of the intestine.

myesthesia (mi-es-the′zĭ-ah) [G. *mys,* muscle, + *aisthēsis,* sensation]. Kinesthetic or muscular sense; the sensation felt in muscle when it is contracting.

myiasis (mi-i′ă-sis) [G. *myia,* fly]. Any infection due to invasion of tissues or cavities of the body by larvae of dipterous insects by larva migrans.

mylohyoid (mi′lo-hi′oyd) [G. *mylē,* a mill; pl. *mylai,* molar teeth]. Relating to the molar teeth, or posterior portion of the lower jaw, and to the hyoid bone.

myo- [G. *mys,* muscle]. Combining form relating to muscle.

myoarchitectonic (mi′o-ar′kĭ-tek-ton′ik) [myo- + G. *architektonikos,* relating to construction]. Relating to the structural arrangement of muscle or of fibers in general.

myoatrophy (mi-o-at′ro-fĭ). Myatrophy; muscular atrophy.

my′oblast [myo- + G. *blastos,* germ]. Sarcoblast; a primitive muscle cell with the potentiality of developing into a muscle fiber.

myoblas′tic. Relating to a myoblast or to the mode of formation of muscle cells.

myoblastoma (mi′o-blas-to′mah) [myo- + G. *blastos,* germ, + *-oma,* tumor]. A tumor of immature muscle cells.

granular cell m., granular cell *tumor.*

myobra′dia [myo- + G. *bradys,* slow]. Sluggish reaction of muscle following stimulation.

myocar′dial. Relating to the myocardium.

myocardiograph (mi-o-kar′dĭ-o-graf) [myo- + G. *kardia,* heart, + *graphō,* to record]. An instrument used to make tracings of the movements of the heart muscle.

myocardiopathy (mi′o-kar-dĭ-op′ă-thĭ) [myocardium + G. *pathos,* suffering]. Cardiomyopathy.

myocardiorraphy (mi′o-kar-dĭ-or′ă-fĭ) [myocardium + G. *raphē,* suture]. Suture of the myocardium.

myocardi′tis. Inflammation of the muscular walls of the heart.

acute isolated m., Fiedler's m., an acute interstitial m. not affecting the endocardium and pericardium.

myocardium, pl. **myocardia** (mi′o-kar′dĭ-um, -kar′dĭ-ah) [myo- + G. *kardia,* heart] [NA]. The middle layer of the heart, consisting of cardiac muscle.

myocardo′sis. 1. Symptomatic signs of cardiac disease without any discoverable pathologic lesion. **2.** Any degenerative condition of the heart muscle, except myofibrosis.

myocele (mi′o-sēl). **1** [myo- + G. *kēlē,* hernia]. Protrusion of muscle substance through a rent in its sheath. **2** [myo- + G. *koilia,* a cavity]. The small cavity that appears in somites.

myocellulitis (mi'o-sel-u-li'tis) [myo- + Mod. L. *cellularis*, cellular (tissue), + G. *-itis*, inflammation]. Inflammation of muscle and cellular tissue.

myocerosis (mi'o-se-ro'sis) [myo- + G. *kēros*, wax]. Waxy degeneration of the muscles.

myoclonia (mi'o-klo'nī-ah) [myo- + G. *klonos*, a tumult]. Any disorder characterized by myoclonus.

myoclon'ic. Showing myoclonus.

myoclonus (mi-o-klo'nus) [myo- + G. *klonus*, tumult]. Clonic spasm or twitching of a muscle or group of muscles.

    m. mul'tiplex, Friedreich's disease; polyclonia; polymyoclonus; paramyoclonus; a disorder marked by rapid contractions occurring simultaneously or consecutively in various unrelated muscles.

    nocturnal m., frequently repeated muscular jerks occurring at the moment of dropping off to sleep.

myocutaneous (mi'o-ku-ta'ne-us). **1.** Musculocutaneous. **2.** Denoting a parcel comprising a muscle and its investments and vascular supply, the overlying skin, and the intervening tissues.

my'ocyte [myo- + G. *kytos*, cell]. A muscle cell.

    Anitschkow m., cardiac *histiocyte.*

myocytoma (mi'o-si-to'mah). A benign neoplasm derived from muscle.

myode'mia [myo- + G. *dēmos*, tallow]. Fatty degeneration of muscle.

myodynia (mi'o-din'ĭ-ah) [myo- + G. *odynē*, pain]. Myalgia.

myodystony (mi-o-dis'to-nĭ) [myo- + G. *dys-*, difficult, + *tonos*, tone, tension]. A condition of slow relaxation, interrupted by a succession of slight contractions, following electrical stimulation of a muscle.

myodystrophy (mi-o-dis'tro-fĭ) [myo- + G. *dys-*, difficult, poor, + *trophē*, nourishment]. Muscular *dystrophy.*

myoedema (mi'o-ĕ-de'mah) [myo- + G. *oidēma*, swelling]. Idiomuscular contraction; mounding; localized contraction of a degenerating muscle, occurring at the point of a sharp blow; the response is independent of the nerve supply.

my'oelas'tic. Pertaining to closely associated smooth muscle fibers and elastic connective tissue.

myoendocarditis (mi-o-en-do-kar-di'tis) [myo- + G. *endon*, within, + *kardia*, heart, + *-itis*, inflammation]. Inflammation of the muscular wall and lining membrane of the heart.

my'oepithe'lial. Relating to myoepithelium.

my'oepithelio'ma [myo- + epithelium, + G. *-ōma*, tumor]. A benign tumor of myoepithelial cells.

myoepithelium (mi'o-ep-ĭ-the'lĭ-um) [myo- + epithelium]. Contractile spindle-shaped cells arranged longitudinally or obliquely around sweat glands and the secretory alveoli of the mammary gland.

myofascitis (mi'o-fă-si'tis) [myo- + fascitis]. *Myositis* fibrosa.

myofi'bril [myo- + Mod. L. *fibrilla*, fibril]. One of the fine longitudinal fibrils occurring in a skeletal or cardiac muscle fiber; in striated muscle, the fibril is made up of ultramicroscopic thick and thin myofilaments.

myofibroblast (mi-o-fi'bro-blast). The cell responsible for contracture of wounds; has characteristics of fibroblasts and smooth muscle.

myofibro'ma. A benign neoplasm that consists chiefly of fibrous connective tissue, with variable numbers of muscle cells forming portions of the neoplasm.

my'ofibrosi'tis. Perimysiitis (1).

myofibro'sis. Chronic myositis with diffuse hyperplasia of the interstitial connective tissue pressing upon and causing atrophy of the muscular tissue.

myofil'aments. Ultramicroscopic threads making up myofibrils in striated muscle.

myogenesis (mi-o-jen'ĕ-sis) [myo- + G. *genesis*, origin]. Formation of muscle cells or fibers.

myogenet'ic, myogen'ic. Myogenous. **1.** Originating in or starting from muscle. **2.** Relating to the origin of muscle cells or fibers.

myogenous (mi-oj'en-us). Myogenetic.

myoglo'bin (Mb). Muscle hemoglobin; the oxygen-transporting protein of muscle, resembling blood hemoglobin in function, but containing only one heme as part of the molecule and with one-fourth of the molecular weight.

my'oglobinu'ria. Excretion of myoglobin in the urine.

myoglob'ulin. Globulin present in muscle tissue.

myoglobulinemia (mi'o-glob'u-lin-e'mĭ-ah). The presence of myoglobulin in the blood.

myoglobulinuria (mi'o-glob'u-lin-u'rĭ-ah). Excretion of myoglobulin in the urine.

my'ogram [myo- + G. *gramma*, a drawing]. Tracing made by a myograph.

my'ograph [myo- + G. *graphō*, to write]. A recording instrument by which tracings are made of muscular contractions.

myograph'ic. Relating to a myogram, or the record of a myograph.

myography (mi-og'ră-fĭ). The recording of muscular movements by the myograph.

my'oid [myo- + G. *eidos*, appearance]. Resembling muscle.

myokinesimeter (mi'o-kin-ĕ-sim'ĕ-ter) [myo- + G. *kinesis*, movement, + *metron*, measure]. A device for registering the time and extent of contraction muscles in response to electric stimulation.

myokymia (mi-o-ki'mĭ-ah) [myo- + G. *kyma*, wave]. Kymatism; a benign condition, often familial, characterized by an irregular twitching of most of the muscles.

myolipo'ma. A benign neoplasm that consists chiefly of fat cells, with variable numbers of muscle cells forming portions of the neoplasm.

myology (mi-ol'o-jĭ) [myo- + G. *logos*, study]. The branch of science concerned with the muscles and their accessories.

myolysis (mi-ol'ĭ-sis) [myo- + G. *lysis*, dissolution]. Dissolution or liquefaction of muscular tissue.

myoma (mi-o'mah) [myo- + G. *-oma,* tumor]. A benign neoplasm of muscular tissue.

myomalacia (mi'o-mă-la'shĭ-ah) [myo- + G. *malakia,* softness]. Pathologic softening of muscular tissue.

myo'matous. Pertaining to or characterized by the features of a myoma.

myomectomy (mi-o-mek'to-mĭ) [myoma + G. *ektomē,* excision]. Operative removal of a myoma, specifically of a uterine myoma.

myomelanosis (mi'o-mel'ă-no'sis) [myo- + G. *melanōsis,* becoming black]. Abnormal dark pigmentation of muscular tissue.

myomere (mi'o-mēr) [myo- + G. *meros,* a part]. The muscular segment within a metamere.

myometri'tis [myo- + G. *mētra,* uterus, + *-itis,* inflammation]. Inflammation of the muscular wall of the uterus.

myometrium (mi-o-me'trĭ-um) [myo- + G. *mētra,* uterus] [NA]. The muscular wall of the uterus.

myom'ter [myo- + G. *metron,* measure]. An instrument for measuring the extent of a muscular contraction.

my'onecro'sis. Necrosis of muscle.

myoneme (mi'o-nēm) [myo- + G. *nēma,* thread]. A muscle fibril.

myoneural (mi-o-nu'ral) [myo- + G. *neuron,* nerve]. Denoting the synapse of the motor neuron with striated muscle fibers: myoneural junction or motor endplate.

myoneuralgia (mi'o-nu-ral'jĭ-ah) [myo- + G. *neuron,* nerve, + *algos,* pain]. Neuralgic pain in a muscle.

myopal'mus [myo- + G. *palmos,* a quivering]. Muscle twitching.

myoparal'ysis. Muscular paralysis.

myoparesis (mi'o-pă-re'sis). Slight muscular paralysis.

myopath'ic. Relating to disease of the muscles.

myop'athy [myo- + G. *pathos,* suffering]. Any abnormal conditions or disease of the muscular tissues, especially involving skeletal muscle.

   carcinomatous m., Lambert-Eaton *syndrome.*

   centronuclear m., myotubular m.; slowly progressive generalized muscle weakness and atrophy beginning in childhood; the nuclei of most muscle fibers are located near the center rather than at the periphery of the fiber; familial incidence.

   distal m., m. affecting predominantly the distal portions of the limbs usually after age 40; autosomal dominant inheritance.

   myotubular m., centronuclear m.

   nemaline m., congenital, nonprogressive muscle weakness most evident in the proximal muscles, with characteristic threadlike rods seen in the muscle cells composed of Z-band material.

   ocular m., a specific type of progressive muscular dystrophy that begins with the gradual onset of ptosis and sequential involvement of the other extraocular muscles.

myopericarditis (mi'o-pĕr-ĭ-kar-di'tis) [myo- + pericarditis]. Inflammation of the muscular wall of the heart and of the enveloping pericardium.

myopia (M, my.), (mi-o'pĭ-ah) [G. fr. *myo,* to shut, + *ōps,* eye]. Shortsightedness; nearsightedness; an error in refraction or of elongation of the globe of the eye, causing parallel rays to be focused in front of the retina.

   curvature m., m. due to refractive errors consequent upon excessive corneal curvature.

   pathologic m., degenerative m., progressive m. marked by fundus changes, posterior staphyloma, and subnormal corrected acuity.

myopic (mi-op'ik, -o'pik). Relating to myopia.

my'oplasm [myo- + G. *plasma,* a thing formed]. The contractile portion of the muscle cell.

myoplas'tic. Relating to the plastic surgery of the muscles, or to the use of muscular tissue in correcting defects.

myoplasty (mi'o-plas-tĭ) [myo- + G. *plassō,* to form]. Plastic surgery of muscular tissue.

myorrhaphy (mi-or'ă-fĭ) [myo- + G. *raphē,* seam]. Suture of a muscle.

myorrhexis (mi-o-rek'sis) [myo- + G. *rhēxis,* a rupture]. Tearing of a muscle.

myosalpinx (mi-o-sal'pingks) [myo- + salpinx]. The muscular tunic of the uterine tube.

myosarcoma (mi'o-sar-ko'mah). A malignant neoplasm derived from muscular tissue.

myosclerosis (mi'o-sklē-ro'sis). Chronic myositis with hyperplasia of the interstitial connective tissue.

my'osin. A globulin in muscle that in combination with actin forms actomyosin, the fundamental contractile unit of muscle.

myosit'ic. Relating to myositis.

myositis (mi-o-si'tis) [myo- + G. *-itis,* inflammation]. Initis (2); inflammation of a muscle.

   epidemic m., epidemic *pleurodynia.*

   m. fibro'sa, myofascitis; induration of a muscle through an interstitial growth of fibrous tissue.

   multiple m., occurrence of multiple foci of acute inflammation in the muscular tissue and overlying skin in various parts of the body, accompanied by fever and other signs of systemic infection.

   m. ossif'icans, ossification or deposit of bone in muscle with fibrosis, causing pain and swelling muscles.

my'ospasm. Spasmodic muscular contraction.

myotac'tic [myo- + L. *tactus,* a touching]. Relating to the muscular sense.

myotasis (mi-ot'ă-sis) [myo- + G. *tasis,* a stretching]. Stretching of a muscle.

myotat'ic. Relating to myotasis.

myotenositis (mi'o-ten'o-si'tis) [myo- + G. *tenōn,* tendon, + *-itis,* inflammation]. Inflammation of a muscle with its tendon.

myotenotomy (mi'o-tĕ-not'o-mĭ) [myo- + G. *tenōn,* tendon, + *tomē,* incision]. Tenomyotomy; cutting through the principal tendon of a muscle, with division of the muscle itself in whole or in part.

my'otome [myo- + G. *tomos*, a cut]. **1.** A knife for dividing muscle. **2.** Muscle plate; in embryos, that part of the somite that gives rise to skeletal muscle. **3.** All muscles derived from one somite and innervated by one segmental spinal nerve.

myotomy (mi-ot'o-mǐ) [myo- + G. *tomē*, excision]. **1.** Anatomy or dissection of the muscles. **2.** Surgical division of a muscle.

myoto'nia [myo- + G. *tonos*, tension, stretching]. Delayed relaxation of a muscle after an initial contraction.

   m. atroph'ica, myotonic *dystrophy*.

   m. congen'ita, Thomsen's disease; a hereditary disease marked by momentary tonic spasms occurring when a voluntary movement is attempted.

   m. dystroph'ica, myotonic *dystrophy*.

myoton'ic. Pertaining to or exhibiting myotonia.

myotonoid (mi-ot'o-noyd) [myo- + G. *tonos*, tone, tension, + *eidos*, resemblance]. Denoting a muscular reaction characterized by a slow contraction and, especially, relaxation.

myot'onus [myo- + G. *tonos*, tension, stretching]. A tonic spasm or temporary rigidity of a muscle or group of muscles.

myot'ony [myo- + G. *tonos*, tension]. Muscular tonus or tension.

myotrophic (mi-o-tro'fik). Relating to myotrophy.

myot'rophy [myo- + G. *trophē*, nourishment]. Nutrition of muscular tissue.

my'otube. A developing skeletal muscle fiber with a tubular appearance; formerly called a myotubule; however, the electron microscopy shows smaller tubular elements.

myringectomy (mǐr-in-jek'to-mǐ) [myringo- + G. *ektomē*, excision]. Myringodectomy; excision of the tympanic membrane.

myringitis (mǐr-in-ji'tis) [myring- + G. *-itis*, inflammation]. Tympanitis; inflammation of the tympanic membrane.

myringo-, myring- [Mod. L. *myringa, q.v.*]. Combining forms denoting the membrana tympani.

myringodectomy (mǐ-ring'go-dek'to-mǐ). Myringectomy.

myringoplasty (mǐ-ring'go-plas'tǐ) [myringo- + G. *plassō*, to form]. Surgical repair of a damaged tympanic membrane.

myringostapediopexy (mǐ-ring'go-sta-pe'dǐ-o-pek-sǐ) [*myringo-* + *L. stapes*, stirrup (stapes), + G. *pēxis*, fixation]. Tympanoplasty in which the drum membrane or grafted drum membrane is brought into functional connection with the stapes.

myringotomy (mǐr-ing-got'o-mǐ) [myringo- + G. *tomē*, excision]. Tympanotomy; paracentesis of the tympanic membrane.

myrinx (mi'ringks, mǐr'ringks) [Mod. L. *myringa*, drum membrane]. *Membrana tympani.*

myrmecia (mǐr-me'shǐ-ah) [G. *murmex*, ant]. A form of verruca simplex in which the lesion has a domed (ant hill) configuration.

mysophilia (mi-so-fil'ǐ-ah) [G. *mysos*, defilement, + *philos*, fond]. Sexual interst in excretions.

mysophobia (mi-so-fo'bǐ-ah) [G. *mysos*, defilement, + *phobos*, fear]. A morbid fear of dirt of defilement.

myx-. See myxo-.

myxadenitis (miks'ad-ĕ-ni'tis) [myx- + G. *adēn*, gland, + *-itis*, inflammation]. Obsolete term for inflammation of the mucous glands.

myxadenoma (miks'ad-ĕ-no'mah). An adenoma, in which the loose connective tissue of the stroma has a resemblance to relatively primitive mesenchymal tissue.

myxasthenia (miks-as-the'nǐ-ah) [myx- + G. *astheneia*, weakness]. Faulty secretion of mucus.

myxedema (miks-ĕ-de'mah) [myx- + G. *oidema*, swelling]. Hypothyroidism characterized by a relatively hard edema of subcutaneous tissue; caused by removal or loss of functioning thyroid tissue.

   circumscribed m., pretibial m.; nodules and plaques of mucoid edema of the skin, usually in the pretibial region, occurring in some patients with hyperthyroidism.

   congenital m., cretinism.

   pituitary m., m. resulting from inadequate secretion of thyrotropic hormone.

   pretibial m., circumscribed m.

myxedem'atoid. Resembling myxedema.

myxedem'atous. Relating to myxedema.

myxemia (mik-se'mǐ-ah) [myx- + G. *haima*, blood]. Mucinemia.

myxo-, myx- [G. *myxa*, mucus]. Combining forms relating to mucus. See also muci-, muco-.

myxochondrofibrosarcoma (mik'so-kon'dro-fi'bro-sar-ko'ma) [myxo- + G. *chondros*, cartilage, + L. *fibra*, fiber, + G. *sarx*, flesh, + *-ōma*, tumor]. A fibrosarcoma, in which there are intimately associated foci of cartilaginous and myxomatous tissue.

myxochondroma (mik'so-kon-dro'mah) [myxo- + G. *chondros*, cartilage, + *-ōma*, tumor]. A chondroma, in which the stroma has a resemblance to relatively primitive mesenchymal tissue.

myxocyte (miks'o-sīt) [myxo- + G. *kytos*, cell]. One of the stellate or polyhedral cells present in mucous tissue.

myxofibro'ma [myxo- + L. *fibra*, fiber, + G. *-ōma*, tumor]. Fibroma myxomatodes; a benign neoplasm of fibrous connective tissue in which focal or diffuse degenerative changes result in portions that resemble primitive mesenchymal tissue.

myxofibrosarcoma (mik'so-fi'bro-sar-ko'mah) [myxo- + L. *fibra*, fiber, + G. *sarx*, flesh, + *-ōma*, tumor]. A fibrosarcoma in which focal or diffuse degenerative changes or growth of less differentiated anaplastic cells results in portions that resemble primitive mesenchymal tissue.

myx'oid [myxo- + G. *eidos*, resemblance]. Mucoid; resembling mucus.

myxolipo'ma [myxo- + G. *lipos*, fat, + *-ōma*, tumor]. A lipoma in which focal or diffuse degenerative changes result in portions that resemble mucoid mesenchymal tissue.

myxoma (mik-so'mah) [myxo- + G. -ōma, consisting. A neoplasm derived from connective tissue, consisting chiefly of polyhedral and stellate cells that are loosely embedded in a soft, mucoid matrix, thereby resembling primitve mesenchymal tissue.

myxomatosis (mik'so-mă-to'sis). 1. Mucoid *degeneration*. 2. Multiple myxomas.

myxo'matous. 1. Pertaining to or characterized by the features of a myxoma. 2. Said of tissue that resembles primitive mesenchymal tissue.

myxopapilloma (mik'so-pap-ĭ-lo'mah) [myxo- + L. *papilla*, a nipple, + G. suffix -ōma, tumor]. A papilloma in which the stroma resembles primitive mesenchymal tissue.

myxopoiesis (mik'so-poy-e'sis) [myxo- + G. *poiēsis*, a making]. Mucus production.

myxorrhea (mik-so-re'ah) [myxo- + G. *rhoia*, a flow]. Blennorrhea (1).

myxosarco'ma [myxo- + G. *sarx*, flesh, + -ōma, tumor]. A sarcoma by immature, relatively undifferentiated, and primitive gross cells that grow rapidly and invade extensively, resulting in tissue that resembles primitive mesenchyme in its gross features.

myx'ovirus. Term formerly used for viruses with an affinity for mucins, now included in the families Orthomyxoviridae and Paramyxoviridae, which include influenza virus, parainfluenza virus, respiratory syncytial virus, and measles virus.

N

ν [nu, thirteenth letter of G. alphabet] Kinematic *viscosity*.

N Newton; nitrogen.

N Normal concentration. See normal (3).

n Nano-; refractive *index*.

NA *Nomina Anatomica.*

Na Sodium (natrium).

nacreous (na'kre-us) [Fr. *nacre*, mother-of-pearl]. Lustrous, like mother-of-pearl.

NAD Nicotinamide adenine dinucleotide.

NAD+ Nicotinamide adenine dinucleotide (oxidized form).

NADH Nicotinamide adenine dinucleotide (reduced form).

NADP Nicotinamide adenine dinucleotide phosphate.

NADP+ Nicotinamide adenine dinucleotide phosphate (oxidized form).

NADPH Nicotinamide adenine dinucleotide phosphate (reduced form).

nail [A.S. *naegel*]. 1. Unguis. 2. A slender rod used in operations to fasten together the divided extremities of a broken bone.

  hippocratic n.'s, the coarse curved n.'s capping hippocratic fingers.

  ingrown n., ingrown toenail; acronyx; a toenail, one edge of which is overgrown by the nailfold, producing a pyogenic granuloma.

  spoon n., koilonychia.

nalorphine (nal'or-fēn, nal-or'fēn). *N*-allylnormorphine; $C_{19}H_{21}NO_3$; an antagonist of most of the depressant and stimulatory effects of morphine and related narcotic analgesics.

nalox'one hydrochloride. 1-*N*-allyl-7,8-dihydro-14-hydroxymorphinone hydrochloride; a potent antagonist of all narcotics, including pentazocine, unique because of the absence of pharmacologic action when administered without narcotics.

nan'ism [G. *nanos*; L. *nanus*, dwarf]. Dwarfism.

nano- [G. *nānos*, dwarf]. 1. Combining form relating to dwarfism (nanism). 2 (n). Prefix used in the SI and metric system to signify one-billionth (10^{-9}).

nanocephalous (nan-o-sef'ă-lus). Microcephalic.

nanocephaly (nan-o-sef'ă-lĭ) [nano- + G. *kephale*, head]. Microcephaly.

nanocormia (nan-o-kor'mĭ-ah) [nano- + G. *kormos*, trunk]. Microsomia.

nan'ogram (ng). One-billionth (10^{-9}) of a gram.

nan'oid [nano- + G. *eidos*, resemblance]. Dwarflike.

nanome'lia [nano- + G. *melos*, limb]. Micromelia.

nanom'eter (nm). One-billionth (10^{-9}) of a meter.

nanophthalmia, nanophthalmos (nan-of-thal'mĭ-ah, -mos) [nano- + G. *ophthalmos*, eye]. Microphthalmia.

Nano'phyetus salmin'cola. *Troglotrema salmincola;* a digenetic fish-borne fluke (family Nanophyetidae) of fish-eating mammals; vector of *Neorickettsia helmintheca,* the agent of salmon poisoning.

na'nous. Dwarfish.

na'nus [L.; G. *nanos*]. Dwarf.

nape. Nucha.

naphtha (naf'thah). *Petroleum* benzin.

naphthalene (naf'thă-lēn). Tar camphor; a carcinogenic and toxic hydrocarbon obtained from coal tar; used for many syntheses in industry and in some moth repellents.

naphthalenol (naf-thal'ĕ-nol). Naphthol.

naphthol (naf'thol). $C_{10}H_7OH$; a phenol of naphthalene.

narcissism (nar-sis'izm, nar'sĭ-sizm) [*Narkissos*, G. myth. char.]. 1. Selflove; sexual attraction toward one's own person. 2. A state in which the individual regards everything in relation to himself and not to other persons or things.

narco- [G. *narkoun*, to benumb, deaden]. Combining form relating to stupor or narcosis.

narcoanal'ysis. Narcosynthesis; psychotherapeutic treatment under light anesthesia.

narcohypnia (nar-ko-hip'nĭ-ah) [narco- + G. *hypnos,* sleep]. General numbness sometimes experienced at the moment of waking.

narcohypnosis (nar'ko-hip-no'sis) [narco- + G. *hypnos,* sleep]. Stupor or deep sleep induced by hypnosis.

nar′colepsy [narco- + G. *lēpsis*, seizure]. Hypnolepsy; a sudden uncontrollable disposition to sleep occurring at irregular intervals, with or without obvious predisposing or exciting cause, usually involving an abnormality in sleep-stage sequencing.

narcosis (nar-ko′sis) [G. a benumbing]. An obsolete synonym for anesthesia; now used to denote general and nonspecific reversible depression of neuronal excitability, produced by a number of physical and chemical agents, usually resulting in stupor rather than in anesthesia.

narcosyn′thesis. Narcoanalysis.

narcother′apy. Psychotherapy conducted with the patient under the influence of a sedative or narcotic drug.

narcot′ic [G. *narkōtikos*, benumbing]. **1.** Any substance producing stupor associated with analgesia; specifically, a drug derived from opium or opium-like compounds, with potent analgesic effects associated with significant alteration of mood and behavior, and with the potential for dependence and tolerance following repeated administration. **2.** Capable of inducing a state of stuporous analgesia.

na′ris, pl. **na′res** [L.] [NA]. Nostril; the anterior opening on either side of the nasal cavity.

nasal (na′zal) [L. *nasus*, nose]. Rhinal; relating to the nose.

nascent (nas′ent, na′sent) [L. *nascor*, pres. p. *nascens*, to be born]. **1.** Beginning; being born or produced. **2.** Denoting the state of a chemical element at the moment it is set free from one of its compounds.

nasion (na′zĭ-on) [L. *nasus*, nose] [NA]. A point on the skull corresponding to the middle of the naso-frontal suture.

naso- [L. *nasus*, nose]. Combining form relating to the nose.

nasoantral (na′zo-an′tral). Relating to the nose and the maxillary sinus.

nasofrontal (na′zo-frun′tal). Relating to the nose and the forehead, or to the nasal cavity and the frontal sinuses.

nasolabial (na′zo-la′bĭ-al) [naso- + G. *labium*, lip]. Relating to the nose and the upper lip.

nasolacrimal (na′zo-lak′rĭ-mal). Relating to the nasal and the lacrimal bones, or to the nasal cavity and the lacrimal ducts.

naso-oral (na′zo-o′ral). Relating to the nose and the mouth.

nasopalatine (na′zo-pal′ă-tīn, -tin). Relating to the nose and palate.

nasopharyngeal (na′zo-fă-rin′jī-al). Relating to the nose or the nasal cavity and the pharynx, or to the rhinopharynx or nasopharynx.

nasopharyngitis (na′zo-făr-in-ji′tis) [naso- + pharynx, + G. *-itis*, inflammation]. Inflammation of the mucous membrane of the posterior nares and upper part of the pharynx.

nasopharyngolaryngoscope (na′zo-fă-ring′go-lă-ring′go-skōp). A fiberoptic endoscope used to visualize the upper airways and pharynx.

nasopharynx (na′zo-făr′ingks). Epipharynx; the part of the pharynx that lies above the soft palate, anteriorly opening into the nasal cavity.

nasoscope (na′zo-skōp). Rhinoscope.

nasosinusitis (na′zo-si-nus-i′tis). Inflammation of the nasal cavities and of the accessory sinuses.

na′sus [L.] [NA]. Nose; the external portion of the respiratory pathway which forms a prominent feature of the face and contains the nasal cavity perforated inferiorly by two nostrils separated by a septum.

na′tal. 1 [L. *natalis*, fr. *nascor*, pp. *natus*, to be born]. Relating to birth. **2** [L. *nates*, buttocks]. Relating to the buttocks or nates.

natal′ity [see natal (1)]. The birth rate; the ratio of births to the general population.

nates (na′tēz) [L. pl. of *natis*] [NA]. The buttocks; breech; clunes; the prominence formed by the gluteal muscles on either side.

natimortality (na′tĭ-mor-tal′ĭ-tĭ) [L. *natus*, birth]. The perinatal death rate; the proportion of fetal and neonatal deaths to the general natality.

National Formulary (NF). An official compendium formerly issued by the American Pharmaceutical Association but now published by the United States Pharmacopeia Convention for the purpose of providing standards and specifications which can be used to evaluate the quality of pharmaceuticals and therapeutic agents.

natremia (na-tre′mĭ-ah) [natrium (sodium) + G. *haima*, blood]. Presence of sodium in the circulating blood.

natriferic (na-trif′er-ik). Tending to increase sodium transport.

na′trium [Ar. *natrūm*, fr. G. *nitron*, carbonate of soda]. Sodium.

natriuresis (na′trĭ-u-re′sis) [natrium + G. *ouron*, urine]. Urinary excretion, especially enhanced, of sodium.

na′triuret′ic. 1. Pertaining to or characterized by natriuresis. **2.** A chemical compound that may be used as a means of retarding the tubular reabsorption of sodium ions from glomerular filtrate, thereby resulting in greater amounts of that ion in the urine.

na′turopath′ic. Relating to or by means of naturopathy.

na′turop′athy. A system of therapeutics in which neither surgical nor medicinal agents are used, dependence being placed only on natural (nonmedicinal) forces.

nausea (naw′ze-ah, naw′zhah) [L. fr. G. *nausia*, seasickness, fr. *naus*, ship]. Sick at the stomach; an inclination to vomit.

 n. gravida′rum, morning *sickness.*

nauseant (naw′ze-ant). Nauseating; causing nausea.

nauseate (naw′ze-āt). To make sick at the stomach.

nauseated (naw′ze-a′ted). Affected with nausea.

nauseous (naw′ze-us, naw′shus). Causing nausea.

na′vel [A.S. *nafela*]. Umbilicus.

navicular (nă-vik'u-lar) [L. *navicularis*, relating to shipping]. Scaphoid.

Nb Niobium.

Nd Neodymium.

Ne Neon.

near'sight'edness. Myopia.

nearthrosis (ne-ar-thro'sis) [G. *neos*, new, + *arthrōsis*, a jointing]. A new joint; *e.g.*, a pseudarthrosis arising in an ununited fracture, or a "new" joint resulting from a total joint replacement operation.

nebula, pl. **neb'ulae** (neb'u-lah) [L. fog, cloud, mist]. **1.** A faint, foglike opacity of the cornea. **2.** A class of oily preparations, intended for application by atomization.

neb'ulizer [L. *nebula*, mist]. A device used to reduce liquid medication to an extremely fine cloud; useful in delivering medication to the deep part of the respiratory tract.

Necator (ne-ka'tor) [L. a murderer]. A genus of nematode hookworms (family Ancylostomatidae, subfamily Necatorine) distinguished by two chitinous cutting plates in the buccal cavity and fused male copulatory spicules. Species include *N. americanus* (New World hookworm), the adults of which attach to villi in the small intestine and suck blood, causing abdominal discomfort, diarrhea (usually with melena) and cramps, anorexia, loss of weight, and anemia. See also *Ancylostoma*.

necatoriasis (ne-ka-to-ri'ă-sis). Hookworm disease caused by *Necator*, the resulting anemia being usually less severe than that from ancylostomiasis.

nec'cropsy [necro- + G. *opsis*, view]. Autopsy.

neck [A.S. *hnecca*]. **1.** Collum. **2.** Any constricted part of a structure having a fancied resemblance to the n. of an animal.

buffalo n., combination of moderate kyphosis with thick heavy fat pad on the n.

bull n., heavy, thick n., caused by hypertrophied muscles or enlarged cervical lymph nodes.

stiff n., wry n., torticollis.

webbed n., the broad n. due to lateral folds of skin extending from the clavicle to the head, as in Turner's syndrome.

necrectomy (nĕ-krek'to-mĭ) [necr- + G. *ektomē*, excision]. Operative removal of any necrosed tissue.

necro-, necr- [G. *nekros*, corpse]. Combining forms relating to death or to necrosis.

nec'robio'sis [necro- + G. *biōs*, life]. Bionecrosis. **1.** Physiologic or normal death of cells or tissues as a result of changes associated with development, aging, or use. **2.** Necrosis of a small area of tissue.

n. lipoid'ica, n. lipoid'ica diabetico'rum, n. in the cutis, not infrequently associated with diabetes, in which one or more atrophic shiny lesions develop on the legs.

nec'robiot'ic. Pertaining to or characterized by necrobiosis.

necrocytosis (nek'ro-si-to'sis) [necro- + G. *kytos*, cell, + *-osis*, condition]. A process that results in, or a condition characterized by, abnormal or pathologic death of cells.

necrogenic, necrogenous (nek-ro-jen'ik, nĕ-kroj'-en-us) [necro- + G. *genesis*, origin]. Relating to, living in, or having origin in dead matter.

necrology (nĕ-krol'o-jĭ) [necro- + G. *logos*, study]. The science of the collection, classification, and interpretation of mortality statistics.

necrolysis (nĕ-krol'ĭ-sis) [necro- + G. *lysis*, loosening]. Necrosis and loosening of tissue.

toxic epidermal n. (TEN), Ritter's disease (1); a syndrome in which a large portion of the skin becomes intensely erythematous and peels off in the manner of a second-degree burn, often simultaneous with the formation of flaccid bullae.

nec'roma'nia [necro- + G. *mania*, frenzy]. **1.** A morbid tendency to dwell with longing on death. **2.** Necrophilia (1).

necrophagous (nĕ-krof'ă-gus) [necro- + G. *phagein*, to eat]. **1.** Living on carrion. **2.** Necrophilous.

necrophilia (nek'ro-fil'ĭ-ah) [necro- + G. *phileō*, to love]. **1.** Necromania (2); a morbid fondness for being in the presence of dead bodies. **2.** The impulse to sexual contact, or the act of such contact, with a corpse.

necrophilous (nĕ-krof'ĭ-lus) [necro- + G. *philos*, fond]. Necrophagous (2); having a preference for dead tissue; denoting certain bacteria.

nec'ropho'bia [necro- + G. *phobos*, fear]. Morbid fear of corpses.

necrose (nĕ-krōz'). **1.** To cause necrosis. **2.** To become the site of necrosis.

necrosis (nĕ-kro'sis) [G. *nekrōsis*, death]. Pathologic death of one or more cells, or of a portion of tissue or organ, resulting from irreversible damage; the most frequent visible alterations are nuclear: pyknosis, karyolysis, or karyorhexis.

aseptic n., n. in the absence of infection.

caseous n., caseation n., caseous degeneration; n. characteristic of certain inflammations, with loss of separate structures of the various cellular and histologic elements; affected tissue manifests the crumbly consistency and dull opaque quality of cheese.

central n., n. involving the deeper or inner portions of a tissue, or an organ or its units.

coagulation n., n. in which the affected cells or tissue are converted into a dry, dull, fairly homogeneous eosinophilic mass as a result of the coagulation of protein.

colliquative n., liquefactive n.

fat n., steatonecrosis; death of adipose tissue, characterized by the formation of small foci representing small quantities of calcium soaps formed in the affected tissue when fat is hydrolyzed into glycerol and fatty acids.

focal n., the occurrence of numerous, relatively small or tiny, fairly well circumscribed, usually spheroidal portions of tissue that manifest coagulative, caseous, or gummatous n.

logic death of cells.

ischemic n., n. caused by hypoxia resulting from local deprivation of blood supply, as by infarction.

liquefactive n., colliquative n.; n. characterized by a circumscribed lesion that consists of the fluid remains of tissue that became necrotic and was digested by enzymes.

subcutaneous fat n. of newborn, *sclerema* neonatorum.

Zenker's n., Zenker's *degeneration.*

zonal n., n. predominantly affecting or limited to a defined anatomical area.

nec'rosper'mia [necro- + G. *sperma*, seed]. A condition in which there are dead or immobile spermatozoa in the semen.

necrot'ic. Pertaining to or affected by necrosis.

necrot'omy [necro- + G. *tomē*, cutting]. **1.** Dissection. **2.** Surgical removal of a sequestrum or necrosed portion of bone.

needle (ne'dl). **1.** A slender, usually sharp-pointed, instrument used for puncturing tissues, suturing, or passing a ligature around an artery, or for injection or aspiration. **2.** To separate tissues by means of one or two n.'s in the dissection of small parts. **3.** To perform discission of a cataract by means of a knife n.

needle-holder, -carrier, -driver. Needle forceps; an instrument for grasping needle in suturing.

need'ling. Discission of a soft or of a secondary cataract.

NEEP Negative end-expiratory *pressure.*

nega'tion. Denial.

negative (−) (neg'ă-tiv) [L. *negativus*, fr. *nego*, to deny]. **1.** Not affirmative; refutative; not positive. **2.** Denoting failure of response, absence of a reaction, or absence of an entity or condition in question.

neg'ativism. A tendency to do the opposite of what one is requested to do, or to stubbornly resist for no apparent reason.

neg'atron. A term used for electron to emphasize its negative charge in contradistinction to the positive charge carried by the otherwise similar positron.

Neisseria (ni-se'rī-ah) [A. *Neisser*]. A genus of aerobic to facultatively anaerobic bacteria (family Neisseriaceae) containing Gram-negative cocci which occur in pairs with the adjacent sides flattened. The type species is *N. gonorrhoeae.*

   N. gonorrhoe'ae, gonococcus; a species that causes gonorrhea and other infections in man; the type species of the genus *N.*

   N. meningit'idis, meningococcus; a species that is the causative agent of meningococcal meningitis; groups are characterized by serologically specific capsular polysaccharides (A, B, C, and D).

nem [Ger. *Nahrung, Einheit, Milch;* nourishment, unit, milk]. The caloric value of 1 of mother's milk of a definite composition; a unit of comparison of food values, equivalent to about 2/3 calorie.

nema-, nemat-, nemato- [G. *nēma*, thread]. Combining forms meaning thread, threadlike.

nemathelminth (nem-ă-thel'minth). A member of the phylum Nemathelminthes.

Nemathelminthes (nem'ă-thel-min'thēz) [nemat- + G. *helmins, helminthos*, worm]. Aschelminthes.

nematoci'dal. Destructive to nematode worms.

nematocide (ne-mat'o-sīd) [nematode + L. *caedo,* to kill]. An agent that kills nematodes.

nematocyst (nem'ă-to-sist) [nemato- + G. kystis, bladder]. A stinging cell of coelenterates, consisting of a poison sac and a coiled barbed sting capable of being ejected and penetrating the skin on contact, as those of jelly fish and the Portuguese man-of-war.

Nematoda (nem'ă-to'dah) [nemat- + G. *eidos,* form]. A class in the phylum Aschelminthes, including species parasitic in man and plant-parasitic and free-living soil or aquatic nonparasitic species; may be classified in two groups, based on their habitat in the human body; **1)** intestinal roundworms (*Ascaris, Trichuris, Ancylostoma, Necator, Strongyloides, Enterobius,* and *Trichinella*); **2)** filarial roundworms of the blood, lymphatic tissues, and viscera (*Wuchereria, Mansonella, Dipetalonema, Loa, Onchocerca,* and *Dracunculus*).

nematode (nem'ă-tōd). Any parasitic worm of the class Nematoda.

nem'atodi'asis. Infection with nematode parasites.

nem'atoid. Relating to nematodes.

neo- [G. *neos,* new]. Prefix meaning new or recent.

neoantigens (ne'o-an'tī-jenz). Tumor *antigens.*

neoarthro'sis. Nearthrosis.

neoblas'tic [neo- + G. *blastos,* germ, offspring]. Developing in or characteristic of new tissue.

neocerebellum (ne'o-sĕr-e-bel'um) [NA]. The large lateral portion of the cerebellar hemisphere receiving its dominant input from the pontine nuclei which, in turn, are dominated by afferent nerves originating from all parts of the cerebral cortex.

neocortex (ne-o-kor'teks). Isocortex. See *cortex* cerebri.

neocystostomy (ne'o-sis-tos'to-mī) [neo- + G. *kystis,* bladder, + *stoma,* mouth]. An operation in which the ureter or a segment of the ileum is implanted into the bladder.

neodymium (ne-o-dim'ī-um) [neo- + didymium]. One of the rare earth elements; symbol Nd, atomic no. 60, atomic weight 144.24.

neogenesis (ne'o-jen'ē-sis) [neo- + G. *genesis,* origin]. Regeneration; new formation of tissue.

neogenet'ic. Pertaining to or characterized by neogenesis.

neokinetic (ne'o-kī-net'ik) [neo- + G. *kinētikos,* relating to movement]. Denoting one of the divisions of the motor system, the function of which is the transmission of isolated synergic movements of voluntary origin.

neologism (ne-ol'o-jizm) [neo- + G. *logos,* word]. A new word or phrase, or an old word used in a new sense.

neomem'brane. False *membrane.*

neomy′cin sulfate. The sulfate of an antibacterial substance produced by the growth of *Streptomyces fradiae*, active against a variety of Gram-positive and Gram-negative bacteria.

ne′on [G. *neos*, new]. An inert gaseous element, symbol Ne, atomic no. 10, atomic weight 20.183.

neona′tal [neo- + L. *natalis*, relating to birth]. Newborn; relating to the period immediately succeeding birth and continuing through the first 28 days of life.

neonate (ne′o-nāt) [L. *neonatus*, newborn]. A neonatal infant.

neonatologist (ne′o-na-tol′o-jist). One specializing in neonatology.

ne′onatol′ogy [neo- + L. *natus*, pp. born, + G. *logos*, theory]. The specialty concerned with disorders of the neonate.

neopal′lium. Isocortex. See *cortex* cerebri.

neoplasia (ne-o-pla′zi-ah) [neo- + G. *plasis*, a molding]. The pathologic process that results in the formation and growth of a neoplasm.

ne′oplasm [neo- + G. *plasma*, thing formed]. Tumor (2); an abnormal tissue that grows by cellular proliferation more rapidly than normal, continues to grow after the stimuli that initiated the new growth cease, shows partial or complete lack of structural organization and functional coordination with the normal tissue, and usually forms a distinct mass of tissue which may be either benign or malignant.

neoplas′tic. Pertaining to or characterized by neoplasia, or containing a neoplasm.

neostriatum (ne′o-stri-a′tum). The caudate nucleus and putamen considered as one and distinguished from the globus pallidus.

neothal′amus. The portion of the thalamus projecting to the neocortex.

nephelometry (nef-ĕlom′ĕ-tri) [G. *nephelē*, cloud, + *metron*, measure]. A technique for estimation of the number and size of particles in a suspension by measurement of light scattering.

nephr-. See nephro-.

nephralgia (nĕ-fral′ji-ah) [nephr- + G. *algos*, pain]. Pain in the kidney.

nephrectasis (nĕ-frek′tă-sis) [nephr- + G. *ektasis*, a stretching]. Dilation or distention of the pelvis of the kidney.

nephrectomy (nĕ-frek′to-mĭ) [nephr- + G. *ektomē*, excision]. Surgical removal of a kidney.

nephrelcosis (nef-rel-ko′sis) [nephr- + G. *helkōsis*, ulceration]. Ulceration of the mucous membrane of the pelvis or calices of the kidney.

nephremorrhagia (nef′rem-o-ra′ji-ah) [nephr- + hemorrhage]. Nephrorrhagia; hemorrhage from or into the kidney.

nephric (nef′rik). Renal; relating to the kidney.

nephrit′ic. Relating to nephritis.

nephritis, pl. **nephritides** (nĕ-fri′tis, -frit′ĭ-dēz) [nephr- + G. *-itis*, inflammation]. Inflammation of the kidneys.

glomerular n., glomerulonephritis.

interstitial n., n. in which the interstitial connective tissue is chiefly affected.

lupus n., glomerulonephritis occurring with systemic lupus erythematosus, characterized by hematuria and a progressive course culminating in renal failure, often without hypertension; sometimes also applied to the nephrotic syndrome in patients with systemic lupus.

salt-losing n., a rare disorder resulting from renal tubular damage of unknown etiology; it mimics adrenocortical insufficiency in that abnormal renal loss of sodium chloride occurs, accompanied by azotemia, acidosis, dehydration, and vascular collapse.

serum n., induced glomerulonephritis; glomerulonephritis occurring in serum sickness.

suppurative n., focal glomerulonephritis with abscess formation in the kidney.

transfusion n., renal failure and tubular damage resulting from the transfusion of incompatible blood; the hemoglobin of the hemolyzed red cells is deposited as casts in the renal tubules.

nephro-, nephr- [G. *nephros*, kidney]. Combining forms denoting the kidney. See also reno-.

nephroblasto′ma. Wilms *tumor.*

nephrocalcinosis (nef′ro-kal-sĭ-no′sis) [nephro- + calcinosis]. Renal lithiasis characterized by diffusely scattered foci of calcification in the kidneys.

nephrocapsectomy (nef′ro-kap-sek′to-mĭ) [nephro- + L. *capsula*, a small box, + G. *ektomē*, excision]. Decortication, or decapsulation, of the kidney.

neph′rocar′diac [nephro- + G. *kardia*, heart]. Cardiorenal.

nephrocele (nef′ro-sēl) [nephro- + G. *kēlē*, hernia]. Hernial displacement of a kidney.

nephrocystanastomosis (nef′ro-sist′an-as-to-mo′sis) [nephro- + G. *kystis*, bladder, + *anastomōsis*, an outlet]. Establishment of a connection between the kidney and the bladder, for correction of a permanent obstruction of the ureter.

nephrocystosis (nef′ro-sis-to′sis) [nephro- + G. *kystis*, cyst, + *-osis*, condition]. Formation of renal cysts.

neph′rogenet′ic, neph′rogen′ic [nephro- + G. *genēsis*, origin]. Giving rise to kidney tissue.

nephrogenous (nef-roj′ĕ-nus). Arising from kidney tissue.

neph′rogram. Radiograph of the kidney after the intravenous injection of a radiopaque substance.

nephrography (nĕ-frog′ră-fĭ) [nephro- + G. *graphō*, to write]. Radiography of the kidney.

neph′roid. (nef′royd) [nephro- + G. *eidos*, resemblance]. Reniform; kidney-shaped; resembling a kidney.

neph′rolith [nephro- + G. *lithos*, stone]. A renal calculus; a calculus occurring within the kidney.

nephrolithiasis (nef′ro-lĭ-thi′ă-sis). The presence of renal calculi.

nephrolithotomy (nef'ro-lĭ-thot'o-mĭ) [nephro- + G. *lithos*, stone, + *tomē*, incision]. Incision into the kidney for the removal of a renal calculus.

nephrology (nĕ-frol'o-jĭ) [nephro- + G. *logos*, study]. The branch of medical science concerned with the kidneys.

nephrolysis (nĕ-frol'ĭ-sis) [nephro- + G. *lysis*, dissolution]. 1. Freeing of the kidney from inflammatory adhesions, with preservation of the capsule. 2. Destruction of renal cells.

nephrolyt'ic. Nephrotoxic (2); pertaining to, characterized by, or causing nephrolysis.

nephroma (nĕ-fro'mah) [nephro- + G. *-oma*, tumor]. A tumor arising from renal tissue.

nephromegaly (nef-ro-meg'ă-lĭ) [nephro- + G. *megas*, great]. Extreme hypertrophy of one or both kidneys.

neph'ron [G. *nephros*, kidney]. The functional unit of the kidney, consisting of the renal corpuscle, the proximal convoluted tubule, the nephronic loop, and the distal convoluted tubule.

nephropathy (nef-rop'ă-thĭ) [nephro- + G. *pathos*, suffering]. Nephrosis (1); renopathy; any disease of the kidney.

nephropexy (nef'ro-pek-sĭ) [nephro- + G. *pēxis*, fixation]. Surgical fixation of a floating or mobile kidney.

nephrophthisis (nef-rof'thĭ-sis, -tĭ-sis) [nephro- + G. *phthisis*, a wasting]. 1. Suppurative nephritis with wasting of the substance of the organ. 2. Tuberculosis of the kidney.

nephroptosis (nef-rop-to'sis) [nephro- + G. *ptōsis*, a falling]. Prolapse of the kidney.

nephropyelitis (nef'ro-pi-ĕ-li'tis). Pyelonephritis.

nephropyeloplasty (nef-ro-pi'el-o-plas-tĭ) [nephro- + G. *pyelos*, trough (pelvis), + *plassō*, to form]. A plastic procedure on the kidney and renal pelvis.

nephropyosis (nef'ro-pi-o'sis) [nephro- + G. *pyōsis*, suppuration]. Suppuration of the kidney.

nephrorrhagia (nef'ro-ra'jĭ-ah) [nephro- + G. *rhēgnymi*, to break forth]. Nephremorrhagia.

nephrorrhaphy (nef-ror'ă-fĭ) [nephro- + G. *raphē*, a suture]. Nephropexy by suturing the kidney.

nephrosclerosis (nef'ro-sklĕ-ro'sis) [nephro- + G. *sklērosis*, hardening]. Induration of the kidney from overgrowth and contraction of the interstitial connective tissue.

    arterial n., arterionephrosclerosis; patchy atrophic scarring of the kidney due to arteriosclerotic narrowing of the lumens of large branches of the renal artery, occurring in old or hypertensive persons and occasionally causing hypertension.

    arteriolar n., arteriolonephrosclerosis; renal scarring due to arteriolar sclerosis resulting from long-standing hypertension; the kidneys are finely granular and mildly or moderately contracted, with hyaline thickening of the walls of afferent glomerular arterioles and hyaline scarring of scattered glomeruli; chronic renal failure develops infrequently.

    malignant n., the renal changes in malignant hypertension: subcapsular petechiae, necrosis in the walls of scattered afferent glomerular arterioles, red blood cells and casts in the urine, and uremia.

neph'rosclerot'ic. Pertaining to or causing nephrosclerosis.

nephrosis (nĕ-fro'sis) [nephro- + G. *-osis*, condition]. 1. Nephropathy. 2. Degeneration of renal tubular epithelium. 3. Nephrotic *syndrome*.

    amyloid n., the nephrotic syndrome due to renal amyloidosis.

    hemoglobinuric n., acute oliguric renal failure associated with hemoglobinuria, due to massive intravascular hemolysis; the kidneys show the morphologic changes of hypoxic n.

    hypoxic n., acute oliguric renal failure following hemorrhage, burns, shock, or other causes of hypovolemia and reduced renal blood flow; frequently associated with patchy tubular necrosis, tubulorrhexis, and distal tubular casts of hemoglobin.

    lipoid n., membranous *glomerulonephritis.*

    toxic n., acute oliguric renal failure due to chemical poisons, septicemia, or bacterial toxemia; frequently associated with extensive necrosis of proximal convoluted tubules.

nephrostomy (nĕ-fros'to-mĭ) [nephro- + G. *stoma*, mouth]. Establishment of an opening between the pelvis of the kidney through its cortex to the exterior of the body.

nephrot'ic. Relating to, caused by, or similar to nephrosis.

nephrotomogram (nef-ro-to'mo-gram). A sectional radiograph of the kidneys following intravenous administration of contrast material to improve visualization of the renal parenchyma.

nephrotomography (nef'ro-to-mog'ră-fĭ). X-ray examination of the kidney by tomography.

nephrotomy (nĕ-frot'o-mĭ) [nephro- + G. *tomē*, incision]. Incision into the kidney.

nephrotox'ic. 1. Pertaining to nephrotoxin. 2. Nephrolytic.

nephrotox'in. A cytotoxin specific for cells of the kidney.

nephrotroph'ic. Renotrophic.

nephrotrop'ic. Renotrophic.

neph'rotuberculo'sis. Tuberculosis of the kidney.

nephroureterectomy (nef'ro-u-re'ter-ek'to-mĭ) [nephro- + ureter + G. *ektomē*, excision]. Surgical removal of a kidney and its ureter.

neph'roure'terocystec'tomy [nephro- + ureter, + G. *kystis*, bladder, + *ektomē*, excision]. Surgical removal of kidney, ureter, and part or all of the bladder.

neptunium (nep-tu'nĭ-um) [planet, *Neptune*]. A transuranian radioactive element; symbol Np, atomic no. 93.

nerve [L. *nervus*]. Microscopically, a bundle composed of one or more fascicles of myelinated or unmyelinated n. fibers, or both, together with accompanying connective tissue and blood vessels.

For gross anatomical description, see nervus.

abducent n., *nervus* abducens.

accelerator n.'s, slender unmyelinated n.'s establishing the sympathetic innervation of the heart, originating from the ganglion cells of the superior, middle, and inferior cervical ganglion of the sympathetic trunk.

accessory n., *nervus* accessorius.

accessory phrenic n.'s, *nervi* phrenici accessorii.

acoustic n., *nervus* vestibulocochlearis.

afferent n., centripetal n.; a n. conveying impulses from the periphery to the CNS.

alveolar n.'s, *nervus* alveolaris inferior and *nervi* alveolares superiores.

ampullar n., *nervus* ampullaris.

anococcygeal n.'s, *nervi* anococcygei.

articular n., a branch of a n. supplying a joint.

auditory n., see *nervus* vestibulocochlearis.

auricular n.'s, *nervi* auriculares anteriores; *nervus* articularis magnus and posterior.

auriculotemporal n., *nervus* auriculotemporalis.

axillary n., *nervus* axillaris.

buccal n., *nervus* buccalis.

cardiac n.'s, *nervus* cardiacus cervicalis; *nervi* cardiaci thoracici.

caroticotympanic n., *nervus* caroticotympanicus.

carotid n.'s, *nervi* carotici externi and *nervus* caroticus internus.

cavernous n.'s, *nervi* cavernosi clitoridis and penis.

centrifugal n., efferent n.

centripetal n., afferent n.

cervical n.'s, n.'s whose nuclei of origin are situated in cervical spinal cord.

ciliary n., nervus ciliaris.

cluneal n., *nervi* clunium.

coccygeal n., *nervus* coccygeus.

cochlear n., see *nervus* vestibulocochlearis.

cranial n.'s, *nervi* craniales.

cubital n., *nervus* ulnaris.

cutaneous n.'s, *nervus* cutaneus antebrachii; cutaneus brachii; cutaneus brachii lateralis; cutaneus dorsalis; cutaneus femoris; cutaneus surae.

deep temporal n.'s, *nervi* temporales profundi.

digital n.'s, *nervi* digitales dorsales and dorsales pedis, digitales palmares, and digitales plantares.

dorsal n.'s, *nervus* dorsalis clitoridis, penis, and scapula.

efferent n., centrifugal n.; a n. conveying impulses from the central nervous system to the periphery.

ethmoidal n., *nervus* ethmoidalis.

excitor n., a n. conducting impulses that stimulate to increased function.

excitoreflex n., a visceral n. that causes reflex action.

facial n., *nervus* facialis.

femoral n., *nervus* femoralis.

fibular n., *nervus* peroneus.

frontal n., *nervus* frontalis.

gangliated n., a n. of the sympathetic nervous system.

genitofemoral n., *nervus* genitofemoralis.

glossopharyngeal n., *nervus* glossopharyngeus.

gluteal n., *nervus* gluteus.

hemorrhoidal n.'s, see *plexus* rectalis superior, medii, and inferiores.

hypogastric n., *nervus* hypogastricus.

hypoglossal n., *nervus* hypoglossus.

iliohypogastric n., *nervus* iliohypogastricus.

ilioinguinal n., *nervus* ilioninguinalis.

inferior rectal n.'s, *nervi* rectales inferiores.

infraorbital n., *nervus* infraorbitalis.

infratrochlear n., *nervus* infratrochlearis.

inhibitory n., a n. conveying impulses that diminish functional activity in a part.

intercostal n., *nervi* intercostales.

intercostobrachial n.'s, *nervi* intercostobrachiales.

intermediary n., intermediate n., *nervus* intermedius.

interosseous n.'s, *nervus* interosseus anterior, cruris, and posterior.

jugular n., *nervus* jugularis.

labial n.'s, *nervi* labiales.

lacrimal n., *nervus* lacrimalis.

laryngeal n., *nervus* laryngeus.

lingual n., *nervus* lingualis.

lumbar n.'s, *nervi* lumbales.

mandibular n., *nervus* mandibularis.

masseteric n., *nervus* massetericus.

median n., *nervus* medianus.

mental n., *nervus* mentalis.

mixed n., a n. containing both afferent and efferent fibers.

motor n., an efferent n. conveying an impulse that excites muscular contraction.

musculocutaneous n., *nervus* musculocutaneus.

mylohyoid n., *nervus* mylohyoideus.

nasociliary n., *nervus* nasociliaris.

nasopalatine n., *nervus* nasopalatinus.

obturator n., *nervus* obturatorius.

occipital n., *nervus* occipitalis.

oculomotor n., *nervus* oculomotorius.

olfactory n., *nervi* olfactorii.

ophthalmic n., *nervus* ophthalmicus.

optic n., *nervus* opticus.

palatine n.'s, *nervus* palatinus major and *nervi* palatini minores.

parasympathetic n., one of the n.'s of the parasympathetic nervous system.

pectoral n., *nervus* pectoralis.

perineal n.'s, *nervi* perineales.

peroneal n., *nervus* peroneus.

petrosal n., *nervus* petrosus.

phrenic n.'s, *nervus* phrenicus and *nervi* phrenici accessorii.

plantar n., *nervus* plantaris.

pneumogastric n., *nervus* vagus.

pressor n., an afferent n., stimulation of which excites a reflex vasoconstriction, thereby raising the blood pressure.

pterygoid n., *nervus* pterygoideus.

n. of pterygoid canal, *nervus* canalis pterygoidei.

pterygopalatine n.'s, *nervi* pterygopalatini.

pudendal n., *nervus* pudendus.

radial n., *nervus* radialis.

saccular n., *nervus* saccularis.

sacral n.'s, *nervi* sacrales.

saphenous n., *nervus* saphenus.

sciatic n., *nervus* ischiadicus.

scrotal n.'s, *nervi* scrotales.

secretory n., a n. conveying impulses that excite functional activity in a gland.

sensory n., an afferent n. conveying impulses that are processed by the CNS so as to become part of the organism's perception of self and its environment.

somatic n., one of the n.'s of sensation or motion.

spinal n.'s, *nervi* spinales.

splanchnic n.'s, *nervus* splanchnicus imus, major, and minor; *nervi* splanchnici lumbales, pelvini, and sacrales.

n. to stapedius muscle, *nervus* stapedius.

subclavian n., *nervus* subclavius.

subcostal n., *nervus* subcostalis.

sublingual n., *nervus* sublingualis.

suboccipital n., *nervus* suboccipitalis.

subscapular n., *nervus* subscapularis.

supraclavicular n., *nervus* supraclavicularis.

supraorbital n., *nervus* supraorbitalis.

suprascapular n., *nervus* suprascapularis.

supratrochlear n., *nervus* supratrochlearis.

sural n., *nervus* suralis.

sympathetic n., one of the n.'s of the sympathetic nervous system.

temporomandibular n., *nervus* zygomaticus.

n. of tensor tympani muscle, *nervus* tensoris tympani.

n. of tensor veli palatini muscle, *nervus* tensoris veli palatini.

terminal n.'s, *nervi* terminales.

thoracic n.'s, *nervi* thoracici.

thoracodorsal n., *nervus* thoracodorsalis.

tibial n., *nervus* tibialis.

transverse n. of neck, *nervus* transversus colli.

trigeminal n., *nervus* trigeminus.

trochlear n., *nervus* trochlearis.

tympanic n., *nervus* tympanicus.

ulnar n., *nervus* ulnaris.

utricular n., *nervus* utricularis.

utriculoampullar n., *nervus* utriculoampullaris.

vaginal n.'s, *nervi* vaginales.

vagus n., *nervus* vagus.

vascular n., a small nerve filament that supplies the wall of a blood vessel.

vasomotor n., a motor n. effecting dilation (vasodilator n.) or contraction (vasoconstrictor n.) of the blood vessels.

vertebral n., *nervus* vertebralis.

vestibular n., see *nervus* vestibulocochlearis.

vestibulocochlear n., *nervus* vestibulocochlearis.

zygomatic n., *nervus* zygomaticus.

ner'vi [L.] [NA]. Plural of nervus.

nervimo'tor. Neurimotor; relating to a motor nerve.

nervon'ic acid. *cis*-15-Tetracosenoic acid; a 24-carbon straight-chain fatty acid that occurs in cerebrosides such as nervone.

nervous (ner'vus) [L. *nervosus*]. 1. Relating to a nerve or the nerves. 2. Easily excited or agitated; suffering from instability.

ner'vousness. A condition of unrest and of irritability.

ner'vus, pl. ner'vi [L.] [NA]. Nerve; a whitish cord, made up of nerve fibers arranged in fascicles held together by a connective tissue sheath, through which stimuli are transmitted from the CNS to the periphery or the reverse. For histological description, see nerve.

n. abdu'cens [NA], abducent nerve; sixth cranial nerve; small motor nerve supplying lateral rectus muscle of eye; originates in dorsal part of tegmentum of pons, passes through cavernous sinus, and enters orbit through superior orbital fissure.

n. accesso'rius [NA], accessory nerve; eleventh cranial nerve; arises by two sets of roots: cranial, from side of medulla, and spinal, from ventrolateral part of first five cervical segments of spinal cord; these roots unite to form the accessory nerve trunk, which divides into two branches: internal, unites with vagus nerve in jugular foramen and supplies muscles of pharynx, larynx, and soft palate, and external, which continues independently through jugular foramen to supply sternocleidomastoid and trapezius muscles.

ner'vi alveola'res superio'res [NA], superior alveolar nerves; three branches (posterior, middle, and anterior) of maxillary nerve that enter maxilla to supply upper teeth and gingiva.

n. alveola'ris infe'rior [NA], inferior alveolar nerve; a terminal branch of mandibular nerve which enters mandibular canal to be distributed to lower teeth, periosteum, and gingiva of mandible.

n. ampulla'ris [NA], ampullar nerve; (1) anterior, branch of utriculoampullar nerve that supplies crista ampullaris of anterior semicircular duct; (2) lateral, branch of utriculoampullar nerve that supplies crista ampullaris of the lateral semicircular duct; (3) posterior, branch of vestibular part of eighth cranial nerve that supplies crista ampullaris of posterior semicircular duct.

ner'vi anococcyg'ei [NA], anococcygeal nerves; several small nerves arising from coccygeal plexus, supplying skin over coccyx.

ner'vi auricula'res anterio'res [NA], anterior auricular nerves; branches of auriculotemporal nerve that supply tragus and upper part of auricle.

n. auricula'ris mag'nus [NA], great auricular nerve; arises from second and third cervical nerves, and supplies skin of part of ear, adjacent portion of scalp, cheek, and angle of jaw.

n. auricula'ris poste'rior [NA], posterior auricular nerve; first extracranial branch of facial nerve which passes behind the ear, supplying auricularis posterior and intrinsic muscles of auricle and, through its occipital branch, innervating occipital belly of occipitofrontal muscle.

n. auriculotempora'lis [NA], auriculotemporal nerve; branch of mandibular nerve that passes through parotid gland, terminating in skin of temple and scalp, and sends branches to external acoustic meatus, tympanic membrane, parotid gland, and auricle, as well as a communicating branch to facial nerve.

n. axilla'ris [NA], axillary nerve; arises from posterior cord of brachial plexus in axilla and supplies deltoid and teres minor muscles.

n. bucca'lis [NA], buccal nerve; a sensory branch of mandibular division of trigeminal nerve which supplies buccal mucous membrane and skin of cheek near the angle of mouth.

n. cana'lis pterygoi'dei [NA], nerve of pterygoid canal; nerve constituting motor and sympathetic roots of pterygopalatine ganglion; formed in foramen lacerum by union of greater and deep petrosal nerves, and runs through pterygoid canal to pterygopalatine fossa.

ner'vi cardi'aci thora'cici [NA], thoracic cardiac nerves; branches from second to fifth segments of the thoracic sympathetic trunk that pass forward to enter cardiac plexus.

n. cardi'acus cervica'lis [NA], cervical cardiac nerve; (1) inferior, nerve passing from cervicothoracic ganglion of sympathetic trunk to cardiac plexus; (2) middle, bundle of fibers running downward from middle cervical ganglion of sympathetic trunk to join the cardiac plexus; (3) superior, nerve that arises from lower part of superior cervical ganglion of sympathetic trunk and passes down to form, with branches of vagus nerve, the cardiac plexus.

ner'vi carot'ici exter'ni [NA], external carotid nerves; sympathetic nerve fibers extending upward from superior cervical ganglion along external carotid artery, forming external carotid plexus.

n. caroticotympan'icus [NA], carotico tympanic nerve; one of two sympathetic branches from internal carotid plexus to tympanic plexus.

n. carot'icus inter'nus [NA], internal carotid nerve; a sympathetic nerve extending upward from superior cervical ganglion along internal carotid artery, forming internal carotid plexus.

ner'vi caverno'si clitor'idis [NA], cavernous nerves of clitoris that correspond to nervi cavernosi penis in the male.

ner'vi caverno'si pe'nis [NA], cavernous nerves of penis; two nerves, major and minor, derived from inferior hypogastric plexus supplying sympathetic and parasympathetic fibers to corpus cavernosum.

n. cilia'ris [NA], ciliary nerve; (1) short, one of a number of branches of ciliary ganglion, supplying ciliary muscles, iris, and tunics of eyeball; (2) long, one of two or three branches of nasociliary nerve,

supplying ciliary muscles, iris, and cornea.

ner'vi clu'nium [NA], cluneal nerves; (1) inferior, branches of posterior femoral cutaneous nerve supplying skin of lower half of gluteal region; (2) middle, terminal branches of dorsal branches of sacral nerves, supplying skin of mid-gluteal region; (3) superior, terminal branches of dorsal branches of lumbar nerves, supplying skin of upper half of gluteal region.

n. coccyg'eus [NA], coccygeal nerve; lowest of the spinal nerves, entering into formation of coccygeal plexus.

ner'vi crania'les [NA], cranial nerves; twelve paired nerves that emerge from, or enter, the brain: olfactory (I), optic (II), oculomotor (III), trochlear (IV), trigeminal (V), abducent (VI), facial (VII), vestibulocochlear (VII), glossopharyngeal (IX), vagus (X), accessory (XI), and hypoglossal (XII).

n. cuta'neus antebra'chii [NA], cutaneous nerve of forearm; (1) lateral, terminal cutaneous branch of musculocutaneous nerve that supplies skin of radial side of forearm; (2) medial, arises from medial fasciculus of brachial plexus and supplies skin of anterior and ulnar surfaces of forearm; (3) posterior, a branch of radial nerve supplying skin of dorsal surface of forearm.

n. cuta'neus bra'chii [NA], cutaneous nerve of arm; (1) medial, arises from medial fasciculus of brachial plexus, unites in axilla with lateral cutaneous branch of second intercostal nerve, and supplies skin of medial side of arm; (2) posterior, a branch of radial nerve supplying skin of posterior surface of arm.

n. cuta'neus bra'chii latera'lis [NA], lateral cutaneous nerve of arm; (1) lower, a branch of radial nerve supplying skin of lower lateral aspect of arm; frequently a branch of posterior antebrachial nerve; (2) upper, a branch of axillary nerve supplying skin over lower portion of deltoid.

n. cuta'neus dorsa'lis [NA], dorsal cutaneous nerve; (1) intermediate, lateral terminal branch of superficial peroneal nerve, supplying dorsum of foot and dorsal nerves to toes; (2) lateral, continuation of sural nerve in foot, supplying lateral margin and dorsum; (3) medial, medial terminal branch of superficial peroneal nerve, supplying dorsum of foot and dorsal nerves to toes.

n. cuta'neus femo'ris [NA], cutaneous nerve of thigh; (1) lateral, arises from second and third lumbar nerves, and supplies skin of anterolateral and lateral surfaces of thigh; (2) posterior, arises from first three sacral nerves and supplies skin of posterior surface of thigh and of popliteal region.

n. cuta'neus su'rae [NA], cutaneous nerve of calf; (1) lateral, arises from common peroneal nerve in popliteal space and is distributed to skin of inferolateral surface of calf; (2) medial, arises from tibial nerve in popliteal space and unites in middle of leg with communicating branch of the common peroneal nerve to form sural nerve; distributed to skin of distal and lateral surfaces of leg and ankle.

ner'vi digita'les dorsa'les [NA], dorsal digital nerves; nerves of hand supplying skin of dorsal surface of fingers.

ner'vi digita'les dorsa'les pe'dis [NA], dorsal digital nerves of foot; nerves of foot supplying skin of proximal and middle phalanges.

ner'vi digita'les palma'res [NA], palmar digital nerves; (1) common, four nerves in palm that send branches to adjacent sides of two digits (three are branches of median, one is from ulnar); (2) proper, ten palmar nerves of digits of hand derived from common palmar digital nerves; each nerve supplies a palmar quadrant of a digit and a part of dorsal surface of distal phalanx.

ner'vi digita'les planta'res [NA], plantar digital nerves; (1) common, three nerves derived from medial nerve plantar and one from lateral plantar nerve that supply skin of ball of foot and terminate as proper plantar digital nerves to side of each toe; (2) proper, ten nerves derived from common plantar digital nerves; each nerve supplies a plantar quadrant of a toe and part of dorsal surface of distal phalanx.

n. dorsa'lis clitor'idis [NA], dorsal nerve of clitoris; deep terminal branch of pudendal nerve, supplying especially the glans clitoridis.

n. dorsa'lis pe'nis [NA], dorsal nerve of penis; deep terminal branch of the pudendal running along dorsum of penis, supplying skin of penis, prepuce, and glans.

n. dorsa'lis scap'ulae [NA], dorsal nerve of scapula; arises from fifth to seventh cervical nerves and passes downward to supply levator scapulae and rhomboideus major and minor muscles.

n. ethmoida'lis [NA], ethmoidal nerve; (1) anterior, branch of nasociliary nerve; (2) posterior, branch of nasociliary nerve.

n. facia'lis [NA], facial nerve; seventh cranial nerve; originates in tegmentum of lower portion of pons, emerges from brain at posterior border of pons, leaves cranial cavity through internal acoustic meatus, traverses facial canal in petrous portion of temporal bone, exits through stylomastoid foramen, passes through parotid gland, and reaches facial muscles through various branches.

n. femora'lis [NA], femoral nerve; arises from second, third, and fourth lumbar nerves in substance of the psoas muscle and supplies muscles and skin of the anterior region of thigh.

n. fronta'lis [NA], frontal nerve; a branch of the ophthalmic nerve which divides within orbit into supratrochlear and supraorbital nerves.

n. genitofemora'lis [NA], genitofemoral nerve; arises from the first and second lumbar nerves, passes distad along the anterior surface of psoas major muscle and divides into genital and femoral branches.

n. glossophoryn'geus [NA], glossopharyngeal nerve; ninth cranial nerve; emerges from the rostral end of medulla and passes through jugular foramen to supply sensation to pharynx and posterior third of tongue; also carries motor fibers to stylopharyngeus muscle and parasympathetic fibers to otic ganglion.

n. glu'teus [NA], gluteal nerve; (1) inferior, arises from fifth lumbar nerve and first and second sacral nerves, and supplies gluteus maximus muscle; (2) superior, arises from fourth and fifth lumbar and first sacral nerves, and supplies gluteus medius and minimus and tensor fasciae latae muscles.

n. hypogas'tricus [NA], hypogastric nerve; one of two nerve trunks (right and left) which lead from superior hypogastric plexus into pelvis to join inferior hypogastric plexuses.

n. hypoglos'sus [NA], hypoglossal nerve; twelfth cranial nerve; arises from medulla, emerges by several roots between pyramid and olive, passes through the hypoglossal canal, and supplies intrinsic muscles of tongue and styloglossus, hyoglossus, and genioglossus muscles.

n. iliohypogas'tricus [NA], iliohypogastric nerve; arises from first lumbar nerve and supplies abdominal muscles and skin of lower part of anterior abdominal wall.

n. ilioinguina'lis [NA], ilioinguinal nerve; arises from first lumbar nerve and passes through superficial inguinal ring to supply skin of upper medial thigh and scrotum or labia majora.

n. infraorbita'lis [NA], infraorbital nerve; continuation of maxillary nerve after it has entered orbit, traversing infraorbital canal to supply upper incisors, canine and premolars, upper gums, inferior eyelid and conjunctiva, part of nose and upper lip.

n. infratrochlea'ris [NA], infratrochlear nerve; branch of nasociliary nerve, supplying skin of eyelids and root of nose.

ner'vi intercosta'les [NA], intercostal nerves; ventral branches of thoracic nerves.

ner'vi intercostobrachia'les [NA], intercostobrachial nerves; branches of the second and third intercostal nerves which pass to skin of medial side of arm.

n. interme'dius [NA], intermediary or intermediate nerve; a root of facial nerve containing sensory fibers whose cell bodies are located in geniculate ganglion and autonomic fibers whose cell bodies are located in superior salivatory nucleus.

n. interos'seus ante'rior [NA], anterior interosseous nerve; a branch of the median nerve supplying the flexor pollicis longus, part of flexor digitorum profundus, and pronator quadratus muscles.

n. interos'seus cru'ris [NA], interosseous nerve of leg; a nerve given off from one of muscular branches of tibial nerve which passes down over posterior surface of interosseous membrane supplying it and the two bones of leg.

n. interos'seus poste'rior [NA], posterior interosseous nerve; deep terminal branch of radial nerve, supplying supinator and all extensor muscles in forearm.

n. ischia'dicus [NA], sciatic nerve; arises from sacral plexus and passes through greater sciatic foramen and down to about middle of thigh where it divides into common peroneal and tibial nerves.

n. jugula'ris [NA], jugular nerve; a communicating branch between superior cervical ganglion of sympathetic trunk and superior ganglion of vagus nerve and inferior ganglion of glossopharyngeal nerve.

ner'vi labia'les [NA], labial nerves; (1) anterior, branches of ilioinguinal nerve distributed to labia majora; (2) posterior, terminal branches of perineal nerve, supplying skin of posterior portion of labia and vestibule of vagina.

n. lacrima'lis [NA], lacrimal nerve; branch of ophthalmic nerve, supplying upper eyelid, conjunctiva, and lacrimal gland.

n. laryn'geus [NA], laryngeal nerve; (1) inferior, terminal branch of recurrent laryngeal nerve; supplies all laryngeal muscles except cricothyroid and mucosa inferior to vocal folds; (2) recurrent, a branch of the vagus nerve that supplies cardiac, tracheal and esophageal branches terminating as inferior laryngeal nerve; (3) superior, branch of vagus nerve at inferior ganglion; at thyroid cartilage it divides into two branches: internal, supplying mucous membrane of larynx superior to vocal folds; external, supplying inferior pharyngeal constrictor and cricothyroid muscle.

n. lingua'lis [NA], lingual nerve; one of branches of mandibular nerve that is distributed to the anterior two-thirds of the tongue; also supplies mucous membrane of floor of mouth.

ner'vi lumba'les [NA], lumbar nerves; five nerves on each side, emerging from lumbar portion of spinal cord; first four enter into formation of lumbar plexus, fourth and fifth into that of sacral plexus.

n. mandibula'ris [NA], mandibular nerve; third division of trigeminal nerve formed by union of sensory fibers from trigeminal ganglion and motor root in foramen ovale, through which the nerve emerges; branches are: meningeal, masseteric, deep temporal, lateral and medial pterygoid, buccal, auriculotemporal, lingual, and inferior alveolar.

n. masseter'icus [NA], masseteric nerve; muscular branch of mandibular nerve passing to medial surface of masseter muscle which it supplies.

n. maxilla'ris [NA], maxillary nerve; second division of trigeminal nerve, passing from trigeminal ganglion through foramen rotundum into pterygopalatine fossa, where it gives off pterygopalatine nerve and continues on to give off zygomatic nerve and enter orbit, where it becomes infraorbital nerve.

n. media'nus [NA], median nerve; formed by union of medial and lateral roots from medial and lateral cords of brachial plexus, respectively; supplies muscular branches in anterior region of forearm and muscular and cutaneous branches in hand.

n. menta'lis [NA], mental nerve; branch of inferior alveolar nerve arising in mandibular canal and passing through mental foramen to chin and lower lip.

n. musculocuta'neus [NA], musculocutaneous nerve; arises from lateral cord of brachial plexus, passes through coracobrachialis and then downward between brachialis and biceps, supplying these three muscles and being prolonged as lateral cutaneous nerve of forearm.

n. mylohyoi'deus [NA], mylohyoid nerve; small branch of inferior alveolar nerve which is distributed to anterior belly of digastric muscle and to mylohyoid muscle.

n. nasocilia'ris [NA], nasociliary nerve; branch of ophthalmic nerve whose branches are long root of ciliary ganglion, long ciliary nerves, infratrochlear nerve, and nasal branches, supplying mucous membrane of nose, tip of nose, and conjunctiva.

n. nasopalati'nus [NA], nasopalatine nerve; branch from pterygopalatine ganglion, supplying mucous membrane of hard palate.

n. obturato'rius [NA], obturator nerve; arises from second, third, and fourth lumbar nerves in psoas muscle, crosses brim of pelvis, and enters thigh through obturator canal; supplies muscles and skin on medial side of thigh.

n. occipita'lis [NA], occipital nerve; (1) greater, medial branch of dorsal ramus of second cervical nerve; sends branches to semispinalis capitis and multifidus cervicis muscles, but is mainly cutaneous, supplying back part of scalp; (2) lesser, arises from second and third cervical nerves; supplies skin of posterior surface of pinna and adjacent portion of scalp; (3) third, medial branch of dorsal ramus of third cervical nerve; usually joined with greater occipital nerve, but may exist as an independent nerve supplying cutaneous branches to scalp and nucha.

n. oculomotor'rius [NA], oculomotor nerve; third cranial nerve; originates in midbrain below cerebral aqueduct; supplies all extrinsic muscles of eye, except lateral rectus and superior oblique; also supplies levator palpebrae superioris, ciliary muscle, and sphincter pupillae.

ner'vi olfacto'rii [NA], olfactory nerve; first cranial nerve; collective term denoting numerous olfactory filaments in the olfactory portion of the nasal mucosa which pass through cribriform plate of ethmoid bone and enter olfactory bulb, where they terminate in synaptic contact with mitral cells, tufted cells, and granule cells.

n. op'ticus [NA], optic nerve, second cranial nerve; originating from retina, it passes out of orbit through optic canal to chiasm, where part of its fibers cross to opposite side and pass through optic tract to geniculate bodies and superior colliculus.

n. ophthal'micus [NA], ophthalmic nerve; ophthalmic branch of trigeminal nerve; through its branches, frontal, lacrimal, and nasociliary, it supplies sensation to orbit and its contents, anterior part of nasal cavity, and skin of nose and forehead.

ner'vi palati'ni mino'res [NA], lesser palatine nerves; usually two branches of pterygopalatine ganglion that contain sensory fibers of the maxillary and facial nerves, and supply mucosa and glands of soft palate and uvula.

n. palati'nus ma'jor [NA], greater palatine nerve; branch of pterygopalatine ganglion that supplies mucosa and glands of hard palate, and anterior part of soft palate.

n. pectora'lis [NA], pectoral nerve; one of two nerves, medial and lateral, that arise from medial and lateral cords of the brachial plexus, respectively, and pass to pectoral muscles.

ner'vi perinea'les [NA], perineal nerves; superficial terminal branches of pudendal nerve, supplying most of muscles of perineum as well as skin of that region.

n. perone'us [NA], peroneal or fibular nerve; (1) common, one of terminal divisions of sciatic nerve, passing through lateral portion of popliteal space to opposite the head of fibula where it divides into superficial and deep peroneal nerves; (2) deep, one of terminal branches of common peroneal nerve, passing into anterior compartment of leg; supplies tibialis anterior, extensor hallucis longus, extensor digitorum longus, and peroneus tertius muscles, and also skin of great toe and medial surface of second toe; (3) superficial, branch of common peroneal nerve which passes downward in front of fibula to supply long and short peroneal muscles and terminate in skin of dorsum of foot and toes.

n. petro'sus [NA], petrosal nerve; (1) greater, parasympathetic root of pterygopalatine ganglion, a branch of facial nerve running on anterior surface of petrous part of temporal bone to reach pterygopalatine ganglion; (2) lesser, parasympathetic root of otic ganglion, derived from tympanic plexus; (3) deep, sympathetic part of greater petrosal nerve which arises from internal carotid plexus and joins the nerve at entrance of pterygoid canal.

ner'vi phren'ici accesso'rii [NA], accessory phrenic nerves; accessory nerve strands that arise from fifth cervical nerve, often as branches of nerve to subclavius, passing downward to join phrenic nerve.

n. phren'icus [NA], phrenic nerve; arises from cervical plexus, chiefly from the fourth cervical nerve; mainly motor nerve of diaphragm but sends sensory fibers to pericardium and branches that communicate with branches from celiac plexus.

n. planta'ris [NA], plantar nerve; (1) lateral, one of two terminal branches of tibial nerve, dividing into superficial and deep branches; supplies skin of lateral aspect of sole and lateral one and one-half toes; innervates intrinsic muscles of plantar part of foot with exception of abductor hallucis and flexor digitorum brevis; (2) medial, one of two terminal branches of tibial nerve, dividing into common and

proper digital branches to innervate skin of medial part of foot and medial three and one-half toes; supplies abductor hallucis and flexor digitorum brevis muscles.

n. pterygoi'deus [NA], pterygoid nerve; one of two motor branches, lateral and medial, of mandibular nerve, supplying lateral and medial pterygoid muscles.

ner'vi pterygopalati'ni [NA], pterygopalatine nerves; two short sensory branches of maxillary nerve in pterygopalatine fossa, which pass through pterygopalatine (Meckel's) ganglion without synapse.

n. puden'dus [NA], pudendal nerve; formed by fibers from second, third, and fourth sacral nerves, it passes through greater sciatic foramen and accompanies internal pudendal artery to terminate as dorsal nerve of penis or of clitoris.

n. radia'lis [NA], radial nerve; arises from posterior cord of brachial plexus and divides into two terminal branches, superficial and deep, which supply muscular and cutaneous branches to dorsal aspect of arm and forearm.

ner'vi recta'les inferio'res [NA], inferior rectal nerves; several branches of pudendal nerve that pass to sphincter ani externus and skin of anal region.

n. saccula'ris [NA], saccular nerve; a branch of vestibular nerve going to macula sacculi.

ner'vi sacra'les [NA], sacral nerves; five nerves issuing from sacral foramina on either side; first three enter into formation of sacral plexus, second two into coccygeal plexus.

n. saphe'nus [NA], saphenous nerve; branch of femoral nerve that supplies cutaneous branches to skin of leg and foot, by way of infrapatellar and medial crural branches.

ner'vi scrota'les [NA], scrotal nerves; (1) anterior, branches of ilioinguinal nerve distributed to skin of root of penis, and anterior surface of scrotum; (2) posterior, several terminal branches of perineal nerve supplying skin of posterior portion of scrotum.

ner'vi spina'les [NA], spinal nerves; 31 pairs of nerves emerging from the spinal cord, each attached to the cord by two roots, anterior and posterior (ventral and dorsal), the latter provided with a spinal ganglion; the two roots unite in the intervertebral foramen and the nerve almost immediately divides again into ventral and dorsal rami, or anterior and posterior primary divisions, the former supplying the foreparts of the body and limbs, the latter the muscles and skin of the back.

ner'vi splanch'nici lumba'les [NA], lumbar splanchnic nerves; branches from lumbar sympathetic trunks that pass anteriorly to join celiac, intermesenteric, aortic, and superior hypogastric plexuses.

ner'vi splanch'nici pelvi'ni [NA], pelvic splanchnic nerves; branches from second, third, and fourth sacral nerves that join inferior hypogastric plexus;

they carry parasympathetic and sensory fibers.

ner'vi splanch'nici sacra'les [NA], sacral splanchnic nerves; branches from sacral sympathetic trunk that pass to inferior hypogastric plexus.

n. splanch'nicus i'mus [NA], lowest splanchnic nerve; a nerve containing sympathetic fibers for renal plexus, usually contained in lesser splanchnic nerve, but occasionally existing as an independent nerve.

n. splanch'nicus ma'jor [NA], greater splanchnic nerve; arises from fifth or sixth to the ninth or tenth thoracic sympathetic ganglia and passes downward along bodies of thoracic vertebrae to join celiac plexus.

n. splanch'nicus mi'nor [NA], lesser splanchnic nerve; arises from last two thoracic sympathetic ganglia and passes to aorticorenal ganglion.

n. stape'dius [NA], nerve to the stapedius muscle; branch of facial nerve arising in facial canal and innervating stapedius muscle.

n. subcla'vius [NA], subclavian nerve; branch from superior trunk of the brachial plexus supplying subclavius muscle.

n. subcosta'lis [NA], subcostal nerve; ventral branch of twelfth thoracic nerve; supplies parts of abdominal muscles and gives off cutaneous branches to skin of lower abdominal wall and to gluteal region.

n. sublingua'lis [NA], sublingual nerve; branch of lingual nerve to sublingual gland and mucous membrane of floor of mouth.

n. suboccipita'lis [NA], suboccipital nerve; dorsal branch of first cervical nerve, sending branches to rectus capitis posterior major and minor, obliquus capitis superior and inferior, rectus capitis lateralis, and semispinalis capitis muscles.

n. subscapula'ris [NA], subscapular nerve; branch of posterior cord of brachial plexus, supplying subscapularis muscle.

n. supraclavicula'ris [NA], supraclavicular nerve; (1) intermediate or middle, one of several nerves arising from cervical plexus which pass down across the clavicle to supply skin in infraclavicular region; (2) lateral or posterior, one of several branches of cervical plexus which descend to skin over acromion and deltoid region; (3) medial or anterior, one of several nerves arising from the cervical plexus which supply the skin over the upper medial part of the thorax.

n. supraorbita'lis [NA], supraorbital nerve; branch of frontal nerve, dividing into branches distributed to forehead and scalp, upper eyelid, and frontal sinus.

n. suprascapula'ris [NA], suprascapular nerve; arises from fifth and sixth cervical nerves to supply supraspinatus and infraspinatus muscles, and also sends branches to shoulder joint.

n. supratrochlea'ris [NA], supratrochlear nerve; branch of frontal nerve supplying medial part of upper eyelid, central part of skin of forehead, and

root of nose.

n. sura'lis [NA], sural nerve; formed by union of medial cutaneous nerve of leg from tibial and peroneal communicating branch of the common peroneal nerve; accompanies small saphenous vein around lateral malleolus to dorsum of foot.

ner'vi tempora'les profun'di [NA], deep temporal nerves; two branches, anterior and posterior, from mandibular nerve, supplying temporal muscle.

n. tenso'ris tym'pani [NA], nerve of the tensor tympani muscle; branch of mandibular nerve passing through otic ganglion without synapse to supply tensor tympani muscle.

n. tenso'ris ve'li palati'ni [NA], nerve of the tensor veli palatini muscle; branch of mandibular nerve passing through otic ganglion without synapse to supply tensor veli palatini muscle.

ner'vi termina'les [NA], terminal nerves; delicate plexiform nerve strands passing parallel and medial to olfactory tracts, distributing peripherally with olfactory nerves and passing centrally into anterior perforated substance; considered to have an autonomic function.

ner'vi thora'cici [NA], thoracic nerves; twelve nerves on each side, mixed motor and sensory, supplying muscles and skin of thoracic and abdominal walls.

n. thora'cicus lon'gus [NA], long thoracic nerve; arises from fifth, sixth, and seventh cervical nerves, descends neck behind brachial plexus, and is distributed to serratus anterior muscle.

n. thoracodorsa'lis [NA], thoracodorsal nerve; arises from posterior cord of brachial plexus; contains fibers from sixth, seventh, and eighth cervical nerves and supplies latissimus dorsi muscle.

n. tibia'lis [NA], tibial nerve; one of two major divisions of sciatic nerve; supplies hamstring muscles, muscles of back of leg and plantar aspect of foot, and skin on back of leg and sole of foot.

n. transver'sus col'li [NA], transverse nerve of neck; branch of cervical plexus that supplies skin over anterior triangle of neck.

n. trigem'inus [NA], trigeminal nerve; fifth cranial nerve; chief sensory nerve of face and motor nerve of muscles of mastication; its nuclei are in mesencephalon and in pons, extending down into cervical portion of spinal cord; emerges by two roots, sensory and motor, from lateral surface of pons, and enters a cavity of dura mater at apex of petrous portion of temporal bone, where its sensory root expands to form trigeminal (gasserian) ganglion; from there, three divisions (ophthalmic, maxillary, and mandibular) branch forth.

n. trochlea'ris [NA], trochlear nerve; fourth cranial nerve; supplies superior oblique muscle of eye; origin is in midbrain below cerebral aqueduct.

n. tympan'icus [NA], tympanic nerve; a nerve from inferior ganglion of glossopharyngeal nerve, passing to tympanic cavity and forming tympanic plexus which supplies mucous membrane of tympanic cavity, mastoid cells, and auditory tube; parasympathetic fibers also pass through tympanic nerve via lesser petrosal nerve to otic ganglion to supply parotid gland.

n. ulna'ris [NA], ulnar or cubital nerve; arises from medial cord of brachial plexus and gives off numerous muscular and cutaneous branches in forearm and supplies intrinsic muscles of hand and skin of medial side of hand.

n. utricula'ris [NA], utricular nerve; branch of utriculoampullar nerve, supplying macula of utricle.

n. utriculoampulla'ris [NA], utriculoampullar nerve; division of vestibular part of eighth cranial nerve; gives off branches to macula of utricle (n. utricularis) and to cristae of ampullae of anterior and lateral semicircular ducts (n. ampullaris anterior and lateralis).

ner'vi vagina'les [NA], vaginal nerves; several nerves passing from uterovaginal plexus to vagina.

n. va'gus [NA], vagus or pneumogastric nerve; tenth cranial nerve; a mixed nerve that arises by numerous small roots from side of medulla oblongata; supplies pharynx; larynx, lungs, heart, esophagus, stomach, and most of abdominal viscera.

n. vertebra'lis [NA], vertebral nerve; branch from cervicothoracic ganglion that ascends along vertebral artery to level of axis or atlas, giving branches to cervical nerves and meninges.

n. vestibulocochlea'ris [NA], vestibulocochlear nerve; eighth cranial nerve; acoustic nerve; a composite sensory nerve emerging from the brainstem at the cerebellopontine angle and innervating receptor cells of membranous labyrinth, consisting of two anatomically and functionally distinct components: **(1)** vestibular nerve, which innervates hair cells of vestibular organ; **(2)** cochlear or auditory nerve, which innervates hair cells of spiral organ.

n. zygomat'icus [NA], zygomatic or temporomandibular nerve; branch of maxillary nerve in inferior orbital fissure through which it passes; divides into zygomaticotemporal and zygomaticofacial branches which supply skin of temporal and zygomatic regions.

net'work. Net; a structure bearing a resemblance to a woven fabric. See also rete; reticulum.

neur-, neuri-, neuro- [G. *neuron*, nerve]. Combining form denoting a nerve or relating to the nervous system.

neural (nūr'al) [G. *neuron*, nerve]. **1.** Relating to any structure composed of nerve cells or their processes, or that on further development will give rise to nerve cells. **2.** Referring to the dorsal side of the vertebral bodies or their precursors, where the spinal cord is located.

neuralgia (nūr-al'jī-ah) [neur- + G. *algos*, pain]. Neurodynia; pain of a severe throbbing, or stabbing character in the course or distribution of a nerve.

n. facia'lis ve'ra, geniculate n.

Fothergill's n., trigeminal n.

geniculate n., n. facialis vera; Hunt's n.; a severe paroxysmal lancinating pain deep in the ear, on the anterior wall of the external meatus, and on a small area just in front of the pinna.

Hunt's n., geniculate n.

idiopathic n., nerve pain not due to any apparent lesion of the nerve itself.

Morton's n., Morton's *syndrome*.

red n., erythromelalgia.

trifacial n., trigeminal n.

trigeminal n., severe paroxysmal bursts of pain in one or more branches of the trigeminal nerve, often induced by touching trigger areas in or about the mouth. Also called trifacial or Fothergill's n.; Fothergill's disease (1); tic douloureux; prosopalgia; prosoponeuralgia.

neural'gic. Relating to, resembling, or of the character of, neuralgia.

neuraminic acid (nūr'ă-min-ik). An aldol product of mannosamine and pyruvic acid; the *N*- and *O*-acyl derivatives are known as sialic acids and are constituents of gangliosides and of the polysaccharide components of muco- and glycoproteins from many tissues, secretions, and species.

neuramin'idase. An enzyme that cleaves terminal acylneuraminic residues from oligosaccharides, glycoproteins, or glycolipids; present as a surface antigen in myxoviruses.

neuranagenesis (nūr'an-ă-jen'ĕ-sis) [neur- + G. *ana*, up, again, + *genesis*, generation]. Regeneration of a nerve.

neurapophysis (nūr-ă-pof'ĭ-sis) [neur- + G. *apophysis*, offshoot]. *Lamina* arcus vertebrae.

neurapraxia (nūr-ă-prak'sĭ-ah) [neur- + apraxia]. Injury to a nerve resulting in paralysis without degeneration and followed by rapid and complete recovery of function.

neurasthenia (nūr-as-the'nĭ-ah) [neur- + G. *astheneia*, weakness]. An ill-defined condition, commonly accompanying or following depression, characterized by vague functional fatigue.

neurasthenic (nūr-as-then'ik). Relating to neurasthenia.

neuraxis (nūr-ak'sis). The axial unpaired part of the CNS: spinal cord, rhombencephalon, mesencephalon, and diencephalon.

neurectasis, neurectasia (nūr-ek'tă-sis, -ek-ta'zĭ-ah) [neur- + G. *ektasis*, extension]. Neurotony; surgical stretching of a nerve or nerve trunk.

neurectomy (nūr-ek'to-mĭ) [neur- + G. *ektomē*, excision]. Excision of a segment of a nerve.

presacral n., Cotte's operation; removal of the presacral plexus to relieve severe dysmenorrhea.

neurectopia, neurectopy (nūr-ek-to'pĭ-ah, -ek'to-pĭ) [neur- + G. *ektopos*, fr. *ek*, out of, + *topos*, place]. **1.** Dislocation of a nerve trunk. **2.** A condition in which a nerve follows an anomalous course.

neurenteric (nūr-en-tĕr'ik) [neur- + G. *enteron*, intestine]. Relating, in the embryo, to both the neural tube and enteric canal.

neurergic (nūr-er'jik) [neur- + G. *ergon,* work]. Relating to the activity of a nerve.

neurexeresis (nūr'ek-sĕr-e'sis) [neur- + G. *exairesis,* a taking out, fr. *haireō,* to grasp, take]. Surgical evulsion of a nerve.

neuri-. See neur-.

neurilemma (nu-rĭ-lem'ah). Neurolemma.

neurilemoma (nu'rĭ-lĕ-mo'mah) [neurilemma + G. *-oma,* tumor]. Neurinoma; schwannoma (2); a benign encapsulated neoplasm in which the fundamental component is structurally identical to Schwann cells; neoplastic cells proliferate within the endoneurium, and the perineurium forms the capsule; may originate from a peripheral or sympathetic nerve, or from various cranial nerves, particularly the eighth nerve;

  acoustic n., a benign neoplasm of the intracranial segment of the eighth cranial nerve, producing cerebellar, lower cranial nerve, and brainstem signs and symptoms.

neurimo'tor. Nervimotor.

neurino'ma. Neurilemoma.

neuritic (nu-rit'ik). Relating to neuritis.

neuritis, pl. **neuritides** (nu-ri'tis, nu-rit'ĭ-dēz) [neuri- + G. *-itis,* inflammation]. Inflammation of a nerve, marked by neuralgia, hyperesthesia, anesthesia or paraesthesia, paralysis, muscular atrophy in the region supplied by the affected nerve, and by abolition of the reflexes.

  adventitial n., inflammation of the sheath of a nerve.

  endemic n., beriberi.

  interstitial n., inflammation of the connective tissue framework of a nerve.

  multiple n., polyneuritis.

  optic n., retrobulbar n.; neuropapillitis; inflammation of the optic nerve.

  parenchymatous n., inflammation of the nervous substance proper, the axons, and myelin.

  retrobulbar n., optic n.

  segmental n., inflammation occurring at several points along the course of a nerve.

  toxic n., n. due to the action of alcohol, lead, arsenic, or some other poison.

  traumatic n., inflammation of a nerve following an injury.

neuro-. See neur-.

neu'roanas'tomo'sis. Surgical formation of a junction between nerves.

neuroanatomy (nu'ro-an-at'o-mĭ). The anatomy of the nervous system.

neuroarthropathy (nu'ro-ar-throp'ă-thĭ) [neuro- + G. *arthron,* joint, + *pathos,* suffering, disease]. A trophoneurosis affecting one or more joints.

neurobiology (nu'ro-bi-ol'o-jĭ). The biology of the nervous system.

neu'roblast [neuro- + G. *blastos,* germ]. An embryonic nerve cell.

neuroblasto'ma. A malignant neoplasm characterized by immature, only slightly differentiated nerve cells of embryonic type arranged in sheets, irregular clumps, cordlike groups, individually, and in pseudorosettes; occurs frequently in infants and children in the mediastinal and retroperitoneal regions, and widespread metastases are common.

neurocar'diac [neuro- + G. *kardia,* heart]. **1.** Relating to the nerve supply of the heart. **2.** Relating to a cardiac neurosis.

neu'rochem'istry. The chemistry of nerve material, metabolism, and function.

neurochorioretinitis (nu'ro-ko'rĭ-o-ret-in-i'tis). Inflammation of the choroid coat of the eye, the retina, and the optic nerve.

neurochoroiditis (nu'ro-ko-roy-di'tis). Inflammation of the choroid coat of the eye and the optic nerve.

neurocladism (nu-rok'lă-dizm) [neuro- + G. *klados,* a young branch]. Outgrowth of axons from the central stump to bridge the gap in a cut nerve.

neurocranium (nu-ro-kra'nĭ-um) [neuro- + G. *kranion,* skull]. The part of the skull enclosing the brain, as distinguished from the bones of the face.

neurocristopathy (nu'ro-kris-top'ă-thĭ) [neuro- + L. *crista,* crest, + G. *pathos,* suffering]. Maldevelopment or neoplasia of tissues of neural crest origin.

neurocyte (nu'ro-sīt) [neuro- + G. *kytos,* cell]. Neuron.

neurocytolysis (nu'ro-si-tol'ĭ-sis) [neuro- + G. *kytos,* cell, + *lysis,* dissolution]. Destruction of neurons.

neurocytoma (nu'ro-si-to'mah) [neuro- + G. *kytos,* cell, + *-oma,* tumor]. Ganglioneuroma.

neu'roden'drite, neu'roden'dron. Dendrite.

neurodermatitis (nu'ro-der-mă-ti'tis) [neuro- + G. *derma,* skin, + *-itis,* inflammation]. Neurodermatosis; a chronic lichenified skin lesion, localized or disseminated.

neu'rodermato'sis. Neurodermatitis.

neurodynamic (nu'ro-di-nam'ik) [neuro- + G. *dynamis,* force]. Pertaining to nervous energy.

neurodynia (nu-ro-din'ĭ-ah) [neuro- + G. *odynē,* pain]. Neuralgia.

neuroectoderm (nu'ro-ek'to-derm). That central region of the early embryo's ectoderm which in further development forms the brain and spinal cord, and also gives rise to the nerve cells and neurolemma of the peripheral nervous system.

neu'roectoder'mal. Relating to the neuroectoderm.

neu'roenceph'alomyelop'athy. Disease of the brain, spinal cord and nerves.

neu'roen'docrine. 1. Pertaining to the anatomical and functional relationships between the nervous system and the endocrine apparatus. **2.** Denoting cells that release a hormone into the circulating blood in response to a neural stimulus.

neu'roen'docrinol'ogy. The study of the anatomical and functional relationships between the nervous system and the endocrine apparatus.

neu'roepithe'lial. Relating to the neuroepithelium.

neuroepithelioma (nu'ro-ep-ĭ-the-lĭ-o'mah). A relatively rare type of glioma (usually of the retina) that consists of cuboidal or columnar ectodermal cells in a trabecular stroma of cellular fibrous tissue; the cells resemble primitive forms that develop into specialized sensory epithelium.

neuroepithelium (nu′ro-ep-ĭ-the′lĭ-um) [NA]. Epithelial cells specialized for the reception of external stimuli.

neurofi′bril. A filamentous aggregation microfilaments and microtubules in the nerve cell's body, dendrites, axon, and sometimes synaptic endings.

neurofi′brillar. Relating to neurofibrils.

neurofibroma (nu-ro-fi-bro′mah). Schwannoma (1); fibroneuroma; a moderately firm, benign, nonencapsulated tumor resulting from proliferation of Schwann cells in a disorderly pattern that includes portions of nerve fibers.

   multiple n.'s, neurofibromatosis.

   plexiform n., plexiform neuroma; a type of n., representing an anomaly rather than a true neoplasm, in which the proliferation of Schwann cells occurs from the inner aspect of the nerve sheath, thereby resulting in an irregularly thickened, distorted, tortuous structure.

neurofibromatosis (nu′ro-fi-bro-mă-to′sis). (von) Recklinghausen's disease; neuromatosis; multiple neurofibromas; small, discrete, pigmented skin lesions (café-au-lait spots, pigmented nevi) that develop into multiple slow-growing neurofibromas, usually subcutaneous, along the course of a peripheral nerve; sometimes associated with acoustic neurinomas or other intracranial neoplasms; autosomal dominant inheritance with marked clinical variability.

neuroganglion. Ganglion (1).

neurogenesis (nu-ro-jen′ĕ-sis) [neuro- + G. *genesis,* production]. Formation of nervous tissue.

neurogen′ic, neurogenet′ic. 1. Neurogenous; originating in, or caused by, the nervous system or nerve impulses. **2.** Relating to neurogenesis.

neurogenous (nu-roj′ĕ-nus). Neurogenic (1).

neuroglia (nu-rog′lĭ-ah) [neuro- + G. *glia,* glue]. Glia; reticulum (2); non-neuronal cellular elements of the central and peripheral nervous system.

neurogliacyte (nu-rog′lĭ-ă-sīt) [neuro- + G. *glia,* glue, + *kytos,* cell]. A cell of the neuroglia.

neurog′lial, neurog′liar. Relating to neuroglia.

neurog′liomato′sis. Gliomatosis.

neu′rogram [neuro- + G. *gramma,* something written]. The engram or physical register of the mental experience, stimulation of which retrieves and reproduces the original experience, thereby producing memory.

neurohistol′ogy. Microscopic anatomy of the nervous system.

neu′rohor′mone. A hormone liberated by nerve impulses formed by neurosecretory cells.

neurohypophysial (nu′ro-hi-po-fiz′ĭ-al). Relating to the neurohypophysis.

neurohypophysis (nu′ro-hi-pof′ĭ-sis) [neuro- + hypophysis] [NA]. *Lobus* posterior hypophyseos. See also hypophysis.

neuroid (ru′royd) [neuro- + G. *eidos,* resemblance]. Resembling a nerve; nervelike.

neurolemma (nu′ro-lem′ah) [neuro- + G. *lemma,* husk]. Neurilemma; sheath of Schwann; a cell that enfolds one or more axons of the peripheral nervous system.

neuroleptanalgesia (nu′ro-lept-an-al-je′sĭ-ah). An intense analgesic and amnesic state produced by administration of narcotic analgesics and neuroleptic drugs.

neuroleptanesthesia (nu′ro-lept-anes-the′zĭ-ah). A technique of general anesthesia based upon intravenous administration of neuroleptic drugs, together with inhalation of a weak anesthetic.

neuroleptic (nu-ro-lep′tik) [neuro- + G. *lēpsis,* taking hold]. Denoting an agent producing analgesia, sedation, and tranquilization or a condition similar to that produced by such an agent.

neurol′ogist. A specialist in neurology.

neurology (nu-rol′o-jĭ) [neuro- + G. *logos,* study]. The branch of medical science concerned with the nervous system and its disorders.

neurolysin (nu-rol′ĭ-sin). Neurotoxin; an antibody causing destruction of ganglion and cortical cells.

neurolysis (nu-rol′ĭ-sis) [neuro- + G. *lysis,* dissolution]. **1.** Destruction of nerve tissue. **2.** Freeing of a nerve from inflammatory adhesions.

neurolyt′ic. Relating to neurolysis.

neuroma (nu-ro′mah) [neuro- + G. *-oma,* tumor]. Old general term for any neoplasm derived from cells of the nervous system; such neoplasms are now classified in more specific categories, *e.g.,* ganglioneuroma, neurilemoma, pseudoneuroma.

   acoustic n., acoustic *neurinoma.*

   amputation n., traumatic n.

   n. cu′tis, neurofibroma of the skin.

   false n., traumatic n.

   plexiform n., plexiform *neurofibroma.*

   n. telangiecto′des, a neurofibroma with a conspicuous number of blood vessels.

   traumatic n., amputation or false n.; the proliferative mass of Schwann cells and neurites that may develop at the proximal end of a severed or injured nerve.

neuromalacia (nu′ro-mă-la′shĭ-ah) [neuro- + G. *malakia,* softness]. Pathologic softening of nervous tissue.

neuromatosis (nu′ro-mă-to′sis). Neurofibromatosis.

neuromere (nu′ro-mēr) [neuro- + G. *meros,* part]. That part of the neural tube within a metamere.

neuromus′cular. Referring to the relationship between nerve and muscle.

neuromyasthenia (nu′ro-mi-as-the′nĭ-ah) [neuro- + G. *mys,* muscle, + *a-* priv. + *sthenos,* strength]. Muscular weakness, usually of emotional origin.

   epidemic n., Iceland disease; an epidemic disease often with insidious onset and characterized by stiffness of the neck and back, headache, diarrhea, fever, and localized muscular weakness.

neuromyelitis (nu′ro-mi-el-i′tis) [neuro- + G. *myelos*, marrow, + *-itis*, inflammation]. Myeloneuritis; neuritis combined with spinal cord inflammation.

n. op′tica, Devic's disease; a demyelinating disorder associated with transverse myelopathy and optic neuritis.

neu′romyop′athy [neuro- + G. *mys*, muscle, + *pathos*, disease]. A disorder of muscle that directly reflects a disease or disorder of nerve supplying the muscle.

neuromyositis (nu′ro-mi-o-si′tis) [neuro- + G. *mys*, muscle, + *-itis*, inflammation]. Neuritis with inflammation of the muscles with which the affected nerve or nerves are in relation.

neuron (nu′ron) [G. *neuron*, a nerve]. Nerve cell; neurocyte; the morphologic and functional unit of the nervous system, consisting of the nerve cell body, the dendrites, and the axon.

bipolar n., a n. that has two processes arising from opposite poles of the cell body.

internuncial n., intercalary n., a n. interposed between and connecting two other n's.

lower motor n., clinical term indicating the final motor n., as opposed to the upper motor n.'s of the motor cortex that contribute to the pyramidal or corticospinal tract.

motor n., motoneuron; a nerve cell in the spinal cord, rhombencephalon, or mesencephalon characterized by having an axon that leaves the CNS to establish a functional connection with an effector tissue; **somatic motor n.'s** directly synapse with striated muscle fibers by motor endplates; **visceral** or **autonomic motor n.'s** (**preganglionic motor n.'s**) innervate smooth muscle fibers or glands only by the intermediary of a second, peripheral, n. (**postganglionic** or **ganglionic motor n.**) located in an autonomic ganglion.

multipolar n., a n. with several processes, usually an axon and three or more dendrites.

unipolar n., a n. the cell body of which emits a single axonal process which divides into a peripheral axon branch extending outward as a peripheral afferent (sensory) nerve fiber, and a central axon branch that enters into synaptic contact with n.'s in the spinal cord or brainstem.

upper motor n.'s, clinical term indicating those n.'s of the motor cortex that contribute to the formation of the pyramidal or corticospinal and corticobulbar tracts.

neuronal (nu′ro-nal, nu-ro′nal). Pertaining to a neuron.

neuronevus (nu′ro-ne′vus). A variety of intradermal nevus in which nests of nevus cells in the lower dermis are hyalinized and resemble nerve bundles.

neuronophage (nu-ron′o-fāj) [neuron + G. *phagein*, to eat]. A phagocyte that ingests neuronal elements.

neuronophagia, neuronophagy (nu′ron-o-fa′ji-ah, nu-ro-nof′a-jī [neuron + G. *phagein*, to eat]. Phagocytosis of nerve cells.

neurooncology (nu′ro-on-kol′o-jī) [neuro- + onco- + G *logos*, study]. The study of tumors of the nervous system.

neuro-ophthalmology (nu′ro-of-thal-mol′o-jī). That branch of medical science pertaining to visual representation in the CNS.

neu′ropapilli′tis. Optic *neuritis*.

neuroparal′ysis. Paralysis resulting from disease of the nerve supplying the affected part.

neuropath′ic. Relating in any way to neuropathy.

neu′ropathogen′esis [neuro- + G. *pathos*, suffering, + *genesis*, origin]. The origin or causation of a disease of the nervous system.

neu′ropathol′ogy. Pathology of the nervous system.

neuropathy (nu-rop′ă-thī) [neuro- + G. *pathos*, suffering]. Any disorder affecting any segment of the nervous system; specifically, a disease involving the cranial or spinal nerves.

diabetic n., a combined sensory and motor n., typically symmetric and segmental, and involving autonomic fibers, seen frequently in older diabetic persons.

entrapment n., a region of traumatic neuritis in which the nerve is maintained in an irritated state by external pressure created by encroachment or impingement from a nearby structure.

hereditary hypertrophic n., Déjérine's or Déjérine-Sottas disease; a progressive chronic sensorimotor polyneuropathy associated with swelling and mucoid degeneration of peripheral nerves; autosomal dominant inheritance.

segmental n., demyelination of scattered segments of peripheral nerves, with relating sparing of axons; noted in diabetes, arsenic poisoning, lead poisoning, diphtheria, and leprosy.

neuropharmacology (nu′ro-far-mă-kol′o-jī). The study of drugs that exert effects on neuronal tissue.

neurophysines (nu-ro-fiz′ēnz). A family of proteins synthesized in the hypothalamus and found associated with vasopressin and oxytocin in the neurosecretory granules; they function as carriers in the transport and storage of neurohypophysial hormones.

neurophysiology (nu′ro-fiz-ī-ol′o-jī). Physiology of the nervous system.

neuropil, neuropile (nu′ro-pil, -pīl) [neuro- + G. *pilos*, felt]. The complex net of axonal, dendritic, and glial arborizations that forms the bulk of the CNS gray matter, and in which the nerve cell bodies lie embedded.

neu′roplasm. The protoplasm of a nerve cell.

neuroplasty (nu′ro-plas′tī) [neuro- + G. *plassō*, to form]. Plastic surgery of the nerves.

neuroplegic (nu-ro-ple′jik) [neuro- + G. *plēgē*, a stroke]. Pertaining to paralysis due to nervous system disease.

neuropodia (nu-ro-po′dī-ah) [neuro- + G. *podion*, little foot]. Axon *terminals*.

neuropore (nu'ro-pōr) [neuro- + G. *poros*, pore]. An opening in the embryo leading from the central canal of the neural tube to the exterior.

neuropraxia (nu-ro-prak'sĭ-ah) [neuro- + G. *praxis*, action]. A state of a nerve in which conduction is blocked across a point but is present in the nerve above and below the lesion.

neuropsychiatry (nu'ro-si-ki'ă-trĭ). The specialty concerned with organic and functional diseases of the nervous system.

neuropsychopathy (nu'ro-si-kop'ă-thĭ). An emotional illness of neurologic and/or functional origin.

neur'oradiol'ogy. Radiology concerned with the study of the nervous system.

neuroretinitis (nu'ro-ret-ĭ-ni'tis). Inflammation of the retina and of the optic nerve.

neurorrhaphy (nu-ror'ă-fĭ) [neuro- + G. *rhaphē*, suture]. Neurosuture; joining together, usually by suture, of a divided nerve.

neurosarcocleisis (nu'ro-sar-ko-kli'sis) [neuro- + G. *sarx*, flesh, + *kleisis*, closure]. Resection of one of the walls of the osseous canal traversed by the nerve and the transportation of the latter into the soft tissues, for the relief of neuralgia.

neurosarco'ma. A malignant neoplasm derived from cells of the nervous system.

neurosciences (nu-ro-si'en-sez). The scientific disciplines concerned with the development, structure, function, chemistry, pharmacology, and pathology of the nervous system.

neu'rosecre'tion. The release of a secretory substance from the axon terminals of certain nerve cells in the brain.

neurosecretory (nu'ro-se-kre'tor-ĭ). Relating to the cells involved in, or the substance produced by, neurosecretion.

neurosis, pl. **neuroses** (nu-ro'sis, -sēz) [neuro- + G. *-osis*, condition]. **1.** A psychological or behavioral disorder in which anxiety is the primary characteristic; in contrast to the psychoses, persons with a n. do not exhibit gross distortion of reality or disorganization of personality. **2.** A functional nervous disease, or one which is dependent upon no evident lesion. **3.** A peculiar state of tension or irritability of the nervous system; any form of nervousness.

anxiety n., anxiety state; chronic abnormal distress and worry to the point of panic.

battle n., war n.

cardiac n., cardioneurosis; anxiety concerning the state of the heart, as a result of palpitation, chest pain, or other symptoms not due to heart disease.

character n., a subclass of personality disorders.

compensation n., development of symptoms of n. believed to be motivated by the desire for, and hope of, monetary gain.

compulsive n., obsessive-compulsive n.

conversion hysteria n., conversion *hysteria*.

obsessive-compulsive n., compulsive n.; a disorder characterized by the persistent and repetitive intrusion of unwanted thoughts, urges, or actions that the

individual is unable to prevent; anxiety or distress is the underlying emotion or drive state, and ritualistic behavior is a learned method of reducing the anxiety.

occupation or **professional n.,** a functional disorder of a group of muscles used chiefly in one's occupation, marked by the occurrence of spasm, paresis, or incoordination on attempt to repeat the habitual movements.

transference n., in psychoanalysis, the phenomenon of the patient's developing a strong emotional relationship with the analyst, symbolizing an emotional relationship with a family figure.

traumatic n., any functional nervous disorder following an accident or injury.

war n., battle n.; a stress condition or mental disorder induced by conditions existing in warfare.

neu'rospasm. Muscular spasm or twitching caused by a disordered nerve supply.

neurosplanchnic (nu-ro-splangk'nik) [neuro- + G. *splanchnon*, a viscus]. Neurovisceral.

Neurospora (nūr-os'por-ah) [neuro- + G. *spora*, seed]. Pink bread mold; a genus of fungi (class Ascomycetes) grown in cultures and used in research in genetics and cellular biochemistry.

neurosthenia (nu-ro-sthe'nĭ-ah) [neuro- + G. *sthenos*, force]. A condition in which the nerves respond with abnormal force or rapidity to slight stimuli.

neurosur'geon. A surgeon specializing in neurosurgery.

neurosur'gery. Surgery of the nervous system.

neurosu'ture. Neurorrhaphy.

neurosyphilis (nu-ro-sif'ĭ-lis). Nervous system manifestations of syphilis, including tabes dorsalis, general paresis, and meningovascular syphilis.

neurotendinous (nu-ro-ten'dĭ-nus). Relating to both nerves and tendons.

neurotic (nu-rot'ik). Relating to a neurosis.

neurotization (nu'ro-tĭ-za'shun). Development of nervous substance; regeneration of a nerve.

neurotmesis (nu-rot-me'sis) [neuro- + G. *tmēsis*, a cutting]. The condition in which there is complete division of a nerve.

neurotomy (nu-rot'o-mĭ) [neuro- + G. *tomē*, a cutting]. Surgical division of a nerve.

neurotonic (nu'ro-ton'ik). **1.** Relating to neurotony. **2.** Strengthening or stimulating impaired nervous action.

neurotony (nu-rot'o-nĭ) [neuro- + G. *tonos*, tension]. Neurectasis.

neurotox'ic. Poisonous to nervous substance.

neurotox'in. Neurolysin.

neurotransmitter (nu'ro-trans-mit'er) [neuro- + L. *transmitto*, to send across]. Any specific chemical agent released by a presynaptic cell, upon excitation, which crosses the synapse to stimulate or inhibit the postsynaptic cell.

neurotrip'sy [neuro- + G. *tripsis*, a rubbing]. Surgical crushing of a nerve.

neurotrophic (nu-ro-trof′ik). Relating to neurotrophy.

neurotrophy (nu-rot′ro-fĭ) [neuro- + G. *trophē*, nourishment]. Nutrition and metabolism of tissues under nervous influence.

neurotropic (nu′ro-trop′ik). Having an affinity for the nervous system.

neurotropy, neurotropism (nu-rot′ro-pĭ, -pizm) [neuro- + G. *tropē*, a turning]. **1.** Affinity of basic dyes for nervous tissue. **2.** The attraction of certain pathogenic microorganisms, poisons, and nutritive substances toward the nerve centers.

neurotubule (nu′ro-tu-būl). One of the microtubules occurring in the cell body, dendrites, axon, and in some synaptic endings of neurons.

neurovaccine (nu-ro-vak′sēn). A fixed or standardized vaccine virus of definite strength, obtained by continued passage through the brain of rabbits.

neurovas′cular. Relating to both nervous and vascular systems; relating to the nerves supplying the walls of the blood vessels.

neurovi′rus. Vaccine virus modified by means of passage into and growth in nervous tissue.

neurovisceral (nu-ro-vis′er-al) [neuro- + L. *viscera*, the internal organs]. Neurosplanchnic; referring to innervation of the internal organs by the autonomic nervous system.

neutral (nu′tral) [L. *neutralis*, fr. *neuter*, neither]. **1.** Exhibiting no positive properties; indifferent. **2.** In chemistry, neither acid nor alkaline.

neu′traliza′tion. **1.** The conversion of the entire amount of an acid or a base into a salt by the addition of an exactly sufficient quantity of a base or of an acid, respectively. **2.** The change in reaction of a solution from acid or alkaline to neutral by the addition of just a sufficient amount of an alkaline or of an acid substance, respectively. **3.** The rendering ineffective of any action, process, or potential.

neutrino (nu-tre′no) [neutron + It. dim. *-ino*]. A subatomic particle having zero rest mass and no charge, traveling always at the speed of light, and interacting with matter only very rarely.

neutro-, neutr- [L. *neutralis*, fr. *neuter*, neither]. Combining forms meaning neutral.

neutron [L. *neuter*, neither]. An electrically neutral particle in the nuclei of all atoms (except hydrogen-1) with a mass approximately that of a proton.

neutropenia (nu-tro-pe′nĭ-ah) [neutrophil + G. *penia*, poverty]. Neutrophilic leukopenia; presence of abnormally small numbers of neutrophils in the circulating blood.

  periodic n., cyclic n., n. recurring at regular intervals, in association with various types of infectious diseases.

neutrophil, neutrophile (nu′tro-fil, -fīl) [neutro- + G. *philos*, fond]. **1.** A mature white blood cell in the granulocytic series, formed by myelopoietic tissue of the bone marrow and released into the circulating blood; characterized by a lobated nucleus and a coarse network of fairly dense chromatin and a cytoplasm that contains numerous fine granules. **2.** Any cell or tissue that manifests no special affinity for acid or basic dyes.

neutrophil′ia. Neutrophilic leukocytosis; an increase of neutrophilic leukocytes in blood or tissues; also frequently used synonymously with leukocytosis, inasmuch as the latter is generally the result of an increased number of neutrophilic granulocytes in the circulating blood, the tissues, or both.

neutrophil′ic. **1.** Pertaining to or characterized by presence of neutrophils. **2.** Characterized by a lack of affinity for acid or basic dyes.

neutrotaxis (nu-tro-tak′sis) [neutrophil + G. *taxis*, arrangement]. A phenomenon in which neutrophilic leukocytes are stimulated by a substance in such a manner that they are either attracted and move toward it (*positive n.*) or they are repelled and move away from it (*negative n.*).

ne′vi [L.]. Plural of nevus.

ne′void [L. *naevus*, mole (nevus), + G. *eidos*, resemblance]. Nevose (2); nevous (2); resembling a nevus.

ne′vose, ne′vous. **1.** Marked with nevi. **2.** Nevoid.

nevoxanthoendothelioma (ne′vo-zan′tho-en′do-the-lī-o′mah) [nevus + G. *xanthos*, yellow, + endothelioma]. Juvenile *xanthogranuloma*.

ne′vus, pl. **ne′vi** [L. *naevus*, mole, birthmark]. **1.** Birthmark; a circumscribed malformation of the skin, especially if colored by hyperpigmentation or increased vascularity. **2.** A benign localized overgrowth of melanin-forming cells arising in the skin early in life.

  basal cell n., a hereditary disease characterized by usually benign lesions of the eyelids, nose, cheeks, neck, and axillae, appearing as uneroded flesh-colored papules histologically indistinguishable from basal cell epithelioma; autosomal dominant inheritance with high penetrance.

  bathing trunk n., Tierfellnaevus; a large hairy congenital pigmented n. with a predilection for the entire lower trunk.

  blue n., Jadassohn-Tièche n.; a dark blue or blue-black n. covered by smooth skin and formed by melanin-pigmented spindle cells in the lower dermis.

  blue rubber-bleb nevi, a syndrome characterized by erectile, easily compressible, thin-walled hemangiomatous nodules, widely distributed in the skin and in the alimentary canal, and sometimes in other tissues.

  n. comedon′icus, comedo n., congenital linear keratinous cystic invaginations of the epidermis, with failure of development of normal pilosebaceous follicles.

  n. flam′meus, port-wine mark or stain; a large n. vascularis having a purplish color, usually found on the head and neck.

  halo n., leukoderma acquisitum centrifugum; Suton's disease (1); a usually benign, sometimes multiple, melanotic n. in which involution occurs with a central brown mole surrounded by a uniformly depigmented zone.

intradermal n., a n. in which nests of melanocytes are found in the dermis, but not at the epidermal-dermal junction.

Ito's n., pigmentation of skin innervated by lateral branches of the supraclavicular nerve and the lateral cutaneous nerve of the arm, due to scattered n. cells in the dermis.

Jadassohn-Tièche n., blue n.

junction n., a n. consisting of nests of n. cells in the basal cell zone, at the junction of the epidermis and dermis, appearing as a small, slightly raised, flat, nonhairy pigmented (dark brown or black) tumor.

Ota's n., oculodermal *melanosis*.

n. pigmento'sus, mole (1); a congenital pigmented lesion of varying size, raised or level with the skin.

n. pilo'sus, hairy mole; a mole covered with an abundant growth of hair.

n. seba'ceus (of Jadassohn), congenital hyperplasia of the sebaceous glands with papillary acanthosis of the epidermis.

spider n., arterial *spider*.

n. spi'lus, a flat mole.

n. spongio'sus al'bus muco'sae, white sponge n.

strawberry n., strawberry mark; a small n. vascularis resembling a strawberry in size, shape, and color.

n. u'nius lat'eris, a congenital linear n. limited to one side of the body or to portions of the extremities on one side.

n. vascula'ris, n. vasculo'sus, a congenital irregular red discoloration of the skin caused by an overgrowth of the cutaneous capillaries.

white sponge n., n. spongiosus albus mucosae; hereditary mucosal keratosis manifested by a thickened white spongy fold of mucosa in the mouth.

woolly-hair n., allotrichia circumscripta; a circumscribed congenital kinking or woolliness of scalp hair.

new'born. Neonatal.

new'ton (N). [I. *Newton*]. Derived SI unit of force, expressed as meters-kilograms per second squared (m kg s^{-2}); equivalent to 10^5 dynes in the CGS system.

newton-meter. A unit of the mks system; energy expended, or work done, by a force of 1 newton acting through a distance of 1 meter; equal to a joule (10^7 ergs).

nexus, pl. **nexus** (nek'sus) [L. interconnection]. Gap *junction.*

NF *National Formulary.*

ng Nanogram.

Ni Nickel.

niacin (ni'ă-sin). Nicotinic acid.

ni'acinam'ide. Nicotinamide.

niche (nitch, nēsh) [Fr.]. **1.** An eroded or ulcerated area detected by contrast radiography. **2.** Ecological term for the "occupation" species in a biotic community, particularly its relationships to various other competitor, predator, prey, and parasite species.

nickel (nik'l) [Ger. *kupfer-nickel*, copper-colored ore from which first obtained]. A metallic element, symbol Ni, atomic no. 28, atomic weight 58.70.

nicotin'amide. Niacinamide; biologically active amide of nicotinic acid.

nicotin'amide adenine dinucleotide (NAD). Nadide; ribosylnicotinamide 5'-phosphate (NMN) and adenosine 5'-phosphate (AMP) linked by pyrophosphate formation between the two phosphoric groups; attached as a prosthetic group to a protein, it serves as a respiratory enzyme (hydrogen acceptor and donor) through alternate oxidation (NAD$^+$) and reduction (NADH).

nicotin'amide adenine dinucleotide phosphate (NADP). A coenzyme of many oxidases (dehydrogenases), in which the reaction NADP$^+$ + 2H $\rightleftharpoons$ NADPH + H$^+$ takes place; the third phosphoric group esterifies the 2'-hydroxyl of the adenosine moiety of NAD.

nicotin'amide mononucleotide (NMN). A condensation product of nicotinamide and ribose 5-phosphate, linking the N of nicotinamide to the (β) C-1 of the ribose; in NAD, the ring is linked by the 5'-P to the 5'-P of AMP.

nicotine (nik'o-tēn). 1-Methyl-2-(3-pyridyl)pyrrolidine; a poisonous volatile alkaloid, derived from tobacco and responsible for many of its effects; it first stimulates (small doses) then depresses (large doses) at autonomic ganglia and myoneural junctions.

nicotin'ic. Nicotine-like; relating to the stimulating action of acetylcholine and other nicotinic agents on autonomic ganglia, adrenal medulla, and the motor-end-plate of striated muscle.

nicotin'ic acid. Niacin; pyridine-4-carboxylic acid, a part of the vitamin B complex; is used in the prevention and treatment of pellagra, as a vasodilator, and as a cholesterol-lowering agent.

nictitation (nik-tĭ-ta'shun) [L. *nicto,* pp. *-atus,* to wink, fr. *nico,* to beckon]. Winking.

ni'dal. Relating to a nidus, or nest.

nidation (ni-da'shun) [L. *nidus,* nest]. Embedding of the early embryo in the uterine mucosa.

ni'dus, pl. **ni'di** [L. nest]. **1.** The nucleus or central point of origin of a nerve. **2.** A focus or point of lodgment and development of a pathogenic organism. **3.** The coalescence of molecules or small particles that is the beginning of a crystal or similar solid deposit.

n. a'vis, n. hirun'dinis, a deep depression on each side of the inferior surface of the cerebellum, between the uvula and the biventral lobe, in which the tonsil rests.

night'mare [*A.S. nyht,* night, + *mara,* a demon]. Incubus (2); a terrifying dream.

night-terrors. A disorder allied to nightmare in which a child awakes screaming with fright, the alarm persisting for a time during a state of semiconsciousness.

ni′gra [L. fr. *niger*, black]. In neuroanatomy, the *substantia* nigra.

nigrities (ni-grish′ĭ-ēz) [L. blackness, fr. *niger*, black]. Black pigmentation.

nigrosin, nigrosine (ni′gro-sin, -sēn). A variable mixture of blue-black aniline dyes; used as a histologic stain for nervous tissue and as a negative stain for studying bacteria and spirochetes.

nigrostriatal (ni′gro-stri-a′tal). Referring to the efferent connection of the substantia nigra (*q.v.*) with the striatum.

NIH National Institutes of Health.

nihilism (ni′ĭ-lizm, ni′hĭ-lizm) [L. *nihil*, nothing]. **1.** In psychiatry, the delusion of the nonexistence of everything especially of the self or part of the self. **2.** Engagement in acts which are totally destructive to one's own purposes and those of one's group.

nillip′arous. Never having borne children.

ninhydrin (nin-hi′drin). 2,2-Dihydroxy-1,3-indanedione; reacts with free amino acids to yield CO_2, NH_3, and an aldehyde, the NH_3 produced yielding a colored product.

niobium (ni-o′bĭ-um) [*Niobe*, G. myth. char.]. A rare metallic element, symbol Nb, atomic no. 41, atomic weight 92.91.

nipple (nip′l) [dim. of A.S. *neb*, beak, nose]. *Papilla* mammae.

nit [A.S. *knitu*]. The ovum of a body, head, or crab louse attached to human hair or clothing by a layer of chitin.

ni′trate. A salt of nitric acid.

nitric acid (ni′trik). HNO_3; a strong acid oxidant.

ni′trida′tion. Formation of nitrogen compounds through the action of ammonia (analogous to oxidation).

ni′tride. A compound of nitrogen and one other element.

ni′trifica′tion. 1. Bacterial conversion of nitrogenous matter into nitrates. **2.** Treatment of a material with nitric acid.

ni′trile. An alkyl cyanide; individual n.'s are named for the acid formed on hydrolysis.

nitrilo-. Prefix indicating the presence of a cyanide group, $-C{\equiv}N$.

ni′trite. A salt of nitrous acid.

nitritu′ria. The presence of nitrites in urine, as a result of the action of microorganisms that may reduce nitrates.

nitro-. Prefix denoting the group $-NO_2$.

nitrocel′lulose. Pyroxylin.

nitrofu′rans. Antimicrobials effective against Gram-positive and Gram-negative organisms.

nitrogen (ni′tro-jen) [L. *nitrum*, niter, + *-gen*, to produce]. **1.** A gaseous element, symbol N, atomic no. 7, atomic weight 14.007, forming about 77 parts by weight of the atmosphere. **2.** Pharmaceutical grade N_2; contains not less than 99.0% by volume of N_2; used as a diluent for medicinal gases, and for air replacement in pharmaceutical preparations.

blood urea n. (BUN), n., in the form of urea, in the blood; the most prevalent of nonprotein nitrogenous compounds in blood; blood normally contains 10 to 15 mg of urea/100 ml.

nonprotein n. (NPN), the n. content of other than protein bodies.

undetermined n., the n. of blood, urine, etc., other than urea, uric acid, amino acids, etc., that can be directly estimated; in blood it amounts to about 25 mg per 100 ml.

urea n., the portion of n. in a biological sample, such as blood or urine, that derives from its content of urea.

urinary n., the n. excreted as urea, amino acids, uric acid, etc., in the urine; each gram of urinary n. indicates the breakdown in the body of 6.25 g of protein.

nitrogenase (ni′tro-jĕ-nās). General term used to describe enzyme systems that catalyze the reduction of molecular nitrogen to ammonia in nitrogen-fixing bacteria.

nitrogen distribution. Nitrogen partition.

nitrogen group. Five trivalent or quinquivalent elements whose hydrogen compounds are basic and oxyacids vary from monobasic to tetrabasic: nitrogen, phosphorus, arsenic, antimony, and bismuth.

nitrogen lag. The length of time after the ingestion of a given protein before the amount of nitrogen equal to that in the protein has been excreted in the urine.

nitrogen mustards. Compounds of the general formula $R-N(CH_2CH_2Cl)$, the prototype of which is HN2 nitrogen mustard (mechlorethamine) in which R is CH_3; some have been used as antineoplastics.

nitrogenous (ni-troj′ĕ-nus). Relating to or containing nitrogen.

nitrogen partition. Nitrogen distribution; determination of the distribution of nitrogen in the urine among the various constituents.

nitroglycerin (ni-tro-glis′er-in). $C_3H_5(NO_3)_3$; an explosive yellowish oily fluid formed by the action of sulfuric and nitric acids on glycerin; used as a vasodilator, especially in angina pectoris.

nitrosamines (ni-trōs-am′ēnz). Amines substituted by a nitroso (NO) group, usually on a nitrogen atom, to yield *N*-nitrosamines (R–NH–NO or R_2N–NO). These compounds can be formed by direct combination of an amine and nitrous acid (which can be formed from nitrites in the acidic gastric juice); some are mutagenic and/or carcinogenic.

nitroso-. Prefix denoting a compound containing nitrosyl.

ni′trosyl. A univalent radical or atom group, $-N{=}O$, forming the nitroso compounds.

ni′trous. Denoting a nitrogen compound containing one less atom than the nitric compounds; one in which nitrogen is present in its trivalent state.

ni′trous acid. HNO_2; a standard biologic and clinical laboratory reagent.

ni′trous oxide. Laughing gas; N_2O; a rapidly acting and reversible, nondepressant, and nontoxic inhalation analgesic to supplement other anesthetics and analgesics.

ni′tryl. The radical −NO₂ of the nitro compounds.

nm Nanometer.

NMN Nicotinamide mononucleotide.

NMR Nuclear magnetic *resonance*.

No Nobelium.

nobelium (no-bel′ĭ-um) [*Nobel*Institute for Physics]. An element, atomic no. 102, symbol No, prepared by bombardment of curium with carbon nuclei.

Nocardia (no-kar′dĭ-ah) [E. *Nocard*]. A genus of aerobic, nonmotile actinomycetes (family Actinomycetaceae), transitional between bacteria and fungi, mainly saprophytic, and may produce disease in man and other animals. The type species is *N. farcinica.*

   N. asteroi′des, a species causing nocardiosis and possible mycetoma in man.

   N. ca′viae, a species, closely resembling *N. asteroides,* that causes mycetoma in man.

   N. farci′nica, a species, closely resembling *N. asteroides,* that is an infrequent cause of systemic nocardiosis and is the type species of the genus.

nocar′dial. Pertaining to or caused by *Nocardia.*

nocardiosis (no-kar′dĭ-o′sis). A generalized disease in man caused by *Nocardia asteroides,* occasionally by *N. farcinica,* characterized by primary pulmonary lesions which may be subclinical or chronic with hematogenous spread, and usually with CNS involvement.

noci- [L. *noceo,* to injure, hurt]. Combining form relating to hurt, pain, or injury.

nociceptive (no-sĭ-sep′tiv) [see nociceptor]. Capable of appreciation or transmission of pain.

nociceptor (no-sĭ-sep′tor) [noci- + L. *capio,* to take]. A peripheral nerve organ or mechanism for the appreciation and transmission of painful or injurious stimuli.

nocifensor (no-sĭ-fen′sor) [noci- + L. *fendo,* to strike, ward off]. Denoting processes or mechanisms that act to protect the body from injury; specifically, a system of nerves in the skin and mucous membranes that react to adjacent injury by vasodilation.

noci-influence. Injurious or harmful influence.

nociperception (no′sĭ-per-sep′shun) [noci- + perception]. Appreciation of injurious influences, as by nerve centers.

noct- [L. *nox,* night]. Combining form meaning night, nocturnal. See also nycto-.

nocturia (nok-tu′rĭ-a) [noct- + G. *ouron,* urine]. Urinating at night, often because of increased nocturnal secretion of urine.

noctur′nal [L. *nocturnus,* of the night]. Pertaining to the hours of darkness; the opposite of diurnal (1).

no′dal. Relating to any node.

node [L. *nodus,* a knot]. **1.** A knob; nodosity; a circumscribed swelling. **2.** A circumscribed mass of differentiated tissue. See nodus. **3.** A knuckle, or finger joint.

atrioventricular n., *nodus* atrioventricularis.

central lymph n.'s, n.'s located around the midportion of the axillary artery; they receive afferent vessels from the brachial, paramammary, and interpectoral n.'s and send efferent vessels to the apical n.'s.

n. of Cloquet, one of the deep inguinal lymph n.'s located in or adjacent to the femoral canal; sometimes mistaken for a femoral hernia when enlarged.

Dürck's n.'s, a small cell infiltration of the perivascular lymphatic tissue, throughout the brain, cord, and meninges, occurring in human trypanosomiasis.

Haygarth's n.'s, exostoses from the margins of the articular surfaces and from the periosteum and bone in the area of the finger joints, leading to ankylosis and associated with lateral deflection of the fingers toward the ulnar side, which occur in rheumatoid arthritis.

Heberden's n.'s, tuberculum arthriticum (1); small exostoses found on the terminal phalanges of the fingers in osteoarthritis, which are enlargements of the tubercles at the articular extremities of the distal phalanges.

Hensen's n., primitive n.

lymph n., lymph gland; nodus lymphaticus; lymphonodus; one of numerous round, oval, or bean-shaped bodies located along the course of lymphatic vessels, usually presenting a depressed area, the hilum, on one side through which blood vessels enter and efferent lymphatic vessels emerge; afferent vessels enter at many points of its periphery. Their structure consists of a fibrous capsule and internal trabeculae supporting lymphoid tissue and lymph sinuses; the lymphoid tissue is arranged in nodules in the cortex and cords in the medulla.

Osler n., a small, raised, and tender cutaneous lesion characteristic of subacute bacterial endocarditis, these n.'s usually appearing in the pads of fingers of toes.

primitive n., primitive knot; Hensen's n.; a local thickening of the blastoderm at the cephalic end of the primitive streak of the embryo.

Ranvier's n.'s, a short interval in the myelin sheath of a nerve fiber, occurring between each two successive segments of the myelin sheath; at the n., the axon is invested only by short, finger-like cytoplasmic processes of the two neighboring Schwann cells or, in the CNS, oligodendroglia cells.

signal n., Virchow's n.; jugular gland; a firm palpable supraclavicular lymph n., especially on the left side, which may be the first recognized *presumptive* evidence of a malignant neoplasm in one of the viscera.

singer's n.'s, small circumscribed beadlike enlargements on the vocal cords, caused by overuse or abuse of the voice.

sinoatrial n., sinus n., *nodus* sinuatrialis.

   Virchow's n., signal n.

no′di [L.]. Plural of nodus.

no'dose [L. *nodosus*]. Nodous; nodular; nodulous; nodulate; nodulated; having nodes or knotlike swellings.

nodos'ity [L. *nodositas*]. **1.** A node; a knoblike or knotty swelling. **2.** The condition of being nodose.

no'dous, nod'ular, nod'ulate, nod'ula'ted. Nodose.

nod'ula'tion. Formation or presence of nodules.

nodule (nod'ūl) [L. *nodulus,* dim. of *nodus,* knot]. A small node. See also nodulus.

    Albini's n.'s, minute fibrous n.'s on the margins of the mitral and tricuspid valves of the heart, sometimes present in the neonate.

    apple jelly n.'s, descriptive term for the papular lesions of lupus vulgaris, as they appear on diascopy.

    Arantius' n., *nodulus* valvulae semilunaris.

    Bianchi's n., *nodulus* valvulae semilunaris.

    cold n., clinical jargon for a thyroid n. with a much lower uptake of radioactive iodine than the surrounding parenchyma.

    Gamna-Gandy n.'s, Gamna-Gandy *bodies.*

    hot n., clinical jargon for a thyroid n. with a much higher uptake of radioactive iodine than the surrounding parenchyma.

    Jeanselme's n.'s, juxta-articular n.'s, a form of tertiary yaws characterized by the occurrence of n.'s on the arms and legs, usually near the joints.

    lymph n., *folliculus* lymphaticus.

    Morgagni's n., *nodulus* valvulae semilunaris.

    pulp n., pulp *stone.*

    rheumatoid n.'s, subcutaneous n.'s, occurring most commonly over bony prominences, in some patients with rheumatoid arthritis.

    siderotic n.'s, Gamna-Gandy *bodies.*

nodulous (nod'u-lus). Nodose.

nodulus, pl. **noduli** (nod'u-lus, -li) [L. dim. of *nodus*] [NA]. **1.** Nodule; a small node. **2.** The posterior extremity of the inferior vermis of the cerebellum, forming with the velum medullare posterius the central portion of the flocculonodular lobe.

    n. lymphat'icus, *folliculus* lymphaticus.

    n. val'vulae semiluna'ris [NA], Arantius, Morgagni's, or Bianchi's nodule; a nodule at the center of the free border of each semilunar valve at the beginning of the pulmonary artery and aorta.

no'dus, pl. **no'di** [L. a knot] [NA]. Node; in anatomy, a circumscribed mass of tissue.

    n. atrioventricula'ris [NA], atrioventricular node; a small node of specialized cardiac muscle fibers, located near the ostium of the coronary sinus, that gives rise to the atrioventricular bundle of the conduction system of the heart.

    no'di lymphat'ici mesenter'ici inferio'res [NA], inferior mesenteric lymph nodes; nodes located along the inferior mesenteric artery and its branches that drain the upper part of the rectum, the sigmoid colon, and the descending colon.

    no'di lymphat'ici mesenter'ici superio'res [NA], superior mesenteric lymph nodes; numerous nodes located in the mesentery along the superior mesenteric artery and its branches to the jejunum and ileum, from which they receive lymph.

    n. lymphat'icus, lymph *node.*

    n. sinuatria'lis [NA], sinoatrial or sinus node; the mass of specialized cardiac muscle fibers that normally acts as the "pacemaker" of the cardiac conduction system; it lies under the epicardium at the upper end of the sulcus terminalis.

no'ma [G. *nomē,* a spreading (sore)]. Stomatonecrosis; a gangrenous stomatitis, usually beginning in the mucous membrane of the corner of the mouth or cheek, and then progressing fairly rapidly to involve the entire thickness of the lips, cheek, or both, with conspicuous necrosis and complete sloughing of tissue. A similar process (**n. pudendi, n. vulvae**) may also involve the labia majora.

nomenclature (no'men-kla-chur, no-men'klă-chur). A set system of names used in any science, as of anatomic structures, organisms, etc.

nom'ogram [G. *nomos,* law, + *gramma,* something written]. A series of scales arranged so that calculations can be performed graphically.

nomotop'ic [G. *nomos,* law, custom, + *topos,* place]. Relating to, or occurring at, the usual or normal place.

non compos mentis [L. *non,* not, + *compos,* participating, competent, + *mens,* gen. *mentis,* mind]. Not of sound mind; mentally incapable of managing one's affairs.

nonconduc'tor. A substance that does not possess conductivity.

non'disjunc'tion. Failure of one or more pairs of chromosomes to separate at the miotic stage of karyokinesis, with the result that both chromosomes are carried to one daughter cell and none to the other.

nonelec'trolyte. A substance with molecules that do not, in solution, dissociate to ions, and, therefore, do not carry an electric current.

nonimmu'nity. Aphylaxis.

non'inva'sive. Denoting diagnostic procedures that do not involve penetration of the skin.

nonproprietary name (non-pro-pri'ĕ-tĕr-ĭ). A short name (often called a generic name) of a chemical, drug, or other substance, that is not subject to trademark (proprietary) rights but is, in contrast to a trivial name, recognized or recommended by government agencies and other organizations; like proprietary names, they are almost always coined designations derived without using set criteria.

nonsecre'tor. An individual whose saliva does not contain antigens of the ABO blood group.

non'union. Failure of normal healing of a fractured bone.

nonva'lent. Having no valency; not capable of entering into chemical composition.

nonvi'able. Incapable of independent existence.

nor-. Chemical prefix denoting: **1.** Elimination of one methylene group from a chain, the highest permissible locant being used. **2.** Contraction of a (steroid) ring by one CH_2 unit, the locant being the capital letter identifying the ring. **3.** "Normal" (*i.e.*, unbranched chain of carbon atoms) in aliphatic compounds, as opposed to branched.

noradren'aline. Norepinephrine.

norepinephrine (nor'ep-ĭ-nef'rin). Noradrenaline; levarterenol; *l*-α-(aminomethyl)-3,4-dihydroxybenzyl alcohol; a catecholamine hormone of which the natural form is D, although the L form has some activity. The base is considered to be the postganglionic adrenergic mediator present in the adrenal medulla which possesses the excitatory actions of epinephrine, but has minimal inhibitory effects.

nor'ethan'drolone. 17α-Ethyl-19-nortestosterone; an androgenic steroid similar chemically and pharmacologically to testosterone.

noreth'indrone. 19-nor-17α-Ethinyltestosterone; a progestational agent with some estrogenic and androgenic activity.

norleucine (nor-lu'sin). Caprine; $CH_3(CH_2)_3$-$CHNH_2COOH$; an α-amino acid, isomeric to leucine and isoleucine, but not found in proteins; a deamination product of lysine, to which it is linked in collagens.

norma, pl. **normae** (nor'man, nor'me) [L. a carpenter's square] [NA]. A line or pattern defining the contour of a part; extended to denote the outline of a surface, referring especially to the various aspects of the cranium.

nor'mal [L. *normalis*, according to pattern]. **1.** Typical; usual; healthy; according to the rule or standard. **2.** In bacteriology, nonimmune; untreated; denoting an animal, or the serum or substance contained therein, that has not been experimentally immunized against any microorganism or its products. **3 (N).** Denoting a solution containing 1 equivalent of replaceable hydrogen or hydroxyl per liter. **4.** In psychiatry and psychology, denoting a state of effective function satisfactory to both the individual and his social milieu.

normetanephrine (nor'met-ă-nef'rin). 3-*O*-Methylnorepinephrine; a catabolite of norepinephrine found, together with metanephrine, in the urine and some tissues; results from the action of catechol-*O*-methyltransferase on norepinephrine.

normo- [L. *normalis*, normal, according to pattern]. Combining form meaning normal, usual.

nor'moblast [normo- + G. *blastos*, sprout, germ]. A nucleated red blood cell, the immediate precursor of a normal erythrocyte in man.

normocapnia (nor-mo-kap'nĭ-ah) [normo- + G. *kapnos,* vapor]. A state in which the arterial carbon dioxide pressure is normal, about 40 mm Hg.

normochromia (nor-mo-kro'mĭ-ah) [normo- + G. *chrōma,* color]. Normal color; referring to blood in which the amount of hemoglobin in the red blood cells is normal.

normocyto'sis. A normal state of the blood with regard to its component formed elements.

normoglycemia (nor'mo-gli-se'mĭ-ah). Euglycemia.

normoglycemic (nor-mo-gli-se'mik). Englycemic.

nor'mokale'mia. A normal level of potassium in the blood.

normoten'sive. Normotonic (2); indicating a normal arterial blood pressure.

normother'mia [normo- + G. *thermē,* heat]. Environmental temperature that does not cause increased or depressed activity of body cells.

normoton'ic. 1. Eutonic; relating to or characterized by normal muscular tone. **2.** Normotensive.

normovolemia (nor'mo-vol-e'mĭ-ah) [normo- + volume + G. *haima,* blood]. A normal blood volume.

noscapine (nos'kă-pēn). An isoquinoline alkaloid, occurring in opium, with papaverine-like action on smooth muscle.

nose (nōz) [A.S. *nosu*]. Nasus.

 saddle n., a n. with markedly depressed bridge.

nose'bleed. Epistaxis.

nose'piece. A microscope attachment, consisting of several objectives surrounding a central pivot.

noso- [G. *nosos,* disease]. Combining form relating to disease.

nosocomial (nos-o-ko'mĭ-al) [G. *nosokomeian,* hospital]. **1.** Relating to a hospital. **2.** Denoting a new disorder (unrelated to the patient's primary condition) associated with being treated in a hospital.

nosogenesis, nosogeny (nos-o-jen'ĕ-sis, nos-oj'ĕ-nĭ) [noso- + G. *genesis,* production]. Pathogenesis.

nosogenic (nos-o-jen'ik). Pathogenic.

nosologic (nos-o-loj'ik). Relating to nosology.

nosology (no-sol'o-jĭ) [noso- + G. *logos,* study]. Nosonomy; nosotaxy; the science of classification of diseases.

nos'oma'nia [noso- + G. *mania,* insanity]. An unfounded, morbid belief that one is suffering from some special disease.

nosonomy (no-son'o-mĭ) [noso- + G. *nomos,* law]. Nosology.

nosophilia (nos'o-fil'ĭ-ah) [noso- + G. *phileō,* to love]. A morbid desire to be sick.

nosophobia (nos'o-fo'bĭ-ah) [noso- + G. *phobos,* fear]. An inordinate dread and fear of disease.

nosopoietic (nos'o-poy-et'ik) [noso- + G. *poiēsis,* a making]. Pathogenic.

Nosopsyllus (nos'o-sil'us) [noso- + G. *psylla,* flea]. A flea genus commonly found on rodents. *N. fasciatus,* the northern rat flea, is a species that infrequently transmits the plague bacillus to man.

nos'otaxy (noso- + G. *taxis,* arrangement]. Nosology.

nostalgia (nos-tal'jĭ-ah) [G. *nostos,* a return (home), + *algos,* pain]. Homesickness; the longing to return home or to familiar surroundings.

nos'tril. Naris.

nostrum [L. neuter of *noster,* our, "our own remedy"]. A therapeutic agent, sometimes patented and usually of secret composition, offered to the general public as a specific remedy for any disease or class of diseases.

no'tal [G. *nōtos,* the back]. Relating to the back.

notancephalia (no'tan-sĕ-fa'lĭ-ah) [G. *nōtos*, back, + *an*- priv. + *kephalē*, head]. A fetal malformation characterized by a deficiency in the occipital region of the skull.

notancephalia (no'tan-en-sĕ-fa'lĭ-ah) [G. *nōtos*, back, + *an*- priv. + *enkephalos*, brain]. A malformation marked by defective development or absence of the cerebellum.

notch. Incisure.

aortic n., the slight n. in the sphygmographic tracing caused by the rebound at the closure of the aortic valves.

cardiac n., a deep n. between the esophagus and fundus of the stomach.

dicrotic n., the n. in a pulse tracing which precedes the second or dicrotic wave.

Hutchinson's crescentic n., the semilunar n. on the incisal edge of the upper middle incisors in Hutchinson's teeth.

parotid n., the space between the ramus of the mandible and the mastoid process of the temporal bone.

notencephalocele (no-ten-sef'al-o-sēl) [G. *nōtos*, back, + *enkephalos*, brain, + *kēlē*, hernia]. A malformation in the occipital portion of the cranium with protrusion of brain substance.

notochord (no'to-kord) [G. *nōtos*, back, + *chordē*, cord, string]. **1.** In primitive vertebrates, the primary axial supporting structure of the body; an important organizer for determining the final form of the nervous system and related structures. **2.** In embryos, the axial fibrocellular cord about which the vertebral primordia develop.

notochordal (no-to-kor'dal). Relating to the notochord.

noxious (nok'shus) [L. *noxius*, injurious, fr. *noceo*, to injure]. Injurious.

Np Neptunium.

NPH insulin. See under insulin.

NPN Nonprotein *nitrogen*.

nRNA Nuclear RNA.

nubile (nu'bil) [L. *nubilis*, fr. *nubo*, pp. *nuptus*, to marry]. Fit for marriage; sexually mature; said of a young woman at puberty.

nucha (nu'kah) [Fr. *nuque*] [NA]. Nape; the back of the neck.

nuchal (nu'kal). Relating to the nucha.

nucl-. See nucleo-.

nuclear (nu'kle-ar). Relating to a nucleus.

nuclease (nū'kle-ās). General term for enzymes that catalyze the hydrolysis of nucleic acid into nucleotides or oligonucleotides by cleaving phosphodiester linkages.

nucleate (nu'kle-āt). A salt of a nucleic acid.

nucleated (nu'kle-a-ted). Provided with a nucleus, a characteristic of all true cells.

nucleation (nu-kle-a'shun). The process of forming a nidus (4).

nuclei (nu'kle-i). Plural of nucleus.

nucleic acid (nu-kle'ik). Linear (unbranched) polymers of nucleotides in which the 5′ phosphate of each is esterified with the 3′ hydroxyl of the preceding nucleotide. A family of substances of large molecular weight, found in chromosomes, nucleoli, mitochondria, and cytoplasm of all cells, and in viruses; in combination with proteins they are called nucleoproteins. On hydrolysis they yield purines, pyrimidines, phosphoric acid, and a pentose, either D-ribose or D-deoxyribose; from the last, the n.a.'s derive their more specific names, ribonucleic acid and deoxyribonucleic acid.

nucleiform (nu'kle-ĭ-form). Nucleoid (1); shaped like or having the appearance of a nucleus.

nucleo-, nucl-. Combining forms for nucleus or nuclear.

nucleocapsid (nu'kle-o-kap'sid). See virion.

nucleofugal (nu'kle-of'u-gal) [nucleo- + L. *fugio*, to flee]. **1.** Moving within the cell body in a direction away from the nucleus. **2.** Moving in a direction away from a nerve nucleus; said of nerve transmission.

nucleohistone (nu'kle-o-his'tōn). A complex of histone and deoxyribonucleic acid, the form in which the latter is usually found in the nuclei of cells.

nucleoid (nu'kle-oyd) [nucleo- + G. *eidos*, resemblance]. **1.** Nucleiform. **2.** A nuclear inclusion body. **3.** Nucleus (2).

nucle'olar. Relating to a nucleolus.

nucle'oli. Plural of nucleolus.

nucle'oliform. Nucleoloid; resembling a nucleolus.

nucleoloid (nu-kle'o-loyd) [nucleolus + G. *eidos*, resemblance]. Nucleoliform.

nucleolonema (nu-kle'o-lo-ne'mah) [nucleolus + G. *nema*, thread]. The irregular network or rows of fine ribonucleoprotein granules or microfilaments forming most of the nucleolus.

nucleolus, pl. **nucleoli** (nu-kle'o-lus, -li) [L. dim of *nucleus*, a nut, kernel]. **1.** A small, usually single, rounded mass within the cell nucleus where ribonucleoprotein is produced. **2.** A more or less central body in the vesicular nucleus of certain protozoa in which an endosome is lacking but one or more Feulgen-positive (DNA+) nucleoli are present.

nu'cleon. One of the subatomic particles of the atomic nucleus; *i.e.,* either a proton or a neutron.

nucleopetal (nu-kle-op'ĕ-tal) [nucleo- + L. *peto*, to seek]. **1.** Moving in the cell body in a direction toward the nucleus. **2.** Moving in a direction toward a nerve nucleus; said of a nervous impulse.

nucleophil, nucleophile (nu'kle-o-fil, -fil) [nucleo- + G. *philos*, fond]. **1.** The electron donor in a chemical reaction in which a pair of electrons is picked up by an electrophil. **2.** Nucleophilic; relating to a nucleophil.

nu'cleophil'ic. Nucleophil (2).

nucleoplasm (nu'kle-o-plazm). The protoplasm of the nucleus of a cell.

nu'cleopro'tein. A complex of protein and nucleic acid, the form in which essentially all nucleic acids exist in nature.

nucleorrhexis (nu'kle-o-rek'sis) [nucleo- + G. *rhēxis*, rupture]. Fragmentation of a cell nucleus.

nu'cleosi'dases. Enzymes that catalyze the hydrolysis of nucleosides, releasing the purine or pyrimidine base.

nu'cleoside. A compound of a sugar usually ribose or deoxyribose) with a purine or pyrimidine base by way of an *N*-glycosyl link.

nucleoside or **nucleotide pair.** See base pair.

nucleotidases (nu'kle-o-ti-da-sez). Enzymes that catalyze the hydrolysis of nucleotides into phosphoric acid and nucleosides.

nu'cleotide. Mononucleotide; originally a combination of a (nucleic acid) purine or pyrimidine, one sugar (usually ribose or deoxyribose), and a phosphate group; by extension, any compound containing a heterocyclic compound bound to a phosphorylated sugar by an *N*-glycosyl link.

nucleotidyltransferase (nu'kle-o-ti'dil-trans'fer-ās). Enzymes (transferases) transferring nucleotide residues (nucleotidyls) from nucleoside di- or triphosphates into dimer or polymer forms.

nu'cleotox'in. A toxin acting upon the cell nuclei.

nucleus, pl. **nuclei** (nu'kle-us, -kle-i) [L. a little nut, a kernel]. **1.** Karyon; in cytology, a rounded or oval mass of protoplasm within the cytoplasm of a cell which is surrounded by a nuclear envelope that encloses euchromatin heterochromatin, and one or more nucleoli, and undergoes mitosis during cell division. **2.** Nucleoid (3); by extension, because of similar function, the genome of microorganisms (microbes) that is relatively simple in structure, lacks a nuclear membrane, and does not undergo mitosis during replication. **3** [NA]. In neuroanatomy, a group of nerve cells in the brain or spinal cord that can be demarcated from neighboring groups on the basis of either differences in cell type or the presence of a surrounding zone of nerve fibers or cell-poor neuropil. **4.** Any substance around which a urinary or other calculus is formed. **5.** The central portion of an atom (composed of protons and neutrons) where most of the mass and all of the positive charge are concentrated.

n. ambig'uus [NA], **ambiguous n.,** a slender longitudinal column of motor neurons in the ventrolateral region of the medulla oblongata; its efferent fibers leave with the vagus and glossopharyngeal nerve and innervate the striated muscle fibers of the pharynx and the vocal cord muscles of the larynx.

    amygdaloid n., *corpus* amygdaloideum.

    nu'clei arcua'ti [NA], **arcuate nuclei,** a variable assembly of small cell groups, probably outlying components of the pontine nuclei, on the ventral and medial aspects of the pyramid in the medulla oblongata.

    atomic n., see nucleus (5).

branchiomotor nuclei, collective term for those motoneuronal nuclei of the brainstem that develop from the branchiomotor column of the embryo and innervate striated muscle fibers developed from the mesenchyme of the branchial arches.

n. cauda'tus [NA], **caudate n.,** caudatum; an elongated curved mass of gray matter, consisting of an anterior thick portion that projects into the anterior horn of the lateral ventricle, a portion extending along the floor of the body of the lateral ventricle, and an elongated curved thin portion that curves downward and backward in the temporal lobes to the wall of the descending horn.

n. centromedia'nus [NA], centromedian n.; the largest and most caudal of the intralaminar nuclei which receives numerous fibers from the internal segment of the globus pallidus by way of the fasciculus thalamicus of the ansa lenticularis, as well as from area 4 of the motor cortex; its major efferent connection is with the putamen.

nu'clei cochlea'res [NA], **cochlear nuclei,** nuclei located on the dorsal and lateral surface of the inferior cerebellar peduncle, in the floor of the lateral recess of the rhomboid fossa, which receive the incoming fibers of the cochlear part of the vestibulocochlear nerve and are the major source of origin of the lateral lemniscus or central auditory pathway.

n. cunea'tus [NA], **cuneate n.,** one of the three nuclei of the posterior column of the spinal cord, located near the dorsal surface of the medulla oblongata, which receives posterior root fibers corresponding to the sensory innervation of the arm and hand of the same side; together with its medial companion, n. gracilis, it is the major source of origin of the medial lemniscus.

n. denta'tus cerebel'li [NA], **dentate n. of cerebellum,** the most lateral and largest of the deep cerebellar nuclei which receives axons of the Purkinje cells of the neocerebellum; together with the more medially located nuclei globosus and emboliformis, it is the major source of fibers composing massive superior cerebellar peduncle.

    dorsal n., n. thoracicus.

n. dorsa'lis ner'vi va'gi [NA], **dorsal n. of the vagus,** the visceral motor n. located in the vagal trigone of the floor of the fourth ventricle; gives rise to the parasympathetic fibers of the vagus nerve innervating the heart muscle and the smooth musculature and glands of the respiratory and intestinal tracts.

n. fasti'gii [NA], the most medial of the deep cerebellar nuclei, near the midline in the white matter underneath the vermis of the cerebellar cortex, which receives axons of Purkinje cells and fibers from the vestibular nerve and nuclei.

n. gra'cilis [NA], the medial of the three nuclei of the dorsal spinal column which receives dorsal-root fibers corresponding to the sensory innervation of the leg.

hypoglossal n., n. nervi hypoglossi.

n. intermediolatera'lis, intermediolateral n., intermediolateral cell column; the cell column that forms the lateral horn of the spinal cord's gray matter. Extending from the first thoracic through the second lumbar segment, the column contains the autonomic motor neurons that give rise to the preganglionic fibers of the sympathetic system.

n. intermediomedia'lis, intermediomedial n., a small group of scattered visceral motor neurons immediately ventral to the n. thoracicus in the thoracic and upper two lumbar segments of the spinal cord; like the larger n. intermediolateralis it gives rise to preganglionic fibers of the sympathetic nervous system.

n. interpeduncula'ris [NA], interpeduncular n., a median ovoid cell group at the base of the midbrain tegmentum between the left and right cerebral peduncles; receives the fasciculus retroflexus from the habenula and projects to the nuclei raphes and central gray substance of the midbrain.

n. lentifor'mis [NA], lentiform n., lenticular n., the large cone-shaped mass of gray matter forming the central core of the cerebral hemisphere; its convex base is formed by the putamen which together with the caudate n. composes the corpus striatum, the apical part consists of the large-celled globus pallidus.

motor nuclei, nuclei originis.

n. ner'vi hypoglos'si [NA], hypoglossal n.; the motor n. innervating the musculature of the tongue, located in the medulla oblongata near the midline.

n. ner'vi oculomoto'rii [NA], oculomotor n.; the composite group of motor neurons innervating all of the external eye muscles except the nusculus rectus lateralis and musculus obliquus superior; lies in the rostral half of the midbrain, near the midline in the most ventral part of the central gray substance.

nu'clei ner'vi vestibulocochlea'ris [NA], the combined nuclei cochleares and vestibulares.

oculomotor n., n. nervi oculomotorii.

n. oliva'ris [NA], olivary n., a large aggregate of small densely packed nerve cells arranged in a folded lamina, corresponding in position to the oliva, projecting to all parts of the contralateral half of the cerebellar cortex by way of the olivocerebellar tract, and believed to be the major source of cerebellar climbing fibers.

nu'clei ori'ginis [NA], nuclei of origin, motor nuclei; collections of motor neurons (forming a continuous column in the spinal cord, discontinuous in the medulla and pons) giving origin to the spinal and cranial motor nerves.

n. paraventricula'ris [NA], paraventricular n., a triangular group of large neurons in the periventricular zone of the anterior half of the hypothalamus, functionally associated with the posterior lobe of the hypophysis.

nu'clei pon'tis [NA], pontine nuclei, the very large mass of gray matter filling the pons; the nuclei are a major way-station in the impulse conduction

from the cerebral cortex to the cerebellum.

n. pulpo'sus [NA], the soft fibrocartilage central portion of the intervertebral disk.

nu'clei raph'es, raphe nuclei, collective term denoting a variety of unpaired nerve cell groups in and along the median plane of the mesencephalic tegmentum; the dorsal, ventral, and anterior ones include neurons with serotonin-carrying axons that extend rostrally to the hypothalamus, septum, hippocampus, and cingulate gyrus.

n. ru'ber [NA], red n., a large, well defined, somewhat elongated cell mass of reddish-gray hue, located in the rostral part of the mesencephalic tegmentum; it receives a massive projection from the contralateral half of the cerebellum by way of the superior cerebellar peduncle, and an additional projection from the ipsilateral motor cortex; its efferent connections are with the contralateral half of the rhombencephalic reticular formation and spinal cord by way of the rubrobulbar and rubrospinal tracts.

secondary sensory nuclei, nuclei terminationis.

n. of solitary tract, n. tractus solitarii.

somatic motor nuclei, collective term indicating the motor nuclei innervating the tongue masculature and external eye muscles.

n. subthalam'icus [NA], subthalamic n., a circumscript n. located in the ventral part of the subthalamus on the dorsal surface of the cerebral peduncle; receives a massive projection from the lateral segment of the globus pallidus, and itself projects to both pallidal segments, as well as to the mesencephalic tegmentum.

n. supraop'ticus hypothal'ami [NA], supraoptic n., a large-celled neurosecretory n. in the hypothalamus, located over the lateral border of the optic tract; its neurons produce vasopressin which is released into the general circulation from the axon terminals in the supraopticohypophysial tract.

nu'clei tegmen'ti [NA], two small round cell groups in the caudal part of the midbrain, associated with the mamillary body by way of the mamillary peduncle and mamillotegmental tract.

nu'clei terminatio'nis [NA], terminal nuclei, secondary sensory nuclei; collective term indicating those nerve cell groups in the rhombencephalon and spinal cord in which the afferent fibers of the spinal and cranial nerves terminate.

n. thorac'icus [NA], thoracic n., dorsal n.; a column of large neurons located in the base of the posterior gray column of the spinal cord, extending from the first thoracic through the second lumbar segment; gives rise to the dorsal spinocerebellar tract of the same side.

n. trac'tus solita'rii [NA], n. of the solitary tract; a slender cell column extending sagittally through the dorsal part of the medulla oblongata which is the visceral sensory n. of the brainstem, receiving the afferent fibers of the vagus, glossopharyngeal, and facial nerves by way of the tractus solitarius.

nu'clei vestibula'res [NA], **vestibular nuclei**, a group of four nuclei (lateral, medial, superior, and inferior) located in the lateral region of the hindbrain closely beneath the floor of the rhomboid fossa; they receive the incoming fibers of the vestibular nerve, are reciprocally connected with the n. fastigii and flocculonodular lobe of the cerebellum, and project by way of the medial longitudinal fasciculus to the abducens, trochlear, and oculomotor nuclei and to the ventral horn of the spinal cord, on both left and right side.

nuclide (nu'klīd). A particular (atomic) nuclear species with defined characteristics and properties.

NUG Necrotizing ulcerative *gingivitis.*

nulligravida (nul-ĭ-grav'ĭ-dah) [L. *nullus,* none, + *gravida,* pregnant]. A woman who has never conceived a child.

nullipara (nul-ip'ă-rah) [L. *nullus,* none, + *pario,* to bear]. A woman who has never borne any children.

nullipar'ity. The condition of having borne no children.

num'ber. 1. A symbol expressive of a certain value or of a specific quantity determined by count. **2.** The place of any unit in a series.

    atomic n., the n. of negatively charged electrons in an uncharged atom, or the number of protons in its nucleus; indicates the position of the element in the periodic system.

    Avogadro's n., Avogadro's constant; the n. of molecules in one gram-molecular weight (mole) of any compound; defined as the number of atoms in 0.0120 kg of pure carbon-12; equivalent to 6.0225×10^{23}.

    mass n., the mass of the atom of a particular isotope relative to hydrogen-1 (or to $1/12$ the mass of carbon-12), generally very close to the whole number represented by the sum of the protons and neutrons in the atomic nucleus of the isotope; not to be confused with the atomic weight of an element, which may include a number of isotopes in natural proportion.

numb'ness. A peculiar sensation due to impaired cutaneous perception.

nummular (num'u-lar) [L. *nummus,* coin]. **1.** Discoid or coin-shaped; denoting the thick mucous or mucopurulent sputum in certain respiratory diseases, so called because of the disc shape assumed when it is flattened on the bottom of a sputum mug containing water or transparent disinfectant. **2.** Arranged like stacks of coins, denoting the association of the red blood corpuscles with flat surfaces apposed, forming rouleaux.

nurse [O. Fr. *nourice,* fr. L. *nutrix,* wet-nurse, fr. *nutrio,* to sucke, to nourish]. **1.** To suckle; to give suck to an infant. **2.** To perform all the necessary offices in the care of the sick. **3.** A woman who has the care of an infant or young child. **4.** One who is professionally trained in the care of a sick person.

    n. anesthetist, a person who, after completing basic educational requirements as a nurse, is additionally trained for 2 years in the administration of anesthetics, in order to function thereafter as an anesthetist under the direction of a physician.

    clinical n. specialist, a n. with advanced knowledge and competence in a particular specialty area.

    general duty n., a n. who does not specialize in a particular area of practice but is available for any duty.

    licensed practical n. (L.P.N.), licensed vocational n. (L.V.N.), a n. who has graduated from a program requiring fewer instructional hours than is required for a graduate n., and who has passed a state examination for licensure.

    private duty n., (1) a n. who is not a member of the hospital staff, but is called upon to take special care of an individual patient; **(2)** one who specializes in the care of patients with diseases of a particular class; *e.g.,* surgical cases, tuberculosis, children's diseases, etc.

    registered n. (R.N.), a n. who has been graduated from an accredited school of nursing, and has been registered and licensed to practice by a state authority.

    scrub n., a n. who assists the surgeon in the operating room.

    wet n., a woman who suckles a child not her own.

nurse-midwife. A person formally educated and certified to practice in the two disciplines of nursing and midwifery.

nurse practitioner. A registered n. with special skills in assessing the physical and psychosocial status of patients, often as a colleague of a physician.

nurs'ing. 1. Feeding an infant at the breast; tending and taking care of a child. **2.** Caring for the ill or infirm; performing the duties of a nurse. **3.** The scientific care of the sick by a professional nurse.

nutation (nu-ta'shun) [L. *annuere,* to nod]. The act of nodding, especially involuntary nodding.

nutrient (nu'trĭ-ent) [L. *nutriens,* fr. *nutrio,* to nourish]. An item of food; may be essential or nonessential.

nutrition (nu-trish'un) [L. *nutritio,* fr. *nutrio,* to nourish]. **1.** A function of living organisms, consisting in the taking in and assimilation through chemical changes (metabolism) of material whereby tissue is built up and energy liberated; its successive stages are: digestion, absorption, assimilation, and excretion. **2.** The study of the food and drink requirements of human beings or animals for maintenance, growth, activity, reproduction, and lactation.

nu'triture [L. *nutritura,* a nursing, fr. *nutrio,* to suckle, nourish]. State or condition of the nutrition of the body; state of the body with regard to nourishment.

nyct-. See nycto-.

nyctalgia (nik-tal'jĭ-ah) [nyct- + G. *algos,* pain]. Night pain, denoting especially the osteoscopic pains of syphilis occurring at night.

nyctalopia (nik-tă-lo'pĭ-ah) [nyct- + G. *alaos*, obscure, + *ōps*, eye]. Night blindness; nocturnal amblyopia; decreased ability to see in reduced illumination.

nycterine (nik'ter-in, -in) [G. *nykterinos*]. **1.** By night. **2.** Dark; obscure.

nycterohemeral (nik-ter-o-he'mer-al) [G. *nykteros*, by night, nightly, + *hēmera*, day]. Both daily and nightly.

nycto-, nyct- [G. *nyx*, night]. Combining forms denoting night, nocturnal. See also noct-.

nyctophilia (nik-to-fil'ĭ-ah) [nycto- + G. *philos*, fond]. Scotophilia; preference for the night or darkness.

nyctophobia (nik'to-fo'bĭ-ah) [nycto- + G. *phobos*, fear]. Scotophobia; morbid fear of night or of the dark.

nympha, pl. **nymphae** (nim'fah, nim'fe) [Mod. L. fr. G. *nymphē*, a bride]. One of the labia minora.

nymphectomy (nim-fek'to-mĭ) [nymph- + G. *ektomē*, excision]. Surgical removal of the hypertrophied labia minora.

nymphitis (nim-fi'tis) [nymph- + G. *-itis*, inflammation]. Inflammation of the labia minora.

nympho-, nymph-. Combining forms denoting the nymphae (labia minora).

nym'phoma'nia [nympho- + G. *mania*, frenzy]. Extreme eroticism or sexual desire in women.

nym'phomani'acal. Pertaining to, or exhibiting, nymphomania.

nymphoncus (nim-fongk'us) [nympho- + G. *onkos*, tumor]. A swelling or hypertrophy of one or both labia minora.

nymphotomy (nim-fot'o-mĭ) [nympho- + G. *tomē*, incision]. An incision into the labia minora or the clitoris.

nystagmic (nis-tag'mik). Relating to nystagmus.

nystag'miform. Nystagmoid.

nystag'mograph. An apparatus for measuring the amplitude and velocity of ocular movements in nystagmus, by measuring the change in the resting potential of the eye as the eye moves.

nystagmography (nis-tag-mog'ră-fĭ). The technique of recording nystagmus.

nystagmoid (nis-tag'moyd) [nystagmus + G. *eidos*, resemblance]. Nystagmiform; resembling nystagmus.

nystagmus (nis-tag'mus) [G. *nystagmos*, a nodding, fr. *nystazō*, to be sleepy, nod]. Rhythmical oscillation of the eyeballs, either pendular or jerky.

caloric n., jerky n. as part of Bárány's *sign.*

central n., reflex from stimulation arising in the CNS.

congenital n., (1) congenitally predetermined n. caused by lesions sustained in utero or at the time of birth; (2) inherited n., usually sex-linked, without associated neurologic lesions and nonprogressive; (3) the n. associated with albinism, achromatopsia, and hypoplasia of the macula.

conjugate n., a n. in which the two eyes move simultaneously in the same direction.

dissociated n., n. in which the movements of the two eyes are dissimilar in direction, extent, and periodicity.

end-position n., a jerky physiologic n. occurring in a normal individual when attempts are made to fixate a point at the limits of the field of fixation.

fixation n., a n. most marked during fixation movements of the eyes, arising as opticokinetic n., or resulting from midbrain lesions.

gaze n., a n. occurring in partial gaze paralysis when an attempt is made to look in the direction of the palsy.

jerky n., n. in which there is a slow drift of the eyes in one direction, followed by a rapid recovery movement, always described in the direction of the recovery movement.

labyrinthine n., vestibular n.

latent n., jerky n. that is brought out by covering one eye.

lateral n., n. in which the eyes oscillate from side to side.

opticokinetic n., optokinetic n., n. induced by looking at moving visual stimuli.

pendular n., a n. that, in most positions gaze, has oscillations equal in speed and amplitude, usually arising from a visual disturbance.

positional n., n. occurring only when the head is in a particular position.

retraction n., irregular, jerky n., either horizontal, vertical, or rotatory, with drawing back of the eye backward into the orbit when the patient attempts to look in one or the other direction.

rotational n., jerky n. arising from stimulation of the labyrinth by rotation of the head around any axis and induced by change of motion.

rotatory n., a slight movement of the eyes around the visual axis.

vertical n., an up-and-down oscillation of the eyes.

vestibular n., labyrinthine n.; n. resulting from physiological stimuli to the labyrinth that may be rotatory, caloric, compressive, or galvanic, or due to labyrinthal lesions.

nyxis (nik'sis) [G.]. A pricking; puncture; paracentesis.

O

O Oxygen; opening (in formulas for electrical reactions); oculus; a blood group in the ABO system.

o- ortho-(2).

obdormition (ob-dor-mish'un) [L. *ob-dormio*, pp. *-itus*, to sleep]. Numbness of an extremity, due to pressure on the sensory nerve.

obe'liac. Relating to the obelion.

obelion (ŏ-be'lĭ-on) [G. *obelos*, a spit]. A craniometric point on the sagittal suture between the parietal foramina near the lambdoid suture.

obese (o-bēs') [L. *obesus*, fat]. Extremely fat or corpulent.

obe'sity [see obese]. Fatness; corpulence; an abnormal increase of fat in the subcutaneous connective tissues.

morbid o., the condition of weighing at least twice the ideal weight.

o'bex [L. barrier] [NA]. The point on the midline of the dorsal surface of the medulla oblongata that marks the caudal angle of the rhomboid fossa or fourth ventricle.

OB/GYN Obstetrics and gynecology.

objec'tive [L. *ob-jicio*, pp. *-jectus*, to throw before]. **1.** The lens or lenses in the lower end of a microscope, by means of which the image of the object examined is brought to a focus. **2.** Viewing events or phenomena as they exist in the external world, impersonally or in an unprejudiced way; opposite of subjective.

achromatic o., an o. that is corrected for two colors chromatically, and one color spherically.

apochromatic o., an o. in which chromatic aberration is corrected for three colors and spherical abberation is corrected for two.

immersion o., a high power o. used with a liquid between the lens and the specimen on the slide.

obligate (ob'lĭ-gāt) [L. *ob-ligo*, pp. *-atus*, to bind to]. Without an alternative pathway.

oblique (ob-lēk') [L. *obliquus*]. Slanting; deviating from the perpendicular or the horizontal.

obliquity (ob-lik'wĭ-tĭ). Asynclitism.

Litzmann o., posterior asynclitism; inclination of the fetal head so that the biparietal diameter is oblique in relation to the place of the pelvic brim, the posterior parietal bone presenting to the parturient canal.

Nägele o., anterior asynclitism; inclination of the fetal head in cases of flat pelvis, so that the biparietal diameter is oblique in relation to the plane of the brim, the anterior parietal bone presenting to the parturient canal.

obliteration (ob-lit'er-a'shun) [L. *oblittero*, to blot out]. Blotting out, especially by filling of a natural space or lumen by fibrosis or inflammation.

oblongata (ob-long-gah'tah) [L. fem. of *oblongatus*, from *oblongus*, rather long]. *Medulla* oblongata.

obsession (ob-sesh'un) [L. *obsideo*, pp. *-sessus*, to besiege]. A condition, usually associated with anxiety and dread, in which one idea constantly fills the mind despite one's efforts to ignore or dislodge it.

impulsive o., an o. accompanied by action, sometimes becoming a mania.

inhibitory o., an o. involving an impediment to action, usually representing a phobia.

obses'sive-compul'sive. Having a tendency to perform certain repetitive acts or ritualistic behavior to relieve anxiety.

obstet'ric, obstet'rical. Relating to obstetrics.

obstetrician (ob-stĕ-trish'un). A specialist in obstetrics.

obstet'rics [L. *obstetrix*, a midwife]. Tocology; the medical specialty concerned with the care of the pregnant woman during pregnancy, parturition, and the puerperium.

ob'stinate [L. *obstinātus*, determined]. **1.** Intractable (2); refractory (2); firmly adhering to one's own purpose, opinion, etc., not yielding to argument, persuasion, or entreaty. **2.** Refractory (1).

obstipation (ob-stĭ-pa'shun) [L. *ob*, against, + *stipo*, pp. *-atus*, to crowd]. Intestinal obstruction; severe constipation.

obstruction (ob-struk'shun) [L. *obstructio*]. Blockage or clogging as by occlusion or stenosis.

obstruent (ob'stru-ent) [L. *ob-struo*, pp. *-structus*, to build against, obstruct]. **1.** Obstructing; blocking; clogging. **2.** An agent that obstructs or prevents a normal discharge, especially a discharge from the bowels.

obtund' [L. *ob-tundo*, to beat against, blunt]. To dull or blunt, especially sensation or pain.

obturation (ob-tu-ra'shun) [see obturator]. Obstruction or occlusion.

ob'turator [L. *obturo*, pp. *-atus*, to occlude or stop up]. **1.** Any structure that occludes an opening. **2.** A prosthesis used to close an opening of the hard palate, usually a cleft palate. **3.** The stylus or removable plug used during the insertion of many tubular instruments.

obtuse (ob-tūs') [see obtund]. **1.** Dull in intellect; of slow understanding. **2.** Blunt; not acute.

obtusion (ob-tu'zhun). Dulling or deadening of sensibility.

occipital (ok-sip'ĭ-tal). Relating to the occiput.

occipitalization (ok'sip'ĭ-tal-ĭ-za'shun). Bony ankylosis between the atlas and occipital bone.

occipito- (ok-sip'ĭ-to-). Combining form for occiput, occipital.

occip'itofa'cial. Relating to the occiput and the face.

occip'itofron'tal. **1.** Relating to the occiput and the forehead. **2.** Relating to the occipital and frontal lobe of the cerebral cortex.

occip'itomen'tal. Relating to the occiput and the chin.

occiput, gen. **occip'itis** (ok'sĭ-put) [L.] [NA]. The back of the head.

occlude (o-klūd') [see occlusion]. **1.** To close or bring together. **2.** To inclose, as in an occluded virus.

occlusal (o-klu'zal). **1.** Pertaining to occlusion or closure. **2.** In dentistry, pertaining to the contacting surfaces of opposing occlusal units (teeth or occlusion rims), or the masticating surfaces of the posterior teeth.

occlusion (o-klu'zhun) [L. *oc-cludo*, pp. *-clusus*, to shut up]. **1.** The act of closing or the state of being closed. **2.** In chemistry, the absorption of a gas by a metal or the inclusion of one substance within another. **3.** Any contact between the incising or

masticating surfaces of the upper and lower teeth.
4. The relationship between the occlusal surfaces of the maxillary and mandibular teeth when they are in contact.

 abnormal o., an arrangement of the teeth not considered to be within the normal range of variation.

 afunctional o., a malocclusion that does not permit normal function of the dentition.

 balanced o., balanced articulation; the simultaneous contacting of the upper and lower teeth on the right and left and in the anterior and posterior occlusal areas in centric and eccentric positions within the functional range.

 centric o., (1) the relation of opposing occlusal surfaces which provides the maximum planned contact and/or intercuspation; (2) the o. of the teeth when the mandible is in centric relation to the maxillae.

 coronary o., blockage of a coronary vessel, usually by thrombosis or atheroma, and often leading to infarction of the myocardium.

 eccentric o., any o. other than centric.

 functional o., (1) any tooth contacts made within the functional range of the opposing teeth surfaces; (2) o. which occurs during function.

 hyperfunctional o., occlusal stress of tooth or teeth exceeding normal physiologic demands.

 mesial o., (1) mesio-occlusion; anterior o. (2) an o. in which the mandibular teeth articulate with the maxillary teeth in a position anterior to normal; (3) mesioclusion.

 normal o., that arrangement of teeth and their supporting structure which is usually found in health and which approaches an ideal or standard arrangement.

 pathogenic o., an occlusal relationship capable of producing pathologic changes in the supporting tissues.

 physiologic o., o. in harmony with functions of the masticatory system.

 protrusive o., o. which results when the mandible is protruded forward from centric position.

 o. of the pupil, the presence of an opaque membrane closing the pupillary area.

 retrusive o., a biting relationship in which the mandible is forcefully or habitually placed more distally than the patient's centric o.

 traumatogenic o., traumatic o., a malocclusion capable of producing injury to the teeth and/or associated structures.

occlu'sive. Serving to close; denoting a bandage or dressing that closes a wound and excludes it from the air.

occult (ŏ-kult', ok'ult) [L. *oc-culo,* pp. *-cultus,* to cover, hide]. **1.** Hidden; concealed. **2.** Denoting a concealed hemorrhage, the blood being so changed as not to be readily recognized. **3.** In oncology, a clinically unidentified primary tumor with recognized metastases.

ochrometer (o-krom'ĕ-ter) [G. *ōchros,* pale yellow, + *metron,* measure]. An instrument for determining the capillary blood pressure by compressing one of two adjacent fingers until blanching of the skin occurs, after which the force necessary to accomplish this color change is read in millimeters of mercury.

ochronosis (o-kron-o'sis) [G. *ōchros,* pale yellow, + *nosos,* disease]. A pathologic condition observed in certain patients with alkaptonuria, characterized by pigmentation of cartilages and sometimes other tissues.

ochronotic (o-kron-ot'ik). Relating to or characterized by ochronosis.

oct-, octa-, octi-, octo- [G. *oktō,* L. *octo,* eight]. Combining forms meaning eight.

octan (ok'tan) [L. *octo,* eight]. Applied to fever, the paroxysms of which recur every eighth day, the day of each paroxysm being included in the count.

ocular (ok'u-lar) [L. *oculus,* eye]. **1.** Ophthalmic. **2.** The eyepiece of a microscope, the lens or lenses at the upper end of a microscope by means of which the image focused by the objective is viewed.

oc'ularist [L. *oculus,* eye]. One skilled in the design, fabrication, and fitting of artificial eyes and the making of prostheses associated with the appearance or function of the eyes.

oculi (ok'u-li) [L.]. Plural of oculus.

oculist (ok'u-list) [L. *oculus,* eye]. Ophthalmologist.

oculo- [L. *oculus,* eye]. Combining form denoting eye, ocular. See also ophthalmo-.

oculocutaneous (ok'u-lo-ku-ta'ne-us). Relating to the eyes and the skin.

oculofacial (ok'u-lo-fa'shal). Relating to the eyes and the face.

oculography (ok-u-log'răfĭ) [oculo- + G. *graphē,* a writing]. A method of recording eye position and eye movements.

oculogyria (ok'u-lo-ji'rĭ-ah) [oculo- + G. *gyros,* circle]. The limits of rotation of the eyeballs.

oculogyric (ok'u-lo-ji'rik). Referring to rotation of the eyeballs; characterized by oculogyria.

oc'ulomo'tor [oculo- + L. *motorius,* moving]. Relating to or causing movements of the eyeball.

oc'ulona'sal. Relating to the eyes and the nose.

oc'ulopu'pillary. Pertaining to the pupil of the eye.

oc'ulozygomat'ic. Relating to the orbit or its margin and the zygomatic bone.

oc'ulus, gen. and pl. **oc'uli (O)** [L.] [NA]. Eye; the organ of vision, consisting of the eyeball and the optic nerve.

O.D. L. *oculus dexter,* right eye; Doctor of Optometry; overdose.

-odes [G. *eidos,* form, resemblance]. Suffix denoting having the form of, like, resembling.

odont-, odonto- [G. *odous* (*odont-*), tooth]. Combining forms denoting a tooth or teeth.

odontalgia (o-don-tal'jĭ-ah) [odont- + G. *algos,* pain]. Toothache.

odontal'gic. Relating to or marked by odontalgia.

odontectomy (o-don-tek'to-mĭ) [odont- + G. *ek-tomē*, excision]. Removal of teeth by the reflection of a mucoperiosteal flap and excision of bone from around the root or roots before the application of force to effect the tooth removal.

odonto-. See odont-.

odontoameloblastosarcoma (o-don'to-am'ĕ-lo-blas'to-sar-ko'mah). A benign ameloblastic fibroma with mesenchymal hard tissue differentiation eventuating in odontoma-like structures.

odon'toblast [odonto- + G. *blastos*, sprout, germ]. One of the dentin-forming cells, derived from mesenchyme, lining the pulp cavity of a tooth, and arranged in a layer peripherally in the dental pulp; forms the dentinal matrix.

odon'toblasto'ma [odontoblast + G. *-oma*, tumor]. 1. A tumor composed of neoplastic epithelial and mesenchymal cells that may differentiate into cells able to produce calcified tooth substances. 2. An odontoma in its early formative stage.

odon'toclast [odonto- + G. *klastos*, broken]. One of the cells believed to produce absorption of the roots of the deciduous teeth.

odontogenesis (o-don'to-jen'ĕ-sis) [odonto- + G. *genesis*, production]. Odontogeny; odontosis; the process of development of the teeth.

   o. imperfec'ta, an odontogenic developmental anomaly characterized by deficient development of enamel and dentin; affected teeth exhibit a marked reduction in radiodensity, so that unusually large pulp chambers with thin enamel and dentin are seen; the tooth assume a "ghostly" or opalescent appearance.

odontogeny (o-don-toj'ĕ-nĭ). Odontogenesis.

odon'toid [odont- + G. *eidos*, resemblance]. Shaped like a tooth.

odontol'ogy [odonto- + G. *logos*, study]. Dentistry.

odontolysis (o-don-tol'ĭ-sis) [odonto- + G. *lysis*, dissolution]. Erosion (3).

odontoma (o-don-to'mah) [odonto- + G. *-oma*, tumor]. 1. A tumor of odontogenic origin. 2. A developmental anomaly of odontogenic origin comprised of enamel, dentin, cementum, and pulp tissue.

   ameloblastic o., ameloblastodontoma; a form of soft o. in which ameloblasts comprise a conspicuous part of the hamartoma.

   complex o., an anomalous singular mass of dental tissues that are irregularly arranged because of abnormal morphodifferentiation even though histodifferentiation is essentially normal.

   compound o., a developmental odontogenic anomaly comprised of two or more anomalous or miniature teeth whose histo- and morphodifferentiation are essentially normal.

   radicular o., an o. positioned on or near the root of a tooth.

odontoneuralgia (o-don'to-nūr-al'jĭ-ah). Facial neuralgia caused by a carious tooth.

odontonomy (o'don-ton'o-mĭ) [odonto- + G. *onoma*, name]. Dental nomenclature.

odontopathy (o'don-top'ă-thĭ) [odonto- + G. *pathos*, suffering]. Any disease of the teeth or of their sockets.

odonto'sis. Odontogenesis.

odontotomy (o-don-tot'o-mĭ) [odonto- + G. *tomē*, incision]. Cutting into the crown of a tooth.

o'dor [L.]. Scent; smell (3); emanation from any substance that stimulates the olfactory cells in the organ of smell.

odyn-, odyno- [G. *odyne*, pain]. Combining forms meaning pain.

odynacusis (o-din-ă-koo'sis) [odyn- + G. *akouō*, to hear]. Hypersensitiveness of the organ of hearing, so that noises cause actual pain.

odynometer (o-dĭ-nom'ĕ-ter) [odyno- + G. *metron*, measure]. Algesiometer.

odynophagia (o-din-o-fa'jĭ-ah) [odyno- + G. *phagein*, to eat]. Dysphagia.

oe-. For words so beginning and not found here, see e-.

oedipism (ed'ĭ-pizm) [*Oedipus*, G. myth. char.]. 1. Self-infliction of injury to the eyes, usually an attempt at evulsion. 2. Manifestation of Oedipus complex.

oestrids (est'ridz) [G. *oistros*, gadfly]. Common name for botflies of the family Oestridae, such as *Oestrus*.

official (ŏ-fish'al) [L. *officialis*, fr. *officium*, a favor, service]. Authoritative; denoting a drug or a chemical or pharmaceutical preparation recognized as standard in the Pharmacopeia.

officinal (ŏ-fis'ĭ-nal) [L. *officina*, shop]. Denoting a chemical or pharmaceutical preparation kept in stock, in contrast to magistral.

ohm (Ω) (ōm) [G. S. *Ohm*]. The practical unit of electrical resistance, the resistance of any conductor allowing 1 ampere of current to pass under the electromotive force (EMF) of 1 volt.

ohne Hauch [Ger. without breath]. A term used to designate the nonspreading growth of nonflagellated bacteria on agar media; also applied to somatic agglutination.

oi-. For words so beginning and not found here, see e-.

-oid [G. *eidos*, form, resemblance]. Suffix denoting resemblance to; equivalent to -form.

oidiomycin (o-id'ĭ-o-mi'sin). An antigen used to demonstrate cutaneous hypersensitivity in patients infected with one of the Candida species; one of a series of antigens used to demonstrate an immunocompromised patient's capacity to react to any cutaneous antigen.

oil [L. *oleum*; G. *elaion*, originally olive oil]. An inflammable liquid, of fatty consistence and unctuous feel, that is insoluble in water, soluble or insoluble in alcohol, and freely soluble in ether; variously classified as animal, vegetable, and mineral o.'s according to their source, into fatty (fixed) and volatile o.'s, and into drying and nondrying (fatty) o.'s.

essential o.'s, plant products, usually somewhat volatile, giving the odors and tastes characteristic of the particular plant, thus possessing the essence.

ethereal o. volatile o.

fatty o., fixed o., an o. derived from both animals and plants; a glyceride of a fatty acid which, by substitution of the glycerine by an alkaline base, is converted into a soap.

volatile o., ethereal o.; a substance of oily consistence and feel, derived from a plant and containing the principles to which the odor and taste of the plant are due (essential o.).

oint'ment [O. Fr. *oignement*; L. *unguo*, pp. *unctus*, to smear]. Salve; unguent; a semisolid preparation usually containing medicinal substances and intended for external application.

-ol. Suffix denoting that a substance is an alochol or a phenol.

oleaginous (o-le-aj'ĭ-nus) [L. *oleagineus*, pertaining to *olea*, the olive tree]. Oily; greasy.

oleate (o'le-āt). **1.** A salt of oleic acid. **2.** A pharmacopeial preparation consisting of a combination or solution of an alkaloid or metallic base in oleic acid.

olecranon (o-lek'ră-non) [G. the head or point of the elbow] [NA]. Tip or point of the elbow; the prominent curved proximal extremity of the ulna.

o'lefin. Any one of a group of hydrocarbons possessing one or more double bonds in the carbon chain. The simplest is ethylene.

ole'ic [L. *oleum*, oil]. Relating to oil.

ole'ic acid. Octadecenoic acid; an organic acid prepared from fats; used in the preparation of oleates and lotions.

oleo- [L. *oleum*, oil]. Combining form relating to oil. See also eleo-.

olfaction (ol-fak'shun) [L. *ol-facio*, pp. *-factus*, to smell]. Osphresis. **1.** Smell (2); the sense of smell. **2.** The act of smelling.

olfac'tory [see olfaction]. Osphretic; relating to the sense of smell.

olig-. See oligo-.

oligemia (ol-ĭ-ge'mĭ-ah) [oligo- + G. *haima*, blood]. Hyphemia; hypovolemia; a deficiency in the amount of blood in the body.

olige'mic. Pertaining to or marked by oligemia.

oligo-, olig- [G. *oligos*, few]. **1.** Combining form denoting a few or a little. **2.** In chemistry, used in contrast to "poly-" in describing polymers.

oligoamnios (ol'ĭ-go-am'nĭ-os) [oligo- + amnion]. Oligohydramnios; deficiency in the amount of the amniotic fluid.

oligocar'dia [oligo- + G. *kardia*, heart]. Bradycardia.

oligocystic (ol'ĭ-go-sis'tik) [oligo- + G. *kystis*, bladder, cyst]. Consisting of only a few cysts, as occasionally observed in certain lesions that ordinarily have numerous cysts.

ol'igodac'tyly, ol'igodactyl'ia [oligo- + G. *daktylos*, finger or toe]. The presence of fewer than five digits on one or more extremities.

oligoden'dria. Oligodendroglia.

oligodendrocyte (ol'ĭ-go-den'dro-sīt). A cell of the oligodendroglia.

oligodendroglia (ol'ĭ-go-den-drog'lĭ-ah) [oligo- + G. *dendron*, tree, + *glia*, glue]. Oligodendria; one of the three types of glia cells that, together with nerve cells, compose the tissue of the CNS; characterized by having a variable number of veil-like or sheetlike processes which, wrapped each around an individual axon, form the myelin sheath of nerve fibers.

oligodendroglioma (ol'ĭ-go-den'dro-gli-o'mah). A relatively rare and slowly growing glioma characterized by numerous, small, round or ovoid oligodendroglial cells rather uniformly distributed in a sparse fibrillary stroma.

ol'igodip'sia [oligo- + G. *dipsa*, thirst]. Abnormal absence of thirst.

oligodontia (ol'ĭ-go-don'shĭ-ah) [oligo- + G. *odous*, tooth]. **1.** Presence of less than a full complement of teeth. **2.** Hypodontia.

oligodynamic (ol'ĭ-go-di-nam'ik) [oligo- + G. *dynamis*, power]. Active in very small quantity.

oligogalactia (ol'ĭ-go-gă-lak'tĭ-ah, -shĭ-ah) [oligo- + G. *gala*, milk]. Slight or scant secretion of milk.

oligo-1, 6-glucosidase. Limit dextrinase; a glucanohydrolase cleaving α-1,6 links in isomaltose and dextrins produced from starch and glycogen by α-amylase.

oligohydramnios (ol'ĭ-go-hi-dram'nĭ-os) [oligo- + G. *hydōr*, water, + amnion]. Oligoamnios.

oligohydruria (ol'ĭ-go-hi-dru'rĭ-ah) [oligo- + G. *hydōr*, water, + *ouron*, urine]. Excretion of small quantities of urine, as seen in dehydration.

oligomenorrhea (ol'ĭ-go-men-o-re'ah) [oligo- + menorrhea]. Scanty menstruation.

oligomor'phic [oligo- + G. *morphē*, form]. Presenting a few changes of form; not polymorphic.

ol'igonu'cleotide. A compound made up of the condensation of a small number of nucleotides.

oligopnea (ol'ĭ-gop'ne-ah) [oligo- + G. *pnoē*, breath]. Infrequent respiration.

oligoptyalism (ol'ĭ-go-ti'ă-lizm) [oligo- + G. *ptyalon*, saliva]. Scanty secretion of saliva.

oligor'ia [G. *oligōria*, negligence, slight esteem, fr. *oligos*, little, + *ōra*, care, regard]. An abnormal indifference toward or dislike of persons or things.

ol'igosac'charide. A compound made up of the condensation of a small number of monosaccharide units.

ol'igosper'mia [oligo- + G. *sperma*, seed]. Oligozoospermia; a subnormal concentration of spermatozoa in the penile ejaculate.

oligosynaptic (ol'ĭ-go-sĭ-nap'tik). Paucisynaptic; referring to neural conduction pathways that are interrupted by only a few synaptic junctions, *i.e.*, made up of a sequence of only few nerve cells.

oligotro'phia, oligot'rophy [oligo- + G. *trophē*, nourishment]. Deficient nutrition.

oligozoospermia (ol'ĭ-go-zo'o-sper'mĭ-ah) [oligo- + G. *zōon*, animal, + *sperma*, seed]. Oligospermatism.

oliguria (ol'ĭ-gu'rĭ-ah) [oligo- + G. *ouron*, urine]. Scanty urination.

oliva, pl. **oli'vae** (o-li'vah, ve) [L.] [NA]. Olive; Corpus olivare; a smooth oval prominence of the ventrolateral surface of the medulla oblongata lateral to the pyramidal tract, corresponding to the nucleus olivaris.

ol'ivary. 1. Relating to the oliva. **2.** Relating to or shaped like an olive.

olive (ol'iv) [L. *oliva*]. Oliva.

olivifugal (ol-ĭ-vif'u-gal) [oliva + L. *fugio*, to flee]. In a direction away from the olive.

olivipetal (ol-ĭ-vip'ĕ-tal) [oliva + L. *peto*, to seek]. In a direction toward the olive.

ol'ivopon'tocerebel'lar. Relating to the olivary nucleus, the basis pontis, and the cerebellum.

-ology. See -logia.

-oma [G. *-ōma*]. Suffix denoting a tumor or neoplasm.

omen'tal. Epiploic; relating to the omentum.

omentec'tomy [oment- + G. *ektomē*, excision]. Resection or excision of the omentum.

omentitis (o-men-ti'tis) [L. *omentum* + G. *-itis*, inflammation]. Peritonitis involving the omentum.

omento-, oment-. Combining forms relating to the omentum. See also epiplo-.

omen'tofixa'tion. Omentopexy.

omen'topexy [omento- + G. *pēxis*, fixation]. Omentofixation **1.** Suture of the great omentum to the abdominal wall to induce collateral portal circulation. **2.** Suture of the omentum to another organ to increase arterial circulation.

omen'toplasty [omento- + G. *plassō*, to form, manipulate]. Use of the great omentum to cover or fill a defect, augment arterial or portal venous circulation, absorb effusions, or increase lymphatic drainage.

omentorrhaphy (o-men-tor'ă-fĭ) [omento- + G. *rhaphē*, suture]. Suture of an opening in the omentum.

omen'tulum [Mod. L. dim. of *omentum*]. Omentum minus.

omen'tum, pl. **omen'ta** [L. the membrane that encloses the bowels] [NA]. A fold of peritoneum passing from the stomach to another abdominal organ.

  o. ma'jus [NA], greater o., gastrocolic o., epiploon; velum (2); a peritoneal fold passing from the greater curvature of the stomach to the transverse colon, hanging like an apron in front of the intestines.

  o. mi'nus [NA], lesser o., gastrohepatic o., omentulum; a peritoneal fold passing from the margins of the porta hepatis and the bottom of the fossa ductus venosi to the lesser curvature of the stomach and to the upper border of the duodenum.

omniv'orous [L. *omnis*, all, + *voro*, to eat]. Living on food of all kinds, upon both animal and vegetable food.

omo- [G. *ōmos*, shoulder]. Combining form indicating relationship to the shoulder.

omphal-, omphalo- [G. *omphalos*, navel (umbilicus)]. Combining form denoting relationship to the umbilicus.

omphalectomy (om-fă-lek'to-my) [omphal- + G. *ektomē*, excision]. Excision of the umbilicus or of a neoplasm connected with it.

omphalelcosis (om'fal-el-ko'sis) [omphal- + G. *helkōsis*, ulceration]. Ulceration at the umbilicus.

omphal'ic [G. *omphalos*, umbilicus]. Umbilical.

omphalitis (om-fă-li'tis). Inflammation of the umbilicus and surrounding parts.

omphalocele (om'fă-lo-sēl) [omphalo- + G. *kēlē*, hernia]. Exomphalos (3); congenital herniation of viscera into the base of the umbilical cord, with a covering membranous sac of peritoneum-amnion.

om'phaloenter'ic. Relating to the umbilicus and the intestine.

om'phalomesenter'ic. Relating to the umbilicus and the mesentery or intestine.

omphalophlebitis (om'fă-lo-flĕ-bi'tis) [omphalo- + G. *phleps*, vein, + *-itis*, inflammation]. Inflammation of the umbilical veins.

omphalorrhagia (om'fă-lo-ra'jĭ-ah) [omphalo- + G. *rhēgnymi*, to burst forth]. Bleeding from the umbilicus.

omphalorrhea (om'fă-lo-re'ah) [omphalo- + G. *rhoia*, flow]. A serous discharge from the umbilicus.

omphalorrhexis (om'fă-lo-rek'sis) [omphao- + G. *rhēxis*, rupture]. Rupture of the umbilical cord during childbirth.

omphalosite (om'fă-lo-sīt) [omphalo- + G. *sitos*, food]. The parasitic member of unequal monochorial twins which derives its blood supply from the placenta of the autosite and is not capable of independent existence after birth and separation from the placenta.

omphalospinous (om'fă-lo-spi'nus). Denoting a line connecting the umbilicus and the anterior superior spine of the ilium, on which lies McBurney's point.

omphalotomy (om'fă-lot'o-mĭ) [omphalo- + G. *tomē*, incision]. Cutting of the umbilical cord at birth.

o'nanism [*Onan*, son of Judah, who practiced it. Genesis 38:9]. **1.** Coitus interruptus; withdrawal of the penis before ejaculation, in order to prevent insemination and fecundation of the ovum. **2.** Incorrectly used when synonymous with masturbation.

oncho-. For words beginning thus, and not found here, see onco-.

Onchocerca (ong'ko-ser'kah) [G. *onkos*, a barb, + *kerkos*, tail]. A genus of elongated filariform nematodes (family Onchocercidae) that inhabit the connective tissue of their hosts, usually within firm nodules in which these parasites are coiled and entangled. *O. volvulus* is a species that causes onchocerciasis in man.

onchocerciasis, onchocercosis (ong'ko-ser-si'ă-sis, -ser-ko'sis). Volvulosis; infection with *Onchocerca* (especially *O. volvulus*), marked by nodular swellings forming a fibrous cyst enveloping the coiled parasites; Ocular complications may develop, with blindness in advanced cases, as a result of the sensitization of the cornea to the microfilariae.

onco- [G. *onkos*, bulk, mass]. Combining form denoting a tumor, some relation to a tumor, bulk, or volume.

oncocyte (ong'ko-sit) [onco- + G. *kytos*, cell]. A large, granular, acidophilic tumor containing numerous mitochondria; a neoplastic oxyphil cell.

on'cocyto'ma. Oxyphil *adenoma*.

oncogene (ong'ko-jĕn). A viral gene, found in certain retroviruses, that may transform the host cell to a neoplastic phenotype but is not required for viral replication.

oncogenesis (ong-ko-jen'ĕ-sis) [onco- + G. *genesis,* production]. Origin and growth of a neoplasm.

oncogenic (ong-ko-jen'ik). Oncogenous; causing, inducing, or being suitable for the formation and development of a neoplasm.

oncogenous (ong-koj'ĕ-nus). Oncogenic.

oncologist (ong-kol'o-jist). A specialist in oncology.

oncology (ong-kol'o-jĭ) [onco- + G. *logos,* study]. The science dealing with the physical, chemical, and biologic properties and features of neoplasms, including causation, pathogenesis, and treatment.

oncolysis (ong-kol'ĭ-sis) [onco- + G. *lysis,* dissolution]. Destruction of a neoplasm; sometimes used with reference to the reduction of any swelling or mass.

oncolytic (ong-ko-lit'ik). Pertaining to, characterized by, or causing oncolysis.

oncor'navi'ruses. Oncovirinae.

oncosis (ong-ko'sis) [G. *onkōsis,* swelling]. Formation of one or more neoplasms or tumors.

oncot'ic. Relating to or caused by edema or any swelling (oncosis).

oncotomy (ong-kot'o-mĭ) [onco- + G. *tomē,* incision]. Incision of an abscess, cyst, or other tumor.

oncotropic (ong'ko-trop'ik) [onco- + G. *tropē,* a turning]. Manifesting a special affinity for neoplasms or neoplastic cells.

on'covi'rus. Any virus of the subfamily Oncovirinae; *i.e.,* an RNA tumor virus. See also oncogenic *virus.*

Oncovirinae (ong-ko-vīr'ĭ-ne). Oncornaviruses; a subfamily of viruses (family Retroviridae) composed of the RNA tumor viruses which contain RNA-dependent DNA polymerases (reverse transcriptases) that can be integrated into the DNA of the host cell where it serves as a cellular gene.

one-carbon-fragment. The formyl group or to the methyl group that takes part in transformylation or transmethylation reactions; by means of these reactions a group containing a single carbon atom is added to a compound being biosynthesized, adding

a methyl group as in thymidine formation, adding a hydroxymethyl group as in serine biosynthesis, or closing a ring as in purine formation.

oneiric (o-ni'rik) [G. *oneiros,* dream]. **1.** Pertaining to dreams. **2.** Pertaining to the clinical state of oneirophrenia.

oneirism (ŏ-ni'rizm) [G. *oneiros,* dream]. A waking dream state.

oneirodynia (o-ni-ro-din'ĭ-ah) [G. *oneiros,* dream, + *odynē,* pain]. An unpleasant or painful dream.

oneirophrenia (o-ni'ro-fre'nĭ-ah) [G. *oneiros,* dream, + *phrēn,* mind]. A state in which hallucinations occur, caused by such conditions as prolonged deprivation of sleep, sensory isolation, and a variety of drugs.

oneiroscopy (o-ni-ros'ko-pĭ) [G. *oneiros,* dream, + *skopeō,* to examine]. Dream analysis; diagnosis of a person's mental state by a study of his dreams.

-onium. Suffix indicating a positively charged radical.

onko-. For words beginning thus, see onco-.

onlay. 1. A restoration of the occlusal surface of a posterior tooth or the lingual surface of an anterior tooth the entire surface of which is in dentin, leaving no side walls. **2.** A graft applied on the exterior of a bone.

onomatomania (on'o-mat'o-ma'nĭ-ah) [G. *onomo,* name, + *mania,* frenzy]. An abnormal impulse to dwell upon certain words and their supposed significance, or to frantically try to recall a particular word.

onomatophobia (on'o-mat'o-fo'bĭ-ah) [G. *onomo,* name, + *phobos,* fear]. Abnormal dread of certain words or names because of their supposed significance.

ontogenesis (on-to-jen'ĕ-sis). Ontogeny.

on'togenet'ic. Relating to ontogeny.

ontogeny (on-toj'ĕ-nĭ) [G. *ōn,* being, + *genesis,* origin]. Ontogenesis; development of the individual, as distinguished from phylogenesis, evolutionary development of the species.

onych-. See onycho-.

onychalgia (on-ĭ-kal'jĭ-ah) [onycho- + G. *algos,* pain]. Pain in the nails.

onychatrophia, onychatrophy (on'ĭ-kă-tro'fĭ-ah, on-ik-at'ro-fĭ) [onycho- + G. *antrophia,* atrophy]. Atrophy of the nails.

onychauxis (on-ĭ-kawk'sis) [onycho- + G. *auxē,* increase]. Marked overgrowth of fingernails or toenails.

onychectomy (on-ĭ-kek'to-mĭ) [onycho- + G. *ectomē,* excision]. Ablation of a toenail or fingernail.

onychia (o-nik'ĭ-ah) [onycho- + G. *-ia,* condition]. Onychitis; inflammation of the nail matrix.

onychitis (on-ĭ-ki'tis). Onychia.

onycho-, onych- [G. *onyx,* nail]. Combining forms denoting a fingernail or toenail.

onychoclasis (on-ĭ-kok'lă-sis) [onycho- + G. *klasis,* breaking]. Breaking of the nails.

onychodystrophy (on'ĭ-ko-dis'tro-fĭ) [onycho- + G. *dys-,* bad, + *trophē,* nourishment]. Dystrophic changes in nails occuring as a congenital defect or due to any illness or injury that may cause a malformed nail.

onychograph (on´ĭ-ko-graf) [onycho- + G. *graphō,* to write]. An instrument for recording the capillary blood pressure as shown by the circulation under the nail.

onychogryposis, onychogryphosis (on-ĭ-ko-grĭ-po´sis, -grĭ-fo´sis). [onycho- + G. *grypōsis,* a curvature]. Enlargement with increased thickening and curvature of the fingernails or toenails.

onychoheterotopia (on´ĭ-ko-het-er-o-to´pĭ-ah) [onycho- + heterotopia]. Abnormal placement of nails.

onychoid (on´ĭ-koyd) [onycho- + G. *eidos,* resemblance]. Resembling in structure or form a fingernail.

onycholysis (on-ĭ-kol´ĭ-sis) [onycho- + G. *lysis,* loosening]. Loosening of the nails, beginning at the free border, and usually incomplete.

onychoma (on-ĭ-ko´mah) [onycho- + G. *-ōma,* tumor]. A tumor arising from the nail bed.

onychomadesis (on´ĭ-ko-mă-de´sis) [onycho- + G. *madēsis,* a growing bald]. Complete shedding of the nails usually associated with a systemic illness.

onychomalacia (on´ĭ-ko-mă-la´shĭ-ah) [onycho- + G. *malakia,* softness]. Abnormal softness of the nails.

onychomycosis (on´ĭ-ko-mi-ko´sis) [onycho- + G. *mykes,* fungus, + *-ōsis,* condition]. Ringworm of the nails; tinea unguium; a fungus infection of the nails, causing thickening, roughness, and splitting, usually caused by *Trichophyton rubrum* or *T. mentagrophytes.*

onycho-osteodysplasia (on´ĭ-ko-os´te-o-dis-pla´zĭ-ah). Nail-patella syndrome; a congenital condition (autosomal dominant inheritance) characterized by a disturbance of growth of the bone and of the toes and fingernails. The lower ends of the femur have a shape very similar to that of the Erlenmeyer flask used by chemists. See also Erlenmeyer flask *deformity.*

onychopathic (on-ĭ-ko-path´ik). Relating to onychopathy.

onychopathy (on-ĭ-kop´ă-thī) [onycho- + G. *pathos,* suffering]. Onychosis; any disease of the nails.

onychophagy, onychophagia (on-ĭ-kof´ă-jī, on-ĭ-ko-fa´jĭ-ah) [onycho- + G. *phagein,* to eat]. Nail-biting.

onychoplasty (on´ĭ-ko-plas-tī) [onycho- + G. *plastos,* formed, shaped]. A corrective or plastic operation on the nail matrix.

onychorrhexis (on´ĭ-ko-rek´sis) [onycho- + G. *rhēxis,* a breaking]. Abnormal brittleness of the nails with splitting of the free edge.

on´ychoschiz´ia [onycho- + G. *schizein,* to divide, + suffix, *-ia,* condition]. Splitting of the nails in layers.

onychosis (on-ĭ-ko´sis). Onychopathy.

onychotillomania (on´ĭ-kot´ĭ-lo-ma´nĭ-ah) [onycho- + G. *tillein,* to pluck, + *mania,* insanity]. A tendency to pick at the nails.

onychotomy (on-ĭ-kot´o-mī) [onycho- + G. *tomē,* cutting]. Incision into a toenail or fingernail.

onyx (on´iks) [G. nail]. **1.** Unguis. **2.** A collection of pus in the anterior chamber of the eye, resembling a fingernail.

oo- [G. *ōon,* egg]. Combining form denoting egg, ovary. See also oophor-, ovario-, ovi-, ovo-.

ooblast (o´o-blast) [G. *ōon,* egg, + *blastos,* germ]. Seldom used term for a primordial cell from which the ovum is developed.

o´ocyst [G. *ōon,* egg, + *kystis,* bladder]. The encysted form of the fertilized macrogamete, or zygote, in coccidian Sporozoa in which sporogonic multiplication occurs, resulting in the formation of sporozoites.

oocyte (o´o-sīt) [G. *ōon,* egg, + *kytos,* a hollow (cell)]. The immature ovum.

  primary o., an o. during its growth phase and prior to completion of the first maturation division.

  secondary o., an o. in which the first meiotic division is completed; the second meiotic division usually stops short of completion unless fertilization occurs.

oogenesis (o-o-jen´ĕ-sis) [G. *ōon,* egg, + *genesis,* origin]. Ovigenesis; formation and development of the ovum.

oogenetic (o´o-jĕ-net´ik). Ovigenetic; producing ova.

oogonium, pl. **oogonia** (o´o-go´nĭ-um, -ah) [G. *ōon,* egg, + *gonē,* generation]. The primitive egg mother cell, from which the oocytes are developed.

ookinesis (o´o-kĭ-ne´sis) [G. *ōon,* egg, + *kinēsis,* movement]. The chromosomal movements of the egg during maturation and fertilization.

ookinete (o´o-kĭ-nēt) [G. *ōon,* egg, + *kinētos,* motile]. The motile zygote of the malarial organism that penetrates the mosquito stomach to form an oocyst under the outer gut lining; the contents of the oocyst subsequently divide to produce numerous sporozoites.

oolemma (o-o-lem´ah) [G. *ōon,* egg, + *lemma,* sheath]. The plasma membrane of the oocyte.

oophor-, oophoro- [Mod. L. *oophoron,* ovary, fr. G. *ōophoros,* egg-bearing]. Combining forms denoting the ovary. See also oo-, ovario-.

oophorectomy (o-of´or-ek´to-mī) [G. *ōon,* egg, + *phoros,* bearing, + *ectomē,* excision]. Ovariectomy.

oophoritis (o-of-or-i´tis) [G. *ōon,* egg, + *phoros,* a bearing, + *-itis,* inflammation]. Ovaritis; inflammation of an ovary.

oophoro-. See oophor-.

oophorocystectomy (o-of´or-o-sis-tek´to-mī). Excision of an ovarian cyst.

oophorocystosis (o-of´or-o-sis-to´sis). Ovarian cyst formation.

oophorohysterectomy (o-of´or-o-his-ter-ek´to-mī). Ovariohysterectomy.

oophoron (o-of´or-on) [Mod. L. ovary, fr. G. *ōon,* egg, + *phoros,* bearing]. Ovary.

oophoropexy (o-of'or-o-pek-sĭ) [oophoro- + G. *pēxis*, fixation]. Surgical fixation or suspension of an ovary.

oophoroplasty (o-of'or-o-plas-tĭ) [oophoro- + G. *plastos*, formed, shaped]. Plastic operation upon an ovary.

oophorostomy (o-of'or-os'to-mĭ) [oophoro- + G. *stoma*, mouth]. Ovariostomy.

oophorotomy (o-of'or-ot'o-mĭ) [oophoro- + G. *tomē*, incision]. Ovariotomy.

ooplasm (o'o-plazm) [G. *ōon*, egg, + *plasma*, a thing formed]. The protoplasmic portion of the ovum.

o'otid [G. *ōotidion*, a diminutive egg]. The nearly mature ovum after the first maturation has been completed and the second initiated.

opacification (o-pas'ĭ-fĭ-ka'shun) [L. *opacus*, shady]. **1.** The process of making opaque. **2.** The formation of opacities.

opacity (o-pas'ĭ-tĭ) [L. *opacitas*, shadiness]. A lack of transparency; an opaque or nontransparent area.

opaque (o-pāk') [Fr. fr. L. *opacus*, shady]. Impervious to light; not translucent.

o'pening. An aperture. See fossa, hiatus; ostium; orifice.

op'erable. Denoting a patient or condition on which a surgical procedure can be performed with a reasonable expectation of cure or relief.

op'erant. Target response; in conditioning, any behavior or specific response chosen by the experimenter.

op'erate [L. *operor*, pp. *-atus*, to work]. To work upon the body by the hands or by means of cutting or other instruments to correct a surgical problem.

opera'tion. 1. Any surgical procedure. **2.** The act, manner, or process of functioning. See also entries under method, procedure, technique.

Abbé o., the transfer of a flap of the full thickness of the middle portion of the lower lip into the upper lip.

Bassini's o., an o. for the radical correction of hernia.

Baudelocque's o., an incision through the posterior cul-de-sac of the vagina for the removal of the ovum, in extrauterine pregnancy.

Beer's o., flap o. for cataract.

Billroth's o. I and II, (1) Billroth I anastomosis; excision of the pylorus with end-to-end anastomosis of stomach and duodenum; **(2)** Billroth II anastomosis; resection of the pylorus with the greater part of the lesser curvature of the stomach, closure of the cut ends of the duodenum and stomach, followed by a posterior gastrojejunostomy.

Blalock-Taussig o., an o. for congenital malformations of the heart, in which an abnormally small volume of blood passes through the pulmonary circuit; blood from the systemic circulation is directed to the lungs by anastomosing the right or left subclavian artery to the right or left pulmonary artery.

bloodless o., an o. performed with negligible loss of blood.

Bowman's o., (1) a double-needle o. for dilaceration of a cataract; **(2)** slitting the canaliculus for the relief of stenosis, to evacuate an abscess of the lacrimal sac, etc.

Bricker o., an o. utilizing an isolated segment of ileum to collect urine from both ureters and conduct it to the skin surface.

Caldwell-Luc o., an intraoral procedure for opening into the maxillary antrum through the supradental (canine) fossa above the maxillary premolar teeth.

Cotte's o., presacral *neurectomy*.

Dandy o., (1) see third *ventriculostomy;* **(2)** a suboccipital trigeminal *rhizotomy*.

Daviel's o., extracapsular cataract extraction.

Dupuy-Dutemps o., a modification of the Toti operation for stenosis of the lacrimal duct.

Elliot's o., trephining of the eyeball, at the corneoscleral margin, to relieve tension in glaucoma.

Estlander o., transfer of a flap of the full-thickness of the lip from one side of one lip to the same side of the opposite lip.

filtering o., a surgical procedure for creation of a fistula between the anterior chamber of the eye and the subconjunctival space in treatment of glaucoma.

flap o., (1) flap *amputation;* **(2)** in dental surgery, an o. in which a portion of the mucoperiosteal tissues is surgically detached from the underlying bone or impacted tooth for better access and visibility in exploring the area covered by the tissue.

Fothergill's o., Manchester o.

Frazier-Spiller o., a subtemporal trigeminal *rhizotomy*.

Fredet-Ramstedt o., pyloromyotomy.

Frost-Lang o., insertion of a gold ball after the enucleation of the eyeball, then union of the superior and inferior recti muscles by a suture including the overlying conjunctiva.

Gifford's o., delimiting *keratotomy*.

Gonin o., closure of a break in the retina through cauterization, in the treatment of detachment of the retina.

Graefe's o., (1) removal of cataract by a limbal incision with capsulotomy and iridectomy; **(2)** iridectomy for glaucoma.

Halsted's o., (1) an o. for the radical correction of inguinal hernia; **(2)** radical *mastectomy*.

Herbert's o., an o. for obtaining a filtering cicatrix in glaucoma by cutting and displacing, without removing, a wedge-shaped scleral flap.

Hill o., a surgical procedure to prevent esophageal reflux.

Hoffa's o., hollowing out the acetabulum and reduction of the head of the femur after severing the muscles inserted into the upper portion of the bone, in cases of congenital dislocation of the hip.

Hofmeister's o., partial gastrectomy with closure of a portion of the lesser curvature and retrocolic anastomosis of remainder to jejunum.

Kasai o., portoenterostomy.

Kelly's o., (1) correction of retroversion of the uterus by plication of uterosacral ligaments; (2) correction of urinary stress incontinence by vaginally placing sutures beneath the bladder neck.

Kondoleon o., excision of strips of subcutaneous connective tissue for the relief of elephantiasis.

Kraske's o., removal of the coccyx and excision of the left wing of the sacrum in order to afford approach for resection of the rectum for cancer or stenosis.

Lagrange's o., a combined iridectomy and sclerectomy performed in glaucoma for the purpose of forming a filtering cicatrix.

Lambrinudi o., a form of triple arthrodesis done in such a manner as to prevent foot drop, usually as occurs in poliomyelitis.

Manchester o. [*Manchester,* England]. Fothergill's o.; a vaginal o. for prolapsus uteri consisting of cervical amputation and parametrial fixation (cardinal ligaments) anterior to the uterus.

Matas o., aneurysmoplasty.

Mayo's o., an o. for the radical correction of umbilical hernia.

McVay's o., repair of femoral hernias by suture of the transversus abdominis muscle and its associated fasciae (transversus layer) to the pectineal ligament.

Meyer-Schwickerath o., photocoagulation of the retina or choroid.

Mikulicz o., excision of bowel in two stages, first, exteriorizing the diseased area, suturing efferent and afferent limbs together, and closing the abdomen around them, after which the diseased part is excised; second, cutting the spur and closing the stoma extraperitoneally.

Motais o., transplantation of the middle third of the tendon of the superior rectus muscle of the eyeball into the upper lid, between the tarsus and skin, to supplement the action of the levator muscle in ptosis.

Naffziger o., orbital decompression for severe malignant exophthalmos by removal of the lateral and superior orbital walls.

Ogura o., orbital decompression by removal of the flow of the orbit through an opening made in the supradental (canine) fossa.

Pancoast's o., division of the trigeminal nerve at the foramen ovale.

Payne o., a jejunoileal bypass for morbid obesity, utilizing end-to-side anastomosis of the upper jejunum to the terminal ileum, with closure of the proximal end of the bypassed intestine.

Pomeroy's o., excision of a ligated portion of the fallopian tubes.

Putti-Platt o., a procedure for recurrent dislocation of shoulder joint.

Ramstedt o., pyloromyotomy.

Saemisch's o., incision of the cornea to evacuate pus.

Scott o., a jejunoileal bypass for morbid obesity utilizing end-to-end anastomosis of the upper jejunum to the terminal ileum, with the bypassed intestine closed proximally and anastomosed distally to the colon.

stapes mobilization o., fracture of tissue immobilizing the stapes to restore hearing, especially used in patients with otosclerosis.

Stookey-Scarff o., see third *ventriculostomy.*

subcutaneous o., an o., as for the division of a tendon, performed without incising the skin other than by a minute opening made by the entering knife.

Wertheim's o., a radical o. for carcinoma of the uterus in which as much as possible of the vagina is excised and there is wide lymph node excision.

Whipple's o., pancreatoduodenectomy.

Whitehead's o., excision of hemorrhoids by two circular incisions above and below involved veins, allowing normal mucosa to be pulled down and sutured to anal skin.

Ziegler's o., a V-shaped iridotomy for the formation of an artificial pupil.

op'era·tive. 1. Relating to, or effected by means of an operation. **2.** Active; effective.

op'erator. In genetics, operator *gene.*

opercular (o-per'ku-lar). Relating to an operculum.

operculitis (o-per'ku-li'tis) [operculum + G. *-itis,* inflammation]. Pericoronitis.

operculum, pl. **opercula** (o-per'ku-lum, -lah) [L. cover or lid]. **1.** Anything resembling a lid or cover. **2** [NA]. In anatomy, the portions of the frontal, parietal, and temporal lobes bordering the lateral sulcus and covering the insula. **3.** A bit of mucus sealing the endocervical canal of the uterus after conception has taken place. **4.** The attached flap in tear of retinal detachment. **5.** The mucosal flap partially or completely covering an unerupted tooth.

op'eron. A genetic functional unit that controls production of a messenger RNA; consists of an operator gene and two or more structural genes located in sequence in the cis position on one chromosome.

ophiasis (o-fi'ă-sis) [G. fr. *ophis,* snake]. Alopecia areata in which the loss of hair occurs in bands partially or completely encircling the head.

ophritis, ophryitis (of-ri'tis, -re-i'tis) [G. *ophrys,* eyebrow, + *-itis,* inflammation]. Dermatitis in the region of the eyebrows.

oph'ryon [G. *ophrys,* eyebrow]. The point on the midline of the forehead just above the glabella (1).

ophryosis (of-re-o'sis) [G. *ophrys,* eyebrow, + *-osis,* condition]. Spasmodic twitching of the upper portion of the orbicularis palpebrarum muscle causing a wrinkling of the eyebrow.

ophthalm-. See ophthalmo-.

ophthalmalgia (of-thal-mal'jĭ-ah) [ophthalmo- + G. *algos,* pain]. Pain in the eyeball.

ophthalmia (of-thal'mĭ-ah) [G.]. Ophthalmitis. **1.** Severe, often purulent, conjunctivitis. **2.** Inflammation of the deeper structures of the eye.

Egyptian o., trachoma.

gonorrheal o., acute purulent conjunctivitis due to gonococcal infection.

granular o., trachoma.

o. neonato'rum, infantile purulent conjunctivitis; a conjunctival inflammation occurring within the first 10 days of life; causes include *Neisseria gonorrhoeae, Staphylococcus, Streptococcus pneumoniae,* and *Chlamydia oculogenitalis.*

purulent o., purulent conjunctivitis, usually of gonorrheal origin.

sympathetic o., a serous or plastic uveitis caused by a perforating wound of the uvea followed by a similar severe reaction in the other eye that may eventuate to bilateral blindness.

ophthal'mic [G. *ophthalmikos*]. Ocular (1); relating to the eye.

ophthalmitis (of-thal-mi'tis). Ophthalmia.

ophthalmo-, ophthalm- [G. *ophthalmos,* eye]. Combining forms denoting relationship to the eye. See also oculo-.

ophthalmodiaphanoscope (of-thal'mo-di-ă-fan'o-skōp) [ophthalmo- + diaphanoscope]. An instrument for viewing the interior of the eye by transmitted light.

ophthal'modynamom'eter [ophthalmo- + G. *dynamis,* power, + *metron,* measure]. **1.** An instrument for determining the power of convergence of the eyes as regards the near point of vision. **2.** An instrument that measures the blood pressure in the retinal vessels.

ophthal'modynamom'etry. Use of an ophthalmodynamometer.

ophthalmograph (of-thal'mo-graf) [ophthalmo- + G. *graphē,* a description]. An instrument that records eye movements during reading by photographing a mark on the cornea or making a tracing of light reflexes.

ophthalmog'raphy. Use of the ophthalmograph.

ophthal'molith [ophthalmo- + G. *lithos,* stone]. Dacryolith.

ophthalmol'ogist. Oculist; a specialist in ophthalmology.

ophthalmology (of-thal-mol'o-jĭ) [ophthalmo- + G. *logos,* study]. The medical specialty concerned with the eye, its diseases, and refractive errors.

ophthalmomalacia (of-thal'mo-mă-la'shĭ-ah) [ophthalmo- + G. *malakia,* softness]. Abnormal softening of the eyeball.

ophthalmometer (of'thal-mom'e-ter) [ophthalmo- + G. *metron,* measure]. Keratometer.

ophthalmomycosis (of-thal'mo-mi-ko'sis) [ophthalmo- + G. *mykēs,* fungus, + *-osis,* condition]. Any disease of the eye or its appendages caused by a fungus.

ophthalmomyitis (of-thal'mo-mi-i'tis) [ophthalmo- + G. *mys,* muscle, + *-itis,* inflammation]. Inflammation of the extrinsic muscles of the eye.

ophthalmopathy (of-thal-mop'ă-thĭ) [ophthalmo- + G. *pathos,* suffering]. Any disease of the eyes.

external o., any disease of the conjunctiva, cornea, or adnexa of the eye.

internal o., any disease of the retina, lens, or other internal structures of the eyeball.

ophthalmoplegia (of-thal-mo-ple'jĭ-ah) [ophthalmo- + G. *plēgē,* stroke]. Paralysis of one or more of the motor nerves of the eye.

exophthalmic o., o. with protrusion of the eyeballs due to orbital edema and contracture of ocular muscles, incidental to thyroid disorders.

external o., paralysis affecting one or more of the nerves supplying the extrinsic eye muscles.

internal o., paralysis affecting only the iris and ciliary muscle.

nuclear o., o. due to a lesion of the nuclei of origin of the motor nerves of the eye.

Parinaud's o., paralysis of conjugate vertical movement upward; less often, downward.

partial o., o. involving only one or two of the extrinsic or intrinsic ocular muscles.

progressive o., progressive upper bulbar palsy, due to degeneration of the nuclei of the motor nerves of the eye.

total o., paralysis of all the motor nerves of the eye.

ophthalmople'gic. Relating to or marked by ophthalmoplegia.

ophthal'moscope [ophthalmo- + G. *skopeō,* to examine]. Funduscope; a device for studying the interior of the eyeball through the pupil.

oph'thalmos'copy. Use of the ophthalmoscope.

ophthal'movas'cular. Relating to the blood vessels of the eye.

ophthalmus (of-thal'mus) [L. fr. G. *ophthalmos*]. The eye; oculus.

-opia [G. *ōps,* eye]. Suffix meaning vision.

opiate (o'pĭ-āt). Any preparation or derivative of opium.

opioid (o'pĭ-oyd). Any synthetic narcotics that resembles opiates in action but is not derived from opium.

opisthenar (o-pis'the-nar) [G. back of the hand]. Dorsum of the hand.

opisthion (o-pis'thĭ-on) [G. *opisthios,* posterior] [NA]. The middle point on the posterior margin of the foramen magnum, opposite the basion.

opistho- [G. *opisthen,* at the rear, behind]. Combining form denoting backward, behind, dorsal.

opisthorchiasis (op'is-thor-ki'ă-sis). Infection with the Asiatic liver fluke, *Opisthorchis viverrini,* or other opisthorchids.

Opisthorchis (op-is-thor'kis) [opistho- + G. *orchis,* testis]. A genus of digenetic trematodes (family Opisthorchiidae) found in the bile ducts or gallbladder of fish-eating mammals, birds, and fish.

O. felin'eus, the cat liver fluke, a parasitic species whose ingested eggs hatch in *Bithynia* snails and cercariae encyst on various species of fish; man acquires the infection by ingesting raw or inadequately cooked fish.

O. viverri'ni, a species closely related to O. *felineus* which also causes opisthorchiasis.

opisthotonic (op'is-tho-ton'ik). Relating to or characterized by opisthotonos.

opisthotonos (op-is-thot'o-nus) [opistho- + G. *tonos,* tension, stretching]. A tetanic spasm in which the spine and extremities are bent with convexity forward, the body resting on the head and the heels.

opium (o'pĭ-um) [L. fr. G. *opion,* poppy-juice]. Meconium (2); the air-dried milky exudation obtained by incising the unripe capsules of *Papaver somniferum* or its variety *P. album* (family Papaveraceae); contains some 20 alkaloids, including morphine, 9 to 16%; noscapine, 4 to 8%; codeine, 0.8 to 2.5%; papaverine, 0.5 to 2.5%; and thebaine, 0.5 to 2%.

opportunistic (op'or-tu-nis'tik). **1.** Denoting an organism capable of causing disease only in a host whose resistance is lowered. **2.** Denoting a disease caused by an o. organism.

op'sin. The protein portion of the rhodopsin molecule.

opsin'ogen. Opsogen; a substance that stimulates the formation of opsonin.

opsiuria (op'sĭ-u'rĭ-ah) [G. *opsi,* late, + *ouron,* urine]. A more rapid excretion of urine during fasting than after a full meal.

opsoclonus (op'so-klo'nus) [G. *ōps, ōpos,* eye, + *klonos,* confused motion]. Rapid, irregular, nonrhythmic movements of the eye in horizontal and vertical directions.

op'sogen. Opsinogen.

opsoma'nia [G. *opson,* seasoning, + *mania,* frenzy]. A longing for a particular article of diet, or for highly seasoned food.

opson'ic. Relating to opsonins or to their utilization.

op'sonin [G. *opsonein,* to cater, prepare food]. A substance that enhances phagocytosis.

normal o., common or thermolabile o.; o. normally present in the blood, without stimulation by a known specific antigen, that reacts with various organisms.

specific o., immune or thermostable o.; o. formed in response to stimulation by a specific antigen, either as a result of a disease or of injections with a suitably prepared suspension of the specific microorganism; it reacts only with microorganisms that contain the specific antigens that stimulated formation of the antibody.

opsoniza'tion. The process by which bacteria are altered in such a manner that they are more readily and more efficiently engulfed by phagocytes.

opsonocytophagic (op'son-o-si'to-fa'jik) [opsonin + G. *kytos,* a hollow (cell), + *phagein,* to eat]. Pertaining to the increased efficiency of phagocytic

activity of the leukocytes in blood that contains specific opsonin.

opsonom'etry. Determination of the opsonic index or the opsonocytophagic activity.

optesthesia (op-tes-the'zĭ-ah) [G. *optikos,* optical, + *aisthēsis,* sensation]. Visual sensibility to light stimuli.

op'tic, op'tical [G. *optikos*]. Relating to the eye, vision, or optics.

optician (op-tish'an). One who practices opticianry.

opticianry (op-tish'an-rī). The professional practice of filling prescriptions for ophthalmic lenses, dispensing spectacles, and making and fitting contact lenses.

optico-. See opto-.

opticociliary (op'tĭ-ko-sil'ĭ-ĕr-ĭ). Relating to the optic and ciliary nerves.

op'ticopu'pillary. Relating to the optic nerve and the pupil.

op'tics [G. *optikos,* fr. *ōps,* eye]. The science concerned with the properties of light, its refraction and absorption, and the refracting media of the eye in that relation.

opto-, optico- [G. *optikos,* optical, from *ōps,* eye]. Combining forms relating to the eye.

optokinet'ic [opto- + G. *kinēsis,* movement]. Pertaining to the occurrence of nystagmus-like twitchings or movements of the eye when the subject looks at moving objects.

optom'eter [opto- + G. *metron,* measure]. An instrument for determining the refraction of the eye.

optom'etrist. One who practices optometry.

optom'etry. 1. The profession concerned with the examination of the eyes and related structures to determine the presence of vision problems and eye disorders, and with the prescription and adaptation of lenses and other optical aids. **2.** Use of an optometer.

optomyometer (op-to-mi-om'ĕ-ter) [opto- + G. *mys,* muscle, + *metron,* measure]. An instrument for determining the relative power of the extrinsic muscles of the eye.

ora (o'rah) [L.]. Plural of L. *os,* the mouth.

ora, pl. **orae** (o'rah, o're) [L.] [NA]. An edge or a margin.

o'rad [L. *os,* mouth, + *ad,* to]. **1.** In a direction toward the mouth. **2.** Situated nearer the mouth in relation to a specific reference point.

o'ral [L. *os* (*or-*), mouth]. Relating to the mouth.

oral'ity. A term used to denote the psychic organization derived from, and characteristic of, the oral period of psychosexual development.

orbicular (or-bik'u-lar) [L. *orbiculus,* a small disk, dim. of *orbis,* circle]. Circular.

orbicula're [L. fr. *orbiculus,* a small disk]. *Processus lenticularis incudis.*

orbic'ulus cilia'ris [Mod. L.] [NA]. Ciliary disk or ring; anulus ciliaris; pars plana; the darkly pigmented posterior zone of the ciliary body continuous with the retina at the ora serrata.

or'bit. Orbita.

orbita, *pl.* **orbitae** (or'bĭ-tah, -te) [L. a wheel-track, fr. *orbis*, circle] [NA]. Orbit; orbital cavity; eye socket; the bony cavity containing the eyeball and its adnexa, formed of parts of seven bones: frontal, maxillary, sphenoid, lacrimal, zygomatic, ethmoid, and palatine.

or'bital. Relating to the orbits.

orbita'le [L. of an orbit]. The lowermost point in the lower margin of the bony orbit that may be felt under the skin.

orbitography (or-bĭ-tog'ră-fĭ) [L. *orbita*, orbit, + G. *graphō*, to write]. A diagnostic technique for radiographic evaluation in suspected blow-out fracture of the orbit, using a water-soluble iodinated compound injected over the orbital floor.

or'bitona'sal. Relating to the orbit and the nose or nasal cavity.

orbitonometer (or'bĭ-to-nom'e-ter) [L. *orbita*, orbit, + G. *metron*, measure]. An instrument for measurement of the resistance offered to pressing the eyeball backwards into its socket.

orbitonom'etry. Use of the orbitonometer.

orbitot'omy [L. *orbita*, orbit, + *tomas*, cut]. Surgical incision into the orbit.

Orbivirus (or'bĭ-vi-rus) [L. *orbis*, ring, + virus]. A genus of viruses of vertebrates (family Reoviridae) that multiply in insects, including the Colorado tick fever virus of man and certain viruses formerly included with the arboviruses. They are antigenically distinct from other groups of viruses and are characterized by an indistinct but rather large outer layer of capsomeres which give the appearance of rings.

orcein (or'se-in). A natural dye derived from orcinol which as a purple dye complex is used in various histologic staining methods.

orchi-, orchido-, orchio- [G. *orchis*, testis]. Combining forms denoting relationship to the testes.

orchialgia (or-kĭ-al'jĭ-ah) [orchi- + G. *algos*, pain]. Didymalgia; testalgia; pain in the testis.

orchidectomy (or-kĭ-dek'to-mĭ). Orchiectomy.

orchidic (or-kid'ik). Relating to the testis.

orchido-. See orchi-.

orchiectomy (or-kĭ-ek'to-mĭ) [orchi- + G. *ektomē*, excision]. Orchidectomy; testectomy; removal of one or both testes.

orchiencephaloma (or'kĭ-en-sef-al-o'ma) [orchi- + G. *enkephalos*, brain, + *-oma*, tumor]. A relatively soft or encephaloid neoplasm of the testes.

orchiepididymitis (or'kĭ-ep'ĭ-did-ĭ-mi'tis) [orchi- + epididymis, + G. *-itis*, inflammation]. Inflammation of the testis and epididymis.

orchio-. See orchi-.

orchiocele (or'kĭ-o-sēl) [orchio- + G. *kēlē*, hernia tumor]. **1.** A tumor of the testis. **2.** A testis retained in the inguinal canal.

orchiopathy (or-kĭ-op'ă-thĭ) [orchio- + G. *pathos*, suffering]. Any disease of a testis.

orchiopexy (or'kĭ-o-pek-sĭ) [orchio- + G. *pēxis*, fixation]. Cryptorchidopexy; surgical treatment of an undescended testicle by freeing it and implanting it into the scrotum.

orchioplasty (or'kĭ-o-plas-tĭ) [orchio- + G. *plassō*, to form]. Plastic surgery of the testis.

orchiotomy (or-kĭ-ot'o-mĭ) [orchio- + G. *tomē*, incision]. Incision into a testis.

orchis, pl. **orchises** (or'kis, or'kĭ-sēz) [G. testis, an orchid]. The testis.

orchit'ic. Denoting to orchitis.

orchitis (or-ki'tis) [orchi- + G. *-itis*, inflammation]. Orchiditis; didymitis; testitis; inflammation of the testis.

ORD Optical rotatory *dispersion.*

or'der [L. *ordo*, regular arrangement]. In biological classification, the division just below the class (or subclass) and above the family.

or'derly. A male attendant in a hospital.

or'dinate. The plane in a Cartesian coordinate system representing the distance from a specified point to the *x* axis (horizontal) measured parallel to the *y* axis (vertical).

orexigenic (o-rek-sĭ-jen'ik). Appetite-stimulating.

or'gan [G. *organon*, a tool, organ]. Any part of the body exercising a specific function.

circumventricular o.'s, structures in or near the base of the brain that differ from normal brain tissue in having capillaries that lack the usual blood-brain barrier and thus are not isolated from certain compounds in the blood.

Corti's o., spiral o.

critical o., the o. or physiologic system that for a given method of administration would furnish the subjected to the legally defined maximum permissible radiation exposure as the dose of radioactive material is increased.

enamel o., mass of ectodermal cells budded off from the dental lamina which develops the ameloblast layer of cells which produce the enamel cap of a developing tooth.

end o., the special structure containing the terminal of a nerve fiber in peripheral tissue.

genital o.'s, genitalia; genitals; the organs of reproduction or generation; **(1)** external feminine: vulva and clitoris; **(2)** internal feminine: ovaries, uterine tubes, uterus, and vagina; **(3)** external masculine: penis and scrotum; **(4)** internal masculine: testes, epididymides, deferent ducts, seminal vesicles, prostate, and bulbourethral glands.

Golgi tendon o., neurotendinous spindle; a proprioceptive sensory nerve ending embedded among the fibers of a tendon, often near the musculotendinous junction.

sense o.'s, o.'s of special sense, including those of sight, hearing, smell, taste, and touch.

spiral o., Corti's organ; a prominent ridge of highly specialized epithelium in the floor of the cochlear duct overlying the basilar membrane; containing one inner row and three or four outer rows of hair cells supported by various columnar cells.

target o., target (3); a tissue or o. upon which a hormone exerts its action; may be an endocrine gland, a nonendocrine gland; or a type of tissue.

vestibular o., collective term for the utricle, saccule, and semicircular ducts of the membranous labyrinth, each having a single patch of ciliated receptor epithelium innervated by the vestibular nerve: macula sacculi, macula utriculi, and cristae of the semicircular ducts.

vestigial o., a rudimentary structure in man corresponding to a functional structure or o. in the lower animals.

o.'s of Zuckerkandl, *corpora paraaortica.*

or′gana. Plural or organum.

organelle (or′gă-nel) [Mod. L. dim. of G. *organon,* organ]. Organoid (3); one of the specialized parts of a cell, including mitochondria, the Golgi apparatus, cell center and centrioles, granular and agranular endoplasmic reticulum, vacuoles, microsomes, lysosomes, plasma membrane, and certain fibrils, as well as plastids of plant cells.

organ′ic [G. *organikos*]. **1.** Relating to an organ. **2.** Relating to an animal or vegetable organism. **3.** Organized; structural. **4.** In chemistry, relating to those compounds in which the atoms are linked by covalent bonds, chiefly the compounds of carbon; originally, relating to compounds of natural origin.

organism (or′gă-nizm). Any living individual, whether plant or animal, considered as a whole.

pleuropneumonia-like o.'s (PPLO), the original name given to a group of bacteria that did not possess cell walls; now assigned to the order Mycoplasmatales.

or′ganiza′tion. 1. An arrangement of distinct but mutually dependent parts. **2.** The conversion of coagulated blood, exudate, or dead tissue into fibrous tissue.

or′ganize. To provide with, or to assume, a structure.

or′ganizer. A group of cells that induces differentiation of cells in the embryo, controlling the growth and development of adjacent parts, through the action of a chemical of a steroid nature called the evocator.

organo-. Combining form denoting organ or organic.

organogel (or-gan′o-jel). A hydrogel with an organic liquid instead of water as the dispersion means.

organogenesis (or′gă-no-jen′ĕ-sis) [organo- + G. *genesis,* origin]. Organogeny; formation of organs during development.

organogenetic, organogenic (or′gă-no-jĕ-net′ik, -jen′ik). Relating to organogenesis.

organogeny (or-gan-oj′ĕ-nī). Organogenesis.

organoid (or′gă-noyd) [organo- + G. *eidos,* resemblance]. **1.** Resembling in superficial appearance or in structure any of the organs or glands of the body. **2.** Composed of glandular or organic elements, and not of a single tissue; pertaining to certain neoplasms that contain cytologic and histologic ele-

ments arranged in a pattern that closely resembles or is virtually identical to a normal organ. **3.** Organelle.

organoma (or′gă-no′mah) [organo- + G. *-oma,* tumor]. A neoplasm that contains cytologic and histologic elements in such an arrangement that specific types of tissue may be identified in various parts. See also teratoma.

or′ganomeg′aly. Visceromegaly.

organ′omercu′rial. Any organic mercurial compound.

or′ganometal′lic. Denoting an organic compound containing one or more metallic atoms in its structure.

organon, pl. **organa** (or′gă-non, -nah) [G. organ]. An organ.

organotrophic (or′gă-no-trof′ik) [organo- + G. *trophē,* nourishment]. Pertaining to the nourishment of an organ.

organotrop′ic. Pertaining to or characterized by organotropism.

organotropism (or-gă-not′ro-pizm) [organo- + G. *tropē,* a turning]. The special affinity of particular drugs, pathogens, or other agents for particular organs or their component parts.

organ-specific. Denoting or pertaining to a serum produced by the injection of the cells of a certain organ or tissue that, when injected into another animal, destroys the cells of the corresponding organ.

organum, pl. **organa** (or′gă-num, -nah) [L. organ] [NA]. An organ.

orgasm (or′gazm) [G. *orgaō,* to swell, be excited]. The acme or climax of the sexual act.

orientation (or′ĭ-en-ta′shun) [Fr. *orienter,* to set toward the East (therefore in a definite position)]. **1.** Recognition of one's temporal, spatial, and personal relationships and environment. **2.** The relative position of an atom with respect to one to which it is connected, *i.e.,* the direction of the bond connecting them.

orifice (or′ĭ-fis) [L. *orificium*]. Any aperture or opening. See also ostium, foramen, meatus.

orificial (or-ĭ-fish′al). Relating to an orifice of any kind.

orificium, pl. **orificia** (or-ĭ-fish′ī-um, -ah) [L.] [NA]. Orifice.

origin (or′ĭ-jin) [L. *origo,* source, beginning]. **1.** The less movable of the two points of attachment of a muscle, that which is attached to the more fixed part of the skeleton. **2.** The starting point of a cranial or spinal nerve; the former have two o.'s: **ental, deep,** or **real o.,** the cell group in the brain or medulla, whence the fibers of the nerve begin; **ectal, superficial,** or **apparent o.,** the point where the nerve emerges from the brain.

Orn Ornithine or its radical.

or′nithine (Orn). $NH_2(CH_2)_3CH(NH_2)COOH$; the amino acid formed when arginine is hydrolyzed by arginase; an important intermediate in the urea cycle.

Ornithodoros (or-nĭ-thod'o-rus) [G. *ornis* (*ornith-*), bird, + *doros*, a leather bag]. A genus of soft ticks (family Argasidae), several species of which are vectors of pathogens of various relapsing fevers.

ornitho'sis [G. *ornis* (*ornith-*), bird, + *-osis*, condition]. A disease of birds and fowl caused by *Chlamydia psittaci* and contracted by man by contact with these birds; generally milder than psittacosis.

Oro Orotic acid or orotate.

oro- [L. *os, oris,* mouth]. Combining form relating to the mouth.

orodigitofacial (o'ro-dij'ĭ-to-fa'shăl). Relating to the mouth, fingers, and face.

orofacial (o-ro-fa'shal). Relating to the mouth and face.

orolingual (o-ro-ling'gwal). Relating to the mouth and the tongue.

orona'sal. Relating to the mouth and the nose.

oropharynx (o-ro-făr'ingks). [L. *os* (*or-*), mouth]. The portion of the pharynx that lies posterior to the mouth and is continuous above with the nasopharynx and below with the laryngopharynx.

orosomucoid (or'o-so-mu'koyd). An α_1-globulin in plasma, 40% carbohydrate.

or'otate (Oro). A salt or ester of orotic acid.

orot'ic acid (Oro). 6-Carboxyuracil; an important intermediate in the formation of the pyrimidine nucleotides.

orot'ic acidu'ria [orotic acid + G. *ouron,* urine]. A disorder of pyrimidine metabolism characterized by megaloblastic anemia, leukopenia, retarded growth, and urinary excretion of orotic acid; recessive inheritance.

orthergasia (orth-er-ga'zĭ-ah) [G. *orthos,* straight, correct, + *ergasia,* work]. Normal intellectual and emotional adjustment.

orthe'sis. An orthopedic brace or appliance.

orthet'ics. Orthotics.

ortho- [Gr. *orthos,* correct, straight]. **1.** Prefix denoting straight, normal, or in proper order. **2** (*o-*). In chemistry, denoting that a compound has two substitutions on adjacent carbon atoms in a benzene ring.

orthochorea (or'tho-ko-re'ah). A form of chorea in which the spasms occur only or chiefly when the patient is in the erect posture.

orthochromatic (or'tho-kro-mat'ic) [ortho- + G. *chrōma,* color]. Denoting any tissue or cell that stains the color of the dye used, *i.e.,* the same color as the dye solution with which it is stained.

orthocytosis (or'tho-si-to'sis) [ortho- + G. *kytos,* cell, + *-osis,* condition]. A condition in which all of the cellular elements in circulating blood are mature forms, irrespective of the proportions of various types and total numbers.

orthodontics, **orthodontia** (or-tho-dont'iks, -don'shĭ-ah) [ortho- + G. *odous,* tooth]. That branch of dentistry concerned with the correction

and prevention of irregularities and malocclusion of the teeth.

orthodont'ist. A specialist in orthodontics.

orthodro'mic [ortho- + G. *dromos,* course]. Denoting the propagation of an impulse along an axon in the normal direction.

orthognathia (or-tho-nath'ĭ-ah) [ortho- + G. *gnathos,* jaw]. The study of the causes and treatment of conditions related to malposition of the bones of the jaws.

orthognathic, **orthognathous** (or'tho-nath'ik, or-thog'nă-thus) [ortho- + G. *gnathos,* jaw]. **1.** Relating to orthognathia. **2.** Having a face without projecting jaw.

or'thograde [ortho- + L. *gradior,* pp. *gressus,* to walk]. Walking or standing erect; denoting the posture of man.

orthokeratology (or'tho-kĕr-ă-tol'o-jĭ) [ortho- + G. *keras,* horn (cornea), + *logos,* science]. A method of improving unaided vision by molding the cornea with contact lenses.

or'thomechan'ical [ortho- + mechanical]. Pertaining to braces, prostheses, orthotic devices, and appliances.

orthom'eter [ortho- + G. *metron,* measure]. An instrument for determining the degree of protrusion or retraction of the eyeballs.

orthomolecular (or'tho-mo-lek'u-lar). Designating the normal chemical constituents of the body, including substances formed endogenously and those acquired through the diet.

Orthomyxoviridae (or-tho-mik'so-vĭr'ĭ-de). The family of viruses that comprises the three groups of influenza viruses (types A, B, and C). The only recognized genus is *Influenzavirus,* which comprises the strains of virus types A and B. Influenza virus type C differs somewhat from types A and B and probably belongs to a separate genus.

orthope'dic, orthopae'dic. Relating to orthopedics.

orthopedics, orthopaedics (or-tho-pe'diks) [ortho- + G. *pais* (*paid-*), child]. The medical specialty concerned with the preservation, restoration, and development of form and function of the extremities, spine, and associated structures by medical, surgical, and physical methods.

orthope'dist, orthopae'dist. A specialist in orthopedics.

orthopercussion (or'tho-per-kush'un). Very light percussion of the chest, not perpendicularly to the wall of the chest, used to determine the size of the heart, the faint percussion sound disappearing when the heart is reached even though that may be overlapped by a layer of the lung.

orthophoria (or-tho-fo'rĭ-ah) [ortho- + G. *phora,* motion]. Binocular fixation in which the lines of sight meet at a distant or near point of reference in the absence of a fusion stimulus.

orthopho'ric. Pertaining to orthophoria.

orthopnea (or-thop-ne'ah) [ortho- + G. *pnoĕ,* breathing]. Discomfort on breathing which is partly or wholly relieved by the erect sitting or standing position.

orthopneic (or-thop-ne′ik). Relating to or suffering from orthopnea.

Orthopox′virus. The genus of the family Poxviridae which comprises the viruses of alastrim, vaccinia, variola, cowpox, ectromelia, monkeypox, and rabbitpox.

orthopsychiatry (or′tho-si-ki′ă-trī). The science relating to the study and treatment of disorders of behavior, especially in children.

orthop′tic. Relating to orthoptics.

orthop′tics [ortho- + G. *optikos,* relating to sight]. The study and treatment of defective binocular vision, of defects in the action of the ocular muscles, or of faulty visual habits.

orthoscope (or′tho-skōp) [ortho- + G. *skopeō,* to view]. An instrument by which water is held in contact with the eye, thereby eliminating corneal refraction.

orthoscop′ic. 1. Relating to the orthoscope. 2. Having normal vision. 3. Denoting an object correctly observed by the eye.

orthoscopy (or-thos′ko-pī). Examination of the eye with the orthoscope.

ortho′sis, pl. **ortho′ses** [G. *orthōsis,* a making straight]. The straightening of a deformity, often by use of orthopedic appliances.

orthostat′ic. Relating to an erect posture or position.

orthot′ics. Orthetics; the science concerned with the making and fitting of orthopaedic appliances.

or′thotist. One skilled in orthotics.

orthot′onos, orthot′onus [ortho- + G. *tonos,* tension]. A form of tetanic spasm in which the neck, limbs, and body are held fixed in a straight line.

orthotop′ic [ortho- + G. *topos,* place]. In the normal or usual position.

orthotrop′ic [ortho- + G. *tropē,* a turn]. Extending or growing in a straight, especially a vertical, direction.

O.S. Oculus sinister [L.], left eye.

Os Osmium.

os, pl. **o′ra** [L. mouth]. **1** [NA]. The mouth. **2.** An opening into a hollow organ or canal, especially one with thick or fleshy edges.

incompetent cervical o., a defect in the muscular ring at the internal o. allowing premature dilation of the cervix.

os, gen. **os′sis,** pl. **os′sa** [L. bone] [NA]. Bone; a portion of osseous tissue of definite shape and size, forming a part of the animal skeleton and consisting of a dense outer layer of compact or cortical substance covered by the periosteum, and an inner, loose, spongy substance; the central portion of a long bone is filled with marrow. See also bone and subentries.

o. bre′ve [NA], short bone; a bone with dimensions that are approximately equal and a layer of cortical substance enclosing spongy substance and marrow.

o. capita′tum [NA], capitate bone; the largest of the carpal bones; located in the distal row.

os′sa car′pi [NA], carpal bones: o. scaphoideum, o. lunatum, o. triquetrum, o. pisiforme, o. trapezium, o. trapezoideum, o. capitatum, o. hamatum. See also carpus (2).

o. coc′cygis [NA], coccyx; the small bone at the end of the vertebral column, formed by the fusion of four rudimentary vertebrae, that articulates above with the sacrum.

o. cox′ae [NA], hip or innominate bone; coxa (1); a large flat bone formed by the fusion of ilium, ischium, and pubis (in the adult), constituting the lateral half of the pelvis; articulates with its fellow anteriorly, with the sacrum posteriorly, and with the femur laterally.

ossa cra′nii [NA], cranial bones; the bones surrounding the brain; the paired parietal and temporal and the unpaired occipital, frontal sphenoid and ethmoid.

o. cuboi′deum [NA], cuboid bone; the lateral bone of the distal row of the tarsus, articulating with the calcaneus, lateral cuneiform, navicular (occasionally), and fourth and fifth metatarsal bones.

o. cuneifor′me interme′dium [NA], intermediate, middle, or second cuneiform bone; a bone of the distal row of the tarsus, articulating with the medial and lateral cuneiform, navicular, and second metatarsal bones.

o. cuneifor′me latera′le [NA], lateral or third cuneiform bone; a bone of the distal row of the tarsus, articulating with the intermediate cuneiform, cuboid, navicular, and second, third, and fourth metatarsal bones.

o. cuneifor′me media′le [NA], medial or first cuneiform bone; the largest of the three cuneiform bones, the medial bone of the distal row of the tarsus, articulating with the intermediate cuneiform, navicular, and first and second metatarsal bones.

os′sa digito′rum ma′nus [NA], bones of the digits of the hand; the phalanges and sesamoid bones of the fingers. See also phalanx (1).

os′sa digito′rum pe′dis [NA], bones of the digits of the foot; the phalanges and sesamoid bones of the toes. See also phalanx (1).

o. ethmoida′le [NA], ethmoid bone; an irregularly shaped bone lying between the orbital plates of the frontal bone and anterior to the sphenoid bone, and articulating with the sphenoid, frontal, maxillary, lacrimal, and palatine bones, the inferior nasal concha, and the vomer; contributes to the formation of the anterior cranial fossa, the orbits, and the nasal cavity.

os′sa fa′ciei [NA], facial bones; the bones surrounding the mouth and nose and contributing to the orbits: the paired maxilla, zygomatic, nasal, lacrimal, palatine, and inferior nasal concha; and the unpaired vomer, mandible, and hyoid.

o. fem′oris [NA], thigh bone; femur (2); the long bone of the thigh, articulating with the hip bone proximally and the tibia and patella distally.

o. fronta′le [NA], frontal bone; the large single bone forming the forehead and the upper margin and roof of the orbit on either side; articulates with the parietal, nasal, ethmoid, maxillary, and zygomatic bones, and with the lesser wings of the sphenoid.

o. hama′tum [NA], hamate or unciform bone; the bone on the medial (ulnar) side of the distal row of the carpus; articulates with the fourth and fifth metacarpal, triquetral, lunate, and capitate.

o. hyoi′deum [NA], hyoid bone; a U-shaped bone lying between the mandible and the larynx, suspended from the styloid processes by ligaments.

o. il′ium [NA], ilium; iliac bone; the broad flaring portion of the hip bone, distinct at birth but later becoming fused with the ischium and pubis; its body joins the pubis and ischium to form the acetabulum and the ala or wing.

o. incisi′vum [NA], incisive intermaxillary, or premaxillary bone; the anterior and inner portion of the maxilla, which in the fetus and sometimes in the adult is a separate bone; the incisive suture runs from the incisive canal between the lateral incisor and the canine tooth.

o. intermetatar′seum, a supernumerary bone at the base of the first metatarsal, or between the first and second metatarsal bones, usually fused with one or the other or with the medial cuneiform bone.

o. irregula′re [NA], irregular bone; one of a group of bones having peculiar or complex forms; *e.g.*, vertebrae, many of the skull bones.

o. is′chii [NA], ischium; ischial bone; the lower and posterior part of the hip bone, distinct at birth but later becoming fused with the ilium and pubis; consists of a body, where it joins the ilium and superior ramus of the pubis to form the acetabulum, and a ramus joining the inferior ramus of the pubis.

o. lacrima′le [NA], lacrimal bone; an irregularly rectangular thin plate, forming part of the medial wall of the orbit behind the frontal process of the maxilla and articulating with the inferior nasal concha, ethmoid, frontal, and maxillary bones.

o. lon′gum [NA], long bone; one of the elongated bones of the extremities, consisting of a tubular shaft (diaphysis) and two extremities (epiphyses) usually wider than the shaft which is composed of compact bone surrounding a central medullary cavity.

o. luna′tum [NA], lunate bone; semilunar bone; one of the proximal row in the carpus between the scaphoid and triquetral; it articulates with the radius, scaphoid, triquetral, hamate, and capitate.

o. metacarpa′le, pl. **os′sa metacarpa′lia** [NA], one of the metacarpal bones, five long bones forming the skeleton of the metacarpus or palm and articulating with the bones of the distal row of the carpus and with the five proximal phalanges.

o. metatarsa′le, pl. **os′sa metatarsa′lia** [NA], one of the metatarsal bones; five long bones forming the skeleton of the anterior portion of the foot and articulating posteriorly with the three cuneiform and the cuboid bones, anteriorly with the five proximal phalanges.

o. nasa′le [NA], nasal bone; an elongated rectangular bone which, with its fellow, forms the bridge of the nose; articulates with the frontal bone superiorly, the ethmoid bone and the frontal process of the maxilla posteriorly, and its fellow medially.

o. navicula′re [NA], navicular bone; a bone of the tarsus on the medial side of the foot, articulating with the head of the talus, the three cuneiform bones, and occasionally the cuboid bone.

o. occipita′le [NA], occipital bone; a bone at the lower and posterior part of the skull, consisting of three parts (basilar, condylar, and squamous) enclosing the foramen magnum; articulates with the parietal and temporal bones on either side, the sphenoid bone anteriorly, and the atlas below.

o. palati′num [NA], palatine bone; an irregularly shaped bone posterior to the maxilla, which enters into the formation of the nasal cavity, the orbit, and the hard palate; articulates with the maxilla, inferior nasal concha, sphenoid and ethmoid bones, the vomer, and its fellow of the opposite side.

o. parieta′le [NA], parietal bone; a flat curved bone of irregular quadrangular shape at either side of the vault of the cranium; ariculates with its fellow medially, with the frontal bone anteriorly, the occipital bone posteriorly, and the temporal and sphenoid bones inferiorly.

o. pisifor′me [NA], pisiform bone; a small bone in the proximal row of the carpus, lying on the anterior surface of the triquetral, with which alone it articulates, and giving insertion to the tendon of the flexor carpi ulnaris muscle.

o. pla′num [NA], flat bone; a type of bone characterized by a thin, flattened shape; *e.g.*, scapula, certain cranial bones.

o. pneumat′icum [NA], pneumatic or hollow bone; a bone that is hollow or contains many air cells; *e.g.*, mastoid process of the temporal bone.

o. pu′bis [NA], pubic bone; pubis (1); anteroinferior portion of the hip bone, distinct at birth but later becoming fused with the ilium and ischium; composed of a body, which articulates with its fellow at the symphysis publis, and two rami: a superior contributing to formation of the acetabulum and an inferior fusing with the ramus of the ischium.

o. sa′crum [NA], sacrum; the segment of the vertebral column forming part of the pelvis and closing in the pelvic girdle posteriorly; formed by the fusion of five originally separate sacral vertebrae; articulates with the last lumbar vertebra, the coccyx, and the hip bone on either side.

o. scaphoi′deum [NA], scaphoid bone; the largest bone of the proximal row of the carpus on the lateral (radial) side, articulating with the radius, lunate, capitate, trapezium, and trapezoid bones.

o. sesamoi'deum, pl. **os'sa sesamoi'dea** [NA], sesamoid bone; a bone formed in a tendon where it passes over a joint.

o. sphenoida'le [NA], sphenoid bone; a bone of irregular shape occupying the base of the skull, articulating with the occipital, frontal, ethmoid, and vomer bones and with the paired temporal, parietal, zygomatic, palatine and sphenoidal concha bones.

os'sa sutura'rum [NA], sutural or wormian bones; small irregular bones found along the sutures of the cranium, particularly related to the parietal bone.

os'sa tar'si [NA], tarsal bones. See tarsus.

o. tempora'le [NA], temporal bone; a large irregular bone situated in the base and side of the skull, articulating with the sphenoid, parietal, occipital, and zygomatic bones, and by a synovial joint with the mandible.

o. trape'zium [NA], trapezium bone; trapezium (2); the lateral (radial) bone in the distal row of the carpus, articulating with the first and second metacarpals, scaphoid, and trapezoid bones.

o. trapezoi'deum [NA], trapezoid bone; a bone in the distal row of the carpus, articulating with the second metacarpal, trapezium, capitate, and scaphoid bones.

o. trigo'num [NA], triangular bone; an independent ossicle sometimes present in the tarsus, usually forming part of the talus and constituting the lateral tubercle of the posterior process.

o. trique'trum [NA], triquetral bone; cuneiform or pyramidal bone; a bone on the medial (ulnar) side of the proximal row of the carpus, articulating with the lunate, pisiform, and hamate bones.

o. zygomat'icum [NA], zygomatic, jugal, or malar bone; zygoma (1); a quadrilateral bone that forms the prominence of the cheek and articulates with the frontal, sphenoid, temporal, and maxillary bones.

osche-, oscheo- [G. *oschē*, scrotum]. Combining forms denoting the scrotum.

oscheal (os'ke-al). Scrotal.

oscheitis (os-ke-i'tis) [osche- + G. *-itis*, inflammation]. Inflammation of the scrotum.

oscheocele (os'ke-o-sēl) [oscheo- + G. *kēlē*, hernia, tumor]. Scrotal *hernia.*

oscheoplasty (os'ke-o-plas-tĭ) [oscheo- + *plassō*, to form]. Scrotoplasty.

oscillation (os'ĭ-la'shun) [L. *oscillatio*, fr. *oscillo*, to swing]. **1.** A to-and-fro movement. **2.** A stage in the vascular changes in inflammation in which the accumulation of leukocytes in the small vessels arrests the passage of blood and there is simply a to-and-fro movement at each cardiac contraction.

oscillometer (os'ĭ-lom'ĕ-ter) [L. *oscillo*, to swing, + G. *metron*, measure]. An apparatus for measuring oscillations of any kind, especially those of the blood stream in sphygmometry.

oscillometric (os'ĭ-lo-met'rik). Relating to the oscillometer or the records made by its use.

oscillom'etry. Use of an oscillometer.

oscillopsia (os'ĭ-lop'sĭ-ah) [L. *oscillo*, to swing, + G. *opsis*, vision]. Oscillating vision; the subjective sensation of oscillation of objects viewed.

osculum, pl. **oscula** (os'ku-lum, -la) [L. dim.of *os*, mouth]. A pore or minute opening.

-ose. 1. In chemistry, a termination usually indicating a carbohydrate. **2** [L. *-osus*, full of, abounding]. Suffix with significance of the commoner -ous (2).

-osis [G.]. Suffix meaning a process, condition, or state, usually abnormal or diseased; denotes primarily any production or increase, physiologic or pathologic, and secondarily an invasion, and increase within the organism of parasites (in the latter sense, similar to and often interchangeable with -iasis).

os'mate. A salt of osmic acid.

osmic acid (oz'mik). Osmium tetroxide; OsO_4; a volatile caustic and strong oxidizing agent; the aqueous solution is a fat and myelin stain and a general fixative for electron microscopy.

osmics (oz'miks) [G. *osmē*, smell]. The science of olfaction.

osmidrosis (oz-mĭ-dro'sis) [G. *osmē*, smell, + *hidrōs*, sweat]. Bromidrosis.

osmium (oz'mĭ-um) [G. *osmē*, smell, because of the strong odor of the tetroxide]. A metallic element of the platinum group, symbol Os, atomic no. 76, atomic weight 190.2.

osmo-. 1 [G. *osmos*, impulsion]. Combining form denoting osmosis. **2** [G. *osme*, smell]. Combining form denoting smell or odor.

os'molal'ity. Osmotic concentration, the number of osmoles (Φn moles) where n is the number of particles or ions formed upon dissociation of a solute in solution; given solution, numerically equal to the molality of an ideal solution of a nonelectrolyte having the same freezing point, approxir ated by the quotient of the freezing point depression of an aqueous solution below that of water (Δ°C) and the molal freezing point depression for water (*ca.* 1.86°C per mol of undissociated solute per kg of water).

osmo'lar. Osmotic.

osmolarity (os'mo-lăr'ĭ-tĭ). The osmotic concentration of a solution expressed as osmols of solute per liter of solution.

os'mole. The molecular weight of a solute, in grams, divided by the number of ions or particles into which it dissociates in solution.

os'morecep'tor. 1 [G. *osmos*, impulsion]. A receptor in the CNS that responds to changes in the osmotic pressure of the blood. **2** [G. *osmē*, smell]. A receptor that receives olfactory stimuli.

os'moreg'ulatory. Influencing the degree and the rapidity of osmosis.

os'mose. To subject to osmosis; to diffuse by osmosis.

osmo'sis [G. *ōsmos*, a thrusting, an impulsion]. The phenomenon of the passage of certain fluids and solutions through a membrane or other porous substance; the net passage of fluid from the less concentrated to the more concentrated side of the membrane.

osmot'ic. Osmolar; relating to osmosis.

osphresio- [G. *osphresis,* smell]. Combining form denoting odor or the sense of smell.

osphre'sis [G. *osphrēsis,* smell]. Olfaction.

osphret'ic. Olfactory.

ossa (os'ah) [L.]. Plural of os (bone).

ossein, osseine (os'e-in) [L. *os,* bone]. Collagen.

osseo- [L. *osseus,* bony]. Combining form denoting bony. See also ossi-, osteo-.

osseocartilaginous (os'e-o-kar-tĭ-laj'ĭ-nus). Osteocartilaginous; relating to, or composed of, both bone and cartilage.

osseomucin (os'e-o-mu'sin). The ground substance of bony tissue.

osseous (os'e-us) [L. *osseus*]. Osteal; bony.

ossi- [G. *os,* bone. OS-]. Combining form denoting bone. See also osseo-, osteo-.

ossicle (os'ĭ-kl) [L. *ossiculum,* dim of *os,* bone]. Ossiculum.

ossicula (ŏ-sik'u-lah) [L.]. Plural of ossiculum.

ossicular (ŏ-sik'u-lar). Pertaining to an ossicle.

ossiculect'omy [L. *ossiculum,* ossicle, + G. *ektomē,* excision]. Removal of the ossicles of the middle ear.

ossiculot'omy [L. *ossiculum,* ossicle, + G. *tomē,* incision]. Division of one of the processes of the ossicles of the middle ear, or of a fibrous band causing ankylosis between any two ossicles.

ossiculum, pl. **ossicula** (ŏ-sik'u-lum, -lah) [L. dim. of *os,* bone] [NA]. Ossicle; bonelet; a small bone; specifically, one of the bones of the middle ear: the malleus, incus, and stapes which are articulated to form a chain for the transmission of sound from the tympanic membrane to the oval window.

ossiferous (ŏ-sif'er-us) [ossi- + L. *fero,* to bear]. Containing or producing bone.

ossif'ic. Relating to a change into or formation of bone.

ossification (os'ĭ-fĭ-ka'shun) [L. *ossificatio,* fr. *os,* bone, + *facio,* to make]. 1. Formation of bone. 2. A change into bone.

    endochondral o., formation of osseous tissue within cartilage, the process by which bones grow in length.

    membranous o., intramembranous o., development of osseous tissue within connective tissue, such as that of the skull.

    metaplastic o., formation of irregular foci of bone (sometimes including bone marrow) in various soft structures and other sites where osseous tissue is abnormal.

ossify (os'ĭ-fi) [ossi- + L. *facio,* to make]. To form bone or change into bone.

ost-, oste-. See osteo-.

osteal (os'te-al) [G. *osteon,* bone]. Osseous.

ostealgia (os-te-al'jĭ-ah) [osteo- + G. *algos,* pain]. Osteodynia; pain in a bone.

osteal'gic. Relating to or marked by bone pain.

ostectomy (os-tek'to-mĭ) [osteo- + G. *ektomē,* excision]. 1. Surgical removal of bone. 2. In dentistry, resection of supporting osseous structure to eliminate periodontal pockets.

ostein, osteine (os'te-in). Collagen.

osteitic (os-te-it'ik). Ostitic; relating to or affected by osteitis.

osteitis (os-te-i'tis) [osteo- + G. *-itis,* inflammation]. Ostitis; inflammation of bone.

    caseous o., tuberculous caries in bone.

    central o., (1) osteomyelitis; (2) endosteitis.

    condensing o., sclerosing o.

    o. defor'mans, Paget's disease (1).

    o. fibro'sa cir'cumscrip'ta, monostotic fibrous dysplasia.

    o. fibro'sa cys'tica or **generalisa'ta,** Recklinghausen's disease of bone; increased osteoclastic resorption of calcified bone with replacement by fibrous tissue, due to primary hyperparathyroidism or other causes of the rapid mobilization of mineral salts.

    o. fungo'sa, chronic o. with dilated Haversian canals filled with a vascular granulation tissue.

    sclerosing o., condensing o.; Garré's disease; fusiform thickening or increased density of bones, of unknown cause; considered a form of chronic nonsuppurative osteomyelitis.

ostempyesis (os'tem-pi-e'sis) [osteo- + G. *empyēsis,* suppuration]. Suppuration in bone.

osteo-, ost-, oste- [G. *osteon,* bone]. Combining forms denoting bone. See also osseo-, ossi-.

osteoanagenesis (os'te-o-an-ă-jen'ĕ-sis) [osteo- + G. *ana,* again, + *genesis,* generation]. Reproduction of bone.

osteoarthritis (os'te-o-ar-thri'tis). Osteoarthrosis; hypertrophic arthritis; degenerative joint disease; degeneration of articular cartilage, either primary or secondary to trauma or other conditions, especially affecting weight-bearing joints.

osteoarthropathy (os'te-o-ar-throp'ă-thĭ) [osteo- + G. *arthron,* joint, + *pathos,* suffering]. Any disorder affecting bones and joints.

    hypertrophic pulmonary o., Bamberger-Marie disease; expansion of the distal ends, or the entire shafts, of the long bones, sometimes with erosions of the articular cartilages, thickening and villous proliferation of the synovial membranes, and frequently clubbing of fingers; occurs in chronic pulmonary disease, in heart disease, and occasionally in other acute and chronic disorders.

    idiopathic hypertrophic o., o., not secondary to pulmonary or other progressive lesions, which may occur alone (acropathy) or as part of pachydermoperiostosis.

osteoarthrosis (os'te-o-ar-thro'sis) [osteo- + G. *arthron,* joint, + *-osis,* condition]. Osteoarthritis.

os'teoblast [osteo- + G. *blastos,* germ]. A bone-forming cell derived from mesenchyme to form the osseous matrix in which it becomes enclosed as an osteocyte.

osteoblas'tic. Relating to osteoblasts.

os'teoblasto'ma. An uncommon benign tumor of osteoblasts, with areas of osteoid and calcified tissue.

osteocartilaginous (os'te-o-kar-tĭ-laj'ĭ-nus). Osseocartilaginous.

osteochondritis (os'te-o-kon-dri'tis) [osteo- + G. *chondros,* cartilage, + *-itis,* inflammation]. Inflammation of a bone with its cartilage.

   o. defor'mans juveni'lis, Legg-Calvé-Perthes *disease.*

   o. defor'mans juveni'lis dor'si, Scheuermann's *disease.*

   o. dis'secans, complete or incomplete separation of a portion of joint cartilage and underlying bone, usually involving the knee, associated with epiphyseal aseptic necrosis.

osteochondrodystrophy (os'te-o-kon'dro-dis'tro-fĭ). Chondro-osteodystrophy.

osteochondroma (os'te-o-kon-dro'mah) [osteo- + G. *chondros,* cartilage, + *-oma,* tumor]. A benign cartilaginous neoplasm that consists of a pedicle of normal bone (protruding from the cortex) covered with a rim of proliferating cartilage cells; multiple o.'s are inherited and referred to as hereditary multiple exostoses.

osteochondromatosis (os'te-o-kon'dro-mă-to'sis). Hereditary multiple *exostoses.*

osteochondrosarcoma (os'te-o-kon'dro-sar-ko'ma) [osteo- + G. *chondros,* cartilage, + *sarx,* flesh, + *-oma,* tumor]. A chondrosarcoma arising in bone.

osteochondrosis (os'te-o-kon-dro'sis) [osteo- + G. *chondros,* cartilage, + *-osis,* condition]. Any of a group of disorders of one or more ossification centers in children, characterized by degeneration or aseptic necrosis followed by reossification; includes the various forms of epiphysial aseptic necrosis.

osteoclasis, osteoclasia (os-te-ok'lă-sis, os'te-o-kla'zĭ-ah) [osteo- + G. *klasis,* fracture]. Diaclasis; diaclasia; intentional fracture of a bone to correct deformity.

os'teoclast [osteo- + G. *klastos,* broken]. **1.** Osteophage; a large multinucleated cell with abundant acidophilic cytoplasm, functioning in the absorption and removal of osseous tissue. **2.** An instrument used to break a misshapen bone to correct the deformity.

os'teoclas'tic. Pertaining to osteoclasts, especially with reference to their activity in the absorption and removal of osseous tissue.

osteoclasto'ma. Giant cell *tumor* of bone.

osteocra'nium [osteo- + G. *kranion,* skull]. The cranium of the fetus after ossification of the membranous cranium has advanced to firmness.

osteocystoma (os'te-o-sis-to'mah). Solitary bone *cyst.*

osteocyte (os'te-o-sīt) [osteo- + G. *kytos,* cell]. Bone cell; a cell of osseous tissue which occupies a lacuna and has processes which extend into canaliculi and make contact by means of gap junctions with other processes.

osteoden'tin [osteo- + L. *dens,* tooth]. A calcified deposit that resembles both bone and dentin in structure.

osteodermatopoikilosis (os'te-o-der'mă-to-poy-kĭ-lo'sis) [osteo- + G. *derma,* skin, + *poikilos,* dappled, + *-osis,* condition]. Osteopoikilosis with skin lesions, most commonly small fibrous nodules on the posterior aspects of the thighs and buttocks; autosomal dominant inheritance with incomplete penetrance.

osteodermia (os'te-o-der'mĭ-ah) [osteo- + G. *derma,* skin]. *Osteosis cutis.*

osteodiastasis (os'te-o-di-as'tă-sis) [osteo- + G. *diastasis,* a separation]. Separation of two adjacent bones, as of the cranium.

os'teodyn'ia [osteo- + G. *odynē,* pain]. Ostealgia.

osteodystrophia (os'te-o-dis-tro'fĭ-ah). Osteodystrophy.

osteodystrophy (os'te-o-dis'trof-ĭ) [osteo- + G. *dys,* difficult, imperfect, + *trophē,* nourishment]. Osteodystrophia; defective formation of bone.

   Albright's hereditary o., Albright's syndrome (2); pseudohypoparathyroidism or pseudo-pseudohypoparathyroidism with diabetes, hypertension, arteritis, and polyarthrosis.

   renal o., generalized bone changes resembling osteomalacia and rickets or osteitis fibrosa, occurring in children or adults with chronic renal failure.

osteoectasia (os'te-o-ek-ta'sĭ-ah) [osteo- + G. *ektasis,* a stretching]. Bowing of bones, particularly of the legs.

os'teofibro'ma. A benign lesion of bone, consisting chiefly of fairly dense, moderately cellular, fibrous connective tissue in which there are small foci of osteogenesis.

osteofibrosis (os'te-o-fi-bro'sis). Fibrosis of bone, mainly involving red bone marrow.

osteogen (os'te-o-jen) [osteo- + G. *-gen,* producing]. The substance forming the inner layer of the periosteum from which new bone is formed.

osteogenesis (os'te-o-jen'ĕ-sis) [osteo- + G. *genesis,* production]. Osteogeny; osteosis (2); the formation of bone.

   o. imperfec'ta, brittle bones; a condition of abnormal fragility and plasticity of bone, with recurring fractures on minimal trauma, deformity of long bones, usually bluish color of sclerae, and, in many cases, the development of otosclerosis; inheritance is autosomal dominant in most families, but a rare autosomal recessive type also exists. In **o. i. congenita,** a more severe form, the fractures occur before or at birth; in **o.i. tarda,** a less severe form, the fractures occur later in childhood.

os'teogen'ic, os'teogenet'ic. Osteogenous; relating to osteogenesis.

osteogenous (os-te-oj'ĕ-nus). Osteogenic.

osteogeny (os-te-oj'ĕ-nĭ). Osteogenesis.

osteohalisteresis (os'te-o-hal'is-ter-e'sis) [osteo- + G. *hals,* salt, + *sterēsis,* privation]. Softening of the bones through absorption or insufficient supply of the mineral portion.

osteoid (os'te-oyd) [osteo- + G. *eidos,* resemblance]. **1.** Relating to or resembling bone. **2.** Osseous tissue prior to calcification.

osteolipochondroma (os'te-o-lip'o-kon-dro'mah) [osteo- + G. *lipos,* fat, + *chondros,* cartilage, + *-oma,* tumor]. A benign neoplasm of cartilaginous tissue, in which metaplasia occurs and foci of adipose cells and osseous tissue are formed.

osteology (os-te-ol'o-jĭ) [osteo- + G. *logos,* study]. Anatomy of the bones; the science concerned with the bones and their structure.

osteolysis (os-te-ol'ĭ-sis) [osteo- + G. *lysis,* dissolution]. Softening, absorption, and destruction of bone tissue.

osteolyt'ic. Pertaining to, characterized by, or causing osteolysis.

osteo'ma [osteo- + G. *-oma,* tumor]. A benign slow-growing mass of mature, predominantly lamellar bone, usually arising from the skull or mandible.

  o. cu'tis, see *osteosis* cutis.

  o. medulla're, an o. containing spaces filled with various elements of bone marrow.

  osteoid o., a painful benign neoplasm, usually originating in one of the bones of the lower extremities, characterized by a nidus that consists of osteoid material, vascularized osteogenic stroma, and poorly formed bone; around the nidus there is a relatively large zone of reactive thickening of the cortex.

  o. spongio'sum, an o. that consists chiefly of cancellous bone tissue.

osteomalacia (os'te-o-mă-la'shĭ-ah) [osteo- + G. *malakia,* softness]. A disease characterized by a gradual and painful softening and bending of the bones; due to the bones containing osteoid tissue which has failed to calcify because of a lack of vitamin D or renal tubular dysfunction.

  infantile o., juvenile o., rickets.

osteomala'cic. Relating to osteomalacia.

osteo'matoid [osteoma + G. *eidos,* appearance, form]. An abnormal nodule or small mass of overgrowth of bone, usually occurring bilaterally and symmetrically, in juxtaepiphysial regions, especially in long bones of the lower extremities.

osteomere (os'te-o-mēr) [osteo- + G. *meros,* a part]. One of the series of bone segments, such as the vertebrae.

osteomyelitis (os'te-o-mi-ĕ-li'tis) [osteo- + G. *myelos,* marrow, + *-itis,* inflammation]. Central osteitis (1); inflammation of the marrow and adjacent bone.

osteomyelodysplasia (os'te-o-mi'ĕ-lo-dis-pla'zĭ-ah) [osteo- + G. *myelos,* marrow, + dysplasia]. A disease characterized by enlargement of the marrow cavities of the bones, thinning of the osseous tissue, large, thin-walled vascular spaces, leukopenia, and irregular fever.

osteon, osteone (os'te-on, -ōn) [G. *osteon,* bone]. Haversian system; a central canal and the concentric osseous lamellae around it occurring in compact bone.

osteonecrosis (os'te-o-nĕ-kro'sis) [osteo- + G. *nekrōsis,* death]. The death of bone in mass, as distinguished from caries or relatively small foci of necrosis in bone.

os'teopath. A practitioner of osteopathy.

osteopath'ia. Osteopathy (1).

  o. conden'sans, osteopoikilosis.

  o. stria'ta, linear striations seen by x-ray in the metaphyses of long bones and also flat bones.

osteopath'ic. Relating to osteopathy.

osteop'athy [osteo- + G. *pathos,* suffering]. **1.** Osteopathia; any disease of bone. **2.** A school of medicine based upon the idea that the normal body when in "correct adjustment" is a vital machine capable of making its own remedies against infections and other toxic conditions; employs the diagnostic and therapeutic measures of ordinary medicine in addition to manipulative measures.

osteope'nia [osteo- + G. *penia,* poverty]. **1.** Decreased calcification or density of bone. **2.** Reduced bone mass due to inadequate osteoid synthesis.

osteoperiostitis (os'te-o-pĕr'ĭ-os-ti'tis). Inflammation of the periosteum and of the underlying bone.

osteopetrosis (os'te-o-pĕ-tro'sis) [osteo- + G. *petra,* stone, + *-osis,* condition]. Albers-Schönberg disease; marble bones; marble bone disease; excessive formation of dense trabecular bone and calcified cartilage, especially in long bones, leading to obliteration of marrow spaces and to anemia, with myeloid metaplasia and hepatosplenomegaly, beginning in infancy and with progressive deafness and blindness; autosomal recessive inheritance.

osteopetrot'ic. Relating to osteopetrosis.

osteophage (os'te-o-fāj) [osteo- + G. *phagein,* to eat]. Osteoclast (1).

osteophlebitis (os'te-o-flĕ-bi'tis) [osteo- + G. *phleps,* vein, + *-itis,* inflammation]. Inflammation of the veins of a bone.

os'teophy'ma [osteo- + G. *phyma,* tumor]. Osteophyte.

osteophyte (os'te-o-fīt) [osteo- + G. *phyton,* plant]. Osteophyma; a bony outgrowth.

os'teoplasty [osteo- + G. *plassō,* to form]. **1.** Bone grafting; reparative or plastic surgery of the bones. **2.** In dentistry, resection of osseous structure to achieve acceptable gingival contour.

osteopoikilosis (os'te-o-poy-kī'-lo'sis) [osteo- + G. *poikilos,* dappled, + *-osis,* condition]. Osteopathia condensans; mottled or spotted bones caused by widespread small foci of compact bone in the substantia spongiosa; autosomal dominant inheritance with incomplete penetrance.

osteoporosis (os'te-o-po-ro'sis) [osteo- + G. *poros,* pore, + *-osis,* condition]. Reduction in the quantity of bone or atrophy of skeletal tissue; occurs in postmenopausal women and elderly men, resulting in bone trabeculae that are scanty, thin, and without osteoelastic resorption.

os'teoporot'ic. Pertaining to, characterized by, or causing a porous condition of the bones.

os'teora'dionecro'sis. Necrosis of bone produced by ionizing radiation.

osteorrhaphy (os-te-or'ă-fĭ) [osteo- + G. *rhaphē*, suture]. Osteosuture; wiring together of the fragments of a broken bone.

os'teosarco'ma. Osteogenic *sarcoma*.

osteosclerosis (os'te-o-skle-ro'sis) [osteo- + G. *sklērōsis*, hardness]. Abnormal hardening or eburnation of bone.

  o. congen'ita, achondroplasia.

osteosclerotic (os'te-o-skle-rot'ik). Relating to, due to, or marked by hardening of bone substance.

osteosis (os-te-o'sis) [osteo- + G. *-osis*, condition].
  1. A morbid process in bone. **2.** Osteogenesis.

  o. cu'tis, osteodermia; bone formed in the skin by osseous metaplasia of calcium deposits; also called osteoma cutis, although not neoplastic.

osteosuture (os'te-o-su'chur). Osteorrhaphy.

osteosynthesis (os'te-o-sin'the-sis). Bringing the ends of a fractured bone into close apposition.

os'teothrombo'sis. Thrombosis in one or more of the veins of a bone.

os'teotome [osteo- + G. *tomē*, incision]. A chisel-like instrument for use in cutting bone.

osteot'omy [osteo- + G. *tomē*, incision]. Cutting a bone, usually by means of a saw or chisel, for any purpose.

osteotribe (os'te-o-trĭb) [osteo- + G. *tribō*, to bruise, to grind down]. An instrument for crushing off bits of necrosed or carious bone.

osteotrite (os'te-o-trīt) [osteo- + L. *tritus*, a grinding, a wearing off]. A grinding instrument, resembling a dental burr, for removing carious bone.

ostia (os'tĭ-ah) [L.]. Plural of ostium.

os'tial. Relating to any orifice, or ostium.

osti'tic. Osteitic.

osti'tis. Osteitis.

ostium, pl. **ostia** (os'tĭ-um, -ah) [L. door, entrance, mouth] [NA]. A small opening, especially as an entrance into a hollow organ or canal.

  o. abdomina'le tu'bae uteri'na [NA], the fimbriated or ovarian extremity of an oviduct.

  o. aor'tae [NA], **aortic o.,** the opening from the left ventricle into the ascending aorta, guarded by the aortic valve.

  os'tia atrioventricula'ria dex'trum et sinis'trum [NA], atrioventricular openings; the two openings, right (tricuspid orifice) and left (mitral orifice), which lead from the atria into the ventricles of the heart.

  o. cardi'acum [NA], cardiac opening; esophagogastric orifice; the opening of the esophagus into the stomach.

  o. ileoceca'le [NA], ileocecal opening; the opening of the terminal ileum into the large intestine at the transition between the cecum and the ascending colon.

  o. pharyn'geum tu'bae auditi'vae [NA], pharyngeal opening of the auditory tube; an opening in the upper part of the nasopharynx behind the posterior extremity of the inferior concha on each side.

  o. pylor'icum [NA], pyloric or gastroduodenal orifice; the opening between the stomach and the superior part of the duodenum.

  o. trun'ci pulmona'lis [NA], the opening of the pulmonary trunk from the right ventricle, guarded by the pulmonary valve.

  o. tympan'icum tu'bae auditi'vae [NA], tympanic opening of the auditory tube; an opening in the anterior part of the tympanic cavity below the canal for the tensor tympani muscle.

  o. ure'teris [NA], ureteral opening or meatus; the opening of the ureter in the bladder, situated one at each lateral angle of the trigone.

  o. ure'thrae exter'num [NA], external urethral opening; **(1)** the slitlike opening of the urethra in the glans penis; **(2)** the external orifice of the urethra (in the female) in the vestibule.

  o. ure'thrae inter'num [NA], internal urethral opening; the internal opening or orifice of the urethra, at the anterior and inferior angle of the trigone.

  o. u'teri [NA], o. of the uterus; the mouth of the womb; the vaginal opening of the uterus.

  o. uteri'num tu'bae [NA], the uterine opening of the oviduct.

  o. vagi'nae [NA], vaginal opening; the narrowest portion of the canal, in the floor of the vestibule posterior to the urethral orifice.

os'tomate [L. *ostium*, mouth]. One who has an ostomy.

os'tomy [L. *ostium*, mouth]. **1.** An artificial stoma or opening into the urinary or gastrointestinal canal, or the trachea. **2.** Any operation by which an opening is created between two hollow organs or between a hollow viscus and the abdominal wall.

OT Occupational *therapy;* Koch's old *tuberculin.*

ot- [G. *ous,* ear]. Combining form denoting the ear. See also auri-.

otalgia (o-tal'jĭ-ah) [ot- + G. *algos,* pain]. Earache.

otal'gic. Relating to otalgia, or earache.

OTC Over the counter; denoting a drug available without a prescription.

othematoma (ōt'he-mă-to'mah) [ot- + G. *haima,* blood, + suffix *-oma,* tumor]. A purplish, rounded, hard swelling of the external ear, resulting from an effusion of blood between the cartilage and perichondrium; it may be caused by an inadvertent trauma; *e.g.,* self-inflicted injury or infection in the mentally ill.

othemorrhagia (ōt'hem-o-raj'ĭ-ah) [ot- + G. *haima,* blood, + *rhēgnymi,* to burst forth]. Bleeding from the ear.

other-directed. Pertaining to a person readily influenced by the attitudes of others.

o'tic [G. *otikos,* fr. *ous,* ear]. Relating to the ear.

otit'ic. Relating to otitis.

otitis (o-ti'tis) [ot- + G. -*itis*, inflammation]. Inflammation of the ear.

  o. exter'na, inflammation of the external auditory canal.

  o. exter'na circumscrip'ta, o. furunculosa; furunculosis of the external auditory canal.

  o. exter'na diffu'sa, inflammation of the entire extent of the external auditory meatus.

  o. furunculo'sa, o. externa circumscripta.

  o. inter'na, labyrinthitis.

  o. me'dia, inflammation of the middle ear.

  o. mycot'ica, a fungous growth in the external auditory meatus, often of *Aspergillus niger.*

  secretory o. me'dia, serous o.

  serous o., secretory o. media; inflammation of middle ear mucosa, often accompanied by accumulation of fluid, secondary to eustachian tube obstruction.

oto- [G. *ous*, ear]. Combining form denoting the ear. See also auri-.

otoantritis (o'to-an-tri'tis). Inflammation of the mastoid antrum.

Oto'bius. A genus of argasid ticks similar to *Ornithodoros* which occur in southwestern parts of the U.S., where it is an important pest; also distributed worldwide.

otocephaly (o-to-sef'ă-lĭ) [oto- + G. *kephalē,* head]. A malformation characterized by markedly defective development of the lower jaw (micrognathia or agnathia) and the union or close approach of the ears (synotia) on the front of the neck.

otocleisis (o-to-kli'sis) [oto- + G. *kleisis,* closure]. **1.** Closure of the auditory tube. **2.** Closure, by a new growth or accumulation of cerumen, of the external auditory meatus.

otoco'nium, pl. **otoco'nia.** Statoconium. See statoconia.

otocra'nial. Relating to the otocranium.

otocranium (o-to-kra'nĭ-um) [oto- + G. *kranion,* cranium]. The bony case of the internal and middle ear, consisting of the petrous portion of the temporal bone.

otocyst (o'to-sist) [oto- + G. *kystis,* a bladder]. The embryonic auditory vesicle.

otodyn'ia [oto- + G. *odynē,* pain]. Earache.

otoencephalitis (o'to-en-sef-ă-li'tis) [oto- + G. *enkephalos,* brain, + -*itis,* inflammation]. Inflammation of the brain by extension of the process from the middle ear and mastoid cells.

otoganglion (o-to-gang'glĭ-on). *Ganglion* oticum.

otogenic, otogenous (o'to-jen'ik, o-toj'ĕ-nus) [oto- + G. *-gen,* producing]. Originating within the ear, especially from inflammation of the ear.

otolaryngologist (o'to-lăr-in-gol'o-jist). A specialist in otolaryngology.

otolaryngology (o'to-lăr-ing-gol'o-jĭ) [oto- + G. *larynx, logos,* study]. The medical specialty concerned with diseases of the ear and larynx, often including the upper respiratory tract and many diseases of the head and neck, tracheobronchial tree, and esophagus.

otolith (o'to-lith) [oto- + G. *lithos,* stone]. **1.** Statoconium. See statoconia. **2.** Otosteon (2).

otologic (o-to-loj'ik). Relating to otology.

otol'ogist. A specialist in otology.

otology (o-tol'o-jĭ) [oto- + G. *logos,* study]. The branch of medical science that embraces the study, diagnoses, and treatment of diseases of the ear and related structures.

otomu'cormyco'sis. Mucormycosis of the ear.

-otomy. See -tomy.

otomycosis (o'to-mi-ko'sis) [oto- + G. *mykēs,* fungus]. An infection due to a fungus in the external auditory canal.

otop'athy [oto- + G. *pathos,* suffering]. Any disease of the ear.

otopharyngeal (o'to-fă-rin'je-al). Relating to the middle ear and the pharynx.

o'toplasty [oto- + G. *plassō,* to form]. Reparative or plastic surgery of the auricle of the ear.

otopolypus (o'to-pol'ĭ-pus) [oto- + L. *polypus,* polyp]. A polyp in the external auditory meatus, usually arising from the middle ear.

otopyorrhea (o'to-pi-o-re'ah) [oto- + G. *pyon,* pus, + *rhoia,* a flow]. Chronic otitis media with perforation of the drum membrane and a purulent discharge.

otorhinolaryngology (o'to-ri'no-lăr-ing-gol'o-jĭ) [oto- + G. *rhis,* nose, + *larynx,* larynx, + *logos,* study]. The medical specialty concerned with diseases of the ear, nose, and larynx.

otorhinology (o'to-ri-nol'o-jĭ) [oto- + G. *rhis,* nose, + *logos,* study]. The branch of medicine concerned with disease of the ear and nose.

otorrhagia (o-to-ra'jĭ-ah) [oto- + G. *rhēgnymi,* to burst forth]. Bleeding from the ear.

otorrhea (o-to-re'ah) [oto- + G. *rhoia,* flow]. A discharge from the ear.

otosclerosis (o'to-skle-ro'sis) [oto- + G. *sklērosis,* hardening]. A new formation of spongy bone about the stapes and fenestra vestibuli (ovalis), resulting in progressively increasing deafness, without signs of disease in the auditory tube or tympanic membrane.

otoscope (o'to-skōp) [oto- + G. *skopeō,* to view]. An instrument for examining the drum membrane or auscultating the ear.

otoscopy (o-tos'ko-pĭ) [oto- + G. *skopeō,* to view]. Inspection of the ear, especially of the drum membrane.

otosteal (o-tos'te-al) [oto- + G. *osteon,* bone]. Relating to the ossicles of the ear.

otosteon (o-tos'te-on) [oto- + G. *osteon,* bone]. **1.** One of the ossicles of the ear. **2.** Otolith (2); a concretion in the ear, larger than a statoconium.

otot'omy [oto- + G. *tomē,* inci sion]. Dissection of the ear.

ototoxic (o'to-tok'sik) [oto- + G. *toxikon,* poison]. Having a toxic action upon the ear.

ototoxici'ty. The property of being ototoxic.

O.U. Oculus uterque [L.], each eye; both eyes.

ouabain (wah'bān, wah'bah-in). $C_{29}H_{44}O_{12}8H_2O$; a glycoside from ouabaio, obtained from the wood of *Acocanthera ouabaio* or from the seeds of *Strophanthus gratus;* its action is qualitatively identical to that of the digitalis glycosides; used for rapid digitalization.

ounce (oz). A weight containing 480 gr., or $1/12$ pound troy and apothecaries' weight, or $437 1/2$ gr., $1/16$ pound avoirdupois. Apothecary o. contains 8 dr. and is equivalent to 31.10349 g; avoirdupois o. is equivalent to 28.35 g.

-ous. 1. A chemical suffix denoting that the element to the name of which it is attached is in one of its lower valencies. **2** [L. *-osus*, full of, abounding]. Suffix for forming an adjective from a noun.

out'let. An exit or opening of a passageway.

out'patient. A patient treated in a hospital, dispensary, or clinic and released in the same day.

out'put. The quantity produced, ejected or excreted of a specific entity in a specified period of time or per unit time.

ova (o'vah) [L.]. Plural of ovum.

ovalbumin (o-val-bu'min). Egg *albumin.*

o'valocyte [L. *ovalis*, oval, + G. *kytos*, cell]. Elliptocyte.

o'valocyto'sis. Elliptocytosis.

ovarialgia (o-vär-ĭ-al'jĭ-ah) [ovario- + G. *algos*, pain]. Ovarian pain.

ovarian (o-vär'ĭ-an). Relating to the ovary.

ovariectomy (o'vär-ĭ-ek'to-mĭ) [ovario- + G. *ektomē*, excision]. Oophorectomy; excision of one or both ovaries.

ovario-, ovari- [L. *ovarium*, ovary]. Combining forms denoting ovary. See also oo-, oophor-, oophoro-.

ovariocele (o-vär'ĭ-o-sēl) [ovario- + G. *kēlē*, hernia]. Hernia of an ovary.

ovariocentesis (o-vär'ĭ-o-sen-te'sis) [ovario- + G. *kentēsis*, puncture]. Puncture of an ovary or an ovarian cyst.

ovariocyesis (o-vär'ĭ-o-si-e'sis) [ovario- + G. *kyēsis*, pregnancy]. Ovarian *pregnancy.*

ovariohysterectomy (o-vär'ĭ-o-his-ter-ek'to-mĭ) [ovario- + G. *hystera*, uterus, + *ektomē*, excision]. Oophorohysterectomy; removal of ovaries and uterus.

ovariorrhexis (o-vär'ĭ-o-rek'sis) [ovario- + G. *rhēxis*, rupture]. Rupture of an ovary.

ovariosalpingectomy (o-vär'ĭ-o-sal-pin-jek'to-mĭ) [ovario- + salpingectomy]. Operative removal of an ovary and the corresponding oviduct.

ovariosalpingitis (o-vär'ĭ-o-sal-pin-ji'tis) [ovario- + salpingitis]. Inflammation of ovary and oviduct.

ovarios'tomy [ovario- + G. *stoma*, mouth]. Oophorostomy; establishment of a temporary fistula for drainage of a cyst of the ovary.

ovariot'omy [ovario- + G. *tomē*, incision]. Oophorotomy; incision into an ovary.

ovaritis (o-vä-ri'tis). Oophoritis.

ovarium, pl. **ovaria** (o-vär'ĭ-um, -ah) [Mod. L. fr. *ovum*, egg[[NA]. Ovary.

ovary (o'vä-rĭ) [Mod. L. *ovarium*, fr. *ovum*, egg]. Ovarium; oophoron; one of the paired female reproductive glands whose stroma is a vascular connective tissue containing numbers of ovarian follicles enclosing the ova; surrounding this is a more condensed layer of stroma called the tunica albuginea.

polycystic o., enlarged cystic o.'s, pearl white in color, thickened tunica albuginea, characteristic of the Stein-Leventhal syndrome; clinical features are abnormal menses, obesity, and evidence of masculinization, such as hirsutism and clitoromegaly.

o'verbite. Vertical *overlap.*

o'vercompensa'tion. 1. An exaggeration of personal capacity to overcome a real or imagined inferiority. **2.** The process in which a psychologic deficiency inspires exaggerated correction.

overden'ture. Overlay *denture.*

o'verdetermina'tion. In psychoanalysis, a term indicating the multiple causation of a single behavioral or emotional reaction, mental symptom, or dream.

o'verdose. 1. An excessive dose. **2.** To administer an excessive dose.

o'verjet, o'verjut. Horizontal *overlap.*

o'verlap. 1. Suturing of one layer of tissue above or under another to gain strength. **2.** An extension or projection of one structure over another.

horizontal o., overjet; overjut; projection of the upper anterior and/or posterior teeth beyond their antagonists in a horizontal direction.

vertical o., overbite; **(1)** extension of the upper teeth over the lower teeth in a vertical direction when the opposing posterior teeth are in contact in centric occlusion; **(2)** the distance that teeth lap over their antagonists vertically.

overriding (o'ver-ri'ding). **1.** The slipping of the lower fragment of a broken long bone up alongside the proximal portion. **2.** Descriptive of a fetal head which is palpable above the symphysis because of cephalopelvic disproportion.

ovi- [L. *ovum*, egg.]. Combining form denoting egg. See also oo-, ovo-.

ovicidal (o-vĭ-si'dal) [ovi- + L. *caedo*, to kill]. Causing death of an ovum.

ovidu'cal. Oviductal.

oviduct (o'vĭ-dukt) [ovi- + L. *ductus*, a leading]. Uterine *tube.*

oviduc'tal. Oviducal; relating to a uterine tube.

ovif'erous [ovi- + L. *fero*, to carry]. Carrying or containing ova.

o'viform. Ovoid (2).

ovigen'esis. Oogenesis.

ovigenet'ic. Oogenetic.

ovo- [L. *ovum*, egg]. Combining form denoting egg. See also oo-, ovi-.

ovoid (o'voyd) [ovo- + G. *eidos*, resemblance]. **1.** An oval or egg-shaped form. **2.** Oviform; resembling an egg.

ovoplasm (o'vo-plazm). The protoplasm of an unfertilized egg.

ovotestis (o-vo-tes'tis). A gonad in which both testicular and ovarian components are present.

o'vover'din. A chromoprotein with a carotenoid prosthetic group found in lobster eggs.

ovular (o'vu-lar). Relating to an ovule.

ovulation (o-vu-la'shun). Release of an ovum from the ovarian follicle.

ovulatory (o'vu-lă-to-rĭ). Relating to ovulation.

ovule (o'vūl) [Mod. L. *ovulum*, dim. of L. *ovum*, egg]. Ovulum. **1.** The ovum of a mammal, especially while still in the ovarian follicle. **2.** A small beadlike structure bearing a fancied resemblance to an o.

ovulocyclic (o'vu-lo-si'klik). Denoting any recurrent phenomenon associated with and occurring at a certain time within the ovulatory cycle.

o'vulum, pl. **o'vula,** Ovule.

ovum, pl. **ova** (o'vum, -vah) [L. egg]. The female sex cell that, when fertilized by a spermatozoon, is capable of developing into a new individual of the same species.

oxa-. Combining form inserted in names of organic compounds to signify the presence or addition of oxygen atom(s).

ox'alate. A salt of oxalic acid.

oxale'mia [oxalate + G. *haima*, blood]. The presence of an abnormally large amount of oxalates in the blood.

oxal'ic acid. HOOC–COOH; an acid found in many plants and vegetables which is toxic when ingested by man; used as a general reducing agent.

oxaloacetic acid (ok'să-lo-ă-se'tik). HOOC–CO–CH$_2$COOH; a ketodicarboxylic acid that is important intermediate in the tricarboxylic acid cycle.

oxalo'sis. Widespread deposition of calcium oxalate crystals in the kidneys, bones, arterial media, and myocardium, with increased urinary excretion of oxalate.

oxalosuccinic acid (ok'să-lo-suk-sin'ik). Oxalourea; HOOC–CO–CH(COOH)–CH$_2$–COOH; the product of the dehydrogenation of isocitric acid under the catalytic influence of isocitrate dehydrogenase; an intermediate of the tricarboxylic acid cycle.

oxalourea (ok'să-lo-u-re'ah). Oxalosuccinic acid.

oxaluria (ok'să-lu'rĭ-ah) [oxalate + G. *ouron*, urine]. Excretion of an abnormally large amount of oxalates, especially calcium oxalate, in the urine.

oxazepam (ok-sa'zĕ-pam). A benzodiazepine chemically and pharmacologically related to chlordiazepoxide and diazepam; an antianxiety agent.

ox'idant. The substance that is reduced and that therefore oxidizes the other component of an oxidation-reduction system.

oxidase (ok'sĭ-dās). Classically, one of a group of enzymes, now termed oxidoreductases, which bring about oxidation by the addition of oxygen to a metabolite or by the removal of hydrogen or of one or more electrons; now used for those cases in which O$_2$ acts as an acceptor.

oxidation (ok-sĭ-da'shun). **1.** Combination with oxygen or increasing the valence of an atom or ion by the loss from it of hydrogen or of one or more electrons, thus rendering it more electropositive. **2.** In bacteriology, the aerobic dissimilation of substrates with the production of energy and water; in contrast to fermentation, the transfer of electrons is accomplished via the respiratory chain, which utilizes oxygen as the final electron acceptor.

oxida'tion-reduc'tion. Any chemical oxidation or reduction reaction, which must, *in toto*, comprise both oxidation and reduction; often shortened to "redox."

oxida'tive. Having the power to oxidize; referring to a processing involving oxidation.

oxide (ok'sĭd). A compound of oxygen with another element or a radical.

ox'idize. To combine or cause an element or radical to combine with oxygen or to lose electrons.

ox'idoreduc'tase. An enzyme catalyzing an oxidation-reduction reaction.

oxime (ok'sim). A compound resulting from the action of hydroxylamine, NH$_2$OH, on a ketone or an aldehyde to yield the group =N–OH attached to the former carbonyl carbon atom.

oxim'eter. A photoelectric instrument used in oximetry.

oxim'etry. Measurement with an oximeter of the oxygen saturation of hemoglobin in a sample of blood.

oxo-. Prefix denoting addition of oxygen; often used in place of keto- in systematic nomenclature.

3-oxoacyl-ACP reductase. An enzyme reducing acetoacetyl-ACP to hydroxybutyryl-ACP, with NADPH as hydrogen donor; part of the synthesis of fatty acids involving ACP.

3-oxoacyl-ACP synthase. An enzyme condensing malonyl-ACP and acetyl-ACP to acetoacetyl-ACP + ACP + CO$_2$, and similar reactions, as steps in fatty acid synthesis.

17-oxosteroids (ok-so-stĕr'oydz). 17-Ketosteroids.

OXT Oxytocin.

oxy- [G. *oxys*, keen]. Combining form denoting: sharp, pointed; acid; acute; shrill; quick (incorrectly used for oxy-); in chemistry, the presence of oxygen, either added or substituted, in a substance.

oxyacid (ok'sĭ-as'ĭd). Oxacid.

oxybarbit'urates. Hypnotics of the barbiturate group in which the atom attached at the carbon-2 position is oxygen.

oxycephal'ic, oxyceph'alous. Acrocephalic; acrocephalous; relating to or characterized by oxycephaly.

oxycephaly (ok-sĭ-sef'ă-lĭ) [G. *oxys*, pointed, + *kephalē*, head]. Acrocephalia; acrocephaly; craniosynostosis in which there is premature closure of the lambdoid and coronal sutures, resulting in an abnormally high, peaked, or conically shaped skull.

oxychromatic (ok'sĭ-kro-mat'ik) [G. *oxys*, sour, acid, + *chrōma*, color]. Acidophilic.

11-oxycor'ticoids. Corticosteroids bearing an alcohol or ketonic group on carbon-11.

oxyesthesia (ok'sĭ-es-the'zĭ-ah) [G. *oxys*, acute, + *aisthēsis*, sensation]. Hyperesthesia.

oxygen (ok'sĭ-jen). **1.** A gaseous element, symbol O, atomic no. 8, atomic weight 16.000; combines with most of the other elements to form oxides. **2.** A medicinal gas that contains not less than 99.0%, by volume, of O_2.

oxygenase (ok'sĭ-jĕ-nās). Direct oxidase; one of a group of enzymes catalyzing direct incorporation of O_2 into the substrates.

oxygenate (ok'sĭ-jĕ-nāt). To accomplish oxygenation.

oxygenation (ok'sĭ-jĕ-na'shun). Addition of oxygen to any chemical or physical system.

oxygeusia (ok'sĭ-gu'sĭ-ah) [G. *oxys*, acute, + *geusis*, taste]. Hypergeusia.

oxyhematoporphyrin (ok'sĭ-he-mă-to-por'fĭ-rin). A derivative of hematoporphyrin sometimes found in the urine; distinguished from urobilin on the basis of a red color reaction.

ox'yheme. Hematin.

ox'yhemochro'mogen. Hematin.

ox'yhemoglo'bin (HbO$_2$). Oxygenated hemoglobin; hemoglobin in combination with oxygen, the form of hemoglobin present in arterial blood.

oxyla'lia [G. *oxys*, swift, + *lalia*, speech]. Abnormally rapid speaking.

oxymyoglobin (ok'sĭ-mi-o-glo'bin). Myoglobin in its oxygenated form, analogous in structure to oxyhemoglobin.

oxyntic (ok-sin'tik) [G. *oxynō*, to sharpen, make sour, acid]. Acid forming, as are the parietal cells of gastric glands.

oxyphil, oxyphile (ok'sĭ-fil, -fīl) [G. *oxys*, sour, acid, + *philos*, fond]. **1.** Oxyphil *cell.* **2.** Eosinophilic *leukocyte.* **3.** Oxyphilic.

oxyphilic (ok-sĭ-fil'ik). Oxyphil (3); having an affinity for acid dyes.

oxypho'nia [G. *oxys*, sharp, + *phōnē*, voice]. Shrillness or high pitch of the voice.

ox'ypolygel'atin. A modified gelatin used as a plasma extender in transfusions.

oxytalan (ok-sit'ă-lan) [G. *oxys*, acid, + *talas*, suffering, resisting; coined term probably intended to mean "resistant to acid hydrolysis"]. A type of connective tissue fiber, histochemically distinct from collagen or elastic fibers, described in the periodontal membrane and gingivae.

ox'ytetracy'cline. Oxytetracycline dihydrate; an antibiotic produced by *Streptomyces rimosus,* with actions and uses similar to those of tetracycline.

oxytocia (ok'sĭ-to'sĭ-ah) [G. *oxys*, swift, + *tokos*, childbirth]. Rapid parturition.

oxytocic (ok-sĭ-to'sik). Hastening childbirth.

oxytocin (ok-sĭ-to'sin) [G. *okytokos*, first birth, prompt delivery]. A nonapeptide hormone of the neurohypophysis that causes myometrial contractions at term and promotes milk release during lactation; used for the induction or stimulation of

labor, in the management of postpartum hemorrhage and atony, and to relieve painful breast engorgement.

oxyuriasis (ok'sĭ-u-ri'ă-sis). Disease manifestations from infection with seatworms or pinworms (oxyurids).

oxyuricide (ok-sĭ-u'rĭ-sī) [oxyurid + L. *caedo*, to kill]. An agent that destroys pinworms.

oxyurid (ok-sĭ-u'rid) [see *Oxyuris*]. Common name for members of the family Oxyuridae.

Oxyu'ridae. A family of parasitic nematodes (superfamily Oxyuroidea), found in the large intestine or cecum of vertebrates and the intestine of invertebrates, including the genera *Aspiculuris, Enterobius, Oxyuris, Passalurus, Syphacia,* and *Thelandros.*

Oxyuris (ok-sĭ-u'ris) [G. *oxys*, sharp, + *oura,* tail]. A genus of nematodes commonly called seatworms or pinworms; the pinworm of man is the closely related form, *Enterobius vermicularis.*

oz. Ounce.

oze'na [G. *ozaina,* a fetid polypus, fr. *ozō,* to smell]. A disease characterized by intranasal crusting, atrophy, and fetid odor.

ozone (o'zōn) [G. *ozō,* to smell]. O$_3$; air containing a perceptible amount of O$_3$ formed by an electric discharge or by the slow combustion of phosphorus, with an odor suggestive of Cl or SO$_2$; a powerful oxidizing agent.

P

P Phosphorus; in nucleic acid terminology, symbol for phosphoric residue; followed by a subscript, refers to the plasma concentration of the substance indicated by the subscript; pressure or partial *pressure,* frequently with subscripts indicating location and chemical species.

P$_1$ Parental *generation.*

p Pupil; optic *papilla;* phosphoric ester or phosphate in polynucleotide symbolism; pico-.

p- para- (3).

P.A. Physician's assistant.

Pa Protactinium; pascal.

PABA *p*-Aminobenzoic acid.

pacchionian (pak-e-o'nĭ-an). Attributed to or described by Pacchioni.

pace'follower. Any cell in excitable tissue that responds to stimuli from a pacemaker.

pace'maker. **1.** Biologically, any rhythmic center that establishes a pace of activity; also used to mean an artificial p. **2.** In chemistry, the substance whose rate or reaction sets the pace for a series of chain reactions; the rate-limiting reaction.

  artificial p., any device that substitutes for an anatomic to p. control the rhythm of the organ; especially a cardiac p.

  demand p., a form of artificial p. usually implanted into cardiac tissue because its output of electrical stimuli can be inhibited by endogenous cardiac electrical activity.

fixed-rate p., an artificial p. that emits electrical stimuli at a constant frequency.

wandering p., a disturbance of the normal cardiac rhythm in which the site of the controlling p. shifts from beat to beat, usually between the sinus and A-V nodes.

pachy- [G. *pachys*, thick]. Prefix denoting thick.

pachyblepharon (pak-ĭ-blef'ă-ron) [pachy- + G. *blepharon*, eyelid]. Thickening of the tarsal border of the eyelid.

pachycephalic (pak'ĭ-sĕ-fal'ik). Relating to or marked by pachycephaly.

pachycephaly (pak-ĭ-sef'ă-lĭ) [pachy- + G. *kephalē*, head]. Abnormal thickness of the skull.

pachycheilia, pachychilia (pak-ĭ-ki'lĭ-ah) [pachy- + G. *cheilos*, lip]. Swelling or abnormal thickness of the lips.

pachychromatic (pak'ĭ-kro-mat'ik). Having a coarse chromatin reticulum.

pachydactyly (pak-ĭ-dak'tĭ-lĭ) [pachy- + G. *daktylos*, finger or toe]. Enlargement of the fingers or toes, especially extremities.

pachyderma (pak-ĭ-der'mah) [pachy- + G. *derma*, skin]. Abnormally thick skin. See also elephantiasis.

p. laryn'gis, a circumscribed connective tissue hyperplasia at the posterior commissure of the larynx.

p. lymphangiectat'ica, elephantiasis due to lymph stasis.

p. vesi'cae, elephantiasis with nodules comprised of lymph vesicles on skin surface.

pachydermatocele (pak'ĭ-der-mat'o-sēl) [pachy- + G. *derma*, skin, + *kēlē* tumor]. **1.** *Cutis* laxa. **2.** A huge neurofibroma.

pachydermoperiostosis (pak-ĭ-der'mo-per'ĭ-os-to'sis) [pachy- + G. *derma*, skin, + periostosis]. A syndrome characterized by clubbing of the digits, periosteal new bone formation especially over the distal ends of the long bones, and coarsening of the facial features with thickening, furrowing, and oiliness of the skin of the face and forehead; probably of autosomal dominant inheritance, usually more severe in males.

pachyglossia (pak-ĭ-glos'ĭ-ah) [pachy- + G. *glōssa*, tongue]. Macroglossia.

pachygyria (pak-ĭ-ji'rĭ-ah) [pachy- + G. *gyros*, circle]. Unusually thick convolutions of the cerebral cortex, related to defective development.

pachyleptomeningitis (pak'ĭ-lep'to-men-in-ji'tis) [G. *pachys*, thick, + *leptos*, thin, + *mēninx* (*mēning-*), membrane, + *-itis*, inflammation]. Inflammation of the membranes of the brain or spinal cord.

pachymeningitis (pak'ĭ-men-in-ji'tis) [pachy- + G. *mēninx*, membrane, + *-itis*, inflammation]. Perimeningitis; inflammation of the dura mater.

pach'ymeningop'athy [pachy- + G. *mēninx* (*mēning-*), membrane, + *pathos*, disease]. Any disease of the dura mater.

pachymeninx (pak'ĭ-me'ningks) [pachy- + G. *mēninx*, membrane]. The dura mater.

pachynsis (pă-kin'sis) [G. a thickening]. Any pathologic thickening.

pachyntic (pă-kin'tic). Relating to pachynsis.

pachyonychia (pak'ĭ-o-nik'ĭ-ah) [pachy- + G. *onyx*, nail]. Abnormal thickness of the fingernails or toenails.

p. congen'ita, Jadassohn-Lewandowsky syndrome; a syndrome characterized by an abnormal thickness and elevation of nail plates with palmar and plantar hyperkeratosis; the tongue is whitish and glazed due to papillary atrophy; autosomal dominant inheritance.

pach'yperiosti'tis [pachy- + periostitis]. Proliferative thickening of the periosteum caused by inflammation.

pachyperitonitis (pak'ĭ-pĕr-ĭ-to-ni'tis) [pachy- + peritonitis]. Inflammation of the peritoneum with thickening of the membrane.

pachypleuritis (pak-ĭ-plu-ri'tis) [pachy- + pleura + G. *-itis*, inflammation]. Inflammation of the pleura with thickening of the membrane.

pachysalpingitis (pak'ĭ-sal-pin-ji'tis). Chronic interstitial salpingitis.

pachysalpingo-ovaritis (pak-ĭ-sal'pin-go-o-var-i'tis) [pachy- + salpinx + Mod. L. *ovarium*, ovary, + G. *-itis*, inflammation]. Chronic parenchymatous inflammation of the ovary and fallopian tube.

pachysomia (pak-ĭ-so'mĭ-ah) [pachy- + G. *sōma*, body]. Pathologic thickening of the soft parts of the body, notably in acromegaly.

pachytene (pak'ĭ-tēn) [pachy- + G. *tainia*, band, tape]. The stage of prophase in meiosis in which pairing of homologous chromosomes is complete and the paired homologues may twine about each other as they continue to shorten; longitudinal cleavage occurs in each chromosome to form two sister chromatids so that each homologous chromosome pair becomes a set of four intertwined chromatids.

pachyvaginalitis (pak'ĭ-vaj'ĭ-nal-i'tis) [pachy- + Mod. L. (tunica) *vaginalis*, + G. *-itis*, inflammation]. Chronic inflammation with thickening of the tunica vaginalis testis.

pachyvaginitis (pak'ĭ-vaj-ĭ-ni'tis) [pachy- + vagina + G. *-itis*, inflammation]. Chronic vaginitis with thickening and induration of the vaginal walls.

pacinian (pă-che'nĭ-an). Attributed to or described by Pacini.

pack. 1. To fill, stuff, or tampon. **2.** To enwrap or envelop the body in a sheet, blanket, or other covering. **3.** In dentistry, to apply a dressing or covering to a surgical site. **4.** The items so used above.

pack'er 1. An instrument for tamponing. **2.** Plugger.

pack'ing. 1. Filling a natural cavity or a wound with some material. **2.** The material so used.

pad. 1. Soft material forming a cushion, to apply or relieve pressure on a part, or fill a depression. **2.** A body of fat or some other tissue serving to fill a space or act as a cushion in the body.

abdominal p., laparotomy p.

dinner p., a p. of moderate thickness placed over the pit of the stomach before the application of a plaster jacket; after the plaster has set the p. is removed, leaving space for varying conditions of abdominal distention.

fat p., see *fat-pad.*

knuckle p.'s, congenital condition, an atavistic trait, in which thick p.'s of skin appear over the proximal phalangeal joints.

laparotomy p., abdominal p.; a p. made from several layers of gauze folded into a rectangular shape; used as a sponge, for packing off the viscera in abdominal operations, etc.

retromolar p., a cushioned mass of tissue, frequently pear-shaped, located on the alveolar process of the mandible behind the area of the last natural molar tooth.

paed-. See ped-.

PAF Platelet-aggregating (or -activating) *factor.*

-pagus [G. *pagos,* something fixed]. A termination denoting conjoined twins, the first element of the word denoting the parts fused. See also -didymus, -dymus.

PAH *p*-Aminohippuric acid.

pain [L. *poena,* a fine, a penalty]. **1.** An unpleasant sensory and emotional experience associated with, or described in terms of, actual or potential tissue damage. **2.** One of the uterine contractions occurring in childbirth.

after-p.'s, see afterpains.

bearing-down p., a uterine contraction accompanied with straining and tenesmus; usually appearing in the second stage of labor.

expulsive p.'s, effective labor p.'s, associated with contraction of the uterine muscle.

false p.'s, ineffective uterine contractions, preceding and sometimes resembling true labor, but distinguishable from it by the lack of progressive effacement and dilation of the cervix.

growing p.'s, aching p.'s, frequently felt at night, in the limbs of growing children.

hunger p., cramp in the epigastrium associated with hunger.

intermenstrual p., (1) pelvic discomfort occurring at midpoint of the menstrual cycle; (2) mittelschmerz.

labor p.'s, rhythmic uterine contractions that under normal conditions increase in quality, frequency, and duration, culminating in vaginal delivery of the infant.

phantom limb p., see phatom *limb.*

referred p., p. perceived as coming from an area or situation remote from its actual origin.

paint. A solution or suspension of one or more medicaments applied to the skin with a brush or large applicator.

palatal (pal'ă-tal). Palatine; relating to the palate or the palate bone.

pal'ate [L. *palatum,* palate]. Uraniscus; the roof of the mouth; the bony and muscular partition between the oral and nasal cavities.

bony p., a concave elliptical bony plate, constituting the roof of the oral cavity, formed by the palatine process of the maxilla and the horizontal plate of the palatine bone on either side.

cleft p., palatoschisis; a congenital fissure in the median line of the p., often associated with cleft lip.

hard p., the anterior part of the palate, consisting of the bony palate covered above by the mucous membrane of the floor of the nose and below by the mucoperiosteum of the roof of the mouth which contains the palatine vessels, nerves, and mucous glands.

soft p., velum palatinum; the posterior muscular portion of the palate, forming an incomplete septum between the mouth and the oropharynx, and between the oropharynx and the nasopharynx.

palatine (pal'ă-tīn). Palatal.

palatitis (pal'ă-ti'tis). Inflammation of the palate.

palato- [L. *palatum,* palate]. Combining form meaning palate.

pal'atoglos'sal. Relating to the palate and the tongue.

palatognathous (pal'ă-tog'nă-thus) [palato- + G. *gnathos,* jaw]. Having a cleft palate.

pal'atomax'illary. Relating to the palate and the maxilla.

palatona'sal. Relating to the palate and the nasal cavity.

palatopharyngeal (pal'ă-to-fă-rin'je-al). Relating to palate and pharynx.

palatopharyngorrhaphy (pal'ă-to-făr'ing-or'ă-phī) [palato- + pharynx + G. *raphē,* suture]. Staphylopharyngorrhaphy.

pal'atoplasty [palato- + G. *plassō,* to form]. Staphyloplasty; uranoplasty; surgery of the palate to restore form and function.

palatoplegia (pal'ă-to-ple'jĭ-ah) [palato- + G. *plēgē,* stroke]. Paralysis of the muscle of the soft palate.

palatorrhaphy (pal-ă-tor'ă-fī) [palato- + G. *rhaphē,* suture]. Staphylorrhaphy; uranorrhaphy; suture of a cleft palate.

palatoschisis (pal-ă-tos'kĭ-sis) [palato- + G. *schisis,* fissure]. Cleft *palate.*

palatum, pl. **pala'ti** (pă-la'tum, -ti) [L.] [NA]. Palate.

paleo-, pale- [G. *palaios,* old, ancient]. Combining forms denoting old, primitive, primary, early.

paleocerebellum (pa'le-o-sĕr'e-bel'um) [paleo- + L. *cerebellum*] [NA]. Spinocerebellum; a phylogenetic term referring to a medial region of the cerebellum comprising most of the vermis and the adjacent medial zone of the cerebellar hemisphere; corresponds to the zone of distribution of the spinocerebellar tracts.

paleocortex (pa'le-o-kor'teks). The phylogenetically oldest part of the cortical mantle of the cerebral hemisphere, represented by the olfactory cortex; the archicortex of the hippocampus is often included.

paleokinetic (pa′le-o-kī-net′ik) [paleo- + G. *kinētikos*, relating to movement]. Denoting the primitive motor mechanisms underlying muscular reflexes and automatic stereotyped movements.

paleopathology (pa-le-o-pă-thol′o-jī) [paleo- + pathology]. The science of disease in prehistoric terms as revealed in bones, mummies, and archaeologic artifacts.

paleostriatal (pa′le-o-stri-a′tal). Relating to the paleostriatum.

paleostriatum (pa′le-o-stri-a′tum) [paleo- + L. *striatum*, neut. of *striatus*, furrowed]. The globus pallidus, denoting that it developed earlier in evolution than did the "neostriatum" or striatum (caudate nucleus and putamen).

paleothalamus (pa′le-o-thal′ă-mus). The intralaminar nuclei, believed to be the components of the thalamus to develop earliest in evolution.

palikinesis (pal-ĭ-kī-ne′zĭ-ah) [G. *palin*, again, + *kinēsis*, movement]. Involuntary repetition of movements.

palilalia (pal-ĭ-la′lĭ-ah) [G. *palin*, again, + *lalia*, a form of speech]. Paliphrasia.

palindrome (pal′in-drōm) [G. *palindromos*, a running back]. In molecular biology, a self-complementary nucleic acid sequence; a sequence identical to its complementary strand, if both are "read" in the same 5′-to-3′ direction.

palindromia (pal-in-dro′mĭ-ah) [G. *palindromos*, a running back, + *-ia*, condition]. A relapse or recurrence of a disease.

palindrom′ic. Relapsing; recurring.

palinopsia (pal-ĭ-nop′sĭ-ah) [G. *palin*, again, + *opsis*, vision]. Abnormal recurring visual imagery.

paliphrasia (pal-ĭ-fra′zĭ-ah) [G. *palin*, again, + *phrasis*, speech]. Palilalia; involuntary repetition of words or sentences in talking.

palla′dium [fr. the asteroid, Pallas]. A metallic element resembling platinum, symbol Pd, atomic no. 46, atomic weight 106.4.

pallanesthesia (pal′an-es-the′zĭ-ah) [G. *pallō*, to quiver, + *anaisthēsia*, insensibility]. Apallesthesia; absence of pallesthesia.

pallesthesia (pal-es-the′zĭ-ah) [G. *pallō*, to quiver, + *aisthesis*, sensation]. The appreciation of vibration, a form of pressure sense most acute when a vibrating tuning fork is applied over a bony prominence.

pal′lesthet′ic. Pertaining to pallesthesia.

pal′lial. Relating to the pallium.

palliate (pal′ĭ-āt) [L. *palliatus*, cloaked]. Mitigate; to reduce the severity of; to relieve somewhat.

pal′liative. Mitigating; reducing the severity of; denoting the alleviation of symptoms without curing the underlying disease.

pal′lidal. Relating to the pallidum.

pallidectomy (pal-ĭ-dek′to-mī) [pallidum + G. *ektomē*, excision]. Excision or destruction of the globus pallidus.

pallidoansotomy (pal′id-o-an-sot′o-mī). Production of lesions in the globus pallidus and ansa lenticularis.

pallidotomy (pal-ĭ-dot′o-mī) [pallidum + G. *tomē*, incision]. A lesion-producing operation on the globus pallidus to relieve involuntary movements or muscular rigidity.

pal′lidum [L. *pallidus*, pale]. *Globus* pallidus.

pallium (pal′ĭ-um) [L. cloak] [NA]. Mantle (2); brain mantle, the cerebral cortex with the subjacent white substance.

pal′lor [L.]. Paleness, as of the skin.

palm (pahm) [L. *palma*]. Palma; the flat of the hand; the flexor or anterior surface of the hand, exclusive of the thumb and fingers.

palma, pl. **palmae** (pahl′mah, -me) [L.] [NA]. Palm.

palmar (pahl′mar) [L. *palmaris*, fr. *palma*]. Volar; referring to the palm of the hand.

palmic (pal′mik). Beating; throbbing; relating to a palmus.

palmit′ic acid. Hexadecanoic acid; $C_{16}H_{32}O_2$; a saturated fatty acid occurring in palm oil and other fats.

palmitoleic acid (pal′mĭ-to-le′ik). 9-Hexadecenoic acid; an unsaturated 16-carbon acid; one of the common constituents of the glycerides of human adipose tissue.

pal′mus, pl. **pal′mi** [G. *palmos*, pulsation, quivering]. **1.** Facial *tic*. **2.** Rhythmical fibrillary contractions in a muscle.

palpable (pal′pă-bl) [see palpation]. **1.** Perceptible to touch; capable of being palpated. **2.** Evident; plain.

pal′pate. To examine by feeling and pressing with the palms of the hands and the fingers.

palpa′tion [L. *palpatio*, fr. *palpo*, pp. *-atus*, to touch, stroke]. **1.** Examination by means of the hands, used to outline the organs or tumors of the abdomen, to determine the degree of resistance of various parts, to feel the heart beat, the vibrations in the chest, etc. **2.** Touching; feeling or perceiving by the sense of touch.

palpe′bra, pl. **palpe′brae** [L.] [NA]. Eyelid; one of the two movable folds of skin, lined with conjunctiva, in front of the eyeball.

pal′pebral. Relating to an eyelid or the eyelids.

palpitation (pal-pĭ-ta′shun) [L. *palpitatio*, to throb]. Perceptible forcible pulsation of the heart, usually with an increase in frequency or force, with or without irregularity in rhythm.

palsy (pawl′zĭ) [a corruption fr. O. Fr. fr. L. and G. *paralysis*]. Paralysis; often used to connote paresis.
  Bell's p., facial p.
  birth p., obstetrical paralysis; paralysis due to cerebral hemorrhage occurring at birth or to anoxic injury of the fetal brain *in utero.*
  cerebral p., defect of motor power and coordination related to damage of the brain.
  Erb's p., Duchenne-Erb paralysis; birth p. in which there is paralysis of the muscles of the upper arm due to a lesion of the brachial plexus or of the

roots of the fifth and sixth cervical nerves.

facial p., Bell's p.; facial paralysis; facioplegia; prosopoplegia; unilateral paralysis of the facial muscles supplied by the seventh cranial nerve.

night p., waking *numbness*.

pampin'iform [L. *pampinus,* a tendril, + *forma,* form]. Having the shape of a tendril; denoting a vinelike structure.

pan- [G. *pas,* all]. Prefix denoting all, entire. See also pant-.

panacea (pan-ă-se'ah) [G. *panakeia,* universal remedy (fr. *Panacea,* G. myth. char.]. A cure-all; a remedy claimed to be curative of all problems or disorders.

panagglu'tinins. Agglutinins that react with all human erythrocytes.

panangiitis (pan'an-jī-i'tis) [pan- + angiitis]. Inflammation involving all the coats of a blood vessel.

panarthri'tis. **1.** Inflammation involving all the tissues of a joint. **2.** Inflammation of all the joints of the body.

panatrophy (pan-at'ro-fī) **1.** Atrophy of all the parts of a structure. **2.** General atrophy of the body.

pancardi'tis. Diffuse inflammation of the heart.

pancolectomy (pan-ko-lek'to-mĭ). Extirpation of the entire colon.

pancreas, pl. **pancreata** (pan'kre-as, -kre-a'tah) [G. *pankreas,* the sweetbread] [NA]. A lobulated gland, devoid of capsule, extending from the concavity of the duodenum to the spleen and consists of a flattened head within the duodenal concavity, an elongated three-sided body extending transversely across the abdomen, and a tail in contact with the spleen; it secretes pancreatic juice, discharged into the intestine, and the internal secretions, insulin and glucagon.

pancreat-, pancreatico-, pancreato-, pancreo- [G. *pankreas,* pancreas]. Combining forms denoting the pancreas.

pancreatalgia (pan'kre-ă-tal'jĭ-ah) [pancreat- + G. *algos,* pain]. Pain arising from, or felt in or near the region of, the pancreas.

pancreatectomy (pan'kre-ă-tek'to-mĭ) [pancreat- + G. *ektomē,* excision]. Excision of the pancreas.

pancreatic (pan-kre-at'ik). Relating to the pancreas.

pancreatico-. See pancreat-.

pancreaticoduodenal (pan-kre-at'ĭ-ko-du-o-de'nal, -du-od'ĕ-nal). Relating to the pancreas and the duodenum.

pancreatitis (pan'kre-ă-ti'tis). Inflammation of the pancreas.

acute hemorrhagic p., acute inflammation of the pancreas accompanied by the formation of necrotic areas on the surface of the pancreas and in the omentum due to the action of the escaped pancreatic enzymes, and, frequently, hemorrhages into the substance of the gland.

pancreato-. See pancreat-.

pancreatoduodenectomy (pan'kre-ă-to-du-o-dĕ-nek'to-mĭ). Whipple's operation; excision of all or part of the pancreas together with the duodenum.

pancreatoduodenostomy (pan'kre-ă-to-du-o-dĕ-nos'to-mĭ). Surgical anastomosis of a pancreatic duct, cyst, or fistula to the duodenum.

pancreatogastrostomy (pan'kre-ă-to-gas-tros'to-mĭ). Surgical anastomosis of a pancreatic cyst or fistula to the stomach.

pancreatogenic (pan'kre-ă-to-jen'ik). Pancreatogenous.

pancreatogenous (pan'kre-ă-toj'e-nus). Pancreatogenic; of pancreatic origin; formed in the pancreas.

pancreatog'raphy (pan'kre-ă-tog'ră-fī) [pancreato- + G. *graphō,* to write]. Radiographic visualization of the pancreatic ducts after injection of radiopaque material into the collecting system.

pancreatolith (pan-kre-at'o-lith) [pancreato- + G. *lithos,* stone]. A pancreatic calculus; a concretion, usually multiple, in the pancreatic duct, associated with chronic pancreatitis.

pancreatolithectomy (pan'kre-ă-to-lĭ-thek'to-mĭ) [pancreato- + G. *lithos,* stone, + *ektomē,* excision]. Pancreatolithotomy.

pancreatolithiasis (pan'kre-ă-to-lĭ-thi'ă-sis). Stones in the pancreas, usually in the pancreatic duct system.

pancreatolithotomy (pan'kre-ă-to-lĭ-thot'o-mĭ) [pancreato- + G. *lithos,* stone, + *tomē,* incision]. Pancreatolithectomy; removal of a pancreatic concretion.

pancreatolysis (pan'kre-ă-tol'ĭ-sis) [pancreato- + G. *lysis,* dissolution]. Destruction of pancreatic tissue.

pancreatolytic (pan'kre-ă-to-lit'ik). Denoting pancreatolysis.

pancreatopathy (pan'kre-ă-top'ă-thĭ) [pancreato- + G. *pathos,* suffering]. Any disease of the pancreas.

pancreatotomy (pan'kre-ă-tot'o-mĭ) [pancreato- + G. *tomē,* incision]. Incision of the pancreas.

pancreatropic (pan'kre-ă-trop'ik) [pancreat- + G. *tropikas,* relating to a turning]. Exerting an action on the pancreas.

pancrelipase (pan-kre-lip'ās). A concentrate of pancreatic enzymes standardized for lipase content; a lipolytic used for substitution therapy.

pancreo-. See pancreat-.

pancytopenia (pan'si-to-pe'nĭ-ah) [pan- + G. *kytos,* cell, + *penia,* poverty]. Pronounced reduction in the number of erythrocytes, all types of white blood cells, and the blood platelets in the circulating blood.

congenital p., Fanconi's p., Fanconi's *anemia.*

pandemic (pan-dem'ik) [pan- + G. *dēmos,* the people]. A widespread epidemic.

panencephalitis (pan'en-sef-ă-li'tis). A diffuse inflammation of the brain.

panendoscope (pan-en'do-skōp) [pan- + G. *endon,* within, + *skopeō,* to view]. **1.** A cystoscope for visualization of the entire interior of the bladder. **2.** An illuminated instrument for inspection of the interior of the urethra as well as the bladder by means of a foroblique lens system.

panesthesia (pan-es-the′zĭ-ah) [pan- + G. *aisthēsis*, sensation]. The sum of all the sensations experienced by a person at one time.

pang. A sudden, sharp, brief pain.

panhypopituitarism (pan′hi-po-pī-tu′ĭ-tă-rizm). A state in which the secretion of all anterior pituitary hormones is inadequate or absent, as a result of destruction of substantially all of the anterior pituitary gland.

pan′ic [fr. G. god *Pan*, presumed to inspire terror]. A violent and unreasoning anxiety and fear.

homosexual p., an acute, severe attach of anxiety based on unconscious conflicts regarding homosexuality.

pan′immu′nity. A general immunity to all infectious diseases.

panmyelophthisis (pan′mi-ē-lof′thĭ-sis). Myelophthisis (2).

panmyelosis (pan′mi-ē-lo′sis) [pan- + G. *myelos*, marrow, + *-osis*, condition]. Myeloid metaplasia with abnormal immature blood cells in the spleen and liver, associated with myelofibrosis.

panniculitis (pă-nik-u-li′tis) [panniculus + G. *-itis*, inflammation]. Inflammation of the panniculus adiposus of the abdominal wall.

nodular nonsuppurative p., Weber-Christian disease; Christian disease (2); a condition of unknown cause; marked by recurring attacks of fever and formation of tender subcutaneous nodules; necrotic areas infiltrated by lipid macrophages are present in subcutaneous fat.

subacute migratory p., erythema nodosum migrans; nodular tender lesions of changing configuration on the lateral aspect of one or both legs, of many months duration.

panniculus, pl. **panniculi** (pă-nik′u-lus, -li) [L. dim. of *pannus*, cloth] [NA]. A sheet or layer of tissue.

p. adipo′sus [NA], the superficial fascia which contains a fatty deposit in its areolar substance.

p. carno′sus, the skeletal muscle layer in the superficial fascia represented by the platysma muscle.

pan′nus, pl. **pan′ni** [L. cloth]. A membrane of granulation tissue covering a normal surface, particularly the articular cartilages in rheumatoid arthritis and the cornea in trachoma, where it occurs in three forms: **p. crassus,** thick, with many blood vessels and very dense opacity; **p. siccus,** dry, with a dry glossy surface; **p. tenuis,** thin, with few blood vessels and slight opacity.

panophthalmia, panophthalmitis (pan′of-thal′mĭ-ah, -of′thal-mi′tis) [pan- + G. *ophthalmos*, eye]. Purulent inflammation of all parts of the eye.

panotitis (pan-o-ti′tis) [pan- + G. *ous*, ear, + *-itis*, inflammation]. General inflammation of the entire ear.

pansinusitis (pan-si-nus-i′tis). Inflammation of all paranasal sinuses on one or both sides.

pansystolic (pan′sis-tol′ik). Holosystolic; lasting throughout systole, extending from first to second heart sound.

pant [Fr. *panteler,* to gasp]. To breathe rapidly and shallowly.

pant-, panto- [G. *pas,* all]. Prefix denoting all, entire. See also pan-.

pantalgia (pan-tal′jĭ-ah) [pant- + G. *algos,* pain]. Pain involving the entire body.

pantomogram (pan′to-mo-gram). A panoramic radiographic record of the maxillary and mandibular dental arches and their associated structures, obtained by a pantomograph.

pantomograph (pan′to-mo-graf). A panoramic radiographic instrument that permits visualization of the entire dentition, alveolar bone, and contiguous structures on a single extraoral film.

pantomography (pan-to-mog′ră-fĭ). Use of a pantomograph.

pantothen′ate. A salt or ester of pantothenic acid.

pantothen′ic acid. $HOCH_2C(CH_3)_2CHOH-CO-NH-CH_2CH_2COOH$; a growth substance widely distributed in plant and animal tissues, and in part of the vitamin B_2 complex part of coenzyme A.

pap. A food of soft consistence, like that of breadcrumbs soaked in milk or water.

papain, papainase (pap-a′in, -ās). A proteolytic enzyme, or a crude extract containing it, obtained from papaya latex; has esterase, thiolase, transamidase, and transesterase activities.

papav′erine. A benzylisoquinoline alkaloid of opium; not narcotic but has mild analgesic action, and is a powerful spasmolytic.

papilla, pl. **papillae** (pă-pil′ah, pă-pil′e) [L. a nipple, dim. of *papula,* a pimple]. [NA]. Any small nipple-like process.

circumvallate p., p. vallata.

papil′lae con′icae [NA], **conical papillae,** numerous projections on the dorsum of the tongue, scattered among the filiform papillae and similar to them, but shorter.

papil′lae co′rii [NA], **papillae of corium,** superficial projections of the corium or dermis that interdigitate with recesses in the overlying epidermis, contain vascular loops and specialized nerve endings, and are arranged in ridgelike lines best developed in the hand and foot.

p. den′tis [NA], **dentinal p.,** a projection of the mesenchymal tissue of the developing jaw into the cup of the enamel organ; its outer layer becomes odontoblasts that form the dentin of the tooth.

p. duod′eni [NA], **duodenal p., (1)** major: the point of opening of the common bile duct and pancreatic duct into the duodenum, located posteriorly in the descending part of the duodenum; **(2)** minor: the site of the opening of the accessory pancreatic duct into the duodenum, located anterior to and slightly superior to the major p.

papil'lae filifor'mes [NA], **filiform papillae**, numerous elongated conical projections on the dorsum of the tongue.

papil'lae folia'tae [NA], **foliate papillae**, folia linguae; numerous projections arranged in several transverse folds upon the lateral margins of the tongue just in front of the palatoglossus muscle.

papil'lae fungifor'mes [NA], **fungiform papillae**, numerous minute elevations on the dorsum of the tongue, of a fancied mushroom shape; the epithelium of many of these papillae have taste buds.

hair p., p. pili.

p. inci'siva [NA], **incisive p.,** a slight elevation of the mucosa at the anterior extremity of the raphe of the palate.

interdental p., the gingiva that fills the interproximal space between two adjacent teeth.

p. lacrima'lis [NA], **lacrimal p.,** a slight projection from the margin of each eyelid near the medial commisure, in the center of which is the opening of the lacrimal duct.

p. lingua'lis, [NA], **lingual p.,** see conical, filiform, fungiform, and vallate p.

p. mam'mae [NA], **nipple;** mamilla (2); teat (1); thelium (3); the projection at the apex of the mamma, on the surface of which the lactiferous ducts open, surrounded by a circular pigmented area, the areola.

optic p., discus nervi optici.

p. paroti'dea [NA], **parotid p.,** the projection at the opening of the parotid duct into the vestibule of the mouth opposite the neck of the upper second molar tooth.

p. pi'li [NA], **hair p.;** a knoblike vascular indentation of the bottom of the hair follicle, upon which the hair bulb fits like a cap.

p. rena'lis [NA], **renal p.,** the apex of a renal pyramid which projects into a minor calyx.

tactile p., one of the papillae of the skin containing a tactile cell or corpuscle.

urethral p., the slight projection in the vestibule of the vagina marking the urethral orifice.

p. valla'ta [NA], **vallate p.,** circumvallate p.; one of eight or ten projections from the dorsum of the tongue forming a row anterior to and parallel with the terminal sulcus.

pap'illary. Relating to, resembling, or provided with papillae.

papillectomy (pap-ĭ-lek'to-mĭ) [papilla + G. ektomē, excision]. Surgical removal of any papilla.

papilledema (pă-pil-ĕ-de'mah) [papilla + edema]. Edema of the optic disk.

papil'liform. Resembling or shaped like a papilla.

papillitis (pap-ĭ-li'tis) [papilla + G. -itis, inflammation]. Inflammation of the optic disk or renal papilla.

papillo- [L. papilla]. Combining form denoting papilla, papillary.

papilloadenocystoma (pă-pil'o-ad'ĕ-no-sis-to'mah). A benign epithelial neoplasm characterized by glands or glandlike structures, formation of cysts, and finger-like projections of neoplastic cells covering a core of fibrous connective tissue.

papillocarcinoma (pă-pil'o-kar-sĭ-no'mah) [papilla + G. karkinōma, cancer]. **1.** A papilloma that has become malignant. **2.** A carcinoma characterized by papillary projections of neoplastic cells in association with cores of fibrous stroma as a supporting structure.

papilloma (pap-ĭ-lo'mah) [papilla + G. -oma, tumor]. Papillary tumor; villoma; a benign epithelial neoplasm consisting of villous or arborescent outgrowths of fibrovascular stroma covered by neoplastic cells.

papillomatosis (pap'ĭ-lo-mă-to'sis). **1.** The development of numerous papillomas. **2.** Papillary projections of the epidermis forming a microscopically undulating surface.

papillo'matous. Relating to a papilloma.

Papillo'mavirus. A genus of viruses (family Papovaviridae) containing DNA, including the papilloma and warts viruses of man and other animals.

papilloretinitis (pap'ĭ-lo-ret-ĭ-ni'tis). Retinopapillitis; papillitis with extension of the inflammation to neighboring parts of the retina.

papillotomy (pă-pil-lot'o-mĭ) [papilla + G. tome, incision]. Incision into the major duodenal papilla.

Papovaviridae (pă-po'vă-vĭr'ĭ-de) [pa(pilloma) + po(lyoma) + va(cuolating)]. A family of small antigenically distinct viruses, comprising the genera Papillomavirus and Polyomavirus, that replicate in nuclei of infected cells; most have oncogenic properties.

papovavirus (pă-po'vă-vi'rus). Any virus of the family Papovaviridae.

pap'ular. Relating to papules.

papula'tion. The formation of papules.

papule (pap'ūl) [L. papula, pimple]. A small, circumscribed, solid elevation on the skin.

papulo- [L. papula, papule]. Combining form denoting papule.

papuloerythematous (pap'u-lo-ĕr-ĭ-them'ă-tus, -the'mă-tus). Denoting an eruption of papules on an erythematous surface.

pap'ulopus'tular. Denoting an eruption composed of papules and pustules.

papulo'sis. The occurrence of numerous widespread papules.

papulosquamous (pap'u-lo-skwa'mus) [papulo- + L. squamosus, scaly]. Denoting an eruption composed of both papules and scales.

pap'ulovesic'ular. Denoting an eruption composed of papules and vesicles.

papyraceous (pap-ĭ-ra'shus) [L. papyraceus, made of papyrus]. Like parchment or paper.

par [L. equal]. A pair; specifically a pair of cranial nerves.

para- [G. alongside of, near]. **1.** Prefix denoting departure from the normal. **2.** Prefix denoting involvement of two like parts or a pair. **3** (p-). In

550

parageusia

chemistry, a prefix designating two substitutions in the benzene ring arranged symmetrically. For words so beginning, see the specific name.

para (păr′ah) [L. *pario,* to bring forth]. A woman who has given birth to an infant or infants, denoted either by a Latin numerical prefix or by a Roman numeral for each occurrence; *e.g.,* **primipara** or **para I,** first infant(s); **secundipara** or **para II,** second infant(s).

paraballism (păr-ă-bal′izm) [para- + G. *ballismos,* jumping about]. Severe jerking movements of both legs.

parabio′sis [para- + G. *biōsis,* life]. **1.** The fusion of whole eggs or embryos, as occurs in conjoined twins. **2.** Surgical joining of the vascular systems of two organisms.

parabiot′ic. Relating to, or characterized by, parabiosis.

parablep′sia [para- + G. *blepsis,* sight]. Perverted vision, as in visual illusions or hallucination.

parabu′lia [para- + G. *boulē,* will]. Perversion of volition or will; one impulse is checked and replaced by another.

paracasein (păr-ă-ka′se-in). The compound produced by the action of rennin upon κ-casein (which liberates a glycoprotein), and that precipitates with calcium ion as the insoluble curd.

paracenesthesia (păr′ă-se-nes-the′zĭ-ah) [para- + G. *koinos,* common, + *aisthestai,* to perceive]. Deterioration in one's sense of bodily well-being.

paracentesis (păr′ă-sen-te′sis) [G. *parakentēsis,* a tapping for dropsy]. The passage into a cavity of a trocar and cannula, needle, or other hollow instrument to remove fluid; variously designated according to the cavity punctured.

paracentet′ic. Relating to paracentesis.

parac′etal′dehyde. Paraldehyde.

paracholera (păr-ă-kol′er-ah). A disease clinically resembling Asiatic cholera but due to a vibrio specifically different from *Vibrio cholerae.*

parachordal (păr-ă-kor′dal) [para- + G. *chordē,* cord]. Alongside the anterior portion of the notochord in the embryo; designating the cartilaginous bars on either side which enter into the formation of the base of the skull.

parachroma (păr′ă-kro′mah) [para- + G. *chrōma,* color]. Parachromatosis; abnormal coloration of the skin.

parachromatopsia (păr′ă-kro-mă-top′sĭ-ah) [para- + G. *chrōma,* color, + *opsis,* vision]. Dichromatism (2).

parachromatosis (păr′ă-kro-mă-to′sis). Parachroma.

Paracoccidioides brasiliensis (păr′ă-kok-sid-ĭ-oy′dēs brā-sil-ĭ-en′sis). A dimorphic fungus that causes paracoccidioidomycosis; grows as large spherical or oval cells which bear single or several buds, occasionally covering the entire surface.

paracoccidioidin (păr′ă-kok-sid-ĭ-oy′din). A filtrate antigen prepared from the filamentous form of *Paracoccidioides brasiliensis;* used for demonstrating

delayed type dermal hypersensitivity in populations and is useful in demonstrating endemic areas in different geographic regions.

paracoccidioidomycosis (păr′ă-kok-sid-ĭ-oy′do-mi-ko′sis). South American blastomycosis; Almeida's or Lutz-Splendore-Almedia disease; paracoccidioidal granuloma; a chronic mycosis caused by *Paracoccidioides brasiliensis* and characterized by primary pulmonary lesions with dissemination to many visceral organs, conspicuous ulcerative granulomas of the buccal and nasal mucosa with extensions to the skin, and generalized lymphangitis.

paracoli′tis. Inflammation of the peritoneal coat of the colon.

paracrine (păr′ă-krin). Referring to the release of locally acting substances from endocrine cells.

paracusis, paracusia (păr′ă-ku′sis, -ku′sĭ-ah) [para- + G. *akousis,* hearing]. **1.** Impaired hearing. **2.** Auditory illusion or hallucination.

paracys′tic [para- + G. *kystis,* bladder]. Alongside or near the urinary bladder.

paracystitis (păr′ă-sis-ti′tis) [para- + G. *kystis,* bladder, + *-itis,* inflammation]. Inflammation of the connective tissue and other structures about the urinary bladder.

paradidymis (păr′ă-did′ĭ-mis) [para- + G. *didymos,* twin, pl. *didymoi,* testes] [NA]. Parepididymis; a small body sometimes attached to the front of the lower part of the spermatic cord above the head of the epididymis; the remnants of tubules of the mesonephros.

paradip′sia [para- + G. *dipsa,* thirst]. Perverted appetite for fluids ingested without relation to bodily need.

paradox (păr′ă-doks) [G. *paradoxos,* incredible, beyond belief]. That which is apparently, though not actually, inconsistent with or opposed to the known facts in any case.

Weber's p., if a muscle is loaded beyond its power to contract it may elongate.

paraffinoma (păr′ă-fĭ-no′mah) A tumefaction, usually a granuloma, caused by the prosthetic or therapeutic injection of paraffin; sometimes referring to similar lesions resulting from the injection of any oil, wax, etc.

paragang′lia. Plural of paraganglion.

par′aganglio′ma. A neoplasm usually derived from the chromoceptor or chromaffin tissue of a paraganglion or the medulla of the adrenal gland; when such a neoplasm produces hormone, it is usually termed a chromaffinoma or pheochromocytoma.

nonchromaffin p., chemodectoma.

paraganglion, pl. **paraganglia** (păr-ă-gang′glĭ-on, -ah). Chromaffin body; a small, roundish body containing chromaffin cells; a number of such bodies may be found retroperitoneally near the aorta and in organs such as the kidney, liver, heart, and gonads.

parageusia (păr-ă-gu′sĭ-ah) [para- + G. *geusis,* taste]. Disordered or perverted sense of taste.

parageu'sic. Relating to parageusia.

paragonimiasis (păr'ă-gon-ĭ-mi'ă-sis). Infection with a worm of the genus *Paragonimus,* especially *P. westermani.*

Paragonimus (păr-ă-gon'ĭ-mus) [para- + G. *gonimos,* with generative power]. A genus of lung flukes, parasitic in man and a wide variety of mammals, that feed upon crustaceans carrying the metacercariae.

P. westerman'i, *P. ringeri;* a species that causes paragonimiasis, found chiefly in Asia in man, excysted worms invade the wall of the gut and migrate through the diaphragm into the lungs, causing an intense inflammatory reaction and eventually forming fibrous-walled nodules that usually contain a pair of adult worms, exudate, eggs, and remains of red blood cells; the fibroparasitic nodules may become contiguous and form multiloculated cystlike structures.

paragram'matism. Paraphasia.

paragranulo'ma. A cellular infiltrate with some features of a granuloma, especially with a relatively good prognosis.

paragraphia (păr-ă-graf'ĭ-ah) [para- + G. *graphō,* to write]. **1.** Loss of the power of writing from dictation, although the words are understood. **2.** Writing one word when another is intended.

parahemophilia (păr'ă-he-mo-fil'ĭ-ah). Owren's *disease.*

parahormone (păr-ă-hor'mōn). A substance, product of ordinary metabolism, not produced for a specific purpose, that acts like a hormone in modifying the activity of some distant organ.

parakeratosis (păr'ă-kĕr-ă-to'sis) [para- + keratosis]. Retention of nuclei in the cells of the stratum corneum of the epidermis, observed in scaly dermatoses such as psoriasis and exfoliative dermatitis.

parakinesia, parakinesis (păr'ă-kĭ-ne'zĭ-ah, -kĭ-ne'sis) [para- + G. *kinēsis,* movement]. Any motor abnormality.

parala'lia [para- + G. *lalia,* talking]. Any speech defect; especially one in which one letter is habitually substituted for another.

paralexia (păr-ă-lek'sĭ-ah) [para- + G. *lexis,* speech]. Misapprehension of written or printed words, other meaningless words being substituted for them in reading.

paralgesia (păr-al-je'zĭ-ah) [para- + G. *algēsis,* the sense of pain]. Painful paresthesia; any disorder or abnormality of the sense of pain.

parallac'tic. Relating to a parallax.

parallax (păr'ă-laks) [G. alternately, fr. *par-allassō,* to make alternate]. The apparent displacement of an object by a change in the position from which it is viewed.

parallergic (păr-ă-ler'jik). Denoting an allergic state in which the body becomes predisposed to nonspecific stimuli following original sensitization with a specific allergen.

paralogia (păr-ă-lo'jĭ-ah) [G. *paralogia,* a fallacy, fr. *para,* beside, + *logos,* reason]. False reasoning, involving self-deception.

paralysis, pl. **paralyses** (pă-ral'ĭ-sis, -sēz) [G. fr. para- + *lysis,* a loosening]. **1.** Palsy; loss of power of voluntary movement in a muscle through injury or disease of its nerve supply. **2.** Loss of any function.

acute ascending p., Landry's p.; a p. of rapid course beginning in the legs and involving progressively the trunk, arms, and neck.

bulbar p., progressive bulbar p.

central p., p. due to a lesion in the brain or spinal cord.

compression p., p. due to compression of a nerve, as by prolonged pressure.

conjugate p., p. of one or more of the external muscles of the eye, resulting in loss of conjugate movement of the eyes.

decubitis p., a form of compression p. due to pressure on a limb during sleep.

Duchenne's p., pseudohypertrophic muscular *dystrophy.*

Duchenne-Erb p., Erb's p., Erb's *palsy.*

facial p., facial *palsy.*

familial periodic p., see hyperkalemic p., hypokalemic p., normokalemic p.

hyperkalemic periodic p., periodic p. in which the serum potassium level is elevated during attacks; onset occurs in infancy, attacks are frequent but relatively mild, and myotonia is often present; autosomal dominant inheritance.

hypokalemic periodic p., periodic p. in which the serum potassium level is low during attacks; onset usually occurs between the ages of 7 and 21 years; attacks may be precipitated by exposure to cold, high carbohydrate meal, or alcohol, and may cause respiratory p.; autosomal dominant inheritance with reduced penetrance in females.

immunological p., lack of specific antibody production after exposure to large doses of the antigen; disappears when the antigen is eliminated.

Klumpke's p., atrophic p. of the forearm and small muscles of the hand together with paralysis of the eighth cervical and first dorsal nerves.

Landry's p., acute ascending p.

mixed p., combined motor and sensory p.

motor p., loss of the power of muscular contraction.

musculospiral p., p. of the muscles of the forearm due to injury of the radial (musculospiral) nerve.

normokalemic periodic p., periodic p. in which the serum potassium level is within normal limits during attacks; onset usually occurs between the ages of 2 and 5 years, often with severe quadriplegia; autosomal dominant inheritance.

obstetrical p., birth *palsy.*

periodic p., term for a group of diseases characterized by recurring episodes of muscular weakness or flaccid p. without loss of consciousness, speech, or sensation; attacks begin when the patient is at rest, and there is apparent good health between attacks.

progressive bulbar p., bulbar p.; Duchenne's disease (3); Erb's disease; progressive atrophy and p. of the muscles of the tongue, lips, palate, pharynx, and larynx, occurring in later life and due to atrophic degeneration of the neurons innervating these muscles.

pseudobulbar p., p. of the lips and tongue, simulating progressive bulbar p., due to cerebral lesions involving the upper motor neurons bilaterally; there is difficulty in speech and swallowing, with emotional instability.

pseudohypertrophic muscular p., pseudohypertrophic muscular *dystrophy.*

sensory p., loss of sensation.

sleep p., sleep dissociation; a condition which upon waking in the morning the person is aware of his surroundings but is unable to move.

spinal p., loss of motor power due to a lesion of the spinal cord.

supranuclear p., p. due to lesions above the primary motor neurons.

tick p., ascending p. caused by the continuing presence of ticks of the genera *Dermacentor* and *Ixodes* attached on the occipital region or on the upper neck.

Todd's p., temporary p. that occurs in the limb(s) involved in the jacksonian convulsions of epilepsy after the attack is over.

vasomotor p., vasoparesis.

paralytic (păr′ă-lit′ĭk) Relating to paralysis.

paralyzant (pă-ral′ī-zant). 1. Causing paralysis. 2. Any agent, such as curare, that causes paralysis.

paralyze (păr′ă-līz). To produce paralysis in.

paramastitis (păr′ă-mas-tī′tis) [para- + G. *mastos,* breast, + *-itis,* inflammation]. Submammary *mastitis.*

Paramecium (păr-ă-me′shī-um, -sī-um) [G. *paramēkēs,* rather long, fr. *mēkos,* length]. A genus of freshwater holotrichous ciliates, characteristically slipper-shaped, commonly used for genetic and other studies.

paramed′ical. Relating to the medical profession in an adjunctive capacity, *e.g.,* denoting allied fields such as physical therapy.

parame′nia [para- + G. *mēn,* mouth]. Any disorder or irregularity of menstruation.

parameter (pă-ram′ĕ-ter) [para- + G. *metron,* measure]. One of many ways of measuring or describing an object or evaluating a subject: 1. In a mathematical expression, an arbitrary constant that can possess different values, each value defining other expressions, and can determine the specific form but not the general nature of the expression. 2. In statistics, a term used to define a characteristic of a population, in contrast to a sample from that population; *e.g.,* the mean and standard deviation of a total population. 3. In psychoanalysis, any tactic, other than interpretation, used by the analyst to

further the patient's progress.

paramet′ric. Relating to the parametrium, or structures immediately adjacent to the uterus.

parametrit′ic. Relating to parametritis.

parametritis (păr-ă-me-trī′tis) [parametrium + G. *-itis,* inflammation]. Pelvic cellulitis; inflammation of the cellular tissue adjacent to the uterus.

parametrium, pl. **parametria** (păr-ă-me′trī-um, -ah) [para- + G. *mētra,* uterus] [NA]. The connective tissue of the pelvic floor extending from the fibrous subserous coat of the supracervical portion of the uterus laterally between the layers of the broad ligament.

paramim′ia [para- + G. *mimia,* imitation]. The use of gestures unsuited to the words which they accompany.

paramnesia (păr-am-ne′zĭ-ah) [para- + G. *amnēsia,* forgetfulness]. False recollection, events being recalled which have never occurred.

paramu′cin. A glycoprotein found in ovarian and certain other cysts, insoluble in water like mucin, but unlike mucin precipitated by tannin.

paramyloidosis (pă-ram′ī-loy-do′sis). A variety of amyloid deposit seen in lymph nodes in some chronic nonspecific inflammations and in primary localized amyloidosis; histologic reactions are the same as in amyloidosis.

paramyoclonus (păr′ă-mi-ok′lo-nus) [para- + G. *mys,* muscle, + *klonos,* a tumult]. *Myoclonus* multiplex.

paramyotonia (păr′ă-mi-o-to′nĭ-ah). An atypical form of myotonia.

congenital p., p. congen′ita, Eulenburg's disease; a nonprogressive disease characterized by myotonia induced by exposure to cold, with episodes of intermittent flaccid paralysis, but no atrophy or hypertrophy of muscles; autosomal dominant inheritance.

Paramyxoviridae (păr-ă-mik′so-vīr′ī-de). A family of RNA-containing viruses similar in morphology to the influenza viruses. Three genera are recognized: *Paramyxovirus, Morbillivirus,* and *Pneumovirus;* all cause cell fusion and produce cytoplasmic eosinophilic inclusions.

Paramyxovirus (păr-ă-mik′so-vi′rus). A genus of viruses (family Paramyxoviridae) that includes Newcastle disease, mumps, and parainfluenza viruses (types 1 to 5); all have hemagglutinating and hemadsorbing activities.

paranephr′ic. Relating to the paranephros.

paranephros, pl. **paranephroi** (păr-ă-nef′ros, -nef′roy) [para- + G. *nephros,* kidney]. *Glandula* suprarenalis.

paranoia (păr-ă-noy′ah) [G. derangement, madness, fr. para- + *noeō,* to think]. A mental disorder characterized by the presence of systematized delusions, often of a persecutory character, in an otherwise intact personality; when symptoms are relatively mild and mental illness is not present, the condition is called paranoid *personality.*

paranoid (păr′ă-noyd). Relating to, or characterized by, paranoia.

parano′mia [para- + G. *onoma*, name]. Aphasia in which objects are called by the wrong names.

paranuclear (păr-ă-nu′kle-ar). **1.** Paranucleate. **2.** Outside of, but near the nucleus.

paranucleate (păr′ă-nu′kle-āt). Paranuclear (1); relating to or having a paranucleus.

paranucleus (păr-ă-nu′kle-us). An accessory nucleus, or small mass of chromatin lying near the nucleus.

par′aop′erative. Relating to the accessories of an operation, the preparation of the patient, asepsis, selection and care of the instruments, etc.

paraparesis (păr-ă-păr′ĕ-sis) [para- + paresis]. A slight degree of paralysis, affecting the lower extremities.

paraparetic (păr′ă-pă-ret′ik). Relating to paraparesis.

paraphasia (păr-ă-fa′zĭ-ah) [para- + G. *phasis*, speech]. Paraphrasia; paragrammatism; jargon (2); aphasia in which the patient has lost the power of speaking correctly, substituting one word for another, and jumbling words and sentences in such a way as to make speech unintelligible.

parapha′sic. Relating to paraphasia.

paraphemia (păr-ă-fe′mĭ-ah) [para- + G. *phēmē*, speech]. Aphasia in which wrong words are constantly used.

paraphia (pă-ra′fĭ-ah) [para- + G. *haphē*, touch]. Parapsia; pseudesthesia (1); any disorder of the sense of touch.

paraphil′ia [para- + G. *philos*, fond]. Sexual practices that are socially prohibited.

paraphimosis (păr′ă-fi-mo′sis) [para- + G. phimosis]. **1.** Capistration; painful constriction of the glans penis by a phimotic foreskin, which has been retracted behind the corona. **2.** A retraction of the lid behind a protruding eyeball.

paraphrasia (păr-ă-fra′zĭ-ah) [para- + G. *phrasis*, speech]. Paraphasia.

paraplec′tic [G. *paraplēktikos*, paralyzed]. Paraplegic.

paraplegia (păr-ă-ple′jĭ-ah) [G. a stroke on one side, fr. *para*, beside, + *plēgē*, a stroke]. Paralysis of both lower extremities and, generally, the lower trunk.

paraple′gic. Paraplectic; relating to or suffering from paraplegia.

parapraxia (păr-ă-prak′sĭ-ah) [para- + G. *praxis*, a doing]. Defective performance of purposive acts; *e.g.*, slips of the tongue, mislaying of objects.

parapro′tein. An abnormal plasma protein, such as macroglobulin, cryoglobulin, and myeloma protein.

par′aproteine′mia. The presence of abnormal proteins in the blood.

parapsia (pă-rap′sĭ-ah) [para- + G. *hapsis*, touch]. Paraphia.

parapsoriasis (păr′ă-so-ri′ă-sis). A chronic dermatosis of unknown origin, with erythematous, papular, and scaling lesions appearing in persistent and often enlarging plaques.

parapsychology (păr′ă-si-kol′o-jĭ). The study of extrasensory perception, such as thought transference (telepathy) and clairvoyance.

parapsychosis (păr′ă-si-ko′sis). A transitory psychotic episode.

parareflexia (păr′ă-re-flek′sĭ-ah). A condition characterized by abnormal reflexes.

pararosanilin (par′ă-ro-san′ĭ-lin). A tri(aminophenyl)methane hydrochloride; a red biologic stain used in Schiff's reagent to detect cellular DNA, mucopolysaccharides, and proteins.

pararrhythmia (păr-ă-rith′mĭ-ah) [para- + G. *rhythmos*, rhythmos, rhythm]. A cardiac dysrhythmia in which two independent rhythms coexist, but not as a result of A-V block; p. thus includes parasystole and A-V dissociation (2), but not complete A-V block.

parasinoidal (păr′ă-si-noy′dal). Near a sinus, particularly a cerebral sinus.

parasite (păr′ă-sit) [G. *parasitos*, a guest, fr. *para*, beside, + *sitos*, food]. **1.** An organism that lives on or in another and draws its nourishment therefrom. **2.** In the case of a fetal inclusion or conjoined twins, the more or less incomplete twin that derives its support from the more nearly normal autosite.

  facultative p., an organism that may either lead an independent existence or live as a p.

  heterogenetic p., a p. whose life cycle involves an alternation of generations.

  heteroxenous p., a p. that has more than one obligatory host in its life cycle.

  incidental p., a p. that normally lives on another than its present host.

  obligate p., an organism that cannot lead an independent nonparasitic existence.

  specific p., a p. that habitually lives in its present host and is particularly adapted for the host species.

  temporary p., an organism accidentally ingested that survives briefly in the intestine.

parasitemia (păr′ă-si-te′mĭ-ah). Presence of parasites in the circulating blood; especially with reference to malarial and other protozoan forms, and microfilariae.

parasit′ic. 1. Relating to or of the nature of a parasite. **2.** Denoting organisms that normally grow only in or on the living body of a host.

parasiticidal (păr′ă-sit-ĭ-si′dal). Destructive to parasites.

parasit′icide [parasite + L. *caedo*, to kill]. An agent that destroys parasites.

parasitism (păr′ă-sĭ-tizm). A symbiotic relationship in which one species (the parasite) benefits at the expense of the other (the host).

par′asitize. To invade as a parasite.

parasitogenic (păr′ă-si-to-jen′ik) [parasite + G. -*gen*, producing]. **1.** Caused by parasite. **2.** Favoring parasitism.

parasitol′ogist. A specialist in parasitology.

parasitology (păr'ă-si-tol'o-jĭ) [parasite + G. *logos*, study]. The branch of biology and of medicine concerned with parasitism.

parasitosis (păr'ă-si-to'sis). Infestation with parasites.

parasitotropic (păr'ă-si-to-trop'ik). Pertaining to or characterized by parasitotropism.

parasitotropism (păr'ă-si-tot'ro-pizm) [parasite + G. *tropē*, turning]. The special affinity of particular drugs or other agents for parasites rather than for their hosts, including microparasites that infect a larger parasite.

paraspadia, paraspadias (păr-ă-spa'dĭ-ah, -us) [G. *para-spaō*, to draw aside]. A congenital opening into the urethra at one side of the normal urethral lumen.

parasympathet'ic. Pertaining to a division of the autonomic nervous system.

parasym'patholyt'ic. Relating to an agent that annuls or antagonizes the effects of the parasympathetic nervous system.

parasympathomimetic (păr-ă-sim'pă-tho-mĭ-met'ik) [para- + G. *sympatheia*, sympathy, + *mimētikos*, imitative]. Relating to an agent having an action resembling that caused by stimulation of the parasympathetic nervous system.

parasynapsis (păr'ă-sĭ-nap'sis) [para- + G. *synapsis*, a connection, junction]. Side-to-side union of chromosomes in the process of reduction.

parasynovitis (păr'ă-sĭ-no-vi'tis) [para- + synovitis]. Inflammation of the tissues immediately adjacent to a joint.

parasystole (păr-ă-sis'to-le) [para- + G. *systolē*, a contracting]. A second automatic rhythm existing simultaneously with normal sinus rhythm, the parasystolic center being protected from the sinus impulses so that its rhythm is undisturbed.

paratene'sis. The passage of an infective agent by one or a series of hosts in which the agent does not undergo further development.

paraten'on [para- + G. *tenōn*, tendon]. The material, fatty or synovial, between a tendon and its sheath.

parathi'on. A highly poisonous organic phosphate insecticide; an irreversible inhibitor of cholinesterases.

parathy'rin. Parathyroid *hormone*.

parathy'roid. *Glandula* parathyroidea.

parathyroidectomy (păr'ă-thi-roy-dek'to-mĭ) [parathyroid + G. *ektomē*, excision]. Excision of the parathyroid glands.

parathyrotropic, parathyrotrophic (păr-ă-thi-ro-trop'ik, -trof'ik) [parathyroid + G. *tropē*, a turning; *trophē*, nourishment]. Influencing the growth or activity of the parathyroid glands.

paratrophic (păr'ătrof'ik) [para- + G. *trophē*, nourishment]. Deriving sustenance from living organic material.

paratuber'culo'sis. A condition marked by symptoms of tuberculosis, in which the presence of the tubercle bacillus cannot be demonstrated.

paratyphoid (păr'ă-ti'foyd). Resembling in some respects, yet not the same as, typhoid.

paravaginitis (păr'ă-vaj-ĭ-ni'tis). Inflammation of the connective tissue alongside the vagina.

paraxial (păr-ak'sĭ-al). By the side of the axis of any body or part.

paraxon (păr-ak'son) [para- + G. *axōn*, axis]. A collateral branch of an axon.

paregor'ic [G. *parēgorkos*, soothing]. Camphorated opium tincture; an antiperistaltic containing powdered opium, anise oil, benzoic acid, camphor, glycerin, and diluted alcohol.

parenchyma (pă-reng'kĭ-mah) [G. anything poured in beside] [NA]. The distinguishing or specific cells of a gland or organ, contained in and supported by the connective tissue framework, or stroma, as of the testis, consisting of the seminiferous tubules located within the lobules.

parenchymal (pă-reng'kĭ-mah). Relating to the parenchyma.

parenchymatitis (pă-reng'kĭ-mă-ti'tis). Inflammation of the parenchyma or differentiated substance of a gland or organ.

paren'teral [para- + G. *enteron*, intestine]. By some other means than through the gastrointestinal tract or lungs; referring particularly to the introduction of substances into an organism; *i.e.*, by intravenous, subcutaneous, intramuscular, or intramedullary injection.

parepididymis (păr'ep-ĭ-did'ĭ-mis). Paradidymis.

paresis (pă-re'sis, păr'ĕ-sis) [G. a letting go, slackening]. **1.** Partial or incomplete paralysis. **2.** Dementia paralytica; a disease of the brain, syphilitic in origin, marked by progressive dementia, tremor, speech disturbances, and increasing muscular weakness.

paresthesia (păr-es-the'zĭ-ah) [para- + G. *aisthēsis*, sensation]. An abnormal sensation, such as of burning, pricking, tickling, or tingling.

paresthet'ic. Relating to or marked by paresthesia; denoting numbness and tingling in an extremity which usually occurs on the resumption of the blood flow to a nerve following temporary pressure or mild injury.

paret'ic. Relating to or suffering from paresis.

pareunia (păr-u'nĭ-ah) [G. *pareunos*, lying beside]. Sexual intercourse.

paries, pl. **parietes** (păr'ĭ-ēz, pă-ri'ĕ-tēz) [L. wall] [NA]. A wall, as of the chest, abdomen, or any hollow organ.

parietal (pă-ri'ĕ-tal). Relating to the wall of any cavity.

parieto- [L. *paries*, wall]. Combining form denoting relationship to a wall (paries) or to the parietal bone.

parietography (pă-ri-ĕ-tog'ră-fĭ) [parieto- + G. *graphē*, a writing]. Radiographic imaging of the walls of an organ.

parity (păr'ĭ-tĭ) [L. *pario*, to bear]. The state of having given birth to an infant or infants, alive or dead; multiple birth is considered as a single parous experience.

parkinso'nian. Relating to parkinsonism.

parkinsonism (par'kin-son-izm). **1.** Parkinson's disease; A neurological syndrome usually resulting from arteriosclerotic changes in the basal ganglia and characterized by rhythmical muscular tremors, rigidity of movement, festination, droopy posture, and masklike facies. **2.** A syndrome to p. appearing as a side effect of certain antipsychotic drugs.

paromphalocele (par-om'fa-lo-sēl) [para- + G. *omphalos*, umbilicus, + *kēlē*, tumor, hernia]. **1.** A tumor near the umbilicus. **2.** A hernia through a defect in the abdominal wall near the umbilicus.

paronychia (par-o-nik'ĭ-ah) [para- + G. *onyx*, nail]. Inflammation of the nail fold with separation of the skin from the proximal portion of the nail.

paronychial (par-o-nik'ĭ-al). Relating to paronychia or to the nail fold.

paroophoron (par-o-of'o-ron) [para- + oophoron, ovary] [NA]. Parovarium; a few scattered rudimentary tubules in the broad ligament between the epoophoron and the uterus; remnants of the tubules and glomeruli of the lower part of the wolffian body.

parophthalmia (par-of-thal'mĭ-ah) [para- + G. *ophthalmos*, eye]. Inflammation of the tissues around the eye.

parop'sia, parop'sis [para- + G. *opsis*, vision]. Disorientation of the perception of direction in hemianopia caused by occipital lesions.

parorchidium (par-or-kid'ĭ-um) [para- + G. *orchis*, testis]. Ectopic *testis.*

parorexia (par'o-rek'sĭ-ah) [para- + G. *orexis*, appetite]. Perverted appetite, especially a craving for items unsuitable for food.

parosmia (par-oz'mĭ-ah) [para- + G. *osmē*, the sense of smell]. Any disorder of the sense of smell, especially the subjective perception of odors that do not exist.

parosteo'sis, paroso'sis [para- + G. *osteon*, bone, + *-osis*, condition]. **1.** Development of bone in an unusual location, as in the skin. **2.** Abnormal or defective ossification.

parotic (pă-rot'ik) [para- + G. *ous*, ear]. Near or beside the ear.

parotid (pă-rot'id) [G. *parōtis* (*parōtid-*), the gland beside the ear, fr. *para*, beside, + *ous* (*ōt-*), ear]. Situated near the ear; usually refers to the p. salivary gland.

parotidectomy (pă-rot-ĭ-dek'to-mĭ) [parotid + *ektomē*, excision]. Surgical removal of the parotid gland.

parotiditis (pă-rot-ĭ-di'tis). Parotitis; inflammation of the parotid gland.

   epidemic p., mumps; an acute infectious and contagious disease caused by Paramyxovirus and characterized by inflammation and swelling of the parotid gland, sometimes of other salivary glands, and occasionally by inflammation of the testis, ovary, pancreas, or meninges.

paroti'tis. Parotiditis.

parous (păr'us) [L. *pario*, to bear]. Pertaining to parity.

parova'rian. 1. Relating to the paroophoron. **2.** Paraovarian.

parova'rium [para- + L. *ovarium*, ovary]. Paroophoron.

paroxysm (păr'ok-sizm) [G. *paroxysmos*, fr. *paroxynō*, to sharpen, irritate]. **1.** A sharp spasm or convulsion. **2.** A sudden onset of a symptom or disease, especially one with recurrent manifestations such as the chills and rigor of malaria.

paroxysmal (păr-ok-siz'mal). Relating to or occurring in paroxysms.

pars, pl. **par'tes** [L. *pars* (*part-*) a part] [NA]. A part or portion of a structure.

   p. amor'pha, the part of the nucleolus which occupies irregular spaces in the nucleonema and contains finely filamentous substance (p. granulosa).

   p. granulo'sa, the granular and filamentous part of the nucleonema of the nucleolus.

   p. mastoi'dea, mastoid part; the portion of the petrous part of the temporal bone bearing the mastoid process.

   p. petro'sa [NA], petrous part of the temporal bone; petrosal petrous bone; petrous pyramid; the part of the temporal bone that contains the structures of the inner ear and the second part of the internal carotid artery.

   p. pla'na, *orbiculus* ciliaris.

   p. tympan'ica [NA], tympanic portion of the temporal bone, forming the greater part of the wall of the external acoustic meatus.

pars-planitis (parz'pla-ni'tis). A clinical syndrome consisting of inflammation of the peripheral retina and/or pars plana, exudation into the overlying vitreous base, and edema of the posterior pole.

part. See pars.

parthenogen'esis [G. *parthenos*, virgin, + *genesis*, product]. A form of asexual reproduction in which the female reproduces its kind without fecundation by the male.

particle (par'tĭ-kl) [L. *particula*, dim. of *pars*, part]. A very small piece or portion of anything.

   alpha p., a p. consisting of two neutrons and two protons, and with a positive charge ($2e^+$), that is emitted energetically from the nucleus of an unstable isotope of high atomic number; its properties are identical to those of the helium nucleus.

   beta p., an electron, either positively (positron) or negatively (negatron) charged, emitted during beta decay of a radionuclide.

   Dane p.'s, the larger spherical forms of hepatitis-associated antigens comprising the virion of hepatitis B virus and containing a "core" in which DNA-dependent DNA polymerase and circular, double-stranded DNA have been found.

   elementary p., (1) platelet; (2) one of the units occurring on the matrical surface of mitochondrial cristae; may be concerned with the electron transport system.

partic'ulate. Relating to or occurring in the form of fine particles.

partic'ulates. Formed elements, discrete bodies, as contrasted with the surrounding liquid or semiliquid material in cells.

parturient (par-tu'rī-ent) [L. *parturio,* to be in labor]. Relating to or being in the process of parturition or childbirth.

parturifacient (par-tu-rī-fa'shent)]L. *parturio,* to be in labor, + *facio,* to make]. Oxytocic; inducing or accelerating labor.

parturiometer (par-tu-rī-om'e-ter) [L. *parturitio,* parturition, + G. *metron,* measure]. A device for determining the force of the uterine contractions in childbirth.

parturition (par-tu-rish'un) [L. *parturitio,* fr. *parturio,* to be in labor]. Childbirth.

parvicellular (par-vī-sel'u-lar) [L. *parvus,* small, + Mod. L. *cellularis,* cellular]. Relating to or composed of cells of small size.

Parvoviridae (par-vo-vīr'ī-de). A family of small viruses containing single-stranded DNA; replication and assembly occur in the nucleus of infected cells. Three genera are recognized: *Parvovirus, Densovirus,* and an officially unnamed genus that includes the adeno-associated satellite virus (unofficially named *Adenosatellovirus*).

Parvovirus (par'vo-vi-rus). A genus of viruses (family Parvoviridae), of which the Kilham rat virus is the type species, whose members replicate autonomously in suitable cells.

PAS *p*-Aminosalicylic acid; periodic acid-Schiff (stain).

PASA *p*-Aminosalicylic acid.

pas'cal (Pa). A derived SI unit of pressure, expressed in newtons per square meter.

passive (pas'iv) [L. *passivus,* fr. *patior,* to endure]. Not active; submissive.

passivism (pas'ī-vizm) [see passive]. **1.** An attitude of submission. **2.** A form of sexual perversion in which the subject, usually male, is submissive to the will of his partner in sexual practices.

paste [L. *pasta*]. A soft semisolid soft enough to flow slowly and not to retain its shape.

Pasteurella (pas-tur-el'ah) [L. *Pasteur*]. A genus of aerobic to facultatively anaerobic, nonmotile bacteria (family Brucellaceae) containing small Gram-negative, rods; parasites of man and other animals. The type species is *P. multocida.*

P. multoci'da, a species that causes fowl cholera and hemorrhagic septicemia in warm-blooded animals; it is the type species of the genus *P.*

P. pes'tis, *Yersinia pestis.*

P. pseudotuberculo'sis, *Yersinia pseudotuberculosis.*

P. tularen'sis, *Francisella tularensis.*

pasteurellosis (pas'tur-ĕ-lo'sis). Infection with bacteria of the genus *Pasteurella.*

pasteurization (pas'tur-ĭ-za'shun) [L. *Pasteur*]. The heating of milk or other liquids for about 30 minutes at 68°C. (154.4°F.) whereby the living bacteria are destroyed, but the flavor or bouquet is preserved; the spores are unaffected, but are kept from developing by immediately cooling the liquid to 10°C. (50°F.) or lower.

patch. A small circumscribed area differing from the surrounding surface.

   cotton-wool p.'s, cotton-wool spots; accumulations of cytoplasmic debris in the retinal nerve fiber layer caused by damage to axons.

   Peyer's p.'s, *folliculi* lymphatici aggregati.

   smoker's p.'s, leukoplakia.

patella, pl. **patellae** (pă-tel'ah, -tel'e) [L. a small plate, the kneecap, dim. of *patina,* a shallow disk, fr. *pateo,* to lie open] [NA]. Kneecap; the large sesamoid bone, in the combined tendon of the extensors of the leg, covering the anterior surface of the knee.

patel'lar. Relating to the patella.

patellectomy (pat'ĕ-lek'to-mĭ) [patella + G. *ektomē,* excision]. Excision of the patella.

patel'liform. Of the shape of the patella.

patency (pa'ten-sĭ). The state of being freely open or patulous.

pa'tent [L. *patens,* pres. p. of *pateo,* to lie open]. Patulous; open; exposed.

path-, patho-, -pathy [G. *pathos,* suffering, disease]. Combining forms meaning disease.

pathergasia (path-er-ga'zī-ah) [G. *pathos,* disease, + *ergasia,* work]. A physiologic or anatomical defect that limits normal emotional adjustment.

pathergy (path'er-jĭ) [G. *pathos,* disease, + *ergon,* work]. A term suggested to include reactions of all kinds resulting from a state of altered activity, both allergic (immune) and nonallergic.

path'finder. A filiform bougie for introduction through a narrow stricture to serve as a guide for the passage of a larger sound or catheter.

patho-. See path-.

path'oanat'omy. Anatomical *pathology.*

path'obiol'ogy. Pathology with emphasis more on the biological than on the medical aspects.

path'oclis'is [patho- + G. *klisis,* bending, proneness]. A specific tendency toward sensitivity to special toxins; a tendency for toxins to attack certain organs.

pathogen (path'o-jen) [patho- + G. *-gen,* to produce]. Any virus, microorganism, or other substance causing disease.

pathogenesis (path'o-jen'ĕ-sis) [patho- + G. *genesis,* production]. Nosogenesis; the mode of origin or development of any disease or morbid process.

pathogen'ic, pathogenet'ic. Morbific; nosogenic; nosopoietic; causing disease.

pathogenicity (path'o-jĕ-nis'ĭ-tĭ). The condition of being pathogenic or of causing disease.

pathognomonic (pă-thog-no-mon'ik) [patho- + G. *gnōmē,* a mark, a sign]. Characteristic or indicative of a disease; denoting especially one or more typical symptoms.

pathologic, pathological (path-o-log'ik, -ik-al). Pertaining to pathology; morbid; diseased; resulting from disease.

pathol'ogist. A specialist pathology and practices chiefly in the laboratory as a consultant to clinical colleagues.

pathology (pă-thol'o-jĭ) [patho- + G. *logos,* study, treatise]. The medical science and specialty practice concerned with all aspects of disease, but with special reference to the essential nature, causes, and development of abnormal conditions, as well as the structural and functional changes that result from the disease processes.

anatomical p., pathological anatomy; the subspecialty of p. that pertains to the gross and microscopic study of organs and tissues removed for biopsy or during postmortem examination.

cellular p., (1) the interpretation of diseases in terms of cellular alterations, *i.e.,* the ways in which cells fail to maintain homeostasis; (2) sometimes used as a synonym for cytopathology.

clinical p., (1) in a strict sense, any part of the medical practice of p. as it pertains to the care of patients; (2) the subspecialty in p. concerned with the theoretical and technical aspects of laboratory technology as pertains to the diagnosis and prevention of disease.

comparative p., the p. of diseases of animals, especially in relation to human p.

oral p., the branch of dentistry concerned with the etiology, pathogenesis, and clinical, gross, and microscopic aspects of disease of oral and paraoral structures including oral soft tissues and mucous membranes, the teeth, jaws and salivary glands.

speech p., the science concerned with functional and organic speech defects and disorders.

surgical p., a field in anatomical p., concerned with examination of tissues removed from living patients for the purpose of diagnosis of disease and guidance in the care of patients.

pathomimesis (path'o-mĭ-me'sis) [patho- + G. *mimēsis,* imitation]. Mimicry of disease, whether intentional or unconscious.

path'ophysiol'ogy. Derangement or alteration of function seen in disease.

pathopsychology (path-o-si-kol'o-jĭ) [patho- + psychology]. The study of deviations from normal psychological processes.

patho'sis [patho- + G. *-osis,* condition]. A state of disease, a diseased condition, or disease entity.

path'way. **1.** A collection of axons establishing a conduction route for nerve impulses from one group of nerve cells to another group or to an effector organ composed of muscle or gland cells. **2.** Any sequence of chemical reactions leading from one compound to another; if taking place in living tissue, usually referred to as a **biochemical p.**

Embden-Meyerhof p., the anaerobic glycolytic p. by which glucose (most notably in muscle) is converted to lactic acid.

pentose phosphate p., Dickens shunt; a secondary p. for the oxidation of glucose, generating reducing power (NADPH) in the cytoplasm outside the mitochondria and synthesizing pentoses; does not occur in skeletal muscle.

-pathy. See path-.

patient (pa'shent) [L. *patiens,* pres. p. of *patior,* to suffer]. One who is suffering from a disease or disorder and is under treatment for it; not to be confused with "case."

patrilineal (pat-rĭ-lin'e-al) L. *pater,* father, + *linea,* line]. Related to descent through the male line.

patulous (pat'u-lus) [L. *patulus,* fr. *pateo,* to lie open]. Patent.

paucisynaptic (paw'sĭ-sĭ-nap'tik) [L. *paucus,* few, + synapse, *q.v.*]. Oligosynaptic.

pause (pawz) [G. *pausis,* cessation]. Temporary stop.

compensatory p., the p. following an extrasystole, when long enough to compensate for the prematurity of the extrasystole.

postextrasystolic p., the somewhat prolonged cycle immediately following an extrasystole.

preautomatic p., a temporary p. in cardiac activity before an automatic pacemaker escapes. See also escape.

sinus p., a spontaneous interruption in the regular sinus rhythm, the p. lasting for a period that is not an exact multiple of the sinus cycle.

Pb Lead (plumbum).

PBG Porphobilinogen.

PBI Protein-bound *iodine.*

p.c. L. *post cibum,* after meals.

PCB Polychlorinated biphenyl, an industrial carcinogen.

PCO₂, pCO₂ Partial pressure (tension) of carbon dioxide.

PCP Phencyclidine.

Pd Palladium.

p.d. Prism *diopter.*

PDLL Poorly differentiated lymphocytic *lymphoma.*

pearl. **1.** A small hollow sphere of thin glass containing amyl nitrite or other fluid for inhalation; the p. is crushed in a handkerchief and its contents are inhaled. **2.** One of a number of small tough masses of mucus occurring in the sputum in asthma.

epithelial p., keratin p.

Epstein's p.'s, multiple small white epithelial inclusion cysts found in the midline of the palate in most newborn infants; probably developmental in origin.

keratin p., epithelial p. or nest; a focus of central keratinization within concentric layers of abnormal squamous cells; seen in squamous cell carcinoma.

peccant (pek'ant) [L. *peccans(-ant-),* pres. p. of *pecco,* to sin]. Morbid; unhealthy; producing disease.

pec'ten [L. comb]. **1** [NA]. A structure with comblike processes or projections.

p. ana'lis [NA], anal p., the middle third of the anal canal.

p. os'sis pu'bis [NA], pectineal line of the pubis, the continuation on the superior pubic ramus of the terminal line, forming a sharp ridge.

pectenitis (pek-ten-i'tis) [L. *pecten*, a comb, + *-itis*]. Inflammation of the sphincter ani.

pecteno'sis. Exaggerated enlargement of the pecten band.

pec'tinate. Pectiniform; combed; comb-shaped.

pectineal (pek-tin'e-al). Ridged; relating to the os pubis or to any comblike structure.

pectin'iform. Pectinate.

pec'toral [L. *pectoralis*; fr. *pectus*, breast bone]. Relating to the chest.

pectoriloquy (pek-to-ril'o-kwĭ) [L.*pectus*, chest, + *loquor*, to speak]. Transmission of the voice sound through the pulmonary structures, so that it is audible with exceptional clarity on auscultation of the chest; it indicates either consolidation of the lung parenchyma or the presence of a large cavity.

pectus, pl. **pec'tora** (pek'tus) [L.] [NA]. The thorax; the chest; especially the anterior wall, the breast.

p. carina'tum, pigeon or chicken breast; a flattening of the chest on either side with forward projection of the sternum resembling the keel of a boat.

p. excava'tum, p. recurva'tum, funnel breast or chest; a hollow at the lower part of the chest caused by a backward displacement of the xiphoid cartilage.

ped-, pedi-, pedo-. **1** [G. *pais*, child]. Combining forms denoting child. **2** [L. *pes*, foot]. Combining forms denoting feet.

ped'al [L. *pedalis*, fr. *pes*(*ped-*), a foot]. Relating to the feet, or to any structure called pes.

pederasty (ped'er'as'tĭ) [G. *paiderastia*; fr. *pais* (*paid*), boy, + *eraō*, to long for]. Anal intercourse, especially when practiced on boys.

pedesis (pe-de'sis) [G. *pēdēsis*, a leaping]. Brownian *movement*.

pedi-. See ped-.

pediatric (pe-dī-at'rik) [ped- (1) + G. *iatrikos*, relating to medicine]. Relating to pediatrics.

pediatrician (pe'dī-ă-trish'an). A specialist in pediatrics.

pediatrics (pe-dī-at'riks) [ped- (1) + G. *iatreia*, medical treatment]. The medical specialty concerned with the development and care of children and the diagnosis and treatment of their diseases.

pedicel (ped'ĭ-sel) [Mod. L. *pedicellus*, dim. of L. *pes*, foot]. Foot process; footplate (2); the secondary process of a podocyte which helps form the visceral capsule of a renal corpuscle.

pedicellate. (ped'ĭ-sel-lāt). Pediculate.

pedicellation (ped-ĭ-sel-la'shun). Formation of a pedicle or peduncle.

pedicle (ped'ĭ-kl) [L. *pediculus*, dim. of *pes*, foot]. **1.** Pediculus. **2.** Peduncle (2); a stalk by which a nonsessile tumor is attached to normal tissue. **3.** A stalk through which a skin flap receives nourishment until its transfer to another site results in the nourishment coming from that site.

pedicular (pĕ-dik'u-lar) [L. *pedicularis*]. Relating to lice.

pediculate (pĕ-dik'u-lāt) [L. *pedicutatus*]. Pedicellate; pedunculate; not sessile, having a pedicle or peduncle.

pedicula'tion [L. *pediculus*, louse]. Infestation with lice.

pedic'uli [L.]. Plural of pediculus.

pediculicide (pĕ-dik'u-lĭ-sīd) [L. *pediculus*, louse, + *caedo*, to kill]. An agent used to destroy lice.

Pediculoi'des ventrico'sus [Mod. L. fr. L. *pediculus*, louse, + *venter*, belly]. *Acarus tritici*; the grain itch mite, a mite infesting straw or grain that causes an acarodermatitis.

pediculosis (pĕ-dik-u-lo'sis) [L. *pediculus*, louse, + G. *-osis*, condition]. The state of being infested with lice.

pedic'ulous. Infested with lice.

Pediculus (pĕ-dik'u-lus) [L.]. A genus of parasitic lice (family Pediculidae) that live in the hair and feed periodically on blood, including *P. humanus*, the species infecting man; *P. humanus* var. *capitis*, the head louse of man; *P. humanus* var. *corporis* (also called *P. vestimenti* or *P. corporis*), the body louse or clothes louse, which lives and lays eggs (nits) in clothing and feeds on the human body; and *P. pubis* (see *Pthirus pubis*).

pediculus, pl. **pediculi** (pĕ-dik'u-lus, -li) [L. pedicle] [NA]. Pedicle (1); a constricted portion or stalk.

pedigree (ped'ĭ-grē) [M.E. *pedegra* fr. O.Fr. *pie de grue*, foot of crane]. An ancestral line of descent, especially as diagrammed on a chart to show ancestral history to analyze mendelian inheritance.

pedo-. See ped-.

pedodontics, pedodontia (pe'do-don'tiks, -don'shī-ah) [ped-(1) + G. *odous*, tooth]. The branch of dentistry concerned with dental care and treatment of children.

pedodon'tist. A dentist who practices pedodontics.

pedodynamometer (ped'o-di-nă-mom'e-tur) [ped-(2) + G. *dynamis*, force, + *metron*, measure]. An instrument for measuring the strength of the leg muscles.

pedomorphism (pe'do-mor'fizm) [G. *pais* (*paid*), child, + *morphē*, form]. Description of adult behavior in terms appropriate to child behavior.

pedophilia (pe-do-fil'ĭ-ah) [G. *pais*, child, + *philos*, fond]. Fondness of children by an adult for sexual purposes.

pe'dophil'ic. Relating to or exhibiting pedophilia.

Pedoviridae (ped-o-vīr'ĭ-de). Provisional name for a family of bacterial viruses with short tails and genomes of double-stranded DNA; includes the T-7 phage group and other genera.

peduncle (pĕ-dung'kl, pe'dung-kl, ped'ung-kl) [Mod. L. *pedunculus*, dim. of *pes*, foot]. **1.** Pedunculus. **2.** Pedicle (2).

cerebellar p., *pedunculus* cerebellaris inferior, medius, and superior.

cerebral p., see *pedunculus* cerebri and *crus* cerebri.

p. of corpus callosum, *gyrus* subcallosus.

thalamic p., *pedunculus* thalami inferior, lateralis, and ventralis.

peduncular (pĕ-dung'ku-lar). Relating to a pedicle or peduncle.

pedunculate (pĕ-dung'ku-lāt). Pediculate.

pedunculotomy (pĕ-dung-ku-lot'o-mĭ) [peduncle + G. *tomē*, incision]. **1.** A total or partial section of a cerebral peduncle. **2.** (Mesencephalic) pyramidal *tractotomy*.

pedunculus, pl. **pedunculi** (pĕ-dung'ku-lus, -ku-li) [Mod. L. dim. of *pes*, foot] [NA]. Peduncle (1); a stalk or stem; in neuroanatomy, a variety of stalklike connecting structures in the brain, composed either exclusively of white matter or of white and gray matter.

p. cerebella'ris infe'rior [NA], inferior cerebellar peduncle; restiform body; a large bundle of nerve fibers extending up under the lateral recess of the rhomboid fossa, then curving steeply dorsalward into the cerebellum; made up of the dorsal spinocerebellar tract and the cerebellar afferents originating in the ipsilateral nucleus cuneatus accessorius, vestibular nuclei, lateral reticular nucleus, and in the contralateral inferior olive; also contains fibers from the nucleus fastigii of the cerebellum to the vestibular nuclei and medullary reticular formation.

p. cerebella'ris me'dius [NA], middle cerebellar peduncle; brachium pontis; the largest of three paired cerebellar peduncles, composed entirely of fibers that originate in the nuclei pontis, cross the midline in the pars basilaris pontis, and emerge on the oppostie side as a massive bundle arching dorsally along the lateral side of the pontine tegmentum into the cerebellum; distributed chiefly to the cortex of the cerebellar hemisphere.

p. cerebella'ris supe'rior [NA], superior cerebellar peduncle; brachium conjunctivum cerebelli; a large bundle of nerve fibers that originates from the nuclei dentatus and interpositus; a large part of the bundle terminates in the red nucleus; the remainder continues rostrally to the nuclei ventralis lateralis, ventralis anterior, and centralis lateralis of the thalamus.

p. cer'ebri [NA], cerebral peduncle; originally denoting either of the two halves of the midbrain (a relatively narrow "neck" connecting the forebrain to the hindbrain), later referring to the crus cerebri together with the midbrain tegmentum, and now used occasionally to indicate the crus cerebri (basis pedunculi): the massive bundle of corticofugal fibers on either side at the ventral surface of the midbrain.

p. of the pineal body, see habenula (2).

p. thal'ami infe'rior [NA], inferior thalamic peduncle; a large fiber bundle emerging from the anterior part of the thalamus in the ventral direction, many of its fibers establish a reciprocal connection of the mediodorsal nucleus of the thala-

mus with the orbital gyri of the frontal lobe, but numerous other fibers constitute a conduction system from the amygdala and olfactory cortex to the mediodorsal nucleus.

p. thal'ami latera'lis, lateral thalamic peduncle; the massive group of fibers that emerges from the laterodorsal side of the thalamus to join the corona radiata; reciprocally connects the lateral nucleus and the geniculate bodies of the thalamus with the corresponding regions of the cerebral cortex.

p. thal'ami ventra'lis, ventral thalamic peduncle; the massive system of fiber bundles emerging through the ventral, lateral, and anterior borders of the thalamus to join the internal capsule; contains the fibers reciprocally connecting the ventral thalamic nuclei with the precentral and postcentral gyri of the cerebral cortex.

PEEP Positive end-expiratory *pressure*.

peliosis (pe-lĭ-o'sis, pel'ĭ-) [G. *peliōsis*, a livid spot]. Purpura.

p. hep'atis, the presence throughout the liver of blood-filled cavities which may become lined by endothelium, or organized.

pellagra (pĕ-lag'rah, -la'grah) [It. *pelle*, skin, + *agro*, rough]. An affection characterized by gastrointestinal disturbances, erythema followed by desquamation, and nervous and mental disorders; may occur because of a poor diet, alcoholism, or some other disease upsetting nutrition; main cause is a deficiency of niacin.

pellag'rous. Relating to pellagra.

pellet (pel'et) [Fr. *pelote*; L. *pila*, a ball]. **1.** A pilule, or minute pill. **2.** A small rod-shaped or ovoid dosage form that is sterile and is composed essentially of pure steroid hormones in compressed form, intended for subcutaneous implantation in body tissues as a depot providing slow release of the hormone over an extended period of time.

pellicle (pel'ĭ-kl) [L. *pellicula,* dim of *pellis,* skin]. A film or scum on the surface of a liquid.

pellucid (pel-lu'sid) [L. *pellucidus*]. Allowing the passage of light.

pelta'tion [L. *pelta,* a light shield]. The prophylactic influence of inoculation with an antitoxic serum or with a vaccine.

pelvi-, pelvio-, pelvo-. Combining forms relating to the pelvis.

pel'vic. Relating to a pelvis.

pelvic direction. The curved line denoting the direction of the axis of the canal of the pelvis.

pelvicephalography (pel'vĭ-sef-ă-log'ră-fĭ) [pelvi- + G. *kephalē,* head, + *graphō,* to write]. Radiographic mensuration of the birth canal and of the fetal head.

pelvicephalometry (pel'vĭ-sef-ă-lom'ĕ-trĭ) [pelvi- + G. *kephalē,* head, + *metron,* measure]. Measurement of the pelvic diameters in relation to those of the fetal head.

pel'vifixa'tion. Surgical attachment of a floating pelvic organ to the wall of the cavity.

pelvilithotomy (pel'vĭ-lĭ-thot'o-mĭ) [pelvi- + G. *lithos,* stone, + *tomē,* incision]. Pyelolithotomy; operative removal of a calculus from the kidney through an incision in the renal pelvis.

pelvim'eter. An instrument shaped like calipers for measuring the diameters of the pelvis.

pelvimetry (pel-vim'ĕ-trĭ) [pelvi- + G. *metron,* measure]. Measurement of the diameters of the pelvis.

pelvio-. See pelvi-.

pel'vioplasty [pelvio- + G. *plassō,* to form]. Symphysiotomy or pubiotomy for enlargement of the pelvic outlet.

pelviotomy (pel-vĭ-ot'o-mĭ) [pelvio- + G. *tomē,* incision]. **1.** Symphysiotomy. **2.** Pubiotomy. **3.** An incision into the pelvis of the kidney.

pelviperitonitis (pel'vĭ-pĕr-ĭ-to-ni'tis). Pelvic *peritonitis.*

pelvis, pl. **pelves** (pel'vis, pel'vēz) [L. basin]. **1** [NA]. The cup-shaped ring of bone, with its ligaments, at the lower end of the trunk, formed of the os coxae (the pubic bone, ilium, and ischium) on either side and in front, and the sacrum, and coccyx posteriorly. **2.** Any basin-like or cup-shaped cavity, as the p. of the kidney.

    android p., a masculine or funnel-shaped p.

    anthropoid p., an apelike p., with a long anteroposterior diameter and a narrow transverse diameter.

    assimilation p., a deformity in which the transverse processes of the last lumbar vertebra are fused with the sacrum, or the last sacral with the first coccygeal body.

    beaked p., osteomalacic p.

    brachypellic p., a p. in which the transverse diameter is longer than the anteroposterior diameter.

    contracted p., a p. with less than normal measurements in any diameter.

    cordate p., cordiform p., a p. with sacrum projecting forward between the ilia, giving to the brim a heart shape.

    dolichopellic p., a p. in which the anteroposterior diameter is longer than the transverse.

    false p., p. major.

    flat p., a p. in which the anteroposterior diameter is uniformly contracted, the sacrum being dislocated forward between the iliac bones.

    frozen p., a condition in which the true p. is indurated throughout, especially by carcinoma.

    funnel-shaped p., a p. in which the inlet dimensions are normal, but the outlet is contracted in the transverse or in both transverse and anteroposterior diameters.

    gynecoid p., the normal female p.

    p. jus'to ma'jor, a gynecoid p. with greater than normal measurements in all diameters.

    p. jus'to mi'nor, a gynecoid p. with all its diameters smaller than normal.

    juvenile p., a p. justo minor in which the bones are slender.

    kyphotic p., backward curvature of lumbar spine causing contraction of pelvic measurements.

    p. ma'jor [NA], large or false p.; the expanded portion of the p. above the brim.

    masculine p., **(1)** a p. justo minor in which the bones are large and heavy; **(2)** in a female, a slight degree of funnel-shaped p. in which the shape approximates that of the male p.

    mesatipellic p., a p. in which the anteroposterior and transverse diameters are equal or the transverse diameter is not more than 1 cm longer than the anteroposterior diameter.

    p. mi'nor [NA], small or true p.; the cavity of the p. below the brim or superior aperture.

    Nägele's p., an obliquely contracted or unilateral synostotic p., marked by arrest of development of one lateral half of the sacrum, usually ankylosis of the sacroiliac joint on that side, rotation of the sacrum toward the same side, and deviation of the symphysis pubis to the opposite side.

    osteomalacic p., beaked p.; a pelvic deformity in osteomalacia, in which the pressure of the trunk on the sacrum and lateral pressure of the femoral heads produce a pelvic aperture that is three-cornered or has the shape of a heart of cloverleaf, while the pubic bone becomes beak-shaped.

    Otto p., an inward bulging of the acetabulum causing the prominence of the femur to be reduced instead of being increased as in rheumatoid arthritis.

    platypellic p., platypelloid p., a flat oval p., in which the transverse diameter is longer than the anteroposterior diameter.

    Prague p., spondylolisthetic p.

    rachitic p., a contracted and deformed p., most commonly a flat p., occurring from rachitic softening of the bones in early life.

    p. rena'lis [NA], **renal p.,** a flattened funnel-shaped expansion of the upper end of the ureter receiving the calices of the kidney, the apex being continuous with the ureter.

    Robert's p., a p. that is narrowed transversely due to the almost entire absence of the alae of the sacrum.

    Rokitansky's p., spondylolisthetic p.

    scoliotic p., a deformed p. associated with lateral curvature of the spine.

    split p., a p. in which the symphysis pubis is absent, the pelvic bones being separated; usually associated with exstrophy of the bladder.

    spondylolisthetic p., Prague or Rokitansky's p.; a p. whose brim is more or less occluded by a dislocation forward of the body of the lower lumbar vertebra.

    true p., p. minor.

pelvit'omy. Pelviotomy.

pelvo-. See pelvi-.

pel'vospondyli'tis ossif'icans [L. *pelvis,* basin, + G. *spondylos,* vertebra, + *-itis;* L. *os,* bone, + *facere,* to make]. Deposit of bony substance between the vertebrae of the sacrum.

pemphigoid (pem'fĭ-goyd) [G. *pemphix*, blister, + *eidos*, resemblance]. **1.** Resembling pemphigus. **2.** A disease resembling pemphigus but significantly distinguishable histologically (nonacantholytic) and clinically (generally benign course).

benign mucosal p., a chronic disease that produces adhesions and progressive cicatrization and shrinkage of the conjunctivae and nonacantholytic vesicles, and denuded areas of oral mucosa.

bullous p., a chronic, generally benign disease, most commonly of old age, characterized by tense nonacantholytic bullae in which serum antibodies are localized to the epidermal basement membrane, causing detachment of the entire epidermis.

ocular p., cicatricial *conjunctivitis.*

pemphigus (pem'fĭ-gus) [G. *pemphix*, a blister]. General term used to designate the chronic bullous diseases: p. foliaceus, p. erythematosus, or p. vegetans; also used with a modifying adjective to designate a variety of blistering skin diseases.

p. erythemato'sus, an eruption involving the scalp, face, and trunk; the lesions are scaling erythematous macules and blebs, combining the clinical features of both lupus erythematosus and p. vulgaris.

familial benign chronic p., Hailey and Hailey disease; recurrent eruption of vesicles and bullae that become scaling and crusted lesions with vesicular borders, predominantly of the neck, groin, and axillary regions; irregular autosomal dominant inheritance.

p. folia'ceus, a generally chronic form of p. in which extensive exfoliative dermatitis, with no perceptible blistering, may be present in addition to the bullae.

p. gangreno'sus, bullous *impetigo* of the newborn.

p. veg'etans, (1) a form of p. vulgaris in which vegetations develop on the eroded surfaces left by ruptured bullae; new bullae continue to form; (2) Hallopeau's disease (2); a chronic benign vegetating form of p., with lesions commonly in the axillae and perineum.

p. vulga'ris, p. in which cutaneous flaccid acantholytic suprabasal bullae and oral mucosal erosions may be localized before becoming generalized; the blisters break easily, leaving new non-breaking areas; results from the action of autoimmune antibodies that localize to intercellular sites of stratified squamous epithelium.

pen'etrance [see penetration]. The frequency, usually expressed as a percentage, with which a mutant gene produces its characteristic effect in those individuals possessing it.

penetrom'eter. A device for measuring the penetrating power of x-rays.

-penia [G. *penia*, poverty]. Suffix denoting deficiency.

penicil'lamine. A degradation product of penicillin; a chelating agent used in the treatment of lead poisoning, hepatolenticular degeneration, and cystinuria, and in the removal of excess copper in Wilson's disease.

penicillin (pen-ĭ-sil'in) [L. *penicillus*, paint brush]. **1.** Originally, an antibiotic substance obtained from cultures of the molds *Penicillium notatum* or *P. chrysogenum*. **2.** One of a family of natural or synthetic variants, mainly bacteriostatic in action, but also slightly bactericidal, especially active against Gram-positive organisms, and with a particularly low toxic action on animal tissue.

p. G (or II), $R = C_6H_5CH_2-$; the most commonly used p. compound, comprising 85% of the p. salts (sodium, potassium, aluminum, and procaine).

p. V, $R = C_6H_5OCH_2-$; a crystalline, nonhydroscopic acid, very stable even in high humidity, that resists destruction by gastric juice.

penicil'linase. 1. Cephalosporinase; an enzyme that brings about the hydrolysis of penicillin to penicilloic acid; found in most staphylococcus strains that are naturally resistant to penicillin. **2.** A purified enzyme preparation obtained from cultures of a strain of *Bacillus cereus;* formerly used in the treatment of slowly developing or delayed penicillin reactions.

Penicillium (pen-ĭ-sil'ĭ-um) [see penicillin]. A genus of fungi (class Ascomycetes, order Aspergillales), species of which yield several antibiotic substances and biologicals.

penicillus, pl. **penicilli** (pen-ĭ-sil'us, -sil'ĭ) [L. paint brush]. **1** [NA]. One of the tufts formed by the repeated subdivision of the minute arterial twigs in the spleen. **2.** In fungi, one of the complex systems of branches bearing conidia-producing organs in *Penicillium* species.

penile (pe'nĭl). Relating to the penis.

pe'nis [L. tail] [NA]. Phallus; the male organ of copulation, formed by three columns of erectile tissue, two arranged laterally on the dorsum (corpora cavernosa) and one median below (corpus spongiosum); the extremity (glans p.) is formed by an expansion of the corpus spongiosum, covered by a free fold of skin (preputium).

penischisis (pe-nis'kĭ-sis) [L. *penis*, + G. *schisis*, fissure]. A fissure of the penis resulting in an abnormal opening into the urethra, either above (epispadia), below (hypospadia), or to one side (paraspadia).

peni'tis. Phallitis; inflammation of the penis.

pen'nate [L. *pennatus*, fr. *penna*, feather]. Penniform; feathered; resembling a feather.

pen'niform [L. *penna*, feather, + *forma*, form]. Pennate.

penta- [G. *pente*, five]. Combining form denoting five.

pentet'ic acid. Diethylenetriamine pentaacetic acid; a pentaacetic acid triamine with affinity for heavy metals; used as the calcium sodium chelate in the treatment of iron-storage disease and poisoning from heavy metals and radioactive metals.

pen'tose. A monosaccharide containing five carbon atoms in the molecule.

pentosu'ria. The excretion of one or more pentoses in the urine.

    alimentary p., the urinary excretion of L -arabinose and L-xylose, as the result of the excessive ingestion of fruits containing these pentoses.

    essential p., primary p., a benign heritable disorder in which the urinary output of L-xylulose is 1 to 4 g per 24 hr; autosomal recessive inheritance.

pentyl (pen'til). Amyl.

peotillomania (pe'o-til-o-ma'nĭ-ah) [G. *peos,* penis, + *tillō,* to pull out (of hair), + *mania,* frenzy]. A nervous tic consisting of a constant pulling of the penis.

peplomer (pep'lo-mer). A subunit of the peplos of a virion, the assemblage of which produces the complete peplos.

peplos (pep'lōs) [G. an outer garment worn by women]. The coat or envelope of lipoprotein material that surrounds certain virions.

pep'sin [G. *pepsis,* digestion]. Former term for **pepsin A,** the principal digestive enzyme (protease) of the gastric juice, formed from pepsinogen; it hydrolyzes peptide bonds at low pH values, preferably adjacent to phenylalanine and leucine residues, thus reducing proteins to smaller molecules (proteoses and peptones).

pepsinogen (pep-sin'o-jen) [pepsin + G. *-gen,* producing]. Propepsin; a proenzyme formed and secreted by the chief cells of the gastric mucosa; acidity of gastric juice and pepsin itself remove 42 amino acid residues from p. to form active pepsin.

pep'tic [G. *peptikos,* fr. *peptō,* to digest]. Relating to the stomach, to gastric digestion, or to pepsin A.

pep'tidase. An enzyme capable of hydrolyzing one of the peptide links of a peptide.

pep'tide. A compound of two or more amino acids in which the α-carboxyl group of one is united with the α-amino group of the other, with the elimination of a molecule of water, thus forming a p. bond, $-CO-NH-$.

peptidergic (pep-tĭ-der'jik) [peptide + G. *ergon,* work]. Referring to nerve cells or fibers believed to employ small peptide molecules as their neurotransmitter.

pep'tidogly'can. A compound containing amino acids (or peptides) linked to sugars, with the latter proponderant.

peptidoid (pep'tĭ-doyd). A condensation product of two amino acids involving at least one condensing group other than the α-carboxyl or α-amino groups.

peptidolytic (pep'tĭ-do-lit'ik) [peptide + G. *lytikos,* solvent]. Causing the cleavage or digestion of peptides.

peptogenic, peptogenous (pep-to-jen'ik, pep-toj'ĕ-nus). **1.** Producing peptones. **2.** Promoting digestion.

peptolysis (pep-tol'ĭ-sis). The hydrolysis of peptones.

peptolyt'ic. 1. Pertaining to peptolysis. **2.** Denoting an enzyme or other agent that hydrolyses peptones.

pep'tone. Descriptive term applied to intermediate polypeptide products formed in partial hydrolysis of proteins; generally soluble in water, diffusible, and not coagulable by heat.

pepton'ic. Relating to or containing peptone.

pep'toniza'tion. Conversion, by enzymic action, of native protein into soluble peptone.

pep'totox'in. 1. A toxic substance obtained from peptone. **2.** A poisonous product formed at a certain stage in the digestion of protein and disappearing at a later stage.

per- [L. through, throughout, extremely]. **1.** Prefix denoting through, conveying intensity. **2.** In chemistry, a prefix denoting: 1) more or most, with respect to the amount of a given element or radical contained in a compound; 2) the degree of substitution for hydrogen.

peracid (per-as'id). An acid containing a peroxide group $(-O-OH)$.

per a'num [L.]. By or through the anus.

percept (per'sept) [L. *perceptum,* a thing perceived]. **1.** That which is perceived; the complete mental image, formed by the process of perception, of an object present in space. **2.** In clinical psychology, a single unit of perceptual report, such as one of the responses to an inkblot in the Rorschach test.

perception (per-sep'shun). The mental process of becoming aware of or recognizing an object; primarily cognitive rather than affective or conative, although all three aspects are manifested.

    depth p., the ability to judge depth or distance in space by vision.

    extrasensory p. (ESP), p. by means other than through the ordinary senses; *e.g.,* telepathy, clairvoyance, precognition.

percep'tive. Relating to or having the power of perception.

perceptiv'ity. The power of perception.

perchloric acid (per-klor'ik). $HClO_4$; the highest in oxygen content of the series of chlorine acids.

percolation (per'ko-la'shun) [L. *percolatio,* fr. per- + *colare,* to strain]. **1.** Filtration. **2.** Extraction of the soluble portion of a solid mixture by passing a solvent liquid through it.

per contiguum (per kon-tig'u-um) [per- + L. *contiguus,* touching, fr. *tango,* to touch]. In contiguity; touching; denoting the mode of spread of an inflammation or other morbid process that passes into an adjacent contiguous structure.

per continuum (per kon-tin'u-um) [per- + L. *continuus,* holding together, continuous]. In continuity; continuous; denoting the mode of spread of an inflammation or other morbid process from one part to another through continuous tissue.

percuss (per-kuss') [see percussion]. To perform percussion.

percussion (per-kush'un) [L. *percussio,* fr. *per-cutio,* pp. *-cussus,* to beat, fr. *quatio,* to shake, beat]. A diagnostic procedure designed to determine the density of a part by means of tapping the surface with the finger or a plessor.

auscultatory p., auscultation of the chest or other part at the same time that p. is made.

immediate p., direct p.; the striking of the part under examination directly with the finger or a plessor, without the intervention of another finger or plessimeter.

mediate p., p. effected by the intervention of a finger or a thin plate of ivory or other substance (plessimeter) between the striking finger or hammer and the part percussed.

palpatory p., finger p. concerned with the resistance of the tissues under the finger as well as upon the sound elicited.

percussor (per-kus'sor). Plessor.

percutaneous (per-ku-ta'ne-us). Denoting the passage of substances through unbroken skin, as in absorption by inunction.

perencephaly (pe-ren-sef'a-lĭ) [G. *pēra*, a purse, a wallet, + *enkephalos*, brain]. A condition marked by one or more cerebral cysts.

perfec'tionism. A tendency to set rigid high standards of performance for oneself.

per'forated [L. *perforatus*, fr. *per-foro*, pp. *-atus*, to bore through]. Pierced with one or more holes.

perforation (per-fo-ra'shun) [see perforated]. An abnormal opening in a hollow organ or viscus.

perfusion (per-fu'zhun) [L. *perfusio*, fr. per- + *fusio*, a pouring]. Passage of blood or other fluid through a vascular bed.

peri- [G. around]. Prefix denoting around, about.

periadenitis (pĕr'ĭ-ad-ĕ-ni'tis) [peri- + G. *adēn*, gland, + *itis*, inflammation]. Inflammation of the tissues surrounding a gland.

p. muco'sa necrot'ica recur'rens, Sutton's disease (2); a severe form of recurrent aphthous stomatitis, marked by recurrent attacks of aphtha-like lesions that begin as small, firm nodules which then enlarge, ulcerate, and heal by scar formation, leaving numerous atrophied scars on the oral mucosa.

periangitis (pĕr'ĭ-an-ji'tis) [peri- + G. *angeion*, a vessel, + *-itis*, inflammation]. Perivasculitis; inflammation of the adventitia of a blood vessel or of the tissues surrounding it or a lymphatic vessel.

periaortitis (pĕr'ĭ-a-or-ti'tis). Inflammation of the adventitia of the aorta and of the tissues surrounding it.

periapical (pĕr'ĭ-ap'ĭ-kal). **1.** At or around the apex of a root of a tooth. **2.** Denoting the periodontal membrane and adjacent bone.

periappendicitis (pĕr'ĭ-ă-pen-dĭ-si'tis). Inflammation of the tissue surrounding the vermiform appendix.

periarteritis (pĕr'ĭ-ar-ter-i'tis). Inflammation of the outer coat, or adventitia, of an artery.

p. nodo'sa, *polyarteritis* nodosa.

periarthritis (pĕr'ĭ-ar-thri'tis). Exarteritis; inflammation of the parts surrounding a joint.

periarticular (pĕr'ĭ-ar-tik'u-lar). Surrounding a joint.

periaxillary (pĕr'ĭ-ak'sĭ-lĕr-ĭ). Around the axilla.

peribronchiolitis (pĕr'ĭ-brong-kī'-o-li'tis). Inflammation of the tissues surrounding the bronchioles.

peribronchitis (pĕr'ĭ-brong-ki'tis). Inflammation of the tissues surrounding the bronchi or bronchial tubes.

pericardia (pĕr'ĭ-kar'dĭ-ah). Plural of pericardium.

pericar'diac, pericar'dial. 1. Surrounding the heart. **2.** Relating to the pericardium.

pericardiectomy (pĕr'ĭ-kar-dĭ-ek'to-mĭ) [pericardium + G. *ektomē*, excision]. Excision of a portion of the pericardium.

pericardiocentesis (pĕr-ĭ-kar'dĭ-o-sen-te'sis) [peri- + G. *kardia*, heart, + *kentēsis*, puncture]. Paracentesis of the pericardium.

pericar'dioperʹitoneʹal. Relating to the pericardial and peritoneal cavities.

pericar'diophren'ic [pericardium + G. *phrēn*, diaphragm]. Relating to the pericardium and the diaphragm.

pericar'diopleur'al. Relating to the pericardial and pleural cavities.

pericardiorrhaphy (pĕr'ĭ-kar-dĭ-or'ă-fĭ) [pericardium + G. *rhaphē*, suture]. Suture of the pericardium.

pericardiostomy (pĕr'ĭ-kar-dĭ-os'to-mĭ) [pericardium + G. *stoma*, mouth]. Establishment of an opening into the pericardium.

pericardiotomy (pĕr'ĭ-kar-dĭ-ot'o-mĭ) [pericardium + G. *tomē*, incision]. Incision into the pericardium.

per'icardit'ic. Relating to pericarditis.

per'icardi'tis. Inflammation of the pericardium.

adhesive p., p. with adhesions between the two pericardial layers, between the pericardium and heart, or between the pericardium and neighboring structures.

constrictive p., tuberculous or other infection of the pericardium, with thickening of the membrane and constriction of the cardiac chambers.

fibrinous p., hairy heart; acute p. with fibrinous exudate.

internal adhesive p., concretio cordis.

p. oblit'erans, inflammation of the pericardium leading to adhesion of the two layers, obliterating the sac.

pericardium, pl. **pericardia** (pĕr-ĭ-kar'dĭ-um, -ah) [L. fr. G. *pericardion*, the membrane around the heart] [NA]. Theca cordis; heart sac; the fibroserous membrane covering the heart and beginning of the great vessels; consists of two layers: visceral (epicardium), immediately surrounding the heart, and the outer parietal layer, forming the sac, composed of strong fibrous tissue (**p. fibrosum**) lined with serous membrane (**p. serosum**).

pericementitis (pĕr'ĭ-se-men-ti'tis). An inflammatory reaction of the periodontium and its adjacent structures. See also periodontitis.

pericholangitis (pĕr-ĭ-ko-lan-ji'tis) [peri- + G. *cholē*, bile, + *angeion*, vessel, + *-itis*, inflammation]. Inflammation of the tissues around the bile ducts.

perichondral, perichondrial (pĕr-ĭ-kon'dral, -kon'drĭ-al). Relating to the perichondrium.

perichondritis (pĕr′ĭ-kon-dri′tis). Inflammation of the perichondrium.

perichondrium (pĕr-ĭ-kon′drĭ-um) [peri- + G. *chondros,* cartilage]. [NA].The dense, irregular connective tissue membrane around cartilage.

perichrome (pĕr′ĭ-krōm) [peri- + G. *chrōma,* a color]. Denoting a nerve cell in which the chromophil substance, or stainable material, is scattered throughout the cytoplasm.

pericolitis, pericolonitis (pĕr-ĭ-ko-li′tis, -co′lon-i′tis). Inflammation of the connective tissue or peritoneum surrounding the colon.

pericolpi′tis [peri- + G. *kolpos,* bosom (vagina), + *-itis,* inflammation]. Perivaginitis.

pericoronitis (pĕr′ĭ-kor-o-ni′tis) [peri- + L. *corona,* crown, + G. *-itis,* inflammation]. Operculitis; inflammation around the crown of a tooth, usually of an incompletely erupted mandibular third molar.

per′icrani′tis. Inflammation of the pericranium.

pericranium (pĕr-ĭ-kra′nĭ-um) [peri- + G. *kranion,* skull] [NA]. The periosteum of the skull.

pericystic (pĕr-ĭ-sis′tik) [peri- + G. *kystis,* bladder]. Perivesical; Surrounding the urinary bladder, the gallbladder, or a cyst.

pericystitis (pĕr′ĭ-sis-ti′tis). Inflammation of the tissues surrounding a bladder, especially the urinary bladder.

pericyte (pĕr′ĭ-sit) [peri- + G. *kytos,* cell]. Adventitial cell; one of the slender, relatively undifferentiated, connective tissue cells in close relationship to the outside of the capillary wall.

per′iderm, perider′ma [peri- + G. *derma,* skin]. Epitrichium; the outermost layer of the epidermis of the embryo and fetus up to the sixth month of intrauterine life.

peridesmitis (pĕr′ĭ-dez-mi′tis) [peri- + G. *desmos,* band, + *-itis,* inflammation]. Inflammation of the connective tissue surrounding a ligament.

peridesmium (pĕr-ĭ-dez′mĭ-um) [peri- + G. *desmion* (*desmos*), band]. The connective tissue membrane surrounding a ligament.

perididymis (pĕr-ĭ-did′ĭ-mis) [G. *didymos,* twin, pl. *didymoi,* testes]. The thick white fibrous membrane forming the outer coat of the testis.

perididymitis (pĕr′ĭ-did-ĭ-mi′tis). Inflammation of the perididymis.

per′idiverticuli′tis. Inflammation of the tissues around an intestinal diverticulum.

peridu′odeni′tis. Inflammation around the duodenum.

periencephalitis (pĕr′ĭ-en-sef′ă-li′tis) [peri- + G. *enkephalos,* brain]. Inflammation of the cerebral membranes.

perienteritis (pĕr′ĭ-en-ter-i′tis). Seroenteritis; inflammation of the peritoneal coat of the intestine.

periesophagitis (pĕr′ĭ-e-sof-ă-ji′tis). Inflammation of the tissues surrounding the esophagus.

perifolliculitis (pĕr′ĭ-fŏ-lik-u-li′tis). The presence of an inflammatory infiltrate surrounding hair follicles, frequently in conjunction with folliculitis.

per′igastri′tis [peri- + G. *gastēr,* belly, stomach, + *-itis,* inflammation]. Inflammation of the peritoneal coat of the stomach.

periglot′tis [G. *periglottis,* covering of the tongue]. The mucous membrane of the tongue.

perihepatitis (pĕr-ĭ-hep-ă-ti′tis) [peri- + G. *hēpar,* liver, + *-itis,* inflammation]. Inflammation of the serous, or peritoneal, covering of the liver.

perijejunitis (pĕr′ĭ-jē-ju-ni′tis). Inflammation around the jejunum.

perikaryon, pl. **perikarya** (pĕr-ĭ-kăr′ĭ-on, -ah) [peri- + G. *karyon,* kernel]. **1.** The cytoplasm around the nucleus, such as that of the cell body of nerve cells. **2.** The body of the odontoblast, excluding the dentinal fiber. **3.** The cell body of the nerve cell, as distinguished from its axon and dendrites.

perilabyrinthitis (pĕr′ĭ-lab′ĭ-rin-thi′tis). Inflammation of the parts about the labyrinth.

perilaryngitis (pĕr′ĭ-lăr-in-ji′tis). Inflammation of the tissues around the larynx.

per′ilymph. Perilympha.

perilympha (pĕr-ĭ-lim′fah) [peri- + L. *lympha,* a clear fluid (lymph)] [NA]. Perilymph; the fluid contained within the osseus labyrinth, surrounding and protecting the membranous labyrinth.

perilymphangitis (pĕr′ĭ-lim-fan-ji′tis). Inflammation of the tissues surrounding a lymphatic vessel.

perilymphatic (pĕr′ĭ-lim-fat′ik). **1.** Surrounding a lymphatic structure (node or vessel). **2.** The spaces and tissues surrounding the membranous labyrinth of the inner ear.

perimeningitis (pĕr′ĭ-men-in-ji′tis). Pachymeningitis.

perim′eter [G. *perimetros,* circumference, fr. *peri,* around, + *metron,* measure]. **1.** A circumference, edge, or border. **2.** An instrument used to measure field of vision.

perimet′ric. 1 [G. *peri,* around, + *mētra,* uterus]. Periuterine; surrounding the uterus; relating to the perimetrium. **2** [G. *perimetros,* circumference]. Relating to the circumference of any part or area. **3.** Relating to perimetry.

perimetrit′ic. Relating to or marked by perimetritis.

perimetritis (pĕr′ĭ-me-tri′tis) [perimetrium + G. *-itis,* inflammation]. Metroperitonitis.

perimetrium, pl. **perimetria** (pĕr′ĭ-me′trĭ-um, -me′trĭ-ah) [peri- + G. *mētra,* uterus] [NA]. The serous (peritoneal) coat of the uterus.

perim′etry [G. *perimetros,* circumference]. The determination of the limits of the visual field.

perimyelitis (pĕr′ĭ-mi-ĕ-li′tis). Endosteitis.

perimyositis (pĕr′ĭ-mi-o-si′tis). Perimysiitis (2); inflammation of the loose cellular tissue surrounding a muscle.

perimysial (pĕr′ĭ-mis′ĭ-al, -miz′ĭ-al). Relating to the perimysium; surrounding a muscle.

perimysiitis, perimysitis (pĕr′ĭ-mis-ĭ-i′tis, -mĭ-si′tis). **1.** Myofibrosiitis; inflammation of the perimysium. **2.** Perimyositis.

perimysium, pl. **perimysia** (pĕr′ĭ-mis′ĭ-um, -miz′ĭ-um, -ĭ-ah) [peri- + G. *mys,* muscle] [NA]. The fibrous sheath enveloping each of the primary bundles of skeletal muscle fibers.

perina'tal [peri- + L. *natus*, pp. of *nascor*, to be born]. Occurring during, or pertaining to, the periods before, during, or after the time of birth; *i.e.,* before delivery from the 28th week of gestation through the first 7 days after delivery.

per'inatol'ogist. A specialist in perinatology.

perinatology (pĕr'ĭ-na-tol'o-jĭ). Subspecialty of obstetrics concerned with care of the mother and fetus during pregnancy, labor, and delivery, especially when the mother and/or fetus are ill or at risk of becoming ill.

perineal (pĕr'ĭ-ne'al). Relating to the perineum.

perineo- [L. fr. G. *perineon, perinaion*]. Combining form denoting the perineum.

perineocele (pĕr-ĭ-ne'o-sēl) [perineo- + G. *kēlē*, hernia]. Perineal hernia; a hernia in the perineal region, either between the rectum and the vagina or the rectum and the bladder, or alongside the rectum.

perineoplasty (pĕr-ĭ-ne'o-plas-tĭ). Reparative or plastic surgery of the perineum.

perineorrhaphy (pĕr-ĭ-ne-or'ă-fĭ). Suture of the perineum, performed in perineoplasty.

perineoscrotal (pĕr-ĭ-ne'o-skro'tal). Relating to the perineum and the scrotum.

perineostomy (pĕr-ĭ-ne-os'to-mĭ) [perineo- + G. *stoma*, mouth]. Urethrostomy through the perineum.

perineotomy (pĕr-ĭ-ne-ot'o-mĭ). Incision into the perineum as in external urethrotomy, lithotomy, etc., or to facilitate childbirth.

perineovaginal (pĕr-ĭ-ne-o-vaj'ĭ-nal). Relating to the perineum and the vagina.

perinephrial (pĕr-ĭ-nef'rĭ-al). Relating to the perinephrium.

perinephritis (pĕr'ĭ-nĕ-fri'tis). Inflammation of the perinephric tissue.

perinephrium, pl. **perinephria** (pĕr-ĭ-nef'rĭ-um, -nef'rĭ-ah) [peri- + G. *nephros*, kidney]. The connective tissue and fat surrounding the kidney.

perineum, pl. **perinea** (pĕr-ĭ-ne'um, -ne'ah) [L. fr. G. *perineon, perinaion*]. **1** [NA]. The area between the thighs extending from the coccyx to the pubis and lying below the pelvic diaphragm. **2.** The external surface of the central tendon of the perineum, lying between the vulva and the anus in the female and the scrotum and the anus in the male.

perineurial (pĕr-ĭ-nu'rĭ-al). Relating to the perineurium.

perineuritis (pĕr-ĭ-nu-ri'tis). Inflammation of the perineurium.

perineurium, pl. **perineuria** (pĕr-ĭ-nu'rĭ-um, -rĭ-ah) [L. fr. peri- + G. *neuron*, nerve]. The connective tissue sheath surrounding a fascicle of nerve fibers in a peripheral nerve.

period (pēr'ĭ-od) [G. *periodos*, a way round, a cycle, fr. *peri*, around, + *hodos*, way]. **1.** A certain duration or division of time. **2.** One of the stages of a disease. See also entries under *stage* and *phase*.

eclipse p., the period of time between infection by (or induction of) bacteriophage, or other virus, and the appearance of mature virus within the cell.

ejection p., sphygmic *interval.*

extrinsic incubation p., the time interval between the acquisition of an infectious agent by a vector and the vector's ability to transmit the agent to other susceptible vertebrate hosts.

incubation p., (1) latent p. (2); (2) incubative *stage.*

induction p., the interval between an initial injection of antigen and the appearance of demonstrable antibodies in the blood.

isoelectric p., the p. occurring in the electrocardiogram between the end of the S wave and the beginning of the T wave during which electrical forces are acting in directions such as to neutralize each other so that there is no difference in potential under the two electrodes.

isometric p. of cardiac cycle, that p. in which the muscle fibers do not shorten although the cardiac muscle is excited and the pressure in the ventricles rises, extending from the closure of the atrioventricular valves to the opening of the semilunar valves.

latency p., latency *phase.*

latent p., (1) the p. elapsing between the application of a stimulus and the obvious response; (2) incubation p.; the p. of incubation of an infectious disease before the appearance of the prodromal symptoms.

postsphygmic p., postsphygmic *interval.*

preejection p., the interval between onset of QRS complex and cardiac ejection; electromechanical systole minus ejection time.

prepatent p., the time interval between infection of an individual by a parasitic organism and first ability to detect a diagnostic stage of the organism from that host.

presphygmic p., presphygmic *interval.*

refractory p., the p. following effective stimulation, during which excitable tissue fails to respond to a stimulus of threshold intensity.

safe p., the p. in the menstrual cycle when conception is least likely to occur, about 10 days before or after the onset of menstruation, since ovulation occurs about midway between two menstrual p.'s.

sphygmic p., sphygmic *interval.*

Wenckebach p., a sequence of cardiac cycles in the electrocardiogram ending in a dropped beat due to A-V block, the preceding cycles showing progressively lengthening P-R intervals; the P-R interval following the dropped beat is again shortened.

periodic (pēr-ĭ-od'ĭk). Recurring at regular intervals; denoting a disease with regularly recurring exacerbations or paroxysms.

periodicity (pēr'ĭ-o-dis'ĭ-tĭ). The tendency to recurrence at regular intervals.

periodontal (pĕr'ĭ-o-don'tal) [peri- + G. *odous*, tooth]. Around a tooth; relating to the periodontium.

periodontia (pĕr'ĭ-o-don'shĭ-ah). **1.** Plural of periodontium. **2.** Periodontics.

periodontics (pĕr'ĭ-o-don'tiks) [peri- + G. *odous*, tooth]. Periodontia (2); the branch of dentistry concerned with the study of the normal tissues and the treatment of abnormal conditions of the tissues immediately about the teeth.

per'iodon'tist. A dentist who specializes in periodontics.

periodontitis (pĕr'ĭ-o-don-ti'tis) [periodontium + G. *-itis*, inflammation]. A disease of the periodontium characterized by inflammation of the gingivae, resorption of the alveolar bone, degeneration of the periodontal membrane (ligament), migration of the epithelial attachment apically, and formation of periodontal pockets.

periodontium, pl. **periodontia** (pĕr'ĭ-o-don'shĭ-um, -shĭ-ah) [L. fr. peri- + G. *odous*, tooth]. [NA]. Alveolodental or peridental membrane; the tissues that surround and support the teeth; includes the gingivae, cementum, periodontal ligament, and alveolar and supporting bone.

periodontoclasia (pĕr'ĭ-o-don'to-kla'zĭ-ah) [periodontium + *klasis*, breaking]. Destruction of periodontal tissues, gingiva, pericementum, alveolar bone, and cementum.

periodontosis (pĕr'ĭ-o-don-to'sis) [periodontium + G. *-osis*, condition]. A noninflammatory degenerative disease of the attachment apparatus characterized by looseness and migration of teeth.

perionychia (pĕr-ĭ-o-nik'ĭ-ah). Inflammation of the perionychium.

perionychium, pl. **perionychia** (pĕr-ĭ-o-nik'ĭ-um, -nik'ĭ-ah) [peri- + G. *onyx*, nail]. Eponychium (2).

perioophoritis (pĕr'ĭ-o-of'o-ri'tis) [peri- + G. *oophoron*, ovary, + *-itis*, inflammation]. Periovaritis; inflammation of the peritoneal covering of the ovary.

perioophorosalpingitis (pĕr'ĭ-o-of'o-ro-sal-pin-ji'tis) [peri- + G. *oophoron*, ovary, + salpingitis]. Inflammation of the peritoneum and other tissues around the ovary and oviduct.

periop'erative. Denoting an event that occurs during the period of an operation.

perior'bit. Periorbita.

periorbita (pĕr-ĭ-or'bĭ-tah) [peri- + L. *orbita*, orbit] [NA]. Periorbit; orbital fascia; the periosteum of the orbit.

perior'bital. Around the orbit; relating to the periorbita.

periorchitis (pĕr'ĭ-or-ki'tis) [peri- + G. *orchis*, testis, + *-itis*, inflammation]. Inflammation of the tunica vaginalis testis.

periostea (pĕr-ĭ-os'te-ah). Plural of periosteum.

perios'teal. Relating to the periosteum.

periosteitis (per'ĭ-os-te-i'tis). Periostitis.

periosteo-. Combining form denoting the periosteum.

periosteoma (pĕr'ĭ-os-te-o'mah). Periosteophyte; a neoplasm derived from the periosteum.

periosteomyelitis (pĕr-ĭ-os'te-o-mi-ĕ-li'tis) [periosteo- + G. *myelos*, marrow, + *-itis*, inflammation]. Inflammation of the entire bone, including the periosteum and marrow.

periosteophyte (pĕr-ĭ-os'te-o-fīt) [periosteo- + G. *phyton*, growth]. Periosteoma.

periosteosis (pĕr'ĭ-os-te-o'sis). Periostosis; formation of a periosteoma.

periosteotomy (pĕr'ĭ-os-te-ot'o-mĭ) [periosteo- + G. *tomē*, incision]. Cutting through the periosteum to the bone.

periosteum, pl. **periostea** (pĕr-ĭ-os'te-um, -te-ah) [Mod. L. fr. G. *periosteon*, fr. *peri*, around, + *osteon*, bone] [NA]. The thick fibrous membrane covering the entire surface of a bone except its articular cartilage. In young bones it consists of two layers: an inner which is osteogenic, forming new bone tissue, and an outer connective tissue layer conveying the blood vessels and nerves supplying the bone; in older bones the osteogenic layer is reduced.

periostitis (pĕr'ĭ-os-ti'tis). Periosteitis; inflammation of the periosteum.

periosto'sis, pl. **periosto'ses.** Periosteosis.

periovaritis (pĕr'ĭ-o-vă-ri'tis). Perioophoritis.

peripachymeningitis (pĕr'ĭ-pak'ĭ-men-in-ji'tis) [peri- + pachymeninx (dura mater) + G. *-itis*, inflammation]. Inflammation of the parietal layer of the dura mater.

peripancreatitis (pĕr'ĭ-pan-kre-ă-ti'tis). Inflammation of the peritoneal coat of the pancreas.

peripherad (pĕ-rif'er-ad) [G. *periphereia*, periphery, + L. *ad*, to]. In a direction toward the periphery.

periph'eral. 1. Relating to or situated at the periphery. **2.** Situated nearer the periphery of an organ or part of the body in relation to a specific reference point.

periphery (per-if'er-ĭ) [G. *periphereia*, fr. *peri*, around, + *pherō*, to carry]. The part of a body away from the center; the outer part or surface.

periphlebitis (pĕr'ĭ-flĕ-bi'tis) [peri- + G. *phleps*, vein, + *-itis*, inflammation]. Inflammation of the outer coat of a vein or of the tissues surrounding it.

per'ipori'tis [peri- + G. *poros*, pore, + *-itis*, inflammation]. Miliary papules and papulovesicles with staphylococcic infection; most frequently on the face and in infants.

periproctitis (pĕr'ĭ-prok-ti'tis). Perirectitis; inflammation of the areolar tissue about the rectum.

periprostatitis (pĕr'ĭ-pros-tă-ti'tis). Inflammation of the tissues surrounding the prostate.

peripylephlebitis (pĕr'ĭ-pi'le-flĕ-bi'tis) [peri- + G. *pylē*, gate, + *phleps*, vein, + *-itis*, inflammation]. Inflammation of the tissues around the portal vein.

perirectitis (pĕr'ĭ-rek-ti'tis). Periproctitis.

perisalpingitis (pĕr'ĭ-sal-pin-ji'tis) [peri- + G. *salpinx*, trumpet, + *-itis*, inflammation]. Inflammation of the peritoneum covering the fallopian tube.

perisalpinx (pĕr-ĭ-sal'pingks) [peri- + G. *salpinx* (*salping-*), trumpet]. The peritoneal covering of the uterine tube.

periscopic (pĕr-ĭ-skop'ĭk) [peri- + G. *skopeō*, to view]. Denoting that which gives the ability to see objects to one side as well as in the direct axis of vision.

perisigmoiditis (pĕr'ĭ-sig-moy-dī'tis). Inflammation of the connective tissues surrounding the sigmoid flexure.

perispermatitis (pĕr'ĭ-sper-mă-tī'tis). Inflammation of the tissues around the spermatic cord.

perisplanchnitis (pĕr'ĭ-splangk-nī'tis) [peri- + G. *splanchna*, viscera, + -*itis*, inflammation]. Inflammation surrounding any viscus or viscera.

perisplenitis (pĕr'ĭ-splen-i'tis). Inflammation of the peritoneum covering the spleen.

perispondylitis (pĕr'ĭ-spon-dī-lī'tis) [peri- + G. *spondylos*, vertebra, + -*itis*, inflammation]. Inflammation of the tissues about a vertebra.

peristalsis (pĕr'ĭ-stal'sis) [peri- + G. *stalsis*, constriction]. Vermicular movement; the movement of the intestine or other tubular structure; the waves of alternate circular contraction and relaxation of the tube by which the contents are propelled onward.

　　mass p., forcible peristaltic movements of short duration that move the contents of the large intestine from one division to the next, as from the ascending to the transverse colon.

　　reversed p., antiperistalsis; a wave of intestinal contraction in a direction the reverse of normal, by which the contents of the tube are forced backward.

peristal'tic. Relating to peristalsis.

peristole (pĕ-ris'tō-le) [peri- + G. *stellō*, to contract]. The tonic activity of the walls of the stomach whereby the organ contracts about its contents.

peristolic (pĕr-ĭ-stol'ĭk). Relating to peristole.

peritectomy (pĕr-ĭ-tek'tō-mĭ) [peri- + G. *ektomē*, excision]. Peritomy (1); the removal of a paracorneal strip of the conjunctiva to correct pannus.

peritendineum, pl. **peritendinea** (pĕr'ĭ-ten-din'e-um, -e-ah) [L. fr. peri- + G. *tenōn*, tendon] [NA]. One of the fibrous sheaths surrounding the primary bundles of fibers in a tendon.

peritendinitis (pĕr'ĭ-ten-dī-nī'tis). Peritenontitis; inflammation of the sheath of a tendon.

peritenontitis (pĕr'ĭ-ten-on-tī'tis). Peritendinitis.

perithelium, pl. **perithelia** (pĕr'ĭ-the'lĭ-um, -lĭ-ah) [peri- + G. *thēlē*, nipple]. The connective tissue that surrounds smaller vessels and capillaries.

perithyroiditis (pĕr'ĭ-thi-roy-dī'tis). Inflammation of the capsule or tissues surrounding the thyroid gland.

peritomy (pe-rit'ō-mĭ) [G. *peritomē*, fr. *peri*, around, + *tomē*, incision]. **1.** Peritectomy. **2.** Circumcision (1).

peritoneal (pĕr'ĭ-to-ne'al). Relating to the peritoneum.

peritonealgia (pĕr-ĭ-to-ne-al'jĭ-ah) [peritoneum + G. *algos*, pain]. Pain in the peritoneum.

peritoneo-. Combining form denoting the peritoneum.

peritoneocentesis (pĕr'ĭ-to-ne'o-sen-te'sis) [peritoneum + G. *kentēsis*, puncture]. Paracentesis of the abdomen. Also called abdominocentesis; celiocentesis; celioparacentesis.

peritoneoclysis (pĕr'ĭ-to-ne-ok'lĭ-sis) [peritoneum, + G. *klysis*, a washing out]. Irrigation of the abdominal cavity.

peritoneopathy (pĕr'ĭ-to-ne-op'ă-thĭ) [peritoneum, + *pathos*, suffering]. Inflammation or other disease of the peritoneum.

peritoneopericardial (pĕr'ĭ-to-ne'o-pĕr'ĭ-kar'dĭ-al). Relating to the peritoneum and the pericardium.

peritoneopexy (pĕr'ĭ-to-ne'o-pek-sĭ) [peritoneum + G. *pēxis*, fixation]. A suspension or fixation of the peritoneum.

peritoneoplasty (pĕr'ĭ-to-ne'o-plas-tĭ) [peritoneum + G. *plassō*, to form]. Loosening adhesions and covering the raw surfaces with peritoneum to prevent reformation.

peritoneoscope (pĕr'ĭ-to-ne'o-skōp) [peritoneum + G. *skopeō*, to view]. Laparoscope; an endoscope for examining the peritoneal cavity.

peritoneoscopy (pĕr'ĭ-to-ne-os'ko-pĭ). Abdominoscopy; celioscopy; laparoscopy; ventroscopy; examination of the contents of the peritoneum with a peritoneoscope passed through the abdominal wall.

peritoneotomy (pĕr'ĭ-to-ne-ot'o-mĭ) [peritoneum + G. *tomē*, incision]. Incision of the peritoneum.

peritoneum, pl. **peritonea** (pĕr'ĭ-to-ne'um, -ne'ah) [Mod. L. fr. G. *peritonaion*, fr. *periteino*, to stretch over] [NA]. The serous sac, consisting of mesothelium and a thin layer of irregular connective tissue, that lines the abdominal cavity (**parietal p.**) and covers most of the viscera contained therein (**visceral p.**); forms two sacs, the peritoneal (or greater) sac and the omental bursa (lesser sac) connected by the foramen epiploicum (of Winslow).

peritonitis (pĕr'ĭ-to-ni'tis). Inflammation of the peritoneum.

　　adhesive p., p. in which a fibrinous exudate occurs, matting together the intestines and various other organs.

　　chemical p., p. due to the escape of bile, contents of the gastrointestinal tract, or pancreatic juice into the peritoneal cavity; shock and peritoneal exudation due to chemical injury may precede any associated infection.

　　p. defor'mans, a chronic p. in which thickening of the membrane and contracting adhesions cause shortening of the mesentery and kinking and retraction of the intestines.

　　gas p., inflammation of the peritoneum accompanied by an intraperitoneal accumulation of gas.

　　meconium p., p. caused by intestinal perforation in the fetus or newborn associated with congenital obstruction or fibrocystic disease of the pancreas.

　　pelvic p., pelviperitonitis; inflammation, more or less strictly localized, of the peritoneum surrounding the uterus and fallopian tubes.

peritonsillitis (pĕr'ĭ-ton-sĭ-li'tis). Inflammation of the connective tissue above and behind the tonsil.

peritrichal, peritrichate (pĕ-rit'rĭ-kal, -rĭ-kat). Peritrichous (2).

peritrichous (pĕ-rit'rĭ-kus) [peri- + G. *thrix,* hair]. 1. Relating to cilia or other appendicular organs projecting from the periphery of a cell. 2. Peritrichal; peritrichate; having flagella uniformly distributed over a cell; especially referring to bacteria.

perituber'culo'sis. Paratuberculosis.

periureteritis (pĕr'ĭ-u-re'ter-i'tis) [peri- + ureter + G. *-itis,* inflammation]. Inflammation of the tissues about a ureter.

periurethritis (pĕr'ĭ-u-re-thri'tis) [peri- + urethra + G. *itis,* inflammation]. Inflammation of the tissues about the urethra.

periuterine (pĕr-ĭ-u'ter-in). Perimetric (1).

perivaginitis (pĕr'ĭ-vaj-ĭ-ni'tis). Pericolpitis; inflammation of the connective tissue around the vagina.

perivasculitis (pĕr'ĭ-vas-ku-li'tis). Periangitis.

perives'ical [peri- + L. *vesica,* bladder]. Pericystic.

perivisceritis (pĕr'ĭ-vis-er-i'tis) [peri- + L. *viscere* + G. *-itis,* inflammation]. Inflammation surrounding any viscus or viscera.

permanganate (per-mang'gă-nāt). A salt of permanganic acid, HMnO₄, derived from manganese.

permeability (per'me-ă-bil'ĭ-tĭ). The property of being permeable.

permeable (per'me-ăbl) [L. *permeabilis* (see permeation)]. Pervious; permitting the passage of substances through a membrane or other structure.

permease (per'me-ās). Any of a group of membrane-bound carriers (enzymes) which effect the transport of solute through a semipermeable membrane.

per'meate [*permeo,* to pass through]. 1. To pass through a membrane or other structure. 2. That which can so pass.

permeation (per-me-a'shun) [L. *per-meo,* pp. *-meatus,* to pass through]. The extension of a malignant neoplasm by proliferation of the cells continuously along the blood vessels or lymphatics.

pernicious (per-nish'us) [L. *perniciosus,* destructive]. Destructive; harmful; denoting a disease of severe character and usually fatal without specific treatment.

pero- [G. *pēros,* maimed]. Combining form meaning maimed or malformed.

perodactyly (pe-ro-dak'tĭ-lĭ) [pero- + G. *daktylos,* finger or toe]. A congenital condition characterized by deformed fingers or toes.

peromelia (pe-ro-me'lĭ-ah) [pero- + G. *melos,* limb]. Severe congenital malformations of extremities, including absence of hand or foot.

peroneal (pĕr-o-ne'al) [L. *peroneus,* fr. G. *peronē,* fibula]. Relating to the fibula, to the lateral side of the leg, or to the muscles there present.

peroral (per-o'ral) [L. *per,* through, + *os* (*or-*), mouth]. Through the mouth.

per os [L.]. By mouth.

peroxi-. See peroxy-.

perox'idases. Hydrogen peroxide reducing oxidoreductases; enzymes in animal and plant tissues that catalyze the dehydrogenation (oxidation) of various substances in the presence of hydrogen peroxide, which acts as hydrogen acceptor, being converted to water in the process.

perox'ide. That oxide of any series that contains the greatest number of oxygen atoms; applied to compounds containing an –O–O– link.

perox'isome [peroxide + G. *sōma,* body]. Microbody; an organelle occuring in animal and plant cells that has an electron-dense core or nucleoid containing urate oxidase and other oxidative enzymes relating to the formation and degradation of H₂O₂.

peroxy-. Prefix denoting the presence of an extra O atom.

peroxyl (per-ok'sil). H–O–O; one of the free radicals presumed formed as a result of the bombardment of tissue by high energy radiation.

per rec'tum [L.]. By rectum.

persalt (per'sawlt). In chemistry, any salt that contains the greatest possible amount of the acid radical.

perseveration (per-sev-er-a'shun). [L. *persevero,* to persist]. 1. Constant repetition of a meaningless word or phrase. 2. In clinical psychology, the repetition of a previously appropriate or correct response, even though the repeated response has since become inappropriate or incorrect.

persis'tence [L. *persisto,* to abide, stand firm]. Obstinate continuation of characteristic behavior, or of existence in spite of opposition or adverse environmental conditions.

persona (per-so'nah) [L. *per,* through, + *sonare,* to sound: from the small megaphone in ancient dramatic masks, to aid in projecting the actor's voice]. In jungian psychology, the outer character as opposed to anima (inner personality); the assumed personality used to mask the true one.

per'sonal'ity. 1. The unique self; the organized system of attitudes and behavioral predispositions by which one impresses and establishes relationships with others. 2. An individual with a particular p. pattern.

  antisocial p., see antisocial personality *disorder.*

  authoritarian p., a cluster of p. traits reflecting a desire for security and order, *e.g.,* rigidity, highly conventional outlook, unquestioning obedience, scapegoating, and a desire for structured lines of authority.

  compulsive p., a p. characterized by rigidity, extreme inhibition, and excessive concern with conformity and adherence to standards of conscience either for himself or others.

  cyclothymic p., a p. disorder in which a person experiences regularly alternating periods of elation and depression, usually not related to external circumstances.

  hysterical p., histrionic p., a condition in which a person, typically immature, dependent, self-centered, and often vain, exhibits unstable, overreactive, and excitable behavior intended to gain attention even though not aware of this intent.

inadequate p., a p. disorder, characterized by ineptness and emotional and physical instability, which renders the individual unable to cope with the normal vicissitudes of life.

multiple p., a dissociative reaction in which two or more distinct conscious p.'s alternately prevail in the same person, without either p. being aware of the other.

paranoid p., a p. disorder characterized by hypersensitivity, rigidity, unwarranted suspicion, jealousy, and a tendency to blame others and ascribe evil motives to them.

passive-aggressive p., a p. disorder in which aggressive feelings are manifested in passive ways, especially through mild obstructionism and stubbornness.

schizoid p., a disorder with characteristics similar to those of schizophrenia but in milder form.

type A p., a behavior pattern characterized by aggressiveness, competitiveness, restlessness, and a sense of time urgency; associated with increased risk for coronary heart disease.

perspiration (pers-pĭ-ra′shun) [L. *per-spiro*, pp. *-atus*, to breathe everywhere]. 1. Sweating; diaphoresis; sudation; excretion of fluid by the sweat glands of the skin. 2. All fluid loss through normal skin, whether by sweat gland secretion or by diffusion through other skin structures. 3. Sweat (1); sudor; the fluid excreted by the sweat glands; it consists of water containing sodium chloride and phosphate, urea, ammonia, ethereal sulfates, creatinine, fats, and other waste products.

insensible p., p. that evaporates before it is perceived as moisture on the skin.

sensible p., p. excreted in large quantity, so that it appears as moisture on the skin.

per tu′bam [L.]. Through a tube.

pertussis (per-tus′is) [L. *per*, very (intensive), + *tussis*, cough]. Whooping cough; an acute infectious disease caused by *Bordetella pertussis*, and characterized by an inflammation of the larynx, trachea, and bronchi producing recurrent bouts of spasmodic coughing that continue until the breath is exhausted, then ending in a noisy inspiratory stridor ("whoop") caused by laryngeal spasm.

perversion (per-ver′zhun, -shun) [L. *perversio*, fr. *per-verto*, pp. *-versus*, to turn about]. A deviation from a societal norm, especially concerning sexual interest or behavior considered medically abnormal, morally wrong, or legally prohibited.

per vi′as natura′les [L.]. Through the natural passages; *e.g.*, denoting a normal delivery, as opposed to cesarean section, or the passage in stool of a foreign body instead of its surgical removal.

per′vious [L. *pervius*, fr. *per*, through, + *vis*, a way]. Permeable.

pes, pl. **pe′des** [L.]. 1 [NA]. The foot. 2. Any footlike or basal structure or part. 3. Talipes. In this sense, p. is qualified by a modifier expressing the specific type.

p. anseri′nus, the tendinous expansions of the sartorius, gracilis, and semitendinosus muscles at the medial border of the tuberosity of the tibia.

p. hippocam′pi [NA], the anterior thickened extremity of the hippocampus.

pessary (pes′ă-rĭ) [L. *pessarium*, fr. G. *pessos*, an oval stone used in certain games]. 1. An appliance of varied form, introduced into the vagina to support the uterus or to correct any displacement. 2. A medicated vaginal suppository.

pest [L. *pestis*]. Plague (2).

pes′ticide. An agent that destroys fungi, insects, rodents, or any other pest.

pes′tilence [L. *pestilentia*]. An epidemic of any infectious disease.

pestilential (pes-tĭ-len′shal). Relating to, or tending to produce, a pestilence.

pestle (pes′l) [L. *pistillum*, fr. *pinso*, or *piso*, to pound]. An instrument in the shape of a rod with one rounded and weighted extremity, used for bruising, breaking, and triturating substances in a mortar.

PET Positron emission *tomography*.

petechiae, sing. **petechia** (pe-te′kĭ-e, pe-te′kĭ-ah; pe-tek′-) [Mod. L. form of It. *petecchie*]. Minute hemorrhagic spots in the skin.

petechial (pe-te′kĭ-al, -tek′ĭ-al). Relating to or accompanied or characterized by petechiae.

pet′iolate, pet′iolated, pet′ioled. Stalked or pedunculate.

petiole (pet′ĭ-ōl) [L. *petiolus*, the stalk of a fruit]. A stem or pedicle.

petit mal (pĕ-te′mal). Absence.

petrifaction (pet-rĭ-fak′shun) [L. *petra*, rock + *facio*, to make]. Fossilization, as in conversion into stone.

pétrissage (pa-tre-sazh′) [Fr. kneading]. A manipulation in massage, consisting in a kneading of the muscles.

petro- [L. *petra*, rock; G. *petros*, stone]. Combining form denoting stone, stone-like hardness.

petroccipital (pet′ro-ok-sip′ĭ-tal). Relating to the petrous portion of the temporal bone and the occipital bone.

petrola′tum. Petroleum jelly; paraffin jelly; a mixture of the softer members of the paraffin or methane series of hydrocarbons, obtained from petroleum as an intermediate product in its distillation; used as a soothing application to burns and abrasions of the skin, and as a base for ointments.

petroleum benzin. Benzin; benzine; naphtha; purified low boiling fractions distilled from petroleum consisting of hydrocarbons, chiefly of the methane series; highly flammable, and its vapors, when mixed with air and ignited, may explode; used as a solvent.

petromas′toid. Relating to the petrous and the mastoid portions of the temporal bone.

petrosa, pl. **petrosae** (pĕ-tro'sah, -se) [L. fr. *petra*, rock]. The petrous portion of the temporal bone.

petro'sal. Petrous (2); relating to the petrosa.

petrositis (pet-ro-si'tis). Inflammation involving the petrous portion of the temporal bone and its air cells.

petrosphenoid (pet-ro-sfe'noyd). Relating to the petrous portion of the temporal bone and to the sphenoid bone.

petrosquamosal, petrosquamous (pet'ro-skwa-mo'sal, -skwa'mus). Relating to the petrous and the squamous portions of the temporal bone.

petrous (pet'rus, pe'trus) [L. *petrosus*, fr. *petra*, a rock]. **1.** Of stony hardness. **2.** Petrosal.

pexis (pek'sis) [G. *pēxis*, fixation]. Fixation, usually surgical, of substances in the tissues.

-pexy [G. *pēxis*, fixation]. Suffix meaning fixation, usually surgical.

pg Picogram.

PGA, PGB, PGE, PGF. Abbreviations, with numerical subscripts according to structure, often used for prostaglandins.

Ph Phenyl.

pH [p (power) of [H$^+$]$_{10}$]. Symbol for the logarithm of the reciprocal of the H ion concentration; a solution with pH 7.00 is neutral, one with a pH of more than 7.0 is alkaline, one with a pH lower than 7.00 is acid.

PHA Phytohemagglutinin.

phaco- (fak'o-) [G. *phakos*, lentil (lens), anything shaped like a lentil]. Combining form usually meaning lens-shaped, or relating to a lens.

phacoanaphylaxis (fak'o-an'-ă-fi-lak'sis). Hypersensitiveness to protein of the lens.

phacocele (fak'o-sēl) [phaco- + G. *kēlē*, hernia]. Hernia of the lens.

phacocystectomy (fak'o-sis-tek'to-mĭ) [phaco- + G. *kystis*, bladder, + *ektomē*, excison]. Surgical removal of a portion of the capsule of the lens.

phacoemulsification (fak'o-e-mul-sĭ-fĭ-ka'shun). A method of emulsifying and aspirating a cataract with the use of a low-frequency ultrasonic needle.

phacoerysis (fak-o-ĕr'ĭ-sis) [phaco- + G. *erysis*, pulling, drawing off]. Extraction of the lens by means of suction.

phacoid (fak'oyd) [phaco- + G. *eidos*, resemblance]. Of lentil shape.

phacolysis (fă-kol'ĭ-sis) [phaco- + G. *lysis*, dissolution]. Operative breaking down and removal of the lens.

phacolytic (fa-ko-lit'ik). Characterized by or referring to phacolysis.

phacoma (fă-ko'mah) [phaco- + G. *-oma*, tumor]. Phakoma; a hamartoma found in phacomatosis.

phacomalacia (fak'o-mă-la'shĭ-ah) [phaco- + G. *malakia*, softness]. Softening of the lens.

phacomatosis (fak'o-mă-to'sis) [Van der Hoeve's coinage fr. G. *phakos*, mother-spot]. Phakomatosis; a group of hereditary diseases characterized by hamartomas involving multiple tissues: Lindau's

disease, neurofibromatosis, Sturge-Weber syndrome, tuberous sclerosis.

phacoscope (fak'o-skōp) [phaco- + G. *skopeō*, to view]. An instrument for observing the changes in the crystalline lens during accomodation.

phage (fāj). Bacteriophage.

-phage, -phagia, -phagy [G. *phagein*, to eat]. Suffixes meaning eating or devouring.

phagedena (faj-ĕ-de'nah) [G. *phagedaina*, a canker]. An ulcer that rapidly spreads peripherally, destroying the tissues as it increases in size.

phagedenic (faj-ĕ-den'ik). Relating to or having the characteristics of phagedena.

phago- [G. *phagein*, to eat]. Prefix denoting eating, devouring.

phagocyte (fag'o-sīt) [phago- + G. *kytos*, cell]. A cell possessing the property of ingesting bacteria, foreign particles, and other cells; divided into two general classes: microphages and macrophages.

phagocytic (fag-o-sit'ik). Relating to phagocytes or phagocytosis.

phagocy'tin. A very labile bactericidal substance isolated from polymorphonuclear leukocytes.

phagocytize (fag'o-si-tīz). Phagocytose.

phagocytolysis (fag'o-si-tol'ĭ-sis) [phagocyte + G. *lysis*, dissolution]. Destruction of phagocytes, or leukocytes, occurring in the process of blood coagulation or as the result of the introduction of certain antagonistic foreign substances into the body.

phagocytolytic (fag'o-si-to-lit'ik). Relating to phagocytolysis.

phagocytose (fag'o-si-tōs). Phagocytize; to engulf and destroy bacteria and other foreign substances denoting the action of phagocytic cells.

phagocytosis (fag'o-si-to'sis) [phagocyte + G. *-osis*, condition]. The process of ingestion and digestion by phagocytes of solid substances, such as other cells, bacteria, bits of necrosed tissue, foreign particles.

phagolysosome (fag-o-li'so-sōm). A body formed by union of a phagosome or ingested particle with a lysosome having hydrolytic enzymes.

phagosome (fag'o-sōm) [phago- + G. *soma*, body]. A vesicle which forms around a particle within the phagocyte that engulfed it, separates from the cell membrane, and then fuses with and receives the contents of cytoplasmic granules (lysosomes), thus forming a phagolysosome in which digestion of the engulfed particle occurs.

phagotype (fag'o-tīp) [phago- + G. *typos*, type]. In microbiology, a subdivision of a species distinguished from other strains therein by sensitivity to certain bacteriophage(s).

-phagy. See -phage.

phako-. See phaco-.

phako'ma. Phacoma.

phak'omato'sis. Phacomatosis.

phalangeal (fă-lan'je-al). Relating to a phalanx.

phalangectomy (fal-an-jek'to-mĭ). Excision of one or more of the phalanges of hand or foot.

phalanx, pl. **phalanges** (fa'langks, fă-lan'jēz) [L. fr. G. *phalanx* (*-ang-*), line of soldiers] [NA]. One of the long bones of the fingers or toes, 14 in number for each hand or foot, two for the thumb or great toe, and three each for the other four digits; designated as proximal, middle, and distal, beginning from the metacarpus.

phall-, phalli-, phallo- [G. *phallos*, penis]. Combining forms denoting the penis.

phallectomy (fal-ek'to-mī) [phall- + G. *ektomē*, excision]. Surgical removal of the penis.

phallic (fal'ik) [G. *phallos*, penis]. Relating to or resembling the penis.

phallitis (fal-i'tis). Penitis.

phallo-. See phall-.

phallocampsis (fal-o-kamp'sis) [phallo- + G. *kampsis*, a bending]. Curvature of the erect penis.

phallodynia (fal-o-din'ī-ah) [phallo- + G. *odynē*, pain]. Pain in the penis.

phalloidin (fă-loy'din). Best known of the toxic cyclic peptides produced by the poisonous mushroom, *Amanita phalloides;* closely related to amanitin.

phalloplasty (fal'o-plas-tī) [phallo- + G. *plassō*, to form]. Reparative or plastic surgery of the penis.

phallotomy (fal-lot'o-mī) [phallo- + G. *tomē*, a cutting]. Surgical incision into the penis.

phallus, pl. **phalli** (fal'us, fal'ī) [L.; G. *phallos*]. Penis.

phantasia (fan-ta'zī-ah) [G. appearance]. Fantasy.

phantasm (fan'tazm) [G. *phantasma*, an appearance]. Phantom (1); the mental imagery produced by fantasy.

phantasmagoria (fan-taz'mă-go'rī-ah). A fantastic sequence of haphazardly associative imagery.

phantom (fan'tom) [G. *phantasma*, an appearance]. 1. Phantasm. 2. A model, especially a transparent one, of the human body or any of its parts.

pharmaceutic, pharmaceutical (far-mă-su'tik, far-mă-su'tĭ-kal) [G. *pharmakeutikos*, relating to drugs]. Relating to pharmacy or to pharmaceutics.

pharmaceutics (far-mă-su'tiks). 1. Pharmacy. 2. The science of pharmaceutical systems, *i.e.,* preparations, dosage forms, etc.

pharmacist (far'mă-sist) [G. *pharmakon*, a drug]. One who prepares and dispenses drugs and has knowledge concerning their properties.

pharmaco- (far'mă-ko-) [G. *pharmakon*, drug, medicine]. Combining form relating to drugs.

phar'macodiagno'sis. Use of drugs in diagnosis.

phar'macodynam'ic. Relating to drug action.

pharmacodynamics (far'mă-ko-di-nam'iks) [pharmaco- + G. *dynamis*, force]. The study of the actions of drugs on the living organism.

phar'macogenet'ics. The study of genetically determined variations in responses to drugs.

pharmacognosy (far-mă-kog'no-sī) [pharmaco- + G. *gnōsis*, knowledge]. A branch of pharmacology concerned with the physical characteristics and botanical sources of crude drugs.

pharmacokinetic (farm'ă-ko-kī-net'ik). Relating to the disposition of drugs in the body.

phar'macokinet'ics [pharmaco- + G. *kinēsis*, movement]. Movements of drugs within biological systems, as affected by uptake, distribution, elimination, and biotransformation.

pharmacol'ogist. One who specializes in pharmacology.

pharmacology (far-mă-kol'o-jī) [pharmaco- + G. *logos*, study]. The science concerned with drugs, their sources, appearance, chemistry, actions, and uses.

pharmacopeia, pharmacopoeia (far'mă-ko-pe'ah) [G. *pharmakopoiia*, fr. *pharmakon*, a medicine, + *poieo*, to make]. A work containing monographs of therapeutic agents, standards for their strength and purity, and directions for making preparations.

pharmacopeial (far'mă-ko-pe'al). Relating to a pharmacopeia; denoting a drug in the list of a pharmacopeia.

pharmacopsychosis (far'mă-ko-si-ko'sis) [pharmaco- + psychosis]. A psychosis causally related to taking a drug.

phar'macother'apy [pharmaco- + G. *therapeia*, therapy]. Treatment of disease by means of drugs. See also chemotherapy.

pharmacy (far'mă-sī) [G. *pharmakon*, drug]. 1. The practice of preparing and dispensing drugs. 2. A place where drugs are prepared and dispensed.

Pharm. D. Doctor of Pharmacy.

pharyng-. See pharyngo-.

pharyngalgia (făr-ing-gal'jī-ah) [pharyng- + G. *algos*, pain]. Pharyngodynia; pain in the pharynx.

pharyngeal (fă-rin'je-al) [Mod. L. *pharyngeus*]. Relating to the pharynx.

pharyngectomy (făr-in-jek'to-mī) [pharyng- + G. *ektomē*, excision]. Excision of a part of the pharynx.

pharyngemphraxis (făr'in-jem-frak'sis) [pharyng- + G. *emphraxis*, a stoppage]. A pharyngeal obstruction.

pharynges (fă-rin'jēz). Plural of pharynx.

pharyngismus (făr-in-jiz'mus). Pharyngospasm; spasm of the muscles of the pharynx.

pharyngitic (făr-in-jit'ik). Relating to pharyngitis.

pharyngitis (făr-in-ji'tis) [pharyng- + G. *-itis*, inflammation]. Inflammation of the mucous membrane and underlying parts of the pharynx.

pharyngo-, pharyng- [Mod. L. fr. G. *pharynx*]. Combining forms denoting the pharynx.

pharyngocele (fă-ring'go-sēl) [pharyngo- + G. *kēlē*, hernia]. A diverticulum from the pharynx.

pharyngodynia (fă-ring'go-din'ī-ah) [pharyngo- + G. *odynē*, pain]. Pharyngalgia.

pharyngoepiglottic, pharyngoepiglottidean (fă-ring'go-ep-ĭ-glot'ik, -glŏ-tid'e -an). Relating to the pharynx and the epiglottis.

pharyngoesophageal (fă-ring'go-e-sof-ă-je'al). Relating to the pharynx and the esophagus.

pharyngoglossal (fă-ring'go-glos'al). Relating to the pharynx and the tongue.

pharyngokeratosis (fă-ring'go-kĕr-ă-to'sis) [pharyngo- + G. *keras* (*kerat-*), horn]. A thickening of the lining of the lymphoid follicles of the pharynx, with the formation of a pseudomembranous exudate.

pharyngolaryngeal (fă-ring'go-lă-rin'je-al). Relating to both the pharynx and the larynx.

pharyngolaryngitis (fă-ring'go-lăr-in-jītis). Inflammation of both the pharynx and the larynx.

pharyngolith (fă-ring'go-lith) [pharyngo- + G. *lithos,* stone]. Pharyngeal calculus; a concretion in the pharynx.

pharyngology (făr'ing-gol'o-jĭ) [pharyngo- + G. *logos,* study]. The medical science concerned with the study, diagnosis, and treatment of the pharynx.

pharyngomycosis (fă-ring'go-mi-ko'sis) [pharyngo- + G. *mykēs,* a fungus]. Fungal invasion of the mucous membrane of the pharynx.

pharyngonasal (fă-ring'go-na'zal). Relating to the pharynx and the nasal cavity.

pharyngopathy (făr'ing-gop'ă-thĭ) [pharyngo- + G. *pathos,* suffering]. Any disease of the pharynx.

pharyngoperistole (fă-ring'go-pĕ-ris'to-le) [pharyngo- + G. *peristolē,* a drawing out]. Narrowing of the lumen of the pharynx.

pharyngoplasty (fă-ring'go-plas-tĭ) [pharyngo- + G. *plassō,* to form]. Plastic surgery of the pharynx.

pharyngoplegia (fă-ring'go-ple'jĭ-ah) [pharyngo- + G. *plēgē,* stroke]. Paralysis of the muscles of the pharynx.

pharyngorhinitis (fă-ring'go-ri-ni'tis). Inflammation of the rhinopharynx, or of the mucous membrane of the pharynx and the nasal fossae.

pharyngoscleroma (fă-ring'go-skle-ro'mah) [pharyngo- + G. *sklērōma,* an induration]. A scleroma, or indurated patch, in the mucous membrane of the pharynx.

pharyngoscope (fă-ring'go-skōp) [pharyngo- + G. *skopeō,* to view]. An instrument, like a laryngoscope, for inspection of the pharynx.

pharyngoscopy (făr-ing-gos'ko-pĭ) [pharyngo- + G. *skopeō,* to view]. Inspection and examination of the pharynx.

pharyngospasm (fă-ring'go-spazm). Pharyngismus.

pharyngostenosis (fă-ring'go-stĕ-no'sis) [pharyngo- + G. *stenōsis,* a narrowing]. Stricture of the pharynx.

pharyngotomy (făr-ing-got'o-mĭ) [pharyngo- + G. *tomē,* incision]. Any cutting operation upon the pharynx either from without or from within.

pharynx, pl. **pharynges** (făr'ingks, fă-rin'jēz) [Mod. L. fr. G. *pharynx* (*pharyng-*), the throat, the joint opening of the gullet and windpipe] [NA]. The upper expanded portion of the digestive tube, between the esophagus below and the mouth and nasal cavities above and in front.

phase (fāz) [G. *phasis,* an appearance]. **1.** One of the stages in which a thing appears during its course of change or development. **2.** A homogeneous, physically distinct, and separable portion of a heterogeneous system. **3.** The time relationship between two or more events. **4.** A particular part of a recurring time-pattern or wave-form. See also stage; period.

anal p., in psychoanalytic personality theory, the stage of psychosexual development occuring when a child's activities, interests, and concerns are centered around his anal zone.

aqueous p., the water portion of a system consisting of two liquid p.'s, one mainly water, the other a liquid immiscible with water.

external p., dispersion medium; the medium or fluid in which a disperse is suspended.

genital p., in psychoanalytic personality theory, the final stage of psychosexual development, occuring during puberty, when the individual's psychosexual development is so organized that sexual gratification can be achieved from genital-to-genital contact and the capacity exists for a mature, affectionate relationship with an individual of the opposite sex.

internal p., the particles contained in a colloid solution.

latency p., in psychoanalytic personality theory, the period of psychosexual development in children, extending from about age 5 to the beginning of adolescence, marked by the apparent cessation of sexual preoccupation; boys and girls are inclined to choose friends and join groups of their own sex.

luteal p., that portion of the menstrual cycle extending from the time of formation of the corpus luteum to the time when menstrual flow begins; usually 14 days in length.

oedipal p., in psychoanalysis, a stage in the psychosexual development of the child, characterized by erotic attachment to the parent of the opposite sex, repressed because of fear of the parent of the same sex.

oral p., in psychoanalytic personality theory, the earliest stage in psychosexual development, during which period the oral zone is the center of the infant's needs, expression, gratification, and pleasurable erotic experiences.

phallic p., in psychoanalytic personality theory, the stage in psychosexual development occurring when a child's interest, curiosity, and pleasurable experiences are centered around the penis in boys and the clitoris in girls.

Ph.D. Doctor of Philosophy.

Phe Phenylalanine or its radical.

phen-, pheno- [fr. G. *phainō,* to appear, show forth]. Combining form denoting appearance; in chemistry, derivation from benzene.

phenaceturic acid (fē-nas-ĕ-tu'rik). Phenylaceturic acid; $C_6H_5CH_2CO-NH-CH_2COOH$; end product of the metabolism of phenylated fatty acids with even numbers of carbon atoms.

phenanthrene (fē-nan'thrēn). $C_{14}H_{10}$; a compound isomeric with anthracene, derived from coal tar; used as a basis for the synthesis of various dyes and drugs.

phe'nate. A salt or ester of phenol (carbolic acid).

phency'clidine (PCP). 1-(1-Phenylcyclohexyl)piperidine hydrochloride; an anesthetic used in veterinary medicine; also abused for its hallucinogenic properties.

phenethicillin potassium (fĕ-neth'ĭ-sil'in). α-Phenoxyethylpenicillin potassium; a penicillin preparation that is stable in gastric acid and is rapidly but only partially absorbed from the gastrointestinal tract.

phenic acid (fe'nik). Phenol.

pheno-. See phen-.

phenobarbital (fe-no-bar'bĭ-tal). $CO(NHCO)_2$ $C(C_2H_5)(C_6H_5)$; a long-acting oral or parenteral sedative and hypnotic.

phenocopy (fe'no-kop-ĭ) [G. *phainō*, to appear, + copy]. **1.** An individual with clinical or laboratory characteristics that would ordinarily assign him to a specific phenotype with respect to genetic abnormality, but whose characteristics are of environmental rather than genetic etiology. **2.** A condition of environmental etiology that mimics a condition usually of genetic etiology.

phe'nol. Phenyl alcohol; phenic or carbolic acid; C_6H_5OH; an antiseptic and disinfectant; locally and internally escharotic in concentrated form, and neurolytic in 3 to 4% solutions.

  p. red, phenolsulfonphthalein.

phenolphthalein (fe-nol-thal'e-in, -thal'ēn). $C_{20}H_{14}O_4$; used as a hydrogen ion indicator and as a laxative.

phenolsulfonphthalein (PSP) (fe'nol-sulf-ōn-thal'e-in, -thal'ēn). Phenol red; occurs as a bright to dark red crystalline powder; used as an indicator in tissue culture media (yellow at pH 6.8, red at pH 8.4) and by parenteral injection as a test for renal function.

phenoluria (fe-nol-u'rĭ-ah). The excretion of phenols in the urine.

phenomenon, pl. **phenomena** (fē-nom'ĕ-non, -nah) [G. *phainomenon,* fr. *phainō,* to cause to appear]. **1.** A symptom; an occurrence of any sort, whether ordinary or extraordinary, in relation to a disease. See also reaction; sign. **2.** Any unusual fact or occurrence.

  Arias-Stella p., Arias-Stella reaction; focal, unusual, decidual changes in endometrial epithelium, consisting of intraluminal budding, and nuclear enlargement and hyperchromatism with cytoplastic swelling and vacuolation.

  declamping p., declamping shock; shock or hypotension following abrupt release of clamps from a large portion of the vascular bed, as from the aorta; apparently caused by transient pooling of blood in a previously ischemic area.

  déjà vu p., the mental impression that a new experience (*e.g.,* a sight, sound, or action) has happened before; a common p. in normal persons that may occur more frequently or continuously in certain emotional or organic disorders.

  diaphragm p., Litten's p.; a lowering of the line of retraction on the side of the chest (marking the insertion of the diaphragm) during inspiration, and elevation of the same during expiration; absent in cases of distention of the pleural sac.

  Donath-Landsteiner p., the hemolysis which results in a sample of blood of a subject of paroxysmal hemoglobinuria when the sample is cooled to around 5°C and then warmed again.

  generalized Shwartzman p., when both the preparative injection of endotoxin-containing filtrate and the provocative injection are given intravenously 24 hours apart, the animal usually dies within 24 hours after the second inoculation; characteristic lesions include widespread hemorrhages and bilateral cortical necrosis of the kidney, associated with a marked fall in the number of circulating leukocytes and platelets.

  gestalt p., see gestalt.

  Goldblatt p., hypertension resulting from partial occlusion of a renal artery.

  Litten's p., diaphragm p.

  Marcus Gunn p., jaw-winking *syndrome.*

  on-off p., a state in the treatment of Parkinson's disease by *l*-dopa, in which there is a rapid fluctuation of akinetic (off) and choreoathetotic (on) movements.

  paradoxical diaphragm p., in pyopneumothorax, hydropneumothrax, and some cases of injury, the diaphragm on the affected side rises during inspiration and falls during expiration.

  psi p., a p. that includes both psychokinesis and extrasensory perception.

  quellung p., Neufeld capsular *swelling.*

  Raynaud's p., spasm of the digital arteries with blanching and numbness of the fingers.

  rebound p., Stewart-Holmes *sign.*

  Shwartzman p., see generalized Shwartzman p.

  staircase p., treppe.

  Tyndall p., the visibility of floating particles in gases or liquids when illuminated by a ray of sunlight and viewed at right angles to the illuminating ray.

phe'nothi'azine. Thiodiphenylamine; the parent compound for synthesis of a large number of antipsychotic compounds, including promethazine, chlorpromazine, mepazine, and prochlorperazine.

phenotype (fe'no-tīp) [G. *phainō,* to display, show forth, + *typos,* model]. In genetics, a category or group to which an individual may be assigned on the basis of one or more characteristics observable clinically or by laboratory means that reflect genetic variation or gene-environment interaction; may include more than one genotype.

phen'otyp'ic. Relating to phenotype.

phenox'yben'zamine hydrochloride. An adrenergic (α-receptor) blocking agent of the β-haloalkylamines, selectively blocking the excitatory response of smooth muscle and exocrine glands to epinephrine.

phenozygous (fe-noz'ĭ-gus) [G. *phainō,* to show, + *zygon,* yoke]. Having a narrow cranium as compared with the width of the face, so that when the skull is viewed from above, the zygomatic arches are visible.

phenyl (Ph) (fen'il). The univalent radical, C_6H_5-, of phenol.

phen'ylace'tic acid. $C_6H_5CH_2COOH$; an abnormal product of phenylalanine catabolism, appearing in the urine in phenylketonuria.

phen'ylacetur'ic acid. Phenaceturic acid.

phenylalaninase (fen-il-al'ă-nin-ās). Phenylalanine 4-monooxygenase.

phenylalanine (Phe) (fen-il-al'ă-nēn). 2-Amino-3-phenylpropionic acid; $C_6H_5CH_2CH(NH_2)COOH$; one of the common amino acids in proteins.

phenylalanine 4-monooxygenase. Phenylalaninase; an enzyme that catalyzes the oxidation of phenylalanine to tyrosine with O_2 and tetrahydrobiopterin, the latter forming the dihydro derivative, which is reduced by NADPH and a reductase to the active form.

phen'yleth'yl alcohol. 2-Phenylethanol; C_6H_5-CH_2CH_2OH; a natural constituent of some volatile oils, used as an antibacterial agent.

phenylketonuria (PKU) (fen'il-ke'to-nu'rĭ-ah) [phenyl + ketone + G. *ouron*, urine]. Congenital deficiency of phenylalanine 4-monooxygenase causing inadequate formation of tyrosine, elevation of serum phenylalanine, urinary excretion of phenylpyruvic acid, and accumulation of phenylalanine and its metabolites; produces brain damage resulting in severe mental retardation, often with seizures, other neurologic abnormalities such as retarded myelination, and deficient melanin formation that predisposes to eczema; autosomal recessive inheritance.

phenyllactic acid (fen-il-lak'tik). $C_6H_5CH_2$-$CHOH-COOH$; a product of phenylalanine catabolism, appearing prominently in the urine in phenylketonuria.

pheo-. **1.** Prefix denoting same substituents on a phorbin or phorbide (porphyrin) residue as are present in chlorophyll, excluding any ester residues and Mg. **2** [G. *phaios*, dusky]. Combining form meaning dusky, gray, or dun.

pheochrome (fe'o-krōm) [G. *phaios*, dusky, + *chrōma*, color]. **1.** Chromaffin. **2.** Staining darkly with chromic salts.

pheochromocyte (fe-o-kro'mo-sīt) [pheochrome + G. *kytos*, cell]. A chromaffin cell of a sympathetic paraganglion, medulla of an adrenal gland, or of a pheochromocytoma.

pheochromocytoma (fe'o-kro-mo-si-to'mah). A functional chromaffinoma, usually benign, derived from cells in the adrenal medullary tissue and characterized by the secretion of catecholamines, resulting in hypertension which may be paroxysmal.

phere'sis. A procedure in which blood is removed from a donor, separated, and a portion retained, with the remainder returned to the donor. See also leukapheresis, plateletpheresis, plasmapheresis.

pher'omones [G. *pherein*, to carry, + *horman*, to excite, stimulate]. Substances secreted externally by an individual, and perceived by a second individual of the same species, thereby producing a change in the sexual or social behavior of that individual.

Ph.G. Graduate in Pharmacy.

Phialophora (fi'ă-lof'o-rah) [G. *phialē*, a broad, flat vessel, + *phoreō*, to carry]. A genus of fungi of which at least four species cause chromomycosis, including *P. verrucosa, P. pedrosoi, P. compacta,* and *P. dermatitidis;* another species, *P. jeanselmei,* causes mycetoma.

-phil, -phile, -philic, -philia [G. *philos,* fond, loving; *phileō,* to love]. Suffix denoting affinity or craving for.

philtrum, pl. **philtra** (fil'trum, -trah) [L. from G. *philtron,* depression on upper lip, fr. *phileo,* to love] [NA]. The infranasal depression; the indentation in the midline of the upper lip.

phimosis, pl. **phimoses** (fi-mo'sis, -sēz) [G. a muzzling, fr. *phimos,* a muzzle]. Narrowness of the opening of the prepuce, preventing its being drawn back over the glans.

phimot'ic. Pertaining to phimosis.

phleb-. See phlebo-.

phlebarteriectasia (fleb'ar-tēr-ĭ-ek-ta'zĭ-ah) [phlebo- + G. *arteria,* artery, + *ektasis,* a stretching]. Vasodilation.

phlebectasia (fleb-ek-ta'zĭ-ah) [phlebo- + G. *ektasis,* a stretching]. Venectasia; vasodilation of the veins.

phlebectomy (flē-bek'to-mī) [phlebo- + G. *ektomē,* excision]. Venectomy; excision of a segment of a vein.

phlebemphraxis (fleb-em-frak'sis) [phlebo- + G. *emphraxis,* a stoppage]. Venous thrombosis.

phlebismus (flē-biz'mus) [phlebo- + G. *-ismos,* condition]. Venous congestion and phlebectasia.

phlebit'ic. Relating to phlebitis.

phlebitis (flē-bi'tis) [phlebo- + G. *-itis,* inflammation]. Inflammation of a vein.

phlebo-, phleb- [G. *phleps,* vein]. Combining forms denoting vein.

phleboclysis (flē-bok'lĭ-sis) [phlebo- + G. *klysis,* a washing out]. Intravenous injection of an isotonic solution of dextrose or other substances in quantity.

phleb'ogram [phlebo- + G. *gramma,* something written]. Venogram (2); a tracing of the jugular venous pulse.

phleb'ograph [phlebo- + G. *graphō,* to write]. A venous sphygmograph; an instrument for making a tracing of the venous pulse.

phlebography (flē-bog'ră-fī) [phlebo- + G. *graphē,* a writing]. **1.** The recording of the venous pulse. **2.** Venography.

phlebolith (fleb'o-lith) [phlebo- + G. *lithos,* stone]. A calcareous deposit in a venous wall or thrombus.

phlebolithiasis (fleb'o-lĭ-thi'ă-sis). The formation of phleboliths.

phlebomanometer (fleb'o-mă-nom'e-ter). A manometer for measuring venous blood pressure.

phlebophlebostomy (fleb'o-flē-bos'to-mī). Venovenostomy.

phleboplasty (fleb'o-plas-tĭ) [phlebo- + G. *plassō,* to fashion]. Surgical repair of a vein.

phleborrhagia (fleb-o-ra'jĭ-ah) [phlebo- + G. *rhēg-nymi,* to burst forth]. Venous hemorrhage.

phleborrhaphy (flĕ-bor'ă-fĭ) [phlebo- + G. *rhaphē,* seam]. Suture of a vein.

phleborrhexis (fleb-o-rek'sis) [phlebo- + G. *rhēxis,* rupture]. Rupture of a vein.

phlebosclerosis (fleb'o-skle-ro'sis) [phlebo- + G. *sklērōsis,* hardening]. Venosclerosis; fibrous hardening of the walls of the veins.

phlebostasis (flĕ-bos'tă-sis) [phlebo- + G. *stasis,* a standing still]. Venostasis. **1.** Abnormally slow motion of blood in veins, usually with venous distention. **2.** Treatment of congestive heart failure by compressing proximal veins of the extremities with tourniquets.

phlebostenosis (fleb'o-stĕ-no'sis) [phlebo- + G. *stenōsis,* a narrowing]. Narrowing of the lumen of a vein from any cause.

phleb'othrombo'sis [phlebo- + G. *thrombōsis*] Thrombosis, or clotting, in a vein without primary inflammation.

Phlebotomus (flĕ-bot'o-mus) [phlebo- + G. *tomos,* cutting]. A genus of very small midges or blood-sucking sand flies (family Psychodidae), various species of which are vectors of kala azar, cutaneous leishmaniasis, and phlebotomus fever.

phlebotomy (flĕ-bot'o-mĭ) [phlebo- + G. *tomē,* incision]. Venesection; venotomy; incision into a vein for the purpose of drawing blood.

phlegm (flem) [G. *phlegma,* inflammation]. **1.** Mucus. **2.** One of the four humors of the body, according to the ancients.

phlegmasia (fleg-ma'zĭ-ah) [G. fr. *phlegma,* inflammation]. Inflammation, especially when acute and severe.

 p. al'ba do'lens, milk leg; an extreme edematous swelling of the leg following childbirth, due to thrombosis of the veins that drain the part.

 p. ceru'lea do'lens, thrombosis of the veins of a limb, with sudden severe pain with swelling, cyanosis, and edema of the part, followed by circulatory collapse and shock.

phlegmatic (fleg-mat'ik) [G. *phlegmatikos,* relating to phlegm]. Relating to the heavier of the four humors (phlegm), and therefore of a calm, apathetic, unexcitable temperament.

phlegmon (fleg'mon) [G. *phlegmonē,* inflammation]. Acute suppurative inflammation of the subcutaneous connective tissue.

phlegmonous (fleg'mon-us). Denoting phlegmon.

phlyctena, pl. **phlyctenae** (flik-te'nah, -ne) [G. *phlyktaina,* a blister made by a burn]. A small vesicle, especially one of a number of small blisters following a first degree burn.

phlyctenar (flik'tĕ-nar). Relating to or marked by the presence of phlyctenae.

phlyctenoid (flik'tĕ-noyd) [G. *phlyktaina,* blister, + *eidos,* resemblance]. Resembling a phlyctena.

phlyctenula, pl. **phlycten'ulae** (flik-ten'u-lah) [Mod. L. dim. of G. *phlyktaina,* blister]. Phlyctenule; a small red nodule of lymphoid cells, with ulcerated apex, occurring in the conjunctiva.

phlyctenular (flik-ten'u-lar). Relating to a phlyctenula.

phlyc'tenule. Phlyctenula.

phlyctenulosis (flik-ten-u-lo'sis). A nodular hypersensitive affection of corneal and conjunctival epithelium due to endogenous toxin.

phobia (fo'bĭ-ah) [G. *phobos,* fear]. Any objectively unfounded morbid dread or fear; used as a termination in many terms expressing the object that inspires the fear, *e.g.,* agoraphobia.

 school p., a young child's sudden aversion to or fear of attending school, usually considered a manifestation of separation anxiety.

phobic (fo'bik). Pertaining to or characterized by phobia.

phobophobia (fo-bo-fo'bĭ-ah) [G. *phobos,* fear]. A morbid dread of developing some phobia.

phocomelia (fo-ko-me'lĭ-ah) [G. *phōkē,* a seal, + *melos,* extremity]. Defective development of arms or legs, or both, so that the hands and feet are attached close to the body, resembling the flippers of a seal.

phon-. See phono-.

phonal (fo'nal). [G. *phōnē,* voice]. Relating to sound or to the voice.

phonasthenia (fo-nas-the'nĭ-ah) [phon- + G. *astheneia,* weakness]. Difficult or abnormal voice production, the enunciation being too high, too loud, or too hard.

phonation (fo-na'shun) [G. *phōnē,* voice]. The utterance of sounds by means of vocal cords.

phonatory (fo'nă-tor-ĭ). Relating to phonation.

phoneme (fo'nēm) [G. *phōnēma,* a voice]. The smallest sound unit which, in terms of the phonetic sequences of sound, controls meaning.

phonendoscope (fo-nend'o-skōp) [phon- + G. *endon,* within, + *skopeō,* to view]. A stethoscope that intensifies auscultatory sounds.

phonetic (fo-net'ik) [G. *phōnētikos*]. Relating to speech or to the voice.

phonetics (fo-net'iks). The science of speech and of pronunciation.

phoniatrics (fo-nī-at'riks) [phon- + G. *iatrikos,* of the healing art]. The study of speech habits; the science of speech.

phonic (fo'nik). Relating to sound or to the voice.

phono-, phon- [G. *phōnē,* sound, voice]. Combining forms denoting sound, speech, or voice sounds.

phonocar'diogram. A record of the heart sounds made by means of phonocardiograph.

phonocard'iograph. An instrument for graphically recording the heart sounds, which are displayed on an oscilloscope or tracing.

phonocardiography (fo'no-kar-dĭ-og'ră-fĭ) [phono- + G. *kardia,* heart, + *graphō,* to record]. **1.** Cardiophony; recording of the heart sounds with a phonocardiograph. **2.** The science of interpreting phonocardiograms.

pho′nocath′eter. A cardiac catheter with diminutive microphone housed in its tip, for recording sounds and murmurs from within the heart and great vessels.

phonogram (fo′no-gram) [phono- + G. *gramma*, diagram]. A graphic curve depicting the duration and intensity of a sound.

phonometer (fo-nom′ĕ-ter) [phono- + G. *metron*, measure]. An instrument for measuring the pitch and intensity of sounds.

phonomyoclonus (fo′no-mi-ok′lo-nus) [phono- + G. *mys*, muscle, + *klonos*, tumult]. A condition in which fibrillary muscular contractions are present, as evidenced by the sound heard on auscultation, even though not visible.

phonopathy (fo-nop′ă-thĭ) [phono- + G. *pathos*, suffering]. Any disease of the vocal organs affecting speech.

pho′nophotog′raphy [phono- + photography]. Recording of the movements imparted to a diaphragm by sound waves.

phonopsia (fo-nop′sĭ-ah) [phono- + G. *opsis*, vision]. A condition in which the hearing of certain sounds gives rise to a subjective sensation of color.

pho′norecep′tor. A receptor for sound stimuli.

phonorenogram (fo-no-re′no-gram). A sound tracing of the renal arterial pulse recorded by means of a phonocatheter placed in the renal pelvis.

phoresis (fōr′e-sis, fo-re′sis) [G. *phorēsis*, a being borne]. **1.** Electrophoresis. **2.** A biological association in which one animal is transported by another, as in the attachment of the eggs of a botfly to the legs of a mosquito, which transports them to the botfly as well as to the mosquito host.

phoria (fōr′ĭ-ah) [G. *phora*, a carrying, motion]. The relative directions assumed by the eyes during binocular fixation of a given object in the absence of an adequate fusion stimulus.

phoro-, phor- [G. *phoros*, carrying, bearing]. Combining forms denoting carrying or bearing, a carrier or bearer, phoria.

phoro-optometer (fo′ro-op-tom′e-ter). An instrument for determining phorias, ductions, and refractive states of the eyes.

phoropter (fo-rop′ter). A device containing different lenses used for refraction of the eye.

phos- [G. *phōs*, light]. Combined form denoting light.

phose (fōz) [G. *phōs*, light]. A subjective perception of a bright spot or patch.

phosgene (fos′jēn) [G. *phōs*, light, + -*gen*, to produce]. Carbonyl chloride; $COCl_2$; a colorless liquid at temperatures below 8°C, but an extremely poisonous gas at ordinary temperatures.

phosph-, phospho-, phosphor-, phosphoro-. Prefixes indicating presence of phosphorus in a compound. See also phospho- (2).

phosphatase (fos′fă-tās). Any of a group of enzymes that liberate inorganic phosphate from phosphoric esters.

   acid p., a p. with an optimum pH of 5.4, notably present in the prostate gland.

   alkaline p., a p. with an optimum pH of 8.6, present ubiquitously.

phosphate (fos′fāt). A salt or ester of phosphoric acid.

   high energy p.'s, those p.'s that, on hydrolysis, yield an unusually high quantity of energy.

phosphatemia (fos-fă-te′mĭ-ah) [phosphate + G. *haima*, blood]. An abnormally high concentration of inorganic phosphates in the blood.

phosphat′ic. Relating to or containing phosphates.

phosphatidylglycerol (fos-fă-ti′dil-glis′er-ol). A phosphatidic acid that is a constituent in human amniotic fluid and denotes fetal lung maturity when present in the last trimester.

phosphaturia (fos-fă-tu′rĭ-ah) [phosphate + G. *ouron*, urine]. Excessive excretion of phosphates in the urine.

phosphene (fos′fēn) [G. *phōs*, light, + *phainō*, to show]. Sensation of light produced by mechanical or electrical stimulation of the peripheral or central optic pathway of the nervous system.

phosphide (fos′fīd). A compound of phosphorus with valence −3.

phospho-. 1. See phosph- **2.** Biochemical term for *O*-phosphono-, a prefix that may replace the suffix "phosphate."

phosphoamidase (fos-fo-am′ĭ-dās). An enzyme catalyzing the hydrolysis of phosphorus-nitrogen bonds, notably the hydrolysis of phosphocreatine to creatine and phosphoric acid.

phosphoam′ides. Amides of phosphoric acid and their salts or esters, of the general formula $(HO)_2$. P(O)—NH$_2$.

phosphocre′atine. Creatine phosphate; a compound of creatine (through its NH_2 group) with phosphoric acid; a source of energy in the contraction of vertebrate muscle, its breakdown furnishing phosphate for the resynthesis of ATP from ADP by creating kinase.

phosphodiesterases (fos′fo-di-es′ter-a-sez). Enzymes cleaving phosphodiester bonds, such as those between nucleotides in nucleic acids, liberating smaller poly- or oligonucleotide units or mononucleotides but not inorganic phosphate.

phospho *enol*/**pyruvic acid** (fos′fo-e-nol-pi-ru′vik). $CH_2=C(OPO_3H_2)$—COOH; the phosphoric ester of pyruvic acid in the latter's enol form; an intermediate in the conversion of glucose to pyruvic acid and an example of a high energy phosphate ester.

phosphoglyc′erides. Phospholipids containing glycerol phosphate.

phospholip′ase. Lecithinase; an enzyme that catalyzes the hydrolysis of a phospholipid.

phospholipid (fos-fo-lip′id). A lipid containing phosphorus, thus including the lecithins and other phosphatidic acids, sphingomyelin, and plasmalogens.

phosphomu'tase. One of a number of phosphotransferases that apparently catalyze intramolecular transfer, because the donor is regenerated.

phosphonecrosis (fos'fo-nĕ-kro'sis) [phosphorus + G. *nekrōsis*, death]. Necrosis of the osseous tissue of the jaw, as a result of poisoning with phosphorus.

phosphoprotein (fos-fo-pro'tēn). A protein containing phosphoric groups attached directly to the side chains of its constituent amino acids, usually to the hydroxyl group of serine.

phosphor (fos'for) [G. *phōs*, light, + *phoros*, bearing]. A chemical substance that transforms incident electromagnetic or radioactive energy into light, as in scintillation radioactivity measurements.

phosphor-, phosphoro-. See phosph-.

phosphorescence (fos-fo-res'ens) [G. *phōs*, light, + *phoros*, bearing]. The quality or property of emitting light without active combustion or the production of heat, generally as the result of prior exposure to radiation; persists after the inciting cause is removed.

phosphorescent (fos'fo-res'ent). Having the property of phosphorescence.

phosphoric acid (fos-fōr'ik). H_3PO_4; $OP(OH)_3$; a solvent, dilute solutions of which have been used as urinary acidifiers and to remove necrotic debris.

phos'phorism. Chronic poisoning with phosphorus.

phosphorolysis (fos-fo-rol'ĭ-sis). A reaction analogous to hydrolysis except that the elements of phosphoric acid, rather than of water, are added in the course of splitting a bond.

phosphorous (fos'fo-rus, -fōr'us). 1. Relating to, containing, or resembling phosphorus. 2. Referring to phosphorus in its lower $+3$ valence state.

phosphorus (fos'fo-rus) [G. *phosphoros*, fr. *phōs*, light, + *phoros*, bearing]. A nonmetallic chemical element, symbol P, atomic no. 15, atomic weight 30.975, occurring as the phosphate in essentially every living cell; its elemental form is extremely poisonous, causing intense inflammation, fatty degeneration, and necrosis of the jaw (phossy jaw).

phos'phorus-32. (^{32}P). Radioactive isotope with atomic weight of 32; beta emitter with half-life of 14.3 days; used as tracer in study of metabolism of nucleic acids, phospholipids, phosphorylated intermediates in carbohydrate catabolism, etc.; also used in the treatment of certain diseases of osseous and hematopoietic systems.

phosphorylase (fos-fōr'ĭ-lās). 1. General term for an enzyme transferring an inorganic phosphate group to some organic acceptor, hence belonging to the transferases. 2. An enzyme that cleaves a single glucose residue from a poly(1,4-α-glucose) as glucose 1-phosphate, the phosphate coming from inorganic orthophosphate.

   p. phosphatase, phosphorylase-rupturing enzyme; PR enzyme (1); an enzyme catalyzing the conversion of p. by splitting it into halves, with release of four phosphates.

phos'phoryla'tion. The addition of phosphate to an organic compound, such as glucose to produce glucose monophosphate, through the action of a phosphotransferase (phosphorylase) or kinase.

   oxidative p., the formation of "high energy" phosphoric bonds (*e.g.*, pyrophosphates) from the energy released by the dehydrogenation (*i.e.*, oxidation) of various substrates; most notably, isocitric acid, α-ketoglutaric acid, succinic acid, and malic acid in the tricarboxylic acid cycle.

phosphosug'ar. A phosphorylated saccharide; any sugar containing an alcoholic group esterified with phosphoric acid.

phosphotransferase (fos-fo-trans'fer-ās). A subclass of transferases transferring phosphorus-containing groups; includes the kinases that transfer phosphate to alcohols, to carboxyl groups, to nitrogenous groups, or to another phosphate group.

phot-. See photo-.

photalgia (fo-tal'jĭ-ah) [photo- + G. *algos*, pain]. Photodynia; pain caused by light, an extreme degree of photophobia.

photic (fo'tik). Relating to light.

pho'tism. Production of a sensation of light or color by a stimulus to another sense organ, such as of hearing, taste, or touch.

photo-, phot- [G. *phōs* (*phōt*-), light]. Combining forms relating to light.

photobiotic (fo'to-bi-ot'ik) [photo- + G. *bios*, life]. Living or flourishing only in the light.

photocatalyst (fo-to-kat'ă-list) [photo- + G. *katalysis*, dissolution (catalysis)]. A substance that helps bring about a light-catalyzed reaction; *e.g.*, chlorophyll.

photocoagulation (fo'to-ko-ag-u-la'shun) [photo- + L. *coagulo*, pp. *-atus*, to curdle]. Direction of an intense light beam to a desired area of the ocular fundus to produce localized coagulation by absorption of light energy and its conversion to heat; used for retinal detachment, peripheral degeneration, neovascularization, and angiomas.

pho'tocoag'ulator. The apparatus used in photocoagulation.

photodermatitis (fo'to-der-mă-ti'tis) [photo- + G. *derma*, skin, + *-itis*, inflammation]. Dermatitis caused or elicited by exposure to ultraviolet light.

photodynia (fo-to-din'ĭ-ah) [photo- + G. *odynē*, pain]. Photalgia.

photofluorography (fo'to-flūr-og'ră-fĭ) [photo- + L. *fluor*, a flow, + G. *graphē*, a writing]. Fluorography; recording by photographs on film of fluoroscopic views; used in mass x-ray study of lungs.

photogastroscope (fo'to-gas'tro-skōp) [photo- + G. *gastēr*, stomach, + *skopeō*, to view]. An instrument for taking photographs of the interior of the stomach.

photogenic (fo'to-jen'ik) [photo- + G. *genesis*, production]. Light-producing; phosphorescent.

photoinactivation (fo'to-in-ak-tĭ-va'shun). Inactivation by light; *e.g.*, as in the treatment of herpes simplex by local application of a photoactive dye followed by exposure to a fluorescent lamp.

photoluminescent (fo'to-lu-mĭ-nes'ent) [photo- + L. *lumen*, light]. Having the ability to become luminescent upon exposure to visible light.

photolysis (fo-tol'ĭ-sis) [photo- + G. *lysis*, dissolution]. Decomposition of a chemical compound by the action of light.

photolytic (fo-to-lit'ik). Pertaining to photolysis.

photomicrograph (fo'to-mi'kro-graf) [photo- + G. *mikros*, small, + *graphē*, a record]. Micrograph (2); an enlarged photograph of an object viewed with a microscope; distinguished from microphotograph.

photomicrography (fo'to-mi-krog'rä-fĭ). Production of a photomicrograph.

photomyoclonus (fo'to-mi-ok'lo-nus) [photo- + G. *mys*, muscle, + *klonos*, confused motion]. Clonic spasms of muscles in response to visual stimuli.

pho'ton. 1. Troland. 2. In physics, a corpuscle of energy or particle of light; a quantum of light.

photoperceptive (fo'to-per-sep'tiv). Capable of both receiving and perceiving light.

photophobia (fo-to-fo'bĭ-ah) [photo- + G. *phobos*, fear]. 1. Abnormal sensitiveness to light, especially of the eyes. 2. Morbid dread and avoidance of light places.

photopho'bic. Relating to photophobia.

photophthalmia (fo-tof-thal'mĭ-ah) [photo- + G. *ophthalmos*, eye]. The inflammatory reaction caused by short-waved light on the external parts of the eye, as in snow blindness.

photopia (fo-to'pĭ-ah) [photo- + G. *opsis*, vision]. Photopic *vision*.

photop'ic. Pertaining to photopic *vision.*

photopsia (fo-top'sĭ-ah) [photo- + G. *opsis*, vision]. Photopsy; a subjective sensation of lights, sparks, or colors due to retinal or cerebral disease.

photop'sin. The protein moiety (opsin) of the pigment (iodopsin) in the cones of the retina.

photop'sy. Photopsia.

photoptarmosis (fo'to-tar-mo'sis) [photo- + G. *ptarmos*, a sneezing, + *-osis*, condition]. Reflex sneezing occurring when bright light reaches the retina.

pho'toradia'tion. Therapeutic exposure to visible light; in cancer therapy, combined with intravenous injection of a photosensitizing agent and for deep-seated tumors by a fiberoptic system.

photoradiometer (fo'to-ra-dĭ-om'ĕ-ter) [photo- + L. *radius*, a ray, + G. *metron*, measure]. An instrument for determining the penetrating power of radiation.

photoreaction (fo'to-re-ak'shun). A reaction caused or affected by light, *e.g.*, photolysis, photosynthesis.

photoreactivation (fo'to-re-ak-tĭ-va'shun). Activation by light of something or of some process previously inactive or inactivated.

photoreceptive (fo'to-re-sep'tiv). Functioning as a photoreceptor.

photoreceptor (fo'to-re-sep'tor) [photo- + L. *re-cipio*, pp. *-ceptus*, to receive]. A receptor that is sensitive to light, *e.g.*, a retinal rod or cone.

photoretinitis (fo'to-ret-ĭ-ni'tis). See photoretinopathy.

photoretinopathy (fo'to-ret-ĭ-nop'ä-thĭ) [photo- + retina, + G. *pathos*, suffering]. A macular burn from excessive exposure to sunlight or other intense light, characterized subjectively by reduced visual acuity.

photoscan (fo'to-skan). Scintiscan.

photoscanning (pho'to-skan-ing). Scanning.

pho'tosensitiza'tion. Sensitization of the skin to light, usually due to the action of certain drugs.

photostable (fo'to-sta'bl). Not subject to change upon exposure to light.

photostethoscope (fo'to-steth'o-skōp). A device that converts sound into flashes of light; used for continuous observation of the fetal heart.

photosynthesis (fo-to-sin'thĕ-sis) [photo- + G. *synthesis*, a putting together]. The compounding or building up of chemical substances under the influence of light; in particular, the process by which green plants, using chlorophyll and the energy of sunlight, produce carbohydrate out of water and carbon dioxide, liberating molecular oxygen in the process.

phototaxis (fo-to-tak'sis) [photo- + G. *taxis*, orderly arrangement]. Reaction of living protoplasm to the stimulus of light, involving bodily motion of the organism toward (**positive p.**) or away from (**negative p.**) stimulus.

photother'apy. Light treatment; treatment of disease by means of light rays.

phototropism (fo-tot'ro-pizm) [photo- + G. *tropē*, a turning]. The movement of an organism toward or away from light, differing from phototaxis in that the motion is of parts of the organism rather than of the organism as a whole.

photuria (fo-tu'rĭ-ah) [photo- + G. *ouron*, urine]. The passage of phosphorescent urine.

phren-. See phreno-.

phrenalgia (frĕ-nal'jĭ-ah) [phren- + G. *algos*, pain]. 1. Psychalgia (1). 2. Pain in the diaphragm.

phrenemphraxis (fren-em-frak'sis) [phren- + G. *emphraxis*, a stoppage]. Phreniclasia.

phrenetic (frĕ-net'ik) [G. *phrenitikos*, frenzied]. Frenzied; maniacal.

phreni-, phrenico-. See phreno-.

-phrenia [G. *phrēn*, the diaphragm, mind, heart (as seat of emotions)]. Suffix denoting the diaphragm or the mind.

phrenic (fren'ik). 1. Relating to the diaphragm. 2. Relating to the mind.

phrenicectomy (fren-ĭ-sek'to-mĭ) [phreni- + G. *ektomē*, excision]. Phrenicoexeresis; exsection of a portion of the phrenic nerve, to prevent reunion such as may follow phrenicotomy.

phreniclasia (fren-ĭ-kla'sĭ-ah) [phreni- + G. *klasis*, a breaking away]. Phrenemphraxis; phrenicotripsy;

crushing of a section of the phrenic nerve as a substitute for phrenicotomy.

phrenicoexeresis (fren-ĭ-ko-eks-er'ĕ-sis) [phrenico- + G. *exairesis,* a taking out]. Phrenicectomy.

phrenicotomy (fren-ĭ-kot'o-mē) [phrenico- + G. *tome,* incision]. Sectioning of the phrenic nerve.

phrenicotripsy (fren'ĭ-ko-trip-sī) [phrenico- + G. *tripsis,* a rubbing]. Phreniclasia.

phreno-, phren-, phreni-, phrenico- [G. *phren,* diaphragm, mind, heart (as seat of emotions)]. Combining forms denoting diaphragm, mind, or phrenic.

phrenocardia (fren-o-kar'dī-ah) [phreno- + G. *kardia,* heart]. Cardiophrenia; precordial pain and dyspnea of psychogenic origin.

phrenocolic (fren-o-kol'ik) [phreno- + G. *kolon,* colon]. Relating to the diaphragm and the colon.

phrenocolopexy (fren-o-kol'o-pek-sī, -ko'lo-) [phreno- + G. *kolon,* colon, + *pexis,* fixation]. Suture of a displaced or prolapsed transverse colon to the diaphragm.

phrenogastric (fren-o-gas'trik) [phreno- + G. *gaster,* stomach]. Relating to the diaphragm and the stomach.

phrenohepatic (fren-o-hĕ-pat'ik) [phreno- + G. *hepar,* liver]. Relating to the diaphragm and the liver.

phrenoplegia (fren-o-ple'jī-ah) [phreno- + G. *plege,* stroke]. **1.** A psychosis of sudden onset. **2.** Paralysis of the diaphragm.

phrenoptosia (fren-op-to'sī-ah) [phreno- + G. *ptosis,* a falling]. An abnormal sinking down of the diaphragm.

phrynoderma (frin-o-der'mah) [G. *phrynos,* toad, + *derma,* skin]. A follicular hyperkeratotic eruption thought to be due to deficiency of vitamin A.

phthalein (thal'e-in). One of a group of highly colored compounds of which phenolphthalein is the best known example.

phthiriasis (thi-ri'ă-sis) [G. *phtheiriasis,* fr. *phtheir,* a louse]. Infestation with the pubic or crab louse, *Pthirus pubis.*

   p. pu'bis, presence of crab lice in the pubis and other hairy areas of the trunk, and in the eyelashes of infants and young children.

Phthirus (thi'rus) [L. *phthir; G. phtheir,* a louse]. See *Pthirus.*

phthisis (ti'sis, te'sis, thi'sis, the'sis) [G. a wasting]. Obsolete term for: **(1)** a wasting or atrophy, local or general, and **(2)** consumption or, specifically, tuberculosis of the lungs.

Phycomycetes (fi'ko-mi-se'tēz) [phyco- + G. *mykes,* fungus]. A general term used to designate a class of saprophobic pathogenic fungi belonging to the orders Mucorales and Entomophthorales.

phycomycosis (fi'ko-mi-ko'sis). An infectious disease caused by fungi of the class Phycomycetes; because these fungi are common saprobes found in nature, infection is usually seen in patients with various predisposing conditions.

phylaxis (fi-lak'sis) [G. a guarding, protection]. Protection against infection.

phylo- [G. *phylon,* tribe]. Combining form denoting tribe, race, or phylum.

phylogenesis (fi-lo-jen'ĕ-sis) [phylo- + G. *genesis,* origin]. Phylogeny; the evolutionary development of any plant or animal species; ancestral history of the individual as opposed to ontogenesis, development of the individual.

phy'logenet'ic, phy'logen'ic. Relating to phylogenesis.

phylogeny (fi-loj'ĕ-nī). Phylogenesis.

phylum, pl. **phyla** (fi'lum, fi'lah) [Mod. L. fr. G. *phylon,* tribe]. The taxanomic division below kingdom and above class.

phyma (fi'mah) [G. a tumor]. A nodule or small rounded tumor of the skin.

phymatosis (fi'mă-to'sis). The growth or the presence of phymas or small nodules in the skin.

physaliform (fī-sal'ĭ-form) [G. *physallis,* bladder, bubble, + L. *forma,* form]. Like a bubble or small bleb.

physalis (fis'ă-lis) [G. *physallis,* a bladder]. A vacuole in a giant cell found in certain malignant neoplasms, such as chondroma.

physeal (fiz'ī-al). Pertaining to the growth cartilage area (physis) separating the metaphysis and the epiphysis.

physi-. See physio-.

physiatrics (fiz-ī-at'riks) [G. *physis,* nature, + *iatrikos,* healing]. Physical *therapy.*

physiatrist (fiz-ī'ă-trist). A physician who specializes in physical medicine.

physi'atry. Physical *medicine.*

physical (fiz'ī-kal) [Mod. L. *physicalis,* fr. G. *physikos*]. Relating to the body, as distinguished from the mind.

physician (fī-zish'un) [Fr. *physicien,* a natural philosopher]. A licensed practitioner of medicine; a doctor.

physician's assistant (P.A.). A person trained and licensed in the diagnosis and treatment of commonly encountered medical problems, and in technical skills, and who thereby extends the physician's capacity to provide medical care.

physicochemical (fiz'ī-ko-kem'ī-kal). Relating to physical chemistry.

physics (fiz'iks). The branch of science concerned with the phenomena of matter, with the changes that matter undergoes without losing its chemical identity.

physio-, physi- [G. *physis,* nature]. Combining forms denoting physical (physiologic) or natural (relating to physics).

physiogenic (fiz-ī-o-jen'ik) [physio- + G. *genesis,* origin]. Related to or caused by physiologic activity.

physiognomy (fiz'ī-og'no-mī) [physio- + G. *gnomon,* a judge,]. **1.** The countenance, as considered an indication of character or a factor in diagnosis.

2. Estimation of one's character and mental qualities by a study of the face and general bodily carriage.

physiologic, physiological (fiz-ĭ-o-loj'ik, -loj'ĭ-kal). **1.** Relating to physiology. **2.** Normal as opposed to pathologic; denoting the various vital processes. **3.** Denoting the action of a drug when given to a healthy person, as distinguished from its therapeutic action.

physiologist (fiz-ĭ-ol'o-jist). A specialist in physiology.

physiology (fiz-ĭ-ol'o-jĭ) [L. or G. *physiologia*, fr. G. *physis*, nature, + *logos*, study]. The science concerned with the normal vital processes of organisms.

phys'iotherapeu'tic. Pertaining to physiotherapy.

physiotherapist (fiz'ĭ-o-thĕr'ă-pist). Physical *therapist*.

physiotherapy (fiz'ĭ-o-thĕr'ă-pĭ) [physio- + G. *therapeia*, treatment]. Physical *therapy*.

physique (fĭ-zēk') [Fr.]. Biotype; constitutional type; the physical or bodily structure; the "build."

physo- [G. *physaō*, to inflate, distend]. Combining form denoting (1) tendency to swell or inflate; (2) relation to air or gas.

physocele (fi'so-sēl) [physo- + G. *kelē*, tumor, hernia]. **1.** A circumscribed swelling due to the presence of gas. **2.** A hernial sac distended with gas.

physohematometra (fi'so-he-mă-to-me'trah) [physo- + G. *haima*, blood, + *mētra*, uterus]. Distention of the cavity of the uterus with gas and blood.

physohydrometra (fi'so-dro-me'trah) [physo- + G. *hydōr*, water, + mētra, uterus]. Distention of the cavity of the uterus with gas and serous fluid.

physometra (fi-so-me'trah) [physo- + G. *mētra*, uterus]. Distention of the uterine cavity with air or gas.

physopyosalpinx (fi'so-pi-o-sal'pingks) [physo- + G. *pyon*, pus, + *salpinx*, trumpet]. Pyosalpinx accompanied by a formation of gas in the tube.

phytan'ic acid. 3,7,11,15-Tetramethylhexadecanoic acid that accumulates in the serum and tissues of patients with Refsum's disease and is attributed to the hereditary absence of phytanate α-oxidase; arises from phytol and acts as an inhibitor of the α-oxidation of palmitic (hexadecanoic) acid.

phyto-, phyt- [G. *phyton*, a plant]. Combining form denoting plants.

phytoagglutinin (fi'to-ă-glu'tĭ-nin). A lectin that causes agglutination of erythrocytes or of leukocytes.

phytobezoar (fi-to-be'zōr) [phyto- + bezoar]. Food ball; hortobezoar; a gastric concretion formed of vegetable fibers, with the seeds and skins of fruits, and sometimes starch granules and fat globules.

phy'tohemagglu'tinin (PHA). Phytolectin; a phytomitogen from plants that agglutinates red blood cells; commonly used for the lectin obtained from the red kidney bean (*Phaseolus vulgaris*) which is also a mitogen that stimulates T lymphocytes more vigorously than B lymphocytes.

phy'tohor'mones. Plant hormones; *e.g.*, auxins.

phytoid (fi'toyd) [G. *phytōdēs*, fr. *phyton*, plant, + *eidos*, resemblance]. Resembling a plant; denoting an animal having many of the biologic characteristics of a plant.

phy'tol. Phytyl alcohol; an unsaturated primary alcohol derived from the hydrolysis of chlorophyll; used for the synthesis of vitamins E and K1.

phytolec'tin. Phytohemagglutinin.

phytomitogen (fi-to-mi'to-jen). A mitogenetic lectin causing lymphocyte transformation accompanied by mitotic proliferation of the resulting blast cells identical to that produced by antigenic stimulation; *e.g.*, phytohemagglutinin.

phytophlyctodermatitis (fi'to-flik'to-der-mă-ti'tis) [phyto- + G. *phlyktaina*, blister, + dermatitis]. Meadow *dermatitis*.

phytotox'ic. 1. Poisonous to plant life. **2.** Pertaining to phytotoxin.

phytotoxin (fi'to-tok'sin) [phyto- + G. *toxikon*, poison]. Any toxin elaborated by plants.

pI The pH value for the isoelectric point of a given substance.

pia (pi'ah) [L. fem. of *pius*, tender]. Pia mater.

pi'al. Relating to the pia mater.

pia-arachnitis (pi'ah-ă-rak-ni'tis). Leptomeningitis.

pia-arachnoid (pi'ah-ă-rak'noyd). Leptomeninges.

pia mater (pi'ah ma'ter) [L. tender, affectionate mother]. Pia; a delicate vasculated fibrous membrane firmly adherent to the glial capsule of the brain and spinal cord; it and the arachnoid are collectively called leptomeninges.

pian (pe-an', pi'an). Yaws.

piarachnoid (pi-ă-rak'noyd). Leptomeninges.

pica (pi'kah, pe'kah) [L. *pica*, magpie]. A depraved or perverted appetite; a hunger for substances not fit for food.

pico- (p) [It. *piccolo*, small]. **1.** Combining form meaning small. **2** (p). Bicro-; prefix denoting one-trillionth (10^{-12}).

picogram (pg) (pi'ko-gram). One-trillionth (10^{-12}) of a gram.

picometer (pm) (pi'ko-me-ter). Bicron; one-trillionth (10^{-12}) meter.

Picornaviridae (pi-kor-nă-vīr'ĭ-de) [It. *piccolo*, very small, + RNA + -viridae]. A family of very small nonenveloped viruses having a core of single-stranded RNA; includes the polioviruses, coxsackieviruses, and echoviruses.

picornavirus (pi-kor-nă-vi'rus). A virus of the family Picornaviridae.

pic'rate. A salt of picric acid.

pic'ric acid [G. *pikros*, bitter]. 2,4,6-Trinitrophenol; carbazotic acid; $C_6H_2(NO_2)_3OH$; has been used as an application in burns, eczema, erysipelas, and pruritus.

picrocarmine (pik-ro-kar'min, -mēn). See under stain.

pic'rotox'in [G. *pikros*, bitter, + *toxican*, poison]. Cocculin; a very bitter neutral principle derived from the fruit of *Anamirta cocculus* (family Menispermaceae); a central nervous system stimulant used as an antidote for poisoning by barbiturates and certain other CNS-depressant drugs.

PID Pelvic inflammatory *disease.*

piebaldness (pi'bawld-ness). Circumscribed or localized albinism; a term usually used to describe patchy absence of pigment of scalp hair, giving a streaked appearance; patches of vitiligo may be present in other areas.

piedra (pe-a'drah) [Sp. a stone]. A fungus disease of hair characterized by the presence of numerous small black or white nodular masses.

piesesthesia (pi'es-es-the'zĭ-ah) [G. *piesis,* pressure, + *aisthēsix,* sensation]. Pressure *sense.*

PIF Prolactin-inhibiting *factor.*

pig'ment [L. *pigmentum,* paint]. **1.** Any coloring matter, as that of the skin, hair, iris, etc., or the stains used in histologic or bacteriologic work, or that in paints. **2.** A medicinal preparation for external use, applied to the skin like paint.

  bile p.'s, coloring matter in the bile derived from porphyrins by rupture of a methane bridge; *e.g.,* bilirubin, biliverdin.

  respiratory p.'s, the oxygen-carrying (colored) substances in blood and tissues; *e.g.,* hemoglobin, myoglobin.

  visual p.'s, the photopigments in the retinal cones (photopsins) and rods (scotopsins) that absorb light and by photochemical processes initiate the phenomenon of vision.

  wear-and-tear p., lipofuscin that accumulates in aging or atrophic cells as residue of lysosomal digestion.

pigmentary (pig'men-tĕr-ĭ). Relating to a pigment.

pigmentation (pig'men-ta'shun). Coloration, either normal or pathologic, of the skin or tissues resulting from a deposit of pigment.

pig'mented. Colored as the result of a deposit of pigment.

pigmentolysin (pig-men-tol'ĭ-sin) [L. *pigmentum,* pigment, + G. *lysis,* a loosening]. An antibody causing destruction of pigment.

pi'lar, pil'ary [L. *pilus,* a hair]. Hairy; relating to pili.

pile [L. *pila,* ball]. An individual hemorrhoidal tumor. See hemorrhoids.

  sentinel p., a circumscribed thickening of the mucous membrane at the lower end of a fissure of the anus.

pileous (pi'le-us) [L. *pilus,* hair]. Hairy.

piles [L. *pila,* a ball]. Hemorrhoids.

pi'li [L.] [NA]. Plural of pilus.

pill [L. *pilula;* dim of *pila,* ball]. A small globular mass of some coherent but soluble substance, containing a medicinal substance to be swallowed.

  pep p.'s, colloquialism for tablets containing a CNS stimulant, especially amphetamine.

pil'lar [L. *pila*]. A structure or part having a resemblance to a column or pillar.

  p.'s of fauces, *arcus* palatoglossus and *arcus* palatopharyngeus.

p.'s of fornix, *columna* fornicis and *crus* fornicis.

pill-rolling. A circular movement of the opposed tips of the thumb and the index finger appearing as a form of tremor in paralysis agitans.

pilo- [L. *pilus,* hair]. Combining form relating to hair.

pilobezoar (pi-lo-be'zōr) [pilo- + bezoar]. Trichobezoar.

pilocystic (pi-lo-sis'tik) [pilo- + G. *kystis,* bladder]. Denoting a dermoid cyst containing hair.

piloerection (pi'lo-e-rek'shun). Erection of hair.

pi'loid [pilo- + G. *eidos,* resemblance]. Hairlike; resembling hair.

pilojection (pi-lo-jek'shun) [pilo- + injection]. The process of shooting shafts of stiff mammalian hair into a saccular aneurysm in the brain in order to produce thrombosis.

pilomatrixoma (pi'lo-ma-trik-so'mah) [pilo- + L. *matrix* + G. *-oma,* tumor]. Malherbe's calcifying epithelioma; a benign tumor of the skin and subcutis, containing cells resembling basal cell carcinoma and areas of coagulation necrosis forming eosinophilic ghost cells with variable calcification and foreign body giant cell reaction in the fibrous stroma.

pi'lomo'tor [pilo- + L. *motor,* mover]. Moving the hair; denoting the arrectores pilorum muscles of the skin and the postganglionic sympathetic nerve fibers innervating them.

pilonidal (pi'lo-ni'dal) [pilo- + L. *nidus,* nest]. Denoting a growth of hair in a dermoid cyst or in the deeper layers of the skin.

pi'lose [L. *pilosus*]. Hairy.

pilosebaceous (pi'lo-se-ba'shus) [pilo- + L. *sebum,* suet]. Relating to the hair follicles and sebaceous glands.

pi'lus, pl. **pi'li** [L.]. **1** [NA]. Hair (1); one of the fine filamentous epidermal growths covering the body, except the palms, soles, and flexor surfaces of the joints, and composed of a bulbous root and cylindrical shaft slanting toward the follicular opening of invaginated epidermis at the skin surface. **2.** Fimbria (2); a fine filamentous appendage, somewhat analogous to the flagellum, that occurs on some bacteria.

  pi'li cunicula'ti, pi'li incarna'ti, ingrown *hairs.*

  pi'li tor'ti, twisted hairs; a condition in which the hair shafts are twisted on the long axis, as a result of distortion of the follicles from a scarring inflammatory process, mechanical stress, or cicatrizing alopecia.

pimelic acid (pĭ-mel'ik). Heptanedioic acid; HOOC-$(CH_2)_5$COOH; an intermediate in the oxidation of oleic acid; a precursor of biotin.

pimeli'tis (pim-ĕ-li'tis) [pimelo- + G. *-itis,* inflammation]. Inflammation of adipose tissue.

pimelo- [G. *pimelē,* soft fat, lard]. Combining form denoting fat or fatty.

pimelopterygium (pim'ĕ-lo-ter-ij'ĭ-um) [pimelo- + pterygium, *q. v.*]. A pterygium containing fat, composed in part of fatty tissue.

pimelosis (pim-ĕ-lo'sis) [pimelo- + G. suffix *-osis*, condition]. **1.** Adiposis. **2.** Fatty *degeneration*.

pimple (pim'pl). A papule or small pustule; usually meant to denote a lesion of acne.

pin. A metal rod used in surgical treatment of fractures.

pincement (pans-moń') [Fr. pinching]. A pinching manipulation in massage.

pineal (pin'e-al) [L. *pineus*, relating to the pine, pinus]. **1.** Piniform; shaped like a pine cone. **2.** Pertaining to the corpus pineale.

pinealectomy (pin'e-ă-lek'to-mĭ) [pineal + G. *ektomē*, excision]. Removal of the pineal body.

pinealocyte (pĭ-ne'al-o-sīt) [pineal + G. *kytos*, cell]. A cell of the pineal body with long processes ending in bulbous expansions.

pinealoma (pin'e-ă-lo'mah) [pineal + G. *-oma*, tumor]. A neoplasm derived from the pineal gland and characterized by relatively large round or polygonal cells with a large nucleus, as well as small cells that resemble lymphocytes.

pineoblastoma (pin'e-o-blas-to'mah) [pineal + G. *blastos*, germ, + *-oma*, tumor]. A poorly differentiated form of pinealoma.

pinguecula, pinguicula (ping-gwek'u-lah) [L. *pinguiculus*, fattish]. A yellowish spot sometimes observed on either side of the cornea in the aged; a connective tissue thickening of the conjunctiva.

piniform (pin'ĭ-form, pi'nĭ-) [L. *pinus*, pine, + *forma*, form]. Pineal (1).

pink'eye. Acute contagious or acute epidemic conjunctivitis.

pinna, pl. **pinnae** (pin'ah, pin'e) [L. *pinna* or *penna*, a feather; pl., a wing]. **1.** Auricula. **2.** A feather, wing, or fin.

pin'nal. Relating to a pinna.

pinocyte (pin'o-sīt, pi'no-) [G. *pineo*, to drink, + *kytos*, cell]. A cell that exhibits pinocytosis.

pinocytosis (pin'o-si-to'sis, pi'no-) [pinocyte + G. *-osis*, condition]. The cellular process of actively engulfing liquid, a phenomenon in which minute incuppings or invaginations are formed in the surface of the cell membrane and close to form fluid-filled vesicles; resembles phagocytosis.

pinosome (pin'o-sōm, pi'no-) [G. *pineō*, to drink, + *sōma*, body]. A fluid-filled vacuole formed by pinocytosis.

pint (pīnt). A measure of quantity, containing 16 fluidounces, 28.875 cubic inches; 473.166 cc; **imperial p.** contains 20 fluidounces, 34.659 cubic inches; 567.94 cc.

pinta (pin'tah, pēn'tah) [Sp. spot, blemish]. Azul; a disease caused by a spirochete, endemic in Mexico and Central America, and characterized by an eruption of patches of varying color that finally become white.

pin'worm. Seatworm; a member of the genus *Enterobius* or related genera of nematodes in the family Oxyuridae, abundant in a large variety of vertebrates, including *Enterobius vermicularis* (the human p.).

piperazine (pī-pĕr'ă-zēn, -zin). Formerly used in gout, based upon its property of dissolving uric acid *in vitro;* its compounds are now used as anthelmintics in oxyuriasis and ascariasis.

piperocaine hydrochloride (pip'er-o-kān, pĭ-pĕr'o-kān). 3-(2-Methyl-1-piperidyl)propyl benzoate hydrochloride; a rapidly acting local anesthetic for infiltration and spinal anesthesia.

pipette, pipet (pī-pĕt') [Fr. dim. of *pipe*, pipe]. Pipet; a graduated tube (marked in ml) used to transport a definite volume of a gas or liquid in laboratory work.

piriform (pĭr'ĭ-form, pi'rī-) [L. *pirum*, pear, + *forma*, form]. Pear-shaped.

Piroplasma (pĭr'o-plaz'mah, pi'ro-) [L. *pirum*, pear, + G. *plasma*, a thing formed]. Former name for *Babesia*.

pir'oplasmo'sis. Babesiosis.

pisiform (pis'ĭ-form) [L. *pisum*, pea, + *forma*, appearance]. Pea-shaped or pea-sized.

pit [L. *puteus*]. **1.** Any natural depression on the surface of the body, such as the axilla. **2.** One of the pinhead-sized depressed scars following the pustule of acne, chickenpox, or smallpox (pockmark). **3.** A sharp-pointed depression in the enamel surface of a tooth, due to faulty or incomplete calcification or formed by the confluent point of two or more lobes of enamel. **4.** To become indented, said of the edematous tissues when pressure is made with the fingertip.

   anal p., proctodeum.

   auditory p.'s, paired depressions, one on either side of the head of the embryo, marking the location of the future auditory vesicles.

   central p., *fovea* centralis retinae.

   iris p.'s, coloboma affecting the stroma of the iris with pigment epithelium intact.

   lens p.'s, paired depressions formed in the superficial ectoderm of the embryonic head as the lens placodes sink in toward the optic cup; the external openings of the p.'s are closed as the lens vesicles are formed.

   nasal p.'s, olfactory p.'s, paired depressions formed when the nasal placodes come to lie below the general external contour of the developing face as a result of the rapid growth of the adjacent nasal elevations.

   p. of the stomach, epigastric *fossa.*

   sublingual p., *fovea* sublingualis.

pith [A.S. *pitha*]. **1.** The center of a hair. **2.** The spinal cord and medulla oblongata.

pithecoid (pith'e-koyd) [G. *pithēkos*, ape, + *eidos*, resemblance]. Resembling an ape.

pit'ting. In dentistry, the formation of well defined, relatively deep depressions in a surface, usually used in describing defects in surfaces.

pituicyte (pĭ-tu'ĭ-sīt) [pituitary + G. *kytos*, cell]. The primary cell of the posterior lobe of the pituitary gland, a fusiform cell closely related to neuroglia.

pituicytoma (pī-tu´ĭ-si-to´mah) [pituicyte + G. *-oma*, tumor]. A gliogenous neoplasm derived from pituicytes, occurring in the posterior lobe of the pituitary gland and characterized by cells with relatively small, round or oval nuclei and long branching processes that form a complex network of cytoplasmic material.

pituitarism (pī-tu´ĭ-tăr-izm). Pituitary dysfunction.

pituitary (pit-u´ĭ-tĕr-ĭ). Relating to the pituitary gland (hypophysis).

pityriasic (pit-ĭ-ri´ă-sik). Relating to pityriasis.

pityriasis (pit-ĭ-ri´ă-sis) [G. fr. *pityron*, bran, dandruff]. A dermatosis marked by branny desquamation.

   p. al´ba, seborrheic *dermatitis.*

   p. ro´sea, a self-limited eruption of macules or papules involving principally the trunk and extremities; lesions are usually oval and follow the lines of cleavage of the skin.

   p. ru´bra, exfoliative *dermatitis.*

   p. ru´bra pila´ris, a chronic eruption of the hair follicles, which become firm, red, surmounted with horny plug, and often confluent to form scaly plaques; associated with erythema, thickening of the palms and soles, and opaque thickening of the nails.

   p. versic´olor, *tinea* versicolor.

pityroid (pit´ĭ-royd) [G. *pityrōdēs*, branlike]. Furfuraceous.

Pityrosporum (pit-ĭ-ros´po-rum) [G. *pityron*, bran, + *sporos*, seed]. A genus of nonpathogenic fungi found in dandruff and seborrheic dermatitis.

pixel (pik´sel). Contraction for picture element, a representation of a single volume element (voxel) of the display of the CT image.

pK Negative logarithm of the ionization constant (K_a) of an acid; the pH at which equal concentrations of the acid and basic forms of a substance (usually a buffer) are present.

PKU Phenylketonuria.

placebo (plă-se´bo) [L. I will please, future of *placeo*]. **1.** An indifferent substance, in the form of a medicine, given for the suggestive effect. **2.** An inert compound, identical in appearance with material being tested in experimental research, where the patient and the physician may or may not know which is which.

placenta (plă-sen´tah) [L. a cake] [NA]. The organ of metabolic interchange between fetus and mother, composed of a portion of embryonic origin, derived from the outermost embryonic membrane (chorion frondosum) and a maternal portion formed by a modification of the part of the uterine mucosa (decidua basalis) in which the chorionic vesicle is implanted. There is no direct mixing of fetal and maternal blood, but the intervening placental membrane is sufficiently thin to permit the absorption of nutritive materials, oxygen, and some harmful substances, like viruses, into the fetal blood and the release of carbon dioxide and nitrogenous waste

from it.

   p. accre´ta, abnormal adherence of the chorionic villi to the myometrium, associated with partial or complete absence of the decidua basalis and, in particular, the stratum spongiosum.

   battledore p., a p. in which the umbilical cord is attached at the border; so-called because of the fancied resemblence to the racquet (racket) used in battledore (precursor to badminton).

   bidiscoidal p., a p. with two separate disc-shaped portions attached to opposite walls of the uterus, normal for certain monkeys and shrews, and occasionally found in humans.

   p. circumvalla´ta, a cup-shaped with raised edges, having a thick, round, white, opaque ring around the periphery of the p.; fetal vessels are limited in their course across the p. by the ring.

   p. fenestra´ta, one in which there are areas of thinning, sometimes extending to entire absence of placental tissue.

   fetal p., the chorionic portion of the placenta, containing the fetal blood vessels, from which the funis arises.

   hemochorial p., the type of p., as in man, in which maternal blood is in direct contact with the chorion.

   hemoendothelial p., the type of p. in which the trophoblast becomes so attenuated that, by light microscopy, maternal blood appears to be separated from fetal blood only by the endothelium of the chorionic capillaries.

   p. incre´ta, a form of p. accreta in which the chorionic villi invade the myometrium.

   p. margina´ta, a p. with raised edges, less pronounced than the p. circumvallata.

   maternal p., that part of the p. derived from uterine tissue.

   p. membrana´cea, an abnormally thin p. covering an unusually large area of the uterine lining.

   p. pre´via, placental presentation; the condition in which the p. is implanted in the lower segment of the uterus, extending to the margin of the internal os of the cervix or partially or completely obstructing the os.

   p. reflex´a, an anomaly of the p. in which the margin is thickened so as to appear turned back upon itself.

   p. spu´ria, a mass of placental tissue that has no vascular connection with the main p.

   p. uteri´na, *pars* uterina placentae.

placen´tal. Relating to the placenta.

placentascan (plă-sen´tă-skan). A method of determining the location of the placenta by means of injected radioactive material and its localization and display by a scintillation detector.

placentation (plas-en-ta´shun). The structural organization and mode of attachment of fetal to maternal tissues in the formation of the placenta.

placentitis (plas-en-ti´tis). Inflammation of the placenta.

placentography (plas-en-tog′ră-fĭ) [placenta + G. *graphō*, to write]. Radiography of the placenta following injection of a radiopaque substance.

placentoma (plas-en-to′mah). Deciduoma.

placode (plak′ōd) [G. *plakōdēs*, fr. *plax*, anything flat or broad, + *eidos*, like]. A local thickening in an embryonic epithelial layer, the cells of which ordinarily constitute a primordial group from which some organ or structure is later developed.

plafond (plă-fon′) [Fr. ceiling]. A ceiling, especially the ceiling of the ankle joint, *i.e.*, the articular surface of the distal end of the tibia.

plagio- [G. *plagios*, oblique]. Combining form denoting oblique, slanting.

plagiocephalic (pla′jĭ-o-sĕ-fal′ĭk). Relating to or marked by plagiocephaly.

plagiocephaly (pla′jĭ-o-sef′ă-lĭ) [G. *plagios*, oblique, + *kephalē*, head]. An asymmetric craniostenosis due to premature closure of the lambdoid and coronal sutures on one side; characterized by an oblique deformity of the skull.

plague (plăg) [L. *plaga*, a stroke, injury]. **1.** Any disease of wide prevalence or of excessive mortality. **2.** Pest; an acute infectious disease caused by *Pastuerella pestis* and marked clinically by high fever, toxemia, prostration, a petechial eruption, lymph node enlargement, and pneumonia, or hemorrhage from the mucous membranes; primarily a disease of rodents and is transmitted to man by fleas that have bitten infected animals.

    bubonic p., the usual form of p. marked by inflammatory enlargement of the lymphatic glands in the groins, axillae, or other parts.

    hemorrhagic p., the hemorrhagic form of bubonic p.

    pneumonic p., a frequently fatal form in which there are areas of pulmonary consolidation, with chill, pain in the side, bloody expectoration, and high fever.

plan-. See plano-.

pla′na [L.]. Plural of planum.

plane (plăn) [L. *planus*, flat]. **1.** A flat surface. See planum. **2.** An imaginary surface formed by extension through any axis or two definite points in reference especially to craniometry and to pelvimetry.

    Addison's clinical p.'s., a series of p.'s used as landmarks in thoracoabdominal topography: **(1)** vertically, the trunk is divided by a *median p.* from the upper border of the manubrium sterni to the symphysis pubis, by a *lateral p.* drawn vertically on either side through a point half way between the anterior superior iliac spine and the median p. at the interspinal p., and by a *spinous p.* passing vertically through the anterior superior iliac spine on either side; **(2)** transversely, the trunk is divided by a *transthoracic p.* passing across the thorax just above the lower border of the corpus sterni, by a *transpyloric p.* midway between the jugular notch of the sternum and the pubic symphysis, and by an

intertubular p. passing through the iliac tubercles and cutting usually the fifth lumbar vertebra.

    coronal p., frontal p.; a vertical p. at right angles to a sagittal p., dividing the body into anterior and posterior portions.

    datum p., an arbitrary p. used as a base from which to make craniometric measurements.

    Frankfort p., Frankfort horizontal p., a standard craniometric reference p. passing through the right and left porion and the left orbitale; it is drawn on the profile radiograph or photograph from the superior margin of the acoustic meatus to the orbitale.

    frontal p., coronal p.

    horizontal p., transverse p.; a p. across the body at right angles to the coronal and sagittal p.'s.

    p. of inlet, *apertura* pelvis superior.

    interspinal p., a horizontal plane passing through the anterior superior iliac spines; it marks the boundary between the lateral and umbilical regions superiorly and the inguinal and pubic regions inferiorly.

    median p., midsagittal p., a vertical p. through the midline of the body that divides the body into right and left halves.

    nuchal p., the external surface of the squamous part of the occipital bone giving attachment to the muscles of the back of the neck.

    orbital p., the orbital surface of the maxilla, lying perpendicular to the Frankfort p. at the orbitale.

    p. of pelvic canal, *axis* pelvis.

    pelvic p. of greatest dimensions, the p. extending from the middle of the posterior surface of the pubic symphysis to the junction of the second and third sacral vertebrae, and laterally passing through the ischial bones over the middle of the acetabulum.

    pelvic p. of least dimensions, the p. that extends from the end of the sacrum to the inferior border of the pubic symphysis, bounded posteriorly by the end of the sacrum, laterally by the ischial spines, and anteriorly by the inferior border of the pubic symphysis.

    sagittal p., the anteroposterior median p., or any p. parallel to it.

    sternal p., a p. indicated by the front surface of the sternum.

    subcostal p., a horizontal plane passing through the inferior limits of the tenth costal cartilages; marks the boundary between the hypochondriac and epigastric regions superiorly and the lateral and umbilical regions inferiorly.

    temporal p., a slightly depressed area on the side of the cranium, below the inferior temporal line, formed by the temporal and parietal bones, the greater wing of the sphenoid, and a part of the frontal bone.

    transverse p., horizontal p.

plani-. See plano.-

planigraphy (plă-nig′ră-fĭ) [L. *planum*, plane, + G. *graphē*, a writing]. Tomography.

plano-, plan-, plani-   1. [L. *planum*, plane; *planus*, flat]. Combining form relating to a plane, or meaning flat or level. 2. [G. *planos*, roaming, wandering]. Combining form meaning wandering.

planocellular (pla-no-sel'u-lar) [L. *planus*, flat, + cellular]. Relating to or composed of flat cells.

planoconcave (pla-no-kon'kăv). Flat on one side and concave on the other; denoting a lens of that shape.

planoconvex (pla-no-kon'veks). Flat on one side and convex on the other; denoting a lens of that shape.

planog'raphy. Tomography.

pla'noval'gus [plano- + L. *valgus*, turned outward]. A condition in which the longitudinal arch of the foot is flattened and everted.

planta, gen. and pl. **plantae** (plan'tah, plan'te) [L.] [NA]. Pelma; the sole of the foot.

plantalgia (plan-tal'jĭ-ah) [L. *planta*, sole of foot, + G. *algos*, pain]. Pain on the plantar surface of the foot over the plantar fascia.

plan'tar [L. *plantaris*]. Relating to the sole of the foot.

plantigrade (plan'tĭ-grād) [L. *planta*, sole, + *gradior*, to walk]. Walking with the entire sole and heel of the foot on the ground, as do man and bears.

planum, pl. **plana** (pla'num, pla'nah) [L. plane]. A plane or a flat surface.

plaque (plak) [Fr. a plate]. 1. Platelet. 2. A patch or small differentiated area on a surface. 3. A sharply defined zone of demyelination characteristic of multiple sclerosis.

    bacterial p., dental p. (2); a mass of filamentous microorganisms and a variety of smaller forms attached to the surface of a tooth which may give rise to caries, calculus, or inflammatory changes in adjacent tissue.

    dental p., (1) the noncalcified accumulation of oral microorganisms and their products that adheres to the teeth; (2) bacterial p.

    Hollenhorst p.'s, glittering orange-yellow atheromatous emboli in the retinal arterioles containing cholesterin crystals, a sign of serious cardiovascular disease.

-plasia [G. *plassō*, to form]. Suffix meaning formation.

plasm (plazm). Plasma.

plasma-, plasmat-, plasmato-, plasmo- [G. *plasma*, something formed]. Combining forms denoting plasma.

plasma (plaz'mah) [G. something formed]. Plasm. 1. Blood p.; the fluid (noncellular) portion of the circulating blood, distinguished from the serum obtained after coagulation. 2. The fluid portion of the lymph.

    antihemophilic p. (human), human p. in which the labile antihemophilic globulin component, present in fresh p., has been preserved; is used to temporarily relieve dysfunction of the hemostatic mechanism in hemophilia.

    blood p., plasma (1).

    fresh frozen p. (FFP), separated p., frozen within 6 hours of collection, used in hypovolemia and coagulation factor deficiency.

    normal human p., sterile p. obtained by pooling approximately equal amounts of the liquid portion of citrated whole blood from eight or more adult humans who have been certified as free from any disease tranmissible by transfusion, and treating it with ultraviolet irradiation to destroy possible bacterial and viral contaminants.

plasmablast (plaz'mă-blast) [plasma + G. *blastos*, germ]. Precursor of the plasma cell.

plasmacrit (plaz'mă-krit) [plasma + G. *krinō*, to separate]. A measure of the percentage of the volume of blood oocupied by plasma, in contrast to a hemocrit.

plasmacyte (plaz'mă-sīt). Plasma *cell.*

plasmacytoma (plaz'mă-si-to'mah) [plasmacyte + G. *-oma*, tumor]. Plasmocytoma; plasmoma; a discrete, presumably solitary mass of neoplastic plasma cells in bone or in one of various extramedullary sites; probably the initial phase of developing plasma cell myeloma.

plas'ma expander. Plasma *substitute.*

plasmacytosis (plaz'mă-si'to 'sis) [plasmacyte + G. *-osis*, condition]. Plasmocytosis. 1. Presence of plasma cells in the circulating blood. 2. Presence of unusually large proportions of plasma cells in the tissues or exudates.

plas'malem'ma [plasma + G. *lemma*, husk]. Cell *membrane.*

plasmalogen (plaz-mal'o-jen). Alk-1-enylglycerophosphate.

plasmapheresis (plaz'mă-fĕ-re'sis) [plasma + G. *aphairesis*, a withdrawal]. Removal of whole blood from the body, separation of its cellular elements by centrifugation, and reinfusion of them suspended in saline or some other plasma substitute, thus depleting the body's own plasma protein without depleting its cells.

plas'mapheret'ic. Relating to plasmapheresis.

plasmat-, plasmato-. See plasma-.

plasmatic (plaz-mat'ĭk). Plasmic; relating to plasma.

plasmic (plaz'mik). Plasmatic.

plasmid (plaz'mid). Extrachromosomal *element.*

    bacteriocinogenic p. s, bacteriocinogens; bacterial p.'s responsible for the elaboration of bacteriocins.

    conjugative p., an extrachromosomal element that can effect its own intercellular transfer by means of conjugation.

    F p., F or fertility factor; the prototype conjugative p. associated with conjugation in the K-12 strain of *Escherichia coli.*

    nonconjugative p., an extrachromosomal element that cannot effect conjugation and self-transfer to another bacterium (bacterial strain); transfer depends upon mediation of conjugative p.

    R p.'s, resistance p.'s, R or resistance factors; p.'s carrying genes responsible for antibiotic (or antibacterial drug) resistance among bacteria; may be conjugative or nonconjugative p.'s, the former possessing transfer genes (resistance transfer factor) lacking in the latter.

plasmin (plaz'min). Fibrinolysin; fibrinase (2); an enzyme hydrolyzing peptides and esters of arginine and histidine, and converting fibrin to soluble products; occurs in plasma as plasminogen and is activated to plasmin by organic solvents.

plasminogen (plaz-min'o-jen). See plasmin.

plasmo-. See plasma-.

plas'mocyte. Plasma cell.

plas'mocyto'ma. Plasmacytoma.

plas'mocyto'sis. Plasmacytosis.

plasmodia (plaz-mo'dĭ-ah) [L.]. Plural of plasmodium.

plasmo'dial. Relating to a plasmodium, or to any species of the genus Plasmodium.

Plasmo'dium (plaz-mo'dĭ-um) [Mid. L. from G. plasma, something formed, + eidos, appearance]. A genus of the family Plasmodiidae (order or suborder Haemosporidia) that are blood parasites of vertebrates; includes the causal agents of malaria in man and other animals, with an asexual cycle occurring in liver and red blood cells of vertebrates and a sexual cycle in mosquitoes.

P. falcip'arum, a species that is the causal agent of falciparum or malignant tertian malaria.

P. mala'riae, a species that is the causal agent of quartan malaria.

P. ova'le, a species that is the agent of the least common form of human malaria; resembles P. vivax in its earlier stages, but often modifies the cell membrane, causing it to form a fimbriated outline, and the cell often assumes an oval shape.

P. vi'vax, the species that is the most common malarial parasite of man.

plasmodium, pl. **plasmodia** (plaz-mo'dĭ-um, -dĭ-ah) [Mod. L. fr. G. plasma, something formed, + eidos, appearance]. A protoplasmic mass containing several nuclei, resulting from multiplication of the nucleus without cell division.

plasmogamy (plaz-mog'ă-mĭ) [plasmo- + G. gamos, marriage]. Union of two or more cells with preservation of the individual nuclei, to form plasmodium.

plasmolysis (plaz-mol'ĭ-sis) [plasmo- + G. lysis, dissolution]. **1.** Dissolution of cellular components. **2.** Shrinking of plant cells by osmotic loss of cytoplasmic water.

plasmolyt'ic. Relating to plasmolysis.

plasmoma (palz-mo'mah). Plasmacytoma.

plasmon (plaz'mon). The total of the genetic properties of the cell cytoplasm.

plasmorrhexis (plaz-mo-rek'sis). The splitting open of a cell from the pressure of the protoplasm.

plasmoschisis (plaz-mos'kĭ-sis) [plasmo- + G. schisis, a cleaving]. The splitting of protoplasm into fragments.

plasmotrop'ic. Pertaining to or manifesting plasmotropism.

plasmotropism (plaz-mot'ro-pizm) [plasmo- + G. tropē, a turning]. A condition in which the bone marrow, spleen, and liver contain strongly hemolytic bodies that cause the destruction of the erythrocytes, although the latter are not affected while in the circulating blood.

plas'ter [L. emplastrum; G. emplastron, plaster or mold]. **1.** A solid preparation which can be spread when heated, and which becomes adhesive at the temperature of the body; used to keep the edges of a wound in apposition, to protect raw surfaces, and, when medicated, to redden or blister the skin or to apply drugs to the surface to obtain their systemic effects. **2.** See p. of Paris.

p. of Paris, exsiccated calcium sulfate from which the water of crystallization has been expelled by heat, but which, when mixed with water, will form a paste which subsequently sets; used for casts and making impressions.

plas'tic [G. plastikos, relating to molding]. **1.** Capable of being formed or molded. **2.** A material that can be shaped by pressure or heat to the form of a cavity or mold.

plasticity (plas-tis'ĭ-tĭ). The capability of being formed or molded; the quality of being plastic.

plastid (plas'tid) [G. plastos, formed, + -id (2)]. **1.** Trophoplast; one of the differentiated structures in cytoplasm of plant cells where photosynthesis or other cellular processes are carried on. **2.** One of the granules of foreign or differentiated matter, food particles, waste material, etc., in cells. **3.** A self-duplicating virus-like particle that multiplies within a host cell.

-plasty [G. plastos, formed, shaped]. Suffix meaning molding or shaping or the result thereof, as of a surgical procedure.

plasty (plas'tĭ) [G. plassō, to fashion]. A surgical procedure for repair of a defect or restoration of form and/or function of a part.

plate (plāt) [O.Fr. plat, a flat object]. **1.** In anatomy, lamina; lamella; a thin, flat, differentiated structure. **2.** A metal bar applied to a fractured bone in order to maintain the ends in apposition. **3.** A denture. **4.** The agar layer within a Petri dish or similar vessel. **5.** To form a very thin layer of a bacterial culture by streaking it on the surface of agar to isolate individual organisms from which a colonial clone will develop.

anal p., the anal portion of the cloacal p.

axial p., the primitive streak of an embryo.

cribriform p. of ethmoid bone, lamina cribrosa ossis ethmoidalis.

cutis p., dermatome (2).

dorsal p. of neural tube, lamina alaris.

epiphysial p., cartilago epiphysialis.

equatorial p., the collected chromosomes at the equator of the spindle in the process of mitosis.

floor p., ventral p.; the thin ventral portion of the embryonic neural tube which merges on either side with the basal portion of the lateral p.'s.

lateral p., a nonsegmented mass of mesoderm on the lateral periphery of the embryonic disk.

medullary p., neural p.

motor p., a motor endplate.

muscle p., myotome (2).

neural p., medullary p; the unpaired neuroectodermal region of the early enbryo's dorsal surface which in later development is transformed into the neural tube and neural crest.

roof p., roofplate; the thin layer of the embryonic neural tube connecting the lateral p.'s dorsally.

tarsal p.'s, *tarsus* superior and inferior.

tympanic p., the bony p. between the anterior wall of the external acoustic meatus and the tympanic cavity and the posterior wall of the mandibular fossa.

ventral p., floor p.

ventral p. of neural tube, *lamina basalis.*

platelet (plāt′let) [see plate]. An irregularly shaped disk found in blood, containing granules in the central part (granulomere) and, peripherally, clear protoplasm (hyalomere), but with no definite nucleus and no hemoglobin. Also called thrombocyte; thromboplastid (1); hemolamella; elementary particle (1) or body (2); blood disk.

plateletpheresis (plāt′let-fē-re′sis) [platelet + G. *aphairesis,* a withdrawal]. Removal of blood from a donor with replacement of all blood components except platelets.

platinum (plat′ĭ-num) [Mod. L., originally *platina,* fr. Sp. *plata,* silver]. A metallic element, symbol Pt, atomic no. 78, atomic weight 195.09.

platy- [G. *platys,* flat, broad]. Combining form denoting width or flatness.

platybasia (plat-ĭ-ba′sĭ-ah) [*platy-* + G. *basis,* ground]. A developmental anomaly of the skull or an acquired softening of the skull bones so that the floor of the posterior cranial fossa bulges upward in the region about the foramen magnum.

platycephalic,   **platycephalous** (plat′ĭ-sĕ-fal′ik, -sef′ă-lus) [platy- + G. *kephalē,* head]. Having a flattened skull.

platyhelminth (plat-ĭ-hel′minth) [platy- + G. *helmins,* worm]. Common name for any flatworm of the phylum Platyhelminthes; any cestode (tapeworm) or trematode (fluke).

Platyhelminthes (plat′ĭ-hel-min′thēz) [see platyhelminth]. A phylum of flatworms that are bilaterally symmetric, flattened, and without a true body cavity; parasitic species of medical and veterinary importance are in the subclass Cestoda (the tapeworms) of the class Cestoidea, and in the subclass Digenea (the flukes) of the class Trematoda.

platypnea (plă-tip′ne-ah) [platy- + G. *pnoē,* a breathing]. Difficulty in breathing when erect, relieved by recumbency.

platysma, pl. **platysmas, platysmata** (plă-tiz′mah, -tiz′mă-tah) [G. *platysma,* a flatplate] [NA]. A muscle: *origin,* subcutaneous layer and fascia covering pectoralis major and deltoid at level of first or second rib; *insertion,* lower border of mandible, risorius and platysma of opposite side; *action,* depresses lower lip, wrinkles skin of neck and upper chest; *nerve supply,* cervical branch of facial.

platyspondylia, platyspondylisis (plat′ĭ-spon-dil′ĭ-ah, -spon-dĭ-li′sis) [platy- + G. *spondylos, vertebra*]. Flatness of the bodies of the vertebrae.

pledget (plej′et). A tuft of wool, cotton, or lint.

-plegia [G. *plēgē,* stroke]. Suffix denoting paralysis.

pleio-. Rarely used alternative spelling for pleo-.

pleiotropy, pleiotropia (pli-ot′o-pī, pli′o-tro′pī-ah) [pleio- + G. *tropos,* turning]. Production by a single mutant gene of apparently unrelated multiple effects at the clinical or phenotypic level.

pleo- [G. *pleiōn,* more]. Combining form denoting more.

pleocytosis (ple′o-si-to′sis) [pleo- + G. *kytos,* cell, + *-ōsis,* condition]. Presence of more cells than normal; often denotes leukocytosis and especially lymphocytosis or round cell infiltration.

pleomas′tia [pleo- + G. *mastos,* breast]. Polymastia.

pleomorphic (ple-o-mor′fik). **1.** Polymorphic. **2.** Among fungi, having two or more spore forms; also used to describe a sterile mutant dermatophyte resulting from degenerative changes in culture.

pleomorphism (ple-o-mor′-fizm) [pleo- + G. *morphē,* form]. Polymorphism.

pleomor′phous. Polymorphic.

pleonasm (ple′o-nazm) [G. *pleonasmos,* exaggeration, excessive, fr. *pleiōn,* more]. Excess in number or size of parts.

pleonosteosis (ple′on-os-te-o′sis) [pleo- + G. *osteon,* bone, + *-osis,* condition]. Superabundance of bone formation.

pless-, plessi- [G. *plessō,* to strike]. Combining forms denoting a striking, especially percussion.

plessimeter (plĕ-sim′e-ter) [G. *plēssō,* to strike, + *metron,* measure]. Pleximeter; a flexible oblong plate used in mediate percussion by being placed against the skin and struck with the plessor.

ples′sor [G. *plēssō,* to strike]. Plexor; percussor; a small hammer, usually with soft rubber head, used to tap the part directly, or with a plessimeter, in percussion of the chest or other part.

plethora (pleth′o-rah) [G. *plēthōrē, fullness*]. Repletion. **1.** Hypervolemia. **2.** An excess of any of the body fluids.

plethoric (plĕ-thor′ik, pleth′o-rik). Sanguine (1); sanguineous (2); relating to plethora.

plethysmograph (plĕ-thiz′mo-graf) [G. *plēthysmos,* increase, + *graphō,* to write]. A device for measuring and recording changes in volume of a part, organ, or whole body.

plethysmography (pleth-iz-mog′ră-fĭ) [G. *plēthysmos,* increase, + *graphē,* a writing]. Use of a plethysmograph.

plethysmometry (pleth-iz-mom′ĕ-trĭ) [G. *plēthysmos,* increase, + *metron,* measure]. Measuring the fullness of a hollow organ or vessel, as of the pulse.

pleur-, pleura-, pleuro- [G. *pleura*, a rib, the side]. Combining forms denoting rib, side, or pleura.

pleura, gen. and pl. **pleurae** (plūr'ah, plūr'ē) [G. *pleura*, a rib, pl. the side] [NA]. The serous membrane enveloping the lungs (**pulmonary p.**) and lining the walls of the pleural cavity (**parietal p.**).

pleuracotomy (plūr-ă-kot'o-mǐ) [pleura + G. *tomē*, a cutting]. Thoracotomy.

pleural (plūr'al). Relating to the pleura.

pleuralgia (plūr-al'jǐ-ah) [pleur- + G. *algos*, pain]. Pleurodynia (2).

pleuralgic (plūr-al'jik). Relating to pleuralgia.

pleurapophysis (plūr'ă-pof'ǐsis) [pleur- + G. *apophysis*, process, offshoot 1]. A rib, or the process on a cervical or lumbar vertebra corresponding thereto.

pleurectomy (plūr-ek'to-mǐ) [pleur- + G. *ektomē*, excision]. Excision of pleura, usually parietal.

pleurisy (plūr'ǐ-sǐ) [L. *pleurisis*, fr. G. *pleuritis*]. Pleuritis; inflammation of the pleura.

    adhesive p., dry p.

    diaphragmatic p., epidemic *pleurodynia.*

    dry p., adhesive, fibrinous, or plastic p.; p. with a fibrinous exudation, without an effusion of serum, resulting in adhesion between the opposing surfaces of the pleura.

    p. with effusion, serous or wet p.; p. accompanied by serous exudation.

    fibrinous p., dry p.

    interlobular p., inflammation limited to the pleura in the sulci between the pulmonary lobes.

    plastic p., dry p.

    purulent p., p. with empyema.

    serofibrinous p., the more common form of p., characterized by a fibrinous exudate on the surface of the pleura and an extensive effusion of serous fluid into the pleural cavity.

    serous p., wet p., p. with effusion.

pleuritic (plūr-it'ik). Pertaining to pleurisy.

pleuritis (plūr-i'tis) [G. fr. *pleura*, side, + *itis*, inflammation]. Pleurisy.

pleuro-. See pleur-.

pleurocele (plūr'o-sēl) [pleuro- + G. *kēlē*, hernia]. Pneumonocele.

pleurocentesis (plūr'o-sen-te'sis) [pleuro- + G. *kentēsis*, puncture]. Thoracentesis.

pleurocentrum (ploor'o-sen'trum) [pleuro- + G. *kentron*, center]. One of the lateral halves of the body of a vertebra.

pleuroclysis (plūr-ok'lǐ-sis) [pleuro- + G. *klysis*, a washing out]. Washing out of the pleural cavity.

pleurodesis (plūr-od'ě-sis) [pleuro- + G. *desis*, a binding together]. Surgical creation of a fibrous adhesion between the visceral and parietal layers of the pleura, thus obliterating the pleural cavity; a treatment in cases of recurrent spontaneous pneumothorax, malignant pleural effusion, and chylothorax.

pleurodynia (plūr'o-din'ǐ-ah) [pleuro- + G. *odynē*, pain]. Costalgia. **1.** Pleuritic pain in the chest. **2.** Pleuralgia; a painful rheumatic affection of the tendinous attachments of the thoracic muscles, usually of one side only.

    epidemic p., an acute infectious disease usually occurring in epidemic form and characterized by paroxysms of pain, usually in the chest; associated with strains of group B coxsackievirus. Also called Bornholm disease; diaphragmatic pleurisy; epidemic myalgia or myositis.

pleurogenic; pleurogenous (plūr-o-jen'ik, -oj'ě-nus) [pleuro- + -*gen*, producing]. Pleurogenous; of pleural origin; beginning in the pleura.

pleurography (plūr-og'răfǐ) [pleuro- + G. *graphō*, to write]. Radiography of the pleural cavity.

pleurohepatitis (plūr'o-hep-ă-ti'tis) [pleuro- + G. *hēpar*, liver, + -*itis*, inflammation]. Hepatitis with extension of the inflammation to the neighboring portion of the pleura.

pleurolith (plūr'o-lith) [pleuro- + G. *lithos, stone*]. Pleural calculus; a concretion in the pleural cavity.

pleurolysis (plūr-ol'ǐ-sis) [pleuro- + G. *lysis*, dissolution]. Surgical division of pleural adhesions.

pleuroparietopexy (plūr'o-pă-ri'ě-to-pek-sǐ) [pleuro- + parietal + G. *pēxis*, fixation]. Suturing of the visceral pleura to the thoracic wall.

pleuropericardial (plūr'o-pěr-ǐ-kar'dǐ-al). Relating to both pleura and pericardium.

pleuropericarditis (plūr'o-pěr'ǐ-kar-di'tis) [pleuro- + pericardium + G. -*itis*, inflammation]. Combined inflammation of the pericardium and of the pleura.

pleuroperitoneal (plūr'o-pěr-ǐ-to-ne'al). Relating to both pleura and peritoneum.

pleuropulmonary (plūr'o-pul'mo-něr-ǐ). Relating to the pleura and the lungs.

pleurotomy (plūr-ot'o-mǐ) [pleuro- + G. *tomē*, incision]. Thoracotomy.

pleurovisceral (plūr-o-vis'er-al). Visceropleural.

plexal (plek'sal). Relating to a plexus.

plexectomy (plek-sek'to-mǐ) [plexus + G. *ektomē*, excision]. Surgical excision of a plexus.

plexiform (plek'sǐ-form) [plexus + L. *forma*, form]. Weblike, or resembling or forming a plexus.

pleximeter (plek-sim'ǐ-ter) [G. *plēxis*, stroke]. Plessimeter.

plexitis (plek-si'tis). Irritation of a plexus.

plexogenic (pleks'o-jen-ik) [plexus + G. -*gen*, producing]. Giving rise to weblike or plexiform structures.

plexometer (plek-som'ě-ter). Plessimeter.

plexor (plek'sor) [G. *plēxis*, a stroke]. Plessor.

plexus, pl. **plexuses, plexus** (plek'sus, -ez) [L. a braid] [NA]. A network or interjoining of nerves and blood vessels or of lymphatic vessels.

    aortic p., (1) a p. of lymph nodes and connecting vessels lying along the lower portion of the abdominal aorta; (2) an autonomic p. surrounding the abdominal aorta, directly continuous with the thoracic aortic p.; (3) an autonomic p. surrounding the thoracic aorta and passing with it through the aortic opening in the diaphragm, to become continuous with the abdominal aortic p.

p. autono′mici [NA], **autonomic p.'s,** p.'s of nerves in relation to blood vessels and viscera, the component fibers of which are sympathetic parasympathetic, and sensory.

p. brachia′lis [NA], **brachial p.,** formed of the anterior branches of the fifth cervical to first thoracic nerves which converge in the posterior triangle of the neck between the scalenus anterior and medius muscles and pass down on the lateral side of the subclavian artery behind the clavicle into the axilla.

p. cardi′acus [NA], **cardiac p.,** a wide-meshed network of anastomosing cords from the sympathetic and vagus nerves, surrounding the arch of the aorta, the pulmonary artery, and continuing to the atria, ventricles, and coronary vessels.

p. carot′icus [NA], (1) common carotid p.; an autonomic p. accompanying the artery of the same name formed by fibers from the middle cervical ganglion; (2) external carotid p.; an autonomic p. formed by the external carotid nerves surrounding the artery of the same name, and giving origin to a number of secondary p.'s along the branches of this artery and to branches to the carotid body; (3) internal carotid p.; an autonomic p. surrounding the internal carotid artery in the carotid canal and cavernous sinus, and sending branches to the tympanic p., sphenopalatine ganglion, abducens and oculomotor nerves, the cerebral vessels, and the ciliary ganglion.

p. celi′acus, celiac p., (1) [NA] solar p.; the largest of the autonomic p.'s, lying in front of the aorta at the level of origin of the celiac artery and behind the stomach; formed by the splanchnic and the vagus nerves and cords from the celiac and superior mesenteric ganglia, and through its connections with the other abdominal p.'s it sends branches to all the abdominal viscera; (2) a lymphatic p. formed of the superior mesenteric lymph nodes and the nodes behind the stomach, duodenum, and pancreas, together with the connecting vessels.

p. cervica′lis [NA], **cervical p.,** a p. lying beneath the sternocleido-mastoid muscle, formed by loops joining the anterior branches of the first four cervical nerves and receiving gray communicating branches from the superior cervical ganglion; sends out numerous cutaneous, muscular, and communicating branches.

p. choroi′deus [NA], **choroid p.,** a vascular proliferation of the cerebral ventricles that serves to regulate intraventricular pressure by secretion or absorption of cerebrospinal fluid.

p. coccyg′eus [NA], **coccygeal p.,** a small p. formed by the fifth sacral and the coccygeal nerves; gives origin to the anococcygeal nerves.

p. denta′lis [NA], (1) inferior: formed by branches of the inferior alveolar nerve interlacing before they supply the teeth; gives off dental and gingival branches; (2) superior: formed by branches of the infraorbital nerve; gives off dental and gingival branches.

p. hypogas′tricus [NA], **hypogastric p.,** (1) inferior: the autonomic p. in the pelvis that is distributed to the pelvic viscera, and receives the hypogastric nerves and the pelvic splanchnic nerves; (2) superior: continuation of the aortic p. into the pelvis where it divides into two hypogastric nerves at the sides of the rectum; these join the inferior hypogastric p.'s to supply pelvic viscera.

p. lumba′lis, lumbar p., (1) [NA], a nervous p., formed by the ventral branches of the first four lumbar nerves, lying in the substance of the psoas muscle; (2) a lymphatic p. formed of about 20 lymph nodes and connecting vessels situated along the lower portion of the aorta and the common iliac vessels.

p. lymphat′icus [NA], **lymphatic p.,** a network of lymphatic capillaries, usually without valves, that opens into one or more larger lymphatic vessels.

p. mesenter′icus [NA], **mesenteric p.,** (1) inferior: an autonomic p., derived from the aortic p., surrounding the inferior mesenteric artery and sending branches to the descending colon, sigmoid, and rectum; (2) superior: an autonomic p., a continuation or part of the celiac p., sending nerves to the intestines and forming with the vagus the subserous, myenteric, and submucous p.'s.

p. myenter′icus [NA], **myenteric p.,** a p. of unmyelinated fibers and postganglionic autonomic cell bodies lying in the muscular coat of the esophagus, stomach, and intestines, and communicating with the subserous and submucous p.'s.

nerve p., a p. formed by the interlacing of nerves by means of numerous communicating branches.

p. pampinifor′mis [NA], **pampiniform p.,** a p. formed, in the male, by veins from the testicle and epididymis lying in front of the ductus deferens and forming part of the spermatic cord; in the female the ovarian veins form this p. between the layers of the broad ligament.

p. periarteria′lis [NA], **periarterial p.,** an autonomic p. that accompanies an artery.

p. pulmona′lis [NA], **pulmonary p.,** one of two autonomic p.'s, anterior and posterior, at the hilus of each lung, formed by branches of the sympathetic and bronchial branches of the vagus nerve; from them various branches accompany the bronchi and arteries into the lung.

p. sacra′lis [NA], **sacral p.,** formed by the fourth and fifth lumbar and first, second, and third sacral nerves, it lies on the inner surface of the posterior wall of the pelvis and supplies the lower limbs.

solar p., p. celiacus (1).

p. submuco′sus [NA], **submucosal p.,** a gangliated p. of unmyelinated nerve fibers, derived chiefly from the superior mesenteric p., ramifying in the intestinal submucosa.

p. tympan′icus [NA], **tympanic p.,** a p. on the promontory of the labyrinthine wall of the tympanic cavity, formed by the tympanic nerve, an anastomotic branch of the facial nerve, and sympathetic branches from the internal carotid p.; supplies the mucosa of the middle ear, mastoid cells, and auditory tube, and gives off the lesser petrosal nerve to the otic ganglion.

plica, pl. **plicae** (pli'kah, pli'se) [Mod. L. a plait or fold]. **1** [NA]. An anatomical structure in which there is a folding over of the parts. **2.** False *membrane.*

p. aryepiglot'tica [NA], aryepiglottic or aryteno-epiglottidean fold; a prominent fold of mucous membrane stretching between the lateral margin of the epiglottis and the arytenoid cartilage on either side to enclose the aryepiglottic muscle.

pli'cae circula'res [NA], circular folds; the numerous folds of the mucous membrane of the small intestine, running transversely for about two-thirds of the circumference of the gut.

p. epiglot'tica, epiglottic fold; one of the three folds of mucous membrane passing between the tongue and the epiglottis.

pli'cae gas'tricae [NA], gastric folds; characteristic folds of the gastric mucosa.

p. interureter'ica [NA], interureteric fold; Mercier's bar; a fold of mucous membrane extending from the orifice of the ureter of one side to that of the other side.

p. lacrima'lis [NA], lacrimal fold; a fold of mucous membrane guarding the lower opening of the nasolacrimal duct.

pli'cae palma'tae [NA], palmate folds; the two longitudinal ridges, anterior and posterior, in the mucous membrane lining the cervix uteri.

p. rectouteri'na [NA], rectouterine or Douglas fold; a fold of peritoneum, containing the rectouterine muscle, passing from the rectum to the base of the broad ligament on either side, forming the lateral boundary of the rectouterine (Douglas) pouch.

p. semiluna'ris conjuncti'vae [NA], semilunar conjunctival fold; the semilunar fold formed by the palpebral conjunctiva at the medial angle of the eye.

p. spira'lis duc'tus cys'tici [NA], spiral fold of the cystic duct; spiral valve; a series of crescentic folds of mucous membrane in the upper part of the cystic duct, arranged in a somewhat spiral manner.

pli'cae transversa'les rec'ti [NA], transverse folds of rectum; the three or four horizontal crescentic folds in the rectal mucous membrane above the anus.

p. vestibula'ris [NA], vestibular or ventricular fold; false vocal cord; one of the pair of folds of mucous membrane stretching across the laryngeal cavity from the angle of the thyroid cartilage to the arytenoid cartilage to enclose the rima vestibuli or false glottis.

p. voca'lis [NA], vocal cord or fold; true vocal cord; the sharp edge of a fold of mucous membrane stretching along either wall of the larynx from the angle between the laminae of the thyroid cartilage to the vocal process of the arytenoid cartilage; vibra-

tion of the f.'s are used in voice production.

plicate (pli'kāt). Folded; pleated; tucked.

plication (pli-ka'shun, plī-) [L. *plico,* to fold]. An operation for reducing the size of a hollow viscus by taking folds or tucks in its walls.

plicotomy (pli-kot'o-mī) [plica + G. *tomē,* incision]. Division of the fold(s) of the tympanic membrane.

-ploid [G. *-plo-,* -fold, + *-ides,* in form; L. *-ploïdeus*]. Adjectival suffix denoting multiple in form.

ploidy (ploy'dī) [see -ploid]. The state of a cell nucleus with respect to the number of genomes it contains; *e.g.,* diploid, haploid.

plombage (plom-bahzh') [Fr. lit. lead-work]. Formerly, the use of an inert material in collapse of the lung in the surgical treatment of pulmonary tuberculosis.

plug. A peg or any mass filling a hole or closing an orifice.

   Dittrich's p.'s, minute, dirty-grayish, ill-smelling masses of bacteria and fatty acid crystals in the sputum in pulmonary gangrene and fetid bronchitis.

   epithelial p., a mass of epithelial cells temporarily occluding an embryonic opening; most commonly used with reference to the nostrils.

   mucous p., a mass of mucus and cells filling the cervical canal between periods or during pregnancy.

plug'ger. Packer (2); an instrument used for condensing material in a cavity.

plumbic (plum'bik) [L. *plumbum,* lead]. **1.** Relating to or containing lead. **2.** Denoting the higher valence of lead ion. Pb^{4+}.

plum'bism [L. *plumbum,* lead]. Lead *poisoning.*

plum'bum [L.]. Lead.

pluri- [L. *plus, pluris,* more]. Combining form denoting several or more. See also multi-, poly-.

plu'riglan'dular. Multiglandular; polyglandular; denoting several glands or their secretions.

plurip'otent, plu'ripoten'tial. 1. Having the capacity to affect more than one organ or tissue. **2.** Not fixed as to potential development.

plutonium (plu-to'nī-um) [planet, *Pluto*]. A transuranic radioactive element, symbol Pu, atomic no. 94; its ions are boneseekers.

Pm Promethium.

pm Picometer.

P-mitra'le. An electrocardiographic syndrome consisting of broad, notched P waves in many leads and with a prominent late negative component to the P wave in leads V_1 and V_2, presumed to be characteristic of mitral valvular disease.

-pnea [G. *pneō,* to breathe]. Suffix denoting breath or respiration.

pneo- [G. *pneō,* to breathe]. Combining form denoting breath or respiration. See also pneum-, pneumo-.

pneograph (ne'o-graph). Pneumograph.

pneum-, pneuma-, pneumat-, pneumato- [G. *pneuma, pneumatos,* air, breath]. Combining forms denoting presence of air or gas, the lungs, or breathing. See also pneo-, pneumo-.

pneumarthro'sis (nu-mar-thro'sis) [G. *pneuma*, air, + *arthron*, joint, + *-osis*, condition]. Presence of air in a joint.

pneumatic (nu-mat'ik) [G. *pneumatikos*]. **1.** Relating to air or gas, or to a structure filled with air. **2.** Relating to respiration.

pneumatization (nu'mă-tĭ-za'shun) [G. *pneuma*, air]. The development of air cells such as those of the mastoid and ethmoidal bones.

pneumato-. See pneum-.

pneumatocardia (nu'mă-to-kar'dĭ-ah). The presence of air bubbles or gas in the blood of the heart, produced by air embolism.

pneumatocele (nu'mă-to-sēl) [G. *pneuma*, air, + *kēlē*, tumor, hernia]. **1.** An emphysematous or gaseous swelling. **2.** Pneumonocele. **3.** A thin-walled cavity forming within the lung, characteristic of staphylococcus pneumonia.

pneumatogram (nu'mă-to-gram). Pneumogram (1).

pneumatograph (nu'mă-to-graf). Pneumograph.

pneumatorrhachis (nu-mă-tor'ă-kis) [G. *pneuma*, air, + *rhachis*, spine]. Pneumorrhachis.

pneumatosis (nu-mă-to'sis) [G. a blowing out]. Abnormal accumulation of gas in any tissue or part of the body.

    p. cystoi'des intestina'lis, intestinal emphysema; a condition characterized by the occurrence of gas cysts in the intestinal mucous membrane; may produce intestinal obstruction.

pneumaturia (nu-mă-tu'rĭ-ah) [G. *pneuma*, air, + *ouron*, urine]. Passage of gas or air from the urethra during or after urination.

pneumectomy (nu-mek'to-mĭ). Pneumonectomy.

pneumo-, pneumon-, pneumono- [G. *pneumōn, pneumonos*, lung]. Combining forms denoting the lungs, air or gas, respiration, or pneumonia. See also pneo-, pneum-.

pneumoangiography (nu'mo-an-jĭ-og'ră-fĭ) [pneumo- + G. *angeion*, vessel, + *graphō*, to write]. Contrast radiography study of the pulmonary and bronchial blood vessels.

pneumoarthrography (nu'mo-ar-throg'ră-fĭ) [G. *pneuma*, air, + *arthron*, joint, + *graphō*, to write]. Radiographic study of a joint after injection of air.

pneumobacillus (nu'mo-bă-sil'us). *Klebsiella pneumoniae.*

pneumocardial (nu'mo-kar'dĭ-al). Cardiopulmonary.

pneumocele (nu'mo-sēl). Pneumonocele.

pneumocentesis (nu'mo-sen-te'sis). Pneumonocentesis.

pneumocephalus (nu-mo-sef'ă-lus) [G. *pneuma*, air, + *kephalē*, head]. Presence of air or gas within the cranial cavity.

pneumococcal (nu-mo-kok'al). Pertaining to or containing the pneumococcus.

pneumococcemia (nu'mo-kok-se'mĭ-ah) [pneumococcus + G. *haima*, blood]. Presence of pneumococci in the blood.

pneumococcidal (nu'mo-kok-sī'dal) [pneumococcus + L. *caedo*, to kill]. Destructive to pneumococci.

pneumococcosis (nu'mo-kok-o'sis). Infection with pneumococci.

pneumococcosuria (nu'mo-kok-o-su'rĭ-ah) [pneumococcus + G. *ouron*, urine]. Presence of pneumococci or their specific capsular substance in the urine.

pneumococcus, pl. **pneumococci** (nu-mo-kok'us, -kok'si) [G. *pneumōn*, lung, + *kokkos*, berry (coccus)]. *Streptococcus pneumoniae.*

pneumoconiosis, pl. **pneumoconioses** (nu'mo-ko-nĭ-o'sis, -sēz) [G. *pneumon*, lung, + *konis*, dust, + *-osis*, condition]. Inflammation commonly leading to fibrosis of the lungs due to irritation caused by inhalation of dust incident to an occupation; the degree of disability depends on the particles inhaled, as well as the level of exposure to them.

pneumocranium (nu-mo-kra'nĭ-um) [G. *pneuma*, air, + *kranion*, skull]. Presence of air between the cranium and the dura mater.

Pneumocystis carinii (nu-mo-sis'tis kah-rī'ne-i) [G. *pneuma*, air, breathing, + *kystis*, bladder, pouch]. A parasite, transitional between fungi and protozoa, frequently occurring as aggregate forms within a rounded cystlike structure with a visible wall; the apparent cause of pneumocystosis.

pneumocystography (nu'mo-sis-tog'ră-fĭ) [G. *pneuma*, air, + *kystis*, bladder, + *graphō*, to write]. Radiography of the bladder following injection of air.

pneumocystosis (nu'mo-sis-to'sis). Interstitial plasma cell pneumonia; pneumonia resulting from infection with *Pneumocystis carinii,* particularly frequent among immunologically compromised or debilitated individuals, characterized by alveoli filled with a network of acidophilic material within which the organisms are enmeshed; throughout the alveolar walls and pulmonary sputa there is a diffuse infiltration of mononuclear inflammatory cells, chiefly plasma cells and macrophages.

pneumoderma (nu-mo-der'mah) [G. *pneuma*, air, + *derma*, skin]. Subcutaneous emphysema.

pneumodynamics (nu'mo-di-nam'iks) [G. *pneuma*, breath, + *dynamis*, force]. The mechanics of respiration.

pneumoencephalogram (nu'mo-en-sef'ă-lo-gram). Radiograph obtained by pneumoencephalography.

pneumoencephalography (nu'mo-en-sef'ă-log'ră-fĭ) [G. *pneuma*, air, + *enkephalos*, brain, + *graphō*, to write]. Radiographic visualization of cerebral ventricles and subarachnoid spaces by use of gas such as air.

pneumogastric (nu-mo-gas'trik) [G. *pneumōn*, lung, + *gastēr*, stomach]. Gastropneumonic; gastropulmonary; relating to the lungs and the stomach.

pneumogram (nu'mo-gram) [G. *pneumōn*, lung, + *gramma*, a drawing]. **1.** Pneumatogram; record or tracing made by a pneumograph. **2.** Radiograph following air injection as in encephalography.

pneumograph (nu'mo-graf) [G. *pneumōn*, lung, + *graphō*, to write]. Pneograph; pneumatograph; an instrument for recording the force and rapidity of the respiratory movements, usually by responding to changes in chest circumference.

pneumography (nu-mog'ră-fĭ) [G. *pneumōn*, lung, + *graphō*, to write]. Radiography of the lungs.

pneumohemopericardium (nu'mo-he'mo-pĕr-ĭ-kar'dĭ-um). Hemopneumopericardium.

pneumohemothorax (nu'mo-he-mo-tho'raks). Hemopneumothorax.

pneumohydrometra (nu'mo-hi-dro-me'trah) [G. *pneuma*, air, + *hydōr* (*hydr-*), water, + *mētra*, uterus]. Presence of gas and serum in the uterine cavity.

pneumohydropericardium (nu'mo-hi'dro-pĕr-ĭ-kar'dĭ-um). Hydropneumopericardium.

pneumohydroperitoneum (nu'mo-hi'dro-pĕr-ĭ-to-ne'um). Hydropneumoperitoneum.

pneumohydrothorax (nu'mo-hi-dro-tho'raks). Hydropneumothorax.

pneumolith (nu'mo-lith) [G. *pneumōn*, lung, + *lithos*, stone]. A calculus in the lung.

pneu'molithi'asis. Formation of calculi in the lungs.

pneumomediastinum (nu'mo-me'dĭ-ă-sti'num) [G. *pneuma*, air, + mediastinum]. Escape of air into the mediastinal tissues, usually from interstitial emphysema or from a ruptured pulmonary bleb.

pneumomyelography (nu'mo-mi-ĕ-log'ră-fĭ) [G. *pneuma*, air, + *myelos*, marrow, + *graphō*, to write]. Radiographic examination of spinal canal after injection of air or gas into it.

pneumon-. See pneumo-.

pneumonectomy (nu-mo-nek'to-mĭ) [G. *pneumōn*, lung, + *ektomē*, excision]. Pneumectomy; removal of all pulmonary lobes, in one operation, from a lung.

pneumonia (nu-mo'nĭ-ah) [G. fr. *pneumōn*, lung, + *-ia*, condition]. Inflammation of the lung parenchyma, excluding the bronchi, in which the affected part is consolidated, the alveolar air spaces being filled with blood cells and fibrin; distribution may be lobar, segmental, or lobular.

    aspiration p., bronchopneumonia resulting from the entrance of foreign material, usually food particles or vomit into the bronchi.

    atypical p., primary atypical p.

    bronchial p., bronchopneumonia.

    desquamative interstitial p., diffuse proliferation of alveolar lining cells, which desquamate into the air sacs, producing a gradual onset of dyspnea and nonproductive cough.

    double p., lobar p. involving both lungs.

    Friedländer's p., a severe form of lobar p. caused by infection with *Klebsiella pneumoniae* (Friedländer's bacillus) and characterized by swelling of the affected lobe.

    hypostatic p., pulmonary congestion due to stagnation of blood in the dependent portions of the lungs in the aged or those debilitated by disease who lie in the same position for long periods.

    influenzal p., (1) p. complicating influenza; **(2)** p. due to *Haemophilus influenzae.*

    interstitial plasma cell p., pneumocystosis.

    lipid p., lipoid p., inflammatory and fibrotic changes in the lungs due to the inhalation of various oily or fatty substances; or from accumulation in the lungs of endogenous lipid material following fracture of a bone; phagocytes containing lipid are usually present.

    lobar p., p. affecting a lobe, lobes, or part of a lobe where the consolidation is homogeneous; commonly due to infection by *Streptococcus pneumoniae.*

    mycoplasmal p., primary atypical p.

    primary atypical p., atypical or mycoplasmal p.; an acute systemic disease with involvement of the lungs, caused by *Mycoplasma pneumoniae* and marked by high fever, cough, and relatively few physical signs; usually associated with development of cold agglutinins.

    progressive p., maedi.

    rheumatic p., p. occurring in severe acute rheumatic fever; consolidation occurs and nodules may be present in the fibrous septa of the lungs.

pneumonic (nu-mon'ĭk). **1.** Pulmonary. **2.** Relating to pneumonia.

pneumonitis (nu-mo-ni'tis) [G. *pneumōn*, lung, + *-itis*, inflammation]. Pulmonitis; inflammation of the lungs.

pneumono-. See pneumo-.

pneumonocele (nu'mo-no-sēl). Pneumatocele (2); pneumocele; pleurocele; protrusion of a portion of the lung through a defect in the chest wall.

pneumonocentesis (nu'mo-no-sen-te'sis) [G. *pneumōn*, lung, + *kentēsis*, puncture]. Pneumocentesis; paracentesis of the lung.

pneumonocyte (nu'mo-no-sit) [G. *pneumōn*, lung, + *kytos*, cell]. A nonspecific term sometimes used in referring to cells characteristic of the respiratory part of the lung.

pneumonopexy (nu'mo-no-pek-sĭ) [G. *pneumōn*, lung, + *pēxis*, fixation]. Fixation of the lung by suturing the costal and pulmonary pleurae or otherwise causing adhesion of the two layers.

pneumonorrhaphy (nu-mo-nor'ă-fĭ) [G. *pneumōn*, lung, + *rhaphē*, suture]. Suture of the lung.

pneumonotomy (nu-mo-not'o-mĭ) [G. *pneumōn*, lung, + *tomē*, incision]. Pneumotomy; incision of the lung.

pneumo-orbitography (nu'mo-or-bĭ-tog'ră-fĭ). Radiographic visualization of the orbital contents utilizing injection of a gas.

pneumopericardium (nu'mo-pĕr-ĭ-kar'dĭ-um) [G. *pneuma*, air, + pericardium]. Presence of gas in the pericardial sac.

pneumoperitoneum (nu'mo-pĕr-ĭ-to-ne'um) [G. *pneuma*, air, + peritoneum]. Presence of air or gas in the peritoneal cavity as a result of disease or produced artificially for the treatment of certain conditions.

pneumoperitonitis (nu'mo-pĕr-ĭ-to-ni'tis) [G. *pneuma*, air, + peritonitis]. Inflammation of the peritoneum, with an accumulation of gas in the peritoneal cavity.

pneumopleuritis (nu'mo-plŭr-i'tis) [G. *pneuma*, air, + pleur- + *-itis*, inflammation]. Pleurisy with air or gas in the pleural cavity.

pneumopyelography (nu'mo-pi-ĕ-log'ră-fĭ) [G. *pneuma*, air, + *pyelos*, pelvis, + *graphō*, to write]. Radiographic examination of the kidney after air or gas has been injected into the kidney pelvis.

pneumopyothorax (nu'mo-pi-o-tho'raks). Pyopneumothorax.

pneumoradiography (nu'mo-ra'dĭ-og'ră-fĭ). Radiographic study of a region after air has been injected into it.

pneumoretroperitoneum (nu'mo-ret'ro-pĕr'ĭ-tone'um). Escape of air into the retroperitoneal tissues.

pneumorrhachis (nu-mor'ă-kis) [G. *pneuma*, air, + *rachis*, spinal column]. Pneumatorrhachis; presence of gas in the spinal canal.

pneumotachogram (nu-mo-tak'o-gram) [G. *pneuma*, air, + *tachys*, swift, + *gramma*, something written]. A recording of respired gas flow as a function of time, produced by a pneumotachograph.

pneumotachograph (nu-mo-tak'o-graf). Pneumotachometer; an instrument for measuring the instantaneous flow of respiratory gases.

pneumotachometer (nu'mo-tă-kom'ĕ-ter) [G. *pneuma*, air, + *tachys*, swift, + *metron*, measure]. Pneumotachograph.

pneumothorax (nu-mo-tho'raks) [G. *pneuma*, air, + thorax]. Presence of air or gas in the pleural cavity.

   artificial p., p. produced by the injection of air or a gas into the pleural space to collapse the lung.

   open p., blowing or sucking wound; a free communication between the atmosphere and the pleural space either via the lung or through the chest wall.

   spontaneous p., p. occurring secondary to parenchymal lung disease.

pneumotomy (nu-mot'o-mi). Pneumonotomy.

PNPB Positive-negative pressure *breathing*.

Po Polonium.

pock [A.S. *poc*, a pustule]. The specific pustular cutaneous lesion of smallpox.

pock'et [Fr. *pochette*]. **1.** A cul-de-sac or pouchlike cavity. **2.** A diseased gingival attachment; a space between the inflammed gum and the surface of a tooth, limited apically by an epithelial attachment. **3.** To enclose within a confined space. **4.** A collection of pus in a nearly closed sac. **5.** To approach the surface at a localized spot, as with the thinned out wall of an abscess which is about to rupture.

pock'mark. The small depressed scar left after the healing of the smallpox pustule.

pod-, podo- [G. *pous, podos*, foot]. Combining forms meaning foot or foot-shaped.

podagra (po-dag'rah) [G. fr. *pous*, foot, + *agra*, a seizure]. Typical gout in the great toe.

podalgia (po-dal'jĭ-ah) [pod- + G. *algos*, pain]. Tarsalgia; pododynia; pain in the foot.

podalic (po-dal'ik) [G. *pous(pod-)*, foot]. Relating to the foot.

podarthritis (pod-ar-thri'tis) [pod- + arthritis]. Inflammation of any of the tarsal or metatarsal joints.

podedema (pod'ĕ-de'mah). Edema of the feet and ankles.

podiatrist (po-di'ă-trist) [pod- + G. *iatros*, physician]. Chiropodist; a practitioner of podiatry.

podiatry (po-di'ă-trĭ) [pod- + G. *iatreia*, medical treatment]. Chiropody; the specialty concerned with the diagnosis and/or medical, surgical, mechanical, physical, and adjunctive treatment of the diseases, injuries, and defects of the human foot.

podo-. See pod-.

pod'ocyte [podo- + G. *kytos*, a hollow (cell)]. An epithelial cell of the renal glomerulus, attached to the outer surface of the glomerular capillary basement membrane by cytoplasmic foot processes, or pedicels.

pododynamometer (pod'o-di-nă-mom'e-ter) [podo- + G. *dynamis*, force, + *metron*, measure]. An instrument for measuring the strength of the muscles of the foot or leg.

pododynia (pod-o-din'ĭ-ah) [podo- + G. *odynē*, pain]. Podalgia.

pod'ogram [podo- + G. *gramma*, written]. An imprint of the sole of the foot, showing the contour and the condition of the arch, or an outline tracing.

podomechanotherapy (pod'o-mek'ă-no-thĕr'ă-pĭ). Treatment of foot conditions with mechanical devices, *e.g.*, arch supports.

pogoniasis (po-go-ni'ă-sis) [G. *pōgōn*, beard, + *-iasis*, condition]. Growth of a beard on a woman, or excessive hairiness of the face in men.

pogonion (po-go'nĭ-on) [G. dim. of *pōgōn*, beard]. The most anterior point on the mandible in the midline.

-poiesis [G. *poiēsis*, a making]. Combining form denoting production.

poikilo- [G. *poikilos*, many colored, varied]. Combining form denoting irregular or varied.

poikiloblast (poy'kĭ-lo-blast) [poikilo- + G. *blastos*, germ]. A nucleated red blood cell of irregular shape.

poikilocyte (poy'kĭ-lo-sīt) [poikilo- + G. *kytos*, cell]. A red blood cell of irregular shape.

poikilocythemia (poy'kĭ-lo-si-the'mĭ-ah) [poikilocyte + G. *haima*, blood]. Poikilocytosis.

poikilocytosis (poy'kĭ-lo-si-to'sis) [poikilocyte + G. *-osis*, condition]. Poikilocythemia; presence of poikilocytes in the peripheral blood.

poikiloderma (poy'kĭ-lo-der'mah) [poikilo- + G. *derma*, skin]. A variegated hyperpigmentation and telangiectasia of the skin, followed by atrophy.

poikilothermic, poikilothermal, poikilothermous (poy'kĭ-lo-ther'mic, -mal, -mus) [poikilo- + G. *thermē*, heat]. Cold-blooded; hematocryal. **1.** Varying in temperature according to the temperature of the surrounding medium; denoting animals such as the reptiles and amphibians. **2.** Capable of existence and growth in mediums of varying temperatures.

point [Fr.; L. *punctum,* fr. *pungo,* pp. *punctus,* to pierce]. **1.** Punctum. **2.** A sharp end or apex. **3.** A slight projection. **4.** A stage or condition reached. **5.** To become ready to open, as an abscess or boil.

p. A, subspinale.

alveolar p., prosthion.

anterior focal p., the p. where rays starting parallel from the retina are focused.

auricular p., auriculare.

p. B, supramentale.

cardinal p.'s, (1) the four p's in the pelvic inlet toward one of which the occiput of the baby is usually directed in case of head presentation: the two sacroiliac articulations and the two iliopectineal eminences corresponding to the acetabula; **(2)** six p.'s in the eye: anterior focal p., posterior focal p., two principal p.'s, and two nodal p.'s (*q. v.* below).

craniometric p.'s, fixed p.'s on the skull used as landmarks in craniometry.

far p., the farthest p. of distinct vision.

p. of fixation, the p. on the retina at which the rays coming from an object regarded directly are focused.

isoelectric p., the pH at which an amphoteric substance such a protein is electrically neutral; below or above this pH, it acts as a base or acid, respectively.

isosbestic p., in applied spectroscopy, a wavelength at which absorbance of two substances, one of which can be converted into the other, is the same.

J p., the p. marking the end of the QRS complex and the beginning of the S-T segment in the electrocardiogram.

jugal p., jugale.

McBurney's p., a p. between $1^1/_2$ and 2 inches above the anterior superior spine of the ilium, on a straight line joining that process and the umbilicus, where pressure of the finger elicits tenderness in acute appendicitis.

mental p., pogonion.

nasal p., nasion.

near p., the nearest p. of distinct vision.

nodal p., one of the two p.'s in a compound optical system, so related that a ray directed toward the first p., before entering the system, will leave the system in a direction as if it had passed through the second p. parallel to its original direction.

posterior focal p., the p. on the retina where parallel rays entering the eye are focused.

pressure p., (1) any of the various locations on the body where pressure may be applied to control bleeding; **(2)** a p. of extreme sensitivity to pressure.

principal p., one of the two p.'s in an optical system where the axis is cut by the two principal planes; lines drawn from these to corresponding p.'s

on the object and the image will be parallel.

trigger p., a specific p. on the body at which touch or pressure will give rise to pain.

Valleix's p.'s, various p.'s in the course of a nerve, pressure upon which is painful in cases of neuralgia: 1) where the nerve emerges from the bony canal; 2) where it pierces a muscle or aponeurosis to reach the skin; 3) where a superficial nerve rests upon a resisting surface where compression is easily made; 4) where the nerve gives off one or more branches; 5) where the nerve terminates in the skin.

zygomaxillary p., zygomaxillare.

pointillage (pwań-te-yazh') [Fr. dotting, stippling]. A massage manipulation with the tips of the fingers.

poise (poyz, pwahz) [J. *Poiseuille*]. The unit of viscosity in the CGS system equal to 1 dyne second per square centimeter.

poison (poy'zun) [Fr. from L. *potio,* potion, draught]. Any substance (taken internally or applied externally) that is injurious to health or dangerous to life.

poisoning (poy'zun-ing). Intoxication (1). **1.** The administering of poison. **2.** The state of being poisoned.

bacterial food p., a term commonly used to refer to conditions limited to enteritis or gastroenteritis (excluding enteric or typhoid fevers and the dysenteries) caused by bacterial multiplication *per se* or a soluble exotoxin.

blood p., see septicemia; pyemia.

carbon monoxide p., carboxyhemoglobinemia; intoxication caused by inhalation of carbon monoxide gas which competes favorably with oxygen for binding with hemoglobin and thus interferes with the transportation of oxygen and carbon dioxide by the blood.

food p., poisoning in which the active agent is contained in ingested food.

lead p., plumbism; intoxication by lead or any of its salts; symptoms of **acute l. p.** are usually those of acute gastroenteritis; **chronic l. p.** is manifested chiefly by anemia, constipation, colicky abdominal pain, paralysis with wrist-drop involving the extensor muscles of the forearm, bluish lead line of the gums, convulsions, and coma.

mercury p., mercurialism; hydrargyria; hydrargyrism; a disease usually caused by the ingestion of mercury or mercury compounds: **acute m. p.** is associated with ulcerations of the stomach and intestine and nephrotoxic changes in the renal tubules; **chronic m. p.** may be related to metallic mercury and primarily involves the CNS, producing an intention tremor, increased tendon reflexes, and emotional instability.

mushroom p., see mycetism.

Salmonella p., gastroenteritis caused by food contaminated with various strains of *Salmonella* which multiply freely in the gastrointestinal tract but do not produce septicemia; symptoms include fever, headache, nausea, vomiting, diarrhea, and abdominal pain.

sausage p., allantiasis.

scombroid p. [G. *skombros*, mackerel], p. from ingestion of heat-stable toxins produced by bacterial action on inadequately preserved dark-meat fish of the order Scombroidea (tuna, bonito, mackerel, albacore, skipjack); characterized by epigastric pain, nausea and vomiting, headache, thirst, difficulty in swallowing, and urticaria.

poison ivy or **oak.** See *Rhus* and *Toxicodendron*.

poi'sonous. Toxic (1); toxicant (1); pertaining to or caused by a poison.

po'lar [Mod. L. *polaris*, fr. *polus*, pole]. **1.** Relating to a pole. **2.** Having poles, said of certain nerve cells having one or more processes.

polarity (po-lăr'ĭ-tĭ) [Mod. L. *polaris*, polar]. **1.** The property of having two opposite poles, as that possessed by a magnet, or opposite properties or characteristics. **2.** The direction or orientation of positivity relative to negativity.

polarization (po'lar-ĭ-za'shun). **1.** In electricity, the coating of an electrode with a thick layer of hydrogen bubbles, with the result that the flow of current is weakened or arrested. **2.** A change effected in a ray of light passing through certain media, whereby the transverse vibrations occur in one plane only, instead of in all planes as in the ordinary light ray. **3.** The development of differences in potential between two points in living tissues, as between the inside and outside of the cell wall.

pole [L. *polus*, the end of an axis, pole, fr. G. *polos*]. **1.** One of the two points at the extremities of the axis of an organ or body. **2.** One of the two points on a sphere at the greatest distance from its equator. **3.** One of the two points in a magnet or an electric battery or cell having the extremes of opposite properties: **negative p.,** cathode; **positive p.,** anode.

animal p., germinal p.; the point in a telolecithal egg opposite the yolk, where most of the protoplasm is concentrated, where the nucleus is located; and from where the polar bodies are extruded during maturation.

cephalic p., the head end of the fetus.

frontal p., the most anterior promontory of each cerebral hemisphere.

germinal p., animal p.

occipital p., the most posterior promontory of each cerebral hemisphere.

pelvic p., the breech end of the fetus.

temporal p., the most prominent anterior part of the temporal lobes.

vegetal p., vitelline p., the part of a telolecithal egg where the bulk of the yolk is situated.

policeman (po-lēs'man). An instrument, usually a rubber-tipped rod, for removing solid particles from a glass container.

polio- [G. *polios*, gray]. Combining form denoting gray or the gray matter (substantia grisea).

polio (po'lĭ-o). Abbreviated term for poliomyelitis.

polioclastic (po'lĭ-o-klas'tik) [polio- + G. *klastos*, broken]. Destructive to gray matter of the nervous system.

po'liodystro'phia. Poliodystrophy.

p. cer'ebri progressi'va infanta'lis, Christensen-Krabbe or Alpers disease; familial progressive spastic paresis of extremities with progressive mental deterioration, with development of seizures, blindness and deafness, beginning during the first year of life, and with destruction and disorganization of nerve cells of the cerebral cortex.

poliodystrophy (po'lĭ-o-dis'tro-fĭ) [polio- + G. *dys-*, bad, + *trophē*, nourishment]. Poliodystrophia; wasting of the gray matter of the nervous system.

polioencephalitis (po'lĭ-o-en-sef'ă-li'tis) [polio- + G. *enkephalos*, brain, + *-itis*, inflammation]. An acute infectious inflammation of the gray matter of the brain, either of the cortex or of the central nuclei.

polioencephalomeningomyelitis (po'lĭ-o-en-sef-ă-lo-mĕ-ning'go-mi-ĕ-li'tis) [polio- + G. *enkephalos*, brain, + *mēninx*, membrane, + *myelon*, marrow, + *-itis*, inflammation]. Inflammation of the gray matter of the brain and spinal cord and of their meningeal covering.

polioencephalomyelitis (po'lĭ-o-en-sef'ă-lo-mi'e-li'tis). Poliomyeloencephalitis.

polioencephalopathy (po'lĭ-o-en-sef'ă-lop'ă-thĭ) [polio- + G. *enkephalos*, brain, + *pathos*, suffering]. Any disease of the gray matter of the brain.

poliomyelitis (po'lĭ-o-mi'ĕ-li'tis) [polio- + G. *myelos*, marrow, + *-itis*, inflammation]. Inflammation of the gray matter of the spinal cord.

acute anterior p., Heine-Medin disease; an acute infectious inflammation of the anterior cornua of the spinal cord caused by the poliomyelitis virus and marked by fever, pains, and gastroenteric disturbances, followed by flaccid paralysis of one or more muscular groups, and later by atrophy.

acute bulbar p., poliomyelitis virus infection affecting nerve cells in the medulla oblongata.

poliomyeloencephalitis (po'lĭ-o-mi'ĕ-lo-en-sef-ă-li'tis) [polio- + G. *myelon*, marrow, + *enkephalos*, brain, + *-itis*, inflammation]. Polioencephalomyelitis; acute anterior poliomyelitis with pronounced cerebral signs

poliomyelopathy (po'lĭ-o-mi-ĕ-lop'ă-thĭ) [polio- + G. *myelon*, marrow, + *pathos*, suffering]. Any disease of the gray matter of the spinal cord.

poliosis (po-lĭ-o'sis) [G. fr. *polios*, gray]. An absence or lessening of melanin in groups of hair of the scalp, brows, or lashes.

po'liovi'rus hom'inis. Poliomyelitis *virus*.

politzerization (pol'it-zer-ĭ-za'shun). Inflation of the auditory tube and middle ear with a Politzer bag.

pol'len [L. fine dust, fine flour]. Microspores of seed plants carried by wind or insects prior to fertilization.

polleno'sis. Pollinosis.

pollex, pl. **pollices** (pol'eks, pol'ĭ-sēz) [L.] [NA]. The thumb.

pollicization (pol'ĭ-sĭ-za'shun) [L. *pollex*, thumb, + *ize*, to make like, + *-ation*, state]. Construction of a substitute thumb.

pollinosis (pol'ĭ-no'sis) [L. *pollen*, pollen, + G. *-osis*, condition]. Pollenosis; hay fever excited by the pollen of various plants.

pollution (pŏ-lu'shun) [L. *pollutio*, fr. *pol-luo*, pp. *-lutus*, to defile]. Rendering unclean or unsuitable by contact or mixture with a dirty or toxic substance.

  air p., contamination of air by smoke and harmful gases, mainly oxides of carbon, sulfur, and nitrogen.

  noise p., annoying or physiologically damaging environmental noise levels.

polonium (po-lo'nĭ-um) [L. fr. Polonia, Poland, native country of Mme. Curie who with her husband discovered it]. A radioactive element, symbol Po, atomic no. 84; one of the disintegration products of uranium.

po'lus, pl. **po'li** [L. pole] [NA]. A pole.

poly- [G. *polys*, much, many]. **1.** Prefix denoting multiplicity; equivalent to *multi-*. See also pluri-. **2.** In chemistry, prefix meaning "polymer of," as in polypeptide.

polyadenitis (pol'ĭ-ă-dĕ-ni'tis). Inflammation of many lymph nodes, especially with reference to the cervical group.

polyadenop'athy, polyadeno'sis. A disorder affecting many lymph nodes.

polyam'ine [G. *polys*, much, many + amine]. Class name for substances of the general formula $H_2N(CH_2)_nNH_2$, $H_2N(CH_2)_nNH(CH_2)_nNH_2$, or $H_2N(CH_2)_nNH(CH_2)_nNH(CH_2)_nNH_2$, where n = 3, 4, or 5; many arise by bacterial action on protein, are normally occurring body constituents of wide distribution, or are essential growth factors for microorganisms.

polyangiitis (pol'ĭan-je-i'tis). Inflammation of multiple blood vessels involving more than one type of vessel, *e.g.*, arteries and veins, or arterioles and capillaries.

polyarteritis (pol'ĭar-ter-i'tis). Simultaneous inflammation of a number of arteries.

  p. nodo'sa, Kussmaul's disease; periarteritis nodosa; segmental inflammation, with infiltration by eosinophils, and necrosis of medium-sized or small arteries, most common in males, with varied symptoms related to involvement of arteries in the kidneys, muscles, gastrointestinal tract, and heart.

polyar'thric. Multiarticular.

polyarthritis (pol'ĭ-ar-thri'tis) [poly- + G. *arthron*, joint, + *-itis*, inflammation]. Simultaneous inflammation of several joints.

  p. chron'ica villo'sa, a chronic inflammation confined to the synovial membrane, involving a number of joints.

  p. rheumat'ica acu'ta, acute articular or inflammatory rheumatism, associated with rheumatic fever.

polyartic'ular [poly- + L. *articulus*, joint]. Multiarticular.

polyba'sic. Having more than one replaceable hydrogen atom, denoting an acid with a basicity greater than 1.

pol'yblast [poly- + G. *blastos*, germ]. One of a group of ameboid, mononucleated, phagocytic cells found in inflammatory exudates.

polychondritis (pol'ĭ-kon-dri'tis) [poly- + G. *chondros*, cartilage, + *-itis*, inflammation]. A widespread disease of cartilage.

  relapsing p., chronic atrophic p., a degenerative disease of cartilage producing an unusual form of arthritis: collapse of the ears, a cartilaginous portion of the nose, and the tracheobronchial tree.

polychromasia (pol'ĭ-kro-ma'zĭ-ah). Polychromatophilia.

polychromat'ic. Multicolored.

polychromatocyte (pol-ĭ-kro'mă-to-sit). Polychromatophil (2).

polychromatophil, polychromatophile (pol-ĭ-kro'mă-to-fil, -fil) [poly- + G. *chrōma*, color, + *phileō*, to love]. **1.** Polychromatophilic; staining readily with acid, neutral, and basic dyes. **2.** Polychromatocyte; a young or degenerating erythrocyte that manifests acid and basic staining affinities.

polychromatophilia (pol-ĭ-kro'mă-to-fil'ĭ-ah). Polychromasia. **1.** A tendency of certain cells to stain with basic and acid dyes. **2.** A condition characterized by the presence of many red blood cells that have an affinity for acid, basic or neutral stains.

polychro'matophil'ic. Polychromatophil (1).

polychromemia (pol'ĭ-kro-me'mĭ-ah). An increase in the total amount of hemoglobin in the blood.

polyclin'ic [poly- + G. *klinē*, bed]. A dispensary for the treatment of diseases of all kinds and their study.

polyclonal (pol-ĭ-klo'nal). In immunochemistry, pertaining to proteins from more than a single clone of cells.

polyclonia (pol-ĭ-klo'nĭ-ah) [poly- + G. *klonos*, tumult]. *Myoclonus* multiplex.

polyco'ria [poly- + G. *korē*, pupil]. The presence of two or more pupils in one iris.

polycrot'ic. Relating to or marked by polycrotism.

polycrotism (pol-ik'ro-tizm) [poly- + G. *krotos*, a beat]. A condition in which the sphygmographic tracing shows several upward breaks in the descending wave.

polycyesis (pol'ĭ-si-e'sis) [poly- + G. *kyēsis*, pregnancy]. Multiple pregnancy.

polycys'tic. Composed of many cysts.

polycythemia (pol'ĭ-si-the'mĭ-ah) [poly- + G. *kytos*, cell, + *haima*, blood]. Erythrocythemia; hyperglobulia; an increase above the normal in the number of red cells in the blood.

  compensatory p., a secondary p. resulting from anoxia, *e.g.*, in congenital heart disease, pulmonary emphysema, or prolonged residence at a high altitude.

  p. hyperton'ica, p. associated with hypertension, but without splenomegaly.

relative p., a relative increase in the number of red blood cells as a result of loss of the fluid portion of the blood.

p. ru'bra, p. ve'ra, erythremia.

polydactyly, polydactylism (pol-ĭ-dak'tĭ-lĭ, -dak'tĭ-lizm). [poly- + G. *daktylos,* finger]. Hyperdactyly; polydactylism; presence of more than five digits on either hand or foot.

polydip'sia [poly- + G. *dipsa,* thirst]. Frequent drinking because of extreme thirst.

polydysplasia (pol'ĭ-dis-pla'zĭ-ah) [poly- + G. *dys-,* bad, + *plasis,* a molding]. Tissue development abnormal in several respects.

polyergic (pol-ĭ-er'jik) [poly- + G. *ergon,* work]. Capable of acting in several different ways.

polyesthesia (pol'ĭ-es-the'zĭ-ah) [poly- + G. *aisthēsis,* sensation]. A disorder of sensation in which a single touch or other stimulus is felt as several.

polyeth'ylene glycols. Condensation polymers of ethylene oxide and water, of the general formula $HO(CH_2CH_2O)_nH$, that are waxlike solids, soluble in water, and used as ointment bases.

polygalactia (pol'ĭ-gă-lak'tĭ-ah, -shĭ-ah) [poly- + G. *gala,* milk]. Excessive secretion of milk, especially at the weaning period.

polygalac'tose. Galactan.

polygalac'turonase. A hydrolase cleaving α-1,4-galacturonide links in pectate and other polygalacturonides.

polygene (pol'ĭ-jēn). One of a group of genes acting together to produce quantitative variations of a particular character.

polygen'ic. Relating to a hereditary disease or normal characteristic controlled by interaction of genes at more than one locus.

polyglan'dular. Pluriglandular.

polygraph (pol'ĭ-graf) [poly- + G. *graphō,* to write]. 1. An instrument to obtain simultaneous tracings from several different pulsations. 2. Lie detector; an instrument for recording physiological changes as indicators of emotional reactions, and thus whether a person is telling the truth.

polygyria (pol-ĭ-ji'rĭ-ah) [poly- + G. *gyros,* circle, gyre]. An excessive number of convolutions in the brain.

polyhidrosis (pol'ĭ-hi-dro'sis). Hyperhidrosis.

polyhydramnios (pol'ĭ-hi-dram'nĭ-os) [poly- + G. *hydōr,* water, + amnion]. An excess in the amount of amniotic fluid.

polyhy'dric. Containing more than one hydroxyl group.

polyidrosis (pol'ĭ-ĭ-dro'sis). Hyperhidrosis.

polylep'tic [poly- + G. *lēpsis,* a seizing]. Denoting a disease occurring in many paroxysms.

polymastia (pol-ĭ-mas'tĭ-ah) [poly- + G. *mastos,* breast]. Hypermastia (1); pleomastia; a condition in which, in the human, more than two breasts are present.

polyme'lia [poly- + G. *melos,* limb]. Presence of supernumerary limbs or parts of limbs.

polymenorrhea (pol'ĭ-men-o-re'ah) [poly- + G. *mēn,* month, + *rhoia,* flow]. The occurrence of menstrual cycles of greater than usual frequency.

polymer (pol'ĭ-mer) [poly- + -mer]. A substance of high molecular weight, made up of a chain of identical repeated "base units."

polymerase (pol'ĭ-mer-ās, po-lim'er-ās). Any enzyme catalyzing a polymerization, as of nucleotides to polynucleotides.

polymeria (pol-ĭ-mēr'ĭ-ah) [poly- + G. *meros,* part]. An excessive number of parts, limbs, or organs of the body.

polymeric (pol-ĭ-měr'ik). 1. Having the properties of a polymer. 2. Relating to or characterized by polymeria.

polymerization (pol'ĭ-mer-ĭ-za'shun, po-lim'er). A reaction in which a molecular weight product is produced by successive additions to or condensations of a simpler compound.

polymerize (pol'ĭ-mer-īz, po-lim'er-īz). To bring about polymerization.

polymorphic (pol-ĭ-mor'fik) [G. *polymorphos,* multiform]. Multiform; pleomorphic (1); pleomorphous; polymorphous; occurring in more than one morphologic form.

polymorphism (pol-ĭ-mor'fizm). Pleomorphism; occurrence in more than one form; the existence in the same species or other natural group of more than one morphologic type.

polymorphocellular (pol'ĭ-mor-fo-sel'u-lar) [G. *polymorphos,* multiform, + L. *cellula,* cell]. Relating to or formed of cells of several different kinds.

polymorphonuclear (pol'ĭ-mor-fo-nu'kle-ar) [G. *polymorphos,* multiform, + L. *nucleus,* kernel]. Having nuclei of varied forms; denoting a variety of leukocyte.

polymor'phous. Polymorphic.

polymyalgia (pol'ĭ-mi-al'jĭ-ah) [poly- + G. *mys,* muscle, + *algos,* pain]. Pain in several muscle groups.

polymyoclonus (pol'ĭ-mi-ok'lo-nus). *Myoclonus* multiplex.

polymyositis (pol'ĭ-mi-o-si'tis) [poly- + G. *mys,* muscle, + *-itis,* inflammation]. Inflammation of a number of voluntary muscles simultaneously.

polymyx'in. A mixture of antibiotic substances obtained from cultures of *Bacillus polymyxa* (*B. aerosporus*), of which there are five different types: A, B, C, D, and E, about equally effective against Gram-negative bacteria but differing in toxicity.

polyne'sic [poly- + G. *nēsos,* island]. Occurring in many separate foci.

polyneu'ral [poly- + G. *neuron,* nerve]. Relating to, supplied by, or affecting several nerves.

polyneuralgia (pol'ĭ-nu-ral'jĭ-ah). Neuralgia of several nerves simultaneously.

polyneuritis (pol'ĭ-nu-ri'tis). Multiple neuritis; simultaneous inflammation of a large number of the spinal nerves, marked by paralysis, pain, and wasting of muscles.

acute idiopathic p., infectious p., Guillain-Barré syndrome; radiculoganglionitis; a neurologic syndrome, seemingly a sequela of certain virus infections, marked by paresthesia of the limbs and muscular weakness or a flaccid paralysis; characteristic finding is increased protein in the cerebrospinal fluid without increase in cell count.

polyneuropathy (pol´ĭ-nu-rop´ă-thĭ) [poly- + G. *neuron,* nerve, + *pathos,* disease]. A disease process involving a number of peripheral nerves.

polynuclear (pol-ĭ-nu´kle-ar). Multinuclear.

polynucleated (pol-ĭ-nu´kle-a-ted). Multinuclear.

polynu´cleoti´dase. An enzyme catalyzing the hydrolysis of polynucleotides to oligonucleotides or to mononucleotides.

polynu´cleotide. A linear polymer containing an indefinite (usually large) number of nucleotides, linked from one ribose (or deoxyribose) to another via phosphoric residues.

polyodontia (pol´ĭ-o-don´shĭah) [poly- + G. *odous,* tooth]. Presence of supernumerary teeth.

polyoncosis (pol´ĭ-ong-ko´sis) [poly- + G. *onkos,* tumor, + *-osis,* condition]. Formation of multiple tumors.

polyonychia (pol´ĭ-o-nik´ĭ-ah) [poly- + G. *onyx,* nail]. Presence of supernumerary nails on fingers or toes.

polyopia (pol-ĭ-o´pĭ-ah) [poly- + G. *ōps,* eye]. Multiple vision; the perception of several images of the same object.

polyorchidism (pol-ĭ-or´kĭ-dizm). Polyorchism.

polyorchism (pol-ĭ-or´kizm) [poly- + G. *orchis,* testis]. Polyorchidism; presence of one or more supernumerary testes.

polyostotic (pol´ĭ-os-tot´ik) [poly- + G. *osteon,* bone]. Involving more than one bone.

polyotia (pol-ĭ-o´shĭ-ah) [poly- + G. *ous,* ear]. The presence of a supernumerary auricle on one or both sides of the head.

polyo´vulatory. Discharging several ova in one ovulatory cycle.

polyp (pol´ip) [L. *polypus;* fr. G. *polys,* many, + *pous,* foot]. Polypus; any mass of tissue that bulges or projects outward or upward from a surface by growing from a broad base (**sessile p.**) or a slender stalk (**pedunculated p.**).

adenomatous p., a p. that consists of benign neoplastic tissue derived from glandular epithelium.

dental p., hyperplastic pulpal tissue growing out of a grossly decayed tooth with wide pulpal exposure.

fibrinous p., misnomer for a mass of fibrin retained within the uterine cavity after childbirth.

juvenile p., retention p., a smoothly rounded mucosal hamartoma of the large intestine, which may be multiple and cause rectal bleeding, especially in the first decade of life.

vascular p., a bulging or protruding angioma of the nasal mucous membrane.

polypec´tomy [polyp + G. *ektomē,* excision]. Excision of a polyp.

polypep´tide. A peptide formed by the union of an indefinite (usually large) number of amino acids.

vasoactive intestinal p. (VIP), a p. hormone secreted most commonly by non-beta islet cell tumors of the pancreas, producing copious watery diarrhea and fecal electrolyte loss, particularly hypokalemia.

polyphagia (pol-ĭ-fa´jĭ-ah) [poly- + G. *phagein,* to eat]. Excessive eating; gluttony.

polyphalangism (pol´ĭ-fă-lan´jizm). Hyperphalangism.

polyphar´macy. The mixing of many drugs in one prescription.

polypho´bia [poly- + G. *phobos,* fear]. Morbid fear of many things; a condition marked by the presence of many phobias.

polyphrasia (pol-ĭ-fra´zĭ-ah) [poly- + G. *phrasis,* speech]. Extreme talkativeness.

polyphyletic (pol´ĭ-fi-let´ik) [poly- + G. *phylē,* tribe]. **1.** Derived from more than one source, or having several lines of descent. **2.** In hematology, relating to the theory that blood cells are derived from several different stem cells, depending on the particular blood cell type.

polypi (pol´ĭ-pi). Plural of polypus.

polyplas´tic [poly- + G. *plastikos,* plastic]. **1.** Formed of several different structures. **2.** Capable of assuming several forms.

polyplegia (pol-ĭ-ple´jĭ-ah) [poly- + G. *plēgē,* a stroke]. Paralysis of several muscles.

polyploid (pol´ĭ-ployd). Characterized by or pertaining to polyploidy.

polyploidy (pol´ĭ-ploy-dĭ) [poly- + -ploid]. The state of a cell nucleus containing three or a higher multiple of the haploid number of chromosomes.

polypnea (pol´ip-ne´ah) [poly- + G. *pnoia,* breath]. Tachypnea.

polypoid (pol´ĭ-poyd) [polyp + G. *eidos,* resemblance]. Resembling a polyp in gross features.

polyporous (pol-ip´or-us) [poly- + G. *poros,* pore]. Cribriform.

polyposia (pol-ĭ-po´zĭ-ah) [poly- + G. *posis,* drinking]. Sustained excessive drinking.

polyposis (pol-ĭ-po´sis) [polyp + G. suffix *-osis,* condition]. Presence of several polyps.

familial or **multiple intestinal p.,** (1) p. of the colon characterized by polyps only of the mucosa, with no associated lesions, which begin to form usually in late childhood, increase in numbers, and may carpet the mucosal surface; autosomal dominant inheritance; (2) p. of the small or large intestine as a feature of Gardner's, Peutz-Jeghers, Turcot, and Zollinger-Ellison syndromes.

pol´ypous. Pertaining to, manifesting the gross features of, or characterized by the presence of a polyp or polyps.

polyptychial (pol-ĭ-tik'ĭ-al) [G. *polyptychos*, fr. poly- + *ptychē*, fold or layer]. Folded or arranged so as to form more than one layer.

polypus, pl. **polypi** (pol'ĭ-pus, -pi) [L.]. Polyp.

polyradic'uli'tis. Inflammation of nerve roots.

polyribosomes (pol-ĭ-ri'bo-sōmz). Polysomes; conceptually, two or more ribosomes connected by a molecule of messenger RNA; active in protein synthesis.

polysaccharide (pol-ĭ-sak'ă-rīd). Glycan; a carbohydrate containing a large number of saccharide groups; *e.g.*, starch.

polyserositis (pol'ĭ-sēr-o-si'tis) [poly- + L. *serum*, serum, + G. *-itis*, inflammation]. Concato's disease; chronic inflammation with effusions in several serous cavities resulting in fibrous thickening of the serosa and constrictive pericarditis.

    familial paroxysmal p., familial Mediterranean fever; Mediterranean fever (2); transient recurring attacks of abdominal pain, fever, pleurisy, arthritis, and rash.

polysinusitis (pol'ĭ-si-nū-si'tis). Simultaneous inflammation of two or more sinuses.

polysomes (pol'ĭ-sōmz). Polyribosomes.

polysomia (pol-ĭso'mĭ-ah) [poly- + G. *sōma*, body]. A fetal malformation involving two or more imperfect and partially fused bodies.

polyso'mic. Pertaining to or characterized by polysomy.

polyso'mus. An individual with polysomia.

polysomy (pol'ĭ-so'mĭ) [poly- + G. *sōma*, body (chromosome)]. The state of a cell nucleus in which a specific chromosome is represented more than twice.

polyspermia (pol-ĭ-sper'mĭ-ah). 1. Polyspermy. 2. An abnormally profuse spermatic secretion.

polyspermy (pol'ĭ-sper-mĭ). Polyspermia (1); the entrance of more than one spermatozoon into the ovum.

polystichia (pol-ĭ-stik'ĭ-ah) [poly- + G. *stichos*, row]. An arrangement of the eyelashes in two or more rows.

polysymbrachydactyly (pol'ĭ-sim-brak-ĭ-dak'tĭ-lĭ) [poly- + symbrachydactyly]. A congenital malformation of the hand or foot in which the shortened digits are syndactylous and polydactylous.

polysynaptic (pol'ĭ-sĭ-nap'tik). Multisynaptic; referring to neural conduction pathways formed by a chain of many synaptically connected nerve cells.

polytendini'tis. Inflammation of several tendons.

polythe'lia [poly- + G. *thēlē*, nipple]. Hyperthelia; presence of supernumerary nipples on the breast or elsewhere.

polytomog'raphy. Body section radiography using a machine specifically designed to effect complex motion.

polytrichia (pol-ĭ-trik'ĭ-ah) [poly- + G. *thrix* (*trich*), hair]. Excessive hairiness.

polyuria (pol-ĭ-u'rĭ-ah) [poly- + G. *ouron*, urine]. Hydruria; excessive excretion of urine, or profuse micturition.

polyvalent (pol-ĭ-va'lent). 1. Multivalent (1,2). 2. Pertaining to a polyvalent (1,2) antiserum.

polyvi'nyl. Referring to a compound containing a number of vinyl groups in polymerized form.

polyvinyl chloride (PVC). Chlorethene homopolymer; used as a rubber substitute in industry and suspected of being carcinogenic.

POMP A cancer chemotherapy drug consisting of Purinethol (6-mercaptopurine), Oncovin (vincristine sulfate), methotrexate, and prednisone.

pompholyx (pom'fo-liks) [G. a bubble, fr. *pomphos*, a blister]. Dyshidrosis.

pons, pl. **pontes** (ponz, pon'tēz) [L. bridge] 1 [NA]. That part of the brainstem intermediate between the medulla oblongata caudally and the mesencephalon rostrally, and composed of a ventral part and the tegmentum. 2. Any bridgelike formation connecting two or more disjoined parts of the same structure or organ.

pon'tic. An artificial tooth on a fixed partial denture, replacing the lost natural tooth.

pontile, pontine (pon'tĭl, -tēn, -tīn). Relating to a pons.

pool [A.S. *pōl*]. A collection of blood in any region of the body, due to a dilation and retardation of the circulation in the capillaries and veins of the part.

poples (pop'lēz) [L. the ham of the knee] [NA]. The posterior region of the knee.

popliteal (pop-lit'e-al, pop-lĭ-te'al). Relating to the poples.

population (pop-u-la'shun) [L. *populus*, a people, nation]. A statistical term denoting all the objects, events, or subjects in a particular class.

por-. See poro-.

pore (pōr) [G. *poros*, passageway]. A hole, meatus, or foramen; one of the minute openings of the sweat glands of the skin.

    external acoustic or **auditory p.,** *porus* acusticus externus.

    internal acoustic or **auditory p.,** *porus* acusticus internus.

    nuclear p., an octagonal opening where the inner and outer membranes of the nuclear envelope are continuous.

    slit p.'s, intercellular clefts between the interdigitating pedicels of podocytes; part of the filtration barrier of renal corpuscles.

porencephalia (pōr'en-sĕ-fa'lĭ-ah). Porencephaly.

porencephalic (pōr'en-sĕ-fal'ik). Porencephalous; relating to or characterized by porencephaly.

porencephalitis (pōr-en-sef-ă-li'tis) [G. *poros*, pore, + *enkephalos*, brain, + *-itis*, inflammation]. Chronic inflammation of the brain with the formation of cavities in the substance of the organ.

porencephalous (pōr'en-sef'ă-lus). Porencephalic.

porencephaly (pōr'en-sef'ă-lĭ) [G. *poros*, pore, + *enkephalos*, brain]. Porencephalia; occurrence of cavities in the brain substance, communicating usually with the lateral ventricles.

po'ri. Plural of porus.

porocele (po'ro-sēl) [G. *pōros*, callus, + *kēlē*, hernia]. A hernia with indurated coverings.

porokeratosis (po'ro-kĕr-ă-to'sis) [G. *poros*, pore, + keratosis]. A rare dermatosis in which there is thickening of the stratum corneum and progressive centrifugal atrophy.

poroma (po-ro'mah) [G. *pōrōma*, callus, fr. *pōros*, stone]. **1.** Callosity. **2.** Exostosis. **3.** Induration following a phlegmon. **4.** A tumor of cells lining the skin openings of sweat glands.

eccrine p., a p. or acrospiroma of the eccrine sweat glands on the sole of the foot.

porosis pl. **poroses** (po-ro'sis, -sēz) [L. *porosus*, porous]. Porosity (1); a porous condition.

porosity (po-ros'ĭ-tĭ) [G. *poros*, pore]. **1.** Porosis. **2.** A perforation.

porotomy (po-rot'o-mī) [G. *poros*, passage, + *tomē*, incision]. Meatotomy.

porous (po'rus). Having pores that pass directly or indirectly through the substance.

porphin, porphine (por'fin). The unsubstituted tetrapyrrole nucleus that is the basis of the porphyrins.

porphobilin (por-fo-bi'lin). General term denoting intermediates between the monopyrrole, porphobilinogen, and the cyclic tetrapyrrole of heme (a porphin derivative).

porphobilinogen (PBG) (por'fo-bi-lin'o-jen). A porphyrin compound found in the urine in large quantities in cases of acute or congenital porphyria.

porphyria (por-fīr'ĭ-ah). A disorder of porphyrin metabolism; may be a heritable disease, of which four types have been described, or may be acquired, as from the effects of certain chemical agents.

acute intermittent p., hepatic p.; p. caused by congenital hepatic overproduction of δ-aminolevulinic acid, with greatly increased urinary excretion of this compound and of porphobilinogen; characterized by intermittent hypertension, abdominal colic, psychosis, and neuropathy; autosomal dominant inheritance.

congenital erythropoietic p., Günther's disease; enhanced porphyrin formation by erythroid cells in bone marrow, leading to severe porphyrinuria, often in conjunction with hemolytic anemia and persistent cutaneous photosensitivity; autosomal recessive inheritance.

p. cuta'nea tar'da, symptomatic p.

erythropoietic p., (1) a relatively mild heritable form of p., characterized by enhanced formation of protoporphyrin III (9α), which leads to increased fecal excretion of this (2) an older name for congenital erythropoietic p.

hepatic p., acute intermittent p.

symptomatic p., p. cutanea tarda; p. occurring in middle-aged and elderly persons who have liver dysfunction, with hyperpigmentation and scleroderma-like changes in skin, neurologic manifesta-

tions, and porphyrinuria.

variegate p., a heritable disorder characterized by dermal sensitivity to light and mechanical trauma, and by increased fecal excretion of proto- and coproporphyrin; autosomal dominant inheritance.

porphyrins (por'fī-rinz). Pigments widely distributed throughout nature (*e.g.*, heme, bile pigments, cytochromes), consisting of four pyrroles joined in a ring (porphin) structure, which are substitution products of porphin and comprise several varieties, differing for the most part in the sidechains present at the eight available positions on the pyrrole rings; they combine with various metals (iron, copper, magnesium, etc.) to form metalloporphyrins, and with nitrogenous substances.

porphyrinuria (por'fī-rin-u'rĭ-ah). Excretion of porphyrins and related compounds in the urine.

porrigo (po-ri'go) [L. scurf, dandruff]. Any disease of the scalp.

porta, pl. **portae** (pōr'tah, -te) [L. gate]. **1.** Hilum. **2.** *Foramen* interventriculare.

p. hep'atis [NA], portal fissure; caudal transverse fissure; a transverse fissure on the visceral surface of the liver between the caudate and quadrate lobes, lodging the portal vein, hepatic artery, hepatic nerve plexus, hepatic ducts, and lymphatic vessels.

portacaval (pōr-tă-ka'val). Concerning the portal vein and the inferior vena cava.

portal pōr'tal) [L. *portalis*, pertaining to a porta (gate)]. **1.** Relating to any porta. **2.** The point of entry into the body of a pathogenic microorganism.

portio, pl. **portiones** (pōr'shī-o, -o'nēz) [L. portion] [NA]. A part.

p. supravagina'lis [NA], the part of the cervix uteri lying above the attachment of the vagina.

p. vagina'lis [NA], the part of the cervix uteri contained within the vagina.

porto- [L. *porta*, gate]. Combining form meaning portal.

por'tobil'ioarte'rial. Relating to the portal vein, biliary ducts, and hepatic artery, which have similar distributions.

portoenterostomy (por'to-en-ter-os'to-mī). Kasai operation; an o. for biliary atresia in which a Roux-en-Y loop of jejunum is anastomosed to the hepatic end of the divided extravascular portal structures, including rudimentary bile ducts.

por'togram [porto- G. *gramma*, a writing]. The image obtained by portography.

portography (por-tog'ră-fī) [porto- + G. *graphō*, to write]. Radiographic delineation of the portal circulation using radiopaque material introduced into the spleen or into the portal vein.

portosystemic (por'to-sis-tem'ik). Relating to connections between the portal and systemic venous systems.

po'rus, pl. **po'ri** [L. fr. G. *poros*, passageway] [NA]. A pore, meatus, or foramen.

p. acus'ticus exter'nus [NA], external acoustic or auditory pore or foramen; the orifice of the external acoustic meatus in the tympanic portion of the temporal bone.

p. acus'ticus inter'nus [NA], internal acoustic or auditory pore or foramen; the inner opening of the internal acoustic meatus on the posterior surface of the petrous part of the temporal bone.

position (po-zish'un) [L. *positio*, a placing, position]. **1.** An attitude, posture, or place occupied. **2.** In obstetrics, the relation of some arbitrarily chosen p. of the fetus to the right or left side of the mother.

anatomical p., the erect p. of the body with the face directed forward, the arms at the side and the palms of the hands facing forward; the terms posterior, anterior, lateral, medial, etc., are applied to the parts as related to each other and to the axis of the body when in this p.

Bozeman's p., knee-elbow p., the patient being strapped to supports.

Brickner's p., by tying the wrist to the elevated head of the bed, traction is obtained in abduction and external rotation.

flank p., a lateral recumbent p., but with the lower leg flexed, the upper leg extended, and convex extension of the upper side of the body; used for nephrectomy.

Fowler's p., an inclined p. obtained by raising the head of the bed to promote better dependent drainage after an abdominal operation.

genucubital p., knee-elbow p.

genupectoral p., knee-chest p.

knee-chest p., genupectoral p.; a prone posture resting on the knees and upper part of the chest, assumed for gynecologic or rectal examination.

knee-elbow p., genucubital p.; a prone p. resting on the knees and elbows, assumed for rectal or vaginal examination or operation.

lateral recumbent p., Sims p.

lithotomy p., a supine p. with buttocks at the end of the operating table, the hips and knees being fully flexed with feet strapped in p.

Mayo-Robson's p., a supine p. with a thick pad under the loins, causing a marked lordosis in this region; used in operations on the gallbladder.

mentoanterior p., a presentation of the fetus with its chin pointing to the right (**right m.p., RMA**) or to the left (**left m.p., LMA**) acetabulum of the mother.

mentoposterior p., a presentation of the fetus with its chin pointing to the right (**right m.p., RMP**) or to the left (**left m.p., LMP**) sacroiliac articulation of the mother.

occipitoanterior p., a presentation with the occiput of the fetus being turned toward the left (**left o.p., LOA**) or right (**right o.p., ROA**) acetabulum of the mother.

occipitoposterior p., a presentation with the occiput of the fetus being turned toward the left (**left o.p., LOP**) or right (**right o.p., ROP**) sacroiliac joint of the mother.

occlusal p., the relationship of the mandible and maxillae when the jaws are closed and the teeth are in contact.

physiologic rest p., the habitual postural p. of the mandible when the patient is resting comfortably in the upright p. and the condyles are in a neutral unstrained p. in the glenoid fossae.

Rose's p., a supine p. with the head over the end of the table; used in operations in the mouth, or the fauces, and on the fauciopharyngeal boundary.

sacroanterior p., a breech presentation of the fetus with the sacrum directed toward the left (**left s.p., LSA**) or to the right (**right s.p., RSA**) acetabulum of the mother.

sacroposterior p., a breech presentation of the fetus with the sacrum pointing to the left (**left s.p., LSP**) or to the right (**right s.p., RSP**) sacroiliac articulation of the mother.

Sims p., lateral recumbent p.; a p. to facilitate a vaginal examination; a semiprone p. with the under arm behind the back, the thighs flexed, the upper one more than the lower.

Trendelenburg p., a supine p. inclined at an angle of 45°, so that the pelvis is higher than the head; used during and after operations in the pelvis or for shock.

Valentine's p., a supine p. on a table with double inclined plane so as to cause flexion at the hips; used to facilitate urethral irrigation.

positive (+) (poz'ĭ-tiv) [L. *positivus*, settled by arbitrary agreement]. Affirmative; definite; not negative.

positron (poz'ĭ-tron). Positive electron; a subatomic particle of the same mass as the electron but of the opposite charge.

posologic (po-so-loj'ik). Relating to posology.

posology (po-sol'o-jī) [G. *posos*, how much, + *logos*, study]. The branch of pharmacology and therapeutics concerned with a determination of the doses of remedies; the science of dosage.

post- [L. *post*, after]. Prefix denoting after, behind, or posterior; corresponding to *meta-*.

postax'ial. 1. Posterior to the axis of the body or any limb, the latter being in the anatomical position. **2.** Denoting the portion of a limb bud which lies caudal to the axis of the limb.

postbra'chial. On or in the posterior part of the upper arm.

postca'va. *Vena* cava inferior.

postca'val. Relating to the inferior vena cava (post-cava).

postcibal (pōst-si'bal) [L. *cibum*, food]. Postprandial.

postcoital (pōst-ko'ĭ-tal) After coitus.

postcoitus (pōst-ko'ĭtus). The time immediately after coitus.

postcor'dial [L. *cor* (*cord-*), heart]. Posterior to the heart.

postcu'bital. On or in the posterior or dorsal part of the forearm.

postduc'tal. Relating to that part of the aorta distal to the aortic opening of the ductus arteriosus.

posterior (pos-tēr'ĭ-or) [L. comparative of *posterus*, following]. **1.** After, in relation to time or space. **2** [NA]. Dorsal (2); in human anatomy, denoting the back surface of the body or nearer the back of the body. **3.** Near the tail or caudal end of certain embryos.

postero- [L. *posterior, q.v.*]. Combining form denoting posterior.

post'eroante'rior. A term denoting the direction of view or progression, from posterior to anterior, through a part.

post'eroexter'nal. Posterolateral.

post'erointer'nal. Posteromedial.

posterolat'eral. Posteroexternal; behind and to one side, specifically to the outer side.

posterome'dial. Posterointernal; behind and to the inner side.

posterome'dian. Occupying a central position posteriorly.

posterosupe'rior. Situated behind and at the upper part.

postganglion'ic. Distal to or beyond a ganglion; referring to the unmyelinated nerve fibers originating from cells in an autonomic ganglion.

posthioplasty (pos'thī-o-plas-tĭ) [G. *posthion*, dim. form of *posthē*, prepuce, + *plassō*, to form]. Reparative or plastic surgery of the prepuce.

posthitis (pos-thī'tis) [G. *posthē*, prepuce, + *-itis*]. Inflammation of the prepuce.

pos'tholith [G. *posthē*, prepuce, + *lithos*, stone]. A preputial calculus; a calculus occurring beneath the foreskin.

posthypnotic (pōst-hip-not'ik). Following hypnotism.

postic'tal. Following a seizure.

postmature (pōst-mă-tūr'). Remaining in the uterus longer than the normal gestational period.

postmenopau'sal. Relating to the period following the menopause.

postmor'tem. 1. Pertaining to or occurring during the period after death. **2.** Colloquialism for autopsy (1).

postna'sal. 1. Posterior to the nasal cavity. **2.** Relating to the posterior portion of the nasal cavity.

postna'tal [L. *natus*, birth]. Occurring after birth.

postop'erative. Following an operation.

posto'ral [L. *os* (*or-*), mouth]. In the posterior part of, or posterior to, the mouth.

post par'tum [L. *partus*, birth (noun), fr. *pario*, pp. *partus*, to bring forth]. After childbirth; as an adjective, usually written postpartum.

postpran'dial [L. *prandium*, breakfast]. Postcibal; following a meal or the taking of food.

postpu'beral, postpu'bertal. Postpubescent.

postpubescent (pōst-pu-bes'ent). Postpuberal; postpubertal; subsequent to the period of puberty.

postsphygmic (post-sfig'mik) [G. *sphygmos*, pulse]. Occurring after the pulse wave.

posttib'ial. On or in the posterior portion of the leg.

post'traumat'ic. Temporally, and implied causally, related to a trauma.

postulate (pos'tu-lāt) [L. *postulo*, pp. *-atus*, to demand]. An unproved assertion or assumption; a statement or formula offered as the basis of a theory.

    Koch's p.'s, to establish the specificity of a pathogenic microorganism, it must be present in all cases of the disease, inoculations of its pure cultures must produce disease in animals (when transmitted to such), and from these it must be again obtained and be propagated in pure cultures.

postural (pos'tu-ral, pos'cher-al). Relating to or effected by posture.

posture (pos'tūr, pos'cher) [L. *positura*, fr. *pono*, pp. *positus*, to place]. The position of the limbs or the carriage of the body as a whole.

postval'var, postval'vular. Relating to a position distal to the pulmonary or aortic valves.

potable (po'tă-bl) [L. *potabilis*, fr. *poto*, to drink]. Drinkable; fit to drink.

pot'ash [E. pot-ashes]. Impure potassium carbonate.

potas'sic. Relating to or containing potassium.

potassium (po-tas'ĭ-um) [Mod. L. fr. E. potash (fr. pot + ashes) + *-ium*]. An alkaline metallic element, symbol K (*kalium*), atomic no 19, atomic weight 39.100, occurring always in combination; its salts are used medicinally.

potassium-40 (⁴⁰K). A naturally occurring radioactive potassium isotope; beta emitter with half-life of 1.3 billion years; chief source of natural radioactivity of living tissue.

potassium-42 (⁴²K). An artificial potassium isotope; beta emitter with half-life of 12.47 hr, used as a tracer in studies of potassium distribution in body fluid compartments.

potassium-43 (⁴³K). An artificial potassium isotope; a beta emitter with a half-life of 22 hr, used as a tracer in myocardial perfusion studies.

potency (po'ten-sĭ) [L. *potentia*, power]. **1.** Power, force, or strength; the condition or quality of being potent. **2.** Specifically, **sexual p.,** the ability to carry out and consummate the sexual act; referring mainly to the male. **3.** In therapeutics, the pharmacological activity of a compound.

po'tent. Denoting potency.

potential (po-ten'shal) [L. *potentia*, power, potency]. **1.** Capable of doing or being; possible, but not actual. **2.** A state of tension in an electric source enabling it to do work under suitable conditions; analogous to temperature in relation to heat; unit: volt.

    action p., the change in membrane p. occurring in nerve, muscle or other excitable tissue when excitation occurs.

    after-p., see afterpotential.

    excitatory postsynaptic p., a local change in the direction of depolarization, produced in the membrane of the next neuron when an impulse which has an excitatory influence arrives at the synapse; summation of these p.'s can lead to discharge of an impulse by the neuron.

inhibitory postsynaptic p., a local change in the direction of hyperpolarization, produced in the membrane of the next neuron when an impulse which has an inhibitory influence arrives at the synapse; the frequency of discharge of a given neuron is determined by the extent to which impulses that lead to excitatory postsynaptic p.'s predominate over those that cause inhibitory postsynaptic p.'s.

membrane p., the p. inside a cell membrane, measured relative to the fluid just outside; it is negative under resting conditions and becomes positive during an action p.

spike p., the main wave in the action p. of a nerve, followed by negative and positive afterpotentials.

visual evoked p., the measurement that results from the recordings of an electroencephalogram from the occipital area of the scalp while the subject fixates a light flashing at quarter-second intervals, as given by a computer that averages the electroencephalogram response of 100 consecutive flashes.

potentiation (po-ten-shǐ-a'shun). In chemotherapy, a degree of synergism that is greater than additive.

potion (po'shun) [L. *potio, potus,* fr. *poto,* to drink]. A draft or large dose of liquid medicine.

pouch (powch). A pocket or cul-de-sac.

branchial p.'s, pharyngeal p.'s.

Douglas p., *excavatio* rectouterina.

pharyngeal p.'s, branchial p.'s; paired evaginations of embryonic pharyngeal entoderm, between the branchial arches, that extend toward the corresponding ectodermally lined branchial grooves; during development they give rise to epithelial tissues and organs such as thymus and thyroid glands.

Rathke's p., pituitary *diverticulum.*

rectouterine p., *excavatio* rectouterina.

rectovesical p., *excavatio* rectovesicalis.

vesicouterine p., *excavatio* vesicouterina.

poudrage (pū-drahzh') [F.]. Powdering, as of the opposing pleural surfaces with a slightly irritating powder in order to secure adhesion.

poultice (pōl'tis) [L. *puls* (*pult-*), a thick pap; G. *poltos*]. A soft, moist mass prepared by wetting various powders or other absorbent substances with fluids, sometimes medicated, and usually applied hot to the surface; exerts an emollient, relaxing, stimulant, or counterirritant effect upon the skin and underlying tissues.

pound (pownd) [A.S. *pund;* L. *pondus,* weight]. A unit of weight, containing 12 ounces apothecaries' weight or 16 ounces avoirdupois.

pow'der [Fr. *poudre;* L. *pulvis*]. **1.** A dry mass of minute separate particles. **2.** In pharmaceutics, a homogenous dispersion of finely divided, relatively dry, particulate matter consisting of one or more substances. **3.** A single dose of a powdered drug.

pow'er. 1. Potency. **2.** In optics, the refractive vergence of a lens. **3.** In physics and engineering, the rate at which work is done.

resolving p., definition of a lens; in a microscope objective lens it is calculated by dividing the wavelength of the light used by twice the numerical aperture of the objective. See also definition.

pox (poks) [variant of the pl. of pock]. **1.** An eruptive disease, usually qualified by a descriptive term; *e.g.,* smallpox, chickenpox. **2.** An eruption, first papular then pustular, occurring in chronic antimony poisoning. **3.** Archaic term for syphilis.

Poxviridae (poks-vīr'ĭ-de). A family of large complex DNA viruses, with an affinity for skin tissue, that are pathogenic for man and other animals; replication occurs entirely in the cytoplasm of infected cells. Six genera are recognized: *Orthopoxvirus, Avipoxvirus, Capripoxvirus, Leporipoxvirus, Parapoxvirus,* and *Entomopoxvirus.*

poxvirus (poks'vi'rus). Any virus of the family Poxviridae.

PP Pyrophosphate.

PPCA Proserum prothrombin conversion *accelerator.*

PPD Purified protein derivative of *tuberculin.*

PPLO Pleuropneumonia-like *organisms.*

ppm Parts per million.

P-pulmona'le. An electrocardiographic syndrome of tall, narrow, peaked P waves in leads II, III, and a VF, and a prominent initial positive P wave component in V_1 and V_2, presumed to be characteristic of cor pulmonale.

Pr Presbyopia; praseodymium.

PRA Plasma renin *activity.*

practice (prak'tis) [Mediev. L. *practica,* business, G. *praktikos,* pertaining to action, fr. *prassō,* to do]. The exercise of the profession of medicine or one of the associated health professions.

family p., the medical specialty concerned with the delivery of comprehensive primary health care to members of the family on a continuing basis.

general p., the provision of continuing comprehensive medical care regardless of the patient's age or of the disorder involved, even if it requires intervention by a specialist.

group p., the p. of medicine by a group, each of whom usually confined to some special field, but shares a common facility.

practitioner (prak-tish'un-er). One who practices medicine or an associated health care profession.

prae-. For words beginning thus, see pre-.

pragmatagnosia (prag'mat-ag-no'sĭ-ah) [G. *pragma* (*pragmat-*), thing done, a deed]. Loss of the power of recognizing objects.

pragmatamnesia (prag'mat-am-ne'zĭ-ah) [G. *pragma,* a thing done, + *amnēsia,* forgetfulness]. Loss of the memory of the appearance of objects.

pragmatism (prag'mă-tizm) [G. *pragma* (*pragmat-*), thing done]. An approach emphasizing practical applications and consequences, that the value of anything derives from its practicality.

prandial (pran′dĭ-al) [L. *prandium*, breakfast]. Relating to a meal.

praseodymium (pra-se-o-dim′ĭ-um) [G. *prason*, a leek, + didymium]. An element of the lanthanide or "rare earth" group; symbol Pr, atomic no. 59, atomic weight 140.92.

pre- [L. *prae*, before]. Prefix denoting anterior or before in space or time. See also ante-, pro-.

preagonal (pre-ag′o-nal) [pre- + G. *agōn*, struggle (agony)]. Immediately preceding death.

pre′anesthet′ic. Before anesthesia.

pre′antisep′tic. Denoting the period, especially in relation to surgery, before the adoption of the principles of antisepsis.

preaseptic (pre-ă-sep′tik). Denoting the period, especially the early antiseptic period in relation to surgery, before the principles of asepsis were known or adopted.

preaxial (pre-ak′sĭ-al). **1.** Anterior to the axis of the body or a limb, the latter being in the anatomical position. **2.** Denoting the portion of a limb bud which lies cranial to the axis of the limb.

precancer (pre-kan′ser). A lesion from which a malignant neoplasm is presumed to develop in a significant number of instances, and which may or may not be recognizable clinically or by microscopic changes in the affected tissue.

precan′cerous. Premalignant; pertaining to any lesion that is interpreted as a precancer.

precap′illary. Preceding a capillary; an arteriole or venule.

precar′tilage. A closely packed aggregation of mesenchymal cells just prior to their differentiation into embryonic cartilage.

preca′va. *Vena cava superior.*

precipitable (pre-sip′ĭ-tă-bl). Capable of being precipitated.

precipitant (pre-sip′ĭ-tant). Anything causing a precipitation from a solution.

precip′itate [L. *praecipito*, pp. *-atus*, to cast headlong]. **1.** To cause a substance in solution to separate as a solid. **2.** A solid separated out from a solution or suspension; a floc or clump, such as that resulting from the mixture of a specific antigen and its antibody. **3.** Punctate keratitis; a punctate opacity on the posterior surface of the cornea, arising from inflammatory cells in the vitreous.

precipitation (pre-sip′ĭ-ta′shun) [see precipitate]. The act of precipitating or the process of forming a precipitate.

precipitin (pre-sip′ĭ-tin). Precipitating antibody; an antibody that under suitable conditions combines with and causes its specific and soluble antigen to precipitate from solution.

precipitinogen (pre-sip-ĭ-tin′o-jen) [precipitin + G. *-gen*, producing]. **1.** An antigen that stimulates the formation of specific precipitin when injected into an animal body. **2.** A precipitable soluble antigen.

preclin′ical. 1. Before the onset of disease. **2.** A period in medical education before the student is involved with patients and clinical work.

precocious (pre-ko′shus) [L. *praecox*, premature]. Developing unusually early.

precocity (pre-kos′ĭ-tĭ) [see precocious]. Unusually early or rapid development of mental or physical traits.

precognition (pre-kog-nish′un) [L. *praecogito*, to ponder before]. Advance knowledge, by means other than the normal senses, of a future event; a form of extrasensory perception.

preconscious (pre-kon′shus). In psychoanalysis, one of the three divisions of the psyche according to Freud's topographical psychology; includes all ideas, thoughts, past experiences, and other memory impressions that with effort can be consciously recalled.

preconvul′sive. Denoting the stage in an epileptic paroxysm preceding convulsions.

precor′dia [L. *praecordia*, the diaphragm, the entrails]. The epigastrium and anterior surface of the lower part of the thorax.

precor′dial. Relating to the precordia.

precor′dium. Singular of precordia.

precu′neate. Relating to the precuneus.

precu′neus [pre- + L. *cuneus*, a wedge] [NA]. Quadrate lobe (2); a division of the medial surface of each cerebral hemisphere between the cuneus and the paracentral lobule.

precursor (pre-ker′ser) [L. *praecursor*, fr. *prae*-, pre- + *curro*, to run]. Anything that precedes another or from which another is derived, applied especially to a physiologically inactive substance that is converted to an active enzyme, vitamin, hormone, etc., or to a chemical substance that is built into a larger structure in the course of synthesizing the latter.

predecidual (pre′de-sid′u-al). Relating to the premenstrual or secretory phase of the menstrual cycle.

preden′tin. The organic fibrillar matrix of the dentin before its calcification.

prediabetes (pre-di-ă-be′tēz). A state in which one or a few of the abnormalities typical of diabetes mellitus can be observed episodically or persistently, and are often mild in nature.

prediastole (pre-di-as′to-le). The interval in the cardiac rhythm immediately preceding the diastole.

prediastol′ic. Relating to the diastole.

prediges′tion. The artificial initiation of digestion of proteins (proteolysis) and starches (amylolysis) before they are eaten.

predispose (pre-dis-pōz′). To render susceptible.

predisposition (pre-dis-po-zish′un). A condition of special susceptibility to a disease.

prednisolone (pred-nis′o-lōn). A dehydrogenated analogue of cortisol with the same actions and uses as cortisol.

prednisone (pred′nĭ-sōn). Deltacortisone; a dehydrogenated analogue of cortisone with the same actions and uses.

preduc'tal. Relating to that part of the aorta proximal to the aortic opening of the ductus arteriosus.

preeclampsia (pre'e-klamp'sĭ-ah) [pre- + G. *eklampsis*, a shining forth (eclampsia)]. The development of hypertension with proteinuria or edema, or both, due to pregnancy or the influence of a recent pregnancy.

pre'excita'tion. Premature activation of part of the ventricular myocardium by an impulse that travels by an anomalous path and so avoids physiological delay in the atrioventricular junction; an intrinsic part of the Wolff-Parkinson-White syndrome.

preganglionic (pre'gang-glĭ-on'ik). Situated proximal to or preceding a ganglion; referring specifically to the preganglionic motor neurons of the autonomic nervous system (located in the spinal cord and brainstem) and the myelinated nerve fibers by which they are connected to the autonomic ganglia.

pregnancy (preg'nan-sĭ) [L. *praegnans*, fr. *prae*, before, + *gnascor*, pp. *natus*, to be born]. Gestation; cyesis, the state of a female after conception until the birth of the baby.

   abdominal p., abdominocyesis (1); implantation and development of the ovum in the peritoneal cavity, usually secondary to an early rupture of a tubal p.

   ampullar p., tubal p. situated near the midportion of the oviduct.

   cervical p., lodgment and development of the impregnated ovum in the cervical canal.

   combined p., coexisting uterine and ectopic p.

   cornual p., the lodgment and development of the impregnated ovum in one of the cornua of the uterus.

   ectopic p., extrauterine p., the development of an impregnated ovum outside the cavity of the uterus.

   false p., pseudocyesis.

   interstitial p., intramural p.

   intraligamentary p., ectopic p. within the broad ligament.

   intramural p., interstitial p.; development of the fertilized ovum in the uterine portion of the fallopian tube.

   multiple p., the state of bearing two or more fetuses simultaneously.

   ovarian p., ovariocyesis; development of an impregnated ovum in an ovarian follicle.

   secondary abdominal p., abdominocyesis (2); a condition in which the embryo or fetus continues to grow in the abdominal cavity after its expulsion from the tube or other seat of its primary development.

   tubal p., development of an impregnated ovum in the oviduct.

   tuboabdominal p., development of an ectopic p. partly in the tube and partly in the abdominal cavity.

   tubo-ovarian p., development of the ovum at the fimbriated extremity of the oviduct and involving the ovary.

preg'nane. Parent hydrocarbon of two series of steroids, stemming from 5α-**pregnane**, found largely in urine as a metabolic product of 5β-pregnane compounds, and 5β-**pregnane,** the parent of the progesterones, pregnane alcohols and ketones, and several adrenocortical hormones.

pregnanediol (preg-nān-di'ol). 5β-Pregnane-3α,20α-diol; a steroid metabolite of progesterone that is biologically inactive and occurs as pregnanediol glucuronidate in the urine.

pregnanedione (preg-nān-di'ōn). 5β-Pregnane-3,20-dione; a metabolite of progesterone, formed in relatively small quantities; occurs in 5α and 5β isomeric forms.

pregnanetriol (preg-nān-tri'ol). 5β-Pregnane-3α,17α,20α-triol; a urinary metabolite of 17-hydroxyprogesterone and a precursor in the biosynthesis of cortisol; its excretion is enhanced in certain diseases of the adrenal cortex and following administration of corticotropin.

preg'nant [see pregnancy]. Gravid; denoting a female bearing within her the product of conception.

prehen'sile [L. *prehendo*, pp. *-hensus*, to lay hold of, seize]. Adapted for taking hold of or grasping.

prehen'sion. The act of grasping, or taking hold of.

prehor'mone. A glandular secretory product, having little or no inherent biological potency, that is converted peripherally to an active hormone in physiologically significant quantities.

preictal (pre-ik'tal) [pre- + L. *ictus,* a stroke]. Occurring before a convulsion or stroke.

preinduction (pre-in-duk'shun) [L. *prae,* before, + *inductio,* a bringing in]. A modification in the third generation resulting from the action of environment on the germ cells of one or both individuals of the grandparental generation.

pre'load. The load to which a muscle is subjected before shortening.

premalig'nant. Precancerous.

premature (pre-mă-tūr', -chūr) [L. *praematurus,* too early, fr. *prae-*, pre- + *maturus,* ripe (mature)]. **1.** Occurring before the usual or expected time. **2.** Denoting an infant born after less than 37 weeks of gestation, birth weight no longer considered a critical criterion.

prematurity (pre'mă-tūr'ĭ-tĭ). The state of being premature.

premedica'tion. 1. Administration of drugs prior to anesthesia to allay apprehension, produce sedation, and facilitate the administration of anesthesia to the patient. **2.** Drugs used for such purposes.

premen'strual. Relating to the period preceding menstruation.

premenstruum (pre-men'stroo-um) [pre- + L. *menstruum,* ntr. of *menstruus,* monthly, pertaining to menstruation]. The period preceding menstruation.

premo'lar. 1. Anterior to a molar tooth. **2.** A bicuspid tooth.

premon'ocyte. Promonocyte; an immature monocyte not normally seen in the circulating blood.

premor'bid [pre- + L. *morbidus*, ill, fr. *morbus*, disease]. Preceding the occurrence of disease.

premunition (pre-mu-nish'un) [Fr. fr. L. *praemunio*, pp. *-munitus*, to fortify beforehand]. Infection *immunity*.

premu'nitive. Relating to premunition.

premyeloblast (pre-mi'ĕ-lo-blast). The earliest recognizable precursor of the myeloblast.

premyelocyte (pre-mi'ĕ-lo-sīt). Myeloblast.

prena'tal [pre- + L. *natus*, born, pp. of *nascor*, to be born]. Antenatal; preceding birth.

preneoplastic (pre'ne-o-plas'tik) [pre- + G. *neos*, new, + *plastikos*, formative]. Preceding the formation of any neoplasm, benign or malignant.

preop'erative. Preceding an operation.

prepotency (pre-po'ten-sĭ) [pre- + L. *potentia*, power]. The ability or power possessed by one parent in greater degree than the other, of transmitting hereditable characteristics to the offspring.

prepo'tent. Possessing prepotency.

prepoten'tial. A gradual rise in potential between action potentials as a phasic swing in electric activity of the cell membrane, which establishes its rate of automatic activity, as in the ureter or cardiac pacemaker.

prepsychotic (pre'si-kot'ik). **1.** Relating to the period antedating the onset of psychosis. **2.** Denoting a potential for a psychotic episode, one that appears imminent under continued stress.

prepu'beral, prepu'bertal. Before puberty.

prepubescent (pre-pu-bes'ent). Immediately prior to the commencement of puberty.

prepuce (pre'pūs) [L. *praeputium*, foreskin]. Preputium.

preputial (pre-pu'shĭ-al). Relating to the prepuce

preputiotomy (pre-pu'shĭ-ot'o-mĭ) [preputium + *tomē*, incision]. Incision of prepuce.

preputium, pl. **prepu'tia** (pre-pu'shĭ-um) [L. *praeputium*] [NA]. Prepuce; foreskin; the free fold of skin that covers the glans penis.

    p. clitor'idis [NA], the external fold of the labia minora, forming a cap over the clitoris.

presby-, presbyo- [G. *presbys*, old man]. Combining forms denoting old age. See also gero-.

presbyacousia (prez'bĭ-ă-kū'sĭ-ah). Presbyacusis.

presbyacusis, presbyacusia (prez'bĭ-ă-kū'sis, kū'-sĭ-ah) [presby- + G. *akousis*, hearing]. Presbyacousia; presbycusis; loss of ability to perceive or discriminate sounds as a part of the aging process.

presbyatrics (prez-bĭ-at'riks) [presby- + G. *iatreia*, medical treatment]. Geriatrics.

presbycusis (prez-bĭ-kū'sis). Presbyacusis.

presbyophrenia (prez'bĭ-o-fre'nĭ-ah) [presbyo- + G. *phrēn*, mind]. Presbyphrenia; one of the mental disorders of old age marked by loss of memory, disorientation, and confabulation, but with relative integrity of judgment.

presbyopia (Pr) (prez-bĭ-o'pĭ-ah) [presby- + G. *ōps*, eye]. The physiologic change in accommodation power in the eyes in advancing age, said to begin when the near point has receded beyond 22cm.

presbyopic (prez-bĭ-op'ik, -o'pik). Relating to or suffering from presbyopia.

presbyphrenia (prez'bĭ-fre'nĭ-ah). Presbyophrenia.

prescribe [L. *prae-scribo*, pp. *-scriptus*, to write before]. To give directions, either orally or in writing, for the preparation and administration of a remedy to be used in the treatment of any disease.

prescrip'tion [L. *praescriptio*; see prescribe]. **1.** A written formula for the preparation and administration of any remedy. **2.** A medicinal preparation compounded according to the directions formulated in a p., said to consist of four parts: *superscription*, consisting of the word *recipe*, take, or its sign; *inscription*, or main part of the p., containing the names and amounts of the drugs ordered; *subscription*, directions for mixing the ingredients and designation of the form in which the drug is to be made (usually begins with *misce*, mix, M); and *signature*, directions to the patient regarding the dose and times of taking the remedy (preceded by *signa*, designate, or S).

pre'secre'tion. Hormone.

presenile (pre-se'nīl). Displaying presenility.

presenility (pre'sĕ-nil'ĭ-tĭ) [pre- + L. *senilis*, old]. Premature old age; the condition of one, not old in years, who displays the physical and mental characteristics of old age.

present (pre-zent') [L. *praesens* (*-sent-*), pres. p. of *prae-sum*, to be before, be at hand]. To precede or appear, as of the part of the fetus at the os uteri that is felt by the examining finger.

presentation (pre-zen-ta'shun, prez-) [see present]. The part of the body of the fetus which is in advance during birth; the occiput, chin, and sacrum are the determining points in vertex, face, and breech p.'s, respectively. See also position.

    breech p., p. of any part of the pelvic extremity of the fetus, the nates, knees, or feet; more properly only of the nates, but the thighs may be flexed and the legs extended over the anterior surfaces of the body (**frank b.p.**), the thighs may be flexed on the abdomen and the legs upon the thighs (**full b.p.**), the feet may be the lowest part (**footling p.**), or one leg may retain the position which is typical of one of the above-mentioned presentations, while the other foot or knee may present (**incomplete foot** or **knee p.**)

    cephalic p., p. usually with the head sharply flexed so that the chin is in contact with the thorax (vertex p.); but more rarely, there may be degrees of deflexion so that the presenting part is the large fontanel, the brow, or the face.

    footling p., foot p., descent of the fetus feet first.

    placental p., *placenta* previa.

shoulder p., p. in which the fetus lies with its long axis transverse to the long axis of the mother's body and the shoulder is the presenting part.

transverse p., an abnormal p., neither of head nor breech, the fetus lying transversely in the uterus, across the axis of the birth canal.

vertex p., the normal cephalic p., of the upper and back part of the fetal head.

preservative (pre-zer'vă-tiv). A substance added to food products or to organic solution to prevent chemical change or bacterial action.

presomite (pre-so'mit). Relating to the embryonic stage before the appearance of somites.

presphygmic (pre-sfig'mik) [pre- + G. *sphygmos,* pulse]. Preceding the pulse beat; denoting a brief interval following the filling of the ventricles with blood before their contraction forces open the semilunar valves.

pres'sor [L. *premo,* pp. *pressus,* to press]. Hypertensor; exciting to vasomotor activity; producing increased blood pressure.

pres'sorecep'tive. Pressosensitive; capable of receiving as stimuli changes in pressure, especially changes of blood pressure.

pres'sorecep'tor. Baroreceptor.

pres'sosen'sitive. Pressoreceptive.

pressure (presh'ur) [L. *pressura,* fr. *premo,* pp. *pressus,* to press]. 1. A stress or force acting in any direction against resistance. 2 (P, frequently followed by a subscript indicating location). In physics and physiology, the force per unit area exerted by a gas or liquid against the walls of its container.

abdominal p., p. surrounding the bladder; estimated from rectal, gastric, or intraperitoneal p.

back p., p. exerted upstream in the circulation as a result of obstruction to forward flow, as when congestion in the pulmonary circulation results from stenosis of the mitral valve or failure of the left ventricle.

blood p., (BP), arteriotony; the p. or tension of the blood within the arteries, maintained by the contraction of the left ventricle, resistance of the arterioles and capillaries, elasticity of the arterial walls, as well as viscosity and volume of the blood; always expressed as relative to the ambient atmospheric p.

central venous p. (CVP), the p. of the blood within the venous system in the superior and inferior vena cava, normally measured between 4 and 10 cm of water; depressed in circulatory shock and deficiencies of circulating blood volume, and increased with cardiac failure and congestion of circulation.

cerebrospinal p., tension of the cerebrospinal fluid, normally 100 to 150 mm of water, relative to the ambient atmospheric p.

diastolic p., the lowest blood p. reached during any given ventricular cycle.

effective osmotic p., that part of the total osmotic p. of a solution that governs the tendency of its solvent to pass across a boundary, usually a semipermeable membrane.

intracranial p, (ICP), p. within the cranial cavity.

intraocular p., the p. of the intraocular fluid within the eye.

negative end-expiratory p. (NEEP), a subatmospheric p. at the airway at the end of expiration.

osmotic p., p. that must be applied to a solution to prevent the passage into it of solvent when solution and pure solvent are separated by a perfectly semipermeable membrane.

partial p., the p. exerted by a single component of a mixture of gases, commonly expressed in mm Hg or torr; for a gas dissolved in a liquid, the partial p. is that of a gas that would be in equilibrium with the dissolved gas. Symbol: P followed by subscripts denoting location and/or chemical species.

positive end-expiratory p. (PEEP), a technique used in respiratory therapy in which p. is maintained in the airway so that the lungs empty less completely in expiration.

pulmonary capillary wedge p., an indirect indication of left atrial p. obtained by wedging a catheter into a small pulmonary artery sufficiently tightly to block flow from behind and thus to sample the p. beyond.

pulse p., the variation in blood p. occurring in an artery during the cardiac cycle; the difference between the systolic or maximum and diastolic or minimum p.'s.

standard p., the absolute p. to which gases are referred under standard conditions (STPD), *i.e.,* 760 mm Hg, 760 torr, or 101,325 newtons/sq m.

systolic p., the highest blood pressure reached during any given ventricular cycle.

wedge p., intravascular pressure reading obtained when a fine catheter is advanced until it completely occludes a small blood vessel or is sealed in place by inflation of a small cuff.

pre'ster'num. *Manubrium* sterni.

presuppurative (pre-sup'u-ra'tiv). Denoting an early stage in an inflammation prior to the formation of pus.

presynaptic (pre'sĭ-nap'tik). Pertaining to the area on the proximal side of a synaptic cleft.

presystole (pre-sis'to-le). Late diastole; that part of diastole immediately preceeding systole.

presystol'ic. Late diastolic; relating to the interval immediately preceding systole.

pretar'sal. Denoting the anterior, or inferior, portion of the tarsus.

prevalence (prev'ă-lens). The number of existing cases of a disease in a given population at a specific time.

preventive (pre-ven'tiv) [L. *prae-venio,* pp. *-ventus,* to come before, prevent]. **1.** Prophylactic (1). **2.** Anything that arrests the threatened onset of disease.

previus (pre'vĭ-us) [L. *prae,* before, + *via,* way]. In the way; referring usually to anything obstructing the passages in childbirth.

priapism (pri'ă-pizm) [L. *priapus* (*q.v.*), penis]. Abnormal persistent erection of the penis.

pri'mal. 1. First or primary. **2.** Primordial (2).

primaquine phosphate (pri'mă-kwin). An antimalarial agent especially effective against *Plasmodium vivax*, terminating relapsing vivax malaria; usually administered with chloroquine.

primary (pri'mĕr-ĭ) [L. *primarius*, fr. *primus*, first]. **1.** The first or foremost, as a disease or symptoms to which others may be secondary or occur as complications. **2.** Relating to the first stage of growth or development. See primordial. **3.** Principal.

primate (pri'māt) [L. *primus*, first]. An individual of the order Primates, the highest order of mammals, including man, monkeys, and lemurs embraced in the two suborders: Anthropoidea and Lemuroidea, or Prosimiae.

primigravida (pri-mĭ-grav'ĭ-dah) [L. fr. *primus*, first, + *gravida*, a pregnant woman]. Unigravida; a woman who is pregnant for the first time.

primipara (pri-mip'ă-rah) [L. fr. *primus*, first, + *pario*, to bring forth]. Unipara; para I; a woman who has given birth for the first time to an infant or infants, alive or dead, weighing 500 g or more and having a length of gestation of at least 20 weeks.

primiparity (pri-mĭ-păr'ĭ-tĭ). The condition of being a primipara.

primiparous (pri-mip'ă-rus). Uniparous; denoting a primipara.

primitive (prim'ĭ-tĭv) [L. *primitivus*, fr. *primus*, first]. Primordial (2).

primor'dial. 1. Relating to a primordium. **2.** Primitive; primal (2); relating to a structure in its first or earliest stage of development.

primor'dium [L. origin, fr. *primus*, first, + *ordior*, to begin]. Anlage (1); an aggregation of cells in the embryo indicating the first trace of an organ or structure.

princeps, pl. **principes** (prin'seps, -sĭ-pēz) [L. chief, fr. *primus*, first, + *capio*, to take, choose]. Principal; a term used to distinguish several arteries.

principle (prin'sĭ-pl) [L. *principium*, a beginning, fr. *princeps*, chief]. **1.** A continuously acting power or force. See also law, theorem. **2.** The essential ingredient in a drug or chemical compound.

   active p., a constituent of a drug, usually an alkaloid or glycoside, upon the presence of which the characteristic therapeutic action of the substance largely depends.

   closure p., in psychology, the p. that when one views fragmentary stimuli forming a nearly complete figure one tends to ignore the missing parts and perceive the figure as whole.

   consistency p., in psychology, the desire of the human being to be consistent, especially in attitudes and beliefs.

   pain-pleasure p., pleasure p., a psychoanalytic concept that, in man's psychic functioning, he tends to seek pleasure and avoid pain.

   reality p., the concept that the pleasure p. in personality development is modified by the demands of external reality.

prism (prizm) [G. *prisma*. A solid whose sides are parallelograms and whose transverse section is a triangle; a triangular p. deflects the ray of light toward the base of the triangle and splits it up into its primary colors; used in spectacles to correct imbalance of the extrinsic ocular muscles.

privacy (pri'vă-sĭ). **1.** Being apart from others; seclusion; secrecy. **2.** Respect for the confidential nature of the physician-patient relationship.

PRL Prolactin.

p.r.n. L. *pro re nata,* as needed.

Pro Proline or its radicals.

pro- [L. and G. *pro,* before]. **1.** Prefix denoting before or forward. See also ante-, pre-. **2.** In chemistry, prefix indicating precursor of. See also -gen.

proaccelerin (pro-ak-sel'er-in). *Factor* V.

proactivator (pro-ak'tĭ-va-tor). A substance that, when chemically split, yields a fragment (activator) capable of rendering another substance enzymically active.

probacteriophage (pro-bak-tēr'ĭ-o-fāj). Prophage; the stage of a temperate bacteriophage in which the genome is incorporated in the genetic apparatus of the bacterial host.

pro'band [L. *probare,* to test, prove]. Propositus (1); in human genetics, the patient or member of the family that brings a family under study.

pro'bang. A slender flexible rod, tipped with a globular piece of sponge or some other material, used chiefly for making applications or removing obstructions in the larynx or esophagus.

probe (prōb) [L. *probo,* to test]. **1.** A slender rod with a blunt bulbous tip, used for exploring an open body part. **2.** To enter and explore a body part, as with a p.

probio'sis [pro- + G. *biōsis,* life]. An association of two organisms that enhances the life processes of both.

probiot'ic. Relating to probiosis.

procaine hydrochloride (pro'kān). 2-Diethylamino-ethyl *p*-aminobenzoate monohydrochloride; a local anesthetic used for infiltration and spinal anesthesia.

procapsid (pro-kap'sid). A protein shell lacking a virus genome.

procarbox'ypep'tidase. Inactive precursor of a carboxypeptidase.

procaryote. Prokaryote.

pro'caryot'ic. Prokaryotic.

proce'dure. Act or conduct of a treatment or an operation. See method; operation; technique.

procentriole (pro-sen'trĭ-ōl). The early phase in development of centrioles or basal bodies from the centrosphere.

procephalic (pro-sĕ-fal'ik) [pro- + G. *kephalē,* head]. Relating to the anterior part of the head.

procercoid (pro-ser'koyd) [pro- + G. *kerkos,* tail, + *eidos,* resemblance]. The first stage in the aquatic life cycle of certain tapeworms, following ingestion of the newly hatched larva (coracidium) by a copepod (water flea).

process (pros'es, pro'ses) [L. *processus,* an advance, progress]. **1.** A method or mode of action used in the attainment of a certain result. **2.** An advance or progress, as of a disease. **3.** A projection or outgrowth. See processus.

acromial p., acromion.

alveolar p., *processus* alveolaris.

caudate p., *processus* caudatus.

ciliary p., *processus* ciliaris.

clinoid p., *processus* clinoideus.

complex learning p.'s, those which require the use of symbolic manipulations, as in reasoning.

condylar p., condyloid p., *processus* condylaris.

coracoid p., *processus* coracoideus.

coronoid p., *processus* coronoideus.

dendritic p., dendrite (1).

ensiform p., *processus* xiphoideus.

falciform p., *processus* falciformis.

foot p., pedicel.

funicular p., the tunica vaginalis surrounding the spermatic cord.

malar p., *processus* zygomaticus (1).

mandibular p., mandibular *arch.*

mastoid p., *processus* mastoideus.

maxillary p., *processus* maxillaris.

odontoid p. of epistropheus, dens (2).

orbital p. *processus* orbitalis.

palatal p.'s, in the embryo, medially directed shelves from the oral surface of the maxillae which develop into the palate after midline fusion.

palatine p., *processus* palatinus.

primary p., in psychoanalysis, the mental p. directly related to the functions of the id and characteristic of unconscious mental activity; marked by unorganized, illogical thinking and by the tendency to seek immediate discharge and gratification of instinctual demands.

pterygoid p., *processus* pterygoideus.

secondary p., in psychoanalysis, the mental p. directly related to the functions of the ego and characteristic of conscious and preconscious mental activities; marked by logical thinking and by the tendency to delay gratification by regulation of the discharge of instinctual demands.

spinous p., (1) *spina ossis* sphenoidalis; (2) *processus* spinosus.

spinous p. of tibia, *eminentia* intercondylaris.

styloid p., see *processus* styloideus radii, styloideus ossis temporalis, and styloideus ulnae.

temporal p., *processus* temporalis.

transverse p., *processus* transversus.

xiphoid p., *processus* xiphoideus.

zygomatic p., *processus* zygomaticus.

proces'sus, pl. **proces'sus** [L. see process] [NA]. Process; a projection or outgrowth.

p. alveola'ris [NA], alveolar process. the projecting ridge on the surface of the maxilla and the mandible containing the tooth sockets.

p. cauda'tus [NA], caudate process; a narrow band of hepatic tissue connecting the caudate and right lobes of the liver posterior to the porta hepatis.

p. cilia'ris [NA], ciliary process; one of the radiating pigmented ridges on the inner surface of the ciliary body which, with the folds (plicae) in the furrows between them, constitute the corona ciliaris.

p. clinoi'deus [NA], clinoid process; one of three pairs of bony projections (anterior, middle, superior) from the sphenoid bone.

p. condyla'ris [NA], condylar or condyloid process; the articular process of the ramus of the mandible.

p. coracoi'deus [NA], coracoid process; a long curved projection from the neck of the scapula that overhangs the glenoid cavity; gives attachment to the short head of the biceps, the coracobrachialis, and the pectoralis minor muscles, and the conoid and coracoacromial ligaments.

p. coronoi'deus [NA], coronoid process; (1) the triangular anterior process of the mandibular ramus, giving attachment to the temporal muscle; (2) a bracket-like projection from the anterior portion of the proximal extremity of the ulna, giving attachment to the brachialis and entering into formation of the trochlear notch.

p. falcifor'mis [NA], falciform process; a continuation of the inner border of the sacrotuberous ligament upward and forward on the inner aspect of the ramus of the ischium.

p. mastoi'deus [NA], mastoid process; (1) mastoid bone; the nipple-like projection of the petrous part of the temporal bone; (2) in the embryo, the part of the first pharyngeal arch that develops into the upper jaw.

p. maxilla'ris [NA], maxillary process; a thin plate projecting from the upper border of the inferior nasal concha, articulating with the maxilla and partly closing the orifice of the maxillary sinus.

p. orbita'lis [NA], orbital process; the anterior and larger of the two processes at the upper extremity of the vertical plate of the palatine bone, articulating with the maxilla, ethmoid, and sphenoid bones.

p. palati'nus [NA], palatine process; the horizontal plate of the maxilla, forming with its fellow the anterior portion of the roof of the mouth.

p. pterygoi'deus [NA], pterygoid process; a long process extending downward from the junction of the body and great wing of the sphenoid bone.

p. spino'sus [NA], spinous process (2); the dorsal projection from the center of a vertebral arch.

p. styloi'deus os'sis tempora'lis [NA], styloid process of temporal bone; a slender pointed projection from the petrous portion of the temporal bone where it joins the tympanic portion; gives attachment to the styloglossus, stylohyoid, and stylopharyngeus muscles and the stylohyoid and stylomandibular ligaments.

p. styloi′deus ra′dii [NA], styloid process of the radius; a thick, pointed projection on the lateral side of the distal extremity of the radius.

p. styloi′deus ul′nae [NA], styloid process of the ulna; a cylindrical, pointed projection from the medial and posterior aspect of the head of the ulna, to the tip of which is attached the ulnar collateral ligament of the wrist.

p. tempora′lis [NA], temporal process; the posterior projection of the zygomatic bone articulating with the zygomatic process of the temporal bone to form the zygomatic arch.

p. transver′sus [NA], transverse process; a p. projecting on either side of the arch of a vertebra.

p. xiphoi′deus [NA], xiphoid or ensiform process or cartilage; xiphisternum; the cartilage at the lower end of the sternum.

p. zygomat′icus [NA], zygomatic process; **(1)** malar process; the rough projection from the maxilla that articulates with the zygomatic bone; **(2)** the projection of the frontal bone that joins the zygomatic bone to form the lateral margin of the orbit; **(3)** the anterior process of the temporal bone that articulates with the temporal process of the zygomatic bone to form the zygomatic arch.

prochondral (pro-kon′dral) [pro- + G. *chondros*, cartilage]. Denoting a developmental stage prior to the formation of cartilage.

prochymosin (pro-ki′mo-sin). Prorennin; renninogen; the precursor of chymosin (rennin).

procidentia (pros-ĭ-den′shĭ-ah, pro-sĭ-) [L. a falling forward, fr. *procido*, to fall forward]. A sinking down or prolapse of any organ or part.

procollagen (pro-kol′ă-jen). Soluble precursor of collagen, presumably formed by the fibroblast in the process of collagen synthesis.

proconver′tin. *Factor* VII.

procreate (pro′kre-āt) [L. *pro-creo*, pp. *-creatus*, to beget]. To beget; to produce by the sexual act; said usually of the male parent.

procreation (pro-kre-a′shun). Reproduction.

procreative (pro′kre-a-tiv). Having the power to beget or procreate.

proct-. See procto-.

proctalgia (prok-tal′jĭ-ah) [proct- + G. *algos*, pain]. Proctodynia; rectalgia; pain at the anus, or in the rectum.

proctatresia (prok-tă-tre′zĭ-ah) [proct- + G. *a-* priv. + *trēsis*, a boring]. Anal *atresia.*

proctectasia (prok-tek-ta′zĭ-ah) [proct- + G. *ektasis*, extension]. Dilation of the anus or rectum.

proctectomy (prok-tek′to-mĭ) [proct- + G. *ektomē*, excision]. Rectectomy; surgical resection of the rectum.

procteurynter (prok-tu-rin′tur) [proct- + G. *eurynō*, to dilate, fr. *eurys*, wide]. An inflatable bag for dilating the rectum.

proctitis (prok-ti′tis) [proct- + G. *-itis*, inflammation]. Rectitis; inflammation of the mucous membrane of the rectum.

procto-, proct- [G. *prōktos*, anus]. Combining forms signifying anus or, more frequently, rectum. See also recto-.

proctocele (prok′to-sēl) [procto- + G. *kēlē, tumor*]. Rectocele; prolapse or herniation of the rectum.

proctoclysis (prok-tok′lĭ-sis) [procto- + G. *klysis*, a washing out]. Murphy drip; slow continuous administration of saline solution by instillation into the rectum and sigmoid colon.

proctococcypexy (prok-to-kok′sĭ-peks-ĭ) [procto- + G. *kokkyx*, coccyx, + *pēxis*, fixation]. Rectococcypexy; suture of a prolapsing rectum to the tissues anterior to the coccyx.

proctocolectomy (prok′to-ko-lek′to-mĭ) [procto- + G. *kolon*, colon, + *ektomē*, excision]. Surgical removal of the rectum and part or all of the colon.

proctocolonoscopy (prok′to-ko-lo-nos′ko-pĭ) [procto- + G. *kolon*, colon, + *skopeō*, to view]. Inspection of interior of rectum and colon.

proctocolpoplasty (prok′to-kol′po-plas-tĭ) [procto- + G. *kolpos*, bosom (vagina), + *plassō*, to form]. Surgical closure of a rectovaginal fistula.

proctocystoplasty (prok′to-sis′to-plas-tĭ) [procto- + G. *kystis*, bladder, + *plassō*, to form]. Surgical closure of a rectovesical fistula.

proctocystotomy (prok′to-sis-tot′o-mĭ) [procto- + G. *kystis*, bladder, + *tomē*, incision]. Incision into the bladder from the rectum.

proctodeum, pl. **proctodea** (prok-to-de′um, -de′ah) [L. fr. G. *prōktos*, anus + *hodaios*, on the way]. Anal pit; an ectodermally lined depression, adjacent to the terminal part of the embryonic hindgut, from which the anal and urogenital external orifices are established.

proctodynia (prok-to-din′ĭ-ah) [procto- + G. *odynē*, pain]. Proctalgia.

proctologic (prok-to-loj′ik). Relating to proctology.

proctologist (prok-tol′o-jist). A specialist in proctology.

proctology (prok-tol′o-jĭ) [procto- + G. *logos*, study]. The surgical specialty concerned with the anus and rectum and their diseases.

proctoparalysis (prok′to-pă-ral′ĭ-sis). Paralysis of the anus, leading to incontinence of feces.

proctopexy (prok′to-pek-sĭ) [procto- + G. *pēxis*, fixation]. Rectopexy; surgical fixation of a prolapsing rectum.

proctoplasty (prok′to-plas-tĭ) [procto- + G. *plassō*, to form]. Rectoplasty; reparative or plastic surgery of the anus or of the rectum.

proctoplegia (prok-to-ple′jĭ-ah) [procto- + G. *plēge*, stroke]. Paralysis of the anus and rectum occurring with paraplegia.

proctoptosia, proctoptosis (prok-top-to′sĭ-ah, -to′sis) [procto- + G. *ptōsis*, a falling]. Prolapse of the rectum and anus.

proctorrhaphy (prok-tor'ă-fĭ) [procto- + G. *rhaphē*, suture]. Suturing of a lacerated rectum or anus.

proctorrhea (prok-to-re'ah) [procto- + G. *rhoia*, a flow]. A mucoserous discharge from the rectum.

proctoscope (prok'to-skōp) [procto- + G. *skopeō*, to view]. Rectoscope; a rectal speculum.

proctoscopy (prok-tos'ko-pĭ). Visual examination of the rectum and anus, as with a proctoscope.

proctosigmoidectomy (prok'to-sig-moy-dek'to-mĭ) [procto- + sigmoid, + G. *ektomē*, excision]. Excision of the rectum and sigmoid colon.

proctosigmoiditis (prok'to-sig-moy-di'tis) [procto- + sigmoid + G. -*itis*, inflammation]. Inflammation of the sigmoid colon and rectum.

proctosigmoidoscopy (prok'to-sig-moy-dos'ko-pĭ) [procto- + sigmoid + G. *skopeō*, to view]. Direct inspection through a sigmoidoscope of the rectum and sigmoid colon.

proctospasm (prok'to-spazm) [procto- + G. *spasmos*, spasm]. **1.** Spasmodic stricture of the anus. **2.** Spasmodic contraction of the rectum.

proctostenosis (prok'to-stě-no'sis) [procto- + G. *stenōsis*, a narrowing]. Stricture of the rectum or anus.

proctostomy (prok-tos'to-mĭ) [procto- + G. *stoma*, mouth]. Rectostomy; formation of an artificial opening into the rectum.

proctotomy (prok-tot'o-mĭ) [procto- + G. *tomē*, incision]. Rectotomy; an incision into the rectum.

proctotresia (prok-to-tre'zĭ-ah) [procto- + G. *trēsis*, a boring]. Surgical correction of an imperforate anus.

proctovalvotomy (prok'to-val-vot'o-mĭ). Incision of the rectal valves.

procumbent (pro-kum'bent) [L. *procumbens*, falling or leaning forward]. In a prone position; lying face down.

prodromal (pro-dro'mal). Prodromic; relating to a prodrome.

prodrome (pro'drōm) [G. *prodromos*, a running before]. An early or premonitory symptom of a disease.

prodrom'ic. Prodromal.

pro'drug. A class of drugs the pharmacologic action of which results from conversion by metabolic processes within the body (biotransformation).

product (prod'ukt) [L. *productus*, fr. *pro-duco*, pp. -*ductus*, to lead forth]. Anything produced or made, either naturally or artificially.

   cleavage p., a substance resulting from the splitting of a molecule into two or more simpler molecules.

   fibrin/fibrinogen degradation p.'s, several poorly characterized small peptides, designated X, Y, D, and E, that result following the action of plasmin on fibrinogen and fibrin in the fibrinolytic process.

   fission p., an atomic species produced in the course of the fission of a massive atom such as U^{235}.

   spallation p., an atomic species produced in the course of the spallation of any atom.

   substitution p., a p. obtained by replacing one atom or group in a molecule with another atom or group.

productive (pro-duk'tiv) [see product]. Producing or capable of producing; denoting especially an inflammation leading to the production of new tissue with or without an exudate.

proenzyme (pro-en'zīm). Zymogen; the precursor of an enzyme, requiring some change (usually the hydrolysis of an inhibiting fragment that masks an active grouping) to render it active.

proerythroblast (pro-ĕ-rith'ro-blast). Pronormoblast.

proerythrocyte (pro-ĕ-rith'ro-sīt). Precursor of an erythrocyte; an immature red blood cell with a nucleus.

proestrogen (pro-es'tro-jen). An estrogen that acts only after it has been metabolized in the body to an active compound.

profibrinolysin (pro-fi'brĭ-nol'ĭ-sin). Plasminogen. See also plasmin.

pro'file [It. *profilo*, fr. L. *pro*, forward, + *filum*, thread, line (contour)]. **1.** An outline or contour, especially one representing a side view of the human head. **2.** A summary, brief account, or record.

   biochemical p., a combination of biochemical tests usually performed with automated instrumentation upon admission of a patient to a hospital or clinic.

   personality p., (1) a method by which the results of psychological testing are presented in graphic form; (2) a vignette or brief personality description.

   test p., a combination of laboratory tests usually performed by automated methods and designed to evaluate organ systems of patients upon admission to a hospital or clinic.

progas'trin. Precursor of gastric secretion in the mucous membrane of the stomach.

progenitor (pro-jen'ĭ-tor) [L.]. A precursor; ancestor; one who begets.

progeny (proj'ě-nĭ) [L. *progenies*, fr. *progigno*, to beget]. Offspring; descendents.

progeria (pro-jēr'ĭ-ah) [pro- + G. *gēras*, old age]. Hutchinson-Gilford disease or syndrome; premature senility syndrome; a condition in which normal development in the first year is followed by gross retardation of growth, with a senile appearance characterized by dry wrinkled skin, total alopecia, and bird-like facies.

progestational (pro-jes-ta'shun-al). **1.** Favoring pregnancy; conducive to gestation; having a stimulating effect upon the uterine changes essential for the implantation and growth of the fertilized ovum. **2.** Referring to progesterone, or to a drug with progesterone-like properties.

progesterone (pro-jes'ter-ōn). Progestational or corpus luteum hormone; luteohormone; 4-pregnene-3,20-dione; a progestin, an antiestrogenic steroid believed to be the active principle of the corpus luteum, isolated from the corpus luteum and placenta or synthetically prepared, and used to correct abnormalities of the menstrual cycle.

progestin (pro-jes'tin). **1.** A hormone of the corpus luteum. **2.** Generic term for any substance, natural or synthetic, that effects some or all of the biological changes produced by progesterone.

progestogen (pro-jes'to-jen). **1.** Any agent capable of producing biological effects similar to those of progesterone. **2.** A synthetic derivative from testosterone or progesterone that has some of the physiologic activity and pharmacologic effects of progesterone.

proglos'sis [pro- + G. *glōssa,* tongue]. Tip of the tongue.

proglottid, pl. **proglottids, proglottides** (pro-glot'id, -idz, -ĭ-dēz) [pro- + G. *glōssa,* tongue]. Proglottis; one of the segments of a tapeworm, containing the reproductive organs.

proglot'tis. Proglottid.

prognathic (prog-nath'ik) [pro- + G. *gnathos,* jaw]. Prognathous. **1.** Having a projecting jaw; having a gnathic index above 103. **2.** Denoting a forward projection of either or both of the jaws relative to the craniofacial skeleton.

prognathism (prog'nă-thizm). The condition of being prognathic.

prognathous (prog'nă-thus). Prognathic.

prognosis (prog-no'sis) [G. *prognōsis,* fr. *pro,* before, + *gignōskō,* to know]. **1.** The foretelling of the probable course of a disease. **2.** A forecast of the outcome of a disease.

prognostic (prog-nos'tik) [G. *prognōstikos*]. **1.** Relating to a prognosis. **2.** A symptom upon which a prognosis is based.

prognosticate (prog-nos'tĭ-kāt). To give a prognosis.

prognostician (prog-nos-tish'un). One skilled in prognosis.

progranulocyte (pro-gran'u-lo-sīt). Promyelocyte

progressive (pro-gres'iv) [L. *pro-gredior,* pp. *-gressus,* to go forth]. Going forward; advancing; denoting the course of a disease, especially, when unqualified, an unfavorable course.

pro'hor'mone. An intraglandular precursor of a hormone.

pro'insulin. A single-chain precursor of insulin.

projec'tion [L. *projectio;* fr. *projicio,* pp. *-jectus,* to throw before]. **1.** A pushing out. **2.** A prominence. **3.** The referring of a sensation to the object producing it. **4.** A defense mechanism involving the referring to another of a repressed complex in the individual, as when one reprobates in others faults to the commission of which he himself has a constant inclination. **5.** Localization of visual impressions; straight ahead, right or left, above or below. **6.** In neuroanatomy, the system or systems of nerve fibers by which a group of nerve cells discharges its nerve impulses ("projects") to one or more other cell groups.

prokaryote (pro-kăr'ĭ-ōt) [pro- + G. *karyon,* kernel, nut]. Procaryote; a unicellular microorganism whose cell does not contain a limiting membrane around the nuclear material.

pro'karyot'ic. Procaryotic; pertaining to a prokaryote.

prola'bium [pro- + L. *labium,* lip]. **1.** The exposed carmine margin of the lip. **2.** The small elevation at the termination of the philtrum.

prolac'tin (PRL). Lactogenic hormone; lactotropin; a hormone of the anterior lobe of the hypophysis cerebri that stimulates the secretion of milk and possibly during pregnancy, breast growth.

prolactostat'in. Prolactin-inhibiting *factor.*

prolamine (pro-lam'ēn, pro'lă-mēn, -min). A protein insoluble in water or neutral salt solutions, soluble in dilute acids or alkalies, and in dilute (70 to 90%) alcohol.

prolapse (pro-laps') [L. *prolapsus,* a falling]. **1.** To sink down, said of an organ or other part. **2.** A sinking of an organ or other part, especially its appearance at a natural or artificial orifice.

   Morgagni's p., chronic inflammation of Morgagni's ventricle.

   p. of umbilical cord, presentation of part of the umbilical cord ahead of the fetus; it may cause fetal death due to compression of the cord between the presenting part of the fetus and the maternal pelvis.

   p. of uterus, descensus uteri resulting from laxity and atony of the muscular and fascial structures of the pelvic floor, usually resulting from injuries of childbirth or advanced age, and occurring in three forms: **first degree p.,** the cervix of the prolapsed uterus is well within the vaginal orifice; **second degree p.,** the cervix is at or near the introitus; **third degree p.** (procidentia uteri), the cervix protrudes well beyond the vaginal orifice.

prolepsis (pro-lep'sis) [G. *prolēpsis,* anticipation]. Recurrence of the paroxysm of a periodical disease at regularly shortening intervals.

prolep'tic. Relating to prolepsis.

pro'lidase. *Proline* dipeptidase.

prolif'erate [L. *proles,* offspring, + *fero,* to bear]. To grow and increase in number by means of reproduction of similar forms.

prolifera'tion. Growth and reproduction of similar cells.

prolif'erative, prolif'erous. Reproductive; increasing the numbers of similar forms.

proligerous (pro-lij'er-us) [L. *proles,* offspring, + *gero,* to bear]. Germinating; producing offspring.

pro'linase. Prolyl dipeptidase.

proline (Pro) (pro'lēn). An amino acid, 2-pyrrolidine-carboxylic acid, found in proteins.

   p. dipeptidase, prolidase; an enzyme cleaving aminoacyl-proline bonds.

   p. iminopeptidase, a hydrolase cleaving L-proline residues from the N-terminal position in peptides.

pro'lyl dipep'tidase. Prolinase; an enzyme cleaving L-prolyl-aminoacid bonds.

promastigote (pro-mas'tĭ-gōt) [pro- + G. *mastix,* whip]. The flagellate stage of a trypanosomatid protozoan, usually an extracellular phase, as in the insect intermediate host (or in culture) of *Leish-*

mania parasites.

promegaloblast (pro-meg'ă-lo-blast). The earliest of four maturation stages of the megaloblast.

prometaphase (pro-met'ă-fāz) [pro- + metaphase]. The stage of mitosis or meiosis in which the nuclear membrane disintegrates, the centrioles reach the poles of the cell, and the chromosomes continue to contract.

promethium (pro-me'thĭ-um) [*Prometheus*, Greek demigod]. A radioactive element of the rare earth series; symbol Pm, atomic no. 61; isolated in 1948 among the fission products of uranium-235.

prominence (prom'ĭ-nens) [L. *prominentia*]. A protuberance or projection.

  laryngeal p., Adam's apple; the projection on the anterior portion of the neck formed by the thyroid cartilage of the larynx.

  thenar p., thenar (1).

promon'ocyte. Premonocyte.

promontory (prom'on-to-rī) [L. *promontorium*, mountain ridge]. An eminence or projection.

promo'ter. 1. In chemistry, a substance that increases the activity of a catalyst. **2.** In molecular biology, a DNA sequence at which RNA polymerase binds and initiates transcription.

promyelocyte (pro-mi'ĕ-lo-sīt) [pro- + G. *myelos*, marrow, + *kytos*, cell]. Progranulocyte **1.** The developmental stage of a granular leukocyte between the myeloblast and myelocyte, when a few specific granules appear in addition to azurophilic ones. **2.** A large uninuclear cell occurring in the circulating blood in myelocytic leukemia.

pronasion (pro-na'zĭ-on) [pro- + L. *nasus*, nose]. The point of the angle between the septum of the nose and the surface of the upper lip.

pro'nate [L. *pronatus*, bent forward]. **1.** To assume, or to be placed in, a prone position. **2.** To perform pronation of the forearm or foot

prona'tion. The condition of being prone; the act of assuming or of being placed in a prone position; *e.g.*, eversion and abduction of foot, causing a lowering of the medial edge, or rotation of the forearm in such a way that the palm of the hand faces backward when the arm is in the anatomical position, or downward when the arm is extended at a right angle to the body.

prona'tor. [L.]. A muscle which turns a part into the prone position.

prone (prōn) [L. *pronus*, bending down or forward]. Denoting the hand or foot in pronation, or the body when lying face downward.

pronephros, pl. **pronephroi** (pro-nef'ros, -roy) [pro- + G. *nephros*, kidney]. In the embryos of higher vertebrates, a vestigial structure consisting of a series of tortuous tubules emptying into the cloaca by way of the primary nephric duct; rudimentary and temporary structure followed by the mesonephros and later by the metanephros.

pro'normoblast. Proerythroblast; rubriblast; the earliest of four stages in development of the normoblast.

pronucleus (pro-nu'kle-us). **1.** One of two nuclei undergoing fusion in karyogamy. **2.** In embryology, the nuclear material of the head of the spermatozoon (**male p.**) or of the ovum (**female p.**), after the ovum has been penetrated by the spermatozoon; each carries the haploid number of chromosomes.

prootic (pro-o'tik) [pro- + G. *ous*, ear]. In front of the ear.

prop'agate [L. *propago*, pp. *-atus*, to generate, reproduce]. **1.** To reproduce; to generate. **2.** To move along a fiber, *e.g.*, a nerve impulse.

propagation (prop-ă-ga'shun). The act of propagating.

propagative (prop'ă-ga-tiv). Relating to or involved in propagation; denoting the sexual part of an animal or plant as distinguished from the soma.

pro'pane. $CH_3CH_2CH_3$; one of the alkane series of hydrocarbons.

propep'sin. Pepsinogen.

proper'din. A normal serum γ_2-globulin that participates, in conjunction with other factors, in an alternate pathway to the activation of the terminal components of complement.

prophage (pro'fāj). Probacteriophage.

prophase (pro'fāz) [G. *prophasis*, from *prophainō*, to foreshadow]. The first stage of mitosis or meiosis, consisting of linear contraction and increase in thickness of the chromosomes (each composed of two chromatids) accompanied by division of the centriole and migration of the two daughter centrioles and their asters toward the poles of the cell.

prophylactic (pro-fĭ-lak'tik) [G. *prophylaktikos*; see prophylaxis]. **1.** Preventive (1); preventing disease; relating to prophylaxis. **2.** An agent that acts as a preventive against disease.

prophylaxis, pl. **prophylaxes** (pro-fĭ-lak'sis, -sēz) [Mod.L. fr. G. *pro-phy-lassō*, to take precaution]. The prevention of disease.

propionate (pro'pĭ-o-nāt). A salt or ester of propionic acid.

Propionibacterium (pro-pĭ-on-ĭ-bak-tēr'ĭ-um). A genus of saprophytic Gram-positive bacteria (family Propionibacteriaceae) that occur in dairy products, on the skin, and in the intestinal tract, and may be pathogenic. The type species is *P. freudenreichii*.

propion'ic acid. Methylacetic or ethylformic acid; CH_3CH_2COOH; found in sweat.

propositus, pl. **propos'iti** (pro-poz'ĭ-tus, -i-ti) [L. fr. *proponere*, to propound]. **1.** Proband. **2.** A premise; an argument.

proprietary name (pro-pri'ĕ-tēr-ĭ) [L. *proprietarius*]. The patented brand name or trademark under which a manufacturer markets his product; written with a capital initial letter and is often further distinguished by a superscript R in a circle.

proprioceptive (pro'prī-o-sep'tiv) [L. *proprius*, one's own, + *capio*, to take]. Capable of receiving stimuli originating in muscles, tendons, and other internal tissues.

proprioceptor (pro'prĭ-o-sep'tor). One of a variety of sensory end organs in muscles, tendons, and joint capsules.

proptosis (prop-to'sis) [G. *proptōsis*, a falling forward]. A forward displacement of any organ, as in exophthalmos.

proptot'ic. Referring to proptosis.

propulsion (pro-pul'zhun) [G. *pro-pello*, pp. *-pulsus*, to drive forth]. The tendency to fall forward that causes the festination in paralysis agitans.

propyl (pro'pil). The radical of propyl alcohol or propane; $CH_3CH_2CH_2-$.

p. alcohol, ethylcarbinol; propanol; $CH_3CH_2-CH_2OH$; a solvent; more toxic than ethyl alcohol.

propylene (pro'pĭ-lēn). Methylethylene; $CH_2=CHCH_3$; a gaseous olefinic hydrocarbon.

propyliodone (pro-pil-i'o-dōn). A radiopaque material used for bronchography.

proren'nin. Prochymosin.

prorubricyte (pro-ru'brĭ-sīt) [pro- + rubricyte]. A basophilic normoblast.

prosecretin (pro-se-kre'tin). Unactivated secretin.

prosect (pro-sekt') [L. *pro-seco*, pp, *-sectus*, to cut]. To dissect a cadaver or any part for a demonstration of anatomy.

prosector (pro'sek'tor). One who prosects, or prepares material for a demonstration of anatomy.

prosencephalon (pros-en-sef'ă-lon) [G. *prosō*, forward, + *enkephalos*, brain] [NA]. Forebrain; the anterior primitive cerebral vesicle, which divides in further development into diencephalon and telencephalon.

prosodemic (pros'o-dem'ik) [G. *prosō*, forward, + *dēmos*, people]. Denoting a disease that is transmitted directly from person to person.

prosop-. See prosopo-.

prosopagnosia (pros'o-pag-no'sĭ-ah) [prosop- + G. *a-* priv. + *gnōsis*, recognition]. Difficulty in recognizing familiar faces.

prosopalgia (pros'o-pal'jĭ-ah) [prosop- + G. *algos*, pain]. Trigeminal *neuralgia*.

prosopal'gic. Relating to trigeminal neuralgia.

prosopectasia (pros'o-pek-ta'zĭ-ah) [prosop- + G. *ektasis*, extension]. Enlargement of the face, as in acromegaly.

prosoplasia (pros-o-pla'zĭ-ah) [G. *prosō*, forward, + *plasis* a molding]. Progressive transformation, such as the change of cells of the salivary ducts into secreting cells.

prosopo-, prosop- [G. *prosōpon*, face, countenance]. Combining forms denoting the face. See also facio-.

prosopodiplegia (pros'o-po-di-ple'jĭ-ah) [prosopo- + diplegia]. Paralysis affecting both sides of the face.

prosoponeuralgia (pros'o-po-nu-ral'jĭ-ah) Trigeminal *neuralgia*.

prosopoplegia (pros'o-po-ple'jĭ-ah) [prosopo- + G. *plēgē*, stroke]. Facial *palsy*.

prosopoplegic (pros'o-po-ple'jik). Relating to facial paralysis.

prosoposchisis (pros-o-pos'kĭ-sis) [prosopo- + G. *schisis*, fissure]. Congenital facial cleft from mouth to orbit.

prosopospasm (pros'o-po-spazm) [prosopo- + G. *spasmos*, spasm]. Facial *tic*.

prospermia (pro-sper'mĭ-ah) [pro- + G. *sperma*, seed]. Premature *ejaculation*.

prostacyclin (pros-tă-si'klin). A derivative of prostaglandin that is a natural inhibitor of platelet aggregation and a vasodilator.

prostaglandin (pros'tă-glan'din) [first found in genital fluids and accessory glands]. Any of a class of physiologically active substances present in many tissues; among effects are those of vasodepressors, stimulation of intestinal smooth muscle, uterine stimulation, and antagonism to hormones influencing lipid metabolism; p.'s are prostanoic acids with ortho side-chains of varying degrees of unsaturation and varying degrees of oxidation, and are abbreviated PGE, PGF, PGA, and PGB with numerical subscripts according to structure.

prostanoic acid (pros'tă-no-ik). 7-[2-(1-Octanyl)cyclopentyl]heptanoic acid; the 20-carbon acid that is the skeleton of the prostaglandins, with various hydroxyl and keto substitutions at positions 9, 11, and 15, and dehydrogenations (double bonds) in the long aliphatic chains.

prostat-. See prostato-.

prostata (pros'tah-tah) [Mod. L. from G. *prostatēs*, one standing before] [NA]. Prostate gland; prostate; a chestnut-shaped body that surrounds the beginning of the urethra in the male, consisting of two lateral lobes connected anteriorly by an isthmus and posteriorly by a middle lobe lying above and between the ejaculatory ducts; its secretion is a milky fluid discharged by excretory ducts into the prostatic urethra at the time of the emission of semen.

prostatalgia (pros-tă-tal'jĭ-ah) [prostat- + G. *algos*, pain]. Prostadodynia; pain in the prostate gland.

prostate (pros'tāt). Prostata.

prostatectomy (pros-tă-tek'to-mĭ) [prostat- + G. *ektomē*, excision]. Removal of part or all of the prostate.

prostatic (pros-tat'ik). Relating to the prostate gland.

pros'tatism. A clinical syndrome caused by enlargement of the prostate gland and characterized by significant obstruction to urinary flow and often a progressive increase in urgency and urinary frequency.

prostatit'ic. Relating to prostatitis.

prostatitis (pros-tă-ti'tis) [prostat- + G. *-itis*, inflammation]. Inflammation of the prostate.

prostato-, prostat-. Combining forms denoting the prostate gland.

prostatocystitis (pros'tă-to-sis-ti'tis) [prostato- + G. *kystis*, bladder, + *-itis*, inflammation]. Inflammation of the prostate and the bladder; cystitis by extension of inflammation from the prostatic urethra.

prostatocystotomy (pros'tă-to-sis-tot'o-mĭ) [prostato- + G. *kystis*, bladder, + *tomē*, incision]. Incision through the prostate and bladder wall with drainage through the perineum.

prostatodynia (pros'tă-to-din'ĭ-ah) [prostato- + G. *odynē*, pain]. Prostatalgia.

prostatolith (pros-tat'o-lith) [prostato- + G. *lithos*, stone]. A prostatic calculus; a concretion formed in the prostate gland.

prostatolithotomy (pros'tă-to-lĭ-thot'o-mĭ, pros-tat'o-) [prostato- + G. *lithos*, stone, + *tomē*, incision]. Incision of the prostate for removal of a calculus.

prostatomegaly (pros'tă-to-meg'ă-lĭ) [prostato- + G. *megas*, large]. Enlargement of the prostate gland.

prostatorrhea (pros'tă-to-re'ah) [prostato- + G. *rhoia*, a flow]. An abnormal discharge of prostatic fluid.

prostatotomy (pros'tă-tot'o-mĭ) [prostato- + G. *tomē*, incision]. An incision into the prostate.

prostatovesiculectomy (pros'tă-to-vĕ-sik'u-lek'to-mĭ). Surgical removal of the prostate gland and seminal vesicles.

prostatovesiculitis (pros'tă-to-vĕ-sik'u-li'tis). Inflammation of the prostate gland and seminal vesicles.

prosthesis, pl. **prostheses** (pros-the'sis, -sēz) [G. an addition]. A fabricated substitute for a diseased or missing part of the body, as a limb, tooth, eye, or heart valve.

    surgical p., an appliance prepared as an aid or as a part of a surgical proceeding, such as a heart valve or cranial plate.

prosthetic (pros-thet'ik). Relating to a prosthesis or to an artificial part.

prosthet'ics. The art and science of making and adjusting artificial parts of the human body.

pros'thetist. One skilled in constructing and fitting prostheses.

prosthion (pros'thĭ-on) [G. ntr. of *prosthios*, foremost]. Alveolar point; the most anterior point on the maxillary alveolar process in the midline.

prosthodontics (pros-tho-don'tiks) [L. *prosthodontia*, fr. G. *prosthesis*, *q.v.*, + *odous* (*odont-*), tooth]. Prosthetic dentistry; the science of and art of providing suitable substitutes for the coronal portions of teeth, or for lost or missing teeth and their associated parts.

prosthodon'tist. A dentist specializing in prosthodontics.

prostra'tion [L. *pro-sterno*, pp. *-stratus*, to strew before, overthrow]. Marked loss of strength, as in exhaustion.

prot-. See (1) proteo-; (2) proto-.

protactinium (pro-tak-tin'ĭ-um). A radioactive element, symbol Pa, atomic no. 91, atomic weight 231.

protamine (pro'tă-mēn, -min). Any of a class of proteins, highly basic because rich in arginine and

simpler in constitution than the albumins and globulins, etc., found in certain fish spermatozoa in combination with nucleic acid; neutralizes anticoagulant action of heparin.

protanopia (pro-tă-no'pĭ-ah) [G. *prōtos*, first, + *a*-priv. + *ōps* (*ōp*-) eye]. A form of dichromatism characterized by absence of the red-sensitive pigment in cones, decreased luminosity for long wavelengths of light, and confusion in recognition of red and bluish-green.

protean (pro'te-an) [*Prōteus*, G. myth. char.]. Changeable in form; having the power to change body form like the ameba.

protease (pro'te-as). Descriptive term for proteolytic enzymes, both endopeptidases and exopeptidases.

protein (pro'tēn) [G. *protein*, fr. *proteios*, primary]. Macromolecules consisting of long sequences of α-amino acids [$R-CH(NH_2-COOH)$] in peptide linkage (elimination of H_2O between the $2-NH_2$ and $1-COOH$ of successive residues); the amino acids involved are generally the 20 common "α-amino acids." P. is three-fourths of the dry weight of most cell matter and is involved in structures, hormones, enzymes, muscle contraction, immunological response, and other essential life functions.

    antiviral p. (AVP), a human or animal factor, induced by interferon in virus-infected cells, which mediates interferon inhibition of virus replication.

    Bence Jones p., p. with unusual thermosolubility found in the urine of patients with multiple myeloma and occasional persons with other diseases of the reticuloendothelial system; similar in size and physical properties to the light chains of the myeloma p. synthesized by a given patient.

    conjugated p., compound p., p. attached to some other molecule or molecules otherwise than as a salt: nucleoproteins, glycoproteins, phosphoproteins, lipoproteins, and chromoproteins or hemoglobins.

    C-reactive p., a β-globulin found in the serum of persons with certain inflammatory, degenerative, and neoplastic diseases; although not a specific antibody, it precipitates *in vitro* the C carbohydrate present in all types of pneumococci.

    nonspecific p., a p. substance that elicits a response not mediated by specific antigen-antibody reaction.

    plasma p.'s, dissolved p.'s of blood plasma (normally 6 to 8 g/100 ml); they hold fluid in blood vessels by osmosis and include antibodies and blood-clotting p.'s.

    receptor p., an intracellular p. (or p. fraction) that has a high specific affinity for binding a known stimulus to cellular activity, such as a steroid hormone or adenosine 3':5'-cyclic phosphate (cyclic AMP).

    simple p., p. that yields only α-amino acids or their derivatives by hydrolysis: albumins, globulins, glutelins, prolamines, albuminoids, histones, and protamines.

proteinaceous (pro'te-ĭ-na'shus) [protein + L. *-aceus*, resembling or characterized by]. Resembling a protein; possessing, to some degree, the physico-chemical properties characteristic of proteins.

proteinases (pro'te-in-ās-ez). Enzymes hydrolyzing native protein, or polypeptides, making internal cleavages.

protein hydrolysate. A sterile solution of amino acids and soft chain peptides prepared from a suitable protein by acid or enzymatic hydrolysis; used intravenously for the maintenance of positive nitrogen balance in severe illness, after surgery involving the alimentary tract, in the diets of infants allergic to milk, or as a supplement when high protein intake from ordinary foods cannot be accomplished.

proteinosis (pro'te-ĭ-no'sis) [protein + G. *-osis*, condition]. A state characterized by disordered protein formation and distribution, particularly as manifested by the deposition of abnormal proteins in tissues.

lipid p., a disturbance of lipid metabolism in which there are deposits of a protein-lipid complex on the labial mucosa and sublingual and faucial areas, and characteristic papillomatous eyelid lesions; autosomal recessive inheritance.

pulmonary alveolar p. a chronic progressive lung disease of adults, characterized by alveolar accumulation of granular proteinaceous material, with little inflammatory cellular exudate.

proteinuria (pro'te-ĭ-nu'ri-ah) [protein + G. *ouron*, urine]. **1.** Presence of abnormal concentrations of urinary protein. **2.** Albuminuria.

gestational p., the presence of p. during or under the influence of pregnancy in the absence of hypertension, edema, renal infection, or known intrinsic renovascular disease.

orthostatic p., postural p., orthostatic *albuminuria*.

proteo-, prot-, Combining forms indicating protein.

pro'teogly'cans. Glycoaminoglycans (mucopolysaccharides) bound to protein chains in covalent complexes occurring in the extracellular matrix of connective tissue.

proteolip'ids. A class of lipid-soluble proteins.

proteolysis (pro-te-ol'ĭsis) [proteo- + G. *lysis*, dissolution]. Protein hydrolysis; the decomposition of protein.

proteolyt'ic. Relating to or effecting proteolysis.

proteometabolic (pro'te-o-met'ă-bol'ik). Relating to protein metabolism.

proteometabolism (pro'te-o-mĕ-tab'o-lizm). Protein metabolism.

proteose (pro'te-ōs). A descriptive term for protein derivatives resulting from further cleavage of metaprotein material; a mixture of intermediate products of proteolysis between protein and peptone.

Proteus (pro'te-us) [*Prōteus*, G. myth. char.]. **1.** A former genus of the Sarcodina, now termed *Amoeba*. **2.** A genus of motile Gram-negative bacteria (family Enterobacteriaceae) occurring primarily in fecal matter and in putrefying materials. The type species is *P. vulgaris*.

P. morgan'ii, Morgan's bacillus; a species found in the intestinal canal and in normal and diarrheal stools.

P. vulgar'is, the type species of the genus *P.,* found in putrefying materials and in abscesses; certain strains are agglutinated by typhus serum and are therefore significant in the diagnosis of typhus.

prothrombin (pro-throm'bin). Factor II; a glycoprotein formed and stored in the parenchymal cells of the liver, and present in blood in a concentration of approximately 20 mg per 100 ml; in the presence of thromboplastin and calcium ion, p. is converted to thrombin, which in turn converts fibrinogen to fibrin, this process resulting in coagulation of the blood.

prothrombinase (pro-throm'bĭ-nās). Factor X; Stuart or Stuart-Power f.; an enzyme hydrolyzing prothrombin to thrombin.

Protista (pro-tis'tah) [G. ntr. pl. of *protistos* (suprl. of *protos,* first), the first of all]. A proposed third kingdom of living things to include the lowest orders of the animal and vegetable kingdoms, the Protozoa and the Protophyta.

protium (pro'tĭ-um). Hydrogen-1.

proto- [G. *prōtos,* first]. Prefix denoting the first in a series or the highest in rank.

protocol (pro'to-kol). A precise and detailed plan for the study of a biomedical problem or for a regimen of therapy.

protodiastolic (pro'to-di-ă-stol'ik). Early diastolic; relating to the beginning of cardiac diastole.

protoduodenum (pro'to-du-o-de'num, -du-od'ē-num). The first part of the duodenum extending from the gastroduodenal pylorus as far as the papilla duodeni major; it has no plicae circulares and is the seat of the duodenal glands.

pro'ton [G. ntr. of *prōtos,* first]. The positively charged unit of the nuclear mass, forming part (in hydrogen-1 the whole) of the nucleus of the atom around which the negative electrons revolve.

protopath'ic [proto- + G. *pathos,* suffering]. Denoting a set or system of peripheral sensory nerve fibers furnishing a low order of sensibility, allowing a generalized appreciation of pain and temperature without definite localization.

protoplasm (pro'to-plazm) [proto- + G. *plasma,* thing formed]. Living matter, the substance of which animal and vegetable cells are formed.

protoplasmic (pro-to-plaz'mik). Relating to protoplasm.

pro'toplast [proto- + G. *plastos,* formed]. **1.** Archaic term meaning the first individual of a type or race. **2.** A bacterial cell from which the rigid cell wall has been completely removed, causing the bacterium to lose its characteristic shape and become round.

protoporphyria (pro'to-por-fir'ĭ-ah). Enhanced fecal excretion of protoporphyrin.

erythropoietic p., a benign disorder of porphyrin metabolism characterized by enhanced fecal excretion of protoporphyrin and elevated quantities of protoporphyrin in red blood cells, plasma, and feces; acute solar urticaria or more chronic solar eczema develops quickly upon exposure to sunlight; autosomal dominant inheritance with variable penetrance.

protoporphyrin (pro-to-por'fĭ-rin). The substituted porphin that, with iron, forms the heme of hemoglobin and the prosthetic groups of myoglobin, catalase, cytochromes, etc.

protospasm (pro'to-spazm) [proto- + G. *spasmos,* spasm]. A spasm beginning in one limb or one muscle and gradually becoming more general.

prototroph (pro'to-trof, -tröf) [proto- + G. *trophē,* nourishment]. A bacterial strain that has the same nutritional requirements as the wild-type strain from which it was derived.

prototrophic (pro'to-trof'ik). **1.** Pertaining to a prototroph. **2.** Denoting the ability to undertake anabolism or to obtain nourishment from a single source, as with nitrifying bacteria or photosynthesizing plants.

pro'totype [proto- + G. *typos,* type]. The primitive form; the first form to which subsequent individuals of the class or species conform.

protovertebra (pro'to-ver'te-brah). Provertebra. **1.** In the older literature, a mesodermic somite. **2.** The sclerotomal concentration that is the primordium of the centrum of a vertebra.

Protozoa (pro-to-zo'ah) [proto- + G. *zōon,* animal]. A phylum (sometimes regarded as a subkingdom) of the animal kingdom, including all of the so-called unicellular forms, consisting of a single functional cell unit or of an aggregation of nondifferentiated cells, loosely held together and not forming tissues.

protozo'al. Protozoan (2).

protozo'an. 1. Protozoon; a member of the Protozoa. **2.** Protozoal; relating to protozoa.

protozoiasis (pro'to-zo-i'ă-sis). Infection with protozoans.

protozoicide (pro-to-zo'ĭ-sīd) [protozoa + L. *caedo,* to kill]. An agent used to kill protozoa.

protozoology (pro'to-zo-ol'o-jĭ) [protozoa + G. *logos,* study]. The science concerned with all aspects of protozoa.

protozoon, pl. **protozoa** (pro-to-zo'on, -zo'ah). Protozoan (1).

protozoophage (pro-to-zo'o-fāj) [protozoa + G. *phagein,* to eat]. A phagocyte that ingests protozoa.

protraction (pro-trak'shun) [see protractor]. Extension of teeth or other maxillary or mandibular structures into a position anterior to normal.

protrac'tor [L. *pro-traho,* pp. *-tractus,* to draw forth]. A muscle drawing a part forward, as antagonistic to a retractor.

protrusion (pro-tru'zhun) [L. *protrusio*]. **1.** The state of being thrust forward or projected. **2.** In dentistry, a position of the mandible forward from centric relation.

protuberance (pro-tu'ber-ans) [Mod. L. *protuberantia*]. A prominence, eminence, or projection.

protuberantia (pro'tu-ber-an'shĭ-ah) [Mod. L. fr. *protubero,* to swell out] [NA]. Protuberance.

proventriculus (pro-ven-trik'u-lus) [L. *pro,* before, + *ventriculus,* dim. of *venter(ventr-)* belly]. **1.** In birds, the thin-walled glandular stomach preceding the muscular gizzard. **2.** In insects, the portion of the stomodeum that lies in front of the ventriculus or stomach; it is modified into a small proventricular valve in many diptera (flies).

prover'tebra. Protovertebra.

Providencia (prov'ĭ-den'sĭ-ah). A genus of motile, peritrichous, nonsporeforming, aerobic or facultatively anaerobic bacteria (family Enterobacteriaceae) containing Gram-negative rods. These organisms do not hydrolyze urea or produce hydrogen sulfide; they produce indole and grow on Simmons' citrate medium. They do not decarboxylate lysine, argine, or ornithine. These organisms occur in specimens from extraintestinal sources, particularly urinary tract infections; they have also been isolated from small outbreaks and sporadic cases of diarrheal disease. The type species is *P. alcalifaciens.*

P. alcalifa'ciens, a species found in extraintestinal sources, particularly in urinary tract infections; it has also been isolated from small outbreaks and sporadic cases of diarrheal disease; it is the type species of the genus *P.*

P. stuar'tii, a species isolated from urinary tract infections, and from small outbreaks and sporadic cases of diarrheal disease.

provirus (pro-vi'rus). The precursor of an animal virus (*q.v.*); theoretically analogous to the prophage in bacteria, the provirus being integrated in the nucleus of infected cells.

provi'tamin. A substance that may be converted into a vitamin.

p. A, a generic name for all carotenoids exhibiting qualitatively the biological activity of β-carotene, *i.e.,* vitamin A precursors (α-, β-, and γ-carotene and cryptoxanthin); they are contained in fish liver oils, spinach, carrots, egg yolk, milk products, and other green leaf or yellow vegetables and fruits.

p. D$_2$, any substance that can give rise to ergocalciferol (vitamin D$_2$); in nature, the chief p. is ergosterol.

proximad (prok'sĭ-mad) [L. *proximus,* nearest, next, + *ad,* to]. In a direction toward a proximal part, or toward the center.

prox'imal [Mod. L. *proximalis,* fr. L. *proximus,* nearest, next]. **1.** Nearest the trunk or the point of origin. **2.** Mesial. **3.** In dental anatomy, denoting the surface of a tooth in relation with its neighbor, nearer to or farther from the anteroposterior median plane.

prox'imate. Immediate; next; proximal.

proximo-, prox-, proxi-. Combining forms denoting proximal.

proximoataxia (prok'sĭ-mo-ă-tak'sĭ-ah) [proximo- + ataxia]. Lack of muscular coordination in the proximal portions of the extremities.

prozone (pro'zōn). In the case of agglutination and of precipitation, the phenomenon in which visible reaction does not occur in mixtures of specific antigen and antibody because of either antibody or antigen excess.

PRPP 5'-Phospho-α-D-ribosyl 1-pyrophosphate.

pruriginous (pru-rij'ĭ-nus) [L. *pruriginosus,* having the itch]. Relating to prurigo.

prurigo (pru-ri'go) [L. itch, fr. *prurio,* to itch]. A chronic disease of the skin marked by a persistent eruption of papules that itch intensely.

p. mi'tis, a mild form of a chronic dermatitis characterized by recurring, intensely itching papules and nodules.

p. nodula'ris, an eruption of hard nodules in the skin, accompanied by intense itching.

p. sim'plex, a mild form having a pronounced tendency to relapse.

prurit'ic. Relating to pruritus.

pruritus (pru-ri'tus) [L. an itching, fr. *prurio,* to itch]. **1.** Itching. **2.** Itch (3).

p. a'ni, itching of varying intensity at the anus.

bath p., bath itch; itching produced by inadequate rinsing off of soap or by overdrying of skin from excessive bathing.

essential p., itching that occurs independently of skin lesions.

p. seni'lis, senile p., itching associated with degenerative changes in the skin of the aged.

symptomatic p., itching occurring as a symptom of some systemic illness.

p. vul'vae, itching of the external female genitalia.

Prussian blue. Berlin blue.

prus'sic acid. Hydrocyanic acid.

psammo- [G. *psammos,* sand]. Combining form denoting sand.

psammocarcinoma (sam'o-kar-sĭ-no'mah). A carcinoma that contains calcified foci resembling psammoma bodies.

psammoma (să-mo'mah) [psammo- + G. *-oma,* tumor]. Sand tumor; a firm cellular neoplasm derived from fibrous tissue of the meninges, choroid plexus, and certain other structures associated with the brain, characterized by the formation of multiple, discrete, concentrically laminated, calcareous bodies (psammoma bodies).

psammous (sam'us) [G. *psammos,* sand]. Sandy.

pseud-. See pseudo-.

pseudagraphia (su-dă-graf'ĭ-ah) [pseud- + G. *a*-priv. + *graphō,* to write]. Pseudoagraphia; partial agraphia in which one can do no original writing, but can copy correctly.

pseudankylosis (su-dang-kĭ-lo'sis). Fibrous *ankylosis.*

pseudarthrosis (su-dar-thro'sis) [pseud- + G. *arthrōsis,* a jointing]. Pseudoarthrosis; false joint; a new, false joint arising at the site of an ununited fracture.

pseudesthesia (su-des-the'zĭ-ah) [pseud- + G. *aisthēsis,* sensation]. Pseudoesthesia. **1.** Paraphia. **2.** A subjective sensation not arising from an external stimulus. **3.** Phantom *limb.*

pseudo-, pseud- [G. *pseudēs,* false]. Prefix denoting a resemblance, often deceptive.

pseudoacanthosis nigricans (su'do-ă-kan-tho'sis ni'grĭ-kanz). Acanthosis nigricans secondary to maceration of the skin from excessive sweating, or occurring in obese and dark-complexioned adults, or in association with endocrine disorders.

pseudoagraphia (su'do-ă-graf'ĭ-ah). Pseudagraphia.

pseudo-ainhum (su'do-in'yŭm). Nonspontaneous amputation of a digit, caused by a variety of disorders.

pseudoallele (su'do-ă-lēl'). A gene exhibiting pseudoallelism.

pseudoallelic (su'do-ă-le'lik). Relating to pseudoallelism.

pseudoallelism (su'do-al'ē-lizm). State of two or more genes that appear to occupy the same locus under certain conditions, but can be shown to occupy closely linked loci under other conditions.

pseudoanemia (su'do-ă-ne'mĭ-ah). False anemia; pallor of the skin and mucous membranes without the blood signs of anemia.

pseudoaneurysm (su'do-an'u-rizm). False aneurysm (2); a dilation of an artery with actual disruption of one or more layers of its walls, rather than with expansion of all layers of the wall.

pseudoarthrosis. Pseudarthrosis.

pseudobulbar (su-do-bul'bar). Denoting a supranuclear paralysis of the bulbar nerves.

pseudocartilage (su-do-kar'tĭ-lij). Chondroid *tissue* (1).

pseudocartilaginous (su-do-kar-tĭ-laj'ĭ-nus). Composed of a substance resembling cartilage in texture.

pseudocast (su'do-kast). False *cast.*

pseudochancre (su-do-shang'ker). A nonspecific indurated sore, usually located on the penis, resembling a chancre.

pseudochorea (su-do-ko-re'ah). A spasmodic affection or extensive tic resembling chorea.

pseudochromesthesia (su'do-kro-mes-the'zĭ-ah) [pseudo- + G. *chrōma,* color, + *aisthēsis,* sensation]. **1.** An anomaly in which each vowel in the printed word is seen as colored. **2.** Color *hearing.*

pseudochromhidrosis (su'do-kro-mĭ-dro'sis) [pseudo- + G. *chrōma,* color, + *hidrōs,* sweat]. Presence of pigment on the skin in association with sweating, but due to the local action of pigment-forming bacteria and not to the excretion of colored sweat.

pseudocirrhosis (su-do-sĭ-ro'sis). Cardiac *cirrhosis.*

pseudocoarctation (su'do-ko-ark-ta'shun). Distortion, often with slight narrowing, of the aortic arch at the level of insertion of the ligamentum arteriosum.

pseudocolloid (su-do-kol'oyd). A colloid-like or mucoid substance found in ovarian cysts, in the lips (Fordyce's *spots*), and elsewhere.

pseudocoloboma (su'do-kol-o-bo'mah). An apparent coloboma, due to heterochromia of the iris.

pseudocoxalgia (su'do-kok-sal'ji-ah) [pseudo- + L. *coxa,* hip, + G. *algos,* pain]. Legg-Calvé-Perthes *disease.*

pseudocroup (su-do-krūp'). *Laryngismus* stridulus.

pseudocryptorchism (su'do-krip'tor-kizm) [pseudo- + G. *kryptos,* hidden, + *orchis,* testis]. A condition in which the testes descend to the scrotum but move up and down, rising high in the inguinal canal at one time and descending to the scrotum at another.

pseudocyesis (su-do-si-e'sis) [pseudo- + G. *kyēsis,* pregnancy]. False pregnancy; pseudopregnancy (1); a condition in which some of the signs and symptoms suggest pregnancy although the woman is not pregnant.

pseudocylindroid (su'do-sil'in-droyd). A shred of mucus or other substance in the urine resembling a renal cast.

pseudocyst (su'do-sist) [pseudo- + G. *kystis,* bladder]. **1.** Adventitious or false cyst; an accumulation of fluid in a cystlike locule, but without an epithelial or other membranous lining. **2.** A cyst whose wall is formed by a host cell and not by a parasite. **3.** A mass of *Toxoplasma* parasites found within a host cell, now considered a true cyst enclosed in its own membrane within the host cell.

pseudodementia (su-do-de-men'shi-ah). A condition of exaggerated indifference to one's surroundings without actual mental impairment.

pseudodiphtheria (su'do-dif-thēr'i-ah). Diphtheroid (1).

pseudoedema (su'do-ĕ-de'ma) [pseudo- + G. *oidēma,* a swelling (edema)]. A puffiness of the skin not due to a fluid accumulation.

pseudofracture (su-do-frak'chur). A condition in which an x-ray shows formation of new bone with thickening of periosteum at site of an injury to bone.

pseudoganglion (su-do-gang'gli-on). A localized thickening of a nerve trunk having the appearance of a ganglion.

pseudogeusesthesia (su'do-gu-ses-the'zi-ah) [pseudo- + G. *geusis,* taste, + *aisthēsis,* sensation]. Color *taste.*

pseudogeusia (su-do-gu'si-ah) [pseudo- + G. *geusis,* taste]. A taste sensation not produced by an external stimulus.

pseudogout (su'do-gowt). Articular *chondrocalcinosis.*

pseudohematuria (su'do-hem'ă-tu'ri-ah, -he'mă-tu'ri-ah). False hematuria; a red pigmentation of urine caused by certain foods or drugs.

pseudohemophilia (su'do-he'mo-fil'i-ah). False hemophilia; a noninherited hemophilia-like syndrome due to some specific disorder or disorders.

hereditary p., von Willebrand's *disease.*

pseudohermaphrodite (su'do-her-maf'ro-dīt). An individual exhibiting pseudohermaphroditism.

pseudohermaphroditism (su'do-her-maf'ro-di-tizm). False hermaphroditism; a state, somewhat resembling true hermaphroditism in which the individual is distinctly of one sex, possessing either testes (**male p.**) or ovaries (**female p.**), although having somatic characteristics of both sexes.

pseudohernia (su-do-her'ni-ah). Inflammation of the scrotal tissues or of an inguinal gland, simulating a strangulated hernia.

pseudohypertrophic (su'do-hi-per-trof'ik). Relating to or marked by pseudohypertrophy.

pseudohypertrophy (su'do-hi-per'tro-fi). False hypertrophy; increase in size of an organ or a part, due not to increase in size or number of the specific functional elements but to that of some other tissue.

pseudohyponatremia (su'do-hi-po-nă-tre'mi-ah). A low serum sodium concentration due to volume displacement by massive hyperlipidemia or hyperproteinemia, or hyperglycemia.

pseudohypoparathyroidism (su'do-hi'po-păr-ă-thi'-royd-izm). Seabright bantam syndrome; a disorder resembling hypoparathyroidism, but with signs and symptoms unresponsive to treatment with parathyroid hormone; characterized by short stature, round face, achondroplasia, calcification of basal ganglia, true ectopic bone in fascial planes and skin, mental deficiency, hypocalcemia, hyperphosphatemia, and parathyroid tissue that is hyperplastic; most commonly inherited as a sex- linked dominant trait.

pseudoicterus (su-do-ik'ter-us). Pseudojaundice; discoloration of the skin not due to bile pigments, as in Addison's disease.

pseudoisochromatic (su'do-i-so-kro-mat'ik). Apparently of the same color; denoting certain charts containing colored spots mixed with figures printed in confusion colors; used in testing for color blindness.

pseudojaundice (su-do-jawn'dis). Pseudoicterus.

pseudologia (su-do-lo'ji-ah) [pseudo- + G. *logos,* word]. Pathological lying in speech or writing.

p. phantas'tica, an elaborate and often fantastic account of a patient's exploits, which are completely false but which the patient himself appears to believe.

pseudoluxation (su'do-luk-sa'shun). Incomplete dislocation.

pseudomania (su-do-ma'ni-ah). **1.** Feigned insanity. **2.** A mental disorder in which the patient alleges to have committed a crime, but of which he is innocent. **3.** Generally, the morbid impulse to falsify or lie.

pseudomembrane (su-do-mem'brān). False *membrane.*

pseudomembranous (su-do-mem'brā-nus). Relating to or marked by the presence of a false membrane.

pseudomonad (su-do-mo'nad). Any member of the genus *Pseudomonas.*

Pseudomonas (su-do-mo'nas) [pseudo- + G. *monas,* unit, monad]. A genus of motile, Gram-negative, strictly aerobic bacteria (family Pseudomonadaceae) that occur commonly in soil and in fresh water and marine environments; some species are plant pathogens, others are occasionally pathogenic to animals. The type species is *P. aeruginosa,* the causative agent of blue pus.

pseudomyxoma (su'do-mik-so'mah). A gelatinous mass resembling a myxoma but composed of epithelial mucus.

p. peritone'i, accumulation of large quantities of mucoid or mucinous material in the peritoneal cavity, either as a result of rupture of a mucocele of the appendix, or rupture of benign or malignant cystic neoplasms of the ovary.

pseudoneoplasm (su-do-ne'o-plazm). 1. Pseudotumor. 2. A circumscribed fibrous exudate of inflammatory origin, temporary in character.

pseudoneuritis (su'do-nu-ri'tis). Congenital reddish appearance of the optic disk simulating optic neuritis.

pseudopapilledema (su'do-pap-il-ĕ-de'mah). Anomalous elevation of the optic disk; seen in high hyperopia and optic nerve drusen.

pseudoparalysis (su'do-pă-ral'ĭ-sis). Pseudoparesis (1); apparent paralysis due to voluntary inhibition of motion because of pain, incoordination, or other cause, but without actual paralysis.

arthritic general p., Klippel's disease; a disease, occurring in arthritic subjects, having symptoms resembling those of general paresis, the lesions of which consist of diffuse changes of a degenerative and noninflammatory character due to intracranial atheroma.

pseudoparaplegia (su'do-păr-ă-ple'jĭ-ah). Apparent paralysis in the lower extremities, in which the tendon and skin reflexes and the electrical reactions are normal.

pseudoparesis (su'do-pă-re'sis). 1. Pseudoparalysis. 2. A condition marked by the pupillary changes, tremors, and speech disturbances suggestive of early paresis, in which, however, the serologic tests are negative.

pseudopelade (su'do-pĕ-lahd) [pseudo- + Fr. *pelade,* disease that causes sporadic falling of hair]. A scarring type of alopecia, usually occurring in small areas preceded by folliculitis.

pseudopod (su'do-pod). Pseudopodium.

pseudopodium, pl. **pseudopodia** (su-do-po'dĭ-um, -po'dĭ-ah) [pseudo- + G. *pous,* foot]. Pseudopod; a temporary protoplasmic process, put forth by an ameboid organism for locomotion or for prehension of food.

pseudopolyp (su-do-pol'ip). A projecting mass of granulation tissue, large numbers of which may develop in ulcerative colitis.

pseudopregnancy (su-do-preg'nan-sĭ). 1. Pseudocyesis. 2. A condition in which symptoms resembling those of pregnancy are present, but which is not pregnancy, occurring after sterile copulation in mammalian species in which copulation induces ovulation.

pseudo-pseudohypoparathyroidism (su'do-su-do-hi'po-păr-ă-thi'royd-ism). A heritable disorder that closely simulates pseudohypoparathyroidism; manifestations of hypoparathyroidism are mild or absent and hypocalcemia is not present, or the consequences thereof, such as tetanic convulsions.

pseudopsia (su-dop'sĭ-ah) [pseudo- + G. *opsis,* vision]. Visual hallucinations, illusions, or false perceptions.

pseudopterygium (su'do-tĕ-rij'ĭ-um). A pterygium of irregular shape following diphtheria, a burn, or other injury of the conjunctiva; may occur at any part of the corneal margin.

pseudoptosis (su-do-to'sis, su-dop'to-sis) [pseudo- + G. *ptōsis,* a falling]. False ptosis; a condition resembling ptosis and due to blepharophimosis, blepharochalasis, or some other affection.

pseudoreaction (su'do-re-ak'shun). A false reaction; one not due to specific causes in a given test.

pseudorickets (su'do-rik'ets). Renal *rickets.*

pseudoscarlatina (su'do-skar-lă-te'nah). Erythema with fever, due to causes other than *Streptococcus pyogenes.*

pseudosclerosis (su'do-skle-ro'sis) [pseudo- + G. *sklērosis,* hardening]. 1. Inflammatory induration or fatty or other infiltration simulating fibrous thickening. 2. Strümpell-Westphal or Westphal-Strümpell disease; the cerebral changes of hepatolenticular degeneration.

pseudosmia (su-doz'mĭ-ah) [pseudo- + G. *osmē,* smell]. Subjective sensation of an odor that is not present.

pseudotruncus arteriosus (su'do-trung'kus ar-tēr'ĭ-o'sus). A congenital cardiovascular deformity in which there is atresia of the pulmonic valve and no main pulmonary artery; the lungs are supplied with blood either through a patent ductus or via bronchial arteries arising from the aorta.

pseudotumor (su'do-tu-mor). Pseudoneoplasm. 1. An enlargement of nonneoplastic character which clinically resembles a true neoplasm. 2. A circumscribed fibrous exudate of inflammatory origin and temporary character. 3. A condition, commonly associated with obesity in young females, of cerebral edema with narrowed small ventricles but with increased intracranial pressure and frequently papilledema.

pseudoxanthoma elasticum (su'do-zan-tho'mah e-las'tĭ-kum). Elastoma; slightly elevated yellowish plaques on the neck, axillae, abdomen, and thighs, associated with angioid streaks of the retina and similar elastic tissue degeneration in other organs.

psi (si). The 23rd letter (Ψ) of the Greek alphabet.

psilocin (si'lo-sin). A hallucinogenic agent related to psilocybin.

psilocybin (si-lo-si'bin, -sib'in). The N',N'-dimethyl derivative of 4-hydroxytryptamine; obtained from the fruiting bodies of the Mexican hallucinogenic fungus *Psilocybe mexicana* and other species of *Psilocybe* and *Stropharia;* a hallucinogenic agent.

P-sinistrocardia′le. An electrocardiographic syndrome characteristic of overloading of the left atrium; often erroneously called P-mitrale, as the syndrome can result from any overloading of the left atrium from any cause.

psittacine (sit′ă-sēn). Referring to birds of the parrot family.

psittacosis (sit-ă-ko′sis) [G. *psittakos*, a parrot, + *-osis*, condition]. Parrot fever; an infectious disease of birds, especially parrots, caused by *Chlamydia psittaci* and sometimes transmitted to man, in whom the symptoms are headache, nausea, epistaxis, constipation, and fever preceded by a chill, and usually with added symptoms of bronchopneumonia.

psorelcosis (so-rel-ko′sis) [G. *psōra*, itch, + *helkōsis*, ulceration]. Ulceration resulting from scabies.

psoriasic (so-ri′ă-sik). Psoriatic.

psoriasiform (so-ri′ă-sĭ-form). Resembling psoriasis.

psoriasis (so-ri′ă-sis) [G. *psōriasis*, fr. *psōra*, the itch]. A condition characterized by the eruption of circumscribed, discrete and confluent, reddish, silvery-scaled maculopapules preeminently on the elbows, knees, scalp, and trunk.

psoriatic (so-rĭ-at′ik). Psoriasic; relating to psoriasis.

PSP Phenolsulfonphthalein.

psych-, psyche-. See psycho-.

psychalgia (si-kal′jĭ-ah) [psych- + G. *algos*, pain]. **1.** Phrenalgia (1); distress attending a mental effort, noted especially in melancholia. **2.** Pain believed to be entirely or primarily of psychological causation.

psychataxia (si-kă-tak′sĭ-ah) [psych- + G. *ataxia*, confusion]. Mental confusion; inability to fix the attention or to make any continued mental effort.

psyche (si′ke) [G. mind, soul]. Obsolete term for the subjective aspects of the mind and of the individual.

psychedelic (si-kĕ-del′ik) [psyche- + G. *dēloun*, to manifest]. **1.** Pertaining to a category of drugs with mainly CNS action, and with effects said to be the expansion or heightening of consciousness. **2.** A drug, visual display, music, or other sensory stimulus having such action.

psychiatric (si-kĭ-at′rik). Relating to psychiatry.

psychiatrist (si-ki′ă-trist). A specialist in psychiatry.

psychiatry (si-ki′ă-rī) [psych- + G. *iatreia*, medical treatment]. **1.** The medical specialty concerned with mental disorders and diseases.

  community p., p. focusing on the detection, prevention, early treatment, and rehabilitation of emotional disorders and social deviance as they develop in the community; particular emphasis is placed on the social-interpersonal-environmental factors that contribute to mental illness.

  contractual p., psychiatric intervention voluntarily assumed by the patient who retains control over his participation with the psychiatrist.

  dynamic p., psychoanalytic p.

  forensic p., the application of p. in courts of law, as in determinations for commitment, fitness to stand trial, responsibility for crime, etc.

  psychoanalytic p., dynamic p.; psychiatric theory and practice emphasizing psychoanalytic principles. See also psychoanalysis.

  social p., an approach to psychiatric theory and practice emphasizing the cultural and sociological aspects of mental disorders and their treatment.

psychic (si′kik) [G. *psychikos*]. **1.** Relating to the phenomena of consciousness, mind, or soul; mental. **2.** A person who is supposed to be endowed with the power of communicating with spirits; a spiritualistic medium.

psycho-, psych-, psyche- [G. *psyche̅*, soul, mind]. Combining forms denoting the mind.

psychoactive (si′ko-ak′tiv). Possessing the ability to alter mood, anxiety, behavior, cognitive processes, or mental tension; usually applied to pharmacologic agents.

psychoanalysis (si′ko-ă-nal′ĭ-sis) [psycho- + analysis, *q.v.*]. **1.** A method of psychotherapy, originated by Freud, designed to bring preconscious and unconscious material to consciousness primarily through analysis of transference and resistance. **2.** A method of investigating the human mind and psychological functioning, especially through free association and dream analysis in the psychoanalytic situation. **3.** An integrated body of observations and theories on personality development, motivation, and behavior. **4.** An institutionalized school of psychotherapy, as in jungian or freudian p.

  freudian p., the theory and practice of p. and psychotherapy as developed by Freud, based on: 1) theory of personality, which postulates that psychic life is made up of instinctual forces (id, ego, and superego) each of which must constantly accommodate to the other; 2) the free association technique of verbalizing which reveals the areas of conflict within a patient's personality; and 3) that the vehicle for gaining this insight and readjusting one's personality is the learning a patient does as he first develops a stormy emotional bond with the analyst (transference relationship) and next successfully learns to break the bond.

  jungian p., analytical psychology; the theory of psychopathology and practice of psychotherapy, according to Jung, emphasizing man's symbolic nature and differing from freudian p. especially in placing less significance upon instinctual (sexual) urges.

psychoanalyst (si-ko-an′ă-list). A psychotherapist, usually a psychiatrist, trained in psychoanalysis and employing its methods in the treatment of emotional disorders.

psychoanalytic (si′ko-an-ă-lit′ik). Pertaining to psychoanalysis.

psychobiology (si′ko-bi-ol′o-jĭ). The study of the biology of the mind.

psychochemistry (si-ko-kem′is-trĭ). The alteration of affect or emotion by chemical means.

psychodiagnosis (si'ko-di-ag-no'sis). **1.** Any method used to discover the factors which underlie behavior, especially malajusted or abnormal behavior. **2.** A subspecialty within clinical psychology that emphasizes the use of psychological tests and techniques for assessing psychopathology.

psychodrama (si'ko-drah'mah). A method of psychotherapy in which patients act out their personal problems by taking roles in spontaneous dramatic performances.

psychodynamics (si'ko-di-nam'iks) [psycho- + G. *dynamis,* force]. The systematized study and theory of human behavior, emphasizing unconscious motivation and the functional significance of emotion.

psychogenesis (si-ko-jen'ĕ-sis) [psycho- + G. *genesis,* origin]. The origin and development of the psychic processes including mental, behavioral, personality, and related psychological processes.

psychogenic (si'ko-jen'ik). **1.** Of mental origin or causation. **2.** Relating to psychogenesis.

psychogram (si'ko-gram) [psycho- + G. *gramma,* a writing]. **1.** Psychograph; a profile or graph indicating the personality traits of an individual. **2.** A subjective visualization of a mental concept.

psychograph (si'ko-graf). Psychogram (1).

psychographic (si-ko-graf'ik). Relating to a psychogram.

psychokinesis (si'ko-kĭ-ne'sis) [psycho- + G. *kinēsis,* movement]. **1.** Impulsive behavior. **2.** The influence of mind upon matter.

psycholepsy (si'ko-lep-sĭ) [psycho- + G. *lepsis,* seizure]. Sudden mood changes accompanied by feelings of hopelessness and inertia.

psycholinguistics (si'ko-lin-gwĭ'stiks) [psycho- + L. *lingua,* tongue]. The study of mental and intellectual factors that affect communication and understanding of language.

psychologic, psychological (si-ko-loj'ik, -loj'ĭ-kal). Relating to psychology or to the mind and its processes.

psychologist (si-kol'o-jist). A specialist in psychology licensed to practice professional psychology, or certified to teach psychology as a scholarly discipline, or whose scientific specialty is a subfield of psychology.

psychology (si-kol'o-jĭ) [psycho- + G. *logos,* study]. The profession (*e.g.*, clinical p.), scholarly discipline (academic p.), and science (research p.) concerned with the behavior of man and animals, and related mental and physiological processes.

   analytical p., jungian *psychoanalysis.*

   behavioral p., behaviorism.

   clinical p., a branch of p. which specializes in both discovering new knowledge and in applying the art and science of p. to persons with emotional or behavioral disorders; subspecialties include clinical child p., pediatric p., and neuropsychology.

   community p., the application of p. to community programs for prevention of mental disorders and promotion of mental health.

   criminal p., the study of the mind and its workings in relation to crime.

   developmental p., the study of the psychological changes in an organism which occur with aging.

   dynamic p., an approach that concerns itself with the causes of behavior.

   environmental p., the study and application by behavioral scientists and architects of how changes in physical space and related physical stimuli impact upon the behavior of individuals.

   experimental p., (1) a subdiscipline within the science of p. that is concerned with the study of conditioning, learning, perception, motivation, emotion, language, and thinking; **(2)** also used in relation to subject-matter areas in which experimental, in contrast to correlational or socio-experiential, methods are emphasized.

   forensic p., the application of p. to legal matters in a court of law.

   genetic p., a science dealing with the evolution of behavior and the relation to each other of the different types of mental activity.

   gestalt p., see gestaltism.

   individual p., a theory of human behavior emphasizing man's social nature, his strivings for mastery, and his drive to overcome, by compensation, feelings of inferiority.

psychometrics (si-ko-mĕ'triks). Psychometry.

psychometry (si-kom'ĕ-trĭ) [psycho- + G. *metron,* measure]. Psychometrics; the discipline pertaining to psychological and mental testing, and to any quantitative analysis of an individual's psychological traits or attitudes or mental processes.

psychomotor (si-ko-mo'tor). **1.** Relating to the mental origin of muscular movement, to the production of voluntary movements. **2.** Relating to the combination of psychic and motor events, including disturbances.

psychoneurosis (si'ko-nu-ro'sis) [psycho- + G. *neuron,* nerve, + *-osis,* condition]. **1.** A mental or behavioral disorder of mild or moderate severity. **2.** Formerly a classification of neurosis including hysteria, psychasthenia, and neurasthenia.

psychoneurotic (si'ko-nu-rot'ik). Pertaining to psychoneurosis.

psychopath (si'ko-path). An obsolete and inexact term for an individual who engages in antisocial behavior, shows no empathy or bonding with others, and manipulates others for his own ends. See sociopath.

psychopathic (si-ko-path'ik). Relating to psychopathy.

psychopathology (si'ko-pă-thol'o-jĭ) [psycho- + G. *pathos,* disease, + *logos,* study]. **1.** The science concerned with the pathology of the psyche or mind. **2.** The science of mental and behavioral disorders, including psychiatry and abnormal psychology.

psychopathy (si-kop'ă-thĭ) [psycho- + G. *pathos,* disease]. An obsolete and inexact term referring to a pattern of antisocial or manipulative behavior. See sociopathy.

psychopharmaceuticals (si'ko-far-mă-su'tĭ-kals). Drugs used in the treatment of emotional disorders.

psychopharmacology (si'ko-far-mă-kol'o-jĭ) [psycho- + G. *pharmakon,* drug, + *logos,* study]. **1.** The use of drugs to influence affective and emotional states. **2.** The science of drug-behavior relationships.

psychophysical (si-ko-fiz'ĭ-kal). **1.** Relating to the mental perception of physical stimuli. **2.** Psychosomatic.

psychophysics (si-ko-fiz'iks). The science of the relation between the physical attributes of a stimulus and the measured, quantitative attributes of the mental perception of the same stimulus.

psychophysiologic (si'ko-fiz-ĭ-o-loj'ik). **1.** Pertaining to psychophysiology. **2.** Denoting a so-called psychosomatic illness or a somatic disorder with significant emotional or psychological etiology.

psychophysiology (si-ko-fiz-ĭ-ol'o-jĭ). The science of the relation between psychological and physiological processes.

psychosensory (si-ko-sen'so-rĭ). **1.** Denoting the mental perception and interpretation of sensory stimuli. **2.** Denoting a hallucination which the mind by an effort is able to distinguish from an actuality.

psychosexual (si-ko-sek'shu-al). Pertaining to the emotional or mental components of sex.

psychosis, pl. **psychoses** (si-ko'sis, -sēz) [G. an animating]. **1.** A mental disorder causing gross distortion or disorganization of a person's mental capacity, affective response, and capacity to recognize reality, communicate, and relate to others to the degree of interfering with the capacity to cope with the ordinary demands of everyday life; divided into two major classifications according to their origins: those associated with organic brain syndromes and functional p.'s. **2.** Generic term for any of the insanities, the most common forms being the schizophrenias. **3.** A severe emotional illness.

   affective p., p. with predominant affective features.

   alcoholic p., mental disorders that result from alcoholism and that involve organic brain damage.

   circular p., see manic-depressive p.

   drug p., p. following or precipitated by ingestion of a drug, *e.g.,* LSD.

   exhaustion p., a confusional emotional state following an exhausting event.

   gestational p., psychotic reaction associated with pregnancy.

   hysterical p., (1) psychotic disturbance with predominantly hysterical symptoms; (2) a mental disorder resembling conversion hysteria but of psychotic severity.

   infection-exhaustion p., a p. following an acute infection, shock, or chronic intoxication; begins as delirium followed by pronounced mental confusion with hallucinations and unsystematized delusions and sometimes stupor.

   involutional p., mental disturbance occurring during the menopause or later life.

   Korsakoff's p., Korsakoff's *syndrome.*

   manic-depressive p., a major mental disorder in which there are severe changes of mood and usually a tendency to remission and recurrence. In the manic state, the patient is over-elated and hyperactive; in the depressed state, he suffers from a depressed mood, anxiety, and possible physical slowing down that can lead to stupor. In the circular form of this disorder, at least one of each type of episode occurs.

   polyneuritic p., Korsakoff's *syndrome.*

   postpartum p., an acute mental disorder in the mother following childbirth.

   schizo-affective p., psychotic disturbance in which there is a mixture of schizophrenic and manic-depressive symptoms.

   senile p., mental disturbance occurring in old age and related to degenerative cerebral processes.

   situational p., a transitory emotional disorder caused in a predisposed person by a seemingly unbearable situation.

psychosocial (si-ko-so'shal). Involving both psychological and social aspects.

psychosomatic (si'ko-so-mat'ik) [psycho- + G. *soma,* body]. Psychophysical (2); pertaining to the influence of the mind or higher functions of the brain upon the functions of the body, especially in relation to bodily disorders or disease.

psychosomimetic (si'ko'so-mĭ-met'ik). Psychotomimetic.

psychostimulant (si-ko-stim'u-lant). An agent with antidepressant or mood-elevating properties.

psychosurgery (si-ko-sur'jer-ĭ). The treatment of mental disorders by operation upon the brain, *e.g.,* lobotomy.

psychotherapeutics (si'ko-thĕr-ă-pu'tiks). Psychotherapy.

psychotherapist (sk-ko-thĕr'ă-pist). A person, usually a psychiatrist or clinical psychologist, professionally trained and engaged in psychotherapy.

psychotherapy (si-ko-thĕr'ă-pĭ) [psycho- + G. *therapeia,* treatment]. Psychotherapeutics; treatment of emotional, behavioral, personality, and psychiatric disorders based primarily upon verbal or nonverbal communication with the patient, in contrast to utilizing chemical and physical measures.

psychotic (si-kot'ik). Relating to or affected by psychosis.

psychotogenic (si-kot-o-jen'ik). Inducing psychosis; particularly referring to drugs of the LSD series and similar substances.

psychotomimetic (si-kot'o-mĭ-met'ik). **1.** Psychosomimetic; a drug or substance that produces psychological and behavioral changes resembling those of psychosis. **2.** Denoting such a drug or substance.

psychotropic (si'ko-trop'ik) [psycho- + G. *tropē,* a turning]. Affecting the mind, denoting drugs used in the treatment of mental illnesses.

psychro- [G. *psychros,* cold]. Combining form relating to cold. See also cryo-, crymo-.

psychroalgia (si-kro-al'jĭ-ah) [psychro- + G. *algos,* pain]. A painful sensation of cold.

psychrometry (si-krom'ĕ-trĭ) [psychro- + G. *metron,* measure]. Hygrometry; the calculation of relative humidity and water vapor pressures from temperature and barometric pressure; whereas relative humidity is the value ordinarily employed, the vapor pressure is the measurement of physiological significance.

psychrophile, psychrophil (si'kro-fĭl) [psychro- + G. *phileō,* to love]. An organism that grows best at a low temperature.

psychrophilic (si-kro-fil'ik). Pertaining to a psychrophile.

psychrophore (si'kro-fōr) [psychro- + G. *phoros,* bearing]. A double lumen catheter through which cold water is circulated to apply cold to a canal or cavity.

Pt Platinum.

PT Physical *therapy.*

PTA Plasma thromboplastin *antecedent.*

pter-, ptero- [G. *pteron,* wing, feather]. Combining forms meaning wing or feather.

pterion (te'rĭ-on) [G. *pteron,* wing]. The junction of the greater wing of the sphenoid, the squamous temporal, the frontal, and the parietal bones.

pteropterin (ter-op'ter-in). Pteroyltriglutamic acid; a folic acid conjugate, a principle chemically similar to folic acid except that it contains three molecules of glutamic acid instead of one, in γ linkage.

pteroylmonoglutamic acid (tĕr'o-il-mon'o-glu-tam'ik). Folic acid (2).

pteroyltriglutamic acid (tĕr'o-il-tri'glu-tam'ik). Pteropterin.

pterygium (tĕ-rij'ĭ-um) [G. *pterygion,* anything like a wing]. **1.** A triangular patch of hypertrophied bulbar subconjunctival tissue, extending from the medial canthus to the border of the cornea or beyond, with apex pointing toward the pupil. **2.** A forward growth of the eponychium with adherence to the proximal portion of the nail. **3.** An abnormal skin web, as of the neck extending from the acromion to the mastoid, usually bilateral.

pterygo- [G. *pteryx, pterygos,* wing]. Combining form denoting wing-shaped.

pterygoid (tĕr'ĭ-goyd) [G. *pteryx* (*pteryg-*), wing, + *eidos,* resemblance]. Wing-shaped; resembling a wing; applied to various anatomical parts in the area of the sphenoid bone.

pterygomandibular (tĕr'ĭ-go-man-dib'u-lar). Relating to the pterygoid process and the mandible.

pterygomaxillary (tĕr'ĭ-go-mak'sĭ-lĕr-ĭ). Relating to the pterygoid process and the maxilla.

pterygopalatine (tĕr'ĭ-go-pal'ă-tĭn). Relating to the pterygoid process and the palatine bone.

PTH Parathyroid *hormone.*

Pthirus (thi'rus) [L. *phthir;* G. *phtheir,* a louse]. A genus of lice (family Pediculidae) formerly grouped in the genus *Pediculus. P. pubis* (*Pediculus pubis*), the crab or pubic louse, is a parasite that infests the pubis and neighboring hairy parts of the body.

ptilosis (tĭ-lo'sis) [G. *ptilōsis,* plumage, inflamed eyelids with falling lashes]. Loss of the eyelashes.

ptomaine (to'mān) [G. *ptōma,* a corpse]. An indefinite term applied to poisonous substances, *e.g.,* toxic amines, formed in the decomposition of protein by the decarboxylation of amino acids by bacterial action.

ptosed (to'zd). Ptotic.

-ptosis [G. *ptōsis,* a falling]. Suffix denoting a falling or downward displacement of an organ.

ptosis, pl. **ptoses** (to'sis, to'sēz) [G. *ptōsis,* a falling]. A sinking down or prolapse of an organ; specifically, a drooping of the upper eyelid.

ptotic (tot'ik). Ptosed; relating to or marked by ptosis.

ptyal-, ptyalo- [G. *ptyalon,* saliva]. Combining forms denoting saliva, or the salivary glands. See also sialo-.

ptyalagogue (ti-al'ă-gog). Sialagogue.

ptyalectasis (ti-ă-lek'tă-sis) [ptyal- + G. *ektasis,* a stretching out]. Sialectasis.

ptyalocele (ti'ă-lo-sēl). Ranula (2).

Pu Plutonium.

pubarche (pu-bar'ke) The onset of puberty, particularly as manifested by the appearance of pubic hair.

pu'beral, pu'bertal. Relating to puberty.

puberty (pu'ber-tĭ) [L. *pubertas,* fr. *puber,* grown up]. The sequence of events by which a child is transformed into a young adult: gametogenesis begins, as well as secretion of gonadal hormones, growth of secondary sexual characters, and development reproductive functions; sexual dimorphism is accentuated. In law, the ages of presumptive puberty are 12 years in girls and 14 years in boys.

precocious p., a state in which pubertal changes begin at an unexpectedly early age; often the result of a pathological process involving a gland capable of secreting estrogens or androgens.

pubes (pu'bēz) [L.]. Plural of pubis.

pubescence (pu-bes'ens). **1** [L. *pubesco,* to attain puberty]. The coming to the age of puberty or sexual maturity. **2** [L. *pubes,* pubic hair]. The presence of downy or fine, short hair.

pubescent (pu-bes'ent). Pertaining to pubescence.

pubic (pu'bik). Relating to the os pubis.

pubiotomy (pu-bĭ-ot'o-mĭ) [L. *pubis,* pubic bone, + G. *tomē,* incision]. Pelviotomy (2); severance of the pubic bone a few centimeters lateral to the symphysis, in order to increase the capacity of a contracted pelvis sufficiently to permit the passage of a living child.

pubis, pl. **pubes** (pu'bis, pu'bēz) [L. *pubes,* the hair on the genitals; the genitals]. **1.** *Os* pubis. **2** [NA]. One of the pubic hairs; the hair of the pubic region just above the external genitals. **3** [NA]. *Mons* pubis.

pubo- Combining form denoting pubis or pubic.

puboprostatic (pu'bo-pros-tat'ik). Relating to the pubic bone and the prostate gland.

puborectal (pu'bo-rek'tal). Relating to the pubis and the rectum.

pubovesical (pu'bo-ves'ĭ-kal). Relating to the pubic bone and the bladder.

puden'dal. Pudic; relating to the external genitals.

pudendum, pl. **pudenda** (pu-den'dum, -dah) [L. ntr. of *pudendus*, fr. *pudeo*, to feel ashamed]. The external genitals, especially the female genitals (vulva).

pu'dic [L. *pudicus*, modest]. Pudendal.

puerile (pu'er-il) [L. *puer*, child]. Childish; pertaining to childhood or children.

puerpera, pl. **puerperae** (pu-er'per-ah, -per-e) [L., fr. *puer*, child, + *pario*, to bring forth]. Puerperant (2); a woman who has just given birth.

puerperal (pu-er'per-al). Puerperant (1); relating to the puerperium, or period after childbirth.

puerperant (pu-er'per-ant). **1.** Puerperal. **2.** A puerpera.

puerperium, pl. **puerperia** (pu'er-pēr'ĭ-um, -ĭ-ah) [L. childbirth, fr. *puer*, child, + *pario*, to bring forth]. The period from the termination of labor to complete involution of the uterus, usually defined as 42 days.

Pu'lex [L. flea]. A genus of fleas (family Pulicidae), including *P. irritans*, the common human flea that infests man and many animals.

pulicicide, pulicide (pu-lis'ĭ-sīd, pu'lĭ-sīd) [L. *pulex* (*pulic-*), flea, + *caedo*, to kill]. A chemical agent destructive to fleas.

pulmo-, pulmon-, pulmono- [L. *pulmo*, lung]. Combining forms denoting the lungs. See also pneum-, pneumo-.

pulmo, gen. **pulmonis,** pl. **pulmones** (pul'mo, pul-mo'-nis, -mo'nēz) [L.] [NA]. Lung.

pulmoaortic (pul'mo-a-or'tik). Relating to the pulmonary artery and the aorta.

pulmonary (pul'mo-nĕr-ĭ) [L. *pulmonarius*, fr. *pulmo*, lung]. Pneumonic (1); pulmonic; relating to the lungs, to the pulmonary artery, or to the aperture leading from the right ventricle into the pulmonary artery.

pulmonic (pul-mon'ik). Pulmonary.

pulmonitis (pul-mo-ni'tis). Pneumonitis.

pulmotor (pul'mo-tor) [L. *pulmo*, lung, + motor]. Denoting volume-limited or, more rarely, pressure-limited devices for the rhythmical inflation of lungs during resuscitation outside of hospitals.

pulp [L. *pulpa*, flesh]. A soft, moist, coherent solid.

  dead p., devital, devitalized, or nonvital p.; dental p. that has died as a result of trauma, chemical action, or infection, and that gives no response to vitality tests such as the electric and thermal tests.

  dental p., tooth pulp; the soft tissue within the pulp cavity, consisting of connective tissue containing blood vessels, nerves and lymphatics, and at the periphery a layer of odontoblasts capable of internal repair of the dentin.

  devital p., devitalized p., nonvital p., dead p.

  red p., the splenic p. seen grossly as a reddish brown substance consisting of splenic sinuses and the tissue intervening between them.

  splenic p., see red p., white p.

  tooth p., dental p.

  vital p., living dental p., either normal or diseased, that responds to electric and thermal tests.

  white p., that part of the spleen that consists of nodules and other lymphatic concentrations.

pulpa (pul'pah) [L. pulp] [NA]. Pulp.

pul'pal. Relating to the pulp.

pulpectomy (pul-pek'to-mĭ) [L. *pulpa*, pulp, + G. *ektomē*, excision]. Removal of the entire pulp structure of a tooth, including that in the roots.

pulpifaction (pul-pĭ-fak'shun) [L. *pulpa*, pulp, + *facio*, pp. *factus*, to make]. Reduction to a pulpy condition.

pulpitis (pul-pi'tis) [L. *pulpa*, pulp, + G. *-itis*, inflammation]. Inflammation of the pulp of a tooth.

pulpotomy (pul-pot'o-mĭ) [L. *pulpa*, pulp, + G. *tomē*, incision]. Pulp amputation; removal of a portion of the pulp structure of a tooth, usually coronal.

pulpy (pul'pĭ). In the condition of a soft, moist solid.

pulsate (pul'sāt) [L. *pulso*, pp. *-atus*, to beat]. To throb or beat rhythmically; said of the heart or an artery.

pulsatile (pul'sā-til). Throbbing; beating.

pulsation (pul-sa'shun) [L. *pulsatio*, a beating]. A throbbing or rhythmical beating, as of the pulse or the heart.

pulse (puls) [L. *pulsus*]. The rhythmical dilation of an artery, produced by the increased volume of blood thrown into the vessel by the contraction of the heart.

  alternating p., *pulsus* alternans.

  anacrotic p., anadicrotic p., a small slow rising p. tracing with a perceptible notch.

  bigeminal p., pulsus bigeminus; coupled beats or p.; a p. in which the beats occur in pairs.

  bisferious p., *pulsus* bisferiens.

  cannonball p., water-hammer p.

  Corrigan's p., the water-hammer-type p. in aortic regurgitation or peripheral arterial dilation, characterized by an abrupt rise and rapid fall away.

  coupled p., bigeminal p.

  dicrotic p., a p. which is marked by a double beat, the second, due to a palpable dicrotic wave, being weaker than the first.

  hard p., a p. that strikes forcibly against the tip of the finger and is with difficulty compressed, indicating hypertension.

  jugular p., the p. in the right internal jugular vein at the root of the neck, due to waves transmitted in the blood stream from the right side of the heart.

  paradoxical p., an exaggeration of the normal variation in the p. volume with respiration, becoming weaker with inspiration and stronger with expiration; characteristic of constrictive pericarditis or pericardial effusion; so called because these changes are independent of changes in p. rate.

plateau p., the slow, sustained p. of aortic stenosis, producing a prolonged flat-topped curve in the sphygmogram.

Quincke's p., Quincke's sign; capillary pulsation, as shown by alternate reddening and blanching of the nailbed with each heart beat; a sign of arteriolar dilation and especially well seen in severe aortic insufficiency.

Riegel's p., a p. that diminishes in volume during expiration.

thready p., a small fine p., feeling like a small cord or thread under the finger.

trigeminal p., pulsus trigeminus; a p. in which the beats occur in threes, a pause following every third beat.

undulating p., a toneless p. in which there is a succession of waves without character or force.

vagus p., a slow p. due to the inhibitory action of the vagus nerve on the heart.

venous p., a pulsation occurring in the veins, especially the internal jugular vein.

vermicular p., a small rapid p., giving a wormlike sensation to the finger.

water-hammer p., cannonball p.; a p. with forcible impulse but immediate collapse, characteristic of aortic incompetency. See also Corrigan's p.

wiry p., a small, fine, incompressible p.

pulsion (pul'shun) [L. *pulsio*]. A pushing outward or swelling.

pul'sus [L. a stroke, pulse]. Pulse.

p. alter'nans, alternating pulse; a pulse regular in time but with alternate beats stronger and weaker, often detectable only with the sphygmomanometer and usually indicating serious myocardial disease.

p. bigem'inus, bigeminal *pulse.*

p. bisfer'iens, bisferious pulse; an arterial pulse with two palpable peaks, the second stronger than the first, as may be found in aortic insufficiency combined with aortic stenosis.

p. cel'er, a pulse beat swift to rise and fall.

p. dif'ferens, a condition in which the pulses in the two radial arteries differ in strength.

p. paradox'us, paradoxical *pulse.*

p. ra'rus, p. tar'dus, a pulse beat slow to rise and fall.

p. trigem'inus, trigeminal *pulse.*

pultaceous (pul-ta'shus) [G. *poltos*, porridge]. Macerated; pulpy.

pulvinar (pul-vi'nar) [L. a couch made from cushions] [NA]. The posterior extremity of the thalamus which forms a cushion-like prominence slung over the posterior aspect of the internal capsule.

pumice (pum'is) [L. *pumex* (*pumic-*), a pumice stone]. Silicates ground to particles of varying sizes; used in dentistry for polishing restorations or teeth.

pump. 1. An apparatus for forcing a gas or liquid from or to any part. **2.** Any mechanism for using metabolic energy to accomplish active transport of a substance.

breast p., a suction instrument for withdrawing milk from the breast.

sodium p., a biologic mechanism that uses metabolic energy from ATP to achieve active transport of sodium across a membrane; sodium p.'s expel sodium from most cells of the body, sometimes coupled with the transport of other substances, and also serve to move sodium across multicellular membranes such as renal tubule walls.

sodium-potassium p., the biochemical mechanism that uses sodium-potassium ATPase to achieve (in most cells) transport of potassium opposite to that of the sodium p.

stomach p., an apparatus for removing the contents of the stomach by means of suction.

pump-ox'ygena'tor. A mechanical device that can substitute for both the heart (pump) and the lungs (oxygenator) during open heart surgery.

punch'drunk. See punchdrunk *syndrome.*

puncta (pungk'tah) [L.]. Plural of punctum.

punctate (pungk'tāt) [L. *punctum,* a point]. Marked with points or dots differentiated from the surrounding surface by color, elevation, or texture.

punctiform (pungk'tĭ-form) [L. *punctum,* a point, + *forma,* shape]. Very small but not microscopic, having a diameter of less than 1 mm.

punctograph (pungk'to-graf) [L. *punctum,* point, + G. *graphō,* to write]. A localizer, by x-ray, of a foreign body.

punctum, pl. **puncta** (pungk'tum, -tah) [L. a prick, point] [NA]. Point (1). **1.** The tip of a sharp process. **2.** A minute round spot differing in color or otherwise in appearance from the surrounding tissues.

p. ce'cum, the blind spot on the visual field where the optic nerve enters the eyeball.

p. lacrima'le [NA], lacrimal p., the minute circular opening of the lacrimal canaliculus, on the margin of each eyelid near the medial commissure.

p. vasculo'sum, one of the minute dots seen on section of the brain, due to small drops of blood at the cut extremities of the arteries.

puncture (pungk'chur) [L. *punctura,* fr. *pungo,* pp. *punctus,* to prick]. **1.** To make a hole with a small pointed object, such as a needle. **2.** A prick or small hole made with a pointed instrument.

cisternal p., passage of a hollow needle through the posterior atlantooccipital membrane into the cisterna cerebellomedullaris.

lumbar p., spinal p., spinal tap; rachicentesis; rachiocentesis; p. into the subarachnoid space of the lumbar region for diagnostic or therapeutic purposes.

sternal p., removal of bone marrow from the manubrium by needle.

PUO Pyrexia of unknown (or uncertain) origin, applied to febrile illness before diagnosis has been established.

pupa, pl. **pupae** (pu'pah, pu'pe) [L. *pupa*, doll]. The stage of insect metamorphosis following the larva and preceding the imago.

pu'pil (p.) [L. *pupilla, q.v.*]. Pupilla.

Adie's p., Holmes-Adie *syndrome.*

Argyll Robertson p., a form of reflex iridoplegia characterized by the loss of reflexes to light, direct and consensual, with normal pupillary contraction on accommodation and convergence; often present in tabes and general paresis.

fixed p., a stationary pupil unresponsive to all stimuli.

Hutchinson's p., an immobile dilation of the p. on the side of the lesion, with contraction of the other p., occurring in meningeal hemorrhage compressing the third nerve at the base of the brain.

neurotonic p., contraction of the p. in response to light, not followed by equivalent redilation.

pinhole p., an extremely contracted p.

tonic p., Piltz sign; Westphal-Piltz; a p. usually large, that responds very slowly, if at all, to light and accommodation.

Westphal-Piltz p., tonic p.

pupilla, pl. **pupillae** (pu-pil'ah, pu-pil'e) [L. dim. of *pupa*, a girl or doll] [NA]. Pupil; the circular orifice in the center of the iris, through which the light rays enter the eye.

pupillary (pu'pĭ-lĕr-ĭ). Relating to the pupil.

pupillo-. Combining form relating to the pupils.

pupillometer (pu-pĭ-lom'ĕ-ter) [pupillo- + G. *metron*, measure]. An instrument for measuring the diameter of the pupil.

pupillometry (pu'pĭ-lom'e-trĭ). Measurement of the pupil.

pupilloplegia (pu'pĭ-lo-ple'jĭ-ah) [pupillo- + G. *plēgē*, stroke]. A condition in which the pupil reacts slowly to light stimuli.

pupilloscopy (pu'pĭ-los'ko-pĭ) [pupillo- + G. *skopeō*, to view]. Retinoscopy.

pupillostatometer (pu'pĭ-lo-stă-tom'ĕ-ter) [pupillo- + G. *statos*, placed, + *metron*, measure]. An instrument for measuring the distance between the centers of the pupils.

pure (pūr) [L. *purus*]. **1.** Unadulterated; free from admixture or contamination with any extraneous matter. **2.** In genetics, referring to an inherited character which is transmitted without a break through an indefinite number of successive generations, or to an individual who is homozygous in respect to a particular pair of unit characters, not hybrid.

purgation (pur-ga'shun) [L. *purgatio*]. Catharsis (1); evacuation of the bowels with the aid of a purgative or cathartic.

purgative (pur'gă-tiv) [L. *purgativus*, purging]. An agent used for purging the bowels.

purge (purj) [L. *purgo*, to cleanse]. **1.** To cause a copious evacuation of the bowels. **2.** A cathartic remedy.

purine (pu'rēn, -rin). The parent substance of naturally occurring purine bases, not known to exist as such in the body. There are three p. groups: oxypurines (hypoxanthine, xanthine, and uric acid), aminopurines (adenine and guanine), and methyl p.'s (caffeine, theophylline, and theobromine).

purpura (pur'pu-rah) [L. fr. G. *porphyra*, purple]. Peliosis; a condition characterized by hemorrhage into the skin, the appearance of the lesions varying with the type of p., duration of the lesions, and acuteness of the onset; the color is first red, gradually darkening to purple and then fading to a brownish yellow and usually disappearing; the color of residual permanent pigmentation depends largely on the type of unabsorbed pigment of the extravasated blood; extravasations may occur also into the mucous membranes and internal organs.

allergic p., anaphylactoid p. (1); nonthrombocytopenic p. due to foods, drugs, and insect bites.

anaphylactoid p., (1) allergic p.; **(2)** Henoch-Schönlein p.

p. annula'ris telangiecto'des, Majocchi's disease; annular lesions, principally of the lower extremities, in which the peripheral portion is composed of purpura or petechiae with brawny staining of hemosiderin deposits and minute telangiectasia.

fibrinolytic p., p. in which the bleeding is associated with rapid fibrinolysis of the clot.

p. ful'minans, a severe and rapidly fatal form of p. hemorrhagica, occurring especially in children, with hypotension, fever, and disseminated intravascular coagulation, usually following an infectious illness.

p. hemorrhag'ica, idiopathic thrombocytopenic p.

Henoch-Schönlein p., anaphylactoid p. (2); eruption of nonthrombocytopenic purpuric lesions associated with joint pains or swelling, colic, vomiting of blood, passage of bloody stools, and sometimes glomerulonephritis, most commonly occurring in male children.

idiopathic thrombocytopenic p. (ITP), Werlhof's disease; p. hemorrhagica; thrombopenic or thrombocytopenic p.; a systemic illness characterized by extensive ecchymoses, hemorrhages from mucous membranes, deficiencies in platelet count, anemia, and prostration.

nonthrombocytopenic p., p. simplex.

p. seni'lis, occurrence of petechiae and ecchymoses on the legs in aged and debilitated persons.

p. sim'plex, nonthrombocytopenic p.; eruption of petechiae or larger ecchymoses, usually unaccompanied by constitutional symptoms and not associated with systemic illness.

thrombocytopenic p., thrombopenic p., idiopathic thrombocytopenic p.

thrombotic thrombocytopenic p., a rapidly fatal or occasionally protracted disease with varied symptoms in addition to p., including signs of CNS involvement, due to formation of fibrin or platelet thrombi in arterioles and capillaries in many organs.

purpuric (pur-pu′rik). Relating to or affected with purpura.

purpurinuria (pur′pur-rĭ-nu′rĭ-ah). Porphyrinuria.

purulence (pūr′u-lens) [L. *purulentia*, a festering, fr. *pus* (*pur-*), pus]. The condition of containing or forming pus.

purulent (pu′ru-lent). Containing, consisting of, or forming pus.

puruloid (pu′ru-loyd). Resembling pus.

pus [L.]. A fluid product of inflammation, consisting of a liquid containing leukocytes and the debris of dead cells and tissue elements liquefied by proteolytic and histolytic enzymes elaborated by polymorphonuclear leukocytes.

  blue p., p. tinged with pyocyanin, a product of *Pseudomonas aeruginosa.*

  laudable p., a term formerly used when suppuration was considered a desirable stage in wound healing.

pustula (pus′tu-lah) [L.]. Pustule.

pustular (pus′tu-lar). Relating to or marked by pustules.

pustulation (pus′tu-la′shun). The formation or presence of pustules.

pustule (pus′tūl) [L. *pustula*]. A small circumscribed elevation of the skin, containing purulent material.

pustulosis (pus-tu-lo′sis) [L. *pustula*, pustule, + G. *-osis*, condition]. An eruption of pustules.

putamen (pu-ta′men) [L. that which falls off in pruning] [NA]. The outer, larger, and darker gray of the three portions into which the nucleus lentiformis is divided by laminae of white fibers; its histological structure is similar to that of the caudate nucleus with which together it composes the striatum.

putrefaction (pu-trĭ-fak′shun) [L. *putre-facio*, pp. *-factus*, to make rotten]. Decay (2); decomposition or rotting, the breakdown of organic matter usually by bacterial action, resulting in the formation of other less complex substances with the evolution of ammonia or its derivatives and hydrogen sulfide; characterized usually by the presence of toxic or malodorous products.

putrefactive (pu-trĭ-fak′tiv). Relating to or causing putrefaction.

putrefy (pu′trĭ-fi). To cause to become, or to become, putrid.

putrescence (pu-tres′ens). The state of putrefaction.

putrescent (pu-tres′ent) [L. *putresco*, to grow rotten]. Denoting, or in the process of, putrefaction.

putrescine (pu-tres′ēn). $NH_2(CH_2)_4NH_2$; a poisonous amine (polyamine) formed from the amino acid, arginine, during putrefaction.

pu′trid [L. *putridus*]. **1.** In a state of putrefaction. **2.** Denoting putrefaction.

PUVA Oral administration of *p*soralen and subsequent exposure to long wavelength ultraviolet light (*uv-a*); used to treat psoriasis.

PVC Polyvinyl chloride.

PVP Polyvinylpyrrolidone.

pyarthrosis (pi-ar-thro′sis) [G. *pyon*, pus, + *arthrōsis*, a jointing]. Suppurative *arthritis.*

pycno-. See pykno-.

pyel-. See pyelo-.

pyelectasis, pyelectasia (pi-ĕ-lek′tă-sis, -lek-ta′zĭ-ah) [pyel- + G. *ektasis*, extension]. Dilation of the pelvis of the kidney.

pyelit′ic. Relating to pyelitis.

pyelitis (pi-ĕ-li′tis) [pyel- + G. *-itis*, inflammation]. **1.** Inflammation of the renal pelvis. **2.** Obsolescent term for pyelonephritis.

pyelo-, pyel- [G. *pyelos*, trough, tub, vat (pelvis)]. Combining forms denoting pelvis, usually the renal pelvis.

pyelocaliceal (pi′ĕ-lo-kal′ĭ-se′al). Relating to the renal pelvis and calices.

pyelocaliectasis (pi′e-lo-kal′ĭ-ek′tă-sis). Calicectasis.

pyelocystitis (pi-ĕ-lo-sis-ti′tis) [pyelo- + G. *kystis*, bladder, + *-itis*, inflammation]. Inflammation of the renal pelvis and the bladder.

pyelofluoroscopy (pi′ĕ-lo-flūr-os′ko-pĭ) [pyelo- + L. *fluo*, to flow, + G. *skopeō*, to view]. Fluoroscopic examination of the renal pelves, usually with a contrast medium.

py′elogram. A radiograph of the renal pelvis and ureter.

pyelography (pi′ĕ-log′ră-fĭ) [pyelo- + G. *graphō*, to write]. Pyeloureterography; ureteropyelography; radiologic study of the kidney and renal collecting system, usually with a contrast agent.

pyelolithotomy (pi′ĕ-lo-lĭ-thot′o-mĭ) [pyelo- + G. *lithos*, stone, + *tomē*, incision]. Pelvilithotomy.

pyelonephritis (pi′ĕ-lo-nĕ-fri′tis) [pyelo- + G. *nephros*, kidney, + *-itis*, inflammation]. Nephropyelitis; inflammation of the renal parenchyma, calyces, and pelvis, particularly due to local bacterial infection.

pyelonephrosis (pi′ĕ-lo-nĕ-fro′sis) [pyelo- + G. *nephros*, kidney, + *-osis*, condition]. Any disease of the pelvis of the kidney.

pyeloplasty (pi′ĕ-lo-plas-tĭ) [pyelo- + G. *plassō*, to fashion]. A plastic or reconstructive operation on the kidney pelvis to correct an obstruction.

pyeloplication (pi′ĕ-lo-pli-ka′shun) [pyelo- + L. *plico*, to fold]. An obsolete procedure of taking tucks in the wall of the renal pelvis when unduly dilated by a hydronephrosis.

pyeloscopy (pi-ĕ-los′ko-pĭ) [pyelo- + G. *skopeō*, to view]. Fluoroscopic observation of the pelvis and calices of the kidney after the injection through the ureter of an opaque solution.

pyelostomy (pi-ĕ-los′to-mĭ) [pyelo- + G. *stoma*, mouth]. Formation of an opening into the kidney pelvis to establish urinary drainage.

pyelotomy (pi-ĕ-lot′o-mĭ) [pyelo- + G. *tomē*, incision]. Incision into the pelvis of the kidney.

pyeloureterectasis (pi′ĕ-lo-u-re′ter-ek′tă-sis) [pyelo- + ureter + G. *ektasis*, a stretching]. Dilation of kidney pelvis and ureter.

pyeloureterography (pi′ĕ-lo-u-re′ter-og′ră-fĭ). Pyelography.

pyelovenous (pi'ĕ-lo-ve'nus) [pyelo- + venous]. Denoting the phenomenon of drainage from the renal pelvis into the renal veins resulting from increased intrapelvic pressure.

pyemesis (pi-em'e-sis) [G. *pyon*, pus, + *emesis*, vomiting]. The vomiting of pus.

pyemia (pi-e'mĭ-ah) [G. *pyon*, pus, + *haima*, blood]. Pyohemia; septicemia due to pyogenic organisms causing multiple abscesses.

pyemic (pi-e'mik). Relating to pyemia.

pyencephalus (pi-en-sef'ă-lus) [G. *pyon*, pus, + *enkephalos*, brain]. Pyocephalus.

pyesis (pi-e'sis) [G. *pyon*, pus, + *-esis*, condition or process]. Suppuration.

pygmalionism (pig-māl'yon-izm) [*Pygmalion*, G. myth. char.]. The state of being in love with an object of one's own creation.

pygmy (pig'mĭ) [G. *pygmaios*, dwarfish]. A physiologic dwarf; especially one of a race of similar people, such as those of Central Africa.

pyknic (pik'nik) [G. *pyknos*, thick]. Denoting a constitutional body type characterized by well rounded external contours and ample body cavities.

pykno-, pyk- [G. *pyknos*, thick, dense]. Combining forms meaning thick, dense, compact.

pyknodysostosis (pik'no-dis-os-to'sis) [pykno- + G. *dys-*, difficult, + *osteon*, bone, + *-osis*, condition]. A condition characterized by short stature, delayed closure of the fontanelles, and hypoplasia of the terminal phalanges.

pyknomorphous (pik-no-mor'fus) [pykno- + G. *morphē*, form, shape]. Denoting a cell or tissue that stains deeply because the stainable material is closely packed.

pyknosis (pik-no'sis) [pykno- + G. *-osis*, condition]. A condensation and reduction in size of the cell or its nucleus, usually associated with hyperchromatosis.

pyknotic (pik-not'ik). Relating to or characterized by pyknosis.

pylemphraxis (pi-lem-frak'sis) [G. *pylē*, gate, + *emphraxis*, a stoppage]. Obstruction of the portal vein.

pylephlebectasis (pi'le-flē-bek'tă-sis) [G. *pylē*, gate, + *phleps* (*phleb-*), vein, + *ektasis*, extension]. Dilation of the portal vein.

pylephlebitis (pi-le-flē-bi'tis) [G. *pylē*, a gate, + *phleps*, vein, + *-itis*, inflammation]. Inflammation of the portal vein or any of its branches.

pylethrombophlebitis (pi'le-throm'bo-phlē-bi'tis) [G. *pylē*, gate, + *thrombos*, a clot, + *phleps*, vein, + *-itis*, inflammation]. Inflammation of the portal vein with formation of a thrombus.

pylethrombosis (pi'le-throm-bo'sis) [G. *pylē*, gate, + *thrombos*, a clot, + *-osis*, condition]. Thrombosis of the portal vein or its branches.

pylor-. See pyloro-.

pylorectomy (pi'lo-rek'to-mĭ) [pylor- + G. *ektomē*, excision]. Gastropylorectomy; pylorogastrectomy; excision of the pylorus.

pylori (pi-lōr-i) [L.]. Plural of pylorus.

pyloric (pi-lōr'ik). Relating to the pylorus.

pyloristenosis (pi-lōr'ĭ-stĕ-no'sis) [pylor- + G. *stenōsis*, a narrowing]. Pylorostenosis; stricture or narrowing of the orifice of the pylorus.

pyloro-, pylor- [G. *pyloros*, gatekeeper]. Combining forms denoting the pylorus.

pylorodiosis (pi-lōr'o-di-o'sis) [pyloro- + G. *diōsis*, pushing apart]. Operative dilation of the pylorus.

pyloroduodenitis (pi-lōr'o-du'o-dĕ-ni'tis) [pyloro- + duodenitis]. Inflammation involving the pyloric outlet of the stomach and the duodenum.

pylorogastrectomy (pi-lōr'o-gas-trek'to-mĭ). Pylorectomy.

pyloromyotomy (pi-lor'o-mi-ot'o-mĭ) [pyloro- + G. *mys*, muscle, + *tomē*, incision]. Ramstedt or Fredet-Ramstedt operation; longitudinal incision through the anterior wall of the pyloric canal to the level of the submucosa, to treat hypertrophic pyloric stenosis.

pyloroplasty (pi-lōr'o-plas-tĭ) [pyloro- + G. *plassō*, to form]. An operation, commonly performed in conjunction with truncal vagectomy to treat peptic ulcer disease, in which an opening into pyloric canal is made in a longitudinal place and closed transversely; the latter destroys the normal closing mechanism at the gastric outlet and facilitates prompt emptying of gastric contents into the duodenum.

pylorospasm (pi-lōr'o-spazm). Spasmodic contraction of the pylorus.

pylorostenosis (pi-lōr'o-stĕ-no'sis). Pyloristenosis.

pylorostomy (pi-lo-ros'to-mĭ) [pyloro- + G. *stoma*, mouth]. Establishment of a fistula from the abdominal surface into the stomach near the pylorus.

pylorotomy (pi-lo-rot'o-mĭ) [pyloro- + G. *tomē*, incision]. Incision of the pylorus.

pylorus, pl. **pylori** (pi-lōr'us, -lōr'i) [L. fr. G. *pylōros*, a gatekeeper] [NA]. **1.** A muscular or myovascular device to open (dilator) and to close (sphincter) an orifice or the lumen of an organ. **2.** The muscular tissue surrounding and controlling the aboral outlet of the stomach.

pyo- [G. *pyon*, pus]. Combining form denoting suppuration or an accumulation of pus.

pyocele (pi'o-sēl) [pyo- + G. *kēlē*, tumor, hernia]. An accumulation of pus in the scrotum.

pyocephalus (pi'o-sef'ă-lus) [pyo- + G. *kephalē*, head]. Pyencephalus; a purulent effusion within the cranium.

pyochezia (pi-o-ke'zĭ-ah) [pyo- + G. *chezō*, to defecate]. A discharge of pus from the bowel.

pyococcus (pi-o-kok'us) [pyo- + G. *kokkos*, berry (coccus)]. One of the cocci causing suppuration, especially *Streptococcus pyogenes*.

pyocolpocele (pi-o-kol'po-sēl) [pyo- + G. *kolpos*, bosom (vagina), + *kēlē*, tumor, hernia]. A vaginal tumor or cyst containing pus.

pyocolpos (pi-o-kol'pos) [pyo- + G. *kolpos*, bosom (vagina)]. An accumulation of pus in the vagina.

pyocyanic (pi′o-si-an′ik) [pyo- + G. *kyanos*, blue]. Relating to blue pus or the organism that causes it, *Pseudomonas aeruginosa.*

pyocyanogenic (pi′o-si-ă-no-jen′ik) [pyo- + G. *kyanos*, blue, + *-gen*, producing]. Causing blue pus.

pyocyst (pi′o-sist) [pyo- + G. *kystis*, bladder]. A cyst with purulent contents.

pyoderma (pi-o-der′mah) [pyo- + G. *derma*, skin]. Any pyogenic infection of the skin.

   p. gangreno′sum, a chronic eruption of spreading, undermined ulcers showing central healing.

pyogenesis (pi-o-jen′ĕ-sis) [pyo- + G. *genesis*, production]. Suppuration.

pyogenic (pi-o-jen′ik). Pus-forming; relating to pus formation.

pyohemia (pi-o-he′mĭ-ah). Pyemia.

pyohemothorax (pi′o-he-mo-tho′raks) [pyo- + G. *haima*, blood, + thorax]. Presence of pus and blood in the pleural cavity.

pyoid (pi′oyd) [G. *pyōdēs*, fr. *pyon*, pus, + *eidos*, resemblance]. Resembling pus.

pyolabyrinthitis (pi′o-lab-ĭ-rin-thi′tis) [pyo- + G. *labyrinthos*, labyrinth, + *-itis*, inflammation]. Suppurative inflammation of the labyrinth of the ear.

pyometra (pi-o-me′trah) [pyo- + G. *mētra*, uterus]. An accumulation of pus in the uterine cavity.

pyometritis (pi′o-me-tri′tis) [pyo- + G. *mētra*, womb, + *-itis*, inflammation]. An inflammation of uterine musculature associated with pus in the uterine cavity.

pyomyositis (pi′o-mi-o-si′tis) [pyo- + G. *mys*, muscle, + *-itis*, inflammation]. Abscesses, carbuncles, or infected sinuses lying deep in muscles.

pyonephritis (pi-o-nĕ-fri′tis) [pyo- + G. *nephros*, kidney, + *itis*, inflammation]. Suppurative inflammation of the kidney.

pyonephrolithiasis (pi′o-nef′ro-lĭ-thi′ă-sis) [pyo- + G. *nephros*, kidney, + *lithos*, stone, + *-iasis*, condition]. Presence in the kidney of pus and calculi.

pyonephrosis (pi′o-nĕ-fro′sis) [pyo- + G. *nephros*, kidney, + *-osis*, condition]. Distention of the pelvis and calices of the kidney with pus, usually associated with obstruction.

pyoovarium (pi′o-o-vār′ĭ-um). Presence of pus in the ovary; an ovarian abscess.

pyopericarditis (pi′o-pĕr-ĭ-kar-di′tis). Suppurative inflammation of the pericardium.

pyopericardium (pi′o-pĕr-ĭ-kar′di-um). An accumulation of pus in the pericardial sac.

pyoperitoneum (pi′o-pĕr-ĭ-to-ne′um). An accumulation of pus in the peritoneal cavity.

pyoperitonitis (pi′o-pĕr-ĭ-tŏ-ni′tis). Suppurative inflammation of the peritoneum.

pyophthalmitis (pi′of-thal-mi′tis) [pyo- + G. *ophthalmos*, eye, + *-itis*, inflammation]. Suppurative inflammation of the eye.

pyophysometra (pi′o-fi-so-me′trah) [pyo- + G. *physa*, air, + *mētra*, uterus]. Presence of pus and gas in the uterine cavity.

pyopneumocholecystitis (pi′o-nu′mo-ko′le-sis-ti′tis) [pyo- + G. *pneuma*, air, + cholecystitis]. Combination of pus and gas in an inflamed gallbladder, caused by gas-producing organisms or by the entry of air from the duodenum through the biliary tree.

pyopneumohepatitis (pi′o-nu′mo-hep-ă-ti′tis) [pyo- + G. *pneuma*, air, + hepatitis]. Combination of pus and air in the liver, usually in association with an abscess.

pyopneumopericardium (pi′o-nu′mo-pĕr-ĭ-kar′dĭ-um) [pyo- + G. *pneuma*, air, + pericardium]. Presence of pus and gas in the pericardial sac.

pyopneumoperitoneum (pi′o-nu′mo-pĕr-ĭ-tŏ-ne′um) [pyo- + G. *pneuma*, air, + peritoneum]. Presence of pus and gas in the peritoneal cavity.

pyopneumoperitonitis (pi′o-nu′mo-pĕr-ĭ-to-ni′tis) [pyo- + G. *pneuma*, air, + peritonitis]. Peritonitis with gas-forming organisms or with gas introduced from a ruptured bowel.

pyopneumothorax (pi′o-nu′mo-tho′raks) [pyo- + G. *pneuma*, air, + thorax]. Pneumopyothorax; presence of gas together with a purulent effusion in the pleural cavity.

pyopoiesis (pi′o-poy-e′sis) [pyo- + G. *poiēsis*, a making]. Suppuration.

pyopoietic (pi′o-poy-et′ik). Pus-producing.

pyoptysis (pi-op′tĭ-sis) [pyo- + G. *ptysis*, a spitting]. Purulent expectoration; spitting of pus.

pyopyelectasis (pi′o-pi-ĕ-lek′tă-sis) [pyo- + G. *pyelos*, pelvis, + *ektasis*, a stretching]. Dilation of the renal pelvis with pus-producing inflammation.

pyorrhea (pi-o-re′ah) [pyo- + G. *rhoia*, a flow]. A purulent discharge.

pyosalpingitis (pi′o-sal-pin-ji′tis) [pyo- + salpingitis]. Suppurative inflammation of the fallopian tube.

pyosalpingo-oophoritis (pi′o-sal′ping-go-o-of′o-ri′tis) [pyo- + G. *salpinx*, trumpet (tube), + oophoritis]. Suppurative inflammation of the fallopian tube and the ovary.

pyosalpinx (pi-o-sal′pingks) [pyo- + G. *salpinx*, trumpet (tube)]. Distention of a fallopian tube with pus.

pyosis (pi-o′sis) [G.]. Suppuration.

pyostatic (pi-o-stat′ik) [pyo- + G. *statikos*, causing to stand]. Arresting the formation of pus.

pyothorax (pi-o-tho′raks). Empyema in a plural cavity.

pyourachus (pi-o-u′ră-kus). A purulent accumulation in the urachus.

pyoureter (pi′o-u-re′ter). Distention of a ureter with pus.

pyramid (pĭr′ă-mid) [G. *pyramis* (*pyramid-*), a pyramid]. An anatomical structure having a pyramidal shape.

   anterior p., *pyramis* medullae oblongatae.

   cerebellar p., *pyramis vermis.*

   Ferrein's p., medullary *ray.*

   p. of light, a triangular area at the anterior inferior part of the drum membrane, running from the umbo to the periphery, where there is seen a bright reflection of light.

malpighian p., *pyramis* renalis.

p. of medulla oblongata, *pyramis* medullae oblongatae.

medullary p., *pyramis* renalis.

posterior p. of medulla, *fasciculus* gracilis.

renal p., *pyramis* renalis.

p. of tympanum, *eminentia* pyramidalis.

pyramidal (pĭ-ram´ĭ-dal). **1.** Of the shape of a pyramid. **2.** Relating to any anatomical structure called pyramid.

pyramis, pl. pyramides (pĭr´ă-mis, pĭ-ram´ĭ-dēz) [Mod. L. fr. G. pyramid] [NA]. Pyramid.

p. medul´lae oblonga´tae [NA], pyramid of the medulla oblongata; anterior pyramid; an elongated white prominence on the ventral surface of the medulla oblongata on either side along the anterior median fissure, corresponding to the pyramidal tract.

p. rena´lis, pl. **pyram´ides rena´les** [NA], renal or malpighian pyramid; one of a number of pyramidal masses, seen on longitudinal section of the kidney, that contain part of the secreting tubules and the collecting tubules.

p. tym´pani, *eminentia* pyramidalis.

p. ver´mis [NA], cerebellar pyramid; a subdivision of the inferior vermis of the cerebellum anterior to the tuber, between it and the uvula.

pyranose (pĭr´ă-nōs, pi´-). A cyclic form of a sugar in which the oxygen bridge forms in such a way as to produce a ring made up of five carbon atoms and an oxygen atom.

pyretic (pi-ret´ik) [G. *pyretikos*]. Feverish; pertaining to fever.

pyreto- [G. *pyretos,* fever]. Combining form denoting fever. See also pyro-.

pyretogenesis (pi´rē-to-jen´ĕ-sis, pĭr´ĕ-to-) [pyreto- + G. *genesis,* origin]. The origin and mode of production of fever.

pyretogenet´ic, pyretogen´ic. Pyrogenic.

pyretogenous (pi-rē-toj´ĕ-nus). **1.** Caused by fever. **2.** Pyrogenic.

pyrexia (pi-rek´sĭ-ah) [G. *pyrexis,* feverishness]. Fever.

pyrexial (pi-rek´sĭ-al). Relating to fever.

pyridine (pĭr´ĭ-dēn, -din). C_5H_5N; a colorless volatile liquid resulting from the dry distillation of organic matter containing nitrogen; used as an industrial solvent, in analytical chemistry, and for denaturing alcohol.

pyridoxal (pĭr-ĭ-dok´sal). The aldehyde of pyridoxine, having a similar physiologic action.

pyridoxal 5´-phosphate. A coenzyme essential to many reactions in tissue, notably transaminations and amino acid decarboxylations.

pyridoxamine (pĭr´ĭ-dok´să-mēn). The amine of pyridoxine (–CH_2NH_2 replacing –CH_2OH at position 4), having a similar physiologic action.

4-pyridoxic acid (pĭr-ĭ-dok´sik). The principal product of the metabolism of pyridoxal in man (–COOH

replaces –CHO at position 4), appearing in the urine.

pyridoxine (pĭr-ĭ-dok´sēn, -sin). 3-Hydroxy-4, 5-bis-(hydroxymethyl)-2-methylpyridine (with CH_2OH replacing CHO); the original vitaman B_6, which term now includes pyridoxal and pyridoxamine; associated with the utilization of unsaturated fatty acids.

pyrimethamine (pĭr-ĭ-meth´ă-mēn). 2,4-Diamino-5-*p*-chlorophenyl-6-ethylpyrimidine; a potent folic acid antagonist used as an antimalarial agent effective against *Plasmodium falciparum;* also used in the treatment of toxoplasmosis.

pyrimidine (pi-rim´ĭ-dēn). A heterocyclic substance, the formal parent of several "bases" present in nucleic acids (uracil, thymine, cytosine) as well as of the barbiturates.

pyro- [G. *pyr,* fire]. **1.** Combining form denoting fire, heat, or fever. See also pyreto-. **2.** In chemistry, combining form denoting derivatives formed by removal of water (usually by heat) to form anhydrides.

pyrocatechol (pi-ro-kat´ĕ-kol). Catechol; *o*-dihydroxybenzene; a constituent of epinephrine and norepinephrine (both "catecholamines") and dopa; used externally as an antiseptic.

pyrogen (pi´ro-jen) [pyro- + -*gen,* producing]. An agent that causes a rise in temperature.

pyrogenic (pi-ro-jen´ik). Pyretogenic; pyretogenetic; pyretogenous (2); causing fever.

pyroglobulins (pi-ro-glob´u-linz). Serum proteins (immunoglobulins), usually associated with multiple myeloma or macroglobulinemia, which precipitate irreversibly when heated to 56°C.

pyrolysis (pi-rol´ĭ-sis) [pyro- + G. *lysis,* dissolution]. Decomposition of a substance by heat.

pyromania (pi-ro-ma´nĭ-ah) [pyro- + G. *mania,* frenzy]. A morbid impulse to set fires.

pyronin (pi´ro-nin). A fluorescent red basic xanthene dye, the chloride of tetramethyldiaminoxanthene or of tetraethyldiaminoxanthene; used in combination with methyl green for differential staining of RNA (red) and DNA (green), and as a tracking dye for RNA in electrophoresis.

pyrophobia (pi´ro-fo´bĭ-ah) [pyro- + G. *phobos,* fear]. A morbid dread of fire.

py´rophos´phatase. Any enzyme cleaving a pyrophosphate between two phosphoric groups, leaving one on each of the two fragments.

py´rophos´phate (PP). A salt of pyrophosphoric acid.

py´rophosphor´ic acid. An acid, $H_4P_2O_7$, that forms pyrophosphates with bases; its esters are important in energy metabolism and in biosynthesis.

pyrosis (pi-ro´sis) [G. a burning]. Heartburn; substernal pain or burning sensation, usually associated with regurgitation of acid-peptic gastric juice into the esophagus.

pyrot´ic. 1. Relating to pyrosis. **2.** Caustic.

pyroxylin (pi-rok´sĭ-lin) [pyro- + G. *xylon,* wood]. Nitrocellulose; consists chiefly of cellulose tetranitrate, obtained by the action of nitric and sulfuric acids on cotton; used in the preparation of collodion.

pyrrole (pĭr'ōl). Azole; imidole; divinylenimine; a heterocyclic compound found in many biologically important substances.

pyrrolidine (pĭr-rol'ĭ-dēn). Pyrrole to which four H atoms have been added, the basis of proline and hydroxyproline.

pyruvate (pi'ru-vāt). A salt or ester of pyruvic acid.

pyruvic acid (pi-ru'vik). CH_3 $\_$ CO–$COOH$; an intermediate compound in the metabolism of carbohydrate; in thiamin deficiency, its oxidation is retarded and it accumulates in the tissues, especially in the nervous structures. The enol form, *enol*pyruvic acid, CH_2=$C(OH)$–$COOH$, plays an important metabolic role.

pyuria (pi-u'rĭah) [G. *pyon*, pus, + *ouron*, urine]. Presence of pus in the urine.

Q

Q Coulomb.

Q̇ [quantity + an overdot denoting the time derivative]. Symbol for blood *flow*.

QCO₂ Microliters of CO_2 given off per milligram of tissue per hour.

q.d. L. *quaque die*, every day.

q.h. L. *quaque hora*, every hour.

q.i.d. L. *quater in die*, four times a day.

QO or QO₂ Oxygen consumption (1).

quack (kwak). Charlatan.

quackery (kwak'er-ĭ). Charlatanism.

quadrant (kwah'drant) [L. *quadrans*, a quarter]. In anatomy, roughly circular areas are divided for descriptive purposes into quarters; *e.g.*, the abdomen is divided by a horizontal and a vertical line intersecting at the umbilicus, the fundus oculi by a horizontal and a vertical line intersecting at the optic disk, the tympanic membrane by a line drawn across the diameter of the drum in the axis of the handle of the malleus and another intersecting the first at right angles at the umbo.

quadrate (kwah'drāt) [L. *quadratus*, square]. Having four equal sides; square.

quadri- [L. *quattuor*, four]. Combining form denoting four.

quadribasic (kwah-drĭ-ba'sik). Denoting an acid having four hydrogen atoms that are replaceable by atoms or radicals of a basic character.

quadriceps (kwah'drĭ-seps) [L. fr. quadri- + *caput*, head]. Having four heads; denoting various muscles.

quadrigeminal (kwah-drĭ-jem'ĭ-nal) [quadri- + L. *geminus*, twin]. Fourfold.

quadrigeminum (kwah-drĭ-jem'ĭ-num). One of the corpora quadrigemina.

quadriplegia (kwah-drĭ-ple'jĭ-ah) [quadri- + G. *plēgē, stroke*]. Tetraplegia; paralysis of all four limbs.

quadriplegic (kwah-drĭ-ple'jik). Pertaining to quadriplegia.

quadrivalent (kwah-drĭ-va'lent, kwah-driv'ă-lent) [quadri- + L. *valeo*, pres. p. *valens*, to have power]. Tetravalent; having the combining power of four atoms of hydrogen.

quadruplet (kwah'drup-let, kwah-dru'plet) [L. *quadruplus*, fourfold]. One of four children born at one birth.

quadrantanopsia (kwah'drant-an-op'sĭ-ah) [quadrant + anopsia]. Quadrantic *hemianopsia*.

quantum, pl. **quanta** (kwahn'tum, -tah) [L. how much]. **1.** A unit of radiant energy (ϵ) varying according to the frequency (ν) of the radiation. **2.** A certain definite amount.

quarantine (kwahr'an-tēn) [It. *quarantina* fr. L. *quadraginta,* forty]. **1.** A period (originally 40 days) of detention of vessels and their passengers coming from an area where an infectious disease prevails. **2.** To detain such vessels and their passengers until the incubation period of the disease has passed. **3.** A place where such vessels and their passengers are detained. **4.** The isolation of a person with a contagious disease.

quart (kwort) [L. *quartus*, fourth]. One fourth of a gallon, equivalent of 0.9468 liter; an **imperial q.** is about 20% more than the ordinary q., or 1.135 liters.

quartan (kwor'tan) [L. *quartanus*, relating to a fourth (thing)]. Recurring every fourth day.

quartz (kworts). A crystalline form of silicon dioxide used in chemical apparatus and in optical and electric instruments.

quaternary (kwah'ter-nĕr'ĭ, kwah-ter'nĕ-rĭ) [L. *qua ternarius*, containing four, fr. *quattuor*, four]. **1.** Denoting a chemical compound containing four elements. **2.** Fourth in a series.

quenching (kwench'ing). **1.** The process of extinguishing, removing, or diminishing a physical property, such as heat or light. **2.** In beta liquid scintillation counting, the shifting of the energy spectrum from a true to a lower energy; caused by a variety of interfering materials in the counting solution, including foreign chemicals and coloring agent.

quick (kwik) [A.S. *cwic*, living]. **1.** Pregnant with a child the movement of which is felt. **2.** A sensitive part, painful to touch. **3.** Eponychium.

quick'ening [A.S. *cwic*, living]. The signs of life felt by the mother as a result of the fetal movements.

quiescent (kwĭ-es'ent). At rest or inactive.

quinacrine hydrochloride (kwin'ă-krēn, -krin). An acridine derivative, $C_{23}H_{30}ClN_3O \cdot 2HCl \cdot 2H_2O$ used as an antimalarial and as an anthelmintic; as a dihydrochloride, used as a stain in cytogenetics to demonstrate Y chromatin by fluorescent microscopy.

quinidine (kwin′ĭ-dēn, -din). β-quinine; one of the alkaloids of cinchona, a stereoisomer of quinine; used as an antimalarial and in the treatment of cardiac arrhythmias.

quinine (kwi′nīn, -nēn, kwin′-ĭn, -ēn). $C_{20}H_{24}N_2O_2$-$3H_2O$; an alkaloid derived from cinchona (family Rubiaceae), used as an antimalarial effective against the asexual and erythrocytic forms of the parasite, but having no effect on the exoerythrocytic (tissue) forms; also used as an antipyretic, analgesic, sclerosing agent, stomachic, and oxytocic (occasionally), and in the treatment of atrial fibrillation and certain myopathies.

quinone (kwin′ōn, kwi′nōn). General name for aromatic compounds bearing two oxygens in place of two hydrogens, usually in the *para* position; the oxidation product of a hydroquinone.

quinsy (kwin′zĭ) [M.E. *quinsie* (*quinesie*), a corruption of L. *cynanche*, sore throat]. Peritonsillar *abscess*.

quintan (kwin′tan) [L. *quintus*, fifth]. Recurring every fifth day.

quintuplet (kwin′tu-plet, kwin, tup′let) [L. *quintuplex*, fivefold]. One of five children born at one birth.

quotidian (kwo-tid′ĭ-an) [L. *quotidianus*, daily]. Amphemerous; daily; occurring every day.

quotient (kwo′shent) [L. *quoties*, how often]. The number of times one amount is contained in another.

    achievement q., a percentile rating of the amount a child has learned in relation to his age, level of education, or peers.

    intelligence q. (IQ), an index of measured intelligence as one part of a two-part determination of intelligence (the other being an index of adaptive behavior) used to denote a person's standing relative to his age peers on a test of general ability, ordinarily expressed as a ratio between the person's score on a given test and the score which the average individual his age attained on the same test.

    respiratory q., (R.Q.), the steady state ratio of carbon dioxide produced by tissue metabolism to oxygen consumed in the same metabolism; for the whole body, normally about 0.82 under basal conditions; in the steady state, equal to the respiratory exchange ratio.

R

R Gas *constant;* electrical resistance; radical (usually an alkyl or aryl group); Réaumur *scale;* L. *recipe;* respiration; respiratory exchange *ratio;* roentgen; unit of resistance in the cardiovascular system.

℞ L. *recipe,* prescription.

r Roentgen; "racemic," occasionally used in naming compounds in place of the more common "*dl.*"

Ra Radium.

rab′beting [Fr. *raboter,* to plane]. Making congruous stepwise cuts on apposing bone surfaces for stability after impaction.

rab′id [L. *rabidus,* raving, mad]. Relating to or affected with rabies.

rabies (ra′bēz) [L. rage, fury, fr. *rabio,* to rave, to be mad]. Hydrophobia; lyssa; a highly fatal infectious disease transmitted by the bite of carnivorous animals and caused by a neurotropic lyssavirus that occurs in the CNS and the salivary glands; symptoms are those of a profound disturbance of the nervous system: excitement, aggressiveness, and dementia, followed by paralysis and death; characteristic cytoplasmic inclusion bodies (Negri bodies) found in many of the neurons are characteristic.

race. A class of animals or individuals having common somatic inherited characteristics.

racemase (ra′se-mās). An enzyme capable of catalyzing racemization, *i.e.,* inversions of asymmetric groups; when more than one center of asymmetry is present, "epimerase" is used.

racemate (ra′se-māt). A racemic compound; also, the salt or ester of such a compound.

raceme (ra-sēm′). An optically inactive chemical compound.

racemic (ra-se′mik, -sem′ik). Denoting a mixture that is optically inactive, being composed of an equal number of dextro- and levorotatory substances, which are separable; compounds internally compensated, and therefore not separable into D and L (or *d* and *l*) forms, are termed "meso."

racemization (ra′se-mĭ-za′shun). Partial conversion of one enantiomorph into another (as an L-amino acid to the corresponding D- form) so that the specific optical rotation is decreased, or even reduced to zero, in the resulting racemate.

racemose (ras′e-mōs) [L. *racemosus,* full of clusters]. Branching, with nodular terminations, resembling a bunch of grapes.

rachi-, rachio- [G. *rachis,* spine, backbone]. Combining form denoting the spine.

rachial (ra′kĭ-al). Spinal.

rachicentesis (ra-kĭ-sen-te′sis) [rachi- + G. *kentēsis,* puncture]. Lumbar *puncture.*

rachidial, rachidian (rā-kid′ĭ-al, -ĭ-an). Spinal.

rachigraph (ra′kĭ-graf) [rachi- + G. *graphō,* to write]. A graph for recording the curves of the vertebrae.

rachilysis (rā-kil′ĭ-sis) [rachi- + G. *lysis,* a loosening]. Forcible correction of lateral curvature by lateral pressure against the convexity of the curve.

rachio-. See rachi-.

rachiocentesis (ra-kĭ-o-sen-te′sis) [rachio- + G. *kentēsis,* puncture]. Lumbar *puncture.*

rachiometer (ra-kĭ-om′ĕ-ter) [rachio- + G. *metron,* measure]. An instrument for measuring the curvature of the spinal column.

rachiotomy (ra-kĭ-ot′o-mī) [rachio- + G. *tomē,* incision]. Laminectomy.

rachis, pl. **rachides, rachises** (ra′kis, ra′kĭ-dēz, rak-) [G. spine, backbone]. *Columna vertebralis.*

rachischisis (ră-kis′kĭ-sis) [G. *rhachis,* spine, + *schisis,* division]. Spondyloschisis.

rachitic (ră-kit′ic). Rickety; relating to rachitis.

rachitis (ră-ki′tis) [G. *rhachitis*]. Rickets.

rachitogenic (ră-kit-o-jen′ik) [rachitis + G. *genesis,* production]. Producing or causing rickets.

rad The unit for absorbed dose, a measure of the dose absorbed from ionizing radiation equivalent to 100 ergs of energy per g.

radarkymography (ra′dar-ki-mog′ră-fī). Video tracking of heart motion by means of image intensification and closed circuit television during fluoroscopy; enables cardiac motion to be measured by reproducible linear graphic tracing.

radectomy (ra-dek′to-mĭ) [L. *radix,* root, + G. *ektomē,* excision]. Root *amputation.*

radiability (ra-dĭ-ă-bil′ĭ-tĭ). The property of being radiable.

radiable (ra′dĭ-ă-bl). Capable of being penetrated or examined by rays, especially x-rays.

radiad (ra′dĭ-ad). In a direction toward the radial side.

radial (ra′dĭ-al) [L. *radialis,* fr. *radius,* ray]. **1.** Relating to the radius (bone of the forearm), to any structures named from it, or to the radial or lateral aspect of the upper limb as compared to the ulnar or medial aspect. **2.** Relating to any radius. **3.** Radiating; diverging in all directions from any given center.

ra′dian (rad) [L. *radius,* ray]. A supplementary SI unit of plane angle.

radiant (ra′dĭ-ant). **1.** Giving out rays. **2.** A point from which light radiates to the eye.

radiate (ra′dĭ-āt) [L. *radio,* pp. *-atus,* to shine]. **1.** To spread out in all directions from a center. **2.** To emit radiation.

radiatio, pl. **radiationes** (ra-dĭ-a′shĭ-o, -shi-o′nēz) [L.]. Radiation (3); in neuroanatomy, a term applied to any one of the thalamocortical fiber systems that together compose the corona radiata of the cerebral hemisphere's white matter.

r. acus′tica [NA], acoustic radiation; the fibers that pass from the medial geniculate body to the transverse temporal gyri of the cerebral cortex, forming part of the sublentiform part of the internal capsule.

r. cor′poris callo′si [NA], radiation of the corpus callosum; the spreading out of the fibers of the corpus callosum in the centrum semiovale of each cerebral hemisphere.

r. op′tica [NA], optic radiation; the massive fanlike fiber system passing from the lateral geniculate body of the thalamus to the visual cortex.

r. pyramida′lis, pyramidal radiation; white fibers passing from the cortex to the pyramidal tract.

radiation (ra-dĭ-a′shun) [L. *radiatio,* fr. *radius,* ray, beam]. **1.** The act or condition of diverging in all directions from a center. **2.** The sending forth of light, short radio waves, ultraviolet or x-rays, or any other rays for treatment or diagnosis or for other purpose; *cf.* irradiation (2). **3.** Radiatio. **4.** Radiant energy or a radiant beam.

acoustic r., *radiatio* acustica.

r. of corpus callosum, *radiatio* corporis callosi.

electromagnetic r., r. originating in a varying electromagnetic field; *e.g.,* visible light, radio waves, x-radiation, etc.

optic r., *radiatio* optica.

pyramidal r., *radiatio* pyramidalis.

radical (rad′ĭ-kal) [L. *radix* (*radic-*), root]. **1.** In chemistry, a group of elements or atoms usually passing intact from one compound to another, but usually incapable of prolonged existence in a free state; in chemical formulas, often distinguished by being enclosed in parentheses or brackets. **2.** Thorough; relating or directed to the extirpation of the root or cause of a morbid process; *e.g.,* a r. operation. **3.** Denoting treatment by extreme, drastic, or innovative measures, as opposed to conservative.

radi′ces. Plural of radix.

radicle (rad′ĭ-kl) [L. *radicula,* dim of *radix,* root]. A rootlet or structure resembling one, as a minute veinlet joining with others to form a vein or a nerve fiber which joins others to form a nerve.

radicotomy (rad′ĭ-kot′o-mĭ) [L. *radix* (*radic-*), root, + G. *tomē,* incision]. Rhizotomy.

radicul-. See radiculo-.

radicula (ră-dik′u-lah) [L. dim of *radix,* root]. A spinal nerve root.

radiculalgia (ră-dik′u-lal′jĭ-ah) [radicul- + G. *algos,* pain]. Neuralgia due to irritation of the sensory root of a spinal nerve.

radicular (ră-dik′u-lar). **1.** Relating to a radicle. **2.** Pertaining to the root of a tooth.

radiculectomy (ră-dik-u-lek′to-mĭ) [radicul- + G. *ektomē,* excision]. Rhizotomy.

radiculitis (ră-dik-u-li′tis) [radicul- + G. *-itis,* inflammation]. Inflammation of the intradural portion of a spinal nerve root prior to its entrance into the intervertebral foramen or of the portion between that foramen and the nerve plexus.

radiculo-, radicul-. Combining forms denoting radicle, radicular.

radiculoganglionitis (ră-dik′u-lo-gang′glĭ-o-ni′tis). Acute idiopathic *polyneuritis.*

radiculomeningomyelitis (ră-dik′u-lo-mĕ-ning′go-mi-ĕ-li′tis). Rhizomeningomyelitis.

radiculomyelopathy (ră-dik′u-lo-mi′ĕ-lop′ă-thĭ). Myeloradiculopathy.

radiculoneuropathy (ră-dik′u-lo-nu-rop′ă-thĭ). Disease of the spinal nerve roots and nerves.

radiculopathy (ră-dik-u-lop′ă-thĭ) [radiculo- + G. *pathos,* suffering]. Disease of the spinal nerve roots.

radiectomy (ra-dĭ-ek′to-mĭ) [L. *radix,* root, + G. *ektomē,* excision]. Root *amputation.*

radii (ra′dĭ-i) [L.]. Plural of radius.

radio- [L. *radius*, ray]. Combining form denoting radiation, chiefly x-ray; the radioactive isotope of the element to which it is prefixed; radius.

ra'dioac'tive. Possessing radioactivity.

radioactivity (ra'dĭ-o-ak-tiv'ĭ-tĭ). The property of some atomic nuclei of spontaneously emitting gamma rays or subatomic particles of matter.

artificial r., induced r., the r. of isotopes that exist only because man-made through the bombardment of naturally occurring isotopes by subatomic particles, or high levels of x- or gamma radiation.

radioautography (ra'dĭ-o-aw-tog'rā-fĭ). Autoradiography.

radiobicipital (ra'dĭ-o-bi-sip'ĭtal). Relating to the radius and the biceps muscle.

ra'diobiol'ogy. The biologic study of the effects of ionizing radiation upon living things.

ra'diocar'diogram. A graphic record of the concentration of injected radioisotope within the cardiac chambers.

ra'diocardiog'raphy. The technique of recording or interpreting radiocardiograms.

ra'diocar'pal. Cubitocarpal. **1.** Relating to the radius and the bones of the carpus. **2.** On the radial or lateral side of the carpus.

radiochemistry (ra'dĭ-o-kem'ĭs-trĭ). The science that uses radionuclides and their properties to study chemical applications and problems.

radiocinematography (ra'dĭ-o-sin'e-mă-tog'rā-fĭ) [radio- + G. *kinēma*, motion, + *graphō*, to write]. Taking a moving picture of the movements of organs as revealed by an radiographic examination.

radiocurable (ra'dĭ-o-kūr'ă-bl). Curable by irradiation.

ra'diodermati'tis. Dermatitis due exposure to ionizing radiation.

ra'diodiagno'sis. Diagnosis by means of x-rays.

radiofrequency (ra'dĭ-o-fre'kwen-sĭ). Radiant energy of a certain frequency.

radiogold colloid. A radioactive isotope of gold emitting negative beta particles and gamma radiation, with a half-life of 2.7 days; used for irradiation of closed serous cavities in the palliative treatment of ascites and pleural effusion due to metastatic malignancies, and for liver scans.

radiogram (ra'dĭ-o-gram) [radio- + G. *gramma*, something written]. Radiograph.

radiograph (ra'dĭ-o-graf) [radio- + G. *graphō*, write]. Radiogram; roentgenogram; the sensitized film or plate upon which a shadow image is produced by radiography.

bitewing r., intraoral dental film adapted to show the coronal portion and cervical third of the root of the teeth in near occlusion.

panoramic r., a radiographic view of the maxillae and mandible extending from the left to the right glenoid fossae.

ra'diograph'ic. Pertaining to a radiograph or to radiography.

radiography (ra'dĭ-og'rā-fĭ). Roentgenography; examination of any part of the body for diagnostic purposes by means of x-rays, the record of the findings being impressed upon a photographic plate or film.

electron r., a radiographic imaging process in which the incident x-radiation is converted to a latent charge image subsequently developed by a special printing process; it improves detail enhancement by the virtual absence of background fog and image noise.

serial r., several x-ray exposures, over a period of time, of a region under study.

radioimmunity (ra'dĭ-o-ĭ-mu'nĭ-tĭ). Lessened sensitivity to radiation.

radioimmunoassay (ra'dĭ-o-im'u-no-as'sā). An immunological procedure in which radioisotope-labeled antigen is reacted with specific antiserum and an aliquant part of the same antiserum previously treated with test fluid; any specific substance in the test fluid sample would have reacted with antibody and, accordingly, a greater quantity of free, labeled antigen in the test fluid, with reference to the specific antiserum, would be a measure of the substance in the test fluid sample.

radioimmunodiffusion (ra'dĭ-o-im'u-no-dī-fu'zhun). A method for the study of antigen-antibody reactions by gel diffusion using radioisotope-labeled antigen or antibody.

radioimmunoelectrophoresis (ra'dĭ-o-im'u-no-e-lek'-tro-fo-re'sis). Immunoelectrophoresis in which the antigen or antibody is labeled with a radioisotope, as, for example, in testing for insulin-binding antibodies by treating the test serum with radioactive iodine-labeled insulin, subjecting the mixture (antigen) to electrophoresis, precipitating the separated immunoglobulins with immunoglobulin-specific antiserum, and, then, with radiosensitive film, testing for bound insulin in the precipitates.

radioisotope (ra'dĭ-o-i'so-tōp). An unstable isotope that decays to a stable state by emitting radiation.

radiolesion (ra'dĭ-o-le'zhun). A lesion produced by ionizing radiation.

radioligand (ra'dĭ-o-lig'and). A molecule with a radionuclide tracer attached; usually used for radioimmunoassay procedures.

radiologic, radiological (ra-di-o-loj'ĭk, -loj'ĭ-kal). Pertaining to radiology.

radiologist (ra-di-ol'o-jist). Roentgenologist; a specialist in the diagnostic and/or therapeutic use of x-rays and other forms of radiant energy.

radiology (ra-dĭ-ol'o-jĭ) [radio- + G. *logos*, study]. Roentgenology; science concerned with radiant energy, with the chemical and other actions of rays proceeding from luminous bodies, and with the sources of these rays.

radiolucency (ra'dĭ-o-lu'sen-sĭ). The state of being radiolucent.

radiolucent (ra'dĭ-o-lu'sent) [radio- + L. *lucens,* shining]. Neither wholly penetrable nor wholly impenetrable by x-rays or other forms of radiation.

radiometer (ra-dĭ-om'ĕ-ter) [radio- + G. *metron,* measure]. A device for determining the penetrative power of x-rays.

radiomimetic (ra'dĭ-o-mĭ-met'ik) [radio- + G. *mimētikos,* imitative]. Imitating the action of radiation, as in the case of chemicals such as nitrogen mustards which affect cells as high-energy radiation does.

ra'dionecro'sis. Necrosis due to excessive exposure to radiation.

radioneuritis (ra'dĭ-o-nu-ri'tis). Neuritis due to excessive exposure to radiation.

radionuclide (ra'dĭ-o-nu'klid). A nuclide of artificial or natural origin that exhibits radioactivity.

radiopacity (ra-di-o-pas'ĭ-tĭ). State of being radiopaque.

radiopaque (ra-dĭ-o-pāk') [radio- + Fr. opaque fr. L. *opacus,* shady]. Exhibiting relative impenetrability by x-rays or any other form of radiation.

radioparency (ra-dĭ-o-păr'en-sĭ). State of being radioparent.

radioparent (ra-dĭ-o-păr'ent). Penetrable by x-rays or other forms of radiation.

ra'diopathol'ogy. A branch of radiology or pathology concerned with the effects of radioactive substances on cells and tissues.

ra'diopelvim'etry. Measurement of the pelvis by radiography.

radiopharmaceuticals (ra'dĭ-o-far-mă-su'tĭ-kalz). Radioactive chemical or pharmaceutical preparations, used as diagnostic or therapeutic agents.

radiophylaxis (ra'dĭ-o-fi-lak'sis) [radio- + G. *phylaxis,* protection]. The lessened effect of radiation after a previous small dose of radiation.

ra'diorecep'tor. A receptor that normally responds to radiant energy such as light or heat.

ra'dioresis'tant. Indicating cells, *e.g.,* of a new growth, that are not destroyed by exposure to radiations.

radioscopy (ra'dĭ-os'ko-pĭ) [radio- + G. *skopeō,* to view]. Fluoroscopy.

radiosens'itive. Affected by radiation.

ra'diosensitiv'ity. The condition of being readily acted upon by radioactive forces.

ra'diotelem'etry. See telemetry; biotelemetry.

ra'diotherapeu'tic. Relating to radiotherapy or to radiotherapeutics.

ra'diotherapeu'tics. The study and use of radiotherapeutic agents.

ra'diother'apist. One who practices radiotherapy or is knowledgable in radiotherapeutics.

ra'diother'apy. The medical specialty concerned with the use of electromagnetic or particulate radiations in the treatment of disease.

ra'diother'my [radio- + G. *thermē,* heat]. Diathermy effected by heat from radiant sources.

radiotoxemia (ra'dĭ-o-tok-se'mĭ-ah) [radio- + G. *toxikon,* poison, + *haima,* blood]. Radiation sickness caused by the products of disintegration produced by the action of x-rays or other forms of activity and by the depletion of certain cells and enzyme systems.

ra'diotranspar'ent. Allowing transmission of radiant energy.

ra'diotrop'ic [radio- + G. *tropē,* a turning]. Affected by radiation.

radisectomy (ra-dĭsek'to-mĭ) [L. *radix,* root, + G. *ektomē,* excision]. Root *amputation.*

ra'dium [L. *radius,* ray]. A metallic element, symbol Ra, atomic weight 226.05, extracted from pitchblende; its therapeutic action is similar to that of x-rays and is applied as one of its salts: the bromide, carbonate, chloride, and sulfate.

radius, pl. **radii** (ra'dĭ-us, ra'dĭ-i) [L. spoke of a wheel, rod, ray]. **1.** A straight line passing from the center to the periphery of a circle. **2** [NA]. The lateral and shorter of the two bones of the forearm.

radix, pl. **radices** (ra'diks, ra'dĭ-sēz) [L.] [NA]. Root; the primary or beginning portion of a part or organ buried in a tissue or by which it arises from another structure.

    ra'dices crania'les [NA], cranial roots; the roots of the accessory nerve which arise from the medulla.

    r. den'tis [NA], root of tooth; that part below the neck of the tooth, covered by cementum rather than enamel, and attached by the periodontal ligament to the alveolar bone.

    r. dorsa'lis [NA], dorsal or posterior root; the sensory root of a spinal nerve.

    r. lin'guae [NA], root of tongue; the posterior attached portion of the tongue.

    r. pe'nis [NA], root of penis; the proximal attached part of the penis, including the two crura and the bulb.

    r. pi'li, hair root; the part of a hair embedded in the hair follicle.

    r. pulmo'nis [NA], root of lung; all the structures entering or leaving the lung at the hilum, forming a pedicle invested with the pleura.

    ra'dices spina'les [NA], spinal roots; the roots of the accessory nerve which arise from the ventrolateral part of the first five segments of the spinal cord.

    r. un'guis [NA], root of nail; the proximal end of the nail, concealed under a fold of skin.

    r. ventra'lis [NA], ventral or anterior root; the motor root of a spinal nerve.

ra'don. A radioactive element, symbol Rn, atomic no. 86, atomic weight 222, resulting from the decay of radium.

rale (rahl) [Fr. rattle]. Ambiguous term for an added sound heard on auscultation of the chest; used by some to denote rhonchus and by others for crepitation.

    amphoric r., a sound associated with the movement of fluid in a lung cavity communicating with a bronchus.

cavernous r., a hollow bubbling sound caused by air entering a cavity partly filled with fluid.

crepitant r., a fine bubbling or crackling sound produced by the presence of a very thin secretion in the smaller bronchial tubes.

dry r., a sound produced by a constriction in a bronchial tube or the presence of a viscid secretion narrowing the lumen.

gurgling r., coarse sound heard over large cavities or over trachea nearly filled with secretions.

moist r., a bubbling sound caused by the pressure of a fluid secretion in the bronchial tubes or a cavity.

sibilant r., a whistling sound caused by the presence of a viscid secretion narrowing the lumen of a bronchus.

sonorous r., a cooing or snoring sound often produced by the vibration of a projecting mass of viscid secretion in a large bronchus.

ra′mal. Relating to a ramus.

rami (ra′mi) [L.]. Plural of ramus.

ramification (ram′ĭ-fĭ-ka′shun). A branching.

ramify (fam′ĭ-fi) [L. *ramus*, branch, + *facio*, to make]. Arborize; to branch.

ramisection (ram-ĭ-sek′shun) [L. *ramus*, branch, + L. *sectio*, section]. Section of the communicating branches of the sympathetic nervous system.

rami′tis [L. *ramus*, branch, + G. suffix *-itis*, inflammation]. Inflammation of a ramus.

ramose, ramous (ra′mōs, ra′mus) [L. *ramosus*, fr. *ramus*, a branch]. Branching.

ramulus, pl. **ramuli** (ram′u-lus, -li) [L. dim. of *ramus*, a branch]. A small branch or twig; one of the terminal divisions of a ramus.

ra′mus, pl. **ra′mi** [L.] [NA]. **1.** A branch. **2.** One of the primary divisions of a nerve or blood vessel. Arterial and nerve branches are also given under the major nerve (see nervus) or artery (see arteria). **3.** A part of an irregularly shaped bone (less slender than a "process") that forms an angle with the main body. **4.** One of the primary divisions of a cerebral sulcus.

r. anastomot′icus, anastomotic branch; a blood vessel that interconnects two neighboring vessels.

ra′mi communican′tes, sing. **ra′mus commu′nicans** [NA], communicating branches; bundles of nerve fibers passing from one nerve to join another.

rancid (ran′sid) [L. *rancidus,* stinking, rank]. Having a disagreeable odor and taste, usually characterizing fat that is undergoing oxidation or bacterial decomposition.

range. A statistical measure of the dispersion or variation of values determined by the endpoint values.

ranine (ra′nīn) [L. *rana,* a frog]. **1.** Relating to a frog. **2.** Relating to the undersurface of the tongue.

ranula (ran′u-lah) [L. tadpole, dim. of *rana,* frog]. **1.** Hypoglottis. **2.** Sublingual cyst; sialocele; ptyalocele; a cystic tumor of the undersurface of the tongue, or floor of the mouth due to obstruction of the duct of the sublingual glands.

r. pancreat′ica, a cystic tumor caused by obstruction of the pancreatic duct.

ran′ular. Relating to a ranula.

rape (rāp) [L. *rapio*, to seize, to drag away]. **1.** Sexual intercourse with a woman by force or without her legal consent. **2.** To perform such an act.

raphe (ra′fe) [G. *rhaphē,* suture seam] [NA]. Rhaphe; the line of union of two contiguous, bilaterally symmetrical structures.

anogenital r., in the male embryo the line of closure of the genital folds and swellings extending from the anus to the tip of the penis; in the adult, differentiated into three regions: perineal, scrotal, and penile r.

median longitudinal r. of tongue, *sulcus* medianus linguae.

r. pala′ti [NA], palatine r.; palatine ridge; a rather narrow, low elevation in the center of the hard palate that extends from the incisive papilla posteriorly over the entire length of the mucosa of the hard palate.

r. pe′nis [NA], continuation of the r. of the scrotum onto the underside of the penis.

r. perine′i [NA], central anteroposterior line of the perineum, most marked in the male, being continuous with the r. of the scrotum.

r. scro′ti [NA], a central line, like a cord, running over the scrotum from the anus to the root of the penis, marking the position of the septum scroti.

rapport (rap-or′) [Fr.]. A feeling of relationship, especially when characterized by emotional affinity.

rapture of the deep. A psychosis seen in deep-sea divers and others subjected to sensory deprivation and disorientation, and excessive blood levels of nitrogen.

rarefaction (rār′ĕ-fak′shun) [L. *rarus,* thin, + *facio,* to make]. Expansion; the condition of becoming or being light or less dense.

RAS Reticular activating *system.*

rash [O. Fr. *rasche,* skin eruption, fr. L. *rado,* pp. *rasus,* to scratch, scrape]. A cutaneous eruption.

butterfly r., a scaling lesion on each cheek, joined by a narrow band across the nose; seen in lupus erythematosus and seborrheic dermatitis.

diaper r., diaper *dermatitis.*

drug r., drug *eruption.*

heat r., *miliaria* rubra.

raspatory (ras′pă-tōr′ĭ) [L. *raspatorium*]. An instrument used for scraping a bone.

RAST Radioallergosorbent *test.*

rate (rāt) [L. *ratum,* a reckoning]. A record of the measurement of an event or process in terms of its relation to some fixed standard; measurement expressed as the ratio of one quantity to another.

basal metabolic r. (BMR), basal *metabolism.*

birth r., the precise number of births for a year related to an exact population and place.

death r., mortality r.

erythrocyte sedimentation r. (ESR), the rate of settling of red blood cells in anticoagulated blood utilizing the Westergren method.

fatality r., mortality r.

glomerular filtration r. (GFR), the volume of water filtered out of the plasma through glomerular capillary walls into Bowman's capsules per unit time; it is considered to be equivalent to inulin clearance.

growth r., absolute or relative growth increase, expressed in units of time.

heart r., r. of the heart's beat, invariably recorded as the number of beats per minute.

infant mortality r., the number of deaths in the first year of life divided by the number of live births occurring in the same population during the same period of time.

morbidity r., the proportion of patients with a particular disease during a given year per given unit of population.

mortality r., mortality (2); death or fatality r.; the ratio of the total number of deaths to the total population of a given community, usually expressed as deaths per 1000, 10,000, or 100,000 population.

neonatal mortality r., the number of deaths in the first 28 days of life divided by the number of live births occurring in the same population during the same period of time.

pulse r., r. of the pulse as observed in an artery; invariably recorded as beats per minute.

respiration r., frequency of breathing, recorded as the number of breaths per minute.

sedimentation r., the sinking velocity of blood cells, *i.e.,* the degree of rapidity with which the red cells sink in a mass of drawn blood.

ratio (ra'shĭ-o) [L. *ratio* (*ration-*) a reckoning, reason]. An expression of the relation of one quantity to another.

albumin-globulin r. (A/G r.), the r. of albumin to globulin in the serum or in the urine in kidney disease; the normal r. in the serum is approximately 1.55.

ALT:AST r., the r. of serum alanine aminotransferase to serum aspartate aminotransferase; elevated serum levels of both enzymes characterize hepatic disease; when both levels are abnormally elevated and the ALT:AST r. is greater than 1.0, severe hepatic necrosis or alcoholic hepatic disease is likely; when the r. is less than 1.0, an acute non-alcoholic condition is favored.

amylase-creatinine clearance r., a test for the diagnosis of acute pancreatitis, determined by measuring amylase and creatinine in serum and urine: in acute pancreatitis the r. is said to be greater than 0.05 or 5% and to be specific for acute pancreatitis.

cardiothoracic r., the transverse diameter of the heart, determined by x-ray, compared with that of the thoracic cage.

‑traction r. (E), the fraction of a substance ‑ved from the blood flowing through the kid-

ney; calculated from the formula $(A-V)/A$, where and V, respectively, are the concentrations of th substance in arterial and renal venous plasma.

IRI/G r., the r. of immunoreactive insulin serum or plasma glucose; in hypoglycemic states r. of less than 0.3 is usual with the exception of th hypoglycemia due to insulinoma, where the r. often higher than 0.3.

lecithin/sphingomyelin r. (L/S r.), a r. used t determine fetal pulmonary maturity, found by test ing the amniotic fluid; when the lungs are mature lecithin exceeds sphingomyelin by two to one.

M:E r., the r. of myeloid to erythroid precursor in bone marrow; normally it varies from 2:1 to 4:1 an increased r. is found in infectious chroni myelogenous leukemia or erythroid hypoplasia; decreased r. may mean a depression of leukopoiesi or normoblastic hyperplasia depending on the over all cellularity of the bone marrow.

respiratory exchange r. (R), the r. of the net output of carbon dioxide to the simultaneous net uptake of oxygen at a given site, both expressed as moles or STPD volumes per unit time; in the steady state, respiratory exchange r. is equal to the respiratory quotient of metabolic processes.

therapeutic r., the r. of the maximally tolerated dose of a drug to the minimal curative or effective dose; LD_{50} divided by ED_{50}.

rational (rash'un-al) [L. *rationalis,* fr. *ratio,* reason]. 1. Pertaining to reasoning or to the higher thought processes; based on objective or scientific knowledge, in contrast to empirical. 2. Influenced by reasoning rather than by emotion. 3. Having the reasoning faculties; not delirious or comatose.

rationalization (ră-shun-al-ĭ-za'shun) [L. *ratio,* reason]. In psychoanalysis, a postulated defense mechanism through which irrational behavior, motives, or feelings are made to appear reasonable.

rat'tlesnake. A member of the crotalid genera *Crotalus* and *Sistrurus,* characterized by possession of cuticular warning rattles at the tip of the tail.

RAV Rous-associated *virus.*

ray [L. *radius*]. 1. A line of light, heat, or other form of radiation. 2. A part or line that extends radially from a structure.

alpha r.'s, fast-moving streams of minute particles of matter consisting of helium nuclei, containing two protons and two neutrons, and consequently carrying a double positive charge, emitted from radioactive bodies with enormous velocity but with less penetrative power than beta r.'s.

beta r.'s, electrons emitted with great velocity in radioactive decomposition; they have properties identical with cathode r.'s and greater penetrative power than alpha r.'s.

cathode r.'s, a stream of electrons emitted from the negative electrode (cathode) in a Crookes tube; their bombardment of the glass wall of the tube or of the anode gives rise to x-rays.

gamma r.'s, electromagnetic radiation emitted from radioactive substances; analogous to the x-rays but originating from the nucleus rather than the orbital shell and are not deflected by a magnet.

grenz r. (grents) [Ger. *Grenze*, borderline, boundary], very soft x-rays closely allied to the ultraviolet r.'s in their wavelength and in their biologic action upon tissues.

hard r.'s, r.'s of short wavelength and great penetrability.

medullary r., Ferrein's pyramid; the center of the renal lobule, consisting of ascending or descending limbs of the nephronic loop or collecting tubules.

roentgen r., x-ray.

soft r.'s, r.'s of relatively long wavelength and slight penetrability.

x-r., see under x.

Rb Rubidium.

rbc, RBC Red blood *cell;* red *blood count.*

RBF Renal blood flow. See effective renal blood *flow.*

R.C.P. Royal College of Physicians.

R.C.S. Royal College of Surgeons.

R.D. *Reaction* of degeneration.

R.E. Right eye.

Re Rhenium.

re-. Prefix fr. L. meaning again or backward.

react (re-akt) [Mod. L. *reactus*]. To take part in or to undergo a chemical reaction.

reactant (re-ak'tant). A substance taking part in a chemical reaction.

reaction (re-ak'shun). **1.** The response of living tissue or an organism to a stimulus. **2.** The color change effected in litmus and certain other organic pigments by contact with various substances (acids or alkalies); also the property that such substances possess of producing this change. **3.** In chemistry, the intermolecular action of two or more substances upon each other, whereby these substances are caused to disappear, new ones being formed in their place. **4.** In immunology, *in vivo* or *in vitro* action of antibody on specific antigen, with or without involvement of complement or other components of the immunological system. See also response; test.

acute situational r., stress r.

adverse r., a result of drug therapy which is neither intended nor expected in normal therapeutic use and which causes significant, sometimes life-threatening morbidity.

alarm r., the various phenomena which the body exhibits as an adaptive response to injury or stress; first phase of the general adaptation syndrome.

allergic r., a local or general r. of an organism to internal or external contact with a specific allergen to which the organism has been previously sensitized.

anamnestic r., augmented production of an antibody due to previous response of the subject to stimulus by the same antigen.

antigen-antibody r., the phenomenon, occurring *in vitro* or *in vivo,* of antibody combining with

antigen of the type that stimulated the formation of the antibody, thereby resulting in agglutination, precipitation, complement fixation, greater susceptibility to ingestion and destruction by phagocytes, or neutralization of exotoxin.

anxiety r., a psychological r. or experience involving the apprehension of danger accompanied by a feeling of dread and such physical symptoms as restlessness and tachycardia, in the absence of a clearly identifiable fear stimulus; when chronic, called anxiety neurosis.

Arias-Stella r., Arias-Stella *phenomenon.*

Bence Jones r., the classic means of identifying Bence Jones protein, which precipitates when urine (from patients with this type of proteinuria) is gradually warmed to 45 to 70°C and redissolves as the urine is heated to near boiling; as the specimen cools, the Bence Jones protein precipitates in the indicated range of temperature, and redissolves as the temperature of the specimen becomes less than 30 to 35°C.

bi-bi r., a r. catalyzed by a single enzyme in which two substrates and two products are involved; the ping-pong mechanism may be involved in such a r.

biuret r., the formation of biuret (NH_2CONH-$CONH_2$), which gives a violet color due to the r. of a polypeptide of more than three amino acids with $CuSO_4$ in strongly alkaline solution; dipeptides and amino acids (except histidine, serine, and threonine) do not so react; used for the detection and quantitation of polypeptides, or proteins, in biological fluids.

catastrophic r., disorganized behavior that is the response to a severe shock or threatening situation with which the person cannot cope.

cell-mediated r., immunological r. of the delayed type, involving chiefly T-lymphocytes.

chain r., a self-perpetuating r. in which a product of one step in the r. itself serves to bring about the next step in the r., and so on.

conjunctival r., ophthalmic r.; a r. analogous to a skin r. when specific antigen (allergen) is placed on the conjunctiva of a subject sensitive to the allergen, convalescent from the specific disease, or chronically infected.

constitutional r., a generalized r. in contrast to a focal or local r.; in allergy the immediate or delayed response, following the introduction of an allergen, occurring at sites remote from that of injection.

conversion r., conversion *hysteria.*

cross r., a specific r. between an antiserum and an antigen complex other than the antigen complex that evoked the various specific antibodies of the antiserum, due to the two complexes including among their respective antigenic determinants at least one that is included also among the determinants of the other complex.

cytotoxic r., an immunologic (allergic) r. in which noncytotropic IgG or IgM antibody combines with specific antigen on cell surfaces; the resulting complex initiates the activation of complement which causes cell lysis or other damage, or which, in the absence of complement, may lead to phagocytosis or may enhance T lymphocyte involvement.

r. of degeneration (D.R. or R.D.), the electrical r. in a degenerated nerve and the muscles supplied by it.

delayed r., a local or generalized response that begins 24 to 48 hours after exposure to an antigen (allergen, immunogen) to which the individual has been sensitized (immunized).

dissociative r., r. characterized by such dissociative behavior as amnesia, fugues, sleepwalking, and dream states.

false-negative r., an erroneous or mistakenly negative response.

false-positive r., an erroneous or mistakenly positive response.

focal r., local r.; a r. which occurs at the point of entrance of an infecting organism or of an injection.

general adaptation r., see general adaptation *syndrome.*

graft versus host r., graft versus host *disease.*

hemiopic pupillary r., Wernicke's r.

Herxheimer's r., Jarisch-Herxheimer r.; an inflammatory r. in syphilitic tissues induced in certain cases by specific treatment with Salvarsan, mercury, or antibiotics; believed to be due to a rapid release of treponemal antigen with an associated allergic reaction in the patient.

immediate r., local or generalized response that begins within a few minutes to about an hour after exposure to an antigen (allergen, immunogen) to which the individual has been sensitized (immunized).

immune r., antigen-antibody r. indicating a certain degree of resistance usually in reference to the 36- to 48-hour reaction in vaccination against smallpox; because the degree of resistance indicated by the r. is not true immunity and may disappear relatively rapidly there is a tendency to refer to the immune r. as an allergic r.

Jarisch-Herxheimer r., Herxheimer's r.

leukemoid r., see *leukemoid reaction.*

local r., focal r.

mixed agglutination r., mixed agglutination; immune agglutination in which the aggregates contain cells of two different kinds but with common antigenic determinants; used to identify isoantigens.

Neufeld r., Neufeld capsular *swelling.*

ninhydrin r., triketohydrindene r.; a test for proteins, peptones, peptides, and amino acids possessing free carboxyl and α-amino groups; a blue color reaction is used to quantitate free amino acids.

ophthalmic r., conjunctival r.

Prausnitz-Küstner r., the classic demonstration of homocytotropic antibody, a test based on passive transfer of allergic sensitivity: blood serum from an allergic individual is injected into the skin of a normal person; 48 hours later the injected site shows an urticarial r. when injected with antigens to which

the donor is allergic, other parts of the recipient's skin show no response.

primary r., vaccinia (2).

quellung r. [Ger. swelling], Neufeld capsular *swelling.*

reversed Prausnitz-Küstner r., the appearance of an urticarial r. at the site of injection when serum containing reaginic antibody is injected into the skin of a person in whom the allergen is already present.

Schultz-Charlton r., the specific blanching of a scarlatinal rash at the site of intracutaneous injection of scarlatina antiserum.

serum r., serum *sickness.*

specific r., the phenomena produced by an agent that is identical with or immunologically related to the one that has already caused an alteration in capacity of the tissue to react.

stress r., acute situational r.; an acute emotional r. related to extreme environmental stress.

symptomatic r., an allergic response similar to the original one, but occurring after the use of a test or therapeutic dose of an allergen or atopen.

vaccinoid r., accelerated r.

Wassermann r. (W.r.), Wassermann *test.*

Weil-Felix r., the agglutination of the X-strains of *Proteus vulgaris,* especially X-19, with serum of patients with certain rickettsial diseases.

Wernicke's r., hemiopic or hemiopic pupillary r.; Wernicke's sign; in hemianopsia, a r. due to injury of the optic tract, consisting in loss of the light reflex when the light is shown on the blind side of the retina, and preservation of the same when the light strikes the sensitive side.

wheal-and-flare r., the characteristic immediate r. observed in the skin test: within 10 to 15 minutes after injection of antigen (allergen), an irregular, blanched, elevated wheal appears, surrounded by an area of erythema (flare).

reactivate (re-ak'tĭ-vāt). To render active again; said of an inactivated immune serum to which normal serum (complement) is added.

reactivity (re-ak-tiv'ĭ-tĭ). 1. The property of reacting, chemically or in any other sense. 2. The process of reacting.

readthrough (rēd'thru). In molecular biology, transcription of a nucleic acid sequence beyond its normal termination sequence.

reagent (re-a'jent) [Mod. L. *reagens*]. Any substance added to a solution of another substance to participate in a chemical reaction.

reality testing. In psychiatry, the ego function by which the objective or real world and one's relationship to it are evaluated and appreciated.

reamer (re'mer) [A.S. *ryman*, to widen]. A rotating finishing or drilling tool used to shape or enlarge a hole.

rebreath'ing. Inhalation of part or all of gases previously exhaled.

recalcification (re-kal-sĭ-fĭ-ka'shun). The restoration to the tissues of lost calcium salts.

re'call. The process of remembering thoughts, words, and actions of a past event in an attempt to recapture actual happenings.

recan'aliza'tion. 1. Restoration of a lumen in a blood vessel following thrombotic occlusion, by organization of the thrombus with formation of new channels. **2.** Spontaneous restoration of the continuity of the lumen of any occluded duct or tube.

receptaculum, pl. **receptacula** (re'sep-tak'u-lum, -lah) [L. fr. *re-cipio,* pp. *-ceptus,* to receive]. Reservoir; a receptacle.

receptor (re-sep'tor) [L. receiver, fr. *recipio,* to receive]. **1.** In Ehrlich's theory of immunity, one of the side chains of the cell which combine with foreign substances, conceived as being of three orders; although much of his theory is now obsolete, the concept of specific sites (*i.e.,* molecular configurations) of attachment continues to play a major role in immunology and pharmacology. **2.** Any one of the various sensory nerve endings in the skin, deep tissues, viscera, and special sense organs.

  adrenergic r.'s, adrenoreceptors; reactive components of effector tissues, most of which are innervated by adrenergic postganglionic fibers of the sympathetic nervous sytem, which can be activated by norepinephrine and/or epinephrine and by various adrenergic drugs, and results in a change in effector tissue function; adrenergic r.'s are divided into α-r.'s and βr.'s, on the basis of their response to various adrenergic activating and blocking agents.

  α-adrenergic r.'s, adrenergic r.'s in effector tissues capable of selective activation and blockade of drugs, conceptually differing from the ability of certain agents, such as phenoxybenzamine, to block only some adrenergic r.'s and of other agents, such as methoxamine, to activate only the same adrenergic r.'s; their activation results in physiological responses such as increased peripheral vascular resistance, mydriasis, and contraction of pilomotor muscles.

  β-adrenergic r.'s, adrenergic r.'s in effector tissues capable of selective activation and blockade by drugs, conceptually derived from the ability of certain agents, such as propranolol, to block only some adrenergic r.'s and of other agents, such as isoproterenol, to activate only the same adrenergic r.'s; their activation results in physiological responses such as increases in cardiac rate and force of contraction (β_1), and relaxation of bronchial and vascular smooth muscle (β_2).

  cholinergic r.'s, chemical sites in effector cells or at synapses through which acetylcholine exerts its action.

  opiate r.'s, regions of the brain which have the capacity to bind morphine; some, along the aqueduct of Sylvius and in the center median, are in areas related to pain, but others, as in the striatum, are not related.

stretch r.'s, r.'s that are sensitive to elongation, especially those in Golgi tendon organs and muscle spindles, but also in visceral organs such as the stomach, small intestine, and urinary bladder.

recess (re'ses) [L. *recessus,* a withdrawing or receding]. A small hollow or indentation.

recession (re-sesh'un) [L. *recessio* (see recessus)]. A withdrawal or retreating of tissue. See also retraction.

recessive (re-ses'iv). **1.** Drawing away; receding. **2.** In genetics, denoting an allele possessed by one parent of a hybrid which is not expressed in the latter because of suppression by a contrasting allele (dominant) from the other parent.

recessus, pl. **recessus** (re-ses'sus) [L. a withdrawing, a receding] [NA]. Recess.

recidivation (re-sid-ĭ-va'shun) [L. *recidivus,* falling back, recurring, fr. *recido,* to fall back, fr. *cado,* to fall]. Relapse of a disease, symptom or behavioral pattern such as an illegal activity for which one was previously hospitalized or imprisoned.

recidivism (re-sid'ĭ-vizm) [L. *recidivus,* recurring]. The tendency of an individual toward recidivation.

recidivist (re-sid'ĭ-vist). A person who tends toward recidivation.

recipe (res'ĭ-pī) [L. imperative *recipio,* to receive]. **1.** Take; the superscription of a prescription, usually indicated by the sign ℞ . **2.** A prescription or formula.

reclination (rek'lĭ-na'shun) [L. *reclino,* pp. *-atus,* to bend back]. Turning the cataractous lens over into the vitreous to remove it from the line of vision; distinguished from couching, in which the lens is simply depressed into the vitreous.

recombinant (re-kom'bĭ-nant). **1.** A microbe, or strain, that has received chromosomal parts from different parental strains. **2.** Pertaining to or denoting such organisms.

recombinant DNA. DNA resulting from the insertion into the chain, by chemical or biological means, of a sequence (a whole or partial chain of DNA) not originally (biologically) present in that chain.

recombination (re-kom'bĭ-ha'shun). In microbial genetics, the inclusion of a chromosomal part or extrachromosomal element of one microbial strain in the chromosome of another; the interchange of chromosomal parts between different microbial strains.

recon (re'kon). In genetics, the smallest unit (corresponding to a single DNA nucleotide) of recombination or crossing-over between two homologous chromosomes.

recrement (rek're-ment). [L. *recrementum,* refuse, filth, fr. re- + *cerno,* to separate]. A secretion, like saliva, that is reabsorbed after having performed its function.

recrementitious (rek're-men-tish'us). Of the nature of a recrement.

recrudescence (re-kru-des'ens) [L. *re-crudesco,* to become raw again, break out afresh]. A recurrence of a morbid process or its symptoms after a period of improvement.

recrudescent (re-kru-des'ent). Becoming active again, relating to a recrudescence.

recruitment (re-krūt'ment) [Fr. *recrutement*, fr. L. *re-cresco*, pp. *-cretus*, to grow again]. **1.** The unequal reaction of the ear to equal steps of increasing intensity, measured in decibels, when such inequality of response results in a greater than normal increment of loudness. **2.** The bringing into activity of additional motor neurons and thus causing greater activity in response to increased duration of the stimulus applied to a given receptor or afferent nerve.

rect-. See recto-.

rectal (rek'tal). Relating to the rectum.

rectalgia (rek-tal'ji-ah). Proctalgia.

rectectomy (rek-tek'to-mī). Proctectomy.

rectify (rek'tĭ-fi) [L. *rectus*, right, straight]. **1.** To correct. **2.** To purify or refine by distillation; usually implies repeated distillations.

rectitis (rek-ti'tis). Proctitis.

recto-, rect-. Combining forms denoting the rectum. See also procto-.

rectocele (rek'to-sēl) [recto- + G. *kēlē*, tumor, hernia]. Proctocele.

rectococcypexy (rek'to-kok'sĭ-pek-sĭ). Proctococcypexy.

rectopexy (rek'to-pek-sĭ). Proctopexy.

rectoplasty (rek'to-plas-tĭ). Proctoplasty.

rectoscope (rek'to-skōp). Proctoscope.

rectosigmoid (rek-to-sig'moyd). The rectum and sigmoid colon considered as a unit; also applied to the junction of the sigmoid colon and rectum.

rectostenosis (rek'to-stē-no'sis). Proctostenosis.

rectostomy (rek-tos'to-mī). Proctostomy.

rectotomy (rek-tot'o-mī). Proctotomy.

rectum, pl. **rectums, recta** (rek'tum, rek'tah) [L. *rectus*, straight, pp. of *rego*, to make straight] [NA]. The terminal portion of the digestive tube, extending from the sigmoid colon to the anal canal.

recumbent (re-kum'bent) [L. *recumbo*, to lie back, recline, fr. *re-*, back, + *cubo*, to lie]. Leaning; reclining; lying down.

recuperate (re-ku'per-āt) [L. *recupero* (or *recip-*), pp. *-atus*, to take again, recover]. To recover; to regain health and strength.

recurrence (re-kŭr'ens) [L. *re-curro*, to run back, recur]. **1.** A return of the symptoms, occurring as a phenomenon in the natural history of the disease, as seen in recurrent fever. **2.** Relapse.

recurrent (re-kŭr'ent). **1.** In anatomy, turning back on itself. **2.** Returned; denoting symptoms or lesions reappearing after an intermission or remission.

recurvation (re-ker-va'shun) [L. *re-curvus*, bent back]. A backward bending or flexure.

redintegration (re-din-tĕ-gra'shun) [L. *red-integro*, pp. *-atus*, to make whole again]. **1.** Restoration of lost or injured parts. **2.** The recalling of a whole experience on the basis of a stimulus representing some item or portion of the original circumstances of the experience.

redox (red'oks). Oxidation-reduction.

reduce (re-dūs') [L. *re-duco*, pp. *-ductus*, to lead back, restore, reduce]. **1.** To perform reduction (1). **2.** In chemistry, to initiate a reaction involving a gain of electrons by the substance in question; the substance supplying the electrons or the hydrogen, or removing the oxygen, is itself oxidized in so doing.

reducible (re-du'sĭ-bl) Capable of being reduced.

reductant (re-duk'tant). The substance oxidized in the course of performing reduction; the reduced component of an oxidation-reduction enzyme system.

reductase (re-duk'tās). An enzyme that catalyzes a reduction.

reduction (re-duk'shun) [L. *reductio*, see reduce]. **1.** Repositioning; restoration, by surgical or manipulative procedures, of a part to its normal anatomical relation. **2.** In chemistry, the gain of one or more electrons by an ion or compound.

  r. of chromosomes, the process occurring during the meiotic cell division in gametogenesis whereby one member of each homologous pair of chromosomes is distributed to each sperm or ovum; union of the sperm and ovum restores the diploid or somatic number in the one-cell zygote.

  closed r. of fractures, r. by manipulation of bone, without incision in the skin.

  open r. of fractures, r. by manipulation of bone, after incision in skin and muscle over the site of the fracture.

reduplication (re'du-plĭ-ka'shun) [L. *reduplicatio*, fr. *re-*, again, + *duplico*, to double]. **1.** A redoubling. **2.** A duplication or doubling, as of the sounds of the heart in certain morbid states or the presence of two instead of a normally, single part. **3.** A fold or duplicature.

reef'ing. Surgically reducing the extent of a tissue by folding it and securing with sutures, as in plication.

reentry (re'en'trĭ). Return of the same impulse into an area of heart muscle that it has recently activated but which is now no longer refractory, as seen in reciprocal rhythms.

refine (re-fin'). To free from impurities.

reflection (re-flek'shun) [L. *reflexio*, a bending back]. **1.** A bending back. **2.** The sending back of light or other form of radiant energy from a surface.

reflector (re-flek'tor). Any surface that reflects the waves of light, heat, or sound.

reflex (re'fleks) [L. *reflexus*, pp. of *re-flecto*, to bend back]. **1.** An involuntary reaction in response to a stimulus applied to the periphery and transmitted to the nervous centers in the brain or spinal cord. **2.** Consensual.

  abdominal r.'s, contraction of the muscles of the abdominal wall upon stimulation of the skin (superficial) or tapping neighboring bony structures (deep).

accommodation r., constriction of the pupil, convergence of the eyes, and increased convexity of the lens when the eyes view a near object.

Achilles r., Achilles tendon r., ankle r.; triceps surae r.; a contraction of the calf muscles when the tendo calcaneus is sharply struck.

anal r., contraction of the internal sphincter gripping the finger passed into the rectum.

ankle r., Achilles r.

auditory r., any r. occurring in response to a sound.

Babinski's r., Babinski's *sign* (1).

basal joint r., finger-thumb or Mayer's r.; opposition and adduction of the thumb with flexion at its metacarpophalangeal joint and extension at its interphalangeal joint, when firm passive flexion of the third, fourth, or fifth finger is made; absent in pyramidal lesions.

Bechterew-Mendel r., Mendel-Bechterew r.; percussion of the dorsum of the foot causes flexion of the toes; present in pyramidal lesions.

biceps r., contraction of the biceps muscle when its tendon is struck.

Brain's r., quadripedal extensor r.

carotid sinus r., carotid sinus *syndrome.*

celiac plexus r., arterial hypotension coincident with surgical manipulations in the upper abdomen during general anesthesia.

Chaddock r., Chaddock *sign.*

chain r., a series of r.s, each serving as a stimulus for the next.

ciliary r., contraction of the pupil in the accommodation r.

ciliospinal r., pupillary-skin r.

cochleopalpebral r., startle r. (2); a form of the wink r. in which there is a contraction of the orbicularis palpebrarum muscle when a sudden noise is made close to the ear; absent in labyrinthine disease with total deafness.

conditioned r. (CR), a r. gradually developed by training and association through frequent repetition of a definite stimulus.

conjunctival r., closure of the eyes in response to irritation of the conjunctiva.

corneal r., a contraction of the eyelids when the cornea is lightly touched.

cough r., the r. which mediates coughing in response to irritation of the larynx or tracheobronchial tree.

cremasteric r., a drawing up of the scrotum and testicle of the same side when the skin over Scarpa's triangle or on the inner side of the thigh is scratched.

crossed r., a r. movement on one side of the body in response to a stimulus applied to the opposite side.

darwinian r., the tendency of young infants to grasp a bar and hang suspended.

deep r., jerk (2); an involuntary muscular contraction following percussion of a tendon or bone.

digital r., Hoffmann's *sign* (2).

diving r., cardiovascular and metabolic adaptations that conserve oxygen in certain animals when diving in water; observed in man in apparent drowning victims who have been successfully resuscitated.

enterogastric r., peristaltic contraction of the small intestine induced by the entrance of food into the stomach.

finger-thumb r., basal joint r.

gag r., retching or gagging caused by contact of a foreign body with the mucous membrane of the fauces.

gastrocolic r., a mass movement of the contents of the colon, frequently preceded by a similar movement in the small intestine, that sometimes occurs immediately following the entrance of food into the stomach.

gastroileac r., entrance of food into the stomach causes opening of the ileocolic valve.

grasping r., grasp r., an involuntary flexion of the fingers to tactile or tendon stimulation on the palm of the hand, producing an uncontrollable grasp; usually associated with frontal lobe lesions.

Hoffmann's r., Hoffmann's *sign* (2).

intrinsic r., a r. muscular contraction elicited by the application of a stimulus, usually stretching, to the muscle itself as opposed to a muscular contraction caused by an extrinsic stimulus.

jaw r., a spasmodic contraction of the temporal muscles following a downward tap on the loosely hanging mandible; seen in corticospinal tract lesions.

knee r., knee-jerk r., patellar r.

latent r., a r. considered a normal one but which, as a rule, appears only under some pathologic circumstance that lowers its threshold.

light r., (1) pupillary r.; **(2)** red r.; a red glow reflected from the fundus of the eye when a light is cast upon the retina, as in retinoscopy; **(3)** *cone* of light.

lip r., a pouting movement of the lips provoked in young infants by tapping near the angle of the mouth.

Mayer's r., basal joint r.

Mendel-Bechterew r., Bechterew-Mendel r.

Moro's r., startle r. (1).

myotatic r., stretch r.; tonic contraction of the muscles in response to a stretching force, due to stimulation of muscle proprioceptors.

nasal r., sneezing caused by irritation of the nasal mucous membrane.

nociceptive r., any r. elicited by a painful stimulus.

orienting r., orienting response; an aspect of attending in which an organism's initial response to a change or to a novel stimulus is such that the organism becomes more sensitive to the stimulation.

palatal r., palatine r., swallowing r. induced by stimulation of the palate.

paradoxical r., any r. in which the usual response is reversed or does not conform to the pattern characteristic of the particular r.

patellar r., knee or knee-jerk r.; quadriceps r.; a sudden contraction of the anterior muscles of the thigh, caused by a smart tap on the patellar tendon while the leg hangs loosely at a right angle with the thigh.

pharyngeal r., (1) swallowing r.; (2) vomiting r.

pilomotor r., contraction of the smooth muscle of the skin resulting in "gooseflesh" caused by mild application of a tactile stimulus or by local cooling.

plantar r., the response to tactile stimulation of the ball of the foot, normally plantar flexion of the toes; the pathologic response is Babinski's *sign* (1).

proprioceptive r.'s, any r. brought about by stimulation of proprioceptors.

protective laryngeal r., closure of the glottis to prevent entry of foreign substances into the respiratory tract, usually abolished in the second state of anesthesia.

pupillary r., light r. (1); change in diameter of the pupil as a reflex response to light or to any type of stimulus.

pupillary-skin r., ciliospinal r.; dilation of the pupil following scratching of the skin of the neck.

quadriceps r., patellar r.

quadripedal extensor r., Brain's r.; extension of the arm of a hemiplegic patient when turned prone as if on all fours.

red r., light r. (2).

righting r.'s, static r.'s; r.'s which through various receptors, in labyrinth, eyes, muscles, or skin, tend to bring the body into its normal position in space and which resist any force acting to put it into a false position.

rooting r., in infants, a puckering of the lips produced by rubbing or scratching about the mouth.

Rossolimo's r., Rossolimo's sign; (1) flicking the tops of the toes from the plantar surface causes flexion of the toes; seen in lesions of the pyramidal tracts; (2) flexion of the fingers by tapping the tips of the fingers on their volar surfaces.

snout r., light tapping of closed lips near the midline causes pouting or pursing of the lips; seen in defective pyramidal innervation of facial musculature.

spinal r., a r. arc involving the spinal cord. See reflex *arc*.

startle r., (1) Moro's r.; the r. response of an infant (contraction of the limb and neck muscles) when allowed to drop a short distance through the air or startled by a sudden noise or jolt; (2) cochleopalpebral r.

static r.'s, righting r.'s.

statokinetic r., a r. that, through stimulation of the receptors in the neck muscles and semicircular canals, brings about movements of the limbs and eyes appropriate to a given movement of the head in space.

statotonic r.'s, r.'s which through labyrinthine (utricular) and muscle receptors influence the tone of the limb muscles; the former brought about by alterations in the position of the head in space, the latter by changes in the position of the head in relation to the body.

stretch r., myotatic r.

sucking r., sucking movements of an infant's lips elicited by touching them or the adjacent skin.

superficial r., any r. elicited by stimulation of the skin.

supporting r.'s, supporting *reactions*.

swallowing r., pharyngeal r. (1); the act of swallowing (second stage) induced by stimulation of the palate, fauces, or posterior pharyngeal wall.

tendon r., a myotatic or deep r. in which the muscle stretch receptors are stimulated by percussing the tendon of a muscle.

toe r., (1) strong passive flexion of the great toe excites contraction of the flexor muscles in the leg; (2) Babinski's *sign* (1).

triceps r., a sudden contraction of the triceps muscle caused by a smart tap on its tendon when the forearm hangs loosely at a right angle with the arm.

triceps surae r., Achilles r.

unconditioned r., an instinctive r. not dependent on previous learning or experience.

vestibulospinal r., the influence of vestibular stimulation on body posture.

vomiting r., pharyngeal r. (2); vomiting (contraction of the abdominal muscles with relaxation of the cardiac sphincter of the stomach and of the muscles of the throat) elicited by a variety of stimuli, especially one applied to the region of the fauces.

wink r., general term for r. closure of eyelids caused by any stimulus.

reflexogenic, reflexogenous (re′flek-so-jen′ik, -soj′ĕ-nus). Causing a reflex.

reflexograph (re-flek′so-graf) [reflex + G. *graphō*, to write]. An instrument for graphically recording a reflex.

reflexometer (re-flek-som′ĕ-ter) [reflex + G. *metron*, measure]. An instrument for measuring the force necessary to excite a reflex.

reflux (re′fluks) [L. *re-*, back, + *fluxus*, a flow]. **1.** A backward flow. See also regurgitation. **2.** In chemistry, to boil without loss of vapor because of the presence of a condenser that returns vapor as liquid.

esophageal r., gastroesophageal r., r. of stomach contents into the esophagus.

hepatojugular r., an elevation of venous pressure visible in the jugular veins and measurable in the veins of the arm, produced in active or impending congestive heart failure by firm pressure with the flat hand over the abdomen.

ureterorenal r., r. of urine from ureter into renal pelvis.

vesicoureteral r., r. of urine from bladder into ureter.

refract (re-frakt') [L. *refringo*, pp. *-fractus*, to brack up]. **1.** To bend a ray of light. **2.** To detect an error of refraction in the media of the eye and to correct it by means of lenses.

refraction (re-frak'shun) [L. *refractio* (see refract)]. Refringence. **1.** Deflection of a ray of light when it passes from one medium into another of different optical density. **2.** The act of determining the nature and degree of the refractive errors in the eye and correction of the same by lenses.

    double r., birefringence; the property of having more than one refractive index according to the direction of the transmitted light.

    dynamic r., r. of the eye during accommodation.

refractionist (re-frak'shun-ist). A person trained to measure the refraction of the eye and to determine the proper corrective lenses.

refractive (re-frak'tiv). Refringent; pertaining to refraction.

refractivity (re'frak-tiv'ĭ-tĭ). Ability of a substance to refract rays of light.

refractometer (re'frak-tom'ĕ-ter) [refraction + G. *metron*, measure]. An instrument for measuring the degree of refraction in translucent substances, especially the eye media.

refractometry (re'frak-tom'ĕ-trĭ). **1.** Measurement of the refractive index. **2.** Use of a refractometer in determining the refractive error of the eye.

refractory (re-frak'to-rĭ) [L. *refractarius*, fr. *refringo*, pp. *-fractus*, to break in pieces]. **1.** Intractable (1); obstinate (2); resistant to treatment, as of a disease. **2.** Obstinate (1).

refracture (re-frak'chur) [re- + fracture]. The breaking again of a bone that has united, after a previous fracture.

refresh (re-fresh') [O. Fr. *re-frescher*]. **1.** To renew; to cause to recuperate. **2.** To perform revivification.

refrigerant (re-frij'er-ant) [L. *re-frigero*, pr. p. *-ans*, to make cold]. **1.** Cooling; reducing slight fever. **2.** An agent that gives a sensation of coolness or relieves feverishness.

refrigeration (re-frij'er-a'shun) [L. *refrigeratio* (see refrigerant)]. The act of cooling or reducing fever.

refringence (re-frin'jens). Refraction.

refringent (re-frin'jent). Refractive.

refusion (re-fu'zhun) [L. *re-fundo*, pp. *-fusus*, to pour back]. The return to the circulation of blood which has been temporarily cut off by ligature of a limb.

regeneration (re'jen-er-a'shun) [L. *re-genero*, pp. *-atus*, to reproduce]. **1.** Reproduction or reconstitution of a lost or injured part. **2.** A form of asexual reproduction, as when a worm is divided into two or more parts, each segment is regenerated into a new individual.

regimen (rej'ĭ-men) [L. direction, rule]. A regulation of the mode of living, diet, sleep, exercise, etc., for a hygienic or therapeutic purpose.

regio, pl. **regiones** (re'jĭ-o, -o'nis, -o'nēz) [L.] [NA]. Region.

region (re'jun) [L. *regio*]. **1.** An arbitrarily defined portion of the body's surface. **2.** A portion of the body having a special nervous or vascular supply, or a part of an organ having a special function.

    abdominal r.'s, topographical subdivisions of the abdomen: right and left hypochondriac, right and left lateral, right and left inguinal, and the unpaired epigastric, umbilical and pubic regions.

    r.'s of back, topographical divisions of the back of the trunk: vertebral, sacral, scapular, infrascapular, and lumbar.

    r.'s of chest, topographical divisions of the chest: presternal, pectoral, mammary, inframammary, and axillary.

    r.'s of face, topographical divisions of the face: nasal, oral, mental, orbital, infraorbital, buccal, and zygomatic.

    r.'s of head, topographical divisions of the cranium in relation to the bones of the cranial vault: frontal, parietal, occipital, and temporal.

    r.'s of inferior limb, topographical divisions of the lower limb: buttock, thigh, knee, leg, ankle, and foot.

    r.'s of superior limb, topographical divisions of the upper limb: deltoid, arm, elbow, forearm, and hand.

regional (re'jun-al). Relating to a region.

regiones (re'jĭ-o'nēz) [L.]. Plural of regio.

regression (re-gresh'un) [L. *re-gredior*, pp. *-gressus*, to go back]. **1.** A subsidence of symptoms. **2.** A relapse; return of symptoms. **3.** Any retrograde movement or action. **4.** Return to a more primitve mode of behavior due to an inability to function adequately at a more adult level. **5.** An unconscious defense mechanism by which there occurs a return to earlier patterns of adaptation.

regres'sive. Relating to or characterized by regression.

regulation (reg'u-la'shun) [L. *regula*, a rule]. **1.** The control of the rate or manner in which a process progresses or a product is formed. **2.** In experimental embryology, the power of what remains of a very young embryo, after part of it has been destroyed, to restore its normal structure.

regurgitant (re-ger'jĭ-tant). Regurgitating; flowing backward.

regurgitate (re-ger'jĭ-tāt) [L. *re-*, back, + *gurgito*, pp. *-atus*, to flood]. **1.** To flow backward. **2.** To expel the contents of the stomach in small amounts, short of vomiting.

regurgitation (re-ger'jĭ-ta'shun) [L. *regurgitatio* (see regurgitate)]. **1.** A backward flow, as of blood through an incompetent heart valve. **2.** The return of contents in small amounts from the stomach.

rehabilitation (re-hă-bil'ĭ-ta'shun) [L. *rehabilitare*, pp. *-tatus*, to make fit]. Restoration, following disease, illness, or injury, of ability to function in a normal or near normal manner.

rehydration (re-hi-dra'shun). The return of water to a system after its loss.

reimplantation (re'im-plan-ta'shun). Replantation.

re'infec'tion. A second infection by the same microorganism, after recovery from or during the course of a primary infection.

re'inforce'ment. 1. An increase of force or strength. **2.** In conditioning, the totality of the process in which the conditioned stimulus is followed by presentation of the unconditioned stimulus which, itself, elicits the response to be conditioned.

reinforcer. Reward; in conditioning, a satisfaction-yielding (positive) or unsatisfying (negative) stimulus, object, or stimulus event that is obtained upon the performance of a desired or predetermined operant.

reinnervation (re'in-ner-va'shun). Restoration of nerve control of a paralyzed muscle or organ by means of regrowth of nerve fibers, either spontaneously or after anastomosis.

reintegration (re'in-tĕ-gra'shun). In psychiatry, the return to well adjusted functioning following disturbances due to mental illness.

rejection (re-jek'shun) [L. *rejectio,* a throwing back]. **1.** The immunological response to incompatibility in a transplanted organ. **2.** A refusal to accept, recognize, or grant; a denial. **3.** Elimination of small ultrasonic echoes from display.

relapse (re'laps) [L. *re-labor,* pp. *-lapsus,* to slide back]. Recurrence (2); the return of the symptoms of a disease after convalescence has begun.

relation (re-la'shun) [L. *relatio,* a bringing back]. **1.** An association or connection between or among people or objects. **2.** In dentistry, the mode of contact of teeth or the positional relationship of oral structures.

relationship (re-la'shun-ship). The state of being related, associated, or connected.

    blood r. consanguinity.

    object r., in psychiatry, the emotional bond between an individual and another person, as opposed to the individual's interest in himself (narcissism).

relax'ant. 1. Relaxing; causing relaxation; reducing tension, especially muscular tension. **2.** An agent that so acts.

relaxation (re'lak-sa'shun) [L. *relaxatio,* fr. *re-laxo,* to loosen]. Dilation; loosening; lengthening or lessening of tension, as in a muscle.

relearn'ing. The process of regaining a skill or ability that has been partially or entirely lost.

relieve (re-lēv') [thru O. Fr. fr. L. *re-levo,* to lift up, lighten]. To free wholly or partly from pain or discomfort, either physical or mental.

REM Rapid eye *movement.*

rem Roentgen-equivalent-man.

remedy (rem'ĕ-dī) [L. *remedium,* fr. *re-,* again, + *medeor,* cure]. An agent that cures disease or alleviates its symptoms.

remineralization (re'min'er-al-ĭ-za'shun). The return to the body of necessary mineral constituents lost through disease or dietary deficiencies; commonly referring to the content of calcium salts in bone.

remission (re-mish'un) [L. *re-mitto,* pp. *-missus,* to send back, slacken, relax]. **1.** Abatement or lessening in severity of the symptoms of a disease. **2.** The period during which such abatement occurs.

remit'tence. A temporary amelioration, without actual cessation, of symptoms.

remit'tent. Characterized by temporary remissions or periods of abatement of the symptoms.

ren, pl. **renes** (ren, re'nēz) [L.] [NA]. Kidney.

re'nal. Nephric.

reni-. See reno-.

ren'iform. Nephroid.

re'nin. An enzyme that converts angiotensinogen to angiotensin.

ren'ipor'tal [reni- + L. *porta,* gate]. **1.** Relating to the hilum of the kidney. **2.** Relating to the portal, or venous capillary circulation in the kidney.

ren'nin. Chymosin.

renninogen (rĕ-nin'o-jen) [rennin + G. *-gen,* producing]. Prochymosin.

reno-, reni- [L. *ren,* kidney]. Combining forms denoting the kidney. See also nephro-.

renogenic (re'no-jen'ik). Originating in or from the kidney.

re'nogram. The assessment of renal function by external radiation detectors after the administration of a radiopharmaceutical with renotropic characteristics.

renography (re'nog'rä-fī). Radiography of the kidney.

renomegaly (re'no-meg'ä-lī). Enlargement of the kidney.

renopathy (re-nop'ä-thī). Nephropathy.

renoprival (re-no-pri'val) [reno- + L. *privus,* deprived of]. Relating to, characterized by, or resulting from total loss of kidney function or from removal of all functioning renal tissue.

renotrophic, renotropic (re-no-trof'ik, -trop'ik) [reno- + G. *trophē,* nourishment]. Nephrotrophic; nephrotropic; relating to any agent influencing the growth or nutrition of the kidney or to the action of such an agent.

renovas'cular. Pertaining to the blood vessels of the kidney, denoting especially disease of these vessels.

Reoviridae (re-o-vīr'ĭ-de) [*R*espiratory *E*nteric *Or*phan + viridae]. A family of double stranded ether-resistant RNA viruses comprising six genera: *Reovirus, Orbivirus,* rotavirus group, cytoplasmic polyhedrosis virus group, and two plant reovirus groups.

Reovirus (re-o-vi'rus). A genus of viruses (family Reoviridae) of three antigenically distinct human types related by a common complement-fixing antigen; recovered from children with mild fever and sometimes diarrhea, and from children with no apparent infection; hosts are vertebrates, but the virus does not multiply in vertebrates.

rep Roentgen-equivalent-physical.

repair (re-pār′). Restoration of diseases or damaged tissues naturally by healing processes or artificially, as by surgical means.

repel′lent [L. *re-pello*, pp. *-pulsus*, to drive back]. **1.** Capable of driving off or repelling; repulsive. **2.** An agent that drives away or prevents annoyance or irritation by insect pests.

repetition-compulsion (rep′ē-tish′un-kom-pul′zhun). In psychoanalysis, the tendency to repeat earlier experiences or actions, in an unconscious effort to achieve belated mastery over them.

re′plant. **1.** To perform replantation. **2.** A part or organ so replaced or about to be so replaced.

replantation (re-plan-ta′shun) [G. *re-*, again, + *planto*, pp. *-atus*, to plant]. Reimplantation; replacement of an organ or part back in its original site and reestablishing its circulation.

repletion (re-ple′shun) [L. *repletio*, fr. *re-pleo*, pp. *-pletus*, to fill up]. Plethora.

rep′licase. An RNA-dependent RNA polymerase associated with replication of RNA viruses.

replicate (rep′lĭ-kāt). **1.** One of several identical processes or observations. **2.** To repeat; to produce an exact copy.

replication (rep′lĭ-ka′shun) [L. *replicatio*, a reply, fr. *replico*, pp. *-atus*, to fold back]. **1.** Repeating a process or observation, commonly used in describing experimental work. **2.** Autoreproduction.

rep′licator. The specific site of bacterial genome (chromosome) at which replication begins.

rep′licon. A segment of a chromosome (or of the DNA of a chromosome or similar entity) that can replicate, with its own initiation and termination points, independently of the chromosome in which it may be located, and that has a unique function.

replisome (rep′lĭ-sōm) [L. *replico*, to repeat + G. *sōma*, body]. Any of the sites on the matrix of a cell nucleus that contain series of enzyme complexes where DNA replication is thought to occur.

repolarization (re′po-lar-ĭ-za′shun). The process whereby the membrane, cell, or fiber, after depolarization, is polarized again, with positive charges on the outer and negative charges on the inner surface.

repositioning (re-po-zish′un-ing). Reduction (1).

repositor (re-poz′ĭ-tor). An instrument used to replace a dislocated part, especially a prolapsed uterus.

repressed (re-prest′). Subjected to repression.

repression (re-presh′un) [L. *re-primo*, pp. *-pressus*, to press back]. In psychoanalysis, the defense mechanism by which ideas, impulses, and affects once available to conscious thought are removed from consciousness.

repres′sor. The product of a regulator or repressor gene.

  active r., a homeostatic mechanism for regulation of inducible enzyme systems: a r. that combines directly with an operator gene to repress activity of the operator and its structural genes, thus repressing

enzyme synthesis; may be inactivated by an inducer, with resulting activation of enzyme synthesis.

  inactive r., a homeostatic mechanism for regulation of repressible enzyme systems: a r. that is unable to combine with an operator gene until it has been activated by combination with a corepressor molecule; after activation the r. stops production of the enzymes controlled by the operator gene.

reproduction (re-pro-duk′shun) [L. *re-*, again, + *pro-duco*, pp. *-ductus*, to lead forth, produce]. **1.** The recall and presentation in the mind of the steps of a former impression. **2.** Procreation; generation (1) the total process by which organisms produce offspring.

  asexual r., r. other than by union of male and female sex cells.

  cytogenic r., r. by means of unicellular germ cells; includes both sexual r. and asexual r. by means of spores.

  sexual r., syngenesis; r. by union of male and female gametes to form a zygote.

  somatic r., asexual r. by fission or budding of somatic cells.

reproductive (re-pro-duk′tiv). Relating to reproduction.

repulsion (re-pul′shun) [L. *re-pello*, pp. *-pulsus*, to drive back]. **1.** The act of repelling or driving apart. **2.** Aversion.

resect (re-sekt′) [L. *re-seco*, pp. *sectus*, to cut off]. **1.** To cut off, especially the articular ends of one or both bones forming a joint. **2.** To excise a segment of a part.

resectable (re-sek′tă-bl). Amenable to resection.

resection (re-sek′shun). **1.** Removal of articular ends of one or both bones forming a joint. **2.** Excision of a segment of a part.

  gum r., gingivectomy.

  root r., apicoectomy.

  transurethral r., endoscopic removal of the prostate gland or bladder lesions, usually for relief of prostatic obstruction or treatment of bladder malignancies.

  wedge r., removal of a wedge-shaped portion of tissue, as of the ovary.

resectoscope (re-sek′to-skōp). A special endoscopic instrument for the transurethral electrosurgical removal of lesions involving the bladder, prostate gland, or urethra.

reserpine (re-ser′pēn, -pin). An ester alkaloid isolated from certain species of *Rauwolfia* which decreases the 5-hydroxytryptamine and catecholamine concentrations in the CNS and in peripheral tissues; used in conjunction with other hypotensive agents in the management of essential hypertension and as a tranquilizer in psychotic states.

reserve (re-zerv′) [L. *re-servo*, to keep back, reserve]. Something available, but held back for later use, *e.g.*, r. strength or carbohydrate r.

  alkali r., the sum total of the basic ions (mainly bicarbonates) of the blood and other body fluids which, acting as buffers, maintain the normal pH of the blood.

breathing r., the difference between the pulmonary ventilation (volume of air breathed under ordinary resting conditions) and the maximum breathing capacity.

cardiac r., the work which the heart is able to perform beyond that required under ordinary circumstances.

reservoir (rez'er-vwor) [Fr.]. Receptaculum.

r. of infection, living or nonliving material in or on which an infectious agent multiplies and/or develops and is dependent for its survival in nature.

r. of spermatozoa, the site where spermatozoa are stored, the distal portion of the tail of the epididymis and the beginning of the ductus deferens.

resident (rez'ĭ-dent) [L. *resideo*, to reside]. A house officer attached to a hospital for clinical training after the intern year; formerly, actually residing in the hospital.

resid'ua. Plural of residuum.

residual (re-zid'u-al). Relating to or of the nature of a residue.

residue (rez'ĭ-du) [L. *residuum*]. Residuum; that which remains after removal of substances.

residuum, pl. **residua** (re-zid'u-um, -u-ah) [L. ntr. of *residuus*, left behind, remaining]. Residue.

resin (rez'in). **1.** An amorphous, brittle substance consisting of the hardened secretion of a number of plants, probably derived from a volatile oil and similar to a stearoptene. **2.** Rosin. **3.** A precipitate formed by the addition of water to certain tinctures. **4.** Organic substances (monomers) soluble in ether, etc., but not in water; named according to their chemical composition, physical structure, and means for activation or curing.

anion-exchange r., see anion exchange; anion exchanger.

cation-exchange r., see cation exchange; cation exchanger.

copolymer r., a synthetic r. produced by joint polymerization of two or more different monomers or polymers.

ion-exchange r., see ion exchange; ion exchanger.

resinous (rez'ĭ-nus). Relating to or derived from a resin.

resistance (re-zis'tans) [L. *re-sisto*, to stand back, withstand]. **1.** The natural ability of an organism to remain unaffected by pathogenic or toxic agents. **2.** The opposition in a conductor to the passage of a current of electricity, whereby there is a loss of energy and a production of heat; specifically, the potential difference in volts across the conductor per ampere of current flow; unit: ohm. **3.** The opposition to flow through one or more passageways. **4.** In psychoanalysis, opposition to the uncovering of the unconscious. **5.** The power residing in the red blood cells to resist hemolysis and to preserve their shape under varying degrees of osmotic pressure.

mutual r., antagonism.

systemic vascular r., an index of arteriolar constriction throughout the body, equal to the blood pressure divided by the cardiac output.

resolution (rez-o-lu'shun) [L. *resolutio*, a slackening]. **1.** The arrest of an inflammatory process without suppuration; the absorption or breaking down and removal of the products of inflammation or of a new growth. **2.** The ability optically to distinguish detail such as the separation of closely approximated objects.

resolve (re-zolv') [L. *resolvo*, to loosen]. To return or cause to return to normal, particularly without suppuration; said of inflammation.

resolvent (re-zol'vent). **1.** Causing resolution. **2.** An agent that arrests an inflammatory process or causes the absorption of a neoplasm.

resonance (rez'o-nans) [L. *resonantia*, echo]. **1.** Sympathetic or forced vibration of air in body cavities above, below, in front of, or behind a source of sound. **2.** The sound obtained on percussing a part that can vibrate freely. **3.** The intensification and hollow character of the voice sound obtained on auscultating over a cavity.

amphoric r., a percussion sound like that produced by blowing across the neck of an empty bottle, obtained by percussing over a pulmonary cavity, the patient's mouth being open.

electron spin r. (ESR), a spectrometric method, based on measurement of electron spins and magnetic moments, for detecting and estimating free radicals in organic reactions.

nuclear magnetic r. (NMR), a method for defining the character of covalent bonds by measuring the magnetic moment of the atomic nuclei involved.

skodaic r. [J. *Shoda*], a peculiar, high-pitched sound, less musical than that obtained over a cavity, elicited by percussion just above the level of a pleuritic effusion.

tympanitic r., a drumlike r. obtained by percussion over a large space filled with air, as the stomach or intestine or a large pulmonary cavity.

vesicular r., the normal pulmonary r.

vesiculotympanitic r., a peculiar, partly tympanitic, partly vesicular, sound obtained on percussion in cases of pulmonary emphysema.

vocal r. (VR), voice sounds as heard on auscultation of the chest.

resorb (re-sorb') [L. *re-sorbeo*, to suck back]. To reabsorb; to absorb what has been excreted, as an exudate or pus.

resorcinol (re-zor'sĭ-nol). *m*-Dihydroxybenzene; used internally for the relief of nausea, asthma, whooping cough, and diarrhea, but chiefly as an external antiseptic in psoriasis, eczema, seborrhea, and ringworm. Pyrocatechol and hydroquinone are isomers of r.

resorption (re-sorp'shun). **1.** The act of resorbing; removal of an exudate, a blood clot, pus, etc., by absorption. **2.** A loss of substance by physiologic or pathologic means.

respirable (rĕ-spīr′ă-bl, res′pī-ră-bl). Capable of being breathed.

abdominal r., breathing effected mainly by the action of the diaphragm.

aerobic r., r. in which molecular oxygen is consumed and carbon dioxide and water are produced.

anaerobic r., r. in which molecular oxygen is not consumed. See nitrate r., sulfate r.

artificial r., artificial *ventilation.*

assisted r., assisted *ventilation.*

Biot's r., abrupt and irregular alternating periods of apnea and constant rate and depth of breathing, as that resulting from lesions due to increased intracranial pressure.

Cheyne-Stokes r., the pattern of breathing with gradual increase in depth and sometimes in rate to a maximum, followed by a decrease resulting in apnea; characteristically seen in coma from affection of the nervous centers of respiration.

cogwheel r., the inspiratory sound being broken into two or three by silent intervals.

controlled r., controlled *ventilation.*

diffusion r., maintenance of oxygenation during apnea by intratracheal insufflation of oxygen at high flow rates.

electrophrenic r., rhythmical electrical stimulation at the motor points of the phrenic nerve; used in paralysis of the respiratory center resulting from acute bulbar poliomyelitis.

external r., the exchange of respiratory gases in the lungs.

internal r., tissue r.

Kussmaul r., deep rapid r. characteristic of diabetic acidosis or coma.

mouth-to-mouth r., a method of artificial ventilation involving an overlap of the patient's mouth (and nose in small children) with the operator's mouth, to inflate the patient's lungs by blowing, followed by an unassisted expiratory phase brought about by elastic recoil of the patient's chest and lungs.

paradoxical r., deflation of the lung during inspiration, and inflation of the lung during the phase of expiration; seen in the lung on the side of an open pneumothorax.

tissue r., internal r.; the interchange of gases between the blood and the tissues.

vesicular r., vesicular murmur; the respiratory murmur heard on auscultation of the normal lung.

respiration (R) (res-pĭ-ra′shun) [L. *respiratio,* fr. *re-spiro,* pp. *-atus,* to exhale, breathe]. **1.** A fundamental process of life in which oxygen is used to oxidize organic fuel molecules, providing a source of energy as well as carbon dioxide and water. **2.** Ventilation (2).

res′pirator. 1. Inhaler (1); an appliance fitting over the mouth and nose, used for the purpose of excluding dust, smoke, or other irritants, or of otherwise altering the air before it enters the respiratory passages. **2.** An apparatus for administering artificial respiration, especially for a prolonged period, in cases of paralysis of inadequate spontaneous ventilation.

Drinker r., iron lung; a mechanical r. in which the whole body except the head is encased within a metal tank, which is sealed at the neck with an airtight gasket; artificial respiration is induced by making the air pressure inside alternately negative and positive.

respiratory (rĕ-spīr′ă-to-rī, res′pī-ră-to-rī). Relating to respiration.

respirometer (res-pĭ-rom′ĕ-ter) [L. *respiro,* to breathe, + G. *metron,* measure]. **1.** An instrument for measuring the extent of the respiratory movements. **2.** An instrument for measuring oxygen consumption or carbon dioxide production, usually of an isolated tissue.

response (re-spons′) [L. *responsus* (noun), an answer]. **1.** The reaction of a muscle or other part to any stimulus. **2.** Any act or behavior, or its constituents, that an organism is capable of emitting.

conditioned r., a r. already in an individual's repertoire but which, through repeated pairings with its natural stimulus, has been acquired or conditioned anew to a previously neutral or conditioned stimulus.

evoked r., an alteration in the electrical activity of a particular part of the nervous system produced by an incoming sensory stimulus.

galvanic skin r. (GSR), a measure of changes in emotional arousal recorded by attaching electrodes to any part of the skin and recording changes in moment-to-moment perspiration and related autonomic nervous system activity.

immune r., (1) the r. of previously sensitized tissue to an antigen; in the case of antigens produced by microbes and other parasitic organisms, the immune r. tends to resist infection; **(2)** the r. of the immunological mechanism to an antigen (immunogen) that leads to the condition of induced sensitivity, especially from the viewpoint of antibody (immunoglobulin) production.

orienting r., orienting *reflex.*

target r., operant.

triple r., triphasic r. to the firm stroking of the skin: phase 1, sharply demarcated erythema that follows a momentary blanching of the skin, and is the result of release of histamine from the mast cells; phase 2, intense red flare extending beyond the margins of the line of pressure but in the same configuration, and is the result of arteriolar dilation; phase 3, appearance of a line wheal in the configuration of the original stroking.

unconditioned r., a r. such as salivation which is a part of the organism's repertoire.

rest. 1 [A.S. *raes*]. Quiet; repose. **2** [A.S. *raestan*]. To repose; to cease from work. **3** [L. *restare,* to remain]. A group of cells or a portion of fetal tissue that has become displaced and lies embedded in tissue of another character. **4.** In dentistry, an extension from a prosthesis that affords vertical support for a restoration.

adrenal r., accessory *adrenal.*

Walthard's cell r., a nest of epithelial cells occurring in the peritoneum of the uterine tubes or ovary.

wolffian r., remnants of the wolffian duct in the female genital tract that give rise to cysts.

re'stenosis [*re-* + G. *stenōsis,* a narrowing]. Recurrence of stenosis after corrective surgery on the heart valve.

res'tiform [L. *restis,* rope, + *forma,* form]. Ropelike; rope-shaped.

restitution (res-tĭ-tu'shun) [L. *restitutio,* act of restoring]. In obstetrics, the return of the rotated head of the fetus to its natural relation with the shoulders after its emergence from the vulva.

restoration (res-to-ra'shun) [L. *restauro,* pp. *-atus,* to restore, to repair]. **1.** Any inlay, crown, bridge, partial denture, or complete denture which restores or replaces lost tooth structure, teeth, or oral tissues. **2.** Any substance used for restoring the missing portion of a tooth.

restor'ative. 1. Renewing health and strength. **2.** An agent with such action.

restraint (re-strānt) [O. Fr. *restrainte*]. In psychiatry, intervention, as by a straitjacket, to prevent an excited or violent patient from doing harm to himself or others.

resuscitate (re-sus'ĭ-tāt) [L. *re-suscito,* to raise up again, revive]. To revive; to restore to life after apparent death.

resuscitation (re-sus-ĭ-ta'shun) [L. *resuscitatio*]. Restoration to life after apparent death. See also artificial *respiration.*

cardiopulmonary r. (CPR), restoration of cardiac output and pulmonary ventilation following cardiac arrest and apnea, using artificial respiration and closed chest massage.

resus'citator. An apparatus that forces gas (usually O_2) into lungs to produce artificial respiration.

retain'er. Any type of clasp, attachment, or device used for the fixation or stabilization of a prosthesis; an appliance used to prevent the shifting of teeth following orthodontic treatment.

continuous bar r., a metal bar, usually resting on lingual surfaces of teeth, to aid in their stabilization and to act as indirect r.'s.

retar'date [L. *retardo,* to delay, hinder]. A mentally retarded individual.

retardation (re-tar-da'shun). A slowness or limitation of development.

mental r., amentia (1); subaverage general intellectual functioning that originates during the developmental period and is associated with impairment in adaptive behavior. The American Association on Mental Deficiency lists 8 medical classifications and 5 psychological classifications (borderline, mild,

moderate, severe, profound); the latter five replace the former classifications of moron, imbecile, and idiot.

retch [A.S. *hraecan,* to hawk]. To make an involuntary effort to vomit.

retch'ing. Vomiturition; dry vomiting; movements of vomiting without effect.

rete, pl. **re'tia** (re'te, re'shī-ah, -tĭ-ah) [L. net] [NA]. **1.** A network of nerve fibers or small vessels. **2.** A structure composed of a fibrous network or mesh.

r. arterio'sum [NA], a vascular network formed by anastomoses between minute arteries just before they become capillaries.

r. articula're, a vascular r. in the neighborhood of a joint, where such arrangements are common.

r. cuta'neum cor'ii, the network of vessels parallel to the surface between the corium and the tela subcutanea.

r. mirab'ile [NA], a vascular network interrupting the continuity of an artery or vein, such as occurs in the glomeruli of the kidney (arterial) or in the liver (venous).

r. ova'rii, a transient network of cells in the developing ovary; homologous to the r. testis.

r. subpapilla're, the network of vessels between the papillary and reticular strata of the corium.

r. tes'tis [NA], the network of canals at the termination of the straight tubules in the mediastinum testis.

r. veno'sum [NA], a venous network.

rete pegs. Rete *ridges.*

retention (re-ten'shun) [L. *retentio,* a holding back, see retain]. **1.** The keeping in the body of what normally belongs there, especially the retaining of food and drink in the stomach, or of what normally should be discharged, as urine or feces. **2.** Retaining that which has been learned so that it can be utilized later as in recall, recognition, or, if r. is partial, relearning.

re'tia [L.]. Plural of rete.

retial (re'shī-al). Relating to a rete.

reticul-. See reticulo-.

retic'ula [L.]. Plural of recticulum.

reticular, reticulated (rĕ-tik'u-lar, -la-ted). Relating to a reticulum.

reticulation (rĕ-tik-u-la'shun). The presence or formation of a reticulum or network.

retic'ulin. An albuminoid or scleroprotein present in the connective tissue framework of the lymphatic tissues.

reticulo-, reticul-. Combining forms denoting reticulum or reticular.

reticulocyte (re-tik'u-lo-sīt) [reticulo- + G. *kytos,* cell]. A young red blood cell with a network of precipitated basophilic substance, occurring during the process of active blood regeneration.

reticulocytopenia (re-tik'u-lo-si-to-pe'nĭ-ah) [reticulocyte + G. *penia,* poverty]. Reticulopenia; paucity of reticulocytes in the blood.

reticulocytosis (re-tik'u-lo-si-to'sis) [reticulocyte + G. *-osis*, condition]. An increase in the number of circulating reticulocytes above the normal (less than 1% of the total number of red blood cells).

reticuloendothelial (re-tik'u-lo-en-do-the'li-al). Denoting or referring to reticuloendothelium.

reticuloendothelioma (re-tik'u-lo-en'do-the-li-o'mah) [reticuloendothelium + G. *-oma*, tumor]. A localized reticuloendotheliosis, or neoplasm derived from reticuloendothelial tissue.

reticuloendotheliosis (re-tik'u-lo-en'do-the-li-o'sis) [reticuloendothelium + G. *-osis*, condition]. Proliferation of the reticuloendothelium in any of the organs or tissues.

   leukemic r., hairy cell leukemia; a rare, usually chronic disorder characterized by proliferation of "hairy" cells (probably B-lymphocytes) in reticuloendothelial organs and blood.

reticuloendothelium (re-tik'u-lo-en-do-the'li-um) [reticulo- + endothelium]. The cells making up the reticuloendothelial system.

reticulohistiocytoma (re-tik'u-lo-his'ti-o-si-to'mah). A solitary skin nodule composed of glycolipid-containing multinucleated large histiocytes.

reticulopenia (re-tik'u-lo-pe'ni-ah). Reticulocytopenia.

reticulosis (re-tik'u-lo'sis) [reticulo- + G. *-osis*, condition]. An increase in histiocytes, monocytes, or other reticuloendothelial elements.

   benign inoculation r., cat-scratch *disease*.

   histiocytic medullary r., a rapidly fatal form of lymphoma, characterized by fever, jaundice, pancytopenia, and enlargement of the liver, spleen, and lymph nodes; the affected organs show focal necrosis and hemorrhage, with proliferation of histiocytes and phagocytosis of red blood cells.

reticulum, pl. **reticula** (re-tik'u-lum, -lah) [L. dim of *rete*, a net]. **1** [NA]. A fine network formed by cells, or formed of certain structures within cells or of connective tissue fibers between cells. **2.** Neuroglia. **3.** The second compartment of the stomach of a ruminant.

   agranular endoplasmic r., endoplasmic r. that is lacking in ribosomal granules; characteristic of cells that secrete steroid hormones.

   endoplasmic r., (ER), the network of tubules or flattened sacs (cisternae) with or without ribosomes on the surface of their membranes.

   granular endoplasmic r., ergastoplasm; endoplasmic r. in which ribosomal granules are applied to the cytoplasmic surface of the cisternae; concerned in secretion of protein and peptides.

   sarcoplasmic r., the endoplasmic r. of skeletal and cardiac muscle; the vesicles and tubules forming a continuous structure around striated myofibrils, with a repetition of structure within each sarcomere.

   stellate r., a network of cells in the center of the enamel organ between the outer and inner enamel epithelium.

   trabecular r., the network of fibers at the iridocorneal angle between the anterior chamber of the eye and the venous sinus of the sclera; involved in drainage of the aqueous humor.

ret'iform [L. *rete,* network]. Resembling a net or network.

retin-. See retino-.

retina (ret'ĭ-nah) [Mediev. L. prob. fr. L. *rete,* a net] [NA]. The innermost tunic of the eyeball, consisting of three parts: optic, ciliary, and iridial. The optic part, the physiologic portion that receives the visual light rays, is further divided into two parts, pigmented and nervous, which are arranged in the following layers: pigment layer, layer of rods and cones, external limiting membrane, outer nuclear layer, outer plexiform layer, inner nuclear layer, inner plexiform layer, layer of ganglion cells, layer of nerve fibers, and internal limiting membrane. The ciliary and iridial parts are forward prolongations of the pigmented layer and a layer of supporting columnar or epithelial cells over the ciliary body and the posterior surface of the iris, respectively.

   leopard r., tesselated *fundus.*

   shot-silk r., shot-silk reflex; the appearance of numerous wavelike, glistening reflexes, like the shimmer of silk, observed sometimes in the r. of a young person.

retinaculum, pl. **retinacula** (ret'ĭ-nak'u-lum, -lah) [L. a band, a halter, fr. *retineo,* to hold back] [NA]. A frenum, or a retaining band or ligament.

   r. cu'tis [NA], r. of the skin; one of the numerous small fibrous strands that attaches the dermis to the underlying tela subcutanea; particularly well developed over the breast where they are known as suspensory ligaments of Cooper.

   retinacula of extensor muscles, r. musculorum extensorum inferius and superius.

   r. extenso'rum [NA], **extensor r.,** a strong fibrous band stretching obliquely across the back of the wrist and binding down the extensor tendons of the fingers and thumb.

   r. of flexor muscles, r. musculorum flexorum.

   r. flexo'rum [NA], **flexor r.,** a strong fibrous band crossing the front of the carpus and binding down the flexor tendons of the digits and the flexor carpi radialis tendon.

   r. musculo'rum extenso'rum infe'rius [NA], inferior r. of the extensor muscles; a V-shaped ligament restraining the extensor tendons of the foot distal to the ankle joint.

   r. musculo'rum extenso'rum supe'rius [NA], superior r. of the extensor muscles; the ligament that binds down the extensor tendons proximal to the ankle joint; it is continuous above with the deep fascia of the leg.

   r. musculo'rum flexo'rum [NA], r. of the flexor muscles; a wide band passing from the medial malleolus to the medial and upper border of the calcaneus and to the plantar surface as far as the navicular bone; it holds in place the tendons of the tibialis posterior, flexor digitorum longus, and flexor hallucis longus muscles.

retinac'ula musculo'rum peroneo'rum [NA], **retinacula of peroneal (fibular) muscles,** superior and inferior fibrous bands retaining the tendons of the peroneus longus and brevis in position as they cross the lateral side of the ankle.

retinacula of peroneal muscles, retinacula musculorum peroneorum.

r. of skin, r. cutis.

r. ten'dinum, the annular ligament of the ankle or wrist.

retinal (ret'ĭ-nal). **1.** Relating to the retina. **2.** Retinaldehyde.

r. isomerase, retinaldehyde isomerase; an isomerase that catalyzes the *cis-trans* conversion of all-*trans*-retinal(dehyde) to 11-*cis*-retinal(dehyde); a reaction of importance in the visual cycle.

11-*cis*-retinal. The isomer of retinaldehyde that can combine with opsin to form rhodopsin; it is formed from all-*trans*-retinal by retinal isomerase.

retinal'dehyde. Retinal (2); retinene; vitamin A₁ aldehyde; retinol oxidized to a terminal aldehyde; a carotene released (as all-*trans*-retinal(dehyde)) in the bleaching of rhodopsin by light and the dissociation of opsin.

retinene (ret'ĭ-nēn). Retinaldehyde.

retinitis (ret-ĭ-ni'tis) [retina + G. *-itis,* inflammation]. Inflammation of the retina.

circinate r., see circinate *retinopathy.*

exudative r., Coats disease; a chronic inflammatory condition characterized by the appearance of white or yellowish raised areas encircling the optic disk due to the accumulation of edematous fluid beneath the retina.

r. pigmento'sa, pigmentary retinopathy; a progressive abiotrophy of the neuroepithelium, with atrophy and pigmentary infiltration of the inner layers.

r. prolif'erans, neovascularization of the retina extending into the vitreous.

retino-, retin-. Combining forms denoting the retina.

retinoblastoma (ret'ĭ-no-blas-to'mah) [retino- + G. *blastos,* germ, + *-oma,* tumor]. A malignant neoplasm composed of primitive retinal cells, occurring sporadically (mainly uniocularly) and as an autosomal dominant trait (mainly binocularly).

retinochoroid (ret'ĭ-no-ko'royd). Chorioretinal.

retinochoroiditis (ret'ĭ-no-ko-roy-di'tis) [retinochoroid + G. *-itis,* inflammation]. Chorioretinitis.

r. juxtapapilla'ris, Jensen's disease; r. close to the optic nerve.

retinodialysis (ret'ĭ-no-di-al'ĭ-sis) [retino- + G. *dialysis,* separation]. Disinsertion.

retinol (ret'ĭ-nol). Vitamin A (2); **r. dehydrogenase** is an oxidoreductase catalyzing interconversion of retinaldehyde and retinol, a reaction of importance in the chemistry of rod vision.

retinopapillitis (ret-ĭ-no-pap-ĭ-li'tis). Papilloretinitis.

retinopathy (ret-ĭ-nop'ă-thĭ) [retino- + G. *pathos,* suffering]. Noninflammatory degenerative disease of the retina, as distinguished from retinitis.

circinate r., a usually bilateral retinal degeneration marked by a girdle of sharply defined white exudates around a grayish macula.

diabetic r., retinal changes occurring in diabetes of long standing, marked by punctate hemorrhages, microaneurysms, and sharply defined waxy exudates.

hypertensive r., a retinal picture occurring in accelerated hypertension, marked by arteriolar constriction, flame-shaped hemorrhages, cotton-wool patches, increased severity of star-figure edema at the macula, and papilledema.

leukemic r., retinal picture in all types of leukemia, characterized by a yellow-orange fundus, engorgement and tortuosity of veins, scattered hemorrhages, and edema of the retina and disk.

pigmentary r., *retinitis* pigmentosa.

sickle cell r., a condition marked by dilation and tortuosity of retinal veins, and by microaneurysms and retinal hemorrhages; advanced stages may show sea fan neovascularization, vitreous hemorrhage, or retinal detachment.

retinopexy (ret'ĭ-no-pek-sĭ) [retino- + G. *pexis,* fixation]. Formation of chorioretinal adhesions surrounding a retinal tear for correction of retinal detachment.

retinoschisis (ret-ĭ-nos'kĭ-sis) [retino- + G. *schisis,* division]. Splitting of the retina due to degeneration, with cyst formation between the two layers.

juvenile r., r. occurring before 10 years of age and within the nerve-fiber layer, with frequent macular involvement; X-linked recessive inheritance.

senile r., r. occurring most often after 40 years of age and affecting the outer plexiform layer.

retinoscope (ret'ĭ-no-skōp) [retino- + G. *skopeō,* to view]. An optical device used in retinoscopy.

retinoscopy (ret-ĭ-nos'ko-pĭ) [retino- + G. *skopeō,* to view]. Pupilloscopy; a method of detecting errors of refraction by illuminating the retina and noting the direction of movement of the light when the mirror is rotated.

retractile (re-trak'tĭl). Retractable; capable of being drawn back.

retraction (re-trak'shun) [L. *retractio,* a drawing back]. **1.** A shrinking, drawing back, or pulling apart. **2.** Posterior movement of teeth, usually with the aid of an orthodontic appliance.

retractor (re-trak'tor). **1.** An instrument for drawing aside the edges of a wound or for holding back structures adjacent to the operative field. **2.** A muscle that draws a part backward.

retreat from reality. Substitution of imaginary satisfactions for relations with the real world.

retrench'ment [F. *re-,* back, + *trancher,* to cut]. The cutting away of superfluous tissue.

retrieval (re-tre'val). The third of three stages in the memory process, involving mental processes associated with bringing stored information back into consciousness.

retro- [L. back, backward]. Prefix, to words formed from Latin roots, denoting backward or behind.

retrocalcaneobursitis (rĕ′tro-kal-ka′ne-o-bur-si′tis) [retro- + L. *calcaneum* heel, + bursitis]. Achillobursitis.

retrocession (rĕ-tro-sesh′un) [L. *retro- cedo*, pp. *-cessus*, to go back, retire]. **1.** A going back; a relapse. **2.** Cessation of the external symptoms of a disease followed by signs of involvement of some internal organ or part. **3.** Denoting a position of the uterus or other organ further back than is normal.

retroclusion (rĕ-tro-klu′zhun) [retro- + L. *claudo* (*cludo*) to close]. A form of acupressure for the arrest of bleeding: the needle is passed through the tissues above the cut end of the artery, is turned around, and then is passed backward beneath the vessel to come out near the point of entrance.

retrocollis (rĕ-tro-kol′is). Retrocollic *spasm*.

retroconduction (rĕ-tro-kon-duk′shun). Retrograde *conduction*.

retrocursive (rĕ-tro-ker′siv) [retro- + L. *cursus*, a running]. Running backward.

retrodeviation (rĕ′tro-de-vī-a′shun). A backward bending or inclining.

retrodisplacement (rĕ′tro-dis-plās′ment). Any backward displacement, such as retroversion or retroflexion of the uterus.

retroflexion (rĕ-tro-flek′shun) [retro- + L. *flecto*, pp. *flexus*, to bend]. Backward bending, as of the uterus when the corpus is bent back, forming an angle with the cervix.

retrognathic (rĕtro-nath′ik). Denoting retrognathism.

retrognathism (rĕ-tro-nath′izm) [retro- + G. *gnathos*, jaw]. A condition of facial disharmony in which one or both jaws are posterior to normal in their craniofacial relationships.

retrograde (rĕ′tro-grād) [L. *retrogradus*, fr. retro- + *gradior*, to go]. **1.** Moving backward. **2.** Degenerating; reversing the normal order of growth and development.

retrogression (rĕ-tro-gresh′un) [L. *retrogressus*, fr. *retro-gradior*, to go backwards]. Degeneration, deterioration, or return to a previous, less complex condition.

retrojection (rĕ-tro-jek′shun) [L. *retro*, backward, + *jacio*, to throw]. The washing out of a cavity by the backward flow of an injected fluid.

retroperitoneum (rĕ′tro-pĕr′ĭ-to-ne′um) [retro- + peritoneum]. *Spatium* retroperitoneale.

retroperitonitis (rĕ′tro-pĕr′ĭ-to-ni′tis). Inflammation of the cellular tissue behind the peritoneum.

retropharynx (rĕ-tro-făr′ingks). The posterior part of the pharynx.

retroplasia (rĕ-tro-pla′zī-ah) [retro- + G. *plasis*, a molding]. That state of cell or tissue in which activity is decreased below normal; associated with retrogressive changes.

retroposed (rĕ′tro-pōzd) [retro- + L. *pono*, pp. *positus*, to place]. Denoting retroposition.

retroposition (rĕ′tro-po-zish′un) [retro- + L. *positio*, a placing]. Simple backward displacement of a structure or organ, as the uterus, without inclination, bending, retroversion, or retroflexion.

retropulsion (rĕ-tro-pul′shun) [retro- + L. *pulsio*, a pushing]. An involuntary backward walking or running, occurring in patients with the parkinsonian syndrome. **2.** A pushing back of any part.

retrospondylolisthesis (rĕ′tro-spon′dĭ-lo-lis-the′sis) [retro- + G. *spondylos*, vertebra, + *olisthēsis*, a slipping]. Slipping backward of the body of a vertebra, bringing it out of line with the adjacent vertebrae.

retroversioflexion (rĕ′tro-ver′sī-o-flek′shun, -ver′-zho-). Combined retroversion and retroflexion of the uterus.

retroversion (rĕ-tro-ver′zhun) [retro- + L. *verto*, pp. *versus*, to turn]. **1.** A turning backward, as of the uterus. **2.** A condition in which the teeth are located in a more posterior position than is normal.

retroverted (rĕ′tro-ver-ted). Denoting retroversion.

Retroviridae (rĕ-tro-vīr′ĭde). A family of viruses resembling the orthomyxoviruses in size and shape, but structurally more complex; they possess RNA-dependent DNA polymerases (reverse transcriptases) and are grouped in three subfamilies: Oncovirinae (RNA tumor viruses), Spumavirinae (foamy viruses), and Lentivirinae (visna and related agents).

retrovirus (rĕ′tro-vi-rus). Any virus of the family Retroviridae.

retrusion (re-tru′zhun) [L. *re-trudo*, pp. *-trusus*, to push back]. **1.** Retraction of the mandible from any given point. **2.** The backward movement of the mandible.

revaccination (re′vak-sĭ-na′shun). Vaccination of a person previously successfully vaccinated.

revascularization (re-vas′ku-lăr-ĭ-za′shun). Reestablishment of blood supply to a part.

reversal (re-ver′sal) [L. *re-verto*, pp. *-versus*, to turn back or about]. **1.** A turning in the opposite direction, as of a disease, symptom, or a state. **2.** Denoting the difficulty of some persons in distinguishing the lower case printed or written letter *p* from *q* or *g*, *b* from *d*, or *s* from *z*. **3.** In psychoanalysis, the change of an instinct of affect into its opposite, as from love into hate.

epinephrine r., the fall in blood pressure produced by epinephrine when given following blockage of α-adrenergic receptors by an appropriate drug.

sex r., a process whereby the sexual identity of an individual is changed from one sex to the other, as by a combination of surgical, pharmacologic, and psychiatric procedures.

reversion (re-ver′zhun) [L. *reversio* (see reversal)]. **1.** The appearance in an individual of certain characteristics, peculiar to a remote ancestor, which have been in abeyance during one or more of the intermediate generations. **2.** The return to the original phenotype, either by reinstatement of the original genotype (true r.) or by a mutation at a site different from that of the first mutation and which cancels the effect of the first mutation (suppressor mutation).

rever′tant. In microbial genetics, a mutant that has reverted to its former genotype (true reversion) or to the original phenotype by means of a suppressor mutation.

revivification (re-viv′ĭ-fi-ka′shun) [L. *re-*, again, + *vivo*, to live, + *facio*, to make]. Vivification (2); refreshening the edges of a wound by paring or scraping to promote healing.

revulsion (re-vul′shun) [L. *revulsio*, art of pulling away]. Counterirritation.

reward. Reinforcer.

RF Releasing *factor;* rheumatoid *factors.*

RFP Right frontoposterior *position.*

RH Releasing *hormone.*

Rh **1.** Rhodium. **2.** Rh blood group.

rhabd-. See rhabdo-.

Rhabditis (rab-di′tis) [G. *rhabdos,* a rod]. A genus of small oxyurid-like nematodes (family Rhabditidae), some of which are parasitic on plants and animals; many of the described species are no longer valid or have been transferred to other genera.

rhabdo-, rhabd- [G. *rhabdos,* rod]. Combining forms denoting rod, rod-shaped.

rhabdoid (rab′doyd) [rhabdo- + G. *eidos,* resemblance]. Rod-shaped.

rhabdomyolysis (rab′do-mi-ol′ĭ-sis) [rhabdo- + G. *mys,* muscle, + *lysis,* loosening]. An acute, fulminating, potentially fatal disease of skeletal muscle which entails destruction of skeletal muscle as evidenced by myoglobinemia and myoglobinuria.

rhabdomyoma (rab′do-mi-o′mah) [rhabdo- + G. *mys,* muscle, + *-oma,* tumor]. A benign neoplasm derived from striated muscle.

rhabdomyosarcoma (rab′do-mi-o-sar-ko′mah) [rhabdo- + G. *mys,* muscle, + *sarkōma,* sarcoma]. Rhabdosarcoma; a malignant neoplasm derived from skeletal (striated) muscle; characterized in adults by poorly differentiated oblong, as well as rounded and bizarre, cells with large hyperchromatic nuclei.

    embryonal r.′s, malignant neoplasms occuring in children, consisting of loose, spindle-celled tissue with rare cross-striations, and arising in many parts of the body in addition to skeletal muscles.

rhabdosarcoma (rab′do-sar-ko′mah). Rhabdomyosarcoma.

Rhabdoviridae (rab′do-vīr′ĭ-de). A family of rod- or bullet-shaped RNA viruses of vertebrates, insects, and plants, including rabies virus; two genera have been assigned: *Vesiculovirus* and *Lyssavirus.*

rhabdovirus (rab′do-vi′rus). Any virus of the family Rhabdoviridae.

rhagades (rag′ă-dēz) [G. *rhagas,* pl. *rhagades,* a crack]. Chaps, cracks, or fissures occurring at mucocutaneous junctions; seen in vitamin deficiency diseases and in congenital syphilis.

rhegma (reg′mah) [G. breakage]. A rent or fissure.

rhegmatogenous (reg-mă-toj′ĕ-nus) [G. *rhegma,* breakage, + *-gen,* producing]. Arising from a bursting or fractionating of an organ.

rhenium (re′nĭ-um) [L. *Rhenus,* Rhine river]. A metallic of the platinum group; symbol Re, atomic weight 186.21, atomic no. 75.

rheo- [G. *rheos,* stream, current, flow]. Combining form usually denoting blood flow or electrical current.

rheobase (re′o-bās) [rheo- + G. *basis,* a base]. The minimal strength of an electrical stimulus of indefinite duration that is able to cause excitation of a tissue.

rheobasic (re-o-ba′sik). Pertaining to or having the characteristics of a rheobase.

rheology (re-ol′o-jĭ) [rheo- + G. *logos,* study]. The study of the deformation and flow of materials.

rheom′etry. The measurement of electrical current or blood flow.

rheostosis (re-os-to′sis) [rheo- + G. *osteon,* bone, + *-osis,* condition]. A hypertrophying and condensing osteitis which tends to run in longitudinal streaks or columns, like wax drippings on a candle, and involves a number of the long bones.

rheotaxis (re-o-tak′sis) [rheo- + G. *taxis,* orderly arrangement]. A form of positive barotaxis, in which a microorganism in a fluid is impelled to move against the current flow of its medium.

rheotropism (re-ot′ro-pizm) [rheo- + G. *tropos,* a turning]. A movement contrary to the motion of a current, involving part of an organism rather than, as in rheotaxis, the organism as a whole.

rhestocythemia (res′to-si-the′mĭ-ah) [G. *rhaiō,* to destroy, + *kytos,* a hollow (a cell), + *haima,* blood]. Presence of broken down red blood cells in the peripheral circulation.

rheum (rūm) [G. *rheuma,* a flux]. A mucous or watery discharge.

rheumatalgia (rū-mă-tal′jĭ-ah) [G. *rheuma,* flux, + *algos,* pain]. Rheumatic pain.

rheumatic (rū-mat′ik) [G. *rheumatikos,* subject to flux]. Relating to or characterized by rheumatism.

rheumatid (rū′mă-tid) [G. *rheum,* flux, + *-id*]. Rheumatic nodules or other eruptions which may accompany rheumatism.

rheumatism (rū′mă-tizm) [G. *rheumatismos,* rheuma, a flux]. Indefinite term applied to various conditions with pain or other symptoms which are of articular origin or related to other elements of the musculoskeletal system.

    acute articular r., *polyarthritis* rheumatica acuta.

    articular r., arthritis.

    inflammatory r., *polyarthritis* rheumatica acuta.

    lumbar r., lumbago.

    nodose r., acute or subacute articular r., accompanied by the formation of nodules on the tendons, ligaments, and periosteum in the neighborhood of the affected joints.

rheumatoid (rū'mă-toyd) [G. *rheuma*, flux, + *eidos*, resemblance]. Resembling rheumatism in one or more features.

rheumatologist (rū'mă-tol'o-jist). A specialist in the diagnosis and treatment of rheumatic conditions.

rhexis (rek'sis) [G. *rhēxis*, rupture]. Bursting or rupture of an organ or vessel.

rhin-, rhino- [G. *rhis*, nose]. Combining form denoting the nose.

rhinal (ri'nal). Nasal.

rhinalgia (ri-nal'ji-ah) [rhin- + G. *algos*, pain]. Rhinodynia; pain in the nose.

rhinedema (rĭn-ĕ-de'mah) [rhin- + G. *oidema*, swelling]. Swelling of the nasal mucous membrane.

rhinencephalic (ri'nen-sĕ-fal'ik). Relating to the rhinencephalon.

rhinencephalon (ri-nen-sef'ă-lon) [rhin- + G. *enkephalos*, brain]. Collective term denoting the parts of the cerebral hemisphere directly related to the sense of smell: the olfactory bulb, olfactory peduncle, olfactory tubercle, and olfactory or piriform cortex including the cortical nucleus of the amygdala.

rhinitis (ri-ni'tis) [rhin- + G. *-itis*, inflammation]. Inflammation of the nasal mucous membrane.

  acute r., coryza; an acute catarrhal inflammation of the mucous membrane of the nose, marked by sneezing, lacrimation, and a profuse secretion of watery mucus; usually associated with infection by one of the common cold viruses.

  allergic r., r. associated with hay fever.

  atrophic r., chronic r. with thinning of the mucous membrane; often associated with crusts and foul-smelling discharge.

  caseous r., chronic r. in which the nasal cavities are more or less completely filled with an ill-smelling cheesy material.

  fibrinous r., membranous r.

  hypertrophic r., chronic r. with permanent thickening of the mucous membrane.

  membranous r., fibrinous r.; a chronic inflammation of the nasal mucous membrane attended with a fibrinous or pseudomembranous exudate.

  purulent r., chronic r. in which pus formation is excessive.

  vasomotor r., congestion of nasal mucosa without infection or allergy.

rhino-. See rhin-.

rhinoantritis (ri'no-an-tri'tis) [rhino- + G. *antron*, cave (antrum) + *-itis*, inflammation]. Inflammation of the nasal cavities and one or both maxillary antrums.

rhinocanthectomy (ri'no-kan-thek'to-mī) [rhino- + G. *kanthos*, canthus, + *ektomē*, excision]. Excision of the inner canthus of the eye.

rhinocele (ri'no-sēl) [rhino- + G. *koilia*, a hollow]. The cavity or ventricle of the rhinencephalon or primitive olfactory part of the telencephalon.

rhinocephaly (ri'no-sef'ă-li) [rhino- + G. *kephalē*, head]. Rhinencephaly; a form of cyclopia in which

the nose is represented by a fleshy, proboscis-like protuberance arising above the slitlike orbits.

rhinocheiloplasty, rhinochiloplasty (ri-no-ki'lo-plas-tī) [rhino- + G. *cheilos*, lip, + *plassō*, to form]. Plastic or reparative surgery of the nose and upper lip.

rhinocleisis (ri-no-kli'sis) [rhino- + G. *kleisis*, a closure]. Rhinostenosis.

rhinodacryolith (ri-no-dak'rĭ-o-lith) [rhino- + G. *dakryon*, tear (duct), + *lithos*, stone]. A calculus in the nasolacrimal duct.

rhinodynia (ri-no-din'ĭ-ah) [rhino- + G. *odynē*, pain]. Rhinalgia.

rhinogenous (ri-noj'ĕ-nus) [rhino- + G. *-gen*, producing]. Originating in the nose.

rhinokyphectomy (ri'no-ki-fek'to-mī) [rhino- + G. *kyphōsis*, humped condition, + *ektomē*, excision]. A plastic operation for rhinokyphosis.

rhinokyphosis (ri'no-ki-fo'sis) [rhino- + G. *kyphōsis*, humped condition]. A humpback deformity of the nose.

rhinolalia (ri'no-la'lĭ-ah) [rhino- + G. *lalia*, talking]. rhinophonia; nasalized speech.

rhinolaryngitis (ri'no-lăr-in-ji'tis) [rhino- + G. *larynx*, larynx, + *-itis*, inflammation]. Inflammation of the nasal and laryngeal mucous membranes.

rhinolaryngology (ri'no-lăr-ing-gol'o-jī). Rhinology and laryngology combined.

rhinolith (ri'no-lith) [rhino- + G. *lithos*, stone]. Nasal calculus; a calcareous concretion in the nasal cavity.

rhinolithiasis (ri'no-lĭ-thi'ă-sis) [rhinolith + G. *-iasis*, condition]. Presence of a nasal calculus.

rhinologist (ri-nol'o-jist). A specialist in rhinology.

rhinology (ri-nol'o-jī) [rhino- + G. *logos*, study]. The branch of medical science concerned with the nose and its diseases.

rhinomanometer (ri'no-mă-nom'ĕ-ter) [rhino- + manometer]. A manometer used to determine the presence and amount of nasal obstruction, and the nasal air pressure and flow relationships.

rhinomanometry (ri'no-mă-nom'ĕ-trī). Use of a rhinomanometer.

rhinomucormycosis (ri'no-mu'kor-mi-ko'sis) [rhino- + mucormycosis]. Rhinophycomycosis; mucormycosis involving the nose, paranasal sinuses, the eye, and sometimes the cranial cavity.

rhinomycosis (ri'no-mi-ko'sis) [rhino- + mycosis]. Fungus infection of the nasal mucous membranes.

rhinonecrosis (ri'no-nĕ-kro'sis) [rhino- + necrosis]. Necrosis of the bones of the nose.

rhinopathy (ri-nop'ă-thī) [rhino- + G. *pathos*, suffering]. Disease of the nose.

rhinophonia (ri-no-fo'nĭ-ah) [rhino- + G. *phōnē*, voice]. Rhinolalia.

rhinophycomycosis (ri'no-fi'co-mi-ko'sis). Rhinomucormycosis.

rhinophyma (ri'no-fi'mah) [rhino- + G. *phyma*, tumor, growth]. Hypertrophy of the nose with follicular dilation, resulting from hyperplasia of sebaceous glands with fibrosis and increased vascularity.

rhinoplasty (ri'no-plas-ti) [rhino- + G. *plassō*, to form]. **1.** Repair of a partial or complete defect of the nose with tissue taken from elsewhere. **2.** A plastic operation to change the shape or size of the nose.

rhinorrhagia (ri-no-ra'ji-ah) [rhino- + G. *rhēgnymi*, to burst forth]. Epistaxis or nosebleed, especially if profuse.

rhinorrhea (ri-no-re'ah) [rhino- + G. *rhoia*, flow]. A discharge from the nasal mucous membrane.

    cerebrospinal fluid r., a discharge of cerebrospinal fluid from the nose.

    gustatory r., watery nasal discharge associated with stimulation of the sense of taste.

rhinosalpingitis (ri'no-sal-pin-ji'tis) [rhino- + G. *salpinx*, tube, + *-itis*, inflammation]. Inflammation of the mucous membrane of the nose and eustachian tube.

rhinoscleroma (ri'no-skle-ro'mah) [rhino- + G. *sklērōma*, an induration (scleroma)]. A chronic granulomatous process involving the nose, upper lip, mouth, and upper air passages; believed to be due to a specific bacterium, possibly a strain of *Klebsiella.*

rhinoscope (ri'no-skōp). Nasoscope; a small mirror with an angled handle, used in posterior rhinoscopy.

rhinoscopic (ri-no-skop'ik). Relating to the rhinoscope or to rhinoscopy.

rhinoscopy (ri-nos'ko-pi) [rhino- + G. *skopeō*, to view]. Inspection of the nasal cavity.

    anterior r., inspection of the anterior portion of the nasal cavity with or without the aid of a nasal speculum.

    median r., inspection of the roof of the nasal cavity and openings of the posterior ethmoid cells and sphenoidal sinus with a long-bladed nasal speculum or nasopharyngoscope.

    posterior r., inspection of the nasopharynx and posterior portion of the nasal cavity with a rhinoscope or a nasopharyngoscope.

rhinosporidiosis (ri'no-spo-rid-i-o'sis). Invasion of the nasal cavity by *Rhinosporidium seeberi*, a yeast-like organism, resulting in a chronic granulomatous disease producing polyps or other forms of hyperplasia on mucous membranes.

rhinostenosis (ri'no-stě-no'sis) [rhino- + G. *stenosis*, a narrowing]. Rhinocleisis; nasal obstruction.

rhinotomy (ri-not'o-mi) [rhino- + G. *tomē*, incision, cutting]. **1.** Any cutting operation on the nose. **2.** Operative procedure in which the nose is incised along one side so that it may be turned away to provide full vision of the nasal passages for radical sinus operations.

Rhinovirus (ri'no-vi'rus). A proposed genus of acid-labile viruses (family Picornaviridae) associated with the common cold in man and foot-and-mouth disease in cattle; there are 100 or more antigenic types classified as M strains (culturable in rhesus monkey kidney cells) and H strains (growing only in cultures of human cells).

Rhipicephalus (ri'pi-sef'ă-lus) [G. *rhipis*, fan, + *kephalē*, head]. A genus of inornate hard ticks (family Ixodidae) that includes vectors of diseases in man and domestic animals.

rhizo- [G. *rhiza*, root]. Combining form denoting root.

rhizoid (ri'zoyd) [rhizo- + G. *eidos*, resemblance]. Rootlike; irregularly branching.

rhizomeningomyelitis (ri'zo-mē-ning'go-mi-ě-li'tis) [rhizo- + G. *mēninx*, membrane, + *myelon*, marrow, + *-itis*, inflammation]. Radiculomeningomyelitis; inflammation of the nerve roots, the meninges, and the spinal cord.

Rhizopodea, Rhizopoda (ri-zo-po'de-ah, -po'dah) [rhizo- + G. *pous* (*pod-*), foot]. A class (superclass Sarcodina) that includes the amebae of man, having pseudopodia of various forms, but without axial filaments.

Rhizopus (ri-zo'pus). A genus of fungi (class Phycomycetes, family Mucoraceae); some species cause mucormycosis in man.

rhizotomy (ri-zot'o-mi) [G. *rhiza*, root, + *tomē*, section]. Radiculectomy; radicotomy; section of the spinal nerve roots for the relief of pain or spastic paralysis.

    trigeminal r., division or section of a sensory root of the fifth cranial nerve, accomplished through a subtemporal (Frazier-Spiller operation), suboccipital (Dandy operation), or transtentorial approach.

rhod-. See rhodo-.

rhodium (ro'di-um) [Mod. L. fr. G. *rhodon*, a rose]. A metallic element, symbol Rh, atomic no. 45, atomic weight 102.91.

rhodo-, rhod- [G. *rhodon*, rose]. Combining forms denoting rose or red color.

rhodogenesis (ro-do-jen'ĕ-sis) [rhodopsin + G. *genesis*, production]. The production of rhodopsin by the combination of 11-*cis*-retinal and opsin in the dark.

rho'dophylac'tic. Relating to rhodophylaxis.

rhodophylaxis (ro'do-fi-lak'sis) [rhodopsin + G. *phylaxis*, a guarding]. The action of the pigment cells of the choroid in preserving or facilitating the reproduction of rhodopsin.

rhodopsin (ro-dop'sin). Visual purple; a red thermolabile protein found in the external segments of the rods of the retina; bleached by the action of light, which converts it to opsin and all-*trans*-retinal, and restored in the dark (see rhodogenesis).

rhombencephalon (rom-ben-sef'ă-lon) [rhombo- + G. *enkephalos*, brain] [NA]. Hindbrain, that part of the brain developed from the posterior of the three vesicles of the embryonic neural tube, secondarily into metencephalon and myelencephalon; it includes the pons, cerebellum, and medulla oblongata.

rhombic (rom'bik). **1.** Rhomboid. **2.** Relating to the rhombencephalon.

rhombocele (rom'bo-sēl). Rhomboidal *sinus*.

rhomboid (rom'boyd) [rhombo- + G. *eidos*, appearance]. Rhombic (1); resembling an oblique parallelogram, but having unequal sides.

rhonchal, rhonchial (rong'kal, rong'kĭ-al). Relating to a rhonchus.

rhonchus, pl. **rhonchi** (rong'kus, -ki) [L. fr. G. *rhenchos*, a snoring]. An added sound with musical pitch occurring during inspiration or expiration, heard on auscultation of the chest, caused by air passing through bronchi that are narrowed by inflammation, spasm of smooth muscle, or by the presence of mucus in the lumen. A similar sound, produced in like manner, heard by air conduction from the mouth, is called a wheeze.

rhythm (rithm) [G. *rhythmos*]. Measured time or motion; the regular alternation of two different or opposite states; especially applied to the pattern of the heart's beat.

  alpha r., alpha wave; a recurring wave pattern in the encephalogram in the frequency band of 8 to 13 Hz.

  atrioventricular (A-V) nodal r., nodal bradycardia; nodal r.; the cardiac r. when the heart is controlled by the A-V node; arising in the A-V node, the impulse ascends to the atria and descends to the ventricles more or less simultaneously.

  beta r., beta wave; the frequency band of the electroencephalogram from 18 to 30 Hz.

  bigeminal r., coupling; coupled r.; that cardiac r. when each sinus beat is followed by a premature beat, with the result that the heart beats occur in pairs (bigeminy).

  cantering r., gallop.

  coupled r., bigeminal r.

  delta r., delta wave (2); a wave pattern in the electroencephalogram that lies in the frequency band of $1\frac{1}{2}$ to 4 Hz.

  escape r., three or more consecutive impulses at a rate not exceeding the upper limit of the inherent pacemaker.

  gallop r., gallop.

  idioventricular r., ventricular r.; a slow independent r. under control of an ectopic ventricular center.

  nodal r., atrioventricular nodal r.

  quadrigeminal r., a cardiac dysrhythmia in which the heart beats are grouped in fours, each usually composed of one sinus beat followed by three extrasystoles.

  sinus r., normal cardiac r. proceeding from the sinoatrial node.

  theta r., theta wave; the frequency band in the electroencephalogram from 4 to 7 Hz.

  trigeminal r., trigeminy; a cardiac dysrhythmia in which the heart beats are grouped in trios, usually composed of a sinus beat followed by two extrasystoles.

  ventricular r., idioventricular r.

rhytidectomy (rit-ĭ-dek'to-mĭ) [G. *rhytis* (*rhytid-*), a wrinkle]. Rhytidoplasty; elimination of wrinkles from, or reshaping of, the face by excising any excess skin and tightening the remainder; the so-called "face-lift."

rhytidoplasty (rit'ĭ-do-plas-tĭ) [G. *rhytis*, a wrinkle, + *plassō*, to fashion]. Rhytidectomy.

rhytidosis (rit-ĭ-do'sis) [G. a wrinkling fr. *rhytis*, a wrinkle, + *-osis*, condition]. **1.** Wrinkling of the face to a degree disproportionate to age. **2.** Laxity and wrinkling of the cornea, an indication of approaching death.

Rib Ribose.

rib [A.S. *ribb*]. Costa (1).

  bicipital r., fusion of first thoracic r. with cervical vertebra.

  cervical r., *costa cervicalis*.

  false r.'s, *costae spuriae*.

  floating r.'s, *costae fluitantes*.

  lumbar r., an occasional r. articulating with the transverse process of the first lumbar vertebra.

  slipping r., subluxation of a r. cartilage, with costochondral separation.

  true r.'s, *costae verae*.

  vertebral r.'s, *costae fluitantes*.

ribo-. **1.** Root of ribose, and thus part of its derivatives, *e.g.*, ribofuranose, ribopyranose. **2.** As an italicized prefix to the systematic name of a monosaccharide, indicative that the configuration of a set of three consecutive CHOH (or asymmetric) groups is that of ribose.

riboflavin(e) (ri-bo-fla'vin). Flavin (1); One of the heat-stable factors of the vitamin B complex; dietary sources include green vegetables, liver, kidneys, wheat germ, milk, eggs, and cheese; used as replacement therapy in araboflavinosis and general vitamin B complex deficiencies.

  r. kinase, an enzyme catalyzing the formation of flavin mononucleotide (riboflavin phosphate) from riboflavin, utilizing ATP or ADP as phosphorylating agent.

ribonuclease (RNase) (ri-bo-nu'kle-ās). A transferase or phosphodiesterase that catalyzes the hydrolysis of ribonucleic acid.

ribonucleic acid (RNA) (ri'bo-nu-kle'ik). A macromolecule consisting of ribonucleoside residues connected by phosphate from the 3′ hydroxyl of one to the 5′ hydroxyl of the next nucleoside; found in all cells, in both nuclei and cytoplasm and in particulate and nonparticulate form, and also in many viruses.

  messenger RNA (mRNA), RNA reflecting the exact nucleoside sequence of the genetically active DNA and carrying the "message" of the latter, coded in its sequence, to the cytoplasmic areas where protein is made in amino-acid sequences specified by the mRNA, and hence primarily by the DNA.

  nuclear RNA (nRNA), RNA found in nuclei, or associated with DNA, or with nuclear structure.

ribosomal RNA (rRNA), the RNA of ribosomes and polyribosomes.

soluble RNA (sRNA), [soluble in molar salt], transfer RNA.

transfer RNA (tRNA), soluble RNA; short-chain RNA molecules present in cells in at least 20 varieties, each variety capable of combining with a specific amino acid. By joining (through their anticodons) with particular spots (codons) along the messenger RNA molecule and carrying their amino acids along, they lead to the formation of protein molecules with a specific amino-acid arrangement — the one ultimately dictated by a segment of DNA in the chromosomes.

ribonucleoprotein (RNP) (ri'bo-nu'kle-o-pro'tēn). A combination of protein and ribonucleic acid.

ri'bonu'cleoside. A nucleoside in which the sugar component is ribose.

ri'bonu'cleotide. A nucleotide in which the sugar component is ribose.

ribose (Rib) (ri'bōs). The pentose present in ribonucleic acid.

ribosephos'phate isom'erase. Phosphoriboisomerase; an enzyme catalyzing interconversion of ribose 5-phosphate and ribulose 5-phosphate; of importance in ribose metabolism.

ribosome (ri'bo-sōm). A granule of ribonucleoprotein that is the site of protein synthesis from aminoacyl-tRNA's as directed by mRNA's.

ribosuria (ri-bo-su'ri-ah) [ribose + G. *ouron,* urine]. Enhanced urinary excretion of D-ribose; a common manifestation of muscular dystrophy.

ribosyl (ri'bo-sil). The radical formed by loss of the hemiacetal OH group from either of the two cyclic forms of ribose (yielding ribofuranosyl and ribopyranosyl compounds), by combination with an H of –NH– or –CH– group.

ricin (ri'sin, ris'in). A phytotoxic protein occurring in the seeds of the castor oil plant, *Ricinus sanguineus;* a violent irritant that may be fatal.

rickets (rik'ets) [E. *wrick,* to twist]. Rachitis; a vitamin-D deficiency disease characterized by overproduction and deficient calcification of osteoid tissue, with associated skeletal deformities, enlargement of the liver and spleen, profuse sweating, and general tenderness of the body when touched.

adult r., late r.; a disease resembling r. in many of its features, occurring in adult life.

hemorrhagic r., bone changes seen in infantile scurvy, consisting of subperiosteal hemorrhage and deficient osteoid tissue formation.

late r., adult r.

renal r., pseudorickets; a form of r. occurring in children in association with and apparently caused by renal disease with hyperphosphatemia.

vitamin D-resistant r., a heritable form of r., characterized by hypophosphatemia due to defective renal tubular reabsorption of phosphate and subnormal absorption of dietary calcium; X-linked recessive inheritance.

Rickettsia (ri-ket'si-ah). A genus of Gram-negative bacteria (order Rickettsiales) that usually occur intracytoplasmically in lice, fleas, ticks, and mites; pathogenic species are parasitic on man and other animals. The type species is *R. prowazekii.*

R. ak'ari, a species that causes human rickettsialpox.

R. austral'is, a species causing a spotted fever in which the patient's serum contains a different antibody from that reacting with *R. rickettsii, R. prowazekii,* and others.

R. conor'ii, R. conori, a species causing boutonneuse fever in man.

R. prowazek'ii, a species causing epidemic typhus fever; the type species of the genus *R.*

R. ricketts'ii, a species causing Rocky Mountain spotted fever, South African tick-bite fever, São Paulo exanthematic typhus of Brazil, Tobia fever of Colombia, and spotted fevers of Minas Gerais and Mexico.

R. tsutsugam'ushi, a species causing tsutsugamuchi disease and scrub typhus.

rickettsial (ri-ket'si-al). Pertaining to or caused by rickettsiae.

rickettsialpox (ri-ket'si-al-poks). Kew garden fever; an acute disease caused by *Rickettsia akari* and transmitted by the mite *Liponnysoides sanguineus;* a papule in the skin of a covered part of the body develops into a deep-seated vesicle and then shrinks to form a black eschar; symptoms develop about a week after the appearance of the papule and consist of fever, chills, headache, backache, sweating, and local adenitis.

rickettsiosis (ri-ket'si-o'sis). Infection with rickettsiae.

ridge (rij) [A. S. *hrycg,* back, spine]. A (usually rough) linear elevation. See also crest; crista.

dental r., the prominent border of a cusp or margin of a tooth.

epidermal r.'s, *cristae* cutis.

genital r., gonadal r.

gonadal r., genital r.; an elevation of thickened mesothelium and underlying mesenchyme on the ventromedial border of the embryonic mesonephros; the primordial germ cells become embedded in it, establishing it as the primordium of the testis or ovary.

mammary r., mammary fold; milk line; a bandlike thickening of ectoderm in the embryo extending on either side from just below the axilla to the inguinal region; the mammary glands arise from primordia in the thoracic part of the r., the balance of the r. disappearing.

mesonephric r., a r. which, in early human embryos, comprises the entire urogenital r.; later in development a more medial genital r., the potential gonad, is demarcated from it.

palatine r., *raphe* palati.

rete r.'s, rete pegs; downward thickenings of the epidermis between the dermal papillae.

skin r.'s, *cristae cutis.*

supraorbital r., *margo* supraorbitalis.

temporal r., *linea* temporalis inferior and superior.

trapezoid r., *linea* trapezoidea.

urogenital r., wolfian r., mesonephric fold; one of the paired longitudinal r.'s developing in the dorsal body-wall of the embryo on either side of the dorsal mesentery.

rif'ampin. An antibacterial agent used in the treatment of tuberculosis.

right-eyed. Dextrocular.

right-footed. Dextropedal.

right-handed. Dextral.

rigidity (rī-jid'ĭ-tĭ) [L. *rigidus,* rigid, inflexible]. **1.** Rigor; stiffness or inflexibility. **2.** In psychiatry and clinical psychology, an aspect of personality characterized by resistance to change.

catatonic r., r. associated with catatonic psychotic states in which muscles exhibit flexibilitas cerea.

clasp-knife r., clasp-knife *spasticity.*

cogwheel r., r. seen as part of Parkinson's disease in which, upon applying force to bend the limb, the muscles yield jerkily.

postmortem r., *rigor* mortis.

rigor (rig'or) [L. stiffness]. Rigidity (1).

r. mortis, postmortem rigidity; stiffening of the body after death, from hardening of the muscular tissues as a result of coagulation of myosinogen and paramyosinogen; disappears when decomposition begins.

rim. A margin, border, or edge, usually circular in form.

rima, pl. **rimae** (ri'mah, ri'me) [L. a slit] [NA]. A slit or fissure, or narrow elongated opening between two symmetrical parts.

r. glot'tidis [NA], the interval between the true vocal cords.

r. o'ris [NA], the aperture of the mouth.

r. palpebra'rum [NA], palpebral fissure; the lid slit, or fissure between the eye lids.

r. puden'di [NA], the cleft between the labia majora.

r. vestib'uli [NA], the interval between the false vocal cords.

rimose (ri-mōs) [L. *rimosus,* fr. *rima,* a fissure]. Fissured; marked by cracks in various directions.

rimula (rim'u-lah) [L. dim. of *rima*]. A minute slit or fissure.

ring [A.S. *hring*]. **1.** A circular band surrounding a wide central opening. **2.** Anulus; any approximately circular structure surrounding an opening or a level area. **3.** The closed (*i.e.,* endless) chain of atoms in a cyclic compound; commonly used for "cyclic" or "cycle."

Albl's r., a curvilinear eggshell shadow arching above the sella turcica, seen in radiographs of intracranial aneurysms.

annular r.'s, pleural r.'s; an opaque area seen in radiographs of lung, indicating cavity of tuberculosis.

anterior limiting r., Schwalbe's r. (1); a landmark in gonioscopy: the periphery of the cornea thickened by a bundle of circular connective and elastic fibers, in front of or in the termination of the lamina limitans posterior corneae.

Bandl's r., pathologic retraction r.

benzene r., the closed-chain arrangement of the carbon and hydrogen atoms in the benzene molecule. See also cyclic *compound.*

Cannon's r., a tonically contracted muscular band in the transverse colon close to the hepatic flexure.

ciliary r., *orbiculus* ciliaris.

conjunctival r., *anulus* conjunctivae.

constriction r., true spastic stricture of the uterine cavity resulting when a zone of muscle goes into local tetanic contraction and forms a tight constriction about some part of the fetus.

deep inguinal r., *anulus* inguinalis profundus.

Kayser-Fleischer r., a greenish yellow pigmented r. encircling the cornea just within the corneoscleral margin, seen in Wilson's syndrome.

pathologic retraction r., Bandl's r.; one of the classic signs of threatened rupture of the uterus: a constriction located at the junction of the thinned lower uterine segment with the thick retracted upper uterine segment, resulting from obstructed labor.

physiologic retraction r., a ridge on the inner uterine surface at the boundary line between the upper and lower uterine segment that occurs in the course of normal labor.

pleural r.'s, annular r.'s.

posterior limiting r., Schwalbe's r.'s (2); a circular bundle of the sclera at the level of the termination of the deep trabeculae.

Schwalbe's r.'s, **(1)** anterior limiting r.; **(2)** posterior limiting r.

superficial inguinal r., *anulus* inguinalis superficialis.

tracheal r., *cartilagines* tracheales.

tympanic r., *anulus* tympanicus.

umbilical r., *anulus* umbilicalis.

vascular r., anomalous arteries congenitally encircling the trachea and esophagus, at time producing pressure symptoms.

ring-knife. A circular or oval ring with internal cutting edge for shaving off tumors in the nasal and other cavities.

ring'worm. Tinea.

ri'sus sardon'icus. Cynic spasm; the semblance of a grin caused by a facial spasm, especially in tetanus.

ritual (rich'u-al) [L. *ritualis,* fr. *ritus,* rite]. Any psychomotor activity sustained by an individual to relieve anxiety or forestall its development.

rivalry (ri'val-rĭ) [L. *rivalis,* competitor, rival]. Competition between two or more individuals for the same object or goal.

sibling r., jealous competition among children, especially for the attention, affection, and esteem of their parents; by extension, a factor in both normal and abnormal competitiveness throughout life.

riz'iform [Fr. *riz*, rice]. Resembling rice grains.

RMA Right mentoanterior position.

RMP Right mentoposterior position.

R.N. Registered *nurse*.

Rn Radon.

RNA Ribonucleic acid.

RNase Ribonuclease.

RNA splicing. Splicing (2).

RNP Ribonucleoprotein.

ROA Right occipitoanterior *position*.

Rochalimaea. A genus of bacteria (family Rickettsiaceae) closely resembling *Rickettsia* in staining properties, morphology, and mode of transmission between hosts; the type species is *R. quintana*, which causes trench fever.

rod [A.S. *rōd*]. **1.** A straight slender cylindrical formation. **2.** Rod cell of retina; the photosensitive, outward-directed process of a rhodopsin-containing rod cell in the external granular layer of the retina.

    basal r., costa (2).

    enamel r.'s, the calcified, microscopic r.'s radiating from the surface of the dentin, forming the substance of tooth enamel.

rodenticide (ro-den'tĭ-sīd) [rodent + L. *caedo*, to kill]. An agent lethal to rodents.

roentgen (r, R) (rent'gen, -jen) [W. K. *Roentgen*]. The international unit of x- or gamma radiation: the quantity of x-radiation or gamma radiation such that the associated corpuscular emission per 0.001293 g of air produces, in air, ions carrying 1 electrostatic unit of quantity of electricity of either sign.

roentgen-equivalent-man (rem). A unit of dose equal to that quantity of ionizing radiation of any type that produces in man the same biologic effect as one roentgen of x-rays or gamma rays; equal to the absorbed dose, measured in rads, multiplied by the relative biologic effectiveness of the radiation in question.

roentgen-equivalent-physical (rep). That quantity of ionizing radiation of any kind which, upon absorption by living tissue, produces an energy gain per gram of tissue equivalent to that produced by 1 roentgen of x-rays or gamma rays.

roentgenism (rent'gĕ-nizm). **1.** The use of x-rays in the diagnosis and treatment of disease. **2.** Any untoward effects of x-rays on tissues.

roentgenogram (rent'gen-o-gram). Radiograph.

roentgenography (rent-gen-og'rä-fī). Radiography.

roentgenologist (rent'gen-ol'o-jist). Radiologist.

roentgenology (rent'gen-ol'o-jī). Radiology.

rolan'dic. Relating to or described by Luigi Rolando.

role (rōl) [Fr.]. The pattern of behavior that one exhibits in relationship to significant persons in his life.

    gender r., the sex of a child assigned by a parent or significant other.

    sex r., a stereotyped masculine or feminine pattern in everyday behavior.

    sick r., the individual regarded, by himself or others, as a patient; may be assumed voluntarily or it may be imposed.

role-playing. A psychotherapeutic method used in psychodrama to understand and treat emotional conflicts through the enactment or re-enactment of stressful interpersonal events.

rom'bergism. Romberg's *sign*.

rongeur (rawn-zher') [Fr. *ronger*, to gnaw]. A strong biting forceps for nipping away bone.

roof [A.S. *hrōf*]. See tectorium; tectum; tegmen; tegmentum; integument.

roof'plate. See roof *plate*.

root [A.S. rot]. Radix.

rosacea (ro-za'she-ah) [L. *rosaceus*, rosy]. Acne rosacea or erythematosa; vascular and follicular dilation involving the nose and contiguous portions of the cheeks; may vary from very mild but persistent erythema to extensive hyperplasia of the sebaceous glands with deep-seated papules and pustules and accompanied by telangiectasia at the affected erythematous sites.

rosanilin (ro-zan'ĭ-lin). A tris(aminophenyl)methyl compound used with pararosanilin as a component of basic fuchsin.

rosary (ro'zĕr-ĭ). A beadlike arrangement or structure.

    rachitic r., beading of the ribs; a row of beading at the junction of the ribs with their cartilages, often seen in rachitic children.

rose bengal (rōz'ben'gal). $C_{20}H_2O_5I_4Cl_4Na_2$, used as a stain for bacteria, as a stain in the diagnosis of keratitis sicca, and in liver function tests.

roseola (ro-ze'o-lah) [Mod. L. dim. of L. *roseus*, rosy]. A symmetrical eruption of small, closely aggregated patches of rose-red color.

    epidemic r., rubella.

    r. infan'tilis, r. infan'tum, exanthema subitum.

    syphilitic r., usually the first eruption of syphilis, occurring 6 to 12 weeks after the initial lesion.

rosette (ro-zet') [Fr. a little rose]. **1.** The quartan malarial parasite of *Plasmodium malariae* in its segmented or mature phase. **2.** A grouping of cells, characteristic of neoplasms of neuroblastic or neuroectodermal origin, in which a number of nuclei form a ring from which neurofibrils extend to interlace in the center.

rosin (roz'in). Resin (2); the solid resin obtained from species of *Pinus* (family Pinaceae); used as an adhesive in plasters and locally stimulating in ointments.

rostellum (ros-tel'um) [L. dim. of *rostrum*, a beak]. The anterior fixed or invertible portion of the scolex of a tapeworm, frequently provided with a row (or several rows) of hooks.

ros'trad [L. *rostrum*, beak, + *-ad*, toward]. In a direction toward or situated nearer a rostrum or the snout end of an organism.

ros'tral [L. *rostralis*, fr. *rostrum*, beak]. Relating to a rostrum.

rostrate [L. *rostratus*]. Having a beak or hook.

rostrum, pl. **rostra**, **rostrums** (ros'trum, -trah) [L. a beak] [NA]. Any beak-shaped structure.

rotation (ro-ta'shun) [L. *roto*, pp. *rotatus*, to revolve, rotate]. 1. Turning or movement of a body round its axis. 2. A recurrence in regular order of certain events, such as the symptoms of a periodical disease.

   molecular r., $1/100$ of the product of the specific r. of an optically active compound and its molecular weight.

   optical r., the change in the plane of polarization of polarized light upon passing through optically active substances; measured in terms of specific rotation by polarimetry.

   specific r., the arc through which the plane of polarized light is rotated by 1 gram of a substance per milliliter of water when the length of the light path through the solution is 1 decimeter.

rotator [L. See rotation]. A muscle by which a part can be turned circularly.

ro'tavirus. Gastroenteritis virus type B; a group of viruses (family Reoviridae) which probably form a separate genus that includes the infantile gastroenteritis viruses of man.

rotoscoliosis (ro'to-sko-li-o'sis) [L. *roto*, to rotate, + G. *skoliōsis*, crookedness]. Curvature of the vertebral column by turning on its axis.

roughage (ruf'ij). 1. Anything in the diet, *e.g.,* fiber, serving as a stimulant of intestinal peristalsis. 2. Hay or other coarse feed fed to cattle and other herbivores.

round'worm. A nematode member of the phylum Nemathelminthes; commonly restricted to the parasitic forms.

RPF Renal plasma flow.

rpm Revolutions per minute.

R.Q. Respiratory *quotient*.

-rrhagia [G. *rhēgnymi*, to burst forth]. Suffix denoting excessive or unusual discharge.

-rrhaphy [G. *rhaphē*, suture]. Suffix denoting surgical suturing.

-rrhea [G. *rhoia*, a flow]. Suffix denoting a flowing or flux.

rRNA Ribosomal RNA.

RSA Right sacroanterior *position*.

RSP Right sacroposterior *position*.

RSV Rous sarcoma *virus*.

Ru Ruthenium.

rub. Friction encountered in moving one body over another.

   friction r., friction *sound*.

   pericardial r., a friction sound produced by the rubbing together of inflamed or roughened pericardial surfaces.

   pleuritic r., a friction sound produced by the rubbing together of the roughened surfaces of the costal and visceral pleurae.

rubedo (ru-be'do) [L. redness, fr. *ruber*, red]. A temporary redness of the skin.

rubefacient (ru-be-fa'shent) [L. *rubi-facio*, fr. *ruber*, red, + *facio*, to make]. 1. Causing a reddening of the skin. 2. A counterirritant that produces erythema when applied to the skin surface.

rubefaction (ru-be-fak'shun) [see rubefacient]. Erythema of the skin caused by local application of a counterirritant.

rubella (ru-bel'ah) [L. *rubellus*, fem. -*a*, reddish]. German or three-day measles; epidemic roseola; third disease; an acute exanthematous disease caused by rubella virus (*Rubivirus*) and marked by enlargement of lymph nodes, usually with little fever or constitutional reaction; of importance because of the high incidence of abnormalities in children from infection during the first several months of fetal life.

rubeola (ru-be'o-lah) [Mod. L. dim. of *ruber*, red, reddish]. Used as a synonym for two different virus diseases of man: measles and rubella.

rubeosis (ru-be-o'sis) [L. *ruber*, red, + G. -*osis*, condition]. Reddish discoloration, as of skin.

   r. i'ridis diabet'ica, neovascularization of the anterior surface of the iris, seen in chronic severe diabetes.

rubescent (ru-bes'ent) [L. *rubesco*, to become red]. Reddening.

rubidium (ru-bid'i-um) [L. *rubidus*, reddish, dark red]. An alkali element, symbol Rb, atomic no. 37, atomic weight 85.48; its salts have been used in medicine for the same purposes as the corresponding sodium or potassium salts.

Ru'bivirus. A genus of viruses (family Togaviridae) that includes the rubella virus.

ru'bor [L.]. Redness, as one of the four signs of inflammation (r., calor, dolor, tumor) enunciated by Celsus.

ru'briblast [L. *ruber*, red, + G. *blastos*, germ]. Pronormoblast.

rubricyte (ru'brī-sit) [L. *ruber*, red, + *kytos*, cell]. A polychromatic normoblast.

rudiment (ru'dī-ment) [L. *rudimentum, a beginning*]. 1. An organ or structure that is incompletely developed. 2. The first indication of a structure in the course of ontogeny.

ru'dimen'tary. Abortive (2); relating to a rudiment.

rudimentum, pl. **rudimenta** (ru-dī-men'tum, -tah) [L.] [NA]. Rudiment.

rufous (ru'fus) [L. *rufus*, reddish]. Erythristic.

ruga, pl. **rugae** (ru'gah, ru'ge) [L. a wrinkle] [NA]. A fold, ridge, or crease; a wrinkle.

rugine (ru-zhēn') [Fr.]. 1. Periosteum *elevator*. 2. Raspatory.

rugose (ru'gōs) [L. *rugosus*]. Rugous; marked by rugae; wrinkled.

rugosity (ru-gos'ī-tī). 1. The state of being rugose. 2. A ruga.

rugous (ru'gus). Rugose.

rule (rūl) [O. Fr. *reule*, fr. L. *regula*, a guide, pattern]. Criterion; standard; guide.

   American Law Institute r., a 1962 test of criminal responsibility: "a person is not responsible for criminal conduct if at the time of such conduct as a result of mental disease or defect he lacks substantial capacity either to appreciate the wrongfulness of his conduct or to conform his conduct to the requirements of law."

Bartholomew's r. of fourths, the duration of pregnancy can be obtained by measuring the height of the fundus of the uterus above the pubic symphysis.

Clark's weight r., an approximate child's dose (2 years or over) obtained by dividing the child's weight in pounds by 150 and multiplying the result by the adult dose.

Durham r., an American test (1954) of criminal responsibility: "an accused is not criminally responsible if his unlawful act was the product of mental disease or mental defect."

M'Naghten r., the classic English test of criminal responsibility (1843): "to establish a defense on the ground of insanity, it must be clearly proved that, at the time of committing the act, the party accused was laboring under such a defect of reasoning, from disease of the mind, as not to know the nature and quality of the act he was doing, or if he did know it, that he did not know he was doing what was wrong."

Nägele's r., a means of estimating date of delivery by counting back three months from the first day of the last menstrual period and adding seven days.

New Hampshire r., pioneering American test of criminal responsibility (1871): "if the [criminal] act was the offspring of insanity–a criminal intent did not produce it."

Ogino-Knaus r., the basis for "rhythm" method of contraception: the time in the menstrual period when conception is most likely to occur is at about midway between two menstrual periods; fertilization of the ovum is least likely just before or just after menstruation.

r. of outlet, an obstetric r. for determining whether the pelvic outlet will permit the passage of a fetus; the sum of the posterior sagittal diameter (internal) and the transverse diameter (external) of the outlet must equal at least 15 cm if a normal-sized baby is to pass.

Young's r., to determine the dose of a medicine suitable for a child, 12 is added to the child's age and the sum is divided by the age; the adult dose divided by the figure so obtained gives the proper dose for the child.

ru'minant. An animal that chews the cud (sheep, cow, deer, antelope).

rupia (ru'pĭah) [G. *rhypos,* filth]. **1.** Ulcers of late secondary syphilis, covered with yellowish or brown crusts. **2.** Yaws, **3.** Term occasionally used to designate a very scaly and secondarily psoriatic lesion.

ru'pial. Relating to rupia.

rupture (rup'chur) [L. *ruptura,* a break, fracture]. **1.** Hernia. **2.** A tear of solution of continuity; a break of any organ or other of the soft parts.

rusts. Species of *Puccinia* and other microbes comprising important pathogens of plants, especially cereal grains, and important allergens for man when inhaled in large numbers.

ruthenium (ru-the'nĭ-um) [Mediev. L. *Ruthenia,* Russia]. A metallic element of the platinum group; symbol Ru, atomic no. 44, atomic weight 101.1.

ruth'erford [E. *Rutherford*]. A unit of radioactivity: that quantity of radioactive material in which a million disintegrations are taking place per second; 37 r. equal 1 mCi.

ru'tido'sis. Rhytidosis.

RV Residual *volume.*

S

σ [18th letter of the Greek alphabet, sigma] Reflection *coefficient;* standard *deviation.*

S Spherical; spherical *lens;* Svedberg *unit;* siemens; sulfur; percentage saturation of hemoglobin, when followed by subscript O_2 or CO_2.

S$_f$ Flotation *constant.*

s L. *sinister,* left; L. *semis,* half; as a subscript, denotes steady *state.*

S-A Sinoatrial.

sab'ulous [L. *sabulosus,* fr. *sabulum,* coarse sand]. Sandy; gritty.

sac (sak) [L. *saccus,* a bag]. **1.** A pouch or bursa. **2.** An encysted abscess at the root of a tooth. **3.** The capsule of a tumor, or envelope of a cyst.

   allantoic s., the dilated distal portion of the allantois.

   alveolar s., air s., *sacculus* alveolaris.

   amniotic s., amnion.

   conjunctival s., *saccus* conjunctivae.

   dental s., the outer connective tissue envelope surrounding a developing tooth; also applied to the mesenchymal concentration that is the primordium of the s.

   endolymphatic s., *saccus* endolymphaticus.

   greater peritoneal s., *cavum* peritonei.

   heart s., pericardium.

   hernial s., the peritoneal envelope of a hernia.

   lacrimal s., *saccus* lacrimalis.

   tear s., *saccus* lacrimalis.

   yolk s., vitelline s., umbilical vesicle; the highly vascular layer of splanchnopleure surrounding the yolk of an embryo.

saccadic (să-kad'ik) [Fr. *saccade,* sudden check of a horse]. Jerky.

saccate (sak'āt) [L. *saccus,* sac]. Relating to a sac.

sacchar-, sacchari-. See saccharo-.

saccharides (sak'ă-rīds). Carbohydrates; classified as mono-, di-, tri-, and polysaccharides according to the number of monosaccharide groups composing them.

sacchariferous (sak-ă-rif'er-us). Producing sugar.

saccharin (sak'ă-rin). Benzosulfimide; in dilute aqueous solution, 300 to 500 times sweeter than sucrose; used as a sweetening agent (sugar substitute).

saccharine (sak'ă-rēn, -rin). Relating to sugar; sweet.

saccharo-, sacchar-, sacchari- [G. *sakcharon*, sugar]. Combining forms denoting sugar.

saccharogalactorrhea (sak'ă-ro-gă-lak'to-re'ah) [saccharo- + G. *gala*, milk, + *rhoia*, a flow]. Excessive secretion of lactose in milk.

saccharolytic (sak'ă-ro-lit'ik) [saccharo- + G. *lysis*, loosening]. Capable of hydrolyzing or otherwise breaking down a sugar molecule.

saccharometabolic (sak'ă-ro-met'ă-bol'ik). Relating to saccharometabolism.

saccharometabolism (sak-ă-ro-mĕ-tab'o-lizm). Metabolism of sugar; the cellular process of utilization of sugar.

saccharum (sak'ă-rum) [Mod. L. fr. G. *sakcharon*]. Sucrose.

sacciform (sak'sĭ-form) [L. *saccus*, sack, + *forma*, form]. Saccular; sacculated; pouched: sac-shaped.

saccular, sacculated (sak'u-lar, -la-ted). Sacciform.

sacculation (sak-u-la'shun). **1.** A structure formed by a group of sacs. **2.** Formation of a sac or pouch.

saccule (sak'ūl). Sacculus.

s. of larynx, *sacculus* laryngis.

sacculocochlear (sak'u-lo-kok'le-ar). Relating to the sacculus and the membranous cochlea.

sacculus, pl. **sacculi** (sak'u-lus, -li) [L. dim. of *saccus*, sac] [NA]. Saccule; the smaller of the two membranous sacs in the vestibule of the labyrinth.

s. alveola'ris [NA], alveolar or air sac; dilation of the ductuli alveolares which give rise to the alveoli of the lung.

s. laryn'gis [NA], saccule of the larynx; a small diverticulum extending upward from the ventricle of the larynx between the vestibular fold and the lamina of the thyroid cartilage.

saccus, pl. **sacci** (sak'us, sak'si) [L. a bag, sack] [NA]. A sac.

s. conjunctivae [NA], conjunctival sac; the space bound by the conjunctival membrane between the palpebral and bulbar conjunctiva.

s. endolymphat'icus [NA], endolymphatic sac; the dilated blind extremity of the endolymphatic duct.

s. lacrima'lis [NA], lacrimal or tear sac; dacryocyst; the upper portion of the nasolacrimal duct into which empty the two lacrimal canaliculi.

sacr-. See sacro-.

sacrad (sa'krad) [sacr- + L. *ad*, to]. In the direction of the sacrum.

sacral (sa'kral). Relating to or in the neighborhood of the sacrum.

sacralgia (sa-kral'ji-ah) [sacr- + G. *algos*, pain]. Sacrodynia; pain in the sacral region.

sacralization (sa'kral-ĭ-za'shun). Lumbar development of the 1st sacral vertebra.

sacrectomy (sa-krek'to-mĭ) [sacr- + G. *ektomē*, excision]. Resection of a portion of the sacrum to facilitate an operation.

sacro-, sacr- [L. *sacrum, q.v.*]. Combining forms denoting the sacrum.

sacrococcygeal (sa-kro-kok-sij'e-al). Relating to both sacrum and coccyx.

sacrodynia (sa'kro-din'ĭ-ah) [sacro- + G. *odyne*, pain]. Sacralgia.

sacroiliac (sa-kro-il'ĭ-ak). Relating to the sacrum and the ilium.

sa'crolum'bar. Lumbosacral.

sacrosciatic (sa'kro-si-at'ik). Relating to both sacrum and ischium.

sacrospinal (sa'kro-spi'nal). Relating to the sacrum and the vertebral column above.

sacrovertebral (sa-kro-ver'tĕ-bral). Relating to the sacrum and the vertebrae above.

sacrum, pl. **sacra** (sa'krum, sa'krah) [L. sacred bone, fr. *sacer*, sacred]. *Os* sacrum.

saddle (sad'l). Sella; a structure shaped like, or suggestive of, a seat or saddle.

sadism (sa'dizm) [Marquis de *Sade*]. A form of sexual perversion in which the subject finds pleasure in inflicting pain.

sa'dist. One who practices sadism.

sadis'tic. Pertaining to or characterized by sadism.

sadomasochism (sa'do-mas'o-kizm, sad'o-) [sadism + masochism]. A form of sexual perversion marked by love of cruelty in its active and/or passive form.

sagittal (saj'ĭ-tal) [L. *sagitta*, an arrow]. **1.** Resembling an arrow. **2.** In the line of an arrow shot from a bow, *i.e.,* in an anteroposterior direction.

sal, pl. **sal'es** [L.]. Salt.

salicyl'amide. The amide of salicylic acid, an analgesic, antipyretic and antiarthritic, similar in action to aspirin.

salicylate (să-lis'ĭ-lāt, sal-ĭ-sil'ăt). A salt or ester of salicylic acid.

salicyl'ic acid. *o*-Hydroxybenzoic acid; a component of aspirin; also used externally as a keratolytic agent, antiseptic, and fungicide.

salicylism (sal'ĭ-sĭ-lizm). Poisoning by salicylic acid or any of its compounds.

salifiable (sal-ĭ-fi'ă-bl). Capable of being made into salts; said of a base that combines with acids to make salts.

saline (sa'lēn, -līn). **1.** Relating to, of the nature of, or containing salt; salty. **2.** A salt solution.

physiological s., an isotonic aqueous solution of salts in which cells will remain alive for a time; contains 0.9% sodium chloride.

saliva (să-li'vah) [L. akin to G. *sialon*]. Spittle; a slightly acid viscid fluid, consisting of the secretion from the parotid, sublingual, and submaxillary salivary glands and the mucous glands of the oral cavity; keeps the mucous membrane of the mouth moist, lubricates food during mastication, and converts starch into maltose.

sal'ivant. 1. Causing a flow of saliva. **2.** Salivator; an agent that increases the flow of saliva.

salivary (sal'ĭ-vĕr-ĭ) [L. *salivarius*]. Sialic; sialine; relating to saliva.

sal'ivate. To cause an excessive flow of saliva.

salivation (sal'ĭ-va'shun). Sialism.

sal'ivator. Salivant (2).

Salmonella (sal'mo-nel'ah) [D. E. *Salmon*]. A genus of aerobic to facultatively anaerobic Gram-negative bacteria (family Enterobacteriaceae) that are pathogenic for man and other animals. The type species is *S. cholerae-suis.*

  S. chol'erae-su'is, a species which occurs in pigs, and occasionally causes acute gastroenteritis and enteric fever in humans; the type species of the genus *S.*

  S. enterit'idis, Gärtner's bacillus; a species that causes gastroenteritis in man.

  S. hirschfeld'ii, a species causing enteric fever in man.

  S. paraty'phi, a species causing enteric fever in man.

  S. schottmülleri, Schottmüller's bacillus; a species causing enteric fever in man.

  S. ty'phi, *S. typhosa;* typhoid bacillus; a species found in cases of typhoid fever and in contaminated water and food.

  S. typhimu'rium, a species causing food poisoning in humans.

  S. typho'sa, *S. typhi.*

salmonellosis (sal'mo-nel-o'sis) [*Salmonella* + G. *-osis*, condition]. Infection with organisms of the genus *Salmonella.*

salping-. See salpingo-.

salpingectomy (sal-pin-jek'to-mĭ) [salping- + G. *ektomē*, excision]. Tubectomy; removal of the fallopian tube.

salpingemphraxis (sal'pin-jem-frak'sis) [salping- + G. *emphraxis*, a stopping]. Obstruction of the eustachian or fallopian tube.

salpingian (sal-pin'jĭ-an). Relating to the uterine (fallopian) tube or to the auditory (eustachian) tube.

salpingitic (sal-pin-jit'ik). Relating to salpingitis.

salpingitis (sal-pin-ji'tis) [salping- + G. *-itis*, inflammation]. Inflammation of the fallopian or the eustachian tube.

  chronic interstitial s., pachysalpingitis; s. in which fibrosis or mononuclear cell infiltration involves all layers of the fallopian or eustachian tube.

  s. isth'mica nodo'sa, adenosalpingitis; nodular thickening of the tunica muscularis of the isthmic portion of the fallopian tube enclosing gland-like or cystic duplications of the lumen.

salpingo-, salping- [G. *salpinx*, trumpet (tube)]. Combining forms denoting a tube, usually the fallopian or eustachian tubes. See also tubo-.

salpingocele (sal-ping'go-sēl) [salpingo- + G. *kēle*, hernia]. Hernia of a fallopian tube.

salpingography (sal-ping-gog'rǎ-fǐ) [salpingo- + G. *graphō*, to write]. Radiographic imaging of the uterine tubes after the injection of a radiopaque substance.

salpingolysis (sal-ping-gol'ĭ-sis) [salpingo- + G. *lysis*, loosening]. Freeing the fallopian tube from adhesions.

salpingo-oophorectomy (sal-ping'go-o-of-o-rek'to-mĭ). Removal of the ovary and its fallopian tube.

salpingo-oophoritis (sal-ping'go-o-of-o-ri'tis). Inflammation of both fallopian tube and ovary.

salpingo-oophorocele (sal-ping'go-o-of'o-ro-sēl). Hernia of both ovary and fallopian tube.

salpingoperitonitis (sal-ping'go-pĕr-ĭ-to-ni'tis) [salpingo- + peritonitis]. Inflammation of the fallopian tube, perisalpinx, and peritoneum.

salpingopexy (sal-ping'go-pek-sĭ) [salpingo- + G. *pēxis*, fixation]. Operative fixation of an oviduct.

salpingoplasty (sal-ping'go-plas-tĭ) [salpingo- + G. *plassō*, to fashion]. Tuboplasty; plastic operation upon the uterine tubes.

salpingorrhaphy (sal-ping-gor'ǎ-fĭ) [salpingo- + G. *rhaphē*, stitching]. Suture of the fallopian tube.

salpingostomy (sal-ping-gos'to-mĭ) [salpingo- + G. *stoma*, mouth]. Establishment of an artificial opening in a fallopian tube in which the fimbriated extremity has been closed by inflammation.

salpingotomy (sal-ping-got'o-mĭ) [salpingo- + G. *tomē*, incision]. Incision into a fallopian tube.

salpinx, pl. **salpinges** (sal'pingks, sal-pin'jēz) [G. a trumpet (tube)]. **1.** Uterine *tube.* **2.** Auditory *tube.*

salt. 1. A compound formed by the interaction of an acid and a base, the hydrogen atoms of the acid being replaced by the positive ion of the base. **2.** Sodium chloride, the prototypical salt. **3.** A saline cathartic (magnesium sulfate, sodium sulfate, or potassium sodium tartrate); often called salts.

  effervescent s.'s, preparations made by adding sodium bicarbonate and tartaric and citric acids to the active s.; when put in water, the acids break up the sodium bicarbonate, setting free the carbonic acid gas.

  Epsom s.'s, *magnesium* sulfate.

  smelling s.'s, ammonium carbonate, scented with aromatic oils and sniffed as a general stimulant.

saltation (sal-ta'shun) [L. *salto*, pp. *-atus*, to dance]. A dancing or leaping, as in a disease (*e.g.*, chorea) or physiologic function (*e.g.*, saltatory conduction).

sal'tatory. Pertaining to, or characterized by, saltation.

salt'ing out. Precipitation of a protein from its solution by saturation or partial saturation with such neutral salts as sodium chloride, magnesium sulfate, or ammonium sulfate.

salubrious (sǎ-lu'brĭ-us) [L. *salbris*, healthy, fr. *salus*, health]. Healthful, usually in reference to climate.

saluresis (sal-u-re'sis) [L. *sal*, salt, + G. *ourēsis*, uresis (urination)]. Excretion of sodium in the urine.

saluretic (sal-u-ret'ik) Facilitating the renal excretion of sodium.

salutary (sal'u-tĕr-ĭ) [L. salutaris]. Healthful; wholesome.

salve (sav) [A.S. *sealf*]. Ointment.

samarium (să-mĕr'ĭ-um) [bands indicating its presence first found in the spectrum of *samarskite*]. A metallic element of the lanthanide group, symbol Sm, atomic no. 62, atomic weight 150.35.

SAN Sinoatrial *node*.

sanatorium (san-ă-tōr'ĭ-um) [Mod. L. neuter of *sanatorius*, curative]. An institution for the treatment of chronic diseases and for recuperation under medical supervision; often improperly called sanitarium.

san'atory [Mod. L. *sanatorius*]. Health-giving; curative.

sand [A.S.]. The fine detritus of quartz and other crystalline rocks.

    brain s., acervulus; psammoma bodies (2); sabulum; a gritty substance present in central nervous tissue or the pineal gland.

    urinary s., multiple small calculous particles passed in the urine, usually too small to cause significant symptoms or to be identified as a true calculus.

sane [L. *sanus*]. Denoting sanity.

sangui-, sanguin-, sanguino- [G. *sanguis*, blood]. Combining forms meaning blood, bloody.

sanguifacient (sang-gwĭ-fa'shĭ-ent) [sangui- + L. *facio*, to make]. Hemopoietic.

sanguiferous (sang-gwif'er-us) [sangui- + L. *fero*, to carry]. Circulatory (2); conveying blood.

sanguification (sang'gwĭ-fĭ-ka'shun) [sangui- + L. *facio*, to make]. Hemopoiesis.

sanguine (sang'gwin) [L. *sanguineus*]. **1.** Plethoric. **2.** Hopeful; full of vitality.

sanguineous (sang-gwin'e-us) [L. *sanguineus*]. **1.** Relating to blood; bloody. **2.** Plethoric.

sanguinolent (sang-gwin'o-lent) [L. *sanguinolentus*]. Bloody; tinged with blood.

sanguinopurulent (sang'gwĭ-no-pu'ru-lent) [sanguino- + G. *purulentus*, suppurative]. Containing blood and pus.

sanguivorous (sang-gwiv'er-us) [sangui- + L. *voro*, to devour]. Bloodsucking, as applied to certain bats, leeches, insects, etc.

sanies (sa'nĭ-ēz) [L.]. A thin, blood-stained, purulent discharge.

saniopurulent (sa'nĭ-pu'ru-lent) [L. *sanies*, thin, bloody matter, + *purulentus*, suppurative]. Characterized by bloody pus.

sa'niose'rous. Characterized by blood-tinged serum.

sanious (sa'nĭ-us). Relating to sanies.

sanitarian (san-ĭ-tĕr'ĭ-an) [L. *sanitas*, health, fr. *sanus*, sound]. One skilled in the science of public health.

sanitarium (san-ĭ-tĕr'ĭ-um) [L. *sanitas*, health]. A health resort, as contrasted with sanatorium.

sanitary (san'ĭ-tĕr-ĭ) [L. *sanitus*, health]. Healthful; conducive to health; usually in reference to a clean environment.

sanitation (san-ĭ-ta'shun) [L. *sanitas*, health]. The establishment and use of measures designed to promote health and prevent disease.

sanitization (san'ĭ-tĭ-za'shun). The process of making something sanitary.

sanity (san'ĭ-tĭ) [L. *sanitas*, health]. Soundness of mind, emotions, and behavior.

saphenous (să-fe'nus) [G. *saphēnēs*, clearly visible]. Relating to or associated with a saphenous vein; denoting a number of structures in the leg.

sapo-, sapon- [L. *sapo*, soap]. Combining forms relating to soap.

saponaceous (sap-o-na'shus). Soapy; relating to or resembling soap.

saponification (să-pon'ĭ-fĭ-ka'shun) [L. *sapo*, soap, + *facio*, to make]. Conversion into soap; denoting the hydrolytic action of an alkali upon fat.

sap'onins. Glycosides of plant origin characterized by properties of foaming in water and of lysing cells.

sapphism (saf'izm) [*Sapphō*, homosexual Greek poetess of Lesbos]. Lesbianism.

sapr-. See sapro-.

sap'rine. A ptomaine from the putrefying abdominal viscera.

sapro-, sapr- [G. *sapros*, rotten]. Combining forms denoting rotten, putrid, decayed.

saprobe (sap'rōb) [sapro- + G. *bios*, life]. An organism that lives upon dead organic material. This term is preferable to saprophyte, since bacteria and fungi are no longer regarded as plants.

saprobic (sap-ro'bik). Pertaining to a saprobe.

saprogen (sap'ro-jen) [sapro- + G. *-gen*, producing]. An organism living on dead organic matter and causing the decay thereof.

saprogenic, saprogenous (sa-pro-jen'ik, să-proj'en-us). Causing or resulting from decay.

saprophyte (sap'ro-fīt) [sapro- + G. *phyton*, plant]. See saprobe.

saprophytic (sap-ro-fit'ik). Relating to a saprophyte.

saprozoic (sap'ro-zo'ik) [sapro- + G. *zōikos*, relating to animals]. Living in decaying organic matter, denoting especially certain protozoa.

saprozoonosis (sap'ro-zo-o-no'sis) [sapro- + G. *zōon*, animal, + *nosos*, disease]. A zoonosis the agent of which requires both a vertebrate host and a nonanimal (food, soil, plant) reservoir or developmental site for completion of its cycle.

Sarcina (sar'sĭ-nah) [L. *sarcina*, a pack, bundle]. A genus of strictly anaerobic Gram-positive bacteria (family Micrococcaceae) in which saprophytic and facultatively parasitic species occur. The type species is *S. ventriculi.*

sarco- [G. *sarx* (*sark-*), flesh]. Combining form denoting muscular substance or a resemblance to flesh.

sar'coblast [sarco- + G. *blastos*, germ]. Myoblast.

sarcocarcinoma (sar'ko-kar-sĭ-no'mah). Carcinosarcoma.

sarcocele (sar'ko-sēl) [sarco- + G. *kēlē*, tumor]. A fleshy tumor or sarcoma of the testis.

Sarcodina (sar'ko-di'nah, -de'nah) [Mod. L. fr. G. *sarx*, flesh]. A superclass of protozoa (subphylum Sarcomastigophora) possessing pseudopodia for locomotion.

sarcoid (sar'koyd) [sarco- + G. *eidos*, resemblance]. **1.** Sarcoidosis. **2.** A tumor resembling a sarcoma.

    Boeck's s., sarcoidosis.

sarcoidosis (sar-koy-do'sis) [sarcoid + G. *-osis*, condition]. Sarcoid (1); Boeck's disease or sarcoid; Besnier-Boeck-Schaumann syndrome or disease; Schaumann's syndrome; a systemic granulomatous disease of unknown cause, especially involving the lungs with resulting fibrosis, but also involving lymph nodes, skin, liver, spleen, eyes, phalangeal bones, and parotid glands; granulomas are composed of epithelioid and multinucleated giant cells with little or no necrosis.

sarcolemma (sar-ko-lem'ah) [sarco- + G. *lemma*, husk]. The plasma membrane of a muscle fiber.

sarcolem'mal, sarcolem'mic, sarcolem'mous. Relating to the sarcolemma.

sarcoma (sar-ko'mah) [G. *sarkōma*, a fleshy excrescence, fr. *sarx*, flesh, + *-oma*, tumor]. A connective tissue neoplasm, usually highly malignant, formed by proliferation of mesodermal cells.

    alveolar soft part s., a malignant tumor formed of a reticular stroma of connective tissue enclosing aggregates of large round or polygonal cells.

    ameloblastic s., a mixed odontogenic tumor in which the mesenchymal component exhibits histocellular features of malignant change.

    botryoid s., a polypoid form of rhabdomyosarcoma which occurs in children, most frequently in the urogenital tract; characterized by the formation of grossly apparent grapelike clusters of neoplastic tissue that consist of rhabdomyoblasts, spindle, and stellate cells in a myxomatous stroma.

    endometrial stromal s., a relatively rare s. in which the lesions form multiple foci in the myometrium and in vascular spaces in other sites, and which consist of histologic and cytologic elements that resemble those of the endometrial stroma.

    giant cell s., a malignant giant cell tumor of bone.

    Kaposi's s., a multifocal malignant or benign neoplasm of primitive vasoformative tissue, occurring in the skin and sometimes in lymph nodes or viscera; consists of spindle cells and small vascular spaces frequently infiltrated by hemosiderin-pigmented macrophages.

    osteogenic s., osteosarcoma; the most common and malignant of bone s.'s, which arises from bone-forming cells and affects chiefly the ends of long bones.

sarcomatoid (sar-ko'mă-toyd) [sarcoma + G. *eidos*, resemblance]. Resembling a sarcoma.

sarcomatosis (sar-ko-mă-to'sis) [sarcoma + G. *-osis*, condition]. Occurrence of several sarcomatous growths on different parts of the body.

sarcomatous (sar-ko'mă-tus). Relating to or of the nature of sarcoma.

sarcomere (sar'ko-mēr) [sarco- + G. *meros*, part]. The part of a cross-striated muscle fiber between two adjacent Z lines.

sarcoplasm (sar'ko-plazm) [sarco- + G. *plasma*, a thing formed]. The nonfibrillar cytoplasm of a muscle fiber.

sarcoplas'mic. Relating to sarcoplasm.

sarcopoietic (sar'ko-poy-et'ik) [sarco- + G. *poiēsis*, a making]. Forming muscle.

Sarcoptes scabiei (sar-kop'tez ska'bī-i) [sarco- + G. *koptō*, to cut; L. *scabies*, scurf]. *Acarus scabiei*; the itch mite, varieties of which affect man and various domestic and wild animals, and cause scabies and mange.

sarcosinemia (sar'ko-sī-ne'mī-ah). Hypersarcosinemia; a disorder of amino acid metabolism due to deficiency of sarcosine dehydrogenase; characterized by elevated sarcosine in blood plasma and excretion in the urine, failure to thrive, irritability, muscle tremors, and retarded motor and mental development; autosomal recessive inheritance.

sarcosis (sar-ko'sis) [G. *sarkōsis*, the growth of flesh]. **1.** An abnormal increase of flesh. **2.** A multiple growth of fleshy tumors. **3.** A diffuse sarcoma involving the whole of an organ.

sarcostosis (sar'kos-to'sis) [sarco- + G. *osteon*, bone, + *-osis*, condition]. Ossification of muscular tissue.

sarcot'ic. 1. Relating to sarcosis. **2.** Causing an increase of flesh.

sarcotubules (sar-ko-tu'būlz). The continuous system of membranous tubules in striated muscle which corresponds to the smooth endoplasmic reticulum of other cells.

sar'cous [G. *sarx*, flesh]. Relating to muscular tissue; muscular; fleshy.

sardon'ic grin [G. *sardanios, sardonios*, an epithet of bitter, scornful laughter]. *Risus* sardonicus.

sat. Saturated.

satellite (sat'ĕ-līt) [L. *satelles* (*satellit-*), attendant]. A minor structure accompanying a more important or larger one.

    chromosome s., a small chromosomal segment separated from the main body of the chromosome by a secondary constriction; in man, usually associated with the short arm of an acrocentric chromosome.

    nucleolar s., a small dot of chromatin found adjacent to the nucleolus in nerve cells of females.

satellitosis (sat'ĕ-lĭ-to'sis) [L. *satelles* (*satellit-*), an attendant, + G. *-osis*, condition]. A condition marked by an accumulation of neuroglia cells around the neurons of the central nervous system; often as a prelude to neuronophagia.

satiation (sa-shī-a'shun) [L. *satio*, pp. *-atus*, to fill, satisfy]. The state produced by having had a specific need fulfilled, such as hunger or thirst.

sat. sol. Saturated *solution*.

saturate (satch'u-rāt) [L. *saturo*, pp. *-atus*, to fill, fr. *satur*, sated]. **1.** To impregnate to the greatest possible extent. **2.** To neutralize; to satisfy all the chemical affinities of a substance. **3.** To dissolve a substance up to that concentration beyond which the addition of more results in two phases.

saturation (satch'u-ra'shun). **1.** The act of saturating or the state of being saturated. **2.** Filling of all the available sites on an enzyme molecule by its substrate, or on a hemoglobin molecule by oxygen (SO_2) or carbon monoxide (SCO).

secondary s., a technique of nitrous oxide anesthesia that consists of an abrupt curtailment of the oxygen in the inhaled mixture in order to produce a deep plane of anesthesia, following which oxygen is administered to correct overdosage and produce muscular relaxation.

saturnine (sat'ur-nin) [L. *saturnus*, lead, fr. *saturnis*, the god and planet Saturn]. **1.** Relating to lead. **2.** Due to or symptomatic of lead poisoning.

satyriasis (sat-ĭ-ri'ă-sis) [G. *satyros*, a satyr]. Excessive sexual excitement and behavior in the male.

saucerization (saw'ser-ĭ-za'shun). Excavation of tissue to form a shallow depression, performed in wound treatment to facilitate drainage from infected areas.

sax'itox'in. A potent neurotoxin found in shellfish, such as the mussel or the clam, produced by the dinoflagellate *Gonyaulax catenella,* which is ingested by the shellfish.

Sb Antimony (stibium).

Sc Scandium

s.c. Subcutaneous or subcutaneously.

scab (skab) [A.S. *scaeb*]. A crust formed by coagulation of blood, pus, serum, or a combination of these, on the surface of an ulcer, erosion, or other type of wound.

scabicidal (ska-bĭ-si'dal). Destructive to itch mites.

scabicide (ska'bĭ-sīd). An agent lethal to itch mites.

scabies (ska'beez) [L. fr. *scabo*, to scratch]. **1.** A skin eruption due to the female *Sarcoptes scabiei* var. *hominis,* which burrows into the skin, producing a vesicular eruption with intense pruritus between the fingers, on the male genitalia, buttocks, and elsewhere on the trunk and extremities. **2.** In animals, usually applied to cutaneous acariasis in sheep, which may be caused by *Sarcoptes, Psoroptes,* or *Chorioptes;* mite infections causing dermatitis in wild and domestic animals are more commonly called mange, and may be caused by members of the genera listed above and of others such as *Demodex, Notoedres,* and *Otodectes.*

scala, pl. **scalae** (ska'lah, -le) [L. a stairway] [NA]. One of the cavities of the cochlea winding spirally around the modiolus.

s. me'dia, *ductus* cochlearis.

s. tym'pani [NA], the division of the spiral canal of the cochlea lying below the lamina spiralis.

s. vestib'uli [NA], vestibular canal; the division of the spiral canal of the cochlea lying above the lamina spiralis and vestibular membrane.

scald (skawld) [L. *excaldo*, to wash in hot water]. **1.** To burn by contact with a hot liquid or steam. **2.** The lesion resulting from such contact.

scale (skāl). [L. *scala*, a stairway] **1.** A strip of metal, glass, or other substance, marked off in lines, for measuring. **2.** A standardized test for measuring psychological, personality, or behavioral characteristics. See also subentries under test. [O.E. *scealu,* fr. O.Fr. *escale,* shell, husk] **3.** Squama. **4.** A small thin plate of horny epithelium, resembling a fish s., cast off from the skin. **5.** To desquamate. **6.** To remove tartar from the teeth.

absolute s., Kelvin s.

Baumé s., one of two hydrometer s.'s for determining the specific gravity of liquids lighter and heavier than water: for liquids lighter than water divide 140 by 130 plus the Baumé degree; for liquids heavier than water divide 145 by 145 minus the Baumé degree.

Binet s., a measure of intelligence designed for both children and adults.

Celsius s., centigrade s., the temperature s. in which there are 100 degrees between the freezing point (0°C) and boiling point (100°C) of water at sea level.

Charrière s., the French s. (Fr) for grading the sizes of urethral catheters or sounds.

coma s., a clinical method to assess impaired consciousness: motor responsiveness, verbal performance, and eye opening, and also dysfunction of cranial nerves.

Fahrenheit s., a thermometer s., in which the freezing point of water is 32°F and the boiling point of water 212°F.

French s. a s. of catheter size, used in the Charrière s.

gray s., see gray-scale *ultrasonography.*

isometric s., a radiopaque strip of metal calibrated in centimeters and placed between the buttocks of the patient; since it is subject to the same distortions as pelvic diameters, it can be used to measure anteroposterior diameters of the pelvis directly.

Kelvin s., absolute s.; temperature measured in degrees Celsius from absolute zero (−273.16°C).

Stanford-Binet intelligence s., Binet or Binet-Simon test; a standardized test for the measurement of intelligence consisting of a series of questions, graded according to the intelligence of normal children at different ages, the answers to which indicate the mental age of the person tested.

Wechsler intelligence s.'s, standardized s.'s for the measurement of general intelligence in preschool children (Wechsler preschool and primary s. of intelligence), in children (Wechsler intelligence s. for children), and in adults (Wechsler adult intelligence s., the successor to the Wechsler-Bellevue s.).

scalenectomy (ska-le-nek'to-mĭ). Resection of the scalene muscles.

scalenotomy (ska-le-not'o-mĭ). Division or section of the anterior scalene muscle.

scaling (ska'ling). In dentistry, removal of accretions from the crowns and roots of teeth by use of special instruments.

scalp (skălp) [M. E. fr. Scand. *skalpr*, sheath]. The skin covering the cranium.

scalpel (skal'pl) [L. *scalpellum;* dim. of *scalprum*, a knife]. A knife used in surgical dissection.

scalprum (skal'prum) [L. chisel, penknife, fr. *scalpo*, pp. *sculptus*, to carve]. **1.** A large strong scalpel. **2.** A raspatory.

scaly (ska'lĭ). Squamous.

scan (skan). **1.** To move a beam in search of a structure; *e.g.*, to move an ultrasonic beam to make a trace follow in synchronism. **2.** In computed tomography, the mechanical motion of the CT machine required to produce the image(s).

scandium (skan'dĭ-um) [L. *Scandia*, Scandinavia, where discovered]. A metallic element, symbol Sc, atomic no. 21, atomic weight 44.96.

scanning (skan'ing) [L. *scando*, to climb]. Scintiscanning; photoscanning; determination of the distribution of a specific radioactive element or compound or an internally administered radiopharmaceutical in the body by recording the emitted ray on a photographic film.

scapha (skaf'ah, ska'fah) [L. fr. G. *skaphē*, skiff] [NA]. **1.** A boat-shaped structure. **2.** The longitudinal furrow between the helix and the antihelix of the auricle.

scapho- [G. *skaphē*, skiff, boat]. Combining form denoting scapha or scaphoid.

scaphocephalic, scaphocephalous (skaf'o-sē-fal'ik, sef'ă-lus) [scapho- + G. *kephalē*, head]. Denoting a long narrow skull with a ridge along the prematurely ossified sagittal suture.

scaphoid (skaf'oyd) [scapho- + G. *eidos*, resemblance]. Navicular; boat-shaped; hollowed.

scapula, pl. **scapulae** (skap'u-lah, -le) [L.] [NA]. The shoulder blade; a large triangular flattened bone lying over the ribs, posteriorly on either side, articulating laterally with the clavicle and the humerus.

s. ala'ta, winged s.

scaphoid s., a s. in which the vertebral border below the level of the spine presents a concavity in place of the normal convexity; the **scaphoid type of s.** (Graves) is one in which the vertebral border between the spine and the teres major process is straight or somewhat concave.

winged s., s. alata; posterior and lateral protrusion of the medial border of the scapula from the thorax as the scapula rotates out; caused by paralysis of the serratus anterior muscle.

scapular (skap'u-lar). Relating to the scapula.

scapulectomy (skap-u-lek'to-mĭ) [scapula + G. *ektomē*, excision]. Excision of the scapula.

scapulo- [L. *scapulae*, shoulder blades]. Combining form denoting scapula or scapular.

scapuloclavicular (skap'u-lo-klă-vik'u-lar). **1.** Acromioclavicular. **2.** Coracoclavicular.

scapulohumeral (skap'u-lo-hu'mer-al). Relating to both scapula and humerus.

scapulopexy (skap'u-lo-pek-sĭ) [scapulo- + G. *pēxis*, fixation]. Operative fixation of the scapula to the chest wall or to the spinous process of the vertebrae.

scapus, pl. **scapi** (ska'pus, -pi) [L. shaft, stalk]. A shaft or stem.

scar (skar) [G. *eschara*, scab]. Cicatrix; the fibrous tissue replacing normal tissues destroyed by injury or disease.

scarification (skăr'ĭ-fī-ka'shun) [L. *scarifico*, to scratch]. The making of a number of superficial incisions in the skin.

scarificator (skăr'ĭ-fī-ka-tor). An instrument for scarification, consisting of concealed spring-projected cutting blades, set closely together, that make superficial incisions in the skin.

scarlatina (skar-lă-te'nah) [through It. fr. Med. L. *scarlatum*, scarlet, a scarlet cloth]. Scarlet fever; an acute exanthematous disease caused by streptococcal erythrogenic toxin and marked by fever and other constitutional disturbances, and a generalized eruption of closely aggregated points or small macules of a bright red color, followed by desquamation.

anginose s., s. angino'sa, Fothergill's disease (2); a form of s. in which the throat affection is unusually severe.

s. hemorrhag'ica, a form in which blood extravasates into the skin and mucous membranes, giving to the eruption a dusky hue; frequently with bleeding from the nose and into the intestine.

scarlatinal (skar-lă-te'nal). Relating to scarlatina.

scarlatinella (skar'lă-tĭ-nel'ah) [dim. of scarlatina]. Fourth *disease*.

scarlatiniform (skar-lă-te'nĭ-form, -tin'ĭ-form). Scarlatinoid; resembling scarlatina; denoting a rash.

scarlatinoid (skar-lă-te'noyd, -lat'ĭ-noyd) [scarlatina + G. *eidos*, resemblance]. Scarlatiniform.

scarlet red. *o*-Tolylazo-*o*-tolylazo-β-naphthol. An azo dye used in medicine as a vulnerary, in histology to stain fat in tissue sections and basic proteins at high pH, and in immunoelectrophoresis.

scatemia (skă-te'mĭ-ah) [scato- + G. *haima*, blood]. Intestinal autointoxication.

scato- [G. *skōr* (*skat-*), feces, excrement]. Combining forms denoting feces. See also copro-, sterco-.

scatologic (skat-o-loj'ik). Pertaining to scatology.

scatology (skă-tol'o-jĭ) [scato- + G. *logos*, study]. **1.** Coprology; the study and analysis of the feces for physiologic and diagnostic purposes. **2.** The study relating to the psychiatric aspects of excrement or the excremental (anal) function.

scatophagy (skă-tof'ă-jĭ) [scato- + G. *phagein*, to eat]. Coprophagy; eating of excrement.

scatoscopy (skă-tos'ko-pĭ) [scato- + G. *skopeō*, to view]. Examination of the feces for purposes of diagnosis.

scat′ter. A change in direction of a photon or subatomic particle, as the result of a collision or interaction.

schema, pl. **schemata** (ske′mah, skĕ-mä′tah) [G. *schēma,* shape, form]. **1.** A plan, outline, or arrangement. **2.** In sensorimotor theory, the organized unit of cognitive experience.

schindylesis (skin-dĭ-le′sis) [G. *schindylēsis,* splintering] [NA]. Wedge-and-groove joint, a form of fibrous joint in which the sharp edge of one bone is received in a cleft in the edge of the other, as in the articulation of the vomer with the rostrum of the sphenoid.

schisto- [G. *schistos,* split]. Combining form denoting split or cleft. See also schizo-.

schistocelia (skis-to-se′lĭ-ah) [schisto- + G. *koilia,* a hollow]. A congenital fissure of the abdominal wall.

schistocormia (skis-to-kor′mĭ-ah) [schisto- + G. *kormos,* trunk of a tree]. Schistosomia; a congenital cleft of the trunk, the lower extremities of the fetus usually being imperfectly developed.

schistocyte (skis′to-sīt) [schisto- + G. *kytos,* cell]. A variety of poikilocyte that owes its abnormal shape to fragmentation occurring as the cell flows through damaged small vessels.

schistocytosis (skis-to-si-to′sis). Schizocytosis; the occurrence of many schistocytes in the blood.

schistoglossia (skis-to-glos′ĭ-ah) [schisto- + G. *glōssa,* tongue]. A congenital fissure or cleft of the tongue.

Schistosoma (skis-to-so′mah) [schisto- + G. *sōma,* body]. A genus of digenetic trematodes, including the important blood flukes of man and domestic animals, that cause schistosomiasis.

    S. **haemato′bium,** the vesical blood fluke, a species with terminally spined eggs that occurs as a parasite in the portal system and mesenteric veins of the bladder (causing human schistosomiasis haematobium) and rectum; found along waterways, irrigation ditches, or streams throughout Africa and in parts of the Middle East; intermediate hosts are snails of the subfamily Bulininae (*Bulinus, Physopsis, Pyrgophysa*).

    S. **japon′icum,** the Oriental or Japanese blood fluke, a species having eggs with small lateral spines, causes schistosomiasis japonicum, with extensive pathology from encapsulation of the eggs, particularly in the liver; intermediate hosts are amphibious snails (species of *Oncomelania,* family Amnicolidae); many domestic animals serve as reservoir hosts.

    S. **manso′ni,** a common species in Africa, parts of the Middle East, the West Indies, South America, and certain Caribbean islands and the cause of human schistosomiasis mansoni; characterized by large eggs with a strong lateral spine and transmitted by snails of the genus *Biomphalaria.*

schistosome (skis′to-sōm). Common name for a member of the genus *Schistosoma.*

schistosomia (skis-to-so′mĭ-ah) [schisto- + G. *sōma,* body]. Schistocormia.

schistosomiasis (skis′to-so-mi′ă-sis). Bilharziasis; infection with a species of *Schistosoma;* manifestations of which vary with the infecting species but depend in large measure upon tissue reaction (granulation and fibrosis) to the eggs deposited in venules and in the hepatic portals, the latter resulting in portal hypertension and esophageal varices, as well as liver damage leading to cirrhosis.

    s. **haemato′bium,** endemic hamaturia; infestation with *Schistosoma haematobium,* the eggs of which invade the urinary tract, causing cystitis and hematuria.

    s. **japon′icum,** Katayama disease; infection with *Schistosoma japonicum,* characterized by dysenteric symptoms, painful enlargement of liver and spleen, dropsy, urticaria, and progressive anemia.

    s. **manso′ni,** Manson's disease; infection with *Schistosoma mansoni,* the eggs of which invade the wall of the large intestine and the liver, causing irritation, inflammation, and ultimately fibrosis.

schistothorax (skis-to-tho′raks) [schisto- + G. *thorāx,* thorax]. Congenital cleft of the chest wall.

schiz-. See schizo-.

schizamnion (skiz-am′nĭ-on) [schiz- + amnion]. An amnion developing, as in the human embryo, by the formation of a cavity within the inner cell mass.

schizaxon (skiz-ak′son) [schiz- + G. *axōn,* axis]. A neuraxon divided into two branches.

schizo-, schiz- [G. *schizō,* to split or cleave]. Combining forms denoting split, cleft, or division. See also schisto-.

schizogenesis (skiz-o-jen′ĕ-sis) [schizo- + G. *genesis,* origin]. Fissiparity; origin by fission.

schizogony (skĭ-zog′o-nĭ) [schizo- + G. *gonē,* generation]. Agamocytogeny; multiple fission in which the nucleus divides first and the cell then divides into as many parts as there are nuclei.

schizogyria (skiz-o-ji′rĭ-ah, -jĭr′ĭ-ah) [schizo- + G. *gyros,* circle (convolution)]. A deformity of the cerebral convolutions marked by occasional interruptions of continuity.

schizoid (skit′zoyd) [schizo(phrenia), + G. *eidos,* resemblance]. **1.** Schizophrenia-like; resembling the personality characteristic of schizophrenia, but in milder form. **2.** Also used to describe the withdrawal or "shut-in-ness" of the introverted personality.

schizomycete (skiz′o-mi-sēt). A member of the class Schizomycetes; a bacterium.

Schizomycetes (skiz-o-mi-se′tēz) [schizo- + G. *mykēs,* fungus]. Fission fungi; a class comprised of all the bacteria; a misnomer, since bacteria are generally not considered to be fungi except as "fungi" is loosely used to include all nonchlorophyllous organisms of low order.

schizont (skiz′ont) [schizo- + G. *ōn (ont-),* a being]. A sporozoan trophozoite (vegetative form) that reproduces by schizogony, producing a varied number of daughter trophozoites or merozoites.

schizonychia (skiz-o-nik′ĭ-ah) [schizo- + G. *onyx,* nail]. Splitting of the nails.

schizophasia (skiz-o-fa′zĭ-ah) [schizo- + G. *phasis*, speech]. The disordered speech of the schizophrenic person; "word-salad."

schizophrenia (skit′so-fre′nĭ-ah, skiz′o-) [schizo- + G. *phrēn*, mind]. A term synonymous with and replacing dementia precox; the most common type of psychosis, characterized by a disorder in the thinking processes, such as delusions and hallucinations, and extensive withdrawal of the individual's interest from other people and the outside world, and the investment of it in one's own; now considered a group of mental disorders rather than as a single entity.

   catatonic s., s. characterized by marked disturbances in activity, with either generalized inhibition or excessive activity.

   hebephrenic s., hebephrenia.

   latent s., a preexisting susceptibility for developing overt s. under strong emotional stress.

   paranoid s., s. characterized predominantly by delusions of persecution and megalomania.

   process s., those forms of severe schizophrenic disorders in which chronic and progressive organic brain changes are considered to be the primary cause and in which prognosis is poor.

   reactive s., those forms of severe schizophrenic disorders that are distinguished from process s. by their more acute onset, greater relation to environmental stress, and better prognosis.

schizophrenic (skit′so-fren′ik, -fre′nik, skiz′o-). Relating to or suffering from one of the schizophrenias.

schizotrichia (skiz-o-trik′ĭ-ah) [schizo- + G. *thrix*, hair]. A splitting of the hairs at their ends.

schwannoma (schwah-no′mah, shvah-) [T. *Schwann*]. **1.** Neurofibroma. **2.** Neurilemoma.

schwannosis (shwah-no′sis). A non-neoplastic proliferation of Schwann cells in the perivascular spaces of the spinal cord.

sciage (se-ahzh′) [Fr. *scie,* saw]. A to-and-fro sawlike movement of the hand in massage.

sciatic (si-at′ik) [Med. L. *sciaticus,* fr. G. *ischion,* the hip joint]. **1.** Ischiadic; ischial; ischiatic; relating to or situated in the neighborhood of the ischium or hip. **2.** Relating to sciatica.

sciatica (si-at′ĭ-kah) [see sciatic]. Pain in the lower back and hip radiating down the back of the thigh into the leg, usually due to herniated lumbar disc.

scinticisternography (sin′tĭ-sis-tern-og′ră-fĭ). Cisternography performed with a radiopharmaceutical and recorded with a stationary imaging device.

scintigram (sin′tĭ-gram) [fr. L. *scintilla,* spark + G. *gramma,* something written]. Scintiscan.

scintigraphy (sin-tig′ră-fĭ). Scintiphotography.

scintillascope (sin-til′ă-skōp) [L. *scintilla,* spark, + G. *skopeō,* to observe]. Scintillation *counter.*

scintillation (sin-tĭ-la′shun) [L. *scintilla,* a spark]. **1.** A flashing or sparkling; a subjective sensation of sparks or flashes of light. **2.** In nuclear medicine, the light emitted when an x- or gamma ray is absorbed by a crystal or liquid radiation detector.

scintillator (sin′tĭ-la-tor) [L. *scintilla,* spark]. Scintillation *counter.*

scintiphotography (sin′tĭ-fo-tog′ră-fĭ). Scintigraphy; the process of obtaining a photographic recording of the distribution of an internally administered radiopharmaceutical with the use of a stationary scintillation detector device, a gamma camera.

scintiscan (sin′tĭ-skan). Gammagram; photoscan; scintigram; the record obtained by scanning; the photographic display of the distribution of an internally administered radiopharmaceutical.

scintiscanner (sin′tĭ-skan′er). The apparatus used to make a scintiscan.

scintiscanning (sin-tĭ-skan′ing). Scanning.

scirrhous (skĭr′us, sĭr-). Hard; indurated.

scission (sish′un) [L. *scissio,* fr. *scindo,* pp. *scissus,* to cleave]. **1.** A separation, division, or splitting, as in fusion. **2.** Cleavage (2).

scissura, pl. **scissurae** (sĭ-su′rah, -re) [L.]. Scissure. **1.** A cleft or fissure. **2.** A splitting.

scissure (sish′ūr). Scissura.

scler-. See sclero-.

sclera, pl. **scleras, sclerae** (sklēr′ah, sklēr′e) [Mod. L. fr. G. *sklēros,* hard] [NA]. Sclerotica; white of the eye; a fibrous tunic forming the outer envelope of the eye, except for its anterior sixth occupied by the cornea.

scleradenitis (sklēr′ad-ĕ-ni′tis) [scler- + G. *adēn,* gland, + -*itis,* inflammation]. Inflammatory induration of a gland.

scleral (sklēr′al). Sclerotic (1); relating to the sclera.

sclerectasia (sklēr-ek-ta′zĭ-ah) [scler- + G. *ektasis,* an extension]. Localized bulging of the sclera lined with uveal tissue.

sclerectoiridectomy (skle-rek′to-ĭr-ĭ-dek′to-mĭ). Sclerectomy and iridectomy used in glaucoma to form a filtering cicatrix.

sclerectoiridodialysis (skle-rek′to-ĭr′ĭ-do-di-al′ĭ-sis). Sclerectomy and iridodialysis for relief of glaucoma.

sclerectomy (skle-rek′to-mĭ) [scler- + G. *ektomē,* excision]. **1.** Excision of a portion of the sclera. **2.** Removal of the fibrous adhesions formed in chronic otitis media.

scleredema (sklēr-ĕ-de′mah) [scler- + G. *oidēma,* a swelling (edema)]. Hard nonpitting edema of the skin, giving a waxy appearance with no sharp demarcation.

   s. adulto′rum, a benign spreading induration of the skin and subcutaneous tissue, appearing first on the head and neck and extending over the trunk; a misnomer, since the disease is not restricted to adults.

sclerema (skle-re′mah) [scler- + edema]. Induration of the subcutaneous fat.

   s. neonato′rum, s. adipo′sum, adiponecrosis neonatorum; subcutaneous fat necrosis appearing at birth or in early infancy as sharply demarcated indurated plaques, usually involving the cheeks, buttocks, shoulders, and calves.

scleriritomy (sklēr-ĭ-rit′o-mĭ). Incising the iris and sclera.

scleritis (skle-ri′tis). Inflammation of the sclera.

   anterior s., an inflammation of the sclera adjoining the limbus of the cornea, appearing as a dark red or bluish swelling.

   posterior s., s. with a tendency to extend posteriorly to Tenon's capsule and causing chemosis.

sclero-, scler- [G. *sklēros*, hard]. Combining forms denoting hardness (induration), sclerosis, or relationship to the sclera.

scleroblastema (sklēr′o-blas-te′mah) [sclero- + G. *blastēma*, sprout]. The embryonic tissue entering into the formation of bone.

sclerochoroiditis (sklēr′o-ko-roy-di′tis). Inflammation of the sclerotic and choroid coats of the eye.

scleroconjunctival (sklēr′o-kon-jungk-ti′val). Relating to the sclera and the conjunctiva.

sclerocornea (sklēr-o-kor′ne-ah). **1.** The cornea and sclera regarded as forming together the hard outer coat of the eye. **2.** A congenital anomaly in which the whole or part of the cornea is opaque and resembles the sclera; other ocular abnormalities are frequently present.

sclerodactyly, sclerodactylia (sklēr-o-dak′tĭ-lĭ, -dak-til′ĭ-ah) [sclero- + G. *daktylos*, finger or toe]. Acrosclerosis.

scleroderma (sklēr-o-der′mah) [sclero- + G. *derma*, skin]. Dermatosclerosis; thickening of the skin caused by swelling and thickening of fibrous tissue, with eventual atrophy of the epidermis; a manifestation of progressive systemic sclerosis and used synonymously for that disease.

   circumscribed s., morphea.

sclerogenous (skle-roj′ĕ-nus) [sclero- + G. *-gen*, producing]. Producing hard or sclerotic tissue; causing sclerosis.

scleroid (sklēr′oyd) [sclero- + G. *eidos*, resemblance]. Sclerous; sclerosal; indurated or sclerotic, of unusually firm texture, leathery, or scar-like texture.

scleroiritis (sklēr′o-i-ri′tis). Inflammation of both the sclera and iris.

sclerokeratitis (sklēr′o-kĕr-ă-ti′tis) [sclero- + G. *keras*, horn]. Inflammatory cellular infiltration of the sclera and cornea.

sclerokeratoiritis (skle′r-o-kĕr′ă-to-i-ri′tis). Inflammation of sclera, cornea, and iris.

scleroma (skle-ro′mah) [G. *sklērōma*, an induration]. A circumscribed indurated focus of granulation tissue in the skin or mucous membrane.

   respiratory s., rhinoscleroma in which the lesion involves the mucous membrane of the greater part or all of the upper respiratory tract.

scleromalacia (sklēr′o-mă-la′shĭ-ah) [sclero- + G. *malakia*, a softening]. Degenerative thinning of the sclera, occurring in persons with rheumatoid arthritis and other collagen disorders.

scleromere (sklēr′o-mēr) [sclero- + G. *meros*, part]. Any metamere of the skeleton, such as a vertebral segment.

scleromyxedema (sklēr′o-mik-se-de′mah). Lichen myxedematosus with diffuse thickening of the skin underlying the papules.

scleronychia (sklēr-o-nik′ĭ-ah) [sclero- + G. *onyx*, nail, + *-ia*, condition]. Induration and thickening of the nails.

sclero-oophoritis (sklēr′o-o-of′o-ri′tis) [sclero- + Mod. L. *oophoron*, ovary + G. *-itis*, inflammation]. Inflammatory induration of the ovary.

sclerophthalmia (sklēr-of-thal′mĭ-ah) [sclero- + G. *opthalmos*, eye]. A congenital condition in which the opacity of the sclera has advanced over the edge of the cornea so that only a small central area of the latter remains transparent.

scle′ropro′tein. Albuminoid (3).

sclerosal (skle-ro′sal). Scleroid.

sclerose (skle-rōz′). To harden; to undergo sclerosis.

sclerosis (skle-ro′sis) [G. *sklērōsis*, hardness]. **1.** Induration of chronic inflammatory origin. **2.** In neuropathy, induration of nervous and other structures by a hyperplasia of the interstitial fibrous or glial connective tissue.

   amyotrophic lateral s., Charcot's disease; a disease of the motor tracts of the lateral columns and anterior horns of the spinal cord, causing progressive muscular atrophy, increased reflexes, fibrillary twitching, and spastic irritability of muscles.

   arterial s., arteriosclerosis.

   lateral spinal s., a degenerative state of the lateral tracts of the spinal cord causing spastic paraplegia; a clinical variant of amyotrophic lateral s.

   Mönckeberg's s., Mönckeberg's *arteriosclerosis.*

   multiple s. (MS), occurrence of patches of s. (plaques) in the brain and spinal cord, causing some degree of paralysis, tremor, nystagmus, and disturbances of speech, the various symptoms depending upon the seat of the lesions; occurs chiefly in early adult life, with characteristic exacerbations and remissions.

   progressive systemic s., scleroderma; a systemic disease characterized by formation of hyalinized and thickened collagenous fibrous tissue, with thickening of the skin and adhesion to underlying tissues, especially of the hands and face.

   tuberous s., Bourneville's disease; multisystem hamartomas producing a typical triad of seizures, mental retardation, and skin nodules of the face; autosomal dominant inheritance with variable penetrance and expression.

sclerostenosis (sklēr-o-stĕ-no′sis) [sclero- + G. *stenōsis*, a narrowing]. Induration and contraction of the tissues.

sclerostomy (skle-ros′to-mĭ) [sclero- + G. *stoma*, mouth]. Surgical perforation of the sclera, as for the relief of glaucoma.

sclerotherapy (sklĕr-o-thĕr′ă-pĭ). Treatment involving the injection of a sclerosing solution into vessels or tissues.

sclerotic (skle-rot′ik). **1.** Relating to or characterized by sclerosis. **2.** Scleral.

sclerot′ica [Mod. L. *scleroticus*, hard]. Sclera.

sclerotome (sklĕr′o-tōm) [sclero- + G. *tomos*, a cutting]. **1.** A knife used in sclerotomy. **2.** The group of mesenchymal cells emerging from the ventromesial part of a mesodermic somite and migrating toward the notochord.

sclerotomy (skle-rot′o-mĭ) [sclero- + G. *tomē*, incision]. An incision through the sclerotic coat of the eye.

sclerous (sklĕr′us) [G. *skleros*, hard]. Scleroid.

scolex, pl. **scoleces**, **scolices** (sko′leks, sko-le′sēz, sko′lĭ-sēz) [G. *skōlēx*, a worm]. The head or anterior end of a tapeworm; attached by suckers and, frequently, by rostellar hooks to the wall of the intestine, the wide variety of the form of the s. characterizes the orders of cestodes.

scoliokyphosis (sko′lĭ-o-ki-fo′sis) [G. *scolios*, curved, + *kyphōsis*, kyphosis]. Lateral and posterior curvature of the spine.

scoliosis (sko-lĭ-o′sis) [G. *skoliōsis*, a crookedness]. A lateral curvature of the spine; depending on etiology, there may be just one curve, or primary and secondary compensatory curves, which may be fixed as a result of muscle and/or bone deformity, or mobile as a result of unequal muscle contraction.

scoliotic (sko-lĭ-ot′ik). Relating to scoliosis.

-scope [G. *skopeō*, to view]. Suffix usually denoting an instrument for viewing but extended to include other methods of examination.

scopolamine (sko-pol′ă-mēn, -min). Hyoscine; an alkaloid found in the leaves and seeds of solanaceous plants; the 6,7-epoxide of atropine.

scopophilia (sko-po-fil′ĭ-ah) [G. *skopeō*, to view, + *philos*, fond]. Voyeurism.

scopophobia (sko′po-fo′bĭ-ah) [G. *skopeō*, to view, + *phobos*, fear]. A morbid dread of being looked at.

-scopy [G. *skopeō*, to view]. Suffix denoting an action or activity involving the use of an instrument for viewing.

scorbutic (skor-bu′tik) [Med. L. *scorbutus*, fr. Teutonic *schorbuych*, scurvy]. Relating to scurvy.

scorbu′tigen′ic. Scurvy-producing.

scordinema (skor-dĭ-ne′mah) [G. *skordinēma*, yawning]. Heaviness of the head with yawning and stretching, occuring as a prodrome of an infectious disease.

Dubowitz s., a clinical assessment of gestational age in the newborn which includes neurological criteria for maturity and other physical criteria.

scoto- [G. *skotos*, darkness]. Combining form denoting darkness.

scotoma (sko-to′mah) [G. *skotōma*, vertigo, fr. *skotos*, darkness]. **1.** An isolated area of varying size and shape, within the visual field, in which vision is absent or depressed. **2.** A blind spot in psychological awareness.

annular s., a circular s. surrounding the center of the field of vision.

cecocentral s., a s. involving the optic disk area (blind spot) and the papillomacular fibers; there are three forms: 1) the cecocentral defect which extends from the blind spot toward or into the fixation area; 2) angioscotoma; 3) glaucomatous nerve-fiber bundle s., due to compression of nerve-fiber bundles at the edge of the optic disk.

central s., a s. involving the fixation point.

color s., an area of color blindness in the visual field.

mental s., blind spot (2); absence of insight into, or inability to grasp, a mental problem.

negative s., a s. that is not ordinarily perceived, but is detected only on examination of the visual field.

peripheral s., a s. outside of the central 30 degrees of the visual field.

physiological s., blind spot (1); a negative scotoma in the visual field, corresponding to the optic disk.

positive s., a s. that is perceived subjectively as a black spot within the field of vision.

relative s., a s. in which the visual impairment is not complete.

ring s., an annular area of blindness in the visual field surrounding the fixation point in pigmentary degeneration of the retina and glaucoma.

scintillating s., a localized area of blindness that may follow the appearance of brilliantly colored shimmering lights; usually a prodromal symptom of migraine.

scotomatous (sko-to′mă-tus). Relating to scotoma.

scotometer (sko-tom′ē-ter). An instrument used in scotometry.

scotometry (sko-tom′ē-trĭ) [scoto- + G. *metron*, measure]. The plotting and measuring of a scotoma.

scotophilia (sko-to-fil′ĭ-ah) [scoto- + G. *philos*, fond]. Nyctophilia.

scotophobia (sko-to-fo′bĭ-ah) [scoto- + G. *phobos*, fear]. Nyctophobia.

scotopia (sko-to′pĭ-ah) [scoto- + G. *opsis*, vision]. Scotopic *vision.*

scotopic (sko-to′pik, -to′ik). Referring to low illumination to which the eye is dark-adapted.

scotopsin (sko-top′sin). The protein moiety of the pigment in the rods of the retina.

screen [Fr. *écran*]. **1.** A thin sheet of any substance used to shield an object from an influence. **2.** That upon which an image is projected. **3.** To make a fluoroscopic examination. **4.** In psychoanalysis, a term meaning concealment, one image or memory concealing another. **5.** To examine, evaluate; to process a group to select or separate certain individuals from it.

screen′ing. 1. Examination of a group of usually asymptomatic individuals to detect those with a high probability of having a given disease, typically by means of an inexpensive diagnositc test. **2.** In psychiatry, initial patient evaluation that includes medical and psychiatric history, mental status evaluation, and diagnostic formulation to determine the patient's suitability or a particular treatment modality.

screw-worm. The larve of the botfly, *Cochliomyia hominivorax*, and other similar forms that cause human and animal myiasis.

scrobiculate (skro-bik'u-lāt) [L. *scrobiculus;* dim. of *scrobis,* a trench]. Pitted; marked with minute depressions.

scrofula (skrof'u-lah) [L. *scrofulae,* glandular swellings]. Obsolete term for cervical tuberculous lymphadenitis.

scrofuloderma (skrof'u-lo-der'mah) [scrofula + G. *derma,* skin]. Cutaneous *tuberculosis.*

scrof'ulous. Relating to scrofula.

scrotal (skro'tal). Oscheal; relating to the scrotum.

scrotectomy (skro-tek'to-mī) [scrotum, + G. *ektomē,* excision]. Removal of part of scrotum.

scrotitis (skro-ti'tis). Inflammation of the scrotum.

scrotocele (skro'to-sēl) [scrotum + G. *kēlē,* hernia]. Scrotal *hernia.*

scro'toplasty [scrotum + G. *plassō,* to form]. Oscheoplasty; reparative or plastic surgery of the scrotum.

scrotum, pl. **scrota, scrotums** (skro'tum, -tah) [L.] [NA]. The musculocutaneous sac containing the testes, formed of skin, a network of nonstriated muscular fibers (dartos), cremasteric fascia, cremaster muscle, and the serous coverings of the testes and epididymides.

scruple (skru'pl) [L. *scrupulus,* a small sharp stone, a weight]. An apothecaries' weight of 20 grains or one-third of a dram.

scurf [A.S.]. Dandruff.

scurvy (skur'vī) [fr. A. S. scurf]. Scorbutus; a disease marked by inanition, debility, anemia, edema of the dependent parts, a spongy condition, sometimes with ulceration, of the gums, and hemorrhages into the skin and from the mucous membranes; due to a deficiency of sources of vitamin C in the diet.

  infantile s., Barlow's disease; a cachectic condition, resulting from the use of improper food, in infants; marked by pallor, fetid breath, coated tongue, diarrhea, and subperiosteal hemorrhages.

scute (skūt) [L. *scutum,* shield]. Scutum (1); a thin lamina or plate.

scu'tiform [L. *scutum,* shield, + *forma,* form]. Shield-shaped.

scutular (sku'tu-lar). Relating to a scutulum.

scutulum, pl. **scutula** (sku'tu-lum, sku'chu-; -lah) [L. dim. of *scutum,* shield]. A yellow saucer-shaped crust, the characteristic lesion of favus, consisting of a mass of hyphae and spores.

scutum, pl. **scuta** (sku'tum, -tah) [L. shield]. **1.** Scute. **2.** In ixodid (hard) ticks, a plate that largely or entirely covers the dorsum of the male and forms an anterior shield behind the capitulum of the female or immature ticks.

scybala (sib'ā-lah). Plural of scybalum.

scybalous (sib'ā-lus). Relating to scybala.

scybalum, pl. **scybala** (sib'ā-lum, -lah) [G. *skybalon,* excrement]. A hard round mass of inspissated feces.

scyphoid (si'foyd) [G. *skyphos,* cup, + *eidos,* resemblance]. Cup-shaped.

SD Streptodornase; standard *deviation.*

SDA Specific dynamic *action.*

Se Selenium.

searcher (ser'cher). A form of sound used to determine the presence of a calculus in the bladder.

seasickness (se'sik-nes). Mal de mer; a form of motion sickness caused by the motion of a floating platform or vessel.

seat'worm. Pinworm.

seb-, sebi-. See sebo-.

seba'ceous (se-ba'shus) [L. *sebaceus*]. Relating to sebum; oily; fatty.

sebiferous, sebiparous (sĕ-bif'er-us, sĕ-bip'-) [sebi- + L. *fero,* to bear]. Producing fatty or sebaceous matter.

sebo-, seb-, sebi- [L. *sebum,* suet, tallow]. Combining forms denoting sebum, sebaceous.

seb'olith [sebo- + G. *lithos,* stone]. A concretion in a sebaceous follicle.

seborrhea (seb-o-re'ah) [sebo- + G. *rhoia,* a flow]. Overactivity of the sebaceous glands, resulting in an excessive amount of sebum.

  s. furfura'cea, s. sicca (1).

  s. sic'ca, (1) s. furfuracea; an accumulation on the skin, especially the scalp, of dry scales; **(2)** dandruff.

seborrheic (seb-o-re'ik). Relating to seborrhea.

se'bum [L. tallow]. Smegma; secretions of the sebaceous glands.

secreta (se-kre'tah) [L. *secretus,* pp. of *se-cerno,* to separate]. Secretions.

secretagogue (se-kre'tă-gog) [secreta + G. *agōgos,* drawing forth]. An agent that promotes secretion.

secrete (se-krēt') [see secreta]. To elaborate or produce and deliver a secretion.

secre'tin. Oxykrinin; a hormone, formed by the epithelial cells of the duodenum under the stimulus of acid contents from the stomach, that incites secretion of pancreatic juice.

  gastric s., gastrin.

secre'tinase. Descriptive name for the agent in serum that destroys the activity of secretin.

secretion (se-kre'shun) [see secreta]. **1.** Production by a cell or gland of some substance differing in chemical and physical properties from the body from which or by which it is produced. **2.** The product, solid, liquid, or gaseous, of cellular or glandular activity that is stored in or utilized by the organism in which it is produced.

secre'toinhib'itory. Restraining or curbing secretion.

secre'tomo'tor, secre'tomo'tory. Stimulating secretion.

secre'tor. An individual whose saliva and other body fluids contain water-soluble form of the antigens of the ABO blood group found in his erythrocytes.

secre′tory. Relating to secretion or the secretions.

sectio, pl. **sectio′nes** (sek′shĭo, sek-shĭ-o′nēz) [L.]. [NA]. Section; in anatomy, a subdivision or segment.

section (sek′shun) [L. *sectio,* a cutting]. **1.** The act of cutting. **2.** A cut or division. **3.** A segment or part of any organ or structure delimited from the remainder. **4.** A cut surface. **5.** A thin slice of tissue, cells, microorganisms, or any material for examination under the microscope.

abdominal s., celiotomy.

cesarean s. [so called not because performed at the birth of Julius Caesar, but because included under *lex cesarea,* Roman law], cesarean operation; incision through the abdominal wall and the uterus (abdominohysterotomy) for extraction of the fetus.

frozen s., a thin slice of tissue cut from a frozen specimen, often used for rapid microscopic diagnosis.

perineal s., any s. through the perineum, either lateral or median lithotomy or external urethrotomy.

Saemisch′s s., procedure of transfixing the cornea beneath an ulcer and then cutting from within outward through the base.

serial s., one of a number of consecutive s.'s (5).

sectiones (sek-shĭ-o′nēz). Plural of sectio.

secundines (sek′un-dēnz) [L. *secundinae,* the afterbirth]. Afterbirth.

sedate (sĕ-dāt) [L. *sedatus;* see sedation]. To bring under the influence of a sedative.

sedation (sĕda′shun) [L. *sedatio,* to calm, allay]. The act of calming, especially by the administration of a sedative, or the state of being calm.

sedative (sed′ă-tiv) [see sedation]. **1.** Calming; quieting. **2.** An agent that quiets nervous excitement, designated according to the part or the organ upon which their specific action is exerted.

sediment (sed′ĭ-ment) [L. *sedimentum* a settling]. **1.** An insoluble material that sinks to the bottom of a liquid, as in hypotasis. **2.** Sedimentate; to cause, or effect, the formation of a sediment or deposit.

sed′imentate. Sediment (2).

sedimentation (sed′ĭ-men-ta′shun). Formation of a sediment.

sed′imentator. A centrifuge.

sedimentometer (sed′ĭ-men-tom′ĕ-ter) [sediment + G. *metron,* measure]. A photographic apparatus for the automatic recording of blood sedimentation rate.

seed [A.S. *soed*]. **1.** The reproductive body of a flowering plant; in man, semen. **2.** In bacteriology, to inoculate a culture medium with microoganisms.

seg′ment [L. *segmentum,* fr. *seco,* to cut]. Segmentum. **1.** A section; a part of an organ or other structure delimited naturally, artificially, or in the imagination from the remainder. **2.** A territory of an organ having independent function, supply, or drainage.

bronchopulmonary s., the largest subdivision of a lobe of the lung, supplied by a direct branch of a lobar bronchus and separated from adjacent segments by connective tissue septa.

internodal s., internode; the portion of a myelinated nerve fiber between two successive nodes.

uterine s.'s, (1) lower, the isthmus of the uterus, the lower extremity of which joins with the cervical canal and, during pregnancy, expands to become the lower part of the uterine cavity; **(2)** upper, the main portion of the body of the gravid uterus, the contraction of which furnishes the chief expulsory force in labor.

segmentum, pl. **segmenta** (seg-men′tum, -tah) [L. segment] [NA]. Segment.

segregation (seg-re-ga′shun) [L. *segrego,* pp. *-atus,* to set apart, separate]. **1.** Separation; removal of certain parts from a mass. **2.** Separation of contrasting characters in the offspring of heterozygotes. **3.** Separation of the paired state of genes which occurs at the reduction division of meiosis.

seg′regator. Separator (2).

seizure (se′zhur) [O. Fr. *seisir,* to grasp, take possession of]. An attack; the sudden onset of a disease or of certain symptoms, such as convulsions.

selection (sĕ-lek′shun) [L. *se-ligo,* to separate, select]. Differential and nonrandom reproduction of individuals of different genotypes, resulting in a change in gene frequency in the population.

artificial s., interference by man with natural s. by purposeful breeding of animals or plants of specific genotype or phenotype to produce a strain with desired characteristics.

natural s., "survival of the fittest"; the process in nature whereby those individuals best able to adapt to their environment survive and reproduce, while those less able die without progeny; the genes carried by the survivors will increase in frequency.

sexual s., a form of natural s. in which the male or female is attracted by certain characteristics, form, color, behavior, etc., in the opposite sex; thus modifications of a special nature are brought about in the species.

selenium (sĕ-le′nĭ-um) [G. *selēnē,* moon]. A metallic element chemically similar to sulfur; symbol Se, atomic no. 34, atomic weight 78.96.

self. 1. A sum of the attitudes and behavioral predispositions that make up the personality. **2.** The individual as represented in his own awareness and in his environment.

self-awareness. Realization of one's ongoing emotional experience; a major goal of all psychotherapy.

self-limited. Denoting a disease that tends to cease after a definite period, as a result of its own processes.

self-love. Narcissism.

sella (sel′ah) [L. saddle]. Saddle (1).

s. tur′cica, [Turkish saddle] [NA], a saddle-like prominence on the upper surface of the sphenoid bone, situated in the middle cranial fossa and dividing it into two halves.

sel'lar. Relating to the sella turcica.

seman'tics [G. *sēmainein,* to show]. **1.** The study of the significance and development of the meaning of words. **2.** The study dealing with the relations between signs and what they refer to (referents); the relations between the signs of a system and human behavioral reaction to signs, including unconscious attitudes, influences of social institutions, and epistomological and linguistic assumptions.

semeio-. For words beginning thus, see semio-.

semelincident (sem-el-in'sĭ-dent) [L. *semel,* once, + *in-cido,* to happen]. Happening once only; said of an infectious disease, one attack of which confers permanent immunity.

se'men, pl. **semi'na, semens** [L. *semen,* seed]. **1** [NA]. Seminal fluid; sperm (2); the penile ejaculate, containing spermatozoa; a mixture of the secretions of the testes, seminal vesicles, prostate, and bulbourethral glands. **2.** A seed.

semenuria (se-mē-nu'rĭ-ah). Seminuria; spermaturia; excretion of urine containing semen.

semi- [L. *semis,* half]. Prefix denoting one-half or partly, corresponding to hemi-.

sem'icanal. A half canal; a deep groove on the edge of a bone which, uniting with a similar groove or part of an adjoining bone, forms a complete canal.

semico'ma. A mild degree of coma from which it is possible to arouse the patient.

semico'matose. Denoting semicoma.

semiconscious (sem-ĭ-kon'shus). Partly conscious.

semilu'nar [semi- + L. *luna,* moon]. Lunar (2).

sem'inal. Relating to the semen.

semina'tion. Insemination.

seminiferous (sem'ĭ-nif'er-us) [L. *semen,* seed, + *fero,* to carry]. Carrying or conducting the semen; denoting the tubules of the testis.

seminoma (sem-ĭ-no'mah) [L. *semen,* seed, + G. *-oma,* tumor]. A malignant testicular neoplasm, arising from the sex cells in young male adults, which metastasizes to the paraortic lymph nodes.

seminuria (se-mĭ-nu'rĭ-ah). Semenuria.

semiper'meable. Permeable to water and small ions or molecules, but not to larger molecules or colloidal matter.

semisulcus (sem'ĭ-sul'kus). A slight groove on the edge of a bone or other structure, which, uniting with a similar groove on the corresponding adjoining structure, forms a complete sulcus.

semisynthet'ic. Describing the process of synthesizing a particular chemical utilizing a naturally occurring chemical as a starting material, thus obviating part of a total synthesis.

semisystematic name (sem'ĭ-sis-tĕ-mat'ik). Semitrivial name; a name of a chemical of which at least one part is systematic and at least one part is not (*i.e.,* is trivial); many generic or nonproprietary names of drugs are semitrivial, although often termed trivial names.

semitrivial name (sem-ĭ-triv'ĭ-al). Semisystematic name.

senescence (se-nes'ens) [L. *senesco,* to grow old, fr. *senex,* old]. The state or process of growing old.

senescent (se-nes'ent). Growing old.

senile (sen'ĭl) [L. *senilis*]. Relating to or characteristic of old age.

se'nilism. Premature senility.

senil'ity. Old age; the sum of the physical and mental changes occurring in advanced life.

senopia (se-no'pĭ-ah) [L. *senilis,* senile, + G. *ōps,* eye]. An improvement in near vision in the aged caused by the myopia of increasing lenticular nuclear sclerosis, a precursor of eventual nuclear cataract.

sensation (sen-sa'shun) [L. *sensatio,* perception, feeling]. A feeling; the translation into consciousness of the effects of a stimulus exciting any of the organs of sense.

   girdle s., zonesthesia.

   objective s., a s. caused by some material object.

   referred s., reflex s., a s. felt in one place in response to a stimulus applied in another.

   subjective s., a s. not readily referrable to verifiable external stimulus.

sense (sens) [L. *sentio,* pp. *sensus,* to feel, to perceive]. Feeling; sensation; consciousness; the faculty of perceiving any stimulus.

   s. of equilibrium, the s. that makes possible a normal physiologic posture.

   kinesthetic s., muscular s., myesthesia.

   posture s., the non-visual ability to recognize the position in which a limb is passively placed.

   pressure s., baresthesia; piesesthesia; the faculty of discriminating various degrees of pressure on the body's surface.

   special s., one of the five senses related to the organs of sight, hearing, smell, taste, and touch.

   visceral s., splanchnesthesia; splanchnesthetic sensibility; the perception of the existence of the internal organs.

sensibility (sen'sĭ-bil'ĭ-tĭ) [L. *sensibilitas*]. The consciousness of sensation; the capability of perceiving sensible stimuli.

   dissociation s., loss of the pain and the thermal senses with preservation of the sense of touch.

   epicritic s., see epicritic.

   proprioceptive s., see proprioceptive.

   protopathic s., see protopathic.

   splanchnesthetic s., visceral sense.

sensible (sen'sĭ-bl) [L. *sensibilis,* fr. *sentio,* to feel, perceive]. **1.** Perceptible to the senses. **2.** Capable of sensation.

sensitive (sen'sĭ-tiv). **1.** Capable of perceiving sensations. **2.** Responding to a stimulus. **3.** Acutely perceptive of interpersonal situations **4.** In immunology, denoting 1) a sensitized antigen; 2) one who has been rendered susceptible to immunological reactions by previous exposure of the immunological system to the antigen concerned.

sensitivity (sen-sĭ-tiv'ĭ-tĭ) [L. *sentio*, pp. *sensus*, to feel]. **1.** The state of being sensitive. **2.** The proportion of individuals with a positive test result for the disease that the test is intended to reveal, *i.e.*, true positive results as a proportion of the total of true positive and false negative results.

sensitiza'tion. Immunization, especially with reference to antigens (immunogens) not associated with infection; the induction of acquired sensitivity or allergy.

   autoerythrocyte s., a peculiar and unusual condition, usually occurring in women, in which the individual is easily bruised (purpura simplex), and the ecchymoses tend to enlarge and involve adjacent tissues, resulting in pain in the affected parts; so-called because similar lesions are produced by the inoculation of the individual's own blood and is assumed to be a form of autosensitization although no specific antibodies have been demonstrable.

sen'sitize. To render sensitive (4); to induce acquired sensitivity, to immunize.

sensori- [L. *sensorius*, sensory]. Combining form denoting sensory.

senso'rial. Relating to the sensorium.

sen'sorimo'tor. Both sensory and motor, denoting a mixed nerve with afferent and efferent fibers.

sensorium, pl. **sensoria, sensoriums** (sen-so'rĭ-um, -ah) [Late L.]. **1.** An organ of sensation. **2.** The hypothetical "seat of sensation" in the cerebral cortex. **3.** In psychiatry, synonymous with consciousness; also sometimes used as a generic term for the intellectual functions.

sensory (sen'so-rĭ) [L. *sensorius*, fr. *sensus*, sense]. Relating to sensation.

sentient (sen'shent, sen'shĭ-ent) [L. *sentiens*, fr. *sentio*, to feel, perceive]. Capable of, or characterized by, sensation.

sepsis, pl. **sepses** (sep'sis, -ēz) [G. *sēpsis*, putrefaction]. Presence of various pus-forming and other pathogenic organisms, or their toxins, in the blood or tissues.

sept-. See septi-; septico-; septo-.

septa (sep'tah) [L.]. Plural of septum.

sep'tal. Relating to a septum.

sep'tate [L. *saeptum*, septum]. Having a septum; divided into compartments.

septectomy (sep-tek'to-mĭ) [L. *saeptum*, septum, + G. *ektomē*, excision]. Operative removal of all or part of the nasal septum.

septi-, sept- [L. *septem*, seven]. Combining forms meaning seven.

septic (sep'tik). Relating to or caused by sepsis.

septicemia (sep-tĭ-se'mĭ-ah) [G. *sēpsis*, putrefaction, + *haima*, blood]. Septic fever; systemic disease caused by the multiplication of microorganisms in the circulating blood.

   cryptogenic s., a form of s. in which no primary focus of infection can be found.

   puerperal s., a severe blood stream infection resulting from an obstetric delivery or procedure.

septice'mic. Relating to or resulting from septicemia.

septico-, septic- [G. *sēptikos*, putrifying]. Combining form meaning septic, septic.

septicopyemia (sep-tĭ-ko-pi-e'mĭ-ah). Pyemia and septicemia occurring together.

septicopye'mic. Relating to septicopyemia.

septo-, sept- [L. *saeptum*, septum]. Combining forms meaning septum.

septomarginal (sep-to-mar'jĭ-nal). Relating to the margin of a septum, or to both a septum and a margin.

sep'tona'sal. Relating to the nasal septum.

septoplasty (sep'to-plas-tĭ) [septo- + G. *plassō*, to fashion]. An operation to correct defects or deformities of the nasal septum, often by alteration or partial removal of supporting structures.

septorhinoplasty (sep-to-ri'no-plas-tĭ) [septo- + G. *rhis*, nose, + *plassō*, to fashion]. A combined operation to repair defects or deformities of the nasal septum and of the external nasal pyramid.

septostomy (sep-tos'to-mĭ) [septo- + G. *stoma*, mouth]. Surgical creation of a septal defect.

septotomy (sep-tot'o-mĭ) [septo- + G. *tomē*, incision]. Incision of the nasal septum.

septulum, pl. **septula** (sep'tu-lum, -lah) [Mod. L. dim. of *septum*]. [NA]. A minute septum.

septum, pl. **septa** (sep'tum, -tah) [L. *saeptum*, a partition]. **1** [NA]. A thin wall dividing two cavities or masses of softer tissue. **2.** In neuroanatomy, the septal area or the septum pellucidum.

   s. atrioventricula're [NA], **atrioventricular s.,** the small part of the membranous s. of the heart just above the septal cusp of the tricuspid valve that separates the right atrium from the left ventricle.

   interalveolar s., (1) the tissue intervening between two adjacent pulmonary alveoli, consisting of a close-meshed capillary network covered on both surfaces by very thin alveolar epithelial cells; **(2)** interdental s.; one of the bony partitions between the tooth sockets.

   s. interatria'le [NA], **interatrial s.,** the wall between the atria of the heart.

   interdental s., interalveolar s.

   s. intermuscula're [NA], **intermuscular s.,** any of the aponeurotic sheets separating various muscles of the extremities: anterior and posterior crural, lateral and medial femoral, lateral and medial humeral.

   s. interventricula're [NA], **interventricular s.,** the wall between the ventricles of the heart.

   s. lu'cidum, s. pellucidum.

   s. na'si [NA], **nasal s.,** the wall dividing the nasal cavity into halves, composed of a central supporting skeleton covered by a mucous membrane.

   s. pe'nis [NA], the portion of the tunica albuginea separating the two corpora cavernosa of the penis.

   s. pellu'cidum [NA], s. lucidum; a thin sheet of brain tissue, containing nerve cells and numerous nerve fibers stretched between the columna and corpus fornicis below and the corpus callosum above and anteriorly.

s. rectovagina'le [NA], **rectovaginal s.,** the fascial layer between the vagina and the lower part of the rectum.

s. rectovesica'le [NA], **rectovesical s.,** a fascial layer that extends from the central tendon of the perineum to the peritoneum between the prostate and rectum.

s. scro'ti [NA], **scrotal s.,** an incomplete wall of connective tissue and nonstriated muscle dividing the scrotum into two sacs, each containing a testis.

sequela, pl. **sequelae** (se-kwel'ah, se-kwel'e) [L. a sequel, fr. *sequor,* to follow]. A morbid condition following as a consequence of a disease.

sequestral (se-kwes'tral). Relating to a sequestrum.

sequestration (se-kwes-tra'shun) [L. *sequestratio,* fr. *sequestro,* pp. *-atus,* to lay aside]. **1.** Formation of a sequestrum. **2.** Loss of blood or of its fluid content into spaces within the body so that it is withdrawn from the circulating volume.

   bronchopulmonary s., a congenital anomaly in which a mass of lung tissue becomes isolated, during development, from the rest of the lung; the bronchi in the mass are usually dilated or cystic and are not connected with the bronchial tree; supplied by a branch of the aorta.

sequestrectomy (se-kwes-trek'to-mī) [sequestrum + G. *ektomē,* excision]. Operative removal of a sequestrum.

sequestrum, pl. **sequestra** (se-kwes'trum, -trah) [Med. L. *sequestrum,* something laid aside]. A piece of necrosed tissue, usually bone, that has become separated from the surrounding healthy tissue.

Ser Serine.

sera (sēr'ah). Plural of serum.

seralbumin (sēr'al-bu'min). Serum *albumin.*

series, pl. **series** (sēr'ēz) [L. fr. *sero,* to join together]. **1.** A succession of similar objects or events following one another in space or time. **2.** In chemistry, a group of substances, either elements or compounds, having similar properties or differing from each other in composition by a constant ratio.

   aromatic s., all compounds derived from benzene, or similar cyclic compounds, distinguished from those that are acyclic or that contain rings that lack the unsaturated conjugated double bond structure characteristic of benzene.

   erythrocytic s., the cells in the various stages of development in the red bone marrow leading to the formation of the erythrocyte.

   granulocytic s., the cells in the several stages of development in the bone marrow leading to the mature granulocyte of the circulation.

   lymphocytic s., the cells at various states in the development in lymphoid tissue of the mature lymphocytes.

   myeloid s., the granulocytic and erythrocytic s.

   thrombocytic s., the cells of successive stages in thrombocytic (platelet) development in the bone marrow.

serine (Ser) (sēr'ēn, sēr'ēn). α-Amino-β-hydroxypropionic acid; one of the amino acids occurring in proteins.

sero- [L. *serum,* whey]. Combining form denoting serum or serous.

serocolitis (sēr'o-ko-li'tis). Pericolitis.

se'rodiagno'sis. Diagnosis by means of a reaction in the blood serum or other serous fluids in the body.

seroenteritis (sēr'o-en-ter-i'tis). Perienteritis.

serofibrinous (sēr-o-fi'brī-nus). Denoting an exudate composed of serum and fibrin.

serofibrous (sēr-o-fi'brus). Relating to a serous membrane and a fibrous tissue.

serologic (sēr-o-loj'ik). Relating to serology.

serology (se-rol'o-jī) [sero- + G. *logos,* study]. The branch of science concerned with serum, especially with specific immune or lytic serums.

seroma (se-ro'mah) [sero- + G. *-oma,* tumor]. A mass or tumefaction caused by the localized accumulation of serum within a tissue or organ.

seromembranous (sēr-o-mem'brā-nus). Relating to a serous membrane.

seromucous (sēr-o-mu'kus). Pertaining to a mixture of watery and mucinous material such as that of certain glands.

seropurulent (sēr-o-pu'ru-lent). Composed of or containing both serum and pus.

seropus (sēr'o-pus). Purulent serum; pus largely diluted with serum.

serosa, pl. **serosae** (se-ro'sah, -se) [fem. of Mod. L. *serosus,* serous]. **1.** *Tunica* serosa. **2.** Membrana serosa (2); the outermost of the extraembryonic membranes that encloses the embryo and all its other membranes.

serosanguineous (sēr'o-sang-gwin'e-us). Composed of or containing serum and blood.

seroserous (sēr'o-sēr'us). **1.** Relating to two serous surfaces. **2.** Denoting a suture, as of the intestine, in which the edges of the wound are infolded so as to bring the two serous surfaces in apposition.

serositis (sēr-o-si'tis). Inflammation of a serous membrane.

serosity (se-ros'ī-tī). **1.** A serous fluid or a serum. **2.** The condition of being serous. **3.** The serous quality of a liquid.

serosynovitis (sēr'o-sin-o-vi'tis). Synovitis attended with a copious serous effusion.

serotherapy (sēr-o-thěr'ă-pī). Serum therapy; treatment of an infectious disease by the injection of an antitoxin or specific serum.

serotonin (sēr-o-to'nin, sēr-). 5-Hydroxytryptamine; a vasoconstrictor, liberated by the blood platelets, that inhibits gastric secretion and stimulates smooth muscle; present in relatively high concentrations in some areas of the CNS, and occurs in many peripheral tissues and cells and in carcinoid tumors.

serotype (sēr'o-tīp). Former name for serovar.

serous (sēr'us). Relating to, containing, or producing serum or a substance having a watery consistency.

serovaccination (sĕr'o-vak-sĭ-na'shun). A process for producing mixed immunity by the injection of a serum, to secure passive immunity, and by vaccination with a modified or killed culture to acquire active immunity later.

serovar (sĕr'o-var). A subdivision of a species of subspecies distinguishable from other strains therein on the basis of antigenic character.

serpiginous (ser-pij'ĭ-nus) [Med. L. *serpigo-* (*-gin*), ringworm]. Creeping; denoting an ulcer or other cutaneous lesion that extends with an arciform border and has a wavy margin.

serpigo (ser-pi'go) [Med. L. *serpigo* (*-gin*), ringworm, fr. L. *serpo*, to creep]. **1.** Tinea. **2.** Herpes. **3.** Any creeping or serpiginous eruption.

serrate, serrated (sĕr'at, -a'ted) [L. *serratus,* fr. *serra,* a saw]. Notched; dentate; toothed.

serration (sĕ-ra'shun) [L. *serra,* saw]. **1.** The state of being serrated or notched. **2.** Any one of the processes in a serrate or dentate formation.

serrefine (sair-fēn') [Fr.]. A small spring forceps used for approximating the edges of a wound or for temporarily closing an artery during an operation.

serumal (sĕr'um-al). Relating to or derived from serum.

serum-fast. Serofast; pertaining to a serum in which there is little or no change in the titer of antibody, even under conditions of treatment or immunologic stimulation.

serum, pl. **serums** or **sera** (sĕr'um, sĕr'ah) [L. whey]. **1.** A clear watery fluid, especially that moistening surface of serous membranes, or exuded in inflammation of any of those membranes. **2.** The fluid portion of the blood obtained after removal of the fibrin clot and blood cells; sometimes used as a synonym for antiserum or antitoxin.

   antilymphocyte s. (ALS), antiserum against lymphoid tissue, the globulin fraction of a heterologous s. usually used in conjunction with other immunosuppressive agents to suppress rejection of grafts or organ transplants.

   immune s., antiserum.

   muscle s., the fluid remaining after the coagulation of muscle plasma and the separation of myosin.

   nonimmune s., a s. from a subject that is not immune; a s. that is free of antibodies to a given antigen.

   normal s., a nonimmune s., usually with reference to a s. obtained prior to immunization.

   polyvalent s., an antiserum obtained by inoculating an animal with several species or strains of the bacterium in question.

   pooled s., the mixed s. from a number of individuals.

sesamoid (ses'ă-moyd) [G. *sēsamoeidēs,* like sesame]. **1.** Resembling in size or shape a grain of sesame. **2.** Denoting the sesamoid bone.

sessile (ses'il) [L. *sessilis,* low-growing, fr. *sedeo,* pp. *sessus,* to sit]. Having a broad base of attachment; not pedunculated.

set. 1. A readiness to perceive or to respond in some way; an attitude which facilitates or predetermines an outcome. **2.** To reduce a fracture; to bring the bones back into a normal position or alinement.

seta, pl. **setae** (se'tah, -te) [L.]. **1.** A bristle. **2.** A slender, stiff, bristle-like structure.

setaceous (se-ta'shus) [L. *seta,* a bristle]. **1.** Having bristles. **2.** Resembling a bristle.

se'ton [L. *seta,* bristle]. A wisp of threads, a strip of gauze, a length of wire, or other foreign material passed through the subcutaneous tissues or a cyst to form a sinus or fistula.

sex [L. *sexus*]. **1.** The character or quality that distinguishes between male and female as expressed in the nature of the sex chromosomes, the gonads, and the accessory sexual organs, as contrasted with gender role. **2.** The physiological and psychological processes within an individual which prompt behavior related to procreation and/or erotic pleasure.

sex'duction. F *duction.*

sex-limited. Occurring in one sex only.

sex-linked. See sex *linkage;* sex-linked *gene.*

sexology (sek-sol'o-jĭ) [L. *sexus,* sex, + G. *logos,* study]. The study of all aspects of sex and, in particular, sexual behavior.

sexual (sek'shu-al) [L. *sexualis,* fr. *sexus,* sex]. **1.** Relating to sex; erotic; genital. **2.** A person considered in his or her s. relation or tendencies.

sexuality (sek-shu-al'ĭ-tĭ). Sex; the sum of a person's sexual behaviors and tendencies, and the latter's strength; the quality of having sexual functions or implications.

   infantile s., the overlapping oral, anal, and phallic phases of psychosexual development during the first 5 years of life.

SGOT Serum glutamic-oxaloacetic transaminase.

SGPT. Serum glutamic-pyruvic transaminase.

SH Serum *hepatitis.*

shaft [A.S. *sceaft*]. An elongated rodlike structure, as the part of a long bone between the epiphysial extremities.

shank [A.S. *sceanca*]. The tibia; the shin; the leg or a leg like part.

shaping. In operant conditioning, when the operant is not in the organism's repertoire, a procedure in which the experimenter breaks down the operant into those parts which appear most frequently, begins reinforcing them, and then slowly and successively withholds the reinforcer until more and more of the operant is emitted.

sheath (shēth) [A.S. *sceath*]. **1.** Any enveloping structure. **2.** Vagina (1).

   carotid s., *vagina* carotica.

   crural s., femoral s.

   dentinal s., a layer of tissue relatively resistant to the action of acids, which forms the walls of the dentinal tubules.

   dural s., an extension of the dura mater which ensheathes the roots of spinal nerves.

   s. of eyeball, *vagina* bulbi.

femoral s., crural s.; the fascia enclosing the femoral vessels, formed by the fascia transversalis anteriorly and the fascia iliaca posteriorly.

Henle's s., endoneurium.

Mauthner's s., axolemma.

myelin s., medullary s., the lipoproteinaceous envelope in vertebrates surrounding most axons of more than 0.5-μm diameter; consists of a double plasma membrane wound tightly around the axon and supplied by oligodendroglia cells (in the brain and spinal cord) or Schwann cells (in peripheral nerves).

root s., one of the epidermic layers of the hair follicle: **external r. s.,** continuous with the stratum basale and stratum spinosum of the epidermis; **internal r. s.,** comprises the cuticle of the internal roots.

s. of Schwann, neurolemma.

synovial s., the membrane lining the cavity of bone through which a tendon moves.

shield (shēld) [A.S. *scild*]. A protecting screen. **1.** A lead sheet for protecting the operator from x-rays. **2.** A watchglass sealed over the sound eye to protect it in a case of gonorrheal ophthalmia.

embryonic s., a thickened area of the embryonic blastoderm within which the primitive streak appears.

nipple s., a cap or dome placed over the nipple to protect it during nursing.

shift. Transfer; change. See also deviation.

axis s., axis *deviation.*

chloride s., when CO_2 enters the blood from the tissues, it passes into the red cell and is converted by carbonate dehydratase to carbonic acid (H_2CO_3); HCO_3^- ion passes out into the plasma while Cl^- migrates into the red cell. Reverse changes occur in the lungs when CO_2 is eliminated from the blood.

Doppler s., the magnitude of the frequency change in hertz when sound and observer are in relative motion away from or toward each other.

s. to the left, a marked increase in the percentage of immature cells in the circulating blood; based on the premise in hematology that the bone marrow with its immature myeloid cells is on the left, while on the right is the circulating blood with its mature neutrophils.

Purkinje s., Purkinje's *phenomenon.*

s. to the right, in a differential count of white blood cells in the peripheral blood, the absence of young and immature forms.

Shigella (she-gel'lah) [K. *Shiga*]. A genus of Gram-negative bacteria (family Enterobacteriaceae) whose normal habitat is the intestinal tract and which produce dysentery. The type species is *S. dysenteriae.*

S. boy'dii, a species that occurs in a low proportion of cases of bacillary dysentery.

S. dysenter'iae, Shiga-Kruse bacillus; a species causing dysentery; the type species of the genus *S.*

S. flexne'ri, Flexner's bacillus; a species that is the most common cause of dysentery epidemics and sometimes of infantile gastroenteritis.

S. son'nei, Sonne bacillus; a species causing mild dysentery and also summer diarrhea in children.

shigellosis (shig'ĕ-lo'sis). Bacillary dysentery caused by bacteria of the genus *Shigella,* often occurring in epidemic patterns.

shin [A.S. *scina*]. The anterior portion of the leg.

saber s., the sharp-edged anteriorly convex tibia in congenital syphilis.

shingles (shing'glz) [L. *cingulum,* girdle]. *Herpes zoster.*

shin-splints. Tenderness and pain with induration and swelling of pretibial muscles, following athletic overexertion by the untrained.

shock. 1. A sudden physical or mental disturbance. **2.** A state of profound mental and physical depression consequent upon severe physical injury or an emotional disturbance. **3.** The abnormally palpable impact, appreciated by a hand on the chest wall, of an accentuated heart sound.

anaphylactic s., a severe, often fatal form of s. characterized by smooth muscle contraction and capillary dilation initiated by cytotropic (IgE class) antibodies.

anaphylactoid s., anaphylactoid crisis; a reaction similar to anaphylactic s., but not requiring the incubation period characteristic of induced sensitivity (anaphylaxis); unrelated to antigen-antibody reactions.

cardiogenic s., s. resulting from decline in cardiac output secondary to serious heart disease, usually myocardial infarction.

chronic s., the state of peripheral circulatory insufficiency that develops in elderly patients with a debilitating disease; there is a subnormal blood volume and the patient is susceptible to hemorrhagic s. as a result of a moderate blood loss, as may occur during an operation.

cultural s., a form of stress associated with an individual's assimilation into a new culture vastly different from that in which he was raised.

declamping s., declamping *phenomenon.*

hemorrhagic s., hypovolemic s. resulting from acute hemorrhage, characterized by hypotension, tachycardia, pale, cold, and clammy skin, and oliguria.

hypovolemic s., s. caused by a reduction in volume of blood, as from hemorrhage or dehydration.

insulin s., hypoglycemic s. produced by overdosage of insulin, characterized by sweating, tremor, anxiety, vertigo, and diplopia, followed by delirium, convulsions, and collapse.

septic s., (1) s. associted with sepsis, usually associated with abdominal and pelvic infection complicating trauma or operations; **(2)** s. associated with septicemia caused by Gram-negative bacteria.

serum s., anaphylactic or anaphylactoid s. caused by the injection of antitoxic or other foreign serum.

shell s., a euphemistic term used especially during and after World War I to denote a type of traumatic neurosis consequent to battle.

shortsightedness. Myopia.

shoulder (shōl'der) [A.S. *sculder*]. The lateral portion of the scapular region, where the scapula joins with the clavicle and humerus and is covered by the rounded mass of the deltoid muscle.

frozen s., adhesive *capsulitis.*

shoulder blade. Scapula.

show (sho) [A.S. *sceáwe*]. An appearance; specifically: (1) the first appearance of blood in beginning menstruation; (2) a sign of impending labor, characterized by the discharge from the vagina of a small amount of blood-tinged mucus which represents the extrusion of the mucous plug that has filled the cervical canal during pregnancy.

shunt. A bypass or diversion of accumulations of fluid to an absorbing or excreting system by fistulation or a mechanical device; nomenclature commonly includes origin and terminus of structures involved.

arteriovenous s., the passage of blood directly from arteries to veins, without going through the capillary network.

Dickens s., pentose phosphate *pathway.*

jejunoileal s., jejunoileal *bypass.*

left-to-right s., a diversion of blood from the left side of the heart to right (as through a septal defect), or from the systemic circulation to the pulmonary (as through a patent ductus arteriosus).

mesocaval s., (1) anastomosis of the side of the superior mesenteric vein to the proximal end of the divided inferior vena cava, for control of portal hypertension; (2) H-graft anastomosis of the inferior vena cava to the superior mesenteric vein, using a synthetic conduit or autologous vein.

peritoneovenous s., a s., usually by a catheter, between the peritoneal cavity and the venous system.

portacaval s., (1) any communication or anastomosis between the portal vein and general circulation, as to the paraumbilical, azygos or esophageal veins; (2) surgical anastomosis between the portal vein and the vena cava, as in an Eck fistula.

right-to-left s., the passage of blood from the right side of the heart into the left (as through a septal defect), or from the pulmonary artery into the aorta (as through a patent ductus arteriosus).

splenorenal s., anastomosis of the splenic vein to the left renal vein, usually end-to-side, for control of portal hypertension.

SI International System of Units.

Si Silicon.

sial-. See sialo-.

sialadenitis (si'al-ad-ĕ-ni'tis) [sial- + G. *adēn*, gland, + *-itis*, inflammation]. Sialoadenitis; inflammation of a salivary gland.

sialagogue (si-al'ă-gog) [sial- + G. *agōgos*, drawing forth]. Sialogogue; ptyalagogue; promoting the flow of saliva.

sialectasis (si'ă-lek'tă-sis) [sial- + G. *ektasis*, a stretching]. Ptyalectasis; dilation of a salivary duct.

sialemesis, sialemesia (si'al-em'e-sis, -ĕ-me'zĭ-ah) [sial- + G. *emesis*, vomiting]. Vomiting of saliva, or vomiting caused by or accompanying an excessive secretion of saliva.

sial'ic acid. Esters and other derivatives of *N*-acetylneuraminic acid; components of various mucoproteins. The radical of sialic acids are sialoyl, if the OH of the COOH is removed, and sialosyl, if the OH comes from the anomeric carbon (C-2) of the cyclic structure.

sialic (si-al'ik). Salivary.

sialidosis, pl. **sialidoses** (si'al-ĭ-do'sis, -sēz). Any of a group of lysosomal storage disorders associated with α-*N*-acetylneuraminidase deficiency and in some cases also β-galactosidase.

sialin (si'ă-lin). Name applied to a tetrapeptide in saliva: Gly-gly-lys-arg.

si'aline. Salivary.

sialism, sialismus (si'ă-lizm, si'ă-liz'mus) [G. *sialismos*]. Hypersalivation; salivation sialorrhea; sialosis; an excess secretion of saliva.

sialo-, sial- [G. *sialon*, saliva]. Combining forms denoting saliva or the salivary glands. See also ptyal-.

sialoadenectomy (si'ă-lo-ad-ĕ-nek'to-mĭ) [sialo- + G. *adēn*, gland, + *ektomē*, excision]. Excision of a salivary gland.

sialoadenitis (si'ă-lo-ad-ĕ-ni'tis). Sialadenitis.

sialoadenotomy (si'ă-lo-ad-ĕ-not'o-mĭ) [sialo- + G. *adēn*, gland, + *tomē*, incision]. Incision of a salivary gland.

sialoangiectasis (si'ă-lo-an-jī-ek'tă-sis) [sialo- + G. *angeion*, vessel, + *ektasis*, a stretching]. Dilation of salivary ducts.

sialoangiitis (si'ă-lo-an-jī-i'tis) [sialo- + G. *angeion*, vessel, + *-itis*, inflammation]. Sialodochitis; inflammation of a salivary duct.

sialocele (si'ă-lo-sēl) [sialo- + G. *kēlē*, tumor]. Ranula (2).

sialodochitis (si'ă-lo-do-ki'tis) [sialo- + G. *dochē*, receptacle, + *-itis*, inflammation]. Sialoangiitis.

sialodochoplasty (si'ă-lo-do'ko-plas-tĭ) [sialo- + G. *dochē*, receptacle, + *plassō*, to fashion]. Surgical repair of a salivary duct.

sialogenous (si'ă-loj'ĕ-nus) [sialo- + G. *-gen*, producing]. Producing saliva.

sialogogue (si-al'ă-gog). Sialagogue.

sialogram (si-al'o-gram) [sialo- + G. *gramma*, a writing]. A radiograph of one or more of the salivary ducts.

sialography (si-ă-log'ră-fĭ) [sialo- + G. *graphō*, to write]. Radiographic examination of the salivary glands and ducts after the introduction of a radiopaque material into the ducts.

sialolith (si'ă-lo-lith) [sialo- + G. *lithos,* stone]. A salivary calculus.

sialolithiasis (si'ă-lo-lĭ-thi'ă-sis) [sialolith + G. *-iasis,* condition]. Formation or presence of a salivary calculus.

sialolithotomy (si'ă-lo-lĭ-thot'o-mĭ) [sialolith + G. *tomē,* incision]. Incision of a salivary duct or gland to remove a calculus.

sialomucin (si'ă-lo-mu-sin). An acid mucopolysaccharide having sialic acid as its acidic component.

sialorrhea (si'ă-lo-re'ah) [sialo- + G. *rhoia,* a flow]. Sialism.

sialoschesis (si-ă-los'ke-sis) [sialo- + G. *schesis,* retention]. Suppression of the secretion of saliva.

sialosis (si'ă-lo'sis). Sialism.

sialostenosis (si'ă-lo-stě-no'sis) [sialo- + G. *stenōsis,* a narrowing]. Stricture of a salivary duct.

sialosyrinx (si'ă-lo-sĭr'ingks) [sialo- + G. *syrinx,* a pipe, fistula]. A salivary fistula between the outside via the skin or oral tissues and the salivary gland or duct.

sib. Sibling.

sib'ilant (sib'ĭ-lant) [L. *sibilans,* pres. p. of *sibilo,* to hiss]. Hissing or whistling in character; denoting a form of rale.

sib'ling [A. S. *sib,* relation]. Sib; one of two or more children of the same parents.

sib'ship. All children of one pair of parents.

siccant (sik'ant) [L. *siccans*]. Siccative; drying.

siccative (sik'ă-tiv). Siccant.

sick [A.S. *seóc*]. **1.** Ill; unwell; suffering from disease. **2.** Nauseated.

sickle-form (sik'el). Malarial *crescent.*

sicklemia (sik-le'mĭ-ah). Presence of sickle- or crescent-shaped erythrocytes in peripheral blood; seen in sickle cell anemia and sickle cell trait.

sick'ling. Production of sickle-shaped erythrocytes in the circulation.

sick'ness. Disease (1).

acute sleeping s., Rhodesian *trypanosomiasis.*

African sleeping s., African *trypanosomiasis.*

altitude s., Acosta's disease; mountain s.; a syndrome caused by low inspired oxygen pressure and characterized by nausea, headache, dyspnea, malaise, and insomnia.

car s., a form of motion s. similar to seasickness and caused by riding on a train or in a bus or automobile.

chronic mountain s., Monge's disease; loss of high altitude tolerance after prolonged exposure, characterized by extreme polycythemia, exaggerated hypoxemia, and reduced mental and physical capacity.

chronic sleeping s., Gambian *trypanosomiasis.*

decompression s., aeroemphysema; bends; caisson disease; a symptom complex caused by the escape from solution in body fluids of nitrogen bubbles absorbed originally at high atmospheric pressure, as a result of abrupt reduction in atmospheric pressure; characterized by headache, pain in the arms, legs, joints, and epigastrium, itching of the skin, vertigo,

dyspnea, coughing, choking, vomiting, weakness and sometimes paralysis, and severe peripheral circulatory collapse.

morning s., nausea gravidarum; the nausea and vomiting of early pregnancy.

motion s., kinesia; the syndrome of pallor, nausea, weakness, and malaise which may progress to vomiting and incapacitation, caused by the stimulation of the semicircular canals during travel or motion.

mountain s., altitude s.

radiation s., the condition that follows x-radiation at levels in excess of about 100 rem; severity of the effect in dose dependent. In mild forms there are anorexia, nausea, vomiting, malaise, and leukopenia; in more severe forms there are reduction or disappearance of platelets with bleeding, reduction or disappearance of leukocytes with risk of infection, and reduction of new red cells leading to anemia.

serum s., serum disease; seroreaction (2); local and general symptoms (urticaria, fever, general glandular enlargement, edema, pains in the joints, and occasionally albuminuria) appearing after an injection of foreign serum.

sleeping s., see Gambian *trypanosomiasis,* Rhodesian *trypanosomiasis.*

side effect. A result of drug or other therapy in addition to or in extension of the desired therapeutic effect; usually connotes an undesirable effect.

sidero- [G. *siderōs,* iron]. Combining form denoting iron.

sideroblast (sid'e-ro-blast) [sidero- + G. *blastos,* germ]. An erythroblast containing granules of ferritin.

siderocyte (sid'er-o-sīt) [sidero- + G. *kytos,* cell]. An erythrocyte containing granules of free iron.

sideroderma (sid'er-o-der'mah) [sidero- + G. *derma,* skin]. Brownish discoloration of the skin on the legs due to hemosiderin deposits.

siderofibrosis (sid'er-o-fi-bro'sis). Fibrosis associated with small foci in which iron is deposited.

sideropenia (sid'er-o-pe'nĭ-ah) [sidero- + G. *penia,* poverty]. An abnormally low level of serum iron.

sid'erope'nic. Characterized by sideropenia.

siderophil, siderophile (sid'er-o-fil, -fil) [sidero- + G. *philos,* fond]. **1.** Siderophilous; absorbing iron. **2.** A cell or tissue that contains iron.

siderophilin (sid'er-o-fil'in, -of'ĭ-lin). Transferrin.

siderophilous (sid-er-of'ĭ-lus). Siderophil (1).

siderophore (sid'er-o-fōr) [sidero- + G. *phoros,* bearing]. A large extravasated mononuclear phagocyte containing a granule of hemosiderin.

siderosilicosis (sid'er-o-sil-ĭ-ko'sis) [sidero- + silicosis]. Silicosiderosis; silicosis due to inhalation of dust containing iron and silica.

siderosis (sid-er-o'sis) [sidero- + G. *-osis,* condition]. **1.** Pneumoconiosis due to the presence of iron dust. **2.** Discoloration of any part by an iron pigment. **3.** An excess of iron in the circulating blood.

siderot'ic. Pigmented by iron or containing an excess of iron.

SIDS Sudden infant death *syndrome.*

siemens (S) (se'menz) [Sir William *Siemens*]. Mho; the SI unit of electrical conductance; the conductance of a body with an electrical resistance of 1 ohm, allowing 1 ampere of current to flow per volt applied.

sight [A.S. *gesihth*]. The ability or faculty of seeing. See also vision; hemeralopia; hyperopia; myopia; myetalopia; presbyopia; senopia.

sigmoid (sig'moyd) [G. *sigma*, S, + *eidos*, resemblance]. Resembling in outline the letter S or one of the forms of the Greek sigma.

sigmoid-. See sigmoido-.

sigmoidectomy (sig-moy-dek'to-mǐ) [sigmoid- + G. *ektomē*, excision]. Excision of the sigmoid colon.

sigmoiditis (sig-moy-di'tis) [sigmoid- + G. *-itis*, inflammation]. Inflammation of the sigmoid colon.

sigmoido-, sigmoid- [G. *sigma*, S, + *eidos*, resemblance]. Combining forms denoting sigmoid, usually the sigmoid colon.

sigmoidopexy (sig-moy'do-pek-sǐ) [sigmoido- + G. *pēxis*, fixation]. Operative attachment of the sigmoid colon to a firm structure to correct rectal prolapse.

sigmoidoproctostomy (sig-moy'do-prok-tos'to-mǐ) [sigmoido- + G. *prōktos*, anus, + *stoma*, mouth]. Sigmoidorectostomy; establishment of an artificial anus by opening into the junction of the sigmoid colon and the rectum.

sigmoidorectostomy (sig-moy'do-rek-tos'to-mǐ). Sigmoidoproctostomy.

sigmoidoscope (sig-moy'do-skōp) [sigmoido- + G. *skopeō*, to view]. A speculum for viewing the cavity of the sigmoid colon.

sigmoidoscopy (sig'moy-dos'ko-pǐ). Use of the sigmoidoscope.

sigmoidostomy (sig-moy-dos'to-mǐ) [sigmoido- + G. *stoma*, mouth]. Establishment of an artificial anus by opening into the sigmoid colon.

sigmoidotomy (sig-moy-dot'o-mǐ) [sigmoido- + G. *tomē*, incision]. Surgical opening of the sigmoid colon.

sign (sīn) [L. *signum*, mark]. **1.** Any abnormality indicative of disease, discoverable by examination; an objective symptom of disease. **2.** In psychology, any object or artifact that represents a specific thing or conveys a specific idea to the person who perceives it.

Abadie's s. (1) of exophthalmic goiter, spasm of the levator palpebrae superioris in Graves disease; (2) of tabes dorsalis, insensibility to pressure over the tendo achillis.

Allis s., in fracture of the neck of the femur, the trochanter rides up, relaxing the fascia lata so that the finger can be sunk deeply between the great trochanter and the iliac crest.

Babinski's s., (1) Babinski's reflex; toe reflex (3); extension of the great toe and abduction of the other toes instead of the normal flexion reflex to plantar stimulation, considered indicative of pyramidal tract involvement; (2) in hemiplegia, weakness of the platysma muscle on the affected side, evident in such actions as blowing or opening the mouth; (3) when the patient is lying upon his back with arms crossed on the front of his chest, and attempts to assume the sitting posture, the thigh on the side of an *organic* paralysis is flexed and the heel raised, whereas the limb on the sound side remains flat; (4) in hemiplegia, the forearm on the affected side when placed in a position of supination turns into the pronated position.

Bamberger's s., (1) jugular pulse in tricuspid insufficiency; (2) dullness on percussion at the angle of the scapula, clearing up as the patient leans forward, indicating pericarditis with effusion.

Bárány's s., in cases of ear disease, in which the vestibule is healthy, injection into the external auditory canal of water 65°F. or lower will cause rotary nystagmus toward the opposite side; when the injected fluid is 106°F. or higher, the nystagmus will be toward the injected side; if the labyrinth is diseased there is no nystagmus.

Barré's s., if the hemiplegic is placed in the prone position with the limbs flexed at the knees, he is unable to maintain the flexed position on the side of the lesion but extends the leg.

Beevor's s., with paralysis of the lower portions of the recti abdominis muscles the umbilicus moves upward.

Biernacki's s., analgesia of the ulnar nerve (the "funny-bone" sensation being absent) in tabes dorsalis and dementia paralytica.

Boston's s., jerky lowering of the upper eyelid on downward rotation of the eye, characteristic of Graves disease.

Braxton Hicks s., irregular uterine contractions occurring after the third month of pregnancy.

Broadbent's s., a retraction of the thoracic wall, synchronous with cardiac systole, visible in the left posterior axillary line; a s. of adherent pericardium.

Brudzinski's s., (1) in meningitis, on passive flexion of the leg on one side, a similar movement occurs in the opposite leg; (2) in meningitis, if the neck is passively flexed, flexion of the legs occurs.

Chaddock s., Chaddock reflex; when the external malleolar skin area is irritated extension of the great toe occurs in cases of organic disease of the corticospinal reflex paths.

Chvostek's s., facial irritability in tetany, unilateral spasm being excited by a slight tap over the facial nerve.

clenched fist s., the gesture of the patient with angina pectoris by pressing a clenched fist against the chest to indicate the constricting, pressing quality of the pain.

Comby's s., an early s. of measles: thin whitish patches on the gums and buccal mucous membrane.

Comolli's s., a typical triangular cushion-like swelling, corresponding to the outline of the scapula, in cases of fracture of that bone.

conventional s.'s, s.'s that acquire their function through social (linguistic) custom; also called symbols.

Cruveilhier's s., *caput* medusae (1).

Cullen's s., periumbilical darkening of the skin from blood, a s. of intraperitoneal hemorrhage especially in ruptured ectopic pregnancy.

Dalrymple's s., in Graves disease, abnormal wideness of the palpebral fissures, the upper lid being retracted.

Delbet's s., in a case of aneurysm of a main artery, efficient collateral circulation if the nutrition of the part below is well maintained, despite the fact that the pulse has disappeared.

doll's eye s., dissociation between the movements of the eyes and those of the head, the eyes being lowered as the head is raised, and the reverse; also characterized by protrusion of the eyeballs and sluggish movements of the eyes and lids; both s.'s may occur in diphtheria.

drawer s., drawer test; the forward or backward sliding of the tibia indicating laxity or tear of the anterior or posterior cruciate ligaments of the knee.

Ebstein's s., obtuseness of the cardiohepatic angle on percussion in pericardial effusion.

Erb's s., (1) increased electric excitability of the muscles in tetany; (2) Erb-Westphal s.

Erb-Westphal s., Erb's s. (2); abolition of the patellar tendon reflex, in tabes and certain other diseases of the spinal cord, and occasionally also in brain disease.

Ewart's s., in large pericardial effusions, an area of dullness with bronchial breathing and bronchophony below the angle of the left scapula.

eyelash s., in a case of apparent unconsciousness due to functional disease, such as conversion hysteria, stroking the eyelashes will occasion movement of the lids, but no such reflex will occur in case of severe organic brain lesion.

Friedreich's s., sudden collapse of the previously distended veins of the neck at each diastole of the heart, in cases of adherent pericardium.

Goldstein's toe s., increased space between the great toe and its neighbor, seen in mongolism and occasionally in cretinism.

Goodell's s., softening of the cervix and vagina as being indicative of pregnancy.

Graefe's s., in Graves disease with exophthalmos, the upper eyelid does not follow evenly the movement of the eyeball downward, but lags or moves jerkily.

Gunn's s., Marcus Gunn's s.; the compression of the underlying vein at arteriovenous crossings seen ophthalmoscopically in arteriolar sclerosis.

halo s., elevation of the subcutaneous fat layer over the fetal skull in a dead or dying fetus.

Hill's s., in aortic insufficiency, the exaggerated excess of femoral over brachial artery systolic pressure.

Hoffmann's s., (1) in latent tetany, mild mechanical stimulation of the trigeminal nerve causes severe pain; (2) Hoffmann's, digital, or snapping reflex; flexion of the terminal phalanx of the thumb and of the second and third phalanges of one or more of the fingers when the volar surface of the terminal phalanx of the fingers is flicked.

Homans' s., slight pain at the back of the knee or calf when the ankle is slowly and gently dorsiflexed (with the knee bent), indicative of incipient or established thrombosis in the veins of the leg.

Hoover's s.'s, (1) a person lying supine on a couch, when asked to raise one leg, involuntarily makes counterpressure with the heel of the other leg; if this leg is paralyzed, whatever muscular power is preserved in it will be exerted in this way; or if the patient attempts to lift a paralyzed leg, counterpressure will be made with the other heel, whether any movement occurs in the paralyzed limb or not; not present in hysteria or malingering; (2) a modification in the movement of the costal margins during respiration, caused by a flattening of the diaphragm; suggestive of empyema or other intrathoracic condition causing a change in the contour of the diaphragm.

Joffroy's s., (1) immobility of the facial muscles when the eyeballs are rolled upward, in exophthalmic goiter; (2) inability to do simple sums in addition or multiplication in the early stages of organic brain disease.

Kernig's s., when the subject lies upon the back and the thigh is flexed to a right angle with the axis of the trunk, complete extension of the leg on the thigh is impossible; present in various forms of meningitis.

Kussmaul's s., the paradoxical increase in venous distention and pressure during inspiration seen in patients with cardiac tamponade.

Lasègue's s., when patient is supine with hip flexed, dorsiflexion of the ankle causing pain or muscle spasm in the posterior thigh indicates lumbar root or sciatic nerve irritation.

Leri's s., voluntary flexion of the elbow is impossible in a case of hemiplegia when the wrist on that side is passively flexed.

Lhermitte's s., sudden electric-like shocks extending down the spine when the patient flexes his head; seen in multiple sclerosis and in compression and other cervical cord disorders.

Macewen's s., percussion of the skull gives a cracked-pot sound in cases of hydrocephalus.

Marcus Gunn's s., Gunn's s.

Möbius s., impairment of ocular convergence in Graves disease.

Musset's s., rhythmical nodding of the head, synchronous with the heart beat, occurring in incompetence of the aortic valve.

Nikolsky's s., a peculiar vulnerability of the skin in pemphigus vulgaris: the apparently normal epidermis may be separated at the basal layer and rubbed off when pressed with a sliding motion.

Osler's s., small circumscribed painful erythematous swellings in the skin and subcutaneous tissues of the hands and feet, in cases of acute bacterial endocarditis.

Payr's s., pain on pressure over the sole of the foot; a s. of thrombophlebitis.

physical s., a s. that is elicited by auscultation, percussion, or palpation.

Piltz s., tonic *pupil.*

Porter's s., tracheal *tugging.*

pyramid s., any of the symptoms indicating a morbid condition of the pyramidal tracts, such as Babinski's s.

Quincke's s., Quincke's *pulse.*

Remak's s., dissociation of the sensations of touch and of pain in tabes dorsalis and polyneuritis.

Romberg's s., rombergism; if a patient standing is more unsteady with the eyes closed it indicates a loss of proprioceptive control.

Rossolimo's s., Rossolimo's *reflex.*

Saenger's s., a lost light reflex of the pupil returns after a short time in the dark, noted in cerebral syphilis but absent in tabes dorsalis.

scimitar s., a curvilinear structure seen in the lung base associated with anomalous pulmonary venous drainage.

Steinberg thumb s., in Marfan's syndrome, when the thumb is held across the palm of the same hand, it projects well beyond the ulnar surface of the hand.

Stellwag's s., infrequent and incomplete blinking in Graves disease.

Stewart-Holmes s., rebound phenomenon; the inability to check a movement when passive resistance is suddenly released, present in cerebellar deficit.

Tinel's s., a sensation of tingling, or "pins and needles," felt in the distal extremity of a limb when percussion is made over the site of an injured nerve, indicating a partial lesion or early regeneration in the nerve; sometimes called "distal tingling on percussion" (DTP).

Trendelenburg's s., in congenital dislocation of the hip, or in hip abductor weakness, if the patient stands on the dislocated leg and flexes the hip and knee on the other side the pelvis on this side will sag, whereas if normal, it will be raised on the side of the flexed hip and knee.

Trousseau's s., in latent tetany, the occurrence of carpal spasm or accoucheur's hand, elicited when the upper arm is compressed, as by a tourniquet or a blood pressure cuff.

vital s.'s, manifestation of breathing, heart beat, and sustained blood pressure.

Wernicke's s., Wernicke's *reaction.*

Westphal's s., Westphal-Erb s., abolition of the patellar reflex.

wrist s., in Marfan's syndrome, when the wrist is gripped with the opposite hand, the thumb and fifth finger overlap appreciably.

signature (sig'nă-chūr, -tür) [L. *signum,* a sign, mark]. The part of a prescription containing the directions to the patient.

silica (sil'ĭ-kah) [Mod. L. fr. L. *silex,* flint]. Silicon dioxide; SiO_2; the chief constituent of sand, hence of glass.

sil'icate. A salt of silicic acid.

sil'icato'sis. Silicosis.

sil'icon dioxide. Silica.

silicon (sil'ĭ-kon). A nonmetallic element, symbol Si, atomic no. 14, atomic weight 28.086.

silicone (sil'ĭ-kōn). A plastic compound of silicon oxides which may be a liquid, gel, or solid, depending on the extent of polymerization.

silicosiderosis (sil'ĭ-ko-sid-er-o'sis). Siderosilicosis.

silicosis [L. *silex,* flint, + -*osis,* condition]. Silicatosis; a form of pneumoconiosis due to the inhalation of dust containing silica; a slowly progressive fibrosis of the lungs is a predominant feature, which may result in restrictive and obstructive impairment of lung function.

silicotuberculosis (sil'ĭ-ko-tu'ber-ku-lo'sis). Silicosis associated with tuberculous pulmonary lesions.

siliquose (sil'ĭ-kwōs). Resembling a long slender pod; denoting a form of cataract resulting in shriveling of the lens with calcareous deposit in the capsule.

sil'ver [A.S. *seolfor*]. Argentum; a metallic element with a specific gravity of 10.4 to 10.7, symbol Ag, atomic no. 47, atomic weight 107.873.

s. nitrate, an antiseptic and astringent; used externally, in solution, in the prevention of ophthalmia neonatorum; also used in the special staining of the nervous system, spirochetes, reticular fibers, Golgi apparatus, and calcium.

silver impregnation. Silver complexes employed to demonstrate reticulin in normal and diseased tissues, as well as neuroglia, neurofibrillae, argentaffin cells, and Golgi apparatus.

simeth'icone. A mixture of dimethyl polysiloxanes and silica gel; antiflatulent.

simil'ia simil'ibus curan'tur [L. likes are cured by likes]. The homeopathic formula expressing the law of similars, or the doctrine that any drug which is capable of producing morbid symptoms in the healthy will remove similar symptoms occurring as an expression of disease; a variation employed by Hahnemann, the founder of homeopathy, is *similia similibus curentur,* let likes be cured by likes.

simulation (sim-u-la'shun) [L. *simulatio,* fr. *simulo,* pp. -*atus,* to imitate]. **1.** Imitation; said of a disease or symptom that resembles another, or of the feigning of illness, as by a malingerer.

Simulium (sĭ-mu'lĭ-um) [L. *simulo,* to simulate]. A genus of biting gnats or midges (family Simuliidae), various species of which transmit *Onchocerca volvulus,* the agent of human onchocerciasis.

sincipital (sin-sip'ĭ-tal). Relating to the sinciput.

sinciput, pl. **sincipita, sinciputs** (sin'sĭ-put, sin-sip'-ĭ-tah) [L. half of the head] [NA]. The anterior part of the head just above and including the forehead.

sin'ew [A.S. *sinu*]. A tendon.

sinis'ter (S) [L.] [NA]. Left.

sinistrad (sin'is-trad, sĭ-nis'trad) [L. *sinister*, left, + *ad*, to]. Toward the left side.

sinistral (sin'is-tral, sĭ-nis'tral). Relating to the left side.

sin'istral'ity. Left-handedness.

sinistro- [L. *sinister*, left]. Combining form denoting left, or toward the left.

sinistrocardia (sin'is-tro-kar'dĭ-ah) [sinistro- + G. *kardia*, heart]. Displacement of the heart beyond the normal position on the left side.

sinistrocer'ebral (sin'is-tro-sĕr'ĕ-bral) [sinistro- + L. *cerebrum*, brain]. Relating to the left cerebral hemisphere.

sinistrocular (sin'is-trok'u-lar) [sinistro- + L. *oculus*, eye]. Left-eyed; denoting use of the left eye by preference in monocular work, as with the microscope.

sinistrogyration (sin'is-tro-ji-ra'shun) [sinistro- + L. *gyratio*, a turning around (gyration)]. Sinistrotorsion.

sinistromanual (sin'is-tro-man'u-al) [sinistro- + L. *manus*, hand]. Left-handed; denoting use of the left hand by preference.

sinistropedal (sin'is-trop'ĕdal) [sinistro- + L. *pes* (*ped*-), foot]. Left-footed; denoting use of the left leg by preference.

sinistrotorsion (sin'is-tro-tor'shun) [sinistro- + L. *torsio*, a twisting (torsion)]. Sinistrogyration; levotorsion (1); a turning or twisting to the left.

sinoatrial (si'no-a'trī-al). Relating to the sinus venosus and the right atrium of the heart.

si'nopul'monary. Relating to the paranasal sinuses and the pulmonary airway.

si'nus, pl. **si'nus, si'nuses** [L. *sinus*, cavity, channel, hollow]. **1** [NA]. A channel for the passage of blood or lymph, which does not have the coats of an ordinary vessel, as in the gravid uterus or the cerebral meninges. **2** [NA]. A hollow in bone or other tissue. **3.** A fistula or tract leading to a suppurating cavity.

s. ana'les, [NA], **anal s.'s,** Morgagni's crypts; the grooves between the anal columns.

s. aor'tae [NA], **aortic s.,** the space between each semilunar valve and the wall of the aorta.

s. carot'icus [NA], **carotid s.,** a dilation of the common carotid artery at its bifurcation into external and internal carotids; contains baroreceptors which, when stimulated, cause slowing of the heart, vasodilation, and a fall in blood pressure.

s. caverno'sus [NA], **cavernous s.,** a paired dural s. on either side of the sella turcica, the two being connected by anastomoses in front of and behind the hypophysis, making a circular s.

cerebral s.'s, s. durae matris.

s. circula'ris, circular s., (1) s. intercavernosi; (2) a venous s. at the periphery of the placenta; (3) s. venosus sclerae.

coccygeal s., a fistula opening in the region of the coccyx, as a result of incomplete closure of the caudal end of the neural tube.

s. corona'rius [NA], **coronary s.,** a short trunk receiving most of the veins of the heart, running in the posterior part of the coronary sulcus and emptying into the right atrium between the inferior vena cava and the atrioventricular orifice.

dermal s., a s. lined with epidermis and skin appendages extending from the skin to some deeper-lying structure, most frequently the spinal cord.

s. du'rae ma'tris [NA], **s.'s of the dura mater,** cerebral or venous s.'s; endothelium-lined venous channels in the dura mater.

s. ethmoida'les [NA], **ethmoidal s.'s,** evaginations of the mucous membrane of the middle and superior meatuses of the nasal cavity; subdivided into s. anterior middle, and posterior s.'s.

s. fronta'lis [NA], **frontal s.,** a hollow formed on either side in the lower part of the squama of the frontal bone; communicates by the ethmoidal infundibulum with the middle meatus of the nasal cavity of the same side.

s. intercaverno'si [NA], **intercavernous s.'s,** s. circularis (1); the anterior and posterior anastomoses between the cavernous s.'s.

s. lactif'eri [NA], **lactiferous s.,** ampulla of milk duct; a circumscribed spindle-shaped dilation of the lactiferous duct just before it enters the nipple.

s. lie'nis [NA], splenic sinus; an elongated venous channel in the spleen, lined by rod-shaped cells.

lymphatic s., the channels in a lymph node crossed by a reticulum of cells and fibers and bounded by littoral cells.

marginal s. of placenta, discontinuous venous lakes at the margin of the placenta.

mastoid s.'s, numerous small intercommunicating cavities in the mastoid process of the temporal bone that empty into the mastoid or tympanic antrum.

s. maxilla'ris [NA], **maxillary s.,** antrum of Highmore; maxillary antrum; an air cavity in the body of the maxilla, communicating with the middle meatus of the nose.

s. occipita'lis [NA], **occipital s.,** an unpaired dural s. commencing at the confluens sinuum and passing downward in the base of the falx cerebelli to the foramen magnum.

s. paranasa'les [NA], **paranasal s.'s,** paired cavities (frontal, sphenoidal, maxillary, ethmoidal) in the bones of the face lined by mucous membrane continuous with that of the nasal cavity.

parasinoidal s.'s, *lacunae* laterales.

s. petro'sus [NA], **petrosal s.,** (1) inferior, a paired s. of the dura mater running in the groove on the petrooccipital fissure connecting the cavernous s. with the superior bulb of the internal jugular vein;

(2) superior, a paired s. of the dura mater in the groove on the superior margin of the petrous part of the temporal bone, connecting the cavernous s. with the transverse s.

pilonidal s., pilonidal fistula; a fistula or pit in the sacral region, communicating with the exterior, containing hair which may act as a foreign body producing chronic inflammation.

s. pocula'ris, *utriculus* prostaticus.

s. prostat'icus [NA], **prostatic s.**, the groove on either side of the urethral crest in the prostatic part of the urethra.

rectal s.'s, s. anales.

s. rec'tus [NA], straight or tentorial s.; an unpaired s. of the dura mater in the posterior part of the falx cerebri.

s. rena'lis [NA], **renal s.**, the cavity of the kidney, containing the calyces and pelvis.

rhomboidal s., rhombocele; a dilation of the central canal of the spinal cord in the lumbar region.

s. sagitta'lis infe'rior [NA], **sagittal s.**, (1) inferior, an unpaired dural s. in the lower margin of the falx cerebri; (2) superior, an unpaired dural s. in the sagittal groove.

s. sigmoi'deus [NA], **sigmoid s.**, the S-shaped dural s. lying on the mastoid process of the temporal bone and the jugular process of the occipital bone.

s. sphenoida'lis [NA], **sphenoidal s.**, one of a pair of cavities in the body of the sphenoid bone communicating with the nasal cavity.

s. sphenoparieta'lis [NA], **sphenoparietal s.**, a paired s. of the dura mater beginning on the parietal bone and emptying into the cavernous s.

splenic s., s. lienis.

straight s., s. rectus.

s. tar'si [NA], tarsal s. or canal; a hollow or canal formed by the groove of the talus and the groove of the calcaneus.

tentorial s., s. rectus.

terminal s., the vein bounding the area vasculosa in the blastoderm.

s. transver'sus [NA], **transverse s.**, a paired dural s. that begins at the confluens sinuum and terminates in the sigmoid s.

s. transver'sus pericar'dii [NA], **transverse s. of the pericardium**, a passage in the pericardium between the origins of the great vessels and the atria.

s. tym'pani [NA], **tympanic s.**, a depression in the tympanic cavity posterior to the tympanic promontory.

s. urogenita'lis, [NA], **urogenital s.**, the ventral part of the cloaca after its separation from the rectum by the growth of the urorectal septum; gives rise to the lower part of the bladder in both sexes, to the prostatic portion of the male urethra, and to the urethra and vestibule in the female.

uterine s., a small irregular vascular channel in the endometrium.

uteroplacental s.'s, irregular vascular spaces in the zone of the chorionic attachment to the decidua basalis.

s. vena'rum cava'rum [NA], **s. of venae cavae**, the portion of the cavity of the right atrium of the heart that receives the blood from the venae cavae and is separated from the rest of the atrium by the crista terminalis.

s. veno'sus [NA], a cavity at the caudal end of the embryonic cardiac tube in which the veins from the intra- and extraembryonic circulatory arcs unite; in the course of development it forms the portion of the right atrium known in adult anatomy as the s. venarum cavarum.

s. veno'sus scle'rae [NA], **venous s. of the sclera**, Schlemm's canal; s. circularis (3); a ringlike vein in the sclera, near its inner edge, encircling the cornea.

venous s.'s, s. durae matris.

sinusitis (si-nŭ-si'tis) [sinus + G. -itis, inflammation]. Inflammation of the lining membrane of any sinus, especially of one of the paranasal sinuses.

sinusoid (si'nŭ-soyd) [sinus + G. eidos, resemblance]. **1.** Resembling a sinus. **2.** A terminal blood vessel having an irregular and larger caliber than an ordinary capillary.

sinusoidal (si-nŭ-soy'dal). Relating to a sinusoid.

sinusotomy (sin-us-ot'o-mī) [sinus + G. tomē, incision]. Incision into a sinus.

siphon (si'fon) [G. siphōn, tube]. A tube bent into two unequal lengths, used to remove fluid from a cavity or vessel by atmospheric pressure.

siphonage (si'fon-ij). Emptying of the stomach or other cavity by means of a siphon.

sirenomelia (si'rĕ-no-me'lĭ-ah) [L. siren, G. seirēn, a siren]. Congenital union of the legs with partial or complete fusion of the feet.

sis'ter. In Great Britain: **1.** The title of a head nurse in a public hospital or in a ward or the operating room of a hospital. **2.** Any registered nurse in private practice.

site [L. situs]. Place; seat; situation; location.

active s., that portion of an enzyme molecule at which the actual reaction proceeds.

allosteric s., the place on an enzyme where a nonsubstrate may bind and influence the activity of the enzyme by changing the enzyme's shape.

fragile s., a non-staining gap at a specific point on a chromosome, usually involving both chromatids, always at the same point on chromosomes of different cells from an individual or kindred; it results in *in vitro* production of acentric fragments, deleted chromosomes, or other chromosome anomalies; inherited as a dominant chromosome marker.

sito- [G. sitos, sition, food, grain]. Combining form relating to food or grain.

sitotaxis (si-to-tak'sis) [sito- + G. taxis, orderly arrangement]. Sitotropism.

sitotoxin (si-to-tok'sin) [sito- + G. toxikon, poison]. Any food poison, especially one developing in grain.

sitotropism (si-tot'ro-pizm) [sito- + G. *tropē*, a turning]. Sitotaxis; turning of living cells to or away from food.

si'tus inver'sus, Visceral inversion; a transposition of the viscera, the liver being on the left side, the heart on the right, etc.

SK Streptokinase.

ska'tole. 3-Methylindole; formed in the intestine by the bacterial decomposition of tryptophan and found in fecal matter, to which it imparts its characteristic odor.

skatox'yl 3-Hydroxymethylindole; formed in the intestine by the oxidation of skatole; some undergoes conjugation in the body with sulfuric or gluronic acids and is excreted in the urine in conjugated form.

skeletal (skel'ĕ-tal). Relating to the skeleton.

skeleton (skel'ĕ-ton) [G. *skeletos*, dried, ntr. *skeleton*, a mummy]. **1.** The bony framework of the body in vertebrates (endoskeleton) or the hard outer envelope of insects (exoskeleton or dermoskeleton). **2.** All the dry parts (ligaments, cartilages, bones) remaining after the destruction and removal of the soft parts. **3.** All the bones of the body taken collectively.

s. appendicula're [NA], **appendicular s.,** the bones of the limbs including the pectoral and pelvic girdles.

s. axia'le [NA], **axial s.,** the bones of the head and trunk excluding the pectoral and pelvic girdles.

skia- [G. *skia*, shadow]. Combining form denoting shadow; in radiology, superseded by radio-.

skiascopy (ski-as'ko-pī). Retinoscopy.

skin [A.S. *scinn*]. Cutis.

  alligator s., ichthyosis.

  elastic s., Ehlers-Danlos *syndrome.*

  fish s., ichthyosis.

  nail s., eponychium (2).

  piebald s., vitiligo.

  shagreen s., an oval-shaped nevoid plaque, skin-colored or occasionally pigmented, smooth or crinkled, appearing on the trunk or lower back in early childhood.

skull [Early Eng. *skulle,* a bowl]. Cranium.

skull'cap. Calvaria.

S.L.E. Systemic *lupus* erythematosus.

sleep [A.S. *slaep*]. A physiologic state of relative unconsciousness and inaction of the voluntary muscles, the need for which recurs periodically.

  paradoxical s., a deep s., with a brain wave pattern more like that of waking states than of other states of sleep, which occurs during the rapid eye movement state of s.

  rapid eye movement (REM) s., that state of deep s. in which rapid eye movements, alert EEG pattern, and dreaming occur.

  twilight s., (1) a stage of anesthesia between s. and wakefulness in which the person is analgesic and amnestic; (2) formerly, a popular method of producing s. for delivery by a combination of morphine and scopolamine.

slide. An oblong glass plate on which is placed an object to be examined under the microscope.

sling. A supporting bandage or suspensory device; especially a loop suspended from the neck and supporting the flexed forearm.

slit'lamp. Biomicroscope.

slough (sluf). **1.** Necrosed tissue separated from the living structure. **2.** To separate from the living tissue, said of a dead or necrosed part.

Sm Samarium.

small'pox [E. *small pocks,* or pustules]. Variola; an acute eruptive contagious disease caused by a poxvirus (*Orthopoxvirus*) and marked at the onset by chills, high fever, backache, and headache, followed by papules which become umbilicated vesicles and develop into pustules; the pustules dry and form scabs which on falling off leave a permanent marking of the skin (pock marks).

smear (smēr). A thin specimen for examination, usually prepared by spreading material uniformly onto a glass slide, fixing it, and staining it before examination.

  cytologic s., cytosmear; a type of cytologic specimen made by smearing a sample, then fixing it and staining it, usually with 95% ethyl alcohol and Papanicolaou stain.

  fast s., an FGT cytologic s. containing material from the vaginal pool and pancervical scrapings, mixed and prepared on one microscopic slide, smeared, and fixed immediately; used principally for routine FGT screening of ovaries, endometrium, cervix, vagina, and hormonal states.

  FGT cytologic s., any cytologic s. obtained from the female genital tract.

  Pap s., Papanicolaou s., a s. of vaginal mucosa obtained for a Pap test.

  VCE s., a cytologic s. of material obtained from the vagina, ectocervix, and endocervix, smeared separately (in that order) on one slide, and fixed immediately; used principally for the detection of cervical cancer and identification of the sites of diseases of those areas, and for hormonal evaluation.

smegma (smeg'mah) [G. unguent]. Sebum; especially the whitish secretion that collects under the prepuce of the foreskin of the penis or of the clitoris, comprised chiefly of desquamating epithelial cells.

smegmalith (smeg'mă-lith) [smegma + G. *lithos,* stone]. A calcareous concretion in the smegma.

smell. 1. To scent; to perceive by means of the olfactor apparatus. **2.** Olfaction (1). **3.** Odor.

smog [smoke + fog]. Air pollution characterized by a hazy and often highly irritating atmosphere resulting from a mixture of smoke and other air pollutants, and fog.

Sn Tin.

snap. A short sharp sound; a click; said especially of cardiac sounds.

closing s., the accentuated first heart sound of mitral stenosis, related to closure of the abnormal valve.

opening s., a sharp, high-pitched click in early diastole, usually best heard between the cardiac apex and the lower left sternal border, related to opening of the abnormal valve in cases of mitral stenosis.

snare [A.S. *snear,* a cord]. A wire loop passed around the base of a polyp or other projection and gradually tightened to remove it.

sneeze [A.S. *fneōsan*]. **1.** To expel air from the nose and mouth by an involuntary spasmodic contraction of the muscles of expiration. **2.** The act so performed.

snore [A.S. *snora*]. **1.** A rough inspiratory noise produced by vibration of the pendulous palate, or sometimes of the vocal cords, during sleep or coma. **2.** To breathe noisily, or with a s.

snuff. **1.** To inhale forcibly through the nose. **2.** Finely powdered tobacco used by inhalation through the nose or applied to the gums. **3.** Any medicated powder applied by insufflation to the nasal mucous membrane.

snuffles (suf'lz). Obstructed nasal respiration, especially in the newborn infant, sometimes due to congenital syphilis.

soap [A.S. *sape,* L. *sapo,* G. *sapōn*]. The sodium or potassium salts of long chain fatty acids; used for cleansing purposes and as an excipient in the making of pills and suppositories.

socialization (so'shă-lĭ-za'shun) [L. *socia,* partner, companion]. The process of learning interpersonal and interactional skills which are in conformity with the values of one's society.

socio- [L. *socius,* companion]. Combining form denoting social, society.

sociocentric (so'sĭ-o-sen'trik) [socio- + L. *centrum,* center]. Outgoing; reactive to the culture.

sociogenic (so'sĭ-o-jen-ic) [socio- + G. *genesis,* origin]. Denoting social behavior originating from past interpersonal experiences.

sociopath (so'sĭ-o-path). A person with antisocial personality disorder.

sociopathy (so-sĭ-op'ă-thĭ) [socio- + G. *pathos,* suffering]. The behavioral pattern exhibited by persons with antisocial personality disorder.

sock'et [thr. O. Fr. fr. L. *soccus,* a shoe, a sock]. **1.** The hollow part of a joint; the excavation in one bone of a joint which receives the articular end of the other bone. **2.** Any hollow or concavity into which another part fits, as the eye or tooth s.

soda (so'dah) [It., possibly fr. Mediev. L. barilla plant]. See bicarbonate, *sodium* carbonate, and hydroxide.

s. lime, a mixture of calcium and sodium hydroxides used to absorb carbon dioxide in rebreathing apparatus and circuits.

sodium (so'dĭ-um) [Mod. L. fr. *soda*]. Natrium; a caustic alkaline metallic element, symbol Na,

atomic no. 11, atomic weight 22.99; its salts are extensively used in medicine.

s. benzoate, C_6H_5COONa; used in chronic and acute rheumatism and as a liver function test.

s. bicarbonate, baking soda; $NaHCO_3$; used as a gastric and systemic antacid, to alkalize urine, and for washes of body cavities.

s. carbonate, washing soda; $Na_2CO_3 \cdot 10H_2O$; used in the treatment of scaly skin diseases; otherwise rarely used in medicine because of its irritant action.

s. chloride, common or table salt; NaCl; used as in making isotonic and physiological salt solutions, as an emetic, and in treatment of salt depletion.

s. cyclamate, the s. salt of cyclamic acid; a noncaloric artificial sweetener.

s. fluoride, used as a dental prophylactic in drinking water, and topically as a 2% solution applied on the teeth.

s. hydroxide, caustic soda; NaOH; used externally as a caustic.

s. nitrite, $NaNO_2$; used to lower systemic blood pressure, to relieve local vasomotor spasms, especially in angina pectoris and Raynaud's disease, to relax bronchial and intestinal spasms, and as an antidote for cyanide poisoning.

s. sulfate, $Na_2SO_4 \cdot 10H_2O$; an ingredient of many of the natural laxative waters, also used as a hydragogue cathartic.

s. thiosulfate, $Na_2S_2O_3 \cdot 5H_2O$; used as an antidote in cyanide poisoning in conjunction with s. nitrite, as a prophylactic agent against ringworm infections in swimming pools and baths, and to measure the extracellular fluid volume of the body.

sodium group. The alkali metals: lithium, sodium potassium, rubidium, and cesium.

sod'omist, sod'omite [G. *sodomitēs,* inhabitant of biblical city of Sodom]. One who practices sodomy.

sod'omy [see sodomist]. A term denoting a variety of sexual practices considered abnormal, especially copulation of man and animal (bestiality), fellatio, and anal intercourse.

sol. **1.** A colloidal dispersion of a solid in a liquid. **2.** Abbreviation for solution.

solation (sol-a'shun). Transformation of a gel into a sol as by melting gelatin.

sole [A.S.]. The under part of the foot; the plantar surface.

sol'id [L. *solidus*]. **1.** Firm; compact; not fluid; without interstices or cavities; not cancellous. **2.** A body that retains its form when not confined; one that is not fluid, neither liquid nor gaseous.

solubility (sol-u-bil'ĭ-tĭ). The property of being soluble.

soluble (sol'u-bl) [L. *solubilis,* fr. *solvo,* to dissolve]. Capable of being dissolved.

solute (so-lūt') [L. *solutus,* dissolved]. The dissolved substance in a solution.

solution (sol.) (so-lu'shun) [L. *solutio*]. **1.** Incorporation of a solid, a liquid, or a gas in a liquid or noncrystalline solid resulting in a homogeneous single phase. **2.** Generally, an aqueous s. of a nonvolatile substance. **3.** Termination of a disease by crisis. **4.** A break, cut, or laceration of the solid tissues.

colloidal s., dispersion (3).

s. of contiguity, the breaking of contiguity; a dislocation or displacement of two normally contiguous parts.

s. of continuity, dieresis; division of bones or soft parts that are normally continuous, as by a fracture, a laceration, or an incision.

Dakin's s., buffered sodium hypochlorite, a bactericidal wound irrigant.

disclosing s., a s. that selectively stains all soft debris, pellicle, and bacterial plaque on teeth; used as an aid in identifying bacterial plaque after rinsing with water.

lactated Ringer's s., a s. containing NaCl, sodium lactate, $CaCl_2$ (dihydrate), and KCl in distilled water; used for the same purposes as Ringer's s.

normal s., see normal (3).

ophthalmic s.'s, sterile s.'s, free from foreign particles and suitably compounded and dispensed for instillation into the eye.

Ringer's s.'s, a s. resembling the blood serum in its salt constituents: 8.6 g of NaCl, 0.3 g of KCl, and 0.33 g of $CaCl_2$ in each 1000 ml of distilled water; used topically for burns and wounds.

saline s., salt s., a s. of any salt; specifically an isotonic sodium chloride s.

saturated s. (sat. sol.), a s. that contains all of a substance capable of dissolving; a solution of a substance in equilibrium with excess undissolved substance.

standard s., standardized s., a s. of known concentration, used as a standard of comparison or analysis.

supersaturated s., a s. containing more of the solid than the liquid would ordinarily dissolve; made by heating the solvent when the substance is added, and on cooling the latter is retained without precipitation.

test s., a s. of some reagent, in definite strength, used in chemical analysis or testing.

volumetric s. (VS), a s. made by mixing measured volumes of the components.

sol'vent [L. *solvens,* pres. p. of *solvo,* to dissolve]. **1.** Capable of dissolving a substance. **2.** Menstruum; a liquid that holds another substance in solution, *i.e.,* dissolves it.

soma (so'mah) [G. *sōma,* body]. **1.** The axial part of a body: head, neck, trunk, and tail. **2.** All of an organism with the exception of the germ cells.

somasthenia (so-mas-the'nĭ-ah). Somatasthenia

somat-, somatico-. See somato-.

somatagnosia (so'mă-tag-no'sĭ-ah) [somat- + G. *a*-priv. + *gnōsis,* recognition]. Inability to identify parts of one's own body and parts of another's body.

somatalgia (so'mă-tal'jĭ-ah) [somat- + G. *algos,* pain]. Pain in the body due to organic causes, as opposed to psychalgia, or psychogenic pain.

somatasthenia (so'mă-tas-the'nĭ-ah) [somat- + G. *asthenia,* weakness]. Somasthenia; a condition of chronic physical weakness and fatigability.

somatesthesia (so'mă-tes-the'zĭ-ah) [somat- + G. *aisthēsis,* sensation]. Somesthesia; bodily sensation, the consciousness of the body.

somatesthet'ic. Relating to somatesthesia.

somatic (so-mat'ik) [G. *sōmatikos,* bodily]. **1.** Relating to the soma or trunk, the wall of the body cavity, or the body in general. **2.** Relating to the vegetative, as distinguished from the generative, functions.

so'matiza'tion. The conversion of anxiety into physical symptoms.

somato-, somat-, somatico- [G. *sōma,* body]. Combining forms denoting the body, bodily.

somatochrome (so'mă-to-krōm) [somato- + G. *chrōma,* color]. Denoting the group of neurons or nerve cells in which there is an abundance of cytoplasm completely surrounding the nucleus.

somatogenic (so'mă-to-jen'ik) [somato- + G. *genesis,* origin]. **1.** Originating in the body under the influence of external forces. **2.** Having origin in body cells.

so'matolib'erin. Somatotropin-releasing factor; growth hormone-releasing factor or hormone; a decapeptide released by the hypothalamus; which induces the release of somatotropin.

somatomammotropin (so'mă-to-mam'o-tro-pin). A peptide hormone closely related to growth hormone in its biological properties, produced by the normal placenta and by certain neoplasms.

human chorionic s. (HCS), human placental *lactogen.*

so'matome'din. A peptide, synthesized in the liver and probably in the kidney, capable of stimulating certain anabolic processes in bone and cartilage; its secretion and/or biological activity is dependent on somatotropin.

somatopathic (so-mă-to-path'ik) [somato- + G. *pathos,* suffering]. Relating to bodily or organic illness, as distinguished from neurologic or psychologic disorder.

somatopathy (so-mă-top'ă-thǐ) [somato- + G. *pathos,* suffering]. Disease of the body.

somatoplasm (so'mă-to-plazm, so-mat'o-) [somato- + G. *plasma,* something formed]. The aggregate of all the forms of specialized protoplasm entering into the composition of the body, other than germ plasm.

somatopleural (so'mă-to-plūr'al). Relating to the somatopleure.

somatopleure (so'mă-to-plūr) [somato- + G. *pleura,* side]. The embryonic layer formed by the association of the parietal layer of the lateral mesoderm with the ectoderm.

somatopsychic (so'mă-to-si'kik) [somato- + G. *psychē,* soul]. Relating to the body-mind relationship, or the study of the effects of the body upon the mind.

somatopsychosis (so'mă-to-si-ko'sis) [somato- + G. *psychōsis*, an animating]. An emotional disorder associated with an organic disease.

so'matosex'ual. Denoting the somatic aspects of sexuality, as distinguished from its psychosexual aspects.

so'matostatin. Somatotropin release-inhibiting factor; a tetradecapeptide capable of inhibiting the release of somatotropin by the anterior lobe of the pituitary gland.

somatostatinoma (so'mă-to-stat-ī-no'mah). A somatostatin-secreting tumor of the pancreatic islets.

so'matother'apy. 1. Therapy directed at bodily or physical disorders. 2. In psychiatry, a variety of therapeutic interventions employing chemical or physical, as opposed to psychological, methods.

somatotonia (so'mă-to-to'nĭ-ah) [somato- + G. *tonos*, tension]. Term for a personality type characterized by vigorous activity and assertiveness.

somatotopic (so-mă-to-top'ĭk). Relating to somatotopy.

somatotopy (so-mă-tot'o-pĭ) [somato- + G. *topos*, place]. The topographic association of positional relationships of receptors in the body via respective nerve fibers to their terminal distribution in specific functional areas of the cerebral cortex.

somatotroph (so'mă-to-trof). A cell of the adenohypophysis that produces somatotropin.

somatotrophic (so'mă-to-trof'ik) [somato- + G. *trophē*, nourishment]. Somatotropic.

somatotropic (so'mă-to-trop'ik) [somato- + G. *tropē*, a turning]. Somatotrophic; having a stimulating effect on body growth.

somatotropin (so'mă-to-tro'pin). Growth hormone; somatotropic hormone; pituitary growth hormone; a protein hormone of the anterior lobe of the pituitary, produced by the acidophil cells; promotes body growth, fat mobilization, and inhibition of glucose utilization.

so'matotype. The constitutional or body type of an individual, especially that associated with a particular personality type.

somesthesia (so-mes-the'zī-ah). Somatesthesia.

somite (so'mīt) [G. *sōma*, body]. One of the 42 paired, metamerically arranged cell masses formed in the early embryonic paraxial mesoderm.

somnambulism (som-nam'bu-lizm) [L. *somnus*, sleep, + *ambulo*, to walk]. 1. Sleepwalking; a disorder of sleep, involving complex motor acts, that occurs primarily during the first third of the night but not during rapid eye movement sleep. 2. A form of hysteria in which purposeful behavior is forgotten.

somnifacient (som'nĭ-fa'shent) [L. *somnus*, sleep, + *facio*, to make]. Soporific.

somniferous (som-nif'er-us) [L. *somnus*, sleep, + *fero*, to bring]. Soporific.

somniloquence, somniloquism (som-nil'o-kwens, -kwizm) [L. *somnus*, sleep, + *loquor*, to talk]. Sleeptalking; talking in one's sleep.

somnipathy (som-nip'ă-thī) [L. *somnus*, sleep, + G. *pathos*, suffering]. Any disorder of sleep.

som'nolence [L. *somnolentia*]. 1. Drowsiness; sleepiness; an inclination to sleep. 2. A condition of semiconsciousness approaching coma.

som'nolent [L. *somnus*, sleep]. 1. Sleepy; drowsy; having an inclination to sleep. 2. In a condition of incomplete sleep; semicomatose.

somnolescent (som-no-les'ent). Inclined to sleep; drowsy.

sonic (son'ik) [L. *sonus*, sound]. Of, pertaining to, or determined by sound.

sonication (son-ĭ-ka'shun). The process of disrupting biologic materials by use of sound wave energy.

sonification (son'ĭ-fĭ-ka'shun). The production of sound, or of sound waves.

sonogram (son'o-gram) [L. *sonus*, sound, + G. *gramma*, a drawing]. Ultrasonogram; the image obtained by ultrasonography.

sonograph (son'o-graf) [L. *sonus*, sound, + G. *graphō*, to write]. Ultrasonograph; the instrument used to create an image using ultrasound.

sonographer (sŏ-nog'ră-fer). Ultrasonographer; one who performs and interprets ultrasonographic examinations.

sonography (sŏ-nog'ră-fī) [L. *sonus*, sound + G. *graphō*, to write]. Ultrasonography.

so'por [L.]. Stupor; an unnaturally deep sleep.

soporific (so'pŏr-if'ik, sop'ōr-) [L. *sopor*, deep sleep, + *facio*, to make]. Somnifacient, somniferous; causing sleep.

so'porous [L. *sopor*, deep sleep]. Relating to or causing sopor.

sorbefacient (sor'bĕ-fa'shent) [L. *sorbeo*, to suck up, + *facio*, to make]. Causing or facilitating absorption.

sor'bic acid. 2,4-Hexadienoic acid; obtained from berries of the mountain ash, *Sorbus aucuparia* (family Rosaceae), or prepared synthetically; used as a preservative.

sordes (sor'dēz) [L. fifth fr. *sordeo*, to be foul]. A dark brown or blackish crustlike collection on the lips, teeth, and gums of a person with dehydration in chronic debilitating disease.

sore (sōr) [A.S. *sār*]. 1. A wound, ulcer, or any open skin lesion. 2. Painful.

   bed s., see bedsore.

   canker s.'s, ulcerative *stomatitis*.

   cold s., colloquialism for *herpes* simplex.

   pressure s., decubitus *ulcer*.

   recurrent canker s.'s, recurrent ulcerative *stomatitis*.

   tropical s., the lesion occurring in cutaneous leishmaniasis.

sorption (sorp'shun). Adsorption or absorption.

s.o.s. L. *sit opus sit*, if needed.

souffle (sū'fl) [Fr. *souffler*, to blow]. A soft blowing sound heard on auscultation.

cardiac s., a soft puffing heart murmur.

fetal s., funic s., funicular s., a blowing murmur, synchronous with the fetal heart beat, sometimes only systolic and sometimes continuous, heard on auscultation over the pregnant uterus.

uterine s., placental s., a blowing sound, synchronous with the cardiac systole of the mother, heard on auscultation of the pregnant uterus.

sound. **1.** Noise; the vibrations produced by a sounding body, transmitted by the air or other medium, and perceived by the internal ear. **2.** An elongated cylindrical, usually curved, instrument used for exploring the bladder or other cavities of the body, dilating strictures of the urethra, esophagus, or other canal, calibrating the lumen of a body cavity, or detecting the presence of a foreign body in a body cavity. **3.** Whole; healthy; not diseased or injured.

bowel s.'s, s.'s caused by the propulsion of intestinal contents through the lower alimentary tract.

ejection s., a sharp s. heard in early systole over the aortic or pulmonic area when the aorta or pulmonary artery is dilated.

friction s., friction rub; the s., heard on auscultation, made by the rubbing of two opposed serous surfaces roughened by an inflammatory exudate.

heart s., one of the s.'s heard on auscultation over the heart **first h. s.,** occurs with ventricular systole and is mainly produced by closure of the atrioventricular valves; **second h. s.,** signifies the beginning of diastole, due to closure of the semilunar valves; **third h. s.,** occurs in early diastole and corresponds with the first phase of rapid ventricular filling; **fourth h. s.,** occurs in late diastole and corresponds with atrial contraction.

hippocratic succussion s., a splashing s. elicited in a patient with hydro- or pyopneumothorax.

Korotkoff s.'s, the s.'s heard over an artery when blood pressure is determined by the auscultatory method.

tambour s., a heart s., usually the aortic or pulmonic valve closure s. when it has a booming and ringing quality like that of a drum.

space (spās) [L. *spatium*, room, space]. Any demarcated portion of the body, either an area of the surface, a segment of the tissues, or a cavity.

alveolar dead s., the difference between physiologic dead s. and anatomical dead s.; represents that part of the physiologic dead s. resulting from ventilation of relatively underperfused or nonperfused alveoli.

anatomical dead s., the volume of the conducting airways from the external environment (at the nose and mouth) down to the level at which inspired gas exchanges oxygen and carbon dioxide with pulmonary capillary blood.

apical s., the s. between the alveolar-wall and the apex of the root of a tooth where an alveolar abscess usually has its orgin.

capsular s., Bowman's s., the slitlike s. between the visceral and parietal layers of the capsule of the renal corpuscle; opens into the proximal tubule of the nephron at the neck of the tubule.

cartilage s., cartilage *lacuna.*

corneal s., lacuna (4); one of the stellate s.'s between the lamellae of the cornea, each of which contains a cell or corneal corpuscle.

dead s., **(1)** a cavity, potential or real, remaining after the closure of a wound not obliterated by the operative technique; **(2)** see anatomical dead s. and physiologic dead s.

epidural s., the s. between the walls of the vertebral canal and the dura mater of the spinal cord.

episcleral s., Tenon's s.; the s. between the vagina bulbi and the sclera.

haversian s.'s, s.'s in bone formed by the enlargement of haversian canals.

intercostal s., the interval between each rib.

interpleural s., mediastinum (2).

interproximal s., the s. between adjacent teeth in a dental arch.

interradicular s., the s. between the roots of multirooted teeth.

intervillous s.'s, the s.'s between placental villi containing maternal blood.

Kiernan's s., interlobular s. in the liver.

Meckel's s., the cleft in the meningeal layer of dura of the middle cranial fossa near the tip of the petrous part of the temporal bone; encloses the roots of the trigeminal nerve and the trigeminal ganglion.

mediastinal s., mediastinum (2).

medullary s., the central cavity and the cellular intervals between the trabeculae of bone, filled with marrow.

palmar s., one of two fascial s.'s in the palm: **middle p. s.,** toward the ulnar side; **thenar s.,** toward the radial side.

perforated s., *substantia perforata.*

perilymphatic s., the s. between the bony and membraneous portions of the labyrinth.

perineal s., **(1)** deep, the cleft between the superior and inferior fascial layers of the urogenital diaphragm occupied by the membranous part of the urethra, the bulbourethral gland (male), the deep transverse perineal and sphincter urethrae muscles, and the dorsal nerve and artery of the penis or clitoris; **(2)** superficial, the space bounded above by the perineal membrane and below by the superficial perineal fascia; contains the root structure of the penis or clitoris.

personal s., the physical area immediately surrounding an individual who is in proximity to one or more others, and which serves as a body buffer zone in interpersonal transactions.

physiologic dead s. (V_D) the sum of anatomic and alveolar dead s.; the dead s. calculated when the CO_2 pressure in systemic arterial blood is used instead of that of alveolar gas in Bohr's equation.

plantar s., one of four areas between fascial layers in the foot.

pleural s., *cavitas* pleuralis.

Poiseuille's s., still *layer.*

retroperitoneal s., retroperitoneum; the space between the parietal peritoneum and the muscles and bones of the posterior abdominal wall.

retropubic s., the area of loose connective tissue between the bladder with its related fascia and the pubis and anterior abdominal wall.

subarachnoid s., the space between the arachnoidea and pia mater, filled with cerebrospinal fluid and containing the large blood vessels supplying the brain and spinal cord.

subchorial s., subchorial lake; the part of the placenta adjacently beneath the chorion.

subdural s., the narrow s. between the dura and arachnoid.

subgingival s., gingival *crevice.*

Tenon's s., *spatium* episclerale.

thenar s., see palmar s.

zonular s.'s, the spaces between the fibers of the zonula ciliaris at the equator of the lens of the eye.

sparganoma (spar-gă-no'mah). A localized mass resulting from sparganosis.

sparganosis (spar-gă-no'sis). Infection with the plerocercoid (sparganum) of certain tapeworms, usually in a dermal sore resulting from infection.

spasm (spazm) [G. *spasmos*]. Spasmus. **1.** An involuntary muscular contraction; if painful, usually referred to as a cramp; if violent, a convulsion. **2.** Muscle s.; increased muscular tension and shortness which cannot be released voluntarily and which prevent lengthening of the muscles involved.

carpopedal s., carpopedal contraction; s. of the feet and hands observed in hyperventilation, calcium deprivation, and tetany: flexion of the hands at the wrists and of the fingers at the metacarpophalangeal joints and extension of the fingers at the phalangeal joints; feet are dorsiflexed at the ankles and toes plantar flexed.

clonic s., alternate involuntary contraction and relaxation of a muscle.

cynic s., *risus* caninus.

facial s., facial *tic.*

habit s., tic.

intention s., a spasmodic contraction of the muscles occurring when a voluntary movement is attempted.

muscle s., spasm (2).

nodding s., salaam convulsions; spasmus nutans (1); **(1)** in infants, a drop of the head on the chest due to loss of tone in the neck muscles as in epilepsy or to tonic spasm of anterior neck muscles as in West's syndrome; **(2)** in adults, a psychogenic nodding of the head from clonic s.'s of the sternomastoid muscles.

retrocollic s., retrocollis; torticollis in which the s. affects the posterior neck muscles.

saltatory s., static convulsion; a spasmodic affection of the muscles of the lower extremities.

tonic s., entasia; entasis; a continuous involuntary muscular contraction.

tonoclonic s., convulsive contraction of muscles.

torsion s., a spasmodic twisting of the body and pelvis.

spasmo- [G. *spasmos*, spasm]. Combining form denoting spasm.

spasmodic (spaz-mod'ik) [G. *spasmōdes*, convulsive]. Relating to or marked by spasm.

spasmolysis (spaz-mol'ĭ-sis) [spasmo- + G. *lysis*, dissolution]. Arrest of a spasm or convulsion.

spasmolytic (spaz-mo-lit'ik). **1.** Relating to spasmolysis. **2.** Antispasmodic; denoting a chemical agent that relieves smooth muscle spasms.

spasmus (spaz'mus) [L. fr. G. *spasmos*, spasm]. Spasm.

s. nu'tans, **(1)** nodding *spasm;* **(2)** nystagmus associated with head-nodding movements.

spastic (spas'tik) [L. *spasticus*, fr. G. *spastikos*, drawing in]. **1.** Hypertonic (1). **2.** Relating to spasm or to spasticity.

spasticity (spas-tis'ĭ-tĭ). A state of increased muscular tone with exaggeration of the tendon reflexes.

clasp-knife s., clasp-knife rigidity; rigidity of the extensor muscles of a joint which offer resistance to passive flexion and then give way suddenly to allow the joint to be easily flexed; due to exaggeration of the stretch reflex.

s. of conjugate gaze, an oblique or horizontal deviation of the eyes evoked during forcible lid closure or while fixating on an object 30 or 40 cm in front, the eyelids being opened and closed at 4- to 5-second intervals; usually associated with a temporal lesion opposite to the direction of deviation.

spatial (spa'shal). Relating to space or a space.

spatium, pl. **spatia** (spa'shĭ-um, -shĭ-ah) [L.] [NA]. A space.

spatulate (spach'u-lāt). **1.** Having a broad flat end. **2.** To incise the cut end of a tubular structure longitudinally and splay it open, to allow creation of an elliptical anastomosis of greater circumference than would be possible with conventional transverse or oblique (bevelled) end-to-end anastomoses.

spay [Gael. *spoth*, castrate, or G. *spadōn*, eunuch]. To remove the ovaries of an animal.

SPCA Serum prothrombin conversion *accelerator.*

specialist (spesh'ă-list). One who devotes himself to the study, research, and treatment of a particular group of diseases.

specialization (spesh'ă-lĭ-za'shun). **1.** Confining attention to a single disease, region of the body, age, or sex of a patient for study, research, and treatment. **2.** Differentiation (1).

specialty (spesh'al-tĭ) [L. *specialitis* fr. *specialis*, special]. The particular group of diseases or branch of medical science on which a health professional concentrates.

speciation (spe-she-a'shun). The evolutionary process by which new species of animals or plants are formed from preexisting species.

species, pl. **species** (spe'shēz) [L. appearance, form, kind, fr. *specio*, to look at]. **1.** A biological division between the genus and variety or the individual; a group of organisms which generally bear a close resemblance to one another in the more essential features of their organization, and with sexual forms which produce fertile progeny. **2.** A class of pharmaceutical preparations consisting of a mixture of dried plants in sufficiently fine division to be used in making extemporaneous decoctions or infusions.

species-specific. Indicating a serum that is produced by the injection of cells, protein, or other material into an animal, and that acts only upon the cells, protein, etc., of a member of the same species as that from which the original antigen was obtained.

specific (spē-sif'ik) [L. *species,* + *facio,* to make]. **1.** Relating to a species. **2.** Denoting specificity.

specific gravity (sp. gr.). The weight of any body compared with that of another body of equal volume regarded as the unit; usually the weight of a liquid compared with that of distilled water.

specificity (spes-ĭ-fis'ĭ-tĭ). **1.** The condition or state of being specific, of having a fixed relation to a single cause or to a definite result; manifested in the relation of a disease to its pathogenic microorganism or the curative remedy, of a reaction to a certain chemical union, or of an antibody to its antigen, or the reverse. **2.** In clinical pathology and medical screening, the proportion of individuals with negative test results for the disease that the test is intended to reveal, *i.e.,* true negative results as a proportion of the total of true negative and false positive results.

  diagnostic s., the probability (P) that, given the absence of disease (D), a normal test result (T) excludes disease; *i.e.,* P(T/D).

specimen (spes'ĭ-men) [L. fr. *specio,* to look at]. A small part, or sample, of any substance or material obtained for testing.

spectacles (spek'tĭ-klz) [L. *specto,* pp. *-atus,* to watch, observe]. Eyeglasses; glasses (1); lenses set in a frame which holds them in front of the eyes, used to correct errors of vision or to protect the eyes.

spectra (spek'trah) [L.]. Plural of spectrum.

spectral (spek'tral). Relating to a spectrum.

spectro-. Combining form denoting a spectrum.

spectrometer (spek-trom'ĕ-ter). An instrument used in spectrometry.

spectrometry (spek-trom'ĕ-trĭ) [spectro- + G. *metron,* measure]. The procedure of observing and measuring the wavelengths of light and other electromagnetic rays.

spectrophotometer (spek'tro-fo-tom'ĕ-ter) [spectro- + photometer]. An instrument for measuring the intensity of light of a definite wavelength transmitted by a substance or a solution, giving a quantitative measure of the amount of material in the solution absorbing the light.

spectrophotometry (spek'tro-fo-tom'ĕ-trĭ). Spectrophotometric *analysis*.

spectroscope (spek'tro-skōp) [spectro- + G. *skopeō,* to view]. An instrument for resolving light from any luminous body into its spectrum, and for the observation of the spectrum so formed.

spec'troscop'ic. Relating to or performed by means of a spectroscope.

spectroscopy (spek-tros'ko-pĭ). The observation and study of spectra of absorbed or emitted light by means of a spectroscope.

spectrum, pl. **spectra, spectrums** (spek'trum, -ah) [L. an image]. **1.** The color image presented when white light is resolved into its constituent colors by being passed through a prism or through a diffraction grating; arranged according to the increasing frequency of vibration or decreasing wavelength: red, orange, yellow, green, blue, indigo, violet. **2.** Figuratively, the pathogenic microorganisms against which an antibiotic or other antibacterial agent is active. **3.** The plot of intensity vs. wavelength of light emitted or absorbed by a substance, usually characteristic of the substance and used in qualitative and quantitative analysis.

  absorption s., the s. observed when light has passed through, and been partially absorbed by a solution or translucent substance.

  broad s., indicative of a broad range of activity of an antibiotic against a wide variety of microorganisms.

  fortification s., in migraine, the zigzag banding of colored light that marks the margin of the scintillating figures retained afer the central figure disappears.

  visible s., that part of the spectrum that is visible to the human eye; extends from extreme red, 7606 Å (760.6 nm), to extreme violet, 3934 Å (393.4 nm).

speculum, pl. **specula** (spek'u-lum, -lah) [L. a mirror, fr. *specio,* to look at]. An instrument for enlarging the opening of any canal or cavity in order to facilitate inspection of its interior.

speech [A.S. *spaec*]. Speaking; talk; the use of the voice in conveying ideas.

  esophageal s., a technique for speaking following total laryngectomy; the swallowing of air and regurgitating of it to produce a vibration in the hypopharynx.

  mirror s., a reversal of the order of syllables in a word, analogous to mirror writing.

  scanning s., measured or metered, often slow, s.

  staccato s., s. in which each syllable is enunciated separately.

  subvocal s., slight movements of the muscles of s. related to thinking but producing no sound.

sperm [G. *sperma*, seed] [NA]. **1.** Spermatozoon. **2.** Semen.

sperma-, spermato-, spermo- [G. *sperma*, seed]. Combining forms denoting semen or spermatozoa.

sperm-aster [sperm + G. *astēr*, a star (aster)]. A cytocentrum with astral rays in the cytoplasm of an inseminated ovum; brought in by the penetrating spermatozoon and gives rise to the mitotic spindle of the first cleavage division.

spermat'ic. Relating to sperm or semen.

spermatid (sper'mă-tid). A cell derived from the secondary spermatocyte and which gives rise by spermiogenesis to a spermatozoon.

spermato-. See sperma-.

sper'matoblast [spermato- + G. *blastos*, germ]. Spermatogonium.

spermatocele (sper'mă-to-sēl) [spermato- + G. *kēlē*, tumor]. A cyst of the epididymis containing spermatozoa.

spermatocidal (sper-mă-to-si'dal). Spermicidal; destructive to spermatozoa.

spermatocide (sper'mă-to-sīd) [spermato- + L. *caedo*, to kill]. Spermicide; an agent destructive to spermatozoon.

sper'matocy'tal. Relating to spermatocytes.

spermatocyte (sper'mă-to-sīt) [spermato- + G. *kytos*, cell]. A cell arising from a spermatogonium and destined to give rise to spermatozoa.

    primary s., the s. arising by a growth phase from a spermatogonium.

    secondary s., the s. derived from a primary s. by the first meiotic division; each secondary s. gives rise by the second meiotic division to two spermatids.

spermatocytogenesis (sper'mă-to-si'to-jen'ĕ-sis). Spermatogenesis.

spermatogenesis (sper'mă-to-jen'ĕ-sis) [spermato- + G. *genesis*, production]. Spermatocytogenesis; formation and development of the spermatozoon.

spermatogenic (sper'mă-to-jen'ik). Spermatopoietic (1); relating to spermatogenesis; sperm-producing.

spermatogonium (sper'mă-to-go'nī-um) [spermato- + G. *gonē*, generation]. Spermatoblast; the primitive sperm cell derived by mitotic division from the germ cell, increasing in size to become primary spermatocytes.

spermatoid (sper'mă-toyd) [spermato- + G. *eidos*, resemblance]. Resembling a sperm or sperm tail.

spermatolysis (sper-mă-tol'ĭ-sis) [spermato- + G. *lysis*, dissolution]. Destruction, with dissolution, of spermatozoa.

sper'matolyt'ic. Relating to spermatolysis.

spermatopoietic (sper'mă-to-poy-et'ik) [spermato- + G. *poieō*, to make]. **1.** Spermatogenic. **2.** Secreting semen.

spermatorrhea (sper'mă-to-re'ah) [spermato- + G. *rhoia*, a flow]. An involuntary discharge of semen, without orgasm.

sper'matozo'al, sper'matozo'an. Relating to spermatozoa.

spermatozoon, pl. **spermatozoa** (sper'mă-to-zo'on, -zo'ah) [G. *sperma*, seed, + *zoōn*, animal]. Sperm (1); the male gamete or sex cell, composed of a head and a tail, which contains genetic information to be transmitted by the male, exhibits autokinesia, and is able to effect zygosis with an ovum.

spermaturia (sper-mă-tu'rī-ah). Semenuria.

spermia (sper'mī-ah). Plural of spermium.

spermicidal (sper-mī-si'dal). Spermatocidal.

spermicide (sper'mī-sīd). Spermatocide.

sper'miduct. 1. *Ductus* deferens. **2.** *Ductus* ejaculatorius.

spermiogenesis (sper'mī-o-jen'ĕ-sis) [sperm- + G. *genesis*, production]. That segment of spermatogenesis during which spermatids are changed into spermatozoa.

spermo-. See sperma-.

sper'molith [spermo- + G. *lithos*, stone]. A concretion in the ductus deferens.

sp. gr. Specific gravity.

sph Spherical; spherical *lens*.

sphacelate (sfas'ĕ-lāt) [G. *sphakelos*, gangrene]. To become gangrenous or necrotic.

sphacelation (sfas-ĕ-la'shun) [G. *sphakelos*, gangrene]. **1.** The process of becoming gangrenous or necrotic. **2.** Gangrene or necrosis.

sphacelism (sfas'ĕ-lizm). The condition manifested by a sphacelus.

sphaceloderma (sfas'ĕ-lo-der'mah) [G. *sphakelos*, gangrene, + *derma*, skin]. Gangrene of the skin.

sphacelous (sfas'ĕ-lus). Sloughing, grangrenous, or necrotic.

sphacelus (sfas'ĕ-lus) [G. *sphakelos*, gangrene]. A mass of sloughing, gangrenous, or necrotic matter.

sphenion (sfe'nī-on) [Mod. L. fr. G. *sphēn*, wedge]. The tip of the sphenoidal angle of the parietal bone; a craniometric point.

spheno- [G. *sphēn*, wedge]. Combining form denoting wedge or wedge-shaped, or the sphenoid bone.

sphenocephaly (sfe-no-sef'ă-lī) [spheno- + G. *kephalē*, head]. The state of having a wedge-shaped head.

sphenoid, sphenoidal (sfe'noyd, sfe-noy'dal) [G. *sphēnoeidēs*, fr. *sphēn*, wedge, + *eidos*, resemblance]. **1.** Relating to the sphenoid bone. **2.** Wedge-shaped.

sphenoiditis (sfe-noy-di'tis) [sphenoid + G. *-itis*, inflammation]. **1.** Inflammation of the sphenoid sinus. **2.** Necrosis of the sphenoid bone.

sphenoidotomy (sfe-noy-dot'o-mī) [sphenoid + G. *tomē*, a cutting]. Surgical creation of an opening in the anterior wall of the sphenoid sinus.

sphenorbital (sfe-nor'bī-tal). Denoting the portions of the sphenoid bone contributing to the orbits.

sphenotic (sfe-no'tik) [spheno- + G. *ous*, ear]. Relating to the sphenoid bone and the bony case of the ear.

sphere (sfēr) [G. *sphaira*]. A ball or globular body.
    attraction s., astrosphere.

sphero-. Combining form denoting spherical or a sphere.

spherocyte (sfēr'o-sīt) [sphero- + G. *kytos,* cell]. A small spherical red blood cell.

spherocytosis (sfēr'o-si-to'sis) [spherocyte + G. *-osis,* condition]. The presence of sphere-shaped red blood cells in the blood.

hereditary s., a congenital defect of the erythrocyte cell membrane, which is abnormally permeable to sodium, resulting in thickened and almost spherical erythrocytes that are fragile and susceptible to spontaneous hemolysis, with decreased survival in the circulation; results in chronic anemia with reticulocytosis, episodes of mild jaundice due to hemolysis, and acute crises with fever and abdominal pain; autosomal dominant inheritance. Also called congenital hemolytic jaundice or anemia; chronic familial jaundice; spherocytic anemia.

spherophakia (sfēr-o-fa'kĭ-ah) [sphero- + G. *phakos,* lens]. Microphakia; a congenital bilateral anomoly in which the lenses of the eye are small, spherical, and subject to subluxation.

sphincter (sfingk'ter) [G. *sphinktēr,* a band or lace]. See anatomical s.

anatomical s., a muscle that encircles an organ or orifice in such a way that its contraction constricts or closes the lumen or orifice; the closing component of a pylorus.

s. a'ni, see *musculus* sphincter ani externus and internus.

cardiac s., a physiological s. at the esophagogastric junction.

extrinsic s., a s. provided by circular muscular fibers extraneous to the organ.

intrinsic s., a thickening of the circular fibers of the tunica muscularis of an organ.

Oddi's s., *musculus* sphincter ampullae hepatopancreaticae.

physiological s., not recognizable in surgical specimens or at autopsy by dissection or by histological techniques, probably because the s. assumes a resting arrangement which cannot be differentiated from adjacent tissues during anesthesia, after removal, or after death.

pyloric s., *musculus* sphincter pylori.

smooth muscular s., lissosphincter.

sphincteral (sfingk'ter-al). Sphincteric; relating to a sphincter.

sphincteralgia (sfingk-ter-al'jĭ-ah) [sphincter + G. *algos,* pain]. Pain in the sphincter ani muscles.

sphincterectomy (sfingk-ter-ek'to-mī) [sphincter + G. *ektomē,* excision]. **1.** Excision of a portion of the pupillary border of the iris. **2.** Dissecting away any sphincter muscle.

sphincter'ic. Sphincteral.

sphincterismus (sfingk-ter-iz'mus). Spasmodic contraction of the sphincter ani muscles.

sphincteritis (sfingk'ter-i'tis). Inflammation of a sphincter.

sphincterolysis (sfingk-ter-ol'ĭ-sis) [sphincter, + G. *lysis,* loosening]. Operation for freeing the iris from the cornea in anterior synechia involving only the pupillary border.

sphincteroplasty (sfingk'ter-o-plas-tĭ) [sphincter + G. *plassō,* to form]. Reparative or plastic surgery of any sphincter muscle.

sphincterotomy (sfingk'ter-ot'o-mī) [sphincter + G. *tomē,* incision]. Incision or division of a sphincter muscle.

sphingolipid (sfing'go-lip-id). Any lipid containing a long chain base like sphingosine; a constituent of nerve tissue.

sphingolipidosis (sfing'go-lip-ĭ-do'sis). Sphingolipodystrophy; collective designation for a variety of diseases characterized by abnormal sphingolipid metabolism.

cerebral s., cerebral lipidosis; any one of a group of inherited diseases characterized by failure to thrive, hypertonicity, progressive spastic paralysis, loss of vision and occurrence of blindness, usually with macular degeneration and optic atrophy, convulsions, and mental deterioration; associated with abnormal storage of sphingomyelin and related lipids in the brain; four types are recognized as clinically and enzymatically distinct: 1) infantile type (Tay-Sachs disease, G_{M2} gangliosidosis); 2) early juvenile type (Jansky-Bielschowsky or Bielschowsky's disease); 3) late juvenile type (Spielmeyer-Vogt disease; Batten-Mayou disease; ceroid lipofuscinosis); 4) adult type (Kufs disease).

sphingolipodystrophy (sfing'go-lip-o-dis'tro-fī). Sphingolipidosis.

sphingomy'elin phosphodiesterase. An enzyme catalyzing hydrolysis of sphingomyelin to ceramide and phosphocholine.

sphingomyelins (sfing-go-mi'ĕ-linz). A group of phospholipids found in the brain, spinal cord, kidney, and egg yolk, containing 1-phosphocholine combined with a ceramide.

sphingosine (sfing'go-sēn). $CH_3(CH_2)_{12}CH = CHCH(OH)CH(NH_2)CH_2OH$; the principal long-chain base found in sphingolipids.

sphygmic (sfig'mik). Relating to the pulse.

sphygmo-, sphygm- [G. *sphygmos,* pulse]. Combining forms denoting pulse.

sphygmochronograph (sfig'mo-kron'o-graf) [sphygmo- + G. *chronos,* time, + *graphō,* to write]. A modified sphygmograph that represents graphically the time relations between the beat of the heart and the pulse.

sphygmogram (sfig'mo-gram) [sphygmo- + G. *gramma,* something written]. Graphic curve made by a sphygmograph.

sphygmograph (sfig'mo-graf) [sphygmo- + G. *graphō,* to write]. An instrument that graphically records the excursions of the radial artery pulse.

sphyg'mograph'ic. Relating to or made by a sphygmograph.

sphygmoid (sfig'moyd) [sphygmo- + G. *eidos*, resemblance]. Pulselike; resembling the pulse.

sphygmomanometer (sfig'mo-mă-nom'ĕ-ter) [sphygmo- + G. *manos*, thin, scanty, + *metron*, measure]. Sphygmometer; an instrument for measuring the blood pressure.

sphygmomanometry (sfig'mo-mă-nom'ĕ-trĭ). Determination of the blood pressure by means of a sphygmomanometer.

sphygmometer (sfig-mom'ĕ-ter). Sphygmomanometer.

sphygmoscopy (sfig-mos'ko-pĭ) [sphygmo- + G. *skopeō*, to view]. Examination of the pulse.

sphyrectomy (sfi-rek'to-mĭ) [G. *sphyra*, malleus, + *ektomē*, excision]. Exsection of the malleus.

sphyrotomy (sfi-rot'o-mĭ) [G. *sphyra*, malleus, + *tomē*, incision]. Section of a part of the malleus.

spicular (spik'u-lar). Relating to or having spicules.

spicule (spik'ūl) [L. *spiculum*, dim. of *spicum*, a point]. A small, needle-shaped body.

spi'der [O. E. *spinnan*, to spin]. 1. An arthropod (subclass Arachnida) characterized by four pairs of legs, a cephalothorax, a globose smooth abdomen, and a complex of web-spinning spinnerets. Among the venomous s.'s found in the New World are the black widow s., *Latrodectus mactans;* red-legged widow s., *Latrodectus bishopi;* pruning s., or Peruvian tarantula, *Glyptocranium gasteracanthoides;* Chilean brown s., *Loxosceles laeta;* Peruvian brown s., *Loxosceles rufiper;* brown recluse s. of North America, *Loxosceles reclusus.* 2. Arterial s.

arterial s., vascular s., spider nevus; a telangiectatic arteriole in the skin with radiating capillary branches simulating the legs of a s.

spider-burst. Radiating dull red capillary lines on the skin of the leg, usually without any visible or palpable varicose veins, due to deep-seated venous dilation.

spigelian (spi-je'lĭ-an). Relating to or described by Adrian Spigelius.

spike. A brief electrical event of 3 to 25 msec that gives the appearance in the electroencephalogram of a rising and falling vertical line.

spina, pl. **spinae** (spi'nah, -ne) [L. a thorn, the backbone, spine] [NA]. Any spine or sharp thornlike process.

s. bif'ida, a limited defect in the spinal column, consisting in absence of the vertebral arches, through which the spinal membranes, with or without spinal cord tissue, may protrude.

s. bif'ida aper'ta, s. bifida occulta.

s. bif'ida cys'tica, s. bifida associated with a meningocele.

s. bif'ida occul'ta, cryptomerorachischis; a bifida aperta; s. bifida with no protrusion of the cord or its membrane.

s. ischiad'ica [NA], ischiadic or sciatic spine; a pointed process from the posterior border of the ischium on a level with the lower border of the acetabulum.

s. menta'lis [NA], mental spine; genial tubercle; a slight projection, sometimes two, in the middle line of the posterior surface of the body of the mandible, giving attachment to the geniohyoid muscle (below) and the genioglossus (above).

s. nasa'lis ante'rior [NA], anterior nasal spine; a pointed projection at the anterior extremity of the intermaxillary suture.

s. nasa'lis os'sis fronta'lis [NA], nasal spine of the frontal bone; a projection from the center of the nasal part of the frontal bone, which lies between and articulates with the nasal bones and the perpendicular plate of the ethmoid.

s. nasa'lis poste'rior [NA], posterior nasal spine; the sharp posterior extremity of the nasal crest.

s. os'sis sphenoida'lis [NA], sphenoidal spine; alar or angular spine; spinous process (1); a posterior and downward projection from the greater wing of the sphenoid bone on either side.

spi'nae palati'nae [NA], palatine spines; the longitudinal ridges along the palatine grooves on the inferior surface of the palatine process of the maxilla.

s. scap'ulae [NA], spine of the scapula; the prominent triangular ridge on the dorsal aspect of the scapula.

s. trochlea'ris [NA], trochlear spine; a spicule of bone arising from the edge of the fovea trochlearis, giving attachment to the pulley of the superior oblique muscle of the eyeball.

s. vento'sa, a condition occasionally seen in tuberculosis or tuberculous dactylitis, in which there is absorption of bone bordering the medulla, with a new deposit under the periosteum, resulting in a change that is suggestive of bone being inflated with gas.

spi'nal [L. *spinalis*]. Rachial; rachidial; rachidian. 1. Relating to any spine or spinous process. 2. Relating to the vertebral column.

spi'nate. Spined; having spines.

spindle (spin'dl) [A.S.]. In anatomy and pathology, any fusiform cell or structure.

central s., a central group of microtubules that course between the asters uninterrupted, in contrast to the microtubules attached to the individual chromosomes.

cleavage s., the s. formed during the cleavage of a zygote or its blastomeres.

Krukenberg's s., a vertical fusiform area of melanin pigmentation on the posterior surface of the cornea in the pupillary area.

mitotic s., nuclear s.; the fusiform figure characteristic of a dividing cell, consisting of microtubules (s. fibers), some of which become attached to each chromosome at its centromere and provide the mechanism for chromosomal movement.

neuromuscular s., muscle s., a fusiform end organ in skeletal muscle in which afferent and a few efferent nerve fibers terminate; sensitive to passive stretch of the muscle in which it is enclosed.

neurotendinous s., Golgi tendon *organ.*

nuclear s., mitotic s.

spine [L. *spina*]. **1.** A short sharp process of bone; a spinous process. **2.** Columna vertebralis.

alar s., angular s., *spina* ossis sphenoidalis.

cleft s., spondyloschisis.

dendritic s.'s, variably long excrescences of certain nerve cell dendrites, varying in shape from small knobs to thornlike or filamentous processes; a preferential site of synaptic axodendritic contact.

ischiadic s., *spina* ischiadica.

mental s., *spina* mentalis.

nasal s.'s, *spina* nasalis anterior, posterior, and ossis frontalis.

neural s., the middle point of the neural arch of the typical vertebra, represented by the spinous process.

palatine s.'s, *spinae* palatinae.

poker s., stiff s. resulting from widespread joint immobility or overwhelming muscle spasm.

s. of the scapula, *spina* scapulae.

sciatic s., *spina* ischiadica.

sphenoidal s., *spina* ossis sphenoidalis.

trochlear s., *spina* trochlearis.

spinnbarkheit (spin'bahr-kīt) [Ger. "spinnability"]. The stringy, elastic character of cervical mucus during the ovulatory period.

spino-. Combining form denoting the spine; spinous.

spi'nobul'bar. Bulbospinal.

spinocerebellar (spi'no-sĕr-ĕ-bel'ar). Relating to the spine and cerebellum.

spinous (spi'nus). Relating to, shaped like, or having a spine or spines.

spir-. See spiro-.

spiradenoma (spi'rad-ĕ-no'mah) [G. *speira*, coil, + *adenoma*]. A benign tumor of sweat glands.

spi'ral [Med. L. *spiralis*, fr. G. *speira*, a coil]. **1.** Coiled; winding around a center like a watch spring; winding and ascending like a wire spring. **2.** A structure in the shape of a coil.

Curschmann's s.'s, spirally twisted masses of mucus occurring in the sputum in bronchial asthma.

spirillar (spi-ril'ar). S-shaped; referring to a bacterial cell with an S shape.

spirit (spĭr'it) [L. *spiritus*, a breathing, life, soul]. **1.** An alcoholic liquor stronger than wine, obtained by distillation. **2.** Any distilled liquid. **3.** An alcoholic or hydroalcoholic solution of volatile substances.

spiro-, spir-. **1** [G. *speira*, a coil]. Combining forms denoting coil or coil-shaped. **2** [L. *spiro*, to breathe]. Combining forms denoting breathing.

spi'rogram. The tracing made by the spirograph.

spi'rograph [L. *spiro*, to breathe, + G. *graphō*, to write]. A device for representing graphically the depth and rapidity of respiratory movements.

spirometer (spi-rom'ĕ-ter) [L. *spiro*, to breathe, + G. *metron*, measure]. A gasometer used for measuring respiratory gases.

Spirome'tra [G. *speira*, coil, + *metra*, womb (uterus)]. A genus of pseudophyllid tapeworms, the

larval form of which (sparganum) may survive in human tissues via active migration from skin infections or from eating any vertebrate harboring these plerocercoids.

spirometry (spi-rom'ĕ-trī). Making pulmonary measurements with a spirometer.

spis'sated [L. *spisso*, pp. *spissatus*, to thicken]. Inspissated; thickened.

spittle (spit'l) [A.S. *spātl*]. Saliva.

splanchn-, splanchni-. See splanchno-.

splanchnapophysial, -physeal (splangk'nă-po-fiz'ī-al). Relating to a splanchnapophysis.

splanchnapophysis (splangk-nă-pof'ī-sis) [splanchn- + G. *apophysis*, offshoot]. An apophysis of the typical vertebra, on the side opposite to the neural apophysis, and enclosing any viscera.

splanchnectopia (splangk'nek-to'pī-ah) [splanchn- + G. *ektopos*, out of place]. Splanchnodiastasis; displacement of any of the viscera.

splanchnesthesia (splangk-nes-the'zĭ-ah) [splanch- + G. *aisthēsis*, sensation]. Visceral *sense.*

splanchnic (splangk'nik). Visceral.

splanchnicectomy (splangk-nĭ-sek'to-mī) [splanchni- + G. *ektomē*, excision]. Resection of the splanchnic nerves and, usually, of the celiac ganglion.

splanchnicotomy (splangk-nĭ-kot'o-mī) [splanchni- + G. *tomē*, incision]. Section of a splanchnic nerve or nerves.

splanchno-, splanchn-, splanchni- [G. *splanchnon*, viscus]. Combining forms denoting the viscera. See also viscero-.

splanchnocele (splangk'no-sēl). **1** [G. *koilos*, hollow]. The primitve body cavity or celom in the embryo. **2** [G. *kēlē*, hernia]. Hernia of any of the abdominal viscera.

splanchnodiastasis (splangk'no-di-as'tă-sis) [splanchno- + G. *diastasis*, separation]. Splanchnectopia.

splanchnography (splangk-nog'ră-fī) [splanchno- + G. *graphō*, to write]. A treatise on or description of the viscera.

splanchnolith (splangk'no-lith) [splanchno- + G. *lithos*, stone]. An intestinal calculus.

splanchnomegaly (splangk-no-meg'ă-lī) [splanchno- + G. *megas*, large]. Visceromegaly.

splanchnopathy (splangk-nop'ă-thī) [splanchno- + G. *pathos*, disease]. Disease of the abdominal viscera.

splanchnopleure (splangk'no-plūr) [splanchno- + G. *pleura*, side]. The embryonic layer formed by the association of the visceral layer of the lateral mesoderm with the entoderm.

splanchnoptosis (splangk'nop-to'sis) [splanchno- + G. *ptosis*, a falling]. Visceroptosis.

splanchnosclerosis (splangk'no-sklēr-o'sis) [splanchno- + G. *sklērōsis*, hardening]. Hardening, through connective tissue overgrowth, of any of the viscera.

splanchnoskeletal (splangk-no-skel'ĕ-tal). Viscero-skeletal.

splanchnoskeleton (splangk-no-skel'ĕ-ton). Visceroskeleton (2).

splanchnotribe (splangk'no-trīb) [splanchno- + G. *tribō*, to rub, bruise]. An instrument used for occluding the intestine temporarily, prior to resection.

splay'foot. *Talipes* planus.

spleen [G. *splēn*]. Lien; a large vascular lymphatic organ between the stomach and diaphragm that acts as a blood-forming organ in early life, a storage organ for red corpuscles, and, because of the large number of macrophages, as a blood filter.

accessory s., *lien* accessorius.

diffuse waxy s., amyloid degeneration of the s., affecting chiefly the extrasinusoidal tissue spaces of the pulp.

floating s., movable s., lien mobilis; a s. that is palpable because of excessive mobility from a relaxed or lengthened pedicle.

sago s., amyloidosis in the s. affecting chiefly the malpighian bodies.

waxy s., amyloidosis of the s.

splen-. See spleno-.

splenalgia (sple-nal'jĭ-ah) [splen- + G. *algos*, pain]. Splenodynia; pain in the spleen.

splenectomy (sple-nek'to-mī) [splen- + G. *ektomē*, excision]. Removal of the spleen.

splenectopia, splenectopy (splen'ek-to'pĭ-ah, sple-nek'to-pī) [splen- + G. *ektopos*, out of place]. **1.** Displacement of the spleen. **2.** Presence of rests of splenic tissue, usually in the region of the spleen.

splen'ic. Lienal; relating to the spleen.

splenitis (sple-ni'tis) [splen- + G. *-itis*, inflammation]. Inflammation of the spleen.

splenium, pl. **splenia** (sple'nĭ-um, -ah) [Mod. L. fr. G. *splēnion*, bandage]. **1.** A compress or bandage. **2** [NA]. A structure resembling a bandaged part.

s. cor'poris callo'si [NA], the thickened posterior extremity of the corpus callosum.

spleno-, splen- [G. *splēn*, spleen]. Combining forms denoting the spleen.

splenocele (sple'no-sēl) [spleno- + G. *kēlē*, tumor, hernia]. **1.** Splenoma. **2.** A splenic hernia.

splenodynia (sple-no-din'ĭ-ah) [spleno- + G. *odynē*, pain]. Splenalgia.

splenography (sple-nog'ră-fī) [spleno- + G. *graphō*, to write]. Radiography of the spleen after injection of contrast material into it.

splenohepatomegaly (sple'no-hep'ă-to-meg'ă-lī) [spleno- + G. *hēpar*, liver, + *megas*, large]. Enlargement of both spleen and liver.

splenoid (sple'noyd) [spleno- + G. *eidos*, resemblance]. Resembling the spleen.

splenoma (sple-no'mah) [spleno- + G. *-oma*, tumor]. Splenocele (1); a general, nonspecific term for an enlarged spleen.

splenomalacia (sple'no-mă-la'shĭ-ah) [spleno- + G. *malakia*, softness]. Softening of the spleen.

sple'nomed'ullary [spleno- + L. *medulla*, marrow]. Splenomyelogenous.

splenomegaly (sple'no-meg'ă-lī) [spleno- + G. *megas* (*megal-*), large]. Megalosplenia; enlargement of the spleen.

congestive s., enlargement of the spleen due to passive congestion.

hemolytic s., s. associated with congenital hemolytic jaundice.

splenomyelogenous (sple'no-mi-ĕ-loj'ĕ-nus) [spleno- + G. *myelos*, marrow, + *-gen*, producing]. Splenomedullary; originating in the spleen and bone marrow.

splenomyelomalacia (sple'no-mi'ĕ-lo-mă-la'shĭ-ah) [spleno- + G. *myelos*, marrow, + *malakia*, softness]. Pathologic softening of the spleen and bone marrow.

splenopathy (sple-nop'ă-thī) [spleno- + G. *pathos*, suffering]. Any disease of the spleen.

splenopexy (sple'no-pek-sī) [spleno- + G. *pēxis*, fixation]. Splenorrhaphy (2); suturing in place an ectopic or floating spleen.

splenoportography (sple'no-pōr-tog'ră-fī) [spleno- + portography]. The introduction of radiopaque material into the spleen to obtain radiographic delineation of the portal vessel of the portal circulation.

splenoptosis (sple'no-to'sis) [spleno- + G. *ptōsis*, falling]. Downward displacement of the spleen.

splenorrhagia (sple-no-ra'jĭ-ah) [spleno- + G. *rhēgnymi,* to burst forth]. Hemorrhage from a ruptured spleen.

splenorrhaphy (sple-nor'ră-fī) [spleno- + G. *rhaphē*, suture]. **1.** Suturing a ruptured spleen. **2.** Splenopexy.

splenotomy (sple-not'o-mī) [spleno- + G. *tomē*, incision]. Incision of the spleen.

sple'notox'in [spleno- + G. *toxikon*, poison]. A cytotoxin specific for cells of the spleen.

splicing (splīs'ing). **1.** Gene s.; attachment of one DNA molecule to another. **2.** RNA s.; removal of introns from mRNA precursors.

splint [Middle Dutch *splinte*]. An appliance for preventing movement of a joint or for the fixation of displaced or movable parts.

air s., a hollow tubular inflatable s.

airplane s., a s. that holds the arm in abduction at about shoulder level with the forearm midway in flexion, generally with an axillary strut for support.

anchor s., a s. used for fracture of jaw, with wires around teeth and held in place by a rod.

Anderson s., a skeletal traction s., with pins inserted into proximal and distal ends of a fracture and reduction obtained by an external plate attached to the pins.

backboard s., a board s. with slots for fixation by straps; shorter ones are used for neck injuries, longer ones for back injuries.

Balkan s., Balkan *frame.*

coaptation s., a short s. designed to prevent overriding of the ends of a fractured bone, usually supplemented by a longer s. to fix the entire limb.

contact s., a slotted plate, held by screws, used in the treatment of fracture of long bones.

Denis Browne s., a light aluminum s. applied to the lateral aspect of the leg and foot; used for clubfoot.

dynamic s., functional s. (1); a s. that aids in movements initiated by the patient by controlling the plane and range of motion.

Frejka pillow s., a pillow s. used for abduction and flexion of the femurs in treatment of congenital hip dysplasia or dislocation in infants.

functional s., (1) dynamic s.; (2) the joining of two or more teeth into a rigid unit by means of fixed restorations that cover all or part of the abutment teeth.

interdental s., a s. for a fractured jaw, consisting of two metal or acrylic resin bands wired to the teeth of the upper and lower jaws, respectively, and then fastened together to keep the jaws immovable.

labial s., an appliance made to conform to the outer aspect of the dental arch and used in the management of jaw and facial injuries.

ladder s., a flexible s. consisting of two stout parallel wires with finer cross wires.

shin s.'s, see shin-splints.

surgical s., one of many devices used to maintain tissues in a new position following surgery.

Thomas s., a rigid bar metal s. extending from a ring at the hip to beyond the foot, allowing traction to a fractured leg, for emergencies and transportation.

split'ting. In chemistry, the cleavage of a covalent bond, fragmenting the molecule involved.

spodogenous (spŏ-doj'ĕ-nus) [G. *spodos,* ashes, + *-gen,* producing]. Caused by waste material.

spondyl-. See spondylo-.

spondylalgia (spon-dĭ-lal'jĭ-ah) [spondyl- + G. *algos,* pain]. Pain in the spine.

spondylarthritis (spon'dil-ar-thri'tis) [spondyl- + G. *arthron,* joint, + *-itis,* inflammation]. Inflammation of the intervertebral articulations.

spondylitic (spon-dĭ-lit'ik). Relating to spondylitis.

spondylitis (spon-dĭ-li'tis) [spondyl- + G. *-itis,* inflammation]. Inflammation of one or more of the vertebrae.

ankylosing s., Strümpell-Marie or Marie-Strümpell disease; rheumatoid s.; arthritis of the spine, resembling rheumatoid arthritis, that may progress to bony ankylosis with lipping of vertebral margins.

s. defor'mans, Bechterew's disease; Strümpell's disease (1); arthritis and osteitis deformans involving the spinal column; marked by nodular deposits at the edges of the intervertebral disks, with ossification of the ligaments and bony ankylosis of the intervertebral articulations; results in a rounded kyphosis with rigidity.

Kümmell's s., late posttraumatic collapse of vertebral body.

rheumatoid s., ankylosing s.

tuberculous s., Pott's disease; tuberculous infection of the spine associated with a sharp angulation of the spine at the point of disease.

spondylo-, spondyl- [G. *spondylos,* vertebra]. Combining forms denoting the vertebrae.

spondylolisthesis (spon'dĭ-lo-lis-the'sis) [spondylo- + G. *olisthēsis,* a slipping and falling]. Forward movement of the body of one of the lower lumbar vertebrae on the vertebra below it, or upon the sacrum.

spondylolisthetic (spon'dĭ-lo-lis-thet'ik). Relating to or marked by spondylolisthesis.

spondylolysis (spon-dĭ-lol'ĭ-sis) [spondylo- + G. *lysis,* loosening]. A defect in the interarticular part of the vertebra.

spondylopathy (spon-dĭ-lop'ă-thĭ) [spondylo- + G. *pathos,* suffering]. Any disease of the vertebrae or spinal column.

spondylopyosis (spon'dĭ-lo-pi-o'sis) [spondylo- + G. *pyōsis,* suppuration]. Suppurative inflammation of one or more of the vertebral bodies.

spondyloschisis (spon-dĭ-los'kĭ-sis) [spondylo- + G. *schisis,* fissure]. Rachischisis; cleft spine; congenital fissure of one or more of the vertebral arches.

spondylo'sis [G. *spondylos,* vertebra]. Vertebral ankylosis; also applied nonspecifically to any degenerative lesion of the spine.

spondylosyndesis (spon'dĭ-lo-sin-de'sis) [spondylo- + G. *syndesis,* binding together]. Spinal *fusion.*

sponge (spunj) [G. *spongia*]. **1.** An absorbent material used to absorb fluids. **2.** A member of the phylum Porifera, the cellular endoskeleton of which is a source of commercial s.'s.

spongiform (spun'jĭ-form). Spongy.

spongin (spun'jin). The fibrous or horny constituent of sponges; a scleroprotein.

spongio- [G. *spongia,* sponge]. Combining form denoting sponge-like, spongy.

spongioblast (spun'jĭ-o-blast) [spongio- + G. *blastos,* germ]. A neuroepithelial, filiform ependyma cell extending across the entire thickness of the wall of the brain or spinal cord.

spongioblastoma (spun'jĭ-o-blas-to'mah) [spongioblast + G. *-oma* tumor]. A glioma derived from spongioblasts, *i.e.,* immature forms of the astrocytic series; sometimes termed gliosarcoma.

spongiocyte (spun'jĭ-o-sit) [spongio- + G. *kytos,* cell]. **1.** A neuroglial cell. **2.** A cell in the zona fasciculata of the adrenal containing many droplets of lipid material which show pronounced vacuolization.

spongioid (spun'jĭ-oyd) [spongio- + G. *eidos,* resemblance]. Spongy.

spongiose (spun'jĭ-ōs) [L. *spongiosus*]. Porous, resembling a sponge.

spongiosis (spun-jĭ-o'sis). Intercellular edema of the epidermis.

spongiositis (spun'jĭ-o-si'tis). Inflammation of the corpus spongiosum, or corpus cavernosum urethrae.

spongy (spun'jĭ). Spongiform; spongioid; of sponge-like texture or appearance.

spor-, spori-. See sporo-.

sporadic (spo-rad'ik) [G. *sporadikos*, scattered]. Occurring singly, not grouped; neither epidemic nor endemic.

sporangium, pl. **sporangia** (spo-ran'ji-um, -ah) [L. fr. G. *sporos*, seed, + *angeion*, vessel]. A cell within a fungus, in which asexual spores are borne by progressive cleavage.

spore (spōr) [G. *sporos*, seed]. **1.** The asexual reproductive body of sporozoan protozoa or of Cryptogamia. **2.** A cell of a plant lower in organization than the seed-bearing spermatophytic plants. **3.** A resistant form of certain species of bacteria.

sporicidal (spōr'ĭ-si'dal) [spori- + L. *caedo*, to kill]. Lethal to spores.

sporicide (spōr'ĭ-sīd). An agent that kills spores.

sporidium, pl. **sporidia** (spo-rid'ĭ-um, -ah) [Mod. L. dim. fr. G. *sporos*, seed]. A protozoan spore; an embryonic protozoan organism.

sporo-, spori-, spor- [G. *sporos*, seed]. Combining forms denoting seed or spore.

sporoagglutination (spōr'o-ă-glu-tĭ-na'shun). A diagnostic method in relation to the mycoses, based upon the fact that the blood in diseases caused by fungi contains specific agglutinins that cause clumping of the spores of these organisms.

sporoblast (spōr'o-blast) [sporo- + G. *blastos*, germ]. An early stage in the development of a sporocyst prior to differentiation of the sporozoites.

sporocyst (spōr'o-sist) [sporo- + G. *kystis*, bladder]. **1.** A larval form of digenetic fluke that develops in the body of its molluscan intermediate host, usually a snail. **2.** A secondary cyst that develops from a sporoblast and produces within itself one or several sporozoites.

sporogenesis (spōr-o-jen'ĕ-sis) [sporo- + G. *genesis*, production]. Sporogeny **1.** Reproduction by means of spores. **2.** The process of spore or sporozoite production.

sporogenous (spo-roj'ĕ-nus). Relating to or involved in sporogenesis.

sporogeny (spo-roj'ĕ-nĭ). Sporogenesis.

sporogony (spo-rog'o-nĭ) [sporo- + G. *goneia*, generation]. Formation of sporozoites in sporozoan protozoa, a process of asexual division within the sporoblast, which becomes the sporocyte within an oocyst.

sporont (spōr'ont) [sporo- + G. *ōn* (*ont-*), being]. The zygote stage within the oocyst wall in the life cycle of coccidia.

Sporothrix (spo'ro-thriks) [Mod. L. fr. G. *sporos*, seed, + *thrix*, hair]. A genus of dimorphic imperfect fungi, including the species *S. schenckii*, the causative agent of sporotrichosis.

sporotrichosis (spōr'o-trĭ-ko'sis). A chronic subcutaneous mycosis spread by way of the lymphatics and caused by *Sporothrix schenckii*; may remain localized or become generalized, involving bones, joints,

lungs, and the CNS; lesions may be granulomatous or suppurative, ulcerative or draining.

Sporozoa (spōr-o-zo'ah) [Mod. L. fr. G. *sporos*, seed, + *zoōn*, animal]. A large class of protozoans consisting of obligatory parasites that includes the gregarines and coccidia.

sporozoan (spōr'o-zo'an). **1.** Sporozoon; an individual organism of the class Sporozoa. **2.** Relating to the Sporozoa.

sporozoite (spōr-o-zo'īt) [sporo- + G. *zoōn*, animal]. Oxyspore; germinal rod; one of the minute elongated bodies resulting from the repeated division of the oocyst; in the case of the malarial parasite, it is the form concentrated in the salivary glands of the mosquito and introduced into the blood by its bite.

sporozoon (spōr'o-zo'on) Sporozoan (1).

sporular (spōr'u-lar). Relating to a spore or sporule.

sporulation (spōr-u-la'shun). Multiple *fission*.

sporule (spōr'ŭl) [Mod. L. *sporula;* dim. of G. *sporos*, seed]. A small spore.

spot. 1. Macula. **2.** To lose a slight amount of blood through the vagina.

Bitot's s.'s, small grayish foamy triangular deposits on the bulbar conjunctiva adjacent to the cornea in the area of the palpebral fissure, associated with vitamin A deficiency.

blind s., (1) physiological *scotoma;* (2) mental *scotoma;* (3) *discus* nervi optici.

blue s., (1) *macula* cerulea; (2) mongolian s.

café au lait s.'s, uniformly light brown, sharply defined, and usually oval-shaped patches of the skin characteristic of neurofibromatosis, but also found in normal individuals.

cherry-red s., the choroid appearing as a red s. through the fovea centralis surrounded by a contrasting white edema; noted in cases of infantile cerebral sphingolipidosis.

cotton-wool s.'s, cotton-wool *patches*.

Fordyce's s.'s, Fordyce's disease; a condition marked by the presence of numerous small yellowish white bodies or granules on the inner surface and vermilion border of the lips.

hypnogenic s., a pressure-sensitive point on the body of certain susceptible persons, which, when pressed, causes the induction of sleep.

Koplik's s.'s, small red s.'s on the buccal mucous membrane, with a minute bluish white speck in the center; regarded as a pathognomonic sign of measles.

liver s., senile *lentigo*.

milk s.'s, (1) white plaques of hyalinized fibrous tissue situated in the epicardium overlying the right ventricle of the heart where it is not covered by lung; (2) white macroscopic areas in the omentum, due to accumulation of macrophages and lymphocytes.

mongolian s.'s, blue s. (2); any of a number of dark bluish or mulberry-colored s.'s on the sacral region, observed as a congenital lesion in children, which do not disappear on pressure; they enlarge for a short time after birth and then gradually recede.

rose s.'s, characteristic exanthema of typhoid fever.

Roth's s.'s, round white s.'s surrounded by hemorrhage, observed in the retina in some cases of bacterial endocarditis.

Soemmering's s., *macula* retinae.

yellow s., *macula* retinae.

sprain (sprān). **1.** An injury to a ligament when the joint is carried through a range of motion greater than normal, but without dislocation or fracture. **2.** To cause a s. of a joint.

spray. A jet of liquid in fine drops, coarser than a vapor.

sprue (spru) [D. *spruw*]. **1.** Psilosis; primary intestinal malabsorption with steatorrhea. **2.** In dentistry, wax or metal used to form the aperture or apertures for molten metal to flow into a mold to make a casting.

nontropical s., s. occurring in persons away from the tropics; usually called celiac disease.

tropical s., tropical diarrhea; s. occuring in the tropics, often associated with enteric infection and nutritional deficiency, and frequently complicated by folate deficiency with macrocytic anemia.

spur [A.S. *spora*]. Calcar.

spu'rious [L. *spurius*]. False; not genuine.

sputum, pl. **sputa** (spu'tum, -tah) [L. *spuo,* pp. *sputus,* to spit]. **1.** Expectorated matter, especially mucus or mucopurulent matter expectorated in diseases of the air passages. **2.** An individual mass of such matter.

nummular s., a thick, coherent mass expectorated in globular shape which does not run at the bottom of the cup but forms a discoid mass resembling a coin.

rusty s., a reddish brown, blood-stained expectoration characteristic of lobar pneumonia.

squama, pl. **squamae** (skwa'mah, skwa'me) [L. a scale]. Square; scale (2). **1** [NA]. A thin plate of bone. **2.** An epidermic scale.

squamate (skwa'māt). Squamous.

squame (skwām). Squama.

squamo-. Combining form denoting squama or squamous.

squamosa, pl. **squamosae** (skwa-mo'sah, -se) [L. *squamosus,* scaly, fr. *squama,* scale]. The squama of the frontal, occipital, or temporal bone, especially the latter.

squamosal (skwa-mo'sal). Relating especially to the squama of the temporal bone.

squamous (skwa'mus) [L. *squamosus*]. Squamate; scaly; relating to or covered with scales.

squamozygomatic (skwa'mo-zi-go-mat'ik). Relating to the squama and the zygomatic process of the temporal bone.

squint (skwint). Strabismus.

Sr Strontium.

SRF Somatotropin-releasing *factor.*

SRF-A Slow-reacting *factor* of anaphylaxis.

SRIF Somatotropin release-inhibiting *factor.*

sRNA Soluble RNA; now known as transfer RNA (tRNA).

SRS, SRS-A Slow-reacting *substance* or slow-reacting *substance* of anaphylaxis.

stabilate (sta'bĭ-lāt). A population of organisms similar to, but more stable than a strain, and maintained in viable condition for a particular purpose or reason.

stabile (sta'bĭl, -bil) [L. *stabilis*]. Stable; steady; resistant to change.

stability (stă-bil'ĭ-tĭ). The condition of being stable or resistant to change.

stabilization (sta'bĭ-lĭ-za'shun). Accomplishment of a stable state.

stable (sta'bl). Stabile; steady; not varying.

staff [A.S. *staef*]. **1.** A specific group of workers. **2.** Director (1).

attending s., the physicians and surgeons who are members of a hospital s. and regularly attend their patients at the hospital; they may also supervise and teach house s., fellows, and medical students.

consulting s., the body of specialists attached to a hospital who serve in an advisory capacity to the attending s.

house s., physicians and surgeons in specialty training at a hospital who care for the patients under the direction and responsibility of the attending s.

staff of Aesculapius [L. *Aesculapius,* G. *Asklēpios,* god of medicine]. A rod with only one serpent encircling it and without wings; correct symbol of medicine and emblem of the American Medical Association, Royal Army Medical Corps (Britain), and Royal Canadian Medical Corps. See also caduceus.

stage (stāj) [M.E. thr. O. Fr. *estage,* standing-place]. **1.** A period in the course of a disease; the distribution and extent of a malignant neoplastic disease. See also period. **2.** The part of a microscope on which the microslide bears the object to be examined. **3.** A particular step, phase, or position in a developmental process.

algid s., the s. of collapse in cholera.

cold s., the s. of chill in a malarial paroxysm.

end s., the late, fully developed phase of a disease.

exoerythrocytic s., developmental s. of the malaria parsite (*Plasmodium*) ouside of the red blood cells of the vertebrate host in liver parenchyma cells.

imperfect s., the asexual life cycle phase of a fungus.

incubative s., incubation period (2); latent or prodromal s.; the primary s. of certain infectious diseases during which the prodromal symptoms are appearing, and usually synchronous with the induction of sensitivity.

intuitive s., in psychology, a s. of development, usually occurring between 4 and 7 years of age, in which a child's thought processes are determined by the most prominent aspects of the stimuli to which he is exposed, rather than by some form of logical thought.

s.'s of labor, see labor.

latent s., incubative s.

perfect s., the sexual life cycle phase of a fungus in which spores are formed after nuclear fusion.

preconceptual s., in psychology, the s. of development in an infant's life in which sensorimotor activity predominates.

prodromal s., incubative s.

psychosexual s.'s, see under phase.

staging. Classification of neoplasms according to the extent of the tumor.

stagnation (stag-na'shun) [L. *stagnum,* a pool]. Retardation or cessation of flow of blood in the vessels, as in passive congestion; accumulation in any part of a normally circulating fluid.

stain (stān) [M.E. *steinen*]. 1. A dye used in histologic and bacteriologic technique. 2. A procedure in which a dye or combination of dyes and reagents is used to color the constituents of cells and tissues.

acid s., a dye in which the anion is the colored component of the dye molecule.

basic s., a dye in which the cation is the colored component of the dye molecule that binds to anionic groups of nucleic acids or acidic mucopolysaccharides.

basic fuchsin-methylene blue s., a s. for intact epoxy sections.

C-banding s., centromere banding s., a selective chromosome s. used in human cytogenetics, employing Giemsa s. after most of the DNA is extracted; only heterochromatic regions close to the centromeres stain, with the exception of the Y chromosome which shows a light diffuse s. throughout.

contrast s., differential s., a dye used to color one portion of a tissue or cell which remained unaffected when the other part was stained by a dye of different color.

double s., a mixture of two dyes, each of which stains different portions of a tissue or cell.

fluorescent s., a s. (or staining procedure) involving the use of a fluorescent dye or substance that will combine selectively with certain tissue components and that will then fluoresce upon irradiation with ultraviolet or violet-blue light.

G-banding s., Giemsa chromosome banding s., a chromosome staining technique, used in human cytogenetics to identify individual chromosomes, which produces characteristic bands; utilizes Giemsa s. after denaturing chromosomes.

Giemsa s., compound of azur II-eosin and azur II used for demonstrating Negri bodies, *Tunga* species, spirochetes and protozoans, and differential staining of blood smears; also used for chromosomes.

Golgi's s., any of several methods for staining nerve cells, nerve fibers, and neuroglia using fixation and hardening in formalin-osmic-dichromate combinations for various times, followed by impregnation in silver nitrate.

Gram's s., a method for differential staining of bacteria in which Gram-positive organisms stain purple black and Gram-negative organisms stain pink; useful in bacterial taxonomy and identification, and also in indicating fundamental differences in cell wall structure.

hematoxylin and eosin s., a general purpose staining method for tissues; nuclei are stained a deep blue-black with hematoxylin, and cytoplasm is stained pink after counterstaining with eosin, usually in water.

immunofluorescent s., s. resulting from combination of fluorescent antibody with antigen specific for the antibody portion of the fluorochrome conjugate.

intravital s., a s. which is taken up by living cells after parenteral adminstration.

iodine s., a s. to detect amyloid, cellulose, chitin, starch, carotenes, and glycogen, and to stain amebas by virtue of their glycogen.

metachromatic s., a s., such as methylene blue, thronin, or azure A, that has the ability to produce different colors with various histological or cytological structures.

multiple s., a mixture of several dyes each having an independent selective action on one or more portions of the tissue.

negative s., forming an opaque or colored background against which the object to be demonstrated appears as a transclucent or colorless area.

neutral s., a compound of an acid s. and a basic s. in which the anion and cation each contains a chromophore group.

nuclear s., a s. for cell nuclei, usually based on the binding of a basic dye to DNA or nucleohistone.

Papanicolaou s., a multichromatic s. used principally on exfoliated cytologic specimens, giving great transparency and delicacy of detail; important in cancer screening, especially of gynecologic smears.

picrocarmine s., a red crystalline powder derived from a solution of carmine, ammonia, and picric acid which is evaporated leaving the powder (soluble in water); it produces excellent staining of keratohyaline granules.

port-wine s., *nevus* flammeus.

positive s., direct binding of a dye with a tissue component to produce contrast.

Q-banding s., quinacrine chromosome banding s., a fluorescent s. for chromosomes which produces specific banding patterns for each pair of homologous chromosomes; centromeric regions of human chromosomes 3, 4, and 13 are specifically stained, as are satellites of some acrocentric chromosomes and the end of the long arm of the Y chromosome.

R-banding s., a reverse Giemsa chromosome banding method that produces bands complementary to G-bands.

selective s., a s. that colors one portion of a tissue or cell exclusively or more deeply than the remaining portions.

silver protein s., a silver proteinate complex used in staining nerve fibers, nerve endings, and flagellate protozoa; also used to demonstrate phagocytosis in living animals by the cells of the reticuloendothelial system.

supravital s., a procedure in which living tissue is removed from the body and cells are placed in a nontoxic dye solution so that their vital processes may be studied.

trichrome s., staining combinations which usually contain three dyes of contrasting colors selected to stain connective tissue, muscle, cytoplasm, and nuclei in bright colors.

vital s., a s. applied to cells or parts of cells while they are still living.

Wright's s., a dry s. mixture of eosinates of polychromed methylene blue used in staining of blood smears.

stain'ing. 1. The act of applying a stain. **2.** In dentistry, modification of the color of the tooth or denture base.

progressive s., a procedure in which s. is continued until the desired intensity of coloring of tissue elements is attained.

regressive s., a type of s. in which tissues are overstained and the excess dye is then removed selectively until the desired intensity is obtained.

staircase (stăr'kās). A series of reactions that follow one another in progressively increasing or decreasing intensity, so that a chart shows a continuous rise or fall. See **treppe**.

stalagmometer (stal-ă-gom'ĕ-ter) [G. *stalagma*, a drop, + *metron*, measure]. An instrument for determining exactly the number of drops in a given quantity of liquid; used as a measure of the surface tension of a fluid, for the lower the tension the smaller the drops, and consequently the more numerous in the given quantity of the fluid.

stalk (stawk). A narrowed connection with a structure or organ.

allantoic s., the narrow connection between the intraembryonic portion of the allantois and the extraembryonic allantoic vesicle.

pineal s., the attachment of the pineal body to the roof of the third ventricle; contains the pineal recess of the third ventricle.

yolk s., omphalomesenteric duct; the narrowed connection between the intraembryonic gut and the yolk sac.

stam'mering. A speech disorder characterized by hesitation and repetition of sounds, or by mispronunciation or transposition of certain consonants, especially *l*, *r*, and *s*.

stanch, staunch [L. *stagno*, to stagnate]. To arrest bleeding.

stan'dardiza'tion. 1. The making of a solution of definite strength so that it may be used for comparison and in tests. **2.** Making any drug or other preparation conform to the type or standard.

stand'still. Arrest; cessation of activity, as of the heart.

stan'nic [L. *stannum*, tin]. Relating to tin, especially when in combination in its higher valency.

stan'nous [L. *stannum*, tin]. Relating to tin, especially denoting compounds containing tin in its lower valency.

stannous fluoride. A preparation containing not less than 71.2% of stannous tin and not less than 22.3% and not more than 25.5% of fluoride; used as a dental prophylactic.

stan'num [L.]. Tin.

stanolone (stan'o-lōn). Dihydrotestosterone; 17β-hydroxy-5α-androstane-3-one; an androgen with the same actions and uses as testosterone.

stapedectomy (sta-pe-dek'to-mĭ) [stapes + G. *ektomē*, excision]. Removal of the stapes in whole or part and replacement with various prostheses and tissues.

stapedial (sta-pe'dĭ-al). Relating to the stapes.

stapediotenotomy (sta-pe'dĭ-o-tĕ-not'o-mĭ) [stapedius + G. *tenōn*, tendon, + *tomē*, incision]. Division of the tendon of the stapedius muscle.

stapes, pl. **stapes, stapedes** (sta'pēz, sta'pe-dēz) [Mod. L. stirrup] [NA]. Stirrup; smallest of the three auditory ossicles; its base, or footpiece, fits into the vestibular (oval) window, while its head is articulated with the lenticular process of the long limb of the incus.

staphyl-. See **staphylo-**.

staphylectomy (staf'ĭ-lek'to-mĭ) [staphyl- + G. *ektomē*, excision]. Uvulectomy.

staphyledema (staf'il-ĕ-de'mah) [staphyl- + G. *oidēma*, swelling (edema)]. Edema of the uvula.

staphyline (staf'ĭ-lĭn, -lēn). Botryoid.

staphylion (stă-fil'ĭ-on) [G. dim. of *staphylē*, a bunch of grapes]. The midpoint of the posterior edge of the hard palate.

staphylo-, staphyl- [G. *staphylē*, a bunch of grapes]. Combining forms denoting resemblance to a grape or a bunch of grapes, hence relating usually to staphylococci. See also **uvulo-**.

staphylococcal, staphylococcic (staf'ĭ-lo-kok'al, -kok'sik). Relating to or caused by any species of *Staphylococcus*.

staphylococcemia (staf'ĭ-lo-kok-se'mĭ-ah) [staphylo- + G. *haima*, blood]. Presence of staphylococci in the circulating blood.

staphylococci (staf'ĭ-lo-kok'si). Plural of staphylococcus.

Staphylococcus (staf'ĭ-lo-kok'us) [staphylo- + G. *kokkos*, a berry]. A genus of Gram-positive bacteria (family Micrococcaceae) that form irregular clusters; found on the skin, in skin glands, on the nasal and other mucous membranes of warm-blooded animals, and in a variety of food products. The type species is *S. aureus*.

S. au'reus, a common species that causes furunculosis, pyemia, osteomyelitis, suppuration of wounds, and food poisoning; it is the type species of the genus

S.

S. pyog'enes al'bus, mutants of *S. aureus* which form white colonies.

staphyloderma (staf'ĭ-lo-der'mah) [staphylo- + G. *derma,* skin]. Pyoderma due to staphylococci.

staphylodermatitis (staf'ĭ-lo-der-mă-ti'tis). Inflammation of the skin due to the action of staphylococci.

staphylodialysis (staf'ĭ-lo-di-al'ĭ-sis) [staphylo- + G. *dialysis,* a separation]. Uvuloptosis.

staph'yloki'nase. Neutral proteinase; a microbial metalloenzyme from *Staphylococcus aureus,* with action similar to that of urokinase and streptokinase.

staphylolysin (staf'ĭ-lol'ĭ-sin). **1.** A hemolysin elaborated by a staphylococcus. **2.** An antibody causing lysis of staphylococci.

staphyloma (staf-ĭ-lo'mah) [G.]. A bulging of the cornea or sclera due to inflammatory softening, usually containing adherent uveal tissue.

anterior s., corneal s.; bulging near the anterior pole of the eyeball.

corneal s., anterior s.

equatorial s., scleral s.; a s. occurring in the area of exit of the vortex veins.

posterior s., a bulging of a weakened sclera, from loss of the choroid lining, at the posterior of the eyeball due to degenerative changes in high myopia.

scleral s., equatorial s.

staphylo'matous. Relating to or marked by staphyloma.

staphylopharyngorrhaphy (staf'ĭ-lo-făr-ing-or'ă-fĭ) [staphylo- + pharynx + G. *rhaphē,* suture]. Palatopharyngorrhaphy; surgical repair of defects in the uvula or soft palate and the pharynx.

staphyloplasty (staf'ĭ-lo-plas-tĭ) [staphylo- + G. *plassō,* to form]. Palatoplasty.

staphyloptosis (staf'ĭ-lop-to'sis) [staphylo- + G. *ptōsis,* a falling]. Uvuloptosis.

staphylorrhaphy (staf-ĭ-lor'ă-fĭ) [staphylo- + G. *rhaphē,* suture]. Palatorrhaphy.

staphyloschisis (staf-ĭ-los'kĭ-sis) [staphylo- + G. *schisis,* fissure]. Bifid uvula with or without cleft of soft palate.

staphylotomy (staf-ĭ-lot'o-mĭ) [staphylo- + G. *tomē,* incision]. **1.** Uvulotomy. **2.** Cutting away of a staphyloma.

staphylotoxin (staf'ĭ-lo-tok'sin) [staphylo- + G. *toxikon,* poison]. The toxin elaborated by any species of *Staphylococcus.* See also staphylohemolysin.

star [A.S. *steorra*]. Any star-shaped structure. See also aster, astrosphere, stella, stellula.

daughter s., polar s.; one of the figures forming the diaster.

lens s.'s. congenital cataracts with opacities along the suture lines of the lens; may be anterior, posterior, or both.

polar s., daughter s.

venous s., a small red nodule formed by a dilated vein in the skin; caused by increased venous pressure.

starch [A.S. *stearc,* strong]. Amylum; a polysaccharide built up of glucose residues in α-1,4 linkage, differing from cellulose in the presence of α- rather than β-glucoside linkages, that exists in most plant tissues; converted into dextrin when subjected to the action of dry heat, and into dextrin and glucose by amylases and glucoamylases in saliva and pancreatic juice.

starve [A.S. *steorfan,* to die]. **1.** To suffer from lack of food. **2.** To deprive of food so as to cause suffering or death.

stasis, pl. **stases** (sta'sis, stas'is, -ēz) [G. a standing still]. Stagnation of the blood or other fluids.

papillary s., papilledema.

pressure s., traumatic *asphyxia.*

stat. Statim.

-stat [G. *statēs,* stationary]. Suffix indicating an agent intended to keep something from changing or moving.

state [L. *status,* condition, state]. Condition; situation. See also status.

anxiety s., anxiety *neurosis.*

dreamy s., the semiconscious s. associated with an epileptic attack.

ground s., the normal, inactivated s. of an atom from which, on activation, the singlet, triplet, and other excited s.'s are derived.

multiple ego s.'s, various psychological organizational s.'s reflecting different life experiences.

refractory s., subnormal excitability immediately following a response to previous excitation; divided into absolute and relative phases.

steady s. (s as a subscript), a s. obtained in moderate muscular exercise, when the removal of lactic acid by oxidation keeps pace with its production, the oxygen supply being adequate, and the muscles do not go into debt for oxygen; more generally, any condition in which the formation of substances just keeps pace with their destruction so that all volumes, concentrations, pressures, and flows remain constant.

twilight s., a condition of disordered consciousness during which actions may be performed without the conscious volition of the individual and without any remembrance of them being retained.

sta'tim (stat.) [L.]. At once; immediately.

statoacoustic (stat'o-ă-kū'stik) [G. *statos,* standing, + *akoustikos,* acoustic]. Vestibulochochlear (2); relating to equilibrium and hearing.

statoconia, sing. **statoconium** (stat'o-ko'nĭ-ah, -nĭ-um) [L. fr. G. *statos,* standing, *konis,* dust] [NA]. Statoliths; otoconia; otoliths (1); crystalline particles of calcium carbonate and a protein adhering to the gelatinous membrane of the maculae of the utricle and saccule.

stat'oliths [G. *statos,* standing, + *lithos,* stone]. Statoconia.

stature (statch'ur) [L. *statuo*, pp. *statutus*, cause to stand]. The height of a person.

status (sta'tus, stat'us) [L. a way of standing]. State; condition.

  s. asthmat'icus, a condition of severe, prolonged asthma.

  s. epilep'ticus, a condition in which one major attack of epilepsy succeeds another with little or no intermission.

  s. thymicolymphat'icus, s. lymphaticus, supposed enlargement of the thymus and lymph nodes in infants and young children, formerly believed to be associated with unexplained sudden death; prominence of these structures is now considered normal in young children, including those who have died suddenly without preceding illnesses that might lead to atrophy of lymphoid tissue. See also sudden death *syndrome.*

staurion (staw'ri-on) [G. dim. of *stauros*, cross]. A craniometric point at the intersection of the median and transverse palatine sutures.

stauroplegia (staw-ro-ple'ji-ah) [G. *stauros*, cross, + *plēgē*, stroke]. Alternate *hemiplegia.*

STD Sexually transmitted disease.

steal (stēl). Diversion of blood via alternate routes or reversed flow, from a vascularized tissue to one deprived by proximal arterial obstruction.

  external carotid s., see external carotid steal *syndrome.*

  subclavian s., obstruction of the subclavian artery proximal to the origin of the vertebral artery; blood flow through the vertebral artery is reversed and the subclavian artery thus "steals" cerebral blood, causing symptoms or cerebrovascular insufficiency.

steapsin (ste-ap'sin). Triacylglycerol lipase.

stear-. See *stearo-.*

stearate (ste'ă-rāt). A salt of stearic acid.

stearic acid (ste'ă-rik). Octadecanoic acid; one of the most abundant fatty acids found in animal lipids; used in pharmaceutical preparations, ointments, soaps, and suppositories.

stearo-, stear- [G. *stear*, tallow]. Combining forms denoting fat. See also *steato-.*

steatitis (ste-ă-ti'tis) [G. *stear* (*stear-*), tallow, + *-itis*, inflammation]. Inflammation of adipose tissue.

steato- [G. *stear* (*stear-*), tallow]. Combining form denoting fat. See also *stearo-.*

steatocystoma (ste'ă-to-sis-to'mah). 1. A cyst with sebaceous gland cells in its wall. 2. Sebaceous *cyst.*

  s. mul'tiplex, widespread, multiple, thin-walled cysts of the skin lined by squamous epithelium, including lobules of sebaceous cells.

steatolysis (ste-ă-tol'ĭ-sis) [steato- + G. *lysis*, dissolution]. Hydrolysis or emulsion of fat in the digestive process.

steatolytic (ste'ă-to-lit'ik). Relating to steatolysis.

steatonecrosis (ste'ă-to-nĕ-kro'sis) [steato- + G. *nekrōsis*, death]. Fat *necrosis.*

steatopyga, steatopygia (ste'ă-to-pi'ga, -pij'ĭ-ah) [steato- + G. *pygē*, buttocks]. An excessive accumulation of fat on the buttocks.

steatopygous (ste-ă-top'ĭ-gus). Having excessively fat buttocks.

steatorrhea (ste-ă-to-re'ah) [steato- + G. *rhoia*, a flow]. Passage of fat in large amounts in the feces, as noted in pancreatic disease and the malabsorption syndromes.

steatosis (ste-ă-to'sis) [steato- + G. *-osis*, condition]. Fatty *degeneration.*

stegnosis (steg-no'sis) [G. stoppage]. 1. A stoppage of any of the secretions or excretions. 2. A constriction or stenosis.

stegnot'ic. Astringent or constipating.

stella, pl. **stellae** (stel'ah, stel'e) [Mod. L.]. A star or star-shaped figure.

stellate (stel'āt) [L. *stella*, a star]. Star-shaped.

stellula, pl. **stellulae** (stel'u-lah, -le) [L. dim. of *stella*, star]. A small star or star-shaped figure.

stenion sten'ĭ-on) [G. *stenos*, narrow]. The termination in either temporal fossa of the shortest transverse diameter of the skull.

steno- [G. *stenos*, narrow]. Combining form denoting narrowness or constriction.

stenocardia (sten-o-kar'di-ah) [steno- + G. *kardia*, heart]. *Angina* pectoris.

stenocephalic (sten-o-sě-fal'ik). Stenocephalous.

stenocephalous (sten-o-sef'ă-lus). Stenocephalic; pertaining to, or characterized by, stenocephaly.

stenocephaly (sten-o-sef'ă-lĭ) [steno- + G. *kephalē*, head]. Marked narrowness of the head.

stenochoria (sten-o-ko'rĭ-ah) [G. *stenochōria*, narrowness, fr. steno- + *chōra*, place, room]. Abnormal contraction of any canal or orifice, especially of the lacrimal ducts.

stenope'ic [steno- + G. *opē*, opening]. Provided with a narrow opening or slit.

stenosed (sten'ōzd'). Narrowed; contracted: strictured.

stenosis, pl. **stenoses** (stĕ-no'sis, -sēz) [G. *stenōsis*, a narrowing]. A stricture of any canal; especially of one of the cardiac valves.

  aortic s., pathlogic narrowing of the aortic valve orifice.

  congenital pyloric s., hypertrophic pyloric s.

  hypertrophic pyloric s., congenital pyloric s.; muscular hypertrophy of the pyloric sphincter, associated with projectile vomiting appearing in the second or third week of life.

  idiopathic hypertrophic subaortic s., muscular subaortic s.; left ventricular outflow obstruction due to hypertrophy of the ventricular septum.

  mitral s., pathologic narrowing of the orifice of the mitral valve.

  pulmonary s., narrowing of the opening into the pulmonary artery from the right ventricle.

  pyloric s., narrowing of the gastric pylorus, especially by congenital muscular hypertrophy or scarring resulting from a peptic ulcer.

subaortic s., subvalvar s.; congenital narrowing of the outflow tract of the left ventricle by a ring of fibrous tissue or by hypertrophy of the muscular septum shortly below the aortic valve.

supravalvar s., narrowing of the aorta above the aortic valve by a constricting ring or shelf, or by coarctation or hypoplasia of the ascending aorta.

tricuspid s., pathologic narrowing of the orifice of the tricuspid valve.

stenostomia (sten-o-sto'mĭ-ah) [steno- + G. *stoma,* mouth]. Narrowness of the oral cavity.

sten'other'mal [steno- + G. *thermē,* heat]. Able to withstand only slight changes in temperature, said of bacteria.

sten'otho'rax [steno- + thorax]. A narrow contracted chest.

stenot'ic. Narrowed; affected with stenosis.

stenoxenous (sten-ok'sen-us) [steno- + G. *xenos,* stranger, foreigner]. Denoting a parasite with a narrow host range.

stent [C. *Stent*]. **1.** A device used to maintain a bodily orifice or cavity during skin grafting, or to immobilize a skin graft after placement. **2.** A slender thread, rod, or catheter placed within the lumen of tubular structures to provide support during or after their anastomosis, or to assure patency of an intact but contracted lumen.

stepha'nial, Pertaining to the stephanion.

stephanion (stě-fa'nĭ-on) [G. dim. of *stephanos,* crown]. A craniometric point where the coronal suture intersects the inferior temporal line.

step'page [Fr.]. The peculiar gait seen in neuritis of the peroneal nerve and from tabes dorsalis; in consequence of this, dorsal flexion of the foot is impossible, and in walking the foot must be raised very high in order to clear the ground with the drooping toes.

sterco- [L. *stercus,* feces, excrement]. Combining form denoting feces. See also copro-; scato-.

stercobilin (ster'ko-bi'lin, -bil'in). A brown degradation product of hemoglobin present in the feces.

stercolith (ster'ko-lith) [sterco- + G. *lithos,* stone]. Fecalith.

stercoraceous (ster'ko-ra'shus). Stercoral; stercorous; relating to or containing feces.

stercoral (ster'ko-ral). Stercoraceous.

stercoroma (ster-ko-ro'mah) [stereo- + G. *-oma,* tumor]. Coproma.

stercorous (ster'ko-rus). Stercoraceous.

stercus (ster'kus) [L. feces, excrement]. Feces.

stereo- [G. *stereos,* solid]. **1.** Combining form denoting a solid, or a solid condition or state. **2.** Prefix denoting spatial qualities, three-dimensionality.

stereoarthrolysis (stěr'e-o-ar-throl'ĭ-sis) [stereo- + G. *arthron,* joint, + *lysis,* loosening]. Production of a new joint with mobility in cases of bony ankylosis.

stereocampimeter (stěr'e-o-kam-pim'ě-ter) [stereo- + L. *campus,* field, + G. *metron,* measure]. An apparatus for studying the central visual fields.

stereochemical (stěr'e-o-kem'ĭ-kal). Relating to stereochemistry.

stereochemistry (stěr-e-o-kem'is-trĭ). The branch of chemistry concerned with atoms in their spatial three-dimensional relations, the positions the atoms in a compound bear in relation to one another in space.

stereocinefluorography (stěr'e-o-sĭn'ě-flūr-og'rǎ-fĭ). Motion picture recording of radiographic images obtained by stereoscopic fluoroscopy; three-dimensional views are obtained.

stereoencephalometry (stěr'e-o-en-sef'ǎ-lom'ě-trĭ). The localization of brain structures by use of three-dimensional coordinates.

stereoencephalotomy (stěr'e-o-en-sef'ǎ-lot'o-mĭ) [stereo- + G. *encephalos,* brain, + *tomē,* a cutting]. Stereotaxy.

stereognosis (stěr'e-og'no'sis) [stereo- + G. *gnōsis,* knowledge]. The appreciation of the form of an object by means of touch.

stereognos'tic. Relating to stereognosis.

stereoisomer (stěr'e-o-i'so-mer) [stereo- + G. *isos,* equal, + *meros,* part]. A molecule containing the same number and kind of atom groupings as another but in a different arrangement in space, by virtue of which it exhibits different properties.

stereoisomeric (stěr'e-o-i-so-měr'ik). Relating to stereoisomerism.

stereoisomerism (stěr'e-o-i-som'er-izm). Stereochemical isomerism; molecular asymmetry; isomerism involving different spatial arrangement of the same groups.

ster'eom'etry. **1.** The measurement of a solid object or the cubic capacity of a vessel. **2.** Determination of the specific gravity of a liquid.

stereopathy (stěr'e-op'ǎ-thĭ). Persistent stereotyped thinking.

stereoradiography (stěr'e-o-ra-dĭ-og'rǎ-fĭ). The taking of an x-ray picture from two slightly different positions so as to obtain a stereoscopic effect.

ster'eoscop'ic [stereo- + G. *skopeō,* to view]. Relating to the three-dimensional appearance of relief presented by a solid body.

stereotaxic (stěr'e-o-tak'sik). Relating to stereotaxis or stereotaxy.

stereotaxis (stěr'e-o-tak'sis) [stereo- + G. *taxis,* orderly arrangement]. **1.** Three-dimensional arrangement. **2.** Stereotropism where the organism as a whole, rather than a part only, reacts. **3.** Stereotaxy.

stereotaxy (stěr'e-o-tak'sĭ). Stereotaxis (3); stereoencephalotomy; stereotactic surgery; a precise method of destroying deep-seated brain structures located by use of three-dimensional coordinates.

ster'eotropic. Relating to or exhibiting stereotropism.

stereotropism (stěr'e-ot'ro-pizm) [stereo- + G. *tropos,* a turning]. Growth or movement of a part of an organism toward (**positive s.**) or away from (**negative s.**) a solid body.

stereotypy (stĕr′e-o-ti-pī) [stereo- + G. *typos*, impression, type]. **1.** Maintenance of one attitude for a long period. **2.** Constant repetition of certain meaningless gestures or movements.

steric (stĕr′ik, stĕr-). Pertaining to stereochemistry.

sterile (stĕr′il) [L. *sterilis*, barren]. Relating to or characrterized by sterility.

sterility (stĕ-ril′ĭ-tĭ) [L. *sterilitas*]. **1.** In general, the incapability of fertilization or reproduction. **2.** The state of being aseptic, or free from all living microorganisms and their spores.

sterilization (stĕr′ĭ-lĭ-za′shun). **1.** The act or process by which an individual is rendered incapable of fertilization or reproduction. **2.** Destruction of all microorganisms in or about an object, as by steam, chemical agents, high-velocity electron bombardment, ultraviolet light radiation.

sterilize (stĕr′ĭ-liz). To produce sterility.

sterilizer (stĕr′ĭ-li-zer). An apparatus for rendering objects aseptic.

stern-. See sterno-.

ster′na. Plural of sternum.

ster′nal. Relating to the sternum.

sternalgia (ster-nal′jĭ-ah) [stern- + G. *algos*, pain]. Sternodynia; pain in the sternum or the sternal region.

sternebra, pl. **sternebrae** (ster′ne-brah, -bre) [Mod. L. fr. stern(um) + (vert-)ebra]. One of the four segments of the primordial sternum of the embryo by fusion of which the body of the adult sternum is formed.

sterno-, stern-. Combining form denoting the sternum.

sternoclavicular (ster′no-klă-vik′u-lar). Relating to the sternum and the clavicle.

sternocleidomastoid (ster′no-kli′do-mas′toyd). Relating to sternum, clavicle, and mastoid process.

sternocostal (ster-no-kos′tal) [L. *costa*, rib]. Relating to the sternum and the ribs.

sternodynia (ster-no-din′ĭ-ah) [sterno- + G. *odynē*, pain]. Sternalgia.

sternoglossal (ster-no-glos′al). Denoting muscular fibers which occasionally pass from the sternohyoid muscle to join the hyoglossal muscle.

sternoid (ster′noyd) [sterno- + G. *eidos*, resemblance]. Resembling the sternum.

sternopagia (ster-no-pa′jĭ-ah) [sterno- + G. *pagos*, something fixed, + -*ia*, condition]. The condition of conjoined twins united at the sterna or more extensively at the ventral walls of the chest.

sternopericardial (ster′no-pĕr-ĭ-kar′dĭ-al). Relating to the sternum and the pericardium.

sternoschisis (ster-nos′kĭ-sis) [sterno- + G. *schisis*, a cleaving]. Congenital cleft of the sternum.

sternotomy (ster-not′o-mĭ) [sterno- + G. *tomē*, incision]. Incision into or through the sternum.

sternovertebral (ster′no-ver′tĕ-bral). Vertebrosternal; relating to the sternum and the vertebrae; denoting the true ribs (seven upper ribs) that articulate with the vertebrae and the sternum.

sternum, pl. **sterna** (ster′num, -nah) [Mod. L. fr. G. *sternon*, the chest] [NA]. The breast bone; a long flat bone, articulating with the cartilages of the first seven ribs and with the clavicle, forming the middle part of the anterior wall of the thorax; consists of three portions: corpus, manubrium, and xiphoid process.

sternutation (ster-nu-ta′shun) [L. *sternutatio*, to sneeze]. The act of sneezing.

sternu′tatory. Causing sneezing.

steroid (stēr′oyd, stĕr′oyd). **1.** Steroidal; pertaining to the steroids. **2.** One of the steroids. **3.** Generic designation for compounds closely related in structure to steroids, such as sterols, bile acids, cardiac glycosides, and precursors of the vitamin D. **4.** Jargon for a compound having biological actions similar to a steroid hormone, of semisynthetic or synthetic origin, and whose structure may or may not resemble that of a steroid.

ster′oidal. Steroid (1).

steroidogenesis (ste′roy′do-jen′ĕ-sis). [steroid + G. *genesis*, production]. The formation of steroids; refers to the biological synthesis of steroid hormones, but not to the production of such compounds in a chemical laboratory.

steroids (stēr′oydz, stĕr′oydz). A large family of chemical substances, comprising many hormones, vitamins, body constituents, and drugs, each containing tetracyclic cyclopenta[α]phenanthrene skeleton.

sterol (stĕr′ol). A steroid of 27 or more carbon atoms with one OH (alcohol) group; systematic names contain either prefix hydroxy- or the suffix -ol.

ster′tor [L. *sterto*, to snore]. A noisy inspiration occurring in coma or deep sleep, sometimes due to obstruction of the larynx or upper airways.

ster′torous. Relating to or characterized by stertor or snoring.

steth-. See stetho-.

stethalgia (stĕ-thal′jĭ-ah) [steth- + G. *algos*, pain]. Pain in the chest.

stetho-, steth- [G. *stēthos*, chest]. Combining forms denoting the chest.

stethogoniometer (steth′o-go-nĭ-om′ĕ-ter) [stetho- + G. *gōnia*, angle, + *metron*, measure]. An apparatus for measuring the curvatures of the thorax.

steth′oscop′ic. **1.** Relating to or effected by means of a stethoscope. **2.** Relating to an examination of the chest.

stethoscope (steth′o-skōp) [stetho- + G. *skopeō*, to view]. An instrument used in auscultation of sounds in the body.

stethoscopy (stĕ-thos′ko-pī). **1.** Examination of the chest by means of auscultation, either mediate or immediate, and percussion. **2.** Mediate auscultation with the stethoscope.

stethospasm (steth′o-spazm). Spasm of the chest.

STH Somatotropic *hormome*.

sthenia (sthe′nĭ-ah) [G. *sthenos*, strength]. A condition of activity and apparent force.

sthen'ic. Strong; active; marked by sthenia; said of a fever with strong bounding pulse, high temperature, and active delirium.

stheno- [G. *sthenos*, strength]. Combining form denoting strength, force, or power.

stibialism (stib′ĭ-ă-lizm) [L. *stibium*, antimony]. Chronic antimonial poisoning.

stigma, pl. **stigmas** or **stigmata** (stig′mah, stig′mă-tah) [G. a mark, fr. *stizō*, to prick]. **1.** Visible evidence of a disease. **2.** Follicular s. **3.** Any spot or blemish on the skin. **4.** A bleeding spot on the skin which is considered a manifestation of conversion hysteria.

    s. of degeneration, one of a number of physical, nervous, or psychic abnormalities occurring solely, or with preponderating frequency, in degenerate constitution.

    follicular s., stigma (2); macula pellucida; the point where the graafian follicle is about to rupture on the surface of the ovary.

    malpighian s.'s, the points of entrance of the smaller veins into the larger veins of the spleen.

stigmat'ic. Relating to or marked by a stigma.

stig′matism. Stigmatization (1); the condition of having stigmas.

stigmatization (stig′mă-tĭ-za′shun). **1.** Stigmatism. **2.** The production of stigmas, especially of hysterical origin.

stil′bene. Toluylene; $C_6H_5CHCHC_6H_5$; an unsaturated hydrocarbon, the nucleus of stilbestrol and other synthetic estrogenic compounds.

still′birth. The birth of an infant who shows no evidence of life.

still′born. Born dead; denoting an infant dead at birth.

stimulant (stim′u-lant) [L. *stimulans*, pres. p. of *stimulo*, pp. *-atus*, to goad, incite]. **1.** Stimulating; exciting to action. **2.** Stimulator; an agent that arouses organic activity, increases vitality, and promotes a sense of well-being; classified, according to the parts upon which they chiefly act.

    diffusible s., a s. that produces a rapid but temporary effect.

    general s., a s. that affects the entire body.

    local s., a s. whose action is confined to the part to which it is applied.

stimulation (stim′u-la′shun) [see stimulant]. **1.** Arousal of the body or any of its parts or organs to increased functional activity. **2.** The condition of being stimulated. **3.** Application of a stimulus to a responsive structure, such as a nerve or muscle, regardless of whether the strength of the stimulus is sufficient to produce excitation.

stimulator (stim′u-la-tor). Stimulant (2).

    long-acting thyroid s. (LATS), a substance found in the blood of hyperthyroid patients that exerts a prolonged stimulatory effect on the thyroid gland; associated in plasma with the IgG fraction.

stimulus, pl. **stimuli** (stim′u-lus, -li) [L. a goad]. **1.** A stimulant. **2.** That which can elicit or evoke action (response) in an excitable tissue, or cause an aug-

menting action upon any function or metabolic process.

    adequate s., a s. to which a particular receptor responds effectively and which gives rise to a characteristic sensation.

    conditioned s., (1) a s. applied to one of the sense organs that is an essential and integral part of the neural mechanism underlying a conditioned reflex; **(2)** a neutral s., when paired with the unconditioned s. in simultaneous presentation to an organism, capable of eliciting a given response.

    discriminant s., a s. that can be differentiated from all other s. in the environment because it has been, and continues to serve as, an indicator of a potential reinforcer.

    heterologous s., a s. that acts upon any part of the sensory apparatus or nerve tract.

    homologous s., a s. that acts only upon the nerve terminations in a special sense organ.

    inadequate s., subthreshold s., a s. too weak to evoke a response.

    threshold s., a s. that is just strong enough to excite.

    unconditioned s., a s. that elicits an unconditioned response.

sting. 1. Sharp momentary pain produced by the puncture of the skin by many species of arthropods, or by contact with venomous species of aquatic life forms. **2.** The venom apparatus of a stinging organism. **3.** To introduce (or the process of introducing) a venom by stinging.

stip′pling. 1. A speckling of a blood cell or other structure with fine dots when exposed to the action of a basic stain, due to the presence of free basophil granules in the cell protoplasm. **2.** An orange peel appearance of the attached gingiva.

stirrup (stur′up) [A.S. *stīrāp*]. Stapes.

stitch [A.S. *stice*, a pricking]. **1.** A sharp sticking pain of momentary duration. **2.** A single suture. **3.** Suture (2).

STM Short term *memory.*

stoichiometry (stoy-kĭ-om′ĕ-trĭ) [G. *stoicheion*, element, + *metron*, measure]. Determination of the relative quantities of the substances concerned in any chemical reaction.

stoke [G. G. *Stokes*]. A unit of kinematic viscosity, that of a fluid with a viscosity of 1 poise and a density of 1 g/ml.

stom-, stoma-. See stomato-.

stoma, pl. **stomas** or **stomata** (sto′mah, sto′mă-tah) [G. a mouth]. **1** [NA]. A minute opening or pore. **2.** The mouth. **3.** An artificial opening between two cavities or canals, or between such and the surface of the body.

stomach (stum′uk) [G. *stomachos*, L. *stomachus*]. Ventriculus (1); gaster; that part of the digestive tract between the esophagus and the small intestine, lying just beneath the diaphragm.

    cascade s., a radiographic diagnosis in which the upper stomach serves as a barium reservoir until sufficient volume is present to spill ("cascade") into the antrum; said to cause symptoms of postprandial distention and inability to belch.

   hourglass s., a condition in which there is an abnormal constriction of the wall of the s. dividing it into two cavities, cardiac and pyloric.

   leather-bottle s., marked thickening and rigidity of the s. wall, with reduced capacity of the lumen although often without obstruction.

   water-trap s., a ptotic and dilated s., having a relatively high (though normally placed) pyloric outlet held up by the gastrohepatic ligament.

stomachal (stum′ă-kal). Stomachic (1); relating to the stomach.

stomachic (sto′mak′ik). **1.** Stomachal. **2.** An agent that improves appetite and digestion.

sto′mal. Relating to a stoma.

stomat-. See stomato-.

sto′mata. Alternate plural of stoma.

stomatalgia (sto-mă-tal′jī-ah) [stomat- + G. *algos,* pain]. Stomatodynia; pain in the mouth.

stomatitis (sto-mă-ti′tis) [stomat- + G. *-itis,* inflammation]. Inflammation of the mucous membrane of the mouth.

   angular s., inflammation at the corners of the mouth usually associated with a wrinkled or fissured epithelium, stopping at the mucocutaneous junction and not involving the mucosa.

   aphthous s., ulcerative s.

   gangrenous s., see noma.

   s. medicamento′sa, allergic inflammatory changes in the oral soft tissues associated with the use of drugs or medicaments, usually taken systemically.

   primary herpetic s., first infection of oral tissues with herpes simplex virus; characterized by gingival inflammation, vesicles, and ulcers.

   recurrent herpetic s., reactivation of herpes simplex virus; characterized by vesicles and ulceration.

   recurrent ulcerative s., recurrent canker sores or aphthous s.; an oral disease characterized by recurrent appearance of single or multiple painful ulcers, centrally depressed, with a grayish yellow coating, and surrounded by a narrow zone of inflammation.

   ulcerative s., canker sores; destructive ulceration of the mucous membrane of the mouth.

stomato-, stom-, stomat- [G. *stoma,* mouth]. Combining forms denoting mouth.

stomatocytosis (sto′mă-to-si-to′sis). A hereditary deformation of red blood cells, which are swollen and cup-shaped, causing congenital hemolytic anemia.

stomatodynia (sto′mă-to-din′ī-ah) [stomato- + G. *odynē,* pain]. Stomatalgia.

stomatomalacia (sto′mă-to-mă-la′shī-ah) [stomato- + G. *malakia,* softness]. Pathologic softening of any of the structures of the mouth.

stomatomenia (sto′mă-to-me′nī-ah) [stomato- + G. *mēn,* month]. Bleeding from the gums as a form of vicarious menstruation.

stomatomycosis (sto′mă-to-mi-ko′sis) [stomato- + G. *mykēs,* fungus, + *-osis,* condition]. A fungal disease of the mouth.

stomatonecrosis (sto′mă-to-nĕ-kro′sis) [stomato- + G. *nekrōsis,* death]. Noma.

stomatopathy (sto-mă-top′ă-thī) [stomato- + G. *pathos,* suffering]. Any disease of the mouth.

sto′matoplas′tic. Relating to stomatoplasty.

stomatoplasty (sto′mă-to-plas-tĭ) [stomato- + G. *plassō,* to form]. Reconstructive or plastic surgery of the mouth.

stomatorrhagia (sto′mă-to-ra′jī-ah) [stomato- + G. *rhēg- nymi,* to burst forth]. Bleeding from any part of the oral cavity.

stomodeal (sto′mo-de′al). Relating to a stomodeum.

sto′mode′um [Mod. L. fr. G. *stoma,* mouth, + *hodaios*]. A midline ectodermal depression ventral to the embryonic brain and surrounded by the mandibular arch which becomes continuous with the foregut and forms the mouth.

-stomy [G. *stoma,* mouth]. Combining form denoting an artificial or surgical opening.

stone [A.S. *stān*]. **1.** Calculus. **2.** An English unit of weight of the human body equal to 14 pounds.

   pulp s., pulp nodule; a calcified mass of dentin within the pulp or projected into it from the cavity wall.

   tear s., dacryolith.

stool [A.S. *stōl,* seat]. **1.** A discharging of the bowels. **2.** Evacuation (2); the matter discharged at one movement of the bowels.

storage (stōr′ij). The second of three stages in the memory process; involves mental processes associated with retention of stimuli that have been registered and modified by encoding.

storm. An exacerbation of symptoms or a crisis in the course of a disease.

   thyroid s., thyrotoxic *crisis.*

STPD A gas volume expressed as if it were at standard temperature (0°C), standard pressure (760 mm Hg absolute), dry.

strabismal, strabismic (stră-biz′mal, -mik). Relating to or affected with strabismus.

strabismometer (stră-biz-mom′ĕ-ter) [G. *strabismos,* a squinting, + *metron,* measure]. A calibrated plate with the upper margin curved to conform with the lower lid; used to measure lateral deviation in squint.

strabismus (stră-biz′mus) [Mod. L. fr. G. *strabismos,* a squinting]. Heterotropia; squint; a manifest lack of parallelism of the visual axes of the eyes.

   concomitant s., s. in which the degree of s. is the same in all directions of gaze.

   convergent s., esotropia.

   s. deor′sum ver′gens, hypotropia; vertical s. in which the visual axis of one eye deviates downward.

   divergent s., exotropia.

   vertical s., a form in which the visual axis of one eye deviates upward or downward.

strabotomy (strā-bot'o-mǐ) [G. *strabismos*, strabismus, + *tomē*, a cutting]. Division of one or more of the ocular muscles or their tendons for the correction of squint.

strain (strān) [A.S. *stryand; streōnan*, to beget]. **1.** A race or stock; in bacteriology, the set of descendants that originates from a common ancestor and retains the characteristics of the ancestor. **2.** A hereditary tendency. **3** [L. *stringere*, to bind]. To make an effort to the limit of one's strength. **4.** To injure by overuse or improper use. **5.** Injury resulting from improper use or overuse. **6.** To filter; to percolate.

strait (strāt) [M.E. *streit* thr. O. Fr. fr. L. *strictus*, drawn together, tight]. In obstetrics, the upper opening (**superior s.** or inlet), or the lower opening (**inferior s.** or outlet), of the pelvic canal.

straitjacket (strāt'jak-et). A garment-like device with long sleeves used to restrain a violent person.

strangle (strang'gl) [G. *strangaloō*, to choke, fr. *strangalē*, a halter]. To suffocate; to choke; to compress the trachea so as to prevent sufficient passage of air.

strangulated (strang'gu-la-ted) [L. *strangulo*, pp. *-atus*, to choke]. Constricted so as to prevent sufficient passage of air, as through the trachea, or to cut off venous return, as in the case a hernia.

strangulation (strang'gu-la'shun). The act of strangulating or the condition of being strangulated.

strangury (strang'gu-rǐ) [G. *stranx*, something squeezed out, + *ouron*, urine]. Difficulty in micturition, the urine being passed drop by drop with pain and tenesmus.

strap [A.S. *stropp*]. **1.** A strip of adhesive plaster. **2.** To apply overlapping strips of adhesive plaster.

strata (stra'tah, strat'ah). Plural of stratum.

stratification (strat'ǐ-fǐ-ka'shun) [L. *stratum*, layer, + *facio*, to make]. An arrangement in layers or strata.

strat'ified. Arranged in the form of layers or strata.

stratigraphy (strā-tig'rāfǐ) [L. *stratum*, layer, + G. *graphē*, a writing]. Tomography.

stratum, pl. **strata** (stra'tum, strat'um; -ah) [L. *sterno*, pp. *stratus*, to spread out, strew] [NA]. One of the layers of differentiated tissue, the aggregate of which forms any given structure. See also lamina.

s. basa'le, basal layer; (**1**) the outermost layer of the endometrium which undergoes only minimal changes during the menstrual cycle; (**2**) the deepest layer of the epidermis.

s. compac'tum, compact layer; the superficial layer of decidual tissue in the pregnant uterus, in which the interglandular tissue preponderates.

s. cor'neum, corneal or horny layer; the outer layer of the epidermis, consisting of several layers of flat keratinized non-nucleated cells.

s. functiona'le, functional layer; the endometrium except for the s. basale; it formerly was believed to be lost during menstruation but is now considered to be only partially disrupted.

s. ganglio'sum cerebel'li, ganglionic layer of the cerebellar cortex; Purkinje's layer; the layer of Purkinje cells formerly described as an individual s. of the cerebellar cortex but currently included in the s. moleculare cerebelli.

s. germinati'vum, germinative or malpighian layer; the combined s. basale epidermidis and s. spinosum epidermidis.

s. granulo'sum [NA], (**1**) of the cerebellar cortex, the deeper of the two layers of the cortex which contains large numbers of granule cells, the dendrites of which synapse with incoming mossy fibers whereas their axons form numerous synapses with the dendrites of Purkinje cells, basket cells, and stellate cells; (**2**) of the epidermis, a layer of somewhat flattened cells containing granules of keratohyalin and eleidin, lying just above the s. spinosum of the epidermis; (**3**) of a vesicular ovarian follicle, the layer of small cells that forms the wall of an ovarian follicle.

s. lu'cidum, clear layer; the layer of the epidermis just beneath the s. corneum; consists of two or three layers of flat clear cells with atrophied nuclei.

s. molecula're cerebel'li [NA], molecular layer of the cerebellar cortex; the outer lamina of the cortex, containing the cell bodies and dendrites of Purkinje cells, the axons of the granule cells, and the cell bodies, dendrites, and axons of basket cells.

s. spino'sum epider'midis, spinous or prickle cell layer; the layer of polyhedral cells in the epidermis whose intercellular bridges give them a spiny or prickly appearance.

s. spongio'sum, spongy layer; the middle layer of the endometrium, formed chiefly of dilated glandular structures, flanked by the s. compactum on the luminal side and the s. basalis on the myometrial side.

streak (strēk) [A.S. *strica*]. A line, stria, or stripe, especially indistinct or evanescent.

angioid s.'s, breaks in the lamina vitrea of the eye occurring in a variety of systemic disorders affecting elastic tissue.

meningitic s., a line of redness following the drawing of the nail or a pencil point across the skin, seen especially in cases of meningitis.

primitive s., an ectodermal ridge in the midline at the caudal end of the embryonic disk from which arises the intraembryonic mesoderm.

strephosymbolia (stref'o-sim-bo'lǐ-ah) [G. *strephō*, to turn, + *symbolon*, a mark or sign]. Perception of objects reversed as if in a mirror; Specifically, difficulty in distinguishing written or printed letters that extend in opposite directions but are otherwise similar, such as *p* and *d*.

strepticemia (strep-tǐ-se'mǐ-ah). Streptococcemia.

strepto- [G. *streptos*, twisted]. Combining form denoting curved or twisted.

Streptobacillus (strep'to-bă-sil'us) [strepto- + bacillus]. A genus of Gram-negative bacteria (family Bacteroidaceae) that are parasitic to pathogenic for rats, mice, and other mammals. Type species is *S. moniliformis,* which is the etiologic agent of Haverhill fever.

streptococcal (strep-to-kok'al). Relating to or caused by any organism of the genus *Streptococcus.*

streptococcemia (strep'to-kok-se'mĭ-ah) [streptococcus + G. *haima,* blood]. Strepticemia; streptosepticemia; presence of streptococci in the blood.

streptococci (strep-to-kok'sī). Plural of streptococcus.

Streptococcus (strep-to-kok'us) [strepto- + G. *kokkus,* berry (coccus)]. *Diplococcus;* a genus of Gram--positive bacteria (family Lactobacillaceae) containing spherical or ovoid cells which occur in pairs or short or long chains; some species are pathogenic. Type species is *S. pyogenes.*

   S. mu'tans, a species associated with the production of dental caries.

   S. pneumo'niae, *Diplococcus pneumoniae;* pneumococcus; a species of Gram-positive diplococci that is the common causative agent of lobar pneumonia, meningitis, sinusitis, and other infections. Type species of the genus *Diplococcus.*

   S. pyog'enes, a species that causes formation of pus and septicemias. Type species of the genus *S.*

   S. vir'idans, a name applied not to a distinct species but rather to the group of α streptococci.

streptococcus, pl. **streptococci** (strep'to-kok'us, -kok'sī). Any member of the genus *Streptococcus.*

   α **streptococci,** those that form a green variety of reduced hemoglobin in the area of the colony on a blood agar medium.

   β-**hemolytic streptococci,** those that produce active hemolysins (O and S) which cause a zone of clear hemolysis on the blood agar medium in the area of the colony and are divided into groups (A to O) on the basis of cell wall C carbohydrate; Group A (strains pathogenic for man) comprises more than 50 types determined by cell wall M protein, which seems to be associated closely with virulence.

streptodor'nase (SD). A deoxyribonuclease obtained from streptococci; used with streptokinase to facilitate drainage in septic surgical conditions.

streptoki'nase (SK). *Streptomyces griseus* neutral proteinase, an extracellular enzyme that cleaves plasminogen, producing plasmin, which causes the liquefaction of fibrin; used usually in conjunction with streptodornase.

streptokinase-streptodornase. A purified mixture containing streptokinase, streptodornase, and other proteolytic enzymes; used by topical application or by injection into body cavities to remove clotted blood and fibrinous and purulent accumulations of exudate.

streptolysin (strep-tol'ĭ-sin). A hemolysin produced by streptococci.

Streptomyces (strep-to-mi'sēz) [strepto- + G. *mykēs,* fungus]. A genus of Gram-positive bacteria (family Streptomycetaceae) that are predominantly saprophytic soil forms; some are parasitic and many produce antibiotics. Type species is *S. albus.*

streptomy'cin. An antibiotic agent obtained from *Streptomyces griseus* that is active against the tubercle bacillus and a large number of Gram-positive and -negative bacteria.

streptosepticemia (strep'to-sep-tĭ-se'mĭ-ah). Streptococcemia.

stress [L. *strictus,* tight]. **1.** Reactions of the animal body to forces of a deleterious nature, infections, and various abnormal states that tend to disturb homeostasis. **2.** The resisting force set up in a body as a result of an externally applied force. **3.** In psychology, a physical or psychological stimulus which, when impinging upon an individual, produces strain or disequilibrium.

stretch'er [A.S. *streccan,* to stretch]. A litter, usually a sheet of canvas stretched to a frame with handles, used for transporting the sick or injured.

stria, pl. **striae** (stri'ah, stri'e) [L. channel, furrow]. **1.** [NA]. Striation (1); a stripe, band, streak, or line, distinguished from the tissue in which it is found. **2.** Striae cutis distensae.

   acoustic striae, striae medullares ventriculi quarti.

   striae atroph'icae, striae cutis distensae.

   striae cu'tis disten'sae, bands of thin wrinkled skin, initially red but becoming purple and white, which occur commonly on the abdomen, buttocks, and thighs during and following pregnancy, and result from atrophy of the dermis and overextension of the skin; also associated with ascites and Cushing's syndrome. Also called lineae atrophicae; linear atrophy; striae (2); striae atrophicae or gravidarum; vergeture.

   striae gravida'rum, striae cutis distensae resulting from pregnancy.

   s. longitudina'lis latera'lis [NA], **lateral longitudinal s.,** a thin longitudinal band of nerve fibers accompanied by gray matter, near each outer edge of the upper surface of the corpus callosum under cover of the gyrus cinguli.

   s. longitudina'lis media'lis [NA], **medial longitudinal s.,** a thin longitudinal band of nerve fibers accompanied by gray matter, running along the surface of the corpus callosum on either side of the median line.

   stri'ae medulla'res ventric'uli quar'ti [NA], **medullary striae of fourth ventricle,** acoustic striae; slender fascicles of fibers extending transversally below the ependymal floor of the ventricle from the median sulcus to enter the inferior cerebellar peduncle.

   s. medulla'ris thal'ami [NA], **medullary s. of thalamus,** a narrow compact fiber bundle that extends along the line of attachment of the roof of the third ventricle to the thalamus on each side and terminates posteriorly in the habenular nucleus.

   s. termina'lis [NA], **terminal s.,** a slender compact fiber bundle that connects the amygdala with the hypothalamus and other basal forebrain regions.

stri'ate, stri'ated [L. *striatus*, furrowed]. Striped; marked by striae.

striation (stri-a'shun). **1.** Stria (1). **2.** A striate appearance. **3.** The act of streaking or making striae.

striatonigral (stri'a-to-ni'gral). Referring to the efferent connection of the striatum with the substantia nigra.

striatum (stri-a'tum) [L. neut. of *striatus*, furrowed]. Collective name for the caudate nucleus and putamen which together with the globus pallidus form the corpus striatum.

stricture (strik'chur) [L. *strictura* drawn tight]. A circumscribed narrowing of a hollow structure.

stricturotomy (strik-chur-ot'o-mĭ) [stricture + G. *tomē*, incision]. Surgical opening or division of a stricture.

stri'dor [L. a harsh, creaking sound]. A high-pitched noisy respiration; a sign of respiratory obstruction.

congenital s., laryngeal s., occurring at birth or within the first few months of life; sometimes without apparent cause and sometimes due to abnormal flaccidity of epiglottis or arytenoids.

expiratory s., a singing sound during general anesthesia due to the semi-approximated vocal cords offering resistance to the escape of air.

inspiratory s., a crowing sound during the inspiratory phase of respiration due to relaxation during general anesthesia of those laryngeal muscles that maintain vocal cord abduction.

stridulous (strid'u-lus) [L. *stridulus*, fr. *strideo*, to creak, to hiss]. Having a shrill or creaking sound.

strip [A.S. *strypan*, to rob]. **1.** Milk (4); to express the contents from a tube or canal by running the finger along it. **2.** Subcutaneous excision of a vein in its longitudinal axis.

stro'bila, pl. **stro'bilae** [G. *stobilē*, a twist of lint]. A chain of segments, less the scolex and unsegmented neck portion, of a tapeworm.

stroke [A.S. *strāc*]. A sudden neurological affliction usually related to the cerebral blood supply; more accurately, a thrombosis, hemorrhage, or embolism.

heat s., see heatstroke.

sun s., see sunstroke.

stroma, pl. **stromata** (stro'mah, stro'mă-tah) [G. *strōma*, bed]. [NA]. The framework, usually of connective tissue, of an organ, gland, or other structure.

stro'mal, stromat'ic. Relating to the stroma.

stromuhr (stro'mūr) [Ger. *Strom*, stream, + *Uhr*, clock]. An instrument for measuring the quantity of blood that flows per unit of time through a blood vessel.

Strongyloides (stron'jĭ-loy'dēz) [G. *strongylos*, round, + *eidos*, resemblance]. The threadworm, a genus of small nematode intestinal parasites (superfamily Rhabditoidea) characterized by a life cycle that involves a generation of free-living adult worms; species include *S. stercoralis*, which causes strongyloidiasis in man.

strongyloidiasis, strongyloidosis (stron-jĭ-loy-di'ă-sis, -do'sis). Infection with the nematode *Strongyloides stercoralis*.

strontium (stron'she-um) [*Strontian*, Scotland]. A metallic element, symbol Sr, atomic no. 38, atomic weight 87.62; one of the alkaline earth series and similar to calcium in chemical and biological properties.

strophulus (strof'u-lus) [L. fr. G. *strophus*, colic]. Miliaria rubra.

struma, pl. **strumae** (stru'mah, -me) [L. fr. *struo*, to pile up]. **1.** Goiter. **2.** Formerly, any enlargement.

Hashimoto's s., s. lymphomato'sa, Hashimoto's *disease.*

s. ova'rii, a rare ovarian tumor in which thyroid tissue has surpassed the other elements.

Riedel's s., a rare fibrous induration of the thyroid, with adhesion to adjacent structures, that may cause tracheal compression.

strumectomy (stru-mek'to-mĭ) [struma + G. *ektomē*, excision]. Surgical removal of all or a portion of a goitrous tumor.

stru'miform [struma + L. *forma*, form]. Resembling a goiter.

strumitis (stru-mi'tus) [struma + G. *-itis*, inflammation]. Inflammation, with swelling, of the thyroid gland.

stru'mous. Denoting or characteristic of a struma.

strychnine (strik'nin, -nēn, -nīn). $C_{21}H_{22}N_2O_2$; a poisonous alkaloid from *Strychnos nux-vomica.*

strychninism (strik'nĭ-nizm). Chronic strychnine poisoning, the symptoms being those that arise from CNS stimulation: tremors and twitching, progressing to severe convulsions and respiratory arrest.

stump. 1. The extremity of a limb left after amputation. **2.** The pedicle remaining after removal of the tumor which was attached to it.

stu'por [L. fr. *stupeo*, to be stunned]. A state of impaired consciousness in which the individual shows a marked diminution in his reactivity to environmental stimuli.

stu'porous. Carotic (2); relating to or marked by stupor.

stut'tering. A phonatory or articulatory disorder, characteristically beginning in childhhod with intense anxiety about the efficiency of oral communications; characterized by difficult enunciation of words with frequent halting and repetition of the initial consonant or syllable.

urinary s., frequent involuntary interruption occurring during the act of urination.

sty, stye, pl. **sties, styes** (stī, stīz). Hordeolum.

stylet, stylette (sti'let, sti-let') [It. *stilletto*, a dagger]. Stylus (3); **1.** A flexible metallic rod inserted in the lumen of a flexible catheter to stiffen it and give it form during its passage. **2.** A slender probe.

stylo- [G. *stylos*, pillar, post]. Prefix denoting styloid; specifically, the styloid process of the temporal bone.

stylohyal (sti-lo-hi'al). Stylohyoid; relating to the styloid process of the temporal bone and to the hyoid bone.

stylohyoid (sti-lo-hi'oyd). Stylohyal.

styloid (sti'loyd) [stylo- + G. *eidos*, resemblance]. Denoting one of several slender bony processes. See *processus* styloideus.

styloiditis (sti-loy-di'tis). Inflammation of a styloid process.

sty'lus [L. *stilus* or *stylus*, a stake or pen]. 1. Any pencil-shaped structure. 2. A pencil-shaped medicinal preparation for external application. 3. Stylet.

stype (stīp) [G. *stypē*, tow]. A tampon.

styp'tic [G. *styptikos*]. Having an astringent or hemostatic effect.

sty'rene. Vinylbenzene; $C_6H_5CH=CH_2$; the monomer from which polystyrenes, plastics, and synthetic rubber are made.

sub- [L. *sub*, under]. Prefix denoting beneath, less than the normal or typical, inferior.

subacute (sub-ă-kūt'). Between acute and chronic; denoting the course of a disease.

subap'ical. Below the apex of any part.

subatom'ic. Pertaining to particles making up the intra-atomic structure.

subax'ial. Below the axis of the body or any part.

subcartilaginous (sub-kar-tĭ-laj'ĭ-nus). 1. Partly cartilaginous. 2. Beneath a cartilage.

sub'class. In biologic classification, a division between class and order.

subclinical (sub-klin'ĭ-kal). Denoting a period prior to the appearance of manifest symptoms in the evolution of a disease.

subconscious (sub-kon'shus). 1. Not wholly conscious. 2. Denoting an idea or impression which is present in the mind, but of which there is at the time no conscious perception.

subconsciousness (sub-kon'shus-nes). 1. Partial unconsciousness. 2. The state in which mental processes take place without the conscious perception of the individual.

subcor'tex. Any part of the brain lying below the cerebral cortex, and not itself organized as cortex.

subcor'tical. Relating to the subcortex; beneath the cerebral cortex.

subcrep'itant. Nearly, but not frankly, crepitant; denoting a rale.

subcul'ture. A culture made by transferring to a fresh medium microorganisms from a previous culture.

subcutaneous (s.c.) (sub-ku-ta'ne-us) [sub- + L. *cutis*, skin]. Hypodermic (1); beneath the skin.

subduce, subduct (sub-dūs', sub-dukt') [L. *sub-duco*, pp. *-ductus*, to lead away]. To pull or draw downward.

sub'endothe'lium. The connective tissue between the endothelium and inner elastic membrane in the intima of arteries.

subfam'ily. In biologic classification, a division between family and tribe or between family and genus.

sub'fertil'ity. A less than normal capacity for reproduction.

subgenus (sub-je'nus). In biologic classification a division between genus and species.

subglos'sal. Sublingual; hypoglossal; below or beneath the tongue.

subgrunda'tion [sub- + A.S. *grund*, bottom, foundation]. Depression of one fragment of a broken cranial bone below the other.

subiculum, pl. **subicula** (su-bik'u-lum, -lah) [L. dim. of *subex*, support]. 1. A support or prop. 2. The zone of transition between the parahippocampal gyrus and Ammon's horn of the hippocampus.

subil'iac. 1. Below the ilium. 2. Relating to the subilium.

subil'ium. The portion of the ilium contributing to the acetabulum.

subinfec'tion. A secondary infection occurring in one exposed to and successfully resisting an epidemic of another infectious disease.

subinvolu'tion. An arrest in the normal involution of the uterus following childbirth, the organ remaining abnormally large.

subja'cent [L. *sub-jaceo*, to lie under]. Below or beneath another part.

subjec'tive [L. *subjectivus*, fr. *subjicio*, to throw under]. Perceived by the individual only and not evident to the examiner.

subking'dom. In biologic classification, a division between kingdom and phylum.

sublation (sub-la'shun) [L. *sublatio*, a lifting up]. Detachment, elevation, or removal of a part.

suble'thal. Not sufficient to cause death.

sublimate (sub'lim-āt) [L. *sublimo*, pp. *-atus*, to raise on high]. 1. Any substance that has been submitted to sublimation. 2. To accomplish sublimation.

ublima'tion. 1. The process of vaporizing a solid substance without passing through a liquid state. 2. In psychoanalysis, an unconscious defense mechanism in which unacceptable instinctual drives and wishes are modified into more personally and socially acceptable channels.

subliminal (sub-lim'ĭ-nal) [sub- + L. *limen* (*limin*-), threshold]. Below the limit of sensory perception or threshold of consciousness.

sublingual (sub-ling'gwal). Subglossal.

subluxation (sub-luk-sa'shun) [sub- + L. *locatio*, dislocation]. An incomplete dislocation; though a relationship is altered, contact between joint surfaces remains.

submaxil'la. Mandibula.

submaxillaritis (sub-mak'sĭ-lă-ri'tis) [sub- + maxilla + G. *-itis*, inflammation]. Inflammation, usually due to mumps virus, affecting the submandibular salivary gland.

submax'illary. Mandibular.

submicroscop'ic. Too minute to be visible under the most powerful light microscope.

submuco'sa. A layer of tissue beneath a mucous membrane.

subnasion (sub-na'zĭ-on). The point of the angle between the septum of the nose and the surface of the upper lip.

subnu'cleus. A secondary nucleus.

subor'der. In biologic classification, a division between order and family.

subpap'ular. Denoting the eruption of few and scattered papules, in which the lesions are very slightly elevated, being scarcely more than macules.

subphylum (sub-fi'lum). In biologic classification, a division between phylum and class.

subscription (sub-skrip'shun) [L. *subscriptio,* to write under]. The part of a prescription preceding the signature, in which are the directions for compounding.

subspina'le. Point A; the most posterior midline point on the premaxilla between the anterior nasal spine and the prosthion.

substance (sub'stans) [L. *substantia,* essence, material]. Matter; stuff; material. See also substantia.

   blood group-specific s.'s A and B, solution of complexes of polysaccharides and amino acids that reduces the titer of anti-A and -B isoagglutinins in serum from group O persons; used to render group O blood reasonably safe for transfusion into persons of group A, B, or AB, but does not affect any imcompatibility that results from various other factors, such as Rh.

   controlled s., any drug or agent whose prescription or dispensing is regulated by the Controlled Substances Act.

   cortical s., *substantia corticalis.*

   gray s., *substantia grisea.*

   ground s., the amorphous material in which structural elements occur; in connective tissue, composed of protein polysaccharides, tissue fluids, and metabolites present between cells and fibers.

   medullary s., substantia medullaris (2); (1) the fatty material present in the myelin sheath of nerve fibers; (2) medulla of bones and other organs.

   Nissl s., Nissl bodies or granules; material consisting of granular endoplasmic reticulum and ribosomes which occurs in nerve cell bodies and dendrites.

   s. P, a tachykinin of eleven amino acids, present in the brain and intestines that affects smooth muscle (dilation of blood vessels and contraction of intestine) and produces pain.

   perforated s., *substantia perforata.*

   reticular s., (1) a filamentous plasmatic material, beaded with granules, demonstrable by vital staining in the immature red blood cells; (2) *formatio reticularis.*

   Rolando's gelatinous s., *substantia gelatinosa.*

   slow-reacting s. (of anaphylaxis) (SRS, SRS-A), a s. released in anaphylactic shock which produces slower and more prolonged contraction of muscle than does histamine.

   threshold s., threshold body; any material excreted in the urine only when its plasma concentration exceeds a certain value.

   white s., *substantia* alba.

substantia, pl. **substantiae** (sub-stan'shĭah, -shĭ-e) [L.] [NA]. Substance.

   s. al'ba [NA], alba; white substance or matter; those regions of the brain and spinal cord largely or entirely composed of nerve fibers and contain few or no neuronal cell bodies or dendrites.

   s. compac'ta [NA], compact bone; the compact noncancellous portion of bone that consists largely of concentric lamellar osteons and interstitial lamellae.

   s. cortica'lis [NA], cortical bone or substance; cortex; the superficial thin layer of compact bone.

   s. gelatino'sa [NA], Rolando's gelatinous substance; the apical part of the posterior horn of the spinal cord's gray matter, composed largely of very small nerve cells very few myelinated nerve fibers.

   s. gris'ea [NA], gray substance or matter; those regions of the brain and spinal cord made up primarily of the cell bodies and dendrites of nerve cells rather than myelinated axons.

   s. medulla'ris, (1) medulla; (2) medullary *substance.*

   s. ni'gra [NA], nigra; a large cell mass extending forward over the dorsal surface of the crus cerebri from the rostral border of the pons into the subthalamus; composed of a dorsal stratum of closely spaced pigmented cells and numerous cells that contain dopamine; destruction or dysfunction of the s. nigra is associated with Parkinson's disease.

   s. perfora'ta [NA], (1) anterior: a region at the base of the brain through which numerous small branches of the anterior and middle cerebral arteries enter the cerebral hemisphere; (2) posterior: the bottom of the interpeduncular fossa at the base of the midbrain containing numerous openings for the passage of branches of the posterior cerebral arteries.

   s. pro'pria [NA], (1) transparent connective tissue, between the layers of which are spaces containing corneal cells; (2) dense white fibrous tissue arranged in interlacing bundles that forms the main mass of the sclera.

   s. spongio'sa [NA], spongy bone (1); cancellous or trabecular bone; bone in which the spicules or trabeculae form a latticework with interstices filled with embryonal connective tissue or bone marrow.

substitution (sub-stĭ-tu'shun) [L. *substitutio*]. **1.** In chemistry, the replacement of an atom or group in a compound by another. **2.** In psychiatry, an unconscious defense mechanism by which the unacceptable or unattainable is replaced by one that which is more acceptable or attainable.

sub'strate [L. *sub-sterno,* pp. *-stratus,* to spread under]. The substance acted upon and changed by an enzyme.

substruc'ture. A tissue or structure wholly or partly beneath the surface.

subthalam'ic. Related to the subthalamus or to the subthalamic nucleus.

subthal'amus. That part of the diencephalon wedged between the thalamus on the dorsal side and the cerebral peduncle ventrally, lateral to the dorsal half of the hypothalamus from which it cannot be sharply delineated; caudally continuous with the midbrain tegmentum.

sub'tribe. In biologic classification, a division between tribe and genus.

subungual, subunguial (sub-ung'gwal, sub-ung'gwĭ-al) [L. *unguis*, nail]. Hyponychial (1); beneath the finger or toe nail.

subvaginal (sub-vaj'ĭ-nal). **1.** Below the vagina. **2.** On the inner side of any sheath.

subvolu'tion [L. *sub*, under, + *volvo*, pp. *volutus*, to turn]. Turning over a flap of mucous membrane to prevent adhesion.

succinate (suk'sĭ-nāt). A salt of succinic acid.

succinic acid (suk-sin'ik). 1,4-Butanedioic acid; HOOC(CH$_2$)$_2$COOH; an intermediate in the tricarboxylic acid cycle.

suc'cinylcho'line chloride. A neuromuscular relaxant with short duration of action; used to produce relaxation during surgical anesthesia.

succinyl-CoA. Succinylcoenzyme A.

succinylcoenzyme (suk'sĭ-nil-ko-en'zīm). Succinyl-CoA; the condensation product of succinic acid and CoA; one of the intermediates of the tricarboxylic acid cycle.

succorrhea (suk'o-re'ah) [L. *succus*, juice, + G. *rhoia*, a flow]. Abnormal increase in the secretion of a digestive fluid.

succubus (suk'u-bus) [L. *succubo*, to lie under]. A demon, in female form, believed to have sexual intercourse with a man during sleep.

succus, pl. **succi** (suk'us, suk'si) [L.]. **1.** The fluid constituents of the body tissues. **2.** A fluid secretion, especially the digestive juices. **3.** Formerly, a pharmacopeial preparation obtained by expressing the juice of a plant and adding to it sufficient alcohol to preserve it.

su'crase. β-Fructofuranosidase.

su'crose. Saccharum; C$_{12}$H$_{22}$O$_{11}$; a nonreducing disaccharide made up of glucose and fructose, obtained from sugar cane, several species of sorghum, and the sugar beet.

sucrosemia (su-kro-se'mĭ-ah) [sucrose + G. *haima*, blood]. Presence of sucrose in the blood.

sucrosuria (su-kro-su'rĭ-ah) [sucrose + G. *ouron*, urine]. Excretion of sucrose in the urine.

suctorial (suk-to'rĭ-al). Relating to or adapted for sucking.

sudamen, pl. **sudamina** (su-da'men, -dam'ĭ-nah) [Mod. L. fr. *sudo*, to sweat]. A minute vesicle due to retention of fluid in a sweat follicle or in the epidermis.

sudam'inal. Relating to sudamina.

Sudan. Any of a variety of dyes used to stain for fats.

sudanophilic (su-dan-o-fil'ik). Staining easily with Sudan dyes, usually referring to lipids in tissues.

sudanophobic (su-dan-o-fo'bik). Denoting tissue that fails to stain with a Sudan dye.

sudation (su-da'shun) [L. *sudatio*, fr. *sudo*, pp. *-atus*, to sweat]. Perspiration (1).

sudomo'tor [L. *sudor*, sweat, + *motor*, mover]. Denoting the nerves that stimulate the sweat glands to activity.

sudor- [L. *sudor*, sweat]. Combining form denoting sweat, perspiration.

su'dor [L.]. Perspiration (3).

su'doral. Relating to perspiration.

sudoresis (su-do-re'sis) [sudor- G. *-ēsis*, condition]. Profuse sweating.

sudoriferous (su-do-rif'er-us) [sudor- L. *fero*, to bear]. Carrying or producing sweat.

sudorific (su-do-rif'ik) [sudor- + L. *facio*, to make]. Causing sweat.

sudoriparous (su-do-rip'ă-rus) [sudo- + L. *pario*, to produce]. Secreting sweat.

suffocate (suf'o-kāt) [L. *suffoco*, pp. *-atus*, to choke, strangle]. **1.** To impede respiration; to asphyxiate. **2.** To suffer from lack of oxygen; to be unable to breathe.

suffocation (suf'o-ka'shun). The act or condition of suffocating.

suffusion (suf-fu'zhun) [L. *suffusio*, to pour out]. **1.** The act of pouring a fluid over the body. **2.** Reddening of the surface. **3.** The condition of being wet with a fluid. **4.** Extravasate (2).

sugar [G. *sakcharon*; L. *saccharum*]. One of the sugars.

    blood s., glucose.

    brain s., galactose.

    deoxy s., desose; a s. containing fewer oxygen atoms than carbon atoms and in which, consequently, one or more carbons in the molecule lack an attached hydroxyl group.

    fruit s., fructose.

    invert s., a mixture of equal parts of glucose and fructose.

sugars. Saccharides; those carbohydrates having the general composition (CH$_2$O)$_n$ and simple derivatives thereof; generally identifiable by the ending -ose or, if in combination with a nonsugar, -oside or -osyl. S.'s, especially glucose, are the chief source of energy and in polymeric form are major constituents of mucoproteins, bacterial cell walls, and plant structural material.

suggestibility (sug-jes'tĭ-bil'ĭ-tĭ). Sympathism; responsiveness or susceptibility to a psychological process whereby an idea is induced into, or adopted by, an individual without argument, command, or coercion.

suggestible (sug-jes'tĭ-bl). Susceptible to suggestion.

suggestion (sug-jes'chun) [L. *sug-gero*, pp. *-gestus*, to bring under]. Implanting of an idea in the mind of another by some word or act, the subject being influenced in his conduct or physical condition.

posthypnotic s., s. given to a subject who is under hypnosis for certain actions to be performed after removal from the hypnotic trance.

suggillation (sug-jĭ-la'shun, suj'i-) [L. *suggillo*, pp. *-atus*, to beat black and blue]. **1.** Ecchymosis; a black and blue mark. **2.** Livedo.

suicide (su'ĭ-sīd) [L. *sui*, self, + *caedō*, to kill]. The act of taking one's own life.

sulcal (sul'kal). Relating to a sulcus.

sulcate (sul'kāt). Grooved; furrowed; marked by a sulcus or sulci.

sulcus, gen. and pl. **sulci** (sul'kus, sul'si) [L. a furrow or ditch]. **1** [NA]. One of the grooves or furrows on the surface of the brain, bounding the several convolutions or gyri; a fissure. See also fissura. **2** [NA]. Any long narrow groove, furrow, or slight depression.

s. calcari'nus [NA], **calcarine s.,** calcarine fissure; a deep fissure on the medial aspect of the cerebral cortex, marking the border between the lingual gyrus below and the cuneus above.

s. centra'lis [NA], **central s.,** fissure of Rolando; a double-S-shaped fissure extending obliquely upward and backward on the lateral surface of each cerebral hemisphere at the border between the frontal and parietal lobes.

s. cin'guli [NA], **cingutate s.,** a fissure on the mesial surface of the cerebral hemisphere, bounding the upper surface of the gyrus cinguli, that curves up to the superomedial margin of the hemisphere and borders the paracentral lobule posteriorly.

s. collatera'lis [NA], **collateral s.,** collateral fissure; a long and deep sagittal fissure on the undersurface of the temporal lobe, marking the border between the fusiform gyrus on its lateral side and the hippocampal and lingual gyri on its medial side.

s. corona'rius [NA], **coronary s.,** atrioventricular groove; a groove on the outer surface of the heart marking the division between the atria and the ventricles.

s. fronta'lis [NA], **frontal s.,** inferior, a sagittal fissure on the outer surface of each frontal lobe of the cerebrum demarcating the middle from the inferior frontal gyrus; middle, a sagittal fissure dividing the middle frontal gyrus into an upper and lower part; superior, a sagittal fissure on the superior surface of each frontal lobe of the cerebrum forming the lateral boundary of the superior frontal gyrus.

s. gingiva'lis [NA], **gingival s.,** the space between the surface of the tooth and the free gingiva.

s. glute'us [NA], **gluteal s.,** gluteal furrow; the furrow between the buttock and thigh.

s. hippocam'pi [NA], **hippocampal s.,** hippocampal fissure; a shallow groove between the dentate gyrus and the parahippocampal gyrus.

s. interventricula'ris [NA], interventricular groove; anterior, a groove on the anterosuperior

surface of the heart indicating the septum between the two ventricles; posterior, a groove on the diaphragmatic surface of the heart indicating the septum between the two ventricles.

s. intraparieta'lis [NA], **intraparietal s.,** a horizontal s. extending back from the postcentral s. and dividing into two branches to form, with the postcentral s., a figure H that divides the parietal lobe into a superior and inferior parietal lobule.

s. latera'lis cer'ebri [NA], **lateral cerebral s.,** fissure of Sylvius; the deepest and most prominent of the cortical fissures, extending between the frontal and temporal lobes, then back and slightly upward over the lateral aspect of the cerebral hemisphere, with the superior temporal gyrus as its lower bank, the insula forming its greatly expanded floor; two short side branches divide the inferior frontal gyrus into three parts.

s. latera'lis poste'rior [NA], posterolateral groove; a longitudinal furrow on either side of the posterior median s. of the spinal cord and medulla oblongata, marking the line of entrance of the posterior nerve roots.

s. ma'tricis un'guis, groove of the nail matrix; the cutaneous furrow in which the lateral border of the nail is situated.

s. media'nus lin'guae [NA], median groove or longitudinal raphe of the tongue; a slight longitudinal depression running forward on the dorsal surface of the tongue from the foramen cecum.

s. media'nus poste'rior, [NA], posterior median s. or fissure; the longitudinal groove marking the posterior midline of the medulla oblongata, continuous below with the posterior median s. of the spinal cord.

s. olfacto'rius [NA], **olfactory s.,** olfactory groove; the sagittal s. on the inferior or orbital surface of each frontal lobe of the cerebrum, demarcating the gyrus rectus from the orbital gyri.

s. parietooccipita'lis [NA], **parietooccipital s.,** parietooccipital fissure; a very deep fissure on the medial surface of the cerebral cortex, marking the border between the parietal lobe and the cuneus of the occipital lobe; its lower part curves forward and fuses with the anterior extent of the calcarine sulcus.

s. poplite'us, popliteal *groove.*

s. postcentra'lis [NA], **postcentral s.,** the s. that demarcates the postcentral gyrus from the superior and inferior parietal lobules.

posterior median s., s. medianus posterior.

s. precentra'lis [NA], **precentral s.,** an interrupted fissure anterior to and in general parallel with the s. centralis, marking the anterior border of the precentral gyrus.

s. rhina'lis [NA], **rhinal s.,** the shallow s. that delimits the anterior part of the hippocampal gyrus from the fusiform or lateral occipitotemporal gyrus, marking the border between the neocortex and the allocortical (olfactory) and juxtallocortical areas medial to it.

s. scle'rae [NA], **s. of the sclera,** a slight groove on the external surface of the eyeball indicating the line of union of the sclera and cornea.

s. tempora'lis infe'rior [NA], **temporal s.,** inferior, the s. on the basal aspect of the temporal lobe that separates the fusiform gyrus from the inferior temporal gyrus on its lateral side; **middle,** the s. between the middle and inferior temporal gyri; **superior,** the longitudinal s. that separates the superior and middle temporal gyri.

s. termina'lis [NA], **terminal s.,** a V-shaped groove, with apex pointing backward, on the surface of the tongue, marking the separation between the oral, or horizontal, and pharyngeal, or vertical, parts.

sulf-, sulfo-. Prefix denoting sulfur, sulfonic acid, or sulfonate.

sulfa (sul'fah). The sulfa drugs, or sulfonamides.

sulfatase (sul'fă-tās). Trivial name for the sulfuric ester hydrolase enzymes, which catalyze the hydrolysis of sulfuric esters (sulfates) to the corresponding alcohols plus inorganic sulfate.

sul'fate. A salt or ester of sulfuric acid (H_2SO_4).

sul'fatidates, sul'fatides. Cerebroside sulfuric esters containing sulfate groups in the sugar portion of the molecule.

sulfation (sul-fa'shun). Addition of sulfate groups as esters to preexisting molecules.

sulfhemoglobin (sulf-he'mo-glo-bin). Sulfmethemoglobin.

sulfhe'moglobine'mia. Presence of sulfhemoglobin in the blood, marked by persistent cyanosis, but the blood count does not reveal any special abnormality in that fluid.

sulfhy'dryl. The radical, –SH.

sul'fide. A compound of sulfur in which sulfur has a valence of –2.

sul'fite. A salt of sulfurous acid (H_2SO_3).

s. oxidase, a liver oxidoreductase (a hemoprotein) catalyzing the oxidation of inorganic sulfate ion with O_2, producing H_2O_2.

sulfmethemoglobin (sulf-met-he'mo-glo-bin). Sulfhemoglobin; the complex formed by H_2S (or sulfides) and ferric ion in methemoglobin.

sulfo-. See sulf-.

sulfobromophthalein sodium (sul'fo-bro-mo-thal'e-in). Bromosulfophthalein; a triphenylmethane derivative excreted by the liver; used in testing hepatic function, particularly of the reticuloendothelial cells.

sulfon'amides. The sulfa drugs; a group of bacteriostatic drugs containing the sulfanilamide group (sulfanilamide, sulfapyridine, sulfathiazole, sulfadiazine, and other derivatives).

sul'fonate. A salt or ester of sulfonic acid.

sul'fone. A compound of the general structure $R'-SO_2-R''$.

sulfon'ic acid. Any compound in which a hydrogen atom of a CH group is replaced by the sulfonic acid group, $-SO_3H$.

sulfonylureas (sul'fo-nil-u-re'ahz). Derivatives of isopropylthiodiazylsulfanilamide, chemically related to the sulfonamides, that possess hypoglycemic action.

sulfosalicylic acid (sul'fo-sal-ĭ-sil'ik). HOC_6H_3-$(CO_2H)SO_3H$; used as a test for albumin and ferric ion.

sulfotrans'ferase. Generic term for enzymes catalyzing the transfer of a sulfate group from 3'-phosphoadenylyl sulfate to the hydroxyl group of an acceptor.

sulfox'ide. The sulfur analogue of a ketone, $R'-SO-R''$.

sul'fur [L. *sulfur, sulphur,* brimstone]. An element, symbol S, atomic no. 16, atomic weight 32.066, that combines with oxygen to form s. dioxide and s. trioxide, and with many of the metals and nonmetallic elements to form sulfides.

sulfur-35 (^{35}S). A radioactive sulfur isotope; a beta emitter with half-life of 87.1 days; used as a tracer in metabolic studies.

sul'furate. To combine with sulfur.

sulfu'ric acid. H_2SO_4; a colorless, nearly odorless, corrosive liquid containing 96% of the absolute acid; used occasionally as a caustic.

sulfurous (sul'fu-rus). Designating a sulfur compound in which sulfur has a valence of +4.

sulfuryl (sul'fu-ril). The bivalent radical, SO_2.

sulph-, sulpho-. See sulf-, sulfo-.

sumac (su'mak) [Ar. *summaq*]. *Rhus glabra.*

summation (sum-a'shun) [Med. L. *summatio,* fr. *summo,* pp. *-atus,* to sum up, fr. L. *summa,* sum]. The aggregation of a number of similars, as the muscular or neural effects produced by the frequent repetition of slight stimuli, one of which alone might be without evident response.

sunburn. Erythema caused by exposure to critical amounts of ultraviolet light, usually within the range of 2600 to 3200 Å.

sunstroke. A form of heatstroke resulting from undue exposure to the sun's rays; symptoms are those of heatstroke, often without fever, but with prostration and collapse.

super- [L. *super,* above, beyond]. Prefix denoting in excess, above, superior, or in the upper part of. See also hyper-, supra-.

superacute (su'per-ă-kūt'). Extremely acute, marked by great severity of symptoms and rapid progress; denoting the course of a disease.

supercil'iary. Relating to or in the region of the eyebrow.

supercilium, pl. **supercilia** (su-per-sil'ĭ-um, -ah) [L. *super,* above, + *cilium,* eyelid] [NA]. **1.** Eyebrow; the line of hairs at the superior edge of the orbit. **2.** An individual hair of the eyebrow.

superduct' [L. *super-duco,* pp. *-ductus,* to lead over]. To elevate or draw upward.

supere'go. In psychoanalytic theory, an outgrowth of the ego that has identified itself unconsciously with important persons from early life, and which results from incorporating the values and wishes of these persons as part of one's own standards to form the "conscience."

su'perexcita'tion. 1. The act of exciting or stimulating unduly. **2.** Overstimulation; a condition of extreme excitement.

superficial (su-per-fish'al) [L. *superficialis,* fr. *superficies,* surface]. **1.** Cursory; not thorough. **2.** Sublimis (2); situated nearer the surface of the body in relation to a specific reference point.

superficies (su-per-fish'ĭ-ēz) [L. the top surface]. Outer surface; facies.

superinduce (su'per-in-dūs). To induce or bring on in addition to something already existing.

su'perinfec'tion. A fresh infection added to one of the same nature already present.

su'perinvolu'tion. Hyperinvolution; an extreme reduction in size of the uterus, after childbirth, below the normal size of the nongravid organ.

superior (su-pe'r'ĭ-or) [L. comparative of *superus,* above]. **1.** Situated above or directed upward. **2** [NA]. Cranial (2); in human anatomy, situated nearer the vertex of the head in relation to a specific reference point.

su'permotil'ity. Hyperkinesis.

supernumerary (su-per-nu'mer-ār-ĭ) [super- + L. *numerus,* number]. Epactal; exceeding the normal number.

su'perolat'eral. At the side and above.

superox'ide. The molecule HO_2, a strong acid, hence often written as $H^+ + O_2^-$, the latter being the superoxide radical.

　s. dismutase, an enzyme decomposing the superoxide radical to $O_2 + H_2O_2$ (with consumption of hydrogen ion).

supersat'urate. To make a solution hold more of a salt or other substance in solution than it will dissolve when in equilibrium with that salt in the solid phase.

superscription (su'per-skrip'shun) [L. *super-scribo,* pp. *-sciptus,* to write upon or over]. The beginning of a prescription, consisting of the injunction, *recipe,* take, usually denoted by the sign ℞.

supersonic (su'per-son'ik) [super- + L. *sonus,* sound]. **1.** Pertaining to or characterized by a speed greater than that of sound. **2.** Pertaining to sound vibrations of high frequency, above the level of human audibility.

superstruc'ture. A structure above the surface.

supinate (su'pĭ-nāt) [L. *supino,* pp. *-atus,* to bend backwards, place on back]. **1.** To assume, or to be placed in, a supine position. **2.** To perform supination.

supination (su'pĭ-na'shun). The condition or act of assuming or of being placed in a supine position, as inversion and abduction of the foot, causing an elevation of the medial edge, rotation of the forearm in such a way that the palm of the hand faces forward when the arm is in the anatomical position, or upward when the arm is extended at a right angle to the body.

supine (su-pīn') [L. *supinus*]. Denoting the hand or foot in supination, or the body when lying face upward.

suppository (sŭ-poz'ĭ-tōr-ĭ) [L. *suppositorius,* placed underneath]. A medicated mass shaped for introduction into one of the orifices of the body other than the oral cavity, solid at ordinary temperatures, and dissolving at body temperature.

suppression (sŭ-presh'un) [L. *sub-primo,* pp. *-pressus,* to press down]. **1.** Deliberately excluding from conscious thought, as distinguished from repression. **2.** Arrest of the secretion of a fluid, as distinguished from retention. **3.** Checking of an abnormal flow or discharge. **4.** The effect of a second mutation which cancels a phenotypic change caused by a previous mutation at a different point on the chromosome.

sup'purant [L. *suppurans,* causing suppuration]. Causing or inducing suppuration.

sup'purate [L. *sup-puro,* pp. *-atus*]. To form pus.

suppuration (sup-u-ra'shun) [L. *suppuratio* (see suppurate)]. Pyesis; pyosis; pyopoiesis; pyogenesis; the formation of pus.

sup'purative. Forming pus.

supra- [L. above]. Prefix denoting a position above. See also super-.

suprabulge (su'prä-bulj'). The portion of the crown of a tooth that converges toward the occlusal surface of the tooth.

suprachoroid (su-prä-ko'royd). On the outer side of the choroid of the eye.

suprachoroidea (su'prä-ko-roy'dĭ-ah). *Lamina* suprachoroidea.

supracos'tal. Above the ribs.

supracris'tal. Above a crest.

supraduc'tion. Sursumduction; the moving upward of one eye independently of its fellow by base-down prisms.

supraliminal (su'prä-lim'ĭ-nal) [supra- + L. *limen,* threshold]. More than just perceptible; above the threshhold for conscious awareness.

supramaxil'la. The maxilla.

supramax'illary. Relating to the maxilla.

supramenta'le [supra- + L. *mentum,* chin]. Point B; the most posterior midline point, above the chin, on the mandibula between the infradentate and the pogonion.

supranuclear (su-prä-nu'kle-ar). **1.** Cranial to the level of the motor neurons of the spinal or cranial nerves; indicating disorders of movement caused by destruction or functional impairment of brain structures other than the motor neurons, such as the motor cortex, pyramidal tract, or corpus striatum. **2.** Denoting the part of a cell between the nucleus and the distal border.

supraocclusion (su'prä-o-klu'zhun). An occlusal relationship in which a tooth extends beyond the occlusal plane.

suprarenalectomy (su'prä-re-nal-ek'to-mĭ). Adrenalectomy.

suprascle'ral. On the outer side of the sclera, denoting the space between the sclera and the fascia bulbi.

su'praventric'ular. Above the ventricles; especially applied to rhythms originating from centers proximal to the ventricles, in the atrium or A-V node.

supravergence (su-pră-ver'jens) [supra- + L. *vergo*, to incline or turn]. Sursumvergence; upward rotation of an eye, the other eye remaining stationary.

supraversion (su-pră-ver'zhun) [supra- + L. *verto*, pp. *versus*, to turn]. **1.** A turning upward. **2.** In dentistry, the position of a tooth when it is out of the line of occlusion in an occlusal direction; a deep overbite. **3.** In opthalmology, binocular conjugate movement upward.

sura (su'rah) [L.] [NA]. Calf; the muscular swelling of the back of the leg below the knee, formed chiefly by the bellies of the gastrocnemius and soleus muscles.

su'ral. Relating to the calf of the leg.

sur'face [F. fr. L. *superficies,* see superficial]. Facies (2); the outer part of any solid structure.

surface-active. Indicating the property of certain agents of altering the physicochemical nature of surfaces and interfaces, bringing about lowering of interfacial tension.

surfactant (sur-fak'tant). **1.** A surface-active agent; includes substances commonly referred to as wetting agents, surface tension depressants, detergents, dispersing agents, emulsifiers. **2.** Term in current use to describe those surface-active agents forming a monomolecular layer over pulmonary alveolar surfaces and stablizing alveolar volume by reducing surface tension and altering the relationship between surface tension and surface area.

surgeon (sur'jun) [G. *cheirourgos;* L. *chirurgus*]. A physician who treats disease, injury, and deformity by operation or manipulation.

  dental s., a general practitioner of dentistry, with the D.D.S. or D.M.D. degree.

surgery (sur'jĕ-rī) [L. *chirurgia;* G. *cheir,* hand, + *ergon,* work]. **1.** The branch of medicine concerned with the treatment of disease, injury, and deformity by operation or manipulation. **2.** The performance or procedures of an operation.

  ambulatory s., operative procedures performed on patients who are admitted to and discharged from the hospital on the same day.

  aseptic s., the performance of an operation under sterilized conditions, utilizing precautions against the introduction of infectious microorganisms.

  closed s., s. without incision into skin, *e.g.,* reduction of a fracture or dislocation.

  cosmetic s., esthetic s., s. in which the principal purpose is to improve the appearance, usually beyond the normal and its acceptable variations.

  open heart s., direct vision correction of intracardiac disease.

  oral s., the branch of dentistry concerned with the diagnosis and surgical and adjunctive treatment of diseases, injuries, and deformities of the oral and maxillofacial region.

  plastic s., the surgical specialty or procedure concerned with the restoration, construction, reconstruction, or improvement in the shape and appearance of body structures that are missing, defective, damaged, or misshapened.

  reconstructive s., see plastic s.

  stereotactic s., stereotaxic s., stereotaxy.

surgical (sur'ji-kal). Relating to surgery.

surrogate (sur'o-gāt) [L. *surrogare,* to put in another's place]. **1.** A person who functions in another's life as a substitute for some third person. **2.** A person who reminds one of another person so that one uses the first as an emotional substitute for the second.

sursumduction (sur-sum-duk'shun) [L. *sursum,* upward, + *duco,* pp. *-ductus,* to draw]. Supraduction.

sursumvergence (sur-sum-ver'jens) [L. *sursum,* upward, + *vergo,* to bend]. Supravergence.

sursumversion (sur-sum-ver'zhun) [L. *sursum,* upward, + *verto,* pp. *versus,* to turn]. The act of moving the eyes upward.

suspen'sion [L. *suspensio,* fr. *sus-pendo,* pp. *-pensus,* to hang up, suspend]. **1.** Fixation of an organ to other tissue for support. **2.** Dispersion through a liquid of a solid in finely divided particles of a size large enough to be detected by purely optical means. **3.** A class of pharmacopeial preparations of finely divided, undissolved drugs dispersed in liquid vehicles for oral or parenteral use.

suspensoid (sus-pen'soyd) [suspension + G. *eidos,* resemblance]. A colloid solution in which the disperse particles are solid and lyophobe or hydrophobe, and are therefore sharply demarcated from the fluid in which they are suspended.

suspen'sory. 1. Suspending; supporting; denoting a ligament, a muscle, or other structure that keeps an organ or other part in place. **2.** A supporter applied to uplift a dependent part, such as the scrotum or a pendulous breast.

sustentac'ular. Relating to a sustentaculum; supporting.

sustentaculum, pl. **sustentacula** (sus-ten-tak'u-lum, -lah) [L. a prop] [NA]. A structure that serves as a stay or support to another.

sutura, pl. **suturae** (su-tu'rah, -re) [L. a sewing, a suture] [NA]. Suture (1); a form of fibrous joint in which two bones formed in membrane are united by a fibrous membrane continuous with the periosteum.

  s. corona'lis [NA], coronal suture; the line of junction of the frontal with the two parietal bones.

  s. fronta'lis [NA], frontal suture; the suture between the two halves of the frontal bone, usually obliterated by about the sixth year.

  s. intermaxilla'ris [NA], intermaxillary suture; the line of union of the two maxillae.

  s. internasa'lis [NA], internasal suture; line of union between the two nasal bones.

s. lambdoi'dea [NA], lambdoid suture; line of union between the occipital and the parietal bones.

s. meto'pica [NA], metopic suture; a persistent frontal suture.

s. pla'na [NA], plane or harmonic suture; harmonia; a simple firm apposition of two smooth surfaces of bones, without overlap.

s. sagitta'lis [NA], sagittal or interparietal suture; line of union between the two parietal bones.

s. serra'ta [NA], serrate or dentate suture; one whose opposing margins present deep sawlike indentations.

s. squamo'sa [NA], squamous suture; a suture whose opposing margins are scalelike and overlapping.

sutural (su'chur-al). Relating to a suture.

suture (su'chŭr) [L. *sutura*, a seam]. **1.** Sutura. **2.** Stitch (3); to unite two surfaces by sewing. **3.** The surgical material so used. **4.** The seam so formed.

absorbable s., a surgical s. material prepared from a substance that can be digested by body tissues.

apposition s., coaptation s.; a s. of the skin only.

approximation s., a s. that pulls together the deep tissues.

atraumatic s., a s. affixed to the end of an eyeless needle.

blanket s., a continuous lock-stitch used to approximate the skin of a wound.

buried s., any s. placed entirely below the surface of the skin.

button s., a s. passed through a button and then tied to prevent the threads cutting through the flesh.

coaptation a., apposition s.

cobbler's s., doubly-armed s.

continuous s., an uninterrupted series of stitches using one s., fastened at each end by a knot.

coronal s., *sutura* coronalis.

cranial s's, the s.'s between the bones of the skull.

Czerny's s., the first row of the Czerny-Lembert intestinal s.: the needle enters the serosa and passes out through the submucosa or muscularis, and then enters the submucosa or muscularis of the opposite side and emerges from the serosa.

Czerny-Lembert s., an intestinal s. in two rows combining the Czerny s. (first) and the Lembert s. (second).

dentate s., *sutura* serrata.

doubly armed s., cobbler's s.; a s. with a needle at both ends.

false s., sutura notha; a s. whose opposing margins are smooth or present only a few ill-defined projections.

far-and-near s., a s. utilizing alternate near and far stitches, used to approximate fascial edges.

figure-8 s., a s. utilizing criss-cross stitches, used to approximate fascial edges.

frontal s., *sutura* frontalis.

glover's s., a continuous s. in which each stitch is passed through the loop of the preceding one.

Halsted's s., a s. placed through the subcuticular fascia; used for exact skin approximation.

harmonic s., *sutura* plana.

implanted s., passage of a pin through each lip of the wound parallel to the line of incision, the pins then being looped together with s.'s.

intermaxillary s., *sutura* intermaxillaris.

internasal s., *sutura* internasalis.

interparietal s., *sutura* sagittalis.

interrupted s., a single stitch fixed by tying ends together.

lambdoid s., *sutura* lambdoidea.

Lembert s., the second row of the Czerny-Lembert intestinal s.; an inverting s. for intestinal surgery, used either as a continuous s. or interrupted s., producing serosal apposition and including the collagenous submucosal layer but not entering the lumen of the intestine.

mattress s., a s. utilizing a double stitch that forms a loop about the tissue on both sides of a wound, producing eversion of the edges when tied.

metopic s., *sutura* metopica.

nonabsorbable s., surgical s. material unaffected by the biological activities of the body tissues therefore permanent unless removed.

plane s., *sutura* plana.

purse-string s., a continuous s. placed in a circular manner either for inversion or closure.

relaxation s., a s. so arranged that it may be loosened if the tension of the wound becomes excessive.

retention s., a heavy reinforcing s. placed deep within the muscles and fasciae of the abdominal wall to relieve tension on the primary s. line and thus obviate postoperative wound disruption.

sagittal s., *sutura* sagittalis.

serrate s., *sutura* serrata.

squamous s., *sutura* squamosa.

tension s., a large s. of heavy material placed through and through both sides of a wound in order to prevent disruption.

transfixion s., (1) a criss-cross stitch so placed as to control bleeding from a tissue surface or small vessel when tied; (2) a s. used to fix the columella to the nasal septum.

uninterrupted s., continuous s.

wedge-and-groove s., schindylesis.

Svedberg of flotation. Flotation *constant.*

swab (swob). A wad of cotton, gauze, or other absorbent material used for applying or removing a substance from a surface.

swallow (swol'o) [A.S. *swelgan*]. To pass anything through the fauces, pharynx, and esophagus into the stomach; to perform deglutition.

somatic s., an adult or mature swallowing pattern with muscular contractions which appear to be under control at a subconscious level.

visceral s., the immature swallowing pattern of an infant or a person with tongue thrust, resembling peristaltic wavelike muscular contractions observed in the gut.

sweat (swet) [*A.S. swāt*]. **1.** Perspiration (3); especially sensible perspiration. **2.** To perspire.

sweat'ing. Perspiration (1).

swell'ing. 1. An abnormal enlargement not due to an increase in cell numbers. **2.** In embryology, a primordial elevation that develops into a fold, ridge, or process.

brain s., a pathologic entity, localized or generalized, characterized by an increase in bulk of brain tissue, due to expansion of the intravascular (congestion) or extravascular (edema) compartments.

cloudy s., isosmotic s., albuminous, hydropic, or parenchymatous degeneration; s. of cells due to injury to the membranes affecting ionic transfer, causing an accumulation of intracellular water.

Neufeld capsular s., Neufeld reaction; quellung reaction or phenomenon; an increase in opacity and visibility of the capsule of capsulated organisms exposed to specific agglutinating anticapsular antibodies.

sycoma (si-ko'mah) [G. *sykon*, fig, + *-oma*, tumor]. A pendulous figlike growth; a large soft wart.

syco'siform. Resembling sycosis.

sycosis (si-ko'sis) [G. *sykōn*, fig, + *-osis*, condition]. Ficosis; a pustular folliculitis, particularly of the bearded area.

lupoid s., ulerythema sycosiforme; a papular or pustular inflammation of the hair follicles of the beard, followed by punctuate scarring and loss of the hair.

syl'vian. Relating to Franciscus or Jacobus Sylvius, or to any of the structures described by either of them.

sym-. See syn-.

symballophone (sim-bal'o-fōn) [G. *symballō*, to throw together, + *phōnē*, sound]. A stethoscope having two chest pieces, designed to lateralize sound.

symbion, symbiont (sim'bī-on, -ont) [G. *symbiōn*, neut. of *symbiōs*, living together]. Mutualist; symbiote; an organism associated with another in symbiosis.

symbiosis (sim-bī-o'sis) [G. *symbiōsis*, state of living together]. **1.** Any intimate association between two species; *e.g.,* mutualism, commensalism, parasitism. **2.** In psychiatry, the mutual cooperation or interdependence of two persons; sometimes denoting excessive or pathological interdependence.

symbiote (sim'bī-ōt). Symbion.

symbiotic (sim-bī-ot'ik). Relating to symbiosis.

symblepharon (sim-belf'ă-ron) [sym- + G. *blepharon,* eyelid]. Adhesion of one or both lids to the eyeball.

symblepharopterygium (sim-blef'ă-ro-tĕ-rij'ĭ-um). Union of the lid to the eyeball through a pterygium-like cicatricial band.

symbolism (sim'bo-lizm). **1.** In psychoanalysis, the process involved in the disguised representation in consciousness of unconscious or repressed contents

or events. **2.** A mental state in which everything that happens is regarded by the individual as symbolic of his thoughts.

symbolization (sim'bo-lĭ-za'shun). An unconscious mental mechanism whereby one object or idea is represented by another.

symbrachydactyly (sim-brak'ĭ-dak'tĭ-lĭ) [sym- + G. *brachys,* short, + *daktylos,* finger]. A condition in which abnormally short fingers are joined or webbed in their proximal portions.

symmetry (sim'ĕ-trĭ) [G. *symmetria,* fr. sym- + *metron,* measure]. Equality or correspondence in form of parts distributed around a center or an axis, at the extremities or poles, or on the opposite sides of any body.

sympath-, sympatheto-, sympathico-, sympatho-. Combining forms relating to the sympathetic part of the autonomic nervous system.

sympathec'tomy [sympath- + G. *ektomē,* excision]. Excision of a segment of a sympathetic nerve or of one or more sympathetic ganglia.

periarterial s., sympathetic denervation by arterial decortication.

presacral s., presacral *neurectomy.*

sympathet'ic [G. *syn,* with, + *pathos,* suffering]. **1.** Relating to or exhibiting sympathy. **2.** Denoting the sympathetic part of the autonomic nervous system.

sympathet'oblast. Sympathoblast.

sympathet'oblasto'ma. Sympathoblastoma.

sympathico-. See sympath-.

sympath'icoblast. Sympathoblast.

sympath'icoblasto'ma. Sympathoblastoma.

sympath'icogonio'ma. Sympathoblastoma.

sympath'icolyt'ic. Sympatholytic.

sympath'icomimet'ic. Sympathomimetic.

sympathicotonia (sim-path'ĭ-ko-to'nĭ-ah) [sympathico- + G. *tonos,* tone]. A condition in which there is increased tonus of the sympathetic system and a marked tendency to vascular spasm and high blood pressure.

sympath'icoton'ic. Relating to or characterized by sympathicotonia.

sympathicotripsy (sim-path'ĭ-ko-trip'sĭ) [sympathico- + G. *tripsis,* a rubbing]. Surgical crushing of the sympathetic ganglion.

sympathicotropic (sim-path'ĭ-ko-trop'ik) [sympathico- + G. *tropikos,* inclined]. Having a special affinity for the sympathetic nervous system.

sympathin (sim'pă-thin). Sympathetic hormone; the substance diffusing into circulation from sympathetic nerve terminals when they are active.

sympatho-. See sympath-.

sym'pathoadre'nal. Relating to the sympathetic part of the autonomic nervous system and the medulla of the adrenal gland.

sympathoblast (sim'pă-tho-blast) [sympatho- + G. *blastos,* sprout]. Sympathetoblast; sympathicoblast; a primitive cell derived from the neural crest glia which enters into the formation of the adrenal medulla.

sympathoblastoma (sim'pă-tho-blas-to'mah) [sympathoblast + G. -oma, tumor]. Sympathicoblastoma; sympathetoblastoma; sympathicogonioma; sympathogonioma; a completely undifferentiated malignant tumor, composed of sympathoblasts, which originates from embryonal cells of the sympathetic nervous system.

sympathogonia (sim'pă-tho-go'nĭ-ah) [sympatho- + G. gonē, seed]. The completely undifferentiated cells of the sympathetic nervous system.

sympathogonioma (sim'pă-tho-go-nĭ-o'mah) [sympathogonia + G. -oma, tumor]. Sympathoblastoma.

sympatholytic (sim'pă-tho-lit'ik) [sympatho- + G. lysis, a loosening]. Sympathicolytic; denoting antagonism to or inhibition of adrenergic nerve activity.

sympathomimetic (sim-păth'o-mĭ-met'ik) [sympatho- + G. mimikos, imitating]. Sympathicomimetic; denoting mimicking of action of the sympathetic system.

sympathy (sim'pă-thĭ) [G. sym- + pathos, suffering]. **1.** The mutual relation, physiologic or pathologic, between two organs, systems, or parts of the body. **2.** Mental contagion, as seen in yawning induced by seeing another person yawn. **3.** An expressed sensitive appreciation or emotional concern for and sharing of the mental and emotional state of another person, as distinguished from empathy (1).

symphalangism, symphalangy (sim-fal'an-jizm, sim-fal'an-jĭ) [sym- + phalanx]. **1.** Syndactyly. **2.** Ankylosis of the finger or toe joints.

symphysial, symphyseal (sim-fiz'e-al). Relating to a symphysis; grown together; fused.

symphysion (sim-fiz'ĭ-on). The most anterior point of the alveolar process of the mandible.

symphysiotomy (sim-fiz'ĭ-ot'-o-mĭ) [symphysis + G. tomē, incision]. Pelviotomy (1); synchondrotomy; division of the pubic symphysis to increase the capacity of a contracted pelvis sufficiently to permit the passage of a living child.

symphysis, pl. **symphyses** (sim'fĭ-sis, -sēz) [G. a growing together]. **1.** [NA]. A form of cartilaginous joint in which union between two bones is effected by means of fibrocartilage. **2.** A union, meeting point, or commissure of any two structures. **3.** A pathologic adhesion or growing together.

    s. menta'lis [NA], **mental s.,** the fibrocartilaginous union of the two halves of the mandible which becomes an osseous union during the first year.

    s. pu'bica [NA], **pubic s.,** the firm fibrocartilaginous joint between the two pubic bones.

sympodia (sim-po'dĭ-ah) [sym- + G. pous, foot]. Fusion of the feet, as in sirenomelia.

sym'port [sym- + L. porto, to carry]. The coupled transport of two different molecules or ions through a membrane in the same direction by a common carrier mechanism (symporter).

symptom (simp'tom) [G. symptōma]. Any morbid phenomenon or departure from the normal in function, appearance, or sensation which is experienced by the patient and indicative of disease. See also sign.

    accessory s., concomitant s.; a s. that usually but not always accompanies a certain disease.

    cardinal s., the primary or major s.

    concomitant s., accessory s.

    constitutional s., a s. indicating that the disease has become general.

    deficiency s., the manifestation of a lack of some substance necessary for normal structure and function of an organism.

    Duroziez s., Duroziez murmur; a double murmur (systolic and diastolic) heard over the femoral artery in cases of aortic insufficiency.

    localizing s., a s. indicating clearly the seat of the morbid process.

    objective s., a s. evident to the observer; a sign.

    pathognomonic s., a s. that, when present, points unmistakably to a certain definite disease.

    reflex s., a disturbance of sensation or function in an organ or part not at the site of the morbid condition giving rise to it.

    subjective s., a s. apparent only to the patient himself.

    withdrawal s.'s, a group of morbid s.'s, predominantly erethistic, occurring in an addict deprived of the accustomed dose of the addicting agent.

symptomatic (simp'to-mat'ik). Indicative; relating to or constituting the semiology of symptoms of a disease.

symptomatology (simp'to-mă-tol'o-jĭ) [symptom + G. logos, study]. **1.** The science of the symptoms of disease, their production, and the indications they furnish. **2.** The aggregate of symptoms of a disease.

symptomatolytic (simp'to-mat'o-lit'ik) [symptom + G. lytikos, dissolving]. Removing symptoms.

symptosis (sim-to'sis) [G. syn, together, + ptōsis, a falling]. A localized or general wasting of the body.

syn- [G. syn, with, together]. Prefix indicating together; sym- before b, p, ph, or m.

synapse, pl. **synapses** (sin'aps, sĭ-naps', sĭ-nap'sēz) [syn- + G. haptein, to clasp]. The functional membrane-to-membrane contact of a nerve cell with another nerve cell, an effector (muscle, gland) cell, or a sensory receptor cell which subserves the transmission of nerve impulses from an axon terminal (presynaptic element) to the receiving cell's axon, dendrite, or plasma membrane (postsynaptic element); in most cases the impulse is transmitted by a chemical transmitter substance released into a synaptic cleft separating the presynaptic from the postsynaptic membrane; in others, transmission takes place by direct propagation of the bioelectrical potential from the presynaptic to the postsynaptic membrane.

synapsis (sĭ-nap'sis) [G. a connection, junction]. The point-for-point pairing of homologous chromosomes during the prophase of meiosis.

synap'tic. Relating to synapse or synapsis.

synarthrodia (sin-ar-thro'dĭ-ah) Articulatio fibrosa.

synarthro′dial. Relating to synarthrosis; denoting an articulation without a joint cavity.

synarthrophysis (sin-ar-thro-fi′sis) [syn- + G. *arthron*, joint, + *physis*, growth]. The process of ankylosis.

synarthrosis, pl. **synarthroses** (sin′ar-thro′sis, -sēz) [G. fr. *syn*, together, + *arthrōsis*, articulation]. *Articulatio fibrosa* or *articulatio cartilaginis*.

syncanthus (sin-kan′thus) [syn- + L. *canthus*, wheel]. Adhesion of the eyeball to orbital structures.

syncephaly (sin-sef′ă-lĭ). Conjoined twins having a single head.

syncheilia, synchilia (sin-ki′lĭ-ah) [syn- + G. *cheilos*, lip]. Congenital adhesion of the lips; atresia of the mouth.

syncheiria, synchiria (sin-ki′rĭ-ah) [syn- + G. *cheir*, hand]. A form of dyscheiria in which a stimulus applied to one side of the body is referred to both sides.

synchondroseotomy (sin-kon′dro-se-ot′o-mĭ) [synchondrosis + G. *tomē*, cutting]. Cutting through a synchondrosis, as through the sacroiliac ligaments and forcibly closing the arch of the pubes.

synchondrosis, pl. **synchondroses** (sin-kon-dro′sis, -sēz) [G. *syn*, together, + *chondros*, cartilage, + *-osis*, condition] [NA]. Synchondrodial joint; a union between two bones formed either by hyaline cartilage or fibrocartilage.

synchondrotomy (sin-kon-drot′o-mĭ). Symphysiotomy.

synchronia (sin-kro′nĭ-ah) [syn- + G. *chronos*, time]. **1.** Synchronism. **2.** Origin, development, involution, or functioning of tissues or organs at the usual time for such an event.

synchronism (sin′kro-nizm) [syn- + G. *chronos*, time]. Sychronia (1); simultaneous occurrence of two or more events.

synchronous (sin′kro-nus) [G. *synchronos*]. Occurring simultaneously.

synchysis (sin′kĭ-sis) [G. a mixing together, fr. syn- + *chysis*, a pouring]. Collapse of the collagenous framework of the vitreous humor with liquefaction of the vitreous body.

  s. scintil′lans, an appearance of glistening spots in the eye, due to cholesterol crystals floating in a fluid vitreous.

synclit′ic. Relating to or marked by synclitism.

synclitism (sin′klĭ-tizm) [G. *syn-klinō*, to incline together]. A condition of parallelism between the planes of the fetal head and of the pelvis, respectively.

synclonus (sin′klo-nus) [syn- + G. *klonos*, tumult]. Clonic spasm or tremor of several muscles.

syncopal (sin′ko-pal). Syncopic; relating to syncope.

syncope (sin′ko-pe) [G. *synkopē*, a cutting short, a swoon]. A fainting or swooning; a sudden fall of blood pressure or failure of the cardiac systole, resulting in cerebral anemia and subsequent loss of consciousness.

  carotid sinus s., s. resulting from overactivity of the carotid sinus; may be spontaneous or produced by pressure on a sensitive carotid sinus.

  laryngeal s., a paroxysmal neurosis characterized by attacks of coughing, with unusual sensations in the throat, followed by a brief period of unconsciousness.

  postural s., s. upon assuming an upright position caused by inadequate blood flow to the brain resulting from failure of normal vasconstrictive mechanisms.

  vasovagal s., vagal *attack.*

syncop′ic. Syncopal.

syncytial (sin-sish′al). Relating to a syncytium.

syncytiotrophoblast (sin-sish′ĭ-o-tro′fo-blast) [syncytium + trophoblast]. Syntrophoblast; the syncytial outer layer of the trophoblast.

syncytium, pl. **syncytia** (sin-sish′ĭ-um, -ah) [L. fr. syn- + G. *kytos*, cell]. A multinucleated protoplasmic mass formed by the secondary union of originally separate cells.

syndactyl′ia, syndac′tylism. Syndactyly.

syndac′tylous. Having fused or webbed fingers or toes.

syndactyly (sin-dak′tĭ-lĭ) [syn- + G. *daktylos*, finger or toe]. Syndactylia; syndactylism; symphalangism (1); any degree of webbing or fusion of the digits, involving soft parts only or including bone structure; usually autosomal dominant inheritance.

syndesis (sin-de′sis) [G. fr. syn- + G. *desis*, a binding]. Arthrodesis.

syndesm-. See syndesmo-.

syndesmectomy (sin-dez-mek′to-mĭ) [syndesm- + G. *ektomē*, excision]. Cutting away a section of a ligament.

syndesmectopia (sin′dez-mek-to′pĭ-ah) [syndesm- + G. *ektopos*, out of place]. Displacement of a ligament.

syndesmitis (sin-dez-mi′tis) [syndesm- + G. *-itis*, inflammation]. Inflammation of a ligament.

syndesmo-, syndesm- [G. *syndesmos*, a fastening]. Combining forms denoting a ligament or ligamentous.

syndesmopexy (sin-dez′mo-pek-sĭ) [syndesmo- + G. *pēxis*, fixation]. Surgical joining of two ligaments, or attachment of a ligament in a new place.

syndesmophyte (sin-dez′mo-fĭt) [syndesmo- + G. *phyton*, plant]. An osseous excrescence attached to a ligament.

syndesmoplasty (sin-dez′mo-plas-tĭ) [syndesmo- + G. *plassō*, to form]. Plastic surgery on a ligament.

syndesmorrhaphy (sin-dez-mor′ă-fĭ) [syndesmo- + G. *rhaphē*, suture]. Suture of ligaments.

syndesmosis, pl. **syndesmoses** (sin′dez-mo′sis, -sēz) [syndesmo- + G. *-osis*, condition] [NA]. Syndesmodial or syndesmotic joint; a form of fibrous joint in which opposing surfaces that are relatively far apart are united by ligaments.

syndesmotomy (sin-dez-mot′o-mĭ) [syndesmo- + G. *tomē*, incision]. Surgical division of a ligament.

syndrome (sin'drōm) [G. *syn*, together, + *dromos*, a running]. The aggregate of signs and symptoms associated with any morbid process and constituting together the picture of the disease.

Aarskog-Scott s., faciodigitogenital *dysplasia.*

abdominal muscle deficiency s., "prune belly" s.; congenital absence of abdominal muscles, in which the outline of the intestines is visible through the protruding abdominal wall.

acquired immunodeficiency s., AIDS.

Adams-Stokes s., Adams-Stokes disease; Stokes-Adams s. or disease; Morgagni's disease; slow or absent pulse, vertigo, syncope, convulsions, and sometimes Cheyne-Stokes respiration; usually as a result of heart block.

Adie s., Holmes-Adie s.

adrenogenital s., a group of disorders caused by adrenocortical hyperplasia or malignant tumors and characterized by masculinization, feminization, or precocious sexual development; representative of excessive or abnormal secretory patterns of adreno-cortical steroids.

adult respiratory distress s. (ARDS), interstitial and/or alveolar edema and hemorrhage as well as perivascular lung edema associated with hyaline membrane, proliferation of collagen fibers, and swollen epithelium with increased pinocytosis.

afferent loop s., obstruction of the duodenum and jejunum proximal to the gastrojejunostomy performed in a Billroth II type gastrectomy.

Ahumada-Del Castillo s., lactation-amenorrhea s. unrelated to a previous pregnancy.

Albright's s., (1) Albright's *disease;* (2) Albright's hereditary *osteodystrophy.*

alcohol amnestic s., an amnestic s. resulting from alcoholism and vitamin deficiency; usually, other neurological complications of alcohol and malnutrition may result, such as peripheral neuropathy and cerebellar ataxia.

Aldrich s., Wiskott-Aldrich s.

Alport's s., progressive nephropathy and nerve deafness, sometimes with ocular defects; autosomal dominant inheritance.

Alström's s., retinal degeneration with nystagmus and loss of central vision, nerve deafness, and diabetes, associated with obesity in childhood; autosomal recessive inheritance.

amenorrhea-galactorrhea s., nonphysiologic lactation from endocrinological causes or from a pituitary tumor.

amnestic s., an organic brain s. with short term (but not immediate) memory disturbance, regardless of the etiology.

anterior tibial compartment s., ischemic necrosis of the muscles of the anterior tibial compartment of the leg, presumed due to compression of arteries by swollen muscles following unaccustomed exertion.

Apert's s., type I *acrocephalosyndactyly.*

Apert-Crouzon s., type II *acrocephalosyndactyly.*

Banti's s., Banti's disease; splenic anemia; chronic congestive splenomegaly that occurs as a sequel to hypertension in the portal or splenic veins; characterized by anemia, splenomegaly, and irregular episodes of gastrointestinal bleeding variously with ascites, jaundice, leukopenia, and thrombocytopenia.

Bardet-Biedl s., mental retardation, pigmentary retinopathy, polydactyly, obesity, and hypogenitalism; a recessive inheritance disorder.

Barrett s., chronic peptic ulcer of the lower esophagus, which is lined by columnar epithelium resembling the mucosa of the gastric cardia.

basal cell nevus s., Gorlin's s.; a dominantly inherited s. of myriad basal cell carcinoma of the skin, cysts of the jaw bones, erythematous pitting of the palms and soles, and frequently skeletal anomalies.

Bassen-Kornzweig s., abetalipoproteinemia.

battered child s., the clinical presentation of child abuse: multiple traumatic lesions of the bones and/or soft tissues willfully inflicted by an adult.

Behçet's s., Behçet's disease; simultaneously or successively occurring recurrent attacks of genital and oral ulcerations (aphthae) and uveitis or irido-cyclitis with hypopyon.

Besnier-Boeck-Schaumann s., sarcoidosis.

Bloch-Sulzberger s., *incontinentia* pigmenti.

Bonnevie-Ullrich s., pseudo-Turner's s.

Börjeson-Forssman-Lehmann s., mental deficiency, epilepsy, hypogonadism, hypometabolism, obesity, and narrow palpebral fissures; X-linked recessive inheritance.

Brown-Séquard's s., hemiparaplegia and hyperesthesia, but with loss of joint and muscle sense on the side of the lesion, and hemianesthesia of the opposite side, in case of a unilateral involvement of the spinal cord.

Budd-Chiari s., Chiari's s.

Caffey's s., infantile cortical *hyperostosis.*

carcinoid s., a combination of symptoms and lesions usually produced by the release of serotonin from carcinoid tumors of the gastrointestinal tract which have metastasized to the liver: irregular mottled blushing, angiomas of the skin, acquired tricuspid and pulmonary stenosis with some minor involvement of valves on the left side of the heart, diarrhea, bronchial spasm, mental aberration, and excretion of 5-hydroxyindoleacetic acid.

carotid sinus s., carotid sinus reflex; stimulation of a hyperactive carotid sinus, causing a marked fall in blood pressure due to vasodilation and cardiac slowing; syncope with or without convulsions or heart block may occur.

carpal tunnel s., pain and paresthesia in the hand in the area of distribution of the median nerve, caused by compression of the median nerve by fibers of the flexor retinaculum.

Carpenter's s. [G. Carpenter], acrocephalopolysyndactyly.

cat-cry s., cri-du-chat s.

cerebrohepatorenal s., muscular hypotonia, incomplete myelinization of nervous tissue, craniofacial malformations, hepatomegaly, and small glomerular cysts of the kidney; possibly autosomal recessive inheritance.

cervical rib s., symptoms due to pressure upon nerves of the brachial plexus by a supernumerary rib which arises from the seventh cervical vertebra: pain and tingling along the forearm and hand over the distribution of the first thoracic nerve root; later, anesthesia with cyanosis and coldness over the ulnar area of the hand.

Cestan-Chenais s., contralateral hemiplegia, hemianesthesia, and loss of pain and temperature sensibility, with ipsilateral hemiasynergia and lateropulsion, paralysis of the larynx and soft palate, enophthalmos, miosis, and ptosis, due to lesions of the brain stem.

Charcot's s., intermittent *claudication.*

Chédiak-Steinbrinck-Higashi s., Chédiak-Steinbrinck-Higashi anomaly; Chédiak-Higashi disease; abnormalities of granulation and nuclear structure of all types of leukocytes with malformation of peroxidase-positive granules, cytoplasmic inclusions, and Döhle bodies, often with hepatosplenomegaly, lymphadenopathy, anemia, thrombocytopenia, radiologic changes of bones, lungs and heart, skin and psychomotor abnormalities, and susceptibility to infection; autosomal recessive inheritance.

Chiari's s., Chiari-Budd s., Chiari's disease; Rokitansky's disease (2); Budd-Chiari s.; thrombosis of the hepatic vein with great enlargement of the liver and extensive development of collateral vessels, intractable ascites, and great portal hypertension.

Chinese restaurant s., development of chest pain, feelings of facial pressure, and sensation of burning over variable portions of the body surface after ingestion of monosodium L-glutamate.

Chotzen s., type III *acrocephalosyndactyly.*

Clarke-Hadfield s., cystic *fibrosis* (of the pancreas).

Cockayne's s., Cockayne's disease; dwarfism, precociously senile appearance, pigmentary degeneration of the retina, optic atrophy, deafness, sensitivity to sunlight, and mental retardation; autosomal recessive inheritance.

compression s., crush s. (1).

Conn's s., primary *aldosteronism.*

Costen's s., temporomandibular joint s.

cri-du-chat s., cat-cry s.; a disorder due to partial deletion of chromosome 5: microcephaly, antimongoloid palpebral fissures, epicanthal folds, micrognathia, strabismus, mental and physical retardation, and a characteristic high-pitched catlike whine.

Crigler-Najjar s., Crigler-Najjar disease; defect in ability to form bilirubin glucuronide, characterized by familial nonhemolytic jaundice and, in its severe

form, by irreversible brain damage that resembles kernicterus; autosomal recessive inheritance.

crocodile tears s., residual facial paralysis with profuse lacrimation during eating, caused by a lesion of the seventh nerve central to the geniculate ganglion.

Cronkhite-Canada s., a sporadically occurring s. of gastrointestinal polyps with diffuse alopecia and nail dystrophy.

CRST s., calcinosis cutis, Raynaud's phenomenon, sclerodactyly, and telangiectasia; usually due to scleroderma.

crush s., (1) compression s.; the shocklike state that follows release of a body part after a prolonged period of compression, as by a heavy weight; characterized by suppression of urine, probably the result of damage to the renal tubules by myoglobin from the damaged muscles; (2) compression fracture of a vertebra as a rare delayed complication of electric shock therapy.

Cruveilhier-Baumgarten s., Cruveilhier-Baumgarten disease; cirrhosis of the liver with patent umbilical or paraumbilical veins and varicose periumbilical veins (caput medusae).

Cushing's s., a disorder resulting from increased adrenocortical secretion of cortisol, caused by adrenocortical hyperplasia or tumor; characterized by centripetal obesity, moon face, acne, abdominal striae, hypertension, decreased carbohydrate tolerance, protein catabolism, psychiatric disturbances, and amenorrhea and hirsutism in females; when associated with a pituitary adenoma, sometimes called Cushing's disease.

Cushing's s. medicamentosus, a variable number of the signs and symptoms of Cushing's s., produced by chronic administration of large doses of glucocorticoids.

DaCosta's s., neurocirculatory *asthenia.*

Dandy-Walker s., hydrocephalus in infants associated with atresia of the foramen of Magendie.

de Lange s., familial growth failure, mental retardation, characteristic facies with eyebrows growing across base of nose and low hairline, depressed bridge of nose with uptilted tip, small head with low-set ears, and flat spadelike hands with short tapering fingers.

Del Castillo s., "Sertoli cell only" s.

dialysis encephalopathy s., dialysis dementia; a progressive diffuse encephalopathy occurring in some patients on chronic hemodialysis.

Down's s., mongolism; trisomy 21 s.; a syndrome of mental retardation associated with a variable constellation of abnormalities caused by representation of at least a critical portion of chromosome 21 three times instead of twice in some or all cells; abnormalities include retarded growth, flat hypoplastic face with short nose, prominent epicanthic skin folds, small rounded ears with prominent antihelix, broad hands and feet, and transverse palmar crease.

Dubin-Johnson s., chronic idiopathic jaundice; familial recurrence of mild jaundice, with impaired dye excretion, iron free pigment in hepatic cells, sulfobromophthalein sodium retention, and nonvisualization of gallbladder.

dumping s., postgastrectomy s.; occurs after eating in patients with shunts of the upper alimentary canal; flushing, sweating, dizziness, weakness, and vasomotor collapse.

Eaton-Lambert s., Lambert-Eaton s.

effort s., neurocirculatory *asthenia.*

Ehlers-Danlos s., cutis hyperelastica; elastic skin; a developmental mesenchymal dysplasia characterized by overelasticity and friability of the skin, excessive extensibility of the joints, and fragility of the cutaneous blood vessels, due to deficient quality or quantity of collagen; commonly inherited as an autosomal dominant trait.

Eisenmenger s., pulmonary hypertension associated with a congenital communication between the two circulations so that a right-to-left shunt results.

EMG s., Beckwith-Wiedemann s.; exomphalos, macroglossia, and gigantism, often with neonatal hypoglycemia; autosomal recessive inheritance.

external carotid steal s., brief ischemic attacks during which dizziness and loss of balance are experienced; caused by vertebrobasilar insufficiency resulting from siphoning of blood from the vertebral artery to the external carotid artery.

Fanconi's s., (1) Fanconi's *anemia:* (2) a group of conditions with characteristic disorders of renal tubular function classified as 1) *cystinosis,* a recessive hereditary disease of early childhood; 2) *adult Fanconi s.,* a rare hereditary form, characterized by the tubular malfunction seen in cystinosis and by osteomalacia, but without cystine deposit in tissues; and 3) *acquired Fanconi s.,* which may be associated with multiple myeloma or may result from damage of proximal tubular epithelium due to various causes, leading to multiple defects of tubular function.

Farber's s., disseminated *lipogranulomatosis.*

Felty's s., rheumatoid arthritis with splenomegaly and leukopenia.

fetal alcohol s., a specific pattern of fetal malformation with growth deficiency, craniofacial anomalies, and limb defects, found among offspring of mothers who are chronic alcoholics; mental retardation is often demonstrated later.

fetal aspiration s., uterine aspiration by the fetus characterized by meconium-stained fetal skin and nails, coarse and irregular streaks of interstitial markings, and areas of aeration focal irregularities.

Franceschetti's s., mandibulofacial *dysostosis.*

Ganser's s., a psychotic-like condition, without the symptoms and signs of a traditional psychosis, occurring typically in in those who feign insanity; *e.g.,* when asked to multiply 6 by 4, will answer 23, or will call a key a lock.

Gardner's s., the development of multiple tumors, inherited as a dominant trait, including osteomas of the skull, epidermoid cysts, and fibromas before 10 years of age, and multiple polyposis predisposing to carcinoma of the colon.

general-adaptation s., the nonspecific reactions of organisms to organic and mental injury or stress: 1) alarm reaction: 2) stage of resistance, which includes all those nonspecific systemic adaptive reactions called forth by prolonged exposure to injurious stimuli: 3) state of exhaustion, in which the adaptation can no longer be maintained.

Gilbert's s., familial nonhemolytic *jaundice.*

Gilles de la Tourette's s., Gilles de la Tourette's *disease.*

Goodpasture's s., glomerulonephritis of the anti-basement membrane type associated with or preceded by hemoptysis.

Gorlin's s., basal cell nevus s.

Gorlin-Chaudhry-Moss s., a rare congenital condition in which are associated craniofacial dysostosis, patent ductus arteriosus, hypertrichosis, hypoplasia of labia majora, and dental and ocular abnormalities.

Greig's s., ocular *hypertelorism.*

Guillain-Barré s., acute idiopathic *polyneuritis.*

Hallervorden s., a pathologic process in which the nerve fibers connecting the striatum and pallidum are completely demyelinated.

Hamman's s., Hamman's disease; spontaneous mediastinal emphysema, resulting from rupture of alveoli.

Hamman-Rich s., acute or chronic interstitial fibrosis of the lung, giving rise to serious right-sided heart failure and cor pulmonale.

happy puppet s., mental retardation, ataxia, hypotonia, epileptic seizures, easily provoked and prolonged spasms of laughter, prognathism, and an open-mouthed expression.

Harada's s., bilateral fundal edema, uveitis, choroiditis, and retinal detachment, with temporary or permanent loss of hearing and visual acuity, graying of the hair, and alopecia.

Hartnup s., Hartnup *disease.*

Hayem-Widal s., icterus and anemia occurring in association with a moderate degree of splenomegaly, increased fragility of red blood cells, and increased amounts of urobilin in the urine.

hemopleuropneumonia s., hemoptysis, sudden dyspnea, moderate tachycardia, and a fever, with tubular breathing over the middle zone of the chest and dullness at the base, indicating pneumonia combined with hemothorax in cases of puncture wounds of the chest.

Holmes-Adie s., Adie's pupil; Adie s.; a s. of unknown etiology and pathology characterized by tonic pupillary reactions; tendon reflexes may be absent or diminished.

Horner's s., ptosis, miosis, anidrosis, and enophthalmos due to a lesion of the cervical sympathetic chain or its central pathways.

Hunt's s., Ramsay Hunt's s.; (1) dyssynergia cerebellaris progressiva; an intention tremor beginning in one extremity, gradually increasing in intensity, and subsequently involving other parts of the body; (2) facial paralysis, otalgia, and herpes zoster resulting from viral infection of the seventh cranial nerve and geniculate ganglion; (3) a form of juvenile paralysis agitans associated with primary atrophy of the pallidal system.

Hunter's s., type II mucopolysaccharidosis; gargoylism (X-linked recessive type); an error of mucopolysaccharide metabolism characterized by deficiency of sulfoid uronate sulfatase, with excretion of chondroitin sulfate B and heparitin sulfate in the urine; clinically similar to Hurler's s. but distinguished by less severe skeletal changes and no corneal clouding; X-linked recessive inheritance.

Hurler's s., an error of mucopolysaccharide metabolism characterized by a deficiency of α-L-iduronidase, an accumulation of an abnormal intracellular material, excretion of chondroitin sulfate B and heparitin sulfate in the urine, severe abnormality in development of skeletal cartilage and bone, corneal clouding, hepatosplenomegaly, mental retardation and gargoyle-like facies; autosomal recessive inheritance. Also called dysostosis multiplex; gargoylism (autosomal recessive type); Hurler's disease; lipochondrodystrophy; type I mucopolysaccharidosis.

hyperkinetic s., a condition marked by pathologically excessive energy, seen sometimes in young children with brain injury or mental defect and in epileptics: hypermotility and emotional instability, accompanied by distractibility, inattention, and lack of shyness and of fear.

Jadassohn-Lewandowsky s., *pachyonychia* congenita.

jaw-winking s., Marcus Gunn phenomenon or syndrome; an increase in the width of the eye lids during chewing, sometimes with a rhythmic elevation of the upper lid when the mouth is open and ptosis when the mouth is closed.

Kanner's s., infantile *autism.*

Kartagener's s., Kartagener's triad; complete situs inversus associated with bronchiectasis and chronic sinusitis.

Katayama s., *schistosomiasis* japonicum.

Kimmelstiel-Wilson s., Kimmelstiel-Wilson *disease.*

Klinefelter's s., XXY s.; a chromosomal anomaly with chromosome count 47, XXY sex chromosome constitution; patients are male in development, but with seminiferous tubule dysgenesis, elevated urinary gonadotropins, variable gynecomastia, and eunuchoid habitus; some patients are chromosomal mosaics, with two or more cell lines of different chromosome constitution.

Klippel-Feil s., a congenital defect manifest as a short neck, extensive fusion of the cervical vertebrae, and abnormalities of the brain stem and cerebellum.

Klumpke-Déjérine s., Klumpke's *paralysis.*

Korsakoff's s., Korsakoff's or polyneuritic psychosis; an alcohol amnestic s. characterized by confusion and severe impairment of memory for which the patient compensates by confabulation; delirium tremens may precede the s., and Wernicke's s. often coexists.

Lambert-Eaton s., carcinomatous myopathy; progressive proximal muscle weakness in patients with carcinoma, in the absence of cutaneous lesions of dermatomyositis.

Laurence-Moon s., a s. of mental retardation, pigmentary retinopathy, hypogenitalism, and spastic paraplegia; recessive inheritance.

Laurence-Moon-Bardet-Biedl s., Laurence-Biedl s.; combination of the Laurence-Moon s. and Bardet-Biedel s.

Leriche's s., aortoiliac occlusive *disease.*

Leri-Weill s., dyschondrosteosis.

Lermoyez s., labyrinthine angiospasm; increasing deafness, interrupted by a sudden attack of dizziness, after which the hearing improves.

Lesch-Nyhan s., a heritable disorder, associated with failure to form hypoxanthine-guanine phosphoribosyl transferase, that occurs only in males and is characterized by hyperuricemia and uric acid urolithiasis, choreoathetosis, mental retardation, spastic cerebral palsy, and self-multilation of fingers and lips by biting; X-linked recessive inheritance.

Libman-Sacks s., Libman-Sacks *endocarditis.*

Lorain-Lévi s., pituitary *dwarfism.*

Lowe's s., oculocerebrorenal s.

Lutembacher's s., a congenital cardiac abnormality consisting of a defect of the interatrial septum, mitral stenosis, and enlarged right atrium.

malabsorption s., a state characterized by diverse features such as diarrhea, weakness, edema, lassitude, weight loss, poor appetite, protuberant abdomen, pallor, bleeding tendencies, paresthesias, muscle cramps, etc., caused by any of several disorders in which there is ineffective absorption of nutrients.

Mallory-Weiss s., laceration of the lower end of the esophagus associated with bleeding, or penetration into the mediastinum, with subsequent mediastinitis; caused usually by severe retching and vomiting.

Marchiafava-Micheli s., paroxysmal nocturnal *hemoglobinuria.*

Marcus Gunn s., jaw-winking s.

Marfan's s., congenital changes in the mesodermal and ectodermal tissues, skeletal changes (arachnodactyly, excessive length of extremities, laxness of joints), bilateral ectopia lentis, and vascular defects (particularly aneurysm of the aorta); autosomal dominant inheritance.

Maroteaux-Lamy s., type VI mucopolysaccharidosis; an error of mucopolysaccharide metabolism characterized by excretion of chondroitin sulfate B in the urine, growth retardation, lumbar kyphosis, sternal protrusion, genu valgum, usually hepatosplenomegaly, and no mental retardation; autosomal recessive inheritance.

Meckel s., *dysencephalia* splanchnocystica.

megacystic s., a combination of a large smooth thin-walled bladder, vesicoureteral regurgitation, and dilated ureters.

Menkes s., kinky-hair *disease*.

middle lobe s., atelectasis with chronic pneumonitis of the middle lobe of the (right) lung; due to compression of the middle lobe bronchus, usually by enlarged lymph nodes.

Mikulicz s., the symptoms characteristic of Mikulicz disease occurring as a complication of some other disease, such as lymphosarcoma, leukemia, or unveoparotid fever.

milk-alkali s., a chronic nephrosis-like disorder of the kidneys, reversible in its early stages, induced by protracted therapy of peptic ulcer with alkalis and a high milk regimen.

Möbius s., a developmental bilateral facial paralysis usually associated with oculomotor or other neurological disorders.

Morgagni's s., metabolic craniopathy; hyperostosis frontalis interna in elderly women, with virilism and obesity of uncertain cause.

Morquio's s., type IV mucopolysaccharidosis; Morquio's or Morquio-Ullrich disease; an error of mucopolysaccharide metabolism with excretion of keratosulfate in urine; characterized by severe skeletal defects with short urine, severe deformity of spine and thorax, long bones with irregular epiphyses but with shafts of normal length, enlarged joints, flaccid ligaments, and waddling gait; autosomal recessive inheritance.

Morton's s., Morton's neuralgia; congenital shortening of the first metatarsal with pain between the heads of two or more of the metatarsals, usually caused by irritation of the nerve between the heads of the metatarsals.

mucocutaneous lymph node s., Kawasaki disease; a polymorphous, erythematous, febrile disease accompanied by conjunctivitis, pharyngitis, cervical lymphadenopathy, perivasculitis and vasculitis, and other systemic toxic involvement; desquamation of fingers and toes, and a furrowing depression of the nails is characteristic.

multiple lentigines s., autosomal dominant inheritance of most or all of the following: multiple lentigines, electrocardiographic abnormalities, ocular hypertelorism, pulmonary stenosis, and retarded growth.

multiple mucosal neuroma s., multiple submucosal neuromas or neurofibromas of the tongue, lips, and eyelids in young persons; sometimes associated with tumors of the thyroid or adrenal medulla, or with subcutaneous neurofibromatosis.

Munchausen s., habitual fabrication of a clinically convincing simulation of disease to seek and maintain hospital treatment.

myeloproliferative s.'s, a group of conditions that result from a disorder in the rate of formation of cells of the bone marrow, including chronic granulocytic leukemia, erythremia, myelosclerosis, panmyelosis, and erythremic myelosis and erythroleukemia.

myofacial pain-dysfunction s., temporomandibular joint pain-dysfunction s.; facial pain originating in the masticatory or cranium-stabilizing muscles, with alteration in mandibular function.

Naegeli s., reticular skin pigmentation, diminished sweating, hypodontia, and hyperkeratosis of the palms and soles; autosomal dominant inheritance.

nail-patella s., onycho-osteodysplasia.

Nelson s., postadrenalectomy s.; a s. of hyperpigmentation, third nerve damage, and enlarging sella turcica caused by development of a pituitary tumor after adrenalectomy for Cushing's s.

nephritic s., the clinical symptoms of nephritis, particularly hematuria, hypertension, and renal failure.

nephrotic s., nephrosis (3); a clinical state characterized by edema, albuminuria, decreased plasma albumin, doubly refractile bodies in the urine, and usually increased blood cholesterol; lipid droplets may be present in the cells of the renal tubules, but the basic lesion is increased permeability of the glomerular capillary basement membranes.

oculocerebrorenal s., Lowe's s.; hydrophthalmia, cataracts, mental retardation, aminoaciduria, reduced ammonia production by the kidney, and vitamin D-resistant rickets; X-linked recessive inheritance.

Oppenheim's s., *amyotonia* congenita.

organic mental s., beaviorial or psychological signs and symptoms caused by transient or permanent dysfunction of the brain.

orodigitofacial s., orodigitofacial *dysostosis.*

Pancoast s., pain and tingling of the arm over the area of distribution of the ulnar nerve, constriction of the pupil, and paralysis of the levator palpebrae superioris muscle, due to pressure on the brachial plexus by a malignant tumor in the region of the superior pulmonary sulcus.

Peutz-Jeghers s., generalized multiple polyposis of the intestinal tract, consistently involving the jejunum, associated with melanin spots of the lips, buccal mucosa, and fingers; autosomal dominant inheritance.

Pfeiffer s., type V *acrocephalosyndactyly.*

pickwickian s., [after the "fat boy" in Dickens' *Pickwick Papers*], grotesque and deforming obesity, hypoventilation, and general debility, theoretically resulting from disability induced by extreme fatness.

Pierre Robin s., micrognathia and abnormal smallness of the tongue, often with cleft palate and bilateral eye defects including high myopia, congenital glaucoma, and retinal detachment.

Plummer-Vinson s., dysphagia due to degeneration of the muscle of the esophagus, atrophy of the papillae of the tongue, and hypochromic anemia.

polycystic ovary s., sclerocystic disease of the ovary; a condition commonly characterized by hirsutism, obesity, menstrual abnormalities, infertility, and enlarged ovaries.

postadrenalectomy s., Nelson s.

postcommissurotomy s., a s. of uncertain cause appearing within a few weeks after a cardiac valvar operation, characterized by fever, chest pain, pericardial rub or effusion, and pleural rub or effusion.

postgastrectomy s., dumping s.

postpartum pituitary necrosis s., Sheehan's s.

postpericardiotomy s., the occurrence of the symptoms of pericarditis, with or without fever and often in repeated episodes, weeks to months after cardiac surgery.

posttraumatic s., a clinical complex, caused by injury to the head, characterized by headache, dizziness, neurasthenia, hypersensitivity to stimuli, and diminished concentration.

posttraumatic neck s., a clinical complex of pain, tenderness, tight neck musculature, vasomotor instability, and ill-defined symptoms such as dizziness and blurred vision. Also variously termed occipital or suboccipital neuralgia or neuritis; tension headache; cervical myospasm; cervical myositis.

Prader-Willi s., a congenital s. of unknown etiology characterized by short stature, mental retardation, polyphagia with marked obesity, and sexual infantilism.

preexcitation s., Wolff-Parkinson-White s.,

premature senility s., progeria.

prune belly s., abdominal muscle deficiency s.

pseudo-Turner's s., Bonnevie-Ullrich s.; a s. characterized by short stature and a webbed neck; unlike Turner's s., patients with this disorder may be of either sex, have normal chromosomes, have no renal abnormalities, are often mentally retarded, and have various forms of congenital heart disease.

pulmonary dysmaturity s., Wilson-Mikity s.; a respiratory disorder occurring in small premature infants incapable of normal pulmonary ventilation; the lungs contain widespread focal emphysematous blebs and the parenchyma has thickened alveolar walls.

punchdrunk s., a condition seen in boxers and alcoholics, presumably caused by repeated cerebral concussions: weakness in lower limbs, unsteadiness of gait, slowness of muscular movements, tremors of hands, hesitancy of speech, and slow cerebration.

Putnam-Dana s., subacute combined *degeneration* of the spinal cord.

Ramsay Hunt's s., Hunt's s.

Reifenstein's s., a familial form of male pseudohermaphroditism characterized by varying degrees of ambiguous genitalia or hypospadias, postpubertal development of gynecomastia, and infertility associated with semeniferous tubular sclerosis; X-linked recessive or autosomal dominant male-linked trait.

Reiter's s., Reiter's disease; a triad of urethritis, iridocyclitis, and arthritis which appear in that order; one or more of these conditions may recur.

Rendu-Osler-Weber s., hereditary hemorrhagic *telangiectasia.*

respiratory distress s. of newborn, hyaline membrane *disease.*

Reye's s., sudden loss of consciousness in children following a prodromal infection, usually resulting in death with cerebral edema and marked fatty change in the liver and renal tubules.

Rh null s., a lack of all Rh antigens, compensated hemolytic anemia, and stomatocytosis.

Riley-Day s., familial *dysautonomia.*

Sanfilippo's s., type III mucopolysaccharidosis; an error of mucopolysaccharide metabolism, with excretion of haparitin sulfate in the urine and severe mental retardation with hepatomegaly; skeleton may be normal or may present mild changes similar to those in Hurler's s.; autosomal recessive inheritance.

scalenus-anticus s., an affection having symptoms identical with those of cervical rib but due to compression of the brachial plexus and subclavian artery against the first thoracic rib by a hypertonic scalenus anticus muscle.

scapulocostal s., pain of insidious development in the upper or posterior part of the shoulder radiating into the neck and occiput with severe headache, down the arm or around the chest; there may be numbness or tingling in the fingers; attributed to an alteration from the normal relationship between the scapula and posterior wall of the thorax.

Schaumann's s., sarcoidosis.

Scheie's s., type IS mucopolysaccharidosis; a variant of Hurler's s. characterized by α-L-iduronidase deficiency, corneal clouding, deformity of the hands, aortic valve involvement, and normal intelligence.

Seabright bantam s., pseudohypoparathyroidism.

"Sertoli cell only" s., Del Castillo s.; absence from the seminiferous tubules of the testes of germinal epithelium, Sertoli cells alone being present, with sterility due to azoospermia.

Sézary s., exfoliative dermatitis with intense pruritus, resulting from cutaneous infiltration by atypical mononuclear cells also found in the peripheral blood, and associated with alopecia, edema, and nail and pigmentary changes.

Sheehan's s., postpartum pituitary necrosis s.; hypopituitarism arising from a severe circulatory collapse post partum, with resultant pituitary necrosis.

Shy-Drager s., a progressive encephalomyelopathy involving the autonomic system, characterized by hypotension, external ophthalmoparesis, atrophy of iris, incontinence, anhidrosis, impotence, tremor, and muscle wasting.

sicca s., Sjögren's s.

sickle cell s., sickle cell *anemia.*

sick sinus s., chaotic atrial activity characterized by continual changes in P wave configuration, with bradycardia alternating with recurring ectopic beats and runs of supraventricular tachycardia.

Sipple's s., pheochromocytoma and medullary thyroid carcinoma with amyloid stroma; parathyroid adenomas may also occur; autosomal dominant inheritance.

Sjögren's s., [H. S. C. Sjögren], sicca s.; keratoconjunctivitis sicca, dryness of mucous membranes, telangiectasias or purpuric spots on the face, and bilateral parotid enlargement, seen in menopausal women, and often associated with rheumatoid arthritis, Raynaud's phenomenon, and dental caries.

Stein-Leventhal s., polycystic ovary s.

Stevens-Johnson s., a bullous form of erythema multiforme which may be extensive, involving the mucous membranes and large areas of the body.

Stewart-Treves s., lymphangiosarcoma arising in arms affected by postmastectomy lymphedema.

Stickler s., hereditary progressive *arthro-ophthalmopathy.*

stiff-man s., a chronic, progressive but variable, disorder of unknown cause associated with fluctuating muscle spasm and stiffness.

Stokes-Adams s., Adams-Stokes s.

Sturge-Weber s., encephalotrigeminal or encephalofacial angiomatosis; Sturge-Weber disease; congenital cutaneous angioma in the distribution of the trigeminal nerve, homolateral meningeal angioma with intracranial calcification and neurologic signs, and angioma of choroid, often with secondary glaucoma; incomplete forms of the s. may exhibit any two of the major features in variable degree, occasionally with angiomas elsewhere.

subclavian steal s., symptoms of cerebrovascular insufficiency resulting from subclavian steal.

sudden infant death s. (SIDS), crib death; abrupt and inexplicable death of an apparently healthy infant; various theories have been advanced to explain such deaths, but none has been generally accepted or demonstrated at autopsy.

Takayasu's s., pulseless *disease.*

tarsal tunnel s., s. produced by entrapment neuropathy of posterior tibial nerve.

Taussig-Bing s., complete transposition of the aorta, which arises from the right ventricle, with a left sided pulmonary artery overriding the left ventricle, and with high ventricular septal defect, right ventricular hypertrophy, anteriorly situated aorta, and posteriorly situated pulmonary artery; compatible with fairly long life.

tegmental s., caused by a lesion in the tegmentum of the midbrain marked by hemiplegia together with paresis or paralysis of the extrinsic occular muscles.

temporomandibular joint s., Costen's s.; various symptoms of discomfort, pain, or pathosis caused by loss of vertical dimension, lack of posterior occlusion, or other malocclusion, trismus, muscle tremor, arthritis, or direct trauma to the temporomandibular joint.

temporomandibular joint pain-dysfunction s., myofacial pain-dysfunction s.

tendon sheath s., limitation of passive movement on attempted elevation of the eye in adduction, appearing clinically as a paresis of the inferior oblique muscle but due to fascial interference with the superior oblique muscle on the same side.

Terry's s., *retinopathy* of prematurity.

testicular feminization s., a type of familial male pseudohermaphroditism characterized by female external genitalia, incompletely developed internal reproductive organs, deficient secondary sex characteristics, and amenorrhea; androgens and estrogens are formed, but target tissues are largely unresponsive to androgens; patients are sex chromatin-negative and have a normal male karyotype.

thoracic outlet s., compression of brachial plexus and subclavian artery by attached muscles in the region of the first rib and clavicle.

Torre's s., multiple sebaceous gland tumors associated with visceral malignancy.

toxic shock s., a staphylococcal endotoxic infection, mostly of the vagina in menstruating women using superabsorbent tampons, characterized by high fever, vomiting, diarrhea, a scarlatinaform rash followed by desquamation, and decreasing blood pressure and shock which can result in death.

trisomy 21 s., Down's s.

Trousseau's s., (1) gastric *vertigo;* (2) thrombophlebitis migrans associated with visceral cancer.

Turcot s., polyps of the colon and brain tumors; inherited as a recessive trait.

Turner's s., XO s.; a chromosomal anomaly with chromosome count 45, including only a single X chromosome; buccal and other cells are usually sex chromatin-negative; anomalies include dwarfism, webbed neck, valgus of elbows, shield-shaped chest, infantile sexual development, and amenorrhea; the ovary has no primordial follicles and may be represented only by a fibrous streak; some patients are chromosomal mosaic, with two or more cell lines of different chromosome constitution.

Usher's s., congenital nerve deafness and retinitis pigmentosa; autosomal recessive inheritance.

Vernet's s., paralysis of the motor components of the glossopharyngeal, vagus, and accessory cranial nerves as they lie in the posterior fossa; most commonly the result of head injury.

Waardenburg s., lateral dystopia of medial canthi and lacrimal punctae, increased width of the root of the nose, heterochromia or hypochromia iridis, cochlear deafness, white forelock, and synophrys; autosomal dominant inheritance.

Waterhouse-Friderichsen s., acute fulminating meningococcal septicemia characterized by vomiting, diarrhea, extensive purpura, cyanosis, toni-clonic convulsions and circulatory collapse, and usually hemorrhage into the adrenal glands.

Weber's s., a form of alternating hemiplegia: paralysis of the oculomotor nerve on the side of the lesion and of the extremities and of the face and tongue on the opposite side due to a lesion in the ventral and internal part of a cerebral peduncle.

Werner's s., scleroderma-like skin changes, bilateral juvenile cataracts, progeria, hypogonadism, and diabetes mellitus; autosomal recessive inheritance.

Wernicke's s., Wernicke's disease or encephalopathy; a condition frequently encountered in chronic alcoholics, largely due to thiamin deficiency and characterized by disturbances in ocular motility, pupillary alterations, nystagmus, and ataxia with tremors; an organic-toxic psychosis is often associated and Korsakoff's s. often coexists.

Wernicke-Korsakoff s., coexistence of Wernicke's and Korsakoff's s.'s.

Wilson-Mikity s., pulmonary dysmaturity s.

Wiskott-Aldrich s., Aldrich s.; an X-linked immunodeficiency disorder occurring in male children and characterized by thrombocytopenia, eczema, melena, and susceptibility to recurrent bacterial infections.

Wolff-Parkinson-White s., preexcitation s.; an electrocardiographic pattern sometimes associated with paroxysmal tachycardia; short P-R interval (0.1 second or less) together with a prolonged QRS complex with a slurred initial component (delta wave).

XO s., Turner's s.

XXY s., Klinefelter's s.

XYY s., a chromosomal anomaly with chromosome count 47, xYY sex chromosome constitution, and sex chromatin-negative buccal and other cells; males are likely to be tall and thin, with less than normal intelligence, and are said to be more likely to commit minor nonagressive crimes than the general population.

Zollinger-Ellison s., peptic ulceration with gastric hypersecretion and non-beta cell tumor of the pancreatic islets, sometimes associated with familial polyendocrine adenomatosis.

syndromic (sin-drom'ik, -dro'mik). Relating to a syndrome.

synechia, pl. **synechiae** (sĭ-nek'ĭ-ah, -ĭ-e) [G. *syn,* together, + *echō,* to have, hold]. Any adhesion; specifically of the iris to the capsule of the lens (anterior) or to the cornea (posterior).

synechiotomy (sĭ-nek-ĭ-ot'o-mĭ) [synechia + G. *tomē,* incision]. Division of a synechia.

synencephalocele (sin-en-sef'ă-lo-sēl) [syn- + G. *enkephalos,* brain, + *kēlē,* hernia]. Protrusion of brain substance through a defect in the skull, with adhesions preventing reduction.

syneresis (sĭ-nĕr'ĕ-sis) [G. *synairesis,* a taking or drawing together]. The contraction of a gel, *e.g.,* a blood clot, by which part of the dispersion medium is squeezed out.

synergetic (sin-er-jet'ik). Synergistic.

synergic (sĭ-ner'jik). Synergistic.

synergism (sin'er-jizm). Synergy.

synergist (sin'er-jist). A structure or drug that aids the action of another.

synergistic (sin'er-jis'tik). Synergic; synergetic. **1.** Pertaining to synergy. **2.** Denoting a synergist.

synergy (sin'er-jĭ) [G. *synergia,* fr. *syn,* together, + *ergon,* work]. Synergism; coordinated or correlated action by two or more structures or drugs.

synesthesia (sin-es-the'zĭ-ah) [syn- + G. *aisthēsis,* sensation]. A condition in which a stimulus, in addition to exciting the usual and normally located sensation, gives rise to a subjective sensation of different character or localization.

synesthesialgia (sin'es-the-zĭ-al'jĭ-ah). Painful synesthesia.

syngamy (sin'gă-mĭ) [syn- + G. *gamos,* marriage]. Conjugation of gametes in fertilization.

syngeneic (sin'jĕ-ne'ik). Isologous.

syngenesis (sin-jen'ĕ-sis) [syn- + G. *genesis,* production]. Sexual *reproduction.*

syngenetic (sin-jĕ-net'ik). Relating to syngenesis.

synizesis (sin-ĭ-ze'sis) [G. collapse]. **1.** Closure or obliteration of the pupil. **2.** The massing of chromatin at one side of the nucleus that occurs usually at the beginning of synapsis.

synkaryon (sin-kăr'ĭ-on) [syn- + G. *karyon,* kernel (nucleus)]. The nucleus formed by the fusion of the two pronuclei in karyogamy.

synkinesis (sin'kĭ-ne'sis) [syn- + G. *kinēsis,* movement]. Involuntary movement accompanying a voluntary one.

synkinet'ic. Relating to or marked by synkinesis.

synophthalmia, synophthalmus (sin'of-thal'mĭ-ah, -mus) [syn- + G. *ophthalmos,* eye]. Cyclopia.

synorchidism, synorchism (sin-or'kĭ-dizm, -or'kizm) [syn- + G. *orchis,* testis]. Congenital fusion of the testes in the abdominal cavity.

synoscheos (sin-os'ke-os) [syn- + G. *oschē,* scrotum]. Partial or complete adhesion of the penis and scrotum.

synosteotomy (sin-os'te-ot'o-mĭ) [syn- + G. *osteon,* bone, + *tomē,* incision]. Arthrotomy.

synostosis (sin-os-to'sis) [syn- + G. *osteon,* bone, + *-osis,* condition]. Bony or true ankylosis; osseous union between the bones forming a joint.

synostotic (sin-os-tot'ik). Relating to synostosis.

synotia (sĭ-no'shĭ-ah) [syn- + G. *ous,* ear]. Fusion or abnormal approximation of the lobes of the ears in otocephaly.

synovectomy (sin-o-vek'to-mĭ) [synovial membrane + G. *ektomē,* excision]. Villusectomy; exsection of a portion or all of the synovial membrane of a joint.

synovia (sĭ-no'vĭ-ah) [L. fr. G. *syn*, together, + *ōon*, egg] [NA]. Joint oil; a clear thixotropic fluid, the function of which is to serve as a lubricant in a joint, tendon sheath, or bursa.

synovial (sĭ-no'vĭ-al). **1.** Relating to, containing, or consisting of synovia. **2.** Relating to a synovial membrane.

synovioma (sĭ-no'vĭ-o'mah) [sinovia + G. *-oma*, tumor]. A tumor of synovial origin involving a joint or tendon sheath.

synovitis (sin-o-vi'tis) [synovial membrane + G. *-itis*, inflammation]. Inflammation of a synovial membrane, especially that of a joint; generally, when unqualified, the same as arthritis.

   bursal s., bursitis.

   dry s., s. sicca; s. with little serous or purulent effusion.

   pigmented villonodular s., diffuse outgrowths of synovial membrane of a joint, usually the knee, composed of synovial villi and fibrous nodules infiltrated by hemosiderin- and lipid-containing macrophages and multinucleated giant cells.

   purulent s., suppurative *arthritis*.

   serous s., s. with a large effusion of nonpurulent fluid.

   s. sic'ca, dry s.

   tendinous s., tenosynovitis.

synovium (sĭ-no'vĭ-um). *Membrana synovialis*.

synten'ic. Pertaining to synteny.

syn'teny [syn- + G. *tainia*, ribbon]. The location of two or more genes on the same chromosome.

synthase (sin'thās). Trivial name for a lyase reaction going in the reverse direction.

synthesis, pl. **syntheses** (sin'thĕ-sis, -sēz) [G. fr. *syn*, together, + *thesis*, a placing, arranging]. **1.** A building up, putting together, composition. **2.** Formation of compounds by the union of simpler compounds or elements. **3.** A period in the cell cycle.

syn'thesize. To make something by synthesis (*i.e.*, synthetically).

synthetase (sin'thĕ-tās). An enzyme catalyzing the synthesis of a specific substance; as a trivial name for the ligases.

synthet'ic. Relating to or made by synthesis.

syntonic (sin-ton'ik) [G. *syntonos*, in harmony]. Having even tone or temperament.

syntrophoblast (sin-tro'fo-blast, -trof'o-). Syncytiotrophoblast.

syntrop'ic. Relating to syntropy.

syntropy (sin'tro-pī) [syn- + G. *tropē*, a turning]. **1.** The tendency sometimes seen in two diseases to coalesce into one. **2.** The state of wholesome association with others. **3.** In anatomy, a number of similar structures inclined in one general direction, as the ribs.

syphilid (sif'ĭ-lid). Any of the several kinds of cutaneous and mucous membrane lesions of secondary and tertiary syphilis.

syphilis (sif'ĭ-lis) [?]. An acute and chronic infectious venereal disease caused by *Treponema pallidum*

(*Spirochaeta pallida*) and transmitted by direct contact, usually through sexual intercourse.

   congenital s., s. acquired by the fetus *in utero*, thus present at birth.

   primary s., the first stage of the disease with the development of the chancre.

   secondary s., the second stage of the disease, beginning with the appearance of the dermatologic eruption, slight fever, and various constitutional symptoms.

   tertiary s., the final stage of the disease, marked by the formation of gummas, cellular infiltration, and cardiovascular and CNS lesions.

syphilitic (sif-ĭ-lit'ik). Luetic; relating to, caused by, or suffering from syphilis.

syphilo-, syphil-, syphili-. Combining forms relating to syphilis.

syphiloma (sif'ĭ-lo'mah) [syphilo- + G. suffix *-oma*, tumor]. Gumma.

syring-. See syringo-.

syringadenoma (sīr'ing-ad-ĕ-no'mah) [syring- + G. *adēn*, gland, + *-oma*, tumor]. Syringoadenoma; a benign sweat gland tumor showing glandular differentiation typical of secretory cells.

syringe (sĭ-rinj', sĭr'inj) [G. *syrinx*, pipe or tube]. An instrument used for injecting or withdrawing fluids.

   chip s., air s., a tapered metal tube through which air is forced to blow debris from, or to dry, a cavity in preparing teeth for restoration.

   control s., ring s.; a type of Luer-Lok s. with thumb and finger rings attached to the proximal end of the barrel and to the tip of the plunger, allowing operation of the s. with one hand.

   dental s., a breech-loading s. into which fits a sealed cartridge containing anesthetic solution.

   fountain s., a reservoir for holding fluid, to the bottom of which is attached a tube with a suitable nozzle; used for vaginal or rectal injections, irrigating wounds, etc., the force of the flow being regulated by the height of the reservoir above the point of discharge.

   hypodermic s., a small s. with a calibrated barrel, plunger, and tip used with a hollow needle for subcutaneous injections and for aspiration.

   Luer s., Luer-Lok s., a glass s. with a metal tip and locking device to secure the needle; used for hypodermic and intravenous purposes.

   probe s., a s. with a slender elongated tip that may also be used as a probe, as in treatment of diseases of the lacrimal passages.

   ring s., control s.

   rubber-bulb s., a s. with a hollow rubber bulb and cannula provided with a check valve, used to obtain a jet of air or water.

syringectomy (sĭr-in-jek'to-mī) [syring- + G. *ektomē*, excision]. Fistulectomy

syringitis (sĭr-in-ji'tis) [syring- + G. *-itis*, inflammation]. Inflammation of the eustachian tube.

syringo-, syring-. Combining forms relating to a syrinx.

syring'oadeno'ma. Syringadenoma.

syringobulbia (sĭ-ring'go-bul'bĭ-ah) [syringo- + L. *bulbus*, bulb (medulla oblongata)]. A fluid-filled cavity of the brainstem, analogous to syringomyelia.

syringocarcinoma (sĭ-ring'go-kar-sĭ-no'mah) [syringo- + carcinoma]. A malignant epithelial neoplasm that has undergone cystic change.

syringocele (sĭ-ring'go-sēl) [syringo- + G. *koilia*, a hollow]. A meningomyelocele in which there is a cavity in the ectopic spinal cord.

syringocystadenoma (sĭ-ring'go-sis-tad-ĕ-no'mah) [syringo- + cystadenoma]. A cystic benign sweat gland tumor.

syringocystoma (sĭ-ring'go-sis-to'mah) [syringo- + cystoma]. Hidrocystoma.

syringoma (sĭr'ing-go'mah) [syringo- + G. *-oma*, tumor]. A benign, often multiple, neoplasm of the sweat glands, composed of very small round cysts.

syringomeningocele (sĭring'go-mĕ-ning'go-sēl) [syringo- + meningocele]. Spina bifida in which the dorsal sac consists chiefly of membranes, with very little cord substance, enclosing a cavity that communicates with a syringomyelic cavity.

syringomyelia (sĭ-ring'go-mi-e'lĭ-ah) [syringo- + G. *myelos*, marrow]. Hydrosyringomyelia; Morvan's disease; presence in the spinal cord of fluid filled longitudinal cavities lined by dense gliogenous tissue not caused by vascular insufficiency; marked clinically by pain and paresthesia followed by muscular atrophy of the hands, analgesia with thermoanesthesia of the hands and arms while the tactile sense preserved, spastic paralysis in the lower extremities, and scoliosis of the lumbar spine.

syringomyelocele (sĭ-ring'go-mĭ'ĕ-lo-sēl) [syringo- + myelocele]. Spina bifida, consisting of a protrusion of the membranes and spinal cord through a dorsal defect in the vertebral column, the fluid of the syrinx of the cord being increased and expanding the cord tissue into a thin-walled sac which then expands through the vertebral defect.

syringotomy (sĭr-ing-got'o-mĭ). Fistulotomy.

syrinx, pl. **syringes** (sĭr'ingks, sĭ-rin'jēz) [G. a tube, pipe]. **1.** Rarely used synonym for fistula. **2.** A pathologic tube-shaped cavity in the brain or spinal cord.

syrup (sĭr'up) [L. *syrupus*, fr. Ar. *sharāb*]. **1.** The uncrystallizable saccharine solution left after the refining of sugar. **2.** Any sweet fluid; a solution of sugar in water in any proportion. **3.** A liquid preparation of medicinal or flavoring substances in a concentrated aqueous solution of a sugar, usually sucrose.

systaltic (sis-tahl'tik) [G. *systaltikos*, contractile]. Pulsating; alternately contracting and dilating; denoting the action of the heart.

system (sis'tem) [G. *systēma*, an organized whole]. A consistent and complex whole made up of correlated and semi-independent parts, as an entire organism; any complex of structures anatomically or functionally related.

alimentary s., digestive s.

autonomic nervous s., that part of the nervous s. which represents motor innervation of the internal organs' smooth muscle, cardiac muscle (heart), and gland cells. It consists of two physiologically and anatomically distinct, mutually antagonistic components: the sympathetic and parasympathetic s.'s whose pathway of innervation consists of a synaptic sequence of two motor neurons, a preganglionic neuron in the spinal cord or brainstem, the myelinated axon of which emerges with a spinal or cranial nerve and synapses with one or more ganglionic neurons composing the autonomic ganglia, whose unmyelinated fibers innervate the internal organs.

cardiovascular s., the heart and blood vessels considered as a whole.

centimeter-gram-second s. (CGS, cgs), the scientific s. of expressing the fundamental physical units of length, mass, and time, and those units derived from them, in centimeters, grams, and seconds.

central nervous s. (CNS), the brain and spinal cord considered as a whole.

circulatory s., vascular s.

conducting s. of the heart, the s. of atypical cardiac muscle fibers comprising the sinoatrial node, internodal tracts, atrioventricular node and bundle, the bundle branches, and their terminal ramifications into the Purkinje network.

digestive s., alimentary s.; the digestive tract from mouth to anus with associated organs and glands concerned with the ingestion, digestion, and absorption of foodstuffs and nutrients.

endocrine s., collective designation for those tissues capable of secreting hormones.

extrapyramidal motor s., literally, all of the brain structures affecting bodily (somatic) movement, excluding the motor neurons, the motor cortex, and the pyramidal (corticobulbar and corticospinal) tract; commonly used to denote in particular the corpus striatum (basal ganglia), its associated structures (substantia nigra; subthalamic nucleus), and its descending connections with the midbrain and, indirectly, with the rhombencephalic and spinal motor neurons.

foot-pound-second (FPS, fps) s., a system of absolute units based on the foot, pound, and second.

genitourinary s., urogenital s.

haversian s., osteon.

hematopoietic s., the blood-making organs, principally the bone marrow and lymph nodes.

heterogeneous s., in chemistry, a s. that contains various distinct and mechanically separable parts or phases; *e.g.,* a suspension or an emulsion.

homogeneous s., in chemistry, a s. whose parts cannot be mechanically separated, and is therefore uniform throughout and possesses in every part identically physical properties; *e.g.,* a solution of sodium chloride.

hypothalamohypophysial portal s., a s. of veins that originate from the capillary tufts of the median eminence, pass downward along the stalk and pars tuberalis of the hypophysis, and enter the anterior lobe of the hypophysis in which they arborize into a secondary capillary bed, the capillary sinusoids; convey releasing factors to the anterior lobe.

limbic s., collective term denoting a heterogeneous array of brain structures at or near the edge (limbus) of the medial wall of the cerebral hemisphere (hippocampus, amygdala, and gyrus fornicatus) also used to include the interconnections of these structures, as well as their connections with the septal area, the hypothalamus, and a medial zone of mesencephalic tegmentum; the s. influences the endocrine and autonomic motor s.'s and appears to affect motivational and mood states.

lymphatic s., the lymphatic vessels, lymph nodes, and lymphoid tissue.

masticatory s., the organs and structures primarily functioning in mastication: jaws, teeth with their supporting structures, temporomandibular articulation, mandibular musculature, tongue, lips, cheeks, and oral mucosa.

metameric nervous s., paleencephalon; that part of the nervous s. which innervates body structures that developed in ontogeny from the segmentally arranged somites or, in the head region, branchial arches.

meter-kilogram-second (MKS, mks) s., an absolute s. based on the meter, kilogram, and second; the basis of the International System of Units (SI).

metric s., a s. of weights and measures based upon the meter as a unit. Fractions (prefixes) are expressed in Latin: deci- (d, 10^{-1}), centi- (c, 10^{-2}), milli- (m, 10^{-3}), micro- (μ, 10^{-6}), nano- (n, 10^{-9}), pico- (p, 10^{-12}), femto- (f, 10^{-15}), atto- (a, 10^{-18}). Multiples (prefixes) are expressed in Greek: deca- (dk, 10), hecto- (h, 10^2), kilo- (k, 10^3), mega- (M, 10^6), giga- (G, 10^9), tera- (T, 10^{12}). The unit of weight is the gram, the weight of one cubic centimeter of distilled water, equivalent to $15.432+$ grains; the unit of volume is the liter or one cubic decimeter, equal to 1.056 quarts.

muscular s., all the muscles of the body collectively, especially the voluntary skeletal muscles.

nervous s., the entire neural apparatus: brain, spinal cord, nerves, and ganglia.

neuromuscular s., the muscles of the body collectively and the nerves supplying them.

parasympathetic nervous s., that part of the autonomic nervous s. whose preganglionic motor neurons compose the visceral motor nuclei of the brainstem and the lateral column of the second to fourth sacral segments of the spinal cord.

peripheral nervous s., that part of the nervous s. other than the central nervous s.

portal s., a s. of vessels in which blood, after passing through one capillary bed, is conveyed through a second capillary network.

properdin s., an immunological s., the alternative pathway for complement, composed of several distinct proteins that react in a serial manner and activate C3 (third component of complement), seemingly without utilizing components C1, C4, and C2; in addition to properdin, the s. includes properdin factors A (native C3), B (C3 proactivator), D (C3 proactivator convertase), and perhaps at least one other, E.

reproductive s., the complex of male or female gonads, associated ducts, and external genitalia concerned with procreation.

respiratory s., the air passages from the nose to the pulmonary alveoli.

reticular activating s (RAS), that part of the brainstem reticular formation that plays a central role in the organism's bodily and behavioral alertness; by its ascending connections it affects the function of the cerebral cortex in the sense of behavioral responsiveness; its descending (reticulospinal) connections transmit its activating influence upon bodily posture and reflex mechanisms.

reticuloendothelial s., collectively, the cells in different organs chiefly concerned with macrophagocytosis: in connective tissue and lymphatic structures, Kupffer cells; in connective tissue, histiocytes; in the lung, alveolar phagocytes; in nervous tissue, microglia.

stomatognathic s., all of the structures involved in speech and in the receiving, mastication, and deglutition of food.

sympathetic nervous s., that part of the autonomic nervous s. whose preganglionic motor neurons lie in the lateral column of the thoracic and upper two lumbar segments of the spinal cord.

urinary s., the kidneys, ureters, bladder, and urethra.

urogenital s., genitourinary s.; the organs involved in the formation and voiding of urine and in reproduction.

vascular s., circulatory s.; the cardiovascular and lymphatic s.'s collectively.

systema (sis'te'mah) [L. fr. G. systēma] [NA]. A complex of anatomical structures functionally related. See also system; apparatus; tract.

systematic name. As applied to chemical substances, a name composed of specially coined or selected words or syllables, each of which has a precisely defined chemical structural meaning, so that the structure may be derived from the name.

Système International d'Unités. International System of Units.

systemic (sis-tem'ik). Relating to a system; specifically somatic, relating to the entire organism as distinguished from any of its individual parts.

systole (sis'to-le) [G. systolē, a contracting]. Miocardia; contraction of the heart, especially of the ventricles, by which the blood is driven through the aorta and pulmonary artery to traverse the systemic and pulmonary circulations, respectively.

aborted s., a loss of the systolic beat in the radial pulse through weakness of the ventricular contraction.

late s., prediastole.

premature s., extrasystole.

systol'ic. Relating to, or occurring during cardiac systole.

systrem'ma [G. anything twisted]. A muscular cramp in the calf of the leg, the contracted muscles forming a hard ball.

syzygial (sĭ-zij'ĭ-al). Relating to syzygy.

syzygy (siz'ĭ-jĭ) [G. *syzygios*, yoked, bound together, fr. *syn*, together, + *zygon*, a yoke]. **1.** The association of gregarine protozoans end-to-end or in lateral pairing (without sexual fusion). **2.** Pairing of chromosomes in meiosis.

T

T Tension (T+, increased tension; T−, diminished tension); tera-; tritium; as a subscript, refers to tidal *volume;* tocopherol.

T Absolute *temperature.*

2,4,5-T (2,4,5-Trichlorophenoxy)acetic acid, a herbicide that is the principal constituent of Agent Orange.

T_m Temperature midpoint (Kelvin).

T_3 3,5,3'-Triiodothyronine.

T_4 Thyroxine.

t Metric ton.

t Temperature on the Celsius scale, and for tritium.

t_m Temperature midpoint (Celsius).

Ta Tantalum.

tabanid (tab'ă-nid) [L. *tabanus*, gadfly]. Any fly of the family Tabanidae, a family of bloodsucking flies that includes the genera *Tabanus* (horsefly) and *Chrysops* (deerfly and mango fly), which are involved in transmission of several blood-borne parasites.

tabes (ta'bēz) [L. a wasting away]. Progressive wasting or emaciation.

t. dorsa'lis, spinal atrophy; a chronic inflammation and progressive sclerosis of the posterior proximal spinal roots, the posterior columns of the spinal cord, and the peripheral nerves; symptoms include muscular incoordination and atrophy, anesthesia, neuralgia, lancinating pains, visceral crises, and trophic disorders of the joints; a tertiary form of syphilis.

t. mesenter'ica, tuberculosis of the mesenteric and retroperitoneal lymph nodes.

tabescent (ta-bes'ent) [L. *tabesco*, to waste away]. Characteristic of tabes.

tabet'ic. Relating to tabes.

tabet'iform. Resembling tabes.

tablature (tab-lă-tūr) [L. *tabula*, tablet]. The cranial bones as two laminae separated by the diploë.

ta'ble [L. *tabula*]. One of the two laminae, separated by the diploë, into which the cranial bones are divided.

ta'blespoon. A measure equivalent to about 4 fluidrams, $1/2$ fluidounce, or 15 ml.

tab'let [Fr. *tablette*, L. *tabula*]. A solid dosage form containing medicinal substances with or without suitable diluents; classed according to the method of manufacture as molded and compressed.

enteric coated t., a t. coated with a substance that delays release of the medication until the t. has passed into the stomach.

hypodermic t., a compressed or molded t. that dissolves completely in water (for injection) to form an injectable solution.

sustained action or **release t.,** a drug product formulation that provides the required dosage initially and then maintains or repeats it at desired intervals.

taboo, tabu (tă-boo') [Tongan, set apart]. Restricted, prohibited, or forbidden as part of a sociocultural tradition.

taboparesis (ta'bo-pă-re'sis, -păr'e-sis). A condition in which the symptoms of tabes dorsalis and general paresis are associated.

tabular (tab'u-lar) [L. *tabularis*, fr. *tabula*, table]. Laminar; table-like.

tache (tash) [Fr. spot]. A circumscribed discoloration of the skin or mucous membrane, as a macule or freckle.

tachetic (tă-ket'ik) [Fr. *tache*, spot]. Marked by bluish or brownish spots.

tachometer (tă-kom'ĕ-ter) [G. *tachos*, speed, + *metron*, measure]. An instrument for measuring speed or rate.

tachy- [G. *tachys*, quick, rapid]. Combining form denoting rapid.

tachyarrhythmia (tak'ĭ-ă-rith'mĭ-ah) [tachy- + G. *a*-priv. + *rhythmos*, rhythm]. Any disturbance of the heart's rhythm resulting in a rate over 100 beats per minute.

tachycardia (tak-ĭ-kar'dĭ-ah) [tachy- + G. *kardia*, heart]. Tachyrhythmia; rapid beating of the heart, usually applied to rates over 100 per minute.

bidirectional ventricular t., ventricular t. in which the QRS complexes in the electrocardiogram are alternately mainly positive and mainly negative.

ectopic t., a t. originating in a focus other than the sinus node.

essential t., persistent rapid action of the heart due to no discernible organic lesion.

paroxysmal t., recurrent attacks of t., with abrupt onset and termination, originating from an ectopic focus.

tachycar'diac. Relating to excessively rapid action of the heart.

tachycrotic (tak-ĭ-krot'ik) [tachy- + G. *krotos*, a striking]. Relating to, causing, or characterized by a rapid pulse.

tachyphagia (tak-ĭ-fa'jĭ-ah) [tachy- + G. *phagein*, to eat]. Rapid eating; bolting of food.

tachyphylaxis (tak-ĭ-fĭ-lak'sis) [tachy- + G. *phylaxis*, protection]. Rapid appearance of progressive decrease in response following repetitive administration of a pharmacologically or physiologically active substance.

tachypnea (tak-ip-ne'ah) [tachy- + G. *pnoĕ(pnoiĕ)*, breathing]. Polypnea; rapid breathing.

tachyrhythmia (tak-ĭ-rith'mĭ-ah) [tachy- + G. *rhythmos*, rhythm]. Tachycardia.

tachysterol (tă-kis'ter-ol). A sterol formed upon ultraviolet irradiation of ergosterol or lumisterol.

tactile (tak'til) [L. *tactilis*]. Relating to touch or to the sense of touch.

tactom'eter [L. *tactus*, touch, + G. *metron*, measure]. Esthesiometer.

tac'tual. Relating to or caused by touch.

Taenia (te'nĭ-ah) [see taenia]. A genus of cestodes that formerly included most of the tapeworms, but is now restricted to those species infecting carnivores with a cysticercus.

    T. sagina'ta, the beef, hookless, or unarmed tapeworm of man, acquired by eating insufficiently cooked flesh of cattle infected with *Cysticercus bovis*.

    T. so'lium, the pork, armed, or solitary tapeworm of man, acquired by eating insufficiently cooked pork infected with *Cysticercus cellulosae*.

taenia (te'nĭ-ah) [L. fr. G. *tainia*, band, tape, a tapeworm]. **1.** See tenia (1). **2.** Tenia (2); common name for a tapeworm, especially of the genus *Taenia*.

taeniid (te-ni'id). Any member of the family Taeniidae, a family of parasitic cestodes that includes the genera *Taenia*, *Multiceps*, and *Echinococcus*.

TAF Tumor angiogenic *factor*.

tag. 1. To incorporate into a compound an element or other substance that is more readily detected, whereby the compound can be detected and its metabolic or chemical history followed. **2.** A small outgrowth or polyp.

    sentinel t., projecting edematous skin at the lower end of an anal fissure.

    skin t., acrochordon; soft wart; an outgrowth of both epidermal and dermal fibrovascular tissue.

tail (tāl) [A.S. *taegl*]. Cauda.

tail'gut. Postanal *gut*.

ta'lar. Relating to the talus.

talc (tălk) [Ar. *talq*]. Talcum; steatite, native hydrous magnesium silicate, sometimes containing small proportions of aluminum silicate, purified by boiling powdered t. with hydrochloric acid in water; used as a dusting powder and in cosmetics.

talcosis (tal-ko'sis). A pneumoconiosis related to silicosis, caused by inhalation of talc mixed with silicates.

talcum (tal'kum) [L.]. Talc.

taliped'ic. Clubfooted.

talipes (tal'ĭ-pēz) [L. *talus*, heel, ankle, + *pes*, foot]. Pes (3); any deformity of the foot involving the talus.

    t. calcaneoval'gus, t. calcaneus and t. valgus combined; a dorsiflexed, everted, and abducted foot.

    t. calcaneova'rus, t. calcaneus and t. varus combined; a dorsiflexed, inverted, and adducted foot.

    t. calca'neus, a deformity, due to weakness or absence of the calf muscles, in which the axis of the calcaneus becomes vertically oriented.

    t. ca'vus, t. pes cavus; an exaggeration of the normal arch of the foot.

    t. equinoval'gus, equinovalgus; pes equinovalgus; t. equinus and t. valgus combined; a plantarflexed, everted, and abducted foot.

    t. equinova'rus, clubfoot; equinovarus; pes equinovarus; t. equinus and t. varus combined; a plantarflexed, inverted, and adducted foot.

    t. equi'nus, permanent extension of the foot so that only the ball rests on the ground.

    t. pla'nus, flatfoot; splayfoot; pes planus; a deformity in which the arch of the foot is broken down, the entire sole touching the ground.

    t. val'gus, pes valgus; permanent eversion of the foot, the inner side alone of the sole resting on the ground.

    t. va'rus, pes adductus or varus; inversion of the foot, with only outer side of the sole touching the ground.

talipomanus (tal-ĭ-pom'ă-nus, -po-ma'nus) [*talipes* + L. *manus*, hand]. Clubhand; a fixed deformity of the hand, either congenital or acquired.

talo- [L. *talus*, ankle, ankle bone]. Combining form denoting the talus.

talocrural (ta-lo-kru'ral). Relating to the talus and the bones of the leg.

ta'lus, pl. **ta'li** [L. ankle bone, heel] [NA]. Ankle bone; ankle (3); astragalus; the bone of the foot that articulates with the tibia and fibula to form the ankle joint.

tam'pon [O. Fr.]. **1.** A cylinder or ball of cotton-wool, gauze, or other loose substance; used as a plug or pack in a canal or cavity to restrain hemorrhage, absorb secretions, or maintain a displaced organ in position. **2.** To insert such a plug or pack.

tamponade, tamponage (tam-pŏ-nād', tam'pŏ-nij). The insertion of a tampon.

    cardiac t., compression of venous return to the heart due to increased volume of fluid in the pericardium.

tangentiality (tan-jen'shĭ-al'ĭ-tĭ) [L. *tangeno*, to touch, take away]. A disturbance in the associative thought process in which one tends to digress readily from one topic under discussion to other topics which arise in the course of associations.

tan'nate. A salt of tannic acid.

tan'nic. Relating to tan (tan-bark) or to tannin.

tan'nic acid. $C_{76}H_{52}O_{46}$, occurring in many plants, used as a styptic, astringent, and in the treatment of diarrhea.

tan'talum [mythical king *Tantalus*]. A heavy non-corroding metal of the vanadium group, symbol Ta, atomic no. 73, atomic weight 180.95.

tan'trum. A fit of bad temper, especially in children.

tap. 1. To withdraw fluid from a cavity by means of a trocar and cannula, hollow needle, or catheter. **2.** To strike lightly with the finger or a hammer-like instrument in percussion or to elicit a tendon reflex. **3.** A light blow.

spinal t., lumbar *puncture*.

tape'toret'inal. Relating to the retinal pigment epithelium and the sensory retina.

tape'toretinop'athy [tapetum + retinopathy]. Hereditary degeneration of the retinal and pigmentary epithelium and of the retinal neurepithelium.

tapetum, pl. **tapeta** (tǎ-pe'tum, -tah) [L. *tapēte*, a carpet]. **1.** Any membranous layer or covering. **2.** A thin sheet of fibers in the lateral wall of the temporal horn of the lateral ventricle, continuous with the fasciculus subcallosus, and largely composed of fibers passing from the temporal cortex to the caudate nucleus.

tape'worm. An intestinal parasitic worm, commonly restricted to members of the class Cestoidea, consisting of a scolex, variously equipped with spined or sucking structures by which the worm is attached to the intestinal wall of the host, and strobila having several to many proglottids that lack a digestive tract at any stage of development.

tapotement (tǎ-pot-moñ') [Fr. fr. *tapoter*, to tap]. A massage movement consisting in striking with the side of the hand, usually with partly flexed fingers.

tardive (tar'div). Late; tardy.

tar'get [It. *targhetta*, a small shield]. **1.** An object of fixation. **2.** In the ophthalmometer, the mire. **3.** Target *organ*.

tars-. See tarso-.

tarsadenitis (tar'sad-ě-ni'tis) [tarsus + G. *adēn*, gland, + *-itis*, inflammation]. Inflammation of the tarsal borders of the eyelids and of the meibomian glands.

tar'sal. Relating to a tarsus in any sense.

tarsale, pl. **tarsalia** (tar-sa'le, -sa'lĭ-ah) [L. fr. G. *tarsos*, sole of the foot]. Any tarsal bone.

tarsal'gia [tarsus + G. *algos*, pain]. Podalgia.

tarsec'tomy [tarsus + G. *ektomē*, excision]. Excision of the tarsus of the foot or of a segment of the tarsus of an eyelid.

tarsi'tis. 1. Inflammation of the tarsus of the foot. **2.** Inflammation of the tarsal border of an eyelid.

tarso-, tars-. Combining forms relating to a tarsus.

tarsochiloplasty (tar-so-ki'lo-plas-tĭ) [tarso- + G. *cheilos*, lip, + *plassō*, to form]. Marginal blepharoplasty.

tarsoclasia, tarsoclasis (tar-so-kla'zĭ-ah, tar-sok'lǎ-sis) [tarso- + G. *klasis*, a breaking]. Instrumental fracture of the tarsus, to correct clubfoot.

tarsomalacia (tar'so-mǎ-la'shĭ-ah) [tarso- + G. *malakia*, softness]. Softening of the tarsal cartilages of the eyelids.

tarsomegaly (tar-so-meg'ǎ-lĭ) [tarso- + G. *megas*, large]. Congenital maldevelopment and overgrowth of a tarsal or carpal bone.

tar'somet'atar'sal. Relating to the tarsal and metatarsal bones.

tarsophalangeal (tar'so-fǎ-lan'je-al). Relating to the tarsus and the phalanges.

tarsophyma (tar-so-fi'mah) [tarso- + G. *phyma*, a tumor, boil]. Any tarsal growth or tumor.

tar'soplasty. Blepharoplasty.

tarsorrhaphy (tar-sor'ǎ-fĭ) [tarso- + G. *rhaphē*, suture]. Blepharorrhaphy; suturing together of the eyelid margins, partially or completely, to shorten the palpebral fissure or to protect the cornea in case of chronic ulcer or paralysis of the orbicularis muscle.

tarsotar'sal. Mediotarsal.

tarsotomy (tar-sot'o-mĭ) [tarso- + G. *tomē*, incision]. **1.** Incision of the tarsal cartilage of an eyelid. **2.** Any operation on the tarsus of the foot.

tar'sus, pl. **tar'si** [G. *tarsos*, a flat surface] [NA]. **1.** Instep; the seven bones of the instep: talus, calcaneus, navicular, three cuneiform, and cuboid. **2.** The fibrous plates giving solidity and form to the edges of the eyelids.

tar'tar [Mediev. L. *tartarum*, ult. etym. unknown]. **1.** A crust on the interior of wine casks, consisting essentially of potassium bitartrate. **2.** Dental calculus; a white or brownish deposit at or below the gingival margin of teeth, chiefly hydroxyapatite in an organic matrix.

tar'trate. A salt of tartaric acid (dihydroxysuccinic acid; HOOC–CHOH–CHOH–COOH).

taste [It. *tastare;* L. *tango*, to touch]. **1.** To perceive through the medium of the gustatory nerves. **2.** The sensation produced by a suitable stimulus applied to the gustatory nerve endings in the tongue.

color t., pseudogeusesthesia; a form of synesthesia in which the color sense and t. are associated, stimulation of either inducing a subjective sensation on the part of the other as well.

TAT Thematic apperception *test*.

tattoo (tǎ-tū') [Tahiti, *tatu*]. **1.** A tinctorial and pictorial effect obtained by implanting or injecting of indelible pigments into the skin. **2.** To produce such an effect.

taurine (taw'rin, -rēn). A crystallizable substance, $NH_2CH_2CH_2SO_3H$, formed by the decomposition of taurocholic acid.

taurocholate (taw-ro-ko'lāt). A salt of taurocholic acid.

taurocholic acid (taw-ro-ko'lik). Cholytaurine; *N*-choloyltaurine; a compound of cholic acid and taurine, involving the –COOH group of the former and the NH_2–of the latter; a common bile salt.

tautomeric (taw-to-mer'ik) [G. *tautos*, the same, + *meros*, part]. **1.** Relating to the same part. **2.** Relating to or marked by tautomerism.

tautomerism (taw-tom'er-izm) [G. *tautos*, the same, + *meros*, part]. A phenomenon in which a chemical compound exists in two forms of different structure (isomers) in equilibrium, the two forms differing, usually, in the position of a hydrogen atom.

taxa (tak′sah). Plural of taxon.

taxis (tak′sis) [G. orderly arrangement]. **1.** Reduction of a hernia or of a dislocation of any part by means of manipulation. **2.** Systematic classification or orderly arrangement. **3.** The reaction of protoplasm to a stimulus, leading an organism to move or act in certain definite ways in relation to its environment.

tax′on, pl. **tax′a.** A particular level or grouping in a systematic classification of natural objects.

taxonom′ic. Relating to taxonomy.

taxonomy (tak-son′o-mī) [G. *taxis,* orderly arrangement, + *nomos,* law]. The classification of various living things or organisms, divided into groups to show degrees of similarity or presumed evolutionary relationships (higher categories being more inclusive and broad, lower categories being more restricted); in descending order: Phylum, Class, Order, Family, Genus, Species, Subspecies (Variety).

Tb Terbium.

tb Tuberculosis; tubercle bacillus.

TBP Thyroxine-binding *protein.*

Tc Technetium.

TDP Ribothymidine 5′-diphosphate.

Te Tellurium.

tear (tār). A discontinuity in substance of a structure.

tear (tēr) [A.S. *teár*]. A drop of the fluid secreted by the lacrimal glands by means of which the conjunctiva is kept moist.

   bucket-handle t., a t. in the central part of a semilunar cartilage.

   crocodile t.'s, see crocodile t.'s *syndrome.*

   Mallory-Weiss t., Mallory-Weiss *lesion.*

tearing (tēr′ing). Epiphora.

tease (tēz) [A. S. *taesan*]. To separate the structural parts of a tissue by means of a needle, in order to prepare it for microscopic examination.

tea′spoon. A measure of about 1 dram or 5 ml.

teat (tēt) [A.S. *tit*]. **1.** *Papilla mammae.* **2.** Breast; mamma. **3.** Papilla.

technetium (tek-ne′shĭ-um) [G. *technetos,* artificial]. An artificial radioactive element, symbol Tc, atomic no. 43.

technetium-99m (⁹⁹ᵐTc). A radioisotope of technetium which decays by isomeric transition, with a physical half-life of 6 hr; used to prepare radiopharmaceuticals for scanning.

technic (tek-nēk′). Technique.

technician (tek-nish′un) [G. *technē,* an art]. Technologist.

technique (tek-nēk′) [Fr. from G. *technikos,* relating to *technē,* art, skill]. Technic; the manner of performance, or the details, of any surgical operation, experiment, or mechanical act. See also method; operation; procedure.

Ficoll-Hypaque t., a density-gradient centrifugation t. for separating lymphocytes from other formed elements in blood.

fluorescent antibody t., a t. used to test for antigen with a fluorescent antibody, performed by one of two methods: **1) direct,** in which immunoglobulin (antibody) conjugated with a fluorescent dye is added to tissue and combines with specific antigen (microbe, or other), the resulting antigen-antibody complex being located by fluorescence microscopy, or **2) indirect,** in which unlabeled immunoglobulin (antibody) is added to tissue and combines with specific antigen, after which the antigen-antibody complex may be labeled with fluorescein-conjugated anti-immunoglobulin antibody, the resulting triple complex then being located by fluorescence microscopy.

open-drop t., a t. for production of inhalation anesthesia by causing drops of a liquid anesthetic, *e.g.,* ether or chloroform, to fall on a gauze mask or cone applied over the mouth and nose.

rebreathing t., a method of producing hypoxia by rebreathing air with carbon dioxide replacing oxygen in the breathing mixture.

technol′ogist. Technician; one trained in and using the techniques of a profession, art, or science.

tec′tal. Relating to a tectum.

tectorial (tek-tōr′ĭ-al). Relating to or characteristic of a tectorium.

tectorium (tek-tōr′ĭ-um) [L. fr. *tego,* pp. *tectus,* to cover]. **1.** An overlaying structure. **2.** *Membrana tectoria ductus cochlearis.*

tectospi′nal. Denoting nerve fibers passing from the tectum mesencephali to the spinal cord.

tectum, pl. **tecta** (tek′tum, tek′tah) [L. fr. *tego,* pp. *tectus,* to cover] [NA]. Any rooflike covering or structure.

   t. mesenceph′ali [NA], *lamina tecti mesencephali.*

teeth. Dentes. See tooth.

teeth′ing. The eruption or "cutting"of the teeth, especially of the dens decidua.

tef′lurane. 2-Bromo-1,1,1,2-tetrafluoroethane; a nonexplosive and nonflammable inhalation anesthetic of moderate potency.

teg′men, pl. **teg′mina** [L. a covering, fr. *tego,* to cover] [NA]. A structure that covers or roofs over a part.

   t. mastoi′deum, the lamina of bone roofing over the mastoid cells.

   t. tym′pani [NA], roof of tympanum; the roof of the middle ear, formed by the thinned anterior surface of the petrous portion of the temporal bone.

   t. ventric′uli quar′ti [NA], roof of the fourth ventricle, formed by the superior medullary velum and by the inferior medullary velum.

tegmen′tal. Relating to, characteristic of, or placed or oriented toward a tegmentum or tegmen.

tegmen'tum, pl. **tegmen'ta** [L. covering structure, fr. *tego,* to cover] [NA]. **1.** A covering structure. **2.** T. mesencephali.

t. mesenceph'ali, mesencephalic t., tegmentum (2); that major part of the substance of the mesencephalon or midbrain that lies between the lamina tecti mesencephali (lamina quadrigemina) dorsally and the pedunculus cerebri (basis pedunculi) ventrally.

t. rhombenceph'ali [NA], **t. of rhombencephalon,** the portion of the pons and medulla oblongata continuous with the t. mesencephali.

tegument (teg'u-ment) [L. fr. *tegmentum*]. Integument.

tegumen'tal, tegumen'tary. Relating to the integument.

teichoic acids (ti-ko'ik). One of two classes (the other being muramic acids or mucopeptides) of polymers in Gram-positive bacteria.

teichopsia (ti-kop'sĭ-ah) [G. *teichos,* wall, + *opsis,* vision]. A transient visual sensation of bright shimmering colors, such as that which precedes scintillating scotoma in migraine.

tel-, tele-, telo- [G. *tēle,* distant; *telos,* end]. Combining forms denoting distance, end, or other end.

te'la, pl. **te'lae** [L. a web] [NA]. **1.** Any thin weblike structure. **2.** A tissue; especially one of delicate formation.

t. choroi'dea ventric'uli quar'ti [NA], **choroid t. of fourth ventricle,** the sheet of pia mater covering the lower part of the ependymal roof of the fourth ventricle.

t. choroi'dea ventric'uli ter'tii [NA], **choroid t. of third ventricle,** diatela; a double fold of pia mater, enclosing subarachnoid trabeculae, between the fornix above and the epithelial roof of the third ventricle and the thalami below.

t. subcuta'nea [NA], superficial fascia; subcutis; hypodermis; a loose fibrous envelope beneath the skin, containing the cutaneous vessels and nerves.

t. submuco'sa [NA], tunica submucosa; the layer of connective tissue beneath the tunica mucosa.

telangiectasia (tel-an'jĭ-ek-ta'zĭ-ah) [G. *telos,* end, + *angeion,* vessel, + *ektasis,* a stretching out]. Telangiectasis; dilation of the previously existing small or terminal vessels of a part.

essential t., (1) localized capillary dilation of undetermined origin; (2) *angioma* serpiginosum.

hereditary hemorrhagic t., Osler's disease (2); Rendu-Osler-Weber disease or syndrome; a disease, with onset usually after puberty, marked by multiple small telangiectases and dilated venules that develop slowly on the skin and mucous membranes; autosomal dominant inheritance.

spider t., arterial *spider.*

telangiectasis, pl. **telangiectases** (tel-an-jĭ-ek'tā-sis, -sēz). Telangiectasia.

telan'giectat'ic. Relating to or marked by telangiectasia.

telangiosis (tel-an'jĭ-o'sis). Any disease of the capillaries and terminal arterioles.

tele-. See tel-.

telecanthus (tel-ĕ-kan'thus) [G. *tēle,* distant, + *kanthos,* canthus]. Increased breadth between the medial canthi of the eyelids.

tel'ediagno'sis. Detection of a disease by evaluation of data transmitted from patient-monitoring instruments and a transfer link to a diagnostic center.

telem'etry [G. *tēle,* distant, + *metron,* measure]. The science of measuring a quantity, transmitting the results to a distant station, and there interpreting, indicating, and/or recording the results.

telencephalic (tel'en-sĕ-fal'ik). Relating to the telencephalon.

telencephalon (tel-en-sef'ă-lon) [G. *telos,* end, + *enkephalos,* brain] [NA]. Endbrain; the anterior division of the prosencephalon corresponding to the cerebral hemispheres; together with the diencephalon it composes the prosencephalon.

teleomitosis (tel'e-o-mi-to'sis) [G. *teleos,* complete, + *mitosis*]. A completed mitosis.

teleopsia (tel-e-op'sĭah) [G. *tēle,* distant, + *opsis,* vision]. An error in judging the distance of objects, arising from lesions in the parietal temporal region.

teleorgan'ic [G. *teleos,* complete, + *organikos,* organic]. Vital; manifesting life.

telep'athy [G. *tēle,* distant, + *pathos,* feeling]. Extrasensory thought transference; mind-reading; the transmittal and reception of thoughts by means other than through the normal senses; a form of extrasensory perception.

teleradiog'raphy [G. *tēle,* distant, + radiography]. Teleroentgenography; radiography with the tube held about 2 m from the body, thereby securing practical parallelism of the rays.

telergy (tel'ur-jī) [G. *tēle,* far off, + *ergon,* work]. Automatism.

teleroentgenography (tel'ĕ-rent-gen-og'ră-fī). Teleradiography.

telether'apy [G. *tēle,* distant, + *therapeia,* treatment]. Radiation therapy administered at a distance from the body.

tellu'ric [L. *tellus,* the earth]. **1.** Relating to or originating in the earth. **2.** Relating to the element tellurium.

tellurium (tel-u'rī-um) [L. *tellus,* the earth]. A rare semimetallic element, symbol Te, atomic no. 52, atomic weight 127.60, belonging to the sulfur group.

telo-. See tel-.

teloden'dron [G. *telos,* end, + *dendron,* tree]. The terminal arborization of an axon.

tel'ogen [G. *telos,* end, + *-gen,* producing]. Resting phase of hair cycle.

telolecithal (tel-o-les'ĭ-thal) [G. *telos,* end, + G. *lekithos,* yolk]. Denoting an ovum in which a considerable amount of deutoplasm accumulates at one pole.

tel'omere [G. *telos,* end, + *meros,* part]. The distal extremity of a chromosome arm.

telophase (tel'o-fāz) [G. *telos*, end, + *phasis*, appearance]. The final stage of mitosis or meiosis beginning when migration of chromosomes to the poles of the cell is complete.

tem'per. 1. Mood; disposition; temperament (2); in general, any characteristic or particular state of mind. **2.** A display of irritation or anger.

temperament (tem'per-ă-ment) [L. *temperamentum*, disposition]. **1.** The psychophysical organization peculiar to the individual, including his character or personality predispositions, which influence his manner of thought and action, and general views of life. **2.** Temper (1).

tem'perance [L. *temperantia*, moderation]. **1.** Moderation in all things, especially abstinence from alcoholic beverages.

tem'perate. Denoting temperance.

temperature (tem'per-ă-chur) [L. *temperatura*, due measure]. The sensible intensity of heat of any substance; the measure of the average kinetic energy of the molecules making up a substance. See also entries under scale.

    absolute t., *(T)*, t. measured in Kelvins from absolute zero.

    critical t., the t. of a gas above which it is no longer possible by use of any pressure, however great, to reduce it to liquid form.

    effective t., a comfort index or scale which takes into account the t. of air, its moisture content, and movement.

    t. midpoint (T_m Kelvin; t_m Celsius), the midpoint in the change in optical properties (absorbance, rotation) of a structured polymer with increasing t.

    standard t., 0°C or 273°absolute (Kelvin).

tem'plate. 1. A pattern or guide that determines the shape of a substance. **2.** Metaphorically, the specifying nature of a nucleic acid or polynucleotide with respect to the primary structure of the nucleic acid or polynucleotide or protein made from it *in vivo* or *in vitro*. **3.** A pattern or guide that determines the specificity of antibody globulins.

temple (tem'pl) [L. *tempus*, time, the temple]. **1.** The area of the temporal fossa on the side of the head above the zygomatic arch. **2.** The part of a spectacle frame passing from the rim backward over the ear.

tempolabile (tem-po-la'bil) [L. *tempus*, time, + *labilis*, perishable]. Undergoing spontaneous change or destruction during the passage of time.

tem'poral [L. *temporalis*, fr. *tempus*, time, temple]. **1.** Relating to time; limited in time; temporary. **2.** Relating to the temple.

temporo- [L. *temporalis*, temporal]. Combining form denoting the temple.

tem'poromandib'ular. Temporomaxillary (2); relating to the temporal bone and the mandible; denoting the articulation of the lower jaw.

tem'poromax'illary. 1. Relating to the regions of the temporal and maxillary bones. **2.** Temporomandibular.

tempostabile, tempostable (tem'po-sta'bil, tem-po-sta'bl) [L. *tempus*, time + *stabilis*, stable]. Not subject to spontaneous alteration or destruction during the passage of time.

tem'pus, pl. **tem'pora** [L.]. **1.** The temple. **2.** Time. TEN Toxic epidermal *necrolysis.*

tenacious (tĕ-na'shus) [L. *tenax*, fr. *teneo*, to hold]. Sticky; glutinous; viscid; not easily diverted.

tenaculum, pl. **tenacula** (tĕ-nak'u-lum, -lah) [L. a holder, fr. *teneo*, to hold]. A surgical clamp designed to hold or grasp tissue during dissection.

tenalgia (tĕ-nal'jĭ-ah) [G. *tenōn*, tendon, + *algos*, pain]. Tenontodynia; tenodynia; pain referred to a tendon.

ten'der [L. *tener*, soft, delicate]. Sensitive; painful on pressure or contact.

ten'derness. The condition of being tender.

    rebound t., t. felt when pressure, particularly abdominal pressure, is suddenly released.

tendini'tis. Tendonitis.

tendinoplasty (ten'din-o-plas-tĭ) [L. *tendo* (*tendin-*), tendon, + G. *plassō*, to form]. Tenontoplasty.

ten'dinosu'ture. Tenorrhaphy.

ten'dinous. Relating to, composed of, or resembling a tendon.

tendo, pl. **tendines** (ten'do, -dĭ-nis, -dĭ-nēz) [L. *tendo*, to stretch out, extend] [NA]. Tendon.

    t. calca'neus [NA], **t. achil'lis** [NA], calcanean, Achilles, or heel tendon; the tendon of insertion of the triceps surae muscle into the tuberosity of the calcaneus.

tendo-. Combining form denoting a tendon. See also teno-.

tendolysis (ten-dol'ĭ-sis) [tendo- + G. *lysis*, dissolution]. Tenolysis; release of a tendon from adhesions.

ten'don [L. *tendo*]. A fibrous cord or band that connects a muscle with its bony attachment; consists of fascicles of very densely arranged, almost parallel collagenous fibers, rows of elongated tendon cells, and a minimum of ground substance.

    Achilles t., calcanean t., *tendo* calcaneus.

    hamstring t., see hamstring.

    heel t., *tendo* calcaneus.

tendoni'tis. Tendinitis; tenonitis (2); tenontitis; tenositis; inflammation of a tendon.

ten'doplasty. Tenontoplasty.

tendosynovitis (ten'do-sĭ-no-vi'tis). Tenosynovitis.

tendot'omy. Tenotomy.

tendovaginal (ten-do-vaj'ĭ-nal) [tendo- + L. *vagina*, sheath]. Relating to a tendon and its sheath.

tendovaginitis (ten-do-vaj-ĭ-ni'tis) [tendo- + L. *vagina*, sheath, + G. *-itis*, inflammation]. Tenosynovitis.

tenectomy (tĕ-nek'to-mĭ) [G. *tenōn*, tendon, + *ektomē*, excision]. Tenonectomy; resection of part of a tendon.

tenesmic (tĕ-nez'mik). Relating to or marked by tenesmus.

tenesmus (tĕ-nez'mus) [G. *teinesmos*, ineffectual effort to defecate]. A painful spasm of the anal sphincter with an urgent desire to evacuate the bowel or bladder, involuntary straining, and passage of little matter.

tenia, pl. **teniae** (te'nĭ-ah, te'nĭ-e) [L. fr. G. *tainia*, band, tape]. **1** [NA]. Any anatomical bandlike structure. **2.** Taenia (2).

　t. choroi'dea [NA], the somewhat thickened line along which a choroid membrane or plexus is attached to the rim of a brain ventricle.

　te'niae co'li [NA], the three bands in which the longitudinal muscular fibers of the large intestine, except the rectum, are collected: **t. mesocolica,** situated at the place corresponding to the mesenteric attachment; **t. libera,** free band, opposite the mesocolic band; **t. omentalis,** at the place corresponding to the site of adhesion of the greater omentum to the transverse colon.

teniacide (te'nĭ-ă-sīd) [L. *taenia*, tapeworm, + *caedo*, to kill]. An agent destructive to tapeworms.

teniafuge (te'nĭ-ă-fūj) [L. *taenia*, tapeworm, + *fugo*, to put to flight]. An agent that causes expulsion of tapeworms.

te'nial. 1. Relating to a tapeworm. **2.** Relating to one of the structures called tenia.

teniasis (te-ni'ă-sis). Presence of a tapeworm in the intestine.

teno-, tenon-, tenonto- [G. *tenōn*, tendon]. Combining forms meaning tendon. See also tendo-.

tenodesis (tĕ-nod'ĕ-sis, ten'o-de'sis) [teno- + G. *desis*, a binding]. Stabilizing a joint by anchoring the tendons that move that joint.

tenodynia (ten-o-din'ĭ-ah) [teno- + G. *odynē*, pain]. Tenalgia.

tenol'ysis. Tendolysis.

tenomyoplasty (ten-o-mi'o-plas-tĭ). Tenontomyoplasty.

tenomyotomy (ten-o-mi-ot'o-mĭ). Myotenotomy.

tenonectomy (ten-o-nek'to-mĭ) [tenon- + G. *ektomē*, excision]. Tenectomy.

tenoni'tis. 1. Inflammation of Tenon's capsule or the connective tissue within Tenon's space. **2.** Tendonitis.

tenonom'eter. Tenometer.

tenon-, tenont-. See teno-.

tenontitis (ten-on-ti'tis) [tenont- + G. *-itis*, inflammation]. Tendonitis.

tenonto-. See teno-.

tenontodynia (tĕ-non-to-din'ĭ-ah). Tenalgia.

tenontomyoplasty (tĕ-non'to-mi'o-plas-tĭ) [tenonto- + G. *mys*, muscle, + *plassō*, to form]. Tenomyoplasty; combined tenontoplasty and myoplasty, used in the radical correction of hernia.

tenontoplasty (tĕ-non'to-plas-tĭ) [tenonto- + G. *plassō*, to form]. Tenoplasty; tendinoplasty; tendoplasty; reparative or plastic surgery of the tendons.

tenophyte (ten'o-fit) [teno- + G. *phyton*, plant]. Bony or cartilaginous growth in or on a tendon.

ten'oplasty. Tenontoplasty.

ten'orecep'tor. Receptor in a tendon, activated by increased tension.

tenorrhaphy (tĕ-nor'ă-fī) [teno- + G. *raphē*, suture]. Tendinosuture; tenosuture; suture of the divided ends of a tendon.

tenosi'tis. Tendonitis.

tenostosis (ten-os-to'sis) [teno- + G. *osteon*, bone, + *-osis*, condition]. Ossification of a tendon.

ten'osuspen'sion. Using a tendon as a suspensory ligament, sometimes as a free graft or in continuity.

tenosu'ture. Tenorrhaphy.

tenosynovectomy (ten'o-sin-o-vek'to-mĭ) [teno- + synovia + G. *ektomē*, excision]. Excision of a tendon sheath.

tenosynovitis (ten'o-sin-o-vi'tis) [teno- + synovia + G. *-itis*, inflammation]. Inflammation of a tendon and its enveloping sheath. Also called tendosynovitis; tendovaginitis; tenovaginitis; tendinous synovitis.

　localized nodular t., giant cell *tumor* of tendon sheath.

　villous t., villonodular pigmented t., a condition resembling pigmented villonodular synovitis but arising in periarticular soft tissue rather than in joint synovia.

tenotomy (tĕ-not'o-mĭ) [teno- + G. *tomē*, incision]. Tendotomy; surgical division of a tendon to correct a deformity caused by congenital or acquired shortening of a muscle.

　curb t., excision of the tendon of the shortened muscle in squint, and fixation of it farther back on the aponeurosis of the globe.

　graduated t., partial incisions of the tendon of an eye muscle to correct a slight degree of strabismus.

tenovaginitis (ten'o-vaj-ĭ-ni'tis) [teno- + L. *vagina*, sheath, + G. *-itis*, inflammation]. Tenosynovitis.

tension [L. *tensio*, to stretch]. **1.** The act or condition of being stretched or tense, or a stretching or pulling force. **2.** The partial pressure of a gas, especially that of a gas dissolved in a liquid such as blood. **3.** Mental, emotional, or nervous strain; strained relations or barely controlled hostility between persons or groups.

　arterial t., the blood pressure within an artery.

　intraocular t. (Tn), the resistance of the tunics of the eye to indentation.

　premenstrual t., the regular monthly experience of physiological and emotional distress, usually during the several days preceding menses, typically involving fatigue, edema, irritability, tension, anxiety, and depression.

　surface t., the expression of intermolecular attraction at the surface of a liquid, in contact with air or another gas, a solid, or another immiscible liquid, tending to pull the molecules of the liquid inward from the surface.

　tissue t., a theoretical condition of equilibrium or balance between the tissues and cells whereby overaction of any part is restrained by the pull of the mass.

ten'sor, pl. **tenso'res** [L. *tendo,* pp. *tensus,* to stretch]. A muscle the function of which is to render a part firm and tense.

tent. 1. A canopy used in various types of inhalation therapy to control humidity and concentration of oxygen in inspired air. **2.** A cylinder of some material, usually absorbent, introduced into a canal or sinus to maintain its patency or to dilate it. **3.** To elevate or pick up a segment of skin, fascia, or tissue at a given point, giving it the appearance of a t.

tentacle (ten'tă-kl) [L. *tentaculum,* a feeler]. A slender process for feeling, prehension, or locomotion in invertebrates.

tento'rial. Relating to a tentorium.

tentorium, pl. **tentoria** (ten-to'rĭ-um, -rĭ-ah) [L. tent, fr. *tendo,* to stretch] [NA]. A membranous cover or horizontal partition.

t. cerebel'li [NA], a fold of dura mater roofing over the posterior cranial fossa but for an anterior median opening, the incisura tentorii, through which the midbrain passes; separates the cerebellum from the basal surface of the occipital and temporal lobes of the cerebral cortex.

t. of hypophysis, *diaphragma sellae.*

tera- [G. *teras,* monster]. **1 (T).** Prefix used in the metric system to signify one trillion (10^{12}). **2.** Combining form denoting a teras. See also terato-.

teras, pl. **terata** (tĕr'as, tĕr'ă-tah) [G.]. A malformed fetus with deficient, redundant, misplaced, or grossly misshapen parts.

terat'ic. Relating to a teras.

teratism (tĕr'ă-tizm) [G. *teratisma,* fr. *teras*]. Teratosis.

terato- [G. *teras,* monster]. Combining form denoting a teras. See also tera- (2).

ter'atoblasto'ma [terato- + G. *blastos,* germ, + *-oma,* tumor]. Teratoma.

ter'atocarcino'ma. 1. A malignant teratoma, occurring most commonly in the testis. **2.** A malignant epithelial tumor arising in a teratoma.

teratogen (tĕr'ă-to-jen) [terato- + G. *-gen,* producing]. An agent that causes abnormal development.

teratogenesis (tĕr'ă-to-jen'ĕ-sis) [terato- + G. *genesis,* origin]. Teratogeny; the origin or mode of production of a malformed fetus.

teratogenic, teratogenetic (tĕr'ă-to-jen'ik, -jĕ-net'ik). **1.** Relating to teratogenesis. **2.** Causing abnormal development.

teratogeny (tĕr-ă-toj'ĕ-nĭ). Teratogenesis.

teratoid (tĕr'ă-toyd) [tera- + *eidos,* resemblance]. Resembling a teras.

teratologic (tĕr'ă-to-loj'ik). Relating to teratology.

teratology (tĕr-ă-tol'o-jĭ) [terato- + G. *logos,* study]. The branch of embryology concerned with the production, development, anatomy, and classification of malformed fetuses.

teratoma (tĕr-ă-to'mah) [terato- + G. *-oma,* tumor]. Teratoblastoma; teratoid tumor; a neoplasm composed of multiple tissues, including tissues not normally found in the organ in which it arises.

teratomatous (tĕr-ăto'mătus). Relating to or of the nature of a teratoma.

teratosis (tĕr'ă-to'sis) [terato- + G. *-osis,* condition]. Teratism; an anomaly producing a teras.

ter'bium [fr. *Ytterby,* a place in Sweden]. A metallic element of the lanthanide or "rare earth" series, symbol Tb, atomic no. 65, atomic weight 158.93.

teres, pl. **teretes** (tĕr'ēz, tĕr'e-tēz; tĕr-) [L. round, smooth, fr. *tero,* to rub]. Round and long; denoting certain muscles and ligaments.

term [L. *terminus,* a limit, an end]. A definite or limited period, as pregnancy.

terminal (ter'mĭ-nal) [L. *terminus,* a boundary, limit]. **1.** Pertaining to the end; final. **2.** Relating to an extremity or end. **3.** A termination, extremity, end, or ending.

axon t.'s, end-feet; terminal or axonal terminal boutons; boutons terminaux; neuropodia; the somewhat enlarged, often club-shaped endings by which axons make synaptic contacts with other nerve cells or with effector cells.

terminatio, pl. **terminationes** (ter'mĭ-na'shĭ-o, -o'nēz) [L.] [NA]. A termination or ending, particularly a nerve ending. See also ending.

terminatio'nes nervo'rum li'berae [NA], free nerve endings, a form of peripheral ending of sensory nerve fibers in which the terminal filaments end freely in the tissue.

ter'nary [L. *ternarius,* of three]. Denoting a chemical compound containing three elements, or a complex formed by three molecules.

ter'pene. One of a class of unsaturated hydrocarbons with an empirical formula of $C_{10}H_{16}$, occurring in essential oils and resins.

ter'race. To suture in several rows, in closing a wound through a considerable thickness of tissue.

territoriality (tĕr'ĭ-to-rĭ-al'ĭ-tĭ). The tendency of individuals or groups to defend a particular domain or sphere of interest or influence.

tertian (ter'shăn) [L. *tertianus,* fr. *tertius,* third]. Occurring every third day (by inclusive reckoning); actually, occurring every 48 hours or every other day.

tes'sellated [L. *tessella,* a small square stone]. Made up of small squares; checkered.

test [L. *testum,* an earthen vessel]. **1.** A trial, examination, or experiment. **2.** To perform such. See also reaction; method; procedure, sign. **3.** A reagent used in making a t. **4.** Testa.

abortus-Bang-ring (ABR) t., milk-ring t.; a special form of agglutination t. done on the mixed milk of many cows, usually entire herds, for the detection of herds containing individuals infected with bovine brucellosis.

achievement t., a standardized t. used to measure acquired learning, in contrast to an intelligence t. as an index of potential learning.

acidified serum t., Ham's t.; lysis of the patient's red cells in acidified fresh serum, specific for paroxysmal nocturnal hemoglobinuria.

acid phosphatase t. for semen, a screening t. for semen by determining acid phosphatase content: seminal fluid contains high concentrations of acid phosphatase, while other body fluids and extraneous foreign materials have very low concentrations.

Adson's t., for thoracic outlet syndrome: patient is seated, with head extended and turned to the side of the lesion; with deep inspiration there is a diminution or total loss of radial pulse on the affected side.

alkali denaturation t., for hemoglobin F, based on the fact that hemoglobins, with the exception of Hb F, are denatured by alkali to alkaline hematin.

Allen t. [E.V. Allen], radial or ulnar patency: either the radial or ulnar artery is digitally compressed by the examiner after blood has been forced out of the hand by clenching it into a fist, and failure of the blood to diffuse into the hand when opened indicates that the artery not compressed is occluded.

alternate binaural loudness balance (ABLB) t., ear: comparison of relative loudness of a series of intensities presented alternately to either ear.

alternate cover t., to detect phoria or strabismus: attention is directed to a small fixation picture, one eye is covered for several seconds, and then the fellow eye is immediately covered; if the eye moves when it is uncovered, a strabismus or phoria is present.

antiglobulin t., Coombs t.

aptitude t., an occupation-oriented intelligence t. used to evaluate a person's abilities, interests, talents, and skills.

association t., a word (stimulus word) is spoken to the subject, who replies immediately with another word (reaction word) suggested to him by the first; a diagnostic aid, clues being given by the length of time (association time) between the stimulus and reaction words, and also by the nature of the reaction words.

Bárány's caloric t., caloric t.; vestibular function: irrigating the external auditory meatus with either hot or cold water normally causes stimulation of the vestibular apparatus, resulting in nystagmus and past-pointing.

Becker's t., a t. for astigmatism, using a diagram of lines radiating in different meridians, in sets of three.

Bender Gestalt t., for measuring visuomotor coordination to detect brain damage by determining a person's ability to visually copy a set of geometric designs.

Benedict's t., a copper-reduction t. for glucose in urine.

bentonite flocculation t., a flocculation t. for rheumatoid arthritis in which sensitized bentonite particles are added to inactivated serum; positive if half of the particles are clumped while the other half remain in suspension.

Betke-Kleihauer t., a slide t. for the presence of fetal red blood cells among those of the mother.

binaural alternate loudness balance (BALB) t., for recruitment in one ear: comparison of relative loudness of a series of intensities presented alternately to either ear.

Binet t., Binet-Simon t., Stanford-Binet intelligence *scale*.

biuret t., for the determination of serum proteins, based on the reaction of an alkaline copper reagent with substances containing two or more peptide bonds to produce a violet-blue color.

breath-holding t., a rough index of cardiopulmonary reserve measured by the length of time that a subject can hold his breath: normally in excess of 30 sec, less than 20 sec with diminished cardiac or pulmonary reserve.

bromphenol t., a colorimetric t. for measurement of protein, albumin, and globulin in urine by use of reagent strips.

caloric t., Bárány's caloric t.

complement-fixation t., an immunological t. for determining the presence of a particular antigen or antibody when one of the two is known to be present, based on the fact that complement is "fixed" in the presence of antigen and its specific antibody.

conjunctival t., conjunctival *reaction.*

Coombs t., antiglobulin t.; a t. for antibodies: **(1) direct:** for detecting sensitized erythrocytes in erythroblastosis fetalis and in acquired hemolytic anemia, indicated by presence of incomplete or univalent antibodies on erythrocytes; **(2) indirect:** in cross matching blood or investigating transfusion reactions, for presence of specific antibodies attached to the antigen of donor erythrocytes.

cover-uncover t., to detect strabismus: attention is directed to a small fixation picture, and one eye is covered; if the uncovered eye moves to see the picture, strabismus is present.

Crampton t., for physical condition and resistance: recording of the pulse and the blood pressure in the recumbent and in the standing position, and grading the difference from theoretical perfection (100) downward; high values indicate a good physical resistance but low ones are said to indicate weakness and a liability to shock after an operation.

Dick t., an intracutaneous t. of susceptibility to the erythrogenic toxin of *Streptococcus pyogenes* responsible for the rash and other manifestations of scarlet fever.

differential ureteral catheterization t., split renal function t.; a study performed to determine various functional parameters of one kidney compared to the contralateral kidney.

dinitrophenylhydrazine t., a screening t. for maple syrup urine disease; the addition of 2,4-dinitrophenylhydrazine in HCl to urine gives a chalky white precipitate in the presence of ketoacids.

direct fluorescent antibody t., see fluorescent antibody *technique.*

Doerfler-Stewart (D-S) t., for differentiating between functional and organic hearing loss: examination of the patient's ability to respond to spondee words in the presence of a masking noise.

drawer t., drawer *sign.*

Dugas t., for an injured shoulder: if the elbow cannot be made to touch the chest while the hand rests on the opposite shoulder, the injury is a dislocation and not a fracture of the humerus.

erythrocyte fragility t., fragility t.

fern t., for estrogenic activity: cervical mucus smears form a fern pattern at times when estrogen secretion is elevated, as at the time of ovulation.

ferric chloride t., for detection of phenylketonuria: addition of ferric chloride to urine gives a blue-green color in the presence of phenylketonuria.

finger nose t., for coordinated movement: the subject is asked to touch the tip of the nose with the finger.

Fishberg concentration t., of renal water conservation: after overnight fluid deprivation, morning urine samples are collected and specific gravity is measured.

flocculation t., see flocculation *reaction.*

fluorescent antinuclear antibody (FANA) t., a t. for antinuclear antibody components, especially for diagnosis of collagen-vascular diseases.

fluorescent treponemal antibody-absorption (FTA-ABS) t., a serologic t. for syphilis using a suspension of the Nichols strain of *Treponema pallidum* as antigen; presence or absence of antibody in the patient's serum is indicated by an indirect fluorescent antibody technique.

Folin's t., (1) for uric acid, by means of the color produced with phosphotungstic acid and a base; (2) for urea, which is decomposed by boiling with magnesium chloride, and the freed ammonia measured.

fragility t., erythrocyte fragility t.; to measure resistance of erythrocytes to hemolysis in hypotonic saline solutions: normal erythrocytes show initial hemolysis at concentrations of 0.45 to 0.39% and complete hemolysis at 0.33 to 0.30%; in hereditary spherocytosis, fragility of erythrocytes is markedly increased; in thalassemia, sickle cell anemia, and obstructive jaundice, fragility of erythrocytes is usually reduced.

Frei t., an intracutaneous diagnostic t. for lymphogranuloma venereum, using antigen prepared from yolk sac preparation of chlamydiae.

galactose tolerance t., a liver function t., based on the ability of the liver to convert galactose to glycogen, measured by the rate of excretion of galactose following ingestion or intravenous injection of a known amount.

gel diffusion precipitin t.'s, precipitin t.'s in which the immune precipitate forms in a gel medium (usually agar) into which one or both reactants have diffused; generally classified in two types: gel diffusion in one dimension and in two dimensions.

glucose tolerance t., a t. for diabetes, based upon the ability of the normal liver to absorb and store excessive amounts of glucose as glycogen: following ingestion of 100 g of glucose, the fasting blood sugar promptly rises, then falls to normal within 2 hours; in a diabetic patient, the increase is greater and the return to normal unusually prolonged.

Guthrie t., bacterial inhibition assay for direct measurement of serum phenylalanine, to detect phenylketonuria in the newborn.

Hallion's t., of collateral circulation: when the main artery and vein of a limb are compressed, in a case of aneurysm, swelling of the veins of the hand or foot will take place only when the collateral circulation is free.

Ham's t., acidified serum t.

head-dropping t., in the diagnosis of disease of the extrapyramidal system: the head of a normal person will drop suddenly like a dead weight, in striatal disease, the head falls slowly.

Histalog t., a t. for measurement of maximal production of gastric acidity or anacidity, using betazole hydrochloride, an analogue of histamine.

histamine t., for maximal production of gastric acidity or anacidity: after preliminary administration of an antihistamine, histamine acid phosphate is injected subcutaneously in a dose of 0.04 mg/kg of body weight, followed by analysis of gastric contents.

17-hydroxycorticosteroid t., a t., dependent on the Porter-Silber reaction of adrenocorticosteroids and phenylhydrazine, used as a measure of adrenocortical function and performed on urine: low values are seen in Addison's disease and hypopituitarism; high values are seen in Cushing's syndrome and extreme stress.

immunologic pregnancy t., general term for t.'s for detection of increased human chorionic gonadotropin in plasma or urine by immunologic techniques including latex particle agglutination, radioimmunoassay, and radioreceptor assays.

indirect fluorescent antibody t., see fluorescent antibody *technique.*

indirect hemagglutination t., passive *hemagglutination.*

Ishihara's t., a t. for color blindness which utilizes a series of pseudoisochromatic cards; all of the figures or letters are easily read by the normal person but not by one with defective color vision.

17-ketosteroid assay t., a colorimetric t. that indicates metabolites or adrenal and testicular steroids excreted as 17-ketones in the urine; increased values are most striking in adrenocortical tumors, decreased values in Addison's disease or in panhypopituitarism.

Korotkoff's t., of collateral circulation: while the artery above an aneurysm is compressed, blood pressure in the distal circulation will be fairly high if the collateral circulation is good.

Kveim t., an intradermal t. for the detection of sarcoidosis, indicated by typical tubercles and giant cell formation.

latex agglutination t., latex fixation t., a passive agglutination t. in which antigen is adsorbed onto latex particles which then clump in the presence of antibody specific for the adsorbed antigen.

lepromin t., utilizes an intradermal injection of a lepromin (*e.g.,* Dharmendra antigen, Mitsuda antigen) to classify the stage of leprosy based on the lepromin reaction (*e.g.,* Fernandez reaction, Mitsuda reaction) differentiates tuberculoid leprosy, in which there is a positive delayed reaction at the injection site, from lepromatous leprosy, in which there is no reaction, but is not diagnostic.

limulus lysate t., a t. for the rapid detection of Gram-negative bacterial meningitis, using *Limulus polyphemus* (horseshoe crab) lysates.

lupus band t. (LBT), a direct immunofluorescent technique for demonstrating a band of immunoglobulins at the dermal-epidermal junction of the skin of patients with lupus erythematosus.

Mantoux t., see tuberculin t.

Master's t., Master's two-step exercise t., two-step exercise t.

McMurray t., rotation of tibia on femur, for injury to meniscal structures.

metabisulfite t., a t. for sickle cell hemoglobin (Hb S); deoxygenation of cells containing Hb S is enhanced by addition of sodium metabisulfite to blood, causing sickling visible on a slide.

migration inhibition t., an *in vitro* method of testing for cellular (delayed type) sensitivity: when specific antigen is present, macrophages from a sensitized animal do not migrate from the capillary tube in which they have been packed in the manner characteristic of similar cells from a normal animal.

milk-ring (MR) t., abortus-Bang-ring t.

Minnesota multiphasic personality inventory t., (MMPI), a questionnaire type of psychological test for ages 16 and over, with true-false statements coded in personality scales in both individual and group forms.

mixed agglutination t., see mixed agglutination *reaction.*

mixed lymphocyte culture (MLC) t., for histocompatibility of HL-A antigens: the degree of incompatibility is indicated by the number of lymphocytes that have undergone transformation and mitosis, or by the uptake of radioactive isotope-labeled thymidine.

Moloney t., to detect a high degree of sensitivity to diphtheria toxoid: more than a minimal local reaction to diluted toxoid given intradermally indicates that prophylactic toxoid should be inoculated in fractional doses at suitable intervals.

Moszkowicz t., for arteriosclerosis: a lower limb is made anemic with a tourniquet that is removed after 5 minutes; color normally reaches the tips of the toes in a few seconds, but in arteriosclerosis with sufficient obstruction the color returns slowly.

multiple puncture tuberculin t., see tuberculin t.

neutralization t., protection t.

nitroblue tetrazolium (NBT) t., a t. to detect the phagocytic ability of polymorphonuclear leukocytes by measuring the capacity of the oxygen-dependent leukocytic bactericidal system.

nitroprusside t., for cystinuria: following the addition of sodium cyanide to urine, further addition of nitroprusside produces a red-purple color if the cyanide has reduced any cystine present to cysteine.

oral lactose tolerance t., a t. for lactose deficiency; the plasma glucose response to an oral lactose load is measured as in the (oral) glucose tolerance t.

Pap t., Papanicolaou smear t., microscopic examination of cells exfoliated or scraped from a mucosal surface after staining with Papanicolaou's stain; used especially for detection of cervical cancer.

parallax t., measurement of the deviation in strabismus by the alternate cover t. combined with prismatic correction of the deviation.

patch t., a t. of skin sensitiveness: a small piece of blotting paper or cloth, wet with the t. fluid, is applied to the skin, and on removal of the patch the area previously covered is compared with the uncovered surface.

Patrick's t., to determine the presence or absence of sacroiliac disease: with the patient supine, the thigh and knee are flexed and the external malleolus is placed above the patella of the opposite leg; on depressing the knee, pain is promptly elicited in sacroiliac disease.

plasmacrit t., a serologic screening method used as an aid in the diagnosis of syphilis: heparinized blood (obtained from a pricked finger) is centrifugated to collect plasma, mixed with antigen, agitated, and the presence or absence of flocculation observed; a positive result is not conclusively diagnostic, but a negative result is exclusive.

platelet aggregation t., a t. of the ability of platelets to adhere to each other and hence form a hemostatic plug to prevent bleeding; conducted by quantitating the decrease in turbidity that occurs in platelet-rich plasma following the *in vitro* addition of one or several platelet-aggregating agents.

precipitin t., an *in vitro* t. in which antigen is in soluble form and precipitates when it combines with added specific antibody in the presence of an electrolyte.

protection t., neutralization t.; to determine the antimicrobial activity of a serum by inoculating a susceptible animal with a mixture of the serum and the virus or other microbe being tested.

protein-bound iodine (PBI) t., of thyroid function: serum protein-bound iodine is measured to provide an estimate of hormone bound to protein in peripheral blood.

prothrombin t., Quick's t. or method; for prothrombin in blood, based on the clotting time of oxalated blood plasma in the presence of thromboplastin and calcium chloride.

pulp t., vitality t.

Queckenstedt-Stookey t., compression of the jugular vein in a healthy person causes a rapid increase in the pressure of the spinal fluid and an equally rapid fall to normal on release of the pressure; when there is a block of subarachnoid channels, compression of the vein causes little or no increase of pressure in the cerebrospinal fluid.

quellung t., Neufeld capsular *swelling.*

Quick's t.'s, prothrombin t.

radioallergosorbent t. (RAST), a radioimmunoassay t. to detect IgE-bound allergens responsible for tissue hypersensitivity: the allergen is bound to insoluble material, and the patient's serum is reacted with this conjugate; if the serum contains antibody to the allergen, it will be complexed to the allergen.

rapid plasma reagin (RPR) t., a group of serologic t.'s for syphilis in which unheated serum or plasma is reacted with a standard test antigen containing charcoal particles; positive t.'s yield a flocculation.

Rapoport t., a differential ureteral catheterization t. used in evaluation of suspected renovascular hypertension; a positive result suggests a decrease in renal blood flow to the involved kidney and correlates well with reduction in blood pressure following corrective surgery.

Rinne's t., (1) *positive t.:* a vibrating tuning fork is held in contact with the skull (usually the mastoid process) until the sound is lost, its prongs are then brought close to the auditory orifice when, if the hearing is normal, a faint sound will again be heard; (2) *negative t.:* a vibrating tuning fork is heard longer and louder when in contact with the skull than when held near the auditory orifice, indicating a disorder of the sound conducting apparatus.

rubella HI t., a hemagglutination inhibition (HI) t. for rubella: presence of any detectable HI titer in the absence of disease indicates previous infection and immunity to reinfection.

Rubin t., tubal insufflation; of patency of the fallopian tubes, using carbon dioxide gas passed through a cannula into the cervix; if the tubes are patent, the escape of gas into the abdominal cavity is evidenced by a high-pitched bubbling sound heard on auscultation over the lower abdomen, or can be demonstrated by x-ray.

Saundby's t., a t. for blood in the stools; on the addition of a 20-volume hydrogen peroxide solution to a mixture of a saturated benzidine solution and a small quantity of feces in a test tube, a persistent dark blue color denotes the presence of blood.

Schick t., an intracutaneous t. for susceptibility to *Corynebacterium diphtheriae* toxin.

Schiller's t., a t. for non-glycogen-containing areas of the cervix, which may be the site of early carcinoma; such areas fail to stain dark brown with iodine solution.

Schilling t., a procedure for determining the amount of vitamin B_{12} excreted in the urine using cyanocobalamine tagged with a radioisotope of cobalt.

scratch t., a form of skin t. in which antigen is applied through a scratch.

screening t., any testing procedure designed to separate people or objects according to a fixed characteristic or property.

sedimentation t., the use in gastric radiology of a nonsuspended mixture of a contrast salt, such as barium or bismuth, in water to coat the stomach wall, thus giving information as to shape and movement of the organ, and also bringing into view lesions on the anterior or posterior wall invisible when the stomach is full.

sex t., a method to determine genetic sex by examination of stained smears of buccal mucosal squamous epithelial cells for the presence and number, or absence, of sex chromatin bodies; normal males have none, normal females have one per cell nucleus.

shadow t., retinoscopy.

sickle cell t., in an anaerobic wet preparation containing equal amounts of blood and 2% sodium bisulfite, erythrocytes containing hemoglobin S undergo a change in shape to a sickle cell form; the number of sickled red cells per 1000 red blood cells is determined, and expressed as a percentage.

SISI (small increment sensitivity index) t., the sounding of a tone 20 db above threshold, followed by a series of 200-msec tones 1 db louder; perception of these is indicative of cochlear damage.

skin t., a method for determining induced sensitivity (allergy) by applying an antigen (allergen) to, or inoculating it into, the skin.

solubility t., a screening t. for sickle cell hemoglobin (Hb S), which is reduced by dithionite and is insoluble in concentrated inorganic buffer; addition of blood showing Hb S to buffer and dithionite causes opacity of the solution.

split renal function t., differential ureteral catheterization t.

spot t. for infectious mononucleosis, a slide t. based on the principle that the heterophil antibodies that occur in the serum of patients with infectious mononucleosis are absorbed by beef red cells but not by guinea pig kidney cells.

sulfosalicylic acid turbidity t., for measurement of protein in urine: sulfosalicylic acid precipitates protein in urine with a turbidity that is approximately proportional to the concentration of protein in a solution.

thematic apperception t. (TAT), a projective psychological t. in which the subject is asked to tell a story about standard ambiguous pictures depicting life-situations to reveal his own attitudes and feelings.

Thompson's t., two-glass t.; the urine, in a case of gonorrhea, is passed into two glasses; if the gonococci and gonorrheal threads are found only in the first glass the probability is that the process is limited to the anterior urethra.

three-glass t., the bladder is emptied by passing urine into a series of 3-ounce test tubes: the first tube contains the washings from the anterior urethra; the second, material from the bladder; the last, material from the posterior urethra, prostate, and seminal vesicles.

tine t., see tuberculin t.

tolbutamide t., to detect insulin-producing tumors: after a 1-g intravenous dose of tolbutamide, plasma insulin and glucose are measured at intervals up to 3 hr; higher insulin responses and lower glucose values are indicative of such tumors.

Trendelenburg's t., of the valves of the leg of the leg veins: the leg is raised above the level of the heart until the veins are empty and is then rapidly lowered; in varicosity and incompetence of the valves the veins will at once become distended.

Treponema pallidum hemagglutination (TPHA) t., for the serologic diagnosis of syphilis: a positive reaction with tanned sheep red blood cells coated with the antigen of *Treponema pallidum* and nonspecific patient serum antibody indicates the presence of specific antibody for *Treponema pallidum* in patient serum.

Treponema pallidum immobilization (TPI) t., a t. for syphilis in which an antibody other than Wassermann antibody is present in the serum of a syphilitic patient, which in the presence of complement causes the immobilization of actively motile *Treponema pallidum* obtained from testes of a rabbit infected with syphilis.

tuberculin t., application of the skin t. to the diagnosis of infection by *Mycobacterium tuberculosis* in which tuberculin or its "purified" protein derivative serves as an antigen (allergen): injection of graduated doses of tuberculin or of purified protein derivative into the skin, most often by means of a needle and syringe (Mantoux t.) or by means of tines (tine t.); the t. is read on the basis of induration and erythema, the former being considered more diagnostic of infection.

two-glass t., Thompson's t.

two-step exercise t., Master's t.; Master's two-step exercise t.; a t. for coronary insufficiency: the subject makes two steps 9 in. high repeatedly for $1^1/_2$ min, the total number of steps to be made in the time being determined by the age, weight, and sex of the subject; significant depression of RS-T in the electrocardiogram is considered abnormal.

vanillylmandelic acid (VMA) t., for catecholamine-secreting tumors (pheochromocytoma and neuroblastoma) performed on a 24-hr urine specimen, based on the fact that vanillylmandelic acid is the major urinary metabolite of norepinephrine and epinephrine.

VDRL t., a flocculation t. for syphilis, using cardiolipin-lecithin-cholesterol antigen as developed by the Venereal Disease Research Laboratory.

vitality t., pulp t.; a group of thermal and electrical t.'s used to aid in assessment of dental pulp health.

Wassermann t., Wassermann reaction; a complement-fixation t. used in the diagnosis of syphilis.

Weber's t., application of a vibrating tuning fork to one of several points in the midline of the head or face, to ascertain in which ear the sound is heard best by bone conduction, that ear being the affected one if the middle ear apparatus is at fault (positive t.), but probably the normal one if the sensorineural apparatus is diseased (negative t.).

Western blot t., a serum electrophoretic analysis used to identify proteins.

Zondek-Aschheim t., Aschheim-Zondek t.

testal'gia [testis + G. *algos,* pain]. Orchialgia.

testec'tomy [testis + G. *ektomē,* excision]. Orchiectomy.

testes (tes'tēz) [L.]. Plural of testis.

testicle (tes'ti-kl) [L. *testiculus,* dim. of *testis*]. Testis.

testicular (tes-tik'u-lar). Relating to the testes.

testis, pl. **testes** (tes'tis, -tēz) [L.] [NA]. Testicle; didymus; one of the two male reproductive glands, located in the cavity of the scrotum.

ectopic t., ectopia testis; parorchidium; a condition in which the t. has descended but occupies an abnormal position.

inverted t., a t. that is rotated in the scrotum, with the epididymis being directed anteriorly.

obstructed t., a t. whose descent has been prevented by fascial bands at the inguinal canal or upper scrotum.

undescended t., retained t., failure of the t. to descend into the scrotum, it being retained in the abdomen or inguinal canal.

testi'tis. Orchitis.

testoid (tes'toyd) [testis + G. *eidos,* resemblance]. **1.** Androgenic. **2.** An androgen.

testos'terone. 17β-Hydroxy-4-androstene-3-one; the male hormone, most potent naturally occurring androgen, formed by the interstitial cells of the testes, possibly secreted also by the ovary and adrenal cortex, and may be produced in nonglandular tissues from precursors such as androstenedione; used in the treatment of hypogonadism, cryptorchism, certain carcinomas, and menorrhagia.

test types. Letters of various sizes printed on a card used to test the acuity of vision.

tetan-. See tetano-.

tetanic (tĕ-tan'ik) [G. *tetanikos*]. **1.** Relating to or marked by tetanus. **2.** An agent that in poisonous doses produces tonic muscular spasm.

tetan'iform. Tetanoid (1).

tetanigenous (tet-ă-nij'ĕ-nus) [tetanus + G. *-gen,* producing]. Causing tetanus or tetaniform spasms.

tetanism (tet'ă-nizm). Neonatal *tetany.*

tetanization (tet'ă-nĭ-za'shun). **1.** Tetanizing the muscles. **2.** A condition of tetaniform spasm.

tet'anize. To stimulate a muscle by a rapid series of stimuli so that the individual muscular contractions are fused into a sustained contraction.

tetano-, tetan-. Combining forms denoting tetanus or tetany.

tet'anode [G. *tetanōdēs*]. The quiet interval between the recurrent tonic spasms in tetanus.

tetanoid (tet'ă-noyd [tetano- + G. *eidos,* resemblance]. **1.** Tetaniform; resembling or of the nature of tetanus. **2.** Resembling tetany.

tetanospasmin (tet'ă-no-spaz'min). The neurotoxin of *Clostridium tetani* which causes the characteristic signs and symptoms of tetanus.

tetanus (tet'ă-nus) [L. fr. G. *tetanos,* convulsive tension]. **1.** A disease marked by painful tonic muscular contractions, caused by the neurotropic toxin (tetanospasmin) of *Clostridium tetani* acting upon the CNS. **2.** A sustained muscular contraction caused by a series of stimuli repeated so rapidly that the individual muscular responses are fused.

    cephalic t., cerebral t., tonic spasms in the face and throat due to head trauma, usually injuring the facial nerve.

    drug t., toxic t.; tonic spasms caused by strychnine or other tetanic.

    intermittent t., tetany.

    t. neonato'rum, t. affecting newborn infants, usually due to infection of the severed umbilical cord.

    puerperal t., postpartum t., t. occurring during the puerperium from obstetric infection.

    toxic t., drug t.

    traumatic t., t. following infection of a wound.

tetany (tet'ă-nī) [G. *tetanos,* tetanus]. Intermittent cramp or tetanus; a disorder marked by intermittent tonic muscular contractions, accompanied by fibrillary tremors, paresthesias, muscular pains, and increased irritability of the motor and sensory nerves to electrical and mechanical stimuli; occurs with gastric and intestinal disorders, alkalosis, or a deficiency of calcium salts.

    duration t. (D.t.), a tonic spasm occurring in degenerated muscles upon application of a strong galvanic current.

    gastric t., t. associated with gastric disorders affecting the muscles of the extremities and of respiration.

    hyperventilation t., t. caused by forced breathing, due to a reduction in the carbon dioxide of blood.

    latent t., t. manifested only when certain diagnostic procedures are used.

    neonatal t., tetanism; a continuous general muscular hypertonicity in neonates or young infants.

    parathyroid t., parathyroprival t., t. following surgical injury to or excision of the parathyroid glands.

tet'artano'pia. Tetartanopsia.

tetartanopsia (tĕ-tar'tă-nop'sĭ-ah) [G. *tetartos,* fourth, + *an-* priv. + *opsis,* vision]. Tetarnopia; a homonymous form of quadrantic hemianopsia.

tetra- [G. four]. Prefix meaning four.

tetracaine hydrochloride (tet'ră-kān). A local anesthetic used for spinal, nerve block, and topical anesthesia.

tet'rachlor'ide. A compound containing four atoms of chlorine to one atom of the other element or one radical equivalent.

tetrachloroethane (tet'ră-klōr'o-eth'ān). Acetylene tetrachloride; cellon; $Cl_2HC-CHCl_2$; a nonflammable solvent used in the manufacture of paint and varnish removers, photographic films, lacquers, and insecticides; toxicity exceeds that of chloroform and carbon tetrachloride, and produces narcosis, liver damage, kidney damage, and gastroenteritis.

tetrachlor'ometh'ane. *Carbon* tetrachloride.

tetracrotic (tet-ră-krot'ik) [tetra- + G. *krotos,* a striking]. Denoting a pulse curve with four upstrokes in the cycle.

tetracycline (tet-ră-si'klēn, -klin). A broad spectrum antibiotic, parent of oxytetracycline, prepared from chlortetracycline and also obtained from the culture filtrate of several species of *Streptomyces;* available as t. hydrochloride and t. phosphate complex.

tet'rad [G. *tetras*(*tetrad-*), the number four]. **1.** Tetralogy; a collection of four things having something in common. **2.** A quadrivalent element. **3.** A bivalent chromosome that divides into four during meiosis.

    Fallot's t., Fallot's *tetralogy.*

tetradactyl (tet-ră-dak'til) [tetra- + G. *daktylos,* finger or toe]. Quadridigitate; having only four fingers or toes on a hand or foot.

tetraethyllead (tet-ră-eth'il-led'). Lead tetraethyl; $Pb(C_2H_5)_4$; an anti-knock compound added to motor fuel; has a toxic action causing anorexia, nausea, vomiting, diarrhea, tremors, muscular weakness, insomnia, irritability, nervousness, and anxiety.

tetrago'num lumba'le. Lumbar quadrangle, a space bounded laterally by the obliquus externus abdominis muscle, medially by the erector spinae muscle, above by the serratus posterior inferior muscle, and below by the obliquus internus abdominis muscle.

tetrahydro-. Prefix denoting attachment of four hydrogen atoms.

tetrahydrocannabinol (tet-ră-hi'dro-kă-nab'ĭ-nol). $C_{21}H_{30}O_2$; the $\Delta1$-3,4-*trans*isomer and the $\Delta6$-3,4-*trans*isomer are believed to be the active isomers present in *Cannabis;* the $\Delta1$-3,4-*trans*isomer has been isolated from marihuana.

tetralogy (tet'ral'o-jī) [G. *tetralogia*]. Tetrad (1).

    Fallot's t., Fallot's tetrad; the most common form of cyanotic congenital heart disease: high pulmonic stenosis, ventricular septal defect, dextroposition of the aorta, and right ventricular hypertrophy.

tetrameric, tetramerous (tet'ră-měr'ik, tě-tram'er-us) [tetra- + G. *meros,* part]. Having four parts, or parts arranged in groups of four, or capable of existing in four forms.

tetrapep'tide. A compound of four amino acids in peptide linkage.

tetraplegia (tet-ră-ple'jĭ-ah) [tetra- + G. *plēgē*, stroke]. Quadriplegia.

tetraploid (tet'ră-ployd) [G. *tetraploos*, fourfold, + *eidos*, form]. See polyploidy.

tet'rasac'charide. A sugar containing four molecules of a monosaccharide.

tetrasomic (tet-ră-so'mik) [tetra- + chromosome]. Relating to a cell nucleus in which one chromosome is represented four times while all others are present in the normal number.

tetravalent (tet'ră-va'lent). Quadrivalent.

tetrodotoxin (tet'ro-do-tok'sin). A potent neurotoxin found in the liver and ovaries of the Japanese pufferfish, *Sphoeroides rubripes*, other species of pufferfish, and certain newts; produces axonal blocks of the preganglionic cholinergic fibers and the somatic motor nerves.

tet'rose. A monosaccharide containing only four carbon atoms in the main chain.

tet'ter [A.S. *teter*]. A colloquial term, popularly applied to ringworm and eczema, and occasionally applied to other skin eruptions.

textiform (teks'tĭ-form) [L. *textum*, something woven]. Weblike.

textural (teks'chur-al). Relating to the texture of the tissues.

texture (teks'chur) [L. *textura*, fr. *texo*, to weave]. The composition or structure of a tissue or organ.

Th Thorium.

thalam-. See thalamo-.

thalamencephalon (thal'ă-men-sef'ă-lon) [thalamus + G. *enkephalos*, brain]. That part of the diencephalon comprising the thalamus and its associated structures.

thalamic (thă-lam'ik). Relating to the thalamus.

thalamo-, thalam. Combining forms relating to the thalamus.

thalamocortical (thal'ă-mo-kor'tĭ-kal). Relating to the efferent connections of the thalamus with the cerebral cortex.

thalamotomy (thal-ă-mot'o-mī) [thalamus + G. *tomē*, incision]. Destruction of a selected portion of the thalamus by stereotaxy for the relief of pain, involuntary movements, epilepsy, and, rarely, emotional disturbances.

thalamus, pl. **thalami** (thal'ă-mus, -mi) [G. *thalamos*, a bed, a bedroom] [NA]. The large ovoid mass of gray matter that forms the larger dorsal subdivision of the diencephalon, located medial to the internal capsule and the body and tail of the caudate nucleus, and is composed of a large number of anatomically and functionally distinct cell groups or nuclei: 1) sensory relay nuclei, each receiving a modally specific sensory conduction system and in turn projecting each to the corresponding primary sensory area of the cortex; 2) secondary relay nuclei receiving fibers from the medial segment of the globus pallidus as well as cerebellothalamic fibers and projecting to the precentral motor cortex; 3) a nucleus associated with the limbic system; 4) association nuclei, each projecting to a large expanse to association cortex; 5) the midline and intralaminar nuclei; and 6) the habenula.

thalassemia (thal-ă-se'mī-ah) [G. *thalassa*, the sea, + *haima*, blood]. Any of a group of inherited disorders of hemoglobin metabolism in which there is a decrease in net synthesis of a particular globin chain without change in the structure of that chain; several genetic types exist, and the corresponding clinical picture may vary from barely detectable hematologic abnormality to severe and fatal anemia.

α **t.,** t. due to one of two or more genes that depress synthesis of α-globin chains by the chromosome with the abnormal gene. Heterozygous state: severe type, t. minor with 5 to 15% of Hb Barts at birth, only traces of Hb Barts in adult; mild type, 1 to 2% of Hb Barts at birth, not detectable in adult. Homozygous state: severe type, erythroblastosis fetalis and fetal death, only Hb Barts and Hb H present; mild type not clinically defined. See also *hemoglobin* H.

β **t.,** t. due to one of two or more genes that depress synthesis of β-globin chains by the chromosome bearing the abnormal gene. Heterozygous state: t. minor with Hb A₂ increased, Hb F normal or variably increased, Hb A normal or slightly reduced. Homozygous state: t. major with Hb A reduced to very low but variable levels, Hb F very high level.

β-δ **t.,** t. due to a gene that depresses synthesis of both β- and δ-globin chains by the chromosome bearing the abnormal gene. Heterozygous state: t. minor with Hb F comprising 5 to 30% of total hemoglobin but distributed unevenly among cells, Hb A₂ reduced or normal. Homozygous state: moderate anemia with only Hb F present, no Hb A or Hb A₂.

Lepore t., t. syndrome due to production of abnormally structured Lepore hemoglobin. Heterozygous state: t. minor with about 10% of Hb Lepore, Hb F moderately increased, Hb A₂ normal. Homozygous state: t. major with only Hb F and Hb Lepore produced, no Hb A or Hb A₂.

t. ma'jor, Cooley's anemia; the syndrome of severe anemia resulting from the homozygous state of one of the t. genes or one of the hemoglobin Lepore genes with onset, in infancy or childhood, of pallor, icterus, weakness, splenomegaly, cardiac enlargement, thinning of inner and outer tables of skull, microcytic hypochromic anemia with poikilocytosis, anisocytosis, stippled cells, target cells, and nucleated erythrocytes; types of hemoglobin are variable and depend on the gene involved.

t. mi'nor, the heterozygous state of a t. gene or a hemoglobin Lepore gene; usually asymptomatic, with leptocytosis, mild hypochromic microcytosis, and often slightly reduced hemoglobin level with slightly increased erythrocyte count; types of hemoglobin are variable and depend on the gene involved.

thalidomide (thă-lid'o-mīd). N-(2,6-Dioxo-3-(piperidyl)phthalimide; a hypnotic drug which, if taken in early pregnancy, may cause the birth of infants with phocomelia and other defects.

thallium (thal'ĭ-um) [G. *thallos*, a green shoot]. A metallic element, symbol Tl, atomic no. 81, atomic weight 204.37.

thal'lus [G. *thallos*, a young shoot]. A simple plant or fungus body which is devoid of roots, stems, and leaves.

thanato- [G. *thanatos*, death]. Combining form denoting death.

thanatobiologic (than'ă-to-bi-o-loj'ik) [thanato- + G. *bios*, life, + *logos*, study]. Relating to the processes concerned in life and death.

thanatognomonic (than'ă-to-no-mon'ik) [thanato- + G. *gnōmē*, a sign]. Of fatal prognosis, indicating the approach of death.

thanatoid (than'ă-toyd) [thanato- + G. *eidos*, resemblance]. **1.** Resembling death. **2.** Mortal; deadly.

thanatology (than'ă-tol'o-jī) [thanato- + G. *logos*, study]. The branch of science concerned with the study of death.

thebaine (the-ba'ēn, -in). $C_{19}H_{21}NO_3$; an alkaloid obtained from opium, resembling strychnine in its action and causing tetanic convulsions.

theca, pl. **thecae** (the'kah, the'se) [G. *thēkē*, a box]. A sheath or capsule.

  t. cor'dis, pericardium.

  t. follic'uli, the wall of a vesicular ovarian follicle.

thecal (the'kal) [see theca]. Relating to a sheath, especially a tendon sheath.

thecitis (the-si'tis) [G. *thēkē*, box (sheath), + *-itis*, inflammation]. Inflammation of the sheath of a tendon.

thecoma (the-ko'mah) [G. *thēkē*, box (theca), + *-oma*, tumor]. Theca cell tumor; a neoplasm derived from ovarian mesenchyme, consisting chiefly of spindle-shaped cells that frequently contain small droplets of fat; generally resembles a granulosa cell tumor and may form considerable quantities of estrogens, thereby resulting in precocious development of secondary sexual features in prepubertal girls, or hyperplasia of the endometrium in older patients.

thecostegnosis (the'ko-steg-no'sis) [G. *thēkē*, box (sheath), + *stegnōsis*, a narrowing]. Constriction of a tendon sheath.

thel-. See thelo-.

thelarche (the-lar'ke) [thel- + G. *archē*, beginning]. The beginning of development of the breasts in the female.

Thelazia (the-la'zĭ-ah) [G. *thēlazō*, to suck]. The eye worms, a genus of spiruroid nematodes that inhabit the lacrimal ducts and surface of the eyes of various domestic and wild animals, but rarely man.

thelaziasis (the-lă-zi'ă-sis). Infection with *Thelazia*.

theleplasty (the'le-plas-tī) [thel- + G. *plassō*, to form]. Mammillaplasty.

thelium, pl. **thelia** (the'lĭ-um, -lĭ-ah) [Mod. L. fr. G. *thēlē*, nipple]. **1.** A papilla. **2.** A cellular layer. **3.** *Papilla* mammae.

thelo-, thel- [G. *thēlē*, nipple]. Combining form denoting the nipples.

thelorrhagia (the-lo-ra'jĭ-ah) [thelo- + G. *rhēgnymi*, to burst forth]. Bleeding from the nipple.

thenal'dine. Thenophenopiperidine; 1-methyl-4-N-2-thenylanilinopiperidine; antihistaminic and antipruritic agent (as the tartrate).

the'nar [G. the palm of the hand] **1** [NA]. The fleshy mass on the lateral side of the palm; the ball of the thumb. **2.** Pertaining to any structure in relation with this part.

theophylline (the-of'ĭ-lēn, -lin). 1,3-Dimethylxanthine; an alkaloid found with caffeine in tea leaves; a smooth muscle relaxant, diuretic, cardiac stimulant, and vasodilator.

theorem (the'o-rem). A proposition that can be proved, or so is established as a law or principle. See also law; principle.

theory (the'o-rī) [G. *theōria*, a beholding, speculation]. **1.** A reasoned explanation of the manner in which something occurs, lacking absolute proof, but more nearly established than hypothesis, which is closer to speculation. **2.** The underlying science, as distinguished from the art or practice, of a profession.

  adsorption t. of narcosis, that a drug becomes concentrated at the surface of the cell as a result of adsorption, and thus alters permeability and metabolism.

  Arrhenius-Madsen t., that the reaction of an antigen with its antibody is a reversible reaction; the equilibrium being determined according to the law of mass action, by the concentrations of the reacting substances.

  Brünsted t., an acid is a substance, charged or uncharged, liberating hydrogen ions in solution; a base is a substance that removes them from solution.

  clonal selection t., that mutation of stem cells produces all possible templates for antibody production; exposure to a specific antigen will then selectively stimulate proliferation of the cell with the appropriate template to form a clone or colony of specific antibody-forming cells.

  colloid t. of narcosis, coagulation or flocculation of protein causes dehydration and reduction of metabolism.

  decay t., a t. of forgetting based on the premise that an engram deteriorates progressively with time during the interval when it is not activated.

  emergency t., that animal and human organisms respond to emergency situations by increased sympathetic nervous system activity including an increased catecholamine production with associated increases in blood pressure, heart and respiratory rates, and skeletal muscle blood flow.

  enzyme inhibition t. of narcosis, that narcotics inhibit respiratory enzymes by suppression of the formation of high energy phosphate bonds within the cell.

gametoid t., that the malignancy of a tumor results from neoplastic cells having developed sexual characteristics, by means of which they multiply and grow autonomously as parasites on the host's tissues.

gate-control t., that afferent stimuli, particularly pain, entering the substantia gelatinosa are modulated by other afferent stimuli and descending spinal pathways so that their transmission to the neurons is blocked (gated) by inhibitory agents.

information t., in the behavioral sciences, a system for studying the communication process: detailed analysis, often mathematical, of all aspects of the process including the encoding, transmission, and decoding of signals.

lipoid t. of narcosis, that narcotic efficiency parallels the coefficient of partition between oil and water, and lipoids in the cell and on the cell membrane absorb the drug because of this great affinity.

omega-oxidation t., that the oxidation of fatty acids commences at the CH_3 group, *i.e.*, the terminal or omega-group; beta-oxidation then proceeds at both ends of the fatty acid chain.

oxygen deprivation t. of narcosis, narcotics inhibit oxidation, which causes the cell to be narcotized.

quantum t., that energy can be emitted, transmitted, and absorbed only in discrete quantities (quanta), so that atoms and subatomic particles can exist only in certain energy states.

recapitulation t., law of recapitulation; the t. formulated by Haeckel that individuals in their embryonic development pass through stages similar in general structural plan to the stages their species passed through in its evolution.

somatic mutation t. of cancer, that cancer is caused by a mutation or mutations in the body cells (as opposed to germ cells), especially nonlethal mutations associated with increased proliferation of the mutant cells.

surface tension t. of narcosis, that substances which lower surface tension of water pass more readily into the cell and cause narcosis by decreasing metabolism.

thermodynamic t. of narcosis, that interposition of narcotic molecules in non-aqueous cellular phase causes changes that interfere with facilitation of ionic exchange.

Young-Helmholtz t. of color vision, that there are three sets of color-perceiving elements in the retina: for red, green, and violet; perception of the other colors arise from the combined stimulation of these elements.

thèque (tek) [Fr. a small box]. A nest or aggregation of nevocytes or other cells in the epidermis.

therapeutic (thĕr-ă-pu'tĭk) [G. *therapeutikos*]. Relating to therapeutics, or to the treatment of disease.

therapeutics (thĕr-ă-pu'tĭks) [G. *therapeutikē,* medical practice]. The practical branch of medicine concerned with the treatment of disease.

therapeu'tist. One skilled in therapeutics.

therapist (thĕr'ă-pist). One skilled in the practice of some type of therapy.

  behavior t., a psychotherapist who practices behavior therapy.

  physical t., a person professionally trained in the practice of physical therapy.

therapy (thĕr'ă-pĭ) [G. *therapeia*, medical treatment]. Treatment of disease by various methods.

  behavior t., an offshoot of psychotherapy involving the use of procedures and techniques associated with conditioning and learning for treatment of a variety of psychological conditions; systematic desensitization, flooding, counter-conditioning, and biofeedback are some techniques employed; distinguished from psychotherapy because specific symptoms are selected as the target for change, planned interventions or remedial steps to extinguish or modify these symptoms are then employed, and the progress of changes are continuously and quantitatively monitored.

  client-centered t., a system of nondirective psychotherapy based on the assumption that the client (patient) both has the internal resources to improve and is in the best position to resolve his own personality dysfunction.

  collapse t., surgical treatment of pulmonary tuberculosis whereby the diseased lung is placed, totally or partially, temporarily or permanently, in a non-functional respiratory state of retraction and immobilization.

  electroconvulsive t. (ECT), electroshock t.

  electroshock t., electroconvulsive t.; a treatment of mental disorders in which convulsions are produced by the passage of an electric current through the brain.

  extended family t., family t. that involves family members outside the nuclear family and who are closely associated with it and affect it.

  family t., group psychotherapy in which a family in conflict meets as a group with the therapist and explores its relationships and processes; focus is on the resolution of current interactions between members rather than on individual members.

  gestalt t., psychotherapy, used with individuals or groups, that emphasizes treatment of the person as a whole: his biological component parts and their organic functioning, his perceptual configuration, and his interrelationships with the external world.

  group t., psychotherapy involving two or more patients participating together with one or more therapists to effect behavioral changes through interpersonal exchanges.

  inhalation t., therapeutic use of gases or aerosols by inhalation.

maintenance drug t., in chemotherapy, systematic dosage reduction to a level at which protection against exacerbation is minimally maintained.

milieu t., psychotherapy employing manipulation of the social environment for the benefit of the patient.

occupational t. (OT), use of avocational or vocational tasks as a form of t., or the training in such as a means of rehabilitation.

physical t. (PT), physiatrics; physiotherapy; treatment of disease by use of natural forces, massage, and therapeutic exercises.

play t., t. used with children in which the young patient reveals his problems and fantasies by playing with dolls, clay, or other toys.

psychoanalytic t., psychoanalysis (1).

radiation t., use of radiant energy in the treatment of disease.

rational t., therapeutic procedures based on the premise that lack of information or illogical thought patterns are basic causes of the patient's difficulties.

replacement t., t. designed to compensate for a lack or deficiency arising from inadequate nutrition, from certain dysfunctions, or from losses; replacement may be physiological or may entail administration of a substitute substance.

shock t., see shock *treatment.*

substitution t., replacement t. when replacement is not physiological but a substance substitute is used.

therm-. See thermo-.

thermacogenesis (ther'mă-ko-jen'ĕ-sis) [G. *thermē,* heat, + *pharmakon,* drug, + *genesis,* production]. Elevation of body temperature by drug action.

ther'mal. Pertaining to heat.

thermalgesia (ther-mal-je'zĭ-ah) [therm- + G. *algēsis,* sense of pain]. Excessive sensibility to heat; pain caused by slight degree of heat.

thermalgia (ther-mal'jĭ-ah) [therm- + G. *algos,* pain]. Burning pain.

thermanalgesia (therm'an-al-je'zĭ-ah) [therm- + analgesia]. Thermoanesthesia.

thermanesthesia (therm'an-es-the'zĭ-ah). Thermoanesthesia.

thermesthesia (therm'es-the'zĭ-ah). Thermoesthesia.

therm'esthesiom'eter. Thermoesthesiometer.

thermo-, therm- [G. *therme,* heat; *thermos,* warm or hot]. Combining forms denoting heat.

thermoanalgesia (ther'mo-an-al-je'zĭ-ah). Thermoanesthesia.

thermoanesthesia (ther'mo-an-es-the'zĭ-ah) [thermo- + G. *an-* priv. + *aisthēsis,* sensation]. Thermanesthesia; thermoanalgesia; thermanalgesia; loss of the temperature sense or of the ability to distinguish between heat and cold.

thermocautery (ther'mo-kaw-ter-ĭ) [thermo- + G. *kautērion,* branding iron]. Use of an actual cautery, such as an electrocautery.

thermochem'istry. The interrelation of chemical action and heat.

thermocoagulation (ther'mo-ko-ag-u-la'shun). The process of converting tissue into a gel by heat.

thermocouple (ther-mo-kup'l). A device for measuring slight changes in temperature, consisting of two wires of different metals, one being kept at a certain low temperature, the other in the tissue or other material whose temperature is to be measured; a thermoelectric current is set up which is measured by a potentiometer.

thermodiffusion (ther'mo-dĭ-fu'zhun). The diffusion of fluids, either gaseous or liquid, as influenced by the temperature of the fluid.

thermoduric (ther-mo-du'rik) [thermo- + L. *durus,* hard, enduring]. Resistant to the effects of high temperature; said of microorganisms.

thermodynamics (ther'mo-di-nam'iks) [thermo- + G. *dynamis,* force]. 1. The branch of physicochemical science concerned with heat and energy and their conversions one into the other involving mechanical work. 2. The study of the flow of heat.

thermoesthesia (ther'mo-es-the'zĭ-ah) [thermo- + G. *aisthēsis,* sensation]. Thermesthesia; the ability to distinguish differences of temperature.

thermoesthesiometer (ther'mo-es-the'zĭ-om'ĕ-ter) [thermo- + G. *aisthēsis,* sensation, + *metron,* measure]. Thermesthesiometer; an instrument for testing the temperature sense.

thermoexcitory (ther'mo-ek-si'to-rĭ). Stimulating the production of heat.

thermogenesis (ther-mo-jen'ĕ-sis) [thermo- + G. *genesis,* production]. The physiologic process of heat production in the body.

thermogenet'ic, thermogen'ic. 1. Relating to thermogenesis. **2.** Calorigenic (2).

ther'mogram [thermo- + G. *gramma,* a writing]. **1.** A regional temperature map of a body or organ obtained, without direct contact, by infrared sensing devices; measures radiant heat, and thus blood flow. **2.** The record made by a thermograph.

ther'mograph [thermo- + G. *graphō,* to write]. A registering thermometer, one form of which records every variation of temperature.

thermography (ther-mog'ră-fĭ). A process for measuring temperature by means of a thermograph.

thermoinhibitory (ther'mo-in-hib'ĭ-to-rĭ). Inhibiting or arresting thermogenesis.

thermolabile (ther'mo-la-bil) [thermo- + L. *labilis,* perishable]. Subject to alteration or destruction by heat.

thermolysis (ther-mol'ĭ-sis) [thermo- + G. *lysis,* dissolution]. **1.** Loss of body heat by evaporation, radiation, etc. **2.** Chemical decomposition by heat.

thermolyt'ic. Relating to thermolysis.

thermomassage (ther'mo-mă-sahzh'). Combination of heat and massage in physical therapy.

ther'momet'ric. Relating to thermometry or to a thermometer reading.

thermometer (ther-mom'ĕ-ter) [thermo- + G. *metron,* measure]. An instrument for indicating the temperature of any substance. For absolute, Celsius, centigrade, Fahrenheit, homigrade, Kelvin, Rankine, and Reamur t. scales, see under scale.

clinical t., a small, self-registering t., consisting of a simple glass tube with etched scale, used for taking the temperature of the body.

resistance t., a device measuring temperature by the change of the electrical resistance of a metal wire.

self-registering t., a t. in which the maximum or minimum temperature, during the period of observation, is registered by means of a special appliance.

thermom'etry [thermo- + G. *metron*, measure]. Measurement of temperature.

thermophile, thermophil (ther'mo-fīl, -fil) [thermo- + G. *phileō*, to love]. An organism which grows best at a temperature of 50°C or higher.

thermophil'ic. Pertaining to a thermophile.

thermophore (ther'mo-fōr) [thermo- + G. *phoros*, bearing]. A device for applying heat to a part.

thermophylic (ther-mo-fi'lik) [thermo- + G. *phylaxis*, protection]. Resistant to heat; said of microorganisms.

thermoplacentography (ther'mo-plă-sen-tog'ră-fī) [thermo- + L. *placenta*, placenta, + G. *graphō*, to write]. Determination of placental position by infrared detection of blood flowing through the placenta.

thermoplegia (ther-mo-ple'jī-ah) [thermo- + G. *plēgē*, stroke]. Sunstroke.

ther'morecep'tor. A nerve ending sensitive to heat.

ther'moregula'tion. Temperature control.

ther'moscope [thermo- + G. *skopeō*, to view]. An instrument for indicating slight differences of temperature, without registering or recording them.

thermostabile, thermostable (ther'mo-sta'bil, -sta'bl) [thermo- + L. *stabilis*, stable]. Not subject to alteration or destruction by heat.

thermosteresis (ther'mo-stē-re'sis) [thermo- + G. *sterēsis*, deprivation, loss]. Abstraction or deprivation of heat.

thermosystaltic (ther'mo-sis-tal'tik) [thermo- + G. *systaltikos*, contractile]. Denoting contraction, as of the muscles, under the influence of heat.

thermotac'tic, thermotax'ic. Relating to thermotaxis.

thermotaxis (ther-mo-tak'sis) [thermo- + G. *taxis*, orderly arrangement]. **1.** Reaction of living protoplasm to the stimulus of heat. **2.** Regulation of the temperature of the body.

thermotherapy (ther-mo-thĕr'a-pī) [thermo- + G. *therapeia*, treatment]. Treatment of disease by application of heat.

thermotonometer (ther'mo-to-nom'ĕ-ter) [thermo- + G. *tonos*, tone, tension, + *metron*, measure]. An instrument for measuring the degree of muscular contraction under the influence of heat.

thermotropism (ther-mot'ro-pizm) [thermo- + G. *tropē*, a turning]. Motion by a part of an organism toward or away from a source of heat.

thia-. Prefix indicating the replacement of carbon by sulfur in a compound. *Cf.* thio-.

thiaben'dazole. 2-(4-Thiazolyl)benzimidazole; a broad spectrum anthelmintic.

thialbar'bital. 5-Allyl-5-(2-cyclohexen-1-yl)-2-thiobarbituric acid; used as the sodium salt for induction of general anesthesia by intravenous injection.

thiamin, thiamine (thi'ă-min). Vitamin B$_1$; a heat-labile vitamin contained in milk, yeast, grains, and also artifically synthesized; essential for growth.

thiam'ylal sodium. A short-acting barbiturate, prepared as a mixture with sodium bicarbonate, used intravenously to produce anesthesia.

thi'azin. C$_{12}$H$_{10}$SN$_2$; parent substance of a family of biological blue dyes.

thiemia (thi-e'mī-ă) [G. *theion*, sulfur, + *haima*, blood]. Presence of sulfur in the circulating blood.

thienylalanine (thi'ĕ-nil-al'ă-nēn). 3-(3-Thienyl)alanine; a compound structurally similar to phenylalanine and inhibiting the growth of *Escherichia coli*, presumably by competitive inhibition of enzymes for which phenylalanine is substrate.

thiethylperazine maleate (thi-eth'il-pĕr'ă-zēn). An antiemetic agent used to control nausea and vomiting.

thigh (thi). Femur (1); the part of the leg between the hip and the knee.

thigmesthesia (thig-mes-the'zĭ-ah) [G. *thigma*, touch, + *aisthēsis*, sensation]. Sensibility to touch.

thigmotaxis (thig-mo-tak'sis) [G. *thigma*, touch, + *taxis*, orderly arrangement]. A form of barotaxis; denoting the reaction of an organism to contact with a solid body.

thigmotropism (thig-mot'ro-pizm) [G. *thigma*, touch, + *tropē*, a turning]. A movement toward or away from a touch stimulus by a part of an organism.

think'ing. The act of reasoning.

abstract t., t. in terms of concepts and general principles.

concrete t., t. of objects as specific items rather than as an abstract representation of a more general concept.

prelogical t., a concrete type of t., characteristic of children and primitives, to which schizophrenic persons are sometimes said to regress.

thinking through. The psychological process of understanding, with insight, one's own behavior.

thio-. Prefix denoting the replacement of oxygen by sulfur in a compound, *Cf.* thia-.

thioacid (thi-o-as'id). An organic acid in which one or more of the oxygen atoms have been replaced by sulfur atoms.

thiobarbit'urates. Hypnotics of the barbiturate group, in which the oxygen atom at carbon-2 is replaced by sulfur.

-thioic acid. Suffix denoting the radical –C(S)OH or –C(O)SH, the sulfur analogue of a carboxylic acid.

thioki'nase. See acyl-CoA synthetase.

thi'ol. 1. The monovalent radical –SH when attached to carbon. **2.** A mixture of sulfurated and sulfonated petroleum oils purified with ammonia; used in the treatment of skin diseases.

thi'olase. Acetyl-CoA acetyltransferase.

thiolysis (thi-ol'ĭ-sis). Cleavage of a chemical bond with the addition to one part of coenzyme A; analogous to hydrolysis and phosphorolysis.

-thione. Suffix denoting the radical $>C=S$, the sulfur analogue of a ketone.

thion'ic. Relating to sulfur.

thionine (thi'o-nin). Amidophenthiazine; a dark green powder, giving a purple solution in water; useful as a basic stain in its histology for chromatin and mucin because of its metachromatic properties.

thiopen'tal sodium. An ultra-short-acting barbiturate administered intravenously or rectally for induction of anesthesia or for general anesthesia.

thiophor'ases. CoA transferases. See under coenzyme A.

thiosul'fate. $S_2O_3=$; a salt of thiosulfuric acid.

thiosulfu'ric acid. $H_2S_2O_3$; sulfuric acid in which an atom of oxygen has been replaced by one of sulfur.

thioxanthene (thi-o-zan'thĕn). A class of tricyclic compounds resembling phenothiazine, but with the central ring nitrogen replaced by a carbon atom; current use emphasizes the antipsychotic and antiemetic properties of this class.

thioxo-. Prefix indicating $=S$ in a thioketone.

thirst [A.S. *thurst*]. A desire to drink, as of water.

thixola'bile. Susceptible to thixotropy.

thixotrop'ic. Pertaining to, or characterized by, thixotropy.

thixotropy (thik-sot'ro-pĭ) [G. *thixis*, a touching, + *tropē*, turning]. The property of certain gels of becoming less viscous when shaken or subjected to sharing forces and returning to the original viscosity upon standing.

thorac-. See thoraco-.

thoracalgia (tho-ră-kal'jĭ-ah) [thoraco- + G. *algos*, pain]. Thoracodynia; pain in the chest.

thoracectomy (tho-ră-sek'to-mĭ) [thoraco- + G. *ektomē*, excision]. Resection of a portion of a rib.

thoracentesis (tho'ră-sen-te'sis) [thoraco- + G. *kentēsis*, puncture]. Pleurocentesis; thoracocentesis; paracentesis of the pleural cavity.

thoracic (tho-ras'ik). Relating to the thorax.

thoracic cage. The skeleton enclosing the thorax, consisting of the thoracic vertebrae, ribs, costal cartilages, and sternum.

thoraco-, thorac-, thoracico- [G. *thōrax*, chest]. Combining forms denoting the chest (thorax).

tho'racoacro'mial. Acromiothoracic.

thoracoceloschisis (tho'ră-ko-se-los'kĭ-sis) [thoraco- + G. *koilia*, belly, + *schisis*, fissure]. Thoracogastroschisis; a congenital fissure of both the thoracic and abdominal cavities.

thoracocentesis (tho'ră-ko-sen-te'sis). Thoracentesis.

thoracocyllosis (tho'ră-ko-sĭ-lo'sis) [thoraco- + G. *kyllōsis*, a crippling]. A deformity of the chest.

thoracocyrtosis (tho'răko-ser-to'sis) [thoraco- + G. *kyrtōsis*, a being crooked]. Abnormally wide curvature of the chest wall.

thoracodyn'ia [thoraco- + G. *odynē*, pain]. Thoracalgia.

thoracogastroschisis (tho'ră-ko-gas-tros'kĭ-sis) [thoraco- + G. *gastēr*, belly, + *schisis*, fissure]. Thoracoceloschisis.

tho'racolum'bar. **1.** Relating to the thoracic and lumbar portions of the vertebral column. **2.** Relating to the sympathetic division of the autonomic nervous system.

thoracolysis (tho-ră-kol'ĭ-sis) [thoraco- + G. *lysis*, dissolution]. Breaking up of pleural adhesions.

thoracom'eter [thoraco- + G. *metron*, measure]. An instrument for measuring the circumference of the chest or its variations in respiration.

thoracomyodynia (tho'ră-ko-mi-o-din'ĭ-ah) [thoraco- + G. *mys*, muscle, + *odynē*, pain]. Pain in the muscles of the chest wall.

thoracopathy (tho-ră-kop'ă-thĭ) [thoraco- + G. *pathos*, suffering]. Any disease of the thoracic organs or tissues.

thoracoplasty (tho'ră-ko-plas-tĭ) [thoraco- + G. *plassō*, to form]. Reparative or plastic surgery of the thorax.

thoracoschisis (tho-ră-kos'kĭ-sis) [thoraco- + G. *schisis*, fissure]. Congenital fissure of the chest wall.

thoracoscope (tho-rak'o-skōp) [thoraco- + G. *skopeō*, to view]. An endoscope for examination of the pleural cavity.

thoracoscopy (tho-ră-kos'ko-pĭ) [thoraco- + G. *skopeō*, to view]. Endoscopic examination of the pleural cavity.

thoracostenosis (tho'ră-ko-stĕ-no'sis). [thoraco- + G. *stenōsis*, narrowing]. Narrowness of the chest.

thoracostomy (tho-ră-kos'to-mĭ). [thoraco- + *stoma*, mouth]. Establishment of an opening into the chest cavity, as for drainage.

thoracotomy (tho-ră-kot'o-mĭ) [thoraco- + G. *tomē*, incision]. Pleuracotomy; pleurotomy; incision into the chest wall.

thorax, pl. **thoraces** (tho'raks; tho'ră-sēz, -ra'sēz) [L. fr. G. *thōrax*, breastplate, the chest] [NA]. The chest; the upper part of the trunk between the neck and the abdomen, encased by the ribs.

thorium (tho'rĭ-um) [*Thor*, Norse god of thunder]. A radioactive metallic element, symbol Th, atomic no. 90, atomic weight 232.05.

Thr Threonine, or its radicals.

thread'worm. Common name for species of the genus *Strongyloides*; sometimes applied to any of the smaller parasitic nematodes.

thre'onine (Thr). 2-Amino-3-hydroxybutyric acid; one of the naturally occurring amino acids, included in the structure of most proteins, and essential to the diet of man and other mammals.

threshold (thresh'old) [A.S. *therxold*]. **1.** The point where a stimulus begins to produce a sensation, the lower limit of perception of a stimulus. **2.** The minimal stimulus that produces excitation of any structure, eliciting a motor response. **3.** Limen.

thrill. The vibration accompanying a cardiac or vascular murmur, which can be felt on palpation.

diastolic t., a t. felt over the precordium or over a blood vessel during ventricular diastole.

hydatid t., hydatid fremitus; the peculiar trembling or vibratory sensation felt on palpation of a hydatid cyst.

presystolic t., a t. sometimes felt, on palpation over the apex of the heart, immediately preceding the ventricular contraction.

systolic t., a t. felt over the precordium or over a blood vessel during ventricular systole.

thrix [G.]. Hair.

throat (thrōt) [A.S. *throtu*]. **1.** Gullet; the fauces and pharynx. **2.** Jugulum; the anterior aspect of the neck.

sore t., angina (1); cynanche; a condition characterized by pain or discomfort on swallowing; may be due to any of a variety of inflammations.

throb. **1.** To pulsate. **2.** A beating or pulsation.

thromb-. See thrombo-.

throm'base. Thrombin.

thrombasthenia (throm-bas-the'nĭ-ah) [thromb- + G. *asthenia*, weakness]. An abnormality of platelets characteristic of Glanzmann's t.

Glanzmann's t., Glanzmann's disease; a hemorrhagic diathesis characterized by normal or prolonged bleeding time, normal coagulation time, defective clot retraction, normal platelet count but morphologic or functional abnormality of platelets; autosomal recessive inheritance.

thrombectomy (throm-bek'to-mĭ) [thromb- + G. *ektomē,* excision]. Excision of a thrombus.

throm'bi. Plural of thrombus.

throm'bin. Thrombase. **1.** An enzyme, formed in shed blood from prothrombin by the action of prothrombinase, that converts fibrinogen into fibrin. **2.** Sterile protein substance prepared from prothrombin through interaction with thromboplastin in the presence of calcium; causes clotting of whole blood, plasma, or a fibrinogen solution.

thrombo-, thromb- [G. *thrombos,* clot (thrombus)]. Combining forms denoting blood clot or relation thereto.

thromboangiitis (throm'bo-an-jĭ-i'tis) [thrombo- + G. *angeion,* vessel, + *-itis,* inflammation]. Inflammation of the intima of a blood vessel, with thrombosis.

t. oblit'erans, Buerger's or Winiwarter-Buerger disease; inflammation of the entire wall and connective tissue surrounding medium-sized arteries and veins, especially of the legs, associated with thrombotic occlusion and commonly resulting in gangrene.

thromboarteritis (throm'bo-ar-ter-i'tis). Arterial inflammation with thrombus formation.

throm'boasthe'nia. Thrombasthenia.

thromboclasis (throm-bok'lă-sis) [thrombo- + G. *klasis,* a breaking]. Thrombolysis.

thromboclas'tic. Thrombolytic.

thrombocyst, thrombocystis (throm'bo-sist, -sis'tis) [thrombo- + G. *kystis,* a bladder]. A membranous sac enclosing a thrombus.

thrombocytasthenia (throm'bo-si-tas-the'nĭ-ah) [thrombocyte + G. *astheneia,* weakness]. A group of hemorrhagic disorders in which the platelets may be only slightly reduced in number, or even within the normal range, but are morphologically abnormal, or are lacking in factors that are effective in the coagulation of blood.

thrombocyte (throm'bo-sīt) [thrombo- + G. *kytos,* cell]. Platelet.

thrombocythemia (throm'bo-si-the'mĭ-ah) [thrombocyte + G. *haima,* blood]. Thrombocytosis.

thrombocytopathy (throm'bo-si-top'ă-thĭ) [thrombocyte + G. *pathos,* suffering]. Any disorder of the coagulating mechanism that results from dysfunction of the blood platelets.

thrombocytopenia (throm'bo-si-to-pe'nĭ-ah) [thrombocyte + G. *penia,* poverty]. Thrombopenia; an abnormally small number of platelets in the circulating blood.

essential t., a primary form of t., in contrast to secondary forms that are associated with metastatic neoplasms, tuberculosis, and leukemia involving the bone marrow, or with direct suppression of bone marrow by the use of chemical agents, or with other conditions.

thrombocytopoiesis (throm'bo-si-to-poy-e'sis) [thrombocyte + G. *poiēsis,* a making]. The process of formation of thrombocytes or platelets.

thrombocytosis throm'bo-si-to'sis) [thrombocyte + G. *-osis,* condition]. Thrombocythemia; an increase in the number of platelets in the circulating blood.

thromboembolism (throm'bo-em'bo-lizm). Embolism from a thrombus.

thromboendarterectomy (throm'bo-end-ar-ter-ek'to-mĭ). Surgical opening of an artery, removing an occluding thrombus along with the intima and atheromatous material, and leaving a clean fresh plane internal to the adventitia.

thrombogenic (throm-bo-jen'ik) [thrombo- + G. *-gen,* producing]. **1.** Relating to thrombogen. **2.** Causing thrombosis or coagulation of the blood.

thromboid (throm'boyd) [thrombo- + G. *eidos,* resemblance]. Resembling a thrombus.

thrombokinase (throm-bo-ki'nās). Thromboplastin.

thrombolymphangitis (throm'bo-lim-fan-ji'tis). Inflammation of a lymphatic vessel with the formation of a lymph clot.

thrombolysis (throm-bol'ĭ-sis) [thrombo- + G. *lysis,* a dissolving]. Thromboclasis; fluidifying or dissolving of a thrombus.

thrombolytic (throm-bo-lit'ik). Thromboclastic; breaking up or dissolving a thrombus.

throm'bon. An all-inclusive term for circulating thrombocytes and the cellular forms from which they arise.

thrombopathy (throm-bop'ăthĭ) [thrombo- + G. *pathos,* disease]. Any disorder of blood platelets resulting in defective thromboplastin, without obvious change in the appearance or number of platelets.

thrombope'nia. Thrombocytopenia.

thrombophilia (throm-bo-fil'ĭ-ah) [thrombo- + G. *philos*, fond]. A disorder of the hemopoietic system in which there is a tendency to the occurrence of thrombosis.

thrombophlebitis (throm'bo-flĕ-bi'tis) [thrombo- + G. *phleps*, vein, + -*itis*, inflammation]. Venous inflammation with thrombus formation.

thromboplas'tid. **1.** Platelet. **2.** A nucleated spindle cell in submammalian blood.

throm'boplas'tin. Thrombokinase; platelet tissue factor; a substance present in tissues, platelets, and leukocytes necessary for the coagulation of blood; in the presence of calcium ions, it is necessary for the conversion of prothrombin to thrombin.

thrombopoiesis (throm-bo-poy-e'sis) [thrombo- + G. *poiēsis*, a making]. The process of a clot forming in blood; generally referring to formation of blood platelets (thrombocytes).

thrombosed (throm'bōsd). **1.** Clotted. **2.** Denoting a blood vessel that is the seat of thrombosis.

thrombosis, pl. **thromboses** (throm-bo'sis, -sēz) [G. *thrombōsis*, a clotting, fr. *thrombos*, clot]. Formation or presence of a thrombus; clotting within a blood vessel which may cause infarction of tissues supplied by the vessel.

   coronary t., coronary occlusion by thrombus formation, usually the result of atheromatous changes in the arterial wall and leading to myocardial infarction.

   mural t., formation of a thrombus in contact with the endocardial lining of a cardiac chamber, or a large blood vessel, if not occlusive.

thrombostasis (throm-bos'tă-sis) [thrombo- + G. *stasis*, a standing]. Local arrest of the circulation by thrombosis.

thrombot'ic. Relating to, caused by, or characterized by thrombosis.

thromboxane (throm'bok-zan). The formal parent of the thromboxanes; prostanoic acid in which the –COOH has been reduced to –CH₃ and an oxygen atom has been inserted between carbons 11 and 12.

throm'boxanes. A group of compounds formally based on thromboxane, but biochemically related to the prostaglandins and formed from them; they influence platelet aggregation and formation of the oxygen-containing six-membered ring.

throm'bus, pl. **throm'bi** [L. fr. G. *thrombos*, a clot]. A clot in the cardiovascular systems formed from constituents of blood; may be occlusive or attached to the vessel or heart wall without obstructing the lumen.

   mural t., a t. formed on and attached to a diseased patch of endocardium, not on a valve or on one side of a large blood vessel.

   obstructive t., a t. due to obstruction in the vessel from compression or other cause.

   parietal t., an arterial t. adhering to one side of the wall of the vessel.

thrush [fr. thrush fungus, *Candida albicans*]. Infection of the oral tissues with *Candida albicans.*

thulium (thu'lĭ-um) [L. *Thule*, island north of Europe]. A metallic element of the lanthanide series, symbol Tm, atomic no. 69, atomic weight 168.94.

thumb [A.S. *thuma*]. Pollex; first finger; the first digit on the radial side of the hand.

   tennis t., tendinitis with calcification in the tendon of the long flexor of the t., caused by exercise in which the t. is subject to much pressure or strain.

thym-. See thymo-.

thymectomy (thi-mek'to-mĭ) [thymus + G. *ektomē*, excision]. Removal of the thymus gland.

thymelcosis (thi'mel-ko'sis) [thymus + G. *helkōsis*, ulceration]. Suppuration of the thymus gland.

thymergasia (thi-mer-ga'zĭ-ah) [G. *thymos*, mind, + *ergazesthai*, to work]. An emotional disorder characterized by excitement or depression.

thymi-. See thymo-.

-thymia [G. *thymos*, the mind or heart as the seat of strong feelings or passion]. Suffix denoting relation to the mind, soul, or emotions. See also thymo-.

thymic (thi'mik). Relating to the thymus gland.

thymicolymphatic (thi'mĭ-ko-lim-fat'ik). Relating to the thymus and the lymphatic system.

thymidine (dThd, dT) (thi'mĭ-dēn). Thymine deoxyribonucleoside; one of the four major nucleosides in DNA.

thymidine 5'-triphosphate (dTTP). Thymidine esterfied at its 5' position with triphosphoric acid; the immediate precursor of thymidylic acid in DNA.

thymidylic acid (thi'mĭ-dil'ik). Thymidine 5'-phosphate; a hydrolysis product of DNA.

thymine (thi'mēn, -min). 5-Methyluracil; a constituent of thymidylic acid and DNA.

thymitis (thi-mi'tis). Inflammation of the thymus gland.

thymo-, thym-, thymi- **1** [G. *thymos*, thymus]. Combining forms denoting the thymus. **2** [G. *thymos*, the mind or heart as the seat of strong feelings or passions]. Combining forms denoting relation to the mind, soul, or emotions.

thymocyte (thi'mo-sīt) [thymo- (1) + G. *kytos*, cell]. A cell that develops in the thymus as the precursor of the thymus-derived lymphocyte (T lymphocyte) that effects cell-mediated (delayed type) sensitivity.

thymogenic (thi-mo-jen'ik) [thymo- (2) + G. *genesis*, origin]. Of affective origin.

thymokinetic (thi'mo-kĭ-net'ik) [thymo- (1) + G. *kinēsis*, movement]. Activating the thymus gland.

thymoma (thi-mo'mah) [thymo- (1) + G. -*oma*, tumor]. A usually benign neoplasm in the anterior mediastinum, originating from thymic tissue and frequently encapsulated.

thymopathy (thi-mop'ă-thī) [thymo- (1) + G. *pathos*, disease]. Any disease of the thymus gland.

thymoprival, thymoprivic, thymoprivous (thi'mo-pri'val, -priv'ik, -pri'vus) [thymo- (1) + L. *privus*, deprived of]. Relating to or marked by premature atrophy or removal of the thymus.

thymus, pl. **thymuses, thymi** (thi'mus, thi'mi) [G. *thymos*, thymus, sweetbread] [NA]. Thymus gland; a lymphoid organ, located in the superior mediastinum and lower part of the neck, that is necessary in early life for the normal development of immunological function; at puberty, it begins to involute and much of the lymphoid tissue is replaced by fat.

thyro-, thyr-. Combining forms denoting the thyroid gland.

thyroadenitis (thi-ro-ad-ĕ-ni'tis) [thyro- + G. *adēn*, gland, + *-itis*, inflammation]. Thyroiditis.

thyroaplasia (thi'ro-ă-pla'zi-ah) [thyro- + G. *a*-priv. + *plasis*, a molding]. Anomalies observed in cases of congenital defects of the thyroid gland and deficiency of its secretion.

thyroarytenoid (thi'ro-ăr'ĭte'noyd). Relating to the thyroid and arytenoid cartilages.

thyrocalcitonin (thi'ro-kal-sĭto'nin). A hypocalcemic polypeptide hormone secreted by the parafollicular cells of the thyroid gland; believed to inhibit the resorption of bone and used in the treatment of Paget's disease.

thyrocele (thi'ro-sēl) [thyro- + G. *kēlē*, tumor]. Enlargement of the thyroid gland.

thyrocricotomy (thi'ro-kri-kot'o-mi). Division of the cricothyroid membrane.

thyroepiglottic (thi'ro-ep-ĭ-glot'ik). Relating to the thyroid cartilage and the epiglottis.

thyrogenic, thyrogenous (thi-ro-jen'ik, -roj'ĕ-nus) [thyro- + G. *-gen*, producing]. Thyrogenous; of thyroid gland origin.

thyroglob'ulin. 1. A thyroid hormone-containing protein, usually stored in the colloid within the thyroid follicles; biosynthesis entails iodination of its tyrosine moieties and the combination of two iodotyrosines to form thyroxine, the fully iodinated thyronine; secretion of thyroid hormone requires proteolytic degradation of t., with the attendant release of free hormone. 2. A substance obtained by the fractionation of thyroid glands from the hog, used as a thyroid hormone in the treatment of hypothyroidism.

thyroglos'sal. Relating to the thyroid gland and the tongue.

thyrohy'al. The greater cornu of the hyoid bone.

thyrohy'oid. Relating to the thyroid cartilage and the hyoid bone.

thyroid (thi'royd) [G. *thyreos*, an oblong shield, + *eidos*, form]. 1. Resembling a shield, scutiform; denoting the t. gland or the t. cartilage. 2. A pharmaceutical preparation of cleaned, dried, and powdered t. gland obtained from a domesticated food animal. It contains 0.17 to 0.23% of iodine; used in the treatment of cretinism and myxedema, in certain cases of obesity, and in skin disorders.

thyroidectomy (thi-roy-dek'to-mi) [thyroid + G. *ektomē*, excision]. Removal of the thyroid gland.

thyroiditis (thi-roy-di'tis). Thyroadenitis; inflammation of the thyroid gland.

    chronic atrophic t., replacement of the thyroid gland by fibrous tissue.

    Hashimoto's t., Hashimoto's *disease.*

thyrolib'erin. Thyrotropin-releasing *hormone.*

thyromegaly (thi-ro-meg'ălĭ) [thyro- + G. *megas*, large]. Enlargement of the thyroid gland.

thyronine (thi'ro-nēn, -nin). An amino acid with a diphenyl ether group in the side chain; occurs in proteins only in the form of iodinated derivatives such as thyroxine.

thyroparathyroidectomy (thi'ro-păr-ă-thi'roy-dek'to-mi). Excision of thyroid and parathyroid glands.

thyroprival, thyroprivic (thi-ro-pri'val, -pri'vik) [thyro- + L. *privus*, deprived of]. Relating to thyroprivia; denoting hypothyroidism produced by disease or thyroidectomy.

thyroptosis (thi-rop-to'sis) [thyro- + G. *ptōsis*, a falling]. Downward dislocation of the thyroid gland.

thyrotomy (thi-rot'o-mi) [thyro- + G. *tomē*, a cutting]. 1. Any cutting operation on the thyroid gland. 2. Laryngofissure.

thyrotox'ic. Designating the state produced by excessive quantities of endogenous or exogenous thyroid hormone.

thyrotoxicosis (thi'ro-tok-sĭ-ko'sis) [thyro- + G. *toxikon*, poison, + *-osis*, condition]. The state produced by excessive quantities of endogenous or exogenous thyroid hormone.

thyrotroph (thi'ro-trof). A cell in the anterior lobe of the pituitary that produces thyrotropin.

thyrotrophic (thi'ro-trof'ik) [thyro- + G. *trophē*, nourishment]. Thyrotropic.

thyrotrophin (thi-rot'ro-fin, thi-ro-tro'fin). Thyrotropin.

thyrotropic (thi'ro-trop'ik) [thyro- + G. *tropē*, a turning]. Thyrotrophic; stimulating or nurturing the thyroid gland.

thyrotropin (thi-rot'ro-pin, thi-ro-tro'pin). Thyrotrophin; thyrotropic hormone; thyroid-stimulating hormone; a glycoprotein hormone produced by the anterior pituitary gland which stimulates the growth and function of the thyroid gland, and is used as a diagnostic test to differentiate primary and secondary hypothyroidism.

thyroxine, thyroxin (T₄) (thi-rok'sēn). 3,3',5,5'-Tetraiodothyronine; the active iodine compound existing normally in the thyroid gland and extracted therefrom in crystalline form for therapeutic use; also prepared synthetically.

Ti Titanium.

TIA Transient ischemic *attack.*

tibia, pl. **tibiae** (tib'ĭ-ah, tib'ĭ-e) [L.] [NA]. Shin bone; the medial and larger of the two bones of the leg, articulating with the femur, fibula, and talus.

    saber t., deformity of the t. occurring in tertiary syphilis or yaws, the bone having a marked forward convexity as a result of the formation of gummas and periostitis.

    t. val'ga, *genu* valgum.

    t. va'ra, *genu* varum.

tibial (tib'ĭ-al) [L. *tibialis*]. Relating to the tibia.

tibio- [L. *tibia*, the large shinbone]. Combining form denoting the tibia.

tic [Fr.]. Habit spasm; an involuntary repeated contraction of a certain group of associated muscles; a habitual spasmodic movement or contraction of any part. See also spasm.

t. douloureux (du-lu-ru') [Fr. painful], trigeminal *neuralgia.*

facial t., involuntary twitching of the facial muscles, sometimes unilateral. Also called palmus (1); facial spasm; prosopospasm.

tick. An acarine of the families Ixodidae (hard t.'s) or Argasidae (soft t.'s), which contain many blood-sucking species that are important pests and vectors of a variety of disease agents; differentiated from the much smaller true mites by possession of an armed hypostome and a pair of tracheal spiracular openings located behind the basal segment of the third or fourth pair of walking legs.

t.i.d. L. *ter in die,* three times a day.

ti'dal. Relating to or resembling the tides, alternately rising and falling.

tide [A.S. *tid,* time]. An alternate rise and fall, ebb and flow, or increase and decrease.

acid t., a temporary increase in the acidity of the urine occurring during fasting.

alkaline t., a period of urinary neutrality or alkalinity after meals due to withdrawal of hydrogen ion for the purpose of secretion of the highly acid gastric juice.

fat t., an increase in the fat content of blood and lymph following a meal.

Tierfellnaevus (tēr'fel-ne-vus) [Ger. a nevus simulating the pelt of an animal]. Bathing trunk *nevus.*

timbre (tam'br, tim'br) [Fr.]. The distinguishing quality of a sound, by which one may determine its source.

time [A.S. *tima*]. **1.** That relation of events which is expressed by the terms past, present, and future, and measured by units such as minutes, hours, days, months, or years. **2.** A certain period during which something definite or determined is done.

activated partial thromboplastin t., the t. needed for plasma to form a fibrin clot following the addition of calcium and a phospholipid reagent; used to evaluate the intrinsic clotting system.

coagulation t., clotting t., the t. required for blood to coagulate.

inertia t., the interval elapsing between the reception of the stimulus from a nerve and the contraction of the muscle.

left ventricular ejection t. (LVET), the t. measured from onset to incisural notch of the carotid pulse.

prothrombin t., the t. required for clotting after thromboplastin and calcium are added in optimal amounts to blood of normal fibrinogen content; if prothrombin is diminished, the clotting t. increases.

reaction t., the interval between the presentation of a stimulus and the response to it.

tin. Stannum; a metallic element, symbol SN, atomic no. 50, atomic weight 118.69.

tinct. Tincture.

tinctorial (tingk-tōr'ĭ-al) [L. *tinctorius,* fr. *tingo,* to dye]. Relating to coloring or staining.

tincture (tinct., tr.) (tingk'chur) [L. *tinctura,* a dyeing]. An alcoholic or hydroalcoholic solution prepared from vegetable materials or from chemical substances. T.'s of potent drugs essentially represent the activity of 10 g of the drug in each 100 ml of t.; most other t.'s represent 20 g of drug in each 100 ml of t.

tinea (tin'e-ah) [L. worm, moth]. Ringworm; serpigo (1); a fungus infection of the hair, skin, or nails.

t. bar'bae, t. sycosis.

t. cap'itis, ringworm of the scalp; a fungus infection of the scalp caused by various species of *Microsporn* and *Trichophyton,* characterized by patches of apparent baldness, scaling, block dots, and occasionally erythema and pyoderma.

t. circina'ta, t. cor'poris, ringworm of the body; a scaling macular eruption that frequently forms annular lesions on any part of the body.

t. cru'ris, jock itch; eczema marginatum; ringworm of the genitocrural region; t. imbricata occurring in the genitocrural region, including the inner side of the thighs, perineum, and groin.

t. imbrica'ta, an eruption consisting of concentric rings of overlapping scales forming papulosquamous patches scattered over the body, caused by the fungus *Trichophyton concentricum.*

t. ke'rion, an inflammatory fungus infection of the scalp and beard, marked by pustules and a boggy infiltration of the surrounding parts, commonly caused by *Microsporum audouini.*

t. pe'dis, athlete's foot; ringworm of the foot, especially of the skin between the toes, caused by a species of *Trichophyton* or *Epidermophyton;* consists of small vesicles, fissures, scaling, maceration, and eroded areas between toes and on the plantar surfaces of the feet.

t. syco'sis, folliculitis or t. barbae; ringworm of the beard, occurring as a follicular infection or as a granulomatous lesion; primary lesions are papules and pustules.

t. un'guium, onychomycosis.

t. versic'olor, pityriasis versicolor; an eruption of tan or brown branny patches on the skin of the trunk, often appearing white in contrast with hyperpigmented skin after exposure to the summer sun; caused by *Malassezia furfur.*

tinnitus (tĭ-ni'tus) [L. *tinnio,* pp. *tinnitus,* to jingle, clink]. The sensation of noises in one or both ears; associated with disease in the middle ear, the inner ear, or the central auditory apparatus.

tiring (tīr'ing). Fixing the fragments of a broken bone by fastening a wire around them.

tissue (tish'u) [Fr. *tissu*, woven, fr. L. *texo*, to weave]. A collection of similar cells and the intercellular substances surrounding them, of four basic types: epithelium, connective tissue, muscle tissue, nerve tissue.

adenoid t., lymphatic t.

adipose t., fat (1); a connective t. consisting chiefly of fat cells surrounded by reticular fibers and arranged in lobular groups or along the course of one of the smaller blood vessels.

areolar t., loose, irregularly arranged connective t. that consists of collagenous and elastic fibers, a protein polysaccharide ground substance, and connective t. cells.

bone t., osseous t.

cancellous t., lattice-like or spongy osseous t.

chondroid t., (1) pseudocartilage; in an adult, t. resembling cartilage; (2) in an embryo, an early stage in cartilage formation.

chromaffin t., a cellular t., vascular and well supplied with nerves, made up chiefly of chromaffin cells and found in the medulla of the suprarenal glands and in the paraganglia.

connective t., interstitial t.; the supporting or framework t. of the animal body, formed of fibrous and ground substance; varieties are: areolar, adipose; fibrous, elastic, mucous, lymphatic, cartilage, and bone; blood and lymph may be regarded as connective t.'s, the ground substance of which is liquid.

elastic t., elastica (2); connective t. in which elastic fibers predominate.

erectile t., t. with numerous vascular spaces that may become engorged with blood.

fibrous t., t. composed of bundles of collagenous white fibers between which are rows of connective t. cells.

granulation t., vascular connective t. forming granular projections on the surface of a healing wound, ulcer, or inflamed t. surface.

indifferent t., undifferentiated, nonspecialized, embryonic t.

interstitial t., connective t.

lymphatic t., lymphoid t., adenoid t.; a three-dimensional network of reticular fibers and cells the meshes of which are occupied by lymphocytes.

mucous t., a gelatinous type of connective t, characteristically supporting the blood vessels of the umbilical cord (Wharton's jelly).

muscular t., flesh (2); t. characterized by the ability to contract upon stimulation, of three varieties: skeletal, cardiac, and smooth. See under muscle.

myeloid t., bone marrow consisting of the developmental and adult stages of erythrocytes, granulocytes, and megakaryocytes in a stroma of reticular cells and fibers, with sinusoidal vascular channels.

nerve t., a highly differentiated t. composed of nerve cells, nerve fibers, dendrites, and neuroglia.

osseous t., bone t.; connective t. whose matrix consists of collagen fibers and ground substance and

in which are deposited calcium salts in the form of an apatite.

reticular t., retiform t., t. in which the argyrophilic fibers form a network and which usually has a network of reticular cells associated with the fibers.

subcutaneous t., a layer of loose, irregular, connective t. immediately beneath the skin, contains fat cells except in the auricles, eyelids, penis, and scrotum.

titanium (ti-ta'nĭ-um) [*Titan*, G. myth, char.]. A metallic element, symbol Ti, atomic no. 22, atomic weight 47.90.

ti'ter [Fr. *titre*, standard]. The standard of strength of a volumetric test solution; assay value of an unknown measure by volumetric means.

TITh Triiodothyronine.

ti'trate. To analyze by titration.

titration (ti-tra'shun) [Fr. *titre*, standard]. Volumetric analysis by means of the addition of definite amounts of a test solution to a solution of the substance being assayed.

titubation (tit'u-ba'shun) [L. *titubo*, pp. *-atus*, to stagger]. **1.** A staggering or stumbling in trying to walk. **2.** Restlessness.

Tl Thallium.

TLC Thin-layer *chromatography;* total lung *capacity.*

TLV Threshold limit *value.*

Tm Thulium; transport or tubular *maximum.*

TMP Ribothymidine 5'-phosphate.

T-mycoplasma. *Ureaplasma.*

Tn Intraocular *tension.*

toco- [G. *tokos*, birth]. Combining form denoting childbirth.

tocodynagraph (to-ko-di'nă-graf) [toco- + G. *dynamis*, force, + *graphē*, a writing]. The recording made by a tocodynamometer.

tocodynamometer (to'ko-di-nămom'ē-ter) [toco- + G. *dynamis*, force, + *metron*, measure]. An instrument for measuring the force of uterine contractions.

tocography (to-kog'ră-fi) [toco- + G. *graphō*, to write]. The process of recording uterine contractions.

to'col. Fundamental unit of the tocopherols; 6-phytylhydroquinone becomes, in the chromanol form, 2-methyl-2-(4,8,12-trimethyltridecyl)chroman-6-ol.

tocolytic (to-ko-lit'ik) [toko- + G. *lysis*, dissolution]. Denoting an agent that arrests uterine contractions in labor.

tocopherol (T) (tok-of'er-ōl). **1.** Generic term for vitamin E and compounds chemically related to it, with or without biological activity. **2.** A methylated tocol or methylated tocotrienol.

α-tocopherol (α-T). Vitamin E (1); 5,7,8-trimethyltocol; obtained from wheat germ oil or by synthesis, and biologically exhibiting the most vitamin E activity of the t.'s.

tocotri'enol. A tocol with three additional double bonds in the phytyl chain.

toe [A.S. *ta*]. Digitus pedis; one of the digits of the feet.

hammer t., permanent flexion at the midphalangeal joint of one or more of the t.'s.

toe-drop. A drooping of the anterior portion of the foot, due to paralysis of the muscles that dorsally flex the foot.

toe'nail. See unguis.

ingrown t., ingrown *nail.*

Togaviridae (to-gă-vĭr'ĭ-de). The family of viruses that includes the antigenic groups A and B arboviruses, which constitute the genera *Alphavirus* and *Flavivirus,* respectively, rubella virus (*Rubivirus*), and *Pestivirus.*

to'gavirus. Any virus of the family Togaviridae.

toko-. See toco-.

tolbu'tamide. 1-Butyl-3-*p*-tolylsulfonylurea; an orally active hypoglycemic agent that appears to stimulate the synthesis and release of endogenous insulin from functional islets; available as t. sodium for injection.

tol'erance [L. *tolero,* pp. *-atus,* to endure]. **1.** The ability to endure or be less responsive to a stimulus, especially over a period of continued exposure. **2.** The power of resisting the action of a poison, or of taking a drug continuously or in large doses without injurious effects.

cross t., the resistance to one or several effects of a compound as a result of t. developed to a pharmacologically similar compound.

immunological t., acquired specific failure of the immunological mechanism to respond, induced by exposure to the given antigen.

tol'erant. Having the property of tolerance.

tolerogenic (tol'er-o-jen'ik). Producing immunologic tolerance.

toluidine blue O (tol-u'ĭ-dēn). $C_{15}H_{16}N_3SCl$; a blue basic dye used as an antibacterial agent, as a nuclear and metachromatic stain, and in electrophoresis to stain RNA, RNase, and mucopolysaccharides; also antagonizes the anticoagulant action of heparin.

-tome [G. *tomos,* cutting, sharp]. Termination denoting a cutting instrument; a segment, part, or section.

tomen'tum, tomen'tum cer'ebri [L. a stuffing for cushions]. The numerous small blood vessels passing between the cerebral surface of the pia mater and the cortex of the brain.

tomogram (to'mo-gram) [G. *tomos,* a cutting (section) + *gramma,* a writing]. The radiograph obtained with a tomograph.

tomograph (to'mo-graf). The device used in tomography.

tomography (to-mog'ră-fĭ) [G. *tomos,* a cutting (section), + *graphō,* to write]. Planigraphy; planography; stratigraphy; laminagraphy; the taking of sectional radiographs in which the image of the selected plane remains clear while the images of all other planes are blurred or obliterated.

computed t. (CT), computerized axial t. (CAT), the gathering of anatomical information from a cross-sectional plane of the body, presented as an image generated by a computer synthesis of x-ray transmission data obtained in many different directions through the given plane.

positron emission t. (PET), tomographic imaging of local metabolic and physiological functions in tissues, as an indicator of the presence or absence of disease, the image being formed by computer synthesis of data transmitted by positron-emitting radionuclides that have been incorporated into natural biochemical substances administered to the patient.

-tomy [G. *tomē,* incision]. Termination denoting a cutting operation. See also -ectomy.

tone (tōn) [G. *tonos,* tone, or a tone]. **1.** A musical sound. **2.** The character of the voice expressing an emotion. **3.** The tension present in resting muscles. **4.** Firmness of the tissues; normal functioning of all the organs.

tongue (tung) [A.S. *tunge*]. Lingua (1).

bifid t., cleft t., a t. whose extremity is divided longitudinally for a certain distance.

black t., melanoglossia; lingua nigra; the presence of a blackish to yellowish brown patch or patches on the t., accompanied by elongation of the papillae; *Candida albicans,* flourishes in this environment, especially after the use of antibiotics.

coated t., a t. with a whitish layer on its upper surface, composed of epithelial debris, food particles, and bacteria.

furrowed t., fissured t., scrotal t.; lingua plicata; a t. marked by numerous longitudinal grooves on the dorsal surface, caused by splitting apart or separation of the papillae.

geographical t., occurrence on the dorsum of the t. of peripherally spreading patches of temporary papillary atrophy or transitory benign migrating plaques. Also called lingua geographica; glossitis areata linguae; erythema migrans; erythema migrans linguae.

hairy t., glossotrichia; trichoglossia; a t. with black hairlike elongations of the papillae.

scrotal t., furrowed t.

smoker's t., leukoplakia.

strawberry t., a t. with a whitish coat through which the enlarged papillae project as red points, characteristic of scarlet fever.

tongue crib. An appliance used to control visceral (infantile) swallowing and tongue thrusting and to encourage the mature or somatic tongue posture and function.

tongue-swallowing. A slipping back of the tongue against the pharynx, causing choking.

tongue thrust. The infantile pattern of the suckle-swallow movement in which the tongue is placed between the incisor teeth or the alveolar ridges during the initial stage of swallowing.

tongue-tie. Ankyloglossia; abnormal shortness of the frenulum linguae.

tonic (ton'ik) [G. *tonikos*, fr. *tonos*, tone]. **1.** In a state of continuous unremitting action; denoting especially a muscular contraction. **2.** Invigorating; increasing physical or mental tone or vigor. **3.** A remedy that restores enfeebled function and promotes vigor and a sense of well being, qualified according to the organ or system on which they act; *e.g.*, cardiotonic.

tonicity (to-nis'ĭ-tĭ) [G. *tonos*, tone]. **1.** Tonus; a state of normal tension of the tissues by virtue of which the parts are ready to function in response to a suitable stimulus. **2.** The osmotic pressure or tension of a solution, usually relative to that of blood.

tonicoclonic (ton'ĭ-ko-klon'ik). Tonoclonic; both tonic and clonic, referring to muscular spasms.

tono- [G. *tonos*, tone, tension]. Combining form relating to tone, tension, pressure.

tonoclonic (ton-o-klon'ik). Tonicoclonic.

tonofibril (ton-o-fi'bril). One of a system of fibers, found in the cytoplasm of epithelial cells.

tonofilament (ton-o-fil'ă-ment). A structural cytoplasmic protein, bundles of which together form a tonofibril.

tonograph (ton'o-graf, to'no-) [tono- + G. *graphō*, to write]. A recording tonometer.

tonography (to-nog'rǎ-fĭ). Continuous measurement of intraocular pressure by means of a recording tonometer, for determining the facility of aqueous outflow.

tonometer (to-nom'ĕ-ter) [tono- + G. *metron*, measure]. Tenonometer; an instrument for determining pressure or tension, especially intraocular tension.

    applanation t., an instrument for determining intraocular tension by application of a small flat disk to the cornea.

    Mueller electronic t., a Schiötz type t. to which is attached an electronic device for indicating the extent of corneal indentation; may also have an attached recorder for continuous pressure readings.

    pneumatic t., a recording applanation t., operated by a gas supply from liquefied Freon.

    Schiötz t., an instrument that measures the indentation of the cornea produced by a facility of aqueous outflow.

tonometry (to-nom'ĕtrĭ). **1.** Measurement of the tension of a part. **2.** Measurement of intraocular tension.

tonoplast (to'no-plast, ton'o-) [tono- + G. *plastos*, formed]. An intracellular structure or vacuole.

ton'sil [L. *tonsilla*, a stake; pl, tonsils]. **1.** Tonsilla. **2.** *Tonsilla* palatina.

    cerebellar t., *tonsilla* cerebelli.

    faucial t., *tonsilla* palatina.

    lingual t., *tonsilla* lingualis.

    palatine t., *tonsilla* palatina.

    pharyngeal t., *tonsilla* pharyngea.

tonsilla, pl. **tonsillae** (ton-sil'ah. ton-sil'e) [L.] [NA]. Tonsil (1); amygdala (2); any collection of lymphoid tissue.

    t. cerebel'li [NA], cerebellar tonsil; amygdala cerebelli; a rounded lobule on the undersurface of each cerebellar hemisphere, continuous medially with the uvula of the vermis.

    t. lingua'lis [NA], lingual tonsil; a collection of lymphoid follicles on the posterior portion of the dorsum of the tongue.

    t. palati'na [NA], faucial or palatine tonsil; tonsil (2); a large oval mass of lymphoid tissue embedded in the lateral walls of the oral pharynx between the pillars of the fauces.

    t. pharyn'gea [NA], pharyngeal tonsil; a collection of aggregated lymphoid nodules on the posterior wall of the nasopharynx, hypertrophy of which constitutes adenoids.

ton'sillar, ton'sillary. Amygdaline (3); relating to a tonsil, especially the palatine tonsil.

tonsillectomy (ton-sĭ-lek'to-mĭ) [tonsil + G. *ektomē*, excision]. Surgical removal of the entire tonsil.

tonsillitis (ton-sĭ-li'tis) [tonsil + G. *-itis*, inflammation]. Inflammation of a tonsil, especially the palatine tonsil.

tonsillo- Combining form denoting a tonsil.

tonsillolith (ton-sil'o-lith) [tonsillo- + G. *lithos*, stone]. Tonsillar calculus; a calcareous concretion in a distended tonsillar crypt.

tonsillotomy (ton-sĭ-lot'o-mĭ) [tonsillo- + G. *tomē*, incision]. The cutting away of a portion of a hypertrophied palatine tonsil.

to'nus [L. fr. G. *tonos*]. Tonicity (1).

tooth, pl. **teeth** [A.S. *tōth*]. Dens (1); one of the hard conical structures set in the alveoli of the upper and lower jaws, used in mastication and assisting also in articulation, composed of dentin encased in cement on the covered portion and enamel on its exposed portion.

    baby t., *dens* deciduus.

    bicuspid t., *dens* premolaris.

    buck t., an anterior t. in labioversion.

    canine t., cuspid t., *dens* caninus.

    deciduous t., *dens* deciduus.

    eye t., *dens* caninus.

    Horner's teeth, incisor teeth having a hypoplastic groove running horizontally across them.

    Hutchinson's teeth, the teeth of congenital syphilis in which the incisal edge is notched and narrower than the cervical area.

    impacted t., a t. whose normal eruption is prevented by adjacent teeth or bone.

    incisor t., *dens* incisivus.

    milk t., *dens* deciduus.

    molar t., *dens* molaris.

    permanent t., *dens* permanens.

    premolar t., *dens* premolaris.

    primary t., *dens* deciduus.

    second t., *dens* permanens.

    temporary t., *dens* deciduus.

wisdom t., *dens* serotinus.

toothache (tūth′āk). Dentalgia; odontalgia; pain in a tooth due to the condition of the pulp or periodontal membrane resulting from caries, infection, or trauma.

top-. See topo-.

topagnosis (top-ag-no′sis) [top- + G. *a-* priv. + *gnosis,* recognition]. Topoanesthesia; inability to localize tactile sensations.

topalgia (to-pal′jĭ-ah) [top- + G. *algos,* pain]. Pain localized in one spot, without evident organic basis.

topesthesia (top′es-the′zĭ-ah) [top- + G. *aisthēsis,* sensation]. Ability to localize tactile sensations.

tophaceous (to-fa′shus) [L. *tophaceus*]. Sandy; gritty; pertaining to or manifesting the features of a tophus.

tophus, pl. **tophi** (to′fus, to′fi) [L. calcareous deposit from springs]. **1.** A deposit of the uric acid and urates in gout. **2.** A salivary calculus, or tartar.

top′ical [G. *topikos,* fr. *topos,* place]. Local; relating to a definite place or locality.

topo-, top- [G. *topos,* place]. Combining forms denoting place, topical.

topoanesthesia (top′o-an-es-the′zĭ-ah, to′po-) [topo- + anesthesia]. Topagnosis.

topography (to-pog′rä-fĭ) [topo- + G. *graphē,* a writing]. In anatomy, the description of any part of the body, especially in relation to a definite and limited area of the surface.

toponarcosis (top′o-nar-ko′sis) [topo- + narcosis]. A localized cutaneous anesthesia.

tor′pid [L. *torpidus,* fr. *torpeo,* to be sluggish]. Inactive; sluggish.

tor′por [L. sluggishness, numbness]. Inactivity, sluggishness.

t. ret′inae, a form of nyctalopia, the retina responding only to strong luminous stimuli.

torque (tork) [L. *torqueo,* to twist]. A rotatory force.

torsade de pointes (tor-sahd-dĕ-pwant′) [Fr. *torsade,* fringe, + *pointe,* point or tip]. Paroxysms of ventricular tachycardia in which the electrocardiogram shows a steady undulation in the QRS axis in runs of 5 to 20 beats with progressive changes in direction.

torsion (tor′shun) [L. *torsio,* fr. *torqueo,* to twist]. **1.** A twisting or rotation of a part upon its long axis. **2.** Twisting of the cut end of an artery to arrest hemorrhage. **3.** Rotation of the eye around its anteroposterior axis.

torsiversion (tor′sĭ-ver-zhun). Torsoclusion (2); a malposition of a tooth in which it is rotated on its long axis.

tor′so [It.]. The trunk; the body without relation to head or extremities.

torsoclusion (tor′so-klu-zhun) [L. *torqueo,* to twist, + *cludo,* to close]. **1.** Acupressure performed by entering a needle in the tissues parallel with the artery, then turning it so that it crosses the artery transversely, and passing it into the tissues on the opposite side of the vessel. **2.** Torsiversion.

torticollar (tor-tĭ-kol′ar). Relating to or marked by torticollis.

torticollis (tor′tĭ-kol′is) [L. *tortus,* twisted, + *collum,* neck]. Wryneck; stiffneck; a contraction, often spasmodic, of the muscles of the neck, chiefly those supplied by the spinal accessory nerve; the head is drawn to one side and usually rotated.

tortuous (tor′chu-us) [L. *tortuosus,* fr. *torqueo,* to twist]. Having many curves, full of turns and twists.

torulopsosis (tor′u-lop′so-sis). An opportunistic infection in man caused by a yeast, *Torulopsis glabrata,* usually seen in patients with severe underlying disease or those treated with antibiotic, corticosteroids, or immunosuppressive agents.

torulus, pl. **toruli** (tor′u-lus, -li) [L. dim. of *torus,* a protuberance, swelling]. A minute elevation in the skin.

torus, pl. **tori** (to′rus, to′ri) [L. swelling, knot, bulge] [NA]. A rounded or swelling, such as that caused by a bone or muscle.

totipotency, totipotence (to-tĭ-po′ten-sĭ, to-tip′o-tens) [L. *totus,* entire, + *potentia,* power]. Ability of a cell to differentiate into any type of cell and thus form a new organism or regenerate any part of an organism.

totip′otent, to′tipoten′tial. Relating to totipotency.

touch (tuch) [Fr. *toucher*]. **1.** Tactile sense; the sense by which contact is appreciated. **2.** Digital examination.

tourniquet (tūr′nĭ-ket) [Fr. fr. *tourner,* to turn]. An instrument for temporarily arresting the flow of blood to or from a distal part by pressure applied with an encircling device.

tox-. See toxico-.

toxemia (tok-se′mĭ-ah) [G. *toxikon,* arrow poison, + *haima,* blood]. **1.** Clinical manifestations observed during certain infectious diseases, assumed to be caused by toxins and other noxious substances elaborated by the infectious agent. **2.** The clinical syndrome caused by toxic substances in the blood.

toxe′mic. Pertaining to, affected with, or manifesting the features of toxemia.

toxi-. See toxico-.

toxic (tok′sik) [G. *toxikon,* arrow poison]. **1.** Poisonous. **2.** Pertaining to a toxin.

toxicant (tok′sĭ-kant). **1.** Poisonous. **2.** Any poisonous agent, specifically an alcoholic poison.

toxicity (tok-sis′ĭ-tĭ). The state of being poisonous.

oxygen t., a condition resulting from breathing high partial pressures of oxygen; characterized by visual and hearing abnormalities, unusual fatigue, muscular twitching, anxiety, confusion, incoordination, and convulsions.

toxico-, tox-, toxi-, toxo-. Combining form denoting a toxin or poison.

Toxicodendron (tok′sĭ-ko-den′dron) [toxico- + G. *dendron,* tree]. A genus of poisonous plants (family Anacardiaceae) comprising members of the genus *Rhus* such as poison ivy and poison oak.

toxicogenic (tok'sĭ-ko-jen'ik) [toxico- + G. -gen, producing]. Producing or caused by a poison.

toxicoid (tok'sĭ-koyd) [toxico- + G. eidos, resemblance]. Having an action like that of a poison.

toxicologic (tok'sĭ-ko-loj'ik). Relating to toxicology.

toxicologist (tok'sĭ-kol'o-jist). One who specializes in toxicology.

toxicology (tok'sĭ-kol'o-jĭ) [toxico- + G. logos, study]. The science of poisons: their source, chemical composition, action, tests, and antidotes.

toxicopath'ic. Denoting any morbid state caused by the action of a poison.

toxicosis (tok'sĭ-ko'sis) [toxico- + G. -osis, condition]. Systemic poisoning; any disease of toxic origin.

tox'igenic. Toxicogenic.

toxin (tok'sin) [G. toxikon, arrow poison]. A noxious or poisonous substance formed or elaborated either as an integral part of the cell (endotoxin) or tissue, as an extracellular product (exotoxin), or as a combination of two, during the metabolism and growth of an organism.

   botulinus t., botuline; a potent neurotoxin from Clostridium botulinum.

   diagnostic diphtheria t., Schick test t.

   Dick test t. streptococcus erythrogenic t.

   erythrogenic t., streptococcus erythrogenic t.

   extracellular t., exotoxin.

   intracellular t., endotoxin.

   Schick test t., diagnostic diphtheria t.; the inoculated dose of Corynebacterium diptheriae t. used in the Schick test.

   streptococcus erythrogenic t., Dick test t.; erythrogenic t.; a culture filtrate of lysogenized group A strains of β-hemolytic streptococci, erythrogenic when inoculated into the skin of susceptible persons, and neutralized by antibodies that appear during scarlet fever convalescence.

   tetanus t., the neurotropic heat-labile exotoxin of Clostridium tetani that causes tetanus.

toxinic (tok-sin'ik). Relating to a toxin.

toxinogenic (tok'sĭ-no-jen'ik) [toxin + G. -gen, producing]. Toxigenic; producing a toxin.

toxipath'ic [toxi- + G. pathos, suffering]. Relating to any diseased state caused by a poison.

toxo-. See toxico-.

toxocariasis (tok'so-kă-ri'ă-sis). Infection with nematodes of the genus Toxocara; parenterally migrating larvae, chiefly of T. canis from dogs, may cause visceral larva migrans in man.

toxoid (tok'soyd) [toxin + G. eidos, resemblance]. A toxin that has been treated so as to destroy its toxic property but retain its antigenicity.

toxophil, toxophile (tok'so-fil, -fīl) [toxo- + G. philos, fond]. Susceptible to the action of a poison.

toxophore (tok'so-fōr) [toxo- + G. phoros, bearing]. Denoting the atomic group of the toxin molecule which carries the poisonous principle.

toxophorous (tok-sof'er-us). Relating to the toxophore group of the toxin molecule.

Toxoplasma gondii (tok-so-plaz'mah gon'dĭ-i) [G. toxon, bow, + plasma, anything formed]. A sporozoan species that is an intracellular, non-host-specific parasite in a great variety of vertebrates but develops its sexual cycle, leading to oocyst production, exclusively in cats and other felids; proliferative stages and tissue cysts develop in other animals that acquire the infection from ingestion of oocysts from cats, tissue cysts from infected meat, or by transplacental migration leading to infection in utero.

toxoplasmosis (tok'so-plaz-mo'sis). Disease caused by presence of or reaction to Toxoplasma gondii. Manifestations vary widely but chorioretinitis and uveitis are common; in prenatal infections, death or severe brain and eye damage usually occur; acute disease may develop, especially in immunologically compromised individuals, leading to generalized infection.

   acquired t. in adults, a form of t. that may result in fever, encephalomyelitis, chorioretinopathy, maculopapular rash, arthralgia, myalgia, myocarditis, and pneumonitis; a lymphadenopathic form is manifested by fever, lymphadenopathy, malaise, and headache.

   congenital t., t. apparently resulting from parasites in an infected mother being transmitted in utero to the fetus; may be observed as three syndromes: 1) acute, most of the organs containing foci of necrosis in association with fever, jaundice, encephelomyelitis, pneumonitis, cutaneous rash, ophthalmic lesions, hepatomegaly, and splenomegaly; 2) subacute, most of the lesions are partly healed or calcified, but those in the brain and eye seem to remain active; 3) chronic, usually not recognized during the newborn period, but chorioretinitis and cerebral lesions are detected later.

TPI Treponema pallidum immobilization test.

TPN Total parenteral nutrition.

tr. Tincture.

trabecula, pl. **trabeculae** (tră-bek'u-lah, -le) [L. dim. of trabs, a beam] [NA]. 1. One of the supporting bundles of fibers traversing the substance of a structure, usually derived from the capsule or one of the fibrous septa. 2. A small piece of the spongy substance of bone usually interconnected with other similar pieces.

trabec'ular, trabec'ulate. Relating to or containing trabeculae.

tra'cer. 1. An element or compound containing atoms that can be distinguished from their normal counterparts and that can thus be used to trace the course of the normal substances in metabolism or similar chemical changes. 2. An instrument used in dissecting out nerves and blood vessels.

trache-. See tracheo-.

trachea, pl. **tracheae** (tra'ke-ah, tra'ke-e) [G. tracheia artēria, rough artery] [NA]. Windpipe; the airway extending from the larynx into the thorax, where it divides into the right and left main bronchi; composed of rings of hyaline cartilage connected by a membrane, the annular ligament.

tracheal (tra′ke-al). Relating to the trachea.

tracheal tugging. 1. A downward pull of the trachea, manifested by a downward movement of the thyroid cartilage, synchronous with the action of the heart and symptomatic of aneurysm of the aortic arch. **2.** A jerky type of inspiration seen when the intercostal muscles and the sternocostal parts of the diaphragm are paralyzed by deep general anesthesia or muscle relaxants, due to the unopposed action of the crura pulling on the dome of the diaphragm and thence on the pericardium, lung roots, and tracheobronchial tree during each inspiration.

tracheitis (tra-ke-i′tis) [trachea + G. *-itis,* inflammation]. Trachitis; inflammation of the lining membrane of the trachea.

trachel-. See trachelo-.

trachelectomy (trak-ĕ-lek′to-mĭ) [trachel- + G. *ektomē,* excision]. Cervicectomy.

trachelematoma (trak′ĕ-le′mă-to′mah) [trachel- + hematoma]. A hematoma of the neck.

trachelism, trachelismus (trak′ĕ-lizm, -liz′mus) [G. *trachēlismos,* a seizing by the throat]. A spasmodic bending backward of the neck, such as sometimes precedes an epileptic attack.

trachelitis (trak-ĕ-li′tis). Cervicitis.

trachelo-, trachel- [G. *trachēlos,* neck]. Combining forms denoting neck.

trachelocystitis (trak′ĕ-lo-sis-ti′tis) [trachelo- + G. *kystis,* bladder, + *-itis,* inflammation]. Inflammation of the neck of the bladder.

trachelodynia (trak + ĕ-lo-din′ĭ-ah) [trachelo- + G. *odynē,* pain]. Cervicodynia.

trachelopexy (trak′ĕ-lo-pek-sĭ) [trachelo- + G. *pēxis,* fixation]. Surgical fixation of the uterine cervix.

tracheloplasty (trak′ĕ-lo-plas-tĭ) [trachelo- + G. *plastos,* formed]. Surgical repair of the uterine cervix.

trachelorrhaphy (trak-ĕ-lor′ă-fĭ) [trachelo- + G. *rhaphē,* suture]. Suture of a laceration of the uterine cervix.

trachelotomy (trak-ĕ-lot′o-mĭ) [trachelo- + G. *tomē,* incision]. Cervicotomy.

tracheo-, trache-. Combining form denoting the trachea.

tracheoaerocele (tra′ke-o-ăr′o-sēl) [tracheo- + G. *aēr,* air, + *kēlē,* hernia]. An air cyst in the neck caused by distention of a tracheocele.

tracheobronchial (tra′ke-o-brong′kĭ-al). Relating to both trachea and bronchi.

tracheobronchitis (tra′ke-o-brong-ki′tis). Inflammation of the mucous membrane of the trachea and bronchi.

tracheobronchoscopy (tra′ke-o-brong-kos′ko-pĭ) [tracheo- + bronchus, + G. *skopeō,* to view]. Inspection of the interior of the trachea and bronchi.

tracheocele (tra′ke-o-sēl) [tracheo- + G. *kēlē,* hernia]. A protrusion of the mucous membrane through a defect in the wall of the trachea.

tracheoesophageal (tra′ke-o-ē-sof-ăje′al). Relating to the trachea and the esophagus.

tracheolaryngeal (tra′ke-o-lă-rin′je-al). Relating to the trachea and the larynx.

tracheomalacia (tra′ke-o-mă-la′shĭ-ah) [tracheo- + G. *malakia,* softness]. Degeneration of elastic and connective tissue of trachea.

tracheopharyngeal (tra′ke-o-fă-rin′je-al). Relating to both trachea and pharynx.

tracheophony (tra-ke-of′o-nĭ) [tracheo- + G. *phōnē,* voice]. The hollow voice sound heard in auscultating over the trachea.

tracheoplasty (tra′ke-o-plas-tĭ) [tracheo- + G. *plassō,* to form]. Reparative or plastic surgery of the trachea.

tracheopyosis (tra′ke-o-pi-o′sis) [tracheo- + G. *pyōsis,* suppuration]. Suppurative inflammation of the trachea.

tracheorrhagia (tra′ke-o-ra′jĭ-ah) [tracheo- + G. *rhēgnymi,* to burst forth]. Hemorrhage from the mucous membrane of the trachea.

tracheoschisis (tra-ke-os′kĭ-sis) [tracheo- + G. *schisis,* fissure]. A fissure into the trachea.

tracheoscopic (tra′ke-o-skop′ik). Relating to tracheoscopy.

tracheoscopy (tra-ke-os′ko-pĭ) [tracheo- + G. *skopeō,* to examine]. Inspection of the interior of the trachea.

tracheostenosis (tra′ke-o-stĕ-no′sis) [tracheo- + G. *stenōsis,* constriction]. Narrowing of the lumen of the trachea.

tracheostomy (tra-ke-os′to-mĭ) [tracheo- + G. *stoma,* mouth]. Surgical creation of an opening into the trachea, or that opening.

tracheotomy (tra-ke-ot′o-mĭ) [tracheo- + G. *tomē,* incision]. Incision into the trachea through the neck.

trachitis (tra-ki′tis). Tracheitis.

trachoma (tră-ko′mah) [G. *trachōma,* fr. *trachys,* rough, harsh]. Contagious granular conjunctivitis; granular or Egyptian ophthalmia; chronic contagious microbial inflammation, with hypertrophy, of the conjunctiva caused by *Chlamydia trachomatis.*

trachomatous (tră-ko′mă-tus). Relating to or suffering from trachoma.

tracing (tra′sing). Any graphic display of electrical or mechanical events, as scribed by a pointed instrument.

tract (trakt) [L. *tractus,* a drawing out, extent]. An elongated assembly of tissue or organs having a common origin, function, and termination, or a serial arrangement serving a common function.

    alimentary t., digestive t.

    digestive t., alimentary t. or canal; the passage leading from the mouth to the anus through the pharynx, esophagus, stomach, and intestine.

    dorsolateral t., *fasciculus* dorsolateralis.

    gastrointestinal t., the stomach, small intestine, and large intestine.

genital t., the genital passages of the urogenital system.

optic t., *tractus* opticus.

pyramidal t., *tractus* pyramidalis.

respiratory t., the air passages from the nose to the pulmonary alveoli, through the pharynx, larynx, trachea, and bronchi.

reticulospinal t., *tractus* reticulospinalis.

solitary t., *tractus* solitarius.

spinocerebellar t.'s, see *tractus* spinocerebellaris anterior and posterior.

spinothalamic t., *tractus* spinothalamicus.

urinary t., the passage from the pelvis of the kidney to the urinary meatus through the ureters, bladder, and urethra.

vestibulospinal t., *tractus* vestibulospinalis.

traction (trak'shun) [L. *traho,* pp. *tractus,* to draw]. **1.** The act of drawing or pulling. **2.** A pulling force.

axis t., t. upon the fetal head in the line of the birth canal by means of forceps.

external t., a pulling force created by using fixed anchorage outside the oral cavity, as in the management of midfacial fractures.

internal t., a pulling force created by using one of the cranial bones, above the point of fracture, for anchorage.

skeletal t., skeletal extension; t. pull on a bone structure mediated through a pin or wire inserted into the bone to reduce a fracture of long bones.

skin t., t. on an extremity by means of adhesive tape or other types of strapping applied to the limb.

tractotomy (trak-tot'o-mĭ) [L. *tractus,* tract, + G. *tomē,* incision]. Interruption of a nerve tract in the brain stem or spinal cord by laminectomy, craniotomy, or stereotaxy.

tractus, pl. **tractus** (trak'tus) [L.] [NA]. Tract.

t. iliotibia'lis [NA], iliotibial band; a fibrous reinforcement of the fascia lata on the lateral surface of the thigh, extending from the crest of the ilium to the lateral condyle of the tibia.

t. op'ticus [NA], optic tract; continuation of the optic nerve beyond its hemidecussation in the optic chiasm; each of the two tracts is composed of fibers originating from the temporal half of the retina of the ipsilateral eye and a nearly equal number of fibers from the nasal half of the contralateral retina.

t. pyramida'lis [NA], pyramidal tract; a massive bundle of fibers originating from the precentral motor cortex, to a lesser extent also in the postcentral gyrus, and emerge on the ventral surface of the medulla oblongata as the pyramis. Most of the fibers cross to the opposite side in the pyramidal decussation to descend throughout the length of the spinal cord to innervate distal extremity muscles subserving in particular hand-and-finger or foot-and-toe movements.

t. reticulospina'lis [NA], reticulospinal tract, a variety of fiber tracts descending to the spinal cord from the reticular formation of the pons and medulla oblongata; some fibers conduct impulses from the neural mechanisms regulating cardiovascular and respiratory functions to the corresponding somatic and visceral motor neurons of the spinal cord; others form links in extrapyramidal motor mechanisms affecting muscle tonus and somatic movement, and convey the influence of the premotor cortex, cerebellum, and corpus striatum upon the spinal motor neurons.

t. solita'rius [NA], solitary tract; a slender compact bundle of primary sensory fibers that accompany the vagus, glossopharyngeal, and facial nerves, and convey information from stretch receptors and chemoreceptors in the walls of the cardiovascular, respiratory, and intestinal tracts, as well as impulses generated by the receptor cells of the taste buds in the mucosa of the tongue.

t. spinocerebella'ris ante'rior [NA], anterior spinocerebellar tract; a bundle of fibers originating in the posterior horn and zona intermedia throughout the length of the spinal cord, crossing to the opposite side and ascending in a peripheral position in the ventral half of the lateral funiculus, through the rhombencephalon to terminate in the cerebellar vermis; conveys largely exteroceptive information from the opposite body half.

t. spinocerebella'ris poste'rior [NA], posterior spinocerebellar tract; a compact bundle of heavily myelinated fibers at the periphery of the dorsal half of the lateral funiculus of the spinal cord, consisting of thick fibers originating in the thoracic nucleus on the same side of the cord and ascending by way of the inferior cerebellar peduncle to terminate in the cerebellar vermis; conveys largely proprioceptive information.

t. spinothalam'icus, spinothalamic tract; a large ascending fiber bundle in the ventral half of the lateral funiculus of the spinal cord, composed of fibers that arise in the posterior horn at all levels of the cord and continue into the brainstem, issuing fibers to the rhombencephalic and mesencephalic reticular formation, to the lateral part of the central gray substance of the mesencephalon, to the deep and intermediate layers of the superior colliculus, and the thalamus; in the spinal cord, it is composed of a lateral part which conveys impulses associated with pain and temperature sensation, and an anterior part involved in tactile sensation.

tra'gal. Relating to the tragus.

tragus, pl. **tra'gi** [G. *tragos,* goat, fr. hairs growing on the part] **1** [NA]. Hircus (3); a tongue-like projection of the cartilage of the auricle in front of the opening of the external acoustic meatus and continuous with the cartilage of this canal. **2** [NA]. Plural, the hairs at the entrance to the external acoustic meatus.

trait (trāt) [Fr. from L. *tratus,* a drawing out, extension]. A characteristic, especially one that distinguishes an individual from others.

dominant t., recessive t., see *dominance* of genes.

sickle cell t., the heterozygous state of the gene for hemoglobin S; heterozygotes produce both Hb S and Hb A, a portion of their erythrocytes assume sickle shape on reduction of oxygen tension.

trance (trans) [L. *trans-eo,* to go across]. An altered state of consciousness as in hypnosis, catalepsy, or ecstasy.

tranquilizer (trang-kwĭ-li'zer). A drug that brings tranquility by calming, soothing, quieting, or pacifying without depression.

trans- [L. *trans,* through, across]. **1.** Prefix meaning across, through, beyond; opposite of cis-. **2.** In genetics, denoting the location of two genes on opposite chromosomes of a homologous pair. **3.** In organic chemistry, denoting a form of isomerism in which the atoms attached to two carbon atoms, joined by double bonds, are located on opposite sides of the molecule. **4.** In biochemistry, prefix to group name in an enzyme name or a reaction denoting transfer of that group from one compound to another.

transacet'ylase. Acetyltransferase.

transacylases (trans-as'ĭ-lāsez). Acyltransferases.

transacetylation (trans'ă-set-ĭ-la'shun). Transfer of an acetyl group (CH_3CO-), from one compound to another.

transal'dola'tion. A reaction involving the transfer of an aldol group ($CH_2OH-CO-CHOH-$) from one compound to another.

transam'idina'tion. A reaction involving the transfer of an amidine group ($NH_2C=NH$) from one compound to another.

transam'inases. Aminotransferases.

transam'ina'tion. The reaction between an α-amino acid and an α-keto acid through which the amino group is transferred from the former to the latter.

transcalent (trans-ka'lent) [trans- + L. *caleo,* to be warm]. Diathermanous.

transcarbamoylases (trans-kar-bam'o-ĭ-lā-sez). Carbamoyltransferases.

transcarbox'ylases. Carboxyltransferases.

transcor'tical. 1. Across or through the cortex of an organ. **2.** From one part of the cerebral cortex to another; denoting the various association tracts.

transcor'tin. Corticosteroid-binding globulin; an α_2-globulin in blood that binds cortisol and corticosterone.

transcriptase (tran-skrip'tās). A polymerase associated with the process of transcription; especially the DNA-dependent RNA polymerase.

reverse t., RNA-dependent DNA polymerase, present in virions of RNA tumor viruses.

transcription (tran-skrip'shun). Transfer of genetic code information from one kind of nucleic acid to another, as the process by which a base sequence of mRNA is synthesized on a template cDNA.

transduction (trans-duk'shun) [trans- + L. *duco,* pp. *ductus,* to lead across]. **1.** The transfer of genetic material (and its phenotypic expression) from one bacterium to another by the mediation of bacterio-

phage. **2.** The conversion of energy from one form to another.

abortive t., t. in which the genetic fragment from the donor bacterium is not integrated in the genome of the recipient bacterium, and, when the latter divides, is transmitted to only one of the daughter cells.

complete t., t. in which the transferred genetic fragment is fully integrated in the genome of the recipient bacterium.

transection (tran-sek'shun) [trans- + L. *seco,* pp. *sectus,* to cut]. Transsection. **1.** A cross section. **2.** Cutting across.

transfec'tion. Infection of a bacterium or cell with DNA or RNA isolated from bacteriophage or animal or plant virus, and that results in replication of complete virus.

trans'fer [L. *trans-fero,* to bear across]. A condition in which learning in one situation influences learning in another situation; may be positive, as when learning one behavior facilitates the learning of something else, or negative, as when one habit interferes with the acquisition of a later one.

transferases (trans'fer-ās-ez). Enzymes transferring one-carbon groups, acyl residues, glycosyl residues, alkyl or aryl groups, nitrogenous groups, phosphorus-containing groups, and sulfur-containing groups.

transfer'ence. 1. The shifting of symptoms from one part of the body to another, as in certain cases of conversion hysteria. **2.** Displacement of affect from one person or one idea to another.

transferrin (trans-fĕr'in). Siderophilin, a β_1-globulin of the plasma, capable of associating reversibly with up to 1.25 μg of iron per g and acting as an iron transporting protein.

transfer-RNA. See under ribonucleic acid.

transfixion (trans-fik'shun) [L. *trans-figo,* pp. *-fixus,* to pierce through]. In amputation, passing the knife from side to side through tissues close to the bone and dividing muscles from within outward.

transformation (trans'for-ma'shun) [L. *trans-formo,* pp. *-atus,* to transform]. **1.** Metamorphosis. **2.** A change of one tissue into another, as cartilage into bone. **3.** Transfer of genetic information between bacteria by means of "naked" intracellular DNA fragments derived from bacterial donor cells and incorporated into a competent recipient cell.

transfuse (trans-fūz). To perform transfusion.

transfusion (trans-fu'zhun) [L. *trans-fundo,* pp. *-fusus,* to pour from one vessel to another]. **1.** Transfer of blood from one individual to another. **2.** Intravascular injection of physiologic saline solution.

direct t., immediate t.; t. of blood from the donor directly to the receptor.

exchange t., substitution or total t.; removal of most of a patient's blood followed by introduction of an equal amount from donors.

immediate t., direct t.

indirect t., mediate t., introduction into a patient of blood previously obtained from a donor and stored in a suitable container.

reciprocal t., an attempt to confer immunity by transfusing blood taken from a donor just recovered from an infectious disease into a receptor suffering from the same affection, the balance being maintained by transfusing an equal amount from the sick to the well person.

substitution t., total t., exchange t.

transilient (tran-sil'yent, -zil-) [L. *trans-silio*, to leap across]. Jumping across; passing over; pertaining to those cortical association fibers in the brain that pass from one convolution to another nonadjacent one.

transketolation (trans'ke-to-la'shun). A reaction involving the transfer of a ketole group from one compound to another.

translation (trans-la'shun) [L. *translatio*, a transferring, fr. irreg. verb. *transfero*, pp. *-latus*, to carry across]. **1.** The process by which mRNA, tRNA, and ribosomes effect the production of protein from amino acids, the specificity of synthesis being controlled by the base sequences of the mRNA. **2.** Movement of a tooth through alveolar bone without change in axial inclination.

translocation (trans-lo-ka'shun). Transposition of two segments between nonhomologous chromosomes as a result of abnormal breakage and refusion of reciprocal segments.

balanced t., t. of the long arm of an acrocentric chromosome to another chromosome, accompanied by loss of the small fragment containing the centromere.

reciprocal t., t. without demonstrable loss of genetic material.

robertsonian t. [W.R.B. *Robertson*], centric fusion; t. in which the centromeres of two acrocentric chromosomes appear to have fused, forming an abnormal chromosome consisting of the long arms of two different chromosomes.

unbalanced t., condition resulting from fertilization of a gamete containing a t. chromosome by a normal gamete; the individual would have 46 chromosomes, but a segment of the t. chromosome would be represented three times in each cell and a partial or complete trisomic state would exist.

transmeth'ylase. Methyltransferase.

transmeth'yla'tion. Transference of a methyl group from one compound to another.

transmigration (trans-mi-gra'shun) [L. *trans-migro*, pp. *-atus*, to remove from one place to another]. Movement from one site to another; may entail the crossing of some usually limiting barrier, as in diapedesis.

transmis'sible. Capable of being conveyed from one person to another, as a t. disease.

transmission (trans-mish'un) [L. *transmissio*, a sending across]. Transfer, as in the conveyance of disease from one person to another, or the passage of a nerve impulse across synapses or at myoneural junctions.

horizontal t., t. of infection by contact, in contradistinction to vertical t.

vertical t., t. of a virus by means of the genetic apparatus of a cell in which the viral genome is integrated.

transmu'ral [trans- + L. *murus*, wall]. Through any wall, as of the body or of a cyst or any hollow structure.

transmutation (trans-mu-ta'shun) [L. *trans-muto*, pp. *-atus*, to change, transmute]. A change; transformation.

transova'rial. Denoting the passage of parasites or infective agents from the maternal body to eggs within the ovaries, as with the infection of larval mites or ticks with rickettsiae or viruses.

transpep'tidase. An enzyme catalyzing a transpeptidation reaction.

transpep'tida'tion. A reaction involving the transfer of one or more amino acids from one peptide chain to another, as by an enzyme, or of a peptide chain itself, as in bacterial cell wall synthesis.

transphos'phatase. Phosphotransferase.

transphosphorylation (trans-fos-fōr'ĭ-la'shun). A reaction involving the transfer of a phosphoric group from one compound to another.

transpiration (tran-spī-ra'shun) [trans- + L. *spiro* pp. *-atus*, to breathe]. Passage of watery vapor through the skin or any membrane.

trans'plant [trans- + L. *planto*, to plant]. **1.** To transfer from one part to another, as in grafting and transplantation. **2.** The tissue or organ so used. See also graft.

transplantation (trans-plan-ta'shun) [L. *trans-planto*, pp. *-atus*, to transplant]. Implanting in one part a tissue or organ taken from another part or from another person.

trans'port [L. *transporto*, to carry over]. Movement or transference of biochemical substances in biologic systems.

active t., passage of ions or molecules across a cell membrane against an electrochemical gradient.

hydrogen t., transfer of hydrogen through the action of an enzyme system from one metabolite (hydrogen donor) to another (hydrogen acceptor); the former is thus oxidized and the latter reduced.

transpose (trans-pōz) [L. *trans-pono*, pp. *-positus*, to place across, transfer]. To transfer one tissue or organ to the place of another and *vice versa*.

transposition (trans-po-zish'un). **1.** Removal from one place to another. **2.** The state of being transposed or of being on the wrong side of the body, as of the viscera.

t. of the great vessels, a cyanotic form of congenital cardiovascular malformation in which the aorta arises from the right ventricle while the pulmonary artery arises from the left ventricle; life requires an associated septal defect or patent ductus arteriosus to permit crossflow between the two circulations.

transpo'son. A segment of DNA, with a repeat of an insertion sequence element at each end, which can migrate from one to another plasmid within the same bacterium, to the bacterial chromosome, or to a bacterial chromosome, or to a bacteriophage.

transsection (trans-sek'shun). Transection.

transsexual (trans-sek'shu-al). **1.** A person with the external genitalia and secondary sexual characteristics of one sex, but whose personal identification and psychosocial configuration is that of the opposite sex. **2.** Denoting or relating to such a person. **3.** Relating to medical and surgical procedures designed to alter a patient's external sexual characteristics so that they resemble those of the opposite sex.

transsexualism (trans-sek'shu-ă-lizm). **1.** The state of being a transsexual. **2.** An overwhelming desire to change one's anatomic sexual characteristics, stemming from the conviction that one is a member of the opposite sex.

transudate (tran'su-dāt) [trans- + L. *sudo*, pp. *-atus*, to sweat]. Transudation (2); any fluid (solvent and solute) that has transuded through a normal membrane as a result of imbalanced hydrostatic and osmotic forces.

transudation (tran-su-da'shun). **1.** Passage of a transudate. **2.** Transudate.

transureteroureterostomy (trans-u-re'ter-o-u're-ter-os'to-mī). Anastomosis of the transsected end of one ureter into the intact contralateral ureter.

transvec'tor. An animal that transmits a toxic substance that it does not produce but is accumulated from other sources.

transverse (trans-vers') [L. *transversus*]. Crosswise; lying across the long axis of the body or of a part.

transversectomy (trans-ver-sek'to-mī) [transverse + G. *ektomē*, excision]. Exsection of the transverse process of a vertebra.

transversion (trans-ver'zhun). In dentistry, eruption of a tooth in a position normally occupied by another.

transvestism (trans-ves'tizm) [trans- + L. *vestio*, to dress]. Transvestitism; dressing or masquerading in the clothes of the opposite sex, especially adoption of feminine mannerisms and costume by a male.

transvestite (trans-ves'tīt). One who practices transvestism.

transvestitism (trans-ves'tī-tizm). Transvestism.

trape'zial. Relating to any trapezium.

trapeziform (tră-pe'zi-form). Trapezoid (1).

trapezium, pl. **trapezia, trapeziums** (tră-pe'zi-um, -ah, umz) [G. *trapezoin*, table, fr. *tra-* (*tetra-*), four, + *pous* (*pod-*), foot]. **1.** A four-sided geometrical figure having no two sides parallel. **2.** *Os* trapezium.

trape'zius. *Musculus* trapezius.

trapezoid (trap'e-zoyd) [G. *trapezōdēs*, fr. *trapezoin*, trapezium, + *eidos*, resemblance]. **1.** Trapeziform; resembling a trapezium. **2.** A trapezium with two of its opposite sides parallel. **3.** *Os* trapezoideum. **4.** *Corpus* trapezoideum.

trauma, pl. **traumata, traumas** (traw'mah, -mă-tah, -mahz) [G. wound]. Traumatism; a wound or injury, accidental or inflicted.

birth t., (1) physical injury to an infant during its delivery; (2) the supposed emotional injury, inflicted by the events incident to birth, upon the psyche of the infant.

psychic t., an upsetting experience precipitating or aggravating an emotional or mental disorder.

traumasthenia (traw-mas-the'ni-ah) [traum- + G. *astheneia*, weakness]. Nervous exhaustion following an injury.

traumata (traw'mă-tah). Plural of trauma.

traumatic (traw-mat'ik) [G. *traumatikos*]. Relating to or caused by a wound or injury.

traumatism (traw'mă-tizm). Trauma (1).

traumato-, traumat-, traum- [G. *trauma*, wound]. Combining forms denoting a wound or injury.

traumatopnea (traw'mă-top-ne'ah) [traumato- + G. *pnoē*, breath]. Passage of air in and out through a wound of the chest wall.

trav'erse. In computed tomography, one complete linear movement of the gantry across the object being scanned, as occurs in translate and rotate CT machines.

treat (trēt) [Fr. *traiter*, fr. L. *tracto*, to drag, handle, perform]. To manage a disease or to care for a patient.

treatment (trēt'ment) [Fr. *traitment* (see treat)]. Medical, surgical, or other management of a patient. See also therapy; therapeutics.

Kenny's t., a method for the t. of anterior poliomyelitis; the affected parts are wrapped in woolen cloth wrung out of hot water; after the acute stage of the disease has passed, the limbs are passively exercised to reeducate the paralyzed muscles.

light t., phototherapy.

palliative t., t. to alleviate symptoms without curing the disease.

prophylactic t., preventive t., institution of measures designed to protect a person from a disease to which he has been, or is liable to be exposed.

shock t., a form of psychiatric t., used in certain types of mental disorders, in which a chemical substance or electric current is employed to produce a convulsive seizure and unconsciousness.

Trematoda (trem-ă-to'dah) [G. *trēmatōdēs*, full of holes]. The flukes; a class of parasites in the phylum Platyhelminthes (flatworms), having a leaf-shaped body and two muscular suckers; flukes of medical interest belong to the subclass Digenea.

trem'atode. Any fluke of the class Trematoda.

trem'or [L. a shaking]. **1.** An involuntary trembling movement. **2.** Minute ocular movement occurring during fixation of an object.

alternating t., a form of hyperkinesia characterized by regular, symmetrical, to-and-fro movements produced by patterned, alternating contraction of muscles and their antagonists.

fibrillary t., isolated twitching of the fine strands or fasciculi of a muscle.

flapping t., asterixis.

intention t., volitional t.; a t. that occurs when a voluntary movement is made.

passive t., a t. that occurs when the subject is at rest, and diminishes or ceases during voluntary movement.

senile t., a t., usually an intention t., but sometimes persistent, occurring in the aged.

volitional t., intention t.

trem'ulous. Characterized by tremor.

trepan (tre-pan') [G. *trepanon*, a borer]. Trephine.

trepanation (trep-ă-na'shun). Trephination.

trephination (tref-ĭ-na'shun). Trepanation; removal of a circular piece of cranium by a trephine.

trephine (tre-fīn', -fēn') [fr. L. *tres fines*, three ends]. Trepan. **1.** A cylindrical or crown saw for the removal of a disc of bone, especially from the skull, or of other firm tissue as that of the cornea. **2.** To remove a disc of bone or other tissue by means of a t.

trep'idant. Characterized by trepidation.

trepidation (trep-ĭ-da'shun) [L. *trepidatio*, fr. *trepido*, to tremble, to be agitated]. **1.** Trembling; tremor. **2.** Anxious fear.

Treponema (trep-o-ne'mah) [G. *trepō*, to turn, + *nēma*, thread]. A genus of anaerobic bacteria (order Spirochaetales) consisting of cells with acute, regular, or irregular spirals and no obvious protoplasmic structure; some species are pathogenic and parasitic for man and other animals. Type species is *T. pallidum*.

    T. pal'lidum, a species that causes syphilis in man; the type species of the genus *T.*

    T. perten'ue, a species that causes yaws.

trep'onemato'sis. Treponemiasis.

treponeme (trep'o-nēm). Any member of the genus *Treponema*.

treponemiasis (trep'o-ne-mi'ă-sis). Treponematosis; infection caused by *Treponema*.

treponemicidal (trep'o-ne-mī-si'dal) [*Treponema* + L. *caedo*, to kill]. Antitreponemal; destructive to any species of *Treponema*.

treppe (trep'eh) [Ger. staircase]. Staircase phenomenon; a phenomenon in cardiac muscle: if a number of stimuli of the same intensity are sent into the muscle after a quiescent period, the first few contractions of the series show a succesive increase in amplitude.

tre'sis [G. *trēsis*, a boring]. Perforation.

TRH Thyrotropin-releasing *hormone*.

tri- [L. and G.]. Prefix denoting three.

triace'tic acid. $CH_3COCH_2COCH_2COOH$; formed by condensation of acetyl and malonyl CoA's in the course of fatty acid synthesis.

triacylglycerol (tri-as'il-glis'er-ol). Triglyceride; glycerol esterified at each of its three hydroxyl groups by a fatty (aliphatic) acid.

t. lipase, steapsin; sometimes called simply lipase; the fat-splitting enzyme in pancreatic juice.

tri'ad [G. *trias* (*triad-*), the number 3]. **1.** A collection of three things having something in common. **2.** The transverse tubule and the terminal cisternae on each side of it in skeletal muscle fibers. **3.** The father, mother, and child relationship projectively experienced in group psychotherapy.

    acute compression t., Beck's t., the rising venous pressure, falling arterial pressure, and decreased heart sounds of pericardial tamponade.

    Charcot's t., in multiple sclerosis: nystagmus, tremor, and scanning speech.

    Fallot's t., trilogy of Fallot.

    Hutchinson's t., parenchymatous keratitis, labyrinthine disease, and Hutchinson's teeth, seen in congenital syphilis.

    Kartagener's t., Kartagener's *syndrome.*

triage (tre'ahzh) [Fr. sorting]. Medical screening of large numbers of patients, to determine priority for treatment, into three groups: those who cannot be expected to survive even with treatment; those who will recover without treatment; and the priority group of those who need treatment in order to survive.

triangle (tri'ang-gl) [L. *triangulum*, fr. *tri-*, three, + *angulus*, angle]. A three-sided area, space, or structure.

    t. of auscultation, space bounded by the lower border of the trapezius, the latissimus dorsi, and the medial margin of the scapula.

    Bryant's t., iliofemoral t.; a line (*a*) drawn around the body at the level of the anterior suprior iliac spines, another (*b*) drawn perpendicular to it to the great trochanter of the femur, and a line (*c*) drawn from the trochanter to the iliac spine; upward displacement of the trochanter, in fracture of the neck of the femur, is measured along line *b*.

    carotid t.'s, see *trigonum* musculare and caroticum.

    digastric t., *trigonum* submandibulare.

    Einthoven's t., an imaginary equilateral t. with the heart at its center, formed by lines representing the three standard limb leads of the electrocardiogram.

    Farabeuf's t., formed by the internal jugular and facial veins and the hypoglossal nerve.

    femoral t., *trigonum* femorale.

    Hesselbach's t., *trigonum* inguinale.

    iliofemoral t., Bryant's t.

    infraclavicular t., *fossa* infraclavicularis.

    inguinal t., *trigonum* inguinale.

    Langenbeck's t., formed by lines drawn from the anterior superior iliac spine to the surface of the great trochanter and to the surgical neck of the femur; a penetrating wound in this area probably involves the joint.

    Lesser's t., the space between the bellies of the digastric muscle and the hypoglossal nerve.

    lumbar t., *trigonum* lumbale.

lumbocostoabdominal t., an irregular area bounded by the serratus posterior inferior, obliquus externus, obliquus internus, and erector spinae muscles.

Macewen's t., suprameatal t.

muscular t., *trigonum* musculare.

omoclavicular t., *trigonum* omoclaviculare.

Petit's lumbar t., *trigonum* lumbale.

t. of safety, the t. at the lower left sternal border where the pericardium is not covered by lung.

Scarpa's t., *trigonum* femorale.

subclavian t., *trigonum* omoclaviculare.

submandibular t., submaxillary t., *trigonum* submandibulare.

suprameatal t., Macewen's t.; formed by the root of the zygomatic arch, the posterior wall of the bony external acoustic meatus, and a line connecting the extremities of the first two; used as a guide in mastoid operations.

vesical t., *trigonum* vesicae.

Triato'ma. A genus of insects (family Reduviidae) that includes important vectors of *Trypanosoma cruzi,* such as *T. dimidiata, T. infestans,* and *T. maculata.*

triba'sic. Having three titratable hydrogen atoms; denoting an acid with a basicity of 3.

tribe [L. *tribus*]. An occasional taxonomic division between family and genus; often same as subfamily.

tribrachia (tri-bra'kĭ-ah) [tri- + G. *brachion,* arm]. A condition seen in conjoined twins when the fusion has merged the adjacent arms to form a single one, so that there are only three arms for the two bodies.

TRIC Trachoma and inclusion conjunctivitis. See *Chlamydia trachomatis.*

tri'ceps [L. fr. *tri-,* three, + *caput,* head]. Three-headed, denoting musculus t. brachii and t. surae.

trich-, trichi-. See tricho-.

-trichia [G. *thrix (trich-),* hair, + *-ia,* condition]. Combining form denoting condition or type of hair.

trichiasis (trĭ-ki'ă-sis) [trich- + G. *-iasis,* condition]. A condition in which hairs around a natural orifice, or eyelashes, turn in and cause irritation.

trichilemmoma (trik'ĭ-lem-mo'mah) [trichi- + G. *lemma,* husk, + *-oma,* tumor]. A benign tumor derived from outer root sheath epithelium of a hair follicle.

trichina, pl. **trichinae** (trĭ-ki'nah, -ne). A larval worm of the genus *Trichinella,* infective form in pork.

Trichinella (trik-ĭ-nel'ah). A parasitic nematode genus in the aphasmid group; *T. spiralis,* the pork or trichina worm, that causes trichinosis.

trichinosis (trik-ĭ-no'sis). The disease resulting from ingestion of raw or inadequately cooked meat of carnivores, especially pork, that contains encysted viable larvae of *Trichinella spiralis.* Signs and symptoms may be related to the following: 1) intestinal phase: abdominal discomfort, nausea, and loose stools, associated with inflammation caused by adult worms in the jejunum and ileum; 2) dissemina-

tion phase: fever, leukocytosis and eosinophilia, and exaggeration of previous symptoms, associated with circulation of large numbers of larvae in the blood; 3) inflammation phase: intense inflammatory reactions in sites where the larvae degenerate and die; 4) phase of recession: decreasing manifestation of previous signs and symptoms, but larvae coiled within oval cysts may be found in biopsies of skeletal muscle.

trichinous (trik'ĭ-nus). Infected with trichina worms.

trichitis (trĭ-ki'tis) [trich- + G. *-itis,* inflammation]. Inflammation of the hair bulbs.

trichlor'ide. A chloride having three chlorine atoms in the molecule.

trichloroethylene (tri-klôr'o-eth'ĭ-lēn). ClCH=CCl₂; an analgesic and inhalation anesthetic used in minor surgical operations and in obstetrics.

tricho-, trich-, trichi- [G. *thrix (trich-),* hair]. Combining form denoting the hair or a hairlike structure.

trichobezoar (trik'o-be'zōr). Pilobezoar; hairball; a hair cast in the stomach or intestinal tract.

trichoclasia, trichoclasis (trik-o-kla'zĭ-ah, trĭ-kok'lă-sis) [tricho- + G. *klasis,* breaking off]. *Trichorrhexis* nodosa.

trichoepithelioma (trik'o-ep-ĭ-the-lĭ-o'mah) [tricho- + epithelioma]. Epithelioma adenoides cysticum; Brooke's tumor; one of multiple small, benign nodules, occurring mostly on the skin of the face, derived from basal cells of hair follicles enclosing keratin pearls; autosomal dominant inheritance.

trichoglossia (trik-o-glos'ĭ-ah) [tricho- + G. *glossa,* tongue]. Hairy *tongue.*

trichoid (trik'oyd) [tricho- + G. *eidos,* resemblance]. Hairlike.

tricholith (trik'o-lith) [tricho- + G. *lithos,* stone]. A concretion on the hair; the lesion of piedra.

trichologia (trik-o-lo'jĭ-ah) [G. *tricho-* + *lego,* to pick out, gather]. A nervous habit of plucking at the hair.

trichomegaly (trik-o-meg'ă-lĭ) [tricho- + G. *megas,* large]. Congenital condition characterized by abnormally long eyelashes.

trichom'onad. Any member of the family Trichomonadidae (*e.g., Trichomonas*).

Trichomonas (trĭ-kom'o-nas) [tricho- + G. *monas,* single (unit)]. A genus of parasitic protozoan flagellates (family Trichomonadidae) that cause trichomoniasis.

T. te'nax, a species that lives as a commensal in the mouth, especially in tartar around the teeth or in defects of carious teeth.

T. vagina'lis, a species found in the vagina and urethra of women and in the urethra and prostate gland of men (only natural hosts), in whom it causes trichomoniasis vaginitis.

trichomoniasis (trik'o-mo-ni'ă-sis). Disease caused by infection with a species of *Trichomonas* or related genera.

t. vagini'tis, acute or subacute vaginitis or urethritis caused by infection with *Trichomonas vaginalis;* infection is venereal or by other forms of contact.

trichomycosis (trik'o-mi-ko'sis) [tricho- + G. *mykēs,* fungus, + -*osis,* condition]. Formerly, any disease of the hair caused by a fungus; presently synonymous with trichonocardiosis or t. axillaris.

t. axilla'ris, lepothrix; trichonodosis; infection of axillary and pubic hairs with development of yellow (flava), black (nigra), or red (rubra) concretions around the hair shafts.

trichonocardiosis (trik'o-no-kar'dī-o'sis) [tricho- + *Nocardia* + G. -*osis,* condition]. An infection of hair shafts, especially of the axillary and pubic regions, with nocardiae; yellow, red, or black concretions develop around the infected hair shafts. See also *trichomyosis* axillaris.

trichonodosis (trik'o-no-do'sis) [tricho- + L. *nodus,* node (swelling), + G. -*osis,* condition]. *Trichomycosis* axillaris.

trichonosis (trik-o-no'sis) [tricho- + G. *nosos,* disease]. Trichopathy.

trichopathic (trik-o-path'ik). Relating to any disease of the hair.

trichopathy (trī-kop'ă-thī) [tricho- + G. *pathos,* suffering]. Trichonosis; trichosis; any disease of the hair.

trichophagy (trī-kof'ă-jī) [tricho- + G. *phagein,* to eat]. Habitual biting of the hair.

trichophytic (trik'o-fit'ik). Relating to trichophytosis.

trichophytid (trī-kof'ī-tid, trik'o-fi'tid) [tricho- + G. *phyton,* plant]. An eruption remote from the site of *Trichophyton* infection, as an expression of allergic response.

trichophytobezoar (trik'o-fi'to-be'zōr) [tricho- + G. *phyton,* plant, + *bezoar*]. A mixed hair- and food-ball in the stomach of man or animals, especially ruminants.

Trichophyton (trik-o-fi'ton) [tricho- + G. *phyton,* plant]. A genus of pathogenic fungi causing dermatophytosis in man and animals. Species may be anthropophilic, zoophilic, or geophilic, and attack hair, skin, and nails. Many of the 20 to 30 species which have been listed are now known to be variants. The three groups of species are characterized by their growth in hair: endothrix species grow from the skin into the hair follicle, penetrate the shaft, and grow into it, producing rows of arthrospores as the hyphae septate; there is no growth on the external surface of the shaft. Ectothrix species are of two kinds, large spored and small spored. In both, the fungus grows into the hair follicle, surrounds the hair shaft, and penetrates it, but continues to grow both within and outside the hair shaft.

T. concen'tricum, an anthropophilic species that causes tinea imbricata.

T. mentagrophy'tes, a zoophilic small-spored ectothrix species that causes infection of hair, skin, and nails.

T. ru'brum, an anthropophilic endoectothrix species that causes persistent infections in the nails that are unusually resistant to therapy.

T. schoenlei'nii, an anthropophilic endothrix species that causes favus.

T. ton'surans, an anthropophilic endothrix species that causes epidemic dermatophytosis.

T. viola'ceum, an anthropophilic endothrix species that causes black-dot ringworm or favus infection of the scalp.

trichophytosis (trik'o-fi-to'sis) [tricho- + G. *phyton,* plant, + -*osis,* condition]. Superficial fungus infection caused by species of *Trichophyton.*

trichoptilosis (trik'o-tī-lo'sis) [tricho- + G. *ptilōsis,* plummage, + *osis,* condition]. A splitting of the shaft of the hair, giving it a feathery appearance.

trichorrhexis (trik-o-rek'sis) [tricho- + G. *thēxis,* a breaking]. Trichoschisis; a condition in which the hairs readily break or split.

t. invagina'ta, bamboo *hair.*

t. nodo'sa, trichoclasia; trichoclasis; clastothrix; a condition in which minute nodes are formed in the hair shafts; splitting and breaking may occur at these points or nodes.

trichoschisis (trī-kos'kī-sis) [tricho- + G. *schisis,* a cleaving]. Trichorrhexis.

trichosis (trī-ko'sis) [tricho- + G. -*osis,* condition]. Trichopathy.

Trichosporon (trī-kos'po-ron) [tricho- + G. *sporos,* seed (spore)]. A genus of imperfect fungi that are part of the normal flora of the intestinal tract of man. *T. beigelii* is the causative agent of trichosporosis.

trichosporosis (trik'o-spo-ro'sis) [*Trichosporon* + G. -*osis,* condition]. A superficial mycotic infection of the hair in which nodular masses of fungi become attached to the hair shafts.

trichostasis spinulosa (trī-kos'tă-sis spi'nu-lo'sah) [tricho- + G. *stasis,* a standing; L. *spinulosus,* thorny]. A condition in which hair follicles are blocked with a keratin plug containing lanugo hairs.

trichotillomania (trik'o-til'o-ma'nī-ah) [tricho- + G. *tillo,* pull out, + *mania,* insanity]. A compulsion to pull out one's own hair.

trichromatic (tri-kro-mat'ik) [tri- + G. *chrōma,* color]. Trichromic. **1.** Having, or relating to, the three primary colors, red, blue, and green. **2.** Capable of perceiving the three primary colors; having normal color vision.

trichromatopsia (tri-kro'mă-top'sī-ah) [tri- + G. *chrōma,* color, + *opsis,* vision]. Normal color vision; the ability to perceive the three primary colors.

trichromic (tri-kro'mik). Trichromatic.

trichuriasis (trik-u-ri'ă-sis). Infection with a species of *Trichuris;* usually asymptomatic and not associated with peripheral eosinophilia, but in massive infections it frequently induces diarrhea or rectal prolapse.

Trichuris (trī-ku'ris) [tricho- + G. *oura,* tail]. Whipworm; a genus of aphasmid nematodes related to the trichina worm, *Trichinella spiralis. T. trichiura* causes trichuriasis in man.

tricipital (tri-sip'ĭ-tal). Having three heads; denoting a triceps muscle.

tricornute (tri-kor'nūt) [tri- + L. *cornutus,* horned, fr. *cornu,* a horn]. Having three cornua or horns.

tricrotic (tri-krot'ik) [tri- + G. *krotos,* a beat]. Marked by three waves in the arterial pulse tracing.

tricus'pid, tricus'pidal, tricus'pidate. Having three points, prongs, or cusps.

triden'tate [tri- + L. *dentatus,* toothed]. Trident; three-toothed; three-pronged.

trider'mic [tri- + G. *derma,* skin]. Relating to or derived from the three primary germ layers of the embryo.

tri'fid [L. *trifidus,* three-cleft]. Split into three.

trifurcation (tri-fur-ka'shun) [tri- + L. *furca,* fork]. A division into three branches.

trigas'tric [tri- + G. *gastēr,* belly]. Having three bellies; denoting a muscle with two tendinous interruptions.

trigeminy (tri-jem'ĭ-nī) [L. *trigeminus,* threefold]. Trigeminal *rhythm.*

triglyceride (tri-glis'er-īd). Triacylglycerol.

trigona (tri-go'nah) [L.]. Plural of trigonum.

trig'onal. Triangular; relating to a trigonum.

trigone (tri'gōn) [L. *trigonum,* fr. G. *trigōnon,* triangle]. **1.** A triangle or trigonum. **2.** The first three dominant cusps of an upper molar tooth.

   t. of the bladder, *trigonum* vesicae.

   inguinal t., *trigonum* inguinale.

   vertebrocostal t., a triangular area in the diaphragm near the lateral arcuate ligament that is devoid of muscle fibers; covered by pleura superiorly and by peritoneum inferiorly.

trigonid (tri-gon'id) [see *trigonum*]. The first three dominant cusps of a lower molar tooth.

trigonitis (tri-go-ni'tis) [trigone + G. *-itis,* inflammation]. Inflammation of the urinary bladder, localized in the mucous membrane at the trigonum vesicae.

trig'onocephal'ic. Pertaining to trigonocephaly.

trigonocephaly (trig'o-no-sef'ă-lī) [trigone + G. *kephalē,* head]. A malformation characterized by a triangular configuration of the skull, due in part to premature synostosis of the cranial bones with compression of the cerebral hemispheres.

trigonum, pl. **trigona** (tri-go'num, -nah) [L. from G. *trigōnon,* a triangle] [NA]. Trigone; any triangular area. See also triangle.

   t. carot'icum [NA], superior carotid triangle; a space bounded by the superior belly of the omohyoid, anterior border of the sternocleidomastoid, and posterior belly of the digastric muscles; contains bifurcation of the common carotid artery.

   t. femora'le [NA], femoral or subinguinal triangle; Scarpa's triangle; a triangular space at the upper part of the thigh, bounded by the sartorius and adductor longus muscles and the inguinal ligament.

   t. inguina'le [NA], inguinal triangle or trigone; Hesselbach's triangle; the triangular area in the lower abdominal wall bounded by the inguinal ligament below, the rectus abdominis muscle medially, and the inferior epigastric vessels laterally; the site of direct inguinal hernia.

   t. lumba'le [NA], lumbar triangle; Petit's lumbar triangle; an area in the posterior abdominal wall bounded by the edges of the latissimus dorsi and external oblique muscles and the iliac crest; herniations occasionally occur here.

   t. muscula're [NA], muscular triangle; inferior carotid triangle; the triangle bounded by the sternocleidomastoid muscle, the superior belly of the omohyoid muscle, and the anterior midline of the neck; the infrahyoid muscles occupy most of it.

   t. omoclavicula're [NA], omoclavicular or subclavian triangle; the triangle bounded by the clavicle, omohyoid muscle, and sternocleidomastoid muscle; contains the subclavian artery and vein.

   t. submandibula're [NA], submandibular, digastric, or submaxillary triangle; the triangle of the neck bounded by the mandible and the two bellies of the digastric muscle; contains the submandibular gland.

   t. vesi'cae [NA], vesical triangle; trigone of the bladder; a triangular smooth area at the base of the bladder between the openings of the two ureters and that of the urethra.

3,5,3'-triiodothyronine (TITh, T₃) (tri-i'o-do-thi'ro-nēn). A thyroid hormone normally synthesized in smaller quantities than thyroxine; present in blood and in thyroid gland and exerts the same biological effects as thyroxine but, on a molecular basis, is more potent and the onset of its effect more rapid.

tri'labe [tri- + G. *labē,* a handle, hold]. A three-pronged forceps for removal of foreign bodies from the bladder.

trilam'inar. Having three layers.

trilo'bate, tri'lobed. Having three lobes.

triloc'ular. Having three cavities or cells.

trilogy of Fallot (tril'o-jī; fal-o'). Fallot's triad; atrial septal defect associated with pulmonic stenosis and right ventricular hypertrophy.

trimester (tri-mes'ter) [L. *trimestris,* of three-month duration]. A period of 3 months; one-third of the length of a pregnancy.

trimethaphan camsylate (tri-meth'ă-fan). A ganglionic blocking agent that produces vasodilation of brief duration; used in surgery, particularly neurosurgery, to produce a relatively bloodless operative field.

trimethylamine (tri-meth'il-am'in). $N(CH_3)_3$; a degradation product probably resulting from decomposition of choline.

trimethylaminuria (tri-meth'il-am-ĭ-nūr'ĭ-ah). Increased excretion of trimethylamine in urine and sweat, with characteristic offensive, fishy body odor.

trinu'cleotide. A combination of three adjacent nucleotides, free or in a polynucleotide or nucleic acid molecule; often used with specific reference to the codon or anticodon specifying a particular amino acid in expression of the genetic code.

tri'ose. A three-carbon monosaccharide.

tri'osephosphate isomerase. Phosphotriose isomerase; an isomerizing enzyme that catalyzes the interconversion of glyceraldehyde 3-phosphate and dihydroxyacetone phosphate, a reaction of importance in glycolysis.

triplegia (tri-ple'jĭ-ah) [tri- + G. *plēgē*, stroke]. Paralysis of an upper and a lower extremity and of the face, or of both extremities on one side and of one in the other.

trip'let. 1. One of three children delivered at the same birth. 2. A set of three similar objects, as a compound lens in a microscope, formed of three planoconvex lenses. 3. Codon.

  nonsense t., a trinucleotide (codon) in which a base change results in premature termination of the growing polypeptide chain and, consequently, incomplete protein molecules.

triploid (trip'loyd) [G. *triploos*, threefold, + *eidos*, form]. See polyploidy.

triploidy (trip'loy-dĭ). Presence of three complete sets of chromosomes, instead of two, in all cells; results in fetal or neonatal death.

triplopia (trip-lo'pĭ-ah) [G. *triploos*, triple, + *opsis*, sight]. A visual defect in which three images are seen of the same object.

-tripsy [G. *tripsis*, a rubbing]. Suffix denoting a surgical procedure in which a structure is crushed, as a calculus.

tris-. Chemical prefix indicating three of the substituents that follow.

trismus (triz'mus) [L. fr. G. *trismos*, a creaking, rasping]. Lockjaw; a firm closing of the jaw due to tonic spasm of the muscles of mastication from disease of the motor branch of the trigeminal nerve; usually associated with and due to general tetanus.

trisomic (tri-so'mik). Relating to or denoting trisomy.

trisomy (tri'so-mĭ) [tri- + (chromo)some]. State of an individual or cell with an extra chromosome; instead of the normal pair of homologous chromosomes there are three of a particular chromosome.

trisplanchnic (tri-splangk'nik) [tri- + G. *splanchnon*, viscus]. Relating to the three visceral cavities: skull, thorax, and abdomen.

tristichia (tri-stik'ĭ-ah) [G. *tristichos*, in three rows]. Presence of three rows of eyelashes.

trisulcate (tri-sul'kāt). Marked by three grooves.

tritanomaly (tri'tă-nom'ă-lĭ) [G. *tritos*, third, + *anōmalia*, irregularity]. Partial color blindness due to a deficiency of retinal photosensitive pigment for blue.

tritanopia (tri'tă-no'pĭ-ah) [G. *tritos*, third, + *an*-priv. + *ōps*, eye]. Deficient color perception in which there is an absence of blue-sensitive pigment in the retinal cones.

tritium (T, *t*) (trit'ĭ-um, trish'ĭ-um). Hydrogen-3.

triturable (trit'u-rā-bl). Capable of being triturated.

triturate (trit'u-rāt). 1. To accomplish trituration. 2. A triturated substance.

trituration (trit-u-ra'shun) [L. *trituratio*, fr. *trituro*, to thresh, fr. *tero*, pp. *tritus*, to rub]. Reducing a substance to a fine powder.

trivalent (tri-va'lent) [tri- + L. *valentia*, strength]. Having a valence of 3.

trivial name. A name of a chemical that gives no clue as to chemical structure; commonly used for drugs, hormones, proteins, and other biologicals, but not officially sanctioned; *e.g.*, aspirin, chlorophyll, caffeine.

tRNA Transfer RNA.

trocar [Fr. *trocart*]. An instrument for withdrawing fluid from a cavity, or for use in paracentesis, consisting of a metal tube (cannula) into which fits an obturator with a sharp three-cornered tip, which is withdrawn after the instrument has been pushed into the cavity; usually applied to the obturator alone, the entire instrument being designated t. and cannula.

trochanter (tro-kan'ter) [G. *trochantēr*, a runner, fr. *trechō*, to run]. One of the bony prominences developed from independent osseous centers near the upper extremity of the femur.

  t. ma'jor [NA], **greater t.,** a strong process overhanging the root of the neck of the femur; gives attachment to the gluteus medius and minimus, piriformis, obturator internus and externus, and gemelli muscles.

  t. mi'nor [NA], **lesser t.,** a pyramidal process projecting from the shaft of the femur at the junction of the shaft and the neck; receives insertion of the psoas major and iliacus (iliopsoas) muscles.

trochanterian, trochanteric (tro-kan-tēr'ĭ-an, -tēr'ik). Relating to a trochanter, especially the trochanter major.

troche (trōk, tro'ke) [L. *trochiscus*, small wheel]. Lozenge; a small disk-shaped or rhombic body containing a drug, used for local treatment of the mouth or throat, being held in the mouth until dissolved.

trochlea, pl. **trochleae** (trok'le-ah, -le-e) [L. pulley] [NA]. 1. A structure serving as a pulley. 2. A smooth articular surface of bone upon which another glides. 3. A fibrous loop in the orbit, near the nasal process of the frontal bone, through which passes the tendon of the superior oblique muscle of the eye.

trochlear (trok'le-ar). Relating to a trochlea.

trochoid (tro'koyd) [G. *trochos*, wheel, + *eidos*, resemblance]. Denoting a revolving or wheel-like articulation.

Trombicula (trom-bik'u-lah). The chigger mite, a genus of mites (family Trombiculidae) whose larvae (chiggers, red bugs) include pests of man and other animals; *T. akamushi* and *T. deliensis* are two species implicated in the transmission of *Rickettsia tsutsuga-*

mushi, agent of tsutsugamushi disease.

trombiculiasis (trom-bik-u-li'ă-sis). Infestation by *Trombicula.*

trombic'ulid. Any member of the family Trombiculidae.

Trombiculidae (trom'bik-u-li'de). A family of mites whose larvae (redbugs, harvest mites, scrub mites, chiggers) are parasitic on vertebrates and whose nymphs and adults are bright red and free-living, living on insect eggs or minute organisms in the soil.

tromethamine (tro-meth'ă-mēn). $H_2N–C(CH_2OH)_3$; a weakly basic compound used as an alkalizing agent and as a buffer in enzymic reactions.

troph-. See tropho-.

trophectoderm (trof-ek'to-derm). The cell layer from which the trophoblast differentiates.

trophedema (trof-ĕ-de'mah) [troph- + edema]. Hereditary *lymphedema.*

trophe'sic. Pertaining to trophesy.

trophesy (trof'e-sĭ). The results of any disorder of the trophic nerves.

-trophic [G. *trophē,* nourishment]. Suffix denoting nutrition.

trophic (trof'ik, tro'fik) [G. *trophē,* nourishment]. **1.** Relating to or dependent upon nutrition. **2.** Resulting from interruption of nerve supply.

tropho-, troph- [G. *trophē,* nourishment]. Combining forms denoting food or nutrition.

trophoblast (trof'o-blast, tro'fo-blast) [tropho- + G. *blastos,* germ]. The mesectodermal cell layer covering the blastocyst which erodes the uterine mucosa and through which the embryo receives nourishment from the mother; it contributes to the formation of the placenta.

trophoblas'tic. Relating to the trophoblast.

trophoblasto'ma. Choriocarcinoma.

trophodermatoneurosis (trof'o-der'mă-to-nu-ro'sis). Cutaneous trophic changes due to neural involvement.

trophoneurosis (trof'o-nu-ro'sis) [tropho- + G. *neuron,* nerve, + *-osis,* condition]. A trophic disorder occurring as a consequence of disease or injury of the nerves of the part.

trophoneurot'ic. Relating to a trophoneurosis.

troph'oplast [tropho- + G. *plastos,* formed]. Plastid (1).

trophotaxis (trof-o-tak'sis) [tropho- + G. *taxis,* arrangement]. Trophotropism.

trophotropic (trof-o-trop'ik). Relating to trophotropism.

trophotropism (tro-fot'ro-pizm) [tropho- + G. *trope,* a turning]. Trophotaxis; chemotaxis of living cells in relation to nutritive material.

trophozoite (trof-o-zo'ĭt) [tropho- + G. *zōon,* animal]. The asexual form of certain Sporozoa, such as the schizont of the plasmodia of malaria and related parasites.

-trophy [G. *trophē,* nourishment]. Suffix meaning food, nutrition.

tro'pia [G. *tropē,* a turning]. Abnormal deviation of the eye. See strabismus.

-tropic [G. *tropē,* a turning]. Suffix denoting a turning toward, having an affinity for.

tro'pine. 3α-Tropanol; the major constituent of atropine and scopolamine, from which it is obtained on hydrolysis.

tro'pism [G. *tropē,* a turning]. The phenomenon observed in living organisms of moving toward (positive t.) or away from (negative t.) a focus of a stimulus; usually applied to movement of a portion of the organism.

tropocollagen (tro'po-kol'ă-jen, trop'o-). Fundamental units of collagen fibrils consisting of three helically arranged polypeptide chains.

Trp Tryptophan and its radicals.

truncal (trung'kal). Relating to the trunk of the body or to any arterial or nerve trunk, etc.

truncate (trung'kāt) [L. *trunco,* pp. *-atus,* to maim, cut off]. Truncated; cut across at right angles to the long axis.

truncus, pl. **trunci** (trung'kus, -ki) [L. stem, trunk] [NA]. **1.** Trunk; the body, excluding the head and extremities. **2.** A primary nerve or vessel before its division. **3.** A large collecting lymphatic vessel.

   t. atrioventricula'ris [NA], atrioventricular trunk or; bundle; His bundle; ventriculonector; the bundle of modified cardiac muscle fibers that begins at the atrioventricular node and passes through the right atrioventricular fibrous ring to the membranous part of the interventricular septum where it divides into right and left branches, which ramify in the subendocardium of their respective ventricles.

   t. brachiocepha'licus [NA], brachiocephalic trunk; innominate artery; *origin,* arch of aorta; *branches,* right subclavian and right common carotid.

   t. celi'acus [NA], celiac trunk or artery; arteria celiaca; *origin,* abdominal aorta just below diaphragm; *branches,* left gastric, common hepatic, splenic.

   t. costocervica'lis [NA], costocervical trunk or artery; a short artery that arises from the subclavian artery on each side and divides into deep cervical and highest intercostal branches.

   persistent t. arterio'sus, a congenital cardiovascular deformity resulting from failure of development of the bulbar septum and consisting of a common arterial trunk opening out of both ventricles, the pulmonary arteries being given off from the ascending common trunk.

   t. pulmona'lis [NA], pulmonary trunk or artery; *origin,* right ventricle of heart; *distribution,* divides into the right and left pulmonary arteries, which enter the corresponding lungs and branch along with the segmental bronchi.

   t. sympath'icus [NA], sympathetic trunk; one of the two long ganglionated nerve strands alongside the vertebral column that are connected to each spinal nerve by gray rami and receive fibers from the spinal cord through white rami connecting with the thoracic and upper lumbar spinal nerves.

t. thyrocervica'lis [NA], thyrocervical trunk; a short arterial trunk arising from the subclavian and dividing generally into three branches: thyroidea inferior, transversa colli, and suprascapularis.

t. vaga'lis [NA], vagal trunk; one of the two nerve bundles, anterior and posterior, into which the esophageal plexus continues as its passes through the diaphragm.

trunk [L. *truncus*]. Truncus.

atrioventricular t., *truncus* atrioventricularis.

brachiocephalic t., *truncus* brachiocephalicus.

celiac t., *truncus* celiacus.

costocervical t., *truncus* costocervicalis.

pulmonary t., *truncus* pulmonalis.

sympathetic t., *truncus* sympathicus.

thyrocervical t., *truncus* thyrocervicalis.

vagal t., *truncus* vagalis.

truss [Fr. *trousser,* to tie up, to pack]. An appliance designed to prevent the return of a reduced hernia or the increase in size of an irreducible hernia.

trypan blue (tri'pan). An acid azo dye used for vital staining of the reticuloendothelial system, uriniferous tubules, and cells in tissue culture.

trypanocidal (trī-pan'o-si'dal). Destructive to trypanosomes.

trypanocide (trī-pan'o-sīd) [trypanosome + L. *caedo,* to kill]. Trypanosomicide; an agent that kills trypanosomes.

Trypanosoma (trī-pan'o-so'mah) [G. *trypanon,* an anger, + *sōma,* body]. A genus of asexual, digenetic, protozoan flagellates (family Trypanosomatidae) that are parasitic in the blood plasma of many vertebrates and have an intermediate host, a blood-sucking invertebrate, such as a leech, tick, or insect; pathogenic species cause trypanosomiasis in man.

T. cru'zi, a species that causes South American trypanosomiasis.

T. gambien'se, a species that causes Gambian or chronic trypanosomiasis (West African sleeping sickness); transmitted by several species of tsetse flies, particularly *Glossina palpalis.*

T. rhodesien'se, a species that causes Rhodesian or acute trypanosomiasis (East African sleeping sickness); chief vector is the tsetse fly, *Glossina morsitans.*

trypanosome (trī-pan'o-sōm). Any member of the genus *Trypanosoma* or its family Trypanosomatidae.

trypanosomiasis (trī-pan'o-so-mi'ă-sis). Any disease caused by a trypanosome.

acute t., Rhodesian t.

African t., African sleeping sickness; see Gambian t., Rhodesian t.

chronic t., Gambian t.

Cruz t., South American t.

Gambian t., chronic t.; chronic sleeping sickness; t. caused by *Trypanosoma gambiense,* transmitted to man by tsetse flies, chiefly *Glossina palpalis;* symptoms are erythematous patches and local edemas;

neuralgic pains, cramps, tremors, and paresthesia; enlargement of the lymph glands, spleen, and liver; emaciation; and an evening elevation of temperature; in later stages (after invasion of trypanosomes into the CNS) there is lethargy, with somnolence deepening to coma in the terminal stage.

Rhodesian t., acute t.; acute sleeping sickness; t. caused by *Trypanosoma rhodesiense,* transmitted by tsetse flies of the species *Glossina morsitans,* and similar to Gambian t. but running a far more rapid, acute course.

South American t., Chagas or Chagas-Cruz disease; Cruz t.; t. caused by *Trypanosoma cruzi* and transmitted by certain species of reduviid bugs in its acute form, there is swelling of the skin at the site of entry, most often the face, with regional lymph node enlargement; in its chronic form it assumes several aspects (cardiac, nervous, or myxedematous) according to the predominating symptoms.

trypanosomic (trī-pan-o-so'mik). Relating to trypanosomes, especially denoting infection by such organisms.

trypanosomicide (trī-pan-o-so'mī-sīd). Trypanocide.

trypanosomid (trī-pan'o-so-mid). A skin lesion resulting from immunologic changes from trypanosome disease.

trypsin (trip'sin). A proteolytic enzyme formed in the small intestine from trypsinogen by the action of enterokinase; a serine proteinase that hydrolyzes peptides, amides, esters, etc., at bonds of the carboxyl groups of L-arginine of L-lysine, and also produces the meromyosins.

trypsinogen, trypsogen (trip-sin'o-jen, trip'so-jen). An inactive substance secreted by the pancreas that is converted into trypsin by the action of enterokinase.

tryptamine (trip'tă-mēn, -min). 3-(2-Aminoethyl)indole; a decarboxylation product of tryptophan that occurs in certain foods and raises the blood pressure through vasocontrictor action by the release of norepinephrine at postganglionic sympathetic nerve endings.

tryp'tic. Relating to or resulting from trypsin.

tryp'tophan (TRP). 2-Amino-3-indolepropionic acid; a component of proteins.

tryptophan 2,3-dioxygenase. Tryptophanase (1); pyrrolase; an adaptive enzyme, an oxidoreductase, the level (in liver) being controlled by adrenal hormones.

tryptophanase (trip'to-fă-nās). 1. Tryptophan 2,3-dioxygenase. 2. An enzyme found in bacteria, that catalyzes the cleavage of tryptophan to indole, pyruvic acid, and ammonia; pyridoxal phosphate is a coenzyme.

tryptophanuria (trip'to-fă-nu'rī-ah). Enhanced urinary excretion of tryptophan.

tsetse (tset'se, tse'tse) [S. African native name]. See *Glossina.*

TSH Thyroid-stimulating *hormone.*

TSTA Tumor-specific transplantation *antigens.*

T.U. Abbreviation for toxic or toxin *unit.*

tuba, pl. **tubae** (tu'bah, tu'be) [L.] [NA]. Tube.

tu'bal. Relating to a tube, especially the uterine tube.

tube [L. *tubua,* straight trumpet]. Tuba. **1.** A hollow cylinder or pipe. **2.** A canal or tubular organ.

auditory t., eustachian t.; salpinx; a t. from the tympanic cavity of the ear to the nasopharynx.

bronchial t.'s, the smaller divisions of the bronchi.

drainage t., a t. introduced into a wound or cavity to facilitate removal of a fluid.

endobronchial t., Carlens *catheter.*

endotracheal t., a catheter inserted into the trachea to provide an airway.

eustachian t., auditory t.

fallopian t., *tuba* uterine t.

feeding t., a flexible t. passed through oral pharynx and into the esophagus and stomach, through which liquid food is fed.

Levin t., a t. introduced through the nose into the upper alimentary canal, to facilitate intestinal decompression.

Miller-Abbott t., a t. with two lumens, used for intestinal decompression.

Moss t., (1) triple-lumen, nasogastric, feeding-decompression t., utilizing a gastric balloon to occlude cardioesophageal junction, with simultaneous esophageal aspiration and intragastric feeding; (2) double-lumen, gastric lavage t., providing continuous delivery of saline via a small bore, with simultaneous aspiration of fluid and some particles via a large bore.

nasogastric t., a stomach tube passed through the nose.

Sengstaken-Blakemore t., a t. with three lumens, one for drainage of the stomach and two for inflation of attached gastric and esophageal balloons; used for emergency treatment of bleeding esophageal varices.

stomach t., a flexible t. passed into the stomach for lavage or feeding.

tracheotomy t., a curved t. used to keep the stoma free after tracheotomy.

uterine t., fallopian t.; gonaduct; oviduct; salpinx (1); a t. from each ovary to the side of the fundus of the uterus, through which the ova pass.

Wangensteen t., Wangensteen *suction.*

tubectomy (tu-bek'to-mī) [L. *tuba,* tube, + G. *ektomē,* excision]. Salpingectomy.

tu'ber, pl. **tu'bera** [L. protuberance, swelling] [NA]. A localized swelling; a knob, tuberosity, or eminence.

t. cine'reum [NA], a prominence of the base of the hypothalamus, extending ventrally into the infundibulum and hypophysial stalk.

tubercle (tu'ber-kl) [L. *tuberculum,* dim. of *tuber,* a swelling]. **1.** In anatomy, tuberculum. **2.** In dentistry, a small elevation arising on the surface of a tooth. **3.** A granulomatous lesion due to infection by *Mycobacterium tuberculosis,* although morphologically indistinguishable lesions may occur in diseases caused by other agents.

auricular t., darwinian t.

darwinian t., a small projection from the upper end of the posterior part of the inward free margin of the helix.

dissection t., postmortem *wart.*

fibrous t., a t. in which fibroblasts proliferate about the periphery (and into the cellular zones), eventually resulting in a rim or wall of cellular fibrous tissue or collagenous material.

genial t., *spina* mentalis.

Ghon's t., Ghon's focus or primary lesion; the pulmonary lesion of primary tuberculosis.

hard t., a t. lacking necrosis.

hyaline t., a fibrous t. in which the cellular fibrous tissue and collagenous fibers become altered and merged into a fairly homogeneous, acellular, firm mass.

intervenous t., the projection on the wall of the right atrium between the orifices of the venae cavae.

pearly t., milium.

t. of rib, the knob on a rib with which it articulates with the transverse process of a vertebra.

soft t., a t. showing caseous necrosis.

tubercul-. See tuberculo-.

tuber'cula. Plural of tuberculum.

tuber'cular, tuber'culate, tuber'culated. Pertaining to or characterized by tubercles or small nodules.

tuberculid (tu-ber'ku-lid). A lesion of the skin or mucous membrane resulting from specific sensitization to the tubercle bacillus.

papular t., lichen scrofulosorum; an allergic manifestation of tuberculous infection in the body, consisting of small to medium-sized papules.

papulonecrotic t., dusky-red papules followed by crusting and ulceration primarily on the extremities; seen in persons with a deep focus of tuberculosis or with a history of preceding infection.

tuberculin (tu-ber'ku-lin). A liquid culture of *Mycobacterium tuberculosis* used chiefly for diagnostic tests; originally known as Koch's old t. (OT).

purified protein derivative of t. (PPD), purified t. containing the active protein fraction; differs from OT chiefly in that the bacteria are grown in a synthetic rather than in a broth medium.

tuberculitis (tu-ber'ku-li'tis) [tubercul- + G. *-itis,* inflammation]. Inflammation of any tubercle.

tuberculo-, tubercul-. Combining forms denoting a tubercle, tuberculosis.

tuberculocele (tu-ber'ku-lo-sēl) [tuberculo- + G. *kēlē,* tumor, hernia]. Tuberculosis of the testes.

tuberculofibroid (tu-ber'ku-lo-fi'broyd). An encapsulated nodule that is formed during the process of healing in a focus of tuberculous granulomatous inflammation.

tuberculoid (tu-ber'ku-loyd) [tuberculo- + G. *eidos,* resemblance]. Resembling tuberculosis, or a tubercle.

tuberculoma (tu-ber'ku-lo'mah) [tuberculo- + G. *-oma,* tumor]. A rounded tumorlike but non-neoplastic mass, usually in the lungs or brain, due to localized tuberculous infection.

tuberculosis (tu-ber'ku-lo'sis) [tuberculo- + G. *-osis*, condition]. A specific disease caused by the presence of *Mycobacterium tuberculosis*, the most common seat being the lungs, which produces a tubercle that undergoes caseation; general symptoms are those of sepsis: fever, sweats, and emaciation.

   acute t., acute miliary t., disseminated t.; a rapidly fatal disease due to the general dissemination of tubercle bacilli in the blood, resulting in the formation of miliary tubercles in various organs and tissues, and producing symptoms of profound toxemia.

   cutaneous t., scrofuloderma; pathologic lesions of the skin caused by *Mycobacterium tuberculosis*.

   t. cu'tis indurati'va, obsolete term for *erythema induratum*.

   t. cu'tis verruco'sa, tuberculous wart; a tuberculous skin lesion having a warty surface with a chronic inflammatory base. See also postmortem *wart*.

   disseminated t., acute miliary t.

   open t., pulmonary t., tuberculous ulceration, or other form in which the bacilli are present in the excretions or secretions.

   primary t., first infection by *Mycobacterium tuberculosis* characterized in the lungs by the formation of a primary complex consisting of small peripheral pulmonary focus and hilar or paratracheal lymph node involvement; may heal with calcification or may progress, sometimes with miliary dissemination.

   secondary t., t. found in adults and characterized by lesions near the apex of an upper lobe, which may cavitate or heal with scarring; may be due to reinfection or to reactivation of a dormant endogenous infection.

tuberculostatic (tu-ber'ku-lo-stat'ik) [tuberculo- + G. *statikos*, causing to stand]. Denoting an agent that inhibits the growth of tubercle bacilli.

tuberculous (tu-ber'ku-lus). Relating to or affected by tuberculosis.

tuberculum, pl. **tubercula** (tu-ber'ku-lum, -lah) [L. dim. of a *tuber*, a knob, swelling, tumor] [NA]. Tubercle (1). **1.** An anatomical nodule. **2.** A circumscribed, rounded, solid elevation on the skin, mucous membrane, or surface of an organ. **3.** A slight elevation from the surface of a bone giving attachment to a muscle or ligament.

   t. arthrit'icum, (1) Heberden's *nodes;* (2) any gouty concretion in or around a joint.

   tuber'cula doloro'sa, multiple cutaneous myomas or neuromas, painful on pressure.

tuberositas (tu-ber-os'ĭtas) [NA]. Tuberosity.

tuberosity (tu-ber-os'ĭ-tĭ) [L. *tuberosus*, full of lumps]. Tuberositas; a large tubercle or rounded elevation, as from the surface of a bone for attachment of a ligament or tendon.

tu'berous [L. *tuberosus*]. Knobby, lumpy, or nodular; presenting many tubers or tuberosities.

tubo-. Combining form denoting tubular or a tube. See also salpingo-.

tubocurarine chloride (tu'bo-kūr-ar'ēn). *d*-Tubocurarine chloride; $C_{38}H_{44}Cl_2N_2O_6\cdot5H_2O$; an alkaloid (from the stems of *Chondodendron tomentosum*) that raises the threshold for acetylcholine at the myoneural junction by occupying the receptors competitively, and that also blocks ganglionic tranmission and releases histamine; used to produce muscular relaxation during surgical operations.

tu'bo-ova'rian. Relating to the uterine tube and the ovary.

tu'boplasty. Salpingoplasty.

tubotorsion (tu'bo-tor-shun) [tubo- + L. *torsio,* torsion]. Twisting of a tubular structure, such as a uterine tube.

tubotympanic, tubotympanal (tu'bo-tim-pan'ik, -tim'pă-nal). Relating to the auditory tube and the tympanic cavity of the ear.

tubouterine (tu'bo-u'ter-in). Relating to a uterine tube and the uterus.

tubule (tu'būl) [L. *tubulus,* dim. of *tubus,* tube]. A small tube.

   collecting t., one of the straight t.'s of the kidney, present in the medulla and pars radiata of the cortex.

   convoluted t., the first, proximal, or primary leads from the capsule of the kidney; the second or distal lead is formed from the ascending limb of Henle's loop which enters the labyrinth and ends in a collecting t.

   dentinal t.'s , *canaliculi* dentales.

   Henle's t.'s, the straight descending and ascending portions of the renal t.'s which form Henle's loop.

   renal t.'s, see collecting t., convoluted t.

   seminiferous t., one of two or three twisted curved t.'s in each lobule of the testis, in which spermatogenesis occurs, which becomes straight just before entering the mediastinum to form the rete testis.

   T t., the transverse t. that passes from the sarcolemma across a myofibril of striated muscle.

tu'buli. Plural of tubulus.

tubulin (tu'bu-lin). Protein molecules of microtubules which exist in two states: X-state, equivalent to material found predominantly in trailing fraction; Y-state in the leading fraction.

tubulocyst (tu'bu-lo-sist). Tubular cyst; a cyst formed by the dilation of any occluded canal or tube.

tubulorrhexis (tu'bu-lo-rek'sis) [tubule + G. *rhēxis,* a breaking]. Necrosis of the epithelial lining in localized segments of renal tubules, with focal rupture or loss of the basement membrane.

tubulus, pl. **tubuli** (tu'bu-lus, -li) [L. dim. of *tubus,* tube] [NA]. Tubule.

tu'bus, pl. **tu'bi** [L.]. Tube; canal.

tularemia (tu-lă-re'mĭ-ah) [*Tulare,* CA, + G. *haima,* blood]. A disease caused by *Francisella tularensis* and transmitted to man from rodents through the bite of a deer fly, *Chrysops discalis*, and other bloodsucking insects, and can also be acquired directly through the bite of or handling of an infected animal; symptoms are similar to those of undulant fever and plague.

tumefacient (tu-mĕ-fa'shent) [L. *tume-facio*, to cause to swell]. Causing or tending to cause swelling.

tumefaction (tu-mĕfak'shun) [see tumefacient]. **1.** A swelling. **2.** Tumescence.

tumefy (tu'mĕ-fi). To swell or to cause to swell.

tumescence (tu-mes'ens) [L. *tumesco*, to begin to swell]. Tumefaction (2); turgescence; the condition of being or becoming tumid.

tumescent (tu-mes'ent). Turgescent; denoting tumescence.

tu'mid [L. *tumidus*]. Turgid; swollen, as by congestion, edema, hyperemia.

tu'mor [L. *tumor*, a swelling]. **1.** Any swelling or tumefaction; one of the four signs of inflammation (t., calor, dolor, rubor) enunciated by Celsus. **2.** Neoplasm.

   adenomatoid t., adenofibromyoma; Recklinghausen's t.; a small benign t. of the male epididymis and female genital tract, consisting of fibrous tissue or smooth muscle enclosing spaces lined by cells; the lining cells may resemble endothelium, epithelium, or mesothelium.

   amyloid t., nodular *amyloidosis.*

   aortic body t., chemodectoma.

   benign t., a t. that does not form metastases and does not invade and destroy adjacent normal tissue.

   Brenner t., a relatively infrequent benign neoplasm of the ovary, consisting chiefly of fibrous tissue that contains nests of cells resembling transitional type epithelium and glandlike structures that contain mucin.

   Buschke-Löwenstein t., giant *condyloma.*

   carcinoid t., argentaffinoma; a small slow-growing neoplasm composed of islands of rounded cells of medium size, with moderately small vesicular nuclei, which can occur in the gastrointestinal tract, lungs, and other sites.

   carotid body t., chemodectoma.

   chromaffin t., paraganglioma.

   connective t., histoid t.; any t. of the connective tissue group, *e.g.*, osteoma, fibroma, sarcoma.

   dermoid t., dermoid *cyst.*

   desmoid t., desmoid (2).

   embryonal t., embryonic t., embryoma; a neoplasm, usually malignant, that arises during intrauterine or early postnatal development from an organ rudiment or immature tissue, forms immature structures characteristic of the part from which it arises, and may form other tissues.

   Ewing's t., endothelial myeloma; a malignant neoplasm which occurs usually before the age of 20 years, about twice as frequently in males, and mostly involves bones of the extremities including the shoulder girdle, with a predilection for the metaphysis.

   giant cell t. of bone, giant cell myeloma; osteoclastoma; a sometimes malignant osteolytic t. composed of multinucleated giant cells and ovoid or spindle-shaped cells, occurring most frequently in an end of a long tubular bone.

   giant cell t. of tendon sheath, localized nodular tenosynovitis; a nodule, possibly inflammatory, arising commonly from the flexor sheath of the fingers and thumb; composed of fibrous tissue, lipid- and hemosiderin-containing macrophages, and multinucleated giant cells.

   glomus t., angiomyoneuroma; angioneuromyoma; glomangioma; a painful neoplasm composed of specialized pericytes and neurites, usually in single encapsulated nodular masses that occur almost exclusively in the skin.

   glomus jugulare t., chemodectoma.

   granular cell t., granular cell myoblastoma; a slow-growing benign t., often involving peripheral nerves in skin, mucosa, or connective tissue, derived from Schwann cells.

   granulosa cell t., folliculoma (1); a benign or malignant t. of the ovary arising from the granular layer of the graafian follicle and frequently secreting estrogen.

   heterologous t., a t. composed of a tissue unlike that from which it springs.

   histoid t., connective t.

   homologous t., a t. composed of tissue of the same sort as that from which it springs.

   Hürthle cell t., a neoplasm of the thyroid gland composed of polyhedral acidophilic cells and which may be benign or malignant, the behavior of the latter depending on the general microscopic pattern, whether follicular, papillary, or undifferentiated.

   Krukenberg t., a metastatic carcinoma of the ovary, usually bilateral and secondary to a mucous carcinoma of the stomach, which contains signet ring cells filled with mucus.

   malignant t., a t. that invades surrounding tissues, is usually capable of producing metastases, may recur after attempted removal, and is likely to cause death unless adequately treated.

   melanotic neuroectodermal t., melanoameloblastoma; pigmented ameloblastoma; a benign t., commonly seen in the maxilla, containing melanin-pigmented cells.

   mixed t., a t. composed of two or more varieties of tissue.

   organoid t., a t. of complex structure, glandular in origin, containing epithelium, connective tissue, etc.

   papillary t., papilloma.

   pearl t., cholesteatoma.

   phantom t., accumulation of fluid in interlobar spaces of the lung, secondary to congestive heart failure, radiologically simulating a neoplasm.

   pontine angle t., a t. growing in the proximal portion of the acoustic nerve, in the angle formed by the cerebellum and the lateral pons.

   Recklinghausen's t., adenomatoid t.

sand t., psammoma.

Sertoli cell t., androblastoma (1).

teratoid t., teratoma.

theca cell t., thecoma.

Warthin's t., adenolymphoma.

Wilms t., adenomyosarcoma; embryoma of the kidney; nephroblastoma; renal carcinosarcoma; a malignant renal mixed t. of young children, composed of small spindle cells and various other types of tissue.

tumoricidal (tu'mor-ĭ-si'dal) [tumor + L. *caedo*, to kill]. Destructive to tumor cells.

tumorigenesis (tu'mor-ĭ-jen'ĕ-sis) [tumor + G. *genesis*, origin]. Production of a new tumor or growths.

tumorigenic (tu'mor-ĭ-jen'ik). Causing or producing tumors.

Tunga penetrans (tung'ah pen'ĕ-tranz). A member of the flea family, Tungidae, commonly known as chigger flea, sand flea, chigoe, or jiggers; the female penetrates the skin, frequently under the toenails, and as she becomes distended with eggs a painful ulcer with inflammation develops.

tung'sten [Swed. *tung*, heavy, + *sten*, stone]. Wolfram; wolframium; a metallic element, symbol W, atomic no. 74, atomic weight 183.85.

tu'nic [L. *tunica*]. Tunica.

tunica, pl. **tunicae** (tu'nĭ-kah, -ke) [L. a coat] [NA]. Tunic; one of the enveloping layers or coats of a part, as of a blood vessel or other tubular structure.

t. adventi'tia [NA], membrana adventita (1); the outermost fibrous coat of a vessel or an organ that is derived from the surrounding connective tissue.

t. albugin'ea [NA], a dense, white, collagenous sheath surrounding a structure.

t. conjuncti'va [NA], conjunctiva.

t. exter'na [NA], the outer of two or more enveloping layers of any structure; specifically, the outer fibroelastic coat of a blood or lymph vessel.

t. fibro'sa any fibrous envelope of a part.

t. in'tima [NA], the innermost coat of a blood or lymphatic vessel, consisting of endothelium, usually a thin fibroelastic subendothelial layer, and an inner elastic membrane or longitudinal fibers.

t. me'dia [NA], media (1); the middle, usually muscular, coat of an artery or other tubular structure.

t. muco'sa [NA], mucous membrane; a lining of epithelium, lamina propria, and (in the digestive tract) a layer of smooth muscle which secretes mucus.

t. muscula'ris [NA], the muscular, usually middle, layer of a tubular structure.

t. pro'pria, the special envelope of a part as distinguished from the peritoneal or other investment common to several parts.

t. reflex'a, the reflected layer of the vascular layer of testis that lines the scrotum.

t. sero'sa [NA], serous tunic or membrane; membrana serosa (1); serosa (1); the outermost coat of a visceral structure that lies in a body cavity; consists of a surface layer of mesothelium reinforced by irregular fibroelastic connective tissue.

t. submuco'sa, *tela* submucosa.

t. vagina'lis tes'tis [NA], the serous sheath of the testis and epididymis, derived from the peritoneum, consisting of an outer and inner serous layer.

t. vasculo'sa, any layer well supplied with blood vessels.

tun'nel. An elongated enclosed passageway, usually open at both ends.

carpal t., *canalis* carpi.

Corti's t., Corti's canal; the spiral canal in the organ of Corti, filled with fluid and occasionally crossed by nonmedullated nerve fibers.

tur'bid [L. *turbidus*, confused, disordered]. Cloudy.

turbidimetry (tur-bĭ-dim'ĕ-trĭ) [turbidity + G. *metron*, measure]. A method for determining the concentration of a substance in a solution by the degree of cloudiness or turbidity it causes or by the degree of clarification it induces in a turbid solution.

turbidity (tur-bid'ĭ-tĭ) [L. *turbiditas*, fr. *turbidus*, turbid]. The quality of being turbid, of losing transparency because of sediment or insoluble matter.

tur'binate. *Concha* nasalis.

tur'binated [L. *tubinatus*, shaped like a top]. Scroll-shaped.

turbinectomy (tur-bĭ-nek'to-mĭ) [turbinate + G. *ektomē*, excision]. Surgical removal of a turbinated bone.

turbinotomy (tur-bĭ-not'o-mĭ) [turbinate + G. *tomē*, incision]. Incision into or excision of a turbinated body.

turgescence (tur-jes'ens) [L. *turgesco*, to begin to swell]. Tumescence.

turgescent (tur-jes'ent). Tumescent.

turgid (tur'jid) [L. *turgidus*, swollen]. Tumid.

tur'gor [L. fr. *turgeo*, to swell]. Fullness.

turista (tu-rēs'tah). Colloquialism for traveler's diarrhea.

tus'sal. Tussive.

tus'sis [L.]. A cough.

tussive (tus'siv) [L. *tussis*, a cough]. Tussal; relating to a cough.

twin [A.S. *getwin*, double]. **1.** One of two children born at one birth. **2.** Double; growing in pairs.

allantoidoangiopagous t.'s, omphaloangiopagous t.'s; unequal monozygotic t.'s with fusion of their allantoic vessels within the placenta.

conjoined t.'s, monozygotic t.'s with varying extent of union and different degrees of residual duplication.

dizygotic t.'s, fraternal or heterologous t.'s; t.'s derived from two separate zygotes.

enzygotic t.'s, identical t.'s, monozygotic t.'s.

fraternal t.'s, heterologous t.'s, dizygotic t.'s.

monoamniotic t.'s, t.'s within a common amnion.

monozygotic t.'s, enzygotic or identical t.'s resulting from a single fertilized ovum that at an early stage of development becomes separated into independently growing cell aggregations giving rise to two individuals of the same sex and identical genetic constitution.

omphaloangiopagous t.'s, allantoidoangiopagous t.'s.

Siamese t.'s, originally, much publicized conjoined t.'s from Siam in the 19th century; now, lay usage for any type of conjoined t.'s.

twinge (twinj). A sudden momentary sharp pain.

twin'ning. The production of equivalent structure by division; the tendency of divided parts to assume symmetrical relations.

twitch [A.S. *twiccian*]. **1.** To jerk spasmodically. **2.** A momentary spasmodic contraction of a muscle fiber.

two-carbon fragment. The acetyl group ($CH_3CO–$) taking in part in transacetylation reactions with coenzyme A as carrier; commonly referred to as acetate or acetic acid, from which it is derived.

tylectomy (ti-lek'to-mĭ) [G. *tylē*, lump, + *ektomē*, excision]. Lumpectomy; surgical removal of a tumor from the breast.

tyloma (ti-lo'mah) [G. a callus]. Callosity.

tylosis, pl. **tyloses** (ti-lo'sis, -sēz) [G. a becoming callous]. Formation of a callosity (tyloma).

tylot'ic. Relating to or marked by tylosis.

tympan-, tympani-. See tympano-.

tympanal (tim'pă-nal). Tympanic.

tympanectomy (tim-pă-nek'to-mĭ) [tympan- + G. *ektomē*, excision]. Excision of the tympanic membrane.

tympanic (tim-pan'ik). Tympanal. **1.** Relating to the tympanic cavity or membrane. **2.** Resonant. **3.** Tympanitic (2).

tympanism (tim'pă-nizm). Tympanites.

tympanites (tim-pă-ni'tēz) [L. fr. G. *tympanitēs*, dropsy in which the belly is stretched like a drum, *tympanon*]. Meteorism; tympanism; abdominal distension from gas in the intestinal or peritoneal cavity.

tympanitic (tim-pă-nit'ik). **1.** Tympanous; referring to tympanites. **2.** Tympanic (3); denoting the quality of sound elicited by percussing over the inflated intestine or a large pulmonary cavity.

tympanitis (tim-pă-ni'tis). Myringitis.

tympano-, tympan-, tympani- [G. *tympanon*, drum]. Combining forms denoting tympanum or tympanites.

tympanocentesis (tim'pă-no-sen-te'sis) [tympano- + G. *kentēsis*, puncture]. Puncture of the tympanic membrane with a needle to aspirate middle ear fluid.

tympanomastoiditis (tim'pă-no-mas-toy-di'tis). Inflammation of the middle ear and the mastoid cells.

tympanoplasty (tim'pă-no-plas-tĭ) [tympano- + G. *plassō*, to form]. Operative correction of a damaged middle ear.

tympanotomy (tim-pă-not'o-mĭ) [tympano- + G. *tomē*, incision]. Myringotomy.

tympanous (tim'pă-nus). Tympanitic (1).

tympanum, pl. **tympanums, tympana** (tim'pă-num, tim'pă-nah) [L. fr. G. *tympanon*, a drum]. *Cavitas tympanica.*

tympany (tim'pă-nĭ). Low-pitched, resonant, drumlike note obtained by percussing the surface of a large air-containing space.

type [G. *typos*, a mark, a model]. The usual form that all others of the class resemble, that is characteristic of the class.

basic personality t., **(1)** an individual's unique, covert, or underlying personality propensities; **(2)** personality characteristics of an individual also shared by a majority of the members of a social group.

blood t., see under B.

typhl-. See typhlo-.

typhlectasis (tif-lek'tă-sis) [G. *typhlon*, cecum, + *ektasis*, a stretching out]. Dilation of the cecum.

typhlectomy (tif-lek'to-mĭ). Cecectomy.

typhlenteritis (tif'len-ter-i'tis). Cecitis.

typhlitis (tif-li'tis). Cecitis.

typhlo-, typhl-. **1** [G. cecum]. Combining form denoting the cecum. See also ceco-. **2** [G. *typhlos*, blind]. Combining form denoting blindness.

typhlodicliditis (tif'lo-dik-lĭ-di'tis) [G. typhlo- + *diklis*, double-folding, + *-itis*, inflammation]. Inflammation of the ileocecal valve.

typhloenteritis (tif-lo-en-ter-i'tis). Cecitis.

typhlolithiasis (tif'lo-lĭ-thi'ă-sis) [G. typhlo- + *lithos*, stone]. Presence of fecal concretions in the cecum.

typhlopexy (tif'lo-pek-sĭ). Cecopexy.

typhlorrhaphy (tif-lor'ă-fĭ). Cecorrhaphy.

typhlosis (tif-lo'sis) [G. *typhlos*, blind]. Blindness.

typhlostomy (tif-los'to-mĭ). Cecostomy.

typhlotomy (tif-lot'o-mĭ). Cecotomy.

typhloureterostomy (tif'lo-u-re'ter-os'to-mĭ). Anastomosis of ureter into cecum.

typhoid (ti'foyd) [typhus + G. *eidos*, resemblance]. **1.** Resembling typhus. **2.** Typhoid *fever.*

typhoid'al. Relating to or resembling typhoid fever.

typhous (ti'fus). Relating to typhus.

typhus (ti'fus) [G. *typhos*, smoke, stupor]. Camp fever; an acute infectious and contagious disease, caused by rickettsiae, and occurring in two chief forms; epidemic t. and murine t.

endemic t., murine t.

epidemic t., t. caused by *Rickettsia prowazekii* and spread by body lice; marked by high fever, mental and physical depression, and a macular and papular eruption.

mite t., tsutsugamushi *disease.*

murine t., endemic t.; caused by *Rickettsia typhi* and transmitted to man by rat or mouse fleas; milder than epidemic t., but otherwise similar.

recrudescent t., Brill-Zinsser *disease.*

scrub t., tsutsugamushi *disease.*

tick t., collective term for tick-borne rickettsial diseases, involving many strains (or species) of the subgenus *Dermacentroxenus;* identified by their immunological reactions and, in some cases, pathogenicity.

tropical t., tsutsugamushi *disease.*

typing (ti'ping). Classification according to type.

blood t., blood grouping.

Tyr Tyrosine and its radicals.

tyramine (ti'ră-mēn, tīr'ă-). Decarboxylated tyrosine, a sympathomimetic amine having an action resembling that of epinephrine.

tyroketonuria (ti'ro-ke-to-nu'rĭ-ah). Urinary excretion of ketonic metabolites of tyrosine.

tyroma (ti-ro'mah) [G. *tyros,* cheese, + *-oma,* tumor]. A caseous tumor.

tyrosine (**Tyr**) (ti'ro-sēn, -sin). (HOC6H4)CH2 - CHNH2COOH; an α-amino acid present in most proteins.

tyrosinemia (ti'ro-sĭ-ne'mĭ-ah) [tyrosine + G. *haima,* blood]. Elevated blood concentrations of tyrosine, enhanced urinary excretion of tyrosine and tyrosyl compounds, hepatosplenomegaly, nodular cirrhosis of the liver, multiple renal tubular reabsorptive defects, and vitamin D-resistant rickets; autosomal recessive inheritance.

tyrosinosis (ti'ro-sĭ-no'sis) [tyrosine + G. *-osis,* condition]. A rare, possible heritable disorder of tyrosine metabolism characterized by enhanced urinary excretion of tyrosyl metabolites upon ingestion of tyrosine.

tyrosinuria (ti'ro-sĭ-nu'rĭ-ah) [tyrosine + G. *ouron,* urine]. Excretion of tyrosine in the urine.

tyrosyluria (ti'ro-sil-u'rĭ-ah). Enhanced urinary excretion of certain metabolites of tyrosine, as in tyrosinosis, scurvy, pernicious anemia.

U

U Unit; uranium; uridine in polymers; urinary *concentration,* followed by subscripts indicating location and chemical species.

ubiquinol (u-bī-kwi'nol, u-bik'wĭ-nol). The reduction product of a ubiquinone.

ubiquinone (u'bī-kwi'nōn, u-bik'wĭ-nōn). 2,3-Dimethoxy-5-methyl-1,4-benzoquinone with a multiprenyl side chain, as in coenzyme Q.

UDP Uridine diphosphate.

ulcer (ul'ser) [L. *ulcus,* a sore]. A lesion on the skin or a mucous surface caused by superficial loss of tissue, usually with necrosis and inflammation.

anastomotic u., u. of jejunum, after gastroenterostomy.

chronic u., a longstanding u. with fibrous scar tissue in its floor.

cold u., a small gangrenous u. on the extremities, due to defective circulation.

Curling's u., u. of the duodenum in a patient with extensive superficial burns or severe bodily injury.

decubitus u., bedsore; pressure sore; a chronic u. that appears in pressure areas in debilitated patients confined to bed or otherwise immobilized, due to a circulatory defect in the area under pressure.

gravitational u., a chronic u. of the leg with impaired healing because of the dependent position of the extremity and incompetence of the valves of the varicosed veins; the venous return stagnates and creates hypoxemia.

hard u., chancre.

Hunner's u., a focal and often multiple lesion involving all layers of the bladder wall in chronic interstitial cystitis.

peptic u., an u. of the alimentary mucosa, usually in the stomach or duodenum, exposed to acid gastric secretion.

perforated u., an u. extending through the wall of an organ.

phagedenic u., a rapidly spreading u. attended by formation of extensive sloughing.

rodent u., a slowly enlarging ulcerated basal cell carcinoma, usually on the face.

soft u., chancroid.

stercoral u., an u. of the colon due to pressure and irritation of retained fecal masses.

stomal u., an intestinal u., occurring after gastrojejunostomy, in the jejunal mucosa near the opening (stoma) between the stomach and the jejunum.

stress u.'s, acute peptic u.'s occurring in association with other conditions, including burns, cor pulmonale, intracranial lesions, and operations.

trophic u., a u. due to impaired nutrition of the part.

varicose u., loss of skin surface in the drainage area of a varicose vein, usually in the leg, resulting from stasis and infection.

venereal u., chancroid.

ul'cera. Plural of ulcus.

ul'cera'tive. Relating to, causing, or marked by an ulcer or ulcers.

ulcerate (ul'ser-āt). To form an ulcer.

ulceration (ul'ser-a'shun). **1.** The formation of an ulcer. **2.** An ulcer or aggregation of ulcers.

ulcerous (ul'ser-us) [L. *ulcerosus,* fr. foll.]. Relating to, affected with, or containing an ulcer.

ulcus, pl. **ulcera** (ul'kus, ul'ser-ah) [L.]. Ulcer.

ule-. See ulo-.

ulerythema (u'lĕr-ĭ-the'mah) [ule- + G. *erythēma,* redness of the skin]. Scarring with erythema.

ulna, pl. **ulnae** (ul'nah, ul'ne) [L. elbow, arm] [NA]. Elbow bone; cubitus (2); the medial and larger of the two bones of the forearm.

ul'nad [ulna + L. *ad,* to]. In a direction toward the ulna.

ul'nar. Relating to the ulna, or to any of the structures named from it.

ulo-, ule- [G. *oulē,* scar]. Combining forms denoting scar or scarring.

ulodermatitis (u'lo-der-mă-ti'tis) [ulo- + G. *derma,* skin, + *itis,* inflammation]. Inflammation of the skin resulting in destruction of tissue and the formation of scars.

u'loid [ulo- + G. *eidos*, resemblance]. **1.** Resembling a scar. **2.** A scarlike lesion due to a degenerative process in deeper layers of skin.

ultra- [L. beyond]. Prefix denoting excess, exaggeration, beyond.

ultracen'trifuge. A high speed centrifuge by means of which large molecules are caused to sediment at practicable rates.

ultradian (ul-tra'dī-an) [ultra- + L. *dies*, day]. Relating to biologic variations or rhythms occurring in cycles more frequent than every 24 hours.

ultrafiltration (ul'tră-fil-tra'shun). Filtration through a semipermeable membrane or any filter that separates colloid solutions from crystalloids or separates particles of different size in a colloid mixture.

ultraliga'tion. Ligation of a blood vessel beyond the point where a branch is given off.

ultramicroscop'ic. Submicroscopic.

ultrasonic (ul-tra-son'ik) [ultra- + L. *sonus*, sound]. Relating to energy waves similar to those of sound but of higher frequencies (above (30,000 Hz).

ultrasonogram (ul-tra-son'o-gram). Sonogram.

ultrasonograph (ul-tra-son'o-graf). Sonograph.

ultrasonography (ul'tră-sŏ-nog'ră-fĭ) [ultra- + L. *sonus*, sound, + G. *graphō*, to write]. Echography; sonography; location, measurement, or delineation of deep structures by measuring the reflection or transmission of high frequency or ultrasonic waves. See also subentries under ultrasound.

   gray-scale u., u. using a display of small differences in a acoustical impedance as different shades of gray, thus improving the quality of the image obtained.

ul'trasound. Sound having a frequency greater than 20,000 Hz.

   diagnostic u., use of u. to obtain images for medical diagnostic purposes, employing frequencies ranging from 1.6 to about MHz.

   real-time u., obtainment of individual B-mode images rapidly, so that a moving video display results.

ultravi'olet. Denoting the electromagnetic rays beyond the violet end of the visible spectrum.

ultravirus (ul'tră-vi'rus). Virus (2).

umbilical (um-bil'ĭ-kal). Omphalic; relating to the umbilicus.

umbil'icate, umbil'icated [L. *umbilicatus*]. Of navel shape; pitlike.

umbil'ica'tion. 1. A pit or navel-like depression. **2.** Formation of a depression at the apex of a papule, vesicle, or pustule.

umbilicus, pl. **umbilici** (um-bil'ĭ-kus, um-bĭ-li'kus, -si, -ki) [L. navel] [NA]. Navel; belly-button; the pit in the center of the abdominal wall marking the point where the umbilical cord entered the fetus.

um'bo, pl. **umbo'nes** [L. boss of a shield, a knob] [NA]. A projection on a surface, such as that on the inner surface of the tympanic membrane at the end of the manubrium of the malleus, corresponding to the most depressed point of the membrane.

UMP *Uridine* phosphate.

un-. Prefix meaning not, akin to in-, a-, and an-; denoting reversal, removal, release, deprivation; expressing an intensive action.

uncal (ung'kal). Denoting or relating to the uncus.

unci (un'si). Plural of uncus.

unciform (un'sĭ-form) [L. *uncus*, hook, + *forma*, form]. Uncinate.

Uncinaria (un-sĭ-năr'ĭ-ah) [LL. *uncinus*, a hook]. A genus of nematode hookworms that infect various mammals; species include *U. americana* (*Necator americanus*) and *U. duodenalis* (*Ancylostoma duodenale*).

uncinariasis (un'sĭ-nă-ri'ă-sis). Ancylostomiasis.

uncinate (un'sĭ-nāt) [L. *uncinatus*]. Unciform; hooklike or hook-shaped.

unconscious (un-kon'shus). **1.** Insensible (1); not conscious. **2.** In psychoanalysis, the psychic structure comprising the drives and feelings of which one is unaware.

   collective u., in jungian psychology, the combined engrams or memory potentials inherited from an individual's phylogenetic past.

unconsciousness (un-kon'shus-ness). A state of impaired consciousness in which one shows a total lack of responsiveness to environmental stimuli, but may respond to deep pain with involuntary movements.

uncovertebral (un-ko-ver'te-bral). Pertaining to or affecting the uncinate process of a vertebra.

unction (ungk'shun) [L. *unctio*, fr. *ungo*, pp. *unctus*, to anoint]. The action of applying or rubbing with an ointment or oil.

unctuous (ungk'shu-us, -chu-us) [L. *unctuosus*, fr. *unctio*, unction]. Greasy; oily.

uncus, pl. **unci** (un'kus, un'si) [L. a hook] [NA]. **1.** Any hook-shaped process or structure. **2.** Uncinate gyrus; the anterior hooked extremity of the parahippocampal gyrus on the basomedial surface of the temporal lobe.

un'derbite. Mandibular underdevelopment or excessive maxillary development.

undifferentiated (un'dif-er-en'shĭ-a-ted). Primitive, embryonic, immature, or having no special structure or function.

undulate (un'du-lāt) [Mod. L. *undula*, dim. of *unda*, wave]. Having an irregular, wavy border; denoting the shape of a bacterial colony.

ung. L. *unguentum*, ointment.

ungual (ung'gwal) [L. *unguis*, nail]. Unguinal; relating to a nail or the nails.

unguent (ung'gwent) [L. *unguentum*]. Ointment.

ungues (ung'gwēz). Plural of unguis.

unguinal (ung'gwĭ-nal). Ungual.

unguis, pl. **ungues** (ung'gwis, -gwēz) [L.] [NA]. Onyx (1); nail; one of the thin, horny, translucent plates covering the dorsal surface at the distal end of each finger and toe; consists of a visible corpus or body and a radix or root concealed under a fold of skin.

uni- [L. *unus,* one]. Prefix denoting one, single, not paired; equivalent to mono-.

unicam′eral. Monolocular.

unicel′lular. Composed of but one cell, as the protozoons.

unicornous (u-nĭ-kor′nus). Having but one horn, or cornu.

uniglan′dular. Involving, relating to, or containing but one gland.

unilat′eral. Confined to one side only.

unilo′bar. Having but one lobe.

uniloc′ular [uni- + L. *loculus,* compartment]. Having but one compartment or cavity, as in a fat cell.

union (u′nyun) [L. *unus,* one]. **1.** The joining or amalgamation of two or more bodies. **2.** The structural adhesion or growing together of the edges of a wound.

    faulty u., u. of fracture by fibrous tissue, without bone formation.

    primary u., *healing* by first intention.

    secondary u., *healing* by second intention.

uniovular (un-ĭ-ov′u-lar). Relating to or formed from a single ovum.

unipen′nate [uni- + L. *penna,* feather]. Denoting a muscle with a lateral tendon to which the fibers are attached obliquely, like one half of a feather.

unipo′lar. 1. Having but one pole; denoting a nerve cell from which the branches project from one side only. **2.** Situated at one extremity only of a cell.

u′niport [uni- + L. *porto,* to carry]. Transport of a molecule or ion through a membrane by a carrier mechanism (uniporter) without known coupling to any other molecule or ion transport.

u′nit [L. *unus,* one]. **1.** One; a single entity. **2** (U). A standard of measure, weight, or any other quality, by multiplications or fractions of which a scale or system is formed. **3.** A group of persons or things considered as a whole because of mutual activities or functions.

    absolute u., a u. whose value is constant regardless of place or time.

    antigen u., the smallest amount of antigen that, in the presence of specific antiserum, will fix one complement u.

    antitoxin u., a u. expressing the strength or activity of an antitoxin.

    atomic mass u. (amu), a u. of mass equal to $1/12$ of the mass of an atom of $^{12}_6C$; in terms of energy; 1 amu = 931 MeV.

    base u., the fundamental u.'s of length (meter), mass (kilogram), time (second), electric current (ampere), thermodynamic temperature (kelvin), amount of substance (mole), and luminous intensity (candela) in the International System of Units (SI).

    Bodansky u., that amount of phosphatase that liberates 1 mg of phosphorus as inorganic phosphate during the first hour of incubation with a buffered substrate containing sodium *β*-glycerophosphate.

    British thermal u. (BTU), the quantity of heat required to raise one point of water from 39°F. to 40°F; equal to 252 calories.

    centimeter-gram-second (CGS, cgs) u., an absolute u. of the centimeter-gram-second system.

    complement u., the smallest amount (highest dilution) of complement that will cause solution of the u. quantity of red blood cells in the presence of a hemolysin u.

    foot-pound-second (FPS, fps) u., an absolute u. of the foot-pound-second system.

    hemolysin u., the smallest quantity (highest dilution) of inactivated immune serum (hemolysin) that will sensitize the standard suspension of erythrocytes so that the standard complement will cause complete hemolysis.

    insulin u. (international), the activity contained in $1/22$ of the international standard of zinc-insulin crystals.

    intensive care u. (ICU), a hospital facility for provision of intensive care of critically ill patients, characterized by high quality and quantity of continuous nursing and medical supervision and by use of sophisticated monitoring and resuscitative equipment.

    international u. (IU), a u. of biological material or of a drug as accepted by an international body.

    International System of Units (SI), see under I.

    Mache u. (M.u.), a u. of measure of radium emanation; one thousand Mache u.'s denote the amount of emanation in equilibrium with $1/2000$ mg of radium; 1 microcurie equals 2670 Mache u.'s.

    meter-kilogram-second (MKS, mks) u., an absolute u. of the meter kilogram-second system.

    motor u., a single somatic motor neuron and the group of muscle fibers innervated by it.

    physiologic u., the smallest division of an organ that will perform its function.

    Somogyi u., a measure of the level of activity of amylase in blood serum, as analyzed by means of the Somogyi method; one u. is equivalent to 1 mg. of reducing sugar liberated as glucose per 100 ml of serum.

    Svedberg u. (S), a sedimentation constant of 1×10^{-13} seconds.

    toxic u., toxin u. (T.U.), a u. formerly synonymous with minimal lethal dose but which, because of the unstability of toxins, is now measured in terms of the quantity of standard antitoxin with which the toxin combines.

    u. of penicillin, (1) USP, the penicillin activity of 0.6 *μ*g of the FDA master standard; (2) international, the penicillin activity of 0.6 *μ*g of penicillin G.

    USP u., a u. as defined and adopted by the *United States Pharmacopeia.*

United States Pharmacopeia (USP). See Pharmacopeia.

univalence (u-nĭ-va′lens). Monovalence.

univalent (u-nĭ-val′lent). Monovalent (1).

unmyelinated (un-mi'ĕ-lĭ-na-ted). Amyelinated; amyelinic; denoting nerve fibers (axons) lacking a myelin sheath.

unofficial. Denoting a drug that is not listed in the *United States Pharmacopeia* or the *National Formulary.*

unphysiolog'ic. Pertaining to conditions in the organism that are abnormal.

unsat'urated. 1. Not saturated; denoting a solution in which the solvent is capable of dissolving more of the solute. 2. Denoting a chemical compound in which all the affinities are not satisfied, so that still other atoms or radicals may be added to it. 3. Denoting compounds containing double and triple bonds.

unstri'ated. Without striations, denoting the structure of the smooth or involuntary muscles.

up'take. The absorption by a tissue of some substance, food material, mineral, etc. and its permanent or temporary retention.

urachal (u'rā-kal). Relating to the urachus.

urachus (u'rā-kus) [G. *ourachos,* the urinary canal of a fetus]. That portion of the reduced allantoic stalk between the apex of the bladder and the umbilicus.

u'racil. 2,4-Dioxopyrimidine; 2,4-(1*H*,3*H*)-pyrimidinedione; a pyrimidine (base) present in ribonucleic acid.

uranisco-. See urano-.

uranium (u-ra'nĭ-um) [G. myth. char. *Uranus*]. A feebly radioactive metallic element, symbol U, atomic no. 92, atomic weight 238.03.

urano- [G. *ouranos,* vault of sky; *ouraniskos,* roof of mouth]. Combining form relating to the hard palate.

uranoplasty (u'rā-no-plas-tĭ). Palatoplasty.

uranorrhaphy (u-ră-nor'ă-fĭ) [urano- + G. *raphē,* suture]. Palatorrhaphy.

uranoschisis (u-rā-nos'kĭ-sis) [urano- + G. *schisis,* fissure]. Cleft of the hard palate.

uranostaphyloschisis (u'rā-no-staf'ĭ-los'kĭ-sis) [urano- + G. *staphylē,* uvula, + *schisis,* fissure]. Cleft of the soft and hard palates.

u'ranyl. The ion, UO^{++}, usually found in such salts as uranyl nitrate, UO$_2$(NO$_3$)$_2$.

urarthritis (u-rar-thri'tis) [urate + arthritis]. Gouty inflammation of a joint.

u'rate. A salt or uric acid.

    u. oxidase, uricase; an oxygen oxidoreductase oxidizing uric acid.

uratemia (u-ra-te'mĭ-ah) [urate + G. *haima,* blood]. Presence of urates, especially sodium urate, in the blood.

urato'sis. Any morbid condition due to the presence of urates in the blood or tissues.

uraturia (u'ra-tu'rĭ-ah) [urate + G. *ouron,* urine]. Passage of an increased amount of urates in the urine.

Urd Uridine.

ur-defenses. Fundamental beliefs essential for man's psychological integrity.

ure-, urea-, ureo- [G. *ouron,* urine]. Combining forms denoting urea or urine. See also urin-; uro-.

urea (u-re'ah) [G. ouron, urine]. Carbamide; carbonyldiamide; the chief end product of nitrogen metabolism in mammals, formed in the liver and excreted in the urine.

urea frost. Minute flakes of urea sometimes observed on the skin, particularly of the face, of patients with uremia.

Ureaplasma (u-re'ā-plaz'mah). *T-mycoplasma;* a genus of nonmotile Gram-negative bacteria (family Mycoplasmataceae) that require urea and cholesterol for growth; in males, associated with nongonococcal urethritis and prostatitis and, in females, with genitourinary tract infections and reproductive failure. The type species is *U. urealyticum.*

ureapoiesis (u-re'ā-poy-e'sis) [urea + G. *poiēsis,* a making]. Production of urea.

urease (u're-ās). An amidohyrolase cleaving urea into CO$_2$ and NH$_3$.

urecchysis (u-rek'ĭ-sis) [G. *ouron,* urine, + *ekchysis,* a pouring out]. Extravasation of urine into the tissues.

uredema (u-re-de'mah) [G. *ouron,* urine, + *oidēma,* swelling]. Uroedema; edema due to infiltration of urine into the subcutaneous tissues.

urelcosis (u-rel-ko'sis) [G. *ouron,* urine, + *helkōsis,* ulceration]. Ulceration of the urinary tract.

uremia (u-re'mĭ-ah) [G. *ouron,* urine, + *haima,* blood]. Azotemia. 1. Excess of urea and other nitrogenous waste in the blood. 2. The complex of symptoms due to severe persisting renal failure that can be relieved by dialysis.

ure'mic. Relating to uremia.

uremigenic (u're-mĭ-jen'ik). 1. Of uremic origin or causation. 2. Causing or resulting in uremia.

ureo-. See ure-.

uresiesthesis (u-re'sĭ-es-the'sis) [G. *ourēsis,* a urinating, + *aisthēsis,* sensation]. Uriesthesis; the sensation prompting urination.

ure'sis [G. *ourēsis*]. Urination.

ureter (u-re'ter, u'rē-ter) [G. *ourētēr,* urinary canal] [NA]. The tube conducting urine from the renal pelvis of the kidney to the bladder.

ure'teral. Ureteric; relating to the ureter.

ureteralgia (u-re-ter-al'jĭ-ah) [ureter + G. *algos,* pain]. Pain in the ureter.

uretercystoscope (u're'ter-sis'to-skōp). Ureterocystoscope; a cystoscope with an attachment for catheterization of the ureters.

ureterectasia (u-re'ter-ek-ta'zĭ-ah) [ureter + G. *ektasis,* a stretching out]. Dilation of a ureter.

ureterectomy (u-re-ter-ek'to-mĭ) [ureter + G. *ektomē,* excision]. Excision of a segment or all of a ureter.

ureter'ic. Ureteral.

ureteritis (u-re-ter-i'tis). Inflammation of a ureter.

uretero- [G. *ourētēr,* urinary canal]. Combining form denoting the ureter.

ureterocele (u-re′ter-o-sēl) [utero- + G. *kēlē*, hernia]. Saccular dilatation of the terminal portion of the ureter which protrudes into the lumen of the urinary bladder, due to a congenital stenosis of the ureteral meatus.

ureterocelorraphy (u-re′ter-o-se-lor′ă-fĭ) [ureterocele + G. *raphē*, suture]. Excision and suturing of a ureterocele performed through an open cystotomy incision.

ureterocolostomy (u-re′ter-o-ko-los′to-mĭ) [ureterocolostomy + G. *kolon*, colon, + *stoma*, mouth]. Implanting of the ureter into the colon.

ureterocystoscope (u-re′ter-o-sis′to-skōp). Uretercystoscope.

ureterocystostomy (u-re′ter-o-sis′tos′to-mĭ) [ureterocystostomy + G. *kystis*, bladder, + *stoma*, mouth]. Ureteroneocystostomy.

ureterodialysis (u-re′ter-o-di-al′ĭ-sis) [ureterodialysis + G. *dialysis*, separation]. Ureterolysis (1).

ureteroenterostomy (u-re′ter-o-en-ter-os′to-mĭ) [ureteroenterostomy + G. *enteron*, intestine, + *stoma*, mouth]. Surgical formation of an opening between a ureter and the intestine.

ureterography (u-re-ter-og′rǎ-fĭ) [ureterography + G. *graphē*, a writing]. Radiography of the ureter after injection of contrast media.

ureteroileoneocystostomy (u-re′ter-o-il′e-o-ne′o-sis-tos′to-mĭ) [ureteroileoneocystostomy + G. *ileum* + G. *neos*, new, + *kystis*, bladder, + *stoma*, mouth]. Restoration of the continuity of the urinary tract by anastomosis of the upper segment of a partially destroyed ureter to a segment of ileum, the lower end of which is then implanted into the bladder.

ureteroileostomy (u-re′ter-o-il-e-os′to-mĭ) [ureteroileostomy + G. *ileum* + G. *stoma*, mouth]. Implantation of a ureter into an isolated segment of ileum which drains through an abdominal stoma.

ureterolith (u-re′ter-o-lith) [ureterolith + G. *lithos*, stone]. A calculus in the ureter.

ureterolithiasis (u-re′ter-o-lĭ-thi′ă-sis) [ureterolith + G. *-iasis*, condition]. Formation or presence of a calculus or calculi in one or both ureters.

ureterolithotomy (u-re′ter-o-lĭ-thot′o-mĭ) [ureterolith + G. *tomē*, incision]. Surgical removal of a stone lodged in a ureter.

ureterolysis (u-re-ter-ol′ĭ-sis) [ureterolysis + G. *lysis*, a loosening]. **1.** Ureterodialysis; rupture of a ureter. **2.** Paralysis of the ureter. **3.** Surgical freeing of the ureter from surrounding disease or adhesions.

ureteroneocystostomy (u-re′ter-o-ne′o-sis-tos′to-mĭ) [ureteroneocystostomy + G. *neos*, new, + *kystis*, bladder, + *stoma*, mouth]. Ureterocystostomy; an operation whereby the upper end of a transected ureter is implanted into the bladder.

ureteroneopyelostomy (u-re′ter-o-ne′o-pi-ĕ-los′to-mĭ) [ureteroneopyelostomy + G. *neos*, new, + *pyelos*, pelvis, + *stoma*, mouth]. Ureteropyeloneostomy; surgical reimplantation of the ureter into the pelvis of the kidney.

ureteronephrectomy (u-re′ter-o-nĕ-frek′to-mĭ) [ureteronephrectomy + G. *nephros*, kidney, + *ektomē*, excision]. Removal of a kidney with its ureter.

ureteropathy (u-re-ter-op′ă-thĭ) [ureteropathy + G. *pathos*, suffering]. Any disease of the ureter.

ureteroplasty (u-re′ter-o-plas-tĭ) [ureteroplasty + G. *plassō*, to form]. Reparative or plastic surgery of the ureters.

ureteropyelitis (u-re′ter-o-pi-ĕ-li′tis) [ureteropyelitis + G. *pyelos*, pelvis, + *-itis*, inflammation]. Ureteropyelonephritis; inflammation of the pelvis of a kidney and its ureter.

ure′teropy′elog′raphy. Pyelography.

ure′teropy′eloneos′tomy. Ureteroneopyelostomy.

ure′teropy′elonephri′tis. Ureteropyelitis.

ureteropyeloplasty (u-re′ter-o-pi′ĕ-lo-plas-tĭ) [ureteropyeloplasty + G. *pyelos*, pelvis, + *plassō*, to form]. Plastic surgery of the ureter and pelvis of the kidney.

ureteropyelostomy (u-re′ter-o-pi-ĕ-los′to-mĭ) [ureteropyelostomy + G. *pyelos*, pelvis, + *stōma*, mouth]. Formation of a junction of the ureter and renal pelvis.

ureteropyosis (u-re′ter-o-pi-o′sis) [ureteropyosis + G. *pyōsis*, suppuration]. Accumulation of pus in the ureter.

ureterorrhagia (u-re′ter-o-ra′jĭ-ah) [ureterorrhagia + G. *rhēgnymi*, to burst forth]. Hemorrhage from a ureter.

ureterorrhaphy (u-re-ter-or′ă-fĭ) [ureterorrhaphy + G. *raphē*, suture]. Suture of a ureter.

ureterosigmoidostomy (u-re′ter-o-sig-moyd-os′to-mĭ). Implantation of the ureters into the sigmoid colon.

ureterostomy (u-re-ter-os′to-mĭ) [ureterostomy + G. *stoma*, mouth]. Surgical establishment of an external opening into the ureter.

ureterotomy (u-re-ter-ot′o-mĭ) [ureterotomy + G. *tomē*, incision]. Surgical incision into a ureter.

ure′teroure′teros′tomy. Establishment of an anastomosis between the two ureters or between two segments of the same ureter.

ureterovesicostomy (u-re′ter-o-ves-ĭ-kos′to-mĭ) [ureterovesicostomy + L. *vesico*, bladder, + *stōma*, mouth]. Surgical joining of a ureter to the bladder.

urethr-. See urethro-.

urethra (u-re′thrah) [G. *ourēthra*]. Urogenital canal; a canal leading from the bladder, discharging the urine externally; in the male, it also conducts spermatic fluid.

ure′thral. Relating to the urethra.

urethralgia (u-re-thral′jĭ-ah) [urethr- + G. *algos*, pain]. Urethrodynia; pain in the urethra.

urethratresia (u-re-thră-tre′zĭ-ah) [urethr- + G. *a*-priv. + *trēsis*, a boring]. Imperforation or occlusion of the urethra.

urethrectomy (u-re-threk′to-mĭ) [urethr- + G. *ektomē*, excision]. Excision of a segment or the entire urethea.

urethremorrhagia (u-re'threm-o-ra'jĭ-ah) [urethr- + G. *haima*, blood, + *rhēgnymi*, to burst forth]. Urethrorrhagia; bleeding from the urethra.

urethremphraxis (u're-threm-frak'sis) [urethr- + G. *emphraxis*, a stoppage]. Urethrophraxis; obstruction of the flow of urine through the urethra.

urethrism, urethrismus (u're-thrizm, -thriz'mus). Urethrospasm; irritability or spasmodic stricture of the urethra.

urethritis (u-re-thri'tis) [ureth- + G. *-itis*, inflammation]. Inflammation of the urethra.

    nonspecific u., u. not resulting from gonococcal or other specific infectious agents.

    u. petrif'icans, u. in which there is a deposit of calcareous matter in the wall of the urethra.

    specific u., gonorrhea.

urethro-, urethr-. Combining forms denoting urethra.

ure'throbul'bar. Bulbourethral.

urethrocele (u-re'thro-sēl) [urethro- + G. *kēlē*, tumor, hernia]. A prolapse of the female urethra.

urethrocystitis (u-re'thro-sis-ti'tis) [urethro- + G. *kystis*, bladder, + *-itis*, inflammation]. Inflammation of the urethra and bladder.

urethrocystometry (u-re'thro-sis-tom'ĕ-trĭ) [urethro- + G. *kystis*, bladder, + *metron*, measure]. A procedure that simultaneously measures pressures in urinary bladder and urethra.

urethrodynia (u-re-thro-din'ĭ-ah) [urethro- + G. *odynē*, pain]. Urethralgia.

urethropexy (u-re'thro-pek-sĭ) [urethro- + G. *pēxis*, fixation]. Surgical suspension of the urethra from the posterior surface of the pubic symphysis, to correct urinary stress incontinence.

urethrophraxis (u-re-thro-frak'sis). Urethremphraxis.

urethrophyma (u-re-thro-fi'mah) [urethro- + G. *phyma*, a tumor]. Any tumor or circumscribed swelling of the urethra.

urethroplasty (u-re'thro-plas-tĭ) [urethro- + G. *plassō*, to form]. Reparative or plastic surgery of the urethra.

urethrorrhagia (u-re-thro-ra'jĭ-ah). Urethremorrhagia.

urethrorrhaphy (u-re-thror'ă-fĭ) [urethro- + G. *rhaphē*, suture]. Suture of the urethra.

urethrorrhea (u-re-thro-re'ah) [urethro- + G. *rhoia*, a flow]. An abnormal discharge from the urethra.

urethroscope (u-re'thro-skōp) [urethro- + G. *skopeō*, to view]. An instrument for viewing the interior of the urethra.

urethroscop'ic. Relating to the urethroscope or to urethroscopy.

urethroscopy (u-re-thros'ko-pĭ). Inspection of the urethra with a urethroscope.

urethrospasm (u-re'thro-spazm). Urethrism.

urethrostaxis (u-re-thro-stak'sis) [urethro- + G. *staxis*, trickling]. Oozing of blood from the mucous membrane of the urethra.

urethrostenosis (u-re'thro-stĕ-no'sis) [urethro- + G. *stenōsis*, a narrowing]. Stricture of the urethra.

urethrostomy (u-re-thros'to-mĭ) [urethro- + G. *stoma*, mouth]. Surgical formation of a permanent opening between the urethra and the skin.

urethrotomy (u-re-throt'o-mĭ) [urethro- + G. *tomē*, incision]. Surgical incision of a stricture of the urethra.

urethrovesicopexy (u-re'thro-ves'ĭ-ko-pek-sĭ) [urethro- + L. *vesica*, bladder, + G. *pexis*, fixation]. Surgical suspension of the urethra and the base of the bladder to correct stress incontinence.

-uretic [G. *ourētikos*, relating to the urine]. Combining form denoting urine.

urhidrosis (u-rĭ-dro'sis). Uridrosis.

uri-, uric-, urico- [G. *ouron*, urine]. Combining forms relating to uric acid.

uric (u'rik). Relating to urine.

u'ric acid. 2,6,8-Trioxypurine; white crystals, poorly soluble, contained in solution in urine; with sodium and other bases it forms urates.

u'ricase. *Urate* oxidase.

urico-. See uri-.

uricolysis (u-rĭ-kol'ĭ-sis) [urico- + G. *lysis*, a loosening]. Decomposition of uric acid.

uricolyt'ic. Relating to or effecting the hydrolysis of uric acid.

uricosuria (u'rĭ-ko-su'rĭ-ah) [urico- + G. *ouron*, urine]. Excessive amounts of uric acid in the urine.

uridine (URD) (u'rĭ-dēn). Uracil ribonucleoside; one of the major nucleosides in RNA; as the pyrophosphate (UDP), it is active in sugar metabolism.

    u. diphosphate (UDP), uridine 5'-diphosphate or -pyrophosphate.

    u. phosphate (UMP), uridylic acid.

    u. triphosphate (UTP), u. esterfied with triphosphoric acid at its 5' position; the immediate precursor of uridylic acid residues in RNA.

uridrosis (u-rĭ-dro'sis) [uri- + G. *hidrōs*, sweat]. Urhidrosis; excretion of urea or uric acid in the sweat.

uridyl'ic acid. Uridine phosphate; uridine esterified by phosphoric acid on one or more sugar hydroxyl groups.

uriesthesis (u-rĭ-es-the'sis). Uresiesthesis.

urin-, urino-. Combining forms denoting urine. See also ure-, uro-.

u'rinal. A vessel into which urine is passed.

urinalysis (u-rĭ-nal'ĭ-sis). Analysis of the urine.

urinary (u'rĭ-nĕr-ĭ). Relating to urine.

urinate (u'rĭ-nāt). Micturate; to pass urine.

urination (u-rĭ-na'shun). Emiction; miction; micturition (1); uresis; the passing of urine.

urine (u'rin) [L. *urina*; G. *ouron*]. The fluid and dissolved substances excreted by the kidney.

    residual u., u. remaining in the bladder at the end of micturition in cases of prostatic obstruction, bladder atony, etc.

urino-. See urin-.

urinogenous (u-rĭ-noj'ĕ-nus). Urogenous. **1.** Producing or excreting urine. **2.** Of urinary origin.

urinoma (u-rĭ-no'mah). A cyst containing urine.

urinom′etry. Determination of the specific gravity of urine.

urinos′copy. Uroscopy.

uro- [G. *ouron*, urine]. Combining form relating to urine. See also ure- and urin-.

urobilin (u′ro-bi′lin, -bil′in). A uroporphyrin, one of the natural breakdown products of hemoglobin; a urinary pigment that gives a varying orange-red coloration to urine according to its degree of oxidation.

urobilinemia (u′ro-bi-li-ne′mi-ah). Presence of urobilins in the blood.

urobilinogen (u′ro-bi-lin′o-jen). Precursor of urobilin.

urobilinuria (u′ro-bi-li-nu′ri-ah). Presence in the urine of excess urobilins.

urocele (u′ro-sēl) [uro- + G. *kēlē*, hernia]. Uroscheocele; extravasation of urine into the scrotal sac.

urochesia (u-ro-ke′zi-ah) [uro- + G. *chezō*, to defecate]. Passage of urine from the anus.

urochrome (u′ro-krōm). The principal pigment of urine, a compound of urobilin and a peptide.

urocystitis (u′ro-sis-ti′tis) [uro- + G. *kystis*, bladder, + *-itis*, inflammation]. Inflammation of the urinary bladder. See also cystitis.

urodynia (u-ro-din′i-ah) [uro- + G. *odynē*, pain]. Pain on urination.

uroedema (u′ro-ĕ-de′mah) [uro- + G. *oidēma*, swelling]. Uredema.

u′rofla′vin. A fluorescent product of riboflavin catabolism, found in urine and feces.

urogas′trone. A fluorescent pigment extracted from urine; an inhibitor of gastric secretion and motility.

urogenital (u-ro-jen′ĭ-tal). Genitourinary.

urogenous (u-roj′ĕ-nus). Urinogenous.

u′rogram. The image obtained by urography.

urography (u-rog′rā-fi) [uro- + G. *graphō*, to write]. Radiography of any part of the urinary tract.

    antegrade u., x-ray examination of the urinary tract utilizing precutaneous injection of a contrast agent into the renal calices or pelvis or into the urinary bladder.

    cystoscopic u., retrograde u.

    excretory u., intravenous u., x-ray examination of the kidneys, ureters, and/or bladder utilizing a contrast agent injected into a vein.

    retrograde u., cystoscopic u.; x-ray examination of the urinary tract utilizing a contrast agent injected directly into the bladder.

uroki′nase. A proteinase found in urine, with the same action (cleaving plasminogen to plasmin) as streptokinase or staphylokinase.

u′rolith [uro- + G. *lithos*, stone]. A calculus in the kidney, ureter, bladder, or urethra.

urolithiasis (u′ro-li-thi′ă-sis). Presence of calculi in the urinary system.

urolith′ic. Relating to urinary calculi.

urologic, urological (u-ro-loj′ĭk, ĭ-kal). Relating to urology.

urol′ogist. A specialist in urology.

urology (u-rol′o-ji) [uro- + G. *logos*, study]. The medial specialty concerned with the study, diagnosis, and treatment of diseases of the urinary tract in females and the genitourinary tract in males.

uroncus (u-rong′kus) [uro- + G. *onkos*, mass (tumor)]. A urinary cyst; a circumscribed area of extravasation of urine.

uronephrosis (u′ro-nĕ-fro′sis). Hydronephrosis.

uropathy (u-rop′ă-thi) [uro- + G. *pathos*, suffering]. Any disorder involving the urinary tract.

urophanic (u-ro-fan′ik) [uro- + G. *phainō*, to appear]. Appearing in the urine.

uroplania (u-ro-pla′ni-ah) [uro- + G. *planē*, a wandering]. Extravasation of urine.

uropoiesis (u′ro-poy-e′sis) [uro- + G. *poiēsis*, a making]. Production or secretion and excretion of urine.

uropoietic (u′ro-poy-et′ik). Relating to or pertaining to uropoiesis.

u′ropor′phyrin. A porphyrin excreted in the urine; *e.g.*, urobilin.

uroscheocele (u-ros′ke-o-sēl) [uro- + G. *oscheon*, scrotum, + *kēlē*, tumor]. Urocele.

uroschesis (u-ros′ke-sis) [uro- + G. *schesis*, a checking]. **1.** Retention of urine. **2.** Suppression of urine.

uroscop′ic. Relating to uroscopy.

uroscopy (u-ros′ko-pi) [uro- + G. *skopeō*, to view]. Urinoscopy; examination of the urine, usually with a microscope.

urosepsis (u-ro-sep′sis) [uro- + G. *sēpsis*, decomposition]. Sepsis resulting from the decomposition of extravasated urine.

urosep′tic. Relating to urosepsis.

urothorax (u-ro-tho′raks). Presence of urine in the thoracic cavity, usually following complex multiple organ trauma.

uroureter (u′ro-u-re′ter). Hydroureter.

urticant (ur′tĭ-kant) [L. *urtica*, nettle]. Producing a wheal or other similar itching lesion.

urticaria (ur-tĭ-kār′ĭ-ah) [L. *urtica*, nettle]. Hives; urtication (2); an eruption of itching wheals, usually of systemic origin; may be due to a state of hypersensitivity to foods or drugs, foci of infection, physical agents, or psychic stimuli.

    bullous u., u. bullo′sa, an eruption of wheals capped with subepidermal vesicles.

    cholinergic u., a form of physical or non-allergic u. initiated by heat or by excitement, consisting of pruritic areas 1 to 2 mm in diameter surrounded by bright red macules.

    u. endem′ica, u. caused by the nettling hairs of certain caterpillars.

    giant u., u. gi′gans, angioneurotic *edema*.

    u. medicamento′sa, an urticarial form of drug eruption.

    papular u., u. papulo′sa, *lichen* urticatus.

    u. pigmento′sa, mastocytosis resulting from congenital excess of mast cells in the superficial dermis; a chronic eruption characterized by brownish papules which urticate when stroked.

solar u., u. resulting from exposure to specific light spectra.

urtica'rial. Relating to or marked by urticaria.

urticate (ur'tĭ-kāt) [L. *urticatus*]. **1.** To perform urtication. **2.** Marked by the presence of wheals.

urtication (ur-tĭ-ka'shun). **1.** A burning sensation resembling that produced by urticaria or resulting from nettle poisoning. **2.** Urticaria.

USAN United States Adopted Names, a designation for nonproprietary names of drugs adopted by the USAN Council in cooperation with the manufacturers concerned.

USP *United States Pharmacopeia.* See Pharmacopeia.

USPHS United States Public Health Service.

uterine (u'ter-in, u'ter-īn). Relating to the uterus.

utero-, uter-. Combining forms relating to the uterus. See also hystero-; metra-; metro-.

uterocystostomy (u'ter-o-sis-tos'to-mĭ) [utero- + G. *kystis*, bladder, + *stoma*, mouth]. Surgical formation of a communication between the uterus (cervix) and the bladder.

u'terofixa'tion. Hysteropexy.

u'terolith [utero- + G. *lithos*, stone]. Hysterolith; a calcified myoma of the uterus.

uterom'eter. Hysterometer.

uteropexy (u'ter-o-pek-sĭ). Hysteropexy.

uteroplasty (u'ter-o-plas-tĭ) [utero- + G. *plassō*, to form]. Metroplasty; hysteroplasty; a plastic operation upon the uterus.

u'terosalpingog'raphy. Hysterosalpingography.

u'teroscope. Hysteroscope.

uteros'copy. Hysteroscopy.

uterot'omy. Hysterotomy.

uterotonic (u'ter-o-ton'ik) [utero- + G. *tonos*, tone, tension]. **1.** Giving tone to the uterine muscle. **2.** An agent that overcomes relaxation of the muscular wall of the uterus.

u'terotubog'raphy. Hysterosalpingography.

uterus, pl. **uteri** (u'ter-us, u'ter-i) [L.] [NA]. Womb; metra; the hollow muscular organ in which the impregnated ovum is developed into the fetus. It consists of a main portion (corpus) with an elongated lower part (cervix), at the extremity of which is the opening (os); the upper-rounded portion of the u., opposite the os, is the fundus, at each extremity of which is the cornu marking the part where the uterine tube joins the u.

bicornate u., u. bicor'nis, a u. that is divided into two lateral horns, as a result of imperfect fusion of the paramesonephric ducts; the cervix may be single or double.

Couvelaire u., extravasation of blood into the uterine musculature and beneath the uterine peritoneum in association with severe forms of abruptio placentae.

u. didel'phys [G. *di-*, two, + *delphys*, womb]. dimetria; double u. with double cervix and double vagina; due to failure of the paramesonephric ducts to unite.

gravid u., the condition of the u. in pregnancy.

septate u., u. sep'tus, a u. that is divided into two cavities by an anteroposterior septum.

unicorn u., u. unicor'nis, a one-horned u. with only one lateral half, the other being undeveloped or absent.

UTP Uridine triphosphate.

utricle (u'trĭ-kl). Utriculus.

prostatic u., *utriculus* prostaticus.

utricular (u-trik'u-lar). Relating to or resembling a utricle.

utriculi (u-trik'u-li). Plural of utriculus.

utriculitis (u'trik-u-li'tis) [utriculus + G. *-itis*, inflammation]. **1.** Inflammation of the internal ear. **2.** Inflammation of the utriculus prostaticus.

utriculosaccular (u-trik'u-lo-sak'u-lar). Relating to the utricle and the saccule of the labyrinth.

utriculus, pl. **utriculi** (u'trik'u-lus, -li) [L. dim. of *uter*, leather bag] [NA]. Utricle; the larger of the two membranous sacs in the vestibule of the labyrinth from which arise the semicircular ducts.

u. prostat'icus [NA], prostatic utricle; sinus pocularis; a minute pouch in the prostate opening on the summit of the seminal colliculus, the analogue of the uterus and vagina, being the remains of the fused caudal ends of the paramesonephric ducts.

uvea (u've-ah) [L. *uva*, grape]. The vascular, pigmentary, or middle coat of the eye comprising the choroid, ciliary body, and iris.

uveal (u've-al). Relating to the uvea.

uveitic (u-ve-i'tik). Relating to or marked by uveitis.

uveitis (u-ve-i'tis) [uvea + G. *-itis*, inflammation]. Inflammation of the uvea.

heterochromic u., pigmentary changes in the iris, with inflammation of the anterior uvea complicated by deposits on Descemet's membrane and by opacities in the vitreous.

sympathetic u., a bilateral inflammation of the uveal tract due to a perforating wound of one eye in which damage to the uveal tract has occurred.

uveoparotitis (u've-o-păr-o-ti'tis). Uveitis associated with parotitis.

uveoscleritis (u've-o-skle-ri'tis). Inflammation of the sclera involved by extension from the uvea.

u'viform [L. uva, grape, + *forma*, form]. Botryoid.

uvul-, uvulo-. Combining forms denoting the uvula, usually the uvula palatina. See also staphylo-.

uvula, pl. **uvuli** (u'vu-lah, -li) [dim. of L. *uva*, a grape] [NA]. A pendant fleshy mass, especially the u. palatina.

u. cerebel'li, u. vermis.

u. palati'na [NA], a conical projection hanging from the posterior edge of the middle of the soft palate.

u. ver'mis [NA], u. cerebelli; a triangular elevation on the vermis of the cerebellum, lying between the two tonsils anterior to the pyramis.

u. vesi'cae [NA], a slight projection into the cavity of the bladder just behind the urethral opening, marking the location of the middle lobe of the prostate.

uvular (u'vu-lar). Relating to the uvula.

uvulectomy (u-vu-lek'to-mī) [uvul- + G. *ektomē*, excision]. Staphylectomy; excision of the uvula.

uvulitis (u'vu-li'tis). Inflammation of the uvula.

uvuloptosis (u'vu-lop-to'sis) [uvulo- + G. *ptōsis*, a falling]. Staphyloptosis; staphylodialysis; relaxation or elongation of the uvula.

uvulotomy (u-vu-lot'o-mī) [uvulo- + G. *tomē*, a cutting]. Staphylotomy (1); incision of the uvula.

V

V Vision or visual acuity; volt; with subscript 1, 2, 3, etc., the unipolar chest electrocardiogram leads; vanadium; volume, frequently with subscripts denoting location, chemical species, and conditions.

V_{max} Maximum *velocity* in an enzymatic reaction and of shortening of a contractile element.

$\dot{V}$ Gas *flow*, frequently with subscripts indicating location and chemical species; ventilation.

$\dot{V}CO_2$ Carbon dioxide *elimination.*

$\dot{V}O_2$ Oxygen *consumption.*

v Volt; as a subscript, venous *blood.*

V-A Ventriculoatrial.

vaccina (vak-si'nah). Vaccinia.

vaccinal (vak'si-nal). Relating to vaccine or vaccination.

vaccinate (vak'si-nāt). To administer a vaccine.

vaccination (vak-si-na'shun). **1.** Inoculation with the virus of cowpox as a means of producing immunity against smallpox. **2.** The injection of a killed culture of a specific microbe as a means of prophylaxis or cure of the disease caused by that microorganism.

vaccine (vak'sēn, vak-sēn') [L. *vaccinus*, relating to a cow]. Originally, the live cowpox virus inoculated in the skin as prophylaxis against smallpox; now, extended to include any preparation intended for active immunological prophylaxis.

autogenous v., a v. made from a culture of the patient's own bacteria.

BCG v., bacillus Calmette-Guérin v.; tuberculosis v.; a suspension of an attenuated strain of *Mycobacterium tuberculosis*, bovine type, inoculated into the skin for tuberculosis prophylaxis.

diphtheria and tetanus toxoids and pertussis v., a v. available in three forms; diphtheria and tetanus toxoids plus pertussis vaccine (DTP), tetanus and diphtheria toxoids, adult type (Td), tetanus toxoid (T); used for active immunization against diphtheria, tetanus, and whooping cough.

heterogenous v., v. that is not autogenous, but is prepared from the same species of bacterium.

influenza virus v.'s, influenza virus grown in embryonate eggs and inactivated; because of the marked and progressive antigenic variation of the influenza viruses, strains included are regularly changed following various outbreaks of influenza in order to include most recently isolated epidemic strains of both type A and B influenza.

live v., prepared from living attenuated organisms.

measles virus v., v. containing live, further attenuated strains of measles virus prepared in chick embryo cell culture.

multivalent v., polyvalent v.

mumps v., mumps virus v., a live, attenuated virus v. prepared in chick embryo cell cultures.

pertussis v., see diphtheria and tetanus toxoids and pertussis v.

plague v., v. prepared from cultures of inactivated *Yersinia (Pasteurella) pestis;* injections are made intramuscularly, and booster inoculations are recommended while individuals remain in an area of risk; live, attenuated bacterial and chemical fraction v.'s are also available.

poliovirus or poliomyelitis v.'s, (1) inactivated poliovirus v. (IPV), an aqueous suspension of inactivated strains of poliomyelitis virus given by injection; largely replaced by the oral v.; **(2) oral poliovirus v. (OPV),** an aqueous suspension of live attenuated strains of poliomyelitis virus given orally for active immunization against poliomyelitis.

polyvalent v., multivalent v.; a v. prepared from cultures of two or more strains of the same species or microorganism.

rabies v., a v. introduced by Pasteur as a method of treatment for the bite of a rabid animal, utilizing daily injections of virus that increased serially from noninfective to fully infective "fixed" virus; largely replaced by rabies v. of duck embryo origin (DEV), prepared from embryonic duck eggs infected with inactivated "fixed" virus.

Rocky Mountain spotted fever v., suspension of inactivated *Rickettsia rickettsii* prepared by growing the rickettsiae in the embryonic yolk sac of fowl eggs.

rubella virus v., a live virus v. prepared from duck embryo or human diploid cell culture infected with rubella virus, and administered as a single subcutaneous injection.

Sabin v., an orally administered v. containing live attenuated strains of poliovirus.

Salk v., the original poliovirus v., composed of virus propagated in monkey kidney tissue culture and inactivated.

smallpox v., vaccinia virus suspensions prepared from cutaneous vaccinial lesions of calves and inoculated subcutaneously.

stock v., a v. made from a stock microbial strain, in contradistinction to an autogenous v.

T.A.B. v., typhoid-paratyphoid A and B v.

tetanus v., see diphtheria and tetanus toxoids and pertussis v.

tuberculosis v., BCG v.

typhoid v., a suspension of inactivated *Salmonella typhi;* the combined typhoid and paratyphoid A and B v.'s have been largely replaced by the monovalent typhoid v.

typhoid-paratyphoid A and B v., T.A.B. v.; a suspension of killed typhoid and paratyphoid A and B bacilli. See typhoid v.

typhus v., an inactivated suspension of *Rickettsia prowazekii* grown in embryonate eggs, effective against louse-borne (epidemic) typhus; booster doses are required as long as the possibility of exposure exists.

whopping-cough v., pertussis v.

yellow fever v., a live attenuated strain of yellow fever virus propagated in embryonate fowl eggs.

vaccinia (vak-sin′ĭ-ah) [L. *vaccinus,* relating to a cow]. Vaccina. **1.** A contagious eruptive disease occurring in cattle, involving chiefly the skin and teats, and caused by the vaccine (vaccinia) virus; lesions are similar to those of smallpox in man, but much milder. **2.** Primary reaction; an infection, primarily local and limited to the site of inoculation, induced in man by inoculation with the vaccinia virus in order to confer resistance to smallpox.

generalized v., secondary lesions of the skin following vaccination which may occur in persons with previously healthy skin but more common in the case of traumatized skin.

progressive v., a severe or even fatal form of v. occurring chiefly in persons with an immunologic deficiency or dyscrasia, characterized by progressive enlargement of the initial and also of secondary lesions.

vaccinial (vak-sin′ĭ-al). Relating to vaccinia.

vacciniform (vak-sin′ĭ-form). Resembling vaccinia.

vaccinization (vak′sĭ-nĭ-za′shun). Vaccination repeated at short intervals until it will no longer take.

vacuolar (vak′u-o-lar). Relating to or resembling a vacuole.

vac′uolate, vac′uolated. Having vacuoles.

vacuolation (vak′u-o-la′shun). Vacuolization. **1.** Formation of vacuoles. **2.** The condition of having vacuoles.

vacuole (vak′u-ōl) [fr. L. *vacuum,* an empty space]. **1.** A minute space in any tissue. **2.** A clear space in the substance of a cell, sometimes degenerative in character, sometimes surrounding an englobed foreign body and serving to digest the body.

vac′uoliza′tion. Vacuolation.

vacuum (vak′u-um) [L. *vacuus,* empty]. An empty space, one practically exhausted of air or gas.

va′gal. Relating to the vagus nerve.

vagi (va′gi, -ji). Plural of vagus.

vagin-. See vagino-.

vagina, pl. **vaginae** (vă-ji′nah, -ne) [L. sheath, the vagina] [NA]. **1.** Sheath (2); any sheathlike structure. **2.** The genital canal in the female, extending from the uterus to the vulva.

v. bul′bi [NA], sheath of the eyeball; Tenon's capsule; a condensation of connective tissue on the outer aspect of the sclera from which it is separated by a narrow cleftlike space.

v. carot′ica [NA], carotid sheath; the dense fibrous investment of the carotid artery, internal jugular vein, and vagus nerve on each side.

vaginal (vaj′ĭ-nal) [Mod. L. *vaginalis*]. Relating to the vagina or to any sheath.

vaginalitis (vaj′ĭ-nă-li′tis). Inflammation of the tunica vaginalis testis.

vaginate (vaj′ĭ-nāt). **1.** To ensheathe; to enclose in a sheath. **2.** Ensheathed; provided with a sheath.

vaginectomy (vaj-ĭ-nek′to-mĭ) [vagina + G. *ektomē,* excision]. Colpectomy; excision of the vagina, or a segment thereof.

vaginismus (vaj-ĭ-niz′mus) [vagina + L. *-ismus,* action, condition]. Painful involuntary spasm of the vagina preventing intercourse.

vaginitis, pl. **vaginitides** (vaj-ĭ-ni′tis, -ni′tĭ-dēz) [vagina + G. *-itis,* inflammation]. Colpitis; inflammation of the vagina.

v. adhesi′va, inflammation of vaginal mucosa with adhesion of the vagina walls to each other.

atrophic v., thinning and atrophy of the vaginal epithelium usually resulting from diminished endocrine stimulation.

desquamative inflammatory v., an acute inflammation of vagina of unknown cause, characterized by grayish psuedomembrane, free discharge containing pus and immature epithelial cells, and easy bleeding on trauma.

v. emphysemato′sa, v. characterized by accumulation of gas in small connective tissue spaces lined by foreign-body giant cells.

v. seni′lis, atrophic v. occurring in old age, often assuming the form of v. adhesiva.

vagino-, vagin-. Combining forms denoting the vagina. See also colpo-.

vaginocele (vaj′ĭ-no-sēl). Colpocele (1).

vaginodynia (vaj′ĭ-no-din′ĭ-ah). Colpodynia; colpalgia; vaginal pain.

vaginofixation (vaj′ĭ-no-fik-sa′shun). Colpopexy; vaginopexy; suture of a relaxed and prolapsed vagina to the abdominal wall.

vaginomycosis (vaj′ĭ-no-mi-ko′sis). Inflammation (infection) of the vagina due to a fungus.

vaginopathy (vaj-ĭ-nop′ă-thĭ) [vagino- + G. *pathos,* suffering]. Any diseased condition of the vagina.

vaginoperineoplasty (vaj′ĭ-no-pĕr′ĭ-ne′o-plastĭ) [vagino- + perineum, + G. *plassō,* to form]. Colpoperineoplasty; plastic surgery for repair of an injury of the perineum involving the vagina.

vaginoperineorrhaphy (vaj′ĭ-no-pĕr′ĭ-ne-or′ă-fĭ) [vagino- + perineum, + G. *raphē,* suture]. Colpoperineorrhaphy; surgical repair of a lacerated vagina and perineum.

vaginoperineotomy (vaj′ĭ-no-pĕr′ĭ-ne-ot′o-mĭ) [vagino- + perineum, + G. *tome,* incision]. Division of the outlet of the vagina and adjacent portion of the perineum to facilitate childbirth.

vaginopexy (vaj′ĭ-no-pek-sĭ). Vaginofixation.

vaginoplasty (vaj′ĭ-no-plas-tĭ). Colpoplasty; plastic surgery involving the vagina.

vaginoscopy (vaj-ĭ-nos'ko-pĭ). Inspection of the vagina, usually with an instrument.

vaginotomy (vaj-ĭ-not'o-mĭ). Colpotomy; a cutting operation in the vagina.

vago-. Combining form denoting the vagus nerve.

vagolysis (va-gol'ĭsis) [vago- + G. *lysis,* a loosening]. Surgical destruction of the vagus nerve.

va'golyt'ic. 1. Pertaining to or causing vagolysis. **2.** An agent that has inhibitory effects on the vagus nerve.

vagomimetic (va'go-mĭ-met'ik). Mimicking the action of the efferent fibers of the vagus nerve.

vagotomy (va-got'o-mĭ) [vago- + G. *tomē,* incision]. Surgical division of the vagus nerve.

vagotonia (va-go-to'nĭ-ah) [vago- + G. *tonos,* strain]. Sympathetic imbalance; irritability of the vagus nerve, often marked by excessive peristalsis and loss of the pharyngeal reflex.

vagotonic (va-go-ton'ik). Relating to or marked by vagotonia.

vagotropic (va-go-trop'ik) [vago- + G. *tropos,* turning]. Acting upon the vagus nerve.

vagovagal (va'go-va'gal). Pertaining to a process that utilizes both afferent and efferent vagal fibers.

vagus, pl. **vagi** (va'gus; va'gi, -ji) [L. wandering, because of its wide distribution]. *Nervus* vagus.

Val Valine and its radicals.

va'lence, va'lency [L. *valentia,* strength]. The combining power of one atom of an element (or a radical), that of the hydrogen atom being the unit of comparison, determined by the number of electrons in the outer shell of the atom.

val'gus [Mod. L. turned outward, fr. L. bowlegged]. Bent or twisted outward; modern accepted usage, particularly in orthopedics, erroneously transposes the meaning of varus (*q.v.*) to v., as in *genu* valgum (knock-knee).

val'ine (Val). 2-Aminoisovaleric acid; $(CH_3)_2$-$CHCH(NH_2)COOH$; a constituent of most proteins.

val'late [L. *vallo,* pp. *-atus,* to surround with]. Cupped; surrounded with an elevation.

vallecula, pl. **valleculae** (vă-lek'u-lah, -le) [L. dim. of *vallis,* valley] [NA]. A crevice or depression on any surface; *e.g.,* v. cerebelli, a deep hollow on the inferior surface of the cerebellum, between the hemispheres, in which the medulla oblongata rests.

value (val'u). A particular quantitative determination. See also index; number.

    buffer v., the power of a substance in solution to absorb acid or alkali without change in pH.

    normal v.'s, a set of laboratory test v.'s used to characterize apparently healthy individuals; now replaced by reference v.'s.

    predictive v., the likelihood that a positive test result indicates disease (diagnostic sensitivity), or that a negative test result excludes disease (diagnostic specificity).

    reference v.'s, a set of laboratory test v.'s obtained from an individual or group in a defined state of health; replaces normal v.'s, since it is based on a defined state of health rather than on apparent health.

    threshold limit v. (TLV), maximum concentration of a chemical allowable for repeated exposure without adverse health effects.

valva, pl. **valvae** (val'vah, -ve) [L. one leaf of a double door] [NA]. Valve.

val'val, val'var. Relating to a valve.

val'vate. Valvular; relating to or provided with a valve.

valve [L. *valva*]. Valva. **1.** A fold of the lining membrane of a canal or other hollow organ serving to retard or prevent a reflux of fluid. **2.** Any reduplication of tissue or flaplike structure resembling a v.

    aortic v., the v. between the left ventricle and the ascending aorta, consisting of three semilunar cusps.

    atrioventricular v.'s, (1) right, tricuspid v.; the v. closing the orifice between the right atrium and the right ventricle of the heart; **(2) left,** bicuspid or mitral v.; the v. closing the orifice between the left atrium and the left ventricle of the heart.

    ball v., any of a variety of prosthetic cardiac v.'s comprised of a ball within a retaining cage affixed to the orifice.

    bicuspid v., left atrioventricular v.

    congenital v., an abnormal lining fold obstructing a passage.

    coronary v., a fold of endocardium at the opening of the coronary sinus into the right atrium.

    Heyer-Pudenz v., a v. used in the shunting procedure for hydrocephaly; a ventricular catheter leads the cerebrospinal fluid into a one-way pump through which the cerebrospinal fluid passes down the distal catheter into the right atrium of the heart.

    ileocecal v., ileocolic v., in cadavers, the bilabial prominence of the terminal ileum into the large intestine at the cecocolic junction; in the living, appears as a truncated cone with a star-shaped orifice.

    mitral v., left atrioventricular v.

    parachute mitral v., congenital deformity of the mitral v. in which there is only one papillary muscle present; the chordae of both v. leaflets converge to insert into this single muscle.

    pulmonary v., a v. with semilunar cusps at the entrance to the pulmonary trunk from the right ventricle.

    pyloric v., a fold of mucous membrane at the gastroduodenal junction enclosing the pylorus.

    semilunar v., one of three semilunar segments serving as the cusps of a v. preventing regurgitation at the beginning of the aorta; a similar v. is the pulmonary v.

    tricuspid v., right atrioventricular v.

    urethral v.'s, folds in the urethral mucous membrane.

vesicoureteral v., a lock mechanism in the wall of the intravesical portion of the ureter that normally prevents urinary reflux.

valvoplasty (val'vo-plas-tĭ) [valve + G. *plassō*, to form]. Valvuloplasty; surgical reconstruction of a deformed cardiac valve.

valvotomy (val-vot'o-mĭ) [valve + G. *tomē*, incision]. **1.** Valvulotomy; cutting through a stenosed cardiac valve to relieve obstruction. **2.** Incision of a valvular structure.

valvula, pl. **valvulae** (val'vu-lah, -le) [L. dim of *valva*] [NA]. Valvule; a valve, especially one of small size.

val'vular. Valvate.

valvule (val'vūl). Valvula.

valvulitis (val-vu-li'tis) [L. *valvula*, valve, + G. *-itis*, inflammation]. Inflammation of a valve, especially a heart valve.

val'vuloplasty. Valvoplasty.

valvulot'omy. Valvotomy (1).

vanadium (vă-na'dĭ-um) [*Vanadis*, Scand. myth. char.]. A metallic element, symbol V, atomic no. 23, atomic weight 50.95.

vanil'lism. 1. Symptoms of irritation of the skin, nasal mucous membrane, and conjunctiva from which workers with vanilla sometimes suffer. **2.** Infestation of the skin by sarcoptiform mites found in vanilla pods.

vanillylmandelic acid (VMA) (van'ĭ-lil-man-del'ik, vă-nil'il-). 4-Hydroxy-3-methoxymandelic acid; the major urinary metabolite of adrenal and sympathetic catecholamines.

va'por [L. steam]. **1.** The molecules in the gaseous phase of a solid or liquid substance exposed to a gas. **2.** A visible emanation of fine particles of a liquid. **3.** A medicinal preparation to be administered by inhalation.

va'poriza'tion. 1. The change of a solid or liquid to a state of vapor. **2.** Therapeutic application of a vapor.

va'porize. To convert a solid or liquid into a vapor.

va'porizer. An apparatus for reducing medicated liquids to a state of vapor fit for inhalation or application to accessible mucous membranes.

variable [L. *vario*, to vary, change, differ]. **1.** That which is inconstant, which can or does change. **2.** Deviating from the type in structure, form, physiology, or behavior.

var'iance. The state of being variable, different, divergent, or deviate.

var'iant. 1. That which, or one who, is variable. **2.** Having the tendency to alter or change, exhibit variety or diversity, not conform, or differ from the type.

variation (văr-ĭ-a'shun) [L. *variatio*, fr. *vario*, to change, vary]. Deviation from the type, especially the parent type, in structure, form, physiology, or behavior.

varication (văr-ĭ-ka'shun). Formation or presence of varices.

variceal (văr-ĭ-se'al, vă-ris'e-al). Of or pertaining to a varix.

varicella (văr-ĭ-sel'ah) [L. dim. of *variola*]. Chickenpox; an acute contagious disease, occurring usually in children, caused by the varicella-zoster virus and marked by a sparse eruption of papules, becoming vesicles and then pustules, like that of smallpox although less severe.

varicel'liform. Resembling varicella.

varices (văr'ĭ-sēz). Plural of varix.

variciform (văr'ĭ-sĭ-form, vă-ris'ĭ-form). Cincoid; resembling a varix.

varico-. Combining form denoting a varix or varicosity.

varicoblepharon (văr'ĭ-ko-blef'ă-ron) [varico- + G. *blepharon*, eyelid]. A varicosity of the eyelid.

varicocele (văr'ĭ-ko-sēl) [varico- + G. *kēlē*, tumor, hernia]. Abnormal dilation of the veins of the spermatic cord, caused by incompetency of valves in the internal spermatic vein and resulting in downward reflux of blood into the spermatic cord veins when the patient assumes the upright position.

varicocelectomy (văr'ĭ-ko-se-lek'to-mĭ) [varicocele + G. *ektomē*, excision]. Ligature and excision and ligation of the dilated veins of a varicocele.

varicography (văr-ĭ-kog'ră-fĭ) [varico- + G. *graphō*, to write]. Radiography of varicose veins after injection of a radiopaque medium.

varicomphalus (văr-ĭ-kom'fă-lus) [varico- + G. *omphalos*, navel]. A swelling formed by varicose veins at the umbilicus.

varicophlebitis (văr'ĭ-ko-flē-bi'tis) [varico- + G. *phleps*, vein, + *-itis*, inflammation]. Inflammation of varicose veins.

varicose (văr'ĭ-kōs). Relating to, affected with, or characterized by varices or varicosis.

varicosis, pl. **varicoses** (văr-ĭ-ko'sis, -sēz) [varico- + G. *-osis*, condition]. A dilated or varicose state of a vein.

varicosity (văr-ĭ-kos'ĭ-tĭ). A varix or varicose condition.

varicotomy (văr-ĭ-kot'o-mĭ) [varico- + G. *tomē*, a cutting]. An operation for varicose veins by subcutaneous incision.

varicula (vă-rik'u-lah) [L. dim. of *varix*]. Conjunctival varix; a varicose condition of the veins of the conjunctiva.

varicule (văr'ĭ-kūl) [L. *varicula*, dim. of *varix*]. A small varicose vein ordinarily seen in the skin; it may be associated with venous stars, venous lakes, or larger varicose veins.

variola (vă-ri'o-lah) [dim. of L. *varius*, spotted]. Smallpox.

variolar (vă-ri'o-lar). Variolous; relating to smallpox.

variolate (văr'ĭ-o-lāt). Pitted or scarred, as if with smallpox.

varioliform (vă-ri'o-lĭ-form, văr-ĭ-o'-). Varioloid (1).

varioloid (văr'ĭ-o-loyd) [variola + G. *eidos*, resemblance]. **1.** Varioliform; resembling smallpox. **2.** A mild form of smallpox occurring in persons who are relatively resistant, usually as a result of a previous vaccination.

variolous (vă-ri'o-lus). Variolar.

varix, pl. **varices** (văr'iks, văr'ĭ-sēz) [L. dilated vein]. **1.** A dilated vein. **2.** An enlarged and tortuous vein, artery, or lymphatic vessel.

   aneurysmal v., dilation and tortuosity of a vein resulting from an acquired communication with an adjacent artery.

   conjunctival v., varicula.

   esophageal varices, longitudinal superficial venous varices at the lower end of the esophagus as a result of portal hypertension; liable to ulceration and massive bleeding.

   lymph v., formation of varices or cysts in the lymph nodes in consequence of obstruction in the efferent lymphatics.

va'rus [Mod. L. bent inward, fr. L. knock-kneed]. Bent or twisted inward; modern accepted usage, particularly in orthopedics, erroneously transposes the meaning of valgus (*q.v.*) to v., as in *genu* varum (bowleg).

vas-. See vaso-.

vas, pl. **va'sa** [L. vessel, dish] [NA]. A vessel; a duct or canal conveying a liquid.

   v. aber'rans, *ductulus* aberrans.

   v. af'ferens, pl. **va'sa affferen'tia** [NA], afferent vessel; (1) any artery conveying blood to a part; (2) the arteriole that enters a renal glomerulus; (3) a lymphatic vessel entering a lymph node.

   va'sa bre'via, *arteriae* gastricae breves.

   v. def'erens, pl. **va'sa deferen'tia,** *ductus* deferens.

   v. ef'ferens, pl. **va'sa efferen'tia** [NA], efferent vessel; (1) a vein carrying blood away from a part; (2) the arteriole that carries blood out of a renal glomerulus; (3) a lymphatic vessel leaving a lymph node.

   va'sa lymphat'ica [NA], absorbent, lymphatic, or lymph vessels; the freely anastomosing vessels that convey lymph.

   va'sa pre'via, umbilical vessels presenting in advance of the fetal head, usually traversing the membranes and crossing the internal cervical os.

   va'sa rec'ta, (1) *arteriolae* rectae; (2) *tubuli* seminiferi recti.

   va'sa vaso'rum [NA], vessels of vessels; small arteries distributed to the outer and middle coats of the larger blood vessels, and their corresponding veins.

vasa (va'sah). Plural of vas.

va'sal. Relating to a vas or to vasa.

vascular (vas'ku-lar) [L. *vasculum,* a small vessel]. Relating to or containing blood vessels.

vascular'ity. The condition of being vascular.

vascularization (vas'ku-lar-ĭ-za'shun). Formation of new blood vessels in a part.

vas'cularized. Rendered vascular by the formation of new vessels.

vasculature (vas'ku-lă-chur). The vascular network of an organ.

vasculitis (vas-ku-li'tis). Angiitis.

vasculo- [L. *vasculum,* a small vessel]. Combining forms denoting a blood vessel. See also vas-; vaso-.

vasectomy (vă-sek'to-mĭ) [vas- + G. *ektomē,* excision]. Deferentectomy; gonangiectomy; excision of a segment of the vas deferens, performed in association with prostatectomy, or to produce sterility.

vasifac'tion. Angiopoiesis.

vasifac'tive. Angiopoietic.

vas'iform. Having the shape of a vas or tubular structure.

vasi'tis. Deferentitis.

vaso-, vas-. Combining forms denoting a vas or blood vessel. See also vasculo-.

vasoac'tive. Influencing the tone and caliber of blood vessels.

vas'oconstric'tion. Narrowing of the blood vessels.

vas'oconstric'tive. Causing narrowing of the blood vessels.

vas'oconstric'tor. 1. An agent that causes narrowing of the blood vessels. **2.** A nerve, stimulation of which causes vascular constriction.

vas'odepress'or. An agent that lowers blood pressure through reduction in peripheral resistance.

vas'odila'tion. Phlebarteriectasia; dilation of the blood vessels.

vas'odila'tive. Causing dilation of the blood vessels.

vas'odila'tor. 1. An agent that causes dilation of the blood vessels. **2.** A nerve, stimulation of which results in dilation of the blood vessels.

vasoepididymostomy (vas'o-ep-ĭ-did-ĭ-mos'to-mĭ). Surgical anastomosis of the vasa deferentia to the epididymis.

vas'oforma'tion. Angiopoiesis.

vasofor'mative. Angiopoietic.

vasoganglion (vas-o-gang'glĭ-on). A mass of blood vessels.

vasography (vă-sog'ră-fĭ). **1.** Radiography of blood vessels. **2.** Radiographic study of the vas deferens, utilizing a contrast agent injected into the lumen, to determine its patency.

vas'ohyperton'ic [vaso- + G. *hyper,* over, + *tonos,* tone]. Relating to increased arteriolar tension or vasoconstriction.

vas'ohypoton'ic [vaso- + G. *hypo,* under, + *tonos,* tone]. Relating to reduced arteriolar tension or vasodilation.

vas'oinhib'itory. Restraining vasomotor action.

vasoinhibitor (vas'o-in-hib'ĭ-tor). An agent that restricts or prevents the functioning of the vasomotor nerves.

vas'oliga'tion. Ligation of the vas deferens.

vasomo'tion. Angiokinesis; change in caliber of a blood vessel.

vasomo'tor. Angiokinetic. Causing dilation or constriction of the blood vessels.

vasoneuropathy (vas'o-nu-rop'ă-thĭ) [vaso- + G. *neuron,* nerve, + *pathos,* suffering]. Any disease involving both nerves and blood vessels.

vaso-orchidostomy (vas'o-or-kĭ-dos'to-mĭ) [vaso- + G. *orchis*, testis, + *stoma*, mouth]. Reestablishment of the interrupted seminiferous channels by uniting the tubules of the epididymis or of the rete testis to the divided end of the vas deferens.

vas'oparal'ysis. Angioparalysis; paralysis, atonia, or hypotonia of blood vessels.

vasoparesis (vas'o-pă-re'sis) [vaso- + G. *paresis*, weakness]. Angioparesis; vasomotor paralysis; a mild degree of vasoparalysis.

vasopressin (VP) (va-zo-pres'in, vas-o-). Antidiuretic hormone; a nonapeptide hormone, related to oxytocin, synthetically prepared or obtained from the neurohypophysis of healthy food animals; acts as a vasopressor and stimulates intestinal motility.

vasopres'sor. Producing vasoconstriction and a rise in blood pressure.

vasopunc'ture. Puncturing a vessel with a needle.

vasore'flex. A reflex that influences the caliber of blood vessels.

vasorelaxation (vas'o-re-lak-sa'shun). Reduction in tension of the walls of the blood vessels.

vasosec'tion. Vasotomy.

vasosen'sory. 1. Relating to sensation in the blood vessels. **2.** Denoting sensory nerve fibers innervating blood vessels.

vas'ospasm. Angiospasm; contraction or hypertonia of the muscular coats of the blood vessels.

vasospas'tic. Angiospastic; relating to or characterized by vasospasm.

vasostim'ulant. 1. Exciting vasomotor action. **2.** An agent that excites the vasomotor nerves to action. **3.** Vasotonic (2).

vasostomy (vă-sos'to-mĭ) [vaso- + G. *stoma*, mouth]. Establishment of an artificial opening into the deferent duct.

vasotomy (vă-sot'o-mĭ) [vaso- + G. *tomē*, incision]. Vasosection; incision into or division of the vas deferens.

vasotonia (vas-o-to'nĭ-ah) [vaso- + G. *tonos*, tone]. Angiotonia; the tone of blood vessels, particularly the arterioles.

vasoton'ic. 1. Angiotonic; relating to vascular tone. **2.** Vasostimulant (3); an agent that increases vascular tension.

vasotripsy (vas'o-trip-sĭ). Angiotripsy.

vasotrophic (vas-o-trof'ik) [vaso- + G. *trophē*, nourishment]. Angiotrophic.

vasotro'pic [vaso- + G. *tropē*, a turning]. Tending to act on the blood vessels.

vasova'gal. Relating to the action of the vagus nerve upon the blood vessels.

vasovasostomy (vas'o-vă-sos'to-mĭ). Surgical anastomosis of vasa deferentia, to restore fertility in a previously vasectomized male.

vasovesiculectomy (vas'o-vĕ-sik-u-lek'to-mĭ) [vaso- + L. *vesicula*, vesicle, + G. *ektomē*, excision]. Excision of the vas deferens and seminal vesicles.

VC Color *vision*; vital *capacity*.

VDRL Venereal Disease Research Laboratories. See VDRL *test*.

vection (vek'shun) [L. *vectio*, conveyance]. Transference of agents of disease from the sick to the well by a vector.

vector (vek'tor) [L. *vector*, a carrier]. **1.** An invertebrate animal capable of transmitting an infectious agent among vertebrates. **2.** Anything having magnitude, direction, and sense which can be represented by a straight line of appropriate length and direction.

 biological v., a v. that is essential in the life cycle of the pathogenic organism.

 mechanical v., a v. that simply conveys pathogens to a susceptible individual without essential development of the pathogenic organisms in the v.

vectorcardiogram (vek'tor-kar'dĭ-o-gram). A graphic representation of the magnitude and direction of the heart's action currents in the form of a vector loop.

vectorcardiography (vek'tor-kar-dĭ-og'ră-fĭ). **1.** A variant of electrocardiography in which the heart's activation currents are represented by vector loops. **2.** The study and interpretation of vectorcardiograms.

vecto'rial. Relating in any way to a vector.

vegetable (vej'tă-bl). **1.** A plant, specifically one used for food. **2.** Vegetal (1); relating to plants, as distinguished from animals or minerals.

vegetal (vej'ĕ-tal). **1.** Vegetable (2). **2.** Denoting the vital functions common to plants and animals, as distinguished from those peculiar to animals.

vegeta'rian. One whose diet consists of foods of vegetable origin.

vegetation (vej-ĕ-ta'shun) [Mod. L. *vegetatio*, growth]. A growth or excrescence of any sort; specifically, a clot, composed largely of fused blood platelets, fibrin, and sometimes bacteria, adherent to a diseased heart valve.

vegetative (vej'ĕ-ta-tiv). **1.** Growing or functioning involuntarily or unconsciously, after the assumed manner of vegetable life. **2.** Not active; denoting the resting stage of a cell or its nucleus.

vehicle (ve'hĭ-kl) [L. *vehiculum*, a conveyance]. A substance, usually without therapeutic action, used as a medium, to give bulk, for the administration of medicines.

veil [L. *velum*]. **1.** Velum (1). **2.** Caul.

Veillonella (va-yon-el'ah) [A. *Veillon*]. A genus of Gram-negative bacteria (family Veillonellaceae) that are parasitic in the mouth and the intestinal and respiratory tracts of man and other animals. The type species is *V. parvula*.

vein (vān) [L. *vena*]. Vena.

 accessory cephalic v., *vena* cephalica accessoria.

 accessory hemiazygos v., *vena* hemiazygos accessoria.

 accessory vertebral v., *vena* vertebralis accessoria.

 accompanying v., *vena* comitans.

 anastomotic v., *vena* anastomotica.

 angular v., *vena* angularis.

anterior vertebral v., *vena* vertebralis anterior.
appendicular v., *vena* appendicularis.
arcuate v.'s of kidney, *venae* arcuatae renis.
auricular v., *vena* auricularis.
axillary v., *vena* axillaris.
azygos v., *vena* azygos.
basal v.'s, see under *vena* basalis.
basilic v., *vena* basilica.
basivertebral v., *vena* basivertebralis.
brachial v.'s, *venae* brachiales.
brachiocephalic v.'s, *venae* brachiocephalicae.
bronchial v.'s, *venae* bronchiales.
v. of bulb of penis, *vena* bulbi penis.
capillary v., venule.
cardiac v.'s, see under *vena* cordis.
cardinal v.'s, major systemic venous channels in adult primitive vertebrates and in embryos of higher vertebrates; anterior c. v.'s are major drainage channels from the cephalic part of the body, posterior c. v.'s, from the caudal part; common c. v.'s, formed by anastomosis of the anterior and posterior c. v.'s, are the main systemic return channels to the heart.
central v.'s of liver, *venae* centrales hepatis.
central v. of retina, *vena* centralis retinae.
central v. of suprarenal gland, *vena* centralis glandulae suprarenalis.
cephalic v., *vena* cephalica.
cerebellar v.'s, *venae* cerebelli.
cerebral v.'s, see under *vena* cerebri.
cervical v., see *vena* cervicalis profunda.
choroid v., *vena* choroidea.
ciliary v.'s, *venae* ciliares.
circumflex v.'s, see under *vena* circumflexa.
v.'s of clitoris, *venae* profundae clitoridis, *vena* dorsalis clitoridis profunda, *venae* dorsales clitoridis superficiales.
v. of cochlear canal, *vena* canaliculi cochleae.
colic v., *vena* colica.
common facial v., union of the facial v. and the retromandibular v., emptying into the jugular v.
conjunctival v.'s, *venae* conjunctivales.
costoaxillary v., one of a number of anastomotic v.'s connecting intercostal v.'s of the first to seventh intercostal spaces with the lateral thoracic or the thoracoepigastric v.
cutaneous v., *vena* cutanea.
cystic v., *vena* cystica.
digital v.'s, *venae* digitales.
diploic v., *vena* diploica.
dorsal scapular v., *vena* scapularis dorsalis.
emissary v., *vena* emissaria.
epigastric v.'s, *vena* epigastrica inferior and superficialis, *venae* epigastricae superiores.
episcleral v.'s, *venae* episclerales.
esophageal v.'s, *venae* esophageae.
ethmoidal v.'s, *venae* ethmoidales.
external nasal v.'s, *venae* nasales externae.
v.'s of eyelids, *venae* palpebrales.
facial v., *vena* facialis, *vena* faciei profunda.

femoral v., *vena* femoralis, *vena* profunda femoris.
fibular v.'s, *venae* peroneae.
gastric v.'s, *venae* gastricae breves, *vena* gastrica dextra and sinistra.
gastroomental v.'s, gastroepiploic v.'s, *vena* gastroomentalis dextra and sinistra.
genicular v.'s, *venae* genus.
gluteal v.'s, *venae* gluteae inferiores and superiores.
hemiazygos v., *vena* hemiazygos.
hemorrhoidal v.'s, *venae* rectales inferiores and mediae, *vena* rectalis superior.
hepatic v.'s, *venae* hepaticae.
hypogastric v., internal iliac v.
ileal v.'s, see *venae* jejunales et ilei.
ileocolic v., *vena* ileocolica.
iliac v., *vena* iliaca.
iliolumbar v., *vena* iliolumbalis.
innominate v.'s, *venae* brachiocephalicae.
intercapitular v.'s, *venae* intercapitales.
intercostal v.'s, see under *venae* intercostales.
interlobar v.'s of kidney, *venae* interlobares renis.
interlobular v.'s, *venae* interlobulares renis and hepatis.
intermediate v.'s, *vena* intermedia antebrachii, basilica, cephalica, and cubiti.
internal auditory v.'s, *vena* labyrinthi.
intervertebral v., *vena* intervertebralis.
jejunal and ileal v.'s, *venae* jejunales et ilei.
jugular v., *vena* jugularis.
v.'s of kidney, *venae* renis.
v.'s of knee, *venae* genus.
labial v.'s, *venae* labiales anteriores and posteriores, *vena* labialis inferior and superior.
labyrinthine v.'s, *venae* labyrinthi.
lacrimal v., *vena* lacrimalis.
laryngeal v., *vena* laryngea.
lingual v.'s, *vena* lingualis, *vena* profunda linguae.
lumbar v.'s, *venae* lumbales, *vena* lumbalis ascendens.
maxillary v., *vena* maxillaris.
median v.'s, see under *vena* intermedia.
mediastinal v.'s, *venae* mediastinales.
meningeal v.'s, *venae* meningeae and meningeae mediae.
mesenteric v., *vena* mesenterica.
metacarpal v., *venae* metacarpeae.
metatarsal v., *venae* metatarseae.
musculophrenic v.'s, *venae* musculophrenicae.
nasofrontal v., *vena* nasofrontalis.
oblique v. of left atrium, *vena* obliqua atrii sinistri.
obturator v., *vena* obturatoria.
occipital v.'s, *vena* occipitalis, *venae* occipitales.
ophthalmic v.'s, *vena* ophthalmica.
ovarian v., *vena* ovarica.
palatine v., *vena* palatina.
pancreatic v.'s, *venae* pancreaticae.
pancreaticoduodenal v.'s, *venae* pancreaticoduodenales.
paraumbilical v.'s, *venae* paraumbilicales.

parotid v.'s, *venae* parotideae.

pectoral v.'s, *venae* pectorales.

v.'s of penis, *vena* dorsalis penis profunda, *venae* dorsales penis superficiales, *vena* profunda penis.

perforating v.'s, *venae* perforantes.

pericardiacophrenic v.'s, *venae* pericardiacophrenicae.

pericardial v.'s, *venae* pericardiacae.

peroneal v.'s, *venae* peroneae.

pharyngeal v.'s, *venae* pharyngeae.

phrenic v.'s, *vena* phrenica.

popliteal v., *vena* poplitea.

portal v., *vena* portae.

posterior v. of left ventricle, *vena* posterior ventriculi sinistri.

prepyloric v., *vena* prepylorica.

v. of pterygoid canal, *vena* canalis pterygoidei.

pudendal v.'s, *venae* pudendae externae, *vena* pudenda interna.

pulmonary v.'s, *venae* pulmonalis inferior and superior.

pyloric v., *vena* gastrica dextra.

radial v.'s, *venae* radiales.

rectal v.'s, *venae* rectales.

renal v.'s, *venae* renales.

retromandibular v., *vena* retromandibularis.

sacral v.'s, *venae* sacrales laterales, *vena* sacralis mediana.

saphenous v., *vena* saphena.

scleral v.'s, *venae* sclerales.

scrotal v.'s, *venae* scrotales.

v. of septum pellucidum, *vena* septi pellucidi.

sigmoid v.'s, *venae* sigmoideae.

spinal v.'s, *venae* spinales.

spiral v. of modiolus, *vena* spiralis modioli.

splenic v., *vena* lienalis.

stellate v.'s, stellate *venules.*

sternocleidomastoid v., *vena* sternocleidomastoidea.

striate v.'s, *venae* thalamostriatae inferiores.

stylomastoid v., *vena* stylomastoidea.

subclavian v., *vena* subclavia.

subcutaneous v.'s of abdomen, *venae* subcutaneae abdominis.

sublingual v., *vena* sublingualis.

submental v., *vena* submentalis.

superior v. of vermis, *vena* vermis superior.

supraorbital v., *vena* supraorbitalis.

suprarenal v., *vena* suprarenalis.

suprascapular v., *vena* suprascapularis.

supratrochlear v.'s, *venae* supratrochleares.

surface thalamic v.'s, *venae* directae laterales.

temporal v.'s, *vena* temporalis media, *venae* temporales.

v.'s of temporomandibular joint, *venae* articulares temporomandibulares.

testicular v.'s, *vena* testicularis.

thalamostriate v., *venae* thalamostriatae inferiores, *vena* thalamostriata superior.

thoracic v., *vena* thoracica.

thoracoacromial v., *vena* thoracoacromialis.

thoracoepigastric v., *vena* thoracoepigastrica.

thymic v.'s, *venae* thymicae.

thyroid v., *vena* thyroidea.

tibial v.'s, *venae* tibiales.

tracheal v.'s, *venae* tracheales.

transverse v. of face, *vena* transversa faciei.

transverse v.'s of neck, *venae* transversae colli.

tympanic v.'s, *venae* tympanicae.

ulnar v.'s, *venae* ulnares.

umbilical v., see *vena* umbilicalis sinistra.

uterine v.'s, *venae* uterinae.

varicose v.'s, permanent dilation and tortuosity of v.'s most commonly seen in the legs.

vertebral v., *vena* vertebralis.

vesical v.'s, *venae* vesicales.

vestibular v.'s, *venae* vestibulares.

v. of vestibular aqueduct, *vena* aqueductus vestibuli.

v. of vestibular bulb, *vena* bulbi vestibuli.

vortex v., vorticose v.'s, *venae* vorticosae.

vela (ve'lah). Plural of velum.

velamen, pl. **velamina** (vē-la'men, vĕ-lam'ĭ-nah) [L. a veil]. Velum (1).

velamen'tous. Expanded in the form of a sheet or veil.

ve'lar. Relating to any velum.

vel'lus [L. fleece]. Fine body hair present before puberty.

velocity (vĕ-los'ĭ-tĭ) [L. *velox,* quick, swift]. Rate of movement, specifically, the distance traveled per unit time.

  maximum v. (V_{max}), **(1)** maximum rate of an enzymatic reaction that can be achieved by progressively increasing the substrate concentration. **(2)** the maximum initial rate of shortening of a myocardial fiber that can be obtained under zero load; used to evaluate the contractility of the fiber.

velopharyngeal (ve'lo-fă-rin'je-al). Pertaining to the soft palate (velum palatinum) and the posterior nasopharyngeal wall.

velum, pl. **vela** (ve'lum, -lah) [L. veil, sail] **1** [NA]. Velamen; veil (1); any structure resembling a veil or curtain. **2.** *Omentum* majus. **3.** Any serous membrane or membranous envelope or covering.

  v. medulla're infe'rius [NA], **inferior medullary v.,** a thin sheet of white matter attached along the peduncle of the flocculus and to the nodulus of the vermis.

  v. medulla're supe'rius [NA], **superior medullary v.,** the thin layer of white matter stretching between the two superior cerebellar peduncles, forming part of the roof of the fourth ventricle.

  v. palati'num, soft *palate.*

ve'nacavog'raphy. Cavography, angiography of a vena cava.

vena, pl. **venae** (ve'nah, -ne) [L.] [NA]. Vein; a blood vessel carrying blood toward the heart; all veins except the pulmonary carry dark unaerated blood.

v. anastomot'ica [NA], (1) inferior, inconstant vein passing from the superficial middle cerebral vein posteriorly over the lateral aspect of the temporal lobe to enter the transverse sinus; (2) superior, large communicating vein between the superficial middle cerebral vein and the superior sagittal sinus; passes upward from the lateral sulcus, often following the line of the sulcus centralis.

v. angula'ris [NA], angular vein; short vein at the anterior angle of the orbit, formed by the supraorbital and supratrochlear veins and continuing as the facial.

v. appendicula'ris [NA], appendicular vein; tributary of the ileocolic vein that accompanies the appendicular artery.

v. aqueduc'tus vestib'uli [NA], vein of vestibular aqueduct; accompanies the endolymphatic duct and terminates in the inferior petrosal sinus.

ve'nae arcua'tae re'nis [NA], arcuate veins of kidney; parallel the arcuate arteries, receive blood from interlobular veins and rectal venules, and terminate in interlobar veins.

v. auricula'ris [NA], (1) anterior, one of several emptying into the retromandibular; (2) posterior, a tributary to the external jugular vein, draining the region posterior to the ear.

v. axilla'ris [NA], axillary vein; continuation of the basilic and brachial veins, running from the lower border of the teres major muscle to the outer border of the first rib where it becomes the subclavian vein.

v. az'ygos [NA], azygos vein; arises from the right ascending lumbar vein or the inferior v. cava, ascends through aortic orifice of the diaphragm, lies in the posterior mediastinum, and terminates in the superior v. cava.

v. basa'lis [NA], basal vein; a large vein passing caudally and dorsally along the medial surface of the temporal lobe and emptying into the vena cerebri magna from the lateral side.

v. basa'lis commu'nis [NA], common basal vein; tributary to the inferior pulmonary vein (right and left) that receives blood from the superior and inferior basal veins.

v. basa'lis infe'rior [NA], inferior basal vein; tributary to the common basal vein, draining the medial and posterior part of the inferior lobe in each lung.

v. basa'lis supe'rior [NA], superior basal vein; tributary to the common basal vein, draining the lateral and anterior part of the inferior lobe of each lung.

v. basil'ica [NA], basilic vein; arises on the back of the hand, curves around the medial side of the forearm, and passes up the medial side of the arm to join the axillary vein.

v. basivertebra'lis [NA], basivertebral vein; one of a number of veins in the spongy substance of the bodies of the vertebrae, emptying into the anterior internal vertebral venous plexus.

ve'nae brachia'les [NA], brachial veins; two veins in either arm accompanying the brachial artery and emptying into the axillary vein.

ve'nae brachiocephal'icae [NA], brachiocephalic veins; innominate veins; formed by union of the internal jugular and subclavian; tributaries are: right brachiocephalic, receives the right vertebral and internal thoracic veins and the right lymphatic duct; left brachiocephalic, receives left vertebral, internal thoracic, superior intercostal, inferior thyroid and various anterior pericardial, bronchial, and mediastinal veins.

ve'nae bronchia'les [NA], bronchial veins; veins running in front of and behind the bronchi and uniting into two main trunks which empty on the right into the azygos vein, on the left into the accessory hemiazygos or left superior intercostal vein.

v. bul'bi pe'nis [NA], vein of bulb of penis; tributary of the internal pudendal vein which drains the bulb.

v. bul'bi vestib'uli [NA], vein of vestibular bulb; a tributary of the internal pudendal vein which drains the bulb.

v. canalic'uli coch'leae [NA], vein of cochlear canal; drains the cochlea and the sacculus, and empties into the superior bulb of the jugular vein by accompanying the cochlear aqueduct through the canal.

v. cana'lis pterygoi'dei [NA], vein of pterygoid canal; accompanies the nerve and artery through the pterygoid canal and empties into the pharyngeal vein.

v. ca'va [NA], (1) inferior, postcava; receives blood from lower limbs and greater part of the pelvic and abdominal organs, and empties into the posterior part of the right atrium of the heart; (2) superior, precava; returns blood from the head and neck, upper limbs, and thorax; formed by union of the two brachiocephalic veins and the azygos vein.

ve'nae caverno'sae pe'nis [NA], cavernous venous spaces in the erectile tissue of the penis.

ve'nae centra'les hep'atis [NA], central veins of liver; terminal branches of the hepatic veins that lie centrally in the hepatic lobules and receive blood from the liver sinusoids.

v. centra'lis glan'dulae suprarena'lis [NA], central vein of suprarenal gland; the single draining vein, which receives a number of medullary veins; on the right, empties directly into the inferior vena cava, on the left into the left renal vein.

v. centra'lis ret'inae [NA], central vein of retina; formed by union of the retinal veins and accompanies artery of the same name in the optic nerve.

v. cephal'ica [NA], cephalic vein; arises at the radial border of the dorsal venous rete of the hand, passes upward in front of the elbow and along the lateral side of the arm, and empties into the upper part of the axillary vein.

v. cephal'ica accesso'ria [NA], accessory cephalic vein; variable vein that passes along the radial border of the forearm to join the cephalic vein near the elbow.

ve'nae cerebel'li [NA], cerebellar veins; veins draining the cerebellum: venae hemispherii inferiores and superiores, v. petrosa, v. precentralis cerebelli, v. vermis inferior and superior.

v. cer'ebri ante'rior [NA], anterior cerebral vein; parallels the anterior cerebral artery and drains into the basal vein.

ve'nae cer'ebri inferio'res [NA], inferior cerebral veins; drain undersurface of the cerebral hemispheres and empty into cavernous and transverse sinuses.

ve'nae cer'ebri inter'nae [NA], internal cerebral veins; two paired veins passing caudally near midline in the tela choroidea of the third ventricle, formed by the union of the choroid vein, superior thalamostriate vein, and v. septi pellucidi, and uniting caudally to form the v. cerebri magna.

v. cer'ebri mag'na [NA], great cerebral vein; formed by junction of the two internal cerebral veins and passes caudally between the splenium of the corpus callosum and the pineal gland to continue into the sinus rectus.

v. cer'ebri me'dia [NA], middle cerebral vein; (1) deep, accompanies the middle cerebral artery in the depths of the sylvian fissure and empties into the v. basalis; (2) superficial, a large vein passing along the line of the sylvian fissure to join the cavernous sinus.

ve'nae cer'ebri superio'res [NA], superior cerebral veins; drain the dorsal convexity of the cortical hemisphere and empty into the superior sagittal sinus.

v. cervica'lis profun'da [NA], deep cervical vein; accompanies artery of same name between the semispinalis capitis and semispinalis cervicis and empties into the brachiocephalic or the vertebral vein.

v. choroi'dea [NA], choroid vein; (1) inferior, drains lower part of the choroid plexus of the lateral ventricle into the basal vein; (2) superior, follows choroid plexus of the lateral ventricle and unites with the superior thalamostriate vein and the anterior vein of the septum pellucidum to form the internal cerebral vein.

ve'nae cilia'res [NA], ciliary veins; several small veins, anterior and posterior, coming from the ciliary body.

v. circumflex'a il'ium [NA], circumflex iliac vein; (1) deep, corresponds to artery of same name and empties, near or in a common trunk with the inferior epigastric, into the external iliac vein; (2) superficial, corresponds to artery of same name and empties usually into the greater saphenous, or sometimes the femoral, vein.

ve'nae circumflex'ae fem'oris [NA], circumflex femoral veins; (1) lateral, accompany the lateral circumflex femoral artery; (2) medial, parallel the medial circumflex femoral artery.

v. col'ica [NA], colic vein; (1) right, parallels the right colic artery and drains blood from the ascending colon and right flexure; (2) middle, tributary of the superior mesenteric vein that accompanies the middle colic artery; (3) left, tributary of the inferior mesenteric vein that accompanies the left colic artery and drains the left flexure and descending colon.

v. com'itans, pl. **ve'nae comitan'tes** [NA], accompanying vein; (1) a vein accompanying another structure; (2) a pair of veins, occasionally more, that closely accompany an artery in such a manner that the pulsations of the artery aid venous return.

ve'nae conjunctiva'les [NA], conjunctival veins; veins draining the conjunctiva.

ve'nae cor'dis anterio'res [NA], anterior cardiac veins; two or three small veins in the anterior wall of the right ventricle opening into the right atrium independently of the coronary sinus.

v. cor'dis mag'na [NA], great cardiac vein; tributary of the coronary sinus, beginning at the apex and running in the anterior interventricular sulcus.

v. cor'dis me'dia [NA], middle cardiac vein; begins at the apex of the heart and passes through the posterior interventricular sulcus to the coronary sinus.

ve'nae cor'dis min'imae [NA], smallest cardiac veins; numerous small venous channels that open directly into the chambers of the heart from the capillary bed in the cardiac wall.

v. cor'dis par'va [NA], small cardiac vein; an inconstant vessel, accompanying the right coronary artery in the coronary sulcus, from the right margin of the right ventricle, and emptying into the coronary sinus or the middle cardiac vein.

v. cuta'nea [NA], cutaneous vein; one of a number of veins that course in the subcutaneous tissue and empty into deep veins.

v. cys'tica [NA], cystic vein; drains the gallbladder, passing along the cystic duct to enter the right branch of the portal vein.

ve'nae digita'les [NA], digital veins; (1) dorsal of toes, receive intercapitular veins from the plantar venous arch, join to form four common dorsal digital veins, and terminate in the dorsal venous arch; (2) palmar, form paired venae comitantes along the proper and common digital arteries and empty into the superficial palmar venous arch; (3) plantar, arise in the toes and pass back to form four metatarsal veins that empty into the plantar venous arch.

v. diplo'ica [NA], diploic vein; one of the veins (frontal, anterior temporal, posterior temporal, occipital) in the diploë of the cranial bones, connected with the cerebral sinuses by emissary veins.

ve'nae dorsa'les clitor'idis superficia'les [NA], superficial dorsal veins of clitoris; paired tributaries to the external pudendal vein on either side.

ve'nae dorsa'les pe'nis superficia'les [NA], superficial dorsal veins of penis; paired tributaries, superficial to the fascia, of the external pudendal veins on each side.

v. dorsa'lis clitor'idis profun'da [NA], deep dorsal vein of clitoris; tributary, deep to the fascia, of the vesical venous plexus.

v. dorsa'lis pe'nis profun'da [NA], deep dorsal vein of penis; tributary, deep to the fascia, of the prostatic plexus.

v. emissa'ria [NA], emissary vein; (1) condylar, connects the sigmoid sinus and the external vertebral venous plexuses through the condylar canal of the occipital bone; (2) mastoid, connects the sigmoid sinus with the occipital vein or one of the tributaries of the external jugular by way of the mastoid foramen; (3) occipital, inconstant vessel connecting the occipital veins with the confluens sinuum; (4) parietal, connects the superior sagittal sinus with the tributaries of the superficial temporal vein and other veins of the scalp.

v. epigas'trica infe'rior [NA], inferior epigastric vein; corresponds to artery of same name and empties into the external iliac vein.

v. epigas'trica superficia'lis [NA], superficial epigastric vein; drains the lower and medial part of the anterior abdominal wall and empties into the great saphenous vein.

ve'nae epigas'tricae superio'res [NA], superior epigastric veins; venae comitantes of artery of same name which are tributaries of the internal thoracic.

ve'nae episclera'les [NA], episcleral veins; a series of small venules in the sclera close to the corneal margin which empty into the anterior ciliary veins.

ve'nae esopha'geae [NA], esophageal veins; several small venous trunks bringing blood from the esophagus and emptying into the brachiocephalic or the azygos vein.

ve'nae ethmoida'les [NA], ethmoidal veins; veins that drain the ethmoidal sinuses and pass into the superior ophthalmic vein.

v. facia'lis [NA], facial vein; (1) anterior, continuation of the angular vein, uniting with the retromandibular vein below the border of the lower jaw before emptying into the internal jugular vein; (2) posterior, v. retromandibularis.

v. facie'i profun'da [NA], deep facial vein; valveless communicating vein that passes from the facial vein to the pterygoid plexus in the infratemporal fossa.

v. femora'lis [NA], femoral vein; accompanies femoral artery in the same sheath, being a continuation of the popliteal vein, and becomes the external iliac vein at the level of the inguinal ligament.

v. gas'trica dex'tra [NA], right gastric vein; pyloric vein; receives veins from both surfaces of the upper portion of the stomach, runs to the right along the lesser curvature, and empties into the portal vein.

v. gas'trica sinis'tra [NA], left gastric vein; arises from a union of veins from both surfaces of the gastric cardia, runs in the lesser omentum, and empties into the portal vein.

ve'nae gas'tricae bre'ves [NA], short gastric veins; veins in the wall of the stomach which empty into the splenic vein.

v. gastroomenta'lis [NA], gastroomental or gastroepiploic vein; (1) right, tributary of the superior mesenteric vein that parallels the right gastroomental artery along the greater curvature of the stomach; (2) left, accompanies the left gastroomental artery along the greater curvature of the stomach and empties into the splenic vein.

ve'nae ge'nus [NA], genicular veins; accompany the genicular arteries, drain blood from structures around the knee, and terminate in the popliteal vein.

ve'nae glu'teae [NA], gluteal veins; (1) inferior, venae comitantes of the inferior gluteal artery uniting at the sciatic foramen to form a common trunk which empties into the internal iliac vein, (2) superior, accompany the gluteal artery, entering the pelvis as two veins which unite into one and empty into the internal iliac vein.

v. hemiaz'ygos [NA], hemiazygos vein; continuation of the left ascending lumbar vein; ascends along the left side of the lower thoracic vertebrae to the eighth vertebra, where it crosses the midline behind the aorta, thoracic duct, and esophagus, and empties into the azygos vein.

v. hemiaz'ygos accesso'ria [NA], accessory hemiazygos vein; formed by the union of the fourth to seventh left posterior intercostal veins, passes along the fifth, sixth, and seventh thoracic vertebrae, then crosses the midline behind the aorta, esophagus, and thoracic duct, and empties into the azygos vein.

ve'nae hemisphe'rii cerebel'li [NA], veins of cerebellar hemisphere; (1) inferior, several veins draining the inferior portion of the cerebellar hemispheres and terminating in the petrosal vein; (2) superior, several veins draining the superior part of the cerebellar hemispheres and terminating in the superior petrosal sinus or the petrosal vein.

ve'nae hepat'icae [NA], hapatic veins; collect blood from the central veins and terminate in three large veins (right, middle, left) opening into the inferior vena cava below the diaphragm and several small inconstant veins entering the vena cava lower down.

v. ileocol'ica [NA], ileocolic vein; tributary of the superior mesenteric vein which runs parallel to the ileocolic artery and drains the terminal ileum, appendix, cecum, and the lower part of the ascending colon.

v. ili'aca [NA], iliac vein; (1) common, formed by union of the external and internal iliac veins at the brim of the pelvis and passes upward to the right of the fifth lumbar vertebra where it unites with its fellow of the opposite side to form the inferior v.

cava; (2) external, direct continuation of the femoral vein above the inguinal ligament, uniting with the internal iliac to form the common iliac; (3) internal, hypogastric vein; runs from upper border of the greater sciatic notch to the brim of the pelvis where it joins the external iliac to form the common iliac; drains most of the territory supplied by the internal iliac artery.

v. iliolumba′lis [NA], iliolumbar vein; accompanies artery of same name, anastomoses with the lumbar and deep circumflex iliac veins, and empties into the internal iliac.

inferior v. cava, see v. cava.

ve′nae intercapita′les [NA], intercapitular veins; veins connecting the dorsal and palmar veins in the hand, or the dorsal and plantar veins in the foot.

ve′nae intercosta′les anterio′res [NA], anterior intercostal veins; tributaries to the musculophrenic or internal thoracic veins from the intercostal spaces.

ve′nae intercosta′les posterio′res [NA], posterior intercostal veins; veins draining the intercostal spaces posteriorly: from the fourth to the eleventh spaces on the right, they are tributaries of the azygos vein; on the left, they empty into either the hemiazygos or accessory hemiazygos veins.

v. intercosta′lis supe′rior [NA], superior intercostal vein; (1) right, tributary of the azygos vein formed by union of the right second, third, and fourth posterior intercostal veins; (2) left, formed by the union of the left second, third and fourth intercostal veins, passes across the arch of the aorta, empties into the left brachiocephalic vein, and frequently communicates also with the accessory hemiazygos vein.

v. intercosta′lis supre′ma [NA], highest intercostal vein; drains first intercostal space into either the vertebral or the brachiocephalic vein.

ve′nae interloba′res re′nis [NA], interlobar veins of kidney; parallel the interlobar arteries, receive blood from arcuate veins, and terminate in the renal vein.

ve′nae interlobula′res hep′atis [NA], interlobular veins of liver; terminal branches of the portal vein that course between the lobules and empty into the liver sinusoids.

ve′nae interlobula′res re′nis [NA], interlobular veins of kidney; parallel the interlobular arteries and drain the peritubular capillary plexus, emptying into arcuate veins.

v. interme′dia antebra′chii [NA], intermediate antebrachial vein; begins at the base of the dorsum of the thumb, curves around the radial side, ascends the middle of the forearm, and just below the bend of the elbow divides into the intermediate basilic and intermediate cephalic veins.

v. interme′dia basil′ica [NA], intermediate basilic vein; medial branch of the intermediate antebrachial vein which joins the basilic.

v. interme′dia cephal′ica [NA], intermediate cephalic vein; lateral branch of the intermediate antebrachial vein which joins the cephalic near the elbow.

v. interme′dia cu′biti [NA], intermediate cubital vein; passes across the bend of the elbow from the cephalic to the basilic vein.

v. intervertebra′lis [NA], intervertebral vein; one of numerous veins accompanying the spinal nerves, emptying in the neck into the vertebral, in the thorax into the intercostal, in the lumbar and sacral regions into the lumbar and sacral veins.

ve′nae jejuna′les et il′ei [NA], jejunal and ileal veins; they drain the jejunum and ileum, and terminate in the superior mesenteric vein.

v. jugula′ris [NA], jugular vein; (1) anterior, arises below the chin from veins draining the lower lip and mental region, descends the anterior portion of the neck superficially, and terminates in the external jugular at the lateral border of the scalenus anterior muscle; (2) external, formed below the parotid gland by junction of the posterior auricular and the retromandibular veins, passes down the side of the neck superficial to the sternocleidomastoid muscle, and empties into the subclavian vein; (3) internal, continuation of the sigmoid sinus of the dura mater, uniting, behind the cartilage of the first rib, with the subclavian to form the brachiocephalic vein.

ve′nae labia′les anterio′res [NA], anterior labial veins; they pass from the labia majora to the external pudendal veins.

ve′nae labia′les posterio′res [NA], posterior labial veins; they pass posteriorward from the labia majora to the internal pudendal veins.

v. labia′lis infe′rior [NA], inferior labial vein; tributary of the facial vein draining the lower lip.

v. labia′lis supe′rior [NA], superior labial vein; it takes blood from the upper lip and empty into the facial vein.

ve′nae labyrin′thi [NA], labyrinthine veins; internal auditory veins; two veins, accompanying each labyrinthine artery, which drain the internal ear, pass out through the internal acoustic meatus, and empty into the transverse sinus or the inferior petrosal sinus.

v. lacrima′lis [NA], lacrimal vein; drains the lacrimal gland, passes through the orbit with the lacrimal artery, and empties into the superior ophthalmic vein.

v. laryn′gea [NA], laryngeal vein; (1) inferior, passes from lower part of the larynx to the plexus thyroideus impar; (2) superior, accompanies the superior laryngeal artery and empties into the superior thyroid vein.

v. liena′lis [NA], splenic vein; arises by the union of several small veins at the hilum on the anterior surface of the spleen, passes to the left kidney, then runs to the neck of the pancreas where it joins the superior mesenteric to form the portal vein.

v. lingua'lis [NA], lingual vein; receives blood from the tongue, sublingual and submandibular glands, and muscles of the floor of the mouth; empties into the internal jugular or the facial vein.

ve'nae lumba'les [NA], lumbar veins; five veins that accompany the lumbar arteries, drain the posterior body wall and lumbar vertebral venous plexuses, and terminate anteriorly as follows: first and second in the ascending lumbar vein, third and fourth in the inferior vena cava, and fifth in the iliolumbar vein.

v. lumba'lis ascen'dens [NA], ascending lumbar vein; arises from the sacral and lumbar veins; at the diaphragm becomes the azygos vein on the right side, the hemiazygos vein on the left.

v. maxilla'ris, [NA], maxillary vein; posterior continuation of the pterygoid plexus, joining the superficial temporal vein to form the retromandibular vein.

ve'nae mediastina'les [NA], mediastinal veins; several small veins from the mediastinum emptying into brachiocephalic vein or the superior v. cava.

ve'nae menin'geae [NA], meningeal veins; accompany the meningeal arteries, communicate with venous sinuses and diploic veins, and drain into regional veins outside the cranial vault.

ve'nae menin'geae me'diae [NA], middle meningeal veins; venae comitantes of the middle meningeal artery which empty into the pterygoid plexus.

v. mesenter'ica [NA], mesenteric vein; (1) inferior, continuation of the superior rectal at the brim of the pelvis, ascending to the left of the aorta behind the peritoneum and emptying into the splenic or into the superior mesenteric vein; (2) superior, begins at the ileum in the right iliac fossa, ascends in the root of the mesentery, and unites behind the pancreas with the splenic vein to form the portal.

ve'nae metacar'peae [NA], metacarpal veins; (1) dorsal, three veins on the dorsum of the hand draining from the four medial digits into the dorsal venous network of the hand; (2) palmar, empties into the deep venous arch from which the radial and ulnar veins arise.

ve'nae metatar'seae [NA], metatarsal veins; (1) dorsal, arises from the dorsal digital veins forming the dorsal venous arch of the foot; (2) plantar, formed from the plantar digital veins constituting the deep plantar venous arch, which empties into the medial and lateral plantar veins.

ve'nae mus'culophren'icae [NA], musculophrenic veins; accompany the musculophrenic artery and drain blood from the upper abdominal wall, lower intercostal spaces, and diaphragm.

ve'nae nasa'les exter'nae [NA], external nasal veins; several vessels that drain the external nose, emptying into the angular or facial vein.

v. nasofronta'lis [NA], nasofrontal vein; located in the anterior medial part of the orbit and connects the superior ophthalmic with the angular vein.

v. obli'qua a'trii sinis'tri [NA], oblique vein of left atrium; tributary of the coronary sinus, on the posterior wall of the left atrium, developed from the left common cardinal vein.

v. obturato'ria, [NA], obturator vein; union of tributaries draining the hip joint and the muscles of the upper and back part of the thigh; enters the pelvis by the obturator canal and empties into the internal iliac vein.

ve'nae occipita'les [NA], occipital veins; superficial veins draining the occipital cortex and emptying into the superior sagittal and transverse sinus.

v. occipita'lis [NA], occipital vein; drains the occipital region and empties into the internal jugular vein or the suboccipital plexus.

v. ophthal'mica [NA], ophthalmic vein; (1) inferior, arises from the inferior palpebral and lacrimal veins, and divides into two terminal branches: one to the pterygoid plexus, the other joining the superior ophthalmic or emptying into the cavernous sinus; (2) superior, begins anteriorly from the nasofrontal vein, passes along the upper part of the medial wall of the orbit and through the superior orbital fissure, and empties into the cavernous sinus.

v. ova'rica [NA], ovarian vein; (1) right, begins at the pampiniform plexus at the hilum of the ovary and opens into the inferior v. cava; (2) left, begins at the pampiniform plexus at the hilum of the ovary and empties into the left renal vein.

v. palati'na [NA], palatine vein; drains the palatine regions and empties into the facial vein.

ve'nae palpebra'les [NA], veins of eyelids; tributaries of the superior ophthalmic vein that drain the superior eyelid; (1) inferior, veins originating in the lower eyelid and emptying into the angular vein; (2) superior, veins draining the upper eyelid into the angular vein.

ve'nae pancreat'icae [NA], pancreatic veins; veins draining the pancreas and emptying into the splenic and the superior mesenteric vein.

ve'nae pancreat'icoduodena'les [NA], pancreaticoduodenal veins; accompany the superior and inferior pancreaticoduodenal arteries, and empty into the superior mesenteric or portal vein.

ve'nae paraumbilica'les [NA], paraumbilical veins; small veins arising from cutaneous veins about the umbilicus, running along the ligamentum teres of the liver and terminating as accessory portal veins in its substance.

ve'nae parotide'ae [NA], parotid veins; parotid branches of the facial vein, draining part of the parotid gland and emptying into the retromandibular vein.

ve'nae pectora'les [NA], pectoral veins; veins draining the pectoral muscles and emptying into the subclavian vein.

ve'nae perforan'tes [NA], perforating veins; accompany the perforating arteries, drain the vastus lateralis and the hamstring muscles, and terminate in the v. profunda femoris.

ve'nae pericardi'acae [NA], pericardial veins; several small veins from the pericardium emptying into the brachiocephalic vein. or superior v. cava.

ve'nae pericardiacophren'icae [NA], pericardiacophrenic veins; accompany the pericardiacophrenic artery and empty into the brachiocephalic vein or superior v. cava.

ve'nae perone'ae [NA], peroneal or fibular veins; accompany the peroneal artery and join the posterior tibial veins to enter the popliteal vein.

ve'nae pharyn'geae [NA], pharyngeal veins; veins from the pharyngeal plexus which empty into the internal jugular.

v. phren'ica [NA], phrenic vein; (1) inferior, drains substance of the diaphragm and empties on the right side into the v. cava, on the left side into the left suprarenal vein; (2) superior, tributaries of the azygos and hemiazygos veins which drain the upper surface of the diaphragm.

v. poplite'a [NA], popliteal vein; arises at the lower border of the popliteus muscle by union of the anterior and posterior tibial veins, ascends through the popliteal space, and enters the adductor magnus muscle to become the femoral vein.

v. por'tae [NA], portal vein; formed by the superior mesenteric and splenic veins behind the pancreas, ascends in front of the inferior v. cava, and divides at the right end of the transverse fissure of the liver into right and left branches, which ramify within the liver.

v. poste'rior ventric'uli sinis'tri [NA], posterior vein of left ventricle; arises on the diaphragmatic surface of the heart near the apex, runs to the left and parallel to the posterior interventricular sulcus, and empties in the coronary sinus.

v. prepylo'rica [NA], prepyloric vein; tributary of the right gastric vein that passes anterior to the pylorus at its junction with the duodenum.

v. profun'da fem'oris [NA], deep femoral vein; accompanies the deep femoral artery, receives perforating veins from the posterior aspect of the thigh, and joins the femoral vein in the femoral triangle, usually with the medial and lateral circumflex femoral veins.

v. profun'da lin'guae [NA], deep lingual vein; accompanies the deep lingual artery, drains the body and apex of the tongue, and joins the lingual vein.

v. profun'da pe'nis [NA], deep vein of penis; the vein, deep to the fascia, that enters the prostatic plexus.

ve'nae profun'dae clitor'idis [NA], deep veins of clitoris; pass from the dorsum of the clitoris to join the vesical plexus.

v. puden'da inter'na [NA], internal pudendal vein; tributary of the internal iliac vein that accompanies the internal pudendal artery as a single or double vessel and drains the perineum.

venae puden'dae exter'nae [NA], external pudendal veins; correspond to arteries of same name, empty into the great saphenous or directly into the femoral vein, and receive the superficial dorsal vein of the penis (clitoris) and anterior scrotal (labial) veins.

v. pulmona'lis infe'rior [NA], inferior pulmonary vein; (1) right, vein returning blood from the inferior lobe of the right lung to the left atrium; (2) left, vein returning blood from the inferior lobe of the left lung to the left atrium.

v. pulmona'lis supe'rior [NA], superior pulmonary vein; (1) right, returns blood from the superior and middle lobes of the right lung to the left atrium; (2) left, returns blood from the left superior lobe of the lung to the left atrium.

ve'nae radia'les [NA], radial veins; several veins continuing the deep palmar veins on the lateral side and accompanying the radial artery.

ve'nae recta'les [NA], rectal or hemorrhoidal veins; (1) inferior, pass to the internal pudendal vein from the venous plexus around the anal canal; (2) middle, pass from the rectal venous plexus to the internal iliac vein; (3) superior, drains the greater part of the rectal venous plexus and ascends between layers of the mesorectum to the brim of the pelvis, where it becomes the inferior mesenteric.

ve'nae rena'les [NA], renal veins; accompany arteries of same name and open at right angles into the v. cava at the level of the second lumbar vertebra.

ve'nae re'nis [NA], veins of kidney; tributaries of the renal vein that parallel the arteries and drain the kidney.

v. retromandibula'ris [NA], retromandibular vein; posterior facial vein; formed by union of the temporal veins in front of the ear, runs behind the ramus of the mandible through the parotid gland, and unites with the facial vein.

ve'nae sacra'les latera'les [NA], lateral sacral veins; accompany corresponding artery and empty into the internal iliac vein on each side.

v. sacra'lis media'na [NA], median sacral vein; an unpaired vein accompanying the middle sacral artery, emptying into the left common iliac vein.

v. saphe'na [NA], saphenous vein; (1) accessory, occasional vein running in the thigh parallel to the great saphenous, which it joins just before the latter empties into the femoral vein; (2) great, formed by union of the dorsal vein of the great toe and the dorsal venous arch of the foot, ascends in front of the medial malleolus behind the medial condyle of the femur, and empties into the femoral vein in the upper part of the femoral triangle; (3) small, arises on the lateral side of the foot from union of the dorsal vein of the little toe with the dorsal venous arch, ascending through the middle of the calf to the lower portion of the popliteal space where it empties into the popliteal vein.

v. scapula'ris dorsa'lis [NA], dorsal scapular vein; tributary to the subclavian or the external jugular vein which accompanies the descending scapular artery.

ve'nae sclera'les [NA], scleral veins; tributaries to the anterior ciliary veins which drain the sclera.

ve'nae scrota'les [NA], scrotal veins; **(1)** anterior, veins passing from the scrotum to the external pudendal veins; **(2)** posterior, veins passing from the scrotum to the internal pudendal veins.

v. sep'ti pellu'cidi [NA], vein of septum pellucidum; **(1)** anterior, drains anterior part of the septum pellucidum and empties into the superior thalamostriate vein; **(2)** posterior, drains posterior part of the septum pellucidum and empties into the superior thalamostriate vein.

ve'nae sigmoi'deae [NA], sigmoid veins; tributaries of the inferior mesenteric vein that drain the sigmoid colon.

ve'nae spina'les [NA], spinal veins; veins that drain the spinal cord, forming a plexus on the surface of the cord from which veins pass along the spinal roots to the internal vertebral venous plexus.

v. spira'lis modi'oli [NA], spiral vein of the modiolus; tributary, in the modiolus of the cochlea, to both the labyrinthine vein and the vein of the cochlear canal.

v. sternocleidomastoi'dea [NA], sternocleidomastoid vein; arises in the sternocleidomastoid muscle and drains into the internal jugular vein.

v. stylomastoi'dea [NA], stylomastoid vein; drains the tympanic cavity and empties into the retromandibular vein.

v. subcla'via [NA], subclavian vein; direct continuation of the axillary vein at lateral border of the first rib; passes medially to join the internal jugular and form the brachiocephalic vein on each side.

ve'nae subcuta'neae abdom'inis [NA], subcutaneous veins of abdomen; network of superficial veins of the abdominal wall that empty into the thoracoepigastric, superficial epigastric, or superior epigastric veins.

v. sublingua'lis [NA], sublingual vein; a tributary of the lingualis.

v. submenta'lis [NA], submental vein; situated below the chin, anastomoses with the sublingual, connects with the anterior jugular and empties into the facial vein.

superior v. cava. see v. cava.

v. supraorbita'lis [NA], supraorbital vein; drains the front of the scalp and unites with the supratrochlear to form the angular vein.

v. suprarena'lis [NA], suprarenal vein; **(1)** right, short vein that passes from the hilum of the right suprarenal to the inferior v. cava; **(2)** left, vein that passes downward from the hilum of the left suprarenal gland to open into the left renal vein.

v. suprascapula'ris [NA], suprascapular vein; accompanies the suprascapular artery and empties into the external jugular vein.

ve'nae supratrochlea'res [NA], supratrochlear veins; drain the front part of the scalp and unite with the supraorbital to form the angular vein.

ve'nae tempora'les [NA], temporal veins; **(1)** deep, corresponding to arteries of same name and emptying into the pterygoid venous plexus; **(2)** superficial, pass from the temporal region to join the retromandibular vein.

v. tempora'lis me'dia [NA], middle temporal vein; arises near the lateral angle of the eye and joins the superficial temporal veins to form the retromandibular vein.

v. testicula'ris [NA], testicular vein; **(1)** right, passes upward from the pampiniform plexus to join the inferior v. cava; **(2)** left, originates from the pampiniform plexus and joins the left renal vein.

v. thalamostria'ta supe'rior [NA], superior thalamostriate vein; a long vein passing forward in the groove between the thalamus and caudate nucleus, and joining the v. choroidea and v. septi pellucidi to form the v. cerebri interna.

ve'nae thalamostria'tae inferio'res [NA], inferior thalamostriate veins; striate veins; tributaries to the basal vein which drain the thalamus and corpus striatum, exiting the anterior perforated substance.

v. thora'cica [NA], thoracic vein; **(1)** internal, usually two veins accompany each artery of the same name, fusing into one at the upper part of the thorax and emptying into the brachiocephalic vein; **(2)** lateral, tributary of the axillary vein that drains the lateral thoracic wall and communicates with the thoracoepigastric and intercostal veins.

v. thoracoacromia'lis [NA], thoracoacromial vein; corresponds to artery of same name and empties into the axillary vein.

v. thoracoepigas'trica [NA], thoracoepigastric vein; one of two veins, sometimes single, arising from the region of the superficial epigastric and opening into the axillary or the lateral thoracic vein.

ve'nae thy'micae [NA], thymic veins; a number of small veins from the thymus emptying into the left brachiocephalic vein.

v. thyroi'dea [NA], thyroid vein; **(1)** inferior, formed by veins from the isthmus and lateral lobe of the thyroid gland and the plexus thyroideus impar, and terminates in the left brachiocephalic vein; **(2)** middle, passes from the thyroid gland across the common carotid artery to empty into the internal jugular vein; **(3)** superior, receives blood from the upper part of the thyroid gland and larynx, accompanies artery of the same name, and empties into the internal jugular.

ve'nae tibia'les [NA], tibial veins; **(1)** anterior, usually two that accompany the anterior tibial artery and empty into the popliteal vein; **(2)** posterior, usually two that accompany the posterior tibial artery and terminate in the popliteal vein.

ve'nae trachea'les [NA], tracheal veins; several small venous trunks from the trachea, emptying into the brachiocephalic vein or the superior v. cava.

v. transver'sa facie'i [NA], transverse vein of face; tributary of the retromandibular, anastomosing with the facial vein.

ve'nae transver'sae col'li [NA], transverse veins of neck; accompany corresponding arteries, emptying into the external jugular or sometimes into the subclavian vein.

ve'nae tympan'icae [NA], tympanic veins; exit from the tympanic cavity and empty into the retromandibular vein.

ve'nae ulna'res [NA], ulnar veins; veins that accompany the ulnar artery.

v. umbilica'lis sinis'tra [NA], left umbilical vein; returns blood from the placenta to the fetus, traversing the umbilical cord to pass into the liver, where it is joined by the portal vein.

ve'nae uteri'nae [NA], uterine veins; two veins on each side which arise from the uterine plexus, pass through a part of the broad ligament and through a peritoneal fold, and empty into the internal iliac vein.

v. vertebra'lis [NA], vertebral vein; derived from tributaries that run through the foramina in the transverse process of the first six cervical vertebrae and form a plexus around the vertebral artery; empties as a single trunk into the brachiocephalic vein.

v. vertebra'lis accesso'ria [NA], accessory vertebral vein; accompanies the vertebral vein but passes through the foramen of the transverse process of the seventh cervical vertebra and opens independently into the brachiocephalic vein.

v. vertebra'lis ante'rior [NA], anterior vertebral vein; accompanies the ascending cervical artery and opens below into the vertebral vein.

ve'nae vesica'les [NA], vesical veins; veins that drain the vesical plexus and join the internal iliac veins.

ve'nae vestibula'res [NA], vestibular veins; tributaries of the labyrinthine veins and the vein of the vestibular aqueduct which drain the saccule and utricle.

ve'nae vortico'sae [NA], vortex or vorticose veins; veins in the tunica vasculosa formed of branches from the posterior surface of the eye and the ciliary body, emptying into the superior or inferior ophthalmic vein.

vene-. **1** [L. *vena*, vein]. Combining form denoting the veins. See also veno-. **2** [L. *venenum*, poison]. Combining form relating to venom.

venectasia (ven-ek-ta'sĭ-ah). Phlebectasia.

venec'tomy. Phlebectomy.

venenation (ven'e-na'shun) [L. *veneno*, pp. *-atus*, to poison]. Poisoning, as from a sting or bite.

ven'enous [L. *venenosus*]. Poisonous.

venereal (vĕ-nēr'e-al) [L. *Venus*, goddess of love]. Relating to or resulting from sexual intercourse.

ven'ery [L. *veneria*, lust]. Excessive, especially illicit, sexual intercourse.

venesec'tion [L. *vena*, vein, + *sectio*, a cutting]. Phlebotomy.

veni-. See ver-o-.

venipuncture (ven'ĭ-punk-chur). Puncture of a vein, usually to withdraw blood or inject a solution.

veno-, veni. Combining forms denoting the veins. See also vene- (1).

ve'nogram [veno- + G. *gramma*, a writing]. **1.** A radiograph of the veins. **2.** Phlebogram.

venography (ve-nog'ră-fĭ) [veno- + G. *grapho*, to write]. Phlebography (2); radiographic visualization or skiagraphic recording of a vein, after injection of a radiopaque substance.

ven'om [L. *venenum*, poison]. A poisonous fluid secreted by snakes, insects, etc.

    Russell's viper v., a v. used as a coagulant in the arrest of hemorrhage from accessible sites in hemophilia.

ve'nomo'tor [veno- + L. *motor*, a move]. Causing change in the caliber of a vein.

venoperitoneostomy (ve'no-pĕr'ĭ-to-ne-os'to-mĭ) [veno- + peritoneum + G. *stoma*, mouth]. Insertion of the saphenous vein into the peritoneal cavity to drain ascitic fluid.

ve'nosclero'sis. Phlebosclerosis.

venosity (ve-nos'ĭ-tĭ). A condition in which the bulk of the blood is in the veins at the expense of the arteries.

venostasis (ve-no-sta'sis) [veno- + G. *stasis*, a standing]. Phlebostasis.

venos'tomy. Cutdown.

venot'omy. Phlebotomy.

venous (ve'nus) [L. *venosus*]. Relating to a vein or to the veins.

venous return. The blood returning to the heart via the great veins.

venovenostomy (ve'no-ve-nos'to-mĭ). Phlebophlebostomy; formation of an anastomosis between two veins.

vent [O. Fr. *fente*, a chink, cleft]. An opening into a cavity or canal, especially one through which contents are discharged.

ven'ter [L. *venter*, belly]. **1.** Abdomen **2** [NA]. Belly (2); the wide swelling part of a muscle. **3.** One of the great cavities of the body. **4.** Uterus.

ventilation (ven'tĭ-la'shun) [L. *ventilo*, pp. *-atus*, to fan, fr. *ventus*, the wind]. **1.** Replacement of the air or other gas in a space by fresh air or gas. **2.** Respiration (2); movement of gas(es) into and out of the lungs. **3** (V̇). In physiology, tidal exchange of air between the lungs and the atmosphere that occurs in breathing.

    alveolar v. (V̇$_A$), the volume of gas expired from the alveoli to the outside of the body per minute; calculated as respiratory frequency (f) multiplied by the difference between tidal volume and the dead space (V$_T$–V$_D$); units: ml/min BTPS.

artificial v., artificial respiration; application of mechanically or manually generated pressures, usually positive, to gas(es) in or about the airway as a means of producing gas exchange between the lungs and surrounding atmosphere.

assist-control v., artificial respiration in which inspiration is produced automatically after a set interval if the patient has not begun to inspire earlier.

assisted v., assisted respiration; application of mechanically or manually generated positive pressure to gas(es) in or about the airway during inhalation as a means of augmenting movement of gases into the lungs.

controlled v., controlled respiration; intermittent application of mechanically or manually generated positive pressure to gas(es) in or about the airway as a means of forcing gases into the lungs in the absence of spontaneous ventilatory efforts.

manual v., use of the hands to generate, directly or indirectly, airway pressures employed in assisted or controlled v.

maximum voluntary v. (MVV), maximum breathing *capacity.*

mechanical v., use of automatically cycling devices to generate airway pressures employed in assisted or controlled v.

pulmonary v., respiratory minute volume: the total volume of gas per minute inspired (V_I) or expired (V_E) expressed in liters per minute.

ven'trad. Toward the ventral aspect.

ven'tral [L. *ventralis*]. **1.** Pertaining to the abdomen or to any venter. **2.** Anterior (2). **3.** In veterinary anatomy, situated nearer the undersurface of an animal body.

ventricle (ven'trĭ-kl) [L. *ventriculus,* dim. of *venter,* belly]. Ventriculus (2); a normal cavity, as of the brain or heart.

    Arantius v., calamus scriptorius.

    fourth v., an irregular cavity, extending from the obex rostalward to a communication with the sylvian aqueduct, enclosed between the cerebellum dorsally and the rhombencephalic tegmentum ventrally.

    lateral v., a horseshoe-shaped cavity conforming with the general shape of each cerebral hemisphere; communicates with the third v. through the foramen of Monro.

    left v., the cavity on the left side of the heart that receives the arterial blood from the left atrium and drives it by the contraction of its walls into the aorta.

    right v., the cavity on the right side of the heart which receives the venous blood from the right atrium and drives it by the contraction of its walls into the pulmonary artery.

    third v., a narrow, vertically oriented cavity in the midplane below the corpus callosum, communicating with each of the lateral v.'s through the foramen of Monro.

ventricular (ven-trik'u-lar). Relating to a ventricle.

ventriculitis (ven-trik-u-li'tis) [ventricle + G. *-itis,* inflammation]. Inflammation of the ventricles of the brain.

ventriculo-. Combining form denoting a ventricle.

ventriculoatrial (V-A) (ven-trik'u-lo-a'trĭ-al). Relating to both ventricles and atria, especially to the passage of conduction.

ventric'ulocisternos'tomy [ventriculo- + L. *cisterna,* cistern, + G. *stoma,* mouth]. A surgical opening between the ventricles of the brain and the cisterna magna.

ventriculography (ven-trik-u-log'ră-fĭ) [ventriculo- + G. *graphē,* a writing]. Radiographic visualization of the ventricular system by direct injection of a contrast or radiopaque agent.

ventriculomastoidostomy (ven-trik'u-lo-mas'toy-dos'to-mĭ) [ventriculo- + mastoid, + G. *stoma,* mouth]. Surgical establishment of a communication between the lateral cerebral ventricle and the mastoid antrum for the relief of hydrocephalus.

ventriculonector (ven-trik'u-lo-nek'tor) [ventriculo- + L. *necto,* to join]. *Truncus* atrioventricularis.

ventriculoplasty (ven-trik'u-lo-plas-tĭ) [ventriculo- + G. *plassō,* to form]. Surgical repair of a defect of one of the cardiac ventricles.

ventric'ulopunc'ture. Insertion of a needle into a ventricle.

ventriculoscopy (ven-trik-u-los'ko-pĭ) [ventriculo- + G. *skopeō,* to view]. Direct instrumental inspection of a ventricle.

ventriculostomy (ven-trik-u-los'to-mĭ) [ventriculo- + G. *stoma,* mouth]. Surgical establishment of an opening in a ventricle, usually from the third to the subarachnoid space to relieve hydrocephalus.

    third v., a v. from the third ventricle to the prechiasmal and interpeduncular cisterns (Stookey-Scarff operation) or to the interpeduncular cistern (Dandy operation).

ventriculosubarachnoid (ven-trik'u-lo-sub-ă-rak'-noyd) [ventriculo- + subarachnoid]. Relating to the space occupied by the cerebrospinal fluid.

ventriculotomy (ven-trik-u-lot'o-mĭ) [ventriculo- + G. *tomē,* incision]. Incision into a ventricle.

ventriculus, pl. **ventriculi** (ven-trik'u-lus, -li) [L. dim. of *venter,* belly]. **1** [NA]. Stomach. **2** [NA]. Ventricle.

ventriduc'tion [L. *venter,* belly, + *duco,* pp. *ductus,* to lead]. Drawing toward the abdomen or abdominal wall.

ventro- [L. *venter,* belly]. Combining form meaning ventral.

ventroscopy (ven-tros'ko-pĭ) [ventro- + G. *skopeō,* to view]. Peritoneoscopy.

ventrot'omy [ventro- + G. *tomē,* incision]. Celiotomy.

venula, pl. **venulae** (ven'u-lah, -le) [L. dim. of *vena,* vein] [NA]. Venule.

ven'ular. Pertaining to venules.

venule (ven'ūl, ve'nūl). Venula; Capillary vein; a minute vein; a venous radicle continuous with a capillary.

postcapillary v.'s, v.'s in the lymph nodes, tonsils, and Peyer's patches with a high-walled endothelium, through which lymphocytes are believed to migrate.

stellate v.'s, stellate veins; star-shaped groups of v.'s in the renal cortex.

verbigeration (ver-bij-er-a'shun) [L. *verbum*, word, + *gero*, to carry about]. Constant repetition of meaningless words or phrases.

verge. An edge or margin.

anal v., transitional zone between the skin of the anal canal and the perianal skin.

vergence (ver'jens) [L. *vergo*, to incline, to turn]. Disjunctive movement of the eyes in which the fixation axes are not parallel, as in convergence or divergence.

vermi- [L. *vermis*, worm]. Combining form denoting a worm or wormlike.

vermicidal (ver-mī-si'dal) [vermi- + L. *caedo*, to kill]. Destructive to parasitic intestinal worms.

vermicide (ver'mī-sīd) [vermi- + L. *caedo*, to kill]. An agent that kills intestinal parasitic worms.

vermicular (ver-mik'u-lar) [L. *vermiculus*, dim. of *vermis*, worm]. Relating to, resembling, or moving like a worm.

vermiculation (ver-mik-u-la'shun). A wormlike movement, as in peristalsis.

vermic'ulose, vermic'ulous. 1. Infested with worms or larvae. **2.** wormlike.

ver'miform [vermi- + L. *forma*, form]. Worm-shaped.

vermifugal (ver-mif'u-gal). Anthelmintic (2).

vermifuge (ver'mī-fūj) [vermi- + L. *fugo*, to chase away]. Anthelmintic (1).

vermilionectomy (ver-mil'yon-ek'to-mī) [vermilion border + G. *ektomē*, cutting out]. Excision of the vermilion border of the lip.

ver'min [L. *vermis*, a worm]. Parasitic insects, such as lice and bedbugs.

vermination (ver'mī-na'shun). **1.** Production or breeding of worms or larvae. **2.** Infestation with vermin.

verminous (ver'mī-nus) [L. *verminosus*, wormy]. Relating to, caused by, or infested with worms, larvae, or vermin.

vermis, pl. **vermes** (ver'mis, -mēz) [L. worm] [NA]. The narrow middle zone between the two hemispheres of the cerebellum.

ver'nix caseo'sa. The fatty substance, consisting of desquamated epithelial cells and sebaceous matter, which covers the skin of the fetus.

verruca, pl. **verrucae** (vĕ-ru'kah, -ke) [L.]. Verruga; wart; a flesh-colored growth characterized by circumscribed hypertrophy of the papillae of the corium, with thickening of the malpighian, granular, and keratin layers of the epidermis, and caused by papilloma virus; also applied to epidermal verrucous tumors of nonviral etiology.

v. acumina'ta, *condyloma* acuminatum.

v. necrogen'ica, postmortem *wart.*

v. perua'na, v. peruvia'na, *verruga* peruana.

v. pla'na, flat or plane wart; a small, smooth, flat, flesh-colored wart, occurring in groups, seen especially on the face of the young.

v. planta'ris, plantar *wart.*

verruciform (vĕ-ru'sī-form) [L. *verruca*, wart, + *forma*, form]. Wart-shaped.

verrucose, verrucous (vĕr'u-kōs, vĕ-ru'kus) [L. *verrucosus*]. Resembling a wart; denoting wartlike elevations.

verruga (vĕ-ru'gah) [Sp.]. Verruca.

v. perua'na, v. peruvia'na, verruca peruana or peruviana; Peruvian wart; a stage or cutaneous form of Oroya fever, characterized by an eruption of soft conical or pedunculated papules.

version (ver'zhun) [L. *verto*, pp. *versus*, to turn]. **1.** Displacement of the uterus, with a tilting of the entire organ without bending upon itself. **2.** Change of position of the fetus in the uterus, occurring spontaneously or effected by manipulation. **3.** Inclination. **4.** Conjugate rotation of the eyes in the same direction.

bimanual v., bipolar v., turning of the baby *in utero,* performed by the hands acting upon both extremities of the fetus; it may be external or combined.

cephalic v., v. in which the fetus is turned so that the head presents.

combined v., bipolar v. by means of one hand in the vagina, the other on the abdominal wall.

external v., v. performed entirely by external manipulation.

internal v., v. performed by means of one hand within the vagina.

pelvic v., v. by means of which a transverse or oblique presentation is converted into a pelvic one.

podalic v., a manual procedure that results in a podalic extraction.

spontaneous v., turning of the fetus effected by the unaided contraction of the uterine muscle.

vertebra, pl. **vertebrae** (ver'te-brah, -bre) [L. joint, fr. *verto*, to turn] [NA]. One of the segments of the spinal column, usually 33: 7 cervical, 12 thoracic, 5 lumbar, 5 fused sacral (sacrum), and 4 fused coccygeal (coccyx).

basilar v., the lowest lumbar v.

cranial v., a segment of the skull regarded as homologous with a segment of the vertebral column.

v. denta'ta, axis (3).

v. pla'na, spondylitis with reduction of vertebral body to a thin disk.

ver'tebral. Relating to a vertebra or the vertebrae.

Vertebrata (ver-te-bra'tah) [L. *vertebratus,* jointed]. The vertebrates, a major division of the phylum Chordata, consisting of those animals with a dorsal nerve cord enclosed in a cartilaginous or bony spinal column; includes several classes of fishes, and the amphibians, reptiles, birds, and mammals.

vertebrate (ver'te-brāt). **1.** Having a vertebral column. **2.** A member of the *Vertebrata*.

vertebrectomy (ver-te-brek'to-mĭ) [vertebra + G. *ektomē*, excision]. Exsection of a vertebra.

vertebro-. Combining form denoting a vertebra or vertebral.

vertebrochondral (ver'te-bro-kon'dral) [vertebro- + G. *chondros*, cartilage]. Vertebrocostal (2); denoting the three false ribs (8th, 9th, and 10th), which are connected with the vertebrae at one extremity and the costal cartilages at the other, these cartilages not articulating directly with the sternum.

ver'tebrocos'tal [vertebro- + L. *costa*, rib]. **1.** Costovertebral. **2.** Vertebrochondral.

ver'tebroster'nal. Sternovertebral.

vertex, pl. **vertices** (ver'teks, ver'tĭ-sēz) [L. whirl, whorl] **1** [NA]. The crown of the head; the topmost point of the vault of the skull. **2.** In obstetrics, the portion of the fetal head bounded by the planes of the trachelobregmatic and biparietal diameters, with the posterior fontanel at the apex.

ver'tical. **1.** Relating to the vertex, or crown of head. **2.** Perpendicular to the horizontal.

verticillate (ver'tĭ-sil'āt). Whorled.

vertiginous (ver-tij'ĭ-nus). Relating to or suffering from vertigo.

vertigo (ver'tĭ-go) [L. *vertigo*, dizziness, fr. *verto*, to turn]. A sensation of irregular or whirling motion, either of oneself (subjective), or of external objects (objective).

auditory v., Ménière's *disease*.

gastric v., Trousseau's syndrome (1); v. symptomatic of disease of the stomach.

labyrinthine v., Ménière's *disease*.

ocular v., v. attributed to refractive errors or imbalance of the extrinsic muscles.

organic v., v. due to a lesion of the brain.

postural v., v. which occurs with change of position, usually from lying or sitting to standing position.

vesic-. See vesico-.

vesica, pl. **vesicae** (ves'ĭ-kah, -ke) [L.] **1** [NA]. A bladder; a distensible musculomembranous organ serving as a receptacle for fluid. **2.** Any hollow structure or sac, normal or pathologic, containing a serous fluid.

v. fel'lea [NA], gallbladder; cholecyst; cholecystis; a pear-shaped receptacle, on the inferior surface of the liver between the right and the quadrate lobes, which serves as a storage reservoir for bile.

v. prostat'ica, *utriculus* prostaticus.

v. urina'ria [NA], urinary bladder; a musculomembranous elastic receptacle serving as a storage place for the urine.

vesical (ves'ĭ-kal). Relating to any bladder, especially the urinary bladder.

ves'icant. An agent that produces blisters.

vesication (ves-ĭ-ka'shun). Vesiculation (1).

vesicle (ves'ĭ-kl) [L. *vesicula,* a blister, dim. of *vesica,* bladder]. **1.** Vesicula; a small bladder-like structure. **2.** A small, circumscribed elevation of the skin, containing serum. See also bleb; blister; bulla. **3.** A small sac containing liquid or gas.

acrosomal v., a v. derived from the Golgi apparatus during spermiogenesis whose limiting membrane adheres to the nuclear envelope; together with the acrosomal granule within, it spreads in a thin layer over the pole of the nucleus to form the acrosomal cap.

allantoic v., the hollow portion of the allantois.

auditory v., otic v.; one of the paired sacs of invaginated ectoderm that develop into the membranous labyrinth of the internal ear.

blastodermic v., blastocyst.

cerebral v., **encephalic v.**, primary brain v.; each of the three divisions of the early embryonic brain; anterior, prosencephalon; middle, mesencephalon, posterior, rhombencephalon.

lens v., **lenticular v.**, in the embryo, the ectodermal invagination that forms opposite the optic cup and is the primordium of the lens.

ocular v., **optic v.**, in the embryo, one of the paired evaginations of the forebrain from which develop the sensory and pigment layers of the retina.

otic v., auditory v.

primary brain v., cerebral v.

seminal v., seminal gland; gonecyst; one of two glandular structures that is a diverticulum of the ductus deferens and secretes a component of semen.

synaptic v.'s small, intracellular, membrane-bound v.'s at a synaptic junction that contain the transmitter substance which, in chemical synapses, mediates the passage of nerve impulses across the junction.

umbilical v., yolk *sac*.

vesico-, **vesic-**. Combining forms denoting a vesica or vesicle. See also vesiculo-.

vesicocele (ves'ĭ-ko-sēl). Cystocele.

vesicoclysis (ves-ĭ-kok'lĭ-sis) [vesico- + G. *klysis,* a washing out]. Washing out, or lavage, of the urinary bladder.

ves'icofixa'tion. Suture of the uterus to the bladder wall.

vesicorectostomy (ves'ĭ-ko-rek-tos'to-mĭ) [vesico- + rectum + G. *stoma,* mouth]. Cystoproctostomy; cystorectostomy; surgical urinary tract diversion by anastomosis of the posterior bladder wall to the rectum.

vesicosigmoidostomy (ves'ĭ-ko-sig-moy-dos'to-mĭ) [vesico- + sigmoid + G. *stoma,* mouth]. Surgical formation of a communication between the bladder and the sigmoid colon.

vesicospi'nal. Denoting the spinal neural mechanisms that control retention and evacuation of urine by the bladder.

vesicostomy (ves-ĭ-kos'to-mĭ) [vesico- + G. *stoma,* mouth]. Surgical creation of a stoma between the anterior bladder wall and the skin of the lower abdomen, for temporary or permanent lower urinary tract diversion.

vesicotomy (ves-ĭ-kot'o-mĭ). Cystotomy.

vesicula, pl. **vesiculae** (vĕ-sik'u-lah, -le) [L.] [NA]. Vesicle (1).

vesic'ular. 1. Relating to a vesicle. **2.** Vesiculous; vesiculate (2); characterized by or containing vesicles.

vesic'ulate. 1. To become vesicular. **2.** Vesicular (2).

vesiculation (vĕ-sik-u-la'shun). **1.** Blistering; vesication; formation of vesicles. **2.** Presence of a number of vesicles.

vesiculectomy (vĕ-sik'u-lek'to-mĭ) [L. *vesicula,* vesicle, + G. *ektomē,* excision]. Resection of a portion or all of each of the seminal vesicles.

vesiculiform (vĕ-sek'u-lĭ-form). Resembling a vesicle.

vesiculitis (vĕ-sik-u-li'tis) [L. *vesicula,* vesicle, + G. *-itis,* inflammation]. Inflammation of any vesicle; especially of a seminal vesicle.

vesiculo-. Combining form denoting vesicle.

vesic'ulocav'ernous. Both vesicular and cavernous; denoting **(1)** an auscultatory sound, and **(2)** the structure of certain neoplasms.

vesiculography (vĕ-sik'u-lo-log'ră-fĭ) [vesiculo- + G. *graphō,* to write]. Radiography of the seminal vesicles.

vesic'ulopap'ular. Pertaining to or consisting of a combination of vesicles and papules.

vesiculoprostatitis (vĕ-sik'u-lo-pros'tă-ti'tis) [vesiculo- + prostate + G. *-itis,* inflammation]. Inflammation of the bladder and prostate.

vesic'ulopus'tular. Pertaining to a mixed eruption of vesicles and pustules.

vesiculotomy (vĕ-sik-u-lot'o-mĭ) [vesiculo- + G. *tomē,* incision]. Surgical division of the seminal vesicles.

vesic'ulotu'bular. Denoting an auscultatory sound having a vesicular and a tubular quality.

vesiculotympanic (vĕ-sik'u-lo-tim-pan'ik). Denoting a percussion sound having a vesicular and a tympanic quality.

vesic'ulous. Vesicular (2).

ves'sel [O. Fr. fr. L. *vascellum,* dim. of *vas*]. Vas; a duct or canal conveying any liquid, such as blood, lymph, chyle, or semen.

    absorbent v.'s, *vasa* lymphatica.

    afferent v., *vas* afferens.

    blood v., see under B.

    chyle v., lacteal (2).

    collateral v., a branch of an artery running parallel with the parent trunk.

    efferent v., *vas* efferens.

    lacteal v., lacteal (2).

    lymph v.'s, lymphatic v.'s, *vasa* lymphatica.

    nutrient v., *arteria* nutricia.

    vitelline v.'s, *arteria* vitellina and *vena* vitellina.

vestibula (ves-tib'u-lah). Plura of vestibulum.

vestibular (ves-tib'u-lar). Relating to a vestibule, especially of the ear.

vestibule (ves'tĭ-būl) [L. *vestibulum,* antechamber]. Vestibulum. **1.** A small cavity or space at the entrance of a canal. **2.** Specifically, of the ear, the central cavity of the osseous labyrinth that communicates with the semicircular canals and the cochlea.

    aortic v., the part of the left ventricle of the heart below the aortic orifice allowing room for segments of the closed aortic valve.

    v. of mouth, buccal cavity; that part of the mouth bounded by the lips, cheeks, and gums.

    v. of nose, the anterior part of the nasal cavity, enclosed by cartilage.

    v. of vagina, the space behind the glans clitoridis, between the labia minora, containing openings of the vagina, urethra, and ducts of the greater vestibular glands.

vestibulo-. Combining form denoting vestibule, vestibulum.

vestibulocochlear (ves-tib'u-lo-kok'le-ar). **1.** Relating to the vestibulum and cochlea of the ear. **2.** Statoacoustic.

vestib'uloplasty [vestibulo- + G. *plassō,* to form]. A surgical procedure to restore alveolar ridge height by lowering muscles attaching to the buccal, labial, and lingual aspects of the jaws.

vestibulotomy (ves-tib-u-lot'o-mĭ) [vestibulo- + G. *tomē,* incision]. Surgical opening into the vestibule of the labyrinth.

vestibulum, pl. **vestibula** (ves-tib'u-lum, -lah) [L.] [NA]. Vestibule.

vestige (ves'tij) [L. *vestigium,* footprint (trace)]. A rudimentary structure, the degenerated remains of which occurs as an entity in the embryo or fetus.

vestigial (ves-tij'ĭ-al). Relating to a vestige.

veterinarian (vet'er-ĭ-nĕr'ĭ-an) [see veterinary]. One who is licensed to practice or who holds an academic degree in veterinary medicine.

veterinary (vet'er-ĭ-nĕr-ĭ) [L. *veterinarius,* fr. *veterina,* beast of burden]. Relating to the diseases of animals.

viability (vi-ă-bil'ĭ-tĭ) [Fr. *viabilité* fr. L. *vita,* life]. Capability of living; the state of being viable.

viable (vi'ă-bl) [Fr. fr. *vie,* life, fr. L. *vita*]. Capable of living; denoting a fetus sufficiently developed to live outside of the uterus.

Vibrio (vib'rĭ-o) [L. *vibro,* to vibrate]. A genus of Gram-negative bacteria (family Spirillaceae) that are saprophytes in salt and fresh water and in soil; others are parasites or pathogens. Type species is *V. cholerae.*

    V. chol'erae, comma bacillus; Koch's bacillus (2); a species that produces a soluble exotoxin (permeability factor) that seems to be the cause of Asiatic cholera in human beings; the type species of genus *V.*

    V. fe'tus, *Campylobacter fetus.*

    V. parahaemolyt'icus, a marine species which may contaminate shellfish and cause human gastroenteritis.

vibriosis (vib-rĭ-o'sis). Infection caused by species of *Vibrio*.

vibrissa, pl. **vibrissae** (vi-bris'ah, -bris'e) [L. *vibrissae*, fr. *vibro*, to quiver] [NA]. One of the hairs growing at the anterior nares.

vibrocardiogram (vi'bro-kar'dĭ-o-gram) [L. *vibro*, to shake, + G. *kardia*, heart, + *gramma*, a drawing]. A graphic record of chest vibrations produced by hemodynamic events of the cardiac cycle; provides an indirect externally recorded measurement of isometric contraction and ejection times.

vicarious (vi-kăr'ĭ-us) [L. *vicarius*, fr. *vicis*, supplying place of]. Acting as a substitute; occurring in an abnormal situation.

vidarabine (vi-dăr'ăbēn). A purine nucleoside obtained from *Streptomyces antibioticus* and used to treat herpes simplex infections.

vid'ian. Named after or described by Vidius.

vigilambulism (vij-ĭ-lam'bu-lizm) [L. *vigil*, awake, alert, + *ambulo*, to walk about]. A condition of unconsciousness regarding one's surroundings, with automatism, resembling somnambulism but occurring in the waking state.

vil'li. Plural of villus.

villiki'nin [L. *villus*, shaggy hair (of beasts), + *kineō*, to move]. A postulated hormone said to stimulate the movement of intestinal villi.

villo'ma. Papilloma.

vil'lose. Villous (2).

villositis (vil-o-si'tis). Inflammation of the villous surface of the placenta.

villosity (vĭ-los'ĭ-tĭ). An aggregation of villi.

vil'lous. 1. Relating to villi. **2.** Villose; covered with villi.

villusectomy (vil-us-ek'to-mĭ) [villus + G. *ektomē*, excision]. Synovectomy.

villus, pl. **villi** (vil'us, vil'i) [L. shaggy hair (of beasts)] **1** [NA]. A projection from the surface, especially of a mucous membrane. See also microvillus. **2.** An elongated dermal papilla projecting into an intraepidermal vesicle or cleft.

   arachnoid villi, *granulationes* arachnoideales.

   chorionic villi, vascular processes of the chorion of the embryo entering into the formation of the placenta.

   intestinal villi, projections of the mucous membrane of the intestine that are leaf-shaped in the duodenum and become shorter, more finger-shaped, and sparser in the ileum; serve as sites of adsorption.

vinblas'tine sulfate. A dimeric alkaloid obtained from *Vinca rosea* that arrests mitosis in metaphase and exhibits antimetabolic activity; used in the treatment of Hodgkin's disease, choriocarcinoma, acute and chronic leukemias, and other neoplastic diseases.

vincaleukoblastine (ving'kă-lu-ko-blas'tēn). Vinblastine sulfate.

vincris'tine sulfate. A dimeric alkaloid obtained from *Vinca rosea*, with antineoplastic activity is similar to that of vinblastine sulfate, but more useful in treating lymphocytic lymphosarcoma and acute leukemia.

vinculum, pl. **vincula** (ving'ku-lum, -lah) [L. a fetter, fr. *vincio*, to bind] [NA]. A frenum, frenulum, or ligament.

   vin'cula ten'dinum [NA], **vincula of tendons,** synovial frenula; fibrous bands that extend from the flexor tendons of the fingers and toes to the capsules of the interphalangeal joints and to the phalanges; convey small vessels to the tendons.

vinegar (vin'e-gar) [Fr. *vin*, wine, + *aigre*, sour]. Acetum; impure dilute acetic acid, made from wine, cider, malt, etc.

vi'nyl. Ethenyl; the hydrocarbon radical, $CH_2 = CH-$.

   v. chloride, a substance used in the plastics industry and suspected of being a potent carcinogen in man.

   v. ether, divinyl ether.

vi'nylben'zene. Styrene.

vi'nyleth'yl ether. Ethylvinyl ether.

violet (vi'o-let) [L. *viola*]. The color evoked by wavelengths of the visible spectrum shorter than 450 nm.

   visual v., iodopsin.

vipoma (vī-po'mah) [*v*asoactive *i*ntestinal *p*olypeptide + G. *-ōma*, tumor]. An endocrine tumor, usually originating in the pancreas, that produces a vasoactive intestinal polypeptide believed to cause profound cardiovascular and electrolyte changes with vasodilatory hypotension, watery diarrhea, hypokalemia, and dehydration.

vi'ral. Pertaining to or caused by a virus.

viremia (vi-re'mĭ-ah) [virus + G. *haima*, blood]. Presence of a virus in the bloodstream.

virgin (ver'jin) [L. *virgo* (*virgin-*), maiden]. **1.** One who has never had sexual intercourse. **2.** Virginal (2); fresh; unused; uncontaminated.

virginal (ver'jĭ-nal) [L. *virginalis*]. **1.** Relating to a virgin. **2.** Virgin (2).

virginity (ver-jin'ĭ-tĭ) [L. *virginitas*]. The state of being a virgin.

-viridae. Suffix denoting a virus family.

virile (vīr'il) [L. *virilis*, masculine, fr. *vir*, man]. **1.** Relating to the male sex. **2.** Manly, strong, masculine. **3.** Possessing virile traits.

virilescence (vīr-ĭ-les'ens). Assumption of male characteristics by the female.

virilism (vīr'ĭ-lizm) [L. *virilis*, masculine]. Possession of mature masculine somatic characteristics by a female.

virility (vĭ-ril'ĭ-tĭ) [L. *virilitas*, manhood]. The condition of being virile.

virilization (vīr-ĭ-lĭ-za'shun). Introduction or development of virilism.

virilizing (vīr'ĭ-li-zing). Causing virilism.

-virinae. Suffix denoting a subfamily of viruses.

virion (vī'rĭ-on, vīr'). An elementary virus particle composed of a central core (nucleoid) containing either DNA or RNA, surrounded by a protein covering (capsid); this nucleic acid-protein complex (nucleocapsid) may be the complete v. (as in adenoviruses and picornaviruses) or may be surrounded by an "envelope" (as in herpetroviruses and myxoviruses).

virol'ogist. A specialist in virology.

virology (vi-rol'o-ji, vī-) [virus + G. *logos*, study]. The study of viruses and of virus disease.

virucidal (vi-ru-si'dal). Destructive to a virus.

virucide (vi'ru-sid) [virus + L. *caedo*, to kill]. An agent active against virus infections.

virulence (vīr'u-lens) [L. *virulentus*, poisonous]. The quality of being poisonous; the disease-evoking power of a microorganism in a given host.

virulent (vīr'u-lent) [L. *virulentus*, poisonous]. Extremely poisonous; denoting a markedly pathogenic microorganism.

viruliferous (vi-ru-lif'er-us). Conveying virus.

viruria (vi-ru-rī'ah) [virus + G. *ouron*, urine]. Presence of living viruses in the urine.

-virus. Suffix denoting a genus of viruses.

vi'rus, pl. **vi'ruses** [L. poison]. **1.** Formerly, the specific agent of an infectious disease. **2.** Filtrable v.; ultravirus; specifically, a term for a group of microbes which with few exceptions are capable of passing through fine filters that retain most bacteria, and are incapable of growth or reproduction apart from living cells. Classification of v.'s depends upon characteristics of virions as well as upon mode of transmission, host range, symptomatology, and other factors. **3.** Relating to or caused by a v.; *e.g.*, virus disease.

adenoidal-pharyngeal-conjunctival (A-P-C) v., adenovirus.

amphotropic v., an oncornavirus that does not produce disease in its natural host but does replicate in tissue culture cells of the host species and also in cells from other species.

attenuated v., a variant strain of a pathogenic v., so modified as to excite the production of protective antibodies, yet not producing the specific disease.

avian leukosis-sarcoma v., avian leukosis-sarcoma *complex.*

bacterial v., a v. which "infects" bacteria; a bacteriophage or a filamentous bacterial v.

Bornholm disease v., epidemic pleurodynia v.

California v., the type strain of a serologic group of the genus *Bunyavirus* which causes *encephalitis.*

CELO v. [chicken embryo *lethal orphan*], a v. with characteristics of adenovirus.

chickenpox v., varicella-zoster v.

Coe v., a v. serologically identical with the A-21 strain of coxsackievirus; causes common cold-like disease.

Colorado tick fever v., a v. (genus *Orbivirus*) transmitted by the tick, *Dermacentor andersoni,* and the cause of Colorado tick fever.

common cold v., any of the numerous strains of v. etiologically associated with the common cold; chiefly the rhinoviruses, but also strains of adenovi-

rus, coxsackievirus, ECHO v., and parainfluenza v.

croup-associated (CA) v., parainfluenza 2 v.

cytopathogenic v., a v. whose multiplication leads to degenerative changes in the host cell.

defective v., a v. particle that contains insufficient nucleic acid to provide for production of all essential viral components; consequently, infection is not produced except under certain conditions.

dengue v., a v. (genus *Flavivirus*), transmitted by *Aedes* mosquitoes, that is the etiologic agent of dengue.

DNA v., a major group of animal v.'s in which the core consists of deoxyribonucleic acid; includes adenoviruses, papovaviruses, herpesviruses, and poxviruses.

EB v., Epstein-Barr v.

Ebola v., a v. that causes viral hemorrhagic fever.

ECHO v. [*enteric cytopathogenic human orphan*], echovirus; an enterovirus belonging to the Picornaviridae, associated with fever and aseptic meningitis; some serotypes appear to cause mild respiratory disease.

ecotropic v., an oncornavirus that does not produce disease in its natural host but does replicate in tissue culture cells derived from the host species.

encephalomyocarditis (EMC) v., a picornavirus that causes febrile illness with CNS involvement.

enteric v.'s, v.'s of the genus Enterovirus.

enteric orphan v.'s, enteroviruses isolated from man and other animals, orphan implying lack of known association with disease when isolated; many are now known to be pathogenic.

epidemic gastroenteritis v., gastroenteritis v. type A; an unclassified v. that is the cause of epidemic nonbacterial gastroenteritis.

epidemic keratoconjunctivitis v., an adenovirus (type 8) causing epidemic keratoconjunctivitis, and associated with swimming pool conjunctivitis.

epidemic parotitis v., mumps v.

epidemic pleurodynia v., Bornholm disease v.; a v. (genus *Enterovirus*) that causes epidemic pleurodynia.

Epstein-Barr v., EB v.; a herpetovirus found in cell cultures of Burkitt's lymphoma; antibodies reactive with this v. have been reported in cases of infectious mononucleosis.

filtrable v., virus (2).

fixed v., rabies v. of the utmost possible virulence for rabbits, obtained by numerous passages through this experimental host.

foamy v.'s., retroviruses (subfamily Spumavirinae), found in primates and other mammals, so named because of lacelike changes produced in monkey kidney cells.

gastroenteritis v. type A, epidemic gastroenteritis v.

gastroenteritis v. type B, rotavirus.

German measles v., rubella v.

HA1 v., HA2 v., see parainfluenza v.'s.

helper v., a v. whose replication renders it possible for a defective v. to develop into fully infectious v.

hemadsorption v. 1, hemadsorption v. 2, see parainfluenza v.'s.

hepatitis A v. (HAV), infectious hepatitis v.; the causative agent of viral hepatitis type A.

hepatitis B v. (HBV), serum hepatitis v.; the causative agent of viral hepatitis type B.

herpes simplex v., herpesvirus (type 1 or 2).

herpes zoster v., varicella-zoster v.

human papilloma v., infectious warts v.

human T-cell lymphocytotrophic v. (HTLV), a group of human retroviruses, of which four types have been identified; HTLV-III is the etiologic agent of AIDS.

infectious hepatitis v., hepatitis A v.

infectious warts v., verruca vulgaris or human papilloma v.; an icosahedral DNA v. (genus *Papillomavirus*) which causes certain kinds of warts.

influenza v.'s, v.'s (family Orthomyxoviridae) that cause influenza and influenza-like infections; v.'s included are types A and B (genus *Influenzavirus*) causing influenza A and B, and type C, which probably belongs to a separate genus and causes influenza C.

Japanese B encephalitis v., a v. of the genus *Flavivirus* (group B arbovirus) normally present as an inapparent infection, but may cause febrile response and sometimes encephalitis; wild birds are probably the natural hosts and culicine mosquitoes the vectors.

Lassa v., an arenavirus that causes Lassa fever.

lymphocytic choriomeningitis (LCM) v., an RNA v. (family Arenaviridae) that causes lymphocytic choriomeningitis; infection may be inapparent, but sometimes the v. causes influenza-like disease, meningitis, or rarely meningoencephalomyelitis.

Marburg v., an unclassified, seemingly RNA-containing v. that causes Marburg disease.

masked v., a v. ordinarily occurring in the host in a noninfective state, but which may be activated and demonstrated by special procedures.

measles v., rubeola v.; an RNA v. (genus *Morbillivirus*) that causes measles in man.

mumps v., epidemic parotitis v.; a v. (genus *Paramyxovirus*) that causes parotitis and is transmitted by infected salivary secretions.

Murray Valley encephalitis (MVE) v., a group B arbovirus of the genus *Flavivirus* that causes Murray Valley encephalitis and transmitted by *Culex* mosquitoes.

naked v., a v. consisting only of a nucleocapsid, that does not possess an enclosing envelope.

negative strand v., a v. the genome of which is a strand of RNA that is complementary to mRNA also carries RNA polymerases necessary for the synthesis of mRNA.

oncogenic v., tumor v.; a v. of one of the two groups of tumor-evoking v.'s: RNA tumor v.'s (oncornaviruses) or DNA v.'s.

orphan v.'s, v.'s, such as enteric orphan v.'s, which are originally not specifically associated with disease but later may be shown to be pathogenic.

papilloma v.'s, DNA v.'s of the genus *Papillomavirus*.

parainfluenza v.'s, v.'s of the genus *Paramyxovirus*, of five types, including **Parainfluenza 1 v.,** which includes hemadsorption v. 2 (HA2) that causes acute laryngotracheitis, **Parainfluenza 2 v.** (croup-associated or CA v.), associated with acute laryngotracheitis or croup and minor upper respiratory infections, and **Parainfluenza 3 v.** (hemadsorption v. 1 or HA1), isolated from cases of pharyngitis, bronchiolitis, and pneumonia, and causes occasional respiratory infection.

phlebotomus fever v.'s, an unclassified serologic group of arboviruses morphologically like *Bunyavirus* but antigenically unrelated, transmitted by *Phlebotomus papatasii* (sandfly), and causing phlebotomus fever.

poliomyelitis v., poliovirus hominis; the picornavirus (genus *Enterovirus*) causing poliomyelitis; serologic types 1, 2, and 3 are recognized, type 1 being responsible for most paralytic poliomyelitis and most epidemics.

rabies v., a rather large bullet-shaped v. of the genus *Lyssavirus* that causes rabies.

respiratory syncytial (Rs) v., an RNA-containing v. (genus *Pneumovirus*) that causes minor respiratory infections in adults, but is capable of causing bronchitis and bronchopneumonia in young children.

RNA v., a group of v.'s in which the core consists of RNA; a major group of animal v.'s that includes the families Picornaviridae, Reoviridae, Togaviridae, Bunyaviridae, Arenaviridae, Paramyxoviridae, Retroviridae, Coronaviridae, Orthomyxoviridae, and Rhabdoviridae.

RNA tumor v.'s, v.'s of the subfamily Oncovirinae.

Rous-associated v. (RAV), a leukemia v. (leukemia-sarcoma complex) which by phenotypic mixing with defective (noninfectious) strain of Rous sarcoma v. effects production of infectious sarcoma v. with envelope antigenicity of the RAV.

Rous sarcoma v. (RSV), a sarcoma-producing v. of the avian leukosis-sarcoma complex.

rubella v., German measles v.; an RNA v. (genus *Rubivirus*) that causes rubella (German measles).

rubeola v., measles v.

serum hepatitis v., hepatitis B v.

slow v., a v., or virus-like agent, etiologically associated with a slow virus disease.

smallpox v., variola v.

St. Louis encephalitis v., a group B arbovirus normally present as inapparent infection, but sometimes a cause of encephalitis.

street v., the virulent rabies v. from a rabid domestic animal which has contracted the disease in the usual way, from a bite or scratch of another animal.

tick-borne encephalitis v., an arbovirus (genus *Flavivirus*) that occurs in two subtypes (Central European, Eastern), causing two forms of encephalitis; vectors are ticks of the genus *Ixodes*.

tumor v., oncogenic v.

vaccinia v., the poxvirus (genus *Orthopoxvirus*) used in the immunization against variola (smallpox); closely related serologically to the v.'s of variola and cowpox, but certain differences indicate that they may be distinct but closely related strains of a variola-vaccinia-cowpox complex.

varicella-zoster v., chickenpox or herpes zoster v.; a herpetovirus, morphologically identical to herpes simplex v., that causes varicella (chickenpox) and herpes zoster.

variola v., smallpox v.; a poxvirus (genus *Orthopoxvirus*) that causes smallpox.

verruca vulgaris v., infectious warts v.

visceral disease v., cytomegalovirus.

xenotropic v., an oncornavirus that does not produce disease in its natural host and replicates only in tissue culture cells derived from a different species.

yellow fever v., an arbovirus, the type species of the genus *Flavivirus*, that is the cause of yellow fever and is transmitted by the *Aedes-Haemagogus* complex of mosquitoes.

viscera (vis'er-ah). Plural of viscus.

viscerad (vis'er-ad) [viscera + L. *ad*, to]. In a direction toward the viscera.

visceral (vis'er-al). Splanchnic; relating to the viscera.

visceralgia (vis-er-al'jĭ-ah) [viscera + G. *algos*, pain]. Pain in any viscera.

viscero- [L. *viscera*, internal organs]. Combining form denoting the viscera. See also splanchno-.

viscerogenic (vis-er-o-jen'ik) [viscero- + G. *-gen*, producing]. Of visceral origin; denoting a number of sensory and other reflexes.

visceroinhibitory (vis'er-o-in-hib'ĭ-to-rĭ). Restricting or arresting the functional activity of the viscera.

visceromegaly (vis'er-o-meg'ă-lĭ) [viscero- + G. *megas*, large]. Splanchnomegaly; organomegaly; abnormal enlargement of the viscera.

vis'ceromo'tor. Relating to or controlling movement in the viscera or a movement having a relation to the viscera.

visceropleural (vis'er-o-plu'ral). Pleurovisceral; relating to the pleural and thoracic viscera.

visceroptosis (vis'er-op-to'sis) [viscero- + G. *ptōsis*, a falling]. Splanchnoptosis; descent of the viscera from their normal positions.

vis'cerosen'sory. Relating to the sensory innervation of internal organs.

visceroskel'etal. Splanchnoskeletal; relating to the visceroskeleton.

vis'ceroskel'eton. 1. Any bony formation in an organ; may also include the cartilaginous rings of the trachea and bronchi. **2.** Splanchnoskeleton; that part of the skeleton protecting the viscera.

viscerosomatic (vis'er-o-so-mat'ik) [viscero- + G. *sōma*, body]. Relating to the viscera and the body.

viscerotrophic (vis'er-o-trof'ik) [viscero- + G. *trophē*, nourishment]. Relating to any trophic change determined by visceral conditions.

viscerotropic (vis'er-o-trop'ik) [viscero- + G. *tropē*, a turning]. Affecting the viscera.

viscid (vis'id) [L. *viscidus*, sticky]. Adhesive; sticky; glutinous.

viscidity (vĭ-sid'ĭ-tĭ). Stickiness; adhesiveness.

viscosity (vis-kos'ĭ-tĭ) [L. *viscositas*, fr. *viscosus*, viscous]. Resistance to flow or alteration of shape by a substance as a result of molecular cohesion.

viscous (vis'kus). Viscid; sticky; adhesive; marked by high viscosity.

viscus, pl. **viscera** (vis'kus, vis'er-ah) [L. the soft parts, internal organs]. An organ of the digestive, respiratory, urogenital, and endocrine systems as well as the spleen, the heart, and great vessels.

vision (vizh'un) [L. *visio*, to see]. The act of seeing. See also sight.

achromatic v., achromatopsia.

binocular v., v. with a single image, by both eyes simultaneously.

central v., direct v.; v. produced by the rays falling on the fovea centralis.

chromatic v., chromatopsia.

direct v., central v.

double v., diplopia.

indirect v., peripheral v.

multiple v., polyopia.

night v., v. that improves in dim light.

oscillating v., oscillopsia.

peripheral v., indirect v.; resulting from retinal stimulation beyond the macula.

photopic v., photopia; v. when the eye is light-adapted.

scotopic v., scotopia; v. when the eye is dark-adapted.

stereoscopic v., the perception of two images as one by means of fusing the impressions on both retinas.

triple v., triplopia.

tunnel v., a narrowing of the visual field, as though one were looking through a hollow cylinder or tube.

visual (vizh'u-al). Relating to vision.

visual purple. Rhodopsin.

visuognosis (vizh'u-og-no'sis) [L. *visus*, vision, + G. *gnōsis*, knowledge]. Recognition and understanding of visual impressions.

visuosensory (vizh'u-o-sen'so-rĭ). Pertaining to the perception of visual stimuli.

vi'tal [L. *vitalis*, fr. *vita*, life]. Relating or necessary to life.

vitality (vi-tal'ĭ-tĭ). Vital force or energy.

vital red. Trisodium salt of a sulfonated diazo dye, used as a vital stain.

vi'tals. Viscera.

vital statistics. Numerical facts concerned with data pertaining to birth, health, disease, and death.

vitamer (vi'tă-mer). One of two or more similar compounds capable of fulfilling a specific vitamin function in the body.

vitamin (vi'tă-min) [L. *vita*, life, + amine]. One of a group of organic substances, present in minute amount in natural foodstuffs, that are essential to normal metabolism.

fat-soluble v.'s, those v.'s soluble in fat solvents (nonpolar solvents) and insoluble in water, marked in chemical structure by the presence of large hydrocarbon moieties in the molecule.

v. A, any β-ionone derivative, except provitamin A carotenoids, possessing qualitatively the biological activity of retinol; deficiency interferes with the production and resynthesis of rhodopsin, thereby causing night blindness, and produces a keratinizing metaplasia of epithelial cells that may result in xerophthalmia, keratosis, susceptibility to infections, and retarded growth.

v. B, a group of water-soluble substance originally considered as one v.

v. B_x, *p*-aminobenzoic acid.

v. B_1, thiamin.

v. B_6, pyridoxine and related compounds.

v. B_{12}, cyanocob(III)alamin; antipernicious anemia factor; generic descriptor for compounds exhibiting the biological activity of cyanocobalamin.

v. B complex, a pharmaceutical term applied to drug products containing a mixture of the B v.'s usually thiamin, riboflavin, nicotinamide, pantolhenic acid, and pyridoxine.

v. C, ascorbic acid.

v. D, generic descriptor for all steroids exhibiting the biological activity of ergocalciferol (or cholecalciferol); promote the proper utilization of calcium and phosphorus, thereby producing growth in young children together with proper bone and tooth formation.

v. D_2, ergocalciferol.

v. D_3, cholecalciferol.

v. E, (1) α-tocopherol; (2) generic descriptor of tocol and tocotrienol derivatives possessing the biological acitivity of α-tocopherol; contained in various oils, whole grain cereals (constitutes the nonsaponifiable fraction) certain animal tissue, and lettuce.

v. K, antihemorrhagic factor; generic descriptor for fat-soluble, thermostable compounds with the biological activity of phylloquinone; found in alfalfa, hog liver, fish meal, and vegetable oils; essential for formation of normal amounts of prothrombin.

v. P, capillary permeability factor; a mixture of bioflavonoids extracted from plants (especially citrus fruits) that reduces the permeability and fragility of capillaries.

vitelline (vĭ-tel'in, -ēn). Relating to the vitellus.

vitellus (vi-tel'us) [L.]. Yolk.

vitiation (vish-ĭ-a'shun) [L. *vitio*, pp. *vitiatus*, to corrupt]. A change that impairs utility or reduces efficiency.

vitiligines (vit-ĭ-lij'ĭ-nēz). Plural of vitiligo.

vitiliginous (vit-ĭ-lij'ĭ-nus). Relating to or characterized by vitiligo.

vitiligo, pl. **vitiligines** (vit-ĭ-li'go, vit-ĭ-lij'ĭ-nēz) [L. a skin eruption, fr. *vitium*, blemish, vice]. Piebald skin; the appearance, on otherwise normal skin, of loss of melanin with white patches of varied sizes, often symmetrically distributed.

vitrectomy (vĭ-trek'to-mĭ) [vitreous + G. *ektomē*, excision]. Removal of the vitreous by means of an instrument which simultaneously removes it by suction and cutting, and replaces it with saline or some other fluid.

vitreo-. Combining form denoting vitreous.

vit'reoden'tin. Dentin of a particular brittle hardness.

vit'reoret'inal. Relating to, or pertaining to, or affecting the limit between the retina and the corpus vitreum.

vitreous (vit're-us) [L. *vitreus*, glassy, fr. *vitrum*, glass]. 1. Glassy; resembling glass. 2. *Corpus* vitreum.

persistent anterior hyperplastic primary v., a unilateral congenital abnormality occurring in full-term infants; characterized by a retrolental fibrovascular membrane, leukocoria, microphthalmos, shallow anterior chamber, and elongated ciliary processes.

persistent posterior hyperplastic primary v., a unilateral congenital anomaly in full-term infants; associated with a congenital retinal fold and a v. membranous stalk containing remnants of hyaloid artery.

vitreum (vit're-um) [L. ntr. of *vitreus*, glassy]. *Corpus* vitreum.

vit'riol [L. *vitreolus*, glassy]. Sulfuric acid.

vivi- [L. *vivus*, alive]. Combining form denoting living, alive.

vivification (viv'ĭ-fĭ-ka'shun) [L. *vivus*, alive, + *fascio*, to make]. 1. The change of protein in food into the living matter of the cells, in the final stage of assimilation. 2. Revivification.

viviparous (vi-vip'ă-rus) [vivi- + L. *pario*, to bear]. Giving birth to living young.

vivisection (viv-ĭ-sek'shun) [vivi- + section]. Any cutting operation on a living animal for purposes of experimentation; often extended to denote any form of animal experimentation.

vivisec'tionist. One who practices vivisection.

VLDL Very low density lipoprotein.

VMA Vanillylmandelic acid.

V.M.D. See D.V.M.

vocal (vo'kal) [L. *vocalis*]. Pertaining to the voice or the organs of speech.

voice [L. *vox*]. The sound made by air passing out through the larynx and upper respiratory tract, the vocal cords being approximated and made tense.

void. To evacuate excrementitious matter.

vola (vo'lah) [L.] [NA]. Palm of the hand or sole of the foot.

vo'lar. Referring to the vola, the palm of the hand or sole of the foot.

volatile (vol'ă-til). **1.** Tending to evaporate rapidly. **2.** Tending toward violence, explosiveness, or rapid change.

volatilization (vol'ă-til-ĭ-za'shun) [fr. L. *volatilis,* volatile, fr. *volo,* pp. *volatus,* to fly]. Evaporation.

volition (vo-lish'un) [L. *volo,* fut. p. *voliturus,* to wish]. The conscious impulse to perform or not perform an act.

volitional (vo-lish'un-al). Voluntary; done by an act of will; relating to volition.

vol'ley [Fr. *volée,* fr. L. *volo,* to fly]. A synchronous group of impulses induced simultaneously by artificial stimulation of either nerve fibers or muscle fibers.

volt (V, v) [A. *Volta*]. The unit of electromotive force that will produce a current of 1 ampere in circuit that has resistance of 1 ohm.

voltage (vōl'tej). Electromotive force, pressure, or potential expressed in volts.

volt'ampere. A unit of electrical power: the product of 1 volt by 1 ampere; equivalent to 1 watt or 1/1000 kilowatt.

volume (V) (vol'yun). The space occupied by any form of matter, expressed usually in cubic millimeters, cubic centimeters, liters, etc.

   closing v., lung v. at which the flow from the lower parts of the lungs becomes severely reduced or stops during expiration.

   expiratory reserve v. (ERV), supplemental or reserve air; the maximal v. of air (about 1000 ml) that can be expelled from the lungs after a normal expiration.

   forced expiratory v. (FEV, with subscript indicating time interval in seconds); the maximal v. that can be expired in a specific time interval when starting from maximal inspiration.

   inspiratory reserve v. (IRV), complemental air; the maximal v. of air that can be inspired after a normal inspiration; inspiratory capacity less tidal v.

   mean cell v. (MCV), the average v. of red cells, calculated from the hematocrit and the red cell count, in erythrocyte indices.

   minute v., the v. of any fluid or gas moved per minute.

   packed cell v., the v. of the blood cells in a sample of blood after it has been centrifuged in a hematocrit.

   partial v,, the actual v. occupied by one species of molecule or particle in a solution; the reciprocal of the density of the molecule.

   residual v. (RV), residual air or capacity; the v. of air remaining in the lungs after a maximal expiratory effort.

   respiratory minute v., the product of tidal v. times the respiratory frequency.

   resting tidal v., the tidal v. under normal resting conditions.

   standard v., the v. of a perfect gas at standard temperature and pressure, 22.414 liters.

   stroke v., the v. pumped out of one ventricle of the heart in a single beat.

   tidal v. (V_T), tidal air; the v. of air inspired or expired in a single breath during regular breathing.

volumetric (vol-u-met'rik). Relating to measurement by volume.

voluntary (vol'un-tĕr-ĭ) [L. *voluntarius,* fr. *voluntas,* will]. Relating to or acting in obedience to the will.

volute (vo-lūt) [L. *voluta,* a scroll, fr. *volvo,* pp. *volutus,* to roll]. Rolled up; convoluted.

volvulosis (vol-vu-lo'sis). Onchocerciasis.

volvulus (vol'vu-lus) [L. *volvo,* to roll]. A twisting of the intestine causing obstruction.

vo'mer [L. ploughshare] [NA]. A flat bone of trapezoidal shape forming the inferior and posterior portion of the nasal septum; articulates with the sphenoid, ethmoid, two maxillae, and two palatine bones.

vo'merine. Relating to the vomer.

vom'it [L. *vomo,* pp. *vomitus,* to vomit]. **1.** To eject matter from the stomach through the mouth. **2.** Vomitus (2); the matter so ejected.

vomiting (vom'ĭ-ting). Emesis; ejection of matter from the stomach through the esophagus and mouth.

   dry v., retching.

   fecal v., stercoraceous v.; copremesis; ejection of fecal matter aspirated into the stomach from the intestine by repeated spasmodic contractions of the gastric muscles.

   pernicious v., uncontrollable v.

   v. of pregnancy, v. occurring in the early months of pregnancy, as in morning sickness.

   projectile v., expulsion of the contents of the stomach with great force.

   stercoraceous v., fecal v.

vom'itive, vom'itory. Emetic.

vomiturition (vom'ĭ-tu-rish'un). Retching.

vomitus (vom'ĭ-tus) [L. a vomiting, vomit]. **1.** Vomiting. **2.** Vomit (2).

vortex, pl. **vortices** (vor'teks, vor'tĭ-sēz) [L. whirlpool, whorl]. Whorl (2).

voxel (vok'sel). Contraction of volume element, the basic unit of CT reconstruction; represented as a pixel in the CT image display.

voyeur (vwah-yer'). One who practices voyeurism.

voyeurism (vwah-yer'izm) [Fr. *voir,* to see]. Scopophilia; the practice of obtaining sexual pleasure by looking the naked body or genitals of another or at erotic acts between others.

VP Vasopressin.

VR Vocal *resonance.*

VS Volumetric *solution.*

vulga'ris [L. fr. *vulgus,* a crowd]. Ordinary; of the usual type.

vul'nerary [L. *vulnerarius,* fr. *vulnus (vulner-),* wound]. Relating to, or healing, a wound.

vulsel'la, vulsel'lum [L. pincers]. Vulsella *forceps.*

vulva, pl. **vulvae** (vul'vah, vul've) [L. a wrapper or covering]. Pudendum; the external genitalia of the female, comprised of the mons pubis, labia majora and minora, clitoris, vestibule of the vagina, and the opening of the urethra and of the vagina.

vul'var, vul'val. Relating to the vulva.

vulvectomy (vul-vek'to-mĭ) [vulva + G. *ektomē,* excision]. Excision of the vulva.

vulvitis (vul-vi'tis) [vulva + G. *-itis,* inflammation]. Inflammation of the vulva.

vulvo-. Combining form denoting the vulva.

vulvovaginitis (vul'vo-vaj-ĭ-ni'tis). Inflammation of both vulva and vagina, or of the vulvovaginal glands.

V-Y-plasty. Lenghtening of tissues in one direction by incising in the lines of a V, sliding the two segments apart, and closing in the lines of a Y.

W

W Tungsten; watt.

waist (wāst) [A.S. *waext*]. The portion of the trunk between the ribs and the pelvis.

w. of the heart, in the chest x-ray, the middle segment of the cardiac silhouette, containing the pulmonary salient.

walk. The characteristic manner in which one moves on foot. See also gait.

wall [L. *vallum*]. An investing part enclosing a cavity, chamber, or any anatomical unit.

cell w., the outer layer or membrane of some animal and plant cells.

chest w., thoracic w.; in respiratory physiology, the total system of structures outside the lungs that move as a part of breathing; it includes the rib cage, diaphragm, abdominal w. and abdominal contents.

parietal w., the body w. or the somatopleure from which it is formed.

splanchnic w., the w. of one of the viscera or the splanchnopleure from which it is formed.

thoracic w., chest w.

walle'rian. Relating to or described by A. V. Waller.

wall-eye. 1. Extropia. **2.** Absence of color in the iris, or leukoma of the cornea.

wan'dering [A.S. *wandrian,* to wander]. Moving about; not fixed; abnormally motile.

ward [A.S. *weard*]. A room or hall in a hospital containing a number of beds.

warfarin sodium (war'fă-rin). An anticoagulant with the same actions as bishydroxycoumarin.

wart (wort). Verruca.

anatomical w., postmortem w.

fig w., *condyloma* acuminatum.

flat w., *verruca* plana.

genital w., *condyloma* acuminatum.

moist w., *condyloma* acuminatum.

mosaic w., plantar growth of numerous closely aggregated w.'s.

necrogenic w., postmortem w.

Peruvian w., *verruga* peruana.

pitch w., a precancerous keratotic epidermal tumor, common among workers in pitch and coal tar derivatives.

plantar w., verruca plantaris; a w. on the sole, often painful.

pointed w., *condyloma* acuminatum.

postmortem w., a tuberculous warty growth (tuberculosis cutis verrucosa) on the hand of one who performs postmortem examinations. Also called verruca necrogenica; dissection tubercle; anatomical or necrogenic w.

soft w., skin *tag.*

telangiectatic w., angiokeratoma.

tuberculous w., *tuberculosis* cutis verrucosa.

venereal w., *condyloma* acuminatum.

wash. A solution for cleansing or soothing bathing of a part.

Wassermann-fast. A term used to designate a case in which the Wassermann test remains positive despite all treatment.

wasting (wāst'ing). Emaciation.

water [A.S. *waeter*]. **1.** H_2O; a clear, odorless, tasteless liquid, solidifying at 32°F (0°C and R) and boiling at 212°F (100°C, 80°R) that is present in all animal and vegetable tissues. **2.** Euphemism for urine. **3.** A pharmacopeial preparation: clear, saturated aqueous solutions of volatile oils or other aromatic or volatile substances.

w. of crystallization, w. that unites with certain salts and is essential to their arrangement in crystalline form.

w. for injection, w. purified by distillation for the preparation of products for parenteral use.

w. of metabolism, w. formed in the body by oxidation of the hydrogen of food, the greatest amount being produced in the metabolism of fat.

mineral w., w. that contains appreciable amounts of certain salts which give to it therapeutic properties.

waterfall. Sluice; flow in vascular beds where lateral pressure tending to collapse vessels greatly exceeds venous pressure; likened to flow from a spillway over a dam, with arterial pressure being height of water behind the dam, lateral pressure being spillway height, and venous pressure being height of outflow stream below the dam.

waters. Colloquialism for amniotic *fluid.*

bag of w., colloquialism for the amniotic sac and contained amniotic fluid.

false w., a leakage of fluid prior to or in beginning labor, before the rupture of the amnion.

watt (W) [J. *Watt*]. The SI unit of electrical power: power available when the current is 1 ampere and the electromotive force is 1 volt; equal to 1 joule (107 ergs) per second or 1 voltampere.

wave [A.S. *wafian,* to fluctuate]. **1.** A movement of particles in an elastic body, solid or fluid, whereby an advancing series of alternate elevations and depressions, or expansions and condensations, is produced. **2.** A graphically represented wavelike pattern. See also entries under rhythm.

alpha w., alpha *rhythm.*

beta w., beta *rhythm.*

brain w., colloquialism for fluctuations of electric potentials recorded by the electroencephalograph.

delta w., (1) a slurring of the initial part of the upstroke of the R wave in the Wolff-Parkinson-White syndrome; (2) delta *rhythm.*

excitation w., a w. of altered electrical conditions propagated along a muscle fiber preparatory to its contraction.

F w.'s, FF w.'s, regular rapid atrial w.'s in the electrocardiogram characterizing atrial flutter.

f w.'s, ff w.'s, irregular undulations of the base line in the electrocardiogram, characterizing atrial fibrillation.

P w., the first complex of the electrocardiogram, representing depolarization of the atria; P' is retrograde or ectopic in form.

postextrasystolic T w., the T w. of the sinus beat immediately following an extrasystole.

pulse w., the progressive expansion of the arteries occurring with each contraction of the left ventricle of the heart.

Q w., the initial deflection of the QRS complex when such deflection is negative (downward).

R w., the first positive (upward) deflection of the QRS complex in the electrocardiogram; successive upward deflections within the same QRS complex are labeled R', R", etc.

S w., a negative (downward) deflection of the QRS complex following an R w; successive downward deflections within the same QRS complex are labeled S', S", etc.

T w., the next deflection in the electrocardiogram following the QRS complex; represents ventricular repolarization.

theta w., theta *rhythm.*

Traube-Herring w.'s, Traube-Herring *curves.*

U w., a positive w. following the T w. of the electrocardiogram.

V w., a large pressure w. visible in recordings from either the atrium or the incoming veins, normally produced by venous return but becoming very large when blood regurgitates through the A-V valve beyond the chamber from which the recording is made.

wave'length. The distance from one point on a wave to the next point in the same phase; *i.e.,* from peak to peak or from trough to trough.

WBC White blood *cell* or *blood count.*

WDLL Well differentiated lymphocytic *lymphoma.*

wean (wēn) [A.S. *wenian*]. **1.** To take from the breast; to deprive permanently of breast milk and to begin to nourish with other food. **2.** To gradually withdraw from a life support system.

web [A.S.]. A tissue or membrane bridging a space.

web'bing. A congenital condition apparent when adjacent structures are joined by a broad band of tissue not normally present to such a degree.

weight (wāt) [A.S. *gewiht*]. The product of the force of gravity, defined internationally as 980.665 cm/s², times the mass of the body.

apothecaries'w. [U.S.P.], a system of w.'s, used in compounding prescriptions, based on the grain; 5760 grains equal 288 scruples, 96 drams, 12 ounces, 1 pound.

atomic w., the mass in grams of 1 mole (6.02 × 10²³, atoms) of an atomic species; the mass of an atom of a chemical element in relation to the mass of an atom of carbon-12 (¹²C), which is set equal to 12.000.

avoirdupois w. [B.P.], a system of w.'s based on the grain; 7000 grains equal 256 drams, 16 ounces, 1 pound.

birth w., in humans, the first w. of an infant obtained within less than the first 60 completed minutes after birth; a full-size infant is one weighing 2500 g or more.

molecular w. (MW, mol wt), the sum of the atomic w.'s of all atoms constituting a molecule; the mass of a molecule relative to the mass of a standard atom, now ¹²C (taken as 12.000).

welt [O.E. *waelt*]. Wheal.

wen [A.S.]. Sebaceous *cyst.*

wheal (wēl) [A.S. *hwēle*]. Welt; a circumscribed evanescent area of edema of the skin, appearing as an urticarial lesion, slightly reddened, and usually accompanied by intense itching.

wheeze [A.S. *hwēsan*]. **1.** To breathe with difficulty and noisily. **2.** A squeaking or puffing sound made in difficult breathing.

whip'lash. See whiplash *injury.*

whip'worm. See *Trichuris.*

white'head. Milium.

whitlow (wit'lo) [M.E. *whitflawe*]. Felon.

herpetic w., painful herpes simplex virus infection of a finger, often accompanied by lymphangitis and regional adenopathy.

melanotic w., a melanoma beginning in the skin at the border of or beneath the nail.

whoop (hūp, hwūp). The sonorous inspiration with which the paroxysm of coughing terminates in pertussis, due to spasm of the larynx (glottis).

whooping cough. Pertussis.

whorl (hwurl). **1.** A turn of the cochlea or of a nasal concha. **2.** Vortex; an area of hair growing in a radial manner. **3.** One of the distinguishing patterns comprising fingerprints.

whorled (hwurld). Verticillate; marked by or arranged in whorls.

wind'burn. Erythema of face due to exposure to wind.

window (win'do). Fenestra.

aortic w., a radiolucent region below the aortic arch in the left anterior oblique view, formed by the bifurcation of the trachea and traversed by the left pulmonary artery.

oval w., *fenestra* vestibuli.

round w., *fenestra* cochleae.

wind'pipe. Trachea.

wing. Ala.

wink [A.S. *wincian*]. **1.** To close and open the eyes rapidly. **2.** An involuntary act by which the tears are spread over the conjunctiva, keeping it moist.

wi'ring. Fastening together the ends of a broken bone by wire sutures.

wi'ry. Filiform and hard; denoting a variety of pulse.

withdraw'al. 1. The act of removal or retreating. **2.** A psychological and/or physical syndrome caused by abrupt cessation of the use of a drug in an habituated individual. **3.** The therapeutic process of discontinuing a drug so as to avoid w. (2). **4.** A pattern of behavior, observed in schizophrenia and depression, characterized by a pathological retreat from interpersonal contact and social involvement, and leading to self-preoccupation.

Wohlfahrtia (vōl-far'tĭ-ah) [P. *Wohlfahrt*]. A genus of dipterous fleshflies (family Sarcophagidae); larvae of some species breed in ulcerated surfaces and flesh wounds.

wolf'fian. Relating to or described by Kaspar Wolff.

wolf'ram, wolfram'ium. Tungsten.

womb (wūm) [A.S. belly]. Uterus.

wood alcohol. *Methyl* alcohol.

word salad. A jumble of meaningless and unrelated words, as emitted by persons with certain kinds of schizophrenia.

working out. In psychoanalysis, the state in the treatment process in which the patient's personal history and psychodynamics are uncovered.

working through. In psychoanalysis, the process of obtaining additional insight and personality changes in a patient through repeated and varied examination of a conflict or problem.

worm (wurm) [A.S. *wyrm*]. Any member of the phyla Annelida (segmented or true worms), the Aschelminthes (roundworms), and the Platyhelminthes (flatworms).

worm'ian. Relating to or described by Ole Worm.

wound (wūnd). **1.** Trauma to any of the tissues of the body, especially that caused by physical means and with interruption of continuity. **2.** A surgical incision.

abraded w., a w. caused by or resulting from abrasion.

avulsed w., a w. caused by or resulting from avulsion.

blowing w., open *pneumothorax.*

contused w., a bruise or contusion.

gutter w., a tangential w. that makes a furrow without perforating the skin.

incised w., a clean cut, as by a sharp instrument.

lacerated w., a w. caused by or resulting from laceration.

nonpenetrating w., injury, especially within the thorax or abdomen, produced without disruption of the surface of the body.

open w., a w. in which the tissues are exposed to the air.

penetrating w., a w. with disruption of the body surface that extends into underlying tissue or into a body cavity.

perforating w., a w. with an entrance and exit opening.

puncture w., a w. in which the opening is relatively small as compared to the depth, as produced by a narrow pointed object.

sucking w., open *pneumothorax.*

W-plasty. A procedure to prevent contracture of a straight-line scar; the edges of the wound are trimmed in the shape of a W, or a series of W's, and closed in a zig-zag manner.

W.r. Wassermann *reaction.*

wrist (rist) [A.S. wrist joint, ankle joint]. Carpus (1).

wrist-drop. Carpoptosia; drop hand; paralysis of the extensors of the wrist and fingers.

wryneck (ri'nek). Torticollis.

Wuchereria (vu-ker-ĕr'ĭ-ah). A genus of filarial nematodes (family Onchocercidae, superfamily Filarioidea) characterized by adult forms that live chiefly in lymphatic vessels and produce large numbers of embryos or microfilariae that circulate in the bloodstream, often appearing in the peripheral blood at regular intervals; the extreme form of this infection (wuchereriasis or filariasis) is elephantiasis.

W. bancrof'ti, a species transmitted to man by mosquitoes (*Culex, Aedes, Anopheles,* and *Mansonia*); adult worms inhabit the larger lymphatic vessels and the sinuses of lymph nodes where they sometimes cause temporary obstruction to the flow of lymph and slight or moderate degrees of inflammation.

wuchereriasis (vu'ker-e-ri'ă-sis). Infestation with worms of the genus *Wuchereria.* See also filariasis.

X

X Xanthosine.

xanth-. See xantho-.

xanthemia (zan-the'mĭ-ah) [xanth- + G. *haima,* blood]. Carotenemia.

xanthic (zan'thik). **1.** Yellow or yellowish in color. **2.** Relating to xanthine.

xanthine (zan'thin). Oxidation product of guanine and hypoxanthine; a precursor of uric acid that occurs in many organs and in the urine.

xanthinuria (zan-thĭ-nu'rĭ-ah) [xanthine + G. *ouron,* urine]. **1.** Excretion of abnormally large amounts of xanthine in the urine. **2.** A disorder resulting from defective synthesis of xanthine oxidase, characterized by urinary excretion of xanthine in place of uric acid, hypouricemia; autosomal recessive inheritance.

xanthism (zan'thizm) [G. *xanthos,* yellowish]. A pigmentary anomaly of Blacks, characterized by red or yellow-red hair color, copper-red skin, and often dilution of iris pigment.

xantho-, xanth- [G. *xanthos*, yellow]. Combining forms denoting yellow or yellowish.

xanthochromatic (zan-tho-kro'mat'ik). Xanthochromic; yellow-colored.

xanthochromia (zan-tho-kro'mĭ-ah) [xantho- + G. *chrōma*, color]. Xanthoderma (1); occurrence of patches of yellow color in the skin, resembling xanthoma, but without the nodules or plates.

xanthochromic (zan-tho-kro'mik). Xanthochromatic.

xanthoderma (zan-tho-der'mah) [xantho- + G. *derma*, skin]. **1.** Xanthochromia. **2.** Any yellow coloration of the skin.

xanthogranuloma (zan'tho-gran-u-lo'mah). An infiltration of retroperitoneal tissue by lipid macrophages, occurring mostly in women.

    juvenile x., nevoxanthoendothelioma; single or multiple reddish papules, usually found in young children, consisting of dermal infiltration by histiocytes and Touton giant cells.

xanthoma (zan-tho'mah) [xantho- + G. *-oma*, tumor]. A yellow nodule or plaque, especially of the skin, composed of lipid-laden histiocytes.

    x. dissemina'tum, xanthomatosis.

    eruptive x., sudden appearance of groups of waxy yellow or yellowish-brown lesions, especially over extensors of the elbows and knees, and on the back and buttocks, on patients with severe hyperlipemia.

    x. mul'tiplex, xanthomatosis.

    x. palpebra'rum, soft yellow-orange plaques found about the eyes; the most common type of x.

    x. pla'num, x. marked by the occurrence of yellow bands or rectangular plates in the corium.

    x. tubero'sum, x. tubero'sum sim'plex, xanthomatosis associated with familial type II, and occasionally type III, hyperlipoproteinemia.

xanthomatosis (zan'tho-mă-to'sis). Xanthoma dissemination or multiplex; widespread xanthomas, especially on the elbows and knees, and sometimes the mucous membranes.

    biliary x., x. with hypercholesterolemia, resulting from biliary cirrhosis.

    x. bulbi, ulcerative fatty degeration of the cornea after injury.

    cerebrotendinous x., a disorder associated with deposition of cholestanol in the brain and other tissues, and elevated levels in plasma but normal cholesterol level; characterized by progressive cerebellar ataxia beginning after puberty, juvenile cataracts, spinal cord involvement, and tendinous or tuberous xanthomas; autosomal recessive inheritance.

xanthomatous (zan-tho'mă-tus). Relating to xanthoma.

xanthopsia (zan-thop'sĭ-ah) [xantho- + G. *opsis*, vision]. Chromatopsia in which all objects appear yellow.

xanthosine (X, Xao) (zan'tho-sēn, -sin). Xanthine ribonucleoside; the deamination product of guanosine (O replacing –NH₂).

xanthosis (zan-tho'sis) [xantho- + G. *-osis*, condition]. A yellowish discoloration of degenerating tissues, especially seen in malignant neoplasms.

Xao Xanthosine.

Xe Xenon.

xeno- [G. *xenos*, stranger, foreign]. Combining form denoting strange or relationship to foreign material.

xenobiotic (zen'o-bi-ot'ik). A pharmacologically, endocrinologically, or toxicologically active substance not endogenously produced.

xenodiagnosis (zen'o-di-ag-no'sis). **1.** A method of diagnosing acute or early *Trypanosoma cruzi* infection (Chagas disease) in man by feeding infection-free triatomid bugs on the suspected person and identifying the trypanosome by microscopic examination of the intestinal contents of the bug after a suitable incubation period. **2.** A method of biological diagnosis based upon exposure of a parasite-free normal host capable of allowing the organism in question to multiply, hence being more easily and reliably detected in the host's tissues.

xenogeneic (zen'o-jen-e'ik). Xenogenic (2); heterologous, with respect to tissue grafts, especially when donor and recipient belong to widely separated species.

xenogenic (zen-o-jen'ik) [xeno- + G. *-gen*, producing]. Xenogenous. **1.** Originating outside of the organism, or from a foreign substance introduced into the organism. **2.** Xenogeneic.

xenogenous (zĕ-noj'ĕ-nus). Xenogenic.

xenograft (zen'o-graft). Heterograft.

xenon (zen'on) [G. *xenos*, a stranger]. A gaseous element, symbol Xe, atomic no. 54, atomic weight 131.30.

xenon-133 (133Xe). A radioisotope with a gamma emission and a physical half-life of 5.27 days; used in the study of pulmonary function and organ blood flow.

xenoparasite (zen'o-păr'ă-sīt). An ecoparasite that becomes pathogenic in consequence of weakened resistance on the part of its host.

xenophobia (zen-o-fo'bĭ-ah) [xeno- + G. *phobos*, fear]. A morbid fear of meeting strangers.

xenophthalmia (zen-of-thal'mĭ-ah) [xeno- + ophthalmia]. Inflammation excited by presence of a foreign body in the eye.

Xenopsylla (zen-op-sil'ah) [xeno- + G. *psylla*, flea]. The rat flea, a genus of fleas parasitic on the rat and involved in the transmission of bubonic plague; *X. cheopis* is a vector of *Yersinia pestis.*

xero- [G. *xeros*, dry]. Combining form meaning dry.

xerochilia (zēr-o-ki'lĭ-ah) [zero- + G. *cheilos*, lip]. Dryness of lips.

xeroderma (zēr-o-der'mah) [xero- + G. *derma*, skin]. A mild form of ichthyosis characterized by excessive dryness of the skin due to a slight increase of the horny layer and diminished cutaneous secretion.

    x. pigmento'sum, an eruption of exposed skin occurring in childhood and characterized by numerous pigmented spots resembling freckles, larger atrophic lesions eventually resulting in glossy white thinning of the skin surrounded by telangiectases, and multiple solar keratoses which undergo malignant change; results from a single-gene autosomal recessive disorder in which DNA repair processes are defective, with consequent hypersensitivity to the carcinogenic effect of ultraviolet light.

xerography (zēr-og′ră-fĭ). Xeroradiography.

xeroma (ze-ro′mah). Zerophthalmia.

xeromenia (zēr-o-me′nĭ-ah) [xero- + G. *mēniaia,* menses]. Occurrence of the usual constitutional symptoms at the menstrual period without show of blood.

xerophthalmia (zēr-of-thal′mĭ-ah) [xero- + G. *ophthalmos,* eye]. Xeroma; extreme dryness of the conjunctiva, due to local disease or to a systemic deficiency of vitamin A.

xeroradiography (zēr′o-ra-dĭ′og′ră-fĭ). Xerography; making of a radiograph by means of a specially coated charged plate and developing with a dry powder rather than liquid chemicals.

xerosis (ze-ro′sis) [xero- + G. *-osis,* condition]. **1.** Pathologic dryness of the skin, conjunctiva, or mucous membranes. **2.** The normal evolutionary sclerosis of the tissues in old age.

xerostomia (zēr-o-sto′mĭ-ah) [xero- + G. *stoma,* mouth]. Dryness of the mouth, resulting from diminished or arrested salivary secretion.

xerotic (ze-rot′ik). Dry; affected with xerosis.

xiphisternal (zif-ĭ-ster′nal). Relating to the xiphisternum (xiphoid process).

xiphisternum (zif-ĭ-ster′num) [xiphoid + G. *sternon,* chest]. *Processus xiphoideus.*

xipho-, xiph-, xiphi- [G. *xiphos,* sword]. Combining forms denoting xiphoid or the processus xyphoideus.

xiphoid (zif′oyd) [xipho- + G. *eidos,* appearance]. Ensiform; sword-shaped; applied especially to the processus xiphoideus.

xiphoiditis (zif-oy-di′tis) [xiphoid + G. *-itis,* inflammation]. Inflammation of the xiphoid process of the sternum.

x-ray. Roentgen ray. **1.** Electromagnetic radiation emitted from a highly evacuated tube excited by the bombardment of the target anode with a stream of electrons from a heated cathode. **2.** Electromagnetic radiation produced by excitation of the inner orbital electrons of an atom.

xylose (zi′lōs). An aldopentose, isomeric with ribose, obtained by fermentation or hydrolysis of naturally occurring carbohydrate substances.

xylulose (zi′lu-lōs). A 2-ketopentose. L-Xylulose appears in the urine in cases of essential pentosuria; D-xylulose 5-phosphate is an intermediate in pentose metabolism.

xysma (ziz′mah) [G. filings, shavings]. Membranous shreds in the feces.

Y

Y Yttrium.

yaw. An individual lesion of yaws.

mother y., buba madre; frambesioma; mamanpian; a large granulomatous lesion, considered to be the initial lesion in yaws, most commonly present on the hand, leg, or foot.

yawn [A.S. *gānian*]. An involuntary opening of the mouth, usually accompanied by a movement of respiration.

yaws [African, *yaw,* a raspberry]. An infectious tropical disease caused by *Treponema pertenue,* characterized by the development of crusted granulomatous ulcers on extremities which may involve bone. Also called pian; rupia (2); boubas; bubas, frambesia; polypapilloma (2); granuloma tropicum.

Yb Ytterbium.

yeast (yēst) [A.S. *gyst*]. General term denoting true fungi of the family Saccharomycetaceae that are widely distributed in substrates that contain sugars, and in soil, animal excreta, vegetative parts of plants, etc.

Yersinia (yer-sin′ĭ-ah) [A. J. E. *Yersin*]. A genus of Gram-negative bacteria (family Enterobacteriaceae) that are parasitic on man and other animals; type species is *Y. pestis.*

Y. enterocolit′ica, a species that causes yersiniosis.

Y. pes′tis, *Pasteurella pestis;* a species causing plague; *Xenopsylla cheopis,* transmitted from rat to man by the rat flea, the type species of the genus *Y.*

Y. pseudotuberculo′sis, *Pasteurella pseudotuberculosis;* a species causing pseudotuberculosis in rodents (rarely in man) and some cases of acute mesenteric lymphadenitis.

yersiniosis (yer-sin′ĭ-o′sis). An infectious disease caused by *Yersinia enterocolitica* and marked by diarrhea, enteritis, pseudoappendicitis, ileitis, erythema nodosum, and sometimes septicemia or acute arthritis.

-yl. Chemical suffix signifying that the substance is a radical by loss of an H atom or OH group.

-ylene. Chemical suffix denoting a bivalent hydrocarbon radical or possessing a double bond.

yoke (yōk) [A.S. *geoc*]. Jugum (1).

yolk (yōk) [A.S. *geolca; geolu,* yellow]. Vitellus; a substance stored in the ovum for nutrition of the embryo.

ytterbium (ĭ-tur′bĭ-um) [*Ytterby,* Sweden]. A metal of the lanthanide group; symbol Yb; atomic no. 70, atomic weight 173.04.

yttrium (it′rĭ-um) [*Ytterby,* Sweden]. A metallic element, symbol Y, atomic no. 39, atomic weight 88.92.

Z

Zeitgeist (zīt′gīst) [Ger. *zeit,* time, + *geist,* spirit]. In psychology, the climate of opinion, conventions of thought, covert influences, and unquestioned assumptions that are implicit in a given culture, the arts, or science at any point in time, and in which the individual operates.

ze′ro [Sp.; Ar. *sifr,* cipher]. **1.** The figure 0, indicating nothingness. **2.** In the Centigrade and Réaumur scales, the freezing point for distilled water; in the Fahrenheit scale, 32° below the freezing point of water.

absolute z., the lowest possible temperature, that at which the form of motion constituting heat is assumed no longer to exist: −273.2°C or 0 Kelvin.

zetacrit (za′tă-krit). Vertical centrifugation of blood in capillary tubes allowing controlled compaction and dispersion of red blood cells; read as a hematocrit.

zinc [Ger. *zink*]. A metallic element, symbol Zn, atomic no. 30, atomic weight 65.38; a number of its salts are used in medicine.

zinc-65 (⁶⁵Z). A radioactive zinc isotope with a half-life of 245 days; used as tracer in studies of zinc metabolism.

zirconium (zir-ko′nĭ-um) [*zircon,* a mineral, fr. Ar. *zarkūn,* cinnabar]. A metallic element, symbol Zr, atomic no. 40 atomic weight 91.22.

Zn Zinc.

zo-. See zoo-.

zoacanthosis (zo′ă-kan-tho′sis) [G. *zōon,* animal, + *acanthosis*]. A cutaneous eruption due to introduction into the human skin of animal hair, bristles, stingers, etc.

zo′anthrop′ic. Relating to or marked by zoanthropy.

zoanthropy (zo-an′thro-pĭ) [G. *zōon,* animal, + *anthrōpos,* man]. A delusion that one is an animal.

zona, pl. **zonae** (zo′nah, zo′ne) [L. fr. G. *zōnē,* a girdle] **1** [NA]. Zone; a segment; any encircling or beltlike structure. **2.** *Herpes zoster.*

z. arcua′ta, arcuate zone; z. tecta; the inner third of the basilar membrane of the cochlear duct, from the tympanic lip of the osseous spiral lamina to the outer pillar cell of the spiral organ (of Corti).

z. fascicula′ta, the layer of radially arranged cell cords in the cortical portion of the suprarenal gland, between the z. glomerulosa and z. reticularis.

z. glomerulo′sa, the outer layer of the cortex of the suprarenal gland just beneath the capsule.

z. hemorrhoida′lis, the part of the anal canal that contains the rectal venous plexus.

z. ophthal′mica, herpes zoster in the distribution of the ophthalmic nerve.

z. orbicula′ris [NA], orbicular zone; zonular band; fibers of the articular capsule of the hip joint encircling the neck of the femur.

z. pectina′ta, pectinate zone; the outer two-thirds of the lamina basilaris ductus cochlearis.

z. pellu′cida, pellucid zone; a layer consisting of microvilli of the oocyte, cellular processes of follicular cells, and an intervening substance rich in glycoprotein.

z. reticula′ris, the inner layer of the cortex of the adrenal gland, where the cell cords anastomose in a netlike fashion.

z. tec′ta, z. arcuata.

z. vasculo′sa, vascular zone; an area in the external acoustic meatus where a number of minute blood vessels enter from the mastoid bone.

zone (zōn) [L. *zona,*]. Zone (1).

arcuate z., *zona arcuata.*

ciliary z., the outer wider area of the anterior surface of the iris, adjacent to the pupillary z.

comfort z., the temperature range between 28 and 30°C at which the naked body is able to maintain heat balance without either shivering or sweating; in the clothed body, 13 to 21°C.

epileptogenic z., a cortical region which on stimulation reproduces the patient's spontaneous seizure or aura.

erogenous z., a part of the body, stimulation of which excites sexual feelings.

orbicular z., *zona orbicularis.*

pectinate z., *zona pectinata.*

pellucid z., *zona pellucida.*

pupillary z., the central region of the anterior surface of the iris.

transitional z., (1) the region of the lens of the eye where the anterior epithelial capsule cells become transformed into the fibers composing the lens substance, (2) that portion of a scleral contact lens that joins the corneal and scleral sections.

trigger z., the area which when stimulated by touch or pressure excites an attack of neurologic pain.

vascular z., *zona vasculosa.*

zonesthesia (zōn-es-the′zĭ-ah) [G. *zōnē,* girdle, + *aisthēsis,* sensation]. Girdle sensation; a sensation as if a cord were drawn around the body, constricting it.

zonifugal (zo-nif′u-gal) [L. *zona,* zone, + *fugio,* to flee]. Passing from within any region outward.

zo′ning. Occurrence of a stronger reaction in a lesser amount of suspected serum, probably the result of high antibody titer.

zonipetal (zo-nip′ĕ-tal) [L. *zona,* zone, + *peto,* to seek]. Passing from without toward and into any region.

zonula, pl. **zonulae** (zo′nu-lah, -le, zon′-) [L. dim. of *zona,* zone] [NA]. Zonule.

zonular (zon′u-lar, zo′nu-lar). Relating to a zonula.

zonule (zo′nūl, zon′ūl). Zonula; a small zone.

ciliary z., Zinn's z., suspensory ligament of lens; a series of delicate meridional fibers arising from the inner surface of the orbiculus ciliaris and diverge into two groups that are attached to the capsule on the anterior and posterior surfaces of the lens close to the equator.

zonuli′tis [zonule + G. *-itis,* inflammation]. Assumed inflammation of the ciliary zonule.

zonulolysis (zo-nu-lol′ĭ-sis) [zonule + G. *lysis,* dissolution]. Disintegration of the ciliary zonule by

zoo-

enzymes instilled into the anterior chamber in selected cases of cataract extraction to facilitate surgical removal.

zoo- [G. *zōon*, animal]. Combining form denoting an animal or animal life.

zooerastia (zo'o-ĕ-ras'tĭ-ah) [zoo- + G. *erastēs*, lover]. Sexual practices with an animal.

zoograft (zo'o-graft). A graft of tissue from one of the lower animals to a human.

zoografting (zo-o-graf'ting). Zooplasty.

zooid (zo'oyd) [G. *zōodēs*, fr. *zōon*, animal, + *eidos*, resemblance]. **1.** Resembling an animal; or an organism or object with an animal-like appearance. **2.** An animal cell capable of independent existence or movement. **3.** An individual of a colonial invertebrate such as coral.

zoolagnia (zo-o-lag'nĭ-ah) [zoo- + G. *lagneia*, lust]. Sexual attraction toward animals.

Zoomastigophorea (zo'o-mas-tĭ-go-fo're-ah) [zoo- + G. *mastix*, whip, + *phoros*, bearing]. A class of flagellates (superclass Mastigophora, subphylum Sarcomastigophorea) with animal-like as opposed to plantlike characteristics; includes parasites such as the trypanosomes and trichomonads.

zoonosis (zo-ŏ-no'sis) [zoo- + G. *nosos*, disease]. An infection or infestation shared in nature by man and lower vertebrate animals.

zoonotic (zo'o-not'ik). Relating to a zoonosis.

zooparasite (zo-o-păr'ă-sīt). An animal parasite.

zoophilia, zoophilism zo-of'ĭ-lizm) [zoo- + G. *philos*, fond, loving]. An extravagant fondness for animals.

zoophobia (zo-o-fo'bĭ-ah) [zoo- + G. *phobos*, fear]. A morbid fear of animals.

zooplasty (zo'o-plas-tĭ). Zoografting; grafting of skin or other tissue from an animal to a human.

zootoxin (zo'o-tok'sin). Animal toxin; a substance, resembling the bacterial toxins in its antigenic properties, found in the fluids of certain animals.

zoster [G. *zōstēr*, a girdle]. Herpes zoster.

zosteriform, zos'teroid. Resembling herpes zoster.

Z-plasty. A procedure to elongate a contracted scar, or to rotate tension 90°; the middle line of the Z-shaped incision is made along the line of greatest tension or contraction, and triangular flaps are raised on opposite sides of the two ends and transposed.

Zr Zirconium.

zwitterions (tsvit'er-i'onz) [Ger. *Zwitter*, hermaphrodite, mongrel]. Dipolar *ions*.

zy'gal. H-shaped; shaped like a yoke.

zygo-, zyg- [G. *zygon*, yoke, *zygōsis*, a joining]. Combining forms denoting yoke, a joining.

zygodactyly (zi-go-dak'tĭ-lĭ). Syndactyly.

zygoma (zi-go'mah) [G. a bar, bolt]. **1.** *Os* zygomaticum. **2.** *Arcus* zygomaticus.

zygomatic (zi-go-mat'ik). Relating to the os zygomaticum.

zygomaxilla're. Zygomaxillary point; a craniometric point located externally at the lowest extent of the zygomaticomaxillary suture.

zy'gon [G. crossbar, yoke]. The short crossbar connecting the branches of a zygal fissure.

zygonema (zi-go-ne'mah) [zygo- + G. *nēma*, thread]. Zygotene.

zygosis (zi-go'sis) [G. a joining]. Conjugation or sexual union of two unicellular organisms, consisting essentially in the fusion of the nuclei of the two cells.

zygosity (zi-gos'ĭ-tĭ). The nature of the zygotes from which individuals are derived.

zygote (zi'gōt) [G. *zygōtos*, yoked]. **1.** The diploid cell resulting from union of a sperm and an ovum. **2.** The individual that develops from a fertilized ovum.

zygotene (zi'go-tēn) [zygo- + G. *tainia* (L. *taenia*), band]. Zygonema; the stage of prophase in meiosis in which precise point for point pairing of homologous chromosomes begins.

zygot'ic. Pertaining to a zygote, or to a zygosis.

zymo-, zym- [G. *zymē*, leaven]. Combining forms denoting fermentation, enzymes.

zymogen (zi'mo-jen). Proenzyme.

zymogenesis (zi-mo-jen'ĕ-sis) [zymo- + G. *genesis*, production]. Transformation of a proenzyme (zymogen) into an active enzyme.

zymogen'ic. 1. Relating to a zymogen or to zymogenesis. **2.** Causing fermentation.

zymogram (zi'mo-gram) [zymo- + G. *gramma*, something written]. A material or substance in which the locations of enzymes are demonstrated by histochemical methods.